Contemporary Authors

Permanent Series

Contemporary
Authors
Permanent Series

A BIO-BIBLIOGRAPHICAL GUIDE TO
CURRENT AUTHORS AND THEIR WORKS

CLARE D. KINSMAN

Editor

volume 1

GALE RESEARCH COMPANY • BOOK TOWER • DETROIT, MICHIGAN 48226

CONTEMPORARY AUTHORS

Published by
Gale Research Company, Book Tower, Detroit, Michigan 48226
Each Year's Volumes Are Cumulated and Revised About Five Years Later

Frederick G. Ruffner, *Publisher*   James M. Ethridge, *Editorial Director*

Clare D. Kinsman, *Editor*
Cynthia R. Fadool and Alexander James Roman, *Associate Editors*
Jane Bowden, Robin Farbman, Christine Nasso, Nancy M. Rusin,
Adele C. Sarkissian, and Frank Michael Soley, *Assistant Editors*
Mary Ann Tennenhouse, Sandra Bunnell, and Roberta Dahlberg, *Contributing Editors*
Laura Bryant, *Operations Supervisor*
Daphne Cox, *Production Manager*

EDITORIAL ASSISTANTS

Frances Carol Locher, Norma Sawaya, Shirley Seip

Library of Congress Card Number 75-13539
ISBN 0-8103-0036-2

PREFACE

Beginning with this volume, a permanent series of *Contemporary Authors* volumes is being established as an adjunct to the ongoing series of new and revised volumes.

The *Permanent Series* will consist of biographical sketches which formerly appeared in regular volumes of *Contemporary Authors*. Sketches in the *Permanent Series* have been removed from regular volumes at the time of revision for one of two reasons:

    1. The subject of the sketch is now deceased.

    2. The subject of the sketch is approaching or has passed normal retirement age and has not reported a recently published book or a new book in progress.

Thus, the *Permanent Series* will make it possible to avoid reprinting in future revisions of regular volumes those sketches which no longer need periodic review and revision. Transferring inactive sketches to the new series will also make it possible to keep the size of revised volumes within economic limits by making available additional space to accommodate the steadily lengthening sketches of those writers who are active and remain in the revised volumes.

REVISION OF SKETCHES IN PERMANENT SERIES

Sketches in the *Permanent Series* are, of course, carefully revised prior to final publication. In revising sketches, the following major steps were taken:

    1. Every sketch was submitted to the author concerned, and all requested changes which were within the scope and purpose of *Contemporary Authors* were made.

    2. If an author failed to submit changes or to approve the sketch as still correct, or if it was learned that the author was deceased, the editors attempted to verify and bring up-to-date the *Personal* and *Career* sections.

    3. Additional research was done on the bibliographies of all authors, both to pick up publications which were not included in the previous versions of the sketches and to assure that all recent works were included.

INDEXING OF AUTHORS IN PERMANENT SERIES

Users of *CA* will locate authors in the *Permanent Series* in the same way as any other authors in the series, i.e., through the Cumulative Index which appears in alternate volumes of *CA*. Volume references pertaining to authors in the *Permanent Series* will be to <u>both</u> the volume in which the author's sketch originally appeared and to the pertinent volume of the *Permanent Series*. A typical reference would read as follows:

Brown, Lloyd Arnold 1907-1966............CAP-1
Earlier sketch in CA 11-12

Occasionally, a revised volume of *CA* and the cumulative index containing *CAP* references for authors transferred from the revised volume will not be available simultaneously. Thus, there will necessarily be periods when the latest sketches for certain inactive authors will not be locatable through the then-current index, or when the sketch will not be available, pending appearance of the next volume in the *Permanent Series*. The editors will work to keep such periods as brief as possible, and will be glad to accept collect telephone calls concerning authors in this interim status.

The editors believe that the *Permanent Series* is a useful innovation in the *CA* concept. As always, suggestions from users concerning revisions or any other aspect of *CA* will be welcomed.

CONTEMPORARY AUTHORS
Permanent Series

ABERNETHY, Thomas Perkins 1890-

PERSONAL: Born August 25, 1890, in Collirene, Ala.; son of Thomas Hines (a broker) and Anne (Rast) Abernethy; married Ida Robertson, December 6, 1917. *Education:* College of Charleston, A.B., 1912; Harvard University, A.M., 1915, Ph.D., 1922. *Politics:* Democrat. *Home:* 39 University Circle, Charlottesville, Va. 22903.

CAREER: Vanderbilt University, Nashville, Tenn., visiting assistant professor of history, 1921; University of Chattanooga, Chattanooga, Tenn., professor of history, 1922-28; University of Alabama, Tuscaloosa, associate professor of history, 1928-30; University of Virginia, Charlottesville, Richmond Alumni Professor of History, 1930-61; retired, 1961. Visiting professor at University of Texas, 1961-62, and University of Arizona, 1963-64. *Military service:* U.S. Army, World War I; became second lieutenant. *Member:* American Historical Association, Southern Historical Association (founder and president), Virginia Historical Society (member of executive committee), Phi Beta Kappa, Pi Kappa Phi, Raven Society, Colonnade Club. *Awards, honors:* Litt.D., Washington and Lee University, 1947; Phi Beta Kappa Award for best historical work, 1961, for *The South in the New Nation.*

WRITINGS: The Formative Period in Alabama, Alabama Department of Archives and History, 1922, 2nd edition, University of Alabama Press, 1965; *From Frontier to Plantation in Tennessee*, University of North Carolina Press, 1932; *Western Lands and the American Revolution*, Appleton, 1937; *Three Virginia Frontiers*, Louisiana State University Press, 1940; *The Burr Conspiracy*, Oxford University Press, 1954; (contributor) Walker D. Wyman and Clifton B. Kroeber, editors, *The Frontier in Perspective*, University of Wisconsin Press, 1957; *The South in the New Nation*, Louisiana State University Press, 1961; (contributor) James L. Bugg, editor, *Jacksonian Democracy: Myth or Reality?*, Holt, 1962; (co-author) George Brown Tindall, editor, *The Pursuit of Southern History*, Louisiana State University Press, 1964; (contributor) Edward T. Jones, editor, *The American Plutarch* (sketches), Scribner, 1964; *The Antecedents of the Abernethy Family in Scotland, Virginia and Alabama*, privately printed, c.1966; *Southern Frontiers of the War of 1812*, University of Alabama Press, 1967. Also editor of Thomas Jefferson's *Notes on the State of*

Virginia, Harper. Contributor to *Encyclopaedia Britannica* and *Dictionary of American Biography.*

BIOGRAPHICAL/CRITICAL SOURCES: Darrett B. Rutman, editor, *The Old Dominion: Essays for Thomas Perkins Abernethy*, University Press of Virginia, 1964.

* * *

ADAIR, Margaret Weeks ?-1971

PERSONAL: Born in Portland, Ore.; daughter of William Stone (a purchasing agent for Great Northern Railroad) and Kate L. (McPherson) Weeks; married Wistar Morris Adair (a retired banker); children: Henry Rodney, Wistar Morris, Jr. *Education:* Oregon State University, student, four years; San Jose State Teachers College, diploma. *Home:* Tigard, Ore.

CAREER: Former teacher in public and private schools, playground supervisor in athletics and crafts, and director of children's theater, all in Oregon. Owner and director of private pre-school. Organizer of public library board and its first voluntary librarian. *Member:* Puppeteers of America, Oregon Society of Artists, Tualatin Valley Writers' League, Portland Arts and Crafts Association. *Awards, honors:* First runner-up in *Boys' Life* book competition.

WRITINGS: Do-It-In-A-Day Puppets, Day, 1964; *A Far Voice Calling*, Doubleday, 1964. Contributor to teachers' magazines and other periodicals.

WORK IN PROGRESS: A novel for boys and girls to age sixteen about a journey from New York to Oregon by way of Panama in the Gold Rush days; three other books.

AVOCATIONAL INTERESTS: Camping, oil painting, clay modeling, the theater, puppets, and children and their pets.

(Died December 19, 1971)

* * *

ADAM, Thomas R(itchie) 1900-

PERSONAL: Born May 7, 1900, in Brechin, Scotland; son of Thomas Beat (a doctor) and Isabella (Robertson) Adam. *Education:* University of Edinburgh, M.A. (honors in history), 1922, LL.B., 1924. *Home:* 610 West 115th St., New York, N.Y. 10025.

CAREER: Commonwealth of Australia, Development and

Migration Commission, 1925-30, began as associate, became chairman; Occidental College, Los Angeles, Calif., associate professor of government, 1930-37; American Association for Adult Education, field representative, 1937-39; New York University, New York, N.Y., associate professor, 1945-54, professor of political science, 1954-69, professor emeritus, 1969—. *Military service:* British Army, 1939-45; became lieutenant colonel; decorated officer of Order of Orange Nassau (with swords). *Member:* American Political Science Association, Conference on Science and Religion (fellow), African Studies Association (fellow).

WRITINGS: The Worker's Road to Learning, American Association for Adult Education, 1940; *Education for International Understanding,* Teachers College, Columbia University, 1948; *Modern Colonialism,* Doubleday, 1955; *Government and Politics in Africa, South of the Sahara,* Random House, 1958, 3rd edition, 1965; *Elements of Government,* Random House, 1960; *Western Interests in the Pacific—Realm,* Random House, 1967.

*   *   *

ADAMS, Harlen M(artin)   1904-

PERSONAL: Born March 15, 1904, in Provo, Utah; son of Walter (a business executive) and Violet (Martin) Adams; married Lois Carman, December 26, 1938; children: Harlene (Mrs. George Beattie), Gordon M., Martin D. *Education:* Brigham Young University, A.B., 1925; Harvard University, A.M., 1928; Princeton University, postgraduate study, 1931-32; Stanford University, Ed.D., 1938. *Religion:* Presbyterian. *Home:* 555 Vallombrosa Ave., Apt. 43, Chico, Calif. 95926. *Office:* California State University, Chico, Calif. 95927.

CAREER: High school teacher in Utah and New Jersey, 1924-26, 1928-35; Menlo Junior College (now Menlo College), Menlo Park, Calif., teacher of English and speech, 1935-39; Stanford University, Stanford, Calif., acting instructor in English and education, 1935-39; Chico State College (now California State University), Chico, Calif., associate professor, 1939-40, professor of speech, 1940-43; Stanford University, assistant professor of speech and education, 1943-46; California State University, Chico, dean of School of Arts and Sciences, 1946-47, dean of School of Education, 1947-50, executive dean, 1950-67, professor of speech and drama, 1967-74. United Presbyterian Church in the U.S.A., member of national council on theological education, 1959—, and of presbytery and other synod bodies. *Member:* National Council of Teachers of English (president, 1953), Speech Association of America, United Presbyterian Men, Phi Delta Kappa, Alpha Psi Omega, Kappa Delta Pi, Theta Alpha Phi, Rotary.

WRITINGS: Junior College Library Program, American Library Association and Stanford University Press, 1940; (with Tom Pollock) *Language Arts and Skills,* Macmillan, 1961; (with Pollock) *Speak Up!,* Macmillan, 1964.

Contributor: *The Challenge of Education,* McGraw, 1937; H. D. Roberts, W. V. Kaulfers, and G. N. Kefauver, editors, *English for Social Living,* McGraw, 1943; Robert C. Pooley, editor, *Perspectives on English,* Appleton, 1960; Alfred H. Grommon, editor, *The Education of Teachers of English for American Schools and Colleges,* Appleton, 1963. Contributor to *English Journal, Quarterly Journal of Speech, Junior College Journal,* and other publications.

ADAMS, Henry Mason   1907-

PERSONAL: Born February 12, 1907, in Fall River, Mass.; son of Martin Hartwell and Mary (Borden) Adams; married Robin Kreutzberg, 1932. *Education:* Lehigh University, A.B., 1930; University of Southern California, M.A., 1934; Stanford University, Ph.D., 1937. *Home:* 1221 Las Canoas Lane, Santa Barbara, Calif.

CAREER: Stanford University, Stanford, Calif., instructor in history, 1937-39; Eastern Washington College, Cheney, assistant professor of social sciences, 1939-42, assistant professor of history, 1946-47; University of California, Santa Barbara, associate professor, 1947-61, professor of history, 1961-74, professor emeritus, 1974—. *Military service:* U.S. Army, Corps of Military Police, 1942-46; served in Europe for thirty-one months; became captain. *Member:* American Historical Association, Ranke Gesellschaft, Phi Alpha Theta, Phi Gamma Delta.

WRITINGS: (Contributor) *The Development of Historiography,* Stackpole, 1954; *Prussian-American Relations, 1775-1870,* Western Reserve University Press, 1960. Contributor to *Military Affairs* and history journals.

WORK IN PROGRESS: A biography of Franz von Papen.

BIOGRAPHICAL/CRITICAL SOURCES: Santa Barbara News Press, September 30, 1954, April 6, 1958, and March 23, 1961.

*   *   *

ADAMS, Leonie (Fuller)   1899-

PERSONAL: Born December 9, 1899, in Brooklyn, N.Y.; daughter of Charles Frederick (a lawyer) and Henrietta (Rozier) Adams; married William E. Troy (a critic), June 3, 1933 (died, 1961). *Education:* Barnard College, A.B., 1922. *Politics:* Liberal Democrat. *Religion:* Roman Catholic. *Home:* Candlewood Mountain, R.R. 2, New Milford, Conn. 06776.

CAREER: Wilson Publishing Co., New York, N.Y., member of editorial staff, 1922-26; Metropolitan Museum of Art, New York, N.Y., editorial worker, 1926-28; Washington Square College, New York University, New York, N.Y., instructor in English, 1930-32; Sarah Lawrence College, Bronxville, N.Y., instructor in English, 1933-34; Bennington College, Bennington, Vt., instructor in English, 1935-37, 1941-44; New Jersey College for Women, lecturer, 1946-48; Columbia University, New York, N.Y., lecturer, 1947-68. Library of Congress, consultant in poetry, 1948-49, fellow in letters, 1949-55. Fulbright lecturer in France, 1955-56. Staff member of Breadloaf Writers Conference, 1956-58. Visiting lecturer, University of Washington, 1969-70. Has served on National Book Committee and Juries, Bollingen Juries, and others. *Member:* Academy of American Poets (fellow), National Institute of Arts and Letters (secretary, 1959-61), P.E.N., Phi Beta Kappa. *Awards, honors:* Guggenheim fellowship, 1928-30; National Institute of Arts and Letters Grant in Literature, 1949; D.Lit., New Jersey College for Women, 1950; Harriet Monroe Poetry Award, 1954; Shelley Memorial Award, 1954; Bollingen Prize, 1955, for *Poems: A Selection;* Academy of American Poets fellowship, 1959; National Council of Arts Grant, 1966-67; Brandeis University Creative Arts Award, 1968-69.

WRITINGS: Those Not Elect (poems), McBride, 1925; *High Falcon and Other Poems,* John Day, 1929; *This Measure* (poems), Knopf, 1933; (translator with others, and author of introduction) Francois Villon, *Lyrics,* Limited Editions, 1933; *Poems: A Selection,* Funk, 1954; (author of introduction) *University and College Poetry Prizes 1957-61,* Academy of American Poets, 1962. Represented in many anthologies, including *Modern American Poetry and Modern British Poetry,* edited by Louis Untermeyer, Harcourt, 1942, enlarged edition, 1962, *A Treasury of Modern Poetry,* edited by Oscar Williams, Scribner, 1946, and *The Criterion Book of Modern American Verse,* edited by W. H. Auden, Criterion, 1956. Contributor to *New Republic, Poetry, Saturday Review, Scribner's* and *Botteghe Oscure* (Rome). Member of editorial board of *The Measure,* 1924.

WORK IN PROGRESS: The Collected Poems and Translations of Leonie Adams.

SIDELIGHTS: About her poetry, Miss Adams has commented: "[It is] Lyric Poetry, in largely traditional forms. At [my] formative period [I was] influenced by Elizabethan, Early Romantic and, through Yeats largely, by Symbolist poetry. . . .My work has been sometimes described as 'metaphysical' and sometimes as 'romantic.' It is perhaps some sort of fusion. Its images are largely from nature (and tradition of Nature) and I have tended in my better work toward a contemplative lyric articulated by some sort of speech music."

In communicating this metaphysical/romantic imagery, she evidences a characteristic which Geoff Hewitt describes as a meticulous craftsmanship. "Nowhere does the reader feel that the poet has abandoned her poem in favor of a digressive second look at the subject. This single-mindedness sometimes results in an almost too-predictable unity to Miss Adams' work, but the energy with which she welds her vision to her art provides an oasis for those who thirst after a time when the poem was a song of life, neither contradictory nor simple."

Though she acknowledges that the body of Miss Adams' work is slight and limited in scope, Babette Deutsch believes that one of its virtues is the awareness that the loveliness it portrays is tenuous. "None of her contemporaries has recorded more subtly the movement of the hours as sky and earth body them forth. She is as no other the poet of light. . . ."

Miss Adams told *CA*: "In addition to writing poems when a poem occurs to me I have pursued and pursue an interest in poetics, especially the preservation and renewed life of poetry as spoken. My viewpoint (or responsibility) on other matters rests with God and my conscience."

Miss Adams has recorded her verse for the Columbia University Press Series of Contemporary Poets and for the Library of Congress.

BIOGRAPHICAL/CRITICAL SOURCES: Horace Gregory and M. A. Zaretzka, *A History of American Poetry, 1900-1940,* Harcourt, 1946; Babette Deutsch, *Poetry in our Time,* Columbia University Press, 1952; *Commentary,* November 24, 1954; *Chicago Review,* fall, 1954; Louise Bogan, *Selected Criticism,* Noonday, 1955; *Yale Review,* spring, 1959.

* * *

ADAMS, Theodore Floyd 1898-

PERSONAL: Born September 26, 1898, in Palmyra, N.Y.; son of Floyd H. Olden (a minister) and Evelyn (Parkes) Adams; married Esther J. Jillson, February 26, 1925; childern: Betsy Ann (Mrs. Frank K. Thompson), Theodore

F., Jr., John Jillson. *Education:* Denison University, B.A., 1921; Rochester Theological Seminary, B.D., 1924. *Office:* First Baptist Church, Richmond, Va.

CAREER: Ordained Baptist minister, 1924. Paster in Cleveland, Ohio, 1924-27, in Toledo, Ohio, 1927-36; First Baptist Church, Richmond, Va., pastor, 1936-1968, pastor emeritus, 1968—. Visiting professor, Southeastern Baptist Seminary, 1968—. Baptist World Alliance, member of executive committee, 1934—, president, 1955-60; Southern Baptist Convention, member of Foreign Mission Board, 1940-50, 1961—. Trustee of Council on Religion and International Affairs and of University of Richmond, Virginia Union University, Richmond Memorial Hospital; member of board of directors of Cooperative for American Relief Everywhere (CARE). *Member:* Phi Beta Kappa, Beta Theta Pi, Phi Mu Alpha, Omicron Delta Kappa. *Awards, honors:* D.D. from University of Richmond, 1938, Denison University, 1940, College of William and Mary, 1940, Baylor University, 1958, Washington and Lee University, 1958, Stetson University, 1959, McMaster University, 1962, Wake Forest University, 1968; L.H.D. from Hampden-Sydney College, 1959; LL.D. from Keuka College, 1964; *Upper Room* citation, 1960, for outstanding leadership in World Christian Fellowship; National Brotherhood Citation, National Conference of Christians and Jews, 1964; Knight of the Order of African Redemption of the Republic of Liberia, 1968.

WRITINGS: Making Your Marriage Succeed, Harper, 1953; *Making the Most of What Life Brings,* Harper, 1957; *Tell Me How,* Harper, 1964; *Baptists Around the World,* Broadman, 1967.

Contributor: *The Living Christ in the Life of Today,* Broadman, 1941; *Faith of Our Fathers Living Still,* Broadman, 1941; G. P. Butler, editor, *Best Sermons of 1944,* Ziff-Davis Publishing Co., 1944; G. P. Butler, editor, *Best Sermons of 1945,* Abingdon-Cokesbury, 1945; Garland Evans Hopkins, editor, *The Mighty Beginnings,* Bethany, 1956; Foy Valentine, editor, *Christian Faith in Action,* Broadman, 1956; H. C. Brown, editor, *Southern Baptist Preaching,* Broadman, 1959; G. Allen West, Jr., editor, *Christ for the World,* Broadman, 1963; J. S. Childers, editor, *A Way Home,* Tupper & Love, 1964.

* * *

ADBURGHAM, Alison Haig 1912-

PERSONAL: Born January 28, 1912, in Yeovil, Somerset, England; daughter of Arthur Norman (a doctor of medicine) and Agnes I. (Stephenson) Haig; married Myles Ambrose Adburgham (a company director); children: Thurstan Haig, Carolyn Ashton (Mrs. D. J. Gimson), Jocelyn Alison (Mrs. C. Hughes), Roland Faulkner. *Education:* Attended Roedean School in England; further education in Switzerland. *Home:* Medlar Tree, Gravel Path, Berkhamsted, Hertfordshire, England. *Agent:* A. D. Peters, 10 Buckingham St., London W.C. 2, England. *Office:* Guardian, 192 Gray's Inn Rd., London W.C. 1, England.

CAREER: Guardian, London and Manchester, England, fashion critic, 1954—. *Member:* National Book League.

WRITINGS: A Punch History of Manners and Modes, 1841-1940, Hutchinson, 1961; *Shops and Shopping, 1800-1914: Where, and in What Manner the Well-dressed Englishwoman Bought Her Clothes,* Allen & Unwin, 1964; *View of Fashion,* Allen & Unwin, 1966; *Writing Women and Women's Magazines: From the Restoration to the Accession of Victoria,* Allen & Unwin, in press. Regular contributor to *Punch*, 1953—; contributor of short stories to *Evening Standard*, *Harper's Bazaar*, and *Good Housekeeping;* occasional contributor of articles and book reviews to *Vogue*, *Queen*, *Town and Country*, *Observer*, *New Statesman*, and *Nation*.

AVOCATIONAL INTERESTS: European travel, gardening.

* * *

ADCOCK, C(yril) John 1904-

PERSONAL: Born June 15, 1904, in England; son of Samuel and Evangeline A. M. (Eggington) Adcock; married Irene Robinson, December 20, 1931; married Ngaire Valmai Sadler (a university lecturer), November 9, 1957; children: Kareen Fleur, Marilyn Rose (Mrs. Ian Macfarlane). *Education:* University of Auckland, B.A., 1935, M.A., 1937; University of London, Ph.D., 1947. *Home:* 7 Oriental Ter., Wellington C. 4, New Zealand. *Office:* Victoria University of Wellington, Wellington, New Zealand.

CAREER: Auckland Education Board, Auckland, New Zealand, assistant teacher, later head teacher, 1925-39; Civil Defence Rescue Depot, Sidcup, England, deputy superintendent, 1940-45; Oxford University Extension, Kent, England, part-time lecturer, 1942-47; Victoria University of Wellington, Wellington, New Zealand, junior lecturer, 1947, lecturer, 1948-50, senior lecturer, 1950-63, associate professor, 1963—. *Member:* British Psychological Association (chairman, New Zealand branch, 1958-59, 1966-67), Royal Society (chairman, social science section, Wellington branch), United Nations Association (member of New Zealand executive board), New Zealand Esperanto Association (president), Wellington Education Association (vice president).

WRITINGS: Problems of Life and Existence, Stockwell, 1929; *Factor Analysis for Non-Mathematicians*, Melbourne University Press, 1954; *Fundamentals of Psychology*, Price Milburn, 1959, revised edition, Penguin, 1964; *Psychology and Nursing*, Methuen, 1960; *Frontal and Occipital Potentials and Personality* (booklet), Department of Psychology, Victoria University of Wellington, 1967; *Humour Preferences and Personality* (booklet), Department of Psychology, Victoria University of Wellington, 1967; (with wife, Ngaire V. Adcock) *Psychology*, Heinemann Educational Books, 1968. Contributor to psychological journals.

WORK IN PROGRESS: Research on personality and ability dimensions.

SIDELIGHTS: Adcock reads French, and has used Esperanto extensively for travel, lecturing, and scientific papers. *Avocational interests:* Theater, ballet, swimming, boating.

* * *

ADLER, Betty 1918-1973

PERSONAL: Born May 13, 1918, in Havana, Cuba. *Education:* Goucher College, A.B., 1937; Drexel Institute of Technology, M.A. in L.S., 1938. *Politics:* Democrat. *Home:* 1701 Eutaw Pl., Baltimore, Md. 21217. *Office:* Enoch Pratt Free Library, Baltimore, Md. 21201.

CAREER: Enoch Pratt Free Library, Baltimore, Md., 1938-40, 1950-73. Consular officer, Office of Coordinator of Inter-American Affairs, 1940-41.

WRITINGS: H.L.M., the Mencken Bibliography, Johns Hopkins Press, 1961; *Census of Ventures into Verse by Henry Louis Mencken*, Enoch Pratt Free Library, 1965.

Compiler of cumulative index to *Maryland Historical Magazine*, 1962—. Reviewer of Latin American fiction for *Baltimore Sun;* editor, *Menckeniana* (a quarterly); translator from Spanish, German, French, and Portuguese.†

(Died March 10, 1973)

* * *

AGAN, (Anna) Tessie 1897-

PERSONAL: Born October 19, 1897, in Silver City, Iowa; daughter of William B. (a farmer) and Margaret J. (Simmons) Agan. *Education:* University of Nebraska, B.Sc., 1927; Kansas State University, M.Sc., 1930; Oregon State University, postgraduate study, 1937-38. *Politics:* Republican. *Religion:* Methodist. *Home:* 4718 Hallmark, Houston, Tex. 77027.

CAREER: Elementary school teacher in St. Edward, Neb., 1916-24; high school teacher of home economics and principal in Dix, Neb., 1927-29; Kansas State University, Manhattan, associate professor of family economics, 1930—. Visiting professor at Auburn University, 1941, Oregon State University, 1959, University of Arkansas, 1965, University of Southern Illinois, 1970, and other universities. Consultant to Institute of Home Economics, U.S. Department of Agriculture, 1945-46; secretary-treasurer, Kansas Citizens Council on Aging, 1966-67; chairman, Riley County Council on Social Agencies, 1966-67; state director, American Association of Retired Persons, 1970-74. *Member:* American Association of Housing Educators (president, 1965-66), American Association of University Women, Delta Kappa Gamma (state vice-president, 1954-56), Phi Kappa Phi.

WRITINGS: The House, Lippincott, 1939, 2nd and 3rd editions published as *The House, Its Plan and Use*, 1945, 1956, 4th edition (with Elaine Luchsinger) as *The House: Principles/Resources/Dynamics*, 1965. Contributor to *Ergonomics, Consumers All, Journal of Home Economics*, and others.

AVOCATIONAL INTERESTS: Photography.

* * *

AGNEW, Edith J(osephine) 1897-
(Marcelino)

PERSONAL: Born October 13, 1897, in Denver, Colo.; daughter of Charles Clinton and Ella (Dunlap) Agnew. *Education:* Park College, Parkville, Mo., A.B., 1921; graduate study at New Mexico Highlands University and Western State College of Colorado. *Politics:* Republican. *Religion:* Presbyterian. *Home:* 532 Columbia St., Delta, Colo.

CAREER: Teacher at high school in Delta, Colo., 1921-24, and Logan Academy, Logan, Utah, 1924-28; New York (N.Y.) Public Library, assistant in children's department, 1928-29; Agua Negra Mission School, Holman, N.M., kindergarten and primary teacher, 1929-39; Ganado Mission, Ganado, Ariz., teacher of English and librarian, 1940-44; Presbyterian Board of National Missions, New York, N.Y., writing assistant, 1945-50; Presbyterian Board of Christian Education, Philadelphia, Pa., editor of *Opening Doors*, 1950-57; Delta High School, Delta, Colo., part-time teacher of English, speech and Latin, 1957-62. *Member:* Shakespeare Study Club, P.E.O. Sisterhood, Delta Kappa Gamma, Sigma Tau Delta.

WRITINGS—All published by Friendship, except as indicated: *The Songs of Marcelino* (poetry), privately printed,

1936, Board of National Missions, Presbyterian Church in the U.S.A., 1953; *The House of Christmas* (play), Eldridge Publishing House, c.1940; *My Alaska Picture Story Book*, 1948; *Sandy and Mr. Jalopy*, 1949; *The Three Henrys and Mrs. Hornicle*, 1950; *The Gray Eyes Family*, 1952; (with Gabino Rendon) *Hand on My Shoulder*, Board of National Missions, Presbyterian Church in the U.S.A., 1953; *Beyond Good Friday* (play), 1953; *Nezbah's Lamb*, 1954; *Leo of Alaska*, 1958; *The Rain Will Stop* (play), 1958; *People of the Way*, Board of Christian Education, United Presbyterian Church in the U.S.A., 1959; (with Margaret Jump) *Edge of the Village* (play), 1959; *Larry*, 1960; *Treasures for Tomas*, 1964. Contributor of poems, articles, and stories to periodicals, including *Horn Book, Opening Doors, Discovery, Presbyterian Life, Stories*, and *New Mexico Magazine*.

WORK IN PROGRESS: A book on Old Testament characters for World Books.

*   *   *

AKHMATOVA, Anna   1888-1966

PERSONAL: Born in 1888, near Odessa, Russia; real name Anna Andreevna Gorenko (she took her great-grandmother's name, Akhmatova, as a pen name); daughter of an officer in the merchant marine; married Nicholas G. Gumilyov (a major Acmeist poet; shot in 1921 for complicity in an anti-Bolshevik plot), 1910 (divorced, 1918); married Vladimir Silejko; married four times in all; children: (with first husband) Lev Nikolaevich, one daughter from a later marriage. *Education:* Attended Carskoe Selo and the Smolny Institute, St. Petersburg (now Leningrad); completed secondary education in Kiev; attended colleges in Kiev and St. Petersburg, including Zhenskie Kursy. *Residence:* Komarovo, on the Gulf of Finland, northwest of Leningrad, U.S.S.R. *Address:* Ulitsa Vorovskovo 52, Moskva, U.S.S.R.

CAREER: Poet and translator. Lived in Paris, France, spring, 1910-11; joined Acmeist movement and the Guild of Poets (Acmeist society), St. Petersburg, 1912; toured northern Italy, 1912, again in 1964; from 1922 to 1940 she was not allowed to publish officially (although some scholarly articles appeared), but her poems re-appeared in state-sanctioned periodicals during World War II; during the siege of Leningrad, 1941, she was evacuated to Tashkent where she remained until 1944; went to Moscow, 1944-45, before returning to Leningrad; in 1946 her work was declared dangerous and subversive by Zhdanov, the Soviet cultural leader; following this attack, she again did not publish and lived in considerable poverty until her work re-appeared in Soviet periodicals in 1953, following the death of Stalin; in 1965 she traveled to England. *Member:* Union of Soviet Writers (expelled, 1946), Writers' Union (honorary; elected to presidium, 1965). *Awards, honors:* Candidate for the Nobel Prize, 1958 (won by Boris Pasternak), and 1965 (won by Mikhail Sholokov); Taormina Prize for poetry (Catagna, Italy), 1964; doctorate in literature, Oxford University, 1965.

WRITINGS—Poetry: *Vecher* (title means "Evening"), Guild of Poets, 1912; *Chetki* (title means "The Rosary"), Izdatelstvo Giperborey (organ of Guild of Poets), 1914, several later editions; *Belaya Staya* (title means "The White Flock"), Izdatelstvo Giperborey, 1917; *Skrizhal Sbornik* (title means "Scratchy Collection"), [Russia], 1918; *U Samovo Morya* (title means "At the Seaside"), [St. Petersburg], 1921; *Podorozhnik* (title means "Buck-

thorn"), Petropolis Printers (St. Petersburg), 1921; *Anno Domini MCMXXI*, Petropolis Printers, 1922; *Anno Domini*, [St. Petersburg], 1923; *Stikhi* (title means "Poems"), [Russia], 1940; *Iz Shesti Knig* (title means "From Six Books"; includes a group of new poems entitled "Iva," which means "The Willow"), Izdatelstvo Sovetskii Pisatel (Moscow), 1940; *Izbrannie Stikhi* (title means "Selected Poems"), Izdatelstvo Sovetskii Pisatel (Tashlcent), 1943; *Tashkentskie Stikhi* (title means "Tashkent Poems"), [Tashkent], 1944; *Izbrannie Stikhotvoreniya* (title means "Selected Poems"), [New York], 1952; *Stikhotvoreniya, 1909-1957*, edited by A. A. Surkov, Izdatelstvo Khudozhestvennaya Literatura (Moscow), 1958; *Poema Bez Geroya; Triptykh* (originally published in *Vozdushnye puti*; title means "Poem Without a Hero; Triptych"), [New York], 1960; *Stikhi, 1909-1960*, [Russia], 1961; *Stikhotvoreniya*, [Moscow], 1961; *Collected Poems: 1912-1963* (Russian language), edited by Virginia E. Van Wynen, privately printed, 1963; *50 Stikhotvorenii*, YMCA Press (Paris), 1963; *Rekviem: Tsikl Stikhotvorenii* (title means "Requiem: A Cycle of Poems"), Possev-Verlag (Frankfurt am Main), 1964; *Poeziya* (title means "Poetry"), Vilnyus Vaga, 1964; *Beg Vremeni* (poems, 1909-1965; title means "Race of Time"; includes poems from *Vecher, Chetki, Belaya Staya, Podorozhnik, Anno Domini MCMXXI*, and two new groups entitled "Trostnik" [means "Cane"] and "Sedmaya Kniga" [means "Seventh Book"]), Izdatelstvo Sovetskii Pisatel, 1965; *Stikhotvoreniya, 1909-1965*, [Moscow], 1965; *Sochineniya*, 2 volumes, Inter-Language Literary Associates (Washington, D.C.), 1965, 1968.

Translator: *Koreiskaya Klassicheskaya Poeziya* (title means "Korean Classical Poetry"), edited by A. A. Kholodovich, Izdatelstvo Khudozhestvennaya Literatura, 1956; (with Vera Potapova) *Lirika Drevnevo Egipta* (title means "Ancient Egyptian Lyrics"), Izdatelstvo Khudozhestvennaya Literatura, 1965; *Golosa Poetov* (anthology; title means "Voices of the Poets"), Izdatelstvo Progress (Moscow), 1965; *Klassicheskya poeziya Vostoka*, [Moscow], 1969. Also translator of works from French, Chinese, Rumanian, Bengali, Polish, Hebrew, and other languages.

English translations: *Forty-Seven Love Poems*, translated by Natalie Duddington, J. Cape, 1927; *Selected Poems*, translation and introduction by Richard McKane, Penguin, 1969; *Poems of Akhmatova*, translation and introduction by Stanley Kunitz and Max Hayward, Little, Brown, 1973; *A Poem Without a Hero*, translated by Carl R. Proffer and Assya Humesky, Ardis Publishers, 1973.

Anthologies: *Modern Poems from Russia*, translated by Gerard Shelley, Allen & Unwin, 1942; *A Book of Russian Verse*, edited by Cecil wm. bowra, Macmillan (London), 1943; *Sbornik Stikhov* (title means "A Collection of Poems"), compiled by Vasilii Kazin and Viktor Pertsov, Goslitizdat (Moscow), 1943; *A Treasury of Russian Verse*, translated and edited by Avrahm Yarmolinsky, Macmillan, 1949; *Soviet Russian Verse* (Russian language), edited by R. R. Milner-Gulland, Pergamon, 1964; *Stikhotvoreniya*, Letchworth, 1965; *Modern European Poetry*, edited by Willis Barnstone, Bantam, 1966.

A collection of short poems originally published in Russian periodicals was published in German as part of *Geschichte der Sowjetliteratur*, three volumes (title means "A History of Soviet Literature"; Volumes 1395-1397 of *Goldmanns Gelbe Taschenbuecher*), edited and translated by Gleb Struve and B. Filippov, Goldmann (Munich), 1966.

Also author of twenty-five essays about Pushkin, written

between 1926 and 1936. Contributor to *Sirus* (edited by her first husband, Nicholas A. Gumilyov), *Apollon, Krasnaya Nov, Zvezda, Novy Mir, Znamya; Ogonyok*, and other periodicals.

SIDELIGHTS: In 1964 R. R. Milner-Gulland noted that Akhmatova had been called "the greatest living Russian poet." When she was young, critics called her work brilliant and original, and while still in her twenties she became, with her husband Gumilyov and the poet Mandelstam, one of the three leading figures in the Acmeist movement, which predominated, with Russian futurism, in Russian poetry from about 1910 to 1917. The movement was a reaction against the mysticism and vagueness of style employed by the symbolists; the precision of Akhmatova's language and her clear, concrete imagery were considered exemplary by Acmeist theoreticians.

Akhmatova's theme was always love. When she was young, she was happy, and the simple lyricism with which she developed her theme is unequaled in contemporary Russian verse. During the revolution and, later, the war years, she became intense and bitter. Her only son was arrested during the thirties and sent to a concentration camp for more than fifteen years, she herself was shamed, and her work was banned in her own country. But her theme was still love, if love turned to hatred and remaining alive only in reminiscence. Deming Brown writes: "Akhmatova, always a patriot, seemed to take a dogged pride in the ability of her people to suffer and endure, and almost to welcome this adversity as a test of will and moral courage." During these years she wrote "Requiem" and "Poem Without a Hero," and the critics, when she was again allowed to publish, called this work great poetry. But she had passed 65 when she wrote her finest poems, those in which she resolved her early lyricism with her mature pathos and despair and finally became, in Alexander Werth's words, the "tragic queen" of Russian poetry.

Akhmatova began writing poems in 1907 and her husband Gumilyov was the first to publish them. Although he considered her earliest work to be the insignificant pastime of a young wife, his review of her second book exemplifies his increasing awareness of her talent and importance. Leonid I. Strakhovsky quotes from Gumilyov's review: "The most outstanding factor in Akhmatova's poetry is her style: she almost never explains, she demonstrates.... There are many definitions of color in Akhmatova's poems and most often these are of yellow and gray, until now the rarest in poetry." Another critic of her early work, according to Strakhovsky, wrote: "Anna Akhmatova knows how to follow the highway of contemporary artistic culture with such primitive independence of her personal life as if this highway were merely a whimsical path in her own private garden.... Revery feeds the poetry of Anna Akhmatova, a deeply sad revery often romantic in its content. However, we call a romantic a man who sees in reality merely a pretext for revery, but a woman who wants to abandon herself to revery is not a romantic but simply—a woman." Werth notes that "her second book, *The Rosary*, ... became immensely popular, especially with women readers who were fascinated by the music of her verse, its epigrammatic conciseness, and by her strangely varying female moods, ranging from feminine humility to haughtiness and feminine arrogance; from timid uncertainty to full self-assurance; from sensuality to a kind of intellectually amorous detachment." Werth continues: "Akhmatova was happiest in her youth, before the revolution, and she scarcely ever made any secret of it. She loved Russia, but was always out of step with the Soviet Union except—and the exception is significant—during World War II when 'Russia' and the 'Soviet Union' became one for her."

Essentially, Akhmatova was an urban poet. Strakhovsky writes: "All told, cities predominate in Akhmatova's poetry. It seems that man-made structures attract her more than nature's landscapes." And throughout her life she wrote with deepest affection for pre-revolutionary St. Petersburg.

But whether her poems spoke of city or country, peace or war, love or hatred (although, Strakhovsky notes, "her hate is only another form of her love"), it was the manner in which she developed her poetic subject that was most distinctive. Her poetry is fundamentally subjective, approaching the fact of the poem by an analysis of her own interpretation of it. The subjective statement is necessarily engendered by perception of the objective correlative but, within the poem, the objective is made significant and fully comprehensible only as a result of subjective experiential analysis. Strakhovsky writes: "She assembles artistically the particulars of a given moment which are often unnoticeable to others; she notices everything anew so that her internal world is not merely framed by the external world, but they combine into one solid and organic wholeness of life."

It was the perfection of this technique—the interpretation of reality in terms of experience—that made her achievement in the last poems truly remarkable. Werth writes: "Unlike her early love lyrics, unlike her tragic, intensely bitter 'Requiem,' unlike her war poems with their exaltation, pathos and infinite human pity—above all, for the martyred children of Leningrad—her last poems are marked by the serenity, wisdom and resignation of old age. They combine a deep love of art, music, nature and, again, St. Petersburg-Leningrad and Tsarskoye Selo, the one associated with her whole life, the other with her happy youth." Akhmatova, citing "Midnight Verses," a cycle of very short poems written between 1963 and 1964, chose her own favorites from among these most recent poems. The last poems, too, were written when she had finally been recognized by her country, and it is possible that the state's acceptance of her after so many years contributed to the inner harmony and peacefulness that is often expressed in these poems. Werth notes: "Even the official obituary published by the Writers' Union paid tribute to a 'remarkable Soviet poet': 'For more than half a century she devoted herself to the noble service of Russian poetic speech, of the homeland, and of Soviet society building a new world.'"

Akhmatova wrote poems for 59 years; certainly her poetry and her life were inseparably fused. Thus, to study the body of her work is to understand the remarkable achievement of her life. The *Books Abroad* reviewer writes: "Akhmatova was one of the first to use the elements of genuine popular speech in Russian poetry; with utmost simplicity and depth she developed the great lyrical theme of love, jealousy, parting and death, as if writing her own diary—though a diary crystallized into art; and what is even more, she introduced a great historiosophic theme. In her last works ... there is a deep perception of the meaning of our times and of our historical trials, as well as perfection of form." Michael Klimenko adds: "Akhmatova did not write much, but everything she wrote bears the stamp of finely-chiseled, most intimate, aesthetic and emotional experience."

BIOGRAPHICAL/CRITICAL SOURCES: (Interview)

Literaturnaya Gazeta (official publication of the Union of Soviet Writers), November 24, 1945; Leonid I. Strakhovsky, *Craftsmen of the Word: Three Poets of Modern Russia*, Harvard University Press, 1949; R. R. Milner-Gulland, editor, *Soviet Russian Verse: An Anthology*, Pergamon, 1964; Willis Barnstone, editor, *Modern European Poetry*, Bantam (original paperback), 1966; *New York Times Book Review*, April 17, 1966; Alexander Werth in *Nation*, August 22, 1966; *Books Abroad*, winter, 1967; *New York Times Magazine*, May 28, 1967.*

(Died March 5, 1966)

* * *

ALBAUGH, Ralph M.   1909-

PERSONAL: Born June 7, 1909, in Mingo Junction, Ohio; son of William A. and Bertha (Smith) Albaugh; married Norma Pfister, October 26, 1945. *Education:* Miami University, Oxford, Ohio, A.B., 1940, M.A., 1942; Ohio State University, Ph.D., 1948. *Home:* 326 South 20th St., Terre Haute, Ind. 47803. *Office:* Department of English, Indiana State University, Terre Haute, Ind. 47809.

CAREER: Ohio State University, Columbus, instructor in English, 1944-48; Ohio University, Athens, assistant professor of English, 1948-51; University of Maryland, College of Special and Continuation Studies, assistant professor of English, Heidelberg, Germany, 1951-56; Indiana State University, Terre Haute, professor of English, 1957—. *Member:* National Council of Teachers of English, Modern Language Association of America, Modern Humanities Research Association, American Association of University Professors, Conference on College Composition and Communication.

WRITINGS: Thesis Writing: A Guide to Scholarly Style, Littlefield, 1951; *English: A Dictionary of Grammar and Structure*, Chandler Publishing, 1964.

* * *

ALBRIGHT, Raymond W(olf)   1901-1965

PERSONAL: Born July 16, 1901, in Akron, Pa.; son of Richard L. and Margaret G. (Wolf) Albright; married Mary Catherine Sherr, 1924 (died, 1932); married Caroline E. Ayer Rising, June 9, 1933; children: (first marriage) Winifred (Mrs. Fritz Oyen), Raymond Jacob; Hawley K. Rising (stepchild). *Education:* Albright College, student, 1919-21; Franklin and Marshall College, A.B., 1923, A.M., 1924; Reformed Theological Seminary, Lancaster, Pa., B.D., 1924; Divinity School of Protestant Episcopal Church, Th.D., 1933. *Home:* 43 Linnaean St., Cambridge, Mass. 02138.

CAREER: Ordained deacon in Evangelical Church, 1923, elder, 1925; ordained deacon and priest in Protestant Episcopal Church, 1952. Pastor in Pennsylvania, 1922-27; Evangelical School of Theology, Reading, Pa., professor of church history, 1926-52; Temple University, Philadelphia, Pa., professor of church history, 1935-45; Episcopal Theological School, Cambridge, Mass., William Reed Huntington Professor of Church History, 1952-65. Visiting professor, University of Marburg, 1956, Boston University, 1960; lecturer, Radcliffe Seminars, 1957-65. Member of board of corporators, Presbyterian Ministers Fund. *Member:* American Society of Church History (president, 1963). *Awards, honors:* Litt.D., Franklin and Marshall College, 1948; LL.D., Albright College, 1964.

WRITINGS: History of Religious Education in Evangel-

ical *Church*, Evangelical Press (Harrisburg, Pa.), 1932; *A History of the Peace Movement*, privately printed, 1935; *A History of the Evangelical Church*, Evangelical Press, 1942, 3rd edition, revised, 1956; *Two Centuries of Reading, Pa., 1748-1948: A history of the County Seat of Berks County*, Historical Society of Berks County, 1948; *Focus on Infinity: A Life of Phillips Brooks*, Macmillan, 1961; *A History of the Protestant Episcopal Church*, Macmillan, 1964. Contributor to *Collier's Encyclopedia, Mennonite Encyclopedia, Encyclopedia of Religion, Encyclopaedia Britannica.* Department editor, *New Schaff-Herzog Encyclopedia;* American editor, *Bibliographie de la Reforme, 1450-1648*, [Lieden], 1960.

(Died, 1965)

* * *

ALDRICH, Frederic DeLong   1899-

PERSONAL: Born November 2, 1899, in Port Huron, Mich.; son of Horace Nathan (an Episcopal clergyman) and Helen Grace (Champlain) Aldrich; married Dorothy May Lindquist, June 19, 1937; children: Frederic DeLong, Jr., John Lindquist, William James, Andrew Lindstrom. *Education:* Willamette University, A.B., 1921; University of Oregon, graduate student, 1923; Western Reserve University (now Case Western Reserve University), M.A., 1931, Ed.D., 1953; Cleveland-Marshall Law School, special law student, 1934-36. *Politics:* Republican. *Religion:* Episcopal. *Home and office:* Route 1, Richmond, Vt. 05477.

CAREER: Collinwood High School, Cleveland, Ohio, coach, and instructor in history and English, 1921-53; Western Reserve University (now Case Western Reserve University), Cleveland, Ohio, lecturer in education, 1953-56; Alderson-Broaddus College, Philippi, W.Va., professor of education and head of department, 1956-57; Chatham College, Pittsburgh, Pa., chairman of education department and director of Audio-Visual Center, 1957-61; retired, 1961. Visiting lecturer at Pennsylvania State University, 1958-61, at University of Vermont, 1962—. Education specialist, Vermont State Department of Education, 1966. Episcopal Church, lay reader, 1921—. Delegate, Vermont State Republican Convention, 1964, 1966, 1968. *Military service:* U.S. Navy, 1918-19. Officers Reserve Corps, 1927-46, serving on active duty with Army Medical Service Corps, 1941-46; became lieutenant colonel. *Member:* Delta Theta Phi, Phi Delta Kappa, Reserve Officers Association (Ohio chapter historian, 1934-35), American Legion, Military Order of Foreign Wars of the U.S.

WRITINGS: A Brief Outline of Church History, William Feather, 1927; *The School Library in Ohio*, Scarecrow, 1959. Writer of Army technical manual, *Army Medical Supply Depot*, U.S. Government Printing Office, 1942, and of *School Newspaper Style Book*, Samsey Press, 1927. Contributor to *Quill and Scroll, School Press Review, Reserve Officer, Educational Administration and Supervision,* and *Curriculum Programs.*

WORK IN PROGRESS: Vermont Mores.

AVOCATIONAL INTERESTS: Legitimate theatre, sports.

BIOGRAPHICAL/CRITICAL SOURCES: Pittsburgh Press, October 6, 1957, February 12, 1961.

* * *

ALLEN, Clifford Edward   1902-

PERSONAL: Born October 23, 1902, in Gravesend, Kent,

England; son of William Thomas (a pilot) and Jane Amelia (Marshall) Allen; married Madeline Jane Lloyd, October 12, 1929. *Education:* Guy's Hospital Medical School, University of London, M.R.C.S., L.R.C.P., M.B., B.S., 1926, D.P.M., 1932, M.D., 1933, M.R.C.P., 1934. *Politics:* Liberal. *Religion:* Humanist. *Home:* The Lodge, Llwyn Offa, Mold, Flintshire, North Wales. *Agent:* Laurence Pollinger Ltd., 18 Maddox St., Mayfair, London W.1, England.

CAREER: Charing Cross Hospital, London, England, honorary chief assistant psychiatrist, 1930-45; Tavistock Clinic, London, honorary psychotherapist, 1933-44; Dreadnought Seamen's Hospital, Greenwich, London, psychiatrist in charge of department, 1937-62; retired from active practice, 1962. Honorary consultant psychiatrist, Seamen's Hospitals. *Member:* Royal Society of Medicine (fellow), Royal Society of Psychiatrists (founding fellow), 1971.

WRITINGS: Modern Discoveries in Medical Psychology, Macmillan, 1937, 3rd edition, 1965; (with others) *The Adrenal Cortex and Intersexuality,* Chapman & Hall, 1938; *The Sexual Perversions and Abnormalities: A Study in the Psychology of Paraphilia,* Oxford University Press, 1940, 2nd edition, 1949; (with Philip M. Bloom and H. J. Blackman) *The Grammar of Marriage,* Ethical Union, 1950; *Homosexuality: Its Nature, Causation and Treatment,* Staples, 1958; (with Charles Berg) *The Problem of Homosexuality,* Citadel, 1958; *A Textbook of Psychosexual Disorders,* Oxford University Press, 1962, 2nd edition, 1969; *Passing Examinations: A Psychological Study of Learning, Remembering and Examination Techniques and the Causes of Failure,* St. Martin's, 1963, revised and enlarged edition, Pan Books, 1966; *Passing School Examinations: A Book for Parents Who Wish Their Children to Pass Examinations,* St. Martin's, 1964; *Planning a Career,* St. Martin's, 1965.

Novels: *The Palm Grows,* Hurst & Blackett, 1943; *The Shorn Lamb,* Ward, Lock, 1950; *The Underlings,* Ward, Lock, 1952; *The Untroubled Wolves, a Provincial Comedy,* Ward, Lock, 1953; *Trampled Pastures, a Country Diversion,* Ward, Lock, 1954; *The Dark Places,* Redman, 1958.

Contributor: *The Psychology of the Growing Child,* Routledge & Kegan Paul, 1937; *Sex, Society and the Individual,* Churchill, 1952; *Colloquia on Endocrinology,* Churchill, 1952; *Psychiatry in General Practice,* Staples, 1956; *The Trial of John George Haigh,* Hodge & Co., 1958. Also contributor to *The Encyclopedia of Sexual Behavior,* Hawthorn, 1961, *Encyclopaedia Britannica,* 1961, and to medical journals.

*   *   *

ALLEN, Edith Marion

PERSONAL: Born in Boonville, Mo.; daughter of Marion and Emma (Don Carlos) Allen. *Education:* University of Missouri, A.B., 1922, B.S. in Ed., 1923, A.M., 1928. *Home:* 4807 Round Lake Rd., Apt. G, Indianapolis, Ind. 46205.

CAREER: High school teacher in Missouri, 1922-24; Mississippi State College for Women, Columbus, instructor in Spanish, 1924-25; Hardin Junior College, Mexico, Mo., head of department of foreign languages, 1925-28; Indianapolis (Ind.) public schools, teacher of Spanish, Arsenal Technical High School, 1928-62, head of department of foreign languages, 1957-62, special assignment in foreign language supervision, 1962-65, supervisor, foreign languages, 1966-70. Member of advisory committee, Indiana State Foreign Language Curriculum Committee, 1962-70.

Member: National Education Association, Modern Language Association of America, American Association of Teachers of Spanish and Portuguese (member of national council, 1964-66), American Council on the Teaching of Foreign Languages, Central States Modern Language Teachers Association, Indiana State Teachers Association, Indiana Foreign Language Teachers Association, Sigma Delta Pi.

WRITINGS: (With L. H. Turk) *El Spanol al Dia,* Book I, Heath, 1949, 4th edition, 1973, Book II, 1950, 4th edition, 1973, Book III, 1968.

*   *   *

ALLEN, Edward J(oseph) 1907-

PERSONAL: Born November 13, 1907, in Erie, Pa.; son of Edward Joseph and Mary (Grant) Allen; married Dorothy Davenport, May 26, 1937; children: John Davenport, Mary Elizabeth. *Education:* Attended FBI National Academy, 1947. *Home:* 2510 French St., Santa Ana, Calif. *Office:* Police Department, Santa Ana City Hall, 511 West Sixth St., Santa Ana, Calif.

CAREER: Union Bank, Erie, Pa., teller, 1928-35; police department, Erie, Pa., detective-sergeant, 1936-47; police department, Youngstown, Ohio, chief of police, 1948-53; State of Ohio, department of liquor control, Columbus, Ohio, chief of the department, 1954-55; police department, Santa Ana, Calif., chief of police, 1955—. Instructor of police administration course, International City Managers' Association, 1958—. Director, Boys' Club, 1956-60, and Salvation Army, 1958—. *Member:* International Association of Chiefs of Police, California Peace Officers' Association, Orange County Peace Officers' Association, Community Chest (director), Rotary Club, Knights of Columbus. *Awards, honors:* Kiwanis Clubs Award, 1945 and 1960; American Legion Award, 1949; Chambers of Commerce Award, 1959; Rotary Club Award, 1965.

WRITINGS: Merchants of Menace: The Mafia, C. C Thomas, 1962. Abstractor for *Excerpta Criminologica.* Regular contributor to national and international police journals.

BIOGRAPHICAL/CRITICAL SOURCES: Reader's Digest, November, 1950; *Look,* December 19, 1950.

*   *   *

ALLEN, G(eorge) Francis 1907-

PERSONAL: Born February 27, 1907, in Yeovil, Somerset, England; son of George Richard (a glover) and Jane Frances (Ewens) Allen. *Education:* Attended Elizabeth College, Guernsey, Channel Islands, and King's College, London. *Religion:* "Adaita Vedanta." *Address:* c/o Chartered Bank, 38 Bishopsgate, London E.C.2, England.

CAREER: Free-lance rating surveyor in London and Sussex, England, prior to 1949; Buddhist monk, member of Sri Ramana Asraman, in India, Ceylon and Burma, 1945-59. *Military service:* Royal Air Force, 1939-45; served in Ceylon.

WRITINGS—Editor and translator: *Buddha's Philosophy: Selections from the Pali Canon and an Introductory Essay,* Macmillan, 1959; *Buddha's Words of Wisdom: The Buddhist's Companion Book Containing 365 Maxims and Utterances Attributed to Gotama Buddha for Each Day and Night of the Year,* Macmillan, 1959. Contributor of Articles on Buddhism and other aspects of oriental philosophy to journals in Ceylon, India, Burma, Great Britain, and America, 1946-51.

WORK IN PROGRESS: Mystics and Sages of India, 1800-1960; Taoist Words of Wisdom.

AVOCATIONAL INTERESTS: Languages (has studied German, Spanish, Italian, Portuguese, Sanskrit, Pali, Sinhala, Tamil, and Malay), movies, radio, and piano recitals.

*   *   *

ALLEN, Geoffrey Francis 1902-

PERSONAL: Born August 25, 1902, in England; son of John Edward Taylor and Mabel (Saunders) Allen; married Madeline Gill, Decemeber 6, 1932. *Education:* Attended University College, Oxford; Ripon Hall, Oxford, first class honors in philosophy, politics, and economics, 1924, second class honors in theology, 1926. *Home:* The Knowle, Deddington, Oxford, OX5 4TB, England.

CAREER: Ordained deacon, Church of England, 1927, priest, 1928. Ripon Hall, Oxford University, Oxford, England, chaplain, 1928-30; Lincoln College, Oxford University, Oxford, England, fellow and chaplain, 1930-35; Church Missionary Society, missionary at Union Theological College, Canton, China, 1935-40; National Christian Council of China, secretary, 1942-44; archdeacon of Birmingham, England, 1944-47; Bishop in Egypt, 1947-52; Ripon Hall, principal, 1952-59; Bishop of Derby, 1959-69. *Member:* English-Speaking Union, Athenaeum Club. *Awards, honors:* D.D. Lambeth, 1959; honorary fellow, Lincoln College, Oxford University, 1959.

WRITINGS: (With others) *Tell John*, Maclehose & Co., 1932; *He That Cometh*, Maclehose & Co., 1932; *Christ the Victorious*, Maclehose & Co., 1935; *The Courage to be Real*, Maclehose & Co., 1938; *The Theology of Missions*, S.C.M. Press, 1941; *Law with Liberty*, S.C.M. Press, 1942; (contributor) R.J.W. Bevan, editor, *The Churches and Christian Unity*, Oxford University Press, 1963.

*   *   *

ALLEN, Irene 1903-

PERSONAL: Born August 16, 1903, in Cornwall, England; daughter of Ernest Edward (an engineer) and Helena (Higham) Allen. *Education:* University College of South Wales and Monmouthshire, B.A., (honors in history), 1926, graduate study, 1927-28; Maria Grey Training College, London, England, teacher's diploma, 1927. *Religion:* Anglican. *Home:* 25 Wootton, Boars Hill, Oxford, England.

CAREER: Assistant mistress at schools in Hatfield, England, 1928-29, Oxford, England, 1929-32; private coaching, 1932-41; Howell's School, Llandaff, Cardiff, Wales, mistress of religious knowledge, 1941-65. Ordained deaconess of Church in Wales, 1961; deaconess at the parish in Llandaff, Cardiff, Wales, 1965-68; now part-time deaconess at St. Peter's parish, Wootton, Boars Hill, Oxford.

WRITINGS: A Short Introduction to the Old Testament, Oxford University Press, 1935, revised edition, 1964; *The Early Church and the New Testament*, Longmans, Green, 1950. Writer of pamphlets on prayer for boys and girls. Collaborator with S. G. Gurney on film strip, "Jericho."

*   *   *

ALLEN, Marjory (Gill) 1897-
(Lady Allen of Hurtwood)

PERSONAL: Born May 10, 1897, in London, England; daughter of George J. and Sarah Shorey (Driver) Gill; married Lord Allen of Hurtwood, December 17, 1922 (died, 1939); children: Polly. *Education:* Attended University of Reading. *Home:* 10 Selwood Ter., London S.W. 7, England.

CAREER: United Nations social welfare adviser for Europe and Middle East, 1950-52; now a landscape architect and playground consultant. Founder of adventure playgrounds in England. Justice of the Peace. British Film Institute Governor. *Member:* Institute of Landscape Architects (honorary vice-president), World Organization for Early Childhood Education (founder), Nursery School Association of Great Britain (president).

WRITINGS: Whose Children?, privately printed, 1945; (with Susan Jellicoe) *Gardens*, Penguin, 1953; *The New Small Garden*, Architectural Press, 1956; *Play Parks*, Housing Centre, 1960; *Design for Play: The Youngest Children*, Housing Centre, 1962; *New Playgrounds*, Housing Centre, 1964, 2nd edition, 1966; (editor with others) *Space for Play: The Youngest Children*, World Organization for Early Childhood Education, 1964; *Planning for Play*, Thames & Hudson, 1968, M.I.T. Press, 1969. Gardening correspondent, *Guardian*, 1921-39. Contributor to architectural publications and to newspapers.

*   *   *

ALLEN, Myron Sheppard 1901-

PERSONAL: Born February 14, 1901, in Lowell, Mass.; son of Franklin (a designer) and Florence (Hamilton) Allen; married Dorothy Ruth Petersen (a public health nurse), May 2, 1926; children: Donald, Richard, David. *Education:* Tufts University, B.S.M.E., 1923; University of Southern California, A.M., 1929, Ed.D., 1942. *Home and office:* Institute for Scientific Creativity, 15850 West Rd., Los Gatos, Calif. 95030.

CAREER: Engineer and sales engineer with various California companies, 1923-26; Long Beach City College, Long Beach, Calif., physics instructor, 1929-62; University of Southern California, Los Angeles, part-time psychology instructor, 1957—, visiting research associate, 1956-60; Ernest L. Loen & Associates (management consultants), Los Angeles, Calif., director of creativity research, 1959-65; Creative Growth Center, Los Gatos, Calif., director, 1965—. Technical Service Research, consulting physicist and psychologist, 1950—. Creative Education Foundation, member of leadership council. *Military service:* U.S. Navy, Bureau of Ordnance, 1943-45; became lieutenant commander. *Member:* American Society of Mechanical Engineers, American Association of Physics Teachers (industry council, 1957-59), National Education Association, California Teachers Association, Phi Delta Kappa.

WRITINGS: Morphological Creativity: The Miracle of Your Hidden Brain Power, Prentice-Hall, 1962; *Morphological Synthesis–Introduction*, Technical Service, 1962; *Psycho-Dynamic Synthesis: The Key to Total Mind Power*, Parker Publishing, 1966. Writer of technical papers; contributor to *American Journal of Physics*.

WORK IN PROGRESS: Break-Through to Personal Power: A Creative Alternative to the Destructive Use of Drugs, Alcohol, Tobacco and Sex.

*   *   *

ALLUM, Nancy (Patricia Eaton) 1920-

PERSONAL: Born May 11, 1920, in London, England; daughter of Alfred John and D.C.M. (Payne) Allum; married J.H.P. Draper (a civil servant), September 22, 1941;

children: Ann, Frances, Charles. *Education:* Attended Haberdashers' Askes Acton School, London, England, and Couvent des Soeurs de Notre Dame, Marche, Belgium. *Religion:* Church of England. *Home:* 24 Gordon Mansions, Huntley St., London, W.C.1, England.

CAREER: British Foreign Office, London, England, journalist and script writer, 1956—. Radio broadcaster as journalist, reporter, and interviewer. *Member:* International P.E.N., Women's Press Club of London, National Book League.

WRITINGS: Monica Joins the WRAC, Parrish, 1961; *A Commission in the WRAC*, Central Office of Information, 1961; *Monica Takes a Commission*, Parrish, 1965. Columnist for *Publisher*. Contributor to *Books and Bookmen*, and other British newspapers and magazines.

* * *

ALTMAN, Wilfred 1927-

PERSONAL: Born October 13, 1927, in Stettin, Pommerania; son of Curt and Alice (Munzer) Altmann; married Mynerva Smith, January 23, 1961; children: Tanya Rebecca, Catherine Belinda, Natasha Louise. *Education:* Attended City Literary Institute and The Polytechnic, London, England, 1947-52. *Politics:* Liberal. *Religion:* Jewish. *Home:* Mortimer House, Graemesdyke Rd., Berkhamsted, Hertfordshire, England. *Office:* 21 Great Portland St., London W.1, England.

CAREER: J. Sainsbury Ltd. (supermarket chain), London, England, various positions in distribution, merchandising and writing, 1943-53; free-lance writer and marketing and public relations consultant, 1953—; Co-ordinated Marketing Services Ltd., London, England, chairman, 1967—. *Member:* Institute of Marketing, Grocers Institute (fellow), Writers Guild.

WRITINGS: (With Denis Thomas and David Sawyer) *TV: From Monopoly to Competition, and Back*, Institute of Economic Affairs, 1961, revised edition, 1962; *Mergers: Bigger and Better?*, Newman Neame Take Home Books, in press. Contributor to *Financial Times, Daily Mail, London Evening Standard, Campaign, Advertising Quarterly, Marketing*, and other publications. Script consultant for BBC-TV series "This Is Marketing."

* * *

ALTROCCHI, Julia Cooley 1893-1972

PERSONAL: Surname is accented on second syllable; rhymes with *rocky;* born July 4, 1893, in Seymour, Conn.; daughter of Harlan Ward and Nellie (Wooster) Cooley; married Rudolph Altrocchi (a professor), August 26, 1920 (deceased); children: John Cooley, Paul Hemenway. *Education:* Vassar College, A.B., 1914. *Agent:* Alex Jackinson, 11 West 42nd St., New York 36, N.Y.

CAREER: Writer and lecturer. *Member:* National League of American Penwomen (president, Piedmont-Oakland branch, 1960-61, secretary, 1964-65), National Poetry Society of America, California Writers' Club (president, 1941, 1942). *Awards, honors:* Commonwealth Club of San Francisco silver medal, 1937, for *Snow Covered Wagons;* California Writers' Guild first prize for poem, 1937; Browning Society of San Francisco first prize for poem, 1962; Stephen Vincent Benet Narrative Poetry Award, 1969, for poem, "Chicago: Narrative of a City."

WRITINGS: Poems of a Child (introduction by Richard Le Gallienne), Harper, 1904; *The Dance of Youth, and Other Poems*, Sherman French & Co., 1917; *Snow Covered Wagons: A Pioneer Epic*, Macmillan, 1936; *Wolves Against the Moon* (historical novel), Macmillan, 1940; *The Old California Trail* (nonfiction), Caxton, 1945; *Spectacular San Franciscans*, Dutton, 1950; *Girl with Ocelot, and Other Poems*, Humphries, 1964. Contributor to *Atlantic, Yale Review, Harper's, Poetry, California Historical Society Quarterly, California Folklore Quarterly*, and other periodicals.

SIDELIGHTS: Mrs. Altrocchi began writing verse at the age of six, and had published a book by the time she was eleven. Her major interests were travel, and reading on literary, historical, and anthropological subjects. She wrote: "Find myself particularly happy in Ireland, Italy, Greece, and the Aegean Islands. Have always lived within the sound of the chapel-chimes of some great university (University of Chicago, Brown, Vassar and the University of California at Berkeley) and can imagine no other life more interesting."

BIOGRAPHICAL/CRITICAL SOURCES: Harper's, September, 1902; Gertrude Atherton, *My San Francisco*, Bobbs, 1946; Ernest E. Leisy, *The American Historical Novel*, University of Oklahoma Press, 1950; *San Francisco Chronicle*, November 24, 1964, page 22.

(Died November 23, 1972)

* * *

AMBROSE, Eric (Samuel) 1908-
(Christopher Rennie, Edgar Vance, Esor B. MacIre)

PERSONAL: Born May 9, 1908, in London, England; son of Philip (a schoolmaster) and Eve Rebecca (Morgan) Ambrose; married Sally Emanuel, March 11, 1936; children: Jill (Mrs. David Bernstein). *Education:* University College, London, B.A., 1933. *Office:* "Maccab," The Ridgeway, Mill Hill, London N.W.7, England.

CAREER: Consultant on domestic architecture, London, England; architectural critic and writer. Consultant, Odhams Press Ltd. and Commercial Plastics Ltd. Director, Eric Ambrose Productions Ltd., London. Architectural advisor to an advertising agency and honorary architect for a youth organization; assessor for architectural competitions. Occasional examiner and representative to British Standards Committees, Royal Institute of British Architects. *Military service:* Royal Engineers (Bomb Disposal), 1939-45; became captain. *Member:* Royal Institute of British Architects (fellow), Institute of Arbitrators (fellow), Arts Club (London), Press Golfing Society, Old Stooges Chapter (past master), Rogues and Vagabonds Society (London; founder; first president). *Awards, honors:* Bronze medal, London Rococo Society, 1937.

WRITINGS: Know Your House, Thames & Hudson, 1954; *A New Approach to Criticism*, The Builder, 1961; *History of the Architectural Competition*, The Builder, 1962.

Radio plays: "Apothecary in Tir na Nog," first broadcast by Radio Eirann, 1948; "The Man Who Died," first broadcast by Radio Eirann, 1950; "The Man Who Was Tomorrow," first broadcast by Radio Eirann, 1952.

Television plays: "The Dullards," "Glad Did I Live." Contributor of short stories to *Evening Standard Great Short Stories, Carlton's Father, The Coward, Beyond the Wall*, and *Architecture Smells*. Contributor of short stories and articles to British newspapers and magazines and of articles on thermal isolation to Spanish publications.

AVOCATIONAL INTERESTS: Photography.

* * *

AMES, Van Meter 1898-

PERSONAL: Born July 9, 1898, in De Soto, Iowa; son of Edward Scribner and Mabel (Van Meter) Ames; married Betty Breneman, June 12, 1930; children: Sanford Scribner, Christine (Mrs. Judson E. Cornish), Damaris. *Education:* University of Chicago, Ph.B., 1919, Ph.D., 1924. *Home:* 448 Warren Ave., Cincinnati, Ohio. *Office:* University of Cincinnati, Cincinnati, Ohio.

CAREER: University of Cincinnati, Cincinnati, Ohio, 1925—, began as instructor, became professor of philosophy, Obed J. Wilson Professor of Ethics, 1960—, head of philosophy department, 1959—. Visiting professor at Cornell University, 1931, University of Texas, 1934-35, University of Hawaii, 1947-48, Faculte des Lettres, University of Aix-Marseille, 1949, Columbia University, 1957. *Member:* American Philosophical Association (president of Western division, 1959-60), American Humanist Association, American Society for Aesthetics (president, 1961-62), *Awards, honors:* Rockefeller grantee, France, 1948; fellow, University of Cincinnati Graduate School, 1957; Fulbright research professor in philosophy, University of Komazawa, Tokyo, 1956-59.

WRITINGS: Aesthetics of the Novel, University of Chicago Press, 1928, reprinted, Gordian, 1966; *Introduction to Beauty*, Harper, 1931, reprinted, Books for Libraries, 1968: *Out of Iowa* (poetry), Henry Harrison, 1936; *Proust and Santayana: The Aesthetic Way of Life*, Willett, Clark, 1937, reprinted , Russell, 1964; *Andre Gide*, New Directions, 1947; (with Max Schoen and H. G. Schrickel) *Understanding the World*, Harper, 1947; (editor) *Beyond Theology: The Autobiography of Edward Schribner Ames*, University of Chicago Press, 1959; (with wife, Betty Breneman Ames) *Japan and Zen*, University of Cincinnati, 1961; *Zen and American Thought*, Univeristy of Hawaii Press, 1962.

* * *

ANDERS, Edith (Mary) England 1899-
(E.M. England)

PERSONAL: Born July 1, 1899, in Townsville, Queensland, Australia daughter of John (a merchant) and Jane (Kelly) England; married Schomberg Montagu Bertie (a farmer), September 5, 1922; married second husband, Harry Anders (a grazier, now retired), March 15, 1941; children: (first marriage) Caroline (Mrs. Gordon Ross), Rose Patricia (Mrs. Harold E. Kleinschmidt). *Education:* Trinity College of Music, London, England, diploma in music; also received a commercial education. *Religion:* Anglican. *Home:* 26 Hooper St., Ipswich, Queensland, Australia.

CAREER: Queensland Times, Ipswich, Queensland, Australia, social editor, beginning, 1959; free-lance writer. *Member:* Society of Australian Authors, Fellowship of Writers (Brisbane); Business and Professional Womens' Club and Countrywomen's Associaion (both Ipswich). *Awards, honors:*—All for poetry: Jubilee Medal (England), 1937; Capel Boake Award, 1948; Coronation Medal (England), 1953; Queensland Centenary Award, 1960; Mattara Festival Award, 1962; Fellowship of Australian Writers, 1964.

WRITINGS—Under name E. M. England: *The Happy Monarch* (verse), Carter Watson, 1927; *The Sealed Temple* (novel), Fenland Press, 1933; *Queensland Days* (verse), Dymocks, 1944; *Tornado* (historical short stories), Worker Press, 1944; *Where the Turtles Dance* (novel), Dymocks, 1950; (with Ray Albion) *Road Going North* (novel), Dymocks, 1952; *House of Bondage* (novel), Dymocks, 1954. Contributor of short stories, serials, and verse to magazines and anthologies.

WORK IN PROGRESS: A nature novel and an autobiography.

AVOCATIONAL INTERESTS: Australian pioneering period, Australian fauna, Polynesian voyages, and history of the American Indian.

* * *

ANDERSEN, Arlow W. 1906-

PERSONAL: Born January 13, 1906, in Neenah, Wis.; son of Carl Andreas (a Methodist minister) and Rakel (Trockstad) Andersen; married Katherine Kolberg, November 23, 1938; children: Arlow W., Jr. *Education:* University of Minnesota, B.A., 1929; Northwestern University, M.A., 1939, Ph.D., 1942. *Office:* Department of History, Wisconsin State University, Oshkosh, Wis. 54901.

CAREER: Evanston Collegiate Institute, Evanston, Ill., teacher of history, 1934-42; Jamestown College, Jamestown, N.D., professor of history, 1946-62; McMurry College, Abilene,. Tex., professor history, 1962-64; Wisconsin State University, Oshkosh, associate professor, 1964-66, professor of history, 1966—. *Military service:* U.S. Army Air Forces, 1943-46; served in Japan, 1945-46. *Member:* American Historical Association, Organization of American Historians, Society for the Advancement of Scandinavian Study, Immigrant History Group, Norwegian-American Historical Association, Wisconsin State Historical Association. *Awards, honors:* Fulbright research scholar at University of Oslo, 1960-61.

WRITINGS: The Immigrant Takes His Stand: The Norwegian-American Press and Public Affairs, 1847-1872, Norwegian-American Historical Association, 1953; *The Salt of the Earth: A History of Norwegian-Danish Methodism in America*, Parthenon, 1962.

WORK IN PROGRESS: Assembling results of research in Norway on reactions of the Norwegian press to American government and politics, 1875 to 1905; a book on Norwegian and Danish immigrants to America, for Twayne.

* * *

ANDERSON, Courtney 1906-

PERSONAL: Born December 22, 1906, in Jamestown, N.Y.; son of Alfred A. (a manufacturer) and Alice (Sundell) Anderson; married Catherine Bullock (a nursery school teacher), June 17, 1931; children: James. *Education:* Dartmouth College, A.B., 1931; Western Reserve University (now Case Western Reserve University), M.A., 1934. *Home:* 12427 Rochedale Lane, Los Angeles, Calif. 90049. *Agent:* Reece Halsey, 8733 Sunset Blvd., Los Angeles, Calif. 90069. *Office:* Elba Corp., P.O. Box 7085, Park Hill Station, Denver, Colo. 80207.

CAREER: Fenn College (now Cleveland State University), Cleveland, Ohio, assistant professor of English, 1931-36; writer for Jam Handy Organization, Detroit, Mich., and Caravel Films, New York, N.Y., 1937-42; free-lance writer, largely of scripts for informational motion pictures, 1945-65; Elba Corp. (audiovisual sales systems), Denver,

Colo., vice-president and director of research and product development, 1965. Lecturer on alcoholism, California State College, Los Angeles, 1964-66; film consultant, Dartmouth College. Chairman of committee on information and research, Los Angeles County Commission on Alcoholism. *Military service:* U.S. Army Air Forces, writer and motion picture technical officer, 1942-45; became first lieutenant.

MEMBER: American Association for the Advancement of Science, Writers Guild of America (West), National Association of Science Writers, Essex Institute. *Awards, honors:* Golden Eagle Award of Council on International Nontheatrical Events, for film, "With Care and Concern"; second prize in general public service films classification, National Visual Presentation Association, for "Television in Education"; both of those films plus "The Hardesty Case" were selected by National Association of Manufacturers to represent American industry at film festivals in London and Madrid.

WRITINGS: To the Golden Shore (biography), Little, Brown, 1956; (contributor) Russell Hitt, editor, *Heroic Colonial Christians*, Lippincott, 1966.

Films: "Cancer in Children" and "Cancer of the Stomach," for American Cancer Society; "Better Your Odds for a Longer Life," for American Heart Association; "With Care and Concern," for Upjohn Co.; "Television in Education," for American Telephone & Telegraph Co.; "The Hardesty Case," Ford Motor Co.; "The File on Henry Royall," for Bank of America; four films on Arizona, including "Arizona Showcase"; and more than 140 other films for General Motors, Prudential Life, Texaco, B. F. Goodrich, U.S. Department of State, and various corporations and organizations.

WORK IN PROGRESS: A book on Jonathan Edwards, for Lippincott; research on alcoholism for a possible book; an American novel, set roughly in the period, 1925-45.

SIDELIGHTS: Anderson told *CA:* "Avocation is really Man—how he got here, what he is, where going. Biographies are more or less buds off this basic interest.... No foreign travel, but average 50,000-100,000 miles a year in U.S."

*   *   *

ANDERSON, Madeleine Paltenghi   1899-
(Madeleine Paltenghi)

PERSONAL: Born November 20, 1899, in New York, N.Y.; daughter of Joseph and Florence (Locke) Paltenghi; married Clarence William Anderson (an artist and author), December 24, 1944; children: (prior marriage) Charles Emile Ruchstuhl. *Education:* Studied at Appleton Academy, at Emerson School of Art, Boston, at Art Students League, New York, at Parsons School of Fine and Applied Arts, New York and Paris, and Ecole Delacroix, Paris; studied voice privately in New York and Paris. *Religion:* Roman Catholic. *Home:* Windy Ledge, Mason, N.H.

CAREER: Onetime song recitalist, presenting concert programs of French, Spanish, Russian, and Italian folk songs at music centers and colleges; poet, and writer of children's books. *Member:* New Hampshire Society of Poetry, Boston Authors Club, Professional Women's Club (Boston).

*WRITINGS—*Children's books, under name Madeleine Paltenghi: *Honey the City Bear*, Garden City Books, 1936; *Remus Goes to Town*, Grosset, 1937; *Honey on a Raft*, Garden City Books, 1938; *Rumpus Rabbit*, Harper, 1940.

Poetry (illustrated in silverpoint by her husband, C. W. Anderson): *Silverpoint*, Wake-Brook, 1962; *Under One Bough*, Wake-Brook, 1965.

SIDELIGHTS: Madeleine Anderson is fluent in French; she speaks some Italian and Spanish.

AVOCATIONAL INTERESTS: Horses, cooking.

*   *   *

ANDRADE, E(dward) N(eville) da C(osta)   1887-1971

PERSONAL: Born December 27, 1887, in London, England; son of Henry S. da Costa (a businessman) and Amy Eliza (Davis) Andrade; married Katherine Barbara Evans (died, 1951); married Mona Wilkinson; children: (first marriage) Trevor John, Edward Anthony. *Education:* University College, London, B.Sc. (first class honors); University of Heidelberg, Ph.D. (summa cum laude); additional study at University of Manchester. *Agent:* David Higham Associates Ltd., 5-8 Lower John St., London WIR 4HA, England. *Office:* Imperial College of Science, London S.W.7, England.

CAREER: Artillery College, Woolwich, England, professor of physics, 1919-26; University of London, London, England, Quain Professor of Physics, 1928-50; Royal Institution, London, director, 1950-52; Imperial College of Science, London, senior research fellow, 1955-71. Wilkins and Rutherford Lecturer, Royal Society. Past Master, Glass Sellers' Company. *Military service:* British Army, 1914-19; became captain; mentioned in dispatches.

MEMBER: Royal Society (fellow; member of council, 1942-44), Institute of Physics (founder fellow), Physical Society (president, 1943-45), Institut de France Academie des Sciences (corresponding), Societe Francaise de Physique (honorary), Athenaeum Club, Chelsea Arts Club, Savage Club. *Awards, honors:* LL.D., University of Edinburgh; D.Sc., University of Durham; Hughes Medal of Royal Society; Mitchell Gold Medal; Grand Medaille Osmond of Societe Francaise de Metallurgie; Holweck Prize of Physical Society and Societe Francaise de Physique; Chevalier Legion d'Honneur (France).

WRITINGS: The Structure of the Atom, G. Bell, 1923, 3rd edition, revised and enlarged, Van Nostrand, 1927; *Airs–for the Hautbois and Other Instruments* (poems), Cecil Palmer, 1924; *The Atom*, Benn, 1927, Farrar & Rinehart, 1928, new edition, revised, Thomas Nelson, 1936; *What Is the Atom*, Harper, 1927; *Engines*, Harcourt, 1928; (author of introductory essay) Titus Lucretius Carus, *T. Lucreti Cari de rerum natura libri sex*, Volume II, Cambridge University Press, 1928; *An Hour of Physics*, Lippincott, 1930 (published in England as *The Mechanism of Nature: Being a Simple Approach to Modern Views on the Structure of Matter and Radiation*, G. Bell, 1930), revised edition published as *An Approach to Modern Physics*, G. Bell, 1956, Doubleday, 1957, 3rd edition, G. Bell, 1962; (with Julian Huxley) *An Introduction to Science* (juvenile), seven books, Basil Blackwell, 1932-35, Harper, 1935-36; *The New Chemistry*, G. Bell, 1936.

(With wife, Mona Andrade) *The Answer Is*, G. Bell, 1941; *Poems and Songs*, Macmillan, 1949; *Isaac Newton*, Chanticleer, 1950; (author of introductory reading guide) *Science*, International University Society, 1952, revised edition published as *Science: A Course of Selected Reading by Authorities*, International University Society, 1957, Philosophical Library, 1960; *From Small Beginnings*, Macmillan, 1954; *Sir Isaac Newton*, Doubleday, 1954.

A Brief History of the Royal Society, Royal Society, 1960; *Physics for the Modern World*, Barnes & Noble, 1962; *Rutherford and the Nature of the Atom*, Doubleday, 1964. Editor, "International Textbooks of Exact Science," G. Bell, 1926—; editor for physics, *Encyclopaedia Britannica*, 14th edition. Contributor of scientific papers to published proceedings and journals in England and abroad.

WORK IN PROGRESS: Experimental research on the creep of metals, metal grains growth, and allied phenomena; memoirs.

SIDELIGHTS: Andrade's books have been translated into Burmese, Polish, French, Italian, Dutch, Danish, and Swedish. *Avocational interests:* History of science, especially in the seventeenth and eighteenth centuries.

BIOGRAPHICAL/CRITICAL SOURCES: New Scientist, June 8, 1961; John H. Durston's introduction to *Rutherford and the Nature of the Atom*, Doubleday, 1964.

(Died June 6, 1971)

*   *   *

ANDREWS, Mark Edwin 1903-

PERSONAL: Born October 17, 1903, in Houston, Tex.; son of Jesse and Celeste (Bujac) Andrews; married Marguerite McLellan (died, 1946); married Lavone Dickensheets (an architect), July 23, 1948; children: (first marriage) Marguerite McLellan; (second marriage) Mark Edwin III. *Education:* Princeton University, A.B. (magna cum laude), 1927; University of Colorado, graduate courses, 1931-34; South Texas College, LL.B. (magna cum laude), 1934. *Religion:* Episcopalian. *Home:* 8 Shadder Way, Houston, Tex.; Sea Wynde, Fisher's Island, N.Y.; River House, New York, N.Y.; and Knappogue Castle, New Market on Fergus, County Clare, Ireland. *Office:* 100 Bank of the Southwest Building, Houston, Tex. 77002.

CAREER: Andrews, Loop & Co., president, 1928-34; South Texas College, Houston, member of law faculty, 1934-42; U.S. Government, Washington, D.C. chief of procurement for the Navy, 1945-46, assistant secretary of the Navy, 1947-49; president of Ryan & Andrews and Westmoreland Manufacturing Co., both Houston, Tex., 1936-42, and of M. E. Andrews Ltd. and Ancon Oil & Gas, Inc. (oil and gas production), both Houston, Tex., 1951—. Chairman of the board, Dixel Manufacturing Co. (oil field equipment and automobile parts), Houston; director and member of advisory committee, Bank of the Southwest, Houston. *Military service:* U.S. Naval Reserve, active duty, 1942-46; became captain; received Legion of Merit.

WRITINGS: Buying a Navy, U.S. Navy, 1946; *Wildcatter's Handbook*, privately printed, 1952; *Law versus Equity in "The Merchant of Venice"*, University of Colorado Press, 1965. Contributor of articles to law journals.

*   *   *

ANDREWS, (Charles) Robert Douglas (Hardy) 1908-
(Robert D. Andrews, Robert Douglas, Douglas Hardy)

PERSONAL: Born October 19, 1908, in Effingham, Kan.; son of Charles R. (a physician and surgeon) and Mary (Hedding) Andrews; married Irene Colman, April 25, 1942; children: Colman Robert, Ann-Merry. *Education:* Attended University of Minnesota, Northwestern University, and University of Chicago. *Politics:* Independent. *Religion:* Roman Catholic. *Office:* Librafilms, Suite 333, 139 South Beverly Dr., Beverly Hills, Calif. 94712.

CAREER: Reporter, then city editor for *Minneapolis Journal*, Minneapolis, Minn., and reporter, then editor of *Midweek* for *Chicago Daily News*, Chicago, Ill., 1923-40; writer-producer for radio, 1930-47; author of books and short stories, 1929—; writer-producer for motion pictures, 1936—, for television, 1950—. Film production executive in India and Egypt. Consultant to U.S. firms in Far East, 1953—; consultant to film companies on overseas production. California lay consultant, 38th International Eucharistic Congress. Lecturer, television commentator. *Member:* Writers Guild (founding), Academy of Motion Picture Arts and Sciences, Academy of TV Arts and Sciences, Authors Club, Rotary (honorary), Ojai Valley Country Club.

WRITINGS: One Girl Found, Grosset, 1930; *Three Girls Lost*, Grosset, 1930; *The Stolen Husband*, Grosset, 1931; *Windfall*, John Day, 1931, published as *If I Had a Million*, Grosset, 1932; (with Anne Ashenhurst) *Just Plain Bill, His Story: The Truth About a Man Millions Love*, McKay, 1935; *Burning Gold*, Doubleday, Doran, 1945; *Legend of a Lady: The Story of Rita Martin*, Coward, 1949; *Great Day in the Morning*, Coward, 1950; *A Corner of Chicago* (autobiographical), Little, Brown, 1963; *The Unbeliever* (life of Buddha), Doubleday, c.1963; *A Lamp for India: The Story of Madame Pandit*, Prentice-Hall, 1967. Also author of a play, "Rebel in the Ranks."

Screenplays: (with Joseph Hoffman and Jonathan Finn) "Jailbreak," Warner Brothers, 1936; (with William Jacobs) "Isle of Fury" (based on *The Narrow Corner*, a novel by W. Somerset Maugham), Warner Brothers, 1936; "The Longest Night" (based on "The Whispering Window," a story by Cortland Fitzsimmons), M-G-M, 1936; (with David Silverstein and John Twist) "Flight from Glory," R.K.O., 1937; (with Karl Brown) Gangster's Boy," Monogram, 1938; (with Martin Mooney) "Mutiny in the Big House," Monogram, 1939; "Streets of New York," Monogram, 1939.

(With Howard J. Green and Barry Trivers) "Dreaming Out Loud," R.K.O., 1940; (with Joseph Carole and Harvey Gates) "Men Without Souls," Columbia, 1940; (with Robert Chapin and Carole) "Babies for Sale," Columbia, 1940; "Girls of the Road," Columbia, 1940; "Island of Doomed Men," Columbia, 1940; (with Brown) "Before I Hang," Columbia, 1940; (with Milton Gunzberg and William Sloane) "The Devil Commands," Columbia, 1941; (with Edmund L. Hartmann) "Sweethearts of the Campus," Columbia, 1941; (with Stanley Roberts) "Under Age," Columbia, 1941; "Road to Happiness" (based on "First Performance," a story by Matt Taylor), Monogram, 1942; (with Lewis Foster and Frank Ryan) "The Mayor of 44th Street" (based on a story of Luther Davis and John Cleveland), R.K.O., 1942; (adapter) "Sherlock Holmes and the Voice of Terror," Universal, 1942; (with Sam Fuller) "Power of the Press," Columbia, 1942; "Bataan," M-G-M, 1943; (with George Bruce) "Salute to the Marines," M-G-M, 1943; (with Deela Dunning) "The Hairy Ape" (based on the play by Eugene O'Neill), United Artists, 1944; (with Michael Kanin, Ring Lardner, Jr., and Alexander Esway) "The Cross of Lorraine," M-G-M, 1944; (with Richard Weil and Ted Thomas) "Talk About a Lady," Columbia, 1946; (with Winston Miller) "Relentless" (based on the novel *Three Were Thoroughbreds* by Kenneth Perkins), Columbia, 1948; (with Ben Maddow and Borden Chase) "The Man from Colorado," Columbia, 1948; (with Tamara Hovey) "Bagdad," Universal, 1949; (with Paul Short) "Bad Boy," Allied Artists, 1949; (with

Charles Grayson, George W. George, and George Slavin) "The Woman on Pier 13," R.K.O., 1949.

(With Harry Essex and Leonard Lee) "Wyoming Mail," Universal, 1950; (with Karl Kamb) "The Kid from Texas," Universal, 1950; (with Samuel Fuller) "The Tanks Are Coming," Warner Brothers, 1951; (with Twist) "Best of the Badmen," R.K.O., 1951; (with Louis Solomon and Johnston McCulley) "Mark of the Renegade," Universal, 1951; (with Harold Shumate and Richard Wormser) "The Half-Breed," R.K.O., 1952; (with Mel Shavelson, Jack Rose, and Douglas Morrow) "Trouble Along the Way," Warner Brothers, 1953; (with Christopher Knopf) "The King's Thief," M-G-M, 1955; (with Robert Smith) "Girls' Town," M-G-M, 1959.

(With John Guillerman) "Tarzan Goes to India" (produced in India), M-G-M, 1962. Also author and co-producer of "Wa Islamah," produced in Egypt, in Arabic and Italian. Also writer of documentary films for Department of State, written and produced in Pakistan.

Also writer of television scripts for "Ford Theater," "Family Theater," "Thriller," "87th Precinct," "Barbara Stanwyck Theater," "The Great Adventure," and other network programs. Originated and wrote radio serials, including "Just Plain Bill," "Helen Trent," "Jack Armstrong," and "Ma Perkins." Contributor to *Liberty, Ladies' Home Journal, This Week, Pakistan Quarterly, Times of India, Los Angeles Times, Catholic Digest,* and other publications.

WORK IN PROGRESS: They Shipped Me East of Suez, a journal of personal experiences during 200,000 miles of working travel in Egypt, Lebanon, Pakistan, India, and Southeast Asia.

SIDELIGHTS: Andrews has traveled ("never as a tourist") more than 250,000 miles since 1953. "Vocation and avocation," he adds, "merged in [my] effort to learn from people, not from politicos, in newly independent nations east of Suez. . . . Harry Hansen says the subjective is my stock in trade. I'll settle for that." Concerning the length of his full name, he told *CA* that James Thurber claimed to have heard it [and] said that "Charles Robert Douglas Hardy Andrews is not a person, but a syndicate!"

Great Day in the Morning was filmed by R.K.O. in 1956.

BIOGRAPHICAL/CRITICAL SOURCES: James Thurber, *The Beast in Me,* Harcourt, 1948; *Punch,* November 15, 1967.†

*   *   *

ANGELL, (Ralph) Norman   1872(?)-1967

PERSONAL: Name legally changed from Ralph Norman Angell Lane; Born December 26, 1872(?), in Holbeach, Lincolnshire, England; son of Thomas Angell (owner of a group of stores) and Mary (Brittain) Lane. *Education:* Attended schools in England and France, and University of Geneva. *Politics:* Socialist in earlier years; Liberal, then non-party. *Religion:* Humanist, agnostic, *Home and office:* Stone Cottage, Fernden Hill, Haslemere, Surrey, England.

CAREER: Emigrated to America at the age of seventeen, working as farm and ranch hand, teamster, homesteader, and reporter for *San Francisco Chronicle, Philadelphia Ledger,* and other newspapers; returned to Europe in 1898 as correspondent for U.S. newspapers; became editor of *Galignani's Messenger* (English-language newspaper), Paris, France, 1899-1903, staff member of *Paris Eclair,* 1903-05, and general manager of Paris edition of Lord Northcliffe's *Daily Mail,* 1905-14; first attracted political attention with *The Great Illusion,* 1909, and when the Garton Foundation was created to promote his thesis for international peace, he took up residence in London, England, 1914, lectured and wrote; editor of *Foreign Affairs,* London, England, 1928-31; Labour member of Parliament for North Bradford, 1929-31; resigned from party politics, 1931, and devoted his remaining years to writing and lecturing on behalf of reason in international affairs. Lecturer on tours in United States, France, and Germany. Member of council, Royal Institute of International Affairs, 1928-42; founding member, Union of Democratic Control. Inventor of "Money Game," a card game that teaches the principles of economics and banking. *Awards, honors:* Knighted, 1931; Nobel Peace Prize, 1933.

WRITINGS: Patriotism Under Three Flags: A Plea for Rationalism in Politics, T. Fisher Unwin, 1903; *Europe's Optical Illusion,* Simpkin, Marshall, 1908, greatly expanded version published as *The Great Illusion: A Study of the Relation of Military Power in Nations to Their Economic and Social Advantage,* Putnam, 1910, 4th edition published as *The Great Illusion: A Study of the Relation of Military Power to National Advantage,* 1913, abridged edition published as *The Great Illusion–Now,* Penguin, 1938, early edition reprinted with A. T. Mahan, *The Place of Force in the International Relations of States,* as *Armaments and Arbitration,* Garland, 1972.

The Foundations of International Polity, Heinemann, 1912, published as *Arms and Industry: A Study of the Foundations of International Polity,* Putnam, 1914; *Peace Treaties and the Balkan War,* H. Marshall, 1912; *War and the Workers,* National Labour Press, 1913; *Prussianism and Its Destruction,* Heinemann, 1914; *The Problems of the War–and the Peace: A Handbook for Students,* Heinemann, 1914; *America and the New World State: A Plea for American Leadership in International Organisation,* Putnam, 1915; *The World's Highway,* George H. Doran, 1915; *The Dangers of Half Preparedness,* Putnam, 1916: *War Aims: The Need for a Parliament of the Allies,* Headley Bros., 1917; *Why Freedom Matters,* National Council for Civil Liberties, 1917, reissued, Penquin, 1940; *The Political Conditions of Allied Success: A Protective Union of the Democracies,* Putnam, 1918; *The British Revolution and the American Democracy,* B.W. Huebsch (New York), 1919; *The Peace Treaty and the Economic Chaos of Europe,* Swarthmore Press, 1919.

The Fruits of Victory: A Sequel to "The Great Illusion", Century, 1921, reprinted, Garland, 1972; *The Press and the Organization of Society,* Labour Publishing, 1922; *If Britain Is to Live,* Putnam, 1923; *Foreign Policy and Our Daily Bread,* Collins, 1925; *Human Nature and the Peace Problem,* Collins, 1925; *Must Britain Travel the Moscow Road?,* Unwin Bros., 1926; *The Public Mind; Its Disorders: Its Exploitation,* Noel Douglas, 1926, Dutton, 1927; *The Money Game: How to Play It,* Dent, 1928, published as *The Money Game, Explaining Fundamental Finance: A New Instrument of Economic Education,* Dutton, 1929; *The Story of Money,* Garden City Publishing, 1929, F. A. Stokes, 1924.

(With Harold Wright) *Can Governments Cure Unemployment?,* Dent, 1931; *From Chaos to Control* (Halley Stewart Lecture), Century, 1932; *The Unseen Assassins,* Harper, 1932; (contributor) Leonard S. Woolf, editor, *The Intelligent Man's Way to Prevent War,* Gollancz, 1933, reprinted, Garland, 1973; *The Menace to Our National Defence,* Hamish Hamilton, 1934; *Peace and the Plain*

Man, Harper, 1935 (published in England as *Preface to Peace: A Guide for the Plain Man*, Hamish Hamilton); *The Mystery of Money* (also issued under title *The Money Mystery: An Explanation for Beginners*), Dent, 1936; *This Have and Have-not Business*, Hamish Hamilton, 1936; *Raw Materials, Population Pressure and War*, World Peace Foundation (New York), 1936; *The Defence of the Empire*, Hamish Hamilton, 1937, Appleton, 1938; (with others) *Problems of Peace, Twelfth Series: Geneva and the Drift to War*, Geneva Institute of International Relations, 1938, reprinted, Books for Libraries, 1970; *Peace with the Dictators?*, Harper, 1938; *Must It Be War*, Labour Book Service, 1939; *For What Do We Fight?*, Hamish Hamilton, 1939, Harper, 1940; (with Dorothy Buxon) *You and the Refugee: The Morals and Economics of the Problem*, Penguin, 1939.

America's Dilemma, Harper, 1941; *Let the People Know* (Book-of-the Month Club selection), Viking, 1943; *The Steep Places*, Hamish Hamilton, 1947, Harper, 1948.

After All (autobiography), Hamish Hamilton, 1951, Farrar, Straus, 1952; *Defence and the English-Speaking Role*, Pall Mall, 1958. Also author of pamphlets and over 2000 articles.

WORK IN PROGRESS: A "farewell book," tentatively titled *Political Sickness in the Nuclear Age*.

SIDELIGHTS: Sir Norman Angell's life-long (and often controversial) battle for lucidity in international relations did not leave him bitter. In his autobiography, written as he neared eighty, he said that he would do it (the crusading) all over again if he had to. And among the collected cuttings on his books, selected letters, and tributes, chosen by him for private distribution to personal friends, there is a message from Ezra Pound. It roasts Angell as an exploiter of pacificism "who has made money and a career bleating about pacifism but contributed nothing to the knowledge of the economic causes of war," and concludes, "And may hell rot your bones."

Sir Norman commented on his books: "The theme running through most of the published books is that collective decisions (those made by nations, states, etc.) are less rational than those made when the individual acts on his individual responsibility.... But the books also insist that the political failure of our cultures, as demonstrated by the persistence of war throughout all ages, could be corrected by better use of the cultural and educational means now available in such abundance."

When he was ninety, Sir Norman undertook a two-month tour of the United States, lecturing on education for the nuclear age; and he flew to New York several months before his death, to discuss a revision of his autobiography.

The Great Illusion has sold about two million copies in twenty-five languages.

BIOGRAPHICAL/CRITICAL SOURCES: Norman Angell, *After All*, Hamish Hamilton, 1951, Farrar, Straus, 1952; *Listener*, January 10, 1963; *Guardian*, February 19, 1963.

(Died October 7, 1967)

* * *

ANSBACHER, Heinz L(udwig) 1904-

PERSONAL: Born October 21, 1904, in Frankfurt am Main, Germany; son of Max (a banker) and Emilie (Dinkelspiel) Ansbacher; married Rowena Ripin, June 23, 1934; children: Max, Benjamin, Theodore, Charles. *Education:* Columbia University, Ph.D., 1937. *Home:* 130 East Ave., Burlington, Vt. 05401. *Office:* Department of Psychology, University of Vermont, Burlington, Vt. 05401.

CAREER: Works Progress Administration, New York, N.Y., psychologist, 1938-39; Yeshiva University, New York, N.Y., instructor in psychology, 1939-40; Brown University, Providence, R.I., assistant editor of psychological abstracts, 1940-43; Brooklyn College (now Brooklyn College of the City University of New York), Brooklyn, N.Y., instructor in psychology, 1945-46; University of Vermont, Burlington, 1946-70, began as assistant professor, became professor of psychology, professor emeritus, 1970—. Field service consultant, U.S. Office of Research and Development, 1945-46. Visiting associate professor, Duke University, 1946; Fulbright lecturer, University of Kiel, Kiel, Germany, 1954-55. *Member:* American Psychological Association (fellow), American Society of Adlerian Psychology (former president), Sigma Xi. *Awards, honors:* U.S. Department of State grant, 1950; U.S. Public Health Service research grant, 1967-68.

WRITINGS—Editor: (With wife, Rowena Ansbacher) *The Individual Psychology of Alfred Adler*, Basic Books, 1956; (with Rowena Ansbacher) Alfred Adler, *Superiority and Social Interest*, Northwestern University Press, 1964; (and author of introduction) Alfred Adler, *The Science of Living*, Doubleday, 1969.

Contributor: N. L. Farberow and E. S. Shneidman, editors, *The Cry for Help*, McGraw, 1961; B. B. Wolman and E. Nagel, editors, *Scientific Psychology: Principles and Approaches*, Basic Books, 1965; *International Encyclopedia of the Social Sciences*, Crowell, 1968. Editor, *Journal of Individual Psychology* (publication of American Society of Adlerian Psychology), 1957—.

* * *

ANSLINGER, Harry Jacob 1892-

PERSONAL: Born May 20, 1892, in Altoona, Pa; son of Robert John and Christina (Fladtt) Anslinger, *Education:* Pennsylvania State University, student, 1913-15; American University, LL.B., 1930. *Politics:* "Unaffiliated." *Religion:* Protestant. *Home and office:* 612 Pine St., Hollidaysburg, Pa. 16648.

CAREER: Served in U.S. Government, 1918-63, under nine presidents; held consular posts in The Netherlands, Germany, Venezuela, and the Bahamas, 1918-26; Treasury Department, chief of Division of Foreign Control, 1926-29, assistant commissioner of prohibition, 1929-30, commissioner, Bureau of Narcotics, 1930-63. U.S. representative at League of Nations conferences on narcotics, and on United Nations Narcotic Drugs Commission. *Member:* Police, pharmaceutical, and allied associations; Dacor House (Washington, D.C.). *Awards, honors:* Proctor Gold Medal, 1952; selected as one of ten outstanding career men in federal government service by National Civil Service League, 1958; Alumni Recognition Award, American University, 1959; distinguished alumnus award, Pennsylvania State University, 1959; LL.D., University of Maryland; Remington Medal; Alexander Hamilton Medal.

WRITINGS: (With William F. Tompkins) *The Traffic in Narcotics*, Funk, 1953; (with Will Oursler) *The Murderers: The Story of the Narcotic Gangs*, Farrar, Straus, 1961; (with J. Dennis Gregory) *The Protectors: The Heroic Story of the Narcotics Agents, Citizens, and Officials in Their Unending, Unsung Battles Against Organized Crime in*

America and Abroad, Farrar Straus, 1964. Contributor of articles to *Reader's Digest, Saturday Evening Post, FBI Bulletin, United Nations Bulletin,* and police and detective magazines.†

*   *   *

ANSTEY, Vera (Powell) 1889-

PERSONAL: Born January 3, 1889, in Reigate, Surrey, England; daughter of James (a merchant) and Mary S. (Higginbothan) Powell; married Percy Anstey, 1913 (died, 1920); children: Mary (Mrs. Harry Henry), Edgar. *Education:* Studied at Hoch Conservatorium, Frankfurt am Main, Germany, for two years; Bedford College, London, Diploma in Public Health, 1913; London School of Economics and Political Science, B.Sc. (first class honors), 1913, D.Sc., 1929. *Home:* Startforth Mews, The Green, Esher, Surrey, England.

CAREER: Lived in Bombay, India, 1914-20; University of London, London School of Economics and Political Science, London, England, member of academic staff, 1921-61, part-time member, 1961-65, chairman of admitting deans and tutors, later chairman of tutors only, 1938-64, Sir Ernest Cassel Reader in Commerce for the University, 1941-54, dean of Faculty of Economics, 1950-54; retired, 1964. Member, Royal Commission on Taxation of Profits and Income, 1950-55. *Member:* Royal Economic Society. *Awards, honors:* Fellow, London School of Economics and Political Science, 1965.

WRITINGS: The Trade of the Indian Ocean, Longmans, Green, 1929; *The Economic Development of India*, Longmans, Green, 1929, 4th edition, 1952; (with Ann Martin) *An Introduction to Economics* (for students in India and Pakistan), Allen & Unwin, 1964.

Contributor: Sir John Cumming, editor, *Modern India: A Cooperative Survey*, Oxford University Press, 1931; *India Analysed*, Volume II: *Economic Facts*, Gollancz, 1934; G. E. Hubbard, compiler, *Eastern Industrialization and Its Effects on the West*, Oxford University Press, for Royal Institute of International Affairs, 1935; L. S. S. O'Malley, editor, *Modern India and the West*, Oxford University Press (New York), 1941; P. Lamartine Yates, editor, *Commodity Control*, J. Cape, 1943. Contributor to *Encyclopaedia Britannica.*

SIDELIGHTS: The Economic Development of India has been translated into Japanese and various Indian languages.

*   *   *

APPLEMAN, Roy Edgar 1904-

PERSONAL: Born April 10, 1904, in Columbus, Ohio; son of Lewis Arthur and Anna Christina (Ribble) Appleman; married Irene White, February 8, 1947; children: Anna Christina, Charlotte O., William Minor. *Education:* Ohio State University, A.B., 1928; Yale University, law student, 1932-33; Columbia University, M.A., 1934. *Home:* 1719 Edgewater Pkwy., Hillandale, Silver Spring, Md. 20903.

CAREER: U.S. Government, Washington, D.C., historian with National Park Service, retired, 1970. *Military service:* U.S. Army, 1942-46, 1951-54; became lieutenant colonel; received Commendation Medal and ribbon for service in Okinawa and U.S. Secretary of the Army certificate of appreciation for work on history of the Korean War.

WRITINGS: Abraham Lincoln: From His Own Words and Contemporary Accounts, U.S. Government Printing Office, 1942; (co-author) *Okinawa: The Last Battle* (official

history of Ryukyus campaign), U.S. Department of the Army, 1948; *South to the Naktong, North of the Yalu* (official history of Korean War, June-November, 1950), U.S. Department of the Army, 1960; (co-author) *Great Western Indian Fights*, Doubleday, 1960; (co-author) *The History of the United States Flag: From the Revolution to the Present, Including a Guide to Its Use and Display*, Harper, 1961; *Charlie Seringo, Cowboy Detective*, Potomac Corral, 1968.

WORK IN PROGRESS: The Lewis and Clark Expedition; a book on the Korean War, November, 1950, to July, 1951.

*   *   *

ARDEN, Gothard Everett 1905-

PERSONAL: Born April 29, 1905, in Wausa, Neb.; married Irene M. Erickson, June 28, 1933; children: Janice (Mrs. R. A. Palmer), Eldon Everett. *Education:* University of Denver, B.A., 1930; Augustana Theological Seminary, B.D., 1933; University of Chicago, Ph.D., 1944. *Politics:* Independent. *Home:* 1602 26th St., Rock Island, Ill. 61201. *Office:* Department of Religion, Lutheran School of Theology, 1100 East 55th St., Chicago, Ill. 60615.

CAREER: Teacher of music before ordination as Lutheran minister, 1933; minister of churches in Granville and Chicago, Ill., 1933-44; Lutheran School of Theology, Rock Island, Ill., professor of historical theology, 1945—; Lutheran School of Theology, Chicago, Ill., dean of graduate studies, 1968—. Augustana Lutheran Church, chairman of Commission on Evangelism, 1956-62, of Liturgical Commission, 1957-62; member, Joint Liturgical Commission (Lutheran), 1956-62; member of Commission on Worship, Lutheran Church in America, 1962-64. Lecturer to U.S. military chaplains in Japan, 1959.

WRITINGS—All published by Augustana Press, except as indicated: (Translator with Eric H. Wahlstrom) Gustaf Aulen, *Faith of the Christian Church*, Muhlenberg, 1948; (translator) Sam Ronnegard, *Prairie Shepherd: Lars Paul Esbjoern and the Beginnings of the Augustana Lutheran Church*, 1952; *History of the Illinois Conference*, 1953; *The School of the Prophets: The Background and History of Augustana Theological Seminary, 1860-1960*, 1960; *Meet the Lutherans: Introducing the Lutheran Church in North America*, 1962; *Augustana Heritage: A History of the Augustana Lutheran Church*, 1963; *Four Northern Lights: Men Who Shaped Scandinavian Churches*, Augsburg, 1964; (editor and translator) Eric Norelius, *The Journals of Eric Norelius, a Swedish Missionary on the American Frontier*, Fortress, 1967. Contributor to *New Schaff-Herzog Encyclopedia* and *Lutheran World Encyclopedia.*

WORK IN PROGRESS: A bibliographical guide to the history of the Augustana Lutheran Church, now merged with the Lutheran Church in America; an account and analysis of the significance of frontier preachers.

AVOCATIONAL INTERESTS: Music, especially piano and symphony; painting and photography.

*   *   *

ARGYLE, Aubrey William 1910-

PERSONAL: Born September 27, 1910, in Reading, Berkshire, England; son of William Albert (a tinsmith) and Edith Louie (Burton) Argyle; married Phyllis Lilian Fowler (a ward secretary in a hospital), August 24, 1940; children: Keith John, Sheila Mary, Irene Joy. *Education:* Oriel College, Oxford, B.A., 1932, M.A., 1937, B.D., 1939. *Politics:*

Socialist. *Home:* 13 Knolles Rd., Cowley, Oxford, England.

CAREER: Baptist minister in England, 1938-51; Oxford University, Oxford, England, lecturer in theology, 1951-64; Oxford University Press, Oxford, England, specialist reader, 1964—.

WRITINGS: (Contributor) E. A. Payne, editor, *Essays in History and Religion*, Lutterworth, 1942; *The Christ of the New Testament*, Carey Kingsgate Press, 1951; (contributor) Alec Gilmore, editor, *Christian Baptism*, Lutterworth, 1960; *The Gospel According to Matthew*, Cambridge University Press, 1963; *God in the New Testament*, Hodder & Stoughton, 1965, Lippincott, 1966; *An Introductory Grammar of New Testament Greek*, Hodder & Stoughton, 1965, Cornell University Press, 1966. Contributor to theological and Biblical journals.

* * *

ARMITAGE, Angus 1902-

PERSONAL: Born July 19, 1902, in Sheffield, England; son of Harold (an author and journalist) and Jeanie (Cameron) Armitage. *Education:* University College, University of London, B.Sc., 1923, M.Sc., 1929, Ph.D., 1947. *Religion:* Presbyterian. *Home:* 52 Parkhill Rd., Hampstead, London N.W.3, England.

CAREER: University College, University of London, London, England, lecturer, 1927-57, reader in history and philosophy of science, 1957-69. *Member:* Royal Astronomical Society, British Society for History of Science, British Society for Philosophy of Science.

WRITINGS: Sun Stand Thou Still, Schuman, 1947, published as, *The World of Copernicus*, New American Library, 1963; *A Century of Astronomy*, Sampson Low, Marston & Co., 1950; *Copernicus, the Founder of Modern Astronomy*, Yoseloff, 1957, reprinted, A. S. Barnes, 1962; *William Herschel*, Nelson, 1962; *John Kepler*, Roy, 1966. Contributor to *Nature, Endeavour, Discovery, Popular Astronomy*, and to scientific journals.

SIDELIGHTS: Armitage is competent in French, German, Latin. *Avocational interests:* Exploring the British countryside.

* * *

ARMITAGE, E(dward) Liddall 1887-

PERSONAL: Born December 11, 1887, in London, England; son of Thomas Liddall (an artist) and Kate (Wells) Armitage; married Ellen Mary Foster, January 19, 1915; children: John Edward Liddall, Denis Edward Liddall. *Education:* Attended University College School, London, England; studied art at Polytechnic Regent Street School of Art, Royal Academy School of Art, and Slade School of Art. *Religion:* Church of England. *Home and office:* 47 Blenheim Crescent, London W.11, England.

CAREER: Portrait painter in Wilno, Russia, 1912-14; stained glass artist in partnership with Karl Parsons, 1921-24, with own studio in London, England, 1924-39; farmer, Suffolk, England, 1942-47; Whitefriars Stained Glass Studios, Wealdstone, England, chief designer, 1949-62. Teacher of stained glass, Central School of Arts and Crafts, 1923-24. Councillor, Royal Borough of Kensington, 1929. *Military service:* British Army, Royal Horse Guards, 1914-15; Royal Garrison Artillery, 1915-18; served in France, Belgium, Germany; became acting major. *Member:* British Society of Master Glass Painters (fellow;

council member and secretary, 1958-62), Art Workers Guild (member of council, 1963), Ecclesiological Society, Society for Protection of Ancient Buildings.

WRITINGS: Stained Glass: History, Technology, and Practice, Hill, 1959, Branford, 1960. Contributor to professional journals.

WORK IN PROGRESS: Autobiography.

AVOCATIONAL INTERESTS: Sailing.

* * *

ARMSTRONG, Ruth Gallup 1891-

PERSONAL: Born May 27, 1891, in Jefferson, Iowa; daughter of George and Stella Gallup, foster daughter of Edgar E. and Julia (McIntyre) Gallup; married William Bruce Armstrong (a physician; deceased); children: William Bruce, Jr., Eugene M. (killed at Anzio, World War II). *Education:* Cornell College, Mount Vernon, Iowa, B.A., 1912; University of Iowa, graduate student, 1927-28. *Home:* 3319 Woodland, Ames, Iowa 50010.

MEMBER: American Association of University Women, P.E.O. Sisterhood, Daughters of the American Revolution.

WRITINGS: Sisters under the Sari, Iowa State University Press, 1964.

WORK IN PROGRESS: A novel.

SIDELIGHTS: During her extended stay in India, Mrs. Armstrong explored the question of the happiness of older people in oriental culture, a topic suggested by her pollster brother, George Gallup of the American Institute of Public Opinion. *Avocational interests:* Collection of Kashmir shawls and other oriental objects.

* * *

ARNOLD, Francena H(arriet Long) 1888-

PERSONAL: Born September 9, 1888, in Jacksonville, Ill.; daughter of James Harvey and Hannah (Cox) Long; married Frank Mitchell Arnold (a Baptist seminary business manager), 1912 (deceased); children: Helen (Mrs. Joel P. Hoel), Frank Mitchell, Jr. (deceased), Harriet (Mrs. Lucas W. Buttry), Shirley (Mrs. Robert Worgul). *Education:* Completed high school in Jacksonville, Ill. *Religion:* Baptist. *Home:* 5518 West Ohio St., Chicago, Ill. 60644.

CAREER: Writer. *Awards, honors:* Third prize in Zondervan's christian novel contest, 1949, for *The Light in My Window.*

WRITINGS: Not My Will, Moody, 1946; *Fruit For Tomorrow*, Zondervan, 1948; *The Light in My Window*, Zondervan, 1949; *Then Am I Strong*, Moody, 1951; *Three Shall Be One*, Moody, 1953; *Jack O'Lantern House*, Moody, 1955; *The Road Winds On*, Moody, 1955; *A Brother Beloved*, Moody, 1957; *Straight Down a Crooked Lane*, Moody, 1959; *The Deepening Stream*, Zondervan, 1963.

* * *

ARNOLD, Thurman Wesley 1891-1969

PERSONAL: Born June 2, 1891, in Laramie, Wyo.; son of Constantine Peter (a lawyer and rancher) and Annie (Brockway) Arnold; married Frances Longan, September 7, 1917; children: Thurman Wesley, Jr., George Longan. *Education:* Princeton University, A.B., 1911; Harvard University, LL.B., 1914; Yale University, M.A., 1931. *Politics:* Democrat. *Religion:* Episcopalian. *Home:* 301

South St. Asaph St., Alexandria, Va. *Office:* Arnold and Porter, 1229 19th St., N.W., Washington, D.C. 20036.

CAREER: Admitted to Illinois bar, 1914; attorney in private practice in Chicago, Ill., 1914-19; sheep rancher and attorney in Laramie, Wyo., 1919-27; University of Wyoming, Laramie, lecturer in law, 1921-26; West Virginia University, Morgantown, dean of College of Law, 1927-30; Yale University, New Haven, Conn., visiting professor, 1930-31, professor of law, 1931-38; U.S. Department of Justice, Washington, D.C., assistant attorney general in charge of anti-trust, 1938-43; U.S. Court of Appeals for District of Columbia, associate justice, 1943-45; Arnold & Porter (formerly Arnold, Fortas & Porter; law firm), Washington, D.C., partner, 1945-69. Member of Wyoming House of Representatives, 1921; mayor of Laramie, Wyo., 1923-24, U.S. Agricultural Adjustment Administration, special assistant to general counsel, 1933; legal adviser to governor general of the Phillipines in administration of sugar control, 1934; Temporary National Economic Committee, representative of U.S. Department of Justice, 1938-41. *Military service:* U.S. Army, Field Artillery, World War I. Wyoming National Guard, 1924-27; became major and judge advocate general. *Member:* American Bar Association, Wyoming State Bar Association, West Virginia State Bar Association, Phi Beta Kappa. *Awards, honors:* LL.D., University of Wyoming, 1943.

WRITINGS: The Symbols of Government, Yale University Press, 1935; (with Fleming James) *Cases on Trials, Judgments and Appeals*, West Publishing, 1936; *The Folklore of Capitalism*, Yale University Press, 1937; *The Bottlenecks of Business*, Reynal & Hitchcock, 1940; *Democracy and Free Enterprise*, University of Oklahoma Press, 1942; *Fair Fights and Foul: A Dissenting Lawyer's Life*, Harcourt, 1965. Contributor to law journals and magazines.

(Died November 7, 1969)

* * *

ARONSON, Joseph 1898-

PERSONAL: Born December 22, 1898, in Buffalo, N.Y.; son of Max (a businessman) and Jennie (Simon) Aronson; married Henriette Mayer, October 24, 1930; children: Joseph Henry. *Education:* Attended University of Buffalo, 1916-19; Columbia University, B.Arch., 1923. *Home:* Townsend Hollow, Pine Hill P.O., N.Y. 12465. *Office:* 118 East 37th St., New York, N.Y. 10016.

CAREER: Joseph Aronson, Inc., New York, N.Y., consultant interior architect, 1933—. Guest critic of interior design, Pratt Institute. *Military service:* U.S. Army, 1918. *Member:* Society of Architectural Historians, International Castles Institute, Architectural League of New York.

WRITINGS: Book of Furniture and Decoration, Crown, 1936, revised edition, 1952; *Encyclopedia of Furniture*, Crown, 1938, revised edition, 1965, published as *The New Encyclopedia of Furniture*, 1967. Contributor to *Encyclopedia of the Arts*, *Book of Knowledge*, and *Popular Science*.

WORK IN PROGRESS: A supplementary guide to *Encyclopedia of Furniture*; a manual of interior design practice; also writing on optical illusion in interior design and nineteenth-century origins of modern design.

* * *

ARTHUR, Percy E. 1910-

PERSONAL: Born June 14, 1910, in Nacogdoches, Tex.;

son of John William and Eugenia (Ashley) Arthur; married Ivy Alice Riu (a registered nurse), November 20, 1940; children: Percine (Mrs. Robert Clark Dorris), Karen Ashley, Richard Addison. *Education:* Rice University, B.S., 1935; Columbia University, M.A., 1936. *Politics:* Independent. *Religion:* Episcopalian. *Home:* 4838 Creekbend, Houston, Tex. 77035.

CAREER: Rice University, Houston, Tex., varsity football end and center coach 1936-40; Great Southern Life Insurance Co., Houston, Tex., agent, 1946-54, agency manager, 1954—. *Military service:* U.S. Air Force, 1940-46. U.S. Air Force Reserve, 1946—, currently deputy commander of Air Force Reserve Recovery Group, with rank of lieutenant colonel. *Member:* Houston Association of Life Underwriters, General Agents and Managers Conference, Association of Rice Alumni, Houston Club.

WRITINGS: You Are the Captain, Steck, 1963.

WORK IN PROGRESS: You Are the Supervisor; How to Become a Captain.

* * *

ASH, Bernard 1910-

PERSONAL: Born October 28, 1910, in Liverpool, England; son of Morris (a watchmaker) and Rose (Myers) Ash; married Josephine Driver, March 6, 1948; children: Alexander Bernard. *Education:* Exeter College, Oxford, B.A. (honors), 1933. *Religion:* Church of England. *Home:* Honeywood, Knowle Park, Cobham, Surrey, England. *Agent:* Laurence Pollinger Ltd., 18 Maddox St., London W. 1, England. *Office:* Pressmark Ltd., Gillow House, Winsley St., London W. 1, England.

CAREER: Advertising copywriter in London, England, 1933-36; Kemsley Newspapers Ltd., London, staff, 1936-39 and 1946-48, became deputy publicity director; Odhams Press Ltd., London, group publicity manager, 1948-62; Pressmark Ltd. (public relations consultants), London, director, 1962—. Metropolitan Borough councillor, London, 1937-42. *Military service:* British Army, 1940-46; became staff captain. *Member:* Society of Authors, Inland Waterways Association, Guilford Diocesan Guild of Church Bell Ringers.

WRITINGS: Silence for His Worship, Staples, 1953, Knopf, 1954; *Omega Street*, Staples, 1954; *Three Men Went to War*, Staples, 1954; *Fitchett's Inn*, Staples, 1955; *Burning Glass*, Staples, 1956; *Too Deep the Sea*, Staples, 1958; *Someone Had Blundered* (the sinking of the "Prince of Wales" and "Repulse"), M. Joseph, 1960, Doubleday, 1961; *Norway 1940* (nonfiction), Cassell, 1964; *The Golden City: London Between the Fires, 1666-1941*, Phoenix House, 1964; *The Lost Dictator: A Biography of Field-Marshall Sir Henry Wilson*, Cassell, 1968.

AVOCATIONAL INTERESTS: Current affairs, local government, and London history.

* * *

ASH, Sarah Leeds 1904-

PERSONAL: Born November 20, 1904, in Cinnaminson, N.J.; daughter of Samuel P. (a hotel proprietor) and Clara (Mulford) Leeds; married H. Dickson Ash (an editor), October 3, 1931. *Education:* Attended Miss Illman's Training School for Teachers (later a unit of University of Pennsylvania). *Politics:* Republican. *Religion:* Society of Friends. *Home:* West Nook, Wyncote, Pa. 19095.

CAREER: Former teacher in Atlantic City Public Schools, Atlantic City, N.J.; conductor of creative writing groups. *Member:* Poetry Society of America, National Society of American Pen Women, Pennsylvania Poetry Society, Colonial Dames of America.

WRITINGS: Little Things (poetry), Folio Press, 1941; *Changeless Shore* (poetry), Haverford, 1962. Contributor to *Saturday Evening Post, Good Housekeeping, New York Times, Yachting, Office Executive,* and other periodicals.

AVOCATIONAL INTERESTS: The sea, sailing, and politics.

* * *

ASHLEY, (Arthur) Ernest 1906-
(Francis Vivian)

PERSONAL: Born March 23, 1906, in East Retford, Nottinghamshire, England; son of Arthur Ernest (a photographer) and Elizabeth (Hallam) Ashley; married Dorothy Wallwork (a schoolteacher), December 26, 1940; children: Susan Elizabeth. *Politics:* Conservative. *Religion:* "Heaven only knows." *Home:* 7 West End Ct., Sutton in Ashfield, Nottinghamshire, England. *Agent:* John Farquharson Ltd., 15 Red Lion Sq., London W.C. 1, England.

CAREER: Full-time author and short story writer, 1932-52; *Nottinghamshire Free Press*, Sutton in Ashfield, Nottinghamshire, England, assistant editor, 1952-71. Former lecturer on literary techniques and psychology. *Military service:* Royal Air Force, 1941-45; seconded to Royal Canadian Air Force, 1941-43; served in North Africa, Sicily, Italy, and Greece. *Member:* British Legion, Nottingham Writers' Club (former president, two terms; honorary life member).

WRITINGS—Detective novels; all under pseudonym Francis Vivian: *Death at the Salutation,* Jenkins, 1937; *The Arrow of Death,* Jenkins, 1938; *Black Alibi,* Jenkins, 1938; *Three Short Men,* Jenkins, 1939; *Dark Moon,* Jenkins, 1939.

The Frog was Yellow, Jenkins, 1940; *The Death of Mr. Lomas,* Jenkins, 1941; *Murder in Angel Yard,* Piccadilly Novels, 1946; *Sable Messenger,* Jenkins, 1947; *The Threefold Cord,* Jenkins, 1947; *The Ninth Enemy,* Hodder & Stoughton, 1948; *The Laughing Dog,* Hodder & Stoughton, 1949.

The Singing Masons, Hodder & Stoughton, 1950; *The Sleeping Islands,* Hodder & Stoughton, 1951; *The Elusive Bowman,* Hodder & Stoughton, 1952; *The Ladies of Locksley,* Jenkins, 1953, Roy, 1957; *Darkling Death,* Jenkins, 1956, Roy, 1957; *Dead Opposite the Church,* Jenkins, 1959.

Nonfiction: *Story Weaving,* Hutchinson, 1940; *Creative Technique in Fiction,* Hutchinson, 1946.

Contributor of short stories to periodicals.

SIDELIGHTS: The manuscript of *The Singing Masons,* which Ashley believes to be the first detective novel written around beekeeping, is in Cornell University's Horticulture Library. In tracing other beekeeping fiction, he found only Gene Stratton Porter's romance, *Keeper of the Bees,* and two short stories, both American. *The Sleeping Island* and *The Elusive Bowman* have been printed in Braille. *Avocational interests:* Beekeeping, archery, Eastern philosophies.

* * *

ASSELIN, E(dward) Donald 1903-1970

PERSONAL: Surname is pronounced Ah-sell-in; born December 19, 1903, in St. Johnsbury, Vt.; son of Edward G. (a merchant) and Rose (Benoit) Asselin; married Valeria Elizabeth Bergmann, February 5, 1935; children: Rosemary (Mrs. Frederick Cameron), Suzanne (Mrs. George Teixiera), Donald, Pierre, Michelle. *Education:* University of Vermont, M.D., 1929; New York University, postdoctoral study in medicine, 1930-31. *Politics:* Democrat. *Religion:* Roman Catholic. *Home:* Meadow Lane, Falmouth, Mass. 02540.

CAREER: Physician in private practice, 1929-70. U.S. Air Force, flight surgeon, 1948-56; became major. *Member:* American Medical Association, Societe des Ecrivains Normands.

WRITINGS: Vermont: Rural Rhymes of a Native Son, Vantage, 1954; (editor) *New England Laughs,* Vermont Books, 1963; *A Portuguese-American Cookbook,* Tuttle, 1966; *A French-Canadian Cookbook,* Tuttle, 1968; *Scandinavian Cookbook,* Tuttle, 1970. Represented in *Japan—Theme and Variations: A Collection of Poems by Americans,* edited by Charles E. Tuttle, Tuttle, 1959. Contributor of historical articles and French poetry to periodicals. Columnist, *Falmouth Enterprise,* 1958-61.

SIDELIGHTS: Asselin was fluent in French, read Spanish and Italian, and knew some Portuguese and German. *Avocational interests:* Music, painting, and building model ships.†

(Died, 1970)

* * *

ATHERTON, James S(tephen) 1910-

PERSONAL: Born December 15, 1910, in England; married Nora Heathcoat; children: four sons, one daughter. *Education:* Attended Strawberry Hill Training College; University of Liverpool, M.A. *Home:* 152 Barnsley St., Wigan, Lancashire, England.

CAREER: Wigan District Mining and Technical College, Wigan, England, lecturer, 1959—. Visiting professor, State University of New York at Buffalo, 1965.

WRITINGS: The Books at the Wake, Faber, 1959, Viking, 1960; (editor, and author of explanatory notes) James Joyce, *A Portrait of the Artist as a Young Man,* Heinemann, 1965.

WORK IN PROGRESS: Satire in England; and *James Joyce: A Literary Interpretation of His Works.*

* * *

ATKINSON, Carroll (Holloway) 1896-

PERSONAL: Born October 24, 1896, in Fairbury, Neb.; son of Charles Raymond (an economist) and Florence B. (Cooper) Atkinson; married Ruby Baker, 1921 (died, 1925); married Mary Hansen, 1926 (died, 1941); married Carol Mary Gonzales, June 1, 1959; children: (first marriage) Yvonne Atkinson Everett, Carroll H., Jr.; (third marriage) Ardith Anne, Alicia Arthurita, Arthur Amigo. *Education:* University of Grenoble, student, 1919; Lawrence College, Appleton, Wis., A.B., 1920; University of Southern California, M.A., 1929; George Peabody College for Teachers, Ph.D., 1938. *Politics:* Republican. *Religion:* Protestant. *Home:* 3021 North Oleander Ave., Daytona Beach, Fla. 32018. *Agent:* Scott Meredith Literary Agency, Inc., 580 Fifth Ave., New York, N.Y. 10036.

CAREER: Instructor and athletic coach in public schools and colleges of Idaho, Oregon, Washington, Texas, Pennsylvania, and New Jersey, 1921-41; director of Nelson Memorial Library and McLucas Memorial Library, Detroit, Mich., 1941-45; public relations work, Oakland, Calif., 1945-46; columnist, "Younger Set and Its Problems," *Honolulu Star-Bulletin*, and radio producer in Honolulu, 1946-47; Southwestern University, Georgetown, Tex., dean of men, 1947-49; Dakota Wesleyan University, Mitchell, S.D., director of teacher training, 1949-51; supervising principal or teaching specialist in New Mexico public schools, 1952-62; Texas Lutheran College, Seguin, visiting professor, 1961-62; Pacific University, Forest Grove, Ore., chairman of psychology department, 1962-64; Florida Memorial College, St. Augustine, visiting professor of social studies, 1964-65; Embry-Riddle Aeronautic Institute, professor of humanities, 1965-66; Bethune-Cookman College, professor of education, 1966-72. Summer professor at universities in five states; radio broadcaster and producer; consulting psychologist in state mental hospitals and training schools in Texas and South Dakota. *Military service:* U.S. Army, American Expeditionary Forces, 1918-19; received Croix de Guerre (France).

MEMBER: National Education Association (life), American Association of University Professors, American Association de Croix de Guerre, Masons, American Legion (past commander of posts in California and Oregon), Phi Delta Kappa.

WRITINGS: Education by Radio in American Schools, George Peabody College Press, 1938; *True Confessions of a Ph.D.*, Edinboro Press, 1939; *American Universities and Colleges That Have Held Broadcast License*, Nelson Memorial Library, 1941; *Radio Extension Courses Broadcast for Credit*, Nelson Memorial Library, 1941; *The New Deal: Will It Survive the War?*, McLucas Memorial Library, 1942; *Public School Broadcasting to the Classroom*, Nelson Memorial Library, 1942; *Radio Network Contributions to Education*, Nelson Memorial Library, 1942; *Broadcasting to the Classroom by Universities and Colleges*, Nelson Memorial Library, 1942; *Radio Programs Intended for Classroom Use*, Nelson Memorial Library, 1942; *Radio in State and Territorial Education Departments*, Nelson Memorial Library, 1942; *I Knew the Voice of Experience*, McLucas Memorial Library, 1944; *Pro and Con of the Ph.D.*, McLucas Memorial Library, 1945; *Intellectual Tramp*, Exposition, 1955; *The Story of Education*, Chilton, 1962, 2nd edition, 1965.

Ghost writer of other books for corporations and individuals. Author of radio scripts, more than fifty articles in professional journals, and some forty short stories and articles in magazines. Columnist for New Mexico newspapers, 1952-53, 1959-60. Editor, *American Educator*, 1931-35; associate editor, *Dictionary of Education*, 1941-42; associate editor, *Modern Language Journal*, 1943-49.

WORK IN PROGRESS: A book on the educational handicaps of the Negro; a series of three textbooks for Embry-Riddle Aeronautic Institute; *The Show Must Go On–Even for Children*, relating the ups-and-downs in getting the "three young Atkinsons" into show business.

SIDELIGHTS: Atkinson is a onetime holder of the National Amateur Athletic Union featherweight and twelve other wrestling titles.

*   *   *

AUSTIN, Lloyd James 1915-

PERSONAL: Born November 4, 1915, in Melbourne, Australia; son of James William Ashurst and Jane (Tymms) Austin; married Jeanne Guerin, August 31, 1939; children: James L., Colin F., Michel M., Suzanne E. *Education:* University of Melbourne, B.A., 1935, M.A., 1947; University of Paris, Dr. Univ., 1940. *Home:* 14 Park Ter., Cambridge, England.

CAREER: University of Melbourne, Melbourne, Victoria, Australia, lecturer in French, 1940-42, 1945-47; University of St. Andrews, St. Andrews, Scotland, lecturer in French, 1947-51; research in Paris, France, 1951-55; Cambridge University, Cambridge, England, fellow of Jesus College, 1955-56; University of Manchester, Manchester, England, professor of modern French literature, 1956-61; Cambridge University, fellow of Jesus College and university lecturer, 1961-66, reader, 1966-67, Drapers Professor of French, 1967—. Herbert F. Johnson Visiting Professor, University of Wisconsin, 1962-63. *Military service:* Royal Australian Naval Volunteer Reserve, 1942-45; became lieutenant. *Member:* Society for French Studies, Association Internationale des Etudes Francaises (president, 1969-72), Modern Languages Association (president of Lancashire and Cheshire branch, 1961), Modern Humanities Research Association, Modern Language Association of America. *Awards, honors:* Fellow of the British Academy, 1968; Chevalier de l'Ordre des Arts et des Lettres, 1972; Dr. honoris causa, Sorbonne, 1973.

WRITINGS: Paul Bourget, E. Droz, 1940; (editor) Paul Valery, *Le Cimetiere marin*, Roissard, 1954; *L'Univers poetique de Baudelaire*, Mercure de France, 1956; (editor with G. Rees and E. Vinaver) *Studies in Modern French Literature Presented to P. Mansell Jones*, Manchester University Press, 1961; (editor with H. Mondor) *Les Gossips de Mallarme*, Gallimard, 1962; (editor with Mondor) *La Correspondence de Mallarme,* Gallimard, Volume II (1872-1885), 1965, Volume III (1886-1889), 1969, Volume IV (1890-1891), 1973, Volume V (1892-1894), 1974; (editor) Charles Baudelaire, *L'Art romantique*, Garnier-Flammarion, 1968. Contributor to language journals. General editor, *French Studies*.

WORK IN PROGRESS: Books on Mallarme and Valery.

AVOCATIONAL INTERESTS: Music, architecture, painting, and sculpture; travel in Europe and the United States to observe landscapes and to visit museums and art galleries.

*   *   *

AUSTIN, Margot

PERSONAL: Born in Portland, Ore.; daughter of Peter and Maude (Campbell) Helser; married Darrell R. Austin (an artist), 1933; children: Darrell D. *Education:* Attended St. Mary's Academy, Portland, Ore., National Academy of Design, New York, N.Y., and Grand Central School of Art, New York, N.Y. *Home address:* R.F.D. 3, Saw Mill Rd., New Fairfield, Conn. 06810.

CAREER: Writer and illustrator of children's books. Chairman of board, New Fairfield Free Public Library.

WRITINGS—Self-Illustrated: Moxie and Hanty and Bunty, Scribner, 1939; *Once Upon a Springtime,* Scribner, 1940; *Tumble Bear,* Scribner, 1940; *Barney's Adventure,* Dutton, 1941; *Peter Churchmouse,* Dutton, 1941; *Willamette Way,* Scribner, 1941; *Effelli,* Dutton, 1942; *Gabriel Churchkitten,* Dutton, 1942; *Trumpet,* Dutton, 1943; *Manuel's Kite String, and Other Stories,* Scribner, 1943; *Lutie,* Dutton, 1944; *Gabriel Churchkitten and the Moths,* Dutton, 1948; *Poppet,* Dutton, 1949; *Look Baby,* Platt, 1949.

The Three Silly Kittens, Dutton, 1950; *Growl Bear,* Dutton, 1951; *First Prize for Danny,* Dutton, 1952; *William's Shadow,* Dutton, 1954; *Brave John Henry,* Dutton, 1955; *Churchmouse Stories: A Collection of Peter Churchmouse, and Other Children's Favorites,* Dutton, 1956; *Archie Angel,* Dutton, 1957; *Cousin's Treasure,* Dutton, 1960.

Illustrator: *Mother Goose Rhymes,* Platt, 1938; Elizabeth Briggs Squires, *David's Silver Dollar,* Platt, 1940; *The Very Young Mother Goose,* Platt, 1963.†

*   *   *

AVEY, Albert E(dwin)   1886-1963

PERSONAL: Born May 29, 1886, in Hannibal, Mo.; son of Edwin Winter (a contractor) and Lucy Alice (Parker) Avey; married Anna Benade Cornuelle, March 20, 1939; children: Margaret (Mrs. Harvey W. Walker, Jr.), Alice Cornuelle (Mrs. William E. Browning, Jr.), Margaret Cornuelle (Mrs. Robert E. Ricketts), Janet Cornuelle (Mrs. Harry E. Ebert). *Education:* Yale University, A.B., 1908, A.M., 1909, Ph.D., 1915; University of Berlin, graduate study, 1912-13. *Politics:* Independent. *Religion:* American Baptist. *Home:* 4705 Olentangy Blvd., Columbus 14, Ohio.

CAREER: High school teacher in Leavenworth, Kan., 1909-10, principal in Salina, Kan., 1910-12; Bryn Mawr College, Bryn Mawr, Pa., associate in philosophy and psychology, 1915-17; Ohio State University, Columbus, assistant professor, 1917-26, professor of philosophy, 1926-54, chairman of department, 1941-52, professor emeritus, 1954-63. Visiting professor, Pierce College, Greece, 1954-56, and College of Wooster, 1961-62; guest professor, Cottey College, 1956-59. Adviser on rural discussion groups to U.S. Government, 1941; member of Ohio Governor's Commission on Democracy, 1942. *Member:* American Philosophical Association (president of Western Division, 1950-51), American Association of University Professors, Phi Beta Kappa, Phi Delta Kappa.

WRITINGS: An Analysis of the Process of Conceptual Cognition, Reuter & Kieneman, 1915; (editor) *Readings in Philosophy,* R. G. Adams, 1921, 2nd edition, Appleton, 1924; *Historical Method in Bible Study,* Scribner, 1924; *The Functions and Forms of Thought,* Holt, 1927; *Re-Thinking Religion,* Holt, 1936; *Handbook in the History of Philosophy,* Barnes & Noble, 1954, 2nd edition published as *Handbook of Philosophy,* 1961; *Primary Questions, Historical Answers,* Christopher, 1968. Also author of *Basic Religious Questions,* 1947. Contributor to journals.

(Died, 1963)

*   *   *

AZOY, A(nastasio) C.M.   1891-

PERSONAL: Surname is pronounced A-thoy; born November 9, 1891, in Merida, Mexico; son of Anastasio C. M. (a businessman) and Mary L. (Bolton) Azoy; married Margaret F. Groves, June 12, 1918; children: Philip Livingston. *Education:* Princeton University, Litt. B., 1914. *Religion:* Protestant.

CAREER: Entered U.S. Army as second lieutenant, Coast Artillery Corps, 1917, and served, 1917-20; advertising writer and executive, New York, N.Y., 1920-39, and instructor in advertising at Columbia University, New York, N.Y., in same period; recalled to Army, 1939, and remained on active duty, 1939-51, with assignments at U.S. Military Academy, West Point, N.Y., as chief of Allied Press Camp, Berlin, Germany, chief of Historical Section,

Frankfurt, Germany, and staff officer, First Army; retired as colonel, 1951. Member, New York State Civil Defense Commission, 1952-63. *Member:* General Society of Colonial Wars (governor-general, 1962—), Colonial Lords of the Manor, Rof-Mar Sports Lodge, Nassau Club, Princeton Club of New York.

WRITINGS: (With F. D. Halsey) *Goal Lines,* Princeton University Press, 1922; *Reserve Officers Handbook,* McBride, 1928; *A Primer of Advertising,* Harper, 1930; *They Were Not Afraid to Die,* Military Service Publishing Co., 1939; *West Point Today,* Coward, 1942, new revised edition, 1963; *Army Officer's Manual,* Appleton, 1942; *Patriot Battles,* U.S. War Department, 1943; *Paul Revere's Horse,* Doubleday, 1949; *Charge! The Story of the Battle of San Juan Hill,* McKay, 1962; *Signal 250! The Fight off Santiago,* McKay, 1964. Contributor to *American Heritage, Esquire, Town and Country, New Yorker,* and other magazines.

AVOCATIONAL INTERESTS: Sailing, photography, travel, and history.

*   *   *

BABB, Hugh Webster   1887-197(?)

PERSONAL: Born March 3, 1887, in Yarmouth, Me.; son of Howard Selden and Margaret (Wagg) Babb; married Persis Loring Conant, June 19, 1915; children: Warren, Richard, Hugh, Jr., Howard. *Education:* Worcester College, Oxford, B.A., 1911; Cambridge University, law tripos, part I, 1913; Harvard University, LL.B., 1916; graduate study at University of Munich, 1930-31, and University of Warsaw, 1937, 1939. *Politics:* Republican. *Religion:* Episcopalian. *Home:* Route 200, C.F., Portland, Me.

CAREER: Boston University, College of Business Administration, Boston, Mass., instructor, 1920-21, assistant professor, 1921-23, associate professor, 1923-26, professor of law, 1926-56, became chairman of department; University of Maine, Portland, lecturer in Law School, 1963-7?. Panel chairman, War Labor Board; public member of Wage Stabilization Board; arbitrator in labor disputes. *Member:* American Business Law Association (honorary president, 1942).

WRITINGS: (With H. L. Perrin) *Commercial Law Cases,* Doran, 1922; *Commercial Law Cases: Partnerships and Corporations,* Blanchard Printing Co., 1933, revised edition, with C.B. Everberg, published as *Commercial Law: Cases and Materials,* Foundation Press, 1949; *Commercial Law Cases: Negotiable Instruments,* Blanchard Printing Co., 1933, 2nd edition published as *Negotiable Instruments: Cases and Materials,* Foundation Press, 1949; (with Charles Martin) *An Outline of Business Law,* Barnes & Noble, 1943, revised edition published as *Business Law,* 1964, 2nd edition, 1969; (with Everberg and Louis DiGiovanni) *Business Law: Cases and Materials,* Foundation Press, 1959.

Translator: A. I. Vyshinsky, editor, *Law of the Soviet State,* Macmillan, 1948; V. I. Lenin and others, *Soviet Legal Philosophy,* Harvard University Press, 1951, Johnson Reprint, 1968; L. I. Petrazycki, *Law and Morality,* Harvard University Press, 1955; *Some Translations of Russian Lyrical Poetry,* Cumberland Foreside, 195?.

WORK IN PROGRESS: Translating *Law and the State: The Soviet Theory.*†

(Deceased)

BACHARACH, Alfred L(ouis) 1891-1966

PERSONAL: Born August 11, 1891; son of Otto Leonhard (a stockbroker) and Alice Eva (Wagner) Bacharach; married Elizabeth Owen, April 13, 1931; children: John P. L., Michael O. L. *Education:* Clare College, Cambridge, B.A., 1912, M.A., 1926. *Politics:* Socialist. *Religion:* Humanist. *Home:* 26 Willow Rd., London N.W. 3, England. *Agent:* David Higham Associates Ltd., 5-8 Lower John St., London W1R 4HA, England.

CAREER: Glaxo Laboratories Ltd. (food and pharmaceutical manufacturers), Greenford, Middlesex, England, chemist, 1920-30, biochemist, 1931-35, head of biochemistry unit, 1935-49, public relations officer for science, 1949-56; Masius & Ferguson Ltd. (advertising agents), consultant, 1958-61; free-lance consultant in editing and preparing scientific books, papers, and review articles for publication, 1961-66. Governor of Borough Polytechnic and of Kyneston School; member of North London Group Hospital Management Committee. *Member:* Nutrition Society (treasurer, 1942-52; president, 1959-62), Society of Chemical Industry (food group chairman, 1951-52), Royal Institute of Chemistry (fellow; former vice-president), Society for Analytical Chemistry, Society of Chemical Industry, Radiowriters Association of the Incorporated Society of Authors, Savage Club (London).

WRITINGS: (Editor) *The Musical Companion: A Compendium for All Lovers of Music,* Gollancz, 1934, revised edition published as *The New Musical Companion,* 1957; (editor) *Lives of the Great Composers,* Gollancz, 1935, Dutton, 1936; *Science and Nutrition,* C. A. Watts, 1938, 3rd edition, 1947; (editor with J. C. Drummond) *Vitamin E: A Symposium,* Society of Chemical Industry, 1939; (translator with F. A. Robinson) Laszlo Zechmeister and Laszlo Cholnoky, *Principles and Practice of Chromatography,* Wiley, 1941, 2nd edition, Chapman & Hall, 1943; (editor) *British Music of Our Time,* Penguin, 1946; (editor with Theodore Rendle) *The Nation's Food,* Society of Chemical Industry, 1946; (editor) *The Music Masters, Including "Lives of the Great Composers,"* Volume I, Maurice Fridberg, 1948, Volumes II-IV, Cassell, 1948-54; (editor with Charles H. Gray) *Hormones in Blood,* two volumes, Academic Press, 1961, 2nd edition, 1967-68; (editor with Desmond Roger Laurence) *Evaluation of Drug Activities: Pharmacometrics,* two volumes, Academic Press, 1964; (editor with Otto G. Edholm) *Exploration Medicine: Being a Practical Guide for Those Going on Expeditions,* Williams & Wilkins, 1965; (with Edholm) *The Physiology of Human Survival,* Academic Press, 1966.

AVOCATIONAL INTERESTS: Bird watching, chess, stamp collecting, music, and reading detective stories.

(Died July 16, 1966)

*   *   *

BACMEISTER, Rhoda W(arner) 1893-

PERSONAL: Surname is pronounced *Bach*-my-ster; born February 28, 1893, in Northampton, Mass.; daughter of Charles Forbes (an editor) and Mary (Dawes) Warner; married Otto Bacmeister, November 7, 1917 (deceased); children: Margaret (Mrs. F. R. Gruger, Jr.), Lucretia (Mrs. Paul F. Harrison), Theodore Warner. *Education:* Vassar College, A.B. (honors), 1914; University of Chicago, A.M., 1915; additional study at University of Iowa, Columbia University, National College of Education, Bank Street College of Education, and University of Minnesota. *Home and office:* 501 West 123rd St., 15H, New York,

N.Y. 10027. *Agent:* McIntosh & Otis, Inc., 18 East 41st St., New York, N.Y. 10017.

CAREER: High school teacher in Toulon, Ill., 1915-16, 1923-27; Flower Hill Nursery School, Plandome, N.Y., teacher-director, 1928-30; Manhasset Bay School, Port Washington, N.Y., teacher, co-director, 1930-37; Works Progress Administration, Indiana state director of Adult Education for Family Living, 1938-41; high school teacher, Annandale, Minn., 1942-43; Lanham Act Centers, supervisor in Philadelphia, Pa., 1943-45; free-lance writer and lecturer, 1945-50; Manhattanville Nursery, New York, N.Y., director, 1950-59; free-lance writer, lecturer, and conductor of conferences and short courses for teachers, 1959—. Instructor in early childhood education at Brooklyn College (now Brooklyn College of the City University of New York), 1947-48, and City College (now City College of the City University of New York), 1959-60; also teacher at other colleges and universities.

MEMBER: National Association for Education of Young Children, National Education Association, National Committee for the Day Care of Children, Child Study Association of America, Association for Childhood Education International, American Association of University Women, American Civil Liberties Union, Early Childhood Education Council (New York state and city), Phi Beta Kappa. *Awards, honors:* Parents' Institute award, 1947, for *Growing Together.*

WRITINGS: Caring for the Runabout Child, Dutton, 1937; *Jet* (story for children), Dutton, 1938; *Stories to Begin On,* Dutton, 1940; *Growing Together* (for parents), Appleton, 1940; *Sing About It* (songs for the very young), Schirmer, 1949; *Your Child and Other People,* Little, Brown, 1950; *All in the Family,* Appleton, 1951; *The People Downstairs,* Coward, 1964; *Voices in the Night,* Bobbs-Merrill, 1965. Contributor of nearly two hundred articles, stories, and poems to professional journals, magazines, and anthologies.

AVOCATIONAL INTERESTS: Weaving.

*   *   *

BACON, Elizabeth E(maline) 1904-

PERSONAL: Born July 29, 1904, in Whittier, Calif.; daughter of Edmund Warren and Ann (Irvine) Bacon; divorced; children: Alfred Bacon Hudson. *Education:* University of Grenoble, diploma, 1925; Sorbonne, University of Paris, diploma (honors), 1926; Smith College, B.A., 1927; Yale University, graduate student, 1936-38; University of California, Berkeley, Ph.D., 1951. *Residence:* East Lansing, Mich. *Office:* Department of Anthropology, Michigan State University, East Lansing, Mich. 48823.

CAREER: Ethnographic field worker in Kazakstan, Soviet Union, under joint auspices of Yale University and USSR Academy of Sciences, 1933-34, and in Iran and Afghanistan as Bayard Dominick traveling fellow, 1938-39; University of Washington, Seattle, instructor in Far East department, 1942-43; Ethnogeographic Board, Washington, D.C., project director, 1943-44; U.S. Department of State, Washington, D.C., research analyst, 1944-46; University of California, Los Angeles, lecturer in anthropology, 1948-49; Washington University, St. Louis, Mo., assistant professor of anthropology, 1949-54; Cornell University, Ithaca, N.Y., director of India Handbook Project, 1955-56, visiting associate professor, 1956-57; *Collier's Encyclopedia,* New York, N.Y., special editor for anthropology, 1957-59; Hofstra University, New College, Hempstead, N.Y., adjunct professor of anthropology, 1965-66; Michigan State University, East Lansing, professor of anthropology and Asian studies and university consultant, 1968—.

MEMBER: American Anthropological Association (fellow), Royal Central Asian Society, Mongolia Society, Society for Ethnomusicology, Phi Beta Kappa, Sigma Xi. *Awards, honors:* Grants from Social Science Research Council, 1940, American Council of Learned Societies, and Wenner-Gren Foundation.

WRITINGS: (Contributor) Leslie Spier and others, editors, *Language, Culture, and Personality*, Sapir Memorial Publication Fund, 1941; (contributor) Donald Wilbur, editor, *Afghanistan*, Human Relations Area File, 1956, 2nd edition, 1962; (editor) *India: A Sociological Background*, Human Relations Area File, 1956; (editor) *Uttar Pradesh: An Area Handbook*, Human Relations Area File, 1956; *Obok: A Study of Social Structure in Eurasia*, Wenner-Gren Foundation for Anthropological Research, 1958; *Central Asians under Russian Rule*, Cornell University Press, 1966. Contributor to *Encyclopedia Americana*, *Encyclopaedia Britannica*, *American Oxford Encyclopedia*, and *Collier's Encyclopedia*, and to journals. Board of advisory editors, *Middle East Journal*, 1946-48, *Encyclopedia Americana*, 1961-63.

WORK IN PROGRESS: Two articles, "Anthropological Research in Afghanistan" and "Peoples of Afghanistan"; writing up field material on the Hazaras of Afghanistan; a study of Tajik culture; a study of Islam across several culture areas.

SIDELIGHTS: Elizabeth Bacon speaks French, Russian, and German, as well as some Persian and Kazak Turkic.

*   *   *

BAILEY, Alice Cooper   1890-

PERSONAL: Born December 9, 1890, in San Diego, Calif.; daughter of Henry Ernest (a judge and first secretary of Territory of Hawaii) and Mary Ellen (Porter) Cooper; married George William Bailey (member of advisory board, Electrical & Electronics Engineers, Inc.), June 16, 1913; children: Mary Alice (Mrs. Luke Hamilton Montgomery), George William, Jr., Richard Briggs, *Education:* Wellesley College, student, one year (taken at Oahu College); Oahu College, graduate; College of Hawaii (now University of Hawaii), special student, one year; Honolulu Normal School, life diploma in teaching; also attended Boston Conservatory of Music. *Politics:* Republican. *Religion:* Episcopalian. *Home:* 255 Lexington Rd., Concord, Mass. 01742.

CAREER: Author; lecturer on Hawaii and Robert Louis Stevenson. Weston School Committee, member, 1931-39, chairman, 1939-40. *Member:* Women's National Book Association, National League of American Pen Women (state president for Massachusetts, 1946-50, Hawaii, 1954-56; president of Honolulu branch, 1952-54), New England Woman's Press Club (past vice-president), Hawaiian Historical Society, Friends of Iolani Palace (Honolulu), Boston Authors Club (president, 1941-43), Weston Community League (life member), Weston Historical Association, Concord Antiquarian Museum, Concord Woman's Club, Friends of the Concord Public Library. *Awards, honors:* Second prize, National League of Pen Women, for *Footprints in the Dust.*

WRITINGS: Katrina and Jan, P. F. Volland, 1923; *The Skating Gander*, P. F. Volland, 1926; *Kimo, the Whistling Boy of Hawaii*, P. F. Volland, 1927; *Sun Gold*, Houghton,

1930: *Footprints in the Dust*, Longmans, Green, 1936; *The Hawaiian Box Mystery*, Longmans, Green, 1960; *To Remember Robert Louis Stevenson*, McKay, 1966. Contributor to *Travel, American Girl, Child Life*, and *Story Parade.*

WORK IN PROGRESS: A book, tentatively titled *Rainbow over Manoa*, on the life of her father during the monarchial, provisional, and annexation periods in Hawaii.

SIDELIGHTS: Mrs. Bailey was taken to Honolulu at the age of six weeks, and lived there until 1913. At one time her father owned fifty-two coral atolls in the South Pacific; she inherited title to one-sixth of two islands she has never seen. Her father's office was in Iolani Palace and she has donated all her Hawaiian possessions, including bronze seals, candelabra, etc., to the committee restoring that landmark. Her present home is a pre-revolutionary house on Concord's famous Historic Mile, within walking distance of the homes of Ralph Waldo Emerson, Louisa May Alcott, and Nathaniel Hawthorne.

Mrs. Bailey's first two books, Dutch folktales, brought a note of appreciation from Queen Wilhelmina. All her galley proofs are part of the de Grummond Collection in the library of the University of Southern Mississippi; one book and all her magazine stories for teen-agers have been transcribed into Braille.

*   *   *

BAILEY, Frederick Marshman   1882-1967

PERSONAL: Born February 3, 1882, in Lahore, India; son of Frederick (a colonel, Royal Engineers) and Florence (Marshman) Bailey; married Irma Cozens-Hardy, April 7, 1921. *Education:* Attended The Edinburgh Academy, Edinburgh, Scotland, 1891-95, Wellington College, Berkshire, England, 1895-99, Royal Military College, Sandhurst, England, 1900. *Politics:* Conservative. *Religion:* Church of Scotland. *Home:* Warborough House, Stiffkey, Wells-Next-Sea, Norfolk, England.

CAREER: Entered Indian Army, 1900, in Indian Political Department, 1905, serving government of India in various civil capacities, 1905-38 (with exception of military service in France and Gallipoli, 1914-15). Member of Younghusband Tibet Expedition, 1903-04; trade agent in Tibet, 1905-09; assistant commissioner, North-West Frontier Province, India, 1916-17; political officer in Mesopotamia and Persia, 1917-18, in Sikkim, Tibet, and Bhutan, 1921-28; political agent for Central India and resident, Baroda, 1930; resident, Kashmir, 1932-33; envoy extraordinary and minister plenipotentiary at Court of Nepal, 1935-38; King's messenger to Central and South America, 1942-43. Explorer.

MEMBER: Royal Geographical Society, Royal Central Asian Society, Zoological Society of London, United Service Club. *Awards, honors:* Gill Medal of Royal Geographic Society, 1912, for explorations in western China and eastern Tibet in 1911; McGregor Medal of Royal United Service Institution of India, 1914, and Gold Medal of Royal Geographical Society, 1916, for explorations in southern Tibet, 1912; Commander of the Indian Empire, 1915; Commander, Crown of Rumania, 1920; Livingstone Gold Medal of Royal Scottish Geographical Society, 1921.

WRITINGS: China-Tibet-Assam, a Journey, J. Cape, 1945; *Mission to Tashkent*, J. Cape, 1946; *No Passport to Tibet*, Hart-Davis, 1957.

WORK IN PROGRESS: Memoirs.

SIDELIGHTS: Bailey spoke French, German, Russian, Tibetan, Persian, and Urdu.

BIOGRAPHICAL/CRITICAL SOURCES: Arthur Swinson, *Beyond the Frontiers: The Biography of Colonel F. M. Bailey, Explorer and Special Agent*, Hutchinson, 1971.

(Died, April 17, 1967)

* * *

BAILEY, Ralph Edgar 1893-

PERSONAL: Born September 24, 1893, in East Greenwich, R.I.; son of George E. (a businessman) and Luella (Haley) Bailey; married Margaret Helen Suba, April 1, 1917; children: Brewster Burrows. *Education:* Attended East Greenwich Academy, East Greenwich, R.I., 1909-13. *Politics:* Independent. *Religion:* Protestant Episcopal. *Home and office:* 25 Sargent Park, Newton, Mass. 02158.

CAREER: Newspaperman in New England for fortyfive years, holding most of the jobs from reporter to managing editor on daily papers in Providence, R.I., and Boston, Mass., prior to 1962; full-time author of junior books, 1962—. Editorial posts with *Providence News* and its successors, *Providence News-Tribune*, and *Providence Star-Tribune*, 1914-37, included city editor, editor, and managing editor; did public relations for Republican State Central Committee of Rhode Island, Providence, 1938-40; variously rewriteman, chief of copy desk, and telegraph editor for *Boston Traveler*, 1941-62. *Military service:* National Guard, with Rhode Island Cavalry on Mexican border, 1916. *Member:* Boston Authors Club (board of directors, 1948-52).

WRITINGS: Argosies of Empire, Dutton, 1947; *Sea Hawks of Empire*, Dutton, 1948; *Tim's Fight for the Valley*, Dutton, 1951; *Tony Sees It Through*, Dutton, 1953; *Indian Fighter: The Story of Nelson A. Miles*, Morrow, 1965; *Fighting Sailor: The Story of Nathaniel Fanning*, Morrow, 1967; *Guns Over the Carolinas*, Morrow, 1967; *Fight for Royal Gorge*, Morrow, 1968; *Wagons Westward: The Story of Alexander Majors*, Morrow, 1969.

WORK IN PROGRESS: A junior book about fur trading.

SIDELIGHTS: Bailey told *CA:* "Of my published books, *Argosies* and *Sea Hawks* are a romanticized history of international trade, from the Phoenicians down to the Portuguese, Dutch and English, and are required reference reading in their fields in many high school libraries."

BIOGRAPHICAL SOURCES: Mildred B. Flagg, *Notable Boston Authors*, Dresser, 1965.

* * *

BAILIE, Victoria Worley 1894-

PERSONAL: Born September 11, 1894, in Nikko, Japan; daughter of Joseph (a Presbyterian minister and professor) and Effie Dean (a doctor of medicine; maiden name Worley) Baillie. *Education:* Attended private and public elementary schools in Shanghai, China, and Berkeley, Calif.; University of California, student, 1914-17, B.A., P.H.N., 1922; Stanford University, R.N., 1921. *Politics:* Republican. *Religion:* Presbyterian. *Home:* 1990 Marin Ave., Berkeley, Calif. 94707.

CAREER: Public health nurse, 1922-55, in Fort Bragg, Calif., and environs, 1922-24, Pleasanton, Sunol, Dublin, and Antone, Calif., 1924-27, Alameda City, Calif., 1927-46, and for California State and Contra Costa health departments, 1946-59.

WRITINGS: Bailie's Activities in China, Pacific Books, 1964; *It Happened Years Ago*, Vantage, 1967.

AVOCATIONAL INTERESTS: Reading, agriculture, and gardening.

* * *

BAIRD, A(lbert) Craig 1883-

PERSONAL: Born October 20, 1883, in Vevay, Ind.; son of William J., (a publisher) and Sarah (Hedden) Baird; married Marion Peirce, June 26, 1923; children: Mary Barbara (Mrs. John Rees, Jr.). *Education:* Wabash College. A.B., 1907; Union Theological Seminary, New York, N.Y., B.D. (magna cum laude), 1910; Columbia University, A.M., 1912. *Religion:* Episcopalian. *Home:* 200 Ferson Ave., Iowa City, Iowa. *Office:* Speech Department, University of Iowa, Iowa City, Iowa.

CAREER: Ohio Wesleyan University, Delaware, instructor in English, 1910-11; Dartmouth College, Hanover, N.H., instructor in English, 1911-13; Bates College, Lewiston, Me., professor of rhetoric and argumentation, 1913-25; University of Iowa, Iowa City, associate professor, 1925-28, professor of speech, beginning, 1928. Visiting professor at Columbia University, University of Illinois, University of Washington, Seattle, University of Missiouri, Michigan State University, Southern Illinois University, and University of Southern California. *Member:* Speech Association of America (president, 1939), Modern Language Association of America, Phi Beta Kappa, Delta Sigma Rho, Pi Kappa Delta. *Awards, honors:* Litt.D., Wabash College, 1932.

WRITINGS: (Compiler) *College Readings on Current Problems*, Houghton, 1925; *Public Discussion and Debate*, Ginn, 1928, revised edition, 1937; (compiler) *Essays and Addresses Toward a Liberal Education*, Ginn, 1934; *Discussion: Principles and Types*, McGraw, 1943; (with Lester Thonssen) *Speech Criticism: The Development of Standards for Rhetorical Appraisal*, Ronald, 1948, 2nd edition, 1970; (with Franklin H. Knower) *General Speech: An Introduction*, McGraw, 1949, 4th edition with Knower and Samuel L. Becker published as *General Speech Communication*, 1971; *Argumentation, Discussion, and Debate*, McGraw, 1950; (with Knower) *Essentials of General Speech*, McGraw, 1952, 4th edition with Knower and Becker published as *Essentials of General Speech Communication*, 1973; (editor) *American Public Addresses, 1940-1952*, McGraw, 1956; (editor) Chauncey Allen Goodrich, *Essays from Select British Eloquence*, Southern Illinois University Press, 1963; *Rhetoric: A Philosophical Inquiry*, Ronald, 1965. Compiler, *Representative American Speeches*, annually, 1937—.

* * *

BAIRD, Forrest J. 1905-

PERSONAL: Born October 19, 1905, in McKeesport, Pa.; son of Thomas W. and Catherine (Forrest) Baird; married Mildred Warburton, June 11, 1938. *Education:* San Jose State College (now California State University), B.A., 1932; Columbia University, M.A., 1933; Stanford University, Ed.D., 1955. *Religion:* Methodist. *Home:* 309 Bookwood Ave., San Jose, Calif. 95116.

CAREER: Teacher at Marysville High School and Yuba College, Marysville, Calif., 1934-46; San Jose State College (now California State University), professor of music, 1946—. Professional trombonist. *Member:* Music Educators National Conference (life), Phi Mu Alpha-Sinfonia (life), Phi Delta Kappa, Masons.

WRITINGS: Music Skills for Recreation Leaders, W. C. Brown, 1963; (editor) Spartan Songs, Informal Music Service, 1966; Sing with Chords, W. C. Brown, 1967. Contributor to music and educational journals.

AVOCATIONAL INTERESTS: Freighter travel.

*　　*　　*

BAKER, Elizabeth Faulkner 1886(?)-1973

PERSONAL: Born in Abilene, Kan.; daughter of Lothrop Hedge (a businessman) and Hattie (Bearce) Faulkner; married Fred J. Baker (deceased). Education: University of California, Berkeley, LL.B., 1914; Columbia University, A.M., 1919, Ph.D. 1925. Politics: Democrat. Home: 601 West 113th St., New York, N.Y. 10025.

CAREER: Served as dean of women at Washington State Normal School and Idaho State Normal School, prior to 1919; Columbia University, Barnard College, New York, N.Y., member of faculty, 1919-73, professor of economics, 1948-52, professor emeritus, 1952-73, chairman of department, 1940-52. Public member and panel chairman, Region II, National War Labor Board, 1942-45. Member of Columbia University Seminar on Labor, 1960-65. Panel member, New York State Mediation Board and American Arbitration Association. Member: American Economic Association, American Civil Liberties Union, National Planning Association. Awards, honors: Made an honorary member of International Printing Pressmen and Assistants' Union following publication of her book about printing history.

WRITINGS: Protective Labor Legislation: With Special Reference to Women in the State of New York, Columbia University Press, 1925, reprinted, AMS Press, 1969; Displacement of Men by Machines: Effects of Technological Change in Commercial Printing, Columbia University Press, 1933; Printers and Technology: History of the International Printing Pressmen and Assistants' Union, Columbia University Press, 1957; Technology and Woman's Work, Columbia University Press, 1964. Contributor of articles and reviews to periodicals.

WORK IN PROGRESS: Professional Women.

(Died January 28, 1973)

*　　*　　*

BAKER, Lawrence M(anning) 1907-

PERSONAL: Born January 23, 1907, in Laurel Creek, Ky.; son of Daniel and Lucy (Caldiron) Baker; married Leeta Derthick (a journalist), August 18, 1934; children: Lois Jean Baker Berger, Linda Carolyn, Martha Gail Baker Halstead. Education: Berea College, A.B., 1929; University of Kentucky, M.A., 1932, Ph.D., 1933. Politics: Democrat. Religion: Protestant. Home: 1204 North Grant, West Lafayette, Ind. Office: Purdue University, West Lafayette, Ind.

CAREER: High school teacher in Kentucky, 1930-31; Berea College, Berea, Ky., associate professor, 1933-37, professor of psychology and head of department, 1937-44, dean of Upper Division, 1943-44; U.S. Veterans Administration, Lexington, Ky., chief clinical psychologist, 1946-47; Purdue University, Lafayette, Ind., associate professor, 1947-51, professor of psychology, 1951—. Trustee, Indiana Mental Health Foundation; Member, Indiana Governor's Commission on Mental Health Planning, 1963—. Military service: U.S. Navy, 1944-46; became lieutenant. Member: American Psychological Association, In-

diana Psychological Association (president, 1963-64), Indiana Association for Mental Health (vice-president, 1962-63), Berea College Alumni Association (president, 1964-65), Sigma Xi, Phi Delta Kappa.

WRITINGS: General Experimental Psychology, Oxford University Press, 1960; Laboratory Experiments in Psychology, Oxford University Press, 1960. Contributor of articles to psychology journals.

*　　*　　*

BAKER, Mary Gladys Steel 1892-197(?)
(Sheila Stuart)

PERSONAL: Born in 1892, in Johnstone, Renfrewshire, Scotland; daughter of William (a clergyman) and E. S. (Thomson) Westwood; married S. Howard Baker (deceased). Education: Attended High School for Girls, Glasgow, Scotland. Religion: Scottish Presbyterian. Home: Clarig, Crieff, Perthshire, Scotland.

CAREER: Author and journalist.

WRITINGS—All under pseudonym Sheila Stuart: Kitty Comes to Stay, J. Leng & Co., 1929; The Morisons of Cleave, J. Leng & Co., 1929; Antiques on a Modest Income, Chambers, 1939; Dictionary of Antiques, DeGraff, 1954; Antiques for the Modern Home, Chambers, 1962, A. S. Barnes, 1964; A Home from Home, Longmans, 1967; Small Antiques for the Small Home, A. S. Barnes, 1969. Contributor to Scottish Field.

"Alison" series of adventure stories for young people (all published by Blackie & Son): Alison's Highland Holiday, 1946; More Adventures of Alison, 1947; Alison's Christmas Adventure, 1948; Well Done, Alison!, 1949; Alison's Easter Adventure, 1950; Alison's Poaching Adventure, 1951; Alison's Kidnapping Adventure, 1952; Alison's Pony Adventure, 1953; Alison's Island Adventure, 1954; Alison's Spy Adventure, 1955; Alison and the Witch's Cave, 1956; Alison's Yacht Adventure, 1957; Alison's Riding Aventure, 1958; Alison's Cliff Adventure, 1959; Riddle of Corran Lodge, 1959, Alison's Caravan Adventure, 1960.

(Deceased)

*　　*　　*

BAKER, Richard St. Barbe 1889-

PERSONAL: Born October 9, 1889, in Southampton, England; son of John R. St. Barbe (a horticulturist) and Charlotte (Purrott) Baker; married Doreen Whitworth Long, 1946 (divorced, 1958); married Catriona Burnett, 1959; children: (first marriage) Angela, Paul. Education: Attended Dean Close School, Cheltenham, England, and University of Saskatchewan; Gonville and Caius College, Cambridge, Forestry Diploma, 1920. Home: Leagate House, Bramley, Surrey, England.

CAREER: Assistant conservator of forests in Kenya, 1920-23, in Nigeria, 1924-29; forestry adviser and silviculturist, 1929—. Lectured on tour in United States and Canada, 1930, on world tour, 1931; recently rode through New Zealand 1200 miles on horseback, speaking about trees to 95,000 schoolchildren. Director of Sahara Reclamation Program. Founder of Men of the Trees, Kenya, 1922, and as a world-wide society, 1932; founder of World Forestry Charter Gatherings, 1945, now supported by more than ninety countries. Organizer of forestry summer schools at Oxford University, 1938, and other universities. Military service: British Army, 1914-18; served in France. Member: Naval and Military Club.

WRITINGS: Among the Trees, privately printed by the Men of the Trees (London), 1935; *Arbor Day Planting* (form of ceremony and instructions with a selected list of trees), [London], 1935; *The Brotherhood of the Trees* (on the founding of a native society to protect the Central African forests), Figurehead, 1930; *Men of the Trees: In the Mahogany Forests of Kenya and Nigeria*, introduction by Lowell Thomas, includes photographs by Baker, Dial, 1931; *Trees: A Book of the Seasons*, Lindsay Drummond, 1940, 2nd edition, 1948; *Africa Drums*, includes 48 photographs by Baker, Lindsay Drummond, 1942, revised edition, with an introduction by Bronislaw Malinowski, George Ronald, 1942, revised edition, George Ronald, 1951; *The Redwoods*, Lindsay Drummond, 1943, revised and enlarged edition, George Ronald, 1959; *I Planted Trees* (autobiography), includes 46 photographs by Baker, Lutterworth, 1944; *Green Glory: The Story of the Forests of the World*, Lutterworth, 1948, published as *Green Glory: Forests of the World*, Wyn, 1949; (with others) *The Lasting Victories*, Lutterworth, 1948; *Trees: A Readers Guide*, National Book League (London), 1948; *New Earth Charter*, Men of the Trees, 1949; *Famous Trees*, Dropmore Press, 1953; *Sahara Challenge* (account of an expedition across the desert), Lutterworth, 1954; *Kabongo: The Story of a Kikuyu Chief*, A. S. Barnes, 1955; *Land of Tane: The Threat of Erosion*, Lutterworth, 1956; *Dance of the Trees: The Adventures of a Forester*, Oldbourne, 1956; *My Life—My Trees*, Friends of Nature, 1956; *Kamiti: A Forester's Dream*, foreword by Dr. Nkrumah, George Ronald, 1958, Duell, Sloan & Pearce, 1960; *Horse Sense: Horses in War and Peace*, Stanley Paul, 1962; *The True Book About Trees*, Muller, 1964; *Famous Trees of New Zealand*, George Ronald, 1965; *Sahara Conquest: Reforestation*, Friends of Nature, 1966. Editor of annual *Tree Lovers' Calendar*, Jarrold & Sons, 1929—; founder and editor, *Trees and Life*, 1940—. Author of pamphlets and articles on forestry.

WORK IN PROGRESS: Trees of Great Britain (American edition of *My Life—My Trees*); *Sapoba—Unless the King: The Birth of Forestry in Nigeria*.

* * *

BAKEWELL, Paul, Jr. 1889-1972

PERSONAL: Born January 26, 1889, in St. Louis, Mo., son of Paul and Eugenia (McNair) Bakewell; married Mary C. M. Fullerton, June 2, 1909 (deceased); married Harriet M. Rodes, December 31, 1956; children: (first marriage) Joseph S. (deceased), Paul III, Claude I., George Morgan, Francis F., Mary Caroline (deceased). *Education:* St. Louis University, A.B., 1908. *Politics:* Conservative. *Religion:* Roman Catholic. *Home:* 10 Portland Pl., St. Louis, Mo. 63108. *Office:* 509 Olive St., St. Louis, Mo. 63101.

CAREER: Admitted to Missouri Bar, 1910; St. Louis University, St. Louis, Mo., professor of corporate law and real property law, 1916-18; U.S. War Trade Board, Washington, D.C., director of Bureau of Enemy Trade, 1918; Government Research Institute, St. Louis, Mo., organizer and chairman, 1922-36; Bakewell, Bakewell & Cramer (law firm), St. Louis, Mo., partner, 1948-72. Director of First National Bank of Clayton, Rock Ridge Land Co., and Philipsburg Coal & Land Co. Chairman of advisory board, St. Louis University; governor of St. Louis Community Fund. *Member:* American Bar Association, St. Louis Bar Association, Academy of Political Science.

WRITINGS: Past and Present Facts About Money in the

United States, Macmillan, 1936; *What Are We Using for Money?*, Van Nostrand, 1952; *Inflation in the United States*, Caxton, 1958; *13 Curious Errors about Money*, Caxton, 1962. Contributor of editorials to *Saturday Evening Post*.

(Died October 1, 1972)

* * *

BALBONTIN, Jose Antonio 1893-

PERSONAL: Born October 8, 1893, in Madrid, Spain; refugee in London, England, 1939, returned to Spain, 1970; son of Adolfo and Flora (Gutierrez) Balbontin; married Maria Munoz. *Education:* University of Madrid, Doctor in Law. *Politics:* Republican-Socialist. ("I am one of those dreamers who wants to harmonize individual liberty and social justice.") *Religion:* "Christian-Humanist." *Home:* Miguel Angel, 17, Madrid 10, Spain.

CAREER: Barrister in Madrid, Spain, 1927-39; Republican member of Cortes Cobstituyentes (Parliament of Spanish Republic), 1931-33; judge of High Court of Spain, 1936-39; minister counsellor for Spanish Republican government in exile, London, England, 1952-70. Writer; Spanish translator for British magazines. *Member:* Ateneo de Madrid, Academia de Jurisprudencia de Madrid. *Awards, honors:* Spanish National Prize of Literature, 1925, for *Inquietudes*.

WRITINGS—Poetry: Albores, Del Amo, 1910; *De la Tierruca*, Del Amo, 1912; *La Risa de la esperanza*, Santafe, 1914; *Inquietudes*, [Madrid], 1925; *Romancero del pueblo*, [Madrid], 1931; *Por el amor de Espana y de la idea*, [Mexico], 1956.

Prose: *El Suicidio del Principe Ariel* (novel), Historia Nueva, 1929; *La Espana de mi experiencia* (autobiography and history), Coleccion Aquelarre, 1952; *Tres poetas de Espana: Rosalis de Castro, Federico Garcia Lorca, Antonio Machado*, [Mexico], 1957, translation published as *Three Spanish Poets*, Alvin Redman, 1961; *Donde esta la verdad?*, Fontanella (Barcelona), 1967; *A La Busca del Dios perdido*, Indice Editorial (Madrid), 1969; *Reflexiones sobre la no-violencia*, Indice Editorial, 1972.

Plays, performed in Madrid in 1936, include "Aqui manda Narvaez!," "La Cancion de Riego," "El Cuartel de la montana," "El frente de Extremadura," "Pionera."

WORK IN PROGRESS: In the London Fog; Jesus y los rollos del Mar Muerto, a Humanist interpretation of the Dead Sea Scrolls; *A La Orilla del Tamesis*, poems in Spanish; *Reflexiones sobre el tiranicidio*, a treatise against tyranny.

SIDELIGHTS: Balbontin writes: "I am more interested in life than in my writings. At this moment, I am very interested in the preservation of Universal Peace. At the same time I should like to see, before becoming insensibilized by old age, the triumph of Universal Revolution. This is another contradiction of my spirit [see *Politics*], which I do not know how to solve. I can read and write Spanish, English, French and Italian; but I only speak with relative perfection my own language: the Spanish spoken in Madrid before 1939. I think the Spanish language has deteriorated, as [has] almost everything."

* * *

BALD, F(rederick) Clever 1897-1970

PERSONAL: Born August 12, 1897, in Baltimore, Md.; son of Frederick William and Elizabeth (Krise) Bald; married Laura M. McGrath, 1921; married Jane R. Howard, 1956; children: Robert E. *Education:* Franklin & Marshall College, student, 1914-17; University of Aix-Marseille, student, 1919; University of Michigan, A.B., 1920; Wayne State University, M.A., 1937; University of Michigan, Ph.D., 1943. *Religion:* Congregationalist. *Home:* 1880 Glenwood Rd., Ann Arbor, Mich. *Office:* Michigan Historical Collections, University of Michigan, 160 Rackham Bldg., Ann Arbor, Mich.

CAREER: The Hudson School, Detroit, Mich., teacher, 1922-29, headmaster, 1929-32; Detroit Institute of Technology, Detroit, Mich., instructor, 1932-43; University of Michigan, Ann Arbor, instructor, 1943-45, war historian, 1945-47, assistant director of Michigan Historical Collections, 1947-60, professor of history and director of Michigan Historical Collections, 1960-67. Member, Michigan Civil War Centennial Observance Commission. *Military service:* Medical service in France in 28th Division, 1917-19. *Member:* American Historical Association, Organization of American Historians, American Association of University Professors, Michigan Academy (secretary, 1960-62), American Association for State and Local History, Historical Society of Michigan (president, 1954-55), Faculty Research Club, University Club, Algonquin Club (vice-president).

WRITINGS: Detroit's First American Decade: 1796-1805, University of Michigan Press, 1948; *Michigan in Four Centuries*, Harper, 1954, revised and enlarged edition, 1961. Author of numerous booklets on Michigan historical subjects. Contributor of articles to historical periodicals.

(Died, 1970)

* * *

BALINT, Michael 1896-1970

PERSONAL: Born December 3, 1896; married Alice Szekely-Kovacs, 1923 (died, 1939); married Enid Albu, 1953; children: J. A. (son). *Education:* University of Budapest, M.D., 1920; University of Berlin, Ph.D., 1924; University of Manchester, M.Sc., 1945. *Home and office:* 7 Park Sq. W., London N.W.1, England.

CAREER: Hungarian Psycho-Analytical Institute, Budapest, Hungary, training analyst and lecturer, 1926-39; Budapest Clinic of Psycho-Analysis, Budapest, organizer and director, 1931-39; British Psycho-Analytical Society, London, England, training analyst and lecturer, 1939; medical director and psychiatrist of child guidance clinics in England, 1942-47; Tavistock Clinic, London, consultant psychiatrist, 1950-61; University College Hospital, London, honorary clinical assistant, department of psychological medicine, 1961-70. Visiting professor of psychiatry, University of Cincinnati College of Medicine, 1956-70. *Member:* British Psychoanalytical Society.

WRITINGS: Primary Love and Psycho-Analytic Technique, Hogarth, 1952, Liveright, 1953; (editor) Sandor Ferenczi, *Final Contribution to the Problems and Methods of Psychoanalysis,* Basic Books, 1955; (editor with Sandor Lorand) *Perversions, Psychodynamics and Therapy,* Randon House, 1956; *The Doctor, His Patient and the Illness,* International Universities Press, 1957, 2nd edition, revised and enlarged, Pitman Medical Publishing Co., 1964; *Problems of Human Pleasure and Behaviour,* Liveright, 1957; (with wife, Enid Balint) *Thrills and Regressions,* International Universities Press, 1959; (with Enid Balint) *Psychotherapeutic Techniques in Medicine,* Tavistock Publications, 1961, C. C Thomas, 1962; (contributor) M.

W. Jongsma, editor. *Psychologie in der hausaerztlichen Praxis,* Hippokrates-Verlag, 1963; *A Study of Doctors: Mutual Selection and the Evaluation of Results in a Training Programme for Family Doctors,* Lippincott, 1966; *The Basic Fault: Therapeutic Aspects of Regression,* Barnes & Noble, 1968; (with others) *Treatment or Diagnosis: A Study of Repeat Prescriptions in General Practice,* Tavistock Publications, 1970. Author of more than seventy scientific papers in English, American, French, Hungarian, and German publications. Editor, ''Mind and Medicine Monographs,'' Tavistock Publications, 1961—.

SIDELIGHTS: Balint's books have been translated into German, French, Hungarian, Italian, and Spanish.

(Died, 1970)

* * *

BALLARD, Lowell Clyne 1904-

PERSONAL: Born December 29, 1904, in Bisbee, Ariz.; son of George Philip (a farmer) and Margaret Delight (Winsor) Ballard; married Margaret Marion Holt, October 25, 1939; children: Roger Lowell, Robert Holt. *Education:* Arizona State University, student; San Diego State College (now California State University), B.A., 1939; Claremont College, M.A., 1943. *Politics:* Democrat. *Religion:* Church of Jesus Christ of Latter-day Saints (Mormon). *Home:* 4533 Highland Ave., San Diego, Calif. 92115. *Office:* Ocean View School, 447 South 47th St., San Diego, Calif. 92113.

CAREER: Elementary school principal in Safford, Ariz., 1929-39, and in San Diego, Calif., 1941—. *Member:* National Education Association, Phi Delta Kappa.

WRITINGS—With Frank L. Beals; all juveniles: *Real Adventure with the Discoverers of America,* Harr Wagner, 1954; *Real Adventure with the Pilgrim Settlers,* Harr Wagner, 1954; *Real Adventure with American Pathfinders: Daniel Boone, Lewis and Clark, Zebulon Pike, David Crockett,* Harr Wagner, 1954; *Real Adventure with American Plainsmen,* Harr Wagner, 1954; *Real Adventure with American Patriots,* Harr Wagner, 1954; *Spanish Adventure Trails,* Naylor, 1960. Contributor to *The Caravan of Verse,* 1938, and *Winston Basic Reader,* fourth grade. Contributor to scholastic and curriculum periodicals and to yearbooks. Publisher of several educational history and arithmetic games for young people.

AVOCATIONAL INTERESTS: Writing verse; golf and camping.

* * *

BANER, Skulda Vanadis 1897-1964

PERSONAL: Born November 23, 1897, in Ironwood, Mich.; daughter of Johan G. R. (a newspaper publisher and poet under the name Asabard) and Mathilda (Bergman) Baner. *Education:* High school graduate; extension courses from University of Wisconsin.

CAREER: Was a prairie teacher in rural North Dakota, a personnel director, a photographer, a dressmaker, a secretary and lecturer on utility subjects for a power company in Ironwood, Mich., worked in radio (as copywriter and announcer) and in advertising in Milwaukee, Wis., and edited a house organ for a milk company.

WRITINGS: Latchstring Out, Houghton, 1944; *Voice of the Lute,* McKay, 1959; *First Parting,* McKay, 1960; *Pims: Adventures of a Dala Horse,* McKay, 1964. Contributor to *Ladies' Home Journal, American Swedish Monthly,* and *American Girl.*

SIDELIGHTS: Blinded by glaucoma, Miss Baner was an insatiable reader in Braille in both Swedish and English, and corresponded with the blind in Sweden.

(Died January 31, 1964)

*   *   *

BANNER, Hubert Stewart   1891-1964
(Vexillum)

PERSONAL: Born August 16, 1891, in Dunham O'th Hill, Cheshire, England; son of Francis Stewart (a clergyman) and Sophia (Townson) Banner; married Peggy Regina Lipton, May 21, 1922; married second wife, Winnifred Van Ess, August 22, 1957; children: Melville Stewart (deceased). *Education:* Attended Haileybury College; Brasenose College, Oxford, B.A., 1913. *Politics:* Conservative. *Religion:* Church of England. *Home:* 1205 Sunnyhills Rd., Oakland, Calif. 94610. *Agent:* Hope Leresche & Steele, 11 Jubilee Pl., London S.W.3, England.

CAREER: Myrtle, Burt & Co., Manchester, England, manager of branches in Java, 1913-25; Far Eastern Political Intelligence, organizer, 1914-25; Government of British Malaya, London Agency, London, England, publicity officer, 1926-34; Editorial Services Ltd., London, account executive, 1935-37; Rotary International in Great Britain and Ireland, general secretary, 1937-39; Ministry of Information, chief Southeast region officer, 1939-43; Netherlands House, London, England, director, 1943-46; Hudson's Bay Co., Vancouver, British Columbia, public relations officer, 1948-49; Vancouver Civic Theatre Society, Vancouver, British Columbia, general manager, 1949-54; sales manager for various real estate firms, Vancouver, British Columbia, 1954-57. Lecture tours in England, Canada, United States. *Military service:* World War I, Intelligence Corps; British Home Guard, 1940-42. *Member:* Authors' Club (London), West Sussex Writer's Club, Authors' Lodge (Masonic order in England; master, 1934-35). *Awards, honors:* First prize for short story, Sussex Writers' Club, 1960.

WRITINGS: Ten Poems, privately printed, 1916; *Guide to Brambanan Temples,* Dutch East Indies Government, 1920; *Horrid Rhymes for Torrid Climes,* privately printed, 1924; *Romantic Java: As It Was and Is,* Seeley Service, 1927; *The Mountain of Terror,* Butterworth & Co., 1928; *A Tropical Tapestry,* Butterworth & Co., 1929; *Red Cobra,* Butterworth & Co., 1929; *Great Disasters of the World,* Hurst & Blackett, 1931; *The Clean Wind,* Hurst & Blackett, 1931; *Flamboyante,* Hurst & Blackett, 1932; *Calamities of the World,* Hurst & Blackett, 1932; *Wanted on Voyage,* Hurst & Blackett, 1933; *Masonry in the Malay Peninsula and Archipelago,* Dorset Masters' Lodge, 1933; *Amy Johnson,* Rich & Cowan, 1933; *These Men Were Masons,* Chapman & Hall, 1934; *Hell's Harvest,* Hurst & Blackett, 1934; *Tidal Wave,* Hurst & Blackett, 1935; *Kentish Fire,* Hurst & Blackett, 1944; *Thus, My Orient* (short stories), Dorothy Crisp, 1945. Author of a radio play, "Raffles of Singapore." Contributor to magazines and newspapers in England and Canada. Founder and editor, *Java Palpitator.*

WORK IN PROGRESS: Was working on a novel, *Pint-Sized Delilah,* at time of death.

SIDELIGHTS: Banner lived in Indonesia twelve years. He spoke fluent French, Dutch, and Malay, and was competent in German, Flemish, and various Malaysian dialects. *Avocational interests:* Oriental mythology, folklore, and comparative religion; also music and art.

(Died May 9, 1964)

BARAL, Robert   1910-

PERSONAL: Born April 2, 1910, in Fort Wayne, Ind. *Education:* Attended Indiana University. *Home:* 354 West 23rd St., New York, N.Y. 10011.

CAREER: Fort Wayne Journal-Gazette, Fort Wayne, Ind., reporter, three years; *Variety,* New York, N.Y., staff reporter, 1937-40, roving reporter, 1940—; U.S. Office of War Information, English control editor, 1945. Free-lance publicity work for Walt Disney Productions, Warner Brothers, Columbia Pictures, and Metro-Goldwyn-Mayer, all New York, N.Y. *Member:* Ziegfeld Club (member of advisory board), Delta Upsilon.

WRITINGS: Revue: A Nostalgic Reprise of the Great Broadway Period, Fleet Press, 1962, revised edition, 1970; *Turn West on 23rd: A Toast to New York's Old Chelsea,* Fleet Press, 1966. Contributor to *Harper's Bazaar, Photoplay, Screenland,* and *Dance.*

BIOGRAPHICAL/CRITICAL SOURCES: Antiquarian Bookman, June 7-14, 1971.

*   *   *

BARBOUR, J(ames) Murray   1897-1970

PERSONAL: Born March 31, 1897, in Chambersburg, Pa.; son of J. Will (a photographer) and Irene (Sears) Barbour; married Mary C. Disert, June 30, 1923 (died January 5, 1964); children: James M., Jr., Margaret D. (Mrs. Philip W. Humer). *Education:* Dickinson College, A.B., 1918, M.A., 1920; Temple University, Mus.B., 1924; graduate study at University of Cologne, 1929, and University of Berlin, 1930; Cornell University, Ph.D., 1932; University of Toronto, Mus.D., 1936. *Politics:* Liberal Republican. *Religion:* Protestant. *Home:* 607 Division St., East Lansing, Mich. 48823. *Office:* Music Department, Michigan State University, East Lansing, Mich. 48823.

CAREER: Haverford School, Haverford, Pa., organist and master, 1919-21, 1922-26; Wells College, Aurora, N.Y., assistant professor of music, 1926-32; Ithaca College, Ithaca, N.Y., associate professor of English and music, 1932-39; Michigan State University, East Lansing, professor of music, 1939-65. University of Vienna, Fulbright research professor, 1953-54. Composer. *Military service:* U.S. Army, Signal Corps, World War I. *Member:* American Musicological Society (president, 1957-59), Acoustical Society of America, Mathematical Association of America, Phi Beta Kappa, Theta Chi, Phi Mu Alpha, Kiwanis Club, Masons. *Awards, honors:* Distinguished Alumnus award, Dickinson College, 1948, Temple University, 1964; Mus.D., Temple University, 1965.

WRITINGS: Tuning and Temperament: A Historical Survey, Michigan State University Press, 1951, 2nd edition, 1953; *The Church Music of William Billings,* Michigan State University Press, 1960; *The Principles of Greek Notation,* American Musicological Society, 1960; *Trumpet, Horns and Music,* Michigan State University Press, 1964; (author of introduction) Robert Smith, *Harmonics; or, The Philosophy of Musical Sounds,* DaCapo Press, 1966; *Poems, Mostly for Mary,* privately printed, 1969. Published musical compositions include "Requiem Mass in G Minor." Author of articles, particularly on mathematics of music.

WORK IN PROGRESS: Was editing selected compositions of F. X. Pokorny, and working on a study of German chorale in seventeenth and eighteenth centuries.

SIDELIGHTS: From time to time Barbour studied and did

research in Germany and Austria; he participated in a musicological congress in Salzburg, 1964. He liked to "dabble in light verse, including the 'clean' limerick."

(Died January 4, 1970)

* * *

BARK, William (Carroll) 1908-

PERSONAL: Born December 10, 1908, in Tacoma, Wash.; son of Nelson and Daisy (Shea) Bark; married Eleanor Carlton; children: Dennis Laistner, Jared Carlton. *Education:* Stanford University, A.B. (with great distinction), 1931, A.M., 1932; Cornell University, Ph.D., 1936. *Politics:* Democrat. *Religion:* Episcopal. *Home:* 721 Alvarado Row, Stanford, Calif. *Office:* Department of History, Stanford University, Stanford, Calif.

CAREER: Stanford University, Stanford, Calif., instructor in history, 1936-40; Lawrence College, Appleton, Wis., associate professor of history, 1940-44; University of Chicago, Chicago, Ill., assistant professor of history, 1945-47; Stanford University, associate professor, 1947-57, professor of history, 1957—. Visiting professor, Stanford-in-Italy, Florence, 1962-63. Member, Carnegie Commission of Educational Inquiry, 1951-56; co-chairman, San Francisco Public Schools Survey Committee, 1959-60. *Member:* American Historical Association, Phi Beta Kappa, Sigma Alpha Epsilon, Bohemian Club (San Francisco). *Awards, honors:* Sterling Fellow at Yale University, 1944-45; Bollingen Foundation Fellow in Europe, 1962-63.

WRITINGS: (Contributor) Max Savelle, editor, *History of World Civilization,* Henry Holt, 1956; *Origins of the Medieval World,* Stanford University Press, 1958. Co-author of published report on San Francisco public schools survey. Contributor to historical and philosophical journals. Member of editorial board, *Medievalia et Humanistica,* 1962—.

WORK IN PROGRESS: Dionysius Exiguus and the Founding of the Middle Ages (tentative title); a book on the development of western civilization.

SIDELIGHTS: Bark's books have been translated into Spanish and Portuguese.

* * *

BARKER, Frank Granville 1923-

PERSONAL: Born June 3, 1923, in York, England; son of Richard Braithwaite (an art dealer) and Violet (Hudson) Barker. *Education:* University of Leeds, B.A., 1950. *Politics:* Socialist. *Home:* 11 Upper Wimpole St., London W.1, England.

CAREER: Carl Rosa Opera Co., London, England, public relations officer, 1952; Hansom Books Ltd., London, editor of *Plays and Players,* 1955-1962, of *Music and Musicians,* 1962-70, of *Books and Bookmen,* 1971—. *Military service:* British Army, Royal Electrical and Mechanical Engineers, 1942-46. *Member:* Union of Journalists.

WRITINGS: Stars of the Opera, Lotus Press, 1949; *Voices of the Opera,* Arthur Unwin, 1951; (with Geoffrey Handley-Taylor) *John Gay and the Ballad Opera,* edited by Max Hinrichsen, Hinrichsen Edition, 1956. Contributor of articles and reviews on theatre and music to *Nine, Everybody's Weekly, Music Journal, Opera News, Yorkshire Post, Topic, Scene,* and other publications in England and the United States; assistant music critic, *Daily Express* (London), 1969—.

AVOCATIONAL INTERESTS: Country walks.

BARKER, Melvern 1907-

PERSONAL: Born November 24, 1907, in Providence, R.I.; son of Joseph Edward (a salesman) and Martha (Anslow) Barker; married Dorothy Wight (a public school art supervisor), June 29, 1935; children: Judith Mayhew (Mrs. Barry Burns Lutender), Karen Ann (Mrs. Richard M. Duffy). *Education:* Rhode Island School of Design, graduate, 1931; studied at Provincetown School of Painting, 1931, Art Students League, New York, N.Y., 1933. *Religion:* Protestant. *Residence:* Chilmark, Mass. *Agent:* Florence Crowther, 350 West 57th St., New York, N.Y. 10019.

CAREER: In 1930's worked as art director of advertising agency in Hartford, Conn., advertising artist for the Macy chain of newspapers, Yonkers, N.Y., taught private classes in painting and drawing, adult education classes in illustration and graphic arts; settled on Martha's Vineyard, off Massachusetts coast, 1941, and went to sea with fishing fleet for almost ten years; resumed teaching as instructor at Vesper George Art School, Boston, Mass., 1949-50, in Saugerties Public Schools, Saugerties, N.Y., 1959-60, at Monroe-Woodbury High School, Monroe, N.Y., 1962-63; Vesper George School of Art, teacher, 1968—. Portrait artist with United Service Organization camp shows during World War II.

WRITINGS: Southeast of Noman's: A Trip Dragging Aboard the Southern Cross (adult fishing story with lithographs), John Day, 1948.

Children's picture books, all self-illustrated: *Little Sea Legs,* Oxford University Press, 1951; *Six O'Clock Rooster,* Oxford University Press, 1953; *Little Island Star,* Oxford University Press, 1954; *Country Fair,* Oxford University Press, 1955; *How Little Boats Grew,* Lippincott, 1955; *The Different Twins,* Lippincott, 1957; *Shipshape Boy,* Scribner, 1961.

WORK IN PROGRESS: Two children's books; adult book on swordfishing.

AVOCATIONAL INTERESTS: Swimming, boating, golf, and walking the beaches.

* * *

BARKER, Roger Garlock 1903-

PERSONAL: Born March 31, 1903, in Macksburg, Iowa; son of Guy (a farmer) and Cora (Garlock) Barker; married Louise Shedd, June 17, 1930; children: Celia Barker Lottridge, Jonathan Shedd, Lucy. *Education:* Stanford University, B.A., 1928, M.A., 1930, Ph.D., 1934. *Religion:* Presbyterian. *Home:* Oskaloosa, Kan. 66066. *Office:* Midwest Psychological Field Station, Oskaloosa, Kan. 66066.

CAREER: Research associate at Stanford University, Stanford, Calif., 1934-36, University of Iowa, Iowa City, 1936-38; Harvard University, Cambridge, Mass., assistant professor of psychology, 1938-39; University of Illinois, Urbana, assistant professor of psychology, 1939-42; Stanford University, Stanford, Calif., acting associate professor of psychology, 1942-46; Clark University, Worchester, Mass., Hall Professor of Genetic Psychology, 1946-47; University of Kansas, Lawrence, professor of psychology, 1947—, chairman of department, 1947-51. Co-founder, Midwest Psychological Field Station, Oskaloosa, Kan., 1947. Summer professor at University of Oregon, Columbia University, University of Colorado, Stanford University, and University of California. National Research Council—National Academy of Sciences, member of Committee on Child Development, 1956-58, member of Committee on Primary Records in the Behavioral Sciences, 1957-61.

MEMBER: American Psychological Association (president, division of developmental psychology, 1952-53; fellow), Society for Research in Child Development (president, 1957-59), Society for the Psychological Study of Social Issues, American Association for the Advancement of Science, Ecological Society of America, Society for General Systems Research, Society for Biological Rhythm, American Association of University Professors, Sigma Xi, Rotary International (Oskaloosa; president, 1960-61). *Awards, honors:* Fellow, Center for Advanced Study in the Behavioral Sciences, 1957-58; U.S. Public Health Service Career award, 1962; Kurt Lewin Award of Society for the Psychological Study of Social Issues, 1963; Research Career award of National Institute of Mental Health, 1963; Distinguished Contribution award from American Psychological Association, 1963.

WRITINGS: (With Jacob S. Kounin and Herbert F. Wright) *Viewpoints on Science and the Psychology of Motivation for Students of Child Psychology*, Stanford University Press, 1942; (editor with Kounin and Wright) *Child Behavior and Development: A Course of Representative Studies*, McGraw, 1943; (with Beatrice A. Wright, L. Meyerson, and Millie R. Gonick) *Adjustment to Physical Handicap and Illness: A Survey of the Social Psychology of Physique and Disability*, Social Science Research Council, 1946, revised edition, 1953; (with H. F. Wright and others) *Methods in Psychological Ecology: A Progress Report*, privately printed, 1950; (with H. F. Wright) *The Midwest and Its Children: The Psychological Ecology of an American Town*, Row, Peterson & Co., 1954; (with Louise S. Barker, H. F. Wright, and Maxine Schoggen) *Specimen Records of American and English Children from the Midwest Psychological Field Station*, University of Kansas Press, 1961; (with Paul V. Gump and others) *Big School, Small School: Studies of the Effects of High School Size upon the Behavior and Experiences of Students*, Midwest Psychological Field Station, 1962, reissued as *Big School, Small School: High School Size and Student Behavior*, Stanford University Press, 1964; (editor and contributor) *The Stream of Behavior: Explorations of Its Structure and Content*, Appleton, 1963; *Ecological Psychology: Concepts and Methods for Studying the Environment of Human Behavior*, Stanford University Press, 1968.

Contributor: Q. McNelmar and Maude A. Merrill, editors, *Studies in Personality*, McGraw, 1942; W. Dennis, editor, *Readings in Child Psychology*, Prentice-Hall, 1951; J. H. Rohrer and M. Sherif, editor, *Psychology at the Crossroads*, Harper, 1951; R. Kuhlen and G. Thompson, editors, *Human Development*, Appleton, 1952; H. Brand, editor, *The Study of Personality*, Wiley, 1954; E. O. Wittkower and R. A. Cleghorn, editors, *Recent Developments in Psychosomatic Medicine*, Pitman (London), 1954; A. P. Coladarci, editor, *Educational Psychology: A Book of Readings*, Dryden Press, 1955; *Clinical Studies of Personality*, Harper, 1955; M. R. Jones, editor, *Nebraska Symposium on Motivation*, University of Nebraska Press, 1960; B. Kaplan, editor, *Studying Personality Cross-Culturally*, Row, Peterson & Co., 1961.

Also author with H. F. Wright, Louise S. Barker, and others of "Full Day Records" series, Midwest Social Psychology Field Station, 1951-52. Contributor to *Encyclopedia of Educational Research*, *Encyclopaedia Britannica*, and to pamphlets and bulletins. Contributor of several dozen articles to psychology, sociology, and education journals.

WORK IN PROGRESS: A follow-up of book on American and British children, under grants from National Science Foundation and National Institute of Mental Health.

*   *   *

BARLOW, James   1921-1973

PERSONAL: Born December 1, 1921, in Birmingham, England; son of Stanley (a bank clerk) and Gladys (Jones) Barlow; married Joyce Margaret Everiss, June 24, 1949; children: Stephen, Gillian, Michael. *Education:* Attended English schools, 1927-37. *Politics:* "Undecided!" *Religion:* Christian. *Home:* Half Year House, West Runton, Norfolk, England. *Agent:* Charles Lavell Ltd., Mowbray House, Norfolk St., London W.C. 2, England.

CAREER: Went to work for Birmingham Corp. Water Department, Birmingham, England, at seventeen; joined the Royal Air Force the following year (1940) and served as a gunnery instructor until invalided out in 1941 with tuberculosis; began to write while convalescing, starting with technical articles for aviation journals, then humorous pieces for *Punch*; returned to Water Department of Birmingham Corp. in 1946, and became a rate inspector and investigator, working on novels (and collecting rejection slips for some years) in his spare time; with the success of *The Patriots* in 1960 he gave up his work in Birmingham and moved to the country to write full time.

WRITINGS: *The Protagonists*, Harper, 1956; *One Half of the World*, Harper, 1957; *The Man with Good Intentions*, Cassell, 1958; *The Patriots* (Book Society choice in England), Harper, 1960; *Term of Trial*, Simon & Schuster, 1961; *The Hour of Maximum Danger*, Simon & Schuster, 1962; *This Side of the Sky*, Simon & Schuster, 1964: *One Man in the World*, Simon & Schuster, 1966; *The Love Chase*, Simon & Schuster, 1968; *The Burden of Proof*, Simon & Schuster, 1968; *Goodbye, England*, Hamish Hamilton, 1969; Devin-Adair, 1970; *Liner*, Simon & Schuster, 1970; *Both Your Houses*, Hamish Hamilton, 1971. Contributor to *Flight, Aeroplane, Punch*, and *Sunday Times* (London).

SIDELIGHTS: Barlow felt he was writing against the entire stream of British fiction, and once told *CA* he "believes (but only just) in the dignity of man but in none of those ceremonials that represent it." He wrote for what he called "the little man," believing that "in a world searching for sensation, the hardest but most dignified thing to be is an ordinary man."

Term of Trial was filmed by Warner Brothers, 1963, *The Burden of Proof* was filmed as "Villain," by Metro-Goldwyn-Mayer, 1971; *The Patriots* was also made into a film, and the book, *Liner*, was adapted for a movie.

(Died January 30, 1973)

*   *   *

BARNES, Henry A.   1906-1968

PERSONAL: Born December 16, 1906, in Newark, N.Y.; son of Herman Myron and Maude Louise (Henion) Barnes; married Hazel Mae Stone, September 1, 1928; children: William Henry, Virginia (Mrs. Wayne Plowman). *Education:* Studied at General Motors Institute of Technology, Flint, Mich., and at University of Michigan and Michigan State University Extension Schools. *Religion:* Protestant. *Home:* 79-33 215th St., Bayside, N.Y. 11364. *Office:* Department of Traffic, 28-11 Bridge Plaza North, Long Island City, N.Y. 11101.

CAREER: Chevrolet Motor Co., Flint, Mich., maintenance engineer, 1933-37; captain of police and traffic engineer, Flint, Mich., 1941-47; director of traffic, Denver, Colo., 1947-53; commissioner of transit and traffic, Baltimore, Md., 1953-62; commissioner of traffic, New York, N.Y., 1962-68. Member of National Highway Research Board; consultant on traffic safety and developer of traffic devices; member of the board of directors of Eno Foundation for Highway Traffic Control, Saugatuck, Conn., 1967-68. *Member:* Institute of Traffic Engineers, American Public Works Association, Institute of Electrical and Electronics Engineers, Brooklyn Engineers Club (honorary), Chi Epsilon (honorary), Masons, Elks. *Awards, honors:* Ph.D., Susquehanna University; Presidential Citation for activities in war transportation; Theodore M. Matson Memorial Award for outstanding contribution to the profession of traffic engineering, 1968.

WRITINGS: The Man with the Red and Green Eyes, Dutton, 1965. Contributor to journals and magazines. Associate editor, *Traffic Engineering* and *Municipal South*; contributing editor, *Street Engineering*.

WORK IN PROGRESS: A textbook for Columbia University Press.

BIOGRAPHICAL SOURCES: New York Herald Tribune, March 1, 1965; *New York Times*, March 3, 1965.

(Died September 16, 1968)

* * *

BARNETT, Leonard (Palin) 1919-

PERSONAL: Born April 11, 1919, in Crewe, Cheshire, England; children: Andrew, Richard. *Education:* Attended University of Manchester; University of London, B.D. (second class honors), 1945. *Home:* 7 Essex Park, Finchley, North London, N.3, England.

CAREER: Methodist minister, 1942—; now superintendent minister, Finchley and Hendon Methodist Circuit, England. Director, Methodist Holiday Homes Ltd.; national secretary, Methodist Youth Department, 1949-58; regular BBC broadcaster on religious programs; also makes occasional television appearances. *Awards, honors:* L.H.D., Pfeiffer College, 1972.

WRITINGS: Adventure with Youth, Methodist Youth Department, 1952; *Starting out in Church Youth Club Work*, Methodist Youth Department; *Prayer-Time with Youth*, Methodist Youth Department, 1954; *A Prayer Diary for Youth*, Methodist Youth Department, 1955; *For Christian Beginners*, Methodist Youth Department, 1955; *Christian Responsibility for World Peace*, Epworth; *Talking to Youth*, National Sunday School Union, 1958.

Talking to Youth Again, National Sunday School Union, 1960; *A Boy's Prayer Diary*, Epworth, 1963; *A Girl's Prayer Diary*, Epworth, 1963; *Live for Kicks*, National Sunday School Union, 1964; (author of introduction) *Here is Methodism: For Church Membership Groups and Other Interested People*, Epworth, 1966; *Sex and Teenagers in Love*, Denholm House Press, 1967; *This I Can Believe*, Denholm House Press, 1969; *The Way to the Stars: Sermons for the Space Age*, Epworth, 1971. Also author of *The High Cost of Loving*, Epworth, *Good Times with God*, Hodder & Stoughton, and *A New Prayer Diary*, Hodder & Stoughton.

Plays: *Ten to Twelve*, Methodist Youth Department; *Boy on the Corner*, Evans; *Windswept Week-end*, Evans; *You've Got to Be Tough*, Methodist Youth Department. Regular columnist, *British Weekly.*

BARNETTE, W(arren) Leslie, Jr. 1910-

PERSONAL: Born July 8, 1910, in LeRoy, N.Y.; son of Warren Leslie (a businessman) and Alice Hart (Kellogg) Barnette. *Education:* University of Buffalo, B.A., 1932, M.A., 1936; New York University, Ph.D., 1949. *Politics:* Liberal. *Home:* 1392 Amherst St., Buffalo, N.Y. 14216. *Office:* Department of Psychology, State University of New York at Buffalo, Buffalo, N.Y. 14214.

CAREER: State University of New York at Buffalo, professor of psychology, and director of Vocational Counseling Center, 1950—. Fulbright visiting professor to India, 1952-53, 1964-65. Consulting psychologist, Veterans Administration. Member of board of directors of Buffalo Chamber Music Society, Young Audiences, Inc., and Community Music School. *Military service:* U.S. Army Air Forces and U.S. Office of Strategic Services 1942-46; served in Southeast Asia. *Member:* American Psychological Association, Association of Measurement and Evaluation in Guidance, American Personnel and Guidance Association, Society for Psychological Study of Social Issues, American Association of University Professors, Eastern Psychological Association, New York State Psychological Association, Psychological Association of Western New York, Western New York Personnel and Guidance Association (president-elect), Buffalo Council on World Affairs.

WRITINGS: Occupational Aptitude Patterns of Selected Groups of Counseled Veterans (monograph), American Psychological Association, 1951; (with John N. McCall) *Validation of the Minnesota Vocational Interest Inventory for Vocational High School Boys*, Department of Psychology, State University of New York, Buffalo, 1963; (editor) *Readings in Psychological Tests and Measurements*, Dorsey, 1964, 3rd edition, in press; (with McCall and Robert R. Carkhuff) *The Counselor's Handbook: Scale and Profit Interpretations of the MMPI*, R. W. Parkinson, 1965. Contributor to psychological journals.

AVOCATIONAL INTERESTS: Music and gourmet food.

* * *

BARNHILL, Myrtle Fait 1896-

PERSONAL: Born July 10, 1896, in Fulton, Mo.; daughter of William Lemuel (an architect) and Elizabeth (Breedlove) Fait; married David Hinds Barnhill, June 9, 1926; children: Fairy Jane (Mrs. Don M. Duncan), Mary (Mrs. Rudy Garcia). *Education:* Southern Baptist Theological Seminary, Bachelor of Missionary Training, 1922; Mississippi College, A.B., 1947; University of Texas, graduate study. *Home:* 1002 Speight, Waco, Tex.

CAREER: Teacher in elementary schools, Waco, Tex., 1947-49; Baylor University, Waco, Tex., librarian, 1949-54; teacher of mathematics in elementary schools, LaMarque, Tex., 1957-62.

WRITINGS: Life's Overtones (poetry), Baylor University Press, 1963; *Afterglow* (poetry), Naylor, 1964. Contributor to newspapers.

* * *

BARR, Stephen 1904-

PERSONAL: Born 1904, in England, son of U.S. nationals; married Anna Keiley. *Education:* Attended schools in England. *Residence:* Woodstock, N.Y.

CAREER: Commerical artist for many years and architectural draftsman; full-time writer, 1955—.

WRITINGS: *Experiments in Topology*, Crowell, 1964; *A Miscellany of Puzzles, Mathematical and Otherwise*, Crowell, 1965; *Second Miscellany of Puzzles, Mathematical and Otherwise*, Macmillan, 1969. Contributor of short stories and articles to *Vogue, Mademoiselle, Atlantic Monthly, Harper's Bazaar, Playboy*, and to detective and science fiction magazines.

AVOCATIONAL INTERESTS: Composing music.

* * *

BARRY, Raymond Walker 1894-

PERSONAL: Born January 1, 1894, in McConnelsville, Ohio; son of George Walker (an attorney) and Mary Florence (Work) Barry; married Mildred Ruth Jayne, December 25, 1922; children: George Hamilton. *Education:* Ohio Wesleyan University, A.B., 1915; Stanford University, A.M., 1916, Ph.D., 1925; additional summer study at University of California, Berkeley and Los Angeles, and University of Southern California. *Home:* 21 East Valerio St. Apt. 8, Santa Barbara, Calif. 93101.

CAREER: High school teacher of German and English in Santa Barbara, Calif., 1916-23; San Jose State College (now University), San Jose, Calif., professor of English, 1924-58, head of department, 1926-58, chairman of Division of Language and Literature, 1951-56; writer of textbooks. Visiting summer professor, Indiana University, 1952. *Military service:* U.S. Army, Infantry, 1918; became second lieutenant. *Member:* Retired Teachers Association, Channel City Club (both Santa Barbara).

WRITINGS: (With A. J. Wright) *Literary Terms—Definitions, Explanations, Examples*, Chandler Publishing, 1966.

WORK IN PROGRESS: *Twentieth Century American Novelists*.

* * *

BARTHOLOMEW, Cecilia 1907-

PERSONAL: Born in 1907, in Canada; married Dwight F. Bartholomew, 1934; children: Mrs. Enrique Suarez del Solar, Mrs. David Newby. *Education:* University of California, A.B., 1931. *Home:* 239 Stanford Ave., Berkeley, Calif. *Agent:* Lurton Blassingame, 10 East 43rd St., New York, N.Y. 10017.

CAREER: University of California, Berkeley, instructor in creative writing, 1957—. *Member:* Authors League of America, California Writers Club, Phi Beta Kappa, Theta Sigma Phi.

WRITINGS: *The Risk*, Doubleday, 1958; *A Touch of Joshua*, Doubleday, 1960. Contributor of short stories to *McCall's, Ladies' Home Journal, Redbook, Woman's Day, The Writer*, and other magazines.

* * *

BARTLETT, Ruhl J. 1897-

PERSONAL: Born January 24, 1897, in Webster, W. Va.; son of Adolphus J. (a farmer) and Mary Anne (Shroyer) Bartlett; married Lela M. Work August 30, 1924. *Education:* Ohio University, A.B., 1920; University of Cincinnati, M.A., 1923; Columbia University, summer graduate study, 1926; Ohio State University, Ph.D., 1927. *Home:* 4-G Lake St., Winchester, Mass. 01890. *Office:* Fletcher School, Tufts University, Medford, Mass. 02155.

CAREER: Teacher of history in Ohio high schools, 1920-23, at State University of Iowa, Iowa City, 1925-26, Ohio State University, Columbus, 1927; Tufts University, Medford, Mass., assistant professor, 1927-32, professor of history and head of department, 1932-56, dean of Graduate School, 1938-39, acting dean of Fletcher School of Law and Diplomacy, 1944-45, professor of diplomatic history in Fletcher School, 1944—. *Military service:* U.S. Navy, 1918-19; served in World War I. *Member:* American Historical Association, Southern Historical Association, Organization of American Historians, Phi Beta Kappa, Phi Kappa Tau.

WRITINGS: *John C. Fremont and the Republican Party*, Ohio State University Press, 1930; *The League to Enforce Peace*, University of North Carolina Press, 1944; (with Mary W. Williams) *People and Politics of Latin America*, revised edition (Bartlett was not associated with earlier editions), Ginn, 1945, 4th edition (by Bartlett and Russell E. Miller), 1955; (editor) *The Record of American Diplomacy*, Knopf, 1947, 5th edition, 1964; *Policy and Power: Two Centuries of American Foreign Relations*, Hill & Wang, 1963; *American Foreign Policy: Revolution and Crisis*, Oglethorpe College, 1966.

WORK IN PROGRESS: Two books, *History and the Historian's Craft*, and *The Presidency and the Congress*.

* * *

BARTON, John Mackintosh Tilney 1898-

PERSONAL: Born May 20, 1898, in Parkstone, Dorsetshire, England; son of Tilney Wallace (a solicitor of the Supreme Court) and Marian Helen (Jowitt) Barton. *Education:* St. Edmund's College, Ware, England, seminarian, 1915-20; Angelico University, Rome, Italy, S.T.B. and S.T.L. (cum laude), 1921, S.T.D. (magna cum laude), 1922; Biblical School of St. Etienne, Jerusalem, postdoctoral study, 1922-24; Pontifical Biblical Commission, Rome, Italy, L.S.S., 1928. *Home and office:* SS. Peter & Edward's Presbytery, 43 Palace St., Westminster, London SWIE 5HL, England.

CAREER: Ordained Roman Catholic priest at Westminster, London, England, 1921; named privy chamberlain to the Pope, with title Very Reverend Monsignor, 1936, and domestic prelate, with title Right Reverend Monsignor, 1952. St. Edmund's College, Ware, Hertfordshire, England, professor of Hebrew and Old Testament, 1924-26, professor of Holy Scripture, 1926-36, chief librarian, 1929-36; House of Higher Studies, Edmonton, Middlesex, England, warden, 1936-37; St. Catherine's parish and House of Studies, West Drayton, Middlesex, England, administrator, 1937-50; SS. Peter & Edward's Presbytery, Westminster, London, England, priest in charge, 1950—. Officiating chaplain, Royal Air Force Reception Depot, West Drayton, 1938-50. English consultor and examiner for Biblical degrees, Pontifical Biblical Commission, 1935-72; member of Westminster Metropolitan Tribunal (Catholic), 1946—; diocesan censor, 1955-72; Canon of Westminster Cathedral, 1971—.

MEMBER: Society of Antiquaries (fellow), Royal Society of Arts (fellow), Society for Old Testament Study (president, 1952), Palestine Oriental Society, Catholic Biblical Association (chairman, 1942-57), Society of St. John Chrysostom (chairman), 1959-65), Newman Association, Arts Theatre Club (London).

WRITINGS: *The Holy Ghost*, Burns & Oates, 1930; (editor and author of introduction) Pere Lagrange, *Catholic Harmony of Four Gospels*, Burns & Oates, 1930; *Semitic*

Religions, Catholic Truth Society, 1933; (editor) D. Buzy, *Life of St. John the Baptist*, Burns & Oates, 1933; (editor) Cardinal Nicholas Wiseman, *Lectures on the Blessed Eucharist*, new edition, Burns & Oates, 1933; *The Religion of Israel*, Catholic Truth Society, 1934; (with Cardinal Joseph MacRory) *New Testament and Divorce*, Burns & Oates, 1934; (editor and author of introduction) John Chapman, *Matthew, Mark and Luke*, Longmans, Green, 1937; (adaptor from the French) Severien Salaville, *Introduction to Eastern Liturgies*, Sands, 1938; *The Phases of the Sacred Passion*, Sands, 1954; *Penance and Absolution*, Hawthorn, 1961; (editor of English translation) J. Bonsirven, *Theology of the New Testament*, Burns & Oates, 1964; (editor) P. Drijvers, *The Psalms: Their Statement and Meanings*, Herder, 1965.

Contributor to four Cambridge Summer School volumes and to journals. Editor, Catholic Truth Society's "Studies in Comparative Religion," 1952—; general editor, Burns & Oates's "Scripture Textbooks for Catholic Schools" series, 1945—.

AVOCATIONAL INTERESTS: Swimming and criminology.

* * *

BARTON, Margaret D(over) 1902-

PERSONAL: Born August 1, 1902, in Fall River, Mass.; daughter of Benjamin H. (a machinist) and Mary (Dover) Barton. *Education:* Pembroke College, A.B., 1923; Rhode Island College, M.Ed., 1940; special courses at Brown University, Middlebury College, Tufts University, and in Europe. *Religion:* Protestant Episcopalian. *Home:* 2928 Pawtucket Ave., East Providence, R.I. 02915.

CAREER: High school teacher of French and history in Deep River, Conn., 1923-26; Barrington (R.I.) public schools, high school teacher of French, 1926-63, coordinator of French language study, grades four-twelve, and supervisor of language laboratory, 1958-63, now retired. Consultant to Modern Language Association of America, 1963—, and to Holt, Rinehart & Winston, Inc., 1964—. Member of Rhode Island advisory committee on French language study, 1962-64. *Member:* American Association of Teachers of French (secretary-treasurer, Rhode Island chapter, 1957-58), American Association of University Women (vice-president and president of local branch, 1954-60), New England Modern Language Association (executive board, Rhode Island chapter, 1962-63).

WRITINGS: (With Camille Bauer and Patricia O'Connor) *Lire Parler et Ecrire*, Holt, 1964, revised edition (with Bauer), 1971, workbook (with Laura B. Gilmore), 1965.

* * *

BASSETT, William B. K. 1908-
(Peter Darien)

PERSONAL: Born December 22, 1908, in Newark, N.J.; son of Carroll Phillips and Margaret (Kinney) Bassett; married Constance Colt, September 15, 1943; children: Carroll Colt, Nancy Lee, Constance K., Eliot J. *Education:* Attended Westminster School and Hun School; Lafayette College, student, 1929-31.

CAREER: Associated with utilities companies, 1931-35; Bassett Foundation, Inc., Summit, N.J., chairman, 1935—; Sterling Security Corp., Summit, N.J., currently president. *Military service:* U.S. Army Air Forces, three years, World War II; served in Pacific theater. *Member:* Successor Society of the Cincinnati.

WRITINGS—All under pseudonym Peter Darien; poetry, except as indicated: *Dust from a Grindstone*, Pacific Book Association, 1933; *Echo and Reflection*, Oriole Press, 1935; *Songs of Season*, Golden Hind Press, 1939; *Sound to the Silent*, Oriole Press, 1940; *Drift*, Rittenhouse Book Store, 1941, reissued in two volumes as *Drift, East and West* and *Drift, North and South*, Oriole Press, 1962; *Flame*, Oriole Press, 1947; *Village of Seven Gates*, Oriole Press, 1958; *The Clock*, Oriole Press, 1960; *Celebrations* (essays), Oriole Press, 1962; *Darien's World: A Compendium of Poems in Ten Slender Volumes*, Oriole Press, 1962, one-volume edition, Liveright, 1964.

WORK IN PROGRESS: A Prudential Founder, projected biography of Allan Lee Bassett.

* * *

BATES, Darrell 1913-

PERSONAL: Born November 10, 1913, in Ashtead, Surrey, England; son of Ernest Stuart (an author) and Edith (Prichard) Bates; married Susan Sinclair, August 3, 1944; children: Christopher, Susan, Nicholas. *Education:* Attended Sevenoaks School; Keble College, Oxford, B.A., 1935. *Home:* Mellinpons, St. Buryan, Cornwall, England. *Agent:* Curtis Brown Ltd., 13 King St., Covent Garden, London W.C. 2, England, and 575 Madison Ave., New York, N.Y.

CAREER: Colonial Administrative Service, district commissioner of Tanganyika Territory, 1936-50, acting governor of Seychelles, 1950-51, deputy chief secretary of Somaliland Protectorate, 1951-53, chief secretary of Gibraltar, 1953-68. *Military service:* British Army, King's African Rifles, 1940-44; became captain; mentioned in dispatches. *Member:* Travellers Club (London). *Awards, honors:* Companion of Victorian Order, 1954; Companion of Order of St. Michael and St. George, 1958; Knight Bachelor, 1968.

WRITINGS: A Fly Switch from the Sultan, Hart-Davis, 1961; *A Shell at My Ear* (autobiography), Hart-Davis, 1961; *The Mango and the Palm*, Hart-Davis, 1962; *A Longing for Quails* (six stories), Hart-Davis, 1964; *Susie*, Hart-Davis, 1964; *A Gust of Plumes*, Hodder & Stoughton, in press. Contributor of short stories and articles to *Argosy* (England), *Blackwoods, Punch, Harper's Bazaar, She, Courier, Saturday Evening Post, Cosmopolitan, Atlantic Monthly*, and other magazines and papers, and to British Broadcasting Corp.

* * *

BATES, Kenneth Francis 1904-

PERSONAL: Born May 24, 1904, in N. Scituate, Mass.; son of Francis Loring and Winnette (Litchfield) Bates; married Charlotte Young, 1931; children: Katharine Freedman, Cornelia Bates Martinez, Benham. *Education:* Massachusetts School of Art, B.S. in Ed., 1926; student at Berkshire School of Art, 1927, Fontainbleau School of Art, 1931; European study, 1954. *Religion:* Congregationalist. *Home:* 7 E. 194th St., Euclid 19, Ohio. *Office:* Cleveland Institute of Art, 11141 East Blvd., Cleveland, Ohio.

CAREER: Cleveland Institute of Art, instructor, design and enamelling, 1927-70. Lecturer on enamelling, design theory, color, horticulture and flower arrangement. Instructor, University of Tennessee, summers 1953, 1955, 1957, 1971-74, and University of Notre Dame, 1958-59, 1960, 1961, 1963, and 1965. *Member:* Archaeological Society of

America, Cleveland Art Association, Craft Guild, Cleveland Society of Artists (president, 1945-46), New York Society of Artists and Craftsmen, Society of Aesthetics (chairman, 1959), Archives of American Art (Washington, D.C.), Business Men's Garden Club, United World Federalists. *Awards, honors:* Harshaw Chemical Award for Best Enamel, 11th National Ceramic Exhibition, 1946; Horace Potter Silver Medal for Excellence in Craftsmanship, Cleveland Museum of Art, 1949, 1957, 1966; Silver Medal, American Rose Society, 1952; Special Honor Award, Mid-West Designer-Craftsman Exhibition, Chicago Art Institute, 1957; 1st prize, National Syracuse Ceramic Exhibition, 1960; Cleveland Fine Arts Prize, 1963; Cleveland Institute of Art faculty grant, 1964; twenty-five first and special awards, Cleveland Museum of Art, 1927-64.

WRITINGS: Enamelling: Principles and Practice, World Publishing, 1951; *Basic Design: Principles and Practice*, World Publishing, 1960; *The Enamelist*, World Publishing, 1967.

* * *

BATH, Philip Ernest 1898-

PERSONAL: Born February 21, 1898, in Wickham Market, Suffolk, England; son of George Philip (a postmaster) and Kate (Barker) Bath; married Minnie Clark, August 15, 1923; children: Mary (Mrs. Andrew Adamson). *Education:* King's College, University of London, B.Sc., 1922; London Day Training College, diploma in pedagogy, 1923. *Home:* Fair View, Yallands Hill, Monkton Heathfield, Taunton, Somerset, England.

CAREER: Northamptonshire Education Committee, assistant master in Irthlingborough, England, 1923-28, lecturer in organic chemistry and teacher of mathematics at Evening Technical College, Wellingborough, 1923-28; West Riding of Yorkshire Education Committee, headmaster in Bramley, Rotherham, 1928-57. *Military service:* British Army, 1915-19. *Awards, honors:* Order of the British Empire, 1957, for work in education; fellow, International Institute of Arts and Letters, 1960.

WRITINGS: Fun with Words: A Book of Puzzles and Quizzes for the Not So Old, Epworth, 1958; *Fun with Figures*, Epworth, 1959; *Great Names in Medicine,* Wheaton & Co., 1960; *Great Names in Industry*, Wheaton & Co., 1960; *Great Names in Exploration*, Wheaton & Co., 1960; *Fun with Words Again*, Epworth, 1960; *How Much Do YOU Know?: A Set of Quizzes for Young and Old*, Epworth, 1961; *A Biblical Quiz, by Which the Bible Is Made Plain*, Epworth, 1961; *More Fun with Figures*, Epworth, 1962; *How's Your General Knowledge?*, Epworth, 1963; *The Quiz-Cross Game*, four books, Wheaton & Co., 1965. Contributor to various anthologies for children, and to *Poetry of Today, Poet, English Illustrated, Nursery World*, and other periodicals, and to *World Book Encyclopedia*. Editor, *Our Magazine* (for physically handicapped and deaf children of West Riding of Yorkshire), 1951-71.

* * *

BATHO, Edith C(lara) 1895-

PERSONAL: Born September 21, 1895, in London, England; daughter of William John and Ellen Clara (Hooton) Batho. *Education:* University College, London, B.A., 1915, M.A. (with distinction), 1921, D.Lit., 1935. *Religion:* Church of England. *Home:* 130 Wood St., Barnet, Hertfordshire, England.

CAREER: Member of staff of Roedean School, Brighton, England, 1918-19, of Down House School, Cold Ash, Newbury, England, 1919-21; University of London, London, England, lecturer, later reader in English literature at University College, 1921-45, principal of Royal Holloway College, 1945-62. Visiting professor, University of Wisconsin, 1963. British Academy, Warton Lecturer. *Member:* International Federation of University Women (third vice-president, 1950-53; first vice-president, 1953-56), British Federation of University Women (president, 1945-50), English Association, Viking Society, English-Speaking Union. *Awards, honors:* Rose Mary Crawshay Prize for English Literature, 1922, for *James Hogg, the Ettrick Shepherd*; honorary doctorate from University of Poitiers, 1962.

WRITINGS: The Art of History (John Oliver Hobbes Memorial Scholarship Essay, 1915), University of London Press, 1915; *The Life of Christ in the Ballads* (originally published in *Essays and Studies by Members of the English Association*), [Oxford], 1924; *The Ettrick Shepherd*, Macmillan, 1927; *Sir Walter Scott and the Sagas: Some Notes* (originally published in *Modern Language Review*), [Cambridge], 1929; *Icelandic Ballads* (originally published in *Saga-Book* of Viking Society for Northern Research), [London], 1929; (contributor) H.J.C. Grierson, editor, *Sir Walter Scott Today*, Constable, 1932; *The Later Wordsworth*, Macmillan, 1933; *Notes on the Bibliography of James Hogg, the Ettrick Shepherd* (originally published in *Library*, December, 1935), [London], 1935; *The Poet and the Past* (Wharton Lecture), Oxford University Press, 1937; (with Bonamy Dobree) *The Victorians and After, 1830-1914*, includes chapter by Guy Chapman, Cresset, 1938, 2nd revised edition, 1950; (editor with R. W. Chambers and H. Winifred Husbands) *The Chronicles of Scotland*, compiled by Hector Boece, Blackwood for Scottish Text Society, Volume 1 (with Chambers), 1938, Volume 2 (with Husbands), 1941; (editor) *A Wordsworth Selection*, Athlone Press, 1962. Contributor to *Essays and Studies by Members of the English Association*, Volume IX, Clarendon Press, 1924, and of articles, reviews and notes to *Modern Language Review, Scottish Historical Review*, other learned journals.

SIDELIGHTS: Batho knows French, German, Swedish, Danish, and some Icelandic and Italian. *Avocational interests:* Reading, travel, needlework.

* * *

BATTISCOMBE, E(sther) Georgina (Harwood) 1905-
(Gina Harwood)

PERSONAL: Born November 21, 1905, in London, England; daughter of George (a master cotton spinner, and member of Parliament) and Ellen (Hopkinson) Harwood; married Christopher Battiscombe (a lieutenant colonel, Grenadier Guards), October 1, 1932 (died, 1964); children: Aurea (Mrs. George Lawrence Morshead). *Education:* Lady Margaret Hall, Oxford, B.A. *Religion:* Anglican. *Home:* 3 Queen's Acre, King's Rd., Windsor, Berkshire, England.

AWARDS, HONORS: James Tait Black Prize for Biography, 1963, for *John Kelbe: A Study in Limitations.*

WRITINGS: (Under name Gina Harwood, with A. W. Hopkinson) *The Mantle of Prayer*, Mowbray, 1931; (under name Gina Harwood) *Haphazard*, Mathews & Marrot, 1932; *Charlotte Mary Yonge: The Story of an Uneventful Life*, Constable, 1943; *Two on Safari*, Muller, 1946; *En-*

glish *Picnics*, Harville, 1949; *Mrs. Gladstone: The Portrait of a Marriage*, Constable, 1956, Houghton, 1957; *John Keble: A Study in Limitations*, Constable, 1963, Knopf, 1964; *Christina Rossetti* (pamphlet), Longmans, Green for British Council and National Book League, 1965; (editor, with Marghanita Laski, and contributor) *A Chaplet for Charlotte Yonge*, Cresset, 1965; *Queen Alexandra*, Houghton, 1969. Contributor of articles and reviews to *Times Literary Supplement*, *Country Life*, *Time and Tide*, *Economist*, other newspapers.

BIOGRAPHICAL/CRITICAL SOURCES: New York Times Book Review, November 30, 1969; *Virginia Quarterly Review*, spring, 1970.

* * *

BAUER, Harry C(harles) 1902-

PERSONAL: Born July 22, 1902, in St. Louis, Mo.; son of Emile George and Jennie Theresa (Cannan) Bauer. *Education:* Washington University, St. Louis, Mo., B.A., 1927, M.S., 1929; St. Louis Library School, diploma, 1931. *Politics:* Democrat. *Religion:* Baptist. *Home:* 3 Pooks Hill Rd., Apt. 315, Bethesda, Md. 20014.

CAREER: University of Missouri, Columbia, library, chief of circulation, 1931-34; Tennessee Valley Authority, Knoxville, Tenn., technical librarian, 1934-42; University of Washington, Seattle, librarian, 1945-59, professor of library science, 1959-67, professor emeritus, 1967—. Board member of Allied Arts of Seattle. *Military service:* U.S. Air Force, 98th Bombardment Group, 1942-45; became colonel in Air Force Reserve; awarded Bronze Star, Purple Heart, Air Medal.

MEMBER: American Library Association, Pacific Northwest Library Association, Washington Library Association, Pacific Northwest International Writers Conference, People's Memorial Association, Bibliographic Dowsers of America (founder, president), American Civil Liberties Union, Seattle Creative Activities Center, Sigma Xi, Pi Mu Epsilon, Kiwanis International (past president, local club, 1951), American Legion, Retired Officers Association, Masons, Phi Kappa Tau, Oval Club, Rainier Club.

WRITINGS: Seasoned to Taste (literary essays), University of Washington Press, 1961. Columnist for *Wilson Library Bulletin*, 1951-61. Contributor to professional journals. Author of *Prose Bowl*, a serial circular issued by the Bibliographic Dowsers of America, 1961—.

WORK IN PROGRESS: The Coordinate Conjunction "And" in Literary Style: Of The I Sing, an exposition on the treatment of the definite article in cataloging and indexing of book titles; essays.

SIDELIGHTS: Interests are reading and writing, chess, motoring.

BIOGRAPHICAL SOURCES: College and Research Libraries, October, 1947; *Bulletin of Bibliography*, January, 1954.

* * *

BAXTER, Edna May 1890-

PERSONAL: Born June 30, 1890, in Nichols, N.Y.; daughter of Fred Harry (an engineer) and Mary Christine (Lurcock) Baxter. *Education:* Boston University, B.R.E., 1921; Northwestern University, M.A., 1923; Garrett Theological Seminary, B.D., 1927; graduate study at University of Chicago, 1927, Yale University, 1927-28, Union Theo-

logical Seminary and Columbia University, 1929, and School of Speech and Drama, London, England, 1937.

CAREER: The Methodist Church, deaconess, beginning, 1916. Folts Missions Institute, New York, N.Y., teacher of Bible, 1915-19; director of experiment in regional supervision of religious education in northern Illinois (under Northwestern University and Garrett Theological Seminary), 1921-26; Hartford Seminary Foundation, Hartford, Conn., professor of religious education, 1926-60, became professor emerita, 1960. Visiting summer professor at Northwestern University, Tufts College, Union Theological Seminary, Garrett Theological Seminary, and Randolph-Macon College; teacher at church conferences and leadership schools; lecturer in Japan, 1935, in Japan and Korea, 1958. *Member:* Religious Education Association (life member), Connecticut Council of Churches (life member), Delta Kappa Gamma, Appalachian Mountain Club (life member), Women's College Club (Hartford), Town and County Club. *Awards, honors:* M.Div., Garrett Theological Seminary, 1972.

WRITINGS: Friendship Enterprise with Our Jewish Neighbors, Pilgrim Press, 1935; *Children and Labor Problems*, Pilgrim Press, 1935; *Living and Working in Our Country*, Abingdon, 1938; *Children and the Changing World*, Abingdon, 1838; *How Our Religion Began*, Harper, 1939; *Teaching the New Testament*, United Press, 1960; *Learning to Worship*, Judson, 1965; *The Beginnings of Our Religion*, Judson, 1968. Writer of religion teacher's guides; contributor to *Encyclopedia of Religious Knowledge*, *Westminster Encyclopedia of Christian Education*, and to religion journals. Member of editorial board, *Religious Education Journal* and *Journal of Bible and Religion*.

* * *

BEACHCROFT, T(homas) O(wen) 1902-

PERSONAL: Born September 3, 1902, in Clifton, Bristol, England; son of Richard Owen (a music professor) and Nina (Cooke) Beachcroft; married Marjorie Evelyn Taylor, November 27, 1926; children: Ellinor, Nina, Gardner. *Education:* Attended Clifton College, 1912-21; Balliol College, Oxford, B.A., 1924. *Religion:* Church of England. *Home:* The White Cottage, Datchworth Green, Hertfordshire, England. *Agent:* Curtis Brown Ltd., 13 King St., London W.C. 2, England.

CAREER: Employed by British Broadcasting Co. (now British Broadcasting Corp.), London, England, 1924-25, Paul Derrick Advertising Agency, 1926-30, Unilever Advertising Service, 1930-41; British Broadcasting Corp., chief publicity officer, Overseas Service, 1941-61. Member of advisory committee on British books overseas, British Council. *Military service:* Home Guard, 1940-45. *Member:* Society of Authors, Institute of Journalists, National Book League (executive committee member, 1944-50).

WRITINGS: A Young Man in a Hurry, and Other Stories, Harper, 1934; *You Must Break Out Sometimes, and Other Stories*, Harper, 1936; *The Man Who Started Clean* (novel), Harper, 1937; *Just Cats*, Country Life, 1938; *The Parents Left Alone, and Other Stories*, Bodley Head, 1940; *Collected Stories*, John Lane, 1946; *Asking for Trouble* (novel), Bodley Head, 1948; *Malice Bites Back* (stories), Bodley Head, 1948; *A Thorn in the Heart* (novel), Bodley Head, 1952; *Goodbye, Aunt Hesther* (stories), Bodley Head, 1955; *The Modest Art: A Survey of the Short Story in English*, Oxford University Press, 1968.

Booklets: *Calling All Nations*, British Broadcasting Corp.,

1942; *British Broadcasting*, Longmans, Green for the British Council, 1946; *The English Short Story*, two booklets, Longmans, Green for the British Council and National Book League, 1964.

Short stories anthologized in Somerset Maugham's *Introduction to Modern English and American Literature*, and in several English editions of Edward O'Brien's *Best Stories of the Year*. Contributor of poetry, literary criticism, and stories to magazines, journals, and broadcasting organizations. Co-editor, "British Writers and Their Work," 1950-54.

BIOGRAPHICAL/CRITICAL SOURCES: Books and Bookmen, February 1969; *London Magazine*, March, 1969.

* * *

BEAMISH, Huldine V. 1904-

PERSONAL: Born November 15, 1904, in Cork, Ireland; daughter of Richard Henrik and Violet (Pitcairn-Campbell) Beamish. *Education:* Educated in English schools. *Politics:* Anti-democratic. *Home:* Relva, Portalegre, Portugal.

CAREER: Farmer and sports woman, living at various periods in Ireland, England, Scottish Isles, Sweden, Spain, and currently, in Portugal.

WRITINGS: Your Puppy–and Mine, Edward Arnold, 1937; *Your Puppy–and How to Train Him*, Sheridan, 1938, latest revised edition, 1963; *A Childhood's Animals*, Edward Arnold, 1938; (translator from the Swedish) Anders Sparrman, *A Voyage Round the World*, Golden Cockerel, 1944; *The Wild and the Tame*, Bles, 1957; *The Hills of Alentejo*, Bles, 1958; *Cavaliers of Portugal*, Bles, 1966, Taplinger, 1969. Contributor to *Country Life, Field, Game and Gun, Dog World, Sport and Country*, and *Anglo-Portuguese News*; translator of articles from the Swedish.

WORK IN PROGRESS: Pousadas of Portugal, about the country inns; an autobiography.

SIDELIGHTS: Ms. Beamish is competent in French, Portuguese, and Swedish. *Avocational interests:* Mediterranean history, culture, and archaeology.

* * *

BEAN, Keith F(enwick) 1911-
(Kay Fenwick, K. Harrington)

PERSONAL: Born December 18, 1911, in Melbourne, Victoria, Australia; son of Albert William (a minister) and Annie Swan Watson (Dougal) Bean; married Margaret Ada Sherman (a writer), January 18, 1945. *Education:* University of Melbourne, diploma in journalism. *Home:* 32 Woodstock Rd., Chiswick, London W.4, England. *Agent:* Alec Harrison and Associates, Oldbourne Hall, Shoe Lane, London E.C. 4, England.

CAREER: Argus, Melbourne, Australia, reporter, 1928-31; *Telegraph,* Brisbane, Australia, feature writer, 1931-34; worked in various agencies, London, England, 1934-40; *Fact,* London, European editor, 1940-54; Keith Bean & Associates, London, 1954—. Science and technology correspondent, National Press Agency, London; Contributing writer, Central Office of Information, London. Special consultant on freedom of information, United Nations, 1946. *Member:* Australian Journalists' Association (former president of London unit), Circle of Wine Writers (London).

WRITINGS: Eternal Footman (play), Leonardo Press, 1930; (co-author) *The Golden Gander* (play), Swiss Cot-

tage, 1935; *History of the Green Howards*, St. Clement's Press, 1945; *Famous Waterways of the World,* Muller, 1956, revised edition, 1963. Co-author of "Youth and Laughter," a revue produced at Comedy Theatre, Melbourne, Australia; author of radio and television scripts. Regular contributor to *Japan Times* and *Good Housekeeping* and to International Wine and Food Society publications.

WORK IN PROGRESS: Research on gastronomy, viniculture, and scientific, technological, and sociological subjects.

AVOCATIONAL INTERESTS: Eating, drinking, and taking photographs to illustrate own writings.

* * *

BEATTY, William Alfred 1912-19(?)
(Bill Beatty)

PERSONAL: Born November 27, 1912, in Sydney, New South Wales, Australia; son of James Joseph (a bookkeeper) and Margaret (Brazil) Beatty. *Education:* Attended Christian Brothers College, Waverley, New South Wales, Australia, and studied at New South Wales Conservatorium of Music. *Religion:* Roman Catholic.

CAREER: Musician and lecturer, specializing in broadcasting, beginning in 1936; author. Presented weekly program, "Australoddities," Australian Broadcasting Commission, 1941-50, and also has been a talent scout for A.B.C. radio Eisteddfod, and adjudicator for City of Sydney Eisteddfod, and others. Pianist, appearing in public and radio recitals in Australia and elsewhere (played in United States in 1939). *Member:* International P.E.N., Australian Society of Authors, Australian Fellowship of Authors, Bread and Cheese Club, Kosciusko Alpine, Northern Ski (former president).

WRITINGS—Under name Bill Beatty: *This Australia*, Angus & Robertson, 1941; *Amazing Australia*, J. Sands, 1942; *Australia the Amazing*, Amazing Australia Publishers, 1944; *Australian Wonders*, Amazing Australia Publishers, 1945; *Unique to Australia*, Ure Smith, 1952; *'Come a-waltzing Matilda': Australian Folk Lore and Forgotten Tales*, Angus & Robertson, 1954; *Beyond Australian Cities*, Cassell, 1956; *The White Roof of Australia*, Cassell, 1958; *Here in Australia*, Cassell, 1959; *A Treasury of Australian Folk Tales and Traditions*, Ure Smith, 1960; *The Awakening Giant*, Cassell, 1961; *With Shame Remembered: Early Australia*, Cassell, 1962; *Tasmania: Isle of Splendour*, Cassell, 1963; *Next Door to Paradise: Australia's Countless Islands*, Cassell, 1965; *Around Australia with Bill Beatty*, Cassell, 1966; *Tales of Old Australia*, Ure Smith, 1966; *Along the Great Divide*, Ure Smith, 1969.

(Deceased)

* * *

BEBELL, Mildred Hoyt 1909-

PERSONAL: Surname is pronounced Be-*bell*; born October 13, 1909, in Sioux Falls, S.D.; daughter of Henry J. (a merchant) and Millie (Robbins) Marquison; married Charles G. Hoyt, July, 1944 (divorced October 1951); married Clifford S. Bebell (a professor), August 23, 1957; children: (first marriage) Julie M. Grant. *Education:* University of Chicago, Ph.B., 1931; Northwestern University, graduate studies, 1942-43; University of Denver, M.A., 1951, Ed.D., 1954. *Home:* Mount Vernon Country Club, Golden, Colo.

CAREER: High school teacher of English in Sioux Falls,

S.D., 1931-34; Scott, Foresman and Co. (publishers), Chicago, Ill., editor and personnel worker, 1934-43; American Council on Education, Washington, D.C., editor of *American Colleges and Universities* and *American Junior Colleges*, 1946-48; University of Denver, Denver, Colo., 1949-64, began as instructor, became professor of elementary education; New York University, New York, N.Y., professor of education, 1964-66; Southern Colorado State College, Pueblo, Colo., professor of reading and head of department, 1966-73. Director, McClelland Center for Child Study, Pueblo, Colo., 1973—. Appointed to President's Commission on Education in Family Finance, 1968. *Member:* International Reading Association, International Platform Association, Association for Supervision and Curriculum Development, Association for Childhood Education, Delta Kappa Gamma, Pi Lambda Theta. *Awards, honors:* Evelyn Hosmer Award as outstanding woman faculty member, University of Denver, 1960.

WRITINGS—All primary books: *Peppermint Fence*, Heath, 1964; *Sky Blue*, Heath, 1964; *Star Bright*, Heath, 1964, revised edition, 1967.

WORK IN PROGRESS: Evaluating, via research, manuscripts on children's literature; developing diagnostic materials for young children with learning disabilities.

AVOCATIONAL INTERESTS: Travel anywhere, reading, collecting biographies and outstanding children's literature.

* * *

BECKER, Beril 1901-

PERSONAL: Born August 24, 1901, in Slonim, Russia; son of Jeremiah and Yetta (Rabinowitz) Becker; married Ruth Ellis. *Education:* Columbia University, B.A., 1926. *Home:* 57 West 75th St., New York, N.Y. 10023.

CAREER: U.S. Merchant Marine, radio operator, 1923-25; Batten, Barton, Durstine & Osborne, New York, N.Y., script writer, 1936; owner-manager of art gallery, New York, N.Y., 1947-51; Consolidated Appraisal Co., New York, N.Y., art appraiser, 1950-51; Yale and Towne Manufacturing Co., New York, N.Y., field researcher, 1952-56; Interstate Industrial Reporting Service, New York, N.Y., industrial reporter, 1957-58; Lewis Gittler Associates, New York, N.Y., public relations work, 1958-63; now full-time writer. *Wartime service:* U.S. Merchant Marine, 1942-45; chief radio operator.

WRITINGS: Paul Gaugin: The Calm Madman, A. & C. Boni, 1931; *Whirlwind in Petticoats* (biography of Victoria Woodhull), Doubleday, 1947, reissued as *The Spitfires*, Pyramid, 1955, 2nd revised edition, 1971; *Mechanical Man*, Putnam, 1959; *Captain Edward L. Beach: Around the World Under Water*, Encyclopaedia Britannica, 1961; *Jules Verne*, Putnam, 1966; *Dreams and Realities of the Conquest of the Skies* (Junior Literary Guild selection), Atheneum, 1967. Contributor to *Reader's Digest* and *Pageant*.

WORK IN PROGRESS: Dreams and Realities of the Conquest of Space, two volumes, to be published by Atheneum.

SIDELIGHTS: Based on his experiences as an industrial reporter and researcher, Becker feels that "technology will prove to be the salvation of man; that we are headed for a future of marvels, and that all the dark fears of over-population and nuclear wars will gradually fade away as the level of technology rises over the world.... By the end of this decade, the space shuttle will prove to be as epoch making

as was Stephenson's rocket locomotive in 1830 and Boeing's jet in 1952." Therefore, he feels that "technology is of more importance today than any other field of human endeavor, and is altogether the most creative aspect of modern man." In attempting to give adequate literary recognition to engineers, however, Becker recognizes that he has a formidable task if he is to make "machines as fascinating to the average reader as murder, slander or sex."

Mechanical Man has been translated into 17 different languages, and is used as a grammar school textbook in Japan.

BIOGRAPHICAL/CRITICAL SOURCES: New York Times Book Review, November 5, 1967; *Young Readers' Review*, February, 1968.

* * *

BECKER, John (Leonard) 1901-

PERSONAL: Born December 12, 1901, in Chicago, Ill.; son of Benjamin V. (an attorney) and Elizabeth (Loeb) Becker; married Virginia Campbell (a painter); children: R. Campbell, Haidee Giovanna. *Education:* Phillips Academy, Andover, Mass., graduate, 1919; Harvard University, B.A., 1924. *Home:* Via della Vita, Rome, Italy; and 46 Glebe Pl., London S.W. 3, England. *Agent:* Curtis Brown Ltd., 60 East 56th St., New York, N.Y. 10022.

CAREER: Chicago Daily News, Chicago, Ill., columnist, 1927; John Becker Gallery, New York, N.Y., owner, 1929-33; Brattleboro Theatre, Brattleboro, Vt., and Brooklyn, N.Y., co-director, 1935-37. Free-lance writer. American Red Cross, field service in Italy, 1943-44. Director of work for Negro advancement, Council Against Intolerance in America. *Member:* Authors League of America.

WRITINGS: The Negro in American Life, Messner, 1944; (with Georgene Faulkner) *Melindy's Medal* (juvenile), Messner, 1945; *New Feathers for the Old Goose* (poems for children), illustrated by wife, Virginia Campbell, Pantheon, 1956; *Near-Tragedy at the Waterfall* (juvenile), illustrated by V. Campbell, Pantheon, 1964. Writer of plays for private marionette theater. Contributor of short stories to literary magazines in Italy.

WORK IN PROGRESS: A children's book entitled *Mirabelle Pirabelle Pickles;* short stories; and commentary for a John Ferno film about Israel, "Tree of Life."

SIDELIGHTS: During the years he owned his art gallery Becker was responsible for introducing to the United States such artists as Arp, Bauchant, Charlot, Noguchi, Helion, Le Corbusier, Leger, and Lurcat. Now, he and his family have in their home in Rome a somewhat internationally known marionette theatre, having taken it to Denmark during the summer of 1964. Becker writes the plays for the theatre, his wife does the costumes and sets, and she and their children are the marionetteers. They hope someday to publish the plays, together with illustrations of the sets and dramatizations.

* * *

BECKLER, Marion Floyd 1889-

PERSONAL: Born May 14, 1889, in National City, Calif.; daughter of Henry Wilson (a rancher) and Lilian (Dimock) Floyd; married William W. Beckler (a builder), June 29, 1917 (deceased); children: Stanworth Russell. *Education:* San Diego State Normal College (now San Diego State University), elementary teacher's certificate, 1907; writing courses at California Western University and University of Southern California. *Politics:* Republican. *Religion:* Christian Scientist. *Home:* 3125 Franklin St., Stockton, Calif. 95204.

CAREER: School teacher, now retired. *Member:* Retired Teachers Association, San Diego Writers Club, San Diego Historical Society. *Awards, honors:* Two prizes for short stories, *Writer's Digest.*

WRITINGS: Carrie: A Story of Early San Diego, Vantage, 1952; *Palomar Mountain, Past and Present,* privately printed, 1958; *The Magic Map,* Reilly & Lee, 1964. Contributor of historical articles to *Desert* and *San Diego,* and of stories and plays to national teachers' magazines.

WORK IN PROGRESS: A story for boys.

*   *   *

BEDELL, L. Frank 1888-

PERSONAL: Born June 4, 1888, in Springville, Iowa; son of Elwood T. and Hannah (Ellyson) Bedell; married Cleora Williams; children: Bennett Elwood, Frances Goodyear. *Education:* Attended Iowa State University of Science and Technology. *Home and office:* 2309 C St., S.W., Cedar Rapids, Iowa 52404.

CAREER: Farm operator and horse show exhibitor; certified judge, American Horse Shows Association. Chairman, senior bureau, Cedar Rapids Chamber of Commerce, 1964. *Member:* Farm Bureau, Professional Agriculture Club, Farm Club. *Awards, honors:* Forty horse show trophies.

WRITINGS: The Shetland Pony, Iowa State University Press, 1959; *Quaker Heritage: Friends Coming into the Heartland of America,* privately printed, 1966. Compiler of genealogies. Contributor to *Wallace's Farmer, Hackney Journal, American Shetland Pony Journal.*

WORK IN PROGRESS: The Hackney; a series of pioneer stories; three genealogies.

*   *   *

BEGGS, David W(hiteford) III 1931-1966

PERSONAL: Born April 1, 1931, in Decatur, Ill.; son of David Whiteford II (a businessman) and Melba Elizabeth (Dunn) Beggs; married JoAnn Lytle, April 3, 1953; children: David W. IV, Katherine Ann, Elizabeth Ann. *Education:* Millikin University, B.S., 1953, M.S., 1954; Indiana University, Ed.D., 1965. *Politics:* Democrat. *Religion:* Roman Catholic. *Home:* 1718 Circle Dr., Bloomington, Ind. *Office:* School of Education, Indiana University, Bloomington, Ind.

CAREER: Lakeview High School, Decatur, Ill., principal, 1957-62; Barrington (Ill.) public schools, assistant superintendent, 1962-63; Indiana University, Bloomington, assistant professor of education, 1963-66. Beggs, Inc., Decatur, Ill., vice-president, 1957-66. Associate director of National Association of Secondary School Principals internship project sponsored by Ford Foundation; consultant to some thirty school districts, 1961-66. *Member:* National Education Association, National Society for the Study of Education, American Educational Research Association, Association for Supervision and Curriculum Development, National Association of Secondary School Principals, National Congress of Parents and Teachers (life member). *Awards, honors:* Named outstanding young man of the year, Illinois Junior Chamber of Commerce, 1960.

WRITINGS—All published by Indiana University Press, except as indicated: *Decatur-Lakeview High School,* Prentice-Hall, 1964; (editor) *Team Teaching: Bold New Venture,* 1964; (editor with E. G. Buffie) *Independent Study: Bold New Venture,* 1965; (with Donald C. Manlove) *Flexible Scheduling: Bold New Venture,* 1965; *Nongraded Schools: Bold New Venture,* 1966; (editor with R. B. McQuigg) *America's Schools and Churches: Partners in Conflict,* 1966; (editor with E. G. Buffie) *Nongraded Schools in Action: Bold New Venture,* 1967; (editor with S. K. Alexander) *Integration and Education,* Rand McNally, 1969. Co-editor, "Bold New Venture" series, Indiana University Press.

WORK IN PROGRESS: Strikes and Sanctions in Education and *Instructional Materials Center,* both for Indiana University Press.

(Died, 1966)

*   *   *

BEHA, Ernest 1908-
(Andrew Bede, Drake Elvin)

PERSONAL: Born December 7, 1908, in London, England; son of Adolf (a mechanical supervisor) and Adelaide (Mayer) Beha; married Daisy Huff, February 14, 1931; children: Erna Adelaide Beha Steeden, Andrea Maud Beha Watson, Judy Beha Garrad, Beverly Margaret. *Education:* Attended schools in London, England. *Religion:* Church of England. *Home:* 59 Riverholme Dr., West Ewell, Epsom, Surrey, England. *Office: Evening News,* Harmsworth House, London E.C. 4, England.

CAREER: Journalist in London, England, with *Sunday Referee, Daily Mail,* and *Sunday Dispatch* at earlier periods; *Freemason,* London, England, managing editor, 1949-52; *Evening News,* London, England, sub-editor and writer, 1958—. Wartime service as police sergeant, City of London, 1939-44. *Member:* National Union of Journalists (branch secretary, London evening papers, 1959-64).

WRITINGS: Comprehensive Dictionary of Freemasonary, Arco Publications, 1962.

WORK IN PROGRESS: Three books, *Not a Double,* about life in London, *Railway Sleeper No. 1,* and *Boulogne with the Lid Off.*

*   *   *

BEHRMAN, S(amuel) N(athaniel) 1893-1973

PERSONAL: Born June 9, 1893, in Worcester, Mass.; son of Joseph and Zelda (Feingold) Behrman; married Elza Heifetz (sister of the violinist, Jascha Heifetz), 1936; children: Arthur David; stepchildren: Harold Stone, Barbara Gelb. *Education:* Attended Clark College (now University), Worcester, Mass., 1912-14; Harvard University, A.B., 1916; Columbia University, A.M., 1918. *Religion:* Jewish. *Home:* 1185 Park Ave., New York, N.Y. 10028. *Agent:* Carol Brandt (literary) and Harold Freedman (dramatic), Brandt & Brandt, 101 Park Ave., New York, N.Y. 10017.

CAREER: Prior to 1927, reviewed books for *New Republic* and *New York Times,* wrote short stories and articles for literary periodicals, and worked as a theatrical press agent for publishing houses and later for Broadway producers; full-time playwright and author, beginning 1927. Co-founder, and for a time, director of Playwright's Co. *Member:* National Institute of Arts and Letters, P.E.N., Writers Guild, Phi Beta Kappa, The Players, Century Club. *Awards, honors:* American Academy of Arts and Letters grant, 1943; New York Drama Critics Award for best foreign play, 1944, for "Jacobowsky and the Colonel";

LL.D., Clark University, 1949; Brandeis University Creative Arts Award, 1962.

WRITINGS—Plays: *The Second Man* (comedy; first produced in New York, N.Y., at Guild Theatre, April 11, 1927), Doubleday, Page, 1927; *Meteor* (first produced at Guild Theatre, December 23, 1929), Brentano, 1930; *Brief Moment* (comedy; first produced in New York at Belasco Theatre, November 9, 1931), Farrar & Rinehart, 1931; *Biography* (comedy; first produced at Guild Theatre, December 12, 1932), Farrar & Rinehart, 1933; *Three Plays by S. N. Behrman* (contains "Serena Blandish" [based on an anonymous English novel; first produced in New York at Morosco Theatre, January 23, 1929], "Meteor," and "The Second Man"), Farrar & Rinehart, 1934; *Rain from Heaven* (first produced in New York at John Golden Theatre, December 24, 1934), Random House, 1935; *End of Summer* (first produced at Guild Theatre, February 17, 1936), Random House, 1936; (adapter) Jean Giradoux, *Amphitryon 38* (comedy; first produced in New York at Shubert Theatre, November 1, 1937), Random House, 1938; *Wine of Choice* (comedy; first produced at Guild Theatre, February 21, 1938), Random House, 1939; *No Time for Comedy* (comedy; first produced in New York at Ethel Barrymore Theatre, April 17, 1939), Random House, 1939.

Mechanical Heart, Random House, 1941; *The Talley Method* (comedy; first produced in New York at Henry Miller's Theatre, February 24, 1941), Samuel French, 1942; (adapter) Ludwig Fulda, *The Pirate* (first produced in New York at Martin Beck Theatre, November 25, 1942), Random House, 1943; *Jacobowsky and the Colonel* (based on the German play by Franz V. Werfel; first produced at Martin Beck Theatre, March 14, 1944), Random House, 1944; *Dunnigan's Daughter* (comedy; first produced, 1945), Random House, 1946. *I Know My Love* (comedy; based on Michel Archard's *Aupres de ma blonde*; first produced at Shubert Theatre, November 2, 1949), Samuel French, 1952; *Jane* (comedy; based on a story by W. Somerset Maugham; first produced in London at Aldwych Theatre, January 29, 1947; produced in New York at Coronet Theatre, February 1, 1952; produced under title "The Foreign Language," 1951), Random House, 1952; *Four Plays: The Second Man, Biography, Rain from Heaven, [and] End of Summer*, Random House, 1955; (with Joshua Logan) *Fanny* (musical; based on Marcel Pagnol's trilogy, *Marious, Fanny [and] Cesar*; first produced in New York at Majestic Theatre, November 4, 1954), Random House, 1955; *The Cold Wind and the Warm* (comedy; first produced at Morosco Theatre, December 8, 1959), Random House, 1959; *Lord Pengo* (comedy; based on Behrman's biography, *Duveen*; first produced in New York at Royale Theatre, November 19, 1962), Random House, 1963; *But for Whom Charlie* (first produced in New York at ANTA Washington Square Theatre, March 12, 1964), Random House, 1964.

Other: *Duveen* (biography), Random House, 1952; *The Worcester Account* (autobiographical sketches), Random House, 1954; *Portrait of Max: An Intimate Memoir of Sir Max Beerbohm*, Random House, 1960 (published in England as *Conversation with Max*, Hamilton, 1960); *The Suspended Drawing Room* (biographies), Stein & Day, 1965; (author of introduction) Carl R. Dolmetsch, *The Smart Set: A History and Anthology*, Dial, 1966; (author of introduction) Horatio Alger, *Strive and Succeed: Julius; or, The Street Boy out West [and] The Store Boy; or, The Fortunes of Ben Barclay*, Holt, 1967; *The Burning Glass* (novel), Little, Brown, 1968; *People in a Diary: A Memoir*, Little, Brown, 1972.

Films: "He Knew Women," RKO, 1930; (scenario only) "Liliom," with dialogue by Sonya Levien, Fox, 1930; (scenario and dialogue with Levien) "Lightnin'," Fox, 1930; (dialogue) "Sea Wolf," Fox, 1930; (scenario with Levien and dialogue with Levien and Maude Fulton) "The Brat," Fox, 1931; (scenario and dialogue with Levien) "Surrender," Fox, 1931; (dialogue with Levien) "Daddy Long Legs," Fox, 1931; (scenario and dialogue with Levien) "Rebecca of Sunnybrook Farm," Fox, 1932; (scenario with Levien and Rupert Hughes) "Tess of the Storm Country," Fox, 1932; "Brief Moment," Columbia, 1933; "Cavalcade," Fox, 1933; (adapter, from a story by Ben Hecht) "Hallelujah, I'm a Bum," United Artists, 1933; (dialogue) "My Lips Betray," Fox, 1933; (dialogue) "Queen Christina," M-G-M, 1933; "Biography of a Bachelor Girl" (based on his play, "Biography"), M-G-M, 1934; (screenplay with Salka Viertel and Clemence Dane) "Anna Karenina," M-G-M, 1935; (screenplay with W. P. Lipscomb) "Tale of Two Cities," M-G-M, 1935; (screenplay with Levien) "As Husbands Go," Fox, 1934; (screenplay with Viertel and S. Hoffenstein) "Conquest," M-G-M, 1937; (screenplay with John Van Druten) "Parnell," M-G-M, 1937; (screenplay with Levien) "Cowboy and the Lady," United Artists, 1938; "No Time For Comedy," Warner Bros., 1940; (screenplay with George Froeschel and Hans Rambeau) "Waterloo Bridge," M-G-M, 1940; (screenplay with Viertel and George Oppenheimer) "Two-Faced Woman," Loew's, Inc., 1941; "The Pirate," M-G-M, 1948; (screenplay with John Lee Mahin and Levien) "Quo Vadis," M-G-M, 1951; (screenplay with Froeschel) "Me and the Colonel" (based on Behrman's adaptation of Werfel's "Jacobowsky and the Colonel"), Columbia, 1958; (with Joshua Logan) "Fanny" (based on Marcel Pagnol's trilogy, *Marious, Fanny, [and] Cesar*), Warner Bros., 1961.

Author of unpublished plays: (With J. Kenyon Nicholson) "Bedside Manners," produced, 1923; (with Owen Davis) "The Man Who Forgot," 1926; (with Nicholson) "Love Is Like That," first produced in New York at Cort Theatre, April 18, 1927; "Let Me Hear the Melody."

Work is represented in anthologies, including: *Representative Modern Plays: American*, edited by Robert Warnock, Scott, Foresman, 1952; *Famous American Plays of the 1930's*, edited by Harold Clurman, Dell, 1959; *Great Scenes from the World Theatre*, edited by James L. Steffensen, Jr., Discus Books, 1968. Wrote radio scripts for war effort. Regular contributor to *New Yorker*, beginning 1928; contributor of short stories and articles to periodicals, including *Smart Set, New Republic, Seven Arts*, and *The Masses*.

WORK IN PROGRESS: Adapting Arnold Bennett's *Buried Alive* into a musical with tentative title, "The Great Adventure."

SIDELIGHTS: Behrman, who has been called the "American Congreve," began his career as a dramatist somewhat inadvertently. He wrote "The Second Man" as a short story and submitted it to *Smart Set*, and, writes Behrman, "they published it. In a doldrum of inactivity something impelled me—I will never know what—to dramatize this story." It was produced in 1927, beginning a steady series of theatrical productions that would last until 1964. Edmund M. Cagey, citing Behrman as one of the first practitioners of American high comedy, noted that "he was well qualified by his dispassionate wit and his sense of epigrammatic style. . . . Behrman must be commended for having so consistently attempted intellectual comedy in a commercial theatre. His influence has been felt, even though high comedy can never hope to become as indigenous to the American stage as her low-life sister."

Lloyd Morris believes that, in the 'thirties and 'forties, Behrman's plays were among the few genuine examples of social criticism. "The society represented in Behrman's plays," wrote Morris, "so far as it corresponded with an existing reality—had its prototype in that super-sophisticated, cosmopolitan 'set' which, according to the fashion magazines and other competent authorities, originate all standards of elegance, and inaugurate the absolutely latest modes in art and literature. If Behrman, in his plays, attributed to them a greater degree of intelligence than they seemed to possess, he probably did not exaggerate either their influence or their often diverting irresponsibility. Like Henry James, he wished to deal with the 'best' society of his time, in which the human spirit might be supposed to flower most liberally, and with the greatest graciousness. But the favor of an aristocracy involves a peril which even Henry James—born in the best society of the United States of his day—did not fully escape." (Morris adds that "Behrman's plays frequently suggest that he had never recovered from exposure to his first duchess, or his first Newport hostess.")

Morris concludes that "intellectually honest, and himself an exemplar of that discriminating intelligence which he valued as the highest of virtues, Behrman confronted his own predicament in *No Time for Comedy*, a play about a playwright. Like his own, the playwright's talent is for high comedy; but the age forces upon him conflicts and issues which the comic spirit is incapable of meeting. . . . As perhaps was inevitable, Behrman failed to solve the problem. In an ideal world, in which discriminating intelligence and tolerant liberalism would be sufficient principles, one might anticipate the emergence of a spirit and an understanding transcending the clamors and ferocities of the marching lustful mobs. In such a world, of course, the problem simply wouldn't arise."

Behrman's books, *Duveen, The Worcester Account, Portrait of Max,* and *Suspended Drawing Room* were all drawn from writings published originally in the *New Yorker*. In the early stages of the production of "Ben Hur" (1958), Behrman collaborated with Karl Tunberg on the script. The film, however, is not listed among his motion picture credits. The 1956 film, "Gaby," was based on his screenplay, "Waterloo Bridge."

BIOGRAPHICAL/CRITICAL SOURCES: John Gassner, *Masters of the Drama,* Random House, 1940; Edmund M. Gagey, *Revolution in American Drama,* Columbia University Press, 1947; Lloyd Morris, *Postscript to Yesterday,* Random House, 1947.

(Died September 9, 1973)

* * *

BELGION, (Harold) Montgomery 1892-1973

PERSONAL: Born September 28, 1892, in Paris, France; son of British nationals, John (in insurance) and Beatrice Annie (Montgomery) Belgion; married Gladys Helen Mattock, February 3, 1945. *Education:* Educated privately in Paris; Oxford University, diploma in English literature (earned while prisoner of war), 1943. *Home:* Highfield Titchmarsh, Kettering, Northampshire, England.

CAREER: New York Herald, Paris, France, editor-in-charge, 1915-16; London *Daily Mail,* foreign sub-editor, 1919-21, 1922-24; member of editorial staff of *New York World,* 1921-22; *Westminster Gazette,* London, England, chief sub-editor, 1924-25; with Harcourt, Brace and Co., New York, N.Y., 1924-28; with *Daily Mirror,* London, England, 1935-37, *Daily Sketch,* London, 1939; Westwood House School Trust, Peterborough, England, secretary, finance and administration, 1950-61. *Military service:* British Army, Honourable Artillery Company, Dorset Regiment, 1916-19, served in France, 1916, 1918-19; Royal Engineers, 1940-45, served in France, later in Greece (prisoner of war); became captain. *Member:* Melville Society (U.S.; associate member), Athenaeum (London).

WRITINGS: Our Present Philosophy of Life, Faber, 1929; *The Human Parrot,* Oxford University Press, 1931; *News of the French,* Faber, 1938; *Reading for Profit,* Penguin, 1945, expanded version, Regnery, 1950; *Introduction to Moby Dick,* Cresset, 1946; (editor, and author of introduction) *Selected Poems of E. A. Poe,* Grey Walls Press, 1948; *Epitaph on Nuremberg,* Falcon Press, 1947, revised and expanded version published as *Victors' Justice,* Regnery, 1949; *A Man After My Own Heart,* Regnery, 1950; *H. G. Wells,* British Council, 1953; *David Hume,* British Council, 1965, Contributor to periodicals and newspapers in Britain, United States, France, and Germany, Assistant editor, *This Quarter,* 1931-32.

WORK IN PROGRESS: A book provisionally titled *Megalopolitics.*

SIDELIGHTS: Two of Belgion's books have been translated into French, one into German. He wrote in French for Paris periodicals.

(Died October 29, 1973)

* * *

BELKNAP, S(ally) Yancey 1895-

PERSONAL: Born March 2, 1895, in Ocala, Fla.; daughter of Thomas Allen (a merchant) and Isabella (Bray) Yancey; married Frazee Lockwood Belknap (deceased); children: Grace (Mrs. Robert Reynolds). *Education:* Studied music at Yale University; Rollins College, A.B.; Columbia University, B.S., M.A., and M.S. in Library Science. *Politics:* "Usually Democrat." *Religion:* Episcopal. *Home:* 1217 Southwest Third Ave., Gainesville, Fla. 32601.

CAREER: Reference librarian in Yonkers, N.Y., for several decades; University of Florida, Gainesville, director of Archives of Dance, Music, and Theatre, 1953—. *Member:* American Association of University Women, American Association of University Professors, Philharmonic Society, Gainesville Art Association (treasurer), Gainesville Little Theatre.

WRITINGS: Ballet Close-Ups, Kamin, 1942.

Compiler and editor: *School Library Report, Westchester County, New York, 1935-36,* School Library Division, Westchester County Teachers Association, 1937; *Guide to Dance Periodicals,* Volumes I-VII, University of Florida Press, 1948-55, Volumes VIII-X, Scarecrow, 1956-63; *Guide to the Performing Arts,* Scarecrow, annually, 1957-68; *Florida Index, 1966,* privately printed, c.1967.

WORK IN PROGRESS: Continuing Guide to Performing Arts, and *Guide to Dance Periodicals.*

AVOCATIONAL INTERESTS: Collecting theatre materials, including television criticism.

BELL, H(arold) Idris 1879-1967

PERSONAL: Born October 2, 1879, in Epworth, Lincolnshire, England; son of Charles Christopher (a chemist) and Rachel (Hughes) Bell; married Mabel Winifred Ayling, June 3, 1911 (died, 1967); children: Idris Christopher, Ernest David (deceased), John Rhys. *Education:* Oriel College, Oxford, M.A.; other study at University of Berlin and University of Halle. *Politics:* Labour. *Religion:* Church of England. *Home:* Bro Gynin, Iorwerth Ave., Aberystwyth, Wales.

CAREER: British Museum, London, England, assistant keeper in department of manuscripts, 1903-27, deputy keeper in department of manuscripts, 1927-29, keeper of manuscripts and Egerton Librarian, 1929-44. Honorary reader in papyrology, Oxford University, 1935-50. Member of Governing body, Church in Wales, 1950-67.

MEMBER: British Academy (fellow; president, 1946-50), International Association of Papyrologists (president, 1947-55; honorary president, 1955-67), Egypt Exploration Society (honorary secretary, 1923-27; vice-president, 1945-67), Society for Promotion of Roman Studies (president, 1937-45; vice-president, 1945-67), Society for Promotion of Helenic Studies (vice-president, 1930-67), Honourable Society of Cymmrodorion (president, 1947-53; vice-president, 1953-67), honorary or corresponding member of other academies and societies in America, Argentina, Austria, Belgium, Egypt, France, Germany, Italy, and Norway. *Awards, honors:* Order of the British Empire, 1920; honorary fellow, Oriel College, Oxford University, 1936; Companion of the Bath, 1936; knighted, 1946; Cymmrodorion Medal for services to Welsh literature, 1946; D. Litt. from University of Brussels, University of Michigan, and University of Wales; LL.D. from University of Liverpool.

WRITINGS: Catalogue of Greek Papyri in the British Museum, British Museum, Volume III (with Frederic Kenyon), 1907, Volume IV (with W. E. Crum), 1910, Volume V, 1907; (editor) *Vita Sancti Tathei and Buchedd Seint y Katrin,* Bangor Welsh Manuscript Society, 1909; (editor) *Traherne's Poems of Felicity,* Clarendon Press, 1910; (with father, Charles C. Bell) *Poems from the Welsh,* Welsh Publishing Co., 1913.

(Editor with W. E. Crum) *Wadi Sarga: Coptic and Greek Texts from the Excavations Undertaken by the Byzantine Research Account,* Gyldendalsk Boghandel-Nordisk Forlag, 1922; *Guide to the Exhibited Manuscripts,* Part II, British Museum, 1923; *Jews and Christians in Egypt,* British Museum, 1924; *Oxyrhynchus Papyri,* Egypt Exploration Society, Part XVI (with B. P. Grenfell and A. S. Hunt), 1924, Part XIX (with E. Lobel, E. P. Wegener, and C. H. Roberts), 1948; (translator with Charles C. Bell, and author of critical essay) *Welsh Poems of the Twentieth Century in English Verse,* Hughes a'i Fab, 1925; *Juden und Griechen im roemischen Alexandreia,* J. C. Hirrichs, 1926; *Dewi a'r Blodyn Llo Mawr* (title means "David and the Fritillary"; written in English and translated into Welsh by Olwen Roberts), Hughes a'i Fab, 1928; *Calon y Dywysoges* (title means "The Heart of the Princess"; written in English and translated into Welsh by Olwen Roberts), Hughes a'i Fab, 1929.

(With A. D. Nock and Herbert Thompson) *Magical Texts from a Bilingual Papyrus in the British Museum,* British Academy, 1931; (editor with T. C. Skeat) *Fragments of an Unknown Gospel and Other Early Christian Papyri,* British Museum, 1935; *The Development of Welsh Poetry,* Clarendon Press, 1936.

(Translator and author of introductory essays, with son, Ernest David Bell) *Dafydd ap Gwilym: Fifty Poems,* Honourable Society of Cymmrodorion, 1942; *Trwy Diroedd y Dwyrain* (title means "Through the Lands of the East"; written in English and translated into Welsh by D. T. LLoyd), two volumes, Clwb LLyfrau Cymreig, 1946; *Egypt from Alexander the Great to the Arab Conquest: A Study in the Diffusion and Decay of Hellenism* (Gregynog Lectures), Clarendon Press, 1948; *A Descriptive Catalogue of the Greek Papyri in the Collection of Wilfred Merton,* Volume I (with C. H. Roberts), Emery Walker, 1948, Volume II (with B. R. Rees and J.W.B. Barnes), Hodges, Figgis & Co., 1959.

Cults and Creeds in Graeco-Roman Egypt (Forwood Lectures), Liverpool University Press, 1953, 2nd edition, enlarged, 1954; *The Crisis of Our Time and Other Papers,* Christopher Davies, 1954; (translator, and author of appendix) Thomas Parry, *A History of Welsh Literature,* Clarendon Press, 1955.

(With V. Martin, E. G. Turner, and D. van Berchem) *The Abinnaeus Archive: Papers of a Roman Officer in the Reign of Constantius II,* Clarendon Press, 1962.

Writer of guides to museum exhibitions. Presidential addresses published in *Proceedings* of British Academy, 1947-50, and separately. Contributor to learned journals.

AVOCATIONAL INTERESTS: Walking.

(Died January 22, 1967)

* * *

BELL, Harry McAra 1899-

PERSONAL: Born April 11, 1899, in Aberdeen, Scotland; son of John Nicol and Isabella (Reith) Bell; married Sophia McDonald Fulton, October 9, 1933; children: John Nicol, Alexander Fulton, Patricia Macdonald (Mrs. John Hossack). *Education:* Robert Gordon's College, student, 1909-15; University of Aberdeen, M.A., 1924; Clare College, Cambridge, M.Ed., 1927. *Religion:* Presbyterian. *Home:* Viewpark, Lawhead Rd., St. Andrews, Fife, Scotland.

CAREER: Glasgow Academy, Glasgow, Scotland, assistant master, 1927-33; Elgin Academy, Elgin, Scotland, rector, 1933-36; Dollar Academy, Dollar, Scotland, rector, 1936-60. Volunteer Scottish educational adviser to Air Training Corps, World War II. *Military service:* British Army, one year overseas, World War I. *Member:* English Association, Historical Association, Scottish Headmasters Association (past president), Scottish Mountaineering Club, Royal and Ancient Club (St. Andrews). *Awards, honors:* Officer of Order of the British Empire; honorary research fellow, St. Andrew's University.

WRITINGS: English for Air Cadets, Nelson, 1943; *English for Army Cadets,* Nelson, 1943; *English for Sea Cadets,* Nelson, 1946; (editor) *Selected English Prose: Malory to Joyce,* Oxford University Press, 1963; *The Story of English Literature,* W. & R. Chambers, 1964. General editor of "Oxford Comprehension Course," five books, Oxford University Press, 1954-56, and author (with N. F. Donald) of Book V, *Planned Interpretation,* 1956. Contributor of articles on literary and educational subjects to periodicals, including *British Journal of Educational Psychology, Scottish Educational Journal,* and *Times Educational Supplement* (Scotland).

WORK IN PROGRESS: Research on literature and education.

AVOCATIONAL INTERESTS: Walking, golf, reading, talking, writing.

* * *

BELL, L. Nelson 1894-1973

PERSONAL: Born July 30, 1894, in Waynesboro, Va.; son of James Harvey and Ruth (McCue) Bell; married Virginia Leftwich, June 30, 1916; children: Rosa (Mrs. C. Donald Montgomery), Ruth (Mrs. Billy Graham), Virginia (Mrs. John N. Somerville), Benjamin Clayton. *Education:* Washington and Lee University, student, 1911-12; Medical College of Virginia, M.D., 1916. *Politics:* Independent. *Religion:* Presbyterian. *Home:* 500 Assembly Dr., Montreat, N.C. 28757.

CAREER: Chief surgeon at Tsingkiangpu General Hospital, operated by Presbyterian Mission in China, 1916-41; surgeon in private practice in Asheville, N.C., 1941-56, and assistant chief of staff at Memorial Hospital, Asheville, 1947-48; *Christianity Today*, Washington, D.C., co-founder and executive editor, 1955-73. Also co-founder and associate editor of *Presbyterian Journal*, beginning 1941. Member of Board of World Missions, Presbyterian Church in the United States, 1948-66, and chairman of Far Eastern Division, beginning 1964; moderator of Presbyterian church in the United States, 1972-73. Board memberships include Billy Graham Evangelistic Association, Blue Ridge Broadcasting Corp., and Christian Broadcasting Association, Honolulu. Delegate to meetings of Royal College of Surgeons in Edinburgh, 1955, and International College of Surgeons in Geneva, 1956.

MEMBER: American College of Surgeons (fellow), American Medical Association, North Carolina Medical Society, Buncombe County Medical Society, Kiwanis Club (Asheville; honorary life member). *Awards, honors:* Editorial writing awards from Freedoms Foundation of Valley Forge, six times between 1945 and 1966, and award for best editorial of the year, 1958; LL.D., King College, Bristol, Tenn., 1964; new library at Montreat-Anderson College is to be named L. Nelson Bell Library.

WRITINGS: Convictions to Live By, Eerdmans, 1966; *While Men Slept*, Doubleday, 1970. Regular contributor to *Presbyterian Journal* and *Christianity Today*; contributor to medical journals, and of several thousand articles to religious magazines.

SIDELIGHTS: Bell spoke Chinese fluently.

(Died August 2, 1973)

* * *

BELL, Louise Price
(Lita Bronson, Ruth Jeffrey)

PERSONAL: Born in Akron, N.Y.; daughter of John H. and Myrtie (Swift) Price; married Don H. Bell (a rodeo manager), December 18, 1925; children: Don H., Jr., Jane Louise. *Education:* Attended State Teachers College, Buffalo, N.Y. (now State University of New York College of Education at Buffalo). *Home and office:* 145 Sierra Vista Dr. E., Tucson, Ariz. 85719.

CAREER: Former advertising copywriter; free-lance writer of magazine articles and books.

WRITINGS: Jane Louise's Cook Book, Coward, 1930; *Sick-A-Bed-Sally*, Crowell, 1932; *The Alphabet that Was Good to Eat*, Harter Publishing 1932; *Kitchen Fun*, Harter Publishing 1932; *Having a Party?*, Revell, 1936; *Successful*

Parties, Revell, 1940; *Parties in Wartime*, Revell, 1943; *Parties on a Budget*, Prentice-Hall, 1951; *What Did Tommy Say?*, Warner, 1960; *Pedro*, Review & Herald, 1961; *Grimpo and Grumpy*, Bethany, 1964. Contributor to *Parent's Magazine, Better Homes and Gardens, Today's Health, American Home, Sunset, Ford Times, Modern Maturity, Redbook, Southern Living, Christian, Christian Science Monitor, Successful Farming, Farm Journal*, and other periodicals.

WORK IN PROGRESS: A book about a family making a mobile-home trip through the West; a patriotic book and an alphabet book for children.

SIDELIGHTS: Kitchen Fun has been issued in Braille.

* * *

BELL, Vicars W(alker) 1904-

PERSONAL: Born January 24, 1904, in Redhill, Surrey, England; son of William Anderson and Jean (Symington) Bell; married Dorothy Edith Carley, 1926. *Education:* Attended Goldsmiths' College and King's College, University of London. *Home:* 5 Ashridge Cottages, Little Gaddesden, Berkhamsted, England. *Agent:* Foyle's Lecture Agency, Charing Cross Rd., London, England.

CAREER: Spaldwick Council School, Huntingdon, England, headmaster, 1927-29; Little Gaddesden Church of England School, Little Gaddesden, Berkhamsted, England, headmaster, 1929-62. Lecturer at University of London, University of Birmingham, Oxford University, and Cambridge University; also lecturer in Isreal and public lecturer in England. Founder of Little Gaddesden Parish Council, lay reader for Diocese of St. Albans. *Member:* Society of Authors, National Council of Local History, Gaddesden Society (president).

WRITINGS—All published by Faber, except as indicated: *Little Gaddesden: The Story of an English Parish*, 1949; *Death Under the Stars*, 1949; *The Dodo: The Story of a Village Schoolmaster*, 1950; *Two by Day and One by Night*, 1950; *Death Has Two Doors*, 1950; *This Way Home: The Story of a Voyage in Search of the Earth*, 1951; *Death Darkens Council*, 1952; *On Learning the English Tongue*, 1953; *Death and the Night Watches*, 1955; *To Meet Mr. Ellis: Little Gaddesden in the 18th Century*, 1956; *That Night* (Nativity play), 1959; *Death Walks by the River*, 1959; *Orlando and Rosaline* (three tales), 1960; *Steep Ways and Narrow* (autobiography), 1963; *The Flying Cat*, 1964, Roy Publishers, 1965.

Contributor to *Listener, Church Times, Use of English*, and other journals.

AVOCATIONAL INTERESTS: Walking, music-making (especially singing), cricket, and gardening.

BIOGRAPHICAL SOURCES: Vicars W. Bell, *Steep Ways and Narrow*, Faber, 1963.

* * *

BENDIT, Gladys Williams 1885-
(John Presland)

PERSONAL: Born September 6, 1885, in Melbourne, Australia; daughter of John Frederick (an importer) and Alice Emily (Presland) Williams; married John Herbert Skelton, February 6, 1907 (died, 1942); married Francis E. Bendit, March 20, 1963; children: (first marriage) Anthony Skelton, Patrick Hugh Skelton. *Education:* Attended private schools and Queen's College; Girton College, Cambridge, B.A.

(honors), 1906. *Religion:* Anglican. *Home:* 130 Hamilton Ter., Flat 4, London N.W.8, England.

CAREER: Author, beginning, 1909, and lecturer. Young Men's Christian Association, London, England, director of employment bureau for disabled soldiers, 1919; Central Council for Economic Information, London, director of women's section, and lecturer, 1920-24; University of London, London, extension lecturer in literature, 1924-27. Seafarer's Education Service, member, 1924-48; British Societies for Relief Abroad, member of council, 1942-45; Save the Children Fund, member of council and chairman of foreign relief and rehabilitation committee.

WRITINGS—All under pseudonym John Presland: *Joan of Arc*, Chatto & Windus, 1909; *Mary Queen of Scots*, Chatto & Windus, 1910; *Manin and the Defence of Venice*, Chatto & Windus, 1911; *The Deluge*, Chatto & Windus, 1912; *Marcus Aurelius*, Chatto & Windus, 1912; *Songs of Changing Skies*, Chatto & Windus, 1915; *King Monmouth* (play; produced in Norwich, 1922), Chatto & Windus, 1915; *Poems of London*, Macmillan, 1925; *Dominion*, Philip Allan, 1926; *Frustration*, Philip Allan, 1927; *The Charioteer*, Appleton, 1928; *Barricade*, Philip Allan, 1928; *Escape Me–Never*, Appleton, 1929; *Mosaic*, Appleton, 1929; *Satni* (play; produced in London, 1937), Noel Douglas, 1929.

Albatross, Appleton, 1931; *Vae Victis: The Life of Ludwig von Benedek*, Hodder & Stoughton, 1934; *Women and the Civilized State*, Routledge & Kegan Paul, 1934; *Deedes Bey: A Study of Sir Wyndham Deedes*, Macmillan, 1942; *The Shaken Reed*, Marsland Publications, 1945; *Selected Poems*, Linden Press, 1961.

SIDELIGHTS: Mrs. Bendit speaks French, some Italian and German.

* * *

BENEDICT, Dorothy Potter 1889-

PERSONAL: Born April 15, 1889, in Chicago, Ill.; daughter of Edward C. (a composer) and Emma (McKinley) Potter; married Charles C. Benedict (a pilot, U.S. Air Service), December 27, 1919 (killed in plane crash, 1925); children: Charles C., Jr. (deceased), Patricia (Mrs. Harrison Lobdell, Jr.), Calvert P. *Education:* Took special courses in playwriting at University of Chicago and in languages at Berlitz Schools in United States, France, and Switzerland. *Home and office:* 6200 Oregon Ave., Washington, D.C. 20015. *Agent:* McIntosh & Otis, Inc., 18 East 41st St., New York, N.Y. 10017.

CAREER: American Red Cross canteen worker in France, World War I; secretary in Headquarters, U.S. Air Service, Washington, D.C., following the war, and translator from the French of a book on air strategy; during World War II worked in Plans Division, Air Staff, Washington, D.C., and later as a consultant to the Air Force (speech writer).

WRITINGS: Pagan the Black, Pantheon, 1960; *Fabulous*, Pantheon, 1961; *Bandoleer*, Pantheon, 1963. Contributor of short stories to *Ladies' Home Journal, Seventeen*, and other magazines.

WORK IN PROGRESS: Three books.

SIDELIGHTS: Mrs. Benedict is competent in French, reads German and Spanish.

* * *

BENJAMIN, Harry 1885-

PERSONAL: Born January 12, 1885, in Berlin, Germany;

came to United States, 1913; son of Julius (a banker) and Bertha (Hoffmann) Benjamin; married Greta Guelzow, 1925. *Education:* Studied at Universities in Berlin, Rostock, and Tubingen (all Germany). *Home:* 113 East 31st St., New York, N.Y. 10016. *Office:* 44 East 67th St., New York, N.Y. 10021.

CAREER: Physician, specializing in gerontology and sexology, in private practice in New York, N.Y., 1915—, and summers in San Francisco, Calif., 1935—; now in semiretirement. *Member:* American Medical Association, Society for the Scientific Study of Sex (fellow), American Geriatrics Society (fellow), Association for Advancement of Psychotherapy (fellow), New York State Medical Society, New York County Medical Society (life member), other medical societies.

WRITINGS: Rejuvenation, Sex Education Society (London), 1937; (with Robert Edward Lee Masters) *Prostitution and Morality*, Julian Press, 1964, reissued as *The Prostitute in Society*, Mayflower, 1966; *The Transsexual Phenomenon*, Julian Press, 1966; (contributor) Richard Green and John Money, editors, *Transsexualism and Sex Reassignment* (Society for the Scientific Study of Sex annual award choice, 1969), Johns Hopkins Press, 1969. Contributor of articles to medical and educational journals.

WORK IN PROGRESS: Research on transsexualism.

* * *

BENNETT, Archibald F. 1896-

PERSONAL: Born March 17, 1896, in Dingle, Bear Lake County, Idaho; son of William David and Emma (Neat) Bennett; married Ann Ella Milner, December 21, 1921; children: Barbara Bennett Roach, Marshall Gordon, Marilyn Bennett Romney, Joan Bennett Farr, David Milner. *Education:* University of Utah, B.A., 1925, M.A., 1926; Brigham Young University, graduate study, 1959-61. *Religion:* Church of Jesus Christ of Latter-day Saints. *Home:* 1674 Yale Ave., Salt Lake City, Utah 84105. *Office:* Genealogical Association, 107 South Main St., Salt Lake City, Utah 84111.

CAREER: Genealogical Association (formerly Society) of the Church of Jesus Christ of Latter-day Saints, Salt Lake City, Utah, secretary and librarian, 1928-61, supervisor of education, beginning, 1963. Brigham Young University, Provo, Utah, special instructor in genealogy, 1951-64. Instructor in classes on genealogy in Utah and elsewhere, beginning, 1928; speaker at genealogical conventions and conferences in United States, Canada, Mexico, and Europe. *Military service:* Canadian Army, Cavalry, 1916-19; served in England and France. *Member:* American Society of Genealogists, Mexican Society of Genealogy and Heraldry (honorary), Phi Kappa Phi.

WRITINGS: A Guide for Genealogical Research, Genealogical Society (now Association) of the Church of Jesus Christ of Latter-day Saints, 1951; *Finding Your Forefathers in America*, Bookcraft Co., 1957; *Advanced Genealogical Research*, Bookcraft Co., 1959; *Searching with Success* (genealogical text), Deseret, 1962. Writer of eighteen other genealogical texts, many published anonymously, and of magazine and newspaper articles on the same subject. Also writer of texts published by Deseret Sunday School Union. Editor, *Utah Genealogical and Historical Magazine*, 1928-40; contributing editor, *Improvement Era*, 1952-61.

WORK IN PROGRESS: Histories of the Schwerdtfeder

family in Germany and America, the Daellenbach-Dillabaugh family in Switzerland and America, the Bennett family in England and America, the Zufelt-Shufelt family in America and Canada, and of descendants of William New and Ann Collins.

*   *   *

BENNETT, Charles   1901-

PERSONAL: Born April 23, 1901, in New York, N.Y.; son of Ben and Fannie (Siebenberg) Bennett; married Rose Slavin, 1925; children: Dorothy Bennett Mitchell, Richard A., Howard P. *Education:* Northwestern University, B.Sc. in Commerce, 1922, M.A., 1924; St. Louis University, Ph.D., 1933. *Home:* 32 Washington Ter., St. Louis, Mo. *Office:* 1108 Olive, St. Louis, Mo.

CAREER: Writer, account executive, and sales counselor, Chicago, Ill., 1925-29; president of Bennett Realty Corp., St. Louis, Mo., 1929—, Bennett Investment Corp., St. Louis, 1945—, and Bennett Building Corp., St. Louis, 1947—. DePaul University, Chicago, Ill., lecturer in business, 1925-29; Washington University, St. Louis, lecturer, then assistant professor of salesmanship, 1935-39; St. Louis University, St. Louis, assistant professor of economics, 1937-42. Sales Age (publishers), member of board of directors. *Member:* International Society for General Semantics, St. Louis Real Estate Board, St. Louis Chamber of Commerce, Rotary.

WRITINGS: Influencing the Buyer's Mind, American Efficiency Bureau, 1936; *Listening Salesmanship,* American Efficiency Bureau, 1955; *Sales Age Tips,* Sales Age, 1957; *How Big Ideas Make Big Money Selling Real Estate,* Prentice-Hall, 1961. Contributor to *Encyclopaedia Britannica,* and to periodicals.

WORK IN PROGRESS: A textbook in salesmanship; a guide for buying real estate to make more after-tax income.

*   *   *

BENNETT, E(thel) M. Granger   1891-

PERSONAL: Born November 11, 1891, in Dorsetshire, England; daughter of James Henry and Julia Ann (Hutchings) Granger; married Harold Bennett (a university professor and administrator) September 2, 1919. *Education:* Attended Collegiate Institute, Collingwood, Ontario, Canada; Victoria College, University of Toronto, B.A., 1915; University of Wisconsin, Ph.D., 1931. *Home:* 27 Thorncliffe Park Dr., Toronto, Ontario, Canada.

CAREER: Ontario Ladies' College, Whitby, instructor in modern languages, 1915-19; Lebanon Valley College, Annville, Pa., professor of French and German, 1922-28; Victoria College, University of Toronto, Toronto, Ontario, special lecturer, 1945-47. *Member:* Canadian Authors' Association, Heliconian Club (Toronto). *Awards, honors:* Ryerson Fiction Award, 1960, for *Short of the Glory.*

WRITINGS: Land for Their Inheritance, Ryerson, 1955; *A Straw in the Wind,* Ryerson, 1958; *Short of the Glory,* Ryerson, 1960. Contributor of short stories for children to *Discovery* (magazine).

WORK IN PROGRESS: Minor biographies for *Dictionary of Canadian Biography,* to be published bilingually; historical research on the explorer, La Verendrye, and on life in the Montreal of his day (1731-1749) for a possible historical novel.

BIOGRAPHICAL/CRITICAL SOURCES: Canadian Literature, Spring, 1961; *Queen's Quarterly,* Spring, 1961; *University of Toronto Quarterly,* July, 1961.

*   *   *

BENNETT, Fredna W(illis)   1906-

PERSONAL: Born August 23, 1906, in Tarrant County, Tex.; daughter of George Bennie (a farmer) and Mary Epps (Lamar) Willis; married Cleve O. Bennett (a farmer), May 19, 1931. *Education:* Attended Hardin-Baylor College, 1924-25, and North Texas State Teachers College (now University), 1928-29. *Politics:* Conservative. *Religion:* Southern Baptist. *Address:* Box 212, Claude, Tex. 79019.

CAREER: Teacher in Tarrant County, Tex., 1925-27, and in Claude, Tex., 1929-31. *Member:* Panhandle Pen Women.

WRITINGS: (Editor) *Moments of Meditation from Matthew Henry,* Zondervan, 1963; *Devotionals for Worship Programs,* Baker Book, 1966; *Devotional Studies in Amos: The Herdsman from Tekoa,* Baker Book, 1966; *Devotional Studies in Luke: Christ, the Son of Man,* Baker Book, 1967; *Christian Living from Isaiah,* Baker Book, 1968. Regular contributor to *Claude News.*

WORK IN PROGRESS: A book, *From My Kitchen Window.*

BIOGRAPHICAL/CRITICAL SOURCES: Sunday News-Globe (Amarillo, Tex.), September 29, 1963.

*   *   *

BENSON, Sally   1900-1972
(Esther Evarts)

PERSONAL: Born Sara Mahala Redway Smith, September 3, 1900, in St. Louis, Mo.; daughter of Alonzo Redway (a cotton broker) and Anna (Prophater) Smith; married Reynolds Benson (an athletics manager), January 25, 1919 (divorced); children: Barbara. *Education:* Attended Mary Institute, St. Louis, Mo., and Horace Mann High School, New York, N.Y.

CAREER: National City Bank, foreign exchange bank teller, 1917-1919; *New York Morning Telegraph,* feature writer; book reviewer ("some 32 a month for a pulp paper house"); film critic; full-time professional writer. *Awards, honors:* Academy Award nomination for her screenplay "Anna and the King of Siam," 1946.

WRITINGS: People Are Fascinating (short stories), Covici, 1936; *Emily* (short stories), Covici, 1938 (published in England as *Love They Neighbour,* Constable, 1939); *Stories of the Gods and Heroes,* Dial, 1940; *Junior Miss* (Book-of-the Month Club selection), Random House, 1941; *Meet Me in St. Louis,* Random House, 1942; *Women and Children First,* Random House, 1943. Contributor of stories, under the pseudonym Esther Evarts, and of reviews of mystery stories to *The New Yorker;* also contributor to other magazines.

Film scripts: "Shadow of a Doubt," Universal, 1943; "Experiment Perilous," RKO, 1944; "National Velvet," M-G-M, 1944; "Anna and the King of Siam," 20th Century-Fox, 1946; "Come to the Stable," 20th Century-Fox, 1949; "No Man of Her Own," Paramount, 1950; "Conspirator," M-G-M, 1950; "The Belle of New York," M-G-M, 1952; "The Farmer Takes a Wife," 20th Century-Fox, 1953; "The Adventures of Huckleberry Finn," M-G-M, 1960; "Bus Stop," 20th Century-Fox, 1961; "Summer Magic," Walt Disney, 1962; "Viva Las Vegas," M-G-M, 1963; "Signpost to Murder," M-G-M, 1963; "The Singing Nun," M-G-M, 1966.

Plays: *Seventeen* (adapted from the novel by Booth Tarkington), French, 1954; *The Young and the Beautiful* (based on F. Scott Fitzgerald's "Josephine" stories in the *Saturday Evening Post*), French, 1956.

SIDELIGHTS: Sally Benson's early contributions to the *New Yorker* were noted for their venomous satire on human foibles. "The lady who takes her swains to the zoo," wrote William Soskin, "the 'man's woman,' who is an expert in picking up gents on the matrimonial rebound—these and many other sad people are tripped by [Mrs.] Benson's tweezers, cut a bit with her scalpel, made to squirm and finally fixed for a microscope slide, most competently." *A Boston Transcript* reviewer added: "They are brilliant with a knife-like cut, ruthless in their satire, and penetrating often to the point of tragedy." Soskin summarized: "The writing of such stories should be forthright, bare and understated. It is."

Thus, it is ironic that the author is best remembered for her awkward, ungainly adolescents—Judy Graves in *Junior Miss* and Tootie Smith in the autobiographical *Meet Me in St. Louis*. Miss Benson wrote her first Judy Graves story for the *New Yorker* and, though she soon tired of the idea, she was encouraged by the late Harold Ross to continue them. The stories were subsequently published in book form, successfully dramatized by Jerome Chodorov and Joseph Fields in 1943, with added episodes, became the popular radio show "Junior Miss," with Barbara Whiting in the lead role, and later made into a movie and a television musical. "Though she has forsworn the sophisticated wit and irony for which she is so well noted," commented E. H. Walton, "these seemingly simple sketches still bear her hallmark and are no less adroit than her earlier stories. In writing of Judy Graves's minor adventures, Mrs. Benson is as pithy and concise as ever, as much a master of the perfect phrase, with an added quality of warmth and gentleness which, until now, she has rather conspicuously lacked."

The *New Yorker* was a steady market for her, "possibly because I haven't tried other markets," she once explained to Robert van Gelder. "My style fits here and it wouldn't most places. Every once in a while editors of some of the national magazines have asked for my stuff, but what they really want are healthy, clean-limbed hearty young people on a raft, and that isn't for me."

Meet Me in St. Louis was filmed by Metro-Goldwyn-Mayer in 1944.

BIOGRAPHICAL/CRITICAL SOURCES: Books, July 5, 1936; *Boston Transcript*, July 18, 1936; *New York Times Book Review*, May 25, 1941; *New York Times*, December 25, 1965.

(Died July 19, 1972)

* * *

BENSON, Thomas Godfrey 1899-

PERSONAL: Born December 7, 1899, in Sheffield, England; son of Reginald (a lawyer) and Madeline (Carey) Benson; married Dorothea Williams, December, 1932; children: Christopher, David, John. *Education:* Sherborne Public School, student, 1912-18; Cambridge University, M.A., 1921; Oxford University, Diploma in Education and Diploma in Anthropology, 1931. *Religion:* Church of England. *Home:* 6 Assheton Rd., Beaconsfield, Buckinghamshire, England.

CAREER: Jeanes School, Kenya, principal, training supervisors of elementary schools, 1927-39; senior education officer, Kenya, 1940-47; assistant director of education, Ghana, 1947-49; University of London, London, England, School of Oriental and African Studies, lecturer, 1952—. Overseas secretary, Institute of Christian Education, 1950-52; chairman, Kwato (Papua) Extension Association, 1961—. *Member:* Race Relations Institute.

WRITINGS: (Editor) *Kikuyu Dictionary*, Clarendon Press, 1964. Contributer to *African Language Studies*, 1964.

WORK IN PROGRESS: First Kikuyu course; first Meru course.

* * *

BENTON, William 1900-1973

PERSONAL: Born April 1, 1900, in Minneapolis, Minn.; son of Charles William (a college professor) and Elma Caroline (Hixson) Benton; married Helen Hemingway, June 12, 1928; children; Charles William, Helen (Mrs. John Nicholas Boley), Louise, John. *Education:* Carleton College, student, 1917-18; Yale University, A.B., 1921. *Politics:* Democrat. *Religion:* Episcopalian. *Home:* Sasco Hill Rd., Southport, Conn. 06490. *Office:* Encyclopaedia Britannica, 342 Madison Ave., New York, N.Y. 10017.

CAREER: Associated with Lord & Thomas (advertising agency), Chicago, Ill., prior to 1929; Benton & Bowles (advertising agency), New York, N.Y., founder, 1929, president, 1929-35, chairman of board, 1935-36; University of Chicago, Chicago, Ill., vice-president, 1937-45, assistant chancellor, 1945, trustee, 1946-65; U.S. government, Washington, D.C., assistant Secretary of State, 1945-47, senator from Connecticut, 1949-53. *Encyclopaedia Britannica*, publisher and chairman of board; Encyclopaedia Britannica Educational Corporation (formerly Encyclopaedia Britannica Films) chairman of board, 1943-73. Coordinator of Inter-American Affairs, member of advisory committee, 1939-45; Committee for Economic Development, vice-chairman of board of trustees, 1942-45, member of executive committee, board of trustees, 1958-63; vice-chairman; U.S. Commission on Inter-American Development, 1943-45; UNESCO, member of U.S. delegation to Constitutional Convention, London, 1945, chairman of U.S. delegations at first General Conference, Paris, 1946, and second General Conference, Mexico City, 1947, chief, U.S. member of executive board with rank of ambassador, 1963-68; United Nations Conference on Freedom of the Press, Geneva, chairman of U.S. delegation, 1948. Trustee or director of over thirty public service organizations, including University of Chicago, University of Connecticut, University of Bridgeport, Carleton College, Eisenhower Exchange Fellowships, American Shakespeare Festival Theatre and Academy, and William Benton Foundation.

MEMBER: American Foreign Service Association (honorary), Union Interalliee (Paris), Fairfield Country Club and Pequot Yacht Club (both Connecticut), Metropolitan Country Club (Washington, D.C.), Paradise Valley Country Club (Phoenix, Ariz.), Yale Club, University Club, and River Club (all New York). *Awards, honors:* LL.D., University of Louisville, 1948, Bard College, 1951, Montana State College, 1957, Knox College, 1960, Carleton College, 1961, University of Notre Dame, 1968, Brandeis University, 1968, Dartmouth College, 1968; Distinguished honor award, Department of State, 1967; Human Relations award, American Jewish Commission; Kajima Peace Award; Distinguished Public Service award, Connecticut Bar Association, 1972.

WRITINGS: This is the Challenge, Associated College Presses, 1958; *The Voice of Latin America*, Harper, 1961; *The Teachers and the Taught in the U.S.S.R.*, Atheneum, 1966. Contributor of about 150 articles to national magazines.

SIDELIGHTS: Benton helped work his way through Yale as a high-stake auction bridge player, later gave up a Rhodes scholarship and disappointed family hopes for a ministerial career to become a salesman, then an advertising copywriter. In the firm he established with Chester Bowles, he pioneered in radio advertising and programs that used studio audiences, and retired a millionaire from Benton & Bowles at 35. As a vice-president of the University of Chicago, he acquired the faltering *Encyclopaedia Brittanica* from Sears, Roebuck and put up $100,000 of his own money as working capital to allay fears of the school's worried trustees. Under his stewardship, the encyclopedia's sales zoomed during the next two decades from $3,000,000 to $125 million, netting the university $25 million in royalties.

Benton was a staunch liberal and a bitter foe of Joe McCarthy in his Senate days (1949-53). As Assistant Secretary of State for Public Affairs he organized the Voice of America broadcasts and was active in the establishment of UNESCO. During the Johnson Administration he was chief United States member of the UNESCO executive board with the rank of Ambassador.

Benton was a serious art collector, and in 1972 the University of Connecticut named the William Benton Museum of Art in his honor.

BIOGRAPHICAL/CRITICAL SOURCES: Sidney Hyman, *The Lives of William Benton*, University of Chicago Press, 1969.

(Died, March 18, 1973)

* * *

BERGER, Klaus 1901-

PERSONAL: Born March 24, 1901, in Berlin, Germany; came to United States in 1941, naturalized in 1943; son of Rudolf (a professor) and Margarete (Mueller) Berger; married Margaret Robinson (a professor), December 22, 1941; children: Margaretta. *Education:* Student at University of Munich, University of Heidelberg, and University of Berlin, 1920-24; University of Goettingen, Ph.D., 1925; Ecole du Louvre, certificate, 1925. *Religion:* Protestant. *Home:* 700 Indiana, Lawrence, Kan. *Office:* Department of Art History, University of Kansas, Lawrence, Kan.

CAREER: University of Berlin Extension, Berlin, Germany, lecturer on art, 1927-33; Berlin Municipal Libraries, Berlin, Germany, head librarian, 1929-33; Free German University, Paris, France, lecturer on art, 1933-39; Northwestern University, Evanston, Ill., lecturer on art, 1943-45; U.S. Army University, Biarritz, France, professor of art, 1945; U.S. Military Government of Bavaria, officer, Monuments, Fine Arts, and Archives Section, 1946; University of Kansas City, Kansas City, Mo., assistant professor of art, 1947-50; University of Kansas, Lawrence, beginning 1950, assistant professor, then professor of art history. Visiting lecturer in museums and universities abroad. *Member:* Renaissance Society of America, Societe Poussin, Societe de l'histoire de l'art francais, Verband Deutscher Kunsthistoriker (honorary). *Awards, honors:* Fulbright Fellow and guest professor at University of Cologne, 1954; cultural exchange scholar in Leningrad on American Council of Learned Societies grant, 1962.

WRITINGS: Gericault: Drawings and Watercolors, Bittner, 1946; (editor) *French Master Drawings of the Nineteenth Century*, Harper, 1950; *Gericault und Sein Werk*, Schroll, 1952, translation by Winslow Ames published as *Gericault and His Work*, University of Kansas Press, 1955; *Odilon Redon: Phantasie und Farbe*, Du Mont Schauberg, 1964, translation by Michael Bullock published as *Odilon Redon: Fantasy and Colour*, Weidenfeld & Nicolson, 1964, McGraw, 1965. Contributor to *World Encyclopedia of Art and Collier's Encyclopedia*. Also contributor of almost sixty articles to English, French, German, and Italian periodicals, including *Gazette des Beaux-Arts, Art News.*

WORK IN PROGRESS: The impact of Japanese art on western painting.

SIDELIGHTS: Berger has been a researcher and traveler in western Europe, Soviet Union, Middle East, India, and Japan.

* * *

BERKOWITZ, Freda Pastor 1910-

PERSONAL: Born October 11, 1910, in Newark, N.J.; daughter of Abe (a builder) and Mary (Lubetkin) Pastor; divorced; children: Ellen (Mrs. Albert S. Carlin), Joan (Mrs. Murray R. Schuman). *Education:* Curtis Institute of Music, B.Mus., 1935. *Politics:* Democrat. *Religion:* Jewish. *Home:* 1530 Locust St., Philadelphia, Pa. 19102. *Agent:* Curtis Brown Ltd., 60 East 56th St., New York, N.Y. 10022. *Office:* Curtis Institute of Music, 18th and Rittenhouse Sq., Philadelphia, Pa.

CAREER: Instructor in piano, Curtis Institute of Music, Philadelphia, Pa., and privately, for twenty-eight years; also faculty member at New School of Music and Settlement Music School, both Philadelphia, Pa.

WRITINGS: Popular Titles and Subtitles of Musical Compositions, Scarecrow, 1962; *Unfinished Symphony, and Other Stories of Men and Music*, Atheneum, 1963; *On Lutes, Recorders, and Harpsichords: Men and Music of the Baroque*, Atheneum, 1967.

WORK IN PROGRESS: Work in music for children, mostly about composers.

BIOGRAPHICAL/CRITICAL SOURCES: Christian Science Monitor, November 2, 1967.

* * *

BERNHARDT, Karl S. 1901-1967

PERSONAL: Born October 14, 1901, in Toronto, Ontario, Canada; son of August Edward (an upholsterer) and Elizabeth (Schofield) Bernhardt; married Dorothy Butcher, September 12, 1931; children: David Karl. *Education:* University of Toronto, B.A., 1926, M.A., 1929; University of Chicago, Ph.D., 1933. *Religion:* United Church of Canada.

CAREER: University of Toronto, Toronto, Ontario, 1929-64, began as instructor, professor of psychology, 1943-64, professor emeritus, 1964-67, assistant director of Institute of Child Study, 1936-60, director, 1960-64. Member of board of educators, Tangley Oaks Educational Center, Lake Bluff, Ill. *Member:* American Psychological Association, Canadian Psychological Association (past president; past honorary president), American Association for the Advancement of Science, Society for Research in Child Development, Ontario Psychological Association. *Awards, honors:* Award of Merit from Canadian Credit Institute.

WRITINGS: Introduction to Psychology, Life Underwriters, 1934, revised and enlarged edition published as *Elementary Psychology*, 1943, 2nd revised edition, 1960; *Practical Psychology*, McGraw, 1945; (with son, D. K. Bernhardt) *Making the Most of Your College Career*, Burns & MacEachern, 1956; (editor with E. E. Sentman) *Your Child's World*, Book House for Children, 1960; (editor) *Training for Research in Psychology*, University of Toronto Press, 1961; *Discipline and Child Guidance*, McGraw, 1964; *Being a Parent: Unchanging Values in a Changing World*, edited by David K. Bernhardt, University of Toronto Press, 1970. Editor, *Institute of Child Study Bulletin*.

(Died, 1967)

*   *   *

BERRYMAN, John   1914-1972

PERSONAL: Surname originally Smith; name changed upon adoption by mother's second husband, John A. Berryman; born October 25, 1914, in McAlester, Okla.; son of John Allyn (a banker) and Martha (a teacher; maiden name, Little) Smith; married Eileen Mulligan, October 24, 1942 (divorced, 1953); married Ann Levine, 1956 (divorced, 1959); married Kate Donahue, 1961; children: (second marriage) Paul; (third marriage) Martha, Sara. *Education:* Columbia University, A.B., 1936; Clare College, Cambridge, B.A., 1938. *Home:* 33 Arthur Ave. S.E., Minneapolis, Minn. 55414. *Office:* Department of Humanities, University of Minnesota, Minneapolis, Minn.

CAREER: Wayne University (now Wayne State), Detroit, Mich., instructor in English, 1939-40; Harvard University, Cambridge, Mass., instructor, 1940-43; Princeton University, Princeton, N.J., fellow, 1943-44, lecturer in creative writing, 1946-49, Hodder fellow, 1950-51; University of Cincinnati, Cincinnati, Ohio, Elliston Lecturer in Poetry, 1951-52; University of Minnesota, Minneapolis, 1955—, began as lecturer, became Regents Professor of Humanities. Lecturer at numerous colleges and universities; poet-in-residence, Trinity College, 1967; made U.S. State Department tour to India to read poetry.

MEMBER: National Institute of Arts and Letters, American Academy of Arts and Sciences, Phi Beta Kappa. *Awards, honors:* Kellett fellowship from Columbia University, 1936-38, to study at Clare College; Oldham Shakespeare Scholar, Clare College, 1937; Rockefeller fellow, 1944-46; *Kenyon Review*-Doubleday short story award, 1945, for "The Imaginary Jew"; Shelley Memorial Award, Poetry Society of America, 1949; Levinson Prize, 1950; National Institute of Arts and Letters grant in literature, 1950; Guggenheim fellow, 1952-53, 1966; *Partisan Review* fellowship, 1957; Harriet Monroe Poetry Award, University of Chicago, 1957; Brandeis University Creative Arts Award, 1959-60; Loines Award, National Institute of Arts and Letters, 1964; Pulitzer Prize, 1965, for *77 Dream Songs*; Academy of American Poets fellowship, 1966; National Endowment for the Arts award, 1967; Emily Clark Balch Award, *Virginia Quarterly Review*, 1968; Bollingen Prize and National Book Award, both 1969, for *His Toy, His Dream, His Rest*; received honorary degrees from Cambridge University and Drake University.

*WRITINGS—*Poetry: (Contributor) *Five Young American Poets*, New Directions, 1940; *Poems*, New Directions, 1942; *The Dispossessed*, Sloane, 1948; *Homage to Mistress Bradstreet*, Farrar, Straus, 1956 (published in England as *Homage to Mistress Bradstreet, and Other Poems*, Faber, 1959); *His Thought Made Pockets and the Plane Buckt*, C.

Fredericks, 1958; *77 Dream Songs*, Farrar, Straus, 1964; *Short Poems* (includes *The Dispossessed* and *His Thoughts Made Pockets and the Plane Buckt*), Farrar, Straus, 1967; *Berryman's Sonnets*, Farrar, Straus, 1967; *His Toy, His Dream, His Rest* (sequel to *77 Dream Songs*), Farrar, Straus, 1968; *The Dream Songs* (includes *77 Dream Songs* and *His Toy, His Dream, His Rest*), Farrar, Straus, 1969; *Love & Fame*, Farrar, Straus, 1970, revised edition, 1972; *Delusions, Etc.*, Farrar, Straus, 1972; *Recovery*, Farrar, Straus, 1973; *Selected Poems, 1938-1968*, Faber, 1972.

Other: *Stephen Crane* (biography), Sloane, 1950; (author of introduction) Mathew Gregory Lewis, *The Monk*, Grove, 1952; (editor) Thomas Nash, *Unfortunate Traveller, or, The Life of Jack Wilton*, Putnam, 1960; (contributor) Howard Nemerov, editor, *Poets on Poetry*, Basic Books, 1966.

Contributor to *Southern Review, Kenyon Review, Partisan Review, Nation, New Republic, New Yorker, Accent, Saturday Review, Poetry*, and other periodicals.

WORK IN PROGRESS: A critical biography of Shakespeare, a life of Christ, and a "semi-autobiographical novel."

SIDELIGHTS: Edmund Wilson and Frank Kermode hailed *Homage to Mistress Bradstreet* as the most important work of poetry since *The Waste Land* and *Four Quartets*. Philip Toynbee believes that Berryman and Robert Lowell "have become the most prominent American poets since the recent deaths of Robert Frost, William Carlos Williams, and Theodore Roethke." When *77 Dream Songs* was published, Lowell called it even greater than *Homage to Mistress Bradstreet*. The dream songs "are dazzling even when they befuddle," writes Frederick Seidel. "But Berryman's mature work is always at least dazzling. One takes enormous pleasure just in the expertise. Here are wonderfully intelligent, witty line-breaks that win one's devotion and get memorized like poems. The unmistakable Berryman rhythm, that came into its own in his great *Homage to Mistress Bradstreet*, is less regular and grand now; it calms or swells within a shorter stanza and within a single eighteen-line song. The rhythm is jazzier, odder, more insisted upon and shown off; a syncopation almost." The idiom is entirely his own, "one of the few unmistakable dictions in modern poetry," according to the *Times Literary Supplement*. Always flexible, at times distorted and experimental, it "puns and plays and twists with words in a dreamlike manner reminiscent of Joyce and Cummings, yet quite Berryman's own," writes Louis L. Martz.

M. L. Rosenthal believes that with *77 Dream Songs* Berryman "seriously enters the post-war current of confessional poetry," distinctive for its naked accounts of private suffering, and represented by such poets as Robert Lowell and W. D. Snodgrass. Berryman is the first poet (except Allen Ginsberg, whom he resembles more than he would like to think, perhaps, but whose writing is essentially of a different cast) to pick up Mr. Lowell's cues on so sweeping a scale." However, unlike most confessional poets, Berryman's songs are often surrealistic. Fred Bornhauser writes: "What would be in other poetry the subtle nuance of feeling is here the hush and slush of painful echo drawing nearer. With the impudence of Auden, the boisterous humor of Joyce, the bluntness of Pound, the exoticism of Stevens, the formal freedom of Cummings, and the imaginative flair of Nabokov in his prose, Berryman has composed spontaneous and staggering verses which demand and deserve a like response."

As Seidel observes, "the humor [in *77 Dream Songs*] is wonderfull, . . . doing for poetry what William Burroughs, in the Dr. Benway passages of *Naked Lunch*, did for the comic novel." The *Times Literary Supplement* reviewer writes: "The seventy-seven ways of triangulating early twentieth-century existence add up to a complex humility, a vigorous, humorous, vicious and disturbing entertainment, whose degree of moral criticism stems from one rather middle-aged virtue—'one virtue,—without which a man can hardly hold his own,' which is 'that a man should always reproach himself. . . .' Mr. Berryman is truly his own 'weary daring man,' 'roiling and babbling & braining.' He has made a tough coherent work, the saga of a de-classed intellectual Prufrock in mid-century. . . ."

BIOGRAPHICAL/CRITICAL SOURCES: Atlantic, January, 1965; *Books and Bookmen*, January, 1965; *Poetry*, January, 1965; *Minnesota Review*, January-April, 1965; *New Statesman*, January 15, 1965; *Virginia Quarterly Review*, winter, 1965; *Yale Review*, winter, 1965; *Encounter*, March, 1965; *Reporter*, March 25, 1965; *American Scholar*, autumn, 1965; *New York Review of Books*, June 29, 1967; *Life*, July 21, 1967; *Chelsea*, June, 1968; *New Leader*, December 2, 1968; *Nation*, February 24, 1969; *Yale Review*, spring, 1969; *New York Times*, January 8, 1972; R. J. Kelly, *John Berryman: A Checklist*, Scarecrow, 1972; Carolyn Riley, editor, *Contemporary Literary Criticism*, Gale, Volume I, 1973, Volume II, 1974, Volume III, 1975, Volume IV, 1975.†

(Died January 7, 1972)

*   *   *

BEST, Rayleigh Breton Amis   1905-
(Breton Amis)

PERSONAL: Born October 1, 1905, in Leigh, Essex, England; son of George Arthur and Mary (Amis) Best; married Charlotte Matthews (a writer), June 27, 1928; children: Terence. *Religion:* Anglican. *Home:* 11 Victoria Ave., Winton, Bournemouth, England. *Agent:* Robert Sommerville Ltd., Mowbray House, Norfolk St., London W.C.2, England.

CAREER: Fleet St. journalist, London, England, 1924-39; free-lance writer, 1939—. *Member:* Society of Authors.

WRITINGS: The House Called Yarrow, British Book Service, 1960; *The Honest Rogue*, British Book Service, 1961; *With Pink Trumpets*, Ward, Lock, 1962; *High Tide*, Ward, Lock, 1962; *Pilot's Height*, Ward, Lock, 1963; *Idle Rainbow*, Ward, Lock, 1965.

Under name Breton Amis: *Tomorrow Will Be Sunday*, Stanley Paul, 1946; *Park Royal*, Jenkins, 1950; *Hive of Glass*, Jenkins, 1950; *Road to the Heart*, Ward, Lock, 1959; *A Touch of Scarlet*, Ward, Lock, 1960; *Such Sweet Sorrow*, Ward, Lock, 1961; *Daughters of the Bride*, Ward, Lock, 1962.

*   *   *

BETHERS, Ray   1902-

PERSONAL: Born April 25, 1902, in Corvallis, Ore.; son of Elmer and Anna (Wells) Bethers; married Peggy Sibley, 1923. *Education:* Studied at University of Oregon, California School of Fine Arts, and at art schools in New York, Paris, London. *Home:* Flat 30, Richmond Ct., Davigdor Rd., Hove 2, Sussex, England.

CAREER: Author-illustrator, formerly residing in Paris, France, now in England. Also designer of type pages, cov-

ers, and jackets for most of his books. *Military service:* U.S. Naval Reserve, World War II; became lieutenant commander. *Member:* Dutch Treat Club (New York). *Awards, honors:* Library of Congress purchase prize for wood engraving.

WRITINGS—All self-illustrated: *Pictures, Painters, and You*, Pitman, 1948; *Can You Name Them?: A Pictorial-Informational Quiz Book*, Aladdin Books, 1948; *Composition in Pictures*, Pitman, 1949, 3rd edition, 1962; *Perhaps I'll Be a Sailor*, Aladdin Books, 1949; *The Magic of Oil*, Aladdin Books, 1949.

Perhaps I'll Be a Farmer, Aladdin Books, 1950; *Perhaps I'll Be a Railroad Man*, Aladdin Books, 1951; *How Paintings Happen*, Norton, 1951; *From Eye to Camera*, Pitman, 1951; *The Story of Rivers*, Sterling, 1957, revised edition, Oak Tree Press, 1963; *Photo-Vision*, St. Martin's, 1957; *How to Find Your Own Style in Painting: What Style Is, and How the Kind of a Person You are Will Influence Your Style*, Hastings House, 1957; *Art Always Changes: How to Understand Modern Painting*, Hastings House, 1958; *Nature Invents, Science Applies*, Hastings House, 1959; *Islands of Adventure*, Hastings House, 1959.

Rivers of Adventure, Hastings House, 1960; *Ships of Adventure*, Constable, 1961, Hastings House, 1962; *What Happens Underground?*, St. Martin's, 1961; *Ports of Adventure*, Constable, 1962, Hastings House, 1963; *What Happens in the Sea?*, Macmillan, 1962; *How Does It Grow?*, St. Martin's, 1963; *Discoveries: Dinosaurs to Rockets*, Constable, 1963; *The Language of Paintings: Form and Content*, Pitman, 1963; *What Happens in the Sky?*, St. Martin's, 1963; *This Is Our World*, St. Martin's, 1964; *How Did We Get Our Names?*, Macmillan, 1966. Former associate editor, *This Week*.

SIDELIGHTS: Bethers is a writer-illustrator in reverse. "Thus I do not write and then illustrate what I have written. But instead [I] use words to fill in what it is not possible to explain in the illustrations. . . . To me there are no single pages in a book, but only facing pages seen as a unit."†

*   *   *

BETT, Walter R(eginald)   1903-

PERSONAL: Born April 8, 1903, in Riga, Latvia; British subject by birth; son of William Edward and Sophie Marie (Thies) Bett; married Ruth Irene King, June 21, 1935. *Education:* Attended schools in Germany and St. Paul's School, London, England; St. Bartholomew's Hospital Medical College, University of London, M.R.C.S. (England) and L.R.C.P. (London), 1929. *Office:* Pfizer Laboratories, 235 East 42nd St., New York, N.Y. 10017.

CAREER: East London Children's Hospital, London, England, resident medical officer, 1932; Columbia University, College of Physicians and Surgeons, New York, N.Y., medical librarian, 1935-37; National Association for Prevention of Tuberculosis, London, England, research librarian, 1945-59; *Medical Digest*, London, England, editor, 1956-59; Eaton Laboratories, Norwich, N.Y., medical editor, 1959-61; Pfizer Laboratories, New York, N.Y., medical editor of *Spectrum*, 1961—. *Military service:* Royal Army Medical Corps, 1939-45; became captain.

MEMBER: Royal Society of Literature (fellow), Royal Society of Medicine (fellow), Royal Society of Arts (fellow), Royal Statistical Society (fellow), Society of Antiquaries of Scotland (fellow), Royal Economical Society (fellow), Royal Anthropological Institute (fellow), Chemical Society of London (fellow), American Medical Writers' Association (honorary), Society for Study of Addiction to Alcohol and Other Drugs (London; president, 1955-58).

WRITINGS: The Short-Lived Spring (poems), Stockwell, 1934; *Osler: The Man and the Legend*, Heinemann Medical Books, 1951; *The Infirmities of Genius*, Philosophical Library, 1952; (editor and contributor) *History and Conquest of Common Diseases*, University of Oklahoma Press, 1954; (with Howells and Macdonald) *Amphetamine in Clinical Medicine*, Williams & Wilkins, 1955; *Sir John Bland-Sutton, 1855-1936*, Williams & Wilkins, 1956; (contributor) R. W. Raven, *Cancer*, Volume I, Butterworth & Co., 1958; *Short History of Nursing*, Faber, 1960. Contributor to medical, pharmaceutical, and nursing journals.

AVOCATIONAL INTERESTS: Collecting stamps of medical interest, collecting everything by and about Somerset Maugham, public speaking, good food and wine (and exploring New York restaurants), art, especially modern. Bett adds that "like G. K. Chesterton I understand music so little that it does not even annoy me."

*   *   *

BETZ, Eva Kelly
(Caroline Peters)

PERSONAL: Born in Fall River, Mass.; daughter of Michael Forestal (a medical doctor) and Caroline (Cantwell) Kelly; married Joseph P. Betz; children: Joseph P., Jr. (deceased). *Home:* 353 Van Houten Ave., Passaic, N.J. 07055.

CAREER: Former elementary teacher in Rhode Island and Massachusetts; later employed in sales promotion in Paterson, N.J.; free-lance writer. *Member:* Authors Guild, New Jersey Historical Society (honorary life member).

WRITINGS: Young Eagles, D. X. McMullen Co., 1947.

Freedom Drums, Abelard, 1950, 2nd edition, St. Anthony Guild Press, 1953; *Desperate Drums,* St. Anthony Guild Press, 1951; *Victory Drums,* St. Anthony Guild Press, 1955; *Knight of Molokai,* St. Anthony Guild Press, 1956; *My Little Counting Books,* Bruce, 1957; *The Amazing John Tabb,* Bruce, 1958; *The Man Who Fought the Devil: The Cure of Ars,* St. Anthony Guild Press, 1958; *Priest on Horseback: Father Farmer, 1720-1786,* Sheed, 1958, 2nd edition, St. Anthony Guild Press, 1965.

David, Sheed, 1960; *Priest, Patriot, and Leader: The Story of Archbishop Carroll,* Benziger, 1960; *Yankee at Molokai,* St. Anthony Guild Press, 1960; *The Web Begun,* Bruce, 1961; *Saint Colum and the Crane,* St. Anthony Guild Press, 1961; *Blessed Sebastian and the Oxen,* St. Anthony Guild Press, 1961; *Saint Germaine and the Sheep,* St. Anthony Guild Press, 1961; *Fanny Allen, Green Mountain Rebel,* Kenedy, 1962; *To Far Places: The Story of Francis X. Ford,* Hawthorn, 1962; (under pseudonym Caroline Peters) *The Story of St. Kevin,* St. Anthony Guild Press, 1962; (under pseudonym Caroline Peters) *The Black Madonna: Our Lady of Czestochowa,* St. Anthony Guild Press, 1962; *The Quiet Flame: Mother Marianne of Molokai,* Bruce, 1963; *Virgil Barber, New England Pied Piper,* Kenedy, 1963; *Saint Martin de Porres and the Mice,* St. Anthony Guild Press, 1963; (under pseudonym Caroline Peters) *St. Michael, God's Warrier Angel,* St. Anthony Guild Press, 1963; *William Gaston, Fighter for Justice,* Kenedy, 1964; *Saint Brigid and the Cows,* St. Anthony Guild Press, 1964; *Story of the Rosary,* St. Anthony Guild

Press, 1964; *Apostle of the Ice and Snow: A Life of Bishop Charles Seghers,* Holy Cross Press, 1964; *Stout Hearts and Holy Hands: The Life of Mother Angela, of the Sisters of the Holy Cross,* Holy Cross Press, 1964; (under pseudonym Caroline Peters) *The Story of Saint Clare,* St. Anthony Guild Press, 1965; (under pseudonym Caroline Peters) *Lives of the Saints, for Boys and Girls,* St. Anthony Guild Press, 1965.

*   *   *

BIBERMAN, Herbert   1900-1971

PERSONAL: Born March 4, 1900, in Philadelphia, Pa.; son of Joseph (a manufacturer) and Eva (Goldich) Biberman; married Gale Sondergaard (an actress), May 8, 1930; children: Joan (Mrs. Joseph Campos), Daniel Hans. *Education:* University of Pennsylvania, B.S., 1921; Yale University, Certificate in Fine Arts, 1927. *Religion:* Jewish. *Home:* 263 West End Ave., New York, N.Y. *Agent:* Barthold Fles Literary Agency, 507 Fifth Ave., New York, N.Y. 10017.

CAREER: Toured Europe studying theater production, 1928; New York Theatre Guild, 1929-33, began as an assistant, became production stage manager, and member of board; writer, director, and associate producer at Hollywood studios, 1935-37, 1940-46, working successively with Columbia Pictures, Paramount Pictures, 20th Century Fox, R.K.O., and Majestic Productions (United Artists); Independent Productions Corp., New York, N.Y., director, 1950-56; Mangaard, Inc. (land developers), New York, N.Y., president, 1956-63. Films directed include "Green Grow the Lilacs," the basis for the musical "Oklahoma," "One Way Ticket," "Meet Nero Wolfe," "Salt of the Earth," and "The Slaves"; associate producer of "Abilene Town" and "New Orleans" *Member:* Directors Guild (founder), Hollywood Anti-Nazi League (founder), Screenwriters Guild, Phi Epsilon Pi, Beta Gamma Sigma. *Awards, honors:* "Salt of the Earth" was named best picture of the year by the Motion Picture Academy of France and the Karlovy Vary Film Festival, Czechoslovakia, 1955.

WRITINGS: Salt of the Earth, Beacon, 1965.

Film scripts: "Road to Yesterday" (original story); "New Orleans" (original story); "King of Chinatown" (original story); "The Master Race" (original story); "Action in Arabia" (screenplay), "The Slaves" (screenplay).

WORK IN PROGRESS: "Journey Around a Room," a play.

SIDELIGHTS: Biberman's book, *Salt of the Earth,* is an account of the years 1947-65, during which he says that he was "subject to the blacklist by the motion picture industry because of his refusal to cooperate with the House Committee on Un-American Activities, [Biberman was convicted of contempt of Congress in 1950, and served a six-month sentence in federal prison], of his participation in the independent production of the film, "Salt of the Earth," and of its suffocation in the market; of an antitrust suit against the industry, of the subsequent trial. Since the past seventeen years have been spent largely in battling the blacklist—this book represents ten of those years in the wake of the aborted effort to achieve independency."

(Died June 30, 1971)

*   *   *

BICKLE, Judith Brundrett   ?-19(?)
(J. Tweedale)

PERSONAL: Born in Manchester, England; daughter of

Charles Austin and Annie (Lancashire) Bower; married William Howard Bickle (a staff officer, British Colonial Service; died 1962); children: Alwyn (son). *Education:* Studied at Marlborough College. *Politics:* Conservative. *Religion.* Christian.

CAREER: Author. *Member:* P.E.N. (London), Lancashire Authors Association (life).

WRITINGS: The Story of a Dog, Morland, 1930; *The Unimaginable Flowers* (novel), Heath Cranton, 1938; *Collected Poems*, Mitre Press, 1948; *Further Poems*, R. Hale, 1959; *This Is My Harvest* (poems), R. Hale, 1962; *Village of Rosemary* (novel), R. Hale, 1965. Writer of talks and stories for British Broadcasting Corp. program, "Listen with Mother." Contributor to *Homes and Gardens, Time and Tide, Country Life, Lady, My Garden.*

WORK IN PROGRESS: Stories for "Listen with Mother" program; a novel.

SIDELIGHTS: Mrs Bickle told *CA:* "Hobby, violinist. Keen gardener, especially roses. Animal welfare in all directions—hatred of battery and mechanical farming, also against chemicals and sprays. Pet geese now seventeen years old. Violent disgust re cruel sports, especially stag hunting."

(Deceased)

* * *

BIDWELL, Percy W(ells)   1888-19?

PERSONAL: Born July 19, 1888, in Manchester, Conn.; son of James C. and Clara (Woodbridge) Bidwell; married Anna Cabot Almy, June 8, 1915; children: John, Mary Almy (Mrs. Elihu Root III), Anne Woodbridge (Mrs. Mario Minafra), Charlotte Almy (Mrs. Donald Ryder), Samuel Cabot (deceased). *Education:* Yale University, B.A., 1910, M.A., 1912, Ph.D., 1915; graduate study at universities in Berlin and Munich, 1910-11. *Politics:* Democrat. *Religion:* Protestant. *Home:* 10 Rockledge Rd., Hartsdale, N.Y. 10530.

CAREER: Yale University, New Haven, Conn., began as instructor, became assistant professor of economics, 1915-21; Carnegie Institution of Washington, Washington, D.C., researcher in agricultural history, 1921-22; U.S. Tariff Commission, Washington, D.C., economist, 1922-30, assigned to European office, 1924-29; University of Buffalo, Buffalo, N.Y., professor of economics, 1930-38; Council on Foreign Relations, New York, N.Y., director of studies, 1938-53, research associate, 1953-58; Carnegie Corporation, New York, N.Y., study of undergraduate education in foreign affairs, 1958-61. Columbia University, visiting professor, 1949-50. World Peace Foundation, trustee emeritus. *Member:* Council on Foreign Relations and Century Association (both New York); Phi Beta Kappa, Thursday Club (Buffalo).

WRITINGS: (With H. L. Falconer) *History of Agriculture in Northern United States, 1620-1860,* Carnegie Institution, 1925; *Tariff Policy of the United States,* Council on Foreign Relations, 1933; *Our Trade with Britain,* Council on Foreign Relations, 1938; *The Invisible Tariff,* Council on Foreign Relations, 1939; (contributor) *America Looks Ahead,* World Peace Foundation, c.1940; (with Harold J. Tobin) *Mobilizing Civilian America,* Council on Foreign Relations, 1940; (editor) *Our Foreign Policy in War and Peace: Some Regional Views,* Council on Foreign Relations, 1942; *The United States and the United Nations: Views on Postwar Relations,* Council on Foreign Relations,

1943; *A Commercial Policy for the United Nations,* Committee on International Economic Policy, 1945; (editor and contributor) *Germany's Contribution to European Economic Life,* M. Riviere (Paris), 1949; (with William Diebold, Jr.) *The United States and the International Trade Organization,* Carnegie Endowment for International Peace, 1949; *What the Tariff Means to American Industries,* published for Council on Foreign Relations by Harper, 1956; *Raw Materials: A Study of American Policy,* published for Council on Foreign Relations by Harper, 1958; *Undergraduate Education in Foreign Affairs,* Columbia University Press, 1962. Contributor to *Atlantic, Harper's,* and *Yale Review.*

WORK IN PROGRESS: Education in foreign affairs, in colleges and secondary schools.

(Deceased)

* * *

BILLINGTON, Dora May   1890-1968

PERSONAL: Born March 19, 1890, in Stoke on Trent, England. *Education:* Royal College of Art, London, England, A.R.C.A. in design, 1916, A.R.C.A., full diploma, 1917. *Home:* 13 Uxbridge Rd., Kingston on Thames, England.

CAREER: Royal College of Art, London, England, pottery instructor, 1917-25; Central School of Arts and Crafts, London, England, pottery instructor, 1925-57. Examiner in drawing and design for school certificate, University of London; examiner in pottery for national diploma, Ministry of Education. *Member:* Society of Designer Craftsmen (president of predecessor organization, Arts and Crafts Exhibition Society, 1946-52; past vice-president).

WRITINGS: The Art of the Potter, Oxford University Press, 1937; *The Technique of Pottery,* Batsford, 1962. Contributor to *Children's Encyclopedia, Studio,* and other publications.

(Died August 12, 1968)

* * *

BIRD, Dorothy Maywood   1899-

PERSONAL: Born July 12, 1899, in Crystal Falls, Mich.; daughter of Ames and Pearl (Field) Maywood; married John Wendell Bird (an attorney), June 13, 1924 (deceased); children: John, Donald, Patricia (Mrs. Robert Sheldon Swanson), Richard. *Education:* Albion College, student, 1917-19; University of Michigan, A.B., 1923. *Religion:* Methodist. *Home:* 343 East Ridge St., Marquette, Mich. 49855.

CAREER: Detroit (Mich.) Public Library, children's librarian, 1923-24; Lansing Business University, Lansing, Mich., dean of women and librarian, 1960-64. Free-lance writer. Member of board of directors, Michigan Society for Mental Health, Ingham County chapter, 1953-59.

WRITINGS: Granite Harbor, Macmillan, 1944; *Mystery at Laughing Water,* Macmillan, 1946, reprinted, 1963; *The Black Opal,* Macmillan, 1949, reprinted, 1963. Contributor of column, book reviews, and feature stories to newspapers; also has done miscellaneous writing for magazines.

WORK IN PROGRESS: Short stories for adolescents.

* * *

BIRD, (Cyril) Kenneth   1887-1965
  (Fougasse)

PERSONAL: Born December 17, 1887, in London, England; son of Arthur and Mary (Wheen) Bird; married Mary Holden Caldwell (a landscape painter), September 16, 1914. *Education:* King's College, London, B.Sc. (honors), 1907. *Home:* 115 Swan Ct., London S.W. 3, England.

CAREER: Artist. *Punch*, London, England, art editor, 1937-49, editor, 1949-53. Former county councilor, Invernesshire, Scotland. Writer and illustrator of posters, leaflets, and general propaganda materials for British Forces and civilian ministries during World War II. *Military service:* Royal Engineers, active duty, World War I; became lieutenant. *Member:* Society of Graphic Artists (council), Society of Industrial Artists (fellow), Art Workers' Guild (past master), Omar Khayyam Club (past president), Garrick Club. *Awards, honors:* Honorary fellow of King's College, University of London; Commander of the British Empire, 1946.

WRITINGS—All under pseudonym Fougasse; all published by Methuen, except as noted: *A Gallery of Games*, 1921; *Draw at a Venture*, 1922; *P.T.O.*, 1926; *E. & O.E.*, 1928; *Fun Fair*, Hutchinson, 1934; *The Luck of the Draw*, 1936; *Many Happy Returns*, British National Safety First Association, 1936; *Drawing the Line Somewhere*, 1937; *Stop or Go*, 1938; *Jotsam*, 1939; *The Changing Face of Britain*, 1940; *And the Game Post*, 1940; *Running Commentary*, 1941; *Sorry—No Rubber*, 1942; *Family Group*, 1944; *Home Circle*, 1945; *A School of Purposes*, 1946; *Us*, 1947; *Fancy Meeting You*, British National Safety First Association, 1947; *You and Me*, 1948; *The Neighbors*, 1954; *The Good Tempered Pencil*, Max Reinhardt, 1956; *Between the Lines*, 1958.

Co-author: (with W.D.H. McCullough) *Aces Made Easy*, 1933; (with McCullough) *You Have Been Warned*, 1934; (with A.W. Bird) *Just a Few Lines*, 1943.

(Died June 11, 1965)

*   *   *

BIRD, W(illiam) Ernest 1890-

PERSONAL: Born July 21, 1890, in Qualla, N.C.; son of Charles Asbury (a farmer) and Sarah Ermina (Terrell) Bird; married Myrtle N. Wells, August 16, 1916; children: Sarah Anne (Mrs. Lloyd J. Engman), Charles Wells, Helen Gertrude (Mrs. James M. Foreman). *Education:* Cullowhee Normal and Industrial School, diploma, 1915; University of North Carolina, A.B., 1917; George Peabody College for Teachers, M.A., 1920. *Politics:* Democrat. *Religion:* Methodist. *Home address:* Box 123, Cullowhee, N.C. 28723.

CAREER: High school principal in Wilkesboro, N.C., 1917-19, Sylva, N.C., 1919-20; Western Carolina College, Cullowhee, vice-president and dean, 1920-47, acting president, 1947-49, dean, 1949-56, president, 1956-57, president emeritus, 1957—, part-time professor of English, 1957-67. President of North Carolina College Conference, 1949-50. Member of board of directors, Southern Highlands Museum, 1965—. *Member:* North Carolina Poetry Society, State Literary and Historical Association (member of executive council, 1966), North Carolina Poetry Council (chairman, 1964-66), Western North Carolina Historical Association (past president). *Awards, honors:* D.Lit., Western Carolina College, 1960; Alumnus of the Year Award, Mars Hill College, 1966.

WRITINGS: Lyrics of a Layman, Piedmont Press, 1962; *History of Western Carolina College: The Progress of an Idea*, University of North Carolina Press, 1963; *Level Paths: New Songs by the Layman*, Biltmore Press, 1964. Also author of *New Springs Overflowing*, 1966.

BIRKET-SMITH, Kaj 1893-

PERSONAL: Born January 20, 1893, in Copenhagen, Denmark; son of Sophus and Ludovica (Nielsen) Birket-Smith; married Minna Hvilsom, July 10, 1920 (died, 1957); children: Erik, Kjeld. *Education:* University of Copenhagen, M.Sc., 1917, Ph.D., 1929. *Home:* Drosselvej 25, Copenhagen F., Denmark.

CAREER: National Museum, Copenhagen, Denmark, curator, 1929-40, ethnographical department, chief curator, 1940-63; University of Copenhagen, Copenhagen, Denmark, reader in ethnography, 1945-63. Conducted field research in Greenland, 1912, 1918; in Canadian Arctic, 1921-23; in Alaska, 1933, in the Philippines and British Solomon Islands, 1951. *Member:* Royal Danish Academy of Letters and Sciences, Royal Anthropological Institute of Great Britain, Norwegian Academy of Letters and Sciences, Finnish Academy of Letters and Sciences, Royal Academy of Letters and Sciences (Sweden). *Awards, honors:* Honorary D.Sc., University of Pennsylvania, 1937; honorary Ph.D., University of Oslo, 1951, University of Basel, 1960, University of Upsala, 1969.

WRITINGS: Ethnography of the Egedesminde District, Reitzel (Copenhagen), 1924; *Eskimoerne*, Gyldendal (Copenhagen), 1927, 3rd revised edition, Rhodos (Copenhagen), 1971, translation published as *The Eskimos*, Dutton, 1936, revised edition, Methuen, 1959, Crown, 1971; *Five Hundred Eskimo Words: A Comparative Vocabulary from Greenland and Central Eskimo Dialects*, Stechert, 1928; *The Caribou Eskimos*, two volumes, Gyldendal, 1929.

Contributions to Chipewyan Ethnology, Gyldendal, 1930; *Den Nye Verden*, Erichsen (Copenhagen), 1931; *Geographical Notes on the Barren Grounds*, Gyldendal, 1933; *Naturmennesker*, two volumes, Erichsen, 1934; *Guld og gronne Skove*, Schultz (Copenhagen), 1935; *Knud Rasmussens Saga*, Erichsen, 1936; (with Frederica de Laguna) *The Eyak Indians of the Copper River Delta, Alaska*, University of Pennsylvania Press, 1938.

Anthropological Observations on the Central Eskimos, Gyldendal, 1940; *Vi Mennesker*, Erichsen, 1940, 3rd edition, 1961; (contributor and author of introduction) *Ethnographical Studies*, Gyldendal, 1941; *Kulturens Veje*, two volumes, Jespersen & Pio (Copenhagen), 1941-42, 3rd revised edition, 1966, translation published as *The Paths of Culture*, University of Wisconsin Press, 1965; *Charles B. Kings Indianerportraetter i Nationalmuseet*, Bianco Luno (Copenhagen), 1942; *Tro og Trolddom*, Jespersen & Pio, 1942; *Origin of Maize Cultivation*, Munksgaard, 1943; *Ethnographical Collections from the Northwest Passage*, Gyldendal, 1945.

(Editor with Ernst Mentze and M. Friis Moeller) *Groenlandsbogen*, Schultz, 1950; *The Rice Civilization and Rice-Harvest Feast of the Bontoc Igorot*, Munksgaard, 1952; *The Chugach Eskimo*, Nationalmuseet (Copenhagen), 1953; *An Ethnological Sketch of Rennell Island: A Polynesian Outlier in Melanesia*, Munksgaard, 1956, 2nd edition, 1969; *Fjaerne Folk*, Jespersen & Pio, 1957, translation published as *Primitive Man and His Ways*, World Publishing, 1960; (editor) *Menneskets magfoldighed*, Wangel (Copenhagen), 1957.

De foerste mennesker, Gyldendal, 1962; *Studies in Circumpacific Culture Relations*, Volume I, *Potlatch and Feasts of Merit*, Munksgaard, 1967; *Strejftog*, Nationalmuseet, 1968.

SIDELIGHTS: Birket-Smith's works have been translated into French, German, Spanish, Finnish, Dutch, Yugoslavian, and several other languages.

*   *   *

BIRLA, Lakshminiwas N.   1909-
(Achyut)

PERSONAL: Born in 1909, in Pilani, Rajasthan, India; son of Ghanshyamdas (an industrialist) and (Durgadebi) Birla; married Sushiladevi, February, 1927; children: Snehalata Maheshwari and Ushadevi Poddar (daughters), Sudharshan-Kumar (son). *Education:* Educated in India. *Religion:* Hindu. *Home:* Birla Niket 3/1 Raja Santosh Rd., Calcutta 27, India. *Agent:* Scott Meredith Literary Agency, Inc., 580 Fifth Ave., New York, N.Y. 10036. *Office:* Birla Brothers Private Ltd., 15 India Exchange Pl., Calcutta 1, India.

CAREER: Birla Brothers Private Ltd., Calcutta, India, managing director, 1956—. Director of jute and cotton textile manufacturing concerns, colleries, and engineering firms managed by Birla Brothers Private Ltd.; trustee, Birla Education Trust; vice-president, Calcutta Citizens' Association; president, Hindi High School. *Member:* Royal Agri-Horticultural Society (former president). *Awards, honors:* Prizes for gardening and horticultural improvement in Calcutta.

WRITINGS: Uma's Tapasya (English verse version of a Sanskrit mythology), Thacker Spink & Co., 1961; *Planning a Landscape Garden*, Royal Agri-Horticultural Society of India, 1962; (compiler) *Folk Tales from Rajasthan* (retold in English), Asia Publishing House, 1964; *Sultan and Nihalde* (novel in English), Grantham, 1964; *Popular Tales of Rajasthan*, Bharatiya Vidya, 1967; *Business Horizons: Speeches and Letters of L. N. Birla, President FICCI, 1967-68*, Hindustan Times Press, 1968; *Struggle for Growth: An Inquiry into the Causes of Poverty and Prosperity of Nations*, World Press, 1969. Also author of *Kahiya Samaya Vichari* (essay collection in Hindi).

*   *   *

BISHOP, Curtis (Kent)   1912-1967
(Curt Brandon, Curt Carroll)

PERSONAL: Born Nov. 10, 1912, in Bolivar, Tenn.; son of David (a lawyer) and Ann (Cornelius) Bishop; married Grace Eyres (now a school teacher), June 13, 1940; children: Barry, Burk, Barbee, Brian. *Education:* University of Texas, student, 1933-35. *Politics:* Conservative. *Religion:* Protestant. *Home:* 2705 Bonnie Rd., Austin, Tex.

CAREER: Variously newspaperman, oil field worker, and rodeo announcer, 1935-42; free-lance writer. *Military service:* Served with Foreign Broadcast Intelligence Service in Latin America and Pacific theater. *Awards, honors:* Winner of eleven (out of thirteen) annual awards of Theta Sigma Phi for best juvenile work of the year in Texas.

WRITINGS: Teamwork (short stories), Steck, 1942; *By Way of Wyoming*, Macmillan 1946; *Sunset Rim*, Macmillan, 1946; *Shadow Range*, Macmillan, 1947; *Lots of Land*, Steck, 1949.

The Lost Eleven, Steck, 1950; *Banjo Hitter*, Steck, 1951; *Saturday Heroes*, Steck, 1951; *Football Fever*, Steck, 1952; *Hero at Halfback*, Steck, 1953; *Larry of Little League*, Steck, 1953; (with wife, Grace Bishop) *Stout Rider*, Steck, 1953; *Fighting Quarterback*, Steck, 1954; *Larry Leads Off*, Steck, 1954; *Goal to Go*, Steck, 1955;

Larry Comes Home, Steck, 1955; *Dribble Up*, Steck, 1956; *Half-Time Hero*, Steck, 1956; *Little Leaguer*, Steck, 1956; *The Little League Way*, Steck, 1957; *Bar-O Gunsmoke*, Muller, 1958; *Lank of the Little League*, Lippincott, 1958; *The First Texas Ranger, Jack Hays*, Messner, 1959.

The Playmaker, Steck, 1960; *Little League Heroes*, Lippincott, 1960; *Sideline Quarterback*, Lippincott, 1960; *Lone Star Leader, Sam Houston*, Messner, 1961; *Rio Grande*, Bouregy, 1961; *Little League Double Play*, Lippincott, 1962; *Rebound*, Lippincott, 1962; *The Big Game*, Steck, 1963; *Lonesome End*, Lippincott, 1963; *Field Goal*, Lippincott, 1964; *Little League Amigo*, Lippincott, 1964; (with Grace Bishop and Clyde Inez Martin) *America: Ideals and Men*, W. S. Benson, 1965; *Little League Stepson*, Lippincott, 1965; *Sideline Pass*, Lippincott, 1965; (with Grace Bishop and Martin) *Trails to Texas*, W. S. Benson, 1965; *Gridiron Glory*, Lippincott, 1966; *Little League Visitor*, Lippincott, 1966; *Fast Break*, Lippincott, 1967; *The Last Outlaw*, Broadman, 1967; *Little League Victory*, Lippincott, 1967; *Little League, Little Brother*, Lippincott, 1968; *Hackberry Jones, Split End*, Lippincott, 1968.

Under pseudonym Curt Brandon: *High, Wide, and Handsome*, Dutton, 1950, *Bugle's Wake*, Dutton, 1952.

Under pseudonym Curt Carroll: *The Golden Herd* (novel), Morrow, 1950; *San Jacinto*, Steck, 1957.

Contributor of several hundred stories and articles to magazines. Writer of syndicated column, "This Day in Texas," published in Texas newspapers.

SIDELIGHTS: Motion pictures have been made from five of Bishop's books; one book was adapted for presentation on "Hallmark Playhouse," and one story for television. For material this juvenile author looked into his own activities—he coached Little League teams and other junior sports groups.

(Died March 17, 1967)

*   *   *

BLACHLY, Lou   1889-

PERSONAL: Born November 5, 1889, in Delta, Colo.; son of Andrew Trew (a banker) and Mary Adelle (Bradley) Blachly; divorced; children: William Norton, Barbara (Mrs. Charles Carpenter). *Education:* University of Wisconsin, A.B., 1918. *Home:* Mitchell Route, Silver City, N.M. *Agent:* Curtis Brown Ltd., 575 Madison Ave., New York, N.Y. 10022.

CAREER: Began as statistician, 1919-20; New York City (N.Y.) Division of Foods and Markets, director, 1921-22; in brokerage and export business, New York, N.Y., 1922-41; U.S. government, served as specialist with War Department, 1941-42, with Office of Price Administration, 1942-43, head mission officer, Lend Lease, in North Africa, 1943-45, chief of Lend Lease in Great Britain, 1945, senior economic analyst for Department of State in Germany, 1945-46, chief of field investigations in Germany, 1946-48; *Silver City Enterprise*, Silver City, N.M., editor, 1949. Vice-president and secretary, Pioneers Foundation, 1950—. *Military service:* U.S. Army, Infantry, 1917-19; became second lieutenant. *Member:* National Audubon Society, American Museum of Natural History, Wilderness Society, Local Identification of Nature Club (Tucson; president, 1962).

WRITINGS: Arizona Wild Flowers, Local Identification of Nature Club, 1963; *Naming the Birds at a Glance*, Knopf, 1964; *Mammals, Snakes and Lizards of the Southwest*, Local Identification of Nature Club, 1964.

WORK IN PROGRESS: Poor Dellie, the story of his mother's life in pioneer Colorado; Insect Guide of the Southwest; a tree guide for the Northeast.

SIDELIGHTS: Blachly is competent in French and German. He traveled entire Southwest in 1951-57, obtaining five hundred tape recordings relating to pioneer events; the tapes are in the University of New Mexico Library.

* * *

BLACK, John Wilson 1906-

PERSONAL: Born February 9, 1906, in Vedersburg, Ind.; son of George Keys and Hattie Let (Wilson) Black; married Helen Mary Harrington, 1936; children: Caroline, Richard, Constance, Charlotte. Education: Wabash College, A.B., 1927; University of Iowa, M.A., 1930, Ph.D., 1935. Home: 1400 Lincoln Rd., Columbus, Ohio 43212. Office: Department of Speech, Ohio State University, 154 North Oval Dr., Columbus, Ohio 43210.

CAREER: Adrian College, Adrian, Mich., professor of speech and rhetoric, 1927-35; Kenyon College, Gambier, Ohio, instructor in English, 1935-36, professor of speech, 1936-49; Ohio State University, Columbus, professor of speech, beginning 1949. Director of U.S. Office of Naval Research project in voice communication, beginning 1949.

MEMBER: International Association of Logopedics and Phoniatrics, International Association of Phonetic Sciences, Speech Association of America (president), American Speech and Hearing Association (vice-president, 1964), Acoustical Society of America (fellow), American Association for the Advancement of Science (fellow), American Psychological Association, National Association of Foreign Student Advisors. Awards, honors: Grants from National Institutes of Health and U.S. Vocational Rehabilitation Administration; National Science Foundation senior postdoctoral study fellowship to Italy; Fulbright research fellowship to Italy; Presidential Certificate of Merit; regents professorship, Ohio Board of Regents.

WRITINGS: A Brief Analysis of General Speech, Edwards Brothers, 1948; (with Wilbur E. Moore) Speech: Code, Meaning and Communication, McGraw, 1955; American Speech for Foreign Students, C. C Thomas, 1963; Voice and Diction, C. E. Merrill, 1969. Contributor to speech and scientific journals, including Journal of Experimental Psychology, Journal of Aviation Medicine, Journal of Prosthetic Dentistry.

WORK IN PROGRESS: Research in speech perception, voice communication, and experimental phonetics.

* * *

BLACK, Misha 1910-

PERSONAL: Born October 16, 1910, in Baku, Russia; married Helen Lilian Evans, 1935 (marriage dissolved, 1952); married Edna Joan Fairbrother, 1955; children: (first marriage) Jacob, Julia; (second marriage) Oliver. Home: 160 Gloucester Rd., London S.W.7, England. Agent: Laurence Pollinger Ltd., 18 Maddox St., London W.1, England. Office: Design Research Unit, 32 Aybrook St., London W.1, England.

CAREER: British Ministry of Information, London, England, principal exhibition architect, 1940-45; Design Research Unit, London, England, senior partner, 1946—; Black, Bayes & Gibson (architects), London, England, partner, 1963—. Royal College of Art, London, England,

professor of industrial design, 1959—. Designer or consultant for British exhibitions in Glasgow, 1938, New York World's Fair, 1939, Ceylon, 1952, Bulawayo, 1953. Industrial design consultant to British Overseas Airways Corp., 1951-56, British Transport Commission, 1956, Beagle Aircraft, 1961—, London Transport Board, 1964—; interior architect for Orient Line, 1957-61. Member of international juries on design. Trustee, British Academy, 1968—. Member: International Council of Societies of Industrial Design (president, 1959-61), Royal Designers for Industry, Society of Industrial Artists and Designers (president, 1954-56), Reform Club, Architectural Association. Awards, honors: Order of the British Empire, 1946; Knight Bachelor, 1972.

WRITINGS: (Contributor) Physical Planning, Architectural Press, 1945; (contributor) The Practice of Design, Lund, Humphries, 1946; (editor) Exhibition Design, Architectural Press, 1950; (editor) Public Interiors: An International Survey, Batsford, 1960; The Architect's Anguish (Harry Hardy Peach Memorial Lecture, 1962), Leicester University Press, 1962; (author of notes) Michael Humfrey Middleton, Group Practice of Design, Architectural Press, 1968. Contributor to architectural and design periodicals.

* * *

BLACKMUR, R(ichard) P(almer) 1904-1965 (Perry Hobbs)

PERSONAL: Born January 21, 1904, in Springfield, Mass.; son of George Edward and Helen (Palmer) Blackmur; married Helen Dickson, June 14, 1930 (divorced, 1951). Education: Self-educated. Home: 53 McCosh Circle, Princeton, N.J. 08540.

CAREER: Worked as a clerk in Dunster House Bookshop, Cambridge, Mass.; free-lance poet and critic, 1928-40; Princeton University, Princeton, N.J., resident fellow, 1940-43, Hodder Fellow, 1944; Institute for Advanced Study, Princeton, N.J., member, 1944-45; Princeton University, resident fellow, 1946-48, associate professor, 1948-51, professor of English, 1951-65. Cambridge University, fellow of Christ's College, 1961, Pitt Professor of American History and Institutions, 1961-62. Member: National Institute of Arts and Letters, American Academy of Arts and Sciences, American Association of University Professors. Awards, honors: Guggenheim fellow, 1936-37, 1937-38; Library of Congress Fellow in American Letters; Litt.D., Rutgers University, 1958; M.A., Cambridge University, 1961.

WRITINGS: For Any Book, privately printed, 1924; A Funeral for a Few Sticks, Lone Gull Press, 1927; T. S. Eliot, [Portland], 1928; Dirty Hands; or, The True-Born Censor (pamphlet; originally published under pseudonym Perry Hobbs in New Republic); Psyche in the South, Tryon Pamphlets, 1934; (author of introduction) Henry James, The Art of the Novel, Scribner, 1935; The Double Agent: Essays in Craft and Elucidation, Arrow Editions, 1935; From Jordon's Delight (poems), Arrow Editions, 1937; The Expense of Greatness (essays), Arrow Editions, 1940; The Second World (poems), Cummington, 1942; The Good European, and Other Poems, Cummington, 1947; Form and value in Modern Poetry, Doubleday, 1952; Language as Gesture: Essays in Poetry, Harcourt, 1952; The Lion and the Honeycomb; Essays in Solicitude and Critique, Harcourt, 1955; Anni Mirabiles, 1921-25: Reason in the Madness of Letters, Library of Congress, 1956; (author of introduction) Henry James, The Wings of the Dove,

Dell, 1958; (author of introduction) Henry James, *Washington Square*, Dell, 1959; *New Criticism in the United States*, Kenkyusha (Tokyo), 1959; (editor) *American Short Novels*, Crowell, 1960; (author of introduction) Henry James, *The American*, Dell, 1960; *Eleven Essays in the European Novel*, Harcourt, 1964; *A Primer of Ignorance*, edited by Joseph Frank, Harcourt, 1967.

Contributor: *Lectures in Criticism*, Pantheon, 1949; Ruth Nanda Anshen, editor, *Language: An Enquiry into Its Meaning and Function*, Harper, 1957; Irving Howe, editor, *Modern Literary Criticism*, Beacon Press, 1958; Lewis Gaston Leary, editor, *American Literary Essays*, Crowell, 1960; James Ward Smith and A. L. Jamison, editors, *Religious Perspectives in America*, Princeton University Press, 1961; Quentin Anderson and Joseph A. Mazzeo, editors, *The Proper Study: Essays on Western Classics*, St. Martin's, 1962; Gerald J. Goldberg and Nancy Marmer Goldberg, editors, *The Modern Critical Spectrum*, Prentice-Hall, 1962; Hugh Kenner, editor, *T. S. Eliot: A Collection of Critical Essays*, Prentice-Hall, 1962; Wilbur Stewart Scott, editor, *Five Approaches of Literary Criticism*, Macmillan, 1962, hardcover edition, 1963; Morton Dauwen Zabel, editor, *Literary Opinions in America*, Harper, 1962.

Represented in many anthologies, including *Criticism: The Foundations of Modern Literary Judgment*, edited by Mark Schorer, Josephine Miles, and Gordon McKenzie, Harcourt, 1948, revised edition, 1958, *The Permanence of Yeats*, edited by James Hall and Martin Steinmann, Macmillan, 1950, and *Literary Criticism in America*, edited by A. D. Van Nostrand, Liberal Arts. 1957.

Former advisory editor, *Kenyon Review;* former editor, with Lincoln Kirstein, of *Hound and Horn*. Contributor to *Atlantic, Yale Review, Virginia Quarterly Review, Poetry, Sewanee Review, American Scholar, Hudson Review, Nation,* and other periodicals.

SIDELIGHTS: Stanley Edgar Hyman, in *The Armed Vision*, contends that Blackmur was "probably the subtlest and most distinguished close reader in American criticism," one who constantly affirmed the value of "'the indifferent mind,' pluralism, skepticism, and the imaginative understanding of man."

Blackmur himself said: "The cost of criticism is, if I may borrow and restrict a little a phrase I have used before, the expense of greatness; as its earnings are in the sense of conviction pervading the job done."

Hyman has said that "Blackmur's weakness for the refined sometimes inhibits his appreciation of the not-so-refined.... [But] to balance the snobbishness there is his eloquent insistence on the social responsibility of the artist ... and the ultimate social function assigned to art and criticism."

Richard Kostelanetz believes that the ideals Blackmur used in evaluating literature and contemporary society are applicable to the modern world, although Blackmur's criticism did not always reflect his own precepts. "He suggests that audiences, as well as critics, should not be monoliterate, which is to say specialists in only one field, but polyliterate, familiar with the 'vocabularies' and traditions of several fields. However, where Blackmur was an advocate of the second style, in practice ... he exemplified the first."

Those who influenced Blackmur included Henry James, T. S. Eliot, George Santayana, I. A. Richards, William Empson, Kenneth Burke, John Crowe Ransom, and Yvor Winters; but with most of them he eventually came to disagree.

Blackmur recorded three poems for the Library of Congress Twentieth Century Poetry in English Series, 1948.

BIOGRAPHICAL/CRITICAL SOURCES—Books: Yvor Winters, *In Defense of Reason*, Morrow, 1947; Stanley Edgar Hyman, *The Armed Vision*, Knopf, 1948, revised edition, Vintage, 1955; Randall Jarrell, *Poetry and the Age*, Knopf, 1953; Louise Bogan, *Selected Criticism: Prose, Poetry*, Noonday, 1955; John Paul Pritchard, *Criticism in America*, University of Oklahoma Press, 1956; Hugh Kenner, *Gnomon: Essays on Contemporary Literature*, McDowell, Oblensky, 1958; Robert Jackson Foster, *The New Romantics*, Indiana University Press, 1962; Joseph Frank, *The Widening Gyre: Crisis and Mastery in Modern Literature*, Rutgers University Press, 1963; Walter Kerr, *The Theatre in Spite of Itself*, Simon & Schuster, 1963; Howard Nemerov, *Poetry and Fiction: Essays*, Rutgers University Press, 1963; John Wain, *Essays on Literature and Ideas*, St. Martin's, 1963; Carolyn Riley, editor, *Contemporary Literary Criticism*, Gale, Volume II, 1974.

Articles: New York Times Book Review, February 12, 1967; *Reporter*, June 1, 1967; *Poetry*, August, 1968.

(Died February 2, 1965)

*　　　*　　　*

BLACKSTONE, Geoffrey Vaughan 1910-

PERSONAL: Born May 9, 1910, in Easton Northamptonshire, England; son of Harold Vaughan and Jessie (Ure) Blackstone; married Joanna Vosper, February 8, 1941; children: Christopher, Tessa, Victoria, Timothy. *Education:* Attended Uppingham School, Rutland, England. *Religion:* Anglican. *Home:* Dasselsbury, Braughing, Hertfordshire, England. *Office:* Hertfordshire Fire Brigade Headquarters, Hertford, Hertfordshire, England.

CAREER: Engineering apprentice, Stamford, Lincolnshire, England, 1927-32; engineer, Bristol, England, 1932-38; served with London Fire Brigade, London, England, 1938-41, National Fire Service, in London and Preston, England, and in Cardiff, Wales, 1941-48; Hertfordshire Fire Brigade, Hertford, England, chief officer, 1948—. *Military service:* Royal Artillery; became captain. *Member:* Chief Fire Officers Association (council), Institution of Fire Engineers. *Awards, honors:* Commander of the Order of the British Empire; Officer of the Order of St. John; George Medal.

WRITINGS: Caroline Matilda: Princess of Great Britain and Queen of Denmark (novel), Heinemann, 1955; *A History of the British Fire Service*, Routledge & Kegan Paul, 1957. Contributor of articles to *Times, Guardian*, and various magazines and a regular contributor to fire service technical journals.

WORK IN PROGRESS: A novel of the London Fire Brigade during the air raids of 1940-41.

AVOCATIONAL INTERESTS: History and all historical matters.

BIOGRAPHICAL/CRITICAL SOURCES: Richard Coller, *The City That Would Not Die*, Collins, 1959.

*　　　*　　　*

BLAICH, Theodore Paul 1902-

PERSONAL: Born February 18, 1902, in Cleveland, Ohio; son of William and Pauline (Keck) Blaich; married Charlotte Grace Gilbert, 1928; children: Dorcas Kelsey Blaich Rice. *Education:* University of Michigan, A.B., 1926;

Western Reserve University (now Case Western Reserve University), M.A., 1932. *Religion:* Congregational. *Home:* 53 Main St., Fryeburg, Me.

CAREER: High school teacher in Cleveland, O., 1926-28, 1933-42; Cleveland (Ohio) Board of Education, assistant director of attendance, 1928-33; Foxcroft Academy, Dover-Foxcroft, Me., principal, 1942-47; Fryeburg Academy, Fryeburg, Me., director of curriculum, 1947-66. *Awards, honors:* Congressional Selective Service Medal, 1947, for rehabilitation work.

WRITINGS: (With Joseph C. Baumgartner) *The Challange of Democracy*, Harper, 1942, McGraw, 5th edition, 1966.

AVOCATIONAL INTERESTS: Photography, gardening, woodcarving.

* * *

BLAIR, Edward Payson 1910-

PERSONAL: Born December 23, 1910, in Woodburn, Ore., son of Oscar Newton and Bertha (Myers) Blair; married Vivian Elizabeth Krisel, 1934; children: Phyllis Marie (Mrs. George W. Belsey III), Sharon Louise. *Education:* Seattle Pacific College, A.B., 1931; Biblical Seminary in New York, S.T.B., 1934; American School of Oriental Research, Jerusalem, graduate study, 1935-36; Yale University, Ph.D., 1939. *Office:* Garrett Theological Seminary, Evanston, Ill.

CAREER: Seattle Pacific College, Seattle, Wash., professor of Bible and dean of School of Religion, 1939-41; Biblical Seminary in New York, New York, N.Y., professor of Old Testament language and literature, 1941-42; Garrett Theological Seminary, Evanston, Ill., professor of New Testament interpretation, 1942-60, Harry R. Kendall Professor of New Testament Interpretation, 1960—. Participated in excavation of Roman Jericho, 1951. *Member:* National Association of Biblical Instructors, Society of Biblical Literature and Exegesis, Chicago Society of Biblical Research (president, 1952-53).

WRITINGS: The Acts and Apocalyptic Literature, Abingdon, 1946; *The Bible and You*, Abingdon, 1953; *Getting to Know the Bible*, Abingdon, 1956; *Jesus in the Gospel of Matthew*, Abingdon, 1960; (contributor) *Interpreter's Dictionary of the Bible*, Abingdon, 1962; *The Book of Deuteronomy, The Book of Joshua*, John Knox, 1964. Also author of *A Study of the Book of Acts*, Abingdon.

* * *

BLANCHARD, Ralph Harrub 1890-1973

PERSONAL: Born December 3, 1890, in Plympton, Mass.; son of Thomas Williams (a businessman) and Clara (Harrub) Blanchard. *Education:* Dartmouth College, A.B., 1911, A.M., 1912; University of Pennsylvania, Ph.D., 1916. *Home:* Prospect Rd., Plympton, Mass.

CAREER: Columbia University, New York, N.Y., instructor, 1917, assistant professor, 1920-23, associate professor, 1923-27, professor of insurance, 1927-57, professor emeritus, 1957-73. Consultant to U.S. Social Security Board and, later, to Social Security Administration, 1936-37, 1942-55, Treasury Department, 1949-53, Department of Defense, 1954-73, and to other public and private organizations and agencies. *Military service:* U.S. Army, 1918-19; became captain.

MEMBER: Insurance Institute of America (fellow), Amer-

ican Risk and Insurance Association (vice-president, 1933-34; president, 1935-36), American Management Association (vice-president in charge of insurance division, 1939-40; director, 1940-43), Casualty Actuarial Society (fellow; vice-president, 1925-26, 1935-36; president, 1942-43), Insurance Society of New York (director, 1929-31, 1946-57), Insurance Underwriters Association of the Pacific (honorary), American Arbitration Association (national panel), Insurance Forum of San Francisco (honorary). *Awards, honors:* Named to Insurance Hall of Fame.

WRITINGS: Liability and Compensation Insurance, Appleton, 1917; *Workman's Compensation in the United States*, International Labour Office, 1926; *Dictionary of Insurance Terms*, U.S. Chamber of Commerce, 1949; (with A. H. Mowbray) *Insurance*, McGraw, 1955, 5th edition, 1961. Author of published report on survey of accident and health insurance, U.S. Social Security Board. Contributor of articles and reviews on insurance topics to periodicals. Editor, McGraw's "Insurance Series," 1922-58.

WORK IN PROGRESS: A 6th edition of *Insurance*; and, a collection of papers.

(Died September 28, 1973)

* * *

BLANCK, Jacob Nathaniel 1906-1974

PERSONAL: Born November 10, 1906, in Boston, Mass.; son of Selig (a tailor) and Mildred Rosenberg (Friedman) Blanck; married Stella Ursula Balicer, August 28, 1938; children: Rosamunde. *Education:* Attended Boston (Mass.) public schools. *Religion:* Jewish. *Home:* 19 Reservior Rd., Chestnut Hill 67, Mass. *Office:* c/o Houghton Library, Harvard University, Cambridge, Mass. 02138.

CAREER: Rare book editor of *Publishers Weekly* and *Antiquarian Bookman,* 1936-52; Library of Congress, Washington, D.C. bibliographer in Americana, 1939-41; Indiana Historical Society, Indianapolis, consultant on bibliography, 1942; *Bibliography of American Literature,* editor, 1943-74. *Member:* American Antiquarian Society, Antiquarian Booksellers Association of America (honorary), Massachusetts Historical Society, Club of Odd Volumes (Boston). *Awards, honors:* L.H.D. from Brown University, 1969; P.B.K. from Harvard University, 1970.

WRITINGS: (Editor) *Merle Johnson's American First Editions,* 3rd edition, Bowker, 1936, 4th edition, 1942, 4th edition revised and enlarged, Research Classics, 1962; (editor) *American Book-Prices Current: A Record of Literary Properties Sold at Auction in the U.S.,* Bowker, 1938-39; *Peter Parley to Penrod: A Bibliographical Description of the Best-Loved American Juvenile Books,* Bowker, 1938, revised edition, 1961; (compiler) *Harry Castlemon, Boys' Own Author,* Bowker, 1942; *Jonathan and the Rainbow,* Houghton, 1948; *The King and the Noble Blacksmith,* Houghton, 1950; (compiler) *Bibliography of American Literature,* Volumes I-V, Yale University Press, 1955-69; *The Title Page as Bibliographical Evidence* (John Howell Lecture, University of California, Berkeley, April 5, 1965), School of Librarianship, University of California, Berkeley, 1966. Contributor to *Encyclopaedia Britannica* year books, *New Colophon, Papers* of the Bibliographical Society of America, and professional journals.

WORK IN PROGRESS: Editing additional volumes of *Bibliography of American Literature.*

(Died December 23, 1974)

BLATTER, Dorothy (Gertrude) 1901-

PERSONAL: Surname is pronounced *Blot*-ter; born July 15, 1901, in Albion, Neb.; daughter of Daniel Victor (a banker) and Gertrude (Letson) Blatter. *Education:* Doane College, A.B., 1925; additional study at University of Colorado, Fontainebleau School of Art, and Columbia University. *Home:* Uskudar Amerikan Kiz Lisesi, Uskudar, Istanbul, Turkey. *Office:* Riza Pasa Yokusu, No. 50, Istanbul, Turkey.

CAREER: American Missionary Association, teacher in New Mexico, 1925-26; Albuquerque Public Schools, Albuquerque, N.M., teacher, 1926-31; American Board of Commissioners of Foreign Missions, Boston (now called the United Church Board for World Ministries, New York), teacher in Turkey, 1931-37, 1939-45, teacher and publication worker in Istanbul, Turkey, 1945-61, children's editor, publication department, Istanbul, 1961—. *Awards, honors:* L.H.D., Doane College, 1959.

WRITINGS: (Self-illustrated) *Uncle Ali's Secret: A Story of New Turkey,* A. Whitman, 1939; *Sleepy Sami,* Sealfield, 1946; (self-illustrated) *The Thirsty Village,* Friendship, 1950; *Futbolcu Fil* (title means "Eddie Elephant"), American Board Publication Department, 1955; (translator into English) Cahit Ucuk, *The Turkish Twins,* J. Cape, 1956; *Cap and Candle,* Westminster, 1961; *Gizli Oyun* (title means "The Secret Game"), American Board Publication Department, 1962; *Parables Re-told,* American Board Publication Department, 1964. Author of short stories for children and articles about Turkish children.

WORK IN PROGRESS: Ibrahim, Friend of the Under-Dog, written in English and being translated into Turkish.

SIDELIGHTS: Cap and Candle, Eddie Elephant, The Secret Game, and *Parables Re-told* were published in both English and Turkish.

*   *   *

BLOOMAN, Percy A. 1906-
(Pab)

PERSONAL: Born January 4, 1906, in Southend, Essex, England. *Education:* Attended Cheltenham College; University of Leeds, B.Com. (with honors). *Home:* Rustlings 7, Auburn Rd., Kenilworth, Cape Town, South Africa. *Office:* National Publishing Co. (Pty) Ltd., P.O. Box 335, Cape Town, South Africa.

CAREER: National Publishing Co. (Pty) Ltd., Cape Town, South Africa, editor-in-chief, 1950—. *Member:* Royal Economic Society (fellow). *Awards, honors:* Gladstone Memorial Prize, University of Leeds.

WRITINGS—Editor: (With W. J. Laite) *Industry and Trade Review of South African Business and Business Legislation,* South African Publishers, monthly, 1939-49; *National Trade-Index and Directory of Southern Africa,* National Publishing, annual; *National Trade Marks Directory of Southern Africa,* National Publishing, annual; *Afrikaanse Handel-Sindeks van S.A.,* National Publishing, annual; *Textile, Clothing, Footwear, and Leather Blue Book,* National Publishing, annual; *National Farm Supply Directory,* National Publishing, annual; *Architects, Builders, and Contractors Blue Book,* National Publishing, annual; (with Charles R. Pask) *Advertising and Press Annual of Africa,* National Publishing, annual; *Business Blue Book of South Africa,* National Publishing, annual. Joint editor and contributor to *Business Executive of Southern Africa, Factory Equipment and Materials, Building Equipment*

and Materials, Business Systems and Equipment (monthly magazines); former editor of *Buyer* and of *Southern African Industry and Trade.*

*   *   *

BLOUGH, Glenn O(rlando) 1907-

PERSONAL: Born September 5, 1907, in Edmore, Mich.; son of Levi and Catherine (Thomas) Blough. *Education:* Central Michigan University, student, 1925-26; University of Michigan, A.B., 1929, M.A., 1932; additional study at University of Chicago and Columbia University. *Home:* 2820 Ellicott St. N.W., Washington, D.C. 20008. *Office:* College of Education, University of Maryland, College Park, Md. 20740.

CAREER: Teacher in secondary schools in Michigan, 1925-27, 1929-31; Eastern Michigan University, Ypsilanti, instructor in education, 1932-36; Colorado State College, Greeley, assistant professor of science education, 1937-38; University of Chicago, Chicago, Ill., instructor in science education, 1939-42; U.S. Department of Health, Education, and Welfare, Washington, D.C., specialist for elementary science, Office of Education, 1946-54; University of Maryland, College Park, 1956—, now professor of education. Writer of books for young people and of textbooks. *Military service:* U.S. Navy, 1942-46; became lieutenant commander. *Member:* National Education Association, National Science Teachers Association (president, 1957-58), National Council for Elementary Science International (president, 1947), Phi Delta Kappa, Phi Sigma. *Awards, honors:* LL.D. from Central Michigan University, 1950; Diamond Award, University of Maryland, 1950.

WRITINGS: (With Wilbur L. Beauchamp and Mary Melrose) *Discovering Our World: A Course in Science for the Middle Grades,* Scott, Foresman, 1937-39, teachers edition, 1948; (with Beauchamp and Melrose) *Teaching Manual* (to accompany Books 1-3 of *Discovering Our World*), Scott, Foresman, 1937-39.

An Aquarium, Row, 1943; *Doing Work,* Row, 1943; *The Insect Parade,* Row, 1943; *Plants Round the Year,* Row, 1943; *Water Appears and Disappears,* Row, 1943; *Animals Round the Year,* Row, 1943; *Teaching Manual* (to accompany the "Basic Science Education" series), Row, 1943; *Animals and Their Young,* Row, 1945; *Animals That Live Together,* Row, 1945; *The Birds in the Big Woods,* Row, 1945; (with Ida B. De Pencier) *How the Sun Helps Us,* Row, 1945; *The Pet Show,* Row, 1945; *Useful Plants and Animals,* Row, 1945; *The Monkey with a Notion,* Henry Holt, 1946; *Beno, the Riverburg Mayor,* Henry Holt, 1948; (with Paul E. Blackwood) *Teaching Elementary Science: Suggestions for Classroom Teachers,* U.S. Office of Education, 1948; (with Blackwood) *Science Teaching in Rural and Small Town Schools,* U.S. Office of Education, 1949.

(With Albert J. Huggett) *Elementary-School Science and How to Teach It,* Dryden Press, 1951, revised edition (with Huggett and Julius Schwartz), 1958, 4th edition (with Scwartz), Holt, 1969; (with Huggett) *Methods and Activities in Elementary-School Science,* Dryden Press, 1951; *The Tree on the Road to Turntown,* McGraw, 1953; *Not Only for Ducks: The Story of Rain,* McGraw, 1954; (with Marjorie H. Campbell) *Making and Using Classroom Science Materials in the Elementary School: Apparatus, Demonstrations, Equipment, Experiments,* Dryden Press, 1954; (with Paul E. Garber) *Masters of the Air,* Smithsonian Institution, 1954; *Wait for the Sunshine: The Story of Seasons and Growing Things,* McGraw, 1954; *Lookout for the Forest: A Conservation Story*, McGraw, 1955; (with Campbell) *When You Go to the Zoo*, McGraw, 1955; *After the Sun Goes Down: The Story of Animals at Night*, McGraw, 1956; *Who Lives in This House?: A Story of Animal Families*, McGraw, 1957; *It's Time for Better Elementary School Science* (report), National Science Teachers Association, 1958; (editor) *Young People's Book of Science*, McGraw, 1958; *Soon after September: The Story of Living Things in Winter*, McGraw, 1959.

Discovering Dinosaurs, McGraw, 1960; *Christmas Trees and How They Grow*, McGraw, 1961; *Who Lives at the Seashore?: Animal Life Along the Shore*, McGraw, 1961; *Who Lives in This Meadow?: A Story of Animal Life*, McGraw, 1961; *You, Your Child, and Science: A Handbook for Parents*, National Education Association, 1963; *Bird Watchers and Bird Feeders*, McGraw, 1963; *Discovering Plants*, McGraw, 1966; *Discovering Insects*, McGraw, 1967.

Contributor of articles on science to national magazines. Chairman of editorial board, *Science and Children* (magazine for elementary science teachers); member of editorial advisory board, *My Weekly Reader* (newspaper for children).

* * *

BLUHM, Heinz 1907-

PERSONAL: Born November 23, 1907, in Halle, Germany; came to United States in 1925, naturalized in 1931; son of Fritz and Louise (Henke) Bluhm; married Helen McClure Berry, August 15, 1938; children: Peter, Louise, Margaret, Christopher. *Education:* Northwestern College, Watertown, Wis., B.A., 1928; University of Wisconsin, M.A., 1929, Ph.D., 1932; Yale University, graduate student, 1930-31. *Office:* Department of Germanic Languages, Boston University, Chestnut Hill, Mass. 02167.

CAREER: University of Wisconsin, Madison, instructor in German, 1931-37; Yale University, New Haven, Conn., instructor, 1937-39, assistant professor, 1939-44, associate professor, 1944-50, professor of German, 1950-57, Leavenworth Professor of German Language and Literature, beginning, 1957, chairman of department of Germanic languages, 1954-63; member of faculty of department of Germanic languages, Boston University, Chestnut Hill, Mass.; fellow of Pierson College. Visiting professor at Middlebury College, summers, 1951-1953, University of Minnesota, summer, 1961, and Dartmouth College, 1964; University of California, Berkeley, summer, 1968. *Member:* Modern Language Association of America. *Awards, honors:* M.A., Yale University, 1950; Guggenheim fellowship, 1957; Newberry Library fellowships, 1958, 1960, 1963; grants from American Philosophical Society and American Council of Learned Societies; Huntington Library and Folger Shakespeare Library fellowships, 1973 and 1974.

WRITINGS: August von Goethe und Ottilie von Pogwisch, H. Boehlau (Weimar), 1962; (editor) Ottilie von Goethe, *Tagebuecher*, Bergland (Vienna), Volume I, 1962, Volume II, 1963, Volume III, 1963, Volume IIIA, 1964; (editor) *Essays in Language and Literature*, Newberry, 1965; *Martin Luther, Creative Translator*, Concordia, 1966. Contributor to professional journals.

WORK IN PROGRESS: Several more volumes of Ottilie von Goethe's diary, to be published over the next few years; research on Luther.

BLUMENTHAL, Walter Hart 1883-

PERSONAL: Born February 9, 1883, in Clinton, Iowa; son of Hart and Ida (Rawitch) Blumenthal; married Claudine B. Brown, January 29, 1919. *Education:* University of Pennsylvania, B.S., 1903; University of Halle, graduate student, 1903-04. *Home:* The Drake, Philadelphia, Pa. 19102.

CAREER: Newspaper feature work, editorial and freelance, 1914-16; author, bibliographer, now doing historical research and book collectors' research. *Member:* Pennsylvania Historical Society, Oklahoma Historical Society.

WRITINGS: Women Camp Followers of the American Revolution, George S. Macmanus, 1952; *Rendezvous with Chance: How Luck Has Shaped History*, Exposition, 1954; *American Indians Dispossessed: Fraud in Land Cessions Forced Upon the Tribes*, George S. Macmanus, 1955; *Bookmen's Bedlam: An Olio of Literary Oddities*, Rutgers University Press, 1955; *Formats and Foibles: A Few Books Which Might Be Called Curious*, Achille J. St. Onge, 1956; *Filigree Lettering and Ornamentation: A Forgotten Book Art*, Pickering Press, 1957; *The Mermaid Myth: Shakespeare Not Among Those Present*, Westholm, 1959.

Paging Mr. Shakespeare: A Critical Challenge, University Publishers, 1961; *Bookmen's Trio: Ventures in Literary Philandering*, Achille J. St. Onge, 1961; *A Charm of Books*, Friends of the Free Library of Philadelphia, 1961; *Brides from Bridewell: Female Felons Sent to Colonial America*, Tuttle, 1962; *American Panorama: Pattern of the Past and Womanhood in Its Unfolding*, Achille J. St. Onge, 1962; *Book Gluttons and Book Gourmets, with a Digression on Hungry Authors*, Black Cat Press, 1962; *Eccentric Typography, and Other Diversions in the Graphic Arts*, Achille J. St. Onge, 1963; *Shakespeare—Veneration Versus Verity: Critical Comments from a Skeptic*, George S. MacManus, 1963; (editor) *Franklin Sampler: A Garner for the Mind's Delight*, Joh. Enschede en Zonen (Haarlem), 1964; *The Pepper Shaker* (poems), privately printed, 1964; *Heaven and Hades: Two Excursions for Bookmen*, Achille J. St. Onge, 1965; *The Jaded Jester: Old Fools and New Follies*, George S. MacManus, 1965; *The Red Shadow: A Tale of the Devil Frustrated*, George S. MacManus, 1965; *Who Knew Shakespeare? What Was His Reputation in His Lifetime?*, Prairie Press, 1965; *Imaginary Books and Phantom Libraries*, George S. MacManus, 1966; *Bookmen's Browse*, George S. MacManus, 1967.

* * *

BLUNSDON, Norman (Victor Charles) 1915-1968

PERSONAL: Born July 11, 1915, in London, England; son of Norman Clyde (a wine-cellarman) and Josephine V. (Pagani) Blunsdon; married Daisy Matilda Bullimore, September 13, 1941; children: Joan Margaret. *Education:* Borough Polytechnic, London, England, G.C.E., 1953; University of London, G.C.E., 1953. *Politics:* "Left wing tendency." *Religion:* Spiritualist. *Home:* 19 Burton Rd., Kilburn High Rd., London N.W. 6, England. *Agent:* Derek Gardner, 130 Sheffield Ter., London W. 8, England.

CAREER: Messrs. Kempson & Mauger (jewelry enamelers and engravers), London, England, miniature enamel painter, 1943-68. British Amateur Weightlifting Association, certified referee, 1937-57, primary and senior instructor; The London County Council, part-time weight-training instructor; Kentish Town Men's Institute, member, 1955-58. Conscientious objector, World War II.

Member: Society for Psychical Research, Astrological Association, Spiritualist Association of Great Britain Ltd. (councilor, 1957-63; vice-president, 1963-65), Faculty of Astrological Studies (honorary secretary, 1957-61).

WRITINGS: A Popular Dictionary of Spiritualism, Arco, 1962, Citadel, 1963. Contributor to *Psychic News* and *Astrological Journal.* Editor, *Spiritualist* (bi-monthly magazine).

WORK IN PROGRESS: Research into validity of predictive astrology; an outline of the philosophy of Spiritualism.

AVOCATIONAL INTERESTS: Photography, art, classical orchestral music, and playing piano.

(Died June 3, 1968)

*   *   *

BOARDMAN, Neil S(ervis)   1907-

PERSONAL: Born January 16, 1907, in Stillwater, Minn.; son of Odessa DeWitt (a lumberman) and Dora (Congdon) Boardman; married Una Louise Watts, December 24, 1936; children: Nancie Shanna (Mrs. Hans Theurer), John Michael. *Education:* University of Minnesota, B.S. *Politics:* "Unenthusiastic Democrat." *Religion:* Episcopalian. *Home:* Bloomington, Ind.; Sturgeon Lake, Minn. *Agent:* Russell & Volkening, Inc., 551 Fifth Ave., Room 1414, New York, N.Y. 10017. *Office:* Undergraduate Library, Indiana University, Bloomington, Ind.

CAREER: St. Paul (Minn.) Public Library, readers adviser, later branch librarian, 1940-48; Indiana University, Bloomington, circulation librarian, 1948-60, head of undergraduate library, 1960—. On leave as expert in library science, Institute of Education and Research, University of the Panjab, Lahore, West Pakistan, 1963-65. *Member:* Masons.

WRITINGS: The Long Home (novel), Harper, 1948; *The Wine of Violence*, Simon & Schuster, 1964. Writer of television script for "Alfred Hitchcock Presents." Contributor of short stories to *Harper's, Cosmopolitan, Argosy*, and other periodicals, and of articles to *Library Journal, Wilson Library Bulletin, Etude*, and *Recreation.*

WORK IN PROGRESS: Gathering material for a book, probably in fiction form, about life in Lahore.

SIDELIGHTS: Boardman was at the University of the Punjab to develop a postgraduate-level library; the title "expert in library science," he explained, was not self-bestowed, but the official label under which he served in Pakistan. In the 1940's he spent nine months in Whitehorse, Yukon Territory, working on the Alaska Highway; also has been a houseparent (for a year) at a school for children from broken homes, in Duchess County, N.Y. *Avocational Interests:* "Fond of music, walking, and the out-of-doors when I don't have to do anything in the outdoors; crazy about trains. Was once active in Little Theater work—end-result, I can't stand Little Theater performances today. Favorite sport, sitting."

*   *   *

BOAS, Guy (Herman Sidney)   1896-1966
(G.B.)

PERSONAL: Born December 9, 1896, in Beckley, Kent, England; son of Frederick S. and Henrietta O'Brien (Owen) Boas; married Cicely Whitehead, April 15, 1923; children: Robert. *Education:* Attended Radley College; Christ Church, Oxford, B.A., 1922, M.A., 1927. *Home:* 73 Murray Rd., Wimbledon, London S.W.19, England.

CAREER: St. Paul's School, London, England, senior English master, 1922-29; Sloane School, Chelsea, England, headmaster, 1929-61. *Military service:* British Army, Oxfordshire Hussars, 1916-18; became lieutenant. *Member:* Royal Society of Literature (fellow), Garrick Club, Oxford and Cambridge Club, University Club.

WRITINGS: Domestic Ditties, Basil Blackwell, 1919; *Short Guide to the Reading of English Literature*, Harrap, 1924; *Traffic and Theatre Rhymes*, Methuen, 1925; *Shelley and Keats Contrasted*, Thomas Nelson, 1925; *Tennyson and Browning Contrasted*, Thomas Nelson, 1925; *Wordsworth and Coleridge Contrasted*, Thomas Nelson, 1925; *Lays of Learning*, Jenkins, 1926; *New English Exercises*, Edward Arnold, 1926; *Selected Poems of Gray, Collins, Goldsmith, and Cowper*, Thomas Nelson, 1926; *Chaucer and Spenser Contrasted as Narrative Poets*, Thomas Nelson, 1926; *New Exercises in Precis Writing*, Longmans, Green, 1928; *The Writing of English*, Longmans, Green, 1928; *New Exercises in Essay Writing*, Longmans, Green, 1929.

English Papers for Preparation or Homework, Longmans, Green, 1931; *Key to English Papers for Preparation or Homework*, Longmans, Green, 1931; (with Cyril Aldred) *New Matriculation English Course, Based on the Study of Literature*, Macmillan, 1935; *Lytton Strachey*, Oxford University Press, 1935; (author of introduction) Shakespeare, *King Henry the Eighth*, edited by St. Clare Byrne, Macmillan, 1937; *Wimbledon: Has It a History?*, John Evelyn Club, 1947; *The Garrick Club, 1831-1947*, Garrick Club, 1948; *Shakespeare and the Young Actor: A Guide to Production*, Rockliff, 1955, 2nd edition, Barrie & Rockliff, 1961, Dufour, 1964; *A Teacher's Story*, St. Martin's, 1963; *Selected Light Verse*, Shakespeare Head Press, 1964.

Editor: (And author of introduction) William Cobbett, *Selections from Cobbett's Rural Rides*, Macmillan, 1926; *Humorous Narratives: An Anthology for Schools*, Edward Arnold, 1927; (and author of introductory biography) Richard Brinsley Sheridan, *Three Plays*, Longmans, Green, 1928; Sheridan, *The Rivals*, Edward Arnold, 1929; Sheridan, *The School for Scandal*, Edward Arnold, 1929; Sheridan, *The Critic*, Edward Arnold, 1929.

Oliver Goldsmith, *She Stoops to Conquer; or The Mistakes of a Night*, Edward Arnold, 1931; *Prose of Today*, Longmans, Green for English Association, 1932; (and author of introduction, notes, and questions) Alexander W. Kinglake, *Eothen*, Macmillan, 1932; *A Punch Anthology*, Macmillan, 1932; *Modern English Prose*, Macmillan, 1933, 2nd series, 1938, 3rd series, 1951, 4th series, 1959; *An Anthology of Wit*, Macmillan, 1934; Shakespeare, *Othello*, Macmillan, 1934; Shakespeare, *Romeo and Juliet*, Macmillan, 1935; Shakespeare, *The Winter's Tale*, Macmillan, 1935; Shakespeare, *Antony and Cleopatra*, Macmillan, 1935; *Short Modern Plays*, Macmillan, 1935; Shakespeare, *Cymbeline*, Macmillan, 1936; *Prose of Yesterday: Dickens to Galsworthy*, Macmillan, 1937; *The School Book of English Verse*, Macmillan, 1938, 2nd edition published as *A New Treasury of English Verse*, 1939; (with Howard Hayden, and author of introduction) *School Drama: Its Practice and Theory*, Methuen, 1938; *American Prose*, Macmillan, 1938.

An English Book of Light Verse, Macmillan, 1944, reissued as *The School Book of Light Verse*, 1945; (with Antony Gilkes) *Selections from the Old Testament, Edited for the Modern Reader*, Macmillan, 1944; (with Gilkes) *Selections from the New Testament, Edited for the Modern Reader*,

Macmillan, 1947; (and author of introduction and notes) Sean O'Casey, *Juno and the Paycock* [and] *The Plough and the Stars*, Macmillan, 1948, St. Martin's, 1954; (with John Tanfield) Richard Harris Barham, *The Ingoldsby Legends*, Macmillan, 1951; *Sir Winston Churchill: Selections from His Writings and Speeches*, Macmillan, 1952, 2nd edition, 1966; *Essays and Studies, 1954*, J. Murray, 1954; Sheridan, *Two Plays: The Rivals, and The School for Scandal*, Edward Arnold, 1961; *The School Book of Modern Verse*, St. Martin's, 1962; (with Margaret Willy) *Two Plays of Goldsmith*, Edward Arnold, 1962; *English Prose of Today*, Macmillan, 1966.

General editor, Macmillan's "Scholar's Library," "The Touchstone Shakespeare," and "The New Eversly Shakespeare," Macmillan; contributor to *Chamber's Encyclopaedia*, and to *Punch*, under initials G.B.

AVOCATIONAL INTERESTS: Music and philately.

(Died March 26, 1966)

*   *   *

BODKIN, Maud   1875-

PERSONAL: Born March 30, 1875, in Chelsmford, Essex, England; daughter of William Bodkin (a physician) and Mrs. Bodkin (maiden name Copland). *Education:* University College of Wales, B.A., M.A.

CAREER: For eleven years, lecturer on educational theory in a training college in Cambridge, England. Later, a writer and occasional lecturer.

WRITINGS: Archetypal Patterns in Poetry: Psychological Studies of Imagination, Oxford University Press, 1934; *The Quest for Salvation in an Ancient and a Modern Play*, Oxford University Press, 1941; *Studies of Type Images in Poetry, Religion, and Philosophy*, Oxford University Press, 1951. Contributor to *British Journal of Medical Psychology, Hibbert Journal, Philosophy*, and other publications.

SIDELIGHTS: Miss Bodkin writes to *CA:* "My writings have required some acquaintance with various languages, especially Greek and German, [and] also wide ranging interests in the human adventure so far as this finds expression in such movements as those for educational and religious reform, birth control, world government, etc."

Stanley Edgar Hyman has praised her for what he calls "probably the best use to date of psychoanalysis in literary criticism." He calls her "an amateur student of literature . . . who happens to have a wide acquaintance with both psychology and imaginative literature, as well as genuine literary sensitivity, sense of proportion, and taste that effectively keep her from all the familiar excesses of psychoanalytic criticism."

BIOGRAPHICAL/CRITICAL SOURCES: Stanley Edgar Hyman, *The Armed Vision*, Vintage, 1955.

*   *   *

BOETTCHER, Henry J.   1893-

PERSONAL: Born October 13, 1893, in Storm Lake, Iowa; son of Ernest (a farmer) and Catherine (Sievers) Boettcher; married Esther Kubbernus, July 30, 1920. *Education:* Attended Concordia Seminary, St. Louis, Mo., and Camrose Normal School (now Junior College), Alberta, Canada; University of Alberta, M.A., 1938; University of Minnesota, Ph.D., 1949. *Home:* Apartment 101, Town House, Springfield, Ill. 62703.

CAREER: Lutheran pastor. Illinois Business College, Springfield, consultant on expansion, beginning, 1966. *Member:* National Education Association, Association for Higher Education, National Society for the Study of Education.

WRITINGS: Instructors Manual, Concordia, 1949; *The New Life* (workbook), Concordia, 1949; *Learning and Living* (workbook), Concordia, 1949; *Self-Appraisal through Self-Examination: Comprehensive Tests on Catechetical Objectives*, Concordia, 1965; *Three Philosophies of Education: A Radical Re-examination of the Basic Assumptions Underlying Education, Matter-centered, Idea-centered, God-centered*, Philosophical Library, 1967; also author of *Adult Education in the Parish*, published by Vantage.

WORK IN PROGRESS: A chapter, "Objectives in Lutheran Education," for *A Lutheran Philosophy of Education.*

*   *   *

BOGERT, L(otta) Jean   1888-1970

PERSONAL: Born June 17, 1888, in Scotland, S.D.; daughter of Taylor O. and Jeanette (Gleason) Bogert. *Education:* Cornell University, A.B., 1910; Yale University, Ph.D., 1916. *Politics:* Republican. *Religion:* Congregational. *Home:* 18 Lagon Rd., Belvedere, Calif.

CAREER: Yale University, New Haven, Conn., instructor in experimental medicine, 1916-19; Kansas State University, Manhattan, professor of food and nutrition, 1919-22; Henry Ford Hospital, Detroit, Mich., research assistant in obstetrical department, 1922-24; University of Chicago, Chicago, Ill., instructor in medicine (research), 1927-29; free-lance writer and nutrition consultant, New York, N.Y., 1929-39. *Member:* American Society of Biological Chemists (honorary), Sigma Xi.

WRITINGS: Fundamentals of Chemistry, Saunders, 1924, 9th edition, 1963; *Laboratory Manual of Chemistry*, Saunders, 1927, 6th edition, 1961; *Nutrition and Physical Fitness*, Saunders, 1931, 8th edition (with George M. Briggs and Doris Howes Callaway), 1966; *Diet and Personality*, Macmillan, 1934; (with M. T. Porter) *Dietetics Simplified*, Macmillan, 1937, 2nd edition, 1940; *Good Nutrition for Everybody*, University of Chicago Press, 1942. Former writer of monthly articles for *Delineator*; contributor to *Ladies' Home Journal, Parent-Teacher*, and of scientific articles to professional journals.

(Died August 23, 1970)

*   *   *

BOGGS, Ralph Steele   1901-

PERSONAL: Born November 17, 1901, in Terre Haute, Ind.; son of Harry and Edna Earl (Patterson) Boggs; married Marian Wells, 1929 (divorced, 1948); married Edna Garrido, June 24, 1948; children: (first marriage) Ralph Karl. *Education:* University of Chicago, Ph.B., 1926, Ph.D., 1930. *Religion:* Baptist. *Home:* 536 Altara Ave., Coral Gables, Fla. 33146.

CAREER: University of Puerto Rico, Rio Piedras, instructor in English, 1926-28; University of North Carolina, Chapel Hill, began as assistant professor, became associate professor and professor of Spanish and folklore, 1929-50; University of Miami, Coral Gables, Fla., visiting professor, 1948-49, professor of Spanish and folklore, 1950-67. Visiting professor, University of Santo Domingo, 1944,

National University of Mexico, 1945-46, University of New Mexico, 1948, University of California, Los Angeles, 1963 and Berkeley, 1970. *Member:* Sociedad Folklorica de Mexico (founding member), American Folklore Society (fellow), Phi Beta Kappa. *Awards, honors:* Medalha Sylvio Romero from Brazil.

WRITINGS: Comparative Surveys of the Folktales of Ten Peoples, Suomalainen Tiedeakatemia, 1930; *Index of Spanish Folktales*, Suomalainen Tiedeakatemia, 1930; (editor with N. B. Adams) *Spanish Folktales*, F. S. Crofts & Co., 1932; (editor with Carlos Castillo) *Leyendas epicas de Espana*, Heath, 1935; (with Mary Gould Davis) *Three Golden Oranges, and Other Spanish Folktales*, McKay, 1936; *An Outline History of Spanish Literature*, Heath, 1937; *Bibliografia del folklore mexicano*, Instituto Panamericano de Geografia e Historia, 1939, translation published in America as *Bibliography of Latin American Folklore*, published for Inter-American Bibliographical and Library Association by Wilson, 1940; (compiler with others) *Tentative Dictionary of Medieval Spanish*, privately printed, 1946; *El Folklore en los Estados Unidos de Norteamerica*, Raigal (Buenos Aires), 1954; *Spanish Pronunciation Exercises*, Latin American Institute Press, 1954, revised edition, Regents Publishing, 1966; (with R. J. Dixson) *English Step by Step with Pictures*, Latin American Institute Press, 1956; *Spanish Folklore in America* [*and*] *Folklore in Panamericanism* [*and*] *Latin American Folklore Awaits Conquistadores* (originally published in *Hispanic-American Studies*, Number 1), [Coral Gables], 1958; (with Dixson) *Sound Teaching: A Laboratory Manual of American English* (tapes), Regents Publishing, 1959; (compiler) *La Camara de comercio de las Americas*, Miami Post Publishing Co., 1959; (with Moritz Adolph Jagendorf) *The King of the Mountains: A Treasury of Latin American Folk Stories*, Vanguard, 1960; (with Julio I. Andujar) *Sound Teaching: A Laboratory Manual of Everyday Spanish*, Regents Publishing, 1961; *Las Adivinanzas en el Libro de Chilam Balam de Chumayel* (originally published in *Folklore Americas*, Volume XXII, numbers 1-2), University of Miami Press, 1962; *Spanish Word Builder: 2000 Basic Spanish Words to Increase Your Vocabulary*, Regents Publishing, 1963; *Basic Spanish Pronunciation*, Regents Publishing, 1969.

Contributor: *The Biography of a Spanish and Folklore Bibliography*, published for Inter-American Bibliographical and Library Association by Wilson, 1938; Charles E. Rush, editor, *Folklore Library Resources of the University of North Carolina*, University of North Carolina Press, 1945; *Homenaje a don Luis de Hoyos Sainz*, [Madrid], 1949; *Mark the Boat: Romance Studies Presented to William Morton Dey*, University of North Carolina Press, 1950; A. Curtis Wilgus, editor, *The Caribbean: Contemporary Trends*, University of Florida Press, 1953; (author of foreword) Aurora Lucero White, *Literary Folklore of the Hispanic Southwest*, Naylor, 1953; *Homenaje a Fritz Kruger*, Universidad Nacional de Cuyo, 1954; Angel de Rio, editor, *Responsible Freedom in the Americas*, Doubleday, 1955; *Miscelanea de estudios dedicados a Fernando Ortiz*, [Havana], 1956; Wayland Debs Hand and G. O. Arit, editors, *Humaniora: Essays in Literature, Folklore, and Bibliography, Honoring Archer Taylor on His 70th Birthday*, Augustin, 1960; *Estudos e ensaios folcloricos em homenagem a Renato Almeida*, [Rio de Janeiro], 1960.

Booklets and bulletins: *Practical Phonetics of the American Language*, University of Puerto Rico Press, 1927; *Folklore: An Outline for Individual and Group Study*, University of North Carolina Press, 1929; *The Halfchick Tale in Spain and France*, Academia Scientiarum Fennica (Finland), 1933.

American collaborator, *Volkskundiche Bibliographie*, volumes for years 1925-26, 1927, 1928, 1929-30, 1931-32, 1933-34, Walter de Gruyter, 1935-39. Also contributor: *Handwoerterbuch des deutschen Marchens*, Volume II, Walter de Gruyter, 1935, "Handbook of Latin American Studies" series, Harvard University Press, 1936-48; *Encyclopedia of Literature*, Philosophical Library, 1946; *Funk and Wagnalls Standard Dictionary of Folklore, Mythology, and Legend*, Funk, 1950; contributor to published reports, proceedings, and yearbooks.

Compiler of annual folklore bibliography for *Southern Folklore Quarterly*, 1937-58. Contributor of more than one hundred articles and reviews to folklore and literary journals in Latin America and in the United States. Editor and director of *Folklore Americas*, 1940-65.

BIOGRAPHICAL/CRITICAL SOURCES: Folklore Americas, December, 1951; *Orlando Sentinel* (Orlando), Fla., March 11, 1962.

*   *   *

BOHLMAN, (Mary) Edna McCaull   1897-
(M. E. McCaull)

PERSONAL: Born July 7, 1897, in Joliet, Ill.; daughter of William Seward (a lawyer) and Nora (Hill) McCaull; married Herbert W. Bohlman (a professor and dean of business administration) September 10, 1924 (deceased); children: Herbert McCaull. *Education:* Kansas City (Mo.) Junior College, A.A., 1917; University of Illinois, B.A., 1920; University of Wisconsin, M.A., 1924; Columbia University, postgraduate student, 1934-35. *Religion:* Congregational. *Home:* 1301 37th St., Des Moines, Iowa 50311.

CAREER: High school teacher in Kansas City, Mo., Madison, Wis., and Des Moines, Iowa, 1921-34; New York Life Insurance Co., New York, N.Y., part-time life insurance salesman, 1925-34, full-time, 1935-41; Washington (D.C.) public schools, assistant to curriculum director, 1942-44; National Education Association, Washington, D.C., consumer education study, 1944-45; Des Moines Technical High School, Des Moines, Iowa, chairman of social science department, 1945-65; Grandview Junior College, Des Moines, Iowa, part-time teacher, 1965-70. *Member:* National Education Association, League of Women Voters (Iowa vice-president, 1939-41; Des Moines president, 1940-41), Pi Gamma Mu, Alpha Kappa Delta.

WRITINGS: (Under name Mary E. McCaull, with E. A. Ross) *Readings in Civic Sociology: A Textbook in Social and Civic Problems for Young Americans*, World Book, 1925; (with William B. Guitteau) *Our Government Today*, Houghton, 1938; (with husband, Herbert W. Bohlman) *Our Economic Problems*, Heath, 1942; *Buying Insurance*, National Education Association, 1946; *Democracy and Its Competitors*, C. E. Merrill, 1963; (with H. W. Bohlman) *Problems of Democracy: The United States in a Changing World*, Holt, 1964.

Books for drop-out students, all published by Follett, 1968-69: (With H. W. Bohlman) *Knowing How to Budget and Buy*, (with H. W. Bohlman) *Understanding Consumer Credit*, (with H. W. Bohlman) *Investing Your Savings*, (with H. W. Bohlman) *Insuring Your Life Income and Property*, (with son, Herbert McCaull Bohlman) *Social Insurance.*

BOHLMAN, Herbert W(illiam) 1896-

PERSONAL: Born December 23, 1896, in Hortonville, Wis.; son of Henry H. and Emilie (Schroeder) Bohlman; married Mary Edna McCaull (a teacher), September 10, 1924; children: Herbert McCaull. *Education:* Lawrence College (now University), A.B., 1919; University of Wisconsin, M.A., 1922, Ph.D., 1936. *Religion:* Congregational. *Home:* 1301 37th St., Des Moines, Iowa 50311. *Office:* Drake University, Des Moines, Iowa 50311.

CAREER: Drake University, Des Moines, Iowa, assistant professor, 1924-26, professor of economics, beginning, 1926, dean of Graduate Division, 1940-54, dean of College of Business Administration, 1954-64. Economist for Twentieth Century Fund, 1934-35, for U.S. government, 1942-45. Member of advisory committee, Iowa State Employment Security Commission, beginning, 1960. *Military service:* U.S. Navy, World War I. *Member:* American Economic Association, Midwest Economic Association, Phi Beta Kappa, Beta Gamma Sigma.

WRITINGS: Labor Market in Iowa, Social Science Research Council, 1937; (with wife, Edna McCaull Bohlman) *Problems of Democracy,* Holt, 1964; (with E. M. Bohlman) *Our Economic Problems,* Heath, 1964.

Also author of economic pamphlets, three with E. M. Bohlman, 1968, and two with son, H. Mac Bohlman, 1969, published by Educational Opportunities Division of Follett.

WORK IN PROGRESS: Research on consumer education and on banking history.

* * *

BOLAND, Daniel 1891-

PERSONAL: Born January 1, 1891, in Lisselton, County Kerry, Ireland; son of John and Bridget (Scanlan) Boland; married Hannah Barton; children: John Anthony. *Education:* Studied at St. Michael's College (Ireland) and at King's College, London. *Religion:* Roman Catholic. *Home:* 12 Cullenswood Gardens, Ranelagh, Dublin 6, Ireland.

CAREER: Appointed to central office of the Supreme Court of Judicature, London, England, 1913; Royal Courts of Justice, London, England, associate, King's Bench Division, 1920-38, secretary of King's Bench Masters, 1938-49, chief clerk, King's Remembrancers Department, 1949-50, clerk of the lists, Queen's Bench Division, 1950-56. Attorney in exchequer to sheriffs and Corporation of City of London, 1949-50. *Military service:* British Army, 1915-19; served in France; mentioned in dispatches. *Awards, honors:* Member of Order of the British Empire, 1949; Coronation Medal, 1953.

WRITINGS: (Editor) *ABC Guide to the Practice of the Supreme Court,* 36th and 37th editions, Sweet & Maxwell, 1949 and 1953; (with B. Sayers) *Oaths and Affirmations,* Stevens & Sons, 1953; (editor with Frank Burnand) *Chitty's Queen's Bench Forms,* 18th edition, Sweet & Maxwell, 1956; (editor) *Civil Procedures in a Nutshell,* 7th edition, Sweet & Maxwell, 1956. Editor, *Diary for Lawyers,* Sweet & Maxwell, 1940-56; assistant editor, *Annual Practice of the Supreme Court,* Sweet & Maxwell, 1949-56. Contributor to *Encyclopaedia of the Laws of England, Encyclopaedia of Forms and Precedents,* and to *Law Times* and other legal publications.

WORK IN PROGRESS: Biographical and autobiographical writings.

BOLITHO, Archie A(rdella) 1886-

PERSONAL: Born May 18, 1886, near Madera, Calif.; daughter of William and Addie Lillian (Terry) Bolitho. *Education:* Anderson College, Anderson, Ind., B.A., 1943. *Home:* 307 Cottage Ave., Anderson, Ind. 46012.

CAREER: Missionary in Tokyo, Japan, 1921-26; Church of God, Bronx, New York, N.Y., pastor, 1927-39; National Woman's Missionary Society of Church of God, Anderson, Ind., publications director and editor, 1941—. *Awards, honors:* Alumna of the Year, Anderson College, 1963.

WRITINGS: To the Chief Singer: A Brief Story of the Work and Influence of Barney E. Warren, Gospel Trumpet, 1942; (with Hazel G. Neal) *Madam President* (biography), Gospel Trumpet, 1951; *At Work for a Christian World: A Study Book on Missions* (leadership text), Warner, 1953; *The Church of God in British Guiana,* Missionary Board of Church of God, 1956. *Consider What God Is Doing,* Warner, 1963. Writer of pamphlets and articles connected with mission of church, and writer of church school materials, 1936—. Editor, *Friends of Missions,* 1948-51, *Church of God Missions Magazine,* 1951-69.

* * *

BOLITHO, (Henry) Hector 1897-1974
(Patrick Ney)

PERSONAL: Born May 28, 1897; son of Henry and Ethelred Frances (Bregman) Bolitho. *Education:* Attended Seddon Memorial College, Auckland, New Zealand. *Home:* No. 1, St. Nicholas Rd., Brighton, Sussex, England. *Agent:* A. M. Heath & Co. Ltd., 35 Dover St., London W.1, England.

CAREER: Author. Lecturer, especially in United States where he has spoken more than a hundred times, beginning 1947. Chairman, Committee for Writing and Reading Aids for the Paralyzed. *Military service:* Royal Air Force, Intelligence Corps, 1939-45; became squadron leader. *Member:* Royal Society of Arts (fellow), Royal Society of Literature (fellow), Athenaeum Club (London).

WRITINGS: The Island of Kawau: A Record, Descriptive and Historical, Whitcombe & Tombs, 1919; *With the Prince in New Zealand,* 1920; *Fiji, Samoa, Tonga, the Islands of Wonder,* Whitcombe & Tombs, 1920; (editor with Albert V. Baillie) *Letters of Lady Augusta Stanley, a Young Lady at Court, 1849-1863,* George H. Doran, 1927; *Solemn Boy* (novel), George H. Doran, 1927; *The New Zealanders,* Dent, 1928; *Thistledown and Thunder, a Higgledy-Piggledy Diary of New Zealand, the South Seas, Australia, Port Said, Italy, Paris, England, Madeira, Africa, Canada, and New York,* J. Cape, 1928; *The Glorious Oyster: His History in Rome and in Britain, His Anatomy and Reproduction, How to Cook Him, and What Various Writers and Poets Have Written in His Praise,* Knopf, 1929; *Judith Silver* (novel), Knopf, 1929; (editor with Baillie) *Later Letters of Lady Augusta Stanley, 1864-1876,* J. Cape, 1929; (editor) *The New Countries: A Collection of Stories and Poems by South African, Australian, Canadian, and New Zealand Writers,* J. Cape, 1929.

The Flame on Ethirdova, Cobden-Sanderson, 1930, Appleton, 1931; (editor with Baillie) Arthur Penrhyn Stanley, *A Victorian Dean: A Memoir of Arthur Stanley, Dean of Westminister,* Chatto & Windus, 1930; *Albert the Good and the Victorian Reign,* Appleton, 1932 (published in England as *Albert the Good,* Cobden-Sanderson, 1932); *Alfred Mond, First Lord Melchett,* Appleton, 1933; *Beside Gal-*

ilee: A Diary in Palestine, Appleton, 1933; (editor) *The Prince Consort and His Brother: Two Hundred New Letters*, Cobden-Sanderson, 1933, Appleton, 1934; *Empty Clothes*, Centaur Press, 1934; (editor, contributor, and author of introduction) *Twelve Jews*, Rich & Cowan, 1934, Books for Libraries, 1967; *The Romance of Windsor Castle*, Evans Brothers, 1934; *Victoria, the Widow and Her Son*, Appleton, 1934; *The Queen's Tact* (poetry), Centaur Press, 1934; *Older People*, Appleton, 1935; *The House in Half Moon Street and Other Stories*, Cobden-Sanderson, 1935, Appleton, 1936; *James Lyle Mackay, First Earl of Inchcape*, J. Murray, 1936; *Marie Tempest*, Eyre & Spottiswoode, 1936, Lippincott, 1937; *King Edward VIII, an Intimate Biography*, Lippincott, 1937 (published in England as *King Edward VIII, His Life and Reign*, Eyre & Spottiswoode, 1937, 4th edition published as *Edward VIII—Duke of Windsor*, P. Own, 1954); *Royal Progress: One Hundred Years of British Monarchy* (includes material from *Albert the Good* and *Victoria, the Widow and Her Son*), Cobden-Sanderson, 1938; *Victoria and Disraeli* (play for radio; first broadcast, 1938), Eyre & Spottiswoode, 1938; (editor) *Letters of Victoria, Queen of Great Britain, 1819-1901*, Yale University Press, 1938 (published in England as *Further Letters of Queen Victoria*, Butterworth & Co., 1938); (with John Mulgan) *The Emigrants: Early Travellers to the Antipodes*, Selwyn & Blount, 1939, Books for Libraries, 1970; *Roumania Under King Carol*, Eyre & Spottiswoode, 1939, Longmans, Green (New York), 1940; *Haywire: An American Travel Diary*, Longmans, Green (New York), 1939, new edition published as *America Expects: A Travel Diary*, Eyre & Spottiswoode, 1940.

War in the Strand: A Notebook of the First Two and a Half Years in London, Eyre & Spottiswoode, 1942; (editor) *A Batsford Century: The Record of a Hundred Years of Publishing and Bookselling, 1843-1943*, Batsford, 1943, 2nd edition, 1945; *Combat Report: The Story of a Fighter Pilot*, Batsford, 1943; *Command Performance: The Authentic Story of the Last Battle of Coastal Command, R.A.F.*, Howell, Soskin, 1946 (published in England as *Task for Coastal Command: The Story of the Battle of the South-West Approaches*, Hutchinson, 1946); *No Humour in My Love, and Two Other Stories*, Jenkins, 1946; (editor) *The British Empire*, Batsford, 1948; *The Reign of Queen Victoria*, Macmillan (New York), 1948.

A Biographer's Notebook, Longmans, Green (New York), 1950; *A Century of British Monarchy*, Longmans, Green (New York), 1951, 2nd edition, 1953; *Their Majesties*, Parrish, 1952, British Book Centre, 1953; (with Derek Peel) *Without the City Wall: An Adventure in London Street-names, North of the River*, J. Murray, 1952, Transatlantic, 1953; *Jinnah, Creator of Pakistan*, J. Murray, 1954, Macmillan, 1955; *A Penguin in the Eyrie: An R.A.F. Diary, 1939-45*, Hutchinson, 1955; *The Wine of the Douro* (booklet), Sidgwick & Jackson, 1956; *No. 10 Downing Street, 1660-1900*, Hutchinson, 1957; *The Glasshouse, Jamestown, Virginia* (booklet), Jamestown Glasshouse Foundation, 1957; *The Angry Neighbours: A Diary of Palestine and Transjordan*, Arthur Barker, 1957.

My Restless Years, Parrish, 1962; *A Summer in Germany: A Diary*, Wolff, 1963; *The Galloping Third: The Story of the 3rd, the King's Own Hussars*, J. Murray, 1963, Transatlantic, 1964; (under pseudonym Patrick Ney) *An Animal Lover's Scrapbook*, Parrish, 1963; *Albert, Prince Consort*, Parrish, 1964, Bobbs-Merrill, 1965, revised edition, David Bruce & Watson, 1970; (with Peel) *The Drummonds of Charing Cross*, Allen & Unwin, 1967. Contributor to maga-

zines in England, United States, Germany, Pakistan, and other countries.

SIDELIGHTS: Bolitho was an inveterate traveler; he went around the world at least three times, and lived for periods in Portugal, Pakistan, United States, Australia, and Germany. One of his interests was to awaken enthusiasm on both sides of the Atlantic (England and America) for the history the two nations share.†

(Died, 1974)

* * *

BOLL, Carl R. 1894-

PERSONAL: Born November 28, 1894, in Bremerhaven, Germany; came to United States, 1908; son of Carl Boll; married Margaret Lofgren; children: Carleton H., Barbara Ann (Mrs. Lewis Herndon). *Education:* Carleton College, B.A., 1920; Harvard University, M.B.A., 1922. *Politics:* Republican. *Religion:* Protestant. *Home:* Tidewater Lane, Nyack, N.Y. *Office:* Carl R. Boll & Co., 151 Broadway, New York, N.Y.

CAREER: Cabin boy aboard ship before coming to United States; employee of Aetna Casualty Insurance Co., Hartford, Conn., 1922-36; Beebe & Boll (insurance brokers), New York, N.Y., partner, 1937-46; Carl R. Boll & Co. (general and life insurance), New York, N.Y., owner, 1946—. Director of Solvents Recovery Service, Spiral Binding Co., Kamket Corp., and Chemirad Corp. Trustee of Village of South Nyack. *Member:* National Association of Life Underwriters, Harvard Business School Alumni Association (former governor), Harvard Business School Club of New York (president, 1938-40; director of placement for more than twenty-five years). *Awards, honors:* Carleton College Achievement Award, 1962; Harvard Business School Club of New York award for quarter century of placement service, 1964.

WRITINGS: Executive Jobs Unlimited, Macmillan, 1965.

BIOGRAPHICAL/CRITICAL SOURCES: Nyack Journal News, August 15, 1957; *HBSC Newsletter*, April 20, 1964.

* * *

BONAVIA-HUNT, Noel Aubrey 1882-1965

PERSONAL: Born December 25, 1882, in Primrose Hill, London, England; son of Henry George Bonavia-Hunt (a clergyman and editor). *Education:* Pembroke College, Oxford University, M.A. (honors in theology). *Politics:* Conservative. *Home:* "Earlsmead," Benenden, Cranbrook, Kent, England.

CAREER: Clergyman, Church of England; vicar of Stagsden, Bedford, England, 1934-54; now retired. Organ-building consultant and designer. *Member:* British Chess Problem Society (president, 1954-56), Organ Club.

WRITINGS: (With Charles H. Pratt) *Some Rhymes to Remember from January to December, for the Use of Voluntary Choirs*, Vincent Music Co., 1908; *Studies in Organ Tone: A Practical, Theoretical, Historical, and Aesthetic Treatise on the Tonal Department of the Organ*, Waterside Music, 1914, 3rd edition, Winthrop Rogers, 1917; *The Church Organ: An Introduction to the Study of Modern Organ-Building*, Faith Press, 1920; *Modern Organ Stops: A Practical Guide*, Musical Opinion, 1923; *Modern Studies in Organ Tone*, Musical Opinion, 1933; *The Organ of Tradition or Its Imitation?*, Roberts & Newton, 1939.

The Modern British Organ: A Theoretical and Practical Treatise on the Tone and Mechanism of the King of Instruments, Weekes & Co., 1947, revised edition, 1950; *Organ Tuning*, revised edition, Musical Opinion, 1950; (with H. W. Homer) *The Organ Reed* (includes *The Voicing and Use of Reed Pipes* by Bonavia-Hunt, and *The Mechanical Properties of Reed Pipes* by Homer), J. Fischer, 1950; (author of metrical appendix with Arthur John Arberry) W. Bonavia-Hunt, *Lateres Fitzgeraldi*, [Bedford], c.1951; *High Fidelity Radio: Design and Construction*, Bernards, 1952; *Horace the Minstrel: A Study of His Sapphic and Alcaic Lyrics*, Musical Opinion, 1954, published in America as *Horace the Minstrel: A Practical and Aesthetic Study of His Aeolic Verse*, Verry, 1969; *Irons in the Fire* (personal memoirs), Musical Opinion, 1959; *Faith and the Mountain: A Discussion and Conclusion*, Bles, 1960; *Death Be Not Proud: The Evidence from Science, Philosophy, Psychology, Paranormal Experience and Theology for Personal Survival*, Musical Opinion, 1963. Author of various organ voluntaries, published in England and the United States. Contributor of articles to *Musical Opinion*, 1898-65, and to *Organ*.

WORK IN PROGRESS: Research on Biblical exegesis and voice production.

(Died August, 1965)

*   *   *

BOND, Nelson S(lade) 1908-

PERSONAL: Born November 23, 1908, in Scranton, Pa.; son of Richard Slade (a publicist) and Mary (Beadle) Bond; married Betty Gough Folsom, October 3, 1934; children: Lynn Nelson and Christopher Kent (sons). *Education:* Marshall University, Huntington, W.Va., student, 1932-34. *Politics:* Democrat ("generally"). *Religion:* Episcopalian. *Home:* 1625 Hampton Ave., S.W., Roanoke, Va. 24015.

CAREER: Public relations field director for province of Nova Scotia, 1934-35; professional writer, best known for fantasy, 1935—. Philatelic researcher and expert on Canadian stamps; active in Roanoke community theater, The Showtimers, 1953—, serving consecutively as treasurer, president, and as comptroller, 1959—. *Member:* Writers Guild of America (East), British North American Philatelic Society (life member), Roanoke Writers' Guild, American Contract Bridge League (national master). *Awards, honors:* Citation for valuable contribution to philatelic literature, International Stamp Exhibition, London, England, 1960, for *The Postal Stationery of Canada*.

WRITINGS—Fiction, except as indicated: *Mr. Mergenthwirker's Lobblies and Other Fantastic Tales*, Coward, 1946, reprinted, Books for Libraries, 1970; *The Thirty-first of February*, (short stories), Gnome Press, 1949, reprinted, Books for Libraries, 1970; *Exiles of Time*, Prime Press, 1949; *Lancelot Biggs: Spaceman*, Doubleday, 1950; *The Postal Stationery of Canada* (nonfiction), Herman Herst, 1953; *No Time Like the Future*, Avon, 1954; *Nightmares and Daydreams* (short story collection), Arkham, 1968.

Plays: *Mr. Mergenthwirker's Lobblies* (three acts), Samuel French, 1957; *State of Mind*, Samuel French, 1958; *Animal Farm* (two act; adapted from the novel by George Orwell), Samuel French, 1964. Other produced plays number more than three hundred for radio (in pre-television days), and several dozen television dramas, mostly produced live on "Philco Playhouse," "Kraft Theatre," "Studio One," and other network programs. Also has written several film scripts for government agencies.

Contributor to the philatelic press in United States and Canada.

SIDELIGHTS: Mr. Mergenthwirker's Lobblies is the most widely circulated of Bond's fantasies—not to be confused with science fiction, he points out, although he has done much work in that area too. The story appeared in his earliest collection, was adapted by Bond for the first full-length three-act play ever produced on network television (at that time a three-city network), subsequently published in play form, and included in anthologies and textbooks. In all, Bond stories have been published in almost fifty anthologies in this country and abroad; his books have been translated and reprinted in more than a dozen foreign editions. *Avocational interests:* Contract and duplicate bridge (working toward life master), travel in America.

*   *   *

BONINE, Gladys Nichols 1907-

PERSONAL: Born April 22, 1907, in Heltonville, Ind.; daughter of Harry Emerson (a farmer) and Daisy (Bailey) Nichols; married Clair A. Bonine (an electrical engineer), April 23, 1955. *Education:* Indiana University, R.N., 1930, B.S. in Nursing Education, 1947; University of Chicago, M.A., 1950. *Home:* 300 Arcadia Dr., Pittsburgh, Pa.

CAREER: Indianapolis General Hospital, Indianapolis, Ind., educational director and instructor in pediatric nursing, 1947-50; University of Pittsburgh, Pittsburgh, Pa., assistant professor, later associate professor of pediatric nursing, 1950-60; Children's Hospital of Pittsburgh, Pittsburgh, Pa., educational director, 1960-68. *Military service:* U.S. Army, Nurse Corps, 1942-45; became first lieutenant. *Member:* American Nurses Association, National League for Nursing.

WRITINGS: (Contributor) *Study Guide for Clinical Nursing*, Lippincott, 1953, revised edition, 1961; (with Lois Pounds) *Workbook in Pediatric Nursing*, Macmillan, 1962. Contributor to *American Journal of Nursing*.

*   *   *

BONNAR, Alphonsus 1895-1968

PERSONAL: Born May 11, 1895, in Glasgow, Scotland; son of Peter Cunlisk (an engineer and architect) and Katherine (McQuade) Bonnar. *Education:* St. Anthony's International College, Rome, Italy, Lector Generalis in theology; Gregorian University, Rome, Italy, D.D.; Trinity College, Cambridge University, M.Sc. *Home:* The Friary, East Bergholt, Suffolk, England.

CAREER: Entered Franciscan Order, 1912; ordained priest in Rome, Italy, 1920; lecturer in theology in Franciscan Order, London, England, 1924-39; guardian of St. Bonaventure's, Cambridge, England, 1939-54; lecturer in theology in Franciscan Order, East Bergholt, Suffolk, England, 1957-68. Lecturer in religious education, University of London's Institute of Education, 1950-62. Fellow Commoner, Trinity College, Cambridge University, 1943-48. *Military service:* Officiating chaplain to U.S. Army Air Forces during World War II, and to Royal Air Force, 1945-54. *Member:* Catholic Record Society (council, 1927-57), Catholic Doctors' Guild (honorary member; local chaplain, 1932-57; national chaplain, 1947-57). *Awards, honors:* Lector Jubilatus in Franciscan Order.

WRITINGS: Over Thirty Years' Work of the Catholic Record Society, privately printed, 1935; *The Catholic Doctor*, Burns, 1937, 6th edition, 1952; *Medicine and Men*, Burns, 1962.

Contributor: *St. Paul and His Teaching*, Sands, 1928; *The Atonement*, Heffer, 1928; *Sermons of the Year 1932*, Faber, 1933; *The Pre-Nicence Church*, Burns, 1935; *Church and State*, Burns, 1936; *Man and Eternity*, Burns, 1937; *The Old Testament*, Burns, 1939.

Contributor of articles to religious, professional, and popular publications. Editor, *Catholic Medical Quarterly*, 1947-50; general editor for volumes of Catholic Record Society, 1940-46.

SIDELIGHTS: Bonnar's activities in the medico-moral field (for thirty years) led to personal contacts all over the world—"from Louisiana to Bagdhad," he said, "and from Buenos Aires to Australia, from South Africa to India."

(Died December 29, 1968)

*   *   *

BOOG WATSON, Elspeth Janet   1900-

PERSONAL: Born May 15, 1900, in Musselburgh, Scotland; daughter of Charles and Jane (Nairn) Boog Watson. *Education:* University of Edinburgh, magister artium (with honors), 1924. *Politics:* Conservative. *Religion:* Christian. *Home:* 24 Garscube Ter., Edinburgh, Scotland.

CAREER: Teacher of history and English, Edinburgh, Scotland, 1927-31; George Watson's Ladies' College, Edinburgh, head of history department, 1931-60; now retired. Director, Borestane Co. *Member:* Historical Association, Society of Antiquaries of Scotland (fellow), Royal Scottish Geographical Society (fellow), Ladies' Caledonian Club (Edinburgh; chairman, 1962-63).

WRITINGS: The Story of Moses, Oxford University Press, 1936; *Stories of the Middle Ages*, Johnston, 1940; *The Siege of Gibraltar*, Oxford University Press, 1941; (adapter) Jacoba Tadema Sporry, *The Story of Egypt*, Thomas Nelson, 1964.

With J. Isabel Carruthers: *Beyond the Sunset: A Book of Explorers*, Oxford University Press, 1935; *West of the Moon: A Book of Explorers*, Oxford University Press, 1938; *How People Lived*, Oxford University Press, 1949; *Teachers' Companion to History Through the Ages*, Oxford University Press, 1949; *Country Life Through the Ages*, Allen & Unwin, 1956; *Houses*, Oxford University Press, 1958; (editor) Margaret Bertha Synge, *Book of Discovery*, new edition, Thomas Nelson, 1962; *An Elizabethan Seaman*, Oxford University Press, 1964; *An Eighteenth Century Scottish Highlander*, Oxford University, 1965.

*   *   *

BOOTH, George C(live)   1901-

PERSONAL: Born September 3, 1901, in Portland, Ore.; son of George Charles (a farmer) and Amanda Mae (Beebe) Booth; married Clara D. Schulz (now a teacher of arts and crafts), May 5, 1940; children: George H., Elizabeth A. Booth Edwards, Katherine A. Booth Pearson, Stanton C., James E., Jeffrey A. *Education:* Oregon Agricultural College (now Oregon State University), B.S., 1925; University of Southern California, M.A., 1933, Ph.D., 1939; studied Spanish at other universities in America and Mexico. *Politics:* Democrat. *Religion:* Protestant. *Home:* 532 Almond Ave., Long Beach, Calif., 90812.

CAREER: Engaged in construction business, 1926-29; Long Beach City College, Long Beach, Calif., teacher of English, 1935-67, retired, 1967. *Military service:* U.S. Marine Corps, 1919-21. U.S. Naval Reserve, 1943-57; now

commander (retired). *Member:* Retired Officers Association, Sigma Delta Chi, Phi Delta Kappa, Beta Phi Gamma (national president, 1938-40).

WRITINGS: Mexico's School-Made Society, Stanford University Press, 1940; *The Food and Drink of Mexico*, Ritchie, 1964. Contributor to *School and Society, Social Education, Education Digest, National Motorist, Sunset, Westways*, and *Phi Delta Kappan*.

WORK IN PROGRESS: Look to the Mexican Sierra.

SIDELIGHTS: A self-described dilettante and "liberal spectator," Booth has been a student of Spanish since 1919; he has lived in or visited all of Central America, and Ecuador, Peru, Colombia, and the Galapagos Islands.

*   *   *

BOOTH, Pat(rick John)   1929-

PERSONAL: Born September 9, 1929, in Levin, New Zealand; son of Frederick Charles and Amelia (Johnson) Booth; married Valerie Lineen, January 24, 1953; children: Grant, Therese, Mark, Sally. *Education:* Attended Sacred Heart College, Auckland, New Zealand. *Religion:* Roman Catholic. *Home:* 18 Koraha St., Remuera, Auckland, New Zealand. *Office: Auckland Star*, Shortland St., Auckland, New Zealand.

CAREER: Hawera Star, Hawera, New Zealand, reporter, 1947-50; *Auckland Star*, Auckland, New Zealand, reporter, aviation correspondent, feature writer, 1950-58, parliamentary correspondent in Wellington, 1954-55; *Sydney Daily Telegraph*, Sydney, Australia, sub-editor, 1958; *Auckland Star*, chief sub-editor, 1960-65, assistant editor, 1965—. New Zealand Press Association, special correspondent in Asia, 1957. *Member:* Auckland Journalists Association (executive, 1956), New Zealand Vintage Car Club.

WRITINGS: All Blacks Book for Boys, Whitcombe & Tombs, 1960; *Bert Sutcliffe Book for Boys*, Whitcombe & Tombs, 1961; *Long Night Among the Stars*, Collins, 1961; *Footsteps in the Sea* (novel), Collins, 1964; *Dear Chevvy*, A. H. & A. W. Reed, 1965; *Sprint from the Bell* (novel), Collins, 1966; (with Don B. Clarke) *The Boot*, A. H. & A. W. Reed, 1966. Author of a radio play, "Long Night Among the Stars," for New Zealand Broadcasting Commission, 1962.

WORK IN PROGRESS: A book.

SIDELIGHTS: Booth toured the United States in 1962, examining effects of television on evening newspapers for a report to New Zealand papers. *Avocational interests:* Restoring vintage cars (owns a 1926 Chevrolet in original condition), aikido (Japanese martial art), collecting Edison phonographs, breeding Afghan hounds.

*   *   *

BORCHERS, Gladys L.   1891-

PERSONAL: Born July 4, 1891, in LaValle, Wis.; daughter of August (a farmer) and Sophie (Gross) Borchers. *Education:* Whitewater Normal School (now University of Wisconsin), diploma, 1918; University of Wisconsin, B.A., 1921, M.A., 1925, Ph.D., 1927. *Politics:* "Vote for man and principles." *Religion:* Unitarian Universalist. *Home:* 4725 Sheboygan Ave., Apt. 246, Madison, Wis. 53705.

CAREER: Teacher in rural, elementary, and high schools prior to 1921; Rockford College, Rockford, Ill., associate professor of speech and chairman of department, 1921-24;

University of Wisconsin, Madison, assistant professor, 1927-34, associate professor, 1934-46, professor of speech, 1947-62, emeritus professor, 1962—, chairman of department, 1958-59. Visiting professor at various universities, including University of Colorado, 1962-63, University of Wisconsin, 1963-64, Brigham Young University, 1964-65 and 1970, Eastern Washington State College, 1966, Taylor University, 1966-67; visiting lecturer at Western Washington State College, 1965-66 and 1968, and Illinois State University, 1965-66. Scholar in Residence for the humanities at University of Wisconsin, Whitewater, 1973. Member of Fulbright Committee for selection of speech specialists for foreign awards.

MEMBER: Speech Association of America (vice-president, 1939; council member, 1961-66), National Collegiate Players, Central States Speech Association, Phi Beta, Delta Sigma Rho, Pi Lambda Theta, Mortar Board, Zeta Phi Eta, Madison Civic Club. *Awards, honors:* Distinguished Alumni Award, Wisconsin State College, Whitewater, (now University of Wisconsin), 1958; A. T. Weaver Outstanding Speech Teacher in Wisconsin, 1973-74.

WRITINGS—High school and college texts: *Living Speech*, Harcourt, 1938, 2nd edition, 1949; (with W. Wilber Hatfield and others) *Senior English Activities*, Book 2, American Book Co., c.1938; (with A. T. Weaver) *The New Better Speech*, Harcourt, 1939; (with Weaver) *Speech*, Harcourt, 1947; (with Claude Wise) *Modern Speech*, Harcourt, 1947; (with Weaver and Donald K. Smith), *Teaching Speech*, Prentice-Hall, 1952; (with Weaver and Smith) *Speaking and Listening*, Prentice-Hall, 1956; (contributor) Karl Wallace, editor, *History of Speech Education in America*, Appleton, 1957; (contributor) Joseph Totaro, editor, *Women in College and University Teaching*, University of Wisconsin Press, 1965; (contributor) Keith Brooks, editor, *The Communicative Arts and Sciences of Speech*, C. E. Merrill, 1967; also contributor to *History of American Pronunciation*. Contributor to speech and other professional journals. Editor, *Speech Teacher*, 1961-63.

WORK IN PROGRESS: Continuing research on speech education in Germany and the United States.

SIDELIGHTS: Gladys Borchers speaks German "with fair fluency."

* * *

BORDEN, Mary 1886-1968
(Bridget Maclagan)

PERSONAL: Born May 15, 1886, in Chicago, Ill.; daughter of William and Mary (Whiting) Borden; married George Douglas Turner; married second husband, Sir Edward Spears (a major general, British Army, member of Parliament, and historian), 1918; children: (first marriage) Joyce Comfort Hart-Davis, Mary Hamilton Hall; (second marriage) Michael (deceased). *Education:* Vassar College, B.A., 1907. *Politics:* Conservative. *Religion:* Protestant. *Home:* 12 Strathearn Pl., London W. 2, England.

CAREER: Author. Organizer and director of field hospitals for the French in both World Wars. Official hostess at British legations in Beirut and Damascus when husband was minister plenipotentiary to Syria and Lebanon, 1942-44. *Member:* Society of Authors. *Awards, honors:* British medals for war service, 1914-18; French Legion of Honor and Croix de Guerre with bar and palm.

WRITINGS: The Romantic Woman, Knopf, 1920; *The Tortoise*, Knopf, 1921; *Jane—Our Stranger*, Knopf, 1923;

Three Pilgrims and a Tinker, Knopf, 1924; *Jericho Sands*, Heinemann, 1925, Knopf, 1926; *Four O'Clock, and Other Stories*, Doubleday, Page, 1927; *Flamingo, or the American Tower*, Doubleday, Page, 1927; *Jehovah's Day*, Heinemann, 1928, Doubleday, Doran, 1929; *The Forbidden Zone*, Heinemann, 1929, Doubleday, Doran, 1930.

A Woman with White Eyes, Doubleday, Doran, 1930; *Sarah Defiant*, Doubleday, Doran, 1931; *Sarah Gay*, Heinemann, 1931; *The Technique of Marriage*, Doubleday, Doran, 1933; *Mary of Nazareth*, Doubleday, Doran, 1933; *The King of the Jews*, Little, Brown, 1935; *Action for Slander*, Heinemann, 1936, Harper, 1937; *The Black Virgin*, Heinemann, 1937, published as *Strange Week-end*, Harper, 1938; *Passport for a Girl*, Harper, 1939.

Journey Down a Blind Alley, Harper, 1946; *No. 2 Shovel Street*, Heinemann, 1949.

Catspaw, Longmans, Green, 1950 (published in England as *For the Record*, Heinemann, 1950); *You, the Jury* (Book-of-the-Month Club selection), Longmans, Green, 1952 (published in England as *Martin Merriedew*, Heinemann, 1952); *Margin of Error*, Longmans, Green, 1954; *The Hungry Leopard*, Longmans, Green, 1956.

Under pseudonym Bridget Maclagan: *The Mistress of Kingdoms; or Smoking Flax*, Duckworth, 1912; *The Romantic Women*, Constable, 1916.

Adapted novel, *Action for Slander*, for motion picture of the same title; writer of scripts for British Broadcasting Corp. "Saturday Night Theatre."

WORK IN PROGRESS: A stage version of *Action for Slander*.

SIDELIGHTS: After her death, the *London Times* commented, "Miss Borden was a writer of very real and obvious gifts. Intelligent, resourceful, and accomplished, not seldom impressive in their sustained narrative power, most of her novels were nevertheless somewhat narrowly confined to the experience of the very rich and exalted and in the result were stamped by a certain conventionality of outlook. She tried in time to broaden the field of her observation and imaginative sympathy, but continued for the most part to make the best use of her talents in keeping to the type of wealthy and fashionable milieu which for many years she knew best."

Miss Borden, in private life Lady Spears, was the wife of Major General Sir Edward Spears who brought Charles de Gaulle out of Nazi-occupied France in 1940.

(Died December 2, 1968)

* * *

BORDEN, Richard Carman 1900-

PERSONAL: Born July 10, 1900, in New York, N.Y.; son of Charles Edgar and Josephine Tillotson (Greene) Borden; married Marie Herdeloff, January, 1923 (divorced); married Laurene Hempstead, October, 1932; children: (first marriage) Richard Wallace. *Education:* Colgate University, B.S., 1920; New York University, A.M., 1924. *Politics:* Republican. *Religion:* Episcopalian. *Home:* 111 South Harrison St., East Orange, N.J.

CAREER: New York University, New York, N.Y., executive chairman of department of public speaking, 1920-38, lecturer, 1922—; American Institute of Homeopathy, New York, N.Y., lay manager, 1928-34; Hearst Newspapers, New York, N.Y., general sales supervisor, 1929-30; Borden Co., New York, N.Y., director of sales promotion and coordination, 1937-47; Westinghouse Electric Corp., Pittsburgh, Pa., sales and management consultant, 1947-50. World Institute of Health Education, senator, 1920-34; Life Extension Institute, vice-president, 1930-32; Community Chests and Councils of America, member of national advisory committee on public relations, 1948—. *Military service:* U.S. Army, 1916-18. U.S. Coast Guard Reserve, 1942-45; became lieutenant commander.

MEMBER: National Association of Teachers of Speech (vice-president), National Academy of Speech Correction (executive officer), National Federation of Sales Executives (executive officer, 1935-38), American Academy of Foreign Relations (president, 1935-40), Phi Beta Kappa, Delta Sigma Rho, Pi Rho Mu, Masons, Union League Club, Advertising Club (director, 1936-40), Sales Executives Club (vice-president, 1936-40).

WRITINGS: Public Speaking as Listeners Like It, Harper, 1935; *How to Deliver a Sales Presentation*, Harper, 1938; *Selling Against Resistance*, Dartnell, 1950; *Closing the Sale*, Dartnell, 1952, revised edition, 1957; *Overcoming Objections*, Dartnell, 1953; *Winning Convictions*, Dartnell, 1955; *Presenting Your Sales Case Convincingly!*, Dartnell, 1955; *How to Up Sales By Better Sales Supervision*, Vision, Inc., 1956; *Opening the Sale*, Dartnell, 1957; *International Tele-Sell on General and Retail Selling*, Tele-Sell, Inc., 1958; *Developing Your Sales Personality*, Dartnell, 1959; *Preventing Sales Objections*, Dartnell, 1960.

With Alvin Busse: *Speech Correction*, Crofts & Co., 1925; *How to Win an Argument*, Harper, 1926, reissued as *How to Win a Sales Argument*, 1935; *The New Public Speaking*, Harper, 1930; *How to Sell*, Harper, 1936; *How to Make a Sales Point Hit!*, Prentice-Hall, 1938. Assistant editor, *Quarterly Journal of Speech Education* and *Journal of American Institute of Homeopathy.*

* * *

BORLAND, Barbara Dodge

PERSONAL: Born in Waterbury, Conn.; daughter of Harry George (a merchant) and Grace (Cross) Dodge; married Hal Borland (an author), August 10, 1945; children: Diana (Mrs. James C. Thomson, Jr.) *Education:* Attended Oberlin College and Columbia University School of Journalism. *Politics:* Independent. *Religion:* Congregationalist. *Home:* Weatogue Rd., Salisbury, Conn. 06089. *Agent:* Willis Kingsley Wing, 24 East 28th St., New York, N.Y. 10016.

CAREER: Various publishers, New York, N.Y., editorial consultant, 1923-35; Writers Workshop, New York, N.Y., founder and conductor, 1934-38. *Member:* Authors League of America.

WRITINGS: The Greater Hunger, Appleton, 1962. Contributor of articles, short stories, and poems to various magazines prior to 1945; collaborated with husband on short stories and novelettes for major magazines in United States and abroad, 1945-55.

WORK IN PROGRESS: Five books, three with tentative titles of *This Is the Way My Garden Grows, This Is the Way My Garden Cooks*, and *Witches' Laughter*, a novel; research on early American Puritan and Pilgrim colonies; research on early and modern horticulture.

AVOCATIONAL INTERESTS: Vegetable gardening, fishing, cooking, nature, the outdoors.

BOROFF, David 1917-1965

PERSONAL: Born March 28, 1917, in New York, N.Y.; son of Philip Louis (a baker) and Alize (Magnun) Boroff; married Zuzana Pick, March 24, 1962; children: Philip. *Education:* Brooklyn College (now Brooklyn College of the City University of New York), A.B., 1938, A.M., 1949; Columbia University, graduate study, 1950-54. *Office:* English Department, New York University, New York, N.Y. 10003.

CAREER: Brooklyn College (now Brooklyn College of the City University of New York), Brooklyn, N.Y., lecturer in English, 1947-60; Adelphi University, Garden City, N.Y., instructor in English, 1948-50; New York University, New York, N.Y., associate professor of English, 1960-65. Assistant to the deputy superintendent of New York City Schools, 1957-58; confidential secretary to the president of the Board of Education of the City of New York, 1958-59; Ford Foundation consultant, 1963. *Military service:* U.S. Army, Tank Destroyers and Military Intelligence, 1942-46. *Member:* Modern Language Association of America, Society of Magazine Writers, American Association of University Professors.

WRITINGS: Campus U.S.A.: Portraits of American Colleges in Action, Harper, 1961; (contributor) Paul Woodring and John Scanlon, editors, *Saturday Review: American Education Today*, McGraw, 1963; (editor) *The State of the Nation*, Prentice-Hall, 1966. Contributor of articles to *Harper's* and *New York Times Magazine*, book reviews to *Saturday Review* and *New York Times*, television reviews to *New Leader*, theatre reviews to *National Observer*. Editor, one hundredth-anniversary edition of *Nation*, September, 1965. Literary and drama critic for *American Judaism.*

WORK IN PROGRESS: A book on Catskill resort area of New York; a book on higher education.

SIDELIGHTS: Campus U.S.A. was praised by the critics for its lack of the usual statistics and descriptions of universities, and for its inclusion of particular characteristics about these institutions which make them unique. F. H. Horn commended Boroff for his "extraordinary insight into the practices and problems, the weaknesses and strengths, of American higher education as a whole."

BIOGRAPHICAL/CRITICAL SOURCES: Booklist, October 15, 1961; *Saturday Review*, October 21, 1961, April 23, 1966; *New York Times Book Review*, October 22, 1961, July 3, 1966; *Library Journal*, December 1, 1961, May 1, 1966, June 15, 1966; *Time*, February 8, 1963; *Christian Century*, March 16, 1966; *Choice*, September, 1966.

(Died May 15, 1965)

* * *

BORTZ, Edward L(eRoy) 1896-1970

PERSONAL: Born February 10, 1896, in Greensburg, Pa.; son of Adam Franklin and Anna Margaret (Wineman) Bortz; married Margaret Sophia Welty, December 27, 1926; children: Walter Michael. *Education:* Harvard University, A.B., 1920, M.D., 1923; additional work at University of Illinois Medical School and Mayo Clinic, 1925, at University of Vienna and University of Berlin, 1925-26. *Home:* 70 West Princeton Rd., Bala Cynwyd, Pa. 19004. *Office:* 2021 West Girard Ave., Philadelphia, Pa. 19130.

CAREER: Diplomate, American Board of Internal Medicine, 1937; Lankenau Hospital, Philadelphia, Pa., intern, 1923-25, chief of medical service B, 1932-61, senior consultant in medicine, 1961-70; University of Pennsylvania

School of Medicine, Philadelphia, began as instructor, 1930, associate professor, Graduate School of Medicine, 1932-70. Private practice as internist, Philadelphia, Pa., 1926-70. Consultant, Committee on Aging, White House Conference. *Military service:* U.S. Army Air Corps, pilot, World War I. U.S. Navy, Medical Corps, World War II; served with Marines on Iwo Jima and in atomic bomb area Nagasaki, Japan.

MEMBER: World Medical Association (founding), American Medical Association (vice-president, 1946-47; president, 1947-48), American Geriatrics Society (president, 1960-61), American Clinical and Climatological Association, American College of Physicians (life), American Gerontological Society, Society of Internal Medicine of the Argentine (corresponding), South African College of Physicians (capital honorary fellow), National Academy of Mexico (honorary), Pennsylvania State Medical Society, Philadelphia County Medical Society (life; president, 1940-41), Pen and Pencil, Alpha Omega Alpha, Union League of Pennsylvania, Bala Golf Club (Philadelphia). *Awards, honors:* Meritorious service medal, Commonwealth of Pennsylvania, 1939, for work on Pneumonia Commission of State Medical Society; LL.D., Hahnemann Medical College, 1948; Sc.D., Pennsylvania Military College, 1950; gold medal, American Geriatrics Society, 1959; gold medal, American Medical Writers' Association, 1961.

WRITINGS: A Diabetic Manual for Practitioners and Patients, F. A. Davis, 1936, 2nd edition, revised and enlarged, published as *Diabetes: Practical Suggestions for Doctor and Patient,* 1940, 3rd edition, revised, 1944; *Diabetes Control,* Lea & Febiger, 1951; *Creative Aging,* Macmillan, 1963. Contributor of articles on nutrition, geriatrics, and metabolism to medical journals. Assistant editor, *The Cyclopedia of Medicine and Surgery and Specialities.*

BIOGRAPHICAL/CRITICAL SOURCES: Washington Post, February 25, 1970.

(Died February 24, 1970)

* * *

BOSTON, Noel 1910-1966

PERSONAL: Born December 24, 1910, in Elmdon, Warwickshire, England; son of Bertram Llewellyn (a merchant) and Violet Caroline Phoebe (Round) Boston; married Mary Christine Moore, April 19, 1939; children: Jonathan Bertram, Anthea Caroline. *Education:* Jesus College, Cambridge, B.A., 1934, M.A., 1938. *Home:* Lamas Manor, Norfolk, England.

CAREER: Clergyman, Church of England; vicar of East Dereham, Norfolk, England, 1945-66, rural dean of Mitford, 1948-65, honorary canon of Norwich Cathedral, 1955-66, canon-residentiary of St. Edmundsbury Cathedral, Suffolk, 1965-66. Director, English Hymnal Co., 1955-66. Consultant to *Country Life. Military service:* British Army, major, Welfare Department, 1946. *Member:* Society of Antiquaries (fellow), Royal Archaeological Institute, Ancient Monuments Society (honorary fellow), London School of Music (honorary fellow), Rotary Club of Dereham (former president). *Awards, honors:* Knight of Honour, Grand priory of Europe of the Sovereign Order of St. John of Jerusalem; member of Memorial of Merit of Charles, King and Martyr; Chevalier of Order of the Cross of Stuart.

WRITINGS: The Monasteries of Warwickshire, Hudson, 1928; *History of Solihull,* Twigg, 1930; *History of Lillesh-*

all, Evans, 1933; (with Puddy) *Dereham: The Biography of a Country Town,* Coleby, 1952; *Yesterday Knocks,* Coleby, 1953; *Old Guns and Pistols,* Benn, 1958; *The Musical History of Norwich Cathedral,* Friends of Norwich Cathedral, 1963; (with Lyndesay Graham Langwill) *Church and Chamber Barrel-Organs: Their Origin, Makers, Music, and Location,* William Heinman, 1967, 2nd revised and enlarged edition, 1970. Author of television scripts for British Broadcasting Corp. and Anglia Television. Editor of *Norwich Diocesan Gazette,* 1945-60.

WORK IN PROGRESS: A history of hymn tunes up to 1860.

(Died, 1966)

* * *

BOTKIN, B(enjamin) A(lbert) 1901-

PERSONAL: Born February 7, 1901, in Boston, Mass.; son of Albert (a barber) and Annie (Dechinick) Botkin; married Gertrude Fritz, August 30, 1925; children: Dorothy Ann (Mrs. Jerome A. Rosenthal), Daniel Benjamin. *Education:* Harvard University, A.B. (magna cum laude), 1920; Columbia University, M.A., 1921; University of Nebraska, Ph.D., 1931. *Home and office:* 45 Lexington Dr., Croton-on-Hudson, N.Y. 10520. *Agent:* Curtis Brown Ltd., 575 Madison Ave., New York, N.Y. 10022.

CAREER: University of Oklahoma, Norman, instructor, 1921-31, assistant professor, 1931-38, associate professor of English, 1938-40; Federal Writers Project, Washington, D.C., national folklore editor, 1938-39; Library of Congress, Washington, D.C., chief editor of writers unit, Library of Congress Project, 1939-41, resident fellow in folklore, 1941-42, assistant in charge, later chief of Archive of American Folk Song (in Music Division), 1942-45; freelance writer and editor, 1945—. Visiting summer professor at University of Montana, 1932, at New Mexico Normal (now New Mexico Highlands) University, 1933. Consultant to committee on population problems, National Resources Committee, 1936; chairman of executive committee, Workshop for Cultural Democracy, 1956-58; committee member, National Folk Festival, 1934—.

MEMBER: American Folklore Society (fellow; president, 1944; delegate to American Council of Learned Societies, 1951-53), International Folk Music Council, Manuscript Society, Northeast Folklore Society, New York Folklore Society (honorary vice-president), Nebraska Folklore Society, Phi Beta Kappa. *Awards, honors:* Julius Rosenwald Foundation Fellow, 1937-38; honorary fellow in folklore, Library of Congress, 1942-55; Guggenheim Fellow, 1951; Litt.D., University of Nebraska, 1956; Centennial Medal of Civil War Round Table of New York, 1963; Louis M. Rabinowitz Foundation grant, 1965.

WRITINGS: The American Play-Party Song, with a Collection of Oklahoma Texts and Tunes, University of Nebraska Press, 1937, 2nd edition with new preface, Ungar, 1963.

Editor: (And contributor) *Folk-Say: A Regional Miscellany,* four volumes, University of Oklahoma Press, 1929-32; *The Southwest Scene: An Anthology of Regional Verse,* Economy Co., 1932; *A Treasury of American Folklore: Stories, Ballads, and Traditions of the People,* Crown, 1944 (published in England as *The American People, in Their Stories, Legends, Tall Tales, Traditions, Ballads, and Songs,* Pilot Press, 1946), selections re-issued as *The Sky's the Limit,* Louis Untermeyer, editor, Editions for the

Armed Forces, 1944, and reissued as *A Pocket Treasury of American Folklore*, Pocket Books, 1950; *Lay My Burden Down: A Folk History of Slavery*, University of Chicago Press, 1945; *A Treasury of New England Folklore: Stories, Ballads, and Traditions of the Yankee People*, Crown, 1947, revised edition published as *A Treasury of New England Folklore: Stories, Ballads, and Traditions of the Yankee Folk*, 1965; *A Treasury of Southern Folklore: Stories, Ballads, Traditions, and Folkways of the People of the South*, Crown, 1949; *A Treasury of Western Folklore*, Crown, 1951; (with Alvin F. Harlow) *A Treasury of Railroad Folklore: The Stories, Tall Tales, Traditions, Ballads and Songs of the American Railroad Man*, Crown, 1953; *Sidewalks of America: Folklore, Legends, Sagas, Traditions, Customs, Songs, Stories and Sayings of City Folk*, Bobbs-Merrill, 1954; *A Treasury of Mississippi River Folklore: Stories, Ballads, Traditions and Folkways of the Mid-American River Country*, Crown, 1955; *New York City Folklore: Legends, Tall Tales, Anecdotes, Stories, Sagas, Heroes and Characters, Customs, Traditions, and Sayings*, Random House, 1956; *A Treasury of American Anecdotes: Sly, Salty, Shaggy Stories of Heroes and Hellions, Beguilers and Buffoons, Spellbinders and Scapegoats, Gagsters and Gossips, from the Grassroots and Sidewalks of America*, Random House, 1957; (with Carl Withers) *The Illustrated Book of American Folklore: Stories, Legends, Tall Tales, Riddles, and Rhymes*, Grosset, 1958; *A Civil War Treasury of Tales, Legends and Folklore*, Random House, 1960.

Contributor: W. T. Couch, editor, *Folk and Folklore: Culture in the South*, University of North Carolina Press, 1934; Caroline F. Ware, editor, *The Cultural Approach to History*, Columbia University Press, 1940; *Round-up: A Nebraska Reader*, University of Nebraska Press, 1957; *Folklore in Action*, American Folklore Society, 1962; Jay Monaghan, editor, *A Sampler of Western Folklore and Songs*, Messner, 1963. Contributor of articles and introductions to other anthologies.

Editorial consultant: "Life Treasury of American Folklore," Time, Inc., 1961; (for book and two records) *The Folklore of the Badmen, the Badmen, Songs, Stories and Pictures of the Western Outlaws from Backhills to Border, 1865-1900*, Columbia Records, Inc., 1963. Consultant on games, *American College Dictionary*, 1963.

Editor, and author of notes for albums 7-10, "Folk Music of the United States from Records in the Archive of American Folk Song," Library of Congress, 1945.

Contributor to *Collier's Encyclopedia*, *Funk & Wagnalls Standard Dictionary of Folklore, Mythology and Legend*, *World Book Encyclopedia*. Contributor to *American Speech*, *Frontier*, *Negro Digest*, *Carleton Miscellany*, *New York Folklore Quarterly*, *Southwest Review*, *Trend*, *Vogue*, *Prairie Schooner*, and other journals and magazines. Contributing editor, *Southwest Review*, 1929-37, *New York Folklore Quarterly*, 1946— (columnist, 1950—); editor and publisher, *Space*, 1934-35; member of publication committee, *Westerners New York Posse Brand Book*, 1954-59.

WORK IN PROGRESS: Americans at Play: The Folklore and Folkways of Leisure in the United States; and *American Myths and Symbols in Social Thought and Action*.

BIOGRAPHICAL/CRITICAL SOURCES: New York Post, May 4, 1944; *Nebraska Alumnus*, March, 1964; Bruce Jackson, editor, *Folklore and Society: Essays in Honor of Benjamin A. Botkin*, Folklore Associates, 1966.

BOUCHER, Paul Edward 1893-

PERSONAL: First syllable of surname rhymes with "couch"; born February 2, 1893, in Bayard, Iowa; son of John Norman (a farmer) and Maggie (Sterrett) Boucher; married Edythe Bloom (a secretary), September 7, 1924; children: Stanley W., Wesley W., Gary W. *Education:* Attended Baker University, 1914-15; Colorado College, B.A., 1918; Dartmouth College, graduate study, 1919-20; Rice University, M.A., 1921, Ph.D., 1928. *Politics:* Republican. *Religion:* Protestant. *Home and office:* 1812 Pejin Ave., Colorado Springs, Colo. 80904.

CAREER: Colorado College, Colorado Springs, Colo., instructor, 1921-23, assistant professor of physics, 1923-24; Rice University, Houston, Tex., instructor in physics, 1924-25; Colorado College, associate professor, 1925-28, professor of physics, 1928-61, chairman of department, 1925-61, professor emeritus, 1961—. Conductor of European tours, 1961, 1963, world tour, 1964. *Military service:* U.S. Army, 1918-19. *Member:* American Association for the Advancement of Science (vice-president of Southwest division, 1953), American Association of Physics Teachers, Colorado-Wyoming Academy of Science (president, 1937-38), Pikes Peak Camera Club.

WRITINGS: Fundamentals of Photography, Van Nostrand, 1940, 4th edition, 1963. Contributor of articles to *American Annual of Photography* and to photography magazines.

WORK IN PROGRESS: Photography research in preparation for 5th edition of *Fundamentals of Photography*.

* * *

BOUDAT, Marie-Louise 1909-
(Louise Bellocq)

PERSONAL: Born January 20, 1909, in Charleville, Ardennes, France; daughter of Jean and Marguerite (Bellocq) Boudat. *Education:* Attended Lycee de Pau. *Religion:* Catholic. *Home:* 17, rue Galos, Pau Basses-Pyrenees, France.

CAREER: Writer. *Awards, honors:* Prix Femina, 1960, for *La Porte retombee*.

WRITINGS—All under pseudonym Louise Bellocq: *Le Passager de la belle aventure*, Editions Gautier-Langueriau, 1952; *La Ferme de l'ermitage* (novel), Gallimard, 1955; *La Porte retombee*, Gallimard, 1960, translation by Anne Carter published as *Fled Is That Music*, Sidgwick & Jackson, 1962; *Contes de mes betes au vent*, Casterman, 1963; *Mesdames Minnigan*, Gallimard, 1963; *Contes de mes betes sous la lune*, Casterman, 1964; *Contes de mes betes a l'aventure*, Casterman, 1968.

* * *

BOURKE-WHITE, Margaret 1904-1971

PERSONAL: Born June 14, 1904, in New York, N.Y.; daughter of Joseph (an engineer and inventor) and Minnie Elizabeth (Bourke) White; married Everett Chapman, 1923 (divorced, 1925); married Erskine Caldwell (an author), 1939 (divorced, 1942). *Education:* Studied at Columbia University, 1922-23, University of Michigan, 1923-25; Cornell University, B.A., 1927; other study at Purdue University, Rutgers University, and Western Reserve University (now Case Western Reserve University). *Home:* Point of Woods Rd., Darien, Conn. 06820.

CAREER: Planned to be a biologist, but became interested

in photography while a student and began a professional career as an architectural photographer in Cleveland, Ohio, 1927; experimental photographs she took in Ohio steel mills at night attracted wide attention (published as *The Story of Steel*) and resulted in job as first staff photographer for *Fortune*, 1929-35; joined *Life* in its planning stage, 1935, took the first cover picture and was a staff photographer, 1935-69, working in thirty-two countries, making three trips to Russia in the early 1930's, and spending long periods in India, 1946-48, South Africa, 1950, Japan, 1952. Accredited to U.S. Air Force as correspondent, 1942 (first woman war photographer), covering Britain and then the invasion of North Africa, 1942-43; correspondent with U.S. Fifth Army in Italy, 1943-45, with General Patton in Germany, 1945; United Nations correspondent in Korea, 1952. Photographs included in permanent collections of Library of Congress, Museum of Modern Art, Cleveland Museum of Art, and Brooklyn Museum; industrial photomurals widely used in business buildings, including Rockefeller Center, New York.

MEMBER: American Society of Magazine Photographers, Society of Women Geographers, National League of American Pen Women, Overseas Press Club, Theta Sigma Phi. *Awards, honors:* Litt. D., Rutgers University, 1948; D.F.A., University of Michigan, 1951; American Women of Achievement award, 1951; American Society of Magazine Photographers award, 1951, honor roll, 1964; Photographic Society of America and Nikon awards for fostering international understanding through photography, both 1960; U.S. Camera Achievement award, 1963; National Association of Independent Schools award for one of ten best adult books for the pre-college reader, 1964, for *Portrait of Myself*; U.S. Camera Achievement award, 1965.

WRITINGS: Eyes on Russia, Simon & Schuster, 1931, reprinted, AMS Press, 1968; (text by Erskine Caldwell) *You Have Seen Their Faces*, Viking, 1937; (text by Erskine Caldwell) *North of the Danube*, Viking, 1939; (text by Erskine Caldwell) *Say! Is This the U.S.A.?*, Duell, Sloan & Pearce, 1941; *Shooting the Russian War*, Simon & Schuster, 1941; *They Called It Purple Heart Valley*, Simon & Schuster, 1944, reissued as *Purple Heart Valley*, 1945; *"Dear Fatherland, Rest Quietly,"* Simon & Schuster, 1946; *Halfway to Freedom*, Simon & Schuster, 1949; *Interview With India*, Phoenix, 1950; (with John LaFarge) *A Report on the American Jesuits*, Farrar, Straus & Cudahy, 1956; *Portrait of Myself*, Simon & Schuster, 1963.

BIOGRAPHICAL/CRITICAL SOURCES: Portrait of Myself, Simon & Schuster, 1963; *Saturday Review*, June 29, 1963; *New York Herald Tribune Books*, June 30, 1963; *Christian Science Monitor*, July 3, 1963; *New York Times Book Review*, July 7, 1963; *Atlantic*, August, 1963; *America*, August 17, 1963; *Virginia Quarterly Review*, winter, 1964; *New York Times*, August 28, 1971; *Washington Post*, August 28, 1971; *Time*, September 6, 1971; *Life*, September 10, 1971.

(Died August 27, 1971)

* * *

BOUSCAREN, T(imothy) Lincoln 1884-

PERSONAL: Born August 17, 1884, in Cincinnati, Ohio; son of L. F. Gustave (an engineer) and Helen S. (Lincoln) Bouscaren. *Education:* St. Xavier's College, Cincinnati, Ohio, B.A., 1902; Yale University, B.A., 1906; University of Cincinnati, LL.B., 1909; St. Louis University, M.A., 1921; Gregorian University, S.T.D., 1928. *Home and of-*

fice: St. Xavier High School, 600 North Bend Rd., Cincinnati, Ohio 45224.

CAREER: Practicing lawyer, 1909-13, and assistant U.S. attorney for Eastern District of Oklahoma, 1911-13. Entered Roman Catholic order, Society of Jesus (Jesuits), 1916, ordained priest, 1925; teacher of canon law at Mundelein Seminary, Mundelein, Ill., 1931-38, at Gregorian University, Rome, Italy, 1938-41, at West Baden College, West Baden, Ind., 1941-47; procurator-general (attorney general) of Society of Jesus, 1947-62. *Member:* Canon Law Society of America (retired, 1967).

WRITINGS: (Translator) Arthur Vermeersch, *What is Marriage?*, America Press, 1932; *Ethics of Ectopic Operations*, Loyola University Press, 1933, revised edition, Bruce, 1944; (compiler) *Canon Law Digest*, six volumes (Volumes IV, V, and VI with James I. O'Connor), Bruce, 1934-69, annual supplements, 1935-66; (translator) Guido Gonella, *World to Reconstruct: Pius XII on Peace and Reconstruction*, Bruce, 1944; (with Adam C. Ellis) *Canon Law: A Text and Commentary*, Bruce, 1946, 4th edition (with Francis N. Korth), 1963, 4th edition revised, 1966; *Reserved Cases: Pocket Outlines for Confessors* (text taken from *Canon Law*), Bruce, c.1946; (with O'Connor) *Canon Law Digest for Religious*, Bruce, 1965.

WORK IN PROGRESS: Collaborating with Francis N. Korth on a revision of *Canon Law* (work suspended during official revision of Code in Rome).

AVOCATIONAL INTERESTS: Gardening (dirt-farming) and bird-watching.

* * *

BOWIE, Robert R(ichardson) 1909-

PERSONAL: Born August 24, 1909, in Baltimore, Md.; son of Clarence Keating and Helen (Richardson) Bowie; married Theodosia Chapman, April 15, 1944; children: Robert Richardson, Jr., William Chapman. *Education:* Princeton University, A.B., 1931; Harvard University, L.L.B., 1934. *Politics:* Independent. *Religion:* Baptist. *Home:* 170 Coolidge Hill, Cambridge, Mass. 02138. *Office:* 6 Divinity Ave., Cambridge, Mass. 02138.

CAREER: Admitted to Maryland Bar, 1934; Bowie & Burke (law firm), Baltimore, Md., partner, 1934-42; Harvard Law School, Cambridge, Mass., professor, 1946-55; U.S. High Commissioner for Germany (Bonn), general counsel, 1950-51; Policy Planning Staff, State Department, Washington, D.C., director, 1953-57; Assistant Secretary of State for policy planning, Washington, D.C., 1955-57; Harvard University, Cambridge, Mass., Dillon Professor of International Affairs, and director of Center of International Affairs, 1957—. State Department, Washington, D.C., counselor, 1966-68. Reporter, Maryland Committee on Civil Procedure, 1939-41; assistant director, Maryland Legislative Council, 1940-41; assistant attorney general, Maryland, 1941-42. *Military service:* U.S. Army, 1942-46; special assistant to deputy military governor for Germany, 1945-46; became lieutenant colonel; awarded Legion of Merit with oak-leaf cluster.

MEMBER: Council on Foreign Relations, American Academy of Arts and Sciences, Academy of Political Science, American Bar Association, American Society of International Law, Atlantic Council of the United States, Century Club, Shop Club, Wranglers, Harvard Club (New York), Tower Club (Princeton).

WRITINGS: (Editor and author, with C. J. Friedrich)

Studies in Federalism, Little, Brown, 1954; (editor with Eugene V. Rostow and Robert H. Bork) *Government Regulation of Business: Cases from the National Reporter System*, Foundation Press, 1955, supplement, 1955; (with Z. K. Brzezinski) *Ideology and Foreign Affairs*, U.S. Government Printing Office, 1960; (contributor) Don K. Price, editor, *The Secretary of State*, Prentice-Hall, 1960; (with Theodore Geiger) *The European Economic Community and the United States*, U.S. Government Printing Office, 1961; (contributor) Louis Henkin, editor, *Arms Control*, Prentice-Hall, 1961; *Communist China, 1955-1959: Policy Documents with Analysis*, Harvard University Press, 1962; (with James Bryant Conant and Eli Whitney Debevoise) *The Issues in the Berlin-German Crisis*, Association of the Bar of the City of New York, 1962; (contributor) F. O. Wilcox and H. F. Haviland, editors, *The Atlantic Community: Progress and Prospects*, Praeger, 1963; (with Stanley Hoffman and others) *A la recherche de la France* (originally written in English but published in French), Editions du Seuil, 1963; *The First Five Years, 1958-63*, Center for International Affairs, Harvard University, 1963; *Shaping the Future: Foreign Policy in an Age of Transition*, Columbia University Press, 1964. Also author of monographs on legal subjects.

*   *   *

BOWLES, Gordon Townsend 1904-

PERSONAL: Born June 25, 1904, in Tokyo, Japan; son of Gilbert (a missionary) and Minnie (Pickett) Bowles; married Jane Thomas, February 6, 1932; children: Anne, Barbara Swann. *Education:* Earlham College, A.B., 1925; Harvard University, Ph.D., 1935. *Religion:* Society of Friends. *Home:* 128 Dorset Rd., Syracuse, N.Y. 13210. *Office:* Department of Anthropology, Syracuse University, Syracuse, N.Y. 13210.

CAREER: Harvard University, Division of Anthropology, Cambridge, Mass., research associate, 1935-38; University of Hawaii, Honolulu, assistant professor of anthropology, 1938-42; with U.S. Foreign Economic Administration, Washington, D.C., 1942-44; with U.S. Department of State, Washington, D.C., 1944-47; with Associated Research Councils, Conference Board, Washington, D.C., 1947-51; University of Tokyo, Tokyo, Japan, visiting professor, 1951-58; Columbia University, New York, N.Y., visiting professor, 1959-60; Syracuse University, Syracuse, N.Y., professor of anthropology, 1961—. Field researcher in West China and East Tibet, 1930-32, and in Himalayas and North Burma, 1935-37. *Member:* American Anthropological Association (fellow), American Association of Physical Anthropologists, Association for Asian Studies, Asiatic Society of Japan, Sigma Chi.

WRITINGS: New Types of Old White Americans (at Harvard and Eastern Women's Colleges), Harvard University Press, 1932; (editor with Earl Wendel Count) *Fact and Theory in Social Science*, Syracuse University Press, 1964.

WORK IN PROGRESS: Completion of a book on the peoples of Asia in a five-volume series, "The Peoples of the World"; comparative racial studies of Central and East Asia; biosocial, microevolutionary studies of isolated communities; other studies on assortive mating patterns in mountain villages and on pastoral nomadic communities of the Tibetan area.

SIDELIGHTS: Bowles lived in Japan for twenty-five years, and in India, Burma, and China a total of four years.

BOWMAN, Henry A(delbert) 1903-

PERSONAL: Born July 19, 1903, in Cleveland, Ohio; son of Harry A. and Anna (Westerweller) Bowman; married Edna Charlotte Kalt, 1930 (died, 1964); married Lucille Bodine Baer, 1966; children: (first marriage) Charles. *Education:* Western Reserve University (now Case Western Reserve University), A.B., 1927, M.A., 1929; Yale University, Ph.D., 1931. *Address:* Route 1, Box 210, Colorado City, Tex. 79512.

CAREER: Stephens College, Columbia, Mo., professor of sociology, 1931-34, professor of marriage education, 1934-55, chairman of Division of Home and Family Living, 1942-45; University of Texas, Austin, associate professor, 1955-59, professor of sociology, 1959-69, professor emeritus, 1969—. *Member:* National Council of Family Relations (president, 1958-59), American Association of Marriage and Family Counselors (fellow), American Sociological Association (fellow), American Social Health Association (honorary life member), Phi Beta Kappa.

WRITINGS: Marriage for Moderns, McGraw, 1942, 7th edition, 1974; *A Christian Interpretation of Marriage*, Westminster, 1959. Contributor to professional and popular periodicals.

AVOCATIONAL INTERESTS: Gardening, photography.

*   *   *

BOYD, Martin a Beckett 1893-

PERSONAL: Born June 10, 1893, in Lucerne, Switzerland; son of Arthur Merric (an artist) and Emma (a Beckett) Boyd. *Education:* Attended St. John's College, Victoria, Australia. *Religion:* Anglican. *Residence:* Rome, Italy. *Address:* c/o Australia and New Zealand Bank, 71 Cornhill, London E.C.3, England. *Agent:* Curtis Brown Ltd., 13 King St., Covent Garden, London W.C.2, England.

CAREER: Trained as an architect, but began to write in 1925. Also painter, with one-man exhibit of work in Cambridge, England, 1964. *Military service:* Royal Flying Corps, pilot, World War I; became lieutenant. *Awards, honors:* Australian Literary Society Gold Medal for *The Montforts*, 1928, and *A Difficult Young Man*, 1956.

WRITINGS—All novels, except as indicated: *The Montforts*, Constable, 1928, revised edition [Adelaide], 1963; *Scandal of Spring*, Dent, 1934; *Lemon Farm*, Dent, 1935; *The Picnic*, Dent, 1936; *The Painted Princess*, Constable, 1936; *Night of the Party*, Dent, 1937; *A Single Flame* (autobiography), Dent, 1939; *Nuns in Jeopardy*, Dent, 1940; *Lucinda Brayford*, Cresset, 1946; *Such Pleasure*, Cresset, 1948.

Cardboard Crown, Cresset, 1952, revised edition, Penguin Books, 1964; *A Difficult Young Man*, Cresset, 1955; *Outbreak of Love*, J. Murray, 1957; *Much Else in Italy* (travel), Macmillan, 1958; *When Blackbirds Sing*, Abelard, 1962; *Day of My Delight: An Anglo-American Memoir*, Newnes, 1966; *The Tea-Time of Love: The Clarification of Miss Stilby*, Bles, 1969. Reviewer for *Times Literary Supplement*, 1931-40.

*   *   *

BOYLAN, Lucile 1906-

PERSONAL: Surname accented on first syllable; born August 26, 1906, in Akron, Ohio; daughter of Thomas Joseph (an office manager) and Kathryn (Masterson) Boylan. *Education:* University of Akron, B.E., 1928, M.E., 1943. *Residence:* Akron, Ohio.

CAREER: Akron (Ohio) public schools, teacher, 1928-70; retired, 1970. Volunteer teacher of American idiom to foreign physicians in an Akron hospital. Member: National Council of Teachers of English, National Retired Teachers Association, American Association of Retired Persons, Ohio Retired Teachers Association, Summit County Retired Teachers Association. Awards, honors: Martha Holden Jennings Scholar; Teacher's Writing Competition prize, National Education Association/Reader's Digest Foundation, 1970.

WRITINGS: (With Robert Sattler) A Catalog of Paperbacks for Grades 7 to 12, Scarecrow, 1963.

* * *

BOYLE, (Emily) Joyce 1901-

PERSONAL: Born April 6, 1901, in Toronto, Ontario, Canada; daughter of William Cather and Charlotte (Fensom) Boyle. Education: University of Toronto, B.A., 1924, B. Paed., 1932, D. Paed., 1933. Religion: Theistic Unitarian. Home: 6 Crofton Rd., Toronto, Canada.

CAREER: Primary and kindergarten teacher in suburban schools, Toronto, Ontario, 1926-63, now retired. Lecturer at teachers' summer schools in Saint John, 1938-39, Montreal, 1944, 1946, 1948, and Ottawa, 1945. Writer of children's books. Member: Federation of Women Teachers' Associations of Ontario (honorary member).

WRITINGS: Timothy's Twelve Months, Abingdon, 1952; Muskoka Holiday, Macmillan (Canada), 1953; Susan's Special Summer, Abingdon, 1954; Try Again Tommy, Abingdon, 1956; Stone Cottage Mystery, Macmillan (Canada), 1958; Bobby's Neighbors, Abingdon, 1959; Adventuring with David, Abingdon, 1961. Contributor to Canadian textbooks, to School (magazine), and to Toronto Globe and Mail. Editorial consultant, "Canadians All" series, Dent.

WORK IN PROGRESS: Research in field of children's literature.

BIOGRAPHICAL/CRITICAL SOURCES: Educational Courier, January-February, 1964.

* * *

BOYLE, Sarah Patton 1906-

PERSONAL: Born May 9, 1906, in Albemarle County, Va.; daughter of Robert Williams (an Episcopal clergyman) and Jane (Stringfellow) Patton; married E. Roger Boyle (an associate professor of speech and drama at University of Virginia), December 26, 1932; children: E. Roger III, Patton Lindsay. Politics: Democrat. Religion: Episcopalian. Home and office: 1134 South Wakefield St., Apt. 2, Arlington, Va. 22204.

CAREER: Former portrait painter; writer and lecturer as southern defender of integration, 1950—. Charter member and vice-president, Virginia Council of Human Relations, 1955; sponsor, Virginia Pilgrimage of Prayer for Public Schools, 1959; member of advisory committee on intergroup relations, National Council of the Protestant Episcopal Church, 1960-62; member of Virginia advisory committee, U.S. Commission on Civil Rights, 1963-66.

MEMBER: Authors Guild, National Association for the Advancement of Colored People (life member; Charlottesville board, 1955), Congress of Racial Equality, Council of Social Action (Charlottesville; president, 1954). Awards, honors—For work on behalf of integration: Named Woman of the Year in Human Relations, National Council of Negro Women, 1956; Russwurm Award of Newspaper Publishers Association, 1958; citation from National Association for the Advancement of Colored People and Special Merit Award from Southern Christian Leadership Conference, 1963; ten other citations and awards, 1956-64.

WRITINGS: The Desegregated Heart: A Virginianian's Stand in Time of Transition, Morrow, 1963; For Human Beings Only, Seabury, 1964. Contributor of more than two hundred articles on integration to magazines and newspapers, including Saturday Evening Post, Nation, and Ebony. Weekly columnist, "From Behind the Curtain," in Charlottesville Tribune (Negro newspaper), 1951-53.

WORK IN PROGRESS: A pamphlet for Public Affairs on why integrationists and segregationists have no meeting of minds.

SIDELIGHTS: A Southerner of traditional background, Mrs. Boyle took part in stand-in demonstrations in Charlottesville, Va., and in St. Augustine, Fla., where she was arrested and jailed for three days. She was one of the authorities interviewed on the American Broadcasting Co. special television series, "The Crucial Summer," 1963. The Desegregated Heart was dramatized on CBS News' "Look up and Live," with Mrs. Boyle as narrator, June, 1965.

* * *

BRABSON, George Dana 1900-

PERSONAL: Born August 7, 1900, in Greeneville, Tenn.; son of John M. and Maria Julia (Harmon) Brabson; married Evelyn R. Bristol (a teacher), August 13, 1930; children: G. Dana, Jr., Bennet B., Margaret M., John M. III. Education: University of Tennessee, B.A., 1916; Yale University, LL.B., 1918; George Washington University, M.A., 1930. Politics: Conservative. Religion: Protestant. Home: 303 Bittersweet Dr., Findlay, Ohio 45840.

CAREER: District of Columbia, special assistant attorney general, 1924-26; U.S. Internal Revenue Service, Washington, D.C., trial attorney, 1930-36; Blair and Korner (law firm), Washington, D.C., member, 1936-41; Marathon Oil Co., Findlay, Ohio, general tax attorney, 1943-63; Ohio Northern University, Ada, professor of law, beginning, 1962. President, Dominion Properties, Inc. Member: American Bar Association (past secretary of tax section; past chairman of state and local tax committee), Law Teachers Association, Symposium Association (president), Inquirendo Society, Ohio Oil and Gas Association (chairman of taxation committee), Phi Kappa Phi, Phi Gamma Delta, Hancock County Historical Association (president).

WRITINGS: Little Tailor from Greeneville, Rosselot, 1960; Federal Taxation: Basic Principles and Procedures, Rosselot, 1965; Tax Planning—Estates, Trusts, Partnerships, Ohio Northern University Press, 1965. Contributor of articles, reviews, and legal and literary notes to journals.

WORK IN PROGRESS: Basic Principles of American Jurisprudence: The Socio-Economic Influences; research on effects of narcotics and nicotines in motor vehicle accidents.

* * *

BRACHER, Marjory (Louise) 1906-

PERSONAL: First syllable of surname rhymes with "frock"; born January 6, 1906, in Connersville, Ind.;

daughter of J. Edgar (a farmer) and Grace (Hill) Scholl; married Edwin W. Bracher (a clergyman), May 6, 1931; children: Peter S., Alice E. (Mrs. Ronald N. Smith). *Education:* Wittenberg University, B.A., 1928. *Religion:* The Lutheran Church in America. *Home:* 2770 83rd St., N.W., Seattle, Wash. 98117.

CAREER: High school teacher of history in Casstown, Ohio, 1928-29; parish worker in Buffalo, N.Y., 1929-30; free-lance writer. Former member of Board of Parish Education, The Lutheran Church in America; delegate to Third Assembly, World Council of Churches, 1961; former member of board of directors, Lutheran Family and Child Service.

WRITINGS: Love Is No Luxury: A Guide to Christian Family Living, Muhlenberg Press, 1951, 2nd revised edition, Fortress, 1968; (with Josie Robbins) *Puppets and Bible Plays*, Muhlenberg Press, 1951; *Church School Prayers*, Muhlenberg Press, 1956; *Family Prayers*, Muhlenberg Press, 1962; *Love, Sex, and Life*, Lutheran Church, 1964; *Anchor of Hope*, Fortress, 1964; *SRO: Overpopulation and You*, Fortress, 1966. Writer of religious education curriculum materials, and of programs and manuals for women's organizations. Contributor of stories and articles to church magazines.

AVOCATIONAL INTERESTS: Oriental art and cultures.

*   *   *

BRADBURY, John M(ason) 1908-1969

PERSONAL: Born August 10, 1908, in Louisville, Ky.; son of William F. Bradbury; married Anne Glenn, August 16, 1939. *Education:* Princeton University, B.A., 1930; Northwestern University, M.A., 1939; University of Iowa, Ph.D., 1949. *Politics:* Liberal *Home:* 213 Green St., Schenectady, N.Y. 12305. *Office:* Union College, Schenectady, N.Y. 12308.

CAREER: University of Iowa, Iowa City, instructor in art and English, 1947-50; University of Louisville, Louisville, Ky., assistant professor of English, 1950-51; Union College, Schenectady, N.Y., assistant professor, 1951-52, associate professor, 1952-56, professor of English and humanities, 1956-69. Fulbright lecturer, University of Istanbul, 1964-65; member of advisory board, Albany (N.Y.) Institute of History and Art, 1958-69; secretary of board of trustees, Schenectady Museum, 1960-64. *Military service:* U.S. Army, 1945-46; served in European Theater. *Member:* Modern Language Association of America, American Association of University Professors, Phi Beta Kappa.

WRITINGS: The Fugitives: A Critical Account, University of North Carolina Press, 1958; *The Southern Renaissance*, University of North Carolina Press, 1963; (contributor) John L. Longley, Jr., editor, *Robert Penn Warren*, New York University Press, 1965. Contributor to *Sewanee Review, Western Review, Poetry, Accent*, and *American Literature*.

(Died May 12, 1969)

*   *   *

BRADE-BIRKS, S(tanley) Graham 1887-

PERSONAL: Born November 2, 1887, in Burnage, Manchester, England; son of Brooklyn (a merchant) and Anne Bates (Swan) Birks; married Hilda Kathleen Brade (a registered medical practitioner, now retired); children: Mary Kathleen, Elizabeth Ann (Mrs. Trevor Joyce). *Education:*

University of Manchester, B.Sc. (honors), 1911, M.Sc., 1914; University of London, D.Sc., 1924. *Home and office:* The Vicarage, Godmersham, Canterbury, Kent, England.

CAREER: Priest of the Church of England, 1915—. Wye College, University of London, Kent, England, lecturer on zoology and geology, 1919-46; proctor in Convocation, 1951-70, now parish priest and rural dean, Godmersham, Canterbury, England. Honorary canon of Canterbury Cathedral. *Member:* Society of Antiquaries of London (fellow), Zoological Society of London (scientific fellow), Linnean Society of London (honorary fellow). *Awards, honors:* Fellow of Wye College, University of London.

WRITINGS: Good Soil, English Universities Press, 1944; *Teach Yourself Archaeology*, English Universities Press, 1954, Roy, 1955; (editor) *Teach Yourself Concise Encyclopedia of General Knowledge*, English Universities Press, 1956, 3rd edition, 1963.

WORK IN PROGRESS: A book on the soil; a manuscript on Jane Austen and the Kentish scene; a short history of Wye, Kent, completion expected in 1975.

AVOCATIONAL INTERESTS: Archaeology and local history, particularly in Kent.

*   *   *

BRADLEY, Kenneth (Granville) 1904-

PERSONAL: Born January 5, 1904, in Dehra Dun, India; son of Hugh Vachell (with Indian Army) and Norah (Foster) Bradley; married Emily Guyon Rea (an American), August 2, 1926 (deceased, 1972); children: Martin, Julian. *Education:* University College, Oxford, B.A. (honors), 1925. *Home:* 10 Benson Pl., Norham Rd., Oxford, England.

CAREER: British Colonial Administrative Service, serving as district officer, then information officer in Northern Rhodesia, 1926-42, colonial and financial secretary for Falkland Islands, 1942-46; under-secretary for Gold Coast (now Ghana), 1946-48; *Corona* (journal of British Colonial Service), London, England, editor, 1948-52; Commonwealth Institute, London, England, director, 1952-69, studying, writing and lecturing on Commonwealth affairs. Chairman, League for the Exchange of Commonwealth Teachers, 1963-74. *Member:* Royal African Society (vice-president), Royal Commonwealth Society (fellow). *Awards, honors:* Companion of Order of St. Michael and St. George, 1946; Knight Bachelor, 1963.

WRITINGS: Africa Notwithstanding, Dickson, 1929; *Hawks Alighting*, Dickson, 1932; *Lusaka*, J. Cape, 1936; *The Story of Northern Rhodesia*, Northern Rhodesia Government, 1938, Longmans, Green, 1941; *Native Courts and Authorities in Northern Rhodesia*, Northern Rhodesia Government, 1938; *Diary of a District Officer*, Harrap, 1942, 4th edition, Macmillan (London), 1966; *The Colonial Service as a Career*, H.M.S.O., 1950; *Copper Venture*, Mufulira Copper Mines, 1952; *Britain's Purpose in Africa*, H.M.S.O., 1955; (editor) *The Living Commonwealth*, Hutchinson, 1961; *Once a District Officer*, St. Martin's, 1966.

WORK IN PROGRESS: What Next?, an autobiographical book.

SIDELIGHTS: Bradley told *CA:* "My interests are all bound up with the Commonwealth and I have served in or visited almost every Commonwealth country and British dependency. Also traveled in U.S.A. . . ."

BRADLOW, Edna Rom

PERSONAL: Married Frank R. Bradlow (a furniture company director and author), November 14, 1945; children: Diana Penelope, Anthony, Hugh Simon. Education: University of Cape Town, B.A., 1943, B.A. in history (honors), 1962, M.A., 1966. Home: Sha-anan, Shetland St., Rondebosch, Cape Town, South Africa.

CAREER: Free-lance journalist and writer. Lecturer in history.

WRITINGS: (With husband, Frank Bradlow) Thomas Bowler of the Cape of Good Hope (biography), A Balkema, 1955, reissued as Thomas Bowler: His Life and Work, with a foreword by William Fehr, 1967; (with F. Bradlow) Here Comes the Alabama: The Career of a Confederate Raider, A. Balkema, 1958; (with J. J. Redgrave) Frederick I'Ons, Artist (biography), Maskew Miller, 1959. Regular contributor of articles and reviews to Cape Times; contributor to Archives Yearbook for South African History.

WORK IN PROGRESS: Research for doctoral thesis, "Immigration into South Africa since Union."

SIDELIGHTS: Mrs. Bradlow and her husband wrote their book about a Confederate raider before visiting the United States, learning Civil War history vicariously in South Africa; they have visited the Eastern Seaboard since its publication.

* * *

BRADLOW, Frank R(osslyn) 1913-

PERSONAL: Born June 19, 1913, in Johannesburg, South Africa; son of David Adolf (a company director) and Anne (Greenberg) Bradlow; married Edna Rom (a professional writer), November 14, 1945; children: Diana Penelope, Anthony, Hugh Simon. Education: University of Witwatersrand, B.Com., 1933. Religion: Jewish. Home: Sha-anan, Shetland St., Rondebosch, Cape Town, South Africa. Office: Bradlow's Stores Ltd., 69 Plein St., Cape Town, South Africa.

CAREER: Bradlow's Stores Ltd. (furniture chain), Cape Town, South Africa, regional director, 1934—. South African Library, trustee. Military service: Imperial Light Horse, South African Infantry, 1939-45; wounded at El Alamein. Member: Friends of South African Library (chairman, 1963—), Cape Town P.E.N. Centre (chairman, 1961—), Chartered Institute of Secretaries, Rotary Club, Civil Service Club.

WRITINGS: (With wife, Edna Bradlow) Thomas Bowler of the Cape of Good Hope (biography), A. Balkema, 1955, reissued as Thomas Bowler: His Life and Work, with a foreword by William Fehr, 1967; (with E. Bradlow) Here Comes the Alabama: The Career of a Confederate Raider, A. Balkema, 1958; Baron von Ludwig and the Ludwig's-burg Garden, A. Balkema, 1965; Thomas Bowler in Mauritius, A. Balkema, 1970.

Contributor: A. Honikman, editor, City of Good Hope, Howard Timmins, 1966; (author of commentary) Thomas Bowler, Pictorial Album of Cape Town, C. Struik, 1966; (author of introduction) Bowler's Four Views of Cape Town, A. Balkema, 1966; (author of biographical and general introduction) Christian I. Latrobe, Journal of a Visit to South Africa in 1815-1816, C. Struik, 1969. Contributor to Africana Notes and News Quarterly Bulletin of the South African Library, Connoisseur, and various newspapers.

WORK IN PROGRESS: Thomas Baines: His Art and Work.

AVOCATIONAL INTERESTS: Troutfishing, Africana book-collecting.

* * *

BRAGG, Arthur N(orris) 1897-

PERSONAL: Born December 18, 1897, in Pittsfield, Me.; son of Nathan M. (a farmer) and Emma (Cates) Bragg; married Mary G. Keirstead, December 24, 1924; children: Betty Lee (Mrs. M. L. James, Jr.), William N., Marita Jean (Mrs. P. M. Lowell, Jr.). Education: Bates College, B.Sc., 1924; Johns Hopkins University, graduate student, 1924-25; Boston University, M.A., 1934; University of Oklahoma, Ph.D., 1937. Politics: Independent. Religion: Protestant. Home: 108 West Symmes, Norman, Okla. 73069.

CAREER: Marquette University, Milwaukee, Wis., assistant professor of zoology, 1925-33; University of Oklahoma, Norman, instructor, 1934-42, assistant professor, 1942-46, associate professor, 1946-53, professor of zoology, beginning, 1953. Member: American Society of Zoologists, American Society of Ichthyologists and Herpetologists, Herpetologists League, Southwest Association of Naturalists, Oklahoma Academy of Science, Sigma Xi, Phi Sigma.

WRITINGS: Gnomes of the Night: The Spadefoot Toads, University of Pennsylvania Press, 1965. Contributor of more than two hundred articles and reviews of scientific books to journals. Abstractor, Biological Abstracts.

WORK IN PROGRESS: Further writing on natural history.

SIDELIGHTS: Bragg has some reading knowledge of French, German and Spanish.

* * *

BRAMER, Jennie (Perkins) 1900-
(Faith Perkins)

PERSONAL: Born October 16, 1900, in Grangeville, Idaho; daughter of Silas (a minister) and Jose (Long) Perkins; married Rudolf H. Bramer (divorced); children: William Rudolf, Baird Louis. Education: University of Oregon, A.B., 1921. Politics: Democrat. Religion: Unitarian. Home: 2140 Taylor, San Francisco, Calif. 94133.

CAREER: Reporter on newspaper in Coos Bay, Ore., 1921-22, and staff member and conductor of "Lonely Hearts" column on San Francisco Call-Bulletin, San Francisco, Calif., 1954-55; advertising writer in New York, N.Y., 1927-32, and San Francisco, Calif., 1934-37; now free-lance writer. Lecturer, San Francisco adult education classes, 1956-58.

WRITINGS—Under name Faith Perkins: Meet More People—Have More Fun, Putnman, 1957; My Fight with Arthritis, Random, 1964. Scriptwriter and conductor of radio show, "Your Child and Mine."

WORK IN PROGRESS: A novel about health resorts in this country and Mexico.

BRANNON, William T.   1906-
(H. W. Barrington, Lawrence Gardner, Jack Hamilton, Peter Hermanns, Randy Lebert, Dwight McGlinn, Peter Oberholtzer, S. T. Peters, William Tibbetts)

PERSONAL: Born March 3, 1906, in Meridian, Miss.; son of Lorena Ezra and Mae (Holliday) Brannon; married Betty Lebert, 1930. *Education:* Northwestern University, student, 1930-33. *Residence:* Chicago, Ill. *Agent:* Anita Diamant, 51 East 42nd St., New York, N.Y. 10017; Mauri Grashin Agency, 8730 Sunset Blvd., Los Angeles, Calif. 90069. *Office:* Box 10901, St. Petersburg, Fla. 33733.

CAREER: St. Petersburg Times, St. Petersburg, Fla., reporter, 1925-28, columnist, 1929-30; *Tourist News,* St. Petersburg, Fla., staff writer, 1925-28, editor, 1929-30; *Real America,* Chicago, Ill., editor, 1933-36; free-lance fiction, nonfiction, and feature writer, mainly on crime subjects. *Member:* Overseas Press Club of America, Mystery Writers of America (regional vice-president, 1946, 1950; director, 1946-60; regional treasurer, 1958-65), Intercontinental Biographical Association (fellow), National Historical Society (founding member), American Security Council (member of national advisory board), Smithsonian Associates. *Awards, honors:* Edgar Allan Poe Award of Mystery Writers of America for outstanding crime writing, 1950 and 1951.

WRITINGS: (With J. R. Weil) *Yellow Kid Weil,* Ziff-Davis Publishing, 1948, abridged edition published as *Con Man,* Pyramid Books, 1957; *The Lady Killers,* Quinn Publishing, 1951; *The Crooked Cops,* Regency, 1962.

Stories anthologized in *Four and Twenty Bloodhounds,* edited by Anthony Boucher, Simon & Schuster, 1955; *Men of the Underworld,* edited by Charles Hamilton, Macmillan, 1959; *Quality of Murder,* edited by Boucher, Dutton, 1963; *Masters of Mayhem,* edited by E. D. Radin, Morrow, 1965; *Scoundrels and Scalawags,* edited by Reader's Digest, Funk, 1967; *Fine Art of Robbery,* edited by W. B. Gibson, Grosset, 1967; *Fine Art of Swindling,* edited by Gibson, Grosset, 1967.

Writer of six stories for "Maverick" television series.

Contributor of more than 5,000 stories and articles to magazines and newspapers in America and abroad, including *Coronet, Reader's Digest, Omnibook, American Weekly, Saga, Ellery Queen's Mystery Magazine, True Police Cases, Evening Standard* (London). Staff writer, with assigned territory in middle west and southern states, for *Official Detective, True Detective, Master Detective;* writer of weekly true mystery for King Features Syndicate.

WORK IN PROGRESS: It's Dangerous to Be a Woman; Journal of a Redneck.

SIDELIGHTS: Brannon keeps up his magazine output under a number of pseudonyms by maintaining offices in both Chicago and St. Petersburg, with research and photography assistants.

*   *   *

BRATTON, Fred Gladstone   1896-19?
PERSONAL: Born March 17, 1896, in Trenton, N.J.; son of William (a potter) and Sarah Ann (Pope) Bratton; married Elizabeth Schuster, December 22, 1957. *Education:* Mount Union College, A.B., 1920; Boston University, S.T.B., 1923, Ph.D., 1927; University of Berlin, diploma, 1925; Harvard University, advanced study, 1922-24, 1925-

27. *Politics:* Independent. *Home:* Riverdale House, 80 Brush Hill Rd., West Springfield, Mass.

CAREER: Congregational minister. Boston University, School of Theology, Boston, Mass., associate professor of Biblical languages and literature, 1927-30; University of Rochester, Rochester, N.Y., professor of religion, 1930-31; Springfield College, Springfield, Mass., professor of the history and literature of religion, 1931-62, professor emeritus after 1962. Lecturer on historical and biographical subjects throughout United States. *Member:* Society of Biblical Literature and Exegesis, American Academy of Religion, Reality Club (Springfield; past president).

WRITINGS: (Contributor) E. P. Booth, editor, *New Testament Studies,* Abingdon, 1942; *The Legacy of the Liberal Spirit: Men and Movements in the Making of Modern Thought,* Scribner, 1943; *A History of the Bible: An Introduction to the Historical Method,* Beacon, 1959; *The First Heretic: The Life and Times of Ikhnaton the King,* Beacon, 1961 (published in England as *The Heretic Pharoah,* R. Hale, 1962); *Maimonides, Medieval Modernist,* Beacon, 1967; *A History of Egyptian Archaeology,* R. Hale, 1967, Crowell, 1968; *The Crime of Christendom: The Theological Sources of Christian Anti-Semitism,* Beacon, 1969; *Myths and Legends of the Ancient Near East,* Crowell, 1970. Contributor of articles to *Humanist, Journal of Biblical Literature, Christian Herald, Journal of Bible and Religion,* and *Christian Century.*

WORK IN PROGRESS: Research for *Moral Values in the Ancient World.*

SIDELIGHTS: Bratton traveled frequently in Egypt and the Near East for research purposes. *Avocational interests:* Archaeology of the ancient Near East.

(Deceased)

*   *   *

BRECHER, Ruth E(rnestine)   1911-1966
PERSONAL: Born February 21, 1911, in Ambler, Pa.; daughter of Ernest Fullerton (a teacher and scientist) and Elida Marguerite (Shaffer) Cook; married Earl N. Stilson (died, 1940); married Edward Moritz Brecher (a free-lance writer), December 27, 1941; children: William Earl, John Samuel, Jeremy Hans. *Education:* Swarthmore College, B.A. (with highest honors), 1933; Radcliffe College, M.A., 1934, part-time postgraduate study, 1934-38. *Politics:* Democrat. *Religion:* Society of Friends. *Home and office:* Yelping Hill, West Cornwall, Conn.

CAREER: Harvard University, Cambridge, Mass., research assistant in department of government, 1937-40; *Executives War Digest,* Washington, D.C., correspondent, 1944-45; *Consumer Reports,* New York, N.Y., assistant editor, 1947-51; free-lance writer in collaboration with husband, Edward M. Brecher, 1952-66. Chairwoman of citizens advisory board, Connecticut Department of Mental Health, Community Services Division. *Member:* National Association of Science Writers, Society of Magazine Writers, Concern (secretary). *Awards, honors*—All jointly with Edward M. Brecher: Albert Lasker Medical Journalism Award for "We Can Save More Babies," in *Saturday Evening Post,* 1962; Russell L. Cecil Award of Arthritis and Rheumatism Foundation for "New Clues to the Arthritis Mystery," in *Family Circle,* 1962; grant from Philip M. Stern Family Fund for study of integration, segregation, and discrimination problems, 1962 (report published in *Harper's,* 1963).

WRITINGS: (With husband, Edward M. Brecher) *Medical and Hospital Benefit Plans*, Prentice-Hall, 1961; (with E. M. Brecher and others) *Consumers Union Report on Smoking and the Public Interest*, Simon & Schuster, 1963; (editor with E. M. Brecher) *An Analysis of Human Sexual Response*, Little, Brown, 1966; (with E. M. Brecher) *The Rays: A History of Radiology*, Williams & Wilkins, 1969. Co-author with husband of two Public Affairs pamphlets and of some two hundred articles on medical, scientific, economic, and sociological subjects in *Good Housekeeping*, *Reader's Digest*, *Saturday Evening Post*, *Harper's*, *Parents' Magazine*, *Redbook*, *Consumer Reports*, and other national magazines.

(Died October, 1966)

* * *

BREDSDORFF, Elias Lunn 1912-

PERSONAL: Born January 15, 1912, in Roskilde, Denmark; son of Thomas Birkedal (a headmaster) and Margrete (Lunn) Bredsdorff; married Anne Lise Neckelmann, January 9, 1954; children: Jan, Eva. *Education:* University College, London, 1934; Copenhagen University, Cand. mag., 1938, Dr.Phil., 1964. *Home:* 35 Millington Rd., Cambridge, England.

CAREER: Vordingborg Training College, Vordingborg, Denmark, teacher of literature and English, 1939-43; Frit Danmark (Danish resistance organization), organizer, 1943-45, editor of weekly newspaper, *Frit Danmark*, 1945-46; University College, University of London, London, England, Queen Alexandra Lecturer in Danish, 1946-49; Cambridge University, Cambridge, England, lecturer in Danish, 1949-60, reader in Scandinavian studies, and head of department of Scandinavian studies, 1960—. Anglo-Danish Students' Bureau, London, England, head, 1946-49. *Awards, honors:* Fellow of Peterhouse, Cambridge, 1963—.

WRITINGS: *D. H. Lawrence: Et Forsoeg paa en politisk Analyse*, Munksgaard, 1937; *Corsaren* (on the periodical edited by E. M. Goldschmidt), Carit Andersen, 1941, expanded version published as *Goldschmidts "Corsaren," med en udfoerlig redegoerelse for striden mellem Soeren Kierkegaard og "Corsaren"*, Sirius, 1962; *John Steinbeck*, Carit Andersen, 1943; *Danish Literature in English Translation: A Bibliography* (includes special Hans Christian Andersen supplement), Munksgaard, 1950; (with Brita Mortensen and Ronald G. Popperwell) *An Introduction to Scandinavian Literature, from the Earliest time to Our Day*, Cambridge University Press, 1951; *H. C. Andersen og Charles Dickens: Et Venskab og dets oploesning*, Rosenkilde & Bagger, 1951, revised translation published as *Hans Christian Andersen and Charles Dickens: A Friendship and Its Dissolution* (includes letters by Andersen and Dickens and Andersen's diary of his visit to Dickens), Heffer, 1956; *H. C. Andersen og England*, Rosenkilde & Bagger, 1952; (author of introduction and supervisor of translations) *Contemporary Danish Plays: An Anthology*, Thames & Hudson, 1955; *Hans Christian Andersen, 1805—2nd April—1955* (catalog of jubilee exhibition held at National Book League, organized by Bredsdorff), [London], 1955; *Danish: An Elementary Grammar and Reader*, Cambridge University Press, 1956; *Drama i Syrakus*, Carit Andersen, 1956, new edition, 1968; *Kinas Vej: Samtaler og rejseindtryk*, Gyldendal, 1957; (author of notes and supervisor of translations) *Contemporary Danish Prose: An Anthology*, Gyldendal, 1958; (editor) Sir Edmund William Gosse, *Correspondence with Scandinavian Writers*, Gyldendal, 1960; *Bag Ibsen's maske: To imaginaere interviews med Henrik*

Ibsen, Hasselbalch, 1962; (editor) Kjeld Abell, *Synskhedens Gave: Prose og vers*, Gyldendal, 1962; *Henrik Pontoppidan og Georg Brandes*, two volumes, Gyldendal, 1964.

Contributor to *Chambers' Encyclopaedia*, *Cassell's Encyclopaedia of Literature*, *Encyclopaedia Britannica*, *Encyclopedia Americana*, Penguin "Companions to World Literature." Also contributor to British and Scandinavian newspapers and journals. Editor, *Scandinavica, An International Journal of Scandinavian Studies*, Academic Press, 1962—. Writer of literary radio features for British Broadcasting Corp. programs, and for Scandinavian and continental radio programs.

* * *

BRELSFORD, W(illiam) V(ernon) 1907-

PERSONAL: Born March 6, 1907, in Chesterfield, England; son of Vernon (a local civil servant) and Emily (Gibson) Brelsford; married Wilma Kathleen Morton, July 26, 1933; children: Erica (Mrs. C.B.S. Telfer), Joan (Mrs. Colin Banks). *Education:* Oxford University, B.A. (honors in English language and literature), 1929. *Home:* Umwindsdale, Highlands, Salisbury, Southern Rhodesia.

CAREER: Entered Colonial Service in Northern Rhodesia (later Federation of Rhodesia and Nyasaland, and now Zambia) in 1930, and was connected with the government in various capacities, 1930-60; member of Parliament, Southern Rhodesia, 1962-65. In Northern Rhodesia established Rhodes-Livingstone Institute and Museum and served as secretary-curator, 1937-38; acting information officer, 1945 and 1948; director of information and in charge of African Broadcasting Services in Northern Rhodesia, 1951-53; director of Information Department, Federation of Rhodesia and Nyasaland, 1953-60. Director, Morton Estates, Lusaka, Zambia. *Member:* Royal Anthropological Institute (London; life member), Northern Rhodesia Society (president, 1951-65), Parliamentary Association (life member). *Awards, honors:* Welcome Medal for sociological research, 1948, for *Fishermen of the Bangweulu Swamps*; Coronation Medal, H.M. Overseas Service, 1953.

WRITINGS: *Primitive Philosophy*, John Bale, 1935; *Handbook to Rhodes-Livingstone Museum*, Rhodes-Livingstone Museum, 1937; *The Succession of Bamba Chiefs*, Northern Rhodesia Government, 1944, 2nd edition, 1948; *Fishermen of the Bangweulu Swamps*, Rhodes-Livingstone Institute, 1946; *Copperbelt Markets*, Northern Rhodesia Government, 1947; *African Dances of Northern Rhodesia*, Rhodes-Livingstone Museum, 1949.

(Editor and contributor) *The Story of the Northern Rhodesia Regiment*, Northern Rhodesia Government, 1954; *The Tribes of Northern Rhodesia*, Northern Rhodesia Government, 1957, 2nd enlarged edition published as *The Tribes of Zambia*, Government Printer, 1965; (editor and contributor) *Handbook to the Federation of Rhodesia and Nyasaland*, Federal Government of Rhodesia and Nyasaland, 1960; *Generation of Men*, Stuart-Manning Ltd., 1965.

Contributor of articles on sociological topics to journals and magazines in Africa and other lands. Editor, *Northern Rhodesia Journal* (history and natural history), 1951-65; editor, *Rhodesiana* (Southern Rhodesia), 1967—.

* * *

BRETT-YOUNG, Jessica (Hankinson) 1883-1970

PERSONAL: Born May 23, 1883, in Cheshire, England; daughter of John and Margaret (Lowe) Hankinson; married

Francis Brett-Young (a physician and author), December 28, 1908 (died, 1954). *Education:* Attended school in Halesowen, Worcestershire, England. *Home:* Mount Nelson Hotel, Capetown, South Africa. *Agent:* David Higham Associates Ltd., 5-8 Lower John St., W1R 4HA, England.

CAREER: Professional singer with orchestra in England, 1913-14. *Member:* English Association, P.E.N. Club.

WRITINGS: Francis Brett-Young: A Biography, preface by C. P. Snow, Fernhill, 1962.

(Died September 2, 1970)

* * *

BREWER, Frances Joan 1913-1965

PERSONAL: Born April 10, 1913, in Vienna, Austria; daughter of Albert and Wilma (Seidner) Werner; married George E. F. Brewer (head, chemistry department, Marygrove College), June 29, 1933. *Education:* Liberal Arts College, Vienna, Austria, B.A., 1934; attended Library School, Rosary College, River Forest, Ill., 1942. *Home:* 28610 Meadowbrook Rd., Novi, Mich. 48050. *Office:* Detroit Public Library, 5201 Woodward Ave., Detroit, Mich. 48202.

CAREER: Public Library, Wilmette, Ill., general assistant, 1942; Northwestern University, Evanston, Ill., cataloger, 1943-44; Climax Molybdenum Co. of Michigan, Detroit, technical librarian, 1944-46; Detroit Public Library, Detroit, Mich., catalog librarian, 1946-51, curator of rare books, 1952-57, chief, gifts and rare books division, 1958-65. Conducted seminars on book collecting. *Member:* American Library Association (chairman, rare books section, ACRL, 1961-62), Special Libraries Association, Catholic Library Association, Bibliographical Society of America, Manuscript Society, Michigan Library Association.

WRITINGS: Catalogue of an Exhibition of Manuscripts, Books and Associated Items of Walt Whitman at the Detroit Public Library, 1955; (with Matthew J. Bruccoli) *James Branch Cabell*, two volumes, University of Virginia Press, 1957; (compiler) *The John S. Newberry Gift Collection of Kate Greenaway Presented to the Detroit Public Library*, Friends of the Detroit Public Library, 1959; *A Short History of the Rare Book Section of the Association of College and Research Libraries*, Detroit Public Library, 1962; (editor) *Book Illustration*, Gebr. Mann Verlag (Berlin), 1963; *The Fables of Jean de la Fontaine*, Dawson's Bookshop, 1964. Regular contributor to *Among Friends* (publication of Friends of the Detroit Public Library); contributor to professional journals.

WORK IN PROGRESS: Manual for book collectors.

SIDELIGHTS: Mrs. Brewer's professional interests were in the history of the book, book collecting, and bibliography. She owned about one thousand slides, depicting all phases of rare books and book collecting, which she used in her lectures. She compiled a bibliography of more than two hundred items written by Dr. Hellmut Lehmann-Haupt to honor the anniversary of his thirty years in the United States; in the introduction to a selection from her bibliography, published in *Publishers Weekly*, it was noted "that, although she had not been privileged to attend classes taught by Dr. Lehmann-Haupt, she had learned much from him informally about 'the book.'"

BIOGRAPHICAL/CRITICAL SOURCES: Publishers Weekly, December 7, 1959; *Detroit Free Press*, November 15, 1965.

(Died November 13, 1965)

BRICK, John 1922-1973

PERSONAL: Born January 1, 1922, in Newburgh, N.Y.; son of John T. and Elizabeth (Connell) Brick; married Mary Yakim, December 4, 1943; children: John W., Martha E., Janice A. (Mrs. Dennis Schreckengast). *Education:* Attended New York University and Columbia University. *Home:* 3604 Albee Lane, Alexandria, Va. *Agent:* Mavis McIntosh, McIntosh, McKee & Dodds, 30 East 60th St., New York, N.Y. 10022.

CAREER: Export Trade, New York, N.Y., managing editor, 1945-49; full-time writer, 1950-60; *Life*, Book Division, New York, N.Y., staff writer, 1960-61; University of Toledo, Toledo, Ohio, assistant to the president, 1962-63; U.S. Senate Permanent Investigating Subcommittee, Washington, D.C., professional staff member, 1963-73. *Military service:* U.S. Army Air Forces, World War II. *Member:* Authors Guild (vice-president). *Awards, honors:* Farrar, Straus regional fellowship, 1950, for *Troubled Spring*.

WRITINGS: Troubled Spring, Farrar, Straus, 1950; *The Raid*, Farrar, Straus, 1951; *Homer Crist*, Farrar, Straus, 1952; *The Rifleman*, Doubleday, 1953; *The King's Rangers*, Doubleday, 1954; *They Ran for Their Lives*, Doubleday, 1954; *Eagle of Niagara* (juvenile), Doubleday, 1955; *Jubilee*, Doubleday, 1956; *Panther Mountain*, Doubleday, 1958; *The Strong Men*, Doubleday, 1959; *Gettysburg*, Popular Library, 1960; *The Raid* (juvenile), Duell, Sloan & Pearce, 1960; *Yankees on the Run* (juvenile), Duell, Sloan & Pearce, 1961; *Tomahawk Trail* (juvenile), Duell, Sloan & Pearce, 1962; *Captives of the Senecas* (juvenile), Duell, Sloan & Pearce, 1963; *The Richmond Raid*, Doubleday, 1963; *Ben Bryan, Morgan Rifleman*, Duell, Sloan & Pearce, 1963; *Rogues' Kingdom*, Doubleday, 1965; *They Fought for New York* (juvenile), Putnam, 1965; *On the Old Frontier*, Putnam, 1966. Staff writer on *Life Picture Atlas* and "Life Nature Library." Contributor of short stories to magazines.

WORK IN PROGRESS: Several novels.

SIDELIGHTS: The screen rights to Brick's first novel, *Troubled Spring*, were purchased by Metro-Goldwyn-Mayer. *Avocational Interests:* Reading and fishing.

(Died October 15, 1973)

* * *

BRIDGES-ADAMS, William 1889-1965

PERSONAL: Born March 1, 1889, in Harrow, Middlesex, England; son of Walter and Mary (Daltry) Bridges-Adams; married Marguerite Doris Wellsted, September 13, 1929 (died, 1963); children: John Nicholas, William. *Education:* Worcester College, Oxford, student, 1908-11. *Home:* Hermitage, Waterfall, Bantry, County Cork, Ireland. *Agent:* A. D. Peters, 10 Buckingham St., Adelphi, London W.C.2, England.

CAREER: Theatrical historian, director, and designer. Started career in England as an actor, 1911; director of Bristol Repertory Theatre, 1914-15, of Repertory Theatre (now Playhouse), Liverpool, 1916-17, of Shakespeare Memorial (now Royal Shakespeare) Theatre, Stratford on Avon, 1919-34; also director of other productions in England during these years, and on transcontinental tours of United States and Canada, 1928-32. Designer of settings for

Gilbert and Sullivan revivals in London, 1918-24. British Council, dramatic adviser in charge of foreign tours, 1937, staff member, World War II. Governor of Royal Shakespeare Theatre, 1934—; member of council, Royal Academy of Dramatic Art. *Member:* Savile Club and Garrick Club (both London). *Awards, honors:* Commander, Order of the British Empire, 1960, for services to the theater.

WRITINGS: The Shakespeare Country, Country Life, 1932; *The British Theatre*, Longmans, Green, 1944; *Looking at a Play*, Phoenix House, 1947; *The Lost Leader*, Sidgwick & Jackson, 1954; *The Irresistible Theatre*, World Publishing, 1957; *To Charlotte While Shaving* (light verse), Barrie & Rockliff, 1957; (contributor) Simon Nowell-Smith, editor, *Edwardian England*, Oxford University Press, 1964. Contributor of essays and reviews to periodicals, including *Drama* and *Theatre Notebook*.

WORK IN PROGRESS: Research in theater history.

AVOCATIONAL INTERESTS: Reading, writing letters, fishing, ships, carpentry, and conversation.

(Died August 17, 1965)

* * *

BRIER, Howard M(axwell)   1903-

PERSONAL: Born March 20, 1903, in River Falls, Wis.; son of Warren Judson and Marion (Royce) Brier; married Grace Kjelstad, December 25, 1926; children: Warren, Nancy (Mrs. Peter Rybock). *Education:* University of Washington, Seattle, B.A., 1925, M.Ed., 1931; University of California, Berkeley, graduate study. *Politics:* Independent. *Religion:* Protestant. *Office:* Communication Building, University of Washington, Seattle, Wash.

CAREER: Seattle, Wash., public schools, teacher of journalism and junior high principal, 1933-47; University of Washington, Seattle, 1947—, now associate professor and executive assistant at School of Communications. Former staff member of newspapers in Everett and Seattle, Wash., including *Seattle Post-Intelligencer*. Writer's consultant for Banff Workshop, Alberta Teachers' Association, 1950-52; director of journalism seminar, University of California, 1961-64; state director, Keep Washington Green Association, 1940-48. *Member:* American Association of University Professors, Sigma Delta Chi, Phi Delta Kappa, Beta Theta Phi.

WRITINGS—All youth books, except where noted; all published by Random House, except as indicated: *Waterfront Beat*, 1937; *Skycruiser*, 1939; *Smoke Eater*, 1941; *Skyfreighter*, 1942; *Swing Shift*, 1943; *Skyblazer*, 1946; *Phantom Backfield*, 1948; *Blackboard Magic*, 1949; *Shortstop Shadow*, 1950; *Cinder Cyclone*, 1952; *Fighting Heart*, Doubleday, 1956; *Sawdust Empire* (adult book), Knopf, 1958. Contributor of stories to more than fifteen anthologies. Also contributor of stories to more than 150 short stories and articles to magazines, including *Boys' Life, American Boy, St. Nicholas, Open Road, Boys' Today, Scholastic Editor*. Editor of *Student and Publisher*, 1955-64.

WORK IN PROGRESS: A novel for young people; short stories.

SIDELIGHTS: Nine of Brier's twelve books have been Junior Literary Guild selections.

BRISTOWE, Anthony (Lynn)   1921-19?

PERSONAL: Born November 17, 1921, in Surrey, England; son of O. C. and Lorna (Hutchinson) Bristowe; married Elizabeth Canning, March 18, 1944; children: Susan, Nicholas, Sarah, John. *Education:* Attended Eton College for four years; University of Grenoble, diploma; University of London, diploma in agriculture. *Home:* 2880 Sea View Rd., Victoria, British Columbia, Canada. *Agent:* Jay Garon, 415 Central Park West, New York, N.Y. 10025. *Office:* Yorkshire Securities Ltd., 737 Fort St., Victoria, British Columbia, Canada.

CAREER: Stephen Aske (literary agent), London, England, editorial assistant, 1946-48; Fairmile Nurseries, Essex, England, managing director, 1948-52; Pemberton Securities Ltd., Victoria, British Columbia, stockbroker, 1952-55; Yorkshire Securities Ltd., Victoria, British Columbia, stockbroker, beginning 1955. Dominion Funds, Victoria, president and director, 1958-63. University of Victoria, instructor in course on fly fishing, 1964. *Military service:* Royal Navy, pilot, then intelligence officer, 1941-46; became lieutenant. *Member:* Union Club (Victoria).

WRITINGS: Japan and the Far East, H.M.S.O., 1945; *Fresh Water Fishing: Your Questions Answered*, Taplinger, 1965; *Tunnel*, Belmont, 1970. Writer of industrial film scripts for British government, 1947-50. Occasional contributor of articles on fishing to magazines.

WORK IN PROGRESS: A Season of Trout.

AVOCATIONAL INTERESTS: Conservation, fisheries management, and all other subjects connected with fishing.

(Deceased)

* * *

BRITTAIN, Vera (Mary)   ?-1970

PERSONAL: Born in city of Newcastle, Staffordshire, England; daughter of Thomas Arthur (a paper manufacturer) and Edith Mary (Bervon) Brittain; married George Edward Gordon Catlin (political scientist and philosopher), June 27, 1925; children: John Edward Jocelyn, Shirley Vivien (Mrs. Bernard Williams). *Education:* Somerville College, Oxford, B.A., 1921, M.A., 1925. *Politics:* Labour Party. *Religion:* Quaker-inclined Anglican. *Home:* 4 Whitehall Ct., London S.W. 1, England.

CAREER: Author, journalist, and lecturer. Speaker on seven lecture tours in United States and Canada, 1934-59, other tours in Holland, 1936, Scandinavia, 1945, Germany, 1947, India, 1949-50, 1963, and South Africa, 1960. *Wartime service:* Voluntary Aid Detachment, nurse in London, Malta, and France, 1915-19. *Member:* Royal Society of Literature (fellow), Royal Commonwealth Society, International League for Peace and Freedom (vice-president, 1945-70), National Peace Council, (vice-president, 1930-70), Society of Women Writers and Journalists (honorary life member; president, 1965-70), P.E.N., Married Women's Association (president, 1962), National Arts Theatre Club. *Awards, honors:* D.Litt, Mills College 1950.

WRITINGS: Verses of a V.A.D., Erskine Macdonald, 1918; *The Dark Tide* (novel), Grant Richards, 1923; *Not Without Honour* (novel), Grant Richards, 1924; *Women's Work in Modern England*, Noel Douglas, 1928; *Halcyon, or the Future of Monogamy*, Kegan Paul, 1929.

Testament of Youth (autobiography), Macmillan, 1933; *Poems of the War and After*, Macmillan, 1934; *Honourable Estate* (novel), Macmillan, 1936; *Thrice a Stranger* (travel),

Macmillan, 1938; *Testament of Friendship* (biography), Macmillan, 1940; *England's Hour*, Macmillan, 1941; *Humiliation with Honour*, Dakers, 1942, Friendship, 1945; *Seed of Chaos*, New Vision Publishing, 1944; (editor, with husband, George Catlin, and Sheila Hodges) *Above All Nations* (anthology), Gollancz, 1945, Harper, 1949; *Account Rendered* (novel), Macmillan, 1945; *On Becoming a Writer*, Hutchinson, 1947; published as *On Being an Author*, Macmillan, 1948; *Born 1925: A Novel of Youth*, Macmillan, 1948.

Valiant Pilgrim, Macmillan, 1950 (published in England as *In the Steps of John Bunyan*, Rich & Cowan, 1950); *The Story of St. Martin's: An Epic of London*, St. Martin-in-the-Fields, 1951; *Search after Sunrise: A Traveller's Story*, Macmillan, 1951; *Lady into Woman: A History of Women from Victoria to Elizabeth II*, Dakers, 1953; *Testament of Experience* (autobiography), Macmillan, 1957; (with G.E.W. Sizer) *Long Shadows*, A. Brown, 1958; *The Women at Oxford*, Harrap, 1960; *Selected Letters of Winifred Holtby and Vera Brittain*, limited edition, A. Brown & Sons, 1960; *The Pictorial History of St. Martin-in-the-Fields*, Pitkin Pictorials, 1962; *Pethick-Lawrence: A Portrait*, Allen & Unwin, 1963; *The Rebel Passion: A Short History of Some Pioneer Peace-Making*, Fellowship Publications, 1964; *Envoy Extraordinary: A Study of Vijaya Lakshmi Pandit and Her Contribution to Modern India*, Allen & Unwin, 1965, A. S. Barnes, 1966; *Radclyffe Hall: A Case of Obscenity?*, Femina, 1968, A. S. Barnes, 1969.

Contributor to *This Week*, *Week-end* (Canada), *Author*, *Books*, and other magazines and newspapers in Great Britain, United States, Canada, and Italy. Chairman emeritus, *Peace News*.

WORK IN PROGRESS: Another biography.

SIDELIGHTS: Vera Brittain once told Mimi Josephson: "I never remember a time when I wasn't certain that I should be an author when I grew up." Her first novel, describing conditions in women's colleges, elicited a storm of protest among Oxford authorities and was banned in Somerville, her own college. The novel, however, was later given extremely favorable reviews.

Another of Miss Brittain's early works, *Testament of Youth*, quickly became a best seller. "Its impact on campus idealists," wrote Helen Beal Woodward, "was extraordinary.... They were ... impressed by her struggle for a university education, and already converted—or thought they were—to her passionate pacifism." The sequel, *Testament of Experience*, published twenty-four years later, was "truly a remarkable book," said Miss Woodward, "searchingly and sensitively written, the distillate of a life richer than most in love, thought, pain, and achievement. It [was] about as far from a religious do-it-yourself as a book could be, but I think it would be difficult to read it thoughtfully without having, oneself, something of a religious experience." Mimi Josephson wrote that "in the future the two 'Testaments' will be considered not only as a vividly written narrative of one women's life, but as a valuable historical and sociological record giving a true, unbiased picture of the first half of the twentieth century."

Miss Brittain's interest in feminism dated back to her reading of Olive Schreiner's *Women and Labour* at the age of sixteen, reported Miss Josephson. "Miss Brittain very early rebelled against the genteel, useless life of a middle-class provincial 'young lady.' She decided that she wanted to be a useful member of society in her own right; she wanted a university education and, above all, she wanted to

write." In all of her work, she was able to combine literary talent and a strong personal and social ideology. Of *Search After Sunrise*, Herbert L. Matthews wrote: "Her calm, sensible, matter-of-fact way of writing does not hide the intensity of her convictions. . . . [She] is impressive because this is such a sensible, honest, careful, unpretentious book, and it is, of course, the work of a keen, trained observer who can set down sights and impressions expertly."

Miss Brittain preferred to work mornings and did all her writing in manuscript. She told Mimi Josephson: "'I can't use a typewriter, except for letters. . . . It gets between me and my thought.'" Miss Josephson commented: "She thinks this is because she has a dislike for mechanical things, even where entertainment is concerned. She does not care for TV, radio or the cinema, but is very fond of the theatre—'I like direct human contact,' she added."

Miss Brittain's travels included forty-seven of the United States; Europe, South Africa, and five Asian countries. She spoke French and German with "reasonable facility."

BIOGRAPHICAL/CRITICAL SOURCES: New York Times Book Review, March 2, 1952; *John O'London's Weekly*, April 30, 1954; *Saturday Review*, August 24, 1957; *New Republic*, October 7, 1957; *New Statesman*, February 6, 1960; *Spectator*, February 26, 1960; *Contemporary Review*, August, 1963; *Antiquarium Bookman*, April 6, 1970.

(Died March 29, 1970)

*   *   *

BROADHURST, Ronald Joseph Callender   1906-

PERSONAL: Born December 25, 1906, in Sidcup, Kent, England; son of J. F. (a captain, British Army) and Florence Ethel (Bennett) Broadhurst; married Annie Doreen Morrison, March 14, 1934; children: John Anthony David. *Education:* Attended Cambridge University. *Politics:* Unionist. *Religion:* Church of England. *Home:* Belvedere, Ballyaughlis, County Down, Northern Ireland.

CAREER: While commanding camelry detachment in Beersheba during early 1930's, was invited to accompany, as second in command to Colonel (later General Sir John) Glubb, a small force of a thousand rifles to keep order in Transjordan; during World War II this force expanded to become Arab Legion; Broadhurst retired in 1948 as deputy commander after having served, in addition, as equerry to late King Abdullah of Jordan for ten years. Vice-president of United Nations, Northern Ireland; chairman of Forces Help Society, Lord Robert's Workshops, Outward Bound Trust, Amateur Fencing Union (Northern Ireland). Director of ceremonies, Order of St. John of Jerusalem. *Member:* Athenaeum Club (London), Ulster Club (Belfast).

WRITINGS: (Author of introduction) *Memoirs of King Abdullah*, J. Cape, 1950; (translator) *The Travels of Ibn Jubayr*, J. Cape, 1952. Writer and narrator for Ulster Television of series on American men of Ulster stock, including James Monroe, Andrew Jackson, Stonewall Jackson, Woodrow Wilson.

WORK IN PROGRESS: A translation of the Arabic *History of the Ayyubid Sultans of Egypt*; a biography of Saladin.

AVOCATIONAL INTERESTS: Formerly polo and fox hunting; now gardening, playing with grandchildren, chess, racing, good conversation, claret and port, country walks, and other rural pursuits.

BROCKETT, Eleanor Hall 1913-1967

PERSONAL: Born April 16, 1913, in London, England; daughter of George Benjamin and Amelia (Waller) Hall; married Charles F. Brockett (a local government official, Westminster City), October 5, 1935; children: Barbara Jane. *Education:* Attended school in London, England, and Ursuline Convent, Konigstein im Taunus, Germany. *Politics:* Socialist. *Religion:* Anglican. *Home:* 39 Sylvan Way, West Wickham, Kent, England. *Agent:* Curtis Brown Ltd., 1 Craven Hill, London W2 3EW, England.

CAREER: *Times* Book Club, London, England, employee, 1932; Ivor Nicholson & Watson Ltd. (publishers), London, England, editorial secretary, 1933-40; Robert Hale Ltd. (publishers), London, England, editorial secretary and reader, 1940-45; Curtis Brown Ltd. (literary agent), London, England, executive, 1952-53, advisory reader, 1960-62. Free-lance reader, editor, translator, and indexer for publishers, authors. *Member:* National Book League.

WRITINGS: *How to Retire and Start Living*, Staples, 1955, revised edition, New English Library, 1963; *Choosing a Career*, Staples, 1959, 2nd revised edition, MacGibbon & Kee, 1966; *Persian Fairy Tales* (retold), Muller, 1962; *Turkish Fairy Tales* (retold), Muller, 1963; *Look at Germany*, Hamish Hamilton, 1964; *Burmese and Thai Fairy Tales* (retold), Muller, 1965.

Translator: (And part author, with Anton Ehrenzweig and Karl Herrligkoffer) *Nanga Parbat*, Elek Books, 1954; Gianni Roghi and Francesco Baschieri Salvadori, *Dahlak*, Nicholas Kaye, 1956; Bruno Traven, *The Cotton Pickers*, R. Hale, 1956; (with Ehrenzweig) Fritz Otto Busch, *The Drama of the Scharnhorst*, R. Hale, 1956; Helen Fischer, *Peril is My Companion*, R. Hale, 1957; Karl Nork, *Hell in Siberia*, R. Hale, 1957; Erich Gimpel, *Spy for Germany*, Hamish Hamilton, 1957; Gabrielle Bertrand, *The Jungle People: Men, Beasts and Legends of the Moi Country*, R. Hale, 1959; Fritz Otto Busch, *The Story of the Prince Eugen*, R. Hale, 1960; Gaston Rebuffat, *On Snow and Rock*, Nicholas Kaye, 1963; Gaston Rebuffat, *Between Heaven and Earth*, Oxford University Press, 1965; Gaston Rebuffat, *Men and the Matterhorn*, Oxford University Press, 1967.

WORK IN PROGRESS: Research on the effect on doctor-patient relationships of the National Health Service in Great Britain.

SIDELIGHTS: Mrs. Brockett told *CA:* "The only remarkable thing about my literary output is its variety. I have a natural curiosity about practically everything, and enjoy inquiring into the mysteries of old age, oriental folklore, Himalayan expeditions, and so on." *Avocational interests:* Playing piano, looking at abstract paintings.

(Died June 21, 1967)

*   *   *

BROCKWAY, (Archibald) Fenner 1888-

PERSONAL: Born November 1, 1888, in Calcutta, India; son of William George (a missionary) and Frances Elizabeth (Abbey) Brockway; married Lilla Harvey-Smith, 1914; married second wife, Edith Violet King, January, 1946; children: (first marriage) Audrey (Mrs. James Wood), Joan (Mrs. Sam Pover), Olive; (second marriage) Christopher. *Education:* Attended School for the Sons of Missionaries (now Eltham College). *Politics:* Socialist. *Religion:* Universalist. *Home:* 67 Southway, London N.20, England. *Office:* House of Lords, London S.W.1, England.

CAREER: Writer or editor in Manchester and London, England, on staffs of *Examiner, Christian Commonwealth, Labour Leader*, 1907-17; Labour member of Parliament for East Leyton, 1929-31, for Eton and Slough, 1950—. Independent Labour Party, organizing secretary, 1922, general secretary, 1928, 1933-39, chairman, 1931-33, political secretary, 1939-46, resigned, 1946, and returned to Labour Party. Sentenced to three terms in prison under Military Service Act, 1916-17. Joint secretary, British Committee of Indian National Congress, 1919; chairman, No More War Movement and War Resister's International, 1923-28; executive member, Labour and Socialist International, 1926-31; chairman, British Center for Colonial Freedom, 1942-47; member, International Committee of Socialist Movement for United Europe, 1947-52; first chairman, Congress of Peoples Against Imperialism, 1948—; chairman, Movement for Colonial Freedom, 1954—; chairman, British Asian and Overseas Socialist Fellowship, 1959—; vice-chairman, Campaign for Nuclear Disarmament, 1964—; executive member, Anti-Apartheid Movement, 1964—; chairman, British Council for Peace in Vietnam, 1965. *Awards, honors:* Order of Republic of Tunisia; honorary chief, Kikuyu Tribe, Kenya.

WRITINGS: *Labour and Liberalism*, National Labour Press, 1913; *The Devil's Business* (one-act comedy), National Labour Press, 1915, new edition, Independent Labour Party Publication Department, 1926; *Is Britain Blameless?*, with a letter by G. Bernard Shaw, National Labour Press, 1915; *Socialism for Pacifists*, National Labour Press, 1917; *The Recruit* (one-act play), National Labour Press, 1919; *Non-Cooperation in Other Lands*, Tagore & Co., 1921; (with Stephen Hobhouse) *English Prisons Today: Being the Report of the Prison System Enquiry Committee*, Macmillan, 1922; *A Week in India—and Three Months in an Indian Hospital*, New Leader, 1928; *A New Way with Crime*, Williams & Norgate, 1928.

The Indian Crisis, Gollancz, 1930; *Hungry England*, Gollancz, 1932; (with Harry Pollitt) *Which Way for Workers?*, Communist Party of Great Britain, 1932; *The Bloody Traffic*, Gollancz, 1933; *Will Roosevelt Succeed?: A Study of Fascist Tendencies in America*, G. Routledge & Sons, 1934; *Purple Plague: A Tale of Love and Revolution* (novel), Low, 1935; *Workers' Front*, Secker & Warburg, 1938; *Pacifism and the Left Wing*, Pacifist Publicity Unit, 1938; *Inside the Left: Thirty Years of Platform, Press, Prison and Parliament*, Allen & Unwin, 1942, post-war edition, 1947; (with Frederic Mullally) *Death Pays a Dividend*, Gollancz, 1944; *German Diary*, Gollancz, 1946; *Socialism Over Sixty Years: The Life of Jowett of Bradford, 1864-1944*, Allen & Unwin, 1946; *Bermondsey Story: The Life of Alfred Salter*, Allen & Unwin, 1949.

Why Mau Mau?, Movement for Colonial Freedom, 1953; *African Journeys* (autobiographical), Gollancz, 1955; *1960: Africa's Year of Destiny—A Political Guide to a Continent in Crisis*, Movement for Colonial Freedom, 1960; *Red Liner: A Novel in TV Form*, Lawrence & Wishart, 1962; *Outside the Right* (autobiography), with a lost play by G. Bernard Shaw, Allen & Unwin, 1963; *African Socialism*, Dufour, 1963; (with H. Fennell) *Immigration: What Is the Answer?*, Routledge & Kegan Paul, 1965; (with Wendy Campbell-Purdie) *Woman Against the Desert*, Gollancz, 1967; *This Shrinking Explosive World: A Study of Race Relations*, Epworth, 1967.

Pamphlets: *India and Its Government*, Labour Publishing Co., 1921; *How to End War: The I.L.P. View on Imperi-*

alism and Internationalism, Independent Labour Party, 1925; *Make the Workers Free!: The Industrial Policy of the I.L.P.*, International Labour Party Publication Department, 1925; *Socialism—with Speed!: An Outline of the I.L.P. "Socialism in Our Time" Proposals*, International Labour Party Publication Department, 1928; (with E.R.A. Seligman and Scott Nearing) *Resolved: That Capitalism Offers More to the Workers of the World Than Socialism or Communism*, Rand Book Store, 1930; *The I.L.P. and the Crisis*, International Labour Party Publication Department, 1931; *A Socialist Plan for Unemployment*, International Labour Party Publication Department, 1931; *Hands off the Railmen's Wages!*, International Labour Party Publication Department, 1931; *The Coming Revolution*, Independent Labour Party, 1932; *Socialism at the Cross-Roads: Why the I.L.P. Left the Labour Party*, Independent Labour Party, 1932; (with others) *Socialism Can Defeat Nazism*, Independent Labour Party, 1940; *The Way Out*, Independent Labour Party, 1942; *The C.O. and the Community*, Fellowship of Conscientious Objectors, 1943; *Empire in Crisis: A Survey of Conditions in the British Colonies Today*, Peace News, 1953; (with Richard Acland) *Waging Peace*, Peace News, 1954; *British Protectorates—Key to South African Freedom*, Union of Democratic Control, 1957. Author of weekly article on colonial affairs published in ten countries. Editor, *India*, 1919, *New Leader*, 1926-29, 1931-46.

WORK IN PROGRESS: Continuing study of problems related to the colonies and emerging nations.

BIOGRAPHICAL/CRITICAL SOURCES: John Macnair, *Beloved Rebel*, Allen & Unwin, 1955.

*   *   *

BROMAGE, Mary Cogan 1906-

PERSONAL: Born October 13, 1906, in Fall River, Mass.; daughter of James Joseph (a clergyman) and Edith (Ives) Cogan; married Arthur W. Bromage (a professor), July 5, 1928; children: Susanna Sarah (Mrs. John Paterson). *Education:* Radcliffe College, B.A. (summa cum laude), 1928; University of Michigan, M.A., 1932. *Home:* 2300 Vinewood Blvd., Ann Arbor, Mich. *Office:* University of Michigan, Ann Arbor, Mich.

CAREER: United Nations Relief and Rehabilitation Administration, Washington, D.C., deputy director of Training Division, 1944-45; University of Michigan, Ann Arbor, associate dean of women, 1945-50, instructor in Graduate School of Business Administration, 1955-62, assistant professor, 1962-72, professor of written communication, 1972—. Consultant on written communication to business firms and government agencies in the United States, Europe, and Far East. President of Ann Arbor Community Fund, 1943; former director of Willow Run Community Council. *Member:* American Business Writing Association, American Committee for British Studies, American Committee for Irish Studies, American Association of University Women, League of Women Voters, Michigan League (board of governors, University of Michigan), Phi Beta Kappa. *Awards, honors:* Freedoms Foundation citation for editorial writing in *Ann Arbor News*; named outstanding instructor of the year by U.S. Department of Commerce Inter-agency Auditor Training Center, 1973.

WRITING: DeValera and the March of a Nation, Hutchinson, 1956, Noonday, 1957; *Writing for Business*, Wahr, 1964; *Cases in Written Communication*, Bureau of Business Research, School of Business Administration, University of Michigan, 1964; *Churchill and Ireland*, University of Notre Dame Press, 1965. Has written radio and television interviews, a film strip, editorials, and articles for periodicals.

WORK IN PROGRESS: Additional writing on Irish public affairs and on functional communication.

BIOGRAPHICAL SOURCES: Nation's Business, May, 1964.

*   *   *

BROOKES, Reuben Solomon 1914-

PERSONAL: Born July 8, 1914, in Buenos Aires, Argentina; son of Abraham and Bela (Posner) Brookes; married Blanche Ackerman; children: Eta (Mrs. Dave Stirzaker). *Education:* Liverpool Theological College, student; Manchester Talmudical College, Minister of Religion; University of London, Inter B.A.; University of Birmingham, diploma of theology, 1962. *Home:* B2, Calthorpe Mansions, Fiveways, Birmingham 15, England. *Office:* Birmingham Hebrew Congregation, Singers Hill, Birmingham 1, England.

CAREER: Assistant minister of Hebrew congregations in Manchester, England, 1937-39, Southport, England, 1939-50; assistant minister and director of education of congregation in Birmingham, England, 1950—. Jewish Chaplain, University of Birmingham. Lecturer on subjects of Jewish interest; lecturer in Hebrew at Birmingham Bible Institute. *Member:* Royal Society of Arts (fellow), Royal Asiatic Society (fellow), Philosophical Society (fellow), Royal Society of Literature, Young Israel Society (president), B'nai B'rith (Birmingham, England; president), Birmingham Zionist Council (chairman).

WRITINGS: (With Chaim Pearl) *A Guide to Jewish Knowledge*, Jewish Chronicle Publications, 1956, 4th edition, 1965; *Dictionary of Judaism*, Shapiro, Vallentine, 1959; (translator and editor with Sidney Gold) *A Children's Prayer Book for Rosh Hashanah and Yom Kippur*, Jewish Chronicle Publications, 1961; (with wife, Blanche Brookes) *A Guide to Jewish Names*, Birmingham Hebrew Congregation, 1967; *Main Events and Personalities in Jewish History, 1750 B.C.E. to 1963 C.E.*, Birmingham Hebrew Congregation, 2nd edition, 1970. Contributor of articles to Jewish publications in England and the United States. Writer of paper on David Kimchi, published by International Congress of Orientalists, Moscow, 1963.

WORK IN PROGRESS: Chronological History of the Jewish People; A Dictionary of Personalities; An Introduction to the Calendar; collaborating with wife, Blanche Brookes, on *A Jewish Gift Book*.

*   *   *

BROOKS, C(larence) Carlyle 1888-

PERSONAL: Born August 6, 1888, in Concord, Ga.; son of William Austin (a minister) and Mary Elizabeth (Prior) Brooks; married Mary Olivia Walters, May 24, 1931. *Education:* Attended high school in Quincy, Ill. *Politics:* Democrat. *Home:* 329 East New York Ave., P.O. Box 2022, DeLand, Fla. 32720.

CAREER: Clerk and printer in various cities, 1905-1919; self-employed evangelistic singer, 1920-35; visitation evangelist and pastor's associate (as licensed Baptist minister), beginning 1935. Lecturer on visitation evangelism at pastors' conferences and church clinics.

WRITINGS: Simple Approach to Soul-Winning, Zondervan, 1962. Contributor of articles to church publications.

*   *   *

BROOMELL, Myron H(enry)   1906-1970

PERSONAL: Surname is accented on second syllable; born February 27, 1906, in Boston, Mass.; son of Clyde Washburn (a clergyman) and Grace E. (Browne) Broomell; married Jeanne Cobourn Root (a teacher), October 8, 1928; children: Martha Elizabeth, Stephen Henry. *Education:* University of Colorado, B.A. (magna cum laude), 1928, M.A., 1931; University of California, Berkeley, teaching fellow in Greek, 1928-29; Ohio State University, graduate study in history, summers, 1938-41. *Politics:* Democrat. *Religion:* Swedenborgian. *Home:* 41 Folsom Pl., Durango, Colo. 81301. *Office: Durango Herald*, P.O. Box 61, Durango, Colo. 81302.

CAREER: High School Latin teacher in Leadville, Colo., 1930-31, Lamar, Colo., 1931-32; Urbana Junior College, Urbana, Ohio, professor of history and classics, 1932-43; Consolidated Steel Corp., Los Angeles, Calif., price analyst and accountant, 1943-47; Fort Lewis A&M College, Hesperus, Colo., associate professor of history, 1947-50; *Durango Herald*, Durango, Colo., business manager, 1954-70; accountant, 1960-70. *Member:* Phi Beta Kappa, Chi Psi, Phi Alpha Theta.

WRITINGS—All poetry: The Time by Dialing, Morrow, 1947; *The City Built on Sand*, A. Swallow, 1948; *The Outdoor Labyrinth*, Herald Press, 1961; *In the Iron Temple*, Prairie Press, 1964. Contributor to anthologies and little magazines, 1930-70.

SIDELIGHTS: Broomell wrote to *CA:* "I once said that I specialized in the didactic lyric, but that is not very specific. My favorite poets include Sophocles, Villon, Housman, e. e. cummings, and Karl Shapiro, but I do not imitate them. My ambition is to write a poem which people who do not care for poetry will enjoy."

BIOGRAPHICAL/CRITICAL SOURCES: Denver Post, March 30, 1952, April 6, 1952; *Yankee*, November, 1958.

(Died December 6, 1970)

*   *   *

BROPHY, John   1899-1965

PERSONAL: Born December 6, 1899, in Liverpool, England; son of John and Agnes (Bodell) Brophy; married Charis Weare Grundy, June 6, 1924; children: Brigid Antonia (Mrs. Michael Levey). *Education:* University of Liverpool, B.A., 1922; University of Durham, Diploma in Education, 1923. *Politics:* "A floating vote." *Religion:* Christian. *Home:* 59 Colcherne Ct., London S.W. 5, England.

CAREER: Taught in Egypt for two years in the 1920's, then worked in a general store and as advertising agency copywriter in England before becoming full-time author. Formerly chief fiction critic in London, England, for *Daily Telepgraph, Time and Tide,* and British Broadcasting Corp.; editor of *John O'London's,* 1940-43. *Military service:* British Army; served in France and Belgium in World War I; writer of Home Guard training manuals in World War II; became captain. *Member:* P.E.N. (London), Society of Authors, National Book League, Reform Club.

WRITINGS: The Bitter End (novel), Dutton, 1928; (editor and author of introduction) *The Soldier's War: A Prose Anthology,* Dent, 1929; *Pluck the Flower* (novel), Dutton, 1929; *Peter Lavelle* (novel), Dutton, 1929.

Fanfare, and Other Papers, Scholartis Press, 1930; (editor with Eric Partridge) *Songs and Slang of the British Soldier, 1914-1918,* Scholartis Press, 1930, 4th edition published as *The Long Trail: What the British Soldier Sang and Said in the Great War of 1914-1918,* British Book Centre, 1965; *Flesh and Blood,* Dent, 1931; *Thunderclap,* Scholartis Press, 1931; *The Rocky Road* (novel), J. Cape, 1932; *English Prose* (literary handbook), Macmillan, 1932; *The World Went Mad* (novel), Macmillan, 1934; (with others) *The Writers' Desk Book,* A. & C. Black, 1934; *Waterfront* (novel), Macmillan, 1934, revised edition, Pan Books, 1950; *I Let Him Go* (novel), J. Cape, 1935; *The Five Years: A Conspectus of the Great War,* Arthur Barker, 1936; *Ilonka Speaks of Hungary: Personal Impressions and an Interpretation of the National Character,* Hutchinson, 1936; *The Ramparts of Virtue* (novel), J. Cape, 1936; *Behold the Judge* (novel), Collins, 1937; *Felicity Greene: The Story of a Success,* J. Cape, 1937; *Man, Woman and Child,* Collins, 1938, reissued as *City of Scandals,* Transworld Publishers, 1955; *The Queer Fellow* (stories), Collins, 1939; *Gentleman of Stratford,* (novel), Collins, 1939, Harper, 1940; *The Ridiculous Hat* (novel), Collins, 1939.

Green Glory (novel), Collins, 1940, revised edition published with revised edition of *Green Ladies* as *Soldier of the Queen,* Transworld Publishers, 1957; *Green Ladies* (novel), Collins, 1940, revised edition (see above); *A Home Guard Drill Book and Field Service Manual* (army manual), Hodder & Stoughton, 1940, revised edition published as *Home Guard Drill and Battle Drill,* 1943; *Home Guard: A Handbook for the L.D.V.* (army manual), Hodder & Stoughton, 1940, revised edition published as *A Home Guard Handbook,* 1943; *Advanced Training for the Home Guard* (army manual), Hodder & Stoughton, 1941, revised edition, 1942; *Solitude Island: An Entertainment,* Collins, 1941; *Immortal Sergeant* (novel), Harper, 1942; *Britain Needs Books,* National Book Council (London), 1942; *Home Guard Proficiency* (army manual), Hodder & Stoughton, 1943; *Spearhead* (novel), Harper, 1943 (published in England as *Spear Head,* Collins, 1943); *Target Island* (novel), Harper, 1944; *The Human Face,* British Book Centre, 1945; *Britain's Home Guard: A Character Study,* Harrap, 1945; *Portrait of an Unknown Lady* (novel), Collins, 1945; *City of Departures* (novel), Collins, 1946; *The Woman from Nowhere,* Collins, 1946; *Selected Stories,* Fridberg, 1946; *Sarah,* Collins, 1948; *Body and Soul: On the Aesthetic and Philosophical Aspects of the Human Body and Soul,* British Book Centre, 1948; *The Mind's Eye: A Twelve-Month Journal* (autobiographical), Arthur Barker, 1949; *Julian's Way* (novel), Collins, 1949.

Windfall: A Diversion, Collins, 1951; *Turn the Key Softly* (novel), Collins, 1951; *Somerset Maugham,* Longmans, Green, 1952, revised edition, 1958; *The Prime of Life* (novel), Collins, 1954; (editor) Sarah Curran, *The Voice of Sarah Curran,* Greene's Library, 1955; *The Nimble Rabbit* (novel), Chatto & Windus, 1955; *The Prince and Petronella,* Chatto & Windus, 1956; *The Day They Robbed the Bank of England* (novel), Chatto & Windus, 1959.

The Front Door Key, Heinemann, 1960; (author of introduction) Holbrooke Jackson, *XX Unpublished Letters of Holbrooke Jackson to Joseph Ishill,* Oriole Press, 1960; *The Human Face Reconsidered,* Harrap, 1962; *The Face in Western Art,* Harrap, 1963; *The Meaning of Murder,* Whiting & Wheating, 1966, Crowell, 1967; *The Face of the Nude: A Study in Beauty,* Tudor, 1969.

SIDELIGHTS: Regarded by critics as a writer in the "English tradition," Brophy is best known for his war novels. Drawing on his own experiences in World War I, Brophy is concerned with the ambivalence which sensitive young men feel when confronting the brutality of war. Critics are divided in their judgments of these novels. Larry Barreto praises Brophy for sacrificing "the drama of battle to the development of the soul....," and a *New York Times* reviewer appreciates Brophy's skill in showing "a sensitive character being shaped and molded under the stress and strain of the most searing and dynamic influences of our time." However, David Tilden believes that Brophy's polemics interfere with his art: "Mr. Brophy is so sincere and so angry, so obsessed by his [war] theme, that he has neglected actually to create his characters. While it is admittedly difficult to give the revealing touch to a character in the space of a short chapter, it is none the less one of the important conceptions of fiction...."

In *Gentleman of Stratford,* Brophy wanted to create a novel of real depth. He related that "for some time I was, subconsciously, unable to trust myself to embark on big schemes in fiction, but I had long made up my mind to write one longish and, I hoped, profound novel.... That was *Gentleman of Stratford.* I rather think it marks the beginning of my real writing career." Critics accord Brophy varying degrees of success. John Mair finds that "the title of the book is all too apt; its hero is merely a gentleman from Stratford and even [Brophy's] habit of quoting Shakespeare at great length cannot make him other than a dull little fellow with a penchant for purple phrases." Maxwell Geismar believes that "Brophy's treatment of the Shakespearean era succeeds and admirably so. From the dim shadows of the past and the dusty pages of forgotten texts, he [has] brought back a host of haunting memories."

On the subject of the relationship between his personal life and his work, Brophy seemed remarkably contented: "I am healthy, not unduly neurotic, and perfectly happy in my home life: to that extent, perhaps, I am not in tune with the age I live in. I write journalism off the surface of my mind, and keep its depths for gestating and producing novels."

Four of Brophy's books, *Immortal Sergeant, Waterfront, Turn the Key Softly,* and *The Day They Robbed the Bank of England,* have been made into motion pictures; those books and others have been translated into a total of sixteen languages.

Brophy's art collection was well-known in Europe, and to some extent in the United States. He started collecting pictures and drawings in 1920, and concentrated, after 1945, in Old Master drawings, chiefly of the sixteenth century.

AVOCATIONAL INTERESTS: The theatre, walking, cricket, and hockey.

BIOGRAPHICAL/CRITICAL SOURCES: Saturday Review (English), May 5, 1928; *New York Times,* June 24, 1928, January 27, 1929, January 26, 1930, May 27, 1934, January 13, 1935, April 14, 1940, June 14, 1942, June 6, 1943, August 20, 1944; *Saturday Review,* July 14, 1928, February 2, 1935, July 18, 1942, May 27, 1967; *Books,* July 29, 1928, March 24, 1929, February 23, 1930, May 27, 1934, January 30, 1935, April 21, 1940; *Nation,* August 15, 1928, December 10, 1932, January 27, 1934, August 26, 1939, June 1, 1946; *New York World,* February 10, 1929; *New York Evening Post,* March 2, 1929; *Times Literary Supplement,* October 31, 1929, January 25, 1934, August 26, 1939, May 9, 1942, May 8, 1943, June 10, 1944, January 19, 1946; *Bookman,* March, 1930; *New Statesman,* December 10,

1932, January 27, 1934, August 26, 1939, June 1, 1946; *Spectator,* December 30, 1932, July 27, 1934, September 15, 1939, June 30, 1944; *Christian Science Monitor,* October 21, 1939; *New Republic,* April 22, 1940; *Manchester Guardian,* May 15, 1942, June 9, 1944; *New Yorker,* June 13, 1942, June 5, 1943; *Commonweal,* June 26, 1942; *Book Week,* June 13, 1943, May 8, 1966; *Atlantic,* August, 1943; *New York Review of Books,* October 6, 1966; *Choice,* March, 1968.

(Died November 13, 1965)

*   *   *

BROWIN, Frances Williams   1898-
(Frances B. Williams)

PERSONAL: First syllable of surname rhymes with "grow"; born September 13, 1898, in Media, Pa.; daughter of John J. (a businessman) and Alice (Roberts) Williams; married Beverly Milton Browin, February 24, 1923 (died September 9, 1962). *Education:* Swarthmore College, A.B., 1919. *Politics:* Independent. *Religion:* Quaker. *Home:* 1321 Spruce St., Philadelphia, Pa. 19107. *Agent:* Lenniger Literary Agency, 18 West 42nd St., New York, N.Y. 10036.

CAREER: Rotogravure Publications, Philadelphia, Pa., editor and art director, 1929-31; Pennsylvania Department of Welfare, Harrisburg, editor, 1932-36; *Friends Intelligencer,* Philadelphia, Pa., assistant editor, 1938-44; J. B. Lippincott Co., Philadelphia, Pa., copy editor, 1944-46; *Friends Journal,* Philadelphia, Pa., editor and manager, 1962-68.

WRITINGS: (With Seale Harris) *Banting's Miracle,* Lippincott, 1946; (with Harris) *Woman's Surgeon,* Macmillan, 1950; *Captured Words,* Aladdin Books, 1954; *Ginger's Cave,* Abelard, 1954; *The Whozits,* Abelard, 1955; (with Florence Aiken Banks) *Coins of Bible Days,* Macmillan, 1955; *Big Bridge to Brooklyn,* Aladdin Books, 1956; *Looking for Orlando,* Criterion, 1961; *Coins Have Tales to Tell,* Lippincott, 1966.

*   *   *

BROWN, Alberta L(ouise)   1894-

PERSONAL: Born January 9, 1894, in Chicago, Ill.; daughter of Hilles T. (a physician) and Mary E. (Willkins) Brown. *Education:* Tabor College, A.B., 1920. *Politics:* Independent. *Religion:* Catholic. *Home:* 3234 Butternut Lane, Kalamazoo, Mich. 49007.

CAREER: Council Bluffs (Iowa) Public Library, cataloger, 1920-24; Creighton University, Omaha, Neb., head librarian, 1925-29; University of North Dakota, Grand Forks, head cataloger, 1929-33; St. Mary's College, Notre Dame, Ind., head librarian, 1933-38; H. A. Brassert & Co. (consulting engineers), Chicago, Ill., librarian, 1938-40; Upjohn Co., Kalamazoo, Mich., head librarian, 1941-59; Western Michigan University, Kalamazoo, associate professor, department of librarianship, 1962-70. Library consultant, 1959—. Michigan Library Association, legislative agent, 1965-69; Kalamazoo County Library Board, chairman, 1965—. *Member:* American Library Association, Special Libraries Association (president, 1957-58), Michigan Library Association (honorary), Altrusa Club (Kalamazoo; president, 1948-50). *Awards, honors:* Special Libraries Association Hall of Fame Award; Upjohn Award.

WRITINGS: (With Lucille Jackson Strauss and I. M. Strieby) *Scientific and Technical Libraries: Their Organization and Administration,* Interscience, 1964, new edition, 1971. Contributor to *Special Libraries.*

BROWN, Constantine 1889-1966

PERSONAL: Born September 27, 1889, in Sheldon, Iowa; son of Alexander (an engineer and farmer) and Anna (Holdenburg) Brown; married Ethel Wheeler, 1906 (died, 1939); married Elizabeth Churchill (a writer), June 17, 1949; children: (first marriage) Alexandra Brown (Mrs. Frank Roudybush), Clover Ann Brown (Mrs. Frank Gannon). *Education:* University of Berlin, Ph.D., 1912. *Politics:* Independent. *Religion:* Catholic. *Home:* Via Martelli 10, Rome, Italy. *Office: Evening Star,* Second and Virginia Aves. S.E., Washington, D.C. 20003.

CAREER: London Times, London, England, war correspondent, 1914-16; *Chicago Daily News,* Chicago, Ill., European correspondent and bureau chief, 1920-30; *Washington Evening Star,* Washington, D.C., foreign affairs editor, columnist, 1941-66, column syndicated by Bell-McClure.

WRITINGS: (With Drew Pearson) *The American Diplomatic Game,* Doubleday, 1934 (published in England as *Diplomatic Game,* Dickson, 1935); *The Coming of the Whirlwind,* Regnery, 1964.

BIOGRAPHICAL/CRITICAL SOURCES: New York Times, February 25, 1966.

(Died February 23, 1966)

*   *   *

BROWN, Donald Eugene 1909-

PERSONAL: Born December 4, 1909, in Gibson, Iowa; son of Eugene L. and Olive (Scaife) Brown; married Sylvia M. Fousek, December 27, 1932; children: Karen Irene, Douglas Eugene. *Education:* William Penn College, student, 1926-28; University of Iowa, B.A., 1938, M.A., 1943. *Religion:* Methodist. *Home:* 500 East Alameda Dr., Tempe, Ariz. *Office:* Arizona State University, Tempe, Ariz.

CAREER: Teacher in Iowa public schools, 1928-38; University of Iowa, Iowa City, instructor in journalism, 1943-44; Radio Station WHO, Des Moines, Iowa, news editor, 1944-47; University of Illinois, College of Journalism and Communications, Urbana, 1947-63, associate professor, 1953-63; Arizona State University, Tempe, professor of mass communications, 1963—, department chairman, 1966—. Lecturer at International Center for the Advanced Training of Journalists, University of Strasbourg, 1959. Secretary, National Council on Radio and Television Journalism. Member, Champaign (Ill.) Public Library Board, 1961-63.

MEMBER: Association for Education in Journalism, Radio-Television News Directors Association, American Association of University Professors, Illinois News Broadcasters Association (executive secretary, 1955-63), Phi Beta Kappa, Kappa Tau Alpha, Sigma Delta Chi, Exchange Club (past president). *Awards, honors:* Gold Key Awards from Columbia Scholastic Press Association and Illinois Association of Teachers of Journalism.

WRITINGS: (With John Paul Jones) *Radio and Television News,* Rinehart, 1955; (with Frank E. Schooley) *Pronunciation Guide for Illinois Place Names,* University of Illinois Press, 1957; *Reference Shelf for Radio and Television Newsmen,* Radio-Television News Directors Association, 1962; *Careers in Radio and Television,* Quill and Scroll Foundation, 1965. Contributor to a number of magazines and professional journals.

AVOCATIONAL INTERESTS: Color photography.

BROWN, Herbert Ross 1902-

PERSONAL: Born February 9, 1902, in Allentown, Pa.; son of Guy Paul and Jennie (Miller) Brown; married Ruth Raker, August 21, 1929. *Education:* Lafayette College, B.Sc., 1924; Harvard University, M.A., 1928; Columbia University, Ph.D., 1939. *Politics:* Democrat. *Religion:* Congregationalist. *Home:* 32 College St., Brunswick, Me. 04011. *Office:* Department of English, Bowdoin College, Brunswick, Me. 04011.

CAREER: Lafayette College, Easton, Pa., instructor in English, 1924-25; Bowdoin College, Brunswick, Me., instructor, 1925-29, assistant professor, 1929-33, associate professor, 1933-39, professor of English, 1939-49, Edward Little Professor of Rhetoric and Oratory, 1949—. Visiting summer professor of English at Columbia University, 1940, 1941, 1945, Duke University, 1940, University of Minnesota, 1947, 1963, Bread Loaf School of English, 1948-55, University of Maine, 1965, Harvard University, 1968. Moderator, town of Brunswick, Maine, 1953—; chairman, Maine State Board of Education. Trustee of Zeta Psi Education Foundation, and Brunswick and Topsham Water District.

MEMBER: Colonial Society of Massachusetts (corresponding member), Century Association (New York), Phi Beta Kappa, Zeta Psi, Cumberland Club (Portland, Me.), *Awards, honors:* Duke University Centennial Award in American literature, 1940; honorary Litt.D. from Lafayette College, 1950, and Bowdoin College, 1963; L.H.D. from Bucknell University, 1951; LL.D. from University of Maine, 1965.

WRITINGS: The Sentimental Novel in America, Duke University Press, 1940; (with L. Richardson and G. Orians) *The Heritage of American Literature,* Ginn, 1950; *Sills of Bowdoin,* Columbia University Press, 1964.

Editor: Hawthorne, *The Snow Image,* Bradford Press, 1933; Hannah Foster, *The Coquette,* Columbia University Press, 1939; Oliver Wendell Holmes, *The Autocrat of the Breakfast Table,* Hill & Wang, 1958; William Brown, *The Power of Sympathy,* Frontier Press (Boston), 1961.

Contributor to *Dictionary of World Literature, Dictionary of Notable American Women,* and *Encyclopaedia Britannica;* also contributor to *American Literature* and *Modern Language Notes.* Managing editor, *New England Quarterly,* 1944—.

*   *   *

BROWN, Huntington 1899-

PERSONAL: Born October 30, 1899, in Utica, N.Y.; son of Leslie Warnick and Anne (Huntington) Brown; married Elizabeth Wentworth, August 20, 1925; children: Elizabeth (Mrs. Henry Melson Stommel), Leslie, Randolph, Martha (Mrs. Robert Burnett McGandy), Jonathan, Christopher (deceased). *Education:* Harvard University, A.B., 1922, Ph.D., 1930; Oxford University, B.Litt., 1926. *Home:* 1606 West 28th St., Minneapolis, Minn. 55408.

CAREER: Harvard University and Radcliffe College, Cambridge, Mass., instructor in English and tutor in Division of Modern Languages, 1927-37; University of Minnesota, Minneapolis, associate professor, 1937-42, professor of English, 1942-65; retired, 1965. Visiting summer professor, University of Chicago, 1946. *Member:* Modern Language Association of America, Council for Basic Education, American Association of University Professors.

WRITINGS: (Editor) Francois Girault, *The Tale of Gar-*

gantua and King Arthur, Harvard University Press, 1932; *Rabelais in English Literature*, Harvard University Press, 1933; (editor) Joseph Hall, *The Discovery of a New World*, Harvard University Press, 1937; *Prose Styles: Five Primary Types*, University of Minnesota Press, 1966. Contributor to *Encyclopedia of Poetry and Poetics*, Princeton University Press, 1965, and professional journals.

SIDELIGHTS: Brown is proficient in French, German, Italian, and Latin; knows some classical Greek, and a little Hebrew. He would like to see public school education in the United States directed by commissions of scholars instead of, "as at present, by specialists in pedagogy," and a federation of NATO nations comparable to that of our states. *Avocational interests:* Forest management.

*   *   *

BROWN, Ina Ladd 1905-

PERSONAL: Born May 14, 1905, in Sebec, Me.; daughter of Walter Scott (a state policeman) and Carolyn M. (Loring) Ladd; married Harold P. Brown (a hospital attendant), December 5, 1931 (deceased). *Education:* Attended Shaw Business College, Portland, Me. *Politics:* Republican. *Religion:* Protestant. *Home:* 14 Garland St., Bangor, Me.

CAREER: Secretary to Maine Supreme Court justices, Bangor, 1930-45, to attorney in private practice, Bangor, 1945-54; Mitchell, Ballou, & Keith (formerly Mitchell & Ballou), Bangor, legal secretary, 1954—. Writer, performer, and past-president, Bangor-Brewer Civic Theatre. *Member:* National League of American Pen Women (vice-president, Pine Tree branch, 1958-64), Poetry Fellowship of Maine (president, three terms; former executive secretary), Maine Writers' Research Club, Maine Press, Radio & Television Women, New Hampshire Poetry Society, Maine Writers Conference (vice-chairman, 1962-64; chairman of poetry tournament, 1966), Bangor-Brewer Soroptimist Club (secretary, 1964). *Awards, honors:* Recchia Medal for poetry and prose, Maine Writers Conference, 1960.

WRITINGS: Merry-go-round (poetry), Falmouth Press, 1943; *Just for Luck* (poetry), Falmouth Press, 1946; *More of the Same* (poetry), Falmouth Press, 1949; *As Time Goes By* (poetry), Falmouth Press, 1951; *Johnny-Cake and Gingerbread* (essays and stories), Falmouth Press, 1953; *Homespun* (poetry), Golden Quill, 1959; *Leaves on the Wind* (poetry), Golden Quill, 1963; *Cross-Roads* (poetry), Golden Quill, 1969.

Plays—all produced by Bangor-Brewer Civic Theatre: "Dear David," 1954; "Dark Music," 1955; "Peace and Quiet," 1957; "Bitter Bread," 1958. Contributor of poetry to magazines.

WORK IN PROGRESS: A second collection of prose shorts and essays; a collection of poetry; a play, "The Shallow Cup."

SIDELIGHTS: Mrs. Brown lectures on poetry before clubs and school groups. *Avocational interests:* The theater, travel, gardening, helping retarded and underprivileged children.

*   *   *

BROWN, John 1887-

PERSONAL: Born November 27, 1887, in Grimsby, Lincolnshire, England; son of George (a justice of the peace) and Ellen S. (Lee) Brown; married Margery Featherstone;

children: G. Spencer, David John. *Education:* Sidney Sussex College, Cambridge, B.A., 1909, *Home:* Bargate House, 34 Bargate, Grimsby, Lincolnshire, England.

CAREER: Elgon Estates Ltd. (coffee growers), Kenya, chairman. Artist, and writer on bridge. *Military service:* British Army, World War I; served in British East Africa, Salonica, and France. *Member:* Lincolnshire Artists' Society, National Liberal Club.

WRITINGS: Winning Tricks, Duckworth, 1947; *Winning Defence*, Duckworth, 1952; *Bidding Craft*, Duckworth, 1962; *Bridge with Dora*, Duckworth, 1965. Contributor of articles to bridge periodicals in England, United States, and South Africa.

*   *   *

BROWN, LeRoy Chester 1908-

PERSONAL: Born May 29, 1908, in Valpen, Ind.; son of Lemuel C. (a telegraph operator) and Bertha (McCormick) Brown; married Anne Roales (an art teacher), May 12, 1943; children: David, Gregory. *Education:* Greenville College, A.B., 1947; University of Illinois, M.A., 1949; Bradley University, Ed.D., 1953. *Home:* Olivet College, Kankakee, Ill. 60901.

CAREER: Dale Carnegie Associates, New York, N.Y., instructor, 1947—; Olivet College, Kankakee, Ill., professor of speech, 1951—; Ethel Burge Associates, Chicago, Ill., public speaker, 1963-64; free-lance writer. Professional speaker. *Military service:* U.S. Army, 1942-45; served in Philippines. *Member:* Pi Kappa Delta. *Awards, honors:* Certificates of merit from Olivet Nazarene College, 1961, for *Speaking to Persuade,* and 1962, for *Christian Go-Givers.*

WRITINGS: Speaking to Persuade: A Practical Textbook for Any Class or Any Person Who Wants to Speak More Effectively, Naylor, 1960; *Christian Go-Givers* (stories), Review & Herald, 1961; *They Stood Tall for God,* Review & Herald, 1963; *How to Make a Good Speech,* Fell, 1964; *How to Use the Power of Enthusiasm,* Fell, 1965; *Champions All,* Review & Herald, 1966; *How to Acquire a Million-Dollar Personality,* Fell, 1968. Contributor of about one thousand short stories, articles, and poems to periodicals for juniors.

WORK IN PROGRESS: A Song in the Night, for Beacon Hill Press; a book of biographical sketches about Christian leaders.

AVOCATIONAL INTERESTS: Pitching horseshoes and playing tennis.

*   *   *

BROWN, Lloyd Arnold 1907-1966

PERSONAL: Born May 5, 1907, in Providence, R.I.; son of Arnold Cleveland and Eva Leone (Corbin) Brown; married Florence Eldred Dragoo (a librarian), August 7, 1935; children: Stephen Seabury. *Education:* Wayne State University, student, 1928-29; University of Michigan, A.B., 1933. *Politics:* Republican. *Religion:* Protestant. *Home:* 326 Grieb Rd., Wallingford, Conn. 06492.

CAREER: Began as co-owner of a rare book business; University of Michigan, William L. Clements Library, Ann Arbor, 1935-42, curator of maps, 1935-40, acting director, 1941; Peabody Institute, Baltimore, Md., librarian, 1942-56; Chicago Historical Society, Chicago, Ill., director, 1956-58; Historic Annapolis, Inc., Annapolis, Md., director of research, 1960-61. Johns Hopkins University, Baltimore, Md., instructor in geography, 1943-47, lecturer in cartography, 1947-56. *Member:* American Association for the Advancement of Science (fellow), Bibliographical Society of America, American Congress on Surveying and Mapping, Grolier Club, Odd Volumes. *Awards, honors:* Guggenheim fellow, 1954-55; Boys' Clubs of America Gold Medal, 1961, for *Map Making: The Art that Became a Science.*

WRITINGS: (Editor with Howard H. Peckham) *The Revolutionary War Journals of Henry Dearborn, 1775-1783,* Caxton Club, 1939, Plenum, 1971; *Notes on the Care and Cataloguing of Old Maps,* Hawthorn, 1940; *Jean Dominique Cassini and His World Map of 1696,* University of Michigan Press, 1941; (contributor of fourteen maps) James T. Adams, editor, *Atlas of American History,* Scribner, 1943; *The Story of Maps,* Little, Brown, 1949; *Early Maps of the Ohio Valley: A Selection of Maps, Plans, and Views Made by Indians and Colonials from 1673 to 1783,* University of Pittsburgh Press, 1959; *Map Making: The Art that Became a Science,* Little, Brown, 1960. Also author of *The Reproduction of Maps and Charts: A Statement,* published by Meriden Gravure Co. Contributor to learned journals and to newspapers. Member of editorial advisory board of *American Neptune,* and of advisory council for *Atlas of American History.*

WORK IN PROGRESS: *The Mapping of America,* for Little, Brown.

AVOCATIONAL INTERESTS: Sailing and other activities connected with the water.

(Died March 30, 1966)

* * *

BROWN, Robert Joseph 1907-
(Bob Brown)

PERSONAL: Born August 19, 1907, in Rockwood, Tenn. *Home:* 20 Vandalia St., Asheville, N.C. 28806.

CAREER: Onetime editor; currently lecturer-demonstrator of "Science Circus," appearing at school assemblies throughout eastern and southern United States. *Member:* American Association for Advancement of Science, National Education Association, National Science Teachers Association, International Platform Association, International Brotherhood of Magicians, North Carolina Academy of Science.

WRITINGS: Science Circus, Fleet, 1960; *Science Circus No. 2,* Fleet, 1964; *Take 100,000 Volts,* Vow Labs, 1964; *Science Treasures: Let's Repeat the Great Experiments,* Fleet, 1968. Author of libretto for a comic opera, "The Superintendent," for which Richard Trevarthen is writing the music. Author of newspaper panel, "Science for You," syndicated by General Features Corp.

SIDELIGHTS: Brown was the inventor, with W. B. Lilly, of an improvement in the automotive air bag safety device.

* * *

BROWNING, Mary 1887-

PERSONAL: Born October 26, 1887, in Todd County, Ky.; daughter of James E. (a farmer and civil engineer) and Mildred Anna (a musician and teacher; maiden name Jones) Browning. *Education:* George Peabody College for Teachers, B.S., 1923; Teachers College, Columbia University, M.A., 1927; summer study at Ohio State University, 1934, University of Chicago, 1936, University of Southern California, 1938, and Greeley Teachers College, 1949. *Politics:* Democrat. *Religion:* Methodist. *Home:* 1267 Cherokee Rd., Louisville, Ky. 40204.

CAREER: Teacher in rural, town, city, and normal schools prior to 1929; Louisville Public Schools, Louisville, Ky., teacher for five years, and supervisor of kindergarten and primary education, 1929-58. Instructor in education classes, University of Louisville, 1939-45. *Member:* National Education Association (first vice-president of supervisors department, 1935-37; member of executive board of elementary-kindergarten-primary department, 1958-61), American Council on Education, Association for Supervision and Curriculum Development, Louisville Education Association, Kappa Delta Pi, Delta Kappa Gamma (chapter president, 1943-45), Crescent Hill Woman's Club.

WRITINGS: (With Marian Walsh) *English Workbook,* Grade 5, American Book Co., 1933; (with Ullen Leavell) *Friendly Hour Readers,* Books 1-8, American Book Co., 1935; *Adventuring with Pioneers,* Heath, 1949; *Apples, a Ball, and Some Catnip: An Alphabet Book,* E. C. Seale, 1963.

WORK IN PROGRESS: Research for a biography of Abraham Lincoln for the elementary grades.

AVOCATIONAL INTERESTS: Gardening, travel, and bridge.

* * *

BRUCE, Robert 1927-

PERSONAL: Born December 20, 1927, in Darlington, County Durham, England; son of Robert and Jessie Maggie (Rae) Bruce; married Elizabeth Margaret Thompson (a doctor), July 17, 1951; children: Elizabeth Lynn. *Education:* King's College, Durham, M.B., B.S., 1951, M.D., 1961, M.R.C.G.P., 1962. *Politics:* Anti-war. *Religion:* Agnostic-humanist. *Home:* "Torrish" Newcastle Rd., Chester le Street, County Durham, England.

CAREER: Royal Victoria Infirmary, Newcastle upon Tyne, England, house physician in dermatological department, 1952; General Hospital, County Durham, England, house physician, 1952-53, medical registrar, 1953-54, 1956-59; medical practitioner, Chester le Street, County Durham, 1959—. *Military service:* British Army, Royal Army Medical Corps, 1954-56; served in Germany; became captain. *Member:* Royal College of General Practitioners (chairman of working party investigating industrial health, 1962), British Medical Association, General Practitioners' Association (chairman), Medical Practitioners Union.

WRITINGS: Cheaper Tackle, A. & C. Black, 1960; *Fly-Fishing: A Practical Introduction,* Soccer, 1963. Contributor of articles to medical and medico-political journals.

WORK IN PROGRESS: Investigation into drug efficacy in disease under general-practice conditions; a novel; a children's novel.

AVOCATIONAL INTERESTS: Fresh-water angling, swimming, shooting, woodwork, and hi-fidelity sound reproduction.

* * *

BRUNER, Margaret E. (Baggerly) 1886-197(?)

PERSONAL: Born September 25, 1886, in West Fork, Ind.; daughter of Vardamon David (minister and farmer) and Henrietta S. (Saunders) Baggerly; married Vate Bruner (retail store department manager), October 7, 1916 (deceased). *Education:* Attended The Academy, Rome, Ind., and Bryant & Stratton Business College, Louisville, Ky. *Politics:* Democrat. *Religion:* Unitarian Universalist. *Home:* 611 Goodwin St., New Castle, Ind. 47362.

CAREER: Poet and columnist. Before 1916, worked as stenographer in Louisville, Ky., and in office of Maxwell-Brisco Motor Co. (now Chrysler Motor Co.); *News Republican* (newspaper), New Castle, Ind., writer of weekly column, "In Thoughtful Mood," for over twenty years. Member of Freedoms Foundation and Community Chest. *Member:* World Poetry Society, National League of American Pen Women, Poets Corner, Indiana Poetry Society (honorary), Saturday Club (New Castle). *Awards, honors:* Honor certificate of Freedoms Foundation, 1960, for newspaper article, "The Constitution and the Bill of Rights"; Indiana University award for best book of poems by an Indiana author, 1960, for *The Road Lies Onward*; first prize in book division of Poets' Corner, Inc., 1962, for *The Hills Were Friends*; named outstanding author of Great Lakes Area by National League of American Pen Women, 1964; first prize in Poets Corner, Inc. annual contest, 1964-65, for *The Unwritten Law*; cash awards from poetry magazines.

WRITINGS—Poems: *The Hill Road*, Kaleidograph Press, 1932; *Mysteries of Earth*, Kaleidograph Press, 1934; *In Thoughtful Mood*, Kaleidograph Press, 1937; *Midstream*, Kaleidograph Press, 1940; *Be Slow to Falter*, Kaleidograph Press, 1941; *The Constant Heart*, Kaleidograph Press, 1952; *Above Earth's Sorrow*, Humphries, 1955; *The Deeper Need*, Christopher, 1957; *The Road Lies Onward*, Christopher, 1960; *The Hills Were Friends*, Christopher 1962; *The Unwritten Law*, Christopher, 1963; *Eternal Quest*, Christopher, 1968.

Poems included in approximately 100 anthologies, among these, *Poems That Touch the Heart* (contributor of twenty nine poems), compiled by A. L. Alexander, Garden City, 1941, revised edition, 1956, *Masterpieces of Religious Verse*, compiled by James D. Morrison, Harper, 1948, and *Poems That Live Forever*, compiled by Hazel Felleman, Doubleday, 1965. Contributor of poetry to textbooks and holograph collections and of articles to *Indianapolis Sunday Star*, *Muncie Evening Press*, *Living Tissue*, *Cats Magazine*, and other periodicals. Former member of editorial committee, *American Poetry Magazine*.

SIDELIGHTS: Mrs. Bruner wrote: "I have not traveled to any extent and speak no foreign language. I remember Emerson once said, 'We must carry the beautiful with us or we find it not.' But I have done much research. . . ." Most of the articles written for her newspaper column were literary essays examining diverse aspects of English and American letters. Many of these articles have been reprinted as guest editorials, and in magazines. Several of her poems have been set to music by the late Dr. Emmet Pendleton.

BIOGRAPHICAL/CRITICAL SOURCES: Arthur W. Schumaker, compiler, *A History of Indiana Literature*, Indiana Historical Society, 1962.

(Deceased)

*   *   *

BRUNNER, Edmund de S(chweinitz) 1889-1973

PERSONAL: Born November 4, 1889, in Bethlehem, Pa.; son of Franklin Henry (a business executive) and Benigna (de Schweinitz) Brunner; married Mary W. Vogler, De-

cember 16, 1912 (deceased); married Lousene Rousseau Fry (an author) November 6, 1948; children: (first marriage) Edmund de S. Jr., Wilfred Robert. *Education:* Moravian College, B.A., 1909, M.A., 1912, Ph.D., 1914. *Politics:* Independent. *Home:* 10 High Ridge Road, Wilton, Conn. 06897.

CAREER: Ordained to ministry of Moravian Church, 1911; pastor in Coopersburg, Pa., 1911-14, and Easton, Pa., 1914-16; Moravian Church, executive secretary of Country Church Commission, 1912-20; Wartime Commission of Churches, New York, N.Y., rural secretary, 1917-19; Institute of Social and Religious Research, New York, N.Y., director of town and country surveys, 1921-31; Columbia University, New York, N.Y., professor of sociology, 1931-64, chairman of Bureau of Applied Social Research, 1951-64. Lecturer at Drew University, 1922-29, at various universities of New Zealand and Australia, summer and fall, 1937, Colorado State University, summer, 1955, Western Connecticut State College, 1958-68. Chairman, Board of Education, Mountain Lake, N.J., 1923-25, member of governor's commission on education and welfare in penal institutions of New York, 1934-35, member of President Roosevelt's advisory committee on education, 1936-38, member of executive board, American Association for Adult Education. U.S. Department of Agriculture (War Food Administration), advisor, 1936-51; member of joint U.S. Department of Agriculture-Land Grant College Association committee (served on postwar policy and program for the extension service), 1946-48; trustee of Moravian College, Bethlehem, Pa., 1948-65, board member of International Development Services, Inc., 1953-65; senior consultant for Institute for Social Research, University of Natal, South Africa, 1945. *Member:* American Sociological Association, Rural Sociological Society (president, 1946), Foreign Policy Association, American Philatelic Association, American Philatelic Congress. *Awards, honors:* L.H.D., Moravian College; M.A., University of Queensland; LL.D., University of Natal.

WRITINGS: History of Moravian Missions to the Indians of Southern California, Moravian Historical Society, 1915; *Cooperation in Coopersburg*, Missionary Education Movement of the U.S. and Canada, 1916; *The New Country Church Building*, Missionary Education Movement of the U.S. and Canada, 1917; *The Country Church in the New World Order*, Association Press, 1919.

A Church and Community Survey of Pend Oreille County, Washington, Doran, 1922; *A Church and Community Survey of Salem County, New Jersey*, Doran, 1922; (with wife, Mary V. Brunner) *Irrigation and Religion: A Study of Religious and Social Conditions in Two California Counties, Orange and Stanislaus*, Doran, 1922; *Church Life in the Rural South*, Doran, 1923; *Churches of Distinction in Town and Country*, Doran, 1923; *Tested Methods in Town and Country Churches*, Doran, 1923; (with Hermann N. Morse) *Town and Country Church in the United States*, Doran, 1923; *Surveying Your Community: A Handbook of Method for the Rural Church*, Doran, 1925; (with Gwendolyn S. Hughes and Marjorie Patten) *American Agricultural Villages*, Doran, 1927; *Village Communities*, Doran, 1927; *The Church and the Agricultural Crisis*, Pilgrim, 1928; *Rural Korea: A Preliminary Survey of Social, Economic and Religious Conditions*, International Missionary Council, 1928; (with Kenyon L. Butterfield, W. J. McKee, and T. J. Jones) *Christian Missions in Relation to Rural Problems*, International Missionary Council, 1929; *Immigrant Farmers and Their Children*, Doubleday, 1929.

Industrial Village Churches, Institute of Social and Religious Research, 1930; (with Irving Lorge) *American Agricultural Villages: 1930*, American Statistical Association, 1933; (with J. H. Kolb) *Rural Social Trends*, McGraw, 1933; *The Larger Parish: A Movement or an Enthusiasm?*, Institute of Social and Religious Research, 1934; (with H. P. Douglas) *The Protestant Church as a Social Institution*, Harper, 1935, Russell, 1972; *Radio and the Farmer*, Radio Institute of the Audible Arts, 1935; (with Kolb) *A Study of Rural Society*, Houghton, 1936, 4th edition, Greenwood Press, 1971; (with Samuel H. Patterson and E. A. Choate) *The School in American Society*, International Textbook, 1936; (with Irving Lorge) *Rural Trends in Depression Years: A Survey of Village Centered Agricultural Communities, 1930-36*, Columbia University Press, 1937, Arno Press, 1971; *Rural Australia and New Zealand: Some Observations of Current Trends*, American Council, Institute of Pacific Relations, 1938.

(With others) *Community Organization and Adult Education: A Five-Year Experiment*, University of North Carolina Press, 1942; *Working With Rural Youth*, American Council on Education, 1942; (editor with others) *Farmers of the World: The Development of Agricultural Extension*, Columbia University Press, 1945; (with Hsun-pao Yang) *Rural America and the Extension Service: A History and Critique of the Cooperative Agricultural and Home Economic Extension Service*, Teachers College, Columbia University, 1949.

(With Wilbur C. Hallenbeck) *American Society: Urban and Rural Patterns*, Harper, 1955; *The Growth of a Science: A Half-Century of Rural Sociological Research in the United States*, Harper, 1957; (with Sloan R. Wayland) *The Educational Characteristics of the American People*, Teachers College, Columbia University, for Bureau of Applied Social Research, 1958; (with William Nicholls II and Sam D. Sieber) *The Role of a National Organization in Adult Education*, Columbia University, for Bureau of Applied Social Research, 1959; (with others) *An Overview of Adult Education Research*, Adult Education Association of the U.S., 1959; (consultant) Stuart Chase, *The Proper Study of Mankind*, Harper, 1956, 2nd revised edition, 1965. Author of over 300 articles to magazines and periodicals in America, England, Australia, South Africa, and Korea. Editor, *Christian Work*, 1921-25.

WORK IN PROGRESS: Two separate philatelic research lines; the problem of definition in sociology and its relation to applied social research.

SIDELIGHTS: Brunner told *CA*: "Have traveled on all continents, done socio-economic field surveys and research in Asia and Africa. Lectured in Fiji, China, New Zealand, Australia, Canada, Britain. Motivation—a faith that with adequate support social sciences [through] research and education can help build a better world."

(Died December 21, 1973)

* * *

BRYANT, Bernice (Morgan) 1908-

PERSONAL: Born April 6, 1908, in St. Louis, Mo.; daughter of Swiney and Augusta (Kuster) Morgan; married Louis Henry Bryant, June 16, 1928 (deceased); children: Bernice. *Education:* Illinois State Teacher's College, summer student, 1924, 1925; University of Illinois, student, 1926-27; Chicago Academy of Fine Arts, summer student, 1934. *Home:* Brymor, Strasburg, Va.

CAREER: Penn Hall Preparatory School and Junior College, Chambersburg, Pa., social dean until retirement in 1968. Author of books for children. *Member:* Authors League of America, Midland Authors, Professional Writer's Club, Children's Reading Round Table. *Awards, honors:* Illinois Women's Press Club Award for *Trudy Terrill, Eighth Grader.*

WRITINGS: Yammy Buys a Bicycle, Albert Whitman, 1941; *Pedie and the Twins: A Read-it-Yourself Story*, Albert Whitman, 1942; *Future Perfect: A Guide to Personality and Popularity for the Junior Miss*, Bobbs-Merrill, 1944, revised edition, 1957; *Trudy Terrill, Eighth Grader*, Bobbs-Merrill, 1946; *Everybody Likes Butch*, Childrens Press, 1947, revised edition published as *Let's Be Friends*, Childrens Press, 1954; *God's Wonder World: A Book of Devotional Readings for Children*, Bethany, 1944; *Trudy Terrill, High School Freshman*, Bobbs-Merrill, 1948; *Fancy Free*, Bobbs-Merrill, 1949; *Follow the Leader*, Houghton, 1950; *Miss Behavior: Popularity, Poise and Personality for the Teen-age Girl*, Bobbs-Merrill, 1948, revised edition, 1960; *Dan Morgan, Boy of the Wilderness*, Bobbs-Merrill, 1952, revised edition published as *Dan Morgan, Wilderness Boy*, 1962; *P's and Q's for Boys and Girls: A Book About Manners*, Bobbs-Merrill, 1953, revised edition, 1963; *Party ABC's: A Guide to Party Planning and Behavior for Beginning Hosts and Hostesses–10 to 14 Years Old*, Bobbs-Merrill, 1954; *George Gershwin: Young Composer*, Bobbs-Merrill, 1965.

WORK IN PROGRESS: Another book for Bobbs-Merrill's "Childhood of Famous Americans" series.

* * *

BUCHANAN, Donald W(illiam) 1908-19?

PERSONAL: Born April 9, 1908, in Lethbridge, Alberta, Canada; son of William A. (a publisher) and Alma (Freeman) Buchanan. *Education:* University of Toronto, B.A., 1930; Oxford University, graduate study, 1930-31. *Home:* 460 Crestview Rd., Ottawa, Canada.

CAREER: Most of career has been linked with Canadian arts and culture. Founder and organizer of National Film Society, 1935-36, supervisor of talks for Canadian Broadcasting Co., 1937-40, supervisor of rural circuits for National Film Board, 1941-44, and supervisor of displays, 1945-47, director of cultural exhibits for Canadian Corporation 1967 World Exhibition, Montreal, Quebec. Photographer, exhibiting work at one-man shows in Italy, France, and in Canadian galleries. Trustee, National Gallery of Canada.

WRITINGS: James Wilson Morrice (biography), Ryerson, 1936; *Educational and Cultural Films in Canada*, National Film Society of Canada, 1936; *Les Sentiments religieux de Victor Hugo de 1825 a 1848*, Imprimerie de l'Est, 1939; (with others) John Willis, editor, *Canadian Boards at Work*, Macmillan (Toronto), 1941; (editor) *This is Canada* (photographs), Ryerson, 1944; *The Growth of Canadian Painting*, Collins, 1950; *Contemporary Canadian Painters* (text for exhibition organized by National Gallery of Canada for circulation in Australia, February-December, 1957), [Ottawa], 1957; *Alfred Pellan*, McClelland & Stewart, 1962; *A Nostalgic View of Canada* (autobiography; includes photographs by Buchanan), McClelland & Stewart, 1962; *Sausages and Roses*, [Ottawa], 1963; (with Ossip Zadkine) *Le Monde secret de Zadkine vu par Donald Buchanan/The Secret World of Zadkine as Seen by Donald Buchanan*, bilingual edition, Maquette de Lional Scanteye, 1966. Editor, *Canadian Art*, 1941-58.

(Deceased)

BUCK, Marion A(shby) 1909-

PERSONAL: Born January 30, 1909, in Watertown, N.Y.; daughter of H. Duane (a retail merchant) and Carrie (Dunbar) Buck. *Education:* Radcliffe College, A.B., 1930, Ph.D., 1953; Syracuse University, M.A., 1931. *Office address:* P.O. Box 2636, Laguna Hills, CA 92653.

CAREER: St. Lawrence University, Canton, N.Y., instructor, 1946-49, assistant professor, 1949-52; New York State Legislature, Albany, director of studies, Joint Legislative Committee on Commerce and Economic Development, 1953-64; Syracuse University, Syracuse, N.Y., assistant professor, 1956-61, associate professor of business administration, 1961-65; Federal Reserve Bank, Cleveland, Ohio, senior economist, 1965-67; California State College, Dominguez Hills, California, professor and chairman of department, 1967-73, professor emeritus, 1973—. Consultant to business and government. *Member:* Economic History Association, Business History Association, Jefferson County Historical Association, Phi Beta Kappa, Beta Gamma Sigma.

WRITINGS: (With S. C. Sufrin and J. H. Thompson) *The Economic Status of Upstate New York at Mid-Century*, Business Research Center, Syracuse University, 1960; (with S. Paul and Sufrin) *Small Sellers and Large Buyers in American Industry*, Business Research Center, Syracuse Univeristy, 1961; (editor) J. C. Myles, *Small Business Suppliers in a Changing Market*, Business Research Center, Syracuse University, 1962; (with Sufrin) *What Price Progress?*, Rand McNally, 1963. Contributor to *Challenge*.

WORK IN PROGRESS: *The Financing of the American Revolution; Money Supply and Economic Growth 1820-1860.*

*   *   *

BUCKINGHAM, Clyde E(dwin) 1907-

PERSONAL: Born December 27, 1907, in Huntington, Ind.; son of Robert E. and Lillian (Parker) Buckingham; married Virginia Converse (an office worker), March 13, 1937; children: David, Lytle, Mary K. *Education:* DePauw University, A.B. (with honors), 1929; Colgate-Rochester Divinity School, B.D., 1932; University of Chicago, graduate study, 1932-33. *Religion:* Baptist. *Home:* 6910 Jefferson Ave., Falls Church, Va.

CAREER: Cook County Bureau of Public Welfare, Chicago, Ill., social worker, 1933-34; Illinois Emergency Relief Commission, administrator in northern Illinois, 1934-41; American National Red Cross, field representative and field director for Midwestern area, St. Louis, Mo., 1941-43, personnel director, then director of research and statistics for Southeastern area, Atlanta, Ga., 1943-51, assistant director, then director of research information, Washington, D.C., 1951-68, historian and research analyst, Washington, D.C., 1968-71. Consultant to writers and researchers in the field of social welfare. *Member:* Academy of Political Science, American Academy of Political and Social Science, International Platform Association, American Historical Association, Columbia Historical Association. *Awards, honors:* Award from American Red Cross for *Red Cross Disaster Relief.*

WRITINGS: *Red Cross Disaster Relief*, Public Affairs, 1955; *For Humanity's Sake*, Public Affairs, 1965. Contributor of about twenty articles to historical journals and other scholarly publications.

WORK IN PROGRESS: *Red Cross During the Johnson Administration*, part of the "Pentagon Papers" project (manuscript completed in 1969 but not released for publication); *Red Cross Park.*

SIDELIGHTS: Buckingham told *CA*, "I am the author of innumerable 'limited distribution' studies requested for the use of Red Cross or governmental agencies. Some of them were useful in providing background information in shaping national or international policies. While not 'published,' frequently thousands of copies were distributed. Frequently these studies involved the use of large collections of information which were computerized or the use of restricted and confidential information."

Avocational Interests: Tournament bridge, gardening.

*   *   *

BUCKLER, Ernest 1908-

PERSONAL: Born July 19, 1908, in Dalhousie West, Nova Scotia, Canada; son of Appleton (a farmer) and Mary (Swift) Buckler. *Education:* Dalhousie University, B.A., 1929; University of Toronto, M.A., 1930. *Home:* Bridgetown, Nova Scotia, Canada. *Agent:* Curtis Brown Ltd., 60 East 56th St., New York, N.Y. 10022.

CAREER: Manufacturers Life Insurance Co., Toronto, Ontario, actuarial work, 1931-36; farmer in Nova Scotia, 1936—; free-lance writer, 1937—. *Awards, honors:* Maclean's Magazine $1,000 prize for fiction, 1948; President's Medal from Governor-General Awards Board for the best Canadian short story, 1957 and 1958; Canada Council fellowships, 1960, 1963, and 1966; D.Litt., University of New Brunswick, 1969.

WRITINGS: *The Mountain and the Valley* (novel), Henry Holt, 1952; *The Cruelest Month* (novel), McClelland & Stewart, 1963; *Oxbells and Fireflies: A Memoir*, Knopf, 1968. Contributor of short stories to several collections, including *Atlantic Anthology*, McClelland & Stewart, *Maclean's Canada*, McClelland & Stewart, *Christmas in Canada*, Dent, and *Canadian Short Stories*, Ryerson. Writer of scripts for radio plays and talks. Contributor of stories and articles to *Coronet*, *Esquire*, *Atlantic Monthly*, *Country Gentlemen*, *Ladies' Home Journal*, *Chatelaine*, *Liberty*, *Star Weekly*, *Los Angeles Times*, and other magazines and newspapers. Former columnist, *Saturday Night.*

WORK IN PROGRESS: Text to accompany a "picture book" of Nova Scotia.

*   *   *

BUDD, Kenneth George 1904-1972

PERSONAL: Born August 9, 1904, in Kew, Surrey, England; son of Henry George and Priscilla (MacDermott) Budd; married Betty Dilnot (a physiotherapist); children: one son. *Education:* Attended King's College, University of London. *Home:* The Rectory, Caterham, Surrey, England.

CAREER: Ordained priest, Church of England, at Canterbury, 1928. Curate or priest-in-charge at Norbury and Streatham, 1928-38; vicar of Holy Trinity, Upper Tooting, 1938-52; rector of Caterham, Surrey, 1952-72, rural dean, 1965-72. *Military service:* Royal Air Force, chaplain, 1941-45. *Member:* Private Libraries Association.

WRITINGS: *A Modern Pilgrimage*, S.C.M. Press, 1931;

The Foundations of Faith, Mowbray, 1935; *The Day Is At Hand*, Allen & Unwin, 1946; *The Last Victorian*, Centaur Press, 1960. Regular religious columnist, *Woman's Weekly*.

(Died August 12, 1972)

* * *

BULL, William E(merson) 1909-1972

PERSONAL: Born October 4, 1909, in Sun Prairie, Wis.; son of George Robinson (a printer and newspaper publisher) and Margaret (Hammond) Bull; married Helen May Langewisch (an artist); children: Kay Sather, Jan Emerson, Guy William. *Education:* University of Wisconsin, B.A. and M.A., 1936, Ph.D., 1940. *Home:* 2321 Pelham Ave., Los Angeles, Calif. 90064. *Office:* University of California, Los Angeles, Calif. 90024.

CAREER: University of Wisconsin, Madison, instructor, 1940, Markham traveling fellow, 1940-41; University of Iowa, Iowa City, instructor in Spanish, 1941-42; Washington University, St. Louis, Mo., 1942-49, began as instructor, became assistant professor of Spanish; University of California, Los Angeles, 1949-72, began as assistant professor, professor of Spanish language and literature, 1959-72. Visiting professor, University of California, summer, 1948, University of Michigan, summer, 1959, University of New Mexico, 1961-62, University of Puget Sound, summer, 1963. *Member:* Linguistic Society of America, Modern Language Association of America, American Association of Teachers of Spanish, West Coast Philological Society, Phi Beta Kappa, Phi Eta Sigma, Sigma Delta Pi.

WRITINGS: (With Harry Williams) *Semeianca del Mundo: A Medieval Description of the World*, University of California Press, 1959; *Time, Tense, and the Verb*, University of California Press, 1960; *A Visual Grammar of Spanish*, University of California Extension, 1962; (with V. A. Chamberlin) *Clarin: The Critic in Action*, Oklahoma State University Publications, 1963; *Spanish for Teachers: Applied Linguistics*, Ronald, 1965. Contributor to *Hispania, Economic Geography, Classical Journal, Modern Language Journal*, and other linguistic periodicals.

WORK IN PROGRESS: A monograph on his work in a new branch of linguistics, systemic linguistics; preparation of linguistically-oriented teaching materials for Spanish in grade and high schools and universities.

SIDELIGHTS: Bull read French, Portuguese, Latin, and German in addition to Spanish, and did research on a total of fifty-five languages.

(Died October 26, 1972)

* * *

BULLEID, H(enry) A(nthony) V(aughan) 1912-
(D. Collins)

PERSONAL: Born December 23, 1912, in Doncaster, Yorkshire, England; son of Oliver V. S. (an engineer) and Marjorie (Ivatt) Bulleid; married Ann McCann, April 11, 1942; children: David, Susan, Hilary. *Education:* Attended Ampleforth College; Pembroke College, Cambridge, B.A., 1933. *Religion:* Roman Catholic. *Home:* Lansdown Rd., Abergavenny, Monmouthshire, England.

CAREER: Vickers-Armstrongs Ltd., Newcastle, England, assistant research manager, 1944-47; British Nylon Spinners Ltd., Pontypool, Monmouthshire, England, deputy chief engineer, 1947-56, production manager, 1956-58, chief engineer, 1961-63, director, 1963—. *Member:* Institute of

Mechanical Engineers (council), Royal Photographic Society (associate).

WRITINGS: Trick Effects with the Cine Camera, Link House Publications, 1936, 9th edition, 1950; *Special Effects in Cinematography*, Fountain Press, 1954; *G. B. Bell and Howell 8mm. Cine Manual*, Fountain Press, 1957; *Master Builders of Steam*, Ian Allan, 1963; *The Aspinall Era*, Sportshelf, 1967. Contributor to *Amateur Photographer*.

WORK IN PROGRESS: Research into railway engineering in the United Kingdom from 1880-1920, and into the postal history of Western Australia from 1840-1912.

* * *

BULMER-THOMAS, Ivor 1905-

PERSONAL: Born November 30, 1905, in Cwmbran, Monmouthshire, England; son of Alfred Ernest and Zipporah (Jones) Thomas; married Dilys Jones (died, 1938); married Margaret Joan Bulmer, December 26, 1940; children: (first marriage) Michael Alcuin Thomas Walker; (second marriage) Jennifer Elizabeth, Miranda Christine, Victor Gerald. *Education:* St. John's and Magdalen Colleges, Oxford, B.A., 1928, M.A., 1937. *Politics:* Conservative. *Religion:* Church of England. *Home:* 12 Edwardes Sq., London W.8, England.

CAREER: Times, London, England, sub-editor, 1930-37; *News Chronicle,* London, England, chief leader writer, 1937-39; member of Parliament for Keighley, 1942-50, serving as parliamentary secretary for civil aviation, 1945-46, under-secretary of state for the colonies; delegate to United Nations, and first United Kingdom representative on the Trusteeship Council, 1946-47; *Daily Telegraph,* London, England, leader writer, later acting deputy editor, 1952-54. Member of House of Laity of National Assembly and General Synod, Church of England, 1950—. Chairman of executive committee, Historic Churches Preservation Trust, 1952-56; honorary director, Friends of Friendless Churches, 1957—; secretary and honorary secretary, Ancient Monuments Society, 1958—; chairman, Redundant Churches Fund, 1969—. *Military service:* British Army, Royal Fusiliers, 1939-40, Royal Norfolk Regiment, 1940-45; became captain. *Member:* Ancient Monuments Society (secretary, 1958—), Athenaeum Club, Vincent's Club, Achilles Club. *Awards, honors:* Stella della Solidarieta Italiana.

WRITINGS: Our Lord Birkenhead: An Oxford Appreciation, Putnam, 1930; *The Buchman Groups,* 2nd edition, Morehouse, 1933; *Coal in the New Era,* Putnam, 1934; *Housing Principles* (pamphlet), Fabian Society, 1935; *Gladstone of Hawarden: A Memoir of Henry Neville, Lord Gladstone of Hawarden,* J. Murray, 1936; *Top Sawyer: A Biography of David Davies of Llandinam,* Longmans, Green, 1938; (editor and translator) *Selections Illustrating the History of Greek Mathematics,* Harvard University Press, 1939-41; *Warfare by Words,* Penguin, 1942; *Who Mussolini Is* (pamphlet), Oxford University Press, 1942; *The Newspapers* (pamphlet), Oxford University Press, 1943; *Great Britain and Poland* (pamphlet), Polish Publications Committee, 1944; (with Mato Vucetic) *The Italo-Jugoslav Frontier,* Slovenian American National Council, 1944; *The Problem of Italy: An Economic Survey,* Routledge, 1946; *The Socialist Tragedy,* Latimer House, 1949, Macmillan (New York), 1951; (editor and author of introduction) Edmund J. Webb, *Names of the Stars,* Nisbet, 1952; *The Party System in Great Britain,* Macmillan (New York), 1953; *The Growth of the British Party System,* two volumes, Baker Publishers, 1965, Humanities, 1966, 2nd edition, Baker Publishers, 1967, Humanities, 1968.

*   *   *

BUNCE, Frank David 1907-

PERSONAL: Born July 31, 1907, in Amberg, Wis.; son of Frank and Stella (Stratton) Bunce. *Education:* Attended Wisconsin public schools. *Address:* P.O. Box 1502, Los Angeles, Calif. 90053.

CAREER: Marinette Eagle Star, Marinette, Wis., reporter, 1924; Chamber of Commerce, Marinette, Wis., secretary, 1924-25; *Green Bay Star,* Green Bay, Wis., editor, 1925-26; Kent Press Service, Detroit, Mich., feature writer, 1927. Copywriting, layout work in midwest and New York advertising agencies, radio writing, free-lance magazine writing. *Military service:* U.S. Army, 1941-45.

WRITINGS: So Young a Body, Simon & Schuster, 1950; *Rehearsal for Murder,* Abelard, 1956. Contributor of stories and articles to more than seventy magazines.

WORK IN PROGRESS: A novel.

*   *   *

BUNNELL, William S(tanley) 1925-

PERSONAL: Born July 21, 1925, in Bradford, England; son of William Frederick (an engineer) and Emily (Fildes) Bunnell. *Education:* Selwyn College, Cambridge, B.A., 1950, M.A., 1953; certificate in education, 1951, diploma in education, 1954. *Religion:* Church of England. *Home:* Bank View House, Flat 5, West Cliffe Lane, Baildon, Shipley, Yorkshire, England. *Office:* Mather College, Whitworth St., Manchester 1, England.

CAREER: Crypt School, Gloucester, England, second English master, 1951-54; Ashville College, Harrogate, England, head of English department, 1955-63; Mather College, Manchester, England, principal lecturer in English, 1963—. Part-time lecturer in English, Bradford Institute of Technology. Fellow, College of Preceptors. Examiner, Royal Society of Arts, Oxford local. *Military service:* British Army, 1943-47; became sergeant.

WRITINGS: A Guide to English Language for the G.C.E. Candidate, Brodie, 1957; (editor) Oscar Wilde, *The Importance of Being Earnest,* University of London Press, 1958; *The Art of Criticism: A Course for Advanced and Scholarship Levels of the General Certificate of Education,* Brodie, 1958; *The Poet's Mind* (commentaries and notes on anthology, *Rhyme and Reason,* edited by Raymond O'Malley and Denys Thompson), Brodie, 1959; *Test Papers in English,* Brodie, 1959; *How to Study a Set-Book,* Brodie, 1961; *Wilkie Collins: The Moonstone,* Brodie, 1961; *H. G. Wells: The First Men in the Moon,* Brodie, 1961; *Ten Twentieth-Century Poets,* Brodie, 1963.

WORK IN PROGRESS: A Guide to English Spelling.

*   *   *

BURBANK, Nelson L(incoln) 1898-

PERSONAL: Born November 11, 1898, in Cincinnati, Ohio; son of Oberst (an insurance man) and Ella (Evans) Burbank; married Alice L. Berger, August 27, 1927; children: Miriam L. (Mrs. John W. Williams), Joyce L. (Mrs. William H. Taylor). *Education:* Miami University, Oxford, Ohio, M.A., 1931; graduate study at Ohio State University, Columbia University, and University of Cincinnati. *Religion:* Presbyterian. *Home:* 527 Wellesley Ave., Cincinnati, Ohio 45224.

CAREER: Cincinnati (Ohio) public schools, teacher of carpentry shop, science, mathematics, English, architectural drafting, and fifth and sixth grades, and principal, 1925-63. *Member:* National Education Association (life), Ohio Education Association, Cincinnati Teachers Association, Cincinnati Schoolmasters Club, Martha Kinney Cooper Ohioana Library Association, Phi Delta Kappa (emeritus; treasurer of Alpha Iota chapter, 1937, vice-president, 1938), Epsilon Pi Tau. *Awards, honors:* Epsilon Pi Tau Laureate Citation for research in vocational education.

WRITINGS: Carpentry and Joinery Work, American Builder, 1936, 5th edition published as *House Carpentry and Joinery,* Simmons-Boardman, 1952, 6th edition published as *House Carpentry Simplified* (revised by Charles Phelps), Simmons-Boardman, 1958, 7th edition, 1963; (compiler) *House Construction Details* (based on reproductions from *American Builder, Building Age,* and other sources; published as companion volume to *Carpentry and Joinery Work*), Simmons-Boardman, 1939, 5th edition (with Oscar Shaftel), 1959, 6th edition (with Herbert R. Pfister), 1968; (compiler) *Practical Job Pointers* (selected from *American Builder* and *Building Age*), Simmons-Boardman, 1940, 2nd revised edition, 1947; (compiler with E. M. Mitchell) *Shopcrafter's Handbook,* Simmons-Boardman, 1942; (with Herbert R. Waugh) *Handbook of Building Terms and Definitions,* Simmons-Boardman, 1954; *Suburban Living,* Simmons-Boardman, 1965.

WORK IN PROGRESS: A compendium of farm machinery and equipment.

*   *   *

BURBY, William E(dward) 1893-

PERSONAL: Born December 25, 1893, in Niles, Mich.; son of John M. (a paper manufacturer) and Mary (McGuirk) Burby; married Allene Zwergel, June 21, 1919; children: Allene (Mrs. C. A. Broderick), William E., Jr. *Education:* University of Michigan, A.B. (with distinction), 1917, J.D., 1923. *Home:* 5771 Rutgers Rd., La Jolla, Calif. 92037. *Office:* School of Law, California Western University, 3902 Lomaland Dr., San Diego, Calif. 92106.

CAREER: University of Notre Dame, Notre Dame, Ind., professor of law, 1922-24; University of North Dakota School of Law, Grand Forks, professor of law, 1924-26; University of Southern California, Los Angeles, professor of law, 1926-64, Legion Lex Distinguished Professor of Law, 1958; California Western University School of Law, San Diego, faculty member, 1964—. Member of California State Bar.

WRITINGS: (Editor) *Cases on Community Property,* Legal Briefing Service, 1931, 4th edition, West Publishing, 1955; *Handbook of the Law of Real Property,* West Publishing, 1943, 3rd edition, 1965; *Illustrative Cases on the Law of Real Property,* West Publishing, 1943; *Law Refresher* (23 subjects summarized), Parker, 1946, subsequent editions on each subject in series, with new additions, published separately, West Publishing, 1956—; *Summary of Business Law,* Law School Press, 1947, 2nd edition published as *Business Law,* 1949.

WORK IN PROGRESS: Completion of "Law Refresher" series.

*   *   *

BURDON, R(andal) M(athews) 1896-

PERSONAL: Born August 4, 1896, in Sussex, England;

son of Cotsford Mathews (a sheep farmer) and Mildred (Yatman) Burdon; married Jean Bowden, 1920 (divorced, 1934); children: John Rowland, Juliet Virginia Hobbs. *Education:* Attended Christ's College, Christchurch, New Zealand, 1911-14. *Religion:* Church of England. *Home:* 222 Karori Rd., Wellington, New Zealand.

CAREER: Served with British Army in France, 1915-17, in Italy, 1917-18, and with Indian Army in Northwest Frontier Province, 1919-22; wounded twice; received Military Cross. High country sheep farmer in New Zealand until disabled by back injury in 1937; writer, 1937—.

WRITINGS: High Country, Whitcombe & Tombs, 1938; *New Zealand Notables,* Caxton Publishing Co. (Christchurch), Series 1, 1941, Series 2, 1945, Series 3, 1951; *The Life and Times of Sir Julius Vogel,* Caxton Publishing Co. (Christchurch), 1948; *24 Battalion,* War History Branch, New Zealand, 1952; *King Dick,* Whitcombe & Tombs, 1955; *Scholar Errant,* Pegasus Press (Christchurch), 1956; *The New Dominian,* Allen & Unwin, 1965.

* * *

BUREN, Martha Margareta Elisabet 1910-

PERSONAL: Born May 19, 1910, in Umea, Sweden; daughter of Bernhard and Elisabet (Hallencreutz) Buren. *Education:* Attended Ecole superieure des etrangers, Switzerland, 1928, a commercial school in Stockholm, Sweden, 1929, and studied in France and England, 1931-32. *Religion:* Protestant. *Home:* Slipgatan 14, Stockholm, Sweden.

CAREER: Royal Medical Board and Royal Veterinary Board, Stockholm, Sweden, secretary, 1934-62. Author. *Member:* Swedish Authors' Society.

WRITINGS: Garnison i norr (title means "Garrison in the North"), Lars Hokerbergs, 1948; *Idag och imorgon* (title means "Today and Tomorrow"), Lars Hokerbergs, 1951; *Den andra Kvinnan,* Lars Hokerbergs, 1955, translation by Joan Tate published as *Camilla,* M. Joseph, 1965; *Att ga vidare,* Lars Hokerbergs, 1959, translation by Tate published as *A Need to Love,* Dodd, 1964; *Var ar Sylvia?* (title means "Where Is Sylvia?"), Lars Hokerbergs, 1963.

SIDELIGHTS: Most of Miss Buren's books have been translated into eight other European languages. *Avocational interests:* Current literature, Swedish and world history, the theater, classical music, and interior decoration.

* * *

BURMEISTER, Eva (Elizabeth) 1899-

PERSONAL: Born May 26, 1899, in Milwaukee, Wis.; daughter of Charles and Emma (Schwann) Burmeister. *Education:* University of Wisconsin, Ph.D., 1924. *Politics:* Democrat. *Religion:* Protestant. *Home:* 4408 South Howell Ave., Milwaukee, Wis. 53207.

CAREER: Social worker, mostly in field of institutional child care, 1924—. Successively caseworker, director of Lakeside Children's Center, Milwaukee, Wis., 1932-54, and conductor of courses (or leader of study groups) in the education of houseparents, child care workers, and counselors, as institutional consultant for Federation of Protestant Welfare Agencies, New York, N.Y., 1956-64; freelance consultant to children's institutions and teacher of course for houseparents at University of Wisconsin Extension Division, Milwaukee, 1964—. Served in Switzerland, Holland, and Sweden under United Nations Technical Assistance Program, 1955, in Greece under Unitarian Service Committee, 1957.

WRITINGS: Forty-five in the Family, Columbia University Press, 1949; *Roofs for the Family,* Columbia University Press, 1954; *The Professional Houseparent,* Columbia University Press, 1960; *Tough Times and Tender Moments in Child Care Work,* Columbia University Press, 1967.

SIDELIGHTS: Ms. Burmeister's books have been translated into German, Dutch and Danish. She is competent in German. *Avocational interests:* The outdoors, and sketching.

* * *

BURN, J(oshua) Harold 1892-

PERSONAL: Born March 6, 1892, in Barnard Castle, England; son of J. George (a grocer) and Mary Josephine (Howson) Burn; married Katharine Pemberton, October 4, 1928; children: George, Isabel Burn Caddy, Josephine Burn Oliver, Margaret Burn Gerrard, Frances Burn Gray, Robert. *Education:* Emmanuel College, Cambridge, student, 1909-13; Guy's Hospital Medical School, University of London, student, 1918-20. *Politics:* Liberal. *Home:* 3 Squitchey Lane, Oxford, England.

CAREER: Oxford University, Oxford, England, professor of pharmacology, 1937-59, emeritus professor, 1959—. Fellow emeritus, Balliol College, Oxford. Visiting professor, Washington University, St. Louis, Mo., 1959-68. *Member:* Royal Society (fellow), National Institute of Sciences of India (honorary fellow). *Awards, honors:* D.Sc., Yale University; M.D., University of Mainz; Gairdner International Award, 1959, for research on cardiovascular system; honorary doctorate, University of Paris; D.Sc., Bradford University.

WRITINGS: (With Henry Hallett Dale) *Reports on Biological Standards,* Medical Research Council, 1922; *Methods of Biological Assay,* Oxford University Press, 1928; *Recent Advances in Materia Medica: Being a Description of the Methods of Preparing and Testing Sera and Vaccines, Hormones and Vitamins, with an Account of Their Properties and Medicinal Uses,* Churchill, 1932; *Biological Standardization,* Oxford University Press, 1937, 2nd edition (with D. J. Finney and L. G. Goodwin), 1950; (reviser with E. R. Withell) William Whitla, *Whitla's Pharmacy, Materia Medica and Therapeutics,* 13th edition, Bailliere, Tindall & Cox, 1939, 14th edition, 1943; *The Background of Therapeutics,* Oxford University Press, 1948; *Lecture Notes on Pharmacology,* C. C Thomas, 1948, 10th edition, F. A. Davis, 1971; *Practical Pharmacology,* C. C Thomas, 1952; *Functions of Autonomic Transmitters,* Williams & Wilkins, 1956; *The Principles of Therapeutics,* C. C Thomas, 1957; *Drugs, Medicine and Man,* Scribner, 1962, 2nd edition, Allen & Unwin, 1963; *The Autonomic Nervous System,* F. A. Davis, 1963, 4th edition, 1971; *Our Most Interesting Diseases,* Scribner, 1964.

* * *

BURNABY, John 1891-

PERSONAL: Born July 28, 1891, in Etton, Beverley, Yorkshire, England; son of John Charles Wellesley (a clergyman) and Louisa Georgina Frances (Battersby) Burnaby; married Dorothy (Lock) Newton, December 9, 1922; children: Thomas Patrick, Jenny Marigold (Mrs. G. Melvill Jones), Geoffrey Valentine. *Education:* Trinity College, Cambridge, B.A., 1913, B.D., 1938. *Home:* 6 Hedgerley Close, Cambridge, England.

CAREER: Ordained deacon, Church of England, 1941,

priest, 1942, Trinity College, Cambridge University, Cambridge, England, junior bursar, 1921-31, tutor, 1931-38, senior tutor, 1938-45, lecturer in theology, 1939-51; Cambridge University, lecturer in divinity, 1945-52, Regius Professor of Divinity, 1952-58, Regius Professor Emeritus, 1958—. University member of Cambridge Borough Council, 1923-31. *Military service:* London Regiment, 1915-18; served at Gallipoli and in France; became captain.

WRITINGS: Amor Dei: A Study of the Religion of St. Augustine (Hulsean Lectures), Hodder & Stoughton, 1938; *Is the Bible Inspired?*, Duckworth, 1949; *Christian Words and Christian Meanings*, Hodder & Stoughton, 1955, Harper, 1956; (editor and translator) Saint Augustine, *Later Works*, Westminster, 1955; *The Belief of Christendom*, S.P.C.K., 1959. Contributor to *Encyclopaedia Britannica* and to theological journals.

SIDELIGHTS: Burnaby reads French, German, and Russian. *Avocational interests:* Classical music and folk song, amateur acting.

*   *   *

BURNS, William A. 1909-

PERSONAL: Born October 7, 1909, in New York, N.Y.; son of William A. and Forence (Willis) Burns; married Adelaide Jordan, October 7, 1955. *Education:* Manhattan College, A.B., 1934; Columbia University, M.A., 1937, Ed.D., 1949. *Office:* Witte Museum, 3801 Broadway, San Antonio, Tex.

CAREER: American Museum of Natural History, New York, N.Y., assistant to director, 1940-61; Witte Museum, San Antonio, Tex., director, 1961—. Consultant or member of advisory boards of other museums in United States. Member, New York Mayor's Golden Jubilee Commission, 1949. Trustee, Metropolitan Educational Television Association, New York, 1957-62, American Red Cross, and other organizations. Member, Texas Historical Survey Commission. *Military service:* U.S. Army, 1943-46; served in Southwest Pacific and Australia; became first lieutenant. *Member:* American Association of Museums (member of council, 1950-53), Mountain-Plains Museum Conference, Texas Art Museums Association, Texas Museums Association, Rotary Club, Manuscript Club.

WRITINGS: A World Full of Homes, McGraw, 1954; *Horses and Their Ancestors*, McGraw, 1955; *Man and His Tools*, McGraw, 1956; *Exploring for Fun: A Young Explorer's Handbook*, Dutton, 1961; (with Frank Debenham) *Illustrated World Geography*, McGraw, 1960; (editor and contributor) *Natural History of the Southwest*, F. Watts, 1960; (with Edwin Harris Colbert) *Digging for Dinosaurs*, new edition, Childrens Press, 1967; *Your Future in Museums*, Rosen Press, 1967; *Noise and Man*, J. Murray, 1968, Lippincott, 1969. Contributor to museum periodicals and to *Field and Stream, Air Force Journal, Rotarian;* conductor of column, "Witte Museum Question Box," carried in San Antonio newspapers. Former editor, "Man and Nature Publications," American Museum of Natural History.

WORK IN PROGRESS: A novel.

SIDELIGHTS: Burns in competent in Dutch, French, Spanish, German, Afrikaans, and Flemish; he knows a little Japanese and Russian. *Avocational interests:* Anthropology, world travel, fishing, making antique furniture; collecting brass, copper, and pewter clocks; writing detective stories for friends (not for publication).

BURT, Alfred LeRoy 1888-

PERSONAL: Born November 28, 1888, in Listowel, Ontario, Canada; son of Christian Kimbal (a merchant) and Sarah Jane (Large) Burt; married Dorothy Duff, August 18, 1915 (died, 1967); children: Dorothy Forrest (Mrs. J. S. Johnson), Mary Duff (Mrs. Arlo Leinback), John Arthur, Joan Elizabeth (Mrs. Stuart Jenness). *Education:* University of Toronto, B.A., 1910; Oxford University, M.A., 1916. *Politics:* Independent. *Religion:* Episcopal. *Home:* 39 Crown Ridge Rd., Wellesley, Mass. 02181.

CAREER: University of Alberta, Edmonton, 1913-30, began as lecturer, became professor of history; University of Minnesota, Minneapolis, professor of history, 1930-57, emeritus professor, 1957—. Visiting professor of history at Carlton University, 1957-58, University of Chicago, 1959-60, University of Manitoba, 1960-61. Khaki University of Canada in Great Britain, staff member, 1918-19. *Military service:* Canadian Army, tank battalion, 1915-18; became lieutenant. *Member:* Canadian Historical Association (president, 1948-49), American Historical Association, Canadian Political Science Association, Campus Club, Larrimac Golf Club (Quebec). *Awards, honors:* Robert Herbert Memorial Prize, and shared Beit Prize, 1913, for *Imperial Architects;* Tyrrell Medal of Royal Society of Canada for research and publications in Canadian history, 1946; LL.D., University of Alberta, 1966.

WRITINGS: Imperial Architects, Basil Blackwell, 1913; *The Romance of the Prairie Provinces*, Gage, 1930; *Guy Carleton, Lord Dorchester, 1724-1808*, Ryerson, 1930, revised edition, Canadian Historical Association, 1957; *The Old Province of Quebec*, University of Minnesota Press, 1933, reissued in two volumes, McClelland & Stewart, 1968; *The Romance of Canada: A New History*, Gage, 1937, revised edition published with *British Columbia*, by Arthur Anstey, Gage, 1944; *The United States, Great Britain, and British North America from the Revolution to the Establishment of Peace after the War of 1812*, Yale University Press, 1940; *A Short History of Canada for Americans*, University of Minnesota Press, 1942, 2nd edition, 1944; (co-author) *The United States and Its Place in World Affairs*, Heath, 1943; *The Evolution of the British Empire and Commonwealth from the American Revolution*, Heath, 1956. Contributor of articles and book reviews to periodicals, including *Toronto Saturday Night, Saturday Review of Literature*, history journals. Writer of script for short film on Canada produced by Coronet Films.

*   *   *

BURT, Cyril (Lodowic) 1883-1971

PERSONAL: Born March 3, 1883, in England; son of Cyril Cecil Barrow (a physician) and Martha Decima (Evans) Burt; married Joyce Woods, May 12, 1931. *Education:* Christ's Hospital, student, 1894-1901; Jesus College, Oxford, M.A., 1906, D.Sc., 1916; University of Wurzburg, graduate research, 1907. *Home:* 9 Elsworthy Rd., Hampstead, London N.W. 3, England. *Office:* University College, University of London, Gower St., London W.C. 1, England.

CAREER: University of Liverpool, Liverpool, England, lecturer in experimental psychology, 1909-13; Cambridge University, Cambridge, England, assistant lecturer, 1912-13, lecturer in psychology, 1917-19; London County Council, London, England, psychologist in education department, 1913-32; University of London, London, England, professor of education, 1924-31, professor of psychology,

1932-53, professor emeritus, 1953-71. British War Office, member of Advisory Committee on Personnel Selection. *Member:* British Psychological Society (president, 1940), British Academy (fellow), Mensa (president, 1960-70), Oxford Union. *Awards, honors:* Knighted, 1946. LL.D., University of Aberdeen; D.Litt., University of Reading; honorary fellow, Jesus College, Oxford University.

WRITINGS: Distribution and Relations of Educational Abilities, P. S. King, 1917; *Mental and Scholastic Tests*, P. S. King, 1921, 4th edition, Staples, 1962; *Handbook of Tests for Use in Schools*, P. S. King, 1923; *The Young Delinquent*, University of London Press, 1925, 4th edition revised, 1944, reprinted, 1957; *The Measurement of Mental Capacities*, 1927; (with Ernest Jones, Emanuel Miller, and William Moodie) *How the Mind Works*, Allen & Unwin, 1933, Appleton, 1934, Books for Libraries, 1970; *The Subnormal Child*, Oxford University Press, 1935, 3rd edition, 1955; *The Backward Child*, University of London Press, 1937, 5th edition, 1961.

The Factors of the Mind, University of London Press, 1940; *The Causes and Treatment of Backwardness*, University of London Press, 1952, 4th edition, 1957; *A Psychological Study of Typography*, Cambridge University Press, 1959; *Psychology and Psychical Research*, Society for Psychical Research (London), 1968. Editor, *British Journal of Statistical Psychology;* consulting editor, *Encyclopaedia Britannica.*

WORK IN PROGRESS: The Gifted Child; The Concept of Consciousness.

SIDELIGHTS: At the time of his death, the *New York Times* noted, "Sir Cyril was one of the first educational psychologists to stress the great importance of understanding the social backgrounds of children investigated. To further his studies on delinquency, he took lodgings in the slums. His fourth book, *The Young Delinquent*, published in 1925, is still considered an outstanding source of information on maladjusted children, as is *The Backward Child*, published in 1937. Perhaps his best known work is *Handbook of Tests for Use in Schools*, published in 1923. Many of the intelligence and attainment tests set forth in this book remain in use."

Burt was competent in Greek, Latin, Hebrew, German, French, and Italian; he also knew some Russian. *Avocational interests:* Astronomy, field botany, quantum physics, music, and watercolor painting.

(Died October 10, 1971)

*   *   *

BURTON, Virginia Lee   1909-1968

PERSONAL: Born August 30, 1909, in Newton Centre, Mass.; daughter of Alfred E. (first dean of Massachusetts Institute of Technology) and Lena Dalkeith (Yates) Burton; married George Demetrios (a sculptor and teacher), March 28, 1931; children: Aristides B., Michael B. *Education:* Studied ballet privately in San Francisco, Calif., and art at California School of Fine Arts and Boston Museum School. *Home:* Folly Cove, Gloucester, Mass.

CAREER: One-time swimming instructor and art counselor in Young Men's Christian Association summer camps; sketcher for music, dance, and theater sections of *Boston Transcript*, Boston, Mass., 1928-31; writer and illustrator of children's books, 1935-68. *Awards, honors:* Caldecott Medal for best-illustrated book, 1943, for children for *The Little House.*

WRITINGS—All self-illustrated; all published by Houghton: *Choo Choo*, 1935; *Mike Mulligan and His Steam Shovel*, 1939; *Calico, the Wonder Horse*, 1941; *The Little House*, 1942; *Katy and the Big Show*, 1943; *Maybelle, the Cable Car*, 1952; *Life Story*, 1962.

Illustrator—All published by Houghton: Arna Bontemps and Jack Conroy, *Fast Sooner Hound*, 1942; Anne Malcolmson, *Song of Robin Hood*, 1947; Hans Christian Anderson, *The Emperor's New Clothes*, 1949.

WORK IN PROGRESS: A book on design.

SIDELIGHTS: "My subject matter, with a few exceptions such as *Calico*, I draw directly from life, and I literally draw my books first and write down the text after.... I pin the sketched pages in sequences on the walls of my studio so I can *see* the book as a whole. Then I make a rough dummy and then the final drawings, and at last when I can put it off no longer, I type out the text and paste it in the dummy."

Her first book manuscript, "Jonnifer Lint," was turned down by thirteen publishers, and she quit trying on *that* one when her son, then three, fell asleep before she finished reading it to him. From then on she worked with her own boys to adjust stories to their interest or lack of it.

(Died October 15, 1968)

*   *   *

BUSCH, Francis X(avier)   1879-

PERSONAL: Born May 9, 1879, in Detroit, Mich.; son of Francis X. (a factory superintendent) and Carolyn (Van Buskirk) Busch; married Jeanette Morrison, 1903 (died, 1912); married Jean Mapes Lucas, April 28, 1933; children: (first marriage) Helen Busch Chapman, Frances Busch Zink, Ruth Busch Pierson, Lorraine Busch McNevin. *Education:* Illinois College of Law, LL.B., 1904, LL.M., 1905; De Paul University, LL.D., 1912. *Politics:* Independent. *Religion:* Presbyterian. *Home:* Wetumpka, Ala.

CAREER: Admitted to Illinois bar, 1901. Attorney in Chicago, Ill., 1901-61, as member of firm of Taylor, Miller, Busch & Magner, 1961—. City of Chicago, assistant corporation counsel and attorney for Civil Service Commission, 1904-06; De Paul University Law School, dean, 1912-23 (now emeritus); Cook County Circuit Court, master in chancery, 1920-23; City of Chicago, corporation counsel, 1923-27, 1931. *Member:* American Bar Association, Illinois Bar Association, Chicago Bar Association (president, 1931).

WRITINGS: Busch-Dixon's Law Examiner, Callaghan & Co., 1903; *Busch Outlines of Common Law Pleading*, Callaghan & Co., 1912; *In and Out of Court*, De Paul University Press, 1942; *Law and Tactics in Jury Trials*, Bobbs-Merrill, 1948; *Guilty or Not Guilty*, Bobbs-Merrill, 1948; *Prisoners at the Bar*, Bobbs-Merrill, 1952; *They Escaped the Hangman*, Bobbs-Merrill, 1952; *Enemies of the State*, Bobbs-Merrill, 1955; *Case Book of the Curious and True*, Bobbs-Merrill, 1958; *Trial Procedure Materials*, Bobbs-Merrill, 1960.

*   *   *

BUTCHER, Thomas Kennedy   1914-

PERSONAL: Born January 13, 1914, in London, England; son of Percy Austen (a woollen merchant) and Winifred (Kennedy) Butcher; married Joyce Mary Whitney (a social worker), September 24, 1939; children: Andrew Donald

Whitney. *Education:* Attended Alleyns School, Dulwich, London, England; University of Sheffield, B.A., 1949. *Home:* Woodman Cottage, Pishill, Henley-on-Thames, Oxford, England. *Office:* Broadcasting House, London W.1, England.

CAREER: Bureau of Current Affairs, London, England, editor, 1949-50; British Broadcasting Corp., London, England, producer, 1951-60; Nigerian Broadcasting Corp., Ibadan, Nigeria, senior producer, 1960-62; acting head of school broadcasting, 1962; British Broadcasting Corp., producer, 1962—. British Council lecturer in Ghana, 1960; script writer and producer for UNESCO, 1963-65, 1970. *Military service:* Royal Navy, 1941-46; received three campaign medals and wound stripe. *Member:* Royal Institute of International Affairs, Institute of Race Relations, Islington Society (London; honorary secretary, 1962-65).

WRITINGS: The Great Explorations: Asia and Australasia, Roy, 1955; *The Great Explorations: Africa,* Roy, 1959; *Country Life,* Batsford, 1970. Writer of radio scripts for British Broadcasting Corp., Nigerian Broadcasting Corp., and for radio in Norway, Denmark, and Sweden. Contributor of articles, reviews, and of translations from the French to periodicals.

*   *   *

BUTLER, James 1904-

PERSONAL: Born August 31, 1904, in Birmingham, England; son of William Henry and Ellen Ann (Jones) Bulter; married Charlotte Gertrude Gill, July 29, 1931; children: Michael John, Peter James. *Education:* Educated at Birmingham College of Technology, Dundee College of Technology, Dundee, Scotland, and University of Birmingham; national certificate of engineering, and associate, Institution of Mechanical Engineering. *Politics:* Conservative. *Religion:* Church of England. *Home:* 22 Sutton Oak Rd., Sutton Coldfield, Warwickshire, England.

CAREER: Streetly Manufacturing Co., Birmingham, England, works manager and chief designer, 1931-43; British Industrial Plastics Ltd., Oldbury, England, chief development engineer, 1943—. Director of British Industrial Plastics Engineering Ltd. and of British Industrial Plastics Chemicals Limited. Examiner in engineering subjects for the Guilds of London Institute and Plastics Institute. *Member:* Institution of Mechanical Engineers, Plastics Institute (fellow; chairman of council, 1949-51), Warwickshire Cricket Club, Sutton Coldfield Golf Club, Beau Desert Golf Club, Langland Bay Golf Club.

WRITINGS: Economical Use of Cooling Water, Clowes, 1947; *Mould Design,* three volumes, Wyman & Sons, 1949-53; *Practical Dos and Don'ts in Mould Design,* British Industrial Plastics Ltd., 1957; *Compression and Transfer Moulding of Plastics,* Iliffe, 1959, Interscience, 1960; *Compression and Transfer Mould Design,* Newnes, 1961; *A Moulder's Notebook,* British Industrial Plastics Ltd., 1961. Author of two book-length serials in house magazines, "A Motor-Cycling History," and "A History of Birmingham." Contributor to engineering journals in Great Britain and in continental Europe.

AVOCATIONAL INTERESTS: Formerly playing football, motorcycling, rifle-shooting, and cricket; now golf, gardening, history, music, drawing and cartooning, writing poetry for fun.

BUTLER, James R(amsay) M(ontagu) 1889-

PERSONAL: Born July 20, 1889, in Cambridge, England; son of H. M. (a clergyman, headmaster of Harrow School, and master of Trinity College, Cambridge University) and Agnata F. (Ramsay) Butler. *Education:* Attended Harrow School; Trinity College, Cambridge, M.A., 1914; *Home:* Trinity College, Cambridge, England.

CAREER: Cambridge University, Cambridge, England, fellow of Trinity College, 1913—, Regius Professor of Modern History, 1947-54; chief historian, official British histories of World War II, 1946—. Member of Parliament for Cambridge University, 1922-23. *Military service:* British Army, Scottish Horse, 1914-19, Intelligence Corps, 1939-44; became lieutenant colonel. *Member:* Royal Historical Society (fellow), United Oxford and Cambridge University Club, Alpine Club. *Awards, honors:* Knighted, 1958.

WRITINGS: The Passing of the Great Reform Bill, Longmans, Green, 1914; (contributor) H.W.V. Temperley, editor, *History of the Peace Conference of Paris,* Volume VI, Oxford University Press, 1924; *Henry Montagu Butler, Master of Trinity College, Cambridge,* Longmans, Green, 1925; *A History of England, 1815-1939;,* T. Butterworth, 1928, second edition, Oxford University Press, 1960; *A History of England, 1815-1918,* Oxford University Press, 1949; *Grand Strategy,* Volume II and Volume III (Part II of official history of World War II), H.M.S.O., 1957; *Lord Lothian (Philip Kerr), 1882-1940,* Macmillan, 1960; *Jawaharlal Nehru: The Struggle for Independence,* Cambridge University Press, 1966. Contributor to *Cambridge History of the British Empire,* Volumes II and III.

*   *   *

BUTTERFIELD, Roger (Place) 1907-

PERSONAL: Born July 29, 1907, in Lyndonville, N.Y.; son of Roy L. (an educator) and Ethel (Place) Butterfield; married Margaret Schnug (an editor), August 13, 1955. *Education:* University of Rochester, A.B., 1927; Columbia University, student at Pulitzer Graduate School of Journalism, 1927-28. *Home:* White House, Hartwick, N.Y. 13348.

CAREER: Newspaperman, Philadelphia, Pa., 1928-35; *Time* and *Life,* New York, N.Y., successively reporter, writer, and editor, 1935-45, 1955-61; Time, Inc., New York, N.Y. consultant, 1961-63; free-lance writer, 1963—. Currently engaged in antiquarian book business. *Member:* New York Historical Society, American Antiquarian Society, Century Association (New York).

WRITINGS: Al Schmid, Marine, Norton, 1944; *The American Past: A History of the United States from Concord to Hiroshima, 1775-1945,* Simon & Schuster, 1947, revised and expanded edition published as *The American Past: A History of the United States from Concord to the Nuclear Age,* 1957, 2nd revised edition published as *The American Past: A History of the United States from Concord to the Great Society,* 1966; (editor with others) *The Saturday Evening Post Treasury,* Simon & Schuster, 1954; (with Robert D. Graff and Robert E. Ginna) *FDR* (text by Butterfield; based on ABC-TV series), Harper, 1963; *Ancient Rome,* Odyssey, 1964; *Henry Ford, the Wayside Inn, and the Problem of "History is Bunk"* (originally published in *Proceedings of Massachusetts Historical Society,* 1965), [Boston], 1965; *Sam Clemens and the American Courier,* privately printed for Antiquarian Booksellers' Association of America, 1967. Contributor of articles to *Saturday Evening Post, Ladies' Home Journal, Collier's, Reader's Digest, American Heritage,* and other magazines.

BIOGRAPHICAL/CRITICAL SOURCES: Nation,
March 16, 1970.

* * *

BYRNE, Muriel St. Clare 1895-

PERSONAL: Born May 31, 1895, in England; daughter of
Harry St. Clare and Artemisia Desdemona (an American;
maiden name, Burtner) Byrne. *Education:* Somerville College, Oxford, honors in English, 1916, B.A. and M.A.,
1920. *Home:* 28 St. John's Wood Ter., London N.W. 8,
England.

CAREER: Teaching, lecturing, and research work, 1916-
18; lecturer in France for Army Education School, 1918-19;
Morley College for Working Men and Women, London,
England, lecturer, 1919-23; Oxford University, Oxford,
England, assistant tutor in English, Somerville College,
1919, coach in English for final honors at Oxford, 1920-25,
university extension lecturer, Oxford and London, 1920-37;
Royal Academy of Dramatic Art, London, England, lecturer, 1923-55; University of London, London, England,
lecturer in English, Bedford College, 1941-45, examiner for
university diploma in dramatic art, 1951-60. Writer; researcher on the Lisle Letters, 1933-41. Governor, Royal
Shakespeare Theatre; member of literary advisory panel for
ten-month British Shakespeare Exhibition, 1964. Friends of
Girls' Public Day School Trust, member of board, beginning 1952, executive, beginning 1959.

MEMBER: Society of Antiquaries (fellow), Malone Society (honorary secretary, 1926-37), Bibliographical Society
(council, 1932-39), British Drama League (council), Society
for Theatre Research. *Awards, honors:* Leverhulme research grant, 1945-46; Order of the British Empire, 1955;
research fellowship, Bedford College, University of London, 1955-56; Pilgrim Trust research grants from British
Academy, 1958, 1959; British Academy awards, 1964, 1965,
1966.

WRITINGS: Aldebaran, Basil Blackwell, 1917; (with
Catherine Mansfield) *Somerville College, 1879-1921,* Ox-
ford University Press, 1922; (editor) Anthony Munday,
John a Kent, Malone Society, 1923; *Elizabethan Life in
Town and Country,* Methuen, 1925, Houghton, 1926, 8th
edition, Methuen, 1961; (editor) Claude de Sainliens and
Pierre Erondelle, *The Elizabethan Home Discovered in
Two Dialogues,* Haslewood Books, 1925, 3rd edition, Me-
thuen, 1949; *Elizabethan Zoo,* Haslewood Books, 1926;
*Havelock the Dane; Childe Horne; William and the Were-
wolf* (told from the originals), J. Cape, 1929.

(Editor) *Letters of King Henry VIII,* Cassell, 1936, reprinted, 1968; (editor) Shakespeare, *King Henry VIII,*
Macmillan, 1937, reprinted, Funk & Wagnalls, 1968; (with
Dorothy Sawyers), *Busman's Honeymoon* (play, produced
in 1936), Gollancz, 1937, acting version, Dramatists Play
Service, 1939; *Common or Garden Child,* Faber, 1942;
(compiler) *A History of Shakespearean Production,* [Lon-
don, England], 1948, published as *A Pictorial History of
Shakespearean Production in England, 1576-1946,* Books
for Libraries, 1970; (editor, and author of introduction)
Philip Massinger, *New Way to Pay Old Debts* (comedy),
Falcon Educational Books, 1949, new edition, Athlone,
1965.

(Editor) *The French Litleton of Claudius Holyband,* Cambridge University Press, 1953; (editor) *Essays and Studies,*
Volume 13, New Series, J. Murray, for English Association, 1960; (illustrator, and author of introductions and
notes) Harley Granville-Barker, *Prefaces to Shakespeare,*

four volumes, Batsford, 1963; *What We Said About the
Meiningers in 1881,* English Association, 1965.

Contributor: *Shakespeare in the Theatre,* Oxford University Press, for the Shakespeare Association, 1927;
Granville-Barker and G. B. Harrison, editors, *A Com-
panion to Shakespeare Studies,* Cambridge University
Press, 1934; *Great Tudors,* Nicholson & Watson, 1935,
new edition, Eyre & Spottiswoode, 1956; *Oxford Com-
panion to the Theatre,* Oxford University Press, 1951;
Shakespeare in His Own Age (Shakespeare Survey 17),
Cambridge University Press, 1964; *Essays and Studies,*
Volume 18, New Series, J. Murray, for English Associa-
tion, 1965; M. Roston, editor, *The Shakespearean World,*
Am Hassifer Publications (Tel-Aviv), 1965; *The Reader's
Encyclopedia of Shakespeare,* Crowell, 1966.

Plays produced but not published: "England's Elizabeth,"
1928, revived, 1953; (with G. Wheeler) "Well Gentlemen
...," 1933; "No Spring Till Now" (centenary play, Bedford College, University of London), 1949.

Contributor to *Enciclopedia dello Spettacolo,* 1955-58, to
*Library, Modern Language Review, Review of English
Studies, Drama, Shakespeare Quarterly, Theatre Note-
book, Times* (London), and other periodicals and newspa-
pers. General editor of publications, Society for Theatre
Research, 1949-59.

* * *

CABEEN, David Clark 1886-19(?)

PERSONAL: Born June 24, 1886, in Baraboo, Wis.; son of
Charles William and Sarah Amelia (Clark) Cabeen; married
Violet Abbott (a librarian), September 2, 1923. *Education:*
Syracuse University, A.B., 1908; Cornell University,
A.M., 1919; University of Pennsylvania, Ph.D., 1923. *Poli-
tics:* Republican. *Religion:* Congregationalist. *Home:* 716
Edmonds Ave., Drexel Hill, Pa.

CAREER: Instructor in French at Dartmouth College,
Hanover, N.H., 1915-16, Cornell University, Ithaca,
N.Y., 1916-17, 1919-20, University of Pennsylvania, Philadelphia, 1920-25; Williams College, Williamstown, Mass.,
assistant professor of French, 1923-25; Vanderbilt University, Nashville, Tenn., professor of French, and head of
department of Romanic languages, 1925-37. Visiting professor, University of Nebraska, 1939-41. *Military service:*
U.S. Army, served in France and Italy, 1917-19; became
2nd lieutenant. *Member:* Modern Language Association of
American, Veterans of Foreign Wars, Phi Gamma Delta.

WRITINGS: Montesquieu: A Bibliography, New York
Public Library, 1947; (general editor and contributor) *A
Critical Bibliography of French Literature,* Syracuse Uni-
versity Press, Volume I: *The Medieval Period,* 1947,
Volume II: *The Sixteenth Century,* 1956, Volume III: *The
Seventeenth Century,* 1961, Volume IV: *The Eighteenth
Century,* 1951. Contributor to modern language periodicals.

(Deceased)

* * *

CADBURY, Henry J(oel) 1883-1974

PERSONAL: Born December 1, 1883, in Philadelphia,
Pa.; son of Joel and Anna Kaighn (Lowry) Cadbury; mar-
ried Lydia Caroline Brown, June 17, 1916; children: Eliza-
beth (Mrs. John K. Musgrave, Jr.), Christopher Joel,
Warder Henry, Winifred (Mrs. Martin M. Beer). *Educa-
tion:* Haverford College, A.B., 1903; Harvard University,
A.M., 1904, Ph.D., 1914. *Religion:* Society of Friends.
Home: 774 Millbrook Lane, Haverford, Pa. 19041.

CAREER: Member of faculty: Haverford College, Haverford, Pa., 1910-19, Harvard University, Cambridge, Mass., 1919-26, Bryn Mawr College, Bryn Mawr, Pa., 1926-34; Harvard University, Hollis Professor of Divinity and Dexter Lecturer on Biblical Literature, 1934-54, professor emeritus, 1954-74. Lecturer at Pendle Hill, 1954-72, and Haverford College, 1954-63; adjunct professor, Temple University, 1962-66. Honorary lecturer at other universities and at divinity schools. Secretary, American Schools of Oriental Research, 1934-54; director, Andover-Harvard Theological Library, 1938-54; chairman of board of directors, Bryn Mawr College, 1956-68. Member, American Standard Bible Committee, 1930-74.

MEMBER: American Academy of Arts and Sciences (fellow), American Oriental Society, Society of Biblical Literature (secretary, 1916-33; president, 1936); American Council of Learned Societies (delegate, 1929-50), American Antiquarian Society, American Philosophical Society, Studiorum Novi Testamenti Societas (president, 1958-59), Oxford Society of Historical Theology (honorary), Phi Beta Kappa. *Awards, honors:* Litt.D. from Haverford College, 1933; D.D. from University of Glasgow, 1937; LL.D. from Whittier College, 1951, Swarthmore College, 1954; LH.D. from Howard University, 1959, and Earlham College, 1967.

WRITINGS: The Style and Literary Method of Luke, Harvard University Press, 1920; *National Ideals in the Old Testament*, Scribner, 1920; *The Making of Luke—Acts*, Macmillan, 1927, 2nd edition, S.P.C.K., 1958; *The Peril of Modernizing Jesus*, Macmillan, 1937, new edition, S.P.C.K., 1962; *Jesus: What Manner of Man*, Macmillan, 1947, 2nd edition, S.P.C.K., 1962; *John Hepburn and His Book Against Slavery, 1715*, American Antiquarian Society, 1949; *The Book of Acts in History*, Harper, 1955; *Quakerism and Early Christianity* (Swarthmore Lecture), Allen & Unwin, 1957; *The Character of a Quaker*, Pendle Hill, 1959; *Jesus and Judaism and the Emphasis of Jesus*, (Shrewsbury Lecture), John Woolman, 1962; *Behind the Gospels*, Pendle Hill, 1968.

Editor: (With others, and contributor to Volumes II-V) *Beginnings of Christianity*, five volumes, Macmillan, 1920-33; *Annual Catalogue of George Fox's Papers (1694-1697)*, Friends Book Store, 1939; *The Swarthmore Documents in America*, Friends Historical Society, 1940; *Letters to William Dewsbury and Others*, Bannisdale Press, 1948; George Fox, *Book of Miracles*, Cambridge University Press, 1948; William C. Braithwaite, *Beginnings of Quakerism*, 2nd edition revised, Cambridge University Press, 1955; William C. Braithwaite, *The Second Period of Quakerism*, 2nd edition, Cambridge University Press, 1961; *Cadbury Pedigree, American Branch*, privately printed, 1965; *John Woolman in England, 1772*, Friends Historical Society, 1971; *Friendly Heritage: Letters from the Quaker Past*, Friends Journal Books, 1972; *Narrative Papers of George Fox*, Friends United Press, 1972.

Author of monographs and articles on Biblical subjects and Quakerism. Editor of *Annual of American Schools of Oriental Research*, 1925-1931.

(Died October 7, 1974)

*   *   *

CAM, Helen Maud   1885-1968

PERSONAL: Born August 22, 1885, in Abingdon, Berkshire, England; daughter of William Herbert (a clerk in Holy Orders and teacher) and Kate (a teacher; maiden name Scott) Cam. *Education:* Royal Holloway College,

London, B.A., 1907, M.A., 1909. *Politics:* Labour Party. *Religion:* Church of England. *Home:* 23 Grassy Lane, Sevenoaks, Kent, England.

CAREER: Bryn Mawr College, Bryn Mawr, Pa., fellow in history, 1908-09; Cheltenham Ladies College, Cheltenham, England, assistant mistress in history, 1909-12; Royal Holloway College, University of London, Surrey, England, lecturer, later senior staff lecturer, 1912-21; Cambridge University, Girton College, Cambridge, England, research fellow, 1922-26, lecturer and director of studies in history, 1926-48, faculty lecturer in history, 1927-48; Harvard University, Cambridge, Mass., Zemurray-Radcliffe Professor of History, 1948-54. President, International Commission for Study of Representative Institutions, 1949-60.

MEMBER: Royal Historical Society (fellow; honorary vice-president), British Academy (fellow), American Academy of Arts and Sciences (fellow), Mediaeval Academy of America (corresponding member), Selden Society (vice-president, 1962). *Awards, honors:* Commander of the Order of the British Empire, 1957. D.Litt. from Cambridge University, 1937, Oxford University, 1962; M.A., Harvard University; LL.D. from Smith College, Mount Holyoke College, and University of North Carolina Women's College; fellow, Someville College, Oxford, 1964.

WRITINGS: Local Government in Francia and England: A Comparison of the Local Administration and Jurisdiction of the Carolinian Empire with that of the West Saxon Kingdom, University of London Press, 1912; *Studies in the Hundred Rolls: Some Aspects of Thirteenth-century Administration*, Oxford University Press, 1921; *The Hundred and the Hundred Rolls: An Outline of Local Government in Medieval England*, Methuen, 1930, reprinted, Merlin Press, 1963; *Liberties and Communities in Medieval England: Collected Studies in Local Administration and Topography*, Cambridge University Press, 1944, Barnes & Noble, 1963; *England Before Elizabeth*, Hutchinson, 1950, Harper, 1960, 3rd revised edition, Hutchinson, 1967; (editor) Gaillard T. Lapsley, *Crown, Community and Parliament in the Later Middle Ages*, Macmillan 1951; (editor) Frederick William Maitland, *Selected Historical Essays*, Cambridge University Press, 1957; *Law-finders and Lawmakers in Medieval England: Collected Studies in Legal and Constitutional History*, Merlin Press, 1962, Barnes & Noble, 1963; (editor) Ada Elizabeth Levett, *Studies in Manorial History*, Oxford University Press, 1963; (editor) *The Eyre of London*, Quaritch, 1968.

Also author of sections on Northampton and Cambridge in Victoria County history. Contributor of articles to history journals in England and America.

SIDELIGHTS: In 1948, Helen Maud Cam became the first woman to hold a full professorship on the faculty of Arts and Sciences at Harvard University. The *London Times* noted that "she could fill a lecture room at 9 o'clock throughout a snowy winter . . . and when absorbed in work could become oblivious to times and seasons: she was once locked into the library of Corpus Christi College, from which she escaped by the medieval stratagem of throwing her glove at a passer-by." Miss Cam read German, French, and Italian. She attended international historical congresses in Oslo, 1928, Warsaw, 1933, Zurich, 1938, Paris, 1950, Rome, 1955, Stockholm, 1960. *Avocational interests:* Walking, water color sketching.

(Died February 9, 1968)

CAMERON, Edna M. 1905-

PERSONAL: Born September 1, 1905, in Fredonia, Tex.; married Howard M. Cameron (a teacher), 1938. *Education:* Southwest Texas Teachers College (now Southwest Texas State University), B.A., 1932; University of Kansas, M.A., 1961. *Religion:* Baptist. *Residence:* De Soto, Kan.

CAREER: Elementary teacher in Texas, 1928-34; home economics teacher in Texas junior high schools, 1934-38; elementary teacher in Indian Service, Alaska, 1938-50, in Alaska public schools, 1958-69. *Member:* National League of American Pen Women (Pacific Northwest division).

WRITINGS: Children of the Tundra (juvenile), Lippincott, 1963.

SIDELIGHTS: Mrs. Cameron has traveled to Aleut, Eskimo, and Indian schools of Alaska by bush pilot planes, outboard river skiffs, dog sleds, and Coast Guard boats.

BIOGRAPHICAL/CRITICAL SOURCES: Elementary English, University of Kansas Press, 1962.

* * *

CAMERON, Frank T. 1909-

PERSONAL: Born August 12, 1909, in Sault Ste. Marie, Mich.; married Ruth Leslie, 1943 (died, 1967); children: Georgia Adlen. *Education:* University of Michigan, B.A., 1931. *Address:* Box 314, Kentfield, Calif. 94909.

CAREER: Miscellaneous jobs, chiefly at sea, 1931-36; Grace Lines, Inc., New York, N.Y., started as able seaman and worked up to chief purser prior to World War II, public relations manager, 1945-46; free-lance writer of filmscripts, brochures, and publicity for American Telephone & Telegraph Co., Matson Lines, and other firms, 1946-64; Dancer-Fitzgerald-Sample, Inc., San Francisco, Calif., senior copywriter, 1964-65; Campbell-Ewald Co., senior copywriter, 1965—; free-lance writer, 1965—. *Military service:* U.S. Maritime Service, 1942-45; became lieutenant; served in South Pacific. *Member:* Society of Magazine Writers, Press Club and Copywriters Club (both San Francisco), Sigma Delta Chi, Kappa Tau Alpha. *Awards, honors:* Commonwealth Club of California award, 1953, for *Cottrell: Samaritan of Science.*

WRITINGS: Cottrell: Samaritan of Science, Doubleday, 1952; *Hungry Tiger* (history of Flying Tiger Line), McGraw, 1964. Contributor of nonfiction to national magazines, including *Life, Saturday Evening Post, Reader's Digest, Sports Illustrated,* and *National Geographic.*

* * *

CAMPBELL, Alistair 1907-1974

PERSONAL: Born December 12, 1907, in Birmingham, England; son of Lauchlan and Sarah (Clark) Campbell; married Kathleen Le Pelley Blackmore, April 23, 1935; children: Alistair John, Neil Francis, Colin Hugh. *Education:* University of Birmingham, B.A., 1929; Balliol College, Oxford, B.Litt., 1932; M.A., 1940. *Home:* 11 Marston Ferry Rd., Oxford, England.

CAREER: Oxford University, Oxford, England, lecturer in English language at Balliol College, 1946-53, and senior research fellow, 1953-63, university lecturer in mediaeval English, 1949-63, Rawlinson and Bosworth Professor of Anglo-Saxon, beginning 1963, fellow of Pembroke College, beginning 1963.

WRITINGS: (Editor) *The Battle of Brunanburh,* Heinemann, 1938; (editor with J. H. Brouwer) *The Early Frisian Studies of Jan Van Vliet,* Van Gorcum, 1939; (editor) *Gysbert Japicx, The Oxford Text of Four Poems,* Fryske Academy (Netherlands), 1948; (editor) *Encomium Emmae reginae,* Royal Historical Society, 1949; (editor) *Fridegodus, Frithegodi monachi Breviloquium vitae Beati Wilfredi, et Wulfstani cantoria Narratio metrica de Sancto Swithuno,* [Turici], 1950; (editor) *Thet Freske riim* [and] *Tractatus Alvini,* Nijhoff, 1952; (editor) *Paulus Orosius, The Tollemache Orosius,* Rosenkilde & Bagger (Copenhagen), 1953; *Old English Grammar,* Clarendon Press, 1959; (editor) *The Chronicle of Aethelweard,* Nelson, 1962; (editor) *Aedilvulfus, De abbatibus,* Oxford University Press, 1967. Contributor of articles on historical and linguistic topics to journals.

(Died, 1974)

* * *

CAMPBELL, Archibald Bruce 1881-

PERSONAL: Born January 31, 1881, in London, England; married May Evelyn Webb, March 31, 1942. *Education:* Attended St. Olave's School, London, England, 1892-96. *Politics:* Labour. *Religion:* Church of England. *Address:* c/o J. M. Dent & Sons Ltd., Aldine House, 10-13 Bedford St., London W.C. 2, England.

CAREER: Served in British Merchant Service, and in Royal Navy; author.

WRITINGS: With the Corners Off, Lippincott, 1938; *The Battle of the Plate,* Jenkins, 1940; *You Have Been Listening to . . .,* Chapman & Hall, 1940; *Bring Yourself to Anchor,* Chapman & Hall, 1941; *Escape of H.M.S. Calliope,* Oxford University Press, 1941; *Zeebrugge, St. George's Day, 1918,* Oxford University Press, 1941; *Yarns of the Seven Seas,* Pitman, 1944; *Come Alongside,* Stanley Paul & Co., 1946; *In the Tracks of the Old Explorers,* Pitman, 1950; *Into the Straight,* Stanley Paul & Co., 1950; *Scrapbook,* W. H. Allen, 1950 (also published as *Commander Campbell's Scrapbook,* W. H. Allen, 1950); *Salute the Red Duster,* Christopher Johnson, 1952; *When I Was in Patagonia,* Christopher Johnson, 1953; *Customs and Traditions of the Royal Navy,* Gale & Polden, 1956; *Great Moments at Sea,* Roy Publishers, 1957; *North American Indians,* Muller, 1961; *Queer Shipmates,* Phoenix House, 1962.

* * *

CAMPBELL, Peter (Walter) 1926-

PERSONAL: Born June 17, 1926, in Poole, Dorsetshire, England; son of Walter Howard (a clerk) and Lillian (Locke) Campbell. *Education:* New College, Oxford, B.A., 1947, M.A., 1951; Nuffield College, Oxford, research student, 1947-49. *Office:* University of Reading, Whiteknights Park, Reading RG62AA, England.

CAREER: University of Manchester, Manchester, England, assistant lecturer, 1949-52, lecturer, in government, 1952-60; University of Reading, Reading, England, professor of politics, 1960—. Visiting lecturer, Victoria University of Wellington, 1954. *Member:* Institute of Electoral Research (chairman, 1959-65), Political Studies Association (secretary, 1955-58), British Association for American Studies, Hansard Society (councilor, 1962—).

WRITINGS: (Editor) *Encyclopaedia of World Politics,* Faber, 1950; *French Electoral Systems and Elections,* Faber, 1958; (with Brian Chapman) *Constitution of the Fifth Republic,* Basil Blackwell, 1958. Contributor to political science journals. Editor, *Political Studies,* 1963-69.

WORK IN PROGRESS: Writing on French politics, and on methodology of political science.

* * *

CAMPION, Sidney R(onald) 1891-
(Geoffrey Swayne)

PERSONAL: Born June 30, 1891, in Leicester, England; son of Walter and Martha (Robinson) Campion; married Claire Armitage, May 12, 1912 (died, 1968); children: Cynthia. *Education:* Educated in England at Teachers' Training College, Chester, Honourable Society of Gray's Inn, Morley College, Wimbledon School of Art, St. Martin's School of Art, Regent Street Polytechnic. *Politics:* Socialist. *Religion:* Humanistic. *Home:* 22 Erridge Rd., Merton Park, Wimbledon, London S.W.19, England.

CAREER: Barrister-at-law and licensed school master. Journalist on newspapers in Leicester, Manchester, Chorley, and Bradford, England, and on *Daily News,* London, England, prior to 1933; Kemsley (now Thompson) Newspapers, parliamentary correspondent in London, 1933-40; General Post Office Headquarters, London, chief press and broadcasting officer, 1940-57; freelance writer. Painter and sculptor, exhibiting in galleries in London, Madrid, and Paris. *Military service:* Royal Flying Corps, Royal Air Force, and Independent Air Force, World War I. *Member:* Royal Society of Arts (fellow), Institute of Journalists (fellow), National Union of Journalists (life), Psychical Research Society, English-Speaking Union, League Against Cruel Sport, Francis Bacon Society. *Awards, honors:* Order of the British Empire for services to the General Post Office.

WRITINGS: Sunlight on the Foothills, Rich & Cowan, 1941; *Towards the Mountains,* Rich & Cowan, 1943; *Reaching High Heaven,* Rich & Cowan, 1944; *Only the Stars Remain,* Rich & Cowan, 1945; *Royal Mail,* Newman Neame, 1960; *World of Colin Wilson: A Biographical Study,* Muller, 1962; *Press Gallery,* Newman Neame, 1963. Contributor to newspapers and periodicals.

WORK IN PROGRESS: Adventures Under the Sycamore Tree, a study in mother fixation and incestuous desire, expressed in fiction.

SIDELIGHTS: Campion's paintings and portrait busts include Bernard Shaw, Colin Wilson, Sir Vyvyan Fuchs, Rupert Brooke, and Oscar Wilde. *Avocational interests:* Ghosts, searching for Shakespeare manuscripts.

* * *

CANFIELD, Kenneth French 1909-

PERSONAL: Born June 1, 1909, in Rahway, N.J.; son of William Albert (a pharmacist) and Martha M. (Dunn) Canfield; married Eleanor Elizabeth France, December 21, 1935; children: David France, Kenneth French, Jr. *Education:* Oberlin College, A.B., 1930; Middlebury College, M.A., 1938. *Religion:* Unitarian Universalist. *Home:* Oak Ridge Rd., West Lebanon, N.H. 03784.

CAREER: North Senior High School, Great Neck, N.Y., teacher of French, 1935-71, head of department of foreign languages, 1958-71; Dartmouth College, Hanover, N.H., instructor in community French courses, 1971—. Fulbright teacher in France, 1952-53; lecturer in Luxembourg schools and on Institut National de Radio-diffusion (Belgian National Radio), 1952-53; lecturer, Queens College of the City University of N.Y., 1965-66. *Member:* American Association of Teachers of French (chapter president, 1956-58),

New York State Teachers Association, Great Neck Teachers Association (president, 1948-49). *Awards, honors:* Chevalier des Palmes Academiques, 1972.

WRITINGS: (Editor) *Selections from French Poetry,* Harvey, 1965.

* * *

CANHAM, Erwin D(ain) 1904-

PERSONAL: Born February 13, 1904, in Auburn, Me.; son of Vincent Walter (a newspaper editor) and Elizabeth (Gowell) Canham; married Thelma Whitman Hart, May 10, 1930 (deceased); married Patience Mary Daltry, 1968; children: (first marriage) Carolyn (Mrs. R. Shale Paul), Elizabeth (Mrs. Lyle H. Davis). *Education:* Bates College, B.A., 1925; Oxford University, B.A. and M.A., 1929. *Religion:* Christian Science. *Home:* 6 Acorn St., Boston, Mass. 02108. *Office:* 1 Norway St., Boston, Mass. 02115.

CAREER: Christian Science Monitor, Boston, Mass., reporter, 1925-26, correspondent in Geneva, Switzerland, 1926-28, and 1930-32, chief of bureau, Washington, D.C., 1932-39, general news editor, Boston, Mass., 1939-42, managing editor, 1942-45, editor, 1945-64, editor in chief, 1964—. Commentator, currently on weekly network radio program and a weekly television program. United Nations, deputy chairman of U.S. delegation to Conference on Freedom of Information, 1948, alternate U.S. delegate to General Assembly, 1949. Chairman of National Manpower Council, 1959—; director, National Bureau of Economic Research, 1961—; board member, Resources for the Future, 1961—. Also director of John Hancock, Mutual Life Insurance Co., Federal Reserve Bank of Boston, Chamber of Commerce of the United States (president, 1959-60, chairman of board, 1960-61, executive committee chairman, 1961-62), Keystone Custodian Funds Inc. Trustee of Twentieth Century Fund, Wellesley College, Bates College, Boston Public Library, Boston Museum of Fine Arts; member of corporation, Simmons College.

MEMBER: American Society of Newspaper Editors (president, 1948-49), American Academy of Arts and Sciences (fellow), Association of American Rhodes Scholars, Phi Beta Kappa, Delta Sigma Rho, Masons, Gridiron Club (Washington, D.C.), National Press Club, Overseas Writers Club, Harvard Club of Boston, Saturday Club and Tavern Club (both Boston). *Awards, honors:* Chevalier, French Legion of Honor, 1946, Officer, 1958; Order of Southern Cross (Brazil), 1951; Commander, Order of Orange-Nassau (Netherlands), 1952; Order of George I (Greece), 1954; Julian Yorks Award of Massachusetts Jewish War Veterans of the U.S., 1954; Order of Merit (German Federal Republic), 1960; honorary commander, Order of the British Empire, 1965. Honorary degrees: Litt.D. from Bates College, 1946, Portia Law School, 1952, Northeastern University, 1953, Franklin College, 1960, Brigham Young University, 1962; L.H.D. from Boston University, 1948, Kenyon College, 1949, Yale University, 1949, Lehigh University, 1950, Principia College, 1951, University of Massachusetts, 1963; LL.D. from Middlebury College, 1956, Springfield College, 1957, Colby College, 1957, Tufts University, 1958, Temple University, 1959, Pratt Institute, 1960, Marlboro College, 1960, Babson Institute, 1960; D.Jour. from Suffolk University, 1960; D.S.S. from University of Maine, 1961.

WRITINGS: (With others) *Awakening: The World at Mid-Century,* Longmans, Green, 1951; *New Frontiers for Freedom,* Longmans, Green, 1954; *Commitment to Freedom:*

The Story of The Christian Science Monitor, Houghton, 1958; (editor) *Man's Great Future*, Longmans, Green, 1959; (with DeWitt John) *The Christian Science Way of Life*, Prentice-Hall, 1962; *The Ethics of United States Foreign Relations*, University of Missouri Press, 1966.

SIDELIGHTS: Canham has covered world conferences, trips of American presidents, written about significant events in many countries, but two occurrences that he considers personally meaningful are these: An address on "The Authentic Revolution" that he delivered as long ago as 1950 and which still is in heavy demand in reprint form (he gave a revision of this address as the annual Fourth of July Oration at Faneuil Hall in Boston in 1962); his part in helping quell the riot in the Massachusetts State Prsion at Charleston in January, 1955.

One of a group chosen by the convicts to mediate for them, Canham wrote in the *Christian Science Monitor:* "To have the privilege of restoring hope to 4 desperate men threatening the lives of 11 others—and perhaps more—is the deeply humbling experience which seven Boston citizens had during the last 24 hours . . .''

He formerly did a great deal of public speaking, but has reduced this drastically. Still travels a good deal, getting abroad either to Europe or Asia every year or two, and sometimes more frequently. He speaks and reads French and German, is "deeply interested in defining and articulating the nature of our [American] changing economic system.''

BIOGRAPHICAL SOURCES: Time, January 8, 1965.

* * *

CANTZLAAR, George La Fond 1906-1967

PERSONAL: Surname is pronounced *Kantz*-lar; born February 28, 1906, in New York, N.Y.; son of Frederick Rudolph and Susan La Fond (Brigham) Cantzlaar; married Mayme Bassett (a printing executive), December 19, 1953. *Education:* Colgate University, B.A., 1930. *Politics:* Republican-Conservative. *Religion:* Protestant.

CAREER: Language teacher, 1930-31; State Hospitals Press, Utica, N.Y., assistant editor of *Psychiatric Quarterly*, 1935-40; W. B. Saunders Co. (publishers), Philadelphia, Pa., medical textbooks editor, 1940-43; New York State Department of Mental Hygiene, Albany, director of public relations, 1946-48; Dade County Medical Association, Miami, Fla., executive secretary, 1948-49; Johnson and Owston, Inc. (printers and publishers), New York, N.Y., president, 1953-66. *Military service:* U.S. Army, 1943. U.S. Navy, writer, 1943-46, editor-in-chief of naval warfare publications, 1950-53; also served extended tours of duty for special projects, mainly as editor for Navy management review study group, and as creator, producer, and host of Navy radio program, "Wings of Gold." *Member:* Navy League (national director, 1963-64), Naval Reserve Association (New York; president), Naval Order of the United States, American Meteorological Society, Militia Association of New York (historian).

WRITINGS: (with Helen F. Bruce) *Your Guide to Photography*, Barnes & Noble, 1955; (with D. J. Kern) *Reservist's Guide and Record*, McKay, 1955; *Your Guide to the Weather*, Barnes & Noble, 1964; (with James Arnold Brussel) *Layman's Dictionary of Psychiatry*, Barnes & Noble, 1967. Writer of several Navy training text books. Editor, *Mental Hygiene News*, 1946-48.

WORK IN PROGRESS: A book on typography, tentatively titled *The Wonderful World of ABC's.*

SIDELIGHTS: Cantzlaar told *CA*: "My principal motivation in writing is the clarification of technical information of interest to the general public. In my association with naval publications I have fought consistently against take-it-or-leave-it professional gobbledygook.''

(Died November 12, 1967)

* * *

CAPRON, Louis (Bishop) 1891-

PERSONAL: Surname rhymes with apron; born July 26, 1891, in Menands, Albany County, N.Y.; son of William White (a merchant) and Helen Miller (Kent) Capron; married Clara Louise Hunter. *Education:* Yale University, Ph.B., 1913. *Politics:* Democrat. *Religion:* Episcopal. *Home:* 218 Westminster Rd., West Palm Beach, Fla. 33405. *Agent:* Monica McCall, Inc., 667 Madison Ave., New York, N.Y. 10021.

CAREER: Reporter or editor for *Oneonta Daily Star*, Oneonta, N.Y., 1913-14, *Knickerbocker-Press*, Albany, N.Y., 1914-15, and *Springfield Republican*, Springfield, Mass., 1915-17; Capron Co., Inc. (department store), Oneonta, N.Y., co-owner, 1919-25; Palm Beach Mercantile Co., Palm Beach, Fla., department manager, merchandising manager, and other posts, 1925-51; full-time writer and researcher, 1951—. Florida Governor's Advisory Committee for Seminoles, member, 1956-60; Florida State Library Board, member, 1957-61. *Military service:* U.S. Army Air Service, World War I; became lieutenant. *Member:* American Library Association, Association of College and Research Libraries, American Library Trustee Association, Southeastern Library Association, Florida Anthropological Society, Florida Historical Society. Historical Association of Southern Florida (vice-president), Palm Beach County Historical Society (vice-president).

WRITINGS: The Gold Arrowhead, Howell, Soskin, 1948; *White Moccasins*, Holt, 1955; *The Blue Witch*, Holt, 1957; *The Red War Pole*, Bobbs-Merrill, 1963. Author of *Medicine Bundles of the Florida Seminoles and the Green Corn Dance*, Smithsonian Institution. Contributor of verse, short stories, and of articles on Seminole Indians to *National Geographic, Florida Anthropologist, Florida Historical Quarterly*, and other periodicals.

WORK IN PROGRESS: An adult book and a juvenile book on the Seminoles; adult fiction; a juvenile book on early Florida.

SIDELIGHTS: For the past thirty years, Capron has had a close connection with the Seminole Indians of Florida, even taking part in their sacred ceremonies. He claims to be the only white man to have ever been present during the whole of their five-day Green Corn Dance. *Avocational interests:* Collecting books on pioneer life in the United States.

* * *

CAPRON, Walter Clark 1904-

PERSONAL: Surname rhymes with "apron"; born September 25, 1904, in Elmira, N.Y.; son of Harold Stearns (a minister) and Mattie (Clark) Capron; married Gertrude Booth, June 30, 1928; children: Walter Clark, Jr., Mrs. Hulon W. Oliver, Mrs. Patricia C. Ward. *Education:* U.S. Coast Guard Academy, B.S., 1928; National War College, student, 1951-52. *Politics:* Independent Republican. *Religion:* Protestant. *Home and office:* 4912 16th Rd. North, Arlington, Va. 22207.

CAREER: U.S. Coast Guard, commissioned officer, 1928-63, retiring as captain, 1963; served on sea duty, 1928-34, 1937-41, 1943-44, 1950-51; stationed at U.S. Coast Guard Headquarters, Washington, D.C., as chief of Enlisted Personnel Division, 1946-50, chief of Program Analysis Division, 1952-55, and deputy chief of staff, 1957-62. Member of finance committee, Navy-Marine Residence Foundation. Member of area and district committees, Boy Scouts of America, 1948-50. *Member:* U.S. Naval Institute. *Awards, honors:* Legion of Merit, Navy Commendation Medal, Army Commendation Medal.

WRITINGS: The Coast Guard: A Year of Progress in Naval Review, 1962-1963, U.S. Naval Institute, 1962; *United States Coast Guard,* F. Watts, 1965. Assisted with editing and preparation of *Coast Guardsman's Manual.* Contributor of short stories to U.S. Coast Guard Alumni Bulletin, 1972.

WORK IN PROGRESS: A book, *Famous Coast Guard Cutters.*

*   *   *

CARHART, Arthur Hawthorne 1892-
(Hart Thorne, V. A. VanSickle)

PERSONAL: Born September 18, 1892, in Mapleton, Iowa; son of George W. (a merchant) and Ella Louise (Hawthorne) Carhart; married Vera Amelia VanSickle, August 16, 1918 (died, 1966). *Education:* Iowa State College (now University), B.S. in Landscape Design and City Planning, 1916. *Politics:* Independent. *Religion:* Protestant. *Home and office:* 6970 Central Ave., Lemon Grove, Calif. 92045.

CAREER: U.S. Forest Service, Denver, Colo., recreational engineer, 1919-22; McCrary, Culley & Carhart (land architects and city planners), Denver, Colo., member of firm, 1923-31; Federal Aid in Wildlife Restoration, Colorado coordinator, 1938-43; U.S. Office of Price Administration, regional information executive for Rocky Mountain Region, 1944-46; Denver (Colo.) Public Library, Conservation Library Center, consultant, 1960-70. Member, Citizens Committee on Natural Resources; trustee, J. N. ''Ding'' Darling Foundation. Member of historical advisory committee, American Forestry Association Centennial Celebration, 1970-72. *Military service:* U.S. Army, Sanitary Corps, 1917-19; became lieutenant. *Member:* Outdoor Writers Association of America (honorary), American Society of Landscape Architects (honorary), American Forestry Association (honorary vice-president, 1970), Desert Protective Association, Colorado Authors League (president, 1931), Westerners (founder, and past president, Denver Posse). *Awards, honors:* Founders Award, Izaak Walton League of America; Jade of Chiefs award, Outdoor Writers Association of America; American Forest Products Industries citation for Conservation; American Motors Conservation award.

WRITINGS: The Ordeal of Brad Ogden (novel), Sears, 1929; *The Last Stand of the Pack* (animal stories), Sears, 1929; *Colorado* (guide), Coward, 1932; (contributor) *Angling Success,* Macmillan, 1935; *How to Plan the Home Landscape,* Doubleday, Doran, 1936; *Trees and Shrubs for the Small Home,* Doubleday, Doran, 1936; *Drum Up the Dawn* (historical novel), Dodd, 1937; (under pseudonym V. A. VanSickle) *The Wrong Body,* Knopf, 1937; (under pseudonym Hart Thorne) *Bronc Buster,* Dodd, 1937; (under pseudonym Hart Thorne) *Saddle Men of the C-Bit Brand,* Dodd, 1937; *The Outdoorsman's Cook Book,*

Macmillan, 1944, revised edition, 1962; *Hunting North American Deer,* Macmillan, 1946; *Men of Power,* Popular Publications, 1949; *Fresh Water Fishing,* A. S. Barnes, 1949; *Hi! Stranger,* Ziff-Davis Publishing Co., 1949.

Fishing Is Fun, Macmillan, 1950; *Fishing in the West,* Macmillan, 1950; *Water–Or Your Life,* Lippincott, 1951; *Pinto the Cowboy Pony,* Nifty, 1953; *Timber in Your Life,* Lippincott, 1955; *Son of the Forest,* Lippincott, 1956; *The National Forests,* Knopf, 1959; *Planning for America's Wildlands,* Audubon Society of America, National Parks Association, Wilderness Society, and Wildlife Management Institute, 1961. Contributor of over four thousand short stories, novelettes, serials, articles, and essays to national magazines.

SIDELIGHTS: While with the Forest Service, Carhart was instrumental in developing the first national forest recreational-use plans for the San Isabel National Forest in Colorado, and later developed a similar plan for the Superior National Forest in Minnesota. In 1960 Carhart and John T. Eastlick conceived the idea of the Conservation Library Center in Denver, believed to be the only one of its kind in existence.

*   *   *

CARMAN, J(ustice) Neale 1897-1972

PERSONAL: Born June 26, 1897, in Herington, Kan.; son of Frederic Douglass and Gay (Neale) Carman; married Maybelle Gordon, March 4, 1918; children: Justice, Robert, Frederic, Elizabeth Ann (Mrs. Herman Derrington Wills). *Education:* University of Kansas, A.B., 1917, M.A., 1921; University of Chicago, Ph.D., 1934. *Religion:* Society of Friends (Quakers). *Home:* F-208 Hampton Ct., Meadowbrook Apts., Lawrence, Kan. 66044. *Office:* Department of Romance Languages, University of Kansas, Lawrence, Kan. 66044.

CAREER: University of Kansas, Lawrence, instructor, 1918-22, assistant professor, 1922-34, associate professor, 1934-44, professor of Romance languages, 1944-67, professor emeritus, 1967-72, acting chairman of department of Romance languages, 1953-54, 1963-67, chairman, 1957-62. Ecole Normale d'Insti26ers, Clermont-Ferrand, France, repetiteur d'anglais, 1924-25. Bank of Herington, Herington, Kan., former employee, then director, 1956-72. *Member:* Modern Language Association of America, American Association of Teachers of French (president, West Central chapter, 1949-51), American Association of University Professors (chapter president, 1951-52), American Studies Association, International Arthurian Society, Mayflower Society, Dante Society of America, Kansas Modern Language Association (vice-president, 1946-47), Kansas Historical Society, Poetry Society of Kansas (president, 1948-50), Phi Delta Thi.

WRITINGS: The Relationship of the Perlesvaus and the Queste del Saint Graal, University of Kansas Press, 1936; *Elementary French,* Farrar & Rinehart, 1943; *Foreign Language Units of Kansas,* Volume I, *Historical Atlas and Statistics,* University of Kansas Press, 1962. Translator into English of *Morte d'Artur,* University of Kansas Press, 1973. Contributor of reviews, six articles on Arthurian subjects, and twelve articles on bilingual communities in the United States and Europe, to learned journals; contributor of poetry to magazines.

WORK IN PROGRESS: Volume II of *Foreign Language Units of Kansas;* a monograph on linguistic displacement in Basque country, Brittany, and Flanders, to be published by

University of Kansas Press; a volume of commentary on the *Perlesvaus*.

(Died November 25, 1972)

* * *

CARMICHAEL, Oliver C(romwell) 1891-1966

PERSONAL: Born October 3, 1891, near Goodwater, Ala.; son of Daniel Monroe (a farmer) and Amanda (Lessley) Carmichael; married Ruth Mae Crabtree, July 13, 1918; children: Oliver Cromwell, Jr., Frederick Henry. *Education:* University of Alabama, B.A., 1911, M.A., 1914; Oxford University, B.Sc. and diploma in anthropology, 1917. *Politics:* Democrat. *Religion:* Presbyterian. *Home:* 27 Hilltop Rd., Asheville, N.C. 28803.

CAREER: High school teacher and principal, college and university instructor in Alabama, 1911-13, 1919-22; Alabama College (now University of Montevallo), Montevallo, dean, 1922-26, president, 1926-35; Vanderbilt University, Nashville, Tenn., dean of Graduate School and Senior College, 1935-37, chancellor, 1937-46; Carnegie Foundation for the Advancement of Teaching, New York, N.Y., president, 1946-53; University of Alabama, Tuscaloosa, president, 1953-57; Ford Foundation Fund for the Advancement of Education, New York, N.Y., educational consultant, 1957-66. American National Bank, Nashville, Tenn., director, 1943-46. Chairman of American Council on Education, 1943-44; board of trustees of State University of New York, 1948-53, board of trustees of Nutrition Foundation, 1953-56, Board of Foreign Scholarships, 1954-56, Learning Resources Institute, 1959-66. Member of President's Commission on Higher Education, 1946-47, and government committees, councils, and advisory bodies. *Military service:* British Army, 1915-16; served in India and East Africa; became honorary captain. U.S. Army, 1917-19; became first lieutenant.

MEMBER: National Education Association (life member), Southern Association of Colleges and Secondary Schools (president, 1955-56), Phi Beta Kappa, Omicron Delta Kappa, Kappa Delta Pi (former member of national council; laureate member), Century Association (New York); Round Table, Mountain City Club, Downtown Club, Biltmore Forest Country Club (all Asheville). *Awards, honors:* Rhodes scholar, 1917; American Council Book award gold medal and $1,000 for best book on higher education, 1961-62, for *Graduate Education: A Critique and a Program.* Recipient of twenty-one honorary degrees, 1937-52, including L.H.D. from University of Hawaii, LL.D. from Duke University, University of Southern California, University of Florida, Furman University, University of Pittsburgh, University of Michigan, and University of Alabama.

WRITINGS: The Changing Role of Higher Education, Macmillan, 1949; *Universities, Commonwealth and American: A Comparative Study,* Harper, 1959; *Graduate Education: A Critique and a Program,* Harper, 1961. Contributor of articles to educational journals.

WORK IN PROGRESS: Research for book, *The University of Tomorrow.*

(Died September 25, 1966)

* * *

CARNAHAN, Walter H(ervey) 1891-

PERSONAL: Born November 2, 1891, in Lynnville, Ind.; son of Gilbert B. (a laborer) and Laura A. (Simpson) Carnahan; married Ethel V. Harper, October 28, 1914 (deceased); children: Walter H., Robert D., Patricia Carnahan Kuney, Gilbert C., Mary Carnahan Orr. *Education:* Indiana State College (now University), student, 1911-13; Oakland City College, A.B., 1919; University of Chicago, graduate study, 1921; Indiana University, M.A., 1932. *Religion:* Methodist.

CAREER: Shortridge High School, Indianapolis, Ind., teacher, 1923-42; Purdue University, Lafayette, Ind., instructor, 1942-55; D. C. Heath & Co., Boston, Mass., editor, 1947-56.

WRITINGS: (With Howard Fehr and Max Beberman) *Algebra Course I* [and] *Algebra Course 2,* Heath, 1955; (with Fehr) *Geometry,* Heath, 1961; (with Glen Vannatta) *Advanced High School Mathematics,* C. E. Merrill, 1961; *Hoffman's Row* (novel), Bobbs-Merrill, 1963; *Summer Journey South,* Adams Press, 1968. Contributor of poetry and fiction to periodicals.

WORK IN PROGRESS: Green Paper.

* * *

CARNAP, Rudolf P. 1891-1970

PERSONAL: Born May 18, 1891, in Ronsdorf-Wuppertal, Germany; came to United States, 1935, naturalized, 1941; son of Johannes S. (a manufacturer) and Anna (Doerpfeld) Carnap; married Elizabeth Ina von Stoeger, February 8, 1933 (died, 1964); children: four. *Education:* Attended University of Freiburg; University of Jena, Dr.Phil., 1921. *Office:* Department of Philosophy, University of California, Los Angeles, Calif. 90024.

CAREER: University of Vienna, Vienna, Austria, lecturer in philosophy, 1926-30; German University, Prague, Czechoslovakia, professor of philosophy, 1931-35; University of Chicago, Chicago, Ill., professor of philosophy, 1936-52; Institute for Advanced Study, Princeton, N.J., fellow, 1952-54; University of California, Los Angeles, professor of philosophy, 1954-62, research philosopher, 1962-70. *Member:* American Academy of Arts and Sciences (fellow), British Academy (corresponding fellow), American Philosophical Association, Association for Symbolic Logic, Philosophy of Science Association, British Academy. *Awards, honors:* Sc.D. from Harvard University, 1936; LL.D. from University of California, 1963; H.L.D. from University of Michigan, 1965; Ph.D. from University of Olso, 1969.

WRITINGS: Der Raum (title means "The Space"), [Berlin], 1922; *Physikalische Begriffsbildung* (title means "Concept Formation in Physics"), Karlsruhe, 1926; *Der logische Aufbau der Welt,* [Berlin], 1928, 2nd edition, F. Meiner, 1960; *Scheinprobleme in der Philosophie,* [Berlin], 1960, translation by Rolf A. George of preceding two books published as *The Logical Structure of the World* and *Pseudoproblems in Philosophy,* University of California Press, 1967; *Albriss der Logistik* (title means "Outline of Symbolic Logic"), J. Springer, 1929; *Logische Syntax der Sprache,* J. Springer, 1934, translation by Amethe Smeaton [Countess von Zeppelin] published in England as *Logical Syntax of Language,* Routledge, 1937; *The Unity of Science,* Kegan Paul, 1934; *Die Aufgabe der Wissenschaftslogik* (title means "The Task of the Logic of Science"), Gerold & Co., 1934; *Philosophy and Logical Syntax,* Kegan Paul, 1935.

Introduction to Semantics, Harvard University Press, 1942; *Formalization of Logic,* Harvard University Press,

1943; *Meaning and Necessity: A Study in Semantics and Modal Logic,* University of Chicago Press, 1947, 2nd edition, enlarged, 1956; *Logical Foundations of Probability,* University of Chicago Press, 1950, 2nd edition, 1962, selections published under title *The Nature and Application of Inductive Logic,* University of Chicago Press, 1951; *The Continuum of Inductive Methods,* University of Chicago Press, 1952; *Einfuehrung in die symbolische Logik,* Springer-Verlag, 1954, 2nd enlarged edition, 1960, published as *Introduction to Symbolic Logic,* Dover, 1958; (with W. Stegmueller) *Induktive Logik und Wahrscheinlichkeit* (title means "Inductive Logic and Probability"), Springer-Verlag, 1958; *Philosophical Foundations of Physics: An Introduction to the Philosophy of Science,* edited by Martin Gardner, Basic Books, 1966; (editor with R. C. Jeffrey) *Studies in Inductive Logic and Probability,* Volume I, University of California Press, 1971.

Contributor: *Factors Determining Human Behavior,* Harvard University Press, 1937; *International Encyclopedia of Unified Science,* Volumes I, II, University of Chicago Press, 1938, 1939; (with Y. Bar-Hillel) *An Outline of the Theory of Semantic Information,* Research Laboratory of Electronics, Massachusetts Institute of Technology, 1952; W. Jackson, editor, *Communication Theory,* Butterworth & Co., 1953; Herbert Feigl and May Brodbeck, editors, *Readings in the Philosophy of Science,* Appleton, 1953; Feigl and M. Scriven, editors, *The Foundations of Science and the Concepts of Psychology and Psychoanalysis,* University of Minnesota Press, 1956; A. J. Ayer, *Logical Positivism,* Free Press of Glencoe, 1959; *Logic, Methodology and Philosophy of Science,* Stanford University Press, 1962; *Essays on the Foundation of Mathematics,* Manes Press, 1961; Paul A. Schilpp, *The Philosophy of Rudolf Carnap,* Open Court, 1964.

Contributor of papers to professional journals in Germany, France, Great Britain, Mexico, Italy, Switzerland, and the United States.

BIOGRAPHICAL/CRITICAL SOURCES: Fred Wilson and Alan Housman, *Carnap and Goodman: Two Formalists,* Nijhoff, 1967.

(Died September 14, 1970)

*   *   *

CARNELL, Edward John   1919-1967

PERSONAL: Born June 28, 1919, in Antigo, Wis.; son of Herbert Claude and Fanny (Carstens) Carnell; married Shirley Martha Rowe, January 1, 1944; children: Jean Elaine, John Paul. *Education:* Wheaton College, Wheaton, Ill., A.B., 1941; Westminster Theological Seminary, Chestnut Hill, Pa., Th.B. and Th.M., 1944; Harvard University, S.T.M., 1945, Th.D., 1948; Boston University, Ph.D., 1949. *Home:* 1161 South Oakland, Pasadena, Calif. *Office:* Fuller Theological Seminary, 135 North Oakland, Pasadena, Calif.

CAREER: Ordained Baptist minister, 1944; pastor in Marblehead, Mass., 1945-46; Gordon College, Boston, Mass., professor of philosophy and the philosophy of religion, 1945-48; Fuller Theological Seminary, Pasadena, Calif., professor of apologetics and systematic theology, 1948-54, president, 1954-59, professor of ethics and the philosophy of religion, 1959-67. *Member:* American Philosophical Association, National Association of Biblical Instructors. *Awards, honors:* Eerdmans Evangelical Book Award ($5,000) for *An Introduction to Christian Apologetics.*

WRITINGS: An Introduction to Christian Apologetics, Eerdmans, 1948 revised edition, 1955; *Television—Servant or Master?,* Eerdmans, 1950; *The Theology of Reinhold Niebuhr,* Eerdmans, 1950, revised edition, 1960; *A Philosophy of the Christian Religion,* Eerdmans, 1952; *Christian Commitment,* Macmillan, 1957; *The Case for Orthodox Theology,* Westminster, 1959; *The Kingdom of Love and the Pride of Life,* Eerdmans, 1960; *The Burden of Soren Kierkegaard,* Eerdmans, 1965; *The Case for Biblical Christianity,* edited by Ronald H. Nash (originally titled *Problem of Religious Authority*), Eerdmans, 1969. Contributor to religious journals.

(Died, 1967)

*   *   *

CARNER, Mosco   1904-

PERSONAL: Surname originally Cohen; born November 15, 1904, in Vienna, Austria; son of Rudolph and Selma (Liggi) Cohen; married Elisabeth Rode (a physician), February 17, 1962. *Education:* Vienna Music Academy, diploma, 1926; University of Vienna, Ph.D., 1928. *Home:* 14 Elsworthy Rd., London N.W. 3, England.

CAREER: State Theatre, Free City of Danzig (now in Poland), operatic conductor, 1930-33; conductor of major symphony orchestras in London, England, 1938-55; musical author and critic, London, 1949—. Member of British Broadcasting Corp. score reading panel, 1944-48, 1957-62, 1963—. *Member:* Society for the Promotion of New Music (executive board, 1948-58), London Critics' Circle.

WRITINGS: Dvorak, Novello, 1940; *A Study of 20th-Century Music,* Joseph Williams, 1942; *Of Men and Music,* Joseph Williams, 1944; *The History of the Waltz,* Parrish, 1948; *Puccini: A Critical Biography,* Duckworth, 1958, Knopf, 1959.

Contributor: G. Abraham, editor, *Schubert Symposium,* Lindsay Drummond, 1946; Abraham, editor, *Schumann Symposium,* Oxford University Press, 1952; R. Hill, editor, *The Concerto,* Penguin, 1952; A. Robertson, editor, *Chamber Music,* Penguin, 1957; A. Jacobs, editor, *Choral Music,* Penguin, 1963.

Music critic of *Time and Tide,* 1949-61, and *Evening News* (London), 1957-61; contributor to *Grove's Dictionary of Music,* 5th edition, and to *Musical Times, Times, Daily Telegraph,* all London, and to other British newspapers and journals.

WORK IN PROGRESS: Alban Berg: A Critical Study, for Duckworth.

SIDELIGHTS: Puccini: A Critical Biography was also issued in Italian and German editions. *Avocational interests:* Reading, travel, motoring, and swimming.

*   *   *

CARR, Harriett Helen   1899-

PERSONAL: Born January 4, 1899, in Ann Arbor, Mich.; daughter of Paul and Nellie (Loomis) Carr. *Education:* Attended Michigan State Normal College (now Eastern Michigan University), University of Michigan, and New York University. *Religion:* Presbyterian. *Home:* 23 Third St. S., St. Petersburg, Fla. 33701.

CAREER: Ypsilanti Daily Press, Ypsilanti, Mich., reporter and news editor, 1920-35; *Detroit News,* Detroit, Mich., feature writer, 1935-39; *Michigan Education Journal,* Lansing, staff writer, 1939-40; *Michigan Vocational*

Out-Look, Lansing, editor, 1940-45; Scholastic Magazines, New York, N.Y., assistant director of field services, 1945-63; full-time writer of fiction, 1963—. *Member:* Women's National Book Association, National League of American Pen Women (Florida branch), Westerners (New York Posse). *Awards, honors:* Junior Literary Guild awards, 1955, 1963; special award of Mystery Writers of America, 1963.

WRITINGS: Gravel Gold, Farrar, Straus, 1953; *Borghild of Brooklyn,* Farrar, Straus, 1955; *Where the Turnpike Starts,* Macmillan, 1955; *Against the Wind,* Macmillan, 1955; *Miami Towers,* Macmillan, 1956; *Sharon,* Hastings House, 1956; *Wheels for Conquest,* Macmillan, 1957; *Valley of Defiance,* Macmillan, 1957; *Confidential Secretary,* Macmillan, 1958; *The Mystery of the Aztec Idol,* Macmillan, 1959; *Mystery of Ghost Valley,* Macmillan, 1962; *Young Viking of Brooklyn,* Viking, 1961; *Rod's Girl,* Hastings House, 1963; *Bold Beginning,* Hastings House, 1964. Contributor of articles on vocational education to newspapers and educational magazines.

WORK IN PROGRESS: Collection of animal stories.

* * *

CARR, Mary Jane

PERSONAL: Born in Portland, Ore.; daughter of James B. Buchanan (a lawyer) and Elizabeth Cecilia (Connor) Carr. *Education:* Attended St. Mary's College (now Marylhurst), Marylhurst, Ore. *Politics:* Democrat. *Religion:* Catholic. *Home and office:* 3564 Southwest Council Crest Dr., Portland, Ore. 97201. *Agent:* McIntosh & Otis, Inc., 18 East 41st St., New York, N.Y. 10017.

CAREER: Associate editor of *Catholic Sentinel,* Portland, Ore., for several years, then joined staff of *Oregonian,* Portland, Ore., which published a serial that became her first book. *Member:* American Heart Association, Oregon Historical Society, Theta Sigma Phi. *Awards, honors:* Runner up, Newbery Award, 1941, for *Young Mac of Fort Vancouver.*

WRITINGS: Children of the Covered Wagon (Junior Literary Guild selection), Crowell, 1934, revised edition, 1957; *Young Mac of Fort Vancouver* (Junior Literary Guild selection), Crowell, 1940; *Peggy, Paul and Laddy,* Crowell, 1943; *Stranger at the Apple Ranch,* Silver Burdett, 1946; *Top of the Morning* (verse), Crowell, 1950.

SIDELIGHTS: Walt Disney motion picture and television series, "Westward Ho, the Wagons," 1955-56, was based on *Children of the Covered Wagon,* a book that also was transcribed into Braille, translated into French and Serbo-Croatian.

* * *

CARRINGTON, William Langley 1900-1970

PERSONAL: Born February 28, 1900, in Melbourne, Australia; son of John (a minister) and Alice (Langley) Carrington; married Kathleen Lorraine Johnson, October 18, 1928; children: Anne (Mrs. William Kotzman). *Education:* Trinity College, University of Melbourne, M.B. and B.S., 1923, M.D., 1925. *Religion:* Church of England. *Home:* 5 Lydia Ct., Balwyn, Melbourne E. 8, Victoria, Australia. *Office:* 174 Union Rd., Surrey Hills, Melbourne E. 10, Victoria, Australia.

CAREER: Alfred Hospital, Melbourne, Australia, medical superintendent, 1926-30; physician specializing in private practice of psychiatry and marriage counseling in Australia.

Founder president of National Marriage Guidance Council of Australia, 1953-57; director of Marriage Guidance Council of Victoria, beginning 1962. Honorary lecturer at colleges in Australia; visiting lecturer at Drew University, Madison, N.J., 1958; public and radio lecturer on marriage, parenthood, and religion. *Member:* Australian Medical Association.

WRITINGS: Helping Troubled People, Epworth, 1954; *The Child and God,* Epworth, 1955; *Psychology, Religion and Human Need,* Channel Press, 1957 reprinted, Epworth, 1969; *The Healing of Marriage,* Channel Press, 1961; *A Practical Handbook of Marriage Counselling,* Epworth, 1961.

AVOCATIONAL INTERESTS: Music, the theater, and tennis.

(Died December 7, 1970)

* * *

CARROLL, Herbert A(llen) 1897-

PERSONAL: Born May 23, 1897, in Greenfield, Mass.; son of Charles Robert and Ina (Allen) Carroll; married Gladys Hasty (a novelist), June 23, 1925; children: Warren Hasty, Sarah Linden (Mrs. Hazen Lee Watson). *Education:* Bates College, A.B., 1923; Brown University, A.M., 1928; Columbia University, Ph.D., 1930. *Politics:* Republican. *Religion:* Protestant. *Home:* Earls Rd., South Berwick, Me. 03908. *Office:* University of New Hampshire, Durham, N.H. 03824.

CAREER: Diplomate in clinical psychology; University of Minnesota, Minneapolis, assistant professor of educational psychology, 1930-36; University of New Hampshire, Durham, associate professor, 1941-43, professor of psychology and chairman of department, 1943-62, psychologist, and professor emeritus, 1962—. First National Bank of Biddeford, member of advisory committee. *Military service:* U.S. Army, 1917-19; became sergeant. *Member:* American Psychological Association (fellow), New Hampshire Psychological Association (charter president), Phi Beta Kappa, Phi Kappa Psi.

WRITINGS: Generalization of Bright and Dull Children, Teachers College, Columbia University, Bureau of Publications, 1930; (with A. C. Eurich) *Educational Psychology,* Heath, 1935; *Genius in the Making,* McGraw, 1940; *Mental Hygiene: The Dynamics of Adjustment,* Prentice-Hall, 1947, 5th edition, 1969. Contributor of articles to psychological and educational journals.

* * *

CARROLL, Phil 1895-1971

PERSONAL: Born June 20, 1895, in Bucyrus, Ohio; son of Phil and Martha Ada (Couts) Carroll; married Margaret Birdsell, March 20, 1920; children: Margaret (Mrs. L. Terry Finch), Jeane Durrell (Mrs. Thomas G. Custin), Phil III, Patricia Anne (Mrs. Martin H. Buehler II). *Education:* University of Michigan, B.S. in Electrical Engineering, 1918, M.E., 1940. *Politics:* Republican. *Home:* 6 Crestwood Dr., Maplewood, N.J.

CAREER: Registered professional engineer in New York and New Jersey. Student engineer, then employee in time-study section of Westinghouse Corp. plants and subsidiary, 1919-23; Dyer Engineers, Inc., Cleveland, Ohio, co-founder, and successively engineer, chief engineer, and vice-president in charge of operations, 1924-40; private practice as professional engineer, specializing in timestudies and cost control, 1940-71. Consultant to more than 250 companies; conductor of more than 190 workshops on cost reduction (illustrated with own slides); lecturer at universities and engineering schools. U.S. Mutual Security Agency, member of advisory group on European productivity, 1952. Member of industrial engineering advisory committee, University of Michigan and Newark College of Engineering. *Military service:* U.S. Army, Signal Corps, 1918.

MEMBER: Society for Advancement of Management (life fellow; secretary, 1947-48; treasurer, 1948-50; vice-president, 1955-57; president, 1958; chairman of board, 1959), American Management Association, American Institute of Industrial Engineers (regional vice-president, 1956). National Society of Professional Engineers, American Society of Mechanical Engineers (life fellow; chairman of management division executive commitee, 1954; chairman of general engineering executive committee, 1961-62); Academy of Management, New Jersey Technical Societies Council (president, 1950-51), Alpha Pi Mu, Tau Beta Pi, Masons. *Awards, honors:* University of Michigan Distinguished Alumnus Citation, 1953; Society for Advancement of Management, Gilbreth Medal, 1950, and 1970, Industrial Incentive Award, 1953.

WRITINGS—All published by McGraw except as noted: *Timestudy for Cost Control*, 1938; *Timestudy Fundamentals for Foremen*, 1944; *Discussion Leaders Manual*, privately printed, 1948; *How to Chart Data*, 1950, revised edition, 1960; *How to Control Production Costs*, 1952; *How Foremen Can Control Costs*, 1955; *Better Wage Incentives*, 1957; *Cost Control through Electronic Data Processing*, Society for Advancement of Management, 1958; *Profit Control*, 1962, *Overhead Cost Control*, 1964; *Practical Production and Inventory Control*, 1966. Contributor to *Foremen's Handbook, Industrial Engineering Handbook, Encyclopedia of Science and Technology.* Also contributor of more than one hundred articles to professional journals. Contributing editor, *Supervision*; member of editorial advisory board, *Advanced Management*; consulting editor, *Journal of Industrial Engineering*, 1949-59.

SIDELIGHTS: Carroll's books have been translated into Spanish, Japanese, Dutch, French, and Italian. *Avocational interests:* Making furniture for own home.

(Died October 23, 1971)

*   *   *

CARTER, (William) Hodding   1907-1972

PERSONAL: Born February 3, 1907, in Hammond, La.; son of William Hodding (farmer) and Irma (Dutartre) Carter; married Betty Werlein (a writer), October 14, 1931; children: Hodding III (editor, *Delta Democrat-Times*), Philip D. (a journalist), Thomas (deceased). *Education:* Bowdoin College, B.A., 1927; attended Graduate School of Journalism, Columbia University, 1928, and Harvard University, 1940. *Politics:* Democrat. *Religion:* Episcopalian. *Home:* Feliciana Farm, Greenville, Miss. 38701. *Agent:* Brandt & Brandt, 101 Park Ave., New York, N.Y. 10017.

CAREER: Tulane University, New Orleans, La., teaching fellow, 1928-29; reporter for *New Orleans Item-Tribune*, 1929; United Press, New Orleans, night bureau manager, 1930; Associated Press, Jackson, Miss., bureau manager, 1931-32; *Daily Courier*, Hammond, La., founder, and editor and publisher, 1932-36; *Delta Star* (daily), Greenville, Miss., founder, and editor and publisher, 1936-38; *Delta Democrat-Times*, (formed by merger), founder, publisher

and editor, 1938 to mid-1960's. Helped establish the experimental daily newspaper *PM*, 1940. Writer-in-residence, Tulane University, 1963-69. Co-owned radio station WDDT, Dixie Poultry Co., and Industrial Supply Co. (all in Greenville). Senior warden, St. James Episcopal Church, Greenville, 1957-60. Has held positions as member of board of directors, Chamber of Commerce, Greenville; member Delta Area Council, Boy Scouts of America; member, reconstruction and advance committee of National Protestant Episcopal Church; member, board of trustees, Peabody College, board of overseers, Bowdoin College, board of visitors, Tulane University; member, National Citizens Committee for Better Schools. Member, Pulitzer Prize Advisory Board, 1951-61. Former director, Southern Regional Council. *Military service:* Mississippi National Guard, 114th Field Artillery, 1940-45; became major; served as officer in charge of Middle East editions of *Yank*, and as editor of *Stars and Stripes*, Middle East edition; received War Department citation, 1945; consultant, Department of State, 1953; civilian aide to secretary of the Army, 1954-60; member of Executive Reserve, beginning 1957.

MEMBER: American Society of Newspaper Editors, Phi Beta Kappa (honorary member), Sigma Delta Chi (fellow). *Awards, honors:* Nieman fellowship, Harvard University, 1940; Guggenheim fellowship, 1945; Pulitzer Prize 1946, for editorials; Elijah Lovejoy Award, 1952; William Allen White Foundation's National Citation of Journalistic Merit, 1961; Bowdoin Prize, 1963; First Federal Award of Mississippi, 1968; Journalism Alumni Award, Columbia University, 1971. Honorary degrees: Doctor of Literature, Bowdoin College, 1947; D.H.L., Washington University, St. Louis, 1954, and Protestant Episcopal Theological Seminary, 1965; M.A., Harvard University, 1947; Doctor of Humanities, Coe College, 1958; Ph.D., Allegheny College, 1960.

WRITINGS: Lower Mississippi, Farrar & Rinehart, 1942; (with Ernest R. Dupuy) *Civilian Defense for the United States*, Farrar & Rinehart, 1942; *The Winds of Fear* (novel), Farrar & Rinehart, 1944; *Flood Crest* (novel), Rinehart, 1947; (contributor) Isabel Leighton, editor, *The Aspirin Age, 1919-1941*, Simon & Schuster, 1949; *Southern Legacy*, Louisiana State University Press, 1950; (with Anthony Ragusin) *Gulf Coast Country*, Duell, Sloan & Pearce, 1951; *John Law Wasn't So Wrong*, Esso Standard Oil Co., 1952; *Where Main Street Meets the River*, Rinehart, 1953; *Robert E. Lee and the Road of Honor* (juvenile), Random House, 1955; (with wife, Betty W. Carter) *So Great a Good*, University Press of Sewanee, 1955; *Marquis de Lafayette: Bright Sword for Freedom* (juvenile), Random House, 1958; *The South Strikes Back*, Doubleday, 1959; *The Angry Scar: The Story of Reconstruction*, Doubleday, 1959.

(Contributor) R. W. Howard, editor, *This is the South*, Rand McNally, 1960; *First Person Rural*, Doubleday, 1963; (with Betty W. Carter) *Doomed Road of Empire: The Spanish Trail of Conquest*, McGraw, 1963; *The Ballad of Catfoot Grimes, and Other Verses*, Doubleday, 1964; (contributor) Thomas C. Wheeler, editor, *A Vanishing America*, Holt, 1964; *So the Heffners Left McComb*, Doubleday, 1965; *The Commandos of World War II*, Random House, 1966; (editor with others) *The Past as Prelude: New Orleans, 1718-1968*, Pelican, for Tulane University, 1968; *Their Words Were Bullets: The Southern Press in War, Reconstruction and Peace*, University of Georgia Press, 1969; *Man and the River: The Mississippi*, Rand

McNally, 1970. Contributor to national magazines, including *Reader's Digest*, *Saturday Evening Post*, *Saturday Review*, *New York Times Magazine*, and *Nation*.

SIDELIGHTS: A liberal Southern newspaper editor in the manner of Ralph McGill, Carter once said, "I would rather be a small city newspaper editor and publisher than anything I know." His small city newspaper editorials on racial intolerance earned him a Pulitzer Prize in 1946. And it is in large part due to his paper's espousal of a moderate racial policy in the south that Greenville, Miss., has been said to be one of the least prejudiced cities in the southern United States.

Early in 1960 Carter's patriotism was attacked by the Mississippi Legislature, which alleged that Carter was a member of three liberal-moderate organizations, one of them (the only one he actually belonged to, he told a *Newsweek* interviewer) being the Southern Regional Council, a widely-respected group founded in 1918 to improve race relations; it fosters the desegregation of various public facilities and the elimination of barriers to Negro registration and voting. In 1955 he was censured by the same legislature for a story wherein he anticipated that the then newly-organized White Citizens Council would become an "uptown Ku Klux Klan."

Due to failing eyesight in recent years, Carter began dictating most of his his writings and gradually delegated many of his editorial duties to his son, Hodding Carter III, who assumed editorship of the *Delta-Democrat Times* in the mid-1960's.

He has at some time traveled to Europe, Middle East, North Africa, India, Southeast Asia, Mexico, and Canada. He was in South Africa in 1959 on a U.S.-South Africa Leader Exchange Program, with sojourns in Southern Rhodesia, Kenya, Ethiopia, and Egypt. *Avocational interests:* Historical research, race relations, sailing, and hunting.

BIOGRAPHICAL/CRITICAL SOURCES: Newsweek, January 11, 1960; *Book Week*, October 20, 1963; *Saturday Review*, January 2, 1965; *U.S. News & World Report*, March 29, 1965.

(Died April 4, 1972)

*   *   *

CARTER, John Stewart   1912-1965

PERSONAL: Born March 26, 1912, in Chicago, Ill.; son of Albert Howard (a physician) and Elizabeth (Stewart) Carter; married Marie Valle, February 12, 1941; children: Elizabeth Francis, Ann Alexandra. *Education:* Northwestern University, B.A., 1931; graduate study, Harvard University, 1931-32; University of Chicago, M.A., 1941, Ph.D., 1941. *Home:* 522 Fair Oaks, Oak Park, Ill. 60302.

CAREER: Chicago Teachers College (now Chicago State University), Chicago, Ill., 1940-65, began as member of English department faculty, became professor of English. Fulbright Professor of American Literature, University of Teheran, 1961-62. *Military service:* U.S. Naval Reserve, 1942-47; became lieutenant. *Awards, honors:* Ford fellowship, 1955-56; Houghton Mifflin literary fellowship, and Chicago Friends of Literature prize, 1965, both for *Full Fathom Five*.

WRITINGS: Full Fathom Five (novel; Book-of-the-Month Club selection), Houghton, 1965; (contributor) *50 Best American Short Stories, 1915-1965*, Houghton, 1965; (editor) James Shirley, *The Traitor*, University of Nebraska

Press, 1965; *Poems: An Handful with Quietness*, Houghton, 1966. Contributor to *Best American Short Stories 1963* and *1964*. Contributor to *Kenyon Review*, *New Republic*, *Harper's Bazaar*, *American Scholar*, *Colorado Quarterly*, *Northwestern Tri-Quarterly*, *Chicago Review*, *Beloit Poetry Journal*, *Western Humanities Review*, and other publications.

WORK IN PROGRESS: The Dooms of Love, a novel; a critical work on Edgar Allan Poe.

BIOGRAPHICAL/CRITICAL SOURCES: New York Times, October 23, 1965; *Times Literary Supplement*, April 22, 1965.

(Died October 21, 1965)

*   *   *

CARTER, Victor A(lbert)   1902-

PERSONAL: Born November 18, 1902; son of Francis (a farmer) and Bessie Louisa (Tucker) Carter; married Lily Sarah Emma Bragg, December 26, 1923; children: Denis Oliver. *Education:* Attended St. Luke's Training College, Exeter, England. *Politics:* Conservative. *Religion:* Anglican. *Home:* Sunnyside, 135 Rush Hill, Bath, Somerset, England.

CAREER: Wincanton County Boys' School, Wincanton, Somerset, England, assistant master, 1923-31; Henstridge Church of England School, Henstridge, Somerset, England, headmaster, 1931-41; Peasedown County Junior School, Peasedown, Somerset, England, headmaster, 1941-63. *Member:* National Union of Teachers.

WRITINGS: I Find Out: Groundwork in English Comprehension, Cassell, Books 1, 2, 1961, Books 3, 4, 1962; *I Work Out: Daily Groundwork in Mental Arithmetic*, Books 1-4, Cassell, 1961.

*   *   *

CARTER, William Ambrose   1899-

PERSONAL: Born January 15, 1899, in Washington, D.C.; son of George Peabody and Bertha Florence (Rich) Carter; married Laura Bumstead Tuckerman, June 30, 1925; children: William Douglas, Katharine Adelaide (Mrs. Douglas Rosander Stevenson). *Education:* Dartmouth College, A.B., 1920; University of Missouri, M.A., 1928; Princeton University, graduate student, 1931-32. *Politics:* Independent. *Religion:* Protestant. *Home:* 2549 East Beryl Ave., Phoenix, Ariz. 85028.

CAREER: Dartmouth College, Hanover, N.H., instructor in economics, 1928-31, 1933-34; National Recovery Administration, Washington, D.C., economic analyst, 1934-35; Dartmouth College, assistant professor, 1936-39, professor of economics, 1939-65, chairman of department, 1945-49, chairman of Social Science Division, 1952-55; Kalamazoo College, Kalamazoo, Mich., Stephen B. Monroe Professor of Money and Banking, 1968-70; Dartmouth College, college ombudsman, 1971-72. Director, member of faculty, Vermont-New Hampshire School of Banking, 1960-70. Economic consultant, U.S. Geological Survey, Department of Interior, 1969-71. Past president, Consumer Cooperative Society, Hanover, N.H., and Community Housing Association of Hanover. Member, Hanover Planning Board, 1965-72. *Military service:* U.S. Army, 1918; became second lieutenant.

WRITINGS: (With H. L. Purdy and M. L. Lindahl) *Corporate Concentration and Public Policy*, Prentice-Hall,

1942, 3rd edition (with Lindahl), 1959. Contributor to *Christian Science Monitor* and *Antitrust Bulletin*; also contributor of numerous reviews to periodicals. Guest editor, *Antitrust Bulletin*, Winter-Spring, 1966.

SIDELIGHTS: Carter has some knowledge of Spanish and German. *Avocational interests:* Travel, gardening, sketching.

* * *

CARVER, Saxon Rowe 1905-

PERSONAL: Born November 12, 1905, in Louisville, Ky.; daughter of George Thomas and Mamie Lee (Rogers) Rowe; married George Alexander Carver (a real-estate broker), September 7, 1928; children: George Alexander, Jr. *Education:* Averett College, student, 1923-25; University of Richmond, B.A., 1927; also studied at College of Chinese Studies, Peking, China, 1935-36. *Religion:* Baptist. *Home:* 3523 Winchester Rd., Louisville, Ky. 40207.

CAREER: University of Shanghai, Shanghai, China, teacher of English, 1931-40; Miss Fine's School, Princeton, N.J., librarian, 1950-53; Hong Kong Baptist College, Hong Kong, teacher of English, 1960. *Member:* American Association of University Women, Louisville Woman's Club.

WRITINGS: Yeoman of Kent, Broadman, 1957; *Ropes to Burma*, Broadman, 1961; *The Shoe-Leather Globe*, Broadman, 1965. Contributor to religious journals and other periodicals.

WORK IN PROGRESS: Short stories.

* * *

CARY, Harold Whiting 1903-

PERSONAL: Born October 4, 1903, in Colrain, Mass.; son of Herbert Francis (a manufacturer) and Elizabeth (Blagbrough) Cary; married Thelma Dorothy Freeman, September 3, 1927; children; Harold David, Helen Elizabeth (Mrs. Robert B. Whitney), Louise Thelma. *Education:* Williams College, A.B., 1925; Harvard University, A.M., 1926; Yale University, Ph.D., 1938. *Home:* 29 Summer, North Amherst, Mass. 01059. *Office:* Herter Hall, University of Massachusetts, Amherst, Mass. 01002.

CAREER: Cushing Academy, Ashburnham, Mass., instructor in history, 1926-29; Yale University, New Haven, Conn., instructor in history, 1930-32; University of Massachusetts, Amherst, instructor, 1933-36, assistant professor, 1936-47, professor of history, 1947—, chairman of department of history and government, 1953-57. Town of Amherst, member of school committee. *Member:* American Historical Association, Phi Kappa Phi.

WRITINGS: University of Massachusetts: A History of One Hundred Years, University of Massachusetts Press, 1963; (contributor) Howard Henry Quint and others, editors, *Main Problems in American History*, Dorsey, 1964.

WORK IN PROGRESS: Research on Anglo-American relations, 1920-1930.

AVOCATIONAL INTERESTS: Travel and hiking.

* * *

CASELEYR, Cam(ille Auguste Marie) 1909-
(Jack Danvers)

PERSONAL: Born September 22, 1909, in Antwerp, Belgium; became an Australian citizen; son of Gustave Pierre and Alice (de Staepeleere) Caseleyr; married Doreen

Felice Nicholson (a bursar), September 12, 1941; children: Alice, Veronique. *Education:* Institut Superieur de Commerce d'Anvers, University of Antwerp, Licencie en Sciences Commerciales, 1930. *Politics:* "Not sufficiently interested to belong to any political party." *Home and office:* All Souls' School, Charters Towers, Queensland, Australia. *Agent:* A. P. Watt & Son, 10 Norfolk St., Strand, London W.C.2, England.

CAREER: British Broadcasting Corp., London, England, foreign language specialist, 1941-43; Government of Belgian Congo (now Zaire), Africa, principal territorial agent, 1943-49; Victorian State Rivers Commission, Victoria, Australia, accounting officer, 1951-53; secondary school teacher in South Australia, 1954-58; All Souls' School, Charters Towers, Queensland, Australia, senior English and French master, 1959—. *Military service:* Belgian Army, Field Artillery, 1931-33.

WRITINGS—Under pseudonym Jack Danvers: *The Living Come First*, Heinemann, 1961; *The End of It All*, Heinemann, 1962.

WORK IN PROGRESS: Three books: *The Wolves Among Us, The Failures*, and a historical novel, *The Freemen*.

SIDELIGHTS: Caseleyr's ambition is to quit teaching and live by writing in some isolated spot on the Queensland coast. He is fluent in English, French, Dutch, and Flemish, and knows some Spanish and German. *Avocational interests:* Reading, classical music, fishing, sailing.

* * *

CASON, Mabel Earp 1892-19(?)
(Emily Mary Bell)

PERSONAL: Born March 7, 1892, in Corpus Christi, Tex.; daughter of William Harrison and Elizabeth (Fowler) Earp; married Ernest A. Cason, December 25, 1913; children: V. Rae (Mrs. C. W. Lindsay), Leonard E., Elizabeth Jeanne (Mrs. Bruce Laing), Walter D. *Education:* Attended San Fernando Academy. *Religion:* Seventh-Day Adventist. *Home:* Springmeadow Ranch, Whitmore, Calif. 96096.

CAREER: School teacher, Mohawk, Ariz., 1912-14; advertising artist, Phoenix, Ariz., 1929-34; high school art teacher, Los Angeles, Calif., 1934-44. Author and illustrator.

WRITINGS: Mary Had Ten Little Lambs, Southern Publishing, 1938; (with E. Oren Arnold) *Desert Plants and Animals*, Arizona Printers, 1940; (under pseudonym Emily Mary Bell) *Wolf at Our Door*, Pacific Press, 1948; (self-illustrated) *Ruggy the Mountain Buck*, Pacific Press, 1949; *Song of the Trail*, Pacific Press, 1953; *Desert Enchantment*, Review & Herald, 1963; *Spotted Boy and the Comanches*, Pacific Press, 1963.

Wrote "Key to the Treasure House," for "Voice of Prophecy" radio program, and five scripts for "Faith for Today" television program. Collaborated with E. O. Arnold on an illustrated weekly feature, "Some Wild Westerners You Should Know," for Los Angeles Times Syndicate, 1928-34. Contributor of juvenile and desert wildlife stories, many self-illustrated, to *Children's Friend, Youth's Instructor, Junior Guide*, and other periodicals.

WORK IN PROGRESS: South to the Californias, a book for youth; *By Sun and Star*, a biography of Edward J. Urquhart, missionary in the Orient and World War II prisoner in the Philippines; an illustrated feature series on wildlife; a biography of a missionary raised in the Congo; material on life of a Russian woman, a captive worker in Germany during World War II.

SIDELIGHTS: Competent in Spanish.

(Deceased)

* * *

CASS, Carl Bartholomew 1901-

PERSONAL: Born December 9, 1901, in Dakota, Minn.; son of Harry Alfred (a builder) and Grace (Brown) Cass; married Dorothy Lyne, December, 1942. *Education:* University of Minnesota, B.A., 1927; University of Wisconsin, Ph.M., 1930, Ph.D., 1946. *Home address:* Route 4, Box 100 A, Norman, Okla. 73069. *Office:* University of Oklahoma, Norman, Okla. 73069.

CAREER: Travis-Newton and United Chautauqua, Des Moines, Iowa, acting manager of play company, 1921-27; Mercersburg Academy, Mercersburg, Pa., teacher of dramatics and forensics, 1927-28; University of Pittsburgh, Pittsburgh, Pa., assistant professor of speech and drama, 1930-38; University of Wisconsin, Madison, associate theatre director, 1938-41; U.S. Air Force Technical Command, Truax Field, Wis., instructor, 1942-43; Purdue University, West Lafayette, Ind., assistant professor of speech and drama, 1943-45; University of Oklahoma, Norman, professor of drama, 1945—. *Member:* Speech Communication Association of America, American Educational Theatre Association, National Collegiate Players, Oklahoma Speech Association (executive vice-president, then president, 1956-59), Theta Alpha Phi.

WRITINGS: A Manner of Speaking, Putnam, 1961. Contributor to professional journals.

WORK IN PROGRESS: A secondary school text in interpretative speech arts.

* * *

CASSOLA, Albert M(aria) 1915-

PERSONAL: Born May 2, 1915, in Valletta, Malta; son of Hector and Mary (Dimech) Cassola; married Ethel Jane Marks, April 28, 1947; children: Arnold. *Education:* University of Milan, diploma (cum laude), 1953; Institute of Linguists, London, England, F.I.L. (with distinction), 1953; further study in Italy at universities in Perugia, 1953, Milan, 1957, Rome, 1959. *Religion:* Roman Catholic. *Home:* 3, Mona Lisa Mansions, Giuseppe Cali St., Ta'xbiex, Malta. *Office:* Lyceum, Hamrun, Malta.

CAREER: Civil servant, Malta, 1936-47; Lyceum, Hamrun, Malta, master of Italian and Maltese, 1947—. Lecturer at Italian academies and universities. Radio and television broadcaster in Malta, England, Italy. Songwriter. *Member:* International Academy of Pontzen (Naples; senator), Accademia de "i 500" (Rome), Gli Amici Dei Sacri Lari (Bergamo), Academy of Maltese Authors, Union of Maltese Authors and Composers (honorary president), Pioneer of Catholic Action in Malta, Performing Right Society (London), Societa Dante Alighieri (Malta), Civil Service Sports Club (Malta). *Awards, honors:* Bronze Medal of Ministero Degli Affari Esteri; knight, Sovereign Order of St. John of Jerusalem.

WRITINGS: Ghadu Kemm Jibda!, Lux Press, 1947; *Gabra ta' Gawhar* (stories and essays), Muscat, 1948; *Vagiti* (poems), M. Gastaldi, 1950; *Gogo Rummiena,* Aquilina, 1954; *Maltese in Easy Stages,* 4th edition, Progress Press (Malta), 1956; *Kif Tikteb Ghall-Palk Ghar-Radjo,* Aquilina, 1957; *Bluzi Bojod,* Lux Press, 1964; *Nina,* Lux Press, 1964.

One-act plays: *Il-Berritta Bajda ta Bil-Lejl,* Aquilina, 1941; *Zwieg il-Mewt,* Guzepp, 1945; *Pape Satan Aleppe,* Guzepp, 1949; *Kapitlu l-Ahhar,* Guzepp, 1950; *Il Penitente,* Muscat, 1953; *Il Dono di Nozze,* Empire Press, 1954; *Suspetti,* Progress Press (Malta), 1962.

Other plays: "The Rompish Rogue," 1949; "IXX(H)IH," 1950; "Zwigijiet Imhallta," 1950; "Doppio Annuncio," 1952; "Qrara," 1957; "Milied ta' Gwerra" (radio play), 1957; "Il-Vizzju Tal-Vjaggi," 1957; "Ponzju Pilatu" (radio play), 1957; "Il-Ghe ruq" (radio play), 1960; "Il-Gejjieni Sabih ta' Ibni," 1960; "Gwida Ckejkna ta' Kotba X'-Taqra," 1960; "Mara tad-Dar" (television play), 1964; Malintero Matrimonio (television play), 1964; Imhabba ta' Mrar (television play), 1964.

Author of novels serialized in Maltese periodicals. Contributor to *Writer, Amateur Stage, Linguist's Review, Apollo, L'Osservatore Romano, Narciso, Visto, L'Aspirante* (Italy), *Quadrante* (Portugal), other English and Italian periodicals, and to most publications of Malta and Gozo, 1929—.

WORK IN PROGRESS: Plays and essays.

SIDELIGHTS: Cassola's writings have been translated into English, Italian, French, Spanish, Hungarian, German, Portuguese. *Avocational interests:* Sports.

BIOGRAPHICAL/CRITICAL SOURCES: Italian Modern Art and Literature, 1963.

* * *

CATO, Nancy (Fotheringham) 1917-

PERSONAL: Born March 11, 1917, in Adelaide, South Australia; daughter of Raymond Herbert and Mabel Edmunds (Pearce) Cato; married Eldred de Bracton Norman, May, 1941 (died, 1971); children: Bronley Margarey, Michael Ashley, William Eldred. *Education:* Educated in Australia at Presbyterian Girls' College, 1923-34, Adelaide University, 1938-39; studied at South Australian School of Art, 1954-55. *Residence:* Noosa Heads, Queensland, Australia. *Agent:* David Higham Associates Ltd., 5-8, Lower John St., Golden Square, London, WIR 4HA, England.

CAREER: News, Adelaide, South Australia, journalist, 1935-40, art critic, 1947-48; free-lance writer. *Member:* Fellowship of Australian Writers (vice-president for South Australia, 1960-61; executive, 1956-64), Australian Society of Authors (council member, 1963-64), Contemporary Art Society (South Australia). *Awards, honors:* Northern Territory Poetry Prize; Poetry Society Award, 1963; Commonwealth Literature Fund fellowship, 1968.

WRITINGS: (Editor) *Jindyworobak Anthology,* Jindyworobak, 1950; *The Darkened Window* (verse), Edwards & Shaw, 1950; *The Dancing Bough* (verse), Angus Heinemann, 1958; *Time Flow Softly: A Novel of the River Murray,* Heinemann, 1960; *Green Grows the Vine* (novel), Heinemann, 1960; *But Still the Stream: A Novel of the Murray River,* Heinemann, 1962; *The Sea Ants, and Other Stories,* Heinemann, 1964; *North-West by South,* Heinemann, 1965. Contributor to Australian newspapers and journals. Assistant editor of *Poetry Australia,* 1947-48; advisory editor of *Overland,* 1960-62, *Southern Festival,* 1960.

WORK IN PROGRESS: Children's fiction, *Nin and Scribblies,* for Jacaranda Press.

SIDELIGHTS: Nancy Cato has explored the Australian outback by car and jeep, traveled twelve hundred miles by paddle steamer and launch on the Murray River, and gone up the Darling River to Queensland to collect material for the three published historical novels that form her river trilogy. On her last European trip in 1961 she and her husband drove through Europe, U.S.S.R., and the Middle East to India and Malaya. She is competent in Italian and French and knows some Spanish. *Avocational interests:* Painting, modern art, translating verse.

BIOGRAPHICAL/CRITICAL SOURCES: Morris Miller and F. T. Macartney, *Outline History of Australian Literature,* Angus & Robertson, 1954; John Hetherington, *Forty-Two Faces,* F. W. Cheshire, 1962.

*   *   *

CAYTON, Horace R.   1903-1970

PERSONAL: Born April 12, 1903, in Seattle, Wash.; son of Horace R. (a newspaperman) and Susie (Revels) Cayton; married Ruby Jordan. *Education:* University of Washington, Seattle, A.B., 1931; graduate study at University of Chicago, 1931-34, New York University, 1956. *Politics:* Independent. *Agent:* Henry Volkening, Russell & Volkening, Inc., 516 Fifth Ave., New York, N.Y. 10017.

CAREER: Deputy sheriff, Seattle, Wash., 1929-31; U.S. Department of the Interior, special assistant, 1934-35; Fisk University, Nashville, Tenn., instructor in economics, 1935-36; University of Chicago, Chicago, Ill., research assistant and instructor in department of anthropology, 1936-37; Parkway Community House, Chicago, Ill., director, 1939-49; American Jewish Committee, New York, N.Y., study of the Jewish family 1950-51; *Pittsburgh Courier,* Pittsburgh, Pa., correspondent to United Nations, 1952-54; National Council of Churches, New York, N.Y., research associate, 1954-58; City College (now City College of the City University of New York), New York, N.Y., lecturer in sociology, 1957-58; Commissioner of Welfare, New York, N.Y., special assistant, 1958-59; Langley Porter Clinic, San Francisco, Calif., research assistant for studies in geriatric mental illness, 1959-60; Institute for the Study of Crime and Delinquency, Berkeley, Calif., international survey of correction, 1960-61; University of California, Berkeley, program coordinator of university extension, 1963-64, project director in Institute of Business and Economic Research, 1965-70; lecturer and writer. Member of board of directors, Council of Social Agencies, 1939-49; secretary, and member of board of directors, Parkway Community House, 1944-48. *Member:* Society of Social Research, American Sociological Association, Institute of Psychoanalysis, Society of Midland Authors, Alpha Kappa Delta, Zeta Phi. *Awards, honors:* Julius Rosenwald Fund fellowship, 1937-39; Anisfeld-Wolf Award (shared with St. Clair Drake) for best scholarly book in field of race relations, 1945, for *Black Metropolis,* also named outstanding race relations book, 1945, by New York Public Library.

WRITINGS: (With George S. Mitchell) *Black Workers and the New Unions,* University of North Carolina Press, 1935; (with St. Clair Drake) *Black Metropolis* (with an introductory chapter by Richard Wright), Harcourt, 1945; (with S. M. Nishi) *Social Work and the Church,* National Council of Churches, 1956; *Long Old Road* (autobiography), Simon & Schuster, 1965.

Contributor to various books. Also contributor of regular column to *Pittsburgh Courier* for twenty years, and articles and reviews to newspapers and magazines, including *New*

Republic, Nation, Holiday, American Journal of Sociology, New York Times, Chicago Tribune, Chicago Sun-Times.

WORK IN PROGRESS: A study of the life of Richard Wright.

SIDELIGHTS: Cayton, the son of a former Mississippi slave and grandson of the United States' first Negro senator, has been described as a sociologist who lived in two worlds—the world of things as they are, and the world of things as they should be—with a type of humor to accommodate each of the worlds. At the age of sixteen, Cayton went to sea as a messman on a steamer bound for Alaska, and spent the next four years traveling in Alaska, California, Wyoming, Hawaii, and Mexico.

When *Black Metropolis* appeared in 1945, it was considered a landmark in American social history. Bucklin Moore commented in the *Nation,* "It offers no short cuts or magic solutions, but it contains the clearest picture of what it means to be a Negro in America that I have ever encountered. It is realistic and far-reaching, probing where other books have glossed over, interpreting where others have merely stated generalities." "From cover to cover," observed Thomas Sancton in *New Republic,* "this is a book of intellectual discipline and talent. It towers high above the slight, journalistic volumes that have been written in recent years. . . ."

Reviewing *Long Old Road* in *Book Week,* Nat Hentoff noted, "The prose is lean and swift; the passages of self-analysis are relentlessly candid without being groaningly masochistic. And the story Cayton tells, while rooted in his consciousness of race, is fundamentally a universal tale of a man's search for his identity and a place in the world that he has freely chosen."

AVOCATIONAL INTERESTS: Collecting books, music, and paintings; special reading interest in Asiatic and African periodical literature dealing with the rise of nationalist movements.

BIOGRAPHICAL/CRITICAL SOURCES: Arna Bontemps, *We Have Tomorrow,* Houghton, 1945; Bontemps and Jack Conroy, *They Seek a City,* Doubleday, 1945; *Monterey Peninsula Herald,* February 1, 1964.†

(Died January 22, 1970)

*   *   *

CHADWICK, Nora Kershaw   1891-1972

PERSONAL: Born January 28, 1891, in England; daughter of James (a cotton manufacturer) and Emma Clara (Booth) Kershaw; married Hector Munro Chadwick (a professor), May, 1922 (died, 1947). *Education:* Newnham College, Cambridge, M.A., 1914. *Home:* 7 Causewayside, Cambridge, England.

CAREER: University of St. Andrews, St. Andrews, Scotland, lecturer in English language and assistant lecturer in English literature, 1914-19; Cambridge University, Cambridge, England, research fellow at Newnham College, 1941-44, university lecturer in early history and culture of British Isles, 1950-58, director of studies in Anglo-Saxon and Celtic subjects at Newnham College, 1950-59, at Girton College, 1951-62. Writer and researcher, 1919-72. Honorary lecturer at universities in Scotland, Wales, Ireland, and England. *Member:* British Academy (fellow), Society of Antiquities (fellow). *Awards, honors:* D.Litt. from University of Wales, 1958, National University of Ireland, 1958; Litt.D., University of St. Andrews, 1958;

named honorary life fellow of Newnham College, Cambridge University, 1958; Commander, Order of the British Empire, 1961.

WRITINGS: (Translator from the Norse) Stories and Ballads of the Far Past, Cambridge University Press, 1921; (editor and translator) Anglo-Saxon and Norse Poems, Cambridge University Press, 1922; Early Irish Reader, Cambridge University Press, 1927; (translator) Russian Heroic Poetry, Cambridge University Press, 1932; (with husband, Hector M. Chadwick) The Growth of Literature, three volumes, Cambridge University Press, 1932-40; Poetry and Prophecy, Cambridge University Press, 1942; The Beginnings of Russian History, Cambridge University Press, 1946, reprinted, 1966; (editor) Hector M. Chadwick, Early Scotland, Cambridge University Press, 1949.

(Contributor) The Heritage of Early Britain, G. Bell, 1952; (editor and contributor with Hector M. Chadwick and others) Studies in Early British History, Cambridge University Press, 1954; Poetry and Letters in Early Christian Gaul, Bowes, 1955; (editor, contributor, and reviser) Hector M. Chadwick, Study of Anglo-Saxon, 2nd edition, Heffer, 1955; (editor and contributor, with others) Studies in the Early British Church, Cambridge University Press, 1958; (contributor) edited by Myles Dillon, Irish Sagas, H.M.S.O., for Radio Eireann, 1959; (contributor) edited by A. J. Roderick, Wales Through the Ages, Christopher Davies, 1959; The Age of the Saints in the Early Celtic Church, Oxford University Press, 1961; (editor and contributor, with others) Celt and Saxon, Cambridge University Press, 1963; Celtic Britain, Thames & Hudson, 1963, Praeger, 1964; The Druids, University of Wales Press, 1966; (with Dillon) The Celtic Realms, New American Library, 1967; Early Brittany, University of Wales Press, 1969; (with Victor Zhirmunsky) Oral Epics of Central Asia, Cambridge University Press, 1969; The Celts, Penguin, 1970.

WORK IN PROGRESS: Research in early British history.

(Died April 24, 1972)

*   *   *

CHAFFEE, Allen

PERSONAL: Born Antoinette Gurney, in Farragut, Iowa; changed name legally, 1919; daughter of George E. and Mary Elizabeth (Chaffee) Gurney. Education: Wellesley College, A.B., 1907; Columbia University, extension courses. Politics: Independent. Religion: Presbyterian. Home: 4135 Park Blvd., Oakland, Calif. 94602.

CAREER: Reporter or department editor on Boston Post and other newspapers in Boston, Mass., prior to 1919; author of juvenile books, 1919—. Grolier Society, New York, N.Y., editorial worker and writer, 1928-30; U.S. Office of Censorship, New York, N.Y., staff member, 1942-45; University of California Extension, teacher of creative writing of juvenile books, 1951-58. Member: Everett Club (literary), Sierra Club.

WRITINGS: The Adventures of Twinkly Eyes, the Little Black Bear, Milton Bradley, 1919; Twinkly Eyes at Valley Farm, Milton Bradley, 1919; Twinkly Eyes and the Lone Lake Folk, Milton Bradley, 1920; Sitka, the Snow Baby, Milton Bradley, 1920; Twinkly Eyes, Milton Bradley, 1921; Trail and Tree Top, Milton Bradley, 1921; Lost! The Adventures of Two Boys in the Big Woods, Milton Bradley, 1921; Unexplored, Milton Bradley, 1922; Mammy Cottontail and Her Bunnies, Milton Bradley, 1923; Fuzzy Wuzz,

Milton Bradley, 1923; The Travels of Honk-a-Tonk, Milton Bradley, 1924; Brownie, the Engineer of Beaver Brook, Milton Bradley, 1925; Tony and the Big Top, Century, 1925; Sully Joins the Circus, Century, 1926; Adventures on the High Trail, Milton Bradley, 1928; Linda's El Dorado, Century, 1929; The Winning Hazard, Century, 1929; The Adventures of Fleet Foot and Her Fawns, Milton Bradley, 1929.

Wild Folk (containing The Adventures of Fleet Foot and Her Fawns and The Adventures of Honk-a-Tonk), Milton Bradley, 1930; The Forest Giant (Children's Book Club of America selection), Milton Bradley, 1930; Penn, the Penguin (Junior Book Club selection), Cape & Smith, 1931; The Zoo Book Toy, Milton Bradley, 1931; Wandy, the Wild Pony, Random House, 1932; Wandy Wins!, Random House, 1933; Heroes of the Shoals, Holt, 1935; The Wilderness Trail, Thomas Nelson, 1936; How to File Business Papers and Records, McGraw, 1937; Western Wild Life, Caxton, 1945.

Adaptations for picture books: Pinocchio, Random House, 1945; The Wizard of Oz, Random House, 1950; Bambi's Children, Random House, 1951; The Story of Hiawatha, Random House, 1951.

Contributor: Lands and Peoples, seven volumes, Grolier Society, 1930; The Book of Texas, Grolier Society, c.1930; This is Our Land, Ginn, 1946; Wide Open Windows (school reader), Copp, 1947; Long Ago and Far Away, Pacific Press, 1958; Creative English, Copp, 1962. Also contributor to More Times and Places, Scott, Foresman.

Contributor of monthly nature study to American Childhood for twenty-five years; also contributor of articles and stories to Child Life, Children's Activities, other magazines.

WORK IN PROGRESS: Adult short stories dealing with E.S.P.

SIDELIGHTS: Most of Allen Chaffee's children's books were first serialized and parts of many have been reprinted in school readers. Wandy, the Wild Pony has been reproduced in Braille in England. Avocational interests: Conservation of wild life.

*   *   *

CHAMBERLAIN, Elinor 1901-

PERSONAL: Born June 21, 1901, in Muskegon, Mich.; daughter of Charles Lovell (president of a manufacturing firm) and Marie (Lambert) Chamberlain; married William Rodney Kuhns, April 14, 1927 (divorced); children: William C., Mary K. (Mrs. Paul S. Fancher, Jr.). Education: University of Michigan, B.A., 1922, M.A., 1951; Columbia University, M.S. in L.S., 1954. Politics: Liberal. Religion: Christian. Home: 308 Northeast 17th Ave., Fort Lauderdale, Fla. 33301. Agent: Don Congdon, Harold Matson Co., Inc., 22 East 40 St., New York, N.Y. 10016.

CAREER: University of the Philippines, Manila, instructor in English, 1923-26; Larchmont Public Library, Larchmont, N.Y., assistant librarian, 1954-56; now writer, editor, and indexer. Former member of school and library boards, Haworth, N.J. Member: Mystery Writers of America, Friends of the Library of Fort Lauderdale (recording secretary, 1963-65). Awards, honors: Red Badge Mystery Prize, Dodd, Mead & Co., 1945, for Appointment in Manila; Hopwood Award (major), 1951, for manuscript, "The Bamboo Plow," later published as The Far Command.

WRITINGS: Appointment in Manila, Dodd, 1945; Manila

Hemp, Dodd, 1947; *Snare for Witches*, Dodd, 1948; *The Far Command*, Ballantine, 1953; *Mystery of the Moving Island*, Lippincott, 1965; *Mystery of the Jungle Airstrip*, Lippincott, 1967.

SIDELIGHTS: Elinor Chamberlain has lived in Peking, China, as well as in the Philippines, and has traveled elsewhere in the Far East. Once competent, now "rusty," in Latin, French, German, and Spanish. *Avocational interests:* Ballroom dancing.

* * *

CHAMBERS, Frank P(entland) 1900-

PERSONAL: Born November 3, 1900, in Bombay, India; married Frances McAdoo, December 16, 1948; children: Marion. *Education:* Dulwich College, student, 1914-19; Clare College, Cambridge, M.A., 1923; graduate study at Harvard University, 1926-27, University of Pennsylvania, 1927-28.

CAREER: McGill University, Montreal, Quebec, assistant professor of architecture, 1930-40; University of London, London, England, senior lecturer in international relations, 1948—. *Member:* Royal Institute of British Architects (associate). *Awards, honors:* Commonwealth Fund fellowships, 1926-28.

WRITINGS: Cycles of Taste: An Unacknowledged Problem in Ancient Art and Criticism, Harvard University Press, 1928, Russell, 1967; *The History of Taste: An Account of the Revolutions of Art Criticism and Theory in Europe,* Columbia University Press, 1932, Greenwood, 1971; *The War Behind the War,* Harcourt, 1939; *Perception, Understanding and Society: A Philosophical Essay on the Arts and Sciences and on the Humane Studies,* Sidgwick & Jackson, 1961, A. C. Book Service, 1962; (with Christina Phelps Grant and Charles C. Bayley) *This Age of Conflict: A Contemporary World History, 1914 to 1943,* Harcourt, 1943, revised edition published as *This Age of Conflict: A Contemporary World History, 1914 to the Present,* 1950, 3rd edition published as *This Age of Conflict: The Western World, 1914 to the Present,* 1962. Contributor of articles and reviews to periodicals.

* * *

CHAMBERS, William Trout 1896-

PERSONAL: Born November 14, 1896, in Oaktown, Ind.; son of Sylvester Marion (a carpenter) and Mary Eloise (Trout) Chambers; married Mabel Louise Terry; children: Dorothy (Mrs. Robert William Kastenmeier), Eloise (Mrs. David Duane Adams), Terry, Marilyn. *Education:* Indiana State Normal School (now Indiana State University), B.A., 1921; University of Chicago, M.S., 1924, Ph.D., 1926. *Politics:* Independent. *Religion:* Methodist. *Home:* 320 Zeno St., Nacogdoches, Tex.

CAREER: University of Tennessee, Knoxville, instructor in geography, 1922-24; Stephen F. Austin State College (now Stephen F. Austin State University), Nacogdoches, Tex., 1926-67, began as associate professor, professor of geography, 1937-67, head of department, 1944-67. *Military service:* U.S. Army, Signal Corps, World War I. *Member:* National Council for Geographic Education, National Geographic Society, Southwestern Social Science Association, Texas Academy of Science.

WRITINGS: The Geography of Texas, Steck, 1946; *Texas, Its Land and People,* Steck, 1952; *Texans and Their Land,* Steck, 1963. Author of Texas history and ge-

ography filmstrips: "Texas, The Land and People," Sets I and II, and "Texans and Their Land," Sets I, II, and III, Texas History Filmstrips.

* * *

CHANDLER, Allison 1906-

PERSONAL: Born March 1, 1906, in Newton, Kan.; son of Earl Percy and Lucile (Shamel) Chandler; married Mildred Rose Marlow, October 17, 1945. *Education:* Bethany College, Lindsborg, Kan., A.B., 1934. *Religion:* Methodist. *Home:* 228 East Jewell, Salina, Kan. 67401.

CAREER: Employed as reporter, advertising salesman or manager, news editor, music editor, sports editor, of newspapers in Kansas, Oklahoma, Texas, and California, 1929-71; *Salina Daily Journal,* Salina, Kan., display advertising salesman, 1951-71. *Military service:* U.S. Army, World War II; served in India. *Member:* Kiwanis.

WRITINGS: Trolley through the Countryside, Sage Books, 1963. Contributor to *Railroad, Round Up, Kansas Historical Quarterly.* Transit editor, *Railroad* magazine.

WORK IN PROGRESS: Reminiscences of boyhood in Newton, Kan.; history of Como, Colo.; *Trolleys of the Great Plains, the Ozarks and the Rockies,* with Stephen D. Maguire, for Swallow Press.

* * *

CHANG, Jen-chi 1903-

PERSONAL: Born August 26, 1903, in Taichow, Kiangsu, China; son of Chih-tsai and Shih (Hu) Chang. *Education:* University of Shanghai, B.A., 1930; Columbia Theological Seminary, Decatur, Ga., M.A., B.E., 1948; Mississippi Southern College (now University of Southern Mississippi), M.A., 1949; University of Dubuque, B.Th., 1950, M.Th., 1951; University of North Dakota, Ed.D., 1951. *Address:* P.O. Box 660, St. Augustine, Fla. *Office:* Division of Education, Florida Normal and Industrial Memorial College, St. Augustine, Fla. 32084.

CAREER: High school teacher, then secretary of Nanatao Christian Institute, Shanghai, China, 1930-33; Kiangsi Rural Welfare Service, Kiangsi, China, secretary, 1935-45; United Nations Relief and Rehabilitation Administration fellowship in service, China, 1946-47; Presbyterian Indian Mission, Pine Ridge, S.D., director of Christian education, 1951-52; Highland Institution, Guerrant, Ky., instructor in social studies and Bible, 1952-53; Claflin College, Orangeburg, S.C., professor of education and chairman of division of education, 1953-59; Tuskegee Institute, Tuskegee, Ala., associate professor of education, 1959-61; Florida Normal and Industrial Memorial College, St. Augustine, professor of education and chairman of division of education, 1961—.

MEMBER: National Education Association, Association for Higher Education, National Society for the Study of Education, American Academy of Political and Social Science, American Sociological Association, National Association of Biblical Instructors, American Association of University Professors, Rural Sociological Society, Southern Sociological Society, Young Men's Christian Association, Phi Delta Kappa.

WRITINGS: Pre-Communist China's Rural School and Community, Christopher, 1960. Contributor of articles to sociological, educational, and religious periodicals, and to newspapers in China and United States.

WORK IN PROGRESS: A study of education in Taiwan.

AVOCATIONAL INTERESTS: Stamp collecting, photography, travel.

BIOGRAPHICAL/CRITICAL SOURCES: St. Augustine Record (St. Augustine, Fla.), November 15, 1961.

* * *

CHAPLIN, Sid(ney) 1916-

PERSONAL: Born September 20, 1916, in Shildon, Durham, England; son of Isaiah (a miner) and Elsie (Charlton) Chaplin; married Irene Rutherford, January 1, 1941; children: Gillian (Mrs. David Parry), Christopher Rutherford, John Michael. *Education:* Attended Workers' Educational Association, University of Durham, extramural, 1932-46; attended Fircroft College for Working Men, Birmingham, 1939. *Home:* 11, Kimberley Gardens, Newcastle upon Tyne NE2 IHJ, Northumberland, England. *Agent:* David Higham Associates, 5-8 Lower John St., London W1R 4HA, England. *Office:* Public Relations Dept., National Coal Board, Hobart House, London S.W.1, England.

CAREER: Mineworker, 1931-50; National Coal Board, writer for *Coal Magazine,* 1950-56, northern division public relations officer, 1956-63, specialist writer, 1964—. Writer for *Coal News,* 1961—, and for *Coal Quarterly.* Branch secretary, Miners Federation of Great Britain, 1943-45; member of North Regional Advisory Council, British Broadcasting Corp. *Member:* Royal Society of Arts (fellow), National Union of Journalists, Author's Society. *Awards, honors:* Atlantic award in literature (Rockefeller Foundation), 1946, for *The Leaping Lad.*

WRITINGS: The Leaping Lad, and Other Stories, Phoenix House, 1946; (with others) *Saturday Saga,* Progress Publishing, 1946; *My Fate Cries Out,* Dent, 1949; *The Thin Seam* (novel), Phoenix House, 1950, edited by Geoffrey Halson, Longmans, Green, 1970; *The Lakes to Tyneside,* Collins, 1951; *The Big Room,* Eyre & Spottiswoode, 1961; *The Day of the Sardine,* Eyre & Spottiswoode, 1961; *The Watchers and the Watched,* Eyre & Spottiswoode, 1962; *Sam in the Morning,* Eyre & Spottiswoode, 1965; (editor with Arthur Wise) *Us Northerners* (anthology), Harrap, 1970; *The Mines of Alabaster* (novel), Eyre & Spottiswoode, 1971. Occasional contributor to *Guardian, Sunday Times,* and other publications.

SIDELIGHTS: Two of Chaplin's books have been adapted for the stage.

* * *

CHAPMAN, Edmund H(aupt) 1906-

PERSONAL: Born August 14, 1906, in West Haven, Conn.; son of Herman H. (a professor) and Alberta (Pinneo) Chapman; married Affa Gray (a teacher), September 15, 1930; children: Frederick Kimball, Gretel. *Education:* Yale University, Ph.B., 1928, M.A., 1930; New York University, Ph.D., 1950. *Home:* 11406 Fowlers Mill Rd., Chardon, Ohio. *Office:* Case Western Reserve University, Cleveland, Ohio.

CAREER: University of Colorado, Boulder, 1930-37, began as instructor, became assistant professor; Goucher College, Baltimore, Md., assistant professor, 1939-42; Western Reserve University (now Case Western Reserve University), Cleveland, Ohio, professor of art history, beginning, 1946. *Military service:* U.S. Naval Reserve, 1942-46; became lieutenant commander. *Member:* Society of Architectural Historians (secretary and member of board of directors, 1948-50), Society of Aesthetics, College Art

Association, American Association of University Professors, Cleveland Art Association (member of board of directors, 1960-62).

WRITINGS: Cleveland: Village to Metropolis, Western Reserve Historical Society Press of Western Reserve University, 1964. Contributor to *Journal of Society of Architectural Historians* and *Art Journal.*

WORK IN PROGRESS: A guide to Cleveland architecture.

SIDELIGHTS: Chapman is competent in French, German, and Spanish.

* * *

CHAPMAN, (Constance) Elizabeth (Mann) 1919-

PERSONAL: Born January 5, 1919, in Barnsley, Yorkshire, England; daughter of Hubert (a timber merchant) and Beatrice (Ward) Mann; married Frank Chapman (a research director), November 22, 1941; children: Stephen Godfrey, Nicholas John, Simon Francis Mann. *Education:* Barnsley Technical College, student, 1935-36. *Religion:* Church of England. *Home:* 88 Grange Gardens, Pinner, Middlesex, England.

CAREER: Secretary, 1936-40; writer for children.

WRITINGS—All published by Brockhampton Press: Marmaduke the Lorry, 1954, *Marmaduke and Joe,* 1955, *Riding With Marmaduke,* 1956, *Merry Marmaduke,* 1957, *Adventures with Marmaduke,* 1958, *Marmaduke and His Friends,* 1959, *Marmaduke and the Elephant,* 1960, *Marmaduke and the Lambs,* 1961, *Marmaduke Goes to France,* 1962, *Marmaduke Goes to Holland,* 1963, *Marmaduke Goes to America,* 1965, *Marmaduke Goes to Italy,* 1970. Writer of story series for *Sunny Stories* (children's magazine), and stories for British Broadcasting Corp. program, "Listen with Mother."

AVOCATIONAL INTERESTS: Walking in Pennine Hills, good food and wine, swimming.

* * *

CHAPMAN, Kenneth F(rancis) 1910-

PERSONAL: Born July 29, 1910, in London, England; son of Percy Maldion and Ada Mary (Preece) Chapman; married Dorothy Mary Kennedy (a schoolteacher), June 11, 1938; children: Jennifer Mary (Mrs. Joseph Richardson), Christopher, Graham. *Education:* Attended school in London, England. *Politics:* Liberal. *Religion:* Congregationalist. *Home:* 2 Stuart Crescent, Shirley, Croydon, Surrey, England. *Office:* Stamp Collecting Ltd., 42 Maiden Lane, London W.C.2, England.

CAREER: British Philatelic Association, London, England, public relations officer, 1948-51; *Stamp Collecting* (weekly), London, England, editor, beginning, 1951. Chairman, Philatelic Congress of Great Britain. *Member:* Royal Philatelic Society, British Philatelic Association (director), Philatelic Traders' Society (director), Masons.

WRITINGS: Stamp Collecting on a Small Income, Hutchinson, 1954; *Good Stamp Collecting,* Routledge & Kegan Paul, 1959; *Commonwealth Stamp Collecting,* Routledge & Kegan Paul, 1961; *Arco Handybook of Stamp Collecting,* Arco Publications, 1962, 2nd edition, 1968; *A Start to Stamp Collecting,* W. Foulsham, 1969. Philatelic correspondent, *Times* (London). Contributor to *Encyclopaedia Britannica Book of the Year* and to philatelic publications.

CHARLESWORTH, John Kaye 1889-

PERSONAL: Born January 3, 1889, in Leeds, England; son of George Charlesworth; married Janet Cumming Gibson, March 14, 1922; children: Marian Louise Kaye (Mrs. Derek Lyddon), Henry Alexander Kaye. *Education:* Attended University of London and University of Munich; University of Breslau, Ph.D., 1914; University of Leeds, D.Sc., 1919. *Home:* Ballycastle, County Antrim, Northern Ireland.

CAREER: Geologist on Scottish Spitzbergen expedition, 1919; University of Manchester, Manchester, England, senior lecturer in geology, 1919-21; Queen's University, Belfast, Ireland, professor of geology, 1921-54, professor emeritus, 1954—, member of Senate, 1938-54. Geological adviser to Ministries of Agriculture, Commerce, and Finance, Northern Ireland, 1924-47. Northern Ireland Scientific Research Grants Advisory Board, member, 1929-32, chairman, 1935-41; National Arbitration Tribunal, member, 1941-59; National Insurance Advisory Committee, member, 1947-60; Senate Certificate Examination Enquiry, chairman, 1948-50. *Member:* Royal Irish Academy, Royal Society of Edinburgh (fellow), Royal Geographical Society (fellow), Geological Society (fellow). *Awards, honors:* Neill Prize of Royal Society of Edinburgh, 1954; Prestwich Medal of Geological Society of London, 1957; D.Sc., Queen's University, Belfast, Northern Ireland, 1957; Commander, Order of British Empire, 1957.

WRITINGS: The Geology of Ireland: An Introduction, Oliver & Boyd, 1953; *The Quaternary Era,* two volumes, Edward Arnold, 1957, St. Martin's, 1966; *Historical Geology of Ireland,* Oliver & Boyd, 1963. Contributor of papers to scientific journals.

WORK IN PROGRESS: A three-volume supplement to *The Quaternary Era.*

*   *   *

CHASE, A(lice) Elizabeth 1906-

PERSONAL: Born April 13, 1906, in Ware, Mass.; daughter of Arthur (a clergyman) and Alice (Rondthaler) Chase. *Education:* Radcliffe College, B.A., 1927; Yale University, M.A., 1943. *Religion:* Episcopal. *Home:* 324 Willow St., New Haven, Conn. 06511.

CAREER: Salem Academy, Winston-Salem, N.C., history teacher, 1927-30; high school teacher, Ware, Mass., 1930-31; Yale University, New Haven, Conn., lecturer at University Art Gallery, 1931-70, assistant professor of history of art, 1947-70. Brooklyn Museum, Brooklyn, N.Y., curator of education, 1946-47. *Member:* Archaeological Institute of America, College Art Association, Phi Beta Kappa.

WRITINGS: Famous Paintings: An Introduction to Art for Young People, Platt, 1950, revised edition, 1962; *Famous Artists of the Past,* Platt, 1964 (published in England with a foreword by Sir John Rothenstein, Macdonald & Co., 1964); *Looking at Art,* Crowell, 1966.

BIOGRAPHICAL/CRITICAL SOURCES: Young Readers Review, December, 1966.

*   *   *

CHASE, Mary Ellen 1887-1973

PERSONAL: Born February 24, 1887, in Blue Hill, Me.; daughter of Edward Everett (a lawyer) and Edith (Lord) Chase. *Education:* University of Maine, B.A., 1909; University of Minnesota, M.A., 1918, Ph.D., 1922; graduate study in Germany, 1913, and postdoctoral study in England, 1923-26. *Religion:* Episcopalian. *Home:* 16 Paradise Rd., Northampton, Mass.

CAREER: University of Minnesota, Minneapolis, instructor, 1918-22, assistant professor of English, 1922-26; Smith College, Northampton, Mass., associate professor, 1926-29, professor of English literature, 1929-55, professor emeritus, 1955-73. *Member:* Phi Beta Kappa. *Awards, honors:* Litt.D. from University of Maine, 1929, Bowdoin College, 1933, Northeastern University, 1948, Smith College, 1949, Wilson College, 1957; L.H.D. from Colby College, 1937; Constance Lindsay Skinner Award, Women's National Book Association, 1956; LL.D. from Goucher College, 1960.

WRITINGS: The Girl from the Big Horn Country (juvenile), Page Co., 1916; *Virginia of Elk Creek Valley* (juvenile), Page Co., 1917; (with Frances K. Del Plaine) *The Art of Narration,* Crofts, 1926; *Mary Christmas* (juvenile), Little, Brown, 1926; *Uplands* (novel), Little, 1927; editor with Margaret E. Macgregor) *The Writing of Informal Essays,* Holt, 1928; *The Golden Ass and Other Essays,* Holt, 1929; *Constructive Theme Writing for College Freshmen,* Henry Holt, 1929, 3rd edition, with Henry W. Sams, published as *Constructive Theme Writing,* Holt, 1957.

The Silver Shell (juvenile), Holt, 1930; *A Goodly Heritage* (autobiography), Holt, 1932; *Mary Peters* (novel), Macmillan, 1934; *Silas Crockett* (novel), Macmillan, 1935; *This England,* Macmillan, 1936 (published in England as *In England Now,* Collins, 1937); *Dawn in Lyonesse* (novel), Macmillan, 1938; *A Goodly Fellowship* (autobiography), Macmillan, 1939; *Windswept* (novel), Macmillan, 1941; *The Bible and the Common Reader,* Macmillan, 1944, revised edition, 1952; *Jonathan Fisher, Maine Parson, 1768-1847* (biography), Macmillan, 1948; *The Plum Tree* (novel), Macmillan, 1949.

Abby Aldrich Rockefeller, Macmillan, 1950; (editor) *Readings from the Bible,* Macmillan, 1952; *The White Gate,* Norton, 1954; (contributor of regional introduction) *Look at the U.S.A.,* Houghton, 1955; *Life and Language in the Old Testament,* Norton, 1955; *The Edge of Darkness,* Norton, 1957; *Sailing the Seven Seas* (juvenile), Houghton, 1958; *Donald McKay and the Clipper Ships* (juvenile biography), Houghton, 1959; *The Lovely Ambition* (novel), Norton, 1960; *The Fishing Fleets of New England* (juvenile), Houghton, 1961; *The Psalms for the Common Reader,* Norton, 1962; *The Prophets for the Common Reader,* Norton, 1963; *Victoria,* Norton, 1963; *Dolly Moses,* Norton, 1963; *Richard Mansfield, the Prince of Donkeys,* Norton, 1964; *Thomas Hardy from Serial to Novel,* Russell, 1964; (editor with others) *Values in Literature,* Houghton, 1965; *A Journey to Boston,* Norton, 1965; *The Story of Lighthouses,* Norton, 1965; *A Walk on an Iceberg,* Norton, 1966; (compiler) Sarah Orne Jewett, *The Country of the Painted Firs,* F. Watts, 1968; (editor with M. E. MacGregor) *The Writing of Informal Essays,* Books for Libraries, 1970.

Contributor of stories and reviews to newspapers and periodicals, including *New York Times, New York Herald Tribune, Atlantic Monthly, Yale Review.*

WORK IN PROGRESS: Books on the Old Testament.

SIDELIGHTS: Miss Chase began writing while in college. The author of over forty titles, she was constantly praised for her wit, human understanding, and scholarship. Lewis Gannet said: "To an extraordinary degree Miss Chase has the true novelist's gift for creating characters, interesting the reader in them, and conveying the conviction that these characters are real people.'' Speaking of *The Lovely Ambition*, Gannet noted that ''sheer joy in living permeates [the novel]. It is a pleasure to read and a pleasure to remember. It leaves a good taste in the mouth.'' Fanny Butcher believed that ''nowadays only the rarest of novels have the quiet acceptance of reality that Miss Chase puts into her pages.'' William Hogan said of her work: ''No violence; no loud noises; no sex or bombast—but a display of craftsmanship that might embarrass a younger generation of novelists if they took time out to read this kind of English prose. . . .''

Dawn in Lyonesse was adapted by Thomas Job for a three-act play. *Avocational interests:* Gardening and bird study.

BIOGRAPHICAL/CRITICAL SOURCES: Chicago Sunday Tribune, June 19, 1960; *New York Herald Tribune Book Review*, June 19, 1960; *San Francisco Chronicle*, July 1, 1960; *Christian Science Monitor*, October 9, 1963; Perry Dickie Westbrook, *Mary Ellen Chase*, Twayne, 1965; Carolyn Riley, editor, *Contemporary Literary Criticism* Volume II, Gale, 1973.

(Died July 28, 1973)

*   *   *

CHESHIRE, Geoffrey Leonard 1917-

PERSONAL: Born September 7, 1917, in Cheshire, England; son of Geoffrey Chevalier (a barrister-at-law and professor of jurisprudence at Oxford University) and Primrose (Barstow) Cheshire; married Sue Ryder (a social worker), April 5, 1959; children: Jeromy Charles, Elizabeth Diana Rose. *Education:* Merton College, Oxford, second class honors, School of Jurisprudence, 1939. *Home:* Cavendish, Suffolk, England. *Agent:* John Farquharson Ltd., 15 Red Lion Sq., London W.C. 1, England. *Office:* Cheshire Foundation Homes, 7 Market News, London W. 1, England.

CAREER: Royal Air Force, regular commissioned officer, 1939-45, retiring as group captain, 1945; Cheshire Foundation Homes for the Sick, London, England, founder-director, 1948—; Mission for the Relief of Suffering, London, England, co-founder, director, 1959—. Served as squadron wing commander in England, 1942-44, at Headquarters, Eastern Air Command, South-East Asia, 1944, as member of British Joint Staff Mission in Washington, D.C., 1945, and as British observer at dropping of atomic bomb on Nagasaki, 1945. *Awards, honors*—Military: Victoria Cross, Distinguished Service Order with two bars, Distinguished Flying Cross. Other: Doctorate of Law, University of Liverpool.

WRITINGS: Bomber Pilot, Hutchinson, 1942; *Pilgrimage to the Shroud*, Hutchinson, 1956; *The Face of Victory*, Hutchinson, 1961.

WORK IN PROGRESS: For Your Tomorrow, a book on the problem of suffering.

BIOGRAPHICAL/CRITICAL SOURCES: Russell Braddon, *Cheshire, V.C.*; Andrew Boyle, *No Passing Glory*; Hughes, *The Life of Leonard Cheshire*.

*   *   *

CHESLOCK, Louis 1898-

PERSONAL: Born September 25, 1898, in London, England; came to United States in 1901, naturalized in 1913; son of Jacob and Rebecca (Neumark) Cheslock; married

Elise Hanline, May 31, 1926; children: Barry. *Education:* Attended Baltimore City College; Peabody Conservatory of Music, certificate in violin, 1917, certificate in harmony, 1919, diploma in composition, 1921. *Home:* 2318 Sulgrave Ave., Baltimore, Md. 21209.

CAREER: Peabody Conservatory of Music, Baltimore, Md., instructor in violin, 1916—, in composition, counterpoint, and orchestration, 1922—, chairman of department of theory, 1950-68. Baltimore Symphony Orchestra, violinist, 1916-37, assistant concert master, 1932-37, sometime guest conductor. Composer of opera, ballet, string quartet, and other ensemble works. Lecturer. *Awards, honors:* Doctor of Musical Arts, Peabody Institute, 1964.

WRITINGS: Introductory Study, Violin Vilvato, Peabody Institute, 1931; *Graded History of Violin Pieces*, Peabody Institute, 1948; (editor) *H. L. Mencken on Music*, Knopf, 1961. Contributor of articles to *American Mercury, Musical America*, and to *Baltimore Sun*.

AVOCATIONAL INTERESTS: Collecting bronze medallions of musicians, and world travel.

*   *   *

CHESTERTON, A(rthur) K(enneth) 1899-

PERSONAL: Born May 1, 1899, in Krugersdorp, Transvaal, South Africa; son of Arthur George and Ethel (Down) Chesterton; married Doris Lucy Terry, 1933. *Education:* Attended schools in Johannesburg, South Africa, and Berkhamsted School, in England. *Politics:* ''Empire Loyalist.'' *Home:* 5 Elmhurst Court, St. Peter's Rd., Croydon, Surrey, England. *Office:* 92 Fleet St., London E.C.4, England.

CAREER: Editor of *Shakespeare Review*, 1928; editor-in-chief of *Torquay Times*, 1928-33; deputy editor for *Truth*, 1944-53; personal literary and journalistic advisor to Lord Beaverbrook, 1953-54; currently editor of *Candour*. *Military service:* British Army, 1915-19, 1940-43; became captain; received Military Cross. *Member:* Institute of Journalists, Society of Authors.

WRITINGS: History of the Shakespeare Memorial Theatre, Werner Laurie, 1932; *Adventures in Dramatic Appreciation*, Werner Laurie, 1933; *No Shelter for Morrison*, Crisp, 1945; *Juma the Great*, Carroll & Nicolson, 1947; *Commissars Over Britain*, Bearfoot Publishing, 1948; (with Joseph Leftwich) *The Tragedy of Anti-Semitism*, Anscombe & Co., 1949; *The New Unhappy Lords: An Exposure of Power Politics*, Candour, 1965, Christian Book Club of America, 1967, 3rd edition, Candour, 1969; *Empire of Eclipse: Grim Realities of the Twentieth Century*, Candour, 1966. Contributor of articles to *Times, Daily Mail, Sunday Express, Evening Standard*, and other publications.

WORK IN PROGRESS: An autobiography.

*   *   *

CHETHAM-STRODE, Warren 1896-
(Michael Hamilton)

PERSONAL: Born January 28, 1896, in Pinner, England; son of Reginald (a physician) and Nette (Andrew) Chetham-Strode; married Moira Hamilton Verschoyle (a writer and reviewer), July 16, 1927; children: Michael Edward. *Education:* Attended Sherborne School, Dorsetshire, England. *Politics:* ''Intelligently Conservative.'' *Religion:* Church of England. *Home:* Oast House, Playden, near Rye, Sussex, England. *Agent:* Scott Meredith Literary Agency, Inc., 580 Fifth Ave., New York, N.Y. 10036.

CAREER: Employed by British American Tobacco Co. in United States and India, 1919-22; other business posts in England, 1922-32; playwright and author, 1932—. With British Ministry of Information and War Office, 1939-45. *Military service:* British Army, 1914-18; became captain; received Military Cross, 1916.

WRITINGS—Novels: (Under pseudonym Michael Hamilton) *Mice and Management*, N. Douglas, 1931; *Three Men and a Girl*, Heinemann, 1958, McGraw, 1960; *Top Off the Milk*, Heinemann, 1959, McGraw, 1961; *The Years of Alison*, Putnam, 1961.

Children's books: *A Cat Called Tootoo*, Heinemann, 1966; *Tootoo's Friends at the Farm*, Heinemann, 1967; *Tootoo the Traveling Cat*, Heinemann, 1968. Also author of *A Short Walk: An Autobiography of Youth*.

Plays, most of them produced in London: "Sometimes Even Now," 1933; "Man Proposes," 1933; "Heart's Content," 1936; "The Day is Gone," 1937; "Strangers Road," 1937; "Young Mrs. Barrington," 1945; "The Guinea-Pig," 1946; "A Play For Ronnie," 1947; "The Gleam," 1947; "Background," 1950; "The Pet Shop," 1954; "Silver and Gold," 1954; "The Stepmother," 1958.

Films: "Odette"; "The Lady with the Lamp"; "The Guinea-Pig"; "Background."

Television plays: "Come Read Me a Riddle"; "The Day Is Gone"; "The Guinea-Pig"; "Background." Also author of television serials, "The Happy Man" and "Sinister Street," and a radio serial, "The Barlowes of Beddington."

SIDELIGHTS: Chetham-Strode told CA: "I have been very lucky, and have had success in the theatre as well as failure. The same goes for books, films, etc. Am now more or less out of the rat race and have never been so happy." Chetham-Strode has lived in Egypt and France in addition to his business years in India and America.

*   *   **

CHICHESTER, Francis (Charles) 1901-1972

PERSONAL: Born September 17, 1901, in Barnstaple, Devonshire, England; son of Charles (a clergyman) and Emily (Page) Chichester; married Eileen Blakiston, 1923 (died, 1929); married Sheila Mary Craven (vice-chairman of Francis Chichester Ltd.), 1937; children: (first marriage) George Beresford; (second marriage) Giles Bryan. *Education:* Attended Marlborough College, Wiltshire, England. *Home:* 9 St. James's Pl., London S.W. 1, England. *Agent:* George Greenfield, John Farquharson Ltd., 15 Red Lion Sq., London W.C. 1, England.

CAREER: Emigrated to New Zealand in 1919, and after a variety of jobs began in real estate, later forming, with partner, timber and aviation transport companies, including Goodwin & Chichester Aviation Co.; after three months' flight instruction in England, became second person to fly solo from England to Australia, 1929, the first to fly solo east to west across the Tasman Sea, 1931, and the first to make a solo long-distance flight by seaplane (from New Zealand to Japan), 1931; writer on navigation instruction for British Air Ministry and chief navigation instructor at Empire Central Flying School in England, 1940-45; founder and owner of Francis Chichester Ltd. (maps and guides), London, England, 1945—. Director, Straight Aviation Training Ltd., 1946-49. Deviser of methods for teaching fighter pilots navigation for low-level flying without maps. Competitor in sixteen ocean-yacht races, 1945-59; winner of first solo transatlantic race, 1960, set new record for

transatlantic crossing, 1962, and placed second in solo transatlantic race, 1964; made record-breaking solo voyage around the world, 1966-67. Trustee, National Maritime Museum.

MEMBER: Guild of Air Pilots and Air Navigators (warden of court, 1945-59), Institute of Navigation (fellow; member of council, 1945-59; past vice-president). *Awards, honors:* Johnston Memorial Trophy for navigation in solo flight across Tasman Sea, 1931; Observer Trophy, presented by His Royal Highness, the Duke of Edinburgh, 1960; named "Yachtsman of the Year," Cruising Club of America, 1960; Blue Water Medal of Cruising Club of America, 1960; Gold Medal of Institute of Navigation, 1961; Commander of Order of the British Empire for services to yachting, 1964; Knight Commander, Order of the British Empire, 1967; Gold Medal, Australian Institute of Navigation; Silver Globe Award, British Institute of Navigation; Achievement Medal, American Institute of Navigation; Gold Medal, Royal Geographic Society; and other awards.

WRITINGS: Solo to Sydney, Hamish Hamilton, 1930; *Seaplane Solo*, Faber, 1930, Harcourt, 1934 (published under title, *Alone Over the Tasman Sea*, Allen & Unwin, 1945); *Ride on the Wind*, Hamish Hamilton, 1936, Harcourt, 1937, new edition, Hamish Hamilton, 1967; *The Observer's Book on Astro-Navigation*, Books, 3, 4, 5, 9, Allen & Unwin, 1940-42, Chemical Publishing Co., 1941-42, one-volume edition (under title *The Complete Observers' Astro-Navigation*), Allen & Unwin, 1944; *Night and Fire Spotting*, Allen & Unwin, 1941; *The Spotter's Handbook*, Allen & Unwin, 1941; *The Observer's Planisphere of Air Navigation Stars*, Allen & Unwin, 1942.

Pocket Map and Guide of the British Isles, Chichester, 1956; (editor) *Pocket Map and Guide of London*, new edition, Chichester, 1960; *Yacht's Log*, Chichester, 1960; *100 Mile Map*, Chichester, 1960; *Alone Across the Atlantic*, Doubleday, 1961; *London Man*, Chichester, 1962; *Atlantic Adventure*, Allen & Unwin, 1962, de Graff, 1963; *The Lonely Sea and the Sky*, Coward, 1964; (editor and contributor) *Along the Clipper Way*, Hodder & Stoughton, 1966, Coward, 1967, abridged edition, Brockhampton, 1967; *Gipsy Moth Circles the World*, Hodder & Stoughton, 1967, Coward, 1968; *How to Keep Fit, by One Who Never Is as Fit as He Would Like to Be*, Coward, 1969; *The Romantic Challenge*, Cassell, 1971, Coward, 1972.

Contributor to *Esquire* and other magazines. Also author of four booklets on navigation, including "Pinpoint the Bomber" and "Star Compass, Longitude Finder, Star Clock and Planisphere," published by Allen & Unwin, 1942-45.

SIDELIGHTS: Chichester set his yachting records in "Gipsy Moth III" named after the Gipsy Moth plane he fitted with floats for the Tasman Sea crossing in 1931. He spanned the Atlantic solo in 40½ days in 1960 (sixteen days faster than the previous record), and later sailed back via the Azores with his wife as crew, completing 8,000 miles in all. In June of 1962 he broke his own record by making the east-to-west crossing in 33 days and 15 hours. In the second solo Atlantic race of 1964, he crossed the Atlantic solo east to west in under 30 days, returning with his son in 25 days, 9 hours. It was during his solo voyage around the world in 1966-67 that Chichester was conferred the title of Knight Commander of the British Empire. His trip lasted 274 days and spanned some 29,600 miles via the Cape of Good Hope and Cape Horn. In June, 1972, at the age of seventy, Chichester began a solo race across the Atlantic, stopped only by his impending ill health.

The dauntless Chichester once wrote: "The only way to live life to the full is to do something that depends on both the brain and on physical sense and action"; "I hate being frightened, but, even more, I detest being prevented by fright." Chichester's adventures bear out these words well. He is featured in the film "Atlantic Adventure," released in 1965.

BIOGRAPHICAL/CRITICAL SOURCES: John Rowland, *Lone Adventurer: The Story of Sir Francis Chichester*, Roy, 1969; *Esquire*, June, 1969; *New York Times*, August 27, 1972; *Chicago Tribune*, August 27, 1972.†

(Died August 26, 1972)

* * *

CHILD, Philip 1898-

PERSONAL: Born January 19, 1898, in Hamilton, Ontario, Canada; son of William Addison (a businessman) and Elizabeth Helen (Harvey) Child; married Gertrude Helen Potts, August 5, 1924; children: John, Elizabeth. *Education:* Trinity College, University of Toronto, B.A., 1921; Cambridge University, graduate study, 1921-22; Harvard University, A.M., 1923, Ph.D., 1929. *Religion:* Anglican Church in Canada. *Office:* Trinity College, Hoskin Ave., Toronto, Ontario, Canada.

CAREER: Trinity College, University of Toronto, Toronto, Ontario, lecturer in English, 1923-26; University of British Columbia, Vancouver, assistant professor of English, 1928-29; Harvard University, Cambridge, Mass., tutor and instructor, 1929-36; writer, 1936-41; Trinity College, University of Toronto, special lecturer, 1941-42, professor of English, beginning 1942. *Military service:* Royal Garrison Artillery, World War I; served in France through 1918; became lieutenant. *Member:* Canadian Authors' Association (vice-president, 1945-47), League of Nations Society (formerly on national executive board, Canada), Modern Language Association of America, Arts and Letters Club (Toronto). *Awards, honors:* Ryerson Fiction Award, 1945, for *Day of Wrath*, and, 1949, for *Mr. Ames Against Time*; Governor General's Literary Award, 1950, for *Mr. Ames Against Time*.

WRITINGS—All novels except as indicated: *The Village of Souls*, Butterworth & Co., 1933; *God's Sparrows*, Butterworth & Co., 1937; *Blow Wind Come Wrack*, Jarrolds, 1945; *Day of Wrath*, Ryerson, 1945; *Mr. Ames Against Time*, Ryerson, 1949; *The Victorian House and Other Poems*, Ryerson, 1951; *The Wood of the Nightingale* (narrative poem), Ryerson, 1965. Also author of *Post-War Organization*, and (in collaboration with John W. Holmes) *Dynamic Democracy*.

Author of one-act plays performed in Canadian theaters, of pamphlets, and radio and television scripts. Contributor of essays on literary and historical subjects to *Dalhousie Review*, *Queen's Quarterly*, *University of Toronto Quarterly*, and other journals. Member of editorial board, *University of Toronto Quarterly*, 1940-49.

* * *

CHILDS, H(alla) Fay (Cochrane) 1890-1971

PERSONAL: Born August 31, 1890, in Chambers, Neb.; daughter of Arthur William (a mailman) and Nellie Shutts) Cochrane; married Wilbur Childs, June 11, 1915 (died, 1950); children: Allen E., Jean H. *Education:* Attended Michigan State Normal College (now Eastern Michigan University), two years. *Politics:* Republican. *Religion:*

Baptist. *Home:* 6814 North Lotus Ave., San Gabriel, Calif. 91775.

CAREER: Teacher in Lenawee County, Mich., 1908-10, Adrian, Mich., 1911-15; began writing in 1960 as the result of an interest in the children of Africa.

WRITINGS: Wacheera, Child of Africa, Criterion, 1965; *The Diamond Trail*, Criterion, in press. Contributor to *Jack and Jill*, *Junior Scholastic*, *Children's Friend*, and several other periodicals.

WORK IN PROGRESS: Stories on Tanzania, Zambia, and Rhodesia; research on Kenya and Congo Republic.

(Died October, 1971)

* * *

CHITTY, Susan Elspeth 1929-

PERSONAL: Born August 18, 1929, in London, England; daughter of Rudolph and Antonia (a novelist; maiden name, White) Glossop; married Thomas Hinde (a novelist), August 23, 1951; children: Andrew, Cordelia, Miranda. *Education:* Attended Godolphin School; Somerville College, Oxford University, student, 1947-51. *Religion:* Roman Catholic. *Home:* Bow Cottage, West Hoathly, Sussex, England. *Agent:* Curtis Brown Ltd., 1 Craven Hill, London W2 3EW, England.

CAREER: Vogue, London, England, staff member, 1952-53; free-lance journalist and author. Radio and television work includes appearances on British Broadcasting Corp. program, "What's in the Picture," interviewer on "Wednesday Magazine," and talks for "Woman's Hour." Lecturer on fashion subjects. *Awards, honors: Vogue* Talent Contest winner, 1952.

WRITINGS: Diary of a Fashion Model, Methuen, 1958; (editor) *An Intelligent Woman's Guide to Good Taste,* MacGibbon & Kee, 1958; *White Huntress,* Methuen, 1963; *My Life and Horses,* Hodder & Stoughton, 1966; *The Woman Who Wrote Black Beauty,* Hodder & Stoughton, 1971. Columnist, *Modern Woman;* former reviewer of novels for *Sunday Telegraph* (London); contributor of articles to *Punch, Observer, Spectator.*

SIDELIGHTS: Susan Chitty spent two years in East Africa, 1958-60. Lives in the country with her author-husband, children, and keeps dogs and ponies. Writes, she says, to provide food for the latter.

BIOGRAPHICAL/CRITICAL SOURCES: Housewife, August, 1962; *Books and Bookmen,* October, 1963; *Smith's Trade News,* October 19, 1963.

* * *

CHITWOOD, Oliver Perry 1874-1971

PERSONAL: Born November 28, 1874, in Franklin County, Va.; son of Henry Clay and Gillie Anne (Divers) Chitwood; married Agnes Cady, December 17, 1910; children: Henry Cady, Elizabeth Anne Chitwood Appel. *Education:* College of William and Mary, A.B., 1899; Johns Hopkins University, Ph.D., 1905. *Politics:* Democrat. *Religion:* Baptist. *Home:* 312 Park St., Morgantown, W. Va. *Office:* 423 Chemistry Building, West Virginia University, Morgantown, W. Va.

CAREER: Teacher in public and private schools in Virginia, 1893-97, 1899-1901; College of William and Mary, Williamsburg, Va., librarian, 1898-99; Richmond Academy, Richmond, Va., headmaster, 1902-03; Mercer University, Macon, Ga., professor of history, economics, and political science, 1905-07; West Virginia University, Morgantown, professor of history, 1907-46, professor emeritus, 1946-71. Visiting professor, Stetson University, 1949-52, Ohio State University, University of North Carolina; visiting summer teacher at Johns Hopkins University. *Member:* American Historical Association, Southern Historical Association, West Virginia Historical Society, Monongalia County Historical Society, Phi Beta Kappa, Kiwanis Club. *Awards, honors:* LL.D. from College of William and Mary, 1926; Litt.D., Concord College, 1962; Order of Vandalia, West Virginia University, 1963.

WRITINGS: (Co-author) *Makers of American History*, Silver Burdett, 1904; *Justice in Colonial Virginia*, Johns Hopkins University Press, 1905; *The Immediate Causes of the Great War*, Crowell, 1917, revised and enlarged edition, 1918; *A History of Colonial America*, Harper, 1931, 3rd edition, 1961; *John Tyler: Champion of the Old South*, Appleton, 1939; (co-author) *A Short History of the American People*, Van Nostrand, Volume I, 1945, 3rd edition, 1962, Volume II, 1948, 2nd edition, 1952; (co-author) *The United States: From Colony to World Power*, Van Nostrand, 1949, revised edition, 1954.

Contributor: J. A. C. Chandler, editor, *Makers of Virginia History*, 1904; J. M. Callahan, editor, *Semi-Centennial History of West Virginia*, 1913. Contributor to *Dictionary of American History*, *Dictionary of American Biography*, and to *Political Science Quarterly*, *American Historical Review*, *Magazine of History*, and other journals.

WORK IN PROGRESS: A biography of Richard Henry Lee.

(Died February 3, 1971)

*   *   *

CHORON, Jacques 1904-1972

PERSONAL: Born January 8, 1904, in Shavli, Russia; son of Naum I. (a banker) and Anna (Landesberg) Choron-Zicky; married third wife, Rose Josefowitz, July 10, 1959 (divorced); children: Victoria Irene. *Education:* University of Leipzig, Ph.D., 1928; New School for Social Research, D.S.Sc., 1960. *Home:* 21 West 86th St., New York, N.Y. 10024.

CAREER: Engaged in various business enterprises in Europe and America, 1928-58; president, Amerpro Machine Products, New York, N.Y., and vice-president and general manager, Applied Chemical Corp., New York, N.Y., 1941-51; Concert Hall Society, New York, N.Y., 1951-53; Second Gotham Corp., New York, N.Y., vice-president, 1953-56; New School for Social Research, New York, N.Y., member of faculty, 1958-65; Los Angeles Suicide Prevention Center, Los Angeles, Calif., fellow, 1965-66; National Institute of Mental Health, Center for the Study of Suicide Prevention, New York, N.Y., senior fellow, 1967-69. *Member:* International Association for Suicide Prevention, American Philosophical Association, American Association of Suicidology, Foundation of Thanotology, Authors Guild, Grand Jury Association of New York County.

WRITINGS: La Doctrine bolcheviste, Riviere, 1935; *L'-Impasse*, Haumont, 1936; *The Romance of Philosophy*, Macmillan, 1963; *Death and Western Thought*, Collier, 1963; *Modern Man and Mortality*, Macmillan, 1964, reissued as *Death and Modern Man*, Collier, 1971; (contributor) Edwin Shneidman, editor, *Essays in Self-Destruction*, Science House, 1967; (contributor) *Dictionary of Ideas*,

Scribner, 1971; *The Problem of Suicide*, Scribner, 1971; *Suicide*, Scribner, 1972.

(Died March 30, 1972)

*   *   *

CHOWDHARY, Savitri Devi (Dumra) 1907-

PERSONAL: Born September 9, 1907, in Multan, Punjab, India (now Pakistan); daughter of Nathu Ram (a schoolmaster) and Thakori (Bai) Dumra; married Dharm Sheel Chowdhary, November, 1927 (deceased); children: George Chowdhary-Best, Shakuntala Chowdhary Bigsby. *Education:* Attended school in Multan, Punjab, India. *Religion:* Hindu. *Home:* 174 Clay Hill Rd., Basildon, Essex, England.

CAREER: Arya Girls' School, Montgomery, Punjab, India, headmistress, 1925-27. Governor of a country secondary school, 1957—; Old Age Pensioners and Darby and Joan, vice-chairman; Old People's Welfare Committee, Basildon, secretary, 1955-59; St. John's Ambulance Brigade Cadets, president. *Member:* Punjabi Society of British Isles.

WRITINGS: Indian Cooking, Deutsch, 1954; *I Made My Home in England*, privately printed, 1961. Contributor to *Times* (London), *Family Doctor*, *Vogue*, *Daily Telegraph*, *Caravan*, other periodicals.

*   *   *

CHRISTENSEN, Erwin O(ttomar) 1890-

PERSONAL: Born June 23, 1890, in St. Louis, Mo.; son of Otto and Ida (Schnuhr) Christensen; married Edna Florance, August 14, 1937; children: Hilda Marie (Mrs. Edward F. McGrath), Edith Anne, James Erwin Florance, Judith Florance. *Education:* University of Illinois, B.S., 1914; Harvard University, M.Arch., 1916, M.A., 1927. *Home:* 9030 Stevens Lane, Lanham, Md. 20801. *Agent:* Ann Elmo Agency, Inc., 545 Fifth Ave., New York, N.Y. 10017. *Office:* American Association of Museums, 2306 Massachusetts Ave., N.W., Washington, D.C. 20008.

CAREER: Instructor in art history at Ohio State University, Columbus, 1915-19, and at University of North Dakota, Grand Forks, 1919-26; Isabella Stewart Gardner Museum, Boston, Mass., assistant director, 1928-31; American Federation of Arts, Washington, D.C., director of educational work, 1931-34; Syracuse University, Syracuse, N.Y., lecturer in art history, 1934-36; University of Pennsylvania, Philadelphia, lecturer in art history, 1937-39; National Gallery of Art, Washington, D.C., curator of decorative arts and Index of American Design, 1940-60; American University, Washington, D.C., lecturer in art history, 1945-46; American Association of Museums, Washington, D.C., consultant, 1960—. *Military service:* U.S. Air Service, Aerial Photography, 1918-19. *Member:* Ethical Society (Washington, D.C.).

WRITINGS: (Contributor) Ben Karpman, *Case Studies in the Psychopathology of Crime*, Medical Science Press, 1948; *Arts and Crafts*, National Gallery of Art in collaboration with Federal Security Agency, 1949; *The Index of American Design*, Macmillan, 1950, 2nd edition, 1959; *Early American Wood Carving*, World Publishing, 1952; *Primitive Art*, Crowell, 1955; *The History of Western Art*, New American Library, 1959; (editor) *Museum Directory of the United States and Canada*, American Association of Museums, 1961; *American Crafts and Folk Arts*, Luce, 1964; *A Pictorial History of Western Art*, New American

Library, 1964; *A Guide to Art Museums of the United States*, Dodd, 1968.

Writer of booklets on early American design in ceramics and toleware, published by Pitman, 1952, of National Gallery of Art handbooks on Chinese porcelains and objects of mediaeval art, and of pamphlets on paintings and other museum subjects. Contributor to the *Concise Encyclopedia of American Antiques*, *Book of Knowledge*, and *Pictured Knowledge*. Contributor of articles to journals and magazines, including *Art in America*, *Antiques*, *Ford Times*, *House Beautiful*, *Art and Archaeology*, *Journal of Educational Psychology*, *Museum News*, *Gazette des Beaux Arts*, *Psychoanalytic Review*.

WORKS IN PROGRESS: (With Carrol Bennor and Karl K. Kindel) *Performing the Visual Arts*; *Design as a Measure of Sensitiveness in Aesthetic Reactions*.

* * *

CHRISTIAN, Garth Hood 1921-1967

PERSONAL: Born August 2, 1921, in Riddings, Derbyshire, England; son of Frederick Ewan (a parson) and Ethel Marian Trower (Rogers) Christian. *Education:* Attended Derby School, England. *Religion:* Church of England. *Home:* Beggars Wood, North Chailey, Lewes, Sussex, England. *Agent:* David Higham Associates Ltd., 5-8 Lower John St., London W1R 4HA, England.

CAREER: Editor of *Plough,* 1947-62, of *Sussex County Review,* 1958-59. Sussex Naturalists' Trust, member of council, 1961-63, press officer, 1962-67. Primary school manager, 1953-63; secondary school governor, 1958-63. *Member:* Institute of Journalists, International P.E.N., Sussex Archaeological Society (council, 1957-63).

WRITINGS: A Place for Animals: A Plea for the Preservation of Wild Life and the Establishment of Nature Sanctuaries, Lutterworth, 1958; *Down the Long Wind: A Study of Bird Migration,* George Newnes, 1961; (editor and author of introduction) *James Hawker's Journal: A Victorian Poacher,* Oxford University Press, 1961; *While Some Trees Stand,* George Newnes, 1963, Transatlantic, 1964; (compiler) *Wings of Light: An Anthology for Bird-Lovers,* George Newnes, 1965; *Tomorrow's Countryside: The Road to the Seventies,* J. Murray, 1966; *Ashdown Forest,* Society of the Friends of Ashdown Forest, 1967; *The Country Life Countryman's Pocket Book,* Country Life, 1967. Contributor to *Country Life, Times, New Scientist, Animals,* and other periodicals.

(Died November 26, 1967)

* * *

CHROUST, Anton-Hermann 1907-

PERSONAL: Born January 28, 1907, in Wuerzburg, Germany; son of Anton Julius (a university professor) and Johanna (Sander) Chroust. *Education:* University of Werzburg, A.B., 1925; University of Erlangen, LL.B., 1928, J.U.D., 1929; University of Munich, M.A., 1930, Ph.D., 1931; Harvard University, S.J.D., 1933; also studied at University of Heidelberg, University of Bologna, University of Paris, and University of London. *Home:* 110 Peashway, South Bend, Ind. 46617. *Office:* P.O. Box 133, University of Notre Dame, Notre Dame, Ind. 46556.

CAREER: Harvard University, Cambridge, Mass., research fellow in Law School, 1934-41; University of Notre Dame, Notre Dame, Ind., associate professor, 1946-51, professor of law, 1951—, University Graduate Research

Professor, 1959—. Senior fellow and visiting professor at Yale Law School, 1962, 1966-67. *Awards, honors:* Grants from Walter E. Meyer Foundation and Rockefeller Foundation.

WRITINGS: Socrates, Man and Myth: The Two Socratic Apologies of Xenophon, University of Notre Dame Press, 1957; (editor) *Aristotle: Protrepticus—A Reconstruction,* University of Notre Dame Press, 1964; *The Rise of the Legal Profession in America,* two volumes, University of Oklahoma Press, 1965. Contributor of more than one hundred and forty articles and about thirty book reviews to legal, philosophical, historical, and classical journals in the U.S. and abroad.

WORK IN PROGRESS: Aristotle: Some New Light on Life and Last Works, a two-volume work.

SIDELIGHTS: Chroust is competent in French, Italian, Latin, Greek, and knows some Spanish.

* * *

CISZEK, Walter 1904-

PERSONAL: Born November 4, 1904, in Shenandoah, Pa.; son of Martin and Mary (Mika) Ciszek. *Education:* St. Cyril and Methodius Seminary, Orchard Lake, Mich., A.B.; received Jesuit training in New York; finished theology course at the Gregorian University, Rome, Italy. *Office:* John XXIII Center, Fordham University, 2546 Belmont Ave., Bronx, N.Y. 10458.

CAREER: Ordained Roman Catholic priest, Society of Jesus (Jesuits), 1938, in the Byzantine rite in Rome; volunteered and was sent to Poland; after the Russians took over his sector of Poland and turned the Jesuit mission into a dance hall, he crossed into Russia in 1940 to work as a priest among those deported to the lumber camps in the Ural Mountains; there he was arrested and sent to Moscow's Lubianka prison, and sentenced to hard labor in the Siberian concentration camp. Until 1955, he had been officially presumed dead. Then news came through devious ways that he was still alive. In October, 1964, he was returned to the United States in exchange for a pair of Soviet agents. Currently, he is a lecturer with the John XXIII Center for Eastern Christian Studies, Fordham University, Bronx, N.Y. *Awards, honors:* National Book Award nomination, 1965, for *With God in Russia.*

WRITINGS: (With Daniel L. Flaherty) *With God in Russia,* McGraw, 1964.

SIDELIGHTS: Father Ciszek recalls that he was "never a writer, never a talker," and the idea of putting his years behind the Iron Curtain on paper never occurred to him. His superiors, however, thought it an excellent idea, and assigned another Jesuit to work with him. He began writing ten hours a day, dramatizing scenes to recall their original impact. When the work was finished and the reluctant author read the first galley proofs, he was pleasantly surprised: "I liked the book myself," he said.

* * *

CLAPP, James Gordon 1909-1970

PERSONAL: Born December 8, 1909, in New York, N.Y.; son of James Gordon (an engineer) and Josephine (Meade) Clapp; married Yolanda Elsasser (a teacher), November 29, 1934; children: Andrea (Mrs. Paul Schneck). *Education:* Columbia University, A.B., 1933, M.A., 1934, Ph.D., 1937. *Home:* 420 East 23rd St., New York, N.Y. 10010. *Office:* Hunter College of the City University of New York, 695 Park Ave., New York, N.Y. 10021.

CAREER: Hunter College (now Hunter College of the City University of New York), New York, N.Y., 1937-70, became professor of philosophy. Lecturer, Karen Horney Institute, 1950-51. *Member:* American Philosophical Association, American Association of University Professors (president, Hunter College chapter, 1955-57), Mind Association. *Awards, honors:* Fellow, American Council of Learned Societies, 1950-51.

WRITINGS: Locke's Conception of the Mind, privately printed, 1937; (editor and author of introduction with Morris Philipson and Henry Rosenthal) *The Foundations of Western Thought: Six Major Philosophers* (readings), Knopf, 1962. Contributor of articles and reviews to professional journals.

WORK IN PROGRESS: An article, "John Locke," for Macmillan's *Encyclopedia of Philosophy;* a book, *Philosophic Examination of Psychoanalytic Thought.*

AVOCATIONAL INTERESTS: The theatre and music.

(Died March 27, 1970)

* * *

CLARK, Catherine Anthony (Smith)   1892-

PERSONAL: Born May 5, 1892, in London, England; daughter of Edgar Francis (an antique expert) and Catherine Mary (Palmer) Smith; married Leonard Clark (a retired rancher), December 29, 1919; children: Leonard Hugh, Margaret. *Politics:* Conservative. *Religion:* Roman Catholic. *Home:* Raynham, Brookleigh Rd., Victoria, British Columbia, Canada.

CAREER: Author. *Member:* Catholic Women's League, Royal Oak Women's Institute. *Awards, honors:* Canadian Librarians' Association Medal, for *The Sun Horse.*

WRITINGS—All published by Macmillan (Toronto), except as indicated: *The Golden Pine Cone,* 1950, *The Sun Horse,* 1953, *The One-Winged Dragon,* 1955, *The Silver Man,* 1959, *The Diamond Feather; or, The Door in the Mountain,* 1962, *The Man with Yellow Eyes,* 1963, St. Martin's, 1964, *The Hunter and the Medicine Man,* 1966.

* * *

CLARK, Samuel Delbert   1910-

PERSONAL: Born February 24, 1910, in Lloydminster, Alberta, Canada; son of Samuel David (a farmer) and Mary Alice (Curry) Clark; married Rosemary J. Landry, December 26, 1939; children: Ellen Margaret, Samuel David, William Edmond. *Education:* University of Saskatchewan, B.A., 1930, M.A., 1931; London School of Economics and Political Science, graduate study, 1932-33; McGill University, M.A., 1935; University of Toronto, Ph.D., 1938. *Office:* University of Toronto, 563 Spadina Ave., Toronto, Ontario, Canada M5S 1A1.

CAREER: University of Manitoba, Winnipeg, lecturer in sociology, 1937-38; University of Toronto, Toronto, Ontario, 1938—, became professor of sociology in 1953, chairman of department, 1963-69. McCulloch Professor, Dalhousie University, 1972-74. *Member:* Canadian Political Science Association, American Sociological Association, Royal Society of Canada.

WRITINGS—All published by University of Toronto Press: *The Canadian Manufacturers' Association: A Study in Collective Bargaining and Political Pressure,* 1939; *Social Development of Canada,* 1942; *Church and Sect in Canada,* 1948; *Movements of Political Protest in Canada,*

1660-1840, 1959; *The Developing Canadian Community,* 1963, revised edition, 1969; *The Suburban Society,* 1968.

WORK IN PROGRESS: Research on the disadvantaged rural society in the developed nation.

* * *

CLARK, Van D(euesen)   1909-

PERSONAL: Born December 26, 1909, in Deming, N.M.; son of William Seward Clark; married Jeanne Paquette (a speech pathologist), May 26, 1939; children: Vandi Jeanne, Carlton Fredric. *Education:* University of New Mexico, A.B., 1932, A.M., 1938; Arizona State University, Ed.D., 1966. *Politics:* "Rather independent but usually Democrat." *Home:* 2326 East Clarendon, Phoenix, Ariz. 85016.

CAREER: Federal Transient Relief, administrative positions in New Mexico, 1933-35; high school teacher of English in Santa Fe, N.M., 1937-42, in Phoenix, Ariz., 1945-48; Clark-Paquette Real Estate and Insurance, Phoenix, Ariz., partner, 1945-48; Camelback High School, Phoenix, Ariz., head counselor, 1955—. *Military service:* U.S. Army Air Forces, 1943-45. *Member:* American Personnel and Guidance Association, National Education Association, Phi Delta Kappa.

WRITINGS: Peetie the Pack Rat (juvenile), Caxton, 1960. Contributor to *Jack and Jill* and to education journals.

WORK IN PROGRESS: A book of stories for children.

* * *

CLARKE, Dudley (Wrangel)   1899-1974

PERSONAL: Born April 27, 1899, in Johannesburg, South Africa; son of Sir Ernest M. Clarke. *Education:* Attended Royal Military Academy, Woolwich, England. *Home:* 802 Raleigh House, Dolphin Square, London S.W. 1, England. *Agent:* Curtis Brown Ltd., 1 Craven Hill, London W2 3EW, England.

CAREER: British Army, regular officer, Royal Artillery, 1916-36, General Staff, 1936-47, retiring as brigadier, 1947; Conservative Central Office, London, England, head of public opinion research department, 1948-52. Served with Royal Flying Corps and (later) Royal Air Force, 1914-18, with Army in Iraq Rebellion, 1920, Palestine Rebellion, 1936, Middle East, 1939-40, Norway, 1940, Mediterranean Theater, 1940-45. Director of SECURICOR Ltd., London. *Awards, honors:* Officer, Order of the British Empire, 1942; Commander, Order of the British Empire, 1943; Companion of the Bath, 1945; Africa Star; Italy medal; Legion of Merit (United States).

WRITINGS: Seven Assignments, J. Cape, 1948; *The Eleventh at War,* M. Joseph, 1952; *Golden Arrow,* Hodder & Stoughton, 1955. Also author of *A Quarter of My Century.*

AVOCATIONAL INTERESTS: The theater and travel.

(Died May 7, 1974)

* * *

CLARKE, J(ohn) F(rederick) Gates   1905-

PERSONAL: Born February 22, 1905, in Victoria, British Columbia, Canada; son of Robert Wilson and Ida Charlotte (Gates) Clarke; married Thelma Blanche Canterbury Miesen, June 14, 1929; children: J. F. Gates, Jr., Carol Canterbury (Mrs. Robert E. Lewis). *Education:* University of Washington, Seattle, student, 1923-24; Washington State University, Ph.C., 1926, B.S., 1930, M.S., 1931; Cornell University, postgraduate study, 1935-36; University of

Paris, research, 1945-46; University of London, Ph.D., 1953. *Home:* 5115 72nd Ave., Glenridge, Hyattsville, Md. 20784. *Office:* Department of Entomology, National Museum, Smithsonian Institution, Washington, D.C. 20560.

CAREER: Offerman Drug Co., Bellingham, Wash., pharmacist, 1926-29; Washington State College (now University), Pullman, instructor and researcher, 1931-35; U.S. Department of Agriculture, Washington, D.C., entomologist, 1936-42, 1946-54; Smithsonian Institution, United States National Museum, Washington, D.C., curator, Division of Insects, 1954-63, chairman of department of entomology, 1963-65, senior entomologist, 1965—. *Military service:* U.S. Army, 1942-46; became captain; received Bronze Star.

MEMBER: Entomological Society of America (fellow), American Entomological Society (honorary life member), Royal Entomological Society (fellow), Sociedad Crucena de Ciencias Naturales (Bolivia; honorary member), Entomological Society of Peru (honorary member), Society for British Entomology, Entomological Society of Washington, Biological Society of Washington, Sigma Xi, Phi Kappa Phi, Rho Chi, Phi Sigma, Phi Delta Theta, Washington Biologists Field Club, Cosmos Club. *Awards, honors:* Grants-in-aid for research from National Research Council, 1934-35, Smithsonian Institution, 1947, American Philosophical Society, 1950, National Science Foundation (totaling $44,000), 1958, 1961, Office of Naval Research, 1961, 1962, Smithsonian Research Fund, 1967, Smithsonian Institution Fluid Research Fund, 1973.

WRITINGS: (Contributor) *Exotic Microlepidoptera,* Volume V, Taylor & Francis, 1951; *Catalogue of the Type Specimens of Microlepidoptera in the British Museum (Natural History) Described by Edward Meyrick,* eight volumes, British Museum, 1955-1970; *Giant Golden Book on Butterflies,* Golden Press, 1963. Also contributor of over eighty scientific articles to museum publications, proceedings of professional societies, yearbooks, and journals.

SIDELIGHTS: Has traveled extensively for study and field work in Europe, Pacific Islands, West Indies, South America, Borneo (Sarawak), Ceylon, Africa, northwest United States and Alaska. *Avocational interests:* Philately, early American pottery, growing iris and chrysanthemums.

* * *

CLARKE, John (Campbell) 1913-19(?)
(Hugh Cleland)

PERSONAL: Born October 4, 1913, in Ashton on Mersey, Cheshire, England; son of Hugh Cleland Campbell (a physician) and Elsie Riley (Dawson) Clarke; married Wilda Ruth McNeile, June 25, 1947; children: Nicholas Campbell, Suzanne St. Clair. *Education:* King's College, London, Diploma in Journalism, 1937. *Politics:* Tory. *Religion:* Church of England. *Home:* Mapleton, Maple Ave., Bishop's Stortford, Hertfordshire, England. *Agent:* Desmond Elliott, 15 Duke St., St. James', London S.W.1, England. *Office: Evening Standard,* 47 Shoe Lane, London E.C.4, England.

CAREER: Daily Express, Manchester, England, reporter, 1937-39; Agencia Hulton Presse, Rio de Janeiro, Brazil, bureau head, 1941-42; Globe Agency, India, manager, 1942-45; war correspondent, South-East Asia Command, World War II; *Evening Standard,* London, England, beginning 1949, feature writer, features editor, columnist ("John Clarke's Casebook"), and cricket writer. *Military service:*

British Army, 1940-45; became major. *Member:* Institute of Journalists, Special Forces Club.

WRITINGS: (Under pseudonym Hugh Cleland) *George Washington in the Ohio Valley,* University of Pittsburgh Press, 1956; *Challenge Renewed: The M.C.C. Tour of Australia,* S. Paul, 1963; *Cricket with a Swing: The West Indies Tour, 1963,* S. Paul, 1963; *The Australians In England, 1964,* S. Paul, 1964; *With England In Australia: The M.C.C. Tour 1965-66,* S. Paul, 1966; (with Brian Scovell) *Everything that's Cricket: The West Indies Tour, 1966,* S. Paul, 1966; *St. Michael's Church, Bishop's Stortford,* British Publishing, 1968, 2nd revised edition by J. G. Smith, 1969. Contributor of short stories to magazines and articles to newspapers in England and abroad.

(Deceased)

* * *

CLAUDIA, Sister Mary 1906-

PERSONAL: Born July 24, 1906, in Detroit, Mich.; daughter of Albert Bernard (a piano technician) and Theresa Mary (Ternes) Carlen. *Education:* University of Michigan, A.B.L.S., 1928, A.M.L.S., 1938; University of Chicago, graduate study, 1951. *Home:* Marygrove College, 8425 West McNichols Rd., Detroit, Mich. 48221. *Office:* Marygrove College Library, 8425 West McNichols Rd., Detroit, Mich. 48221.

CAREER: Roman Catholic nun, member of Sisters of Immaculate Heart of Mary; Marygrove College, Detroit, Mich., assistant librarian, 1929-44, librarian, 1944—, on leave of absence to Catholic University of America, Washington, D.C., as index editor for *New Catholic Encyclopedia,* 1963-70. Responsible for plans, building, and furnishings of Marygrove College Library, erected, 1961-62. Immaculate Heart of Mary Board of Education, chairman of library committee. Member of Michigan Week Cultural Activities Committee, 1958-59, and Michigan Curriculum Study Committee on Instructional Materials, 1959-62. *Member:* American Library Association (member of council, 1959-62, 1968-71), Catholic Library Association (vice-president and president-elect, 1963-65; president, 1965-67), Bibliographical Society of America, Catholic Association for International Peace, Michigan Library Association, Phi Beta Kappa, Phi Kappa Phi, Beta Phi Mu.

WRITINGS: Guide to the Encyclicals of the Roman Pontiffs, H. W. Wilson, 1939; *Guide to the Documents of Pius XII,* Newman, 1951; *Dictionary of Papal Pronouncements,* Kenedy, 1958; (contributor) S. M. Regis, editor, *Catholic Bookman's Guide,* Hawthorn, 1961. Contributor to *New Catholic Encyclopedia, Catholic Youth Encyclopedia,* and to magazines and journals. Bibliographical assistant for *Marygrove College Research Annual,* 1939-49, director, 1950-63, 1967—; editor of book columns in *National Catholic Rural Life Conference,* 1952-60, and *Catholic Library World,* 1950-63; member of advisory board, *The Pope Speaks* (an American quarterly), 1954-69; editorial adviser, *The Way.* Consultant, *World Book Encyclopedia.*

WORK IN PROGRESS: Guide to the Documents of Pius XII, 1949-58; Checklist of Encyclicals from Benedict XIV to the Present Time.

* * *

CLEGG, Reed K. 1907-

PERSONAL: Born June 27, 1907, in Heber City, Utah; son of Frederick Lewis (a rancher) and Emma Caroline

(Luke) Clegg; married Irene Lockwood, February 16, 1941; children: Trevor C. *Education:* University of Utah, B.S., 1931, M.S., 1938; American Extension School of Law, LL.B., 1941. *Home:* 5747 Waverly Lane, Fresno, Calif. *Office:* Fresno County Welfare Department, Fresno, Calif.

CAREER: California Youth Authority, parole officer, later field representative supervisory parole officer, 1945-48; Fresno State College, Fresno, Calif., assistant professor of criminology, 1947—; Fresno County Department of Public Welfare, Fresno, Calif., director, 1953—. Director, Community Service Center, Fresno, 1948-53. *Military service:* U.S. Army Air Forces, 1943-45. *Member:* American Academy of Political and Social Science, National Council on Crime and Delinquency, American Management Association, California Probation and Parole Association, California County Welfare Directors Association (president, 1947).

WRITINGS: Probation and Parole, Principles and Practices, C. C Thomas, 1964; *The Welfare World*, C. C Thomas, 1968. Editor, *Confidential Bulletin* (publication of California County Welfare Directors Association), 1953—.

*   *   *

CLEMENTS, E(ileen) H(elen)   1905-

PERSONAL: Born April 20, 1905, in London, England; daughter of Alfred Vivian and Eveline May (Barefoot) Clements; married Taylor Shipley George Hunter (director of *Financial Times*); children: Jennifer Lucy Hunter Ripper. *Education:* Attended Sutton High School for Girls. *Religion:* Anglican. *Home:* White Oaks, Deepdene Park Rd., Dorking, Surrey, England. *Agent:* David Higham Associates Ltd., 5-8, Lower John St., Golden Square, London W1R 4HA, England.

CAREER: National Central Library, London, England, member of staff, 1925-45; free-lance writer. *Member:* Detection Club.

WRITINGS—All published by Hodder & Stoughton, unless otherwise indicated: *Let Him Die*, 1939, *Make Fame a Monster*, 1940, *Bright Intervals*, 1940, *Rain Every Day*, 1941, *Perhaps a Little Danger*, 1942, *Cherry Harvest*, 1943, J. Messner, 1944, *Berry Green*, 1945, *Weathercock*, 1949, *Sea Change*, 1951, *Over and Done With*, 1952, *Parcel of Fortune*, 1954, *Chair Lift*, 1954, *Discord in the Air*, 1955, *The Other Island*, 1956, *Back in Daylight*, 1957, *Uncommon Cold*, 1958, *High Tension*, 1959, *Honey for the Marshal*, 1960, *A Note of Enchantment*, 1961, *Let or Hindrance*, R. Hale, 1963. Contributor to *Lilliput, Housewife*, and *Homes and Gardens*.

*   *   *

CLEMENTS, Julia   1906-

PERSONAL: Lady Seton in private life; born April 10, 1906, in London, England; daughter of Frank Clements; married Sir Alexander Hay Seton, (10th Baronet of Abercorn; died, 1963). *Education:* Attended schools on Isle of Wight and in Brussels, Belgium. *Home:* 122 Swan Court, London S.W.3, England. *Agent:* Hughes Massie Ltd., 18 Southampton Pl., London W.C.1, England.

CAREER: Writer, lecturer, and demonstrator on modern flower arrangements in England and abroad, 1947—. Flower show judge (including international shows in New York and Paris), organizer of the first British course for flower show judges, 1952, and teacher of judging. Lecturer on U.S. tour, 1948, on tour of New Zealand, Australia,

Japan, Belgium, France, Italy, and West Germany. *Member:* Royal Horticultural Society (fellow; judge), London and Home Counties Association of Flower Clubs (president), Women's Press Club (London), Anglo Belge Club.

WRITINGS—All published by Pearson except as indicated: *Fun With Flowers*, 1950, 2nd edition, 1956; *Pictures With Flowers*, 1951; *More Pictures With Flowers*, 1952; *101 Ideas for Flower Arrangement*, 1953; *My Roses*, Collingridge, 1958; *Treasury of Rose Arrangements*, Hearthside Press, 1959; *Floral Roundabout*, 1959; *Party Pieces*, 1960; *Fun Without Flowers*, 1961; *Show Pieces*, 1962; *First Steps With Flowers*, 1962; *A.B.C. of Flower Arranging*, 1963, Van Nostrand, 1964; *The Julia Clements Colour Book of Flower Arrangements*, 1964; *Flower Arrangements in Stately Homes*, Newnes, 1966; *Julia Clement's Gift Book of Flower Arranging*, Newnes, 1969. Contributor to horticulture journals and women's magazines. Regular columnist, *Popular Gardening*.

*   *   *

CLEMONS, Harry   1879-19(?)

PERSONAL: Born September 9, 1879, in Corry, Pa.; son of Henry Dwight and Harriet E. (Barber) Clemons; married Jeannie Cooper Jenkins, May 21, 1918 (died, 1962); children: Henry Jenkins (died on active duty with U.S. Army Air Forces, 1943), Emily (Mrs. George Southall Vest). *Education:* Wesleyan University, Middletown, Conn., B.A., 1902, M.A., 1905; Princeton University, M.A., 1905; Oxford University, graduate student, 1906-07; Columbia University, graduate student (in library science), 1927. *Politics:* Democrat. *Religion:* Presbyterian. *Home:* McCormick Rd., Charlottesville, Va.

CAREER: Princeton University, Princeton, N.J., instructor in English, 1905-06, reference librarian, 1908-13; Nanking University, Nanking, China, professor of English, 1914-20, librarian, 1914-27; University of Virginia, Charlottesville, librarian, 1927-50, consultant on library resources, 1950-57, librarian emeritus, 1957—. Representative of American Library Association, in charge of Library War Service for American Expeditionary Forces in Siberia and Asia, 1918-19; special cataloguer, Chinese Section, Library of Congress, 1922; member of Virginia State Board for Certification of Libraries, 1936-48; honorary trustee, Woodrow Wilson Birthday Foundation. *Member:* American Library Association, Virginia Library Association (president, 1931-32), Psi Upsilon, Phi Beta Kappa, Omicron Delta Epsilon, Pi Delta Epsilon. *Awards, honors:* D.Litt., Wesleyan University, 1942; Thomas Jefferson Award, University of Virginia, 1956.

WRITINGS: An Essay toward a Bibliography of the Published Writings and Addresses of Woodrow Wilson, Princeton University Press, 1912; (editor with M. W. Croll) John Lyly, *Euphues: The Anatomy of Wit* [and] *Euphues and His England*, Dutton, 1916; *The American Library Association in Siberia*, American Library Association, 1919; *A Survey of Research Materials in Virginia Libraries*, University of Virginia Press, 1937; *University of Virginia Library: Story of a Jeffersonian Foundation*, University of Virginia Press, 1954; *The Home Library of the Garretts of Elmwood*, University of Virginia Press, 1957; *Notes on the Professors for Whom the University of Virginia Halls and Residences Are Named*, University of Virginia Press, 1961.

(Deceased)

CLEOBURY, Frank Harold 1892-

PERSONAL: Born November 6, 1892, in London, England; son of William (a brass founder) and Laura (Thompson) Cleobury; married Winifred Clara Sindall, April 29, 1922 (died, 1949); children: John Frank, Audrey Winifred (Mrs. Norman Sunderland). Education: University of London, B.A., 1932, Ph.D., 1941. Politics: Socialist. Home: 20 Desborough Close, Bengeo, Hertford, Hertfordshire, England.

CAREER: Served in H. M. Foreign Office, 1911-46, in H. M. Commonwealth Relations Office, 1946-50; ordained minister, Church of England, 1950. Member: Society for Psychical Research, Modern Churchmen's Union. Awards, honors: Order of the British Empire; Imperial Service Order.

WRITINGS: God, Man, and the Absolute, Hutchinson, 1947; The Armour of Saul, J. Clarke, 1957; Christian Rationalism and Philosophical Analysis, J. Clarke, 1959; Liberal Christian Orthodoxy, J. Clarke, 1963; (contributor) Ian T. Ramsey, Biology and Personality: A Symposium, Basil Blackwell, 1965, Barnes & Noble, 1966. Contributor to Philosophical Quarterly, Modern Churchman, and other religious and philosophical journals.

WORK IN PROGRESS: A study of the metaphysical basis of Christian theology.

*   *   *

CLIFFORD, Harold B(urton) 1893-
(Burt Farnham)

PERSONAL: Born May 21, 1893, in Winthrop, Me.; son of Edwin T. (a salesman) and Stella Mae (Farnham) Clifford; married Gladys L. Mower, July 3, 1917; children: Stella Dorothy Clifford Gray, George Edwin, Flora Elsie Clifford Majumder. Education: Bates College, A.B., 1916, M.A., 1941. Politics: Independent. Religion: Methodist. Residence: East Boothbay, Me.

CAREER: Elementary school teacher, Franklin, Me., and secondary school teacher, Alfred, Me., 1912-13, 1916-17; school administrator in Hartland Union, Me., 1917-25, in Boothbay Union, Me., 1925-56. Member: National Education Association, American Association of School Administrators, Maine Teachers Association, Maine School Superintendents Association, Phi Beta Kappa, Rotary. Awards, honors: Ed.D., University of Maine, 1956; Distinguished Service Award, American Association of School Administrators, 1960.

WRITINGS: America My Home, Scribner, 1940; Canada My Neighbor, Scribner, 1944; Yesterday in America, American Book Co., 1949; American Leaders, American Book Co., 1953; Maine and Her People, Wheelwright, 1957, 2nd edition, with a supplement by Charlotte L. Melvin, 1963; Boothbay Region, 1906 to 1960, Wheelwright, 1961; Exploring New England, Follett, 1961; You and Your Job in Maine, Wheelwright, 1964.

AVOCATIONAL INTERESTS: Gardening, stamp collecting, music, history.

*   *   *

CLINTON, Iris A. (Corbin) 1901-
(Iris Corbin)

PERSONAL: Born September 20, 1901, in London, England; daughter of John Tomlinson (an engineer) and Florence Mary (Clark) Corbin; married Desmond Kenilworth Clinton, June, 1935 (deceased). Education: Westfield College, London, B.A. (honors), 1923. Religion: Congregationalist. Address: c/o Barclay's Bank, Abbey House, Westminster, London S.W.1, England.

CAREER: London Missionary Society, London, England, member of editorial department, 1925-35; Congregational Union of South Africa, Cape Town, office secretary, 1945-53; free-lance writer.

WRITINGS—Under name Iris Corbin: Tanganyika Trail, Livingstone Press, 1925; Kuma of the South Sea, Religious Tract Society, 1930; Wang the Patriot, Religious Tract Society, 1930; Tamate the Fearless, Independent Press, 1932; People of the Buried Book, Independent Press, 1933; Yang the Mystery Man, Edinburgh House Press, 1934; Into the Breakers, Edinburgh House Press, 1935.

Under name Iris A. Clinton: The Hold Up, Edinburgh House Press, 1936; Wong's Wife, Edinburgh House Press, 1938; The Clarkes Go South, Edinburgh House Press, 1948; They Seek a Country, Edinburgh House Press, 1955; Ridge of Destiny, Edinburgh House Press, 1956; Beyond China's Frontiers, Edinburgh House Press, 1958; Friend of the Chiefs, Lutterworth, 1958; These Vessels, Stuart Manning, 1959; Young Man in a Hurry: The Story of William Carey, Lutterworth, 1960, Christian Literature Crusade, 1961; Hope Fountain Story, Mambo Press (Gwelo, Rhodesia), 1969.

*   *   *

CLOUGH, Francis F(rederick) 1912-

PERSONAL: Born October 8, 1912, in Wimbledon, Surrey, England; son of Frederick Harold (a civil engineer) and Lydia (Suddards) Clough; married Clara Elisabeth Robinson, June 26, 1937. Education: Attended Manchester Grammar School; University of Manchester, LL.B. (with honors), 1933. Home: Kingswood, Pen-y-bryn Rd., Upper Colwyn Bay, North Wales.

CAREER: Admitted as solicitor, Supreme Court, 1936. Member: Chester and North Wales Incorporated Law Society, Cambrian Ornithological Society, Stephenson Locomotive Society, North Wales Naturalists' Trust, Festiniog Railway Society.

WRITINGS: (Compiler with G. J. Cuming) The World's Encyclopedia of Recorded Music (incorporating first supplement), Sidgwick & Jackson, 1952, second supplement, 1953, third supplement, 1957; (contributor of discography) Joachim Kaiser, Great Pianists of Our Time, translated from the German by David Wooldridge and George Unwin, Allen & Unwin, 1971. Contributor to Gramophone, American Record Guide, and other musical and historical journals; contributor to Music Year Book, Macmillan, 1972-73.

WORK IN PROGRESS: Further supplements, as consulting editor, to The World's Encyclopedia of Recorded Music.

AVOCATIONAL INTERESTS: Watching cricket, travel.

*   *   *

CLUVER, Eustace Henry 1894-

PERSONAL: Born August 28, 1894, in Robertson, South Africa; son of Fred Albert (a doctor of law) and Ida (Brown) Cluver; married Eileen Ledger, June 28, 1928; children: Ann (Mrs. Alan Weinberg), Helen (Mrs. Alistair Craig Stewart), Sibyl Jane (Mrs. Gorden Stewart). Educa-

tion: Victoria College, University of the Cape of Good Hope, B.A., 1913; Hertford College, Oxford, B.A., 1916; Magdalen College, Oxford, M.A., D.M., 1922; College of Physicians, London, England, D.P.H., 1925. *Home and office:* Motrhill Farm, Walkerhill, Transvaal, South Africa.

CAREER: University of the Witwatersrand, Johannesburg, South Africa, professor of physiology, 1919-26; South Africa Defence Force, director general of medical services, 1932-38; South Africa government, secretary for health and chief health officer, 1938-40; South Africa Institute for Medical Research, director, 1940-59; University of the Witwatersrand, professor of preventive medicine, 1940-59, dean of the faculty of medicine, 1960-63. *Military service:* South Africa Medical Corps, served with British Expeditionary Force in France, 1918; became captain. South Africa Medical Corps, director of pathology, World War II; became colonel.

MEMBER: Royal Institute of Health (fellow), South Africa Medical Association (past president, Southern Transvaal branch), Health Officials Association of South Africa (past president), Council of Allied Medical Professions (past president), South African Medical and Dental Council, Royal Society of Health (fellow). *Awards, honors:* Rhodes Scholar, Oxford University, 1914-17; Knight of St. John of Jerusalem; Efficiency Decoration.

WRITINGS: Birthright (novel), Central News Agency, 1945; *Social Medicine,* Central News Agency, 1951; *Recent Medical and Health Legislation,* Central News Agency, 1955; *Public Health in South Africa,* Central News Agency, 6th edition, 1959; *Medical and Health Legislation in South Africa,* Central News Agency, 2nd edition, 1960. Contributor of papers to scientific and medical journals.

WORK IN PROGRESS: Research on the prevention of sun trauma.

*   *   *

CLYMER, Reuben Swinburne   1878-

PERSONAL: Born November 25, 1878, in Quakertown, Pa.; son of Lewis and Emma (Stevenback) Clymer; married Laura Edith Bowers, December 30, 1898 (deceased); married Gertrude Lucy Cosgrove, November 9, 1932 (deceased). *Education:* College of Medicine and Surgery, Chicago, Ill., M.D., 1902. *Home:* Beverly Hall, Quakertown, Pa. 18951.

CAREER: Registered as osteopath, New York, 1910. Physician and writer. Founder of Philosophical Publishing Co., 1900, Royal Fraternal Association, Inc., 1909, Beverly Hall Corp., 1921, Confederation of Initiates, 1929, Beverly Hall Foundation, 1941, Academy of Comparative Religion and Philosophy, 1941; co-founder and director of La Federation Universelle des Ordres, Societes et Fraternites des Initiates Internationales. Director-general, Church of Illumination. *Member:* Fraternitas Rosae Crucis (grand master), Priests and Princes of Melchizedek and Merged Occult Fraternities (grand master), Supreme Council Brotherhood of America (most venerable grand master), Masons, Shrine, Royal Order of Scotland, Red Cross of Constantine, Orden Constructores Masones (honorary), Lehigh Valley Club, Lehigh Country Club.

WRITINGS—All published by Philosophical Publishing, unless otherwise indicated: *The Fraternity of the Rosicrucians: Their Teachings and Mysteries According to the Manifestoes Issued at Various Times by the Fraternity It-*

self, 1902, 4th edition, completely revised, published as *The Rosicrucians: Their Teachings, the Fraternitatis Rosae Crucis, American—The Manifestoes Issued by the Brotherhood, Order, Temple, and Fraternity of the Rosicrucians Since Its Foundation in America,* 1941, 6th edition, completely revised, published as *The Rosy Cross: Its Teachings . . . The Fraternitatis Rosae Crucis Since Its Foundation Now Made Applicable to Present Day Conditions, and for the Guidance of Those Seeking a More Perfect (Balanced) Life,* Beverly Hall Corp., 1965; *Vaccination Brought Home to You,* C. H. Hebb, 1904; *The Thomsonian System of Medicine, with Complete Rules for the Treatment of Disease,* 1906, 3rd edition published as *The Medicines of Nature: The Thomsonian System,* Humanitarian Society, 1960, 4th edition published as *Nature's Healing Agents: The Medicines of Nature; or, The Natura System,* Dorrance, 1963; *True Spiritualism: Also, a Contradiction of the Work by John E. Roberts, Entitled "Spiritualism; or, Bible Salvation vs. Modern Spiritualism",* 1906; *Alchemy and the Alchemists: Giving the Secret of the Philosopher's Stone, the Elixir of Youth, and the Universal Solvent,* four volumes, 1907; *Ancient Mystic Oriental Masonry: Its Teachings, Rules, Laws, and Present Usages Which Govern the Order at the Present Day,* 1907, revised edition published as *The Mysticism of Masonry,* 1924; *The Philosophy of Fire,* 2nd edition, 1907, 5th edition, completely revised, published as *The Philosophy of Fire: Arcanum of the Spiritual Light,* c.1964; *Divine Alchemy,* c.1907; *The International System of Direct Medication: Giving the Causes and Symptoms of Different Diseases and Their Treatment by Ozone, Direct Medication, the Diet, Internal Bath, and the Nature Cure,* two volumes, privately printed, 1907; *The Mystery of Osiris; or, Egyptian Initiation,* privately printed, 1909, revised edition published as *The Mysteries of Osiris; or, Ancient Egyptian Initiation,* Philosophical Publishing, 1951; *The International System of Magnetic (Alchemic) Therapeutics,* privately printed, 1909.

The Gods; The Immaculate Conception: Setting Forth the Mystery of the Ages, and How This Supposed Impossible Condition is Really Under Natural and Divine Laws, 1910; *The Divine Mystery; The Gods, Known in Early Ages as the Incubi and Succubi, Now Known as the Elementals: Solving the Mystery of the Immaculate Conception and How It Was, and Is, Possible,* 1910; *Instead of Medicine,* c.1910; (with F. E. Gariner) *Christhood and Adeptship,* 1910; *Christisis: Higher Soul Culture—Prepared for the Use of Our Teachers in the Great Work,* 1911, revised edition published as *Christisis: A Course of Study in Higher Soul Culture as a Means to Awaken the Mind to the Truth, the Way and the Life,* 1945; *International Esoteric and Illuminated Bible Lessons,* 1911; *Soul Science and Immortality: The Art of Building a Soul; The Secret of the Coming Christ,* 1911; *The Illuminated Faith: The Christic Interpretation of the Gospel of St. Matthew, in Harmony with Soul Culture and in Accordance with the New Revelation,* 1912; *The Illuminated Faith: Mystical Interpretation of the Gospel of St. John, in Harmony with Higher Soul Culture and in Accordance with the New Revelation,* 1913; *The Priesthood of AEth: Course in AEth Healing,* 1913; *The Son of God: The Mystical Teachings of the Masters, or the Christic Interpretation, Giving a Short Sketch of the Early Life of Jesus and of His Training by the Essenean Order, and Interpretation of Some of His Teachings, in Harmony with the Fundamental Principles of the Temple of Illumination, Known as the "Christic Inter-*

pretation'', 1913; *Temple of Illuminati Instructions: Soul Science and Success*, 1913; *The AEth Mystery; Includes the AEth Drills, the AEth Body and the AEth World, the Divine Science of the Soul, the Highest Development of Soul Powers, and the Divine Mystery of Sex*, 1914; *The Divine Spark, and The Great Pyramid, A Temple of Initiation* (two articles originally published in the magazine *The Initiates*, 1914; *The Imperialistic Council of the Magi*, 1914; *The Way of Life and Immortality: A Text-Book on the New Life That Shall Lead Man from Weakness, Disease, and Death, to Freedom from These Things*, 1914, enlarged edition published as *The Way to Life and Immortality: A Positive Philosophy Leading Man Away from "Sin" . . . and to Manhood, Successful Achievement, Godliness and Immortality*, 1948; *The Way to Godhood* (companion text to *The Way to Life and Immortality*), 1914; *Dietetics: A Complete Course of Instructions in the Correct Use and Combination of Food in Health and Disease*, Rose Cross Aid, 1917, 2nd edition published as *Diet, the Way to Health: A Complete Course of Instructions in the Correct Use and Combination of Food in Health and Disease*, 1919, 3rd edition published as *Diet, a Key to Health: A Series of Lessons in the Selection and Combination of Foods for the Prevention or Cure of Disease*, Humanitarian Society, 1930, 4th edition published as *Diet, A Key to Health: The Selection and Combination of Foods for the Prevention or Cure of Disease*, Franklin Publishing (Philadelphia), 1966; *Higher Race Development: A Course of Instructions on the Right Use of Sex*, 1919, 2nd edition published as *Race Regeneration, the Mystery of Sex: A Course of Instruction on the Right Use of Sex*, Humanitarian Society, 1921, 4th edition published as *The Mystery of Sex and Race Regeneration*, Philosophical Publishing, 1950.

The Way to Happiness: A Positive Inspirational Philosophy Developing an Optimism That Even Misfortune Cannot Obliterate, Humanitarian Society, 1920; *Making Health Certain: A Philosophical and Inspirational Treatise on the Establishment and Maintenance of Health Through a Constructive Mental Attitude*, Humanitarian Society, 1921; *The Science of the Soul: The Art and Science of Building a Soul*, 1922, enlarged edition published as *The Science of the Soul: The Art and Science of Building an Illuminated and Immortal Soul—The Method for the Attainment of Soul or Cosmic Consciousness and Oneness with God; The Spiritual Ethics for the New Age*, 1944; *Soul Consciousness is the Way to Christhood: The Mystical Interpretation of the Teachings of the Illuminati*, 1925; *Soul Science: A Series of Lessons Setting Forth the Divine Laws Applicable to Every Man and Woman Living in the Flesh*, privately printed, 1925; *Initiates and the People*, five volumes, 1928.

The Secret Schools: Members of the Confederation of Initiates, Beverly Hall Foundation, 1930; *The Fraternity of Rosicrucians: Preliminary Information Originally Prepared for Russian Students of Mysticism and Rosicrucian Occultism* (excerpts from Clymer's writings), compiled by Dimitri Valdimirovitch Stranden, Beverly Hall Association, 1933; *Natura Physician*, 1933; *Divine Law Mastership: Fundamental Text Book for All Students Enrolled in the Secret Schools*, Caspar, 1935; *Audi alteram partem/Hear the Other Side* (answer to charges brought against the Ancient Mystical Order Rosae Crucis), National A.M.O.R.C. Rosicrucian Convention, 1935; *A Compendium of Occult Laws: The Selection, Arrangement and Application of the Most Important of Occult Laws Taught by the Masters of Initiation of the Great Secret Schools of the Past and Present—Hermetic, Rosicrucian, Alchemic and AEth Priesthood, and the Practice of the Laws in the Development of the Fourfold Nature of Man in Attaining Success and Mastership on All Planes of Activity*, 1938, 2nd edition, revised, published as *A Compendium of Occult Laws: The Selection, Arrangement and Application of the Most Important of Occult and Arcane Laws Taught by the Masters of the August Fraternities of Initiation, and the Practice of the Laws in the Development of the Fourfold Nature of Man*, Beverly Hall Corp., 1966.

The Interpretation of St. Matthew: An Impartial Interpretation of the Divine Laws Taught in the Book of St. Matthew Directing the Seeker on the Path to the Way of Life, to Spiritual Light, and the Ultimate Complete Freedom of Man, two volumes, 1945; *The Book of Rosicruciae: A Condensed History of the Fraternitas Rosae Crucis or Rosy Cross, the Men Who Made the Order Possible, and Those Who Maintained the Fraternity Throughout the Centuries, Together with the Fundamental Teachings of These Men According to the Actual Records in the Archives of the Fraternity*, three volumes, 1946-49; *The Divine Law, the Path to Mastership: A Full Explanation of the Laws Governing the Inner Development Necessary to Attain to Philosophic Initiation or Mastership, Together with a Detailed Account of the Priests of AEth or Priesthood of Melchizedek*, 1949.

How to Create the Perfect Baby by Means of the Art or Science Generally Known as Stirpiculture; or, Prenatal Culture and Influence in the Development of a More Perfect Race, 1950; *Manual, Order of Service and Ritual* (of Church of Illumination), privately printed, 1952; *The Teachings of the Masters: The Wisdom of the Ages*, revised and enlarged edition, 1952, reissued as *The Hidden Teachings of the Initiate Masters: The Simplified Arcane, Esoteric and Occult Teachings of the Initiates and Masters in the Initiatory Schools of Past Ages—The Interpretation of the Divine Law Which Governs in the New Order of the Ages*, 1957; *The Interpretation of St. John: An Exposition of the Divine Drama*, 1953; *Manisis: The Interpreter of the Divine Law for the Manistic Dispensation*, 1955; *Soul Consciousness or Philosophic Initiation: An Interpretation of the Teachings and the Way of Life, Followed by All Master Initiates of the Authentic Secret Schools Since the Time of Egypt*, 1955; *The Age of Treason: The Carefully and Deliberately Planned Methods Developed by the Vicious Element of Humanity for the Mental Deterioration and Moral Debasement of the Mass as a Means to Their Enslavement, Based on Their Own Writings and Means Already Confessedly Employed—Destroy the Mind and Feelings of Man and Nothing Else Matters*, Humanitarian Society, 1957, 2nd edition published as *Your Health, Your Sanity in the Age of Treason: Food and Liquids Used as a Medium in Deliberately and Carefully Planned Methods Developed by the Vicious Element of Humanity, for the Mental Deterioration and Moral Debasement of the Mass*, 1958, excerpts published as *The Creators of Cancer*, 1958, 3rd edition of entire volume published under original title, with subtitle *Destroy a Man's Reason and Feelings and He Will No Longer Be a Human Being*, 1959; *The Science of Spiritual Alchemy: A Semi-Private Text Especially Prepared for Neophytes Entering the August Fraternity for Study and Training*, 1959.

The Philosophy of Immortality: Known Also as the Philosophy of a Beautiful Life (originally published in *The Son of God*), revised and enlarged edition, 1960; *The Great Work:*

Spiritual Initiation—A Text Prepared for Those No Longer Satisfied with the World of Matter, c.1961.

Editor—All published by Philosophical Publishing, unless otherwise indicated: *The Book of Constitutions of the Grand Lodge of the Universe, Ancient, Free and Accepted Masons,* privately printed, 1906; *The Constitution of Temple Supreme Grand Lodge of the Universe, Ancient and Mystic Oriental Masons and Mystic Masonic Jurisdiction Thereunto Belonging, Governing the First, Second and Third Temple,* privately printed, 1907; (compiler under name Pythagoras 38, supreme master of the temple) *The Imperial Ritual of Magic: Including Full Instruction in the Genuine Kaballa, the Making of Talismans and Amulets, and Other Secret Matter Concerning the Imperialistic Council and Vulnerable Order of Magicians,* 1909, reissued as The "Grand Grimore"; or, *Imperial Ritual of Magic, including Full Instructions in Making of the Magic Rod, Talismans, Amulets and Rings,* 1910; (and author of introduction and notes) *The Rose Cross Order: A Short Sketch of the History of the Rose Cross Order in America, Together with a Sketch of the Life of Dr. P. B. Randolph, the Founder of the Order,* 1916; *The Fraternitatis Rosae Crucis: An Attempt to Harmonize the Spirit of the Writings of Those Who Are Known to Have Been Rosicrucians and a Comparison of the Statements of Those Recognized as Authorities,* 1929; (and author of introduction and notes) P. B. Randolph, *Eulis, Affectional Chemistry: The History of Love—Its Wondrous Magic, Chemistry, Rules, Laws, Moods, Modes and Rationale,* 5th edition, Confederation of Initiates, 1930; (and author of introduction and notes) P. B. Randolph, *Seership: Guide to Soul Sight—A Practical Guide for Those Who Aspire to Develop the Vision of the Soul,* new edition, Confederation of Initiates, 1930; (and author of introduction and notes) P. B. Randolph, *Soul!: The Soul-World—The Homes of the Dead,* Confederation of Initiates, 1932; George Lippard, *Brotherhood of the Rosy Cross,* 1935; *The Rosicrucian Fraternity in America: Authentic and Spurious Organizations as Considered and Dealt with in Treatises Originally Published and Issued in Monograph Form ... with Important Additions,* two volumes, Rosicrucian Foundation, 1935-36; (and author of prologue, introduction, notes, and epilogue) William P. Phelon, *Our Story of Atlantis Written Down for the Hermetic Brotherhood and the Future Rulers of America,* 1937; (and author of prologue, notes and epilogue) B. Randolph, *Ravalette: The Rosicrucians' Story,* 1939; L. H. Anderson and Gerard Encausse, *Occult Science: The Republication, Completely Revised, and Reinterpretation of Two Important Texts— "Occult Science," by L. H. Anderson* [and] *"Occult Science," by Gerard Encausse, Known as Papus,* 1954.

*   *   *

COAKLEY, Mary Lewis

PERSONAL: Born in Baltimore, Md.; daughter of Charles Edward and Rosina (Kerchner) Lewis; first husband deceased; married William Dummond Coakley (an insurance man), 1939; children: (first marriage) Joseph A. *Education:* Attended Sacred Heart Convent, San Francisco, Calif., 1921-25, Dominican College of San Rafael, 1925-28. *Politics:* Republican. *Religion:* Catholic. *Home:* 110 Hewett Rd., Wyncote, Pa. 19095.

CAREER: Writer, 1949—. *Member:* Authors Guild, Bucks County Writers' Guild, Wyncote Players, Republican Neighbors (Wyncote; president).

WRITINGS: Fitting God into the Picture, Bruce, 1950; *Our Child—God's Child,* Bruce, 1953; *Mister Music Maker* (biography of Lawrence Welk), Doubleday, 1958; *Never Date Women,* Bruce, 1964. Writer of four booklets for Doubleday's "Know Your Bible" series, 1959-61, and of pamphlets for Catholic publishing houses. Contributor to Catholic magazines.

SIDELIGHTS: Mrs. Coakley said: "Since writing is nothing more than the 'application of the seat of the pants to the seat of the chair,' it leaves me with little time for other pursuits. However ... I do occasionally address women's clubs etc. and I have recently signed with a lecture agency.

"Also, when I can manage it, I travel. Europe, Mexico, Canada, Alaska—I have made them all. I find it great fun to try out my poor Spanish and poorer French on taxi drivers, waiters, or—whoever will listen."

Mister Music Maker (Bishop Fulton Sheen recommended her to Lawrence Welk as his biographer) ran serially in a number of metropolitan newspapers, and made the bestseller lists.

*   *   *

COBURN, Walt   1889-

PERSONAL: Born October 23, 1889, in White Sulphur Springs, Mont.; son of Robert (a cattleman) and Mary (Blessing) Coburn; married July 7, 1927 (wife's maiden name Acheson). *Education:* Manzinata Hall Preparatory School, student, 1910. *Religion:* Roman Catholic. *Agent:* Donald MacCampbell, Inc., 12 East 41st St., New York, N.Y. 10017.

CAREER: Cattleman; free-lance writer, 1922—. *Military service:* U.S. Army Air Service, Signal Corps, 1917-19; became sergeant first class. *Member:* Westerners, Montana Historical Society, Arizona Historical Society, Arizona Cattle Growers, Prescott Press Club.

WRITINGS: The Ringtailed Rannyhans, Century, 1927; *Mavericks,* Century, 1929; *Barb Wire,* Century, 1931; *Walt Coburn's Action Novels,* Fiction House, 1931; *Law Rides the Range,* Century, 1935; *Sky-Pilot Cowboy,* Appleton, 1937.

Pardners of the Dim Trails, Lippincott, 1951; *The Way of a Texan,* Star Guidance, 1953; *Drift Fence,* Hammond, Hammond, 1953, Macfadden, 1970; *The Burnt Ranch,* Hammond, Hammond, 1954, Macfadden, 1970; *Gun Grudge,* Hammond, Hammond, 1955; *Wet Cattle,* Hammond, Hammond, 1955; *The Square Shooter,* Hammond, Hammond, 1955, Macfadden, 1970; *Cayuse,* Hammond, Hammond, 1956; *Border Jumper,* Hammond, Hammond, 1956, Macfadden, 1970; *Beyond the Wild Missouri,* Arcadia House, 1956; *One Step Ahead of the Posse,* Ace Books, 1956; *The Night Branders,* Ace Books, 1956; *Violent Maverick,* Avon, 1957; *Stirrup High,* Messner, 1957; *Fear Branded,* Hammond, Hammond, 1957, Avon, 1971; *Buffalo Run,* Hammond, Hammond, 1958; *Free Rangers,* Hammond, Hammond, 1959; *Invitation to a Hanging,* Avon, 1959.

La Jornada, World Distributors, 1960; *Feud Valley,* Hammond, Hammond, 1960, Tower, 1969; *Guns Blaze on Spiderweb Range,* Hammond, Hammond, 1961, Avon, 1971; *Pioneer Cattleman: The Story of the Circle C Ranch,* University of Oklahoma Press, 1968. Contributor of between eight and nine hundred novelettes and short stories to thirty-seven pulp magazines, 1924-1950. Two pulp magazines were at one time published as *Walt Coburn's Action Novels* and *Walt Coburn's Western Magazine.*

WORK IN PROGRESS: A novel of the Whoop Up country and Hudson's Bay fur trade; Assiniboine Indian legends; an autobiography.

SIDELIGHTS: Coburn gave this summary to CA: "I started writing Western stories in 1922 and after two years of rejection slips I sold around 900 novelettes to 37 different pulp paper magazines and had the cover and feature story in each magazine over those years. The pulps folded around 1950 and since then I have been writing novels.

"I do little research. I knew the early day cow country about which I write, cowmen, cowpunchers, sheepmen, outlaws, Indians, freighters, et al, before barbwire fenced the free range.

"I have never read another Western author's work in my lifetime of writing. I work four or five hours a day, in the mornings. I take Sundays off and a day or two between stories. I ride horseback for relaxation, and swim when I am near the ocean.

"Born and raised in the cattle business, both in Montana and Arizona, I am still interested in the cattle industry. I am proud to say I have many friends among the cattlemen and old time cowhands who are fast becoming a vanishing breed of man.

"As for myself, I have lived a full life and taken my share of hard knocks along with the good fortune that is my writing career. As the late lamented cowboy artist, Charlie Russell, who was my good friend and neighbor in Great Falls, Montana, from the time I was six years old, once remarked; 'If I cash in my chips tonight, I'm ahead of the game.' I feel the same way."

BIOGRAPHICAL/CRITICAL SOURCES: Madeline Matzen, *Writers' Markets and Methods,* [Hollywood], 1939; *Denver Post,* July 4, 1948; *Phoenix Republic,* October 19, 1952.

*   *   *

COCKERELL, H(ugh) A(nthony) L(ewis)   1909-

PERSONAL: Born May 16, 1909, in London, England; son of Lewis (an estate agent) and Winifred Martha Cockerell; married Fanny Jochelman, April 6, 1939; children: Michael, David, Helen. *Education:* King's College, London, B.A., 1936. *Home:* 22 Mapesbury Rd., London N.W.2, England. *Office:* Graduate Business Centre, Gresham College, City University, E.C.2, England.

CAREER: Chartered Insurance Institute, London, England, secretary, 1945-71; City University, Graduate Business Centre, London, England, senior research fellow in insurance studies, 1971—. Visited Israel, 1958, Nigeria, 1960, and North America, 1964, to investigate insurance education. Senator, University of London, 1956—; chairman, British Association for Commercial and Industrial Education, 1962-64; member of United Kingdom National Advisory Council on Education for Industry and Commerce, 1964—. *Military service:* Royal Naval Volunteer Reserve; became lieutenant. *Member:* Chartered Insurance Institute (fellow), British Insurance Law Association (vice-president). *Awards, honors:* Officer, Order of the British Empire.

WRITINGS: Sixty Years of the Chartered Insurance Institute, Chartered Insurance Institute, 1957; *Insurance,* English Universities Press, 1957, 2nd edition, 1970. Contributor to insurance and legal journals.

WORK IN PROGRESS: Studies in insurance law; survey of British insurance records.

SIDELIGHTS: Cockerell speaks French.

*   *   *

COFFMAN, Barbara Frances   1907-

PERSONAL: Born April 3, 1907, in Vineland, Ontario, Canada; daughter of Samuel Frederick (a minister) and Ella (Mann) Coffman. *Education:* McGill University, student, 1929; Goshen College, B.A., 1931. *Religion:* Mennonite. *Home:* Victoria Ave., Vineland, Ontario, Canada.

CAREER: Goshen College, Goshen, Ind., assistant librarian, 1931-34; local correspondent for *St. Catharines Standard,* St. Catharines, Ontario, *Hamilton Spectator,* Hamilton, Ontario, and *Beamsville Express* (weekly), Beamsville, Ontario, 1944-60; now piano teacher. Charter member and secretary of the board, Jordan Historical Museum of the Twenty, 1953-65. *Member:* Pennsylvania German Folklore Society (branch executive and director), Ontario Genealogical Society (director, 1963-64), Ontario Historical Society, Lincoln County Historical Council.

WRITINGS: (Editor with R. Janet Powell) *Lincoln County 1856-1956.* Lincoln County Council, 1956; *His Name was John,* Herald, 1964. Contributor of articles on historical subjects to *Ontario History, Canadian-German Folklore, Mennonite Quarterly Review,* and newspapers.

WORK IN PROGRESS: Story of the Jacob Fry family and the settlement of Pennsylvania Mennonites in Lincoln County, Ontario, in the early 1800's.

*   *   *

COHEN, Benjamin Victor   1894-

PERSONAL: Born September 23, 1894, in Muncie, Ind.; son of Moses and Sarah (Ringold) Cohen. *Education:* University of Chicago, Ph.B., 1914, J.D., 1915; Harvard University, S.J.D., 1916. *Home:* 1727 Massachusetts Ave. N.W., Washington, D.C. 20036.

CAREER: Admitted to Illinois Bar, 1916. Counsel, American Zionist Conferences in London and Paris, 1919-21; attorney in private practice, New York, N.Y., 1922-33; U.S. government posts, 1933-52, serving as associate general counsel of Public Works Administration, 1933-34, general counsel of National Power Policy Commission, 1934-41, assistant to congressional committees in drafting the Securities Act of 1933, the Securities and Exchange Act of 1934, the Public Utility Holding Act of 1935, and the Fair Labor Standards Act of 1937, general counsel of Office of War Mobilization, 1943-45, counselor of Department of State, 1945-47, member of U.S. delegation to United Nations General Assemblies in Paris, and New York, 1948-52, U.S. representative before International Court of Justice, The Hague, 1950, and U.S. representative on United Nations Disarmament Commission, 1952. Member of American delegations to Dumbarton Oakes Conference, Berlin Conference, Council of Foreign Ministers, and Paris Peace Conference in period, 1944-46; legal adviser at other international conferences. Holmes Lecturer, Harvard University, 1961; Niles Lecturer, Hebrew University, 1965. *Member:* Phi Beta Kappa.

WRITINGS: The United Nations: Constitutional Developments, Growth and Possibilities, Harvard University Press, 1961.

COLBY, Elbridge   1891-

PERSONAL: Born October 4, 1891, in New York, N.Y.; son of Charles Edwards and Emily (Carrington) Colby; married Margaret Egan, November 7, 1917; children: William Egan. *Education:* Columbia University, A.B. (magna cum laude), 1912, A.M., 1913, Ph.D., 1922; also graduate of U.S. Army Command and General Staff School. *Religion:* Catholic. *Home:* 4560 Indian Rock Ter., N.W., Washington, D.C. 20007.

CAREER: Instructor in English at Columbia University, New York, N.Y., 1914-15 and University of Minnesota, Minneapolis, 1916-17, 1919-20; U.S. Army, regular officer, 1917-19, 1920-48, serving overseas in Panama, China, and Europe (with headquarters staff, First U.S. Army, in England, France, Belgium, and Germany, 1943-45), and retiring as colonel; George Washington University, Washington, D.C., associate in English, 1939-41, associate professor, 1948-50, professor of journalism, 1950-57. Reporter and feature writer for *St. Paul Pioneer Press*, *Minneapolis Tribune*, and *Washington Post*, 1920-25; editor and writer, *Army-Navy Register*, 1932-42.

MEMBER: American Military Institute, Phi Beta Kappa, Pi Delta Epsilon, Cosmos Club (Washington, D.C.), Naval and Military Club (London; honorary). *Awards, honors*—Civilian: Serbian Red Cross Gold Medal, 1935, for work as member of Mercy Expedition to Serbia in 1915; Order of Mercy (Yugoslavia), 1938; Toulmin Medal of American Society of Military Engineers, 1938; University Medal of Columbia University, 1940; Pi Delta Epsilon Medal of Merit, 1957; Moncado Award of American Military Institute, 1959. Military: Bronze Star, Legion of Merit, and Commendation Ribbon.

WRITINGS: Echo Device in Literature, New York Public Library, 1920; *Life of Thomas Holcroft*, Constable, 1925; *American Militarism*, Society of American Military Engineers, 1934; *English Catholic Poets*, Bruce, 1935; *Army Talk*, Princeton University Press, 1942; *Masters of Mobile Warfare*, Princeton University Press, 1943; *Theodore Winthrop*, Twayne, 1965; *The First Army in Europe*, Government Printing Office, 1969. Contributor to *Dictionary of American Biography*, *Encyclopedia of Social Sciences*, *Dictionary of American History*, *World Book Encyclopedia*, *Encyclopedia Americana*; also contributor to *Best Sellers*, 1959—, *Infantry Journal*, *American Mercury*, and to law reviews (articles on military affairs).

WORK IN PROGRESS: History of the National Guard of the United States.

*   *   *

COLE, J(ohn) A(lfred)   1905-

PERSONAL: Born April 21, 1905, in London, England; son of John (an engineer) and Edith Alice (Turner) Cole; married Joan Doris Read, May 23, 1929. *Education:* University of London, Diploma in Social Studies. *Home:* 4 Crane Ct., Fleet St., London E.C. 4, England.

CAREER: Self-employed writer, 1930-41; British War Office, London, England, civilian assistant to General Staff, 1943-46; Control Commission for Germany, British Element, intelligence officer in Germany, 1946-50; British Foreign Office, official in Berlin, Germany, 1950-56; British Broadcasting Corp., London, England, head of German audience research department, 1958-73. Part-time writer for the British Broadcasting Corp. German Service, 1973—. *Military service:* British Army, Intelligence Corps, 1941-43; became sergeant.

WRITINGS: Come Dungeon Dark, Faber, 1935; *This Happy Breed*, Faber, 1937; *A Stranger Myself*, Faber, 1938; *Just Back from Germany*, Faber, 1938; *To Make Us Glad*, Faber, 1941; *My Host Michel*, Faber, 1956, published as *Germany My Host*, Abelard, 1957; *Nobody Got Into Trouble*, Faber, 1962; *Lord Haw-Haw—and William Joyce*, Faber, 1964, Farrar, Straus, 1965; (contributor) A. S. Osley, editor, *Calligraphy and Palaeography*, Faber, 1965.

WORK IN PROGRESS: A book tentatively titled *Credit Neither Given Nor Asked*.

SIDELIGHTS: Cole is competent in German.

*   *   *

COLE, Luella (Winifred)   1893-19(?)

PERSONAL: Born April 1, 1893, in Haverhill, Mass.; daughter of Harry Joshua (a lawyer) and Bessie (Garland) Cole; married Robert H. Lowie (a professor of anthropology), August 23, 1933 (deceased). *Education:* Vassar College, A.B., 1916; Indiana University, M.A., 1920, Ph.D., 1922. *Religion:* Episcopalian. *Home:* 2521 Benvenue Ave., Berkeley, Calif.

CAREER: Ohio State University, Columbus, 1921-31, began as instructor, became associate professor of educational psychology; University of Utah, Salt Lake City, professor of educational psychology, 1933; editor and writer of textbooks in educational psychology, beginning, 1933. Adviser to veterinarians on the psychology of animals.

WRITINGS: (With S. L. Pressey) *Essential Preparation for College*, Farrar & Rinehart, 1932; *Psychology of the Elementary School Subjects*, Farrar & Rinehart, 1934; (with J. M. Ferguson) *Students' Guide to Efficient Study*, new edition, Farrar & Rinehart, 1935, 4th edition, Holt, 1960; *Psychology of Adolescence*, Farrar & Rinehart, 1936, workbook, Rinehart, 1954, 7th edition, with Irma Nelson Hall, Holt, 1970; *Improvement of Reading*, Farrar & Rinehart, 1938; *Teaching in the Elementary School*, Farrar & Rinehart, 1939; *Background for College Teaching*, Farrar & Rinehart, 1940; *Teacher's Handbook of Technical Vocabulary*, Public-School, 1940; *Attaining Maturity*, Farrar & Rinehart, 1944; (with J. J. B. Morgan) *Psychology of Childhood and Adolescence*, Rinehart, 1947; *History of Education: From Socrates to Montessori*, Rinehart, 1950; (with husband, Robert H. Lowie) *Practical Handbook for Planning a Trip to Europe*, Vantage, 1957. Ghost writer of other books, and compiler of intelligence and achievement tests.

SIDELIGHTS: Luella Cole once told *CA* that she maintained "a clinic for cats with emotional problems (sent me by vets, since I'm an animal psychologist). Recently I published a small book on cats and people, in which I show how cats can be placed so as to help solve human problems or meet human needs."

(Deceased)

*   *   *

COLES, Cyril Henry   1899-1965
(Manning Coles, Francis Gaite, joint pseudonyms)

PERSONAL: Born June 11, 1899, in London, England; son of David and Rose Elizabeth (Gaite) Coles; married Dorothy Cordelia Smith, 1934; children: Peter, Michael. *Education:* Attended school in Petersfield, Hampshire, England. *Home:* Gaite House, East Meon, Petersfield, Hampshire, England. *Agent:* Curtis Brown Ltd., 60 East 56th St., New York, N.Y. 10022.

CAREER: Apprenticed to shipbuilding firm, John I. Thornycroft, Southampton, England, became manager of millfitting department; left in mid-twenties to travel around the world, staying for a long period in Australia where he worked as a garage manager, railway employee, and daily columnist on a Melbourne newspaper; returned to England in 1928, and in 1936 began writing detective stories and thrillers with a neighbor, Adelaide Frances Oke Manning, a partnership that continued until her death in 1959. Military service: British Army, Infantry and Intelligence, World War I; served in France and Germany; became major.

WRITINGS—All mystery novels (except as otherwise noted) with Adelaide Frances Oke Manning under joint pseudonym, Manning Coles: Drink to Yesterday, Hodder & Stoughton, 1940, Knopf, 1941, reissued with an introduction by James Nelson, Norton, 1967; Pray Silence, Hodder & Stoughton, 1940, published in America as A Toast to Tomorrow, Doubleday, 1941; They Tell No Tales, Hodder & Stoughton, 1941, Doubleday, 1942; This Fortress, Doubleday, 1942; Great Caesar's Ghost (juvenile), Doubleday, 1943 (published in England as The Emperor's Bracelet, University of London Press, 1947); Without Lawful Authority, Doubleday, 1943; Green Hazard, Doubleday, 1945; The Fifth Man, Doubleday, 1946; Let the Tiger Die, Doubleday, 1947; With Intent to Deceive, Doubleday, 1947 (published in England as A Brother for Hugh, Hodder & Stoughton, 1947); Among Those Absent, Doubleday, 1948; Diamonds to Amsterdam, Doubleday, 1949; Not Negotiable, Doubleday, 1949.

Dangerous by Nature, Doubleday, 1950; Now or Never, Doubleday, 1951; Alias Uncle Hugo, Doubleday, 1952; Night Train to Paris, Doubleday, 1952; A Knife for the Juggler, Hodder & Stoughton, 1953, Doubleday, 1964, reissued as The Vengeance Man, Pyramid Publications, 1967; All that Glitters, Doubleday, 1954 (published in England as Not For Export, Hodder & Stoughton, 1954); Brief Candles, Doubleday, 1954 (published in England under pseudonym Francis Gaite, Hodder & Stoughton, 1954); Happy Returns, Doubleday, 1955 (published in England as Family Matter, Hodder & Stoughton, 1956); The Man in the Green Hat, Doubleday, 1955; The Basle Express, Doubleday, 1956; Birdwatcher's Quarry, Doubleday, 1956; The Far Traveller, Doubleday, 1956; Death of an Ambassador: A Tommy Hambledon Story, Doubleday, 1957 (also published in Hugh-a-Bye Murder, by David Alexander, Walter J. Black, 1957); Three Beans, Hodder & Stoughton, 1957; Come and Go, Doubleday, 1958 (published in England under pseudonym Francis Gaite, Hodder & Stoughton, 1958); No Entry, Doubleday, 1958; Duty Free, Doubleday, 1959 (published in England under pseudonym Francis Gaite, Hodder & Stoughton, 1959); The Exploits of Tommy Hambledon (includes Drink to Yesterday, A Toast to Tomorrow, and Alias Uncle Hugo), Doubleday, 1959; Crime in Concrete, Hodder & Stoughton, 1959, published in America as Concrete Crime, Doubleday, 1960; Nothing to Declare (short stories), Doubleday, 1960.

Novels with Tom Hammerton, under joint pseudonym Manning Coles: Search for a Sultan, Doubleday, 1961 (also published in The Cup, the Blade, or the Gun, by Mignon Eberhart, Walter J. Black, 1961); The House at Pluck's Gutter, Hodder & Stoughton, 1963.

Contributor of articles on engineering, travel, and model making to magazines.

SIDELIGHTS: The Manning Coles books have been translated into Japanese, Lebanese, and a number of European languages. Avocational interests: Model making, travel, flying.

BIOGRAPHICAL/CRITICAL SOURCES: New York Times, October 15, 1965.

(Died October 9, 1965)

*   *   *

COLES, Kaines Adlard   1901-

PERSONAL: Born September 1, 1901, in London, England; son of Henry Verney and Ethel (Adlard) Coles; married Lilian Mabel Clegg, 1923; children: Arnaud Mary, Robert Ross Adlard. Education: Clare College, Cambridge, B.A., 1923, M.A., 1928. Politics: Conservative. Religion: Church of England. Home: Ailsa Croft, Poles Lane, Lymington, England.

CAREER: Chartered accountant. Cash Stone & Co., England, partner, 1926-42; Adlard Coles Ltd., (publishers), London, England, managing director, 1933-61, chairman and advisory editor, 1961-68. Chairman, Southern Counties Hotels Ltd., Southampton, 1948—. Yachtsman, London, England, editor and proprietor, 1937-52; competitor in ocean races, and winner of Transatlantic Race, 1950. Military service: Royal Naval Volunteer Reserve, 1942-45; became lieutenant. Member: Royal Cruising Club, Royal Ocean Racing Club, other yachting clubs. Awards, honors: Named Yachtsman of the Year, 1957; Gold Medal, Royal Institute of Navigation, 1971.

WRITINGS: In Broken Water, Seeley, Service & Co., 1925, De Graff, 1956; Close Hauled, Seeley, Service & Co., 1926; Income Tax and the Business Man, Crosby Lockwood & Son, 1931; Income Tax and the Professional Man, Crosby Lockwood & Son, 1931; In Finnish Waters: From Estonia to Sweden, Edward Arnold, 1932; Emergency Finance for Small Business, Crosby Lockwood & Son, 1932; Good Investing, Jordan & Sons, 1933; Incomplete Records: The Preparation and Audit of Accounts, Gee & Co., 1935; Creeks and Harbours of the Solent, Edward Arnold, 1933, 7th edition, 1963; Norie's Summary of the Yacht Racing Rules, Imray, Laurie. Norie & Wilson, 1936; Sailing and Cruising, Scribner, 1937, 2nd edition, Batsford, 1949; Mary Anne Among 10,000 Islands, Witherby, 1938; (with John Macdonald) Income Tax Explained, Jordan & Sons, 1938; Sailing on the South Coast, Faber, 1939, revised edition published as Pocket Pilot for the South Coast 1950, 3rd edition published as South Coast Harbours, 1962.

Sailing Days, Ross & Co., 1944, 5th edition, 1950; Accountancy, Ross & Co., 1946; More Sailing Days, Ross & Co., 1947, 2nd edition, 1951; Accountancy Careers, Gee & Co., revised edition, 1948; North Atlantic: Boat Against Boat Over 3,000 Miles, Ross & Co., 1950, Norton, 1951; Merchant Ships: British Built, Coles, 1952; (with Douglas Phillips-Burt) Yachts and Their Recognition (also see below), Coles, 1953; (editor) Merchant Ships: World Built, 1952-, Coles, 1954; Channel Harbours and Anchorages: Solent to Portland; Barfleur to St. Malo, Including the Channel Islands, Edward Arnold, 1956, 2nd edition, 1963; Sailing Yachts: Types and Classes (incorporating Yachts and Their Recognition), Coles with Harrap, 1958; (with John Fisher) Sailing: Handling and Craft, Coles with DeGraff, 1958; Biscay Harbours and Anchorages, two volumes, Coles with Harrap, 1959; North Brittany Harbours and Anchorages, Coles, 1965; North Biscay Pilot: Brest to La Gironde, Coles 1970.

Editor, *Yachtsman's Annual and Who's Who*, 1938-51, later editions published as *The Yachtsman's Annual* and *The Yachting World Annual*, and two editions, 1949-50 and 1950-51, edited jointly with I. Proctor. Inventor of yachting games "Ship-a-Hoy," "Flotilla," and others. Contributor to yachting magazines.

WORK IN PROGRESS: Heavy Weather Sailing.

* * *

COLLINS, F(rederick) Herbert 1890-

PERSONAL: Born February 2, 1890, in London, England, son of Herbert (a business executive) and Elizabeth Jane (Campsill) Collins; married Winifred Smith, August 16, 1919. *Education:* Latymer Upper School, student, 1900-1908; University of Paris, student, 1909-11; University of London, B.A. (with honors), 1914, M.A. (with distinction), 1924. *Politics:* Conservative. *Religion:* Church of England. *Home:* 45 Arlington Ave., Goring-on-Sea, Sussex, England.

CAREER: Manchester Grammar School, Manchester, England, head of modern side, 1920-28; high school principal in Chichester, England, 1928-34; Ministry of Education, H.M. Inspector of Schools, London, England, staff inspector for modern languages, 1934-51. British Institute in Paris, member of council of administration, 1937—. *Military service:* Derbyshire Yeomanry Regiment, 1914-18; became lance sergeant. *Member:* Authors Club, English-Speaking Union. *Awards, honors:* Companion of Order of St. Michael and St. George, 1949; Medal of Honour, University of Dijon, 1954; honorary Docteur de l'Universite, University of Strasbourg, 1956.

WRITINGS: Conteurs Francis, Macmillan (London), 1950; *Le Charmant Pays de France*, Macmillan, 1953; *La France au Travail*, Macmillan, 1957; *Talma: Biography of an Actor*, Hill & Wang, 1964.

WORK IN PROGRESS: A critical edition of Victor Hugo's *Ruy Blas*, publication expected by Macmillan (London).

AVOCATIONAL INTERESTS: British, American, and French theatre.

* * *

COLLINS, Frederica Joan Hale 1904-
(Freda Collins)

PERSONAL: Born May 15, 1904, in Richmond, Surrey, England; daughter of Frederic Hale and Naomie (Crispin) Collins. *Education:* Attended St. Paul's Girls' School, London, England. *Religion:* Church of England. *Home:* 26A Addison Gardens, London W. 14, England.

CAREER: Author and playwright, writing mainly for children. Lecturer on children's drama and religious drama; former drama adviser, Children's Council, Church of England. *Member:* Religious Drama Society. *Awards, honors:* First prize of the Playwrights Club for "The Fortieth Man," produced at Fortune Theatre, 1937.

WRITINGS—All under name Freda Collins: *Acting Games from History*, Pearson, 1935, revised edition published as *Put On the Armour of Light*, S.P.C.K., 1955; *Children in the Market Place*, University of London Press, 1943, 2nd edition, J. Garnet Miller, 1968; *Christian Playmaking*, University of London Press, 1952; *The Mountain of Prayer*, Church Information Board, 1955; *The Voice of God*, Faith Press, 1959; *Yes, God*, Mowbray & Co., 1959.

Juvenile books—All published by University of London Press except as indicated: *The Brownies at No. 9*, Harrap, 1936; *Goodnight Bible Stories*, Mowbray & Co., 1946; *Every Child's Saint Stories*, Mowbray & Co., 1948; *Jesus in Palestine*, 1949; *Pow-Wow Stories*, 1949.

The Beauty Quest Book, 1954; *The Pack That Ran Itself*, 1956; *The Puffing Billy*, Dolphin Book Co., 1956; *The Woodland Pack*, 1957; *The Brownie Year*, 1957; *Barny and the Big House Pack*, 1958; *The Shrove-Tide Fair*, Faith Press, 1960; *Do My Best Brownie Book*, 1960; *The Silent Three*, 1961; *Pack Tales*, 1962; *A Year Book of Modern Heroes*, Mowbray & Co., 1963; *The Good Turn Hunters*, Brockhampton Press, 1963; *The Brownies and the Fam-Pig*, Brockhampton Press, 1964.

Plays: *The Fortieth Man* (one-act), J. Garnet Miller, 1937; *The Foolishness of God* (one-act), Samuel French, 1938; *The Centurion* (one-act), Nelson, 1940; *Eight Folk Tale Plays*, Harrap, 1940; *Acting Games*, A. Pearson, 1947, revised edition, University of London Press, 1947; *Adventures in Burma* (juvenile), S.P.G., 1948; *Cyprian*, S.P.C.K., 1949; *The Blind Witness* (one-act), Edinburgh House Press, 1949.

The Christmas Story (juvenile), Mowbray & Co., 1950; *Not Martyrs* (one-act), S.P.C.K., 1951; *My Plays—Then Yours* (with production notes), Harrap, 1951; *Redemption* (one-act, in verse), Mowbray & Co., 1952; *Five More Christian Plays* (juvenile), S.P.C.K., 1952; *Five Modern Christian Plays*, Mowbray & Co., 1955; (with Alison G. Campbell) *No Room* (one-act), J. Garnet Miller, 1955; *Let's Prepare a Nativity Play* [with] *The Angels at Bethlehem*, J. Garnet Miller, 1955, also separate edition of *The Angels at Bethlehem* (juvenile), 1955; *Christmas with Saint Francis* (juvenile), Mowbray & Co., 1956; *Simple Bible Plays* (juvenile), Mowbray & Co., 1958; *Outside the Stable* (juvenile), Faith Press, 1958; *Folk Tale Plays* (juvenile), Samuel French, 1958.

Also author of six plays produced on British Broadcasting Corp. "Schools Religious Broadcast" and on Canadian Broadcasting Corp. programs. Contributor of short stories and articles to British periodicals.

WORK IN PROGRESS: The Pack Mascot, a Brownie book and sequel to *The Good Turn Hunters*; *The Green Packet*, a children's adventure story based on author's tour of New Zealand.

SIDELIGHTS: Frederica Collins began writing at eight, had her first fairy story published at fifteen, and is best known for her plays and Brownie stories. She owned a brindled Cairn for eleven years and after his death featured the dog in several Brownie books (*The Pack That Ran Itself*, *Barny and the Big House Pack*, etc.).

* * *

COLLINS, L(ewis) John 1905-

PERSONAL: Born March 23, 1905, in Hawkhurst, Kent, England; son of Arthur and Hannah Priscilla Collins; married Diana Clavering Elliot, October, 1939; children: Andrew, Richard, Peter, Mark. *Education:* Attended Sidney Sussex College, Cambridge, and Wescott House; M.A. (Cambridge) and M.A. (Oxford). *Home:* 2 Amen Ct., London E.C. 4, England.

CAREER: Clergyman, Church of England. Curate of Whitstable, 1928-29; Sidney Sussex College, Cambridge University, Cambridge, England, chaplain, 1929-31, vice-principal, 1934-37; Oriel College, Oxford University, Oxford, England, dean, 1938-48; St. Paul's Cathedral, London, England, minor canon, 1931-34, canon, 1948—. Christian Action, chairman, 1946-73, president, 1959—; chairman, Campaign for Nuclear Disarmament, 1958-64; president of International Defense and Aid Fund, 1964—. *Military service:* Royal Air Force Volunteer Reserve, chaplain, 1940-45. *Member:* Savile Club (London).

WRITINGS: The New Testament Problem, Unicorn Press, 1937; *The Theology of Christian Action*, Hodder & Stoughton, 1949; (contributor) *Three Views on Christianity*, Gollancz, 1962; *Faith Under Fire*, Nelson, Foster & Scott, 1966.

* * *

COLLINS, Myron D(ean) 1901-

PERSONAL: Born November 15, 1901, in Maquoketa, Iowa; son of Charles M. (a physician) and Fannie (Dean) Collins; married Diane G. Skinner, June 10, 1960; children: Jimi St. Leger. *Education:* University of Pennsylvania, student, 1920-23; studied music privately and at University of Chicago Conservatory. *Home:* 1631 Rubenstein Ave., Cardiff-by-the-Sea, Calif. *Office:* San Diego Military Academy, P.O. Box 608, Del Mar, Calif.

CAREER: Professional musician (symphonies, concert bands, light opera, and radio and television), 1917—; also teacher of band instruments, percussion, piano, and theory. Brown Military Academy, San Diego, Calif., assistant director of music, 1937-42; San Diego State College (now San Diego State University), San Diego, Calif., director of bands, 1948-50, then part-time teacher; Army and Navy Academy, Carlsbad, Calif., assistant director of music, 1950-53; Brown Military Academy, bandmaster, 1953-58; San Diego Military Academy, Del Mar, Calif., co-founder and director of music, 1958—. San Diego Civic Light Orchestra, percussionist, 1948—. *Military service:* U.S. Army, 1918-20, 1942-45. *Member:* Music Educators National Conference. All America Association of Contest Judges of Band Music and Drum Corps Percussion, National Association of Rudimental Drummers, National Association of College Wind and Percussion Instructors, American Federation of Musicians, Masons, Shrine, Phi Mu Alpha-Sinfonia.

WRITINGS: "The Snare Drum at School" series, ten books, Highland Music Co., 1950; *Rhythm and Counting*, Pro-Art, 1958; (co-author) *Playing and Teaching Percussion Instruments*, Prentice-Hall, 1962; (co-author) *Stage and Dance Band Drumming*, Kendor Music Co., 1963; *The Snare Drum Instructor*, two volumes, Highland Music Co., 1965.

WORK IN PROGRESS: A book of instructional material for teaching marimba, xylophone, and orchestra bells.

* * *

COLLIS, William Robert Fitzgerald 1900-

PERSONAL: Born February 16, 1900; son of William S. and Edith (Barton) Collis; married Johanna Hogerzeil (a medical doctor); children: Dermot, Robert, Sean, Niall; Edita Zynn and Zsoltan Zynn (adopted). *Education:* Educated at Rugby School, and at Trinity College, Cambridge, 1919-21, Yale University, 1921, King's College Hospital Medical School; M.R.C.S. and L.R.C.P. (London), 1924, M.A. and M.D. (Cambridge), 1929, D.P.H. (Dublin), 1929. *Religion:* Church of Ireland. *Home:* Bo-Island, Newtownmountkennedy, Wicklow, Ireland. *Agent:* Mavis Mc-

Intosh, McIntosh, McKee & Dodds, 30 East 60th St., New York, N.Y. 10022. *Office:* Collis & Ward, 1 Lower Merrion St., Dublin, Ireland.

CAREER: Physician at National Children's Hospital and director of pediatrics at Rotunda Hospital, Dublin, Ireland, 1932-57; physician in Nigeria, 1957—, serving as first director of pediatrics at University College Hospital, Ibadan, 1959-61, later director of Institute of Child Health (research institution), chairman of pediatrics for city of Lagos, and professor of pediatrics; now full-time writer. Member of Red Cross staff at Belsen Concentration Camp, 1945. *Member:* Royal College of Physicians (London; fellow), Royal College of Physicians (Ireland; fellow). *Awards, honors:* Rockefeller Foundation fellowship at Johns Hopkins University Hospital.

WRITINGS: Silver Fleece, Doubleday; *Marrowbone Lane* (play), Runa, 1943; *Straight On,* Methuen, 1947; *The Ultimate Value,* Methuen, 1951; *The Lost and the Found,* Woman's Press (New York), 1953; *Neo-Natal Pediatrics,* Grune, 1959; *A Doctor's Nigeria,* Secker & Warburg, 1960; *African Encounter,* Scribner, 1961; (with O. Adeniyi-Jones) *You and Your Baby,* African Universities Press (Lagos), 1964. Contributor of seventy articles to medical journals. Editor of four textbooks on pediatrics.

WORK IN PROGRESS: A book on Africa; study of wider social and economic problems of Nigeria and other African countries.

* * *

COLSON, Greta (Scotchmur) 1913-

PERSONAL: Born July 3, 1913, in London, England; daughter of Percy Robert and Marion Edith (Clerk) Scotchmur; married C. E. Webber (a dramatist); married second husband, John Nugee Colson (an actor), September 15, 1947; children: (first marriage) Trimnel Felicity Webber. *Education:* Central School of Speech and Drama, London, diploma. *Religion:* Anglican. *Home:* 137 Albert St., London N.W.1, England. *Agent:* John Johnson, 26 Sackville St., London W.1, England. *Office:* New College of Speech and Drama, Ivy House, North End Rd., London N.W.11, England.

CAREER: New College of Speech and Drama, London, England, director.

WRITINGS: Voice Production and Speech, Museum Press, 1963; *Speech Practice,* Museum Press, 1967, 2nd edition, 1970.

* * *

CONDLIFFE, John B(ell) 1891-

PERSONAL: Born December 23, 1891, in Melbourne, Australia; naturalized U.S. citizen, 1945; son of Alfred B. (a potter) and Margaret (Marley) Condliffe; married Olive Grace Mills, June 20, 1916. *Education:* Canterbury University College (now University of Canterbury), Christchurch, New Zealand, B.A., 1914, M.A. (first class honors in economics), 1915, D.Sc., 1928; Gonville and Caius College, Cambridge, graduate study, 1919-20. *Office:* Stanford Research Institute, Menlo Park, Calif. 94025.

CAREER: Canterbury University College (now University of Canterbury), Christchurch, New Zealand, professor of economics, 1920-26; Institute of Pacific Relations, Honolulu, Hawaii, research secretary, 1927-30; University of Michigan, Ann Arbor, professor of economics, 1930-31; League of Nations Secretariat, Geneva, Switzerland, member of Economic Intelligence Service, 1931-37; London School of Economics and Political Science, University of London, London, England, professor of economics, 1940-58; National Council of Applied Economic Research, adviser in India, 1959-60; Stanford Research Institute, Menlo Park, Calif., senior economist 1960—. Visiting professor at Yale University, 1943-44, at Australian National University, Delhi University, and The American University of Beirut, 1950-51; Fulbright professor at Gonville and Caius College, Cambridge University, 1951. Rapporteur, International Studies Conference and International Chamber of Commerce, 1937-39; assistant director, Carnegie Endowment for International Peace, 1943-47. Consultant to U.S. Board of Economic Warfare, 1944, National Bank of Mexico, 1944, Ford Foundation, 1951-52, Reserve Bank of New Zealand, 1958. *Military service:* New Zealand Army, 1916-19; served on Western front, 1917-18.

MEMBER: American Economic Association, Royal Economic Society (England; life member), Economic Society of Australia and New Zealand, American Association for the Advancement of Science (vice-president, 1948). Western Economic Association (president, 1946), Commission for the Organization of Peace, World Affairs Council of Northern California (trustee), Phi Beta Kappa, Sierra Club, Cosmos Club (Washington, D.C.), Bohemian Club (San Francisco).

AWARDS, HONORS: Henry E. Howland Prize of Yale University, 1939, for League of Nations world economic surveys; LL.D., Occidental College, 1942; Wendell L. Willkie Prize of American Political Science Association, 1950, for best international book of the year, *The Commerce of Nations*; Royal Order of the Phoenix (Greece), 1955; D.Litt., University of New Zealand, 1958.

WRITINGS: Short History of New Zealand, Whitcombe & Tombs (Christchurch, New Zealand), 1923; *New Zealand in the Making: A Study of Economic and Social Development*, Allen & Unwin, 1928, 2nd revised edition, 1963; *Problems of the Pacific*, University of Chicago Press, 1928; *China Today*, The World Peace Foundation (Boston), 1929; *Problems of the Pacific, 1929*, University of Chicago Press, 1930; *Reconstruction of World Trade*, Norton, 1940; *Agenda for a Post-War World*, Norton, 1942; *The Commerce of Nations*, Norton, 1950; *The Welfare State in New Zealand* (sequel to *New Zealand in the Making*), Allen & Unwin, 1959; *The Development of Australia*, Ure Smith (Sydney), 1964; *The Economic Outlook for New Zealand*, Whitcombe & Tombs, for the New Zealand Institute of Economic Research, 1969. Author of *Annual World Economic Survey*, League of Nations (Geneva), 1931-37. Editor, Institute of Pacific Relations, 2nd and 3rd conferences, published proceedings, 1969.

WORK IN PROGRESS: Research in economic planning.

* * *

CONLAY, Iris 1910-

PERSONAL: Born January 4, 1910, in Hythe, Kent, England; daughter of W. Lance (a colonial administrator) and G. Maude (Archbold) Conlay. *Education:* Attended Convent of Sacred Heart, Hove, Sussex, England. *Religion:* Roman Catholic. *Home:* 17 Holy Hill, Hampstead, London N.W.3, England.

CAREER: Catholic Herald, art critic, 1950—; Geoffrey Bles Ltd. (publishers), London, England, advertising and publicity manager, 1954—. *Member:* International Art Critics Association.

WRITINGS: (With Peter F. Anson) *The Art of the Church*, Hawthorn, 1964.

WORK IN PROGRESS: Development of modern religious art.

* * *

CONN, Stetson 1908-

PERSONAL: Born October 29, 1908, in Lakewood, Ohio; son of Wallace Thompson (a chemist) and Florence (Stetson) Conn; married Mary Alice Stadden, June 16, 1936; children: Judith Winslow (Mrs. Donald C. Lockerson), Margaret Elizabeth (Mrs. Peter R. Buehler). *Education:* George Washington University, B.A., 1933, M.A., 1934; Yale University, Ph.D., 1938. *Home:* 2513 North Ninth St., Arlington, Va. 22201. *Office:* Office of the Chief of Military History, Department of the Army, Washington, D.C.

CAREER: Department of the Army, Office of the Chief of Military History, historian, 1946-58, chief historian, 1958—. *Member:* American Historical Association, Organization of American Historians, Southern Historical Association, American Military Institute (trustee, 1964—).

WRITINGS: Gibraltar in British Diplomacy in the Eighteenth Century, Yale University Press, 1942; (with Byron Fairchild) *The Framework of Hemisphere Defense*, Government Printing Office, 1960; (with Rose C. Engleman and Fairchild) *Guarding the United States and Its Outposts*, Office of Chief of Military History, Department of the Army, 1964. General editor of series, "U.S. Army in World War II," and other Army publications.

* * *

CONNELL, Francis J. 1888-

PERSONAL: Born January 31, 1888, in Boston, Mass.; son of Timothy J. and Mary (Sheehan) Connell. *Education:* Studied at Boston College, 1905-07, Mount St. Alphonsus Seminary, Esopus, N.Y., 1908-14; Pontifical University of the Angelio, Rome, Italy, S.T.D., 1923. *Home:* 3112 Seventh St., N.E., Washington, D.C. 20017. *Office:* Catholic University of America, Washington, D.C. 20017.

CAREER: Entered Redemptorist Order (Roman Catholic), 1907, ordained priest, 1913. Mount St. Alphonsus Seminary, Esopus, N.Y., professor of dogmatic theology, 1915-21, 1924-40; Catholic University of America, Washington, D.C., associate professor, 1940-48, professor of moral theology, 1948-58, dean of School of Sacred Theology, 1949-57, dean for religious communities, beginning 1957. Consultor, Congregation of Universities and Seminaries, Rome, Italy, beginning 1956. *Member:* Catholic Theological Society of America (president, 1946-47), Knights of Columbus. *Awards, honors:* Pro Ecclesia et Pontifice, 1952; Cardinal Spellman Award, 1955, for theological writings; LL.D., University of Notre Dame, 1952; Seminary of Notre Dame, New Orleans, La., 1957; L.H.D., St. John's University, Brooklyn, N.Y., 1958.

WRITINGS: Reverend Michael J. Sheehan, Mission Church Press, 1926; (editor) Franciscus Ter Haar, *Mixed Marriages and Their Remedies*, Pustet, 1933; (translator) Clement Henze, *Our Lady of Perpetual Help*, Catholic Books, 1940; *Morals in Politics and Professions*, Newman, 1946; (author of text, summarizations, and study helps) *Baltimore Catechism No. 3*, revised edition, Benziger, 1949, new Confraternity edition, 1954; *Outlines of Moral Theology*, Bruce, 1953, 2nd edition, 1958; *Sunday Sermon Out-*

lines, Pustet, 1955; *Father Connell Answers Moral Questions*, edited by E. P. Weitzel, Catholic University of America Press, 1959; *Spiritual and Pastoral Conferences to Priests*, Newman, 1962; (with E. P. Weitzel) *More Answers to Today's Moral Problems*, Catholic University of America Press, 1964; (contributor) J. P. Lerhinan, editor, *Background to Morality*, Desclee, 1964; *The Seven Sacraments: What They Are, What They Do* (first published as pamphlet series), Paulist Press, 1965. Author of pamphlets on theological subjects. Contributor to *American Ecclesiastical Review*, 1943—.

WORK IN PROGRESS: Studies in moral theology.

BIOGRAPHICAL/CRITICAL SOURCES: American Ecclesiastical Review, June, 1958.

* * *

CONNETT, Eugene Virginius III 1891-1969 (Virginius)

PERSONAL: Born March 8, 1891, in South Orange, N.J.; son of Eugene V., Jr. (a manufacturer) and May (Brewer) Connett; married Kathryn Elise Underhill, November 5, 1913; children: Elise Brewer (Mrs. Donald W. Baker), Eugene Virginius IV. *Education:* Princeton University, Litt.B., 1912. *Politics:* Republican. *Religion:* Episcopalian. *Home:* 170 Turrell Ave., South Orange, N.J. 07079.

CAREER: E. V. Connett & Co., New York, N.Y., vice-president, 1912-25; James N. Johnston, Inc., New York, N.Y., vice-president, 1926-27; Derrydale Press, New York, N.Y., president, 1927-42; New Jersey State Highway Department, Trenton, deputy commissioner, 1942-46; D. Van Nostrand Co., Inc., Princeton, N.J., editor of sporting books, 1947-64; retired, 1964. *Military service:* U.S. Army, Chemical Warfare Service, 1918; became sergeant first class. *Member:* Grolier Club, Royal Philatelic Society (London), Collectors Club (New York; former governor), Anglers' Club (New York; president, 1921-22), New York Yacht Club, Dutch Treat Club (New York), Bellport Bay Yacht Club (commodore, 1941-42). *Awards, honors:* Collectors Club Medal for best contribution to club journal; Boston Museum Medal for best photograph in salon.

WRITINGS: Wing Shooting and Angling, Scribner, 1922; *Magic Hours*, Derrydale Press, 1927; *Any Luck?*, Doubleday, 1933; *Fishing a Trout Stream*, Derrydale Press, 1934; *Random Casts*, Derrydale Press, 1939; *The Small Boat Skipper and His Problems*, Norton, 1952; *Duck Decoys: How to Make Them, How to Paint Them, How to Rig Them*, Van Nostrand, 1953; *Adventures in Cover Collecting*, Van Nostrand, 1955; *My Friend the Trout*, Van Nostrand, 1961.

Editor: *Duck Shooting Along the Atlantic Tidewater*, Morrow, 1947; *Yachting in North America Along the Atlantic and Pacific and Gulf Coasts and on the Great Lakes and on the Western and Canadian Lakes and Rivers*, Van Nostrand, 1948; *American Sporting Dogs*, Van Nostrand, 1948; *Wildfowling in the Mississippi Flyway*, Van Nostrand, 1949.

Editor of more than two hundred books. Contributor to *Sportsman, Country Life, English Field, Collier's, Field and Stream, American Angler, Yachting*, and other magazines and newspapers.

BIOGRAPHICAL SOURCES: Time, December 19, 1938.

(Died September 20, 1969)

CONNETTE, Earle 1910-

PERSONAL: Surname rhymes with "bonnet"; born July 30, 1910; son of Claude Christopher and Ara (Wright) Connette; married Ann Muehler (a librarian), August 10, 1935. *Education:* Indiana State College (now Indiana State University), B.S., 1933, M.S., 1935; Indiana University, Ph.D., 1944; University of Denver, M.A., 1963. *Politics:* Democrat. *Religion:* Protestant. *Home:* 903 East C St., Moscow, Idaho.

CAREER: Murray State College, Murray, Ky., assistant professor of music, 1933-36; Columbia University, New York, N.Y., visiting instructor, 1936-37; North Texas State University, Denton, assistant professor of music, 1940-41; University of Missouri, Columbia, associate professor of music, 1944-46; Syracuse University, associate professor of music, 1947-49; Washington State University, Pullman, associate professor of music, 1949-50, social science librarian, 1963-65, librarian, and chief of manuscripts-archives division, 1966—. *Military service:* U.S. Army, Infantry, 1941-44; served as captain. *Member:* Society of American Archivists, Pacific Northwest Library Association.

WRITINGS: (Compiler) *Pacific Northwest Quarterly Index*, Shoestring, 1963. Contributor of about sixty monographic essays and research reports to scholarly periodicals, 1935-44.

WORK IN PROGRESS: Compiling *Idaho Yesterdays Index*, Volumes I-X; a 2nd cumulation of *Pacific Northwest Quarterly Index*.

AVOCATIONAL INTERESTS: Trout fishing, mountain climbing, amateur photography.

* * *

CONNOLLY, Francis X(avier) 1909-1965

PERSONAL: Born June 24, 1909, in New York, N.Y.; son of Thomas (a post office superintendent) and Lillian (Flynn) Connolly; married Mary T. Kennedy, September 7, 1940; children: Katharine Connolly Menze, Elisabeth Connolly Leser, Joseph. *Education:* Fordham University, A.B., 1930, M.A., 1933, Ph.D., 1937. *Politics:* Democrat. *Religion:* Roman Catholic. *Home:* 14 N. Chatsworth Ave., Larchmont, N.Y. *Office:* Fordham University, Bronx, N.Y.

CAREER: Fordham University, Bronx, N.Y., instructor, 1930-36, associate professor, 1936-50, professor of English, 1951-65. Member of editorial board, Catholic Book Club; committee member of National Catholic High School Book Report Program. Word authority on National Broadcasting Co. television program, "Word for Word." *Military service:* U.S. Naval Reserve, 1943-46; became lieutenant. *Member:* Catholic Poetry Society of America (founder; chairman of board of directors, 1940-48), Catholic Renascence Society (former president two terms), Catholic Writers Guild (chairman of Golden Books Award Committee), Modern Language Association of America, Catholic Conference on Intellectual and Cultural Affairs, College English Association, Irish Historical Society. *Awards, honors: Spirit* Award for Poetry, Catholic Poetry Society of America, 1957; Fordham College Alumni Association Achievement Award for Education, 1961.

WRITINGS: Literature: The Channel of Culture, Harcourt, 1948; (editor with John G. Brunini) *Stories of Our Century by Catholic Authors*, Lippincott, 1949, reprinted by Doubleday, 1959; *Give Beauty Back*, Dutton, 1950; (with John C. Hodges) *Harbrace College Handbook*, Harcourt, 1951; *A Rhetoric Case Book*, Harcourt, 1953, 3rd edition (edited by Gerald Levin), 1969; (editor) *The Types of Literature*, Harcourt, 1955; *St. Philip of the Joyous Heart*, Farrar, Straus, 1957; (editor and author of introduction) Robert H. Benson, *The King's Achievement*, Kenedy, 1957; (editor with Donald Sears) *The Sentence in Context: Essentials of Grammar and Rhetoric*, Harcourt, 1959; *Poetry: Its Power and Wisdom*, Scribner, 1960; (with John E. Warriner and Richard M. Ludwig) *Advanced Composition: A Book of Models for Writing*, Harcourt, 1961, 2nd edition, 1968; *Wisdom of the Saints*, Pocket Books, 1963; (editor) *A Newman Reader*, Doubleday, 1964; (editor) *Man and His Measure*, Harcourt, 1964; (editor) *Newman's 'Apologia': A Classic Reconsidered*, Harcourt, 1964; (editor) *Adventures in Reading*, Harcourt, 1968; (compiler) *The Art of Rhetoric*, completed and edited by Gerald Levin, Harcourt, 1968. Editor of critical essays on poetry for *Spirit* magazine.

(Died November 17, 1965)

*   *   *

CONRAD, Will C.   1882-

PERSONAL: Born September 25, 1882, in Clarks Hill, Ind.; son of William H. (a farmer) and Martha (Cross) Conrad; married Vida Clover, November 17, 1907 (deceased); children: Evelyn Conrad Brown, William Ross. *Education:* Indiana University, A.B., 1906. *Home:* 12065 North Lake Shore Dr., Mequon, Wis. 53092 (June to September); 2161 Via Escalera, Los Altos, Calif. 94022 (October to May).

CAREER: High school teacher in Richmond, Ind., 1910-13, in Milwaukee, Wis., 1914-15; *Milwaukee Journal*, Milwaukee, Wis., 1915-59, began as reporter, successively assistant city editor, feature editor, Sunday editor, editorial writer, and contributing editor. *Member:* National Conference of Editorial Writers (founding member), Milwaukee Press Club.

WRITINGS: The Newspaper in the Classroom, Milwaukee Journal, 1938, revised edition, 1948; *A Layman Views the Atom*, Milwaukee Journal, 1950; (with Dale Wilson and Kathleen Wilson) *The Milwaukee Journal—The First Eighty Years*, University of Wisconsin Press, 1964.

WORK IN PROGRESS: A novel with a newspaper background.

*   *   *

CONRADIS, Heinz   1907-

PERSONAL: Born September 9, 1907, in Bremen, Germany; son of Heinrich and Elizabeth (Picker) Conradis; married Irmgard Bach; children: Anke, Ulrike, Wolfgang. *Education:* Technische Hochschule Muenchen, Diplom-Vorexamen, 1928; Technische Hochschule Berlin, Diplom-Ingenieur, 1931, Doktor-Ingenieur, 1939. *Religion:* Evangelisch. *Home:* Verdener Strasse 61, 2133 Ottersberg/Kreis, Verden, West Germany.

CAREER: Worked for Bremer Kreditbank AG, Bremen, Germany, 1932; Focke-Wulf-Flugzeugbau G.m.b.H. (aircraft works), Bremen, Germany, staff leader concerned with wind tunnels, aerodynamics, patents, and research, 1932-45; City of Bremen, Germany, Senator fuer das Bauwesen, 1947-60, Regierungsrat, Senator fuer Wirtschaft und Aussenhandel, 1960—. *Member:* Verein Deutscher Ingenieure. *Awards, honors:* Max Eyth-Preisausschreiben, 1949, for short story "Der verhaengnisvolle Dreikantschaber."

WRITINGS: Die Nassabaggerung bis zur Mitte des 19. Jahrhunderts, VDI (Duesseldorf), 1940; *Nerven, Herz und Rechenschieber*, Musterschmidt (Goettingen), 1955, 2nd edition published as *Forschen und Fliegen*, 1959, translation by Kenneth Kettle published as *Design for Flight: The Kurt Tank Story*, Macdonald, 1960. Has written a great number of short stories for newspapers, magazines, and radio broadcasting.

*   *   *

COOKE, Gilbert William   1899-

PERSONAL: Born December 4, 1899, in Hammond, Minn.; son of Thomas William (a farmer) and Anna Franceska (Pfeiffer) Cooke; married Lottie M. Herman, July 9, 1926; children: Dean W., Wayne T., Janet F. (Mrs. Thomas Benbrook), Allen J., Daniel L., James L. *Education:* University of Minnesota, B.S., 1923, M.A., 1926; University of Wisconsin, Ph.D., 1936. *Politics:* Democrat. *Home:* 27 Ranch Ct., Bowling Green, Ohio 43402.

CAREER: Public school teacher in Grand Rapids, Minn., and Hudson, Wis., 1923-29; University of Pittsburgh, Uniontown Center, Pa., instructor in political science, 1929-33; University of North Dakota, Grand Forks, assistant professor of economics, 1934-37; Bowling Green State University, Bowling Green, Ohio, assistant professor, 1937-39, associate professor, 1939-48, professor of business administration, 1948-69. Trustee, Bowling Green Chamber of Commerce, 1939-42; Board of Education, member, 1955-63, president, 1960-61; City Planning Commission, member, 1956-61, chairman, 1958-59. Boy Scouts of America, Toledo Area Council member, 1939—. *Member:* American Economic Association, American Finance Association, American Political Science Association, Financial Analysts of Toledo, Wood County Democratic Club (treasurer). *Awards, honors:* Silver Beaver award, Boy Scouts of America; Sigma Alpha Epsilon alumni award, 1960.

WRITINGS: (Contributor) *Introduction to Modern Economics*, Dryden Press, 1952; (chief author) *An Introductory Survey of Business Management*, W. C. Brown, 1955; (contributor) *Public Finance*, Pitman, 1959; (editor and chief author) *Financial Institutions: Their Role in the American Economy*, Simmons-Boardman, 1962; *The Stock Markets*, Simmons-Boardman, 1964, revised edition, Schenkman, 1969; (with Edwin C. Bomeli) *Business Financial Management*, Houghton, 1967.

*   *   *

COOPER, Alfred Morton   1890-
(Morley Cooper)

PERSONAL: Born June 12, 1890, in Kankakee, Ill.; son of Edward Lawson and Louisa Armilda (Riggs) Cooper; married Madge Ringland (a school teacher), April 27, 1937; children: Eugene Walter, William Edward, Elsie Lawson. *Education:* University of Washington, Seattle, student, 1918-20. *Politics:* Republican. *Religion:* Protestant. *Home and office:* P.O. Box 1442, Indio, Calif. 92202. *Agent:* Howard E. Hill, P.O. Box 628, Culver City, Calif. 90230.

CAREER: Puget Sound Power & Light Co., Seattle, Wash., chief operator, 1912-20; Kansas City (Mo.) public schools, teacher, 1920-23; Western Electric Co., Chicago, Ill., training supervisor, 1923-26; consultant in industrial training, 1926-31; University of Southern California, Los Angeles, instructor in School of Government, 1931-34; Los Angeles (Calif.) Department of Water & Power, educational expert, 1934-38; free-lance writer, 1938—. Administrative assistant with California State Department of Employment. *Military service:* U.S. Navy, 1907-11. *Member:* National Writers Club, Authors League of America.

WRITINGS: How to Supervise People, McGraw, 1941, 4th edition, 1963; *How to Conduct Conferences,* McGraw, 1942, 2nd edition, 1946; *Employee Training,* McGraw, 1942; *Supervision of Governmental Employees,* McGraw, 1943; *Cruising to Florida,* McGraw, 1946; *The Cruising Yacht,* McGraw, 1947; *The Trailer Book,* Harper, 1950; (compiler) *Audubon Book of True Nature Stories* (anthology), Crowell, 1958. Contributor of three thousand articles to some one hundred magazines, including *Harper's* and *U.S. News and World Report.* Contributing editor and columnist, *Modern Machine Shop.*

WORK IN PROGRESS: In Quest of a Grandfather; a novel, *Desert of Waters.*

SIDELIGHTS: How to Supervise People has been in print continuously since 1941; it appeared in hardcover for twenty-three years, then was issued as a paperback in 1963. Cooper was a ranking yachtsman for some years, and also is considered an authority on such diverse subjects as safety, trailering, and animal life of the desert.

* * *

COPE, (Vincent) Zachary 1881-
(Zeta)

PERSONAL: Born February 14, 1881, in Hull, England; son of Thomas John and Celia Ann (Truscott) Cope; married Agnes Dora Newth, 1909 (died, 1922); married Alice May Watts, 1923 (died, 1944); children: Philippa Agnes Lois (Mrs. Michael Grace). *Education:* St. Mary's Hospital Medical School, University of London, B.A., 1899, M.B., B.S. (honors), 1905, M.D., 1907, M.S., 1909. *Home:* 13 Blausford Ave., Oxford, England.

CAREER: Fellow of Royal College of Surgeons, 1909; former surgeon at St. Mary's Hospital, Paddington, London, England, and Bolingbroke Hospital, Wandsworth Common, London, England; now consulting surgeon at both hospitals. Royal College of Surgeons, Hunterian Professor, 1916, 1920, 1925, 1927, Bradshaw Lecturer, 1949, Tomes and Vicary Lecturer, 1952. Medical Manpower Committee, former chairman. Pitman Medical Publishing Co. Ltd., director. Royal Medical Benevolent Fund, president. *Military service:* Royal Army Medical Corps, 1916-19; became captain; served in Iraq; mentioned in dispatches; sector hospital officer, London, World War II. *Member:* British Medical Association (vice-president), Royal Society of Medicine, Association of Surgeons, Royal College of Surgeons (former member of council and vice-president). *Awards, honors:* Knighted, 1953.

WRITINGS: Minor Gynaecology, John Lane, 1909; *The Surgical Aspects of Dysentery,* Oxford University Press, 1920; *The Early Diagnosis of the Acute Abdomen,* Oxford University Press, 1921, 13th edition, 1968; *Clinical Researches in Acute Abdominal Disease,* Oxford University Press, 1925; *The Treatment of the Acute Abdomen,* Oxford University Press, 1926; *Some Principles of Minor Surgery,* Oxford University Press, 1929; *Actinomycosis,* Oxford University Press, 1938; (under pseudonym Zeta) *The Acute Abdomen in Rhyme,* Lewis & Co., 1947, 4th edition, 1962.

The Versatile Victorian (life of Sir Henry Thompson), Harvey & Blythe, 1951; *Human Actinomycosis,* Heinemann, 1952; *William Cheselden,* E. & S. Livingstone, 1953; *History of St. Mary's Hospital Medical School,* Heinemann, 1954; *A Hundred Years of Nursing,* Heinemann, 1955; *Florence Nightingale and the Doctors,* Museum Press, 1958; *History of the Royal College of Surgeons of England,* Anthony Blond, 1959, C.C Thomas, 1960; *Sir John Tomes* (biography), Dawson & Sons, 1961; *Six Disciples of Florence Nightingale,* Pitman, 1961; *Some Famous General Practitioners, and Other Historical Essays,* Pitman, 1961; *How the Society of Apothecaries Moulded Medical Practice in England,* Faculty of the History of Medicine and Pharmacy, Apothecaries Hall, c.1963; *A History of the Acute Abdomen,* Oxford University Press, 1965; *Almroth Wright: Founder of Modern Vaccine-Therapy,* Thomas Nelson, 1966.

Editor: *Medical History of the Second World War: Medicine and Pathology,* H.M.S.O., 1952; *Medical History of the Second World War: Surgery,* H.M.S.O., 1953; *Sidelights on the History of Medicine,* Butterworth & Co., 1957.

* * *

COPELAND, Morris A(lbert) 1895-

PERSONAL: Born August 6, 1895, in Rochester, N.Y.; son of Albert E. (a realtor) and Jenny (Morris) Copeland; married Mary Enders (an attorney), December 25, 1929; children: Helen (Mrs. R. Elwyn Grattidge), Robert E. *Education:* Amherst College, A.B., 1917; University of Chicago, Ph.D., 1921. *Address:* Box 295, Sodus, N.Y. 14551; and 633 Alhambra Rd., Venice, Fla. 33595 (summer).

CAREER: Cornell University, Ithaca, N.Y., instructor, 1921-25, assistant professor, 1925-28, professor of economics, 1928-30; on leave with Brookings Graduate School, National Bureau of Economic Research, University of Wisconsin Experimental College, and Federal Reserve Board, 1927-29; University of Michigan, Ann Arbor, professor of economics, 1930-36; U.S. government, Washington, D.C., executive secretary of Central Statistical Board, 1933-39, director of research, Bureau of the Budget, 1939-40, chief of Munitions Branch, War Production Board, 1940-44, economist, National Bureau of Economic Research, 1944-60; Cornell University, professor of economics, 1949-57, Robert J. Thorne Professor of Economics, 1957-65, professor emeritus, 1966—. Fulbright lecturer at Indian Statistical Institute and Delhi School of Economics, 1951. Visiting professor at University of Missouri, 1966-67, and State University of New York at Albany, 1968-71. *Military service:* U.S. Army, 1917-18; became sergeant first class.

MEMBER: American Economic Association (distinguished fellow; president, 1957), American Statistical Association (fellow; vice-president, 1936), Phi Beta Kappa, Phi Delta Theta. *Awards, honors:* L.H.D., Amherst College, 1957; Guggenheim fellow, 1964.

WRITINGS: The Keynesian Reformation, Ranjit Publishers (Delhi), 1952; *A Study of Moneyflows in the United States,* National Bureau of Economic Research, 1952; *Fact and Theory in Economics,* Cornell University Press, 1958; *Trends in Government Financing,* Princeton University Press, 1961; *Our Free Enterprise Economy,* Macmillan, 1965; *Toward Full Employment in Our Free Enterprise Economy,* Fordham University Press, 1966. Contributor to professional journals.

SIDELIGHTS: Copeland told *CA:* "I have been greatly influenced by Thorstein Veblen and John Dewey. My approach to economics is institutionalist, to psychology behavioristic.'' He has traveled around the world twice, mostly by freighter.

*   *   *

COPER, Rudolf   1904-

PERSONAL: Born August 20, 1904, in Berlin, Germany; now an American citizen; son of Max and Rose (Casper) Coper; married Freda Gertrude Batchelor, 1947. *Education:* Friedrich Wilhelms Universitat, Ph.D., 1930. *Home:* 106 McClung, Pass Christian Isles, Miss.

CAREER: Stockbroker in Berlin, Germany, 1923-31; Reichs-Kredit-Ges., Berlin, Germany, economist, 1932-33; Rand Mining Timber Co., Johannesburg, South Africa, economist, 1934-38; University of Toronto, Toronto, Ontario, Canada, lecturer in department of German, 1939-47; Loyola University, New Orleans, La., professor of economics, 1948-73. Political commentator, Canadian Broadcasting Corp., 1942-47. *Member:* American Economic Association, Southwestern Social Science Association.

WRITINGS: Failure of a Revolution, Cambridge University Press, 1956. Correspondent in Canada for *Saturday Night,* 1939-47. Contributor to *South African Journal of Economics, University of Toronto Quarterly,* and to other journals, magazines, and newspapers in Germany and United States.

WORK IN PROGRESS: Psychological Aspects of the Business Cycle.

*   *   *

CORBETT, Pearson H(arris)   1900-

PERSONAL: Born October 22, 1900, in Mammoth, Utah; son of Walter S. (a businessman) and Mary Emily (Harris) Corbett; married Gladys Brimhall, June 2, 1926; children: Pearson Starr, Connie (Mrs. Clayne Ricks), Cecelia Ann. *Education:* Brigham Young University, B.S., 1935, M.S., 1944. *Politics:* Republican. *Religion:* Church of Jesus Christ of Latter-day Saints. *Home and office:* 3122 South 2440th East, Salt Lake City, Utah 84109.

CAREER: In early career was bishop of Mormon Church and principal of seminaries at Mesa, Ariz., and Ferron, Utah; Dixie College, St. George, Utah, director of Latter-day Saints Institute of Religion for eighteen years; University of Utah, Salt Lake City, associate director of Latter-day Saints Institute of Religion, 1959; Latter-day Saints Department of Education, Salt Lake City, Utah, assistant editor, 1962—.

WRITINGS: Jacob Hamblin, the Peacemaker, Deseret, 1952; *Hyrum Smith, Patriarch,* Deseret, 1963; *Arthritis and I: A Clinical History and an Autobiography,* Vantage, 1963.

WORK IN PROGRESS: The Tenth Son, an autobiography; *History of Tintic.*

SIDELIGHTS: Arthritis and I developed from Corbett's thirty-year battle with the disease. He became a victim of rheumatoid arthritis at the start of his career, but carried on through several decades of teaching—from a chair.

BIOGRAPHICAL/CRITICAL SOURCES: Utah Historical Quarterly, fall, 1952; *University of Utah Humanities Review,* April, 1953; *Deseret News Telegram,* Salt Lake City, Utah, December 30, 1963.

*   *   *

CORBETT, Richmond McLain   1902-

PERSONAL: Born August 9, 1902, in Chicago, Ill.; son of Henry R. and Jennie (McLain) Corbett; married Marjorie Stassen, 1928; children: Barbara Corbett Riedel (deceased), Judith Corbett Bartow. *Education:* Northwestern University, A.B., 1924; Chicago Kent College of Law, LL.B., 1931; Rutgers University, graduate in banking, 1957. *Home:* 1500 Chicago Ave., Evanston, Ill.

CAREER: Corbett Associates (actuaries), Chicago, Ill., vice-president, 1931-39; attorney in private practice, Chicago, Ill., 1939-45; Radium Industries, Inc., Chicago, Ill., president, 1939-47; with Chicago Title & Trust Co., Chicago, Ill., 1947-63; Northwest National Bank of Chicago, Chicago, Ill., vice-president and head of trust department, 1966-73. Vice-chairman by appointment of Supreme Court of Illinois, Committee on Character and Fitness, 1962-63. Suburban chairman, Chicago Heart Association, 1953-54. *Member:* American Bar Association, Conference of Actuaries, Midwest Pension Conference, Illinois Bar Association, Chicago Bar Association, Alpha Delta Phi, Phi Delta Phi, University Club (Chicago), University Club (Evanston).

WRITINGS: Pension Trends and the Self Employed, Rutgers University Press, 1961. Contributor to legal and trust periodicals.

AVOCATIONAL INTERESTS: Swimming, tennis.

*   *   *

CORKE, Helen   1882-

PERSONAL: Born January 26, 1882, in Hastings, Sussex, England; daughter of Alfred E. and Louisa (Gallop) Corke. *Education:* Took acting teachers' training course; additional private study in history, literature, and music. *Home:* Ingate, Kelvedon, Colchester, England.

CAREER: Croydon Education Committee, Croydon, England, assistant mistress, 1905-1919; Essex County Education Committee, headmistress at Kelvedon, England, 1919-28, history specialist at Witham, Essex, England, 1944-48. Member of panel, D. H. Lawrence Festival, New Mexico, 1970. *Member:* P.E.N. (London center).

WRITINGS: The Class Books of World History, four volumes, Oxford University Press, 1927-31; *A Book of Ancient Peoples,* Clarendon Press, 1933; *Neutral Ground* (novel), Arthur Barker, 1933, Haskell House, 1966; *Lawrence and "Apocalypse"* (criticism), Heinemann, 1933; *A Book of Modern Peoples,* Clarendon Press, 1934; *Towards Economic Freedom,* Methuen, 1936; *Lawrence's Princess* (memoir), Merle Press, 1951; *Songs of Autumn* (poems), University of Texas Press, 1960; *D. H. Lawrence: The Croyden Years,* University of Texas Press, 1965.

WORK IN PROGRESS: A two volume autobiography, *In Our Infancy* and *The Light of Common Day.*

SIDELIGHTS: The Class Books of World History, designed for self study in one-class English rural schools, was translated into Norwegian and adopted by the Norwegian State Education Authority. All copies disappeared from the schools during the Nazi occupation of Norway. *Avocational interests:* Gardening, music.

*   *   *

CORKEY, R(obert)   1881-1966

PERSONAL: Born March 26, 1881, in Londonderry, Northern Ireland; son of J. (a clergyman) and Elizabeth (Sloane) Corkey; married Nina Frances Allison; children: Denise Ingham (Mrs. Terence T. Fulton), Hazel Allison

(Mrs. Glyn Walters). *Education:* Educated at Foyle College, Londonderry, Northern Ireland, and at University of Edinburgh, and The Queen's University of Belfast; M.A., D.Phil., 1908. *Politics:* Unionist. *Home:* 44 Deramore Dr., Belfast 9, Northern Ireland.

CAREER: Minister of the Presbyterian Church in Ireland, Ballygawley, 1906-10, Monaghan, 1910-17; Presbyterian College, Belfast, Northern Ireland, professor of ethics and practical theology, 1917-51; Government of Northern Ireland, member of Parliament for The Queen's University of Belfast, 1929-43, Minister of Education, 1943-44; moderator, General Assembly of the Presbyterian Church in Ireland, 1945-46. *Member:* Irish Philosophical Club. *Awards, honors:* D.D., Theological Faculty of Ireland.

WRITINGS: Paths to Power in Education, National Sunday School Union, 1920; *War, Pacifism and Peace*, Macmillan, 1940; *Can World Peace Be Won?*, H. R. Allenson; *A Philosophy of Christian Morals for Today*, Allen & Unwin, 1962, Transatlantic, 1964. Contributor to *Philosophy* and *Hibbert Journal*.

WORK IN PROGRESS: A book, *Assurance of the Truth about Nature, Morals and God*.

SIDELIGHTS: A Philosophy of Christian Morals for Today was selected by the United Nations education authorities as an official textbook.

(Died January 26, 1966)

* * *

CORMACK, James Maxwell Ross   1909-

PERSONAL: Born July 20, 1909, in Aberdeen, Scotland; son of Benjamin and Frances Helen (Ross) Cormack; married Isabel Ogg Catto, April 19, 1938; married second wife, Sybil Phyllis Dadley, August 14, 1968; children: Andrew James Ross. *Education:* Attended Robert Gordon's College, Aberdeen, Scotland, 1921-28; University of Aberdeen, M.A. (first class honors in classics), 1932; Trinity College, Cambridge, B.A., 1935; advanced study at University of Vienna, 1935, British School of Archaeology, Athens, Greece, 1935-37. *Home:* 5 Royfold Crescent, Aberdeen AB2 6BH, Scotland. *Office:* King's College, University of Aberdeen, Aberdeen AB2 2UB, Scotland.

CAREER: University of Reading, Reading, England, lecturer in classics, 1937-46, professor of classics, 1946-65, dean of faculty of letters, 1948-54, deputy vice-chancellor, 1954-63, acting vice-chancellor, 1963-65; University of Aberdeen, Aberdeen, Scotland, professor of Greek, 1965—. *Member:* Classical Association, Society for Promotion of Hellenic Studies, Society for Promotion of Roman Studies, Royal Numismatic Society (fellow), British School at Athens.

WRITINGS: The Inscribed Monuments of Aphrodisias, University of Reading Press, 1955; (with William Calder) *Monumenta Asiae Minoris Antiqua*, Volume VIII, Manchester University Press, 1962. Contributor of articles on Greek epigraphy to archaeological and other learned journals. Review editor of *Journal of Hellenic Studies*, 1948-51.

WORK IN PROGRESS: Fascicules of Inscriptiones Graecae X, Deutsche Akademie der Wissenschaften.

SIDELIGHTS: Cormack knows French, German, Italian, Spanish, modern Greek, Russian, Serbo-Croatian, and Bulgarian.

CORNELIUS, Temple H.   1891-1964

PERSONAL: Born March 4, 1891, in Indian Territory (now Oklahoma); son of John M. (a stockman) and Nannie V. (McDow) Cornelius; married Olive F. Frazier (a school teacher), June 29, 1917; children: Royce O., Hugh L. (deceased), Myrle, Maurice E., Valerie (Mrs. William Whitney). *Education:* Attended University of Colorado for three years. *Home:* 1919 Grove St., National City, Calif. 92050.

CAREER: Former hard rock miner, packer, stockman, forester, range appraiser, and newspaperman in southwestern Colorado.

WRITINGS: (With John B. Marshall) *Golden Treasures of the San Juan*, Sage Books, 1961; *Sheepherder's Gold*, Sage Books, 1964. Writer of feature articles for newspapers.

SIDELIGHTS: Cornelius was fluent in Spanish, and knew Navajo and Ute dialects.

(Died August 4, 1964)

* * *

COSTIGAN, Giovanni   1905-

PERSONAL: Born February 15, 1905, in Kingston on Thames, England; son of John Francis and Helen (Warren) Costigan; married Amne Macmillan Johnson. *Education:* Oxford University, B.A., 1926, M.A. and B.Litt., 1930; University of Wisconsin, M.A., 1928, Ph.D., 1930. *Home:* 5223 21st, N.E., Seattle, Wash. 98105.

CAREER: University of Idaho, Pocatello, associate professor of history, 1930-34; University of Washington, Seattle, assistant professor, 1934-42, associate professor, 1942-48, professor of history, 1948—. *Military service:* U.S. Army Air Forces, 1943-45; became captain. *Member:* Phi Beta Kappa (honorary).

WRITINGS: Sir Robert Wilson: A Soldier of Fortune in the Napoleonic Wars, University of Wisconsin Press, 1932; *Sigmund Freud: A Short Biography*, Macmillan, 1965; *Makers of Modern England: The Force of the Individual Genius in History*, Macmillan, 1967; *A History of Modern Ireland With a Sketch of Earlier Times*, Pegasus, 1969.

SIDELIGHTS: Costigan has traveled in all countries of western and eastern Europe, U.S.S.R., and in Middle East, Africa, Southeast Asia, Central America, and South America.

* * *

COTTAM, Walter P(ace)   1894-

PERSONAL: Born March 3, 1894, in St. George, Utah; son of Thomas P. and Emaline (Jarvis) Cottam; married Effie Frei, 1915; children: Fae (Mrs. C. H. Olson), Grant, Beatrice (Mrs. W. L. Fowler), Richard, George. *Education:* Brigham Young University, A.B., 1916, A.M., 1918; University of Chicago, Ph.D., 1926. *Home:* 1114 McClelland St., Salt Lake City, Utah. *Office:* University of Utah, Salt Lake City, Utah.

CAREER: High school science teacher in Sandy, Utah, 1918-19; Brigham Young University, Provo, Utah, 1919-31, became professor of botany; University of Utah, Salt Lake City, professor of botany, beginning 1931. Professor of botany, University of Chicago, summer, 1930; civilian botany teacher, U.S. Army, Division of Education, Shrivenham American University, England, 1945; vice-chairman, Salt Lake City Shade Commission, 1940-60. *Member:* American

Botanical Society, Ecological Society of America (president of Pacific division, 1949-51), American Association for the Advancement of Science, California Botanical society, Utah Academy of Science, Arts, and Letters. *Awards, honors:* Utah State University Conservation Award, 1957; named Ecologist of the Year by Ecological Society of America, 1960.

WRITINGS: Our Renewable Wild Lands: A Challenge, University of Utah Press, 1961. Contributor to ecology, botany, and forestry journals.

WORK IN PROGRESS: Phytosociology of the Wasatch Mountains, Utah.

AVOCATIONAL INTERESTS: Flower and scenic photography, hiking, gardening.

*   *   *

COURTNEY, Gwendoline

PERSONAL: Born in Southampton, Hampshire, England; daughter of Edwin and Mary J. (Potter) Courtney. *Education:* Attended high school in Wallasey, Cheshire, England. *Religion:* Church of England. *Home:* Carigluz, Cadgwith, Helston, Cornwall, England.

CAREER: Writer. Lecturer throughout southern England. Temporary civil servant, World War II, doing classified work, mainly in connection with D-Day invasion. *Member:* Society of Authors (honorary secretary, West of England group), West Country Writers Association.

WRITINGS: Torley Grange, Thomas Nelson, 1935; *The Grenville Garrison,* Thomas Nelson, 1940; *The Denehurst Secret Service,* Oxford University Press, 1940; *Well Done, Denehurst!,* Oxford University Press, 1941; *Sally's Family,* Oxford University Press, 1946; *Stepmother,* Oxford University Press, 1948, published as *Those Verney Girls,* F. Watts, 1957, reissued in England as *Elizabeth of the Garret Theatre,* Collins, 1961; *Long Barrow,* Oxford University Press, 1950, reissued as *The Farm on the Downs,* Collins, 1961; *A Coronet for Cathie,* Thomas Nelson, 1950; *At School with the Stanhopes,* Thomas Nelson, 1951; *The Girls of Friar's Rise,* Thomas Nelson, 1952; *The Chiltons,* Thomas Nelson, 1953; *The Wild Lorings at School,* Hutchinson, 1954; *The Wild Lorings—Detectives!,* Hutchinson, 1956. Also author of television play, "Passage of Arms." Contributor of short stories, articles, and reviews to magazines.

AVOCATIONAL INTERESTS: Reading, growing cacti, fencing; natural history, particularly flowers and birds; her two pets, a Sealyham and a Siamese cat.

*   *   *

COWAN, Robert Granniss   1895-

PERSONAL: Born December 14, 1895, in San Francisco, Calif.; son of Robert Ernest (a librarian and bibliographer) and Marie M. (Fleissner) Cowan; married Georgia Harvey, October 4, 1919 (divorced, 1955); children: Robert Harvey, William Alfred. *Education:* Educated in San Francisco (Calif.) public schools. *Home:* 1650 Radcliff St., Los Angeles, Calif. 90026.

CAREER: Clerk, salesman, auto ferry cashier in and about San Francisco, Calif., 1919-26; author with father, 1926-32; LaCal Stamp & Coin Co., Los Angeles, Calif., proprietor, 1933-42; retired, 1942. *Military service:* U.S. Army, World War I. *Member:* California Historical Society, Southern California Historical Society, Stamp Dealers' Association

of Southern California (honorary; former secretary for eighteen years; former president), Friends of U.C.L.A. Library, Friends of Huntington Library, Westerners (Los Angeles Corral).

WRITINGS: (With father, Robert Ernest Cowan) *A Bibliography of the History of California, 1510-1930,* Nash, 1933; (with R. E. Cowan) *Booksellers of Early San Francisco,* privately printed, 1953; *Ranchos of California,* Academy Library, 1956; *Admission of the 31st State by the 31st Congress: An Annotated Bibliography of Congressional Speeches Upon the Admission of California,* privately printed, 1962; *Bibliography of the History of California,* Volume IV, privately printed, 1964; *A Backward Glance: Los Angeles, 1901-1915,* privately printed for the Historical Society of Southern California, 1969.

AVOCATIONAL INTERESTS: "Books—read them, write them, bind them, and repair them."

*   *   *

COWIE, Mervyn (Hugh)   1909-

PERSONAL: Born April 13, 1909, in Nairobi, Kenya; son of Herbert Hugh and Ada Evelyn (Harries) Cowie; married Erica Beaty, February 24, 1934 (died, 1956); married Valori Hare-Duke, April 13, 1957; children: Hugh, Ian, Mitzi (Mrs. Christopher Marley), Bruce, Virginia. *Education:* Brighton College, Sussex, England, student, 1922-26; Brasenose College, Oxford, student, 1930-32. *Home address:* Kikenni, P.O. Box 505, Nairobi, Kenya.

CAREER: Royal National Parks of Kenya, Nairobi, director, 1946-66. Kenya Legislative Council, member, 1950-60, director of manpower, Mau-Mau emergency, 1953-56. National Parks Commission, member. *Military service:* King's African Rifles, Reserve of Officers, 1932-38; Kenya Regiment, 1939; war service, 1939-45; became lieutenant colonel. *Member:* International Union for Conservation of Nature, Institute of Chartered Accountants (London), Zoological Society of London (fellow), Explorers Club (New York), Shikar Club (London), East Africa Tourist Travel Association (vice-president), Mountain Club (East Africa), Rotary Club of Nairobi (past president). *Awards, honors:* Efficiency Decoration, 1945; Commander, Order of the British Empire, 1961.

WRITINGS: Fly, Vulture, Harrap, 1961; *I Walk with Lions: The Story of Africa's Great Animal Preserves,* (autobiography), Macmillan, 1964; *The African Lion,* Golden Press, 1966. Contributor to journals and to British Broadcasting Corp. programs. Editor, *Royal National Parks of Kenya Annual Reports,* 1946-66.

WORK IN PROGRESS: A book on rhinos.

SIDELIGHTS: Cowie holds a private aircraft pilot's license. A film on his work, "Ivory Hunter," was made in 1950.

*   *   *

COWLING, Ellis   1905-

PERSONAL: Born June 15, 1905, in Marshall, N.C.; son of Ira E. and Flora Maude (Wires) Cowling; married Marion Gertrude Brevier (a music teacher), June 17, 1927; children: Ellis Brevier, Jo Ann (Mrs. Charles Rowell), Grayson Boyer, Neil Douglas. *Education:* DePauw University, A.B., 1927; Chicago Theological Seminary, D.B., 1930. *Politics:* Republican. *Home:* Poseyville, Ind. 47633.

CAREER: Ordained minister, Disciples of Christ, 1930;

currently pastor of Christian Pastoral Unity, Posey County, Ind.

WRITINGS: Cooperatives in America, Coward, 1938; *Let's Think About Money*, Abingdon, 1957; *Mind Your Own Spending: A Christian Approach to Family Budgeting*, Bethany, 1964.

* * *

COX, Hebe 1909-

PERSONAL: Born January 10, 1909, in Cheshire, England; daughter of Samuel James and Ethel (Neill) Cox; married George Ronald Webb-Portway (company director), May 14, 1940; children: Nicolas. *Education:* Attended a French convent; Central School of Arts and Crafts, London, England, student, 1932-36. *Home:* Cricketers, Forward Green, Stowmarket, Suffolk, England.

CAREER: Designer and craftsman in embroidery; work has been exhibited in United States, Sweden, Italy, and many parts of Britain, including a one-man showing at Crafts Centre of Great Britain, 1962; work also included in public and private collections in Britain, Australia, and United States.

WRITINGS: (Contributor) John Farleigh, editor, *Fifteen Craftsmen on Their Craft*, Sylvan Press, 1945; *Simple Embroidery Design*, Studio, 1948; *Embroidery Technique and Design*, Dryad, 1954, 2nd edition, 1964; *Canvas Embroidery*, Mills & Boon, 1960.

BIOGRAPHICAL/CRITICAL SOURCES: John Farleigh, *The Creative Craftsman*, G. Bell, 1950.

* * *

COX, Reavis 1900-

PERSONAL: Born September 2, 1900, in Guadalajara, Mexico, of American parentage; son of Jackson Berry and Julia (Barcus) Cox; married Rachel LaVerne Dunaway, 1928; children: David Jackson, Rosemary. *Education:* University of Texas, A.B., 1921; Columbia University, Ph.D., 1932. *Home:* 219 Sykes Lane, Wallingford, Pa. *Office:* Marketing Department, Wharton School of Finance and Commerce, University of Pennsylvania, Philadelphia, Pa. 19174.

CAREER: Newspaperman in various sections of United States, 1921-25; *Journal of Commerce*, New York, N.Y., staff member, 1926-31, marketing editor, 1927-31; Columbia University, New York, N.Y., instructor, 1931-35; University of Pennsylvania, Wharton School of Finance and Commerce, Philadelphia, Pa., associate professor, 1935-38, professor of marketing, 1938-71, Food Fair Stores Foundation Professor of Marketing, 1954-60, Kresge Professor of Marketing, 1967-71, professor emeritus, 1971—, chairman of department, 1935-41. Staff member, U.S. Office of Price Administration and War Production Board, 1941-43; director of research projects, Retail Credit Institute (later National Foundation for Consumer Credit), 1943-45; consultant at various times to many business enterprises, trade organizations, and government agencies. Has conducted seminars at many colleges and universities in the United States and abroad; visiting professor, Canterbury University, New Zealand, 1965, University of Sherbrooke, Canada, 1969-72, and Manchester Business School, 1971-72. *Military service:* U.S. Army.

MEMBER: American Marketing Association (president, 1959-60), American Economics Association, American Academy of Political and Social Science, American Statis-

tical Association, American Association for the Advancement of Science, American Association of University Professors, Beta Gamma Sigma, Cosmos Club (Washington, D.C.). *Awards, honors:* Charles Coolidge Parlin Award, 1948; named to Hall of Fame in Distribution by Boston Conference, 1959; Paul D. Converse Award, 1961.

WRITINGS: Competition in the American Tobacco Industry, 1911-1932, Columbia University Press, 1933; *The Marketing of Textiles*, Textile Foundation, 1938; *Installment Buying by City Consumers in 1941*, Bureau of Labor Statistics, U.S. Department of Labor, 1944; (with Ralph F. Breyer) *Consumer Plant and Equipment*, Retail Credit Institute of America, 1944; *The Economics of Installment Buying*, Ronald, 1948; (editor with Wroe Alderson) *Theory in Marketing* (essays), Irwin, 1950, 2nd edition (with Wroe Alderson and Stanley J. Shapiro), 1964; (co-author) *Consumer Installment Credit*, Federal Reserve System, 1957; (co-author) *Historical Statistics of the United States*, U.S. Department of Commerce, 1960; *Distribution in a High-Level Economy*, Prentice-Hall, 1964. Also co-author of *Marketing in the American Economy*, 1952, and *Channels and Flows in Marketing of House-Building Materials*, three volumes, 1954.

Contributor of articles and reviews to periodicals. Managing editor, *Journal of Marketing*, 1941-42, editor in chief, 1943-44.

WORK IN PROGRESS: A study of the management of marketing channels; a review of major developments in the theory and practice of marketing since 1900.

* * *

CRABB, Alfred Leland 1884-

PERSONAL: Born January 22, 1884, in Warren County, Ky.; son of James Wade (a farmer) and Annie (Arbuckle) Crabb; married Bertha Gardner, August 16, 1911; children: Alfred Leland, Jr. *Education:* Attended Bethel College, Russellville, Ky., 1904-05, Southern Normal School and Western Kentucky State Normal School (both now Western Kentucky University), 1906-10; George Peabody College for Teachers, B.S., 1916, Ph.D., 1925; Columbia University, M.A., 1921. *Religion:* Baptist. *Home:* 1701 18th Ave. South, Nashville, Tenn. *Office:* George Peabody College for Teachers, Nashville, Tenn.

CAREER: Public school teacher and principal in Kentucky and Louisiana, 1901-16; Western Kentucky State Normal School (now Western Kentucky University), Bowling Green, teacher, later dean, 1916-27; George Peabody College for Teachers, Nashville, Tenn., professor of education, 1927-50, professor emeritus, beginning 1950. *Member:* National Society of Sons of the American Revolution, Shakespeare Club, Old Oak Club, Kiwanis Club.

WRITINGS: (With A. C. Ferguson and August Dvorak) *Standard Speller*, second-seventh grades, Southern Publishing, 1931-34; *The Genealogy of George Peabody College for Teachers*, George Peabody College for Teachers, 1935; (with M. F. Altstetter and L. W. Newton) *America Yesterday and Today*, Southern Publishing, 1937; (with L. E. Broaddus and J. P. Cornette) *Modern English Handbook with Exercises*, Johnson Publishing, 1941; *Dinner at Belmont* (novel), Bobbs-Merrill, 1942; *Supper at the Maxwell House* (novel), Bobbs-Merrill, 1943; *Breakfast at the Hermitage* (novel), Bobbs-Merrill, 1945; *Lodging at the St. Cloud* (novel), Bobbs-Merrill, 1946; *Home to the Heritage* (novel), Bobbs-Merrill, 1948; *A Mockingbird Sang at Chickamauga* (novel), Bobbs-Merrill, 1949.

Reunion at Chattanooga (novel), Bobbs-Merrill, 1950; *Home to Tennessee* (novel), Bobbs-Merrill, 1952; *Home to Kentucky* (novel), Bobbs-Merrill, 1953; *Peace at Bowling Green* (novel), Bobbs-Merrill, 1955; *Journey to Nashville* (novel), Bobbs-Merrill, 1957; *Nashville: Personality of a City*, Bobbs-Merrill, 1960.

WORK IN PROGRESS: "Dabbling" in the history of cookery.

SIDELIGHTS: Most of Crabb's books of fiction have to do with the history of Nashville, and incidentally with cookery.

* * *

CRABB, E(dmund) W(illiam) 1912-

PERSONAL: Born October 28, 1912, in Bridport, Dorsetshire, England; son of Charles James and Sarah Jane (Willmott) Crabb; married Eva Woolf, April 22, 1935. *Education:* Goldsmiths' College, University of London, teacher's certificate (honors), 1933; Gresham College and University of London, diploma in literature (with distinction), 1938, diploma in theology, 1945. *Religion:* Christian Brethren. *Home:* 36 The Ridgeway, Kenton, Harrow, Middlesex, England. *Office:* Stanburn School, Abercorn Rd., Stanmore, Middlesex, England.

CAREER: Hyde School, Hendon, London, England, headmaster, 1948-53; Stanburn School, Stanmore, Middlesex, England, headmaster, 1953—. Chairman, Logos Educational Institute in Cyprus. Member of literature committee, Inter-Varsity Fellowship and Tyndale Press. Executive chairman of Covenanter Union, 1960-69. *Military service:* British Army, 1942-45. *Member:* National Association of Schoolmasters, Victoria Institute (council, 1950-57).

WRITINGS: Good News From God, E. J. Arnold, 1948; *Workers For God*, E. J. Arnold, 1948; *Telling the Good News*, E. J. Arnold, 1949; *The Founders of the Faith*, E. J. Arnold, 1949; *Men on the Tower*, Inter-Varsity Fellowship, 1950; *Jesus and the Chosen Nation*, E. J. Arnold, 1951; *Way of Life*, E. J. Arnold, 1951; *Heralds of the Way*, E. J. Arnold, 1952; *Christian Faith*, E. J. Arnold, 1952; *Train Up a Child*, Paternoster, 1954; *The Challenge of the Summit*, Paternoster, 1957; *The Secret of the Plateau*, Evangelical Publishers, 1961; *Living in the Old Testament Days*, E. J. Arnold, 1962; *Living in New Testament Days*, E. J. Arnold, 1963; *Religious Education for the C.S.E. Year*, E. J. Arnold, 1966; *Shadow in the Sunshine*, Evangelical Publishers, 1968. Contributor of articles to religious and educational periodicals.

WORK IN PROGRESS: Europe by Instalments: The Complete Bible Book; Sub; The Towers Trio; Guide to Education.

AVOCATIONAL INTERESTS: European travel, mountain lore, and camps for young people.

* * *

CRAGO, T(homas) Howard 1907-

PERSONAL: Born February 23, 1907, in Ballarat, Victoria, Australia; son of William Albert (a boot-maker) and Judith (Thompson) Crago; married Phyllis Mary Hinde, May 5, 1934; children: Neville, Bruce. *Education:* Baptist College of Victoria, Licentiate in Theology, 1934; also studied at University of Melbourne two years. *Home:* 63 Springfield Rd., Box Hill, Victoria, Australia.

CAREER: Baptist minister. Australian Baptist Board of Christian Education, Auburn, Victoria, Australia, publication director, 1956—.

WRITINGS: Real Discipleship, Marshall, Morgan & Scott, 1940; *The Voice of Friendship*, Banner Publishing, 1941; *Facing Today*, Robertson & Mullens, 1942; (with W. J. Bligh) *Champions of Liberty*, Clifford Press, 1946; *Wind in the Tree Tops*, Epworth, 1954; *The Road Winds Up Hill*, Epworth, 1956; *The Story of F. W. Boreham*, Marshall, Morgan & Scott, 1961. Contributor to *Spectator*, *Melbourne Age*, *Australian Baptist*, and *Revelation*. Editor, *Christian Education*.

AVOCATIONAL INTERESTS: Gardening, printing, and photography.

* * *

CRAIG, Alexander George 1897-
(Alec Craig, Arthur Craik)

PERSONAL: Born April 23, 1897, in London, England; son of George (a relieving officer) and Ellen (North) Craig; married Kathleen Victoria Styles, May 22, 1924; children: Marjorie Thomsen, Charles. *Education:* Educated at St. George's College, London, England, 1913-15, King's College, London, 1919-21, London School of Economics, London, 1921-22. *Politics:* Labour. *Religion:* Church of England. *Home:* 4 Princess Court, Worsley Rd., London N.W.3, England.

CAREER: Public Record Office, London, England, boy clerk, 1912-15, supplementary clerk, 1915-19; Exchequer and Audit Department, London, England, assistant auditor, 1919-22, auditor, 1922-39 (in Cairo, Egypt, 1922-27), senior auditor, 1939-47, deputy director of audit, 1947-58 (in Cairo, Egypt, 1947-50). *Military service:* British Army, 1915-19; became lieutenant. *Member:* Society of Authors, Progressive League, Anglican Pacifist Fellowship, Eugenics Society, Society of Civil Servants, Civil Service Club, Contemporary Poetry and Music Circle (poetry organizer, 1943—), Poetry Society, Victory Ex-Services Club.

WRITINGS—Under name Alec Craig: *Sex and Revolution*, Allen & Unwin, 1934; *The Banned Books of England*, Allen & Unwin, 1937; *Above All Liberties*, Allen & Unwin, 1942, Books for Libraries, 1972; *The Aspirin Eaters* (verse), Fortune Press, 1943; *The Voice of Merlin* (verse), Fortune Press, 1946; *The Prometheans* (verse), Fortune Press, 1955; *The Banned Books of England and Other Countries: A Study of the Conception of Literary Obscenity*, Allen & Unwin, 1962, published in America as *Suppressed Books*, World Publishing, 1963.

Under pseudonym Arthur Craik: *Dumb Gods* (verse), Southern Publishing, 1924.

Contributor: *Experiments in Sex Education*, Federation of Progressive Societies and Individuals, 1935; *Freedom of Expression*, Hutchinson, 1945; *Sex, Society and the Individual*, International Journal of Sexology, 1953; Rex Warner and others, editors, *New Poems, 1954: A P.E.N. Anthology*, M. Joseph, 1954; *The Encyclopedia of Sexual Behavior*, Hawthorn, 1961.

WORK IN PROGRESS: Collecting current material relating to the censorship of literature on the ground of obscenity.

SIDELIGHTS: Craig has been engaged in socialist and left-wing propaganda with particular reference to sex reform since the early thirties. From that time until recently he has always been a member of one or more nudist clubs.

CRAIG, John H(erbert) 1885-

PERSONAL: Born February 9, 1885, in Londonderry, Northern Ireland; son of Robert James and Maria Anne (Miller) Craig; married Vera Worsfold, August 19, 1921. *Education:* Attended Foyle College, Londonderry, Northern Ireland, and Trinity College, Dublin, Ireland. *Home:* 8 Clareville Court, Clareville Grove, London S.W.7, England.

CAREER: Treasury of United Kingdom, principal assistant secretary, 1908-38; Royal Mint, London, England, deputy master, 1938-49. Royal Institution, manager in sundry years, 1940-50; Sir John Cass College, governor, 1939-57, chairman and treasurer, 1950-57. *Member:* City of London Society (vice-president, 1956—). *Awards, honors:* Knight Commander of Victorian Order; Companion of the Bath; LL.D. from Trinity College, Dublin.

WRITINGS: Newton at the Mint, Cambridge University Press, 1946; *The Mint, 287-1948 A.D.,* Cambridge University Press, 1953; *History of Red Tape,* Macdonald & Evans, 1955; *Catalogue of Newton Manuscripts in Royal Mint Library,* privately printed, 1957. Occasional contributor to journals.

WORK IN PROGRESS: A detailed study of Sir Isaac Newton's five-year campaign against counterfeiters.

AVOCATIONAL INTERESTS: Mountain climbing, mostly in French and Spanish Pyrenees.

*   *   *

CRAMER, John Francis 1899-1967

PERSONAL: Born September 13, 1899, in Kansas City, Mo.; son of John Lyman (an attorney) and Josephine (Coffman) Cramer; married Mabel Oesterling, May 30, 1922; children: John F., Jr., William D., Richard S. *Education:* Willamette University, B.A., 1920, M.A., 1921; University of Oregon, M.Ed., 1932, D.Ed., 1937. *Politics:* Republican. *Religion:* Presbyterian. *Home:* 2705 Southeast River Rd., Portland, Ore. 97222. *Office:* Portland State University, Box 751, Portland, Ore. 97207.

CAREER: High school teacher and principal in Oregon, 1920-27; superintendent of school systems in four Oregon cities, 1927-44; Oregon State System of Higher Education, Salem, dean of General Extension Division, 1944-55; Portland State College (now University) Portland, Ore., president, 1955-58, professor of education, 1958-67. Fulbright professor at University of Melbourne, 1955-58, University of Hong Kong, 1958-59; visiting summer professor at University of British Columbia, 1961; U.S. Department of State specialist in Australia, 1965. Member of advisory council, Mount Hood National Forest, 1955-67; member of Oregon Governor's Advisory Council on Education, 1960-67. *Military service:* U.S. Army, 1918. U.S. Army Reserve, 1926-43, with active duty, 1943; became captain. *Member:* Rotary Club, Masons, City Club, and University Club (all Portland). *Awards, honors:* Carnegie traveling fellow to Australia and New Zealand, 1935; John Smythe Silver Medal of University of Melbourne, 1951.

WRITINGS: Australian Schools Through American Eyes, University of Melbourne Press, 1936; (with George S. Browne) *Contemporary Education: A Comparative Study of National Systems,* Harcourt, 1956, 2nd edition, 1965. Contributor to journals.

(Died October 12, 1967)

CRARY, Catherine S. 1909-

PERSONAL: Born February 12, 1909, in Rochester, N.Y.; daughter of Albert C. (a physician) and Cora (Nell) Snell; married Calvert Horton Crary (in securities business), June 30, 1932; children: Peter, Susan, Caroline (Mrs. J. T. Terry Brune), Calvert D. *Education:* Mount Holyoke College, A.B. (cum laude), 1930; Radcliffe College, M.A., 1931, Ph.D., 1934; also studied German at University of Heidelberg, and French at University of Geneva. *Politics:* Variable. *Religion:* Protestant. *Home:* Underhill Rd., Scarsdale, N.Y. *Office:* Finch College, 52 East 78th St., New York, N.Y.

CAREER: Part-time teacher of history at Barnard College, New York, N.Y., 1955-59, at Finch College, New York, N.Y., 1957—. Former member of national board and of White Plains board of Young Women's Christian Association; former member of board of Packard Junior College, United Service Organization, Scarsdale Community Fund and Council, and Scarsdale Girl Scout Council. *Member:* American Historical Association, New York State Historical Association, Phi Beta Kappa, Scarsdale Junior League (president, 1948-50). *Awards, honors:* Fellow, Bread Loaf Writers' Conference, 1965.

WRITINGS: (Editor) Tully McCrea, *Dear Belle: Letters from a Cadet and Officer to His Sweetheart, 1858-1865,* Wesleyan University Press, 1965. Contributor to historical journals.

WORK IN PROGRESS: Peter Jay, Colonial Merchant; and *Revolutionary War Orderly Books.*

*   *   *

CREIGHTON, Luella Bruce 1901-

PERSONAL: Born August 25, 1901, in Stouffivlee, Ontario, Canada; daughter of James Walter (a manufacturer) and Luella (Sanders) Bruce; married Donald Grant Creighton (a historian and writer), June 23, 1926; children: Philip, Cynthia (Mrs. Maurice Jerome Flood) *Education:* Victoria University in the University of Toronto, B.A., 1926. *Religion:* Protestant. *Home:* 15 Princess St., Brooklin, Ontario, Canada.

CAREER: Teacher in rural school before attending university; free-lance writer. *Member:* Heliconian Club (Toronto).

WRITINGS: High Bright Buggy Wheels, McClelland & Stewart, 1950, Dodd, 1951; *Turn East, Turn West,* Dodd, 1954; *Struggle for Empire* (textbook) Dent, 1960; *Trial and Triumph* (textbook), Dent, 1963; *Tecumseh, the Story of the Shawnee Chief,* Macmillan (Canada), 1965; *Miss Multipenny and Miss Crumb* (juvenile), Blackie & Son, 1966; *The Elegant Canadians,* McClelland & Stewart, 1967; *The Hitching Post,* McClelland & Stewart, 1969.

WORK IN PROGRESS: A novel.

AVOCATIONAL INTERESTS: Village people, roses, and cats.

*   *   *

CRESWELL, K(eppel) A(rchibald) C(ameron) 1879-

PERSONAL: Born September 13, 1879; son of Keppel and Margaret (Henderson) Creswell. *Education:* Attended Westminster School, London, England, 1891-96, City and Guilds Technical College, 1896-98. *Politics:* Conservative. *Religion:* Church of England. *Home:* 2 rue Baehler, Qasr en-Nil, Cairo, Egypt. *Office:* American University at Cairo, Cairo, Egypt.

CAREER: Inspector of monuments in occupied territory, Syria and Palestine, 1919-20; domiciled in Cairo, Egypt, 1921—; Egyptian University, Giza, director of Institute of Muslim Art and Archaeology, and professor, 1931-51; American University in Cairo, Cairo, Egypt, Distinguished Professor, 1956—. Trustee, Palestine Museum of Antiquities, 1949-54; member of Higher Council of Arabic Monuments, Comite de Conservation des Monuments de l'Art Arabe (Egypt), Museum of Muslim Art, and Council of Coptic Museum. *Military service:* Royal Flying Corps, 1916-19; became staff captain.

MEMBER: Royal Asiatic Society, Society of Antiquaries (fellow), Royal Central Asian Society (honorary member), American Oriental Soviety (honorary member), Deutsches Archaeologisches Institut (honorary member), Archaeological Survey of India (honorary corresponding member), Coptic Archaeological Society, American Research Center in Egypt (honorary vice-president), Athenaeum Club, (London). *Awards, honors:* Sir Percy Sykes Memorial Medal, Royal Central Asian Society, 1948; Rockefeller Foundation fellowship, 1952-54; Commander, Order of the British Empire, 1955; Order of Ismail, third class; Syrian Order of Merit, first class; fellow, British Academy; Triennial Gold Medal, Royal Asiatic Society, 1959; D.Litt., Oxford University; Hon.D.Litt., Princeton University; Knight Commander, Order of the British Empire, 1970.

WRITINGS: A Brief Chronology of the Muhammadan Monuments of Egypt to A.D. 1517, Institut Francais d'Archeologie Orientale du Caire, 1919; *A Provisional Bibliography of the Muhammadan Architecture of India* (originally published in *Indian Antiquary,* 1922), British India Press, 1922; *The Origin of the Plan of the Dome of the Rock* (supplementary paper, British School of Archaeology in Jerusalem), British Council, 1924; *A Provisional Bibliography of the Moslem Architecture of Syria and Palestine,* published for Pro-Jerusalem Society by Luzac, 1924; *Early Muslim Architecture,* Clarendon Press, Volume I: *Umayyads, A.D. 622-750,* includes material by Marguerite Gautier van Berchem, 1932, 2nd edition, Oxford University Press, 1969, Volume II: *Early 'Abbasids, Umayyads of Cordova, Aghlabids, Tulunids, and Samanids, A.D. 751-905,* 1940; *The Muslim Architecture of Egypt,* Clarendon Press, Volume I: *Ikhshids and Fatimids, A.D. 939-1171,* 1952, Volume II: *Ayyubids and Early Bahrite Mamluks, A.D. 1171-1326,* 1959; *A Bibliography of Painting in Islam,* Institut Francais d'Archeologie Orientale du Caire, 1953; *A Bibliography of Muslim Architecture in North Africa, Excluding Egypt,* Librarie Larose, 1954; *A Bibliography of the Muslim Architecture of Egypt,* Institut Francais d'Archeologie Orientale du Caire, 1955; *A Bibliography of Arms and Armour in Islam,* published for Royal Asiatic Society by Luzac, 1956; *A Short Account of Early Muslim Architecture,* Penguin, 1958; *A Bibliography of the Architecture, Arts and Crafts of Islam to 1st Jan. 1960,* American University at Cairo Press, 1961, supplement in press.

Contributor: E. Denison Ross, editor, *Persian Art,* Luzac, 1930; (contributor of translations) M. Gaston Wiet, *Album de Musee Arabe du Caire,* Publications du Musee Arabe du Caire, 1930; E. Denison Ross, editor, *The Art of Egypt Through the Ages,* Studio Publications, 1931; (author of preface) *The Mosques of Egypt from 21 H. to 1365 H.,* Ministry of Waqfs, Survey of Egypt, 1949; *Aus der Welt der Islamischen Kunst: Festschrift fuer Ernst Kuehnel,* Mann, 1959. Also contributor to *Encyclopaedia Britannica,* and to *Burlington Magazine, Indian Antiquary, Byzantion,*

Proceedings of British Academy and of Congress of Orientalists, and other professional publications.

WORK IN PROGRESS: Updating of bibliographies.

BIOGRAPHICAL/CRITICAL SOURCES: Charles L. Geddes and others, *Studies in Islamic Art and Architecture in Honour of Professor K. A. C. Creswell,* American University in Cairo Press, for Center for Arabic Studies, 1965.

* * *

CRISWELL, Cloyd M. 1908-

PERSONAL: Born December 8, 1908, in Columbia, Pa.; son of James Sylvester and Sarah E. (Rawhauser) Criswell; married Frances Mae Unruh (a librarian at Moravian Academy, Bethlehem, Pa.), July 15, 1942; children: Olivia Ann. *Education:* Millersville State College, B.S., 1933; New York University, M.A., 1937. *Home:* 2304 East Fairmont St., Allentown, Pa. 18103.

CAREER: Teacher of English at high schools in Millersville, Pa., 1933-38, and Mamaroneck, N.Y., 1938-42; Lehigh University, Bethlehem, Pa., professor of English, 1947—. *Military service:* U.S. Navy, 1942-46; served in Atlantic and Pacific theaters; became lieutenant commander; received Navy Commendation. *Member:* Pennsylvania Academy of Fine Arts (fellow), Baltimore Watercolor Society, Woodmere Art Gallery (Philadelphia), Lehigh Art Alliance, Bethlehem Palette Club. *Awards, honors:* Honorable mention at Baltimore Watercolor Society annual show, 1951; Garth Howland Award from Lehigh Art Alliance, 1965, for best painting.

WRITINGS: (With brothers, Carl Criswell and Gardiner Criswell) *Onion Snow,* Serif Press, 1942; *Asiatic Station,* Decker Press, 1946; (self-illustrated) *High Twelve,* Kaleidograph Press, 1950; *Three Stones* (poems), Golden Quill Press, 1955; (self-illustrated) *The Arrow by Day* (short stories), Marshall Jones, 1962.

SIDELIGHTS: Criswell writes: "As an artist and an author, I have been a captive of the seasons ever since childhood, a believer in Thoreau's dictum: 'The morning wind forever blows, the poem of creation is uninterrupted....Olympus is but the outside of the earth everywhere.' I am ever caught by the reality of beginnings; when poetry or prose, or a new painting follows, or when I meet human dignity, I know the romance of rewards. Therefore, 'work in progress' is another way of saying 'the daily search' for meaningful detail and dramatic action in the lives that are taking place in the country of my sketching jaunts."

* * *

CRNJANSKI, Milos 1893-
(C. R. Mill)

PERSONAL: Born October 26, 1893, in Csongrad, Hungary; became British citizen in 1951; son of Thomas (a notary) and Mary (Vujitsch) Crnjanski; married Vida Ruzic (a maker of doll dresses), November 10, 1921. *Education:* Studied at University of Vienna, University of Paris, University of Berlin; University of Belgrade, B.M., 1926; University of London, Diploma in Foreign Affairs, 1951. *Religion:* Serbian Orthodox. *Home and office:* 83, Queen's Ct., Queen's Way, London W.2, England. *Agent:* Verlag Kurt Desch, Roman Strasse 9, Munich, Germany.

CAREER: Professor of history in Belgrade, Yugoslavia, 1922-27, 1930-35; *Politika* (daily), Belgrade, Yugoslavia, staff member, 1922-24; Royal Yugoslav Legation, Berlin, Germany, cultural attache, 1928-29, press attache, 1935-38;

Vreme (daily), Belgrade, Yugoslavia, staff member, 1930-35; Royal Yugoslav Legation, Rome, Italy, press counselor, 1938-41; Royal Yugoslav Government in War, London, England, press counselor, 1941-45. *Military service:* Austro-Hungarian Army, 1914-18. *Member:* P.E.N. *Awards, honors:* Serbian Academy Prize, 1930, for *Seobe.*

WRITINGS: Maska: Poeticna komedija, [Zagreb], 1918, also published in *Sabrana dela* (see below); *Lirika Itake* (poetry), Cvijanovic, 1919, also published in *Sabrana dela* (see below); *Price o muskom,* 1920, also published in *Sabrana dela* (see below); *Seobe* (novel), Kohn, 1929, also published with *Dnevnik o Carnojevicu,* Minerva, 1956, also published in *Sabrana dela* (see below); *Ljubav u Toscani,* Kohn, 1930, also published in *Sabrana dela* (see below); *A Book on Germany,* Kohn, 1930; *A Drop of Spanish Blood* (novel), Vreme, 1932; *Belgrade* (short history and guide), Bureau Central de Presse, 1936; *Konak* (novel), Minerva, 1958, also published in *Sabrana dela* (see below); *Itaka i komentari* (poetry and prose), Prosveta (Belgrade), 1959, also published in *Sabrana dela* (see below); *Seobe i druga knjiga seoba* (first and second books of *Seobe*), two volumes, Serbian Literary Cooperative, 1962, also published in *Sabrana dela* (see below); *Kod hyperborejaca,* Martica Srpska, 1964, also published in *Sabrana dela* (see below); *Lirika, proza, esefi* (poetry, prose, and essays), Matica Srpska, 1965, `also published in *Sabrana dela* (see below); *Serbia, Seobe, Lament nad Beogradom,* Matica Srpska, 1965, also published in *Sabrana dela* (see below); *Tri poeme,* Prosveta, 1965; *Sabrana dela* (collected works), ten volumes, compiled by Riksanda Njegus and Stevan Raickovic, edited by Nikola Milosevic, Prosveta, Volumes 1-3: *Seobe,* 1966, Volume 4: *Peozija, Lirika Itake, Komentari, Antologija kineske lirike, Pesme starog Japana, Lament nad Beogradom,* 1966, Volume 5: *Proza: Dnevni o Carnojevicu, Price o muskom, Suzni krokodil,* 1966, Volume 6: *Putopisi,* 1966, Volumes 7-8: *Kod hyperborejaca,* 1966, Volume 9: *Drame, Maska, Konak, Tesla,* 1966, Volume 10; *Eseji,* 1966; *Lirika,* Prosveta, 1968.

Editor and publisher, *Ideas* (anti-Marxist weekly), 1933-34. Author of many essays, articles, other writings; contributor to *El Economista.*

SIDELIGHTS: Reportedly regarded in Belgrade as the greatest living writer among Serbs, Crnjanski told *CA* that he "was once a political suspect in Austria, suffered much in the First World War, and was a Serbian Nationalist. These few facts speak for themselves." He added: veta (Belgrade), 1959, also published in *Sabrana dela* "Entirely disillustioned."†

* * *

CROCKETT, G(eorge) Ronald 1906-

PERSONAL: Born February 4, 1906, in Belfast, Northern Ireland; son of William Robertson and Victoria (Bowers) Crockett; married Vera Edith Brunton Phillips, October 10, 1936; children: Philip Ronald, Nigel Stephen. *Education:* Attended Belfast Royal Academy. *Politics:* Conservative (left bias). *Home:* 23a Canadian Ave., London S.E.6, England.

CAREER: Asiatic Steam Navigation Co., Calcutta, India, deck officer, 1925-38; Barker & Howard Ltd. (publishers), London, England, secretary and director, 1939, 1946-62. *Military service:* Royal Air Force, 1940-45; became squadron leader; named officer of Order of the British Empire. *Member:* Honourable Company of Master Mariners.

WRITINGS: Crockett's Freight Reckoner, Warne, 1952.

WORK IN PROGRESS: Malta's an Island, a book based on high-speed launch rescue work during World War II.

AVOCATIONAL INTERESTS: Sailing small boats, golf, tennis, scrambling up mountains.

* * *

CROFFORD, Lena H(enrichson) 1908-

PERSONAL: Born January 20, 1908, in San Patricio, Tex.; daughter of Horace Comley (a rancher) and Jurdena (Poole) Henrichson; married Verner Reives Crofford (a college teacher), August 26, 1928; children: Clara Vernelle (Mrs. Jimmy D. Whitson). *Education:* Texas College of Arts and Industries, B.A., 1929, M.A., 1949; summer study at University of Colorado, 1958-59, and University of Wyoming, 1960-62. *Religion:* Baptist. *Home address:* P.O. Box 1016, Ingleside, Tex. 78362.

CAREER: English teacher in Aqua Dulce, Tex., 1928-55; Wichita Falls (Tex.) public schools, elementary English teacher, 1955-70. *Member:* Wichita Falls Poetry Society (president, 1964), Delta Kappa Gamma.

WRITINGS: Pioneers on the Nueces, Naylor, 1963.

BIOGRAPHICAL/CRITICAL SOURCES: Witchita Times and Record News, September 6, 1963.

* * *

CROMPTOM, Margaret (Norah Mair) 1901-
(Margaret Mair)

PERSONAL: Born September 14, 1901, in Clifton, Bristol, England; daughter of Robert John Byford (a career soldier) and Norah Frances (George) Mair; married Geoffrey Roger Crompton, June 10, 1937. *Education:* Educated privately at home and at Badminton School, Bristol, England. *Politics:* Liberal Conservative. *Religion:* Church of England. *Home:* Ashling, 88, The Street, Shalford, Guildford, Surrey, England.

CAREER: Author. *Member:* Society of Women Writers and Journalists (member of council, 1962—), Society of Authors, National Book League, Bronte Society.

WRITINGS—Under name Margaret Mair; all published by Jenkins: *Stay With Me Always,* 1943, *No More Goodbyes,* 1944, *This Was My Father,* 1948, *The Questioning Heart,* 1951, *Bring Back Delight,* 1953, *Let Us Be True,* 1954, *Half Sister,* 1956, *Spring of Love,* 1956.

Under name Margaret Crompton: *Passionate Search: A Life of Charlotte Bronte,* Cassell, 1955, McKay, 1956; *George Eliot: The Woman,* Yoseloff, 1960; *Shelley's Dream Women,* A. S. Barnes, 1967.

* * *

CROOK, Margaret Brackenbury 1886-

PERSONAL: Born May 5, 1886, in Dymock, Gloucestershire, England; became U.S. citizen, 1938; daughter of Leopold George Harris (a Unitarian minister) and Ellen (Brackenbury) Crook. *Education:* St. Anne's College, Oxford, B.A. (London; first class honours), 1913. Diploma in Anthropology (with distinction), 1914; Manchester College, Oxford, England, Certificate in Theology (first class honours), 1917. *Home and office:* 30 Washington Ave., Northampton, Mass. 01060.

CAREER: Ordained Unitarian minister, 1917; Octagon Chapel, Norwich, England, minister, 1918-20; Smith College, Northampton, Mass., assistant professor of religion and Biblical literature, 1921-23, associate professor, 1923-54, associate professor emeritus, beginning 1954. Honorary lecturer, American Schools of Oriental Research, Jerusalem, 1934; visiting lecturer in Old Testament, Manchester College (theology), Oxford, England, 1954, 1955. *Member:* American Academy of Religion, Society of Biblical Literature, American Association of University Professors, Northampton Council of Churches. *Awards, honors:* Sophia Smith fellowship, Smith College, 1963-64, and renewed, 1964-65, 1965-66.

WRITINGS: The Track of the Storm, Headley Bros., 1917; (editor and contributor) *The Bible and Its Literary Associations*, Abingdon, 1937; *The Cruel God: Job's Search for the Meaning of Suffering*, Beacon Press, 1959; *Women and Religion*, Beacon Press, 1964. Contributor to professional journals, 1931-54.

WORK IN PROGRESS: Articles on women in the field of religion; a project on St. Paul, leading to a book, under auspices of Unitarian Universalist Commission on Education; more research on Job, for a book for young people.

SIDELIGHTS: Margaret Crook is competent in Hebrew (taught Hebrew at Smith College), Greek, Latin, and French.

* * *

CROSS, K(enneth) G(ustav) W(alter) 1927-1967

PERSONAL: Born September 5, 1927, in Diss, Norfolk, England; son of Walter George (a farmer) and Alice (Shipp) Cross. *Education:* Trinity College, Dublin, B.A. (first class honors), 1951, Diploma in Education, 1952, Ph.D., 1956. *Religion:* Church of England. *Office:* Department of English, University of Newcastle, New South Wales, Australia.

CAREER: Rhodes University, Grahamstown, South Africa, lecturer in English, 1952-55; University of Adelaide, Adelaide, South Australia, lecturer in English, 1955-57; University of Sydney, Sydney, Australia, senior lecturer in English, 1957-64; University of Newcastle, Newcastle, Australia, professor of English and dean of Faculty of Arts, 1964-67. Visiting professor, University of Leeds, 1963; Carnegie traveling fellow in United States, Canada, and Mexico, 1963. *Military service:* British Army, Educational Corps, 1945-47; became sergeant. *Member:* Australasian Universities Literature and Language Association, Australia and New Zealand American Studies Association, Pacific Modern Language Association.

WRITINGS: F. Scott Fitzgerald, Grove, 1964; (editor with A. Norman Jeffares) *In Excited Reverie: A Centenary Tribute to William Butler Yeats*, Macmillan, 1965; (with D. R. C. Marsh) *Poetry: Reading and Understanding*, F. W. Cheshire, 1965; (editor) William Shakespeare, *Titus Andronicus*, Penguin, 1965; *A Bibliography of Yeats Criticism, 1887-1965*, Macmillan, 1971. Contributor of articles, mainly on Jacobean drama, to scholarly publications.

WORK IN PROGRESS: Macbeth and the Critics; The Elizabethan Sonnet; An Anthology and a Study; John Marston: The Dramatic Works.

SIDELIGHTS: "Trinity College, Dublin, a place of peace and scholarship unchanged since the 18th century, gave me a feeling for the past and its values, and a sense of the importance of humane letters in a scientific age. Through its literature a nation discovers its identity, and the emergence of American and Australian literatures interests me as it illuminates the development of national conscious-

ness." *Avocational interests:* Painting abstract pictures with house paint.

(Died, 1967)

* * *

CROTHERS, George D. 1909-

PERSONAL: Born January 8, 1909, in Fort Morgan, Colo.; son of William H. (a clergyman) and Nina (Morris) Crothers; married Ruth Irene Kinney, August 3, 1932; children: George Michael, Joel Anthony. *Education:* Wooster College, A.B., 1929; Columbia University, A.M., 1931, graduate study, 1932-33, 1937-38, Ph.D., 1941. *Home:* 116 Pinehurst Ave., New York, N.Y. 10033.

CAREER: Knoxville News-Sentinel, Knoxville, Tenn., reporter, 1929-30; Maryville College, Maryville, Tenn., instructor in history, 1932-33; Western College, Oxford, Ohio, assistant professor of history, 1933-41; Columbia University, New York, N.Y., instructor in history, 1941-46; Columbia Broadcasting System News, New York, N.Y., producer-broadcaster, 1945-74; City College of the City University of New York, New York, N.Y., adjunct associate professor of education, 1974—. Member of board of managers, Radio Station WRVR-FM; member of board of directors, National Public Relations Council, 1960-64; member of Adult Education Council, New York State Board of Regents, 1960-64. *Member:* Adult Education Association of the U.S.A. (chairman, adult basic education section, 1962-65; member of executive committee, 1965-68, 1971-74), National Association of Public School Adult Educators. *Awards, honors:* Award of Merit, National Association of Public School Educators, 1962.

WRITINGS: The German Elections of 1907, Columbia University Press, 1941; (with others) *The U.S. and Its Place in World Affairs*, Heath, 1943; (with Jacques Barzun, E. Golob, and Paul Beik) *Introduction to Naval History*, Lippincott, 1944; *American History*, Holt, 1964; (editor) *Invitation to Learning: English and American Novels*, Basic Books, 1966. Editor, *Invitation to Learning Reader* (quarterly), Muschel, 1951-54.

WORK IN PROGRESS: Adult basic education readers.

SIDELIGHTS: Crothers told CA: "I speak halting German and a unique French of my own devising, would rather play golf than work, and prefer doing nothing to either.... Became interested in adult education (through) professional concern with the techniques and content of 'communication.'"

* * *

CROW, Alice (von Bauer) 1894-1966

PERSONAL: Born July 20, 1894, in New York, N.Y.; daughter of Alois (an engineer) and Anne (Metzger) von Bauer; married Lester D. Crow (a professor of education), June 11, 1927. *Education:* New York University, B.Sc., 1921, M.A., 1922, Ph.D., 1924. *Home:* 633 East 19th St., Brooklyn, N.Y. 11230.

CAREER: Teacher in New York (N.Y.) public schools, 1912-22; Maxwell Teachers College, Brooklyn, N.Y., teacher of psychology, 1922-33; Girls High School, Brooklyn, N.Y., dean, 1933-46; Brooklyn College (now Brooklyn College of the City University of New York), Brooklyn, N.Y., assistant professor, 1946-56, associate professor of education, 1956-58. Served as part-time instructor at New York University, Brooklyn College, and City College, New York, N.Y., 1925-40. *Member:* National Retired

Teachers Association (life member), Pi Lambda Theta (life; past president), Kappa Delta Pi (honorary). *Awards, honors:* New York University Alumni Meritorious Award, 1930; Alice Crow Guidance Award was established in her honor by New York Board of Higher Education, 1958.

WRITINGS—All with husband, Lester D. Crow: (Contributor) *An Outline of Educational Psychology*, Barnes & Noble, 1934, revised edition, 1961.

Mental Hygiene in School and Home Life, McGraw, 1942, 2nd edition published as *Mental Hygiene*, 1951; *Learning to Live with Others*, Heath, 1944; *Our Teen-Age Boys and Girls*, McGraw, 1945, reprinted by Books for Libraries, 1969; *An Introduction to Education*, American Book Co., 1947, 5th edition, 1966; *Educational Psychology*, American Book Co., 5th revised edition edited by Francesco Cordasco, Littlefield, 1972; *Eighteen to Eighty: Adjustment Problems of Adults*, Christopher, 1949.

High School Education, Odyssey, 1951; *An Introduction to Guidance*, American Book Co., 1951, 2nd edition, 1960; *Child Psychology*, Barnes & Noble, 1953, revised edition, 1960; (with Charles E. Skinner) *Psychology in Nursing Practice*, 2nd edition (Alice Crow and Lester Crow not associated with first edition), Macmillan, 1954, 3rd edition published as *Understanding Interrelations in Nursing*, 1961; (editor) *Readings in General Psychology*, Barnes & Noble, 1954; *Adolescent Development and Adjustment*, McGraw, 1956, 2nd edition, 1965; *An Outline of Educational Psychology*, Littlefield, 1956; (editor) *Readings in Educational Psychology*, Littlefield, 1956; *Understanding Our Behavior*, Knopf, 1956; *Human Development and Learning*, American Book Co., 1956, revised edition, 1965; (editor) *Readings in Abnormal Psychology*, Littlefield, 1958, *An Outline of General Psychology*, Littlefield, 1958; *Sex Education for the Growing Family*, Christopher, 1959.

(Editor) *Readings in Child and Adolescent Psychology*, McKay, 1961; (editor with Walter Murray) *Teaching in the Elementary School: Readings in Principles and Methods*, McKay, 1961; (with Harry E. Ritchie) *Education in the Secondary School*, American Book Co., 1961; (editor) *Readings in Guidance*, McKay, 1962; *Child Development and Adjustment*, Macmillan, 1962, workbook, 1963; (editor) *Readings in Human Learning*, McKay, 1963; (editor) *Educating the Academically Able: A Book of Readings*, Macmillan, 1963; *How to Study*, Collier, 1963; (editor) *Vital Issues in American Education*, Bantam, 1964; *The Student Teacher in the Secondary School*, and workbook, McKay, 1964; *Organization and Conduct of Guidance Services*, McKay, 1965; *Being a Good Parent*, Christopher, 1966; *Psychology of Human Adjustment*, Knopf, 1967.

Contributor of over twenty articles and reviews to *Better Homes and Gardens*, and education and social hygiene journals.

(Died January 24, 1966)

*   *   *

CROW, Lester D(onald) 1897-

PERSONAL: Born March 31, 1897, in Beach City, Ohio; son of William C. (a farmer and businessman) and Mary (Olmstead) Crow; married Alice von Bauer (a professor of education), June 11, 1927 (died January 24, 1966). *Education:* Ohio University, A.B., 1923; New York University, M.A., 1924, Ph.D., 1927. *Home:* 633 East 19th St., Brooklyn, N.Y. 11230.

CAREER: Principal of schools in Ohio, 1918-21; teacher of

biology, Pelham, N.Y., 1924-26; member of faculty of Mary Washington College, Fredericksburg, Va., 1926-27, Lehigh University, Bethlehem, Pa., 1927-28, New York University, New York, N.Y., 1928-29; Brooklyn College (now Brooklyn College of the City University of New York) Brooklyn, N.Y., tutor and instructor, 1932-40, assistant professor, 1940-46, associate professor, 1948-56, professor of education, beginning, 1956, chairman of department, 1946-49. Visiting expert for U.S. in Teacher Education Program in Japan, 1950-51. *Member:* American Personnel and Guidance Association (life member), International Platform Association, New York Schoolmasters Club (vice-president, beginning, 1963), New York Academy of Science (life member), Guidance and School Counselors Association of Brooklyn College (faculty adviser, beginning, 1958), Midwood Property Owners Association (president, 1954-64), Phi Delta Kappa (emeritus member), Kappa Delta Pi (honor member).

WRITINGS—All with wife, Alice Crow: (Contributor) *An Outline of Educational Psychology*, Barnes & Noble, 1934, revised edition, 1961.

Mental Hygiene in School and Home Life, McGraw, 1942, 2nd edition published as *Mental Hygiene*, 1951; *Learning to Live with Others*, Heath, 1944; *Our Teen-Age Boys and Girls*, McGraw, 1945, reprinted by Books for Libraries, 1969; *An Introduction to Education*, American Book Co., 1947, 5th edition, 1966; *Educational Psychology*, American Book Co., 5th revised edition edited by Francesco Cordasco, Littlefield, 1972; *Eighteen to Eighty: Adjustment Problems of Adults*, Christopher, 1949.

High School Education, Odyssey, 1951; *An Introduction to Guidance*, American Book Co., 1951, 2nd edition, 1960; *Child Psychology*, Barnes & Noble, 1953, revised edition, 1960; (with Charles E. Skinner) *Psychology in Nursing Practice*, 2nd edition (Alice Crow and Lester Crow not associated with first edition), Macmillan, 1954, 3rd edition published as *Understanding Interrelations in Nursing*, 1961; (editor) *Readings in General Psychology*, Barnes & Noble, 1954; *Adolescent Development and Adjustment*, McGraw, 1956, 2nd edition, 1965; *An Outline of Educational Psychology*, Littlefield, 1956; (editor) *Readings in Educational Psychology*, Littlefield, 1956; *Understanding Our Behavior*, Knopf, 1956; *Human Development and Learning*, American Book Co., 1956, revised edition, 1965; (editor) *Readings in Abnormal Psychology*, Littlefield, 1958, *An Outline of General Psychology*, Littlefield, 1958; *Sex Education for the Growing Family*, Christopher, 1959.

(Editor) *Readings in Child and Adolescent Psychology*, McKay, 1961; (editor with Walter Murray) *Teaching in the Elementary School: Readings in Principles and Methods*, McKay, 1961; (with Harry E. Ritchie) *Education in the Secondary School*, American Book Co., 1961; (editor) *Readings in Guidance*, McKay, 1962; *Child Development and Adjustment*, Macmillan, 1962, workbook, 1963; (editor) *Readings in Human Learning*, McKay, 1963; (editor) *Educating the Academically Able: A Book of Readings*, Macmillan, 1963; *How to Study*, Collier, 1963; (editor) *Vital Issues in American Education*, Bantam, 1964; *The Student Teacher in the Secondary School*, and workbook, McKay, 1964; *Organization and Conduct of Guidance Services*, McKay, 1965; *Being a Good Parent*, Christopher, 1966; *Psychology of Human Adjustment*, Knopf, 1967.

Works authored without Alice Crow: (With others) *Educating the Culturally Disadvantaged Child: Principles and Program*, McKay, 1966; (with Walter Murray and Irving

Bloom) *Teaching Language Arts in the Elementary School*, W. C. Brown, 1968. Compiler or co-compiler of twelve sets of standardized achievement tests published by Acorn Publishing, 1945-59. Contributor of over twenty articles and reviews to education journals.

*   *   *

CROW, William Bernard   1895-

PERSONAL: Born September 11, 1895, in Stratford, West Ham, England; son of William Crow (a justice of the peace) and Ellen (a justice of the peace; maiden name Moule) Crow; married Alice Maud Whalley Welsh, November 7, 1934; children: Pamela Margaret Welsh Botterill, Angela Rosemary. *Education:* University of London, B.Sc., 1915, M.Sc., 1920, Ph.D., 1923, D.Sc., 1929; University of Wales, M.Sc., 1926. *Politics:* Monarchist. *Religion:* Ancient Orthodox Catholic. *Home:* 78 Broadmead Rd., Woodford Green, Essex, England.

CAREER: University College of South Wales and Monmouthshire, Cardiff, assistant lecturer, then lecturer, 1917-28; Huddersfield Technical College (affiliated with University of Leeds), Huddersfield, Yorkshire, England, head of department of biology, 1928-38; South West Essex Technical College, Walthamstow, England, senior lecturer in biology, 1938-44; Leicester College of Technology and Commerce, Leicester, England, senior lecturer in biology, 1944-60; Messrs. Davies, Laing and Dick Ltd., London, England, head of department of biology, 1960-68. Examiner for degrees in science and medicine, University of Wales, 1923-28; honorary professor, London College of Physiology, 1930. Priest and patriarch, Ancient Orthodox Catholic Church, 1943—. Grand master, Apostolate of the Holy Wisdom, 1939—; co-founder and life president, Institute of Cosmic Studies, 1934—.

MEMBER: Royal Society of Medicine (London; fellow), Linnean Society (fellow), Zoological Society of London (scientific fellow).

WRITINGS: Contributions to the Principles of Morphology, Kegan Paul, 1929; *Voice and the Vocal Apparatus*, Heffer, 1930; *The Science of Dreams*, Theosophical Publishing House, 1935; *Mysteries of the Ancients*, eighteen parts, Houghton, 1941-45; *A Synopsis of Biology*, Wright & Sons, 1960, 2nd edition, Williams & Wilkins, 1964; *Precious Stones: Their Occult Power and Hidden Significance*, Aquarian, 1968; *A History of Magic, Witchcraft and Occultism*, Aquarian, 1968; *The Occult Properties of Herbs*, Aquarian, 1969; *The Arcana of Symbolism*, Aquarian, 1970. Editor, *Proteus* and *Iao.* Contributor of articles to biological psychological, historical, and theological journals.

WORK IN PROGRESS: Research on depth psychology, history of magic, mythology, anthropology, and evolution.

*   *   *

CROWDER, Richard (Henry)   1909-

PERSONAL: Born October 7, 1909, in Remington, Ind.; son of Richard Horatio (a minister) and Mary Jane (Isaacs) Crowder; married Esther Mae Haber, August 20, 1951. *Education:* DePauw University, A.B., 1931, M.A., 1933; Yale University, graduate student, 1936-37; University of Iowa, Ph.D., 1944. *Politics:* Independent. *Religion:* Episcopal. *Home:* 1525 Sheridan Rd., West Lafayette, Ind. 47906. *Office:* Heavilon Hall, Purdue University, Lafayette, Ind. 47907.

CAREER: High school teacher of Latin and English, Lowell, Ind., 1934-35; Valparaiso University, Valparaiso, Ind., instructor in English, 1935-36; Purdue University, Lafayette, Ind., instructor, 1937-45, assistant professor, 1945-50, associate professor, 1950-57, professor of English, 1957—. Fulbright lecturer in American poetry, University of Bordeaux, 1963-65, University of Nice, summer, 1965. Member of board, United Episcopal Charities of Diocese of Indianapolis, 1973—. *Member:* Modern Language Association of America, Midwest Modern Language Association, Indiana College English Association (secretary-treasurer, 1953-54; vice-president, 1954-55), Lafayette Drama Club (president, 1956-57), Phi Mu Alpha-Sinfonia (life member), Phi Gamma Delta (educational director, 1950-61; historian, 1961-71), Parlor Club of Lafayette (president, 1974-75), Lafayette Country Club. *Awards, honors:* American Philosophical Society fellow, 1955; Episcopal Church Society fellow, 1958; American Council of Learned Societies grant, 1970; Distinguished Alumnus Award, DePauw University, 1971.

WRITINGS: Those Innocent Years: The Inheritance and Legacy of a Victorian Hero, James Whitcomb Riley, Bobbs-Merrill, 1957; *No Featherbed to Heaven: Michael Wigglesworth, 1631-1705*, Michigan State University Press, 1962; *Carl Sandburg*, Twayne, 1964; (editor with others) *Frontiers of American Culture*, Purdue University Studies, 1967; (editor with others) *American Literary Manuscripts: A Checklist of Holdings in Academic, Historical and Public Libraries in the United States*, revised edition (Crowder was not associated with earlier edition), University of Texas Press, 1968. Contributor to an annual, *American Literary Scholarship*, published by Duke University Press, and *Reader's Encyclopedia of American Literature*; contributor of about thirty articles and reviews to *Poetry, New England Quarterly, Bucknell Review, Modern Language Notes, South Atlantic Quarterly, Chicago Review*, and other publications.

WORK IN PROGRESS: A book, *Twentieth-Century American Women Poets*; research on the letters to George Washington Cable from his editors, Richard Watson Gilder and Robert Underwood Johnson.

AVOCATIONAL INTERESTS: Music (church organist and choir director), amateur dramatics.

*   *   *

CROWE, John   1906-

PERSONAL: Born September 18, 1906, in Jhelum, India; son of Osborne (a minister) and Sarah (Burns) Crowe; married Ruth Luckman. *Education:* Westminster College, New Wilmington, Pa., B.A., 1926; University of Pittsburgh, M.Ed., 1939. *Politics:* Republican. *Religion:* Episcopalian. *Home:* 207 Diamond Blvd., Johnstown, Pa. 15905.

CAREER: Erie (Pa.) public schools, teacher, 1928-44; University of Pittsburgh at Johnstown, Pa., 1947-69, began as instructor, became associate professor of English.

WRITINGS: The Book of Trout Lore, A. S. Barnes, 1947; *The Modern ABC's of Fresh Water Fishing*, Stackpole, 1965; *What a Supervisor Should Know About Increasing His Word Power* (booklet), Dartnell, 1971; *What an Executive Should Know About Better English Usage* (booklet), Dartnell, 1971. Contributor to *Field & Stream* and *Outdoor Life*, 1937-49; weekly outdoors columnist, *Johnstown Tribune-Democrat*, 1949-69.

CROWE, Sylvia 1901-

PERSONAL: Born September 15, 1901, in Banbury, England; daughter of Eyre (an engineer) and Beatrice (Stockton) Crowe. *Education:* Swanley Horticultural College, diploma, 1922. *Home:* Flat B, 59 Ladbroke Grove, London W.11, England. *Office:* 182 Gloucester Pl., London N.W.1, England.

CAREER: Cutbush Ltd., England, landscape designer, 1926-38; private practice as landscape architect, London, England, 1945—. Consultant on projects for Central Electricity Generating Board, Harlow New Town, City of Bristol, County of Bedford, Borough of Swansea, among others. *Military service:* British Army, 1939-45. *Member:* Institute of Landscape Architects (past president), Royal Institute of British Architects (honorary fellow), Royal Society of Arts (fellow), International Federation of Landscape Architects, American Society of Landscape Architects (corresponding member), Town Planning Institute (honorary). *Awards, honors:* Commander Order of the British Empire.

WRITINGS: Tomorrow's Landscape, Architectural Press, 1956; *Garden Design,* Country Life, 1958, Hearthside, 1959; *Landscape of Power,* Architectural Press, 1958; *Landscape of Roads,* Architectural Press, 1960; (editor) *Space for Living: Landscape Architecture and the Allied Arts and Professions,* Djambatan, 1961; (editor with Zvi Miller) *Shaping Tomorrow's Landscape,* two volumes, Humanities, 1964; *Forestry in the Landscape,* H.M.S.O., 1966.

WORK IN PROGRESS: Landscape of reservoirs.

* * *

CRUICKSHANK, Helen Gere 1907-

PERSONAL: Surname is pronounced *Crook*-shank; born February 20, 1907, in Brooklyn, Pa.; daughter of Charles Edward and Hilda May (Alworth) Gere; married Allan D. Cruickshank (an editor, lecturer, and photographer on staff of National Audubon Society), February 1937. *Education:* Pennsylvania State College (now University), B.S., 1927. *Home and office:* 1925 Indian River Rd., Rockledge, Fla. 32955.

CAREER: Schoolteacher in Rye, N.Y., during World War II; wildlife photographer and writer, and assistant to husband on field trips for National Audubon Society. Photographer for "Pastures of the Sea," used in Audubon Lecture Series, and assistant producer of other wildlife films; nature photographs also have been used in filmstrips and as book and magazine illustrations and covers. Member of awards committee, Brevard County Board of Conservation, 1962-64; member of Governor's Natural Resources Committee, 1969-71. *Member:* National Audubon Society, Nature Conservancy, Wilderness Society, National Parks Association, Society of Woman Geographers, John Burroughs Association, Florida Audubon Society, Indian River Audubon Society (conservation chairman, 1954-64), Florida Federation of Garden Clubs (state bird chairman, 1959-61), Cocoa-Rockledge Garden Club (founder's circle; conservation chairman, 1958-74). *Awards, honors:* John Burroughs Medal, 1949, for *Flight Into Sunshine*; medal from Societe Provancher d'Histoire Naturelle du Canada, 1949; Brevard County Conservationist of the Year, 1968; "Oppie" award for the best nature book of the year, 1968, for *A Paradise of Birds.*

WRITINGS: Bird Islands Down East, Macmillan, 1941; *Flight Into Sunshine,* Macmillan, 1948; *Water Birds,* Doubleday, 1955; *Wonders of the Bird World,* Dodd, 1956; (editor) *John and William Bartram's America,* Devin, 1957; (with husband, Allan D. Cruickshank) *1001 Questions Answered About Birds,* Dodd, 1958; *Wonders of the Reptile World,* Dodd, 1959; (editor) *Thoreau on Birds,* McGraw, 1964; *A Paradise of Birds,* Dodd, 1968.

Contributor to *Natural History, Audubon Magazine, American Girl, Collier's Woman's Day,* and other magazines.

WORK IN PROGRESS: A book about bird adventures in Texas, with husband, Allan D. Cruickshank.

* * *

CRUMP, Geoffrey (Herbert) 1891-

PERSONAL: Born October 29, 1891, in Sawston, Cambridgeshire, England; son of Charles Edward (an Episcopal priest) and Georgina (Andrewes) Crump; married Barbara Helen Tatham, October 2, 1917; children: Elizabeth Thornycroft, Graeme Peter. *Education:* Queens' College, Cambridge, M.A., 1912. *Home:* Oakhurst, Steep, Petersfield, Hampshire, England.

CAREER: Assistant master of Sherborne Preparatory School, Sherborne, Dorsetshire, England, 1912-16, and Cheltenham College, Cheltenham, Gloucestershire, England, 1916-18; Bedales School, England, senior English master, 1918-49; Royal Academy of Music, London, England, professor of speech and drama, 1949-50, director, 1950-62; New College of Speech and Drama, England, codirector, 1962-63; Royal Schools of Music, examiner in speech and drama, 1962-74. Director of English Amateur Players and Steep Shakespeare Players, 1923-61. *Member:* Society of Teachers of Speech and Drama (honorary secretary, 1946-60), Royal Academy of Music (honorary).

WRITINGS: Mattins and Other Poems, Erskine Macdonald, 1918; *Guide to the Study of Shakespeare's Plays,* Harrap, 1925; *For Weal of All,* Heffer, 1926; *Poets of the Romantic Revival,* Harrap, 1927; *Selections from English Dramatists,* Harrap, 1927, new edition, Dobson, 1950; *English for Schools,* Thomas Nelson, 1929; *Bible Prose and Poetry,* Thomas Nelson, 1929; *A Shorter Malory,* Thomas Nelson, 1930; *Signposts,* privately printed, 1932; *The Lovers and Other Poems,* privately printed, 1935; *Bedales Since the War,* Chapman & Hall, 1936; *A Manual of English Speech,* Pitman, 1947, new edition, Dobson, 1960; *Speaking Poetry,* Methuen, 1953, new edition, Dobson, 1964.

AVOCATIONAL INTERESTS: Gardening, music, tapestry, painting, carpentry, travel.

* * *

CULP, Louanna McNary 1901-1965

PERSONAL: Born July 11, 1901, in Pennsylvania; daughter of Thomas B. (a farmer) and Jennie (Moore) McNary; married David Howard Culp (an orchardist), February 11, 1938; children: Margaret (Mrs. Joseph Crnkovich), David P., John H. *Education:* Occidental College, student; San Jose State College (now University), Teacher's Diploma, 1924. *Politics:* Democrat. *Religion:* Baptist. *Home:* 900 Pine Tree Lane, Aptos, Calif.

CAREER: Teacher at Presbyterian mission schools in India, 1924-30; also taught at public school in Palo Alto, Calif., and at Indian reservation school, Yuma, Ariz., prior to 1938.

WRITINGS: Langurni, Little Monkey of India, Golden Gate Junior Books, 1964.

WORK IN PROGRESS: A book on village life in India.

(Died November 26, 1965)

* * *

CUMBERLAND, Marten 1892-1972
(R. Laugier, Kevin O'Hara; James Bevis, a joint pseudonym)

PERSONAL: Born July 23, 1892, in London, England; son of Alfred (a member of London Stock Exchange) and Ada Frances (Fletcher) Cumberland; married Kathleen Walsh, November 28, 1928. *Education:* Attended Cranleigh School, Surrey, England. *Home:* Wasdale House, Rathfarnham Rd., Dublin 6, Ireland. *Agent:* Stephen Aske, Chansitor House, Chancery Lane, London W.C.2, England; (plays) Suzanne Czech, International Copyright Bureau, Suite 8, D & E, 26 Charing Cross Rd., London W.C.2, England.

CAREER: Ran away from home and stock exchange job at eighteen; trained as wireless operator and went to sea on an Argentine ship in 1913; after service in British Merchant Navy, 1914-18, his short stories brought offer of assistant editorship of *New Illustrated* (weekly paper), London, England; when paper failed, joined staff of *Harmsworth Encyclopaedia*, London, 1919-20, resigning to become one of first advertising consultants, 1920-22; assistant fiction editor of Sir Edward Hulton Press (later Allied Newspapers), London, 1922-24; free-lance writer in England, Paris, France, and Dublin, Ireland, 1924-1972.

WRITINGS: (With Raymond Harrison) *The New Economics*, Cecil Palmer, 1922, 2nd edition, Stanley Nott, 1936; (with B. V. Shann) *Behind the Scenes* (novel), Cecil Palmer, 1923, 2nd edition; published under joint pseudonym James Bevis, 1933; (with Shann) *Loaded Dice*, Methuen, 1926, 2nd edition, published under joint pseudonym James Bevis, 1933; (with Michael Joseph) *How to Write Serial Fiction*, Henry Holt, 1928, published as Part 4 of omnibus volume *The Complete Writing for Profit*, Hutchinson, 1930; (with Granville Hill) *Spoils and Stratagems* (one-act play; reproduced from typewritten script), G. Hill, 1931; *The Sin of David* (novel), Selwyn & Blount, 1932; (with Shann) *Murder at Midnight*, Mellifont, 1935; *Birds of Prey*, Gramol, 1937; *Climbing* (three-act comedy; produced in London, 1937, later in United States), W. H. Baker, 1937; *The Testing of Tony*, Macdonald, 1943.

Mystery novels: *The Perilous Way*, Jarrolds, 1926; *The Dark House*, Gramol, 1935; *The Devil's Snare*, Gramol, 1935; *The Imposter*, Gramol, 1935; *Shadowed*, Mellifont, 1936; *Someone Must Die*, Hurst & Blackett, 1940; *Questionable Shape*, Hurst & Blackett, 1941; *Quislings Over Paris*, Hurst & Blackett, 1942; *The Knife Will Fall*, Hurst & Blackett, 1943, Doubleday, Doran, 1944; *Everything He Touched*, Macdonald, 1945; *Not Expected to Live* (originally announced as "The Lorrain-Prad Affair"), Hurst & Blackett, 1945; *Steps in the Dark*, Doubleday, Doran, 1945; *A Dilemma for Dax*, Doubleday, 1946 (published in England as *Hearsed in Death*, Hurst & Blackett, 1947); *A Lovely Corpse*, Hurst & Blackett, 1946; *Darkness as a Bride*, Hurst & Blackett, 1947; *Hate Will Find A Way*, Doubleday, 1947 (published in England as *And Worms Have Eaten Them*, Hurst & Blackett, 1948); *And Then Came Fear*, Doubleday, 1948; *The Crime School*, Eldon, 1949; *The Man Who Covered Mirrors*, Doubleday, 1949;

Policeman's Nightmare, Doubleday, 1949; *The House in the Forest*, Doubleday, 1950 (published in England as *Confetti Can Be Red*, Hurst and Blackett, 1951); *On The Danger List*, Hurst & Blackett, 1950; *Fade Out The Stars*, Doubleday, 1952; *Grave Consequences*, Doubleday, 1952 (published in England as *Booked for Death*, Hurst & Blackett, 1952); *One Foot in the Grave*, Hurst & Blackett, 1952; *Etched in Violence*, Hurst & Blackett, 1953, McGraw, 1955; *Nobody is Safe*, Doubleday, 1953 (published in England as *Which Of Us Is Safe?*, Hurst & Blackett, 1953); *The Frightened Brides*, Hurst & Blackett, 1954; *Unto Death Utterly*, Hurst & Blackett, 1954, McGraw, 1955; *The Charge Is Murder*, Hurst & Blackett, 1955; *Lying At Death's Door*, Hurst & Blackett, 1956; *Far Better Dead!*, Hutchinson, 1957; *Hate for Sale*, British Book Centre, 1957; *Out Of This World*, Hutchinson, 1958; *Murmurs in the Rue Morgue*, London House & Maxwell, 1959; *Remains to be Seen*, Hutchinson, 1960; *There Must Be Victims*, Hutchinson, 1961; *Attention! Saturnin Dax!*, Hutchinson, 1962; *Postscript to a Death*, Hutchinson, 1963; *Hate Finds A Way*, Hutchinson, 1964; *The Dice Were Loaded* (not the same as *Loaded Dice*), Hutchinson, 1965; *No Sentiment In Murder*, Hutchinson, 1966.

Mystery novels, under pseudonym Kevin O'Hara: *The Customer's Always Wrong*, Hurst & Blackett, 1951; *Exit and Curtain*, Hurst & Blackett, 1952; *Sing, Clubman, Sing!*, Hurst & Blackett, 1952; *Always Tell The Sleuth*, Hurst & Blackett, 1953; *It Leaves Them Cold*, Hurst & Blackett, 1954; *Keep Your Fingers Crossed*, Hurst & Blackett, 1955; *The Pace That Kills*, Hurst & Blackett, 1955; *Danger: Women At Work*, John Long, 1958; *Women Like To Know*, Jarrolds, 1958; *And Here is the Noose*, John Long, 1959; *Well, I'll Be Hanged!*, John Long, 1960; *Taking Life Easy*, John Long, 1961; *If Anything Should Happen*, John Long, 1962; *Don't Tell The Police*, John Long, 1963; *Don't Neglect The Body*, John Long, 1964; *It's Your Funeral*, John Long, 1966.

Other plays produced: "Inside the Room," London, 1934; (adaptor from the French) Louis Verneuil, "No Ordinary Lady," London, 1936; "Men and Wife," London, 1937; "Believe It or Not," London, 1938; (with Claude Houghton) "Baxter's Second Wife," London, 1949. Also author of ballet, "The Golden Bell of Ko," with music by Aloys Fleischmann, produced at Cork Opera House.

Stories included in Edward O'Brien's *Best Short Stories of the Year* series, Dodd, 1927-32, and in *Best Detective Stories of the Year*, Faber, 1933.

Contributor: Verse, short stories, and essays to *New Age* (and later to *New English Weekly*), some under pseudonym R. Laugier, 1920-39; humorous essays to *Daily Herald* (London), 1921; short stories and a "Paris Letter," to *Daily Dispatch* (Manchester), 1930-31; stories and essays to *Ideas*, and stories to *Truth*, both for a twenty-year period; serials to King Features Syndicate, *Montreal Standard*, and *Toronto Star*; reviews, stories, and articles to *Dublin Magazine* for ten years; also contributor at various times to most London newspapers, and to *Men Only*, *Argosy*, *Adelphi*, *Everybody's Weekly*, *Theatrical World*, *Strand*, *Mystery Stories Magazine* (United States), *Lilliput*, *Irish Digest*, *Time and Tide*, *Criminology*, *Kilkenny*, and other magazines; short stories and plays to Radio Eireann.

WORK IN PROGRESS: Autobiography, *Hereinafter Called The Author;* plays.

SIDELIGHTS: Despite the considerable (and international) success of his detective novels, Cumberland considered himself essentially a man of the theatre. He first became aware of this leaning in 1932, and set about working ten hours a day (when writing) for almost two years before the London production of "Inside the Room" established his reputation as a playwright. He wrote plays until his death, but believed that the interruption of the war took the edges off his full potential as a playwright.

"As a dramatist was knocked out by War II," he said, "and started writing this stuff." *Stuff* refers to the detective novels dealing with Saturnin Dax, the French commissaire featured in some thirty books, and the Chico Brett series.

If not the completely doting creator of Dax and Brett, Cumberland had to admit that they were gainful. The thrillers have appeared in thirty countries in fifteen languages. More than a million and a half of the Dax stories have been sold in Germany alone in the past decade, and as many of the Brett books in less time. Eleven of the Dax stories have borne the Doubleday Crime Club imprint.

"Inside the Room" was sold to Ambassador Films in England, and adapted for television production in America.

* * *

CUMMINGS, Parke 1902-

PERSONAL: Born October 8, 1902, in West Medford, Mass.; son of Henry Irving (a lawyer) and Adeline (Parke) Cummings; married Mary Virginia Obear, April 6, 1935; children: John (deceased), Patricia Ann. *Education:* Harvard University, B.S., 1925. *Home:* 178 South Compo Rd., Westport, Conn. 06880. *Office:* Famous Writers School, Wilton Rd., Westport, Conn.

CAREER: Writer, specializing in sports and humor, 1925—; Famous Writers School, Westport, Conn., instructor and editor, 1961—.

WRITINGS: The Whimsey Report: or, Sex Isn't Everything, Crowell, 1948; *The Dictionary of Sports*, A. S. Barnes, 1948; *The Dictionary of Baseball*, A. S. Barnes, 1950; *I'm Telling You Kids for the Last Time*, Schuman, 1951; *American Tennis: The Story of a Game and Its People*, Little, Brown, 1957; *Baseball Stories*, Hill & Wang, 1959; *The Fly in the Martini*, Hill & Wang, 1961. Contributor of humor and verse to *New Yorker, Esquire, Saturday Evening Post, Redbook, Pageant, Atlantic Monthly*, and other national magazines.

* * *

CUMMINS, Geraldine Dorothy 1890-1969

PERSONAL: Born January 24, 1890, in Cork, Ireland; daughter of Ashley (a professor of medicine, National University of Ireland) and Jane (Constable) Cummins. *Education:* Educated privately. *Religion:* Church of Ireland. *Home:* 25 Jubilee Pl., Chelsea, London S.W.3, England; (summer and autumn) Woodville, Glanmire, County Cork, Ireland.

CAREER: Employed at National Library, Dublin, Ireland, during World War I; journalist in London during 1920's; free-lance writer. *Member:* Authors Society.

WRITINGS: The Land They Loved (novel), Macmillan, 1919; *The Scripts of Cleophas: A Reconstruction of Primitive Christian Documents*, Rider, 1928, 4th edition, Psychic Press, 1961; *Paul in Athens*, Rider, 1930; *The Great Days of Ephesus*, Rider, 1933; *The Road to Immortality: Being a Description of the After-Life Purporting to Be Communicated by the Late F. W. H. Myers Through G. Cummins*,

Nicholson & Watson, 1933, 4th edition, Aquarian Press, 1955; *Beyond Human Personality: Being a Detailed Description of the Future Life Purporting to be Communicated by the Late F. W. H. Myers*, Nicholson & Watson, 1935, 2nd edition, Psychic Press, 1952; *Fires of Beltane* (novel), M. Joseph, 1936; *The Childhood of Jesus*, Muller, 1937, 4th edition published as *The Childhood of Christ*, Psychic Press, 1949; *When Nero Was Dictator*, Muller, 1939; *The European Crises: Accurate Prophecies Given Through G. Cummins*, Goodmount Press, 1939.

After Pentecost (the Alexandrian Chronicle of Cleophas), Rider, 1944; *They Survive: Evidence of Life Beyond the Grave from Scripts of Geraldine Cummins*, compiled by E. B. Gibbes, Rider, 1946; *The Resurrection of Christ: An Explanation of This Mystery Through Modern Psychic Evidence*, L.S.A. Publications, 1947; *Travellers in Eternity*, compiled by E. B. Gibbes, Psychic Press, 1948; *The Manhood of Jesus: His Early Adult Years, His Trial and Crucifixion*, Andrew Dakers, 1949; *I Appeal Unto Caesar*, Psychic Press, 1950; *Unseen Adventures* (semi-autobiographical), Rider, 1951; *Dr. E. OE Sommerville: A Biography*, Andrew Dakers, 1952; (with Gibbes) *The Fate of Colonel Fawcett: A Narrative of His Last Expedition*, Aquarian Press, 1955; *Mind in Life and Death: Review of Recent Evidence of the Survival of Franklin Roosevelt and Others*, Aquarian Press, 1956; (with R. C. Connell) *Healing the Mind: How Extra-Sensory Perception Can Be Used in the Investigation and Treatment of Psychological Disorders*, Aquarian Press, 1957; *Variety Show* (novel), Barrie & Rockliff, 1959.

(With Signe Toksvig) *Swan on a Black Sea: A Study in Automatic Writing—The Cummins-Willett Scripts*, Routledge & Kegan Paul, 1965, revised edition, 1970.

Plays: (With Susanne R. Day) "Broken Faith," produced at Abbey Theatre, 1912; (with Day) "The Way of the World," produced at Cork Theatre, 1914; (with Day) "Fox and Geese," produced at Abbey Theatre, Dublin, 1917, Court Theatre, London, 1917; "Till Yesterday Comes Again," produced at Chanticleer Theatre, London, 1938. Contributor of about two hundred articles to periodicals in Great Britain and United States.

AVOCATIONAL INTERESTS: Tennis, light gardening, occasional swim in Atlantic on warm days.

(Died August 24, 1969)

* * *

CUNNINGHAM, Floyd F(ranklin) 1899-

PERSONAL: Born December 24, 1899, in Flat Rock, Ill.; son of Carl Homer (a farmer) and Lillie (Seitzinger) Cunningham; married Helen B. Espy, September 1, 1925; children: Jo Ann (Mrs. Jack Jungers), Floyd Espy. *Education:* Eastern Illinois University, student, 1916-18; Illinois State Normal University (now Illinois State University), B.Ed., 1926; University of Chicago, graduate study, 1926-27; Clark University, A.M., 1928, Ph.D., 1930. *Religion:* Methodist. *Address:* P.O. Box 267, Carbondale, Ill. 62901. *Office:* 612 West Elm St., Carbondale, Ill. 62901.

CAREER: Teacher in Illinois schools, 1918-22, and principal, 1925-27; Florence State Teachers College (now University of North Alabama), Florence, Ala., professor and head of department of geography, 1929-47, director of visual education, 1938-47; Biarritz American University, Biarritz, France, professor of geography, 1945-46; U.S. Army, Information and Education Division, lecturer on geography in Germany and Austria, 1946; Southern Illinois University, Carbondale, professor of geography, 1947-58, director of laboratory of climatology, 1958-66, professor emeritus, 1966—, head of department of geography, 1947-58. Fulbright lecturer in geography, Cairo, Egypt, 1953-54; conductor of field courses in geography in Mexico, Canada, Alaska, western Europe, and on world tour, 1958; Distinguished Visiting Professor of Geography, Western Kentucky University, 1966-70.

MEMBER: Association of American Geographers, National Council for Geographic Education (fellow; member of board of directors, 1934-35; member of executive committee, 1936; secretary, 1937-40; president, 1942-44), American Geographical Society (fellow), American Association for the United Nations, Soil Conservation Society of America, American Association of University Professors, Illinois Academy of Science, Illinois Geographical Society (president, 1948-49), National Travel Club, Kappa Delta Pi, Gamma Theta Upsilon.

WRITINGS: Laboratory Manual in the Geography of North America, Wiley, 1930; (with C. F. Jones) *Laboratory Manual in the Geography of South America,* Holt, 1931; (contributor) Lester D. Crow, Alice V. Crow, and others, editors, *Teaching in the Elementary School,* Longmans, Green, 1961; (with Clarence D. Samford and others) *You and Regions Near and Far,* Benefic, 1964; (with Samford and others) *You and the United States,* Benefic, 1964; (with Samford and others) *You and the Americas,* Benefic, 1965; *1,001 Questions Answered about Water Resources,* Dodd, 1967. Member of editorial board, *Kappa Delta Pi Record,* 1964—.

WORK IN PROGRESS: Research for a five-volume series, "An Adventure in Learning About Peoples and Places"; geography of Illinois.

*   *   *

CUNNINGHAM, H(orace) H(erndon)   1913-1969

PERSONAL: Born January 20, 1913, in Warren, Ind.; son of James William (a banker) and Margaret (Settle) Cunningham; married Mary Shaw Robeson, December 19, 1942; children: Anne Chalmers, Margaret Settle, Jama Rhett. *Education:* Atlantic Christian College, A.B., 1936; University of North Carolina, M.A., 1940, Ph.D., 1952. *Politics:* Independent Democrat. *Religion:* Disciples of Christ. *Home address:* Box 815, Elon College, N.C. 27244.

CAREER: High school teacher in North Carolina, 1936-42; North Carolina State College of Agriculture and Engineering, Raleigh, instructor in history and political science, 1946-47; University of North Carolina, Chapel Hill, part-time instructor in social science and history, 1947-52; Elon College, Elon College, N.C., chairman of department of social sciences and William S. Long Professor of History, 1952-69. North Carolina Confederate Centennial Commission, member. *Military service:* U.S. Army Air Forces, 1942-46; became captain. *Member:* Society of American Historians, Organization of American Historians, Southern Historical Association, Historical Society of North Carolina (secretary-treasurer), State Literary and Historical Association, Owen County Historical Society, Pi Gamma Mu (vice-chancellor of Atlantic region), Burlington Rotary Club (president, 1963-64). *Awards, honors:* R. D. W. Connor Award for best article in *North Carolina Historical Review,* 1958.

WRITINGS: Doctors in Gray: The Confederate Medical Service, Louisiana State University Press, 1958, 2nd edi-

tion, 1960; (contributor) Arthur S. Link and W. Patrick Rembert, editors, *Writing Southern History,* Louisiana University Press, 1965; *Field Medical Services at the Battles of Manassas,* University of Georgia Press, 1968. Contributor to medical and historical journals. Member of board of editors, *Social Science.*

(Died November 5, 1969)

*   *   *

CURIE, Eve   1904-

PERSONAL: Born December 6, 1904, in Paris, France; daughter of Pierre and Marie (Sklodowska) Curie, discoverers of radium, and recipients of Nobel Prize; married Henry Richardson Labouisse (American Ambassador to Greece), November 19, 1954. *Education:* College Sevigne, B.S., Ph.B. *Home:* 1 Sutton Pl.S., New York, N.Y. 10022. *Agent:* Curtis Brown Ltd., 575 Madison Ave., New York, N.Y. 10022.

CAREER: Concert pianist in earlier years, appearing in France and Belgium, then music critic and writer of other articles for *Candide* (weekly); after the fall of France went to England in 1940 to work for cause of Free France, later served in Europe with Fighting French as officer of women's division of army; became co-publisher of *Paris-Presse* (daily newspaper), Paris, France, 1945-49. Lecturer on seven U.S. tours, 1939-49. Special adviser to Secretary General, North Atlantic Treaty Organization (NATO), 1952-54. Executive director, United Nations Childrens Fund, Greece, 1962-65. *Awards, honors:* National Book Award for non-fiction, 1937, for *Madame Curie;* Chevalier de la Legion d'Honneur, 1939; Polonia Restituta, 1939; Croix de Guerre, 1944; D.H.L., Mills College, 1939, Russell Sage College, 1941; D.Litt., University of Rochester, 1941.

WRITINGS: Madame Curie (selection of Literary Guild, Book-of-the-Month Club, Junior Guild, Scientific Book of the Month), Doubleday, 1937, annotated school edition, Houghton, 1963; *Journey Among Warriors* (Literary Guild selection), Doubleday, 1943.

SIDELIGHTS: Eve Curie speaks Polish, and some Greek and Spanish. Her books have been translated into many languages. *Madame Curie* was made into a film by M.G.M. in 1943. *Avocational interests:* Skiing, skating, and swimming.

*   *   *

CURREY, R(onald) F(airbridge)   1894-

PERSONAL: Born October 23, 1894, in London, England; son of Harry Latham (a barrister) and Ethel (Fairbridge) Currey; married Dorothy White, August 28, 1924; children: Harry, Charles, Hilary. *Education:* St. Andrews College, Grahamstown, South Africa, student; Rhodes University, B.A., 1913; Oxford University, M.A., 1920. *Politics:* Progressive Party of South Africa. *Religion:* Anglican. *Home and office:* 34, Hill St., Grahamstown, South Africa.

CAREER: Michaelhouse, Natal, South Africa, rector, 1930-38; St. Andrews College, Grahamstown, South Africa, headmaster, 1939-55; Ruzawi School, Marandellas Southern Rhodesia, headmaster, 1956-61; Rhodes University, Grahamstown, South Africa, lecturer in classics, 1962-68. *Military service:* British Army; became lieutenant; received Military Cross and bar. *Awards, honors:* LL.D. from Rhodes University.

WRITINGS: (With J. F. Hofmeyer and others) *Coming of*

Age, Maskew Miller, 1930; *Rhodes: A Biographical Footnote,* privately printed, 1946; (with others) *The South African Way of Life,* UNESCO, 1951; *Christian National Education in South Africa,* Anglican Church Press, 1963; *Rhodes University 1904-1970,* Rustica Press, 1970.

* * *

CUTHBERT, Eleonora Isabel (McKenzie)   1902-

PERSONAL: Born October 22, 1902, in Wagga Wagga, New South Wales, Australia; daughter of James Thomas (a draftsman) and Eva Isabel (Morrison) McKenzie; married Percy Oakden Cuthbert (an engineer-surveyor), July 11, 1928; children: Janet (Mrs. Wilfred Brandt). *Education:* University of Sydney, B.A., 1938. *Politics:* "Variable." *Religion:* Presbyterian. *Home:* 91 Kameruka Rd., Northbridge, New South Wales, Australia.

CAREER: Public Library of New South Wales, Sydney, Australia, mainly employed as cataloguer, 1921-62. *Member:* Australian Library Association.

WRITINGS: Index of Australian and New Zealand Poetry, Scarecrow, 1963; *The Australian Quarterly: The Journal of the Australian Institute of Political Science, Decennial Index, 1954-63,* Australian Institute of Political Science, 1964. Contributor to *Australian Library Journal.*

WORK IN PROGRESS: Historical research for interstate and overseas readers.

* * *

DABBS, James McBride   1896-1970

PERSONAL: Born May 8, 1896, in Mayesville, S.C.; son of Eugene Whitefield (a farmer) and Maude (McBride) Dabbs; married Jessie Armstrong, May 11, 1918 (deceased); married Edith Mitchell, June 11, 1935; children: Maude (Mrs. Robert Haas), Carolyn (Mrs. Richter Moore), James, Jr., Dorothy, Richard. *Education:* University of South Carolina, A.B., 1916; Clark University, Worcester, Mass., M.A., 1917; Columbia University, graduate study, 1924-25, 1929-30. *Politics:* Democrat. *Religion:* Presbyterian. *Home and office:* Route 1, Mayesville, S.C. 29104.

CAREER: University of South Carolina, Columbia, instructor in English, 1921-24; Coker College, Hartsville, S.C., member of English faculty, 1925-42, head of department, 1925-37; farmer in Sumter County, S.C., 1942-70. Writer and lecturer. Member of executive committee; Fellowship of Southern Churchmen, 1955-63; member of board of directors, South Carolina Council on Human Relations, 1957-63; Southern Regional Council, president, 1957-63, member of executive committee, 1963-70; chairman of board of trustees, Penn Community Services, Inc., Beaufort, S.C., 1964-70; ruling elder of U.S. Presbyterian Church; member of Delta Ministry of Mississippi. *Military service:* U.S. Army, Field Artillery, 1917-19, with overseas duty, 1918-19; became first lieutenant. *Member:* Societe Europeanne de Culture, Phi Beta Kappa (honorary). *Awards, honors:* Brotherhood Award of National Conference of Christians and Jews, 1958, for *Southern Heritage;* citation from National Association for the Advancement of Colored People (Detroit chapter); honorary L.H.D., Morehouse College, 1959; LL.D., Tuskegee Institute, 1964.

WRITINGS: (Author of introduction) *Pee Dee Panorama* (picture book of eastern South Carolina), University of South Carolina Press, 1951; (contributor) Louis Rubin, Jr., and James J. Kilpatrick, editors, *The Lasting South,* Reg-

nery, 1957; *The Southern Heritage,* Knopf, 1958; (contributor) R. W. Howard, editor, *This Is the South,* Rand McNally, 1959; *The Road Home,* Christian Education Press, 1960; (contributor) Hoke Norris, editor, *We Dissent,* St. Martins, 1962; *Who Speaks for the South?,* Funk, 1964; *Civil Rights in Recent Southern Fiction,* Southern Regional Council, 1969; *Haunted by God,* John Knox, 1972.

Contributor of several hundred articles to American journals, including *Scribner's, Yale Review, Virginia Quarterly Review, Christian Century, Presbyterian Outlook,* and *South Atlantic Quarterly.*

WORK IN PROGRESS: Lectures on the race issue in the South; a new book on Southern culture and religion.

SIDELIGHTS: Dabbs at one time told *CA:* "Went abroad at government expense in 1918-19; had enough travel. In 1937 I moved back to my farm from the Coker College community; since 1942 I have been making my living mainly by farming. My chief interest for some fifteen years has been the race situation. . . . I see the South as a region of magnificent resources, especially human resources, but sadly confused and inclined to think of its resources as liabilities." Nationally known as a leading Southern exponent of integration, he told an interviewer: "Segregation is not the Southern way of life. That's a myth. It's the very opposite of our historical tradition. Today the South is moving into a new world and it's afraid it may lose something of value. But the thing of value is not segregation."

Although Dabbs called himself a farmer, that farm was 175 acres of cotton and tobacco plantation, remnant of the 10,000 acres his grandfather had owned. It was his rearing as a Southern gentleman, he maintained, that first involved him in civil rights. It was "such bad manners," he said, "talking publicly about taking the vote from Negroes." Shortly before his death, he felt "the ice was breaking throughout the South," with the old way of life giving way to a new.

Reviewer T. H. Williams wrote, of *Who Speaks for the South,* that "no other writer has so related the currents in Southern thought to the mainstream of human thought throughout the ages." *South Today* called him "one of the South's great voices of common sense and poetic insight."

(Died May 30, 1970)

* * *

DAEHLIN, Reidar A.   1910-

PERSONAL: Born December 9, 1910, in Honan Province, China; son of Ingvald (a missionary) and Emma (Hasle) Daehlin; married Marion Borstad, June 20, 1935; children: Sharon, Douglas, Steven. *Education:* Concordia College, Moorhead, Minn., B.A., 1932; Luther Theological Seminary, St. Paul, Minn., B.Th., 1935; College of Chinese Studies, Peking, China, graduate student, 1935-36; Union Theological Seminary, New York, N.Y., S.T.M., 1942. *Home:* 821 Eighth Ave. W., Kalispell, Mont. 59901.

CAREER: Lutheran minister. Missionary in China, 1935-50; pastor of churches in Missoula, Mont., 1942-45, Great Falls, Mont., 1945-49, and Brooklyn, N.Y., 1949-53; The American Lutheran Church, president of Rocky Mountain District, with headquarters in Great Falls, Mont., 1953—. *Awards, honors:* D.D., Concordia College, Moorhead, Minn., 1954.

WRITINGS: Pastor to Pastor, Augsburg, 1966.

SIDELIGHTS: Daehlin speaks Norwegian, Danish, Chinese, and reads Swedish and German.

DAHL, Murdoch Edgcumbe 1914-

PERSONAL: Born March 11, 1914, in Newcastle Upon Tyne, England; son of Oscar Horace (a timber merchant) and Gladys Edith (Edgcumbe) Dahl; married Joan Woollaston, March 30, 1940; children: Daniel, Philip, Jeremy. *Education:* University of Durham, B.A., 1936, M.A., 1956. *Home:* 2 Sumpter Yard, St. Albans, Hertfordshire, England.

CAREER: Clergyman, Church of England; curate in Bolton, Manchester, and Harpenden, England, 1937-49; vicar and rector in Bedfordshire, England, 1949-51; priest-in-charge, Croxley Green, Hertfordshire, England, 1951-56; vicar of Great Hormead and rector of Wydehall, Hertfordshire, 1956-65; canon theologian of St. Alban's Cathedral, Hertfordshire, 1965—. Examining chaplain to Bishop of St. Albans, 1959—; director of clerical studies, Diocese of St. Albans, 1960; part-time lecturer, Anglican Theological College, Cheshunt, 1960; honorary canon of St. Alban's Cathedral, 1963-65.

WRITINGS: The Resurrection of the Body: A Study of I Corinthians 15, Allenson, 1962; *Sin Streamlined,* Mowbray, 1966; *The Christian Materialist,* Smythe, 1968.

WORK IN PROGRESS: Two semi-satirical works on parochial life in the Church of England; translating *Jerusalem zur Zeit Jesu,* for S.C.M. Press.

SIDELIGHTS: In a review of *The Christian Materialist,* Michael Bootham finds in Dahl's book "a remarkable and poetic use of language. Dahl's main desire," Bootham continues, "is to show the world as intrinsically beautiful, and to stress that its beauty is the result of its having been created by God.... It is an extraordinary and memorable book and ... beautifully produced." *Avocational interests:* Walking, music, and keeping white fan-tail pigeons.

BIOGRAPHICAL/CRITICAL SOURCES: Books and Bookmen, February, 1969.

* * *

DAME, Lawrence 1898-
(Baron Pomfret)

PERSONAL: Born July 2, 1898, in Portland, Me.; son of Edward L. (a chemist) and Katherine (a poet; maiden name, Gunn) Dame; married Rachel Wells (an artist), September 24, 1958; children: Thai. *Education:* Studied at Harvard University and University of Paris. *Politics:* Liberal. *Religion:* Episcopal. *Home:* 245 Worth Ave., Palm Beach, Fla. 33480 (winter); Horse Guards Plantation, Maidstone P.O., Jamaica (summer). *Office address:* P.O. 2392, Palm Beach, Fla. 33480.

CAREER: Career, in United States and abroad, has been linked with writing and the arts, 1919—. Editorial work for various publications, 1919-39; director of Harvard University News Office, Cambridge, Mass., 1943-45, 1946-47; staff critic of *Art News,* London, England, 1950-53; special writer for newspapers in Turkey and Italy, 1952-53; associate editor of *Nantucket Inquirer and Mirror,* Nantucket, Mass., 1953-54; art, book, and arts editor, *Sarasota Herald-Tribune,* Sarasota, Fla., during the fifties; arts and book critic for *Palm Beach Illustrated,* Palm Beach, . Fla., under name Baron Pomfret, arts critic for Stations WQXT (radio) and WPTV, Palm Beach, Fla., social correspondent for *Boston Herald,* Boston, Mass., and special correspondent, U.S. Navy; currently art editor, *Palm Beach Post.* Lecturer on art and travel. *Military service:* U.S. Army, Artillery, 1917-18. *Member:* Society of Colonial Wars,

Wine and Food Society of Palm Beach (founder; president), Harvard Clubs of Boston and Palm Beach. *Awards, honors:* Decorated by French and Portuguese governments for war work, 1941.

WRITINGS: New England Comes Back, Random House, 1940; *Yucatan,* Random House, 1941; (contributor) John N. Makris, editor, *Boston Murders,* Duell, Sloan & Pearce, 1948; *Maya Mission,* Doubleday, 1968. Contributor to *New York Times, All-Florida Weekly,* and about twenty-five other magazines and newspapers in United States and Europe.

WORK IN PROGRESS: Return to Yucatan; Backabush Jamaica.

AVOCATIONAL INTERESTS: Cycling, mountain-climbing, swimming, and exploring.

* * *

DAMON, Virgil Green 1895-1972

PERSONAL: Born January 19, 1895, in Medina, Ohio; son of George J. (a physician) and Perlea E. (Green) Damon; children: James S., Mary (Mrs. Peter Reed), Diane (Mrs. George Morang), Sandra (Mrs. William Pritchett). *Education:* Ohio State University, A.B., M.D., 1921. *Politics:* Republican. *Religion:* Protestant. *Home:* 9 East 93rd St., New York, N.Y. 10028. *Agent:* Helen Strauss, William Morris Agency, 1350 Avenue of the Americas, New York, N.Y. 10019. *Office:* 1088 Park Ave., New York, N.Y. 10028.

CAREER: Columbia University, College of Physicians and Surgeons, New York, N.Y., clinical professor of obstetrics and gynecology, 1923-66; attending physician at Sloane Hospital for Women, Columbia Presbyterian Medical Center, and Vanderbilt Clinic, all New York, N.Y.; private practice of medicine, New York, N.Y., 1926-66. Consultant to Midtown Hospital, New York, N.Y., Tuxedo Hospital, Tuxedo, N.Y., Good Samaritan Hospital, Suffern, N.Y. Ramapo Valley Concert Association, former president, and president emeritus. *Member:* American Medical Association, American Academy of Medicine, American College of Surgeons, New York Obstetrical Society; Economic Club, University Club, Columbia University Club, Tuxedo Club, Players Club (all New York).

WRITINGS: (With Isabella Taves) *I Learned about Women from Them,* foreword by Helen Hayes, McKay, 1962. Contributor to *Harper's Bazaar* and to medical journals.

BIOGRAPHICAL/CRITICAL SOURCES: New York Times, July 11, 1972.

(Died July 9, 1972)

* * *

DANBY, Hope (Smedley) 1899-

PERSONAL: Born March 21, 1899; daughter of John (an architect) and Anna-Maria (Casement) Smedley; married Charles Gilbert Danby (deceased); children: Charles Richard Dexter. *Education:* Attended Ecole Vinet in Lausanne, Switzerland. *Religion:* Church of England. *Home:* The Little Manor, Hawkhurst, Kent, England.

CAREER: Lived for almost twenty years in Peking, China, where she was interned by the Japanese during World War II.

WRITINGS: The Illustrious Emperor, Ziff-Davis Publishing Co., 1947; *The Garden of Perfect Brightness,* Williams & Norgate, 1951; *My Boy Chang*, Gollancz, 1955. Contributor of articles to *Dictionary of National Biography, Everybody's, Architectural Review, North China Daily News*, and to other journals and Chinese newspapers (before the war).

WORK IN PROGRESS: Additional books on China.

* * *

DANFORD, Howard G(orby) 1904-

PERSONAL: Born January 5, 1904, in Ohio; son of Morris (a farmer) and May (Gorby) Danford; married, wife's name, Irma, July 9, 1957; children: Gene, Ardath, Howard, Martha, Rudi. *Education:* Ohio University, B.S., 1928; New York University, M.A., 1938, Ed.D., 1940. *Home:* 809 19th St., Greeley, Colo. 80631. *Office:* Colorado State College, Greeley, Colo. 80631.

CAREER: Colorado State College, Greeley, professor of recreation and physical education, 1959—. Conductor of volleyball clinics for U.S. Armed Forces in Europe, 1955, 1956, 1957. *Member:* American Association for Health, Physical Education and Recreation, National Recreation Association, American Recreation Society.

WRITINGS: Recreation in the American Community, Harper, 1953; *Creative Leadership in Recreation,* Allyn & Bacon 1964, 2nd edition, revised by Max Shirley, 1970.

WORK IN PROGRESS: Revising *Recreation in the American Community,* in collaboration with Dan Dyer.

AVOCATIONAL INTERESTS: Reading history; playing golf and volleyball.

* * *

DARLINGTON, William Aubrey (Cecil) 1890-

PERSONAL: Born February 20, 1890, in Taunton, Somersetshire, England; son of Thomas (an inspector of schools) and Edith (Bainbridge) Darlington; married Marjorie Sheppard, October 3, 1918 (died October, 1973); children: Anne (Mrs. Peter Ryde; deceased), Phoebe Joanna (Mrs. Hugh Boyle). *Education:* Cambridge University, B.A., 1912, and M.A. *Religion:* Church of England. *Home:* Monksdown, Bishopstone, Sussex, England. *Agent:* Curtis Brown Ltd., 13 King St., Covent Garden, London W.C.2, England.

CAREER: Schoolmaster at Westgate-on-Sea, Kent, England, 1913-14; *World*, London, England, editor, 1919; *Daily Telegraph*, London, England, chief dramatic critic, 1920-68, also writer of weekly column, "About the Theatre." London drama correspondent, *New York Times*, 1939-60. Lecturer, East London College, 1931; member, advisory committee for drama diploma, University of London. *Military service:* British Army, 1915-19; became captain. *Member:* Institute of Journalists, Guild of Adjudicators, Society of Authors, League of Dramatists, London Critics Circle (president, 1930); Garrick Club and Dramatists' Club (both London). *Awards, honors:* Commander of the British Empire, 1967.

WRITINGS: Alf's Button (novel), Stokes, 1920; *Wishes Limited* (novel), Jenkins, 1922; *Through the Fourth Wall*, Brentano, 1922, reprinted, Books for Libraries, 1968; *Egbert* (novel), Jenkins, 1924, Penn Publishing, 1925; *Literature in the Theatre and Other Essays*, Henry Holt, 1925, reprinted, Books for Libraries, 1968; *Alf's Carpet* (novel), Jenkins, 1930; *Sheridan*, Macmillan, 1933, reprinted, Longmans, 1966; *Mr. Cronk's Cases* (novel), Jenkins, 1934; *Carpet Slippers* (three-act play; sometimes titled *Magic*

Slippers), Baker International Play Bureau, 1937; *J. M. Barrie*, Blackie & Son, 1938; *Alf's New Button* (novel), Jenkins, 1940; *I Do What I Like* (autobiography), Macdonald & Co., 1947, 2nd edition, Rockliff, 1950; *The Actor and His Audience*, Phoenix House, 1949; *The World of Gilbert and Sullivan*, Crowell, 1950, reprinted, Books for Libraries, 1970; (with others) *The Approach to Dramatic Criticism* (published with Christopher Fry, *An Experience of Critics*), Perpetua, 1952; *Six Thousand and One Nights: Forty Years a Critic* (theater autobiography), Harrap, 1960; *Laurence Olivier*, Morgan, 1968.

Adaptor of *Alf's Button* for silent motion picture, 1920, stage, 1924, talking motion picture, 1929, and television play, 1937. Also author of several other plays and play adaptations, including "Marcia Gets Her Own Back" and "The Key of the House."

Short stories (published originally in London magazines) have been anthologized in *A Century of Humor, Second Century of Humour*, and *My Funniest Story*. Contributor to *Punch* and other humorous weeklies.

SIDELIGHTS: Darlington told *CA* he "began with the idea of becoming a writer of comedy, in novels, short stories, and plays; carried this on with success until 1940 (novel, *Alf's Button*, sold over 300,000 copies). Meanwhile became a drama critic almost by chance, and in the end made of it [my] main career."

BIOGRAPHICAL/CRITICAL SOURCES: I Do What I Like, Macdonald & Co., 1947, 2nd edition, Rockliff, 1950; *Six Thousand and One Nights; Forty Years a Critic*, Harrap, 1960.

* * *

DART, Raymond A(rthur) 1893-

PERSONAL: Born February 4, 1893, in Toowong, Brisbane, Queensland, Australia; son of Samuel (a farmer and tradesman) and Eliza Ann (Brimblecombe) Dart; married Dora Tyree, 1921 (divorced); married Marjorie Gordon Frew (an assistant at University of the Witwatersrand Press), November 11, 1936; children: Diana Elizabeth, Galen Alexander. *Education:* University of Queensland, B.Sc. (honors), 1913, M.Sc., 1915; University of Sydney, M.B. and Ch.M. (honors), 1917, M.D., 1927. *Home:* 20 Eton Park, Eton Road, Sandhurst, Johannesburg, South Africa. *Office:* Bernard Price Institute for Palaeontological Research, University of the Witwatersrand, Johannesburg, South Africa.

CAREER: University of London, University College, London, England, senior demonstrator in anatomy, 1919-21; lecturer in histology and embryology, 1921-22; University of the Witwatersrand, Johannesburg, South Africa, professor of anatomy, 1923-58, professor emeritus, 1959—, dean of medical faculty, 1926-43. Discoverer of the first of the fossil man-apes, *Australopithecus africanus*, at Taungs, Bechuanaland, South Africa, 1924; excavated and developed the Makapansgat fossil site in mid-Transvaal, 1945-55. Lecturer at Viking Fund Seminar, New York, and Lowell Institute, Boston, 1949; honorary lecturer at University of Sydney, 1950, Yale University and University of Toronto, 1958, Washington University, St. Louis, 1971, and other institutes and scientific societies worldwide; United Steelworkers of America Professor of Anthropology in the Institute of Man, and in the Institute for the Achievement of Human Potential, 1966—. Member of International Commission on Fossil Man, 1929; member of South African Medical Council, 1934-38; Pan African Congress of Prehistory, president of anthropological section, 1947-51, vice president, 1959-63; founder of South African Nursing Council, 1944; member of Johannesburg Museum Advisory Committee, and of Johannesburg Municipal Library Advisory Committee. *Military service:* Australian Army, Medical Corps, 1917-19; became captain. South African Army, Medical Corps, Reserve of Officers; served in Field Ambulance Training Corps during World War II; became lieutenant colonel.

MEMBER: International Primatological Committee, Institute of Biology (London; fellow), South African Association for the Advancement of Science (president, 1952-53), South African Society of Physiotherapy (president, 1960-68), Royal Society of South Africa (fellow; vice-president, 1938-40, 1950-51), Association of Scientific and Technical Societies of South Africa (vice-president, 1961-63; president, 1963-64), South African Institute for Medical Research (board member, 1934-48), South African Archaeological Society (president, 1951), Anatomical Society of Great Britain and Ireland, South African Museums Association (president, 1961-62), Linnaeum Society (foreign fellow). *Awards, honors:* Rockefeller Foundation fellow in New York, 1920-21; Gold Medal and grant, South African Association for the Advancement of Science, 1939; Coronation Medal, 1953; Senior Captain Scott Medal, South African Biological Society, 1955; Commemorative Medal, Association for the Advancement of Science (France), 1956; Viking Fund Medal for Physical Anthropology, Wenner-Gren Foundation of New York, 1957; Simon Biesheuvel Medal, National Institute of Personnel Research, 1961; Award of the International Forum for Neurological Organization, 1966; Gold Medal, South African Nursing Association, 1970; Silver Medal from Medical Association of South Africa, 1972; D.Sc. (honoris causa), Natal University, 1956, and University of the Witwatersrand, 1959.

WRITINGS: (Contributor) Isaac Schapera, editor, *The Bantu-Speaking Tribes of South Africa*, Routledge & Kegan Paul, 1937; (contributor) John David R. Jones and Clement M. Doke, editors, *Bushmen of the Southern Kalahari*, University of the Witwatersrand Press, 1937; (editor) *Africa's Place in the Human Story*, South African Broadcasting Corp., 1954; (editor) *The Oriental Horizons of Africa*, privately printed, 1955; *Cultural Status of South African Man-Apes* (excerpt from *Annual Report, 1955*, Smithsonian Institution), [Washington], 1956; *The Osteodontokeratic Culture of Australopithecus Prometheus*, Transvaal Museum (Pretoria), 1957; (with Dennis Craig) *Adventures with the Missing Link*, Harper, 1959; (author of foreword) Alexander Galloway, *The Skeletal Remains of Bambandyanalo*, University of Witwatersrand Press, 1959; (editor) *Africa's Place in the Emergence of Civilization*, South African Broadcasting Corp., 1959; *Beyond Antiquity*, South African Broadcasting Corp., 1965. Contributor of over 200 articles on anatomical, anthropological, and archaeological subjects to scientific journals.

SIDELIGHTS: The fossil dentition of *Australopithecus africanus*, the Taungs baby, who lived 500,000 years before the first known stone implements, convinced Dart this primitive man was a flesh eater. The appearance of a hunter without the use of stone weapons led Dart to excavate in the Makapansgat Valley in South Africa in order to learn something of Australopithecine culture. After finding bone, tooth, and horn tools and weapons and some 28,000 skeletal fragments, Dart developed his osteodontokeratic (bone, tooth, and, horn) theory on pre-stone age culture. His first

detailed explanation of this theory was published in *Cultural Status of the South African Man-Apes* in 1956.

AVOCATIONAL INTERESTS: Swimming, music.

BIOGRAPHICAL/CRITICAL SOURCES: "Dart Festschrift," *Leech*, Volume XXVIII, numbers 3-5, 1958; Robert Ardrey, *African Genesis*, Atheneum, 1961; *Life*, Volume LI, number 85, November 24, 1961; *South African Panorama*, April, 1965; *Johannesburg Star*, February 9, 1966.

*   *   *

DASHWOOD, Robert Julian   1899-
(Julian Hillas)

PERSONAL: Born October 12, 1899, in Leicestershire, England; son of Robert Carthew (a vicar, Church of England) and Eileen (Hillas) Dashwood; third wife, Kopurere (manager of a trading store); children: (first marriage) David; (second marriage) Vaana, Vahua; (third marriage) Burma, Jean, Julian. *Education:* Attended Thames Nautical Training College, 1913-15, Trinity College, Dublin, Ireland, 1922. *Residence:* Mauke, Cook Islands.

CAREER: Teacher in English preparatory schools, 1919-22, and in a boys' high school in Constantinople, Turkey, 1922-23; sales representative of motor company in Birmingham, England, 1924; farmer in northern Transvaal, South Africa, 1925-28, went to South Seas, 1929, and has lived on Mauke; elected Mauke representative to Cook Island Legislative Assembly, 1963; Minister for Health, Justice, Police, and Social Development in Cook Islands transitional government, 1964. *Military service:* Royal Navy, 1916-19, became flight sub-lieutenant, received Greek Order of Military Valour; Australian Imperial Forces, became flying officer (lieutenant), Royal Air Force.

WRITINGS—Under pseudonym Julian Hillas: *I Know an Island* (novel), Hutchinson, 1934; *Today is Forever*, (autobiography), Doubleday, 1964; *South Seas Paradise* (travel), R. Hale, 1965. Contributor of short stories and articles to periodicals in England and Australia.

WORK IN PROGRESS: A book about political activity in Cook Islands and the advent of internal self-government.

*   *   *

DAVEY, Gilbert W(alter)   1913-

PERSONAL: Born June 7, 1913, in London, England; son of Walter (a director of an advertising company) and Ethel (Franklin) Davey; married Angela Gross, October 7, 1939; children: Claire. *Education:* Attended Stationers' Company's School. *Religion:* Church of England. *Home:* 36 Hillbury Ave., Kenton, Harrow, Middlesex, England. *Office:* Pearl Assurance Co. Ltd., North London Regional Office, Edgeware, Middlesex, England.

CAREER: Worked in insurance field prior to World War II, including a period with Lloyd's of London; Pearl Assurance Co., Ltd., West End Branch, London, England, assistant branch manager, 1947-67, assistant manager of North London region, 1967—. Auxiliary Fire Service, Watford, Hertfordshire, England, commandant, 1939-41; Chief Regional Fire Officer, Cambridge, England, staff officer, 1941-44. *Military service:* British Army, 1943-47; served on staff of military governor, Berlin, Germany; became major.

WRITINGS—Edited by Jack Cox: *Fun with Radio*, Edmund Ward, 1957, revised edition, 1969; *Fun with Short Waves*, Edmund Ward. 1960, revised edition published as

Fun with Short Wave Radio, 1968; *Fun with Electronics*, Edmund Ward, 1962; *Fun with Transistors*, Edmund Ward, 1964, revised edition, edited by Jack Cox, Kaye & Ward, 1971. Radio correspondent, *Boy's Own Paper*, 1946-67; contributor of articles to *Practical Wireless* and other periodicals.

WORK IN PROGRESS: A history of radio receiver home-construction in United Kingdom.

* * *

DAVIES, (George) Colliss (Boardman) 1912-

PERSONAL: Born December 7, 1912, in Loddon, Norfolk, England; son of George Middlecott (an archdeacon, Church of England) and Berta Mary (Boardman) Davies; married Edith Mavis Maitland-Kirwan, April 5, 1951; children: Loraine Mary. *Education:* St. Catharine's College, Cambridge, B.A., 1934, M.A., 1938, B.D., 1947, D.D., 1951. *Home:* 10 College Yard, Worcester, England.

CAREER: Priest, Church of England. Canon Residentiary of Worcester Cathedral.

WRITINGS: The Early Cornish Evangelicals, 1735-60: A Study of Walker of Truro and Others, S.P.C.K. for Church History Society, 1951; *Henry Phillpotts, Bishop of Exeter, 1778-1869*, S.P.C.K. for Church History Society, 1954; *The First Evangelical Bishop: Some Aspects of the Life of Henry Ryder*, Tyndale Press, 1958; *Men for the Ministry: The History of the London College of Divinity*, Hodder & Stoughton, 1963. Contributor to religion journals.

WORK IN PROGRESS: Henry Ryder, Bishop of Coventy and Lichfield, 1824-36.

* * *

DAVIES, Ebenezer Thomas 1903-

PERSONAL: Born October 28, 1903, in Pontycymer, Glamorganshire, Wales; son of David Arnold (a businessman) and Caroline (Thomas) Davies; married Winifred Mary Thomas, July 27, 1940; children: Hilary, Robert Hugh Thomas. *Education:* University College, Cardiff, University of Wales, B.A. (first class honors in history), 1928; St. Michael's College, Llandaff, M.A., 1940. *Politics:* Liberal. *Home:* 11 Ty Brith Gardens, Usk, Ginent, England.

CAREER: Clergyman, Church of Wales; director of religious education in the diocese of Monmouth, 1948-73; canon of Monmouth, 1953—; examining chaplain to the Archbishop of Wales, 1953—. Consultant archivist to the Church in Wales, 1955—. Member of court of governors, National Library of Wales, 1957—.

WRITINGS: The Political Ideas of Richard Hooker, University of London Press, 1945; *Episcopacy and the Royal Supremacy*, Oxford University Press, 1951; *An Ecclesiastical History of Monmouthshire*, Starsons (Newport), 1953; *Monmouthshire Schools and Education*, Starsons, 1957; (editor and contributor) *The Story of the Church in Glamorgan*, S.P.C.K., 1962; *Religion in the Industrial Revolution in South Wales*, University of Wales Press, 1965. Also contributor to *Glamorgan County History*. Honorary editor, Church in Wales Historical Society, 1953-73.

* * *

DAVIES, Eileen Winifred 1910-
(Eileen Elias)

PERSONAL: Born July 26, 1910, in England; daughter of Owyn Aubrey and Marian (Carey) Elias; married Albert Thomas Davies (a civil engineer), June 22, 1940; children: Hugh, Allison, Richard. *Education:* Lady Margaret Hall, Oxford, B.A., 1933, M.A., 1936; Institute of Education, University of London, graduate study, 1963-64. *Religion:* Quaker. *Home:* Down Green, Wheathampstead, Hertfordshire, England. *Agent:* Charles Lavell, Norfolk St., London, England.

CAREER: Free-lance journalist and author. *Member:* Society of Women Writers and Journalists (council member, beginning 1964), Women's Press Club of London.

WRITINGS—All under name Eileen Elias: *Enjoy Your Baby*, Evans, 1942; *Happy Families*, National Magazine, 1944; *Fun With Your Family*, Hutchinson, 1955; *Bringing Up Children*, Hutchinson, 1957; *Entertaining*, Hutchinson, 1958; *Your Child at School*, Museum Press, 1962. Contributor of articles on children, education, and travel to *Parents' Magazine* (United States), *Good Housekeeping, Ideal Home, Women's Realm*, and *Homes and Gardens* (England).

WORK IN PROGRESS: Magazine articles.

SIDELIGHTS: Mrs. Davies studied children's activities and education on tour of United States, 1962, in Denmark and the Soviet Union, 1964.

BIOGRAPHICAL/CRITICAL SOURCES: Ideal Home, April, 1961; *Presswoman*, June 1964; *Homes and Gardens*, July, 1964.

* * *

DAVIES, T(refor) Rendall 1913-

PERSONAL: Born September 21, 1913, in Maindy, Wales; son of Thomas William and Mary Elizabeth (Rendall) Davies; married Beryl Nancy Hudson, August 14, 1943; children: Branwen, Megan, Glenys, Nesta (daughters). *Politics:* Socialist. *Religion:* Methodist. *Home:* 1 Greenwood Gardens, London N.13, England.

CAREER: Educational Interchange Council, London, England, deputy secretary, 1950-60, general secretary, 1960—. *Member:* Peace Pledge Unicn (chairman, 1959-61).

WRITINGS: Dealers in Books, Sheppard Press, 1951, 7th edition, 1969; *A Book of Welsh Names*, Sheppard Press, 1953; *Book Dealers in North America*, Sheppard Press, 1954, 5th edition, 1969; *European Book Dealers*, Sheppard Press, 1966, 2nd edition 1971. Author of articles on antiquarian book trade, Celtic nomenclature, peace and politics, educational travel.

WORK IN PROGRESS: Welsh Record, a general reference book.

* * *

DAVIS, Arthur Kennard 1910-

PERSONAL: Born January 15, 1910, in Marlborough, England; son of Rushworth Kennard (a schoolmaster) and Maude (McNamara) Davis; married Margaret Elinor Gray; children: James, Juliet, David and Margaret (twins). *Education:* Attended Birkenhead School and studied architecture at University of Liverpool. *Politics:* Conservative. *Religion:* Church of England. *Home:* 5 Noel St., Taybank, Port Elizabeth, South Africa. *Agent:* Laurence Pollinger Ltd., 18 Maddox St., London W.1, England.

CAREER: British Merchant Navy, cadet, later navigation officer; farmer in Kenya. Former swimming instructor, schoolteacher, hotelier, and stevedore. *Military service:*

Royal Navy Volunteer Reserve, 1939-42; became chief petty officer.

WRITINGS: Isle of Adventure (juvenile), Basil Blackwell, 1937; *A Farm in Cedar Valley* (juvenile), Basil Blackwell, 1947; *Dingdong on Little Hurricane* (juvenile), Kenya Weekly News, 1950; The Gentle Captain *(sea novel),* J. Cape, 1954; The Thee-Yard Ensign *(sea novel), Barrie & Rockliff, 1963.*

AVOCATIONAL INTERESTS: Sailing ships, painting in oil and water color.

* * *

DAVIS, John King   1884-1967

PERSONAL: Born February 19, 1884, in London, England; son of James Green and Marion Alice (King) Davis. *Education:* Attended schools in England. *Home:* 492 St. Kilda Rd., Melbourne S.C.2, Victoria, Australia.

CAREER: Master mariner holding extra master's certificate; lieutenant commander, Royal Australian Naval Reserve, retired. Began sea career as apprentice on fullrigged ship "Celtic Chief" of Liverpool, England; second mate of four-masted barque "Port Jackson," 1906; chief officer of "Nimrod" on British Antarctic Expedition under E. H. Shackleton, 1907-09; master of "Aurora" and second in command of Australasian Antarctic Expedition under Douglas Mawson, 1911-14; commander of Ross Sea Relief Expedition, 1916-17; appointed director of navigation for Australia, 1920; on leave to act as second in command and master of the "Discovery" on an expedition under Sir Douglas Mawson, 1929-30; retired, 1949.

MEMBER: Honorable Company of Master Mariners (London; life), Royal Geographical Society (life fellow), Royal Society of Victoria, Royal Historical Society of Victoria. *Awards, honors:* Bronze and silver Polar medals with two clasps; Murchison Award, Royal Geographical Society, 1914; named Commander, Order of the British Empire, 1964.

WRITINGS: History of St. John's College, Tamaki, Auckland, N.Z., Abel, Dykes (Auckland), 1911; *"Aurora" Relief Expedition: Report of Voyage,* Aurora Advisory Committee, 1918, *With the "Aurora" in the Antarctic, 1911-1914,* Melrose, 1919; *Willis Island: A Storm Warning Station in the Coral Sea,* Critchley Parker, 1923; *High Latitude,* Melbourne University Press, 1962. Contributor to *Journal of Circumnavigators Club* and other periodicals.

BIOGRAPHICAL/CRITICAL SOURCES: Oxford Mail, April 18, 1963.

(Died May 7, 1967)

* * *

DAVIS, Margaret Banfield   1903-

PERSONAL: Born September 28, 1903, in Westmoor (now Kingston), Pa.; daughter of Thomas Hopkin (a mine foreman) and Margaret (Jones) Davis. *Education:* Syracuse University, A.B., 1924; Pennsylvania State University, M.A., 1933; Sorbonne, University of Paris, graduate study, summer, 1935. *Home:* 816 Quincy Ave., Scranton, Pa. 18510.

CAREER: Scranton (Pa.) public schools, teacher, 1924-68, head of French department at Central High School, 1935-68; Marywood College, Scranton, Pa., assistant professor of French, 1968—. American National Red Cross, co-organizer and first director of Junior Red Cross Unit, Scran-

ton, 1943-57, member of chapter board of directors, 1957-68, honorary board member, 1968—; honorary board member, Scranton-Pocono Girl Scout Council, 1967—; Girl Scout leader for thirty years. *Member:* American Association of University Professors, National Education Association, American Association of Teachers of French, American Association of University Women, Pennsylvania State Education Association, Pennsylvania State Modern Language Association, Women Teachers Club of Scranton, Welsh Women's Society, Chi Omega, Delta Kappa Gamma, Alpha Mu Gamma.

WRITINGS: The Blue Book of French, Regents Publishing, 1964.

BIOGRAPHICAL/CRITICAL SOURCES: Scranton Tribune, March 24, 1964, December 3, 1968.

* * *

DAVISON, Gladys Patton   1905-
(Gladyn Condor)

PERSONAL: Born May 15, 1905, in Peoria, Ill.; daughter of William Spencer and Grace (Adlington) Patton; married Lyman P. Davison (a lieutenant colonel, U.S. Air Force, now retired), August 2, 1930; children: Phyllis Anne, Curwood L., Duane R. *Education:* Studied at Bradley College of Music, 1924, Thomas School of Voice, Piano and Organ, 1926, University of Chicago, 1928, Valdosta Women's College, 1943-44, University of New Mexico, 1952. *Religion:* Protestant. *Address:* P.O. Box 2744, Las Vegas, New Mexico 87701.

CAREER: Boys' State, Peoria, Ill., variously adviser, secretary, publicity chairman, during period 1936-40; *Our Army,* staff writer in Georgia, Illinois, and Tennessee, 1941-46; Fifth Army Chapel, Chicago, Ill., organist, 1958-63; free-lance writer. United Press correspondent to *Chicago Tribune,* 1942-45. *Member:* National Writers Club.

WRITINGS: (Under pseudonym Gladyn Condor) *Escape to Life,* Concordia, 1964. Contributor to *Parents' Magazine, Holiday, Reader's Digest, Farm Journal, Saturday Evening Post, Baby Post, Glamour, Russian Review, Church Musician, Camping World,* and other magazines. Columnist, *Ohio Chronicle, Rocky Mountain News, Atlanta Journal,* and other newspapers, 1941-48; radio scriptwriter and producer in Georgia, 1942-44. Article to *London Post* on British flyers stationed in the U.S., 1944.

WORK IN PROGRESS: West—To the Spanish Peaks (historical non-fiction); twenty or more articles based on data acquired through extensive travel.

BIOGRAPHICAL/CRITICAL SOURCES: Needles Desert Star, Needles, Calif., February 25, 1965.

* * *

DAY, George Harold   1900-
(Peter Quince)

PERSONAL: Born 1900, in London, England; married Phyllis Evaline Edmundson; children: three sons, one daughter. *Education:* Attended Bishop's Stortford College; Sidney Sussex College, Cambridge, M.A.; St. Bartholomew's Hospital Medical College, University of London, M.D. *Home:* Mudesley House, Mundesley, Norwich, England.

CAREER: Rural general practitioner; Mundesley Rehabilitation Unit, Mundesley, Norwich, England, medical director, 1957-65. Consulting physician; lecturer on tour in

United States and Canada, 1962, 1968, 1973. *Military service:* British Army, World War I. Royal Army Medical Corps, World War II; psychiatric consultant. *Member:* Hunterian Society, Samaritans, Inc. (vice-chairman). *Awards, honors:* Hunterian Orator, 1952.

WRITINGS: (Under pseudonym Peter Quince) *Left Handed Doctor*, Dent, 1957; (under pseudonym Peter Quince) *At Dr. Mac's*, Dent, 1958. Contributor to *Encyclopaedia Britannica, Chambers's Encyclopaedia.* Contributor of articles to *Lancet, British Medical Journal, Perspectives.*

WORK IN PROGRESS: Studies in suicide prevention.

SIDELIGHTS: "Aim in life," Day told *CA*, "[is] to make people laugh at themselves and deter them from committing suicide."

* * *

DAY, Gwynn McLendon 1908-

PERSONAL: Born February 23, 1908, in Manchester, Ky.; daughter of Henry Reese (a minister) and Ada (McArthur) McLendon; married Thurman Oscar Day, April 24, 1943 (deceased). *Education:* Attended Bethel College, Hopkinsville, Ky.; Coker College, B.S., 1930; Baptist Woman's Missionary Union Training School, Louisville, Ky., M.R.E., 1932; Baylor University, M.A. (honors), 1935. *Politics:* Independent. *Religion:* Baptist. *Home:* 1003 Roxbury Rd., Richmond, Va. 23226.

CAREER: Teacher in Kentucky mountain mission school and at high school in Thomasville, Ga.; Colorado Woman's College, Denver, Bible teacher, 1935-36; educational secretary at Baptist churches in Richmond, Va., 1937-39, Hot Springs, Ark., 1939-42, in Norfolk, Va., 1942-43; teacher of history at schools in Henrico County, Va., 1955-57, 1962—. *Member:* American Bible Society, Virginia Education Association.

WRITINGS: God Lit a Candle: A Volume of Religious Verse, Exposition, 1951; *Path of the Dawning Light,* Broadman, 1952; *The Wonder of the Word,* Revell, 1957; *The Joy Beyond,* Baker Book, 1960; *Gleams of Glory,* Broadman, 1964. Contributor to Baptist periodicals.

AVOCATIONAL INTERESTS: Music, swimming, and bicycle riding.

BIOGRAPHICAL/CRITICAL SOURCES: Richmond News Leader, July 15, 1964.

* * *

DAY LEWIS, C(ecil) 1904-1972
(Nicholas Blake)

PERSONAL: Born April 27, 1904, in Ballintubber, Ireland; son of F. C. (a minister) and Kathleen Blake (Squires; a collateral descendant of Oliver Goldsmith) Day Lewis; married Constance Mary King, 1928 (divorced, 1951); married Jill Angela Henriette Balcon, April 27, 1951; children: (first marriage) Sean Francis, Nicholas Charles; (second marriage) Lydia Tamasin, Daniel Michael. *Education:* Attended Wadham College, Oxford. *Home:* 6 Crooms Hill, Greenwich, London S.E. 10, England. *Office:* Chatto & Windus Ltd., 40 William IV St., London W.C.2, England.

CAREER: Assistant master, Summerfields, Oxford, England, 1927-28, Larchfield, Helensburgh, Scotland, 1928-30, Cheltenham College, England, 1930-35; editor with Ministry of Information, 1941-46; Trinity College, Cambridge, Clark Lecturer, 1946; Oxford University, Oxford, England,

professor of poetry, 1951-56; Harvard University, Cambridge, Mass., Charles Eliot Norton Professor of Poetry, 1964-65. Appointed Poet Laureate of Britain by Queen Elizabeth II, in 1968. Member of Arts Council, 1962-72; member of board of directors, Chatto & Windus Ltd. (publishers). *Member;* Royal Society of Literature (fellow; vice-president, 1958-72), Royal Society of Arts (fellow), American Academy of Arts and Letters (honorary member), Athenaeum. *Awards, honors:* Companion, Order of British Empire, 1950; D.Litt., University of Exeter, 1965, University of Hull, 1970; Litt.D., Trinity College, Dublin, 1968.

WRITINGS: Beechen Vigil, and Other Poems, Fortune Press, 1925; *Country Comets* (poetry), 1928; *Transitional Poem,* Hogarth, 1929.

From Feathers to Iron (poetry), Hogarth, 1932; *Dick Willoughby* (fiction), Basil Blackwell, 1933, Random House, 1938; *The Magnetic Mountain* (poems), Hogarth, 1933; *A Hope for Poetry* (criticism), Basil Blackwell, 1934, reprinted with a postscript, Folcroft, 1969; *Collected Poems, 1929-1933,* Hogarth, 1935, 2nd edition, Hogarth, 1945 (preceding two books published as *Collected Poems, 1929-1933* [*and*] *A Hope for Poetry,* Random House, 1935); *Revolution in Writing* (commentary), Hogarth, 1935, reprinted, Folcroft, 1969; *A Time to Dance, and Other Poems,* Hogarth, 1935; *We're Not Going to Do Nothing* (commentary), Left Review, 1936, reprinted, Folcroft, 1970; *The Friendly Tree* (novel), J. Cape, 1936, Harper, 1937; *Noah and the Waters* (modern morality play), Hogarth, 1936; *A Time to Dance; Noah and the Waters, [poems, and] Revolution in Writing,* Random House, 1936; (with L. S. Stebbing) *Imagination and Thinking,* Life and Leisure, 1936; *Starting Point* (novel), J. Cape, 1937, Harper, 1938; *Overtures to Death, and Other Poems,* J. Cape, 1938; *Child of Misfortune* (novel), J. Cape, 1939.

Selected Poems, Hogarth, 1940, revised edition, Penguin, 1969; *Poems in Wartime,* 1940; *Word Over All* (poems), J. Cape, 1943, Transatlantic, 1944; *Poetry for You: A Book for Boys and Girls on the Enjoyment of Poetry,* Basil Blackwell, 1944, Oxford University Press (New York), 1947, reissued, Soccer, 1966; *Short is the Time: Poems, 1936-1943* (previously published as *Overtures to Death and Word Over All*), Oxford University Press (New York), 1945; *The Poetic Image* (criticism), Oxford University Press, 1947; *Enjoying Poetry,* Cambridge University Press for National Book League, 1947, reprinted, Folcroft, 1970; *The Colloquial Element in English Poetry* (criticism), Literary and Philosophical Society of Newcastle-upon-Tyne, 1947; *Poems, 1943-1947,* Oxford University Press, 1948; *The Otterbury Incident* (adaptation of the French film "Nous le gosses," seen in England as "Us Kids"), Putnam, 1948, reissued, 1963.

The Poet's Task (criticism), Clarendon Press, 1951, reprinted, Folcroft, 1970; *The Grand Manner* (criticism), University of Nottingham, 1952; *An Italian Visit* (narrative poem), Harper, 1953; *Collected Poems,* J. Cape, 1954, published as *Collected Poems, 1954,* 1970; *Christmas Eve,* Faber, 1954; *Notable Images of Virtue: Emily Bronte, George Meredith, W. B. Yeats,* Ryerson, 1954, reprinted, Folcroft, 1969; *Pegasus, and Other Poems,* J. Cape, 1957, Harper, 1958; *The Poet's Way of Knowledge,* Cambridge University Press, 1957.

The Buried Day (autobiography), Harper, 1960; *English Lyric Poems, 1500-1900,* Appleton, 1961 (published in England as *A Book of English Lyrics,* Chatto & Windus, 1961); *The Gate, and Other Poems,* J. Cape, 1962; *Re-*

quiem for the Living (poems), Harper, 1964; The Lyric Impulse (Charles Eliot Norton lectures), Harvard University Press, 1965; The Room, and Other Poems, J. Cape, 1965; Selected Poems, Harper, 1967, revised edition, Penguin, 1969; Selections from His Poetry [by] C. Day Lewis (also published as C. Day Lewis: Selections from His Poetry), edited by Patric Dickinson, Chatto & Windus, 1967; A Need for Poetry?, University of Hull, 1968; The Whispering Roots, and Other Poems, Harper, 1970 (published in England as The Whispering Roots, Cape, 1970).

Detective novels under pseudonym Nicholas Blake: A Question of Proof, Harper, 1935, reissued, Collins, 1969; Shell of Death, Harper, 1936 (British edition published as Thou Shell of Death, Collins, 1936, reissued, 1971); There's Trouble Brewing, Harper, 1937; The Beast Must Die, Harper, 1938; The Smiler With the Knife, Harper, 1939, reissued, Collins, 1972; The Summer Camp Mystery, Harper, 1940 (British edition published as Malice in Wonderland, Collins, 1940; American paperback edition published as Malice with Murder); The Corpse in the Snowman, Harper, 1941 (British edition published as The Case of the Abominable Snowman, Collins, 1941); Minute for Murder, Harper, 1947; Head of a Traveler, Harper, 1949; The Dreadful Hollow, Harper, 1953; The Whisper in the Gloom, Harper, 1954; A Tangled Web, Harper, 1956, reissued, Chivers, 1973; End of Chapter, Harper, 1957; A Penknife in My Heart, Collins, 1958, Harper, 1959; The Widow's Cruise, Harper, 1959; The Worm of Death, Harper, 1961; The Deadly Joker, Collins, 1963; The Sad Variety, Harper, 1964; The Morning after Death, Collins, 1966; The Nicholas Blake Omnibus, Collins, 1966; The Private Wound, Harper, 1968; Shell of Death, Harper, 1971 (published in England as Thou Shell of Death, Collins, 1971).

Editor: (With W. H. Auden) Oxford Poetry, Basil Blackwell, 1927-32; The Mind in Chains: Socialism and the Cultural Revolution, Muller Ltd., 1937, reprinted, Folcroft, 1972; (with John Lehmann, T. A. Jackson Fox, and Ralph Winston) Ralph Fox: Writer in Arms, International Publishers, 1937; (with Charles Fenby) Anatomy of Oxford: An Anthology, J. Cape, 1938; (with L.A.G. Strong) An Anthology of Modern Verse, 1920-1940 (also published as A New Anthology of Modern Verse, 1920-1940), Methuen, 1941, reissued, 1963; The Echoing Green: An Anthology of Verse, Basil Blackwell, 1941-43, reissued, 3 volumes, 1960-63; (and author of introduction) Francis T. Palgrave, The Golden Treasury of the Best Songs and Lyrical Poems in the English Language, Collins, 1954; (with John Lehmann) The Chatto Book of Modern Poetry, 1915-1955, Chatto & Windus, 1956; Charles Dickens, The Mystery of Edwin Drood, Collins, 1956; A Book of English Lyrics, Chatto & Windus, 1961; (and author of introduction and notes) Wilfred Owen, Collected Poems, amended edition, New Directions, 1964; (and author of introduction) Edmund Charles Blunden, The Midnight Skaters: Poems for Young Readers, Bodley Head, 1968; George Crabbe, Crabbe, Penguin, 1973.

Translator: Virgil, Georgics, J. Cape, 1940; Paul Valery, Le Cimetiere marin, Secker & Warburg, 1947; Virgil, Aeneid, Oxford University Press, 1952, Doubleday Anchor, 1953; Virgil, Eclogues, J. Cape, 1963; The Eclogues and Georgics of Virgil, Doubleday Anchor, 1964 (published in England as The Eclogues: Georgics and Aeneid, Oxford University Press, 1966).

Author of introduction: Selected Poems of Robert Frost, J. Cape, 1936; Julius Lipton, Poems of Strife, Lawrence,

1936; Collected Poems of Lilian Bowes Lyon, Dutton, 1948; George Meredith, Modern Love, Hart-Davis, 1948.

SIDELIGHTS: When Day Lewis was appointed Poet Laureate, a reviewer in the Beloit Poetry Journal commented: "If one may judge by his past performance, it is an honor that he will fill with a good deal more distinction than most of his predecessors. As this volume [Selected Poems] quickly demonstrates, he is a poet of superb range. Three themes seem to recur over the years: an admiration for all that is truly heroic, a feeling for the ephemeral quality of life, and a quest for pure and true identity. But there are other themes, too—lighter, less cerebral. But everything he writes is touched with a sense of the truly poetic. He is a major figure."

This regard has not always been shared by critics, nor have his poems been considered of uniformly high quality. Philip Booth offered an explanation: "To look to these poems for the verbal energy of Ted Hughes or the imagistic precision of Philip Larkin is to miss the personal perspective which characterizes this collection [Selected Poems].... Day Lewis is not everyone's cup of tea, especially in an America where stronger, colder, and more bitter drinks are now more fashionable. But to ask these poems to be other than they are would be to deny the very civilization to which they are native; the collection is a wholly honorable brew."

Day Lewis' own history provides other clues to diversity. The late Poet Laureate was once a poet of revolution, inextricably linked with the avant-garde Oxford poets of the Thirties, W. H. Auden, Stephen Spender, and Louis MacNeice. His poems of that period were mostly parodies, and considered highly imitative. Brian Jones wrote that it was not until 1943 that Day Lewis published verse "which gives the authentic shock of originality.... Since then, Day Lewis has continued in this much more personal vein ... which seems to arise geniunely from his own personality. And it is clear from his 'Thirties verse that he could not at that time find a satisfactory voice because he knew only too well what it naturally was—a late Romantic's, words which it was a disgrace to utter at that time. And so he hid it, became a mimic, or at best used his true voice when he was pretending it was somebody else's, as in his parodies."

His prose, on the other hand, was always highly regarded, from his early political essays, to his quite successful "Nicholas Blake" novels, which he began as pot-boilers. "From most of the news stories about the appointment of Cecil Day Lewis as Poet Laureate of Great Britain," noted Anthony Boucher, "you would gather that he is one of those lyric dons who dash off an occasional detective story in their lighter moments. In fact the poet is ... a hard-working professional in crime, who ... is also one of England's two or three leading reviewers of crime fiction. Blake's stature among mystery novelists is at least as high as that of Day Lewis among poets; he has excelled both in the straight detective puzzle and in the broader study of crime and character, as well as in happy blends of the two methods."

Often classified as a Georgian, Day Lewis was a skilled craftsman, excelling at highly disciplined traditional verse forms, at his best in meditative poems. "I always wished to be lucid," he once commented, and his best poems are noted for lucidity, simplicity, and quiet lyricism. "He is a quiet writer," observed John Wain, "with a preference for ordered syntax and regular form, who likes to brood rather than to exclaim." He called himself a member of the "derriere garde,'' and, according to Peter Gellatly, ''derided his 'too meticulous words,' and disclaimed for his works that 'divine incontinence' which he considers an essential element in good poetry. He obviously admires the roistering, Dylan-like figure ... but cannot emulate him. Wild singing is not for Day Lewis. On the other hand, his temperateness and steadiness of outlook sometimes invest his poems with a glossy perfection that is rarely seen elsewhere.''

As Poet Laureate—a position paying somewhat more than $230 per year—he turned out official verse not noted for literary distinction. Yet he could still write in another vein; his last collection elicited this reassurance from Derek Stanford: ''It is good to see Mr. Day Lewis in such a fine and charming fettle.... Those ... who may have feared this poet would be throttled by his chain of office can breathe a deep sigh of relief and get down to enjoying *The Whispering Roots*.''

BIOGRAPHICAL/CRITICAL SOURCES: Clifford Dyment, *C. Day Lewis*, Longmans, Green, for the British Council, 1955; *New Statesman*, June 14, 1958; *New York Times Book Review*, June 22, 1958; *Poetry*, August, 1958; *Times Literary Supplement*, March 6, 1959; *New Republic*, March 28, 1964; *New York Review of Books*, June 25, 1964; Carolyn Riley, editor, *Contemporary Literary Criticism*, Volume I, Gale, 1973.

(Died May 22, 1972)

*   *   *

DEAN, Yetive H(ornor) 1909-

PERSONAL: Born September 6, 1909, in Webb City, Mo.; daughter of Logan Henry (a carpenter) and Ethel (Mosier) Hornor; married Winfield Irving Dean (an electrician), July 3, 1927; children: Lila Yetive (Mrs. Lee Bruckner), Winfield Albert. *Education:* Attended Grossmont Community College. *Politics:* Republican. *Religion:* Protestant. *Home:* 4425 Carmen Dr., LaMesa, Calif. 92041.

CAREER: Bookkeeper, presently employed in auditor's office of San Diego County. Sometime columnist and feature writer for local newspaper.

WRITINGS: *'Neath Texas Stars*, Eerdmans, 1955; *By Pacific Waters*, Zondervan, 1959; *The Circling Prairie*, Zondervan, 1963. Contributor of short stories to juvenile magazines.

WORK IN PROGRESS: A juvenile book, *My Slain Children; Mud and Paper*, based on experiences in the circulation department of a small newspaper; research for a historical novel, *Cave in the Coulee*, with Montana as a setting.

AVOCATIONAL INTERESTS: Travel and taking color slides.

*   *   *

de BANKE, Cecile 1889-1965

PERSONAL: Born August 12, 1889, in London England. *Education:* Educated in England. *Home:* 25 Cottage St., Wellesley, Mass. 02181.

CAREER: Left England in 1915 to join a repertory company in South Africa, where she later had her own school of speech and drama and directed the Cape Town Repertory Theatre; came to United States in 1930, and taught at Wellesley College, Wellesley, Mass., 1932-55, becoming associate professor of speech and drama. Lecturer and writer; speech therapist at various times at Cushing Veterans Administration Hospital, Framingham, Mass., at

Neurological Clinic, Massachusetts General Hospital, Boston, and Bellevue Rehabilitation Center, New York, N.Y. *Member:* English-Speaking Union.

WRITINGS: *The Art of Choral Speaking*, Baker Co., 1937; *The A.B.C. of Speech Sounds*, Baker Co., 1942; *Shakespearean Stage Production: Then and Now*, McGraw, 1953; *Hand over Hand: An Autobiography* (years in England), Hutchinson, 1957; *Bright Weft* (autobiography; years in South Africa), Hutchinson, 1958; *Tabby Magic* (juvenile), Hutchinson, 1959; *American Plaid* (autobiography; years in America), Hutchinson, 1961; *More Tabby Magic* (juvenile), Hutchinson, 1961. Author of four booklets on choral speaking published by Baker Co., 1942-47. Contributor to *Shakespeare Quarterly*, *Queen's Quarterly*, and other literary journals.

BIOGRAPHICAL SOURCES: Cecile de Banke, *Hand over Hand*, Hutchinson, 1957, *Bright Weft*, Hutchinson, 1958, *American Plaid*, Hutchinson, 1961.

(Died January 2, 1965)

*   *   *

De BEER, E(smond) S(amuel) 1895-

PERSONAL: Born September 15, 1895, in Dunedin, New Zealand; son of I. S. and Emily (Bendix-Hallenstein) de Beer. *Education:* New College, Oxford, M.A.; University College, London, M.A. *Home:* 31 Brompton Sq., London S.W.3 2AE, England.

CAREER: Private scholar in England, specializing in seventeenth-century English history. Trustee of National Portrait Gallery, 1959-67; independent member, Reviewing Committee on Export of Works of Art, 1965-70; active on committees of London Library, Friends of the National Libraries, Friends of Lambeth Palace Library. *Member:* British Academy (fellow, 1965), Society of Antiquaries (fellow), Royal Society of Literature (fellow), Royal Historical Society (fellow), Historical Association (member of council), Hakluyt Society (president, 1972—), London Topographical Society (member of council), Athenaeum Club (London). *Awards, honors:* Commander of the British Empire, 1969; D. Litt., University of Durham and Oxford University; Litt.D., University of Otago; fellow, University College, London, 1967; honorary fellow, New College, Oxford.

WRITINGS: (Editor) *The Diary of John Evelyn*, Clarendon Press, 1955. Contributor of articles and reviews to learned journals.

WORK IN PROGRESS: Editing the correspondence of John Locke.

*   *   *

de BEER, Gavin R(ylands) 1899-1972

PERSONAL: Born November 1, 1889, in Malden, London, England; son of Herbert Chaplin and Mabel (Rylands) de Beer; married Cicely Glyn Medlycott, 1925. *Education:* Magdalen College, Oxford, B.A., 1921, M.A., 1924, D. Sc., 1932. *Home:* 3 West Close, Alfriston, Polegate, Sussex, England. *Office:* Thomas Nelson & Sons Ltd., 36 Park St., London W 1, England.

CAREER: Oxford University, Oxford, England, fellow of Merton College, 1923-38, university reader in zoology and Jenkinson Lecturer in Embryology, 1926-38; University College, University of London, London, England, professor of embryology, 1939-50; British Museum (Natural

History), London, England, director, 1950-60; Thomas Nelson & Sons Ltd. (publishers), London, England, director, 1960-67, editorial consultant, 1967-72. President, XV International Congress of Zoology, 1958; trustee, National Portrait Gallery, 1961-67. *Military service:* British Army, Grenadier Guards, 1918-19, becoming lieutenant; General Staff officer (serving on staffs of General Eisenhower and Field Marshal Montgomery), 1939-45, and becoming lieutenant colonel; mentioned in dispatches twice.

MEMBER: Royal Society of London (fellow), Society of Antiquaries of London (fellow), British Council, Institut International d'Embryologique, Linnean Society (president, 1946-49), Academie des Sciences, Institut de France (corresponding member), Societe d'Histoire de Neuchatel (corresponding member), Societe d'histoire et d'archeologie de Geneve (corresponding member), Societe vaudoise d'histoire et d'archeologie (corresponding member), Societe Royale Zoologique de Belgique (honorary), Societe Zoologique de France (honorary), and other honorary memberships. *Awards, honors:* Knighted, 1954; Geoffroy-St-Hilaire Gold Medal of Societe d'Acclimation de France, 1954; Darwin Medal of Royal Society of London, 1958; Gold Medal of Linnean Society, 1958; Chevalier, Legion d'honneur, 1961; Mendel Medal of Moravian Museum, 1965; Kalinga Prize from UNESCO, 1968; D.-es-L., University of Lausanne; Sc.D., Cambridge University; D.Sc., Oxford University; D. de l'universite, University of Bordeaux.

WRITINGS: Growth, E. J. Arnold, 1924; *Introduction to the Study of Genetics,* J. Murray, 1924; *The Comparative Anatomy, Histology and Development of the Pituitary Body,* Oliver & Boyd, 1926; *An Introduction to Experimental Embryology,* Clarendon Press, 1926, 2nd edition, 1934; *Vertebrate Zoology: An Introduction to the Comparative Anatomy, Embryology, and Evolution of Chordate Animals,* Sidgwick & Jackson, 1928, 2nd edition University of Washington Press, 1951, 3rd revised and enlarged edition, 1967.

Early Travellers in the Alps, Sidgwick & Jackson, 1930, reprinted, October House, 1966; *Embryology and Evolution,* Clarendon Press, 1930, revised edition published as *Embroyos and Ancestors,* Oxford University Press, 1940, 4th revised edition, 1962; *Alps and Men,* E. J. Arnold, 1932; (editor with H. G. Fiedler) *A German Reader for Biology Students,* Oxford University Press, 1933; (with Julian S. Huxley) *The Elements of Experimental Embryology,* Cambridge University Press, 1934, Hafner, 1963; *The Development of the Vertebrate Skull,* Clarendon Press, 1937, reprinted, 1971; (editor, and author of notes and commentary) *Le Voyage en Suisse de Mme. Roland, 1787,* Editions de la Baconniere, 1937; (editor and contributor) *Evolution: Essays Presented to E. S. Goodrich,* Clarendon Press. 1938; (with Edmund Blunden and Sylvia Norman) *On Shelley,* Oxford University Press, 1938.

Escape to Switzerland, Penguin, 1945; (with Leonard Woolley) *The Army at War: Tunisia,* H.M.S.O., 1945; (editor) Thomas Pennant, *Tour on the Continent 1765,* Ray Society, 1948; *Travellers in Switzerland,* Oxford University Press, 1949.

(Editor) Harriet Charlotte Beaujolois Campbell, *A Journey to Florence in 1817,* Bles, 1951; *Speaking of Switzerland,* Eyre & Spottiswoode, 1952; (with Georges Bonard) *Edward Gibbon: Journal de mon Voyage dans Quelques Endroits de la Suisse, 1755,* Publications de la Faculte des Lettres, University of Lausanne, 1952; *Sir Hans Sloane and the British Museum,* Oxford University Press, 1953;

Archaeoptery-Lithographica: A Study Based on the British Museum Specimen, British Museum, 1954; *Alps and Elephants: Hannibal's March,* Bles, 1955, Dutton, 1956, published as *Hannibal's March,* Sidgwick & Jackson, 1967; (with T. Graham Brown) *The First Ascent of Mont Blanc,* Oxford University Press, 1957; *A Handbook on Evolution,* British Museum, 1958, 3rd edition, 1964.

(Compiler) *The Sciences Were Never at War,* Nelson, 1960; *Reflections of a Darwinian,* Nelson, 1962; *Charles Darwin: Evolution by Natural Selection,* Nelson, 1963, Doubleday, 1964, published as *Charles Darwin: A Scientific Biography,* Doubleday, 1965; *Atlas of Evolution,* Nelson, 1964; *Genetics and Prehistory* (Rede Lecture), Cambridge University Press, 1965; (compiler with Andre-Michel Rousseau) *Voltaire's British Visitors,* Institut et Musee Voltaire (Geneva), 1967; *Gibbon and His World,* Viking, 1968; *Hannibal: Challenging Rome's Supremacy,* Viking, 1969 (published in England as *Hannibal: The Struggle for Power in the Mediterranean,* Thames & Hudson, 1969); *Streams of Culture,* Lippincott, 1969; *Jean-Jacques Rousseau and His World,* Thames & Hudson, 1972.

Contributor: *The New Systematics,* edited by Julian S. Huxley, Clarendon Press, 1940; *A Century of Science,* edited by Herbert Dingle, Hutchinson, 1951; *Studies in Fossil Vertebrates Presented to D.M.S. Watson,* edited by T. S. Westoll, Athlone Press, 1958; *A Century of Darwin,* edited by S. A. Barnett, Heinemann, 1958; *The Reader's Guide,* Penguin, 1960; *The Evolution of Living Organisms,* edited by G. W. Leeper, Melbourne University Press, 1962; *Shelley and His Circle,* edited by Kenneth Neill Cameron, Oxford University Press, 1970.

Author of preface or introduction: Charles Darwin, *The Origin of Species,* Oxford University Press, 1951; Charles Darwin, *Journal of Researches,* Limited Editions Club (New York), 1956; Charles Darwin, *Journal of Researches into the Geology and Natural History of the Various Countries Visited by H.M.S. Beagle, 1832-1836,* limited edition, Cambridge University Press, 1956; Charles Darwin and Alfred Russell Wallace, *Evolution by Natural Selection,* Cambridge University Press, 1958.

Editor of *Darwin's Notebooks on Transmutation of Species,* published by British Museum (Natural History), 1960; *British Men of Science,* Nelson, 1962-67. Writer of other museum bulletins. Contributor to *Standard Encyclopaedia of the World's Mountains,* Weidenfeld & Nicolson, 1962, *New Dictionary of Birds,* Nelson, 1964, *Encyclopaedia Britannica,* and *Chambers's Encyclopaedia.*

Author of published addresses, lectures, monographs, articles, and papers on zoology, biology, evolution, Alpine history, literary history, and other subjects. More than 400 have appeared in proceedings and journals of learned societies, and in such periodicals as *Listener, London Calling, Geographical Magazine, Country Life, Alpine Journal, British Ski Year Book, Army Quarterly, Revue des Arts* (Paris), *Nature,* and *Cavalry Journal* (United States).

General editor of Methuen "Monographs on Biological Subjects," 1932-46, Clarendon Press "Monographs on Animal Biology," 1939-45, and of "Home University Library," 1945-50; editor of *Notes and Records of the Royal Society of London,* 1946-52.

WORK IN PROGRESS: A critical chronology of the life and works of Charles Darwin; a bibliography to Darwin's *Origin of Species;* writing several volumes for "Oxford Biological Readers" series; editing Darwin's and Huxley's autobiographies in "Oxford Modern Texts" series.

SIDELIGHTS: De Beer was fluent in French, German, and Italian. *An introduction to Experimental Embryology* was published in Greek, several books as well as numerous papers, in French, other books in Italian, German, and Dutch editions.

BIOGRAPHICAL/CRITICAL SOURCES: G. R. de Beer: Publications, Part I: *1922-52,* Private Press of Guido Morris, 1952, Part II: *1952-60,* Nelson, 1960, Part III: *1960-65,* Worden Marazion, 1965.

(Died June 21, 1972)

* * *

de BLANK, Joost 1908-1968

PERSONAL: Born November 14, 1908, in Rotterdam, Netherlands; son of Joost and Louisa Johanna (Quispel) de Blank. *Education:* Ridley Hall, B.A., 1930; Queen's College, Cambridge, M.A., 1933. *Home:* 1 Little Cloister, Westminster Abbey, S.W.1, England.

CAREER: Ordained deacon, Church of England, 1931, priest, 1932. Assistant curate in Bath, 1931-34, Worcester, 1934-37; vicar at Forest Gate, 1937-41, Harrow, 1948-52; Suffragan Bishop of Stepney, 1952-57; Archbishop of Cape Town, Cape Town, South Africa, 1957-63; Canon of Westminster, 1964-68; Assistant Bishop, Diocese of Southwart, 1966-68. Chairman, Greater London Conciliation Committee, 1966-68. *Military service:* Chaplain to the forces, 1940-46; served in Middle East, 1941-44, wounded, 1944. *Member:* Athenaeum Club, Garrick Club, Reform Club. *Awards, honors:* D.D., Lambeth, 1957; D.D., Trinity College, Hartford, Conn., 1961; honorary fellow, Queen's College, Cambridge, 1961.

WRITINGS: Is It Nothing to You?, Mowbray, 1953; *The Parish in Action,* Mowbray, 1954; *Saints at Sixty Miles an Hour,* Faith Press, 1955, Morehouse, 1956; *Members of Christ,* Morehouse, 1956; *Call of Duty,* Oxford University Press, 1956; *This is Conversion,* Hodder & Stoughton, 1957, Morehouse, 1958; *Uncomfortable Words,* Longmans, Green, 1958; *A Working Faith: Sermons for the Man in the Street,* Eerdmans, 1960; *Out of Africa,* Hodder & Stoughton, 1964. Regular contributor of feature stories to *Star* (London) until 1957. Also contributor of articles to periodicals.

SIDELIGHTS: During his tenure in South Africa, de Blank was an outspoken opponent of apartheid, saying, "...the churchman cannot keep silence even if he would, because the honour of God Himself is at stake." He refused to preach in any church not open to black as well as white, and he willingly confronted both the Dutch Reformed Church and the Government of South Africa. At last, the physical stress of his position became too great and, following medical advice, he returned to England.

The Dean of Westminster wrote to the *London Times* after his death, concluding: "Above all, perhaps, we were conscious that we had in our midst one of this century's great witnesses to the Faith, and we are thankful that the end of his life and ministry should have been at Westminster Abbey to which he imparted both his prophetic vision and his love of life in all its colour and drama and excitement."

(Died January 1, 1968)

* * *

DEELMAN, Christian Felling 1937-1964

PERSONAL: Born September 13, 1937, in Johannesburg, South Africa; son of Franciscus P.S. (a company director) and Marie (Felling) Deelman; married Auriol Roberts, August 15, 1958; children: Suzannah, Sarah. *Education:* Early schooling in South Africa; New College, Oxford, B.A. (honors), 1959, M.A., 1962. *Home:* 22 Salisbury Crescent, Oxford, England. *Agent:* Harold Matson Co., Inc., 22 East 40th St., New York, N.Y. 10016. *Office:* St. Peter's College, Oxford University, Oxford, England.

CAREER: Advertising executive in London, England, 1959-60; Oxford University, Oxford, England, research lecturer at Christ Church, 1962-64, fellow and tutor in English literature at St. Peter's College, 1963-64.

WRITINGS: The Great Shakespeare Jubilee, Viking 1964. Contributor to scholarly journals.

(Died July 31, 1964)

* * *

DEFERRARI, Roy J(oseph) 1890-1969

PERSONAL: Born June 1, 1890, in Stoneham, Mass.; son of Austin John (a fruit dealer) and Mary (Crovo) Deferrari; married Evelyn Mary Biggi, December 27, 1920; children: Austin John, Mary Evelyn (Sister Teresa Mary). *Education:* Dartmouth College, A.B., 1912; Princeton University, M.A., 1913, Ph.D., 1915. *Religion:* Catholic.

CAREER: Princeton University, Princeton, N.J., instructor in classics, 1916-17; Catholic University of America, Washington, D.C., associate professor of classics, 1919-21, head of department of Greek and Latin, 1919-49, Margaret H. Gardiner Professor of Greek and Latin, 1922-60, dean of Graduate School, 1930-37, secretary-general, 1937-67, director of Program of Affliation, beginning, 1938. Member of U.S. Educational Mission to Japan, 1946, and of managing committee of American Schools for Classical Studies in Athens, *Military service:* U.S. 814th Aero Squadron, 1917-18.

MEMBER: American Philological Association, National Catholic Educational Association, Linguistic Society of America, Mediaeval Academy of America, Classical Association of Middle Atlantic States (member of commission on higher education), Phi Beta Kappa. *Awards, honors:* LL.D. from St. John's University, Brooklyn, N.Y., 1945, University of Notre Dame, 1945; Ed.D. from Seton Hall University, 1954, Villanova University, 1961; other honorary degrees from nine Catholic colleges. Gold Medal Award of Italian-American Charitable Society of Boston, 1949; created Knight of Sylvester by Pope John XXIII, 1959; St. John Baptist de la Salle Medal, Manhattan College, 1960.

WRITINGS: Lucian's Atticism, Princeton University Press, 1916, reprinted, A. M. Hakkert, 1969; *A First Latin Book for Catholic Schools,* Catholic Education Press, 1921.

(Compiler with James Marshall Campbell) *A Concordance of Prudentius,* Mediaeval, 1932; (with Sister M. Inviolata Barry and Martin R. P. McGuire) *A Concordance of Ovid,* Catholic University of America Press, 1939, reprinted, G. Olms, 1968; (with Sister Maria Walburg Fanning and Sister Anne Stanislaus Sullivan) *A Concordance of Lucian,* Catholic University of America Press, 1940, reprinted, G. Olms, 1965; *Joy in Reading,* Sadlier, 1941; *Appreciation Through Reading,* Sadlier, 1942; (with Sister Mary Clement Eagen) *Concordance of Statius,* privately printed, 1943, G. Olms, 1966; *English Voices,* Sadlier, 1946; (with Sister Francis Joseph) *Second Year Latin,* Bruce, 1948; (with Sister M. Inviolata Barry) *A Lexicon of St. Thomas*

Aquinas Based on the Summa Theologica and Selected Passages of His Other Works, five volumes, Catholic University of America Press, 1948-53.

(With Sister Francis Joseph) *Third Year Latin,* Bruce, 1950, and *Fourth Year Latin,* Bruce, 1953; (with Sister M. Inviolata Barry and Roy J. Deff) *A Complete Index of the Summa Theologica of St. Thomas Aguinas,* Catholic University of America Press, 1956; *A Latin-English Dictionary of St. Thomas Aguinas,* Daughters of St. Paul, 1960; *Memoirs of the Catholic University of America, 1918-60,* Daughters of St. Paul, 1962; *Some Problems of Catholic Higher Education in the United States,* Daughters of St. Paul, 1963; *A Complete System of Catholic Education Is Necessary,* Daughters of St. Paul, 1964; *A Layman in Catholic Higher Education: His Life and Times* (autobiography), Daughters of St. Paul, 1966; (with Rita Watrin) *A Handbook for Catholic Higher Education,* Daughters of St. Paul, 1966.

Editor—All published by Catholic University of America Press, except as indicated: (With Lindley R. Dean) *Selections from Roman Historians,* Allyn & Bacon, 1916; *Vital Problems of Catholic Education in the United States,* 1939; *Essays on Catholic Education in the United States,* 1942, reprinted, Books for Libraries, 1969; *College Organization and Administration,* 1947; *The Philosophy of Catholic Higher Education,* 1948; *Guidance in Catholic Colleges and Universities,* 1949.

Integration in Catholic Colleges and Universities, 1950; *The Organization and Administration of the Minor Seminary,* 1951; *Discipline and Integration in the Catholic College,* 1951; *The Curriculum of the Catholic College,* 1952; *Early Christian Biographies,* Fathers of the Church, 1952; *Theology, Philosophy and History as Integrating Disciplines in the Catholic College of Liberal Arts,* 1953; *Latin and English Syllabi in the Minor Seminary,* 1953; *Latin and Religion Syllabi in the Minor Seminary,* 1954; *The Social Sciences in Catholic College Programs,* 1954; *Curriculum of the Minor Seminary: Religion, Greek and Remedial Reading,* 1955; *St. Augustine: Treatises on Marriage and Other Subjects,* Fathers of the Church, 1955; *The Problems of Administration in the American College,* 1956; *Curriculum of the Minor Seminary,* 1956; *Functions of the Dean of Studies in Higher Education,* 1957; *Self-Evaluation and Accreditation in Higher Education,* 1959; *Quality of Teachers and Staff,* 1961.

Translator: *Saint Basil: The Letters with an English Translation,* four volumes, Putnam, 1926-34; Hugo of St. Victor, *On the Sacraments of the Christian Faith,* Mediaeval, 1951; Eusebius Pamphili, *Ecclesiastical History,* Volumes I-V, Fathers of the Church, 1953; Heinrich J. D. Denzinger, *Sources of Catholic Dogma,* Herder, 1957; (and editor) St. Cyprianus, *Treatises,* Fathers of the Church, 1958; *Saint Ambrose: Theological and Dogmatic Works,* Catholic University of America Press, 1963; Paulus Orosius, *The Seven Books of History Against the Pagans,* Catholic University of America Press, 1964.

Also editor: "Catholic University Patristic Studies," one hundred volumes, 1922-45; "Catholic University Studies in Mediaeval and Renaissance Latin," thirty volumes; "Catholic University Classical Studies," five volumes. Member of editorial committee, "Fathers of the Church" series, fifty volumes, beginning, 1949. Associate editor, *Hesperia* (Journal of American School for Classical Studies at Athens).

(Died August 24, 1969)

DeGERING, Etta Fowler 1898-

PERSONAL: Born January 7, 1898, in Arcadia, Neb.; daughter of Charles Henry and Beryl (Brown) Fowler; married Claud DeGering, July 22, 1917; children: Harvey, Trudy-Anne (Mrs. Dean R. Johnson). *Education:* Walla Walla College, student, 1912-17; Colorado University, extension classes, 1963-64. *Home:* 2945 16th St., Boulder, Colo. 80302.

CAREER: Elementary teacher in British Columbia, 1917-25; instructor in French and English in Battleford, Saskatchewan, 1925-30; *Children's Friend* (Braille magazine), Lincoln, Neb., editor, 1951-60. *Member:* Authors League of America, Colorado Authors League. *Awards, honors:* Children's book award of Thomas Alva Edison Foundation, 1962, for *Seeing Fingers: The Story of Louis Braille.*

WRITINGS: My Bible Friends, ten books, Review & Herald, 1953-58; *Seeing Fingers: The Story of Louis Braille* (Junior Literary Guild selection), McKay, 1962; *Gallaudet, Friend of the Deaf,* McKay, 1964; *Christopher Jones, Captain of the Mayflower,* McKay, 1965; *Wilderness Wife: The Story of Rebecca Bryan Boone,* McKay, 1966. Also author of "'Old Second Reader,' William Holmes McGuffey" as yet unpublished.

WORK IN PROGRESS: William Brewster in *How America's Freedoms Began; Miracle Children of the Bible.*

SIDELIGHTS: Mrs. DeGering told *CA:* "My husband and I have retired in the mile high university city of Boulder, Colorado—a city that pushes hard against the base of the Rocky Mountains. Periods of leave often find us far away absorbing the background sights and sounds of the next biography. There is nothing that I enjoy quite so much as researching an historical episode, and recreating the lives of the men and women who brought it about."

BIOGRAPHICAL/CRITICAL SOURCES: Boulder Camera, January 30, 1963; *Denver Post,* February 7, 1963; *Rocky Mountain News,* March 21, 1963.

* * *

DEGHY, Guy (Stephen) 1912-
(Herald Froy, Lee Gibb, joint pseudonyms)

PERSONAL: Born October 11, 1912, in Budapest, Hungary; son of Ernest and Hermy (Pressburger) Deghy; married Mari Stuart Hooper, December 17, 1956; children: (second marriage) Patrick, Charles; (third marriage) Nicolette, Julian. *Education:* Professor Tschulok (Zurich, Switzerland), Kantonales Maturitatszeugniss, 1931; University of Budapest, student, 1932; Royal Hungarian Academy of Dramatic Art, Budapest, diploma, 1932. *Home:* 45 Fitzgeorge Ave., London W14 0SZ, England.

CAREER: British Broadcasting Corp., London, England, monitor, later broadcaster and drama producer, 1944-52; now writer and stage, television, and film actor.

WRITINGS: (With Keith Waterhouse) *Cafe Royal: Ninety Years of Bohemia,* Hutchinson, 1955; *Noble and Manly: The History of the National Sporting Club, Incorporating the Posthumous Papers of the Pelican Club,* Hutchinson, 1956; *Paradise in the Strand: The Story of Romano's,* Richards Press, 1958; *Fire Next Door,* Wingate, 1958.

With Waterhouse under joint pseudonym Herald Froy: *How to Avoid Matrimony: The Layman's Guide to Laywoman,* Muller, 1957, John Day, 1959; *How to Survive Matrimony,* Muller, 1958; *Can This Be Love; or, Look, Darling, They've Written Our Book,* Muller, 1960; *Maybe*

You're Just Inferior: Head Shrinking for Fun and Profit, Muller, 1961; *O Mistress Mine; or, How to Go Roaming,* Arthur Barker, 1962.

With Waterhouse under joint pseudonym Leo Gibb: *The Joneses: How to Keep Up With Them,* Muller, 1959; *The Higher Jones,* Muller, 1961.

Contributor to many London papers and journals, including *Observer, Evening News, Punch,* and *New Statesman,* and of film scripts and television plays to Granada and British Broadcasting Corp.

WORK IN PROGRESS: An autobiography, *Minority View;* a biography, *The Unicorn: The Life and Times of the Marchesa Luisa Cassati.*

* * *

DeGRE, Muriel (Harris) 1914-1971

PERSONAL: Born May 15, 1914; daughter of Charles Bernard and Frances (Pelcyger) Harris; married Gerard DeGre (a college professor), December 13, 1933; children: Erica (Mrs. Guy Ducornet). *Education:* Attended New York University and New School for Social Research. *Politics:* "Flexible." *Religion:* Quaker. *Home:* Bard College, Annandale-on-Hudson, N.Y. 12504. *Agent:* Robert P. Mills, 20 East 53rd St., New York, N.Y. 10022.

CAREER: Former copywriter in New York, N.Y.; Fashion Promotion Consultants, New York N.Y., president, 1946-49; broadcaster on daily programs, WEOK radio, Poughkeepsie, N.Y., 1949-53, and WKNY radio and television, Kingston, N.Y. 1954-57; *Dutchess County Journal,* Dutchess County, N.Y., editor, 1957-59; free-lance writer.

WRITINGS: (With Paris Leary) *The Jack Sprat Cook Book,* Doubleday, 1965. Contributor of reviews to *Panorama* and *Chicago Daily News.*

WORK IN PROGRESS: Two novels, *Olivia Queen* and *Salt for a Lady's Tail;* a cookbook, *A Cook's Tour of Literature,* with Ellen Burr.

SIDELIGHTS: Mrs. DeGre told *CA:* "My supreme passion is 20th century literature and my greatest worry is the state of the world....[I] agree with Saul Bellow (whose work I admire) that the 'mass audience' is not to be feared—tastes are improving. It is governments we have to fear, and the men who run them." Mrs. DeGre lived in Cairo for a year, and for other periods in Chile and Peru.

(Died, 1971)

* * *

de LAGUNA, Grace A(ndrus) 1878-

PERSONAL: Born September 28, 1878, in East Berlin, Conn.; daughter of Wallace R. (a businessman) and Annis (Mead) Andrus; married Theodore de Laguna, September 9, 1905 (deceased); children: Frederica, Wallace. *Education:* Cornell University, A.B., 1903, Ph.D., 1906. *Politics:* Democrat. *Home:* 221 North Roberts Rd., Bryn Mawr, Pa. 19010. *Office:* Bryn Mawr College, Bryn Mawr, Pa. 19010.

CAREER: Bryn Mawr College, Bryn Mawr, Pa., associate, 1912-22, associate professor, 1922-29, professor of philosophy, 1929-44, professor emeritus, 1944—. Democratic committeewoman for West Bryn Mawr, 1947-51. *Member:* American Philosophical Association (vice-president of Eastern Division, 1938, and president, 1941), Phi Beta Kappa.

WRITINGS: (With husband, Theodore de Laguna) *Dog-*

matism and Evolution, Macmillan, 1909; *Speech: Its Function and Development,* Yale University Press, 1927, revised edition, Indiana University Press, 1963; *On Existence and the Human World,* Yale University Press, 1966. Contributor of articles to philosophical and scientific journals.

WORK IN PROGRESS: Philosophical essays.

* * *

de la WARR, George Walter 1904-1969

PERSONAL: Surname pronounced "Delaware"; born August 19, 1904, in Southwick, Sussex, England; son of George Walter Warr; married Gertrude Marjorie Scholes (partner with husband in research and director of radionic company); children: Elizabeth Anne Hudak, Diane Rosalie (Mrs. Mario di Pinto); *Education:* Attended Brighton Technical College. *Home:* Kingston, Yarnells Hill, Oxford, England. *Office:* Delawarr Laboratories Ltd., Raleigh Park Rd., Oxford, England.

CAREER: County engineer for roads and bridges, Somersetshire, England, 1930-35; assistant county surveyor in Oxfordshire, England, 1935-53; Delawarr Laboratories, Oxford, England, co-owner, 1943-52; Delawarr Laboratories Ltd., Oxford, England, managing director, 1952-69. Developer of thought energy detector, an art appreciation apparatus, the Psychoplot, and the Vibrograph, which detects molecular changes. *Military service:* British Army, Royal Engineers; served in France; became captain. *Member:* Royal Society of Arts (fellow), Institute of Civil Engineers (associate member), Institute of Mechanical Engineers (graduate member).

WRITINGS: (With Langston Day) *New Worlds beyond the Atom,* Stuart, 1956, Devin-Adair, 1963; *The Power of Thought,* Delawarr Laboratories, 1961; *The Network of the Ether,* Delawarr Laboratories, 1962; *The Psycho-Somatic Forcefield,* Delawarr Laboratories, 1963; (with Day) *Matter in the Making,* Stuart, 1966; (with Douglas Baker) *Biomagnetism,* Delawarr Laboratories, 1967. Also author of *A Study of the Ether,* 1963, and *Biomagnetics,* 1969. Contributor to *Mind and Matter.*

WORK IN PROGRESS: Research on the phenomenon of mind and matter, broadcast therapy, the power of thought, techniques of diagnosis involving instrumentally assisted thought scanning, magnetic therapy, sonic and vibrational therapy, and color therapy in association with radionic therapy.

(Died March 31, 1969)

* * *

DEMUTH, Norman (Frank) 1898-1968

PERSONAL: Born 1898, in South Croydon, Surrey, England; son of Alfred Francis and Edith Alice (Davison) Demuth; married Estelle Morris, May 22, 1921 (died, 1962); married Marjorie Hardwick (a professor of piano), September 17, 1964; children: (first marriage) one son, four daughters. *Education:* Studied at Royal College of Music, and studied music privately. *Religion:* Church of England. *Home:* 4 Elfin Grove, Bognor Regis, Sussex, England. *Office:* Royal Academy of Music, Marylebone Rd., London N.W. 1, England.

CAREER: Royal Academy of Music, London, England, professor of composition, 1931-68. Composer, whose works include five operas, three symphonies, four ballets, six concertos, organ music, choral pieces, theater music, and music for British Broadcasting Corp. Examiner for Royal

Academy of Music, London, Paris Conservatoire, and Reine Elizabeth Concours, Brussels. *Military service:* British Army, rifleman, World War I; wounded, 1916; regimental officer, World War II, instructing in camouflage and guerilla warfare. *Member:* Composers Guild of Great Britain (council member), Incorporated Society of Musicians, Royal College of Organists (associate member), Academie Des Beaux Arts. *Awards, honors:* R.A.M., Royal Academy of Music; A.R.C.M., Royal College of Music; Chevalier de la Legion d'Honeur (France), Officer d'Academie (France).

WRITINGS: Ravel, Pellegrini & Cudahy, 1947; *Albert Roussel*, United Music Publishers, 1947; (compiler) *An Anthology of Musical Criticism*, Eyre & Spottiswoode, 1948; *Cesar Franck*, Philisophical Library, 1949; *Vincent d'Imlay*, Barrie & Rockcliff, 1951; *A Course in Musical Composition*, five volumes, Bosworth & Co., 1951-56; *Musical Trends in the Twentieth Century*, Macmillan, 1952; *French Piano Music*, Museum Press, 1959; *French Opera: Its Development to the Revolution*, Artemis Press, 1963, Dufour, 1964; *Musical Forms and Textures*, Dufour, 1963. Contributor to British, French, and American periodicals.

WORK IN PROGRESS: Styles in Harmony; musical compositions.

SIDELIGHTS: Demuth once told *CA* he was a, "Sociable, gregarious fellow. Rather (too) fond of making people rise. Loves home and armchair and occasional solitude. Analytical mind. Rebel. Emotional, quick-tempered, but patient and tolerable. Attracted by youth when it is clean and polite. Fair knowledge of French. Gets on well with other nationals. Deeply, but *cheerfully*, religious." *Avocational interests:* Reading history, dead silence, wine, smoking pipe, conversation, arguing.

(Died April 21, 1968)

*   *   *

DENHAM, Reginald   1894-

PERSONAL: Born January 10, 1894, in London, England; became U.S. citizen, 1947; son of Harry Barton and Emily Constance (Chapman) Denham; married Mary Orr (an actress, dramatist, and novelist), March 26, 1947; children: (previous marriages) Isolde (Mrs. Derek Dempster), Imogen. *Education:* Attended school in England. *Politics:* Liberal. *Home:* 100 West 57th St., New York, N.Y. 10019.

CAREER: Playwright and theatrical director in England and America. Directed more than two hundred plays in London before coming to United States in 1940; director of more than fifty plays in New York, 1940—, with presentations including "Dial M for Murder," 1952, "The Bad Seed," 1954, "Janus," 1955, "Hide and Seek," 1957, "Stranger in the Tea," 1960, and "Hostile Witness," 1965. Also director of films in Europe, film writer in Hollywood, and television writer, the last in collaboration with wife, Mary Orr. *Military service:* British Army, Royal Irish Rifles, World War I; became second lieutenant; later promoted to acting captain. *Member:* Oxford University Dramatic Society (honorary life member).

WRITINGS: (Contributor) R. D. Charques, editor, *Footnotes to the Theatre*, P. Davies, 1938; *Stars in My Hair* (autobiography), Crown, 1958; (with wife, Mary Orr) *Footlights and Feathers: A Logbook of a Theatrical Tour Down Under*, Pageant, 1967.

Plays: (With Edward Percy) *Suspect*, Samuel French (London), 1937, Dramatists Play Service, 1940; (With Percy) *The Dressing Gown* (one-act), H. F. W. Deane & Sons, 1939; (with Percy) *The Harum* (one-act farce), Samuel French (London), 1939; (with Percy) *Trunk Crime*, Dramatists Play Service, 1940; (with Percy) *Ladies in Retirement*, Random, 1940, acting version, Dramatists Play Service, 1941 (also adapted by Denham with Garrett Fort for motion picture, "The Mad Room," Columbia, 1969); (with Percy) *Give Me Yesterday*, English Theatre Guild, 1941; (with Mary Orr) *Wallflower*, Dramatists Play Service, 1943, revised edition, 1944; (with Mary Orr) *Be Your Age*, Dramatists Play Service, 1946; (with Mary Orr) *Dark Hammock*, Dramatists Play Service, 1946; (with Conrad Sutton Smith) *Dash of Bitters*, Dramatists Play Service, 1955; (with Mary Orr) *The Wisdom of Eve*, Dramatists Play Service, 1964; (with Mary Orr) *Minor Murder*, Samuel French, 1967, Dramatists Play Service, 1968.

Translator of three of Alfonso Paso's Spanish plays, published separately as *Blue Heaven, Recipe for a Crime*, and *Oh, Mama!, No, Papa!*, Dramatists Play Service, 1962.

Writer with Mary Orr of some one hundred scripts for television plays produced in New York. Author of short stories in *London Mystery Magazine* and *John Creasy Magazine.*

BIOGRAPHICAL/CRITICAL SOURCES: Stars in My Hair, Crown, 1958.

*   *   *

DENNY, John Howard   1920-

PERSONAL: Born February 26, 1920, in Wellingborough, England; son of George and Kate (Ambridge) Denny. *Education:* Attended Wellingborough School. *Religion:* Baptist. *Home:* Ivy Cottage, Barrowby-Stenwith, Sedgebrook, Grantham, England.

CAREER: Building and civil engineering contracts manager, 1946—. *Military service:* Royal Engineers, served in India and Burma, 1940-46; became captain; awarded Burma Star.

WRITINGS: Chindit Indiscretion, Johnson Publications, 1956. Contributor to *True* and *Storyteller.*

WORK IN PROGRESS: Ffoulkes' Ghost, a novel of Lincolnshire in the early nineteenth century.

BIOGRAPHICAL/CRITICAL SOURCES: Grantham Journal, October, 1956, September, 1963; *Northamton Chronicle and Echo*, October, 1956.

*   *   *

DENTON, H(arry) M.   1882-

PERSONAL: Born December 29, 1882, near Corydon, Ky. *Education:* Southern Normal College (now Western Kentucky State College), B.S., 1904, A.B., 1907; Yale University, LL.B., 1912. *Politics:* Republican. *Religion:* Unitarian. *Home:* 1607 New Cut Rd., Louisville, Ky. 40214.

CAREER: Private law practice, 1914-64. University of Louisville, lecturer in criminal law, 1922-35; University of Louisville Medical School, lecturer, 1927-34. Member, Louisville draft board, 1939-45. *Military service:* U.S. Army, World War I. *Member:* American Bar Association, Kentucky State Bar Association, Louisville Bar Association.

WRITINGS: The Redemption of Preacher Bull (novel), Humphries, 1963.

AVOCATIONAL INTERESTS: Travel and hunting.

DERRICK, Paul 1916-

PERSONAL: Born June 26, 1916, in Congresbury, Somerset, England; son of Thomas and Margaret (Clausen) Derrick; married Peggy Pickering, November 17, 1956. *Education:* University of Reading, diploma in horticulture, 1938. *Politics:* Labour. *Religion:* Roman Catholic. *Home:* 30 Wandworth Bridge Rd., London S.W.6, England. *Office:* International Co-operative Alliance, 11 Upper Grosvenor St., London W. 1, England.

CAREER: Fruitgrower. With British Broadcasting Corp., London, England; *Sunday Citizen,* London, member of research department, 1959-66; International Co-operative Alliance, London, member of research department, 1966—. Prospective Labour Parliamentary candidate for Sutton and Cheam. *Member:* Fabian Society.

WRITINGS: Lost Property, Dobson, 1947; *Production and the Person,* Personalist Group, 1950; *A Co-operative Approach to Socialism,* Socialist Christian League, 1956; *Christian Socialism: Economic Crisis and Common Ownership,* Christian Socialist Movement, 1962; *The Company and the Community,* Fabian Society, 1964; (editor with J. F. Phipps) *Co-ownership, Co-operation and Control: An Independent Objective,* Longmans, Green, 1969; *Socialism in the Seventies,* Co-operative Party, 1970. Contributor of about one thousand articles, mainly on economic problems, to sixty journals in six countries, including *New English Weekly, Liberal, Commonweal, Quarterly Review, Contemporary Review,* and *Christian Democrat.*

WORK IN PROGRESS: A book on inflation and incomes policy.

*   *   *

DERUM, James Patrick 1893-

PERSONAL: Born December 6, 1893, in Bay City, Mich.; son of James and Elizabeth (Kearns) Derum; married Dorothy MacDowell, 1950; children: James, Mary, Daniel. *Education:* Attended Detroit College (now University of Detroit).

CAREER: Most of working life spent in advertising business with agencies in Detroit, New York, and Chicago (for Cadillac Motor Co., Fisher Body, Kroger Grocery and Baking Co., and other products). *Awards, honors:* Christopher Award, 1961.

WRITINGS: Apostle in a Top Hat, Doubleday, 1960.

AVOCATIONAL INTERESTS: Golf.

*   *   *

de SANTILLANA, Giorgio Diaz 1902-

PERSONAL: Born May 30, 1902, in Rome, Italy; came to United States in 1936, naturalized in 1945; son of David (a professor of law) and Emily (Maggiorani) de Santillana; married Dorothy Hancock Tilton, September 1, 1948; children: Ludovico, Gerald. *Education:* University of Rome, Ph.D., 1925; additional study at Sorbonne, University of Paris. *Home and office:* 32 Prince St., Beverly, Mass.

CAREER: University of Rome, Rome, Italy, instructor in physics, 1929-32; New School for Social Research, New York, N.Y., lecturer, 1936-37; Harvard University, Cambridge, Mass., visiting lecturer, 1937-39; Massachusetts Institute of Technology, Cambridge, instructor, 1941-42, assistant professor, 1942-48, associate professor, 1948-54, professor of history and philosophy of science, beginning, 1954, now professor emeritus. *Member:* American

Academy of Art and Sciences, History of Science Society, Examiner Club, Somerset Club. *Awards, honors:* Fulbright Fellow in Italy, 1954-55; Guggenheim Fellow, 1958; National Science Foundation Fellow, 1958; Bollingen Award, 1961.

WRITINGS: (with F. Enriques) *Storia de pensiero scientifica antichita* (title means "A History of Scientific Thought in Antiquity"), Tumminell, 1933; (editor) *I Problemi dell'Asia Centrale* (title means "Historical Problems of Central Asia"), 1934; (translator) Arthur Eddington, *L'-Universo in espansione,* [Bologna], 1934; (with Enriques) *Breve Storia del pensiero scientifica* (title means "A Brief History of Scientific Thought"), Zanichelli (Bologna),1937; (editor) Salusbury's translation, *Galileo's Dialogue on the Great World Systems,* University of Chicago Press, 1953, abridged edition, 1955; *The Crime of Galileo,* University of Chicago Press, 1955; *The Age of Adventure, Renaissance Philosophy,* Houghton and Mentor Books, 1957; (with H. A. Reiche) *Aristotle and Science, a Critical Controversy,* Hall for Massachusetts Institute of Technology, 1959; *The Origins of Scientific Thought,* University of Chicago Press and New American Library, 1961; *Reflections on Men and Ideas,* M. I. T. Press, 1968; (with Hertha von Dechend) *Hamlet's Mill: An Essay on Myth and the Frame of Time,* Gambit, 1969.

Contributor: *Studies and Essays in the History of Science and Learning* (in honor of George Sarton), 1946; Carl J. Friedrich, editor, *Totalitarianism,* Harvard University Press, 1954; La Baconniere, editor, *Recontres de Geneve,* [Geneva], 1954; G. Holt, editor, *Science and the Modern Mind* (Symposium), Beacon, 1959; M. Clagett, editor, *Critical Problems in History of Science,* University of Wisconsin Press, 1959; *New World Writing, No.13,* New American Library, 1959; *La Science Seizieme Siecle,* Colloques de royaumont, 1960; Alistair Crombie, editor, *Scientific Change* (symposium), Basic Books, 1961; *Melanges Koyre,* Hermann (Paris), 1965.

Also contributor: *International Encyclopedia of Unified Science,* Volume II, University of Chicago Press, 1941; *Columbia Biographical Dictionary,* 1944; *Encyclopaedia Britannica,* 1960 Pauly's *Realencyclopaedie.* Contributor of articles to *Isis, Atlantic Monthly, Atlantic Reports, Tech Engineering News, Harper's, Reporter, Saturday Review, Tangent,* and other journals in the United States, France, Italy and of reviews to *American Scientist, Scientific American, American Historical Review,* and others.

SIDELIGHTS: de Santillana is competent in French, German, and Spanish. The *Crime of Galileo* has been published in French, Italian, Swedish, and German translations; two other books also have appeared in translations.

*   *   *

de SAUSMAREZ, (Lionel) Maurice 1915-1969

PERSONAL: Born October 20, 1915, in Sydney, New South Wales, Australia; son of Clarence Montgomery (a marine engineer) and Jessie Rose (Bamford) de Sausmarez; married Kate Elizabeth Lyons, 1939; married second wife, Jane Boswell (an artist and teacher), May 11, 1963; children; (first marriage) Philippa Judith; (second marriage) Emma Louise. *Education:* Royal College of Art, London, England, A.R.C.A., 1939; University of Leeds, M.A. (conferred). *Home:* 16 Leaside Ave., Fortes Green, N.10, England. *Office:* Byam Shaw School of Art, 70 Campden St., London W. 8, England.

CAREER: University of Leeds, Leeds, England, head of

department of fine art, 1950-59; Byam Shaw School of Art, London, England, principal, 1962-69. Painter, lecturer, and writer on the visual arts. Member, National Council for Diplomas in Art and Design, 1968-69. *Member:* Artists' International Association (chairman of central committee, 1945-47), Royal Society of British Artists, Society for Education Through Art, Royal Academy of Arts (associate).

WRITINGS: An Introduction to Paintings (pamphlet), National Association of Girls' Clubs and Mixed Clubs, 1950; (with Jon Silkin) *Isaac Rosenberg, 1890-1918* (catalogue of an exhibition), University of Leeds, 1959; *Basic Design: The Dynamics of Visual Form,* Reinhold, 1964; (editor) *Ben Nicholson,* Studio International, 1969; *Maurice de Sausmarez, A.R.A., on Poussin's Orpheus Eurydice,* Cassell, 1969; *Bridget Riley,* New York Graphic Society, 1970. Contributor to *Universities Quarterly, Connoisseur,* and *Motif.*

WORK IN PROGRESS: Technical Handbook of Modern Painting, for Studio Vista.

SIDELIGHTS: de Sausmarez spent part of each year in Vaucluse, France, where he owned property.

BIOGRAPHICAL/CRITICAL SOURCES: Times Literary Supplement, July 24, 1969; *Listener,* November 26, 1970.

(Died October 27, 1969)

*   *   *

DETJEN, Mary (Elizabeth) Ford   1904-

PERSONAL: Born April 27, 1904, in Cave City, Ky.; daughter of Garland Hopkins (a salesman) and Settie (Parker) Ford; married Ervin W. Detjen (an elementary school principal), June 14, 1938; children: Ervin W., Jr. *Education:* Bowling Green College of Commerce, A.C.A., 1928; University of Kentucky, A.B., 1932; Pennsylvania State College (now University), graduate study, 1944; University of Louisville, M.A., 1946. *Politics:* Independent. *Religion:* Methodist. *Home:* 1956 Deer Park Ave., Louisville, Ky.

CAREER: Teacher of commerce in Clinton, La., 1928, in Glasgow, Ky., 1928-29; Eastern Junior High School, Louisville, Ky., teacher of commerce and guidance counselor, 1929-38; Alex G. Barret Junior High School, Louisville, Ky., counselor, 1938-71. Louisville Council of Parent-Teacher Associations, director of student loans, 1938-63. *Member:* National Education Association, Kentucky Education Association, Kentucky Personnel and Guidance Association, Kappa Delta Pi.

WRITINGS—All with husband, Ervin W. Detjen: *Home Room Guidance Programs for the Junior High School Years,* Houghton, 1940; *Your Plans for the Future,* McGraw, 1947; *Your High School Days,* McGraw, 1947, revised edition for Canadian schools, 1950, 2nd revised edition, 1958; *Elementary School Guidance,* McGraw, 1952, revised edition, 1963; *So You're in High School,* Whittlesey House, 1958. Contributor of articles to Commonwealth of Kentucky educational bulletins and to *Child-Family Digest* and *Vocational Education News.*

SIDELIGHTS: Elementary School Guidance has been translated for use in Argentina.

BIOGRAPHICAL/CRITICAL SOURCES: Louisville Courier Journal, June 18, 1939, May 17, 1952, May 17, 1963; *Better Homes and Gardens,* April, 1950.

DETZER, Karl   1891-
(Michael Costello)

PERSONAL: Born September 4, 1891, in Fort Wayne, Ind.; son of August J. and Laura (Goshorn) Detzer; married Clarice Nissley, November, 1921; children: Karl, Jr. (deceased), Mary Jane (Mrs. John C. Moench). *Politics:* Democrat. *Religion:* Unitarian. *Residence:* Leland, Mich. *Office: Reader's Digest,* Pleasantville, N.Y. 10570.

CAREER: Newspaper reporter and photographer in Fort Wayne, Ind., 1908-16; advertising writer and manager of department stores in Chicago, Ill., 1921-24; script writer and assistant director at film studios in Hollywood, Calif., 1935-37; *Reader's Digest,* Pleasantville, N.Y., roving editor, 1938—. *Enterprise-Tribune,* Leland, Mich., publisher, 1947-51. Michigan State Corrections Commission, member, 1947-48; Michigan Citizens Committee on Reorganization of State Government, chairman, 1949-50. *Military service:* U.S. Army, Mexican Border Campaign, 1916-17, Infantry, 1917-18, Division of Criminal Investigation, 1919; became captain; World War II, General Staff Corps, 1942-46; became colonel; awarded Distinguished Service Medal. Special assistant to Allied military governor of Germany during Berlin airlift. *Member:* Authors Guild of Authors League of America, International City Managers Association (affiliate), National Municipal League (former board member), National Press Club, Overseas Press Club, Deadline Club, Fraternal Order of Police (life), Veterans of Foreign Wars, Sigma Delta Chi. *Awards, honors:* Freedoms Foundation gold medallion; medal of merit, Michigan State Police; citation for promotion of brotherhood, National Council of Christians and Jews; certificate of appreciation, Chicago Police Department; Old Masters Testimonial, Purdue University.

WRITINGS: True Tales of the D.C.I., Bobbs-Merrill, 1925; *The Marked Man,* Bobbs-Merrill, 1927; *Pirate of the Pine Lands,* Bobbs-Merrill, 1929; *The Broken Three,* Bobbs-Merrill, 1929; *Contrabando,* Bobbs-Merrill, 1937; *Carl Sandburg: A Study in Personality,* Harcourt, 1941; (editor) *The Army Reader,* Bobbs-Merrill, 1943; *The Mightiest Army,* Reader's Digest, 1945; (with H. P. Harrison) *Culture under Canvas,* Hastings House, 1958; *Myself When Young,* Funk, 1968. Author of motion picture scripts. Contributor of more than 150 articles to *Reader's Digest,* and 1,000 short stories, serials, and articles to *Saturday Evening Post, American Century, Liberty, Collier's,* and other magazines.

WORK IN PROGRESS: Several books.

*   *   *

DEVI, Indra   1899-

PERSONAL: Born May 12, 1899, in Riga, Russia; daughter of Wilhelm Paul (a bank director) and Alexandra (Zitovich) Petersen; formerly married to a diplomat (deceased); married Sigfrid Knauer (a medical doctor), March 14, 1953. *Education:* Attended school in St. Petersburg (now Leningrad), Russia. *Politics:* Non-partisan. *Home:* Rancho el Cuchuma, Tecate, Baja California, Mexico.

CAREER: Teacher, writer, and lecturer on yoga. Indra Devi Yoga Foundation, Los Angeles, Calif., founder and president, 1958—. Consultant, Instituto de Filosofia Yoga, Mexico; president, S.A.I. Foundation, Los Angeles and Tecate, Calif.; founder, Sai Yoga Academy, Baja, Calif. and Mexico.

WRITINGS: Yoga—The Technique of Health and Happi-

ness, Kitabistan, 1948; *Forever Young, Forever Healthy*, Prentice-Hall, 1953; *Yoga for Americans*, Prentice-Hall, 1959; *Renew Your Life Through Yoga*, Prentice-Hall, 1963. Contributor of monthly articles to *Jueves Exelcior* (Mexico).

WORK IN PROGRESS: A book on Sai Yoga.

SIDELIGHTS: Indra Devi speaks twelve languages. She lived in India for twelve years, in Shanghai, China, for seven; and states she introduced yoga to the U.S.S.R. in 1960. Her three most recent books have been translated into eight languages.

BIOGRAPHICAL/CRITICAL SOURCES: People Today, June, 1950; *Holiday*, October, 1957; *Newsweek*, November 7, 1960; *Life*, February 14, 1964; *Pageant*, December, 1964.

* * *

DEVOR, John W(esley) 1901-

PERSONAL: Born July 19, 1901, in Broken Bow, Neb.; son of John William (a teacher) and Rhoda Ann (Gilmore) Devor; married Lois Blanche Batchedler (a singer), December 25, 1924. *Education:* Central College, McPherson, Kan., student, 1920-22; University of Kansas, A.B., 1924, M.A., 1929; University of Chicago, Ph.D., 1952. *Politics:* Republican. *Religion:* Methodist. *Home:* 6560 Montezuma Rd., Apt. 312, San Diego, Calif. 92115.

CAREER: Teacher, mainly of science and mathematics, at elementary and secondary schools in Oklahoma and Kansas, 1919-48; Asbury College, Wilmore, Ky., 1948-56, started as associate professor, became professor of education and chairman of division of education and psychology; American University, Washington, D.C., professor of education and chairman of division of education, 1959-67, professor emeritus, 1971—. *Member:* Association for Higher Education, American Association of School Administrators, National Education Association (committee on teacher education and professional standards), American Association of University Professors, Association for Supervision and Curriculum Development, National Science Teachers Association (regional director, 1949-52), Association for Student Teaching (Kentucky president, 1954-55; chairman, committee on arrangements for national workshop, 1955), National Society for the Study of Education, District of Columbia Education Association, Federal Schoolmen's Club. *Awards, honors:* National Science Teachers Association medal; Pi Sigma Rho Key for work with Future Teachers of America.

WRITINGS: Learning Experiences for Student Teachers, privately printed, 1955, revised edition, 1958; *The Experience of Student Teaching*, Macmillan, 1964. Contributor of articles to education journals.

AVOCATIONAL INTERESTS: Travel and group singing.

* * *

DEY, Joseph C(harles), Jr. 1907-

PERSONAL: Surname is pronounced Die; born November 17, 1907, in Norfolk, Va.; son of Joseph Charles and Martha Lillian (Holt) Dey; married Rosalie Moran Knapp, January 29, 1937; children: Edward Knapp. *Education:* University of Pennsylvania, student, 1925-27. *Politics:* Republican. *Religion:* Episcopalian. *Home:* 171 Factory Pond Rd., Locust Valley, N.Y. 11560. *Office:* P.G.A. Tournament Players Division, 60 East 42nd St., New York, N.Y. 10017.

CAREER: Sports writer for newspapers, 1923-34; U.S. Golf Association, New York, N.Y., executive director, 1934-69; P.G.A. Tournament Players Division, New York, N.Y., commissioner, 1969—. Honorary Secretary, World Amateur Golf Council, 1958-69. Former president, Nassau County Christian Council. *Military service:* U.S. Naval Reserve, 1944-46; became lieutenant. *Member:* Union League Club (New York), Creek Club (Locust Valley, N.Y.), Royal and Ancient Golf Club (St. Andrews, Scotland), Sigma Alpha Epsilon. *Awards, honors:* William D. Richardson Award, Golf Writers Association of America.

WRITINGS: (Editor) *Golf Rules in Pictures*, Grosset, 1962, revised edition, 1964; (editor) *USGA Golf Handbook, 1964*, United States Golf Association, 1964. Contributor to *Collier's, Sports Illustrated*, and other sports magazines. Former editor, *Golf Journal* (publication of U.S. Golf Association).

* * *

DIAMOND, Arthur Sigismund 1897-

PERSONAL: Born December 23, 1897, in Leeds, England; son of Solomon (a rabbi) and Henrietta (Beckerman) Diamond; married Sybil Grace Mocatta (a gynecologist), April 8, 1952; children: Anthony Edward John, Joan Henriette Diamond Solomon, Susan Flora Diamond Loewe. *Education:* Trinity College, Cambridge, M.A. and LL.M., 1924, LL.D., 1936. *Religion:* Jewish. *Home:* 51 Maresfield Gardens, London N.W.3, England.

CAREER: Called to the bar, 1921; in practice, London, England, 1921-52; a master of the Supreme Court, London, 1952-69. President of various religious, charitable, and educational bodies. *Military service:* British Army, Honourable Artillery Company, 1917-19. *Member:* Royal Anthropological Institute (member of council), Jewish Historical Society (England; president).

WRITINGS: The Law of Master and Servant, Stevens, 1931, 2nd edition, 1946; *Primitive Law*, Longmans, Green, 1935, 3rd edition, Barnes & Noble, 1972; *Evolution of Law and Order*, C. A. Watts, 1951; *The History and Origin of Language*, Philosophical Library, 1959. Editor of *Annual Practice*, 1953-65.

WORK IN PROGRESS: Sociological research.

* * *

DICKIE, Edgar P(rimrose) 1897-

PERSONAL: Born August 12, 1897, in Dumfries, Scotland; son of William and Jane (Paterson) Dickie; married Ishbel Graham Holmes Johnston (a writer), August 31, 1927. *Education:* University of Edinburgh, M.A. and B.D.; Christ Church, Oxford, B.A.; also studied at University of Marburg and University of Tuebingen. *Home:* Surma, 19 Hepburn Gardens, St. Andrews, Fife, Scotland. *Office:* University of St. Andrews, St. Andrews, Scotland.

CAREER: Clergyman, Church of Scotland; minister in Lockerbie, Dumfriesshire, Scotland, 1927-33, and in Edinburgh, Scotland, 1933-35; University of St. Andrews, St. Andrews, Scotland, professor of divinity, 1935-67, professor emeritus, 1967—. Governor of St. Leonard's School; formerly convener of Kate Kennedy Hospital trustees and of Gifford Lectureship committee. Chaplain to Her Majesty in Scotland, 1956—. *Military service:* King's Own Scottish Borderers, 1915-19; received Military Cross. Officers' Training Corps, University of St. Andrews, captain and company commander, 1939-46; mentioned in dispatches (Normandy). *Awards, honors:* D.D., University of Edinburgh, 1946; Commander of Merit of the Order of St. Lazarus of Jerusalem, 1961; D.D., University of St. Andrews, 1969; Companion of the Order, 1970.

WRITINGS: The Seven Words from the Cross, Stockwell, 1930; (contributor) *Asking Them Questions,* Oxford University Press, 1935, new edition, 1971; (author of introduction) Karl Heim, *The Power of God,* translated by L.M. Stalker, Lutterworth, 1935; *Revelation and Response,* Scribner, 1936; (contributor) *The Professor as Preacher,* John Clarke, 1938.

One Year's Talks to Children, Revell, 1940; *Scottish Life and Character,* Oliver & Boyd, 1942; *A Second Year's Talks to Children,* Revell, 1943; *The Obedience of a Christian Man,* S.C.M. Press, 1944; (contributor) *In Our Tongues,* S.P.C.K., 1944; *Ever in the Light,* Church of Scotland, 1945; *It Was New to Me,* Church of Scotland, 1946; *Normandy to Nijmegen,* Church of Scotland, 1946; *The Fellowship of Youth,* Hodder & Stoughton, 1947; (editor) *Christian Leadership,* Christian Leadership Committee, 1947; *What We Believe,* Church of Scotland, 1948; *I Promise: Notes on the Promise and the Law Offered to Guides and Guiders,* Church of Scotland, 1949.

A Call to the Ministry, Church of Scotland, 1950; *God Is Light,* Scribner, 1953; *Thou Art the Christ: The Gospel Witnesses,* Hodder & Stoughton, 1954; *A Safe Stronghold: Studies in Christian Apologetics,* Religious Education Press, 1955; (author of introduction) J. McLeod Campbell, *The Nature of the Atonement,* John Clarke, 1959.

The Unchanging Gospel, St. Andrew Press, 1960; *The Everlasting Father: Studies in Christian Doctrine,* Religious Education Press, 1964; *Remembrance,* Hodder & Stoughton, 1966.

Translations of Karl Heim's books: *The New Divine Order (Die neue welt Gottes),* Harper, 1930; *God Transcendent (Glaube und Denken),* Nisbet & Co., 1934; *Spirit and Truth (Das Wesen des evangelischen Christentums),* Lutterworth, 1935.

Nonsense stories: *Psammy for Short,* Methuen, 1929; *The Paper Boat,* Hodder & Stoughton, 1943; *Mister Bannock,* Hodder & Stoughton, 1947.

Contributor of articles and reviews to theological journals, occasional articles to *Punch,* and poems to *Scotsman* and to newspapers in Scotland.

SIDELIGHTS: Holder of the oldest university chair in Scotland (the Chair of Divinity established in 1537), he has also been honorary president of the University of St. Andrews Madrigal Group, Athletic Club, Cross-Country Club, and Rifle Club. *Avocational interests:* Winter sports, hill-walking, bird-watching.

BIOGRAPHICAL/CRITICAL SOURCES: Times Literary Supplement, April 13, 1967.

*   *   *

DICKS, Russell Leslie 1906-1965

PERSONAL: Born September 30, 1906, in Stillwater, Okla; married Dorothy Smith (assistant dean of women, Wesleyan College, Macon, Ga.); children: James, William, JoAnne. *Education:* University of Oklahoma, A.B., 1930, Union Theological Seminary, New York, N.Y., B.D., 1933.

CAREER: Ordained minister of Methodist Church, 1933; chaplain at Massachusetts General Hospital, Boston,

Mass., 1933-37, Presbyterian Hospital, Chicago, Ill., 1937-40, Wesley Memorial Hospital, Chicago, Ill., 1944-48; Duke University, Durham, N.C., professor of pastoral care, 1948-58; Central Florida Counseling Center, Orlando, director, 1958-65. Lecturer to clergymen and physicians. *Member:* American Association of Marriage Counselors, American Association of Hospital Chaplains. *Awards, honors:* D.D. from Southwestern College, Winfield, Kan., 1944; Litt.D. from Adrian College, 1949; one of four Americans cited by National Council of Churches of Christ in America for outstanding work for the welfare of the people.

WRITINGS: (With Richard C. Cabot) *The Art of Ministering to the Sick,* Macmillan, 1936, 2nd edition, 1961; *Meditations for the Sick,* Willett, Clark Co., 1937; *When You Call on the Sick: A Layman's Guidebook,* Harper, 1938; *Your Self and Health,* Harper, 1939; *And Ye Visited Me; Source Book for Ministers in Work With the Sick,* Harper, 1939.

Who Is My Patient?: A Religious Manual for Nurses, Macmillan, 1941; *Pastoral Work and Personal Counseling,* Macmillan, 1944, revised edition, 1949; *Thy Health Shall Spring Forth; Readings in Religion and Health,* Macmillan, 1945; *Comfort Ye My People: A Manual of the Pastoral Ministry,* Macmillan, 1947; *My Faith Looks Up,* Westminster, 1949.

You Came Unto Me: A Guidebook in Pastoral Calling for Ministers and Laymen, Religion and Health Press, 1951, 2nd revised edition published as *How to Make Pastoral Calls, for Ministers and Laymen,* Bethany, 1962; (with Thomas S. Kepler) *And Peace at Last: A Study of Death, the Unreconciled Subject of Our Times,* Westminster, 1953; *Meet Joe Ross,* Abingdon, 1957.

Toward Health and Wholeness, Macmillan, 1960; *Principles and Practices of Pastoral Care,* Prentice-Hall, 1963; *Premarital Guidance,* Prentice-Hall, 1963.

General editor of "Successful Pastoral Aid" series, Prentice-Hall, 1963-64. Contributor to journals. Founder and editor, *Religion and Health,* 1952-56.

(Died March 8, 1965)

*   *   *

DIEHL, Katharine Smith 1906-

PERSONAL: Born May 16, 1906, in Manheim, Pa.; daughter of Reuben O. (a physician) and Emma C. (Smith) Diehl. *Education:* Millersville Normal School (now Millersville State College), student, 1923-26; Boston University, B.R.E., 1928; Emory University, A.B. in L.S., 1938; University of Michigan, M.A. in L.S., 1954; additional study at three other universities. *Religion:* Episcopalian. *Office:* Graduate School of Library Service, Rutgers University, New Brunswick, N.J. 08903.

CAREER: High school mathematics teacher, Delta, Pa., 1929-35; Texas Lutheran College, Seguin, librarian, 1938-53; full-time writer, 1954-55; University of Tennessee, Knoxville, head of department of library services, 1958-59; University of Dacca, Dacca, East Pakistan, senior Fulbright professor of library science, 1959-61; Serampore College, Serampore, West Bengal, India, bibliographer in William Carey Historical Library under grant from Lilly Endowment, 1961-62; Graduate School of Library Service, Rutgers University, New Brunswick, assistant professor of library service, 1963—. Summer teacher at other university and college library schools. Church organist in Seguin, Tex., and Dacca, East Pakistan. *Member:* American Library Association (life), American Theological Library Association, Bibliographical Society of America, Association for Asian Studies, American Association of University Women, East Pakistan Geographical Society (life), Southeastern Library Association.

WRITINGS: One Librarian, Scarecrow, 1956; *Religions, Mythologies, Folklores: An Annotated Bibliography,* Scarecrow, 1956, 2nd edition, Scarecrow, 1962; (with Hemendra Kumar Sircar) *Early Indian Imprints: A Catalogue from the William Carey Historical Library of Serampore,* Council of Serampore College, 1962; (with Sircar) *Early Indian Imprints* (not the same as 1962 publication), Scarecrow, 1964; *Hymns and Tunes: An Index,* Scarecrow, 1966. Other Diehl-Sircar work under general title of "Early Indian Imprints" includes a microfilmed catalogue and a microfilm on the William Carey Historical Library exhibition.

WORK IN PROGRESS: Editing *The Tale of the Four Durwesh,* by Amir Khusrau.

* * *

DIENSTEIN, William 1909-

PERSONAL: Born May 9, 1909, in Chicago, Ill.; son of Joseph and Fannie (Heda) Dienstein; married Roslyn Robbins (an attorney-at-law), July 13, 1947. *Education:* Stanford University, A.B., 1931, Ph.D., 1959; University of California, Berkeley, M.A., 1939. *Home:* 1800 Gough St., San Francisco, Calif. 94109.

CAREER: Teacher in public schools, 1935-41; California State University, Fresno, assistant professor, 1946, associate professor, 1947-50, 1953-60, professor of sociology and criminology, 1960-74, professor emeritus, 1974—, chairman of department of criminology, 1946-50. Member of California Governor's Special Study Commission on Juvenile Justice, member, 1957-60; Board of Education, Fresno City Unified School District, member, 1961-69, president, 1964-66. *Military service:* U.S. Army, Military Police, 1941-46, 1950-52; received Asiatic-Pacific and Philippine Liberation medals; now major (retired), U.S. Army Reserve. *Member:* International Society of Criminology, American Society of Criminology (fellow; president, 1953-54), International Association of Chiefs of Police, Phi Kappa Phi, Pi Gamma Mu, Phi Delta Kappa.

WRITINGS: Technics for the Crime Investigator, C. C Thomas, 1952; *Are You Guilty? An Introduction to the Administration of Criminal Justice in the U.S.,* C. C Thomas, 1954; *How to Write a Narrative Investigation Report,* C. C Thomas, 1964. Contributor of reviews and articles to journals. Editorial consultant, *Quaderni di Criminologia Clinica.* Book review editor, *Police,* 1955-73.

* * *

DILKE, Annabel (Mary) 1942-

PERSONAL: Surname rhymes with "milk"; born April 28, 1942, in London, England; daughter of Christopher Wentworth (a writer) and Alice Mary (Best) Dilke. *Education:* Attended Francis Holland School, London, England. *Religion:* Church of England. *Home:* 22 Thurloe St., London W. 8, England. *Agent:* Curtis Brown Ltd., 1 Craven Hill, London W2 3EW, England. *Office: Daily Telegraph,* 135 Fleet St., London E.C. 4, England.

CAREER: Daily Telegraph, London, England, research assistant on "Way of the World" column, 1961-68; subsequently worked for United Nations and then went on ar-

chaeological expedition in Guatemala; full-time writer in England, 1969—.

WRITINGS: Rule Three: Pretend to Be Nice (novel), Chatto & Windus, 1964.

WORK IN PROGRESS: Another novel; a television play.

SIDELIGHTS: Miss Dilke writes to *CA:* "I am only interested in writing, but like traveling and love Greece best of the places I have visited. . . . I think there is no such thing as inspiration, or if there is it is fairly rare, and that the only way to work is to establish a routine, then *perhaps* inspiration will come."

BIOGRAPHICAL/CRITICAL SOURCES: Daily Express (London), October 10, 1964; *Daily Telegraph* (London), October 17, 1964; *Listener,* October 24, 1964.

* * *

DISHER, Maurice Willson 1893-1969

PERSONAL: Born January 10, 1893, in London, England; son of Thomas Joseph (a civil servant) and Emily Sarah Henrietta (Rhodes) Disher. *Education:* Attended Latymer Upper School, London, England. *Politics:* "Votes for man, not doctrine." *Religion:* Christian. *Home:* Villa Salvador, Campamento, San Roque, Spain. *Agent:* A. P. Watt & Son, 10 Norfolk St., Strand, London W.C. 2, England.

CAREER: Standard and *Evening Standard,* London, England, music hall and drama critic, 1911-22; *Variety* and *Clipper,* New York, N.Y., theatre, music hall, and circus critic, 1923-24; *Observer,* London, England, film critic, 1927-28; *Daily Mail,* London, England, drama critic, 1930-37; *Times Literary Supplement,* London, England, reviewer of books on public entertainment, 1937-51. *Member:* Royal Society of Literature (fellow), Critics' Circle. *Awards, honors:* Cafe Royal Prize, for *Melodrama.*

WRITINGS: Clown (novel), Parsons, 1924; *Clowns and Pantomimes,* Constable, 1925, Benjamin Blom, 1968; (editor) *The Cowells in America,* Benjamin Blom, 1934; *About Nothing Whatever,* Chapman & Hall, 1935; *Winkles and Champagne,* Batsford, 1935; *Greatest Show on Earth,* Benjamin Blom, 1937; *Fairs, Circuses and Music-Halls,* Collins, 1942; *The Last Romantic,* Hutchinson, 1948; *Blood and Thunder,* Muller, 1949; *Pleasures of London,* R. Hale, 1950; *Mad Genius,* Hutchinson, 1950; *Whitely-Wanton,* Hutchinson, 1951; *Melodrama,* Rockliff, 1954; *Victorian Song,* Phoenix House, 1955; *Pharoah's Fool,* Heinemann, 1958.

Plays: "Joan of Memories," 1920; "There Remains a Gesture," 1920; "Rupert's Revenge" (juvenile), 1923; "Having No Hearts," 1934; "Harlequinade," 1940. Contributor to *Encyclopaedia Britannica, Chambers's Encyclopaedia, Oxford Companion to the Theatre, Book of the Horse.* Also contributor to *Quarterly Review, Edinburgh Review, Nineteenth Century,* and other periodicals. Author of radio scripts for British Broadcasting Corp.

WORK IN PROGRESS: Research on Goya.

SIDELIGHTS: Disher's life's ambition to write a major work on public entertainments ended in the breakdown of his health in 1951. He sold prints and books in 1960, and later traveled in Italy, Spain, and Greece.

(Died November 24, 1969)

* * *

DISRAELI, Robert 1903-

PERSONAL: Born November 16, 1903, in Cologne, Germany; son of Samuel and Sophia (Jonas) Disraeli; married Edith Plitt Waldman (a librarian); children: A. Stephen. *Education:* Attended Cooper Union, 1920-23, College of City of New York (now City College of City University of New York), 1924-27, and Columbia University, 1927-29. *Home:* 206 East 17th St., New York, N.Y. 10003. *Office address:* P.O. Box 343, Cooper Station, N.Y. 10003.

CAREER: Creator and producer of more than twenty-five educational films.

WRITINGS—Juvenile: *Seeing the Unseen* (Juvenile Literary Guild selection), John Day, 1932, revised edition, 1939; *Uncle Sam's Treasury*, Little, Brown, 1939; *Here Comes the Mail*, Little, Brown, 1939; *New Worlds Through the Microscope*, Viking, 1961.

* * *

DIXON, H(arry) Vernor 1908-

PERSONAL: Born October 30, 1908, in Sacramento, Calif.; son of Harry Vernor (in real estate) and Esther (Icanberry) Dixon; married Dorothy Lorraine Moriaty, September 19, 1934; Bradley T., Pamela H. (Mrs. Daryl Hadley). *Education:* California School of Fine Arts, student, 1926. *Politics:* Republican. *Religion:* Protestant. *Home and office:* 2950 Fulton St., San Francisco, Calif. 94118. *Agent:* Curtis Brown Ltd., 60 East 56th St., New York, N.Y. 10022.

CAREER: Professional writer, 1929—, writing exclusively for magazines, 1935-50. Prior to 1934 also appeared in vaudeville, musical comedies, and motion pictures, was an aircraft pilot, deep-sea diver.

WRITINGS: Laughing Gods, Eerdmans, 1935; *Something for Nothing*, Harper, 1950; *To Hell Together*, Gold Medal, 1951; *The Marriage Bed*, Red Seal, 1952; *Up a Winding Stair*, Gold Medal, 1953; *Deep Is the Pit*, Gold Medal, 1953; *Too Rich to Die*, Gold Medal, 1953; *A Lover for Cindy*, Gold Medal, 1954; *The Hunger and the Hate*, Fawcett, 1955; *Cry Blood*, Gold Medal, 1956; *Killer in Silk*, Gold Medal, 1957; *That Girl Marian*, Monarch, 1962; *The Pleasure Seekers*, Monarch, 1963; *Guerilla*, Monarch, 1963; *The Rag Pickers*, McKay, 1966. Writer of motion picture scripts. Contributor of hundreds of short stories and serials to *Saturday Evening Post, Collier's, Liberty, Cosmopolitan*, other magazines.

WORK IN PROGRESS: An essay on American mores; several books.

SIDELIGHTS: When Dixon was concentrating on magazine writing, he had four different short stories and a serial appearing in five magazines on one date. His books have been republished in England, some translated into French and Italian.

* * *

DIXON, Pierson (John) 1904-1965

PERSONAL: Born November 13, 1904, in Englefield Green, Surrey, England; son of Pierson John (a landowner) and Harriet Barbara (Beales) Dixon; married Alexandra Ismene Atchley, 1928; children: Piers, Jennifer (Mrs. Peter Blaker), Corinna. *Education:* Attended Bedford School, 1916-23; Cambridge University, B.A., Pembroke College, 1927, M.A., 1932; also studied at British School of Archaeology, Athens, Greece, 1927-28, Ecole des Sciences Politiques, Paris, France, 1928-29. *Home:* British Embassy, Paris 8e, France.

CAREER: British Foreign Service, 1929-65, served at embassies in Madrid, Ankara, and Rome, 1932-40; principal private secretary to Foreign Secretary, 1943-48; Ambassador to Czechoslovakia, 1948-50; deputy Under-secretary of State, 1950-54; permanent representative of United Kingdom to United Nations, 1954-60; Ambassador to France, 1960-64; Westminster Bank, London, England, director, 1965. Freeman of Drapers Company. *Member:* Society of Authors, Society for the Promotion of Hellenic Studies, Lotos Club (New York), Jockey Club (Paris); Brooks's Club and Union Club (both London). *Awards, honors:* Companion of St. Michael and St. George, 1945; Companion of the Bath, 1948; Knight Commander of St. Michael and St. George, 1950; Knight Grand Cross of St. Michael and St. George, 1957. Cambridge University, honorary fellow of Pembroke College, 1949, honorary LL.D.

WRITINGS: The Iberians of Spain and Their Relations with the Aegean World, Oxford University Press, 1939; *Farewell, Catullus*, Hollis & Carter, 1953; *The Glittering Horn*, J. Cape, 1958; (contributor) Stephen D. Kertesz and Matthew A. Fitzsimmons, editors, *Diplomacy in a Changing World*, University of Notre Dame Press, 1959; *Pauline, Napoleon's Favourite Sister*, Collins, 1964, McKay, 1965. Contributor to *Reader's Digest, Saturday Review, This Week, Christian Science Monitor, New York Times, New York Herald Tribune, Times Literary Supplement, Country Life, Field*, and *Connoisseur*.

BIOGRAPHICAL/CRITICAL SOURCES: Piers Dixon, *Double Diploma: The Life of Sir Pierson Dixon*, Hutchinson, 1968.

(Died April 22, 1965)

* * *

DOANE, Gilbert H(arry) 1897-

PERSONAL: Born January 28, 1897, in Fairfield, Vt.; son of Harry Harvey (a teacher, mailman, and farmer) and Charlotte Maude (Gilbert) Doane; married Susan Howland Sherman, June 23, 1923; children: Cynthia Gilbert (Mrs. Donald Edgar Nickerson, Jr.), John Philip. *Education:* Colgate University, B.A., 1918; graduate study at University of Arizona, 1921-22, University of Michigan, 1923-24. *Home:* 2725 Lynn Ter., Madison, Wis. 53705. *Office:* New England Historic Genealogical Society, 101 Newbury St., Boston, Mass. 02111.

CAREER: New York State Library, Albany, assistant, 1920-21; University of Michigan, Ann Arbor, assistant librarian, 1922-25; University of Nebraska, Lincoln, librarian, 1925-37, professor of bibliography, 1930-37; University of Wisconsin, Madison, director of libraries, 1937-56, university archivist, 1957-62, professor emeritus, 1962—. Protestant Episcopal Church, ordained deacon, 1943, priest, 1956, assistant at Grace Episcopal Church, Madison, Wis., 1951—, historiographer of Milwaukee (Wis.) Diocese, 1955—. *Military service:* U.S. Navy, 1918-19. U.S. Army, 1943-45, became major.

MEMBER: American Society of Genealogists (fellow), New England Historic Genealogical Society (life), State Historical Society of Wisconsin (life), Vermont Historical Society (life), Church Historical Society (Episcopal), Newport (R.I.) Historical Society. *Awards, honors:* LL.D. from Nashotah House Seminary, 1954.

WRITINGS: (With Eloise White Street) *The Legend of the Book*, Bookfellows, 1924; *Classification*, American Correspondence School of Librarianship, 1925; *Sale Catalogue of the Library of the Late Lord Byron,* privately printed, 1929; *Searching for Your Ancestors,* McGraw, 1937, 3rd edition, University of Minnesota Press, 1960; *Some Early Records of Fairfield, Vermont,* [Fairfield], 1938; *About Collecting Bookplates,* Black Mack, 1941; (editor) George B. Utley, *Librarian's Conference of 1853,* American Library Association, 1951; *Grace Episcopal Church, Madison, Wisconsin* (history), 1958; *En-megah-bow of the Chippewas,* Protestant Episcopal Church National Council, 1962.

Contributor to *Dictionary of American Biography, Dictionary of American History,* and to *New England Short Stories,* edited by Paul G. Conway, 1934, 1936. Also contributor to historical, library, and literary journals. Editor of *Nebraska and Midwest Genealogical Record,* 1928-31. Member of editorial board of *Historical Magazine of the Protestant Episcopal Church,* 1963—; editor, *New England Historical and Genealogical Register,* 1960—.

WORK IN PROGRESS: In Journeyings Often, the expansion of the Episcopal Church as reflected in the life and correspondence of Jackson Kemper, first missionary bishop.

BIOGRAPHICAL/CRITICAL SOURCES: Addison Erwin Sheldon, *Nebraska: The Land and the People,* Volume II, 1931.

*   *   *

DOBBINS, Charles G(ordon)   1908-

PERSONAL: Born August 15, 1908, in Greensboro, Ala.; son of John Gordon (a minister) and Mantie (Wolf) Dobbins; married second wife, Sylvie Buffet, December 21, 1963; children: (first marriage) Peter Y. *Education:* Howard College (now Samford University), A.B., 1929; Columbia University, M.A., 1931; University of Wisconsin, graduate study, 1931-33. *Politics:* Democrat. *Religion:* Baptist. *Home:* 1545 18th St. N.W., Washington, D.C. 20036. *Office:* Academy for Educational Development, 1424 16th St. N.W., Washington, D.C. 20036.

CAREER: Newspaper reporter and college field representative, 1929-30; University of Wisconsin, Madison, instructor in English, 1931-33; Federal Emergency Relief Administration, rehabilitation officer in Virginia, 1934, director of Transient Camp, Fort McClellan, Ala., 1935; National Youth Administration, Gadsden, Ala., district director, 1936; Alabama College (now University of Montevallo), Montevallo, assistant professor of English and assistant to the president, 1936-39; *Anniston Times,* Anniston, Ala., editor and publisher, 1939-42; *Montgomery Advertiser,* Montgomery, Ala., editor, 1946-47; *Montgomery Examiner,* Montgomery, Ala., editor and publisher, 1947-55; U.S. Office of Price Stabilization, director for Alabama, 1951-52; American Council on Education, Washington, D.C., staff associate and director of public relations, 1956-61, director of Commission on Federal Relations, 1961-63, executive secretary, 1963-73, director of Academic Administration Internship Program, 1967-73; Academy for Educational Development, Washington, D.C., assistant director of management division, 1974—. Assistant administrator, War Savings Program for Alabama, 1942; trustee of Judson College, 1942-58; member of Alabama State Board of Education, 1951-59; member of board of directors, National Home Library Foundation, 1963—. *Military service:* U.S. Navy, 1942-46. *Member:* Omicron Delta Kappa, Kappa Phi Kappa, Sigma Delta Chi, Pi Gamma Mu, Sigma Nu, Cosmos Club (Washing-

ton, D.C.), Army & Navy (Washington, D.C.). *Awards, honors:* L.H.D., Judson College, 1967; Litt.D., Jamestown College, 1971; LL.D., College of St. Francis, 1973.

WRITINGS—Editor; all published by American Council on Education: *The Strength to Meet Our National Needs,* 1956; *Expanding Resources for College Teaching,* 1956; *Higher Education and the Federal Government: Programs and Problems,* 1963; *The University, the City, and Urban Renewal,* 1964; (with Calvin B. T. Lee) *Whose Goals for American Higher Education?,* 1968; *American Council on Education: Leadership and Chronology, 1918-1968,* 1968. Author of monograph, *An Alabama Forum,* published by the University of Alabama, and of "Life of Corra Harris," serialized in *Atlanta Journal.*

Contributor to *Encyclopedia International* and *Encyclopedia Americana*; also contributor of articles on education and public affairs to newspapers, magazines, and professional journals, including *Educational Record, London Economist, New Republic, Collier's,* and *College and University Business.* Editor, *Educational Record,* 1968-73.

*   *   *

DOBELL, I(sabel) M(arian) B(arclay)   1909-
(Isabel Barclay)

PERSONAL: Born July 17, 1909, in Montreal, Quebec, Canada; divorced. *Education:* McGill University, B.A., 1930; Radcliffe Institute of Historical and Archival Management, certificate, 1956. *Agent:* Mrs. Deryck Waring, 25 West 43rd St., New York, N.Y.

CAREER: McGill University, McCord Museum, Montreal, Quebec, archivist of Canadian history, 1956-68, chief curator, 1968-70, director, 1970—.

WRITINGS—Children's books, under name Isabel Barclay: *Worlds Without End,* Doubleday, 1956; *O Canada,* Doubleday, 1964; *Art of the Canadian Indians and Eskimos,* Queen's Printer (Ottawa), 1969.

WORK IN PROGRESS: Native Land, an ethnography commissioned by the National Museum of Man in Ottawa, projected publication, 1976.

*   *   *

DOBRACZYNSKI, Jan   1910-
(Hozjusz, Eugeniusz Kurowski)

PERSONAL: Born April 20, 1910, in Warsaw, Poland; son of Antoni (director of public assistance in Warsaw) and Waleria (Markiewicz) Dobraczynski; married Maria-Danuta Kotowicz (a journalist), June 2, 1935; children: Joan Dobraczynska-Kus, Aleksandra. *Education:* Attended High School of Commerce, Warsaw, Poland, received degree, 1932. *Religion:* Roman Catholic. *Home:* Hetmanska St. 42, Warsaw 44, Poland. *Agent:* Agencja Autorska, Hipoteczna St. 2, Warsaw, Poland.

CAREER: Author. Member of Parliament, 1952-56. *Military service:* Polish Army, 1939; Polish Underground Army, 1939-44; became captain of cavalry; awarded silver cross of merit with swords. *Awards, honors:* Awarded gold cross of merit; awarded Officers Cross (twice) and Commanders Cross of Polonie Restituta; literary prize of Polish Catholic Action, 1938; Wlodzimierz Pietrzak Prize, 1949, 1953, and 1970; State's Prize of Literature, 1970.

WRITINGS: Bernanos—Powiesciopisarz (essays; title means "Bernanos—Novelist"), Catholic University of Lublin, 1937; *Lawa Gorejaca* (essays; title means "Lava

Ardent''), St. Adalbert, 1938; *Dwa Stosy* (novel; title means "Two Stakes''), Panteon, 1947; *Szata Godowa* (novel; title means "Festival Clothing''), Gustowski, 1947; *Mocarz* (novel; title means "Potentate''), Niepokalanow, 1947; *Przedziwo Jolanty* (play; title means "Jolanta's Yarn''), Bak, 1947; *W rozwalonym Domu* (novel; title means "In the Demolished House''), Czytelnik, 1947; *Najezdzcy* (novel; title means "Invaders''), Officyna Ksiegarska, 1947; *Skapiec Bozy* (biography of Maximilian Kolbe; title means "God's Miser''), Niepokalanow, 1948; *Straszny Dom* (stories; title means "Terrible House''), Gustowski, 1948; *Wybrancy Gwiazd* (novel; title means "Elect of the Stars''), Gustowski, 1949; *Lepsza Czastka* (biography of Mother Franciszka Siedliska; title means "Better Part''), Sisters of the Holy Family of Nazareth, Chicago, 1949; *Swiety Miecz* (novel) Gustowski, 1949, translation by H. C. Stevens published as *The Sacred Sword,* Heinemann, 1959.

Najwieksza Milosc (stories; title means "Greatest Love''), Pax, 1950; *Klucz Madrosci* (novel; title means "The Keys of Wisdom''), Pax, 1951; *Listy Nicodema* (novel), Pax, 1952, translation by Stevens published as *The Letters of Nicodemus,* Heinemann, 1958, Newman, 1960; *Drzewa Chodzace* (novel; title means "Trees in March''), Pax, 1953; *Jezus Chrystus i Jego Apostolowie* (essays; title means "Jesus and His Apostles''), Pax, 1953; *Manna i Chleb* (essays; title means "Manna and Bread''), Pax, 1954; *Kosciol w Chocholowie* (novel: title means "The Church of Chocholow''), Pax, 1955; *Ksiazki, Idee i Czlowiek* (essays; title means "Books, Ideas, and Man''), Pax, 1955; *Notatnik Podrozny* (essays; title means "Journey's Notebook''), Pax, 1955; *Opowiadania* (title means "Short Stories''), Pax, 1955; *Pustynia* (novel; title means "The Desert''), Pax, 1955; *Dwudziesta Brygada* (novel; title means "Twentieth Brigade''), Pax, 1956; *Stworzenie i Naprawa* (essays; title means "Creation and Redress''), Pax, 1956; *Wielkosc i Swietosc* (essays; title means "Greatness and Holiness''), Pax, 1957; *A Znak nie Bedzie Mu Dany* (novel; title means "But a Sign Will Not Be Given Him''), Pax, 1957; *Gwaltownicy* (essays; title means "Men of Violence''), Pax, 1957; *Powiesci Biblijne* (title means "Bible Stories''), Pax, 1957; *Utwory Wybrane* (title means "Selected Works''), Pax, 1958; *Przyszedlem Rozlaczyc* (novel; title means "I Come to Divide''), Pax, 1959.

Niezwyciezona Armada (novel; title means "Invincible Armada''), Pax, 1960; *Dlonie na Murze,* published in one volume with Barbara Przestepska's English translation, *Hands on the Wall,* Pax, 1961; *Wyczerpac Morze* (novel), Pax, 1961, translation by Stevens published as *To Drain the Sea,* Heinemann, 1964; *Piaty Akt* (novel; title means "Fifth Act''), Pax, 1962; *Gra w wybijanego* (autobiography; title means "Chase-Ball Game''), Pax, 1963; *Judyta i Klocki* (novel; title means "Judith and the Toy Blocks''), Pax, 1963; *Moje boje i Niepokoje* (essays; title means "My Fights and Anxieties''), Pax, 1964; *Niepotrzebni* (novel; title means "Useless Men''), Pax, 1964; *Blekitne Helmy na Tamie* (novel; title means "Blue Helmets on the Dam''), Pax, 1965; *Doscigniety* (novel; title means "Overtaken''), Pax, 1967; *Marcin powraca z daleka* (novel; title means "Martin Come Back from Afar''), Pax, 1967; *Spalone mosty* (novel; title means "The Burnt Bridges Left Behind''), Pax, 1969; *Doba Krucjat: szkice historyczne z XI-XIII w.* (essays on church history), Pax, 1968; *Tylko w jedm zyciu* (autobiography; title means "Only in One Life''), Pax, 1970; *W co wierze* (meditations; title means "What I Believe In''), Pax, 1970; *Rozdarty Kosciol: szkice*

historyczne z XIV w.-pol. XVI w. (essays on church history: sequel to *Doba Krucjat*), Pax, 1970.

WORK IN PROGRESS: Further essays on the history of the church; a novel, *Tak bialy jak czerwona jest krew* ("As White as the Blood Is Red'').

SIDELIGHTS: Dobraczynski's books have been translated into English, French, Italian, Spanish, Portuguese, Dutch, Czech, Slovak, German, Swedish, Croat, Hungarian, and Afrikaans.

BIOGRAPHICAL/CRITICAL SOURCES: Zygmut Lichniak, *Szkic do Portretu Jana Dobraczynskiego* (monograph), Pax, 1963; Aleksandr Rogalski, *Dobraczynski* (monograph), Agencja Autorska, 1970.†

* * *

DOBSON, E. Philip 1910-

PERSONAL: Born March 20, 1910, in Hull, Yorkshire, England; son of C. Ernest Dobson (a wood broker); married May Spring, 1938. *Education:* Attended Elmfield College, York, England, 1919-25. *Home:* 67 Hawthorn Ter., New Earswick, York, England.

CAREER: Hull College of Commerce, Hull, England, lecturer in timbers, 1935-37; William Sessions Ltd., Ebor Press, York, England, advertising manager, 1945-55, publications editor, 1955— . Free-lance writer, 1942— .

WRITINGS: (With John B. Ives) *Century of Achievement: The History of James Ives and Company Limited,* Sessions, 1948; (editor with Margaret Kornitzer) *Berisfords: The Ribbon People,* Sessions, 1958; (with Francis W. Garnett) *The Garnett Story,* Sessions, 1962. Author of other commercial histories. Free-lance contributor to British Broadcasting Corp. and to periodicals, newspapers, and trade journals.

WORK IN PROGRESS: A travel book, *Mediterranean Ventures*; a company history.

* * *

DOBZHANSKY, Theodosius 1900-

PERSONAL: Born January 25, 1900, in Nemirov, Russia; came to United States, 1927; naturalized, 1937; son of Gregory (a teacher) and Sophia (Voinarsky) Dobzhansky; married Natalie Siverzev, August 8, 1924; children: Sophia (Mrs. M. D. Coe). *Education:* University of Kiev, diploma, 1921. *Home:* 2122 Espana Ct., Davis, Calif. 95616.

CAREER: Polytechnique Institute, Kiev, Russia, assistant professor of zoology, 1921-24; University of Leningrad, Lenigrad, Russia, lecturer in genetics, 1924-27; Rockefeller Foundation, N.Y., fellow of International Education Board, 1927-29; California Institute of Technology, Pasadena, assistant professor of genetics, 1930-36, professor, 1936-40; Columbia University, New York, N.Y., professor of zoology, 1940-62, Da Costa Professor of Zoology, 1959-62; Rockefeller Institute (now Rockefeller University), New York, N.Y., professor, 1962-71; University of California, Davis, adjunct professor, 1971— . University of Sao Paulo, Sao Paulo, Brazil, exchange professor, 1943, 1948-49.

MEMBER: National Academy of Sciences, American Philosophical Society, American Society of Zoologists, American Society of Genetics, American Society of Naturalists, American Society for the Study of Evolution, Academia Leopoldina, Accademia dei Lincei; Royal Danish, Royal Swedish, and Brazil academies of science; Royal

Society (London), Century Club. *Awards, honors:* D.Sc. from University of Sao Paulo, College of Wooster, University of Munster, University of Montreal, University of Chicago, University of Sydney, Columbia University, Oxford University, Catholic University of Louvain, Clarkson College of Technology, Kalamazoo College, University of Michigan, Syracuse University, University of Padua, University of California at Berkeley, and Northwestern University (Ill.); G. Elliot Prize and Medal from National Academy of Sciences, 1946; Kimber Prize, 1958; Darwin Medal, 1959; Anisfield-Wolf Award, 1963; Pierre Lecomte du Nouy Award, 1963; National Medal of Science, 1965; Addison Emery Verrill Medal, 1966.

WRITINGS: Genetics and the Origin of Species, Columbia University Press, 1937, 3rd edition, 1951; (with L. C. Dunn) *Heredity, Race and Society*, New American Library, 1946; *Biological Basis of Human Freedom*, Columbia University Press, 1956; *Evolution, Genetics and Man*, Wiley, 1956; (with B. Wallace) *Radiation, Genes and Man*, Holt, 1959; *Mankind Evolving*, Yale University Press, 1962; *Heredity and the Nature of Man*, Harcourt, 1964; (with Isaac Asimov) *The Genetic Effects of Radiation*, Atomic Energy Commission, 1966; *The Biology of Ultimate Concern*, New American Library, 1967; *A Genetics Program Library*, University of Hawaii Press, 1969.

BIOGRAPHICAL/CRITICAL SOURCES: Essays in Evolution and Genetics in Honor of Theodosius Dobzhansky, Appleton, 1970.

* * *

DODSON, Richard S(licer), Jr. 1896-

PERSONAL: Born March 20, 1896, in Saint Michaels, Md.; son of Richard (a farm operator and politician) and Florence (Kronau) Dodson; married Edna E. Rawls, April 18, 1926. *Education:* Johns Hopkins University, student, 1914-17. *Politics:* Independent. *Religion:* Non-affiliated. *Home:* Farrington Mill Rd., Route 6, Chapel Hill, N.C. 27514. *Office:* Morehead Planetarium, University of North Carolina, Chapel Hill, N.C. 27514.

CAREER: Newspaper reporter in Baltimore, Md., 1919-24; copy editor, *New York Evening Graphic,* New York, N.Y., 1926-27, *New York Herald Tribune Sunday Magazine,* New York, N.Y., 1927-35; *This Week,* New York, N.Y., rewrite and editing, 1935-44, managing editor, 1944-57, director of special projects, and space editor, 1957-59; retired, 1959; University of North Carolina, lecturer at Morehead Planetarium, 1959—. *Military service:* U.S. Army, American Expeditionary Forces in France, 1918-19. *Member:* Royal Astronomical Society of Canada, Astronomical Society of the Pacific, Amateur Astronomers Association, Dutch Treat Club (New York), Faculty Club (Chapel Hill).

WRITINGS: (Editor) Joseph Miles Chamberlain, *This Week's Key Guide to Outer Space,* Rand McNally, 1958; (editor) *This Week's See-America Vacation Guide,* Rand McNally, 1959, 2nd edition, 1960; (editor) George Clyde Fisher, *Exploring the Heavens: The Original Work of the First Head of the Hayden Planetarium,* Crowell, 1964. Also writer of booklet on meteors and meteorites, published by Morehead Planetarium.

SIDELIGHTS: An enduring interest in astronomy ("since Halley's Comet appeared in 1910") led to Dodson's second vocation. "[I am a] firm believer in star-gazing's therapeutic value," he explains, "[as] a way of easing ulcer-creating tensions that surround New York life."

He has studied astronomy most of his life, intensified his studies from 1935 on, and taught classes for the Amateur Astronomers Association in New York.

"[I've] also spent many hours on my belly in Yellowstone and other National Parks, and everywhere, taking closeups of little wild flowers in color for my wife, who loves them as I love the stars. Once had a one-man show of some of these flower prints at a Chapel Hill gallery."

* * *

DOELL, Charles E(dward) 1894-

PERSONAL: Born May 8, 1894, in Minneapolis, Minn.; son of George Ernst (a millwright) and Emma (Abel) Doell; married Olga Nelson, May 22, 1918; children: James Franklin, Marian (Mrs. Thomas Anderson). *Education:* University of Minnesota, B.S., 1916, civil engineer, 1917. *Home:* 11740 Wilshire Blvd., Apt. A-806, Los Angeles, Calif. 90025.

CAREER: Minneapolis (Minn.) Park Board, 1911-59, began as draftsman, became superintendent, 1945; self-employed park and recreation consultant, Minneapolis, Minn., beginning 1959. Former teacher at Michigan State University and Texas Technological College (now Texas Tech University), lecturer at University of Minnesota. Member of survey teams for National Capital Parks, Washington, D.C., Westchester County (N.Y.) Park System, and Tulsa (Okla.) Municipal Park System, 1957. Member of Minneapolis advisory board, Volunteers of America. *Military services:* U.S. Army Transportation Corps, 1918-19; became first sergeant.

MEMBER: American Recreation and Park Association (member of first board of trustees), American Institute of Park Executives (past president; honorary fellow), American Society of Civil Engineers, Minnesota Society of Professional Engineers (past president), Engineers' Club of Minneapolis (past president; life member), Hennepin County Historical Society (life), Tau Beta Pi, Theta Xi, Masons, Shrine, Minnesota Rose Society (past president), Minneapolis Athletic Club (past president). *Awards, honors:* Certificate from National Recreation Association, 1954, for outstanding service in interest of recreation; Cornelius Amory Pugsley Bronze Medal of American Scenic and Historic Preservation Society, 1957, for outstanding service in field of municipal parks; Everly Gold Medal, 1964, for outstanding service in park and recreation field.

WRITINGS: (With Paul J. Thompson) *Public Park Policies,* Minneapolis Parks and Recreation, 1930; (with Gerald B. Fitzgerald) *A Brief History of Parks and Recreation in the United States,* Athletic Institute (Chicago), 1954; (with Felix K. Dhainin) *A System of Parks for Hennepin County,* Hennepin County Park Reserve District, 1958; *Elements of Park and Recreation Administration,* Burgess, 1963, 3rd revised edition (with Louis Twardzik), 1973. Contributor to *Parks,* by L. H. Weir; also contributor to *Parks and Recreation, Recreation,* and to English and Canadian journals in those fields. Former editor of *Minnesota Engineer.*

* * *

DOMKE, Helmut Georg 1914-1974

PERSONAL: Born April 19, 1914, in Recklinghausen, Germany; son of Alfred and Henrike (Huitink) Domke; married Anne Buedding, April 18, 1956. *Education:* Attended classical college at Recklinghausen and Hannover and University of Goettingen; University of Kiel, Ph.D.,

1939. *Religion:* Lutheran. *Home:* Prinzenweg 25, 818 Tegernsee, Bavaria, Germany.

CAREER: Full-time writer. *Military service:* German Army during Second World War; became lieutenant; received several German decorations, including Iron Cross, Tank-Battle Medal, and Russia Medal. *Member:* P.E.N.

WRITINGS: Fuenfzehn Gedichte, Wester, 1949; *Schneckenreise durch einen Landkreis*, Wester, 1949; *Der Maler Heinz Hehmann* (a tale), Wester, 1951; *Alter Berg und feuchtes Thal*, Prestel, 1957; (author of commentaries on illustrations) Berhnard Lohse and Harald Busch, editors, *Kleinodien*, Umschau Verlag, 1958, translation published as *Art Treasures of Germany*, Batsford, 1958; (author of commentaries on illustrations) Busch and Lohse, editors, *Baukunst der Gotik in Europa*, Umschau Verlag, 1958, translation published as *Gothic Europe*, Batsford, 1958; (author of commentaries on illustrations) Busch and Lohse, editors, *Baukunst der Romanik in Europa*, Umschau Verlag, 1959, translation published as *Romanesque Europe*, Batsford, 1959; *Feuer, Erde, Rote Rose*, Prestel, 1959; *Duisburg*, Prestel, 1960; *Provence*, Prestel, 1961; *Burgund*, Prestel, 1963; *Flandern*, Prestel, 1964; *Maria: die Lebensgeschichte der Mutter Jesu* (a tale), Prestel, 1965; *Spaniens Norden: Der Weg nach Santiago*, Prestel, 1967; (with Josef Mueller-Marein) *Schloesser an der Loire* (essay), Niemeyer, 1967; *Dichter in ihrer Landschaft* (essays), Prestel, 1969; *Der Rhein im Farbbild*, Umschau Verlag, 1969, translation published as *The Rhine: A Panorama in Colour*, Hastings House, 1969.

Also author of texts for about 15 photographic books published by Umschau Verlag. Contributor of several hundred tales, stories, critiques, poems, and feature articles to periodicals and radio programs.

WORK IN PROGRESS: Das kathedralen buch; Bagatellen.

SIDELIGHTS: Domke was competent in French, Spanish, and Flemish. He traveled widely. *Advocational interests:* Painting.

(Died April 30, 1974)

* * *

DOMKE, Martin 1892-

PERSONAL: Born September 11, 1892, in Berlin, Germany; son of Leopold (a merchant) and Meta (Lebram) Domke; came to U.S., 1941, naturalized citizen, 1947; married Eva Charlotte Jacoby (a physician), June 22, 1960; children: George W. *Education:* University of Berlin, student, 1911-14; University of Greifswald, LL.D., 1915. *Home:* 370 East 76th St., New York, N.Y. 10021.

CAREER: Practiced law in Germany, 1922-33; New York University, New York, N.Y., adjunct professor of law, 1950—. American Arbitration Association, vice-president, 1943-67, editor-in-chief of *Arbitration Journal*, 1946-73. *Member:* American Foreign Law Association, (member of board of directors), Consular Law Society (member of board of trustees), International Law Association (member of executive committee, American branch). *Awards, honors:* First recipient of the Sylvan Gotshal Medal for exceptional service in the field of international arbitration, 1967.

WRITINGS: Trading with the Enemy in World War II, Central, Book, 1943; *The Control of Alien Property*, Central Book, 1947; *American-German Private International Law*, Oceana, 1956; (editor) *International Trade Arbitra-*

tion, Greenwood, 1958; *Commercial Arbitration*, Prentice-Hall, 1965; *The Law and Practice of Commercial Arbitration*, Callaghan, 1968, cumulative supplements, 1974. Contributer of more than two hundred articles to legal periodicals in the United States and abroad.

WORK IN PROGRESS: International Commercial Arbitration: A Guide to Current Practice.

* * *

DONALDSON, Malcolm 1884-

PERSONAL: Born April 27, 1884; son of John (an engineer and shipbuilder) and Frances Sarah (Thornycroft) Donaldson; married Evelyn Helen Marguerite Gilroy, 1919; married second wife, 1940; children: John Hamo. *Education:* Attended Charterhouse; Trinity College, Cambridge, M.A., M.B., B.C.L.; St. Bartholomew's Hospital, F.R.C.S., F.R.C.O.S. *Home:* 337 Woodstock Rd., Oxford, England. *Office:* Cancer Information Association, 6 Queen St., Oxford, England.

CAREER: St. Bartholomew's Hospital, London, England, consulting gynecologist, 1919-47; Cancer Information Association, Oxford, England, honorary secretary, 1956—. Consulting gynecologist to numerous hospitals. *Military service:* British Army, 1914-18; became major; mentioned in dispatches. *Member:* Royal Society of Medicine (vice-chairman, national radium committee, 1944-45), Royal College of Obstetrics and Gynaecology (fellow; member of council, 1937-43), Royal College of Surgeons (fellow), Athenaeum Club (London).

WRITINGS: (With Henry C. Simon, Archer Ryland, and J. F. Cunningham) *A Synopsis of Special Subjects, for the Use of Practitioners* (contains *Diseases of the Skin* by Simon, *Obstetrics and the Diseases of Women* by Donaldson, *The Ear, Nose and Throat* by Ryland, and *The Eye* by Cunningham), H. K. Lewis, 1924; *Radiotherapy in the Diseases of Women*, Hodder & Stoughton, 1934; (editor and contributor) *The Early Diagnosis of Malignant Diseases*, Oxford University Press, 1936; *What Every Woman Should Know*, Heinemann, 1950; *The Cancer Riddle: A Message of Hope*, Arthur Barker, 1962. Also author of "All About Life Saving," a series of pamphlets on cancer. Contributor of articles to various lay and medical journals.

* * *

DONATO, Anthony 1909-

PERSONAL: Born March 8, 1909, in Prague, Neb.; son of Anthony Z. (an attorney) and Milada (Maresh) Donato; married Carolyn C. Scott, December 30, 1931. *Education:* Eastman School of Music, B.Mus., 1931, M.Mus., 1937, Ph.D., 1947. *Home:* 9317 Kedvale Ave., Skokie, Ill. *Office:* School of Music, Northwestern University, Evanston, Ill.

CAREER: Violinist with Rochester Philharmonic Orchestra, 1927-31, Hochstein Quartet, 1929-31; also engaged in performing, conducting, and radio broadcasting, 1929-37; Drake University, Des Moines, Iowa, head of violin department and orchestra conductor, 1931-37; Iowa State Teachers College (now University of Northern Iowa), Cedar Falls, head of violin department, 1937-39; University of Texas, Austin, head of violin department and instructor in composition, 1939-46; Northwestern University, Evanston, Ill., professor of theory and composition, 1947—, conductor of chamber orchestra, 1947-58. Composer; touring concert violinist. *Member:* American Society of Composers, Authors and Publishers, National Association of American Composers and Conductors, American Association of University Professors, Masons, Phi Mu Alpha, Pi Kappa Lambda, Sigma Phi Epsilon. *Awards, honors:* Fulbright award to lecture on American music in England and Scotland, 1951-52; Huntington Hartford Foundation fellowship, 1961; various prizes for musical compositions, and commissions to compose music.

WRITINGS: Preparing Music Manuscript, Prentice-Hall, 1963. Has published numerous musical compositions for orchestra, band, chamber music, various instruments, solo voice, chorus, and opera. Contributor to encyclopedias and professional journals.

* * *

DONOHUE, John K. 1909-

PERSONAL: Born January 28, 1909, in St. Paul, Minn.; son of John R. (a lawyer) and Anne (Lang) Donohue; married Mari Iacobelli, August 15, 1945; children: Katherine, Margaret, John III. *Education:* University of Minnesota, B.A., 1930; University of Virginia, graduate study, 1945; Northwestern University, M.A., 1946. *Home:* 711 Fairmount Ave., St. Paul, Minn. 55105. *Agent:* William Coulter, 2642 University, St. Paul, Minn. 55114.

CAREER: Ramsey County Probation Department, St. Paul, Minn., assistant chief probation officer, 1930-38; Boy Scouts of America, St. Paul, Minn., assistant executive, 1938-41; Thirteenth Judicial District of Montana, Billings, probation officer, 1941-46; Ramsey County Probation Department, chief probation officer, 1946—. Formerly member of faculty at Rocky Mountain College, Billings, Mont., St. Thomas College, St. Paul, Minn., and currently, University of Minnesota, as lecturer in criminology. Member of board, Minnesota Prisoners Aid Society and St. Paul Art Center. *Military service:* U.S. Air Force, World War II; became first lieutenant. *Member:* National Association of Social Workers, National Council on Crime and Delinquency, American Judicature Society, American Society of Criminology, Midwest Sociological Association, American Legion (adjutant, 1948—; post commander, 1952). *Awards, honors:* Silver Beaver award, Boy Scouts of America; Leadership Book award ($1,500), Association Press.

WRITINGS: Meet the Gang, Young Men's Christian Association, 1940; *Less Juvenile Delinquency Through Scouting,* Boy Scouts of America, 1952; *Baffling Eyes of Youth,* Association Press, 1957; (author of introduction) *Tales of Hoffman,* Denison, 1961; *My Brother's Boy,* Bruce, 1963. Contributor of articles to *Journal of Criminal Law, Minnesota Medicine,* and to welfare and scouting magazines.

WORK IN PROGRESS: Texts on juvenile delinquency and on probation administration.

* * *

DORIAN, Edith M(cEwen) 1900-

PERSONAL: Born May 5, 1900, in Newark, N.J.; daughter of George Floy (a physician) and Antoinette (Currier) McEwen; married Donald Dorian (a professor of English), June 19, 1924 (deceased); children: Donald McEwen, Nancy Currier. *Education:* Smith College, B.A., 1921; Harvard University, research, 1922; Columbia University, M.A., 1927. *Politics:* Democrat. *Religion:* Congregational. *Home:* 39 Elm St., Topsham, Me. 04086.

CAREER: Rutgers University, Douglass College, New Brunswick, N.J., instructor, later assistant professor of English, 1922-32, lecturer in English, 1959-60; Macmillan Co., New York, N.Y., literary adviser, 1938-48. Highland Park (N.J.) Public Library, chairman of board of trustees, 1945-55; New Brunswick (N.J.) Child and Family Service Bureau, director, 1945-63; New Jersey Library Trustees Association, member of executive committee, 1952-54; Family Service Association of America, member of national personnel committee, 1957-61; School Library Committee, Topsham, Me., chairman, 1962—; Whitten Memorial Library, Topsham, Me., member of board of trustees, 1964—. *Member:* Authors Guild, Phi Beta Kappa, Harpswell Garden Club, Pejepscot Historical Society, Maricnoeeg Yachting Association. *Awards, honors:* National Council of Christians and Jews citation for *Ask Dr. Christmas;* Boys' Clubs of America Junior Book Award, 1958, for *Hokahey: American Indians Then and Now.*

WRITINGS—All published by Whittlesey House: *High-Water Cargo* (Catholic Book Club selection), 1950, new edition, Rutgers University Press, 1965; *Ask Dr. Christmas,* 1951; *No Moon on Graveyard Head* (Teen-Age Book Club Selection), 1953, reissued as *Mystery on Graveyard Head,* Berkley, 1955; *Trails West and Men Who Made Them,* 1955; *The Twisted Shadow,* 1956; *Hokahey: American Indians Then and Now,* 1957; (with W. N. Wilson) *Animals that Made U.S. History,* 1964. Contributor of short stories, articles, and reviews to *Sewanee Review* and other periodicals, and of stories to pulps under pseudonyms in earlier days.

WORK IN PROGRESS: The Blackfeet Indians, for Garrard; *New World, New Man: The Colonial Melting Pot; The House on Crooked Lane;* writing on American Indians, especially the Penobscots of Maine.

SIDELIGHTS: Mrs. Dorian began writing professionally in high school, stayed with the pulps ("everything from *I Confess* to *True Detective*") straight through college; stopped writing except for critical articles when she began teaching, but was prodded back into it by Lois Cole of Macmillan. "If you've always scribbled, the disease eventually becomes chronic anyhow," she admits. *Hokahey, Trails West,* and *Animals that Made U.S. History* were published in Swedish editions.

BIOGRAPHICAL/CRITICAL SOURCES: Lewiston Journal, November 28, 1953.

* * *

DORIAN, Frederick 1902-

PERSONAL: Surname was originally Deutsch; born July 1, 1902, in Vienna, Austria; came to United States in 1936, naturalized in 1940; son of Alois (a merchant) and Therese (Neumann) Deutsch; married Sadie Pearlman, August 9, 1940. *Education:* State Academy of Music, Vienna, Austria, student; University of Vienna, Ph.D., 1925. *Religion:* Jewish. *Home:* 4921 Forbes Ave., Pittsburgh, Pa. 15213.

CAREER: Music critic of *Berlin Morgenpost,* Berlin, Germany, 1930-34, of *Frankfurter Zeitung,* Paris, France, 1934-35, of *Neues Wiener Journal,* Vienna, Austria, 1935-36; Carnegie-Mellon University (formerly Carnegie Institute of Technology), Pittsburgh, Pa., professor of music, 1936—. *Member:* American Musicological Society, International Musicological Society. *Awards, honors:* Andrew W. Mellon grant for research, 1958, 1961; Pittsburgh Foundation research grant, 1966-67.

WRITINGS: Die Fuge in den Werken Bethovens, [Austria], 1925; *The History of Music in Performance: The Art of Musical Interpretation from the Renaissance to Our Day,* Norton, 1942; *The Musical Workshop,* Harper, 1947; *Commitment to Culture: Art Patronage in Europe—Its Significance for America,* University of Pittsburgh Press, 1964. Contributor to *Encyclopedia of Arts,* and to *Notes, Journal of Aesthetics,* other scholarly journals. Music editor of Pittsburgh Symphony *Program Magazine,* 1952—.

SIDELIGHTS: The Musical Workshop has been published in French and Spanish editions; *The History of Music in Performance* has been translated into Japanese. Dorian is competent in German, French, Italian, Latin, and Greek.

* * *

DORMANDY, Clara 1905-

PERSONAL: Born July 10, 1905, in Dormand, Hungary, daughter of Louis and Iren Dormandy; married Paul Szeben (a managing director), September 3, 1923; children: Thomas, Louis, Daisy, John, Adam. *Education:* Educated in Budapest, Hungary. *Home:* Flat A, 4 Lyndhurst Gardens, Hampstead, London N.W.3, England.

CAREER: Writer. *Member:* Romantic Novelist's Association, Writers' Association. *Awards, honors:* Ward, Lock's Book and Literary award for *Resistance to Love.*

WRITINGS: Resistance to Love, Ward, Lock, 1959; *The Doctors,* Avalon Books, 1959; *Diary of a Marriage,* Ward, Lock, 1960; *Image of a Hero,* Ward, Lock, 1962; *Hungary in Pictures,* Sterling, 1970.

Plays: "Poppy Seed," produced in Budapest, 1939; "Malice Afterthought," first produced by British Broadcasting Corp., 1959, and later in Canada, 1960. Author of several books in Hungarian. Contributor to *Psychology,* and other periodicals.

WORK IN PROGRESS: Voice analysis.

* * *

DORNBUSCH, C(harles) E(mil) 1907-

PERSONAL: Born November 17, 1907, in New York, N.Y.; son of Rudolph E. and Emma Rhodes (McClure) Dornbusch. *Education:* Columbia University, student. *Politics:* Republican. *Religion:* Methodist. *Home:* Strong Rd., Cornwallville, N.Y. 12418.

CAREER: New York (N.Y.) Public Library, librarian and bibliographer in reference department, 1926-63; Hope Farm Press (publishers of military books; now Hope Farm Press & Bookshop), Cornwallville, N.Y., founder-manager, 1959—. Green County Historical Society, librarian, 1963-65. *Military service:* U.S. Army, Infantry, World War II; served in European theater; became staff sergeant. *Member:* Company of Military Historians, American Military Institute, Military Historical Society of England, Military Research and Collectors Society of Australia.

WRITINGS—Compiler: Stars and Stripes: Check List of the Several Editions, New York Public Library, 1948; *The G.I. Stories: A Check List,* New York Public Library, 1950; *Yank, the Army Weekly: A Check List,* New York Public Library, 1950; *Post-war Souvenir Books and Unit Histories of the Navy, Marine Corps, and Construction Battalions,* Office of Naval History, 1953; *Histories of American Army Units, World Wars I and II and Korean Conflict, with Some Earlier Histories,* Department of the Army, Special Services Division, Library and Service Club Branch, 1956, revised edition published as *Histories, Personal Narratives, United States Army: A Checklist,* Hope Farm, 1967; *Unit Histories of the United States Air Forces, Including Privately Printed Personal Narratives,* Hampton Books, 1958; *The Canadian Army, 1855-1958: Regimental Histories and a Guide to the Regiments,* Hope Farm, 1959, 2nd edition published as *The Lineages of the Canadian Army, 1855-1961: Armour, Cavalry, Infantry,* 1961, third edition published as *The Canadian Army, 1855-1965: Lineages, Regimental Histories,* 1966; *The New Zealand Army: A Bibliography,* Hope Farm, 1961; *Military Bibliography of the Civil War,* New York Public Library, Volume I: *The Northern States,* 1962, Volume II: *The Southern and Border States,* 1967, Volume III: *General Reference and Index,* 1969; Frederick Phisterer, *The Communities of New York and the Civil War: The Recruiting Areas of the New York Civil War Regiments,* New York Public Library, 1962; *Australian Military Bibliography,* Hope Farm, 1963; Charles King, *American Army Novelist: A Bibliography,* Hope Farm, 1963.

WORK IN PROGRESS: Another volume in *Military Bibliography of the Civil War,* for publication by New York Public Library through the E. F. Skeel Fund and various grants-in-aid.

SIDELIGHTS: Dornbusch's "multiple careers" were listed in a New York Public Library bulletin (at the time of his retirement) as "librarian, bibliographer, writer, publisher, bookseller, traveler, scout master, antiques collector, and last but not least, baker of home made bread." He has visited libraries and research centers in Australia, New Zealand, England, Canada, Hawaii, and in almost every state of the Union to inspect source works for his bibliographies.

* * *

DOUGALL, Herbert E(dward) 1902-

PERSONAL: Born October 20, 1902, in Merriton, Ontario, Canada; came to United States, 1925, naturalized, 1936; son of Hugh Shaw (a minister) and Eleanor (Taylor) Dougall; married Louise Perkins, August 21, 1929, children: Eleanor L. (Mrs. L. Neel Hall), Jean A. (Mrs. J. F. Boydston). *Education:* University of Toronto, B.A., 1925; Northwestern University, M.B.A., 1926, Ph.D., 1930. *Politics:* Republican. *Religion:* Presbyterian. *Home:* 15 Holden Ct., Portola Valley, Calif. 94025. *Office:* Graduate School of Business, Stanford University, Stanford, Calif. 94305.

CAREER: Northwestern University, Evanston, Ill., 1927-46, began as instructor in economics and finance, professor of finance, 1942-46, director of Undergraduate Division, School of Commerce, 1939-44; Stanford University, Graduate School of Business, Stanford, Calif., professor of finance, 1946-53, C. O. G. Miller Professor of Finance, 1953-68. Director of American Express Investment Funds; consultant in finance.

MEMBER: American Economic Association, American Finance Association (vice-president, 1949), Western Economic Association, Western Finance Association, Delta Sigma Pi, Beta Gamma Sigma. *Awards, honors:* Social Science Research Council fellow in France and England, 1932-33; Ford Foundation fellow, 1959-60.

WRITINGS: (With Harold Torgerson) *One Hundred Short Problems in Corporation Finance,* Ronald, 1937, 3rd edition, 1951; (with H. G. Guthmann) *Corporate Financial Policy,* Prentice-Hall, 1940, 4th edition, 1962; (with D. F.

Jordon) *Investments*, Prentice-Hall, 1952, 9th edition (sole author), 1973; *Capital Markets and Institutions*, Prentice-Hall, 1965, 2nd edition, 1970. Contributor to *Encyclopaedia Britannica* and to economic and finance journals.

* * *

DOUGHTY, Oswald   1889-

PERSONAL: Born July 4, 1889, in Kingston-upon-Hull, Yorkshire, England; son of Walter and Sophia (Lamplough) Doughty; married Marcelle Henriette Spitz, 1923; children: Odile Sophia. *Education:* Educated privately and at Kingston-upon-Hull College; University of Durham, B.A., 1915, M.A., 1918; Oxford University, B.Litt., 1921. *Home:* Kelmscott, 132 Camp Ground Rd., Newlands, Cape Town, South Africa.

CAREER: Schoolmaster and vice-principal in grammar school in Lincolnshire, England, 1918-20; University College, University of London, London, England, lecturer in English literature, 1920-21; senior lecturer, 1921-29; University of Cape Town, Cape Town, South Africa, Arderne Professor of English Literature, 1929-54; professor emeritus, 1954—. Has been extension lecturer at University of London, University of Florence, Royal Society of Literature, 1950, and elsewhere in Europe and South Africa. Radio lecturer on literature in London, England, and Cape Town, South Africa. Delegate from University of Cape Town and other South African universities to conferences in England and Europe. *Member:* Royal Society of Literature (fellow).

WRITINGS: English Lyric in the Age of Reason, O'Connor, 1922, 2nd edition, Russell, 1971; *Forgotten Lyrics of the Eighteenth Century*, Witherby, 1924; *A Victorian Romantic: D. G. Rossetti*, Yale University Press, 1949, revised edition, Oxford University Press, 1960; *Dante Gabriel Rossetti*, British Council, 1957; *Early Diamond Days: The Opening of the Diamond Fields in South Africa*, Longmans, Green, 1963; *William Collins*, Longmans, Green, 1964; (editor with John Robert Wahe) *The Letters of D. G. Rossetti*, four volumes, Clarendon Press, 1965-67.

Editor and author of introduction: John Gay, *The Beggar's Opera*, O'Connor, 1922; John Gay, *Polly: An Opera*, O'Connor, 1922; Oliver Goldsmith, *The Vicar of Wakefield*, Scholartis Press, 1928; Horace Walpole, *The Castle of Otranto*, Scholartis Press, 1929; *The Letters of D. G. Rossetti to His Publisher, F. S. Ellis*, Scholartis Press, 1929; *The Poems of Dante Gabriel Rossetti*, Dent, 1957, 2nd edition, Dent, 1961.

Contributor: John Buchan, editor, *A History of English Literature*, Thomas Nelson, 1923; F. C. Slater, editor, *New Century Book of South African Verse*, 1945; *Cambridge History of the British Empire*, Volume VIII: *South Africa*, Cambridge University Press, 1963. Contributor to "English Miscellany," edited by Mario Praz. Contributor of poetry, articles, and reviews to scholarly and literary journals in England, South Africa, Italy, and Holland, and of non-literary articles to newspapers.

AVOCATIONAL INTERESTS: Country walks and drives, private motor tours at home and abroad, listening to good music, seeing good acting.

BIOGRAPHICAL/CRITICAL SOURCES: New Statesman, June 2, 1967; *Listener*, July 13, 1967.

DOW, Emily R.   1904-

PERSONAL: Born May 26, 1904, in Exeter, N.H.; daughter of Albert N. and Florence (Griffin) Dow; married Winslow Eddy (an engineer), November 8, 1947; children: Carolyn (stepdaughter; Mrs. William Timbers). *Education:* Wheelock College, graduate, 1924; special courses at Rachel McMillian Nursery School (London, England), Columbia University, Vesper George Art School. *Religion:* Episcopalian. *Home and office:* Brumble Farm, Walnut Ave., North Hampton, N.H. 03862.

CAREER: Nursery school and kindergarten teacher before marriage; writer of books for children. *Member:* New Hampshire Arts and Crafts Society, Guild of Strawberry Banke.

WRITINGS—Self-illustrated: What Can I Do Now?, Aladdin Books, 1950; *How to Make Doll Clothes: A Book for Daughters, Mothers, and Grandmothers*, Coward, 1953; *Brooms, Buttons, and Beaux: A World of Facts for Girls in Their Teens*, Barrows, 1957; *Of Parties and Petticoats: A World of Wonderful Things for Girls in Their Teens*, Barrows, 1960; *Toys, Toddlers, and Tantrums: The Baby Sitters Book*, Barrows, 1962; *Crafts for Fun and Fairs*, Barrows, 1964; *Now What Shall We Do?: The Family Book of Things to Do and Games to Play*, Barrows, 1966.

* * *

DOWNER, Alan S(eymour)   1912-1970

PERSONAL: Born July 15, 1912, in Syracuse, N.Y.; son of Harry Vincent (an accountant) and Mary Louese (Bliss) Downer; married Florence Marcia Walsh, September 7, 1941; children: Alan Seymour, Jr. *Education:* Harvard University, A.B., 1934, A.M., 1939. *Home:* 294 Nassau St., Princeton, N.J. 08540. *Agent:* The Sterling Lord Agency, 75 East 55th St., New York, N.Y. 10022. *Office:* 22 McCosh Hall, Princeton University, Princeton, N.J. 08540.

CAREER: Wells College, Aurora, N.Y., 1939-46, began as instructor, became assistant professor of English; Princeton University, Princeton, N.J., 1946-70, began as assistant professor, professor of English, 1957-70, chairman of department, 1963-68. Fulbright lecturer on American drama at University of Copenhagen, 1953-54; lecturer on American drama at Salzburg Seminar for American Studies, 1958, 1961, and for U.S. Information Service in Europe, 1961. *Member:* International Federation for Theatre Research (plenary committee, 1954—). Modern Language Association of America, American Society for Theatre Research (chairman, 1955-58), English Institute (secretary, 1947-53).

WRITINGS: (Editor) *25 Modern Plays*, revised edition, Harper, 1948, 3rd edition, 1953; *The British Drama: A Handbook and Brief Chronicle*, Appleton, 1950; *50 Years of American Drama 1900-1950*, Regnery, 1951; (editor and author of introduction) Shakespeare, *Five Plays*, Holt, 1951; (editor) *The Art of the Play: An Anthology of Nine Plays*, Holt, 1955; (editor and author of introduction) Shakespeare, *As You Like It, Julius Caesar, Macbeth*, Rinehart, 1958; (editor and author of introduction) Shakespeare, *Twelfth Night, Othello*, Rinehart, 1958; (editor and author of introduction) *Oxberry's 1822 edition of King Richard III*, Society for Theatre Research, 1959; (editor) Booth Tarkington, *On Plays, Playwrights and Playgoers: Selections from the Letters of Booth Tarkington to George C. Tyler and John Peter Toohey 1918-1925*, Princeton University Library, 1959.

(Editor) *American Drama,* Crowell, 1960; *The Theatre of Bernard Shaw,* Dodd, 1961; *Recent American Drama* (pamphlet), University of Minnesota Press, 1961; (translator and editor) Ibsen, *Hedda Gabler,* Crofts, 1961; (editor) *Autobiography of Joseph Jefferson,* Harvard University Press, 1964; (editor and author of introduction) *The Great World Theatre: An Introduction to Drama,* Harper, 1964; (editor and author of introduction with Arthur C. Kirsch) *Restoration,* Dell, 1965; (editor and author of introduction) *American Drama and Its Critics: A Collection of Critical Essays,* University of Chicago Press, 1965; *The Eminent Tragedian: W. C. Macready and the Victorian Stage,* Harvard University Press, 1966; (editor) *The Memoir of John Durang,* University of Pittsburgh Press, 1966; (editor) *The American Theatre Today,* Basic Books, 1967; *Conference on Theatre Research,* [Columbia, Mo.], 1967.

Contributor of articles on the theatre to professional journals.

BIOGRAPHICAL/CRITICAL SOURCES: New Statesman, June 23, 1967; *Observer,* July 2, 1967; *Punch,* July 12, 1967; *New York Times Book Review,* July 23, 1967, September 3, 1967; *Shenandoah,* spring, 1968.

(Died January 20, 1970)

*   *   *

DRAKE, William E(arle)   1903-

PERSONAL: Born September 25, 1903, in Asheville, N.C.; son of John Robert (an electrical engineer) and Arlene (Ingle) Drake; married Zelma Paxton (a teacher), August 20, 1926; children: William Earle, Jr., Dennis C., Carole Jean Drake Baker. *Education:* University of North Carolina, B.A., 1924, M.A., 1928, Ph.D., 1930. *Home:* 5806 Trailridge Circle, Austin, Tex. *Office:* 219 Sutton Hall, University of Texas, Austin, Tex.

CAREER: Murphry (N.C.) public schools, principal, 1924-26; Columbia (N.C.) public schools, superintendent, 1926-28; Pennsylvania State College (now University), University Park, assistant professor, 1930-39; University of Missouri, Columbia, associate professor, 1939-44, professor, 1944-57; University of Texas, Austin, professor of history and philosophy of education, 1957—, chairman of department, 1959-69. Visiting professor, U.S. Army, Shrivenham American University, England, 1945-46; summer lecturer at University of North Carolina, 1936, University of Illinois, 1953, University of Texas, 1955, Michigan State University, 1966, and Auburn University, 1968. Public panel member of National War Labor Board, Region IX, 1944-45; arbitrator in Industrial Disputes for American Board of Arbitration.

MEMBER: American Historical Society, History of Education Society, Philosophy of Education Society (executive secretary, 1950-60), Comparative Education Society, American Association of University Professors, Southwestern Philosophy of Education Society (president, 1961-62), Texas Society of College Teachers of Education, Phi Delta Kappa, Kiwanis International (president, Columbia, Mo., 1954; lieutenant governor, Missouri-Arkansas District, 1955). *Awards, honors:* Medal, French Teachers of English, Strasbourg, France, 1946; U.S. Army Meritorious Service Award, 1946, for teaching at Shrivenham University.

WRITINGS: (With J. S. Roucek and others) *Sociological Foundations of Education,* Crowell Collier, 1942; *The*

American School in Transition, Prentice-Hall, 1955; *Higher Education in North Caroline Before 1860,* Carlton, 1964; *Intellectual Foundations of Modern Education,* C. E. Merrill, 1967; (editor) *Sources for Intellectual Foundations of Modern Education,* C. E. Merrill, 1967.

Contributor: J. S. Roucek, editor, *The Challenge of Science Education,* Philosophical Library, 1959; William Reavis, editor, *Significant Aspects of American Life and Postwar Education,* Volume VIII, University of Chicago Press, 1944; S. Everett and C. O. Arndt, editors, *Teaching World Affairs in American Schools,* Harper, 1956; Bower Aly, editor, *American Education, The Thirty-Second Discussion and Debate Manual, 1958-59,* Volume I, Lucas Brothers, 1958; H. B. Jacobson and Roucek, editors, *Automation and Society,* Philosophical Library, 1959; R. E. Gross, editor, *The Heritage of American Education,* Allyn & Bacon, 1961; Frederick Gruber, editor, *Teaching in America,* University of Pennsylvania Press, 1962.

Contributor to professional journals and other periodicals. Member of review board, *Educational Theory,* 1964—.

WORK IN PROGRESS: Is Freedom Dying in the United States?; an autobiography; other writings on the philosophy of higher educcation.

SIDELIGHTS: Drake has reading knowledge of Spanish and French. *Avocational interests:* Outdoor life and camping, landscape gardening, ranching.

*   *   *

DRAPER, John William   1893-

PERSONAL: Born July 23, 1893, in Hastings-on-Hudson, N.Y.; son of Daniel and Ann Maury (Ludlow) Draper; married Lulu Clay, June 6, 1919; children: Daniel Clay, John Christopher, Charles Ludlow. *Education:* New York University, B.A., 1914, M.A., 1915; Harvard University, M.A., 1918, Ph.D., 1920. *Politics:* Democrat. *Religion:* Episcopal. *Home:* 100 McLane Ave., Morgantown, W.Va. 26505. *Office:* Department of English, West Virginia University, Morgantown, W.Va. 26505.

CAREER: Instructor in English at New York University, New York, N.Y., 1915-16, University of Minnesota, Minneapolis, 1920-21; Bryn Mawr College, Bryn Mawr, Pa., lecturer in English literature, 1921-22; University of Maine, Orono, associate professor, 1922-24, professor of English, 1924-29; West Virginia University, Morgantown, professor of English, 1929-64, professor emeritus, 1964—. Visiting professor at Harvard University, summer, 1925, 1930, University of Iowa, summer, 1929, Duke University, 1939, University of Munich, 1949. Fulbright lecturer at University of Toulouse, 1952. *Military service:* U.S. Army, 1918-19; became sergeant. *Member:* Modern Language Association of America, Modern Humanities Research Association, West Virginia Philological Society, Phi Beta Kappa, XX Club (Morgantown). *Awards, honors:* Guggenheim fellowship for research in England, 1927-28.

WRITINGS: Poems, Poet Lore Co., 1913; *Exotics,* Bruno, 1913; *William Mason: A Study in Eighteenth-Century Culture,* New York University Press, 1924; (editor and author of introduction and notes) *A Century of Broadside Elegies: Being Ninety English and Ten Scotch Broadsides Illustrating the Biography and Manners of the Seventeenth Century,* Ingpen & Grant, 1928; *The Funeral Elegy and the Rise of English Romanticism,* New York University Press, 1929; *Eighteenth Century English Aesthetics: A Bibliogra-*

phy, C. Winter, 1931; *The Hamlet of Shakespeare's Audience*, Duke University Press, 1938; *The Humors and Shakespeare's Characters*, Duke University Press, 1945.

The Twelfth Night of Shakespeare's Audience, Stanford University Press, 1950; *The Othello of Shakespeare's Audience*, Didier, 1950; *Shakespeare and the Turk*, University of Illinois, 1956; *The Early Troubadours and Persian Poetry*, G. C. Sansoni (Florence), 1957; *The Tempo-Patterns of Shakespeare's Plays*, C. Winter, 1957; *Rhyme in the Pacific*, West Virginia University Press, 1959; *Stratford to Dogberry: Studies in Shakespeare's Earlier Plays*, University of Pittsburgh Press, 1961.

Contributor of more than a hundred articles to journals in United States and Europe. Editor-in-chief, *Colonnade*, 1913-17, 1921-25; editor, *West Virginia Philological Bulletin*, 1937; editorial consultant, *Revista di Letterature e Comparate*, 1953—.

WORK IN PROGRESS: Further studies on Shakespeare; Iranian and Parsi subjects.

AVOCATIONAL INTERESTS: Gardening.

BIOGRAPHICAL/CRITICAL SOURCES: Festschrift Dedicated to John W. Draper, West Virginia University Press, 1961.

* * *

DROWER, E(thel) S(tefana May) 1879-1972
(E. S. Stevens)

PERSONAL: Born December 1, 1879, in London, England; daughter of Silas William (a clerk in holy orders) and Susan Ellen (Carpenter) Stevens; married Sir Edwin Mortimer Drower (a barrister and adviser to Iraq Ministry of Justice); children: Margaret (Mrs. Hackforth Jones), William Mortimer, John Dens Lewis. *Education:* Studied at private schools, at home, and through travel. *Politics:* "A hope for international agreement and tolerance." *Religion:* Open-minded agnostic. *Home:* 8 Willenhall Ave., New Barnet, Hertfordshire, England.

CAREER: Author, who spent a large part of her life in travel and residence in Middle East. Lecturer on Mandaean culture in England, Italy, and Switzerland. *Member:* Royal Asiatic Society (fellow), other societies connected with Middle East. *Awards, honors:* Honorary fellow, School of Oriental and African Studies, University of London; D.Litt., Oxford University; D.D., Uppsala University.

WRITINGS—Under name E. S. Stevens: *The Veil: A Romance of Tunis*, Stokes, 1909; *The Mountain of God*, Press of W. G. Hewitt, 1911; *The Earthen Drum*, Mills & Boon, 1911; *The Lure*, John Lane, 1912; *The Long Engagement*, George H. Doran, 1912; *My Sudan Year*, Mills & Boon, 1912, George H. Doran, 1913; *Sarah Eden*, Dodd, 1914; *Allward; A Story of Gypsy Life*, Dodd, 1915 (published in England as *Allward*, Mills & Boon, 1915); *"–And What Happened," Being an Account of Some Romantic Meals*, Mills & Boon, 1916; *The Safety Candle*, Cassell, 1917; *Magdalene: A Study in Methods*, Cassell, 1919; *By Tigris and Euphrates*, Hurst & Blackett, 1923; *Sophy: A Tale of Baghdad*, Hurst & Blackett, 1924; *The Losing Game*, Hurst & Blackett, 1926; *Cedars, Saints and Sinners in Syria*, Hurst & Blackett, 1926; *Ishtar*, Hurst & Blackett, 1927; *Garden of Flames*, Stokes, 1927; (translator from the vernacular) *Folk-Tales of Iraq*, Oxford University Press, 1931; *Water into Wine: A Study of Ritual Idiom in the Middle East*, J. Murray, 1956, Verry, 1957.

Under name E. S. Drower: *The Mandaeans of Iraq and Iran: Their Cults, Customs, Magic, Legends and Folklore*, Clarendon Press, 1937; *Peacock Angel: Being Some Account of Votaries of a Secret Cult and Their Sanctuaries*, J. Murray, 1941; (translator) *The Book of the Zodiac*, *Sfar Malwasia*, Luzac for Royal Asiatic Society, 1949; (editor, translator, and author of notes) *Diwan Abatur. . .; or, Progress Through the Purgatories*, Biblioteca Apostolica Vaticana, 1950; (editor, translator, and author of notes and commentary) *The Haran Gawaita and the Baptism of Hibil-Ziwa*, Biblioteca Apostolica Vaticana, 1953; (editor and translator) *The Canonical Prayer Book of the Mandaeans*, E. J. Brill (Leiden), 1959; (editor and translator) Alf Trisar Suialia, *The Thousand and Twelve Questions*, Akademie-Verlag (Berlin), 1960; *The Secret Adam, a Study of Nasoraean Gnosis*, Clarendon Press, 1960; *Coronation of Sislam-Rba*, E. J. Brill, 1962; (translator) Alam Risaia Rba, *A Pair of Nasoraean Commentaries: Two Priestly Documents, The Great First World, and the Lesser First World*, E. J. Brill, 1963; (with R. Macuch) *A Mandaic Dictionary*, Oxford University Press, 1963. Contributor of articles and translations to *Journal of the Royal Asiatic Society*, and *Orientalia;* contributor of articles and reviews to other journals, to popular periodicals, and to newspapers.

(Died January 27, 1972)

* * *

DRUMMOND, Edith Marie Dulce Carman 1883-1883-1970
(Dulce Carman)

PERSONAL: Born October 2, 1883, in Norwich, Norfolk, England; daughter of Samuel John (a farmer) and Edith Mary (Balls) Carman; married David Drummond, November 29, 1911; children: Kenneth, Richard, Denzil, Audrey (Mrs. Jamie Rutherford) Streiff. *Education:* Attended schools in New Zealand. *Religion:* Anglican.

CAREER: Writer. *Member:* Romantic Novelist's Association (honorary founder).

WRITINGS—All under name Dulce Carman, except as indicated; all published by Wright & Brown, except as indicated: (Author of introduction with G. Dawes Hicks; under name Edith Drummond) *Pauline Meditations*, Lindsey Press, 1919; *The Broad Stairway*, Ouseley, 1924; *'Neath the Maori Moon*, 1949; *The Riddle of the Ranges*, 1950; *Golden Windows*, 1951; *Where Kowhais Bloom*, 1952; *Colours in the Sun*, 1952; *The Wind from the Hill*, 1953; *The Tapu Tree*, 1954; *The Witching Hour*, 1955; *A Million Dreams Away*, Hutchinson, 1956; *Dream of the Dark*, 1956; *The Devil's Rosebowl*, 1958; *The Loveliest Night of the Year*, 1958; *The Moon Witch*, 1959; *The Shining Hill*, 1960; *Golden Flower*, 1960; *The Magic of the Hills*, 1961; *The Wailing Pool*, 1961; *The Miracle of Tane*, 1962; *The False Dawn*, 1962; *The Maori Gateway*, 1963; *Tomorrow's Sun*, 1964; *The Pool of Wisdom*, 1964; *The Youngest One*, 1965; *The Guiding Star*, 1966; *The Necklace of El-Haya*, 1967; *The Star-Child*, 1967. Contributor of five hundred short stories and serials, many for children, to magazines.

(Died October 1, 1970)

* * *

DRZAZGA, John 1907-

PERSONAL: Born December 27, 1907, in Jamaica, N.Y.; son of Michael (a carpenter) and Mary (Orlowska) Drzazga. *Education:* Blackstone College of Law, LL.B.,

1936, J.D., 1937; studied forensic medicine at New York University, 1937. *Home address:* Route 2, Westville, Fla. 32464.

CAREER: New York (N.Y.) Police Department, member, 1937-57; now retired. Liberty Amendment Committee of Queens County, secretary. Chairman, Holmes County Liberty Amendment Committee. *Member:* American Revenue Association, National Audubon Society, National Consumers Union, National Geographic Society, National Philatelic Society, Audubon Society of Florida, Holmes County Republican Party. *Awards, honors:* LL.M. and LL.D. from Blackstone College of Law.

WRITINGS: Sex Crimes, C. C Thomas, 1960; *Wheels of Fortune,* C. C Thomas, 1963. Contributor of articles to *Law and Order, Police, International Criminal Police Review, Journal of Criminal Law, Criminology and Police Science.*

SIDELIGHTS: Drzazga was a candidate for the U.S. House of Representatives from Florida in 1968.

*   *   *

DuBOSE, Louise Jones   1901-

PERSONAL: Born April 15, 1901, in Columbus, Ga.; daughter of F. Dudley (clergyman and college teacher) and Rowena (Gunby) Jones; married W. Howard DuBose, 1923 (divorced); children: Rowena Gunby (Mrs. Erskine Dendy Betts). *Education:* University of South Carolina, A.B., 1920, M.A., 1932; also attended Agnes Scott College, Chicora College, and Presbyterian College, Clinton, S.C.; University of Chicago, graduate study. *Religion:* Presbyterian. *Home:* 611 Ermine Rd., West Columbia, S.C. 29169.

CAREER: South Carolina Writers' Project, 1935-41, assistant director, then director; University of South Carolina, Columbia, teacher of sociology, English, and airplane navigation, 1941-45, 1949-50; *South Carolina Magazine,* editor, 1946-48; University of South Carolina Press, director, 1950-65. *Member:* South Carolina Historical Society, Poetry Society of South Carolina, South Caroliniana Society, Columbia Art Association, Phi Beta Kappa, Alpha Psi Omega, Pi Gamma Mu, Chi Delta Phi.

WRITINGS: History of Columbus, Georgia, Historical Publishing Co. (Columbus), 1929; *The Woman from Off* (play), Baker & Co., 1934; (editor) *South Carolina Folk Tales,* Works Progress Administration, 1941; *Windstar* (poems), Bostick & Thornley, 1943; *Enigma: The Career of Blondelle Malone in Art and Society, 1879-1951,* University of South Carolina Press, 1963; (editor) *Palmetto Lives,* University of South Carolina Press, 1963. Author of four one-act plays presented in Columbia, and script writer of some 250 radio programs.

WORK IN PROGRESS: Compiler and editor, "Popular Beliefs and Superstitions from South Carolina," a unit of *The Dictionary of American Popular Beliefs and Superstitions;* a biography of Christopher Gadsden.

*   *   *

DUBS, Homer H(asenpflug)   1892-1969

PERSONAL: Born March 28, 1892, in Deerfield, Ill.; son of Charles Newton (a clergyman and missionary in China) and Emma Matilda (Hasenpflug) Dubs; married Florence Arnold, 1918; married second wife, Grace Dorothy Lowry Lamb, 1951 (died, 1953); married Margaret Wilkinson Soothill, August 3, 1954; children: (first marriage) Charles

William, Mrs. W. E. Eberle, Ann Louise Dubs Samberg. *Education:* Yale University, B.A., 1914; Columbia University, M.A., 1916; Union Theological Seminary, New York, N.Y., B.D., 1917; University of Chicago, Ph.D., 1925; Oxford University, M.A., 1947. *Home:* 133A Banbury Rd., Oxford, England.

CAREER: Ordained minister of Evangelical Church, 1917; China Mission of Evangelical Church, Hunan, China, missionary, 1918-24; University of Minnesota, Minneapolis, instructor in philosophy, 1925-27; Marshall College (now Marshall University), Huntington, W.Va., professor of philosophy, 1927-34; American Council of Learned Societies, New York, N.Y., director of Translation of Chinese Histories Project, 1934-37; Duke University, Durham, N.C., acting professor of philosophy, 1937-43; Columbia University, New York, N.Y., visiting professor of Chinese, 1944-45; Hartford Seminary Foundation, Hartford, Conn., professor of Chinese studies, Kenney School of Missions, 1945-47; Oxford University, Oxford, England, professor of Chinese, 1947-59, professor emeritus, 1959-69. *Awards, honors:* Stanislas Julien Prize of Academie des Belles Lettres et Inscriptions, Institut de France, 1947; honorary D. Litt., Oxford University, 1958.

WRITINGS: Hsuntze: The Molder of Ancient Confucianism, Probsthain, 1927; (editor, and translator from the Chinese) *Hsuntze: The Works,* Probsthain, 1928; *Rational Induction: An Analysis of the Method of Philosophy and Science,* University of Chicago Press, 1930; *China, the Land of Humanistic Scholarship,* Clarendon Press, 1949.

Translator, and author of critical notes and annotations: Pan Ku, *The History of the Former Han Dynasty,* Volume 1, Probsthain, 1938, American Council of Learned Societies, 1939, Volume II, American Council of Learned Societies and Probsthain, 1944 (also published under title *A Roman City in Ancient China,* China Society, London, 1957), Volume III, American Council of Learned Societies and Probsthain, 1956.

WORK IN PROGRESS: Additional volumes for projected ten-volume "Han Dynasty" series.

SIDELIGHTS: Dubs was competent in Chinese, French, and German.

(Died August 16, 1969)

*   *   *

DUFFIELD, Anne (Tate)   1893-

PERSONAL: Born November 20, 1893, in Orange, N.J.; daughter of A. D. (in electrical research) and Eliza (Dean) Tate; married Edgar Duffield, May 19, 1922. *Education:* Attended private school in Toronto, Ontario, and Sorbonne, University of Paris. *Religion:* Church of England. *Home:* 10 The Green, Aldbourne, Wiltshire, England. *Agent:* Hughes Massie Ltd., 18 Southampton Pl., London W.C.1, England.

CAREER: Novelist.

WRITINGS: Miss Mayhew and Ming Yun, Stokes, 1928; *Predestined,* J. Murray, 1929.

Lacquer Couch, J. Murray, 1931; *Passionate Interlude,* J. Murray, 1931; *Phantasy,* Cassell, 1932; *Lantern-Light,* Cassell, 1933, Arcadia House, 1943; *Stamboul Love,* Knopf, 1934 (published in England as *Fleeting Shadows,* Cassell, 1934); *Golden Horizons,* Cassell, 1935, Arcadia House, 1942; *Silver Peaks,* Cassell, 1935, Arcadia House, 1941; *Flaming Felicia,* Cassell, 1936; *Glittering Heights,*

Cassell, 1936; *Love's Memory*, Arcadia House, 1936 (published in England as *Wild Memory*, Cassell, 1937); *Moon Over Stamboul*, Cassell, 1936, Arcadia House, 1937; *Paradise*, Cassell, 1936, published as *Enchantment*, Hillman-Curl, 1937; *Bitter Rapture*, Cassell, 1937, published as *Brief Rapture*, Arcadia House, 1938; *The House on the Nile*, Cassell, 1937, published as *Gossip*, Hillman-Curl, 1938; *Gay Fiesta*, Arcadia House, 1938 (published in England as *The Dragon's Tail*, Cassell, 1939); *Grecian Rhapsody*, Cassell, 1938, published as *High Heaven*, 1939; *Desert Moon*, Cassell, 1939, Arcadia House, 1940; *False Star*, Arcadia House, 1939; *Karen's Memory*, Arcadia House, 1939.

Bubbling Springs, Arcadia House, 1940; *Sweeping Tide*, Arcadia House, 1940; *The Shadow of the Pines*, Cassell, 1940, Arcadia House, 1941; *Bevy of Maids*, Cassell, 1941, published as *Volunteer Nurse*, Arcadia House, 1942; *Old Glory*, Cassell, 1942, Arcadia House, 1943; *This Alien Heart*, Arcadia House, 1942 (published in England as *The Inscrutable Nymph*, Cassell, 1942); *Sunrise*, Cassell, 1943, Arcadia House, 1944; *Turn to the Sun*, Arcadia House, 1944 (published in England as *Out of the Shadows*, Cassell, 1944); *Taffy Came to Cairo*, Cassell, 1944, Arcadia House, 1945; *Repent at Leisure*, Arcadia House, 1946; *Forever Tomorrow*, Cassell, 1947, Arcadia House, 1951; *Lonely Bride*, Arcadia House, 1947 (published in England as *Song of the Mocking Bird*, Cassell, 1948); *Wise is the Heart*, Arcadia House, 1947; *Arkady*, Cassell, 1948; *Duty Dawn*, Cassell, 1949, Arcadia House, 1953; *Lovable Stranger*, Macrae Smith, 1949.

Beloved Enemy, Cassell, 1950; *Love Deferred*, Macrae Smith, 1951 (published in England as *Tomorrow Is Theirs*, Cassell, 1952); *Sugar Island*, Cassell, 1951; *Harbor Lights*, Cassell, 1953, Arcadia House, 1954; *The Golden Summer*, Cassell, 1954, Arcadia House, 1955; *The Grand Duchess*, Arcadia House, 1954; *Come Back, Miranda*, Cassell, 1955; *Fiametta*, Arcadia House, 1955; *Castle in Spain*, Cassell, 1958.

Violetta, Cassell, 1960.

*   *   *

DUFFIN, Henry Charles   1884-

PERSONAL: Born July 2, 1884, in London, England; son of Henry William Duffin; married Dorothy Mullinger, August 1, 1910; *Education:* Manchester University, M.A., 1908. *Politics:* Liberal-Socialist. *Home:* 24 Reynolds Rd., Hove 3, Sussex, England.

CAREER: Schoolmaster, 1907-35; writer, 1935—. *Member:* Authors' Society, English Association, Shaw Society.

WRITINGS: Thomas Hardy: A Study of His Wessex Novels, Longmans, Green, 1916, 4th edition, Barnes & Noble, 1963; *The Quintessence of Bernard Shaw*, Allen & Unwin, 1920, 2nd edition, 1939; *The Way of Happiness: A Reading of Wordsworth*, Sidgwick & Jackson, 1946; *Walter de la Mare: A Study of His Poetry*, Sidgwick & Jackson, 1949, Books for Libraries, 1969; *Amphibian: A Reconsideration of Browning*, Bowes, 1956; *The Novels and Plays of Charles Morgan*, Hillary, 1959; *Arnold the Poet*, Bowes, 1962, Barnes & Noble, 1963. Contributor to *Hibbert Journal* and other publications.

WORK IN PROGRESS: A second book on Wordsworth.

DULLES, Foster Rhea   1900-1970

PERSONAL: Born January 24, 1900, in Englewood, N.J.; son of William (a businessman) and Sophea (Rhea) Dulles; married Marion Richardson, August 7, 1926; children: Mary Rhea (Mrs. John E. Waller), Connie Anne (Mrs. Benjamin F. Weems III), Sara W. (Mrs. Howard C. Taylor III), Lynn. *Education:* Princeton University, A.B., 1921; Columbia University, M.A., 1926, Ph.D., 1940. *Politics:* Democrat. *Religion:* Protestant. *Home:* Dorset, Vt.

CAREER: Foreign correspondent for *Christian Science Monitor* in Peking, China, 1922, for *New York Herald Tribune* in Paris, France, 1925-26; member of editorial staff of *New York Herald*, 1923, of *Foreign Affairs* (quarterly), 1924; with *New York Evening Post*, 1927-33; visiting professor at Bennington College, Bennington, Vt., 1938-39, Smith College, Northampton, Mass., 1939-40, Swarthmore College, Swarthmore, Pa., 1940-41; Ohio State University, Columbus, professor of history, 1941-65. Visiting summer professor at Colgate University, 1944, Columbia University, 1954, Salzburg Seminar in American Studies, 1953, 1960, University of Oregon, 1956. U.S. Department of State, participant in International Education Exchange Program in India, 1957, in Soviet Union, 1958; Fulbright lecturer, Japan, 1961-62.

MEMBER: American Historical Association, Organization of American Historians, Phi Beta Kappa, Phi Alpha Theta (honorary). *Awards, honors:* Guggenheim Fellow, 1938-39; Ohioana Book Award in non-fiction, 1945, for *The Road to Teheran;* Ohio Academy of History Award, 1947, 1950.

WRITINGS: The Old China Trade, Houghton, 1930, reprinted, AMS Press, 1970; *Eastwood Ho: The First English Adventurers to the Orient: Richard Chancellor, Anthony Jenkinson, James Lancaster, William Adams, Sir Thomas Roe*, Houghton, 1931, reprinted, Books for Libraries, 1969; *America in the Pacific: A Century of Expansion*, Houghton, 1932, 2nd edition, 1938, reprinted, De Capo Press, 1969; *Lowered Boats: A Chronicle of American Whaling*, Harcourt, 1933; *Harpoon: The Story of a Whaling Voyage*, Houghton, 1935; *Forty Years of Japanese-American Relations*, Appleton, 1937.

America Learns to Play: A History of Popular Recreation, 1607-1940, Appleton, 1940, 2nd edition published as *A History of Recreation*, 1965; *The Road to Teheran*, Princeton University Press, 1944; *Twentieth Century America*, Houghton, 1945, reprinted, Books for Libraries, 1972; *China and America: The Story of their Relations since 1784*, Princeton University Press, 1946, reprinted, Kennikat Press, 1967; *Labor in America*, Crowell, 1949, 3rd edition, 1966.

The American Red Cross, Harper, 1950, reprinted, Greenwood Press, 1971; *America's Rise to World Power*, Harper, 1955; *The Imperial Years*, Crowell, 1956; *The United States Since 1865*, University of Michigan Press, 1959, 2nd edition, revised and enlarged, 1969.

Americans Abroad, University of Michigan Press, 1964; *Prelude to World Power: American Diplomatic History, 1860-1900*, Macmillan, 1965; *Yankees and Samurai: America's Role in the Emergence of Modern Japan, 1791-1900*, Harper, 1965; *The Civil Rights Commission, 1957-1965*, Michigan State University Press, 1968; *American Policy Toward Communist China, 1949-1969*, Crowell, 1972.

SIDELIGHTS: Dulles' books have been translated into French, German, Italian, Hindi, and Japanese. A Talking Books edition of *The Road to Teheran* has been issued.

Avocational interests: Travel, country living; general outdoor activities, from gardening to bird watching.

(Died September 11, 1970)

*   *   *

DUNKERLEY, Roderic   1884-

PERSONAL: Born July 20, 1884, in London, England; son of William Arthur (a writer under pseudonym John Oxenham) and Margery (Anderson) Dunkerley; married Daphne Gammer, June 1, 1920; children: Malcolm Roderic (deceased), John Desmond, Gregor Hamilton, Elspeth Wendy. *Education:* New College, London, B.A., 1907, B.D. (honors), 1909, Ph.D., 1927. *Home:* Inverkip, 45 The Glen, Worthing, Sussex, England.

CAREER: Congregational minister, beginning 1919, retiring from active work, 1958. Westhill College, Birmingham, England, principal, 1935-45. Lecturer and author.

WRITINGS: The Great Awakening, Headgate Press, 1915; *The Arm of God,* Oliphants, 1916; *Postman's Knock,* Oliphants, 1918; *The Proclamation,* Swarthmore Press, 1920; *The Unwritten Gospel,* Allen & Unwin, 1925; *First Prayers,* Methuen, 1929; *Treasure Trove,* Religious Education Press, 1948; *The Secret Moment,* Lutterworth, 1949; *The Hope of Jesus,* Longmans, Green, 1953; *At the House of the Interpreter,* Independent Press, 1956; *Beyond the Gospels,* Penguin, 1957; (with son, Gregor Dunkerley) *Prayer Time in the Junior School,* University of London Press, 1958. Contributor of articles and poems to *British Weekly, London Quarterly, New Testament Studies,* and other periodicals in England and abroad.

WORK IN PROGRESS: Collections of poems and articles.

AVOCATIONAL INTERESTS: Psychical research, child psychology, history, and English literature.

*   *   *

DUNLAP, Orrin E(lmer), Jr.   1896-1970

PERSONAL: Born August 23, 1896, in Niagara Falls, N.Y.; son of Orrin E. and Agnes (Stevenson) Dunlap; married Louise M. Leggett, August 2, 1924. *Education:* Colgate University, B.S., 1920; Harvard University, graduate study, 1921. *Home:* 151 Buffalo Ave., Niagara Falls, N.Y. 14303.

CAREER: New York Times, New York, N.Y., radio-television editor, 1922-40; Radio Corporation of America, New York, N.Y., vice-president, in charge of advertising and publicity, 1940-61. *Military service:* U.S. Navy, radio operator, World War I. *Member:* Institute of Electronic and Electrical Engineers (senior member), Sigma Nu, Harvard Club (New York). *Awards, honors:* Marconi Memorial Medal of History from Veteran Wireless Operators Association, 1945.

WRITINGS: Dunlap's Radio Manual, Houghton, 1924; *The Story of Radio,* Dial, 1927; *Advertising by Radio,* Ronald, 1929; *Radio in Advertising,* Harper & Brothers, 1931; *The Outlook for Television,* Harper & Brothers, 1932; *Talking on the Radio,* Greenberg, 1936; *Marconi: The Man and His Wireless,* Macmillan, 1937; *The Future of Television,* Harper & Brothers, 1942, revised edition, 1947; *Radio's 100 Men of Science,* Harper & Brothers, 1944; *Radar,* Harper & Brothers, 1946, revised edition, 1948; *Understanding Television,* Greenberg, 1948; *Dunlap's Radio and Television Almanac,* Harper & Brothers,

1951; *Communications in Space: From Wireless to Satellite Relay,* Harper, 1962, new and expanded edition, 1970. Corresponding radio editor for *Scientific American,* 1925-28, and *Boys' Life,* 1926-33.

WORK IN PROGRESS: Freedom of the Air; and *The History of Radio Broadcasting.*

SIDELIGHTS: Dunlap's interest in radio dated from 1912, when he built an amateur radio station, 8LQ, at his home in Niagara Falls, N.Y. A charter member of the American Amateur Radio League in 1913, he collected historic radio tubes and other apparatus, and his autograph collection of outstanding radio pioneers included Marconi, DeForest, Armstrong, and Jack Binns.

(Died February 1, 1970)

*   *   *

DUNNE, Philip   1908-

PERSONAL: Born February 11, 1908, in New York, N.Y.; son of Finley Peter (a writer) and Margaret (Abbott) Dunne; married Amanda Duff, July 15, 1939; children: Miranda, Philippa, Jessica. *Education:* Middlesex School, student, 1920-25; Harvard University, student, 1925-29. *Agent:* William Morris Agency, 1740 Broadway, New York, N.Y. 10019. *Office:* 259 South Beverly Dr., Beverly Hills, Calif. 90212.

CAREER: 20th Century-Fox Film Corp., and other studios, writer, producer, and director, 1933—. U.S. Office of War Information, Overseas Branch, chief of production in Motion Picture Bureau, 1942-45. *Member:* Writers Guild of America, West (former vice-president), Academy of Motion Picture Arts and Sciences (former governor). *Awards, honors:* Laurel Award of Writers Guild of America, 1962; Academy Award nominations in 1942, 1951.

WRITINGS: (Editor and author of introduction and commentary) Finley Peter Dunne, *Mr. Dooley Remembers,* Little, Brown, 1963.

Screenplays: (With Dan Totheroh and Rowland V. Lee) "The Count of Monte Cristo," United Artists, 1934; (with Ralph Spence) "Student Tour" (original story by George Seaton, Arthur Bloch, and Samuel Marx), Metro-Goldwyn-Mayer, 1934; (with Ralph Block) "The Melody Lingers On" (based on the novel by Lowell Brentano), Reliance Productions, 1935; "Last of the Mohicans" (based on the novel by James Fenimore Cooper), United Artists, 1936; (author of screen story with Finley Peter Dunne, Jr.) "Breezing Home," screenplay by Charles Grayson, Universal, 1937; "Lancer Spy" (based on the novel by Marthe McKenna), Fox, 1937; (with Julien Josephson and Sam Duncan) "Suez," Fox, 1938; (with Josephson) "Stanley and Livingstone," Fox, 1939; (with Josephson) "The Rains Came" (based on the novel by Louis Bromfield), Fox, 1939; (with John Taintor Foote) "Swanee River" (based on the life and career of Stephen Foster), Fox, 1939; (with Roland Brown, Samuel G. Engel and Hal Long) "Johnny Apollo," Fox, 1940; "How Green Was My Valley" (based on the novel by Richard Llewellyn), Fox, 1941; "Son of Fury" (based on the novel *Benjamin Blake* by Edison Marshall), Fox, 1942; "The Late George Apley" (based on the novel by J. P. Marquand and the play by Marquand and George S. Kaufman), Fox, 1947; (with Ring Lardner, Jr.) "Forever Amber" (based on the novel by Kathleen Winsor), Fox, 1947; "The Ghost and Mrs. Muir" (based on the novel *The Ghost of Captain Gregg and Mrs. Muir* by R. A. Dick), Fox, 1947; "Escape" (based on the play by John

Galsworthy), Fox, 1948; "The Luck of the Irish" (based on the novel by Guy and Constance Jones), Fox, 1948; (with Dudley Nichols) "Pinky" (based on the novel by Cid Ricketts Summer), Fox, 1949; "David and Bathsheba," Fox, 1951; (with Arthur Caesar) "Anne of the Indies" (based on a short story by Herbert Ravenal Sass), Fox, 1951; (with Michael Blankfort) "Lydia Bailey" (based on the novel by Kenneth Roberts), Fox, 1952; "Way of a Gaucho" (based on the novel by Herbert Childs), Fox, 1952; "The Robe" (based on the novel by Lloyd C. Douglas), Fox, 1953; "Demetrius and the Gladiators" (based on a character from Lloyd C. Douglas's *The Robe*), Fox, 1954; (with Casey Robinson) "The Egyptian" (based on the novel by Mika Waltari), Fox, 1954; "The View from Pompey's Head" (based on the novel by Hamilton Basso), Fox, 1955; "Hilda Crane" (based on the play by Samuel Raphaelson), Fox, 1956; "Three Brave Men" (based on Pulitzer Prize newspaper articles by Anthony Lewis), Fox, 1957; "Ten North Frederick" (based on the novel by John O'Hara), Fox, 1958; (with Edith Sommer) "Blue Denim" (based on the play by James Leo Herlihy and William Noble), Fox, 1959; "The Agony and the Ecstasy" (based on the novel by Irving Stone), Fox, 1965; (with W. H. Menger) "Blindfold" (based on the novel by Lucille Fletcher), Universal, 1966.

Contributor of short stories and articles to *New Yorker*, *Atlantic*, and other magazines.

* * *

DUNSTERVILLE, G(alfrid) C. K.   1905-

PERSONAL: Born February 18, 1905, in Bishopsteignton, England; son of Lionel C. (a major general, British Army), and Emily (Keyworth) Dunsterville; married, September 4, 1929 (wife's maiden surname, Freeman); children: Jennifer Fernandez, Hilary Branch. *Education:* University of Birmingham, B.Sc., 1925. *Home:* Quinta Colibri, Urb, Oripoto, El Hatillo, Caracas, Venezuela; (mail address) Apartado 89658, Caracas, Venezuela 108.

CAREER: Shell Group, engineering and management posts in England, United States, Egypt, Holland, Rumania, Columbia, Trinidad, and Venezuela, 1925-59; retired, 1959. *Member:* American Orchid Society (life member), Asociacion Venezolana de Ciencias Naturales. *Awards, honors:* Research associate, Harvard University.

WRITINGS: (With Leslie A. Garay) *Venezuelan Orchids Illustrated*, Museum Books, Volume I, 1959, Volume II, 1961, Volume III, 1965, Volume IV, 1966; *Introduction to the World of Orchids*, Doubleday, 1964. Regular contributor, *Orchid Review*.

WORK IN PROGRESS: Volume V of *Venezuelan Orchids Illustrated*.

SIDELIGHTS: Dunsterville is determined, by exploring tropical forests, to get to know each of Venezuela's thousand or more species of orchids, an interest shared by his wife.

BIOGRAPHICAL/CRITICAL SOURCES: Orchid Review, January, 1963; *Ideal Home*, August, 1963.

* * *

DUPEE, F(rederick) W(ilcox)   1904-

PERSONAL: Born June 25, 1904, in Chicago, Ill.; son of Leroy Church and Frances B. (Wilcox) Dupee; married Barbara Hughes, June 24, 1946; children: Joanna, Anthony. *Education:* Attended University of Illinois, 1922, University of Chicago, 1923-24; Yale University, Ph.B., 1927. *Home:* 25704 Tierra Grande Dr., Carmel, Calif. 93921. *Office:* Columbia University, New York, N.Y.

CAREER: Instructor in English at Bowdoin College, Brunswick, Me., 1927-29, at Columbia University, New York, N.Y., 1940-44; Bard College, Annandale-on-Hudson, N.Y., assistant professor of English, 1944-48; Columbia University, 1948-71, began as associate professor, became professor of English, now professor emeritus. Visiting professor of English at Harvard University, 1957. *Member:* P.E.N., Elizabethan Club (Yale University), Delta Kappa Epsilon. *Awards, honors:* Guggenheim Fellowship, 1951-52; Litt.D. Bard College, 1965.

WRITINGS: (Editor) *The Question of Henry James*, Henry Holt, 1945; *Henry James*, Sloane, 1951; (editor) *Great French Short Novels*, Dial, 1952; (editor) *Pleasures and Days and Other Stories by Marcel Proust*, Anchor Books, 1955; (editor) *The Selected Letters of Charles Dickens*, Farrar, Straus, 1960; *The King of the Cats* (essays and reviews), Farrar, Straus, 1965; (editor with George Stade) *Selected Letters of E. E. Cummings*, Harcourt, 1969. Contributor to *Nation, Commentary, Kenyon Review*, other journals. Editor, *Partisan Review*, 1937-41.

WORK IN PROGRESS: A short critical biography of W. B. Yeats.

* * *

DURKIN, Joseph Thomas   1903-

PERSONAL: Born May 17, 1903, in Philadelphia, Pa.; son of Joseph Leo and Anna (Gaffney) Durkin. *Education:* Boston College, A.B., 1928, M.A., 1930; Fordham University, Ph.D., 1942. *Office:* Department of History, Georgetown University, Washington, D.C. 20007.

CAREER: Entered Society of Jesus (Jesuits), 1920; ordained Roman Catholic priest, 1933; Loyola High School, Baltimore, Md., instructor in English and classics, 1927-30; University of Scranton, Scranton, Pa., professor of history, 1942-44; Georgetown University, Washington, D.C., professor of history, 1944—.

WRITINGS: (Editor) Adam Marshall, *Journal, 1824-25*, University of Scranton Press, 1943; (editor) *John Dooley, Confederate Soldier: His War Journals* (Catholic Book Club selection), preface by Douglas S. Freeman, Georgetown University Press, 1945; *Stephen R. Mallory: Confederate Navy Chief*, University of North Carolina Press, 1954; *General Sherman's Son* (Catholic Book Club selection) Farrar, Straus, 1959; *Armorer of the Confederacy, Secretary Mallory*, Benziger, 1960; (editor) *Confederate Chaplain: A War Journal*, preface by Bruce Catton, Bruce, 1960; *William Matthews, Priest and Citizen*, Benziger, 1963; *Georgetown University: The Middle Years, 1840-1900*, Georgetown University Press, 1963; *Georgetown University: First in the Nation's Capital*, Doubleday, 1964; *Hope for Our Time: Alexis Carrel on Man and Society*, Harper, 1965.

* * *

DURRANI, Mahmood Khan   1914-

PERSONAL: Born July 1, 1914, in Multan, Pakistan; son of Hafuzullah Khan (a landlord) and Hayat (Bibi) Durrani; married Shahzadi Razia, November 10, 1946; children Shahzad (son), Ayaz (son), Mahjabeen (daughter), Yasmueen (daughter), Fayaz (son), Ryaz (son), Nazneen (daughter). *Religion:* Islam. *Home:* Durrani House, Abdali Rd., Multan, Pakistan.

CAREER: Professional soldier in Indian Army, 1936-48, becoming lieutenant colonel; manufactuer of handloomed textiles, Karachi, Pakistan, 1960—. *Awards, honors*—Military: George Cross; mentioned in dispatches.

WRITINGS: The Sixth Column, Cassel, 1955.

WORK IN PROGRESS: Research for a book.

SIDELIGHTS: Durrani was serving in Malaya at the time of Japanese invasion, was captured and imprisoned at Singapore where he conceived and put into operation a plan for thwarting Japanese designs to flood India with fifth columnists. His book is an account of this doublecross and the Japanese torture that followed its discovery. In addition to his native language, he speaks English and Persian.

BIOGRAPHICAL/CRITICAL SOURCES: Time and Tide, November 19, 1955; *Daily Mail*, November 17, 1956.

*   *   *

DUSENBERRY, William Howard 1908-

PERSONAL: Born June 6, 1908, in Carmichaels, Pa; son of William Smith (a miller) and Edith A. (Miller) Dusenberry. *Education:* Waynesburg College, A.B., 1932; University of Michigan, A.M., 1936, Ph.D., 1941. *Politics:* Registered Republican. *Religion:* Presbyterian. *Home:* 53 South Morris, Waynesburg, Pa. 15370.

CAREER: Teacher in Pennsylvania public schools, 1930-38; University of Michigan, Ann Arbor, lecturer in history, 1941; instructor in history at Fresno State College (now California State University), Fresno, Calif., 1942, and University of California, Los Angeles, 1946-48; University of Pittsburgh, Pittsburgh, Pa., associate professor of history, 1948-61; Waynesburg College, Waynesburg Pa., professor of history and chairman of department, 1962-73. *Military service:* U.S. Army Air Forces, 1942-46; became major. *Member:* Agricultural History Society (member of executive committee), American Historical Association, Conference on Latin American History, Pennsylvania Historical Association, Greene County (Pa.) Historical Society. *Awards, honors:* Book award of Agricultural History Society, 1962.

WRITINGS: The Mexican Mesta: Administration of Ranching in Colonial Mexico, University of Illinois Press, 1963. Contributor to historical journals.

WORK IN PROGRESS: A history of the rodeo from its beginning to the present.

AVOCATIONAL INTERESTS: Strawberry culture (cultivates about one and one-half acres), hunting small and big game.

*   *   *

DUTT, R(ajani) Palme 1896-

PERSONAL: Born June 19, 1896, in Cambridge, England; son of Upendra Krishna (a doctor of medicine) and Anna (Palme) Dutt; married Salme Murrik, August 5, 1924. *Education:* Attended Perse School, Cambridge, and Balliol College, Oxford. *Politics:* Communist. *Home:* 8 Highfield Ct., Highfield Rd., London N.W.11, England. *Agent:* Hope Leresche, 11 Jubilee Pl., London S.W.3, England. *Office:* 134 Ballards Lane, London N.3, England.

CAREER: Expelled from Oxford University for Marxist propaganda activities, 1917, and imprisoned 1916, 1925; *Labour Monthly*, London, England, editor, 1921—. Also editor of *Workers' Weekly*, 1922-24, and *Daily Worker*, 1936-38. Communist Party, chairman of reorganization committee, 1922, member of political committee, 1922—. *Awards, honors:* Doctor of history, Moscow University, 1962.

WRITINGS: The Two Internationals, Allen & Unwin, 1920; *The Labour International Handbook*, Allen & Unwin, 1921; *Modern India*, Sunshine Publishing House (Bombay), 1926; *Socialism and the Living Wage*, Communist Party of Great Britain, 1927; *Lenin*, Hamish Hamilton, 1933, published as *Life and Teachings of V.I. Lenin*, International Publishers, 1934; *Fascism and Social Revolution*, International Publishers, 1934, 3rd revised edition published as *Fascism and Social Revolution: A Study of the Economics and Politics of the Extreme Stages of Capitalism in Decay*, 1935; *World Politics, 1918-1936*, Random House, 1936; *India Today*, Gollancz, 1940, 2nd revised edition, People's Publishing House, 1949, revised and abridged edition published as *India, Today and Tomorrow*, Lawrence & Wishart, 1955; *Leninism*, Lawrence & Wishart, 1941; *Britain in the World Front*, Lawrence & Wishart, 1942, International Publishers, 1943; *A Guide to the Problem of India*, Gollancz, 1942, published as *The Problem of India*, International Publishers, 1943; *Britain's Crisis of Empire*, Lawrence & Wishart, 1949, International Publishers, 1950; *The Crisis of Britain and the British Empire*, International Publishers, 1953, new and revised edition, Lawrence & Wishart, 1957; *Problems of Contemporary History*, International Publishers, 1963; *The Internationale*, Lawrence & Wishart, 1964.

Pamphlets: *Capitalism or Socialism in Britain?*, [London], 1931; *Crisis: Tariffs: War*, Communist Party of Great Britain, 1932; *The Political and Social Doctrine of Communism*, Hogarth, 1938, 2nd edition, 1942; (with Ivor Montagu) *Ruby Star*, Labour Monthly, 1941; *The "New Order" in Britain*, Labour Monthly, 1941; *New Chapter in Divide and Rule*, People's Publishing House, 1941; *India: What Must Be Done*, Labour Monthly, 1942; *25 Years*, Labour Monthly, 1942; *The Road to Labor Unity*, Labour Monthly, 1943; *Fascism: An Analysis*, India Publishers, 1943; *Freedom for India: The Truth About the Cabinet Mission*, Communist Party of Great Britain, 1946; *How to Save Peace*, Communist Party of Great Britain, 1948; *Whither India?*, Labour Monthly, 1949; *Empire War Plans*, Trinity Trust, 1949; (with George Bernard Shaw) *George Bernard Shaw: A Memoir [and] The Dictatorship of the Proletariat* (the former by Dutt, the latter by Shaw), Labour Monthly, 1951; *Stand By Congo*, Communist Party of Great Britain, 1960; *Whither China?*, Communist Party of Great Britain, 1967.

*   *   *

DYMENT, Clifford (Henry) 1914-1971

PERSONAL: January 20, 1914, in Alfreton, Derbyshire, England; son of William Clifford and Elizabeth (Riding) Dyment; married Marcella Salzer (an actress), 1947 (died, 1968). *Education:* Attended school in Loughborough, England. *Home:* 53 Harrington Gardens, London S.W. 7, England.

CAREER: Free-lance literary journalist and critic, 1934-40; scriptwriter of documentary films, 1941-42; director of documentary and military training films, 1943-48; free-lance writer and broadcaster, 1948-71. Lecturer and reader of poetry in public recital halls. English Festival of Spoken Poetry, judge, 1953-56. *Member:* Royal Society of Literature (fellow), P.E.N. *Awards, honors:* Rockefeller Foundation Atlantic Award, 1950; Arts Council grant, 1967.

WRITINGS: First Day, Dent, 1935; *Straight or Curly?*, Dent, 1937; *The Axe in the Wood*, Dent, 1944; *Poems 1935-48*, Dent, 1949; *C. Day Lewis* (critical monograph), British Council, 1944, 3rd edition, 1969; *Experiences and Places*, Dent, 1955; *The Railway Game* (autobiography), Dent, 1962; *Fur, Feather and Fin*, Carre Four, 1969; *Collected Poems*, introduction by C. Day Lewis, Dent, 1970. Contributor of commentaries to British Broadcasting Corp. television series, "The Face of Britain," 1951.

WORK IN PROGRESS: Commentaries for Granada television series, "Another World"; radio scripts; a continuation of autobiography begun in *The Railway Game*, with provisional title, *Trains to London*.

SIDELIGHTS: According to Tony Harrison, Dyment's poetry "represents some thirty years of freehold withdrawal. It is a poetry of exclusion, of urban noise, as of definite articles if they don't fit the metre, and ultimately of almost all sense of life, now and in England. From the first poems in 1935, where his art is 'retreat' and 'sanctuary' up to the poems of 1955-56, where he is 'wombed in elm' and even night is 'Dominican', his poetry is resolutely monastic, gleaming with what John Milton called an 'excremental whiteness.'"

Tape recordings of his poems are included in the Yale University collection; *The Railway Game* was made into a talking book for the blind.

AVOCATIONAL INTERESTS: Playing harmonica, collecting cigarette cards, listening to 78 r.p.m. records, drinking cheap wine, and collecting wine lists and miscellaneous catalogues.

BIOGRAPHICAL/CRITICAL SOURCES: London Magazine, November, 1970; *Bookseller*, June 19, 1971.

(Died, 1971)

*   *   *

EASTMAN, Edward Roe   1885-

PERSONAL: Born September 29, 1885, in Berkshire, N.Y.; son of Charles R. (a farmer) and Elizabeth (Roe) Eastman; married Belle V. Rockefeller, April 8, 1906; children: Donald D., Stewart (deceased), Dorothy (deceased), George, Robert. *Education:* Studied at Keuka College and Cornell University. *Politics:* Republican. *Religion:* Protestant. *Home and office:* 515 North Tioga St., Ithaca, N.Y. 14850.

CAREER: Farmer, teacher (including vocational agriculture), school principal, and county agent at earlier periods, then a writer, and general counselor at Ithaca College, Ithaca, N.Y. Former member of board of directors, U.S. Farm Credit Board, Northeastern region. Member of National Commission for Public Schools; New York State Council on Rural Education, president emeritus, also member of committee initiating legislation for centralization of rural schools. Cornell University, former trustee, regent, beginning 1946; New York State Board of Regents, member, 1946-56, serving as vice-chancellor of State University of New York, 1951-56. Member of National Council of Boy Scouts of America.

MEMBER: National Society of Sons of the American Revolution, National Grange (and local unit), New York State Agricultural Society (past president), Friends of Ithaca College, Masons, Rotary. *Awards, honors:* LL.D., Alfred University, 1946; Litt.D., Keuka College, 1952. Silver Antelope Award from National Council, Boy Scouts of America, 1944; Alfred E. Smith Award from New York

State Teachers Association, 1945, for "distinguished service to education"; Freedoms Foundation Award, 1951; award from Cornell Dairy Science Association, 1954, "for lasting contribution to the dairy industry of New York State"; Award of Merit from American Vocational Association, 1960; citations from the National Citizens Commission for the Public Schools, 1956, Four-H Clubs of the United States, 1957, and the National Vocational Teachers Association, 1959.

WRITINGS: The Trouble Maker, Macmillan, 1925; *These Changing Times*, Macmillan, 1927; (with Carl E. Ladd) *Horse and Buggy Days*, Nesterman, 1943; *Tough Sod*, American Agriculturist, 1944; *The Destroyers*, American Agriculturist, 1946; *The Settlers*, Century House, 1950; *No Drums*, American Agriculturist, 1951; *Not with Dreams*, American Agriculturist, 1954; *Walking the Broad Highway*, American Agriculturist, 1956; *Hostages to Fortune*, Interstate, 1958; *The Words and the Music*, Interstate, 1959; *How to Speak and Write for Rural Audiences*, Interstate, 1960; *Why Study Vocational Agriculture in High School*, State University of New York Press, 1961; *Journey to Day Before Yesterday*, Prentice-Hall, 1963. Author of *Eastman's Chestnuts*, Volumes I-V, American Agriculturist, 1930—. Former editor, *Dairymen's League News* and *American Agriculturist*. Regular contributor to *American Agriculturist* and *Ithaca Journal*.

*   *   *

EBLANA, Sister   1907-

PERSONAL: Secular name, Phyllis Margaret McEvoy; born February 22, 1907, in Dublin, Ireland; daughter of William John (a landlord) and Ellen (Conaty) McEvoy. *Education:* Attended Dominican College, Dublin, Ireland. *Politics:* "Benevolently disposed to all progressives." *Home:* Carmelite Monastery, Ranelagh, Dublin 6, Ireland.

CAREER: Roman Catholic nun, member of Carmelite Order, 1925—.

WRITINGS: A Modern Mystic: Mother Mary Teresa of the Angels, 1855-1930, Burns & Oates, 1938; *The Vocation of Lady Christine*, Bruce, 1964.

WORK IN PROGRESS: A book on the life of Princess Louise of France; a biography of the sixteen martyrs of Compiegne.

*   *   *

ECCLES, Henry E.   1898-

PERSONAL: Born December 31, 1898, in Bayside, N.Y.; son of George Warrington (an Episcopal clergyman) and Lydia (Lawrence) Eccles; married Isabel A. McCord, November 12, 1924; children: Frank McCord. *Education:* Columbia University, M.S. in Mechanical Engineering, 1930; U.S. Naval Academy, B.S., 1922. *Religion:* Episcopalian. *Home:* 101 Washington St., Newport, R.I. 02840.

CAREER: U.S. Navy, commissioned ensign, 1922, retired as rear admiral, 1952; commanded two submarines prior to World War II, and a destroyer in the Asiatic Fleet, 1942; served in Office of Vice-Chief of Naval Operations, 1942-43, on staff of Commander, Service Force Pacific, 1944-45, on Joint Operations Review Board, 1946, and on staff of Naval War College, 1947-51. Consultant on Logistics Research Project, George Washington University, 1952—; consultant on systems and logistics, U.S. Air Force, 1957-63. *Member:* American Society of Naval Engineers, U.S. Naval Institute, Academy of Political Science. *Awards, honors*—Military: Navy Cross, Silver Star, Legion of Merit, Order of the Bronze Lion (Netherlands).

WRITINGS: Operational Naval Logistics, U.S. Government Printing Office, 1950; *Logistics in the National Defense*, Stackpole, 1959; *Military Concepts and Philosophy*, Rutgers University Press, 1965. Contributor to military journals. Editor, *Naval Research Logistics Quarterly*, 1954—.

WORK IN PROGRESS: Research in strategy, command, and logistics.

AVOCATIONAL INTERESTS: Music, art, chess, photography, and travel.

*   *   *

EDDISON, Roger (Tatham) 1916-

PERSONAL: Born September 16, 1916; son of Edwin (an electrical engineer) and Hilda (Leadam) Eddison; married Rosemary Land, 1941; children: Charles, Sally, Hugh. *Education:* Cambridge University, B.A., 1938, M.A., 1943. *Home:* Horstedpond Farm, Uckfield, Sussex, England.

CAREER: Rothamsted Experimental Station, England, statistician, 1945-47; British Iron and Steel Research Association, England, head of operational research department, 1947-55; NAAFI (wholesale-retail distribution), England, manager of plans and methods department, 1955-61; Science in General Management Ltd., director, 1961-70; Novy, Eddison, Partners Ltd., Park Lodge, Iver Heath, England, director, 1970—. Visiting professor, University of Sussex, 1968—. *Member:* Operational Research Society, Royal Statistical Society, Operations Research Society of America, Institute of Management Science.

WRITINGS: (with K. Pennycuick and B.H.P. Rivett) *Operational Research in Management*, English Universities Press, 1961, Wiley, 1962; (editor with D. Hertz) *Progress in Operational Research*, Volume II, Wiley, 1964. Editor of *Operational Research Quarterly*, 1949-63.

*   *   *

EDMAN, Marion (Louise) 1901-

PERSONAL: Born April 25, 1901, in St. Paul, Minn.; daughter of Charles M. (a farmer) and Mathilda Edman. *Education:* Gustavus Adolphus College, B.A., 1926; University of Minnesota, M.A., 1935, Ph.D., 1938. *Home:* 50 Moss Avenue, Highland Park, Mich. 48203.

CAREER: Instructor at Gustavus Adolphus College, St. Peter, Minn., University of Minnesota, Minneapolis, and University of Chicago, Chicago, Ill., prior to 1938; Wayne State University, Detroit, Mich., 1938—, professor of education, 1950-71, professor emeritus, 1971—, Franklin Memorial lecturer, 1961. Visiting professor at University of Michigan, Ohio State University, University of California, and other universities. Education specialist (civilian) with U.S. Office of Military Government in Bavaria, 1946-50; consultant to International Cooperation Administration in Lebanon and Vietnam, 1955-57; consultant to Royal Board of Education, Sweden, 1960-61, and Central Education Research Institute, Korea, 1961-62.

MEMBER: Women's International League for Peace and Freedom (chairperson of Peace Education committee, 1970—), American Association for the United Nations (member of state board), Michigan Congress of Parents and Teachers (former chairperson of world citizenship committee), Metropolitan YMCA (president, 1972), Pi Lambda Theta, Alpha Kappa Alpha, Delta Kappa Gamma. *Awards, honors:* L.H.D., Gustavus Adolphus College, 1951, and Alumni Award, 1957; Distinguished Service Award, University of Minnesota, 1951; Alumni Service Award, Wayne State University, 1957; Fulbright research scholar in Korea, 1961-62; Eleanor Fishburn International Understanding Award, 1965, for article, "The Teacher as World Citizen," in *Childhood Education*.

WRITINGS: (Editor) *The Horizons of Man*, Wayne State University Press, 1963; *Primary Teachers of Korea Look at Themselves*, Central Education Research Institute (Korea), 1963; *A Self-Image of Primary School Teachers: A Cross Cultural Study of Their Role and Status in Twelve Cities*, Wayne State University Press, 1968. Also co-author of "Reading Is Fun," series, Harcourt, 1944, and "Adventures in Reading," series, Houghton, 1955, new edition, 1963. Contributor of articles to education journals.

*   *   *

EDMONDS, C(ecil) J(ohn) 1889-

PERSONAL: Born October 26, 1889, in Osaka, Japan; son of Walter John (a clergyman) and Laura (Radermacher) Edmonds; married Alison Hooper, 1935; married second wife, Phyllis Stephenson, 1947; children: (first marriage) one son, two daughters; (second marriage) one son. *Education:* Attended Pembroke College, Cambridge, 1910-12. *Religion:* Church of England. *Home:* 5 Longslip, Langton Green, Tunbridge Wells, Kent, England.

CAREER: Entered British Foreign Service, 1912, retiring with rank of minister, 1950; political officer with British forces in Iraq and Persia, 1915-22; Civil Administration of Iraq, 1922-45, adviser to Ministry of Interior, 1935-45. United Kingdom delegate, International Refugee Organization, 1946-51. Lecturer in Kurdish in School of Oriental and African Studies, University of London, 1951-57. President, British School of Archaeology in Iraq, 1966—. *Member:* Royal Geographical Society, Royal Central Asian Society (member of council and vice-president, 1946-53, 1959-66), Royal Asiatic Society, Royal Institute of International Affairs, Athenaeum Club (London). *Awards, honors—Military:* Mentioned in dispatches three times. *Civilian:* Officer, Order of the British Empire, 1925; Commander, Order of the British Empire, 1930; Companion of St. Michael and St. George, 1941; Rafidain Class II (Iraq), 1945; Burton Memorial Medal, Royal Asiatic Society, 1962; Sykes Memorial Medal, Royal Central Asian Society, 1966.

WRITINGS: Kurds, Turks and Arabs, Oxford University Press, 1957; (with Taufiq Wahby) *A Kurdish-English Dictionary*, Clarendon Press, 1966, revised edition, 1971; *A Pilgrimage to Lalish*, Royal Asiatic Society, 1967. Contributor to *Geographical Journal, Journal of the Royal Central Asian Society, Journal of the Royal Asiatic Society, Bulletin of the School of Oriental and African Studies* (London), and *Iraq* (British School of Archaeology in Iraq).

SIDELIGHTS: Edmonds speaks French, German, Arabic, Persian, and Kurdish.

*   *   *

EDWARDS, Christine 1902-

PERSONAL: Born August 13, 1902, in New York, N.Y.; daughter of Leonard (a manufacturer) and Anna Madeleine (Seidler) Edwards. *Education:* Hunter College (now Hunter College of the City University of New York),

B.A., 1922; Columbia University, M.A., 1930; New York University, Ph.D., 1960. *Home:* 315 East 68th St., New York, N.Y. 10022.

CAREER: Actress on radio and television, and director in community theater and summer stock; Vera Soloviova Studio of Acting, New York, N.Y., co-director, 1951-67. Long Island University, Brooklyn, N.Y., assistant professor, 1961-63, associate professor, 1963-70, professor of speech and theater, 1970-72, professor emeritus, 1972—.

WRITINGS: The Stanislavky Heritage: Its Contribution to the Russian and American Theatre, New York University Press, 1965.

* * *

EDWARDS, (H. C.) Ralph 1894-

PERSONAL: Born June 24, 1894, in England; son of W. A. (a Church of England clergyman) and Edith Lilian (Prichard) Edwards; married Marjorie Inghan Brooke, 1926; children: three sons. *Education:* Hertford College, Oxford, B.A. (war degree). *Home:* Suffolk House, Chiswick Mall, London W. 4, England.

CAREER: Country Life, London, England, member of editorial staff, 1921-26; Victoria and Albert Museum, London, England, assistant, department of woodwork, 1926-28, assistant keeper, 1928-37, keeper, 1937-54, retired, 1954. Adviser on works of art to Ministry of Works and Historic Buildings Council, 1954; member of the court of governors council and art and archeology committee of National Museum of Wales; member of Slade School advisory committee. *Military service:* British Army, 1917-18; served as second lieutenant. *Member:* Athenaeum Club (London), Society of Antiquaries (fellow). *Awards, honors:* Commander of the Order of the British Empire.

WRITINGS: (With Percy Macquoid) *The Dictionary of English Furniture from the Middle Ages to the Late Georgian Period*, three volumes, Scribner, 1924-27, 2nd edition, revised and enlarged, Country Life, 1954; (with Margaret Jourdain) *Georgian Cabinet-makers*, Country Life, 1944, 3rd edition, 1955; *Hepplewhite Furniture Designs from the Cabinet-Maker and Upholsters Guide, 1794*, Transatlantic Book Service, 1947.

(With Peter Ward-Jackson) *Ham House*, H.M.S.O., 1950, 4th edition, 1959; *A History of the English Chair*, H.M.S.O., 1951; *Early Conversation Pictures from the Middle Ages to about 1730*, Country Life, 1954; (editor with L. Ramsey) *The Connoisseur Period Guides to the Houses, Decorations, and Chattels of the Classic Periods*, six volumes, Connoisseur, 1956-58; (author of introduction) *English Chairs*, H.M.S.O., 1957; *Georgian Furniture*, 2nd edition, H.M.S.O., 1958; (editor) William Ince, *The Universal System of Household Furniture*, Quadrangle, 1960; *The Shorter Dictionary of English Furniture from the Middle Ages to the Late Georgian Period*, Country Life, 1964.

Author of museum publications; contributor of articles on painting and decorative art to periodicals.

* * *

EDWARDS, William 1896-

PERSONAL: Born April 6, 1896, in Portland, Dorsetshire, England; son of William and Rosa H. (Towell) Edwards; married Marjorie King Warry, August 3, 1923; children: Jean Mary, Philip John. *Education:* Studied at Trinity College, Cambridge, 1919-20, and St. Bartholomew's Hospital

Medical College, 1920-23, received B.A. and M.D. *Home:* 9 Greville Park Ave., Ashtead, Surrey, England.

CAREER: General medical practitioner, 1923-58; physician to Leatherhead Hospital, 1939-58. *Military service:* British Army, 1915-18; became lieutenant. *Member:* British Medical Association, National Union of Journalists, Royal College of Surgeons, Royal College of Physicians (licentiate).

WRITINGS: The Art is Long: The Work of Every Type of Doctor, Melrose, 1947, 2nd edition, 1949; (contributor) Arthur Massey, editor, *Modern Trends in Public Health*, Butterworth & Co., 1949; *Here's Your Medicine*, Macmillan, 1960; *Home First Aid*, Pelham Books, 1969.

* * *

EHRLICH, Bettina Bauer 1903- (Bettina)

PERSONAL: Born March 19, 1903, in Vienna, Austria; daughter of Eugen (director of an Austrian coal mining company) and Lily (Mauthner) Bauer; married Georg Ehrlich (an artist and sculptor), November 29, 1930. *Education:* Attended Wiener Kunstgewerbeschule (art school), Vienna, Austria, three years. *Religion:* Jewish (not Orthodox). *Home:* 22 Palace Gardens Ter., London W. 8, England. *Agent:* H. J. Fybel, 54 West 74th St., New York, N.Y.

CAREER: Painter in oils and water colors; has done etching, lithography, textile hand-printing, and designing for industry in England and United States. Writer for children; book illustrator. *Awards, honors:* Silver Medal, Paris Exposition Internationale des Arts el Industries, 1937, for handprinted and painted textiles.

WRITINGS—Under name Bettina, all self-illustrated: *Poo-Tsee, the Water Tortoise*, Chatto & Windus, 1943; *Show Me Yours*, Chatto & Windus, 1945; *Cocolo*, Chatto & Windus, 1945, Harper, 1948; *Carmello*, Chatto & Windus, 1946; *Cocolo Comes to America*, Harper, 1949; *Cocolo's Home*, Harper, 1950; *Castle in the Sand*, Harper, 1951; *A Horse for the Island* (adult), Harper, 1952; *Piccolo*, Harper, 1954; *Pantaloni*, Harper, 1957; *Trovato*, Farrar, Strauss, 1959; *Paolo and Panetto*, F. Watts, 1960; *For the Leg of a Chicken*, F. Watts, 1960; *Francesco and Francesca*, Oxford University Press, 1962; *Dolls*, Farrar, Strauss, 1963; *Of Uncles and Aunts*, Oxford University Press, 1963, Norton, 1964; *The Goat Boy*, Oxford University Press, 1965, Norton, 1966; *Sardines and the Angel*, Oxford University Press, 1967; *Neretto*, Oxford University Press, 1969.

Illustrator: Walter Hackett, *The Swans of Ballycastle*, Farrar, Straus, 1954; Lee Kingman, *The Magic Christmas Trees*, Farrar, Straus, 1956; Gilles Saint Cerere, *Pirnwayu and the Rainbow*, Oxford University Press, 1958; Virginia Haviland, *Favorite Fairytales Told in England*, Little, 1959; Eva Lis-Wuorio, *Tal and the Barruget*, Bodley Head, 1969.

SIDELIGHTS: Bettina Ehrlich wrote: "I truly cannot say why I write for children. Maybe because I can feel what they feel. I have such a vivid recollection of what it is like to be a child. Never do I feel their problems or desires are odd." Ms. Ehrlich speaks French and Italian. Ten of her books have been published in more than one country.

* * *

EICHHORN, David Max 1906-

PERSONAL: Born January 6, 1906, in Columbia, Pa.; son

of Joseph (a merchant) and Anna (Zivi) Eichhorn; married Zelda Socol, June 23, 1935; children: Jonathan, Michael, Jeremiah, Judith Ann. *Education:* University of Cincinnati, A.B., 1928; Hebrew Union College, Rabbi, 1931, D.D., 1938, D.H.L., 1956. *Politics:* Liberal. *Home:* 85-14 66th Ave., Rego Park, N.Y. 11374; and 311 Somerset Arms, Satellite Beach, Fla. 32935

CAREER: Rabbi in Springfield, Mass., and Texarkana, Ark., 1932-38; Hillel Foundations, Florida director, 1939-42; National Jewish Welfare Board, New York, N.Y., director of field activities of Commission on Jewish Chaplaincy, 1945-68. *Military service:* U.S. Army, 1942-45; became lieutenant colonel; received Bronze Star. U.S. Army Reserve, 1945—; toured Caribbean, 1950, Europe, 1952 and 1963, and Far East, 1954 and 1958, on preaching missions to Jewish personnel. *Member:* Association of Jewish Chaplains of the Armed Forces (president, 1953-55), Alumni Association of Hebrew Union College (Cincinnati, Ohio; president, 1962-63).

WRITINGS: Cain: Son of the Serpent, Whittier, 1957; *Musings of the Old Professor: The Meaning of Koheles, David*, 1963; (editor) *Conversion to Judaism: A History and Analysis*, Ktav, 1965. Contributor to *Rabbis in Uniform* and other books. Also contributor of articles to magazines.

WORK IN PROGRESS: A commentary on the Book of Daniel; a history of Christian attempts to convert the Jews of the United States, tentatively titled *Christianizing America's Jews*.

SIDELIGHTS: "My writings on the Bible and Talmud reflect a rationalistic rather than a mystical approach to the philosophy and theology of Judaism."

*   *   *

EIDELBERG, Ludwig   1898-1970

PERSONAL: Born December 27, 1898, in Austria; came to United States in 1940; son of Ithamar (a lawyer) and Helen (Selzer) Eidelberg; married first wife, 1924; married second wife, Marthe Elkan, September 6, 1939; children: (second marriage) Philippe. *Education:* University of Vienna, M.D., 1925. *Religion:* Jewish. *Home and office:* 25 East 86th St., New York, N.Y.

CAREER: State University of New York, Downstate Medical Center, Brooklyn, beginning, 1951 as clinical professor of psychiatry, became president. *Member:* New York Psychoanalytic Association (president, 1959-60).

WRITINGS: Take Off Your Mask, International Universities, 1948; *Studies in Psychoanalysis*, International Universities, 1952; *Outline of Comparative Pathology of the Neuroses*, International Universities, 1954; *The Dark Urge*, Pyramid Books, 1961. Editor-in-chief of *Encyclopedia of Psychoanalysis* published by Macmillan.

SIDELIGHTS: Ludwig Eidelberg was fluent in Polish, French, German, and English.

(Died November, 1970)

*   *   *

EISNER, Gisela (Spanglet)   1925-

PERSONAL: Born April 3, 1925, in Berlin, Germany; daughter of Manes and Sara (Pufeles) Spanglet; married Herbert Sigmund (a research physicist), July 17, 1948; children: David, Thomas, Clare, Harriet. *Education:* University of Nottingham, B.Com., 1946; University of Manches-

ter, Ph.D., 1956. *Religion:* Jewish. *Home:* 69 Macclesfield Rd., Buxton, Derbyshire, England.

CAREER: University of Southampton, Highfield, Southampton, England, research, 1946-48; Institute of Economic and Social Research, London, England, research, 1948-50; University of Manchester, Manchester, England, research, 1951-56. Governor, Buxton College of Further Education. Member, Buxton Youth Service Committee.

WRITINGS: Jamaica, 1830-1930: A Study in Economic Growth, Manchester University Press, 1961.

*   *   *

ELDRIDGE, Retha Hazel (Giles)   1910-

PERSONAL: Born August 1, 1910, in Middletown, N.Y.; daughter of Henry Clarence (a clergyman) and Jennie (Quackenbush) Giles; married Paul Herbert Eldridge (now a clergyman of Seventh-day Adventist Church), August 15, 1933; children: Norma Evelyn, Lawrence Allen. *Education:* Atlantic Union College, B.A., 1934. *Religion:* Seventh-day Adventist. *Home:* 800 Thomson Rd., Singapore 11, Malaysia. *Office:* Far Eastern Division of Seventh-day Adventists, 800 Thomson Rd., Singapore 11, Malaysia.

CAREER: Accompanied missionary-husband to Japan in 1937, and taught music and conversational English at a school near Tokyo, 1937-40; interned with family in Philippine Islands during World War II; returned to Japan in 1947, and directed Voice of Prophecy Bible Correspondence School, Tokyo, 1950-60. Resident of Singapore, 1963—.

WRITINGS: Bombs and Blessings, Review & Herald, 1946; *From the Rising of the Sun*, Review & Herald, 1963.

*   *   *

ELLIOTT, Leonard M.   1902-

PERSONAL: Born July 15, 1902, in Dover, N.J.; son of Leonard (in real estate) and Stella (Munson) Elliott; married Helene McQuillan; children: David W., Stephen W. *Education:* Attended public schools in Dover, N.J. *Politics:* Democrat. *Religion:* Episcopalian (non-practicing). *Home:* 27 Madison St., Glen Ridge, N.J. *Office: Newark News*, 215 Market St., Newark, N.J.

CAREER: Newark News, Newark, N.J., sports editor, 1939—. *Member:* Golf Writers Association of America, Metropolitan Golf Writers Association.

WRITINGS: (With Jim Dante and Leo Diegel) *The Nine Bad Shots of Golf*, McGraw, 1947; (with Dante) *Stop That Slice*, McGraw, 1953; (with Dante) *The Four Magic Moves to Winning Golf*, McGraw, 1962.

*   *   *

ELLIOTT, Spencer H(ayward)   1883-1967

PERSONAL: Born June 27, 1883, in Glasgow, Scotland; son of William Hayward (a clergyman) and Mary Alice (Thompson) Elliot; married Hilda Mary Hawley (died, 1947); married Sheila Mabel Elliot, February 5, 1949; children: (first marriage) Jean (Mrs. Robert Orchard), Margaret (Mrs. Charles Ulch), George Spencer. *Education:* University of Manchester, B.A. (honors), 1904, M.A., 1906; University of Leeds, B.A., 1905, M.A., 1927; theological study at Ripon Clergy College. *Home:* 1007 13th St. S.W., Calgary, Alberta, Canada.

CAREER: Ripon School, English and divinity master,

1904-06; ordained priest of the Church of England, 1907; curate in Leeds and in Barrow-in-Furness, England, 1906-11; diocesan minister of Manchester, England, 1911-16, of Sheffield, England, 1916-27; vicar in Sheffield, in Mansfield, and in Bolton, England, 1916-33; rural dean in Mansfield and in Winwick, England, 1927-38; rector of Warrington, England, and canon diocesan of Liverpool, England, 1933-38; Christ Church Cathedral, Victoria, British Columbia, rector, 1938-48; dean of British Columbia, 1938-48; St. John's College, Winnipeg, Manitoba, professor of church history, 1948-56; Emmanuel College, Saskatoon, Saskatchewan, professor of liturgies and practical theology, 1956-60. Missioner to troops, England and France, 1914-16. Extension lecturer, Oxford University, 1925; member of examining board, University of Manitoba, 1948-54. Member, Mission of Help to India, 1922-23. Examining chaplain to Bishop of British Columbia, 1938-48, to Archbishop of Rupert's Land, 1948-56; prolocuter to Provincial Synod of British Columbia, 1938-56. Honorary canon of Sheffield, 1922, of Southwell, 1929, of Manchester, 1930. *Member:* Ancient Monuments Society (fellow), Mansfield Rotary Club (founder-president, 1928). *Awards, honors:* D.D., Trinity College, University of Toronto, 1939.

WRITINGS: The Message of a Mission, Richard Jackson, 1913, 3rd edition, 1926; *The Gospel of the Father,* Richard Jackson, 1922, 2nd edition, 1923; *A Missioner Abroad: Being Letters Written While Engaged Upon the Mission of Help to India,* Richard Jackson, 1923; *Religion and Dramatic Art,* S.C.M. Press, 1927; *The Romance of Marriage,* Macmillan (New York), 1929; *The Romance of Death,* S.P.C.K., 1931; *The Missing Link: Studies in Genesis,* Group Publications, 1934; *When Trouble Comes,* S.P.C.K., 1939; *Members of Christ,* Church of England in Canada, 1946. Author of pamphlets. Reviewer for *Sheffield Daily Telegraph,* 1916-37, *Winnipeg Free Press,* 1948-56; Canadian correspondent for *Living Church,* 1955-64. Author of literary and other articles appearing in journals.

WORK IN PROGRESS: Letters to Young Clergymen; Emmanuel's Land; The Problem of Tragedy; My Web of Time (memoirs); an introduction to the Bible for teenagers.

SIDELIGHTS: Elliot had links with the stage, including being honorary chaplain of Actors Church Union, 1916-27, and appearing with professionals in Shakespearean performances. His register of lectures, sermons, and addresses shows, 18,430 entries, covering churches and universities in many lands.

(Died December 27, 1967)

* * *

ELLIOTT, William M(arion), Jr. 1903-

PERSONAL: Born March 18, 1903, in Charlestown, Ind.; son of William M. and Charlotte (Crump) Elliott; married Helen Hargis, May 4, 1928; children: Joe M., Carol (Mrs. Edward C. Kirby), Jeannette (Mrs. James D. Logan). *Education:* Park College, B.A., 1925; Presbyterian Theological Seminary, Louisville, Ky., B.D., 1928; University of Edinburgh, Ph.D., 1937. *Home:* 6916 Hunters Glen Rd., Dallas, Tex. 75205. *Office:* Highland Park Presbyterian Church, 3821 University, Dallas, Tex. 75205.

CAREER: Presbyterian Seminary, Louisville, Ky., instructor in homiletics and church history, 1929-30; ordained to ministry of Presbyterian Church, 1930; pastor of churches in Knoxville, Tenn., 1930-35, in Atlanta, Ga., 1935-44; Highland Park Presbyterian Church, Dallas, Tex., pastor, 1944—. Presbyterian Church in United States,

chairman of Board of World Missions, 1954-57, moderator of general assembly, 1957-58. Member of board, Austin College. *Member:* Rotary Club.

WRITINGS: Coming to Terms with Life, John Knox, 1944; *For the Living of These Days,* John Knox, 1946; *Lift High That Banner!,* John Knox, 1950; *Two Sons,* John Knox, 1955; *Power to Master Life: The Message of Philippians for Today,* Abingdon, 1964; *The Cure for Anxiety,* John Knox, 1964.

* * *

ELLIS, Charles Howard 1895-

PERSONAL: Born February 13, 1895, in Sydney, Australia; son of William Edward (an artist) and Lilian (Hobday) Ellis; married Barbara Mary Burgess-Smith, 1933 (marriage dissolved, 1947); married Alexandra Surtees Wood, 1954; children: (first marriage) Olick C., Ann Veronica Ellis Salway. *Education:* Studied at Melbourne Business College, 1909-11, University of Melbourne, 1912-13, St. Edmund Hall, Oxford, 1914-15, 1920-21, and at Sorbonne, University of Paris, 1921. *Politics:* Independent. *Religion:* Christian. *Address:* c/o Travellers' Club, Pall Mall, London S.W. 1, England.

CAREER: British Army, served in France, Italy, Egypt, India, Iran, and South Russia, 1914-18, in Afghan War, 1919, in Caucasus and Black Sea, 1919-20; British Foreign Service, consular and embassy posts in Germany, Far East, and United States, 1921-39; British Army, colonel on military missions in United States, Canada, and Far East, 1939-45; British Foreign Service, consular and embassy posts, mainly in Far East, 1946-53; retired, 1953. Former press correspondent for League of Nations Secretariat. *Member:* Royal Central Asian Society; Travellers' Club and Royal Automobile Club (both London). *Awards, honors:* Order of British Empire (military), 1919; Commander of Order of British Empire (military), 1941; Legion of Merit (United States), 1946; Companion of Order of St. Michael and St. George, 1953; Territorial Decoration, 1953.

WRITINGS: The Origin, Structure and Working of the League of Nations, Allen & Unwin, 1928; *The British "Intervention" in Transcaspia,* University of California Press, 1963 (published in England as *The Transcaspian Episode,* Hutchinson, 1963); *The Expansion of Russia,* Ilmgau Verlag, 1964; *The New Left in Britain,* Common Cause Publications, 1968. Contributor of articles to newspapers and to *Journal of Royal Central Asian Society.*

SIDELIGHTS: Ellis has traveled on all the continents. He speaks and writes Russian, German, and French.

* * *

ELLIS, Richard White Bernard 1902-

PERSONAL: Born August 25, 1902, in Leicester, England; son of Bernard and Isabel (Evans) Ellis; married Audrey Russell, January 18, 1941; children: Stephen, Tessa Mary. *Education:* King's College, Cambridge, B.A., 1923, M.A., M.B., and B.Ch., 1927, M.D., 1930. *Religion:* Quaker. *Home:* Glebe House, Hawridge, Berkhamsted, England.

CAREER: Guy's Hospital, London, England, physician for children's diseases, 1937-46; University of Edinburgh, Edinburgh, Scotland, professor of child life and health, 1946-64, professor emeritus, 1964—. Blackadder Lecturer, Canadian Medical Association, 1952; Blackfan Lecturer, Harvard University, 1957. *Military service:* Royal Air

Force, 1940-45; served in North Africa, Italy, and Belgium; became wing commander; received Order of the British Empire (military). *Member:* Royal College of Physicians (London and Edinburgh; fellow), Royal Society of Edinburgh (fellow), British Pediatric Association (president, 1965-66), Scottish Pediatric Society (president, 1962-64), American Academy of Pediatrics (honorary fellow); honorary member of pediatric societies in America, Canada, Turkey, and Paris.

WRITINGS: (Editor) *Child Health and Development*, Churchill, 1949, 4th edition, Grune, 1966; *Disease in Infancy and Childhood*, E. & S. Livingston, 1951, 7th edition, Williams & Wilkins, 1973; *Health in Childhood*, Penguin, 1960. Contributor to *Chambers's Encyclopaedia*, *Encyclopaedia of Medical Practice*, and professional journals.

* * *

ELLISON, Gerald Alexander 1910-

PERSONAL: Born August 19, 1910, in Windsor, England; son of John Henry and Dorothy (Crum) Ellison; married Jane Elizabeth Gibbon, 1947; children: Sara, Elizabeth, Jonathan. *Education:* New College, Oxford, B.A., 1932, Diploma in Theology, 1934, M.A., 1936; D.D. (Lambeth), 1955. *Home:* London House, 19 Cowley St., London SW1P 3LZ, England.

CAREER: Clergyman, Church of England. Assistant curate, Sherborne Abbey, Sherborne, 1935-37; domestic chaplain to Bishop of Winchester, 1937-39, to Archbishop of York, 1943-46; vicar of St. Mark's, Portsea, 1946-50; Bishop of Willesden, 1950-55; Bishop of Chester, 1955-73; Bishop of London, 1973—. *Military service:* Royal Naval Volunteer Reserve, chaplain, 1940-43; mentioned in dispatches. *Member:* Army and Navy Club, Leander Club.

WRITINGS: The Churchman's Duty, Hodder & Stoughton, 1957; *The Anglican Communion*, Seabury, 1960.

AVOCATIONAL INTERESTS: Rowing and walking.

* * *

ELMSLIE, William Alexander Leslie 1885-1965

PERSONAL: Born March 6, 1885, in London, England; son of W. Gray (a clergyman and professor of theology) and Kate (Ross) Elmslie; married Edith Clara Shufflebotham (died, 1935). *Education:* Christ's College, Cambridge, M.A., 1909; Westminster College, Cambridge, England, theological study, 1909-12. *Home:* 8 Aubrey Walk, Kensington, London W. 8, England.

CAREER: Presbyterian minister. Christ's College, Cambridge University, Cambridge, England, fellow, 1911-16; St. John's Presbyterian Church, Kensington, London, England, minister, 1917-22; Cambridge University, Westminster College, Cambridge, England, professor of Old Testament theology, 1922-54, principal, 1935-54, professor emeritus, 1954-65. *Awards, honors:* M.A. and D.D., Cambridge University, 1948; D.D., University of Aberdeen and University of Edinburgh.

WRITINGS: (Editor and translator) *The Mishnah on Idolatry* (text and studies), Cambridge University Press, 1911, Kraus Reprint, 1967; *Chronicles*, Cambridge University Press, 1911; *Chronicles*, Cambridge University Press, 1916; *Jewish Proverbs*, J. Clarke, 1917; *Five Great Subjects* (broadcast addresses), S.C.M. Press, 1943; *How Came Our Faith?*, Cambridge University Press, 1948, Abingdon, 1964; *Chronicles* (volume in *Interpreter's Bible*), Abingdon, 1952.

WORK IN PROGRESS: A Search for Truth.

(Died November 15, 1965)

* * *

ELVIN, (Herbert) Lionel 1905-

PERSONAL: Born August 7, 1905, in Buckhurst Hill, Essex, England; son of Herbert Henry and Mary Jane (Hill) Elvin; married Mona Bedortha Dutton (an educational psychologist), April 3, 1934; children: John Mark Dutton. *Education:* Cambridge University, B.A., 1928, M.A., 1931; Yale University, graduate study, 1928-30. *Politics:* Labour. *Home:* Dundridge Cottage, St. Leonards, near Tring, Hertfordshire, England. *Office:* Institute of Education, University of London, Malet St., London W.C. 1, England.

CAREER: Cambridge University, Trinity Hall, Cambridge, England, fellow, 1930-45; Oxford University, Ruskin Hall, Oxford, England, principal, 1945-50; UNESCO, Paris, France, director of department of education, 1950-56; University of London, Institute of Education, London, England, professor of education in tropical areas, 1956-58, director, 1958—. Temporary civil servant with Air Ministry, 1940-42, Ministry of Information, 1944-45. Consultant to Organization for Economic Cooperation and Development and to UNESCO International Institute of Educational Planning; member of British government committees for education.

WRITINGS: Man of America, Pelican, 1941; *An Introduction to the Study of Poetry*, Sylvan Press, 1949; *Education and Contemporary Society*, C. A. Watts, 1965. Contributor to education journals.

* * *

ELWOOD, Muriel 1902-

PERSONAL: Born April 11, 1902, in London, England; came to United States in 1927, naturalized in 1946; daughter of Arthur William and Gertrude (Porter) Elwood. *Education:* Attended Clarks College, London, 1918-20. *Religion:* Protestant. *Home:* Ojai, Calif. 93023.

CAREER: Secretary prior to 1934; writer, 1934—.

WRITINGS: Pauline Frederick: On and Off the Stage, A. Kroch, 1939; *So Much as Beauty Does*, Liveright, 1941; *Heritage of the River: An Historical Novel of Early Montreal*, Scribner, 1945; *Deeper the Heritage*, Scribner, 1946; *Towards the Sunset*, Scribner, 1947; *Against the Tide*, Bobbs-Merrill, 1950; *Web of Destiny*, Bobbs-Merrill, 1951; *The Deluge*, Bobbs-Merrill, 1959; *The Bigamous Duchess: A Romantic Biography of Elizabeth Chudleigh, Duchess of Kingston*, Bobbs-Merrill, 1960; *Dorothea*, Bobbs-Merrill, 1962.

* * *

EMERSON, Caroline D. 1891-1973

PERSONAL: Born March 14, 1891, in Amherst, Mass.; daughter of Benjamin Kendall (a geologist) and Mary Annette (Hopkins) Emerson. *Education:* Columbia University, B.S., 1930. *Home:* R.F.D. 2, Southbridge, Mass.

CAREER: Brearley School, New York, N.Y., elementary teacher, 1918-35; Spence School, New York, N.Y., elementary director, 1935-49; writer for children. *Member:* Pen and Brush Club (New York).

WRITINGS: A Merry-go-round of Modern Tales, Dutton, 1927; *A Hat-tub Tale: or On the Shores of the Bay of Fundy*, Dutton, 1928; *Mr. Nip and Mr. Tuck*, Dutton,

1930; *Old New York for Young New Yorkers*, Dutton, 1932; revised edition published as *New York City: Old and New*, 1953; *Father's Big Improvements*, Stokes, 1936; *Indian Hunting Grounds*, Stokes, 1938; *School Days in Disneyville*, Heath, 1939; *Magic Tunnel*, Stokes, 1940, reprinted with new illustrations, Four Winds, 1968; *Mickey Sees the U.S.A.*, Heath, 1944; *The Little Green Car*, Grosset, 1946; *Mr. Nip and Mr. Tuck in the Air*, Dutton, 1946; *Pioneer Children of America*, Heath, 1950, revised edition, 1965; (with Ralph Preston, Elizabeth Penn, and Arthur Schrader) *Four Lands, Four Peoples*, Heath, 1966; *New Amsterdam: Old Holland in the New World*, Gerrard, 1967.

(Died December 19, 1973)

* * *

EMERSON, Laura S(alome) 1907-

PERSONAL: Born August 11, 1907, in Clarence, Iowa; daughter of Waldo R. (a clergyman) and Jennie (Lindsey) Emerson. *Education:* Marion College, A.B. (magna cum laude) and B.S. in Ed., 1930; University of Wisconsin, M.A., 1939; Emerson College, graduate study, 1953. *Home:* 223 East 42nd St., Marion, Ind.

CAREER: Elementary teacher in Charles City, Iowa, 1926-27; junior high school teacher, Lake View, Iowa, 1928-29; high school and junior college teacher in Miltonvale, Kan., 1931-35; Marion College, Marion, Ind., 1935-72, became associate professor of speech; Kingsley College, Melbourne, Australia, member of faculty, 1973—. Delegate to World Sunday School Convention, Mexico City, 1941. *Member:* Speech Association of America, National League of American Pen Women, Delta Kappa Gamma.

WRITINGS: (Editor) *Twenty-Five Inspiring Readings*, Lillenas Publishing, 1952; *Storytelling: The Art and Purpose* (text), Zondervan, 1959; (editor) *Effective Readings for Special Days and Occasions*, Zondervan, 1961. Contributor of articles to church magazines, and of a regular column to *Adult Teachers Quarterly*.

SIDELIGHTS: Miss Emerson made a recording, "Aunt Laura's Storyhour," for Diadem in 1968. *Avocational interests:* Cooking, rose-growing, teaching at youth camps, and travel.

* * *

EMMANUEL, Philip D. 1909-

PERSONAL: Born October 5, 1909, in Epirus, Greece; married Artemis Demetriades, 1955. *Education:* Attended Zosimaia Classical Gymnasium and Teachers School, Jannina, (Greece); University of Athens, diploma, 1935; Columbia University, B.Sc., 1948, M.A., 1949.

CAREER: University of Thessaloniki Experimental School, Thessaloniki, Greece, staff, 1935-36; Hellenic Community Schools, Alexandria, Egypt, director, 1936-46; Greek Archdiocese Institute of St. Basil, Garrison, N.Y., professor of education, 1947-63, dean, 1949-52; Columbia University, New York, N.Y., lecturer on the history and civilization of modern Greece, 1958-62; U.S. Information Agency, Washington, D.C., writer, 1963—. Greek Archdiocese of North and South America, New York, N.Y., director of education, 1956-60, member of board of education and adviser on educational matters. *Member:* American Historical Association, Modern Language Association of America, Hellenic University Club (New York).

WRITINGS: (with George Christos Pappageotes) *Cortina's Modern Greek in 20 Lessons*, Cortina, 1959, 3rd edition, 1967; (with Pappageotes) *Modern Greek in Record Time*, Institute for Language Study, 1961; (with Pappageotes) *Modern Greek in a Nutshell*, Institute for Language Study, 1961; (co-author) *Gems of Modern Greek Literature*, Institute for Language Study, 1962. Also author of "Textbooks for Hellenic Schools in Egypt," Daphotis (Alexandria), 1938-45, and "Program of Study for the Greek-American Schools," Greek Archdiocese (New York), 1958. Contributor to Greek-American periodicals, and to *Collier's Encyclopedia*.

WORK IN PROGRESS: Herodotus, for Twayne.

* * *

ENGLAND, Martha Winburn 1909-

PERSONAL: Born September 14, 1909, in Arkadelphia, Ark.; daughter of Hardy Lathan (a pastor) and Elena (Barnes) Winburn; married Farmer Stanford England, December 28, 1933 (deceased). *Education:* Ouachita Baptist College, B.A., 1930; Radcliffe College, M.A., 1950, Ph.D., 1953. *Politics:* Democrat. *Religion:* Baptist. *Home:* 687 Lexington Ave., New York, N.Y. 10022. *Office:* Department of English, Queens College of the City University of New York, 65-30 Kissena Blvd., Flushing, N.Y. 11367.

CAREER: Smith College, Northampton, Mass., instructor in English, 1953-56; Queens College of the City University of New York, Flushing, N.Y., assistant professor of English, 1956—. Member of national program committee, Girl Scouts of America. *Member:* English Institute (Columbia University), Phi Beta Kappa. *Awards, honors:* Folger Shakespeare Library fellowship, 1954; Distinguished Alumna citation, Ouachita College, 1958; American Association of University Women fellowship, 1963-64.

WRITINGS: (Translator) Andre Gide, *Le Voyage d'Urien*, New Directions, 1952; *Garrick and Stratford*, New York Public Library, 1962; *Garrick's Jubilee*, Ohio State University Press, 1964; *Reba* (opera libretto), Boosey & Hawkes; *The Maletroit Door* (opera libretto), Boosey & Hawkes; (with John Sparrow) *Hymns Unbidden: Donne, Herbert, Blake, Emily Dickinson, and the Hymnographers*, New York Public Library, 1966. Translator, adapter, or writer of ten other opera and oratorio libretti, including "La Cenerentola" for New York City Center, "Aida" for Central City Opera Association, "Christus am Oelberg" for Washington National Cathedral, "L'Enfance du Christ" for Minneapolis Symphony. Writer of album notes for Decca Records, 1962-64. Contributor of articles to *Enciclopedia della Spettaculo, Opera News, Spectrum*, and to library and literary periodicals.

WORK IN PROGRESS: The hymns of Isaac Watts and the Wesleys; Emily Dickinson and Isaac Watts; Puritan hymnodists; explication of William Faulkner.

BIOGRAPHICAL/CRITICAL SOURCES: Times Literary Supplement, May 25, 1967.

* * *

ENGLISH, Ronald (Frederick) 1913-

PERSONAL: Born August 19, 1913, in Grantham, Lincolnshire, England; son of Frederic Charles (a baker) and Martha (Papworth) English; married Gladys Mary Elmer, September 11, 1940. *Home:* 24 Barrowby Rd., Grantham, Lincolnshire, England.

CAREER: General Post Office employee in England for

thirty-five years, working as sorting clerk, telegraphist, and overseer at Grantham, Lincolnshire, and Mansfield, Nottinghamshire; assistant head postmaster at Grantham, 1959—. *Military service:* Royal Corps of Signals, 1942-46; served in France, Holland, and Germany. *Member:* Society of Authors.

WRITINGS: Adventure Cycling, Kaye & Ward, 1959; *Cycling for You,* Lutterworth, 1964. Regular contributor of articles on health to *Bicycle,* 1935-36; columnist, *Cyclist,* 1936; regular contributor on cycling to *Boy's Own Paper,* 1947-67, on travel and topographical articles for motoring press; some twenty short stories in periodicals.

WORK IN PROGRESS: Modern Cycling; Cycling Sport; a book on historic journeys; an adventure book for boys.

AVOCATIONAL INTERESTS: Painting in watercolors, classical music.

* * *

ENSLEY, Francis Gerald 1907-

PERSONAL: Born August 12, 1907, in Chesterville, Ohio; son of Louis Alfred (a clergyman) and Nellie (McConnell) Ensley; married Eunice LeBourveau, July 6, 1935; children: Frederick Louis, Philip Chalfant, Elizabeth, Charlotte. *Education:* Ohio Wesleyan University, A.B., 1927; Boston University, S.T.B., 1931, Ph.D., 1938. *Home:* 31 Meadow Park Ave., Columbus, Ohio 43209. *Office:* Ohio West Area Methodist Church, 395 East Broad St., Columbus, Ohio. 43214.

CAREER: Ordained Methodist minister. Served as minister in Norwood, Mass., 1935-44, and in Columbus, Ohio, 1944-52; Boston University, School of Theology, Boston, Mass., instructor in homiletics, 1938-44, professor of systematic theology, 1944; consecrated bishop of Methodist Church, 1952; assigned to Iowa area, 1952-64, to Ohio West area, 1964—. *Member:* Delta Sigma Rho, Omicron Delta Kappa, Masons. *Awards, honors:* Jacob Sleeper Fellow at University of Berlin, 1931-32.

WRITINGS—All published by Abingdon: *John Wesley, Evangelist,* 1955; *Paul's Letters to Local Churches,* 1956; *The Marks of Christian Education,* 1958; *Persons Can Change,* 1964.

* * *

EPSTEIN, Morris 1921-1973

PERSONAL: Born July 7, 1921, in Newark, N.J.; son of Isaac (a wholesale grocer) and Gittel (Minzter) Epstein; married Shifra R. Herschfus, May 29, 1949; children: Guita Eve, Sherry Lee. *Education:* Yeshiva University, B.A., 1942; Columbia University, M.A., 1944; New York University, Ph.D., 1957. *Home:* 207 West 86th St., New York, N.Y. 10024. *Office:* Jewish Education Committee, 426 West 58th St., New York, N.Y. 10019.

CAREER: Board of Jewish Education, New York, N.Y., managing editor of *World Over* (magazine), 1947-49, editor of *World Over,* 1949-73, director of public relations for the organization, 1958-66, and literary editor of publications; Yeshiva University, Stern College for Women, New York, N.Y., 1955-73, began as assistant professor, became professor of English and chairman of department, 1966. Drama and book critic for radio station WEVD. Writer of books for Jewish young people. *Member:* National Council for Jewish Education, American Jewish Public Relations Society (president), American Association of University Professors, Modern Language Association, Radio Writers

Guild, English Graduates Association (New York University), Yeshiva College Alumni Association (president, 1956-58). *Awards, honors:* Revel Award, Yeshiva College Alumni; Horeb Award, Teachers Institute Alumni of Yeshiva University; American Council of Learned Societies travel grants to Israel, 1961, 1965; Memorial Foundation for Jewish Culture fellowship for research at Oxford University and the British Museum, 1970.

WRITINGS: My Holiday Story Book, Ktav, 1952; *Tell Me about God and Prayer,* Ktav, 1953; *All about Jewish Holidays and Customs,* Ktav, 1958, revised edition, 1970; *A Pictorial Treasury of Holidays,* Ktav, 1959; *A Book of Torah Readings,* Ktav, 1960; *A Picture Parade of Jewish History,* Shengold, 1963; (editor and translator), *Mishle Sendebar: The Hebrew Version of the Seven Sages,* Jewish Publication Society, 1967; (with Ezekiel Schloss) *More World Over Stories,* Bloch, 1968. Also associate editor of the *Samuel K. Mirsky Memorial Volume,* 1970 and contributor to *Encyclopedia Judaica.* Editorial advisory board member of *In Jewish Bookland, Jewish Digest.*

SIDELIGHTS: In August 1972, Epstein presented a paper on his research of the fate of the "lost" ten tribes of Israel at the World Congress of Jewish Studies in Jerusalem.

BIOGRAPHICAL/CRITICAL SOURCES: Jerusalem Post, August 2, 1965.

(Died November 18, 1973)

* * *

ERB, Alta Mae 1891-

PERSONAL: Born February 23, 1891, in Kinzer, Pa.; daughter of Abram and Salome (Denlinger) Eby; married Paul Erb (a Mennonite minister and author), May 26, 1917; children: Winifred (Mrs. Milford Paul), John Delbert. *Education:* Goshen College, A.B., 1912; State University of Iowa, M.A., 1924; other study at University of Kansas, George Peabody College for Teachers. *Politics:* Independent. *Religion:* Mennonite. *Home:* Mennonite Apartments, Scottdale, Pa. 15683.

CAREER: Hesston College, Hesston, Kan., instructor in education, 1912-41; Goshen College, Goshen, Ind., instructor in education, 1941-45; Mennonite Publishing House, Scottdale, Pa., librarian, 1945—.

WRITINGS: Christian Nurture of Children, Herald Press, 1943, 2nd edition, 1955; *Christian Family Living: A Selected Book List,* Herald Press, 1952; (with daughter, Winifred Erb Paul) *Christian Parent's Baby Book,* Herald Press, 1955; *Christian Education in the Home,* Herald Press, 1963.

* * *

ERNST, Margaret Samuels 1894-

PERSONAL: Born December 4, 1894, in Natchez, Miss.; daughter of Emanuel (a merchant) and Helen (Lowenburg) Samuels; married Morris L. Ernst (an attorney and author), March 1, 1923; children: Constance (Mrs. Simon Michael Bessie), Roger, Joan (Mrs. Irving Goldstein). *Education:* Stanton College, student; Wellesley College, B.A., 1916. *Politics:* Democrat. *Home:* 2 Fifth Ave., New York, N.Y. 10011. *Agent:* Curtis Brown Ltd., 60 East 56th St., New York, N.Y. 10022.

CAREER: New Orleans Times-Picayune, New Orleans, La., feature writer, 1918-22; City and Country School, New York, N.Y., librarian and teacher of etymology, 1930-

50. Lexington School for Deaf, member of board. *Member:* Phi Beta Kappa, Wellesley Club of New York.

WRITINGS: (With Adele G. Nathan) *The Iron Horse,* Knopf, 1931, 2nd edition, 1937; (with James Thurber) *In a Word,* Knopf, 1939, 2nd edition, Channel Press, Manhasset, N.Y., 1960; *Words: English Roots and How They Grow,* Knopf, 1939, 3rd revised edition, 1954; *More About Words,* Knopf, 1951.

AVOCATIONAL INTERESTS: Gardening in Nantucket, sailing.

* * *

ESPER, Erwin A(llen) 1895-19(?)

PERSONAL: Born August 14, 1895, in Columbus, Ohio; son of Jacob D. and Minna (Drobisch) Esper; married Ethel M. Cooke, August 27, 1918; children: Hildegard (Mrs. Mircea Enesco). *Education:* Ohio State University, B.A., 1917, M.A., 1920, Ph.D., 1923; University of Vienna, postdoctoral study, 1924. *Address:* P.O. Box 118, Index, Wash. 98256.

CAREER: Ohio State University, Columbus, instructor in psychology, 1920-25; University of Illinois, Urbana, assistant professor of psychology, 1925-27; University of Washington, Seattle, associate professor, 1927-34, professor of psychology, 1934-60, became professor emeritus, 1960. *Member:* American Psychological Association (fellow), American Association for the Advancement of Science (fellow), Linguistic Society of America (founding member), American Association of University Professors.

WRITINGS: A Technique for the Experimental Investigation of Associative Interference in Artificial Linguistic Material (monograph), Linguistic Society of America, 1925, Kraus Reprint, 1966; (contributor) C. Murchison, editor, *A Handbook of Social Psychology,* Clark University Press, 1935; *A History of Psychology,* Saunders, 1964; *Mentalism and Objectivism in Linguistics: The Sources of Leonard Bloomfield's Psychology of Language,* American Elsevier, 1968. Contributor to psychology journals.

WORK IN PROGRESS: A biography of Max Meyer.

(Deceased)

* * *

ESTELLE, Sister Mary 1907-
(Estelle Casalandra)

PERSONAL: Born August 22, 1907, in New Castle, Pa. *Education:* College of St. Mary of the Springs (now Ohio Dominican College), B.A., 1937; Ohio State University, M.A., 1944. *Office:* Ohio Dominican College, Columbus, Ohio 43219.

CAREER: Roman Catholic nun, member of Order of Preachers (Dominican Sisters); teacher of English in various high schools, 1929-40; Ohio Dominican College (formerly College of St. Mary of the Springs), Columbus, professor of English and business education, 1940-45; Albertus Magnus College, New Haven, Conn., professor of English, 1945-47, 1955-65, chairman of the department, 1955-65; Ohio Dominican College, professor of English, 1965—. *Member:* National Council of Teachers of English. *Awards, honors:* Knight's Cross, Order of Merit (Italy), 1968; Amita award for distinguished service, 1969.

WRITINGS: True Devotion to the Blessed Sacrament; or, Devotion to Jesus in all Tabernacles of the World, F. Pustel, 1946; *Wheat and Cockle: The Life of Blessed Margaret of Savoy,* Alba, 1960; (under name Estelle Casalandra) *Nuptials Without Love: The Life of Princess Clotilde of Savoy,* Kenedy, 1963. Contributor of poems to three anthologies and various periodicals; contributor of critical articles to journals.

* * *

ESTES, Rice 1907-

PERSONAL: Born April 27, 1907, in Spartanburg, S.C.; son of Elliott (in insurance business) and Sadie (Smith) Estes; married Eleanor Rosenfeldt (a writer), December 8, 1932; children: Helena. *Education:* University of South Carolina, A.B., 1928; Pratt Institute, B.L.S., 1932; University of Southern California, A.M., 1941; Columbia University, postgraduate study, 1945-47. *Politics:* Independent. *Religion:* Episcopalian. *Home:* 175 Steuben, Brooklyn, N.Y. 11205.

CAREER: Brooklyn College (now Brooklyn College of the City University of New York), Brooklyn, N.Y., reference librarian, 1938-43; Pratt Institute, Brooklyn, N.Y., alumni secretary, 1944, assistant professor of library science, 1944-48; University of Southern California, Los Angeles, assistant librarian, 1948-52; Fairfield (Conn.) Public Library, librarian, 1952-53; George Washington University, Washington, D.C., assistant librarian, 1953-55; Pratt Institute, librarian and secretary, 1955—. *Member:* American Library Association, Special Libraries Association, Association of College and Research Libraries, New York Library Association, New York Library Club, Phi Beta Kappa.

WRITINGS: A Study of Seven Academic Libraries in Brooklyn and Their Cooperative Potential, Council of Higher Education Institutions in New York City, 1963. Book reviewer, *Los Angeles News,* 1949-51.

* * *

EVANS, A(lfred) Alexander 1905-

PERSONAL: Born August 22, 1905, in Bristol, England; son of James Symes (an engineer) and Minnie (Nicholls) Evans; married wife, Irene, July 30, 1933 (a free-lance lecturer); children: Michael Alexander. *Education:* University of Bristol, B.A. (first class honors), 1927, diploma in education (first class honors), 1928, M.A., 1937. *Religion:* Anglican. *Home and office:* 24 Mingle Lane, Stapleford, Cambridge, England.

CAREER: Teacher of English in Portsmouth, England, 1928-38, Middlesex, England, 1938-45, Hampshire, England, 1945-47; His Majesty's Inspector of Schools, Essex, England, 1948; Institute of Education, University of Leeds, Leeds, England, deputy director, 1948-55; College of Education, London, England, principal, 1955-65. Director, London Center for English Studies, Antioch College, 1970-71. President, College of Preceptors. Examiner to Universities of Liverpool and Nottingham. Free-lance lecturer in education and English literature. *Member:* Association of Teachers in Colleges of Education (chairman, 1963; general secretary, 1965-70), Savile Club (London).

WRITINGS: (Contributor) *Teaching Poetry* (symposium), Oxford University Press, 1937; (contributor) *Poetry in Sixth Form,* Macdonald & Co., 1940; (editor) *Poet's Tale* (anthology), University of London Press, 1957; (editor) *Victorian Poetry* (anthology), University of London Press, 1958; (editor) Shakespeare, *Henry IV,* University of London Press, Part 1, 1962, Part 2, 1963; *Contemporary: An Anthology of the Contemporary Poetry of Our Time,*

1940-1964, University of London Press, 1965; (editor) Shakespeare, *A Midsummer Night's Dream,* University of London Press, 1967. Contributor to *Times* (London), *Twentieth Century,* educational journals.

WORK IN PROGRESS: An edition of Shakespeare's *Richard III,* for University of London Press.

AVOCATIONAL INTERESTS: The visual arts.

* * *

EVANS, (Jean) Cherry (Drummond) 1928-

PERSONAL: Born December 17, 1928, in London, England; daughter of John and Violet Margaret Florence (Jardine) Drummond; married Humphrey ap Evans (an author, farmer, and falconer), June 2, 1952; children: Adam Humphrey Drummond, Charlotte Cherry Drummond, Humphrey John Jardine, Amelie Margaret Mary, John Humphrey Hugo, Catherine Star Violetta. *Education:* Guildford Secretarial College, student, 1945-46; University of St. Andrews, M.A., 1951; Cambridge University, graduate student, 1951-52. *Politics:* Conservative. *Religion:* Anglican. *Home and office:* Megginch Castle, Errol, Perthjaice, Perthshire, Scotland.

CAREER: Megginch Estate (agriculture), Perth, Perthshire, Scotland, secretary, 1946-48; *College Magazine,* Dundee, Angus, Scotland, advertising staff, 1949-51. University of St. Andrews archaeological rescue team, member, 1949-51. Scotland's Gardens Scheme, local organizer, 1956-61. Glencarse Junior Unionists, chairman, 1948-52. *Member:* Romantic Novelists Association, P.E.N.

WRITINGS: Love from Belinda, Hodder & Stoughton, 1962; *Lalage in Love,* Hodder & Stoughton, 1962; *Creatures Great and Small,* Hodder & Stoughton, 1968. Contributor of stories, poems, and articles to *Woman's Journal, Honey, Woman and Home, Lady, Scotsman,* newspapers in Scotland. Author of children's stories for British Broadcasting Corp. programs, some recorded for overseas transcript broadcasts.

WORK IN PROGRESS: A family history; a projected book on magic; *Castle of Dreams;* in collaboration with her husband, a biography of her ancestor, General Sir Gordon Drummond.

SIDELIGHTS: Lives in an old castle, basically fourteenth and fifteenth century, but with later exterior additions. "There are forty-two rooms," she writes, "but we don't use all of them." Her first novel was serialized in *Woman's Journal. Avocational interests:* Painting, growing vegetables and flowers, furniture, architecture, dogs, cooking, falconry.

* * *

EVANS, Stanley G(eorge) 1912-1965

PERSONAL: Born January 2, 1912, in London, England; son of Sidney P. and Maude (Thompson) Evans; married Anastasia Nicholson (a school teacher), September 2, 1939; children: two daughters. *Education:* Kings College, London, 1929-30; University of Leeds, B.A., 1933, M.A., 1949; College of the Resurrection, Mirfield, England, theology study; 1933-35. *Politics:* Christian Socialist. *Home:* St. Stephen's Lodge, Hankey Place, London S.E.1, England. *Office:* Southwark Ordination Course, Empire Building, Duke of Hill, London S.E.1, England.

CAREER: Clergyman, Church of England, 1935-65; curate in Shepherd's Bush, in Barnsbury, in Plaistow, and in Port-

land Town, England, 1935-46; Diocese of London, London, England, licensed preacher, 1947-55; Holy Trinity Church, Dalston, London, vicar, 1955-60; Diocese of Southwark, Southwark, London, canon residentiary and chancellor of Southwark Cathedral, 1960-65, director of junior clergy, 1960, director of training, 1961-65. Extramural lecturer, University of Oxford, 1948-55; lecturer in social studies, City Literary Institute. Examining chaplain to Bishop of Southwark, 1959-65. Chaplain, International Circus Clowns Club, 1959. *Military service:* Royal Air Force, officiating chaplain, 1943-46. *Member:* P.E.N.

WRITINGS: The Churches in the U.S.S.R., Cobbett Publishing Co., 1943; *East of Stettin-Trieste,* Fore Publications, 1951; (editor) *Return to Reality: Some Essays on Contemporary Christianity,* Zeno Publishers, 1954; *A Short History of Bulgaria,* Lawrence & Wishart, 1960; (compiler) *The General Communion: As It Is Used in the Church of the Holy Trinity, Dalston,* Holy Trinity with St. Philip, 1960; *The Church in the Back Streets,* Mowbray, 1962; *The Social Hope of the Christian Church,* Hodder & Stoughton, 1965; *In Evening Dress to Calvary: A Few Days in Palestine and Greece,* S.C.M. Press, 1965.

Pamphlets: *How the USSR Is Governed: Soviet Democracy in Practice,* Russia Today Society, 1943; *Religion in the USSR,* Russia Today Society, 1944; *Soviet Churches and the War,* Russia Today Society, 1944; *Christians in the World Struggle,* Council of Clergy and Ministers for Common Ownership, 1944; *Christians and Foreign Affairs,* Society of Socialist Clergy & Ministers, 1946; *Frontier of Dollar Imperialism: The Story of Soviet Armenia,* British Soviet Society, 1947; *The Vatican and the Post-War World,* Religion and the People, 1947; *Soviet Story: The USSR Through Thirty Years,* British Soviet Society, 1948; *Christians and Communists,* Society of Socialist Clergy & Ministers, 1949; *Michael Scott of Africa,* Religion and the People, 1949; *Russia and the Atomic Bomb,* British Soviet Society, 1949; *The Trial of Cardinal Mindszenty: An Eye Witness Account,* Religion and the People, 1949; *The USSR and UNO,* British Soviet Society, 1949; *Christians and the General Election,* Council of Clergy and Ministers for Common Ownership, 1952; *Christians and World Peace,* Society of Socialist Clergy & Ministers, 1952; *Hungary's Churches Today,* Hungarian News & Information Service, 1952; *Joseph Stalin,* Society of Socialist Clergy & Ministers, 1953; *The Russian Church Today,* Zeno Publishers, 1955; *Russia Reviewed,* Zeno Publishers, 1956; *Christian Socialism: A Study Outline and Bibliography,* Christian Socialist Movement, 1962; *The First Tawney Memorial Lecture: Equality,* Christian Socialist Movement, 1964. Contributor of articles to periodicals and learned journals. Editor, *New Central European Observer,* 1950-53.

(Died September 11, 1965)

* * *

EXMAN, Eugene 1900-

PERSONAL: Born July 1, 1900, in Warren County, Ohio; son of Emmet (a farmer) and Mary Etta (Smith) Exman; married Gladys Miller, June 6, 1929; children: Frank (adopted), Wallacc, Judith. *Education:* Denison University, Ph.B., 1922; University of Chicago, A.M., 1925. *Residence:* Barnstable, Mass. 02630. *Office:* 10 East 53rd St., New York, N.Y. 10022.

CAREER: University of Chicago Press, Chicago, Ill., correspondent and salesman, 1925-28; Harper & Row Publishers, Inc. (formerly Harper & Brothers), New York, N.Y., manager of religious book department, 1928-65, director, 1944-65, vice-president, 1955-65. Lecturer on authors, books, and publishers. Trustee, Denison University, 1944; Edgemont School Board, Scarsdale, N.Y., member, 1947-51, president, 1949-51; chairman of the board of trustees, Wainwright House, 1954; Sturgis Library, trustee, 1967-73, president, 1969-73. *Member:* American Bible Society (board, 1944), Century Association (New York), *Awards, honors:* D.R.E., Middlebury College, 1952.

WRITINGS: (With Erica Anderson) *The World of Albert Schweitzer*, Harper, 1955; *The Brothers Harper, 1817-1853*, Harper, 1965; (contributor) Chandler B. Grannis, editor, *What Happens in Book Publishing*, Columbia University Press, 1957, 2nd edition, 1967; *The House of Harper*, Harper, 1967. Contributor of articles to periodicals including *Harper's* and *Saturday Review*.

AVOCATIONAL INTERESTS: Reading, painting, and gardening.

* * *

FABIAN, Josephine C(unningham) 1903-

PERSONAL: Born December 6, 1903, in Sheridan, Wyo.; daughter of Joseph Henry and Mary Elizabeth (Landrigan) Cunningham; married Harold P. Fabian (a lawyer and conservationist), February 14, 1938. *Education:* Lincoln (Neb.) School of Business, student, 1921-22; courses at Newspaper Institute of America, Columbia University, University of Chicago, and University of Utah. *Religion:* Roman Catholic. *Home and office:* Belvedere, #415, 29 South State St., Salt Lake City, Utah 84111; (summer) Moose Post Office, Jackson Hole, Wyo. 83001.

CAREER: Waring & Waring (lawyers), Geneva, Neb., secretary, 1922; Fabian & Clendenin (lawyers), Salt Lake City, Utah, secretary, 1924-37. President, Colonel Andrew S. Rowan Reading Room for Blind. *Member:* National League of American Penwomen (chapter vice-president). *Awards, honors:* Fine Arts Institute of Utah first prizes, 1962 and 1963, for *The Jackson's Hole Story* and "The Old Salt Lake Theatre"; honorable mention, Fine Arts Institute of Utah, 1965, for "Carmen Was A Blonde."

WRITINGS: Jackson Hole: How to Discover and Enjoy It, Service Press, 1949, 11th edition, 1966; *Fifty Years of Reading*, Reading Room for Blind, 1958; *The Jackson's Hole Story*, Deseret, 1963. Author of musical plays, "The Old Salt Lake Theatre," "Night Operator," "Carmen Was a Blonde," and "An Affair at Old Saltair." Contributor to magazines and historical periodicals.

WORK IN PROGRESS: A sequel to *The Jackson's Hole Story;* a musical play based on women in the Stock Market.

SIDELIGHTS: The Jackson's Hole Story has been issued in Braille, and will be made into a Talking Book for the blind.

* * *

FAGOTHEY, Austin 1901-

PERSONAL: Born June 23, 1901, in San Francisco, Calif.; son of Joseph A. and Katherine (McDade) Fagothey. *Education:* Gonzaga University, A.B., 1923, M.A., 1924; Weston College, S.T.L., 1932; Gregorian University, Rome, Italy, Ph.D., 1949. *Office:* University of Santa Clara, Santa Clara, Calif. 93153.

CAREER: Roman Catholic priest, member of Society of Jesus (Jesuits). University of Santa Clara, Santa Clara, Calif., instructor, 1932-34, 1935-36, professor of philosophy, 1938—. Alma College, Los Gatos, Calif., instructor in theology, 1936-38. *Member:* American Philosophical Association, American Catholic Philosophical Association, Jesuit Philosophical Association (president, 1953-54), Metaphysical Society of America.

WRITINGS: Right and Reason: Ethics in Theory and Practice, Mosby, 1953, 5th edition, 1972.

* * *

FAINSOD, Merle 1907-1972

PERSONAL: Born May 2, 1907, in McKees Rocks, Pa.; son of Louis and Frieda (Marcus) Fainsod; married Elizabeth Stix (a news writer), April 27, 1933; children: Elizabeth (Mrs. Frederick Alasdair Fitzpayne), Mary (Mrs. Peter Katzenstein). *Education:* Washington University, St. Louis, Mo., A.B., 1928; Harvard University, M.A., 1931, Ph.D., 1932. *Office:* Widener Library, Harvard University, Cambridge, Mass. 02138.

CAREER: Harvard University, Cambridge, Mass., Sheldon traveling fellow, 1932-33, instructor, 1933-38, assistant professor, 1938-44, associate professor, 1944-46, professor of government, 1946-72, Carl H. Pforzheimer University Professor, 1964-72, chairman of department of government, 1946-49, director of Russian Research Center, 1959-64, director of university library, 1964-72. U.S. Office of Price Administration, Washington, D.C., price executive, 1941-42, director of Retail Trade and Services Division, 1942-43. Staff member of President Franklin D. Roosevelt's Committee on Administrative Management, 1936; consultant, Temporary National Economics Committee, 1940. Trustee of East European Fund. *Military service:* U.S. Army, Specialists Reserve, captain, 1943.

MEMBER: American Philosophical Society, American Council of Learned Societies, American Academy of Arts and Sciences, American Political Science Association (former president; member of executive council, 1948-50), Massachusetts Historical Society. *Awards, honors:* Co-winner of Woodrow Wilson Foundation Award, 1953, for *How Russia Is Ruled;* LL.D., Washington University, 1956; Faculty Prize of Harvard University Press, 1958, for *Smolensk Under Soviet Rule.*

WRITINGS: (With A. J. Lien) *American People and Their Government,* Appleton, 1933; *International Socialism and the World War,* Harvard University Press, 1934; (With A. L. Gordon) *Government and the American Economy,* Harvard University Press, 1941; *How Russia Is Ruled,* Harvard University Press, 1953, revised edition, 1963; *Smolensk Under Soviet Rule,* Harvard University Press, 1958 (contributor) Robert A. Goldwin, editor, *The Communist Bloc,* Public Affairs Conference Center, University of Chicago, 1962. Contributor to professional journals. Associate editor of *American Political Science Review,* 1951.

(Died February 10, 1972)

* * *

FALLS, Cyril Bentham 1888-

PERSONAL: Born March 2, 1888, in Dublin, Ireland; son of Sir Charles Fausset (a lawyer) and Claire (Bentham) Falls; married Elizabeth Heath, 1915; children: Anne (Mrs. Peter Harris), Julia (Mrs. Peter Carlyon). *Education:* Attended Bradfield College, Portora Royal School, and the

University of London. *Politics:* Conservative. *Home:* 16 Archery Close, Hyde Park, London W. 2, England. *Agent:* Curtis Brown Ltd., 1 Craven Hill, London W2 3EW, England.

CAREER: Committee of Imperial Defence, London, England, official military historian of World War I, 1923-39; *Times*, London, England, military correspondent, 1939-53; Oxford University, Oxford, England, Chichele Professor of Military History and fellow of All Souls College, 1946-53, professor emeritus, beginning, 1953. *Military service:* British Army, 1914-19; became captain, General Staff; received Croix de Guerre (France), two citations, mentioned in dispatches twice. *Member:* Turf Club (London).

WRITINGS: Rudyard Kipling: A Critical Study, Secker & Warburg, 1915; *The Critic's Armoury* (essays), R. Cobdens-Sanderson, 1924; (compiler) *Military Operations, Macedonia*, H.M.S.O., 1933, Macmillan, 1940; (editor) *War Books: A Critical Guide*, Davies, 1934; *The Birth of Ulster*, Methuen, 1936; *Marshal Foch*, Blackie & Son, 1939.

The Nature of Modern Warfare, Oxford University Press, 1941; *Ordeal by Battle*, Methuen, 1943, Oxford University Press, 1944; *The Man for the Job* (novel), Methuen, 1947; *A Short History of the Second World War*, Methuen, 1948, 3rd edition, Methuen, 1950.

Elizabeth's Irish Wars, Methuen, 1950; *A Hundred Years of War*, Duckworth, 1953; *Mountjoy: Elizabethan General*, Odhams, 1955; *Life of a Regiment: The Gordon Highlanders in the First World War*, University Press, Aberdeen, 1958; *The Great War*, Putnam, 1959 (published in England as *The First World War*, Longmans, Green, 1960).

The Art of War: From the Age of Napoleon to the Present Day, Oxford University Press, 1961; *Armaggedon, 1918*, Lippincott, 1963; (editor) *Great Military Battles*, Macmillan, 1964; *The Battle of Caporetto*, Lippincott, 1966, published in England as *Caporetto 1917*, Weidenfeld & Nicolson.

Also co-author of several volumes of British official history of the First World War, 1917.

WORK IN PROGRESS: The Impact of the War on Europe, a book for Knopf's "Impact Series" on the Civil War in America, edited by Allan Nevins.

SIDELIGHTS: Falls once told *CA*, "My favorite recreation still is watching horse-racing on the flat—I now find steeplechasing too cold. Former pastimes: Shooting, fishing, riding, and lawn tennis. Now, being less mobile and perhaps more sophisticated, reading—history, fiction (but not the most modern), and poetry, with walking and a little gardening my only exercises. Favorite authors are Wordsworth, Byron, Maurice Barries, Kipling."

*   *   *

FANCUTT, Walter 1911-

PERSONAL: Born February 22, 1911, in Blackburn, Lancashire, England; son of James (a baker) and Bertha (Fletcher) Fancutt; married Amy F. M. Hawkins, December 29, 1933. *Education:* Attended All Nations Bible College, 1928-31, and Central School of Arts, London, England, 1957-60. *Politics:* Liberal. *Home:* 4 B St. Boniface Gardens, Ventnor, Isle of Wight, England.

CAREER: Baptist minister in London, England, 1933-45; officiating chaplain to Armed Forces, 1942-50; minister of churches in Andover, Hampshire, England, 1945-52, Isle of Wight, England, 1952-57; Mission to Lepers, London, England, editorial secretary, 1957-69, editorial consultant, 1969— . Member of council, Baptist Union of Great Britain, 1948; president, Southern Baptist Association, 1950. *Member:* Society of Authors, Rotary Club (Mill Hill). *Awards, honors:* National prize, Centre of Religious Journalism, 1942, for patriotic poem.

WRITINGS: The Royal Review: A Poem, Newman Watts, 1942; *The Kingsgate Pocket Poets*, eight volumes, Kingsgate Press, 1943-46; (editor) *Then Came Jesus*, Kingsgate Press, 1944; *From Vision to Advance*, Holmes (Andover), 1950; *The Story of Whitchurch Baptist Church*, Holmes (Andover), 1952; *In This Will I Be Confident: A Little Book of Confident Living for Every Day*, Kingsgate Press, 1957; *Beyond the Bitter Sea*, Mission to Lepers, 1958; (editor) *Escaped as a Bird*, Mission to Lepers, 1962; *Present to Heal*, Mission to Lepers, 1964; *The Mission to Lepers: 90 Years of Leprosy Service, 1874 Despair, 1964 Hope*, Mission to Lepers, 1966; *Daily Remembrance: A Prayer Cycle for the Leprosy Mission*, Mission to Lepers, 1966; *The Imprisoned Splendour*, Mission to Lepers, 1970. Contributor to *Poetry Review*, and to religious journals. Editor, *Without the Camp, Lamplighter*, 1957-70.

WORK IN PROGRESS: The biography of Wellesley C. Bailey, founder of The Mission to Lepers; the history of the Southern Baptist Association.

AVOCATIONAL INTERESTS: Collection of portrait engravings from sixteenth century onwards.

*   *   *

FARJEON, Eleanor 1881-1965 (Chimaera, Tomfool)

PERSONAL: Born February 13, 1881, in London, England; daughter of Benjamin Leopold (a novelist) and Margaret Jane (Jefferson) Farjeon. *Religion:* Catholic (convert, 1951). *Home:* 20 Perrins Walk, London N.W. 3, England. *Agent:* David Higham Associates Ltd., 76 Dean St., London W.1V. 6A.H., England.

CAREER: Writer for seventy-odd years, probably best known for her children's fantasies, verse, and plays. Literally grew up in her father's library, in a London household frequented by the literary and dramatic set of the day ("education, such as it was, also occurred among the books," she said); began to compose verse and stories at seven, was co-librettist of an opera produced by the Royal Academy of Music when she was sixteen, made excursions into other types of writing before finding her metier with *Nursery Rhymes of London Town*, 1916, and *Martin Pippin in the Apple Orchard* (fantastic fiction), 1921; visited her maternal grandfather, the actor Joseph Jefferson, in America for a year following her father's death in 1903, continued writing in London on her return to England in 1904, later lived in Hampstead, and occasionally in Sussex.

MEMBER: P.E.N., Society of Authors. *Awards, honors:* First recipient of International Hans Christian Andersen Award, 1956, for *The Little Bookroom* (the medal is presented biennially by the International Board on Books for Young People, in cooperation with UNESCO, for the best book of fiction for children); Carnegie Medal of Library Association (England), 1956, for the same book; first Regina Medal of Catholic Library Association, 1959 (the award is made annually to an individual whose lifetime dedication to children's literature best exemplifies the words of Walter De La Mare—"only the rarest kind of best in anything can be good enough for the young.").

WRITINGS: Floretta: Opera in Two Acts (based on a story by Heinrich Zschoekke), Henderson & Spaulding, 1899.

The Registry Office: An Original Comic Opera in One Act, Henderson & Spaulding, 1900; *Panworship* (poems), Elkin Matthews, 1908; *Dream-Songs for the Beloved*, Orpheus Press, 1911; *Trees*, Fellowship Books, 1913, Batsford, 1918; *Nursery Rhymes of London Town*, Duckworth, 1916; *All the Way to Alfriston*, Morland Press, 1918; *Singing Games for Children*, Dent, 1918; *Poems and Sonnets*, Blackwell, 1918.

Gypsy and Ginger, Dutton, 1920; *Martin Pippin in the Apple Orchard*, Collins, 1921, Stokes, 1922, Lippincott, 1961; *Songs for Music and Lyrical Poems*, Selwyn & Blount, 1922; *Tunes of a Penny Piper*, Selwyn & Blount, 1922; *The Soul of Kol Nikon*, Stokes, 1923; *All the Year Round* (verse), Collins, 1923; *The Town Child's Alphabet*, Poetry Bookshop (London), 1924; *The Country Child's Alphabet*, Poetry Bookshop, 1924; *Mighty Men*, Book 1, *From Achilles to Julius Caesar*, Basil Blackwell, 1924, Appleton, 1925, Book 2, *From Beowulf to William the Conqueror*, Basil Blackwell, 1924, Appleton, 1925; *Young Folk and Old*, High House Press, 1925; *Tom Cobble*, Basil Blackwell, 1925; *Faithful Jenny Dove, and Other Tales*, Collins, 1925, reissued as *Faithful Jenny Dove, and Other Illusions*, M. Joseph, 1963; *Joan's Door*, Collins, 1926, Stokes, 1927; *Nuts and May, a Medley for Children*, Collins, 1926; *Italian Peepshow and Other Tales*, Stokes, 1926; *Come Christmas*, Collins, 1927, Stokes, 1928; *The Mill of Dreams; or, Jennifer's Tale*, Collins, 1927; *The King's Barn; or, Joan's Tale*, Collins, 1927; *The Wonderful Knight*, Basil Blackwell, 1927; *Young Gerard; or, Joyce's Tale*, Collins, 1927; *Open Winkins; or, Jessica's Tale*, Collins, 1928; *Kaleidoscope*, Collins, 1928, Stokes, 1929, Walck, 1963; *The A.B.C. of the B.B.C.* (verse), Collins, 1928; *An Alphabet of Magic*, Medici Society (London), 1928; *A Bad Day for Martha*, Basil Blackwell, 1928; *Mighty Man from Achilles to Harold*, Basil Blackwell, 1928; *First Chap-Book of Rounds*, Dutton, c.1928; *Second Chap-Book of Rounds*, Dutton, c.1928; *The Perfect Zoo*, McKay, 1929; *A Collection of Poems*, Collins, 1929; *The King's Daughter Cries for the Moon*, Basil Blackwell, 1929; *The Tale of Tom Tiddler*, Collins, 1929, published as *Tale of Tom Tiddler; with Rhymes of London Town*, Stokes, 1930.

Proud Rosalind and the Hart-Royal, Collins, 1930; *King's Barn*, Collins, 1930; *Westwoods*, Basil Blackwell, 1930, Artists and Writers Guild (Poughkeepsie, N.Y.), 1935; *Tales from Chaucer; The Canterbury Tales Done into Prose*, R. Hale, 1930, reissued as *Tales from Chaucer, Re-Told*, Oxford University Press, 1960; *Ladybrook*, Stokes, 1931; *The Old Nurse's Stocking-Basket*, Stokes, 1931, reprinted, University of London Press, 1949; *Perkin the Pedlar*, Faber, 1932, reprinted, Oxford University Press, 1956; *The Fair of St. James*, Stokes, 1932 (published in England as *The Fair of St. James; a Fantasia*, Faber, 1932); *Katy Kruse at the Seaside; or, The Deserted Islanders*, McKay, 1932; *Pannychys*, High House Press, 1933; *Ameliaranne and the Magic Ring*, McKay, 1933; *Over the Garden Wall* (poems for children), Stokes, 1933; *Ameliaranne's Prize Packet*, Harrap, 1933; *Jim at the Corner and Other Stories*, Basil Blackwell, 1934, Walck, 1958; *The Old Sailor's Yarn Box*, Stokes, 1934; *Ameliaranne's Washing Day*, McKay, 1934; *The Clumber Pup*, Basil Blackwell, 1934; *The Children's Bells; a Selection of Poems*, Basil Blackwell, 1934, reprinted, Oxford University Press, 1957, Walck, 1960; *A*

Nursery in the Nineties (autobiographical), Gollancz, 1935, published as *Portrait of a Family*, Stokes, 1936, reprinted, Oxford University Press, 1960; *And I Dance Mine Own Child*, Basil Blackwell, 1935; *Ten Saints*, Oxford University Press, 1936, Walck, 1958; *Jim and the Pirates*, Basil Blackwell, 1936; *Humming Bird* (novel), M. Joseph, 1936, Stokes, 1937; *Paladins in Spain*, Nelson, 1937; *The Wonders of Herodotus*, Nelson, 1937; *Martin Pippin in the Daisy Field*, M. Joseph, 1937, Stokes, 1938, 3rd edition, Lippincott, 1963; *Love Affair*, M. Joseph, 1937, Macmillan, 1949; *Sing For Your Supper* (verse for children), Stokes, 1938; *One Foot in Fairyland*, Stokes, 1938; *Grannie Gray* (children's plays and games; illustrated by Joan Jefferson Farjeon), Dent, 1939, reprinted, Oxford University Press, 1956; *A Sussex Alphabet*, Pear Tree Press, 1939.

Miss Granby's Secret; or, The Bastard of Pinsk, M. Joseph, 1940, Simon & Schuster, 1941; *Brave Old Woman*, M. Joseph, 1941; *Magic Casements*, Allen & Unwin, 1941; *The New Book of Days*, Oxford University Press, 1941, Walck, 1961; *Songs from Punch; Set to Music*, Saville, c.1941; *Cherrystones* (poems for children), M. Joseph, 1942, Lippincott, 1944; *The Fair Venetian*, M. Joseph, 1943; *Golden Coney*, M. Joseph, 1943; *Dark World of Animals*, Sylvan Press, 1945; *A Prayer for Little Things* (verse), Houghton, 1945; *... Ariadne and the Bull*, M. Joseph, 1945; *The Mulberry Bush*, M. Joseph, 1945; *First and Second Love: Sonnets*, M. Joseph, 1947, reprinted, Oxford University Press, 1959; *The Starry Floor* (verses), M. Joseph, 1949.

Mrs. Malone (narrative poem), M. Joseph, 1950, Walck, 1962; *Poems for Children*, Lippincott, 1951; *Silver-Sand and Snow*, M. Joseph, 1951; *The Silver Curlew* (play for children; produced in England, 1948; illustrated by Ernest Shepard), Oxford University Press, 1953, Viking, 1954, acting version, Samuel French, 1953; *The Little Bookroom* (short stories for children), Oxford University Press, 1955; *Elizabeth Myers*, St. Albert's Press, 1957; *Then There Were Three: Being Cherrystones, The Mulberry Bush, The Starry Floor*, M. Joseph, 1958; *Memoirs: Book I* (of a projected 4), *Edward Thomas: The Last Four Years*, Oxford University Press, 1958.

Eleanor Farjeon's Book, edited by Eleanor Graham, Penguin, 1960; (editor with William James Carter Mayne) *The Hamish Hamilton Book of Kings*, Hamish Hamilton, 1964, published as *A Cavalcade of Kings*, Walck, 1965; (editor and author of introduction) Edward Thomas, *The Green Roads: Poems*, Holt, 1965; (editor with Mayne) *A Cavalcade of Queens*, Walck, 1965; *Mr. Garden*, Walck, 1966; *Around the Seasons* (poems), Walck, 1969.

With brother, Herbert Farjeon: (Translator) Carlo Goldoni, *Comedies*, 1922; *Kings and Queens* (in verse), Gollancz, 1932, Dutton, 1933, revised edition, Lippincott, 1953; *Heroes and Heroines* (in verse), Dutton, 1933; *Two Bouquets* (play), Gollancz, 1936; *The Glass Slipper* (play with music; produced, 1944), Wingate, 1946, Viking, 1955; *Two Bouquets* (novel), M. Joseph, 1948; *A Room at the Inn: A Christmas Masque*, Samuel French (London), 1957.

Topical and nonsense poet of *Daily Herald* (London) under pseudonym Tomfool, 1919-32. Contributor to *Time and Tide* under pseudonym Chimaera, and to *Punch* and other periodicals. Two selections of "Nonsense Poems," "Tomfooleries," and "Moonshine" were published by Labour Press, 1920, 1921.

WORK IN PROGRESS: At time of death, planned to write three more volumes of *Memoirs*, dealing in turn with her professional, personal, and religious backgrounds.

SIDELIGHTS: Miss Farjeon has been described as having had a joy for living, which comes through in her poems and stories, still read and enjoyed by children. Since 1949, Oxford University Press has been reprinting at intervals the most popular of Miss Farjeon's children's books—with new illustrations.

BIOGRAPHICAL/CRITICAL SOURCES: Eileen Colwell, *Eleanor Farjeon*, Walck, 1962.†

(Died June 5, 1965)

* * *

FARNSWORTH, Jerry 1895-

PERSONAL: Born December 31, 1895, in Dalton, Ga.; son of Samuel (a merchant) and Lavinia (Pou) Farnsworth; married Helen Sawyer (an artist), August 26, 1924. *Education:* Studied art at Corcoran School, and privately with Charles W. Hawthorne. *Home:* 3482 Flamingo, Sarasota, Fla.

CAREER: Artist, with work represented in permanent collections of Metropolitan Museum of Art, and in twenty museums across the country; exhibitor at shows in New York, Washington, Philadelphia, and other metropolitan centers. University of Illinois, Carnegie visiting professor of art, and artist in residence, 1942-43; Farnsworth School of Art, Truro, Mass., and Sarasota, Fla., director. *Military service:* U.S. Navy, World War I. *Member:* National Academy of Design, Provincetown Art Association, Sarasota Art Association, National Arts Club (New York). *Awards, honors:* Twenty-four awards for painting, including honorable mention, Chicago Art Institute, 1940, purchase prize, Los Angeles Museum, 1945, and Maynard Portrait Prize, National Academy of Design, 1952.

WRITINGS: Painting with Jerry Farnsworth, Watson, 1947; *Learning to Paint in Oil*, Watson, 1954, revised and enlarged edition published as *Portrait and Figure Painting*, 1962.

AVOCATIONAL INTERESTS: Gardening, reading, boating, and sailing.

* * *

FARQUHAR, Francis P(eloubet) 1887-

PERSONAL: Surname is pronounced *Far*-kwar; born December 31, 1887, in Newton, Mass.; son of David Webber (in roofing business) and Grace Thaxter (Peloubet) Farquhar; married Marjory Bridge, December 21, 1934; children: Peter, Suzanne, Roger Peloubet. *Education:* Harvard University, A.B., 1909. *Home:* 2930 Avalon Ave., Berkeley, Calif. 94705.

CAREER: Certified public accountant, with own office and in partnership, San Francisco, Calif., 1922-59; retired, 1959. Varian Associates, Palo Alto, Calif., director, 1948-68. University of California, Davis Extension, lecturer on Sierra Nevada history. California State Board of Accountancy, member, 1951-59, president, 1953-54. *Military service:* U.S. Navy, 1917-19; became lieutenant.

MEMBER: Royal Geographical Society (fellow), American Antiquarian Society, American Alpine Club, Sierra Club (president, 1933-35, 1948-49), California Society of Certified Public Accountants (president, 1942-43), California Historical Society (president, 1960-62), California Academy of Sciences (president, 1950-53; honorary trustee, beginning, 1960), Save-the-Redwoods League, Alpine Club (London), Greek Mountaineering Society (honorary mem-

ber), Appalachian Mountain Club (honorary member), Appalachian Mountain Club (honorary member). *Awards, honors:* John Muir Award for conservation, Sierra Club, 1965; Wagner Memorial Medal, California Historical Society, 1966; L.H.D., University of California, 1967.

WRITINGS: Place Names of the High Sierra, Sierra Club, 1926; (with Aristides E. Phoutrides) *Mount Olympus*, [San Francisco], 1929; (editor) *Up and Down California in 1860-1864: The Journal of William H. Brewer*, Yale University Press, 1930, 3rd edition, 1966; *Yosemite, the Big Trees, and the High Sierra: A Selective Bibliography*, University of California Press, 1948; *History of the Sierra Nevada*, University of California Press, 1965. Author of prefaces and introductions to several other books. Contributor to *Encyclopaedia Britannica* and to journals. Editor, *Sierra Club Bulletin*, 1926-46, and *American Alpine Journal*, 1956-59.

SIDELIGHTS: Farquhar's travels include world trips in 1951 and 1959, a flight over the North Pole as a civilian guest of the U.S. Air Force, extensive travel in Greece (including ascents of Mount Olympus, 1914 and 1951), a photographing safari in East Africa, 1959, travel in Europe, New Zealand, Istanbul, and Baja California. He has climbed in the Canadian Rockies and the Selkirk Mountains.

* * *

FAWCETT, Clara Hallard 1887-

PERSONAL: Born January 10, 1887, in Crewe, England; daughter of Arthur William and Emily Virginia (Mizen) Hallard; married James Waldo Fawcett (a writer), June 4, 1917 (deceased); children: Claire Hallard (deceased). *Politics:* Republican. *Religion:* "Broad" Episcopalian. *Home:* 776 Third Ave. N., St. Petersburg, Fla.

CAREER: Writer about dolls and doll history and former consultant in dollology to Smithsonian Institution. Active in Camp Fire Girls organization almost since its inception; instructor in marionettes and other hobbies at Camp Kiwanee (Camp Fire Girls), Hanson, Mass., 1930-67. *Member:* Dollology Club (Washington, D.C.; president, 1946-47), honorary member of Boston and Detroit dollology clubs. *Awards, honors:* Camp Fire Girls first Wohelo Artist award, 1964.

WRITINGS: Dolls: A Guide for Collectors, Lindquist, 1947; *On Making, Mending and Dressing Dolls*, Lindquist, 1949, new edition, Hobby House Press, 1963; *Paper Dolls: A Guide to Costume*, Lindquist, 1951; *Dolls: A New Guide for Collectors*, Branford, 1964. Also author of *Dolls: Ramblings of a Vagabond Collector*, 1973. Contributor to Grolier's *Book of Knowledge*. Contributor of about one hundred articles on dolls and paper dolls to *Hobbies*; also contributor to *Children's Activities* and other youth magazines.

WORK IN PROGRESS: A book on marionettes.

* * *

FAWCETT, F(rank) Dubrez 1891-1968
(Henri Dupres, Madame E. Farra, Eugene Glen, Griff, Coolidge McCann, Elmer Eliot Saks, Ben Sarto, Simpson Stokes)

PERSONAL: Born November 13, 1891, in Great Driffield, Yorkshire England; son of Frank Burlington and Lydia (Dubrez) Fawcett; married Betty Harwood, June 22, 1923; children: June. *Education:* Attended Hymers College and

Collingwood Private School. *Politics:* Liberal. *Home:* 310 Pickhurst Rise, West Wickham, Kent, England.

CAREER: Started as office boy at Gale & Polden Ltd. (publishers), London, England, 1906-08; newspaper reporter, free-lance journalist, and advertising copywriter, London, 1908-15; Meerloo Publicity Service, London, director, 1918-24; Imperial Advertising and Dorland Advertising, London, chief copywriter, 1924-40; also free-lance writer, 1912-68. *Military service:* British Army, 1915-1918; served in France, wounded in Macedonia. *Member:* National Liberal Club, Press Club (London), Society of Authors.

WRITINGS: Court Ceremonial, Gale & Polden, 1937; *The Wonderful Isle of Ulla-Gapoo*, Modern Fiction, 1946; *Dickens the Dramatist, on Stage, Screen and Radio*, W. H. Allen, 1952, British Book Center, 1953; *Hole in Heaven*, Sidgwick & Jackson, 1954; *The King of All the Seagulls* (monograph), Newnes, 1960; (editor) *Cyclopaedia of Initials and Abbreviations*, Business Publications, 1963.

Under pseudonym Simpson Stokes: *Air-Gods' Parade*, Arthur Barron, 1935; (editor and author of introduction) *Gods and Ghouls of the French Revolution*, Modern Fiction, 1946; (editor and author of introduction) *The Dubious Adventures of Baron Munchausen*, Modern Fiction, 1946; (editor and author of introduction) *Mr. Pepys in Plague and Fire*, Modern Fiction, 1947.

Under pseudonym Henri Dupres: *Loose Love*, Federation Press, 1923; *White Slaves of Two Cities*, Federation Press, 1924; *Shop Soiled*, Federation Press, 1924; *Artists' Wives*, Gramol Publications, 1925; *Fallen Youth*, Gramol Publications, 1925; *Endurance*, Gramol Publications, 1926; *Secret Rendezvous*, Modern Fiction, 1943; *Her Last Love*, Modern Fiction, 1944; *Desperate Love*, Modern Fiction, 1945.

Under pseudonym Ben Sarto, "Miss Otis Series"—all published by Modern Fiction: *Miss Otis Comes to Piccadilly*, 1940, *"Jews" Pellegrini*, 1941, *Miss Otis Throws a Come-Back*, 1941, *Miss Otis Has a Daughter*, 1945, *Miss Otis Goes Up*, 1945; all published by Milestone Publications: *Miss Otis Takes the Rap*, 1953, *Miss Otis Blows Town*, 1953, *Miss Otis Moves In*, 1953, *Miss Otis Plays Eve*, 1953, *Miss Otis Hits Back*, 1953, *Miss Otis Says Yes*, 1953, *Miss Otis Makes a Date*, 1953, *Miss Otis Goes French*, 1953, *Miss Otis Desires*, 1954, *Miss Otis Plays Ball*, 1954.

Under pseudonym Ben Sarto—all published by Modern Fiction: *Bowery Birdie*, 1942, *Duchess of Dope*, 1942, *Chicago Dames*, 1942, *Rebecca of the Snach Racket*, 1943, *Queen of the Crook's Harem*, 1943, *Grand Graft Hotel*, 1945, *City of Sin*, 1946, *Snake Hips*, 1946, *Sidewalk Floozie*, 1946, *Death Rides the Train*, 1949, *Beech on the Boulevard*, 1949, *Floozie Takes Lawman*, 1949, *They Burn for Me*, 1950; all published by Beacon Publishing: *Dames for Hire*, 1953, *Susie Comes to Soho*, 1953, *Dynamite Doll*, 1954, *Bodies Fetch Good Prices*, 1954, *Call Me Shameless*, 1954, *Chain-Gang Queenie*, 1955, *Decoy Babes*, 1956.

Under pseudonym Griff—all published by Craig-Mitchell: *Some Rats Have Two Legs*, 1949, *That Room in Camden Town*, 1949, *Good-Bye Tomorrow*, 1950, *Dance Hall to Opium Dive*, 1951; all published by Modern Fiction: *Back-Alley Blonde*, 1952, *Manhattan Terrors*, 1952, *Hot-Shot Rita*, 1952, *Crooked Coffins*, 1952.

Under pseudonym Eugene Glen: *Romance Ashore*, Modern Fiction, 1948; *Passion Adrift*, Modern Fiction, 1949.

Under pseudonym Coolidge McCann: *Thunder on the Rio Grande*, Brown, Watson, 1955; *Ghost Rangers*, Bear Hudson, 1956; *Bad Man's Burro*, Bear Hudson, 1956.

Under pseudonym Elmer Eliot Saks: *The Case of the Indiana Torturer*, Bear Hudson, 1957.

Under pseudonym Madame E. Farra: *You and Your Stars*, Modern Fiction, 1957.

Writer of brochures for business firms, on topics ranging from vitamins to fishing gear. Contributor of a daily feature series, "Detectographs," and another series, "World's Strangest Stories," to *Evening News* (London). Other articles and more than forty short stories in magazines and newspapers, including *Punch, Blighty, Factor Salesman, Men Only, Passing Show, Everybody's, Sunday Express*, (London), *Illustrated, London Opinion, Guardian*. Former editor, *True Romances, Musico's Club*. Co-editor, *Football Pictorial*. Book reviewer for *History Today, John O'London's*.

WORK IN PROGRESS: The Collector's Book of Cliches; King Stork, a satirical novel; *Live to Be 126; Books About Napoleon*, a major work; reviving paperback character, "Miss Otis," in hardcover editions; the life of Colonel Blood; a three-act stage play, "One Two Six With P.O.F."; three television plays, "The Man Whom God Disobeyed," "My Name is Beechable," "The Nemo."

SIDELIGHTS: Fawcett, who was at first reluctant to supply titles for the numerous paperbacks he had written, later noted that "at one time I was writing at the rate of a book every fortnight, straight on my typewriter without even a read-through till I got the printer's proofs. So, though very big sales resulted, the quality is not high from a literary point of view."

He preferred to write between 4 A.M. and noon. Neither eats nor drinks ("not even a glass of water") until lunch. "If inspiration does not come," he told *CA*, "I sit at the typewriter or scribble on paper anything that comes into my head. [I] never let a day go by (even on vacation) without writing something—from 50 to 1000 words."

Enjoyed research work. Liked to read history, biography, and memoirs, "especially those concerning Napoleonic eras, 1769-1871." He had done amateur acting in Dickensian plays, and had lectured on same. Favorite cities: Paris and Rome. Favorite island: Elba. *Avocational interests:* Chess and travel.

(Died, 1968)

*   *   *

FAY, Gerard (Francis Arthur) 1913-1968

PERSONAL: Born October 13, 1913, in Rochdale, England; son of Francis John (a co-founder of Abbey Theatre, Dublin) and Freda (Curley) Fay; married Alice Mary Bentley, 1935; children: Stephen Francis John, Elizabeth Shelagh. *Home:* 12 Stanford Ct., London S.W.7, England. *Office: Guardian*, 192 Gray's Inn Rd., London W.C.1, England.

CAREER: Oldham Evening Chronicle, Oldham, England, editorial writer, prior to World War II; *Manchester Guardian & Evening News Ltd.*, London and Manchester, England, reporter and reviewer in Manchester, 1939-46, and in London, 1946-54, London editor of *Guardian*, 1954-66, member of board of directors. *Military service:* British Army, South Wales Borderers, World War II; became major.

WRITINGS: The Abbey Theatre: Cradle of Genius, Clonmore & Reynolds, 1958, Macmillan (New York), 1960; *Passenger to London*, Macmillan (New York), 1961; *Fay's Third Book*, Hutchinson, 1964. Contributor to *Encyclopaedia Britannica*, and to *Spectator, Punch, Realities*.

(Died March 15, 1968)

* * *

FEARON, George Edward 1901-

PERSONAL: Born March 3, 1901, in London, England; son of George Margoliouth (a parson) and Marian Fearon; married Barbara Midlen, July 10, 1947; children: Peter Dermot (stepson). *Education:* St. Dunstan's College, London, student, 1913-17. *Politics:* Conservative. *Religion:* Church of England. *Home:* Old Rectory Cottage, Folkington, Polegate, Sussex, England. *Agent:* Curtis Brown Ltd., 1 Craven Hill, London W2 3EW, England. *Office:* William A. Sutton & George Fearon Ltd., 37 Bury St., London S.W.1, England.

CAREER: Royal Canadian Mounted Police, constable, 1919-22; Ford Motor Co., Manchester, England, employee, 1923-26; actor, then theatre manager, 1926-36; Shakespeare Memorial Theatre, Stratford on Avon, England, publicity manager, 1936-39; publicist for various theatres, London, England, 1945—; William A. Sutton & George Fearon Ltd. (public relations), London, England, director, 1955—. *Military service:* Royal Air Force, public relations, 1939-45; became squadron leader. *Member:* Association of London Theatre Press Representatives (founding member; former chairman), Institute of Public Relations, Naval and Military Club.

WRITINGS: (With Ivor Brown) *This Shakespeare Industry: Amazing Monument*, Harper, 1939 (published in England as *Amazing Monument: A Short History of the Shakespeare Industry,* Heinemann, 1939), reissued as *This Shakespeare Industry,* Haskell House, 1970, and as *Amazing Monument,* Kennikat, 1970; (with Brown) *The Shakespeare [and] The Birthplace* (the former by Brown, the latter by Fearon), Edward Fox, 1939; *You Owe Me Five Farthin's: An Adventure with St. Martin-in-the-Fields,* Skeffington & Sons, 1961. Contributor to magazines.

* * *

FECHTER, Alyce Shinn 1909-

PERSONAL: Surname is pronounced *Fek*-ter; born October 11, 1909, in Grafton, Ill.; daughter of Herbert Stanley and Eva Irene (Hubbard) Shinn; married James L. Fechter (an aircraft executive), September 4, 1937. *Education:* Studied at Rawson School of Dance, Whitmer School of Dance, and Clara LaVilla Camp School for Girls.

CAREER: Writer. District chairman, American Cancer Society, 1956-63. *Member:* Sigma Phi Gamma.

WRITINGS: M'Toto, the Adventures of a Baby Elephant, McGraw, 1965. Contributor of short stories and articles to periodicals. International editor, Sigma Phi Gamma, 1931.

WORK IN PROGRESS: Researching life in the 1870's around Fort Colville, Washington Territory; studying African wildlife for further books.

SIDELIGHTS: Alyce Fechter did research on elephants during visit to Kenya, 1960; she had continued correspondence with Africans since.

FEIGL, Herbert 1902-

PERSONAL: Surname is pronounced *Fi*-gl; born December 14, 1902, in Reichenberg, Austria (now Czechoslovakia); came to United States in 1930, naturalized in 1937; son of Otto (an industrialist) and Camilla (Beck) Feigl; married Maria Kasper (a school psychologist), June 30, 1931; children: Eric Otto. *Education:* University of Munich, student, 1921-22; University of Vienna, Ph.D., 1927. *Religion:* Humanist. *Office:* Department of Philosophy, University of Minnesota, Minneapolis, Minn.

CAREER: People's Institute, Vienna, Austria, lecturer, 1927-30; University of Iowa, Iowa City, lecturer, 1931-32, assistant professor, 1932-38, associate professor of philosophy, 1938-40; University of Minnesota, Minneapolis, professor of philosophy, beginning 1940, Regents Professor, beginning 1967, professor emeritus, 1971—, director of Minnesota Center for Philosophy of Science, 1953—. Visiting professor at University of Puerto Rico, 1957; Carnegie visiting professor at University of Hawaii, 1958; Fulbright professor at Australian universities, 1965. *Member:* Philosophy of Science Association (member of governing board, 1961-63), American Philosophical Association (president, 1962-63), American Association for the Advancement of Science (fellow; vice-president, 1959), American Academy of Arts and Sciences, Mind Association (England), American Humanist Association, Minnesota State Philosophical Society (president, 1961-62). *Awards, honors:* Rockefeller Foundation fellow, 1930-31, 1940; Guggenheim fellow, 1947.

WRITINGS: (With Wilfrid Sellars) *Readings in Philosophical Analysis,* Appleton, 1949; (with May Brodbeck) *Readings in the Philosophy of Science,* Appleton, 1953; (co-editor) *Minnesota Studies in the Philosophy of Science,* University of Minnesota Press, Volume I (with Michael Scriven), 1956, Volume II (with Scriven and Grover Maxwell), 1958, Volume III (with Maxwell), 1962; (editor with Maxwell) *Current Issues in the Philosophy of Science,* Holt, 1961; *The "Mental" and the "Physical,"* University of Minnesota Press, 1967. Contributor to philosophy and science periodicals. Member of advisory board, *International Encyclopedia of Unified Science*; associate editor, *Philosophical Studies* (journal), 1949—.

WORK IN PROGRESS: Research in epistemology and the philosophy of science.

SIDELIGHTS: Feigl has traveled often to Europe. He also has visited India, Australia, Brazil, and Mexico. *Avocational interests:* Music.

* * *

FEIS, Herbert 1893-1972

PERSONAL: Surname rhymes with "size"; born June 7, 1893, in New York, N.Y.; son of Louis J. (a businessman) and Louise (Waterman) Feis; married Ruth Stanley-Brown, March 25, 1922; children: Mary Felicia Feis Gomes. *Education:* Harvard University, A.B., 1916, Ph.D., 1921. *Residence:* York, Me. *Agent:* Gerard McCauley, 159 West 53rd St., New York, N.Y. 10019.

CAREER: University of Kansas, Lawrence, associate professor of economics, 1922-25; University of Cincinnati, Cincinnati, Ohio, head of department of economics, 1926-29; Council on Foreign Relations, New York, N.Y., staff member, 1930-31; U.S. Government, Washington D.C., economic adviser to Department of State, 1931-37, adviser on international economic affairs, Department of State,

1937-43, special consultant to Secretary of War, 1944-46, member of policy planning staff, Department of State, 1950-51; Institute for Advanced Study, Princeton, N.J., member, 1948-50, at other intervals, 1951-63. Visiting professor at universities, including Harvard University, 1957, 1965-66, Columbia University, 1961. Special consultant to presidents of International Telephone & Telegraph and Anaconda Copper Co., at intervals, 1921-31; adviser on American industrial relations at International Labor Office, League of Nations, at intervals, 1922-27; adviser to U.S. delegation at World Economic and Monetary Conference, London, 1933, to Inter-American Conference for the Maintenance of Peace, Buenos Aires, 1936, and conferences of American States in Lima, 1938, and Panama, 1939. Consultant to National Broadcasting Co., 1964. *Military service:* U.S. Naval Reserve, World War I; became lieutenant junior grade. *Awards, honors:* Guggenheim fellow, 1926; American Library Association Liberty and Justice Award, 1958, for *Churchill-Roosevelt-Stalin;* Pulitzer Prize in history, 1960, for *Between War and Peace;* D.Litt., Princeton University, 1960.

WRITINGS: The Settlement of Wage Disputes, Macmillan, 1921; (editor and author of introduction) *A Collection of Decisions Presenting Principles of Wage Settlement,* H. W. Wilson, 1924; *International Finance and Commerce* (booklet), League of Nations Non-Partisan Association, 1928; *Labor Relations: A Study Made in the Proctor & Gamble Company,* Adelphi Co., 1928; *Research Activities of the League of Nations,* Old Lyme Press, 1929; *Europe, the World's Banker, 1870-1914: An Account of the European Foreign Investment and the Connection of World Finance with Diplomacy Before the War,* Yale University Press, 1930, Augustus M. Kelley, 1961, *The International Trade of Manchuria,* Carnegie Endowment for International Peace, 1931.

The Changing Pattern of International Economic Affairs, Harper, 1940; *Economics and Peace,* Foreign Policy Association, 1944; *Petroleum and American Foreign Policy,* Stanford University, Food Research Institute, 1944; *The Sinews of Peace,* Harper, 1944; *American Trade Policy and Position: An Outline of Principles,* American Enterprise Association, 1945; *Seen from E.A.: Three International Episodes,* Knopf, 1947, reissued as *Three International Episodes Seen from E.A.,* Norton, 1966; *Franco and the Nations at War,* Knopf, 1948; *The Diplomacy of the Dollar: First Era, 1919-1932,* Johns Hopkins Press, 1950; *Diplomatic History of World War II,* Princeton University Press, Volume I: *The Road to Pearl Harbor: The Coming of War Between the United States and Japan,* 1950, Volume II: *The China Tangle: The American Effort in China from Pearl Harbor to the Marshall Mission,* 1953, Volume III: *Churchill, Roosevelt, Stalin: The War They Waged and the Peace They Sought,* 1957, 2nd edition, 1967, Volume IV: *Between War and Peace: The Potsdam Conference,* 1960, Volume V: *Japan Subdued: The Atomic Bomb and the End of the War in the Pacific,* 1961, revised edition published as *The Atomic Bomb and the End of World War II,* 1966.

Foreign Aid and Foreign Policy, St. Martin's, 1964; *1933: Characters in Crisis,* Little, Brown, 1966; *Contest Over Japan: The Soviet Bid for Power in the Far East,* Norton, 1967; (contributor) Francis L. Lowenheim, editor, *The Historian and the Diplomat: The Role of History and Historians in American Foreign Policy,* Harper, 1967; *The Birth of Israel: The Tousled Diplomatic Bed,* Norton, 1969;

From Trust to Terror: The Onset of the Cold War, Norton, 1970.

Contributor of articles to *Foreign Affairs, Atlantic, New York Times Magazine, Yale Review,* and other periodicals.

WORK IN PROGRESS: Reminiscences.

BIOGRAPHICAL/CRITICAL SOURCES: New York Review of Books, June 15, 1967; *Nation,* November 27, 1967; *Library Journal,* September 1, 1970; *Best Sellers,* December 15, 1970; *New York Times,* December 26, 1970, March 3, 1972; *New Leader,* December 28, 1970; *National Review,* February 9, 1971; *Newsweek,* March 13, 1972; *Time,* March 13, 1972; *Publishers Weekly,* March 20, 1972.

(Died March 2, 1972)

* * *

FELDMAN, George J(ay) 1904-

PERSONAL: Born November 6, 1904, in Boston, Mass.; son of Harry and Bessie (Alpert) Feldman; married Marion Schulman, May 29, 1948; children: George Jay, Jr., Margo. *Education:* Boston University, LL.B., 1925. *Politics:* Democrat. *Religion:* Jewish. *Home:* 1010 Fifth Ave., New York, N.Y. 10028.

CAREER: Admitted to bars of Massachusetts, 1926, District of Columbia, 1936, and New York, 1948; office of U.S. Senator David I. Walsh, Washington, D.C., secretary, 1926-30; Federal Trade Commission, Washington, D.C., attorney, 1930-32; Boston University, Boston, Mass., lecturer in trade regulation and federal anti-trust law, concurrent with private practice, 1932-34; National Recovery Administration, Washington, D.C., litigation counsel, 1934-35; Feldman, Kittelle, Campbell, and Ewing (attorneys-at-law), Washington, D.C., lawyer, 1935-48; private practice of law, 1935-65; U.S. Department of State, Ambassador to Malta, 1965-67, Ambassador to Luxembourg, 1967-69, consultant to assistant secretary for European affairs, 1970. Counsel, vice-president, and member of board of directors, Mastan Co., Inc., New York, N.Y., 1950—; member of executive committee and board of directors, Columbia Mills, Syracuse, N.Y., 1954—; incorporator and director, Communications Satellite Corp., Washington, D.C., 1962-65; director, Atlantic Council of the United States, Inc., Lecturer, Practicing Law Institute, New York, N.Y., 1947-50. Has served as counsel or legal consultant to Democratic Platform Drafting Committee, 1952, U.S. Department of State, 1959-60, and U.S. delegation to United Nations, 1959-60; director and chief counsel, Select Committee on Astronautics and Outer Space, U.S. House of Representatives, 1958-59; member of U.S. NATO Citizens Committee, 1961-62; finance chairman, U.S. Committee for Refugees, 1962; member of advisory committee, Select Committee on Government Research, 1963-64. President of council, Holy Cross College; member of board of fellows, Boston University. *Military service:* U.S. Army Air Forces, 1942-45; became major. *Member:* American Bar Association, American Legion, American Foreign Service Association, National Democratic Club, New York State Bar Association, City Athletic Club (New York, N.Y.), Sands Point Golf Club. *Awards, honors:* LL.D. from Holy Cross College, 1967, and from Boston University, 1968.

WRITINGS: (Co-author) *Does Trade Need Anti-Trust Laws?,* Long & Smith, 1932; *Anti-Trust Laws and Unfair Competition,* U.S. Government, 1935; (co-author) *Business Under the New Price Laws,* Prentice-Hall, 1937; (co-author) *Advertising and Promotional Allowances*, Bureau of National Affairs, 1948; (with Frank Gibney) *The Coming Struggle for Space*, New American Library, 1964. Contributor of articles to journals.

*   *   *

FELTER, Emma K. (Schroeder) 1896-

PERSONAL: Born April 17, 1896, in New York, N.Y.; daughter of John and Bertha (Wittenborg) Schroeder; married Harold D. Felter, 1929. *Education:* New York Teachers Training School, diploma, 1916; City College (now City College of the City University of New York), B.S., 1932; Columbia University, M.A., 1934. *Home:* Smith Rd., Pleasant Valley, N.Y.

CAREER: Teacher in New York, N.Y., and Pasadena, Calif., 1916-39; Walton High School, New York, N.Y., teacher of business education and chairman of department, 1939-64. Lecturer on teaching methods at University of Tennessee, University of Maryland, City College (now City College of the City University of New York), New York University, and Hunter College. Pleasant Valley Township Health Committee, member. *Member:* Protestant Teachers Association, National Retired Teachers Association, Association of Retired Teachers of New York, Commercial Education Association of New York (former president; member of advisory council; life member), Dutchess County Art Association, Dutchess County Historical Society. *Awards, honors:* Business Educator of the Year award, Commercial Education Association of New York, 1962.

WRITINGS: Personal and Clerical Efficiency, Basic, Gregg Publishing Division, McGraw, 1949; *Personal and Clerical Efficiency, Advanced*, Gregg Publishing Division, McGraw, 1950; (co-author) *Basic Clerical Practice*, Gregg Publishing Division, McGraw, 1959. Contributor to most commercial education magazines.

AVOCATIONAL INTERESTS: Travel, the theater, literature, music, oil painting.

*   *   *

FENNER, Kay Toy

PERSONAL: Born in Utica, N.Y.; daughter of W. Henry (a coal merchant) and Elizabeth (McIntyre) Toy; married C. Lawrence Fenner (vice-president of wholesale building materials firm); children: Constance Fay (Mrs. John M. Keough), Lawrence Brian. *Education:* Attended Elmira College; Columbia University, B.Litt. *Politics:* Republican. *Religion:* Roman Catholic. *Home:* 14 Campus View Dr., Loudonville, N.Y. 12211.

MEMBER: Elmira College Club (Albany, N.Y.), Theta Sigma Phi (former chapter president).

WRITINGS: American Catholic Etiquette, Newman, 1961. Contributor to magazines.

WORK IN PROGRESS: A book tentatively titled, *Faces in Shadow*.

SIDELIGHTS: Mrs. Fenner began writing "to keep my mind off my son serving in front lines in Korean War." She admits to being "a bug on local history, preservation of old buildings, *correct* use of English language and simple courtesy. Scared to death by current rash of meaningless violence; bored with fad to explain everything psychologically. And who decided that adjectives and adverbs are outlawed from our language and that symbolism is ALL?"

FENSCH, Edwin A. 1903-

PERSONAL: Born August 16, 1903, in Mansfield, Ohio; son of Charles F. and Rosalie A. (Lander) Fensch; married Heloise Moore (deceased); married Flossie Hoover, 1966; children: (first marriage) Thomas C., Timothy M. *Education:* Ashland College, A.B., 1933; Ohio State University, M.A., 1938, Ph.D., 1942. *Religion:* United Church of Christ. *Home:* 474 Parkview St., Mansfield, Ohio 44903. *Office:* Y.M.C.A. Bldg., 455 Park Ave. W., Mansfield, Ohio 44903.

CAREER: Journalist before entering education field; Ashland College, Ashland, Ohio, faculty member, 1945-73, became professor of psychology, 1968; Young Men's Christian Association, child psychologist, 1973—. Assistant superintendent, Mansfield (Ohio) Board of Education, 1958-68. Member of board of trustees, Young Men's Christian Association, 1961-65. *Member:* American Association of School Administrators, Ohio Psychological Association, Ohio School Psychologists, Ohio Education Association, Ohio Association of School Administrators.

WRITINGS: (With Robert E. Wilson) *The Superintendency Team*, C. E. Merrill, 1965. Contributor of articles to journals in his field.

*   *   *

FENTON, John C(harles) 1921-

PERSONAL: Born June 5, 1921, in Liverpool, England; son of Cornelius O'Connor (an Anglican priest) and Claudine (Harris) Fenton; married Linda Winifred Brandham; children: Thomas, Elizabeth, James, Charlotte, Katherine, Mark. *Education:* Attended St. Edward's School, Oxford, England; Queen's College, Oxford, B.A., 1943, M.A., 1947; Lincoln Theological College, B.D., 1953. *Politics:* Socialist. *Office:* St. Chad's College, Durham, England.

CAREER: Anglican priest; assistant curate in Wigan, England, 1944-47; Lincoln Theological College, Lincolnshire, England, chaplain, 1947-51, sub-warden, 1951-54; vicar in Wentworth, Yorkshire, England, 1954-58; Lichfield Theological College, Lichfield, Staffordshire, England, principal, and lecturer on New Testament, 1958-65; St. Chad's College, Durham, England, principal, 1965—. Part-time lecturer in theology, University of Durham, 1965—.

WRITINGS: Preaching the Cross: The Passion According to St. Mark, S.P.C.K., 1958; *Crucified with Christ: Three Meditations for Holy Week*, S.P.C.K., 1961; *The Passion According to St. John*, S.P.C.K., 1961; *The Gospel of St. Matthew*, Penguin, 1963; *The Gospel According to John in the Revised Standard Version*, Clarendon Press, 1970; *What Was Jesus' Message?*, S.P.C.K., 1971.

*   *   *

FERGUSON, Howard 1908-

PERSONAL: Born October 21, 1908, in Belfast, Northern Ireland; son of Stanley (a banker) and Frances (Carr) Ferguson. *Education:* Educated in London, England, at Westminster School, 1922-24, and Royal College of Music, 1924-28; also studied piano privately. *Home:* 106 Wildwood Rd., London N.W.11, England.

CAREER: Royal Academy of Music, London, England, professor of composition, 1948-63. Composer, with first public performance of a work, "Two Ballads for Baritone and Orchestra," at Gloucester Festival, 1934. *Member:* International Musicological Society, Composers Guild. *Awards, honors:* D. Mus., Queen's University of Belfast.

WRITINGS—Editor: (With R. O. Morris) *Preparatory Exercises in Score-Reading*, Oxford University Press, 1931; Bach, *Fuga Rucercata, Arranged for String Sextet or String Orchestra*, Boosey & Hawkes, 1939; Bach, *Lute Suite in C Minor, Arranged for Keyboard*, Schoot & Co., 1950; Bach, *Fugue in G Minor, for Violin and Continuo*, Oxford University Press, 1951; Mozart, *Sonata in C, for Piano Duet*, Oxford University Press, 1952; Bach, *Sonata in E Minor, for Violin and Continuo*, Schott & Co., 1954; William Tisdall, *Complete Keyboard Works*, Stainer & Bell, 1958; Purcell, *Sonata in G Minor, for Violin and Continuo*, Hunrichsen, 1958; *Style and Interpretation*, six volumes, Oxford University Press, 1963-71; Purcell, *Complete Harpsichord Works*, two volumes, Stainer & Bell, 1964, 2nd edition, 1968; John Blow, *Six Suites, for Keyboard*, Stainer & Bell, 1965; *Early French Keyboard Music*, two volumes, Oxford University Press, 1966; (with Denise Lassimonne) *Myra Hess, by Her Friends*, Vanguard, 1966; *Early Italian Keyboard Music*, two volumes, Oxford University Press, 1968; *Early German Keyboard Music*, two volumes, Oxford University Press, 1969; Francois Dagincour, *Pieces de Clavecin*, Heugel, 1969; Schubert, *Prayer, Freely Adapted for Cello or Viola and Piano*, Oxford University Press, 1969; *Early English Keyboard Music*, two volumes, Oxford University Press, 1971.

Musical compositions—All published by Boosey & Hawkes, except as indicated: *Five Irish Folk-Tunes, for Cello or Viola and Piano*, Oxford University Press, 1928; *Sonata No. 1, for Violin and Piano*, 1933; *Two Ballads, for Baritone and Orchestra*, 1934; *Three Mediaeval Carols, for Voice and Piano*, Curwen, 1934; *Octet, for Clarinet, Bassoon, Horn, String Quartet and Double-bass*, 1934; *Five Pipe Pieces, for Three Bamboo Pipes*, Cramer, 1935; *Partita, for Orchestra*, 1937; *Partita, for Two Pianos*, 1937; *Four Short Pieces, for Clarinet or Viola and Piano*, 1937; *Sonata in F Minor, for Piano*, 1940; *Five Bagatelles, for Piano*, 1945; *Four Diversions for Orchestra on Ulster Airs*, 1949; *Sonata No. 2, for Violin and Piano*, 1949; *"Discovery": Five Songs for Voice and Piano* (words by Denton Welch), 1952; *Three Sketches, for Flute and Piano*, 1953; *Two Fanfares, for Four Trumpets and Three Trombones*, 1953; *Overture for an Occasion, for Orchestra*, 1955; *Five Irish Folksongs, for Voice and Piano*, 1956; *"Amore Langueo," for Tenor Solo, Semi-Chorus, Chorus and Orchestra*, 1956; *"The Dream of the Rood," for Soprano or Tenor Solo, Chorus and Orchestra*, 1959; *Concerto, for Piano and String Orchestra*, 1962.

WORK IN PROGRESS: *Keyboard Interpretations*, and *Haydn: A Selection*, both for Oxford University Press.

BIOGRAPHICAL/CRITICAL SOURCES: *Book World*, October 8, 1967; *Christian Science Monitor*, April 26, 1968.

* * *

FERGUSSON, Erna 1888-1964

PERSONAL: Born 1888, in Albuquerque, N.M.; daughter of Harvey Butler and Clara (Huning) Fergusson. *Education:* University of New Mexico, B.Pd., 1912; Columbia University, M.A., 1913. *Home:* 2704 Veranda Rd., NW, Albuquerque, N.M.

CAREER: American Red Cross, Home Service supervisor for New Mexico, 1918; later operated a tourist bureau before she began writing about her own travels. *Member:* Business and Professional Women's Club, Phi Mu. *Awards, honors:* D.Litt., University of New Mexico, 1943.

WRITINGS: *Dancing Gods: Indian Ceremonials of New Mexico and Arizona*, Knopf, 1931, reissued, University of New Mexico Press, 1958; *Fiesta in Mexico*, Knopf, 1934; *Mexican Cookbook*, Rydal, 1934, reissued, Doubleday, 1961; *Guatemala*, Knopf, 1937; *Venezuela*, Knopf, 1939; *Our Southwest*, Knopf, 1940; *Our Hawaii*, Knopf, 1942; *Chile*, Knopf, 1943; *Cuba*, Knopf, 1946; *Albuquerque*, Copp, 1947; *Murder and Mystery in New Mexico*, Copp, 1948; *Let's Read about Hawaiian Islands*, Fideler, 1950, published as *Hawaii*, Fideler, 1962, new edition, 1964; *New Mexico: A Pageant of Three People*, Knopf, 1951, revised edition, 1964; *Mexico Revisited*, Knopf, 1955.

(Died July 30, 1964)

* * *

FEST, Thorrel B(rooks) 1910-

PERSONAL: Born August 23, 1910, in Audubon, Iowa; son of Albert F. and Augusta C. (Boers) Fest; married Lucille C. Etzler, June 5, 1934; children: Stephen G., Bruce F. *Education:* Iowa State Teachers College (now University of Northern Iowa), B.A., 1932; University of Wisconsin, M.Ph., 1938, Ph.D., 1952. *Politics:* Democrat. *Religion:* Protestant. *Home:* 1546 Sunset Blvd., Boulder, Colo. 80302.

CAREER: High school teacher in Griswold and Spencer, Iowa, 1932-39; University of North Dakota, Grand Forks, assistant professor of speech, 1939-40; Albion College, Albion, Mich., assistant professor of speech, 1940-42, assistant professor of physics, 1942-44; Manhattan Project, Oak Ridge, Tenn., classified work on atom bomb project, 1944-45; University of Tennessee, Knoxville, member of extension faculty, 1944-45; University of Colorado, Boulder, assistant professor, 1945-53, associate professor, 1953-58, professor of speech and drama, 1958—, chairman of department of speech, 1960-68. Visiting summer professor at Western State College of Colorado, Gunnison, 1956, Syracuse University, 1961, University of Hawaii, 1959, 1963. Visiting lecturer at University of New South Wales (Australia), spring, 1970. Beginning 1956, consultant to North American Defense Command Headquarters Staff. Member of advisory committee, Alexander Hamilton Bicentennial Commission, 1956-59.

MEMBER: International Communication Association (president, 1961), International Society for General Semantics, International Platform Association, National Center of Communication Arts and Sciences (vice-president, 1965—; program director, 1966—), American Forensic Association (chairman of public relations committee, 1951-53), Speech Communication Association (member of legislative assembly, 1957-60, 1963-66; member of council, 1958-61; chairman of committee on curricula and certification, 1962-64), Industrial Communication Council, American Theatre Association, National Collegiate Players, American Association of University Professors (president, 1960-62), National University Extension Association, Adult Education Association of the U.S.A., Izaak Walton League of America, Delta Sigma Rho (executive secretary, 1959-53; president, 1953-57; chairman of committee on distinguished alumni awards, 1963-65), Kappa Delta Phi, Lambda Delta Lambda, Theta Alpha Phi. *Awards, honors:* Citation from War Department for contributions to Manhattan Project.

WRITINGS: (With Martin Cobin) *Speech and Theatre*, Library of Education, 1963; (with R. Victor Harnack) *Group Discussion: Theory and Technique*, Appleton, 1964. Contributor to professional journals. Editor, *Gavel*, 1949-53.

SIDELIGHTS: Fest has traveled to New Zealand, Australia, the Philippines, Samoa, Fiji, Japan, and South America.

* * *

FIELD, Hazel E(lizabeth) 1891-19(?)

PERSONAL: Born February 25, 1891, in Princeton, Ill.; daughter of Charles Wilson (a farmer) and Carrie (Lathrop) Field. *Education:* Western College for Women (now Western College) B.A., 1912; University of Chicago, M.S., 1915; University of California, Berkeley, Ph.D., 1927.

CAREER: Belhaven College, Jackson, Miss., teacher of science, 1912-14; Randolph-Macon Women's College, Lynchburg, Va., instructor in biology, 1915-16; Milwaukee-Downer College (now Lawrence University), Milwaukee, Wis., instructor in zoology, 1916-17; Tulane University of Louisiana, Sophie Newcomb College, New Orleans, instructor in biology, 1917-19, 1921-24; Occidental College, Los Angeles, Calif., assistant professor, 1927-32, associate professor, 1932-45, professor of biology, 1945-56, became professor emeritus, 1956. *Member:* American Association for the Advancement of Science, American Association of University Professors, Western Society of Naturalists. *Awards, honors:* D.Sc., Western College for Women, 1962.

WRITINGS: The Fetal Pig: An Introduction to Mammalian Anatomy, Stanford University Press, 1939; (with Mary E. Taylor) *An Atlas of Cat Anatomy*, University of Chicago Press, 1950; *Foods in Health and Disease*, Macmillan, 1964.

(Deceased)

* * *

FIENE, Ernest 1894-1965

PERSONAL: Surname sounds like *Fee*-neh; born November 2, 1894, in Rhineland, Germany; son of William Henry and Maria (Egger) Fiene; married Alicia Wiencek (an artist), 1945 (died, 1961); children: Paul R., Maria L. *Education:* Studied art at National Academy of Design, Art Students League of New York, and Beaux Arts Institute. *Agent:* Brandt & Brandt, 101 Park Ave., New York, N.Y.

CAREER: Art Students League, New York, N.Y., instructor, 1938; National Academy School of Fine Art, instructor, 1958; member of the guiding faculty of fine arts, Famous Artists Schools, Westport, Conn. *Member:* Art Students League (life member), National Academy of Design, Artists Equity Association (honorary president), International Artists Association (treasurer, American committee), Century Association (New York, N.Y.). *Awards, honors:* Guggenheim fellow, 1932; Norman Waite Harris prize, Chicago Art Institute, 1937; W. A. Clark Prize, Corcoran Gallery, Washington, D.C., 1938; Ada S. Garret prize, Chicago Art Institute, 1940; Pennell Purchase prize, Library of Congress, 1940; first Penell award, 1944; Edwyn Palmer Memorial Prize, National Academy of Design, 1961.

WRITINGS: Complete Guide to Oil Painting, Watson, 1964.

(Died, 1965)

* * *

FILLMORE, Lowell 1882-

PERSONAL: Born January 4, 1882; son of Charles

(founder and president of Unity School of Christianity) and Myrtle (Page) Fillmore; married Alice Lee, February 14, 1926. *Education:* Attended Kansas City Business College. *Home:* Unity Village, Lee's Summit, Mo. 64063. *Office:* Unity School of Christianity, Unity Village, Lee's Summit, Mo. 64063.

CAREER: Unity School of Christianity, Lee's Summit, Mo., manager prior to 1948; president, 1948—.

WRITINGS—All published by Unity School of Christianity, except as indicated: *Remember*, 1929; *New Ways to Solve Old Problems*, 1938, 2nd edition, 1939; *Things to be Remembered* (compilation of articles), 1952; (editor) *The Unity Treasure Chest: A Selection of the Best Unity Writing*, Hawthorn, 1956; *The Prayer Way to Health, Wealth, and Happiness*, 1964. Editor, *Weekly Unity*.

* * *

FINBERG, H(erbert) P(atrick) R(eginald) 1900-1974

PERSONAL: Born March 21, 1900, in England; son of Alexander Joseph Finberg; married Joscelyne Henrietta Prideaux Payne, June 17, 1933; children: two sons. *Education:* St. John's College, Oxford, B.A., 1923, M.A., 1941. *Religion:* Roman Catholic. *Home:* 151 Park Rd., Chiswick, London W.4, England.

CAREER: Alcuin Press Ltd., Campden, Gloucestershire, England, founder and director, 1928-36; Broadwater Press Ltd., Welwyn, England, director, 1936-44; Burns, Oates & Washbourne Ltd. (publishers), London, England, director, 1944-49; University of Leicester, Leicester, England, reader, 1952-63, professor of English local history, 1963-65, professor emeritus, 1966-74, head of department of English local history, 1952-65. *Member:* Royal Historical Society, British Agricultural History Society (president, 1965-68), Society of Antiquaries, International Commission for English in the Liturgy. *Awards, honors:* D.Litt. from St. John's College, Oxford, 1957; Prix Graphica Belgica, 1965.

WRITINGS: (Translator from the French) Villiers de l'Isle-Adam, *Axel*, Jarrolds, 1925; (with J. O'Connell) *The Missal in Latin and English*, Sheed, 1949, 2nd edition, Newman Press, 1958; *Tavistock Abbey*, Cambridge University Press, 1951; (with W. G. Hoskins) *Devonshire Studies*, J. Cape, 1952; *The Local Historian and His Theme*, Leicester University Press, 1953; *The Early Charters of Devon and Cornwall*, Leicester University Press, 1953; *Roman and Saxon Withington*, Leicester University Press, 1955; *Gloucestershire*, Hodder & Stoughton, 1955; *The Gostwicks of Willington*, Bedfordshire Historical Record Society, 1956; (editor) *Gloucestershire Studies*, Leicester University Press, 1957; *The Early Charters of the West Midlands*, Leicester University Press, 1961; (editor) *Approaches to History*, Routledge & Kegan Paul, 1962; *The Manual of Catholic Prayer*, Burns & Oates, 1962; *The Early Charters of Wessex*, Leicester University Press, 1964; *Lucerna*, Macmillan, 1964; (with V. H. T. Skipp) *Local History: Objective and Pursuit*, David & Charles, 1967; *West Country Historical Studies*, David & Charles, 1969. Editor, *Agricultural History Review*, 1953-64.

WORK IN PROGRESS: General editor, *The Agrarian History of England and Wales;* member of commission appointed in 1964 by the Hierarchy of England and Wales to prepare an English translation of the Latin liturgy.

AVOCATIONAL INTERESTS: Conversation, music.

(Died November 1, 1974)

FINDLAY, Bruce Allyn 1895-1972

PERSONAL: Born February 23, 1895, in Los Angeles, Calif.; son of John James (a minister) and Emma (Berry) Findlay; married Esther Blair (a writer), August 1, 1930. *Education:* Pomona College, A.B., 1917; Yale University, graduate study; University of Southern California, M.A., 1920. *Politics:* Republican. *Religion:* Protestant. *Home:* 3336 Punta Alta, Apt. 1C, Laguna Hills, Calif. 91711.

CAREER: Los Angeles (Calif.) city schools, 1921-60, began as teacher, became head of audio-visual department, later assistant superintendent, then associate superintendent. Broadway Department Stores, Los Angeles, Calif., superintendent, 1929-31; Los Angeles Chamber of Commerce, Los Angeles, Calif., director of publicity, 1931-38. *Awards, honors:* Freedoms Foundations Award, shared with Esther B. Findlay; Colonial Dames Award; honorary M.B.A., Woodbury College; National Graphic Arts award.

WRITINGS: (With wife, Esther B. Findlay) *Key$ and Cue$*, Gregg Publishing Division, 1933; (with E. B. Findlay) *Tell-A-Vision Plays*, Row Peterson & Co., 1935; *Participation, Last Word in Films*, Los Angeles Board of Education, 1942; *Films That Teach for Keeps*, Los Angeles Board of Education, 1944; *See Your Grammar*, University Publishing, 1947; (with E. B. Findlay) *Your Rugged Constitution*, Stanford University Press, 1951, 2nd revised edition, 1969; *Guaranteed for Life*, Prentice-Hall, 1955; (with E. B. Findlay) *See What You Say*, 2nd edition, Prentice-Hall, 1957; (with E. B. Findlay) *Your Magnificent Declaration*, Holt, 1961. Author with E. B. Findlay of "Liberty, the Pursuit," a visual text series on film. Author of 85 radio scripts. Also author with E. B. Findlay, of *This Person Called You, Your P.Q. (Personality Quotient): How to Raise It*, and *Watch Your Manners! Others Do*, published by Educational Services, 1970.

(Died August 18, 1972)

* * *

FINDLAY, David K. 1901-

PERSONAL: Born August 15, 1901, in Carleton Place, Ontario, Canada; son of David (a manufacturer) and Effie (Hamilton) Findlay; married Kathleen Seaton, October, 1930; children: four. *Education:* University of Toronto, B.A., 1923; Osgoode Hall, law student, 1924-27. *Home and office:* 62 Mohawk Crescent, Qualicum, Ottawa, Ontario, Canada. *Agent:* Collins-Knowlton-Wing, 60 East 56th St., New York, N.Y.

CAREER: Called to the bar, 1927; lawyer in private practice, Carleton Place, Ontario, Canada, 1927-42; writer. *Member:* Canadian Authors Association.

WRITINGS—Novels: *Search for Amelia*, Lippincott, 1958; *Third Act*, Collins, 1961; *Northern Affair*, Morrow, 1964. Also author of about sixty short stories published in *Saturday Evening Post, Collier's*, and other magazines in United States, Great Britain, and Canada.

* * *

FINK, Z(era) S(ilver) 1902-

PERSONAL: Born August 8, 1902, in Holdrege, Neb.; son of Daniel J. and Nellie May (Silver) Fink; married Lucille E. McDannell, March 12, 1927; children: Carlotta Lucille Fink Bogart. *Education:* Grinnell College, A.B., 1924; Northwestern University, M.A., 1928, Ph.D., 1931; University of Chicago, graduate study, 1930. *Politics:* Independent. *Religion:* Presbyterian. *Home:* 2414 Hartzell St.,

Evanston, Ill. 60201. *Office:* Department of English, Northwestern University, Evanston, Ill. 60201.

CAREER: Grinnell College, Grinnell, Iowa, instructor in English, 1925-27; Northwestern University, Evanston, Ill., 1927—, began as instructor, became professor of English, professor, 1945—, acting chairman of department of English, 1954, 1957, 1958. Former member of advisory board, Salvation Army, Evanston, Ill. *Member:* Modern Language Association of America, Milton Society of America, Modern Humanities Research Association, Midwest Renaissance Conference (president, 1954), Phi Beta Kappa. *Awards, honors:* American Council of Learned Societies grant, 1959-60.

WRITINGS: *The Classical Republicans: An Essay in the Recovery of a Pattern of Thought in Seventeenth-Century England*, Northwestern University Press, 1945, 2nd edition, 1962; (editor) *The Early Wordsworthian Milieu: A Notebook of Christopher Wordsworth, with a Few Entries by William Wordsworth*, Clarendon Press, 1958. Contributor of articles and reviews to more than a dozen learned journals.

WORK IN PROGRESS: A book, *Literature and Politics: The Romantic Pattern*.

* * *

FINNEY, Gertrude Elva (Bridgeman) 1892-

PERSONAL: Born May 13, 1892, in Morocco, Ind.; daughter of George Elmer (a hardware merchant) and Lilian Gay (Rolls) Bridgeman; married John Montfort Finney (a physician), March 25, 1913 (died, 1966); children: John M., Jr., Joseph Bertrand, Ruth (Mrs. William S. Laughlin), David Stanley. *Education:* State College of Washington (now Washington State University), extension student, 1949-50. *Politics:* Republican. *Religion:* Methodist. *Home:* 2946 Grandview Ave., Spokane, Wash. 99204. *Agent:* Lurton Blassingame, 60 East 42nd St., New York, N.Y. 10017.

CAREER: Writer. *Member:* Authors Guild, Northwest Writers Conference (panelist, 1965), Eastern Washington Historical Society, Spokane Writers, Women in Communications, Amethyst Club, Delta Kappa Gamma. *Awards, honors:* Outstanding Hoosier Author award from Indiana University, 1967, for *To Survive We Must be Clever*.

WRITINGS: *Sleeping Mines* (Junior Literary Guild selection), Longmans, Green, 1951; *Muskets Along the Chickahominy* (Junior Literary Guild selection), Longmans, Green, 1953; *The Plums Hang High* (Junior Literary Guild selection; Family Reading Club selection), Longmans, Green, 1955; *Is This My Love* (Junior Literary Guild selection), Longmans, Green, 1956; *Life Is a Journey*, Longmans, Green, 1959; *Stormy Winter*, Longmans, Green, 1959; *Yes, a Homestead*, McKay, 1964; *One Woman's Land*, McKay, 1965; *To Survive We Must be Clever*, McKay, 1966.

* * *

FISCHER, Louis 1896-1970

PERSONAL: Born February 29, 1896, in Philadelphia, Pa.; son of David and Shifrah (Kantzapolsky) Fischer; married Bertha Mark (a writer), November 22, 1922; children: George, Victor. *Education:* Philadelphia School of Pedagogy, graduate, 1916. *Home:* 42 South Stanworth Dr., Princeton, N.J. 08540. *Office:* Woodrow Wilson School, Princeton University, Princeton, N.J. 08540.

CAREER: Teacher in public schools, Philadelphia, Pa., 1916-17; *Evening Post*, New York, N.Y., European correspondent, 1921; free-lance correspondent in U.S.S.R., 1922; *Nation*, New York, N.Y., correspondent, 1923-44, based in Moscow, U.S.S.R. until 1936, went to Spain in 1937, returned to U.S. in 1939, went to India in 1942; Institute for Advanced Study, Princeton, N.J., member, 1959-61; Woodrow Wilson School of Public and International Affairs, Princeton University, Princeton, N.J., research associate and lecturer, 1961-70. Visiting professor, University of Washington, Seattle, 1957; lecturer at New School for Social Research. *Military service:* British Army, 1917-20; served in Palestine; joined International Brigade in Spain, 1937. *Awards, honors:* Watumull Prize, American Historical Association, 1951, for *The Life of Mahatma Gandhi*; National Book Award in history and biography category, 1965, for *The Life of Lenin*.

WRITINGS: Oil Imperialism: The International Struggle for Petroleum, International Publishers, 1926; *The Soviets in World Affairs: A History of Relations Between the Soviet Union and the Rest of the World, 1917-1939*, two volumes, J. Cape and H. Smith, 1930, 2nd edition, Princeton University Press, 1951, abridged edition, Vintage, 1960; *Why Recognize Russia?: The Arguments For and Against the Recognition of the Soviet Government by the United States*, J. Cape & H. Smith, 1931; (with George Soule and Edward A. Filene) *Can We Have National Planning Without a Revolution* (pamphlet), Foreign Policy Association, 1932; *Machines and Men in Russia*, photographs by Margaret Bourke-White, H. Smith, 1932; *Soviet Journey*, H. Smith & P. Haas, 1935, Greenwood, 1973; *The War in Spain*, The Nation, 1937 (published in England as *Why Spain Fights On*, Union of Democratic Control, 1937).

Stalin and Hitler: The Reasons for and the Results of the Nazi-Bolshevik Pact, The Nation, 1940; *Men and Politics: An Autobiography*, Duell, Sloan & Pearce, 1941, reissued as *Men and Politics: Europe Between the World Wars*, Harper, 1966; *Dawn of Victory*, Duell, Sloan & Pearce, 1941; *A Week with Gandhi*, Duell, Sloan & Pearce, 1942 (published in England with an introduction by Carl Heath, Allen & Unwin, 1943); *Empire*, Duell, Sloan & Pearce, 1943; *The Great Challenge*, Duell, Sloan & Pearce, 1946; *Gandhi and Stalin: Two Signs at the World's Crossroads*, Harper, 1947; (editor) *Thirteen Who Fled*, Harper, 1949; (contributor) Richard Howard Crossman, editor, *The God That Failed*, Harper, 1950; *The Life of Mahatma Gandhi*, Harper, 1950; *The Life and Death of Stalin*, Harper, 1952; *Two Days That Shook the Soviet World: The Impossible Revolution in East Germany*, Popular Book Depot (Bombay), 1954; *Gandhi: His Life and Message for the World*, New American Library, 1954; *This Is Our World*, Harper, 1956; *Russia Revisited: A New Look at Russia and Her Satellites*, Doubleday, 1957; *On Some Recent Changes in the Communist World* (speech), Office of Asian Affairs, Congress for Cultural Freedom (New Delhi), 1958; *The Story of Indonesia*, Harper, 1959.

(Editor and author of introduction) Abul Kalam Azad, *India Wins Freedom: An Autobiographical Narrative*, Longmans, Green, 1960; *Russia, America and the World*, Harper, 1961; (editor) *The Essential Gandhi: An Anthology*, Random House, 1962, reissued as *The Essential Gandhi: His Life, Work, and Ideas*, Vintage, 1963; *The Life of Lenin*, Harper, 1964; *Fifty Years of Soviet Communism: An Appraisal*, Popular Library, 1968; *Russia's Road from Peace to War: Soviet Foreign Relations, 1917-1941*, Harper, 1969; *The Road to Yalta: Soviet Foreign Relations, 1941-1945*, Harper, 1972; (with David Schimmel) *Civil Rights of Teachers*, Harper, 1973. Contributor to American, European, and Asian periodicals and newspapers.

SIDELIGHTS: Stephen F. Cohen writes: "Students of Soviet affairs are deeply indebted to Louis Fischer. For five decades, in dispatches, essays and books, he has reported and researched the history of the Bolshevik revolution with unflagging energy and enduring results. A foreign correspondent at the outset, his journalistic skills and first-hand experiences in Soviet Russia have not distorted but enriched his scholarly work."

Though they may disagree with Fischer on certain points, most critics generally acknowledge him as one of America's greatest journalists and most knowledgeable authorities on Soviet history and foreign affairs. Cohen states that *Russia's Road from Peace to War* "is written with the author's customary verve, mastery of detail, gift of characterization, and sure instinct for the dramatic and illuminating episode." Theodore H. Von Laue believes that the book "has all the qualities of journalistic grand history, the flashbulb authenticity of personal observation, the human anecdote, the newsman's political and spiritual involvement in contemporary affairs, and of course, an aggressive factualness." Alexander Dallin adds: "His study is rich in texture, reliable in facts, and reflects many years of first-hand experience."

Fischer was, at one time, highly sympathetic to the cause of Soviet Russia. However, after the purge trials of the 1930's, the Russo-German pact, and the Soviet invasion of Poland in 1939, he became disillusioned and later disavowed the concept of a strict political structure. In *Men and Politics* Fischer wrote: "I have never been a member of any political party or of a trade union or, after my youth, of a club. I am essentially a libertarian and resent shackles, even personal ones. I can impose discipline upon myself, but would fight its imposition on me by others." In the same book he stated the political philosophy which derived from his involvement in contemporary events: "I have lived in all the major dictatorships—Russia, Germany and Italy. My experience teaches me that democracy, with all its faults is better than any of these. My experience teaches me that the maintenance of personal freedom should be the primary consideration of every human being."

The Life of Mahatma Gandhi was used as the basis of a Hollywood motion picture.

BIOGRAPHICAL/CRITICAL SOURCES: Newsweek, June 11, 1945; *Saturday Review*, October 4, 1947, September 16, 1950, August 23, 1952, July 9, 1969; Julien Steinberg, editor, *Verdict of Three Decades*, Duell, Sloan & Pearce, 1950; *New York Times*, May 31, 1969, January 17, 1970; *Library Journal*, July, 1969; *Book World*, September 7, 1969; *New York Times Book Review*, September 7, 1969; *Publishers Weekly*, February 23, 1970.

(Died January 15, 1970)

*   *   *

FISHBURN, Hummel 1901-

PERSONAL: Born March 18, 1901, in Washington, D.C.; son of Mosheim Ross (a minister) and Emma (Hummel) Fishburn; married Rebecca Clingerman, October 16, 1930; children: David R., H. Ross, Peter C. *Education:* Pennsylvania State College (now University), B.A., 1922, M.A., 1925; University of Montreal, D.Mus., 1950. *Politics:* Republican. *Religion:* Methodist. *Home:* 1301 Park Hills Ave., State College, Pa. 16801.

CAREER: Pennsylvania State University, University Park, assistant dean of men, 1922-26, member of music faculty, 1929-65, head of departments of music and music education, 1942-65; now retired. *Member:* Music Educators National Conference (president, Eastern division, 1945-47), Pennsylvania Music Educators Association (president, 1944-45), Phi Gamma Delta, Phi Mu Alpha, Phi Delta Kappa, Delta Sigma Pi, Kappa Gamma Psi, Rotary Club (State College).

WRITINGS: Fundamentals of Music Appreciation, Longmans, Green, 1955, revised edition, McKay, 1964. Music consultant and editor, "Songbook of Rotary International," 1965-66.

* * *

FISHER, Lillian Estelle 1891-

PERSONAL: Born May 1, 1891, in Selinsgrove, Pa.; daughter of George P. (a farmer) and Etta R. (Siegfried) Fisher. *Education:* Susquehanna University, A.B. (cum maxima laude), 1912; University of Southern California, M.A., 1918; University of California, Berkeley, Ph.D., 1924. *Religion:* Methodist. *Home:* 1717 Oxford St., Berkeley, Calif. 94709.

CAREER: Whittier College, Whittier, Calif., instructor in history, 1925; Oklahoma College for Women (now Oklahoma College of Liberal Arts), Chickasha, associate professor, 1926-42; University of California, Berkeley, teacher in Extension Division, 1943-45. Visiting professor of Latin American history at Hunter College (now Hunter College of the City University of New York), 1942. Lecturer at George Washington University Seminar Conference, 1935, Institute of Inter-American Affairs, Brazil and Argentina, summer, 1940. *Member:* American Association of University Women (examiner for fellowships in the Southwest, 1935-42), American Historical Association (secretary, conference on Latin American history, 1934-39), General Federation of Women's Clubs (honorary member), National Woman's Party (secretary, northern California branch, 1943-53), Franciscan Society of America (honorary). *Awards, honors:* Fellowship from King of Spain, 1929.

WRITINGS: Viceregal Administration in the Spanish American Colonies, Berkeley Press, 1926; *The Intendant System in Spanish America*, Berkeley Press, 1929; *The Background of the Revolution for Mexican Independence*, Christopher, 1934; (editor) Herbert I. Priestley, *Franciscan Exploration in California*, Glendale Clark, 1946; *Champion of Reform: Manual Abad y Queipo*, Library Publishers, 1955; *The Last Inca Revolt in Peru 1780-1783*, University of Oklahoma Press, 1966. Contributor to books and to historical reviews.

WORK IN PROGRESS: Completion of a book started by Herbert I. Priestly, on Mexico, from early civilization to emergence as a strong nation; a book on modern Mexico since Porfirio Diaz.

* * *

FISHER, Miles Mark 1899-1970

PERSONAL: Born October 29, 1899, in Atlanta, Ga.; son of Elijah John (a minister) and Florida (Neeley) Fisher; married Ada Virginia Foster, September 6, 1930; children: Florida (Mrs. Herbert G. Parker), Miles Mark IV, Alfred Foster, Elijah John III, Christopher Tennant, Ada Markita. *Education:* Morehouse College, A.B., 1918; Northern Baptist Theological Seminary, B.D., 1922; University of Chicago, A.M., 1922, Ph.D., 1948. *Home:* 1219 Fayetteville, Durham, N.C. 27707. *Office:* White Rock Baptist Church, 606 Fayetteville, Durham, N.C. 27701.

CAREER: Baptist minister, 1922-70. Early pastorates in Chicago, Ill., and Racine, Wis.; pastor of churches in Charles City and New Kent counties, Va., 1923-28, and Huntington, W.Va., 1928-33; White Rock Baptist Church, Durham, N.C., pastor, 1933-64, pastor emeritus, 1965-70. Professor at Virginia Union University, Richmond, Va., 1922-28; Shaw University, Raleigh, N.C., lecturer in history of religion, 1933-65. *Member:* American Historical Association, American Society of Church History, Association of the Study of Negro Life and History, Organization of American Historians. *Awards, honors:* D.D. from Shaw University, 1941; National Recreation Association Golden Anniversary Award, 1958.

WRITINGS: The Master's Slave–Elijah John Fisher, Judson, 1922; *Virginia Union University and Some of Her Achievements*, Virginia Union University, 1924; *A Short History of the Baptist Denomination*, National Baptist Sunday School Board, 1933; *Negro Slave Songs in the United States*, Cornell University Press, 1953.

(Died December 14, 1970)

* * *

FLANDERS, Helen Hartness 1890-1972

PERSONAL: Born May 19, 1890, in Springfield, Vt.; daughter of James (an inventor and Governor of Vermont) and Lena (Pond) Hartness; married Ralph Edward Flanders (a U.S. senator), November 1, 1911; children: Helen Elizabeth (Mrs. William Whitney Ballard), Anna Hartness (Mrs. Henry P. Balivet; deceased), James H. *Religion:* Congregational. *Home:* Smiley Manse, Springfield, Vt. 05156.

CAREER: Folk song collector, lecturer, and author. *Member:* Poetry Society of America, National League of American Pen Women, American Folklore Society, American Association for the Advancement of Science, International Folk Music Council, Society for Ethnomusicology, Poetry Society of Vermont, Northeast Folklore Society, Daughters of the American Revolution. *Awards, honors:* M.A. from Middlebury College, 1942.

WRITINGS: (Editor with George Brown) *Vermont Folk-Songs and Ballads*, S. Daye, 1931, 2nd edition, 1932, 1st edition reprinted, Folklore Associates, 1968; (editor) *A Garland of Green Mountain Song*, A. W. Peach, 1934; (compiler) *Country Songs of Vermont*, Schirmer, 1937; (editor with others) *The New Green Mountain Songster: Traditional Folk Songs of Vermont*, Yale University Press, 1939, reprinted, Folklore Associates, 1966; (editor with Enid Pierce) *Green Mountain Verse*, Farrar & Rinehart, 1943; (compiler with Marguerite Olney) *Ballads Migrant in Vermont*, Farrar, Straus, 1953; (editor) *Ancient Ballads Traditionally Sung in New England*, four volumes, University of Pennsylvania Press, 1960-65; *Country News Items, and Other Poems*, 1965.

SIDELIGHTS: An accomplished musician, Mrs. Flanders spent years completing a collection of over 9,000 early ballads, particularly those of New England. She drove from one out-of-the-way district to another in search of ballad singers who might add to her repertoire. Her standard equipment, according to *Washington Post* columnist Jean

R. Hailey, was a recording machine, a notebook, and a persuasive manner. Her collection of recordings, given to Middlebury College, is considered one of the most valuable archives of folk material in the country.

(Died May 23, 1972)

*   *   *

FLANDERS, Ralph Edward   1880-1970

PERSONAL: Born September 28, 1880, in Barnet, Vt.; son of Albert Wellington and Mary Lizzie (Gilfillan) Flanders; married Helen Edith Hartness (an author, lecturer, and folk song authority), November 1, 1911; children: Helen Elizabeth (Mrs. William W. Ballard), Anna Hartness (Mrs. Henry P. Balivet, Jr.; deceased), James Hartness. *Education:* Studied mechanical engineering, International Correspondence School. *Politics:* Republican. *Religion:* Congregationalist. *Address:* Smiley Manse, P.O. Box 479, Springfield, Vt. 65156.

CAREER: Machinist apprentice, draftsman, and designer in New England, 1897-1903; *Machinery*, New York, N.Y., associate editor, 1905-10; Jones & Lamson Machine Co., Springfield, Vt., director and manager, 1921-33, president, 1933-46; Bryant Chuck and Grinder Co., Springfield, Vt., president, 1934-46; appointed U.S. Senator from Vermont to fill unexpired term, 1946, returned to Senate, 1946-58. President, Federal Reserve Bank of Boston, 1944-46; American Research & Development Corp., Boston, president, 1946, former director; also director of National Life Insurance Co. Holder of twenty patents in machine tool field. Member, Economic Stabilization Board, 1943-44; member of research committee and trustee, Committee for Economic Development (non-government). Life member, Massachusetts Institute of Technology Corp.; trustee, St. Johnsbury Academy and Sterling School, 1959-70. *Member:* American Engineering Council (vice-president, 1937), American Society of Mechanical Engineers (president, 1934), National Machine Tool Builders Association (president, 1923), American Academy of Political and Social Science, American Economic Association, Institution of Mechanical Engineers (London; honorary), Tau Beta Pi (honorary), Phi Beta Kappa, Engineers' Club (New York), Union Club (Boston), Cosmos Club (Washington, D.C.).

AWARDS, HONORS: Co-recipient with brother, Ernest Flanders, of Edward Longstreth Medal, Franklin Institute, 1934; Worcester-Warner Medal, American Society of Mechanical Engineers, 1938; Hoover Medal, American Engineering Council, 1944; Howard Coonley Medal, American Standards Association, 1953. Honorary degrees: Dartmouth College, M.A., 1932, LL.D., 1951; M.E., Stevens Institute, 1932; D.Sc., Middlebury College, 1934, Rose Polytechnical Institute, 1935, Norwich University, 1939, Northwestern University, 1940; Eng.D., Polytechnic Institute of Brooklyn, 1934, University of Vermont, 1935, Northeastern University, 1942, Clarkson Institute of Technology, 1949, University of Rhode Island, 1951, Allegheny College, 1953, Rollins College, 1954, University of New Hampshire, and Boston Univeristy; LL.D., Marlboro College, 1949, Harvard University, 1950.

WRITINGS: (With others) *Drafting Room Practice*, Industrial Press, 1908; *Gear Cutting Machinery: Comprising a Complete Review of Contemporary American and European Practice, Together with a Logical Classification and Explanation of the Principles Involved*, Wiley, 1909; *Bevel Gearing*, Industrial Press, 1909, 3rd edition, 1912; *Construction and Manufacture of Automobiles*, Industrial Press, 1910, 2nd edition, 1912; *Locomotive Building*, six parts, Industrial Press, 1911-12; *The Fay Automatic Lathe: A Machine for the Automatic Turning of Work on Centers or on Centered Arbors*, Jones & Lamson Machine Co., 1913; *Spur and Bevel Gearing*, Machinery Publishing, 1914; *The Hartness Automobile Die*, Jones & Lamson Machine Co., 1915; *Design, Manufacture and Production Control of a Standard Machine*, American Society of Mechanical Engineers, 1924; *Taming Our Machines: The Attainment of Human Values in a Mechanized Society*, Richard R. Smith, 1931; *The Management Point of View of Economic Planning* (pamphlet), American Management Association, 1932; *Platform for America*, Whittlesey House, 1936; (with others) *Toward Full Employment*, Whittlesey House, 1938.

(With William E. Wickenden) *The University and Industry: Addresses*, Engineering Experiment Station, Ohio State University, 1941; (with Jesse P. Wolcott and others) *Temporary Extension of Certain Provisions of Second Decontrol Act of 1947*, U.S. Government Printing Office, 1948; *The Function of Management in American Life* (lectures), Graduate School of Business, Stanford University, 1949; *The American Century*, Harvard University Press, 1950; (contributor) *Increasing Productivity Thru Simplification, Standardization, Specialization*, U.S. Economic Cooperation Administration, 1951: *Letter to a Generation*, Beacon Press, 1956; *Senator from Vermont* (autobiography), Little, Brown, 1961; *A Search For Meaning*, privately printed, 1963; *Kingdom Come*, privately printed, 1965. Contributor to technical journals.

SIDELIGHTS: In his long career in the U.S. Senate, Flanders was deeply involved in the areas of rent control and inflationary rises in the cost of housing and consumer goods. He became most well-known, however, when in 1954 he led a successful movement to censure the late Senator Joseph R. McCarthy. At that time, McCarthy was involved in the controversial hunts for Communists in government and in other influential positions in the U.S. Flanders, who compared McCarthy to Adolph Hitler, denounced the Senator from Wisconsin and introduced a resolution of censure against him.

Despite his identification with conservative Republican causes, Flanders refused to be categorized. Despite his dislike for President Franklin Delano Roosevelt and many of his methods, Flanders generally supported the New Deal. He also supported the late Senator Robert Taft's "liberal" measures in federal aid to health, education, and public housing. And though he was once described as "the liberal conservative," Flanders characterized himself as "a large collection of unspectacular things."

BIOGRAPHICAL/CRITICAL SOURCES: Washington Post, February 21, 1970.

(Died February 19, 1970)

*   *   *

FLANNERY, Harry W.   1900-

PERSONAL: Born March 13, 1900, in Greensburg, Pa.; son of John V. (a salesman) and Catherine (Flynn) Flannery; married Ruth Carmody, July 4, 1937; children: Patricia Ann. *Education:* University of Notre Dame, Ph.B., 1923. *Politics:* Democrat. *Religion:* Roman Catholic. *Home:* 4823 Yuma St. N.W., Washington, D.C. 20016. *Agent:* Curtis Brown Ltd., 575 Madison Ave., New York, N.Y. 10022. *Office:* 815 16th St. N.W., Washington, D.C. 20006.

CAREER: Newspaper reporter in Hagerstown, Md., Baltimore, Md., Chicago, Ill., and Albany, N.Y., 1916-25; secretary to J. P. McEvoy, 1925-26; newspaper editor and radio station news editor, Fort Wayne, Ind., 1931-32; WOWO, Ft. Wayne, Ind., radio news editor, 1932-33; KMOX, St. Louis, Mo., news editor and analyst, 1935-40; Columbia Broadcasting System, correspondent in Berlin, Germany, 1940-41, news analyst in Los Angeles, Calif., 1942-48; Los Angeles Examiner, Los Angeles, Calif., makeup editor, 1948-49; Catholic Digest, foreign affairs and labor editor, 1951; AFL News Reporter, Washington, D.C., editor, 1952-56; AFL-CIO, Washington, D.C., radio coordinator, 1956—, and producer of network programs, including "Washington Reports to the People." Member, Archdiocesan Committee on Papal Peace Proposals. Member: Catholic Association for International Peace (president, 1956-58, 1962-63; now on board of directors).

WRITINGS: Assignment to Berlin, Knopf, 1942; (contributor) Jerome Lawrence, editor, Off Mike: Radio Writing by the Nation's Top Radio Writers, Essential Books, 1944; (editor) Pattern for Peace: Catholic Statements on International Order, Newman, 1962; (with John Francis Cronin) The Church and the Workingman, Hawthorn, 1965 (published in England as Labour and the Church, Burns & Oates, 1966); (with Gerhart H. Seger) Which Way Germany?, Hawthorn, 1968.

*   *   *

FLEMING, Sandford 1888-

PERSONAL: Born May 2, 1888, in Adelaide, Australia; son of Joseph Higginson and Mary Jane (Brown) Fleming; married Clarice Ethel Crossing, August 23, 1915. Education: South Australian Baptist College, graduate, 1912; Yale University, B.D., 1917, A.M., 1926, Ph.D., 1929; Berkeley Baptist Divinity School, Th.M., 1924, M.A., 1925. Politics: Republican. Office: 2606 Dwight Way, Berkeley, Calif. 94704.

CAREER: Baptist minister; Berkeley Baptist Divinity School, Berkeley, Calif., professor of church history, 1926-27, president, 1937-57, now president emeritus and professor emeritus of church history. President of Pacific Coast Regional Conference of Theological Schools, 1937-39, Evangelical Fellowship of Northern California, 1939-40, Northern California Council of Churches, 1943-44, American Association of Theological Schools, 1944-46, American (Northern) Baptist Convention, 1948-49, American Society of Church History, and Bible Land Foundation, 1960. Trustee, American Association of Theological Schools Fund, Inc., 1954-57.

MEMBER: American Society of Church History, Religious Education Association. Awards, honors: D.D., University of Redlands, 1944; Litt.D., Berkeley Baptist Divinity School, 1951, S.T.D., 1957.

WRITINGS: Children and Puritanism: The Place of Children in the Life and Thought of New England Churches, 1620-1847, Yale University Press, 1933; Living Portraits of Jesus: Devotional Studies of New Testament Portraiture, Professional Press, 1939; Ninety-five Years Beside the Golden Gate, First Baptist Church (San Francisco), 1944; God's Gold: The Story of Baptist Beginnings in California, Judson, 1949; Where Jesus Walked: Journeys with Jesus in the Land He Loved, Judson, 1953; For the Making of Ministers: A History of Berkeley Baptist Divinity School, 1871-1961, Judson, 1963; American Baptists and Higher Education, Judson, 1965. Contributor of articles to educational and historical periodicals.

FLETCHER, Adele (Whitely) 1898-
(Roberta Ormiston)

PERSONAL: Born November 16, 1898, in New York, N.Y.; daughter of William D. C. (a buyer) and Helen (Clarke) Fletcher; married Robert Ormiston (deceased); children: Susan (Mrs. Darryl Bridson). Religion: "Attend Quaker meetings." Home: 83-09 Talbot St., Kew Gardens, N.Y. 11415. Agent: Bertha Klausner, 71 Park Ave., New York, N.Y. 10016.

CAREER: Photoplay, New York, N.Y., editor, 1943-53; American Weekly, New York, N.Y., women's feature editor, 1953-62; full-time free-lance writer, 1962—. Awards, honors: Named best feature writer of 1960 by New York Newspaper Women.

WRITINGS: How to Give Successful Dinner Parties, Doubleday, 1963; How to Decorate with Accessories, Doubleday, 1963; (with Hildegarde) Over Fifty, So What?, Doubleday, 1963; The Mystery of Blue Star Lodge, Doubleday, 1965; The Six Way Diet Book, Grosset, 1967; How to Stretch Your Dollar, Benjamin Co., 1968. Also author with Rebecca Liswood of book on marriage problems. Contributor to McCall's, Family Weekly, and Lady's Circle.

*   *   *

FLOWER, Harry A(lfred) 1901-

PERSONAL: Born June 16, 1901, in London, England; son of Harry Alfred and Angelina Louisa (Bloomfield) Flower; married Ethelinda Graham, August 29, 1925; children: Harry Graham. Education: Attended London County Council schools. Politics: "Worldwide social justice." Religion: Roman Catholic. Home: 25 Waddington Ave., Old Coulsdon, Surrey, England.

CAREER: Variously employed as police constable in Shanghai, China, as salesman, and as assistant manager of Parisienne Cafe, Shanghai, China, 1919-23; Shanghai Times, Shanghai, China, sports editor, 1923-24; South London News Service, London, England, reporter on Sunday Worker, 1925-26; Daily Express, London, England, reporter, sub-editor, caption writer, 1928-34; Daily Telegraph, London, England, war correspondent, reporter, sub-editor, caption writer, 1934-45; Ludgate Press (trade publications), London, England, editor, 1945-48. Military service: Royal Navy, 1917-18. Member: National Union of Journalists, National Boxing Association (co-founder; secretary; national organizer, 1934-45).

WRITINGS: Boxing from the Inside, National Union of Boxers, 1936. Contributor to British national and provincial newspapers, and to Boxing, Sporting Life, Weekly Sporting Review, Small Trader, other periodicals.

WORK IN PROGRESS: British Bird Song at Eventide; a life of Christ; children's stories from the Bible.

*   *   *

FOAT TUGAY, Emine 1897-

PERSONAL: Born August 19, 1897, in Istanbul, Turkey; daughter of Mahmud Muhtar Katircioglu Pasha (an army general, later governor general, and ambassador) and Princess Nimetullah of Egypt; married Ahmed Hulusi Foat Tugay (a retired ambassador). Education: Educated at home by governesses and private tutors, with accent on history, literature, art, and music; also attended art school in Zurich, Switzerland, 1918-19. Politics: Non-aligned progressive.

CAREER: Occupied with the duties of a Turkish diplomat's wife for thirty-two years. Volunteer welfare worker for Anti-Tubercular Association of Turkey and Society for Protection of Animals, Istanbul.

WRITINGS: Three Centuries (autobiography), Oxford University Press, 1963.

WORK IN PROGRESS: Continuation of reminiscences from 1913 to the present time.

* * *

FOLEY, Charles 1908-

PERSONAL: Born November 29, 1908, in Jhelum, India; son of Maurice John (an engineer) and Eileen Blanche (Bennett) Foley; married Elsie Irene Dixon; children: Sean, Julian, Caroline. *Education:* Attended University College, London. *Home:* Via Gramsci 77A, Nettuno, Rome, Italy. *Agent:* David Higham Associates Ltd., 76 Dean St., London W.1, England.

CAREER: Journalist. *Times of Cyprus* (independent English-language daily), founder, and editor during liberation struggle, 1955-59; *Sunday Express*, London, England, correspondent, chief European correspondent, 1964—, based at present in Italy. *Member:* Reform Club, Press Club (London), Foreign Press Club (Rome).

WRITINGS: Commando Extraordinary, Longmans, Green, 1954, Putnam, 1955; *Island in Revolt*, Longmans, Green, 1962; *Legacy of Strife*, Penguin, 1964; (editor) *The Memoirs of General Grivas*, Longmans, Green, 1964, Praeger, 1965. Contributor to *New Statesman, Christian Science Monitor, Sunday Citizen*, and other publications.

WORK IN PROGRESS: A definitive study of the Eoka underground struggle in Cyprus, 1955-59.

SIDELIGHTS: As an objective observer in Cyprus, Foley became acquainted with "Terrorist" warfare as practiced by Col. Grivas in his campaign against British rule, 1955-59. "After the peace settlement," Foley wrote, "[Grivas] explained to me his plans, methods and techniques. It is notable that *The Memoirs of General Grivas*, which I edited, have been banned in territories where they 'might give the natives ideas.'"

Foley believes that the "secret of success" in warfare "is always to be found in the audacious, imaginative use of the one unanswerable weapon: man."

* * *

FOORD, Archibald Smith 1914-1969

PERSONAL: Born August 13, 1914, in Stamford, Conn.; son of William Malcolm (a lawyer) and Madeleine (Smith) Foord; married Mary Banks Sullivan, June 29, 1940; children: William Malcolm III, Mary Bankhead. *Education:* Yale University, B.A., 1937, Ph.D., 1942; Worcester College, Oxford, graduate study, 1937-38. *Politics:* Republican. *Religion:* Congregational. *Home:* 36 Laurel Rd., Hamden, Conn. 06514.

CAREER: Yale University, New Haven, Conn., instructor, 1940-42, 1946-48, assistant professor, 1948-51, associate professor, 1951-65, professor of history, 1965-69, master of Calhoun College, 1955-64. *Military service:* U.S. Naval Reserve, 1942-46; became lieutenant commander; received Presidential Unit Citation. *Member:* American Historical Association, Conference on British Studies, Phi Beta Kappa, Elizabethan Club (Yale). *Awards, honors:* Guggenheim fellow, 1949-50; senior faculty fellow, Yale University, 1961-62.

WRITINGS: (With T. C. Mendenhall and B. D. Henning) *The Quest for a Principle of Authority in Modern Europe, 1715-Present*, Holt, 1948; (with Barbara Mathias and Henning) *Crises in English History, 1066-1945*, Holt, 1949; (with Mendenhall and Henning) *Ideas and Institutions in European History, 800-1715*, Holt, 1950; *His Majesty's Opposition, 1714-1830*, Clarendon Press, 1964.

WORK IN PROGRESS: Georgian Britain.

(Died, 1969)

* * *

FORBES, Esther 1891-1967

PERSONAL: Born June 28, 1891, in Westborough, Mass.; daughter of William Trowbridge (a judge) and Harriette (Marrifield) Forbes; married, 1926 (divorced, 1933). *Education:* Bradford Junior College, graduate, 1912; University of Wisconsin, student, 1916-18. *Home:* Worcester, Mass.

CAREER: Author. Houghton Mifflin Co., Boston, Mass., member of editorial staff, 1920-26, 1942-46. *Member:* American Academy of Arts and Sciences, American Antiquarian Society, Society of American Historians. *Awards, honors:* Pulitzer Prize in history, 1942, for *Paul Revere and the World He Lived In*; John Newbery Medal, 1944, for most distinguished contribution of year to children's literature for *Johnny Tremain: A Novel for Young and Old*; Metro-Goldwyn-Mayer Novel Award, 1948. Litt.D. from Clark University, 1943, University of Maine, 1943, University of Wisconsin, 1949, Northeastern University, 1949, Wellesley College, 1959; LL.D. from Tufts University.

WRITINGS: O Genteel Lady!, Houghton, 1926; *A Mirror for Witches*, Houghton, 1928; *Miss Marvel*, Houghton, 1935; *Paradise*, Harcourt, 1937; *The General's Lady*, Harcourt, 1938; *Paul Revere and the World He Lived In*, Houghton, 1942; *Johnny Tremain: A Novel for Young and Old*, Houghton, 1943; (with Arthur Griffin) *The Boston Book*, Houghton, 1947; *The Running of the Tide*, Houghton, 1948; (with Lynd Ward) *America's Paul Revere*, Houghton, 1948; *Rainbow on the Road*, Houghton, 1959.

WORK IN PROGRESS: A history of witchcraft in Massachusetts.

SIDELIGHTS: Esther Forbes's books have been translated into at least ten languages, and issued in a number of paperback editions; sections also have appeared in anthologies. Walt Disney made a movie of *Johnny Tremain, The Running of the Tide* was also filmed, and the Sadler Wells Ballet of London performed a ballet based on *A Mirror for Witches*. A musical, "Come Summer," based on *Rainbow on the Road*, was first produced at the Lunt-Fontanne Theatre on Broadway, March 11, 1969.

(Died August 12, 1967)

* * *

FORD, Alice 1906-

PERSONAL: Born August 22, 1906, in Fort Dodge, Iowa; daughter of John Francis (Iowa state conservationist and city official) and Ellen (Howard) Ford. *Education:* University of Michigan, B.A., 1928, M.A., 1931; New York University, graduate study. *Religion:* Roman Catholic. *Address:* c/o University of Oklahoma Press, Norman, Okla.

CAREER: Writer and editor. During World War II served with Office of War Information and U.S. Information Service as writer-editor in New York, N.Y., and China, and as press attache in Dublin, Ireland (first woman of any nationality to be diplomatically accredited to Ireland). *Awards, honors:* Institute of International Education grant, 1934, for study at Institut d'Art, University of Paris.

WRITINGS: Pictorial Folk Art, New England to California, Studio-Crowell, 1949; (editor and compiler) *Audubon's Animals,* Studio-Crowell, 1951; *Aubudon's Butterflies, Moths, and Other Studies,* Studio-Crowell, 1952; *Edward Hicks, Painter of the Peaceable Kingdom,* University of Pennsylvania Press, 1952, revised and augmented edition, Kraus Reprint Co., 1973; (editor and compiler) *Bird Biographies of John James Audubon,* Macmillan, 1957; *John James Audubon* (biography), University of Oklahoma Press, 1964; (transcriber, and author of introduction and notes) *1826 Journal of John James Audubon,* University of Oklahoma Press, 1967; (editor and compiler) *Audubon, By Himself,* Natural History Press, 1969.

WORK IN PROGRESS: Editing more Audubon material, previously unpublished; an expanded edition of the Audubon biography.

SIDELIGHTS: Alice Ford has lived abroad and travels extensively.

* * *

FORD, Edsel 1928-1970

PERSONAL: Born December 30, 1928, in Eva, Ala.; son of James Tilden (a farmer) and Nora Louisa (Chunn) Ford. *Education:* University of Arkansas, A.B., 1952. *Politics:* Democrat, "but not dyed-in-the-wool." *Religion:* Methodist. *Home:* 2021 South R. St., Fort Smith, Ark. 72901.

CAREER: Worked as a farmer until 1952; former newspaperman in Fort Smith, Ark.; free-lance writer. Poetry consultant and lecturer, Kansas University Writers Conference, 1961-64; member, State-wide Advisory Committee on the Arts and Humanities (Arkansas). *Military service:* U.S. Army, 1952-54; first began writing poetry for *Stars and Stripes. Member:* Poetry Society of America. *Awards, honors:* New York State Poetry Day Award, 1955; Norfolk Prize, Virginia Poetry Society, 1958, for a sonnet sequence; Monday Prize, Georgia Poetry Society, 1959 and 1960, for "delicate lyrics"; Arthur Davison Ficke Memorial Award, Poetry Society of America, 1961, for a sonnet sequence; Lowell Mason Palmer Award, Poetry Society of America, 1963; Stanley Corprew Paul Memorial Award, Poetry Society of Virginia, 1964; Conrad Aiken Prize, Poetry Society of Georgia, 1964 and 1968; Alice Fay di Castagnola Award ($3,500), Poetry Society of America, 1965, for group of sonnets, "A Landscape for Dante"; Devins Memorial Award, 1968, for *Looking for Shiloh.*

WRITINGS—All poetry except as noted: (With Carl Selph) *Two Poets,* privately printed, 1951; *The Stallion's Nest,* privately printed, 1952; *This Was My War,* privately printed, 1955; *The Manchild From Sunday Creek,* Kaleidograph Press, 1956; *One Leg Short From Climbing Hills* (humor), privately printed, 1959; *A Thicket of Sky,* Homestead House, 1961; *Love is the House It Lives In,* Homestead House, 1965; *Looking for Shiloh,* University of Missouri Press, 1968. Author of column, "The Golden Country," in *The Ozarks Mountaineer,* Branson, Mo. (monthly). Contributor to *New York Times* and numerous periodicals.

SIDELIGHTS: Ford called himself "a plain Arkansawyer" and his poems were about the harshness of pastoral life, as well as the beauty. His characters in "A Landscape for Dante" were Dante's, transferred from the Inferno to a contemporary village in the Ozarks.

He was often confused with the automobile magnate, Edsel Ford, to whom he was not related.

(Died February 19, 1970)

* * *

FORD, James Allan 1920-

PERSONAL: Born June 10, 1920, in Auchtermuchty, Scotland; son of Douglas and Margaret (Allan) Ford; married Isobel Dunnett, June 3, 1948; children: Allan Douglas, Elizabeth Ann. *Education:* University of Edinburgh, student, 1946-47. *Home:* 29 Lady Rd., Edinburgh EH165PA, Scotland.

CAREER: Ministry of Labour, Edinburgh, Scotland, clerical officer, 1938-39; Board of Inland Revenue, London, England, executive officer, 1939-47; Department of Agriculture and Fisheries for Scotland, Edinburgh, assistant principal, 1947-53, principal, 1953-58, assistant secretary, 1958-66, registrar general for Scotland, 1966-69; Office of Establishments, Edinburgh, Scotland, director, 1969—. *Military service:* British Army, Royal Scots, 1940-46; became captain; awarded Military Cross. *Member:* P.E.N., Society of Authors.

WRITINGS: The Brave White Flag (novel), Hodder & Stoughton, 1961; *Season of Escape* (novel), Hodder & Stoughton, 1963; *A Statue for a Public Place* (novel), Hodder & Stoughton, 1965; *A Judge of Men* (novel), Hodder & Stoughton, 1968. Author of radio and television play, "The Miraculous Letter." Contributor of short stories and articles to Scottish periodicals.

WORK IN PROGRESS: A novel.

SIDELIGHTS: Ford writes in the margins of his days and relaxes as little as possible; as a writer, he is interested in all serious but not too solemn fiction; as a reader, he is "less often disappointed in the old than in the new."

BIOGRAPHICAL/CRITICAL SOURCES: Observer Review, September 8, 1968.

* * *

FORSTER, E(dward) M(organ) 1879-1970

PERSONAL: Born January 1, 1879, in London, England; son of Edward Morgan Llewellyn and Alice Clara (Whichelo) Forster. *Education:* King's College, Cambridge, B.A. (second-class honors in classics), 1900, B.A. (second-class honors in history), 1901, M.A., 1910. *Home:* King's College, Cambridge University, Cambridge, England.

CAREER: Lived in Greece and Italy after leaving Cambridge in 1901, remaining there until 1907, except for a brief visit to England in 1902; lectured at Working Men's College, London, for a period beginning in 1907; made first trip to India in 1912; Red Cross volunteer in Alexandria, 1915-19; returned to England after the war where he was literary editor of the Labor Party's *Daily Herald* for a time, and contributed reviews to journals including *Nation* and *New Statesman;* served as private secretary to the Maharajah of Dewas State Senior, 1921; lived in England, writing and lecturing, 1921-70. Gave annual Clark Lectures at Cambridge University, 1927, Rede Lecturer, 1941, W. P. Ker Lecturer, 1944; made lecture tour of United States in 1947. Member of general advisory council, British Broadcasting Corp., and writer of numerous broadcasts; was a vice-president of the London Library.

MEMBER: American Academy of Arts and Letters (honorary corresponding member), Bavarian Academy of Fine

Arts (honorary corresponding member), Cambridge Humanists (president), Reform Club. *Awards, honors:* James Tait Black Memorial Prize, and Prix Femina Vie Heureuse, both 1925, both for *Passage to India*; LL.D., University of Aberdeen, 1931; Benson Medal, Royal Society of Literature, 1937; honorary fellow, King's College, Cambridge, 1946; Litt.D., University of Liverpool, 1947, Hamilton College, 1949, Cambridge University, 1950, University of Nottingham, 1951, University of Manchester, 1954, Leiden University, 1954, University of Leicester, 1958; Tukojimo III Gold Medal; Companion of Honour, 1953; Companion of Royal Society of Literature; Order of Merit, 1969.

WRITINGS: Where Angels Fear to Tread (novel), Blackwood, 1905, Knopf, 1920; *The Longest Journey* (novel), Blackwood, 1907, Knopf, 1922; *A Room With a View* (novel), Edward Arnold, 1908, Putnam, 1911; *Howards End* (novel), Putnam, 1910; *The Celestial Omnibus, and Other Stories*, Sidgwick & Jackson, 1911, Knopf, 1923.

The Story of the Siren (short story), Hogarth Press, 1920; *The Government of Egypt* (history), Labour Research Department, 1921; *Alexandria: A History and a Guide*, W. Morris, 1922, 3rd edition, Doubleday-Anchor, 1961; *Pharos and Pharillon* (history), Knopf, 1923, 3rd edition, Hogarth Press, 1943; *A Passage to India* (novel), Harcourt, 1924; *Anonymity: An Enquiry*, V. Woolf, 1925; *Aspects of the Novel* (Clark Lecture, 1927), Harcourt, 1927; *The Eternal Moment, and Other Stories*, Harcourt, 1928.

A Letter to Madan Blanchard (belles lettres), Hogarth Press, 1931, Harcourt, 1932; *Goldsworthy Lowes Dickinson* (biography), Harcourt, 1934, new edition, Edward Arnold, 1945; *Abinger Harvest* (essays), Harcourt, 1936; *What I Believe* (political), Hogarth Press, 1939; *Reading as Usual* (criticism), 1939.

Nordic Twilight (political), Macmillan, 1940; *England's Pleasant Land* (pageant play), Hogarth Press, 1940; *Virginia Woolf* (criticism; Rede Lecture, 1941) Harcourt, 1942; *The Development of English Prose Between 1918 and 1939* (criticism; W. P. Ker Lecture, 1944), Jackson & Co. (Glasgow), 1945; *The Collected Tales of E. M. Forster* (previously published as *The Celestial Omnibus* and *The Eternal Moment*), Knopf, 1947 (published in England as *Collected Short Stories of E. M. Forster*, Sidgwick & Jackson, 1948).

(Author of libretto with Eric Crozier) *Billy Budd* (based on the novel by Herman Melville; music by Benjamin Britten), Boosey & Hawkes, 1951, revised edition, 1961; *Two Cheers for Democracy* (essays), Edward Arnold, 1951; *Desmond MacCarthy*, Mill House Press, 1952; *The Hill of Devi*, Harcourt, 1953 (published in England as *The Hill of Devi: Being Letters from Dewas State Senior*, Edward Arnold, 1953); *Battersea Rise* (first chapter of *Marianne Thornton*), Harcourt, 1955; *Marianne Thornton: A Domestic Biography, 1797-1887*, Harcourt, 1956.

E. M. Forster: Selected Writings, edited by G. B. Parker, Heinemann Educational, 1968; *Albergo Empedocle and Other Writings* (previously unpublished material, written 1900-15), edited by George H. Thomson, Liveright, 1971; *Maurice* (novel), Norton, 1971; *The Life to Come and Other Stories*, Norton, 1973.

Author of unfinished novel, "Arctic Summer," published in *Tribute to Benjamin Britten on His Fiftieth Birthday*, edited by Anthony Gishford, Faber, 1963. Also author of plays, "The Heart of Bosnia," 1911, and "The Abinger Pageant," 1934, and script for film, "Diary for Timothy."

Contributor: Arnold W. Lawrence, editor, *T. E. Lawrence by His Friends*, J. Cape, 1937; Hermon Ould, editor, *Writers in Freedom*, Hutchinson, 1942; George Orwell, editor, *Talking to India*, Allen & Unwin, 1943; *Peter Grimes: Essays*, John Lane, for the governors of Sadler's Wells Foundation, 1945; Hermon Ould, editor, *Freedom of Expression: A Symposium*, Hutchinson, 1945; S. Radhakrishnan, *Mahatma Gandhi: Essays and Reflections on His Life and Work*, 2nd edition, Allen & Unwin, 1949; *Hermon Ould: A Tribute*, [London], 1952; *The Fearful Choice: A Debate on Nuclear Policy*, conducted by Philip Toynbee, Wayne State University Press, 1959. Also contributor to *Aspects of England*, 1935, and *Britain and the Beast*, 1937.

Author of introduction: (And notes) Virgil, *The Aeneid*, translated by E. Fairfax Taylor, Dent, 1906; (and notes) Eliza Fay, *Original Letters from India, 1799-1815*, Harcourt, 1925; Constance Sitwell, *Flowers and Elephants*, J. Cape, 1927; George Crabbe, Jr., *The Life of George Crabbe*, Oxford University Press, 1932; Maurice O'Sullivan, *Twenty Years A-Growing*, Chatto & Windus, 1933; Mulk Raj Anand, *Untouchable*, Wishart, 1935; Alec Craig, *The Banned Books of England*, Allen & Unwin, 1937; K. R. Srinivasa Iyengar, *Literature and Authorship in India*, Allen & Unwin, 1943; Goldsworthy Lowes Dickinson, *Letters from John Chinaman and Other Essays*, Allen & Unwin, 1946; Huthi Singh, *Maura*, Longmans, Green, 1951; Zeenuth Futehally, *Zohra*, Hind Kitabs (Bombay), 1951; Peter Townsend, editor, *Cambridge Anthology*, Hogarth Press, 1952; Forrest Reid, *Tom Barber*, Pantheon, 1955; Dickinson, *The Greek View of Life*, University of Michigan Press, 1958; D. Windham, *The Warm Country*, Hart-Davis, 1960; Guiseppe Tomasi di Lampedusa, *Two Stories and a Memory*, translated by A. Colquhoun, Pantheon, 1962; Frank Sargeson, *Collected Stories*, MacGibbon & Kee, 1965.

Author of notes: William Golding, *Lord of the Flies*, Coward, 1955.

Work is represented in collections, including *The Challenge of Our Time*, Percival Marshall, 1948, and *Fairy Tales for Computers*, Eakins Press, 1969.

Contributor to journals and periodicals, including *Listener, Independent Review, Observer, New Statesman, Nation, Albany Review, Open Window, Athenaeum, Egyptian Mail*. and *Horizon*.

SIDELIGHTS: Forster's talent is now labeled "genius" as a matter of course—Graham Greene calls it "the gentle genius"; another critic once wrote: "So erratically and spasmodically has he worked that one cannot think of his genius as in course of development; it comes and goes, apparently as it wills."

His production of novels has been sparse—he had published five by 1924, and the sixth, *Maurice*, was issued posthumously after a hiatus of almost fifty years. Yet what Rose Macaulay concludes of his position is undoubtedly true: "If you asked a selection of educated English readers of fiction to pick out our most distinguished living novelist, nine out of ten, I should say, would answer E. M. Forster."

It was once said that "his reputation goes up with every book he doesn't write." Morton Dauwen Zabel once wrote that Forster has "no stylistic followers and perhaps few disciples in thought, yet if one were fixing the provenance of Auden's generation, Forster's name—whatever the claim of James, Lawrence, or Eliot—would suggest the most accurate combination of critical and temperamental forces, the only one stamped by the peculiarly English skeptical sensibility that survived the war with sanity. . . .''

He has had no wide popular audience. Though his novels have been established as classics, "even now Forster offers few of the appeals that qualify a novelist for urgent 'importance' or timely respect: no dogmatic beliefs in politics or religion, no radical stylistic novelty or aesthetic oddity, no yearly appeal to his public with a new book," writes Zabel. "He suggests few tags of easy distinction; perhaps only one—that he has practiced the difficult strategy of writing little but making it count for much. . . .''

Forster's writings are concerned with the complexity of human nature. What he calls the "Primal Curse" is not the knowledge of good and evil, but the knowledge of good-and-evil in its inextricable and unknowable complexity. Such a complex relationship cannot be explained by dogma. In 1939, Forster wrote: "I do not believe in Belief. Faith, to my mind, is a stiffening process, a sort of mental starch, which ought to be applied as sparingly as possible. I dislike the stuff. . . . My law givers are Erasmus and Montaigne, not Moses and St. Paul. My temple stands not upon Mount Moriah, but in that Elysian Field where even the immoral are admitted. My motto is: 'Lord, I disbelieve—help thou my unbelief.'''

Another time Forster wrote: "Truth, being alive, is not halfway between anything." Seeking the wholeness of truth he has searched for a "synthesis of matter and essence, of civilization with its inhibitions and nature with its crude energy," writes Zabel. "And like Andre Gide, whom he respected, he is one of the 'free minds'. . . . He too makes it his task to transmit not 'life's greatness,' which he has called 'a Nineteenth Century perquisite, a Goethean job,' but 'life's complexity, and the delight, the difficulty, the duty of registering that complexity and conveying it.'''

In 1941, at a time when such tenets were losing influence, he proclaimed his support of art for art's sake. He wrote: "The work of art stands by itself, and nothing else does. It achieves something which has often been promised by society but always delusively. Ancient Athens made a mess—but the Antigone stands up. Renaissance Rome made a mess—but the ceiling of the Sistine got painted; Louis XIV made a mess—but there was Phedre; Louis XV continued it, but Voltaire got his letters written."

Forster's style is meticulous. Miss Macaulay writes that "his presentment of people . . . is most delicately exact. Tones of speech, for instance. He is perhaps the only novelist, apart from Jane Austen, none of whose characters could, when speaking, be confused with any others in the book. And this without any of the obvious tricks and slogans which those whom he calls 'flat' characters in fiction fly like identifying flags."

Austin Warren, however, observes certain shortcomings: "Neither at wholeness nor at steadiness do his novels completely succeed. There are wide and deep *lacunae*: except for the Basts [in *Howards End*], there are no poor. From poverty, hunger, lust, and hate, his people are exempt. Love between the sexes, though recognized with sympathy, is never explored and is central to none of his novels. Except in *A Passage to India*, the individual is not portrayed in relation to society. . . .''

Forster told his *Paris Review* interviewers that he wrote only under inspiration, but that the act of writing inspired him. His childhood was very literary—"I was the author of a number of works between the ages of six and ten," he recalled. He thought highly of his own works and read them

often. ("I go gently over the bits I think are bad.") He also said: "I have always found writing pleasant, and don't understand what people mean by 'throes of creation.' I've enjoyed it, but believe that in some ways it is good. Whether it will last, I have no idea."

Forster is the only honorary fellow of King's College to have been offered permanent rooms there; he had lived at the college since the mid-1940's.

"A Passage to E. M. Forster," a play based on his works, was compiled by William Roerick and Thomas Coley, and produced in New York, N.Y. at Theatre de Lys in October, 1970.

A Room With a View was adapted as a play by Stephen Tait and Kenneth Allott, produced in Cambridge, February, 1950, and published by Edward Arnold, 1951. *A Passage to India* was adapted for the stage by Santha Rama Rau, and published by Edward Arnold, 1960; it was produced in London in 1960 and on Broadway in 1962; the television adaptation by John Maynard was produced by the BBC, and broadcast by NET in 1968. *Where Angels Fear to Tread* was adapted as a play by Elizabeth Hart, S. French, 1963. *Howards End* was adapted for stage by Lance Sieveking and Richard Cottrell and produced in London in 1967; the BBC production, adapted by Pauline Macaulay, was broadcast in 1970.

AVOCATIONAL INTERESTS: Forster was greatly interested in music, and is said to have been an accomplished amateur pianist.

BIOGRAPHICAL/CRITICAL SOURCES—Books: Frank Swinnerton, *The Georgian Literary Scene*, Dent, 1938, revised edition, 1951; Rose Macaulay, *Writings of E. M. Forster*, Harcourt, 1938, new edition, Barnes & Noble, 1970; Lionel Trilling, *E. M. Forster*, New Directions, 1943, 2nd revised edition, 1965; Austin Warren, *Rage for Order*, University of Michigan Press, 1948; J. K. Johnstone, *The Bloomsbury Group*, Noonday, 1954; Morton Dauwen Zabel, *Craft and Character*, Viking, 1957; Malcolm Cowley, editor, *Writers at Work: The Paris Review Interviews*, first series, Viking, 1958.

H. J. Oliver, *The Art of E. M. Forster*, Cambridge University Press, 1960; Mark Schorer, editor, *Modern British Fiction*, Oxford University Press, 1961; Karl Watts Gransden, *E. M. Forster*, Grove, 1962, revised edition, Oliver & Boyd, 1970; F. C. Crews, *E. M. Forster: The Perils of Humanism*, Princeton University Press, 1962; J. B. Beer, *The Achievement of E. M. Forster*, Barnes & Noble, 1963; K. Natwar-Singh, editor, *E. M. Forster: A Tribute*, Harcourt, 1964; David Shusterman, *The Quest for Certitude in E. M. Forster's Fiction*, Indiana University Press, 1965; Wilfred Stone, *The Cave and The Mountain*, Oxford University Press, 1966; Malcolm Bradbury, editor, *Forster*, Prentice-Hall, 1966; George H. Thomson, *The Fiction of E. M. Forster*, Wayne State University Press, 1967; Norman Kelvin, *E. M. Forster*, Southern Illinois University Press, 1967; Vasant Anant Shahane, editor, *Perspectives on E. M. Forster's A Passage to India*, Barnes & Noble, 1968; Laurence Brander, *E. M. Forster*, Hart-Davis, 1968; Denis Godfrey, *Forster's Other Kingdom*, Barnes & Noble, 1968; H. H. Anniah Gowda, *A Garland for E. M. Forster*, Literary Half-Yearly (Mysore, India), 1969; Oliver Stallybrass, editor, *Aspects of E. M. Forster*, Harcourt, 1969.

Andrew Rutherford, *Twentieth Century Interpretations of A Passage to India*, Prentice-Hall, 1970; June P. Levine, *Creation and Criticism: A Passage to India*, University of

Nebraska Press, 1971; Alfred Borrello, *An E. M. Forster Dictionary,* Scarecrow, 1971; James McConkey, *The Novels of E. M. Forster,* Archon Books, 1971; Martial Rose, *E. M. Forster,* Arco, 1971; Borrello, *An E. M. Forster Glossary,* Scarecrow, 1972; Carolyn Riley, editor, *Contemporary Literary Criticism,* Gale, Volume I, 1973, Volume II, 1974, Volume III, 1975, Volume IV, 1975.

Periodicals: *Forum,* December, 1927; *Criterion,* October, 1934; *Scrutiny,* September, 1938; *Theology,* April, 1940; *Yale Review,* June, 1944; *Dublin Review,* 1946; *Encounter,* Volume IX, 1957; *New Yorker,* September, 1959; *New Republic,* October 5, 1949, January 11, 1964; *Times Literary Supplement,* June 22, 1962; *Mademoiselle,* June, 1964; *Vogue,* January 1, 1965; *New York Times Book Review,* December 29, 1968; *Washington Post,* June 8, 1970; *Observer,* June 14, 1970; *Christian Science Monitor,* June 18, 1970; *Time,* June 22, 1970; *Newsweek,* June 22, 1970; *Nation,* June 29, 1970; *Listener,* July 9, 1970; *Christian Century,* July 22, 1970; *New York Review of Books,* July 23, 1970; *Books and Bookmen,* August, 1970.†

(Died June 7, 1970)

*   *   *

FOSTER, H. Lincoln   1906-

PERSONAL: Born February 12, 1906, in Newark, N.J.; son of Harry Walter (a businessman) and Harriet (Edwards) Foster; married Laura Louise James (an artist and author), December, 1948; children: Harriet Rebecca (Mrs. Robert Light), Benjamin G. *Education:* Williams College, A.B., 1928; Trinity College, Hartford, Conn., M.A., 1950; Yale University, graduate study, 1954-55. *Politics:* Republican. *Home:* Under Mountain Rd., Falls Village, Conn. 06031.

CAREER: Williams College Alumni Magazine, Williamstown, Mass., assistant editor, 1928-30; *Living Age* (magazine), New York, N.Y., general assistant, 1930-32; Morristown School, Morristown, N.J., teacher of English and Latin, 1932-37; Norfolk School, Norfolk, Conn., assistant headmaster and teacher, 1937-42; carried out horticultural experiments in Great Mountain Forest, Norfolk, Conn., 1944-49; high school teacher of English and Latin, Falls Village, Conn., 1950-62; landscape designer and gardener, 1962—. Representative in Connecticut General Assembly, 1947-49. Director of Root Glen Foundation, 1960—. *Member:* American Rock Garden Society (president, 1964-68), American Primrose Society, American Rhododendron Society, American Fern Society, Alpine Garden Society (England), Scottish Rock Garden Club, Litchfield County University Club. *Awards, honors:* De Bevoise Medal of Garden Clubs of America, for hybridizing; Merit Award from American Rock Garden Society; Award of Excellence from Federated Garden Clubs of Connecticut.

WRITINGS: (Contributor) Boughton Cobb, *Field Guide to the Ferns,* Houghton, 1956; (editor) *Contemporary American Poetry,* Macmillan, 1962; (editor) *Moby Dick,* Macmillan, 1962; *Rock Gardening: A Guide to Growing Alpines and Other Wildflowers in the American Garden,* Houghton, 1968. Contributor to botanical journals. Founder, *Connecticut Plantsman.*

*   *   *

FOWLER, Helen Rosa Huxley   1917-
   (Helen Foley)

PERSONAL: Born July 23, 1917, in Birkenhead, Cheshire,

England; daughter of Thomas Hugh and Olwen (Roberts) Huxley; married Arthur Laurence Fowler (a brigadier general in British Army), May 29, 1945; children: Richard, Catherine, Lucinda. *Education:* Newnham College, Cambridge, B.A., 1939, M.A., 1943. *Politics:* "Middle of the Road." *Religion:* Church of England. *Address:* c/o National & Grindlay's Bank Ltd., St. James Sq., London S.W.1, England. *Agent:* Curtis Brown Ltd., 1 Craven Hill, London W2 3EW, England.

CAREER: Cambridge University, Cambridge, England, researcher and teacher of medieval English literature, 1939-42; with British Ministry of Information, London, England, 1942-45; Cambridge University, Local Examinations Syndicate, a chief examiner in English, 1945—; Political and Economic Planning, London, England, case worker, 1953-55.

WRITINGS—Under pseudonym Helen Foley: *Between the Parties,* Hodder & Stoughton, 1958; *The Traverse,* Hodder & Stoughton, 1960; *A Handful of Time* (Book Society choice), Hodder & Stoughton, 1961, Lippincott, 1962; *Fort of Silence,* Hodder & Stoughton, 1963; *The Granddaughter,* Hodder & Stoughton, 1965; *The Bright Designs,* Hodder & Stoughton, 1969; *The Pitcher Plant,* Hodder & Stoughton, 1973.

SIDELIGHTS: Mrs. Fowler told *CA:* "[I] like conversation and gossip, Bach and Bartok, memoirs (written or recalled), landscapes, cooking, and France; [I] dislike motor bicycles, suburban mores and manners, sports commentaries, and lack of feeling and compassion."

*   *   *

FOWLER, Wilfred   1907-

PERSONAL: Born July 29, 1907, in Barry, South Wales; son of William Charles and Lucy (Wood) Fowler; married Agnes Muirhead Browning, July 27, 1940; children: Hugh, Margaret, William. *Education:* University of Wales, Bachelor of Science, 1928; Cambridge University, graduate study, 1933. *Politics:* Variable. *Religion:* Protestant. *Home:* 10 Hughenden Rd., Clifton, Bristol, England. *Agent:* Curtis Brown Ltd., 1 Craven Hill, London, W2 3EW, England.

CAREER: British Colonial Administrative Service, district officer in Solomon Islands, 1929-36, various posts ranging from district officer to senior resident and acting administrator of Lagos, in Nigeria, 1936-57; South Western Electricity Board, Bristol, England, assistant secretary, 1958-64; retired. County Scout Commissioner, Bristol.

WRITINGS: This Island's Mine, Constable, 1959; *Harama,* Cresset, 1963 published as *The Old Order and the New: A Novel of Africa,* Macmillan, 1965. Writer of radio scripts, short stories, and articles.

WORK IN PROGRESS: A novel based on the conflict of the labor trade, Christian missions, and the Royal Navy in the western Pacific, circa, 1880, completion expected in 1965; research into small ship seafaring.

SIDELIGHTS: Fowler told *CA:* "My interests are in the behavior of people under primitive physical conditions and subject to the stress of demanding circumstances. I prefer overseas administrators, soldiers, missionaries, explorers and so on to high-powered business executives."

*   *   *

FOX, Adam   1883-

PERSONAL: Born July 15, 1883, in London, England; son

of William Henry and Ellen (Frost) Fox. *Education:* Attended Winchester College, 1897-1902; University College, Oxford, B.A., 1906, M.A., 1909. *Home:* 4 Little Cloister, London SW1P 3PL, England.

CAREER: Ordained deacon, Church of England, 1911, priest, 1913; Lancing College, Sussex, England, assistant master, 1906-18; Radley College, Berkshire, England, headmaster, 1918-24; Diocesan College, Rondebosch, South Africa, assistant master, 1925-29; Oxford University, Oxford, England, fellow of Magdalen College, 1929-42, professor of poetry, 1938-42; Westminster Abbey, London, England, canon, 1942-63, sub-dean, 1959-63. Canon of Chichester Cathedral, 1936-42. Master, Worshipful Company of the Skinners of London, 1947-48. *Member:* Athenaeum Club (London). *Awards, honors:* Sacred Poem Prize, Oxford University, 1929; honorary D.D., University of St. Andrews, 1947; James Tait Black Memorial Prize for best biography of the year published in Great Britain, 1960, for *Dean Inge.*

WRITINGS: Dominus Virtutum, Faith Press, 1936; *Old King Coel*, Oxford University Press, 1937; *Plato for Pleasure*, West House, 1945, new edition, J. Murray, 1962; (editor) T. Collinson, *Poems Old and New*, St. Catherine Press, 1945; *English Hymns and Hymn Writers*, Collins, 1947; *Meet the Greek Testament*, S.C.M. Press, 1952, Allenson, 1954; *John Mill and Richard Bentley*, Basil Blackwell, 1954; (editor and translator) *Plato and the Christians*, S.C.M. Press, 1957; *God Is an Artist*, Bles, 1957; *Dean Inge*, J. Murray, 1960. Contributor to *Cassell's Encyclopedia of Literature.*

SIDELIGHTS: "I have lived in a college since 1897. . . . I am an amateur author. I do not earn my living by my writings, and I try to persuade myself that I shall best please the public by first pleasing myself. This sometimes succeeds, but *God Is an Artist*, which I like very well, has not proven a success. It expresses some of my dearest convictions, but along a line which is perhaps not familiar. I read Plato, Greek tragedies, and the Greek New Testament with immense pleasure, also books about them, and much English poetry.

"I am called Adam because I had a twin sister called Eve."

*   *   *

FOX, Charles Elliot   1878-

PERSONAL: Born October 1, 1878, in Stalbridge, Dorsetshire, England; son of John Elliot (an Anglican priest) and Emma (Phillips) Fox. *Education:* University of New Zealand, M.A. (first class honors). *Religion:* Christian. *Home:* Taroaniara, British Solomon Islands.

CAREER: Early career included periods as schoolmaster in New Zealand and on Norfolk Island, then missionary in Solomon Islands; Native Melanesian Brotherhood, member, 1932-43; missionary in Malaita, Solomon Islands, 1946-52; schoolmaster and chaplain, 1952. *Member:* Polynesian Society (life), Overseas League. *Awards, honors:* Member, Order of British Empire, 1952; Litt.D., University of New Zealand; fellow, St. John's College, Auckland.

WRITINGS: Introduction to Oceanic Languages, Melanesian Mission, 1910; *The Threshold of the Pacific: An Account of the Social Organization, Magic and Religion of the People of San Cristoval in the Solomon Islands*, Kegan Paul, 1924, Knopf, 1925; *A Dictionary of Nggela Language*, Unity Press, 1955; *Lord of the Southern Isles: Being the Story of the Anglican Mission in Melanesia,*

1849-1949, Mowbray & Co., 1958; *Kakamora*, Hodder & Stoughton, 1962. Contributor to *Grammar of Gela Language*, Polynesian Society. Also contributor to journals, including *Royal Anthropological Society Journal*, *Southern Cross Log*. Editor, *Melanesian Messenger.*

WORK IN PROGRESS: Studies of Melanesian languages, conchology, and chess.

SIDELIGHTS: Fox speaks the Melanesian languages Mota, Arosi, Lau, Ulawa, Gela, and others.

*   *   *

FRAENKEL, Gerd   1919-1970

PERSONAL: Born December 25, 1919, in Frankfurt, Germany; son of Adolf (a physician) and Trude (Neugarten) Fraenkel; married Miriam Cohen (a teacher of Hebrew), May 17, 1949; children: Eran. *Education:* The Hebrew University, Jerusalem, M.A., 1951; Indiana University, Ph.D., 1961. *Religion:* Jewish. *Home:* 1424 Barnsdale St., Pittsburgh, Pa. 15217.

CAREER: Indiana University, Bloomington, assistant director of U.S. Air Force Language program, 1959-61; University of Pittsburgh, Pittsburgh, Pa., lecturer in linguistics, 1961-62, chairman of committee on linguistics, 1962-64, associate professor, 1964-70. Yeshiva University, linguist at Summer Institute for High School Teachers of Hebrew, 1961, 1963. *Member:* Linguistic Society of America, American Oriental Society, National Society for the Study of Communication, Association for a World Language, American Association of University Professors, Union Mundial pro Interlingua, Societas Ural-Altaica, Israel Archaeological Society, Israel Oriental Society, Delta Phi Alpha.

WRITINGS—All published by Ginn: *Today's World in Focus: Israel*, 1963; *What is Language?*, 1965; *Writing Systems*, 1965; *Language in Culture*, 1967; *Languages of the World*, 1967. Contributor to *Encyclopaedia Hebraica* (Israel). Contributor of other articles to *International Language Review* and to journals of Oriental societies.

WORK IN PROGRESS: Parts V-X of "New Aspects of Language" series; *A Linguistic Bibliography of Interlinguists*, for Mouton & Co.; a generative grammar of Azerbaijani.

SIDELIGHTS: Fraenkel had been a resident of Israel since 1944; he was fluent in German, English, and Hebrew, competent in Turkish and Azerbaijani.

(Died, 1970)

*   *   *

FRANCE-HAYHURST, Evangeline (Chaworth-Musters)   1904-
(Evangeline France)

PERSONAL: Born February 25, 1904, in London, England; daughter of Arthur Henry and Reinette J. M. (Duminy) Chaworth-Musters; married Fergus Munro Innes (divorced); married Basil Walter France-Hayhurst (deceased); children: (first marriage) Jane (Mrs. Charles Legh), Ruth Evangeline (Mrs. Arthur Vincent). *Education:* Attended Maynard School. *Home:* 83 Halsford Park Rd., East Grimstead, Sussex, England. *Agent:* Curtis Brown Ltd., 1 Craven Hill, London W2 3EW, England.

WRITINGS—Under pseudonym Evangeline France; all published by Collins: *Happy Summer*, 1955; *Leave it to Louise*, 1956; *Company for Caroline*, 1957; *Blackberry*

Lane, 1958; *The Girl from Town*, 1961; *Nigella*, 1962; *Night Enchantment*, 1966.

WORK IN PROGRESS: A novel.

SIDELIGHTS: As a child Mrs. France-Hayhurst lived in Canary Islands, South Africa, Madeira, and in Argentina, where her father bred horses; she also resided in India, 1930-36. She started writing when her husband died and daughters married; she now writes only in winter, devoting her summers to gardening and country horse shows.

*   *   *

FRANCIS, Basil (Hoskins) 1906-
(Austen Rhode)

PERSONAL: Born November 22, 1906, in Bournemouth, England; son of Walter Henry and Rhoda (Hoskins) Francis; married Barbara Chapman; children: one daughter. *Politics:* Conservative. *Religion:* Congregationalist. *Agent:* Fosters Agency, Piccadilly Circus, London, England.

CAREER: Banking positions; Midland Bank Ltd., London and branches, member of head office staff, beginning 1947. Free-lance author and journalist. *Military service:* Royal Air Force, 1941-45; served in Southeast Asia as flying officer. *Member:* Society of Authors, Society for Theatre Research (founder-member; honorary treasurer, beginning 1949), Charles Lamb Society (member of council, 1938), Arts Theatre Club, R.A.F. Reserves Club. *Awards, honors:* Television play award, Cheltenham Festival of Contemporary Literature, 1955, for ''Rendezvous at Kensal Green.''

WRITINGS: Death at the Bank, Constable, 1937; *Slender Margin*, Constable, 1938; *The Holiday Camp Murder*, Constable, 1938; *Death for Safe Custody*, Quality Press, 1944; *Death on the Roof*, Quality Press, 1946; *Death on the Atoll*, Quality Press, 1948; *Fanny Kelly of Drury Lane*, Rockliff Publishing Corp., 1950; *Death in Act IV*, Jenkins, 1954.

Plays: ''What a Lass''; ''Chinese Crackling''; ''Harriot.'' Author of screen play, ''The Strange Case of Blondie,'' and television play, ''Rendezvous at Kensal Green.'' Contributor to ''Shadow Squad'' series, Granada Television.

Writer of ''World's Strangest Stories'' series, *Evening News* (London), of short stories for magazines and newspapers, and literary and dramatic criticism for *Stage, Theatre World, Theatre*, and *Theatre Notebook*.

WORK IN PROGRESS: A biography of Harriot Mellon, Duchess of St. Albans, with proposed title, *Mistress of Stratton Street*; a life of Sir Francis Burdett; a series on first ladies of the stage; a history of the battleship, H.M.S. ''Barham.''

AVOCATIONAL INTERESTS: Reading, talking, cricket, and collecting eighteenth-century playbills.

*   *   *

FRANK, Goldalie 1908-

PERSONAL: Born August 6, 1908, in Jacksonville, Texas; daughter of Louis E. (a merchant) and Tillie (Mandelstamm) Frank; married Solomon Balsam (a handbag manufacturer), November 22, 1945. *Education:* Dallas Art Institute, Dallas, Tex., student one year. *Religion:* Jewish. *Home address:* P.O. Box 1725, Jacksonville, Tex. 75766. *Office:* Contempo Agency, Inc., 551 Fifth Ave., New York, N.Y. 10017.

CAREER: Cramer-Tobias-Meyer, New York, N.Y., vice-president, 1937-46; Contempo Advertising Agency, Inc., New York, N.Y., president, 1946—. East Texas Handbag Co., Jacksonville, vice-president. Member of board of Medical Research Foundation Jacksonville, Tex., 1968—. *Awards, honors*, Jacksonville, Tex., Woman of the Year, 1972.

WRITINGS: Mother, I'd Rather Buy It Myself!, Macfadden, 1965. Also author of *How to Furnish a New Home* published by Macfadden, and centennial book for Jacksonville, Tex. Monthly columnist, *Department Store Economist*, 1948-50; contributor to other trade journals. Editor of home fashions section, *Singer Showcase*, 1966-68.

*   *   *

FRANK, Josette 1893-

PERSONAL: Born March 27, 1893, in New York, N.Y.; daughter of Leo (a merchant) and Hattie (Brill) Frank; married Henry Jacobs; children: Judith Jacobs Rosen, Stephen Frank. *Home:* 201 West 54th St., New York, N.Y. 10019. *Office:* 50 Madison Ave., New York, N.Y. 10010.

CAREER: Child Study Association of America, New York, N.Y., director for children's books and mass media, 1923—. Editor, lecturer, and writer. Member of book selection committee of National Conference of Christians and Jews.

WRITINGS: What Books for Children?: Guideposts for Parents, Doubleday, 1937, revised edition, 1941; (with Clara Lambert) *From the Records: An Adventure in Teacher Training*, Play Schools, 1939; *Your Child's Reading Today*, Doubleday 1954, 2nd revised edition, 1969; *Comics, TV, Radio, Movies: What Do They Offer Children?*, Public Affairs Committee, 1955; (editor) *Peter Pan* (adaptation of *Peter Pan and Wendy*, by J. M. Barrie), Random House, 1957; (editor) *Poems to Read to the Very Young*, Random House, 1961; *Children and TV*, Public Affairs Committee, 1962; *Television: How to Use It Wisely With Children*, Child Study Association of America, 1965, revised edition, 1969; (compiler) *More Poems to Read to the Very Young*, Random House, 1968.

Supervisory editor—All published by Random House: Anna Sewell, *Black Beauty*, 1949; Daniel Defoe, *The Life and Adventures of Robinson Crusoe*, 1952; David McDowell, *Robert E. Lee*, 1953; *Big Black Horse* (adaptation of *The Black Stallion*, by Walter Farley), 1953; Estelle Schneider, *King Arthur and the Knights of the Round Table* (adaptation of *The Story of King Arthur and His Knights*, by Howard Pyle), 1954; Lewis Carroll (pseudonym of Charles Lutwidge Dodgson), *Alice in Wonderland*, 1955; Shirley Temple, compiler, *Storybook*, 1958; Andrew Lang, compiler, *Blue Fairy Book*, 1959.

WORK IN PROGRESS: ''Sexuality in Children's Books'' for *Issues in Children's Book Selections* to be published by Bowker.

*   *   *

FRANKAU, Mary Evelyn Atkinson 1899-
(M. E. Atkinson)

PERSONAL: Born June 20, 1899, in Highgate, London, England; daughter of George Thomas (a schoolmaster) and Edith Jessie (Howard) Atkinson; married George Neuberg Frankau, April 16, 1951. *Education:* Privately educated, and at Leeson House, Langton, Matravers, Dorsetshire, England. *Politics:* Conservative. *Religion:* Anglican.

Home: Storey's Close, Wiveliscombe, near Taunton, Somerset, England.

CAREER: Playwright and author of children's books. Red Cross nurse in both World Wars; currently does welfare work among ex-servicemen for British Red Cross. *Member:* British Legion.

WRITINGS—Under name M. E. Atkinson: (Editor with father, George Thomas Atkinson) *A Book of Giants and Dwarfs*, Dent, 1929; *August Adventure*, J. Cape, 1936; *Mystery Manor*, Bodley Head, 1937; *The Compass Points North*, John Lane, 1938; *Smugglers' Gap*, John Lane, 1939; *Going Gangster*, John Lane, 1940; *Crusoe Island*, Bodley Head, 1941; *Challenge to Adventure*, Bodley Head, 1941; *The Monster of Widgeon Weir*, Bodley Head, 1943; *The Nest of the Scarecrow*, John Lane, 1944; *Problem Party*, John Lane, 1945; *Chimney Cottage*, Bodley Head, 1947; *The House on the Moor*, Bodley Head, 1948; *The 13th Adventure*, Bodley Head, 1949; *Steeple Folly*, Bodley Head, 1950; *Castaway Camp*, Bodley Head, 1951; *Hunter's Moon*, Bodley Head, 1952; *The Barnstormers*, Bodley Head, 1953; *Riders and Raids*, Bodley Head, 1955; *Unexpected Adventure*, Bodley Head, 1955; *Horseshoes and Handle Bars*, Bodley Head, 1958, A. S. Barnes, 1959; *Where There's a Will*, Thomas Nelson, 1961.

One-act plays: *Here Lies Matilda* (comedy), Baker Plays, 1931; *Beginner's Luck* (comedy), Baker Plays, 1932; *Patchwork*, Baker Plays, 1933; *The Chimney Corner*, Baker Plays, 1934; *The Day's Good Cause* (comedy), Baker Plays, 1935; *Crab-Apple Harvest*, Baker Plays, 1936; *Going Rustic* (comedy), Baker Plays, 1936; *Little White Jumbo* (comedy), J. B. Pinker, 1937; *Can the Leopard?* (comedy), Baker Plays, 1939; *The Lights Go Up* (comedy), H. F. W. Deane, 1945.

Contributor of stories to British Broadcasting Corp. "Children's Hour."

*   *   *

FRANKLIN, Burt 1903-1972

PERSONAL: Born November 3, 1903, son of Adolph and Emma (Franklin) Franklin; married Ethel Slomon, 1933; children: John (deceased), Thomas Richard. *Education:* Attended Amherst College; Cornell University, LL.B., 1927. *Home:* 124 East Hunting Ridge Rd., Stamford, Conn. *Office:* 235 East 44th St., New York, N.Y. 10017.

CAREER: Lawyer. Burt Franklin, Publisher, New York, N.Y., director. *Member:* Cavendish Club (New York), Rockrimmon Country Club (Stamford).

WRITINGS: (With G. Legman) *David Ricardo and Ricardian Theory*, B. Franklin, 1949; (with F. Cordasco) *Adam Smith: An International Record of Critical Writings . . . Relating to Smith and Smithian Theory 1876-1950*, B. Franklin, 1950. Contributor to *Cornell Law Review* and *Book Production*.

WORK IN PROGRESS: Continuing work started fifteen years ago on compilation of a bibliography of bibliographies of economics, economic history, and social history.

AVOCATIONAL INTERESTS: Golf, travel, research, bridge.

(Died, 1972)

*   *   *

FRANKLIN, George E. 1890-1971

PERSONAL: Born June 19, 1890, in Whiteshill, Gloucestershire, England; son of Edward George and Martha (Cooke) Franklin; married Florence Batts, May 18, 1945. *Education:* International Correspondence School, M.E., 1915. *Politics:* Republican. *Religion:* Protestant. *Home:* 1133 Pahor Dr., Las Vegas, Nev. 89102.

CAREER: Came to the United States at the age of twelve and worked as a ranch hand in Idaho, 1903-15; Fisher Body Co., mechanical and aeronautical engineer, 1915-20; operated own auto and experimental engine business, 1920-33; Federal Housing Administration, field representative in Nevada, 1934-37; Franklin Realty & Development Co., Las Vegas, Nev., owner and manager, 1938-63. Member of board of review, Building Department, City of Las Vegas, 1941-42; former president of Builders Exchange, Real Estate Board, and Associated General Contractors, all Las Vegas. *Member:* National Society of Professional Engineers, Masons, Knife and Fork Club (Las Vegas).

WRITINGS: From Cotswolds to High Sierras (autobiographical), Caxton, 1966; *The Fallacy of Appeasement*, Carlton, 1968.

SIDELIGHTS: Franklin designed and built a sixteen-cylinder aircraft engine, 1928-30, and worked in home machine shop after retirement.

*   *   *

FRANKLIN, Harry 1906-

PERSONAL: Born January 20, 1906, in London, England; son of Frederick L. (an engineer) and Isabella (Masterman) Franklin; married Hilda Hadfield, August 30, 1928; children: Clive Henry, Tonice Margaret Franklin Tilbey. *Education:* Exeter College, Oxford, B.A., 1927, Dip. Ed., 1928; Lincoln's Inn, Barrister-at-Law, 1938. *Religion:* Church of England. *Home:* Valley Farm, Leopards Hill Rd., Lusaka, Zambia.

CAREER: Colonial Service, Northern Rhodesia (now Zambia), 1929-51, serving variously as inspector of education, district commissioner, and resident magistrate, 1929-41, director of Information and Broadcast Services, 1941-45; Northern Rhodesia government, Minister of Education and Social Services, 1954-59, member of Legislative Council, 1959-60, Minister of Transport and Works, 1961-62; farmer, near Lusaka, Zambia. War correspondent, 1942-45. *Member:* Commonwealth Parliamentary Association, Zambia National Affairs Association. *Awards, honors:* Order of the British Empire.

WRITINGS: Ignorance Is No Defence, Longmans, Green, 1941; *Unholy Wedlock: The Failure of the Central African Federation*, Allen & Unwin, 1963. Author of radio and television scripts for Canadian Broadcasting Corp., British Broadcasting Corp., and National Broadcasting Co. Contributor of short stories to magazines, articles to *Spectator, Guardian, Sunday Times, Times*, and other newspapers.

WORK IN PROGRESS: Several novels.

SIDELIGHTS: Franklin commented, "Writing is hard work. I don't know why I do it." His travels cover all of Africa, most of Europe, the Middle East, Southeast Asia, Canada, and America.

*   *   *

FRASER, Conon 1930-

PERSONAL: Born March 8, 1930, in Cambridge, England; son of Ronald G. J. Isobel (Shaw) Fraser; married Jacqueline Amanda Stearns, March 17, 1955; children: Graham, Derek, John, Michael, Peter. *Education:* Attended Marlborough College and Royal Military Academy at Sandhurst. *Religion:* Anglican. *Home:* 25 Boundary Rd., Kelburn, Wellington, New Zealand. *Agent:* Curtis Brown Ltd., 1 Craven Hill, London W2 3EW, England.

CAREER: British Army, regular officer in Royal Artillery, 1950-53, becoming lieutenant; resigned commission to give more time to writing; was writer and part-time gardener "to make ends meet," for eight years; New Zealand Broadcasting Corp. Television, producer of various programs, including series "Looking at New Zealand," for three years; New Zealand National Film Unit, film director, 1969—.

WRITINGS: Dead Man's Cave, Blackie & Son, 1954; *The Green Dragon*, Blackie & Son, 1955; *Shadow of Danger*, Blackie & Son, 1956; *The Underground Explorers*, Blackie & Son, 1957; *The Underground River*, Blackie & Son, 1959; *The Scoter Island Adventure*, Collins, 1959; *Lim of Hong Kong*, Blackie & Son, 1960; *Oystercatcher Bay*, Blackie & Son, 1962; *With Captain Cook in New Zealand*, Muller, 1963; *A Brave Rescue*, Hamish Hamilton, 1964; *Looking at New Zealand*, Whitcombe & Tombs, 1969. Contributor of *Argosy* (England), *Listener* (New Zealand), and other magazines.

WORK IN PROGRESS: Travel articles on New Zealand.

SIDELIGHTS: The Green Dragon has been translated into Dutch, *Dead Man's Cave* into French.

*   *   *

FRASER, Edith Emily Rose Oram   1903-

PERSONAL: Born January 14, 1903, in London, England; daughter of Bruce (a builder) and Elizabeth (Rye) Oram; married Peter Fraser (an artist), June 7, 1933 (died, 1950); children: Donald Peter and Frederick Rodney (stepsons). *Education:* Attended Stockwell Training College. *Home:* Grunnavoe, Admiralty Walk, Seasalter, Whitstable, Kent, England.

CAREER: Writer for children. Member, Women's Voluntary Service.

WRITINGS: The Voyage to There and Back, Hutchinson, 1939; *Chuffy*, Franklyn Ward & Wheeler, 1942; *Buster Bunny's Birthday*, Burrow & Co., 1944; *Duckling the Dunce*, Burrow & Co., 1944; *Flippity-Hop*, Franklyn Ward & Wheeler, 1944; *Helping Mrs. Wigglenose*, Burrow & Co., 1944; *Sandy's Silver Sixpence*, Burrow & Co., 1944; (with husband, Peter Fraser) *Jack and Jock's Great Discovery*, Partridge Publications, 1944; *Billy Bobtail Goes to School and Small Town Sports: Two Stories for Children*, Art & Education Publishers, 1945; (with Peter Fraser) *Bunky the Bear Cub and Peter the Penguin: Two Stories for Children*, Art & Educational Publishers, 1945; *Jack and Jock: The Mischievous Puppies*, Miller, c.1945; *The New Recruit*, Burrow & Co., 1945; (with Peter Fraser) *Camping Out*, Pocket Editions, 1945; *John and Ann*, Childrens Press, 1949.

David John, Epworth, 1958; *God So Loved the World*, Brockhampton Press, 1960; *Heroes of God*, Brockhampton Press, 1960; *In the Beginning*, Brockhampton Press, 1960; *Jesus and His Work*, Brockhampton Press, 1960; *The Bible Tells Me So: 32 Stories from the Old and New Testaments* (contains *God So Loved the World, Heroes of God, In the Beginning*, and *Jesus and His Work*), Brockhampton Press, 1960, World Publishing, 1965; *David John Hears about Jesus*, Epworth, 1961, published as *A Boy Hears about Jesus*, Abingdon, 1965; *David John Again*, Epworth, 1962; *Nelson's New Job*, Epworth, 1963; *Before Jesus Came: More Stories for David John*, Epworth, 1964, published as *A Boy Hears Stories from the Old Testament*, Abingdon, 1967; *David John Finds Out*, Epworth, 1965. Represented in several anthologies, *Read Aloud Tales*, edited by Malcolm Saville, George Newnes, 1956, and *Tell Me a Story*, edited by Eileen Colwell, Penguin, 1962. Contributor of stories and verse to children's magazines and annuals.

WORK IN PROGRESS: An adventure book for children, with local background.

AVOCATIONAL INTERESTS: Swimming, sailing, gardening, reading, and music.

*   *   *

FRASER, Gordon Holmes   1898-

PERSONAL: Born January 8, 1898, in Lachute, Quebec, Canada; son of James Kemp (a farmer) and Kathleen (Hilsden) Fraser; married Thelma Lucille Corbett, February 11, 1921; children: Martha Anne (Mrs. David McMinn), Ruth (Mrs. Kenneth Davis), James Howard. *Education:* Attended University of Oregon and California Baptist Theological Seminary; Arizona State College, B.S.; Northern Arizona University, M.A. *Politics:* Republican. *Religion:* Plymouth Brethren. *Address:* Box A, Flagstaff, Ariz. 86002.

CAREER: Student Missionary Council, Tacoma, Wash., executive secretary, 1937-56; Southwestern School of Missions, Flagstaff, Ariz., professor of journalism, anthropology, and missions, beginning, 1959; retired; now serving as chancellor.

WRITINGS: Elijah, the Pilgrim Prophet, Moody, 1954; *Is Mormonism Christian?*, Moody, 1957; (with Peter Gunther) *The Fields at Home*, Moody, 1963; *What the Book of Mormon Teaches*, Moody, 1964; *No Dark Valley*, Southwestern School of Missions Press, 1965; *Rain on the Desert*, Moody, in press. Contributor to *Symposium on Creation*, edited by Donald Patten, Baker Book. Also author of *Why Can't Joe Begay Read?*, and *Indians of the Rain Forest*, both published by Southwestern School of Missions. Contributor to religious journals.

WORK IN PROGRESS: Indian Bible Translations; Age of Man in America; Myths of Mormonism; and *Molly Lou, Tales of the Lower Columbia*.

AVOCATIONAL INTERESTS: Indian anthropology, North American archaeology.

*   *   *

FRASER, W(illiam) Lionel   18?-1965

PERSONAL: Born in London, England; married Cynthia Elizabeth Walter, 1931; children: Nicholas A., Robert H. *Home:* 30 Charles St., London W.1, England. *Office:* Crewe House, Curzon St., London W.1, England.

CAREER: Served in H.M. Treasury, 1939-45; Issuing Houses Association, London, England, chairman, 1946-48; chairman of Helbert, Wagg & Co. Ltd., Thomas Tilling Ltd., Cornhill Insurance Co., Scandinvest Trust Ltd., and Banque de Paris et des Pays-Bas Ltd; deputy chairman, Triarch Corp. Ltd., Atlas Assurance Co. Ltd., and Tube Investments Ltd. President, Babcock & Wilcox Ltd. Liveryman of Fishmongers Company. Trustee, Tate Gallery; member, Chelsea Borough Council, 1949-50. *Military ser-*

vice: British Army, 1914-19; served in Dardanelles, Egypt, and France. *Member:* Garrick Club, St. James' Club, White's Club, Portland Club, City of London Club (all London), Travellers Club (Paris).

WRITINGS: All to the Good (autobiography), Heinemann, 1963, Doubleday, 1964.

(Died January 2, 1965)

* * *

FRASER HARRISON, Brian 1918-

PERSONAL: Born September 6, 1918, in Liverpool, England; son of James (a county court judge) and Betty (Broadhurst) Fraser Harrison; married Constance Kathleen Bennion (formerly a fashion boutiquiere); children: James. *Education:* Liverpool College, student, 1931-36. *Home:* Mouldsworth House, Mouldsworth, Chester CH3 8AP, England. *Office:* Mace & Jones, 19 Water St., Liverpool L2 ORP, England.

CAREER: Solicitor of Supreme Court of Judicature. Mace & Jones, Liverpool, England, partner, 1945—. *Military service:* British Army, 1938-44; became captain.

WRITINGS: Advocacy at Petty Sessions, Sweet & Maxwell, 1956, 2nd edition, 1959; *Work of a Magistrate*, Shaw & Sons, 1964, 2nd edition, 1969; *A Business of Your Own*, World's Work, 1969.

* * *

FRAZER-HURST, Douglas 1883-

PERSONAL: Born January 7, 1883, in Walker-on-Tyne, Northumberland, England; son of Hugh (a medical practitioner) and Maria (Smyth) Frazer-Hurst; married Margaret Annetta Steen, January 7, 1914; children: Zoe Margaret (Mrs. Alan Wood), Mary (Mrs. William Rowan), Eva (Mrs. Noel Donaghy). *Education:* University of Durham, M.A., 1909; additional divinity study at Westminster College, Cambridge, England; Trinity College, Dublin, Ireland, Ph.D., 1948. *Politics:* Liberal. *Home:* 280 Merville Garden Village, Newtownabbey, County Antrim, Northern Ireland.

CAREER: Presbyterian minister in Manchester, Sunderland, and Southport, England; Elmwood Church, Belfast, Northern Ireland, minister, 1924-51. World Council of Churches, preacher in United States, 1949. *Member:* Society of Authors, Churches' Fellowship for Psychical Study, Belfast Literary Society (president, 1935), Belfast Poetry Society (president, 1945-63), Belfast Shakespeare Society (president, 1925—), Belfast Psychical Society.

WRITINGS: Wylie Blue: The Life of the Rev. A. Wylie Blue, James Clarke, 1957; *The Bridge of Life: A Clerical Autobiography*, Mullan & Son, 1962. Regular columnist, *Belfast Telegraph*, 1950—.

* * *

FREEMAN, Ira Henry 1906-

PERSONAL: Born August 12, 1906, in New York, N.Y.; son of Arthur J. (a businessman) and Rachel (Abrams) Freeman; married Beatrice Oppenheim (a free-lance writer), September 21, 1937. *Education:* Columbia University, B.Litt., 1928. *Politics:* Independent. *Home and office:* Harkaway, Woodbury Rd., Woodbury, Long Island, N.Y.; and Edgartown, Martha's Vineyard, Mass. (summer). *Agent:* Curtis Brown Ltd., 60 East 56th St., New York, N.Y. 10022.

CAREER: New York Times, New York, N.Y., reporter on general staff, 1928-61; full-time free-lance writer, 1961—. Instructor in journalism, City College (now City College of the City University of New York), 1950-51. *Military service:* U.S. Army, 1943-45; staff writer on New York edition of *Yank, The Army Weekly*, 1943-44, on Mediterranean edition, 1944-45. *Member:* American Newspaper Guild (charter member, New York). *Awards, honors:* Honorable mention, *Best Short Stories of 1941*, for "The Fall of Little Ajax"; George Polk Memorial Award of Long Island University for outstanding national reporting, 1951.

WRITINGS: (Editor) *White Sails Shaking* (anthology of true sailing stories), Macmillan, 1948; *Out of the Burning: The Story of a Boy Gang Leader*, Crown, 1960; (with Beatrice Freeman) *Careers and Opportunities in Journalism*, Dutton, 1966. Articles anthologized in *Yank: The G.I. Story of the War*, edited by Debs Meyers, Duell, Sloan & Pearce, 1947; *Great Reading from Life*, Harper, 1960; *Death Penalty in America*, edited by Hugo Adam Bedau, Aldine, 1964; *Detail and Pattern*, compiled by Robert Baylor, McGraw, 1969. Contributor of articles and short stories, a number of them on sailing, skiing, juvenile delinquency, and travel, to *Life, Esquire, Atlantic Monthly, Woman's Home Companion, Story, New York Times Magazine, Pan Am Clipper, Long Island Press, Prairie Schooner*, and other publications.

WORK IN PROGRESS: A novel, *A Noisy Desperation*; a film script, as yet untitled.

AVOCATIONAL INTERESTS: Sailing, drawing and painting, skiing, figure skating, travel.

* * *

FREEMAN, Ruth L. Sunderlin 1907-

PERSONAL: Born April 17, 1907, in Penn Yan, N.Y.; daughter of George L. (a merchant) and Edith May (Crosby) Sunderlin; married G. L. Freeman (a professor and publisher), June 22, 1929; children: James L., John Crosby, Peter S. *Education:* Attended University of Chicago, 1930, and Columbia University; State University of New York College at Cortland, B.S., 1931. *Politics:* Republican. *Religion:* Protestant. *Home and office:* Yorker Yankee Preservation Museum, Watkins Glen, N.Y.

CAREER: Century House Americana, Inc. (book publishers), Watkins Glen, N.Y., business manager, 1942—; Yorker Yankee Preservation Museum, Old Irelandville, N.Y., educational director, 1950—. Trustee, American Life Foundation. *Member:* Zonta International (former local president).

WRITINGS: (With husband, G. L. Freeman) *Child and His Picture Book*, Northwestern University Press, 1933; (with G. L. Freeman) *Child's First Picture Book*, Northwestern University Press, 1933, revised edition, 1946; (with G. L. Freeman) *Cavalcade of Toys*, Century House, 1942; (with G. L. Freeman) *Victorian Furniture*, Century House, 1952; *American Dolls*, Century House, 1952, new edition, Century House, 1962; *Frugal Housewife*, Century House, 1957; *How To Mend and Dress Old Dolls*, Century House, 1960; *Yesterday's School Books*, Century House, 1960; *Yesterday's Schools*, Century House, 1962; (with G. L. Freeman) *Yesterday's Toys*, Century House, 1962; *Children's Picture Books Yesterday and Today*, Century House, 1967.

WORK IN PROGRESS: A doll book for collectors; developing the Ruth Freeman Museum of Childhood.

FREEMAN, Walter (Jackson, Jr.) 1895-1972

PERSONAL: Born November 14, 1895, in Philadelphia, Pa.; son of Walter Jackson (a physician) and Corinne (Keen) Freeman; married Marjorie Franklin, November 3, 1924; children: Marjorie Lorne (Mrs. Donald Canter), Walter J. III, Franklin, Paul, William (deceased), Robert FitzRandolph. *Education:* Yale University, A.B., 1916; University of Pennsylvania, M.D., 1920; graduate student in neurology in Paris and Rome, 1923-24; Georgetown University, M.S., 1929, Ph.D., 1931. *Home:* 24203 Hillslope Pl., Los Altos, Calif. *Office:* 877 West Fremont Ave., Sunnyvale, Calif. 94087.

CAREER: St. Elizabeth's Hospital, Washington, D.C., director of laboratories, 1924-33; Georgetown University, Washington, D.C., associate in pathology, 1924-33; George Washington University, Washington, D.C., professor of neurology, 1929-54; Santa Clara County Hospital, San Jose, Calif., chief of neurology, 1956-72; private practice in Sunnyvale, Calif., 1961-72. Diplomate of National Board of Medical Examiners and of American Board of Psychiatry and Neurology. Consultant in neurology to California State hospitals in Agnews, Stockton, Modesto, Napa, and Mendocino. *Military service:* U.S. Army, Medical Corps, 1918.

MEMBER: American Medical Association (fellow; secretary of section on nervous and mental diseases, 1927-30, chairman of section, 1931), American Board of Psychiatry and Neurology (secretary, 1934-46; president, 1946-47), American Neurological Association, American Psychiatric Association (fellow), American Association of Neuropathologists (president, 1944-45), Royal Medico-Psychological Association (corresponding member), Academia das Ciencias de Lisbon (corresponding member), Santa Clara-Monterey Counties Psychiatric Society (president, 1958-59), Santa Clara County Medical Society, Sigma Xi. *Awards, honors:* Bronze Medal, American Medical Association Scientific Exhibit, 1931.

WRITINGS: Neuropathology, Saunders, 1933; (with James W. Watts) *Psychosurgery*, C. C Thomas, 1942, 2nd edition, 1950; (with Mary F. Robinson) *Psychosurgery and the Self*, Grune, 1954; *The Psychiatrist: Personalities and Patterns*, Grune, 1968. Contributor to professional journals.

SIDELIGHTS: Freeman, who pioneered in the introduction of prefrontal lobotomy, once told *CA*: "When Watts and I presented our first paper on prefrontal lobotomy in 1936, Adolf Meyer, professor of psychiatry at Johns Hopkins University, urged us to 'follow each case.' I have engaged in this study for nearly thirty years." Freeman spoke French, German, and some Spanish; he read Italian and Portuguese. *Avocational interests:* Hiking in the mountains, trout fishing.

(Died May 31, 1972)

*   *   *

FREEMAN-ISHILL, Rose 1895-

PERSONAL: Born November 28, 1895, in New York, N.Y.; daughter of Abe Yehiel (a tailor) and Tillie (Freeman) Goldstein; married Joseph Ishill (head of Oriole Press), April 22, 1917; children: Crystal (Mrs. Simon Mendelsohn). *Education:* Attended schools in New York, N.Y. *Residence:* Berkeley Heights, N.J.

CAREER: Writer and translator.

WRITINGS: Rain Among the Bamboos (Japanese poems), Little Nirvana, 1917; *Petals Blown Adrift* (poems), Joseph Ishill, 1918; (editor with others) *Peter Kropotkin*, Free Spirit, 1924; (contributor) Joseph Ishill, editor, *Elisee and Elie Reclus*, Oriole Press, 1927; *Dream and Advent* (prose and verse), Oriole Press, 1929; (contributor) Joseph Ishill, editor, *Havelock Ellis: In Appreciation*, Oriole Press, 1929; *Poems*, Oriole Press, 1930; *Abraham Friedland: In Memoriam*, Oriole Press, 1942; *Tillie Freeman Goldstein: In Memoriam*, Oriole Press, 1948; *Dedication: A Group of Poems*, Oriole Press, 1948; *Rose Freeman-Ishill* (reviews and comments), Oriole Press, 1951; *O-Jin-San: From "Rain Among the Bamboos,"* Oriole Press, 1958; *Havelock Ellis, 1859-1959: Centennial*, Oriole Press, 1959; *To the Unknown Martyrs*, Oriole Press, 1959; *Collected Works* (contains *Petals Blown Adrift*, *Rain Among the Bamboos*, *Poems*, *Dedications: A Group of Poems*, *Translations from the French, German, Italian and Yiddish*, *Carved Crosses*, *Views and Reviews*, and *Miscellanea: Reviews and Comments on "Petals Blown Adrift"*), Oriole Press, 1962; (author of tribute) *The Story of Oscar Wilde's Experience in Reading Gaol*, Oriole Press, 1963; *Ishill's Variorum*, Oriole Press, 1963; *Seer in Darkness: A Group of Three Poems*, Oriole Press, 1964; *Wellspring and Later Poems*, Oriole Press, 1965; (contributor of poem) *Jerusalem by Moonlight* [and] *The Hebrew Race: Two Excerpts from the Writings of Benjamin Disraeli*, Oriole Press, 1965; (contributor of poem) Tolstoi, *Preliminary Sketch of "The Kreutzer Sonata,"* Oriole Press, 1965; (contributor of poem) Shelley, *The Divinity of Poetry*, Oriole Press, 1966.

Translator: Basil Dahl, *To the Toilers, and Other Verses*, Oriole Press, 1927; Elle Faure, *The Soul of Japan*, Oriole Press, 1930; Elie Reclus, *Plant Physiognomies*, Oriole Press, 1931; (and editor with others) *Free Vistas: An Anthology of Life and Letters*, Oriole Press, Volume I, 1933, Volume II, 1937; Jacques Mesnil, *Frans Masereel*, Oriole Press, 1934; Eugene Relgis, *Muted Voices*, Oriole Press, 1938; Itzchok Katzenelson, *Elegy*, Oriole Press, 1948; Jacques Mesnil, *Joseph Ishill and the Oriole Press*, Oriole Press, 1958; Maximo Jose Kahn, *Andalusian Popular Chant and Synagogue Music*, Oriole Press, 1958; (and editor) *A Group of Poems: Translated from the French, German, Italian, and Yiddish*, Oriole Press, 1960. Contributor to *Open Vistas*. Co-editor, *Free Spirit* (monthly), 1919.

*   *   *

FRENCH, William Marshall 1907-

PERSONAL: Born February 18, 1907, in Bodine, Pa.; son of Harry H. and Mary (Pray) French; married Florence Smith, April 9, 1936; children: Geoffrey. *Education:* State University of New York at Albany, A.B., 1929; University of Michigan, extension courses, 1930-32; Yale University, Ph.D., 1934. *Politics:* Independent. *Religion:* Lutheran. *Home:* 1200 Hibiscus, Apt. 305, Pompano Beach, Fla. 33062.

CAREER: High school teacher, Grosse Pointe, Mich., 1929-32; Yale University, New Haven, Conn., instructor in education, 1932-34; State University of New York at Albany, instructor in education, 1934-39; Muskingum College, New Concord, Ohio, dean, 1939-43; Hastings College, Hastings, Neb., president, 1943-52; Muhlenberg College, Allentown, Pa., professor of education, 1953-72, professor emeritus, 1972—. Visiting professor of psychology, Macalester College, 1953. *Member:* Pennsylvania Institutional Teacher Placement Association, Pennsylvania Association of Liberal Arts Colleges for Advancement of Teaching, Phi Delta Kappa, Kappa Phi Kappa, Pi Gamma Mu. *Awards, honors:* Distinguished Alumnus Award from State University of New York at Albany, 1969.

WRITINGS: (With wife, Florence S. French) *College of Empire State*, State College for Teachers (Albany, N.Y.), 1944; *Education for All*, Odyssey, 1955; *American Secondary Education*, Odyssey, 1957, revised edition, 1966; *America's Educational Tradition*, Heath, 1964. Contributor to *New York Times* and *School and Society.*

* * *

FRIENDLICH, Richard J. 1909-
(Dick Friendlich)

PERSONAL: Surname is pronounced *Frend*-lick; born January 20, 1909, in San Francisco, Calif.; son of Samuel J. (a salesman) and Josephine (Schoenfeld) Friendlich; married Elisabeth Turner (a writer); children: Francia Ann. *Education:* Stanford University, A.B., 1932. *Politics:* Democrat. *Home:* 2465½ Onion St., San Francisco, Calif. *Agent:* Curtis Brown Ltd., 575 Madison Ave., New York, N.Y., 10022. *Office: San Francisco Chronicle*, San Francisco, Calif.

CAREER: Held a series of odd jobs that included work for a short-lived literary magazine, selling classified ads for *New York Times*, and work as shipping clerk; *San Francisco Chronicle*, San Francisco, Calif., sports writer 1935—. *Military service:* U.S. Army, Signal Corps, 1942-45; became master sergeant; received Bronze Star and three battle stars for Italian campaigns. *Member:* U.S. Basketball Writers Association (president, 1965-66), Baseball Writers of America, Authors Guild, Sigma Delta Chi.

*WRITINGS—*Youth books; under name Dick Friendlich; all published by Westminster except as indicated: *Pivot Man*, 1949, *Warrior Forward*, 1950, *Goal Line Stand*, 1951, *Line Smasher*, 1952, *Play Maker*, 1953, *Baron of the Bull Pen* (Junior Literary Guild selection), 1955, *Left End Scott*, 1956, *Clean Up Hitter*, 1957, *Gridiron Crusader*, 1958, *Backstop Ace*, 1959, *Lead Off Man*, 1960, *Full Court Press*, 1961, *All Pro Quarterback*, 1962, *Relief Pitcher*, 1964, *Pinch Hitter* (Junior Literary Guild selection), 1965, (editor) *An Anthology of Sports Stories*, Scholastic Book Services, 1965, *Touchdown Maker*, Doubleday, 1966; *Fullback from Nowhere*, 1967.

WORK IN PROGRESS: An untitled juvenile, for Westminster.

AVOCATIONAL INTERESTS: Bridge.

* * *

FROMAN, Elizabeth Hull 1920-1975

PERSONAL: Born April 26, 1920, in Minneapolis, Minn.; daughter of George Eliot (a civil engineer) and Elsie (Booth) Hull; married Robert Froman (a free-lance writer), May 30, 1942. *Education:* Attended Minnesota public schools. *Residence:* Tompkins Cove, New York, 10986.

WRITINGS: Eba, the Absent-Minded Witch, World Publishing, 1965; *Mr. Drackle and His Dragons*, F. Watts, 1971. Contributor to *Saturday Review* and *Atlantic Monthly.*

(Died January 11, 1975)

* * *

FROST, Gerhard Emanuel 1909-

PERSONAL: Born January 17, 1909, in Sheyenne, N.D.; son of Hemming Hansen (a minister) and Gena Eliza (Ellingson) Frost; married Ivern Lorraine Johnson, October 17, 1934; children: Mariam, Naomi, Ruth, John. *Education:* Luther College, B.A., 1931; Luther Theological Seminary, B.Th., 1934; Princeton Theological Seminary, M.Th., 1950; advanced study at University of Chicago, 1954, Union Theological Seminary, 1962-63. *Home:* 2375 Como Ave. W., St. Paul, Minn. 55108. *Office:* Department of Practical Theology, Luther Theological Seminary, 2775 Como Ave. W., St. Paul, Minn. 55108.

CAREER: Lutheran minister; pastor at Nashua, Mont., 1934-37, at Whitefish, Mont., 1937-40, at Williston, N.D., 1940-44; Luther College, Decorah, Iowa, head of religion department, 1944-56; Luther Theological Seminary, St. Paul, Minn., professor of practical theology and dean of students, 1956—. *Member:* Society of Biblical Literature and Exegesis, National Association of Biblical Instructors, Lions International, Rotary International. *Awards, honors:* D.D., Concordia College, 1955.

WRITINGS: A Savior, a Song and a Star, Augsburg, 1945; (contributor) *We Beheld His Glory*, Augsburg, 1945; *The Law Perfect: Ten Studies on the Commandments*, Augsburg, 1952; (contributor) J. C. K. Preus and others, editors, *Norsemen Found a Church: An Old Heritage in a New Land*, Augsburg, 1953; (with Gerhard L. Belgum) *Chapel Time*, Augsburg, 1956; *This Book in Your Hand*, Augsburg, 1961; (with others) *That Men May Live in Christ*, Augsburg, 1963; *These Things I Remember*, Augsburg, 1963. Contributor of articles to religious and educational journals.

WORK IN PROGRESS: A devotional approach to the Book of Job; a devotional approach to the Sermon on the Mount.

* * *

FROST, Helen 1898-
(Dave Nichols)

PERSONAL: Born October 4, 1898, in Chandlerville, Ill.; daughter of John and Eva (Leeper) Goodell; married Jack L. Frost. *Education:* Special courses on part-time basis at University of Illinois, Washington University, St. Louis, Mo., Chicago Art Institute, Chicago Academy of Fine Arts, Northwestern University. *Religion:* Protestant. *Home address:* P.O. Box 5642, Tucson, Ariz. *Agent:* Bertha Klausner, International Literary Agency, Inc., 130 East 40th St., New York, N.Y. 10016.

CAREER: One-time operator, with husband, of dude ranches, stock ranches, and of a machine shop working on Air Force contracts.

WRITINGS: (Under pseudonym Dave Nichols) *Cowman's Son*, Chilton, 1960.

WORK IN PROGRESS: Western for young adults; a book of poetry.

AVOCATIONAL INTERESTS: Traveling in western mountainous states.

* * *

FROST, M(ax) Gilbert 1908-

PERSONAL: Born March 18, 1908; son of Ralph (a master printer) and Edyth (Gilbert) Frost; married Katrina Hansen, April 17, 1934; children: Janet Loraine Ford, Monica Jane Drosi. *Education:* London College of Printing, student, 1925-27. *Politics:* Liberal. *Religion:* Church of England. *Home:* 7 Multon Rd., Wandsworth Common,

London S.W. 18, England. *Office:* S. H. Benson Ltd., 129 Kingsway, London W.C. 2, England.

CAREER: J. Miles & Co. Ltd. (printers), London, England, director and manager, 1927-41; Trepur Paper Tube Co. Ltd., London, personnel manager, 1941-45; S. H. Benson Ltd. (advertising), London, staff manager, 1945—. Lecturer in management studies at London College of Printing, The Polytechnic, London, and Wandsworth Technical Institute, 1947-54. Lay reader for Diocese of Southwark, Church of England, 1959—. Home visitor, London County Council Child Care Committee, 1959—. *Member:* Institute of Personnel Management, Institute of Cost and Works Accountants (associate member), Institute of Practitioners in Advertising (associate member), Corporation of Secretaries (fellow).

WRITINGS: (Editor) *What Cheer?*, Laurie, 1932; (editor) *800 Merry Stories*, Laurie, 1934; (editor) *Merry Stories Omnibus Book*, Laurie, 1935; (editor) *Ask me Another*, Laurie, 1936; *Teach Yourself Management*, English Universities Press, 1951, revised edition, 1962; *God in Acacia Grove*, S.P.C.K., 1959. Contributor to technical journals.

WORK IN PROGRESS: A novel dealing with the advertising world.

AVOCATIONAL INTERESTS: Motoring.

*   *   *

FROST, Richard T.   1926-1972

PERSONAL: Born December 30, 1926, in Burlington, Vt.; son of Harold Putnam (a physician) and Ruth (Hallingby) Frost; married Jean Groschupf, July 12, 1952; children: Daniel P., Barbara J., Peter M. K., Sarah H. *Education:* Wesleyan University, Middletown, Conn., B.A., 1949; Syracuse University, Ph.D., 1956. *Politics:* Democrat. *Religion:* Protestant. *Home:* 6721 Southeast 34th Ave., Portland, Ore. *Office:* Reed College, Portland, Ore.

CAREER: Princeton University, Princeton, N.J., assistant professor of politics, 1956-61; Reed College, Portland, Ore., professor of political science, and vice-president, 1961-72. Member of Portland League for Effective City Government; board member of Portland Urban League. *Military service:* U.S. Air Force, 1951-54; became first lieutenant. *Member:* American Society for Public Administration, American Political Science Association.

WRITINGS: (Editor) *Cases in State and Local Government*, Prentice-Hall, 1961; (editor with Rocco J. Tresolini) *Cases in American National Government and Politics*, Prentice-Hall, 1966. Contributor to journals.

(Died November 9, 1972)

*   *   *

FRYER, Holly C(laire)   1908-

PERSONAL: Born December 6, 1908, in Carlton, Ore.; son of Lewis Eugene (a farmer) and Daisy Claire (Nichols) Fryer; first wife deceased; married E. Beth Alsup; children: (first marriage) Gaye (Mrs. Roger W. Badeker), Claire (Mrs. J. David Farris). *Education:* University of Oregon, B.S., 1931; Oregon State University, M.S., 1933; Iowa State University of Science and Technology, Ph.D., 1940. *Home:* 1430 Legore Lane, Manhattan, Kan. 66502.

CAREER: Iowa State University of Science and Technology, Ames, instructor in mathematics, 1937-40; Kansas State University, Manhattan, assistant professor, 1940-42, associate professor and statistician, Experiment Station,

1942-44, professor of statistics, 1945—, director of statistical laboratory, 1946—, head and director of department of statistics, 1959—Columbia University, associate research statistician, 1944-45. Mayor of Manhattan, Kan., 1966; member of City Commission. *Member:* American Statistical Association (fellow), Institute of Mathematical Statistics, Biometric Society, Royal Statistical Society (fellow), American Association of University Professors, Kansas Academy of Science.

WRITINGS: *Elements of Statistics*, Wiley, 1954; *Basic Concepts and Methods of Experimental Statistics*, Allyn & Bacon, 1966. Contributor of forty scientific articles to journals.

AVOCATIONAL INTERESTS: Nature and outdoor activities.

*   *   *

FUERER-HAIMENDORF, Christoph von   1909-

PERSONAL: Born July 27, 1909, in Vienna, Austria; now British subject; son of Rudolf (a civil servant) and Ida (Kurzbauer) von Fuerer-Haimendorf; married Elizabeth Barnado (a bibliographer), 1938; children: Nicholas. *Education:* University of Vienna, Ph.D., 1931; London School of Economics and Political Science, postdoctoral research, 1935-36. *Religion:* Roman Catholic. *Home:* 32 Clarendon Rd., London W.11, England. *Office:* School of Oriental and African Studies, University of London, London, W.C.1, England.

CAREER: University of Vienna, Vienna, Austria, research assistant, 1931-34, lecturer, 1937-38; Indian Government, External Affairs Department, special officer in Subansiri and assistant political officer, Balipara Frontier Tract, 1944-45; Osmania University, Hyderabad, India, professor of anthropology, 1945-49, and adviser to government for tribes and backward classes; School of Oriental and African Studies, University of London, London, England, reader in anthropology, 1949-51, professor of Asian anthropology, 1951—. Anthropological field work in India, 1936-37, 1939-49, 1953, 1962, in Nepal, 1953-54, 1957-58, 1962, and Ceylon, 1960. *Member:* Royal Anthropological Institute, Royal Geographical Society. *Awards, honors:* Rockefeller fellow, 1935-37; Rivers Memorial Medal of Royal Anthropological Institute, 1949.

WRITINGS: *The Naked Nagas*, Methuen, 1939; *The Chenchus*, Macmillan, 1943; *The Reddis of the Bison Hills*, Macmillan, 1945; *Tribal Hyderabad: Four Reports*, Revenue Department, Hyderabad Government, 1945; *Ethnographic Notes on the Tribes of the Subansiri Region*, Assam Government, 1947; *The Raj Gonds of Adilabad*, Macmillan, 1948; *Himalayan Barbary*, J. Murray, 1956; *The Apa Tanis and Their Neighbours: A Primitive Civilization of the Eastern Himalayas*, Free Press of Glencoe, 1962; *The Sherpas of Nepal: Buddhist Highlanders*, University of California Press, 1964; (editor and contributor) *Caste and Kin in Nepal, India, and Ceylon: Anthropological Studies in Hindu-Buddhist Contact Zones*, Asia Publishing, 1966; *Morals and Merit: A Study of Values and Social Controls in South Asian Societies*, University of Chicago Press, 1967; *The Konyak Nagas: An Indian Frontier Tribe*, Holt, 1969.

Contributor: *Custom is King* (essays presented to R. R. Marett), Hutchinson, 1936; *Die heutigen Naturvolker im Kampf und Ausgleich mit der neuen Zeit*, edited by D. Westerman, F. Enke, 1939; F. M. Schnitger, *Forgotten Kingdoms in Sumatra*, Brill (Leiden), 1939; *Essays in An-*

thropology Presented to Sarat Chandra Roy, Maxwell & Co. (Lucknow), 1942; (author of appendix) *Census of India 1941*, Volume XXI, 1945; (author of foreword) Stephen Fuchs, *The Children of Hari*, Herold (Vienna), 1950; (author of foreword) S. C. Dube, *The Kamar*, Universal Publishers (Lucknow), 1951; *Historia Mundi*, Volume II, 1953; (author of foreword) Elizabeth von Fuerer-Haimendorf, *An Anthropological Bibliography of South Asia*, Mouton (Paris), 1958-70; *Mount Everest: Formation, Population and Exploration of the Mount Everest Region*, Oxford University Press, 1963.

Contributor to *Yearbook of Anthropology*, 1955, and to the *Proceedings* of the 37th Indian Science Congress. Also contributor of about thirty articles to professional journals.

WORK IN PROGRESS: Research on the anthropology of Nepal.

SIDELIGHTS: Fuerer-Haimendorf is competent in French, Hindi, Assamese; moderately competent in Latin, Greek, Gondi, and Nepali. *Avocational interests:* Music.

* * *

FULLER, John (Harold)

PERSONAL: Born in Oldham, Lancashire, England; son of Leopold Charles (a manufacturer) and Nellie (Broadbent) Fuller; married Pamela Honor Stewart, July 5, 1945; children: Charles Roy Stewart, Julia Evelyn Honor, James Frederick Broadbent. *Education:* King William's College, Isle of Man, student, 1930-33. *Home:* Holly Lodge, The Green, Adderbury near Branbury, Oxfordshire, England. *Office:* Department of Catering, Oxford Polytechnic, Gypsy Lane, Headington, Oxford, England.

CAREER: Hotel and Catering Institute, London, England, deputy secretary, 1950-54; Battersea College of Technology, Department of Hotel Management, London, England, head, 1954-59; University of Strathclyde, Glasgow, Scotland, Rank Organization Professor of Management and director of Scottish Hotel School, 1959-70; Oxford Polytechnic, Oxford, England, principal lecturer in hotel and catering management, 1970—. Consultant in hotel training to governments of India, 1956, Israel, 1962, Cyprus, 1963, North Ireland, 1966, Gibraltar, 1967, Ethiopia, 1969, National Economic Commission, United Kingdom, 1971; also consultant in hotel management and catering to commercial firms. Lecturer at Cornell University's School of Hotel Administration, 1961; visiting professor, Michigan State University, 1968-69, University of Surrey, 1970—.

WRITINGS: Cuisine au beurre (monograph), British Hotel and Restaurant Association, 1959; *The Chef's Manual of Kitchen Management*, Batsford, 1962, 2nd edition, 1966; *The Caterer's Potato Manual*, Pitman, 1963; *Hotel Training in Cyprus*, Republic of Cyprus, Ministry of Commerce and Industry, 1963; (with Edward Renold) *The Chef's Compendium of Professional Recipes*, Heinemann, 1963; *Gueridon and Lamp Cookery: A Complete Guide to Side-Table and Flambe Service*, Ahrens, 1964 (published in England as *The Restaurateur's Guide to Gueridon and Lamp Cookery*, Barrie & Rockliff, 1964); (with Alexander J. Currie) *The Waiter*, Barrie & Rockliff, 1965; *Hotelkeeping and Catering as a Career*, Batsford, 1965; (editor) *Catering Management in the Technological Age*, Barrie & Rockliff, 1967; (editor) Henri Paul Pellaprat, *L'Art culinaire moderne*, Collins, 1967; (editor with James Steel) *Productivity and Profit in Catering*, University of Strathclyde, Scottish Hotel School, 1968; *The Waiter's Compendium*, Heinemann, in press.

Occasional contributor to *Harper's Bazaar, Wine and Food, Hotel Review*; formerly regular columnist in *Home Economics, Hotel Management, School and College*. Editor, *Journal* of the Hotel and Catering Institute, 1950-54, and of *Food and Cookery*, 1958-59.

* * *

FULLER, John Frederick Charles 1878-1966

PERSONAL: Born September 1, 1878, in Chichester, England; son of Alfred (a clergyman) and Selma (de la Chevallerie) Fuller; married Margret Sonia Karnatski, December 4, 1906. *Education:* Royal Military College at Sandhurst, and Staff College, Camberley. *Agent:* David Higham Associates Ltd., 76 Dean St., London, W.1, England.

CAREER: British Army, career officer, 1898-1933, retiring as major general. Served in Boer War, 1899-1902, then in India; General Staff officer throughout World War I, becoming chief General Staff Officer of newly-organized Tank Corps; assigned to War Office, London, and as brigade commander in Germany and England in post-World War I period; became major general, 1930. Military correspondent in Abyssinian War, 1935-36 and Spanish Civil War, 1936-39. Writer on military subjects for half a century. *Member:* United Service Institution. *Awards, honors*—Military: Queen's Medal and three clasps and King's Medal and two clasps, Boer War; Distinguished Service Order, Legion of Honor (France), Order of Leopold (Belgium), and mentioned in dispatches, World War I; Commander, Order of the British Empire, 1926; Companion of the Bath, 1930. Civilian: Royal United Service Institution Gold Medal, 1919; Chesney Gold Medal, 1963.

WRITINGS: Training Soldiers for War, H. Rees, 1914.

Tanks in the Great War, 1914-1918, J. Murray, 1920; *Reformation of War*, Dutton, 1923; *British Light Infantry in the Eighteenth Century*, Hutchinson, 1925; *Sir John Moore's System of Training*, Hutchinson, 1925; *Yoga*, McKay, 1925; *Atlantis: America and the Future*, Dutton, 1926; *The Foundations of the Science of War*, Hutchinson, 1926; *Imperial Defence, 1588-1914*, Sifton Praed, 1926; *Pegasus; or Problems of Transportation*, Dutton, 1926; *On Future Warfare*, Sifton Praed, 1928; *The Generalship of Ulysses S. Grant*, Dodd, 1929, 2nd edition, Indiana University Press, 1958.

India in Revolt, Eyre & Spottiswoode, 1931; *Lectures on Field Service Regulations, II*, Sifton Praed, 1931; *The Dragon's Teeth: A Study of War and Peace*, Constable, 1932; *General Grant: A Biography for Young Americans*, Dodd, 1932; *Lectures on Field Service Regulations, III*, Sifton Praed, 1932, annotated edition published in United States as *Armored Warfare*, Military Service Publishing Co., 1943; *War and Western Civilization, 1832-1932: A Study of War as a Political Instrument and the Expression of Mass Democracy*, Duckworth, 1932; *Generalship: Its Diseases and Their Cure*, Faber, 1933, Military Service Publishing Co., 1936; *Grant and Lee: A Study in Personality and Generalship*, Scribner, 1933, 2nd edition, Indiana University Press, 1957; *Empire Unity and Defense*, Arrowsmith, 1934; *The Army in My Time*, Rich & Cowan, 1935; *The First of the League Wars: Its Lessons and Omens*, Eyre & Spottiswoode, 1936; *Memoirs of an Unconventional Soldier*, Nicholson & Watson, 1936; *The Last of the Gentlemen's Wars; a Subaltern's Journal of the War in South Africa, 1899-1902*, Faber, 1937; *The Secret Wisdom of the Qabalah*, Rider, 1937; *Towards Armageddon: The Defense Problem and Its Solution*, Dickson,

1937; *Decisive Battles: Their Influence Upon History and Civilization*, Eyre & Spottiswoode, 1939, Scribner, 1940.

Machine Warfare, Hutchinson, 1942; *Decisive Battles of the U.S.A.*, Harper, 1942, 2nd edition, Beechhurst Press, 1953; *Watchwords*, Skeffington & Sons, 1944; *Armament and History*, Scribner, 1945; *Thunderbolts*, Skeffington & Sons, 1946; *The Second World War, 1939-1945: A Strategical and Tactical History*, Eyre & Spottiswoode, 1948, Duell, Sloan & Pearce, 1949.

Russia Is Not Invincible, Eyre & Spottiswoode, 1951; *A Military History of the Western World*, three volumes, Funk, 1954-56 (published in England as *The Decisive Battles of the Western World and Their Influence Upon History*, Eyre & Spottiswoode, 1954-56); *The Generalship of Alexander the Great*, Eyre & Spottiswoode, 1958, Rutgers University Press, 1961.

The Conduct of War, 1789-1961: A Study of the Impact of the French, Industrial, and Russian Revolutions on War and its Conduct, Rutgers University Press, 1961; *Julius Caesar: Man, Soldier, and Tyrant*, Rutgers University Press, 1965.

Contributor of over four hundred articles to English and American periodicals.

SIDELIGHTS: As military correspondent, Fuller had occasion to meet Hitler, Mussolini, Franco, and leading German generals.

BIOGRAPHICAL/CRITICAL SOURCES: Military Affairs, winter, 1959; B. H. Liddell Hart, *The Tanks*, Volume I, 1959.

(Died February 10, 1966)

*   *   *

FULTON, Paul C(edric) 1901-

PERSONAL: Born May 10, 1901, in Dixon, Ill.; son of Robert E. and Vallie (Miller) Fulton; married Esther Weyer, September 15, 1925; children: Patricia Anne (Mrs. Nathaniel S. Eek), Mary Elizabeth (Mrs. James P. Rothermel). *Education:* University of Illinois, B.S., 1923. *Politics:* Republican. *Religion:* Episcopalian.

CAREER: Chicago Tribune, Chicago, Ill., advertising salesman, 1924-34, manager of neighborhood advertising sales, 1934-45, assistant manager of retail advertising, 1945-47, manager of retail advertising, 1947-61, advertising manager, 1961-62, advertising director, 1962-66. Treasurer, Chicago Tribune Co., 1955-62. *Member:* Sales Marketing Executives (director, 1956-58), Masons, University of Illinois Alumni Association (director, 1956-61), Chi Phi, Chicago Athletic Association, Sunset Ridge Country Club (Winnetka, Ill.), Chicago Club.

WRITINGS: (With Leslie W. McClure) *Advertising in the Printed Media*, Macmillan, 1964.

*   *   *

GABRIELSON, Ira N(oel) 1889-

PERSONAL: Born September 27, 1889, in Sioux Rapids, Iowa; son of Frank August (a businessman) and Ida (Jansen) Gabrielson; married Clara Speer, August 7, 1912; children: June (Mrs. Dave N. Martin), Iris (Mrs. Robert A. Nesbitt; deceased), Jean (Mrs. David Holmes), Gail (Mrs. N. Sherwood Ferris). *Education:* Morningside College, B.A., 1912. *Home address:* Route 1, Box 349, Oakton, Va. 22124. *Office:* Wildlife Management Institute, 709 Wire Building, Washington, D.C. 20005.

CAREER: High school biology teacher in Marshalltown, Iowa, 1912-15; U.S. Department of Agriculture, Bureau of Biological Survey, 1915-40, started as assistant in economic ornithology and worked in various research, management, and administrative posts up to chief of bureau, 1935-40; U.S. Department of the Interior, Fish and Wildlife Service, Washington, D.C., director, 1940-46; Wildlife Management Institute (dedicated to wildlife restoration), Washington, D.C., president, 1946-71. Consultant at various times to U.S. Departments of Agriculture, Interior, Defense, and Health, Education, and Welfare. Trustee, International World Wildlife Fund, 1961; president of U.S. World Wildlife Fund, 1962—. Chairman of Northern Virginia Regional Park Authority, 1960—; member of Virginia Outdoor Recreation Study Commission, 1964-65.

MEMBER: American Ornithologists' Union (fellow), American Society of Mammalogists, American Forestry Association, Wildlife Society, Cooper Ornithological Society, Washington Academy of Science, Wilson Ornithological Club, and other scientific societies. *Awards, honors:* Audubon Conservation Award; Distinguished Service Award of both Department of the Interior and American Forestry Association; Leopold Medal of Wildlife Society; Sc.D., Oregon State University, 1936, Middlebury College, 1959, Colby College, 1969; LL.D., Morningside College, 1941.

WRITINGS: Food Habits of Some Winter Bird Visitants, U.S. Government Printing Office, 1924; (with Stanley Gordon Jewett) *Birds of the Portland Area*, The Club (Berkeley), 1929; (with E. E. Horn) *Porcupine Control in the Western States*, U.S. Government Printing Office, 1930; *Controlling Rodents and Other Small Animal Pests in Oregon*, Oregon State Agricultural College, 1932; *Western American Alpines*, Macmillan, 1932; (with Jewett) *Birds of Oregon*, Oregon State College Press, 1940, reissued as *Birds of the Pacific Northwest, with Special Reference to Oregon*, Dover, 1970; *Wildlife Conservation*, Macmillan, 1941, 2nd edition, 1969; *Wildlife Refuges*, Macmillan, 1943; *Concepts in Conservation of Land, Water, and Wildlife*, U.S. Government Printing Office, 1949; (with Herbert Spencer Zim) *Birds: A Guide to the Most Familiar American Birds*, Simon & Schuster, 1949, revised edition, 1956; (editor) *The Fisherman's Encyclopedia*, Stackpole, 1950, 2nd, revised edition, 1963; *Wildlife Management*, Macmillan, 1951; *Report to the Idaho Fish and Game Commission*, Idaho Fish and Game Commission, 1953; (with Frederick C. Lincoln) *The Birds of Alaska*, published by Stackpole for Wildlife Management Institute, 1959. Author of several hundred popular and scientific papers.

WORK IN PROGRESS: An autobiography.

SIDELIGHTS: Gabrielson has traveled all over North America in work and research since 1915, and has made other trips to Europe, South America, and Africa. *Avocational interests:* Gardening, fishing, hunting.

*   *   *

GALBRAITH, Georgie Starbuck 1909-
(G. S. Page, Ann Patrice, Penny Pennington, Stuart Pennington)

PERSONAL: Born December 15, 1909, in Brownington, Mo.; daughter of Harry (a grocer) and Eathel (Munson) Starbuck; divorced. *Education:* Attended Bakersfield Junior College, two years. *Politics:* Republican. *Religion:* Agnostic. *Home:* 1319 Terrace Way, Bakersfield, Calif. 93304.

CAREER: Former clerk in department store; also has worked professionally in pop song field; semi-professional painter, specializing in florals; free-lance writer since the 1940's. *Awards, honors:* Chaparral Poet of the Year, 1959.

WRITINGS: Have One On Me (poems), Lippincott, 1963. Contributor of nearly two thousand pieces of writing, both verse and light essays, some under various pseudonyms, to more than 100 magazines in the United States, Canada, and England; some of these writings have been anthologized in textbooks and anthologies. Also has done special material for night club singers.

WORK IN PROGRESS: A book of light poetry, *A Touch of the Frivolous.*

SIDELIGHTS: Miss Galbraith told *CA* she believes "verse, serious or light, is for people, not for pedants, critics, and little cliques. . . . I try to write my own best, not somebody else's. . . . As a professional writer, my main motivation has been and is money. I write to sell, and keep abreast of editorial requirements. I feel if you are a good writer, Art will take care of itself. And to make a living at writing today, one has to be a pretty good writer."

BIOGRAPHICAL/CRITICAL SOURCES: Bakersfield Californian, May 21, 1966.

* * *

GALE, Herbert M(orrison) 1907-

PERSONAL: Born March 28, 1907, in Macon, Mo.; son of Edward Justus and Anna Maxwell (Morrison) Gale; married Winifred Rannells; children: Herbert M., Jr., Winifred M., Edward R. *Education:* Missouri Wesleyan College, student, 1925-27; University of Iowa, A.B., 1929; Boston University, M.A., 1931, S.T.B., 1932, Ph.D., 1939; University of Berlin, graduate study, 1932-33. *Politics:* Democrat. *Address:* R.F.D., Wolcott, Vt. 05680.

CAREER: Minister of Methodist church, Carrollton, Mo., 1933-35, of Congregational church, Pelham, N.H., 1935-38, of Methodist church, Westboro, Mo., 1938-39; Northfield School for Girls, East Northfield, Mass., teacher of Bible, 1939-44; Wellesley College, Wellesley, Mass., lecturer, 1944-47, assistant professor, 1947-50, associate professor, 1950-58, professor of biblical history, 1958-72, professor emeritus, 1972—. *Member:* American Academy of Religion, Society of Biblical Literature, Studiorum Novi Testamenti Societas, Phi Beta Kappa. *Awards, honors:* Fulbright Research grant to Germany, 1953-54.

WRITINGS: A Study of the Old Testament, Northfield Schools, 1943; revised edition, Nelson, 1958; (contributor) G. Paul Butler, editor, *Best Sermons, 1947-48,* Harper, 1948; *The Use of Analogy in the Letters of Paul,* Westminster, 1964. Contributor to religious journals.

WORK IN PROGRESS: A study of the Sermon on the Mount; a second volume on the letters of Paul.

AVOCATIONAL INTERESTS: Farming, music.

* * *

GALLMAN, Waldemar J(ohn) 1899-

PERSONAL: Born April 27, 1899, in Wellsville, N.Y.; son of John (a merchant) and Henrietta (Engelder) Gallman; married Marjorie Gerry, July 29, 1925; children: John Gerry, Philip Gerry. *Education:* Cornell University, B.A., 1921; Georgetown Law School, student, 1923-24. *Religion:* Unitarian. *Home:* 3312 Woodley Rd. N.W., Washington, D.C. 20008.

CAREER: Cornell University, Ithaca, N.Y., instructor in English, 1921-22; various assignments with U.S. career diplomatic service in Havana, Cuba, 1922, San Jose, Costa Rica, 1925, Quito, Ecuador, 1926, Riga, Latvia, 1930, Warsaw, Poland, 1934, Danzig, 1934, London, 1942; ambassador to Poland, 1948-50; National War College, deputy for Foreign Affairs, 1950-51; ambassador to Union of South Africa, 1951-54; ambassador to Iraq, 1954-59; Foreign Service, director-general, 1959-61; retired from Foreign Service with rank of ambassador, 1961. Adviser to South Korean and South Vietnamese Foreign Offices in Foreign Service training; currently with Foreign Service Research, Inc., Washington, D.C.

WRITINGS: Iraq Under General Nuri: My Recollections of Nuri Al-Said, 1954-1958, Johns Hopkins Press, 1964.

WORK IN PROGRESS: Our Foreign Relations: Thoughts from Retirement.

* * *

GAMBLE, Frederick (John) 1904-

PERSONAL: Born in 1904, in Belfast, Northern Ireland; son of John and Elizabeth (Wilkinson) Gamble; married Elizabeth Spray; children: Barbara, Hilary. *Religion:* Presbyterian. *Home:* 49 Waterloo Gardens, Belfast 15, Northern Ireland. *Office: Belfast Telegraph,* Belfast, Northern Ireland.

CAREER: Belfast Telegraph, Belfast, Northern Ireland, assistant editor, 1922—; also weekly columnist and reviewer of thrillers. Vice-chairman and honorary treasurer, Belfast District Newspaper Press Fund.

WRITINGS: A Man and a Half, Arthur Barker, 1956; *My Coat is Travel Stained,* Arthur Barker, 1957; *The Frightened One,* Arthur Barker, 1958.

WORK IN PROGRESS: Ulsterisms, a collection of Ulster dialect sayings.

AVOCATIONAL INTERESTS: Reading thrillers.

* * *

GAMBLE, Sidney David 1890-1968

PERSONAL: Born July 12, 1890, in Cincinnati, Ohio; son of David Berry and Mary (Huggins) Gamble; married Elizabeth Lowe, January 18, 1924; children: Catherine (Mrs. J. A. Curran, Jr.), Louise (Mrs. Edward B. Harper), David Lowe, Anne (Mrs. Paul S. Symchych). *Education:* Princeton University, Litt.B., 1912; University of California, Berkeley, M.A., 1916. *Politics:* Independent. *Religion:* Presbyterian. *Home:* 4730 Fieldston Rd., New York, N.Y. 10071. *Office:* 347 Madison Ave., New York, N.Y. 10017.

CAREER: Escondido Land and Town Co., Escondido, Calif., secretary and treasurer, 1913-15; University of California, Berkeley, assistant in department of economics, 1916-17; Princeton University Center in China, Peking, member of staff, 1918-19; International Committee, Young Men's Christian Association, New York, N.Y., research secretary for China, 1924-27, recording secretary, 1944-68. Research secretary, Chinese National Association of the Mass Education Movement, Peking, 1927-32. President, Princeton in Asia, 1929-68. Chairman of board of managers of central department of Church World Service, National Council of Churches of Christ in the U.S.A.; treasurer, National Committee on Maternal Health. Director of Agricultural Missions, Inc., of Josiah Macy, Jr. Foundation, and of Riverdale Neighborhood and Library Association;

trustee of United Board for Christian Higher Education in Asia and of World University Service. *Member:* Phi Beta Kappa. *Awards, honors:* LL.D., Hanover College, 1932; L.H.D., Susquehanna Univeristy, 1964.

WRITINGS: (With J. S. Burgess) *Peking: A Social Survey*, R. R. Smith, 1921; *Peking Wages*, edited by Maxwell S. Stewart, Department of Sociology and Social Work, Yenching University, 1929; *The Household Accounts of Two Chinese Families*, China Institute in America, 1931; *How Chinese Families Live in Peiping: A Study of the Income and Expenditure of 283 Chinese Families Receiving from $8 to $550 Silver Per Month*, Funk, 1933; *Ting Hsien: A North China Rural Community*, International Secretariat, Institute of Pacific Relations, 1954; *North China Villages: Social, Political, and Economic Activities Before 1933*, University of California Press, 1963; (editor and author of introduction and notes) *Chinese Village Plays from the Ting Hsien Region (Yang Ke Hsuean): A Collection of Forty-eight Chinese Rural Plays as Staged by the Villagers from Ting Hsien in Northern China*, Philo Press (Amsterdam), 1970, new edition, Schram, 1972.

BIOGRAPHICAL/CRITICAL SOURCES: New York Times, March 30, 1968.

(Died March 29, 1968)

* * *

GANNON, Robert I(gnatius) 1893-

PERSONAL: Born April 20, 1893, in Staten Island, N.Y.; son of Frank S. and Marietta (Burrows) Gannon. *Education:* Georgetown University, A.B., 1913; Woodstock College, M.A., 1919; Gregorian University, Rome, Italy, S.T.D., 1927; Christ's College, Cambridge, M.A., 1930. *Politics:* Republican. *Home and office:* Fordham University, New York, N.Y. 10058.

CAREER: Entered Society of Jesus (Jesuits), 1913, ordained priest, 1926, Fordham University, New York, N.Y., instructor, 1919-23; St. Peter's College, Jersey City, N.J., dean, 1930-36; Hudson College of Commerce and Finance, Jersey City, N.J., organizer, 1933, dean, 1933-36; Fordham University, president, 1936-39; Mount Manresa Retreat House, Staten Island, N.Y., superior, 1949-52; St. Ignatius Loyola Church, New York, N.Y., pastor, 1952-58; Loyola School and Regis High School, New York, N.Y., president, 1952-58; Jesuit Missions House, New York, N.Y., superior, 1958-64; Fordham University, researcher, 1964—. Lecturer or preacher in thirteen countries. Member of advisory committees, U.S. Department of Defense and Department of State, 1941-46. Former trustee of Free Europe University in Exile, Strasbourg, France and Town Hall, New York; currently trustee of Netherlands-America Foundation, Notre Dame College of Staten Island, New York Zoological Society. Former member of advisory committee of Ford Foundation; currently member of advisory council of Robert A. Taft Institute of Government, New York Academy of Public Education, and Century Association; former regional director, Boy Scouts of America.

MEMBER: Pan American Society (honorary vice-president), Royal Society of Arts (England; fellow), Newcomen Society (England; honorary member). *Awards, honors:* Doctorates from twenty-two universities and colleges, including Columbia University, Bowdoin College, New York University, and Catholic University of America, Knight Commander, Order of Polonia Restituta, 1944; Knight of the Order of Orange-Nassau (Netherlands), 1949; Silver

Antelope, Boy Scouts of America, 1950; Freedoms Foundation Award, 1958; Master Knight, Sovereign Military Order of Malta, 1963.

WRITINGS: The Technique of the One-Act Play, Fordham University Press, 1925; *After Black Coffee*, Farrar, Straus, 1945; *The Ten Commandments*, Doubleday, 1958; *The Cardinal Spellman Story*, Doubleday, 1962; *The Poor Old Liberal Arts*, Farrar, Straus, 1962; *After More Black Coffee*, Farrar, Straus, 1964; *Up to the Present: The Story of Fordham*, Doubleday, 1967.

* * *

GARBETT, Colin (Campbell) 1881-

PERSONAL: Born May 22, 1881, in Dalhousie, India; son of Hubert (a civil engineer) and Henrietta Maria (Stokes) Garbett; married Abra Faith Hughes, 1911 (died, 1911); married Marjorie Josephine Maynard, January 20, 1919; children: Jacynthe Mary Suzanne. *Education:* Jesus College, Cambridge, B.A. and M.A. (first class honors in classics), 1903, LL.B., 1904. *Religion:* Church of England. *Home:* 16, Bel Air, Whiteriver, Transvaal, South Africa.

CAREER: Indian Civil Service, 1904-41, except for World War I years and period as assistant secretary of India Office, and then secretary to high commissioner of Iraq, 1919-22; started as an assistant commissioner in India, 1905, became chief secretary to government of Punjab, 1931, commissioner of Multan Division, 1935, financial commissioner of Punjab, 1937-38, chairman of Provincial Transport Authority and of Land Reclamation Board of Punjab; retired, 1941. Government of India, chairman of Interview Board Emergency Commissions (Defense), 1941-43, minister for agriculture, Bhopal, 1944-46, other posts; retired, 1946. Member of missions to Pakistan and India for Raw Cotton Commission, 1948, 1949. Hilton College, Natal, Union of South Africa, classics master, 1951-52. *Wartime service:* Revenue commissioner and administrator of Agricultural Development Scheme (military) in Mesopotamia, 1917; twice mentioned in dispatches. *Member:* Royal Geographical Society, Royal Commonwealth Society (fellow), Royal Society of Arts (fellow). *Awards, honors:* Companion of Order of the Indian Empire and Companion of Order of St. Michael and St. George for wartime service in Mesopotamia; Companion of the Order of Star of India, 1935; Officer of Order of St. John of Jerusalem, 1938; Knight Commander of Order of the Indian Empire, 1941.

WRITINGS: Riwaj-i-Am of Panipat Tahsil and Karnal Pargana in the Karnal District, Punjab Government, 1910; *Friend of Friend* (reminiscences), Oxford University Press (Bombay), 1943, 2nd edition, 1944; *The Hundred Years* (history of Christ Church in Simla, India), Simla Press, 1944; (translator from the Persian, and author of foreword) Jalal al-Din Rumi, *Sun of Tabriz* (selected poems), R. Beerman, 1956, 2nd edition, 1956; *The Ringing Radiance*, Satsang Beas Press, 1968.

* * *

GARDNER, William Henry 1902-1969

PERSONAL: Born September 7, 1902, in London, England; son of Henry George (a landscape gardener) and Annie (Oxenham) Gardner; married Winifred Millicent Markby, July 28, 1928; children: Paul Markby, Colin Oxenham, Susan Janet. *Education:* University of London, B.A. (with honors), 1925, Ph.D., 1942. *Religion:* Roman Catholic. *Office:* University of Natal, Pietermaritzburg, Natal, South Africa.

CAREER: King's Norton Grammar School, and later, Shene Grammar School, London, England, senior English master, 1926-47; University of Natal, Pietermaritzburg, Natal, South Africa, senior lecturer in English, 1947-54; University of the Orange Free State, Bloemfontein, South Africa, professor of English, 1955-61; University of Natal, professor and head of English department, 1962-67, dean of Faculty of Arts, 1962-64. *Member:* English Association, P.E.N., English Academy of Southern Africa.

WRITINGS: Some Thoughts on "The Mayor of Casterbridge," Oxford University Press, for English Association, 1930; *Salamander in Spring and Other Poems,* Duckworth, 1933; *Gerard Manley Hopkins: A Study of Poetic Idiosyncrasy in Relation to Poetic Tradition,* Volume I, Secker & Warburg, 1944, Volume II, Yale University Press, 1948-49, new edition of both volumes, Oxford University Press, 1962; (editor) *Poems of Gerard Manley Hopkins,* 3rd edition, incorporating the selection and notes of Robert Bridges, Oxford University Press, 1948, 4th edition (with N. H. MacKenzie), 1967; (editor) *Selected Poems and Prose of Gerard Manley Hopkins,* Penguin, 1953; *The Teaching of English Through Literature,* National Council for Social Research, 1955.

Writings included in other books, among them *Essays and Studies by Members of the English Association,* 1936, *The Wind and the Rain, Dictionary of National Biography,* and *South African P.E.N. Yearbook.* Contributor of critical articles or poems to *Scrutiny, Month, Standpunte,* and other journals. Editor, *Theoria,* 1951-54.

WORK IN PROGRESS: A critical biography of Roy Campbell.

SIDELIGHTS: Reviewing the fourth edition of the *Poems of Gerard Manley Hopkins,* Norman MacCaig noted in *The Listener,* "The famous first edition of Hopkins's work, published by Robert Bridges in 1918, was re-edited and enlarged first by Charles Williams and then again by W. H. Gardner. Now comes a fourth edition, a book which quite supersedes its predecessors.... It includes the 'latest known versions of all his extant poems and verse fragments' ... as near as may be, the complete corpus.... The other important thing about the book is the careful establishing of the true texts, not only on the work of previous scholars ... but on a thorough examination of the extant manuscripts of Hopkins and transcriptions made from them."

Gardner had a working knowledge (for literary work) of Greek, Latin, Italian, Spanish, French, German, Welsh, and Old English; he also knew some Afrikaans.

(Died January 18, 1969)

*   *   *

GARRARD, L(ancelot) A(ustin)   1904-

PERSONAL: Born May 31, 1904, in Skelbroke, Yorkshire, England; son of William Austin and Muriel Eveline (Winckworth) Garrard; married Muriel Walsh (a schoolteacher), August 13, 1932; children: Anthony Rupert, Rodney Paul. *Education:* Attended Felsted School, 1918-23; Manchester College, Oxford, student, 1928-31; Wadham College, Oxford, M.A., 1930, B.D., 1935; University of Marburg, postgraduate study, 1931-32. *Home and office:* 13 Holmlea Rd., Goring, Reading, England.

CAREER: Assistant master at Edinburgh Academy, Edinburgh, Scotland, 1927, St. Paul's School, London, England, 1928; Unitarian minister in Dover, England, 1932-33; Man-chester College, Oxford, England, tutor and bursar, 1933-43, tutor and librarian, 1952-56, principal, 1956-65; minister in Bristol, England, 1941-43, in Liverpool, England, 1943-52; Unitarian College, Manchester, England, tutor, 1945-51; Emerson College, Boston, Mass., professor of philosophy and religion, 1965-71, professor emeritus, 1971—. *Member:* Studiorum Novi Testamenti Societas, Society for Study of Theology, Athenaeum Club. *Awards, honors:* LL.D. from Emerson College, 1963.

WRITINGS: Duty and the Will of God, Basil Blackwell, 1935; *The Interpreted Bible,* Lindsey Press, 1946; *The Gospels Today,* Lindsey Press, 1953; *The Historical Jesus: Schweitzer's Quest and Ours after Fifty Years,* Lindsey Press, 1956; *Athens or Jerusalem?: A Study in Christian Comprehension* (Minns Lectures 1963), Verry, 1965; (translator) Albert Schweitzer, *The Kingdom of God and Primitive Christianity,* A. & C. Black, 1968. Editor, *Hibbert Journal* (quarterly review of religion, theology, and philosophy), 1951-62. Translator of several German theological works.

BIOGRAPHICAL/CRITICAL SOURCES: Hibbert Journal, July, 1951.

*   *   *

GARRETT, William   1890-1967

PERSONAL: Born September 17, 1890, in Coatbridge, Scotland; son of George and Jessie (Laurie) Garrett; married Mary McNaught, September, 1915; children: George Alan, Marion Morton (Mrs. A. Hume). *Education:* Attended Fettes College, Edinburgh, Scotland; Cambridge University, B.A., LL.B., 1911; University of Glasgow, LL.B., 1914. *Home:* 21 Blackford Rd., Edinburgh, Scotland.

CAREER: Lawyer and advocate, Scots Bar, and Queen's Counsel; now retired. University of Edinburgh, Edinburgh, Scotland, former lecturer in law. Sheriff (judge) in Ayrshire, Scotland, 1940-48, in Edinburgh, Scotland, 1948-60.

WRITINGS—All novels: Saint Antony's Grove, Jarrolds, 1919; *The Secret of the Hills,* Jarrolds, 1920; *The Spirit of Destiny,* Jarrolds, 1922; *Friday to Monday,* Appleton, 1923; *Doctor Ricardo,* Appleton, 1925; *Treasure Royal: Being the Romance of a Modern Hunt for Treasure and an Adventure of James Drew, Detective,* Appleton, 1926; *The Grand Buffalo: An Adventure at the Back of Beyond for Big and Little Folk* (youth book), Appleton, 1926; *The Multitude,* Appleton, 1927; *The Professional Guest,* Appleton, 1928; *From Dusk till Dawn,* Appleton, 1929; *The Man in the Mirror* (biographical reflection), Appleton, 1931.

SIDELIGHTS: A silent motion picture was made of *The Secret of the Hills,* and talking pictures of *The Man in the Mirror* and *The Professional Guest.*

(Died October 17, 1967)

*   *   *

GAVIN, James M(aurice)   1907-

PERSONAL: Born March 22, 1907, in Brooklyn, N.Y.; son of Martin and Mary (Terrell) Gavin; married second wife Jean Emert, July 31, 1948; children: (first marriage) Barbara (Mrs. Clarence G. Fauntleroy); (second marriage) Caroline A., Patricia C., Marjorie A., Chloe J. *Education:* U.S. Military Academy, B.S., 1929; Command and General Staff College, graduate. *Home:* 85 Yarmouth Rd., Chestnut Hill, Mass. 02167. *Office:* Arthur D. Little, Inc., 25 Acorn Pk., Cambridge, Mass. 02140.

CAREER: U.S. Army, career service, 1924-58, retiring as lieutenant general; Arthur D. Little, Inc. (industrial research and engineering consultants), Cambridge, Mass., 1958-61, executive vice-president, 1959-60, president, 1960-61; U.S. Ambassador to France, 1961-62; Arthur D. Little, Inc., chairman of the board and chief executive officer, 1962—. During World War II served in Europe as airborne adviser to General Eisenhower (prior to Normandy landings), as commander of the 82nd Airborne Division, and at war's end as U.S. member of the Allied Command in Berlin. Director of John Hancock Mutual Life Insurance Company, American Electric Power Co., Atomic Industrial Forum, and International Executive Service Corp., and Mitre Corp.; advisory director, New England Merchants National Bank, Boston, Mass. Member of Military Naval and Air Science Board; sponsor of Atlantic Council, New York, N.Y. Life trustee of Tufts University, chairman of board of visitors, Fletcher School of Law and Diplomacy; member of board of visitors, Harvard University. Member: West Point Society of New England. Awards, honors—Military: Distinguished Service Cross with oak leaf cluster, Silver Star, Purple Heart; Legion of Honor and Croix de Guerre with palm (France); Distinguished Service Order (British).

WRITINGS: Airborne Warfare, Harper, 1947; War and Peace in the Space Age, Harper, 1958; (contributor of section of text) An Album of Civil War Drawings by the Prince de Joinville, Atheneum, 1964; (with Arthur T. Hadley) Crisis Now, Random House, 1968. Contributor to New York Times Magazine, and Atlantic Monthly.

*   *   *

GAVIN-BROWN, Wilfred A(rthur)   1904-

PERSONAL: Born March 10, 1904, in Southampton, Hampshire, England; son of Arthur Leopold (a bank accountant) and Isobel (Wood) Brown; married Pamela Wilson, August 10, 1935; children: Gillian Mary, Ian. Education: Attended Merchant Taylor's School. Religion: Anglican. Home: Ridgeway, Claremont Rd., Claygate, Surrey, England. Agent: Alec Harrison, 118 Fleet St., London E.C. 4, England.

CAREER: E. Hulton & Co., London, England, sub-editor, 1922-24; Bystander, London, sub-editor, 1926-29; Times, London, sub-editor of foreign news, 1929—. Military service: Territorial Army, 1922-26. Member: Artists' Rifles Association, Royal Automobile Club, Forty Club, Burhill Golf Club.

WRITINGS: My River, and Some Other Waters, Muller, 1947; Angler's Almanac: Some Leaves on a River, Muller, 1949; Their Village, Ludgate Press, 1958; Successful Coarse Fishing, Oldbourne Press, 1964; Death from the Hills, and Other Verses, Downes, 1966. Contributor of verse, articles, and reviews to Country Life, Field, Spectator, Nash's Magazine, Argosy, and other periodicals.

AVOCATIONAL INTERESTS: Most field sports; golf, cricket, rugby football; reading.

*   *   *

GEARY, Herbert Valentine (Rupert)   1894-1965

PERSONAL: Born May 21, 1894, in London, England; son of Henry Valentine and Ellen Mary Ann (Dovaston) Geary; married Edwina Elizabeth Jones, May 23, 1945. Education: Attended Christ's Hospital; University of London, B.Sc.(Econ.), 1934. Home: 1 Aberdeen Court, Aberdeen Park, London N. 5, England.

CAREER: Indian Army, regular officer in 2nd Punjab Regiment, 1914-23, serving in France, 1915, Aden, 1916-17, in Third Afghan War, 1919, in Pakistan, 1919-22; received Military Cross for service in France; discharged as major. Farmer in Natal, South Africa, 1923-26, merchant banker in Dublin, Ireland, and London, England, 1926-31; teacher in England, at Army College at Farnham, Beaumont College, Malvern College, City of London College, 1931-39, 1945-58. British Army, Intelligence, 1939-45. Royal Society of Arts, senior examiner, 1947-65.

WRITINGS: Notes on Elementary Economics, Farnham Herald, 1933; Your Money and Your Life: An Economic Introduction to Everyday Affairs, Edward Arnold, 1938; The Background of Business, Oxford University Press, 1953, 3rd edition, 1963; (with Geoffrey Betham) The Golden Galley: The Story of the Second Punjab Regiment, 1761-1947, Oxford University Press, 1956. Editor of Industry and Commerce, Volume VII, Oxford Junior Encyclopedia. Contributor to Journal of the Royal United Service Institution (India), Economist, Irish Times, Irish Independent, Irish Statesman, 1919-65.

WORK IN PROGRESS: The Foundations of Bookkeeping.

AVOCATIONAL INTERESTS: Yachting.

(Died June 1, 1965)

*   *   *

GEOGHEGAN, Sister Barbara   1902-

PERSONAL: Surname is pronounced Gay-gen; born June 11, 1902, in New York, N.Y.; daughter of Patrick H. (an importer) and Mae B. (Schwalbert) Geoghegan. Education: College of Mount St. Joseph-on-the-Ohio, A.B., 1928; Loyola University, Chicago, Ill., M.A., 1938; Fordham University, Ph.D., 1950. Politics: Independent. Residence: Mount St. Joseph, Ohio. Office: College of Mount St. Joseph, Mount St. Joseph, Ohio 45051.

CAREER: Roman Catholic nun, member of Sisters of Charity; teacher or principal of Catholic schools in Cleveland, Ohio, 1928-38, Chicago, Ill., 1938-41, Royal Oak, Mich., 1941-47; Sisters of Charity, Cincinnati, Ohio, director of studies and supervisor of high schools, 1951-62; College of Mount St. Joseph-on-the-Ohio, Mount St. Joseph, Ohio, professor of education and psychology, head of department of secondary education, and director of division of special services, 1962-70, chairman of department of education, 1970—. Fordham University, New York, N.Y., adjunct associate professor, 1958—. Member: American Psychological Association, American Personnel and Guidance Association, American Catholic Psychological Association, National Catholic Education Association, Ohio Psychological Association.

WRITINGS: (With Sister Mary Baptista Pollard and William A. Kelly) Developmental Psychology: A Study of the Human Life Spiral, Bruce, 1963; (With Sister Pollard) The Growing Child in Contemporary Society, Bruce, 1969. Author of two original dances for piano, "The Lonely Piper" and "The Daisy Chain," included in Girl's Book of Ballet, edited by Arthur Henry Franks, Burke, 1953, 4th revised edition, 1966. Contributor to journals. Editorial consultant, Harcourt's "Insight Series," 1958-65.

WORK IN PROGRESS: Research in changing attitudes of college students before and after professional courses and experiences; a book, Psychology of the Middle-School Child.

GEORGE, M(ary) Dorothy

PERSONAL: Born in Cheam, Surrey, England; daughter of Alexander (a barrister-at-law) and Emily (Tabor) Gordon; married Eric Beardsworth George (a painter), October 14, 1913 (died, 1961). *Education:* Girton College, Cambridge, M.A.; London School of Economics and Political Science, research scholar. *Home:* 51 Paulton's Sq., Chelsea, London, S.W.3, England.

CAREER: Served in British War Office, London, England, in Intelligence Division, 1915-19; British Museum, researchist, 1930-53; writer. *Member:* Royal Historical Society (fellow; council member, 1944-45), Economic History Society, Historical Association, English-Speaking Union. *Awards, honors:* Litt.D., Cambridge University, 1936; Order of British Empire, 1954; honorary fellow of Girton College.

WRITINGS: English Social Life in the Eighteenth Century, [London], 1923; *London Life in the XVIII Century,* Kegan Paul, 1925, revised edition, London School of Economics and Political Science, 1951, Capricorn, 1965; *England in Jonson's Day,* Methuen, 1928; *England in Transition: Life and Work in the Eighteenth Century,* Routledge, 1931, revised edition, Penguin, 1964; *Catalogue of Political and Personal Satires,* Volumes V-XI *(1771-1832),* Trustees of British Museum, 1935-54; *English Political Caricature,* two volumes, Clarendon Press, 1960; *Hogarth to Cruickshank: Social Change in Graphic Satire,* Walker, 1967; (contributor) Eric Beardsworth George, *Life and Death of Benjamin Robert Haydon,* 2nd edition (Mary George not associated with earlier edition), Clarendon Press, 1967. Contributor of articles and reviews to historical journals.

* * *

GEORGE, Robert Esmonde Gordon 1890-1969
(Robert Sencourt, Robert Esmonde Sencourt)

PERSONAL: Born September 8, 1890, in New Zealand; son of James Cartwright (a merchant) and Annie (Nicholls) George. *Education:* Attended St. John's College, Auckland, New Zealand; St. John's College, Oxford, M.A., B.Litt., 1918. *Religion:* Roman Catholic. *Home:* 10 Manor Rd., Oxford, England. *Agent:* Lawrence Pollinger Ltd., 18 Maddox St., London W.1, England.

CAREER: During academic career was professor of English at University of Lisbon, Lisbon, Portugal, at Punjab University, Lahore, India (now Pakistan), and in Egypt, 1933-36; also taught at Harrow School, Middlesex, England, and Royal Naval College, Dartmouth, England. Visiting lecturer, Yale University, 1965. *Military service:* Indian Cavalry, officer, General Staff, 1915-18. *Member:* Cercle Interalliee (Paris), Royal Automobile Club (London).

WRITINGS—All under pseudonym Robert Sencourt, except as indicated: *Purse and Politics,* Allen & Unwin, 1921; *Outflying Philosophy: A Literary Study of the Religious Element in the Poems and Letters of John Donne and in the Works of Sir Thomas Browne and of Henry Vaughan the Silurist, Together with an Account of the Interest of These Writers in Scholastic Philosophy, in Platonism, and in Hermetic Physic, with Also Some Notes on Witchcraft,* Simpkin, Marshall, Hamilton, Kent & Co., 1925, Haskell House, 1966; *India in English Literature,* Simpkin, Marshall, Hamilton, Kent & Co., 1925, Kennikat, 1970; (under pseudonym Robert Esmonde Sencourt) *The Life of George Meredith,* Scribner, 1929; *The Life of Empress Eugenie,* Scribner, 1931; *The Spanish Crown, 1808-1931: An Intimate Chronicle of a Hundred Years,* Scribner, 1932 (published in England as *Spain's Uncertain Crown: The Story of the Spanish Sovereigns, 1808-1931,* Benn, 1932); *Napoleon III: The Modern Emperor,* Appleton, 1933; (editor and author of introduction with Victor Wellesley) *Conversations with Napoleon III: A Collection of Documents, Mostly Unpublished and Almost Entirely Diplomatic,* Benn, 1934; *The Genius of the Vatican,* J. Cape, 1935; *Spain's Ordeal: A Documented Survey of Recent Events,* Longmans, Green, 1939, enlarged edition, 1940; *Italy,* Arrowsmith, 1938.

Winston Churchill, Faber, 1940; *King Alfonso: A Biography,* Faber, 1942; *Carmelite and Poet: A Framed Portrait of St. John of the Cross,* Hollis & Carter, 1943, Macmillan, 1944; *The Consecration of Genius: An Essay to Elucidate the Distinctive Significance and Quality of Christian Art by Analysis and Comparison of Certain Masterpieces,* Hollis & Carter, 1947, Kennikat, 1970; *The Life of Newman,* Dacre Press, 1948; *Saint Paul, Envoy of Grace,* Sheed, 1948; *Heirs of Tradition: Tributes of a New Zealander,* Carroll & Nicholson, 1949, Books for Libraries, 1971; *The Slavatorians and Their Founder,* 1953; (editor and author of introduction) George Meredith, *The Ordeal of Richard Feveral,* Dutton, 1954; *The Reign of King Edward VIII,* Gibbs Library, 1962; *T. S. Eliot: A Memoir,* edited by Donald Adamson, Dodd, 1971. Contributor to *Revue de Deux Mode, Times* (London), *Edinburgh Review, Discovery, Catholic Herald, Search, Irish Times, Royal Geographical Journal,* and other reviews and newspapers in Great Britain and United States.

WORK IN PROGRESS: A work on the Vatican Council; a study of Wordsworth and Shelley; studies of the way World War II was exploited in the interests of Moscow.

SIDELIGHTS: A well-known and respected critic, biographer, and historian, Sencourt won his reputation in the 1930's, though in later years his output and abilities had been thought by some to diminish. The *Times* (London) obituary described Sencourt's "temper of mind" as "essentially conciliatory. His political views were conservative, yet he welcomed social change and contrived, despite his years, to remain surprisingly modern in outlook. His last years were devoted to ecumenical efforts befitting a man of his vision. . . . Robert Sencourt was the most fervent and devout of religious men, with the same personal mysticism as makes his life of St. John of the Cross a joy to read. Never fearing to speak his mind in religious matters, even when (as often) his views ran counter to the church's, he was intolerant of any form of ecclesiastical cant or humbug.''

Sencourt was fluent in French, German, Italian, and Spanish, and had some knowledge of Arabic and Hindustani.

BIOGRAPHICAL/CRITICAL SOURCES: Times (London), May 24, 1969.

(Died May 23, 1969)

* * *

GERSHOY, Leo 1897-

PERSONAL: Born September 27, 1897, in Krivoi Rog, Russia; brought to United States, 1903; naturalized, 1913; son of Morris and Miriam (Lioubarski) Gershoy; married Ida Elizabeth Prigohzy, September 24, 1924. *Education:* Cornell University, A.B., 1919, A.M., 1920, Ph.D., 1925. *Home:* 29 Washington Square, New York, N.Y. 10011.

CAREER: University of Rochester, Rochester, N.Y., assistant professor of history, 1924-26; Long Island University, Brooklyn, N.Y., assistant professor, 1929-30, associate professor of history, 1930-38; Sarah Lawrence College, New York, N.Y., member of social science department, 1938-46; New York University, New York, New York, professor of European history, 1946-73, professor emeritus, 1969—. Visiting professor at Columbia University, 1947-48, University of California, Los Angeles, 1953-55; visiting summer professor at Cornell University, 1932-34, 1936, University of Chicago, 1938, University of California, Los Angeles, 1948. Consultant to Office of Strategic Services, 1942; principal analyst, Foreign Broadcast Intelligence Service, 1943-44; regional specialist for French Overseas Branch of Office of War Information, 1944-45.

MEMBER: American Historical Association (member of council, 1953-57), Societe des Etudes Robespierristes, Society of American Historians, Societe d'Histoire Moderne, Phi Beta Kappa. Awards, honors: Social Science Research Council fellow, 1927-28; Guggenheim Foundation fellowships, 1936-37, 1939, 1946, 1959; Fulbright grant for research in France, 1952-53; fellow, Center for Advanced Study in the Behavioral Sciences, 1963-64.

WRITINGS: The French Revolution, 1789-1799, Holt, 1932; The French Revolution and Napoleon, Crofts, 1933; From Despotism to Revolution, 1763-1789, Harper, 1944; The Era of the French Revolution, 1789-1799: Ten Years That Shook the World, Van Nostrand, 1957; Bertrand Barere: A Reluctant Terrorist, Princeton University Press, 1962. Contributor of articles to professional journals and to other periodicals. Member of board of editors, American Historical Review, 1959-63.

* * *

GERVASI, Frank H(enry) 1908-

PERSONAL: Born February 5, 1908, in Baltimore, Md.; son of Eugene Leone (a mechanic) and Teresa (Guarnera) Gervasi; separated; children: Sean David, Eugene Michael. Education: Attended Drexel Institute of Technology, 1927-28, University of Pennsylvania, 1928-30. Politics: Independent liberal. Religion: Christian. Residence: New York, N.Y. Agent: (Lectures) Jonas Silverstone, Silverstone & Rosenthal, 250 West 57th St., New York, N.Y.

CAREER: Reporter for Philadelphia Record, Philadelphia, Pa., 1929-30, Associated Press, New York, N.Y., 1930-34; Hearst Newspapers, Madrid correspondent, 1934-35, London correspondent, 1935; International News Service, chief of Rome bureau, 1935-39; Collier's, roving war correspondent, 1939-45, associate editor, 1939-49; U.S. Department of State, chief of information for Marshall Plan, Rome, Italy, 1950-52; New York Post, foreign correspondent based in Rome, Italy, with column, "Dateline Your World," syndicated by Worldwide Press Service, 1954-57; Motion Picture Export Association, New York, N.Y., director of Mediterranean area, Rome, Italy, 1957-60; Fairbanks-Whitney Corp., vice-president of European operations, 1960-61; consultant and speechwriter on staff of Governor Nelson Rockefeller, New York, N.Y., 1961-63; full-time professional writer, 1963—. Lecturer on international affairs. Member: Overseas Press Club (New York).

WRITINGS: War Has Seven Faces, Doubleday, 1942; But Soldiers Wondered Why, Doubleday, 1943; To Whom Palestine?, Appleton, 1945; Big Government, Whittlesey House, 1949; The Real Rockefeller, Atheneum, 1964; The Case for Israel, foreword by Abba Eban, Viking Press, 1967.

Writer and narrator of eight half-hour television films, American Broadcasting Co., 1953-54, and of "Zero Hour in Greece," Columbia Broadcasting System "Twentieth Century" program.
Contributor to national magazines, including Business Week, Atlantic Monthly, Reporter, Cosmopolitan, and Show.

WORK IN PROGRESS: A full-length biography of Guiseppe Garibaldi.

SIDELIGHTS: Gervasi is fluent in Italian, Spanish, and French.

* * *

GIBSON, Reginald Walter 1901-

PERSONAL: Born October 29, 1901, in Oxford, England; son of John Thomas and Edith Annie (Brooks) Gibson; married Gwendolin Lilian Plested, April 12, 1928; children: Trevor Anthony. Education: Educated at schools in Oxford, England. Politics: "Inclined to Labour." Religion: Church of England. Home: 44 Margaret Rd., Headington, Oxford, England.

CAREER: Bodleian Library, Oxford, England, junior assistant, worked on the catalogue of Hebrew printed books, 1916-22; Blackwell's (booksellers), Oxford, manager of Oriental and African departments, 1923-31; bookseller in St. Aldate's, Oxford, 1931-35; Sotheby & Co., London, England, cataloguer and appraiser of literary properties for auction, 1936-38; Blackwell's, manager of Oriental and African departments, 1936-65.

WRITINGS: Francis Bacon, A Bibliography of His Works and of Baconiana to 1750, [Oxford], supplement, privately printed, 1959; St. Thomas More, a Preliminary Bibliography of His Works and of Moreana to 1750, Yale University Press, 1961. Contributor of articles and reviews, mainly on Baconiana, to literary journals. Member of editorial advisory committee, Yale University's St. Thomas More Project.

WORK IN PROGRESS: A life of young Francis Bacon and the story of his times; a definitive edition of the Yale More bibliography; a select bibliography of St. Thomas More, 1751-1965; research into the bibliography of John Milton.

SIDELIGHTS: Gibson owns a large collection of the early editions of the works of Francis Bacon.

* * *

GIDDINGS, James Louis 1909-1964

PERSONAL: Born April 10, 1909, in Caldwell, Tex.; son of James Louis and Maude (Matthews) Giddings; married Ruth Warner; children: James, Ann, Russell. Education: Attended Rice Institute for three years; University of Alaska, B.S., 1931; University of Arizona, M.A., 1941; University of Pennsylvania, Ph.D., 1951. Home: Mount Hope Grant, Bristol, R.I. 02809.

CAREER: University of Alaska, College, researcher in dendrochronology, 1938-40, instructor and associate professor, 1940-50; University of Pennsylvania, Philadelphia, began as visiting assistant professor, became assistant professor of anthropology, 1950-56; Brown University, Providence, R.I., associate professor, 1956-59, professor, 1959-64, director of Haffenreffer Museum. Danish National Museum, Copenhagen, Denmark, Fulbright research professor and Guggenheim fellow, 1962-63. Field work in Alaska and Canada, at intervals, 1934-64, in Greenland, summer, 1963. *Military service:* U.S. Naval Reserve, 1945-54; active duty, 1943-45; became lieutenant. *Member:* Society for American Archaeology (executive committee, 1962-63), American Anthropological Association, American Association for the Advancement of Science, Tree-Ring Society, Arctic Institute, American Geographical Society, Committee for the Recovery of Archaeological Remains (former liaison member for National Research Council).

WRITINGS: Dendrochronology in Northern Alaska, University of Arizona Press, 1941; *The Arctic Woodland Culture of the Kobuk River*, University Museum, University of Pennsylvania, 1952; (with David Moody Hopkins) *Geological Background of the Iyatayet Archaeological Site, Cape Denbigh, Alaska*, Smithsonian Institution, 1953; *"Pillows" and Other Rare Flints*, University of Alaska, 1956; *Forest Eskimos: An Ethnographic Sketch of Kobuk River People in the 1880's*, University Museum, 1956; *Kobuk River People*, University of Alaska Press, 1961; *The Archaeology of Cape Denbigh*, Brown University Press, 1964; *Ancient Men of the Arctic*, Knopf, 1967. Contributor to *American Antiquity*, *Arctic Anthropology*, *Natural History*, other journals. Assistant editor, *Abstracts of New World Archaeology*.

WORK IN PROGRESS: Beach Ridge Archaeology in Alaska; archaeological field work in Alaska.

BIOGRAPHICAL/CRITICAL SOURCES: Atlantic, August, 1967; *Book World*, September 10, 1967.

(Died December, 1964)

* * *

GILDEN, Bert   1915(?)-1971
(K. B. Gilden, joint pseudonym)

PERSONAL: Born in Los Angeles, Calif.; married wife, Katya (writer and researcher with whom he collaborated), 1947; children: David Ethan, Jairus Matthew, Daniel Mordecai. *Education:* Brown University, A.B., 1936. *Home:* 250 Algonquin Rd., Bridgeport, Conn. 06604. *Agent:* Peter Matson, 30 Rockefeller Plaza, New York, N.Y.

CAREER: Formerly publicist, plastic moulding machine operator, paint inspector and touch up man in electrical applicance plant, and assistant to the comptroller in aerosol filling plant; during three year stay in Georgia, helped to initiate G.I. farm training classes for veterans. Founder, New York Screen Publicists Guild. Chairman, Van Wyck Brooks Memorial Awards for best works by Connecticut authors, given each year. *Military service:* U.S. Army, Armored Force, World War II, served as lieutenant; received Silver Star, Bronze Star, Purple Heart with Oak Leaf Cluster, Croix de Guerre with Vermillion Star.

WRITINGS—With Katya Gilden, under pseudonym K. B. Gilden: *Hurry Sundown* (novel; Literary Guild selection), Doubleday, 1965; *Between the Hills and the Sea* (novel; Literary Guild alternate selection), Doubleday, 1971. Also author of a novel, "The Race," published in *Liberty* magazine. Collaborator with Katya Gilden on short stories, four television scripts, and an original screenplay.

SIDELIGHTS: Hurry Sundown was filmed by Paramount, 1967; "The Race" is being produced by Wabash Films.

BIOGRAPHICAL/CRITICAL SOURCES: Time, January 8, 1965; *New York Times Book Review*, January 10, 1965; *Commonweal*, May 7, 1965; *Variety*, April 7, 1971; *Publishers Weekly*, May 3, 1971; *Antiquarian Bookman*, May 17, 1971.

(Died April 4, 1971)

GILL, Traviss   1891-
(Gill Odell, a joint pseudonym)

PERSONAL: Born July 4, 1891, in London, England; son of Marmaduke Fletcher (a business manager) and Kate (Barnes) Gill; married Nellie Baldam, June 2, 1918; children: Pamela Coral (Mrs. J. Beaumont Bissell). *Education:* Attended schools in England until fifteen. *Politics:* Conservative. *Religion:* Church of England. *Home:* The Lodge, 52 Lee Ter., Blackheath, London S.E. 3, England.

CAREER: British Army, volunteer in Territorial Army, 1909-13, Infantry and Machine Gun Corps, 1914-19, becoming second lieutenant; Limehouse Paperboard Mills Ltd., London, England, sales manager, 1923-40; Royal Air Force, Movements Branch, 1941-50, becoming flight lieutenant; also worked in advertising and for Gallup Poll at later periods. *Member:* Rotary International, Royal Air Force Reserves Club (London).

WRITINGS: Recipe for Fame (play), Garamond Press, 1932; (with Carol Odell under joint pseudonym Gill Odell) *Mr. Ozzle of Withery Wood* (juvenile), Angus & Robertson, 1959.

WORK IN PROGRESS: Mr. Ozzle and the Silver Key (as sole author).

SIDELIGHTS: Gill told *CA*: "[I] love people and places. Have cottage in Devon, England. Find motoring relaxing and never tire of it."

* * *

GILMOUR, Garth (Hamilton)   1925-

PERSONAL: Born December 24, 1925, in Dunedin, New Zealand; son of Norman Hamilton (a farmer) and Edith (Veale) Gilmour; married Ann Fraser, October 1, 1949; children: Simon Fraser, Jan Carol. *Education:* Attended schools in New Zealand. *Home:* 46 Kensington Ave., Auckland, New Zealand. *Office:* Advertising Associates (N.Z.) Ltd., 10 Newton Rd., Auckland, New Zealand.

CAREER: Journalist on newspapers in Dunedin, New Zealand, 1941-44, Wanganui, New Zealand, 1946-49, and New Plymouth, New Zealand, 1949-56; *Auckland Star*, Auckland, New Zealand, columnist, 1956-62; Gordon Dryden Ltd., Auckland, public relations consultant, 1962-64; Barfoot and Thompson Real Estate, Auckland, advertising consultant, 1964-66; Spanjer Murdock Advertising, Auckland, copywriter, 1966-68; Clegg Bowler Associates Ltd., Auckland, public relations consultant, 1968-70; Advertising Associates (N.Z.) Ltd., Auckland, public relations manager, 1970—. *Military service:* Royal New Zealand Air Force, 1944-45.

WRITINGS: (With Arthur Leslie Lydiard) *Run to the Top*, A. H. & A. W. Reed, 1962, 2nd edition, Athletics Arena, 1967; (with Murray Halberg) *A Clean Pair of Heels*, A. H. & A. W. Reed, 1963, Jenkins, 1964; (with Lydiard) *Run for Your Life: Jogging with Arthur Lydiard*, Minerva Publishing, 1965; (with Peter Snell) *No Bugles, No Drums*, Hodder & Stoughton, 1966; (with Dardir El Bakary) *Dardir on Squash*, Gilmour Associates Ltd., 1971.

SIDELIGHTS: Gilmour's books have been published in England, Japan, and Russia.

GINNS, Ronald 1896-

PERSONAL: Surname is pronounced *Jinnz*; born March 1, 1896, in Desborough, England; son of John Allen (a farmer) and Kate (Tailby) Ginns; married Dolcina Clothilde Pesaresi, January 24, 1953. *Education:* Wellingborough School, student, 1908-13; University of Manchester, student, 1914-15; University of London, B.Sc. (honors), 1925. *Religion:* Church of England. *Home:* 112 Rothwell Rd., Desborough, Northamptonshire, England.

CAREER: Central School, Kettering, England, head of science department, 1955-59. Lecturer on cacti, and judge of flower shows. Member of convocation, University of London. *Military service:* British and Indian Armies, 1915-21; became captain; 1940-44; became major. *Member:* National Cactus and Succulent Society (fellow; executive member), Alpine Garden Society (assistant show secretary).

WRITINGS: Cacti and Other Succulents, Penguin, 1963; (editor) *Gymnocalyciums: Some Observations on the Genus by a Study Group of the Institute*, Succulent Plant Institute, 1967. Contributor to *Gardeners' Chronicle* and other gardening periodicals. Member of editorial staff, National Cactus and Succulent Society.

WORK IN PROGRESS: Showing and Judging Succulents.

* * *

GLASHEEN, Patrick 1897-

PERSONAL: Born April 6, 1897, in Doon, County Limerick, Eire; son of Thomas (a farmer) and Ellen (O'Dwyer) Glasheen. *Education:* Studied at Belcamp College, Dublin, Eire, 1914-16, and Belmont House, Blackrock, Dublin, 1917-20; National University of Ireland, B.A., 1920, higher diploma in education, 1924, M.A., 1925. *Home:* Sacred Heart Church, St. Aubin, Jersey, Channel Islands.

CAREER: Roman Catholic priest, member of Order of Mary Immaculate. Teacher of Gaelic and other subjects, 1924-33; Belcamp College, Dublin, Eire, bursar and preacher, 1933-40; parish priest at Colwyn Bay, Eire, 1940-46; St. Mary's College, Colwyn Bay, founder and president, 1946-54; parish priest in Leeds, England, 1954-60, at Sacred Heart Church, St. Aubin, Jersey, Channel Islands, beginning 1961. British Forces in North Wales, chaplain, 1940-46. *Member:* Academy of Christian Art (Dublin; Latin secretary, 1935-40).

WRITINGS: Preacher's Concordance, Newman Press, 1963. Contributor of articles to magazines.

* * *

GLASSBERG, B(ertrand) Y(ounker) 1902-19(?)

PERSONAL: Born May 26, 1902, in St. Louis, Mo.; son of Isaac (a salesman) and Gertrude (Younker) Glassberg; married Helen Dub, October 7, 1929; children: Ann (Mrs. Richard Landman), Jane (Mrs. Arthur Young). *Education:* Washington University, St. Louis, Mo., student, 1919-25, B.S. and M.D. *Religion:* Jewish. *Home:* 1001 North McKnight Rd., St. Louis, Mo. 63132. *Office:* 8631 Delmar Blvd., St. Louis, Mo. 63124.

CAREER: Physician, specializing in internal medicine, St. Louis, Mo., beginning 1925, and marriage counselor. Washington University, St. Louis, Mo., faculty member of College of Medicine, beginning 1928. St. Louis (Mo.) Board of Education, lecturer on personal and family living, 1945-

1960; broadcaster of weekly radio program, "Ask the Marriage Counselor," Station KMOX, beginning 1962. *Member:* American Medical Association, American Association of Marriage Counselors, National Council on Family Relations, Groves Conference on Marriage and Family, Missouri Medical Association, St. Louis Medical Association, Missouri Social Health Association.

WRITINGS: Know Yourself, Oxford Book Co., 1954; *Barron's Teen Age Sex Counselor*, Barron's, 1965, revised edition, 1970. Contributor of articles to professional and semi-professional journals.

WORK IN PROGRESS: A book on marriage and its problems, prepared from anonymous questions posed on radio program, "Ask the Marriage Counselor."

SIDELIGHTS: Glassberg traveled in Europe, South America, and Alaska to study marriage and family patterns. He lectured occasionally.†

(Deceased)

* * *

GLASSON, Thomas Francis 1906-

PERSONAL: Born October 8, 1906, in Derby, England; son of Thomas Gundry and Eliza (Trewhella) Glasson; married Rita Corisande Benbow, July 29, 1937; children: Ruth. *Education:* Richmond College, London, B.D., 1933, B.D. (honors), 1936, M.A., 1940, D.D., 1944. *Home:* 50 Millway, Mill Hill, London NW7 3RA, England.

CAREER: After some years in a bank, including three years as a branch manager, was ordained to Methodist ministry, 1933; served in Methodist missions in Manchester and Bradford, England, 1933-39; pastor of churches in the Midlands and south of England, including London, 1939-60; New College, University of London, London, England, lecturer in New Testament studies and biblical theology, 1960—. *Member:* Studiorum Novi Testamenti Societas.

WRITINGS: Thomas Glasson, Lay Preacher, Epworth, 1943; *The Second Advent: The Origin of the New Testament Doctrine*, Epworth, 1945, 3rd edition, 1963; *His Appearing and His Kingdom: The Christian Hope in the Light of Its History*, Epworth, 1953; *Fundamentalism and the Bible*, Epworth, 1956; *Greek Influence in Jewish Eschatology, with Special Reference to the Apocalypses and Pseudepigraphs*, Allenson, 1961; *Moses in the Fourth Gospel*, Allenson, 1963; (editor and author of commentary) *The Revelation of John*, Cambridge University Press, 1965. Contributor to *Expository Times, Journal of Theological Studies, New Testament Studies*.

AVOCATIONAL INTERESTS: Music.

* * *

GLASSOP, (Jack) Lawson 1913-1966

PERSONAL: Born January 30, 1913, in Lawson, New South Wales, Australia; son of John (town clerk) and Lilian (Witney) Glassop; married Alison Esau, January 5, 1962. *Education:* Attended schools in New South Wales, Australia. *Home:* 46A Northgate St., Unley Park, Adelaide, South Australia. *Office: Advertiser*, King William St., Adelaide, South Australia.

CAREER: Journalist for newspapers in New South Wales, Australia, 1930-55, writing for *Newcastle Morning Herald*, 1930-40, 1945, *Sydney Morning Herald*, 1946-51, (war correspondent in Korea, 1950-51), *Daily Mirror*, Sydney, 1951-55; *Truth*, Melbourne, Victoria, Australia, journalist, 1955-

57; *Truth*, Adelaide, South Australia, journalist and chief of staff, 1957-60; *Advertiser*, Adelaide, South Australia, journalist, columnist, and feature writer, 1960-66. Former district senior running champion. *Military service:* Australian Imperial Forces, 1940-45; served in Middle East on Army newspaper two years; became staff sergeant. *Member:* Australian Journalists' Association.

WRITINGS: We Were the Rats, Angus & Robertson, 1944; *Susan and the Bogeywomp*, Angus & Robertson, 1947; *Lucky Palmer*, Shepherd & Newman, 1949; *The Rats in New Guinea*, Horwitz, 1963. Contributor of articles to Australian magazines.

WORK IN PROGRESS: A novel on Captain Cook; a book on writing English.

SIDELIGHTS: Glassop's first book, *We Were the Rats*, had brisk sales in Australia until it was banned as obscene by the New South Wales government in 1946, eighteen months after publication.

While the New South Wales ban meant virtually the end of sales throughout Australia, Glassop had some slight consolation. When the publishers, Angus & Robertson, appealed the verdict, the appeals judge described the book "as a first-rate war book and a first-rate novel; book III covering the seven months siege and defense of Tobruk is particularly stirring and attains, I think, great heights in literary art." He also said "certain pages are just plain filth." The Australian press lampooned the government in editorials and cartoons, and John Dos Passos wrote from America praising the book. But the ban held, until a somewhat modified version of the book was published in 1961.

"I was a compulsive gambler for twenty-seven years," Glassop says, "but have not had a bet for four years and will never bet again."

BIOGRAPHICAL/CRITICAL SOURCES: Melbourne Age, March 18, 1961.

(Died April 11, 1966)

* * *

GLEASON, Harold 1892-

PERSONAL: Born April 26, 1892, in Jefferson, Ohio; son of Cassius M. (an accountant) and Cora (Gillis) Gleason; married Catherine Crozier (a concert organist), April 9, 1942; children: (former marriage) Alan H., Charles N., David T., Peter G. *Education:* California Institute of Technology, student, 1910-1912; University of Rochester, M.M. in Composition, 1932. *Politics:* Republican. *Religion:* Episcopalian. *Home:* 16450 Caminito Vecinos, San Diego, Calif. 92128.

CAREER: Boston Music School Settlement, Boston, Mass., director, 1917-19; Fifth Avenue Presbyterian Church, New York, N.Y., organist and choirmaster, 1918-19; David Hochstein Music School, Rochester, N.Y., director, 1919-29; University of Rochester, Eastman School of Music, Rochester, N.Y., professor of organ, 1921-53, of musicology, 1932-55, of music literature, 1939-55, director of graduate studies, 1953-55; Rollins College, Winter Park, Fla., consultant in music. Private organist for George Eastman, Rochester, N.Y., 1919-32; organist and choirmaster at St. Paul's Church, Rochester, N.Y., 1932-49. Appeared in organ recitals in Europe and United States. Designer of organs. *Member:* American Guild of Organists, American Musicological Society, Phi Mu Alpha (Sinfonia), Phi Kappa Lambda.

WRITINGS: Method of Organ Playing, Eastman School of Music, University of Rochester, 1937, 5th edition, Appleton, 1962; (editor) *Examples of Music Before 1400*, Eastman School of Music, University of Rochester, 1942, 2nd edition, Crofts, 1945; (compiler with Albert T. Luper) *A Bibliography of Books on Music and Collections of Music: Selected from Works in the English Language Generally Available in the United States with Emphasis on Those Recently Published Together with Certain Other Standard Works*, privately printed, 1948; *Music in the Middle Ages and Renaissance*, Levis Music Store, 1949, 2nd edition, 1951; *Music in the Baroque*, Levis Music Store, 1950, 2nd edition, 1951; *Chamber Music from Haydn to Ravel*, Levis Music Store, 1950, 2nd edition, c.1951; *American Music from 1620 to 1920*, Levis Music Store, 1955; *Contemporary American Music*, Levis Music Store, c.1958; (editor with W. T. Marrocco), *Music in America: An Anthology from the Landing of the Pilgrims to the Close of the Civil War, 1620-1865*, Norton, 1964. Contributor of articles to musical journals and bulletins.

WORK IN PROGRESS: Translations of Arnolt Schlick's *Spiegel der Orgelmacher*, "Robin et Marion," a medieval French play with music, and *A Guide to Organ Music*.

AVOCATIONAL INTERESTS: Photography, art, and travel.

* * *

GLEDHILL, Alan 1895-

PERSONAL: Born October 26, 1895, in Leeds, Yorkshire, England; son of Owen and Anne (Watson) Gledhill; married Mercy Harvey, February 17, 1922 (died, 1963); married Marion Glover, 1967; children: (first marriage) Anne Cecile (Mrs. George Merrels), Hugh, Peter. *Education:* Educated at Rugby School, at Corpus Christi College, Cambridge, and Gray's Inn. *Politics:* Liberal. *Religion:* Anglican. *Home:* 24 Chichester Ct., Church Farm Estate, Rustington, Sussex, England. *Office:* School of Oriental and African Studies, University of London, London W.C.1, England.

CAREER: Indian Civil Service, Burma, 1920-48, serving as district and sessions judge, 1927-46, judge of High Court, Rangoon, 1946-48; University of London, London, England, lecturer, 1948-54, reader, 1954-55, professor of oriental laws, 1955-63, professor emeritus, 1963—. Lecturer, Council of Legal Education, 1955-67. *Military service:* British Army, 1914-18; became lieutenant; 1944-45; became lieutenant colonel; mentioned in dispatches. *Member:* Society of Public Teachers of Law, Royal Commonwealth Society.

WRITINGS: The Republic of India: The Development of Its Laws and Constitution, Stevens & Sons, 1951, 2nd edition, 1964, reprint, Greenwood Press, 1970; *Fundamental Rights in India*, Stevens & Sons, 1955; *Whither Indian Law?* (lecture), School of Oriental and African Studies, University of London, 1956; *Pakistan: The Development of Its Laws and Constitution*, Stevens & Sons, 1957, 2nd edition, 1967; *The Penal Codes of Northern Nigeria and the Sudan*, Sweet & Maxwell, 1963; (contributor) J. N. D. Anderson, editor, *Changing Law in Developing Countries*, Praeger, 1963; (contributor) J. N. D. Anderson, editor, *Family Law in Africa and Asia*, Praeger, 1968. Contributor *Modern Law Review, S.D.A.S. Bulletin, Indian Yearbook of International Affairs*, and *International and Corporation Law Quarterly*.

GLEN, J(ohn) Stanley

PERSONAL: Born in Saskatchewan, Canada; the son of John and Minabel (Wyatt) Glen; married Winifred Mac-Dougall, December 23, 1931; children: Eleanor (Mrs. Ramsey Cooke), Gwynneth (Mrs. James Scott), Catherine (Mrs. George Collard). *Education:* University of Toronto, B.A., 1930, M.A., 1933, Ph.D., 1937; University of Saskatchewan, B.Ed., 1931; Knox College, Toronto, Ontario, graduate diploma, 1937; Victoria University, B.D., 1941, Th.D., 1945. *Office:* Knox College, 59 St. George St., Toronto 5, Ontario, Canada.

CAREER: Presbyterian minister; Glenview Presbyterian Church, Toronto, Ontario, minister, 1938-45; Knox College, Toronto, Ontario, professor of New Testament, 1945—, principal, 1952—. World Presbyterian Alliance, North American area chairman, 1957-58, member of central executive, 1954-59. *Awards, honors:* D.D., Presbyterian College (Montreal), 1955.

WRITINGS: The Recovery of the Teaching Ministry, Westminister, 1960; *The Parables of Conflict in Luke*, Westminister, 1962; *Pastoral Problems in First Corinthians*, Westminister, 1964; *Erich Fromm: A Protestant Critique*, Westminister, 1966; *Recovery of the Teaching Ministry*, Westminister, 1967.

* * *

GLIDDEN, Horace Knight 1901-

PERSONAL: Born June 21, 1901, in Colorado Springs, Colo.; son of John William (a contractor) and Lucy (Knight) Glidden; married Mona Bithell, July 24, 1961; children: (prior marriage) Horace Kay, Marianne (Mrs. Frank Provenzano); (stepchildren) Gary Ewing, Camille (Mrs. Robert Wright). *Education:* University of Kansas, B.S. in Industrial Engineering, 1925. *Home:* 2149 East 1700 South, Salt Lake City, Utah. *Office:* Merrill Engineering Building, University of Utah, Salt Lake City, Utah.

CAREER: Engineer and cost accountant in Kansas, 1925-28; U.S. Department of Commerce, assistant civil engineer, working on federal airways system, Washington, D.C., and Milwaukee, Wis., 1928-33; Kansas Emergency Relief Corp., resident engineer on dam construction, 1933-37; U.S. Civil Aeronautics Administration, airport construction and design, Santa Monica, Calif., and New York, N.Y., 1937-45, district airport engineer for state of Idaho, Boise, 1947-50; private engineering practice in Boise and Dubois, Idaho, and manager of Glidden Wood Products Co., 1950-55; University of Utah, Salt Lake City, assistant professor of civil engineering, beginning 1955. Registered civil engineer in Idaho (formerly registered in four other states). *Member:* American Society of Civil Engineers, American Association of University Professors, Elks.

WRITINGS: (With Cowles and Law) *Airports—Design, Construction and Management*, McGraw, 1946; *Reports, Technical Writing, and Specifications*, McGraw, 1964. Contributor of almost sixty articles to periodicals, most of them appearing in *Roads and Streets*. Eastern editor, *Roads and Streets*, 1946; field editor, summers, 1956-59, and 1961-65.

* * *

GODE von AESCH, Alexander (Gottfried Friedrich) 1906-1970
(Alexander Gode)

PERSONAL; Gode is pronounced *Go*-da; born October 30, 1906, in Bremen, Germany; became naturalized American citizen, 1927; son of Heinrich and Anna (von Aesch) Gode; married Johanna Roeser, 1930; married second wife, Janet Alison Livermore, 1963; children: (first marriage) Anna Johanna (Mrs. Richard Merritt), Marilyn; (second marriage) Alison Louise, Heinrich. *Education:* Columbia University, M.A., 1929, Ph.D., 1939. *Home:* Finney Farm, Croton-on-Hudson, N.Y. 10520. *Office:* Interlingua Division, Science Service, Inc., 80 East 11th St., New York, N.Y. 10003.

CAREER: T. Y. Crowell Co. (publishers), New York, N.Y., editor of linguistic works, 1943-46; International Auxiliary Language Association, New York, N.Y., director of research, 1949-53; Storm Publishers, Inc., New York, N.Y., president, 1946-70; Science Service, Inc., Interlingua Division, New York, N.Y., chief, 1953-70. New York University, New York, N.Y., adjunct professor of German, 1959-70.

MEMBER: International Society for General Semantics, International Society of Aviation Writers, Modern Language Association of America, American Medical Writers Association, American Association for Advancement of Science, National Society for Study of Communication, American Translators Association (founding member and first president; executive director), American Interlingua Society, Association of Technical Writers and Publishers (past president, New York chapter), Union Mundial pro Interlingua (president). *Awards, honors:* American Medical Writers Association citation and award for distinguished contributions to medical communication, 1959; First International Translation Prize, Federation Internationale des Traducteurs, 1970.

WRITINGS: Natural Science in German Romanticism, Columbia University Press, 1941; (with E. Clark Stillman) *Spanish at Sight*, Crowell, 1943, 2nd edition, Ungar, 1962; *Portuguese at Sight*, Crowell, 1943; (with Chassia Heldt) *French at Sight*, Crowell, 1945, 2nd revised edition, Ungar, 1963; (with Hugh E. Blair) *Interlingua: A Grammar of the International Language*, Storm, 1951, 2nd edition, 1955; *El Romanticismo aleman y las ciencias naturales*, Espasa-Calpe, 1953; *Interlingua: A prime vista*, Storm, 1954; (with Merrill Moore) *Homo Sonetticus Moorensis*, Storm, 1956; *Dece contos: Bibliotheca de textos in Interlingua*, Storm, 1958.

Editor: *Roget's Thesaurus*, Crowell, 1946; *Bulfinch's Mythology*, Crowell, 1946; (with Frederick Ungar) *An Anthology of German Lyric Poetry Through the 19th Century* (in German and English), Ungar, 1950, 2nd edition, 1972; *Interlingua-English: A Dictionary of the International Language*, Storm, 1951, 2nd edition, Ungar, 1971.

Translator: (With Erika Fueloep-Miller) Rene Fueloep-Miller, *Saints That Moved the World*, Crowell, 1945; Oscar Benjamin Frankl, *Theodore Herzl: The Jew and the Man*, Storm, 1949; Carola Giedion-Welcker, *Paul Klee*, Viking, 1952; Hans Selye, *Le Major phases de recerca in la historia del syndrome de adaptation*, Science Service, 1953; Paul Nettl, *National Anthems*, Storm, 1958, 2nd edition, Ungar, 1967; (and author of introduction) Friedrich Wilhelm Christian Gerstaecker, *Germelshausen*, Barron's, 1958; (and editor, with John H. Moran, and author of introduction) *On the Origin of Language* (essays by Rousseau and Herder), Ungar, 1967; Johann J. Winckelmann, *History of Ancient Art*, two volumes, Ungar, 1968; Wilifried Engler, *The French Novel from 1800 to the Present*, Ungar, 1968; Carol Peterson, *Albert Camus*, Ungar, 1969;

Gerhard Szczesny, *The Case Against Bertolt Brecht: With Arguments Drawn from His "Life of Galileo,"* Ungar, 1969; Wilifried Daim, *The Vatican and Eastern Europe*, Ungar, 1970. Also translator of volumes of abstracts of various international congresses into Interlingua.

Columnist, "Just Words," *Journal of American Medical Association*, "Of Words and Things," Science Service, and "Live Chitchat," *Lebende Sprachen*. Contributor to more than twenty linguistic and science journals, including *Scientific Monthly, International Medical Digest, Language Forum, International Language Review*. Editor, *Translation Inquirer, Buten und Binnen, Der Reading Deutsche*, 1932-35, *Scientia International*, 1952-70, *Novas de Interlingua*, 1954-70, *ATA Notes*, 1960-70.

WORK IN PROGRESS: Translating summaries for some twenty medical journals into Interlingua.

(Died August 11, 1970)

* * *

GODFREY, Frederick M. 1901-1974

PERSONAL: Born 1901, in Berlin, Germany; married, wife's name, Margaret. *Education:* University of Heidelberg, Ph.D., 1927. *Home:* Exeland Cottage, Bickleigh near Tiverton, Devonshire, England.

CAREER: Member of staff, Blundell's School, 1936-39, Mill Hill School, 1945-62. Part-time lecturer in history of art at Exeter College of Art, 1963-73.

WRITINGS: Early Venetian Painters (1415-1495), Tiranti, 1954; *Child Portraiture from Bellini to Cezanne*, The Studio, 1956; *Christ and the Apostles*, The Studio, 1956; *A Students' Guide to Italian Painting (1250-1750)*, Tiranti, Volume 1, 1956, Volume II, 1958, revised one-volume edition, [London], 1965; *Italian Sculpture (1250-1700)*, Tiranti, 1967; *Italian Architecture up to 1750*, Tiranti, 1971. Contributor to *Connoisseur, Apollo, History To-Day*, and other journals. Art critic of *John O'London's*.

WORK IN PROGRESS: Dictionary of Italian Artists, for publication by Academy Editions, London.

AVOCATIONAL INTERESTS: Italy—the country, people, language, and art.

(Died March, 1974)

* * *

GOETZ, Billy E. 1904-

PERSONAL: Surname is pronounced Gets; born January 17, 1904, in Chicago, Ill.; son of Albert and Cora (Maier) Goetz; married Isabelle Reed, September 1, 1928; children: Elizabeth (Mrs. Owen Hedden), Margaret L. (Mrs. Thomas Atkinson), Carolyn (Mrs. Richard Linberg). *Education:* University of Chicago, Ph.B., 1924, Ph.D., 1949; Cornell University, graduate study, 1926-28. *Politics:* Independent. *Office:* Department of Business Administration, Florida Atlantic University, Boca Raton, Fla. 33432.

CAREER: J. O. McKinsey Co., Chicago, Ill., staff member, 1933-35; Sessions Engineering Co., Chicago, Ill., senior associate, 1935-42, director of management division, 1943-45, 1953-54; Illinois Institute of Technology, Chicago, Ill., instructor in economics, 1935-42; University of Chicago, Chicago, Ill., instructor in accounting, 1936-39; The American University, Washington, D.C., assistant professor of business policies and management, 1942-43; Antioch College, Yellow Springs, Ohio, professor, and head of department of business administration, 1945-54; Massa-

chusetts Institute of Technology, Cambridge, professor of industrial management, 1954-69; Florida Atlantic University, Boca Raton, Fla., adjunct professor of accounting, 1969—. *Member:* Society for Advancement of Management (former chapter president), Academy of Management (secretary-treasurer, 1954-56, vice-president, 1957, president, 1958), American Accounting Association, National Accounting Association.

WRITINGS: Management Planning and Control, McGraw, 1949; (with F. R. Klein) *Accounting in Action*, Houghton, 1960; *Quantitative Methods: A Survey for Managers*, McGraw, 1965.

* * *

GOLD, Douglas 1894-

PERSONAL: Born March 24, 1894, in Newburgh, Ind.; son of James Douglas (a Presbyterian minister) and Mary (Love) Gold; married Bertha Levengood, July 2, 1948; children: Marylee (Mrs. Charles Bales). *Education:* Waynesburg College, B.A., 1914; University of California, summer graduate study, 1922, 1933; University of Montana, M.A., 1934; Columbia University, Ed.D., 1952. *Home:* 28 Indian Rd., Hampton, Va. 23369. *Office:* Testing Bureau, Hampton Institute, Hampton, Va. 23368.

CAREER: Schoolteacher on Blackfeet Indian Reservation in Montana, 1914-34; worked for city schools in Butte, Mont., 1934-39, and Office of State Superintendent of Schools, Helena, Mont., 1940-43; U.S. Veterans Administration, Washington, D.C., and USVA Hospital, Dublin, Ga., clinical and counseling psychologist, 1943-64; Hampton Institute, Hampton, Va., member of faculty, 1964—. *Military service:* U.S. Navy, 1918. *Member:* American Psychological Association (fellow), American Personnel and Guidance Association (former president, Georgia chapter), Georgia Psychological Association, District of Columbia Psychological Association.

WRITINGS: Course of Study for Montana Elementary Schools, State Publishing Co. (Helena, Mont.), 1942; *A Schoolmaster with the Blackfeet Indians*, Caxton, 1963.

WORK IN PROGRESS: A book, *Profiles in Persistence*, including some twenty-five actual stories of Negro students at Hampton Institute who have overcome great obstacles; research on Bible beliefs of American and British students, with sampling of fifteen hundred students in forty-one colleges and universities.

SIDELIGHTS: Gold went to the Blackfeet Reservation to spend the summer of 1914 (his father was a missionary there), and remained for a quarter of a century. During that time he kept notes on happenings, and wrote up a few stories for publication, but the bulk of his material waited almost twenty years for the writing. At seventy (compulsory government retirement age), he returned to academic life, specializing in psychology and education at Hampton Institute.

* * *

GOLDING, Louis 1907-

PERSONAL: Born December 4, 1907, in London, England; son of Maurice and Amelia (Bernberg) Golding; married Emmy Kaufmann (a volunteer social worker), October 18, 1942; children: Anthony Michael, Helen Regina. *Education:* Attended London School of Economics and Political Science, University of London. *Politics:* Conservative. *Religion:* Jewish. *Home:* 27 Northwick Circle, Kenton, Harrow, Middlesex, England.

CAREER: Inner London Education Authority, London, England, administrative officer; retired, 1968. University of London, extension lecturer in local government, 1946-51. Examiner to British Air Ministry, Civil Service commissioners, Greater London Council, and other bodies. Willesden Borough Council, member, 1960-63; Brent Borough Council, member, 1964—; Rent Tribunals, member, 1968—; Immigration Appeal Tribunal, member, 1970—: *Member:* Royal Institute of Public Administration.

WRITINGS: Teach Yourself Local Government, English Universities Press, 1955, 4th edition, 1970; *A Dictionary of Local Government in England and Wales,* Verry, 1962; *Local Government,* English Universities Press, 1964.

*   *   *

GORDON, Albert I(saac)   1903-1968

PERSONAL: Born May 11, 1903, in Cleveland, Ohio; son of Hyman Samuel and Martha (Rosenzweig) Gordon; married Dorothy Davis, November 28, 1929; children: Judith R. (Mrs. Lennard Wharton), David Eliot. *Education:* New York University, A.B., 1927; Jewish Theological Seminary of America, Rabbi and M.H.L., 1929; University of Minnesota, M.A., 1938, Ph.D., 1949. *Home:* 510 Ward St., Newton, Mass. 02159.

CAREER: Adath Jeshurun Synagogue, Minneapolis, Minn., rabbi, 1930-46; United Synagogue of America, New York, N.Y., executive director, 1946-50; Temple Emanuel, Newton, Mass., rabbi, 1950-68. Lecturer in Judaism, Andover Newton Theological School, 1949-68; lecturer in sociology and anthropology, Boston University, 1964-68. Panel member, Federal Mediation and Conciliation Service, 1949-68. President, Northeast Region of Rabbinical Assembly, 1950-68; president, Massachusetts Board of Rabbis, 1960, 1966. *Awards, honors:* D.D., Jewish Theological Seminary of America, 1964.

WRITINGS: Jews in Transition, University of Minnesota Press, 1949; *Jews in Suburbia,* Beacon Press, 1959; *Intermarriage: Interfaith, Interracial, Interethnic,* Beacon Press, 1964; *The Nature of Conversion: A Study of Forty-five Men and Women Who Changed Their Religion,* Beacon Press, 1967. Author of booklet series, "How to Celebrate the Jewish Holy Days," 1946-47.

BIOGRAPHICAL/CRITICAL SOURCES: Commentary, January, 1968; *New York Times,* November 7, 1968.

(Died November 5, 1968)

*   *   *

GORDON, Caroline   1895-

PERSONAL: Born October 6, 1895, in Trenton, Ky.; daughter of James (director of a school for boys) and Nancy Minor (Meriwether) Morris; married Allen Tate (a poet and critic), November 2, 1924 (divorced, 1954); children: Nancy Meriwether (Mrs. Percy H. Wood, Jr.). *Education:* Bethany College, A.B., 1916. *Religion:* Roman Catholic. *Home:* The Red House, Princeton, N.J. 08540.

CAREER: Chattanooga News, Chattanooga, Tenn., reporter, 1920-24; University of North Carolina, Woman's College, Greensboro, professor of English, 1938-39; Columbia University, School of General Studies, New York, N.Y., lecturer in creative writing, 1946—. Visiting professor of English at University of Washington, Seattle, 1953, University of Kansas, 1956, Purdue University; writer-in-residence at University of California, Davis, 1962-63; lecturer in creative writing at New School for Social Research, University of Utah, University of Virginia. *Member:* Alpha Xi Delta. *Awards, honors:* Guggenheim fellowship for creative writing, 1932; second prize, O. Henry Memorial Awards, 1934; Litt.D., Bethany College, 1946; National Institute Grant in Literature, 1950; D.Litt., St. Mary's College, Notre Dame, Ind., 1964; grants from National Arts Council, 1966, National Endowment for the Arts, 1966-67.

WRITINGS: Penhally (novel), Scribner, 1931; *Aleck Maury, Sportsman* (novel), Scribner, 1934 (published in England as *The Pastimes of Aleck Maury: The Life of a True Sportsman,* Dickson, 1935); *The Garden of Adonis* (novel), Scribner, 1937; *None Shall Look Back* (novel), Scribner, 1937 (published in England as *None Shall Look Back: A Story of the American Civil War,* Constable, 1937); *Green Centuries* (novel), Scribner, 1941; *The Women on the Porch* (novel), Scribner, 1944; *The Forest of the South* (stories), Scribner, 1945; (editor with former husband, Allen Tate) *The House of Fiction: An Anthology of the Short Story, With Commentary,* Scribner, 1950, 2nd edition, 1960; *The Strange Children* (novel), Scribner, 1951; *The Malefactors* (novel), Harcourt, 1956; *How to Read a Novel,* Viking, 1957; (contributor) Thomas E. Connolly, editor, *Joyce's Portrait: Criticism and Critiques,* Appleton, 1962; *Old Red and Other Stories,* Scribner, 1963; *A Good Soldier: A Key to the Novels of Ford Madox Ford,* University of California Library (Davis), 1963.

Associated with Ford Madox Ford in the original *Transatlantic Review.* Contributor to periodicals, including *Harper's, Sewanee Review,* and *Kenyon Review.* Represented in numerous anthologies.

SIDELIGHTS: Although she has never attained great public prominence, Miss Gordon has received critical praise for her novels. Focusing primarily on historical and modern changes facing the South, her books deal with the effect of these transitions on the people of that area of America. As a representative writer of her native region, Miss Gordon has received almost unqualified acclaim. A *Nation* reviewer described *Aleck Maury* as "one of the most distinguished and beautiful novels to come out of the South . . . and, as a document supporting the Southern Idea . . . it is worth tons of polemic literature, agrarian, libertarian, unreconstructivist, or what not."

One aspect of Miss Gordon's writings which has been particulary appreciated by critics is her method of creating a pervasive mood with an impressionistic style suggesting, rather than directly stating, her themes. Evelyn Scott writes: "The story of *Penhally* is told in impressionistic flashes, episodically. An immediacy of sense-perception pervades the style, giving an illusion of equal contemporaneity to nineteenth and twentieth-century happenings. . . . [Her] method demands close-ups and dwarfs perspective, which becomes difficult for the reader as for a person in the midst of events."

The objectivity with which Miss Gordon portrays her characters and themes has led critics like Andrew Lytle to ascribe a certain "coldness" to her writing. "Her tension at times seems too severe, as if her image as mask penetrates the passion and, instead of objectifying, freezes it. It causes her characters at times to appear immobile or cold. . . ." E. H. Walton believes that "Miss Gordon fails to interest one crucially in any of her characters. She portrays them perfunctorily and without real warmth. . . ."

It is, however, critics like D. B. Collins who best exemplify the literary attitude toward Miss Gordon's writing. "[Her work] is shapely, it has vitality, it illuminates a major aspect of American life, it is written in a style so perfectly suited to its matter that it goes straight to that heaven of all lovers of style: although . . . one feels a constant quiet reassurance running so deep that it rarely emerges into conscious appreciation; it is overlooked, and only seen in retrospect for the remarkable literary feat that it really is."

BIOGRAPHICAL/CRITICAL SOURCES: New York Times, Spetember 20, 1931, December 2, 1934, February 21, 1937, November 2, 1941, May 21, 1944, October 7, 1945, July 30, 1950, March 4, 1956, October 27, 1957; *Books*, September 27, 1931, November 4, 1934, February 21, 1937, November 2, 1941; *Nation*, October 7, 1931, January 9, 1935, March 20, 1937; *New Republic*, November 4, 1931, January 2, 1935, March 31, 1937, January 5, 1942, April 20, 1956; *Saturday Review*, November 21, 1931, February 20, 1937, May 27, 1944, October 27, 1945, June 17, 1950, November 16, 1957; *Christian Science Monitor*, March 8, 1937; *Times Literary Supplement*, August 7, 1937; *Southern Review*, summer, 1937, *Wilson Library Bulletin*, September, 1937; *New Yorker*, November 1, 1941, June 3, 1944, September 22, 1945, March 17, 1956; *Book Week*, May 21, 1944, October 20, 1963; *Commonweal*, October 26, 1945; *Library Journal*, September 15, 1957; Louis D. Rubin and Robert D. Jacobs, editors, *South: Modern Southern Literature in Its Cultural Setting*, Doubleday, 1961; William Van O'Connor, *The Grotesque: An American Genre and Other Essays*, Southern Illinois University Press, 1962; *New York Times Book Review*, October 20, 1963, *National Review*, December 31, 1963; William Edward Walker and Robert L. Welker, editors, *Reality and Myth: Essays in American Literature*, Vanderbilt University Press, 1964; Frederick P. W. McDowell, *Caroline Gordon*, University of Minnesota Press, 1966.

*　　*　　*

GORDON, Gerald 1909-

PERSONAL: Born January 19, 1909, in Kimberley, South Africa; son of Solomon and Frances (Fine) Gordon; married Nancy Muriel Baines (a literary critic), 1960; children: Stephen Michael, Vanessa Helen. *Education:* University of Cape Town, B.A. (with distinction) and LL.B., 1930. *Politics:* Progressive. *Religion:* Jewish. *Home:* Still Point, 88 The Ridge, Clifton, Cape Town, South Africa.

CAREER: Practiced as advocate at Cape bar, Cape Town, South Africa, 1931-73; queen's counsel, 1949-73. Director, Purnell & Sons (publishers), South Africa; chairman, *Contrast* (South African literary journal). *Military service:* South African Infantry, served in East Africa and Egypt, 1940-45; became captain. *Member:* P.E.N. (Cape; vice-chairman).

WRITINGS: South Africa Law of Insurance, Juta, 1936, 2nd Edition 1969; *Let the Day Perish* (novel), Methuen, 1952, published as *Dark Brother*, Pyramid Books, 1954; *The Crooked Rain* (novel), Macdonald, 1954; (with A. Suzman) *Law of Compulsory Motor Vehicle Insurance*, Juta, 1954, 2nd edition 1970; *Four People* (novel), Macdonald, 1964.

Translator from Afrikaans to English, with W. Gordon: Venter, *Dark Pilgrim*, Collins, 1959. Regular contributor of articles on political and sociological topics to South African press.

SIDELIGHTS: Gordon's first novel, *Let the Day Perish*, was translated into seven languages, including Hebrew, Rumanian, and Russian. Gordon made a nine-thousand-mile safari south of the Sahara, in 1954-55, has traveled widely, particularly in Africa.

*　　*　　*

GOULD, Felix

PERSONAL: Born in New York, N.Y. *Education:* New York University, B.S., 1925; Columbia University, graduate courses; studied sculpture in United States and Italy. *Home:* 243 Derrom Ave., Paterson, N.J., 07504.

CAREER: Sometime lecturer on art and travel. *Military service:* U.S. Navy.

WRITINGS: The Marsh Maiden, and Other Plays (one-acts), Four Seas Co., 1918; *Silence, Please!* (one-act comedy), Baker's Plays, 1928; *Sister Cat* (novel), Lyle Stuart, 1963. Contributor of short stories and verse to magazines.

WORK IN PROGRESS: A novel, *The Devil Sends a Gift;* revision of three completed novels, *Late Spring, Master of the Wolves,* and *Blue Cavalier.*

AVOCATIONAL INTERESTS: Travel, playing harp and piano; studying art, archaeology, and church history; collecting Chinese art, fine books, and baroque paintings.

*　　*　　*

GOULLART, Peter 1902-

PERSONAL: Born June 17, 1902, in Moscow, Russia; son of Nicholas (a museum curator) and Maria (Rastorgueva) Goullart. *Education:* Educated privately at home by tutors. *Address:* c/o John Murray (Publishers) Ltd., 50 Albemarle St., London W.1, England.

CAREER: Fled with mother from Russian Revolution into China, 1919; learned Chinese, lived and studied among Chinese people and in Taoist monasteries; cooperative expert for Chinese Industrial Co-operatives in China and Eastern Tibet, 1939-49 (until Chinese Communist takeover); co-operative expert for International Labour Office, Geneva, Switzerland, 1952-61; has continued to travel, work, and live at intervals in Southeast Asia from 1949 until present time. *Member:* Society of Authors (London).

WRITINGS: Forgotten Kingdom, J. Murray, 1955; *Land of the Lamas*, Dutton, 1959 (published in England as *Princes of the Black Bone*, J. Murray, 1959; *The Monastery of Jade Mountain*, J. Murray, 1961; *River of the White Lily*, J. Murray, 1965. Contributor to *Cornhill Magazine* (London).

WORK IN PROGRESS: Research, principally into Taoism, but also into Zen and other forms of Buddhism; answering inquiries from pupils.

SIDELIGHTS: Goullart knows English, French, Russian, Chinese, and Italian.

BIOGRAPHICAL/CRITICAL SOURCES: Peter Goullart, *The Monastery of Jade Mountain*, J. Murray, 1961; *Times*, London, England, November 30, 1961.

*　　*　　*

GOURLIE, Norah Dundas

PERSONAL: Born in Helensburgh, Dumbartonshire, Scotland; daughter of William and Elizabeth (Dalglish) Gourlie. *Education:* Studied at London School of Art. *Politics:* Conservative. *Home:* Chichester Backs, Hurstpierpoint, Sussex, England. *Agent:* E.P.S. Lewin & Partners, 7 Chelsea Embankment, Chelsea, London S.W.3, England.

MEMBER: P.E.N. (London).

WRITINGS: A Winter with Finnish Lapps, Blackie & Son, 1939; *The Prince of Botanists, Carl Linnaeus*, Witherby, 1953; *Where Is It Still Pleasant to Live in the U.S.A.?*, Garden Way Publishers, 1972. Contributor to journals.

WORK IN PROGRESS: Life and voyages of Archibald Menzies, Scottish botanist, for Witherby.

SIDELIGHTS: Miss Gourlie speaks French, Italian, Swedish, Norwegian, and Danish. *Avocational interests:* Skiing, climbing, and travel.

* * *

GOVE, Philip Babcock 1902-1972

PERSONAL: Born June 27, 1902, in Concord, N.H.; son of John McClure (a physician) and Florence (Babcock) Gove; married Grace Potter, August 17, 1929; children: Norwood B., Susan (Mrs. Rosser A. Rudolph, Jr.), Doris. *Education:* Dartmouth College, A.B., 1922; Harvard University, A.M., 1925; Columbia University, Ph.D., 1941. *Politics:* Independent. *Religion:* Protestant. *Home:* Old Patrick Rd., Warren, Mass. 01083. *Office:* G. & C. Merriam Co., 47 Federal St., Springfield, Mass. 01101.

CAREER: Instructor in English at Rice Institute (now University), Houston, Tex., 1924-27, at New York University, New York, N.Y., 1927-42; G. & C. Merriam Co., Springfield, Mass., assistant editor of Merriam-Webster dictionaries, 1946-51, managing editor, 1951-52, general editor, 1952-60, editor-in-chief, 1961-67, consultant, 1967-72. William Bayard Cutting traveling fellow, Columbia University, 1939-40. Member of advisory board, Center for Documentation and Communication Research of Case Western Reserve University; member of board of directors, Warren Library; member of board of editors, *Encyclopaedia Britannica*. *Military service:* U.S. Naval Reserve, 1942-46; became lieutenant commander. *Member:* National Council of Teachers of English, Linguistic Society of America, American Standards Association, Modern Language Association of America, International Society of General Semantics, College English Association, Johnson Society of London, North Carolina English Teachers Association (honorary member), English Graduate Union (Columbia University), Phi Gamma Delta. *Awards, honors:* Litt.D., Dartmouth College, 1963.

WRITINGS: The Imaginary Voyage in Prose Fiction, Columbia University Press, 1941; (editor) *The Role of the Dictionary*, Bobbs-Merrill, 1967.

Editor-in-chief—All published by Merriam: *Webster's Elementary Dictionary*, 1956; *Webster's New Secondary School Dictionary*, 1959; *Webster's Third New International Dictionary*, 1961; *Webster's Seventh New Collegiate Dictionary*, 1963.

Contributor to *American Speech, Word Study, Library* (London), *Review of English Studies, Maryland Historical Magazine, College English*, and *Reading Teacher*.

SIDELIGHTS: Dr. Gove, an internationally known lexicographer, was perhaps best known as the editor of the controversial *Webster's Third New International Dictionary*. The work reflected his philosophy that the "spoken language is the language" and that "correctness rests upon usage." Some critics attacked his policy of accepting many words and word usages previously considered by scholars to be substandard. Summing up his views in an address at Phillips Academy in Andover, Mass., Dr. Gove said, "The most fundamental thing about language is not

whether it is good or bad, but how it behaves, how it is used." In reporting his death, the *New York Times* observed, "Dr. Gove, a studious New Englander, championed the cause of greater freedom in both spoken and written English based on a continuously growing language. Many of his innovations, developed for Webster's Third, have been adopted by dictionary-makers today."

AVOCATIONAL INTERESTS: Farming.

BIOGRAPHICAL/CRITICAL SOURCES: Dartmouth Alumni Magazine, May, 1959; *New York Times*, March 1, 1962.

(Died November 16, 1972)

* * *

GOWEN, (Samuel) Emmett 1902-

PERSONAL: Born September 10, 1902, in Nashville, Tenn.; son of George Washington and Nona Elizabeth (Duffel) Gowen; married Claire Loeb, May 31, 1941. *Home and office address:* R.F.D., Lavergne, Tenn. 37086.

CAREER: U.S. Marine Corps, 1919-23; reporter for newspapers in Memphis, Tenn., 1923-25, for *Bronx Home News*, Bronx, N.Y., 1926; Better Business Bureau, New York, N.Y., publicity director, 1927-29; free-lance writer, 1929—; operator of outfitting, and hunting, fishing, and exploring services in Mexico and Central America, 1959—, as president of Emmett Gowen Ltd., Belize, British Honduras, 1963—. Club de Exploraciones y Deportes Acquaticoes de Mexico, explorer, consultant, and publicity work, 1959—; founder and executive secretary, Club Caribbean West (exploring; Belize, British Honduras), 1961—. Participant in archaeological diving expedition of Quintana Roo coast of Mexico, 1959; leader of expedition in Quintana Roo jungle, 1916. *Member:* Authors League of America, Cannon Hunters Association of Seattle.

WRITINGS: A True Expose of Racketeers and Their Methods, Popular Book Co., 1930; *Mountain Born*, Bobbs-Merrill, 1932; *Dark Moon of March*, Bobbs-Merrill, 1933; *Old Hell*, Modern Age Books, 1937; *The Joys of Fishing*, Rand McNally, 1961. Contributor of short stories and articles to *Scribner's, Story, Yale Review, Atlantic, Pictorial Review, Field and Stream, True, Argosy, Sports Afield, Sports Illustrated, Outdoor Life, Ford Times*, and other magazines.

WORK IN PROGRESS: The Adventure Coast, reminiscences of six years of operating an outfitting service and organizing expeditions in Central America.

BIOGRAPHICAL/CRITICAL SOURCES: True, February, 1962.

* * *

GRACE, William Joseph 1910-

PERSONAL: Born July 3, 1910, in New York, N.Y.; son of William Joseph (a foreign service officer) and Catherine (Hickey) Grace; married Eva Susanna Buchholz (a teacher), August 16, 1952; children: Elizabeth Carroll, William Joseph, Michael John, Marianna Joan, Catherine Anne, George Edward. *Education:* Balliol College, Oxford, B.A., 1933, M.A., 1937. *Home:* 254 Prospect Ave., Staten Island, New York, N.Y. *Office:* School of Education, Fordham University, 302 Broadway, New York, N.Y.

CAREER: Fordham University, New York, N.Y., 1937—, became associate professor of English. Participated in a seminar of Russian studies, State University of New York, summer, 1962. *Military service:* U.S. Navy, 1943-46. *Member:* Modern Language Association of America, American Society of Composers, Authors, and Publishers, Oxford Union. *Awards, honors:* Fordham faculty fellowship, 1961; Bene Merenti medal.

WRITINGS: Triple City (poems), A. D. Publishing Co., 1951; *How to Be Creative With Words,* Fordham University Press, 1952; (with Joan Grace) *The Art of Communicating Ideas,* Devin-Adair, 1952; *Approaching Shakespeare,* Basic Books, 1964; *Response to Literature,* McGraw, 1965; (editor, with others) *The Complete Prose Works of John Milton,* Volume IV, Yale University Press, 1965; *Ideas in Milton,* University of Notre Dame Press, 1968. Author of cantatas, "Requiem to War," 1963, and "Triple City," 1964, composed by Paul Reif, performed at Carnegie Hall and Philharmonic Hall, New York, N.Y.

WORK IN PROGRESS: And the Pursuit of Happiness.

SIDELIGHTS: Grace's competency in languages includes Italian, French, German. *Avocational interests:* Art, music, photography, gardening.

* * *

GRAEBNER, Walter 1909-

PERSONAL: Born December 16, 1909, in Columbus, Ohio; son of John Reynolds (a Lutheran clergyman) and Hedwig (Sievers) Graebner; married Constance Lailey, October 8, 1948; children: Gretchen (Mrs. Justin Morgan), John. *Education:* University of Wisconsin, student, 1928-31. *Politics:* Democrat. *Home:* 34 Albion St., London W.2, England. *Agent:* Curtis Brown Ltd., 1 Craven Hill, London, W.2, England.

CAREER: Time, New York, N.Y., reporter in Chicago, Ill., 1931-35, chief of Chicago bureau, 1935-37, chief of London bureau, 1937-46, war correspondent, 1939-45; Time-Life Ltd., London, England, European area director, 1946-53; Erwin Wasey Ltd., London, England, chairman, 1953-63; Interpublic Ltd. (advertising and public relations), London, England, director, 1964-66.

WRITINGS: (Editor with Allan Michie) *Their Finest Hour,* Harcourt, 1941; (editor with Michie) *Lights of Freedom,* Allen & Unwin, 1941; (with Stephen Laird) *Conversation in London,* Morrow, 1942 (published in England as *Hitler's Reich and Churchill's Britain,* Batsford, 1942); *Roundtrip to Russia,* Lippincott, 1942; *My Dear Mister Churchill,* Houghton, 1965.

AVOCATIONAL INTERESTS: Gardening, skiing, poodles, antiques.

* * *

GRAHAM, Grace 1910-

PERSONAL: Born October 23, 1910, in Bamberg, S.C.; daughter of Harry Malcolm and Jennie Lawton (Kirkland) Graham. *Education:* University of South Carolina, A.B., 1933, M.A., 1936; Stanford University, Ed.D., 1952. *Politics:* Democrat. *Home:* 315 East 36th Ave., Eugene, Ore. *Office:* School of Education, University of Oregon, Eugene, Ore.

CAREER: History teacher in South Carolina, 1934-42; University of South Carolina, Columbia, vocational counselor in Personnel Bureau, 1946; Punahou School, Honolulu, Hawaii, director of guidance, 1946-49; U.S. Armed Forces Education Center, Tokyo, Japan, instructor in his-

tory, 1949-50; Chico State College (now California State University, Chico), Chico, Calif., assistant professor of education, 1953-54; University of Oregon, Eugene, began 1954, became professor of education. Visiting assistant professor at Stanford University, 1952-53, summer 1954, 1955. *Military service:* U.S. Navy Women's Reserve, 1942-64, active duty, 1942-46; became lieutenant commander. *Member:* American Association of University Professors, Association for Supervision and Curriculum Development, Pi Lambda Theta.

WRITINGS: The Public School in the American Community, Harper, 1963, published as *The Public School in the New Society: The Social Foundations of Education,* 1969. Contributor of about thirty articles to periodicals.

WORK IN PROGRESS: Helping Children Learn to Think, in collaboration with Lloyd Lovell; pamphlets on education for Oregon Education Association and National Association of Student Councils.

* * *

GRAHAM, Rachel (Metcalf) 1895-

PERSONAL: Born November 26, 1895, in Wurzburg, Germany; daughter of Wilmot Vernon and Caroline (Soule) Metcalf; married Walter N. Hess (a professor of biology), 1924; children: Wilmot N. Hess, Carroll N. Hess. *Education:* Oberlin College, B.A., 1918; Columbia University, M.A., 1924. *Home:* 309 Aiken Ave., Rock Hill, S.C.

CAREER: Poet. Teacher of biology at Oberlin College, Oberlin, Ohio, 1918, Mount Holyoke College, South Hadley, Mass., 1923-24, De Pauw University, Greencastle, Ind., 1925-26. Chairman of town and county War Council offices, 1941-46. *Member:* American Poetry League, Poetry Society of America, Maine Poetry Fellowship.

WRITINGS: Headlands, Golden Quill, 1960. Poetry included in anthologies and published in magazines and newspapers, including *Saturday Evening Post* and *Christian Science Monitor.*

SIDELIGHTS: Ms. Graham began to write poetry while recuperating from a heart attack in 1950. Since then she has won several dozen prizes for magazine poetry.

* * *

GRANGE, Cyril 1900-
(Onlooker, Quill)

PERSONAL: Born April 17, 1900, in March, Cambridgeshire, England; son of George (a farmer) and Margaret (Jackson) Grange; married Phyllis Swan, June, 1926 (deceased). *Education:* Attended grammar schools in March, England. *Religion:* Church of England. *Home and office:* West Hill House, Bury St. Edmunds, Suffolk, England.

CAREER: Eastern Counties Poultry Society, England, secretary, 1930-46; National Poultry Club, England, secretary, 1935-46; Suffolk Agriculture and Poultry Producers Association, Suffolk, England, managing director, 1939-51. Mayor of Bury St. Edmunds, Suffolk, England, 1961-62. Agricultural photographer with 41,000 published photographs. *Wartime service:* Served with "Diehards" in World War I: served as head warden in World War II. *Member:* Institute of Travel Agents, Farmers' Club (London).

WRITINGS: Poultry Doctoring, Pearson, 1930; *The Book of the Villiers Engine,* Pitman, c. 1930-32, 12th edition, 1964; *Home Bottling and Canning,* Cassell, 1934; *Poultry Keeping Today,* Pearson, 1938; *Poultry Keeping,* Jordan &

Sons, 1943; *Home Made Jams and Jellies*, Free Press, 1946; *Poultry Feeding*, Bates, 1946; *Home Food Preservation*, Cassell, 1951; *Poultry Farming for a Living*, Macmillan, 1958. Illustrator of six books. Writer and illustrator of poultry section of *Smallholder* (weekly newspaper), 1926-46; editor of *Eastern Counties Poultry Journal* and *National Poultry Club Year Book*, 1930-47.

* * *

GRANVILLE, W. Wilfred 1905-

PERSONAL: Born March 11, 1905, in York, England; son of Thomas Henry (a soldier) and Helen (McTurk) Granville; married Audrey Quinton-Fulford (marriage dissolved). *Education:* Attended Royal Naval College, Greenwich, England. *Religion:* Church of England. *Home:* Shakspere Cottage, 8 Eastern Rd., East Finchley, London N.2, England. *Address:* c/o George G. Harrap & Co. Ltd., 182 High Holborn, London W.C.1, England.

CAREER: Royal Navy, 1918-23; took up theatre work—acting, management, and direction—in London, England, and provinces, 1923-38; Royal Navy, 1938-44, with staff appointments including British Admiralty, 1940-42, naval liaison, Royal Air Force; left Navy to write full time, 1944—. *Member:* Royal Naval Sailing Association, Royal Naval Club, Royal Navy Volunteer Reserve Club (honorary), Whitefriars Club.

WRITINGS: (Editor with Eric Partridge and Frank Roberts) *A Dictionary of Forces' Slang, 1939-1945*, Secker & Warburg, 1948; *Sea Slang of the Twentieth Century: Royal Navy, Merchant Navy, Yachtsmen, Fishermen, Bargemen, Canalmen, Miscellaneous*, introduction by Eric Partridge, Winchester Publications, 1949, Philosophical Library, 1950; *The Theatre Dictionary: British and American Terms in the Drama, Opera, and Ballet*, Philosophical Library, 1952 (published in England as *A Dictionary of Theatrical Terms*, Deutsch, 1952); (contributor) *The Book of the Sea*, Winchester Publications, 1952; (with J. Lennox Kerr) *R.N.V.R.: A Record of Achievement*, Harrap, 1957; (with Robin A. Kelly) *Inshore Heroes: The Story of H.M. Motor Launches in Two World Wars*, W. H. Allen, 1961; *A Dictionary of Sailors' Slang*, Oxford University Press, 1962. Anthologized in *Wavy Navy by Some Who Served*, edited by Lennox Kerr and James David, Harrap, 1950. Contributor to *Oxford English Dictionary Supplement*.

WORK IN PROGRESS: A dictionary of outdoor sports and games; *Sea Idioms in the English Language*.

AVOCATIONAL INTERESTS: English etymology, music, sailing, beachcombing, and customs and traditions of fishermen.†

* * *

GRAVES, W(illiam) Brooke 1899-

PERSONAL: Born May 4, 1899, in Charlottesville, Va.; son of William Clayton and Lina Elizabeth (Barber) Graves; married Hazel Wallace, August 31, 1922; children: Wallace Barbour. *Education:* Cornell University, A.B., 1921; University of Pennsylvania, M.A., 1923, Ph.D., 1936. *Home:* 2940 Newark St. N.W., Washington, D.C. 20008. *Office:* Legislative Reference Service, Library of Congress, Washington, D.C. 20025.

CAREER: University of Pennslyvania, Philadelphia, instructor in political science, 1921-25; Temple University, Philadelphia, Pa., 1925-42, became professor of political science; U.S. Civil Service Commission, Philadelphia, Pa.,

various administrative positions, 1942-45; Legislative Reference Service, Library of Congress, Washington, D.C., chief of state law section, 1946-48, chief of government division, 1950-57; American University, Washington, D.C., adjunct professor of political science, 1947—. Visiting professor at Swarthmore College, 1936-37, Bryn Mawr College, 1945-46, Haverford College, 1945, Wayne University, 1946-50, Florida State University, 1951-52, University of Mississippi, 1954, University of Minnesota, 1955, and University of Alaska, 1959-60.

MEMBER: Civil Service Assembly of the United States and Canada, American Political Science Association (life; chairman of program committee, 1940), American Historical Association, American Academy of Political and Social Science, National Civil Service League (director, 1946—), National Municipal League (chairman of committee on state government, 1938—), American Society for Public Administration, Society for Personnel Administration, National Legislative Conference (founding member; member of executive committee, 1950-51), Federal Professional Association (founding member; member of executive council, 1962—), American Association of University Professors, Pi Gamma Mu, Pi Sigma Alpha, Masons.

WRITINGS: (Editor) *Readings in Public Opinion: Its Formation and Control*, Appleton, 1928.

Uniform State Action: A Possible Substitute for Centralization, University of North Carolina Press, 1934; (with others) *A Survey of the Government of Pennsylvania*, Pennsylvania Joint Legislative Committee of Finances, 1934; *American State Government*, Heath, 1936, 4th edition, 1953; *Reference List on Interstate Compacts and Interstate Cooperation*, Department of Political Science, Temple University, 1938; (editor) *Our State Legislators*, American Academy of Political and Social Science, 1938.

(Editor) *Intergovernmental Relations in the United States*, American Academy of Political and Social Science, 1940; (editor and contributor) *Model State Constitution, with Explanatory Articles*, Committee on State Government, National Municipal League, 1941, 5th edition, 1948; *Efficiency Rating System*, Legislative Reference Service, Library of Congress, 1947; (compiler) *The Governors of the States, 1900-1950*, Council of State Governments, 1948; *Anti-Discrimination Legislation in the American States*, Legislative Reference Service, Library of Congress, 1948; (compiler with Norman J. Small and E. Foster Dowell) *American State Government and Administration: A State-by-State Bibliography of Significant General and Special Works*, Council of State Governments, 1949; *Facts and Figures about the Federal Government, Its Departments and Agencies and Their Activities*, Legislative Reference Service, Library of Congress, 1949; (compiler) *Reorganization of the Executive Branch of the Government of the United States: A Compilation of Basic Information and Significant Documents, 1912-1948*, Legislative Reference Service, Library of Congress, 1949.

Public Administration in a Democratic Society, Heath, 1950; *Administration of the Lobby Registration Provision of the Legislative Reorganization Act of 1946: An Analysis of Experience During the Eightieth Congress*, U.S. Government Printing Office, 1950; (compiler) *Public Administration: A Comprehensive Bibliography*, Legislative Reference Service, Library of Congress, 1951; *Fair Employment Practice Legislation in the United States: Federal—State—Municipal*, Legislative Reference Service, Library of Congress, 1951; *Intergovernmental Relations in the United States: A Selected Bibliography*, Legislative Reference Service, Library of Congress, 1953, expanded edition published as *Intergovernmental Relations in the United States: A Selected Bibliography on Interlevel and Interjurisdictional Relations*, U.S. Commission on Intergovernmental Relations, 1955; *Some Current Problems in State and Local Government*, Bureau of Public Administration, University of Mississippi, 1955; *Summaries of Survey Reports on the Administrative and Fiscal Impact of Federal Grants-in-Aid*, U.S. Government Printing Office, 1955; *The Coming Challenge in Federal-State Relations*, State Chamber of Commerce Service Department, 1957; *The Legislative Auditor: His Powers and Duties*, Council of State Governments, 1957; *Public Service Training for Local Government Personnel in 1956: A Survey of Current Programs and Practices*, [Washington, D.C.], 1957; (with H. A. Stieber) *The American State Governments: Their Political Complexion During the Twentieth Century*, Legislative Reference Service, Library of Congress, 1958; *Establishing Local Government in Alaska*, Alaska Legislative Council, 1959.

(Editor) *Major Problems in State Constitutional Revision*, Public Administration Service (Chicago), 1960; *Centralization of Government in Hawaii*, Legislative Reference Service, Library of Congress, 1962; *Interlocal Cooperation: The History and Background of Intergovernmental Agreements*, National Association of Counties Research Foundation, c.1962; *American Intergovernmental Relations: Their Origins, Historical Development, and Current Status*, Scribner, 1964.

General editor of "American Commonwealth" series, twelve volumes on government and administration in the states and territories, Crowell, 1953-55. Author or editor of *Public Affairs Bulletins* and Government reports. Contributor to *Dictionary of American History*, Scribner, 1940. Contributor of more than fifty articles to symposia and to political science, government, law, and personnel journals, and of some fifty book reviews to journals. Member of board of editors, *State Government*, 1939-50, of American Political Science Science Association, 1940-42.

*   *   *

GRAY, Basil 1904-

PERSONAL: Born July 21, 1904, in London, England; son of Charles (a surgeon-major, British Army) and Florence (Cowell) Gray; married Nicolete Binyon (an author), 1932; children: Marius, Camilla, Edmund, Cecilia Sophia. *Education:* Oxford University, B.A., M.A. *Religion:* Church of England. *Home:* Dawber's House, Long Wittenham, Abingdon, Berkshire, England.

CAREER: Participated in British Academy excavations in Constantinople, 1928; British Museum, London, England, 1928-69, in charge of oriental antiquities, 1938-69, deputy keeper, 1940-46, keeper, 1946-69. Arts Council, member of art panel, 1952-57, 1959-68. *Member:* British Academy (fellow), Savile Club. *Awards, honors:* Companion, Order of the British Empire, 1957; Companion, Order of the Bath, 1969.

WRITINGS: (With Stanley Casson and others) *Second Report Upon the Excavations Carried Out In and Near the Hippodrome of Constantinople*, British Academy, 1929; *Persian Painting*, Benn, 1930; (with J.V.S. Wilkinson and Laurence Binyon) *Persian Miniature Painting*, Oxford University Press, 1933; (with Leigh Ashton) *Chinese Art*, Faber, 1935, Hale, Cushman & Flint, 1937, revised edition, Faber, 1952, Beechhurst Press, 1953; (editor with others) *The Chinese Exhibition* (catalogue of International Exhibition of Chinese Art, Royal Academy of Arts, November, 1935-March, 1936), Faber, 1936; *The English Print*, A. & C. Black, 1937.

(Author of introduction) *Persian Painting from the Miniatures of the XIII-XVI Centuries*, Batsford, 1940, 2nd edition, 1947; *Indian Painting*, British Museum, 1947; (editor) *The Faber Gallery of Oriental Art*, Faber, 1948; *The Work of Hokusai* (catalogue of exhibition held on centenary of his death), British Museum, 1948; (author of introduction and notes) *Rajput Painting*, Faber, 1948, Pitman, 1949; (contributor) Leigh Ashton, editor, *The Art of India and Pakistan* (catalogue of exhibition held at Royal Academy of Arts, 1947-48), Faber, 1950; (author of introduction and notes) *Treasures of Indian Miniatures in the Bikaner Palace Collection*, Cassirer, 1951, 2nd edition, 1955; *Early Chinese Pottery and Porcelain*, Pitman, 1952; *Japanese Screen Painting*, Faber, 1955; *Arts of T'ang Dynasty*, Oriental Ceramic Society, 1955; (author of preface) Andre Godard, *Iran: Persian Miniatures—Imperial Library*, New York Graphic Society, 1956; *Japanese Woodcuts*, Citadel, 1957; (with others) *The Arts of the Ming Dynasty*, Oriental Ceramic Society, 1958; *Buddhist Cave Paintings at Tun-Huang*, University of Chicago Press, 1959.

(Editor) Laurence Binyon and J.J. O'Brien Sexton, *Japanese Colour Prints*, 2nd edition (Gray was not associated with earlier edition), Boston Book & Art Shop, 1960; (editor) *The Arts of the East*, Faber, 1961; (with others) *The Arts of the Sung Dynasty* (catalogue of exhibition, Arts Council Gallery, London, June 16-July 23, 1960), International Publishers, 1961; *Persian Painting*, Skira, 1961; (author of introduction) *Persian Miniatures from Ancient Manuscripts*, New American Library of World Literature, 1962; (with Douglas E. Barrett) *Painting of India*, Skira, 1963; *Admonitions of the Instructress of the Ladies in the Palace, a Painting Attributed to Ku K'aichih*, Trustees of the British Museum, 1966; *A Chinese Painter's Choice: Some Paintings from the 14th to the 20th Century from the Collection of Ling Su-hua* (catalogue of exhibition, Arts Council Gallery, February 24-March 25, 1967), Arts Council of Great Britain, 1967. Contributor to *Proceedings of Iran Society*.

*   *   *

GRAYLAND, Eugene C(harles)

PERSONAL: Born in Wellington, New Zealand; son of Charles Henry and Anne (Mawhinney) Grayland; married Valerie Merle Spanner (an author), November 13, 1948. *Education:* Attended New Zealand schools. *Religion:* Anglican. *Home:* 55 Athens Rd., One Tree Hill, Auckland, New Zealand. *Office:* New Zealand Newspapers Ltd., Shortland St., Auckland, New Zealand.

CAREER: Reporter or sub-editor for newspapers in Hastings, Auckland, New Plymouth, and Palmerston North, New Zealand, 1947-53; chief-of-staff of magazine group, *Newsview, Better Business, Women's Choice*, Auckland, New Zealand, 1953-54; *Auckland Star*, Auckland, New Zealand, education and science reporter, 1954-64, medical and science reporter, 1965—. *Military service:* New Zealand Army, four years; served mostly with War History and Archives Branch. *Member:* New Zealand Journalists' Association, Auckland Institute and Museum, Royal Society of New Zealand, New Zealand Association of Scientists (associate), Medical Journalists' Association (Great Britain).

WRITINGS: *Private Presses: Their Contributions to Literature and Typography*, Colenso Press, 1947; *The Newspaper Morgue*, Colenso Press, 1947; *The Value of Newspaper Sources for Historical and Other Research*, Colenso Press, 1947; *Special Uses of Press Clippings Material*, Colenso Press, 1949; *Research As an Aid to Writing*, Colenso Press, 1949; *The Newspaper Reference Library and the Filing and Uses of Clippings*, Colenso Press, 1950; *There was Danger on the Line: Stories of Disastrous Train Smashes*, Belvedere Books, 1954; *New Zealand Disasters*, A.H. & A.W. Reed, 1957, 3rd edition, 1963; (with J.C.M. Cresswell) *Auckland, Queen City of New Zealand*, A.H. & A.W. Reed, 1961; *Coasts of Treachery*, A.H. & A.W. Reed, 1963; (with wife, Valerie Grayland) *Coromandel Coast*, A.H. & A.W. Reed, 1965, revised edition, 1968; *Famous New Zealanders*, Whitcombe & Tombs, 1968; *Unusual Newspapers of New Zealand and Australia*, Colenso Press, 1969; (with Valerie Grayland) *Historic Coromandel*, A.H. & A.W. Reed, 1969; (with Valerie Grayland) *Tarawera*, Hodder & Stoughton, 1971; *More Famous New Zealanders*, Whitcombe & Tombs, 1971. Joint editor, *Hearing News*, 1969—.

WORK IN PROGRESS: Several feature and travel books on New Zealand subjects.

*   *   *

GREEN, A(dwin) Wigfall 1900-1971(?)

PERSONAL: Born September 21, 1900, in Washington, D.C.; son of Adwin Wigfall and Lillie (Gray) Green; married Mary Moore Dooley, May 22, 1949. *Education:* Georgetown University, LL.B., 1921; College of William and Mary, A.B., 1925; University of Virginia, M.A., 1927, Ph.D., 1930. *Politics:* Democrat. *Religion:* Episcopal. *Office address:* Box 22, University of Mississippi, Oxford, Miss. 38655.

CAREER: Admitted to bar of the District of Columbia, 1921, Bar of the U.S. Supreme Court, Bar of the U.S. Court of Appeals, and Bar of the Supreme court of Mississippi; practiced law in Washington, D.C., 1921-24; Gettysburg College, Gettysburg, Pa., assistant professor of English, 1926-27; University of Mississippi, Oxford, professor of English, 1930-c.1971, dean of Graduate School, 1941-46. Fulbright Professor at University of the Philippines, 1949-50; visiting professor at University of Virginia, 1938, University of Puerto Rico, 1947, and U.S. Army Command and General Staff College, 1948, 1950. *Military service:* U.S. Navy, 1917-18; became chief petty officer. U.S. Army, Judge Advocate General's Department, World War II; graduate of Judge Advocate General's School and Command and General Staff College; became colonel; received Bronze Star. *Member:* Modern Language Association of America, Raven Society, Phi Beta Kappa.

WRITINGS: *The Inns of Court and Early English Drama*, preface by Roscoe Pound, Yale University Press, 1931; (with Dudley R. Hutcherson and Pete Kyle McCarter) *Complete College Composition*, F. S. Crofts, 1940, 2nd edition, 1945; (translator and author of commentary) *The Will of Aelfred, King of West Saxons*, Dublin University Press, 1944; *Sir Francis Bacon: His Life and Works*, Syracuse University Press, 1948; *The Epic of Korea*, Public Affairs Press, 1950; (contributor) F. J. Hoffman and O. W. Vickery, editors, *William Faulkner: Two Decades of Criticism*, Michigan State College Press, 1951; (contributor) Fredson Bowers, editor, *English Studies in Honor of James Southall Wilson*, Alderman Library, University of

Virginia, 1951; (editor with J. W. Hebel, Hogt H. Hudson, and Francis R. Johnson) *Prose of the English Renaissance*, Appleton, 1952; (editor with Hebel and others) *Tudor Poetry and Prose*, Appleton, 1953; *The Man Bilbo*, Louisiana State University Press, 1963; (editor with James W. Webb) *William Faulkner of Oxford*, Louisiana State University Press, 1965; *Sir Francis Bacon*, Twayne, 1966. Contributor of fifteen articles to *World Book Encyclopedia*, 1958, and of articles to educational, literary, and law journals.

WORK IN PROGRESS: *Life of Louis Trezevant Wigfall; Historical and Critical Analysis of Shakespeare's Sonnets;* translation of *The Book of the Knight of LaTour Landry.*

SIDELIGHTS: Green traveled extensively in Europe, South America, Canada, Mexico, and the Far and Near East and had a knowledge of Japanese, Spanish, Italian, Portuguese, French, and some ancient languages. *Avocational interests:* Architecture and language.

(Deceased)

*   *   *

GREEN, Bryan S(tuart) W(estmacott) 1901-

PERSONAL: Born January 14, 1901, in London, England; son of Hubert Westmacott and Kathleen (Brockwell) Green; married Winifred Annie Bevan, August 5, 1926; children: Gillian Mary (Mrs. Julian Bell), Mark. *Education:* University of London, B.D., 1923. *Politics:* Liberal. *Home:* West Field, Southern Rd., Thame, England. *Agent:* David Higham Associates Ltd., 76 Dean St., Soho, London W. 1, England.

CAREER: Ordained priest, Church of England, 1924; curate at New Malden, England, 1924-28; Children's Special Service Mission, staff member, 1928-31; Oxford University, Oxford, England, chaplain, 1931-34; vicar of churches in Crouch End, England, 1934-38, and Brompton, England, 1938-48; rector of parish church in Birmingham, England, 1948; honorary canon of Birmingham Cathedral, 1950—. Traveling lecturer and preacher two months each year, 1949—. Conducted evangelistic campaigns in the United States and Canada, 1936, 1944, 1947-63, and in Australia, Africa, and India. *Military service:* British Army Signals, chaplain, 1939-44. *Member:* National Club (London). *Awards, honors:* D.D. from St. John's College, Winnipeg, Manitoba, Canada.

WRITINGS: *The Practice of Evangelism*, Hodder & Stoughton, 1951; *Being and Believing*, Hodder & Stoughton, 1956; *Saints Alive!*, Epworth, 1959. Regular weekly contributor to *Woman* and *Birmingham Post*.

*   *   *

GREEN, Mary Moore 1906-

PERSONAL: Born March 17, 1906, in Romulus, Mich.; daughter of George W. (a farmer) and Letitia (Bush) Moore; married A. Wendell Green (a horticulturist), June 30, 1937; children: George Arthur, James Wendell, Robert Moore. *Education:* Eastern Michigan University, B.S., 1931. *Home:* 37800 Fourteen Mile Rd., Walled Lake, Mich.

CAREER: Pontiac (Mich.) public schools, elementary teacher, 1936-43, 1950-55, elementary teacher consultant, 1955—. *Member:* National Education Association, Association for Childhood Education, Michigan Education Association, Pontiac Education Association.

WRITINGS: *About Apples From Orchard to Market*,

Melmont, 1960; (with Irma Johnson) *Three Feathers*, Follett, 1960; *Is it Hard, Is it Easy*, Addison-Wesley, 1960; *Everybody Has a House and Everybody Eats*, Addison-Wesley, 1961; *Whose Little Red Jacket*, F. Watts, 1965; *When Will I Whistle*, F. Watts, 1967; *Everybody Grows Up*, F. Watts, 1969.

Contributor of articles to *Science Review* and *Education*.

BIOGRAPHICAL/CRITICAL SOURCES: Pontiac Press, May 28, 1960; *Detroit Free Press*, November 5, 1960.

* * *

GREENBLATT, Robert Benjamin 1906-

PERSONAL: Born October 12, 1906, in Montreal, Quebec, Canada; son of Louis and Anne Greenblatt; married Gwen Lande; children: Nathaniel, Edward, Deborah Ann. *Education:* McGill University, B.A., 1928, M.D. and C.M., 1932. *Religion:* Hebrew. *Home:* 3011 Bransford Rd., Augusta, Ga. 30904. *Office:* Medical College of Georgia, Augusta, Ga. 30902.

CAREER: Physician, specializing in endocrinology. Medical College of Georgia, Augusta, assistant professor of pathology, 1936-37, of pathology and gynecology, 1937-39, professor of experimental medicine, 1939-43, professor of endocrinology and head of department, 1945—. Special consultant to U.S. Public Health Service, 1941. U.S. Army and U.S. Veterans Administration, 1946. *Military service:* U.S. Coast Guard, 1943; served with Pacific Fleet; became commander. *Member:* American Medical Association; honorary member of obstetrical and gynecological societies, United States, Canada, South America, Mexico, and other countries; Rotary International. *Awards, honors:* Crawford W. Long Award, Medical Association of Georgia, for original research, 1941; Billings Silver Medal, American Medical Associaiton, 1965; Barren Foundation Gold Medal, 1970; Docteur, University of Bordeaux, 1970.

WRITINGS: Office Endocrinology, School of Medicine, University of Georgia, 1941, 4th edition, C. C Thomas, 1952; *The Management of the Minor Venereal Diseases*, U.S. Government Printing Office, 1942; (with others) *Management of Chancroid, Granuloma Inguinale, Lymphogranuloma Venereum in General Practice*, U.S. Public Health Service, 1953, revised edition, 1958; (contributor) Thaddeus Lemert Montgomery, editor, *Fetal Physiology and Distress*, Hoeber, 1960; *A Physician's Quest for Answers in the Bible*, Les Freres des Ecoles Chretiennes, 1962, reissued as *Search the Scriptures: A Physician Examines Medicine in the Bible*, with a foreword by Ralph McGill, Lippincott, 1963, 2nd enlarged edition published as *Search the Scriptures: Modern Medicine and Biblical Personages*, introduction by Walter C. Alvarez, 1968; (editor) *Hirsute Female*, introduction by M. F. Ashley Montagu, C. C Thomas, 1963; (editor and author of introduction) *Progress in Conception Control: The Sequential Regimen*, Lippincott, 1966; *Ovulation: Stimulation, Suppression, and Detection*, Lippincott, 1966; (compiler and editor with Wladimiro Inguilla) *Endocrinologic and Morphologic Correlations of the Ovary*, C. C Thomas, 1969. Contributor of articles to magazines, including *Reader's Digest* and *McCall's*.

* * *

GREENE, Herbert 1898-

PERSONAL: Born April 25, 1898; son of Charles Henry (a headmaster) and Marion (Carleton) Greene; married Audrey Nutting, March 25, 1927. *Education:* Attended Berkhamsted School, Hamilton House Prep, and Marlborough College. *Religion:* Church of England. *Home:* Oak Cottage, Plumpton, Sussex, England. *Agent:* John Connell, 6 Old Bond St., London W.1, England.

CAREER: Kermit Rooseveldt Shipping Line, Santos, Brazil, agent, 1919-23; farmer in Southern Rhodesia, 1925-32; British Broadcasting Corp. Club, London, England, secretary, 1936; member of Yugo-Slav mission to Middle East, 1944; free-lance journalist, 1945-64. *Military service:* British Army, Suffolk Regiment, 1916-19; became second lieutenant; Middlesex Yeomanry, 1939-42. *Member:* Club XV (Santos), Victory Club (London).

WRITINGS: Secret Agent in Spain, R. Hale, 1938; *Wanted a Lead and Other Trifles*, Nicol, 1949; *Big Ben, and Other Verses*, Connell, 1960, 2nd edition, 1961. Former regular columnist, *Kent Express*; contributor of articles to journals throughout the world.

WORK IN PROGRESS: Television plays.

* * *

GREENWOOD, Julia Eileen Courtney 1910-
(Francis Askham)

PERSONAL: Born November 4, 1910, in London, England; married Antony Terry; second husband, Cecil John Greenwood; children: one son. *Home:* 29 Blashford Tower, Adelaide Rd., London NW3 3RX, England. *Agent:* A. M. Heath & Co. Ltd., 40 William IV St., London WC2 4DF, England.

CAREER: Journalist and broadcaster.

WRITINGS—All under pseudonym Francis Askham: *The Heart Consumed* (novel), Bodley Head, 1943; *A Foolish Wind* (novel), Bodley Head, 1945; *The Gay Delavals*, J. Cape, 1955; *The Mayor Makers*, Secker & Warburg, 1963.

* * *

GREER, Carlotta C(herryholmes) 1879-1965

PERSONAL: Born 1879, in Akron, Ohio; daughter of John F. and Louise (Cherryholmes) Greer. *Education:* Buchtel College (now University of Akron), Ph.B., 1903; graduate study at Drexel Institute of Technology, 1904-05, and Columbia University. *Home:* 2300 Overlook Rd., Cleveland Heights, Ohio.

CAREER: Kansas State Manual Training Normal School (now Kansas State College of Pittsburg), Pittsburg, head of department of foods, 1903-08; Cleveland, Ohio, public schools, head of home economics departments at East Technical High School, 1908-29, John Hay High School, 1929-39, coordinator of home economics curriculum center, 1939-42, head of home economics department, John Hay High School, 1942-46. *Member:* American Home Economics Association (charter and life member), Ohio Home Economics Association, Omicron Nu (honorary), Women's City Club (Cleveland). *Awards, honors:* LL.D., Drexel Institute of Technology, 1950.

WRITINGS—All published by Allyn & Bacon: *A Text-book of Cooking*, 1915; *Food and Victory* (war supplement to *A Text-book of Cooking*), 1918; *School and Home Cooking*, 1920, revised edition, 1925; (with J. Cora Bennett) *Chemistry for Boys and Girls*, 1925, published as *Chemistry*, 1926; *Teachers' Handbook for Chemistry*, 1928; *Foods and Home Making*, 1928, revised edition, 1937; *Workbook in Home-Making*, with teacher's manual, 1932; *Your Home and You: Unit Course in Home Economics*, 1942, revised edition with Ellen P. Gibbs published as *Your Home and You*, 1960; *Foods for Home and School*, 1944, revised edition, 1946.

(Died January 5, 1965)

* * *

GREER, Louise 1899-

PERSONAL: Born August 29, 1899, in Lodi, Va.; daughter of John Smith and Bettie (Keyes) Greer. *Education:* Martha Washington College, student, 1916-18; Emory and Henry College, A.B., 1925; University of Virginia, M.A., 1928, graduate study, 1930-31, 1934-37, Ph.D., 1953. *Religion:* Methodist. *Address:* Box 31, Chilhowie, Va. 24319.

CAREER: Teacher of English at high schools in Virginia, 1918-23, 1925-27, at Logan College, Russellville, Ky., 1928-30, at high schools in Virginia and Maryland, 1940-45; East Carolina College, Greenville, N.C., assistant professor, 1945-53, associate professor, 1953-59, professor of English, 1959-65, professor emeritus, 1965—. *Member:* Modern Language Association of America, North Carolina English Teachers Association, Bibliographical Society of the University of Virginia, Edgar Allan Poe Society of Baltimore.

WRITINGS: Browning and America, University of North Carolina Press, 1952; (contributor) *English Studies in Honor of James Southall Wilson*, Alderman Library, 1951.

WORK IN PROGRESS: Further writing on Browning and on Poe.

* * *

GRIERSON, (Monica) Linden 1914-

PERSONAL: Born September 14, 1914, in Bradford, Yorkshire, England; daughter of Horace Corps and Kathleen (Linden) Wilder; married Leslie Grierson, June 16, 1938; children: Donald, Barry. *Education:* Educated at schools in Bradford, England, and Sydney, New South Wales, Australia. *Home:* Beach Rd., Batemans Bay, NSW 2536, Australia. *Agent:* Christy & Moore Ltd., 52 Floral St., Covent Garden, London W.C.2, England.

CAREER: Writer, residing in Australia, 1949—. West Dubbo Progress Association, president, 1959-61. *Member:* International P.E.N., Australian Society of Authors, Central Western Horticultural Society (secretary, 1962-64).

WRITINGS—All novels; all published by R. Hale: *The Bond Between*, 1950; *The Beloved Fool*, 1951; *Coveted Country*, 1952; *The Pathway Through the Woods*, 1954; *Rising River*, 1954; *The Delightful Journey*, 1955; *The Whisper of the Night Winds*, 1955; *Peppertree Lane*, 1956; *The Edge of Nowhere*, 1957; *The Sunken Garden*, 1958; *The Senorita Penny*, 1959; *The Far Away Bride*, 1960; *The Adventuresome Spirit*, 1962; *Sea Jewel*, 1962; *Sparkling Enemy*, 1963; *The Return of Elizabeth*, 1965; *Fifth Time Lucky*, 1966; *Wild Harvest*, 1966; *The Dreaming Hills*, 1970.

WORK IN PROGRESS: Storm, completed and awaiting publication.

SIDELIGHTS: Mrs. Grierson lived in Australia for a period before World War II, and spent war years in England. Many of her books have been serialized and published as paperbacks in the Scandinavian countries, France, Belgium, Denmark, Italy. When asked whether all her books were romantic novels she replied: "Yes, but not *too* romantic." *Avocational interests:* Gardening and exhibiting at flower shops.

* * *

GRISWOLD, Erwin N(athaniel) 1904-

PERSONAL: Born July 14, 1904, in East Cleveland, Ohio; son of James Harlan (a lawyer) and Hope (Erwin) Griswold; married Harriet Ford, December 30, 1931; children: Hope Eleanor (Mrs. Daniel Murrow), William Erwin. *Education:* Oberlin College, A.B. and A.M., 1925; Harvard University, LL.B., 1928, S.J.D., 1929. *Office:* 1100 Connecticut Ave. N.W., Room 1200, Washington, D.C. 20036.

CAREER: Admitted to Ohio bar, 1929, Massachusetts bar, 1935, District of Columbia bar, 1973; U.S. Department of Justice, Washington, D.C., attorney, later special assistant to the Attorney General, 1929-34; Harvard University Law School, Cambridge, Mass., assistant professor, 1934-35, professor, 1935-46, Charles Stebbins Fairchild Professor of Law, 1946-50, Langdell Professor of Law, 1950-67, dean, 1946-67; Solicitor General of the United States, 1967-73. Member of U.S. Civil Rights Commission, 1961-67. Trustee, Oberlin College, 1936—.

MEMBER: American Bar Association, American Bar Foundation (president of board of directors, 1971—), American Philosophical Society, American Council of Learned Societies, American Academy of Arts and Sciences (fellow; vice-president, 1946-48), British Academy (fellow), Inner Temple (United Kingdom; honorary bencher), Phi Beta Kappa, Cosmos Club (Washington, D.C.), Century Association (New York), Harvard Club (Boston and New York), Charles River Country Club. *Awards, honors:* Honorary degrees from twenty-nine universities and colleges, including University of Sydney, University of Melbourne, Harvard University, Columbia University, Northwestern University, and Oxford University.

WRITINGS: Spendthrift Trusts, Matthew Bender, 1936, 2nd edition, 1947; *Cases on Federal Taxation*, Foundation Press, 1940, 6th edition, Foundation Press, 1966; (with others) *Cases on Conflict of Laws*, Foundation Press, 1941, 5th edition, Foundation Press, 1962; *The Fifth Amendment Today*, Harvard University Press, 1954; *Law and Lawyers in the United States*, Harvard University Press, 1964. Contributor to legal journals.

* * *

GROSS, Irma H(annah) 1892-

PERSONAL: Born July 21, 1892, in Omaha, Neb.; daughter of David and Addie (Gladstone) Gross. *Education:* University of Chicago, S.B., 1915, M.A., 1924, Ph.D., 1931.

CAREER: High school teacher, Omaha, Neb., 1915-21; Michigan State University, East Lansing, 1921-59, became professor of home management, professor emeritus, beginning 1959, University of Ryukus, consultant, 1959. U.S. Bureau of Home Economics, regional supervisor, Consumer Purchases Study, 1936, field supervisor, Study of Family Spending and Saving in Wartime, 1942. Michigan Youth Commission, member, 1949-58, secretary, 1949-51. *Member:* American Sociological Association, American Home Economics Association (president of Michigan branch, 1939-40), National Council on Family Relations, American Association of University Women, League of

Women Voters, Phi Beta Kappa, Omicron Nu, Phi Kappa Phi. *Awards, honors:* Ellen H. Richards fellow, American Home Economics Association.

WRITINGS: (With Mary Lewis) *Home Management*, F. S. Crofts, 1938; (with Elizabeth W. Crandall) *Home Management in Theory and Practice*, F. S. Crofts, 1947; (with Crandall) *Management for Modern Families*, Appleton, 1954, revised edition, 1963; (editor) *Potentialities of Women in the Middle Years*, Michigan State University Press, 1956. Writer of technical articles and bulletins.

* * *

GROSS, William Joseph 1894-

PERSONAL: Born April 2, 1894, in South Boston, Mass.; son of Nicholas John and Elizabeth (Letzelter) Gross; married Louise M. Hucksam, July 3, 1922; children: Jean Marie. *Education:* Boston College, A.B., 1918; additional study at Boston University and Boston State Teachers' College. *Politics:* Republican. *Religion:* Roman Catholic. *Home:* 12 Avalon Rd., West Roxbury, Mass. 02132.

CAREER: Mechanic Arts High School, Boston, Mass., junior master of English, 1921-29; Roxbury Memorial High School, Roxbury, Mass., master of English and German, 1929-59; Catholic Memorial High School, West Roxbury, Mass., teacher of English and German, and guidance counselor, 1959-62. *Member:* St. Vincent de Paul Society (West Roxbury; treasurer, 1948-57), Knights of Columbus.

WRITINGS: (Editor with Charles L. Hanson) *Short Stories of Today*, Ginn, 1928; (editor and author of introduction with Hanson) *Travel Sketches of Today*, Ginn, 1929; *Herod the Great*, Helicon, 1962. Ghost writer; author of brochures, and of notes for revised editions of standard works.

WORK IN PROGRESS: A biography of Nero; a fantasy for children; an adventure story for boys.

AVOCATIONAL INTERESTS: Travel, reading, choral music of muscular male German type, and loafing in garden.

* * *

GROVES, Francis Richard 1889-

PERSONAL: Born August 18, 1889, in Birmingham, England; son of Richard John and Jessie Louise (Jenkinson) Groves; married Edith May Clifford, May 18, 1918; children: Eric R. C., Rodney F. D. *Education:* University of Birmingham, student, 1903-07. *Politics:* Conservative. *Religion:* Christian. *Home:* Upton Court, Slough, Buckinghamshire, England.

CAREER: One-time editor of *Business*, and *West London Chronicle*, London, England, and *West Kent Advertiser* and *Dartford Borough News*, Kent, England; Groves, Brodie & Co. Ltd., Slough, England, chairman, 1927; Printeries Holdings Ltd., Slough, England, managing director, 1955. Speaker on industrial personnel relations at conferences in France, Switzerland, Denmark, and Norway. Councillor, on Dartford Borough Council and Slough Borough Council. *Military service:* Royal Air Force, 1914-19; mentioned in dispatches. *Member:* Society of Authors (London), Institute of House Organ Editors.

WRITINGS: House Organ Handbook, Windsor Press, 1940; *In Search of a Creator*, Windsor Press, 1946. Contributor of articles to *Printers Ink* (United States). Editor of *House Organ Journal*.

WORK IN PROGRESS: Three books, *The Elusive Gold, The Inquest*, and *Saga of a Small Heathen*.

* * *

GRUBB, Kenneth George 1900-

PERSONAL: Born September 9, 1900, in Oxton, Nottinghamshire, England; son of Harry Percy (a clergyman) and M.A. (Crichton-Stuart) Grubb; married Eileen Knight, 1926 (died, 1932); married Nancy Mary Arundel, December 8, 1936; children: Martyn, Frederick, Richard, Margaret (Mrs. Robert Jackson). *Education:* Attended Marlborough College. *Religion:* Protestant (Anglican). *Home:* The Moot Farm, Downton, Salisbury, Wiltshire, England.

CAREER: Missionary in South America, 1923-28; researcher and free-lance writer, 1928-39; British Ministry of Information, London, England, head of Latin-American section, 1939-41, controller of foreign publicity, 1941-42, controller of overseas publicity, 1942-46; Hispanic and Luso-Brazilian Councils, secretary-general, 1946-54. Director of Argentine Club Ltd., Ashmount Properties Ltd., C.S. Services Ltd., Leomark Ltd., Hooker, Craigmyle & Co. Ltd. United Kingdom Delegate to UNESCO, 1954, to Atlantic Congress, 1959. World Council of Churches, member of executive board; other posts on British Council of Churches; Commission of the Churches on International Affairs, chairman, 1946-68; president of Church Missionary Society, 1944-69, House of Laity, 1959-70. Trustee of St. Peter's College, Oxford University, 1946; executive trustee of Survey Application Trust, 1954—; governor of Monkton Combe School, 1957—. *Military service:* Royal Navy, 1918.

MEMBER: Royal Institute of International Affairs, Institute of Linguists (honorary life member), Institute for Strategic Studies (chairman, 1958-63), American Geographical Society (life), Asian Christian Colleges Association (vice-president, 1953; chairman, 1959—; president, 1969), British and Foreign Bible Society (vice-president), United Society for Christian Literature (vice-president), Canning Club (vice-chairman), Author's Club, Naval and Military Club. *Awards, honors:* Companion of the Order of St. Michael and St. George for public services, 1942; LL.D. from Muhlenberg University, 1951; knighted for services to Church Missionary Society, 1953; honorary fellow of St. Peter's College, Oxford University, 1961; Knight Commander of the Order of St. Michael and St. George, for service to the Church of England, 1970.

WRITINGS: The Lowland Indians of Amazonia: A Survey of the Location and Religious Condition of the Indians of Colombia, Venezuela, the Guianas, Ecuador, Peru, Brazil and Bolivia, World Dominion Press, 1927; *Amazon and Andes*, Dial, 1930; *The West Coast Republics of South America*, World Dominion Press, 1930; *The Northern Republics of South America: Ecuador, Colombia, and Venezuela*, World Dominion Press, 1931; *The Need for Non-Professional Missionaries* (originally published in *World Dominion*), World Dominion Press, 1931; *South America, the Land of the Future*, World Dominion Press, 1931; *Parables from South America*, includes photographs by Grubb, Methuen, 1932; (with Erasmo Braga) *The Republic of Brazil: A Survey of the Relgious Situation*, World Dominion Press, 1932; *The Republics of South America*, Royal Institute of International Affairs, 1933; (translator with E. R. Holden) Eduardo Moreira, *The Significance of Portugal: A Survey of Evangelical Progress*, World Dominion Press, 1933; (with Carlos Araujo Garcia) *Religion in the Republic of Spain*, World Dominion Press, 1933; *From Pacific to Atlantic: South American Studies*, Methuen, 1933; *Time's Winged Chariot*, New Mildmay Press, 1934; *Missions Rethought*, New Mildmay Press, 1934; (with G. Baez Camargo) *Religion in the Republic of Mexico*, World Dominion Press, 1935; *An Advancing Church in Latin America*, World Dominion Press, 1936; *Evangelical Handbook of Latin America*, published for Committee on Co-operation in Latin American by World Dominion Press, 1937 edition, 1937, Volume 2, 1939; *Religion in Central America*, World Dominion Press, 1937; *The Christian Handbook of South Africa*, World Dominion Press, 1938; (contributor) "Madras Series," seven volumes, International Missionary Council, 1939; *The Lowland Indians of Amazonia: Review of Ten Years Evangelical Progress to 1938*, World Dominion Press, 1939; *The Northern Republics of South America: Review of Ten Years Evangelical Progress to 1938*, World Dominion Press, 1939; *The West Coast Republics of South America: Review of Ten Years Evangelical Progress to 1938*, World Dominion Press, 1939; (with M.A.C. Warren) *Bridge Builders into a New Age* (two articles originally published in *The C.M.S. Outlook*), Church Missionary Society, 1947; (editor with Ernest John Bingle) *World Christian Handbook*, World Dominion Press, 1949, 5th edition (with H. Wakelin Coxill), 1968; (editor with Bingle) *A Digest of Christian Statistics Based on World Christian Handbook, 1952*, World Dominion Press, 1953; *Coexistence and the Conditions of Peace* (lecture given in Church House, Westminster, February 20, 1957), S.C.M. Press, 1957; *A Layman Looks at the Church*, Hodder & Stoughton, 1964. Chairman of board of management, 1954, and member of editorial board, *Frontier*.

WORK IN PROGRESS: *Crypts of Power*, an autobiography, to be published by Hodder & Stoughton.

*   *   *

GRUBB, Norman (Percy) 1895-

PERSONAL: Born August 2, 1895, in London, England; son of Harry Percy (a minister) and Margaret (Crichton-Stuart) Grubb; married Pauline Studd, November 24, 1919; children: Paul, Priscilla, Daniel. *Education:* Attended Cambridge University. *Home:* 209 Pennsylvania Ave., Fort Washington, Pa.

CAREER: Worldwide Evangelization Crusade, Congo missionary, 1919-31, international secretary, Fort Washington, Pa., beginning 1931. *Military service:* British Army, Infantry, 1914-18; became lieutenant; received Military Cross.

WRITINGS: *C. T. Studd, Cricketer and Pioneer*, Lutterworth, 1934, published as *C. T. Studd, Athlete and Pioneer*, Zondervan, 1935, 5th edition, Lutterworth, 1970; *Touching the Invisible*, Zondervan, 1940; *After C. T. Studd*, Lutterworth, 1942, Zondervan, 1946; *Alfred Buxton of Abyssinia and Congo*, Lutterworth, 1942; *Christ in Congo Forests*, Lutterworth, 1945 published as *C. T. Studd in Congo Forests*, Zondervan, 1947; *The Law of Faith*, Lutterworth, 1947; *Successor in C. T. Studd* (about Jack Harrison), Lutterworth, 1949; *Rees Howells, Intercessor*, Lutterworth, 1952; (editor) *J. D. Drysdale, Prophet of Holiness*, Lutterworth, 1955; *The Liberating Secret*, Lutterworth, 1955; *The Deep Things of God*, Lutterworth, 1958; *Modern Viking: The Story of Abraham Vereide*, Zondervan, 1961; *God Unlimited*, Lutterworth, 1962; *Once Caught, No Escape: My Life Story*, Lutterworth, 1969.

SIDELIGHTS: Grubb's first book about the pioneer Congo missionary, C. T. Studd, has gone into more than twenty editions and reprints in a number of languages, with sales reaching 150,000. That and other of Grubb's writings have been translated into a dozen languages.

*   *   *

GRUBE, Georges M(aximilien) A(ntoine) 1899-

PERSONAL: Born March 8, 1899, in Antwerp, Belgium; son of Antoine and Marie (Reiners) Grube; married Gwenyth Deen Macintosh, July 8, 1924; children: Antonia Joan (Mrs. C. S. Swalgen), John Deen, Jennifer Julia (Mrs. A. J. Podlecki). *Education:* Emmanuel College, Cambridge, B.A., 1922, M.A., 1925. *Politics:* New Democratic Party (Canada). *Home:* 5 Washington Ave., Toronto, Ontario, Canada. *Office:* Trinity College, Toronto, Ontario, Canada.

CAREER: University College of Swansea, Swansea, Wales, lecturer in classics, 1923-28; Trinity College, University of Toronto, Toronto, Ontario, professor of classics, beginning 1928, head of department, 1931-65. *Member:* American Philological Association, Classical Association of Canada (past president), Royal Society of Canada (fellow).

WRITINGS: *Plato's Thought*, Methuen, 1935, Beacon, 1958; *The Drama of Euripides*, Methuen, 1941; *Longinus on Great Writing*, Bobbs-Merrill, 1957; (translator) Aristotle, *On Poetry and Style*, Bobbs-Merrill, 1958; (editor) *A Greek Critic: Demetrius on Style*, University of Toronto Press, 1961; *The Meditations of Marcus Aurelius*, Bobbs-Merrill, 1963; *The Greek and Roman Critics*, Methuen, 1965. Contributor of some thirty articles to classical journals.

*   *   *

GRUBER, Frank 1904-1969
(Stephen Acre, Charles K. Boston, John K. Vedder)

PERSONAL: Born February 2, 1904, in Elmer, Minn.; son of Joseph and Susanna (Reisinger) Gruber; married Lois Mahood, May 21, 1931; children: Robert James. *Education:* Chiefly self-educated after high school. *Religion:* Roman Catholic. *Home:* 521 North Bristol Ave., Los Angeles 49, Calif.

CAREER: Held a variety of jobs while free-lance writing, 1921-34, including editing trade journals in the Midwest, and teaching fiction-writing by mail, in New York, N.Y.; full-time writer, 1934-69. Lecturer on writing at University of Southern California, Santa Monica City College, San Diego State College, and other schools. *Military service:* U.S. Army, Infantry, 1920-21.

WRITINGS: *Peace Marshal*, Morrow, 1939; *The French Key*, Farrar & Rinehart, 1940 (published under title *The French Key Mystery*, Avon, 1942); *The Laughing Fox*, Farrar & Rinehart, 1940; *The Hungry Dog*, Farrar & Rinehart, 1941 (published under title *The Hungry Dog Murders*, Avon, 1943); *The Navy Colt*, Farrar & Rinehart, 1941; *Outlaw*, Farrar & Rinehart, 1941; *Simon Lash, Private Detective*, Farrar & Rinehart, 1941; *The Talking Clock*, Farrar & Rinehart, 1941; (under pseudonym John K. Vedder) *The Last Doorbell*, Holt, 1941; (under pseudonym Charles K. Boston) *The Silver Jackass*, Reynal Hitchcock, 1941; (under pseudonym Stephen Acre) *The Yellow Overcoat*, Dodd, 1942; *The Buffalo Box*, Farrar & Rinehart,

1942; *The Gift Horse*, Farrar & Rinehart, 1942; *Gunsight*, Dodd, 1942; *The Mighty Blockhead*, Farrar & Rinehart, 1942 (reprinted as *The Corpse Moved Upstairs*, Belmont, 1964); *The Silver Tombstone*, Farrar & Rinehart, 1945; *Beagle Scented Murder*, Rinehart, 1946; *The Fourth Letter*, Rinehart, 1947; *The Honest Dealer*, Rinehart, 1947; *The Whispering Master*, Rinehart, 1947; *Fighting Man*, Rinehart, 1948; *The Lock and the Key*, Rinehart, 1948; *Murder '97*, Rinehart, 1948; *The Scarlet Feather*, Rinehart, 1948; *Broken Lance*, Rinehart, 1949; *The Leather Duke*, Rinehart, 1949; *Smoky Road*, Rinehart, 1949 (reprinted as *Lone Gunhawk*, Monarch, 1964).

Fort Starvation, Rinehart, 1953; *Bitter Sage*, Rinehart, 1954; *Bugles West*, Rinehart, 1954; *Johnny Vengeance*, Rinehart, 1954; *The Limping Goose*, Rinehart, 1954; *The Lonesome Badger*, Rinehart, 1954; *The Highwayman*, Rinehart, 1955; *Buffalo Grass*, Rinehart, 1956; *Lonesome River*, Rinehart, 1957; *The Marshal*, Rinehart, 1958; *Tales of Wells Fargo*, Bantam, 1958; *Town Tamer*, Rinehart, 1958; *The Bushwackers*, Holt, Rinehart & Winston, 1959; *The Whispering Master*, New American Library, 1959.

Twenty Plus Two, Dutton, 1961; *Horatio Alger, Jr., a Biography and Bibliography*, Grover Jones Press, 1961; *Brothers of Silence*, Dutton, 1962; *Bridge of Sand*, Dutton, 1963; *The Greek Affair*, Dutton, 1964; *Swing Low, Swing Dead*, Belmont, 1964; *Little Hercules*, Dutton, 1965; *Run, Fool, Run*, Dutton, 1966; *The Pulp Jungle*, Sherbourne, 1967; *The Twilight Man*, Dutton, 1967; *The Gold Gap*, Dutton, 1968; *The Etruscan Bull*, Dutton, 1969; *The Spanish Prisoner*, Dutton, 1969.

Zane Grey: A Biography, World Publishing, 1970.

Author of more than fifty feature motion picture scripts, and of over two hundred television scripts; creator of television series, "Tales of Wells Fargo," "The Texan," and "Shotgun Slade." Contributor of several hundred short stories to fifty magazines.

SIDELIGHTS: Gruber's books have been translated into twenty-four languages, including Japanese, Hebrew, and most western European languages; total sales of American and foreign editions run over eighty million; twenty-four books have been made into motion pictures. His chief hobby was studying archaeology and ancient history—a hobby that provided material for several of his books.

He has been described both as a "one-man mystery factory" and as the writer who did "more to glorify the Wild West for domesticated Americans than anyone since Zane Grey." He began writing Westerns, he said, to keep from starving. He told an interviewer he had talked to many cowboys in every Western state, and learned, unfortunately, "that quite a lot of these oldtimers are great liars." Gruber read hundreds of murder mysteries each year and never, he maintained, became surfeited.

(Died December 9, 1969)

*   *   *

GRUENBERG, Benj(amin) C(harles)   1875-1965

PERSONAL: Born August 15, 1875, in Novo Sielitz, Rumania; brought to United States in 1883; son of John Benedict and Charlotte (Mayberg) Gruenberg; married Sidonie Matsner (a writer and lecturer on child study and parent education), June 30, 1903 (died March 11, 1974); children: Herbert M., Richard M. Gruen, Hilda Sidney (Mrs. David Krech; a writer), Ernest M. *Education:* University of Minnesota, B.S., 1896; graduate study at New York University, 1901-02, New York Botanical Gardens, 1902-09; Columbia University, A.M., 1908, Ph.D., 1911. *Home and office:* 100 Central Park South, New York, N.Y. 10019.

CAREER: Chemist in New York, N.Y., 1895-1902; New York, N.Y. high schools, 1902-20, began as teacher of biology, became head of biology department, and later, coordinator in school and of job project; U.S. Public Health Service, New York, N.Y., director of educational programs, 1920-22; Urban Motion Picture Industries, New York, N.Y., director of educational films, 1922-23; New York State Dental Society, researcher and editor, 1923-24; American Association for Medical Progress, New York, N.Y., managing director, 1925-29; Viking Press, New York, N.Y., educational editor, 1929-32; researcher, and consultant to government agencies and educational organizations on public health education, welfare projects, and medical economics, 1918-45; writer and editor, 1945-65. Lecturer at colleges and universities, including Rand School for Social Science, 1907-24 (also co-founder and president), and New School for Social Research, 1928-29, 1932-33.

MEMBER: American Association for the Advancement of Science (fellow), American Public Health Association (fellow), American Social Hygiene Association (honorary life member), National Association for Research in Science Teaching (honorary life member), National Vocational Guidance Association (co-founder), National Association of Biology Teachers, New York Biology Teachers' Association (honorary life member), New York Academy of Science. *Awards, honors:* Outstanding Achievement Award, University of Minnesota; Science Education Recognition Award, National Association for Research in Science Teaching, 1957.

WRITINGS: Elementary Biology: An Introduction to the Science of Life, Ginn, 1919, *Manual of Suggestions for Teachers*, 1919.

(With Frank M. Wheat) *Student's Manual of Exercises in Elementary Biology*, Ginn, 1920; (editor) *Outlines of Child Study*, Macmillan, 1922, 2nd edition, 1927; (editor and contributor) *High Schools and Sex Education*, U.S. Public Health Service, 1922, revised edition, 1939; *Parents and Sex Education*, American Social Hygiene Association, 1923, 3rd edition, Viking, 1932; *Biology and Human Life*, Ginn, 1925; (with N. E. Robinson) *Experiments and Projects in Biology*, Ginn, 1925; (editor and contributor) *Modern Science and People's Health*, Norton, 1926; (editor and contributor) *Guidance of Childhood and Youth*, Macmillan, 1926; *The Story of Evolution: Facts and Theories on the Development of Life*, Van Nostrand, 1929.

(With Earl R. Glenn) *Instructional Tests in General Science*, World Book, 1932; (contributor) Sidonie Matsner Gruenberg and Dorothy Canfield Fisher, editors, *Our Children*, Viking, 1932; (contributor) Samuel D. Schmalhausen, editor, *Our Neurotic Age: A Consultation*, Farrar & Rinehart, 1932; (with wife, S. M. Gruenberg) *Parents, Children, and Money: Learning to Spend, Save, and Earn*, Viking, 1933; *Science and the Public Mind*, McGraw, 1935; (with Samuel P. Unzicker) *Science in Our Lives*, World Book, 1938; (with others) *Science in General Education*, Appleton, 1938; (with Unzicker) *Activities in General Science*, World Book, 1939; (with Unzicker) *Teachers Manual for the Teaching of General Science*, World Book, 1939.

Instructional Tests in Fundamentals of Electricity, World Book, 1943; *Instructional Tests in Fundamentals of Ma-*

chinery, World Book, 1943; (with N. E. Bingham) *Biology and Man*, Ginn, 1944, *Teacher's Manual*, 1946; (editor and co-author) *Voluntary Health Agencies*, Ronald, 1945; (with Emily E. Snyder and Jesse V. Miller) *Workbook in Biology*, Ginn, 1946; *How Can We Teach About Sex?*, Public Affairs, 1946.

(With Leone Adelson) *Your Breakfast and the People Who Made It*, Doubleday, 1954.

(With S. M. Gruenberg) *The Wonderful Story of You: Your Body, Your Mind, Your Feelings*, Doubleday, 1960.

Contributor of chapters to books, and of articles to encyclopedias and magazines, including *Plant World, Atlantic Monthly, Forum, Success, Popular Science Monthly, Scientific Monthly, Child Study, New Era* (London), *Journal of Heredity*, and *Science Education*. Editor of motion picture shorts and of full-length film, "Evolution." Co-founder and managing editor, *American Teacher*, 1911-18.

SIDELIGHTS: The Wonderful Story of You has been translated into Swedish and Spanish and published in England.

BIOGRAPHICAL SOURCES: Science Education, April 1937, February, 1958.

(Died July 1, 1965)

* * *

GRUENBERG, Sidonie Matsner 1881-1974

PERSONAL: Born June 10, 1881, near Vienna, Austria; daughter of Idore and Augusta Olivia (Basseches) Matzner; married Benjamin C. Gruenberg (an author, educator, and editor), June 30, 1903 (died, 1965); children: Herbert M., Richard M., Hilda S. (Mrs. David Krech), Ernest M. *Education:* Attended Ethical Culture School, New York, N.Y., 1895-97, 1905-06, and Columbia University, 1906-10. *Home:* 100 Central Park South, New York, N.Y. 10019.

CAREER: Child Study Association of America, New York, N.Y., 1906-74, director, 1923-50, special consultant, 1950-74. Lecturer on parent education at Teachers College, Columbia University, 1928-36, 1946-47, New York University, 1936-37, 1940, New York School of Social Work, Temple University, University of Colorado, and other universities. Member of technical advisory committee, National Conference on Family Life, 1948, of preparatory commission, International Congress on Mental Health, London, 1948, of Midcentury White House Conference, 1950, and of National Commission on Children and Youth, U.S. Children's Bureau; also member of advisory boards or special committees of National Council on Family Relations, National Association of Day Nurseries, National Organization of Public Health Nurses, and Social Legislation Information Service; president of League School for Seriously Disturbed Children, 1956-60. Consultant to Educational Policies Commission of National Education Association, and to Doubleday & Co., 1950-74. Member of editorial board of Junior Literary Guild, 1929-74.

MEMBER: American Association for the Advancement of Science (fellow), Association for Childhood Education, American Social Health Association (honorary life member). *Awards, honors:* Parents' Magazine medals for *Our Children: A Handbook for Parents*, 1932, *Parents' Questions*, 1936, and *We, the Parents*, 1939.

WRITINGS: Your Child Today and Tomorrow, Lippincott, 1913; *Sons and Daughters*, Henry Holt, 1916; (with husband, Benjamin C. Gruenberg) *Parents, Children and*

Money, Viking, 1933; *The Use of Radio in Parent Education*, University of Chicago Press, 1939; *We, the Parents*, Harper, 1939, revised edition, 1948.

Your Child and You, Gold Medal Books, 1950; (with daughter, Hilda S. Krech) *The Many Lives of Modern Women*, Doubleday, 1952; *The Wonderful Story of How You Were Born*, Doubleday, 1952, revised edition, 1959, 2nd revised edition, 1970; (with Benjamin C. Gruenberg) *Children for the Childless*, Doubleday, 1954; *Guiding Your Child From Five to Twelve*, Random House, 1958; *Parent's Guide to Everyday Problems of Boys and Girls*, Random House, 1958; (with Benjamin C. Gruenberg) *The Wonderful Story of You*, Doubleday, 1960.

Editor: (With Dorothy Canfield Fisher) *Our Children: A Handbook for Parents*, Viking, 1932; *Parents' Questions*, Harper, 1936, revised edition, 1948; *The Family in a World at War*, Harper, 1942; *Favorite Stories Old and New*, Doubleday, 1942, revised edition, 1955; *More Favorite Stories Old and New*, Doubleday, 1948, revised edition, 1960; *Our Children Today: A Guide to Their Needs*, Viking, 1952; *Encyclopedia of Child Care and Guidance*, Doubleday, 1954, revised edition published as *The New Encyclopedia of Child Care and Guidance*, 1968; *Let's Read a Story*, Doubleday, 1957; *Let's Read More Stories*, Doubleday, 1960; *Let's Hear a Story*, Doubleday, 1961; *Kinds of Courage*, Doubleday, 1962; *The New Illustrated Encyclopedia of Child Care and Guidance*, Stuttman, 1967.

Contributor to *Encyclopaedia Britannica, Social Work Year Book* and *Annals* of American Academy of Political and Social Science. Also contributor to *Childcraft, Family Circle, Family Weekly, Woman's Day, Redbook, New York Times Magazine*, and other periodicals. Member of editorial board of *Parent's Magazine*, 1926-43.

SIDELIGHTS: Your Child and You has been published in Hebrew, and *The Wonderful Story of How You Were Born* in Japanese, Norwegian, and Swedish.

(Died March 11, 1974)

* * *

GRUHN, Carrie Myers 1907-

PERSONAL: Born April 3, 1907, in Clarinda, Iowa; daughter of Frank R. (a researcher) and Clara (DeVoe) Myers; married Stanley G. Gruhn (a printer), May 18, 1929; children: Edward L., Gerald L. *Education:* Attended Iowa State Teachers College, one year; special courses at Oregon Bible College, 1954-59. *Home:* 2930 Miller Trunk, Duluth, Minn. 55811; Route 3, McGregor, Minn. 55760.

MEMBER: Women's Christian Temperance Union (branch president, Mt. Morris, Ill., 1939-59).

WRITINGS—Fiction: A Trumpet in Zion, Moody, 1951, revised edition published as *Lost City*, 1969; *Unwanted Legacy*, Van Kampen Press, 1953; *Happy Is the Man*, Moody, 1963.

WORK IN PROGRESS: The Great Babylon, dealing with Jewish and Babylonian history during period 605-498 B.C., completed and awaiting publication; a biography.

AVOCATIONAL INTERESTS: Bible study, teaching Sunday School, music (accordion, piano, organ), boating, agate hunting, ice fishing, reading.

* * *

GRUSKIN, Alan D(aniel) 1904-1970

PERSONAL: Born December 28, 1904, in Manorville, Pa.;

son of Arthur S. (a department store proprietor) and Jennie (Pollock) Gruskin; married Mary J. Bovio (an art dealer), July 16, 1940; children: Richard, Robert. *Education:* Attended Harvard University. *Residence:* Stockton, N.J. *Office:* Midtown Galleries, 11 East 57th St., New York, N.Y. 10022.

CAREER: Midtown Galleries (contemporary American art), New York, N.Y., director and owner, 1932-70. *Member:* Art Dealers Association of America, Metropolitan Museum, Municipal Art Society, American Federation of Arts, Drawing Society, Archives of American Art, National Art Museum of Sport, Harvard Club (New York).

WRITINGS: Painting in the U.S.A., Doubleday, 1946; (with Dong Kingman) *The Watercolors of Dong Kingman, and How the Artist Works*, introduction by William Saroyan, text by Gruskin, Crowell, 1958; *The Painter and His Technique: William Thon*, includes notes by Thon, Viking, 1964. Also writer, during 1930's, of radio series, "Story Behind the Picture," for WOR, and "Art Appreciation for All," for NBC.

WORK IN PROGRESS: A book dealing with the art of William Palmer, for Viking.

SIDELIGHTS: Active in the promotion and sale of contemporary American art for over 35 years, Gruskin gave first exhibitions to several artists prominent today. Among the outstanding painters and sculptors he represented have been William Palmer, Bishop, Paul Cadmus, Waldo Peirce, Doris Rosenthal, and William Thon. His touring shows, sent on circuit to museums and universities, included "Fine Art in Industry" and "Art in Interiors."

BIOGRAPHICAL/CRITICAL SOURCES: New York Times, October 8, 1970.

(Died October 7, 1970)

* * *

GUILLAUME, Alfred 1888-19(?)

PERSONAL: Born November 8, 1888, in England; son of Alfred Guillaume; married Margaret Woodfield Leadbitter, 1916; children: two sons, two daughters. *Education:* Oxford University, M.A. and D.D. *Home:* High View, Streatley, Berkshire, England.

CAREER: Clergyman, Church of England. Cuddesdon College, curate and lecturer in Hebrew, 1919-20; University of Durham, Newcastle upon Tyne, England, professor of Hebrew and Oriental languages, 1920-30; Culham College, Abingdon, England, principal, 1930-45; University of London, London, England, Davidson Professor of Old Testament Studies, 1945-47, fellow of King's College, 1947, professor of Arabic, School of Oriental and African Studies, and head of the university department of the Near and Middle East, 1947-55, professor emeritus, 1955—. Visiting professor at American University of Beirut, 1944-45, Princeton University, 1955-57, University of Leeds, 1958-59. Examining chaplain to bishop of Oxford, 1937-46; select preacher, Cambridge University, 1955. *Military service:* British Army, 1914-18; served in France and Egypt; became captain; mentioned in dispatches. *Member:* Athenaeum Club (London).

WRITINGS: The Traditions of Islam: An Introduction to the Study of the Hadith Literature, Clarendon Press, 1924; (contributor) *The Legacy of Israel*, Clarendonss, 1927; *Prophecy and Divination Among the Hebrews and Other Semites*, Hodder & Stoughton, 1938, Harper, 1939; *Islam*, Penguin, 1954, 2nd revised edition, 1961, Barnes &

Noble, 1964; (contributor) John Pickrell, compiler, *The Divine Initiative of the Old Testament*, San Francisco Theological Seminary, 1957; *New Light on the Life of Muhammad*, Manchester University Press, 1960; *Hebrew and Arabic Lexicography*, E. J. Brill, 1963; *Studies in the Book of Job*, edited by John Macdonald, E. J. Brill, 1968.

Editor: (With H. L. Goudge and Charles Gore, and contributor) *New Commentary on Holy Scripture, Including the Apocrypha*, Macmillan, 1928; (with Thomas Arnold) *The Legacy of Islam*, Oxford University Press, 1931, 2nd edition, 1960; (and translator) Abu al-Fath Muhammad-al, *Kitabu nihayati 'l iqdam fi 'ilmi 'l kalam*, Part I, Oxford University Press, 1931; (and translator) 'Abd al-Malik Ibn Hisham, *The Life of Muhammad*, Oxford University Press, 1955.

Contributor to *Encyclopaedia of Islam*.

AVOCATIONAL INTERESTS: Walking.

(Deceased)

* * *

GUMP, Richard (Benjamin) 1906-

PERSONAL: Born January 22, 1906, in San Francisco, Calif.; son of Abraham Livingston and Mabel (Lichtenstein) Gump; married Agnes Marie Fraser, August 31, 1945 (divorced December 16, 1960); children: Peter. *Education:* Attended Stanford University, 1924-25, and California School of Fine Arts, 1931. *Office:* Gump's Inc., 250 Post St., San Francisco, Calif. 94108.

CAREER: S. & G. Gump Co., San Francisco, Calif., stock boy, 1925-26, draftsman 1926-27, European buyer, 1929-30, director of gallery, 1930-32; free-lance writer, songwriter, and actor, Hollywood, Calif., 1932-38; S. & G. Gump Co. (later Gump's Inc.), head designer at branch in Honolulu, Hawaii, 1939-41, vice-president and general manager, 1944-47, president, 1947—. Member of import advisory committee, U.S. Department of Commerce 1946-48; Member of world trade committee, San Francisco Chamber of Commerce, 1948, 1949, 1950. Professional lecturer throughout United States; watercolorist; composer; leader and organizer of Guckenheimer Sour Kraut Band. Member of committee for art, Stanford University Board of Governors. *Member:* American Academy of Asian Studies (treasurer, 1957), American Institute of Decorators (associate), American Society of Composers, Authors & Publishers, World Trade Club, Press Club, Redwood Empire Association (director, 1947-48, 1949-52), San Francisco Art Association, Rotary International, Union League Club, Lake Merced Golf and Country Club, Marin Country Club. *Awards, honors:* Star of Italian Solidarity, 1954, for contribution to commercial and cultural relations between United States and Italy.

WRITINGS: Good Taste Costs No More, Doubleday, 1951; *Jade: Stone of Heaven*, Doubleday, 1962.

BIOGRAPHICAL/CRITICAL SOURCES: Time, May 20, 1949, September 29, 1961; *Where*, April 6, 1963; *Business Week*, December 21, 1963.

* * *

GURWITSCH, Aron 1901-1973

PERSONAL: Born January 17, 1901, in Wilna, Russia; son of Meyer (a businessman) and Eva (Bloch) Gurwitsch; married Alice Stern, April, 1929. *Education:* Studied at University of Berlin, 1919-1921, and University of Frankfurt, 1921-28; University of Gottingen, Ph.D., 1928. *Religion:* Jewish. *Home:* 820 West End Ave., New York, N.Y. 10025. *Office:* New School for Social Research, 66 West 12th St., New York, N.Y. 10011.

CAREER: Prussian Ministry for the Sciences, the Arts, and Public Instruction, Berlin, Germany, research fellow in philosophy, 1929-33; Sorbonne, University of Paris, Paris, France, lecturer in philosophy, Institut d'Histoire des Sciences, 1933-40; Caisse Nationale de la Recherche Scientifique, Paris, France, research fellow, 1939-40; Johns Hopkins University, Baltimore, Md., visiting lecturer in philosophy, 1940-42; Harvard University, Cambridge, Mass., instructor in physics, 1943-46; Wheaton College, Norton, Mass., visiting lecturer in mathematics, 1947-48; Brandeis University, Waltham, Mass., assistant professor of mathematics, 1948-51, associate professor of philosophy, 1951-59; New School for Social Research, New York, N.Y., professor of philosophy, Graduate Faculty of Political and Social Science, 1959-73, co-founder and director of Husserl Archives. Fulbright professor of philosophy, University of Cologne, 1958-59; visiting professor at Columbia University, 1962, University of Puerto Rico, 1963, and University of Mainz, 1968.

MEMBER: International Phenomenological Society (member of council, 1940-73), American Metaphysical Society, American Philosophical Association, History of Science Society, Society for Phenomenology and Existential Philosophy, Societe Francaise de Philosophie (foreign correspondent), American Association of University Professors.

WRITINGS: Theorie du champ de la conscience, Desclee de Brouwer, 1957, published in English as *The Field of Consciousness*, Duquesne University Press, 1964; *Studies in Phenomenology and Psychology*, Northwestern University Press, 1966; *Phenomenology and the Theory of Science*, Northwestern University Press, 1974; *Leibniz: Philosophie des Panlogismus*, De Gruyter, 1974. Contributor of over fifty articles to American, French, and German professional journals.

SIDELIGHTS: Gurwitsch was fluent in French and German.

BIOGRAPHICAL/CRITICAL SOURCES: Tijdschrift voor Philosophie, Volume XX, 1958.

(Died June 25, 1973)

*   *   *

GUTTMACHER, Manfred S(chanfarber)   1898-1966

PERSONAL: Born May 19, 1898, in Baltimore, Md.; son of Adolf and Laura (Oppenheimer) Guttmacher; married 3rd wife, Carola Blitzman (a medical doctor), 1946; children: Jonathan, Richard, Laurence, Alan. *Education:* Johns Hopkins University, A.B., 1919, M.D., 1923. *Home:* Englemeade Rd., Stevenson, Md. 21153. *Office:* 819 Park Ave., and Courthouse, Baltimore, Md. 21201.

CAREER: Psychiatrist. Chief medical officer of Supreme Bench, Baltimore, Md., 1930-66; University of Maryland, Baltimore Campus, associate professor of psychiatry, 1952-66; Johns Hopkins University, Baltimore, Md., assistant professor of psychiatry, 1954-66. U.S. Veterans Administration, consultant, 1946-66; member of U.S. Surgeon General's advisory board, 1955-66. Stanford University, Gimbel Lecturer, 1950; University of Minnesota, Isaac Ray Lecturer, 1958. Legal Aid Bureau, member of board, 1932-50. *Military service:* U.S. Army, Medical Corps,

World War II; became lieutenant colonel; received Legion of Merit. *Member:* American Psychiatric Association (fellow), Group for the Advancement of Psychiatry, Maryland Mental Hygiene Society (president, 1934), Laurel on the Severn Club.

WRITINGS: America's Last King, Scribner, 1942; *Sex Offenses: The Problem, Causes and Prevention*, Norton, 1951; (with Henry Weihofen) *Psychiatry and the Law*, Norton, 1952; *The Mind of the Murderer*, Farrar, Straus, 1960; *The Role of Psychiatry in Law*, C. C Thomas, 1968. Contributor of articles to medical journals. Member of editorial board; *Journal of Nervous and Mental Diseases*, and of *Psychiatry Digest*.

SIDELIGHTS: Guttmacher was a principal witness for the defense in the trial of Jack Rudy for the murder of Lee Harvey Oswald, accused assassin of President Kennedy. He testified that Ruby was insane at the time he shot Oswald.

Guttmacher's twin brother, Dr. Alan F. Guttmacher, a well-known obstetrician, is national president of Planned Parenthood-World Population. *Avocational interests:* Tennis and badminton.

BIOGRAPHICAL/CRITICAL SOURCES: New York Times, November 9, 1966.

(Died November 4, 1966)

*   *   *

GWYNN, Denis (Rolleston)   1893-

PERSONAL: Born March 6, 1893, in Bristol, England; son of Stephen (an author) and Mary L. Gwynn; married Alice Trudeau, April 30, 1963. *Education:* National University of Ireland, B.A., 1914, D.Litt., 1934. *Religion:* Roman Catholic. *Home:* Rosenallis, Seamount Rd., Malahide, County Dublin, Ireland.

CAREER: Following World War I was assistant editor or editor of several Irish periodicals, then a journalist in France, 1920-23; London editor of *Freeman's Journal*, 1924; writer for *Westminster Gazette*, 1925; editor of *Dublin Review*, 1935-39; Burns, Oates & Washbourne Ltd. (now Burns & Oates Ltd.; publishers), London, England, literary director, 1933-39; University College, Cork, Ireland, research professor of modern Irish history, 1947-63, editor of Cork University Press, 1952-63; retired. *Military service:* Royal Munster Fusiliers, served in France, 1917; became lieutenant. *Member:* Irish Academy of Letters, Royal Historical Society (fellow), Royal Irish Academy, Authors' Club, National Liberal Club, Reform Club (London), Cork and County Club (Cork), Kildare Street Club (Dublin).

WRITINGS: (Editor) Walter McDonald, *Reminiscences of a Maynooth Professor*, J. Cape, 1924, 2nd edition, Mercier Press, 1967; *The Catholic Reaction in France*, Macmillan, 1925; *The Action Francaise Condemnation*, Burns, 1928; *The Irish Free State, 1922-27*, Macmillan (London), 1928; *The Struggle for Catholic Emancipation*, Longmans, Green, 1928; *A Hundred Years of Catholic Emancipation*, Longmans, Green, 1929.

Daniel O'Connell, Hutchinson, 1930; *Edward Martyn and the Irish Revival*, J. Cape, 1930; *The Life and Death of Roger Casement*, J. Cape, 1930; *John Keogh*, Talbot Press, 1930; *Cardinal Wiseman*, Burns, 1931; *The Life of John Redmond*, Harrap, 1932, reprinted, Books for Libraries, 1971; *Pius XI*, Medici Press, 1932; *De Valera*, Jarrolds, 1933; *The O'Gorman Mahon*, Jarrolds, 1934.

The Vatican and War in Europe, Browne & Nolan, 1940; *The Second Spring*, Burns, 1942; *Lord Shrewsbury, Pugin and the Catholic Revival*, Burns, 1946; *Bishop Challoner*, Organ, 1946; *Father Dominic Barberi*, Burns, 1946; (editor) W. B. Yeats, *Tribute to Thomas Davis*, Cork University Press, 1947; *Young Ireland and 1848*, Cork University Press, 1949; *O'Connell, Davis, and the Colleges Bill*, Cork University Press, 1949.

The History of Partition, Browne & Nolan, 1950; *Father Luigi Gentili*, Clonmore & Reynolds, 1951.

(With Thomas Bodkin) *Tribute to Sir Hugh Lane*, Cork University Press, 1961; *Thomas Francis Meagher*, National University Press, 1962. Contributor to *Encyclopaedia Britannica*, *Encyclopedia Americana*, and other encyclopedias. Author of pamphlets and of essays appearing in monthly and quarterly reviews; bi-weekly columnist, *Cork Examiner*, 1951—. Editor, *Cork University Record*, annually, 1951-63.

WORK IN PROGRESS: Modern Irish History.

* * *

HAAR, Franklin B. 1906-

PERSONAL: Born April 15, 1906, in Lancaster, Pa.; son of E. Miller and Ella (Weise) Haar; married Lillian E. Proctor, June 16, 1928; children: Franklin Robert. *Education:* Springfield College, B.S., 1928; University of Pittsburgh, M.A., 1933, Ph.D., 1946. *Religion:* Protestant. *Home:* 1472 Cal Young Rd., Eugene, Ore. 97401. *Office:* University of Oregon, Eugene, Ore. 97403.

CAREER: Teacher in public schools in Pittsburgh, Pa., 1928-42; University of Florida, Gainesville, associate professor of health education, 1946-49; University of Oregon, Eugene, professor of health education and department chairman, 1949—. *Member:* American Public Health Association (fellow), American Association for the Advancement of Science (fellow), American School Health Association, American Association for Health, Physical Education and Recreation, Royal Society of Health, Rotary, Elks.

WRITINGS: (With Jack Smolensky) *Principles of Community Health*, Saunders, 1961, 3rd edition, 1971; (with Henry H. Clarke) *Health and Physical Education for the Elementary Classroom Teacher*, Prentice-Hall, 1964; (with Miriam L. Tuck) *Health*, Harper, 1969.

AVOCATIONAL INTERESTS: Photography.

* * *

HAARHOFF, Theodore Johannes 1892-1971

PERSONAL: Born April 30, 1892, in Paarl, South Africa; son of Barend Johannes (a clergyman and inspector of schools of Cape Province) and Magdalena Johanna (Marais) Haarhoff; married Jessie Kilburn Davis, February 7, 1919; children: Felix Johannes Julian, John Theodore. *Education:* South African College (now University of Cape Town), B.A., 1912; University of Berlin, graduate study; Oxford University, B.Litt., 1918; University of Amsterdam, Litt.D., 1931. *Politics:* Conservative-Liberal. *Religion:* Christian-Universal. *Home:* Almondbury, Stanford Rd., Rondebosch, Cape Town, South Africa.

CAREER: University of Cape Town, Cape Town, South Africa, lecturer in English literature, 1916, and in classics, 1919; University of the Witwatersrand, Johannesburg, South Africa, 1922-57, became professor of classics; then professor emeritus. Burge Memorial Lecturer, London,

England, 1952. On governing body of South African Broadcasting Corp., 1927-57. South African representative to UNESCO, 1946. Former member of Johannesburg Hospital Board, Johannesburg School Board, and Johannesburg University Council. *Member:* Royal Astronomical Society (London; fellow), Royal Society of Arts (London; fellow), South Africa Academy (Afrikaans; fellow), Ancient Monuments Society (fellow), P.E.N. (Afrikaans and English groups). *Awards, honors:* Rhodes Scholar, 1913; D.Litt. from University of Natal and University of Cape Town.

WRITINGS: Schools of Gaul, Oxford University Press, 1920, 2nd edition, Witwatersrand University Press, 1958; *Primi Gradus*, M. Miller, 1923; *Die Romeinse Boer*, van Schaik, 1925; *Die Klassieke in Suid-Afrika*, van Schaik, 1930; *Tria Corda* (Afrikaans verse), deBussy (Amsterdam), 1930; (with J. H. Hofmeyr and others) *Coming of Age: Essays in Souta African Citizenship and Politics*, M. Miller, 1930; *Vergil in the Experience of South Africa*, Blackwell, 1931; (contributor) *The Holistic Attitude in Education*, Witwatersrand University, 1932; (with C. M. van den Heever) *The Achievement of Afrikaans*, Central News Agency (South Africa), 1934; (editor) *Die Kortverhaal van die Grieke en Romeine*, two volumes, J. H. de Bussy, 1935; *Afrikaans, Its Origin and Development* (lectures), Clarendon Press, 1936; *The Stranger at the Gate*, Longmans, Green, 1938, 2nd edition, Basil Blackwell, 1948.

(With Max Cary) *Life and Thought in the Greek and Roman World*, Methuen, 1940; *The ABC of Afrikaans*, Central News Agency, 1941, 7th edition, 1957; (author of introduction) Ernst G. Malherbe, *The Bilingual School*, Longmans, 1943; (translator into English) Christian Maurits van den Heever, *Harvest Home*, A.P.B. Publishers, 1945; *Spiritual Evolution in South Africa*, Central News Agency, 1946; (editor and translator) *Die antieke Drama*, Afrikaanse Persboekhandel, 1946; *Vergil, the Universal*, Basil Blackwell, 1949; *The Unity of Mankind*, International University Society, revised edition, 1958; *Smuts the Humanist*, Blackwell, 1970.

Writer of published narrative poem and booklets. Contributor of articles to *Chambers's Encyclopaedia*, and *Acta Classica, Encyclopedia of Poetry and Poetics*, and *Oxford Classical Dictionary*. Assistant editor of *Forum* during World War II.

WORK IN PROGRESS: Bilingualism in the Classical World; Classical Literature for the Modern World.

(Died August 30, 1971)

* * *

HAAS, Mary Odin 1910-

PERSONAL: Born July 29, 1910, in Biloxi, Miss.; daughter of George Frances (a machinist) and Olympe (Roch) Haas. *Education:* Dominican College, New Orleans, La., student, 1928-30; Loyola University, New Orleans, La., Ph.D., 1949; summer study at Tulane University, University of Mississippi, The American University, and at several colleges. *Religion:* Roman Catholic. *Home:* 644 Lameuse St., Biloxi, Miss.

CAREER: Biloxi (Miss.) public schools, junior high school history teacher, 1933—. National Education Association (fifth vice-president, 1952-53), Mississippi Education Association (vice-president, 1953-54; president, 1954-55), Mississippi Department of Classroom Teachers (president, 1947-48, 1956-57), Pilot Club (international president, 1948-49), Beta Sigma Phi, Alpha Delta Kappa.

WRITINGS: Workbook for Mississippi History for High School, Steck, 1961. Contributor to *Mississippi Educational Advance*.

AVOCATIONAL INTERESTS: Flower gardening, needlepoint, sewing, reading, fishing, travel, bridge.

*   *   *

HADFIELD, Miles H(eywood) 1903-

PERSONAL: Born October 15, 1903, in Birmingham, England; son of Heywood George (a lawyer) and Hilda (Bragg) Hadfield. *Education:* Attended Bradfield College, Berkshire, England, 1918-21, University of Birmingham, 1921-23, Birmingham College of Art, 1930-33. *Home:* Dillon's Orchard, Wellington Heath, Ledbury, England. *Agent:* David Higham Associates Ltd., 5-8 Lower John St., London W1R 4HA, England.

CAREER: Trained as an electrical engineer and worked in the electrical industry in England, 1923-29; abandoned that career in 1929 to become a full-time author and illustrator, writing mainly about former spare-time interests—horticulture, arboriculture, and art. *Member:* Royal Forestry Society of England, Wales and Northern Ireland.

WRITINGS—Largely self-illustrated with drawings: (Editor) *Gardener's Companion*, Dent, 1936; *Every man's Wild Flowers*, Dent, 1938.

An English Almanac, Dent, 1950; *Gardening on a Small Income*, Hutchinson, 1954; (editor) *Gardener's Album*, Hulton, 1954; *Pioneers of Gardening*, Routledge & Kegan Paul, 1955; *British Trees—A Guide for Everyman*, Dent, 1957.

Gardening in Britain, Hutchinson, 1960; (with John Hadfield) *The Twelve Days of Christmas*, Cassell, 1961, Little, Brown, 1962; *Gardens*, Weidenfeld & Nicholson, 1962; *Your Book of Trees*, Faber, 1964; (with John Hadfield) *Gardens of Delight*, Little, Brown, 1964; *One Man's Garden*, Phoenix House, 1966. Contributor to *Country Life, Gardener's Chronicle*, and *House and Garden*.

WORK IN PROGRESS: Research on world history of gardening.

*   *   *

HADLEY, Hamilton 1896-

PERSONAL: Born January 13, 1896, in New Haven, Conn.; son of Arthur Twining (a university president) and Helen Harrison (Morris) Hadley; married Emily Hammond Morris, July 13, 1929; children: Anne (Mrs. John Keith Howat). *Education:* Yale University, B.A., 1919, LL.B. (cum laude), 1923. *Religion:* Congregationalist. *Home:* Orchard Dr., Armonk, N.Y. 10504.

CAREER: Winthrop, Stimson, Putnam & Roberts (law firm), New York, N.Y., partner, 1929-40; former director and vice-president of several power companies; director emeritus of Research Corp. Brearley School, director and trustee, 1930-54; Society of New York Hospital, director, 1947—, president, 1953-57. *Military service:* U.S. Air Service, American Expeditionary Forces, 1917-19; became captain. *Member:* American Geographical Society (former councillor), American Museum of Natural History (life), Academy of Political Science (life), American Bar Association, New York State Bar Association, Association of Bar of City of New York; Century Association, Down Town Association, and Yale Club (all New York); New Haven Lawn Club, Graduates Club, and Elizabethan Club (all New Haven).

WRITINGS: The United States: Guardian of Atomic Weapons, privately printed, 1947; *A Free Order: National Goal and World Goal*, Dodd, 1963.

*   *   *

HADLOW, Leonard Harold 1908-

PERSONAL: Born July 9, 1908, in Rainham, Kent, England; son of Sydney and Florence (Rayfield) Hadlow; married Evelyn Hitchock, July 31, 1935; children: Angela. *Education:* King's College, London, B.A. (honors) and Diploma of Associateship, 1930. *Home:* 7 Merwood Ave., Long Lane, Cheadle, Cheshire, England.

CAREER: King James Grammar School, Almondbury, Huddersfield, England, senior geography master, 1930-35; Burnage High School, Manchester, England, head of geography department, 1935-69. *Member:* Geographical Association (vice-president; former president of Manchester branch), National Geographic Society (United States), Incorporated Association of Assistant Masters in Secondary Schools (associate member).

WRITINGS: Climate, Vegetation, and Man, University of London Press, 1952, Philosophical Library, 1953; (with R. Abbott) *Regional Geography of Asia*, Book III of "London Geography Series," University of London Press, 1969.

AVOCATIONAL INTERESTS: Amateur dramatics.

*   *   *

HAIME, Agnes Irvine Constance (Adams) 1884- (Persis)

PERSONAL: Born October 29, 1884, in Wandsworth, London, England; daughter of Henry James (in civil service) and Harriet M. (Irvine) Adams; married Bertram Frederic Haime, July 26, 1919; children: John Wilfred. *Education:* Attended Southampton University; University of St. Andrews, Lady Literate of Arts. *Politics:* Liberal. *Religion:* Congregationalist. *Home and office:* 24 Collamore Ave., London S.W.18, England. *Agent: E. Walters Page, 95 Geraldine Rd., London S.W.18, England.*

CAREER: London County Council Schools, London, England, assistant teacher of singing, English literature, history, 1906-49. During World War II worked with evacuated children in several sections of England. *Member:* Society for Abolition of Cruel Sports (honorary press secretary), Anti-Vaccination Society, Anti-Vivisection Society, Crusade of Beauty without Cruelty, Rehabilitation of Convicts Society, Society against Performing Animals.

WRITINGS: The Pencil Falls, and Other Stories, Stockwell, 1942; *The Red Earth*, Mitre Press, 1945; *Dare to Be a Daniel*, Stockwell, 1945; *Reflections in Verse*, Richard Tilling, 1949; *Hope Is the Window* (poetry), P. R. Macmillan, 1960. Contributor to anthologies. Regular contributor to *East Hill Record*.

WORK IN PROGRESS: Poems.

AVOCATIONAL INTERESTS: Travel, card-reading, needlework.

*   *   *

HAINES, William Wister 1908-

PERSONAL: Born September, 1908, in Des Moines, Iowa; son of Diedrich Jansen (an engineer) and Ella (Wister) Haines; married Frances Tuckerman, September, 1934; children: William Wister, Jr., Laura Tuckerman.

Education: University of Pennsylvania, B.S., 1931. *Address:* P.O. Box 401, South Laguna, Calif. 92677. *Agent:* Harold Ober Associates, 40 East 49th St., New York, N.Y. 10017.

CAREER: Free-lance writer. *Military service:* U.S. Army, 1942-45; became lieutenant colonel. *Member:* Authors Guild and Dramatists Guild of Authors League of America, Writers Guild of America, West, Western Writers of America, Franklin Inn Club (Philadelphia).

WRITINGS: Slim, Atlantic-Little, Brown, 1934; *High Tension*, Atlantic-Little, Brown, 1938; *Command Decision*, (novel; based on his play; originally appeared in serialized version in *Atlantic*), Atlantic-Little, Brown, 1947; *Command Decision* (three-act play; first produced in Cleveland at Cleveland Playhouse, November, 1946; produced on Broadway at Fulton Theatre, October 1, 1948), Random House, 1948; *The Hon. Rocky Slade*, Atlantic-Little, Brown, 1957; *The Winter War*, Atlantic-Little, Brown, 1961; *Target*, Atlantic-Little, Brown, 1964; *The Image*, Simon & Schuster, 1968.

Screenplays: "Alibi Ike" (based on a story by Ring Lardner), Warner Brothers, 1935; "Slim" (based on his novel), Warner Brothers, 1937; (with Abem Finkel) "The Black Legion," Warner Brothers, 1937; (with Elaine Ryan) "Mr. Dodd Takes the Air" (based on *The Great Crooner*, a novel by Clarency Buddington Kelland), Warner Brothers, 1937; (with Bertram Millhauser and Paul Sloane) "The Texans" (based on *North of '36*, a novel by Emerson Hough), Paramount, 1938; (with Jonathan Latimer and Charles Marquis Warren) "Beyond Glory," Paramount, 1948; (with W. R. Burnett) "The Racket" (based on a play by Bartlett Cormack), RKO, 1951; (with Milton Krims) "One Minute to Zero," RKO, 1952; (author of screen story) "The Eternal Sea," Republic, 1955; (with Frank Fenton) "The Wings of Eagles" (based on the life of Frank W. Wead), M-G-M, 1957; (with Richard Sale) "Torpedo Run" (based on stories by Sale), M-G-M, 1958.

Contributor of stories and articles to magazines.

BIOGRAPHICAL/CRITICAL SOURCES: Library Journal, June 1, 1968; *New York Times Book Review*, June 30, 1968; *Best Sellers*, July 1, 1968.

*   *   *

HALE, (Charles) Leslie   1902-

PERSONAL: Born July 13, 1902, in England; son of Benjamin George (a managing director) and Mary Ann (Wood) Hale; married Dorothy Ann Latham, 1926 (died, 1971); children: Dorothy Lesley, Ian William. *Education:* Formal schooling ended at fifteen when he was expelled from Ashby de la Zouch Grammar School, Leicestershire, England. *Politics:* Socialist. *Home:* 92 College Rd., London S.E. 21, England.

CAREER: Articled to Evan Barlow (solicitor), Leicester, England; was a practicing solicitor, as senior partner in firms of Hale, Ringrose and Morrow in London, of Hale & Kauntze in Burton on Trent, of Hale & Mander in Coalville, and of Hale, Randle, & Stevenson in Nuneaton; Labour member of Parliament for Oldham, Lancashire, 1945-50, for West Division of Oldham, 1950-68, served on Joint Committee of the House of Lords and of the House of Commons on the Peerage, among other posts. Member of Leicestershire County Council, 1925-50. *Military service:* British Army. *Awards, honors:* Created Baron of Oldham (life peer), 1972.

WRITINGS: Thirty Who Were Tried, Gollancz, 1955; *John Philpot Curran: His Life and Times*, J. Cape, 1956; *Blood on the Scales*, J. Cape, 1959, McBride, 1962; *Hanging in the Balance*, J. Cape, 1961, Dufour, 1962; *Hanged in Error*, Penguin, 1961; *None So Blind* (novel), Gollancz, 1963.

WORK IN PROGRESS: A biography of Pierre Antoine Berryer, a French advocate.

AVOCATIONAL INTERESTS: Chess, trying to paint.

*   *   *

HALEY, Andrew G(allagher)   1904-

PERSONAL: Born November 11, 1904, in Tacoma, Wash.; son of Christopher Joseph and Kathleen (Gallagher) Haley; married Delphine Delacroix, 1934 (died, 1963); children: Delphine Delacroix, Andrew Gallagher, Jr. *Education:* Georgetown University, L.L.B., 1928, and graduate study; George Washington University, B.A., 1934.

CAREER: Admitted to bar of Washington, D.C., 1928, state of Washington, 1929; private practice of law, Tacoma, Wash., 1929-33; counsel for Federal Radio Commission and Federal Communications Commission, Washington, D.C., 1933-39; private practice of law as specialist in radio, television, and space law, Washington, D.C., 1939—, now as senior partner of Haley, Bader & Potts. General counsel of American Rocket Society (now American Institute of Aeronautics and Astronautics), 1950-63, International Astronautical Federation, 1958—, International Academy of Astronautics, and International Institute of Space Law. Co-founder, president, and managing director of Aerojet Engineering Corp., Pasadena and Azusa, Calif., 1942-45; president and director of KAGH, Inc., Pasadena, Calif., 1949-50; vice-president and director of Axe Science Management Co., Inc.; executive vice-president of Theodore von Karman Foundation, Inc.; director of Axe Science Corp. Adviser to U.S. Senate Special Committee investigating National Defense Program, 1945-48; chairman and organizer of First Colloquium on the Law of Outer Space, The Hague, 1958, and participant in subsequent Space Law Colloquiums in London, Stockholm, Washington, Varna, and Paris; delegate, adviser, or counsel at other international conferences on radio, rocketry, astronautics, and telecommunication. Lecturer at first Jet Propulsion School, 1943; speaker on space law and the peaceful uses of outer space at scientific meetings throughout America, in Canada, Africa, South America, and most countries of Europe. Charter member of World Peace Through Law Center and co-chairman on the law of space, 1963—. *Military service:* U.S. Army Air Forces, Judge Advocate General's Department, 1942-43; became major.

MEMBER: American Bar Association (vice-chairman, 1958-65, chairman of committee on the law of outer space, 1965—), International Law Association, International Bar Association, Federal Law Association, International Academy of Astronautics (founder member), American Institute of Aeronautics and Astronautics (fellow; director, 1951-52; president, 1954; chairman of board, 1955), British Interplanetary Society (fellow), South African Interplanetary Society (fellow), American Society of International Law, American Society for Legal History, American Ordnance Association, American Television Society, Astronautical Society of Canada, Armed Forces Communications and Electronics Association, National Aeronautics Association, International Radio and Television Society, London Institute of World Affairs; member or honorary member of other U.S. and foreign law and communications societies; Delta Theta, National Press Club, Congressional Country Club.

AWARDS, HONORS: American Rocket Society Special Award, 1954; Grotius Medal of International Grotius Foundation for the Propagation of the Law of Nations (Munich), 1958; British Interplanetary Society Medal, 1962; G. Edward Pendray Award of American Institute of Aeronautics and Astronautics, 1963, for *Space Law and Government.*

WRITINGS: Rocketry and Space Exploration, Van Nostrand, 1958; *Space Law and Government,* Appleton, 1963. Co-editor and contributor, *Proceedings of the Colloquium on the Law of Outer Space,* I-VIII, published by various presses in Europe and America for International Institute of Space Law, 1959-65. Contributor to *Dictionary of American History* and *Handbuch der Astronautik.* Contributor of about seventy articles on the legal, sociological, and economic aspects of the space age to *Astronautics, Foreign Policy Bulletin, Foreign Service Journal, This Week, Signal,* and other journals in America, Netherlands, France, Switzerland, Brazil, Germany and Spain.

WORK IN PROGRESS: Continued research and writing on various aspects of astronautics, domestic communications law, and the problems and potentials of satellite communications.

* * *

HALL, Anna Gertrude   1882-1967

PERSONAL: Born February 9, 1882, in West Bloomfield, N.Y.; daughter of Myron Edwin (a farmer) and Anna (Sterling) Hall. *Education:* Leland Stanford Junior University, A.B., 1906; New York State Library School, B.L.S., 1916. *Politics:* Democrat. *Religion:* Presbyterian. *Home:* Apartment 209, 850 Webster St., Palo Alto, Calif. 94301.

CAREER: Stanford University, Palo Alto, Calif., library cataloger, 1906-14; Endicott (N.Y.) Free Library, librarian, 1915-18; New York State Department of Education, Albany, library organizer, 1918-21; librarian of county library, Pendleton, Ore., 1923-27, of public library, Longview, Wash., 1929-32, of Palo Alto Medical Clinic, Palo Alto, Calif., 1948-62. *Member:* American Library Association.

WRITINGS: The Library Trustee, American Library Association, 1937; *Nansen,* Viking, 1940; *Cyrus Holt and the Civil War,* Viking, 1964. Author of pamphlets and articles in library field.

(Died February 8, 1967)

* * *

HALL, Clifton L.   1898-

PERSONAL: Born October 28, 1898, in Cowansville, Quebec, Canada; son of Frederick R. (a farmer) and Ella (Foss) Hall. *Education:* Bishops University, B.A. (with honors), 1921; McGill University, MA., 1932; Columbia University, M.A., 1941; University of North Carolina, Ph.D., 1949. *Politics:* Independent. *Religion:* Unitarian. *Home:* 1410 17th Ave. S., Nashville, Tenn. 37212. *Office:* George Peabody College for Teachers, Nashville, Tenn. 37205.

CAREER: Began teaching career in public schools of Quebec; University of North Carolina, Chapel Hill, lecturer in education, 1948-49; George Peabody College for Teachers, Nashville, Tenn., 1949—, now professor of edu-

cation. Simon Visiting Professor, University of Manchester, Manchester, England, 1956-57. *Military service:* Canadian Army, World War II; became major. *Member:* National Education Association, Tennessee Education Association, Phi Delta Kappa, Old Oak Club (Nashville).

WRITINGS: (Editor with Edgar W. Knight) *Readings in American Educational History,* Appleton, 1951; (editor with Holton, Kershner, and Savage) *Readings in American Education,* Scott, Foresman, 1963. Contributor to educational journals.

AVOCATIONAL INTERESTS: Listening to music (also plays several instruments) and reading.

* * *

HALL, Geoffrey Fowler   1888-1970

PERSONAL: Born March 9, 1888, in Surbiton, Surrey, England; son of Percival Ledger (a manufacturer) and Margaret (Fowler) Hall; married Nellie Kate Pidduck, December 10, 1910; children: Geoffrey Peter. *Education:* Attended Marlborough College, Wiltshire, England, 1901-06, and University of London, 1907-09. *Home:* Greenhills, Drumconrath, Navan, County Meath, Ireland.

CAREER: Government of India, Public Works Department, Bihar, engineer in Irrigation section, 1911-14, 1919-22, in Roads and Buildings section, 1923-43, became chief engineer and department secretary; retired, 1943. *Military service:* British Army, Royal Engineers, 1915-18; became captain; wounded; received Military Cross, mentioned in dispatches. *Awards, honors:* Companion of the Eminent Order of the Indian Empire for services in Bihar Earthquake, 1934.

WRITINGS: The Guru's Ring, Heath Cranton, 1933; *Moths Round the Flame,* Methuen, 1935; *The Dragon and the Twisted Stick,* Thacker (Bombay), 1944; (with Joan Sanders) *D'Artagnan, the Ultimate Musketeer: A Biography,* Houghton, 1964.

SIDELIGHTS: Hall had knowledge of French and Hindustani.

(Died August 8, 1970)

* * *

HALL, Jerome   1901-

PERSONAL: Born February 4, 1901, in Chicago, Ill.; son of Herbert (a businessman) and Sarah (Rush) Hall; married Marianne Cowan, July 2, 1941; children: Heather Adele. *Education:* University of Chicago, Ph.B., 1922, J.D., 1923; Columbia University, Jur.Sc.D., 1935; Harvard University, S.J.D., 1935. *Politics:* Republican. *Religion:* Unitarian. *Office:* Hastings College of Law, San Francisco, Calif. 94102.

CAREER: Admitted to Illinois Bar, 1923. Practicing attorney with law firm, 1923-26, privately, 1926-29; University of North Dakota, Grand Forks, professor of law, 1929-32; Louisiana State University, Baton Rouge, professor of criminal law and criminology, 1935-39; Indiana University, Bloomington, professor of law, 1939-57, Distinguished Service Professor of Law, 1957-70; Hastings College of Law, San Francisco, Calif., professor of law, 1970—. Fulbright lecturer in United Kingdom, 1954-55, at University of Freiburg, 1961; U.S. Department of State specialist in India and Far East, 1954 and 1968; Ford Foundation lecturer in Mexico and South America, 1960; lecturer at universities in United States, Canada, and Europe.

MEMBER: American Bar Association, American Society for Legal History (director, 1959—), American Foreign Law Association (director, 1964—), South American Sociological Society (honorary president, 1960—), Korean Legal Institute (honorary director, 1954—), American Society for Political and Legal Philosophy (president, 1966-68), Societe Europeenne de Culture, China Academy, *Awards, honors:* Lieber Award for distinguished teaching, 1956; LL.D. from University of North Dakota, 1958.

WRITINGS: Theft, Law and Society, Little, Brown, 1935, 2nd edition, Bobbs-Merrill, 1952; *General Principles of Criminal Law*, Bobbs-Merrill, 1947, 2nd edition, 1960; *Living Law of Democratic Society*, Bobbs-Merrill, 1949; *Studies in Jurisprudence and Criminal Theory*, Oceana, 1958; *Reason and Reality in Jurisprudence*, University of Buffalo, School of Law, 1958; *The Purposes of a System for the Administation of Criminal Justice*, Georgetown University Law Center, 1963; *Science, Common Sense, and Criminal Law Reform*, College of Law, State University of Iowa, 1963; *Comparative Law and Social Theory*, Louisiana University Press, 1963; *From Legal Theory to Integrative Jurisprudence*, College for Law, University of Cincinnati, 1964.

Editor: *Readings in Jurisprudence*, Bobbs-Merrill, 1938; *Cases and Readings on Criminal Law and Procedure*, Bobbs-Merrill, 1949, 2nd edition (with Gerhard O. W. Mueller), 1965. Editor of "20th Century Legal Philosophy" series, seven volumes, Harvard University Press, 1945-55. Member of board of editors, *Estudios de Sociologia* and *Archiv fuer Rechts-und-Sozial Philosophie*.

BIOGRAPHICAL/CRITICAL SOURCES: Estudios de Sociologia, Volume III, 1964.

*   *   *

HALLBERG, Charles William 1899-

PERSONAL: Born November 13, 1899, in New Britain, Conn.; son of John Charles (a businessman) and Ida Caroline (Esberg) Hallberg; married Eleanore R. Kohlhaupt, July 20, 1929; children: Ingrid (Mrs. F. Whitman Haggerson). *Education:* Trinity College, Hartford, Conn., B.S., 1923; Columbia University, M.A., 1924, Ph.D., 1931. *Politics:* Republican. *Religion:* Episcopalian. *Home:* 45-53 251 St., Little Neck, N.Y. 11362.

CAREER: Instructor or lecturer in history at Purdue University, Lafayette, Ind., 1926-28, Syracuse University, Syracuse, N.Y., 1929-31, University of Minnesota, Minneapolis, 1931-32; University of Missouri, Columbia, assistant professor of history, 1933-34; Brooklyn College (now Brooklyn College of the City University of New York), Brooklyn, N.Y., lecturer in history, 1933-37; Queens College of the City University ofNew York, New York, N.Y., beginning, 1937, professor of history, 1956-70, professor emeritus, 1970—, chairman of department, 1949-64. *Member:* American Historical Association, International Platform Association, New England Society of New York, University Club (New York).

WRITINGS: The Suez Canal—Its History and Diplomatic Importance, Columbia University Press, 1931; (contributor) Mathew A. Fitzsimons, Charles Nowell, and Alfred Pundt, editors, *The Development of Historiography*, Stackpole, 1954; *Franz Joseph and Napoleon III, 1852-1864*, Twayne, 1955.

WORK IN PROGRESS: A book, *Anglo-Austrian Relations, 1820-1870.*

HALLETT, Ellen Kathleen 1899-

PERSONAL: Born December 21, 1899, in Bristol, England; daughter of Frederick (a grocer) and Ellen (Perrett) Hallett. *Education:* West of England College of Art, part-time study, 1917-34; City and Guilds of London Institute, needlework (first class), 1937, teacher's qualifying certificate, 1945. *Politics:* Conservative. *Religion:* Christian. *Home:* 3 Logan Rd., Bristol BS7 8DU, England.

CAREER: Fairfield Grammar School, Bristol, England, 1916-65, began as assistant secretary to principal, became part-time teacher of art, 1917-37, full-time teacher of art, needlework, and games, 1937-65. Part-time teacher of arts and crafts, Tower House (private school), Almondsbury, Bristol, England, 1934-36. Paintings, drawings, and other craft work included in exhibitions of Royal Academy, Royal Society of British Artists, Royal Cambrian Academy, and in other shows and galleries. *Member:* Association of Assistant Mistresses in Secondary Schools, National Society for Art Education (fellow), Old Fairfieldians' Society (president, 1949-50; co-treasurer, 1931-73; honorary vice-president, 1966; honorary life treasurer, 1974), Clifton Arts Club (Bristol).

WRITINGS: Blue Print and Dyeline for Schools, Faber, 1963, Transatlantic, 1964. Contributor of poems and articles to journals and magazines, including *Art and Craft in Education, This England*, and *Somerset Life*.

WORK IN PROGRESS: Research for a book about alcoholism and some of its effects on families, provisionally titled *A Newcomer to Al-Anon.*

AVOCATIONAL INTERESTS: Nature study, photography, motoroing, antiques, archaeology and geology.

BIOGRAPHICAL/CRITICAL SOURCES: Eugenie Alexander, *Fabric Pictures*, Mills & Boon, 1959.

*   *   *

HAMELL, Patrick Joseph 1910-

PERSONAL: Born December 11, 1910, in Cloughjordan, County Tipperary, Ireland; son of Patrick (a merchant) and Margaret Mary (McCraith) Hamell. *Education:* Attended St. Flannan's College, Ennis, County Clare, Ireland; National University of Ireland (with study at St. Patrick's College), B.A., 1931, M.A., 1940 (first class honours); St. Patrick's College, S.T.L., 1936, D.D., 1937; also studied at Catholic University of Louvain and Catholic University of Fribourg. *Home and office:* St. Brendan's Parish, Birr, County Offaly, Ireland.

CAREER: Roman Catholic priest. St. Patrick's College of National University of Ireland (the college also is a Pontifical University), Maynooth, professor of ancient classics in the college, 1937-43, became professor of dogmatic theology in the Pontifical University, 1943, and vice-president of the college, 1959; St. Brendan's Parish, Birr, County Offaly, Ireland, parish priest, 1968—. Canon theologian of Killaloe diocesan chapter, 1958—; vicar general, Killaloe diocese, 1969—; appointed Prelate of Honor to the Pope, 1969; peritus (theological expert) at Vatican Council II; lecturer on patrology.

WRITINGS: Eastern Catholic Churches, Catholic Truth Society (Ireland), 1951; *The Sacred Heart Encyclical*, Catholic Truth Society, 1957; *Membership of the Mystical Body*, Browne & Nolan, 1958; *Index to the Irish Ecclesiastical Record, 1864-1917*, Browne & Nolan, 1962; (editor and contributor) *Sermons for Sundays and Feast Days*, Verry, 1962; *Index to the Irish Ecclesiastical Record, 1917-*

1963, Browne & Nolan, 1964; (editor and contributor) *Sunday and Feast Homilies*, Browne & Nolan, 1965; *Patrology: An Introduction*, Mercier Press, 1968. Also author of *Maynooth Students and Ordinations 1795-1895 Index*, published in 1967-68 and 1973.

Contributor of articles to *New Catholic Encyclopedia, Irish Ecclesiastical Record, Irish Theological Quarterly*, and *Christus Rex*. Editor, *Irish Ecclesiastical Record* (monthly journal), 1948-64. Joint editor, *Irish Theological Quarterly*, 1950—.

* * *

HAMILTON, Earl J(efferson) 1899-

PERSONAL: Born May 17, 1899, in Houlka, Miss.; son of Joseph William and Frances Regina Anne (Williams) Hamilton; married Gladys Olive Dallas, June 2, 1923; children: Sita (Mrs. Joseph Halperin). *Education:* Mississippi State University, B.S. (honors), 1920; University of Texas, M.A., 1924; Harvard University, A.M., 1925, Ph.D., 1929. *Politics:* Independent. *Home:* 1438 Bunker Ave., Flossmoor, Ill. 60422. *Office:* 212 Kelley, University of Chicago, Chicago, Ill. 60637.

CAREER: Duke University, Durham, N.C., assistant professor, 1927-29, professor of economics, 1929-44; Northwestern University, Evanston, Ill., professor of economics, 1944-47; University of Chicago, Chicago, Ill., professor of economics, 1947-68, professor emeritus, 1968—; State University of New York at Binghamton, Distinguished Professor of Economic History, 1966-69, professor emeritus, 1969—; now devoting full time to research. Military Government Fiscal School, director of civilian staff, 1943-44. Rapporteu, Committee on World Regions, Social Science Research Council, American Council of Learned Societies, and National Research Council, 1943; rapporteur, International Congress of Historical Sciences, Stockholm, Sweden, 1960. Social Science Research Council, member of committee on research in economic history, 1951-54, trustee of committee, 1953-63, fellow, 1963—.

MEMBER: American Association for the Advancement of Science (fellow), American Economic Association (vice-president, 1955), Economic History Association (president, 1951-52), American Historical Association, Economic History Society, Hispanic Society of America, Royal Economic Society (fellow), American Academy of Arts and Sciences (fellow), Phi Beta Kappa. *Awards, honors:* Social Science Research fellow, 1930; Guggenheim fellow, 1937-38; Ford Foundation fellow, 1956-57; Doctor Honoris Causa, University of Paris, 1952, University of Madrid, 1967; LL.D., Duke University, 1966.

WRITINGS: American Treasure and the Rise of Capitalism (1500-1700), London School of Economics and Political Science, 1929; *American Treasure and the Price Revolution in Spain, 1501-1650*, Harvard University Press, 1934; *Money, Prices and Wages in Valencia, Aragon, and Navarre, 1351-1500*, Harvard University Press, 1936; *War and Prices in Spain, 1651-1800*, Harvard University Press, 1947; *El Florecimiento del capitalism y otros ensayos de historia economica*, Revista de Occidente, 1948; (editor with Albert Rees and Harry G. Johnson) *Landmarks in Political Economy*, University of Chicago Press, 1962. Contributor to American, English, and French economics and historical journals. Member of board of editors of *Journal of Modern History*, 1941-43, *Journal of Economic History*, 1941-52; editor, *Journal of Political Economy*, 1948-54.

WORK IN PROGRESS: Writing from original European manuscript sources, an account of John Law's System, popularly known as the Mississippi Bubble, and a biography of John Law of Lauriston; *History of Interest Rates in Holland, 1610-1810*.

SIDELIGHTS: Hamilton speaks French, German, Dutch, Spanish, Italian, reads Portuguese; he has spent about one-third of the time in the peace years since 1926 gathering research data in archives and manuscript divisions of libraries in eight European countries, Peru, Colombia, and Mexico. *Avocational interests:* Gardening.

* * *

HAMILTON, Edward G. 1897-

PERSONAL: Born February 25, 1897, in Newtonville, Mass.; son of Franklin E. E. (an Episcopal bishop) and Mary (Pierce) Hamilton; married Leonora Bemis, June 28, 1924 (deceased); children: Leslie L. (Mrs. William A. M. Burden III). *Education:* Harvard University, A.B., 1918. *Politics:* Republican. *Religion:* Episcopal. *Home:* 145 Dudley Lane, Milton, Mass. 02186. *Office:* Fort Ticonderoga, Ticonderoga, N.Y. 12883.

CAREER: Water power engineer in New England, 1921-30; investment manager in Boston, Mass., 1931-56; Fort Ticonderoga, Ticonderoga, N.Y., director, 1957—. Consultant to Colonial Williamsburg, Sturbridge Village, and other historical sites. Selectman, Town of Milton. *Military service:* U.S. Army, served in France, 1918; became second lieutenant, U.S. Army, Field Artillery, World War II, served in Italian campaign; became colonel; received Legion of Merit, Croix de Guerre (France), Croce al Valor Militare (Italy). *Member:* American Society of Civil Engineers, American Antiquarian Society, Massachusetts Historical Society, Colonial Society of Massachusetts, Vermont Historical Society (trustee).

WRITINGS: History of Milton, Massachusetts, Milton Historical Society, 1957; *Lake Champlain and Upper Hudson Valley*, Fort Ticonderoga Association, 1959; *The French and Indian Wars: The Story of Battles and Forts in the Wilderness*, Doubleday, 1962; (editor and translator) Louis Antoine de Bougainville, *Adventure in the Wilderness: American Journals, 1756-1760*, University of Oklahoma Press, 1964; *Fort Ticonderoga: Key to a Continent*, Little, Brown, 1964; (with S. R. Baudouin) *The French Army in America* [and] *The Musketry Drill* (the former by Hamilton, the latter by Baudouin), Museum Restoration Society (Ottawa), 1967. Contributor of reviews and articles to periodicals.

WORK IN PROGRESS: Siege of Louisbourg, 1745.

* * *

HAMILTON, (Muriel) Elizabeth (Mollie) 1906-

PERSONAL: Born April 3, 1906, in County Wicklow, Ireland; daughter of John Douglas and Mary (Garnett) Hamilton. *Education:* University of London, B.A. (first class honors in classics), 1928, M.A. (with distinction), 1932. *Religion:* Roman Catholic. *Home:* 84 Vicarage Ct., Kensington Church St., London W.8, England. *Agent:* Curtis Brown Ltd., 13 King St., Covent Garden, London W.C.2, England.

MEMBER: P.E.N.

WRITINGS: The Year Returns, M. Joseph, 1952, Transatlantic, 1953; *A River Full of Stars*, Deutsch, 1954, Norton, 1955; *Simon* (novel), Deutsch, 1956; *Put Off Thy*

Shoes: A Journey to Palestine and Jordan, Deutsch, 1957, published as *Put Off thy Shoes: A Journey Through Palestine*, Scribner, 1958; *Saint Teresa: A Journey to Spain*, Scribner, 1959 (published in England as *The Great Teresa*, Chatto & Windus, 1960); *An Irish Childehood* (autobiography), Chatto & Windus, 1963; *Heloise*, Hodder & Stoughton, 1966, Doubleday, 1967. Contributor to *New York Times*, *John O' London*, and *Catholic World*.

* * *

HAMILTON, J(ames) Wallace 1900-1968

PERSONAL: Born May 4, 1900, in Pembroke, Ontario, Canada; son of John W. (a farmer) and Elizabeth N. (Warren) Hamilton; married Florence Newlan, June 24, 1930; children: John W., Joan Elizabeth, James R. *Education:* Attended Moody Bible Institute, 1920-24. *Politics:* Democrat. *Residence:* St. Petersburg, Fla.

CAREER: Methodist minister. Pasadena Community Church, St. Petersburg, Fla., senior minister, 1929-68. Chaplain, Florida Military Academy, 18 years. *Member:* Kiwanis Club (St. Petersburg). *Awards, honors:* D.D., Florida Southern College, 1940; Freedoms Foundation Award, 1960, for magazine article, "The Battle for the Free Mind."

WRITINGS—All published by Revell: *Ride the Wild Horses!* (sermons), 1952; *Horns and Halos in Human Nature*, 1954; *Who Goes There?: What and Where is God?*, 1958; (co-author) *He Speaks From the Cross*, 1963; *The Thunder of Bare Feet* (sermons), 1964; *Serendipity*, 1965; *Where Now is Thy God?*, 1969; *Still the Trumpet Sounds*, 1970; *What about Tomorrow?*, 1972. Contributor of articles to periodicals, including *American*, *Christian Herald*, *Reader's Digest*, and *Christian Century*.

(Died, 1968)

* * *

HAMILTON, Milton W(heaton) 1901-

PERSONAL: Born July 8, 1901, in Fabius, N.Y.; son of William L. and Annie B. (Wheaton) Hamilton; married Margaret L. Gatchel, August 30, 1927 (died April, 1965); children: Gwendolyn L., Mary Elizabeth. *Education:* Syracuse University, A.B., 1924, A.M., 1925; Columbia University, Ph.D., 1936. *Religion:* Episcopalian. *Home:* 6 South Helderberg Pkwy., Slingerlands, N.Y. 12159. *Office:* New York State Education Department, Albany, N.Y. 12224.

CAREER: Albright College, Reading, Pa., professor of history, 1926-49; New York State Education Department, Division of Archives and History, Albany, senior historian, beginning 1949, acting director, beginning 1963. *Member:* American Historical Association, American Antiquarian Society, World Affairs Council, New York State Historical Association, Pennsylvania Historical Association.

WRITINGS: *The Country Printer: New York State, 1785-1830*, Columbia University Press, 1936; *Adam Ramage and His Presses*, Southworth Anthoensen, 1942; (editor) *The Papers of Sir William Johnson*, Volumes X-XIII, University of the State of New York, 1951-62; *Henry Hudson and the Dutch in New York*, University of State of New York, 1959; *Sir William Johnson and the Indians of New York*, University of the State of New York, for the Office of State History, 1967. Editor, *Historical Review of Berks County*, 1941-50, *Pennsylvania History*, 1944-50.

HAMILTON, W(illiam) B(askerville) 1908-1972

PERSONAL: Born March 7, 1908, in Jackson, Miss.; son of William Baskerville (a hardware salesman) and Bessie (Cavett) Hamilton; married Mary Elizabeth Boyd, May 27, 1938 (died, 1954); children: Elizabeth Cavett (Mrs. William Barker French). *Education:* University of Mississippi, B.A., 1928, M.A., 1931; Duke University, Ph.D., 1938. *Office:* Department of History, Duke University, Box 6727, College Station, Durham, N.C.

CAREER: Duke University, Durham, N.C., instructor, 1936-42, assistant professor, 1942-47, associate professor, 1947-51, professor of history, 1951-72. *Member:* American Historical Association, African Studies Association, Council on British Studies, Canadian Historical Association, American Association of University Professors, Southern Historical Association, Mississippi Historical Society, North Carolina Literary and Historical Association, Phi Beta Kappa. *Awards, honors:* Faculty study fellowship, American Council of Learned Societies, 1950-51; grants-in-aid, American Philosophical Society and Huntington Library.

WRITINGS: (Editor) *Fifty Years of the South Atlantic Quarterly*, Duke University Press, 1952; *Anglo-American Law on the Frontier*, Duke University Press, 1953; (editor) Daniel Lerner and others, *The Transfer of Institutions*, Duke University Press, 1964; (editor with Kenneth Robinson and C.D.W. Goodwin) *A Decade of the Commonwealth*, Duke University Press, 1966. Contributor of reviews to *New York Times Book Review* and more than a score of articles to professional journals. Managing editor, *South Atlantic Quarterly*, 1957-72.

WORK IN PROGRESS: A life of Lord Grenville, 1759-1834.

SIDELIGHTS: Hamilton's career was shifted from American history to English by the happenstance of his being sent to England in 1935 to do research for an attorney; he traveled extensively in England on eight visits and in other Commonwealth nations—Australia, New Zealand, West Africa, and Canada. *Avocational interests:* Building the history collections in the Duke Library (formerly gardening and fishing).

(Died July 17, 1972)

* * *

HANCOCK, Ralph Lowell 1903-

PERSONAL: Born November 23, 1903, near Plainville, Ind.; son of John Hiram (a farmer) and Nancy (Cunningham) Hancock; married Julia Ellen F. Ross, 1924 (divorced); married Frances Fester Iversen, 1948; children: (first marriage) David Lowell (killed in action, World War II); (second marriage) Nancy Lowell, Bret Hiram. *Education:* Attended Springfield Business College, Springfield, Mo., 1923-24, Washington University, St. Louis, Mo., 1924-27. *Politics:* Republican. *Home and office:* 16527 Avenida Florencia, Poway, San Diego County, Calif. 92101.

CAREER: Reporter on newspapers in St. Louis, Mo., and Los Angeles, Calif., 1925-30; foreign news correspondent in Cental America and Caribbean, 1930-41; Transportes Aereos Centro Americanos, Central America, publicity director, 1940-42; Board of Economic Warfare, Washington, D.C., senior economic analyst and specialist on Caribbean area, 1942-43; adviser and Latin American editor for publishers, 1943-45; free-lance writer and lecturer on annual tour, 1945—. *Member:* Authors Guild.

WRITINGS: *Our Southern Neighbors*, Follett, 1942; *Mexico and Central America*, Ideal School Supply, 1942; *Let's Look at Latin America*, American Education Press, 1942, revised edition, 1947; *Latin America: Land and People*, Ideal School Supply, 1942; *Understanding Central America*, Allen & James, 1943; *Handbook of Central America*, Board of Economic Warfare, 1943; *Latin America*, Encyclopedia Americana, 1944; *Foods from Central America* (juvenile), C. E. Merrill, 1946; *Opportunities in Latin America*, Duell, Sloan & Pearce, 1946; *Exploring Latin America* (juvenile), C. E. Merrill, 1946; *Sports and Fiesta of Latin America* (juvenile), C. E. Merrill, 1946; *Travel in Latin America* (juvenile), C. E. Merrill, 1946; *Latin American Heroes* (juvenile), C. E. Merrill, 1946; *Peoples of Latin America* (juvenile), C. E. Merrill, 1946; *The Rainbow Republics: Central America*, Coward, 1947; (with Eleanor M. Johnson) *America's Southern Neighbors*, C. E. Merrill, 1947; *The Magic Land: Mexico*, Coward, 1948; *Fabulous Boulevard*, Funk, 1949.

When I Make a Garden, Garnett, 1950; *Our American Neighbors*, Follett, 1953; (with Letitia Fairbanks) *Douglas Fairbanks: The Fourth Musketeer*, Holt, 1953; (with others) *Baja California: Hunting, Fishing, and Travel in Lower California, Mexico*, Academy Publishing, 1953; *The Comemoral*, Academy Publishing, 1954; *The Forest Lawn Story*, Academy Publishing, 1955; *Exploring American Neighbors*, Follett, 1956; (with Joe E. Brown) *Laughter is a Wonderful Thing*, A. S. Barnes, 1956; (contributor) A. Curtis Wilgus, editor, *The Caribbean*, University of Florida Press, 1957; (with others) *Blondes, Brunettes, and Bullets*, McKay, 1957; *Desert Living*, Academy Publishing, 1958.

Puerto Rico: A Success Story, Van Nostrand, 1960; (with Julian A. Weston) *The Lost Treasure of Cocos Island*, Thomas Nelson, 1960; *Puerto Rico: A Travelers' Guide*, Van Nostrand, 1962; *Mexico*, Macmillan, 1964; (contributor) Hoagy Carmichael, *Sometimes I Wonder*, Farrar, Straus, 1965; (contributor) Henry Tobias, *The Borscht Belt*, Bobbs-Merrill, 1966; (with Henry Chafetz) *The Compleat Swindler*, Macmillan, 1968.

WORK IN PROGRESS: Ghost writing.

BIOGRAPHICAL/CRITICAL SOURCES: *Newsweek*, March 11, 1968; *National Observer*, April 1, 1968.

* * *

HANKINSON, Cyril (Francis James) 1895-

PERSONAL: Born November 4, 1895, in Bournemouth, Hampshire, England; son of Charles James (an author under pseudonym Clive Holland) and Violet (Downs) Hankinson; married Lillian Louise Read, August 4, 1942; children: Peter Clive Downs. *Education:* Attended Winbourne Grammar School, England. *Politics:* Conservative. *Religion:* Church of England. *Home:* 13 Welsby Ct., Eaton Rise, Ealing, London W.5, England.

CAREER: *National Roll of the Great War*, assistant editor, 1919-21; *Debrett's Peerage*, London, England, assistant editor, 1921-35, editor, 1935-62. *Military service:* Royal Air Force, 1914-18. *Member:* Society of Genealogists.

WRITINGS: *My Forty Years with Debrett*, R. Hale, 1963; *A Political History of Ealing*, R. Hale, 1971. Contributor to *Encyclopaedia Britannica, Collier's Encyclopedia, Chamber's Encyclopaedia, New York Herald Tribune, Christian Science Monitor*, London dailies, and to Canadian, Australian, South African, and New Zealand periodicals.

HANNAK, Johann Jacques 1892-

PERSONAL: Born March 12, 1892, in Vienna, Austria; son of Hermann and Fanny (Gluecklich) Hannak; married. *Education:* University of Vienna, LL.D., 1920. *Politics:* Socialist Party of Austria. *Religion:* Independent Catholic. *Home:* Vienna 18, Poetzleinsdorfstrasse 156, Austria.

CAREER: *Arbeit und Wirtschaft* (Austrian trade-union paper), editor-in-chief, 1921-34; *Wiener Schachzeitung*, editor, 1935-38; came to United States as refugee, 1941; U.S. Office of War Information, associate editor in German section, 1944-45; Garment Workers Union, statistician for retirement fund, 1945-46; returned to Austria, 1946; *Arbeiterzeitung*, Vienna, Austria, associate editor, 1946-60; retired, 1960. *Military service:* Austrian Army, 1914-18; became lieutenant. *Member:* Concordia. *Awards, honors:* Preis der Stadt Wien for literary works.

WRITINGS: *Vier Jahre Zweite Republik: Ein Rechenshaftsbericht der Sozialistischen*, Volksbuchhandlund, 1949, revised edition published as *Vorposten der Freiheit: Oesterreich 1950 bis 1953*, 1954; *Im Sturm eines Jarrhunderts, eine volkstuemliche Geschichte der Sozialistischen Partei Oesterreichs*, Volksbuchhandlund, 1952; *Emanuel Lasker: Biographie eines Schachweltmeisters*, Engelhardt, 1952, translation by Heinrich Fraenkel, published as *Emanuel Lasker: The Life of a Chess Master*, Simon & Schuster, 1959; (author of biographical sketch) Aron Nimzowitsch, *Mein System: Ein Lehrbuch des Schachspiels auf ganz neuartiger Grundlage*, Engelhardt, 1958.

Manner und Taten: Zur Geschichte der oesterreichischen Arbeiterbewegung, Volksbuchhandlund, 1963; (editor) Oskar Helmer, *Ausgewaehlte Reden und Schriften*, Europa-Verlag, 1963; (editor) *Bestandaufnahme Oesterreich, 1945-1963*, Forum Verlag, 1963; (editor) Karl Renner, *Die Nation: Mythos und Wurklichkeit*, [Vienna], 1964; *Karl Renner und seine Zeit: Versuch einer Biographie*, Europa-Verlag, 1965; (editor) *Die Weg ins Heute: Zwanzig Jahre Zweite Republik 1945-1965*, Europa-Verlag, 1965; (editor) Adolph Schaerf, *Die Teil und das Ganz*, Europa-Verlag, 1965; (editor) Ernst Haeusserman, *Im Banne des Burgtheaters: Reden und Aufsaetze*, Europa-Verlag, 1966; *Johannes Schober: Mittelweg in die Katastrophe*, Europa-Verlag, 1966; *Vom Untertan zum Mitbuerger: 100 Jahre Staatsgrundgesetze*, Oesterreichischer Gewerkschaftsbund, 1967. Contributor to periodicals.

* * *

HANSEN, Alvin H(arvey) 1887-

PERSONAL: Born August 23, 1887, in Viborg, S.D.; son of Niels B. (a farmer) and Marie Bergita (Nielsen) Hansen; married Mabel Lewis, August 25, 1916; children: Marian Grace (Mrs. L.S. Merrifield), Mildred Jean (Mrs. George Furiya). *Education:* Yankton College, B.A., 1910; University of Wisconsin, M.A., 1915, Ph.D., 1918. *Home:* 56 Juniper Rd., Belmont, Mass.

CAREER: High school principal and superintendent in Preston, S.D., 1910-13; Brown University, Providence, R.I., instructor in economics, 1916-19; University of Minnesota, Minneapolis, associate professor of economics, 1919-23, professor, 1923-37; U.S. Department of State, Washington, D.C., chief economic analyst, 1935-37; Harvard University, Cambridge, Mass., Lucius N. Littauer Professor of Political Economy, 1937-56, became professor emeritus, 1956. University of Bombay, visiting professor, 1957-58; Smith College, William Allen Neilson researcher, 1960. Commission of Inquiry on National Policy in International Economic Relations, secretary and director of research, 1933-34; Advisory Council on Social Security, member, 1938-39; U.S.-Canadian Joint Economic Commission, chairman, 1941-43; Federal Reserve Board, special economic adviser, 1940-45.

MEMBER: American Economic Association (vice-president, 1937; president, 1938), American Statistical Association (vice-president, 1937). *Awards, honors:* Guggenheim fellowship, 1928-29; LL.D., Yankton College, 1936; knighted (honorary) by Denmark, 1956; Gold Medal Award of Swedish Academy of Science, 1964, Francis A. Walker Medal from American Economic Association, 1967.

WRITINGS: Cycles of Prosperity and Depression, University of Wisconsin Press, 1921; *Business Cycle Theory*, Ginn, 1927; *Fiscal Policy and Business Cycles*, Norton, 1941; *America's Role in the World Economy*, Norton, 1945; *Economic Policy and Full Employment*, McGraw, 1947; (with Paul Samuelson) *Economic Analysis of Guaranteed Wages*, U.S. Government Printing Office, 1947; *Monetary Theory and Fiscal Policy*, McGraw, 1949; *Business Cycles and National Income*, Norton, 1951, expanded edition, 1964; *A Guide to Keynes*, McGraw, 1953; *The American Economy*, McGraw, 1957; *Economic Issues of the 1960's*, McGraw, 1961; *The Postwar American Economy: Performance and Problems*, Norton, 1964; *The Dollar and the International Monetary System*, McGraw, 1965.

Associate editor, *Econometrics*, 1933-38. Member of editorial board, *Review of Economics and Statistics*, 1938—, *Inter-American Economic Affairs*, 1947—, *Kylos*, 1947—.

BIOGRAPHICAL/CRITICAL SOURCES: Newsweek, February 8, 1971.

*   *   *

HARDING, D(enys Clement) W(yatt)   1906-

PERSONAL: Born July 13, 1906, in Lowestoft, England; son of Clement George (an accountant) and Harriet (Wyatt) Harding; married Jessie Ward, December 18, 1930. *Education:* Emmanuel College, Cambridge, B.A., 1928, M.A., 1930. *Office:* Ashbocking Old Vicarage, Ipswich IP6 9LG, England.

CAREER: National Institute of Industrial Psychology, London, England, scientific investigator, 1928-33; London School of Economics and Political Science, London, England, lecturer in social psychology, 1933-38; University of Liverpool, Liverpool, England, senior lecturer in psychology, 1938-45; University of London, Bedford College, London, England, professor of psychology, 1945-68. Part-time lecturer in psychology, University of Manchester, 1940-41, 1944-45; Clark lecturer, Trinity College, Cambridge, 1971-72. *Member:* British Psychological Society (honorary general secretary, 1944-48).

WRITINGS: (Translator with Erik Mesterton) Par Lagerkvist, *Guest of Reality*, J. Cape, 1936; (editor with Gordon Bottomley) *The Complete Works of Isaac Rosenberg*, Chatto & Windus, 1937; *The Impulse to Dominate*, Norton, 1941; *Social Psychology and Individual Values*, Hutchinson, 1953; *Experience into Words: Essays on Poetry*, Chatto & Windus, 1963, Horizon, 1964. Contributor to journals. Member of editorial board, *Scrutiny*, 1933-47; editor, *British Journal of Psychology*, 1948-54.

WORK IN PROGRESS: Preparing for publication his Clark lectures on rhythm in English literature.

HARDINGHAM, John (Frederick Watson)   1916-

PERSONAL: Born June 15, 1916, in Auckland, New Zealand; son of Frederic and Eliza (Pick) Hardingham; married Mabel A. Johns, April 7, 1950. *Education:* University of Auckland, Diploma in Journalism, 1934; Diploma in Social Science, 1935. *Home:* 45 Allendale Rd., Mount Albert, Auckland, New Zealand. *Office: New Zealand Herald*, Auckland C.1, New Zealand.

CAREER: Waikato Times, Hamilton, New Zealand, reporter, 1934-37; *New Zealand Herald*, Auckland, reporter, 1937-40, parliamentary and political correspondent, 1949-52, special correspondent in Middle East, 1949, editorial writer, 1952-59, deputy editor, 1959-69, editor, 1969—. *Military service:* Royal Navy, 1940-46; became lieutenant commander, Royal Naval Volunteer Reserve. *Member:* Commonwealth Press Union, Auckland Club.

WRITINGS: The Queen in New Zealand, A. H. & A. W. Reed, 1954; *New Zealand Travel Guide*, A. H. & A. W. Reed, 1959; (editor) *Bold Century*, Wilson & Horton, 1959; (editor) *The New Zealand Herald Manual of Journalism*, A. H. & A. W. Reed, 1967. Foundation editor, *New Zealand Family Doctor*.

*   *   *

HARDY, Edward R(ochie)   1908-

PERSONAL: Born June 17, 1908, in New York, N.Y.; son of Edward Rochie (an insurance rater) and Sarah (Belcher) Hardy; married Marion Dunlap, September 14, 1939; children: Stephen Minear. *Education:* Columbia University, B.A., 1923, M.A., 1924, Ph.D., 1931; Union Theological Seminary, New York, N.Y., S.T.M., 1932; General Theological Seminary, S.T.B., 1933, S.T.M., 1934. *Office:* 12 St. Mark's Court, Jesus College, Cambridge, England.

CAREER: The Protestant Episcopal Church, ordained deacon, 1929, priest, 1932. General Theological Seminary, New York, N.Y., fellow and tutor, 1929-45, instructor in Hebrew, 1940-45; Berkeley Divinity School, New Haven, Conn., associate professor, 1945-47, professor of church history, 1947-69; Cambridge University, Cambridge, England, university lecturer, 1969—, fellow and dean of Jesus College, 1972—. Paddock Lecturer at General Theological Seminary, 1950. Member of Dumbarton Oaks Symposium, Cambridge University, 1967. Member of Joint Commission on Ecumenical Relations of the Episcopal Church, 1955-61, 1964-70; World Council of Churches, delegate to Near East, 1947, 1955, 1959, member of Commission on Faith and Order, 1961—. *Member:* American Historical Society, American Society of Church History (president, 1942), American Oriental Society, Society of Biblical Literature, United Oxford, Cambridge University Club (London). *Awards, honors:* S.T.D., General Theological Seminary, 1950; D.Th., Russian Theological Academy in Paris, 1953; M.A., Cambridge University, 1969.

WRITINGS: (Editor with W. N. Pittinger) *This Holy Fellowship: The Ancient Faith in the Modern Parish*, Morehouse, 1939; *Militant in Earth: Twenty Centuries of the Spread of Christianity*, Oxford University Press, 1941; (with T. J. Bigham) *Christ With Us: Lessons on the Holy Eucharist*, Holy Cross Press (West Park, New York), 1941; (editor) *Orthodox Statements on Anglican Orders for the Advisory Council to the Presiding Bishop on Ecclesiastical Relations*, Morehouse, 1946; (reviser) Frank Elmer Wilson, *Outline of the Episcopal Church*, fifth edition, Morehouse, 1949; *Christian Egypt: Church and People*, Oxford University Press, 1952; (editor with C. C. Richardson) *Christology of the Later Fathers*, Westminster, 1954; (editor) *Faithful Witnesses: Records of Early Christian Martyrs*, Association Press, 1960; (with E. R. Fairweather) *The Voice of the Church: The Ecumenical Council*, Seabury, 1962. Contributor to *Church History, Anglican Theological Review, Eastern Church Review*, and other religious periodicals.

WORK IN PROGRESS: Studies in liturgical history; research on the origins of Christian liturgy in it's Jewish context.

* * *

HARE, Eric B. 1894-

PERSONAL: Born October 12, 1894, in Hawthorn, Victoria, Australia; son of Robert (a minister) and Henrietta (Johnson) Hare; married Agnes T. Fulton, June 24, 1915; children: Eileen N. Hare Higgins, Leonard N., Verna May Hare Feigner, P. Edgar. *Education:* Attended Australasian Missionary College, 1909-13, and Sydney Sanitarium and Hospital Nursing School, 1913-15. *Home:* 8012 Barron St., Takoma Park, Md. 20012.

CAREER: Minister of Seventh Day Adventist Church. Medical missionary in Burma, 1915-34; Sabbath school and youth worker in California, 1934-46, in Washington, D.C., 1946-62; now retired and writing.

WRITINGS: Jungle Stories, Review & Herald, 1927; *Jungle Heroes*, Pacific Press Publishing, 1932; *Clever Queen: A Tale of the Jungle and of Devil Worshipers*, Pacific Press Publishing, 1936, reprinted, 1967; *Those Juniors*, Review & Herald, 1946; *Treasure from the Haunted Pagoda*, Review & Herald, 1948; *Fullness of Joy*, Review & Herald, 1952; *Jungle Flower*, Review & Herald, 1960; *Make God First*, Review & Herald, 1964; *An Irish Boy and God: The Biography of Robert Hare*, Review & Herald, 1965; (editor of revised and enlarged edition) Arthur W. Spalding, *Christian Story Telling*, Pacific Press Publishing, 1965; *Jungle Story Teller*, Review & Herald, 1967; *Fulton's Footprints in Fiji*, Review & Herald, 1969. Also author of *Doctor Rabbit*, published in 1969.

SIDELIGHTS: Pacific Press Publishing has issued twelve of Hare's children's stories as recordings.

BIOGRAPHICAL/CRITICAL SOURCES: Treasure from the Haunted Pagoda, Review & Herald, 1948; *Advancing Together*, Pacific Press Publishing, 1964.

* * *

HARE, Richard (Gilbert) 1907-1966

PERSONAL: Born September 5, 1907, in London; England; son of fourth Earl of Listowel; married Dora Gordine (a sculptor), 1936. *Education:* Attended Balliol College, Oxford, and Sorbonne, University of Paris. *Office:* University of London, London, England.

CAREER: Oxford University, Queen's College, Oxford, England, Laming fellow, 1929; H.M. Diplomatic Service, secretary in London, England, and Paris, France, 1930-34; British Ministry of Information, London, England, 1939-46, became director of Russian division; Stanford University, Stanford, Calif., Rockefeller Foundation fellow at Hoover Institute, 1947; University of London, London, England, lecturer, 1949-59, reader; 1959-62, professor of Slavonic studies, 1962-66. Visiting professor at Indiana University, 1959.

WRITINGS: Russian Literature from Pushkin to the

Present Day, Methuen, 1947, reprinted by Books for Libraries, 1970; *Pioneers of Russian Social Thought*, Oxford University Press, 1951; *Portraits of Russian Personalities Between Reform and Revolution*, Oxford University Press, 1959; *Maxim Gorky*, Oxford University Press, 1962; *The Art and Artists of Russia*, Methuen, 1965. Translator of works of Turgenev and Ivan Bunin. Contributor of articles to *Encyclopaedia Britannica* and *Collier's Encyclopedia*. Also contributor to *Slavonic Review* (England), *Russian Review* (United States), *Connoisseur, History Today*, and to other periodicals.

AVOCATIONAL INTERESTS: Gardening.

(Died September 14, 1966)

* * *

HARGREAVES, Reginald (Charles) 1888-
(Aiguillette)

PERSONAL: Born February 5, 1888, in London, England; son of Henry and Sarah (Squire) Hargreaves. *Education:* Attended Cheltenham College and Royal Military College at Sandhurst. *Politics:* "Good old-fashioned Tory." *Home and office:* Beech Cottage, Wootton St. Lawrence, near Basingstoke, Hampshire, England. *Agent:* Anthony Sheil Associates Ltd., 6 Grafton St., London W.1, England.

CAREER: Career officer in British Army, with service in England, India, and Egypt, 1908-14, in France and Gallipoli, 1914-18; invalided, 1922; recalled to military duty, 1939-45; received Military Cross, 1916, mentioned in dispatches, 1918. Writer, 1922-39, 1945—. *Member:* Royal United Service Institution, United States Naval Institute (associate), Savage Club (London).

WRITINGS: (With Lewis Melville) *In the Days of Queen Anne*, Hutchinson, 1927; (editor with Melville) *Great French Short Stories*, Liveright, 1928; (editor with Melville) *Great German Short Stories*, Liveright, 1929; (with Melville) *Famous Duels and Assassinations*, Jarrolds, 1929, Sears Publishing, 1930; (with Melville) *"Mr. Crofts, the King's Bastard": A biography of James, Duke of Monmouth*, Hutchinson, 1929; (editor with Melville) *Great English Short Stories*, Viking, 1930; *Women-at-Arms: Their Famous Exploits Throughout the Ages*, Hutchinson, 1930; *The Enemy at the Gate: A Book of Famous Sieges, Their Cause, Their Progress, and Their Consequences*, Macdonald & Co., 1946, Military Service Publications, 1948; (self-illustrated) *This Happy Breed: Sidelights on Soldiers and Soldiering*, Skeffington & Son, 1951; *The Narrow Seas*, Sidgwick & Jackson, 1959; *Red Sun Rising: The Siege of Port Arthur*, Lippincott, 1962; *Beyond the Rubicon: A History of Early Rome*, New American Library, 1967; *The Bloodybacks: The British Serviceman in North America and the Caribbean, 1655-1783*, Walker & Co., 1968.

Contributor to *Encyclopaedia Britannica* and *Chamber's Biographical Dictionary*, and to *Quarterly Review, National Review* (Great Britain), *National Review* (United States), *Blackwood's Magazine, American Heritage, Daily Telegraph*, other newspapers, periodicals, and military journals in United States and Great Britain.

WORK IN PROGRESS: Wards of Destiny, A Survey of Anglo-American Relations to 1763.

SIDELIGHTS: Hargreaves told *CA:* "History has always fascinated me as the story of mankind in transition. But there is such a lot of it, and the more you personnaly uncover, the more there seems to be still unexplained. I have a liking for large canvasses, a big theme.... Fully conscious of the fact that it is useless to await inspiration, unless you are a genius—which I am not—I regard writing as a job of work, to be got on with regularly five days a week. This still leaves time for reading, music, a little mid equitation, gardening and just sitting still doing nothing.''

BIOGRAPHICAL/CRITICAL SOURCES: Books and Bookmen, February, 1969.

* * *

HARLOW, Lewis A(ugustus) 1901-

PERSONAL: Born May 5, 1901, in Milton, Mass.; son of Louis and Minna' (Wagner) Harlow. *Education:* Harvard University, A.B. (cum laude), 1923. *Office:* 62 Long Wharf, Boston, Mass. 02110.

CAREER: Author, editor, and publisher, Boston, Mass., 1923-43; advertising writer and editor, Chicago, Ill., 1943-58; self-employed writer, Boston, Mass., beginning 1958.

WRITINGS: Covered Bridges Can Talk, Wake-Brook, 1963. Author of textbooks on music, electronics, thermodynamics, and other subjects. Contributor of articles on music and electronic subjects to magazines.

WORK IN PROGRESS: A study of the semantics of the Russian language.

* * *

HARMS, Ernest 1895-1974

PERSONAL: Born September 12, 1895, in Alsfeld, Germany; son of Karl and Paula (Neuman) Harms; married Elizabeth Scott. *Education:* University of Wuerzburg, Ph.D., 1919; postdoctoral study at University of Paris, 1921-23, University of London, 1924-26, Harvard University and Duke University, 1927-28. *Home:* 158 East 95th St., New York, N.Y. 10028.

CAREER: Internationales Voelkerpsychologisches Institut, director, 1929-34; editor of *Jahrbuch fuer Idealistische Philosophie* and ''Bibliothek des Idealismus'' (a series), 1934-36; clinical psychologist, lecturer, and director of child guidance clinics and conferences in United States, 1936-74. Director of child guidance clinics at Beth David and Grand Central Hospital (New York), 1943-62; New York State Department of Mental Health and Remedial Education, New York, N.Y., psychotherapist, 1962-68; Addiction Service Agency, New York, N.Y., consultant, 1968-72. *Member:* International Society of Analytical Psychology, American Association for the Advancement of Science, American Psychological Association, Society for the Advancement of Education, American Association of University Professors, British Royal Medical Society (fellow), Metropolitan Museum of Art (fellow).

WRITINGS: Hegel und das Zwanzigstejahrhundert, C. Winter (Heidelberg), 1933; *Psychologie und Psychiatrie der Conversion*, A.W. Sijthoff (Leiden), 1939; (editor) *Handbook of Child Guidance*, Child Care Publications, 1947; *Essentials of Abnormal Psychology*, Julian Press, 1953; (editor) *The Psychology of Thinking*, New York Academy of Sciences, 1960; (editor) *The Psychology of the Self*, New York Academy of Sciences, 1962; (editor) *Somatic and Psychiatric Aspects of Childhood Allergies*, Macmillan, 1963; (editor, with Paul Schrieber) *Handbook of Counseling Techniques*, Macmillan, 1964; (editor) *Problems of Sleep and Dream in Children*, Macmillan, 1964; (editor) *Drug Addiction in Youth*, Macmillan, 1965; *Understanding Mental Disorders in Childhood*, Interstate, 1971; *Drugs in Youth*, Pergamon, 1973.

Editor, *Nervous Child, Journal of Child Psychiatry*, 1940-58, *International Monographs on Child Psychology*, 1960-74, *International Journal of Art Therapy*, 1973-74.

(Died July 4, 1974)

* * *

HARNETT, Cynthia (Mary)

PERSONAL: Born in London, England; daughter of William O'Sullivan and Clara (Stokes) Harnett. *Education:* Studied at Chelsea School of Art. *Religion:* Roman Catholic. *Home:* Little Thatch, Binfield Heath, Henley-on-Thames, England.

CAREER: Author and illustrator of children's books, 1930-49, and of historical novels for young people, 1949—. Served in British Censorship during both world wars. *Awards, honors:* Carnegie Medal for outstanding children's book of the year, 1951, for *The Wool-Pack*.

WRITINGS—Self-illustrated, except as indicated: (Compiler) *In Praise of Dogs: An Anthology in Prose and Verse*, illustrated by G. Vernon Stokes, Country Life, 1936; *Velvet Masks*, illustrated by Stokes, Medici Society, 1937; *Getting to Know Dogs*, illustrated by Stokes, Collins, 1947, British Book Centre, 1951; *The Great House*, Methuen, 1949, World Publishing, 1968; *The Wool Pack*, Methuen, 1951, published in America as *Nicholas and the Wool-Pack*, Putnam, 1953; *Ring Out Bow Bells*, Methuen, 1953, published in America as *The Drawbridge Gate*, Putnam, 1954; *The Green Popinjay*, Basil Blackwell, 1955; *Stars of Fortune*, Putnam, 1956; *The Load of Unicorn*, Methuen, 1959, published in America as *Caxton's Challenge*, World Publishing, 1960; *A Fifteenth Century Wool Merchant*, Clarendon Press, 1962; *Monasteries and Monks*, Batsford, 1963, Sportshelf, 1965; *Stars of Fortune*, Longmans Canada, 1966.

Written and illustrated with G. Vernon Stokes: *Junk, the Puppy*, Blackie & Son, 1937; *David's New World: The Making of a Sportsman*, Country Life, 1937; *The Pennymakers*, Eyre & Spottiswoode, 1937; *Banjo, the Puppy*, Blackie & Son, 1938; *To Be a Farmer's Boy*, Blackie & Son, 1940; *Mudlarks*, Collins, 1940; *Mountaineers*, Collins, 1941; *Ducks and Drakes*, Collins, 1942; *Bob-tail Pup*, Collings, 1944; *Sand Hoppers*, Collins, 1946; *Two and a Bit*, Collings, 1948; *Follow My Leader*, Collins, 1949; *Pets Limited*, Collins, 1950.

WORK IN PROGRESS: A historical novel of England in the fifteenth century; a book on historical characters of medieval London.

AVOCATIONAL INTERESTS: Painting, music, gardening, exploring historic places, tombs, and heraldry.

* * *

HARPER, Wilhelmina 1884-1973

PERSONAL: Born April 21, 1884, in Farmington, Me.; daughter of William (an educator) and Bertha (Tauber) Harper. *Education:* Special courses at New York University, New York State Library School, and Columbia University. *Politics:* Democrat. *Religion:* Congregationalist. *Home:* 2385 Waverley St., Palo Alto, Calif. 94301.

CAREER: Queensboro Public Library, New York, N.Y., children's librarian and branch librarian, 1908-18; Pelham Bay Naval Training Station, New York, N.Y., camp library assistant, 1918-19; Young Men's Christian Association, library organizer at Brest, France, 1919, assistant to director of Overseas Service, 1920; American Red Cross, Chicago, Ill., field representative, 1920-21; Kern County Free Library, Bakersfield, Calif., organizer and supervisor of children's work, 1921-28; Redwood City Public Library, Redwood City, Calif., organizer and librarian, 1929-54. Instructor in children's literature at University of California and San Jose State College (now California State University), 1929, and at Riverside Library School, 1929, 1932. Compiler of books for children. *Member:* American Library Association, California Library Association, Redwood City Woman's Club, Palo Alto Woman's Club.

WRITINGS—Anthologies compiled: *Story Hour Favorites*, Century, 1918; *Off Duty: A Dozen Yarns for Soldiers and Sailors*, Century, 1919; *Magic Fairy Tales*, Longmans, Green, 1926; *Fillmore Folk Tales*, Harcourt, 1926; *Stowaway and Other Stories for Boys*, Atlantic, 1928; *The Girl of Tiptop and Other Stories*, Atlantic, 1928; *More Story Hour Favorites*, Century, 1929.

A Little Book of Necessary Ballads, Harper, 1930; *Around the Hearthfire*, Appleton, 1931; *Merry Christmas to You!*, Dutton, 1935, revised edition, 1965; *The Selfish Giant*, McKay, 1935; *Ghosts and Goblins*, Dutton, 1936, revised edition, 1965; *The Gunniwolf and Other Merry Tales* (Junior Literary Guild selection), McKay, 1936; *The Lonely Little Pig* (Junior Literary Guild selection), McKay, 1938; *The Harvest Feast*, Dutton, 1938, revised edition, 1965; *Flying Hoofs*, Houghton, 1939; *Brownie of the Circus* (Junior Literary Guild selection), McKay, 1941; *Wings of Courage*, Appleton, 1941; *Easter Chimes*, Dutton, 1942, revised edition, 1965; *For Love of Country*, Dutton, 1942; *Uncle Sam's Story Book*, McKay, 1944; *Yankee Yarns*, Dutton, 1944; *Where the Redbird Flies*, Dutton, 1946; (with Aimee M. Peters) *The Best of Bret Harte*, Houghton, 1947; *Down in Dixie*, Dutton, 1948; *Dog Show*, Houghton, 1950; *The Gunniwolf*, Dutton, 1967.

School readers with Aymer J. Hamilton; all published by Macmillan: *Treasure Trails*, Volume I: *Pleasant Pathways*, 1928, new edition, 1933, Volume II: *Winding Roads*, 1928, new edition, 1933, Volume III: *Far Away Hills*, 1928, new edition, 1933, Volume IV: *Heights and Highways*, 1929, new edition, 1933; *Mountain Gateways*, 1933; *Journey's End*, 1933.

School readers with Helen Heffernan and Gretchen Waulfing; all published by Sanborn: *All Aboard for Story Land*, 1941, new edition, 1953; *Sails Set for Treasure Land*, 1941, new edition, 1953; *One to Adventure*, 1943, new edition, 1953.

WORK IN PROGRESS: Compiling more books for children.

(Died December 23, 1973)

*   *   *

HARRAR, E(llwood) S(cott)   1905-

PERSONAL: Born January 18, 1905, in Pittsburgh, Pa.; son of Ellwood Scott and Lucetta (Sterner) Harrar; married Marion Green, September 10, 1927; children: Joanne, Carolyn. *Education:* Oberlin College, student, 1922-24; State University of New York College of Forestry, B.S., 1927, M.S., 1928, Ph.D., 1936. *Politics:* Independent. *Religion:* Presbyterian. *Home:* 2228 Cranford Rd., Durham, N.C. 27706. *Office:* School of Forestry, Duke University, Durham, N.C. 27706.

CAREER: University of Washington, Seattle, instructor, 1928-33, assistant professor of forest products, 1933-36;

Duke University, Durham, N.C., associate professor, 1936-45, professor of wood technology, 1945-57, dean of School of Forestry, 1957-67, James B. Duke Professor of Wood Science, 1967—. Consultant to U.S. Army Corps of Engineers, 1952—, and U.S. Army Biological Laboratories, 1960—. *Member:* Society of American Foresters (fellow), Forest Products Research Society (president, 1959-61), International Association of Wood Anatomists (secretary-treasurer, 1938-45), North Carolina Forest Council (president, 1958-59; secretary, 1963-64), Forest Farmers Association, American Forestry Association, North Carolina Forestry Association, Rotary, Torch International. *Awards, honors:* Sc.D., Syracuse University, 1961.

WRITINGS: (With C. J. Hogue) *Douglas-Fir Use Book*, West Coast Lumberman's Association, 1930; *Forest Dendrology*, George E. Minor, 1934; (with William M. Harlow) *Textbook of Dendrology: Covering the Important Forest Trees of the United States and Canada*, McGraw, 1937, 5th edition, 1968; (with J. George Harrar) *Guide to Southern Trees*, McGraw, 1946, 2nd edition, Dover, 1962; (with others) *Forest Products: Their Sources, Production and Utilization*, McGraw, 1950, 2nd edition, 1962; (editor) *Hough's Encyclopaedia of American Woods*, Speller, Volume I, 1957, Volume II, 1958, Volume III, 1963, Volume IV, 1963, Volume V, 1967; *The Major Defects in Southern Hardwood Veneer Logs and Bolts*, U.S. Forest Service, 1966. Contributor to forestry, wood science, and botanical journals.

WORK IN PROGRESS: Research on tropical woods; handbook on the microscopy and identification of the common timbers of Puerto Rico and the Virgin Islands; further volumes in projected fourteen volume *Hough Encyclopaedia of American Woods*.

AVOCATIONAL INTERESTS: Photography and photomicrography.

*   *   *

HARRIS, Chester W(illiam)   1910-

PERSONAL: Born April 27, 1910, in Denver, Colo.; son of Clark J. and Jessie (Nesbit) Harris. *Education:* University of Denver, A.B., 1931; University of Chicago, Ph.D., 1946. *Office:* University of California, Santa Barbara, Calif. 93106.

CAREER: Teacher in public schools in Colorado, 1934-42; University of Chicago, Chicago, Ill., assistant professor of education, 1946-48; University of Wisconsin, Madison, professor of educational psychology, 1948-70; University of California, Santa Barbara, professor of education, 1970—. *Member:* American Psychological Association, American Educational Research Association (president, 1960), Psychometric Society (president, 1967), American Association for the Advancement of Science.

WRITINGS: Measurement of Comprehension of Literature, privately printed, 1948; (editor) Walter Scott Monroe, *Encyclopedia of Educational Research*, 3rd edition (Harris was not associated with earlier editions), Macmillan, 1960; (editor) *Problems in Measuring Change*, University of Wisconsin Press, 1963; (with Herbert J. Klausmeier) *Strategies of Learning and Efficiency of Concept Attainment by Individuals and Groups*, University of Wisconsin, 1964; (editor with Klausmeier) *Analyses of Concept Learning*, Academic Press, 1966.

HARRIS, Cyril 1891-

PERSONAL: Born May 5, 1891, in LaHave, Nova Scotia; Canada; son of George D. and Susan W. (Owen) Harris; married, wife's name, Emily, September 17, 1919; children: Philip, Emily Katharine. Education: Harvard University, A.B., and graduate study; General Theological Seminary, New York, N.Y., B.D. Home: 451 Guinnip Ave., Elmira, N.Y. 14905.

CAREER: Episcopal priest; professor of English, 1926-56, now professor emeritus. Military service: U.S. army, chaplain, 1917-18; became first lieutenant.

WRITINGS: The Religion of Undergraduates, Scribner, 1925; Trumpets at Dawn, Scribner, 1938; Richard Pryne: A Novel of the American Revolution, Scribner, 1941; One Braver Thing, Scribner, 1942; Street of Knives, Little, Brown, 1950; The Trouble at Hungerfords, Little, Brown, 1953; Northern Exposure: A Nova Scotia Boyhood, Norton, 1963.

* * *

HARRIS, Marion Rose (Young) 1925-
(Rose Young)

PERSONAL: Born July 12, 1925, in Cardiff, South Wales; daughter of Robert and Marion (Phillips) Young; married Kenneth Mackenzie Harris (director of a furnishing company), August 18, 1943; children: Roger Mackenzie, Pamela Daphne, Keith Mackenzie. Education: Attended Gillingham School and Cardiff Technical College. Home and office: 29 Pipers Close, Burnham, Buckinghamshire, England.

CAREER: Private secretary to managing director of builder's merchant, 1942-46; free-lance journalist, 1946—; Regional Feature Service, editor, 1964-71. Child care consultant for Here's Health; London correspondent for Irish Leather and Footwear Journal and Futura (fashion trade magazine). Furnishing consultant to builders, architects, and magazines, designing interiors for show houses at Ideal Homes Exhibition, Olympia, London, England, 1963-64, and for building estates in England. Member: Institute of Journalists, Romantic Novelists Association, Society of Authors, Women's Press Club of London.

WRITINGS: Fresh Fruit Dishes, Jenkins, 1963; Making a House a Home, Pan Books, 1963; The Awful Slimmer's Book, Wolfe, 1967; Teach Your Mum Flower Arranging, Wolfe, 1968; (contributor) Dairy Book of Home Management, Milk Marketing Board, 1969. Scriptwriter for British Broadcasting Corp. schools broadcast, "Do Manners Matter," and for "Home This Afternoon" series. Contributor of short stories to magazines; contributor of articles on variety of subjects, including home, fashion, child care, furnishings, and beauty, to provincial newspapers and magazines, trade publications, and women's magazines, including Top Secretary, Homefinder, Cupid Chronicle, Home Overseas, Moneymaker, and Writer's Review.

WORK IN PROGRESS: Flying without an Engine, for David & Charles; Modern Approach to Homemaking, for David & Charles.

BIOGRAPHICAL/CRITICAL SOURCES: Furniture Today, November, 1963.

* * *

HARRIS, Marjorie Silliman 1890-

PERSONAL: Born June 6, 1890, in Wethersfield, Conn.; daughter of George Wells and Elizabeth (Mills) Harris. Education: Mount Holyoke College, A.B., 1913; Cornell University, Ph.D., 1921. Religion: Congregationalist.

CAREER: Teacher in New York and Connecticut, 1913-17; University of Colorado, Boulder, instructor in philosophy, 1921-22; Randolph-Macon Woman's College, Lynchburg, Va., adjunct professor, 1922-25, associate professor, 1925-30, professor of philosophy, 1930-58, became professor emeritus, chairman of department of philosophy, 1934-58. Visiting summer professor, College of William and Mary, 1945. Member: American Philosophical Association, American Society for Aesthetics, American Association of University Women, Association for Symbolic Logic, Royal Institute of Philosophy, Mind Association, Southern Society for Philosophy and Psychology (member of council, 1937-41; president, 1940; life member), Virginia Philosophical Association (member of executive committee, 1945-46; president, 1946), Phi Beta Kappa, Washington Philosophical Club.

WRITINGS: Francisco Romero on Problems of Philosophy, Philosophical Library, 1960. Reviewer for Journal of Philosophy, 1930-33; contributor of articles and reviews to other journals.

AVOCATIONAL INTERESTS: Birds.

* * *

HARRIS, Mary K. 1905-1966

PERSONAL: Born September 22, 1905, in Harrow, Middlesex, England; daughter of Roland E. and Mary (Mackey) Harris. Education: Attended Harrow County School for Girls, 1916-22. Religion: Roman Catholic. Home: 18 Rosslyn Rd., Watford, England.

CAREER: Writer.

WRITINGS: Fear at My Heart, Sheed, 1951; The Wolf, Sheed, 1955; Thomas, Sheed, 1956; I Am Julie (novel), Crowell, 1956 (published in England as My Darling From the Lion's Mouth, Chatto & Windus, 1956; Emily and the Headmistress (juvenile), Faber, 1958; Lucia Wilmot (novel), Chatto & Windus, 1959; Seraphina (juvenile), Faber, 1960; Elizabeth, Sheed, 1962; Helena, Sheed, 1964; Penny's Way (juvenile), Faber, 1964; The Bus Girls (juvenile), Faber, 1965; Jessica On Her Own (juvenile), Faber, 1968.

AVOCATIONAL INTERESTS: History, painting, the Ecumenical Movement.

(Died, 1966)

* * *

HARRISON, Everett F(alconer) 1902-

PERSONAL: Born July 2, 1902, in Skagway, Alaska; son of Norman Baldwin (a clergyman) and Emma (Smith) Harrison; married Arline Prichard (a substitute teacher), June 30, 1930; children: Estelle (Mrs. Richard C. Anderson; deceased), Everett, Jr., James, Arline (Mrs. Robert V. Jones), Ruth (Mrs. James W. Cole). Education: University of Washington, Seattle, B.A., 1923; Princeton University, A.M., 1927; Princeton Theological Seminary, Th.B., 1927; Dallas Theological Seminary, Th.D., 1938; University of Pennsylvania, Ph.D., 1950. Home: 2320 Lambert Dr., Pasadena, Calif. 91101. Office: Fuller Seminary, 135 North Oakland Ave., Pasadena, Calif. 91101.

CAREER: Ordained Presbyterian minister, 1927. Dallas Theological Seminary, Dallas, Tex., instructor in Old Testament, 1928-30, 1932-35, professor of New Testament, 1936-40, 1944-47; Third Presbyterian Church, Chester, Pa., pastor, 1940-44; Fuller Theological Seminary, Pasadena, Calif., professor of New Testament, 1947—. *Member:* Society of Biblical Literature and Exegesis, Evangelical Theological Society, Studiorum Novi Testamenti Societas.

WRITINGS: The Son of God Among the Sons of Men: Studies of the Gospel According to John, W. A. Wilde, 1949, reissued as *Meditations on the Gospel of John: The Son of God Among the Sons of Men*, 1958, reissued as *Jesus and His Contemporaries*, Baker Book, 1970; (reviser) Henry Alford, *Greek Testament*, two volumes, Moody, 1958; (editor) *Baker's Dictionary of Theology*, Baker Book, 1960; (editor with Charles F. Pfeiffer) *The Wycliffe Bible Commentary*, Moody, 1962; *John: A Brief Commentary*, Moody, 1962; *John: The Gospel of Faith*, Moody, 1962; *Introduction to the New Testament*, Eerdmans, 1964; *A Short Life of Christ*, Eerdmans, 1968. Writer of Sunday school lesson materials for American Sunday School Union for twenty-five years.

WORK IN PROGRESS: New Testament editor for revision of *International Standard Bible Encyclopaedia; A Commentary on Acts.*

SIDELIGHTS: Harrison is competent in Greek, Hebrew, Aramaic, German, Latin, and French.

*   *   *

HARRISON, Louise C(ollbran)   1908-

PERSONAL: Born October 13, 1908, in Seoul, Korea; daughter of Herbert Edward and Augusta (Coors) Collbran; married Joseph Quincy Harrison, May 19, 1934 (divorced; former husband now deceased). *Education:* Attended Bennett Junior College, 1926, and Finch College, 1927-28. *Home and office:* Hotel Splendide, Empire, Colo. 80438.

CAREER: Hotel Splendide, Empire, Colo., co-owner, 1955—. President, Empire Street of Flags Association, 1958-64, and Empire Conservation Society, 1964.

WRITINGS: Empire and Berthoud Pass, Big Mountain Press, 1964.

WORK IN PROGRESS: Research in Colorado history; restoration of early buildings in Empire, an early Colorado gold mining town.

*   *   *

HARRISON, Wilfrid   1909-

PERSONAL: Born May 30, 1909, in Glasgow, Scotland; son of William Thomas (in insurance business) and Amy (Livesey) Harrison; married Elizabeth Sara Sweeny, September 25, 1943; children: Linda Caroline, Jean Elizabeth. *Education:* University of Glasgow, M.A., 1931; Queen's College, Oxford, B.A., 1933, M.A., 1937. *Home:* 73, Coten End, Warwick, England. *Office:* University of Warwick, Coventry, Warwickshire, England.

CAREER: Oxford University, Queen's College, Oxford, England, lecturer in politics, 1935-39, fellow and tutor, 1939-57; University of Liverpool, Liverpool, England, professor of politics, 1957-64; Warwick University, Coventry, England, professor of politics and pro-vice-chancellor, 1964-70. Ministry of Supply, temporary civil servant, 1940-45. Local Government Training Board (formerly Local Government Examination Board), member, 1957—. *Member:* Political Studies Association (executive committee, 1953-63; chairman, 1963), American Political Science Association, Royal Institute of Public Administration.

WRITINGS: The Government of Britain, Hutchinson, 1948, Rinehart, 1950, 9th edition, Hutchinson, 1964; (editor and author of introduction) Jeremy Bentham, *A Fragment on Government, and An Introduction to the Principles of Morals and Legislation*, Macmillan, 1948, Barnes & Noble, 1967; *Conflict and Compromise: A History of British Political Thought, 1593-1900*, Free Press, 1965; *Sources in British Political Thought, 1593-1900*, Free Press, 1965. General editor, Basil Blackwell's political texts, 1963—. Contributor of articles to encyclopedias and academic journals. Editor, *Political Studies*, 1953-65.

WORK IN PROGRESS: A study of political concepts and futher work on British government.

AVOCATIONAL INTERESTS: Music and cooking.

*   *   *

HART, Henry Hersch   1886-1968

PERSONAL: Born September 27, 1886, in San Francisco, Calif.; son of Henry Hersch and Etta (Harris) Hart; married Alice Patek Stern, 1912 (died, 1936); married Helen Kramer Ach, August 21, 1941; children: (first marriage) Peggy, Virginia Hart Page (both deceased) *Education:* University of California, Berkeley, A.B., 1907, J.D., 1909. *Home:* 210 Post St., San Francisco, Calif. 94108. *Agent:* Curtis Brown Ltd., 60 East 56th St., New York, N.Y. 10022. *Office:* 2090 Broadway, San Francisco, Calif. 94115.

CAREER: Assistant city attorney, San Francisco, Calif., 1911-18; collector of oriental art, Far East and San Francisco, Calif., 1921-37; University of California, Berkeley, lecturer on Chinese culture, 1932-60; San Francisco State College, San Francisco, Calif., lecturer on Chinese culture, great writers, world history, 1960-68. Guest lecturer at other colleges and universities. Professional public lecturer, 1950-60, with tours including United States, England, Jamaica, and Mexico. Friends of the San Francisco Public Library, president, 1952-60. *Military service:* U.S. Army, Military Police, 1942-43; became major. *Member:* Royal Geographical Society (fellow), Institute of Coimbra, Portugal (medalist), French Academy (officer), American Oriental Society, Classical Association of Canada, Sociedad de Geografia of Lisbon (corresponding member), Hispanic Society of America, Faculty Club of University of California, Commonwealth Club (San Francisco). *Awards, honors:* Gold medal and chain of Institute of Coimbra, Portugal, 1958; gold medal of Commonwealth Club of California for *Sea Road to the Indies*, 1951.

WRITINGS: (Compiler and translator) *A Chinese Market: Lyrics from the Chinese in English Verse*, Routledge, 1931, J. J. Newbegin, 1932; (compiler and translator) *The Hundred Names: A Short Introduction to the Study of Chinese Poetry*, University of California Press, 1933, 3rd edition published as *Poems of the Hundred Names: A Short Introduction to Chinese Poetry*, Stanford University Press, 1954; (translator) Hsi Hsiang Chi, *The West Chamber: A Medieval Drama*, Stanford University Press, 1936; (compiler and translator) *Seven Hundred Chinese Proverbs*, Stanford University Press, 1937; (translator) *A Garden of Peonies* (Chinese poems), Stanford University Press, 1938; *Venetian Adventurer: Being an Account of the Life and Times and of the Book of Messer Marco Polo*, Stanford University Press, 1942, new edition published as *Marco Polo, Venetian Adventurer*, University of Oklahoma Press, 1967; *Sea Road to the Indies: An Account of the*

Voyages and Exploits of the Portuguese Navigators, Macmillan, 1950; *Luis de Camoens and the Epic of the Lusiads*, University of Oklahoma Press, 1962.

Also co-author of *Tamalpais—Enchanted Mountain*, 1946. Contributor to magazines, 1919-68.

WORK IN PROGRESS: A biography of Manuel I of Portugal.

SIDELIGHTS: Hart's books have been translated into Spanish, German, and Polish. *Avocatinal interests:* Photography—he won several blue ribbons in exhibitions.

(Died, 1968)

* * *

HART, Richard (Harry) 1908-

PERSONAL: Born January 5, 1908, in Baltimore, Md.; son of Harry Hassell (a physicist) and Margaret (Murphy) Hart; married Evelyn Linthicum (a librarian and writer), September 4, 1946. *Education:* Attended Baltimore City College, 1923-25, and Pratt Institute School of Library Science, Brooklyn, N.Y., 1930-31. *Home:* 42 East 26th St., Baltimore, Md. 21218. *Office:* Enoch Pratt Free Library, Baltimore, Md. 21201.

CAREER: With U.S. Merchant Marine, 1926-29; with New York Public Library, 1930-31; Enoch Pratt Free Library, Baltimore, Md., assistant, 1931-33, head of literature and language department, 1933-65, program coordinator and moderator of Pratt Library Noon-Hour Forum, 1943—, head of humanities department, 1965—. Historical services board member, U.S. War Department, 1942-46; occasional consultant for various publishers; president, Children's Educational Theatre, 1958—; board member, Vagabond Theatre, 1959-64; member of Governor's commission on outdoor drama, 1962-68, Governor's Commission on Educational Television, 1963-66; first vice-president, Maryland Council for Educational Television; founder and advisor, Baltimore Writers' Forum; chairman, literary awards committee, The Robert Lindner Foundation; honorary member, Johns Hopkins Theatre. *Member:* American Library Association, Adult Education Association of the United States (board member, 1959-61), Edgar Allan Poe Society (vice-president), American Educational Theatre Association, American National Theatre and Academy, Society for Theatre Research, Maryland Library Association, Maryland Association for Adult Education (former president), Tudor and Stuart Club, History of Ideas Club (both Johns Hopkins University), Johns Hopkins Faculty Club.

WRITINGS: (With Charles McCombs) *Currier & Ives, Print Makers to the American People*, New York Public Library, 1931; *Enoch Pratt: The Story of a Plain Man*, Enoch Pratt Free Library, 1935; *Lewis Henry Steiner and His Son, Bernard Christian Steiner*, Enoch Pratt Free Library, 1936; *The Supernatural in Edgar Allan Poe*, Poe Society, 1936; (editor with Arthur H. Quinn) *Edgar Allan Poe: Letters and Documents in the Enoch Pratt Free Library*, Scholars' Facsimiles and Reprints, 1941; *A Winter's Journey* (poems), Contemporary Poetry, 1945; *What Shall Be Done About Japan?*, U.S. Government Printing Office, 1945; *Eclipse of the Rising Sun*, Foreign Policy Association, 1946; *Papers of Identity* (poems), Contemporary Poetry, 1963.

Opera and ballet libretti: "One Thing is Certain" (ballet, by Hugo Weisgall); "The Stronger" (opera, by Weisgall); "Tancred and Clorinda" (opera, by Monteverdi); "The Mistress of the House" (ballet, by various composers); "Picnic at Fontainebleau" (ballet, by various composers); "The Resurrection of Don Juan" (dance play, by Dominick Argento).

Former editor, *Maryland Libraries*. Author of television scripts. Contributor to anthologies and to *Saturday Review, American Historical Review, Poetry, Journal of Adult Education, Adult Leadership, Library Journal, Wilson Library Bulletin, Contemporary Poetry, Johns Hopkins Review, Baltimore Evening Sun, Encyclopedia of the Social Sciences*, and other publications.

WORK IN PROGRESS: Research on a reader's guide to Europe; long-term research interest in Edgar Allan Poe, H. L. Mencken, community theatre development in the United States, and adult education in the humanities.

AVOCATIONAL INTERESTS: Travel (has visited England, Ireland, France, Italy, Spain, Germany, Austria, Switzerland, Canada, Mexico, and most of the states east of the Mississippi), cinema, sailing in the Chesapeake Bay ("I owned a succession of sailing craft from about 1930 until 1958"), riding, skiing, and country walking.

BIOGRAPHICAL/CRITICAL SOURCES: Poetry, September, 1945; *Spirit*, March, 1946, March, 1964; *Contemporary Poetry* (annual), Volume 14, 1954; *Baltimore Sun*, September 23, 1956, October 27, 1970; *Baltimore News-American*, February 2, 1964; *Baltimore Evening Sun*, February 24, 1964.

* * *

HARTENDORP, A(bram) V(an) H(eyningen) 1893-

PERSONAL: Born September 3, 1893, in Haarlem, Holland; came to United States in 1904, became U.S. citizen while a minor; son of Siebe (a painter) and Clasina (van Heyningen) Hartendorp; married second wife, Segunda Amoy, December 23, 1953; children: (first marriage) Esther, Edward, Lilian, Richard, Henry; (second marriage) Paul, Catherine. *Education:* Attended University of Colorado. *Home:* 25 Acacia Rd., Rosario Heights, Quezon City, Philippines.

CAREER: Teacher in Colorado and Wyoming before going to the Philippine Islands as a high school instructor and supervising teacher, 1917-20; *Manila Times*, Manila, Philippines, editor, 1920-23; *Philippine Education* (later *Philippine Magazine*; a monthly), Manila, editor, 1925-33, publisher, 1933-41; part-time adviser and technical assistant to President Quezon and to President Osmena during period 1934-46; *American Chamber of Commerce Journal*, Manila, editor, 1947-67; *Bulletin, American Historical Collection*, Manila, editor, 1972—. Variously professor of English and psychology at University of Manila, University of the Philippines, and University of Santo Tomas. Introduced use of intelligence tests to Philippine schools. *Member:* American Historical Committee, American Association of the Philippines.

WRITINGS: A Few Poems and Essays, privately published, 1951; *Short History of Industry and Trade of the Philippines from Pre-Spanish Times to the End of the Roxas Administration*, American Chamber of Commerce of the Philippines, 1953, enlarged and updated edition published as Volume I: *History of Industry and Trade of the Philippines*, American Chamber of Commerce of the Philippines, 1958, Volume II: *The Magsaysay Administration*, Philippine Education Co., 1961; *Santo Tomas Story*, McGraw, 1964; *The Japanese Occupation of the Philippines*, two volumes, Bookmark, (Manila), 1967.

WORK IN PROGRESS: I Have Lived, an autobiography; *This Mortal Coil*, a collection of poems.

SIDELIGHTS: Santo Tomas Story is taken from Hartendorp's "History of the Santo Tomas Internment Camp and of the Japanese Occupation of the Philippines," a daily record kept at personal peril during his three years of internment. Hartendorp has returned to the United States only once—for a brief visit in 1946—during his fifty-seven years as a resident of the Philippines. His seven children and their descendents (some sixty in all) are Filipinos, but he remains an American citizen; his U.S. citizenship was nullified at one point because of long residence abroad, but restored by special act of Congress.

*   *   *

HARTFORD, Ellis F(ord) 1905-

PERSONAL: Born March 13, 1905, in Fordsville, Ky.; son of Ellis Casnor (a farmer) and Attella (Ford) Hartford; married Alma Barker, December 29, 1939; children: Jane Barker (Mrs. Don Witt Hadley, Jr.), Ellis Ford, Jr. *Education:* University of Kentucky, A.B., 1930, M.A., 1934; Harvard University, Ed. D., 1942. *Religion:* Episcopalian. *Home:* 401 Holiday Rd., Lexington, Ky. 40502. *Agent:* Ann Elmo Agency, Inc., 545 Fifth Ave., New York, N.Y. 10017. *Office:* University of Kentucky, 112 Frazee Hall, Lexington, Ky.

CAREER: High school teacher, principal, and superintendent of schools in Kentucky, 1930-39; Tennessee Valley Authority, Knoxville, Tenn., specialist in instructional materials, 1939-42; University of Kentucky, Lexington, associate professor, 1942-46, professor of education, and chairman of Division of Foundations of Education, 1946-62; Kentucky Council on Public Higher Education, Frankfort, executive secretary, 1962-64; University of Kentucky, dean of Community College System, 1964-70, vice-president for community colleges, 1970, professor of history of education, 1970-74, professor emeritus, 1974—. Educational adviser to Coronet Films, Inc.; member of Governor's Commission on Aging, 1958-63, of White House Conference on Children and Youth, 1960, and of White House Conference on Aging, 1961; member of State Advisory Council on Vocational Education, 1968—; member of board of trustees, Lincoln Foundation, 1968—. *Military service:* U.S. Naval Reserve, 1943-46; became lieutenant commander. *Member:* Philosophy of Education Society, National Council for the Social Studies, National Education Association, History of Education Society, Kentucky Association of Colleges, Secondary, and Elementary Schools (president, 1960-61), Kentucky State Historical Society, Kentucky Civil War Round Table, Filson Club, Kappa Delta Pi, Phi Delta Kappa.

WRITINGS: (With others) *Citizenship Problems for Young Americans*, Lincoln University Publishing Co., 1938; *Our Common Mooring*, University of Georgia Press, 1941; *Moral Values in Public Education*, Harper, 1958; *Teaching as a Career*, Burgess, 1958; *A Plan Book for Future Teachers*, Row, Peterson & Co., 1961; *Education in These United States*, Macmillan, 1964. Author or co-author of six educational bulletins, and of articles on education subjects.

WORK IN PROGRESS: Research for a two-volume work on Kentucky's educational history; other research on the Green River region of Kentucky, on folk expressions related to distance and other subjects, and on the Civil War as it affected the life of common folk.

AVOCATIONAL INTERESTS: Ornithology, tree-planting, poetry, Kentuckiana, Confederate history, regionalism, especially in the South.

*   *   *

HARTWELL, Dickson Jay 1906-

PERSONAL: Born May 1, 1906, in Portland, Ore.; married Patricia Lochridge (a lecturer in international relations), 1953; children: (previous marriage) Kent; (present marriage) Jay, Ware; two stepsons. *Education:* University of Pennsylvania, student, 1924-25. *Politics:* Republican. *Religion:* Presbyterian. *Home:* 6402 East Hummingbird Lane, Paradise Valley, Ariz. 85253.

CAREER: Senior partner in public relations firm, New York, N.Y., 1937-42; vice-president of Robinson Hannagan Associates (public relations), New York, N.Y., 1954-55, member of management committee, 1955-57, after firm was merged into Hill & Knowlton; *Arizonian* (weekly newspaper), Scottsdale, Ariz., contributing editor, 1962-68; now community relations consultant to local business and municipal organizations. *Military service:* U.S. Army Air Forces, 1942-46; became lieutenant colonel. *Member:* Society of Magazine Writers, Overseas Press Club of America, National Press Club, Alpha Tau Omega, Coffee House (New York), University Club (Phoenix), Rotary. *Awards, honors:* First prize for outstanding reporting, Arizona Press Club, 1963; awards for top economic reporting, University of Missouri, School of Journalism, 1965, 1966.

WRITINGS: Dogs Against Darkness: The Story of the Seeing Eye, Dodd, 1942, 3rd edition, 1968; (editor with Andrew Rooney) *Off the Record*, Doubleday, 1952. Nationally syndicated columnist for North American Newspaper Alliance and for Spadea Syndicate. Contributor of more than 150 articles to *Reader's Digest, Saturday Evening Post, This Week, Collier's*, and other national magazines.

WORK IN PROGRESS: A book on land selling schemes.

*   *   *

HARVEY, Ian Douglas 1914-

PERSONAL: Born January 25, 1914, in Fort Wellington, India; son of Douglas (a major, Indian Army) and Ursula (Cundall) Harvey; married Clare Mayhew, 1949; children: Margaret Aylwin, Amanda, Clare. *Education:* Christ Church, Oxford, B.A., 1937, M.A., 1940. *Politics:* Conservative. *Religion:* Church of England. *Home:* Pitwell House, Edington, Bridgwater, Somerset, England.

CAREER: Mather & Crowther (advertising firm), London, England, personal assistant to vice-chairman, 1937-39; W. S. Crawford Ltd. (advertising firm), London, executive, 1945-49, director, 1949-56; British Foreign Office, London, parliamentary secretary to Ministry of Supply, 1956-57, parliamentary under-secretary of state, 1957-58; Colman, Prentis & Varley Ltd. (advertising firm), advertising and public relations consultant, 1959-60, manager of international division, 1960-62, executive director, 1961-62, director, 1962-63; Yardley & Co. Ltd. (perfumers), London, advertising controller, 1963-64, advertising director, 1964-66. Member of Parliament for Harrow East, 1950-58; member of Parliamentary Select Committee for Reform of the Army and Air Force Acts, 1952-54; member of Advisory Committee on Publicity and Recruitment for Civil Defence, 1952-56. Member of council, Royal Borough of Kensington, 1947-52; member of London County Council for South Kensington, 1949-52. Governor, Birbeck College, 1949-52. Delegate of Advertising Association to Advertising Federation of America Convention, Detroit, Mich., 1950; chairman of Press Relations Committee, International Advertising Conference, 1951. *Military service:* Royal Artillery Territorial Regiment, 1939-45; became lieutenant colonel. *Member:* Institute of Practitioners in Advertising, Institute of Public Relations, Royal Automobile Club, Society of Authors, Advertising Association, Writers Guild of Great Britain, London Society of Rugby Union Football Referees.

WRITINGS: Talk of Propaganda, Falcon Press, 1947; *The Technique of Persuasion: An Essay in Human Relationships*, Falcon Press, 1951; *Arms and Tomorrow*, Clowes, 1954; *To Fall Like Lucifer*, (autobiography), Sidgwick & Jackson, 1971. Contributor to *Handbook of Institute of Public Relations*, and to advertising journals.

WORK IN PROGRESS: Public Diplomacy; Portrait of a Party.

* * *

HASLEY, Lucile (Charlotte Hardman) 1909-

PERSONAL: Surname is pronounced *Haze*-lee; born August 6, 1909, in South Bend, Ind.; daughter of H. Monroe (a coal dealer) and Charlotte (Rennoe) Hardman; married Louis Hasley (a professor at University of Notre Dame), June 19, 1935; children: Susan (Mrs. Albert Ysordia), Janet (Mrs. Paul F. Lombardi), Daniel. *Education:* Studied at Milwaukee-Downer College (now Lawrence University), 1927-29, University of Wisconsin, 1930-31, and at South Bend Art Center. *Politics:* Democrat. *Religion:* Roman Catholic. *Home:* 3128 Wilder Dr., South Bend, Ind. 46615.

CAREER: Writer; lecturer on humor, writing, religion, and other topics, 1949—. Founder, Blessed Martin de Porres Society. *Member:* Northern Indiana Artists Association, Gamma Phi Beta. *Awards, honors:* First prize, Catholic Press Association national short story contest, 1948; Christopher Award, 1959.

WRITINGS: Reproachfully Yours, Sheed, 1949; *The Mouse Hunter*, Sheed, 1953; *Saints and Snapdragons*, Sheed, 1958; *Play It Cool, Sister*, Sheed, 1959; (with Betty Mills) *Mind If I Differ?: A Catholic-Unitarian Dialogue*, Sheed, 1964. Contributor to five anthologies and to magazines.

SIDELIGHTS: Mrs. Hasley resided in Europe, 1964-65. *Avocational interests:* Painting.

* * *

HAUSER, Margaret L(ouise) 1909-
(Gay Head)

PERSONAL: Born May 13, 1909, in High Point, N.C.; daughter of Charles Merrimon (a banker) and Annie (Tomlinson) Hauser. *Education:* Salem College, Winston-Salem, N.C., B.A. (magna cum laude), 1929; American Academy of Dramatic Arts, student, 1929-30. *Religion:* Quaker. *Home:* 30 East 38th St., New York, N.Y. 10016. *Office:* Scholastic Magazines and Book Services, 50 West 44th St., New York, N.Y. 10036.

CAREER: High Point Enterprise, High Point, N.C., feature writer, 1933-37; Scholastic Magazines and Book Services (educational publishers), New York, N.Y., 1937-46, editor of *Practical English*, 1946-62, editor of *Co-ed*, 1956—, director of home economics and guidance, 1962—, director of language arts, 1963-66.

WRITINGS—Under pseudonym Gay Head: *Boy Dates Girl: Question and Answer Book*, Scholastic Book Services, 1949, revised edition, 1952; *Hi There, High School: Tips on How to Be Counted in the Crowd, and How to Make Yourself Count in School Life*, Scholastic Book Services, 1953, revised edition, 1955; *Etiquette for Young Moderns: How to Succeed in Your Social Life*, Scholastic Book Services, 1954; *Dear Gay Head* (originally published as *You're Asking Me?*, 1958), Scholastic Book Services, 1958; (with editors of *Co-ed*) *Party Perfect*, Scholastic Book Services, 1959; (with editors of *Co-ed*) *The Co-ed Book of Charm and Beauty*, Scholastic Book Services, 1962; (editor) *First Love* (anthology of short stories), Scholastic Book Services, 1963.

* * *

HAUSER, Marianne 1910-

PERSONAL: Born December 11, 1910, in Strasbourg, France; married Frederic Kirchberger (a concert pianist); children: Michael. *Agent:* Curtis Brown Ltd., 60 East 56th St., New York, N.Y. 10022.

CAREER: Writer. Lecturer, Queen's College. *Awards, honors:* Rockefeller fellowship.

WRITINGS: Dark Dominion (novel), Random House, 1947; *The Living Shall Praise Thee* (novel), Gollancz, 1957, published as *The Choir Invisible*, McDowell, Obolensky, 1958; *Prince Ishmael* (novel), Stein & Day, 1963; *A Lesson in Music* (short stories), Texas University Press, 1964. Contributor of short stories to *Harper's Bazaar*, *Mademoiselle*, and other magazines, and of book reviews to *New York Times, New York Herald Tribune*, and *Saturday Review*.

WORK IN PROGRESS: Fiction.

* * *

HAVELOCK, Eric A. 1903-

PERSONAL: Born June 3, 1903, in London, England; became U.S. citizen, 1955; son of Alfred Henry and Annie Louise (Williams) Havelock; married Ellen Parkinson; married second wife, Christine Mitchell; children: (first marriage) Joan Ellen (Mrs. Richard Wheeler-Bennet), John Eric, Ronald Geoffrey. *Education:* Cambridge University, B.A., 1926, M.A., 1929. *Home:* R.F.D. 1, Merryall, New Milford, Conn. *Office:* 852 Branford College, Yale University, New Haven, Conn.

CAREER: Acadia University, Wolfville, Nova Scotia, assistant professor, later associate professor of classics, 1926-29; Victoria College, Toronto, Ontario, associate professor of classics, 1929-47; Harvard University, Cambridge, Mass., visiting lecturer, 1946-47, associate professor, 1947-51, professor of Greek and Latin, 1951-63, chairman of classics department, 1955-60; Yale University, New Haven, Conn., Sterling Professor of Classics and chairman of classics department, beginning 1963. Princeton University, visiting professor, 1960, 1962. Candidate for South Wellington in Ontario provincial election, 1945. Trustee of Radcliffe College, 1959-63.

MEMBER: American Academy of Arts and Sciences, American Philological Association (life member), Canadian Classical Association (founder; first president, 1945-46). *Awards, honors:* Guggenheim fellow, 1941-42, 1943; honorable mention, Harvard University Book Prize, for *Preface to Plato*, 1962; senior fellow, Center for Hellenic Studies, 1965-66.

WRITINGS: *Lyric Genius of Catullus*, Basil Blackwell, 1939, Russell & Russel, 1967; *Crucifixion of Intellectual Man*, Beacon, 1950, published as *Prometheus, With a Translation of Aeschylus' "Prometheus Bound,"* University of Washington Press, 1968; *The Liberal Temper in Greek Politics*, Yale University Press, 1957; *Preface to Plato*, Harvard University Press, 1963. Contributor to professional journals. Associate editor, *Canadian Forum*, 1936-38; co-founder and associate editor, *Phoenix*.

WORK IN PROGRESS: *Greek Drama*, for Houghton's "Riverside Series"; *Classical Scholarship in America*, for Prentice-Hall; *History of the Greek Mind*, for Harvard University Press.

* * *

HAVIGHURST, Marion Boyd ?-1974

PERSONAL: Daughter of William Waddell (a college president) and Mary (Gates) Boyd; married Walter Havighurst (a writer and professor of English), December 22, 1930. *Education:* Smith College, A.B., 1916; Yale University, M.A., 1926. *Politics:* Independent. *Religion:* Presbyterian. *Home:* Shadowy Hills, Oxford, Ohio.

CAREER: The Western College for Women (now The Western College), Oxford, Ohio, instructor in English, 1920-23; Miami University, Oxford, Ohio, instructor in English, 1926-34; author and poet. *Member:* Ohio Valley Poetry Society, Martha Kinney Cooper Ohioana Library Association, Women's Faculty Club (Miami University). *Awards, honors:* Ohioana Book Award, 1949, for *Song of the Pines*, written with Walter Havighurst.

WRITINGS: *Silver Wands* (poems), Yale University Press, 1923; *Murder in the Stacks*, Lothrop, 1934; (with husband, Walter Havighurst) *High Prairie*, Farrar & Rinehart, 1944; (with Walter Havighurst) *Song of the Pines*, Holt, 1949; (with Walter Havighurst) *Climb a Lofty Ladder*, Holt, 1952; *Strange Island*, World Publishing, 1957; *The Sycamore Tree*, World Publishing, 1960. Contributor of poetry and stories to magazines.

(Died February 24, 1974)

* * *

HAW, Richard Claude 1913-

PERSONAL: Born June 17, 1913, in Estcourt, Natal, South Africa; son of Cyril and Mabel (Visick) Haw; married Vivienne Myra Beater (a teacher), December 27, 1937; children: Julian, Neil, Diane, Martyn. *Education:* Natal University College (now University of Natal), B.A.; University of South Africa, B.A. (with honors). *Home:* 5 Cecil Rd., Greendale, Salisbury, South Rhodesia.

CAREER: Sir J. L. Hulett & Sons Ltd. (sugar industry), Natal, South Africa, research chemist, 1935-37; Tanganyika Government, topographical surveyor, 1937-40; Southern Rhodesia Government, 1946—, land development officer, then teacher and vice-president at Domboshawa School, Salisbury; senior information officer, Southern Rhodesia Information Service, 1964—. *Military service:* H.M. Armed Forces, East African Engineers, 1939-40. *Member:* Royal Geographical Society (fellow), Henderson Research Station Scientific Society, Economic Research Council.

WRITINGS: *The Conservation of Natural Resources*, Faber, 1959; *No Other Home: The Colour Conflict Resolved*, Stuart Manning, 1961, revised edition published as *No Other Home: Co-existence in Africa*, 1962; *Progress in*

African Education (pamphlet), Southern Rhodesia Information Service, 1965; *Land Apportionment in Rhodesia* (pamphlet), Southern Rhodesia Information Service, 1965; *Rhodesia, the Jewel of Africa*, Heinemann, 1966, 3rd edition, 1967. Writer of articles for periodicals.

WORK IN PROGRESS: Community Development.

AVOCATIONAL INTERESTS: Photography, art, music, and sports.

* * *

HAWES, Frances Cooper (Richmond) 1897-

PERSONAL: Born June 22, 1897, in Albany, N.Y.; daughter of Charles Alexander (president of Union College, Schenectady, N.Y.) and Sarah (Locke) Richmond; married Claude MacKinnon Hawes (an Army officer), December 7, 1922; children: Margaret Locke (Mrs. Alan Glendining), Hubert William Richmond. *Education:* Bryn Mawr College, student, 1914-16; Radcliffe College, A.B., 1918. *Home:* Balfour Pl., St. Andrews, Fife, Scotland.

WRITINGS: *Henry Brougham*, J. Cape, 1957, St. Martin's, 1958. Contributor to *Collier's Encyclopedia*.

WORK IN PROGRESS: Research in late eighteenth- and early nineteenth-century English history.

* * *

HAWTHORNE, (Ivy Ellen) Jennie Crawley 1916-

PERSONAL: Born October 28, 1916, in London, England; daughter of James and Susan (Cole) Crawley; married J. F. Hawthorne (squadron leader, Royal Air Force, retired; a lecturer) October 10, 1940; children: Francine, Jennifer, Michael, Jeremy, Katharine, Stephanie, John. *Education:* Plater Hall, Oxford, diploma in economics, 1939. *Politics:* "Uncommitted." *Religion:* Roman Catholic. *Home:* 18 Hawthorn Rd., Wallington, Surrey, England.

CAREER: Lincoln Technical College, Lincoln, England, lecturer, 1944-45; British War Office, London, England, correspondence tutor in economics for armed forces, 1945-47; Nordwest Deutsches Rundfunk, Cologne, Germany, script writer in English for Schools Broadcasting Service, 1954-56; Institute of Further Education, Carshalton, Surrey, England, lecturer in English literature, 1962-65; Southwest London College, London, England, lecturer in economics, 1965—. *Member:* Institute of Journalists.

WRITINGS: *The Mystery of the Blue Tomatoes*, Harrap, 1958; *David and the Penny Red*, Harrap, 1962; *All About Money*, W. H. Allen, 1970. Contributor to technical magazines, religious papers, and periodicals.

WORK IN PROGRESS: A novel, entitled *Wo-man*.

SIDELIGHTS: Ms. Hawthorne told *CA*: "[I] would like to be a novelist, but am simply a writer, writing on anything from dustbins to infant feeding, from church architecture to camping holidays—anything that provides interest, enlightenment, or amusement for readers and will be paid for, preferably munificently, by a perspicacious editor. My seven children have supplied me with seven good reasons for writing for money, and seven good causes on which to spend it. Now that the last child has started school, and I no longer have anybody to provide copy or noises, I shall have to fall back on the empty resources of my own mind, and work in the frightening quietude of an empty house."

* * *

HAY, Sara Henderson 1906-

PERSONAL: Born November 13, 1906, in Pittsburgh, Pa.;

daughter of Ralph Watson and Daisy Henderson (Baker) Hay; married Nikolai Lopatnikoff (a composer and professor of musical composition at Carnegie-Mellon University), January 27, 1951. *Education:* Attended Brenau College, 1926-1928, and Columbia University, 1928-31. *Home:* 5448 Bartlett St., Pittsburgh, Pa. 15217.

CAREER: Poet. Charles Scribner's Sons, New York, N.Y., staff member in rare book department, 1935-42. *Member:* Alpha Gamma Delta, Sigma Alpha Iota (patroness). *Awards, honors:* Kaleidograph Book Award, 1933, for *Field of Honor*; Edna St. Vincent Millay Memorial Award of Poetry Society of America for outstanding volume of poetry published in 1951, for *The Delicate Balance*; John David Leitch Memorial Award, 1955; *Lyric* Award, 1959; Pegasus Award, 1960, for *The Stone and the Shell*; named Distinguished Daughter of Pennsylvania, 1963.

WRITINGS—Poetry: Field of Honor, Kaleidograph Press, 1933; *This, My Letter*, Knopf, 1939; *The Delicate Balance*, Scribner, 1951; *The Stone and the Shell*, University of Pittsburgh Press, 1959; *Story Hour*, Doubleday, 1963; *A Footing on This Earth: New and Selected Poems*, Doubleday, 1966.

Editor: *Stevenson Home Book of Shakespeare Quotations*, Scribner, 1937.

Poems published in anthologies, textbooks, and in journals, including *Atlantic Monthly, Harper's, New Yorker, Voices, Saturday Review*, and *Lyric*.

SIDELIGHTS: Describing Miss Hay's poetry, *Booklist* reviewers wrote: "Nature, children, gardens, friendship, and woman's lot figure prominently in poems lighted occasionally by a sparkle of ironic wit or an unexpected wry humor." Although Ray Smith feels that the poems "lack ... tension or poetic excitement," other critics believe that such qualities would be an imposition on the familiar, "fragile" subjects about which she writes. "What is memorable to her," wrote E. L. Walton, "is not any moment of illumination, but the daily event; the small communications between people or animals which make for a kind of wholeness."

BIOGRAPHICAL/CRITICAL SOURCES: Booklist, July 1, 1959; *New York Herald Tribune Book Review*, July 19, 1959; *Poetry*, January, 1960.

* * *

HAYDN, Hiram   1907-1973

PERSONAL: Born November 3, 1907, in Cleveland, Ohio; son of Howell Merriman (a college professor) and Mary (Olmstead) Haydn; married Rachel Hutchinson Norris, September 14, 1935; married second wife, Mary Wescott Tuttle, June 5, 1945; children: (first marriage) Mary (Mrs. M. H. Webb); (second marriage) Michael Wescott, Jonathan Olmstead, Miranda Merriman. *Education:* Amherst College, A.B., 1928; Western Reserve University (now Case Western Reserve University), M.A., 1938; Columbia University, Ph.D., 1942. *Home:* 3620 Walnut St., Philadelphia, Pa. 19104. *Office:* Harcourt, Brace, Jovanovich, 757 Third Ave., New York, N.Y. 10017; also *American Scholar*, 1811 Q St. N.W., Washington, D.C. 20009.

CAREER: Hawken School, Cleveland, Ohio, instructor in English, 1928-41; Western Reserve University (now Case Western Reserve University), Cleveland College, Cleveland, Ohio, lecturer in English, 1938-41; University of North Carolina, Greensboro, assistant professor, 1942-43,

associate professor of English, 1943-44; United Chapters of Phi Beta Kappa, New York, N.Y., executive secretary, 1944-45; *American Scholar*, Washington, D.C., editor, 1944-73; Crown Publishers, New York, N.Y., associate editor, 1945-48, editor-in-chief, 1948-50; Bobbs-Merrill Co., Inc., Indianapolis, Ind., New York editor, 1950-54; Random House, New York, N.Y., senior editor, 1955-56, editor-in-chief, 1956-59; Atheneum Publishers, New York, N.Y., co-founder, 1959, member of executive committee and a director, 1959-64; associated with William Jovanovich, chairman of Harcourt, Brace, Jovanovich, in the publication of a dozen books yearly under Haydn's editorship and Harcourt's imprint, 1964-73. New School for Social Research, instructor, 1946-60; University of Pennsylvania, Philadelphia, professor of communications, 1965-73.

MEMBER: Modern Language Association of America, American Association of University Professors, Phi Beta Kappa, Alpha Delta Phi. *Awards, honors:* Litt.D., Western Reserve University (now Case Western Reserve University), 1962; Ohioana Award for the best book of fiction published by an Ohioan, 1963, for *The Hands of Esau*.

WRITINGS: The Fool's Christmas: A Christmas Play for Boys (three-act), Samuel French, 1937; (editor with Winfield H. Rogers and Ruby V. Redinger) *Explorations in Living: A Record of the Democratic Spirit*, two volumes (also a one-volume edition), Reynal, 1941, briefer edition without novel *Fathers and Sons*, 1941; *By Nature Free* (novel), Bobbs-Merrill, 1943; *Manhattan Furlough* (novel), Bobbs-Merrill, 1945; (editor and author of introduction) *The Portable Elizabethan Reader*, Viking, 1946; (editor with John Cournos) *A World of Great Stories*, Crown, 1947; *The Time Is Noon* (novel), Crown, 1948; (editor with Edmund Fuller) *A Thesaurus of Book Digests: Digests of the World's Permanent Writings from the Ancient Classics to Current Literature*, Crown, 1949; *The Counter-Renaissance*, Scribner, 1950; (editor with John Charles Nelson) *A Renaissance Treasury: A Collection of Representative Writings of the Renaissance on the Continent of Europe*, Doubleday, 1953; (editor with Katherine Gauss Jackson) Christian Gauss, *Papers*, Random House, 1957; (editor with Betsy Saunders) *The American Scholar Reader*, Atheneum, 1960; *The Hands of Esau* (novel; first in projected trilogy, "The Generations of Adam"), Harper, 1962; *Report from the Red Windmill* (novel), Harcourt, 1967.

General editor, with Donald Bigelow, of the "Makers of American Tradition" series, Bobbs-Merrill; general editor of Scribner's "Twentieth Century Library" series.

Contributor to *Collier's, Reader's Digest, New York Times Magazine, Sewanee Review* and other periodicals.

WORK IN PROGRESS: Words and Faces, an autobiography, for Harcourt; *Q's Trip*, a novel; a play, "The Garden."

SIDELIGHTS: Haydn was known as an editor who worked closely with his authors, some of whom included Anais Nin, William Faulkner, William Styron, Mario Puzo, Pearl Bailey, and Martha Graham.

Haydn told *CA:* "In my later novels, my consuming interest has been with the themes of the relation of reality and illusion and that of commitment and mortality."

(Died December 2, 1973)

* * *

HAYDON, Glen   1896-1966

PERSONAL: Born December 9, 1896, in Inman, Kan.; son

of William Leslie (a businessman) and Ursula (Parker) Haydon; married Helen Bergfried, September 14, 1922; children: Glen Bergfried, Valeska (Mrs. David M. Howell). *Education:* University of California, Berkeley, A.B., 1918, M.A., 1921; University of Vienna, Ph.D., 1932. *Home:* 303 Laurel Hill Rd., Chapel Hill, N.C. 27514. *Office:* Department of Music, University of North Carolina, Chapel Hill, N.C. 27514.

CAREER: Berkeley High School, Berkeley, Calif., instructor in music, 1920-25; University of California, Berkeley, instructor, 1920-23, assistant professor of music, 1925-28, chairman of the department, 1928-34; University of North Carolina, Chapel Hill, professor of music, 1934-51, Kenan Professor, 1951-66, chairman of the department, 1934-66, chairman of division of humanities, 1950-56. Louis C. Elson Lecturer, Library of Congress, 1947; visiting professor at University of Michigan, 1947, University of California, Los Angeles, and Harvard University, 1956. *Military service:* U.S. Army, Infantry, 1917-19; became sergeant.

MEMBER: International Musicological Society, International Music Library Association, International Folk Music Council, American Musicological Society (president, 1942-44), Music Teachers National Association (president, 1940-42), College Music Society, Music Library Association, American Association of University Professors, National Association of Schools of Music (member of graduate committee, 1942-47), National Association for Music in Liberal Arts Colleges, Music Educators National Conference (member of national board, 1937-41), Royal Musical Society, American Council of Learned Societies (member of committee on musicology, 1934-48, chairman, 1941-48), Mediaeval Academy of America, Society for Ethnomusicology, Southern Humanities Conference, North Carolina State Music Teachers Association (president, 1937-40), Phi Mu Alpha, Phi Delta Kappa, Pi Kappa Lambda.

WRITINGS: A Graded Course of Clarinet Playing, Fischer, 1927; *Fundamentals of Music,* University of California Radio Service, 1933; *The Evolution of the Six-Four Chord: A Study in the History of Dissonance Treatment,* University of California Press, 1933; (translator and author of introduction) Knud Jeppesen, *Counterpoint: The Polyphonic Vocal Style of the Sixteenth Century,* Prentice-Hall, 1939; *Introduction to Musicology: A Survey of the Fields, Systematic and Historical, of Musical Knowledge and Research,* Prentice-Hall, 1941, 2nd edition, University of North Carolina Press, 1959; (contributor) Max Schoen, editor, *The Enjoyment of the Arts,* Philosophical Library, 1944; *On the Meaning of Music* (lecture), U.S. Government Printing Office, 1948; (transcriber and editor) Constanzo Festa, *Hymni per totum annum,* Pontificum Institutum Musicae Sacrae (Rome), 1958, University of North Carolina Press, 1959; (editor) F. Corteccia, *Hinnario secondo l'uso della chiesa romana et fiorentina,* World Library of Sacred Music, numbers 1-5, 1958, numbers 6-10, 1960. Contributor to *Collier's Encyclopedia,* and of about thirty-five articles to music publications.

WORK IN PROGRESS: Study of the history of the polyphonic hymn.

SIDELIGHTS: Haydon visited Russia in 1961 under U.S. State Department Cultural Exchange Program. He was competent in Latin, German, French, Spanish, Italian, and Russian. *Avocational interests:* Golf, chamber music, and foreign languages.

BIOGRAPHICAL/CRITICAL SOURCES: Friedrich Blume, editor, *Die Musik in Geschichte und Gegenwart,* Barenreiter, 1949; Almonte C. Howell, *Kenan Professorships,* University of North Carolina Press, 1956; *New York Times,* May 9, 1966.

(Died May 8, 1966)

*   *   *

HAYES, John F. 1904-

PERSONAL: Born August 5, 1904, in Dryden, Ontario, Canada; son of John George (a merchant) and Jeannette (Houck) Hayes; married Helen Eleen Casselman; children: John Terrence, William Frederick, Nancy Diane (Mrs. J. Nicolson). *Education:* Attended University of Toronto evening classes for twelve years. *Politics:* Liberal. *Religion:* United Church of Canada. *Home and office:* 53 Bennington Heights Dr., Toronto, Ontario, Canada.

CAREER: Writer, Maclean-Hunter Publishing Co., Toronto, Ontario, 1925-27, Saturday Night Press, Toronto, 1928; General Motors of Canada, sales promotion writer, 1929-30; Brigdens Ltd., head of creative department, 1930-34, assistant sales manager, 1935; Moffats Ltd., sales promotion manager, 1937-40; Southam Press Ltd., Toronto, Ontario, 1940-54, sales manager 1943-46, vice-president and general manager, 1947-50, vice-president and general manager of Montreal branch, 1950-54, later member of board of directors and of executive committee; Southam Printing Co., Toronto, Ontario, managing director, 1954-60; retired because of ill health, 1961. Member of board of directors, Toronto Graphic Arts Association.

MEMBER: Canadian Authors Association, Canadian Historical Society, National Club (Toronto). *Awards, honors:* Governor General's Literary Award for best juvenile book of the year, 1952, for *A Land Divided,* and, 1954, for *Rebels Ride at Night;* Quebec Scientific and Literary Award, 1955; Book-of-the-Year for Children Medal from Canadian Library Association, 1958, for *The Dangerous Cove;* Vicky Metcalf Award ($1,000), 1964, for inspirational writing for Canadian youth.

WRITINGS—Juvenile: *Buckskin Colonist,* Blackwell, 1949; *Treason at York,* Copp, 1949; *A Land Divided,* Copp, 1951; *Rebels Ride at Night,* Copp, 1953; *Bugles in the Hills,* Messner, 1956; *The Dangerous Cove: A Story of the Early Days in Newfoundland,* (Junior Literary Guild selection), Copp, 1957, Messner, 1960; *Quest in the Cariboo,* Copp, 1960; *The Flaming Prairie,* Copp, 1965; *The Steel Ribbon,* Copp, 1967; *The Nation Builders,* Copp, 1968; *Wilderness Mission: The Story of Sainte-Marie-Among-the-Hurons,* Ryerson, 1969.

Also author of *The Renovation Industry,* 1960, and *Bookkeeping for the Small Printer,* 1962. Writer of several school plays for Canadian Broadcasting Corp. and a six-month radio series on industry familiarization. Article anthologized in *The Atlas Christmas Anthology of Canadian Stories;* other articles contributed to ethnic newspapers in Canada.

SIDELIGHTS: Hayes's youth books have been published in United States, England, and West Germany, and in school editions for Canadian classroom study. They also have been dramatized on Canadian Broadcasting Corp. radio and television.

*   *   *

HAYES, Wayland J(ackson) 1893-1972

PERSONAL: Born November 30, 1893, in Morgantown,

W. Va.; son of Ulysses S. and Mary Etta (Evans) Hayes; married Mary Lulu Turner, July 13, 1916; children: Wayland Jackson, Jr., Mary Virginia, Carolyn Turner (Mrs. Martin L. Ball, Jr.), Sarah Elizabeth (Mrs. Nat Swann, Jr.). *Education:* University of Virginia, B.S., 1919, M.S., 1921; Columbia University, Ph.D., 1930. *Politics:* Independent. *Religion:* Presbyterian. *Home:* 223 Lauderdale Rd., Nashville, Tenn.

CAREER: Teacher and principal in Virginia rural schools, 1914-15, and in Charlottesville (Va.) high school, 1916-25; Jamaica Teachers College, Jamaica, Long Island, N.Y., teacher of education, 1927-28; Vanderbilt University, Nashville, Tenn., assistant professor, 1928-38, associate professor, 1938-41, became professor of sociology, 1941, and professor in School of Nursing, 1935, also served as chairman of department of sociology. *Member:* American Sociological Society, American Statistical Association, National Education Association, Southern Sociological Society (chairman of committee on teaching sociology, 1937-44; president, 1948-49), Phi Delta Kappa.

WRITINGS: Some Factors Influencing Participation in Voluntary School Group Activities, Bureau of Publications, Teachers College, Columbia University, 1930; (with Irwin V. Shannon) *Visual Outline of Introductory Sociology*, Longmans, Green, 1935; (with Anthony Netboy) *The Small Community Looks Ahead*, Harcourt, 1947; (with Rena Gazaway) *Human Relations in Nursing*, Saunders, 1955, 3rd edition, 1964. Contributor of articles to encyclopedias and professional journals.

(Died June 18, 1972)

* * *

HAYS, Brooks 1898-

PERSONAL: Born August 9, 1898, in London, Ark.; son of A. Steele (an attorney) and Sallie (Butler) Hays; married Marion Prather, February 2, 1922; children: Betty Brooks (Mrs. William E. Bell), M. Steele. *Education:* University of Arkansas, B.A., 1919; George Washington University, J.D., 1922. *Politics:* Democrat. *Religion:* Baptist. *Home:* 314 Second St. S.E., Washington, D.C. 20003. *Office:* Wake Forest University, Box 7227, Winston-Salem, N.C. 27109.

CAREER: Admitted to Arkansas Bar, 1922; attorney in Russellville, Ark., 1922-25; assistant attorney-general of Arkansas, 1925-27; Hays & Turner (law firm), Little Rock, Ark., member and partner, 1928-34; U.S. Department of Agriculture, various posts, including assistant director of rural rehabilitation, Farm Security Administration, 1935-42; elected to U.S. Congress in 1942 and served as Representative from Fifth District of Arkansas, 1943-59; Tennessee Valley Authority, Knoxville, Tenn., a director, 1959-61; U.S. Department of State, assistant secretary of state for congressional relations, 1961; special assistant to the President of the United States, 1962-64; Rutgers University, New Brunswick, N.J., Arthur T. Vanderbilt Professor of Public Affairs, 1964-66. Distinguished visiting professor of government, University of Massachusetts, 1966-67. Consultant to President Lyndon B. Johnson. Democrat national committeeman for Arkansas, 1932-39; delegate to United Nations General Assembly, 1955. President of Arkansas Conference of Social Work, 1932-34, of Southern Baptist Convention, 1957-59. Member of governing board of George Peabody College for Teachers and George Washington University. National chairman of Brotherhood Week, 1964; chairman, Governor's Good Neighbor

Council of North Carolina, 1970—. *Military service:* U.S. Army, 1918.

MEMBER: American Bar Association, Former Members of Congress (chairman), Phi Beta Kappa, Lions Club (Arkansas district governor, 1925-27), Masons. *Awards, honors:* Honorary degrees from colleges and universities, including Stetson University, University of the Pacific, Mercer University, College of the Ozarks, William Jewell College; Silver Buffalo award, Boy Scouts of America; named layman of the year by Religious Heritage Foundation, 1959.

WRITINGS: This World: A Christian's Workshop, Broadman, 1958; *A Southern Moderate Speaks*, University of North Carolina Press, 1959; (with John E. Steely) *The Baptist Way of Life*, Prentice-Hall, 1963; *Hotbed of Tranquility: My Life in Five Worlds*, Macmillan, 1968. Contributor of articles to *Look, New York Times Magazine*, and to civic and religious periodicals.

BIOGRAPHICAL/CRITICAL SOURCES: New York Times Book Review, June 28, 1968; *Christian Century*, February 19, 1969.

* * *

HAYWARD, Richard 1893-

PERSONAL: Born October 24, 1893, in Larne, Northern Ireland; son of Walter Scott and Louise (Ivy) Hayward; married Elma Nelson (an actress), July 12, 1916 (deceased); married Dorothy Gamble (a poet and archivist), February 27, 1962; children: Dion Nelson, Richard Scott. *Education:* Attended Belfast College of Technology. *Politics:* Union/Conservative. *Religion:* Church of Ireland. *Home:* 352 Antrim Rd., Belfast 15, Northern Ireland. *Office:* 7 Bedford St., Belfast 2, Northern Ireland.

CAREER: Lecturer, broadcaster, journalist, singer of Irish ballads, recording artist, harpist, and folklore specialist. Justice of the peace, Belfast, Ireland. Committee member, Belfast City Libraries and Transport Museum. *Member:* P.E.N. (former chairman, Belfast), Young Ulster Society (former president), Belfast Naturalists Field Club (former president), Belfast Gramophone Society (former president). *Awards, honors:* D.Litt., Lafayette College, Easton, Pa.; officer, Order of the British Empire.

WRITINGS: The Jew's Fiddle, Talbot Press, 1917; *Love in Ulster*, Talbot Press, 1922; *Ulster Songs and Ballads*, Duckworth, 1925; *Sugarhouse Entry: A Novel of the Ulster Countryside*, Arthur Barker, 1936; *In Praise of Ulster*, Arthur Barker, 1938, 5th edition, Mullan & Son, 1946; *Where the River Shannon Flows*, Harrap, 1940, 2nd edition, Arthur Barker, 1950; *The Corrib Country*, Dundalgan Press, 1943; *In the Kingdom of Kerry*, Dundalgan Press, 1946; *This Is Ireland*, Arthur Barker, Volume I: *Leinster and the City of Dublin*, 1949, Volume II: *Ulster and the City of Belfast*, 1950, Volume III: *Connacht and the City of Galway*, 1952, Volume IV: *Mayo, Sligo, Leitrim and Roscommon*, 1955; *Belfast Through the Ages*, Dundalgan Press, 1952; *The Story of the Irish Harp*, Arthur Guiness, 1954; *Border Foray*, Arthur Barker, 1957; *Munster and the City of Cork*, Phoenix House, 1964.

WORK IN PROGRESS: Research in Irish dialects, ballads, archaeology, and history.

AVOCATIONAL INTERESTS: History of wine and viniculture, geology, botany, folklore, and field studies.

HAZEN, Allen T(racy)   1904-

PERSONAL: Born November 4, 1904, in Portland, Conn.; son of Carleton (a clergyman) and Julia (Trask) Hazen; married Edith Patterson (an editor), September 6, 1945; children: Allen Patterson. *Education:* Yale University, B.A., 1927, Ph.D., 1935; Harvard University, M.A., 1932. *Religion:* Presbyterian. *Home:* 460 Riverside Dr., New York, N.Y. 10027.

CAREER: American College, Tarsus, Turkey, tutor, 1927-30; Romford School, Washington, Conn., master, 1930-31; Yale University, New Haven, Conn., instructor in English, 1935-40, research assistant in bibliography in university library, 1940-42; Hunter College (now Hunter College of the City University of New York), New York, N.Y., instructor in English, 1942-45; University of Chicago, Chicago, Ill., associate professor of English and bibliographer in university library, 1945-46, professor of English and director of library, 1946-48; Columbia University, New York, N.Y., professor of English, 1948-71, professor emeritus, 1971—. *Member:* American Library Association, Modern Language Association of America, Bibliographical Society of America, Bibliographical Society (London), Cambridge Bibliographical Society, Oxford Bibliographical Society, Phi Beta Kappa. *Awards, honors:* Guggenheim fellow, 1952-53.

WRITINGS: Samuel Johnson's Prefaces and Dedications, Yale University Press, 1937; (with R. W. Chapman) *Johnsonian Bibliography*, 1939; *Bibliography of the Strawberry Hill Press*, Yale University Press, 1942; *Bibliography of Horace Walpole*, Yale University Press, 1948; *Catalogue of Walpole's Library*, three volumes, Yale University Press, 1969. Contributor of articles on literary and bibliographical topics to periodicals. General editor, "Yale Edition of Samuel Johnson's Works," 1958-66.

*   *   *

HEAL, Jeanne (Bennett)   1917-

PERSONAL: Born May 25, 1917, in Cambridge, England; daughter of Victor (an architect) and Florence (Reynolds) Heal; married Philip Bennett (an architect); children: Christopher, Louise. *Education:* Attended Benenden School, Ecole du Louvre, and Architectural Association School, London, England. *Politics:* Socialist. *Religion:* Church of England. *Home:* 7 Park Village West, London N.W.1, England. *Office:* c/o British Broadcasting Corp., London W.1, England.

CAREER: Staff reporter for *Oxford Mail*, Oxford, England, 1937-38, *Birmingham Gazette*, Birmingham, England, 1938-39; Armstrong-Warden Ltd. (advertising), London, England, copywriter, 1939-41; *Picture Post*, London, England, staff writer, 1941-45; *Sunday Graphic* and *Sunday Chronicle*, London, England, columnist, 1945-50. Freelance reporter and interviewer for British Broadcasting Corp., London, England, 1940—, with own regular television program, 1947-58. Public lecturer; qualified scientific graphologist. During World War II served as Land Girl, canteen worker, and in Auxiliary Territorial Service. *Member:* National Union of Journalists, International P.E.N. (London).

WRITINGS: Interior Decorating—Your Career, Jordan & Sons, 1946; *Planning the Ideal Home*, Daily Mail Press, 1956; *Jeanne Heal's Book of Careers for Girls*, Bodley Head, 1958; *A Thousand and One Australians*, M. Joseph, 1959; *New Zealand Journey*, Heinemann, 1963.

WORK IN PROGRESS: Writing about graphology and practicing as a handwriting consultant.

AVOCATIONAL INTERESTS: Natural history, especially butterflies and seashells; opera, botanical watercolor painting, gardening, embroidery.

*   *   *

HEAP, Desmond

PERSONAL: Son of William (an architect) and Minnie (Robinson) Heap; married Adelene Mai Lacey, October 27, 1945; children: Sally, Joanna, John. *Education:* Victoria University of Manchester, LL.B. (honors), 1929, LL.M., 1937. *Home:* Quarry House, Oakhill Rd., Sevenoaks, Kent, England. *Office:* Guildhall, London E.C.2, England.

CAREER: Admitted as solicitor, Supreme Court (honors), 1933; City of Leeds, England, 1933-47, successively assistant solicitor, prosecuting solicitor, and deputy town clerk; Corporation of City of London, England, comptroller and city solicitor, 1947—. Colonial Office Town Planning Advisory Panel, member, 1953—; examiner in law for Town Planning Institute and University of London. British Foreign Office, lecturer in Germany, 1946, 1947; lecturer on town planning in Uganda, 1955, Trinidad, 1959, 1960; also lecturer at Harvard University, Cornell University, and University of Pennsylvania, 1960, at University of Chicago, University of California (Los Angeles and Berkeley), University of Utah, University of Wisconsin, 1965 and 1968, at Washington University, Arizona State University, University of Oklahoma, University of North Carolina, Georgia Institute of Technology, Tulane University, 1971. *Member:* American Bar Association (fellow), Law Society (member of council; vice-president, 1971), Royal Institution of Chartered Surveyors (council), Town Planning Institute (president, 1955), Worshipful Company of Solicitors of City of London (junior warden), Worshipful Company of Carpenters of City of London (liveryman), British Red Cross Society (deputy president, City of London branch). *Awards, honors:* Appointed Knight Bachelor, 1970.

*WRITINGS—*All published by Sweet & Maxwell, except as indicated: *Planning Law for Town and Country*, 1939; *Planning and the Law of Interim Development*, 1944; *The Town and Country Planning Act, 1944*, 1945; *An Outline of Planning Law 1943-1945*, 1945; *The New Town Act, 1946*, 1947; *Introducing the Town and Country Planning Act, 1947*, Law Society, 1947; *Encyclopedia of Planning, Compulsory Purchase and Compensation*, Volume I, 1949; *An Outline of the New Planning Law*, 1949, 2nd edition published as *An Outline of Planning Law*, 1955, 5th edition, 1969; (with Philip Ernest Ricardo) *Heap on the Town and Country Planning Act, 1954*, 1955; (with others) *Town Planning Appeals*, Law Society, 1957; *Title on "Housing," Halsbury's Laws of England*, 3rd edition, Butterworth & Co., 1958; (editor) *Encyclopedia of the Law of Town and Country Planning*, 1959; *Development Plans—Their Status, Making, Review and Effect*, Law Society, 1961; (contributor) *Law and Land—Anglo-American Practice*, Harvard University Press, 1963; *Introducing the Land Commission Act, 1967*, 1967; (editor) *Encyclopedia of Betterment Levy and Land Commission Law and Practice*, 1967; *The New Town Planning Procedures: How They Affect You*, 1968. Member of editorial board, *Journal of Planning and Property Law*, 1948—.

*   *   *

HEASMAN, Kathleen Joan   1913-

PERSONAL: Born June 24, 1913, in Southsea, England;

daughter of Thomas William and Gladys R. (Salmon) Archer; married Roy Ernest Heasman (a banker), June, 1941. *Education:* Walthamstow Hall, student, 1928-32; Girton College, Cambridge, economics tripos, 1935; Bedford College, London, Ph.D., 1960. *Home:* High-and-Over, West View Rd., Warlingham, Surrey, England. *Office:* Queen Elizabeth College, University of London, Campden Hill, London W.8, England.

CAREER: University of Hong Kong, Hong Kong, lecturer in economics, 1936-45; Queen Elizabeth College, University of London, London, England, lecturer in social studies, 1947—. Held in civilian internment camp, Hong Kong, 1941-45. *Member:* British Sociological Association.

WRITINGS: Evangelicals in Action: An Appraisal of Their Social Work in the Victorian Era, Bles, 1962; *Christians and Social Work*, S.C.M. Press, 1965; *Army of the Church*, Lutterworth, 1968; *An Introduction to Pastoral Counselling for Social Workers, the Clergy, and Others*, Constable, 1969.

WORK IN PROGRESS: The Study of Society, for Allen & Unwin; *The Social and Human Aspects of Home Economics*, for Routledge & Kegan Paul.

* * *

HEATH, (Charles) Monro   1899-1966

PERSONAL: Born October 6, 1899, in Colorado Springs, Colo.; son of Charles J. and Kathryn E. (Halligan) Heath. *Education:* Colorado College, A.B., 1921; Harvard University, M.A., 1922. *Politics:* Republican. *Religion:* Episcopalian. *Home:* 129 Emerson No. 8, Palo Alto, Calif. 94301. *Office:* Pacific Coast Publishers, Campbell Ave. at Scott Dr., Menlo Park, Calif. 94025.

CAREER: Henry Holt & Co. (publishers), New York, N.Y., college representative, 1925-33; Thomas Nelson & Sons (publishers), New York, N.Y., college representative, 1935-43; Alexander Film Co., Colorado Springs, Colo., editor, 1943-47; Stanford University Press, Stanford, Calif., education department, 1947-50; Pacific Coast Publishers, Menlo Park, Calif., editor and sales manager, 1951-66. Sometime drama reviewer, *Palo Alto Times*. *Military service:* U.S. Army, 1918. *Member:* International Benjamin Franklin Society, Phi Beta Kappa, Kappa Sigma, Tau Kappa Alpha. *Awards, honors:* George Washington Honor Medal from Freedoms Foundation, 1957, for *Great American Events at a Glance*.

WRITINGS: (With Gatenby Williams) *William Guggenheim*, Lone Voice, 1934; *Beyond This Hour* (poetry), Pacific Coast Publishers, 1953.

"Great American" series, published by Pacific Coast Publishers: *Great Americans at a Glance*, four volumes, 1955-57; *Great American Scientists and Inventors*, 1956; *Great American Authors at a Glance: Poetry, Novel, Essay, Drama, Short Story*, 1956, revised edition, 1962; *Great American Women*, 1957; *Great American Events at a Glance: Thirty Principal Events of United States History*, 1957; *Our 48 States at a Glance*, 1958, revised edition published as *Our 49 States at a Glance*, 1959, 2nd revised edition published as *Our 50 States at a Glance*, 1959; *Our National Parks at a Glance*, 1959, revised edition, 1963; *Great American Rivers at a Glance*, 1960; *Our American Indians at a Glance*, 1961; *Great American Mountains at a Glance*, 1962; (editor with C. F. McIntosh) *Great American Documents at a Glance*, 1965.

(Died May 6, 1966)

HEDGEMAN, Anna Arnold   1899-

PERSONAL: Born July 5, 1899, in Marshalltown, Iowa; daughter of William James and Marie (Parker) Arnold; married Merritt A. Hedgeman (a concert artist and director of Hedgeman Consultant Service), November 1, 1933. *Education:* Hamline University, B.A.; additional study at University of Minnesota and New York School of Social Work. *Religion:* Methodist. *Home and office:* 10 West 135th St., New York, N.Y. 10037. *Office:* National Council of Churches, 475 Riverside Dr., New York, N.Y. 10027.

CAREER: Began career as teacher in Mississippi; Young Women's Christian Association, executive in Ohio, Pennsylvania, New Jersey, and New York, 1924-34, 1938-43; National Council for a Permanent Fair Employment Practices Commission, executive director, 1944-46; Federal Security Agency, Washington, D.C., assistant to administrator, 1949-53; assistant to Mayor Robert F. Wagner, New York, N.Y., 1954-58; *New York Age*, New York, N.Y., associate editor, 1958-60; United Church of Christ Board for Homeland Ministries, consultant, 1960-63; National Council of Churches of Christ in the U.S.A., New York, N.Y., 1963-68, serving at various times as director of Ecumenical Action and as co-ordinator of special events for Commission on Religion and Race; Hedgeman Consultant Service, New York, N.Y., consultant on urban affairs and African American studies, 1967—; lecturer. Exchange leader for U.S. State Department in India, 1953; participated in International Conference on Social Work in Munich, 1956, Tokyo, 1958; keynote speaker for first Conference of Women of Africa and of African Descent, Ghana, 1960. Conductor of radio program, "One Woman's Opinion," New York, N.Y., 1962-63; appeared weekly on WRVR program, "There Are Things to Do," 1964. Member of United Nations Speakers Research Committee, National Advisory Council on Vocational Rehabilitation of U.S. Department of Health, Education and Welfare, and National Committee on Alcoholism; member of boards of directors, National Conference of Christians and Jews, United Seaman's Service, and National Committee on Employment of Youth; member of advisory board, New York City Department of Mental Health and Mental Retardation Services.

AWARDS, HONORS: D.H.L., Hamline University, 1948; Litt.D., Benedict College, 1970; L.L.D., Upsala College, 1970; portrait included in Harmon Foundation national traveling exhibit, "Distinguished American Negroes"; Leadership for Freedom Award, Women's Scholarship Association of Roosevelt University, 1965; Frederick Douglass Award, New York Urban League, 1974; National Human Relations Award, State Fair Board of Texas; other citations include those from National Urban League, National Association for the Advancement of Colored People, AFL-CIO, U.S. Department of Health, Education, and Welfare, United Church Women for Christian Political Leadership, Southern Christian Leadership Conference, Guardians Association of the New York City Police Department, and Montana Farmers Union.

WRITINGS: The Trumpet Sounds (autobiographical), Holt, 1964. Contributor to newspapers and journals.

SIDELIGHTS: Dr. Hedgeman told *CA* that she "came to New York during the 'Harlem Renaissance' and was privileged to hear and discuss the history, achievements, and problems of African Americans around the world with such 'greats' as Carter G. Woodson, James Weldon Johnson,

W.E.B. DuBois, Walter White, William Pickens, Channing H. Tobias, Langston Hughes, Countee Cullen ... and others.''

*   *   *

HEGARTY, Reginald Beaton   1906-1973

PERSONAL: Born August 5, 1906, in Somerset, Mass.; son of William (a whaler) and Sarah C. (Parlow) Hegarty; married Georgiana Lawrence, February 18, 1933 (deceased); children: William Russell. *Education:* Attended high school in New Bedford, Mass. *Politics:* Republican. *Religion:* Congregationalist. *Home:* 77 Adams St., Fairhaven, Mass. 02719. *Office:* New Bedford Free Public Library, New Bedford, Mass. 02740.

CAREER: Grew up aboard whaleships, making three voyages (more than eight years at sea) before he was thirteen, and undergoing training in all phases of whaling during the final voyage; grocery store manager, 1927-40; machinist (precision grinder), 1940-45; worked in a shipyard, 1945-54; operator of New Bedford (Mass.) Public Library bookmobile, 1954; New Bedford (Mass.) Free Public Library, curator of Melville Whaling Room, 1962-73. Consultant to Kendall Whaling Museum, 1955-73, and Mystic Seaport. Member of town meeting, Fairhaven, Mass.

WRITINGS: Returns of Whaling Vessels Sailing from American Ports, 1876-1928, Reynolds Printing, 1959; *New Bedford and American Whaling* (fourth-grade textbook), Reynolds Printing, 1960; *Addendum to Starbuck and Whaling Masters*, Reynolds Printing, 1964; *Birth of a Whaleship*, Reynolds Printing, 1964; *Rope's End* (juvenile), Houghton, 1965. Contributor of articles to newspapers.

WORK IN PROGRESS: Five books, all pertaining to some phase of whaling.

SIDELIGHTS: The Melville Whaling Room is believed to house the largest and most comprehensive collection on whaling in existence. In recent years Hegarty had been occupied with indexing and cataloging some 67,000 items. One item alone, the crew lists, covers some 6,900 voyages representing about 160,000 names. "It is almost a certainty," he wrote, "that any family having four generations in this country had someone go whaling out of New Bedford."

(Died January 18, 1973)

*   *   *

HEICHER, Merlo K. W.   1882-1967

PERSONAL: Surname is pronounced *Hi*-ker; born May 31, 1882, in Highspire, Pa.; son of Truman N. (a steel worker) and Independence (Winchester) Heicher; married Margaret S. Hallock, June 28, 1906; children: Winchester Hallock. *Education:* Susquehanna University, B.S., 1902, M.S., 1904; New York University, M.A., 1913, Ph.D., 1915; Drew Theological Seminary, B.D., 1914. *Politics:* Republican. *Home and office:* 692 West Eighth St., Claremont, Calif.

CAREER: Teacher and high school principal in North Plainfield, N.J., 1903-06; teacher and missionary in Nagasaki, Japan, 1906-11; ordained Presbyterian minister, 1914; minister of churches in New York, Cedar Falls, Iowa, and Corvallis, Ore., 1914-25; San Francisco Theological Seminary, San Anselmo, Calif., professor of missions, 1925-34; Westminster Presbyterian Church and Altadena Community Church, Altadena, Calif., minister, 1934-54. *Member:* University Club (Claremont). *Awards, honors:* Th.D., Susquehanna University, 1926.

WRITINGS: Living on Tiptoe, Richard R. Smith, 1931; *Meditations for Days and Seasons*, Harper, 1942; (editor with G. B. F. Hallock) *The Ministers Manual*, annually, 1943-54, (sole editor) annually, beginning 1955. Plays anthologized in *Modern Treasury of Christmas Plays* and *Religious Plays for Amateur Players*.

WORK IN PROGRESS: The Ministers Manual.

SIDELIGHTS: Heicher made three trips around the world, traveling in twenty-five countries, with extensive stays in Australia and New Zealand. He was competent in Japanese.

(Died, 1967)

*   *   *

HEIGES, P. Myers   1887-1968

PERSONAL: Born December 2, 1887, in York County, Pa.; son of Eli Myers and Catherine (Myers) Heiges; married E. Elizabeth Bollinger, 1911. *Education:* Shippensburg State Normal School (now College), graduate, 1909; Drexel Institute (now University), graduate, 1911; New York University, B.C.S., 1916, graduate study, 1917-18. *Home:* 344 Elm Ave., Hershey, Pa. 17033.

CAREER: High school teacher and assistant principal in Shippensburg, Pa., Haddonfield, N.J., and East Orange, N.J., 1909-15; Central High School, Newark, N.J., teacher and chairman of department of business education, 1915-53; Upsala College, East Orange, N.J., instructor, 1953-54. New York University, School of Commerce, New York, N.Y., part-time instructor, 1916-41; *American Business Education* (magazine), co-founder, 1944, business manager, 1944-48. *Member:* Eastern Business Teachers Association (treasurer, 1940-44), Beta Gamma Sigma (honorary), Delta Pi Epsilon (honorary).

WRITINGS: (With G. H. Dalrymple) *General Record Keeping for Personal and Business Use*, Gregg, 1939, 5th edition (with others), published as *General Record Keeping*, McGraw, 1965. Contributor to professional journals.

(Died March 18, 1968)

*   *   *

HEILBRUNN, Otto   1906-1969

PERSONAL: Born March 7, 1906, in Frankfurt am Main, Germany; married Therese Obermeier. *Education:* Attended Universities of Berlin, Frankfurt, and Munich, LL.D., 1929. *Home:* Fairmount, Top Park, Gerrards Cross, Buckinghamshire, England.

MEMBER: Royal United Service Institution.

WRITINGS: (With C. A. Dixon) *Communist Guerrilla Warfare*, Praeger, 1955; *The Soviet Secret Services*, Praeger, 1956; *Partisan Warfare*, Praeger, 1962; *Warfare in the Enemy's Rear*, Praeger, 1963; *Conventional Warfare in the Nuclear Age*, Praeger, 1965. Contributor to American and British military journals.

WORK IN PROGRESS: A book on the Burma Campaign.

SIDELIGHTS: After World War II, Heilbrunn served as a U.S. Assistant Counsel at the Nuremburg War Crimes trials, and later with the British War Office. He gained international recognition for his studies of the Soviet Secret Service and the problems of national security in the nuclear age. Heilbrunn was regarded as one of the leading authorities on Communist insurgency tactics.

(Died January 6, 1969)

HEINSOHN, A(ugereau) G(ray), Jr. 1896-

PERSONAL: Born April 2, 1896, in Palestine, Tex.; son of Augereau Gray and Ada (Hearne) Heinsohn; married Margaret Lylburn, June 20, 1922; children: Richard Gilmer, Douglas Lylburn. *Education:* Princeton University, War Degree, 1919. *Politics:* Independent. *Religion:* Episcopal. *Office address:* P.O. Box 152, Sevierville, Tenn. 37862.

CAREER: Cherokee Textile Mills, Sevierville, Tenn., president, 1939—; Spindale Mills, Spindale, N.C., president, 1939—. *Military service:* American Expeditionary Forces, pilot in France, World War I.

WRITINGS: One Man's Fight for Freedom, Caxton, 1957; (editor and author of commentary) *Anthology of Conservative Writing in the United States, 1932-1960*, Regnery, 1962; *St. Augustine: Rape of the Ancient City*, Claar Associates, 1964.

* * *

HELLER, David (A.) 1922-1968

PERSONAL: Born August 10, 1922, in Sheridan, Wyo.; son of Augustus and Brunhilde (Manger) Heller; married Deane Heller (an author), September 1, 1943; children: David, Jr., Douglas. *Education:* University of Chicago, A.B., 1943, L.L.B., 1948. *Home and office:* 612 Ellsworth Dr., Silver Spring, Md. 20901; and 1501 Vernon Ave., Key West, Fla. 33040. *Agent:* Scott Meredith Literary Agency, 580 Fifth Ave., New York, N.Y. 10036.

CAREER: Reporter for *Chicago Sun*, Chicago, Ill., before going to Washington, D.C., as attorney for U.S. Department of Justice, 1948; full-time free-lance writer, in collaboration with wife, 1948-68. *Military service:* U.S. Navy, Supply Corps, World War II; became lieutenant, junior grade.

WRITINGS—All with wife, Deane Heller: *John Foster Dulles, Soldier for Peace*, Holt, 1960; *Jacqueline Kennedy: The Complete Story of America's Glamorous First Lady*, Monarch, 1961, enlarged edition published as *Jacqueline Kennedy: The Warmly Human Life Story of the Woman All Americans Have Taken to Their Heart*, 1963; *The Kennedy Cabinet: America's Men of Destiny*, Monarch, 1961; *The Berlin Crisis: Prelude to World War III?*, Monarch, 1961; *The Cold War*, Monarch, 1962; *The Berlin Wall*, Walker & Co., 1962; *Events 1941*, Monarch, 1964; *Paths of Diplomacy: America's Secretaries of State*, Lippincott, 1967. Author, also in collaboration with wife, of some two thousand articles for magazines and newspapers, including *Redbook* and *Coronet*; former ghostwriter of articles and speeches for Washington figures.

WORK IN PROGRESS: The Florida Keys, and *America's Foreign Alliances* both with Deane Heller.

SIDELIGHTS: Heller and his wife worked as a team, dividing research, interviewing, writing, and editing. *The Berlin Crisis* was translated into a number of African and Asian languages for distribution by the U.S. Information Agency; other books have appeared in Japanese, Norwegian, and several other foreign editions. *Avocational interests:* Photography.

BIOGRAPHICAL/CRITICAL SOURCES: Washington Post, May 31, 1968.

(Died May 28, 1968)

* * *

HELLERSTEIN, Jerome R. 1907-

PERSONAL: Born July 30, 1907, in Denver, Colo.; son of Meyer (a jeweler) and Ida (Rosenthal) Hellerstein; married Pauline Lefkowitz (a social worker), August 25, 1935; children: Judith (Mrs. Robert Weisberg), David, Walter, Cindy. *Education:* University of Denver, B.A., 1927; University of Iowa, M.A., 1928; Harvard University, LL.B., 1931. *Religion:* Jewish. *Home:* 285 Central Park West, New York, N.Y. 10024. *Office:* 80 Pine St., New York, N.Y. 10024.

CAREER: Admitted to bar, 1931. Hellerstein, Rosier & Minkin (law firm; formerly Hellerstein, Rosier & Brudner), New York, N.Y., partner, 1946—; New York University, New York, N.Y., 1946—, began as lecturer, became professor of law, 1959-71, adjunct professor, 1971—. Consultant to federal, state, and local governments on tax matters.

WRITINGS: State and Local Taxation, Prentice-Hall, 1952, 3rd edition, West Publishing, 1969; *Taxes, Loopholes and Morals*, McGraw, 1963. Contributor to *Encyclopaedia Britannica*; also contributor of articles to tax and legal periodicals.

BIOGRAPHICAL/CRITICAL SOURCES: New York University Law Center Bulletin, April 1964.

* * *

HELSON, Harry 1898-

PERSONAL: Born November 9, 1898, in Chelsea, Mass.; son of William and Ida Helson; married Lida Anderson (a remedial reading teacher), September 3, 1926; children: Henry Berge, Martha Alice (Mrs. W. A. Wilson, Jr.). *Education:* Bowdoin College, B.A., 1921; Harvard University, M.A., 1922, Ph.D., 1924. *Home:* 87 Columbia Dr., Amherst, Mass. 01002. *Office:* University of Massachusetts, Amherst, Mass. 01002.

CAREER: Instructor in psychology at Cornell University, Ithaca, N.Y., 1924-25, at University of Illinois, Urbana, 1925-26; University of Kansas, Lawrence, assistant professor of psychology, 1926-28; Bryn Mawr College, Bryn Mawr, Pa., associate professor, 1928-32, professor of psychology, 1933-49; Brooklyn College, Brooklyn, N.Y., professor of psychology and head of department, 1949-51; University of Texas, Austin, professor of psychology, 1951-61; Kansas State University, professor of psychology, 1961-67; University of Massachusetts, Amherst, professor of psychology, 1968—. Acting professor at Stanford University, 1948-49; visiting summer professor at University of Southern California, Harvard University, University of California, and University of Colorado; visiting professor, York University, Toronto, 1967-68.

MEMBER: American Psychological Association (division president), Optical Society of America, Society of Experimental Psychologists, Midwestern Psychological Association, Phi Beta Kappa, Sigma Xi. *Awards, honors:* Howard Crosby Warren Medal of Society of Experimental Psychologists, 1959; American Psychological Association award for distinguished scientific contribution, 1962; I. H. Godlove Award, Inter-Society Color Council, 1969.

WRITINGS: The Psychology of Gestalt, American Journal of Psychology, 1926; (editor with others) *Theoretical Foundations of Psychology*, Van Nostrand, 1951; *Adaptation-Level Theory: An Experimental and Systematic Approach to Behavior*, Harper, 1964; (editor with William Bevan and others) *Contemporary Approaches to Psychology*, Van Nostrand, 1967. Contributor to scientific journals. Editor, *Psychological Bulletin*, 1959-64.

WORK IN PROGRESS: Research in psychophysics, perception, role of illumination and background on pleasantness of object colors; adaptation-level theory.

* * *

HENDEL, Charles William 1890-

PERSONAL: Born December 16, 1890, in Reading, Pa.; son of Charles William and Emma (Stoltz) Hendel; married Elizabeth Jones, September 23, 1916; children: James Norman, Charles William III. Education: Princeton University, Litt.B., 1913, Ph.D., 1917; additional study at University of Marburg, 1913-14, and College de France, 1914. Home: 245 East Rock Rd., New Haven, Conn.

CAREER: Williams College, Williamstown, Mass., instructor, 1919-20; Princeton University, Princeton, N.J., assistant professor, 1920-26, associate professor, 1926-29; McGill University, Montreal, Quebec, Macdonald Professor of Moral Philosophy, 1929-40, dean of Faculty of Arts and Science, 1937-40; Yale University, New Haven, Conn., Clark Professor of Moral Philosophy and Metaphysics, 1940-59, chairman of department of philosophy, 1940-45, 1950-59, professor emeritus, 1959—. Gifford Lecturer in Natural Theology, University of Glasgow, 1962, 1963. Military service: Army of the United States, 1917-18; became second lieutenant. Member: American Philosophical Association (president of Eastern division, 1940), American Association for Legal and Political Philosophy (president, 1960-61), Metaphysical Society of America. Awards, honors: M.A., Yale University, 1940.

WRITINGS: Studies in the Philosophy of David Hume, Princeton University Press, 1925, revised edition, Bobbs-Merrill, 1963; (contributor) Idealism in America, Macmillan, 1930; Jean Jacques Rousseau: Moralist, Oxford University Press, 1934, revised edition, Bobbs-Merrill, 1963; Citizen of Geneva, Oxford University Press, 1937; (contributor) Preface to Philosophy, Macmillan, 1946; (contributor) Philosophy in American Education, Harper, 1946; Civilization and Religion, Yale University Press, 1948.

(Contributor) Goals for American Education, Harper, 1950; (author of introduction and translator with William H. Woglom) Ernst Cassirer, Problem of Knowledge: Philosophy, Science and History since Hegel, Yale University Press, 1951; (author of introduction) Cassirer, Philosophy of Symbolic Forms, three volumes, Yale University Press, 1953; (contributor) Freedom and Authority in Our Time, Harper, 1953; (editor) David Hume, Political Essays, Liberal Arts Press, 1953; (editor) Hume, An Inquiry Concerning Human Understanding, Liberal Arts Press, 1955; (editor) Hume, Inquiry Concerning the Principles of Morals, Liberal Arts Press, 1957; (editor and contributor) The Philosophy of Kant and Our Modern World, Liberal Arts Press, 1957; (editor and contributor) John Dewey and the Experimental Spirit in Philosophy, Liberal Arts Press, 1960; (editor) Cassirer, The Myth of the State, Yale University Press, 1961. Contributor to Fortune and to journals in the fields of education and philosophy.

AVOCATIONAL INTERESTS: Music, hiking, and photography.

* * *

HENDERSON, Alexander (John) 1910-

PERSONAL: Born January 20, 1910, in Romford, England; son of Alexander and Adeline (Turnbridge) Henderson; married Elizabeth Wilhelm (a translator), September 22, 1947. Education: Attended University College School, London, England, 1921-28, University College, London, 1928-30. Agent: David Higham Associates Ltd., 76 Dean St., London W.1, England.

CAREER: Newspaper and news agency correspondent, 1930-38; Daily Herald, London, England, correspondent in Prague, 1938-39; British Ministry of Information, head of Istanbul office, 1940-44, head of Balkans section, 1944-45; Daily Express, London, England, associate foreign editor, 1945-53; United Nations Food and Agriculture Organization, Rome, Italy, chief editor, 1953—. Member: Royal Institute of International Affairs, P.E.N., Press Club.

WRITINGS: Aldous Huxley, Harper, 1935; Freedom's Crooked Scars, Hamish Hamilton, 1937; Eyewitness in Czechoslovakia, Harrap, 1939; The Dangerous World, Dent, 1947; The Tunnelled Fire: Poems, Secker & Warburg, 1956; (translator from the German with wife, Elizabeth Henderson) I. G. Seume, A Stroll to Syracuse, Wolff, 1964. Contributor to Listener, Wine & Food Quarterly, Poetry Quarterly, Asiatic Review, and other periodicals.

WORK IN PROGRESS: Seven Faces of Byzantium, a book about Byzantine art and civilization; another book of poems.

SIDELIGHTS: Henderson is competent in French, German, and Italian. Avocational interests: Landscape and art of Italy.

* * *

HENDERSON, Bert C. 1904-

PERSONAL: Born November 8, 1904, in Troy, Ala.; son of Albert Holloway and Gertrude (Faulkner) Henderson; married Mary Middleton Smith, March 2, 1947. Education: Attended State Teachers College (now Troy State University) and University of Alabama. Home: 1103 South Perry St., Montgomery, Ala. 36104. Office: Whitley Hotel, 231 Montgomery St., Montgomery, Ala. 36101.

CAREER: Writer. Military service: U.S. Army Air Corps, 1943. Member: United Poets International, Poetry Society of America, Poetry Society of Alabama, Alabama Writers Conclave. Awards, honors: Appointed poet laureate of Alabama, 1959; national poetry prize in Columbia Broadcasting System contest; recipient of numerous poetry prizes in national contests.

WRITINGS—All poetry: House of Paradoxes, Banner Press, 1941; Blame Noah, Dierkes Press, 1952; Bright Armor, Banner Press, 1956; Eternal Symphony, Banner Press, 1962; The Immortal Legions, American Southern, c.1966. Also author of two unpublished novels. Contributor of more than five hundred poems to New York Times, American Mercury, and other publications.

WORK IN PROGRESS: The Ultimate Harvest, poems; a long narrative poem for possible adaptation on television; poems for another volume of poetry.

* * *

HENDERSON, K(enneth) D(avid) D(ruitt) 1903-

PERSONAL: Born September 4, 1903, in London, England; son of George (a physician) and Helen Ethel (Druitt) Henderson; married Margery Grant Atkinson, June 10, 1935; children: Alison Jane (Mrs. Robert Crole), Robert David, Katharine Charlotte (Mrs. Colin McEachran). Education: Attended Trinity College, Glenalmond, Scotland, 1917-22; University College, Oxford, B.A., 1926, M.A., 1932. Religion: Church of England. Home: Orchard House, Steeple Langford, Wiltshire, England.

CAREER: Sudan Political Service, 1926-53, serving as deputy governor of Kassala Province, 1945, and governor of Darfur Province, 1949-53; general secretary of Spalding Educational Trust, Oxford, England, and of Union for the Study of Great Religions, 1953—. Vice-president, World Congress of Faiths, 1963. Military service: Sudan Auxiliary Defence Force, 1940-44; became lieutenant colonel; mentioned in dispatches. Member: Association of British Orientalists, International Association for the History of Religion, Anglo-Sudanese Association. Awards, honors: Order of the Nile (fourth class), 1937; Companion of St. Michael and St. George, 1951.

WRITINGS: History of the Hamar Tribe, Sudan Government, 1935; Survey of the Anglo-Egyptian Sudan, 1898-1944, Longmans, Green, 1945; The Making of the Modern Sudan, Faber, 1952; Sudan Republic, Benn, 1965; Short History of the Parish of Steeple Langford, privately printed, 1973. Contributor to Encyclopaedia Britannica, Chambers's Encyclopaedia, and Encyclopedia Americana. Editor, Sudan Notes and Records, 1939-44.

SIDELIGHTS: Henderson has visited universities on four continents in connection with his interest in the study of world religions—traveling in many parts of India, Australia, United States, and Canada. He speaks Arabic and French.

*   *   *

HENDERSON, Philip (Prichard) 1906-

PERSONAL: Born February 17, 1906, in Barnes, Surrey, England, married Millicent Rose, 1938 (marriage dissolved, 1947); married Belinda Hamilton (a painter), 1948; children: John Sebastian, Julian Urskwick. Education: Attended Bradfield College. Agent: A. M. Heath & Co., 35 Dover St., London W.1, England.

CAREER: Everyman's Library, assistant editor, 1929-32; British Book News, London, England, co-editor, 1943-46; British Council, London, England, editor of feature articles, 1959-63, assistant editor of publications and recorded sound section, 1963-64; Chatto & Windus, London, England, editor, 1964-66. Wartime service: National Fire Service, fireman, 1939-43. Awards, honors: Arts Council award, 1967.

WRITINGS: (Editor) Shorter Novels, Dutton, Volume I: Elizabethan and Jacobean, 1929, Volume II: Jacobean and Restoration, 1930, Volume III: Eighteenth Century, 1930; (editor) Thomas Nash, The Unfortunate Traveller, Verona Society, 1930; First Poems, Dutton, 1930; (editor) John Skelton, The Complete Poems, Dutton, 1931, 4th edition, 1946; A Wind in the Sand (poems), Boriswood, 1932; (editor and author of introduction) Edmund Spenser, The Shepherd's Calendar, and Other Poems, Dutton, 1932; Events in the Early Life of Anthony Price (novel), Boriswood, 1935; (author of additional selections) Thomas Caldwell, The Golden Book of Modern English Poetry, 1870-1920, Dent, 1935; Literature and a Changing Civilization, John Lane, 1935; The Novel Today: Studies in Contemporary Attitudes, John Lane, 1936; And Morning in His Eyes: A Book About Christopher Marlowe, Boriswood, 1937; The Poet and Society, Secker & Warburg, 1939.

(Editor and author of introduction) George Crabbe, Poems, Lawson & Dunn, 1946; (editor and author of introduction) Emily Bronte: Poems, Lawson & Dunn, 1947; (editor) The Letters of William Morris to His Family and Friends, Longmans, Green, 1960; (editor and author of introduction) Emily Bronte, Complete Poems, Folio Society, 1951; (editor) Emily Bronte, Wuthering Heights and Selected

Poems, Dent, 1951; William Morris, Longmans, Green, 1952, revised edition, 1963; Christopher Marlowe, Longmans, Green, 1952, revised edition, 1962; (editor) Shorter Novels of the Eighteenth Century, Dutton, 1953; Samuel Butler: The Incarnate Bachelor, Cohen & West, 1953, Indiana University Press, 1954; The Life of Laurence Oliphant, Traveller, Diplomat and Mystic, R. Hale, 1956; Richard Coeur de Lion: A Biography, R. Hale, 1958, Norton, 1959.

(With Oswald Doughty) William Morris and Gabriel Rosetti (the former by Henderson, the latter by Doughty), University of Nebraska Press, 1965; (with J. B. Bamborough, Ian Scott-Kilvert, and Clifford Leech) Christopher Marlowe, Ben Jonson, John Webster, John Ford (the first by Henderson, the second by Bamborough, the third by Scott-Kilvert, the fourth by Leech), University of Nebraska Press, 1966; William Morris: His Life, Work and Friends, McGraw, 1967.

AVOCATIONAL INTERESTS: Music, architecture, English medieval churches, painting, bird life, getting away from cities as often as possible.

BIOGRAPHICAL/CRITICAL SOURCES: Observer Review, November 5, 1967; New Statesman, November 24, 1967; Spectator, November 24, 1967; Listener, December 7, 1967; Time, December 8, 1967; Punch, December 20, 1967; New York Times Book Review, January 21, 1968; Commonweal, February 23, 1968; Art Education, March, 1968; New York Review of Books, May 23, 1968; Virginia Quarterly Review, spring, 1968; Sewanee Review, summer, 1968; New Yorker, September 14, 1968.

*   *   *

HENDERSON, Randall 1888-

PERSONAL: Born April 12, 1888, in Clarinda, Iowa; son of Nelson Rankin and Mary Catherine (Thomas) Henderson, married second wife, Cyria Allen, March 23, 1949; children: (first marriage) Rand (deceased), Evonne Louise Henderson Riddell. Education: University of Southern California, B.A., 1911. Politics: Democrat. Religion: Unitarian Universalist. Home: 74-555 Old Prospector Trail, Palm Desert, Calif.

CAREER: Blythe Herald, Blythe, Calif., editor and publisher, 1912-22; Daily Chronicle, Calexico, Calif., editor and publisher, 1922-36; Desert Magazine, Palm Desert, Calif., founder, editor, and publisher, 1937-58. President, then director, Desert Protective Council, Inc. Military service: Signal Corps Air Service pilot, World War I. U.S. Army Air Forces, Air Transport Command, World War II; became captain. Member: Sierra Club of California (honorary vice-president), Death Valley '49ers (director), Rotary Club. Awards, honors: Conservation Award, Sierra Club of California, 1962.

WRITINGS: On Desert Trails Today and Yesterday, Westernlore, 1960; Sun, Sand, and Solitude: Vignettes From the Notebook of a Veteran Desert Reporter, Westernlore, 1968. Feature writer for Desert Magazine and Westways.

WORK IN PROGRESS: In the Sunlight of Tomorrow, a layman's formula for reconciling the religious dogmas of today with Darwinian theory.

SIDELIGHTS: Henderson told CA: "During fifty-two years as editor and reporter on the great American desert my quest has been for the answers to the basic problems of the species homo sapiens—the primary problem being the evolutionary destiny of mankind."

HENDRICK, Ives   1898-1972

PERSONAL: Born March 10, 1898, in New Haven, Conn.; son of Burton J. (an author) and Bertha Jane (Ives) Hendrick; divorced; children: Bertha Jane (Mrs. James Rumsey), Martha Hannica (Mrs. Robert Rusnak). *Education:* Yale University, B.A., 1921, M.D., 1925; Berlin Psychoanalytic Institute, postdoctoral study, 1928-30. *Politics:* Unaffiliated. *Religion:* Protestant. *Office:* 84 Mount Vernon St., Boston, Mass. 02108.

CAREER: Harvard University, Medical School, Boston, Mass., 1930-64, started as assistant in department of psychiatry, assistant clinical professor, 1948-51, associate clinical professor, 1951-53, clinical professor, 1954-64, professor emeritus, 1964-72; Massachusetts Mental Health Center, Boston, chief of Harvard teaching unit, 1943-64, later clinical director emeritus; private practice of psychoanalysis and psychiatry, Boston, Mass., 1930-72. Boston Psychoanalytic Institute, former president, member of educational committee. Instructor, Boston Family Society, Philadelphia Family Society, Smith College, 1930-38; lecturer, Duquesne University, 1935, Radcliffe College, 1940-42. Consultant, Massachusetts General Hospital, 1930-33, McLean Hospital, 1931-34. *Member:* American Psychoanalytic Association (chairman, member of board of professional standards, 1951-53; president, 1953-55), American Medical Association, American Psychiatric Association (life fellow), Group for Advancement of Psychiatry, Boston Psychoanalytic Society (past president), Harvard Music Association, Harvard Faculty Club, Harvard Club (Boston), Yale Club (New York).

WRITINGS: Facts and Theories of Psychoanalysis, Knopf, 1934, 3rd edition, 1958; *The Birth of an Institute,* Wheelwright, 1961; *Psychiatry Education Today,* International Universities Press, 1965. Contributing editor, *Encyclopaedia Britannica.* Contributor of articles to technical journals and popular magazines. Associate editor, *Psychoanalytic Review;* former editor, *Journal of American Psychoanalytic Association;* associate editor, *Psychoanalytic Forum.*

AVOCATIONAL INTERESTS: Study of music theory, sailing.

(Died May 28, 1972)

*   *   *

HERMANN, (Theodore) Placid   1909-19(?)

PERSONAL: Born January 8, 1909, in Indianapolis, Ind.; son of Edward A. and Anna (Ernst) Hermann. *Education:* Our Lady of Angels Seminary, Cleveland, Ohio (now in Quincy, Ill.), A.B., 1931; Western Reserve University (now Case Western Reserve University), M.A., 1941. *Home:* 203 East Main St., Teutopolis, Ill. 62467.

CAREER: Ordained Roman Catholic priest, 1934; member of Franciscan order, beginning 1927; teacher of English in Catholic seminaries (at high school and college level), 1936-63; retired as teacher; writer and editor of works on Franciscan topics, and confessor for novices in Franciscan novitiate, beginning 1963.

WRITINGS: Via Seraphica (annotated anthology), Franciscan Herald, 1959; *Seraph of Love* (biography of St. Francis of Assisi, in iambic pentameter), Franciscan Herald, 1959; (translator) *XIIIth Century Chronicles,* Franciscan Herald, 1961; (translator and author of introduction and footnotes) Brother Thomas of Celano, *St. Francis of Assisi,* Franciscan Herald, 1962; *The Way of St. Francis,*

Franciscan Herald, 1964; (translator with Nesta de Robeck) *St. Francis of Assisi: His Holy Life and Love of Poverty,* Franciscan Herald, 1964; (author of introduction and notes) *The Writings of St. Francis,* Franciscan Herald, 1964; (editor with Marion A. Habig) *Catholic Concise Dictionary,* revised edition, Franciscan Herald, 1966.

WORK IN PROGRESS: Introduction and notes to St. Bonaventure's life of St. Francis.

(Deceased)

*   *   *

HERMANS, Willem Frederik   1921-

PERSONAL: Born September 1, 1921, in Amsterdam, Holland; son of Johannes (a high school teacher) and Hendrika Hillegonda (Eggelte) Hermans; married Emelie Henriette Meurs, July 4, 1950; children: Rupert. *Education:* University of Amsterdam, Dr. Sc. *Home:* Spilsluizen 17a, Groningen, Holland.

CAREER: University of Groningen, Groningen, Holland, lecturer in physical geography, 1958—. Author. Pulpwood expert in Newfoundland, Canada, and United States, 1948. Geological expeditions in northern Scandinavia, 1960, 1961. *Member:* Royal Geological and Mining Society of Netherlands, Royal Dutch Geographical Society.

WRITINGS: Horror coeli en andere gedichten (poetry), J. M. Meulenhoff (Amsterdam), 1946; *Conserve* (novel), Salm, 1947, revised edition published in *Drei melodrama's* (see below); *Hypnodrome* (poetry), A. S. M. Stols ('s-Gravenhage), 1947; *Moedwil en misverstand* (short stories; title means "Malice and Misunderstanding"), J. M. Muelenhoff, 1948; *De Tranen der Acacia's* (novel; title means "The Tears of the Acacias"), G. A. van Oorschot (Amsterdam), 1949; *De Phenomenologie van de Pin-up Girl* (essay), G. A. van Oorschot, 1950; *Ik heb altijd gelijk* (novel; title means "I Am Always Right"), G. A. van Oorschot, 1951; *Het Behouden huis* (novella), De Bezige Bij (Amsterdam), 1952, translation published as "The House of Refuge," *Odyssey Review,* December, 1961; *Paranoia* (short stories), G. A. van Oorschot, 1953; *Description et Genese des depots meubles de surface et du relief de l'Oesling,* Geological Services (Luxembourg), 1955; *De God denkbaar, denkbaar de god* (novel), G. A. van Oorschot, 1956; *Drie melodrama's: Conserve, De Lepros van Molokai, Hermans in hier geweest,* G. A. van Oorschot, 1957; *Een Landingspoging op Newfoundland en andere verhalen,* G. A. van Oorschot, 1957; *De Donkere kamer van Damocles,* G. A. van Oorschot, 1958, translation by Roy Edwards published as *The Dark Room of Damocles,* Heinemann, 1962; *Het zonale beginsel in de geografie,* Wolters (Groningen), 1958.

Erosie, Heijnis (Zaandijk), 1960; *Drie drama's* (plays), De Bezige Bij, 1962; *De Woeste wandeling: Een Scenario* (film story), De Bezige Bij, 1962; *Mandarijnen op zwavelzuur* (essays), University of Groningen Press, 1963, 2nd edition, Thomas Rap (Amsterdam), 1967; *Het Sadistische universum,* De Bezige Bij, 1964; (contributor) H. U. Jessurum d'Oliveira, editor, *Scheppen, riep hij gaat van Au: 10 Interviews,* Polak & Van Gennep (Amsterdam), 1965, 3rd edition, Em Querido (Amsterdam), 1967; *Nooit meer slopen,* De Bezige Bij, 1966; *Wittgenstein in de mode,* De Bezige Bij, 1967; *Hermans is hier geweest,* G. A. von Oorschot, 1967; *Een Wonderkind of een total loss,* De Bezige Bij, 1967; *Overgebleven gedichten,* Thomas Rap, 1968; *Fotobiografie,* Thomas Rap, 1969; *De Laatste resten tropisch Nederland,* De Bezige Bij, 1969; *Van Wittgenstein tot*

Weinreb: Het Sadistische Universum, De Bezige Bij, 1970; *Herinneringen van een engelbewaarder: De Wolk van niet weten*, De Bezige Bij, 1971. Co-editor, *Criterium*, 1946-48, *Podium*, 1949-50, 1963—.

WORK IN PROGRESS: A drama.

SIDELIGHTS: A controversial and icolonclastic writer, Hermans was brought to trial in 1951 for his novel *Ik heb altijd gelijk*. Although it was ruled that a novelist could not be held responsible for the ideas of his characters, Hermans reasserted that his writings accurately reflected his own attitudes. And, as Manfred Wolf writes: "He has not mellowed since. His novels continue to infuriate, and so do his estimates of other writers and critics. In books of criticism as well as in magazine pieces, he has become Holland's most devoted polemicist, attacking the reputations of friend and foe, the living and the dead. He has skillfully probed the weaknesses of others, and many a previously inflated reputation will not recover. At best Hermans' sensitivity to posturing, hypocrisy, and vanity is unequaled, at worst his personal abusiveness is not to be taken seriously."

Hermans' recurring themes are uncertainty, homelessness, the illusory quality of freedom and other revered absolutes, and the total absurdity and chaos present in contemporary life. The bitterness and disillusionment of his characters has caused Hermans to be compared with John Osborne and George Orwell, although Wolf maintains that Hermans' cynicism runs even deeper than in those writers. In the introduction to *Paranoia*, Hermans writes: "What we remember and keep has accidentally not been lost, what we call our life is nothing but a remnant, the odor of a fire that has been put out long ago. . . . Because our words are limited in number (and must be limited), there is repetition, true, but no reality. We live in a falsified world. The same words are repeated but they express nothing. In our language there is one truthful word only: chaos.''

Hermans' books have been translated into six languages; *De Donkere kamer van Damocles* was made into the French film, "Inconnu aux services secrets," 1963, and the English film, "The Spitting Image," released in 1964.

BIOGRAPHICAL/CRITICAL SOURCES: London Magazine, October, 1961; *Odyssey Review*, December, 1961; *Literary Review*, winter, 1961-62; *France-Observateur*, November 22, 1962; W. S. B. Klooster, editor, *Kritisch akkoord 1967*, Manteau (Brussels), 1967; *Books Abroad*, summer, 1967.

* * *

HEROLD, J(ean) Christopher 1919-1964

PERSONAL: Born May 11, 1919, in Brunn, Czechoslovakia; came to United States, 1939, naturalized, 1943; son of Carl M. and Elisabeth (Schnabel) Herold; married Barbara A. Chapman, 1943; married second wife, Luba Sharoff (an actress), April 8, 1963; children: (first marriage) Christopher D. *Education:* University of Geneva, student, 1938-39; Columbia University, B.S., 1941, M.A., 1942. *Religion:* Roman Catholic. *Address:* 145 East 35th St., New York, N.Y. 10016; and P.O. Box 112, Readfield, Me. 04355.

CAREER: Columbia University Press, New York, N.Y., editor, 1946-56; Stanford University Press, Stanford, Calif., editor-in-chief, 1956-60. *Military service:* U.S. Army, Military Intelligence, 1942-45; became staff sergeant. *Member:* Society of American Historians (fellow), Royal Society of Literature (fellow), P.E.N., Authors League, Society of Authors (England). *Awards, honors:* National Book Award

and California Gold Medal for Literature, 1959, for *Mistress to an Age: A Life of Madame de Stael*; Guggenheim fellowship, 1960.

WRITINGS: The Swiss without Halos, Columbia University Press, 1948; *Joan, Maid of France*, Aladdin Books, 1952; (editor and translator) *The Mind of Napoleon*, Columbia University Press, 1955; *Mistress to an Age: A Life of Madame de Stael* (Book-of-the-Month Club selection), Bobbs-Merrill, 1958, reissued with an introduction by Rebecca West, Time, Inc., 1964; *Love in Five Temperaments*, Atheneum, 1961; *Bonaparte in Egypt* (History Book Club selection), Harper, 1963; *The Age of Napoleon* (Book-of-the-Month Club selection), American Heritage Press, 1963; *The Battle of Waterloo*, American Heritage Press, 1967. Contributor of articles and reviews to magazines. Section editor, *Columbia Encyclopedia*, 2nd edition.

WORK IN PROGRESS: The Romantic Movement.

SIDELIGHTS: Herold's books have been published in Great Britain, and translated into six languages, including German, Spanish, and Finnish.

BIOGRAPHICAL/CRITICAL SOURCES: Saturday Review, October, 1958; *Book-of-the-Month Club Bulletin*, October, 1958, October, 1963; *New York Times Book Review*, May 21, 1967; *Times Literary Supplement*, May 25, 1967; *Best Sellers*, June 1, 1967.

(Died December 3, 1964)

* * *

HERRESHOFF, L. Francis 1890-1972

PERSONAL: Born November 11, 1890, in Bristol, R.I.; son of Nathanael Greene and Clara (DeWolf) Herreshoff. *Education:* Attended University of Rhode Island. *Politics:* Independent. *Religion:* Episcopalian. *Home and office:* 2 Crocker Park, Marblehead, Mass.

CAREER: Yacht designer and free-lance writer of books on yachting. *Military service:* U.S. Navy, 1917-21; commanded patrol boats and worked on underwater sound detection at U.S. Navy Experimental Station; became ensign.

WRITINGS: Writings of L. Francis Herreshoff, Rudder Publishing, 1946; *Commonsense of Yacht Design*, two volumes, Rudder Publishing, 1946; *Captain Nat Herreshoff* (biography of father), Sheridan, 1953; *The Compleat Cruiser*, Sheridan, 1963; *An Introduction to Yachting*, Sheridan, 1963; (with Boris L. Leonardi) *Yachts: Designs, and Much Miscellaneous Information*, Poseidon, 1967.

(Died December 3, 1972)

* * *

HERSEY, William Dearborn 1910-

PERSONAL: Born December 3, 1910, in Somerville, Mass.; son of Harry Adams (a minister) and Lottie May (Champlin) Hersey; married Fairlee H. Towsley (a newspaper editor), August 11, 1935; children: Donna Lee, Glen Alden. *Education:* Tufts University, B.S. in psychology, 1932. *Politics:* Independent. *Residence:* Norton, Mass.

CAREER: Socony Mobil Oil Co., various sales and staff positions, 1932-50; Eastern Gas and Fuel Associates, Boston, Mass., assistant training director, 1951-53; Investors Diversified Services, Inc., zone manager in eastern Massachusetts, 1953—. Northeastern University, Boston, Mass., consultant to, and lecturer for, Bureau of Business and Industrial Training. Conductor of memory training institutes for business and industrial firms.

WRITINGS: Hersey's Short Course for Short Memories, privately printed, 1959; *How to Cash in on Your Hidden Memory Power*, Prentice-Hall, 1964. Recorded "How to Remember Names and Faces," Creative Associates, 1962.

SIDELIGHTS: Hersey, who prefers to be known as a memory specialist rather than as a memory expert, developed his skill with a mental filing system when he was past forty. In 1958 he won $30,000 in prizes in ten minutes on the network television show, "Concentration."

* * *

HESKETH, Phoebe Rayner 1909-

PERSONAL: Born January 29, 1909, in Preston, Lancashire, England; daughter of Arthur Ernest (a physician and radiologist) and Amy Gertrude (Fielding) Rayner; married Aubrey Hesketh, September 30, 1931; children: Martin, Richard, Catherine. *Education:* Attended Cheltenham Ladies' College. *Religion:* Church of England. *Home:* Fisher House, Rivington near Bolton, Lancashire, England.

CAREER: Bolton Evening News, Bolton, England, women's page editor, 1942-45; poet and free-lance writer for magazines and radio; Arts Council lecturer for schools, colleges and other institutions. *Member:* Society of Authors, P.E.N. *Awards, honors:* Greenwood prize of Poetry Society of London, 1946 and 1963.

WRITINGS—Poetry, except as indicated: *Poems*, Sheratt & Hughes, 1939; *Lean Forward Spring!*, Sidgwick & Jackson, 1948; *No Time for Cowards*, Heinemann, 1950; *Out of the Dark*, selected by Richard Church, Heinemann, 1954; *Between Wheels and Stars*, Heinemann, 1956; *The Buttercup Children*, Hart-Davis, 1958; *Prayer for Sun*, Hart-Davis, 1966; *My Aunt Edith* (biography), P. Davies, 1966; *Roundabout*, Pergamon, 1971. Contributor of articles and poems to *Country Life, Times Literary Supplement, Time and Tide, John O'London's, Contemporary Review, Observe, Poetry Review*, other journals. Radio scripts include "Lift Up Your Hearts" and "The Way of Life."

WORK IN PROGRESS: A story of her village; poems, entitled *Preparing to Leave.*

* * *

HESS, Albert G(unter) 1909-

PERSONAL: Born March 1, 1909, in Pirna, Germany; son of Gustav and Hermine (Bauer) Hess; married Julia Keh-Fang Kao (a librarian with United Nations), 1960; children: Marie Elisabeth. *Education:* University of Leipzig, Dr. jur. utr. (magna cum laude), 1933; also studied at Universities of Bonn, Hamburg, and London, and Cornell University. *Home:* 30 Winston Woods, Brockport, N.Y. 14420.

CAREER: Juvenile Court Agency, Germany, caseworker, 1930-32; Ministry of Justice, Dresden, Germany, district court judge, 1932-33; Chemische Fabrik, Pirna, Germany, corporation lawyer, 1933-37; Bureau Central d'Exportation Budex, Brussels, Belgium, manager, 1937-40; Goddard College, Plainfield, Vt., staff member, 1942-43; Mohawk College and Cazenovia Junior College, Cazenovia, N.Y., teacher, 1946-50; University of Minnesota, Duluth Campus, assistant professor of humanities, 1950-55; United Nations, New York, N.Y., social affairs officer, 1956-60; National Council on Crime and Delinquency, New York, N.Y., assistant director of Information Center, and director of juvenile court study, 1964-70; State University of New York College at Brockport, professor of sociology, 1970—. *Military service:* U.S. Army, 1944-45; became staff sergeant.

MEMBER: International Society for Criminology (United Nations representative), International Association of Penal Law (United Nations representative), American Society of Criminology (vice-president), American League to Abolish Capital Punishment, American Sociological Association, American Civil Liberties Union, Society for the Psychological Study of Social Issues, Authors Guild. *Awards, honors:* Research grants from Greater University Fund, 1953, from Ford Foundation, 1961, for the study of narcotics addiction in Hong Kong, and 1968, for a study of volunteers in probation in Japan.

WRITINGS: Die Kinderschaendung, Ernst Wiegandt (Leipzig), 1934; *Criminal Statistics: Standard Classification of Offences*, United Nations, 1959; *The Young Adult Offender: A Review of Current Practices and Programmes in the Prevention and Treatment*, United Nations, 1965; *Chasing the Dragon: A Report on Drug Addiction in Hong Kong*, Free Press of Glencoe, 1965; (with wife, Julia K. Hess and Franco Ferracuti) *The Young Adult Offender: A Bibliography*, Giuffre (Milan), 1966. Contributor to *The American Peoples Encyclopedia Yearbook*, 1966; also contributor to professional journals in America and Europe. Managing editor, Musurgia Publishers, 1946-50; executive editor, *Excerpta Criminologica* (Amsterdam), 1960-64.

WORK IN PROGRESS: A History of Juvenile Delinquency, completion expected in 1976.

SIDELIGHTS: Hess is competent in French, German, Spanish, Japanese, and Latin. *The Young Adult Offender* has been translated into French, Russian, and Spanish, and the bibliography on the same topic was published simultaneously in five languages.

* * *

HEUSS, John 1908-1966

PERSONAL: Born July 30, 1908, in Hastings-on-Hudson, N.Y.; son of John and Elizabeth (Norton) Heuss; married Elizabeth Beck, May 20, 1935; children: Gwenith Ann (Mrs. John B. Severance), William Beresford, John Craig. *Education:* Bard College, B.A., 1929; graduate study at University of Cologne, University of Frankfurt, and University of Berlin; Seabury Western Theological Seminary, B.D., 1931; S.T.M., 1937, D.D., 1947. *Home:* 133 East 64th St., New York, N.Y. 10021. *Office:* Trinity Parish, 74 Trinity Pl., New York, N.Y. 10006.

CAREER: Ordained to Episcopal ministry, 1932; assistant priest and rector of churches in Evanston, Ill., 1932-47; chaplain to students at Northwestern University, 1937-43; instructor in homiletics at Seabury-Western Theological Seminary, 1944-47; National Council of Episcopal Church, director of department of Christian education, 1947-52; Trinity Parish, New York, N.Y., rector, 1952-66. Director, Seabury Press. Trustee of Columbia University (emeritus), General Theological Seminary, Sailors' Snug Harbor, Cathedral of St. John the Divine, and South Kent School. Member of board of directors of Seamen's Church Institute, Leake & Watts Children's Home, Church Literature Foundation, and Anglican Congress.

MEMBER: Newcomen Society, St. George's Society, New York Chamber of Commerce, Phi Beta Kappa, University Club, Columbia University Club, Century Club, Union Club, Pilgrims Club, British Luncheon Club, Authors' Club (London), Down Town Club, Downtown Athletic Club, Stage Harbor Yacht Club, Chatham Beach Club. *Awards, honors:* S.T.D., General Theological Seminary, 1950; D.D., University of the South, 1951, Trinity

College, 1952, Springfield College, 1953, Bard College, 1953; L.H.D., Ripon College, 1952; Canon of Cathedral, Madrid, Spain, 1963.

WRITINGS: Do You Want Inward Power?, Seabury, 1953; *Our Christian Vocation*, Seabury, 1955; *Have a Lively Faith*, Morehouse, 1963; *The Implications of the Toronto Manifesto*, Seabury Western Theological Seminary, 1966.

Editor: *Victory of Faith*, Harper, 1935; *Authority in Religious Education*, Religious Education, 1945; *Democracy and the Family*, Living Church, 1946; *Future Development of Christian Education*, National Council of Protestant Episcopal Church, 1948; *Retarded State of Christian Education*, National Council of Protestant Episcopal Church, 1949; ''Church's Teaching'' series, Seabury, 1951-57; *Christian Education*, Seabury, 1953; *A Book of Prayers*, Morehouse, 1957. Contributor to *Reader's Digest, Living Church*, and other religious periodicals.

BIOGRAPHICAL/CRITICAL SOURCES: New York Times, March 22, 1966; *New York Herald Tribune*, March 23, 1966.

(Died March 20, 1966)

* * *

HEWINS, Geoffrey Shaw   1889-

PERSONAL: Born October 26, 1889; son of Alfred John and Anne Louisa (Allen) Hewins; married Elsie Vera Abraham, July 28, 1930. *Education:* University College of Wales, B.A., 1913; further study at Lichfield Theological College. *Politics:* Conservative. *Home:* Silvington Rectory, Cleobury Mortimer, Shropshire, England.

CAREER: Ordained deacon of Church of England, 1914, priest, 1915; curate at Stanley, Derbyshire, England, 1914-24; priest-in-charge at Weston-Under-Redcastle, Shropshire, England, 1925-30, at Tallarn Green, Flintshire, Wales, 1931-34; rector of Hamstall Ridware with Pipe Ridware, Staffordshire, England, 1934-39; vicar at Easton Maudit, Northamptonshire, England, 1939-40; rector of Oxhill with Whatcote, Warwickshire, England, 1940-44, Exhall with Wixford, Warwickshire, 1944-50, Silvington with Cleeton St. Mary, Shropshire, England, 1950—. Served with Young Men's Christian Association in Salonika, Greece, 1918-19. *Member:* Council for the Preservation of Rural England (co-founder of Staffordshire branch), Staffordshire Society (honorary).

WRITINGS: A Bibliography of Shropshire, Stockwell, 1922; *Byways of Shropshire History*, Ludlow Advertiser, 1927; *Salopian Rambles*, Advertiser Printing Works, 1933; *Midland Wanderings*, Advertiser Printing Works, 1937; *Notes on Ancient Tithe Barns*, Mitre Press, 1938; *By Midland Ways*, Newport Advertiser, 1939; *Famous Trees of the Midlands*, Newport Advertiser, 1944; *Shropshire Glimpses*, Newport Advertiser, 1948; *Shropshire Streams*, Newport Advertiser, 1950; *Round and About the Titterstone*, Newport Advertiser, 1955; *Shropshire Village Annals*, Newport Advertiser, 1961; *Villages of the Clee Hills*, Ludlow Advertiser, 1967. Contributor of articles to county magazines and local papers.

WORK IN PROGRESS: Research in local history and antiquarian subjects.

AVOCATIONAL INTERESTS: Preservation of countryside of rural England.

HEWINS, Ralph Anthony   1909-

PERSONAL: Born February 16, 1909, in Broadway, Worcestershire, England; son of Harold Preece and Margaret Elizabeth (Britton) Hewins. *Education:* Studied at Winchester College and University of Poitiers; Christ Church, Oxford, B.A., 1930. *Politics:* Conservative. *Religion:* Church of England. *Home:* 1474 Nordbyhagen, Akershus, Norway. *Agent:* David Higham Associates Ltd., 76 Dean St., London W.1, England.

CAREER: S. H. Benson's Ltd. (advertising firm), London, England, copywriter, 1930-34; *Observer*, London, athletics correspondent, 1932-38; *Daily Mail*, London, reporter, 1933-38; British Foreign Office, London, press attache to Finland and Baltic States, 1939; *Daily Mail*, correspondent in Scandinavia and Middle East, 1937-47; *News of the World*, Kemsley Newspapers and *Daily Express*, London, England, foreign correspondent, 1948-55. *Member:* Institute of Incorporated Practitioners in Advertising (associate), Press Club (London), Junior Carlton Club, Achilles Club, Ski Club of Great Britain.

WRITINGS: Counte Folke Bernadotte: His Life and Work, Denison, 1950; *Mr. Five Per Cent: The Biography of Calouste Gulbenkian*, Hutchinson, 1957, published as *Mr. Five Per Cent: The Story of Calouste Gulbenkian*, Rinehart, 1958; *The Richest American: J. Paul Getty*, Dutton, 1960 (published in England as *J. Paul Getty: The Richest American*, Sidgwick & Jackson, 1961); *A Golden Dream: The Miracle of Kuwait*, International Publications Service, 1963; *Quisling: Prophet Without Honor*, W. H. Allen, 1965, John Day, 1966; *The Japanese Miracle Men*, Secker & Warburg, 1967. Contributor to Swedish biographies of Count Bernadotte and King Gustav V; author of life of Barbara Hutton appearing in *Daily Mail*.

AVOCATIONAL INTERESTS: Athletics, especially winter sports.

* * *

HEYDON, Peter Richard   1913-1971

PERSONAL: Surname rhymes with ''maiden''; born September 9, 1913, in Croydon, New South Wales, Australia; son of Vigar Crawford (a teacher) and Emily (Sinclair) Heydon; married Muriel Naomi Slater, March 7, 1942; children: John Dyson, Julia Lynne, Pamela Ann. *Education:* University of Sydney, B.A., 1933, LL. B., 1936. *Religion:* Presbyterian. *Home:* 18 Tennyson Crescent, Forrest, Australian Capital Territory, Australia. *Office:* Australian Department of Immigration, Canberra, Australian Capital Territory, Australia.

CAREER: Admitted to practice as barrister-at-law, Sydney, 1936; Australian Department of External Affairs, 1936-61, private secretary to minister, Canberra, 1936-37, served in Washington, D.C., 1940-42, Kuibyshev and Moscow, 1942-44, London, 1947-50, and The Hague, 1950, minister to Brazil, 1951-53, high commissioner to New Zealand, 1953-55, and to India, 1955-58, first assistant department secretary, Canberra, 1960-61; Australian Department of Immigration, Canberra, secretary, beginning, 1961. Member of Australian delegation to United Nations General Assembly, 1948-49, 1957. *Member:* Australian Institute of International Affairs (secretary of Commonwealth Council, 1935-36), Royal Institute of Public Administration. *Awards, honors:* Commander, Order of the British Empire, 1959.

WRITINGS: Quiet Decision (study of George Foster

Pearce), Cambridge University Press, 1965. Contributor to *Public Administration* (Australia) and to *Australian Dictionary of Biography*.

(Died May 15, 1971)

* * *

HEYWOOD, Terence

PERSONAL: Born in Johannesburg, South Africa; son of Percy George (a company director) and Eleanor Dora (Liddle) Heywood. *Education:* Worcester College, Oxford, B.A., M.A.; Uppsala University, graduate student. *Home:* 40 Egerton Gardens, Chelsea, London S.W.3, England.

CAREER: Left South Africa in teens and has been a resident of England since, working in southern part of country prior to 1956, in London, 1956—. *Member:* Poetry Society, English Association, Oxford Society (life), National Film Theatre, Youth Hostels (life), New Cinema Club, Civil Service Lawn Tennis Club, Ski Club of Great Britain.

WRITINGS: Background to Sweden, Constable, 1950; *How Smoke Gets into the Air* (poetry), Fortune Press, 1952; *Architectonic: A Poem in VI Parts with Interludes*, Fortune Press, 1953; (with Edward Lowbury) *Facing North*, Mitre Press, Part I: *Poems and Pictures of the North* (by Heywood), 1960, Part II: *Trolls: A Fairy Tale* (by Lowbury), 1960, Part III: *Northern Discoveries: An Anthology* (compiled by Heywood), 1960. Anthologized in *Little Treasury of Modern Poetry*, edited by Oscar Williams, Scribner, 1948, *20th Century Scandinavian Poetry: The Development of Poetry in Iceland, Denmark, Norway, Sweden, Finland, 1900-1950*, edited by Martin Samuel Allwood, Knud K. Mogensen, 1951, *New Poems: A P.E.N. Anthology*, edited by Rex Warner and others, M. Joseph, 1954, *New Orlando Poetry Anthology*, edited by Anna Vrborska, 1958, *A Book of South African Verse*, edited by Guy Butler, Oxford University Press, 1959, *Poetry for Peace*, edited by Ken Geering, Breakthru Publications, 1963, *Verse for You, III*, edited by J. G. Brown, Longmans, 1964, *Commonwealth Poems of Today*, edited by H. Sergeant, J. Murray, 1967, and *The South African Schools Book of Verse*, edited by Hugh Brown and Peter Randall, Juta, 1970. Contributor of poetry to more than 250 periodicals in many countries; contributor of criticism, essays, and other articles to *Horizon, Anglo-Swedish Review, Norseman, Geographical, British Ski Year Book*, and other periodicals.

AVOCATIONAL INTERESTS: Tennis, gardening, travel, country walking, skiing, sailing, photography (illustrates some of his own books), and international cinema.

* * *

HIBBS, Paul 1906-

PERSONAL: Born October 21, 1906, in Ottumwa, Iowa; son of Orville C. (a railroad official) and Gertrude Agnes (Daly) Hibbs. *Education:* Missouri Wesleyan College (now merged with Baker University, Baldwin, Kan.), A.B., 1928; University of Wisconsin, A.M., 1942; graduate study, University of Illinois and Southern Illinois University. *Religion:* Roman Catholic. *Home:* 311 East Main St., Du Quoin, Ill. 62832. *Office:* Department of Speech, Southern Illinois University, Carbondale, Ill.

CAREER: Du Quoin Township (Ill.) High School, teacher of English, Spanish, Latin, dramatics, and psychology, and head of department of English and speech, 1928-47, superintendent, 1947-65; Southern Illinois University, Carbon-

dale, summer opera workshop production director, 1957-65, associate professor, beginning 1965, became professor of speech and chairman of department. News editor, radio station WJPF, 1944, 1945; production director of musical comedies at Egyptian Music Camp, Du Quoin, Ill., summers, 1951-57. *Member:* Speech Association of America, National Forensic League, Illinois Speech Association, Pi Kappa Delta, Phi Delta Kappa, Schoolmasters Club. *Awards, honors:* Tau Kappa Alpha National Sweepstakes Award for excellence in coaching national speech contestants, 1936, 1948; National Forensic League Distinguished Service Award (three times) and diamond key; honoree of endowed annual debate scholarships at Northwestern University, 1971; Distinguished Citizen Award, 1971.

WRITINGS: (Principal author and editor) *Speech for Today*, McGraw, 1965. Contributor of articles to educational and non-professional publications.

* * *

HILDEBRAND, Joel H(enry) 1881-

PERSONAL: Born November 16, 1881, in Camden, N.J.; son of Howard Ovid and Sara Regina (Swartz) Hildebrand; married Emily J. Alexander, December 17, 1908; children: Louise (Mrs. Fred Klein), Alexander, Milton, Roger Henry. *Education:* University of Pennsylvania, B.S., 1903, Ph.D., 1906; University of Berlin, postdoctoral study, 1906-07. *Politics:* Democrat. *Home:* 500 Coventry Rd., Berkeley, Calif. 94707.

CAREER: University of Pennsylvania, Philadelphia, instructor in physical chemistry, 1907-13; University of California, Berkeley, assistant professor, 1913-17, associate professor, 1917-18, professor of chemistry, 1918-52, professor emeritus, 1952—, dean of men, 1923-26, dean of College of Letters and Science, 1939-43, dean of College of Chemistry, 1949-51, now administrator of research contracts between university, U.S. Atomic Energy Commission, and National Science Foundation. Guthrie Lecturer, University of London, 1944; Walker Memorial Lecturer, 1944, and Romanes Lecturer, 1953, University of Edinburgh; Spiers Memorial Lecturer, Faraday Society, 1953; Bampton Lecturer, Columbia University, 1956; Treat B. Johnson Lecturer, Yale University; other lectureships in United States, Canada, and England. Liaison officer for Office of Scientific Research and Development, attached to U.S. Embassy, London, England, 1943-44; consulting chemist, U.S. Bureau of Mines, 1924-26; consultant to Quartermaster General and to War Production Board at intervals during World War II; member of Chemical Referee Board of Office of Production Research and Development, 1942-43. Member of Citizens Advisory Commission to Joint Committee of Education of California Legislature, 1958-60; member of advisory board, California Board of Education, 1966. *Military service:* U.S. Army, Chemical Warfare Service, 1917-18; became lieutenant colonel; received Distinguished Service Medal.

MEMBER: American Chemical Society (president, 1955), National Academy of Sciences (council member, 1949-52), American Physical Society (fellow), American Institute of Chemists (honorary life member), American Association for the Advancement of Science (vice-president, Pacific division, 1924-27, executive committee member, 1929-35; president, Pacific division, 1933-34), American Philosophical Society, Royal Society of Edinburgh (honorary fellow), Faraday Society (honorary life member), Sierra Club (president, 1937-40), California Academy of Science (honorary fellow), Phi Beta Kappa, Sigma Xi, Faculty Club.

AWARDS, HONORS: D.Sc., University of Pennsylvania, 1939; William H. Nichols Medal, 1939, for work on solubility on non-electrolytic solutions; King's Medal (Great Britain), 1948; Remsen Award, 1949; American Chemical Society prize, 1952, for contributions to chemical education; Willard Gibbs Medal, Chicago section of American Chemical Society, 1953; LL.D., University of California, 1954; James Norris Flack Award, 1961; Priestley Medal, American Chemical Society, 1962, for distinguished services to chemistry; William Proctor Prize, Scientific Research Society of America, 1962, for scientific achievement.

WRITINGS: Principles of Chemistry, Macmillan, 1918, 6th edition (with Richard E. Powell), 1952, 7th edition (with Powell), 1964; *Solubility* (monograph), Chemical Catalog Society, 1924, 2nd edition published as *Solubility of Non-Electrolytes*, Reinhold, 1936, 3rd edition (with R. L. Scott), Reinhold, 1950; (with Wendell M. Latimer) *Reference Book of Inorganic Chemistry*, Macmillan, 1929, 3rd edition, 1951; (with daughter, Louise Hildebrand Klein) *Camp Catering; or, How to Rustle Grub for Hikers, Campers, Mountaineers, Packers, Canoeists, Hunters, Skiers, and Fishermen*, Stephen Daye Press, 1938, 2nd edition, 1941.

Principles of Chemistry, 4th edition, [*and*] *Reference Book of Inorganic Chemistry*, 2nd edition, two volumes in one, Macmillan, 1941; *The Lowdown on Higher Education* (limericks), privately printed, 1942; (with others) *Ski Mountaineering*, 2nd edition, University of California Press, 1945; (contributor) D. R. Brower, editor, *Going Light, with Backpack or Burro*, Sierra Club, 1951; *Science in the Making*, Columbia University Press, 1957; (with Scott) *Regular Solutions*, Prentice-Hall, 1962, 2nd edition (with Scott and John M. Prausnitz) published as *Regular and Related Solutions: The Solubility of Gases, Liquids, and Solids*, Van Nostrand, 1970; *An Introduction to Molecular Kinetic Theory*, Reinhold, 1963; *Is Intelligence Important?*, Macmillan, 1963. Author of more than two hundred papers on scientific subjects, and of other articles on education, mountaineering, and skiing.

SIDELIGHTS: As a scientist Hildebrand is best known for his work with intermolecular forces, liquid structure, and the general theory of solubility in non-electrolytic solutions. He is also a "terror" (*Chemical Bulletin*, December 1953) on the harmonica while accompanying himself on the Spanish guitar, a composer of limericks while dressing, good at swinging Indian clubs, and a better baker of biscuits than most professional camp cooks. His philosophy: Real adventure is a matter of the mind and spirit and is not necessarily to be found in getting to some distant place.

Hildebrand was manager of the 1936 U.S. Olympic Ski Team, and retains his interest in all outdoor recreations, particularly mountaineering and skiing.

He knows how whales can dive without getting the bends. The U.S. Navy meanwhile is using the artifical atmosphere he suggested to the U.S. Bureau of Mines to prevent "the bends"—a mixture of helium and oxygen in place of air—for divers. This permits deeper dives and swifter ascents.

BIOGRAPHICAL/CRITICAL SOURCES: California Monthly, March, 1951; *Chemical Bulletin*, December, 1953; *Chemical and Engineering News*, April 2, 1962; *American Scientist*, March, 1963; *Perspectives in Biology and Medicine*, volume 16, 1972.

HILL, Brian (Merrikin) 1896-
(Marcus Magill)

PERSONAL: Born May 2, 1896, in London, England; son of Leonard Erskine (a physiologist) and Janet C. (Alexander) Hill. *Education:* Studied at Merchant Taylors' School and Wadham College, Oxford University. *Home:* 2 Grove Rd., London N.W.2, England.

CAREER: Gas Council (headquarters of British gas industry), London, England, executive, later assistant publicity manager, 1932-63. W.P.R. Ltd. (public relations), London, England, consultant. Executor with Sir Geoffrey Keynes of Samuel Butler's literary estate. *Military service:* British Army, 1915-19; became captain. *Member:* Incorporated Society of Authors, Faculty of the History of Medicine and Pharmacy.

WRITINGS: Youth's Heritage (poems), Erskine Macdonald, 1917; *Wild Geese* (poems), privately printed, 1923; (editor with Geoffrey Keynes) *Letters between Samuel Butler and Miss E. M. A. Savage, 1871-1885*, J. Cape, 1935; *Gas Heating for Public and Commercial Libraries, Museums*, A. J. Philip, 1937; *Take All Colours* (poems), Favil Press, 1943; *The Sheltering Tree* (poems), Favil Press, 1945; *Eighteen Poems*, Abbotsholme Press, 1947; *Inn-Signia*, Whitbread & Co., 1948, 2nd edition, Naldrett Press, 1949; (editor with Keynes) *Samuel Butler's Notebooks*, Dutton, 1951; (translator and author of introduction) Jean Rimbaud, *The Drunken Boat*, Hart-Davis, 1952; (compiler) *Pleasure Garden: An Anthology of Prose and Verse*, Hart-Davis, 1956; (translator and author of introduction) Paul Verlaine, *The Sky Above the Roof*, Macmillan, 1957; *Eight Poems*, privately printed, 1958; (translator and author of introduction) Gerard Labrunie de Nerval, *Fortune's Fool*, Dufour, 1959; (translator and author of introduction) Theophile Gautier, *Gentle Enchanter*, Hart-Davis, 1960, Dufour, 1961; (translator and author of introduction) Jose Maria de Heredia, *The Trophies*, Hart-Davis, 1962; *The Enchanter*, privately printed, 1962; (compiler) *The Greedy Book* (anthology), Hart-Davis, 1966; (compiler) *Such Stuff as Dreams*, Hart-Davis, 1967; *Gates of Horn and Ivory: An Anthology of Dreams*, Taplinger, 1968; *Last Poems*, Fuller & Smith, 1969.

Under pseudonym Marcus Magill: *Who Shall Hang?*, Lippincott, 1929; *Death in the Box*, Knopf, 1929; *I Like a Good Murder*, Lippincott, 1930; *Murder out of Tune*, Lippincott, 1931; *Murder in Full Flight*, Hutchinson, 1932, Lippincott, 1933; *Hide, and I'll Find You*, Hutchinson, 1933.

Contributor to *Bookman*, *Times* (London), and other periodicals and newspapers.

SIDELIGHTS: Hide, and I'll Find You was filmed under the title, "It's a Bet."

BIOGRAPHICAL/CRITICAL SOURCES: Listener, July 27, 1967; *Virginia Quarterly Review*, winter, 1969.

* * *

HILL, George E(dward) 1907-

PERSONAL: Born July 15, 1907, in Bellaire, Mich.; son of George (a clergyman) and Ellen (Couch) Hill; married Beatrice Kraft, August 29, 1934; children: Janet Hill Ball, Judith Hill Veney, Daniel B., Charlotte, May. *Education:* Albion College, A.B. (cum laude), 1929; Northwestern University, M.A., 1930, Ph.D., 1934. *Politics:* Republican. *Religion:* Methodist. *Home:* 38 Briarwood Dr., Athens, Ohio 45701. *Office:* McCracken Hall, Ohio University, Athens, Ohio 45701.

CAREER: Morningside College, Sioux City, Iowa, professor of education, 1934-36; University of Pennsylvania, Philadelphia, assistant professor of education, 1936-41; Kansas State Teachers College, Emporia, director of Graduate Division, 1946-48; Ohio University, Athens, professor, beginning, 1948, now distinguished professor of education. Visiting lecturer at University of Minnesota, Florida State University, University of Hawaii, University of Chicago, and other universities. *Member:* American Educational Research Association, American Personnel and Guidance Association, Association for Measurement in Education, National Society for the Study of Education, North Central Association of Colleges and Secondary Schools (honorary life member), Phi Beta Kappa, Kappa Delta Pi, Psi Chi, Delta Sigma Phi.

WRITINGS: (With Edward F. Potthoff) *Improvement of Teacher Education*, W. C. Brown, 1957; *Management and Improvement of Guidance*, Appleton, 1965, 2nd edition, Prentice-Hall, 1974; *Staffing Guidance Programs*, Houghton, 1968; *Guidance for Children*, Appleton, 1969. Author of four monographs published by Center for Educational Research and Service, Ohio University, 1959-61. Contributor of some one hundred articles to education and guidance journals.

SIDELIGHTS: Hill told *CA*, "My chief interest is the guidance of children and youth and the preparation of counselors to provide this."

*   *   *

HILL, Jim Dan 1897-

PERSONAL: Born February 4, 1897, in Leon County, Tex.; son of Dan Chapman (a merchant and rancher) and Alma A. (Hill) Hill; married Christine W. Cantwell, May 30, 1925; children: Dana Miltia (Mrs. Norman T. Budde). *Education:* Baylor University, A.B., 1922; University of Colorado, M.A., 1924; University of Minnesota, Ph.D., 1931. *Home address:* P.O. Box 228, Madison, Wis. 53701. *Office:* State Coordinating Committee on Higher Education, 333 University of Wisconsin Center Building, Landon Ave., Madison, Wis. 53703.

CAREER: High school principal, assistant commandant of military academy, and college teacher, 1921-24; Michigan College of Mines (now Michigan Technological University), Houghton, assistant professor, 1924-26, associate professor of English and economics, 1926; Wisconsin State College, River Falls (now University of Wisconsin-River Falls), chairman of department of social sciences, 1926-31; Wisconsin State College, Superior (now University of Wisconsin-Superior), president, 1931-64, with periods of leave for military duty; Wisconsin State Coordinating Committee on Higher Education, Madison, co-director, 1964—. Chairman of Committee on National Guard and Reserve Policy, Department of the Army, 1949-53; member of Reserve Forces Policy Board, Department of Defense, 1950-55, of advisory committee, U.S. Coast Guard Academy, 1959—.

MILITARY SERVICE: U.S. Navy, World War I. Officers Reserve Corps and National Guard, 1923-57, with active duty, 1940-46; graduate of Army Command and General Staff College, 1940, commanding officer of 190th Field Artillery Regiment, 1942-45, major general commanding 32nd Infantry Division, Wisconsin National Guard, 1946-56; World War II decorations include European theater medal with five campaign stars and arrowhead (Omaha Beach), Bronze Star, Legion of Merit (Battle of the Bulge), Chevalier de la Legion d'Honneur, Croix de Guerre with palm.

MEMBER: American Historical Association, Wisconsin Historical Society (governing board), Rotary Club, Masons, Army and Navy Club (Washington, D.C.). *Awards, honors:* D.Litt., Baylor University, 1948.

WRITINGS: Sea Dogs of the 'Sixties: Farragut and Seven Contemporaries, North and South, University of Minnesota Press, 1935; *The Texas Navy: Forgotten Battles and Shirtsleeve Diplomacy*, University of Chicago Press, 1937; *The Minute Man in Peace and War: A History of the National Guard*, Stackpole, 1964; (co-author) *Bayonets in the Streets: The Use of Troops in Civil Disturbances*, University of Kansas Press, 1968. Writer of weekly column, "News in Review," appearing in ten daily newspapers in United States, 1950-67.

WORK IN PROGRESS: Co-authoring a book on civil strife, past and present; a book-length series of memoir-like essays.

*   *   *

HILL, Knox C(alvin) 1910-

PERSONAL: Born December 15, 1910, in Oak Park, Ill.; son of Howard Copeland (a professor) and Hermione (Ireland) Hill; married Pauline Willis (an elementary teacher), June 19, 1939; children: Virginia (Mrs. Thomas Carpenter), Maureen, Thomas, Susan. *Education:* University of Chicago, B.S., 1930, M.A., 1936, Ph.D., 1954. *Home:* 6024 South Kimbark Ave., Chicago, Ill. 60637.

CAREER: University of Chicago, Chicago, Ill., 1939—, began as instructor, professor of philosophy, 1962-69, secretary of the faculties, 1969—. Visiting Professor, University of Puerto Rico, 1957. Member of woodlawn Citizens Committee on Urban Renewal. *Military service:* U.S. Army, 1942-46; received Bronze Star. U.S. Army Reserve, 1946-65; became colonel. *Member:* American Philosophical Association, Quadrangle Club (University of Chicago). *Awards, honors:* Ford Foundation fellowship, 1952-53; Quantrell Prize from University of Chicago, 1952, for excellence in teaching.

WRITINGS: Interpreting Literature, University of Chicago Press, 1966. Contributor to professional journals. Managing editor, *Journal of General Education*, 1956-61.

SIDELIGHTS: Hill has reading competency in French and Spanish, and some in German. *Avocational interest:* Music (received M.A. in music, formerly played piano and organ professionally, and directed choirs), photography.

*   *   *

HILL, Lorna 1902-

PERSONAL: Born February 21, 1902, in Durham, England; daughter of G. H. and Edith (Rutter) Leatham; married V. R. Hill (a clergyman); children: Shirley Victorine (Mrs. E. F. Emley). *Education:* University of Durham, B.A., 1926. *Religion:* Anglican. *Home:* Brockleside, Keswick, Cumberland, England. *Agent:* A. M. Heath & Co. Ltd., 35 Dover St., London W.1, England.

CAREER: Author of children's books.

WRITINGS: The Vicarage Children, Evans Brothers, 1961; *More About Mandy*, Evans Brothers, 1963; *The Secret*, Evans Brothers, 1964; *The Vicarage Children in Skye*, Evans Brothers, 1966; *La Sylphide: The Life of Maria Taglioni*, Evans Brothers, 1967.

"Marjorie" series: *Marjorie & Co.*, Art & Education, 1948, Thomas Nelson, 1956; *Stolen Holiday*, Art & Education, 1948, Thomas Nelson, 1956; *Border Peel*, Art & Education, 1950, Thomas Nelson, 1956; *No Medals for Guy*, Thomas Nelson, 1962.

"Sadler's Wells" series: *A Dream of Sadler's Wells*, Evans Brothers, 1950, Holt, 1955; *Veronica at the Wells*, Evans Brothers, 1951, published as *Veronica at Sadler's Wells*, Holt, 1954; *Masquerade at the Wells*, Evans Brothers, 1952, published as *Masquerade at the Ballet*, Holt, 1957; *No Castanets at the Wells*, Evans Brothers, 1953, published as *Castanets for Caroline: A Story of Sadler's Wells*, Holt, 1956; *Jane Leaves the Wells*, Evans Brothers, 1953; *Ella at the Wells*, Evans Brothers, 1954; *Return to the Wells*, Evans Brothers, 1955; *Rosanna Joins the Wells*, Evans Brothers, 1956; *Principal Role*, Evans Brothers, 1957; *Swan Feather*, Evans Brothers, 1958; *Dress Rehearsal*, Evans Brothers, 1959; *Back Stage*, Evans Brothers, 1960; *Vicki in Venice*, Evans Brothers, 1962.

"Patience" series, published by Burke Publishing: *They Called Her Patience*, 1951; *It Was All Through Patience*, 1952; *Castle in Northumbria*, 1953; *So Guy Came Too*, 1954; *The Five Shilling Holiday*, 1955.

"Dancing Peel" series, published by Thomas Nelson: *Dancing Peel*, 1954; *Dancer's Luck*, 1955; *The Little Dancer*, 1956; *Dancer in the Wings*, 1958; *Dancer in Danger*, 1960; *Dancer on Holiday*, 1962.

AVOCATIONAL INTERESTS: Scottish dancing, fell walking, swimming, gardening, photography, and music.

* * *

HILL, Rosalind M(ary) T(heodosia) 1908-

PERSONAL: Born November 14, 1908, in Neston, England; daughter of Arthur Norman and Mary (Danson) Hill. *Education:* St. Hilda's College, Oxford, B.A. (first class honors), 1931, B.Litt., 1936, M.A., 1937. *Politics:* Liberal. *Religion:* Anglican. *Home:* 7 Loom Lane Radlett, Hertfordshire, England. *Office:* Westfield College, University of London, London N.W.3, England.

CAREER: University of Leicester, Leicester, England, assistant lecturer in medieval history, 1932-37; Westfield College, University of London, London, England, lecturer in medieval history, 1937-55, reader, 1955-70, professor of history, 1971—. Director, Universities Federation for Animal Welfare; member of committee, Greek Animal Welfare Fund. *Member:* Royal Historical Society, Society of Antiquaries, Ecclesiastical History Society (secretary, 1963—), Canterbury and York Society treasurer, 1949-59; general editor, 1959-69, chairman, 1969—).

WRITINGS: The Rolls and Register of Bishop Olive Sutton, six volumes, Lincoln Record Society, 1949-56; *Oliver Sutton, Dean of Lincoln, Later Bishop of Lincoln* (pamphlet), Friends of Lincoln Cathedral, 1950; *Both Small and Great Beasts*, Universities Federation for Animal Federation Welfare, 1953; (translator and editor) *Anonymi Gesta Francorum: The Deeds of the Franks and the Other Pilgrims to Jerusalem*, Thomas Nelson, 1962; *The Labourer in the Vineyard: The Visitations of Archbishop Melton in the Archdeaconry of Richmond*, Borthwick Press, 1969.

WORK IN PROGRESS: More volumes of *The Rolls and Register of Bishop Oliver Sutton*; *History of the Manor and Borough of Stockbridge*; *The Register of Archbishop Melton of York*.

AVOCATIONAL INTERESTS: Animal welfare, mountaineering.

HILTON, Richard 1894-
(Zakhmi Dil)

PERSONAL: Born January 18, 1894, in Rawalpindi, Pakistan; son of John Edward (in Indian Service) and Reca (Higgins) Hilton; married Phyllis Martha Woodin, January 16, 1917; children: Peter, John Richard. *Education:* Attended Malvern College, 1907-11, Royal Military Academy, Woolwich, England, 1912-13. *Politics:* National Front. *Religion:* Church of England. *Home:* Little Tysoe, St. John's Ave., Leatherhead, Surrey, England.

CAREER: British Army Officer, 1913-48, with assignments in sixty-three countries; retired as major general. Served on Western front in World War I, with Royal Artillery, Royal Flying Corps, Royal Air Force. Peacetime service included fifteen years in Indian Service, three years as staff officer in War Office. In World War II served in Dunkirk campaign, as chief instructor (air) at School of Artillery, 1940-41, commander of royal artillery of 15th Scottish Division, 1941-44, in Normandy Landing, 1944, as brigadier of General Staff for Norway liberation, 1945, chief of British Mission to Soviet Zone of Germany, 1945-46, British military attache in Moscow, 1946-48; wounded at Caen, 1944. Chairman, True Tories, 1960—; chairman, Patriotic Party, 1963-65. *Awards, honors*—Military: Distinguished Service Order, Military Cross, Distinguished Flying Cross and bar, Commander of Order of St. Olav (Norway).

WRITINGS: Military Attache in Moscow, Hollis & Carter, 1949, Beacon Press, 1951; *Nine Lives: The Autobiography of an Old Soldier*, Hollis & Carter, 1955; *The Indian Mutiny: A Centenary History*, Hollis & Carter, 1957; *The North-West Frontier: A True Story for Boys*, Hollis & Carter, 1957; *The Thirteenth Power: The Middle East and the World Situation*, Johnson Publishers, 1958; *Imperial Obituary: The Mysterious Death of the British Empire*, Britons Publishing, 1968. Contributor to *Blackwood's Magazine* under pseudonym Zakhmi Dil; regular contributor of articles on foreign events to *Coventry Evening Telegraph*, 1952-62; contributor to military journals and to other newspapers.

WORK IN PROGRESS: The Big Feet of Ghulam Rasul.

SIDELIGHTS: Hilton has traveled on foot through Tibet. He is competent in French, Spanish, Italian, Portuguese, Russian, German, Norwegian, Urdu, Pushtu, Persian, and Punjabi. *Avocational interests:* Mountaineering, yachting, riding, rough camping, argument, and chess.

* * *

HINDE, Richard Standish Elphinstone 1912-

PERSONAL: Born April 28, 1912, in Dublin, Ireland; son of Richard and Agnes Margaret (Elphinstone) Hinde. *Education:* Peterhouse, Cambridge, B.A., 1934, M.A., 1938; St. Peter's College, Oxford, M.A., 1939, B.Litt., 1948; Wycliffe Hall, theological study; Trinity College Dublin, M.A. (ad eundem), 1962. *Home:* 17 St. Stephen's Green, Dublin 2, Ireland.

CAREER: Clerk in Holy Orders, Church of Ireland, 1935—; Oxford Prison, chaplain, 1939-43; Hertford College, Oxford University, Oxford, England, fellow, 1951-61, senior tutor, 1948-61, chaplain, 1947-61; St. Andrew's Church, Dublin, Ireland, rector, 1961-65. *Military service:* Royal Air Force, chaplain, 1943-46. *Member:* Royal Commonwealth Society, University Club (Dublin).

WRITINGS: The British Penal System, 1773-1950, Duckworth, 1951.

WORK IN PROGRESS: Crofton and the Irish Convict System, 1854-1862; John Howard: His Life and Letters.

* * *

HINRICHSEN, Max (Henry)   1901-1965

PERSONAL: Born July 6, 1901, in Leipzig, Saxony, Germany; son of Henri Robert (a music publisher) and Martha (Bendix) Hinrichsen; married Carla H. Eddy (a music publisher), March 27, 1956; children: Irene Henriette Elisabeth Hinrichsen Lawford. *Education:* Attended Schola Nicolaitana, Leipzig, Germany.

CAREER: C. F. Peters, Leipzig, Germany, manager of U.S. distribution agency, Peters Edition, New York, N.Y., 1924-27, managing editor of Peters Edition, Leipzig, 1928-37, administrator of Peters Musik Bibliothek (library), Leipzig, 1931-37, director of Peters Edition, London, England, 1949-65; Hinrichsen Edition Ltd., London, England, chairman and managing director, 1937-65. Director of Hinrichsen Concert Direction and Artists Management, London, England, 1942-65, C. F. Peters Musik-Verlag, Frankfurt, Germany, 1950-65, Cranbrook Tower Press, London, 1957-65, Musia Export & Import, Frankfort, 1957-65, London, 1959-65. Committee member, London Council of Social Service Arts, 1948-65; deputy member, Conseil d'Administration du Bureau International de l'Edition Mecanique, 1963-65.

MEMBER: British Copyright Protection Association (vice-president, 1962-65), Hymn Society of Great Britain, National School Brass Band Association, Association of Organists, International Association of Music Libraries, Music Publishers' Association, Mechanical Copyright Protection Society, National Book League, Royal Musical Association, Society of Authors, Performing Right Society, Organ Music Society, Viola da Gamba Society (vice-president, 1962-65), Galpin Society.

WRITINGS: Anno Verdiano, Hinrichsen, 1952; *Compositions Based on the Motive B-A-C-H*, Hinrichsen, 1952; *The Beggar's Opera Playing Cards*, Hinrichsen, 1957; *Some Poetry and Prose of Purcell's Time*, Hinrichsen, 1961; *Samuel Wesley and Dr. Mendelssohn*, Hinrichsen, 1963.

Co-editor of *Jahrbuch der Musicbibliothek Peters*, 1931-37; editor of *Hinrichsen's Musical Year Books* (now titled "music Book Series"), 1944-65. Editor, London Regional Committee for Education among H. M. Forces, University of London, 1943-48; member of editorial committee, *Music, Libraries and Instruments*, 1961, *Dictionary of International Biography*, 1963. Contributor to "Music Book Series" and to music journals.

AVOCATIONAL INTERESTS: Copyright.

BIOGRAPHICAL SOURCES: Music Trades Review, June, 1950, June, 1955; *Times* (London), February 22, 1951; *Author*, autumn, 1951.

* * *

HINTERHOFF, Eugene   1895-

PERSONAL: Born March 3, 1895, in Korea; son of Louis and Angela (de Werbno-Slonczynska) Hinterhoff; married Margaret Countess Arz-Vasegg, June 26, 1939. *Education:* School of Economics and Political Science, Warsaw, Poland, student, 1922; University of Warsaw, Magister Juris, 1924. *Religion:* Roman Catholic. *Home:* 10 Victoria Grove, London W.8, England. *Office: Tablet*, 14 Howick Pl., London S.W.1, England.

CAREER: Polish Army, regular officer, 1918-33; graduate of General Staff College, Warsaw, 1924; became captain; served with Polish Forces under British Command, 1939-42; received Virtuti Militari Vclass. Polish Telegraph Agency, foreign and diplomatic correspondent in Vienna and Prague, 1934-39; Polish Ministry of Information, London, England, staff member, 1942-45; Polish Telegraph Agency, foreign and diplomatic correspondent in London, 1945-49; *Tablet*, London, England, defense correspondent, 1957—. *Member:* International P.E.N., Royal Institute of International Affairs, Institute for Strategic Studies, National Union of Journalists, Military Commentator's Circle (founder; honorary secretary, 1942—), Foreign Press Association (London). *Awards, honors:* Literary Prize, Polish Commbaants' Association, 1960; North Atlantic Treaty Organization fellowship, 1962-63.

WRITINGS: Disengagement, Stevens & Sons, 1959; *Plaene fuer ein militaerisches Auseinanderruecken der Weltmaechte in Deutschland in Scheuer, Gernot*, [Frankfurt am Main], 1960; (translator with Philip Windsor) W. Bader, *Civil War in the Making: The Combat Groups of the Working Class in East Germany*, Independent Information Center (London), 1964. Contributor to military and political journals in England, Holland, France, Germany, and United States, and to British Broadcasting Corp. and Radio Free Europe programs.

WORK IN PROGRESS: Comparative study of the North Atlantic Treaty Organization and the Warsaw Pact.

SIDELIGHTS: Hinterhoff speaks French, German, Russian, Italian, Czech, Polish, and English.

* * *

HIRSCHFELD, Herman   1905-

PERSONAL: Born December 7, 1905, in New York, N.Y.; married Roslyn Nelson, December 26, 1945; children: Seth, Michael. *Education:* New York University, B.S., 1933; University of Oklahoma, M.D., 1935. *Politics:* Liberal. *Religion:* Hebrew. *Home:* 220 East 63rd St., New York, N.Y. 10022.

CAREER: Physician in private practice as specialist in allergy and dermatology, 1935—. Le Roy Hospital, New York, N.Y., consultant, 1955—. *Military service:* U.S. Navy, 1942-44; became lieutenant senior grade. *Member:* International Allergy Association (president), American Geriatric Society, Industrial Medical Association, American Academy of Compensation Medicine (board member), Queens County Medical Society.

WRITINGS: The Whole Truth About Allergy, Arco, 1963; *Your Allergic Child*, Arco, 1964.

WORK IN PROGRESS: A new book on allergy.

* * *

HITSMAN, J(ohn) Mackay   1917-1970

PERSONAL: Born April 19, 1917, in Kingston, Ontario, Canada; son of Samuel A. and Minnie (Mackay) Hitsman; married Catherine Munro, March 6, 1954; children: George, Edward, Anthony. *Education:* Queen's University, Kingston, Ontario, B.A., 1939, M.A., 1940; University of Ottawa, Ph.D., 1964. *Office:* Directorate of History, Canadian Forces Headquarters, Ottawa, Ontario, Canada.

CAREER: Canadian Army, Historical Section, Ottawa, Ontario, civilian archivist and historian, 1947-68. *Military service:* Canadian Army, 1941-47; became captain. *Member:* Royal Historical Society (fellow), Royal United Service Institution, Society for Army Historical Research, American Military Institute, Company of Military Historians, Canadian Historical Association, Ontario Historical Society.

WRITINGS: Military Inspection Services in Canada, 1855-1950, Queen's Printer, 1962; *The Incredible War of 1812: A Military History*, University of Toronto Press, 1965; *Safeguarding Canada, 1763-1871*, University of Toronto Press, 1968. Contributor to history and military journals.

WORK IN PROGRESS: Research for a book on the Canadian Militia.

(Died February, 1970)

*   *   *

HOBSON, Harry   1908-
(Hank Hobson, Hank Janson)

PERSONAL: Born 1908, in Sheffield, England; son of Charles J. and Sarah (Brooksbank) Hobson; married Ivie Hinsby. *Education:* Attended school in Sheffield, England. *Home:* 8 Eastmearn Rd., West Dulwich, London S.E. 21, England. *Agent:* Hughes Massie Ltd., 18 Southampton Pl., London W.C.1, England.

CAREER: Began as professional musician, making two trips around the world, appearing in capital cities in Europe, on radio and television; full-time writer, 1958—. *Military service:* Royal Air Force, 1940-46. *Member:* Crime Writers' Association, Mystery Writers of America.

WRITINGS—Under name Hank Hobson; all published by Cassell: *The Gallant Affair*, 1957, *Death Makes A Claim*, 1958, *The Mission House Murder*, 1959, *The Big Twist*, 1959, *Beyond Tolerance*, 1960.

Under pseudonym Hank Janson; all published by Roberts & Vinter: *Janson Go Home*, 1961; *Crowns Can Kill*, 1961; *Mastermind*, 1961; *Beauty and the Beat*, 1962; *Chicago Chick*, 1962; *Uncover Agent*, 1962; *Take This Sweetie*, 1962; *Like Crazy*, 1962; *Like Poison*, 1962; *Like Lethal*, 1962; *Grape Vine*, 1963; *Uncommon Market*, 1963; *Dateline Diane*, 1963; *Dateline Darlene*, 1963; *Dateline Debbie*, 1963; *The Love Makers*, 1963; *Fast Buck*, 1963; *Visit From a Broad*, 1963; *Lake Loot*, 1963; *Crime Beat Crisis*, 1964; *Fan Fare*, 1964; *Doctor Fix*, 1964; *That Brain Again*, 1964.

AVOCATIONAL INTERESTS: Golf and bridge.

*   *   *

HOCKING, William Ernest   1873-1966

PERSONAL: Born August 10, 1873, in Cleveland, Ohio; son of William Francis (a physician) and Julia Carpenter (Pratt) Hocking; married Agnes Boyle O'Reilly (a schoolteacher), June 28, 1905 (died May 15, 1955); children: Richard, Hester (Mrs. Donald Campbell), Joan, (Mrs. Edward Kracke). *Education:* Iowa State Agricultural College and Farm (now Iowa State University of Science and Technology), engineering student, 1894-95; Harvard University, A.B., 1901, A.M., 1902, Ph.D., 1904; graduate study at University of Goettingen, University of Berlin, and University of Heidelberg, 1902-03. *Politics:* Mugwump. *Religion:* "Suitable to an ecumenical era—world faith in a Christian congregational wrapping." *Home and office:* Eaton Rd., Madison, N.H.

CAREER: Surveyor and engineer in Illinois, 1889-93; Dav-

enport (Iowa) public schools, principal, 1896-99; Harvard University, Cambridge, Mass., instructor in philosophy, 1904-05; Andover (now Andover-Newton) Theological Seminary, Newton Center, Mass., instructor in the philosophy and history of religion, 1904-06; University of California, Berkeley, instructor, 1906-07, assistant professor of philosophy, 1907-08; Yale University, New Haven, Conn., assistant professor, 1908-13, professor of philosophy, 1913-14; Harvard University, Cambridge, Mass., professor of philosophy, 1914-20, Alford Professor of Natural Religion, Moral Philosophy, and Civil Polity, 1920-43; became Alford Professor Emeritus, chairman of division of philosophy and psychology, 1935-37, chairman of philosophy department, 1937-43. Founder with wife of experimental school, Shady Hill School, Cambridge, Mass. Mahlon Powell Lecturer at University of Indiana; Gifford Lecturer at University of Glasgow, 1938-39; William James Lecturer at Harvard University, 1947; visiting professor or lecturer at other universities and colleges in United States and abroad. Laymen's Foreign Mission Inquiry Commission in Far East, chairman, 1931-32; member of Commission on Freedom of the Press, 1944-47.

MEMBER: American Academy of Arts and Letters, American Academy of Arts and Sciences, American Philosophical Association (president, 1925-26), American Philosophical Society, Metaphysical Society of America (president, 1957), American Political Science Association, American Association for the Advancement of Science, American Oriental Society, Faculty Club (Cambridge); Harvard Club and Century Association (both New York); Rotary Club, Grange, Farm Bureau. *Awards, honors:* Lecomte du Nouy Award, 1957, for *The Coming World Civilization*; Knight commander's cross of Order of Merit, Federal Republic of Germany; L.H.D. from Williams College, 1923; Th.D. from University of Glasgow, 1933; D.D. from University of Chicago, 1933; LL.D. from Oberlin College, 1934, Duke University, 1941, Colby College, 1950, University of California, 1952, Yale University, 1959; Litt. et Phil.D. from University of Leyden, 1948.

WRITINGS: Two Extensions of the Use of Graphs in Elementary Logic, University of California Press, 1909, reprinted, Johnson Reprint, 1969; *On the Law of History*, University of California Press, 1909, reprinted, Johnson Reprint, 1969; *The Meaning of God in Human Experience*, Yale University Press, 1912; *Human Nature and Its Remaking*, Yale University Press, 1918, 3rd edition, 1929; *Morale and Its Enemies*, Yale University Press, 1918.

Immanuel Kant and International Policies, American Peace Society, 1924; *Man and the State*, Yale University Press, 1926 reprinted, Archon Books, 1968; *Present Status of the Philosophy of Law and Rights* , Yale University Press, 1926; *The Self, Its Body and Freedom*, Yale University Press, 1928; *Types of Philosophy*, Scribner, 1929, 3rd edition, in collaboration with son, Richard Boyle O'Reilly Hocking, 1959.

(Editor) Charles Andrew Bennett, *Dilemma of Religious Knowledge*, Yale University Press, 1931; (editor and contributor) *Re-Thinking Missions: A Layman's Inquiry After One Hundred Years*, Harper, 1932; *The Spirit of World Politics: With Special Studies of the Near East*, Macmillan, 1932; (with Charles M. Bakewell) *George Herbert Palmer, 1842-1933: Memorial Addresses*, Harvard University Press, 1935; *The Lasting Elements of Individualism* (Mahlon Powell Lectures), Yale University Press, 1937; *Thoughts on Death and Life*, Harper, 1937 (also see below).

Living Religions and a World Faith, Macmillan, 1940; *What Man Can Make of Man*, Harper, 1942; (with others) *Church and the New World Mind: the Drake Lectures for 1944*, Christian Board, 1944, reprinted, Books for Libraries, 1968; *Science and the Idea of God*, University of North Carolina Press, 1944; (with others) *Preface to Philosophy* (textbook), Macmillan, 1946; *Freedom of the Press: a Framework of Principle*, University of Chicago Press, 1947.

Experiment in Education; What We Can Learn from Teaching Germany, Regnery, 1954; *The Coming World Civilization*, Harper, 1956; *The Meaning of Immortality in Human Experience* (including *Thoughts on Death and Life*, revised), Harper, 1957, section published as separate volume, *The Relativity of Death*, Harper, 1957; *Strength of Men and Nations: A Message to the U.S.A. vis-a-vis the U.S.S.R.*, Harper, 1959.

WORK IN PROGRESS: Preparing William James Lectures on Law at Harvard University, 1947, and Gifford Lectures at University of Glasgow, 1938-39, for publication; a summary guide toward a foreign policy for the United States, "neither appeasing nor rigid, involving creative risk."

SIDELIGHTS: "I am not attempting to make these lists complete," Hocking wrote *CA*, listing only half a dozen books, ranging from *The Meaning of God in Human Experience*, 1912, to *Strength of Men and Nations*, 1959. "Busy man.... Besides which: the object of life—which should show a certain productivity—could easily be buried in a sandpile of details. In a well-ordered state, there is a limit which one should not be allowed to exceed, of works of art, Platonic Dialogues, opera magna, finalities in philosophy. The one achievement worth noting is the creation of a certain individual beauty in living and in the environment of living—one's Task."

AVOCATIONAL INTERESTS: Painting, farming, family music.

BIOGRAPHICAL/CRITICAL SOURCES: Wisdom for Our Time, edited by James Nelson, Norton, 1961. *Philosophy, Religion, and the Coming World Civilization*, edited by Leroy S. Rouner, 1966.

(Died June 12, 1966)

*　　*　　*

HODGSON, Leonard 1889-1969

PERSONAL: Born October 24, 1889, in London, England; son of Walter and Lillias Emma (Shaw) Hodgson; married Ethel Margaret du Plat Archer, 1920 (died, 1960); children: Brigid Mary (Mrs. Guy S. Somerset). *Education:* Hertford College, Oxford, B.A., 1912, D.D., 1938; St. Michael's College, Llandaff, Wales, post-doctoral study. *Home:* 24 Newbold Ter., Leamington Spa, Warwickshire, England.

CAREER: Church of England, clergyman, 1913-69; St. Mark's Church, Portsmouth, England, curate, 1913-14; St. Edmund Hall, Oxford University, Oxford, England, vice-principal, 1914-19; Magdalen College, Oxford University, Oxford, fellow and dean of divinity, 1920-25; General Theological Seminary, New York, N.Y., professor of Christian apologetics, 1925-31; Winchester Cathedral, Winchester, England, canon, 1931-38; Christ Church, Oxford University, Oxford, England, canon, 1938-69, Regius Professor of Moral and Pastoral Theology, 1938-44, Regius Professor of Divinity, 1955-58. Examining chaplain to the Bishop of Lichfield, 1917-25; warden, William Temple College, Rugby, England, 1954-66. Theological secretary to the Commission on Faith and Order, World Council of Churches, 1933-52. Fellow, St. Edmund Hall, Oxford University, 1944, and Selwyn College, Cambridge University, 1957. *Awards, honors:* D.C.L., Bishop's College, 1929; S.T.D., General Theological Seminary, 1931; D.D., University of Edinburgh, 1943, University of Glasgow, 1957.

WRITINGS: The Place of Reason in Christian Apologetic: Four Lectures, Appleton, 1925; (translator, editor, and author of introduction and notes with G. R. Driver) Nestorius, *The Bazaar of Heracleides*, Clarendon Press, 1925, Oxford University Press (New York), 1926; *Has Criticism Destroyed the Bible?*, S.P.C.K., 1926; *And Was Made Man: An Introduction to the Study of the Gospels*, Longmans, Green, 1928; *Essays in Christian Philosophy*, Longmans, Green, 1930; (editor) *God and the World Through Christian Eyes*, two volumes, S.C.M. Press, 1933-34 published as *Radio Talks on Religion: God and the World Through Christian Eyes*, Morehouse, 1934; *Eugenics*, Centenary Press, 1933; *The Lord's Prayer: Six Sermons*, Longmans, Green, 1934; (editor with H. N. Bate and Ralph W. Brown) *Convictions: A Selection from the Responses of the Churches to the Report of the World Conference on Faith and Order*, Macmillan (New York), 1934; *Democracy and Dictatorship in the Light of Christian Faith: Two Sermons*, Basil Blackwell, 1935; *The Grace of God in Faith and Philosophy* (lectures), Longmans, Green, 1936; (editor) *The Second World Conference on Faith and Order*, Macmillan (New York), 1938; *This War and the Christian: Four Sermons*, Morehouse, 1939.

The Christian Idea of Liberty, S.C.M. Press, 1941; (editor) *Christian Teaching About Sex*, S.P.C.K., 1942; *Towards a Christian Philosophy*, Nisbet, 1942; *The Doctrine of the Trinity: Croall Lectures, 1942-43*, Nisbet, 1943, Scribner, 1944; *Anglicanism and South India*, Cambridge University Press, 1943; *Theology in an Age of Science*, Oxford University Press (New York), 1944; *The Doctrine of the Church as Held and Taught in the Church of England*, Basil Blackwell, 1946; *Biblical Theology and the Sovereignty of God* (lecture), Macmillan (New York), 1947; *Christian Faith and Practice: Seven Lectures*, Basil Blackwell, 1950, Scribner, 1951, new edition, Eerdmans, 1965; *The Ecumenical Movement: Three Lectures*, University of the South, 1951; *The Doctrine of the Atonement* (lectures), Scribner, 1951; *For Faith and Freedom: The Gifford Lectures, 1955-57*, two volumes, Basil Blackwell, 1956-57, Scribner, 1957, one volume edition, S.C.M. Press, 1968; *Church and Sacraments in Divided Christendom: Three Lectures*, S.P.C.K., 1959; (with Arthur Lichtenberger) *Mary Fitch Page Lecture [and] Commencement Address* (the former by Hodgson, the latter by Lichtenberger), Berkeley Divinity School, 1959; *How Can God Be One and Three?*, S.P.C.K., 1960; (with others) *On the Authority of the Bible: Some Recent Studies*, S.P.C.K., 1960; *The Bible and the Training of the Clergy*, Darton, Longman & Todd, 1963; *Sex and Christian Freedom: An Enquiry*, Seabury, 1967.

AVOCATIONAL INTERESTS: Reading and walking.

BIOGRAPHICAL/CRITICAL SOURCES: Times (London), July 16, 1969, July 18, 1969.

(Died July 15, 1969)

*　　*　　*

HODGSON, Phyllis 1909-

PERSONAL: Born June 27, 1909, in Bradford, Yorkshire,

England; daughter of Herbert Henry and Annie Gertrude (Proctor) Hodgson. *Education:* Bedford College, London, B.A. (honors), 1932; Lady Margaret Hall, Oxford, B.Litt., 1935, D.Phil., 1936. *Religion:* Church of England. *Home:* 48 St. Thomas Rd., St. Annes-on-Sea, Lancashire, England.

CAREER: University of Durham, St. Mary's College, Durham, England, tutor, 1936-38; Cambridge University, Cambridge, England, Jex-Blake Fellow at Girton College, 1938-40; lecturer in English at Homerton College, 1940-42; University of London, London, England, lecturer in English at Queen Mary College, 1940-42, lecturer at Bedford College, 1942-49, university reader in English language, 1949-55, professor of English language and medieval literature at Bedford College, 1955—. External examiner, University of Reading, 1955-57, 1961—; Sir Israel Gollancz Memorial Lecturer, British Academy, 1964.

WRITINGS: (Editor) *The Cloud of Unknowing and the Book of Privy Counselling*, Oxford University Press, for Early English Text Society, 1944, 2nd edition, 1958; (editor) *Deonise hid diuinite and Other Treatises on Contemplative Prayer related to the "Cloud of Unknowing,"* Oxford University Press, for Early English Text Society, 1955, 2nd edition, 1958; (editor) Geoffrey Chaucer, *The Franklin's Tale*, Athlone Press, 1960; (editor with Gabriel M. Liegey) Catherine of Siena, *The Orcherd of Syon*, Volume I, Oxford University Press, for the Early English Text Society, 1966; (editor) Chaucer, *General Prologue to the Canterbury Tales*, Athlone Press, 1969. Contributor of articles to *Modern Language Review*, *Contemporary Review*, *Review of English Studies*, other journals in field.

* * *

HOFFMAN, Hester R(osalyn) 1895-

PERSONAL: Born June 1, 1895, in Terre Haute, Ind.; daughter of George W. J. (a druggist) and Margaret (Miller) Hoffman. *Education:* Smith College, A.B., 1917. *Politics:* Republican. *Religion:* Presbyterian. *Home:* 153 Elm St., Northampton, Mass. 01060. *Office:* R. R. Bowker Co., 1180 Avenue of the Americas, New York, N.Y. 10036.

CAREER: Hampshire Bookshop, Inc., Northampton, Mass., 1917-45, began as assistant, became assistant manager, director, and treasurer; R. R. Bowker Co. (publisher), New York, N.Y., editor, 1945—. Secretary and director, Maine's Massachusetts House Workshop, Inc., Lincolnville, Me., 1949—; director, L. A. Bigelow, Inc., Boston, Mass., 1960—. *Member:* Women's National Book Association.

WRITINGS: (Editor) *The Bookman's Manual: A Guide to Literature*, Bowker, 6th edition (Miss Hoffman was not associated with earlier editions), 1948, 9th edition published as *The Reader's Adviser and Bookman's Manual*, 1960, 10th edition published as *The Reader's Adviser*, 1964.

AVOCATIONAL INTERESTS: Collecting first editions by modern authors, music, drama, ballet, herb gardening, and promoting Maine arts and handicraft.

* * *

HOFFMANN, Eleanor 1895-

PERSONAL: Born December 21, 1895, in Belmont, Mass.; daughter of Ralph and Gertrude (Wesselhoeft) Hoffmann. *Education:* Radcliffe College, A.B., 1917; also studied at Massachusetts Agricultural College and University of North Carolina. *Politics:* Democrat. *Home:* 2653 Glendessary Lane, Santa Barbara, Calif.

CAREER: Author.

WRITINGS: *Melika and Her Donkey*, Stokes, 1937; *Travels of a Snail*, Stokes, 1939; *A Cat of Paris*, Stokes, 1940; *Mischief in Fez*, Holiday, 1943; *Feeding Our Armed Forces*, Nelson, 1943; *The Four Friends*, Macmillan, 1943; *Sierra Sally*, Nelson, 1944; *The Lion of Barbary*, Holiday, 1946; *Princess of the Channel Isles*, Nelson, 1947; *White Mare of the Black Tents*, Dodd, 1949.

The Tall Stallion, Dodd, 1950; *The Search for the Gold Fishhook*, Dodd, 1951; *The Mystery of the Lion Ring*, Dodd, 1953; *Trouble at Sweet Springs Ranch*, Dodd, 1954; *Summer at Horseshoe Ranch*, Dodd, 1957; *The Charmstone*, McNalley & Loftin, 1964; *Realm of the Evening Star: A History of Morocco and the Lands of the Moors*, Chilton, 1965.

Contributor of stories and articles to periodicals, including *Harper's Bazaar*, *Town and Country*, *Asia*, and many juvenile magazines.

WORK IN PROGRESS: Research on nineteenth-century exploration of Africa, and on a special phase of Captain Cook's first voyage.

AVOCATIONAL INTERESTS: Travel and oceanography.

* * *

HOFINGER, Johannes 1905-

PERSONAL: Born March 21, 1905, in St. Johann, Tirol, Austria; son of Josef and Maria (Bichler) Hofinger. *Education:* Studied philosophy at Gregorian University, Rome, 1924-25, at Berchmanskolleg, Munich, 1927-29; studied theology at University of Innsbruck, 1932-36; awarded doctorate in theology, 1940. *Address:* East Asian Pastoral Institute, Box 1815, Manila, Republic of the Philippines.

CAREER: Ordained Roman Catholic priest, 1935; member of Society of Jesus (Jesuit); Regional Seminary of Kinghsien, China, professor of dogmatic theology and catechetics, 1940-49; with St. Joseph's Chinese Seminary, Manila, Philippines, 1949-58; with East Asian Pastoral Institute, Manila, Philippines, 1953-65, director, 1957-65.

WRITINGS: *Geschichte des Katechismus in Oesterreich*, [Innsbruck], 1937; (with Joseph Kellner) *Der priesterlose Gemeindegottesdienst in den Missionen*, Administration der Neuen Zeitschrift fuer Missionswissenschaft, 1956; *The Art of Teaching Christian Doctrine*, University of Notre Dame Press, 1957, 2nd edition, 1962, adaptation published as *Imparting the Christian Message*, 1961; (with Kellner) *Liturgische Erneuerung in der Weltmission*, Tyrolia-Verlag, 1957; (author with others) *Worship: The Life of the Missions*, University of Notre Dame Press, 1958; (with Paul Brunner and Jean Seffer) *Pastorale liturgique en chretiente missionnaire*, Lumen Vitae, 1959; (editor) *Mission und Liturgie*, Matthias-Gruenewald-Verlag (Mainz), 1960, translation published as *Liturgy and the Missions: The Nijmegen Papers*, Kenedy, 1960; (editor) *Katechetik heute: Grundsaetze und Anregungen zur Erneuerung der Katechese in Mission und Heimat*, Herder (Freiburg), 1961, translation by Clifford Howell published as *Teaching All Nations: A Symposium on Modern Catechetics*, Herder & Herder, 1961; (with William J. Reedy) *The ABC's of Modern Catechetics*, W. Sadlier, 1962; (editor with Theodore C. Stone) *Pastoral Catechetics*, Herder & Herder, 1964. Contributor to theological reviews, including *Lumen Vitae*, *Liturgisches Jahrbuch*, and *Chicago Studies*. Editor, 1962-69, of *Good Tidings*, published in Manila with special editions published in the United States, England, and Ireland; editor, 1964-69, of *Teaching All Nations*, a quarterly review of mission catechetics and liturgy, published in Manila.

*   *   *

HOGG, Quintin McGarel 1907-
(Lord Hailsham of St. Marylebone)

PERSONAL: Born October '9, 1907, in England; son of first Viscount Hailsham and Elizabeth (Trimble Brown); married Mary Evelyn Martin, April 18, 1944; children: Douglas Martin, Mary Claire, Frances Evelyn, James Richard Martin, Katharine Amelia. *Education:* Christ Church, Oxford, first class honors, moderations, 1928, first class honors, literae humaniores, 1930. *Politics:* Conservative. *Religion:* Church of England. *Home:* The Corner House, 13 Heathview Gardens, Putney Heath, London S.W. 15, England. *Office:* 4 Paper Buildings Temple, London E.C.4, England.

CAREER: Succeeded father as second Viscount and Baron Hailsham, 1950. Barrister, Lincoln's Inn, 1932; Queen's Counsel, 1953; bencher of Lincoln's Inn, 1956. Member of Parliament for Oxford City, 1938-50; undersecretary of state for air, in coalition and caretaker government, 1945; First Lord of the Admiralty, 1956-57; Minister of Education, 1957; deputy leader of the House of Lords, 1957-60; Lord Privy Seal, 1959-60; Minister for Science and Technology, 1959-63; chairman of Conservative Party, 1959; Lord President of the Council and leader of the House of Lords, 1960-64; member of Parliament for St. Marylebone, London, 1963-70; Secretary of State for Education and Science, 1964; Lord Chancellor, 1970. Fellow, All Soul's College, Oxford University, 1931-38, 1961—; rector, University of Glasgow, 1959. *Military service:* British Army, Rifle Brigade, 1939-45; served in Africa (wounded), and in Middle East; became major. *Member:* Classical Association (president, 1960-61), Institute of Civil Engineers (honorary), Carlton Club, Alpine Club, Marylebone Cricket Club. *Awards, honors:* D.C.L., Westminster College, Fulton, Mo., University of Newcastle, 1964; LL.D., Cambridge University, 1963.

WRITINGS: The Law of Arbitration, Butterworth & Co., 1936; *One Year's Work*, Hurst & Blackett, 1944; *The Law and Employers' Liability*, Stevens & Sons, 1944; *The Times We Live In* (booklet), Signpost, 1944; *Making Peace*, S.C.M. Press, 1945; *The Left Was Never Right*, Faber, 1945; *The Purpose of Parliament*, Blandford, 1946; *The Case for Conservatism*, Penguin, 1947, revised edition published as *The Conservative Case*, 1959; (with W. R. Inge and Walter Elliot) *God, King and Empire*, Hutchinson, 1947; *Parliament: A Reader's Guide*, Cambridge University Press, 1948; (contributor) Tudor Rees and H. V. Usill, editors, *They Stand Apart: A Critical Survey of Homosexuality*, Macmillan, 1955; (with Robert McEwen) *The Law Relating to Monopolies, Restrictive Trade Practices and Resale Price Maintenance*, Butterworth & Co., 1956; *Toryism and Tomorrow* (pamphlet), Conservative Political Centre, 1957; *A New Faith in Ourselves*, Conservative and Unionist Central Office, 1957; *Shaftsbury: A New Assessment*, Shaftsbury Society, 1958; *Interdependence: A Policy for Free Peoples*, Conservative Political Centre, 1960; *Vos Exemplaria Graeca*, J. Murray, 1961; (with Winston Churchill) *The Iron Curtain, Fifteen Years After 1960* [and] *The Sinews of Peace* (the former by Hogg, the latter by Churchill), Westminster College, 1961; *The*

Need for Faith in a Scientific Age, Glasgow University, 1961; *Science and Government*, University of Southampton, 1961; *National Excellence*, Conservative Political Centre, 1963; *Science and Politics*, Faber, 1963, Encyclopaedia Britannica Press, 1964; *The Human Intellect on the Throne of Society*, University of New Brunswick, 1965; *The Brain Drain*, Conservative Political Centre, 1967; *The Devils Own Song, and Other Verses*, Hodder & Stoughton, 1968.

AVOCATIONAL INTERESTS: Shooting, walking, and other outdoor pursuits.

*   *   *

HOGREFE, Pearl

PERSONAL: Born in Holt County, Mo.; daughter of John Henry and Rosanna (Van Gundy) Hogrefe. *Education:* Southwestern College, Winfield, Kan., B.A., 1910; University of Kansas, M.A., 1913; University of Chicago, Ph.D., 1927. *Home:* 1801 Twentieth St., Ames, Iowa. *Office:* Department of English, Iowa State University, Ames, Iowa.

CAREER: Iowa State Teachers College, Cedar Falls, instructor, 1921-25, professor of English, 1925-28; Louisiana Polytechnic Institute, Ruston, professor of English and chairman of department, 1928-31; Iowa State University, Ames, associate professor, 1931-44, professor of English, 1944—. *Member:* Modern Language Association of America, Shakespeare Association of America, American Association of University Professors, American Association of University Women (president of Iowa State Division, 1946-48; member of national committee on higher education, 1954-60), Phi Kappa Phi, Delta Kappa Gamma. *Awards, honors:* Folger Shakespeare Library fellow, 1951, 1961; American Association of University Women, Founders fellow, 1952-53. The Pearl Hogrefe Endowment Fellowship has been established at Iowa State University; and the Wood-Hogrefe National AAUW Fellowship was established for the American Association of University Women.

WRITINGS: (Editor with others) *Interpreting Experience*, 1935; *Renewal: Poems*, Prairie Press, 1940; *The Process of Creative Writing*, Harper, 1947, 3rd edition, Harper, 1963; *The Sir Thomas More Circle*, University of Illinois Press, 1959; *Life and Times of Sir Thomas Elyot*, Iowa State University Press, 1967. Contributor to professional journals.

WORK IN PROGRESS: Tudor Women: Commoners and Queens, a monograph; *Nine Tudor Women*, biographical sketches.

AVOCATIONAL INTERESTS: Gardening (herbs and flowers), cooking.

*   *   *

HOLBECHE, Philippa Jack 1919-
(Philippa Shore)

PERSONAL: Born November 4, 1919, in Loughton, Essex, England; daughter of Robert Hunter (a clergyman, Church of England) and Phyllis Mary (Tanner) Jack; married Brian H. Holbeche (a school headmaster), July 16, 1945; children: Sarah Halcyon, Barnaby John. *Education:* Attended St. Mary's Hall, Brighton, England. *Religion:* Church of England. *Home:* Nelson House, Beechen Cliff, Bath, Somerset, England. *Agent:* Laurence Pollinger Ltd., 18 Maddox St., London W.1, England.

CAREER: Writer.

WRITINGS—Under pseudonym Philippa Shore; all published by Wright & Brown: *House by the Water*, 1958; *Into the Light*, 1959; *Two Hearts, One Spade*, 1959; *Second String*, 1961; *Leaf in the Wind*, 1963.

WORK IN PROGRESS: A novel on contemporary life in a "red brick" university.

* * *

HOLBROOK, Stewart Hall 1893-1964

PERSONAL: Born August 22, 1893, in Newport, Vt.; son of Jesse William (a businessman) and Kate (Stewart) Holbrook; married Katherine Stanton Gill, June 12, 1924 (deceased); married Sibyl Walker, May 1, 1948; *children:* Sibyl Morningstar, Bonnie Stewart. *Education:* Attended Colebrook Academy, Colebrook, N.H. *Religion:* Unitarian. *Home and office:* 2670 Northwest Lovejoy, Portland, Ore. 97210.

CAREER: Early career includes period as cub reporter and semi-pro baseball player in Winnipeg, Manitoba, and actor in touring Canadian stock company, 1911-14; returned to New England and worked in lumber camps, 1914-17, 1919-20; logged in British Columbia, Canada, 1920-23; *Lumber News*, Portland, Ore., associate editor, 1923-25, editor, 1926-34; free-lance writer, Portland, Ore., 1934-64. Lecturer at Harvard University and Boston University during two years' temporary residence in Cambridge, Mass. *Military service:* U.S. Army, 1917-19; served in France; awarded two battle stars. *Member:* American Antiquarian Society. *Awards, honors:* D.H.L., Pacific University, 1957; D.Litt., Willamette University, 1959.

WRITINGS: Holy Old Mackinaw: A Natural History of the American Lumberjack, Macmillan, 1938, 2nd edition, 1956, enlarged edition published as *The American Lumberjack*, Collier, 1962; *Let Them Live*, Macmillan, 1938; *Iron Brew: A Century of American Ore and Steel*, Macmillan, 1939.

Ethan Allen, Macmillan, 1940, illustrated edition, Binfords, 1958; *Tall Timber*, Macmillan, 1941; *Murder out Yonder: An Informal Study of Certain Classic Crimes in Back-Country America*, Macmillan, 1941; *None More Courageous: American War Heroes of Today*, Macmillan, 1942; *Burning an Empire: The Story of American Forest Fires*, Macmillan, 1943; (editor) *Promised Land: A Collection of Northwest Writing*, McGraw, 1945; *Lost Men of American History*, Macmillan, 1946; *The Story of American Railroads*, Crown, 1947; *Little Annie Oakley and Other Rugged People*, Macmillan, 1948; (author of introduction and commentary) Henry Hargrave Sheldon, *Northwest Corner: Oregon and Washington, the Last Frontier*, Doubleday, 1948; *America's Ethan Allen*, Houghton, 1949.

The Yankee Exodus: An Account of Migration from New England, Macmillan, 1950; *Far Corner: A Personal View of the Pacific Northwest*, Macmillan, 1952; *Wild Bill Hickok Tames the West*, Random House, 1952; *The Age of the Moguls*, Doubleday, 1953; *Down on the Farm: A Picture Treasury of Country Life in America in the Good Old Days*, Crown, 1954; *James J. Hill: A Great Life in Brief*, Knopf, 1955; *Machines of Plenty: Pioneering in American Agriculture*, Macmillan, 1955; *Davy Crockett*, Random House, 1955; *Santa's North Pole Circus*, Pageant, 1955; *The Columbia*, Rinehart, 1956, reissued as *The Columbia River*, Holt, 1965; *Wyatt Earp, U.S. Marshal*, Random House, 1956; *The Rocky Mountain Revolution*, Holt, 1956; *Dreamers of the America Dream*, Doubleday, 1957; *Mr. Otis*, Macmillan, 1958; *Hoosiers Start a Railroad: The*

Monon, Fort Wayne Public Library, 1958; *Robbing the Steamcars*, Fort Wayne Public Library, 1958; *War Comes to a "Neutral" Line*, Fort Wayne Public Library, 1958; *The Swamp Fox of the Revolution*, Random House, 1959 (published in England as *Swamp Fox: The Story of General Francis Marion*, E. M. Hale, 1959); *The Golden Age of Quackery*, Macmillan, 1959.

The Golden Age of Railroads, Random House, 1960 (published in England as *Age of Railroads*, E. M. Hale, 1960); *The Old Post Road; The Story of Boston Post Road*, McGraw, 1962; (contributor) Anthony Netboy, editor, *Pacific Northwest*, Doubleday, 1963; *The Wonderful West*, Doubleday, 1963.

Business histories: *Green Commonwealth: A Narrative of the Past and a Look at the Future of One Forest Products Community*, Simpson Logging Co., 1945; *A Narrative of Schafer Bros. Logging Company's Half Century in the Timber*, Schafer Bros. Logging Co., 1945; *Saga of the Saw Filer*, Armstrong Manufacturing Co., 1952; *Personalities of the Woods*, 3rd edition, San Francisco Bethlehem Pacific Coast Steel Corp., c.1957; *Yankee Loggers: A Recollection of Woodsmen, Cooks, and River Drivers*, International Paper Co., 1961.

Contributor of essays and articles to magazines and newspapers, including *American Heritage*, *New Yorker*, *Portland Oregonian*, *New York Times*, *Saturday Evening Post*, *American Mercury*, and *New York Herald Tribune*.

AVOCATIONAL INTERESTS: Painting.

BIOGRAPHICAL/CRITICAL SOURCES: Boston Herald, May 26, 1940; *Denver Post*, August 12, 1947; *New York Herald Tribune*, June 25, 1950; *American Heritage*, April, 1959.

(Died September 3, 1964)

* * *

HOLDING, Charles H. 1897-

PERSONAL: Born August 24, 1897, in Ridgeway, Mo.; son of Ben F. (an attorney) and Mary Alice (Collins) Holding; married Zana Singleton, June 22, 1920; children: Mary Alice Holding Manning, Billy Ben, Zana B. Holding Wood. *Education:* Educated in Oklahoma schools. *Politics:* Democrat. *Religion:* Methodist. *Home:* 1401 South 20th St., Chickasha, Okla. 73018.

CAREER: One-time worker in oil fields; farmer, 1921-41; Oklahoma State, gasoline inspector, 1943-55, with State Employment Service, 1956-61. Lay leader in Methodist church.

WRITINGS: The Scar, Eerdmans, 1946; *The Rustle of Wings*, Eerdmans, 1964.

WORK IN PROGRESS: A children's book, *Glory in Galilee*; a prison story, *Forgive Me for Forgetting*; a story of modern life, *Where Do We Go from Here?*

* * *

HOLDSWORTH, Irene

PERSONAL: Born in Cheshire, England. *Education:* Attended Downs School in England. *Home:* 2 Chelsea Studios, 410 Fulham Rd., London S.W.6, England.

CAREER: Writer. Broadcaster of travel talks for British Broadcasting Corp.

WRITINGS: Yes Ma'am, Hutchinson, 1943; *A Taste for Travel*, Seeley Service, 1956; *Little Masks*, Seeley Service,

1956; *Polio is Not for Pity*, Allen & Unwin, 1963. Contributor to *Times* (London), *The Queen, Go*, and *Sketch*.

AVOCATIONAL INTERESTS: Foreign travel and Siamese cats.

*   *   *

HOLDSWORTH, Mary (Zvegintzov)   1908-

PERSONAL: Born October 24, 1908, in Voronezh, Russia; daughter of Alexander (an army officer) and Catherine (Sverbeev) Zvegintzov; married Richard Holdsworth (a Royal Air Force pilot), September 21, 1940 (died April, 1942); children: Diana Holdsworth Hervey. *Education:* St. Hugh's College, Oxford, B.A., 1930, M.A., 1946. *Politics:* Liberal-Labour. *Religion:* Orthodox. *Home and office:* St. Mary's College, University of Durham, Durham, England.

CAREER: Banking and industrial secretary, London, England, 1930-37; Oxford University, University College, Oxford, England, research assistant and secretary to William Beveridge, 1937-40; British Air Ministry, technical officer, 1942-44; tutor for Education in the Forces, Northern Ireland, 1944-45, and for Workers' Educational Association, 1945-48; Oxford University, Institute of Commonwealth Studies, secretary and senior research officer, 1948-62; University of Durham, St. Mary's College, Durham, England, principal, beginning 1962, and part-time lecturer in department of politics. Manager of Primary and Secondary Schools, Oxfordshire, 1948-62, of Aycliffe Approved School, Durham County, beginning 1962. *Member:* Royal Institute of International Affairs, Congress on Oriental and Islamic Studies, Commonwealth Services Club (Oxford).

WRITINGS: Turkestan in the Nineteenth Century, Central Asia Research Centre, 1959; *Soviet African Studies, 1918-1959* (annotated bibliography), Oxford University Press, 1961; (contributor) Frederick Madden and Kenneth Robinson, editors, *Essays on Imperial Government*, Basil Blackwell, 1963; (contributor) E. Luard, editor, *The Cold War*, Thames & Hudson, 1964.

WORK IN PROGRESS: A study of minorities in the Union of Soviet Socialist Republics, with special emphasis on Soviet Central Asia and Azerbaijan; research on political, constitutional, and cultural problems of minorities.

SIDELIGHTS: Mrs. Holdsworth reads French, Russian, and German. *Avocational interests:* Gardening, walking.

*   *   *

HOLLOWAY, Brenda W(ilmar)   1908-
(Sarah Verney)

PERSONAL: Born October 7, 1908, in Moseley, Worcestershire, England; daughter of William Henry and Martha Patti (Hirst) Holloway. *Education:* Attended Moseley College, Birmingham, England. *Religion:* Church of England. *Home:* 17 Anderton Park Rd., Moseley, Birmingham B13 9BQ, England.

CAREER: Private secretary to the Bishop of Birmingham, Birmingham, England, 1953—. Director of Wilmar Holloway Ltd. *Member:* Society of Authors, Italic Handwriting Society.

WRITINGS: Timothy Richard of China: A Pageant, Carey Press, 1946; *Prayers for Children*, University of London Press, 1951; *Prayers for Younger Children*, University of London Press, 1954; *Prayers for the Home*, Hodder & Stoughton, 1957. Correspondent, *Church Times*;

editor, and contributor to Bible Reading Fellowship Ladder Books; editor, *Birmingham Diocesan Directory*, 1958-63.

WORK IN PROGRESS: Welsh language study and research into Welsh history and culture.

*   *   *

HOLM, Sven (Aage)   1902-
(Farmacevten)

PERSONAL: Born July 15, 1902, in Copenhagen, Denmark; son of Aage Peter Christian and Elizabeth (Hauberg) Holm; married Ingeborg Marie Nimb Lassen, September 11, 1927; children: Kirsten Holm Lassen, Grethe Gale, Christian. *Education:* Studied pharmacy in Copenhagen, Denmark. *Politics:* Conservative. *Religion:* Lutheran. *Home:* Ahlmanns Alle 27 Helleru p, Copenhagen, Denmark. *Office:* Silkegade 1, Copenhagen, Denmark.

CAREER: One-time actor and cameraman, films and television; later pharmacist in Copenhagen, Denmark. Freelance writer. Broadcaster on chemical and pharmaceutical subjects on Danish television, fifteen years, and on radio, thirty years. Violinist. *Member:* Danish Chemists, Danish Scouts.

WRITINGS: Farmaceuts gode raad, Berlingske, 1936; *Drinks* (published in Danish), Berlingske, 1937; *Kosmetik: Instruktiv laerebog og receptsamling for professionelle og amatorer*, Gyldendal, 1939; *Year in Radio* (published in Danish), Frimodt, 1939, 1940, 1941; *Alt om pletter og masser og andre raad*, 1942, translation by Inger O'Hanlon published as *Stains and How to Remove Them*, Deutsch, 1959; *Farmacevtens leksikon*, S. Vendelkaer, 1957; *Jeg renser alt*, Politikens Forlag, 1959; *Jeg blev Farmacevt* (autobiography), J. Frimodt, 1961; (editor) *Delige Mallorca*, S. Vendelkaer, 1962. Contributor of pharmaceutical and chemical articles to Danish newspapers and magazines.

SIDELIGHTS: As a motion picture cameraman, Holm helped produce the first Danish talking picture, "Petersen and Poulsens," and as an actor was one of the first to appear on Danish television. *Stains and How to Remove Them* has been translated into eight languages.

*   *   *

HOLMES, Parker Manfred   1895-

PERSONAL: Born November 15, 1895, in Winona, Minn.; son of Manfred James (a professor) and Jeannette (McCool) Holmes; married Dorothy Thomas; children: Anita Claire, James Parker, Jeannette Elizabeth. *Education:* Illinois State Normal University (now Illinois State University), B.Ed., 1922; University of Chicago, A.M., 1924. *Politics:* Republican. *Religion:* Presbyterian.

CAREER: J. Walter Thompson Co. (advertising), Chicago, Ill., assistant director of research, 1929-34; A. C. Neilsen Co., Chicago, Ill., client service executive, 1934-44; Plough, Inc., Memphis, Tenn., director of marketing research, 1944-47; St. Louis University, St. Louis, Mo., associate professor of marketing, 1947-52; Marquette University, Milwaukee, Wis., professor of marketing, beginning 1952. *Military service:* U.S. Naval Reserve, 1918-22. *Member:* American Marketing Association, Acacia, Alpha Delta Sigma, Pi Sigma Epsilon, Delta Sigma Pi.

WRITINGS: Marketing Research: Principles and Readings, South-Western Publishing, 1960, revised edition, 1965; (senior editor) *Readings in Marketing*, C. E. Merrill, 1963.

WORK IN PROGRESS: Research in trends in population, retail sales, and net effective buying power, and in the decentralization movement in major metropolitan markets.

* * *

HOLMES, William Kersley 1882-
(F. O. O. Serrifile)

PERSONAL: Born June 15, 1882, in Harborne, Staffordshire, England; son of William Charles and Amy Eleanor (Kersley) Holmes. *Education:* Attended Dollar Academy, Dollar, Scotland. *Politics:* Conservative. *Religion:* Episcopal. *Home:* 9 McNabb St., Dollar, Clackmannanshire, Scotland.

CAREER: Clydesdale Bank Ltd., employee in Dollar, Edinburgh, and Glasgow, Scotland, prior to 1941; Blackie & Son Ltd. (publishers), Glasgow, Scotland, editor, beginning in 1919, now retired. Onetime broadcaster of stories for children. *Military service:* British Army, Royal Field Artillery, 1915-19; became captain; served in north Russia, 1919.

WRITINGS: Ballads of Field and Billet, Alexander Gardner, 1915; *More Ballads of Field and Billet*, Alexander Gardner, 1915; *In the Open* (verses), Gowans & Gray, 1925; *A Pocketful of Rhymes*, Blackie & Son, 1929; (with Richard F. Patterson) *How to Write and What to Read*, Gresham, 1933; *The Stolen Trophy, and Other Stories*, Blackie & Son, 1934; (author of introduction and notes) John Milton, *Comus*, Blackie & Son, 1943; *Tramping Scottish Hills*, Eneas Mackay, 1946, revised edition published as *On Scottish Hills*, Oliver & Boyd, 1962; (with Robert Aitchen) *The Pied Piper of Dogs*, Blackie & Son, 1946; *Jimmy and Janet on the Farm*, Blackie & Son, 1954; *Zoo Animals*, Blackie & Son, 1954; *The Life I Love* (verses), Blackie & Son, 1958.

Adapter—All published by Blackie & Son: Robert Louis Stevenson, *Treasure Island*, 1948; *Stories from Grimm*, 1949; *Stories from Hans Andersen*, 1949; Hans Christian Andersen, *Thumbkin, and Other Stories*, 1951; Andersen, *The Tinder-Box and Other Stories*, 1951; *The Gift of the Little People, and Other Stories from Grimm*, 1951; *Snow-White and Rose-Red, and Other Stories from Grimm*, 1951; *Tales from Andersen and Grimm*, 1957.

Translator—All published by Blackie & Son, except as indicated: Friedrich Feld, *The Musical Umbrella*, 1958; Feld, *The Runaway Echo*, 1960; Feld, *The Talking Cat*, 1960; Feld, *The Marvellous Matches*, 1961; Feld, *The Silver Flamingo*, 1962; *Tales from Grimm*, 1963; *Tales from Andersen*, Arco, 1964; Feld, *The Parrot of Isfahan*, 1964.

Contributor of about twelve thousand pieces of verse and many articles to newspapers and magazines, including *Punch, Country Life, Glasgow Herald*, and *Scotsman*.

AVOCATIONAL INTERESTS: Walking in the hills, sketching in water colors.

* * *

HOLMSTROM, (John) Edwin 1898-

PERSONAL: Born February 25, 1898, in Birkdale, Lancashire, England; children: one son and three daughters. *Education:* University of London, Imperial College of Science and Technology, B.Sc., 1920, London School of Economics, Ph.D., 1932. *Address:* c/o National Liberal Club, London S.W. 1, England.

CAREER: Served as assistant engineer for Chinese Government Railways, 1921-24, as section engineer for Federated Malay States Railways, 1925-29, and in engineering posts in London, England, and Northern Ireland, 1930-34; Imperial Chemical Industries Ltd., London, England, developmental research, 1934-39, 1946-49; UNESCO, Paris, France, member of natural sciences department, 1949-58; University of Innsbruck, Innsbruck, Austria, translator in a university institute, 1962-64; now freelance scientific and technical translator from German, French, Italian, and Scandinavian languages, indexer, and consultant. *Military service:* British Army, 1916-19, 1939-45; became major. *Member:* Institution of Civil Engineers (fellow), Institute of Linguists (fellow), Institute of Information Scientists (fellow), Society of Indexers.

WRITINGS: Railways and Roads in Pioneer Development Overseas: A Study of Their Comparative Economics, King, 1934; *Records and Research in Engineering and Industrial Science: A Guide to the Sources, Processing and Storekeeping of Technical Knowledge*, Chapman & Hall, 1940, 3rd edition, 1956; *How to Take, Keep and Use Notes* (pamphlet), Aslib, 1947; *Facts, Files and Action*, Chapman & Hall, Volume I: *Sources and Backgrounds of Facts*, 1950, Volume II: *Filing, Indexing and Circulation*, 1953; *Bibliography of Interlingual Scientific and Technical Dictionaries*, UNESCO, 1951, 4th edition, 1961; *Report of Interlingual Scientific and Technical Dictionaries*, UNESCO, 1951; *Scientific and Technical Translating and Other Aspects of the Language Problem*, UNESCO, 1958; *Multilingual Terminology of Information Processing* (in German, English, Spanish, French, and Russian), Provisional International Computation Center (Rome), 1959; (translator) Martin Scheele, *Punch-Card Methods in Research and Documentation*, Interscience, 1961; (co-author and co-translator) *Modern Documentation and Information Services*, International Federation for Documentation, 1961. Author of more than one hundred articles, papers, and reports, mainly on questions of technical documentation and language. Editor of conference papers.

WORK IN PROGRESS: Translations of current articles in *Scientia*; index to first fifty volumes, *Proceedings* of British Academy; current indexes to publications of Institution of Civil Engineers and of Science Policy Foundation.

* * *

HOLT, William 1897-

PERSONAL: Born September 1, 1897, in Todmorden, Yorkshire, England; son of Arthur and Elizabeth (Egerton) Holt; married Florence Silman (divorced, 1971); children: Florence Dolores, Maureen Elizabeth, Vincent William, Silvia. *Education:* Educated at boarding school and privately; studied art at Anglo-French Art Centre, London, England. *Home:* Kilnhurst, Todmorden, Yorkshire, England.

CAREER: Sailed around the world as able seaman, 1920-21; between that time and his latest odyssey (via horseback) in 1964-65, roamed through thirty-odd countries and worked as a teacher of languages, lumberjack, war correspondent, professional artist, radio commentator, and tutor to Duke of Monteperto; author and journalist. Inventor of a locked pirn alignment for improving automatic weaving, patented in United States and Canada. *Military service:* British Army, Lancashire Fusiliers, 1914-18; became second lieutenant. *Member:* Savage Club (London). *Awards, honors:* British Arts Council award, 1974, for service to literature.

WRITINGS: Under a Japanese Parasol (autobiographical), King & Co. (Halifax), 1933; *Backwaters* (fiction), Nicholson & Watson, 1934; *The Price of Adventure* (fiction), Nicholson & Watson, 1934; *I Was a Prisoner* (autobiographical), John Miles, 1935; *I Haven't Unpacked* (autobiographical), Harrap, 1939; *I Still Haven't Unpacked* (autobiographical), Harrap, 1953; *The Weaver's Knot* (fiction), Laurie, 1956; *The Wizard of Whirlaw* (fiction), privately printed, 1959; *Trigger in Europe* (autobiographical), M. Joseph, 1966, published as *Ride a White Horse*, Dutton, 1967. Contributor to *Listener, Strand, Picture Post, Reader's Digest, Guardian, London Calling*, and other magazines and newspapers.

WORK IN PROGRESS: A novel; further autobiography; a children's book about his horse, Trigger; drawings and sketches for those books; an opera based on *The Wizard of Whirlaw*; a nonfiction book, *They Changed the Face of the World*.

SIDELIGHTS: Holt's most recent book, *Trigger in Europe (Ride a White Horse)*, is an account of his travels by horseback through six European countries, 1964-65; he spent fifteen months on that tour, sleeping in the open without a tent for more than four hundred nights. Holt appeared in a film of his life, "The All or Nothing Man," televised by I.T.V., 1972. He speaks French, Spanish, German, and Italian, and has broadcast for British Broadcasting Corp. in all four languages.

* * *

HOLZAPFEL, Rudolf Patrick   1938-
(Rudi Holzapfel; pseudonyms: rooan hurkey, R. Patrick Ward)

PERSONAL: Born December 11, 1938, in Paris, France; son of Rudolf Melander (a writer and art expert) and Mary Mona Charlotte (Trew) Holzapfel; married Ulla Stroucken (an artist), May 16, 1962; children: Francis Rudolf. *Education:* Attended Santa Barbara Catholic High School, 1952-56; Trinity College, Dublin, Ireland, student, 1957—. *Religion:* Catholic. *Address:* Altis, Ballinclea Rd., Killiney, County Dublin, Ireland.

CAREER: Writer.

WRITINGS: (With Brendan Kennelly) *Cast a Cold Eye* (poetry), Dolmen Press, 1959; (under pseudonym rooan hurkey) *Romances*, Dolmen Press, 1960; (with Kennelly) *The Rain, The Moon* (poetry), Dolmen Press, 1961; (with Kennelly) *The Dark About Our Loves* (poetry), privately printed, 1962; (with Kennelly) *Green Townlands: Poems*, Leeds Bibliographical Press, 1963; *The Leprechaun*, privately printed, 1963; *Transubstantiations*, privately printed, 1963; *Soledades* (poems), privately printed, 1964; *Translations from the English*, privately printed, 1965; (compiler) *An Index of Contributors to the Dublin Magazine*, Museum Bookshop (Dublin), 1966; *The Rebel Bloom*, privately printed, 1967; *James Clarence Morgan: A Checklist of Printed and Other Sources*, privately printed, 1969. Contributor to *Icarus, Dubliner, Kilkenny Magazine, T.C.D., Trinity News, Manana, Quagga, Modern Languages Review, Irish Times, Kerryman*, and other publications.

WORK IN PROGRESS: Nessaycitos, a book of short essays; two novels, *Wangerooge* and *Outrigger*; another experimental novel; a proposed book of poems, *The Ballad of the Leftover Kid*; a book of epitaphs, mostly comic.

HOOD, F(rancis) C(ampbell)   1895-1971

PERSONAL: Born March 30, 1895, in Edinburgh, Scotland; son of Alexander (a dock treasurer) and Agnes Marshall (Cunningham) Hood; married Mary Horsley, 1921 (marriage dissolved, 1939); married Muriel Dodds, December 17, 1940; children: (first marriage) son (deceased); (second marriage) Virginia Agnes. *Education:* Educated at University of Edinburgh, 1912-1916, Balliol College, Oxford, 1916-18. *Politics:* Independent. *Religion:* Christian. *Home:* Kingsgate, Bow Lane, Durham, England.

CAREER: Temporary civil servant with British Board of Trade and Ministry of Labour, 1918-19; University of Birmingham, Birmingham, England, lecturer in history, 1919-20; National Federation of Iron and Steel Manufacturers, in England, intelligence officer, 1920-22; University of Durham, Durham, England, lecturer, 1922-40, reader in history, 1940-45, professor of political theory and institutions, 1946-55, professor emeritus, 1955-71.

WRITINGS: The Divine Politics of Thomas Hobbes, Oxford University Press, 1964.

(Died November 22, 1971)

* * *

HOOVER, Calvin Bryce   1897-1974

PERSONAL: Born April 14, 1897, in Berwick, Ill.; son of John Calvin (a railway foreman) and Margaret (Roadcap) Hoover; married Faith Sprole, July 5, 1919; children: Carol Faith, Sylvia Joan Hoover Schrack. *Education:* Monmouth College, Monmouth, Ill., A.B., 1922; University of Minnesota, graduate study, 1923-25; University of Wisconsin, Ph.D., 1925. *Politics:* Democrat. *Home:* 1515 West Pettigrew St., Durham, N.C. *Office:* Duke University, Durham, N.C.

CAREER: University of Minnesota, School of Business, Minneapolis, instructor, 1923-25; Duke University, Durham, N.C., assistant professor, 1925-27, professor of economics, 1927-50, James B. Duke Professor of Economics, 1950-67, dean of graduate school, 1937-47. Economic adviser to U.S. government agencies, beginning, 1933. *Military service:* U.S. Army, Field Artillery, 1917-19; served in France. U.S. Army, Office of Strategic Services, 1941-45; received Medal of Freedom, 1946. *Member:* American Economic Association (president, 1953), Association for Comparative Economics (president, 1964), Southern Economic Association (president, 1936-37), Phi Beta Kappa. *Awards, honors:* D.Litt., Columbia University, 1934, Monmouth College, Monmouth, Ill., 1935; LL.D., Case Western Reserve University, 1970.

WRITINGS: The Economic Life of Soviet Russia, Macmillan, 1931; *Germany Enters the Third Reich*, Macmillan, 1933; *Dictators and Democracies*, Macmillan, 1937; *International Trade and Domestic Employment*, McGraw, 1944; *Economic Resources and Policies of the South*, Macmillan, 1950; *The Economy, Liberty and the State*, Twentieth Century, 1959; *Memoirs of Capitalism, Communism, and Nazism*, Duke University Press, 1965. Contributor of articles to professional periodicals.

WORK IN PROGRESS: Continuing research in fields of economic systems and economic theory.

SIDELIGHTS: Hoover studied Soviet economic system first-hand, 1929-30, and made return visits in 1933, 1939, 1956, and 1958; he studied Hitler's rise to power in Germany, 1932-33.

(Died June 23, 1974)

HOPE, C(harles) E(velyn) G(raham)   1900-1971

PERSONAL: Born December 6, 1900, in Cheltenham, Gloucestershire, England; son of Graham Archibald (a writer) and Ruby Evelyn (Murray) Hope; married Beryl Maud Daly, March 29, 1930; children: Michael and John (twins; died in infancy). *Education:* Attended Marlborough College, Wiltshire, England, 1914-18 and Royal Military College, Wellington, India, 1918-20. *Politics:* Independent. *Religion:* Roman Catholic. *Home:* 93 Barkston Gardens, London S.W.5, England. *Office:* D. J. Murphy (Publishers) Ltd., 19 Charing Cross Rd., London W.C.2, England.

CAREER: Army officer, 1920-32, 1940-45; writer and editor, 1932—; publisher, 1949—. Cavalryman in Indian Army, 1920-32; returned to active duty with British Army, 1940-45, serving mainly in India and with Allied Land Forces, Southeast Asia; became lieutenant colonel. Freelance journalist, playwright, and novelist, 1932-37, and founder of *Wessex Magazine*, 1935; assistant editor of *Riding* (monthly), 1937, 1945-49; founder and editor of *Pony* (children's monthly), 1949—, and *Show Jumping* (a monthly, now published as *Light Horse*), 1950—. D. J. Murphy (Publishers) Ltd., London, England, director, 1949-55, chairman, 1955—. *Member:* Institute of Directors, British Horse Society, National Pony Society, Hunters Improvement and National Light Horse Breeding Society, Royal Automobile Club.

WRITINGS: Fortress of Ashes (novel), Hodder & Stoughton, 1936; *Summons to Adventure* (novel), Hodder & Stoughton, 1937; *The Second Plan* (novel), Hodder & Stoughton, 1938; *Riding*, Pitman, 1947, published as *Riding for Boys and Girls*, English Universities Press, 1949, new edition published as *Riding*, Brockhampton Press, 1968; *Send Him Victorious* (novel), Hodder & Stoughton, 1949.

Dogs as Pets for Boys and Girls, English Universities Press, 1950; *Teach Yourself Horse Management*, English Universities Press, 1951; (with Cavesson) *Ponies and Riding in Pictures*, Pitman, 1952; (with Charles Harris) *Riding Technique in Pictures*, Hulton, 1956; *Tackle Riding This Way*, Stanley Paul, 1959; *A to Z of Horses*, Parrish, 1960; *Riding Handbook*, Foyle, 1963; *The Pony Owner's Encyclopaedia*, Pelham Books, 1965; *Learn to Ride*, Pelham Books, 1965; (compiler) *The Horse-Lover's Book*, Frewin, 1967, Regnery, 1970; *So They Want to Learn Riding: A Guide for Parents Whose Children Want to Learn Riding*, Darwen Finlayson, 1967; *The Perfect Pony Owner*, SportShelf, 1968; (author of revision) Matthew Horace Hayes, *Points of the Horse: A Treatise on the Conformation, Movements, Breeds, and Evolution of the Horse*, Stanley Paul, 7th edition (Hope was not associated with earlier editions), 1969; *The Horse Trials Story*, Pelham Books, 1969; (with Reginald Sherriff Summerhays) *Horse Shows: The Judges, Stewards, Organisers*, Pelham Books, 1969.

The Book of Riding, Barker, 1970; *The Horseman's Manual*, Scribner, 1972; (editor with G. N. Jackson) *The Encyclopedia of the Horse*, Viking, 1973.

Editor: *Percy's Pony Annual*, D. J. Murphy, 1952; *Horse and Pony Annual*, Guilford Press, 1954-60; *The Beauty of Horses*, Pitman, 1959; *Pony Magazine Annual*, Parrish, 1962—.

Plays: "Misconduct," 1932; "Local Thunder," 1934; "No Way Back," 1934, all produced in London.

Contributor to *Country Life*, *Field*, *Times of India*, *Punch*, *Men Only*, *Fighting Forces*, *Game and Gun*, *Homes and Gardens*, *Chronicle*, and other periodicals and newspapers in England.

SIDELIGHTS: "Misconduct," was filmed as "Taxi to Paradise."

(Died, 1971)

*   *   *

HOPLEY-WOOLRICH, Cornell George   1903-1968
(George Hopley, William Irish, Cornell Woolrich)

PERSONAL: Born December 4, 1903, in New York, N.Y.; son of Genaro and Claire (Tarler) Hopley-Woolrich. *Education:* Attended Columbia University, 1921-25. *Address:* c/o Chase Manhattan Bank, 2099 Broadway, New York, N.Y. 10023.

CAREER: Writer, 1926-68. *Awards, honors:* $10,000 1st prize from College Humor and First National Pictures, 1927, for *Children of the Ritz*; Mystery Writers of America Edgar Allen Poe Award, 1949; Best Motion Picture of the Year Award of Mystery Writers of America, 1950, for "The Window," based on the novelette, "The Boy Cried Murder"; Screen Writers Guild Award, 1954, for "Rear Window," based on short story; French Mystery Prize, 1954, for short story, "One Foot in the Grave"; first prize in Ellery Queen Short Story Contest, 1962.

WRITINGS—Under name George Hopley: *Night Has a Thousand Eyes*, Farrar & Rinehart, 1945; *Fright*, Rinehart, 1950.

Under pseudonym William Irish: *Phantom Lady*, Lippincott, 1942 new edition, Norton, 1967; *I Wouldn't Be in Your Shoes: Short Stories*, Lippincott, 1943; *After-dinner Story*, Lippincott, 1944; *Deadline at Dawn*, Lippincott, 1944; *Borrowed Crime, and Other Stories*, Avon, 1946; *The Dancing Detective*, Lippincott, 1946; *Dead Man Blues: Short Stories*, Lippincott, 1947; *Waltz into Darkness*, Lippincott, 1947; *I Married a Dead Man*, Lippincott, 1948; *The Blue Ribbon: Short Stories*, Lippincott, 1949; *Six Nights of Mystery: Tales of Suspense and Intrigue*, Popular Library, 1950; *Somebody on the Phone: Short Stories*, Lippincott, 1950 (published in England as *Night I Died*, Hutchinson, 1951); *Strangler's Serenade*, Rinehart, 1951; *Eyes That Watch You*, Rinehart, 1952; *The Best of William Irish: Including Phantom Lady, After-dinner Story, and Deadline at Dawn*, Lippincott, 1960.

Under name Cornell Woolrich: *Cover Charge*, Boni & Liveright, 1926; *Children of the Ritz*, Boni & Liveright, 1927; *Times Square*, Liveright, 1929; *A Young Man's Heart*, Mason Publishing, 1930; *The Time of Her Life*, Liveright, 1931; *Manhattan Love Song*, Godwin, 1932; *The Bride Wore Black*, Simon & Schuster, 1940, new edition, with introduction by Anthony Boucher, Collier, 1964; *The Black Curtain*, Simon & Schuster, 1941; *Black Alibi*, Simon & Schuster, 1942; *The Black Angel*, Doubleday, Doran, 1943; *The Black Path of Fear*, Doubleday, Doran, 1944; *Rendezvous in Black*, Rinehart, 1948; *Savage Bride*, Fawcett, 1950; *Nightmare*, Dodd, 1956; *Hotel Room*, Random House, 1958; *Violence*, Dodd, 1958; *Beyond the Night*, Avon, 1959; *Death Is My Dancing Partner*, Pyramid Books, 1959; *The Ten Faces of Cornell Woolrich: An Inner Sanctum Collection of Novelettes and Short Stories*, Simon & Schuster, 1965; *The Dark Side of Love: Tales of Love and Death*, Walker & Co., 1965; *Nightwebs: A Collection of Stories By Cornell Woolrich*, edited by Francis M. Nevins, Jr., Harper, 1971. Work represented in many anthologies, including Erle Stanley Gardner, *The Case of the Cal-*

endar Girl, Walter J. Black, for Detective Book Club, 1958; *With Malice Toward All*, edited by Robert L. Fish, Macmillan, 1969.

SIDELIGHTS: The film, "Rear Window" (Paramount, 1954), adapted from a Hopley-Woolrich short story was the top box-office attraction of 1954. The cast included James Stewart, Grace Kelly, Thelma Ritter, Wendell Corey, and Raymond Burr. Francois Truffaut has directed two adaptations, "The Bride Wore Black" (Lopert, 1968), from the novel by the same title, and "Mississippi Mermaid" (United Artists, 1969), based on the novel, *Waltz into Darkness*. Other screen adaptations are "The Window" (RKO, 1949), from the novelette, "The Boy Cried Murder," and "No Man of Her Own" (Paramount, 1950), from the novel, *I Married a Dead Man*.

(Died September 25, 1968)

* * *

HOPWOOD, Robert R.   1910-

PERSONAL: Born November 25, 1910, in Newcastle upon Tyne, England; son of Robert (a clerk) and Isabella (Page) Hopwood; married Nella Armstrong, August 1, 1935; children: Hazel Ann Hopwood Charlton, Robert Wilfrid. *Education:* Armstrong College, Durham, B.Sc., 1932, Diploma in Theory and Practice of Teaching, 1933. *Home:* Houghton Ave., Cullercoats, North Shields, England. *Office:* Headmaster, Jarrow Central School, Jarrow on Tyne, England.

CAREER: Began as science teacher in North Shields, England; Jarrow Grammar School, Jarrow on Tyne, England, physics master, 1945-59; Jarrow Central School (secondary school), Jarrow on Tyne, headmaster, 1960—. *Military service:* Royal Air Force Volunteer Reserve, 1940-63, active duty, 1940-45, becoming pilot officer; finished service as flight lieutenant. *Member:* National Union of Teachers, South Shields Sailing Club.

WRITINGS: Science Model Making, J. Murray, 1952, 2nd edition, 1962, Macmillan, 1963, 3rd edition, J. Murray, 1968.

SIDELIGHTS: A polio victim at the time, Hopwood had to dictate parts of his book on making science models; now fully recovered, his hobbies are sailing and glider-flying.

* * *

HORIE, Shigeo   1903-

PERSONAL: Born January 28, 1903, in Kakishimacho, Oegun, Tokushima-ken, Japan; son of Arazo Horie; married Ayako Makino (died, 1961); children: Mitsuo and Yukio (sons), Mariko Horie Osawa (daughter). *Education:* Received LL.B. from Tokyo Imperial University, D.Econ. from Tokyo University. *Home:* Shinsaka 40 Building No. 703, 10-24 Akasaka 8-chome, Minato-ku, Tokyo, Japan. *Office:* Japan Institute for International Studies and Training, Kotohira-Kaikan, 1 Shiba Kotohira-cho, Minato-ku, Tokyo, Japan.

CAREER: Bank of Tokyo Ltd., Tokyo, Japan, member of staff and later chairman of board and president, 1929-67, now advisor. Chairman of Japan Institute for International Studies and Training of Ministry of International Trade and Industry, International Economic Committee of Japan Chamber of Commerce and Industry. President of Japan Association for Promotion of Trade with USSR and Socialist Countries of Europe. Director of International Development Center, Asia Research Association, Japan Eco-

nomic Research Center, Japan Olivetti Corp., Family Welfare Association of Ministry of Health and Welfare. Advisor to Japan External Trade Organization of Ministry of International Trade and Industry, Federation of Economic Organizations, Komatsu Manufacturing Co. Ltd., Teijn and Co. Ltd., Idemitsu Kosan Ltd. Member of Foreign Trade Council, Price Stabilization Policy Council, Customs and Tariff Council of Finance Ministry, Export Insurance Council, Industrial Structure Council of Ministry of International Trade and Industry, Economic Deliberation Council of Economic Planning Agency, International Board of Chemical Bank of New York. Arbitrator for International Bank for Reconstruction and Development of Washington, D.C.

AWARDS, HONORS: First Order of the Sacred Treasure (Japan); Sitara i Pakistan; Grand Officier de l'Ordre de la Couronne (Belgium); Grande Ufficiale Al Merito della Republica Italiana (Italy); Knight Commander of the Order of St. Gregory (Vatican); Grand Cross of the Yugoslav Flag (Yugoslavia); Order of Madarski Konnik (Bulgaria).

WRITINGS: Theory of International Finance, Tokyo University Press, 1960; *Economic Travelogue of the World*, Tokyo University Press, 1961; *Study on International Monetary Fund*, Iwanami Shoten, 1962; *International Monetary Fund*, St. Martin's 1964. Also author of *International Economy*, Japan Financial Paper Co. Press.

* * *

HORN, Stefan F.   1900-

PERSONAL: Born January 4, 1900, in Vienna, Austria; became U.S. citizen; son of Paul and Theresa (Strisower) Horn; married Nancy Christensen, July 3, 1951. *Education:* University of Vienna, doctor rerum politicarum, 1922; University of Geneva, Diploma of Conference Interpreter, 1946. *Religion:* Roman Catholic. *Home:* 7109 Central Ave., Takoma Park, Md. 20012.

CAREER: Merrimack College, North Andover, Mass., instructor in German, French, and political science, 1948-49; Georgetown University, Institute of Languages and Linguistics, Washington, D.C., assistant professor of German, 1949-52, associate professor, 1952-66, professor of interpretation and translation, 1966-72, professor emeritus, 1972—, head of Division of Interpretation and Translation, 1956-72. Lecturer on translation and interpretation at universities and before professional groups in United States, Germany, and Switzerland. *Awards, honors:* Golden Cross of Honor, Republic of Austria, 1958, for meritorious services; 175th Anniversary Medal of Honor, Georgetown University, 1964; Distinguished Service Citation, American Austrian Society, 1964.

WRITINGS: Glossary of Financial Terms, Elsevier (Amsterdam), 1965.

SIDELIGHTS: Horn is competent in German and French; he knows some Spanish, Italian, Russian. *Avocational interests:* Baroque art.

* * *

HORWICH, Frances R(appaport)   1908-
(Miss Frances)

PERSONAL: Born July 16, 1908, in Ottawa, Ohio; daughter of Samuel and Rosa (Gratz) Rappaport; married Harvey L. Horwich (an attorney), June 11, 1931. *Education:* University of Chicago, Ph.B., 1929; Columbia University, M.A., 1933; Northwestern University, Ph.D.,

1942. *Home and office:* 6801 E. Camelback Rd., G-103, Scottsdale, Ariz. 85251.

CAREER: Primary teacher, nursery schools supervisor, and director of junior kindergarten in Chicago, Ill., and suburbs, 1929-38; Pestolozzi Froebel Teachers College, Chicago, Ill., dean of education, 1938-40; Chicago Teachers College, Chicago, Ill., counselor of student teachers, 1940-43; Hessian Hills School, Croton-on-Hudson, N.Y., director, 1943-45; University of North Carolina, Chapel Hill, visiting professor of education, 1945-46; Roosevelt University, Chicago, Ill., associate professor, 1946-47, professor of education and chairman of department, 1947-52; National Broadcasting Co., New York, N.Y., supervisor of children's programs, 1955-56; Curtis Publishing Co., Philadelphia, Pa., director of children's activities, 1962-63, educational director and author of bimonthly letter to parents, 1963-64, consultant, 1965; television personality as Miss Frances, conducting, writing, and producing "Ding Dong School," beginning 1952, and "Parents Time With Miss Frances," 1955; Educational consultant, Field Enterprises Educational Corp., beginning 1965. Visiting summer professor or lecturer at Northwestern University, University of North Carolina, University of California, and other universities, 1942-60; conductor of workshops and lecturer for organizations throughout America. Member of board of directors, Girl Scouts of Chicago, beginning 1965.

MEMBER: National Association for the Education of Young Children (secretary, 1944-47; director, 1944-56; president, 1948-51), National Society for the Study of Education, Association for Childhood Education International, Association for Supervision and Curriculum Development, International Reading Association, National Association of Educational Broadcasters, American Association for Gifted Children, National Association for Mental Health, National Academy of Television Arts and Sciences (director, Chicago chapter, 1958-59), American Federation of Television and Radio Artists, American Women in Radio and Television, International Platform Association, Authors League of America, Chicago Unlimited (director, beginning 1965), Delta Kappa Gamma.

AWARDS, HONORS: More than sixty awards and citations for "Ding Dong School," including Woman of the Year in Education, Associated Press, 1953, George Foster Peabody Award, 1953, National Association for Better Radio and Television Award, 1953, 1954, *Parents' Magazine* Medal Award, 1955, Silver Trophy Award of National Audience Board, 1956. P.D. (Doctor of Pedagogy), Bowling Green State University, 1954; Alumni Award of Merit, Northwestern University, 1954; Alumni Medal, University of Chicago, 1957.

WRITINGS: Nursery School First, Then Kindergarten (curriculum material), Hinds, 1947; (contributor) *Portfolio on More and Better Schools for Children Under Six*, Association for Childhood Education, 1949; *Have Fun With Your Children*, Prentice-Hall, 1954; (contributor) *Understanding Yourself and Your Child*, National Society for Crippled Children and Adults, 1955; (author of foreword) Winthrop M. Phelps, Thomas W. Hopkins, and Robert Cousins, editors, *The Cerebral-Palsied Child: A Guide for Parents*, Simon & Schuster, 1958; *The Magic of Bringing Up Your Child*, McGraw, 1959.

Children's books: *Miss Frances' Ding Dong School Book*, Rand McNally, 1953, and twenty-six other "Ding Dong School Books," Rand McNally, 1953-56; *Miss Frances'*

All-Day-Long Book, Rand McNally, 1954; *Miss Frances' Ding Dong School Piano Book*, Hanson Music Corp., 1954; *Miss Frances' Storybook of Manners for the Very Young*, Rand McNally, 1955; *Miss Frances' Storybook of Pets for the Very Young*, Rand McNally, 1956; *Stories and Poems to Enjoy*, Doubleday, 1962.

Writer and narrator for "Ding Dong School Records," issued by RCA-Victor, 1953-56, Golden Records, 1960.

Associate editor, "Junior Life Series" of *Teacher Guides*, Science Research Associates, 1951-52; member of editorial advisory board, *Childcraft*, 1956-60. Contributor to *Jack and Jill*, *Chicago Sunday Tribune Magazine*, and to educational and television periodicals.

SIDELIGHTS: "Ding Dong School," which was nominated for television's Emmy Awards four times, 1954-59, provided material for the nation's cartoonists for many years. A "Peanuts" comic strip character found solace in "Miss Frances likes me!" in 1954, and its creator, Charles M. Schulz, continued to draw on the Miss Frances' theme for other United Feature Syndicate cartoons. Cartoonists for the *New Yorker*, Post-Hall Syndicate, New York Herald Tribune Syndicate, and other syndicates also have used "Ding Dong School." *Avocational interests:* Knitting, working in ceramics and other crafts, cooking and baking.

* * *

HOSSENT, Harry 1916-
(Sean Gregory, Kevin O'Malley)

PERSONAL: Born November 12, 1916, in London, England; son of Joseph Henry (a union official) and Betsy Evelyn (Bolton) Hossent; married Geraldine Mollie Isabel Usher, February 4, 1950. *Education:* Attended schools in London, England. *Politics:* Socialist. *Religion:* Anglican. *Home:* 75 Abbots Park, London Rd., St. Albans, Hertfordshire, England. *Agent:* Rupert Crew Ltd., King's Mews, Gray's Inn Rd., London W.C.2, England. *Office:* Sonostrips Ltd., 49B Station Rd., Edgware, Middlesex, England.

CAREER: Associated Press (United States), telephone editor in London, England, 1937-40; United Press International, London, England, sub-editor, 1945-47; Mason-Peacock Ltd. (advertising agency), London, England, publications manager, 1947-50; Irish News Agency, London, England, manager, 1950-55; Shell-Mex and B. P. Ltd., London, England, film script writer, 1955-59; Sonostrips Ltd. (filmstrip producers), London, England, managing director, 1959—; Cine Sport Ltd., London, England, director, 1970—. *Military service:* Royal Air Force, flight engineer, 1940-45; became sergeant. *Member:* Institute of Journalists, Association of Cinematograph and Television Technicians, Crime Writers' Association, Press Club, British Association of Industrial Editors.

WRITINGS: (Under pseudonym Kevin O'Malley) *Copper Smoke*, T. V. Boardman, 1953; *Spies Die at Dawn*, John Long, 1958; *No End to Fear*, John Long, 1959; *Memory of Treason*, John Long, 1961; *Spies Have No Friends*, John Long, 1963; *Run for Your Death*, John Long, 1965; *This Fear Business*, John Long, 1967. Writer of scripts for documentary and industrial films, including "It's Fun to Fly," 1959, "The Story of the Oil Engine," 1961, "The Road to Everywhere," 1962. Editor of *A.D.*, *L.P.G.*, and *B.P. Progress*.

* * *

HOUGHTON, Walter Edwards 1904-
PERSONAL: Born September 21, 1904, in Stamford,

Conn.; son of Walter Edwards and Nancy Semple (Acheson) Houghton; married Esther Lowrey Rhoads (a researcher), June 22, 1929; children: Nancy Acheson Brown, Esther Edwards Foxworth. *Education:* Yale University, Ph.B., 1924, M.A., 1927, Ph.D., 1931. *Home:* 19 Summit Rd., Wellesley, Mass. 02181. *Office:* Wellesley College Library, Wellesley, Mass. 02181.

CAREER: Instructor at Hill School, Pottstown, Pa., 1924-25, at Phillips Academy, Andover, Mass., 1927-29; Harvard University and Radcliffe College, Cambridge, Mass., instructor and tutor, 1931-38, assistant professor and tutor in history and literature, 1938-41; Wellesley College, Wellesley, Mass., associate professor, 1942-48, professor of English literature, 1948-57, Sophie C. Hart Professor of English, 1957-69, professor emeritus, 1969—. *Member:* Modern Language Association of America, American Academy of Arts and Sciences.

WRITINGS: The Formation of Thomas Fuller's Holy and Profane States, Harvard University Press, 1938; *The Art of Newman's Apologia,* Yale University Press for Wellesley College, 1945; *The Victorian Frame of Mind, 1830-1870,* Yale University Press for Wellesley College, 1957; (editor with Hazelton Spencer and Herbert Barrows) *British Literature from Blake to the Present Day,* Heath, 1952, 2nd edition, with David Ferry and Barrows, Heath, 1973; (editor with G. Robert Stange) *Victorian Poetry and Poetics,* Houghton, 1959, 2nd edition, 1968; *The Poetry of Clough: An Essay in Revaluation,* Yale University Press, 1963. General editor, *Wellesley Index to Victorian Periodicals, 1824-1900,* University of Toronto Press, 1966—. Advisory editor of *Victorian Poetry.*

BIOGRAPHICAL/CRITICAL SOURCES: Times Literary Supplement, January 12, 1967.

*   *   *

HOUSE, Robert Burton   1892-

PERSONAL: Born March 19, 1892, in Thelma, N.C.; son of Joseph Anderson (a sheriff) and Susan (Drake) House; married Harriet Palmer, May 4, 1918; children: Robert Burton (deceased), Caroline Twitty (Mrs. William S. Stewart). *Education:* University of North Carolina, A.B., 1916; Harvard University, A.M., 1917. *Politics:* Democrat. *Religion:* Methodist. *Home and office:* 501 East Franklin St., Chapel Hill, N.C. 27514.

CAREER: University of North Carolina, Chapel Hill, executive secretary, 1926-34, dean of administration, 1934-45, chancellor, 1945-57, professor of English and classics, 1957-62, now professor emeritus. *Military service:* U.S. Army, Infantry, served with American Expeditionary Forces, 1917-18; became first lieutenant. *Member:* North Carolina State Literary and Historical Association, Phi Beta Kappa, Tau Kappa Alpha. *Awards, honors:* LL.D. from Catawba College, 1938, from Bowdoin College, 1948; Doctor of Letters, University of North Carolina, 1970.

WRITINGS: (Editor) *Letters and Papers of Thomas Walter Bickett, Governor of North Carolina, 1917-1921,* Edwards & Broughton, 1923; *Miss Sue and the Sheriff,* University of North Carolina Press, 1941; *Our Faculty and Undergraduate Education* (speech), University of North Carolina, 1956; *Worlds and Music* (speech), Phi Beta Kappa, 1959; *The Light That Shines: Chapel Hill, 1912-1916.* University of North Carolina Press, 1964; *Great and Important Changes,* University of Nortn Carolina, 1967. Contributor to North Carolina historical journals and other periodicals.

AVOCATIONAL INTERESTS: Reading, speaking, music, religion.

*   *   *

HOWARD, Edwin J(ohnston)   1901-

PERSONAL: Born July 10, 1901, in Pittsburgh, Pa.; son of William Bakewell and Elizabeth (Johnston) Howard; married Miriam Elizabeth White, September 7, 1934; children: Elizabeth Ann. *Education:* Cornell University, A.B., 1924, M.A., 1925, Ph.D., 1929. *Home:* M.R. 50, 5035 Bonham Rd., Oxford, Ohio 45056.

CAREER: Miami University, Oxford, Ohio, 1930—, professor of English, 1941-68, professor emeritus, 1968—. Visiting professor at University of Washington Summer School, Seattle, 1941. Former nature photographic salon exhibitor and judge. *Member:* Audubon Society, Wilderness Society, National Parks Society.

WRITINGS: (Editor and author of introduction) *Ten Elizabethan Plays,* Thomas Nelson, 1931; (editor with Gordon D. Wilson) *Chaucer's Canterbury Tales,* Prentice-Hall, 1937; (editor) Thomas Elyot, *The Defence of Good Women,* Anchor Books, 1940; (editor) Thomas Elyot, *Of the Knowledge Which Maketh a Wise Man,* Anchor Books, 1946; (editor) *The Squyr of Low Degree,* Miami University (Oxford, Ohio), 1962; (editor) John Gower, *Confessio amantis,* Miami University, 1964; *Geoffrey Chaucer,* Twayne, 1964. Contributor of several hundred articles on photography and fishing to magazines. Editor, *Fisherman,* 1957-59.

WORK IN PROGRESS: Editing Miami University "Middle English" series of reprints; studies on philosophical poetry of the English Renaissance.

AVOCATIONAL INTERESTS: Fishing, travel.

BIOGRAPHICAL/CRITICAL SOURCES: Sewanee Review, spring, 1967.

*   *   *

HOWARD, Peter D(unsmore)   1908-1965
(Cato, a joint pseudonym)

PERSONAL: Born December 20, 1908, in Maidenhead, England; son of E. Cecil and Evangeline (Bohm) Howard; married Doris Metaxa, 1932; children: Philip, Anne (Mrs. Patrick Wolrige Gordon), Anthony. *Education:* Attended Mill Hill School, and Wadham College, Oxford University. *Home:* Hill Farm, Brent Eleigh, Sudbury, Suffolk, England.

CAREER: With Godden, Holme and Ward (solicitors), London, England, 1932-33; Express Newspapers Ltd., columnist, 1933-41; farmer, 1937-65. *Member:* National Farmers' Union, Liveryman Worshipful Company of Wheelwrights. *Awards, honors:* Member of Court, 1961-65, honorary senator, State of Mississippi; Freedom award, City of Atlanta, Ga.

WRITINGS: (With Frank Owen and Michael Foote, under pseudonym Cato) *Guilty Men,* Gollancz, 1940; *Fighters Ever,* Heinemann, 1941; *Innocent Men,* Heinemann, 1941; *Ideas Have Legs,* Muller, 1945, Coward, 1946; *Men on Trial,* Blandford, 1945; *That Man Frank Buchman,* Blandford, 1946; *The World Rebuilt: The True Story of Frank Buchman and the Achievements of Moral Re-armament,* Duell, Sloan & Pearce, 1951 (published in England as *The World Rebuilt: The True Story of Frank Buchman and the Men and Women of Moral Re-armament,* Blandford,

1951); (with Paul Campbell) *Remaking Men*, Arrowhead Books, 1954; *An Idea to Win the World*, Blandford, 1955, Arrowhead Books, 1956 ; (with Campbell) *A Story of Effective Statesmanship*, Blandford, 1955; *A Renaissance Man That Unites East and West*, Moral Re-armament, 1956; (with Campbell) *America Needs an Ideology*, Muller, 1957; *Frank Buchman's Secret*, Heinemann, 1961, Doubleday, 1962; (with L. P. Collins and T. S. Gregory) *Three Views of Christianity*, Gollancz, 1962; *The Secret of Christian Revolution* (speech), Oxford Group, 1963; *Beyond Communism to Revolution*, Oxford Group, 1963; *Statesmen and Statesmanship* (speech), J. M. Dyce, 1963; *Britain and the Beast*, Heinemann, 1963; *It's Got to Stop!*, Oxford Group, 1963; *Design for Dedication: Selections from a Series of Addresses*, Regnery, 1964; *Election 1964*, Oxford Group, 1964; *Tomorrow Will Be Too Late*, Moral Re-armament, 1964; *Beaverbrook: A Study of Max the Unknown*, Hutchinson, 1964; *Sex and the Oriental*, New International Library, 1965; (with Alan Thornhill) *Give a Dog a Bone: The Story of Pantomime*, Westminster Productions, 1965.

Plays: *The Real News*, Blandford, 1954; *The Dictators' Slippers*, Blandford, 1954; *The Boss*, Blandford, 1954; *We Are Tomorrow*, Blandford, 1954; "The Man with the Key," 1954; (with Cecil Broadhurst) *The Vanishing Island*, Moral Re-armament, 1956; "Rumpelsnits," 1956; "The Man Who Would Not Die," 1957; "Miracle in the Sun," 1959; "Pickle Hill," 1959; (with Thornhill) *The Hurricane*, Blandford, 1960; *The Ladder*, Blandford, 1960; (with Thornhill) *Music at Midnight*, Blandford, 1962; (with Herbert Philip Allen) *Space Is So Startling*, Moral Re-armament, 1962; *Through the Garden Wall*, Blandford, 1963; "The Diplomats," 1963; *Mr. Brown Comes Down the Hill*, Blandford, 1964; "Happy Death Day," 1965; *Give a Dog a Bone* (produced on the West End at Westminster Theatre), Westminster Productions, 1965.

Also author of screenplay, "Decision at Midnight."

SIDELIGHTS: A world leader of Moral Re-armament, Howard described its aim as "to modernize man, to equip his character to meet the challenge of the century." He described himself as "a revolutionary," adding: "My life does not belong to myself. I have no preconception of any kind, any day, for the rest of my life, where I will go or what I will do, or will not do, what I will say or will not say. I want to be used by God if He will use me."

He believed that Moral Re-armament proposes four moral standards: Absolute Honesty, Absolute Purity, Absolute Unselfishness, and Absolute Love. He once stated: "Very simply, I believe in purity. I don't think that God, who gave a man or woman instincts, is so impotent that He cannot teach them to control them. I believe that men should be absolutely free to decide. But I think that they need absolute moral standards to decide by. That is why, in my view, absolute morality is the only answer to absolute totalitarianism. It is a perilous track, when once you start on the path of relative morality. Furthermore, no one with relative standards can point a finger of scorn or blame at Hitler or Stalin who were the great modern apostles of relative morality. Moral absolutism, its traditional standards of honesty, purity, unselfishness and love that spring from our Judeo-Christian heritage, are the only answer to political absolutism and the absolute finality of atomic war. Unless we face the fundamental challenge of our times, unless we decide once and for all that Almighty God and His absolute morality are to reign on earth rather than Almighty Man and his relative amorality, our children will

certainly be Red, and we shall experience a totalitarian tyranny across the earth that will make Hitler's mass butchery look like a picnic in a park."

Howard was once Rugby football captain for England, and represented Britain in the Olympics on bobsleigh. He was a candidate in 1931 for Parliament for the New Party, headed by Sir Oswald Mosley.

BIOGRAPHICAL/CRITICAL SOURCES: Pace, July-August, 1965; Anne Wolrige-Gordon, *Peter Howard: Life and Letters*, Hodder & Stoughton, 1969.

(Died February 25, 1965)

*   *   *

HOWES, Raymond F(loyd) 1903-

PERSONAL: Born April 28, 1903, in Ithaca, N.Y.; son of Charles Henry (a photographer) and Eleanor (Titchener) Howes; married Louise Riley, June 18, 1927; children: Raymond Titchener, Bradford Riley. *Education:* Cornell University, B.A., 1924; University of Pittsburgh, M.A., 1926. *Politics:* Democrat. *Home:* 149 Nisbet Way, Riverside, Calif. 92507.

CAREER: University of Pittsburgh, Pittsburgh, Pa., instructor in English, 1924-26; Washington University, St. Louis, Mo., instructor, 1926-29, assistant professor of English, 1929-36, director of news bureau and director of forensics, 1931-36; Cornell University, Ithaca, N.Y., administrative posts, 1936-51, including assistant to dean of engineering, 1937-41, assistant to provost, 1941-42, administrative assistant to vice-president, 1946-48, secretary of university, 1948-51; American Council on Education, Washington, D.C., staff associate, 1951-62; University of California, Riverside, assistant to chancellor, 1962-66; Claremont Graduate School, and Claremont University Center, Claremont, Calif., director of publicity and publications, 1966-68. *Military service:* U.S. Naval Reserve, active duty, 1943-46; became commander. *Member:* Sigma Delta Chi, Delta Sigma Rho, Omicron Delta Kappa, Alpha Phi Omega, Quill and Dagger Club, Town and Gown. *Awards, honors:* L.H.D., Northeastern University, 1960.

WRITINGS: (Editor and compiler) *Debating*, Heath, 1931; (editor and author with others) *Our Cornell*, Cayuga Press, 1939; (with Richard W. Armour) *Coleridge the Talker*, Cornell University Press, 1941, reprinted, with addenda, Johnson Reprint, 1969; (editor) *Women in the Defense Decade*, American Council on Education, 1952; (editor) *Causes of Public Unrest Pertaining to Public Education*, American Council on Education, 1953; (editor) *Toward Unity in Educational Policy*, American Council on Education, 1953; (editor) *Higher Education and the Society It Serves*, American Council on Education, 1957; (editor) *Historical Studies of Rhetoric and Rhetoricians*, Cornell University Press, 1961; (editor) *Vision and Purpose in Higher Education*, American Council on Education, 1962; *A Cornell Notebook*, Cornell Alumni Association, 1973.

Author or editor of numerous folders and pamphlets for universities and educational organizations, most of them anonymous. Contributor to *American Mercury, Outlook, Social Forces*, and other journals. Associate editor, *Quarterly Journal of Speech*, 1933-36; editor, *Educational Record*, 1951-62.

*   *   *

HOWORTH, Muriel

PERSONAL: Born in Bishop Auckland, Durham, England; daughter of Charles Smith (a lawyer) and Mary (Dunn) Edgar; married Sheldon Wilkinson (a surgeon, Royal Navy); married second husband, Humphrey Howorth (an army officer); children: (first marriage) Darrell Sheldon Wilkinson. *Education:* Royal Academy of Music, London, England, L.R.A.M.; also studied in France and Austria. *Home:* 5 Old Orchard Rd., Eastbourne, England. *Office:* Fawley Office, 320 Regent St., London W.1, England.

CAREER: Writer and lecturer, mainly on atomic subjects. President of Layman's Institute of Atomic Information; director of Seed Mutation Research Laboratories and of World's International Film Association. Chairman of Soddy Memorial Trust. Holder of recording patents. *Military service:* Auxiliary Territorial Service, World War II, with assignments in Army Film Unit, Ministry of Information, Ministry of Supply, and at Royal Aircraft Establishment at Farnborough. *Member:* Royal Academy of Music, Royal Astronomical Society (fellow), Royal Horticultural Society (fellow), Royal Society of Art (fellow), British Nuclear Energy Society, British Society for the History of Science, Physical Society.

WRITINGS: This Is Armageddon, Stockwell, 1939; *Poems and Translations*, Fortune Press, 1946; *Learning About the Atom*, New World Publications, 1948; *Isotopia: An Exposition on Atomic Structure*, privately printed, 1949; *Atom in Wonderland*, New World Publications, 1950; *Atomic Transmutations: The Greatest Discovery Ever Made*, William Heinman, 1953; *Quiet Waters*, New World Publications, 1953; *Atom and Eve*, William Heinman, 1955; *Pioneer Research on the Atom: Rutherford and Soddy in a Glorious Chapter of Science*, William Heinman, 1958; *Atomic Gardening*, New World Publications, 1960; *Impact of a Million Stars*, New World Publications, 1963; *A Panorama of Poems*, New World Publications, 1968. Editor, *Atomic Digest, Atom Review, Mutagenetics Broadsheet*, and *New Parthenon*.

WORK IN PROGRESS: A film, "The Great Tomorrow"; research on galvanizing British technology and air colleges to give television training to wide areas.

*   *   *

HROMADKA, Josef L(ukl) 1889-1971

PERSONAL: Born June 8, 1889, in Hodslavice, Czechoslovakia; son of Josef (a farmer) and Rosina (Palacka) Hromadka; married Nadeje Luklova, 1924; children: Nadia Eunike Mikulkova, Alena Zikmundova. *Education:* Studied at University of Vienna, University of Basel, University of Heidelberg, and University of Aberdeen; University of Prague, Ph.Dr., 1920. *Relgion:* Evangelical Church of Czech Brethren. *Home:* Moravska 45, Prague 2, Czechoslovakia. *Office:* Comenius Faculty of Protestant Theology, Jungmannova 9, Prague 1, Czechoslovakia.

CAREER: John Hus Faculty of Theology, Prague, Czechoslovakia, professor of systematic theology, 1919-39, 1947-50; Princeton Theological Seminary, Princeton, N.J., professor of apologetics and Christian ethics, 1939-47; Comenius Faculty of Protestant Theology, Prague, Czechoslovakia, dean and professor of systematic theology, 1950-71. President, Christian Peace Conference; member of executive and central committees, World Council of Churches; member, World Council of Peace. *Awards, honors:* Lenin Prize, 1958; D.D., Princeton University, University of Aberdeen, Theological Academy of Debrecen, Humboldt University of Berlin, Moravian College, Wooster College; Dr. of History, University of Warsaw.

WRITINGS: Masaryk as European, [Prague], 1936; *Doom and Resurrection*, Madrus House, 1945; *The Church and Theology in Today's Troubled Times: A Czechoslovak Contribution to Ecumenical Discussions*, Ecumenical Council of Churches in Czechoslovakia (Prague), 1956; *Theology Between Yesterday and Tomorrow*, Westminster, 1957; (author of introduction) Johann Amos Comenius, *A Perfect Reformation: An Anthology*, edited by Amedeo Molnar, Ecumenical Institute of the Comenius Faculty of Protestant Theology (Prague), 1957; *My Covenant Is Life and Peace* (address), International Secretariat of the Christian Peace Conference, 1964.

In German: *Kirche und Theologie im Umbruch der Gegenwart*, [Prague], 1956; *Evangelium fuer Atheisten*, Kathe Vogt, 1958; *Sprung ueber die Mauer*, Kathe Vogt, 1961; *Das Evangelium auf dem Wege zum Menschen*, Evangelische Verlagsanstalt, 1961; *Friede aud Erden: Hauptreferat auf der I. Allchristlichen Friedensversammlung*, Hefte aus Burgscheidengen, 1962; (author of afterword) Hans Ruh, *Geschichte und Theologie: Grundlinien der Theologie Hromadkas*, [Zurich], 1963; *Rettet den Menschen: Frieden ist moeglich*, All Christian Peace Assembly (Dortmund), 1968; *Das Evangelium bricht sich Bahn: Predigten, Betrachtungen*, Evangelische Verlagsanstalt, 1968.

In Czech: *Krestanstvi a vedecke mysleni* (title means "Christianity and Scientific Thought"), Valasske Mezirici, 1922; *Katolicism a boj o krestanstvi* (title means "Catholicism and Struggle for Christianity"), 1925; *Cesty protestantskeho theologa* (title means "A Protestant Theologian on His Way"), Nakl. v Horaka (Prague), 1927; *Masaryk*, YMCA, 1930; *Dostojevskij a Masaryk* (title means "Dostoevsky and Masaryk"), 2nd edition, YMCA, 1931; *Krestanstvi v mysleni a zivote* (title means "Christianity in Thought and Life"), Laichter, 1931; *Lide a programy* (title means "Men and Programmes"), 1939; *Masaryk mezi vierejskem a zitrkem: Ceskoslovensky boj o novou Evropu*, Nakladem Narodni Jednoty Csl. Evangeliku v Americe (Chicago), 1940; *Don Quijote ceske filosofie* (title means "Don Quixote of Czech Philosophy"), Vytiskla Tiskarna (New York), 1943; *Kommunismus a krestanstvi* (title means "Communism and Christianity"), 1946; *Zasady ceskobratrske cirkve evangelicke*, 4th edition, [Prague], 1945; *O Nove Ceskoslovensko*, YMCA, 1946; *Theologie a cirkev*, [Prague], 1949; (compiler) *Kniha modliteb: Volame z hlubokosti*, Kalich, 1953; *Smyal bratrske reformace*, 2nd edition, Kalich, 1954; *Od reformace k zitrku* (title means "From the Reformation to the Day of Tomorrow"), Kalich, 1956; (with Frantisek Michalek Bartos) *Jednota bratrska, 1457-1957; Sbornik k petistemu vyroci zalozeni*, [Prague], 1956; *Evangelium na ceste za clovekem: Uvod do studia Pisem a cirkevnich vyznani* (title means "The Gospel on the Way to Man"), Kalich, 1958; *Pole je tento svet*, Kalich, 1964; *Pravda a zivot*, UCN, 1969.

In French: *Pour quoi je vis*, translated from Czech by F. Masarik, Editions du Cerf, 1968, translation from Czech by Monika Page and Benjamin Page published as *Impact of History on Theology: Thoughts of a Czech Pastor*, Fides, 1970 (published in England as *Thoughts of a Czech Pastor*, S.C.M. Press, 1970). Editor, *Krestanska Revue* (title means "Christian Review") and *Communio Viatorum*.

(Died December 26, 1971)

*   *   *

HUBBARD, Thomas Leslie Wallan 1905-

PERSONAL: Born February 23, 1905, in Cambridge, England; married Edith Irving; children: Janine, Diana. *Education:* Sorbonne, University of Paris, Licence-es-Lettres. *Agent:* William Morris Agency, Inc., 1740 Broadway, New York, N.Y. 10019.

CAREER: Before World War II, taught in schools in England and Egypt; after the war was assistant master of French, Marlborough College, Wiltshire, England, and headmaster, Pitmans College, Croydon, England; Surrey Higher Secretarial College, Croydon, England, principal, 1965—. *Military service:* British Army, Intelligence Corps, 1939-47; served at Dunkirk, in United States, Southeast Asia, and Austria; became lieutenant colonel. *Member:* Rotary International (Croydon).

WRITINGS: Poems—1925-34, Basil Blackwell, 1934; *Trois Heros,* Oxford University Press, 1951; (editor) *Trois Explorateurs,* Oxford University Press, 1955; *A Baton for the Conductor,* Faber, 1957, Houghton, 1958.

SIDELIGHTS: A Baton for the Conductor was adapted for radio, and was filmed. Hubbard knows French, Italian, German, Arabic. *Avocational interests:* Travel, music, and painting.

* * *

HUBBELL, Lindley Williams 1901-

PERSONAL: Born June 3, 1901, in Hartford, Conn.; son of Lindley Dodd and Nettie (Stone) Hubbell. Became Japanese citizen in 1960; legal name became Hayashi Shuseki. *Education:* Educated by tutors.

CAREER: With New York Public Library, 1925-46; with Randall School, Hartford, Conn., 1946-53; Doshisha University, Kyoto, Japan, professor of English literature, 1953—. *Awards, honors:* Litt.D, Doshisha University.

WRITINGS—Under name Lindley Williams Hubbell; poetry: Dark Pavilion, Yale University Press, 1927; *The Tracing of a Portal,* Yale University Press, 1931; *Winter Burning,* Knopf, 1938; *The Ninth Continent,* A. Swallow, 1947; *Long Island Triptych,* A. Swallow, 1947; *The Birth of a Diatom,* Banyan, 1949; *Seventy Poems,* A. Swallow, 1965.

Other: *Lectures on Shakespeare,* Nan'un-Do, 1958, AMS Press, 1972; *Shakespeare and the Classic Drama,* Nan'un-Do, 1962; (translator from Japanese) *Aki no Hi,* Nan'un-Do, 1963.

* * *

HUBLER, Edward L(orenzo) 1902-1965

PERSONAL: Born November 29, 1902, in Gordon, Pa.; son of Henry Winfield and Elizabeth (Kaufman) Hubler. *Education:* Wesleyan University, Middletown, Conn., B.A., 1927, M.A., 1928; Princeton University, Ph.D., 1934. *Politics:* Democrat. *Religion:* Protestant. *Home:* 61 Stanworth Lane, Princeton, N.J. *Office:* 22 McCosh Hall, Princeton University, Princeton, N.J.

CAREER: Franklin and Marshall College, Lancaster, Pa., instructor in English, 1928-31; University of Rochester, Rochester, N.Y., instructor, 1934-35, assistant professor of English, 1935-36; Princeton University, Princeton, N.J., 1936-65, associate professor, 1942-64, professor of English, 1964-65. Visiting professor, Haverford College, 1938; teacher, U.S. Army schools in Europe, 1945-46; Fulbright professor at Universities of Bordeaux and Toulouse, 1950-51; Fulbright lecturer at University of Algiers, 1951. *Member:* Modern Language Association of America, Re-

naissance Society of New York, Princeton Club of New York.

WRITINGS: (Editor with T. M. Parrott) *Shakespeare: 23 Plays and the Sonnets,* Scribner, 1938; *The Sense of Shakespeare's Sonnets,* Princeton University Press, 1952; (editor with Parrott) *Shakespeare: Six Plays and the Sonnets,* Scribner, 1956; (editor) William Shakespeare, *Songs and Poems,* McGraw, 1959; (editor) Shakespeare, *Hamlet,* New American Library, 1964.

WORK IN PROGRESS: Shakespeare's serious comedy.

SIDELIGHTS: "All drama and all poetry interest me," Hubler told *CA,* "But I am especially interested in Shakespeare and Elizabethan poetry. I have a smattering of several foreign languages, but the only one I have a competence is in French, which is, perhaps, why I am a Francophile. In my younger days my hobbies were cycling and cooking. Alas, I am now on a diet."

(Died December 27, 1965)

* * *

HUFFARD, Grace Thompson 1892-

PERSONAL: Born May 30, 1892, in Paris Crossing, Ind.; daughter of Amos Garrett (a farmer and salesman) and Demetria (Eador) Thompson; married Robert Boyd Huffard, May 24, 1926. *Education:* Attended Indiana public schools. *Politics:* Independent. *Religion:* Presbyterian. *Home:* 6707 Costello Ave., Van Nuys, Calif. 91405.

CAREER: W. K. Stewart (book sellers), Indianapolis, Ind., saleswoman, 1913-21; L. S. Ayres (department store), Indianapolis, Ind., book buyer, 1921-33; worked for Sears Roebuck in North Hollywood, Calif. 1950-59. *Member:* American Booksellers Association, Daughters of the American Revolution (San Fernando chapter). *Awards, honors:* Medal from French government, 1923, for work with Anne Morgan's Committee for Devastated France.

WRITINGS: (Editor with Laura Mae Carlisle) *My Poetry Book: An Anthology of Modern Verse for Boys and Girls,* Winston, 1934, revised edition, Holt, 1956; *When Rebels Rode,* Bobbs-Merrill, 1963.

WORK IN PROGRESS: A children's book on early Indiana history.

* * *

HUGGINS, Alice Margaret 1891-1971

PERSONAL: Born September 19, 1891, in Overbrook, Kan.; daughter of Harry Hubert (a farmer) and Jessie Margaretta (Mannen) Huggins. *Education:* Washburn University, B.A., 1912; Columbia University, M.A., 1924; University of Chicago, graduate study, 1939-40. *Politics:* Republican. *Religion:* United Church of Christ (Congregational). *Home:* 1630 College Ave., Topeka, Kan. 66604.

CAREER: Goodrich Girls School (missionary school), T'unghsien, Peking, China, teacher, 1917-52. U.S. Office of War Information, San Francisco, Calif., member of staff, 1944; Yale University, New Haven, Conn., teacher of Chinese, 1945. *Member:* National League of American Pen Women, Kansas Historical Society, Kansas Authors' Club, Soroptimist International, Theta Sigma Phi, Delta Kappa Gamma. *Awards, honors:* Alumni award, Washburn University, 1952.

WRITINGS: Fragrant Jade, Broadman, 1948; *The Red Chair Waits,* Westminster, 1948; *Day of the False Dragon,* Westminster, 1953; (with Hugh Laughlin Robinson) *Wan-*

Fu: Ten Thousand Happinesses, Longmans, Green, 1957; (with Robinson) *Spend Your Heart*, Westminster, 1965; *Shan Min's One Wish*, Beacon Hill Press (Kansas City), 1972. Compiler of *Stories We Like to Hear* (in Chinese), Christian Literature Society (Shanghai), 1948, and of ten books of songs and anthems published in Chinese in Peking, 1932-50.

SIDELIGHTS: Alice Higgins spent two war years, 1941-43, in Manila; was in Peking at time of Communist takeover, and was held under house arrest for four months before being released to return to America in March, 1952. She spoke Mandarin Chinese.

(Died May 19, 1971)

*   *   *

HUGHES, Merrit Y(erkes) 1893-1970

PERSONAL: Born May 24, 1893, in Philadelphia, Pa.; son of Adoniram Judson and Annabelle (Yerkes) Hughes; married Grace J. Dedman, August 10, 1923; children: David Yerkes, Elspeth Baillie (Mrs. John F. Benton). *Education:* Boston University, B.A., 1915, M.A., 1916; University of Edinburgh, M.A., 1918; Harvard University, Ph.D., 1921; University of Paris, postdoctoral study, 1921-22. *Politics:* Independent. *Religion:* Society of Friends (Quaker). *Home:* 150 North Prospect Ave., Madison, Wis. 53705.

CAREER: Boston University, Boston, Mass., instructor in English, 1919-20; University of California, Berkeley, assistant professor 1922-26, associate professor of English, 1926-36; University of Wisconsin, Madison, professor of English, 1936-63, professor emeritus, 1963-70, chairman of department at intervals, 1938-55. Visiting member, Insititue for Advanced Study, Princeton, N.J., 1965-66. Visiting summer professor at a number of universities; Taft lecturer at University of Cincinnati, 1962. *Military service:* U.S. Army, infantry, 1918-19, Military Government, 1943-46, serving in France and Germany; became lieutenant colonel.

MEMBER: American Academy of Arts and Sciences (fellow), Modern Language Association of America (member of council, 1948-52), Modern Humanities Research Association, International Association of University Professors of English (member of executive board, beginning, 1956), Wisconsin Academy of Sciences, Arts, and Letters (president, 1960-61). *Awards, honors:* Guggenheim fellow in Rome, 1925-26; fellow of Henry E. Huntington Library and Art Gallery, 1941-42; Fulbirght grantee in London, 1949-50; D. Litt., University of Edinburgh, 1950, Boston University, 1954; fellow of Folger Shakespeare Library, 1964-65.

WRITINGS: Virgil and Spenser, University of California Press, 1929; (editor) *Milton: Complete Poems and Major Prose*, Odyssey, 1957; (editor) *Complete Prose of John Milton*, Volume III, Yale University Press, 1962; *Ten Perspectives on Milton*, Yale University Press, 1965; (general editor) *A Variorum Commentary on the Poems of John Milton*, Columbia University Press, Volume I: *The Greek and Latin Poems* and *The Italian Poems*, 1970, Volume II: *The Minor English Poems*, 1972.

*   *   *

HULL, Helen (Rose) 1888(?)-1971

PERSONAL: Born in Albion, Mich.; daughter of Warren C. and Minnie (McGill) Hull. *Education:* Studied at Michigan State University and University of Michigan; University of Chicago, Ph.B., 1912. *Home:* 872 West End Ave., Apt. 13, New York, N.Y. 10025. *Agent:* Brandt & Brandt, 101 Park Ave., New York, N.Y. 10017.

CAREER: Wellesley College, Wellesley, Mass., instructor in English, 1912-14; Columbia University, New York, N.Y., 1914-58, instructor, then assistant and associate professor, professor of English 1954-58, professor emeritus, 1958-71. *Member:* Authors Guild (president, 1950-54; member of council), P.E.N. (executive council). *Awards, honors:* Guggenheim fellowship in fiction, 1930; College Faculty Mystery prize for *A Tapping on the Wall.*

WRITINGS: Quest, Macmillan, 1922; *Labyrinth*, Macmillan, 1923; *The Surry Family*, Macmillan, 1925; *Islanders*, Macmillan, 1927; (author of introduction) *Copy, 1927* (collection), Appleton, 1927; (with Mabel L. Robinson and Roger S. Loomis) *The Art of Writing Prose*, R. Smith, 1930, revised edition, Farrar, Straus, 1936; *The Asking Price*, Coward, 1930; (author of introduction) *New Copy, 1931* (collection), Columbia University Press, 1931; (with Robinson) *Creative Writing: The Story Form*, American Book Co., 1932; *Heat Lightning*, Coward, 1932; *Hardy Perennial*, Coward, 1933; *Morning Shows the Day*, Coward, 1934; *Uncommon People* (short stories), Coward, 1936; *Candle Indoors*, Coward, 1936; *Frost Flower*, Coward, 1939.

Through the House Door, Coward, 1940; *Experiment: Four Short Novels*, Coward, 1940; *A Circle in the Water*, Coward, 1943 (published in England as *Darkening Hill*, Jarrolds, 1943); *Mayling Soong Chiang*, Coward, 1943; *Hawk's Flight*, Coward, 1946; *Octave: A Book of Stories*, Coward, 1947; (editor) *The Writer's Book*, Harper, 1950, Barnes & Noble, 1956; *Landfall*, Coward, 1953; *Wind Rose*, Coward, 1958; (editor with Michael Drury) *Writer's Roundtable*, Harper, 1959; *A Tapping on the Wall*, Dodd, 1960; *Close Her Pale Blue Eyes*, Dodd, 1963. Contributor of short stories, serials, and novelettes to magazines.

SIDELIGHTS: One of Miss Hull's works was broadcast as a television play on "U.S. Steel Hour," October 22, 1958.

BIOGRAPHICAL/CRITICAL SOURCES: Harry R. Warfel, *American Novelists of Today*, American Book Co., 1951.

(Died, 1971)

*   *   *

HULME, Kathryn 1900-

PERSONAL: Born January 6, 1900, in San Francisco, Calif.; daughter of Edwin Page and Julia Frances (Cavarly) Hulme. *Education:* University of California, student, 1918-21; studied at Columbia University, 1922, and Hunter College (now Hunter College of the City University of New York), 1923. *Religion:* Roman Catholic convert, 1951. *Home:* Kapaa, Kauai, Hawaii.

CAREER: Reporter for *Daily Californian*; recreation director of San Francisco Associated Charities; Ask Mr. Foster Travel Service, publicity director, 1935-43; electric welder in Kaiser Shipyards during World War II; United Nations Relief and Rehabilitation Administration (UN-RRA), U.S. Occupied Zone in Germany, deputy director, 1945-47, helped to organize, and became deputy director of, Wildflecken, a Bavarian camp for displaced Poles, 1947-51. Author. *Awards, honors: Atlantic* $5,000 Non-Fiction Award, 1953, for *The Wild Place;* awards for *The Nun's Story*, 1957, includes Commonwealth Club of California Gold Medal, National Council of Women of the United States Book Award, Brotherhood Award of National Conference of Christians and Jews, National Association of Independent Schools Award, Rupert Hughes Award of Authors Club of Los Angeles.

WRITINGS: *How's the Road*, privately printed, 1928; *Arab Interlude*, Macrae Smith, 1930; *Desert Night* (novel), Macaulay, 1932; *We Lived as Children* (fictional autobiography), Knopf, 1938; *The Wild Place* (non-fiction), Little Brown, 1953; *The Nun's Story* (biography; Book-of-the-Month Club selection; Catholic Book-of-the-Month Selection), Little Brown, 1956; *Annie's Captain* (fiction), Little Brown, 1961; *Undiscovered Country: A Spiritual Adventure* (autobiography), Little Brown, 1966.

SIDELIGHTS: *The Nun's Story* was filmed by Warner Brothers in 1959.

BIOGRAPHICAL/CRITICAL SOURCES: Christian Science Monitor, October 29, 1953; *Atlantic*, November, 1953, October, 1956; *New York Times*, November 1, 1953, September 9, 1956; *Booklist*, November 15, 1956; *Kirkus*, July 1, 1956; *Commonweal*, September 7, 1956; *Saturday Review*, September 8, 1956; *Wilson Library Bulletin*, November, 1962; *New York Times Book Review*, November 20, 1966; *Best Sellers*, December 15, 1966; *Books and Bookmen*, October, 1967; *New Statesman*, December 1, 1967; *Times Literary Supplement*, December 7, 1967.

* * *

HULTGREN, Thor 1902-

PERSONAL: Born September 2, 1902, in New York, N.Y.; son of William (a shopkeeper) and Sara Maria (Johanson) Hultgren. *Education:* Columbia University, A.B., 1923, M.A., 1925; Robert Brookings Graduate School of Economics and Government, advanced study, 1925-27. *Politics:* Independent. *Religion:* Agnostic. *Home:* 2529 East Webster Pl., Milwaukee, Wis.

CAREER: Rutgers University, New Brunswick, N.J., instructor in economics, 1927-28; U.S. Department of Agriculture, Washington, D.C., economist, 1928-37; U.S. Interstate Commerce Commission, Washington, D.C., economic and statistical analyst, 1937-40; National Bureau of Economic Research, New York, N.Y., member of research staff, 1940-63; University of Wisconsin, Milwaukee, 1963—, began as visiting associate professor of economics and lecturer, now lecturer emeritus.

WRITINGS—All published by National Bureau of Economic Research: *American Transportation in Prosperity and Depression*, 1948; *Transport and the State of Trade in Britain*, 1953; *Changes in Labor Cost during Cycles in Production and Business*, 1960; *Cost, Prices and Profits: Their Cyclical Relations*, 1965. Contributor to *Saturday Review* and to economic journals.

WORK IN PROGRESS: Studies on the disequilibrium theory of business fluctuations, and on utility regulation during inflation.

SIDELIGHTS: Hultgren is competent in French, German, and Swedish.

* * *

HULTS, Dorothy Niebrugge 1898-

PERSONAL: Born September 6, 1898, in Brooklyn, N.Y.; daughter of Frank Bernard (an insurance broker) and Mary (Spink) Niebrugge; married Charles Voorhees Hults (a physician), February 22, 1938; children: Marjory Hults Negus (stepdaughter). *Education:* Wellesley College, B.A., 1921; Pratt Institute Library School, M.L.S., 1951. *Politics:* Republican. *Religion:* Protestant. *Home:* 1908 Ditmas Ave., Brooklyn, N.Y. 11226.

CAREER: Brooklyn (N.Y.) Public Library, children's librarian, 1922-24, 1926-38, 1949-60. *Member:* Long Island Historical Society, Brooklyn Botanic Garden, Garden Club of Flatbush (first vice-president, 1970—), Brooklyn Wellesley Club (president, 1944-46), Mardi Club (president, 1963-65).

WRITINGS: *New Amsterdam Days and Ways: The Dutch Settlers of New York*, Harcourt, 1963; (co-author) *Story of the Brevoort Family from Farm to Savings Bank* (booklet), Brevoort Savings Bank of Brooklyn, 1964.

AVOCATIONAL INTERESTS: Oil painting of landscapes and boats, and other creative arts and crafts.

* * *

HUME, Lotta Carswell

PERSONAL: Married Edward Hicks Hume; children: Charlotte Hume Freeman. *Home:* White Sands, 7450 Olivetas Ave., LaJolla, Calif. 92037.

WRITINGS: *Songs Along the Way*, privately printed, 1957; *Drama at the Doctor's Gate: The Story of Doctor Edward Hume of Yale-in-China*, Yale-in-China Association, 1961; *Favorite Children's Stories from China and Tibet*, Tuttle, 1962.

SIDELIGHTS: Mrs. Hume is a former longtime resident of China, with special interest in collecting and publishing Chinese legends as a cultural bond between American and Chinese children.

* * *

HUMPHRIES, Adelaide M. 1898-
(Kathleen Harris, Wayne Way, Token West)

PERSONAL: Born October 31, 1898, in Columbus, Ohio; daughter of William Lee and Lorena (Way) Morris; married George Merrall Humphries ; children: Joyce Humphries Faulkner, William Lee. *Education:* Attended Rye Seminary and Columbia University. *Religion:* Methodist. *Residence:* North Palm Beach, Fla.

CAREER: Author.

WRITINGS—All published by Arcadia House, except as indicated: *Business Marriage*, Chelsea House, 1933; *Skyrocket*, Greenberg, 1936; *Gallant Gesture*, 1937; *Steps to the Moon*, Hillman-Curl, 1937; *Always Another Spring*, 1938; *Trial Flight*, 1938; *Bright Pattern*, 1940; *Inconstant Star*, 1940; *Draft Bride*, 1941; *Happily Ever After*, 1942; *You're the One*, 1942; *Uncertain Glory*, 1943; *Ann Star, Nurse*, 1944; *Then Came Romance*, 1944; *Substitute Nurse*, 1944; *Ann Star: Senior Nurse*, 1945; *Ann Star: Staff Nurse*, 1946; *Double Wedding*, 1946; *Office Nurse*, 1947; *Ann Star at Warm Springs*, 1947.

Glamour Nurse, 1950; *Nurses Are People*, Bouregy & Curl, 1951; *Home Front Nurse*, Bouregy & Curl, 1952; *Nurse Landon's Challenge*, Bouregy & Curl, 1952; *The Nurse Knows Best*, Avalon, 1953; *Nurse Lady*, Bouregy & Curl, 1953; *Ocean Wedding*, 1953; *Navy Nurse*, Avalon, 1954; *Nurse Barclay's Dilemma*, Avalon, 1954; *Orchids for the Nurse*, Avalon, 1955; *Nurse with Wings*, Avalon, 1955; *Nurse Laurie's Cruise*, Avalon, 1956; *New England Nurse*, Avalon, 1956; *Park Avenue Nurse*, Avalon, 1956; *The Nurse Had Red Hair*, Avalon, 1957; *A Case for Nurse Marian*, Avalon, 1957; *Clinic Nurse*, Avalon, 1958; *A Nurse on Horseback*, Avalon, 1959.

Nurse Had a Secret, Bouregy, 1960; *Swamp Nurse*, Avalon, 1961; *Lady Doctor*, Avalon, 1963; *Doctor of the Keys*,

Bouregy, 1963; *A Feather in Her Cap*, Bouregy, 1964; *The Other Love*, Bouregy, 1964; *Luxury Nurse*, Bouregy, 1966; *Chesapeake Doctor*, Avalon, 1966; *Nurse in Flight*, Avalon, 1968; *The Nurse Made Headlines*, Dell, 1969.

Under pseudonym Kathleen Harris—All published by Arcadia House, except as indicated: *Make Way for Romance*, 1940; *Summer of Enchantment*, 1940; *Stand By for Romance (Stand by for Love)*, 1941; *Without Benefit of Headlines*, 1941; *Leave My Heart Alone*, 1943; *Visiting Nurse*, 1944; *Navy Blue Lady*, 1945; *Young Dr. Bob*, 1945; *Robert Gordon, M.D.*, 1946; *The Doctor's Name was Mary*, 1947; *Change of Heart*, 1949; *Let Love Alone*, 1951; *No Other Love*, 1952; *Rehearsal for Love*, 1953; *Jane Arden, Student Nurse*, Avalon, 1955; *Jane Arden, Registered Nurse*, Avalon, 1956; *Jane Arden, Staff Nurse*, Avalon, 1957; *Jane Arden, Surgery Nurse*, Avalon, 1958; *Jane Arden, Head Nurse*, Bouregy, 1959; *Flight Nurse*, Avalon, 1960; *Camp Nurse*, Avalon, 1961; *Jane Arden, Space Nurse*, Avalon, 1962; *Jane Arden's Homecoming*, Avalon, 1963; *Nurse on Holiday*, Bouregy, 1964; *Nurse Barbara*, Avalon, 1965.

Under pseudonym Token West: *Three Gals a Week*, Phoenix Press, 1942; *Conquered*, Woodford Press, 1950; *Fast Girl*, Woodford Press, 1952; *Georgia Girl*, Woodford Press, 1953.

Contributor of articles and short stories to *Cosmopolitan*, *McClure's*, and *Collier's*.

* * *

HUMPHRIES, Helen Speirs Dickie 1915-

PERSONAL: Born May 27, 1915, in Clydebank, Scotland; daughter of Samuel Lamont and Helen Speirs (Hair) Dickie; married Andrew Humphries, November 10, 1945; children: Archibald Samuel, Catherine Helen Hair. *Education:* Glasgow Bible Training Institute, diploma; Bennet College, diploma; Skerry's College, business diploma. *Religion:* Baptist. *Home:* Stuartlea, 137 Sandy Rd., Renfrew, Scotland.

CAREER: Secretary in agents' offices, Glasgow, Scotland, three years; in nursing service in London, England, two years; accounting chief of engineering company, Glasgow, Scotland, three years; tutor in Clydebank, Scotland, eleven years, and at Ladyburn Secondary School, Greenock, four years. Active in church work and Bible classes.

WRITINGS—All published by Pickering & Inglis: *Margaret the Rebel*, 1957; *Margaret of St. Margaret's*, 1959; *Changes for St. Margaret's*, 1960; *St. Margaret's Girls Branch Out*, 1961; *Return to St. Margaret's*, 1962; *St. Margaret's Triumphs and Trials*, 1964; *The Strange New Girl*, 1964; *Prudence Becomes Prudent*, 1966; *Secrets of the Castle*, 1967; *The Twins Who Weren't*, 1970.

* * *

HUNT, Edgar H(ubert) 1909-
(Fidelio)

PERSONAL: Born June 28, 1909, in Clifton, Bristol, England; son of Hubert Walter (a cathedral organist) and Clara Harriet (Clements) Hunt; married Elizabeth Willingham Voss, June 11, 1938; children: Rosemary Elizabeth. *Education:* Attended Bristol Grammar School, 1918-26; Trinity College of Music, London, England, F.T.C.L. and L.R.A.M., 1931. *Religion:* Church of England. *Home:* Rose Cottage, Bois Lane, Chesham Bois, Buckinghamshire, England. *Office:* Trinity College of Music, Mandeville Pl., London W.1, England.

CAREER: Trinity College of Music, London, England, professor of recorder and flute, 1935—. Schott & Co. Ltd. (music publishers), London, England, designer of recorders, editorial work, 1937—; Froebel Educational Institute, Roehampton, England, visiting teacher of flute and clarinet, 1956-64; Queens' College, London, England, visiting teacher of recorder, 1958-65; Royal Masonic School for Girls, Rickmansworth, England, visiting teacher of flute and clarinet, 1958-65. *Military service:* British Army, 1941-46; became captain. *Member:* Incorporated Society of Musicians, Royal Musical Association, Society of Recorder Players (chairman), Galpin Society, Royal Society of Teachers.

WRITINGS: The Recorder or English Flute, Atheneum, 1936; *Twelve National Airs*, Schott & Co., 1938; *Method for Group Instruction for Recorders*, Schott & Co., 1939; (arranger) *Third Ensemble Book*, Schott & Co., 1940; (arranger) *Six Elizabethan Trios*, Associate Music Publishers, 1947; (arranger) *Trio Movements for Recorders*, Schott & Co., 1948; (arranger) Herbert Arthur Chambers, editor, *A Shakespeare Song Book*, Blandford, 1957; *The Recorder: A Handbook of Useful Information*, Schott & Co., 1957; (author of introduction) Christopher Welch, *Lectures on the Recorder in Relation to Literature*, Oxford University Press, 1961; (editor) *Instructions and Tunes for the Treble Recorder from the Modern Music Master*, Schott & Co., 1963; *The Recorder and Its Music*, Jenkins, 1962, Norton, 1963. Contributor to journals.

WORK IN PROGRESS: A student's guide to early instruments; a history of the flute; writing on the training of recorder teachers; a biography of R. L. Pearsall.

AVOCATIONAL INTERESTS: Typography, printing, foreign travel.

* * *

HUNT, Inez Whitaker 1899-

PERSONAL: Born August 21, 1899, in Willow Hill, Ill.; daughter of Andrew Buck (a teacher) and Minnie (Steers) Whitaker; married Nelson V. Hunt (a manufacturer), September 20, 1919; children: Dorothy Frances (Mrs. Kenneth Kiester). *Education:* Studied at Colorado State College (now University of Northern Colorado), 1919, and Colorado University Extension, 1959, 1963. *Religion:* Presbyterian. *Home:* 707 Prospect Pl., Manitou Springs, Colo.

CAREER: Professional lecturer at conventions in Colorado Springs, Denver, Colo., and elsewhere, and professional book reviewer; also does weekly radio broadcast on books. Teacher with University of Colorado Extension, Colorado Springs, 1963-66. *Member:* National League of American Pen Women, Authors Guild of America, Historical Society of the Pike's Peak Region (past president), Colorado Authors League, Poetry Society of Colorado, Poetry Fellowship of Colorado Springs (past president), Portia Study Club, Manitou Women's Club. *Awards, honors:* National League of American Pen Women first prize for lecture, 1962, and first prize ($500) in nonfiction, 1966, for *Lightning in His Hand*; Hafen Award for poetry, 1966.

WRITINGS—With Wanetta Draper; all published by Sage Books: *Ghost Trails to Ghost Towns*, 1958; *Horse Feathers and Applesause*, 1959; *To Colorado's Restless Ghosts*, 1960; *Lightning in His Hand: The Life Story of Nikola Tesla*, 1964.

Poetry: *Windows Through the Wall*, Big Mountain Press, 1956; *High Country*, Big Mountain Press, 1962. Author of weekly column, "Behind the Kitchen Curtain," for *Manitou Springs Journal*; also author of news features for Colorado Springs newspapers. Contributor of poetry to newspapers and farm magazines.

WORK IN PROGRESS: Further research on Nikola Tesla and western Colorado history.

* * *

HUNT, Mabel Leigh 1892-

PERSONAL: Born November 1, 1892, in Coatesville, Ind.; daughter of Tighlman (a physician) and Amanda (Harvey) Hunt. *Education:* Studied at DePauw University, 1910-12, Western Reserve University Library School, 1923-24. *Politics:* Republican. *Religion:* Quaker. *Home:* 4525 Marcy Lane, #252, Indianapolis, Ind. 46205.

CAREER: Indianapolis (Ind.) Public Library, children's librarian, then branch librarian, 1926-38; free-lance writer, mainly for children, 1938—. *Member:* Altrusa International, Alpha Phi, Theta Sigma Phi. *Awards, honors:* New York Herald Tribune honor award for *Billy Button's Butter'd Biscuit*, 1941, and *The Peddler's Clock*, 1943; second runner-up for Newberry Medal, 1943, for *"Have You Seen Tom Thumb?"*; runner-up for Newberry Medal, 1951, for *Better Known as Johnny Appleseed*; Indiana Author's Day awards of Indiana University Writers Conference for *Stars for Cristy*, 1957, and *Cupola House*, 1962.

WRITINGS: Lucinda, a Little Girl of 1860, Stokes, 1934; *The Boy Who Had No Birthday*, Stokes, 1935; *Little Girl with Seven Names*, Stokes, 1936; *Susan, Beware!*, Stokes, 1937; *Benjie's Hat*, Stokes, 1938; *Little Grey Gown*, Stokes, 1939; *Michel's Island*, Stokes, 1940; *John of Pudding Lane*, Stokes, 1941; *Billy Button's Butter'd Biscuit*, Stokes, 1941; *Corn Belt Billy*, Grosset, 1942; *"Have You Seen Tom Thumb?,"* Stokes, 1942; *Peter Piper's Pickled Peppers*, Stokes, 1942; *The Peddler's Clock*, Grosset, 1943; *Young Man of the House*, Lippincott, 1944; *Sibby Botherbox*, Lippincott, 1945; *Such a Kind World*, Grosset, 1947; *The Double Birthday Present*, Lippincott, 1947; *Matilda's Buttons*, Lippincott, 1948.

Better Known as Johnny Appleseed, Lippincott, 1950; *The Wonderful Baker*, Lippincott, 1950; *The Sixty-Ninth Grandchild*, Lippincott, 1951; *Ladycake Farm*, Lippincott, 1952; *Singing among Strangers*, Lippincott, 1954; *Miss Jellytot's Visit*, Lippincott, 1955; *Stars for Cristy*, Lippincott, 1956; *Tomorrow Will Be Bright*, Ginn, 1958; *Cristy at Skippinghills*, Lippincott, 1958; *Cupola House*, Lippincott, 1961; *Johnny-Up and Johnny-Down*, Lippincott, 1962; *Beggar's Daughter*, Lippincott, 1963. Contributor of short stories, articles, and poetry to anthologies, readers, and magazines.

SIDELIGHTS: Miss Hunt told *CA*: "I have never written a book that completely satisfied me as to craftsmanship. When the book is in print, and it is too late to make changes, I wish I could do it, even if only one sentence. There is one exception. I would not change one word in *'Have You Seen Tom Thumb?'*

"The circumstances of my life, my temperament, my inheritance, my education, my preference, and all that I am have made me a writer. Professionally, a remarkable series of most fortunate coincidences have helped me along through all my years of writing. The thing I need comes to me. The jigsaw falls into place. It has been amazing."

Miss Hunt's books have been published in England, and translated into German.

AVOCATIONAL INTERESTS: Travel, reading, driving, cooking.

* * *

HUNTER, Dard 1883-1966

PERSONAL: Born November 29, 1883, in Steubenville, Ohio; son of William Henry (a newspaper owner and editor) and Harriet (Rosemond-Browne) Hunter; married Helen Edith Cornell, March 24, 1908 (died, 1951); children: Dard, Jr., Cornell Choate. *Education:* Attended Ohio State University, 1901-02, Kunstgewerbe Schule, Vienna, 1908, Graphische Lehr and Versuchs-Anstalt, Vienna, 1909-11 (graduate), and Royal Technical College, London, 1912-13. *Home:* Mountain House, Chillicothe, Ohio 45601.

CAREER: Traveled throughout United States as magician's assistant, 1898-1901; associated with Elbert Hubbard (editor and publisher) at Roycroft Press, East Aurora, N.Y., 1903-08; while attending school in Vienna, worked evenings in a stained-glass studio; while studying in London worked as decorative designer in The Carlton Studio, Strand, and The Norfolk Studio, London; book maker and publisher, 1914-50; in 1928, in Lime Rock, Conn., he established Dard Hunter Associates (a mill for making handmade paper, the only mill of its kind in the western hemisphere), president, 1928-32; in 1928, established Dard Hunter Paper Museum at Massachusetts Institute of Technology, Cambridge, Mass., moved collection to Institute of Paper Chemistry, Appleton, Wis., 1954, where it will remain permanently. Vice-president, News-Advertiser Co., Chillicothe, Ohio, 1914-38; honorary curator of graphic arts at Harvard University, 1950-66; spent winter months at La Casa del Libro, a graphic arts library, San Juan, Puerto Rico, where he was assistant to director, 1960-66. *Member*—All honorary life memberships: Technical Association of Pulp and Paper Industry, American Institute of Graphic Arts, American Antiquarian Society, Forest History Foundation, Club of Odd Volumes (Boston), Ohio State Historical Society, Rowfant Club (Cleveland). *Awards, honors:* Gold Medal, American Institute of Graphic Arts, 1931; Ohioana Medal, 1944; Rosenbach Fellowship, University of Pennsylvania, 1949; Gold Medal, Gutenberg Museum (Mainz, Germany), 1954. Honorary degrees: Litt.D., Lawrence College, 1931, Ohio State University, 1939; L.H.D., Wooster College, 1947; M.A., Lehigh University, 1949.

WRITINGS: Old Papermaking, Mountain House Press, 1923; *The Literature of Papermaking, 1390-1800*, Mountain House Press, 1925; *Primitive Papermaking*, Mountain House Press, 1927; *Papermaking Through Eighteen Centuries*, William Edwin Rudge Press (New York), 1930; *Papermaking in the Classroom*, Manual Arts Press (Peoria), 1931; *Old Papermaking in China and Japan*, Mountain House Press, 1932; *A Papermaking Pilgrimage to Japan, Korea and China*, Pynson Printers (New York), 1935; *Papermaking in Southern Siam*, Mountain House Press, 1936; *Chinese Ceremonial Paper*, Mountain House Press, 1937; *Papermaking by Hand in India*, Pynson Printers, 1939; *Before Life Began: An Autobiography*, Rowfant Club (Cleveland), 1941; *Papermaking: The History and Technique of an Ancient Craft*, Knopf, 1942, enlarged edition, 1947; *Papermaking in Indo-China*, Mountain House Press, 1947; *Papermaking by Hand in America, 1690-1820*, Mountain House Press, 1950; (with T. K. Tindale) *The Handmade Papers of Japan*, [Tokyo], 1950; *Papermaking in Pioneer America*, University of Pennsylvania Press, 1952; *My Life With Paper* (autobiography), Knopf, 1958. Contributor to *Encyclopaedia Britannica* and *Colliers Encyclopedia*, to pamphlets, and to technical and popular magazines, all on the history of paper.

SIDELIGHTS: Hunter's great-grandfather set up a printing-office in the wilds of Ohio in 1812; his grandfather and his father owned and edited newspapers. While still a boy, Hunter could set type and was fascinated by the art of fine bookmaking.

The eight books printed by the Mountain House Press were all made entirely by Hunter, and are said to be the only books in the history of printing to be so made, their author being also papermaker, typefounder, typesetter, and printer. One copy of one of his rare editions, *Papermaking by Hand in America, 1690-1820*, published at $175 was sold in 1965 for $1600; the market price in 1974 was $2500 per copy—when available. In 1973, this book was included in an exhibition entitled "Art of the Printed Book—1455-1955; Masterpieces of Typography through Five Centuries," at the Pierpont Morgan Library in New York.

In the twenties and thirties Hunter visited China, Japan, Korea, India, Indochina, Siam, and the remote sections of other Asiatic countries where, at the time, paper continued to be made by hand.

Hunter has said that "the origin and development of papermaking . . . is the basis of all civilization, and that had it not been for this craft the world could not possibly have existed. For without paper there would have been no scientists." This realization, noted Frances J. Brewer, is his real contribution to posterity.

BIOGRAPHICAL/CRITICAL SOURCES: Saturday Evening Post, February 27, 1954; *Among Friends*, Friends of the Detroit Public Library, Fall, 1960.

(Died February 20, 1966)

*   *   *

HUNTER, J(ames) A(lston) H(ope)   1902-

PERSONAL: Born February 12, 1902, in Tigre, Argentina; son of James Hope (an industrialist) and Mamuela Leopoldina (Luna) Hunter. *Education:* Educated at private schools in England, and at Royal Naval Colleges at Osborne and Dartmouth, England. *Address:* c/o Westminster Bank Ltd., 96 Kensington High St., London W.8, England.

CAREER: Royal Navy, 1918-45, midshipman to commander; Control Commission for Germany, chief finance officer for German sea and inland water shipping, 1946-52. *Member:* British Mathematical Association, Mathematical Association of America.

WRITINGS: Fun with Figures, Oxford University Press, 1956; *Figures for Fun*, Phoenix House, 1957; *Figurets: More Fun with Figures*, Oxford University Press, 1958, reissued as *More Fun with Figures*, Dover, 1966 (published in England as *More Figures for Fun*, Phoenix House, 1959); *Figures Are Fun*, five books and manual for elementary grades four to eight, Copp, 1959; (with J. S. Madachy) *Mathematical Diversions*, Van Nostrand, 1963; *Hunter's Math Brain Teasers*, Bantam, 1965. Author of daily newspaper feature, "Fun with Figures," with almost 3500 mathematical teasers published, 1952—, and of monthly magazine feature, "Puzzler." Former associate editor, *Recreational Mathematics*.

*   *   *

HUNTER, Leslie S(tannard)   1890-

PERSONAL: Born May 2, 1890, in Glasgow, Scotland;

son of John (a clergyman) and Marion (Martin) Hunter; married Grace Marion McAulay, 1919. *Education:* Oxford University, B.A. (honors), 1913, M.A., 1917. *Home:* Moorholme, Bakewell, Derbyshire, England.

CAREER: Ordained to ministry of Church of England, 1915; member of staff, Student Christian Movement of Great Britain, 1913-21, and Army and Religion Inquiry Commission, 1917-19, also holding curateships in England during that time; residentiary canon of Newcastle on Tyne, 1922-26, 1931-39; vicar of Barking, Essex, 1926-30; archdeacon of Northumberland, 1931-39; chaplain to the king, beginning, 1936; bishop of Sheffield, 1939-62; retired, 1962. Member of House of Lords, 1944-62. Chairman of Inter-Church Aid and Refugee Service, British Council of Churches, 1948-64; member of Praesidium of European Conference of Churches, 1959-67. Select preacher at Universities of Glasgow, Edinburgh, Aberdeen, St. Andrews, and Oxford University and Cambridge University. Chairman of William Temple College, Rugy, beginning, 1948, and of British Council of Churches from inception to 1967. *Awards, honors:* D.C.L., University of Durham; D.D., Lambeth and University of Toronto; L.L.D., University of Sheffield; Kommander of the Dannebrog (Denmark), 1952.

WRITINGS: John Hunter, D.D.: A Life, Hodder & Stoughton, 1921; (editor) *A Revised Prayer Book*, Oxford University Press, 1923; *A Parson's Job*, S.C.M. Press, 1931; (editor) *Men, Money and the Ministry*, Longmans, Green, 1937; *A Church Militant*, S.C.M. Press, 1939; (editor) *Putting Our Houses in Order*, Longmans, Green, 1941; *Planning Ahead*, British Broadcasting Corp., 1942; *Let Us Go Forward*, S.C.M. Press, 1944; *Church Strategy in a Changing World*, Longmans, Green, 1950; *The Seed and the Fruit*, S.C.M. Press, 1953; *The Mission of the People of God*, S.P.C.K., 1961; *A Diocesan Service Book*, Oxford University Press, 1965; (editor) *Scandinavian Churches*, Augsburg, 1965; (editor) *The English Church*, Penguin, 1966.

WORK IN PROGRESS: A book on Christian ministry.

AVOCATIONAL INTERESTS: Music, hill-walking, travel, and reading.

*   *   *

HUNTLEY, H(erbert) E(dwin)   1892-

PERSONAL: Born December 31, 1892, in England; son of Herbert James (a hotel proprietor) and Selena Browne (Couch) Huntley; married Gladys Kathleen Page, October 28, 1924; children: Rosemary Joan Huntley McMahon, Alison Ruth. *Education:* University of Bristol, B.Sc. (honors), 1932; University of the Witwatersrand, Ph.D., 1949. *Politics:* Socialist (Labour Party). *Religion:* Methodist. *Home:* Nethercombe Cottage, Canada Combe, Hulton, Weston-super-Mare, England.

CAREER: University of Bristol, Bristol, England, member of research team, 1932-38; headmaster of high school, Clarkebury, Cape Province, South Africa, 1942-45; University of Witwatersrand, Johannesburg, South Africa, lecturer in physics, 1945-49; University of Ghana, Legon, Accra, professor of physics, 1949-57; retired, but became full-time grammar school teacher in Weston-super-Mare, England, 1957—. Inventor of the Self-tutor, a programmed teaching aid. *Member:* Institute of Physics (fellow).

WRITINGS: Dimensional Analysis, Macdonald & Co., 1952; *Nuclear Species*, Macmillan, 1954; *The Faith of a*

Physicist, Bles, 1960; *Programmed Trigonometry*, privately printed, 1964. Contributor to *Nature*, *New Scientist*, *Fibonacci Quarterly* (United States), and other journals.

WORK IN PROGRESS: A book, *Beauty Wax the Bait: The Scientist Looks Back*; programmed texts for use with the Self-tutor.

*   *   *

HURD, Charles (Wesley Bolick)   1903-1968

PERSONAL: Born May 11, 1903, in Tonkawa, Okla.; son of Arthur A. (a farmer) and Katherine (Bolick) Hurd; married Eleanor Branson, March 17, 1934. *Education:* Extension courses at Washington University, St. Louis, Mo., 1918-19, Northwestern University, 1920-23. *Politics:* Democrat. *Religion:* Christian Science. *Home:* 177 East 75th St., New York, N.Y. 10021. *Office:* Charles Hurd & Associates, 630 Fifth Ave., New York, N.Y. 10020.

CAREER: Reporter for newspapers in St. Louis, Mo., and Des Moines, Iowa, 1918-19; Associated Press, reporter in Chicago, Ill., and New York, N.Y., 1920-25; *Liberty*, New York, N.Y., associate editor, 1926-28; *New York Times*, New York, N.Y., Washington correspondent, 1929-49, except for one year, 1937, on European assignments; Carl Byoir & Associates, New York, N.Y., public relations, 1949-54; Charles Hurd & Associates (industrial public relations firm), New York, N.Y., founder, 1954-68. Consultant on public relations to American National Red Cross and League of Red Cross Societies (international). *Member:* Authors League of America (member of board of directors of league and of Authors Guild, 1950-52), Overseas Press Club of America (New York), Sigma Delta Chi (honorary), Metropolitan Club (Washington, D.C.).

WRITINGS: The White House: A Biography, Harper, 1940; *A Veteran's Program: A Complete Guide to Its Benefits, Rights and Options*, Whittlesey House, 1946; *Washington Cavalcade*, Dutton, 1948; *The Compact History of the American Red Cross*, Hawthorn, 1959; (with Arthur E. Summerfield) *U.S. Mail: The Story of the United States Postal Service*, Holt, 1960; *When the New Deal Was Young and Gay*, Hawthorn, 1965; *The White House Story*, Hawthorn, 1966.

Compiler of anthologies: *A Treasury of Great American Speeches: Our Country's Life and History in the Words of Its Great Men*, Hawthorn, 1959; (with Lowell Thomas) *Cavalcade of Europe: A Handbook of Information on 22 Countries*, Doubleday, 1959; (with wife, Eleanor A. Hurd) *A Treasury of Great American Letters: Our Country's Life and History in the Letters of Its Men and Women*, Hawthorn, 1961; *A Treasury of Great American Quotations: Our Country's Life and History in the Thoughts of Its Men and Women*, Hawthorn, 1964, also published as *Words That Inspire: A Treasury of Great American Quotations*, J. G. Ferguson, 1964.

WORK IN PROGRESS: Compiling *Treasury of American Heroes*; memoirs of six years as a White House correspondent.

AVOCATIONAL INTERESTS: Collected works of younger European painters, particularly from Spain, France, and Italy.

(Died May 16, 1968)

*   *   *

HURST, Fannie   1889-1968

PERSONAL: Born October 18, 1889, in Hamilton, Ohio; daughter of Samuel (owner of a shoe factory) and Rose (Koppel) Hurst; married Jacques S. Danielson (a pianist), 1915, though kept a secret for five years (died, 1952). *Education:* Washington University, St. Louis, Mo., B.A., 1909; Columbia University, graduate study, 1910-12. *Politics:* Democrat. *Home:* 1 West 67th St., New York, N.Y. 10023.

CAREER: Novelist and short story writer. Grew up in St. Louis, Mo.; went to New York in 1910 to gain experience for writing, taking bit parts in plays, working in department stores, restaurants, and factories and poking around in tenement districts, trying to observe life "the way Dickens did"; wrote for two years before her short stories began appearing in magazines, with the first story collection published in 1914. Sometime lecturer and television commentator. Chairman of National Housing Commission, 1936-37; member of National Advisory Committee to Works Progress Administration, 1940-41; delegate to World Health Organization Assembly, Geneva, 1952. Trustee of Heckscher Foundation, 1949-60, Ecole des Hautes Etudes, 1960; associate trustee, Russell Sage College, 1947. *Member:* Authors Guild (president, 1937; vice-president, 1944-46, 1947). *Awards, honors:* D.Litt., Washington University, St. Louis, Mo., 1953, and Fairleigh Dickinson University.

WRITINGS: Just Around the Corner (stories), Harper, 1914; *Every Soul Hath Its Song* (stories), Harper, 1916; *Gaslight Sonatas* (stories), Harper, 1918; *Humoresque* (stories), Knopf, 1919; *Star-dust: The Story of an American Girl*, Harper, 1921; *The Vertical City* (stories), Harper, 1922; *Lummox*, Harper, 1923; *Appassionata*, Knopf, 1926; *Mannequin*, Knopf, 1926; *Song of Life* (stories), Knopf, 1927; *A President Is Born*, Harper, 1928; *Five and Ten*, Harper, 1929; *Procession* (stories), Harper, 1929.

Back Street, Cosmopolitan Book Corp., 1931; *Imitation of Life*, Harper, 1933; *Anitra's Dance*, Harper, 1934; *No Food with My Meals*, (nonfiction), Harper, 1935; *Great Laughter*, Harper, 1936; *We Are Ten* (stories), Harper, 1937; *Lonely Parade*, Harper, 1942; *White Christmas*, Doubleday, Doran, 1942; *Hallelujah*, Harper, 1944; *The Hands of Veronica*, Harper, 1947.

Anywoman, Harper, 1950; *The Man with One Head*, J. Cape, 1953; *Anatomy of Me: a Wonderer in Search of Herself* (autobiography), Doubleday, 1958; *Family!*, Doubleday, 1960; *God Must Be Sad*, Doubleday, 1961; *Fool Be Still*, Doubleday, 1964.

Plays: *Four Daughters* (three-act comedy), Longmans, Green, circa 1950; other plays produced include "Land of the Free," 1919, and "Back Pay," 1921. Twelve filmscripts include "Humoresque," "Four Daughters," "Back Street," "Imitation of Life," and "Symphony of Six Million."

Contributor to *Cosmopolitan*, *Redbook*, and other magazines.

SIDELIGHTS: Fannie Hurst did not enter easily into the world of letters. She had to overcome the disapproval of a domineering mother and an old-fashioned father, and the persistent dubiosity of magazine editors. Her enthusiasm never faltered, however, and she could claim authorship of over thirty volumes. At fourteen she submitted her first manuscript for publication—a masque in blank verse to the *Saturday Evening Post*. The rejection slip was the first of some thirty-five slips to come from the *Post* before the fiction editor bought "Power and Horse Power" and asked for first chance at all future manuscripts. But her first literary success came with the publication of a story entitled "Ain't Life Wonderful" by *Reedy's Mirror*, a popular St. Louis weekly, while she was in college at Washington University.

Also while in college, Miss Hurst wrote and acted in a play entitled "Home," which was produced by the Keith Vandeville Theatre in St. Louis. The play was a failure, but she received sufficient encouragement to begin dramatic lessons in New York, where she later appeared in numerous bit parts. Her first Broadway performance, in the hit play, "The Music Master," required four single-line speeches—all the same. She was given the part because she was heavy enough to close an over-stuffed suitcase by sitting on it, but she swallowed her pride and accepted the job at twenty-five dollars a week.

During the years of the rejection slips, her work was not wholly unappreciated, however. She was continually praised for her excellent "character delineation." In 1961, M. B. Snyder noted that the characters in *Family!* were "as alive as only her characters can be. They are people you want to know and know more. In fact, you can't avoid knowing them rather completely. . . ." Her autobiography was also praised for its "value as a human document."

During the frustrating early years of her career, Miss Hurst most frequently read Boccaccio, Maeterlinck, Smollett, Gertrude Atherton, Gilbert Chesterton, D'Annunzio, Upton Sinclair, and Thomas Hardy, but it was the then unknown Edgar Lee Masters to whom she was most attracted. Her reading of the newly published *Spoon River Anthology* became for her "a major literary experience," and thereafter continued to recognize Masters' influence on her writings.

Of her novels, Miss Hurst chose *Lummox* as her favorite. It is, perhaps, the epitome of her literary crusade for the downtrodden woman. In her autobiography she says of the novel: "*Lummox* symbolized my complete breakthrough, by what might be termed the short method, from the circumscribed world in which I had been reared into a new social consciousness." Her work continued to be characterized by an acute social awareness. Although frequently criticized for her continual "plucking of heart strings," she was nevertheless recognized as a master of warm, sympathetic, and viable prose.

Her books have been translated into eighteen languages and reissued in a number of paperback editions. Over a dozen of her short stories and novels were made into films. Her film scripts, "Symphony of Six Million," was novelized by John Adams (a pseudonym) and published by A. L. Burt in 1932.

Several days before her death, Miss Hurst delivered two novels to her publisher, one, "Lonely Is Only a Word," the other untitled.

A Fanny Hurst Professorship was endowed at Brandeis and Washington (St. Louis) Universities as a provision of her will.

BIOGRAPHICAL/CRITICAL SOURCES: Anatomy of Me: A Wanderer in Search of Herself, Doubleday, 1958; *Kirkus*, August 1, 1958; *Times Literary Supplement*, October 23, 1959; *Chicago Sunday Tribune*, October 2, 1960; *New York Times Book Review*, October 16, 1960; *New York Herald Tribune Books*, January 7, 1962.

(Died February 23, 1968)

HUTCHINSON, G(eorge) Evelyn   1903-

PERSONAL: Born January 30, 1903, in Cambridge, England; came to United States in 1928, naturalized in 1941; son of Arthur (a mineralogist) and Eviline (Shipley) Hutchinson; married July 30, 1933. *Education:* Cambridge University, B.A., 1924, M.A., 1928. *Home:* 269 Canner St., New Haven, Conn.

CAREER: University of the Witwatersrand, Johannesburg, Transvaal, Republic of South Africa, senior lecturer in zoology, 1926-28; Yale University, New Haven, Conn., instructor in biology, 1928-31, assistant professor, 1931-41, associate professor, 1941-45, professor, 1945, Sterling Professor of Zoology, 1946-71, professor emeritus, 1971—, fellow of Saybrook College. *Member:* National Academy of Sciences, American Philosophical Society, American Society of Zoologists, Ecological Society of America, Limnology Society of America (vice-president, 1938; president, 1948), International Limnology Society (president, 1964-65). *Awards, honors:* L.H.D., Lawrence College, 1954; D.S., Princeton University, 1961, Niagara University, 1970, Washington University (St. Louis), 1972; Tyler Award for Ecology, 1974.

WRITINGS: The Clear Mirror, Cambridge University Press, 1937; *The Itinerant Ivory Tower*, Yale University Press, 1952; *A Treatise on Limnology*, Volume I, Wiley, 1957, Volume II, 1967; *Enchanted Voyage and Other Studies*, Yale University Press, 1963; *The Ecological Theater and the Evolutionary Play*, Yale University Press, 1965. Author of scientific papers on various topics in his field.

WORK IN PROGRESS: Research in limnology, theoretical aspects of ecology, and medieval origins of the study of natural history.

SIDELIGHTS: Hutchinson was biologist for Yale expedition to northern India in 1932, and has taken part in other scientific investigations in Italy, England, South Africa, and the United States.

*   *   *

HUTCHINSON, Margaret Massey   1904-

PERSONAL: Born December 18, 1904, in Haslemere, Surrey, England; daughter of Herbert (an architect) and Elizabeth (Woods) Hutchinson. *Education:* Brunnaker Froebel Training Department, Birmingham, England, higher certificate of National Froebel Union. *Religion:* Quaker. *Home:* Croft House, Inval, Haslemere, Surrey, England.

CAREER: Yafflesmead Kindergarten and Junior School, Haslemere, Surrey, England, principal, 1930-55. Cubmaster and commissioner, Boy Scouts' Association, 1923-35. *Member:* School Natural Science Society, Haslemere National History Society.

WRITINGS: Children as Naturalists, Allen & Unwin, 1947, Macmillan, 1948, 2nd edition, Allen & Unwin, 1966; *What Can You Find in a Wood?*, Educational Supply Association, 1952; *What Can You Find in Hedge and Field?*, Educational Supply Association, 1953; *Making and Keeping a Bird Table*, Educational Supply Association, 1958; *Making and Keeping a Box Garden*, Educational Supply Association, 1960; *What Can You Find Along a River Bank?*, Educational Supply Association, 1962; *Making and Keeping a Vegetable Garden*, Ward, Lock, 1965. Writer of leaflets published by National Froebel Foundation and School Natural Science Society.

WORK IN PROGRESS: Developments in primary education method; a history and ecology of the Inval estate.

AVOCATIONAL INTERESTS: All nature study, but particularly birds (traveled in Australia and New Zealand, observing birds).

* * *

HUTTO, Nelson (Allen) 1904-

PERSONAL: Born December 12, 1904, in Nuevo Laredo, Mexico; son of John Renfroe (a teacher) and Rebecca (Nelson) Hutto; married Pauline Hardesty, June 4, 1928; children: Emily (Mrs. J. W. Frederick), Nell (Mrs. D. K. Usiak). *Education:* Hardin-Simmons University, B.A., 1925; Columbia University, M.S., 1927. *Politics:* Democrat. *Religion:* Baptist. *Home:* 2442 Salerno Dr., Dallas, Tex. 75224. *Agent:* Lenninger Literary Agency, 437 Fifth Ave., New York, N.Y. 10016.

CAREER: Hardin-Simmons University, Abilene, Tex., associate professor of journalism and director of publicity, 1927-35; Abilene (Tex.) High School, journalism adviser, 1935-36; Sunset High School, Dallas, Tex., journalism adviser, 1936-39.

WRITINGS: Breakaway Back, Harper, 1963; *Goal Line Bomber*, Harper, 1964; *Victory Volley*, Harper, 1967. Author of short history of Dallas, *From Buckskins to Top Hat*, 1953. Contributor of more than eighty short stories and novelettes to magazines.

WORK IN PROGRESS: Sophomore Quarterback.

AVOCATIONAL INTERESTS: Sports, music (listening to good music and playing the piano).

BIOGRAPHICAL/CRITICAL SOURCES: Best Sellers, May 1, 1967; *Christian Science Monitor*, May 4, 1967; *Commonweal*, May 26, 1967.

* * *

HUTTON, J(ohn) H(enry) 1885-1968

PERSONAL: Born June 27, 1885, in Yorkshire, England; son of Joseph Henry (a clergyman) and Clarissa (Barwick) Hutton; married Stella Bishop Stewart, 1920 (died, 1944); married Maureen Margaret O'Reilly, 1946. *Education:* Worcester College, Oxford, B.A., 1908, M.A., 1920. *Home:* New Radnor, Presteigne, Radnorshire, Wales.

CAREER: Indian Civil Service, 1909-36, serving in Bengal, Assam, and Delhi; Cambridge University, Cambridge, England, lecturer, 1936-37, William Wyse Professor of Social Anthropology and fellow of St. Catharine's College, 1937-50; Frazer Lecturer, Oxford University, 1938. President, Indian Science Congress, 1935. Master and huntsman, Delhi Foxhounds, 1932; Sheriff of Radnorshire, 1943. *Member:* Royal Anthropological Institute (president, 1943-45), Folklore Society (president, 1939-42), Anthropologische Gesellschaft (Vienna; honorary member). *Awards, honors:* Companion of Order of the Indian Empire, 1920; D.Sc., Oxford University, 1922; Rivers Memorial Medal of Royal Anthropological Institute, 1929; Silver Medal of Royal Society of Arts, 1932; Annadale Memorial Medal of Asiatic Society of Bengal, 1937; honorary fellow, St. Catharine's College, Cambridge University, 1951.

WRITINGS: The Angami Nagas: With Some Notes on Neighbouring Tribes, Macmillan, 1921, 2nd edition, Oxford University Press, 1969; *The Sema Nagas*, Macmillan, 1921, 2nd edition, Oxford University Press, 1968; *Report on the Census of India, 1931*, Government of India, 1933; *Caste in India*, Cambridge University Press, 1946, 4th edition, Oxford University Press, 1963; *Pictures in the Posses-*

sion of St. Catharine's College, Cambridge (monograph), Cambridge University Press, 1950. Contributor of articles to *Folklore*, *Enquiry*, and various journals in his field.

SIDELIGHTS: Hutton was noted for his scholarly approach and his insight into historical problems of his chosen area. His first two publications, considered pioneering anthropological studies, were based, like his other works, on first-hand knowledge acquired during his years of service.

Caste in India has been translated into French and Gujarati.

(Died May 23, 1968)

* * *

HYDE, L(ouis) K(epler, Jr.) 1901-

PERSONAL: Born October 5, 1901, in Titusville, Pa.; son of Louis Kepler and Verna (Emery) Hyde; married Penelope W. Overton, September 9, 1924; children: Louis Kepler III, Richard Witherington. *Education:* Groton School, diploma, 1919; Yale University, B.A., 1923; Corpus Christi College, Cambridge, graduate study, 1923-24. *Home:* Airlie Farm, Bedford, N.Y. *Office:* E. W. Axe & Co., Inc., 730 Fifth Ave., New York, N.Y. 10019; and Tarrytown, N.Y.

CAREER: Union County Investment Co., Plainfield, N.J., vice-president, 1924-32; Time, Inc., New York, N.Y., writer and various other posts on *Fortune*, 1932-34; Wasserman, Nelson, Barringer & Hyde, Inc., Philadelphia, Pa., vice-president and partner, 1934-42; U.S. government, Washington, D.C., posts with Lend-Lease Administration, 1942-43, and Foreign Economic Administration, 1943-44, assistant to Secretary of State, 1945, member of permanent U.S. Mission to United Nations, 1946-51; E. W. Axe & Co., Inc., New York, N.Y., and Tarrytown, N.Y., vice-president, 1950—. President and director of other corporations, financial institutions, and trusts, 1926—. *Member:* Century Association, Coffee House Club, Yale Club, British Luncheon Club (all New York), Cosmos Club (Washington, D.C.), Elizabethan Club (New Haven, Conn.).

WRITINGS: The United States and the United Nations: Promoting the Public Welfare, Carnegie Endowment for International Peace, 1960. Writer and editor for government and company publications.

* * *

HYNEMAN, Charles S(hang) 1900-

PERSONAL: Born May 5, 1900, in Gibson County Ind.; son of Willis Smith and Harriet (Ford) Hyneman; married Frances Tourner, August 31, 1926; children: Richard F., Ruth Anne Hyneman McDaniel, Betty Harriet Hyneman Morrison. *Education:* Indiana University, A.B., 1923, A.M., 1925; University of Pennsylvania, graduate study, 1925-26; University of Illinois, Ph.D., 1929. *Home:* 2320 Fritz Dr., Bloomington, Ind. 47401.

CAREER: High school teacher, 1923-28; Syracuse University, Syracuse, N.Y., instructor in political science, 1928-30; University of Illinois, Urbana, assistant professor of political science, 1930-37; Louisiana State University, Baton Rouge, professor of government and chairman of department, 1937-42; U.S. government, Washington, D.C., administrative analyst, Bureau of the Budget, 1942-43, branch chief, Office of Provost Marshal General, 1943-44, director of Foreign Broadcast Intelligence Service, Federal Communications Commission, 1944-45, assistant to chairman, Federal Communications Commission, 1945-47; Northwestern University, Evanston, Ill., professor of political science, 1947-56; Indiana University, Bloomington, professor of government, 1956-61, Distinguished Professor of political science, 1961-71. Adjunct Scholar, American Enterprise Institute for Policy Research, 1971-73; fellow, Woodrow Wilson International Center for Scholars, 1973—. *Member:* American Political Science Association (president, 1961-64). *Awards, honors:* D.H.L., Ohio Northern University, 1961; LL.D., Wabash College, 1971; commendation for meritorious civilian service, Army Service Forces, U.S. War Department.

WRITINGS: The First American Neutrality: A Study of the American Understanding of Neutral Obligations during the Years 1792 to 1815, University of Illinois Press, 1934, reprinted, Porcupine Press, 1973; *Bureaucracy in a Democracy*, Harper, 1950; *The Study of Politics*, University of Illinois Press, 1959; *The Supreme Court on Trial*, Atherton, 1963; (editor uith George W. Carey) *A Second Federalist: Congress Creates a Government*, Appleton, 1967; (with Charles E. Gilbert) *Popular Government in America: Foundations and Principles*, Atherton, 1968.

WORK IN PROGRESS: Continued examination of the institutions, practices, and popular beliefs and behaviors which are essential to the maintenance of self-government with special attention to the original design for republican government in the United States and the political thought of the founders.

*   *   *

IND, Allison 1963-1974
(Phil Stanley, Richard Wallace)

PERSONAL: Surname rhymes with "wind"; born November 23, 1903, in Lead, S.D.; son of Walter Downing and Suzannah (Blythe) Ind; married Helen M. Leonard (a part-time writer), July 3, 1954; children: (previous marriage) Stanley B., Shirley Anne (Mrs. Carl Koenen). *Education:* University of Michigan, B.S., 1926, graduate student, 1927-28. *Religion:* Episcopalian. *Agent:* Paul R. Reynolds, Inc., 599 Fifth Ave., New York, N.Y. 10017; John Farquharson Ltd., 15 Red Lion Sq., London W.C. 1, England.

CAREER: Ann Arbor Daily News, Ann Arbor, Mich., reporter, movie critic, and columnist, 1926-34; U.S. Army Reserve, Military Intelligence, 1930-60, retiring as colonel after continuous active duty, 1940-60; free-lance writer at earlier periods and 1960-74. Co-founder and deputy director of espionage and sabotage unit of Allied Intelligence Bureau, Far East Command, under General MacArthur. *Member:* Authors Guild of Authors League of America, Reserve Officers Association, Overseas Press Club (Manila); Press Club and Special Forces Club (both London); Maryland Society for Clinical and Experimental Hypnosis (honorary associate). *Awards, honors*—Military: Legion of Merit with oak leaf cluster, Commendation Medal with oak leaf cluster, three battle stars for Pacific service, Order of Orange Nassau (Netherlands).

WRITINGS—All under name Allison Ind: *Bataan: The Judgment Seat*, Macmillan, 1944; *The Fires of Tjepo*, Vantage, 1955; *Allied Intelligence Bureau*, McKay, 1958; *A Short History of Espionage*, McKay, 1964 (modified and expanded version published in England as *A History of Modern Espionage*, Hodder & Stoughton, 1965); *The Sino-Variant*, McKay, 1969. Writer of about one hundred short stories published in America, Asia, and England, 1926-74; writer and technical director of "Australian Bride," ninety-

two-episode radio serial for Australian Broadcasting Corp., 1947-48.

WORK IN PROGRESS: A book on codes and ciphers.

SIDELIGHTS: Ind told *CA*: "(I) hate sports, TV, and road traffic. Love music, cats, dogs and most other animals.... Short wave 'ham' fan (but have no transmitting license in Great Britain) and like cycling in quiet English countryside. Can write best in trains. But like sound of typewriters in our flat when both wife and I are punishing them."

(Died April 16, 1974)

*   *   *

INGERSOLL, Ralph McAllister 1900-

PERSONAL: Born December 8, 1900, in New Haven, Conn.; son of Colin Macrae and Theresa (McAllister) Ingersoll; married Mary Elizabeth Carden, 1925 (divorced, 1935, died, 1964); married Elaine Brown Keiffer, 1945 (died, 1948); married Mary Hill Doolittle, 1948 (divorced, 1962); married Thelma Bradford, July 16, 1964; children: (second marriage) Ralph McAllister III, Jonathan VIII. *Education:* Yale University, B.S., 1921; Columbia University, graduate study, 1923. *Politics:* Democrat. *Home:* Cornwall Bridge, Conn. 06754. *Office:* Newspaper Management, Inc., 641 Lexington Ave., New York, N.Y. 10022.

CAREER: Mining engineer; *New Yorker*, New York, N.Y., reporter, 1925, managing editor, 1925-30; *Fortune*, New York, N.Y., associate editor, 1930, managing editor, 1930-35; Time, Inc., New York, N.Y., vice-president and general manager, 1935-38, publisher of *Time* magazine, 1937-39; *PM* (daily newspaper), New York, N.Y., founder and publisher, 1940-45; R. J. Co., Inc. (principally newspaper properties in New York State), Middletown, N.Y., president, 1948-59; New England Newspapers, Inc. (publisher of Pawtucket, R.I. *Times*), president and director, 1957—; Mid-Atlantic Newspapers, Inc. (publisher of *Daily Journal*, Elizabeth, N.J.), president, 1959—; Central States Publishing, Inc. (publisher of Delaware County, Pa. *Daily Times*), vice-president and director, 1961—. Also president of Capital City Publishing Co., Inc., and of General Publications, Inc. (newspaper consultants), 1957—. *Military service:* U.S. Army, Engineer Amphibian Command and General Staff Corps, 1942-45; served in Africa and Europe; became lieutenant colonel; received Legion of Merit, Bronze Arrowhead (Normandy landing), seven battle stars, and Order of the Crown (Belgium). *Member:* Overseas Press Club, Racquet and Tennis Club, Brook Club, and Yale Club (all New York), Essex Club (Newark, N.J.).

WRITINGS: In and Under Mexico, Century, 1923; *Report on England*, Simon & Schuster, 1940; *Action on All Fronts*, Harper, 1941; *America Is Worth Fighting For*, Bobbs-Merrill, 1941; *The Battle Is the Payoff*, Harcourt, 1944; *Top Secret*, Harcourt, 1946; *The Great Ones*, Harcourt, 1948; *Wine of Violence*, Farrar, Strauss, 1951; *Point of Departure* (autobiography), Harcourt, 1961. Contributor to magazines and newspapers.

WORK IN PROGRESS: Volume II of autobiography, covering the years 1930-40, for Harcourt.

*   *   *

INGLE, Dwight Joyce 1907-

PERSONAL: Born September 4, 1907, in Kendrick, Idaho; son of David J. and Mattie (Self) Ingle; married Geneva

McGarvey, October 25, 1930; children: David, Ann, Jane. *Education:* University of Idaho, B.S., 1929, M.S., 1931; University of Minnesota, Ph.D., 1941. *Home:* 5514 Wood-lawn Ave., Chicago, Ill. 60637.

CAREER: Upjohn Co., Kalamazoo, Mich., senior research scientist, 1941-53; University of Chicago, Chicago, Ill., professor of physiology, 1953—, chairman of department, 1959-68. Consultant to American Cancer Society. *Member:* American Academy of Arts and Sciences (fellow), American Physiological Society, Society for Experimental Biology and Medicine (vice-president, 1963-65; president, 1965-67), National Academy of Sciences, Endocrine Society (president, 1959-60), Sigma Xi, Phi Beta Kappa. *Awards, honors:* Roche-Organon Award of Laurentian Hormone Conference; D.Sc., University of Idaho, 1962; Koch Award, Endocrine Society, 1963.

WRITINGS: (With Burton L. Baker) *Physiological and Therapeutic Effects of Corticotropin and Cortisone*, C. C Thomas, 1953; *Principles of Research in Biology and Medicine*, Lippincott, 1958; (editor with Robert S. Harris) *Vitamins and Hormones: Advances in Research and Applications*, Volume 17 of 27 volumes, Academy Press, 1959; (editor) *A Dozen Doctors: Autobiographic Sketches* (originally published in *Perspectives in Biology and Medicine*), University of Chicago Press, 1963; *I Went to See the Elephant* (autobiography), Vantage, 1963; (editor) *Life and Disease: New Perspectives in Biology and Medicine*, Basic Books, 1963. Editor, *Perspectives in Biology and Medicine*, University of Chicago Press, 1957—. Contributor of more than 350 articles to scientific journals.

WORK IN PROGRESS: A book, *Biological Bases of Social Problems.*

* * *

INGLES, G(lenn) Lloyd 1901-

PERSONAL: Born March 28, 1901, in Camden, Ill.; son of Robert (a businessman) and Ada (Bowers) Ingles; married Elizabeth Walker (a teacher), June 8, 1934; children: Helen (Mrs. William Brubaker), John Allison. *Education:* University of Redlands, A.B., 1925; Claremont College, M.A., 1928; University of California, Berkeley, Ph.D., 1932. *Home:* 409 Rialto, Fresno, Calif. 93704. *Office:* California State University, Fresno, Calif.

CAREER: High school teacher in California, 1925-27; Bakersfield Junior College, Bakersfield, Calif., instructor, 1928-30; Chico State College (now California State University), Chico, Calif., associate professor, later professor of biology, 1932-43; Fresno State College (now California State University), Fresno, Calif., professor of zoology, 1945-66, and head of Life Sciences Division and chairman of biology department, distinguished lecturer, 1965; now retired. *Military service:* U.S. Naval Reserve, 1943-45; became lieutenant. *Member:* American Society of Mammalogists, Photographic Society of America, California Academy of Science (fellow), Sigma Xi, Phi Kappa Phi. *Awards, honors:* Penrose Fund research grant, American Philosophical Society, 1948; named outstanding professor, California State Colleges Trustees, 1965.

WRITINGS: Mammals of California, Stanford University Press, 1947; *Mammals of California and Its Coastal Waters*, Stanford University Press, 1954; *Mammals of the Pacific States*, Stanford University Press, 1966.

WORK IN PROGRESS: Research in the behavior of mammals.

AVOCATIONAL INTERESTS: Nature photography.

INGRAM, (Archibald) Kenneth 1882-1965

PERSONAL: Born June 7, 1882, in London, England; son of Archibald Brown and Kate (Francis) Ingram. *Education:* Attended Charterhouse School. *Religion:* Church of England. *Home:* 31 Queens Gate Ter., London S.W. 7, England.

CAREER: Called to the Bar, London, England, 1909; barrister-at-law, Inner Temple, London; British Ministry of Labour, Appointments Department, secretary of Grants Committee, 1919-23. National Peace Council, vice-chairman, beginning 1951. *Military service:* British Army, 1914-18; became lieutenant; mentioned in dispatches. *Member:* Reform Club (London).

WRITINGS: England at the Flood Tide, Daimon Press, 1924; *Out of Darkness* (fiction), Chatto & Windus, 1927, Stokes, 1928; *Has the Church Failed?*, Allan & Co., 1929.

Romance of Christmas, P. Allan, 1930; *Sun-Worshipper*, H. Walker, 1930; *The Modern Attitude to the Sex Problem*, Stokes, 1930; *The Church of Tomorrow*, P. Allan, 1931, Macmillan, 1932; *The Steep Steps; a Detective Story*, P. Allan, 1931; (editor) *Youth Looks at Religion*, P. Allan, 1932; *Portrait of Six Christian Heroes: St. Appian, St. Alban, St. Athanasius, St. Francis de Sales, St. Ignatius Loyola, George Elton Sedding*, P. Allan, 1932; *Symbolic Island* (fiction), P. Allan, 1932; *The Man Who Was Lonely* (fiction), P. Allan, 1932; *Midsummer Sanity*, P. Allan, 1933; *Modern Thought on Trial*, P. Allan, 1933; *John Keble*, P. Allan, 1933; *Road to Easter*, P. Allan, 1933; *Lay Devotion*, P. Allan, 1934; *Death Comes at Night* (fiction), Sears, 1934; *Adventure of Passiontide*, Bles, 1935; *The Coming Civilization: Will It Be Capitalist, Will It Be Materialist?*, Allen & Unwin, 1935; *It is Expedient* (fiction), Bles, 1936; *Basil Jellicoe*, Centenary Press, 1936; *Christianity—Right or Left?*, Allen & Unwin, 1937; *And He Shall Come Again*, Heinemann, 1938; *The Christian Challenge to Christians*, Allen & Unwin, 1938; *Towards Christianity, the Religious Process of the World*, S.C.M. Press, 1939; *The Ambart Trial* (fiction), Quality Press, 1939; *The Defeat of War: Can Pacifism Achieve It?*, Allen & Unwin, 1939.

Sex-Morality Tomorrow, Allen & Unwin, 1940; *The Night Is Far Spent*, Allen & Unwin, 1941; *Return of Yesterday* (fiction), Quality Press, 1942; *Taken at the Flood*, Allen & Unwin, 1943; *The Premier Tells the Truth* (fiction), Quality Press, 1944; (editor) Kate Agnes Ingram, *Towards Old Age; with a Memoir of the Author by Her Son, Kenneth Ingram*, Quality Press, 1945; *Guide to the New Age*, Allen & Unwin, 1945; *Years of Crisis: An Outline of International History, 1919-1945*, Allen & Unwin, 1946, Macmillan, 1947; *Communist Challenge (Good or Evil)*, Quality Press, 1948.

Christianity, Communism and Society, Rider, 1951; *Easter Journey*, Longmans, Green, 1953; *Storm in a Sanctuary* (fiction), Benn, 1954; *History of the Cold War*, Philosophical Library, 1955.

Is Christianity Credible? A Plain Guide for Intelligent Inquirers, Morehouse, 1963.

Founder and editor, *Green Quarterly*, 1924-32, and *Police Journal*, 1929-32.

AVOCATIONAL INTERESTS: Music, international affairs (Ingram believed "mankind will choose the path of survival rather than the highway which leads to wholesale destruction"), the study of the attitude of contemporary society to fundamental religious issues, travel (he had visited most of the countries of Europe, "except Greece, alas," and traveled in India).

(Died June 28, 1965)

*   *   *

IRVING, R(obert) L(ock) Graham   1877-1969

PERSONAL: Born February 17, 1877, in Liverpool, England; the son of Robert (a clergyman) and Anne H. (Tasker) Irving; married Oriane Sophy Tyndale, April 4, 1908 (deceased); children: Francis, Mary (deceased), Robert, Clare Irving Mysticki. *Education:* New College, Oxford, M.A., 1900. *Religion:* Church of England. *Home:* 18 Ranelagh Rd., Winchester, England.

CAREER: Tutored abroad, 1899-1900; Winchester College, Winchester, England, assistant master, 1900-09, housemaster, 1909-37, assistant master, 1939-44. Winchester City Council, member, 1920-31, alderman, 1950-58; member of education committee of Hampshire County Council, 1944-63. *Member:* Alpine Club (vice-president, 1948; honorary member), Free Foresters.

WRITINGS: (Editor) Horace de Saussure, *La Cime du Mont Blanc*, Oxford University Press, 1933; *The Romance of Mountaineering*, Dent, 1935, 2nd edition, 1946; *The Mountain Way*, Dutton, 1939; *The Alps*, Batsford, 1939, Scribner, 1940, 3rd edition, Batsford, 1947; *Ten Great Mountains*, Dent, 1940; (editor) Guido Rey, *Matterhorn*, Basil Blackwell, 1946; *The Mountains Shall Bring Peace*, Basil Blackwell, 1947; (editor) Norbert Casteret, *Cave Men: New and Old*, Dent, 1951; *A History of British Mountaineering*, Batsford, 1955. Contributor to *Alpine Journal*.

Translator: Norbert Casteret, *My Caves*, Dent, 1947; Casteret, *Darkness Under the Earth*, Holt, 1955; Jean Cadoux, *One Thousand Metres Down*, Allen & Unwin, 1957.

(Died April 10, 1969)

*   *   *

IRWIN, Raymond   1902-

PERSONAL: Born March 14, 1902, in Huddersfield, Yorkshire, England; son of John T. and Lily (Pollard) Irwin; married Ivy Summerville Viggers, August 31, 1929. *Education:* St. John's College, Oxford, B.A., 1923, M.A., 1931. *Home:* 13 Furzefield Crescent, Reigate, Surrey, England.

CAREER: County librarian in Northhamptonshire, England, 1924-34, in Lancashire, England, 1934-44; University of London, London, England, director of School of Librarianship and Archives at University College, 1944-70, professor of library studies, 1957-70, professor emeritus, 1970—. *Member:* Library Association (treasurer, 1947-54; vice-president, 1954-57; president, 1958; honorary fellow, 1963).

WRITINGS: The National Library Service, Grafton & Co., 1947; *Librarianship: Essays on Applied Bibliography*, Grafton & Co., 1949; (editor) *The Libraries of London* (17 lectures given at University of London School of Librarianship, April, 1948), Library Association, 1949, 2nd edition (with Ronald Staveley), 1961; *British Bird Books: An Index to British Ornithology, A.D. 1481 to A.D. 1948*, Grafton & Co., 1951; *British Birds and Their Books* (catalogue of National Book League exhibition), Cambridge University Press, 1952; *The Origins of the English Library*, Allen & Unwin, 1958; *The Golden Chain: A Study in the History of Libraries* (inaugural lecture given at University College,

London, November 21, 1957), published for University College by H. K. Lewis, 1958; *The Heritage of the English Library*, Allen & Unwin, 1964; *The English Library: Sources and History*, Verry, 1966.

*   *   *

ISE, John   1885-196(?)

PERSONAL: Born June 5, 1885, in Downs, Kan.; son of Henry Christian (a farmer) and Rosa (Haag) Ise; married Lillie Bernhard, August 4, 1921; children: John Jr., Charles (deceased). *Education:* University of Kansas, Mus.B., 1908, A.B., 1910, LL.B., 1911; Harvard University, A.M., 1912, Ph.D., 1914. *Politics:* Democrat. *Religion:* Unitarian. *Home and office:* 1208 Mississippi St., Lawrence, Kan.

CAREER: University of Kansas, Lawrence, 1916-55, began as assistant professor, professor of economics, 1920-55. *Member:* American Economic Association (member of executive committee, 1937; vice-president, 1939).

WRITINGS: U.S. Forest Policy, Yale University Press, 1920; *U.S. Oil Policy*, Yale University Press, 1926; *Sod and Stubble: Story of a Kansas Homestead*, Wilson & Erickson, 1936; (editor) *Sod House Days: Letters of a Kansas Homesteader*, Columbia University Press, 1937; *Economics* (textbook), Harper, 1945, revised edition, 1950; *The American Way*, School of Business, University of Kansas, 1955; *Our National Park Policy*, Johns Hopkins Press, 1961. Member of board of editiors, American Economic Association, 1939.

SIDELIGHTS: Ise was competent in German. *Avocational interests:* Music, pioneer life, and the American West.

(Deceased)

*   *   *

ISRAEL, Saul   1910-

PERSONAL: Born September 6, 1910, in New York, N.Y.; son of David and Celia (Mott) Israel; married Silvya Samilson (a teacher), March 24, 1940. *Education:* City College (now City College of the City University of New York), B.S.S., 1931, M.S. in Ed., 1932; also studied at University of London, Cornell University, and University of Wisconsin. *Home:* 42 Beaumont St., Brooklyn, N.Y. 11235.

CAREER: Erasmus Hall High School, Brooklyn, N.Y., teacher of social studies, 1938-48; Seward Park High School, New York, N.Y., chairman of social studies, 1948-58; Haaren High School, New York, N.Y., principal, 1958-65; Erasmus Hall High School, principal, 1965-72; Fordham University, Bronx, N.Y., adjunct assistant professor of education, 1973—. *Military service:* U.S. Army, 1943-45; received Bronze Star. *Member:* American Geographical Society (fellow), National Council for Geographic Education (fellow), History Teachers Association of New York City (former president), Teachers of Social Studies of New York City (former vice-president).

WRITINGS: (with Norma H. Roemer and Loyal Durand, Jr.) *World Geography Today*, Holt, 1960, 3rd edition, 1966; *Introduction to Geography*, Holt, 1964. Contributor to education journals.

*   *   *

IZANT, Grace Goulder   1893-
(Grace Goulder)

PERSONAL: Born March 27, 1893, in Cleveland, Ohio;

daughter of Charles (a businessman) and Marion (Clements) Goulder; married Robert James Izant (a bank officer, now retired), October 18, 1919; children: Robert J., Jr., Jonathan Goulder (deceased), Mary (Mrs. Eugene D. White). *Education:* Vassar College, A.B., 1914; Western Reserve University (now Case Western Reserve University), graduate study, 1931. *Religion:* Society of Friends (Quaker). *Home:* Great Elm, 250 College St., Hudson, Ohio 44236. *Office:* Cleveland Plain Dealer, 1801 Superior Ave., Cleveland, Ohio 44114.

CAREER: Cleveland Plain Dealer, Cleveland, Ohio, staff member, 1914-18, special writer, 1940—. Photographer. Young Women's Christian Association worker in France, Germany, and England, World War I. Former Trustee of Ohioana Library, Columbus, and Rainbow Hospital for Crippled Children, Cleveland. *Member:* American Association for State and Local History, Women's National Book Association, Ohio Historical Society (honorary life member), Ohio Folklore Society, Western Reserve Historical Society, county historical societies, Cleveland Vassar Club (president), garden clubs. *Awards, honors:* Ohio Governor's Award for distinguished service to state, 1949; American Association for State and Local History awards (twice), second time, 1963; awards from Ohio Historical Society, Western Reserve Historical Society, Ohioana Library, and other historical organizations; Cleveland Award for Literature ($500), 1965, for *Ohio Scenes and Citizens.*

WRITINGS—Under name Grace Goulder: *This is Ohio: Ohio's 88 Counties in Words and Pictures*, World Publishing, 1953, revised edition, 1965; *The Cow That Pumped Water* (originally published in *Cleveland Plain Dealer Sunday Magazine*, July 2, 1961), Ross County Historical Society, 1962; *Ohio Scenes and Citizens*, World Publishing, 1964. Writer and photographer of weekly series, "Ohio Scenes and Citizens," in *Cleveland Plain Dealer Sunday Magazine*, 1940—.

WORK IN PROGRESS: Glimpses of John D. Rockefeller in Cleveland.

SIDELIGHTS: Mrs. Izant makes periodic trips to Europe, writing and illustrating series for *Cleveland Plain Dealer Sunday Magazine* with her own photographs.

* * *

JACKMAN, E(dwin) R(ussell) 1894-19(?)

PERSONAL: Born February 14, 1894, in Stillwater, Minn.; son of James Edwin (a farmer) and Emily (Fairbanks) Jackman; married Charlotte Harris, September 4, 1918; children: Sarah (Mrs. Oscar Lee Wilson), James L. *Education:* Montana State College (now Montana State University), student at intervals, 1914-17; Oregon State University, B.S., 1920. *Politics:* Republican. *Home:* 3555 Polk, Corvallis, Ore.

CAREER: Oregon State University, Corvallis, agriculture specialist, 1920-60; full-time writer, 1960-19? *Military service:* U.S. Army, Field Artillery, 1918-19; became first lieutenant. *Member:* American Society of Agronomy, American Society of Range Management, Epsilon Sigma Phi.

WRITINGS: (Editor) Herman Oliver, *Gold and Cattle Country*, Binsfords, 1962; *Oregon, A State of Mind*, Friends of the Library, Oregon State University, 1963; (with R. A. Long) *The Oregon Desert*, Caxton, 1964; (with Charles D. Simpson) *Blazing Forest Trails*, Caxton, 1967; (with John Scharff and Charles Conkling) *Steens Mountain*

in Oregon's High Desert Country, Caxton, 1967. Contributor of several hundred articles to national and regional magazines.

(Deceased)

* * *

JACKSON, C(hester) O(scar) 1901-

PERSONAL: Born February 2, 1901, in DeKalb, Ill.; son of Louis and Hulda (Carlson) Jackson; married Beulah Firkins (a writer), December 19, 1925; children: Willard Lewis, Mary Louise (Mrs. Val S. Jones), Margaret Ann (Mrs. Marcus B. Crotts). *Education:* University of Illinois, B.S., 1926, A.M., 1933; New York University, Ed.D., 1944. *Politics:* Republican. *Religion:* Methodist. *Home:* 1004 South Foley Ave., Champaign, Ill.

CAREER: Menominee (Mich.) public schools, director of physical education, 1926-29; University of Illinois, Urbana, 1929-66, professor of physical education, 1949-66, head of department, 1959-64. Visiting professor at University of Arkansas, University of Oregon, University of Havana, University of Missouri, New York University, University of Washington, Wake Forest University, and University of Bridgeport. Member of Illinois Governor's Advisory Committee on Youth Fitness, 1957—, chairman, 1957-60. *Member:* National College Physical Education Association (past president), American Academy of Physical Education (fellow), American Association for Health, Physical Education and Recreation (fellow), American Association of University Professors, Phi Epsilon Kappa, Phi Delta Kappa, Kappa Delta Pi, Kiwanis Club, American Association of Retired Persons (president, Champaign County chapter). *Awards, honors:* Phi Epsilon Kappa Honor Award; award from Illinois Association for Health, Physical Education and Recreation, 1948; award from American Association for Health, Physical Education and Recreation, 1949; diploma de honor, Colegio Nacional de Profesores de Educacion Fisica, Universitarios Havana, Cuba.

WRITINGS: (With Hilda Kozman and Rosalind Cassidy) *Methods in Physical Education*, Saunders, 1947, 5th edition, W. C. Brown, 1969. Contributor of more than two hundred articles to periodicals. Editor, *Physical Educator*, 1950-73.

SIDELIGHTS: Jackson spends two hours daily taping textbooks for blind students. *Avocational interests:* Gardening, hiking, fishing, writing, and traveling.

* * *

JACKSON, Don(ald) D(e Avila) 1920-1968

PERSONAL: Born January 2, 1920, in Oakland, Calif.; son of Lincoln Grant (in pharmaceuticals) and Caroline (De Avila) Jackson; married Mary Angelina Griffiths, October 6, 1951; children: Paige, Scott. *Education:* University of California, Berkeley, student, three years; Stanford University, A.B., 1941, M.D., 1943. *Office:* Mental Research Institute, 777 Bryant St., Palo Alto, Calif. 94301.

CAREER: Stanford University Hospital, Stanford, Calif., assistant resident in psychiatry, 1944-45; Chestnut Lodge Sanitarium, Rockville, Md., resident in psychiatry, 1947-49, staff member, 1949-51; Palo Alto Medical Clinic, Palo Alto, Calif., chief of psychiatry, 1951-63; Stanford University, School of Medicine, Stanford, Calif., associate clinical professor of psychiatry, 1954-68; Mental Research Institute, Palo Alto, Calif., director, 1959-68. Member of Governor's Advisory Committee on Mental Health, State of

California, 1959-63. Chief of staff, psychiatry, Palo Alto-Stanford Hospital, 1963-64; consultant to Veterans Administration Hospital, Palo Alto, Calif., 1951-68, Letterman General Hospital (Army), San Francisco, Calif., 1954-68. Science and Behavior Books, Inc., Palo Alto, Calif., editor-in-chief. *Military service:* U.S. Army, Medical Corps, 1945-47; became captain.

MEMBER: American Psychiatric Association (fellow), Academy of Psychoanalysis (fellow; council, 1960-64), American Medical Association, American Board of Neurology and Psychiatry, Northern California Psychiatric Society, Midpeninsula Psychiatric Society, Santa Clara County Medical Society. *Awards, honors:* Frieda Fromm-Reichmann Award of Academy of Psychoanalysis, 1961-62, for significant contribution to understanding of schizophrenia; Institute of Pennsylvania Hospital Award in memory of Edward A. Strecker, 1964, for outstanding contribution in field of psychiatric patient care.

WRITINGS: (Editor and contributor) *The Etiology of Schizophrenia*, Basic Books, 1960; *Schizophrenia* (originally published in *Scientific American*, August, 1962), W. H. Freeman, 1962; *Myths of Madness: New Facts for Old Fallacies*, Macmillan, 1964; (with Paul Watzlawick) *Pragmatics of Human Communication*, Norton, 1967; (with Albert Haas, Jr.) *Bulls, Bears, and Dr. Freud*, World Publishing, 1967; (with William J. Lederer) *The Mirages of Marriage*, Norton, 1968; (compiler) *Communication, Family, and Marriage* (Volume I), Science & Behavior Books, 1968; (compiler) *Therapy, Communication, and Change* (Volume II), Science & Behavior Books, 1968.

Contributor: Frieda Fromm-Reichman and J. L. Moreno, editors, *Progress in Psychotherapy*, Grune, 1956; Edwin Shneidman and Norman Farberow, editors, *Clues to Suicide*, McGraw, 1957; Carl Whitaker, editor, *The Psychotherapy of Chronic Schizophrenic Patients*, Little, Brown, 1958; Jules Massermann, editor, *Individual and Familial Dynamics*, Grune, 1959; Arthur Burton, editor, *Case Studies in Counseling and Psychotherapy*, Prentice-Hall, 1959; Nathan Ackerman, Frances Beatman, and Sanford Sherman, editors, *Exploring the Base for Family Therapy*, Family Service Association, 1961; Arthur Burton, editor, *Psychotherapy of the Psychosis*, Basic Books, 1961; Morris I. Stein, editor, *Contemporary Psychotherapies*, Free Press, 1962; Jules Massermann, editor, *Science and Psychoanalysis*, Grune, 1962; Jules Massermann, editor, *Current Psychiatric Therapies*, Volume IV, Grune, 1964; David McKenzie Rioch and Edwin A. Weinstein, editors, *Disorders of Communication* (proceedings of Association for Research of Nervous and Mental Disease, December 7-8, 1962), Williams & Wilkins, 1964. Contributor of about forty articles to professional journals.

(Died January 29, 1968)

*   *   *

JACKSON, George S(tuyvesant) 1906-

PERSONAL: Born February 22, 1906, in Portland, Me.; son of Stuyvesant Ten Broeck (an insurance man) and Elizabeth (Thrasher) Jackson; married Sarah White (a librarian), November 28, 1933; children: Margaret Ten Broeck (Mrs. Robert W. Heussler), Stuyvesant Ten Broeck II. *Education:* Bowdoin College, A.B., 1927; Harvard University, M.A., 1931; Columbia University, postgraduate study, 1940-41. *Politics:* Independent. *Religion:* Episcopalian. *Home:* Surf Rd., Cape Elizabeth, Me.

CAREER: Harvard University, Cambridge, Mass., in-

structor in English, 1928-31; Washington and Lee University, Lexington, Va., assistant professor of English, 1931-41; Central Intelligence Agency, Washington, D.C., 1946-58; University of Maine in Portland, associate professor, 1958-64, professor of English, 1964-71. Teacher of University of Virginia and Georgetown University extension courses while in Washington, D.C., 1946-58. Member of board of reviewers for "World in Books," United Publishers Association. *Military service:* U.S. Navy, 1942-45; served in South Pacific; became lieutenant commander. U.S. Naval Reserve, 1945-65. *Member:* Maine Historical Society, Portland Fraternity Club.

WRITINGS: (Editor) *Early Songs of Uncle Sam*, Humphries, 1932 reprinted, Gale, 1971; *Uncommon Scold, the Story of Anne Royall*, Humphries, 1935; *Hamlet Scene by Scene*, Humphries, 1964; *A Maine Heritage, History of Union Mutual Life Insurance Company, 1848-1963*, Union Mutual Life Insurance Co., 1964; (contributor) *People and Places in the U.S.A.*, Country Women's Council, 1968. Contributor to *Dictionary of American Biography*. Contributor to professional journals.

AVOCATIONAL INTERESTS: Painting (occasionally exhibits and sells oils and watercolors).

*   *   *

JACKSON, Joseph 1924-

PERSONAL: Born August 21, 1924, in London, England; son of Samuel and Hetty Jackson; married Marjorie Henrietta Lyons (a barrister), August 10, 1952; children: Louise Melanie, Madeleine Annette, Samantha Jane. *Education:* Cambridge University, B.A., 1945, LL.B., 1946, M.A., 1948; Middle Temple, Barrister-at-Law, 1947; University of London, LL.M., 1949. *Home:* Brook House, 28 Uxbridge Rd., Stanmore, Middlesex, England. *Office:* 1 Mitre Court Buildings, Temple, London E.C.4, England.

CAREER: Barrister-at-law, London, England, 1947—. Queen's Counsel, 1967. Lecturer, primarily on legal subjects, in England and to U.S. bar associations.

WRITINGS: (Editor) Ronald H. Graveson, *Examination Note-Book of the English Legal System*, 2nd edition (Jackson was not associated with earlier edition), Sweet & Maxwell, 1951; *The Law Relating to the Formation and Annulment of Marriage, and Allied Matters, in English Domestic and Private International Law*, Sweet & Maxwell, 1951, 2nd edition published as *The Formation and Annulment of Marriage*, Butterworth & Co., 1969; (editor) *English Legal History in a Nutshell*, Sweet & Maxwell, 1951, 2nd edition, 1955; (editor with others) William Rayden, *Practice and Law in the Divorce Division of the High Court of Justice and on Appeal Therefrom*, Butterworth & Co., 6th edition (with F. C. Ottway), including supplements, 1953, 7th edition (with D. H. Colgate), including supplement, 1958, supplements to 8th edition (with C. F. Turner), 1960, 9th edition (with Turner and D. R. Ellison) published as *Rayden's Practice and Law of Divorce*, includes supplement, 1964, 10th edition (with R. B. Rowe and Margaret Booth), including supplements, 1967, 11th edition, 1971; (editor) Daniel Huntley Redfearn, *Wills and Administration in Georgia, Including Estate Planning, Guardian and Ward, Trusts and Forms*, 3rd edition, Harrison Co., 1964. Contributor to *Punch, Law Quarterly Review, Law Journal, Modern Law Review*, and other legal journals.

WORK IN PROGRESS: Further work on marriage and divorce law.

JACKSON, Paul R. 1905-

PERSONAL: Born September 27, 1905, in El Paso, Tex.; married Margaret F. Moss, August 10, 1929; children: Karen Willene. *Education:* Stanford University, B.A., 1926; University of Southern California, M.A., 1932. *Home:* 682 Luton Dr., Glendale, Calif. 91206.

CAREER: High school and junior college teacher in California, 1929-36; Charles R. Hadley Co. (publishers), Los Angeles, Calif., editorial director, 1937-39, 1941-42; Arizona State University, Tempe, assistant professor of commerce, 1939-40; began association with Sawyer Schools of Business, Pasadena, Calif., in 1942, became president in 1952, now retired. *Member:* National Association of Business Schools (vice-president, 1957), National Office Management Association (vice-president of Los Angeles branch, 1955), California Council of Business Schools (president, 1965), Stanford Club of Los Angeles (president, 1965), Rotary Club.

WRITINGS: Elementary College Accounting, Prentice-Hall, 1947; *How to Study*, Pacific Books, 1955; *The Right Job*, Vocational Research Bureau, 1957; (with J. P. Ellsworth) *Applied Bookkeeping*, McGraw, 1965. Contributor to magazines.

SIDELIGHTS: Jackson is competent in Spanish. *Avocational interests:* Reading, travel.

* * *

JACOBI, Carl (Richard) 1908-

PERSONAL: Born July 10, 1908, in Minneapolis, Minn.; son of Richard Cleveland and Matie (Hoffman) Jacobi. *Education:* University of Minnesota, B.A., 1931. *Residence:* Minneapolis, Minn. *Agent:* Scott Meredith Literary Agency, Inc., 580 Fifth Ave., New York, N.Y. 10036.

CAREER: Formerly, reporter for *Minneapolis Star*, editor of *Midwest Media* (advertising trade journal), in public relations with Key Center of War Information. Full-time freelance writer.

WRITINGS—Short stories: Revelations in Black, Arkham, 1949; *Portraits in Moonlight*, Arkham, 1964.

Contributor: August Derleth, editor, *Sleep No More*, Farrar & Rinehart, 1944; Bennett Cerf, editor, *The Unexpected*, Bantam, 1948; Derleth, editor, *Far Boundaries*, Pellegrini & Cudahy, 1951; Derleth, editor, *Worlds of Tomorrow*, Farrar, Straus, 1953; Derleth, editor, *Dark Mind, Dark Heart*, Arkham, 1962; Derleth, editor, *Over the Edge*, Arkham, 1964. Contributor of short stories, novelettes, and serials to more than fifty magazines.

WORK IN PROGRESS: A collection of short stories in macabre vein, for Arkham; *The Mystery of French Key*, a juvenile novel; *Gentleman of the Forest*, the life of Daniel Duluth; writing on the life of Doctor Mesmer, and on the Caribbean area.

SIDELIGHTS: Jacobi sold every fantasy story he wrote. *Avocational interests:* His lakeside cabin.

BIOGRAPHICAL/CRITICAL SOURCES: Imagination, August, 1954.

* * *

JAGGER, John Hubert 1880-

PERSONAL: Born August 30, 1880, in Manchester, England; son of John (a Wesleyan minister) and Catherine (Crowther) Jagger; married Nora Kellaway, December 27, 1910; children: Winifred, Gladys (Mrs. William Rae). *Education:* Oxford University, diploma in education, 1906; University of Edinburgh, M.A., 1908, D.Litt., 1914; University of London, M.A., 1909. *Home:* 34 Hamilton Ave., Glasgow WG1 4JD, Scotland. *Agent:* John Farquharson Ltd., 15 Red Lion Sq., London W.C.1, England; Ann Elmo Agency, Inc., 52 Vanderbilt Ave., New York, N.Y. 10017.

CAREER: Various teaching posts, 1899-1903; Royal High School, Edinburgh, Scotland, senior English master, 1909-19; London County Council, London, England, inspector of schools and colleges and district inspector, 1919-30, divisional inspector, 1930-45. Member, Joint Board of Examiners of Scottish Universities, 1915-17; other examining posts in Great Britain. *Military service:* British Army, Royal Garrison Artillery, 1917-19; became lieutenant. *Member:* National Association of Inspectors (president, 1921-22).

WRITINGS: (Author of introduction) Tennyson, *The Princess*, Blackie & Son, 1910; (editor) *Selections from Tennyson*, Dent, 1921; (editor) *Shakespeare's As You Like It*, Dent, 1922; (editor) *A Book of English Poems Graded for Use in Schools*, University of London Press, 1924-26; *Modern English*, University of London Press, 1925; *Poetry in School*, University of London Press, 1928; *The Sentence Method of Teaching Reading*, Grant Educational Co., 1929; (with Ernest James Kenny) *The Westminster Readers*, University of London Press, 1933-34; (editor) *Realms of Adventure*, University of London Press, 1933; (with Kenny) *The New Foundation Readers*, four parts, University of London Press, 1937; (with Kenny) *Reading in Senior Schools: The Problem of the Backward Pupil*, University of London Press, 1937; *English in the Future*, Thomas Nelson, 1940; (editor) *The Poet's Progress: An Anthology of English Lyrical Verse*, Blackie & Son, 1949; *A Handbook of English Grammar*, University of London Press, 1960.

WORK IN PROGRESS: Episodes in the Life of William Shakespeare; research into linguistics.

* * *

JAKSCH, Wenzel 1896-1966

PERSONAL: Born September 25, 1896, in Langstrobnitz, Sudeten, Austria-Hungary; son of Wenzel (a bricklayer) and Maria (Sicko) Jaksch; married Joan Simeon, June 24, 1945; children: George, Mary. *Education:* Attended elementary school in Strobnitz, Sudeten, Austria-Hungary. *Politics:* Social Democrat (since 1913). *Religion:* Roman Catholic. *Home:* Gehrnerweg 32, Wiesbaden, West Germany.

CAREER: Editor in Komotau, Sudeten, Czechoslovakia, and Prague, Czechoslovakia, 1921-29; member of Czechoslovak Parliament, 1929-38; *Der Sozialdemokrat* (exile newspaper), London, England, editor, 1939-49; government of Hesse, West Germany, deputy-minister, 1950-53; member of West German Bundestag, 1953-66. *Member:* League of Expellees (Bonn, West Germany; president, 1964-66). *Awards, honors:* Grosses Bundesverdienstkreuz, 1961; honorary degree from Park College, 1963.

WRITINGS: Volk und Arbeiter, Eugen Praeger (Bratislava), 1936; *Die Fackeltraeger, Hans Vegel: Gedenkblaetter*, Bollwerk-Verlag K. Drott, 1946; *Sozialistische Moeglichkeiten in unserer zeit, eine studie*, Bollwerk-Verlag, 1947; *Europas Weg nach Potsdam: Schuld und schicksal im donauraum*, Deutsche Verlaganstalt, 1958, version translated and edited by Kurt Glaser published as *Europe's Road to*

Potsdam, Thames & Hudson, 1963, Praeger, 1964; *Germany and Eastern Europe: Two Documents of the Third German Bundestag, 1961*, Atlantic Forum (Bonn), 1962; *Westeuropa-Osteuropa Sowjetunion*, Atlantic Forum, 1965; *Sucher und kuender*, Verlag Die Bruecke, 1967; *Patriot und Europaer* (continuation of *Sucher und kuender*), Verlag Die Bruecke, 1967.

(Died November 27, 1966)

* * *

JAMES, Edwin Oliver 1889-1972

PERSONAL: Born March 30, 1889, in London, England; son of William and Sophia Mary (Bowtell) James; married Clarese Augusta Copeland, 1911; children: Basil Edwin Spencer. *Education:* Exeter College, Oxford, B.Litt., 1916; D.Litt., 1934; University College, London, Ph.D., 1924. *Home:* Hidsfield House, Cumnor Hill, Oxford, England.

CAREER: Clergyman, Church of England, serving as curate, rector, and then vicar, 1911-33; University of Cambridge, Cambridge, England, lecturer and tutor in anthropology, 1928-33; University of Leeds, Leeds, England, professor of the history and philosophy of religion, 1933-45; University of London, London, England, professor of the philosophy of religion, King's College, 1945-48, university professor of the history and philosophy of religion, 1948-55, professor emeritus, 1955-72, fellow of University College, 1946-72, fellow of King's College, 1950-72. Wilde Lecturer in Natural and Comparative Religion, Oxford University, 1938-42, chaplain of All Soul's College, beginning 1960. Forwood Lecturer at University of Liverpool, 1949-50; visiting lecturer at University of Amsterdam, 1949, and University of Marburg, 1960. Examiner in comparative religion at universities in England, beginning 1931. *Member:* Society of Antiquaries (fellow), Folklore Society (president, 1930-32), British Association for the Advancement of Science (president, Section H, 1958; member of council, 1960), Athenaeum Club (London). *Awards, honors:* D.D., University of St. Andrews.

WRITINGS: Primitive Ritual and Belief, Methuen, 1917; *Introduction to Anthropology*, Macmillan, 1919; *The Stone Age*, Macmillan, 1927; *The Beginnings of Man*, Doubleday, 1928.

The Christian Faith in the Modern World, Morehouse, 1930; *The Origins of Sacrifice*, J. Murray, 1933, reprinted, Kennikat Press, 1971; *Christian Myth and Ritual*, J. Murray, 1933, Meridan, 1965; *The Old Testament in Light of Anthropology*, Macmillan, 1935; *In the Fulness of Time*, Macmillan, 1935; *Origins of Religion*, Unicorn Press, 1937; *Introduction to Comparative Study of Religion*, Methuen, 1938, revised edition published as *Comparative Religion*, Barnes & Noble, 1961, 2nd revised edition, Methuen, 1969; *The Social Function of Religion*, Hodder & Stoughton, 1940, 2nd edition, 1948; *A History of Christianity in England*, Hutchinson University Library, 1948, 2nd edition, 1950; *The Beginnings of Religion*, Hutchinson University Library, 1948, 2nd edition, 1950, 2nd edition reprinted, Greenwood, 1973; (editor) Herbert Rose, *Ancient Roman Religion*, Hutchinson, 1948.

The Concept of Deity, Hutchinson University Library, 1950; *Marriage and Society*, Hutchinson, 1952, Barnes & Noble, 1955, published as *Marriage Customs through the Ages*, Collier, 1965; *The Nature and Function of Priesthood*, Thames & Hudson, 1956; *The History of Religions*, English Universities Press, 1956, Harper, 1959; *Prehistoric Religion*, Praeger, 1957; *Myth and Ritual in the Ancient*

Near East, Praeger, 1958; *The Cult of the Mother-Goddess*, Praeger, 1959; *The Ancient Gods*, Weidenfeld & Nicholson, 1959, Putnam, 1960; *Seasonal Feasts and Festivals*, Barnes & Noble, 1961; *Prehistoric Religion: A Study in Prehistoric Archaeology*, Barnes & Noble, 1961; *Sacrifice and Sacrament*, Barnes & Noble, 1962; *From Cave to Cathedral*, Thames & Hudson, 1962, Praeger, 1965; *The Worship of the Sky-God*, Athlone Press, 1963; (editor) Harold Rowley, *The Growth of the Old Testament*, Harper, 1963; *The Tree of Life: An Archaeological Study*, E. J. Brill, 1966; *Christianity and Other Religions*, Lippincott, 1968; *Creation and Cosmology: A Historical and Comparative Inquiry*, E. J. Brill, 1969.

Contributor to *Encyclopaedia of Religion and Ethics*, *Encyclopaedia Britannica*, *Chambers's Encyclopaedia*, and *Dictionary of National Biography*. Contributor of articles to theological and scientific journals. Editor, *Folklore*, 1932-56.

(Died, 1972)

* * *

JAMES, Eric Arthur 1925-

PERSONAL: Born April 14, 1925, in England; son of John Morgan and Alice Amelia James. *Education:* King's College, London, B.D.; Trinity College, Cambridge, M.A. *Home:* Holywell Close, 43 Holywell Hill, St. Albans, Hertfordshire, England.

CAREER: Clergyman, Church of England. *Member:* Royal Commonwealth Society.

WRITINGS: The Double Cure: How to Receive Forgiveness, Hodder & Stoughton, 1957; *Odd Man Out?: The Shape of the Ministry Today*, Hodder & Stoughton, 1962; *The Roots of the Liturgy* (pamphlet), Prism Publications, 1962; *Beyond Paul* (pamphlet), Prism Publications, 1964; (contributor) B. Moss, editor, *Crisis for Baptism*, Morehouse, 1965; *The Nature of the Pastoral Ministry* (pamphlet), Prism Publications, 1966; (editor) *Spirituality for Today: The Report of the Parish and People Conference*, S.C.M. Press, 1968; (contributor) Lawrence Bright, editor, *The Christian Community*, Sheed, 1971; (contributor) *More Sermons from St. Mary's*, Hodder & Stoughton, 1971. Contributor to *Prism*.

* * *

JAMES, Fleming, Jr. 1904-

PERSONAL: Born March 26, 1904, in Shanghai, China; son of Fleming (a clergyman and professor of Old Testament) and Rebecca (Godwin) James; married second wife, Ruth Kaubisch (owner-director of nursery school), November 23, 1948; children: (first marriage) Fleming III, Sarah Fairchild. *Education:* Yale University, B.A., 1925, LL.B., 1928. *Politics:* Democrat. *Religion:* Episcopalian. *Home:* 117 Upper State St., North Haven, Conn. 06473. *Office:* Yale Law School, New Haven, Conn.

CAREER: Admitted to Connecticut bar, 1929; Watrous, Hewitt, Sheldon & Gumbart (law firm), New Haven, Conn., clerk, 1928-29; New York, New Haven & Hartford Railroad Co., New Haven, Conn., assistant attorney, 1929-33; Yale University, New Haven, Conn., associate professor, 1933-38, professor of law, 1938-41, Lafayette S. Foster Professor of Law, 1941-68, Sterling Professor of Law, 1968-72, Sterling Professor of Law emeritus, 1972—. University of Utah, visiting lecturer, 1938-39, acting dean of School of Law, 1939-40; director of Litigation Division, U.S. Office of Price Administration, Washington, D.C., 1942-45; chairman, Connecticut State Board of Labor Relations, beginning 1955; visiting professor of law, Harvard University, 1957-58, at University of Stockholm, University of Uppsala, and University of Lund, all 1968, Institute of Advanced Legal Studies, 1971, University of Connecticut, beginning, 1972. Member of North Haven (Conn.) Zoning Board, 1936-39, Town Planning Commission, 1946-47, and Board of Education, 1938-42. *Member:* American Bar Association, American Judicature Society, Connecticut State Bar Association.

WRITINGS: (With T. Arnold) *Cases on Trials, Judgments and Appeals*, West, 1936; (with H. Shulman) *Cases and Materials on Torts*, Foundation, 1942, 2nd edition, 1952; (with Fowler Harper) *Law of Torts*, three volumes, Little, Brown, 1956, *Supplement to Volume II*, 1968; *Civil Procedure*, Little, Brown, 1965. Contributor of articles and reviews to legal journals.

* * *

JAMES, Philip S(eaforth) 1914-

PERSONAL: Born May 28, 1914, in Croydon, England; son of Philip William (a medical practitioner) and Muriel Lindley (Rankin) James; married Wybetty Gerth, January 4, 1954; children: Philip Nicholas Lindley, Edward Peter Hilary. *Education:* Trinity College, Oxford, B.A., 1936, M.A., 1943; Yale University research fellow law, 1937-38. *Religion:* Church of England. *Home:* Hillside, Banks Lane, Riddlesden, near Keighley, Yorkshire, England. *Office:* Faculty of Law, University of Leeds, Leeds 2, Yorkshire, England.

CAREER: Exeter College, Oxford University, Oxford, England, fellow and tutor in law, 1946-49; Inner Temple, London, England, barrister, 1949-51; University of Leeds, Leeds, England, professor and head of department of law, 1951—. University of Louisville, Louisville, Ky., visiting professor, 1961. Hamlyn Trust, trustee; chairman, Yorkshire Real Assessment Panel. *Military service:* British Army, Royal Artillery, 1940-46; became major; mentioned in dispatches. *Member:* Society of Public Teachers of Law (vice-president, 1971), National Liberal Club, Leeds Club.

WRITINGS: Introduction to English Law, Butterworth & Co., 1950, 7th edition, 1969; *General Principles of the Law of Torts*, Butterworth & Co., 1959, 3rd edition, 1969; *A Shorter Introduction to English Law*, Butterworth & Co., 1969. Regular contributor to *Journal of Business Law*.

WORK IN PROGRESS: An 8th edition of the *Introduction to English Law*; a 4th edition of *General Principles of the Law of Torts*; a projected work on tort and the Scottish law of debit, for Collins.

* * *

JAMES, William Milbourne 1881-
(T. B. D.)

PERSONAL: Born December 22, 1881, in Farnborough, Surrey, England; son of W. C. James (a major, 16th Lancers); married Lady Dorothy Alexandra Duff, 1915; children: Christopher Alexander. *Education:* Studied at Trinity College, Glenalmond, Pertshire, Scotland. *Religion:* Church of England. *Home:* Wynd House, Elie, Fife, Scotland.

CAREER: Royal Navy, 1901-44, retiring as admiral. Director of Royal Naval Staff College, 1925-26; chief of staff, Atlantic Fleet, 1929-30, of Mediterranean Fleet, 1930;

commander of Battle Cruiser Squadron, 1932-34; lord commissioner of Admiralty and deputy chief of naval staff, 1935-38; commander-in-chief, Portsmouth Naval Base, 1939-42; chief of naval information, 1943-44. Member of Parliament for North Portsmouth, 1943-45. *Member:* United Service Club. *Awards, honors:* Companion of the Bath, 1919; Knight Commander of the Bath, 1936; Grand Cross of the Bath, 1944.

WRITINGS: New Battleship Organisations, and Notes for Executive Officers, Giene's, 1916; (under pseudonym T. B. D.) *Songs of the Sailor Men*, Hodder & Stoughton, 1916; *The British Navy in Adversity: A Study of the War of American Independence*, Longmans, Green, 1926; *Blue Water and Green Fields* (essays), Methuen, 1939; *Admiral Sir William Fisher*, Macmillan (London), 1943; *The Portsmouth Letters*, Macmillan (London), 1946; *The British Navies in the Second World War*, Longmans, Green, 1946; (editor) *John Ruskin and Effie Gray: The Story of John Ruskin, Effie Gray and John Everett Millais, Told for the First Time in Their Unpublished Letters*, Scribner, 1947 (published in England as *The Order of Release: The Story of John Ruskin, Effie Gray and John Everett Millais, Told for the First Time in Their Unpublished Letters*, J. Murray, 1947); *The Durable Monument: Horatio Nelson*, Longmans, Green, 1948; *The Influence of Sea Power on the History of the British People* (lectures), Macmillan (New York), 1948; *Old Oak: The Life of John Jervis, Earl of St. Vincent*, Longmans, Green, 1950; *The Sky Was Always Blue* (autobiography), Methuen, 1951; *The Eyes of the Navy: A Biographical Study of Admiral Sir Reginald Hall*, Methuen, 1955, published as *The Code Breakers of Room 40: The Story of Admiral Sir William Hall, Genius of British Counter-Intelligence*, St. Martin's, 1956; *A Great Seaman: The Life of Admiral of the Fleet Sir Henry F. Oliver*, Witherby, 1956. Naval editor, *Chambers's Encyclopedia*.

* * *

JAMIESON, Paul F(letcher) 1903-

PERSONAL: Born August 1, 1903, in Des Moines, Iowa; son of John M. (a book-bindery owner) and Stella M. (Young) Jamieson; married Ruth Kirby (a professor of French, now retired), June 10, 1931. *Education:* Drake University, B.A., 1925; Columbia University, M.A., 1926; Cornell University, Ph.D., 1950. *Home:* 13 Jay St., Canton, N.Y. 13617.

CAREER: Drake University, Des Moines, Iowa, instructor in English, 1926-28; St. Lawrence University, Canton, N.Y., instructor, 1929-36, assistant professor, 1936-52, associate professor, 1952-59, professor of English, 1959-65; retired, 1965. Editorial consultant, Adirondack Museum, Blue Mountain Lake, N.Y., 1966—. *Military Service:* U.S. Army, 1942-45; became sergeant. *Member:* Modern Language Association of America, Wilderness Society, Phi Beta Kappa, Adirondack Mountain Club, Adirondack Forty-Sixers.

WRITINGS: (Editor) *The Adirondack Reader: The Best Writings on the Adventurous and Contemplative Life in One of America's Most Loved Regions*, Macmillan, 1964; (author of introduction and notes) Mildred Phelps Hooker, *Camp Chronicles*, Adirondack Museum, 1964; (with Atwood Manley) *Rushton and His Times in American Canoeing*, Syracuse University Press, 1968. Contributor to *New York History, New England Quarterly, Conservationist, Appalachia, Adirondac, Encyclopedia Americana*.

WORK IN PROGRESS: Articles on conservation and forest recreation.

AVOCATIONAL INTERESTS: Mountain climbing, tramping, camping, canoeing.

*   *   *

JARVIS, William Don(ald) 1913-

PERSONAL: Born January 16, 1913, in Salt Lake City, Utah; son of William W. and Lillian (Moore) Jarvis; married Lucille Borgnis, 1936; children: Glen William, Camilla M., Joanna Theresa, Rian Don. *Education:* Attended University of California, Los Angeles. *Home:* 965 Maltman Ave., Los Angeles, Calif. *Office:* William Don Jarvis Interior Design, 13063 Ventura Blvd., Studio City, Calif. 91604.

CAREER: Employed in Los Angeles, Calif., as journeyman painter, 1931-39, tool designer in aircraft plant, 1942-43, technical orders editor in manufacturing plant, 1943-44, and industrial designer with Walter Dorwin Teague, 1944-45; Metro-Goldwyn-Mayer, Culver City, Calif., set designer, 1945-46; self-employed interior designer, Los Angeles, Calif., 1946—. Instructor in painting and decorating, Los Angeles Trade-Technical College. *Member:* American Institute of Interior Designers (member, board of governors, Southern California chapter, 1960-62), American Institute of Decorators.

WRITINGS: Encyclopedia of Painting and Decorating, Goodheart, 1957.

WORK IN PROGRESS: A revision of above.

AVOCATIONAL INTERESTS: Art, literature, fishing.

*   *   *

JASHEMSKI, Wilhelmina Feemster 1910-

PERSONAL: Born July 10, 1910, in York, Neb.; daughter of Howard Calvin (a professor of mathematics) and Emma (Groelz) Feemster; married Stanley A. Jashemski (a physicist), July 18, 1945. *Education:* York College, York, Neb., A.B., 1931; University of Nebraska, A.M., 1933; University of Chicago, Ph.D., 1942. *Religion:* Presbyterian. *Home:* 415 Pershing Dr., Silver Spring, Md. *Office:* Department of History, University of Maryland, College Park, Md.

CAREER: Indiana Central College, Indianapolis, instructor in ancient history, Latin, and Greek, 1935-37, 1938-40; Lindenwood College, St. Charles, Mo., professor of history and humanities, 1942-45; University of Maryland, College Park, 1946—, began as assistant professor, became professor of ancient history, 1965. *Member:* American Historical Association, Archaeological Institute of America, American Philological Association, Society for the Promotion of Roman Studies, Association Internationale d'Epigraphie Latine, American Association of University Professors, Phi Beta Kappa. *Awards, honors:* Tatiana Warsher Award in Archaeology, American Academy in Rome, 1968; National Endowment for the Humanities senior fellowship, 1968-69; National Endowment for the Humanities research grants, 1972-74.

WRITINGS: The Origins and History of the Proconsular and Propraetorian Imperium, University of Chicago Press, 1950; *Letters from Pompeii* (youth book illustrated with drawings by M. Sasek and color photographs by husband, Stanley A. Jashemski), Ginn, 1963; *Pompeii, and the Region Destroyed by Vesuvius in A.D. 79* (illustrated with color photographs by S. A. Jashemski), Wilhelm Andermann Verlag, 1965. Contributor to *Archaeology, Natural History, History Today, Classical Journal, American Journal of Archaeology,* and *American Journal of Science.*

WORK IN PROGRESS: A book, *The Gardens of Pompeii, Herculaneum, and Stabiae.*

SIDELIGHTS: Mrs. Jashemski has done research at Pompeii since 1955, and has excavated there since 1964, besides studying other ancient Greek and Roman sites. Photograph records of the sites have been made by her husband on these trips.

*   *   *

JASNY, Naum 1883-

PERSONAL: Born January 25, 1883, in Kharkov, Russia; son of Michael and Rosa (Poyurovskii) Jasny; wife deceased; children: Natasha Naum, Brunswick, Tatyana (Mrs. Milton Moss). *Religion:* Atheist. *Home:* 2101 16th St. N.W., Washington, D.C. 20009.

CAREER: Specialist and writer on economic research, particularly international agricultural economics and economics of grain, prior to 1948; specialist in Soviet economy, 1948—. *Awards, honors:* A symposium, *Soviet Planning,* was published by Basil Blackwell in honor of Jasny's eightieth birthday, 1964.

WRITINGS: Elevatory v Severnoi Amerike i v Rossii, Tsentrosoyuza, 1925; *Die neuzeitliche Umstellung der ueberseeischen Getreideproduktion und ihr Einfluss auf den Weltmarkt* (title means "The Modern Reorganization of Overseas Grain Production and Its Effect on the World Market"), Reimar Hobbing, 1930; *Die Zukunft des Roggens* (title means "The Future of Rye"), Reimar Hobbing, 1930; *Der Schlepper in der Landwirtschaft, seind Wirtschaftlichkeit und weltwirtschaftliche Bedeutung* (title means "The Tractor in Agriculture, Its Profitability, and Its Significance in World Economy"), P. Parey, 1932; *Research Methods on Farm Use of Tractors,* Columbia University Press, 1938; *Competition Among Grains,* Food Research Institute, Stanford University, 1940; *The Wheats of Classical Antiquity,* Johns Hopkins Press, 1944; *The Socialized Agriculture of the U.S.S.R.: Plans and Performance,* Stanford University Press, 1949.

The Soviet Economy During the Plan Era, Stanford University Press, 1951; *The Soviet Price System,* Stanford University Press, 1951; *Soviet Prices of Producers' Goods,* Stanford University Press, 1952; *Indices of Soviet Industrial Production, 1928-1954,* Council for Economic and Industry Research, 1955; *The Soviet 1956 Statistical Handbook: A Commentary,* Michigan State University Press, 1957; (with others) *The Economy of the U.S.S.R.* (proceedings of annual sessions of National Academy of Economics and Political Science, 1957), George Washington University, 1958; *Soviet Industrialization, 1928-1952,* University of Chicago Press, 1961; *Essays on the Soviet Economy,* Praeger, 1962; *Khrushchev's Crop Policy* (monograph), George Outram, 1965; *Soviet Economists of the Twenties: Names to Be Remembered,* Cambridge University Press, 1972. Contributor of articles on economic subjects to periodicals, including *Soviet Studies.*

BIOGRAPHICAL/CRITICAL SOURCES: Jane Degras and Alec Nove, editors, *Soviet Planning: Essays in Honor of Naum Jasny,* Basil Blackwell, 1963, Praeger, 1964.

JAWORSKI, Leon 1905-

PERSONAL: Born September 19, 1905, in Waco, Tex.; son of Joseph (a clergyman) and Marie (Mira) Jaworski; married Jeannette Adams, May 23, 1931; children: Joan Jaworski Moncrief, Claire Jaworski Draper, Joseph III. *Education:* Baylor University, LL.B., 1925; George Washington University, LL.M., 1926. *Religion:* Presbyterian. *Home:* 3655 Ella Lee Lane, Houston, Tex. 77027. *Office:* Fulbright, Crooker, Freeman, Bates & Jaworski, Bank of the Southwest Building, Travis and Walker, Houston, Tex. 77002.

CAREER: Admitted to Texas bar, 1925; Fulbright, Crooker, Freeman, Bates & Jaworski, Houston, Tex., partner, beginning 1935. Director and member of executive committee of Bank of the Southwest; director of Gulf Publishing Co., Gulf Printing Co., Anderson Clayton & Co., and Benjamin Franklin Savings Association. Chairman of joint administrative committee of Texas Medical Center and Baylor University College of Medicine; Protestant chairman of Houston chapter, National Conference of Christians and Jews, 1955-61. President of Baylor Medical Foundation; trustee, M. D. Anderson Foundation, Houston Symphony Society, United Fund, and other foundations. Special assistant, U.S. Attorney General, 1962-65; special counsel, Attorney General of Texas, 1963-65; member, President's Commission on Law Enforcement and Administration of Justice; U.S. member, Permanent Court of Arbitration (The Hague); chairman, Governor's Committee on Public Education; director, Office of Watergate Special Prosecution Force, U.S. Department of Justice, 1973-74. *Military service:* U.S. Army, Judge Advocate General's Department, 1942-46; served as chief of War Crimes Trial Section in Europe; became colonel; received Legion of Merit.

MEMBER: American College of Trial Lawyers (member of board of regents, 1959-66; president, 1961-62), American Bar Association (standing committee on the federal judiciary, 1960-63), American Law Institute, State Bar of Texas (president, 1962), Texas Civil Judicial Council (president, 1951-53), Houston Bar Association (president, 1949), Houston Chamber of Commerce (president, 1960), Houston Rotary Club, Houston Club, Coronado Club, Headliners Club, International Club, Houston Country Club, Phi Delta Phi. *Awards, honors:* LL.D., Baylor University, 1960; Brotherhood Award, Houston chapter of National Conference of Christians and Jews; distinguished alumnus award, Baylor University School of Law, 1964; alumni achievement award, George Washington University, 1965.

WRITINGS: After Fifteen Years, Gulf, 1961. Contributor of articles to legal journals.

* * *

JEFFERIES, Susan Herring 1903-

PERSONAL: Born August 14, 1903, in Tai Shan, Shantung Province, China; daughter of David Wells (a missionary) and Alice (Rea) Herring; married Clinton L. Jefferies, November 15, 1928 (divorced); married Mark Taynton (a mining engineer and author), 1972; children: Susan J. (Mrs. Rolf Westad), Theodore Rea, Clinton LeRoy. *Education:* Meredith College, A.B., 1924. *Politics:* Democrat. *Religion:* Baptist. *Residence:* Falls Church, Va.

CAREER: North Carolina State College of Agriculture and Engineering (now North Carolina State University), Raleigh, statistical analyst, 1953-59; Douglas Aircraft Co.,

Charlotte, N.C., statistician, 1959-61; North Carolina State University at Raleigh, statistical analyst, 1961-72. Coordinator of Annual Giving Program, Meredith College, 1964-72.

WRITINGS: Papa Wore No Halo, Blair, 1963.

WORK IN PROGRESS: A novel about missions in China, *Pagoda Passage*.

SIDELIGHTS: Susan Jefferies, who speaks Chinese, told *CA* she and her husband have tried, thus far unsuccessfully, for visas to the People's Republic of China, to update research on *Pagoda Passage*.

* * *

JENKS, Almet 1892-1966

PERSONAL: Born April 18, 1892, in Brooklyn, N.Y.; son of Almet Francis (a judge) and Lena (Barre) Jenks; married Charlotte Williams Fenner, December 4, 1923. *Education:* Yale University, B.A., 1914; Columbia University, LL.B., 1917. *Home:* Palm Beach, Fla. *Agent:* Russell & Volkening, Inc., 551 Fifth Ave., New York, N.Y. 10017.

CAREER: Attorney in private practice in New York, N.Y., 1919-27. Author. *Military service:* U.S. Army, Cavalry, 1917-19; served with American Expeditionary Forces, 1918-19. U.S. Marine Corps Reserve, active duty, 1942-45; served in Okinawa campaign; became major. *Member:* Racquet and Tennis Club (New York).

WRITINGS: The Huntsman at the Gate, Lippincott, 1952; *The Second Chance*, Lippincott, 1959. Author of short stories and serials in *Harper's*, *Harper's Bazaar*, *Saturday Evening Post*, and in foreign magazines.

SIDELIGHTS: While a member of the Marine Corps. Historical Division during World War II, Jenks wrote histories of the Tarawa operation and the Battle of Okinawa.

(Died February 2, 1966)

* * *

JENNINGS, John (Edward, Jr.) 1906-1973
(Bates Baldwin, Joel Williams)

PERSONAL: Born December 30, 1906, in Brooklyn, N.Y.; son of John E. (a surgeon) and Florence (Thistle) Jennings; married Virginia Lee Storey, June 20, 1931 (divorced, 1959); married Elise Durrin Dunlap (an artist), January 9, 1960; children: (first marriage) John E. III. *Education:* Attended Colorado School of Mines, 1924-25, New York University, 1925-26, Columbia University, 1927-28; Washington Diplomatic and Consular Institute, graduate, 1935. *Home and office:* P.O. Box U, Pipestave Hollow Rd., Miller Place, N.Y. 11764. *Agent:* Oliver G. Swan, Paul R. Reynolds, Inc., 599 Fifth Ave., New York, N.Y. 10017.

CAREER: Free-lance author, 1929-73, writing short stories for magazines, 1934-38, historical novels, 1939-73. *Military service:* U. S. Naval Reserve, 1942-54; on active duty as officer in charge of Naval Aviation History Unit, 1942-45; became lieutenant commander, 1948.

WRITINGS: Our American Tropics (nonfiction; self-illustrated), Crowell, 1938; *Next to Valour*, Macmillan, 1939; *Call the New World*, Macmillan, 1941; *Gentleman Ranker*, Reynal & Hitchcock, 1942; *The Shadow and the Glory*, Reynal & Hitchcock, 1943; *Boston, Cradle of Liberty, 1630-1776* (nonfiction), Doubleday, 1945; *The Salem Frigate*, Doubleday, 1946; *River to the West: A Novel of the Astor Adventure*, Doubleday, 1948.

The Sea Eagles: A Story of the American Navy during the Revolution, Doubleday, 1950; *The Pepper Tree: A Story of New England and the Spice Islands*, Little, Brown, 1950; *The Strange Brigade: A Story of the Red River and the Opening of the Canadian West*, Little, Brown, 1952; *Clipper Ship Days* (juvenile), Random House, 1952; *Rogue's Yarn*, Little, Brown, 1953; *Banners Against the Wind*, Little, Brown, 1954; *Shadows in the Dusk*, Little, Brown, 1955; *Chronicle of the Calypso, Clipper*, Little, Brown, 1955; *The Wind in His Fists*, Holt, 1955; *The Tall Ships*, McGraw, 1958; *The Golden Eagle*, Putnam, 1959; *The Raider: A Novel of World War I*, Morrow, 1963 (published in England as *The Emden*, Redman, 1964); *Tattered Ensign*, Crowell, 1966.

Under pseudonym Joel Williams: *The Coasts of Folly*, Reynal & Hitchcock, 1942.

Under pseudonym Bates Baldwin: *The Sultan's Warrior*, Holt, 1951; *Tide of Empire*, Holt, 1952.

Author of serial, "Wheel of Fortune," published in *Liberty*, 1943; contributor of short stories during the 1930's to *Saturday Evening Post*, *Cosmopolitan*, *Doc Savage Magazine*, and other periodicals.

WORK IN PROGRESS: A novel about the Revolutionary War, during the period 1776-80, in New York, Connecticut, Long Island, etc.

SIDELIGHTS: Jennings told *CA*, "I made my first voyage abroad in 1925 as a foremast hand in a tramp steamer calling at ports in the Eastern Mediterranean, Turkey and the Black Sea and the Aegean. Even then I had travelled extensively in the U.S. and in Canada, and the experience only whetted my appetite for further journeys. Since then I have travelled widely in Europe and Africa, Mexico and all of South America. In my younger years I spoke French and Spanish fairly fluently and had a working knowledge of Portuguese and Arabic."

Jennings described himself as a mediocre student (but "able to memorize the names of all the railroads whose freight cars passed the study hall windows"), who specialized in college in mining engineering, advertising, sales, and navigation, in that order. He said he learned two things at college: "(a) I was not cut out to be an engineer, and (b) Billy Minsky's Burlesque [was] more interesting than Principles of Business Management III, which I cut every Thursday at NYU."

"As a writer," Jennings noted, he was "born of the Great Depression." When he could find no "respectable" job and observed newsstands "heavily loaded down with all manner of popular magazines," he decided to try writing to earn his living. And to his surprise, his stories sold well, as did his later novels. His first novel, *Next to Valour*, was a best seller, published in England, and translated into seven other European languages; a later book, *The Salem Frigate*, ran into a dozen translations, including Japanese, Korean, and Arabic. In all, thirteen of his novels were best sellers.

AVOCATIONAL INTERESTS: Fishing, camping, and hunting ("all of which involve a considerable amount of travel, which is actually the basic attraction for me").

(Died December 4, 1973)

JENNINGS, Leslie Nelson 1890-1972
(A. B. Brooke, Cyril Carfagne, James McGregor Cartwright, Baroness Julie Desplaines, Judith James, Paul Rayson)

PERSONAL: Born September 6, 1890, in Ware, Mass.; son of Roscoe Leslie (a business executive) and Susan Bryant (Dwight) Jennings. *Education:* Studied under private tutors; otherwise self-educated. *Politics:* Democrat. *Religion:* Protestant. *Home and office:* 45 East 55th St., New York, N.Y. 10021.

CAREER: Formerly associate editor of *Current Opinion*; former editor, *Poetry Chap-Book*; literary consultant, critic, and agent for prose material, and editor of poetry collections.

WRITINGS: Mill Talk, and Other Poems, Fine Editions Press, 1942; *Footsteps of Departure* (poems), Prairie Press, 1963. Contributor to poetry anthologies in England and America. Wrote a series of essays for *Christian Science Monitor*; contributor of social satire (verse) to *New Yorker* for ten years. Formerly contributor to pulp magazines, under pseudonyms.

(Died March 27, 1972)

*   *   *

JENSEN, John Martin 1893-

PERSONAL: Born March 24, 1893, in Toledo, Ohio; son of Rasmus (a salesman) and Margrethe (Sorensen) Jensen; married Ragnhild Gotsche; children: Ronald, Margrethe (Mrs. B. B. Rasmussen), Frederic V. *Education:* Augsburg College, B.A., 1920; Biblical Seminary in New York, student, 1920-21; Lutheran Theological Seminary, Philadelphia, Pa., graduate, 1922; United Theological College, McGill University, B.D., 1934. *Home and office:* 390 26th St. S.E., Cedar Rapids, Iowa.

CAREER: Lutheran pastor at Salmonhurst, New Brunswick, 1922-26, Montreal, Quebec, 1926-37, Spencer, Iowa, 1937-59, and Viborg, S.D., 1959-60. *Awards, honors:* Knighted by King of Denmark, 1955; honorary D.D., Wartburg Theological Seminary, 1957.

WRITINGS: (Translator) Kaj Munk, *By the Rivers of Babylon*, Lutheran, 1945; (translator) Walter Luthe, *Daniel Speaks to the Church*, Augsburg, 1947; (translator) Regin Prenter, *Spiritus Creator*, Fortress Press, 1953; (translator) Kaj Jensen, *The Answer of Faith*, Augsburg, 1961; (editor with Carl E. Linder and Gerald Giving) *Biographical Directory of Pastors in the American Lutheran Church*, Augsburg, 1962; (translator) Peder Olsen, *Healing through Prayer*, Augsburg, 1963; *United Evangelical Lutheran Church: An Interpretation*, Augsburg, 1964. Contributor of articles to encyclopedias. Editor of *Ansgar Lutheran*, 1936-60.

WORK IN PROGRESS: Two books, both translations from the Danish.

SIDELIGHTS: Jensen speaks Danish and Norwegian.

*   *   *

JEWETT, Alyce Lowrie (Williams) 1908-

PERSONAL: Born November 25, 1908, in Oakland, Calif.; daughter of Robert Vincent (a woolens company representative) and Ethel (DeMaranville) Williams; married Lindsay M. Jewett, November 25, 1962. *Education:* University of California, Davis, B.S., 1931; University of California, Berkeley, M.S., 1934; Harvard University, postgraduate study, 1936-37. *Religion:* Presbyterian. *Home address:* P.O. Box 905, Nevada City, Calif.

CAREER: U.S. Farm Security Administration, San Francisco, Calif., regional section chief, 1938-43; Poultry Producers of Central California, San Francisco, administrative assistant and poultry department manager, 1945-55; Agricultural Council of California, Sacramento, director of information, 1955-61; University of California, Davis, public affairs officer and instructor, 1961-62. Official judge of dairy and beef cattle, sheep, and dairy goats. *Member:* American Association of University Women (district officer), Sutter district Federation of Women's Clubs (district officer), Phi Beta Kappa, Prytanean, 4-H Club (honorary). *Awards, honors:* Distinguished Service Plaque from Future Farmers of America, 1964, and honorary state farmer (California and Nevada).

WRITINGS: (With Edwin C. Voorhies) *Agricultural Cooperatives: Strength in Unity*, Interstate, 1963. Contributor to *Encyclopaedia Britannica* and to periodicals. Author of booklet, "Exploring Farmer Cooperatives," Agricultural Council of California, 1958.

WORK IN PROGRESS: A history of the almond industry.

AVOCATIONAL INTERESTS: Internationalism, mountain lakes, wildlife, and horseback riding.

*   *   *

JOBES, Gertrude Blumenthal   1907-

PERSONAL: Born October 5, 1907, in Brooklyn, N.Y.; daughter of Henry and Frances (Scheff) Blumenthal; married James Addison Jobes (an interior decorator), September 1, 1935. *Education:* New York University, Certificate in General Education, 1952; graduate studies at New School for Social Research, Columbia University, and China Institute. *Home:* 408 West 25th St., Miami Beach, Fla. 33140. *Agent:* Augusta Cantor, Park Sheraton Hotel, 870 Seventh Ave., New York, N.Y. 10019.

CAREER: Aborn Operas, New York, N.Y., assistant and secretary to Milton Aborn, 1925-29; Stanley Co. of America (later Warner Brothers Theatres), New York, N.Y., 1929-32, became secretary to George Skouras; Hearst Metronome News, New York, N.Y., assistant to editor, 1932-45. Writer and lecturer, 1956—. Traveled across United States and Canada with Abbott Collection of War Paintings, shown in major museums and galleries. Teacher of literature, Young Men's Christian Association, 1961. Member, American Theatre Wing, 1941-45. *Member:* Authors Guild, American Contract Bridge League, Modern Etchers Group (president), Florida State Poetry Society, New Haven Poetry Society.

WRITINGS: One Happy Family (novel), Pageant, 1955; (editor) *Writers Festival*, Taylor Library, c.1960; *Dictionary of Mythology, Folklore and Symbols*, two volumes, Scarecrow, 1961, index, 1962; (with husband, James Addison Jobes) *Outer Space: Myths, Name Meanings, Calendars from the Emergence of History to the Present Day*, Scarecrow, 1964; *Motion Picture Empire*, Archon Books, 1966. Anthologized in *American Vanguard, 1956*, edited by J. Ernest Wright and Frederic Morton, Cambridge Publishing Co., 1956, and in other publications. Writer of motion picture documentaries, World War II. Contributor of poetry to avant garde journals, and of articles to *American Weekly*. Editor, New Haven Poetry Society *Journal*, 1959-63.

BIOGRAPHICAL/CRITICAL SOURCES: Bridgeport Post, February 19, 1956, May 21, 1961, August 11, 1961; *New Haven Register*, April 2, 1956, June 25, 1961, July 28, 1963, August 30, 1964; *New York World Telegram*, March 14, 1960, May 12, 1961; *American Weekly*, August 13, 1961; *Broderline*, October, 1964.

*   *   *

JOHANSEN, Dorothy O.   1904-

PERSONAL: Born May 19, 1904, in Seaside, Ore. *Education:* Reed College, B.A., 1933; University of Washington, M.A., 1934, Ph.D., 1941. *Home:* 3650 Southeast Knight St., Portland, Ore. 97202. *Office:* Reed College, Portland, Ore. 97202.

CAREER: Reed College, Portland, Ore., instructor, 1938-43, assistant professor of history, 1943-48, associate professor of history and humanities, 1948-57, professor of history, 1957-69, professor emeritus, 1969—. Member of Portland Public School Board, 1950-58. *Member:* American Historical Association (vice-president of Pacific Coast branch, 1964-65; president, 1966). *Awards, honors:* L.H.D. from Reed College, 1973.

WRITINGS: (With Charles M. Gates) *Empire of the Columbia*, Harper, 1957; sole author of revised edition, 1967.

General editor, "Beaver Books" series—all published by Champoeg: Robert Newell, *Memoranda*, 1959; *The Voyage of the Columbia: John Boit's Narrative of a Journey Around the World 1790-1793*, 1960; Constance Bordwell, *March of the Volunteers: Soldiering with Lewis and Clark*, 1961; Luther Cressman, *The Sandal and the Cave*, 1963. Contributor to *Pacific Historical Review*.

WORK IN PROGRESS: Reed College: The Formative Years (tentative title).

*   *   *

JOHNSON, Arnold W(aldemar)   1900-

PERSONAL: Born June 24, 1900, in Buffalo, N.Y.; son of Sam R. and Hulda F. (Nelson) Johnson. *Education:* University of Washington, Seattle, B.B.A., 1927; Harvard University, M.B.A., 1929. *Office:* 633 S.W. 4th St., Boca Raton, Fla. 33432.

CAREER: Certified public accountant. Employed by Ford Motor Co., 1922-26, Gillette Safety Razor Co., 1929; West Virginia University, Morgantown, 1929-33, began as instructor, became assistant professor of accounting; West Virginia Institute of Technology, Montgomery, associate professor of accounting, 1933-35; University of Oklahoma, Norman, 1935-42, began as assistant professor, became professor of accounting; Tulane University of Louisiana, New Orleans, professor of accounting, 1942-46; Syracuse University, Syracuse, N.Y., professor of accounting, and chairman of department, 1946-51; New York University, School of Accounting, New York, N.Y., professor of accounting and chairman of department, 1954-65. Visiting professor, University of Florida, 1966-68, Florida Atlantic University, 1968—. Assistant director of budget, State of West Virginia, 1935; consultant to U.S. Navy, 1948. *Member:* American Institute of Certified Public Accountants, American Accounting Association (vice-president, 1956-57). *Awards, honors:* Citation, School of Commerce, New York University, 1965; Centennial Medal, Syracuse University, 1970; Outstanding Educators of America award, 1970.

WRITINGS: Principles of Accounting, Farrar, 1937, 4th

edition published as *Elementary Accounting*, Holt, 1962; *Intermediate Accounting*, Rinehart, 1947, 3rd edition (with Oscar M. Kreigman), Holt, 1964; *Case Problems in Auditing*, Rinehart, 1950; *Auditing: Principles and Case Problems*, Holt, 1959; (with Evroul S. Germain) *CPA Problems and Solutions*, Allyn & Bacon, 1959; *Advanced Accounting*, Holt, 1960, 3rd edition, Vantage Press, 1968. Contributor to journals in his field.

* * *

JOHNSON, E(dgar) A(ugustus) J(erome)   1900-1972

PERSONAL: Born January 31, 1900, in Orion, Ill.; son of Klaes August and Hannah Charlotte (Carlson) Johnson; married Virginia Gravelle, August 8, 1922; children: Edgar A. J., Jr. *Education:* University of Illinois, B.S., 1922; Harvard University, A.M., 1924, Ph.D., 1929, postdoctoral study at Oxford University and Cambridge University, 1929-30. *Home:* 6622 32nd St., N.W., Washington, D.C. 20015. *Office:* School of Advanced International Studies, Johns Hopkins University, Washington, D.C.

CAREER: University of Oklahoma, Norman, instructor, 1922-23, assistant professor of economics, 1924-26; Harvard University, Cambridge, Mass., instructor, 1926-29; George Washington University, Washington, D.C., associate professor, 1930-31; Cornell University, Ithaca, N.Y., assistant professor, 1931-37; New York University, New York, N.Y., associate professor, 1937-40, professor of economic history, 1940-43; South Korean interim government, director of Department of Commerce, 1946, civil administrator, 1946-47, chief adviser, 1947-48; Economic Cooperation Administration, director of Korea Program, Washington, D.C., 1948-51, adviser, Mission to Greece, 1951; U.S. Aid Program in Yugoslavia, deputy chief, 1952-55; University of Maryland, College Park, and University of Pennsylvania, Philadelphia, visiting professor of economics, 1955-56; Johns Hopkins University, School of Advanced International Studies, Washington, D.C., professor of international economics, 1956-62, professor of economic history, 1962-69, professor emeritus, 1969-72, Center for Cultural and Technical Interchange Between East and West, Honolulu, Hawaii, senior specialist, 1968-69. Lecturer at University of Madrid, Mysore University, University of Ankara, University of Turin, University of Oslo, University of Padova, Yale University, and other universities in America and abroad. Consultant to General Motors, 1940-41, National Council of Applied Economic Research (India), 1952-55, Agency for International Development, Mission to India, 1966-67. *Military service:* U.S. Army Reserve, Cavalry, 1922-37; active duty, 1943-46, serving in England and with Allied Land Forces in Norway; became lieutenant colonel; received Bronze Star, Order of the British Empire, and Cross of King Haakon (Norway). *Member:* Economic History Association (president, 1960-62). *Awards, honors:* Social Science Research Council fellowship in England, 1929-30; L.L.D., Johns Hopkins University, 1972.

WRITINGS: American Economic Thought in the Seventeenth Century, P. S. King, 1932; *Some Origins of the Modern Economic World*, Macmillan, 1935; (translator) Ernst Teilhac, *Pioneers of American Economic Thought*, Macmillan, 1935; *Predecessors of Adam Smith*, Prentice-Hall, 1937; *An Economic History of Modern England*, Nelson, 1939; (with Herman Kroos) *The Origins and Development of the American Economy: An Introduction to Economics*, Prentice-Hall, 1953, published as *The American Economy, Its Origin, Development and Transformation*,

1960; (editor) *The Dimensions of Diplomacy*, Johns Hopkins Press, 1964; *Market Towns and Spatial Development in India*, National Council of Applied Economic Research, 1965; *The Organization of Space in Developing Countries*, Harvard University Press, 1970; *American Imperialism in the Image of Peer Gynt: Memoirs of a Professor-Bureaucrat*, University of Minnesota Press, 1971; *The Foundations of American Economic Freedom: Government and Enterprise in the Age of Washington*, University of Minnesota Press, 1973.

Editor of "Economic Series," published by Prentice-Hall, 34 volumes, 1937-66. Contributor of over fifty articles to American, European, and Asian journals. Editor of *Journal of Economic History*, 1940-43.

WORK IN PROGRESS: Pluralism and Public Policy.

(Died August 17, 1972)

* * *

JOHNSON, Gaylord   1884-

PERSONAL: Born February 8, 1884, in Adrian, Mich.; son of Jacob Schuyler (a dentist) and Celeste (Barrette) Johnson; married Alice Bagley Hall (a Christian Science practitioner), August 31, 1947. *Education:* University of Michigan, student, 1902-04. *Politics:* Republican. *Religion:* Christian Scientist. *Home:* 11 Fifth Ave., New York, N.Y. 10003.

CAREER: Copy writer, specializing in mail order copy for books and educational courses, with five advertising agencies in New York, N.Y., 1920-47, with agency in Minneapolis, Minn., 1947-48; independent consultant on mail order advertising copy, 1948—. Author and illustrator.

*WRITINGS—*All self-illustrated, except as indicated: *The Star People*, Macmillan, 1921; *The Sky Movies*, Macmillan, 1922; *Nature's Program*, Doubleday, 1926; *The Stars for Children* (contains *The Star People* and *The Sky Movies*), Macmillan, 1934; *Discover the Stars*, Leisure League of America, 1935, revised edition (with Irving Adler) published as *Discover the Stars: A Beginner's Guide to the Science of Astronomy and the Earth Satellite*, Sentinel Books, 1954; *Hunting with the Microscope*, Leisure League of America, 1936, revised edition (with Maurice Bleifeld and Charles Tanzer) published as *Hunting with the Microscope: A Beginner's Guide to Exploring the Micro-World of Plants and Animals*, Sentinel Books, 1956; *The Story of Earthquakes and Volcanoes*, Messner, 1938; *How Father Time Changes the Animals' Shapes*, Messner, 1939; *Our Solar System*, Doubleday, 1955; *The Story of Animals: Mammals Around the World*, illustrated by Don Bolognese, Harvey House, 1958; *The Story of Planets, Space and Stars*, illustrated by Frank Angelini, Harvey House, 1959. Contributor of some forty articles on astronomy and natural history to *Popular Science Monthly*, 1932-39.

WORK IN PROGRESS: Biographies of Antoni Van Leeuwenhoek, Robert Hooke, and Christopher Wren; research on Lafayette's triumphal tour of United States in 1824-25; research for brief biographies of Biblical characters.

AVOCATIONAL INTERESTS: Watercolor painting; Biblical archaeology and its effects on Bible history.

* * *

JOHNSON, Geoffrey   1893-1966

PERSONAL: Born December 29, 1893, in England; son of

Charles Thomas (a clerk) and Elizabeth (Dickinson) Johnson; married Agnes Allbut (an artist), December 30, 1922. *Education:* University of London, B.A. (first class honors), 1921; Oxford University, Teacher's Diploma (with distinction), 1927. *Politics:* Labour. *Religion:* Belief in God, no specific creed. *Home and office:* Byways, Springhill, 84 Higher Blandford Rd., Broadstone, Dorsetshire, England.

CAREER: Poet. Grammar School master (sixth form), in England, 1928-53. Member of advisory council, English-Speaking Board, Liverpool. *Member:* Society of Authors, Poetry Society, West Country Writers' Association.

WRITINGS—Poetry: *The Quest Unending*, Selwyn & Blount, 1930; *Changing Horizons*, Daniel Co., 1932; *Mother to Son*, Williams & Norgate, 1935; *The Scholar*, Williams & Norgate, 1936; *The New Road*, Williams & Norgate, 1939; *The Timeless Land*, Poetry Lovers' Fellowship (Manchester), 1941; *The Mountain and Other Poems*, Williams & Norgate, 1946; *The Ninth Wave*, Harrap, 1948; *The Iron Harvest*, Williams & Norgate, 1950; *The Heart of Things*, Williams & Norgate, 1952; *The Magic Stone*, R. Hale, 1955; *A Man of Vision and Other Poems*, R. Hale, 1958.

Verse translations: (Contributor) Harry H. Mayer, editor, *The Lyric Psalter*, Liveright, 1940; (contributor) L. R. Lind, *Latin Poetry in Verse Translation*, Houghton, 1957; *The Pastorals of Vergil* (metrical version), University of Kansas Press, 1960.

Other books: (With others) *Poetic Technique*, Poetry Lovers' Fellowship (Manchester), 1949; (editor with others) *An Anthology of Spoken Prose and Verse*, two volumes, Oxford University Press, 1957; (editor with John Byrne) *Three Modern Plays*, Methuen, 1957.

Poems anthologized in *Albermarle Book of Modern Verse*, J. Murray, and in other anthologies published in Britain and America. Contributor of poetry to *Listener*, *Observer*, *Sunday Times*, *Punch*, *Irish Times*, and other periodicals and newspapers in Britain, and to more than twenty foreign journals and newspapers, including *Poetry* (Chicago), *Harper's*, *Atlantic Monthly*, *Shenandoah*, *New Republic*, *Nation*, *Canadian Author and Bookman*, *Meanjin Quarterly* (Australia), *Arena* (New Zealand), *Thought* (India). Co-editor of *Poetry Review* (publication of Poetry Society of London), 1952-61; former British editor of *Lyric* (Virginia); former European editor of *Poetry Chapbook* (New York) and *Flame* (Texas).

WORK IN PROGRESS: Four in Hand, a collection of verse translations from the French, German, Italian, and Latin; *The Anniversary* and *Lyric Interval*, two collections of original poems.

SIDELIGHTS: Johnson was competent in French, German, Italian, and Latin. *Avocational interests:* Gardening, walking, foreign travel, reading in foreign languages, antiquities (particularly Roman); "devoted lover of Wordsworth and Hardy and their respective landscapes."

(Died April, 1966)

* * *

JOHNSON, Lois Smith 1894-

PERSONAL: Born July 26, 1894, in Parkersburg, W. Va.; daughter of Robert Bruce (a minister) and Carrie E. (Smith) Smith; married George Virgil Johnson, June 29, 1920 (deceased); children: Janet Elizabeth (Mrs. Russell Little), William Bruce (deceased). *Education:* Marietta College,

student, 1912-14; Colorado College, A.B., 1916; graduate work at San Jose State College (now California State University, San Jose), 1930, and University of California, 1936. *Religion:* Baptist. *Home:* 3000 39th St. N.W., Washington, D.C. 20016.

CAREER: Elementary school teacher in Colorado Springs, Colo., 1916-18; junior high school teacher in Springfield, Ohio, 1918-20; elementary and high school teacher in Monterey, Calif., 1930-43; American National Red Cross, Washington, D.C., 1943-59, editor of Junior Red Cross periodicals, 1946-59. Consultant, American National Red Cross Office of International Relations, 1960. *Member:* Women's National Press Club, Women's National Book Association, Children's Book Guild (president, 1954-55), P.E.O. Sisterhood, Phi Beta Kappa.

WRITINGS—All juveniles: (Editor) *Christmas Stories Round the World*, Rand McNally, 1960, 2nd edition, 1970; *Happy Birthdays Round the World*, Rand McNally, 1963; *Happy New Year Round the World*, Rand McNally, 1966; *What We Eat: The Origins and Travels of Foods Round the World*, Rand McNally, 1969.

SIDELIGHTS: Mrs. Johnson traveled in Japan, 1956, Europe, 1958, 1969, around the world, 1960-61.

BIOGRAPHICAL/CRITICAL SOURCES: Young Readers' Review, December, 1966.

* * *

JOHNSON, Mary Ritz 1904-

PERSONAL: Born March 15, 1904, in Szamosdob, Szatmar, Hungary; daughter of George (a mechanic) and Mary (Zaharia) Ritz; married John Johnson (a tool engineer), June 24, 1925; children: Marilyn Johnson Mannion. *Education:* Studied at Booth and Baylis Commercial School and Ecole Guerre-Lavigne, Paris, France. *Home:* 291 Grovers Ave., Bridgeport, Conn. 06605. *Office:* 83 Fairfield Ave., Bridgeport, Conn. 06603.

CAREER: Town and Country Clothes by Mary Johnson, Bridgeport, Conn., proprietor, 1926-43; Mary Johnson Fashion Education, Bridgeport, Conn., founder, owner, director, 1948—. Instructor in sewing, D. M. Read Co., 1943-49, Bridgeport Public School adult classes, 1947-49. *Member:* Quota Club (Bridgeport).

WRITINGS: Sewing the Easy Way, Dutton, 1958, revised and enlarged edition, 1966; *Sew for Your Children*, Dutton, 1961, reissued as *The Easier Way to Sew for Your Family*, 1972; *Mary Johnson's Guide to Altering and Restyling Ready-Made Clothes*, Dutton, 1964. Contributing editor, *Woman's Day*, 1958—.

* * *

JOHNSTON, George Burke 1907-

PERSONAL: Born September 8, 1907, in Tuscaloosa, Ala.; son of George Doherty and Eleanor (McCorvey) Johnston; married Mary Tabb Lancaster, 1936; children: Elizabeth Carrington (Mrs. C. L. Lipscomb III), Thomas McCorvey, George Burke, Jr., Mary Tabb. *Education:* University of Alabama, B.A., 1929; Columbia University, M.A., 1930, Ph.D., 1943. *Home:* 804 Gracelyn Ct., Blacksburg, Va.

CAREER: Virginia Polytechnic Institute and State University, Blacksburg, Va., instructor in English, 1930-33; University of Alabama, Tuscaloosa, instructor, 1935-41, assistant professor, 1941-46, associate professor, 1946-50, professor of English, 1950, assistant dean of College of Arts and Sciences, 1946-50; Virginia Polytechnic Institute and State University, Blacksburg, Va., dean of School of Applied Sciences and Business Administration, 1950-61, dean of School of Science and General Studies, 1961-63, dean of the College of Arts and Sciences, 1963-65, Miles Professor of English, 1965-74. *Military service:* U.S. Army Reserve, beginning, 1929; active duty, 1941-46; now lieutenant colonel (retired). *Member:* Modern language Association of America, Shakespeare Association of America, *Awards, honors:* Whitney Memorial Prize, Keats Memorial Sonnet Prize, and Duff Memorial Prize from Poetry Society of Virginia.

WRITINGS: Ben Jonson: Poet, Columbia University Press, 1945; (editor) *Poems of Ben Jonson*, Routledge & Kegan Paul, 1954, Harvard University Press, 1955, 3rd edition, 1962; (editor) T. C. McCorvey, *Alabama Historical Sketches*, University Press of Virginia, 1960; *Reflections* (poems), White Rhinoceros Press, 1965. Contributor of biographical essays to *Masterplots Cyclopedia of World Authors* and *Collier's Encyclopedia*; also contributor of articles to scholarly journals, and poems to newspapers and magazines, including *Wings, Lyric, Washington Evening Star*, and *New York Times*.

WORK IN PROGRESS: Studies in Philology, Texts and Studies Issue, for University of North Carolina Press; editing *Poems by William Camden*.

*   *   *

JOLIVET, R(egis)   1891-1966

PERSONAL: Born November 8, 1891, in Lyons, France. *Education:* Educated at Catholic University of Lyons and University of Grenoble; Docteur en philosophie, 1921, Docteur es lettres, 1929. *Home:* 11 Rue de Trion, Lyons-5, France.

CAREER: Roman Catholic priest, now a monsignor; Catholic University of Lyons, Lyons, France, professor of metaphysics and history of philosophy, 1926-61, dean of School of Philosophy, 1933-61. Lecturer at universities in France, Belgium, Holland, England, Italy, Spain, Czechoslovakia, Poland, Argentina, and Brazil; Center for Carthage Studies, Tunis, Tunisia, director, 1957-66. *Military service:* Served with French Forces, 1914-18, 1939-45; received Croix de Guerre. *Member:* Society of Professors of Philosophy of Catholic Universities of France (president), Roman Academy of Saint Thomas, International Institute of Philosophy, Academy of Messine, Philosophy Society of Genoa, Philosophy Society of Louvain, International Society of Rosminien Studies (president). *Awards, honors:* Laureate of Academie des Sciences Morales et Politiques, Paris, 1930, of Academie Francaises, Paris, 1933; honorary doctorate, University of Louvain, 1960; Chevalier de la Legion d'Honneur, 1961.

WRITINGS: La Notion de substance: Essai historique et critique sur le developpement des doctrines d'Aristote a nos jours, Beauchesne (Paris), 1929; *Le Probleme du mal d'apres saint Augustin* (originally published in *Archives de Philosophie*, Volume 7, no. 2), Beauchsne, 1930, 2nd edition, 1936; *A la recherche de Dieu: Notes critiques sur la theodicee de m. Edouard Le Roy*, Beauchesne, 1931; *Essai sur le bergsonisme*, Vitte (Paris and Lyon), 1931; *Essai sur les rapports entre la pensee grecque et la pensee chretienne*, Vrin (Paris), 1931, 2nd edition, 1955; *Etudes sur le probleme de Dieu dans la philosophie contemporaine*, Vitte, 1932; *Saint Augustin et le neo-platonisme chretien*,

Denoel & Steele (Paris), 1932; *Le Thomisme et la critique de la connaissance*, Desclee, de Brouwer (Paris), 1933; *L'Intuition intellectuelle et le probleme de la metaphysique*, Beauchesne, 1934; *Dieu, soleil des esprits; ou, La Doctrine augustinenne de l'illumination* (originally published in *Revue de Philosophie*, July-December, 1930), Desclee, de Brouwer, 1934; *Les Sources de l'idealisme*, Desclee, de Brouwer, 1936; (translator and author of notes) Saint Augustine, *Dialogues philosophiques: Problemes fondamentaux; Contra academicos; De beata vita; De ordine* (*Ouevres de saint Augustin*, Part 4, series 1), Desclee, de Brouwer, 1936; (translator and author of notes with M. Jourjon) Saint Augustine, *Dieu et son oeuvre: Six traites anti-manicheens* (*Oeuvres de saint Augustin*, Part 17, series 2), Desclee, de Brouwer, 1936; *Traite de philosophie*, four volumes, Volume I: *Introduction generale, logique, cosmologie*, Volume II: *Psychologie*, Volume III: *Metaphysique*, Volume IV: *Morale*, Vitte, 1939-41, 7th edition, 1964.

Vocabulaire de la philosophie, suivi d'un tableau historique des ecoles de philosophie, Vitte, 1942, 5th edition, 1962; *Introduction a Kierkegaard*, Editions de Fontenelle (Paris), 1946, translation by W. H. Barber published as *Introduction to Kierkegaard*, Muller, 1950, Dutton, 1951, 2nd French edition published as *Aux Sources de l'existentialisme chretien: Kierkegaard*, Fayard (Paris), 1958; *Les Doctrines existentialistes de Kierkegaard a J.-P. Sartre*, Editions de Fontenelle, 1948; *Essai sur le probleme et les conditions de la sincerite*, Vitte, 1950; *Le Probleme de la mort chez M. Heidegger et J.-P. Sartre*, Editions de Fontenelle, 1950; *De Rosmini a Lachelier: Essai de philosophie comparee* (includes "L'Idee de la sagesse," by Rosmini), Vitte, 1953; *Introduction a Rosmini*, Vitte, 1954; *Le Dieu des philosophes et des savants*, Fayard, 1956, translation by Mark Pontifex published as *The God of Reason*, Hawthorn, 1958; *L'Homme metaphysique*, Fayard, 1958, translation by B. M. G. Reardon published as *Man and Metaphysics*, Hawthorn, 1961; *Cours de philosophie*, 6th edition, Vitte, 1959.

Le Courant neo-augustinien, Volume II of the collective work "La Philosophie mondiale," Marzorati, 1962; *Les Activites de l'homme et la sagesse*, Vitte, 1963; *Sarte* (in Spanish), Colomba, 1963; *Sartre; ou, La Theologie de l'absurde*, Fayard, 1965; translation by Wesley C. Piersol published as *Sartre: The Theology of the Absurd*, Newman, 1967.

Contributor to more than twenty-five philosophy, theology, and religious journals in France, Italy, Portugal, Argentina, Canada, Denmark, and Spain.

BIOGRAPHICAL/CRITICAL SOURCES: La Philosophie et ses problemes: Recueil d'etudes de doctrine et d'histoire, offert a Mgr. R. Jolivet, Vitte, 1960.

(Died August 4, 1966)

*   *   *

JOLLY, Cyril Arthur   1910-

PERSONAL: Born December 16, 1910, in Cairo, Egypt; son of Arthur Anthony (a postman) and Millicent (Howard) Jolly; married Hilda Joyce Barber, September 11, 1940; children: Elizabeth, Deborah. *Education:* Attended Dereham National School. *Religion:* Methodist. *Home:* Teazel Patch, Gressenhall, Dereham, Norfolk, England. *Agent:* A. P. Watt & Son, 10 Norfolk St., Strand, London W.C. 2, England.

CAREER: East Dereham Foundry Ltd., Dereham, Norfolk, England, manager, 1947-63; Dereham Property Co. Ltd., Dereham, Norfolk, manager, 1963—. Managing director, Mid-Norfolk Farm Supply Co. Lay preacher, Methodist Church. Lecturer on lifeboat service and Norfolk humor. *Military service:* Royal Air Force, 1939-45; became flight sergeant; mentioned in dispatches. *Member:* Society of Authors.

WRITINGS: History of Dereham Methodist Circuit, Reeve, 1955; *The Vengeance of Private Pooley*, Heinemann, 1956; *Henry Blogg of Cromer: The Greatest of the Life-Boat Men*, Harrap, 1958; *S.O.S.: The Story of the Life-Boat Service*, Cassell, 1961. Contributor of articles to papers and journals.

WORK IN PROGRESS: Great Life-Boat Rescues.

SIDELIGHTS: Jolly is a former football player and has cycled through Europe.

* * *

JOLY, Cyril Bencraft 1918-

PERSONAL: Born September 9, 1918, in Mengtzu, South China; son of Cecil Henry Bencraft (a China customs agent) and Gladys Edith May (Bradgate) Joly; married Joan Evelyn Turbett, October 10, 1939; children: Vivien Oenone, David Nicholas, Peter William. *Education:* Attended Clifton College, and Royal Military Academy, Sandhurst, England. *Politics:* Conservative. *Religion:* Church of England. *Home:* Tregatillian, St. Columb, Cornwall, England.

CAREER: British Army, career service, 1939-61; became lieutenant colonel; received Military Cross and bar. Company director of Caravan Park, Cornwall, England, and several commercial firms.

WRITINGS: Take These Men, Constable, 1955.

WORK IN PROGRESS: The New Pattern of War.

* * *

JONES, A(rthur) Morris 1899-

PERSONAL: Born June 4, 1899, in London, England; son of William David (a priest, Church of England) and Bernetta Scoones (Cullum) Jones; married Nora Margaret Hill (an editor), July 25, 1952. *Education:* Keble College, Oxford, B.A., 1921, M.A.; Wells Theological College, student, 1921-22; London Day Training College, Dip.Ed., 1929.

CAREER: Priest, Church of England. Assistant priest in Ashford, Kent, England, 1922-24, and in Maidstone, Kent, England, 1924-29; St. Mark's College, Mapanza, Northern Rhodesia, warden, 1929-50; School of Oriental and African Studies, University of London, London, England, lecturer in African music, 1951—. Member of advisory committee of Horniman Museum. *Military service:* British Army, 1917-19. *Member:* Royal Anthropological Institute, International African Institute, International Folk Music Society, Society for Ethnomusicology, African Music Society (Johannesburg). *Awards, honors:* D.Litt. from Oxford University, 1960.

WRITINGS: A Book of Saints, Longmans, Green, 1937, children's edition, 1944; *African Music*, Rhodes-Livingstone, 1943, 4th edition, 1958; *The Music Makers-Suggestions on Music Teaching for African Teachers*, Longmans, Green, 1943, 2nd edition, 1948; *A Simple Practical Grammar*, Books 1-2, Longmans, Green, 1944; (with G. I. Fiennes) *Songs for Fun: Twenty-nine Part Songs for African Schools*, Longmans, Green, 1945; (with Fiennes) *Writing and Writing Patterns* (overseas edition), University of London Press, 1951; (with L. Kombe) *The Icila Dance*, African Music Society, 1952; *Road Safety*, Longmans, Green, 1954, Southern Rhodesia edition, 1956; *Studies in African Music*, two volumes, Oxford University Press, 1959; *Africa and Indonesia: The Evidence of the Xylophone and Other Musical and Cultural Factors*, E. J. Brill, 1964; (editor with David G. Temple) *Africa Praise: Hymns and Prayers for Schools*, Lutterworth, 1968. Contributor to *Encyclopaedia Britannica* and *Collier's Encyclopedia*. Contributor of about twenty articles to *African Studies*, *Presence Africaine*, *Ethnomusicology*, and other journals.

WORK IN PROGRESS: Pursuing additional evidence of Indonesian influence in Africa; writing on African music.

* * *

JONES, Archie N(eff) 1900-

PERSONAL: Born September 20, 1900, in Atlantic, Iowa; son of Archie Israel (a minister) and Edith Lorraine (Neff) Jones; married Rosalie Corrine Cartier, January 1, 1932; children: Catherine (Mrs. John B. Longenecker), Elizabeth (Mrs. Allen Ray Moers), Archie Alan. *Education:* University of Nebraska, Diploma in Music, 1925; University of Minnesota, B.S., 1929, M.A., 1931.

CAREER: Marshall (Minn.) public schools, supervisor of music, 1924-27; State Teachers College (now University of Wisconsin—La Crosse), La Crosse, Wis., director of music, 1927-28; University of Minnesota, Minneapolis, head of department of music education, 1928-35; University of Idaho, Moscow, director of music, 1935-40; University of Texas, Austin, professor of music education, 1940-59; University of Missouri, Kansas City Campus, dean of Conservatory of Music, beginning 1959. Visiting professor at University of Southern California, Michigan State University, University of Montana, and other universities and colleges in the West. Concert singer for nine seasons; composer of choral works; conductor of music festivals and choruses or judge of music contests in thirty-six states. President, Sinfonia Foundation, 1960-64; chairman of National Music Council-Department of Defense Overseas Tours Committee, beginning 1961.

MEMBER: Music Educators National Conference (life member; former president of Southwestern division), American Choral Directors Association (president, 1958-60), International Association of Concert Managers (president, 1958-61), Phi Mu Alpha (national president, 1950-60). *Awards, honors:* Mus.D., MacPhail College, 1940; Man of Music award, Phi Mu Alpha, 1964; citation of merit, Mu Phi Epsilon, 1964.

WRITINGS: (With Floyd Barnard) *Introduction to Musical Knowledge*, Paul A. Schmitt, 1935; (with R. Walls and M. Smith) *Pronouncing Guide to French, German, Italian, and Spanish*, Carl Fischer, 1948; *Techniques in Choral Conducting*, Carl Fischer, 1949; *Jones Music Recognition Tests*, Carl Fischer, 1949; (with L. Rhea and R. Rhea) *First Steps to Choral Music*, Bourne, 1955; (editor) *Music Education in Action*, Allyn & Bacon, 1960. Composer of 19 published works for mixed chorus. Contributor of more than one hundred articles to magazines.

* * *

JONES, Charles 1910-

PERSONAL: Born February 6, 1910, in Merthyr Tydfil, Glamorganshire, Wales; son of Rhys (a coal miner) and

Margaret May Jones; married Delia Griffin; children: Delia. *Education:* Attended school in Wales. *Religion:* Agnostic. *Home:* 6 West Grove, Merthyr Tydfil, Glamorganshire, South Wales.

CAREER: Writer; former director of three companies. *Military service:* Royal Marines, 1940-43. *Member:* Recluse Club.

WRITINGS: A Dose of Salts (200 aphorisms), Rock & Fountain Press, 1957; *Come Another Washing Day*, H. G. Walters, 1959; *Chief Petty Officer Kosco Ross*, H. G. Walters, 1959; *Land of Song* (verse), Rock & Fountain Press, 1960; *Sand in My Shoes*, Herald of Wales (Swansea), 1960; *Defeat*, Aryan Path, 1961; *The Challenger* (poems), H. G. Walters, 1963. Also author of *The Jingle* (long poem), Rock & Fountain Press. Short stories published in *Adelphi, Lilliput, Wales, Time and Tide, John O'London's*. Writer of radio and television scripts.

WORK IN PROGRESS: A collection of short stories, to be published by Rock & Fountain Press; a modern novel, *The Field of Glass*; a television play, based on the life of Victorian eccentric Joseph Leycester Lyne, "alias Brother Joseph, a somewhat mad and spiritually twisted Englishman."

SIDELIGHTS: Jones told *CA:* "I take any job that comes along; by doing so I retain my individuality, with no fears of becoming another hack writer. To me writing is my whole life, what I intend to say means so much that much of my work is outspoken to the point of brutality."

He adds: "Throughout the U.K. even in this so-called enlightened age, it is the autocratic belief of the academicians that unless a person has been to a Public School or University, then he or she has no right whatsoever to even contemplate the composition of poetry. And such is their power, that ninety-nine times out of a hundred they succeed in nullifying all one's efforts at recognition. But I happen to be the one man who has proved too tough and resilient for their ruthless dictatorship."

BIOGRAPHICAL/CRITICAL SOURCES: Liverpool Post, August 8, 1960; *Sunday Times* (London), September 15, 1963; *Times* (London), October 5, 1963; *South Wales Echo*, September, 1963, November, 1963.

*   *   *

JONES, Felix Edward Aylmer 1889-
(Felix Aylmer)

PERSONAL: Born February 21, 1889, in Corsham, Wiltshire, England; son of Thomas Edward Aylmer (a lieutenant colonel of Royal Engineers) and Lilian (Cookworthy) Jones; married Cecily Byrne; children: Ian (deceased), Jennifer, David (deceased). *Education:* Exeter College, Oxford, B.A., 1911. *Home:* 6 Painshill House, Cobham, Surrey, England.

CAREER: Actor on stage and in films. *Military service:* Royal Navy Volunteer Reserve, 1914-18. *Member:* British Actors' Equity Association (president), Royal Academy of Dramatic Art (vice-president), Garrick Club, Beefsteak Club, Green Room Club. *Awards, honors:* Officer of Order of the British Empires, 1950; Knighted, 1965.

WRITINGS—Under pseudonym Felix Aylmer: *Dickens Incognito*, Hart-Davis, 1959; *The Drood Case*, Hart-Davis, 1964, Barnes & Noble, 1965.

WORK IN PROGRESS: Shakespeare and Ann Lucy.

JONES, Robert Epes 1908-

PERSONAL: Born January 4, 1908, in Blackstone, Va.; son of Robert Edward (a merchant) and Isie (Epes) Jones; married Lucile Cox, December 20, 1969. *Education:* Randolph-Macon College, B.A., 1930; University of Virginia, M.A., 1931, graduate study, 1931-32; Johns Hopkins University, Ph.D., 1934; American Academy in Rome, postdoctoral study, 1949. *Politics:* Democrat. *Religion:* Methodist. *Home:* 504 Caroline St., Ashland, Va. 23005. *Office:* Randolph-Macon College, Ashland, Va. 23005.

CAREER: Johns Hopkins University, Baltimore, Md., assistant in Latin, 1934-36; Randolph-Macon College, Ashland, Va., assistant professor, 1936-38; University of Alabama, Tuscaloosa, assistant professor, 1938-46, associate professor, 1946-49, professor of classical languages, 1949-50; Randolph-Macon College, professor of Latin, 1950-65, professor of classics, 1965—, chairman, area of arts and letters, 1970—. Treasurer of Hanover County Chapter, American Red Cross, 1952-55. *Military service:* U.S. Army Air Forces, 1943-46; became first lieutenant. *Member:* American Philological Association, Archaeological Institute of America (president of Richmond branch, 1959-60), American Classical League, Classical Association of Middle West and South, Classical Association of Virginia (vice-president, 1958-60; president, 1960-62).

WRITINGS: (Editor and translator, with Bernerd Clarke Weber) *Letters of Ogier Ghislain de Busbecq to the Holy Roman Emperor Maximilian II*, Bookman Associates, 1961. Contributor of articles to professional periodicals.

*   *   *

JONES, Ruby Aileen Hiday 1908-

PERSONAL: Born October 29, 1908, in Fortville, Ind.; daughter of James W. (a blacksmith and gasoline service station operator) and Ora C. (James) Hiday; married Harry Paul Jones (a farmer), September 26, 1934; children: James, David, Jon. *Education:* Attended Butler University, 1928-29, and University of Indiana Extension, 1929-30; Earlham College, A.B., 1930; Ball State University, graduate study, 1960. *Politics:* Republican. *Religion:* Methodist. *Home:* Maplestone Farm, R.R. 1, Daleville, Ind. 47334. *Agent:* Kenneth Hall, 1200 East Fifth St., Box 2499, Anderson, Ind. 46012.

CAREER: McCordsville High School, McCordsville, Ind., English and history teacher, 1930-34; Madison Heights Senior High School, Anderson, Ind., English and journalism teacher, 1959—. *Awards, honors:* Poets of Indiana award, 1963.

WRITINGS: The Searching Wind, Warner Press, 1964. Contributor to *National Poetry Anthology for Teachers, College Professors and Librarians*, 1961, 1963, 1964, 1965, 1966, to *Guideposts Anthology*, and *When Youth Sings* (hymnal). Author of *Notes of a Journey* (European safari), published serially, 1965-66. Columnist, "As I See It," for *Middletown News*, Middletown, Ind., 1958—; columnist, *Alexandria* (Ind.) *Times Tribune*, 1964; guest columnist, *Anderson* (Ind.) *Bull*. Contributor to professional and religious journals, including *Hoosier Schoolmaster* and *English Journal*.

WORK IN PROGRESS: A second book, *Brief Candle*; *Westward, Ho!*, a travelogue of the journey taken on the Vanishing Iron Horse.

JONES, W(alter) Paul 1891-

PERSONAL: Born August 22, 1891, in Larwill, Ind.; son of Oliver Perry (a real estate agent) and Elsie Eliza (Barber) Jones; married Mildred Victoria Demaree, August 30, 1916; children: Barbara (Mrs. Robert Paul Radebaugh), Betty (Mrs. Claude E. McAlpin). *Education:* Wabash College, A.B., 1913; Cornell University, Ph.D., 1925. *Politics:* Registered Republican. *Religion:* Presbyterian. *Home:* 211 Beach Ave., Apartment 3, Ames, Iowa 50012.

CAREER: Instructor for Telluride Association, Ithaca, N.Y., 1913-17, Vincennes University, Vincennes, Ind., 1917-18, and at Potter School for Boys, San Francisco, 1918-20; Cornell University, Ithaca, N.Y., instructor in English, 1920-26; University of Louisville, Speed Scientific School, Louisville, Ky., associate professor of English, 1926-31; Iowa State University, Ames, professor of English, 1932-65. *Military service:* U.S. Army, Infantry, 1917. *Member:* National Council of Teachers of English, American Association of University Professors, Phi Beta Kappa.

WRITINGS: (Editor with Dugald Caleb Jackson) *The Profession of Engineering* (essays), Wiley, 1929; (editor with Jackson) *This Scientific Age: Essays in Modern Thought and Achievement*, Wiley, 1930; (editor and author with Pearl Hogrefe) *Interpreting Experience: Narrative and Descriptive Types for College Use*, Ginn, 1934; (editor with Keith Huntress and Fred W. Lorch) *Of Time and Truth*, Dryden Press, 1941; *Writing Scientific Papers and Reports* (textbook), W. C. Brown, 1945, 5th edition, 1965; (editor) *Essays on Thinking and Writing*, W. C. Brown, 1949, 3rd edition (with Quentin Johnson), published as *Essays on Thinking and Writing in Science, Engineering, and Business*, 1963; (editor with Huntress and Lorch) *Ideas and Backgrounds*, American Book Co., 1958, 2nd edition, 1964; (editor with Huntress and Lorch) *Design for Reading*, American Book Co., 1964, 2nd edition, 1969. Contributor of articles to professional periodicals, including *English Journal* and *Iowa English Yearbook*.

AVOCATIONAL INTERESTS: Woodworking; weaving, including the design and construction of looms.

* * *

JOOS, Martin (George) 1907-

PERSONAL: Surname rhymes with "gross"; born May 11, 1907, near Fountain City, Wis.; son of Alfred and Charlotte (Rather) Joos; married Jennie Mae Austin, September 8, 1938; children: Sharon Kay. *Education:* University of Wisconsin, M.A., 1935, Ph.D., 1938. *Home:* 5501 Raymond Rd., Madison, Wis. 53711.

CAREER: Western Electric Co., Hawthorne, Ill., engineer, 1928-29; University of Toronto, Toronto, Ontario, lecturer in German, 1938-42; U.S. War Department, Washington, D.C., classified work, 1942-46; University of Wisconsin, Madison, associate professor, 1946-49, professor of German and linguistics, 1949-67; University of Toronto, director of Centre for Linguistic Studies, 1967-70, professor of linguistics, 1970-72. Visiting director, Center for Applied Linguistics, Washington, D.C., 1964-65. Visiting professor at University of Alberta, 1958, Academy of Sciences, Belgrade, Yugoslavia, 1958-59, and at numerous linguistic institutes. *Member:* Linguistic Society of America (vice-president, 1952), Canadian Linguistic Association, Phi Eta Sigma, Kappa Eta Kappa, Tau Beta Pi. *Awards, honors:* Citation with medal for exceptional civilian service, U.S. War Department, 1946.

WRITINGS: (With A. R. Hohlfeld and W. F. Twaddell) *Wortindex zu Goethes Faust*, University of Wisconsin, 1940; *Acoustic Phonetics*, Linguistic Society of America, 1948; (with F. R. Whitesell) *Middle High German Courtly Reader*, University of Wisconsin Press, 1951, 3rd edition, 1963; (editor) *Readings in Linguistics*, American Council of Learned Societies, 1957, 4th edition, University of Chicago Press, 1966; *The Five Clocks*, Indiana University Press, 1962; *The English Verb*, University of Wisconsin Press, 1964.

Editor of language books for American Council of Learned Societies, 1953-54. Contributor of linguistic articles and reviews to *Harvard Educational Review*, *Language*, and other professional journals.

WORK IN PROGRESS: A history of the Linguistic Society of America.

SIDELIGHTS: Joos has been described as precocious, lazy, and inventive. He does not join either the traditions or the new fads, but observes them all with fascination. He left the electrical engineering communications field because of insufficient stimulation—after election to an engineering honor society and with two patents in communications engineering.

Joos speaks Spanish, Italian, French, German, Norwegian, and Serbian and reads seven additional languages. He considers his most important book *The Five Clocks*, a technical treatise written in variegated literary forms, dealing with the kinds of English we use for various purposes, from intimate murmuring to literature.

* * *

JORDAN, Gerald Ray 1896-1964

PERSONAL: Born November 11, 1896, in Kinston, N.C.; son of Charles Marion and Sophia (Faulkner) Jordan; married Caroline Moody, March 7, 1922; children: Gerald Ray, Jr., Terrell Franklin. *Education:* Duke University, A.M. (magna cum laude), 1917, D.D., 1935; Emory University, B.D. (summa cum laude), 1920; Yale University, A.M., 1921; postgraduate study at Union Theological Seminary, New York, N.Y., and University of Chicago.

CAREER: Ordained to ministry of Methodist Episcopal Church, 1921. Pastor of churches in North Carolina at Black Mountain, 1921-23, Asheville, 1923-24, Greensboro, 1924-26, Charlotte, 1926-30, High Pointe, 1930-33, Winston-Salem, 1933-40, Charlotte, 1940-45; Emory University, School of Theology, Atlanta, Ga., professor of homiletics and chapel preacher, 1945-60, Charles Howard Candler Professor of Preaching, 1960-64. Honorary lecturer at other universities and theological schools. Trustee of High Point College; former trustee of Scarritt College for Christian Workers; representative of Methodist Episcopal Church to World Conference on Faith and Order and World Conference on Life and Work, 1937, and to various conferences in United States, 1938-60. *Member:* Association of Seminary Professors in Practical Fields, American Association of University Professors, Phi Beta Kappa, Omicron Delta Kappa, Kappa Alpha, Pi Gamma Mu, Theta Phi, Masons, Atlanta Athletic Club, East Lake Country Club. *Awards, honors:* Litt.D., Lincoln Memorial University, 1950.

WRITINGS: What Is Yours?, Revell, 1930; *The Intolerance of Christianity*, Revell, 1931; *Intimate Interests of Youth*, Cokesbury, 1931; *Courage That Propels*, Cokesbury, 1933; *Faith That Propels*, Cokesbury, 1934; *We Face*

Calvary—and Life!, Cokesbury, 1936; *Adventures in Radiant Living*, Round Table, 1938; *Why the Cross?*, Abingdon-Cokesbury, 1941; *Look at the Stars*, Abingdon, 1942; *We Believe: A Creed That Sings*, Abingdon, 1944; *The Supreme Possession*, Abingdon, 1945; *The Emerging Revival*, Abingdon, 1946; *The Hour Has Come*, Abingdon, 1948. *You Can Preach!*, Revell, 1951; *Beyond Despair*, Macmillan, 1955; *Prayer That Prevails*, Macmillan, 1958; *Religion That Is Eternal*, Macmillan, 1960; *Preaching during a Revolution*, Warner, 1962; *Christ, Communism, and the Clock*, Warner, 1963; *Life-Giving Words: Thoughts on the Prayer Jesus Gave Us*, Warner, 1964.

Contributor: W. P. King, editor, *After Pentecost, What?*, Cokesbury Press, 1931; B. C. Hall, editor, *The Spiritual Diary*, Jordan House, 1940; T. O. Nall, editor, *These Prophetic Voices*, Abingdon-Cokesbury, 1942; *A Minute of Prayer*, Blue Ribbon, 1943; G. C. Speer, editor, *Talks to Youth*, Abingdon-Cokesbury, 1949; G. Foote, *Communion Meditations*, Abingdon-Cokesbury, 1951; F. S. Mead, editor, *Pulpit in the South*, Revell, 1951; C. L. Wallis, editor, *The Funeral Encyclopedia*, Musson, 1953; C. L. Wallis, editor, *Worship Resources for the Christian Year*, Musson, 1954. Also contributor to "American Pulpit" series, published by Abingdon-Cokesbury, 1945.

Writer of television series, "Understanding Religion Today," for Emory University station, WAGA-TV. Contributor of more than 200 articles and 250 book reviews to religious periodicals. Editor, homiletics department, *Expositor*, 1931; literary editor, *Pulpit Digest*, 1941-45.

SIDELIGHTS: Jordan preached in many foreign countries and made six study trips to Middle East and Central Europe, 1933-61. These travels allowed him to interview political, religious, and military leaders in Middle and Near East, Europe, Central America, Canada, and Mexico. *Avocational interests:* Football, golf, other sports.

(Died November 15, 1964)

*   *   *

JUDD, Deane B(rewster) 1900-1972

PERSONAL: Born November 15, 1900, in South Hadley Falls, Mass.; son of Horace (a professor of mechanical engineering) and Etta (Gerry) Judd; married Elizabeth Melamed, August 7, 1926; children: Dean Burritt, Audrey Lois (Mrs. Arthur Vaughan, Jr.). *Education:* Ohio State University, B.A., 1922, M.A., 1923; Cornell University, Ph.D., 1926. *Politics:* Democrat. *Religion:* Unitarian Universalist. *Home:* 3115 Leland St., Chevy Chase, Md.

CAREER: National Bureau of Standards, Washington, D.C., optics physicist specializing in color measurement, 1927-70, guest worker, 1970-72. Munsell Color Foundation, president, 1943-72. Instituto de Optica, Madrid, Spain, professor invitado, 1956-57; lecturer on color in Delft, 1948, Madrid, 1949, Stockholm, 1951, London, 1955, 1961, Berlin, 1957. *Member:* Optical Society of America (vice-president, 1951-53; president, 1953-55), American Society for Testing and Materials, Illuminating Engineering Society; Kenwood Golf and Country Club and Cosmos Club (both Washington, D.C.). *Awards, honors:* Society of Motion Picture Engravers Journal Award for paper, "Color Blindness and Anomalies of Vision," 1936; U.S. Department of Commerce Gold Medal for exceptional services, 1950; Godlove Award from Inter-Society Color Council, 1957; Frederick Ives Medal from Optical Society of America, 1958; Gold Medal from Illuminating Engineering Society,

1961; Samuel Wesley Stratton Award, National Bureau of Standards, 1966.

WRITINGS: Color in Business, Science, and Industry, Wiley, 1952, 2nd edition (with Gunter Wyszecki), 1963. Contributor of articles on color measurement, color blindness, and allied topics to professional journals and trade periodicals. Editor, *Journal of Optical Society of America*, 1961-63.

WORK IN PROGRESS: Research on uniform color scales.

SIDELIGHTS: Judd was competent in French, had reading knowledge of Spanish and German.

BIOGRAPHICAL/CRITICAL SOURCES: Journal of Optical Society of America, Volume XLIX (1959), 317.

(Died October 15, 1972)

*   *   *

JUTIKKALA, Eino Kaarlo Ilmari 1907-

PERSONAL: Born October 24, 1907, in Saekmaeki, Finland; son of Kaarle Fredrik and Hilma Maria (Hagelberg) Rinne. *Education:* University of Helsinki, M.A., 1928, Ph.D., 1932. *Home:* Merikatu 3B, Helsinki, Finland. *Office:* University of Helsinki, Helsinki, Finland.

CAREER: University of Helsinki, Helsinki, Finland, docent 1933-47, assistant professor, 1947-50, professor of economic history, 1950-54, professor of Finnish history, 1954—, dean of faculty of humanities, 1966-69, academician, 1972. Foundation for Culture in Sweden and Finland, government-appointed member of directors, 1960-71; Committee for the History of the Town of Helsinki, secretary, 1946-54, chairman, 1964; Comite International des Sciences Historiques, Finnish section chairman, 1955-67; chairman, State Commission for Humanities, 1967-70; chairman, Scandinavian Society for Economic History, 1972—. *Member:* Finnish Historical Society (chairman, 1947), Finnish Academy of Science and Letters (chairman, 1968-70), Union Internationale pour l'Etude Scientifique de la Population, Societas Scientiarum Fennica. *Awards, honors:* Honorary doctor of political faculty, University of Helsinki, 1956, Commercial University of Helsinki, 1966, University of Stockholm, 1966.

WRITINGS: Laentisen Suomen kartanolaitos Ruotsin vallan viimeisenae aikana (title means "Manorial Economy in Finland in the Eighteenth Century"), two volumes, [Helsinki], 1932; *Saeksmaen Pitaejaen Historia*, Jyvae Skylae, 1934; *Suomen postilaitoksen historia, I: Ruotsin vallan aika* (title means "The History of Postal Service in Finland, I: The Swedish Period"), 1938; *Befolknings foerhaallandena i Tavastland fran freden i Nystad till tabellverkets uppkomst, 1721-49* (title means "Population Movement in Finland, 1721-49"), Central Statistical Office, Finland, 1939; *Vaaksyn Kartanon Historia* (title means "The History of the Manor of Vaeksy"), [Helsinki], 1939; *Suomen talonpojan historia* (title means "The History of Finnish Farmers"), Soederstroem, 1942, 2nd edition, Finnish Literary Society, 1958; *Die Bevoelkerung Finnlands in den Jahren 1721-49*, Annales Academiae Scientiarum Fennicae, 1945; *Puoli Nuosistataa Elintarviketeollisuutta* (title means "Finland's Food Industries Through Half a Century"), [Helsinki], 1945; *Atlas of Finnish History*, Soederstroem, 1949, 2nd edition, 1959; *Uudenajan taloushistoria* (title means "Economic History of the Modern Age"), Soederstroem, 1953, 2nd edition, 1965; *Turun kaupungin historia, 1856-1917* (title means "The History of the Town of Turku,

1856-1917"), Turku Municipality, 1957; (with Kauko Pirinen) *A History of Finland*, translation by Paul Sjoeblom, Praeger, 1962, revised edition, 1973; *Saetyvaltiopaeivien valitstjakunta, vaalit ja koostumus* (title means "The Parliamentary Elections in Finland 1863-1906"), 1692; *Tomtbesittningen och kampen om regulariteten i Sverige-Finlands staeder* (title means "Possession of House Plots and the Struggle of Regular Plans in the Towns of Sweden-Finland"), Societas Scientiarum ennica, 1963; *Pohjoismaisen yhteiskunnan historiallisia juuria* (title means "The Historical Roots of Scandinavin Society"), Soederstroem, 1965; (compiler with other) *Itseneisen Suomen talousihtorsiaa, 1919-1950*, Soederstroem, 1967; *Suomen talousja sosiaalihistorian kehityslinjoja*, Soederstroem, 1968.

Editor of a social history of Finland, four volumes published in Finnish, 1933-36, and, with G. Nikander, of a three-volume series on great estates in Finland, published in Finnish and Swedish, 1938-45. Finnish editor, *Scandinavian Economic History Review*, 1953—; editor, *Historiallinen Aikakauskirja*, 1970—. Contributor to *Handbook in Finnish History* and to various periodicals.

BIOGRAPHICAL/CRITICAL SOURCES: Naekoekulmia menneisyyteen, Soederstroem, 1967.

* * *

KABRAJI, Fredoon 1897-

PERSONAL: Both names accented on first syllable; born February 10, 1897, in Nasik, Bombay State, India; son of Jehangier K.N. (with Indian Civil Service) and Puttibai D. (Wadia) Kabraji; married Eleanor Margaret Wilkinson, February 6, 1926; children: Robin Christopher, Cynthia (Mrs. Idries Shah), David Michael. *Education:* Attended Leeds University and London University during the twenties. *Politics:* "Inclined to be Left without being doctrinaire." *Religion:* Zoroastrian. *Home:* 48 Huntington Rd., East Finchley, London N2 9DU, England.

CAREER: At one time was free-lance journalist in London, England, later a staff member on English-language newspapers in India; did publicity and advertising in India, 1932-35; resumed free-lance journalism in London, 1935-45; has held various jobs in England, including snow-sweeping and game beating.

WRITINGS: A Minor Georgian's Swan Song (poems 1921-44), Fortune Press, 1945; (editor) *This Strange Adventure* (anthology of Indian poetry in English), New India Publications, 1947; *The Cold Flame* (poems 1922-53), Fortune Press, 1956. Contributor of poems, reviews, and features to *English Review, Spectator, Time and Tide, London Mercury, Atlantic, New Statesman, Times of India, Bookman, Guardian, Political Quarterly, Christian Science Monitor, Unity*, and other publications.

WORK IN PROGRESS: A book of poems with commentary for Enitharmon Press.

SIDELIGHTS: Kabraji told *CA* that two of his unpublished works, an autobiography and an autobiographical novel, were highly praised by L.P. Hartley, in whom, "while he was alive, I had an untiring friend and champion." He also cited a voluntary tribute from the novelist Celia Fremlin for his unpublished work.

* * *

KACZER, Illes 1887-

PERSONAL: Born October 10, 1887, in Szatmarnemeti, Hungary; son of Joseph and Fanny (Roth) Kaczer; married Dina Zelinger (divorced); married Ara Ehrenthal, 1948; children: Anna (Mrs. Thomas Zador), Jan, Peter. *Education:* Studied in Szatmarnemeti and Nagyverad, Hungary, 1893-1906. *Religion:* Jewish. *Home:* 11, Ido St., Ramat-Chen, Israel.

CAREER: Editor of daily newspapers in Szatmarnemeti, Hungary, 1907-11, Budapest, Hungary, 1911-19, Vienna, Austria, 1919-20, Cluj-Kolozsvar, Rumania, 1920-23, Vienna, 1923-24, Bratislava, Czechoslovakia, 1924-27; Keystone View Co., Berlin, Germany, editor-in-chief of *Illustrated Features*, 1927-33; *Magyar Ujasag*, Bratislava-Prague, Czechoslovakia, editor, 1933-38; *Central-European Observer* and other papers, London, England, collaborator, 1939-46; *Uj Kelet*, Tel Aviv, Israel, London editor, 1948-57; permanent collaborator of *Uj Kelet* and other papers in Israel and abroad, 1958—. *Member:* World Federation of Jews of Hungarian Descent (honorary president), Hitachdut Oley Hungaria (Israel; honorary president), Authors Society, P.E.N. (English center), Max Nordau Literary Society (Tel-Aviv; chairman). *Awards, honors:* Nordau Prize, 1960.

WRITINGS—Novels: *Khafrit*, Biro, 1915; *A fekete kakas*, Grill, 1917; *Ezustfuvola*, Kultura, 1918; *Zsuzsanna es a venek*, Becsi Kiado, 1921; *Az alomtelepes*, Fisher, 1922, 2nd edition, Berenike Kiado, 1967; *Der Traumsiedler*, Menora, 1923; *Sarkanyolo*, 1925; *Die Fahrt der Drei nach Uxenbux* (juvenile), Hagenmeyer, 1929; *Ikongo*, Masaryk Kiado, 1936; *Fear Not, My Servant Jacob*, translation by Lawrence Wolfe, Methuen, 1947; *The Siege of Jericho*, translation by Wolfe, Methuen, 1949; *The Siege* (contains *Fear Not, My Servant Jacob* and *The Siege of Jericho*), translation by Wolfe, Dial, 1953; *Harom a csillag*, Uj Kelet, 1955; *Kossuth Lajos Szidaja*, Uj Kelet, 1956; *Al tira avdi Takov*, Massada, 1969.

Story collections: *A kiraly aludni akar*, Biro, 1916; *A vakember tukre*, Lapkiado, 1923; *Jancsi*, Brasso, 1925; *Dr. Hulla*, Renaissance, 1927; *Godolyet, godolyet*, Graficka, 1937; *Kotojasbol komadar*, Graficka, 1937.

Plays: *A fust* (comedy in verse), Szabadsajto, 1909; *Megjott a Messias*, Lapkiado, 1923; *Golem ember akar Lenni*, Kadima, 1923; "Sziami ikrek" (comedy), 1927.

WORK IN PROGRESS: Three Are the Stars, third novel in Jewish saga including *Fear Not* and *The Siege*; *Ramatcheni Remese*; *The Dreamseller*; *Ranofru*, a tale for everybody.

SIDELIGHTS: Ikongo has been published in eleven languages, *Fear Not My Servant Jacob* published in England, Israel, and Argentina, and *The Siege of Jericho* in England, Israel, and the United States. *Avocational interests:* Pottery, ceramics, gardening.

* * *

KALIJARVI, Thorsten V(alentine) 1897-

PERSONAL: Surname is pronounced Call-i-*jar*-vi; born December 22, 1897, in Gardner, Mass.; son of Gustaf (a pattern maker) and Ida Christina (Kuniholm) Kalijarvi; married Dorothy Corbett Knight, September 4, 1926; children: June (Mrs. Hugh Conway). *Education:* University, A.B., 1920, A.M., 1923; graduate study at Harvard University, 1920-24, Geneva School of International Studies, 1929; University of Berlin, A.L.M., Ph.D., 1936. *Home:* 1552 33rd St., N.W., Washington, D.C., and Seascape, Popponesset Beach, Mass.

CAREER: University of New Hampshire Durham, 1923-

45, began as instructor, professor of government, 1939-45; New Hampshire State Planning and Development Commission, Concord, executive director, 1942-47; Library of Congress, Legislative Reference Service, Washington, D.C., research counsel in international relations, 1947-50, senior specialist for foreign affairs, 1950-52; U.S. Department of State, Washington, D.C., deputy assistant secretary of state for economic affairs, 1953-57, assistant secretary, and acting deputy under secretary of state for economic affairs, 1957, U.S. Ambassador to El Salvador, 1957-61; Pennsylvania State University, University Park, professor of international and public affairs, 1961-64; Cape Cod Community College, Hyannis, Mass., dean, 1964-69. Public panel member, War Labor Board, 1940-45; consultant to and member of staff of U.S. Senate Committee on Foreign Relations, 1947-54. Lecturer on history and government at American University, 1947-53, and Johns Hopkins University, 1952-53.

MEMBER: American Association for the Advancement of Science (fellow), American Society of International Law, National Academy of Economics and Political Science, American Political Science Association, American Arbitration Association, Diplomatic and Consular Officers, Retired (DACOR), Phi Kappa Phi, Pi Gamma Mu, Cosmos Club (Washington, D.C.).

WRITINGS: Der Memel Statut, Ebering (Berlin), 1937, translation published as *The Memel Statute*, R. Hale, 1937; (with W. C. Chamberlin) *Government of New Hampshire*, University of New Hampshire Press, 1939; *Town Management in New England*, University of New Hampshire, 1940; (editor and co-author) *Modern World Politics*, Crowell, 1942, 3rd edition, 1953; *Soviet Power and Policy*, Crowell, 1952; (with Francis Orlando Wilcox) *Recent American Foreign Policy*, Appleton, 1952; *Central America*, Van Nostrand, 1963.

Contributor: Roy Victor Peel and Joseph S. Roucek, editors, *Introduction to Politics*, Crowell, 1941; Roucek, editor, *Twentieth Century Political Thought*, Philosophical Library, 1946; Francis James Brown and Roucek, editors, *One America*, Prentice-Hall, 1946; Roucek, editor, *Central-Eastern Europe*, Prentice-Hall, 1946; Roucek, editor, *Contemporary Europe*, Van Nostrand, 1947; F. Cross, editor, *European Ideologies*, Philosophical Library, 1948. Contributor to *Vital Speeches* and law and government journals.

SIDELIGHTS: Kalijarvi is competent in French, Spanish, German, Swedish, Danish, and Norwegian.

* * *

KAPPEL, Philip 1901-

PERSONAL: Born February 10, 1901, in Hartford, Conn.; son of Morris and Anna (Superior) Kappel; married Theresa M. Pentz, April 10, 1935 (died, 1962). *Education:* Pratt Institute, graduate, 1924; also studied art abroad. *Home address:* R.F.D. 3, Roxbury, Conn.

CAREER: Artist and illustrator. Prints and etchings included in permanent collections of Bibliotheque Nationale, Paris, and in Metropolitan Museum of Art, Carnegie Art Institute, Corcoran Gallery, National Gallery of Art, Congressional Library, and in other museums and collections throughout the country; former roving artist for U.S. steamship lines, doing series of prints on deep-water subjects; illustrator of more than thirty books by other writers. Member of Connecticut Commission on the Arts, 1966—.

MEMBER: National Academy of Design, (associate member), Society of American Etchers, Society of American Graphic Artists, Connecticut Academy of Fine Arts, Marblehead Art Association, Washington Art Association (Washington, Conn.; president, 1955—), Kent Art Association (vice-president), Salmagundi Club (New York). *Awards, honors:* Exhibition prizes, 1925—, include purchase prize in First Annual National Art Competition of Associated American Artists, New York, 1946, prize for best print in Salmagundi Club exhibition in New York, 1947, first prize, Meriden Art Association, 1955; awards by Hudson Valley Art Association, 1969-73; D.F.A., Trinity College, Hartford, Connecticut.

WRITINGS—Illustrations and text: *Boothbay Harbor, Maine*, privately published, 1924; *Louisiana Gallery*, Putnam, 1950; *Jamaica Gallery*, Little, Brown, 1961; *New England Gallery*, Little, Brown, 1966. Illustrator of other books. Writer and illustrator of travel booklets. Contributor to *Pictorial Review*, *Yachting*, *Rudder*, and other magazines.

* * *

KARLGREN, (Klas) Bernhard (Johannes) 1889-

PERSONAL: Born October 5, 1889, in Jonkoping, Sweden; son of Johannes (a high school teacher) and Ella (Hasselberg) Karlgren; married Elin Nilsson, 1916; children: Ella Karlgren Kohler. *Education:* University of Uppsala, Dr.Phil., 1915. *Home:* Mosebacketorg 6, Stockholm, Sweden. *Office:* Museum of Far Eastern Antiquities, Stockholm 100, Sweden.

CAREER: University of Uppsala, Uppsala, Sweden, assistant professor in Sinology, 1915-18; University of Gothenburg, Gothenburg, Sweden, professor of Far Eastern languages, 1919-1939; Museum of Far Eastern Antiquities, Stockholm, Sweden, director, 1939-59; University of Stockholm, Stockholm, Sweden, adjunct professor of Sinology, 1945-65. *Member:* Academy of History and Belles-Lettres (Stockholm; praeses, 1955-64), Academy of Sciences (Copenhagen), Academy of Sciences (Copenhagen), Academy of Sciences (Oslo), Royal Asiatic Society of Great Britain and Ireland (honorary member), British Academy (honorary member), Societe Asiatique (Paris; honorary member), Academie des Inscriptions (Paris; corresponding member), and other academies and learned societies in Sweden, Norway, Denmark, Finland, England, Germany, Holland, France, United States. *Awards, honors:* Grand Cross of the Northern Star Order.

WRITINGS: Folksaegner fraan Tveta ock Mo Haerader, [Stockholm], 1908; *Etudes sur la phonologie chinoise*, four parts, K. W. Appelberg, (Uppsala), 1915-26; *A Mandarin Phonetic Reader in the Pekinese Dialect*, P. A. Norstedt (Stockholm), 1918; *Ordet och pennan i Mittens Rike*, [Stockholm], 1918, translation published as *Sound and Symbol in Chinese*, Oxford University Press, 1923, revised Swedish edition, Wahlstroem & Widstrand, 1965; *Ostasien under nittonde arhundradet*, P. A. Norstedt, 1920; *Kinesiska noveller om mandariner, kurtisaner och andre skalmar*, Hugo Gebers Forlag, 1921; *Analytic Dictionary of Chinese and Sino-Japanese*, P. Geuthner (Paris), 1923, Paragon, 1966; *Asiens Kulturer*, [Copenhagen], 1923; *Philology and Ancient China*, Harvard University Press, 1926; *On the Authenticity and Nature of the Tso Chuan*, Elanders Boktryckeri Aktiebolag (Gothenburg), 1926, Paragon, 1968; *The Romanization of Chinese*, China Society (London), 1928; *Fraan Kinas tankevaerld*, P. A. Norstedt,

1929; *The Poetical Parts in Lao-tsi*, Elanders Boktryckeri Aktiebolag, 1932; *The Rimes in the Sung Section of the Shi King*, Elanders Boktryckeri Aktiebolag, 1935; *Japans vaeg och maal*, Kooperativa Foerlagets Bokfoerlag (Stockholm), 1940; *Fraan Kinas spraakvaerld*, Bonnier (Stockholm), 1946, translation by Karlgren and A. F. P. Hulsewe published as *The Chinese Language: An Essay on Its Nature and History*, Ronald, 1949; *Kinesisk Elementarbok*, Hugo Gebers Forlag, 1948; *A Catalogue of the Chinese Bronzes in the Alfred F. Pillsbury Collection*, University of Minnesota Press, 1952; *Easy Lessons in Chinese Writing*, Naturmetodens Spraak-institut (Stockholm), 1958; *Religion i Kina: Antiken*, Bonnier, 1964.

Studies published by the Museum of Far Eastern Antiquities, Stockholm: *Some Fecundity Symbols in Ancient China*, 1930; *The Early History of the Chou Li and Tso Chuan Texts*, 1931; *Shi King Researches*, 1932; *Word Families in Chinese*, 1933; *Early Chinese Mirror Inscriptions*, 1934; *Yin and Chou in Chinese Bronzes*, 1935; *New Studies on Chinese Bronzes*, 1937; *Grammata serica: Script and Phonetics in Chinese and Sino-Japanese*, 1940, Paragon, 1966; *Glosses on the Kuo Feng Odes*, 1942; (editor and translator) *The Book of Odes* (text of the *Shih Ching*), 1944; *Once Again the A and B Styles in Yin Ornamentation*, 1946; *Legends and Cults in Ancient China*, 1946; (translator) *The Book of Documents* (text of the *Shu Ching*), 1950; *Cognate Words in the Chinese Phonetic Series*, 1956; *Marginalia on Some Bronze Albums*, 1959; *Tones in Archaic Chinese*, 1960; *Compendium of Phonetics in Ancient and Archaic Chinese*, 1963; *Loan Characters in Pre-Han Texts*, five volumes, 1963-67; *Grammata serica recensa*, 1964; *Glosses on The Book of Odes*, 1964; *Index to Glosses on The Book of Odes and Glosses on the Book of Documents*, 1964; *Chinese Agraffes in Two Swedish Collections*, 1966; *Glosses on the Tso Chuan*, 1969; (with Jan Wirgin) *Chinese Bronzes: The Natanael Wessen Collection*, 1969. Also author of *Chung-kuo yin yun hsueh yen chiu*, 1940. Voluminous contributor to the *Bulletin* of the Museum of Far Eastern Antiquities, and to *T'oung Pao*. Translator into Swedish, with K. Michaeelsson, of *Mr. Britling Sees It Through*, by H. G. Wells, published in Stockholm in 1917.

BIOGRAPHICAL/CRITICAL SOURCES: Soeren Egerod and Else Glabn, *Sinological Studies Dedicated to Bernhard Karlgren on His 70th Birthday*, Munksgaard, 1960.

* * *

KARLSSON, Elis (Viktor) 1905-

PERSONAL: Born February 24, 1905, in Vardo, Aland, Finland; son of Leander Viktor (a master mariner) and Maria (Vennstrom) Karlsson; married Alina Cameron MacFadyen, September 29, 1939; children: Elva Mairi, Catherine Cecilie, Alison Svea, Margaret Gerda. *Education:* Attended local schools in Vardo, Finland, until thirteen; School of Navigation, Mariehamn, Aland, Finland, master, 1933. *Home:* Admiral's Cabin, P.O. Norton, Southern Rhodesia.

CAREER: Served as second mate, later first mate, on Finnish ships, 1929-36; moved to Southern Rhodesia and became boat-builder near Lake McIlwaine, beginning 1948. *Military service:* British Army, Royal Artillery, bombardier, 1939-45. *Member:* Association Amicale Internationale des Capitaines au Long Cours Cap-Horniers (Aland Island section).

WRITINGS: Abandon Ship!, W. Blackwood, 1959; *Mother Sea* (alternate Book Society choice in England), Oxford University Press, 1964; *Pully-Haul: The Story of a Voyage*, Oxford University Press, 1966; (self-illustrated) *Cruising off Mozambique*, Oxford University Press, 1969.

WORK IN PROGRESS: A book, *A Ship, Her Crew, and the Sea*.

* * *

KARVE, Irawati (Karmarkar) 1905-1970

PERSONAL: Born December 15, 1905, in Myingyan, Burma; daughter of Ganesh Hari (an engineer) and Bhagirathi (Limaye) Karmarkar; married Dinakar D. Karve (an administrator), May 8, 1926; children: Mrs. Jai Nimbkar, Anand, Mrs. Gauri Deshpande. *Education:* Fergusson College, Poona, India, B.A., 1926; University of Bombay, M.A., 1928; University of Berlin, Ph.D., 1930. *Religion:* Hindu. *Home:* 473/17B Gultekdi, Poona 9, India.

CAREER: Deccan College, Poona, India, member of department of anthropology and sociology, beginning 1939.

WRITINGS: Kinship Organization in India, Deccan College, 1953, 3rd edition, Asia Publishing, 1968; *The Bhils of West Khendesh*, Anthropological Society of Bombay, 1960; *Hindu Society*, Deccan College, 1961, 2nd edition, Deshmukh Prakashan, 1968; (with Yashwant Bhaskar Damle) *Group Relations in Village Community*, Deccan College, 1963; (with Jayant Sadahiv Ranadive) *The Social Dynamics of a Growing Town and its Surrounding Area*, Deccan College, 1965; *Maharastra: Land and its People*, Directorate of Government Printing, 1968; (with Jai Nimbkar) *A Survey of the People Displaced Through the Koyna Dam, July 1965 to January 1967*, Deccan College, 1969; *The Role of Weekly Markets in the Tribal, Rural and Urban Setting*, Deccan College, 1970. Also author of *Mahabharata Studies*, 1969.

Writings in Marathi, all published by Deshmukh and Co., Poona, unless otherwise noted: *Paripurti*, 1949, 5th edition, 1965; *Marathi Lokanchi Sanskriti*, 1951, 2nd edition, 1962; *Bhovara*, 1960; *Hindunchi Samajarachana*, Nagpur University, 1964; *Yuganta*, 1967.

WORK IN PROGRESS: Research on blood groups in India.

SIDELIGHTS: Karve spoke English and German.

(Died August 11, 1970)

* * *

KASTER, Joseph 1912-19(?)

PERSONAL: Born November 24, 1912, in Brockton, Mass; son of Barnet and Esther (Rosenbloom) Kaster; married Zipporah Sommer (a teacher), October 19, 1946; children: Baruch Shlomo, Miriam Judith. *Education:* Brooklyn College (now Brooklyn College of the City University of New York), B.A., 1934; Jewish Theological Seminary of America, B.H.L., 1938; Dropsie College, Ph.D., 1954. *Residence:* Brooklyn, N.Y. *Office:* New School for Social Research, 66 West 12th St., New York, N.Y. 10011.

CAREER: New School for Social Research, New York, N.Y., lecturer in classics and anthropology, beginning, 1960; New York University, New York, N.Y., lecturer in anthropology, beginning, 1965. Organizer and director of tours to American places of historical interest, and to museum collections of Egyptian, classical, and anthropological interest. *Member:* American Historical Association, Association for Applied Psychoanalysis, Classical Association of the Atlantic States, Long Island Historical Society, Essex Institute (Salem, Mass.).

WRITINGS: *Putnam's Concise Mythological Dictionary* (based on *Gods* by Bessie Gordon Redfield), Putnam, 1963; (editor) *An Anthology of Ancient Egyptian Literature*, Holt, 1967; (editor and translator) *Wings of the Falcon: Life and Thought of Ancient Egypt*, Holt, 1968, (published in England as *The Literature and Mythology of Ancient Egypt*, Allen Lane, 1970). Contributor to *Interpreters Dictionary of the Bible*, Abingdon, 1962.

WORK IN PROGRESS: *Witchcraft and Diabolism in America*.

(Deceased)

* * *

KATZ, Milton 1907-

PERSONAL: Born November 29, 1907, in New York, N.Y.; son of Morris (a manufacturer) and Clara (Schiffman) Katz; married Vivian Greenberg, July 2, 1933; children: John, Robert, Peter. *Education:* Harvard University, A.B., 1927, LL.B., 1931. *Home:* 6 Berkeley St., Cambridge, Mass. 02138. *Office:* Harvard Law School, Cambridge, Mass. 02138.

CAREER: Admitted to New York Bar, 1932; U.S. Government, various posts, 1931-39, soliciter with War Production Board and with Combined Production and Resources Board, 1941-43, with Office of Strategic Services, 1943, deputy special representative in Europe, 1949-50, special representative in Europe with rank of ambassador, U.S. representative on Economic Commission for Europe, and chairman of Financial and Economic Committee of North Atlantic Treaty Organization, 1950-51; Harvard University Law School, Cambridge, Mass., member of faculty, 1939-41, Byrne Professor of Administrative Law, 1946-48, Henry L. Stimson Professor of Law, director of international legal studies, and director of the international program in taxation, 1954—; Ford Foundation, New York, N.Y., associate director, 1951-54, consultant, 1954—. Chairman of the board of trustees, Carnegie Endowment for International Peace; trustee, World Peace Foundation, Citizens' Research Foundation, Brandeis University, Case Western Reserve University. President, Cambridge Community Services, 1958-60. *Military service:* U.S. Naval Reserve, 1944-46; became lieutenant commander; received Legion of Merit. *Member:* American Academy of Arts and Sciences (fellow; councilor), American Society of International Law, American Bar Association, Council on Foreign Relations.

WRITINGS: *Cases and Materials in Administrative Law*, West Publishing, 1947; *The Community of Europe and American Policy* (speech), privately printed, 1956; *Domestic, Political and Economic Aspects of National Strategy* (speech), privately printed, 1956; *Economic Aspects of National Security Policy* (speech), privately printed, 1956; (with others) *The Bricker Amendment: Views of Deans and Professors of Law*, Committee for Defense of the Constitution by Preserving the Treaty Power, 1957; (editor with others, and contributor) *Government Under Law and the Individual*, American Council of Learned Societies, 1957; (with Kingman Brewster, Jr.) *Preliminary Selection of Primary Materials for a Course on the Law of International Transactions and Relations*, Foundation Press, 1958; *The International Legal Order: Variations on a Theme*, Harvard Law School Association of New Jersey, 1960; (with

Brewster) *The Law of International Transactions and Relations: Cases and Materials*, Foundation Press, 1960; *The Role of Law in International Affairs as Illustrated by the Eichmann Case*, New Jersey Institute for Practicing Lawyers, 1961; *The Things That Are Caesar's*, Knopf, 1966; *The Modern Foundation: Its Dual Character, Public and Private*, Foundation Library Center, 1968; *The Relevance of International Adjudication*, Harvard University Press, 1968. Contributor of articles to legal, business, and foreign affairs periodicals.

* * *

KAVLI, Guthorm 1917-

PERSONAL: Born May 15, 1917, in Trondheim, Norway; son of Wilhelm (a merchant) and Marie (Sevaldson) Kavli; married Ursula Joan Power, September 18, 1934; children: Pal Guthorm, John Dennis. *Education:* Norwegian Technical University, M.Arch., 1941, Dr.Sc., 1967. Uppsala University, Degree in History of Art, 1946. *Home and office:* Royal Palace, Drammensveien 1, Oslo, Norway.

CAREER: Practice of architecture, Oslo, Norway, 1945-49; Oslo Museum of Applied Arts, Oslo, Norway, curator, 1949-51, deputy director, 1951-61; Royal Palace, Oslo, Norway, architect and director, 1962—. *Military service:* Norwegian Army, 1942-45; Supreme Headquarters, Allied Expeditionary Forces, monuments and fine arts officer; became captain. *Awards, honors:* Herman Schirmer Award, 1958; Officer, Norwegian Order of St. Olav.

WRITINGS: (With Thor Keilland) *Om Museumsbygg, Innredning, Montering*, Kunstindustrimuseet, 1953; *Norwegian Architecture, Past and Present*, Batsford, 1958; (with others) *Byborgerens Hus i Norge*, Dreyer, 1963; (with Widerberg, Christie, and Opstad) *Halden, Byen og Festningen*, Aschehoug, 1963; *Troenderske trepaleer: Borgerlig panelarkitektur nordenfjells*, Cappelen, 1966; *The Royal Palace in Oslo*, Dreyer, 1970.

* * *

KAWIN, Ethel ?-1969

PERSONAL: Born in Peoria, Ill.; daughter of Nathan and Lottie (Goldstein) Kawin. *Education:* University of Chicago, Ph.B., 1921, M.A., 1925. *Home:* 1545 East 60th St., Chicago, Ill. 60637. *Office:* American Foundation for Continuing Education, 19 South LaSalle St., Chicago, Ill. 60603.

CAREER: Diplomate, American Board of Examiners in Professional Psychology; Illinois Institute for Juvenile Research, Chicago, director of preschool department, 1925-34; consultant in child development and guidance to Illinois Public Schools and Illinois Association for Supervision and Curriculum Development, 1934-53; University of Chicago, Chicago, Ill., lecturer in education, 1938-61, director of Parent Education Project, 1953-61; American Foundation for Continuing Education, Chicago, Ill., consultant in parent education, 1961-69. Psychologist, Behavior Research Fund, 1925-34; coordinator for Expanded Parent Education Program, National Congress of Parents and Teachers, 1948-53. *Member:* American Psychological Association (fellow), American Orthopsychiatric Association (fellow), Society for Research in Child Development (fellow), Illinois Association for Supervision and Curriculum Development (honorary). *Awards, honors:* Citation for public service, University of Chicago Alumni Association, 1946.

WRITINGS: (With others) *A Comparative Study of a Nursery School Versus a Non-Nursery School Group*, University of Chicago Press, 1931; *Problems of Preschool Age: Nine Case Studies*, University of Chicago Press, 1933; *Children of Preschool Age: Studies in Socio-Economic Status, Social Adjustment and Mental Ability*, University of Chicago Press, 1934; *The Wise Choice of Toys*, University of Chicago Press, 1934, revised edition, 1938; (contributor) John R. Yale, editor, *Frontier Thinking in Guidance: An Anthology of Significant Thought in the Field of Guidance*, Science Research Associates, 1945; *A Guide for Child-study Groups*, Science Research Associates, 1952; *Middle Childhood: An Age-period Course for Parenthood in a Free Nation*, Parent Education Project, University of Chicago, 1957; *Later Childhood: An Age-period Course for Parenthood in a Free Nation*, Parent Education Project, University of Chicago, 1959; *Adolescence: An Age-period Course for Parenthood in a Free Nation*, Parent Education Project, University of Chicago, 1960; *Parenthood in a Free Nation*, three volumes, Macmillan, 1963. Contributor to education and psychology journals.

WORK IN PROGRESS: Another version of *The Wise Choice of Toys*.

(Died March 24, 1969)

* * *

KEATS, Charles B. 1905-

PERSONAL: Born July 21, 1905, in Bridgeport, Conn.; son of Abraham M. and Jeanette (Boges) Keats; married Katherine Hamilton Kane, August 21, 1937 (deceased); married Kathleen Kenton, February 27, 1967. *Education:* Syracuse University, B.F.A., 1931.

CAREER: Free-lance artist and writer, New York, N.Y., 1931-33; reporter, city editor, and columnist for newspapers in Bridgeport, Conn., 1933-41; Republican State Central Committee of Connecticut, publicity director, 1941-50; State of Connecticut, Hartford, executive secretary to governor, 1947-49, deputy secretary of state, 1950-53, secretary of state, 1953-55; Keats, Allen & Keats (public relations), Hartford, Conn., and Washington, D.C., partner, 1953-65. Member of advisory committee, Connecticut Civil Defense, 1953-55; Republican presidential elector, 1956. *Member:* Authors Guild of the Authors League of America.

WRITINGS: Lucky Luciano, Avon, 1955; *Marked Woman*, Avon, 1956; *Modigliani: The Body of Love*, Berkley, 1957; *Wake Up to Tomorrow*, Heritage Hall, 1959; *Magnificient Masquerade: The Strange Case of Dr. Coster and Mr. Musica*, Funk, 1964.

* * *

KEECH, William J(ohn) 1904-

PERSONAL: Born November 23, 1904, in San Salvador, El Salvador; son of William (a minister) and Martha (Hoffman) Keech; married Clara Louise Robertson, February 21, 1935; children: William Robertson. *Education:* Occidental College, A.B., 1927; Southern Baptist Theological Seminary, M.Th., 1931. *Home:* 227 Avon Rd., Narberth, Pa. 19072. *Office:* American Baptist Convention, Valley Forge, Pa. 19481.

CAREER: Baptist minister; pastor of churches in California, 1931-43; Tri-State Baptist Convention, Idaho, Utah, and Montana, director of Christian education, 1943-47;

American Baptist Convention Board of Education and Publication, Valley Forge, Pa., director of Department of Missionary and Stewardship Education, 1947-69. National Council of Churches, Commission on Missionary Education, chairman of board of managers and member of executive committee, 1957-63. *Awards, honors:* D.D., Occidental College, 1963.

WRITINGS—All published by Judson: *Why Tithe*, 1957; *The Church School of Missions: A Manual*, 1960; *Our Church Plans for Missionary and Stewardship Education*, 1963; *The Life I Owe: Christian Stewardship as a Way of Life*, 1963. Contributor to religious journals.

* * *

KEELING, Jill Annette (Shaw) 1923-

PERSONAL: Born January 29, 1923, in Chesterfield, Derbyshire, England; daughter of Thomas Kenyon (an engineer) and Ileene Vera (Foster) Shaw; married Clinton Harry Keeling (a self-employed zoologist), August 24, 1953; children: Anthony, Jeremy, Diana, Phoebe. *Education:* Bedford College for Women, London, B.A., (honors), 1944. *Politics:* None. *Religion:* Agnostic. *Home:* Ileene Cottage, Upper Town, Ashover, Chesterfield, Derbyshire, England. *Office:* Pan's Garden, Ashover, Chesterfield, Derbyshire, England.

CAREER: St. George's School, Ascot, Berkshire, England, English teacher, 1944-45; private zoo superintendent, Ashover, Derbyshire, England, 1954—. Breeder and exhibitor of English sheep dogs and bearded collies. *Member:* Kennel Club.

WRITINGS: Variations on a Theme, Stockwell, 1957; *Ask of the Beasts*, Anthony Blond, 1960; *The Old English Sheepdog*, W. & G. Foyle, 1961; (with husband, C. H. Keeling) *Keeling's Ark*, Harrap, 1970. Contributor to *Countryman, Chambers's Journal, International Zoo Year Book*, and other journals.

WORK IN PROGRESS: With C. H. Keeling, *Caravan in the Highlands*, for Harrap.

* * *

KEENE, J(ames) Calvin 1908-

PERSONAL: Born July 29, 1908, in Enders, Pa.; son of James E. (a clergyman) and Nora (Kershner) Keene; married Elsa Feichtinger, April 20, 1934; children: Lenore (Mrs. Stephen Congdon), James, Joan (Mrs. Dale Smith). *Education:* Lebanon Valley College, B.A., 1930; Yale University, Ph.D., 1937. *Religion:* Society of Friends. *Home address:* R.D. 1, Box 134, Lewisburg, Pa. 17837.

CAREER: International College, Izmir, Turkey, instructor in mathematics, 1931-34; Colgate University, Hamilton, N.Y., instructor in philosophy and religion, 1937-43; Howard University, School of Religion, Washington, D.C., 1943-58, began as assistant professor, became professor of philosophy of religion and theology; St. Lawrence University, Canton, N.Y., professor and chairman of department of religion, 1958-74. Visiting professor, American University of Beirut, 1949-50. *Member:* American Theological Society (secretary, 1963-72), American Academy of Religion (vice-president, 1947-48), Rotary Club (Canton; president, 1965-66).

WRITINGS: Meditations on the Gospels, Abingdon, 1949; (editor and reviser) *The Western Heritage of Faith and Reason*, Harper, 1963. Contributor of articles and reviews to journals. Editor, *Journal of Religious Thought*, 1953-58, *Quaker Religious Thought*, 1959-64.

WORK IN PROGRESS: A book on modern understanding of Christian thought.

* * *

KEENLEYSIDE, Hugh Llewellyn 1898-

PERSONAL: Born July 7, 1898, in Toronto, Ontario, Canada; son of Ellis William and Margaret (Irvine) Keenleyside; married Katherine Pillsbury, August 12, 1924; children: Mary (Mrs. Sydney Segal), Miles, Anne (Mrs. James A. McCullum), Lynn (Mrs. Gordon C. Jackson). Education: University of British Columbia, B.A., 1920; Clark University, M.A., 1921, Ph.D., 1923. Religion: Unitarian. Home and office: 3470 Mayfair Dr., Victoria, British Columbia, Canada V8P 1P8.

CAREER: University of British Columbia, Vancouver, lecturer in history, 1925-27; Canadian Department of External Affairs, staff member, Ottawa, Ontario, 1928, first secretary of legation in Tokyo, Japan, 1929-36, counsellor, 1940-41, assistant Undersecretary of State for External Affairs, Ottawa, 1941-44, Ambassador to Mexico, 1944-47; Deputy Minister of Mines and Resources, 1947-50; United Nations, delegate to General Assembly, 1946, head of Canadian delegation to scientific Conference on Conservation and Utilization of Resources, 1949, chief of Technical Assistance Mission to Bolivia, 1950, director general of Technical Assistance Administration, 1950-58, Undersecretary for Public Administration, 1959; British Columbia Power Commission, chairman, 1959-62; British Columbia Hydro and Power Authority, Vancouver, chairman, 1962-69. Member of international councils and commissions, including Canada-U.S. Joint Defense Board, 1940-45, and War Technical and Scientific Development Committee, 1941-45. Chairman and commissioner, Northwest Territories Council, 1947-50; trustee, Clark University, 1953-56; member of senate, University of British Columbia, 1963-69. Notre Dame University of Nelson, Chancellor, 1968—, chairman of the board of governors, 1973—. Military service: Canadian Army, Field Artillery and 2nd Tank Battalion, World War I.

MEMBER: Royal Geographical Society (Great Britain; fellow), Institute of Public Administration (Canada), Royal Institute of Public Administration (Great Britain), Canadian Institute on Public Affairs (president, 1953-58), Society for International Development (president, 1959), Arctic Institute of North America (founder; board of governors, 1944-50), Royal Canadian Geographical Society, Asiatic Society (Japan), Association of Canadian Clubs (president, 1959). Awards, honors: Haldane Medal of Royal Institute of Public Administration, 1954; Vanier Medal of Institute of Public Administration (Canada), 1962; Companion of Canada, 1969. Honorary degrees from University of British Columbia, 1945, McMaster University, 1949, Clark University, 1951, and four Canadian and U.S. Colleges, 1947-58.

WRITINGS: Canada and the United States, Knopf, 1929, revised edition, 1952; (with A. F. Thomas) History of Japanese Education, Hokuseido Press, 1937; (with others) The Growth of Canadian Policies in External Affairs, Duke University Press, 1960; International Aid: A Summary, McClelland & Stewart, 1966. Contributor of articles on literary and international topics to periodicals.

* * *

KEESLAR, Oreon 1907-

PERSONAL: Born December 19, 1907, in Orland, Ind.; son of Glenn L. (a salesman) and Janette (Gillis) Keeslar; married Julia May Hackett (a registered nurse), February 22, 1936; children: Peter Terrence, Daniel Curtis, Mary Judith. Education: Attended Hillsdale College, 1926-27, Western State Teachers College (now Western Michigan University), 1929; Ohio State University, B.S., 1938, M.A., 1939; University of Michigan, Ph.D., 1945; University of California, Los Angeles, postdoctoral study, summers, 1951-52. Politics: "I prefer to vote for the man, not the party." Religion: Protestant. Home: 2854 Kring Dr., San Jose, Calif. 95125.

CAREER: Elementary and high school teacher in Indiana, Ohio, and Michigan, 1929-44; Kern County schools, Bakersfield, Calif., audio-visual director and high school coordinator, 1946-53; Inyo County schools, Independence, Calif., director of education, 1953-54; Santa Clara County Schools, San Jose, Calif., high school coordinator, 1954-73. College extension instructor in audio visual education, Fresno State College and University of California, Santa Barbara, 1947-53; visiting summer instructor, University of California, Los Angeles, 1950-55. Military service: U.S. Navy, 1944-46. Member: National Science Teachers Association (program committee chairman for national convention, 1961), California State Science Teachers Association (president, 1959-60), California Association for Supervision and Curriculum Development (secretary, 1948-49), Santa Clara Valley Science Fair Association (executive secretary), Phi Delta Kappa.

WRITINGS: (Contributor) Godfrey Elliott, editor, Film and Education, Philosophical Library, 1948; College Scholarships and Entrance Requirements, Santa Clara County Schools and California State Department of Education, 1957, 3rd edition, 1959; (editor and contributor) Leadership for Science in the Elementary School, California Association for Supervision and Curriculum Development, 1960; A National Catalog of Scholarships and Other Financial Aids for Students Entering College, W. C. Brown, 1963, 6th edition published as Financial Aids for Higher Education: 1974-75 Catalog, 1974. Author of educational bulletins and contributor to educational journals.

WORK IN PROGRESS: Various projects in fiction, nonfiction, and poetry, providing both the text and photography.

AVOCATIONAL INTERESTS: Advanced amateur photography and darkroom work, particularly color print enlargements; construction of a recreational cabin on the Mojave Desert; travel in the U.S. and abroad.

* * *

KEEVILL, Henry J(ohn) 1914-
(Clay Allison, Bill Bonney, Virgil Earp, Wes Hardin, Frank McLowery, Johnny Ringo)

PERSONAL: Born October 5, 1914, in England; son of Walter James (an engineer) and Beatrice Ellen (Sharpe) Keevill; married Gladys May Simpson, February 26, 1940; children: Gillian, Jacqueline. Education: Attended schools in Aylestone and Leicester, England. Religion: Church of England. Home: 165 Worplesdon Rd., Guildford, Surrey, England. Agent: J. F. Gibson's Literary Agency, 17 Southampton Pl., London W.C.1, England.

CAREER: Dispatch clerk and truck driver for English firm, 1931-1933; British Air Ministry, London, England, account clerk, 1937-39; employed in local government, 1945-60; British Civil Service, London, England, clerical officer, 1960—. *Military service:* British Army, Coldstream Guards, 1934-37, 1939-45; became sergeant.

WRITINGS—Under pseudonym Clay Allison: *No Rest for Lawmen*, Ward, Lock, 1955; *Branded*, Ward, Lock, 1956; *Brand of a Cowboy*, Brown, Watson, 1960; *Gun Gold of the West*, Brown, Watson, 1961; *The Drifting Gun*, Wright & Brown, 1963; *The Bounty Hunter*, Wright & Brown, 1963; *He Rode Alone*, R. Hale, 1963; *Outlaw Trail*, R. Hale, 1963; *Gunsmoke Over Wyoming*, R. Hale, 1964; *Guns Across the Rio Grande*, R. Hale, 1964; *Six Guns for Water*, R. Hale, 1964; *Six Guns in Sundance*, R. Hale, 1966; *The Wandering Gun*, R. Hale, 1966; *North From Texas*, R. Hale, 1969; *Trail of the Iron Horse*, R. Hale, 1971.

Under pseudonym Wes Hardin: *Trail from Yuma*, Arthur Barker, 1956; *Trouble at Gunsight Pass*, R. Hale, 1963; *Gun Law in Toledo*, R. Hale, 1964.

Under pseudonym Frank McLowery: *Missouri Man*, Macdonald & Co., 1955; *Herds North*, Macdonald & Co., 1956; *Guns for the Sioux*, Brown, Watson, 1961.

Under pseudonym Johnny Ringo: *Lonely Gun*, Mills & Boon, 1954; *Action in Abilene*, Mills & Boon, 1966; *A Gun for Vengeance*, Mills & Boon, 1966.

Under pseudonym Bill Bonney: *Colorado Gunsmoke*, R. Hale, 1964.

Under pseudonym Virgil Earp: *Hatchet Rides High*, R. Hale, 1964.

Contributor of short stories and articles to *Evening News* (London), *Parade, John O'London's*, and to other newspapers and magazines in England and abroad.

WORK IN PROGRESS: Continuing study of American frontier history for a nonfiction trilogy, underway since 1957.

* * *

KEIR, David E(dwin) 1906-1969

PERSONAL: Born March 12, 1906, in Lauder, Berwickshire, Scotland; son of Thomas (a clergyman) and Lily Jane (Cross) Keir; married Thelma Cazalet (former member of Parliament and government minister, later a governor of British Broadcasting Corp.), August 3, 1939. *Education:* University of Edinburgh, M.A., 1927, graduate study, 1928-29. *Home:* Raspit Hill, near Sevenoaks, Kent, England; 90 Eaton Sq., London S.W.1, England. *Agent:* A. D. Peters, 10 Buckingham St., Adelphi, London W.C.2, England.

CAREER: Liberal candidate for Parliament for North Midlothian, Scotland, in by-election and general election, 1929, Roxburgh and Selkirk, in general election, 1931, and East Fife by-election, 1933; *News Chronicle*, London, England, political correspondent, 1933-40; British Broadcasting Corp., London, England, regular current affairs broadcaster, 1948-56; writer on social and industrial history, 1948-69. Chairman, Parliamentary Lobby Correspondents, 1938; chairman, Parliamentary Press Gallery, 1939-40. *Military service:* Royal Navy Volunteer Reserve, 1940-46; Member of Order of British Empire, received commendation by Commander-in-Chief Nore, 1946. *Member:* Society of Authors, Newspaper Press Fund (life member), Savile Club and Press Club (both London); New Club, Scottish Arts Club, and Scottish Liberal Club (all Edinburgh).

WRITINGS: Poems, Darien Press, 1928; *The Desolation of the Highlands* (social and economic study), Fact Ltd.,

1938; *Newspapers* (short history), Edward Arnold, 1948; *The Younger Centuries: The Story of William Younger & Co. Ltd., 1749 to 1949*, (history of Edinburgh brewing), William Younger & Co., and McLagan & Cumming, 1951; *The House of Collins: The Story of a Scottish Family of Publishers from 1789 to the Present Day*, Collins, 1952; (editor with Bryan Morgan) *Golden Milestone: 50 Years of the A.A.* (jubilee history and contemporary account of British Automobile Association), Newman Neame, 1955; *The Bowring Story* (history of C. T. Bowring & Co.), Bodley Head, 1962; (editor) *The City of Edinburgh*, Collins, 1966.

Monographs: *Guide to the Indian Problem*, News Chronicle, 1935; *Defence and Disarmament*, News Chronicle, 1936. Also editor, with W. P. Kennedy, of an anthology of University of Edinburgh verse, *Our Tounis College*. Contributor to *Encyclopaedia Britannica*, and to newspapers and periodicals, including *New Statesman, Scotsman*, (London) *Times, Daily Telegraph, Edinburgh Evening News, Listener*. Editor of *Student* (University of Edinburgh magazine), 1928.

WORK IN PROGRESS: A history of W. H. Smith & Sons, British booksellers, 1967 or 1968; a biography of Victor Cazalet, British parliamentarian and sportsman.

BIOGRAPHICAL/CRITICAL SOURCES: (London) *Times*, June 14, 1969.

(Died June 9, 1969)

* * *

KELLY, Thomas 1909-

PERSONAL: Born January 25, 1909, in Blackpool, England; son of James Denison and Agnes (Hamilton) Kelly; married Edith Winstanley, August 5, 1933; children: Sheila, Margaret. *Education:* University of Manchester, B.A. (honors), 1929, M.A., 1947; University of Liverpool, Ph.D., 1957. *Home:* 55 Freshfield Rd., Formby, near Liverpool, England. *Office:* University of Liverpool, Liverpool, England.

CAREER: Schoolmaster in Devonshire, England, then publisher's educational editor in Edinburgh, Scotland; University of Manchester, Manchester, England, member of adult education staff, 1940-48; University of Liverpool, Liverpool, England, director of extra-mural studies, 1948—, professor of adult education, 1967—. *Member:* Universities Council for Adult Education (secretary), Royal Historical Society (fellow).

WRITINGS: (with Robert M. Rayner) *A Middle School History of England*, two volumes, J. Murray, 1934-35; (editor) St. Francis of Assisi, *Little Flowers of St. Francis*, W. & R. Chambers, 1936; *The Adventures of Prince Charles After the Battle of Worcester*, W. & R. Chambers, 1936; "The Mayflower Histories: Junior Series," four volumes, W. & R. Chambers, 1937, revised edition edited by Joan Stewart published as "The Mayflower Histories: First Course," 1962-64; *The Story of Robert Bruce*, W. & R. Chambers, 1938; (with Robert B. Mowat) "The Mayflower Histories: Secondary Course," four volumes, W. & R. Chambers, 1939-42; *History of King Edward VI Grammar School, Totnes, and Its Famous Old Boys*, King Edward VI Grammar School, 1947; *Sources for Visual Aid Material*, National Foundation for Adult Education, 1948; *Griffith Jones, Llanddowror, Pioneer in Adult Education*, University of Wales Press, 1950; *Outside the Walls: Sixty Years of University Education at Manchester, 1886-1946*,

Manchester University Press, 1950; (editor) *A Select Bibliography of Adult Education in Great Britain*, National Institute of Adult Education, 1952, 2nd edition, 1962; *George Birkbeck, Pioneer of Adult Education*, Liverpool University Press, 1957; (editor with wife, Edith Kelly) David Winstanley, *A Schoolmaster's Notebook*, Chetham Society, 1957; *Adult Education in Liverpool: A Narrative of Two Hundred Years*, Liverpool University, 1960; *A History of Adult Education in Great Britain*, Liverpool University Press, 1962, 2nd edition, 1970; *Early Public Libraries: A History of Public Libraries in Great Britain Before 1850*, Library Association, 1966, reissued as pamphlet as *Public Libraries in Great Britain Before 1850*, 1966.

Contributor of articles to professional journals. Editor, *Studies in Adult Education*, 1969—.

* * *

KEMP, Diana Moyle 1919-

PERSONAL: Born February 1, 1919, in Stalbridge, Dorsetshire, England; daughter of Henley Hamblin (a medical doctor) and Alice Thorpe (Darnell) Moyle; married Neil McIntyre Kemp (died in World War II); married Robert R. Wyckcliffe Simpson, 1949 (deceased); children: (first marriage) Ian Malcolm McIntyre. *Education:* Educated privately and at Sherborne School for Girls. *Politics:* Conservative. *Religion:* Church of England. *Home:* Spadgers, Kilmington, Warminster, Wiltshire, England. *Agent:* A. M. Heath & Co. Ltd., 35 Dover St., London W.1, England.

CAREER: Whitehall Secretarial College, East Knoyle, Salisbury, England, office worker, 1944; publishers reader, 1957-60. *Member:* Romantic Novelists' Association.

WRITINGS—All published by R. Hale: *Reel of Three*, 1955; *My Mother's Keeper*, 1956; *The Day of the Rowan*, 1956; *The Fencers*, 1957; *A Reed from the River*, 1959; *Firebird*, 1960; *Wings of the Wind*, 1961; *No More Peacocks*, 1962; *Touch Wood*, 1964; *The Same Boat*, 1966; *The Small Hours*, 1968. Contributor to *Woman's Own, Woman's Weekly, Modern Woman*, and other magazines.

SIDELIGHTS: Some of Mrs. Kemp's books have been translated into Norwegian, Dutch, Swedish, Italian, and French. *Avocational interests:* Cooking, especially foreign dishes; the countryside, reading American novels.

* * *

KEMP, Robert 1908-1967

PERSONAL: Born February 25, 1908, in Orkney, Scotland; son of Arnold Low (a minister) and Robina Jane (Simpson) Kemp; married Meta Strachan (a teacher), December 30, 1932; children: David, Arnold, Robert, Christina Margaret. *Education:* University of Aberdeen, M.A., (honors in English), 1929. *Religion:* Christian. *Home:* 18 Warriston Crescent, Edinburgh 3, Scotland. *Agent:* Derek Glynne, 115 Shaftesbury Ave., London W.C. 2, England.

CAREER: Manchester Guardian, Manchester, England, reporter, 1929-37; British Broadcasting Corp., London, England, producer and writer, 1937-47; free-lance writer and playwright. Co-founder and first chairman, Edinburgh Gateway Co. Former member of Arts Council of Great Britain, Scottish Committee of the Arts Council, and Scottish Advisory Panel of the British Council. *Member:* Society of Authors, Screenwriters' Guild, Scottish Arts Club (Edinburgh).

WRITINGS—Plays: *A Trump for Jericho*, St. Giles Press, 1948; *The Saxon Saint*, St. Giles Press, 1950; *The King of* *Scots*, St. Giles Press, 1951; (co-author) *Four One-Act Plays*, Heinemann, 1952; *The Other Dear Charmer*, Duckworth, 1957; *Master John Knox*, St. Andrew Press, 1960; *Off a Duck's Back*, Samuel French, 1961.

Novels: *Malacca Cane*, Duckworth, 1954; *The Maestro*, Duckworth, 1956; *The Highlander*, Duckworth, 1957; *The Campaigns of Captain MacGurk*, Duckworth, 1958; *Gretna Green*, Chambers, 1961.

Adaptor of "The Three Estates" for Edinburgh International Festival of Music and Drama. Contributor to *Glasgow Herald*, periodicals, and British Broadcasting Corp. programs.

(Died November 27, 1967)

* * *

KEMPER, Inez 1906-

PERSONAL: Born May 10, 1906, in Blocton, Ala.; daughter of Charlie and Lottie (Wilson) Kemper. *Education:* Educated in public schools. *Religion:* Baptist. *Address:* P.O. Box 1055, Birmingham 3, Ala.

CAREER: Registered nurse.

WRITINGS: (Compiler) *Highways to the Hills* (anthology of religious poems), Loizeaux, 1947; *The Doorway to Heaven*, Baker Book, 1957; (compiler) *In Touch with Heaven* (devotional selections), Eerdmans, 1964.

* * *

KEMPSTER, Mary Yates 1911-

PERSONAL: Born August 12, 1911, in Bolton, Lancashire, England; daughter of Stanley (a patternmaker) and Sarah Yates; married Albert Kempster (a teacher), June 10, 1939; children: Virginia Margaret. *Education:* Attended St. Katharine's Training College and University of Manchester; B.A. (London), L.R.A.M. and A.T.C.L. (musical diplomas); University of Barcelona, diploma in Spanish. *Religion:* Church of England. *Home:* 23 Devonshire Rd., Bolton, Lancashire, England.

CAREER: Former head teacher at Howe Bridge School, Atherton, Lancashire, England, and at Blackrod Church of England Infant's School, Lancashire, England; Hill Top Infant's School, Rochdale, Lancashire, England, head teacher, 1959—. Bolton Technical College, part-time teacher of French and Spanish, 1953—. *Member:* National Association of Head Teachers.

WRITINGS: Twenty Number Activity Songs, University of London Press, 1958.

WORK IN PROGRESS: The Teacher's Christmas Book; Songs for Young Children.

AVOCATIONAL INTERESTS: Travel, music, modern languages.†

* * *

KENDALL, Paul Murray 1911-1973

PERSONAL: Born March 1, 1911, in Philadelphia, Pa.; son of Oscar B. (a businessman) and Helen (Murray) Kendall; married Carol Seeger (a writer), June 15, 1939; children: Carol, Gillian. *Education:* University of Virginia, A.B., 1932, A.M., 1933, Ph.D., 1939. *Home:* 928 Holiday Dr., Lawrence, Kansas 66044.

CAREER: Ohio University, Athens, instructor, 1937-42, assistant professor, 1942-49, associate professor, 1949-54, professor, 1954-59, Distinguished Professor of English,

1958-66, Regents Professor of English, 1966-70; University of Kansas, Lawrence, visiting professor, 1970-71, professor of English, 1971-73. Rose Morgan Visiting Professor, University of Kansas, 1969. *Member:* Modern Language Association of America, American Historical Association, Renaissance Society of America, Royal Historical Society (fellow). *Awards, honors:* Ford Foundation fellow, 1952-53; Guggenheim fellow, 1957-58, 1961-62; grants from American Philosophical Society, 1959, and Rockefeller Foundation, 1965-67; L.H.D. from Ohio University, 1970.

WRITINGS: Richard the Third, Norton, 1955; *Warwick the Kingmaker*, Norton, 1957; *The Yorkist Age*, Norton, 1962; *The Art of Biography*, Norton, 1965; *The Great Debate*, Folio Society (London), 1965; *Louis XI: The Universal Spider*, Norton, 1970; (editor and translator with Vincent Ilardi) *Dispatches of Milanese Ambassadors*, Ohio University Press, Volume I, 1970, Volume II, 1971; (editor and translator) Philippe de Commyne, *The Universal Spider*, Folio Society, 1973.

WORK IN PROGRESS: A work on sixth century Gaul; *The Complete Works of Shakespeare*, edited in collaboration with Charlton Hinman.

(Died November 21, 1973)

* * *

KENNARD-DAVIS, Arthur (Shelley) 1910-

PERSONAL: Born January 15, 1910, in Marlborough, Wiltshire, England; son of Rushworth (a schoolmaster) and Maude Agnes (Mack) Kennard Davis; married Margaret Elinor Gray, December 16, 1933; children: James, Juliet, Margaret and David (twins). *Education:* Attended Birkenhead School, 1922-27, University of Liverpool, 1927-28. *Politics:* Liberal. *Religion:* Anglican. *Home address:* P.O. Box 5148, Port Elizabeth, South Africa. *Agent:* Laurence Pollinger Ltd., 18 Maddox St., London W.1, England.

CAREER: Left school to go to sea with British Merchant Service as apprentice, later navigating officer, 1928-33; variously farmer, private tutor, teacher, stevedore, hotelier, flax mill operator; part-time writer. *Military service:* Royal Naval Volunteer Reserve, World War II; became chief petty officer.

WRITINGS: Isle of Adventure (juvenile), Basil Blackwell, 1937; *Dingdong on Little Hurricane* (juvenile), Kenya Weekly News, 1939; *A Farm in Cedar Valley* (juvenile), Basil Blackwell, 1947; *The Gentle Captain* (novel), J. Cape, 1954; *The Three-Yard Ensign* (novel), Barrie & Rockliff, 1963. Writer of articles.

WORK IN PROGRESS: A children's book, *The Night-Riders*; story of the author's Kenya farm, *A Field of Daisies*.

AVOCATIONAL INTERESTS: Painting, sailing ships, astronomy, swimming, sailing.

* * *

KENNEY, George Churchill 1889-

PERSONAL: Born August 6, 1889, in Yarmouth, Nova Scotia, Canada; son of Joseph Atwood and Louise (Churchill) Kenney; married Hazel Dell Richardson; married second wife, Alice Steward Maxey, 1922; married third wife, Sarah Schermerhorn, December 13, 1955; married fourth wife, Jeannette C. Stehlin, October 26, 1971; children: (first marriage) William Richardson; (second marriage) Alice Steward (Mrs. Edward C. Hoagland). *Education:* Massachusetts Institute of Technology, student, 1907-

11. *Home:* 10180 West Bay Harbor Dr., Bay Harbor Islands, Fla. 33154.

CAREER: Surveyor and engineer, then head of construction firm in Boston, Mass., 1911-17; enlisted as flying cadet in Aviation Section of Signal Corps, 1917, and served more than three decades as regular commissioned officer in the U.S. Army and U.S. Air Force, retiring in 1951 as a four-star general; National Arthritis and Rheumatism Foundation, New York, N.Y., president, 1951-63. Flew with aero squadrons in France and Germany, 1917-19, returning to United States as a captain; graduated from Army Command and General Staff College, 1927, Army War College, 1933; became chief of production at Wright Field, Ohio, 1939; assumed command of Fourth Air Force, 1942; commanded Allied Air Forces in the Southwest Pacific, 1942-45, and Far East Air Forces, 1944-45; senior U.S. representative on Military Staff Committee of United Nations, 1945-46; commanding general of Strategic Air Command with headquarters at Andrews Air Force Base, Md., 1946-48, and of the Air University, Maxwell Air Force Base, Ala., 1948-51.

MEMBER: Air Force Association, Military Order of World Wars, American Legion, Masons, Lotus Club (New York), Dutch Treat Club. *Awards, honors:* Distinguished Service Cross with oak leaf cluster, Distinguished Service Medal with two clusters, Silver Star, Distinguished Flying Cross, Legion of Merit, Bronze Star, Purple Heart, Knight Commander Order of the British Empire (military), Philippine Star, Order of Military Merit First Class (Guatemala), Grand Officer Leopold with palm and Croix de Guerre (Belgium), Commander, Legion of Honor, and Croix de Guerre (France), Order of Orange-Nassau with Swords (Netherlands); LL.D. from University of Notre Dame, 1947.

WRITINGS—All published by Duell, Sloan & Pearce, unless otherwise noted: (with Horace Moss Guilbert) *History of the 91st Aero Squadron, Air Service, U.S.A.*, Gebrueder Breuer (Coblenz), 1919; *General Kenney Reports: A Personal History of the Pacific War*, 1949; *The MacArthur I Know*, 1951; *The Saga of Pappy Gunn*, 1959; *Dick Bong: Ace of Aces*, 1960.

* * *

KENNEY, Sylvia W. 1922-19(?)

PERSONAL: Born November 27, 1922, in Tampa, Fla; daughter of Arthur W. (a physicist) and Marion L. (Coes) Kenney. *Education:* Wellesley College, B.A., 1944; Yale University, B. Mus., 1945, M.A., 1948, Ph.D., 1955. *Office:* Department of Music, Smith College, Northampton, Mass. 01060.

CAREER: Bryn Mawr College, Bryn Mawr, Pa., assistant professor, 1957-63, associate professor of music, 1963-64; University of California, Santa Barbara, associate professor of music, 1965-66; Smith College, Northampton, Mass., professor of music, beginning, 1966. Visiting associate professor, Yale University, 1963-64.

WRITINGS: (Editor) *Collected Works of Walter Frye*, American Institute of Musicology, 1960; (compiler of catalogue), *Riemenschneider Memorial Bach Library*, Columbia University Press, 1960; *Walter Frye and the "Contenance Angloise,"* Yale University Press, 1965.

WORK IN PROGRESS: An edition of a fifteenth century music manuscript, for Yale University Press; a book on the motet, for Princeton University Press.

(Deceased)

KENT, Nora 1899-

PERSONAL: Born February 20, 1899, in Lewes, Sussex, England; daughter of George Pollington (a farmer) and Bessie Mary (Elphick) Kent. *Education:* Educated at private school in Lewes, England. *Politics:* "Inclining to the right." *Religion:* Church of England. *Home:* 89 Nunney Rd., Frome, Somerset, England. *Agent:* Christy & Moore Ltd., 52 Floral St., Covent Garden, London W.C.2, England.

CAREER: Novelist. Ministry of Agriculture and Fisheries, stenographer, 1943-45. *Member:* Society of Authors.

WRITINGS: The Greater Dawn, Leonard Parsons, 1920; *The Quest of Michael Harland*, Leonard Parsons, 1921; *Constancy*, Leonard Parsons, 1922; *Peter Thurstan*, Robert Holden, 1925; *The Vintage*, Robert Holden, 1925; *Barren Lands*, Robert Holden, 1926; *The Substance of His House*, Robert Holden, 1927; *Endless Furrows*, Hodder & Stoughton, 1928; *Starveacres*, Hodder & Stoughton, 1930; *Fire among Thorns*, Hodder & Stoughton, 1931; *Annabel Verinder*, Hodder & Stoughton, 1931; *Rainbow at Night*, Hodder & Stoughton, 1932; *Pennycocks in Paradise*, Hodder & Stoughton, 1933; *Cornish Excursion*, Hodder & Stoughton, 1934; *Trumpets Sound for the Victor*, George Newnes, 1935; *The Armoured Virgin*, George Newnes, 1938; *Unto Us a Child*, Macdonald & Co., 1943; *Fear No More*, Macdonald & Co., 1944; *The Fingerpost*, Macdonald & Co., 1945; *Creeping Jenny*, Macdonald & Co., 1946; *Landscape under Snow*, Macdonald & Co., 1948; *The Disenchanted*, Macdonald & Co., 1948.

All published by Macdonald & Co. except as indicated: *The Sufficient Beauty*, 1950; *Laggard Spring*, 1951; *I Am a Wanderer*, 1952; *Cousin Trudi*, 1953; *Candles for a Journey*, 1954; *The Face of the Enemy*, 1955; *The Captive Dreamers*, 1956; *There Is a Country*, 1957; *Flight from a Shadow*, 1958; *The Wish That Is Granted*, 1958; *The Hour Before Sunset*, 1960; *The Little Immortality*, 1961; *A Charm of Nieces*, 1962; *A Summer Pilgrimage*, 1963; *Held in Suspense*, 1964; *The Twilight of Hester Lorimer*, 1965; *Rogue's Mantle*, 1966; *A Hint of Murder*, 1967; *Vendetta in Connemara*, R. Hale, 1968; *Late Flowering for Mc-Farthing*, R. Hale, 1970; *Albatross Aunt*, R. Hale, 1971.

WORK IN PROGRESS: Next Door to the Savages, a novel.

AVOCATIONAL INTERESTS: Reading, knitting, canasta, tapestry work, watercolor painting.

*   *   *

KENYON, James William 1910-

PERSONAL: Born February 20, 1910, in London, England; son of James and Jessica (Howard) Kenyon; married Phyllis Mary Copson; children: Alexandra Patricia (Mrs. Carl Porter), Roger James Nelson, James Wynant Stephen. *Education:* Educated in London, England. *Politics:* Liberal. *Religion:* Church of England. *Home:* 31, Stonehill Dr., Great Glen, Leicestershire, England. *Office:* Holt/Blond Ltd., Iliffe House, Iliffe Ave., Oadby, Leicestershire, England.

CAREER: Librairie Hachete (publishers), London, England, general clerk in education department, 1927-37; Oliver & Boyd Ltd. (publishers), Edinburgh, Scotland, educational representative and associate editor, 1937-40;

Edward Arnold Ltd. (publishers), London, England, field editor and associate editor, 1945-62; Blond Educational Ltd. (publishers), now Holt/Blond Ltd., London, England, 1963—, began as sales director and associate editor, became director. Free-lance reader for publishing houses. *Wartime service:* National Fire Service, company officer. *Member:* Association of Publishers' Educational Representatives (president, 1958-59), Institute of Directors' Club, Children's Book Circle.

WRITINGS: (Editor with Maurice Thiery) *Recits comiques et dramatiques*, Oliver & Boyd, 1939; *On My Right*, Thomas Nelson, 1940; *Racing Wheels*, Thomas Nelson, 1941; *The Boy's Book of Modern Heroes*, Harrap, 1942; *Peter Trant, Cricketer-Detective*, Methuen, 1944; *Alan of the Athletic*, Methuen, 1945; *The Fighting Avenger*, Mellifont Press, 1945; *Beau Nash, Heavyweight Champion*, Mellifont Press, 1946; *Mystery at Brinsford*, Thomas Nelson, 1946; *Peter Trant, Heavyweight Champion*, Methuen, 1946; *Lightweight Honours*, Thomas Nelson, 1947; *The Fourth Arm: A Survey of Fire-Fighting, Past, Present, and Future*, Harrap, 1948; *Peter Trant, Speed King*, Methuen, 1949; *Traitor's Gold*, Thomas Nelson, 1952; (with J. G. Colson) *Five Plays for Seniors*, McDougall's Educational Co., 1953; *Easter Egg*, Thomas Nelson, 1960; *Black Flash*, McDougall's Educational Co., 1961; *Fire Sleuth and Moon Rocket*, McDougall's Educational Co., 1961; *Boxing History*, Methuen, 1962; *Children of the American West*, McDougall's Educational Co., 1963; *Focus on Cars*, McDougall's Educational Co., 1964; *Ann of Appleby's*, McDougall's Educational Co., 1964; *Cornish Adventure*, Thomas Nelson, 1964; *Enemies of Outer Space*, McDougall's Educational Co., 1964.

Contributor to *Leicester Mercury, Eagle Annual, Boxing News, Fire, Bookseller, British Books, Higher Education Journal*, and *Times Educational Supplement*. Editor of *NFS Journal* (publication of National Fire Service), and of *News and Views* (journal of Association of Publishers' Educational Representatives). Editor, "Emergency Ward-10" novels, Blond, 1965-66.

SIDELIGHTS: The Boy's Book of Modern Heroes has been transcribed into Braille. *Avocational interests:* Sports, particularly cricket and boxing; collecting oil paintings by unknowns.

*   *   *

KETCHUM, Marshall D(ana) 1905-

PERSONAL: Born December 16, 1905, in Buffalo, N.Y.; son of Dorr Mason (an industrial executive) and Maude (Moore) Ketchum; married Clara Whitten, September 1, 1931; children: Marshall Dorr, Richard Jennings. *Education:* Syracuse University, B.S., 1928, M.S., 1929; University of Chicago, Ph.D., 1937. *Home:* Chicago, Ill. *Office:* Graduate School of Business, University of Chicago, Chicago, Ill. 60637.

CAREER: Syracuse University, Syracuse, N.Y., registrar, 1929-30; Duke University, Durham, N.C., instructor, 1931-32; Utah State University, Logan, 1932-38, began as assistant professor, became associate professor; University of Kentucky, Lexington, 1938-46, began as assistant professor, became professor; University of Chicago, Graduate School of Business, Chicago, Ill., associate professor, 1945-50, professor of finance, 1950-71, professor emeritus and professorial lecturer in finance, 1971—. Director of Life Officers Investment Seminar, Financial Analysts Seminar. *Member:* American Economic Association, American

Finance Association, American Association of University Professors, Institute of Chartered Financial Analysts.

WRITINGS: *The Fixed Investment Trust*, University of Chicago Press, 1937; (with Ralph Russell Pickett) *Investment Principles and Policy*, Harper, 1954; (editor with Leon T. Kendall) *Readings in Financial Institutions*, Houghton, 1965. Editor, *Journal of Finance*, 1946-56.

* * *

KEYS, Thomas Edward 1908-

PERSONAL: Born December 2, 1908, in Greenville, Miss.; son of Thomas Napoleon (an accountant) and Margaret (Boothroyd) Keys; married Elizabeth Schaack, November 2, 1934; children: Thomas Frederick, Charles Edward. *Education:* Beloit College, A.B., 1931; University of Chicago, M.A., 1934. *Religion:* Episcopalian. *Home:* Sunny Slopes, Rochester, Minn. 55901. *Office:* Mayo Clinic, 200 First St., Rochester, Minn. 55901.

CAREER: Mayo Clinic, Rochester, Minn., assistant librarian, 1934-35, reference librarian, 1935-42, librarian, 1946-69, senior library consultant, 1969—; University of Minnesota, Minneapolis, associate professor, 1960-69, professor of history of medicine, 1969—. Lecturer, University of Tokyo, 1961. Member of board of regents, National Library of Medicine, 1959-62; honorary consultant, Army Medical Library, 1946-50. *Military service:* U.S. Army, 1942-46; became lieutenant colonel; received Army Commendation Ribbon. *Member:* International Society for the History of Medicine, American Association for the History of Medicine, Medical Library Association (president, 1957-58; director, 1959-59), Phi Beta Kappa, Beta Phi Mu, Pi Kappa Alpha. *Awards, honors:* Distinguished Service Citation, Beloit College Alumni, 1956.

WRITINGS: *The Colonial Library and the Development of Sectional Differences in the American Colonies*, [Chicago], 1938; (editor with F. A. Willius) *Cardiac Classics: A Collection of Classic Works on the Heart and Circulation*, Mosby, 1941, 2nd edition published as *Classics of Cardiology: A Collection of Classic Works on the Heart and Circulation*, two volumes, Dover, 1961; *The Development of Anesthesia*, privately printed, 1943; (with Chauncy D. Leake and Noel A. Gillespie) *The History of Surgical Anesthesia*, Schuman, 1945, 2nd edition, with an appendix by John F. Fulton, Dover, 1963; (with C. Wilbur Rucker) *The Atlases of Ophthalmoscopy: A Bibliography, 1850-1950*, privately printed, 1950, revised edition, 1960; *The "Salmonia" of Sir Humphry Davy*, privately printed, 1956; (with Catherine Kennedy and Ruth M. Tews) *Applied Medical Library Practice*, C. C Thomas, 1958; *Thomas James Holmes, Bibliographer, Bookbinder and Librarian, 1875-1959*, [Baltimore], 1959; *Sir William Osler and the Medical Library*, [Baltimore], 1961; *Diary of a Trip to the Far East*, privately printed, 1961; *Edmund Revere Osler, 1895-1917*, [Chicago], 1964; (editor with Albert Faulconer, Jr.) *Foundations of Anesthesiology*, two volumes, C. C Thomas, 1965.

Member of editorial board, *New Gould Medical Dictionary*, Blakiston, 1949. Contributor to professional journals in medical history and librarianship. Editor, *Bulletin of the Medical Library Association*, 1942-45.

WORK IN PROGRESS: With R. V. Randall, *Foundations of Endocrinology*, for Warren H. Green; *Books and Friends at Mayo and Elsewhere*, an autobiography.

KHARE, Narayan Bhaskar 1882-
(Bapu)

PERSONAL: Born March 16, 1882, in Kolaba District, India; son of Bhaskar Ballal (a lawyer) and Durga (Gokhale) Khare; married Sundar, 1900 (died, 1911); married Amba, 1912 (died, 1918); married Mathura, 1919; children: Vidyadhar, Usha (Mrs. Ramchandra Damle), Jamuna (Mrs. Shridhar Dongre), Snehlata (Mrs. Ramkrishna Karve), Vimal, Kusum (Mrs. Hadhusudan Kane), Mukta (Mrs. Satish Vartak), Suryakant, Meenaxi. *Education:* Government College, Jabalpur, India, B.A., 1902; Punjab University, M.B., 1907, M.D., 1913. *Politics:* Hindu Maha Sabha. *Religion:* Hindu. *Home:* Indira Mahal Dhantoli, Nagpur, Maharashtra, India.

CAREER: Civil assistant surgeon in Central Provinces, India, 1907-16; private medical practice, Nagpur, India, 1916—. Joined Indian National Congress, 1918, elected prime minister, Government of Central Provinces, 1937, expelled from Congress, 1938; appointed member of Government of India, 1943, resigned, 1946; appointed prime minister, Alwar State, 1947, suppressed Muslim attempt to join the area to Pakistan, resigned after Ghandhi's assassination, 1948; joined all-India Hindu Maha Sabha 1949, presided over annual sessions at Calcutta, 1949, Poona, 1950, and Jaipur, 1951, member of House of the People from Gwalior, 1952-57.

WRITINGS: *My Past Twelve Years* (in Marathi and Hindi), G. M. Joshi, 1956; *My Political Memoirs; or, Autobiography* (in English), J. R. Joshi, 1959; *Khare Darshan* (in Marathi), Vikram Sawarker, 1964.

Pamphlets in English: *My Defense*, A. G. Sheorey, 1938; *Khare versus Nehru*, privately printed, 1961.

* * *

KIDDELL-MONROE, Joan 1908-

PERSONAL: Born August 9, 1908, in Clacton-on-Sea, Essex, England; daughter of William and Lallah Ethel Frances (Lloyd) Kiddell-Monroe; married Webster Murray (a portrait painter and illustrator; deceased); children: James Euan. *Education:* Attended Willesden and Chelsea Schools of Art. *Home:* Ca'n Murray, Camino del Murtara, Soller, Mallorca, Baleareas, Spain.

CAREER: Began working in an advertising studio at eighteen; left after a number of years ("the soul-destroying work almost finished me as an artist") to freelance as an artist and illustrator.

WRITINGS—All self-illustrated: *In His Little Black Waistcoat*, Longmans, Green, 1939; *In His Little Black Waistcoat to China*, Longmans, Green, 1940; *Little Skunk*, Nicholson & Watson, 1942; *Ingulabi*, Nicholson & Watson, 1943; *Wau-Wau the Ape*, Methuen, 1947; *The Irresponsible Goat*, Methuen, 1948; *In His Little Black Waistcoat to India*, Longmans, Green, 1948; *In His Little Black Waistcoat to Tibet*, Longmans, Green, 1949.

Illustrator: Thomas Wyatt Bagshawe, *Pompey Was a Penguin*, Oxford University Press, 1940; David Severn, *Rick Afire*, John Lane, 1942; Patricia Lynch, *Longears: The Story of a Little Grey Donkey*, Dent, 1943; David Severn, *Wagon for Five*, John Lane, 1944; Pearl S. Buck, *The Water-Buffalo Children*, Methuen, 1945; Mary Norton, *The Magic Bed-Knob*, Dent, 1945; Buck, *The Dragon Fish*, Methuen, 1946; Dorothy Martin, *Munya the Lion*, Oxford University Press, 1946; Severn, *Forest Holiday*, John Lane, 1946; Severn, *Ponies and Poachers*, John Lane,

1947; Patricia M. Donahue, *Whiskery Jinks and the Donkey Cart*, Methuen, 1948, British Book Center, 1953; Severn, *The Cruise of the "Maiden Castle,"* Bodley Head, 1948; Frank F. Darling, *Sandy the Red Deer*, Oxford University Press, 1949; Hugh Gardner, *Tales from the Marble Mountain*, Oxford University Press, 1949, Meredith, 1969; Severn, *Hermit in the Hills*, John Lane, 1949; Severn, *Treasure for Three*, Bodley Head, 1949.

Maribel Edwin, *This Way to Greenacres*, Longmans, Green, 1950; E. Dixon, editor, *Fairy Tales from the Arabian Nights*, Dent, 1951, Dutton, 1952; (with others) Buck, *One Bright Day, and Other Stories for Children*, Methuen, 1952; R. Forbes-Watson, *Ambari!*, Oxford University Press, 1952; Rene Guillot, *Sama*, translation by Gwen Marsh, Oxford University Press, 1952; Homer, *The Odyssey*, retold by Barbara L. Picard, Walck, 1952; Lynch, *The Boy at the Swinging Lantern*, Dent, 1952; Severn, *Burglars and Bandicoots*, Bodley Head, 1952; Edwin, *Curlew Jon*, Thomas Nelson, 1953; Guillot, *Sirga, Queen of the African Bush*, translation by Marsh, Oxford University Press, 1953, Criterion, 1959; Lynch, *Delia Daly of Galloping Green*, Dent, 1953; Guillot, *Oworo*, translation by Marsh, Oxford University Press, 1954; Lynch, *Orla of Burren*, Dent, 1954; Mary Elwyn Patchett, *Tam, the Untamed*, Lutterworth, 1954; Barbara Ker Wilson, *Scottish Folk-Tales and Legends*, Walck, 1954; Lorna Wood, *People in the Garden*, Dent, 1954; Edwin, *Zigzag Path*, Thomas Nelson, 1955; Margherita Fanchiotti, *Stories from the Bible*, Oxford University Press, 1955; Emmeline Garnett, *Hills of Sheep*, Hodder & Stoughton, 1955; Guillot, *Kpo the Leopard*, translation by Marsh, Oxford University Press, 1955; Gwyn Jones, *Walsh Legends and Folk-Tales*, Oxford University Press, 1955, Walck, 1965; Patchett, *Treasure of the Reef*, Lutterworth, 1955; Patchett, *Undersea Treasure Hunters*, Lutterworth, 1955; Jones, *Scandinavian Legends and Folk-Tales*, Oxford University Press, 1956; Patchett, *Return to the Reef*, Lutterworth, 1956; Muriel Sherrington, *Poetical Pig*, Brockhampton Press, 1956; Wood, *Rescue by Broomstick*, Dent, 1956; Nada Curcija-Prodanovic, *Yugoslav Folk-Tales*, Oxford University Press, 1957; Guillot, *Animal Kingdom*, translation by Marsh, Oxford University Press, 1957; Fritz Mueller-Guggenbuehl, *Swiss-Alpine Folk-Tales*, translation by Katharine Potts, Walck, 1958.

Eulenspiegel, *The Owl and the Mirror*, edited and translated by Godfrey Freeman, Basil Blackwell, 1960, Duell, Sloan & Pearce, 1961; Homer, *The Iliad*, retold by Barbara L. Picard, Oxford University Press, 1960; Henry Wadsworth Longfellow, *Song of Hiawatha*, Dutton, 1960; Aesop, *Fables*, translation by John Warrington, Dent, 1961, Dutton, 1966; Robert Graves, *Myths of Ancient Greece*, Cassell, 1961; Eugenie Fenton, *Sher, Lord of the Jungle*, Benn, 1962; Homer, *The Adventures of Odysseus*, retold by Andrew Lang, Dutton, 1962; Ogden Nash, *Girls Are Silly*, Dent, 1964; James Reeves, *English Fables and Fairy Stories*, Walck, 1966; Philip Manderson Sherlock, *West Indian Folk-Tales*, Walck, 1966; Charles Downing, *Russian Tales and Legends*, Walck, 1968; Ivan Southall, *The Curse of Cain*, Angus & Robertson, 1968; Southall, *The Sword of Esau*, Angus & Robertson, 1968; Strate Tsirka, *Aisopeioi mythoi*, Chryses Ekdoseis (Athens), 1968; Hester Burton, *The Great Gale*, Oxford University Press, 1969; Lorna Wood, *Hags by Starlight*, Dent, 1970.

WORK IN PROGRESS: Illustrating books; a novel set in Mallorca; reminiscences.

SIDELIGHTS: Mrs. Kiddell-Monroe told *CA:* "[I] am my own architect, remaking two houses. My son and I have two Ibizian hounds—tall, incredibly narrow dogs—descendents of the old Egyptian hunting dogs, an enormous red Setter, and the offspring of one of the hounds and the Setter.... You will notice that I cannot spell also—a drawback for an author—like the Spanish typewriter. I speak a very bad Spanish, with no grammar, but in some extraordinary way seem to get by unless it is a serious matter."

BIOGRAPHICAL/CRITICAL SOURCES: Illustrators of Children's Books, 1946-56, Horn Book, 1958.

*   *   *

KILGOUR, Raymond L(incoln)   1903-

PERSONAL: Born July 27, 1903, in Lexington, Mass.; son of Ashburn C. (a salesman) and Fannie L. (McKay) Kilgour; married Sarah Vance, August 24, 1933; children: Katharine Vance. *Education:* Harvard University, A.B., 1925, A.M., 1927, Ph.D., 1930; University of Michigan, A.B. in L.S., 1942. *Politics:* Independent Republican. *Home:* 1926 South 25th St., Lincoln, Neb. 68502.

CAREER: Harvard University, Cambridge, Mass., Sheldon traveling fellow, 1930-31, instructor and tutor, 1931-41; Carleton College, Northfield, Minn., assistant librarian and assistant professor, 1942-43; Escuela de Bibliotecarios Biblioteca Nacional del Peru, Lima, professor of bibliography and co-director of Library School, 1943-44; University of Michigan, Ann Arbor, assistant professor, 1945-50, associate professor, 1950-55, professor of library science, 1955-68, professor emeritus, 1968—.

WRITINGS: The Decline of Chivalry as Shown in the French Literature of the Late Middle Ages, Harvard University Press, 1937; *Messrs. Roberts Brothers, Publishers*, University of Michigan Press, 1952; *Estes and Lauriat, A History, 1872-1898*, University of Michigan Press, 1957; *Lee and Shepard, Publishers for the People*, Shoe String, 1965. Contributor of articles to professional journals and other periodicals.

SIDELIGHTS: Kilgour is competent in Latin, French, Spanish, Italian, and German. *Avocational interests:* Fine arts, music, nineteenth-century cultural and social history.

*   *   *

KIM, Helen   1899-1970

PERSONAL: Born February 27, 1899, in Inchon, Korea; daughter of Chin Yawn and Dora (Pak) Kim. *Education:* Ewha College, diploma, 1918; Ohio Wesleyan University, B.A., 1924; Boston University, M.A., 1925; Columbia University, Ph.D., 1931; Centro Escolar University, Manila, Phillippines, postdoctoral study, 1963. *Home:* 85-1 Daeshin-Dong, Sudaemoon-Ku, Seoul, Korea. *Office:* Ewha Woman's University, Seoul, Korea.

CAREER: Ewha College, Seoul, Korea, teacher, 1918-22, professor, 1929-30, dean, 1929-39, vice-president, 1932-39, president, 1939-45; Ewha Woman's University, Seoul, Korea, president, 1945-61, president emeritus, 1961-70, president of board of trustees, 1945-70. Publisher of *Korea Times*, Seoul, 1952-55. Member of Korea executive committee, UNESCO, 1953-70, and of Korean missions to United Nations, 1949, 1956-59. Vice-president, International Missionary Council, 1954-61, and of Korean Red Cross, 1955-60; chairman of board of directors, International Night College, 1958-70; member of board of directors, Korean Methodist Church, 1954-66, Korean Research

Institute, 1955-67, Methodist Theological Seminary, Seoul, 1955-56, 1962-70, Korean Anti-Communist League, 1955-65; member of American-Korean Scholarship Selection Committee, 1955-61; president, National Council of Women of the Republic of Korea, 1959-70, and of Upper Room Evangelistic Association, Seoul, 1960-70; roving ambassador of the Republic of Korea, 1965-70. Delegate or observer at more than fifty conferences of church, professional, and international organizations in America, Asia, and Europe, 1922-69.

MEMBER: Korean Association of University Women (president, 1950-66), Korean Christian Teachers Association (president, 1956-70), Columbia Alumni Association of Korea (president, 1955-70). *Awards, honors:* LL.D., Boston University, 1949, Ohio Wesleyan University, 1951, Ewha Woman's University, 1966; L.H.D., Cornell University, 1954, Centro Escolar University, 1963; Order of Cultural Merit, Republic of Korea, 1963; Ramon Magsaysay Award (Philippines), 1963; citation from Upper Room Evangelistic Association, 1963; Christian Leadership Award (Texas), 1966; named honorary citizen of Dallas and Fort Worth, Tex., 1966; Order of Diplomatic Service Merit, first class, Republic of Korea, 1970 (posthumous); citation from Korean Housewives Club's Foundation, 1971 (posthumous).

WRITINGS: Grace Sufficient, Upper Room, 1964.

(Died February 10, 1970)

* * *

KING, Archdale Arthur 1890-1972

PERSONAL: Born April 10, 1890, in Kensington, London, England; son of Charles Blakiston (a clerk in Holy Orders) and Helen E. (Wilson) King. *Education:* Keble College, Oxford, B.A. (honors). *Politics:* Conservative. *Home:* Weston Manor, Totland, Isle of Wight, England.

CAREER: Clergyman of Church of England prior to 1937; held several curacies and served as vicar of Holy Trinity Church, Reading, England, and as chaplain at Valescure, in the south of France; in 1937 received into the Roman Catholic Church; writer. *Member:* Oxford and Cambridge Club (London).

WRITINGS: Notes on the Catholic Liturgies, Longmans, Green, 1930; *Coteaux and Her Elder Daughters*, Burns & Oates, 1954; *Liturgies of the Religious Orders*, Longmans, Green, 1955; *Liturgy of the Roman Church*, Bruce, 1957; *Liturgies of the Primatial Sees*, Longmans, Green, 1957; *Liturgies of the Past*, Bruce, 1959; *Eucharistic Reservation in the Western Church*, Sheed, 1965; *Concelebration in the Christian Church*, Moybray, 1966; *The Rites of Eastern Christendom*, two volumes, AMS Press, 1972. Reviewer for *Catholic Herald, Duckett's Register*, and *Dublin Review*.

WORK IN PROGRESS: The Cistercian Order in the Baroque Centuries.

SIDELIGHTS: King spoke French and Italian. He traveled extensively in Europe, Africa, and the Near East, and stayed in many monasteries, especially Cistercian.

(Died July 10, 1972)

* * *

KING, Homer W. 1907-

PERSONAL: Born March 12, 1907, in Upland, Ind.; son of Charles Austin and Dora (Pierce) King; married Pauline Painter, June 6, 1931; children: David, Donald V. *Education:* Ball State University, A.B., 1929; University of Wisconsin, graduate study, 1930-32. *Office: Rochester Democrat and Chronicle*, Rochester, N.Y. 14614.

CAREER: High school teacher in Indiana, 1929-33; *Marion Chronicle*, Marion, Ind., city editor, 1935-37, 1939-41; Grant County (Ind.) Welfare Department, director, 1937-39; *Protestant Voice*, Fort Wayne, Ind., editor, 1941-46; *Fort Wayne News Sentinel*, Fort Wayne, Ind., chief editorial writer, 1946-52; *Geneva Times*, Geneva, N.Y., managing editor, 1952-54; *Rochester Democrat and Chronicle*, Rochester, N.Y., editorial writer, 1954—. *Member:* Sigma Delta Chi, Rochester Press Club. *Awards, honors:* Freedoms Foundation Award for editorial writing; award for distinguished service in journalism from Ball State University.

WRITINGS: Pulitzer's Prize Editor: A Biography of John A. Cockerill, Duke University Press, 1965. Writer of series of newspaper articles during tour of Europe, Middle East, and Africa, 1958, later reprinted as booklet.

* * *

KING, Spencer B(idwell), Jr. 1904-

PERSONAL: Born February 19, 1904, in Birmingham, Ala.; son of Spencer Bidwell (a minister) and Lizzie (Dodson) King; married Caroline Paul (a violinist), December 26, 1934; children: Spencer B. III, Janet Paul, Margaret Caroline. *Education:* Mercer University, A.B., 1929; George Peabody College for Teachers, M.A., 1936; University of North Carolina, Ph.D., 1950; also studied at Emory University, Vanderbilt University, and University of Michigan. *Politics:* Independent. *Religion:* Baptist. *Home:* 570 El Dorado Dr., Macon, Ga. 31204. *Office:* Mercer University, Macon, Ga. 31207.

CAREER: Mars Hill College, Mars Hill, N.C., instructor in history, 1933-44; Mercer University, Macon, Ga., associate professor, 1946-48, professor of history, 1948—, chairman of department, 1946—. Visiting summer professor at Furman University, 1940-44, Emory University, 1960, University of Georgia, 1963. Chairman of board of editors, Ardivan Press, Macon, 1960-62; Member of board of curators, Georgia Historical Society; trustee of Macon Museum of Arts and Sciences and Georgia Writers Association. *Member:* American Historical Association, American Association of University Professors, Southern Historical Association, Georgia Historical Society, Georgia Society of Historical Research (president, 1953). *Awards, honors:* Carnegie grant, 1950; United Daughters of the Confederacy Award, 1962, for contribution to Southern literature; Dixie Council of Authors and Journalists Award, 1968; Georgia Writers Association First Prize, 1969, for an unpublished manuscript; Daughters of Colonial Wars Teacher Award, 1973.

WRITINGS: Selective Service in North Carolina in World War II, University of North Carolina Press, 1949; (with Ellis Merton Coulter and A. B. Saye) *History of Georgia*, American Book Co., 1954; *Ebb Tide as Seen Through the Diary of Josephine C. Habersham*, University of Georgia Press, 1958; (editor) *John C. Butler's Historical Record of Macon and Central Georgia*, J. W. Burke, 1958; (editor) *Eliza Andrews' Wartime Journal of a Georgia Girl*, Ardivan Press, 1960; (editor) *Rebel Lawyer: The Letters of Theodorick W. Montfort*, University of Georgia Press, 1965; *Georgia Voices: A Documentary History to 1872*, University of Georgia Press, 1966. Contributor to *Encyclo-*

pedia Britannica, *Collier's Encyclopedia*, and professional journals.

Columnist, *Macon Telegraph and News*, 1960-65. Georgia editor, *Encyclopedia of Southern Baptists*.

WORK IN PROGRESS: Darien: The Death and Rebirth of a Southern Town.

* * *

KING-HALL, Magdalen 1904-1971
(Cleone Knox)

PERSONAL: Born July 22, 1904, in London, England; daughter of George Fowler (an admiral, Royal Navy) and Olga (Ker) King-Hall; married Patrick Perceval Maxwell (a landowner), January 19, 1929; children: Richard Stephen, Alastair Patrick, Brigid Louise King-Hall Walker. *Education:* Attended Downe House and St. Leonards School, St. Andrews, Scotland. *Politics:* Independent Conservative. *Religion:* Church of Ireland. *Home:* Headborough, Knockanore, County Waterford, Ireland. *Agent:* A. P. Watt & Son, Hastings House, Norfolk St., Strand, London W.C.2, England.

CAREER: Writer. First woman to take part in British Broadcasting Corp. program, "Round Britain Quiz."

WRITINGS: (Under pseudonym Cleone Knox) *The Diary of a Young Lady of Fashion in the Year 1764-1765*, Thornton Butterworth, 1925, Appleton, 1926, reissued under own name, Meredith, 1967; (under pseudonym Cleone Knox) *I Think I Remember: Being the Random Recollections of Sir Wickham Woolicomb, an Ordinary English Snob and Gentleman*, Appleton, 1927; (with Luise King-Hall) *The Well-Meaning Young Man*, Appleton, 1930; *Gay Crusader*, Appleton, 1934 (published in England as *Gay Crusaders*, P. Davies, 1934); *Jehan of the Ready Fists*, Newnes, 1936, Penguin, 1945; *Maid of Honour*, P. Davies, 1936; *Lady Sarah*, P. Davies, 1939; *Sturdy Rogue*, Thomas Nelson, 1941, Winston, 1945; *Somehow Overdone: A Sudan Scrapbook*, P. Davies, 1942; *Lord Edward*, P. Davies, 1943; *Life and Death of the Wicked Lady Skelton*, P. Davies, 1944, Rinehart, 1946, reissued as *The Wicked Lady*, May Fair Books, 1961; *How Small a Part of Time*, P. Davies, 1945, published as *The Lovely Lynchs*, Rinehart, 1947; *Lady Shane's Daughter*, P. Davies, 1947; *Tea at Crumbo Castle*, P. Davies, 1949; *The Fox Sisters*, P. Davies, 1950; *The Edifying Bishop: The Story of Frederick Hervey, Earl of Bristol and Bishop of Derry*, P. Davies, 1951; *The Venetian Bride*, P. Davies, 1954; *Hag Khalida*, P. Davies, 1954; *18th Century Story*, P. Davies, 1956; *The Story of the Nursery*, Routledge & Kegan Paul, 1958; (contributor) Eric Duthie, editor, *Stirring Stories for Girls*, Transatlantic, 1960; *The Noble Savages*, Bles, 1962. Author of radio plays, short stories, and articles.

SIDELIGHTS: Universal produced a motion picture of *The Life and Death of the Wicked Lady Skelton* in 1947, entitled "The Wicked Lady." *Avocational interests:* Dogs, reading, conversation; ghost stories and mysteries (the Shakespeare claimants, the Loch Ness monster); ballet, travel, old houses.

(Died March 1, 1971)

* * *

KIRK, Clara M(arburg) 1898-

PERSONAL: Born May 10, 1898, in Philadelphia, Pa.; daughter of Edgar and Fanny Dulany (Moncure) Marburg; married Rudolf Kirk (a professor of English), 1930; chil-

dren: Frances J. (deceased), Susanne B., Geoffrey (deceased), Donald. *Education:* Vassar College, A.B., 1920; University of Pennsylvania, A.M., 1921; University of Chicago, Ph.D., 1929. *Politics:* Democrat. *Religion:* Episcopalian. *Home:* 402 Balcones Apartments, San Marcos, Tex. 78666.

CAREER: Vassar College, Poughkeepsie, N.Y., instructor, 1923-26, 1928-29, assistant professor of English, 1929-33; Bryn Mawr College, Bryn Mawr, Pa., associate professor, 1933-36; Rutgers University, New Brunswick, N.J., lecturer in English, 1937-49, 1954, lecturer at Douglass College, 1956-63. *Member:* Modern Language Association of America, League of Women Voters (president, New Brunswick, N.J., 1955-57), Phi Beta Kappa. *Awards, honors:* Commission for Relief in Belgium, fellow in Belgium, 1921-23; Fulbright scholar in art at University of Liege, 1955-56.

WRITINGS: Sir William Temple: A Seventeenth Century "Libertin," Yale University Press, 1932; *Mr. Pepys and Mr. Evelyn*, University of Pennsylvania Press, 1935; *W. D. Howells: A Traveler from Altruria*, Rutgers University Press, 1962; (editor) Susanna Rowson, *Charlotte Temple*, Twayne, 1964; *W. D. Howells and Art in His Time*, Rutgers University Press, 1965; *Oliver Goldsmith*, Twayne, 1967; (editor) William Dean Howells, *The Altrurian Romances*, Indiana University Press, 1968.

With husband, Rudolf Kirk: (Editor) *Types of English Poetry*, Macmillan, 1940; (editor) William Dean Howells, *Representative Selections*, American Book Co., 1950, revised edition, Hill & Wang, 1961; *Authors of New Jersey: A Checklist*, New Jersey Department of Education, 1955; (editor and author of introduction and notes) W. D. Howells, *"Criticism and Fiction," and Other Essays*, New York University Press, 1959; (author of introduction) W. D. Howells, *The Letters of an Altrurian Traveller*, Scholars' Facsimiles, 1961; *The Church of St. John the Evangelist: A Parish History*, published by the church, New Brunswick, N.J., 1961; (author of introduction) W. D. Howells, *The Rise of Silas Lapham*, Collier, 1962; *W. D. Howells*, Twayne, 1962; (editor) W. D. Howells, *European and American Masters*, Collier, 1963.

Contributor of articles, notes, and reviews to professional journals; reviewer for *Survey Graphic* in the 1930s. Editor, *Vassar Alumnae Monthly*, 1937-39.

SIDELIGHTS: A friend described Mrs. Kirk's varied roles in some doggerel that began: "Lady scholar, critic, cook/Educator by the book." Although retired from teaching she still is very much involved in the academic world, still is an exponent of the idea that a teacher cannot escape having a place in society (that his political and social views *do* matter). *Avocational interests:* Art history, travel.

* * *

KIRKPATRICK, Ivone Augustine 1897-1964

PERSONAL: Born February 3, 1897, in Wellington, India; son of Ivone (a colonel) and Lady Mary (Hardinge) Kirkpatrick; married Violet Caulfeild Cottell, January 10, 1929; children: Ivone Peter, Cecilia Sybil. *Education:* Attended Downside School, Bath, England. *Religion:* Roman Catholic. *Agent:* David Higham Associates Ltd., 5-8 Lower John St., London WIR 4HA, England. *Office:* National Bank, 13 Old Broad St., London E.C.2, England.

CAREER: Entered British Diplomatic Service, 1919, serving as second secretary, 1921-28, first secretary, 1928-

30, first secretary, British Embassy, Rome, Italy, 1930-32, Charge d'Affaires, Vatican, Rome, Italy, 1932-33, first secretary, British Embassy, Berlin, Germany, 1933-38, director, Foreign Division, Ministry of Information, 1940, counsellor of Embassy, 1941, controller (European services), British Broadcasting Corp., 1941-44, deputy commander (civil), Control Commission Germany (British Element), 1944, Foreign Office, assistant under-secretary of state, 1945, deputy under-secretary of state, 1948-50, British High Commissioner in Germany, 1950-53, and permanent under-secretary of state, Foreign Office, 1953-57; Independent Television Authority, chairman, 1957-62; National Bank Ltd., London, England, chairman, 1963-64. Channel Tunnel Study Group, joint president, 1959-64. *Military service:* British Army, 1914-19; became captain; received Belgian Croix de Guerre, twice mentioned in dispatches.

MEMBER: St. James' Club (London), Kildare Street Club (Dublin). *Awards, honors:* Companion of St. Michael and St. George, 1939; Knight Commander of St. Michael and St. George, 1948; Knight Commander of the Bath, 1951; Knight Grand Cross of St. Michael and St. George, 1953; Knight Grand Cross of the Bath, 1956.

WRITINGS: The Inner Circle (memoirs), St. Martin's, 1959; *Mussolini: A Study in Power*, Hawthorn, 1964 (published in England as *Mussolini: Study of a Demagogue*, Odhams, 1964). Contributor to London newspapers and to *New York Times.*†

(Died May 25, 1964)

* * *

KIRSCHTEN, Ernest 1902-1974

PERSONAL: Born October 21, 1902, in Chicago, Ill.; son of Joseph J. and Mathilda (Heno) Kirschten; married Jo Nattinger, 1932; children: Peter Baile, Joseph Dicken. *Home:* 4523 Maryland Ave., St. Louis, Mo. 63108.

CAREER: Former editorial writer.

WRITINGS: Catfish and Crystal: The Story of St. Louis, U.S.A., Doubleday, 1960, revised edition, 1965. Author of various magazine articles.

WORK IN PROGRESS: A history of the Busch family and the Anheuser-Busch brewery.

(Died July 26, 1974)

* * *

KIRWAN, Molly (Morrow) 1906-
(Charlotte Morrow)

PERSONAL: Born May 29, 1906, in England; daughter of Robert Alexander and Mary (Thompson) Morrow; children: Christopher, Elizabeth (Mrs. Nicholas Monck), Richard. *Education:* Studied at King's College and London School of Economics and Political Science, University of London, B.A. (honors), 1929. *Politics:* Labor/liberal. *Religion:* Agnostic. *Home:* Long House, Snape, Saxmundham, Suffolk, England. *Agent:* A. M. Heath & Co. Ltd., 35 Dover St., London W.1, England.

CAREER: Began writing in middle age "when a small temporary patch of leisure enabled a long-suppressed ambition to be attempted"; currently engaged in establishing library in Suffolk, England, for the local educational authority.

WRITINGS—Under pseudonym Charlotte Morrow: *The Singing and the Gold*, Hutchinson, 1960; *The Noonday Thread*, Hutchinson, 1962; *The Watchers*, Hutchinson, 1963.

WORK IN PROGRESS: A novel, *Out of the Park*; a children's book, *The Glory House*.

SIDELIGHTS: Molly Kirwan speaks and reads French. Her novel, *The Watchers* has been translated into German. *Avocational interests:* Music, painting, archaeology; travel, particularly in Finland and Greece.

* * *

KISH, Leslie 1910-

PERSONAL: Born July 27, 1910, in Hungary; son of Albert (an engineer) and Serena (Spiegel) Kiss; married Rhea Kuleske (a pianist), March 3, 1947; children: Carla, Andrea. *Education:* University of Michigan, M.A., 1948, Ph.D., 1952. *Home:* 702 Sunset Rd., Ann Arbor, Mich. 48103. *Office:* University of Michigan, Ann Arbor, Mich. 48106.

CAREER: Section head for U.S. Bureau of Census, 1940-41, and statistician for U.S. Department of Agriculture, 1941-42, 1945-47; University of Michigan, Ann Arbor, assistant head of survey research center, 1947-50, lecturer, 1950-55, associate professor, 1955-60, professor of sociology, 1960—, head of sampling section of Institute for Social Research, 1951-62, and program director, 1963—. Visiting professor at London School of Economics and Political Science, 1969, 1972, and 1973. Consultant to World Fertility Survey. *Military service:* U.S. Army Air Forces, 1942-45; became technical sergeant. *Member:* International Statistical Institute, American Statistical Association, American Sociological Association (fellow), Royal Statistical Society, Sociological Research Association, Population Association of America, International Union for Scientific Study of Population, Phi Beta Kappa, Sigma Xi.

WRITINGS: Survey Sampling, Wiley, 1965. Contributor of articles to scientific journals including *American Statistical Association Journal*, *American Sociological Review*, and *Royal Statistical Society Journal*.

WORK IN PROGRESS: Research designs for measuring changes and comparison; and analytical statistics for complex samples.

* * *

KISINGER, Grace Gelvin (Maze) 1913-196(?)

PERSONAL: Surname is pronounced *Ki*-singer, first syllable as in "kite"; born May 14, 1913, in Ridgway, Pa.; daughter of Henry Riley and Labelle (Sutton) Maze; married Harry Elliott Kisinger (a businessman), April 16, 1938. *Education:* Indiana State College, Indiana, Pa., B.S., 1934. *Home:* 920 College Ave., Pittsburgh, Pa. *Agent:* Ruth Cantor, 120 West 42nd St., New York, N.Y. 10036.

CAREER: Worked in sales promotion and selling, principally with West Penn Power Co., Pittsburgh, Pa., and Ringgold Corp., Kittanning, Pa., 1936-55; began to write verse for greeting cards in 1944 and sold more than five hundred items to about ten different firms; switched to short stories and articles, and then to novels for teen-age girls.

WRITINGS: The Enchanted Summer, Random House, 1956; *More than Glamour*, Nelson, 1957; *The New Lucinda* (Junior Literary Guild selection), Nelson, 1958; *Bittersweet Autumn*, Macrae Smith, 1960; *Too Late Tomorrow*, Macrae Smith, 1962. Contributor to periodicals.

WORK IN PROGRESS: A novel for teenage girls, about student nursing.

SIDELIGHTS: The Enchanted Summer was published in a Japanese edition. *Avocational interests:* Reading, square dancing, swimming, politics.

BIOGRAPHICAL/CRITICAL SOURCES: Pittsburgh Press, March 12, 1956, October 30, 1957, December 8, 1957; *Miami Herald*, March 5, 1961.

(Deceased)

* * *

KISSEN, Fan(ny) 1904-

PERSONAL: Born December 6, 1904, in New York, N.Y.; daughter of Bernard and Sonia (Cross) Kissen. *Education:* Hunter College (now Hunter College of the City University of New York), B.A., 1923; additional writing courses at New York University and Columbia University. *Politics:* Democrat. *Religion:* Jewish. *Home:* 601 East 20th St., New York, N.Y. 10010.

CAREER: Former elementary teacher in New York City public schools; Station WNYE (Board of Education), New York, N.Y., scriptwriter for radio series, "Tales from the Four Winds," 1945-61, and consultant; also worked for other radio programs; free-lance writer. Publicity director for Teachers Volunteer Service Organization. New York City, 1942-45. *Member:* American Association for the United Nations. *Awards, honors:* Seven first awards, Ohio State Institute for Educational Radio Programs, for "Tales from the Four Winds."

WRITINGS—Books for children; all published by Houghton, except as noted: *The Straw Ox, and Other Plays*, 1948, reprinted 1964 (published in England as part of *Plays for the Loud Speaker*, two volumes, Harrap, 1952); *The Bag of Fire, and Other Plays*, 1949, reprinted 1964 (published in England as part of *Plays for the Loud Speaker*, see above); *The Crowded House, and Other Plays*, 1950, reprinted 1964 (published in England as part of *Plays for the Loud Speaker*, see above); *They Helped Make America* (plays), 1958; *The Golden Goose, and Other Plays*, 1963; *John Bowne, Defender of Freedom of Thought*, American Book Publishing Co., 1964.

WORK IN PROGRESS: Biographies of lesser-known men and women who fought for ideals or service, as a sort of juvenile *Profiles in Courage* series.

SIDELIGHTS: Most of Miss Kissen's books are collections of plays for eight, nine, and ten-year-olds, written in radio script format, including instructions for music and sound effects. Her seventeen-year radio series, "Tales from the Four Winds," dramatized world folk tales and legends, and was rebroadcast by WNYE and other radio stations through exchange programs of the National Association of Educational Broadcasting. Miss Kissen has traveled widely in Europe, the Near East, and South America. She speaks French, German, and "tourist" Italian. *Avocational interests:* Reading, music, art (mainly representational), painting.

BIOGRAPHICAL/CRITICAL SOURCES: Voice of America (magazine), November-December, 1950.

* * *

KITCHEN, Herminie B(roedel) 1901-1973

PERSONAL: Born May 14, 1901, in Arlington, N.J.; daughter of Frank A. (a contractor) and Herminie (Chaineux) Broedel; married Harvey B. Kitchen, July 31, 1926. *Education:* Rutgers University, Litt.B., 1922, M.A., 1933. *Home and office:* South Royalton, Vt. 05068.

CAREER: High school teacher of mathematics and biology, Asbury Park, N.J., 1922-24; Rutgers University, New Brunswick, N.J., editor of technical publications, 1924-50, associate specialist of agricultural information, 1950-56, specialist emeritus, 1956-73; free-lance editor and writer, beginning, 1956. Editor, U.S. Department of Agriculture, Washington, D.C., 1937; co-chairman of public relations during World War II for New Brunswick Defense Council. *Member:* American Association of Agricultural College Editors (life; director for two terms), American Association of University Women, Phi Beta Kappa, Civic Club (Royalton, Vt.).

WRITINGS: (Editor) *Diagnostic Techniques for Soils and Crops*, American Potash Institute, 1948; *Tips for Scientific Writers*, Rutgers Agricultural Experimental Station, 1949; (with Carroll Lane Fenton) *Plants That Feed Us*, Day, 1956, revised edition published as *Plants We Live On: The Story of Grains and Vegetables*, 1971; (with Fenton) *Animals That Help Us*, Day, 1959, revised edition, 1973; (with Fenton) *Fruits We Eat*, Day, 1961; (with Fenton) *Birds We Live With*, Day, 1963. Contributor to scientific periodicals and to magazines, including *Journal of American Pharmaceutical Association, Alaska Sportsman, Country Gentlemen, Farm Journal*. Associate editor, *Soil Science*, 1925-56, honorary consulting editor, beginning 1956.

WORK IN PROGRESS: Editorial work for Belgian and Dutch institutes of medical research and for Rutgers Institute of Microbiology.

(Died February 8, 1973)

* * *

KITTO, H(umphrey) D(avy) F(indley) 1897-

PERSONAL: Born February 6, 1897, in Stroud, Gloucester, England; son of Humphrey Davy (a schoolmaster) and Caroline (Findley) Kitto; married Ann Kraft (a pianist), January 6, 1928; children: Jane, John. *Education:* St. John's College, Cambridge, B.A., 1920. *Home:* 9 Southfield Rd., Bristol 6, England.

CAREER: University of Glasgow, Glasgow, Scotland, lecturer in Greek, 1921-44; University of Bristol, Bristol, England, professor of Greek, 1945-62, professor emeritus, 1962—. Visiting professor, Cornell University, 1954; Brandeis University, visiting professor, 1959, Ziskind Professor, 1962-63; University of California, Santa Barbara, Sather Professor, 1960-61, Regents' Professor, 1963-64. *Member:* British Academy (fellow), Royal Society of Literature (fellow). *Awards, honors:* Dr.-es-Lettres, University of Aix, 1961.

WRITINGS: In the Mountains of Greece, Methuen, 1933; *Greek Tragedy: A Literary Study*, Methuen, 1939, Barnes & Noble, 1952, 3rd revised edition, Barnes & Noble, 1966; *The Greeks*, Penguin, 1951, 2nd revised edition, 1961, with new preface by the author, Aldine, 1964; *Form and Meaning in Drama: A Study of Six Greek Plays and of "Hamlet,"* Methuen, 1956, Barnes & Noble, 1957, 2nd edition, Methuen, 1964; *Sophocles, Dramatist and Philosopher: Three Lectures Delivered at King's College, Newcastle-upon-Tyne*, Oxford University Press, 1958; (contributor) John Garrett, editor, *More Talking of Shakespeare*, Theatre Arts, 1959; (contributor) Claire Sacks and Edgar Whan, editors, *Hamlet: Enter Critic*, Appleton, 1960; (contributor) Whitney J. Oates, editor, *From Sophocles to Picasso: The Present-day Vitality of the Classical Tradition*, Indiana University Press, 1962; (translator into English verse) Sophocles, *Three Tragedies: Antigone,*

Oedipus the King, Electra, Oxford University Press, 1962; (contributor) Quentin Anderson and Joseph Mazzeo, editors, *The Proper Study: Essays on Western Classics*, St. Martin's, 1962; (contributor) John Gassner and Ralph Allen, editors, *Theatre and Drama in the Making*, Houghton, 1964; *Poiesis: Structure and Thought*, University of California Press, 1966. Contributor of articles and reviews to classical journals.

SIDELIGHTS: Kitto's analyses of classical literature are those of an Aristotelian. He believes that both Victorian and modern criticism of ancient Greek literature have diverted attention from the true intentions of the authors of these plays. Striving to re-emphasize the poetical and mythic background of the Greek tragedies, Kitto rejects the arguments of modern critics who tend to analyze these works in a political or historical context. According to Rosemary Harriott, "Professor Kitto maintains that a play means something, or at least that it has a central area of meaning, and he leads his reader out of critical chaos following no newly fashionable guide, but Aristotle." Elspeth Barker believes that "Kitto's first principle is that a critic should promote contact between the minds of reader and writer. That this contact has too seldom occurred with Greek literature is abundantly evident, and Kitto offers several explanations as to why it has not. First, the failure of critics to distinguish between original myth and a given author's deliberate use of it; second, such critics' personal formulae and *idees recues*; third, the variety in the association of the collective mind of any given period; last, failure in paying attention to the texts themselves."

Miss Barker agrees with Kitto's thesis. "All these [recent interpretations] have led to criticism becoming only too frequently a mere exchange of opinions, producing fruitless statements like: 'A poem is what you choose to make of it,' or the delightful but evasive game of spotting levels of meaning. While some of these tricks might profitably be applied to the examination of modern literature, they can only be damaging to any serious consideration of Greek tragic poetry. For in fifth-century Athens there was no prose literature; poetry was the only literary medium and Greek tragic drama was a public, popular art. A poet was also a teacher, not merely a purveyor of aesthetic luxuries, and he acknowledged heavy responsibilities to his audience. It seems highly likely that the poets actually meant what they said, and said it quite clearly."

Kitto also seems to have avoided the esoteric quality common in classical criticism. Miss Barker states that *Poiesis* "is a fascinating book, brilliantly convincing, very funny and very modest too...." W. J. Roscelli believes that "the demonstration [of Kitto's thesis] is brilliant and the style is witty and urbane." Acceptance of Kitto's work appears to be nearly universal among critics. The *Times Literary Supplement* reviewer praises *Form and Meaning in Drama* as "something of a classic of its kind. One may apply to it the simplest of critical questions: has the author anything to say that throws fresh light on the *Oresteia*, on *Hamlet*, on the dramatic art of the Greeks and the Elizabethans? There is no doubt that he has, and says it, within his chosen field, with learning and force allied to a true dramatic sensibility."

BIOGRAPHICAL/CRITICAL SOURCES: Times Literary Supplement, December 14, 1956, January 4, 1968; *Classical World*, October, 1966; *Choice*, January, 1967; *New Statesman*, June 9, 1967; *Listener*, July 13, 1967; *Comparative Literature*, summer, 1968.

KLAPPER, Charles F(rederick) 1905-

PERSONAL: Born March 29, 1905, in Bromley-by-Bow, London, England; son of Charles James and Edith Isabel (Moffat) Klapper; married Eileen Ethel Papineau, September 14, 1935. *Education:* Attended schools in London, England; Institute of Transport, graduate, 1937. *Home:* 45 Crest Rd., Hayes, Bromley, Kent RR2 7JA, England. *Office:* Ian Allan Ltd., Terminal House, Shepperton, Middlesex, England.

CAREER: Capon & Sons Ltd., London, England, road haulage clerk, 1924-27, 1932; Modern Transport Publishing Co. Ltd., London, editorial assistant on *Modern Transport* (newspaper), 1935-41, assistant editor, 1941-53, editor, 1953-68, director of firm, 1953-70. Consultant, *Passenger Transport and Modern Railways*, 1963-70. *Member:* Chartered Institute of Transport (fellow; vice-president, 1962-63), Railway and Canal Historical Society (president, 1964-65), Omnibus Society (president, 1950), Transport Tutorial Association (chairman, 1962-72).

WRITINGS: (Editor with David R. Lamb) *Modern Railway Operation*, 3rd edition (Klapper was not associated with earlier editions), Pitman, 1941; (editor) *Road Transport*, Staples, 1945; (editor) *Buses and Trams*, Ian Allan, 1949; *The Golden Age of Tramways*, Routledge & Kegan Paul, 1961; *The Trent Story* (Golden Jubilee of a bus operator), published by Trent Motor Traction Co. Ltd. for private circulation, 1963. Contributor to *Railway Magazine, Financial Times, Chambers' Encyclopaedia, Chambers' Annual Review, Buses, Modern Railways, Dock and Harbor Authority*, and other newspapers and journals. Editor, *Omnibus Magazine*, 1929-46; assistant editor, *Furniture Manufacturer*, 1934.

WORK IN PROGRESS: Studies on railway history, high-speed railways, future high-speed land transport, road and rail coordination; a history of the omnibus industry; *British Lorries, 1900-1945*; and a study of railway management under Sir Herbert Walker, general manager of Southern Railway (England), 1923-37, for Ian Allan.

AVOCATIONAL INTERESTS: Walking (has walked in every county in Great Britain); archeology, especially industrial archeology; ancient road systems, Roman and pre-Roman, photography.

*   *   *

KLETT, Guy S(oulliard) 1897-

PERSONAL: Born November 8, 1897, in Rexmont, Pa.; son of Irwin Henry and Kate Ellen (Soulliard) Klett; married Catharine Isabel Robbins, June 26, 1924; children: Gerald S. (deceased). *Education:* Lafayette College, Ph.B., 1920; Gettysburg College, A.M., 1923; graduate study at University of Michigan and University of Pennsylvania. *Religion:* Presbyterian. *Home:* 321 Mill Rd., Oreland, Pa. 19075.

CAREER: Gettysburg College, Gettysburg, Pa., instructor in English and history, 1921-23; Pennsylvania State College (now University), University Park, instructor in English, 1924-25; Heidelberg College, Tiffin, Ohio, instructor in history, 1925-29; United Presbyterian Church in U.S.A., Philadelphia, Pa., research historian, 1936-62. Lecturer on historic Philadelphia. *Military service:* U.S. Army, World War I, 1918. *Member:* American Society of Church History (treasurer, 1951—), Historical Society of Pennsylvania, Pennsylvania Historical Association. *Awards, honors:* Distinguished Service Award from Presbyterian Historical Society, 1961.

WRITINGS: Presbyterians in Colonial Pennsylvania, University of Pennsylvania Press, 1937; *Scotch-Irish in Pennsylvania*, Pennsylvania Historical Association, 1948; (editor) *Journals of Charles Beatty, 1762-1769*, Pennsylvania State University Press, 1962. Contributor of articles to encyclopedias and historical journals.

WORK IN PROGRESS: A book of the minutes of the Presbyterian Church, U.S.A., from 1706 to 1788.

*   *   *

KLOSS, Phillips   1902-

PERSONAL: Born July 11, 1902; son of Charles Luther (a minister) and Mary (Phillips) Kloss; married Alice Geneva Glasier (an artist), May 19, 1925. *Education:* University of California at Berkeley, A.B., 1925. *Politics:* Independent. *Religion:* Congregationalist. *Home:* Box 33, Taos, N.M.

CAREER: Newspaper reporter, ranch hand, and house builder at various times; poet, composer, and naturalist. *Member:* New Mexico Ornithological Society, Wilderness Society, Cooper Ornithological Club. *Awards, honors:* Silver Poetry Medal of Commonwealth Club of California, 1951, for *Dominant Seventh*.

WRITINGS: Arid, Macmillan, 1932; *Realization* (poems), Caxton, 1942; *Dominant Seventh* (poems), Caxton, 1950; *Forever Now*, Naylor, 1964; *Force and Fate* (poems), Naylor, 1968.

WORK IN PROGRESS: A new book of poems about Taos; piano compositions.

SIDELIGHTS: Kloss wrote: "As a naturalist poet I am naturally interested in natural subjects, such as ornithology, botany, geology, and anthropology. My wife and I have explored the West by car and foot for forty years, and hope to keep at it another twenty. My writing is emotionally and intellectually honest, free from faddistic tricks. Which emancipates it, and me, from either commercialism or ballyhoo by modernistical critics."

*   *   *

KNAPLUND, Paul (Alexander)   1885-1964

PERSONAL: Born February 5, 1885, in Bodo, Norway; came to United States in 1906, naturalized in 1913; son of Martinus Johnsen and Kristine (Andreassen) Knaplund; married Dorothy King, June 19, 1926; children: Katherine Barbara (Mrs. K. K. Turman), Paul W. *Education:* Red Wing Seminary, B.A., 1913; University of Wisconsin, M.A., 1914, Ph.D., 1919. *Religion:* Lutheran. *Home:* 2930 Arbor Dr., Madison, Wis. 53711.

CAREER: Teacher, Decorah, Iowa, 1914-16; University of Wisconsin, Madison, instructor, 1917-21, assistant professor, 1921-25, associate professor, 1925-27, professor of history, 1927-55, chairman of the department of history, 1932-38, 1942-49, professor emeritus, 1955-64. Whitney Professor at Wells College, 1955-56; Fulbright lecturer at University College of West Indies, 1956-57; visiting professor at University of Michigan, Columbia University, University of Colorado, and Duke University. *Member:* American Historical Association (member of council, 1946-51), Phi Beta Kappa, University Club and Maple Bluff Country Club (Madison). *Awards, honors:* Guggenheim fellow, 1926-27; knight first class, Order of St. Olav (Norway); D.Litt., St. Olaf College, 1951.

WRITINGS: Sir James Stephen and British North American Problems, 1840-1847, [Toronto], 1924; *Gladstone and*

Britain's Imperial Policy, Allen & Unwin, 1927, Archon Books, 1966; *Gladstone's Foreign Policy*, Harper, 1935; *The British Empire, 1815-1939*, Harper, 1941, new edition, Fertig, 1970; *James Stephen and the British Colonial System, 1813-1847*, University of Wisconsin Press, 1953; *Britain: Commonwealth and Empire, 1901-1955*, Hamish Hamilton, 1956, Harper, 1957; *Moorings Old and New: Entries in an Immigrant's Log* (memoirs), State Historical Society of Wisconsin, 1963.

Editor and author of introduction: Sir Edward Grey, *Speeches on Foreign Affairs, 1904-1914*, Allen & Unwin, 1931, Harvard University Press, 1932; *Letters from Lord Sydenham, Governor General of Canada, 1830-1841, to Lord John Russell*, Allen & Unwin, 1931; (with Carolyn M. Clewes) *Private Letters from the British Embassy in Washington to the Foreign Secretary, Lord Granville, 1880-1885*, American Historical Association, 1941; *Letters from the Berlin Embassy, 1871-1874, 1880-1885*, U.S. Government Printing Office, 1944; *British Views on Norwegian-Swedish Problems, 1880-1895*, Norsk Historisk Kjeldeskrift Institutt, 1952; *Gladstone-Gordon Correspondence, 1851-1896*, American Philosophical Society, 1961. Contributor to *Cambridge History of the British Empire*, 1939, and to *New Cambridge Modern History*, Volume XI, 1962. Member of board of editors, *Journal of Modern History*, 1946-51.

(Died April 8, 1964)

*   *   *

KNIGHT, Charles W.   1891-

PERSONAL: Born April 14, 1891; married Mattie Belle Stanton, 1915; children: Virginia Wendell Ridlon, David. *Education:* Attended public schools, and three years of prep school, New York. *Politics:* Republican. *Religion:* Baptist. *Home:* 698 Gray Rd., South Windham, Me. 04082.

CAREER: Worked at many trades prior to 1946; landscape designer and adviser, 1946—.

WRITINGS: Hurricane Haven, Moody, 1961; *Secrets of Green Thumb Gardening*, Fell, 1964.

WORK IN PROGRESS: Peace—Will Surely Come, a biblical prophesy in novel form.

SIDELIGHTS: Knight is interested in the welfare of abandoned children who are growing up in foster homes, as he did.

*   *   *

KNIGHT, Clayton   1891-1969

PERSONAL: Born March 30, 1891, in Rochester, N.Y.; son of Frederick Clayton and Elizabeth (Brooks) Knight; married Katharine Sturges (an artist and writer), July 28, 1922; children: Clayton, Jr. (deceased), Hilary. *Education:* Attended schools in Rochester, N.Y., and Chicago Art Institute. *Home and office:* Umpawaug Rd., West Redding, Conn. 06896. *Agent:* Lurton Blassingame, 60 East 42nd St., New York, N.Y. 10017.

CAREER: Writer and illustrator on aviation subjects. Special correspondent for Associated Press in England and Iceland, 1942; combat historian with U.S. Air Forces in Alaska, Aleutians, and central Pacific, 1943-45. Flew around South America, 1937; circled globe as passenger on first Pan American Airways world flight, 1947; circled globe, visiting air bases of the Military Air Transport Service, 1955. *Military service:* U.S. Air Service, pilot, 1917-

19. *Member:* Artists Guild, Wings Club (vice-president), Dutch Treat Club. *Awards, honors:* New York Herald Tribune Children's Spring Book Festival Award, 1946, for *The Quest of the Golden Condor*; Officer (civil division), Order of the British Empire, 1946.

WRITINGS—Chiefly self-illustrated: (With Harold Platt) *Ships Aloft: A Construction Book for Future Flyers*, Harper, 1936; *The Quest of the Golden Condor*, Knopf, 1946; *The Aviator*, McKay, 1947; *The Secret of the Buried Tomb*, Knopf, 1948; *Skyroad to Mystery*, Knopf, 1949; (with Robert C. Durham) *Hitch Your Wagon: The Story of Bernt Balchen*, Bell Publishing Co., 1950; *The Big Book of Real Jet Planes*, Grosset, 1952; *The Story of Flight*, Grosset, 1954; *The Big Book of Real Helicopters*, Grosset, 1955; *We Were There at the Normandy Invasion*, Grosset, 1956; *Lifeline in the Sky: The Story of the U.S. Military Transport Service*, Morrow, 1957; *Plane Crash: The Mysteries of Major Air Disasters and How They Were Solved*, Greenberg, 1958; *Rockets, Missiles and Satellites*, Grosset, 1958, expanded edition published as *The How and Why Book of Rockets and Missiles*, 1960; (with wife, K. S. Knight) *We Were There at the Battle of Britain*, Grosset, 1959; (with K. S. Knight) *The Real Book About Our Armed Forces*, Garden City Books, 1959; (with K. S. Knight) *We Were There at the Lafayette Escadrille*, Grosset, 1961; *The History of the Wings Club, 1942-1967: The First Twenty Five Years*, M. W. Lads, 1967.

Illustrator: John M. Grider, *War Birds: Diary of an Unknown Aviator*, Doran, 1926; Floyd Phillips Gibbons, *The Red Knight of Germany: The Story of Baron von Richthofen, Germany's Great War Bird*, Doubleday, 1927; Norman Shannon Hall, *The Balloon Buster, Frank Luke of Arizona*, Doubleday, 1928; Bert Hall and John J. Niles, *One Man's War: The Story of the Lafayette Escadrille*, Holt, 1929; *Pilot's Luck* (includes excerpts from stories by Elliott White Springs, Captain A. Roy Brown, Floyd Gibbons, and Norman S. Hall), McKay, 1929.

WORK IN PROGRESS: Articles on aviation and astronautics for *Grolier International Encyclopedia*.

(Died July 17, 1969)

*   *   *

KNIGHT, Margaret K(ennedy) Horsey 1903-

PERSONAL: Born November 23, 1903, in Waltham Cross, Hertfordshire, England; daughter of Ernest Percival (a headmaster) and Katherine (Edwards) Horsey; married Arthur Rex Knight (a professor of psychology), July 4, 1936 (died, 1963). *Education:* Girton College, Cambridge, B.A., 1926, M.A., 1948. *Politics:* "Floating voter (left-center)." *Home:* Hope House, Bucksburn, Aberdeen, Scotland. *Agent:* Curtis Brown Ltd., 1 Craven Hill, London W2 3EW, England.

CAREER: National Institute of Industrial Psychology, London, England, librarian, information officer, and editor of journal, 1926-36; University of Aberdeen, Aberdeen, Scotland, lecturer in psychology, 1936-70. *Member:* British Psychological Society, British Humanist Association.

WRITINGS: (With husband, Rex Knight) *A Modern Introduction to Psychology*, University Tutorial Press, 1948, 7th edition, 1966; (editor) *William James: A Selection from His Writings*, Penguin, 1950; *Morals without Religion, and Other Essays*, Dobson, 1955; *Physique and Personality* (lecture), [London], 1957; (editor) *Humanist Anthology, from Confucius to Bertrand Russell*, Barrie & Rockliff,

1961; (contributor) John Brierly, editor, *Science in Its Context*, Heinemann Educational Books, 1964; (contributor) A. J. Ayer, editor, *The Humanist Outlook*, Pemberton Publishing, 1968. Contributor to *New Statesman, Spectator, Humanist*, and other journals.

*   *   *

KNIGHT, Maxwell 1900-

PERSONAL: Born July 9, 1900, in London, England; son of Hugh Coleraine (a solicitor) and Ada Phyllis (Hancock) Knight; married Susan Mary Durell Barnes, 1943. *Education:* Attended schools in England. *Agent:* A. P. Watt & Son, Hastings House, 10 Norfolk St., London W.C. 2, England.

CAREER: Author, lecturer, and broadcaster on zoological and other natural history subjects. British Broadcasting Corp., regular broadcaster on natural history programs, beginning 1946; also has done television features for British Broadcasting Corp. and Independent Television. *Military service:* Royal Naval Reserve, 1917-19; British War Office, attached to General Staff, 1939-46. *Member:* Institute of Biology, British Naturalists' Association (president), Royal Society for the Protection of Birds (fellow; council member, 1961-64), Zoological Society of London (fellow; former council member), Linnean Society of London (fellow). *Awards, honors:* Order of the British Empire, 1943.

WRITINGS—For children: *Pets Usual and Unusual*, Routledge & Kegan Paul, 1951; *Keeping Reptiles and Fishes*, Nicholson & Watson, 1952; *The Young Field Naturalist's Guide*, G. Bell, 1952; *Letters to a Young Naturalist*, Collins, 1955; *British Reptiles: Amphibians, and Pond Dwellers*, Museum Press, 1956; *Maxwell Knight Replies: 255 Natural History Questions Answered*, Routledge & Kegan Paul, 1959; *Frogs, Toads and Newts in Britain*, Brockhampton Press, 1962; *Tortoises and How to Keep Them*, Brockhampton Press, 1964, revised edition, edited and enlarged by John Bell, Brockhampton Press, 1970; *Birds as Living Things: An Introduction to the Study of Birds*, Collins, 1964; *The Small Water Mammals*, Bodley Head, 1967, McGraw, 1968.

For adults and young adults: *Bird Gardening: How to Attract Birds*, Routledge & Kegan Paul, 1954; *Some of My Animals*, G. Bell, 1954; *A Cuckoo in the House*, Methuen, 1955; *Animals After Dark*, Routledge & Kegan Paul, 1956; *How to Observe Our Wild Mammals*, Routledge & Kegan Paul, 1957; *Taming and Handling Animals*, G. Bell, 1959; *Talking Birds*, G. Bell, 1961; *Animals and Ourselves*, Hodder & Stoughton, 1962; (with L. Harrison Matthews) *The Senses of Animals*, Museum Press, 1963, Philosophical Library, 1964; *My Pet Friends*, Warne, 1964; *Reptiles in Britain*, Brockhampton Press, 1965; *How to Keep a Gorilla*, Wolfe, 1968. Contributor to British journals, including *Field, Country Life*, and *Country Fair*.

WORK IN PROGRESS: A book on the threats to wildlife and on conservation problems; studies of animals in captivity and observations of animals in nature.

*   *   *

KNOX, John Ballenger 1909-

PERSONAL: Born September 16, 1909, in Mayesville, S.C.; son of Hubbard Allen and Eunice (Ballenger) Knox. *Education:* Davidson College, B.A., 1930; University of North Carolina, M.A., 1934; Harvard University, Ph.D., 1939; also studied at Columbia University and New York

University. *Religion:* Episcopalian. *Home:* 4627 Wye Way Rd., Knoxville, Tenn. 37920. *Office:* Department of Sociology, University of Tennessee, Knoxville, Tenn. 37916.

CAREER: American University, Beirut, Lebanon, instructor, 1930-32; Standard Oil Co., Elizabeth, N.J., personnel assistant, 1938-40; University of Tennessee, Knoxville, 1946—, now professor of sociology. Visiting professor at University of Buenos Aires, Argentina, 1957; visiting lecturer at National University of Colombia, Bogota, 1959. *Military service:* U.S. Navy, 1942-46; became lieutenant commander. *Member:* International Sociological Association, American Sociological Association, Industrial Relations Research Association, American Association of University Professors, Southern Sociological Society.

WRITINGS: (With others) *The People of Tennessee: A Study of Population Trends*, introduction by William E. Cole, University of Tennessee Press, 1949; *The Sociology of Industrial Relations: An Introduction to Industrial Sociology*, Random House, 1955; (editor) *The Ballenger Family of Oconee County, South Carolina*, G. W. Ballenger, 1956. Contributor of articles and reviews to professional journals.

WORK IN PROGRESS: Research on industry in Latin America; study of social isolation.

AVOCATIONAL INTERESTS: Archaeology, fishing, gardening.†

*   *   *

KOBER, Arthur 1900-

PERSONAL: Born August 25, 1900, in Brody, Austria-Hungary (now Ukrainian Soviet Socialist Republic); brought to United States in 1904; son of Adolph Mayer and Tillie (Ballison) Kober; married Lillian Hellman, 1925 (divorced, 1932); married Margaret Frohnknecht, January 11, 1941 (died, 1951); children: Catherine. *Education:* Attended public schools in New York, N.Y. *Home:* 241 Central Park West, New York, N.Y. 10024.

CAREER: Left High School of Commerce after one semester and worked as stock clerk for Gimbels in New York, N.Y.; took a business course and became a stenographer for an automobile company, then for Grenville Kleiser (an author), 1915-22; theatrical press agent for the Shuberts, Jed Harris, Edgar Selwyn, Guthrie McClintic, and Marc Connelly, 1922-29 (produced a play, "Me," by Henry Myers, in this period); columnist for *New York Morning Telegraph*, *New York Evening Sun*, *Theatre* (magazine), 1927-30; screenwriter for Paramount, Fox, R.K.O., Metro-Goldwyn-Mayer, and Columbia Pictures, 1930-50, with credits on more than thirty films, including "Wintertime," "The Little Foxes," and "My Own True Love"; author and playwright. *Member:* P.E.N., Dramatists Guild of the Authors League of America. *Awards, honors:* Roi Cooper Megrue Prize (for best comedy), 1937, for "Having Wonderful Time."

WRITINGS: Thunder Over the Bronx (also see below), Simon and Schuster, 1935; *Having Wonderful Time* (play; produced in 1937), Random House, 1937; *Pardon Me for Pointing*, Simon and Schuster, 1939; *My Dear Bella* (also see below), Random House, 1941; *Parm Me* (includes *Thunder Over the Bronx* and *My Dear Bella*, published in two volumes), Constable, 1945; *That Man Is Here Again*, Random House, 1946; *Bella, Bella, Kissed a Fella*, Random House, 1951; *Oh, What You Said!*, Simon & Schuster, 1958.

Other plays produced: (With Joshua Logan and Harold

Rome) "Wish You Were Here" (musical), 1952; (with George Oppenheimer) "A Mighty Man Is He" (comedy), 1959.

Contributor to *New Yorker*, including "Bella" stories, 1926-58.

WORK IN PROGRESS: Having a Terrible Time, a memoir, or a book of fiction based on fact, for Doubleday.

BIOGRAPHICAL/CRITICAL SOURCES: New York Times Book Review, October 28, 1951.

*   *   *

KOJIMA, Takashi 1902-

PERSONAL: Born February 27, 1902; son of Yubi and Shige (Utagawa) Kojima; married Yuki Nakamura; children: Keiko (Mrs. Eisuke Kondo), Sakiko (Mrs. Takeshi Hirata), Noriko (Mrs. Donald Iwamura), Makoto (son). *Education:* Aoyamagukuin University, student, 1919-21. *Religion:* Christian. *Home:* 483 Josuiminamicho, Kodaira City, Tokyo Prefecture, Japan.

CAREER: Meiji University, Tokyo, Japan, instructor, 1928-42, assistant professor, 1952-56, professor of literature, 1956-68; Broadcasting Corporation of Japan, Tokyo, translator, 1942-52; Yamawaki College, Tokyo, professor of English, 1968—. *Member:* Association of Japanese Translators, International Abacus Association (Japanese committee).

WRITINGS: (Translator) Ryunosuke Akutagawa, *Rashomon and Other Stories*, Liveright, 1952; *The Japanese Abacus: Its Use and Theory*, Tuttle, 1954; *Japanese Short Stories*, Liveright, 1961; *Advanced Abacus: Japanese Theory and Practice*, Tuttle, 1963; (translator with John McVittie) Akutagawa, *Japanese Exotic Stories*, Liveright, 1964.

SIDELIGHTS: The Japanese Abacus: Its Use and Theory was tape-recorded for use by the American blind, and transcribed into braille for use in England. Kojima believes it likely that the abacus will eventually replace braille in teaching arithmetic to the blind of all countries.

*   *   *

KOMARNICKI, Tytus 1896-

PERSONAL: Born January 15, 1896, in Warsaw, Poland; son of Tytus (an industrialist) and Josephine (Suszycka) Komarnicki; married Countess Chiara Asinary Sigray di San Marzano, October 4, 1930; children: Teresa (Mrs. Andre Autin), Juliusz. *Education:* Imperial University of Yurev (now University of Dorpat), Tartu, Estonia, student of law, 1914-15; University of Warsaw, Magister juris, 1920; University of Paris, Doctor in Law, 1923; Ecole Libre des Sciences Politiques, Paris, France, diploma, 1923. *Religion:* Roman Catholic. *Home:* 27 Hazlewell Rd., London S.W.15, England.

CAREER: Polish Diplomatic Service, 1918-45, serving in Belgrade, Yugoslavia, 1924, with Department of League of Nations in Warsaw, Poland, 1925-27, and Berlin, Germany, 1928, at the Vatican, 1929-30, The Hague, Netherlands, 1930-31, as delegate to disarmament conference in Geneva, Switzerland, 1932-34, minister plenipotentiary and permanent Polish delegate to League of Nations, 1934-38, member of governing body of International Labor Office, 1937-40, minister to Switzerland, 1938-40, delegate of Polish Government in France, 1942-43, minister to Royal Dutch Government in exile, 1944-45, secretary general of

Polish Institute of International Affairs, 1946-50; Polish Research Centre, London, England, director of research and library. Professor of international law at Polish University Abroad in London, England; lecturer in international law and relations and diplomatic history at The Hague Academy of International Law, and in Paris, France. Broadcaster on Radio Free Europe, Munich, Germany. *Military service:* Polish Army, 1918-20; became lieutenant; awarded Cross for Valour and Cross of Independence. *Member:* Polish Society of Arts and Science (London), Polish Historical Society (London), Polish Institute of Arts and Science in America, Historical and Literary Society (Paris). *Awards, honors:* Commander of Polonia Restituta; Legion d'Honneur; Great Cross of the Hungarian Order of Merit; Knight Commander of the Order of St. Sylvestre.

WRITINGS: Obrono Chelmszczyzny w Dumie (a defense of the Kholm District, in the Russian Douma), Budowa Panstwa Polskeigo (Warsaw), 1918; *Powstawanie Reprezentacja Dyplomatycznej Nowych Panstw* (on the origins of the diplomatic representation of the New States), Przeglad Dyplomatyczny (Warsaw), 1921; *La Question de l'integrite territoriale dans le pacte de la Societe des Nations*, Presses Universitaires de France, 1923; *Pilsudski a Polityka Wielkich Mocarstw Zachodnich* (title means "Pilsudski and the Great Powers' Policy"), Instytut Jozefa Pilsudskiego (London), 1950; *The Place of Neutrality in the Modern System of International Law* (five lectures), Recueil des Cours de l'Academie de Droit International (The Hague), 1952; *The Satellite State: A Modern Case of Intervention*, Polish Juridical Association in the U.S.A., 1956; *L'Intervention en droit internationale moderne: Revue generale de droit international public*, Recueil Sirey (Paris), 1957; *L'Evolution de la communaute internationale depuis le Traite de Versailles jus qu'a nos jours*, Institut des Hautes Etudes Internationales, l'Universite de Paris, 1957; *Rebirth of the Polish Republic: A Study in the Diplomatic History of Europe, 1914-1920*, Heinemann, 1957; (editor) Jan Szembek, *Diariusz i Teki Jana Szembeka*, Volume 1, Polish Research Centre (London), 1964. Contributor of articles to historical, legal, and political reviews, and to *Dictionnaire Diplomatique*.

WORK IN PROGRESS: A book, *Between Versailles and Locarno, 1920-1924*; editing Szembek's diary and files, Volume 2; research on the diplomatic history of Europe between the two world wars.†

*   *   *

KOMAROVSKY, Mirra

PERSONAL: Born in Russia; came to United States in 1922, naturalized in 1933; daughter of Emmanuel and Anna (Steinberg) Komarovsky; married Marcus A. Heyman, October 2, 1940. *Education:* Barnard College, A.B., 1926; Columbia University, M.A., 1927, Ph.D., 1940. *Religion:* Jewish. *Home:* 340 Riverside Dr., New York, N.Y. 10025. *Office:* Barnard College, Columbia University, New York, N.Y. 10027.

CAREER: Skidmore College, Saratoga Springs, N.Y., 1928-29, began as instructor, became assistant professor; research assistant at Yale University Institute of Human Relations, New Haven, Conn., 1930-31, research associate at Columbia University, New York, N.Y., 1931-33, and International Institute of Social Research, New York, N.Y., 1934-37; Columbia University, Barnard College, instructor, 1938-45, assistant professor, 1945-47, associate professor, 1947-54, professor of sociology, 1954-74, pro-

fessor emeritus, 1974—, chairman of department, 1949-68. Visiting professor, New School for Social Research; Buel G. Gallagher visiting professor, City College of the City University of New York, 1965. *Member:* American Sociological Association (fellow; vice-president, 1972-73; president, 1973-74), American Association of University Professors, Eastern Sociological Society (president, 1955-56).

WRITINGS: (with George Andrew Lindberg and M. A. McInerny) *Leisure: A Suburban Study*, Columbia University Press, 1934; *The Unemployed Man and His Family*, Dryden Press, 1940; *Women in the Modern World: Their Education and Their Dilemmas*, Little, Brown, 1953; (editor) *Common Frontiers of the Social Sciences*, Free Press of Glencoe, 1957; *Blue-Collar Marriage*, Random House, 1964. Contributor to *Harper's*, and to sociology journals.

*   *   *

KOTSUJI, Abraham S(etsuzau) 1899-1973

PERSONAL: Born February 3, 1899, in Kyoto, Japan; son of Kisabrow and Fukuko (Odani) Kotsuji; married Mineko Iwane, October 1, 1923; children: Mary, Julie. *Education:* Attended Meiji Gakuin University and Seminary, Tokyo, Japan; Pacific School of Religion, Th.D., 1931. *Home:* 16-6 Omachi 1-chome, Kamakura, Japan. *Office address:* P.O.B. 18, Kamakura, Japan.

CAREER: Presbyterian minister, 1923-27; Aoyama Gakuin University, Tokyo, Japan, professor of Old Testament and Semitic languages, 1931-34; Institute of Biblical Research, Tokyo, Japan, director, 1934-38; ethnological adviser to president of South Manchuria Railway, 1939-41; converted to Jewish faith, 1959, became rabbi, 1960; Institute of Hebrew Culture, Inc., Kamakura, Japan, chairman, beginning in 1960. *Member:* Creative Culture Association (past president), Agudah L'ma'an Gerei Zedek, United Israel World Union. *Awards, honors:* Litt.D., Kyoto Imperial University, 1947.

WRITINGS: Fire in the Bible (monograph), Myo Bun Kwan, 1935; *A Hebrew Grammar* (in Japanese), Nichieido, 1936, 3rd edition, Seishin Shobo, 1965; *The Origin and Evolution of the Semitic Alphabets* (in English), Kyo-Bun-Kwan, 1937; *True Image of the Jewish Nation* (in Japanese), Meguro Shoten, 1943; *The Jewish Nation* (in Japanese), Seishin Shobo, 1965; *From Tokyo to Jerusalem* (in English), Bernard Geis Associates, 1965. Author of monographs.

WORK IN PROGRESS: A translation of "Song of Songs of Solomon" into Japanese traditional verse, with introduction and commentary.

SIDELIGHTS: Rabbi Kotsuji wrote to *CA*: "Descendant of age-old Shinto priest lords by heritage at Kamo Shrine in Kyoto, the Imperial capital for 1,000 years.... Started English at ten. At thirteen found the whole Bible at second-hand bookshop the late autumn right after Emperor Meiji's grand funeral which was duetted by the loyal self-immolation by General and Mrs. M. Nogi. This finding decided [my] whole life. Nineteen years thereafter, was ... a Semitic scholar holding Th.D. degree. [Though] christened at sixteen, this religion did not finally satisfy life-long aspiration, partly [due to] its sanguinary history and its polytheistic contents. Volunteered to aid thousands of Jewish refugees during World War II that ... found their way to Japan. Later, summoned by Japanese gestapo and tortured. In 1959, after I was examined at Chief Rabbinate Court, I converted to the Jewish faith."†

(Died October 31, 1973)

KRAMER, A(lfred) T(heodore)   1892-

PERSONAL: Born September 8, 1892, in Frohna, Missouri; son of Gottlob Theodore Johannes and Mathilde (Burfeind) Kramer; married Elisa von Lengriesser, 1928. *Education:* Attended St. Paul's College, Concordia, Mo., 1907-13, Concordia Seminary, St. Louis, Mo., 1913-15. *Home:* Guemes 686, Bahia Blanca, Argentina.

CAREER: Evangelical Lutheran Church—Missouri Synod, missionary-pastor in Buenos Aires, Argentina, 1917-29, professor at Colegio Concordia, Crespo, Entre Rios, Brazil, 1929-37, missionary-pastor in Bahia Blanca, Buenos Aires, Argentina, 1937—. *Awards, honors:* D.D., Concordia Seminary, 1955.

WRITINGS: Catecismo menor del Dr. M. Lutero, Rosso, 1927, new translation, Concordia, 1942, revised edition, Martinez, 1961; *Confesion de Augsburgo,* Concordia, 1942; *El Ritual luterano,* Martinez, 1945; *Preguntas y respuestas, catecismo,* Martinez, 1946; *Historias Biblicas,* Martinez, 1953-60; *Brosamlein von des Herrn tisch,* Concordia, 1960. Various devotional booklets in German for Concordia. Has contributed to religious journals and periodicals.

*   *   *

KRAMER, Frank Raymond   1908-

PERSONAL: Born January 2, 1908, in Baraboo, Wis.; son of Chris Edward and Mabel (Shaw) Kramer; married Hetty Louise Eising (a teacher), December 20, 1935; children: Bryce Allen, Anita Louise (Mrs. James C. Shaw). *Education:* University of Wisconsin, B.H., 1929, M.A., 1931, Ph.D., 1936. *Politics:* "Independent locally, Democrat nationally." *Religion:* United Church of Christ. *Home:* 25 Lincoln Rd., Tiffin, Ohio 44883. *Office:* Department of Classical Languages, Heidelberg College, Tiffin, Ohio 44883.

CAREER: Senior high school instructor in Wisconsin, 1934-38; Heidelberg College, Tiffin, Ohio, head of department of classical languages, 1938—. Visiting professor, Ohio State University, summer, 1962, American School of Classical Studies, Athens, 1965. *Member:* American Philological Association, Classical Association of Middle West and South, Ohio Classical Conference (president, 1948-49). *Awards, honors:* Rockefeller Foundation grants, 1948-49, 1951-52; Social Science Research Council grant, 1951.

WRITINGS: Voices in the Valley: Mythmaking and Folk Belief in the Shaping of the Middle West, University of Wisconsin Press, 1964. Contributor to classical journals.

WORK IN PROGRESS: Folk belief in the Middle Ages; *The Athenian Polis: A Cultural and Historical Synthesis.*

SIDELIGHTS: Kramer has traveled extensively in Europe. *Avocational interests:* Chess, photography.

*   *   *

KRETZMANN, Adalbert Raphael   1903-

PERSONAL: Born April 15, 1903, in Stamford, Conn.; son of Karl and Thekla (Hueschen) Kretzmann; married Josephine Marie Heidelberg, October 1, 1927; children: Norman John Karl, Joan Anita. *Education:* Concordia College, Bronxville, N.Y., graduate, 1923; Concordia Seminary, St. Louis, Mo., B.D., 1927. *Home:* 1501 West Melrose St., Chicago, Ill. *Office:* Evangelical Lutheran Church of St. Luke, 1500 West Belmont Ave., Chicago, Ill. 60657.

CAREER: Ordained minister of Evangelical Lutheran Church, 1927. Concordia College, Fort Wayne, Ind., pro-

fessor of German, 1925-26; vacancy pastor in Philadelphia, Pa., 1926, and supply pastor in St. Louis, Mo., 1926-27; Evangelical Lutheran Church of St. Luke, Chicago, Ill., assistant pastor, 1927-30, chief pastor, beginning 1930. Liturgical consultant in architecture and stained glass; lecturer at seminaries and colleges on church art, liturgy, and youth work; radio speaker on "Chicago Lutheran Hour." Member of board of directors of Augustana Hospital, beginning 1954, Lutheran General Hospital, beginning 1959, Ministers Life and Casualty Union, and Lutheran Brotherhood Life Insurance Society.

MEMBER: American Society for Church Architecture, Church Architectural Guild of America (honorary), American Federation of Art, American Institute of Graphic Arts (member of advisory council for religious teaching pictures), Concordia Historical Institute, Chicago Art Institute (life member), Chicago Bible Society. *Awards, honors:* Litt.D., Concordia College, Seward, Neb., 1953; LL.D., Valparaiso University, 1959.

WRITINGS: (Compiler) *Symbols: A Practical Handbook,* Walther League, 1944; (editor) *The Pastor at Prayer,* Augsburg, 1957; *The Message of the Symbols,* Concordia, 1958; (with George Buttrick and Caryl Micklen) *Prayers for Special Seasons,* Cathedral Publishers, 1970. Also author of *History of Evangelical Lutheran Church of St. Luke, 1884-1934,* 1934; *Festival and Occasional Sermons,* 1941; *The Christian Way,* 1941; *Service Prayer Book,* 1942; *Service Stars for Lutheran Youth,* 1943; *In Season, Out of Season,* 1945; *Liturgy and Church Art,* 1959; *The Symbols of the Church,* 1960; *The Arts for Every Christian,* 1961; *Pastoral Theology,* 1962; *The Pastor and the Arts,* 1963; *Guide Book to Saint Luke,* 1965. Art editor, *Cresset.*

*   *   *

KREUZER, James R.   1913-1971

PERSONAL: Born October 27, 1913, in New York, N.Y.; son of Walter (an accountant) and Jeannette (Katz) Kreuzer; married Alice Drasner (a bookkeeper), August 18, 1937; children: Judith Anne, Paul Geoffrey. *Education:* College of the City of New York (now City College of the City University of New York), B.A., 1934, M.S., 1934; New York University, Ph.D., 1946. *Office:* Dean of Faculties, Herbert H. Lehman College, City University of New York, Bedford Park Blvd., Bronx, N.Y. 10468.

CAREER: City College (now City College of the City University of New York), New York, N.Y., tutor in English, 1935-38; Queens College (now Queens College of the City University of New York), Flushing, N.Y., tutor in English, 1938-42, instructor, 1942-49, assistant professor, 1949-57, associate professor, 1958-62, professor of English, 1963-67, director of student activities, 1960-62, associate dean of students, 1962-67; Herbert H. Lehman College of the City University of New York, Bronx, N.Y., dean of faculties, 1967-71. Editorial consultant, Bobbs-Merrill Co., Inc. *Military service:* U.S. Army, 1943-45; became sergeant. *Member:* Modern Language Association of America, National Association of Student Personnel Administrators.

WRITINGS: Elements of Poetry, Macmillan, 1955; (editor and author of introduction) *Sir Gawain and the Green Knight,* translated by James L. Rosenberg, Rinehart, 1959; (editor with Lee Cogan) *Studies in Prose Writing,* Rinehart, 1960, alternate edition, 1961, revised edition, 1966, revised alternate edition, 1967; (editor with Cogan) *The Bobbs-Merrill Reader,* Bobbs-Merrill, 1962; (editor with Cogan)

Modern Writings on Major English Authors, Bobbs-Merrill, 1963; (with Cogan) *Literature for Composition*, Holt, 1965. Contributor of articles to professional journals.

(Died December 13, 1971)

* . * *

KROGER, William S. 1906-

PERSONAL: Born April 14, 1906, in Chicago, Ill.; son of Charles Mandel and Rose (Ziskin) Kroger; married Jimmy Louise Burton, 1953; children: Carol Lynn, Deborah Sue, Lisa Robin, William S., Jr. *Education:* Northwestern University, B.S. and B.M., 1926, M.D., 1930. *Home:* 1701 Lexington Rd., Beverly Hills, Calif. *Agent:* Alex Jackinson, 11 West 42nd St., New York, N.Y. 10036.

CAREER: Diplomate of American Board of Clinical Hypnosis. Physician specializing in obstetrics and gynecology (especially as related to psychosomatic medicine and hypnotherapy), in Chicago, Ill., 1932-59, in Beverly Hills, Calif., 1959—. Institute for Comprehensive Medicine, Beverly Hills, Calif., executive director, 1964—. Former staff member of Edgewater Hospital, Chicago, Ill.; former director of Psychosomatic Clinic, Mount Sinai Hospital, Chicago, Ill. Instructor in obstetrics and gynecology, University of Illinois Medical School, Chicago, Ill., 1944-54; associate professor of obstetrics and gynecology, Chicago Medical School, 1950-60. Lecturer on aspects of hypnosis and psychosomatic medicine at medical schools and before medical groups throughout America, 1947—.

MEMBER: American Medical Association, American Academy of Psychotherapists, International Fertility Association, American Psychosomatic Society, Academy of Psychosomatic Medicine (president, 1958), International Society for Clinical and Experimental Hypnosis, American Society of Clinical Hypnosis (vice-president, 1964), National Association of Science Writers, International Society for Study of Sex, British Society of Medical Hypnotists, Pacific Coast Fertility Society, New York Academy of Sciences, California State Medical Society, Los Angeles County Medical Society, Los Angeles Society for Clinical and Experimental Hypnosis (president, 1960); honorary member of other medical societies and organizations.

WRITINGS: (With S. C. Freed) *Psychosomatic Gynecology, Including Problems of Obstetrical Care*, Saunders, 1951; (with E. Bergler) *Kinsey's Myth of Female Sexuality: The Medical Facts*, Grune, 1953; *Modern Clinical Hypnosis*, Lippincott, 1961; *Childbirth with Hypnosis*, Doubleday, 1961; *Psychosomatic Obstetrics, Gynecology and Endocrinology: Including Diseases of Metabolism*, C. C Thomas, 1962; *Clinical and Experimental Hypnosis in Medicine, Dentistry, and Psychology*, Lippincott, 1963; (with Robert Libott) *Thanks, Doctor, I've Stopped Smoking: A Modern Doctor-Patient Approach to Smoking Control*, C. C Thomas, 1967.

Contributor: Raphael Rhodes, editor, *Therapy Through Hypnosis*, Citadel, 1952; J. Schneck, editor, *Hypnosis in Modern Medicine*, C. C Thomas, 1953; Gordan Ambrose and George Newbold, editors, *Handbook of Medical Hypnosis*, Williams & Wilkins, 1956; Alfred Cantor and A. N. Foxe, editors, *Psychosomatic Aspects of Surgery*, Grune, 1956; H. Rosen, editor, *Therapeutic Abortion*, Julian, 1956; W. J. Reich and M. J. Nechtow, editors, *Practical Gynecology*, Lippincott, 1957; Davis and Carter, editors, *Obstetrics and Gynecology*, W. F. Prior, 1959; Davis and Carter, editors, *Hypnoanesthesia in Obstetrics*, W. F. Prior, 1959; J. P. Greenhill, editor, *Clinical Obstetrics and*

Gynecology, Hoeber Medical Division, 1962. Author of forewords to other medical books.

Contributor of more than forty articles to *American Practitioner*, *Medical Times*, *State of Mind*, and other medical journals; collaborator with science writers on popular articles dealing with hypnosis and psychosomatics. Editor-in-chief, International Society for Comprehensive Medicine; consulting editor and columnist on hypnosis, *Western Journal of Surgery, Obstetrics and Gynecology*; associate editor, *Journal of Existentialist Psychiatry* and *Journal of Psychosomatics*; advisory editor of other medical journals.

WORK IN PROGRESS: What Price Womanhood; *Frigidity and Impotency*; *New Perspectives in Obesity*; with E. Bergler, *Mid-Century Sex: Psychosexuality of Masochism*; with Jules Steinberg, *Hypnosis in Obesity*; *The Giant Within*.

AVOCATIONAL INTERESTS: Collecting French antiques; golf, fishing, horticulture, and history.

* * *

KROLL, Francis Lynde 1904-1973

PERSONAL: Born November 9, 1904, in Fairbury, Neb.; son of August (a farmer and politician) and Maude (Lynde) Kroll; married Viola Hathaway, August 17, 1926; children: Francis L., Jr., Stanley H., Keith D. *Education:* University of Nebraska, student, 1923-26; Chadron State College, A.B., 1959, M.A., 1962; University of Wyoming, graduate study. *Politics:* Democrat. *Religion:* Presbyterian. *Home:* 927 B St., Fairbury, Neb. 68352. *Agent:* Lurton Blassingame, 10 East 43rd St., New York, N.Y. 10017.

CAREER: Teacher in Helvey, Parks, Dodge, Valentine, and Crawford, Neb., 1927-42, 1955-64; U.S. Department of Agriculture, Meat Inspection Service, Omaha, Neb., inspector, 1942-55; Sunol (Neb.) Consolidated School, superintendent, 1964-65; Palisade (Neb.) public schools, superintendent, 1965-68; Orleans (Neb.) public schools, superintendent, 1968-71. *Member:* National Education Association, Nebraska State Teachers Association, Nebraska Writers Guild (vice-president, 1954-55), Sigma Nu.

WRITINGS: Young Sioux Warrior (Junior Literary Guild selection), Lantern, 1952; *Young Sand Hills Cowboy*, Lantern, 1952; *Young Crow Raider*, Lantern, 1953; *Young Medicine Man*, Lantern, 1956; *Top Hand*, McKay, 1965. Author of fifty one-act plays for children. Contributor to *Encyclopaedia Britannica*; contributor of about fifty short stories and a few articles to *Story Parade*, *Plays*, *Stag*, *Man's Life*, and other magazines and newspapers.

WORK IN PROGRESS: Juvenile fiction about settlement of Nebraska near the Oregon Trail; a historically-based novel about the Sioux; a basketball sports story.

SIDELIGHTS: Kroll's first book grew out of one of his short stories, widely reprinted in anthologies and in the *Tokyo Times*, portraying the Sioux Indians apart from their contact and conflict with white men. He writes, "I am trying to find a plane between the Romantics and those now termed Realists, aiming to portray life more nearly as it is. A story-teller's task is to tell a story." Kroll's writing is collected at the Oregon University Research Library in Eugene, Ore.

(Died November 12, 1973)

* * *

KUHN, Irene Corbally

PERSONAL: Born in New York, N.Y.; daughter of Patrick J. and Josephine A. (Connor) Corbally; married Bert L. Kuhn (deceased); children: Rene L. (Mrs. Douglas W. Bryant). *Education:* Attended Marymount College, Tarrytown, N.Y., and Columbia University. *Politics:* Republican. *Home:* 45 Christopher St., New York, N.Y. 10014. *Agent:* Oscar Collier, 280 Madison Ave., New York, N.Y. 10016. *Office:* Columbia Features, Inc., 36 West 44th St., New York, N.Y. 10036.

CAREER: Started as reporter for newspaper in Syracuse, N.Y.; member of staff of European Edition of *Chicago Tribune* in Paris, France, 1921-22, *China Press* in Shanghai, China, 1922-26, *Honolulu Star Bulletin*, Honolulu, Hawaii, 1929-30, *New York World Telegram-Sun*, 1934-35; also foreign correspondent for Hearst Wire Service and International News Service in Far East and Honolulu, reporter for *New York Mirror* and *New York Daily News* prior to 1945; King Features Syndicate, columnist, "It's My Opinion," 1953-69; Columbia Features, Inc., New York, N.Y., columnist, 1970—. Executive and commentator, National Broadcasting Co., 1940-49; radio commentator, Mutual Broadcasting System. Scenario writer for 20th Century-Fox, 1931-32, Metro-Goldwyn-Mayer, 1932-33, Paramount, 1939.

MEMBER: Overseas Press Club (founder member; twice elected vice-president; member, board of governors), Women's National Press Club, Society of Magazine Writers, Society of American Travel Writers, Shanghai Tiffin Club. *Awards, honors:* War Department citation for reporting in China-Burma-India theater; journalism award of Finlandia Foundation, 1959, for contributing to better understanding between the peoples of the United States and Finland.

WRITINGS: Assigned to Adventure, Lippincott, 1939; (contributor) *Inside Story*, Overseas Press Club, 1946; (contributor) *Deadline Delayed*, Overseas Press Club, 1946; (with Raymond J. DeJaegher) *The Enemy Within*, Doubleday, 1953. Contributor of articles to *Reader's Digest, Town and Country, Cosmopolitan, Good Housekeeping, Sign, American Legion, Co-ed, Paradise of the Pacific, Vista*, and *Signature*. Travel editor, *American Labor Magazine*.

*   *   *

KUNCEWICZ, Maria (Szczepanska) 1899-
(Maria Kuncewiczowa)

PERSONAL: Surname is pronounced Koon-*se*-vitch; born October 31, 1899, in Samara, Russia; daughter of Joseph Dionizy (a mathematician) and Roza Adela (Dziubinska) Szczepanski; married Jerzy Karol Kuncewicz (a lawyer and writer), May 14, 1921; children: Witold Wiktur. *Education:* Attended the University of Krakow, and University of Nancy, 1918-22; studied music at Warsaw Conservatoire and in Paris, France, 1922-26. *Politics:* "Not interested." *Religion:* Roman Catholic. *Agent:* Ruth Maxwell Aley, 145 East 35th St., New York, N.Y. 10016. *Office:* Slavic Department, University of Chicago, Chicago, Ill. 60637.

CAREER: Singer in Poland, 1924-39; novelist, essayist, and playwright in Poland, 1926-39, England, 1940-55, and United States, 1955—. Radio Free Europe, New York, N.Y., writer, and broadcaster in Polish, 1955-56; University of Chicago, Chicago, Ill., visiting professor of Polish literature, 1961-64. *Member:* Authors Guild, International P.E.N. (London and New York; founder and first president of Centre for Writers in Exile), Polish Writers' Union (Warsaw), Polish Institute of Arts and Sciences (New

York), Kosciuszko Foundation (New York), Quadrangle Club (Chicago). *Awards, honors:* Polish Golden Cross of Merit and Golden Laurel of Polish Academy of Letters, 1938; Literary Prize of City of Warsaw, 1939.

WRITINGS: Przymierze z Dzieckiem (short stories; title means "Covenant with a Child"), Mortkowicz (Warsaw), 1927; *Twarz Mezczyzny* (novel; title means "The Face of a Man"), Mortkowicz, 1928; *Tseu-Hi* (historical essay), Roj (Warsaw), 1929; *Milose Panienska* (play; title means "Maiden Love"), Roj, 1931; *Dwa Ksiezyce* (short stories; title means "Two Moons"), Roj, 1933, 3rd edition, Orbis (London), 1954; *Cudzoziemka* (novel), Roj, 1935, translation by B. W. A. Massey published as *The Stranger*, Hutchinson, 1944, L. B. Fischer, 1945, 3rd Polish edition, Czytelnik, 1965; *Dylizans Warszawski* (essays; title means "Warsaw Stagecoach"), Roj, 1937, 3rd edition, revised and enlarged, Pax (Warsaw), 1958; *Dni Powszednie Panstwa Kowalskich* (novel; title means "The Daily Life of the Kowalskis"), Roj, 1937; *Miasto Heroda* (travel; title means "The City of Herod"), Roj, 1939; *Polish Millstones* (essays originally written in Polish but published in English), translated by Stephen Garry, P. S. King & Staples, 1942; *Klucze*, Nowa Polska (London), 1943, translation by Harry Stevens published as *The Keys: Journey Through Europe at War*, Hutchinson, 1945, 4th Polish edition, Pax, 1964; *Modern Polish Prose*, Polish Publications Committee (Birkenhead, England), 1945; *Zmowa Nieobecnych* (novel), Swiatowy Zwiazek Polakow (London), 1946, translation by Harry Stevens and Maurice Michael published as *The Conspiracy of the Absent*, Hutchinson, 1950, Roy, 1951, 2nd Polish edition, Pax, 1957.

Lesnik (novel), Kultura, 1952, translation by Harry Stevens published as *The Forester*, Roy, 1954, 2nd Polish edition, Pax, 1962; *Ratunek i Inne Opowiadania*, Wydawnictwo Literackie, 1957; *Odkrycie Patusanu* (essays; title means "Discovery of Patusan"), Pax, 1958; *Kowaiscy w Anglii* (novel; title means "The Kowalskis in England"), Przekroj, 1959; *Gaj Oliwny* (novel), Pax, 1961, English version by Kuncewicz published as *The Olive Grove*, Walker & Co., 1963, 2nd Polish edition, Pax, 1968; (editor and author of preface) *The Modern Polish Mind* (anthology of short stories), Little, Brown, 1962; *Don Kichote i Nianki*, Pax, 1965, 2nd edition, 1967; *Tristan 1946*, Czytelnik, 1967, 2nd edition, 1968; *Twarz Mezczyzny i Trzy Nowele*, Czytelnik, 1969. Also author of plays, "Mitosc Panienska," and "Thank You for the Rose," the latter produced by a London theatre group in 1955.

Youth books: *Przyjaciele Ludzkosci* (title means "Friends of Men"), Roj, 1938; *Serce Kraju* (title means "Heart of the Country"), Roj, 1939; *W Domu i Swiecie* (title means "At Home and Abroad"), Roj, 1939; *Zagranica* (title means "Abroad"), Roj, 1939; *W Domu i w Polsce* (title means "At Home and in Poland"), Czytelnik, 1959.

SIDELIGHTS: In *The Writer's Situation*, Storm Jameson says of this Polish author: "If you believe the signs the writer makes from behind her words, human loneliness, disappointment, unassuaged hunger, have, all of them, the taste and colours of a long, happy life. It is not for a poet to write of defeat."

One of Mrs. Kuncewicz's hopes in the post-war period was world citizenship for displaced persons like herself. She wrote an appeal to the United Nations, but, she says, "the nations stuck by their national guns." However, since the 1956 liberalization of the Polish regime, nine of her books have been published in Poland. *The Stranger*, translated into a total of eleven languages, has been brought out by three Polish publishers since 1948. Part of her series for Radio Free Europe in 1955-56 also has been published in Poland, in the magazine, *Przekroj*.

AVOCATIONAL INTERESTS: Music and travel.

BIOGRAPHICAL/CRITICAL SOURCES: Storm Jameson, *The Writer's Situation, and Other Essays*, Macmillan, 1950.

* * *

KURZWEIL, Zvi Erich 1911-

PERSONAL: Born July 29, 1911, in Pirnitz, Moravia, Czechoslovakia; son of Abraham (a rabbi) and Rachel (Eckfeld) Kurzweil; married Paula Rosner. *Education:* University of Frankfurt, student, 1931-33; German University of Prague, Ph.D. (summa cum laude), 1936; University of London, B.A. (honors). *Politics:* "Unaffiliated." *Religion:* Jewish. *Home:* 4 Aaron Lane, Ahuza, Haifa, Israel.

CAREER: Inspector of Jewish Schools, London, England, 1947-50; Hugim High School, Haifa, Israel, director of English studies, 1950-57; Israel Institute of Technology, Haifa, senior lecturer in education, 1957-70, head of department of general studies, 1961—, head of department of teacher education, 1965—, professor of education, 1970—.

WRITINGS: (With J. S. Steinberg) *English for Science and Engineering Students*, Giradet, 1963; (with Kushner) *English for Students of Technology*, Giradet, 1964; *Modern Trends in Jewish Education*, Yoseloff, 1964; *Ha-Hinukh ba-herrag ha-tekhnologit* (title means "Education in a Technological Society"), Rubin Maas, 1964; *Janusz Korczak's Educational Activities* (published in Hebrew), Tarbut We-Chinuch, 1968; *Anxiety and Education*, Yoseloff, 1968.

WORK IN PROGRESS: Work on progressive education.

AVOCATIONAL INTERESTS: Swimming.

* * *

LAMAN, Russell 1907-

PERSONAL: Surname is pronounced *Lay*-man; born May 19, 1907, in Concordia, Kan.; son of George Washington and Anna (Detrixhe) Laman; married Jane McKee (a writer), August 31, 1953. *Education:* Kansas State University, B.S., 1931; State University of Iowa, M.A., 1933; University of Wisconsin, postgraduate study, summers, 1950-54. *Politics:* Independent. *Religion:* Protestant. *Home:* 2008 Stillman Dr., Manhattan, Kan. 66502. *Agent:* McIntosh & Otis, Inc., 18 East 41st St., New York, N.Y. 10017. *Office:* Department of English, Kansas State University, Manhattan, Kan. 66502.

CAREER: Rural grade school teacher, 1926-28; Kansas State University, Manhattan, 1935-41, 1946—, now assistant professor of English. *Military service:* U.S. Army Air Corps, intelligence and cryptographic security officer with assignments in Mexico, Caribbean Theater, and China-Burma-India Theater, 1942-45; became captain; received Bronze Star.

WRITINGS: Manifest Destiny (novel), Regnery, 1963. Assistant editor, *Kansas Magazine*.

WORK IN PROGRESS: A novel with a Midwest setting, covering the period from 1930 to America's entrance into World War II.

SIDELIGHTS: Laman writes during summers in Montana mountains, spending half of day at his typewriter. *Avocational interests:* Fishing, hunting, hiking, and camping.†

LAMBERT, Eric 1918-1966
(Frank Brennand, George Kay)

PERSONAL: Born January 19, 1918, in London, England; son of Frank (an industrialist) and Marian Lambert; married Phyllis Pamplin (a painter), March 5, 1961; children: Virginia, Francesca. *Education:* University of Sydney, B.Sc., 1937; Oxford University, Ph.D., 1946. *Home:* Red House, Little Maplestead, Halstead, Essex, England. *Agent:* Richmond Towers & Benson Ltd., 14 Essex St., Strand, London W.C. 1, England.

CAREER: Biologist, 1946-49; former professional cricket player, and coach in Essex, England; free-lance writer. *Military service:* Australian Army, 1940-46; served in North Africa, South Pacific, and Malaya; became sergeant; mentioned in dispatches. *Member:* Society of Authors, Fleet Street Column Club. *Awards, honors:* Australian Commonwealth Literary fellowship, 1950.

WRITINGS—All published by Muller, except as noted: *The Twenty Thousand Thieves*, Newmont (Melbourne), 1951; *The Five Bright Stars*, Australasian Book Society (Melbourne), 1954; *The Veterans*, 1954; *Watermen*, 1956; *The Dark Backward*, 1958; *Glory Thrown In*, 1959; *The Rehabilitated Man*, 1960; *Ballarat*, 1962; *The Drip Dry Man*, 1963; *Dolphin*, 1963; *A Short Walk to the Stars*, 1964; *Kelly*, 1964; *The Tender Conspiracy*, 1965; *The Long White Night*, 1965; *MacDougal's Farm*, 1965; *Hiroshima Reef*, Norton, 1967; *Mad with Heart: A Life of the Parents of Oscar Wilde*, 1967.

Under pseudonym Frank Brennand; all published by Four Square Books: *Sink the Bismarck*, 1960; *Oscar Wilde*, 1961; *North to Alaska*, 1962; *Winston S. Churchill*, 1965.

Under pseudonym George Kay: *The Siege of Pinchgut*, Four Square Books, 1960.

Author of motion picture and television scripts. Contributor to periodicals all over the world.

SIDELIGHTS: Lambert spoke French, Arabic, Malay.†

(Died, 1966)

* * *

LAMBURN, John Battersby Crompton 1893-
(John Crompton, John Lambourne)

PERSONAL: Born April 3, 1893, in England; son of Edward John Sewell (a clerk in Holy Orders) and Clara (Crompton) Lamburn; married Doris Joan Mariott, 1932; children: David John Crompton, Sarah Crompton. *Education:* Attended Bury Grammar School and University of Manchester. *Home:* Little Boxhurst, Sandhurst, Hawkhurst, Kent, England.

CAREER: British South Africa Police, member, 1913-19; Butterfield & Swire (shipping firm), China, employee, 1919-32. *Military service:* Royal Air Force, 1940-43; became flight lieutenant.

WRITINGS—Under pseudonym John Lambourne: *The White Kaffir*, Hodder & Stoughton, 1927; *Trooper Fault*, J. Murray, 1931; *The Kingdom That Was*, J. Murray, 1931; *Strong Waters*, J. Murray, 1932; *The Second Leopard*, J. Murray, 1932; *The Unmeasured Place*, J. Murray, 1933; *Squeeze: A Tale of China*, J. Murray, 1935; *Inky Wooing*, J. Murray, 1935; *Trooper in Charge*, R. Hale, 1939.

Under pseudonym John Crompton: *The Hive*, W. Blackwood, 1947; *The Hunting Wasp*, Collins, 1948, Houghton, 1955; *The Spider*, Collins, 1950, published as *The Life of the Spider*, Houghton, 1951; *Ways of the Ant*, Houghton,

1954; *The Living Sea*, Doubleday, 1957; *A Hive of Bees*, Doubleday, 1958; *The Snake*, Faber, 1963, published as *Snake Lore*, Doubleday, 1964.

WORK IN PROGRESS: Autobiography of years with the Royal Air Force.

*   *   *

LAMBURN, Richmal Crompton   1890-1969
(Richmal Crompton)

PERSONAL: Born November 15, 1890, in Bury, Lancashire, England; daughter of Edward John Sewell (a clerk in Holy Orders) and Clara (Crompton) Lamburn. *Education:* Royal Holloway College, London, B.A. (honors), 1914. *Politics:* Conservative. *Religion:* Church of England. *Home:* Beechworth, Orpington Rd., Chislehurst, Kent, England. *Agent:* A. P. Watt & Sons, Hastings House, 10 Norfolk St., Strand, London W.C.2, England.

CAREER: St. Elphin's School, Darley Dale, Derbyshire, England, classical mistress, 1914-17; Bromley High School, Bromley, Kent, England, classical mistress, 1917-24; writer, 1922-69. *Member:* Authors' Society, National Book League.

WRITINGS—All under pseudonym Richmal Crompton: "Just William" series for children; all published by George Newnes: *Just William*, 1922; *More William*, 1923; *William Again*, 1923; *William—the Fourth*, 1924; *Still—William*, 1925; *William—The Conqueror*, 1926; *William—in Trouble*, 1927; *William—the Outlaw*, 1927; *William—the Good*, 1928; *William*, 1929; *William—the Bad*, 1930; *William's Happy Days*, 1930; *William's Crowded Hours*, 1931; *William—the Pirate*, 1933; *William—the Gangster*, 1934; *William—the Detective*, 1935; *Sweet William*, 1936; *William—the Showman*, 1937; *William—the Dictator*, 1938; *William and the A.R.P.*, 1939, reissued as *William's Bad Resolution*, 1956; *Just William: The Story of the Film*, 1939.

William and the Evacuees, 1940, reissued as *William the Film Star*, 1956; *William Does His Bit*, 1941; *William Carries on*, 1942; *William and the Brains Trust*, 1945; *Just William's Luck*, 1948; *William—the Bold*, 1950; *William and the Tramp*, 1952; *William and the Moon Rocket*, 1954; *William and the Space Animal*, 1956; *William's Television Show*, 1958, abridged edition, 1965; *William—the Explorer*, 1960; *William's Treasure Trove*, 1962; *William and the Witch*, 1964; *William and the Pop Singers*, 1965; *William and the Masked Ranger*, 1966; *William the Superman*, 1968; *William the Lawless*, 1970.

Other children's books under pseudonym Richmal Crompton: *Jimmy*, George Newnes, 1949; *Jimmy Again*, George Newnes, 1951.

Novels; all under pseudonym Richmal Crompton: *The Innermost Room*, Andrew Melrose, 1923; *The Hidden Light*, Hodder & Stoughton, 1924; *Anne Morrison*, Jarrolds, 1925; *The Wildings*, Hodder & Stoughton, 1925; *David Wilding*, Hodder & Stoughton, 1926; *Dread Dwelling*, Boni & Liveright, 1926 (published in England as *The House*, Hodder & Stoughton, 1926); *Millicent Dorrington*, Hodder & Stoughton, 1927; *Leadon Hill*, Hodder & Stoughton, 1927; *The Thorn Bush*, Hodder & Stoughton, 1928; *Roofs Off!*, Hodder & Stoughton, 1928; *The Four Graces*, Hodder & Stoughton, 1929; *Abbot's End*, Hodder & Stoughton, 1929.

Blue Flames, Hodder & Stoughton, 1930; *Naomi Godstone*, Hodder & Stoughton, 1930; *Portrait of a Family*, Macmillan, 1931; *The Odyssey of Euphemia Tracy*, Mac-

millan, 1932; *Marriage of Hermione*, Macmillan, 1932; *The Holiday*, Macmillan, 1933; *Chedsy Place*, Macmillan, 1934; *The Old Man's Birthday*, Macmillan, 1934, Little, Brown, 1935; *Quartet*, Macmillan, 1935; *Caroline*, Macmillan, 1936; *There Are Four Seasons*, Macmillan, 1937; *Journeying Wave*, Macmillan, 1938; *Merlin Bay*, Macmillan, 1939; *Steffan Green*, Macmillan, 1940; *Narcissa*, Macmillan, 1941; *Mrs. Frensham Describes a Circle*, Macmillan, 1942; *Weatherley Parade*, Macmillan, 1944; *Westover*, Hutchinson, 1946; *The Ridleys*, Hutchinson, 1947; *Family Roundabout*, Hutchinson, 1948.

Frost at Morning, Hutchinson, 1950; *Linden Rise*, Hutchinson, 1952; *The Gypsy's Baby*, Hutchinson, 1954; *Four in Exile*, Hutchinson, 1955; *Matty and the Dearingroydes*, Hutchinson, 1956; *Blind Man's Buff*, Hutchinson, 1957; *Wiseman's Folly*, Hutchinson, 1959; *The Inheritor*, Hutchinson, 1960.

Short story collections under pseudonym Richmal Crompton: *Kathleen and I, and Of Course, Veronica*, Hodder & Stoughton, 1926; *A Monstrous Regiment*, Hutchinson, 1927; *Enter—Patricia*, George Newnes, 1927; *Mist, and Other Stories*, Hutchinson, 1928; *The Middle Things*, Hutchinson, 1928; *Felicity—Stands By*, George Newnes, 1928; *Sugar and Spice*, Ward, Lock, 1929; *Ladies First*, Hutchinson, 1929; *The Silver Birch, and Other Stories*, Hutchinson, 1931; *First Morning*, Hutchinson, 1936.

SIDELIGHTS: The "Just William" books about an eleven-year-old boy originally were written for adults but were enjoyed by children so much that they came to be classed as children's fiction.

BIOGRAPHICAL/CRITICAL SOURCES: Variety, January 29, 1969.

(Died January 11, 1969)

*   *   *

LAMONT, William D(awson)   1901-

PERSONAL: Born February 3, 1901, on Prince Edward Island, Canada; son of Murdoch (a Church of Scotland minister) and Euphemia Ann (Hume) Lamont; married Ann Fraser Christie, June 19, 1930. *Education:* University of Glasgow, M.A. (first class honors), 1924; Balliol College, Oxford, D.Phil., 1930. *Home:* 37 Kirklee Rd., Glasgow W. 2, Scotland.

CAREER: University of Glasgow, Glasgow, Scotland, assistant lecturer, 1926-28, lecturer in philosophy, 1929-42; University of Cairo, Cairo, Egypt, professor of philosophy, 1942-45; Makerere College, Kampala Uganda, principal, 1946-49. *Military service:* Royal Navy, served with Clyde River Patrol and as intelligence liaison officer, 1939-42. *Member:* Royal Institute of International Affairs (vice-chairman of Cairo group, 1942-45), Anglo-Egyptian Union (honorary secretary, 1944. *Awards, honors:* D.Litt., University of East Africa, 1965.

WRITINGS: Introduction to Green's Moral Philosophy, Allen & Unwin, 1934, Longmans, Green (New York), 1935; *The Principles of Moral Judgment*, Clarendon Press, 1946, Oxford University Press (New York), 1947; *The Value Judgment*, Philosophical Library, 1955; *The Early History of Islay (500-1726)*, Burns & Harris, 1966; *Ancient and Mediaeval Stones of Islay*, Oliver & Boyd, 1968. Contributor of articles and reviews to *Mind*, *Scottish Studies*, and other professional journals.

AVOCATIONAL INTERESTS: Scottish history and antiquities, walking, and sailing.

LAMPRECHT, Sterling P(ower) 1890-1973

PERSONAL: Born January 8, 1890, in Cleveland, Ohio; son of George O. (a businessman) and Emma S. (Power) Lamprecht; married Edith Taber, August 22, 1922. *Education:* Williams College, A.B., 1911; Harvard University, A.M., 1912; Union Theological Seminary, New York, N.Y., B.D. (converted to M.Div.), 1915; Columbia University, Ph.D., 1918; postdoctoral study at University of Poitiers, 1919, University of Berlin, 1931. *Home:* 5 Brockway Rd., Hanover, N.H. 03755.

CAREER: Columbia University, New York, N.Y., instructor in philosophy, 1919-21; University of Illinois, Urbana, assistant professor, 1921-25, associate professor of philosophy, 1925-28; Amherst College, Amherst, Mass., professor of philosophy, 1928-56, professor emeritus, 1956-73. Visiting professor at Johns Hopkins University, 1958, University of North Carolina, 1960-61. Howison lecturer, University of California, 1938; Woodbridge lecturer, Columbia University, 1949. Philosophy editor, Appleton-Century-Crofts, Inc., 1927-67. President, Peacham Library, 1959-63. *Military service:* U.S. Army, Infantry, 1918-19.

MEMBER: American Philosophical Association (vice-president, 1938), Peacham Historical Association (president, 1955-59), Phi Beta Kappa, Delta Sigma Rho. *Awards, honors:* Butler Medal in Philosophy, Columbia University, 1934; A.M., Amherst College, 1934; Litt.D., Williams College, 1957; Fulbright fellow.

WRITINGS: Moral and Political Philosophy of John Locke, Columbia University Press, 1918, new edition, Russell & Russell, 1962; (editor) John Locke, *Selections*, Scribner, 1928; (editor) Henry More, *Enchiridion Ethicum*, Facsimile Text Society, 1930; (editor) Hobbes, *The Citizen*, Appleton, 1949; *Our Religious Traditions*, Harvard University Press, 1950; *Nature and History*, Columbia University Press, 1950; *Our Philosophical Traditions*, Appleton, 1955; *The Metaphysics of Naturalism*, Appleton, 1967. Contributor of articles and reviews to philosophy and religion journals.

AVOCATIONAL INTERESTS: Rereading Shakespeare and Dickens; visiting Shakespeare Festival at Stratford, Ontario, as often as possible, and attending other Shakespeare performances; record-playing, particularly of classical piano music.

(Died October 16, 1973)

* * *

LANCASTER, Bruce 1896-1963

PERSONAL: Born August 22, 1896, in Worcester, Mass.; son of Walter Moody and Sarah Jenkins (Hill) Lancaster; married Jessie Bancroft Payne, December 12, 1931. *Education:* Harvard University, A.B., 1919. *Politics:* Republican. *Religion:* Episcopalian. *Home:* 67 Grover St., Beverly, Mass. 01915.

CAREER: Businessman in Worcester, Mass., 1919-27; U.S. Department of State, foreign service officer in Kobe and Nagoya, Japan, 1927-33; Board of Governors, Society of New York Hospital, New York, N.Y., assistant secretary, 1934-38; author, mainly of historical novels, 1938-63. Trustee, Beverly Public Library, 1958-63. *Military service:* 1st Massachusetts Field Artillery, served on Mexican border, 1916. American Expeditionary Forces, Field Artillery, 1917-19; received five battle stars. *Member:* Company of Military Collectors and Historians (fellow), Authors League of America, P.E.N., Cambridge Historical Society, St. Botolph Club (Boston), Harvard Club (New York).

WRITINGS: The Wide Sleeve of Kwannon, Frederick A. Stokes, 1938; *Guns of Burgoyne*, Frederick A. Stokes, 1939 (published in England as *Gentleman Johnny*, Heinemann, 1939), revised and condensed edition published as *Guns in the Forest*, Atlantic-Little, Brown, 1952; (with Lowell Brentano) *Bride of a Thousand Cedars*, Frederick A. Stokes, 1939; *For Us the Living*, Frederick A. Stokes, 1940; *Bright to the Wanderer*, Little, Brown, 1942; *Trumpet to Arms*, Atlantic-Little, Brown, 1944; *The Scarlet Patch*, Atlantic-Little, Brown, 1947; *No Bugles Tonight*, Atlantic-Little, Brown, 1948.

Phantom Fortress, Atlantic-Little, Brown, 1950; *Venture in the East*, Atlantic-Little, Brown, 1951; *The Secret Road*, Atlantic-Little, Brown, 1952; *Blind Journey*, Atlantic-Little, Brown, 1953; *From Lexington to Liberty: The Story of the American Revolution*, Doubleday, 1955; *Roll, Shenandoah*, Atlantic-Little, Brown, 1956; *The American Revolution* (juvenile), Garden City Books, 1957; (author of narrative) *The American Heritage Book of the Revolution*, American Heritage Press, 1958; *Night March*, Little, Brown, 1958; *Ticonderoga: The Story of a Fort* (juvenile), Houghton, 1959; *The Big Knives*, Little, Brown, 1964. Annotated *Orderly Books and Letter Books of Col. Christian Febiger (1777-1783)*. Contributor of articles and book reviews to *Atlantic* and *Saturday Review*. Editor, *Old-Time New England*, published by Society for the Preservation of New England Antiquities, 1951-56.

SIDELIGHTS: All but four of Lancaster's books deal with American history. He described his work pattern thusly: "I choose my period or setting first of all, then set about learning all that I can about it and the people who figured in it. Not until all of this is as solid as I can make it, do I begin the fictional part.... I have been as careful as is humanly possible to bring about a blending of fact and fiction without any distortion of fact." As soon as actual writing begins, each day's work is read back to him by his wife. "This began with the first book," Lancaster explained, "and for me [it is] an essential part of the whole writing process."

Football was a major interest. He was a member of the Harvard team in 1916, coached there in the fall of 1919, coached the line (as an avocation) at Worcester Polytechnic Institute, 1920-26, and played with a British Rugby team in Kobe, Japan, for three seasons.

(Died June 20, 1963)

* * *

LANDIS, Benson Y. 1897-1966

PERSONAL: Born October 12, 1897, in Center Valley, Pa.; son of Myron S. (a telegrapher) and Emily (Young) Landis; married Dorothea S. Oppenlander; children: Jeanette (Mrs. Walter Starkey), Carolyn Louise (Mrs. Raymond F. Henry). *Education:* Moravian College, B.A., 1918; Columbia University, M.A., 1923, Ph.D., 1927. *Politics:* Liberal Party (New York). *Religion:* Moravian. *Home:* 124 Brambach Rd., Scarsdale, N.Y.

CAREER: Institute of Social and Religious Research, New York, N.Y., associate director of rural surveys, 1919-21; *Christian Work* (periodical), New York, N.Y., managing editor, 1921-23; Federal Council of Churches, New York, N.Y., associate director of research, 1923-50; National Council of Churches, New York, N.Y., editor of research publications, 1951-63; retired, 1963. Field worker, American Association for Adult Education, 1932-33. *Member:* Religious Research Association. *Awards, honors:* LL.D., St. Francis Xavier University, Antigonish, Nova Scotia, and L.H.D., Moravian College, both 1953.

WRITINGS: Rural Church Life in the Middle West, Doubleday, Doran, 1922; *Sedgwick County Kansas: A Church and Community Survey*, Doubleday, Doran, 1922; (with Hubert C. Herring) *The Church and Social Relations*, Pilgrim Press, 1926; (editor with Henry Israel) *Handbook of Rural Social Resources*, University of Chicago Press, 1926, (sole editor) 2nd edition, 1928; *Professional Codes*, Teachers College, Columbia University Bureau of Publications, 1927; (with John D. Willard) *Rural Adult Education*, Macmillan, 1933; *The Third American Revolution: An Interpretation*, Association Press, 1933; *Must the Nation Plan? A Discussion of Government Programs*, Association Press, 1934.

A Cooperative Economy: A Study of Democratic Economic Movements, Harper, 1943; *Rural Welfare Services*, Columbia University Press, 1949; (contributor) J. Frederic Dewhurst and associates, *America's Needs and Resources*, Twentieth Century Fund, 1955; *Poetry and Rural Life*, National Council of Churches, 1956; (compiler) *A Rauschenbusch Reader*, Harper, 1957; *World Religions*, Dutton, 1957, revised edition, 1965.

Clergyman's Fact Book, M. Evans and Co., 1963; *Outline of the Bible, Book by Book*, Barnes & Noble, 1963; *Careers of Service in the Church*, M. Evans and Co., 1964; *Religion in the United States*, Barnes & Noble, 1965; *The Roman Catholic Church in the United States: A Guide to Recent Developments*, Dutton, 1966.

Editor: *Proceedings of the American Country Life Association*, annually, 1929-40; *Yearbook of American Churches*, National Council of Churches, semi-annually, 1941-47, annually, 1952-53.

Author or co-author of more than forty pamphlets published by National Conference of Christians and Jews, Federal Council of Churches, American Library Association, and other organizations. Weekly articles, "The Week in Religion" and "Religion and World Events," syndicated by Religious News Service, 1936-38. Contributor of some eighty-five articles to religious, sociological, and other specialized periodicals and yearbooks, including *Rural America*, *Adult Teacher*, *Decentralist*, *Commonweal*, *Social Action*, *Home Quarterly*, *Christian Century*, and *Advance*.

AVOCATIONAL INTERESTS: Credit unions and cooperatives in rural areas, the poetry of rural life, herb gardening, painting landscapes, and baking special breads.

(Died November 10, 1966)

*   *   *

LANDON, Margaret (Dorothea Mortenson)   1903-

PERSONAL: Born September 7, 1903, in Somers, Wis.; daughter of Annenus Duabus (for many years in the business department of *Saturday Evening Post*) and Adelle Johanne (Estburg) Mortenson; married Kenneth Perry Landon (a Presbyterian missionary in Siam, 1927-37; associate dean of area and language studies, U.S. Department of State Foreign Service Institute), June 16, 1926; children: Margaret Dorothea (Mrs. Charles W. Schoenherr), William Bradley II, Carol Elizabeth (Mrs. Lennart Pearson), Kenneth Perry, Jr. *Education:* Wheaton College, Wheaton, Ill., A.B., 1925; journalism courses at Northwestern Univer-

sity, 1937-38. *Religion:* Protestant. *Home:* 4711 Fulton St., N.W., Washington, D.C. 20007. *Agent:* William Morris Agency, 1740 Broadway, New York, N.Y. 19100.

CAREER: Taught English and Latin in Bear Lake, Wis., 1925-26 ("an agonizing year—soon discovered that I disliked teaching"), and accompanied her missionary husband to Siam in 1927; after a year in Bangkok, largely spent studying Siamese, the Landons were stationed at Nakon Sritamarat, 1927-28, and in Trang (where they often were the only non-Siamese), 1928-31, 1932-37; began to write *Anna and the King of Siam* in 1939 in Richmond, Ind., where her husband was teaching, and finished the book in Washington, D.C., in 1943; a serious bout with rheumatic fever in 1946 interfered with her writing for an extended period of time.

WRITINGS: Anna and the King of Siam, Day, 1944, version for young people, Day, 1947, abridged edition, Square Press, 1963; *Never Dies the Dream* (novel), Doubleday, 1949.

WORK IN PROGRESS: A history of Southeast Asia in the pre-colonial period, in progress for a number of years; research on nineteenth-century Siam.

SIDELIGHTS: Mrs. Landon still reads Siamese with ease, but has lost some of her fluency in speaking it. The three older Landon children spoke Siamese before they learned English (and their father mastered three years' study of the language in one), but Mrs. Landon says, "It is a difficult tonal language, highly idiomatic, so although I spoke it a great deal, I never lost my American accent or learned to speak it perfectly."

Her recollections of writing *Anna and the King of Siam* appeared in *Town and Country*, December, 1952. The best-selling book has been made into a movie, and the Rogers and Hammerstein musical, "The King and I," which was based on *Anna*, was published by Random in 1951, and was also filmed.

BIOGRAPHICAL/CRITICAL SOURCES: Town and Country, December, 1952.

*   *   *

LANGMAN, Ida Kaplan   1904-

PERSONAL: Born February 7, 1904, in Borzna, Russia; daughter of Hyman (an insurance agent) and Dora (Shidlovsky) Kaplan; married Oscar Langman (a musician). *Education:* Philadelphia Normal School, student, 1920-22; University of Pennsylvania, B.S. in Ed., 1930, M.S., 1947. *Politics:* Independent. *Religion:* Humanist. *Home:* 5515 Wissahickon Ave., Apt. B-202, Philadelphia, Pa. 19144.

CAREER: Philadelphia (Pa.) School District, elementary teacher, 1922-26, general science teacher, 1926-34, biology teacher, 1934-50, museum teacher, 1950-56; University of Pennsylvania, Philadelphia, research fellow, 1956-64; International Association for Plant Taxonomy, bibliographer for Index Nominum Genericorum project, 1965-69; Carnegie-Mellon University, Hunt Institute for Botanical Documentation, bibliographer for Bibliographia Huntiana project, 1970-73. *Member:* American Association for the Advancement of Science, Association for Tropical Biology, Sociedad Botanica de Mexico, Academia Nacional de Ciencias de Mexico (corresponding member), Philadelphia Botanical Club. *Awards, honors:* Oberly Memorial Award of American Library Association for best bibliography in agriculture and related sciences, 1963-64; grants from U.S. Office of Education, National Science Foundation, and

American Philosophical Society, for work in Mexico; gold medal of merit from Sociedad Botanica de Mexico, 1972, for *A Selected Guide to the Literature on the Flowering Plants of Mexico*.

WRITINGS: (Translator) *Flores de Mexico*, Mizrachi, 1962; *A Selected Guide to the Literature on the Flowering Plants of Mexico*, University of Pennsylvania Press, 1964. Contributor to botanical journals in United States and Mexico. Translator, *Biological Abstracts*, 1961—.

SIDELIGHTS: Mrs. Langman is fluent in Spanish; she reads, and speaks "haltingly," French, Portuguese, and Yiddish. *Avocational interests:* Hiking, travel, reading, concerts, plays.

* * *

LANOUE, Fred Richard 1908-1965

PERSONAL: Born February 15, 1908; son of Arthur M. (a shoe-worker) and Susan Mary Lanoue; married; children: Susan, Ricky, Nancy. *Education:* Springfield College, Springfield, Mass., B.S., 1932, M.Ed., 1934. *Home:* 1730 North Druid Hills Rd., Atlanta, Ga. *Office:* Georgia Institute of Technology, Atlanta, Ga.

CAREER: Georgia Institute of Technology, Atlanta, 1936-68, became professor of physical education and head swimming coach. Consultant to U.S. Peace Corps, U.S. Marine Corps, Outward Bound Schools of America, and to private firms. Member of Georgia Governor's Council on Physical Fitness. *Member:* College Swimming Coaches Association of America (former president), National Education Association. *Awards, honors:* Creative Award of American Academy of Physical Education for development of "drownproofing."

WRITINGS: Downproofing: A New Technique for Water Safety, Prentice-Hall, 1963.

WORK IN PROGRESS: Physics and Physiology of Drowning.

SIDELIGHTS: Lanoue's "drownproofing" dealt with swimming for survival in natural waters. He felt that the glut of private pools had led to superficial swimming techniques which were inadequate in real water emergencies, particularly for older people in poor physical condition.

BIOGRAPHICAL/CRITICAL SOURCES: Life, June 11, 1951; *Coronet*, July, 1952; *Saturday Evening Post*, May 21, 1955; *Family Circle*, June, 1960; *Reader's Digest*, July, 1960; *World Scouting*, November, 1960; *Boys' Life*, July, 1962.

(Died, 1965)

* * *

LANYON, Carla 1906-

PERSONAL: Born January 16, 1906, in County Down, Northern Ireland; daughter of Charles James (a flax broker) and Helen (Redfern) Lanyon; married Edward Sidney Hacker, July 30, 1927 (deceased); children: George Lanyon, Carlotta Leyla, Edward Arthur. *Education:* Privately. *Religion:* Anglican. *Home:* Shortheath House, Shortheath Crest, Farnham, Surrey, England.

CAREER: Poet. Lecturer, and reader of poetry. *Member:* Poetry Society, English Association, P.E.N., Society of Women Writers and Journalists. *Awards, honors:* Greenwood Prize for poetry, 1961.

WRITINGS—All poetry, except as indicated: *The Wanderer*, Sidgwick & Jackson, 1924; *Second Voyage*, Sidg-

wick & Jackson, 1930; *Far Country*, Basil Blackwell, 1932; *The Crag*, Basil Blackwell, 1934; *Full Circle*, Basil Blackwell, 1938; *Penelope* (novel), Foyle, 1945; *Salt Harvest*, Williams & Norgate, 1947; *Selected Poems*, Guild Press, 1953; *Flow and Ebb*, Cambridge Press, 1955; *Unfamiliar Mountain*, Outposts Publications, 1960; *Trusty Tree*, Mitre Press, 1964; *Uncompromising Gladness*, Outposts Publications, 1968. Contributor of poetry to anthologies and journals; poems also recorded on long-playing records.

* * *

LAPAGE, Geoffrey 1888-

PERSONAL: Born October 5, 1888, in Nantwich, Cheshire, England; son of Charles Clement and Emily Sophia (Simpson) Lapage; married Enid Oldham, September 6, 1927; children: David John (deceased), Jennifer Ann. *Education:* Attended Ellesmere College and Bradfield College; University of Manchester, B.Sc. (first class honors), M.Sc., M.B., Ch.B., M.D. *Politics:* Independent. *Religion:* Church of England. *Address:* Selwyn College, Cambridge, England.

CAREER: University of Manchester, Manchester, England, lecturer in zoology, 1912-16, 1919-24; University of Exeter, Exeter, England, head of department of zoology, 1928-30; Cambridge University, Cambridge, England, parasitologist, Institute of Animal Pathology, later lecturer in animal pathology, 1930-54, retired, 1954. *Military service:* Royal Army Medical Corps, pathologist, 1916-19; served in Iraq; became captain. *Member:* British Medical Association, Institute of Biology, Society of Authors, Playwrights and Composers (life member), English Association, Poetry Society.

WRITINGS: Parasites, Benn, 1929; *Shoes for the Gosling* (poetry), Noel Douglas, 1932; *Pursuit, in Sixty Sonnets*, Heffer, 1935; *The Bearing of the Physiology of Parasitic Nematodes on Their Treatment and Control*, Imperial Bureau of Agricultural Parasitology, 1935; *Nematodes Parasitic in Animals*, Methuen, 1937; *The Effects of Some Natural Factors on the Second Ecdysis of Nematode Infective Larvae* (originally published in 4th report of University of Cambridge Institute of Animal Pathology, 1934-35), Imperial Bureau of Agricultural Parasitology, 1937; *Parasitic Animals*, Cambridge University Press, 1951, 2nd edition, Heffer, 1958; (editor) Hermann Otto Moennig, *Veterinary Helminthology and Entomology*, 4th edition, Williams & Wilkins, 1956, 5th edition, Bailliere, Tindall, 1962; *Veterinary Parasitology*, C. C Thomas, 1956, 2nd edition, 1968; *The Potato-Root Eelworm* (originally published in *School Science Review*), J. Murray, 1957; *Animals Parasitic in Man*, Penguin, 1957, revised edition, Dover, 1963; *Achievement: Some Contributions of Animal Experiment to the Conquest of Disease*, Heffer, 1960; *Art and the Scientist*, John Wright, 1961; *Man Against Disease*, Abelard, 1964.

Children's books: *The Ladybird Book of Bedtime Rhymes*, Wills & Hepworth, 1946; *Strange Holiday*, Blackie & Son, 1956; *A Red Rosette*, Burke Books, 1957; *A Pony Every Time*, Burke Books, 1958. Contributor to *Nature, Discovery, Guardian, Lancet*, other general and scientific periodicals.

AVOCATIONAL INTERESTS: Cycling, walking, motoring.

LARIAR, Lawrence 1908-
(Adam Knight, Michael Lawrence, Michael Stark)

PERSONAL: Original name, Lawrence Rosenblum; born December 25, 1908, in Brooklyn, N.Y.; son of Marcy and Ella (Poll) Rosenblum; married Susan Meyer, October 21, 1935; children: Linda Webb, Stephen. *Education:* Studied at New York School of Fine and Applied Arts, 1926-29; also studied at Art Students League, New York, N.Y., and Academie Julien, Paris, France. *Home:* 57 West Lena Ave., Freeport, N.Y. 11520.

CAREER: Commercial advertising artist, 1930-33; Freelance illustrator and political cartoonist, 1933—; Walt Disney Studios, Hollywood, Calif., story man, 1938-39; *Liberty*, New York, N.Y., cartoon editor, 1941-48; Merryday House, New York, N.Y., editor, 1944-45; *Parade*, New York, N.Y., cartoon editor, 1957—. Director, Professional School of Cartooning, 1927. *Member:* Cartoonists Guild (president, 1942-43), American Society of Magazine Cartoonists (former president), Authors League of America, Long Island Craftsman's Guild (founder; president, 1957). *Awards, honors:* Red Badge Mystery award, 1944, for *Man with the Lumpy Nose.*

WRITINGS: Cartooning for Everybody, Crown, 1941; *The Army Fun Book*, Crown, 1943; *He Died Laughing*, Phoenix Press, 1943; *Death Paints the Picture*, Phoenix Press, 1943, reissued as *Death Is the Host*, Red Circle Magazines, 1943; *The Man with the Lumpy Nose*, Dodd, 1944; (with Colonel Stoopnagle) *Father Goosenagle: Nonsense and Fun for Everyone* (poems), Crown, 1945; (self-illustrated) *Bed and Bored*, McGraw, 1945; *The Girl with the Frightened Eyes*, Dodd, 1945; (self-illustrated) *Careers in Cartooning*, Dodd, 1949; *Friday for Death*, Crown, 1949; *The Easy Way to Cartooning*, Crown, 1950; *You Can't Catch Me*, Crown, 1951; *The Day I Died*, Appleton, 1952; (self-illustrated) *Fish and Be Damned; or, The Night Crawler's Companion*, Prentice-Hall, 1953; *Naked and Alone*, Popular, 1954; *Oh! Dr. Kinsey!: A Photographic Reaction to the Kinsey Report*, Cartwrite, 1953; *Win, Place, and Die!*, Appleton, 1953; (with Michael Morris) *Yankee Yiddish*, Cartwrite, 1953; (self-illustrated) *Golf and Be Damned*, Prentice-Hall, 1954; (self-illustrated) *Fix it and Be Damned*, Prentice-Hall, 1955; *How Green Was My Sex Life*, Pippin Press, 1955; (self-illustrated) *Hunt and Be Damned*, Prentice-Hall, 1956; *The Real Lowdown*, Brown & Bigelow, 1956; (self-illustrated) *Boat and Be Damned*, Prentice-Hall, 1957.

Under pseudonym Adam Knight: *Murder for Madame*, Crown, 1951; *Stone Cold Blonde*, Crown, 1951; *Knife at My Back*, Crown, 1952; *The Sunburned Corpse*, Crown, 1952; *Kiss and Kill*, Crown, 1953; *I'll Kill You Next!*, Appleton, 1954; *Girl Running*, New American Library, 1956.

Under pseudonym Michael Stark: *Run for Your Life!*, Crown, 1946, reissued as *Kill-box*, Ace Books, 1954.

Editor: *Liberty Laughs Out Loud: A Collection of Hilarious Cartoons from Liberty Magazine*, Avon Comics, 1946; *The Salesman's Treasury*, Crown, 1951; *You've Got Me in Stitches: A Collection of Gay Cartoons About Doctors, Patients, and Hospitals*, Dodd, 1954; *You've Got Me on the Hook: A Catch of the Funniest Cartoons About Fish and Fishermen*, Dodd, 1954; *You've Got Me—and How!: A Collection of the Best Marriage Cartoons by the Foremost Comic Artists*, Dodd, 1955; *You've Got Me in a Hole: A Collection of the Best Golfing Cartoons By the Foremost Comic Artists*, Dodd, 1955; *Happy Holiday: A Traveler's Treasury of Humorous Writings and Cartoons*,

Dodd, 1956; *You've Got Me from 9 to 5: The Best Cartoons about the Office by the Nation's Top Comic Artists*, Dodd, 1956; *You've Got Me on the Rocks: A Comic Cocktail of the Funniest Cartoons About Drinks and Drinking by the Foremost Comic Artists*, Dodd, 1956 (published in England as *You've Got Me Seeing Double: A Comic Cocktail of the Funniest Cartoons About Drinks and Drinking by the Foremost Comic Artists*, Hammond, Hammond, 1957); *A Treasury of Sports Cartoons*, A. S. Barnes, 1957; *You've Got Me Behind the Wheel: A Traffic Jam of Automotive Laughs by the Nation's Top Comic Artists*, Dodd, 1957; *You've Got Me in the Suburbs: The Best Cartoons About Suburbanites and Commuters by the Nation's Top Artists*, Dodd, 1957 (published in England as *You've Got Me in the Suburbs: A Collection of Humorous Adventures in the Suburbs as Seen by Well-Known Cartoonists*, Hammond, Hammond, 1958); *You've Got Me in the Nursery: The Best Cartoons About Babies and Parents by the Nation's Top Artists*, Dodd, 1958; *Teensville, U.S.A.: The Best Cartoons About Teenagers by the Top Comic Artists*, Dodd, 1959; *The Best of the Best Cartoons*, Crown, 1961; *The Teen Scene: A Hilarious Cartoon Journey Through the Teen-Age World*, Dodd, 1966.

Illustrator: Gregor Fleshen, *Doctor—It Tickles*, Prentice-Hall, 1953. Also editor of annual series, *Best Cartoons of the Year*, Crown, 1942—, and *Best Cartoons from Abroad*, Crown, 1955-60. Television credits include Columbia Broadcasting System program, "Happy Headlines." Work has appeared in *College Humor, Country Gentleman, Saturday Evening Post, American, Judge, New Yorker*, and in other magazines. Creator of comic strip, "Ben Friday," for New York Herald Tribune Syndicate.

*   *   *

LARRABEE, Harold A(tkins) 1894-

PERSONAL: Born August 20, 1894, in Melrose, Mass.; son of John and Mary Edna (Atkins) Larrabee; married Doris Kennard, December 27, 1917 (died, 1965); married Dorcas Morgan, October 1, 1965; children: (first marriage) Eric, Sylvia (Mrs. Hollis J. Wyman, Jr.). *Education:* Harvard University, A.B. (cum laude), 1916, Ph.D., 1925; Columbia University, M.A., 1918. *Home:* 3303 Tom Green, Austin, Tex. 78705.

CAREER: Syracuse University, Syracuse, N.Y., assistant professor of philosophy, 1920-21; Harvard University and Radcliffe College, Cambridge, Mass., assistant in philosophy, 1921-23; University of Vermont, Burlington, assistant professor of psychology, 1924-25; Union College and University, Schenectady, N.Y., started as assistant professor, 1925, Ichabod Spencer Professor of Philosophy, 1940-60, professor emeritus, 1960—, chairman of Division of Social Studies, 1945-50, chairman of college's sesquicentennial celebration, 1945. Visiting professor of philosophy at Columbia University, summers, 1945, 1953-55, and at Syracuse University, 1962. U.S.A. Bibliography of Philosophy, director of editorial center, 1953-58. Schenectady County Public Library, president of board of trustees, 1959-61; Mohawk Valley Library Association, first president of board, 1960-62. *Military service:* U.S. Army, psychological examiner, 1918-19; became sergeant.

MEMBER: American Philosophical Association (secretary-treasurer of Eastern Division, 1932-34; vice-president, 1941), American Association of University Professors (chapter president, 1951-52, 1958-59), Societe des Americanistes de Paris, Phi Beta Kappa (chapter president, 1930-

32), Club Alpin Francais, Appalachian Mountain Club (life). *Awards, honors:* D.H.L., Union College and University, 1960.

WRITINGS: What Philosophy Is, Vanguard, 1928; *Joseph Jacques Ramee and America's First Unified College Plan*, American Society of French Legion of Honor, 1934; *Lafayette at Schenectady, March, 1778; September-October, 1784; June, 1825* (verse), privately printed, 1934; *Rhymes About College*, Gazette Press, 1936; *Reliable Knowledge: Scientific Methods in the Social Studies*, Houghton, 1945, revised edition, 1964; (editor) *Selections From Bergson*, Appleton, 1949; (translator) Charles Mayer, *Men: Mind or Matter?*, Beacon Press, 1951; (editor) *Bentham's Handbook of Political Fallacies*, John Hopkins Press, 1952; (translator) Charles Mayer, *In Quest of a New Ethics*, Beacon Press, 1953; (translator) Charles Mayer, *Sensation: The Origin of Life*, Antioch, 1961; (with Leon Edel) *Henry James, Sr., Class of 1830*, Union College, 1963; *Decision at the Chesapeake*, C. N. Potter, 1964. Contributor to *Encyclopedia Americana Annual* and other encyclopedias. Also contributor of articles and verse to *American Heritage, Harper's, New Yorker, New York Times Book Review*, and many philosophical periodicals. Member at various times of board of editors of *Journal of Philosophy, Humanist, New England Quarterly*.

* * *

LA SPINA, (Fanny) Greye 1880-

PERSONAL: Born July 10, 1880, in Wakefield, Mass.; daughter of Lorenzo Dow (a clergyman) and Ella Celia (Perkins) Bragg; married, 1899 (husband deceased); married Robert La Spina, April, 1910; children: (first marriage) Celia Geissler (Mrs. Edoardo LaSpina). *Education:* Attended schools in Connecticut. *Politics:* Democrat.

CAREER: Free-lance author. Has also been commercial photographer, private secretary, office manager, and weaver of tapestries, rugs, linens, and other fabrics of her own design. Democratic committeewoman, Quakertown, Pa., 1925-50. *Awards, honors:* Photography prize ($2,500) for short story, "A Seat on the Platform."

WRITINGS: Invaders from the Dark, Arkham, 1960. Contributor of more than one hundred serials, novelettes, and short stories to *Metropolitan, Photoplay, Weird Tales, Black Mask, Action Stories, Modern Marriage, All-Story*, and other periodicals in United States and abroad.

SIDELIGHTS: Invaders from the Dark first ran as a serial in *Weird Tales*. Mrs. La Spina has had a lifelong interest in the supernatural and the occult.

* * *

LATHAM, Harold Strong 1887-1969

PERSONAL: Born February 14, 1887, in Marlboro, Conn.; son of Charles Arthur (a business executive) and Minnie Alice (Strong) Latham. *Education:* Columbia University, B.A., 1909. *Children:* Jerold P. (adopted). *Politics:* Republican. *Religion:* Unitarian-Universalist. *Home:* 17 Pleasant Pl., Kearny, N.J. 07032.

CAREER: Macmillan Co. (publishers), New York, N.Y., 1909-53, head of trade department, 1919, director, 1920, vice-president, 1931-53. Universalist Church of America, president, 1947-51, president of Universalist Publishing House, 1950-52. West Hudson Hospital, Kearny, N.J., president of hospital association for three years, chairman of board of governors, 1960-64; chairman of advisory

board, Salvation Army, Kearny, N.J., 1961-62. *Member:* Columbia University Club, Century Club (New York).

WRITINGS: The Perry Boys: A "Social Center-Historical" Play in 3 Scenes for 10 Boys, Samuel French, 1913; *Little Rebel: Sane Fourth of July Play*, Werner, c.1913; *Thirteen Domino: A Play in One Act*, Samuel French, c.1913; *The Making of Larry: A Boy Scout Play in Two Scenes*, Samuel French, 1914; *Under Orders: The Story of Time and "the Club,"* Macmillan, 1918; *Marty Lends a Hand*, Macmillan, 1919; *Jimmy Quigg, Office Boy*, Macmillan, 1920; *My Life in Publishing* (autobiography), Dutton, 1965. Contributor of articles to magazines.

AVOCATIONAL INTERESTS: Travel and photography.

BIOGRAPHICAL/CRITICAL SOURCES: Times Literary Supplement, January 12, 1967; *New York Times*, March 8, 1969; *Times* (London), March 11, 1969.

(Died March 6, 1969)

* * *

LATHAM, Peter 1910-

PERSONAL: Born October 24, 1910, in Chakrata, India; son of Henry and Anne (Walshe) Latham; married Phoebe G. Ashburner (an editor), December 3, 1954; children: (previous marriage) Peter Floyd, Anne Floyd. *Education:* Privately educated. *Politics:* Conservative. *Religion:* Roman Catholic (non-practicing). *Home:* The Old Mill House, Stanstead, Suffolk, England.

CAREER: Career officer in Indian Army, 1929-47; freelance journalist, 1947-58; *Sunday Times*, London, England, staff member, 1958-63. *Member:* National Book League (council member), Enterprise for Youth (Adventure Unlimited; council member).

WRITINGS: Young Europeans Travel Guide, 1961, MacGibbon & Kee, 1961, new edition, 1964, International Publications, 1965; *Students' Guide to Europe*, MacGibbon & Kee, 1962, new edition, Blackie & Son, 1964; *Guide to Studying in Europe*, London House & Maxwell, 1963, revised edition, 1964; *Holiday Courses in Europe*, Blackie & Son, 1964; *Travel, Business, Study and Art in the U.S.A.*, Blackie & Son, 1964, International Publications, 1965; *Travel, Business, Study and Art in France*, Blackie & Son, 1964, International Publications, 1965; *The German Federal Republic*, Blackie & Son, 1964, International Publications, 1965; *The United Kingdom*, Blackie & Son, 1964, International Publications, 1965; *Italy*, International Publications, 1965; *Travel, Business, Study, and Art in the U.S.S.R.*, International Publications, 1966; *Romania: A Complete Guide*, International Publications, 1967. Contributor of travel articles aimed at young people to *Sunday Times* (London), *Elizabeth, Go*, and other journals and newspapers.

AVOCATIONAL INTERESTS: Fishing ("a keen but inefficient angler").

* * *

LAUBACH, Frank Charles 1884-1970

PERSONAL: Born September 2, 1884, in Benton, Pa.; son of John Britain and Harriet (Derr) Laubach; married Effa Seely, May 15, 1912; children: Robert S. *Education:* Princeton University, A.B., 1909; Columbia University, M.A., 1912, Ph.D., 1915; diploma from Union Theological Seminary, 1913, fellowship, 1920-21. *Home:* 753 James St., Syracuse, N.Y. 13203. *Office:* Laubach Literacy, Inc., 1011 Harrison St., Syracuse, N.Y. 13210.

CAREER: Minister of United Church. Grade school teacher, 1901-04; Spring Street Presbyterian Church, New York, N.Y., assistant, 1909-10; Charity Organization Society, New York, N.Y., staff member, 1913-14; missionary in Cagayan, Misamis, Philippine Islands, 1915-20; teacher, Union Theological Seminary, New York, N.Y., dean Union College, Manila, Philippine Islands, and dean of College of Education, Manila University, 1922-28; Lanao Folk School, Dansalan, Lanao, Philippine Islands, founder and head, 1930-41; World Literacy and Christian Literature Committee of Federal Council of Churches of America, New York, N.Y., traveling representative throughout the world, 1941-54; Laubach Literacy Fund (now Laubach Literacy, Inc.), Syracuse, N.Y., founder, and executive director, 1955-63, president and world representative, 1964-70. Awards, honors: Doctorates from Princeton University, Columbia University, Temple University, Syracuse University, Marietta College, Muskingan College, Wooster College, and Lafayette College.

WRITINGS: Why There Are Vagrants: A Study Based Upon an Examination of One Hundred Men, Columbia University Press, 1916; Religious Problems of Philippine Young Men, Silliman Press, 1918; People of the Philippines: Their Religious Progress and Preparation for Spiritual Leadership in the Far East, Doran, 1925; Seven Thousand Emeralds, Friendship, 1929; Dictionary of the Maranaw Language, Lanao Press, 1933; Rizal, Man and Martyr, Community Publishers (Manila), 1936; Letters by a Modern Mystic (excerpts from letters written at Dansalan, Lake Lanao, Philippine Islands, to his father), Student Volunteer Movement for Foreign Missions, 1937; Toward a Literate World, published for World Literacy and Christian Literature Committee, Foreign Missions Conference of North America, by Columbia University Press, 1938; India Shall Be Literate, National Christian Council, 1940; The Silent Billion Speak, Friendship, 1943, enlarged edition, 1945; Prayer, the Mightiest Force in the World, Revell, 1946; Story of Jesus, Books 1-12, published for World Literacy and Christian Literature Committee, Foreign Missions Conference of North America, by Friendship, 1947; Teaching the World to Read: A Handbook for Literacy Campaigns, published for World Literacy and Christian Literature Committee, Foreign Missions Conference of North America, by Friendship, 1947.

Streamlined English: The New Easier Way to Learn, includes teacher's manual, Macmillan, 1951; Wake Up or Blow Up! America: Lift the World or Lose It!, Revell, 1951; Channels of Spiritual Power, Revell, 1954; Pray for Others, Upper Room, 1954; Literacy as Evangelism, Laubach Literacy Fund, 1955; The Greatest Life: Jesus Tells His Story (based on Edgar J. Goodspeed's translation of harmonies of the Gospels), Revell, 1956, also published as The Master Speaks: Jesus Tells His Own Story, Arthur James, 1956, reissued as The Autobiography of Jesus, Harper, 1962; (editor) Inspired Letters, in Clearest English (New Testament Epistles), Thomas Nelson, 1956; Learning the Vocabulary of God, Upper Room, 1956; The Game with Minutes, privately printed, 1956 (published in England as The Game with Minutes: Practising the Presence of God, Lutterworth, 1959); Making Everybody's World Safe, Committee on World Literacy and Christian Literature, 1957; (with son, Robert S. Laubach) How to Make the World Literate: The Each One Teach One Way, Part 1, Teaching Illiterates, Part 2, Writing for New Literates, Syracuse University Press, 1957, reissued as Toward

World Literacy: The Each One Teach One Way, 1960; The World is Learning Compassion, Revell, 1958.

Thirty Years with the Silent Billion: Adventuring in Literacy (first eight chapters originally published in The Silent Billion Speak—see above), Revell, 1960; Christ Liveth in Me [and] Game with Minutes, Revell, 1961; (with Pauline Jones Hord) A Door Opens, Macmillan, 1962; English the New Way, two books, New Readers Press, 1962; (with Hord) Going Forward, Macmillan, 1963; Frank Laubach's Prayer Diary, Revell, 1964; CIHU, New Readers Press, 1964; How to Teach One and Win One for Christ: Christ's Plan for Winning the World, Zondervan, 1964; War of Amazing Love, Revell, 1965; What Jesus Had to Say About Money, Zondervan, 1966; Living Words (selections from writings), compiled by F. Elmo Robinson, Zondervan, 1967; Long Vowel Sounds, Macmillan, 1967; Did Mary Tell Jesus Her Secret?, Revell, 1970; Forty Years with the Silent Billion: Adventuring in Literacy, Revell, 1970.

Collaborator in publishing primers in 312 languages or dialects, and in preparation of literacy textbooks and charts in more than a hundred countries.

BIOGRAPHICAL/CRITICAL SOURCES: Literacy, Laubach and the Missionary Society, Lutterworth, 1944; Gordon Hewitt, Nothing Can Stop It Now: Frank Laubach and World Literacy, Lutterworth, 1948; New Yorker, February 16, 1952; Marjorie Medary, Each One Teach One: Frank Laubach, Friend to Millions, Longmans, Green, 1954; Saturday Evening Post, April 17, 1954; Atlantic, October, 1957; Saturday Review, May 24, 1959; Christian Herald, September, 1960; Helen M. Roberts, Champion of the Silent Billion: The Story of Frank C. Laubach, Apostle of Literacy, Macalester Park, 1961; David E. Mason, Frank C. Laubach, Teacher of Millions (juvenile), Denison, 1967.

(Died June 11, 1970)

*   *   *

LAURITZEN, Elizabeth Moyes   1909-

PERSONAL: Born December 4, 1909, in Thatcher, Ariz.; daughter of Joseph and Anna (Plumb) Moyes; married Richard Dawn Lauritzen, March 4, 1932; children: JoAnn (Mrs. John Robinson), Richard, Hope (Mrs. Niel S. Dickson), Marion, Karl, Arthur. Education: Gila Junior College, student, 1926-30; Arizona State College (now Arizona State University), A.B., 1934; Utah State University, M.S., 1961; additional study at University of Utah and University of Denver. Politics: Republican. Religion: Church of Jesus Christ of Latter-Day Saints. Home: 686 South Fourth West, Brigham City, Utah 84302.

CAREER: Teacher in rural, elementary, and high schools in Arizona and Utah, 1930-56; Intermountain School (Bureau of Indian Affairs school), Brigham City, Utah, librarian, 1956—. Member: Utah Library Association (secretary of school library section, 1964-65), Utah Penwomen, Utah Folklore Society, Thoreau Society.

WRITINGS: Shush'ma, Caxton, 1964. Author of "Enjoy Books," a column in Box Elder News-Journal.

WORK IN PROGRESS: Yannabah, a fictional story about a Navajo girl in cultural transition; Look, Mamma I Have Bought Us a Hotel!, a travel book about a trip to the New York World's Fair.

LAWLOR, Patrick Anthony 1893
(Pat Lawlor; pseudonyms, Shibli Bagarag, Christopher Penn)

PERSONAL: Born February 12, 1893, in Wellington, New Zealand; son of David Roche and Mary Ellen (Dennehy) Lawlor; married Amy Martha Lambert, December 7, 1917; children: Ruth Josephine, Peter Francis, Naomi, Margaret. *Education:* Attended St. Patrick's College, Wellington, New Zealand. *Religion:* Roman Catholic. *Home:* 6 Hawker St., Wellington, New Zealand.

CAREER: Began career on literary staff of *Evening Post*, Wellington, New Zealand, later did literary work in Australia; left news field in 1922 to become a publisher's representative and to devote spare time to writing. *Member:* P.E.N. (founder of New Zealand center; past president; honorary life member, London center), Friends of the Turnbull Library (past president), New Zealand Ex-Libris Society (founder).

*WRITINGS—*Under name Pat Lawlor: *Maori Tales*, New Century Press, 1926; (editor) *The Poetry of Dick Harris*, New Century Press, 1927; *More Maori Tales*, New Century Press, 1929; *Still More Maori Tales*, New Century Press, 1930; *Confessions of a Journalist, with Observations on Some Australian and New Zealand Writers*, Whitcombe & Tombs, 1935; *Murphy's Moa and Other Sketches*, Simpson & Williams, 1936; *The House of Templemore*, A. H. & A. W. Reed, 1938; (editor and author of introduction) *Wellington in Verse and Picture*, A. H. & A. W. Reed, 1939, 2nd edition, 1955; *The Last First Friday* (verse), Beltane Book Bureau, 1946; *The Mystery of Maata: A Katherine Mansfield Novel*, Folcroft, 1946; *The Best New Zealand Books: A List for Libraries, Students and Collectors*, Beltane Book Bureau, 1948; *Mansfieldiana: A Brief Katherine Mansfield Bibliography* (monograph), Beltane Book Bureau, 1948.

The Loneliness of Katherine Mansfield, Beltane Book Bureau, 1950; *A Katherine Mansfield Enthusiast: The Work of Guy N. Morris*, Beltane Book Bureau, 1951; *The Caxton Press: Some Impressions and a Bibliography*, Beltane Book Bureau, 1951; *Books and Bookmen, New Zealand and Overseas*, Whitcombe & Tombs, 1954; *Wellington Characters of the Long Ago* (originally published in *Evening Post*, December 1, 1956), [Wellington], 1956; *Old Wellington Days: An Intimate Diary, to Which is Appended the Ships of Wellington, the Wellington of Katherine Mansfield and Other Literary Associations: also James Cowan and His Wellington Place-Names*, Whitcombe & Tombs, 1959; *More Wellington Days: A Further Selection of Items from the Old Wellington Diary of the Author, with Sundry Other Memories and Revelations About the Wellington of Yesterday and Today*, Whitcombe & Tombs, 1962; *Saint Joseph and Pope John*, Futuna Press, 1964; *The Froth-Blowers' Manual: Some Confessions, Some Beer Ballads, a Dash of History, Froth of Personalities and an Encyclopedia*, Whitcombe & Tombs, 1965.

Under pseudonym Shibli Bagarag: *New Zealand Book-Plates: Illustrated History and Bibliography*, Beltane Book Bureau, 1948. Also writer of *Collectors' Monographs*, numbers 1-6, Beltane Book Bureau, 1947-51, and of ten booklets published under pseudonym, Christopher Penn. Editor, *New Zealand Artists' Annual*, 1926-32.

WORK IN PROGRESS: An anthology of prayers; and *The Brotherhood of Paris*.

BIOGRAPHICAL/CRITICAL SOURCES: Zealandia, May 23, 1963.

LAWRENCE, H(enry) L(ionel) 1908-

PERSONAL: Born April 22, 1908, in London, England. *Home:* 19 Inholmes Park Rd., Burgess Hill, Sussex, England. *Agent:* Winant Towers Ltd., 1 Furnival St., London E.C.4, England. *Office:* T. B. Browne Ltd., 117 Piccadilly, London W.1, England.

CAREER: Copywriter in advertising agencies in London, England, and at one period, in Sydney, Australia, 1933—. *Military service:* Royal Air Force, 1940-45. *Member:* International P.E.N., Crime Writers Association, Television and Screen Writers Guild, Institute of Practitioners in Advertising.

WRITINGS: The Children of Light, Macdonald & Co., 1960; *The Sparta Medallion*, Macdonald & Co., 1961. Contributor of short stories to *Guardian* and to periodicals; author of pilot script for motion picture, "The Damned," based on *The Children of Light*.

WORK IN PROGRESS: Noxie Comsall, a novel, study of a sex killer.

SIDELIGHTS: Lawrence told *CA:* "[I am] mostly a working hack. [I] would like (who wouldn't?) to write a best seller. [I am] very cynical—and sentimental. Advertising gives me a living. My spare-time writing gives me kicks—and headaches, and income tax demands." Lawrence's books have been published in Finland, Germany, Denmark, and Italy. *Avocational interests:* Being lazy, traveling, reading, and music—classical and popular.†

* * *

LAWSON, John Howard 1894-

PERSONAL: Born September 25, 1894, in New York, N.Y.; son of Simeon Levy (a journalist) and Belle (Hart) Lawson; married Katharine Drain, 1918 (divorced, 1923); married Susan Edmond, September 25, 1925; children: (first marriage) Alan Drain; (second marriage) Jeffery Edmond, Susan Amanda. *Education:* Williams College, B.A., 1914. *Home:* 5726 Camellia Ave., North Hollywood, Calif. 91601.

CAREER: Author and playwright. Began as cable editor for Reuters Press in New York, N.Y., 1914-15, then served with an ambulance unit in France and Italy, 1917-19; film writer in Hollywood from 1928 until 1947, when he was indicted for contempt of Congress following the House Committee on Un-American Activities hearings; found guilty, 1948, and sentenced to one-year term. *Member:* Authors League of America, Writers Guild of America (West; formerly Screen Writers Guild; first president, 1933), Society of Cinematologists.

WRITINGS: Theory and Technique of Playwrighting, Putnam, 1936, enlarged edition published as *Theory and Technique of Playwriting and Screenwriting*, Putnam, 1949; *The Hidden Heritage: A Rediscovery of the Ideas and Forces That Link the Thought of Our Time with the Culture of the Past*, Citadel, 1950, 1st revised edition, 1968; *Film in the Battle of Ideas*, Masses & Mainstream, 1953; *Film, The Creative Process: The Search for an Audio-Visual Language and Structure*, Hill and Wang, 1964, 2nd revised edition, 1967.

Plays: *Roger Bloomer*, Thomas Seltzer, 1923; *Processional*, Thomas Seltzer, 1925; *Loudspeaker*, Macaulay, 1927; *The International*, Macaulay, 1928; *Success Story*, Farrar & Rinehart, 1932; *With a Reckless Preface* (containing *The Pure in Heart* and *Gentlewoman*), Farrar & Rinehart, 1934; *Marching Song*, Dramatists Play Service, 1937.

Film Scripts: "Blockade," 1938; "Algiers," 1938; "They Shall Have Music," 1939; "Four Sons," 1940; "Action in the North Atlantic," 1943; "Sahara," 1943; "Counterattack," 1945; "Smashup," 1947.

WORK IN PROGRESS: First volume of an autobiography, not yet titled.

BIOGRAPHICAL/CRITICAL SOURCES: New York Times, June 10, 1950.

* * *

LAWSON, Marion Tubbs 1896-

PERSONAL: Born August 8, 1896, in Elkhorn, Wis.; daughter of Henry H. (a civil engineer) and Helen Marion (Andrus) Tubbs; married Philip C. Lawson (a salesman), December 6, 1927. *Education:* Carroll College, Waukesha, Wis., A.B., 1919. *Politics:* Republican. *Religion:* Protestant. *Home:* 160 Cabrini Blvd., New York, N.Y. 10033.

CAREER: Worked in Milwaukee, Wis., for printing and publishing companies and an investment house, 1919-27. *Member:* American Association of University Women. *Awards, honors:* Award of merit, State Historical Society of Wisconsin, 1969, for *Proud Warrior: The Story of Black Hawk.*

WRITINGS: Solomon Juneau, Voyageur, Crowell, 1960; *Proud Warrior: The Story of Black Hawk,* Hawthorn, 1968. Contributor of articles to *National Business Woman, Wisconsin Magazine of History,* of short stories to literary magazines.

AVOCATIONAL INTERESTS: Contemporary American Indian art, antiques, bird watching.

BIOGRAPHICAL/CRITICAL SOURCES: Milwaukee Journal, August 24, 1960.

* * *

LAY, Bennett 1910-

PERSONAL: Born November 11, 1910, in Hallettsville, Tex.; son of Hugh and Willie May (Clayton) Lay; married George Tidd, 1942; children: Jane, John B. *Education:* University of Texas, student, 1928-31; South Texas College of Law, LL.B., 1937. *Religion:* Methodist. *Home:* 1802 Albans Rd., Houston, Tex. 77005. *Office:* 3505 Fannin, Houston, Texas 77004.

CAREER: Admitted to Bar of State of Texas, 1937; practice of law, Houston, Tex., 1937—; City of Houston, Houston, Tex., assistant city attorney, 1947-49; assistant U.S. District Attorney, Houston, Tex., 1950. *Military service:* U.S. Army Air Corps, 1942-45, became captain; received Bronze Star. *Member:* State Bar of Texas, Texas State Historical Association, Harris County Historical Society (president, 1956), Harris County Historical Survey Commission, Houston Bar Association. *Awards, honors:* Book selected by Writer's Roundup (Austin, Tex.) as one of twenty best books published by Texans in 1960.

WRITINGS: The Lives of Ellis P. Bean, University of Texas Press, 1960.

* * *

LEAR, Floyd Seyward 1895-

PERSONAL: Born July 7, 1895, in Corfu, N.Y.; son of William Seyward (a merchant) and Harriet (Mann) Lear; married Elsie Mann, December 25, 1920. *Education:* University of Rochester, A.B., 1917; Harvard University, A.M., 1920, Ph.D., 1925. *Home:* 2236 North Blvd., Hous-

ton, Tex. 77006. *Office:* 427 Fondren Library, Rice University, Houston, Tex. 77001.

CAREER: High school teacher, Louisville, Ky., 1920-22; Harvard University, Cambridge, Mass., instructor in history, 1924-25; Rice University, Houston, Tex., began as instructor, 1925, professor of history, 1945-53, Harris Masterson, Jr. Professor of History, 1954-65, Trustee Distinguished Professor of History, 1965-74, Distinguished Lecturer, 1974—, chairman of department, 1933-60. *Military service:* U.S. Army, Air Service, 1917-19; became sergeant. *Member:* Mediaeval Academy of America (council member, 1953-56), American Geographical Society (fellow), American Historical Association, Academy of Political Science, American Military Institute, Renaissance Society of America, U.S. Naval Institute, Classical Association of the Middle West and South, Southern Historical Association, Western Social Science Association, Texas State Historical Association, Houston Philosophical Society (president, 1949-50), Phi Beta Kappa.

WRITINGS: Treason in Roman and Germanic Law, University of Texas Press, 1965. Contributor of articles and reviews to journals. Member of advisory boards, *Speculum,* 1937-40; consulting editor, *Corpus Juris Romani.*

WORK IN PROGRESS: Continuing research in Roman and Germanic law.

SIDELIGHTS: Lear reads German, French, Latin.

* * *

LEDBETTER, Virgil C. 1918-19(?)

PERSONAL: Born March 7, 1918, in Bagley, Ala.; son of Joe Martin (a coal miner) and Mary (Savage) Ledbetter; married Dorothy L. Copple, December 24, 1946; children: Gary Thomas. *Education:* Howard College (now Samford University), student, 1939-42; Arkansas State College (now University), 1963. *Politics:* Democrat. *Religion:* Baptist. *Home:* 1725 Grant Ave., S.W., Birmingham, Ala. *Office:* Howard College, Birmingham, Ala.

CAREER: High school coach in Alabama, 1942-55; Howard College, Birmingham, Ala., football, basketball, and baseball coach, beginning 1955. Professional baseball player with Brooklyn Dodgers farm teams, 1946-55; scout for Los Angeles Dodgers, beginning 1955. Conductor of athletic clinics in several states; public lecturer. *Military service:* U.S. Army Air Forces, 1942-45; served in Italy; received Air Medal with oak leaf clusters. U.S. Army, Special Services officer in Korea, 1951-52. Alabama National Guard, 1945-51, 1952—; became major. *Member:* American Association for Health, Physical Education and Recreation, American Association of College Baseball Coaches, American Association of University Professors, National Guard Association of the United States, Veterans of Foreign Wars of the U.S.A.

WRITINGS: Coaching Baseball, W. C. Brown, 1964. Regular columnist, *Mountain Eagle.* Contributor to *Athletic Journal, First Aider.*

WORK IN PROGRESS: Coaching Basketball.

(Deceased)

* * *

LEDUC, Violette 1907-1972

PERSONAL: Born April 8, 1907, in Arras, Pas de Calais, France; illegitimate daughter of a servant girl and the son of the house where she was employed; married, now divorced. *Education:* Attended small-town boarding schools; received no diploma. *Residence:* Paris, France.

CAREER: Before World War II worked as a switchboard operator, a messenger girl, and a reader for a publisher in Paris, France; during the war she supported herself by trading in the black market in Normandy; turned seriously to writing after World War II.

WRITINGS: L'Asphyxie, Gallimard, 1946, translation by Derek Coltman published as *In the Prison of Her Skin*, Hart-Davis, 1970; *L'Affamee*, Gallimard, 1948; *Ravages* (exclusive of a lesbian interlude which Gallimard published separately as *Therese et Isabelle*), Gallimard, 1955, translation by Coltman (which includes the text of *Therese and Isabelle*) published as *Ravages*, Arthur Barker, 1966; *La Vieille Fille et le mort* (including "Les Boutons dores"), Gallimard, 1958, translation by Coltman included in *The Woman with the Little Fox: Three Novellas* (containing "The Old Maid and the Dead Man," "The Golden Buttons," and "The Woman with the Little Fox"; also see below), Farrar, Straus, 1966, a separate translation of "Les Boutons dores" by Dorothy Williams published as *The Golden Buttons*, P. Owen, 1961, Transatlantic, 1962; *Tresors a prendre*, Gallimard, 1960; *La Batarde* (first part of autobiography), foreword by Simone de Beauvoir, Gallimard, 1964, translation by Coltman published under same title, Farrar, Straus, 1965; *La femme au petit renard*, Gallimard, 1965, translation by Coltman published as *The Lady and the Little Fox Fur*, P. Owen, 1967; *Therese et Isabelle*, Gallimard, 1966, translation by Coltman published as *Therese and Isabelle*, Farrar, Straus, 1967; *La Folie en tete* (second part of autobiography), Gallimard, 1970, translation by Coltman published as *Mad in Pursuit*, Farrar, Straus, 1971; *Le Taxi*, Gallimard, 1971, translation by Helen Weaver published as *The Taxi*, Farrar, Straus, 1972. Contributor to *Les Temps Modernes* and to *Vogue*.

SIDELIGHTS: Violette Leduc first gained public recognition with her autobiography, *La Batarde*, which became a *succes de scandale* early in 1965. Her career as a writer, however, began almost two decades earlier when she was encouraged to write by Maurice Sachs, a young homosexual writer and adventurer whom she loved. Her early efforts earned the praise of France's first rank of critics—Genet, Jouhandeau, Sartre. And on the recommendation of Simone de Beauvoir, Albert Camus published her first novel, *L'Asphyxie*, in his Gallimard "Espoir" series. It was de Beauvoir's suggestion that she write an autobiography since all her writing tended to be autobiographical in nature. But Leduc remained virtually unknown to the public, and dependent on the financial support of her literary mentors, until 1965.

With the publication of *La Batarde* Leduc became not only a bestselling author, but a controversial one. The Paris edition of the *New York Times* wrote that "no one has more to admit than Violette Leduc: promiscuity and perversion, thievery and betrayal, hysteria and chaos." She had, in effect, turned her back on society and its opinions of her. Madeleine Chapsal wrote: "In *La Batarde* there are cries and groans, some quite ovarian (to use her language) wails of ratiocination, justifications vis-a-vis the world of the others, the world of men. But there are, on the other hand, new accents, sudden penetrations, merciless focusings, visions, strange confessions, and, above all, eroticism." Chapsal added: "That which Violette Leduc explores to its limits is solitude, feminine solitude which becomes human solitude in general."

Mlle Leduc told an interviewer for *Le Figaro Litteraire*: "In my actual life I am very modest. But in my books I tell all." (She was reputed to be cursed with total recall.) She once told Chapsal: "I very much liked Colette, who was a good writer and very wise. But, in reading her, I had the feeling that she had not dared, that she withheld things.... As for me, I am going to dare."

If the explicit sexual content of her writing is the attraction for some readers, critics draw attention to the over-riding artistry of her work. Elizabeth Janeway, writing in the *New York Times Book Review*, noted Leduc's "ability to take her readers with her into her constant confrontation with reality." Rejecting labels like "bizarre" and "eccentric," Janeway finds Leduc's writing "profoundly involved with ordinary reality and minute-by-minute living.... If she shocks her audience, it is in the same sense that the first Impressionist and Fauves did: in order to make the viewers look, the hearers listen freshly to the world around them."

As a woman writing about other women, Leduc is often measured against Colette, but she has also been favorably compared with Maupassant, Flaubert, and Beckett. Some critics have taken her to task for being completely wrapped up in herself; but Etienne Lalou points out in *L'Express* that her small world is the "projection of an inner universe—a tragic inner universe." *La Folie en tete* (the second part of her autobiography) reveals how writing became for her a kind of salvation, allowing her to accept the depths of loneliness and frustration that seemed predestined for her.

Unrecognized by her father and hated by her mother, Mlle Leduc had early in life known humiliation, poverty, and defeat, and was disgraced by her ugliness. She once told an interviewer: "I'm always afraid of finding myself above the humble. You see, the worst thing in the world is to humiliate. Death lasts but one second, while humiliation is without end."

Naturally withdrawn, she lived her later years "like a nun," she said, going out infrequently and receiving few visitors. "I would so much like to be taken seriously," she said. "I would so much like to be conventional." She spent her summers and autumns in the south of France where she reportedly wrote beneath a particular apple tree beside the peasant house she had finally been able to afford to buy. Following surgery for cancer in 1969, Mlle Leduc's health declined. In 1972 she died at her home in Faucon in Southern France.

Therese and Isabelle, adapted for the screen by Jess Vogel, was filmed by the Amsterdam Film Corp. and released in the United States through Audubon Films in 1968.

BIOGRAPHICAL/CRITICAL SOURCES: Figaro Litteraire, 1-7 octobre, 1964; *L'Express*, 19-25 octobre, 1964, 30 mars-5 avril, 1970; *Publishers' Weekly*, December 14, 1964; *New Yorker*, January 23, 1965.

(Died May 28, 1972)

* * *

LEE, Austin 1904-19(?)
(John Austwick, Julian Callender)

PERSONAL: Born July 9, 1904, in Cowling, Yorkshire, England; son of Joseph Nicholas and Gertrude (Kershaw) Lee. *Education:* Trinity College, Cambridge, B.A., 1926, M.A., 1928. *Politics:* Liberal. *Home:* Great Paxton Vicarage, Huntingdonshire, England. *Agent:* Ursula Winant, 14 Essex St., Strand, London W.C.2, England.

CAREER: Ordained priest, Church of England, 1928. Royal Navy, chaplain, 1931-36; vicar of Pampisford, Cambridge, England, 1935-38; chaplain to Middlesex Hospital, London, England, 1938-39, to Royal Air Force Motorboats Crew, 1940; rector of Claxby, and of Willoughby, Alford, Lincolnshire, England; vicar of Great Paxton, Huntingdonshire, England, beginning 1963. Author of mystery novels. *Member:* Society of Authors, Crime Writers Association, Mystery Writers of America, National Liberal Club (London).

WRITINGS—All published by J. Cape, except as indicated: *Round Many a Bend* (autobiographical), 1954; *Sheep's Clothing*, 1955; *Call in Miss Hogg*, 1956; *Miss Hogg and the Bronte Murders*, 1957; *Miss Hogg and the Squash Club Murder*, 1957; *Miss Hogg Flies High*, 1958; *Miss Hogg and the Dead Dean*, 1958; *Hubberthwaite Horror*, R. Hale, 1958; *Miss Hogg and the Covent Garden Murders*, 1960; *Miss Hogg and the Missing Sisters*, 1961; *Miss Hogg's Last Case*, 1963.

Under pseudonym John Austwick; all published by R. Hale: *Highland Homicide*, 1957; *Murder in the Borough Library*, 1959; *The County Library Murders*, 1962; *The Mobile Library Murders*, 1963.

Under pseudonym Julian Callender: *Company of Heaven*, Wingate, 1956; *St. Dingan's Bones*, Wingate, 1957, Vanguard, 1958.

WORK IN PROGRESS: A life of the Rev. Doctor Bradford, Edwardian poet; a biography of Archdeacon Wakeford of Stowe, Lincoln.

SIDELIGHTS: Lee wrote: "I read, on an average, ten books a week, buy 150 a year (hard covers), and write two a year. I dabble a little in philately (was once a member of the Royal Philatelic Society), but it's become too much of a racket." *Avocational interests:* Cooking.

(Deceased)

*   *   *

LEE, Carvel (Bigham) 1910-

PERSONAL: Born April 2, 1910, in Minneapolis, Minn.; daughter of A. Lincoln (a printing company owner) and Rebecca (Lung) Bigham; married Kermit Anton Lee (an office manager), May 18, 1934; children: Kermit Anton, Jr., Lorita Gail. *Education:* Attended Minneapolis (Minn.) public schools and Minneapolis School of Art. *Politics:* Unaffiliated. *Religion:* Lutheran. *Home:* 7329 Colfax Ave. S., Minneapolis, Minn. 55423.

CAREER: Strutwear Knitting Co., Minneapolis, Minn., advertising manager and head artist, 1928-40; Carvel Lee Studios, Minneapolis, Minn., owner, 1940—. Free-lance writer and artist; illustrator of science, art, craft, and children's books and of educational materials. University of Minnesota, artist for experimental teaching methods for handicapped children in special education department. *Member:* Woman's Christian Temperance Union (state visual education director, 1962-64), Friends of the Minneapolis Library (vice-president, 1964), Richfield Art Group (organizer and president, 1955-58), Richfield Garden Clubs (president, 1946-47).

WRITINGS: *Kindergarten Activities*, F. A. Owen Publishing Co., 1958; *The Art Guide*, Denison, 1959; *Tender Tyrant* (novel), Augsburg, 1961.

Author and artist with daughter Lorita Lee, of "Bulletin Board Guide" series, nine books for schools, (kindergarten

through senior high), an instructor's manual, and other special guides, Denison, 1963-67.

WORK IN PROGRESS: A novel; research for additional series of educational books.

*   *   *

LEE, Florence Henry 1910-

PERSONAL: Born May 21, 1910, in New Brunswick, N.J.; daughter of William and Frances (May) Henry; married George W. Lee, Jr. (a cost accountant), July 17, 1943 (divorced, 1969); children: Alfred W., Dorothy H. *Education:* Rutgers University, A.B., 1929, M.A., 1932, Ed.D., 1943; Columbia University, M.A. and Diploma in Psychological Counseling, 1940. *Religion:* Episcopalian. *Home:* 23 Delevan St., New Brunswick, N.J. 08902.

CAREER: Christ Episcopal Church, New Brunswick, N.J., director of religious education and parish secretary, 1930-35; Highland Park (N.J.) public schools, teacher, 1935-42; Maplewood-South Orange (N.J.) public schools, school psychologist, 1942-43; Rutgers University, Douglass College, New Brunswick, N.J., lecturer, 1949-57, associate professor, 1957-69, professor of education and chairman of department, 1969-74, professor emeritus, 1974—, coordinator of teacher education, 1966-69. *Member:* American Psychological Association, National Education Association, American Educational Research Association, New Jersey Psychological Association, New Jersey Education Association, Phi Beta Kappa, Kappa Delta Pi, Pi Lambda Theta.

WRITINGS: (Editor) *Principles and Practices of Teaching in Secondary Schools: A Book of Readings*, McKay, 1965. Contributor to educational journals.

*   *   *

LEE, Roy Stuart 1899-

PERSONAL: Born March 28, 1899, in Stuart Town, New South Wales, Australia; son of K. S. (a shopkeeper) and M. A. E. (Dong) Lee; married Catherine Macauley Doyle (a teacher), December 3, 1930; children: Rosemary Susan, Elizabeth Leslie. *Education:* University of Sydney, B.A., 1920, M.A., 1922; Oxford University, B.Litt., 1927, D.Phil., 1947, M.A., 1949. *Home:* Mill St., Islip, Oxford, England. *Office:* Nuffield College, Oxford, England.

CAREER: Clergyman, Church of England; curate in Forbes, New South Wales, Australia, 1923-24; St. Johns College, Morpeth, New South Wales, Australia, vice-warden, 1928-38; curate in London, England, 1938-40; British Broadcasting Corp., London, producer of overseas religious broadcasts, 1940-47; University Church, Oxford, England, incumbent, 1947-61; Oxford University, Oxford, England, chaplain of Nuffield College, 1947—, fellow and chaplain of St. Catherine's College, 1961—. University extension lecturer, 1928-38.

WRITINGS: *Freud and Christianity*, James Clarke, 1948, A. A. Wyn, 1949; *Psychology and Worship*, S.C.M. Press, 1955, Philosophical Library, 1956; *Your Growing Child and Religion: A Psychological Account*, Macmillan, 1963; *Principles of Pastoral Counseling*, S.P.C.K., 1968. Contributor to periodicals.†

*   *   *

LEEMING, John F(ishwick) 1900-

PERSONAL: Born January 8, 1900, in Chorlton, England;

son of Henry Heatley and Edith (Lowe) Leeming; married Gladys Birch, June 25, 1920; children: John Birch, David Christopher. *Education:* Educated in English schools. *Politics:* "Detest politics of any kind." *Religion:* Roman Catholic. *Home and Office:* Badger's, Bowdon, Cheshire, England.

CAREER: Full-time professional writer, 1923—. *Military service:* Royal Air Force, 1939-45. *Member:* Royal Aero Club (member of racing committee, 1925-34), Lancastershire Aero Club (chairman, 1927-33; president, 1962-64), Manchester Chamber of Commerce (member of air transport committee, 1949-64).

WRITINGS: (Compiler) *Pilots "A" License*, Pitman, 1927, 9th edition, 1939; *The Book of the Delphinium*, Pitman, 1932; *The Garden Grows: A Story*, Harcourt, 1935; *Airdays*, Harrap, 1936; *Claudius the Bee*, Harrap, 1936, Viking, 1937; *Thanks to Claudius*, Harrap, 1937, Viking, 1939; (with Gordon Bell) *Claudius the Bee* (three-act play; based on his book; first produced in 1937), Samuel French, 1945; *Always Tomorrow*, Harrap, 1951, published as *The Natives Are Friendly*, Dutton, 1952; *It Always Rains in Rome*, Harrap, 1960, Farrar, Straus, 1961; *A Girl Like Wigan*, Harrap, 1961, published as *A Girl Like Scranton*, Farrar, Straus, 1962; *Arnaldo My Brother*, Harrap, 1962. Author of film and television scripts and magazine articles.

WORK IN PROGRESS: Intended Treason, based on the Gunpowder Plot of 1602-1606.

SIDELIGHTS: Some of Leeming's books have been translated into fourteen languages; sales of *Claudius the Bee, Always Tomorrow,* and *It Always Rains in Rome* have passed 300,000. The play version of *Claudius the Bee* is still being revived at intervals on the stage and radio.

* * *

LEGGE-BOURKE, (Edward Alexander) Henry 1914-

PERSONAL: Born May 16, 1914, in England; son of Nigel Walter Henry and Lady Victoria (Carrington) Legge-Bourke; married Catherine Jean Grant, June 10, 1943; children: William Nigel Henry, Heneage, Victoria. *Education:* Educated at Eton College and at Royal Military College at Sandhurst. *Politics:* Conservative. *Religion:* Anglican. *Home:* 9 Wilbraham Pl., London S.W.1, England. *Office:* Grant Production Co. Ltd., 4 Rathbone Pl., Oxford St., London W.1, England.

CAREER: Grant Production Co. Ltd., London, England, chairman, 1954—. Member of Parliament for Isle of Ely, 1945—; Conservative Party, former chairman of science and technology committee, former chairman of defense committee; chairman, Conservative "1922" Backbenchers Committee, all-party Parliamentary Scientific Committee, sub-committees on Coastal Pollution and Natural Environmental Research Council; member of Select Committee on Science and Technology, 1964—. Page of honor to King George V, 1924-30. *Military service:* British Army, Royal Horse Guards, 1934-45; became major; served as liaison officer with British troops in Greece, 1941, aide-de-camp to British ambassador in Cairo, Egypt, 1941-42. *Member:* Carlton Club (London). *Awards, honors:* Knight Commander, Order of the British Empire, 1960.

WRITINGS: Defence of the Realm, Falcon Press, 1949; *Master of the Offices: An Essay and Correspondence on the Central Control of His Majesty's Civil Service*, Falcon Press, 1950; *The King's Guards, Horse and Foot*, Mac-

donald & Co., 1952, revised edition published as *The Queen's Guards, Horse and Foot*, 1965; *The Household Cavalry on Ceremonial Occasions* [and] *The Brigade of Guards on Ceremonial Occasions*, twin volumes, Macdonald & Co., 1952. Contributor to *Spectator* and *Eastern Daily Press.*

AVOCATIONAL INTERESTS: Historical reading and research, farming (has farmed in Ireland and in Isle of Ely).

* * *

LEHMAN, Milton 1917-1966

PERSONAL: Born December 24, 1917, in Pittsburgh, Pa.; son of Milton G. (a foundry president) and Helen (Nusbaum) Lehman; married Mildred B. Kharfen (a writer-editor), April 28, 1945; children: Ann Helen, John Milton, Betsy Amanda. *Education:* University of Pittsburgh, B.A. (magna cum laude), 1939; graduate study at Columbia University, 1939-40, and New School for Social Research, 1940. *Politics:* Democrat. *Religion:* Jewish. *Home:* 6106 Neilwood Dr., Rockville, Md. 20852. *Agent:* Dorothy Olding, Harold Ober Associates, Inc., 40 East 49th St., New York, N.Y. 10017. *Office:* U.S. Office of Education, Washington, D.C. 20202; also at home address.

CAREER: Free-lance writer for national magazines, 1945—. Motion Picture Association of America, Washington, D.C., assistant to president, 1956-60; U.S. Department of Health, Education, and Welfare, Washington, D.C., assistant to commissioner of education, 1963—. Consultant and writer for various government agencies. *Military service:* U.S. Army, 1941-45; combat correspondent, also editor of *Stars and Stripes* (Mediterranean edition), 1942-45; became technical sergeant; received Legion of Merit. *Member:* National Press Club, National Congress of Parents and Teachers. *Awards, honors:* Sigma Delta Chi Distinguished Service Award for editorial writing, 1943.

WRITINGS: This High Man: The Life of Robert H. Goddard, Farrar, Straus, 1963. Contributor of about 250 articles to *Saturday Evening Post, Life, Reader's Digest, McCall's, Look, Collier's, Cosmopolitan, Esquire, Coronet, New York Times,* and other periodicals, books and newspapers. Associate editor, *Collier's,* 1950.

WORK IN PROGRESS: Television documentaries; writing for Office of Education; articles; a book, possibly autobiographical.

SIDELIGHTS: Lehman spoke "halting" German, French, and Italian.

(Died, 1966)

* * *

LEHRMAN, Simon Maurice 1900-

PERSONAL: Born December 15, 1900, in Russia; son of Isaac Jonah Lehrman (a businessman); married Betty Jacob; children: Jonas Benzion, Faith Roston. *Education:* University College, London, B.A., 1922; Emmanuel College, Cambridge, B.A., 1926, M.A., 1929; Jew's College, London, England, Rabbi, 1934. *Home:* 50 Warwick Grove, London E.5, England.

CAREER: United Synagogue, London, England, rabbi, 1948—. Lecturer at Jews' College and extra-mural lecturer at University of London, 1950-60.

WRITINGS: (Translator with others) I. Epstein, editor, *The Babylonian Talmud*, Soncino Press, 1935-48; *The Jewish Festivals*, Shapiro, Vallentine & Co., 1936, 2nd edition, 1938; *The Sabbath Hour* (essays), Soncino Press, 1936; *The Solemn Festivals*, Bachad Fellowship, 1943; *Sukkoth*, Bachad Fellowship, 1943; *The Jewish Year: Outstanding Days and Their Significance*, 2nd edition, Jewish Religious Educational Publications, 1945; *Rambles in Storyland*, Shapiro, Vallentine & Co., 1946; *Jewish Customs and Folklore*, Shapiro, Vallentine & Co., 1950; *The Jewish Design for Living*, Bloch Publishing, 1951; *Rabbi Joseph Karo: His Life and Times*, Jewish Religious Educational Publications, 1953; (translator and annotator) *The Hagadah for Passover*, A to Z Printers & Publishers, 1954; *Gateways to Sidra*, United Synagogue, 1957; *A Guide to Hanukkah and Purim*, Jewish Chronicle Publications, 1958; *Everyman's Judaism: Essays on Jewish Life and Practice*, Shapiro, Vallentine & Co., 1960; *The World of the Midrash*, Yoseloff, 1962. Contributor to Soncino Press versions in English of *Bible* and *Midrash*, and to *Vallentine's Encyclopaedia*. Regular contributor to *Jewish Chronicle, Jewish Review*, several newspapers in England, and to journals in Israel, United States, and South Africa.

WORK IN PROGRESS: Research into history of Jewish homiletics from the Midrashic period (circa 200 B.C.E.) until the present day; autobiography; a popular exposition of Jewish ritual, custom, and folkways.

AVOCATIONAL INTERESTS: Travel, walking, people, and study of comparative religions.†

*   *   *

LEIBY, Adrian C(oulter)   1904-

PERSONAL: Born December 16, 1904, in Bergenfield, N.J.; son of Elias B. and Mamie (Coulter) Leiby; married Emorie M. Atkins, July 8, 1932; children: Adrian Atkins (Mrs. John L. Shelton, Jr.) *Education:* Middlebury College, B.S., 1925; Columbia University, LL.B., 1929. *Politics:* Republican. *Religion:* Presbyterian. *Home:* 138 West Church St., Bergenfield, N.J. 07621. *Office:* 1 Chase Manhattan Plaza, New York, N.Y. 10005.

CAREER: Law clerk to Justice Harlan F. Stone, 1929-30; admitted to bar of New York State, 1930; private practice of law, New York, N.Y., 1930—, as senior partner in firm of LeBoeuf, Lamb, Leiby & MacRae, 1952—. Director and secretary, Hackensack Water Co., Weehawken, N.J.; director, St. Regius Paper Co., Sentinel Income Fund, and Sentinel Growth Fund. *Member:* American Bar Association, Revolutionary War Round Table, New Jersey Historical Society (honorary fellow), Bergen County Historical Society (fellow; trustee), Delta Upsilon.

WRITINGS: *The Revolutionary War in the Hackensack Valley: The Jersey Dutch and the Neutral Ground, 1775-1783*, Rutgers University Press, 1963; *The Huguenot Settlement of Schraalenburgh: The History of Bergenfield, N.J.*, Bergenfield Free Public Library, 1964; *The Early Dutch and Swedish Settlers of New Jersey*, Van Nostrand, 1964; *The Hackensack Valley and the Tercentenary*, Hackensack Water Co., 1964; *The Buildings of the South Church, Bergenfield, N.J.*, Sorg Printing Co., 1968; (with Nancy Wickman) *The Hackensack Water Company, 1869-1969*, Bergen County Historical Society, 1969.

WORK IN PROGRESS: Writing on Jersey Dutch settlers, Dutch Reformed Church, and the Revolutionary War in New York and New Jersey area.†

*   *   *

LEITNER, Moses J.   1908-

PERSONAL: Born July 9, 1908, in Brooklyn, N.Y.; son of Jonas and Ida (Gillman) Leitner; married Betty Miller, May 6, 1932; children: Barbara Leitner Samet, Carol Leitner Duvoisin. *Education:* University of Wisconsin, B.A., 1929; Long Island College of Medicine, M.D., 1932. *Home:* 120 South Green St., East Stroudsburg, Pa. 18301. *Office:* General Hospital of Monroe County, East Stroudsburg, Pa. 18301.

CAREER: General Hospital of Monroe County, East Stroudsburg, Pa., pathologist, 1946—. *Military service:* U.S. Army, Medical Corps, 1942-46; became captain. *Member:* American Medical Association, American Society of Clinical Pathologists, College of American Pathologists.

WRITINGS: (With J. R. Lanen) *Dictionary of French American Slang*, Crown, 1965 (published in England as *Dictionary of French and English Slang*, Harrop, 1966).

*   *   *

LENSKI, Lois   1893-1974

PERSONAL: Born October 14, 1893, in Springfield, Ohio; daughter of Richard Charles Henry (a Lutheran minister) and Marietta (Young) Lenski; married Arthur S. Covey, 1921 (died, 1960); children: Stephen. *Education:* Ohio State University, B.S. in Ed., 1915; additional study at Art Students League, New York, N.Y., and Westminster School of Art, London, England. *Residence:* Tarpon Springs, Fla.

CAREER: Artist and author. In addition to illustrating all of her own works, has illustrated numerous children's books by others. *Awards, honors:* Litt.D., Wartburg College, 1959; Capital University, 1966, Southwestern College, Winfield, Kan., 1968; L.H.D., University of North Carolina at Greensboro, 1962; Ohioana Medal, 1944, for *Bayou Suzette*; John Newbery Medal for most distinguished contribution to literature for American children, 1946, for *Strawberry Girl*; Child Study Association of America Children's Book Award, 1947, for *Judy's Journey*; Catholic Library Association Regina Medal, 1967; University of Southern Mississippi Special Children's Collection Medallion, 1969.

*WRITINGS—*All self-illustrated: *Skipping Village*, Stokes, 1927; *Jack Horner's Pie* (nursery rhymes), Harper, 1927; *A Little Girl of Nineteen Hundred*, Stokes, 1928; *Alphabet People*, Harper, 1928; *The Wonder City, a Picture Book of New York*, Coward, 1929; *Two Brothers and Their Animal Friends*, Stokes, 1929.

Two Brothers and Their Baby Sister, Stokes, 1930; *The Washington Picture Book*, Coward, 1930; *Spinach Boy*, Stokes, 1930; *Grandmother Tippytoe*, Stokes, 1931; *Benny and His Penny*, Knopf, 1931; *Arabella and Her Aunts*, Stokes, 1932; *The Little Family*, Doubleday, Doran, 1932; *Johnny Goes to the Fair, a Picture Book*, Minnton, Balch, 1932; *The Little Auto*, Oxford University Press, 1934, Walck 1959; *Surprise for Mother*, Stokes, 1934; *Gooseberry Garden*, Harper, 1934; *Sugarplum House*, Harper, 1935; *Little Baby Ann*, Oxford University Press, 1935; *The Easter Rabbit's Parade*, Oxford University Press, 1936; *Phebe Fairchild, Her Book*, Stokes, 1936; *A-Going to the Westward*, Stokes, 1937; *Baby Car*, Oxford University Press, 1937; *The Little Sail Boat*, Oxford University Press, 1937, Walck 1960; *The Little Airplane*, Oxford University Press, 1938, Walck 1959; *Bound Girl of Cobble Hill*, Lippincott, 1938; *Oceanborn Mary*, Stokes, 1939; *Susie Mariar*, Oxford University Press, 1939, Walck, 1968.

The Little Train, Oxford University Press, 1940; *Blueberry*

Corners, Stokes, 1940; *Indian Captive: The Story of Mary Jemison*, Stokes, 1941; *Animals for Me*, Oxford University Press, 1941; *The Little Farm*, Oxford University Press, 1942; *Davy's Day*, Oxford University Press, 1943, Walck, 1959; *Bayou Suzette*, Stokes, 1943; *Puritan Adventure*, Lippincott, 1944; *Let's Play House*, Oxford University Press, 1944; *Spring is Here*, Oxford University Press, 1945, Walck, 1960; *Strawberry Girl*, Lippincott, 1945; *Blue Ridge Billy*, Lippincott, 1946; *The Little Fire Engine*, Oxford University Press, 1946; *Judy's Journey*, Lippincott, 1947; *Surprise for Davy*, Oxford University Press, 1947, Walck, 1959; *Boom Town Boy*, Lippincott, 1948; *Mr. and Mrs. Noah*, Crowell, 1948; *Now It's Fall*, Oxford University Press, 1948; *Cowboy Small*, Oxford University Press, 1949, Spanish-language edition, Walck, 1960; *Cotton in My Sack*, Lippincott, 1949.

Texas Tomboy, Lippincott, 1950; *I Like Winter*, Oxford University Press, 1950, Walck, 1960; *Papa Small*, Oxford University Press, 1951, Spanish-language edition, Walck, 1961, French-language edition, Walck, 1963; *Prairie School*, Lippincott, 1951; (with Clyde R. Bulla) *We Are Thy Children* (hymns), Crowell, 1952; *We Live in the South* (four short stories), Lippincott, 1952; *Peanuts for Billy Ben*, Lippincott, 1952; *Mama Hattie's Girl*, Lippincott, 1953; *On a Summer Day*, Oxford University Press, 1953; *Corn-Farm Boy*, Lippincott, 1954; *We Live in the City*, Lippincott, 1954; (with Bulla) *Songs of Mr. Small*, Oxford University Press, 1954; *Project Boy*, Lippincott, 1954; (with Bulla) *A Dog Came to School*, Oxford University Press, 1955; *San Francisco Boy*, Lippincott, 1955; *Flood Friday*, Lippincott, 1956; *Big Little Davy*, Oxford University Press, 1956; *Berries in the Scoop*, Lippincott, 1956; *We Live by the River*, Lippincott, 1956; (with Bulla) *Songs of the City*, E.B. Marks, 1956; *Davy and His Dog*, Oxford University Press, 1957; *Houseboat Girl*, Lippincott, 1957; (with Bulla) *Little Sioux Girl*, Lippincott, 1958; (with Bulla) *I Went for a Walk* (read-and-sing book), Walck, 1958; (with Bulla) *At Our House* (read-and-sing book), Walck, 1959; *Coal Camp Girl*, Lippincott, 1959.

We Live in the Country, Lippincott, 1960; (with Bulla) *When I Grow Up* (read-and-sing book), Walck, 1960; *Davy Goes Places*, Walck, 1961; *We Live in the Southwest*, Lippincott, 1962; *Policeman Small*, Walck, 1962; *Shoo-Fly Girl*, Lippincott, 1963; *The Life I Live: Collected Poems*, Walck, 1965; *We Live in the North*, Lippincott, 1965; *High Rise Secret*, Lippincott, 1966; *Debbie and Her Grandma*, Walck, 1967; *To Be a Logger*, Lippincott, 1967; *Lois Lenski's Christmas Stories*, Lippincott, 1968; *Adventures in Understanding*, Friends of Florida State University Library, 1968; *Debbie Herself*, Walck, 1969; *Debbie and Her Family*, Walck, 1969; *City Poems*, Walck, 1971; *Florida, My Florida*, Florida State University Press, 1971; *Journey into Childhood: Autobiography of Lois Lenski*, Lippincott, 1972.

AVOCATIONAL INTERESTS: Gardening.

(Died September 11, 1974)

* * *

LEONARD, Edith Marian

PERSONAL: Born in San Bernardino, Calif.; daughter of Willis Edwin (a realtor and insurance broker) and Nettie (McCullough) Leonard. *Education:* National College of Education, B.A., 1924; Claremont Graduate School, M.A., 1930; Northwestern University, graduate study, 1939. *Politics:* Republican. *Religion:* Presbyterian. *Office address:*

P.O. Drawer FF, c/o Trust Department, Santa Barbara, Calif. 93105.

CAREER: San Bernardino (Calif.) city schools, kindergarten director, 1920-22, kindergarten-primary supervisor, 1922-25; University of California, Santa Barbara, primary supervisor, 1925-32, founder of department of early childhood education, 1932, and director, 1932-44, professor of education, 1942-64, professor emeritus, 1964—. *Member:* International Association for Childhood Education, Association for Supervision and Curriculum Development, National Education Association, American Association of University Women, International Platform Association, California Association for Childhood Education, California State Employees Association, Delta Kappa Gamma, Delta Phi Upsilon.

WRITINGS: (With Lillian E. Miles) *The Child at Home and School* (college textbook), American Book Co., 1942; (contributor) P. F. Valentine, editor, *Twentieth Century Education*, Philosophical Library, 1946; (with Dorothy D. VanDeman) *Say It and Play It* (children's plays), Harper, 1950; (contributor) *Guiding the Young Child*, Heath, 1951, 2nd revised edition, 1959; (with VanDeman and Miles) *Counseling With Parents* (college textbook), Macmillan, 1954; (contributor) *Teacher's Guide to Early Childhood Education*, State Department of Education (Sacramento), 1956; (with VanDeman and Miles) *Foundations of Learning in Childhood Education* (college textbook), C. E. Merrill, 1963; (with VanDeman and Miles) *Basic Learning in the Language Arts* (college textbook), Scott, 1965. Contributor to professional journals.

WORK IN PROGRESS: Collaborating with Dorothy D. VanDeman and Lillian E. Miles, on three books—*Living Mathematics in the Elementary School*, a college textbook, *Creative Aids to Teaching*, a college textbook, and *A Child Goes Forth*, a parent handbook; with Dorothy D. VanDeman, a series of musical plays with songs and dances for children's theater and school programs.

SIDELIGHTS: The Leonard-VanDeman writing partnership evolved easily, since the two women were professors at Santa Barbara. They once owned and lived in a mountain home and commuted to their classes and now are traveling together in retirement. The collaboration with Lillian E. Miles, who lives in San Bernardino, involved some long night sessions and meetings at a midway point.

* * *

LEONARD, Justin W(ilkinson) 1909-

PERSONAL: Born October 28, 1909, in Moulton, Iowa; son of Ira Jay and Edna (Wilkinson) Leonard; married Fannie Divelbess, May 30, 1936. *Education:* Grinnell College, A.B., 1931; University of Michigan, A.M., 1932, Ph.D., 1937; Wayne State University, Certificate in Executive Development, 1959. *Religion:* Protestant. *Home:* 1041 Arlington, Ann Arbor, Mich. 48104. *Office:* School of Natural Resources, University of Michigan, Ann Arbor, Mich. 48104.

CAREER: Michigan Department of Conservation, Institute for Fisheries Research, research biologist and director of experiment station, 1939-51, Lansing headquarters, research administrator, 1951-56, assistant deputy director for research, 1956-64, chief of research and development, 1964; University of Michigan, Ann Arbor, professor of natural resources and zoology, 1964—, chairman of department of wildlife and fisheries, 1965-67, chairman of department of resource planning and conservation, 1967-70, acting dean of

School of Natural Resources, 1974, research scientist, Museum of Zoology, 1964—. Michigan State University, lecturer in department of forestry, 1957-64. Visiting professor, Hekkaido University, 1969. U.S. Public Health Service, special consultant, 1956; Michigan Governor's Committee on Control of Botulism, member, 1963—. *Military service:* U.S. Army, Sanitary Corps, 1943-46; became major.

MEMBER: American Association for the Advancement of Science (fellow), American Institute of Fishery Research Biologists (fellow), American Fisheries Society (honorary member), American Institute of Biological Sciences, American Society of Limnology and Oceanography (vice-president, 1951), Entomological Society of America (fellow), Society of Systematic Zoology, Soil Conservation Society of America, Wildlife Society (president, 1956), Michigan Academy of Science, Arts and Letters (president, 1962), Michigan Natural Resources Council (chairman, 1958, 1959), Sigma Xi. *Awards, honors:* Alumni Achievement Award, Grinnell College, 1961; Iowa Conservation Hall of Fame, 1970.

WRITINGS: (With wife, Fannie A. Leonard) *Mayflies of Michigan Trout Streams*, Cranbrook Press, 1962; (with Shirley W. Allen) *Conserving Natural Resources: Principles and Practice in a Democracy*, 3rd edition (Leonard not associated with earlier editions), McGraw, 1966. Contributor to *McClane's Standard Fishing Encyclopedia*, *Encyclopaedia Britannica*, and of about ninety articles, on conservation, fisheries management, and the adverse effects of pesticides, to professional journals. Associate editor, American Fisheries Society, 1941-56.

SIDELIGHTS: Leonard has done biological field work in Alaska, Solomon Islands, the Caribbean, Fiji, Australia, and Thailand. In 1966 he prepared a series of survey reports on the predicted effects of the proposed Rampart Dam (in Alaska) on fisheries and wildlife resources.

*　　　*　　　*

LEONTIEF, Wassily 1906-

PERSONAL: Born August 5, 1906, in Leningrad, Russia; son of Wassily W. and Eugenia (Bekker) Leontief; married Estelle Marks, December 25, 1932; children: Svetlana Eugenia (Mrs. Paul Alpers). *Education:* University of Leningrad, Learned Economist (M.A.), 1925; University of Berlin, Ph.D., 1928. *Home:* 14 Ash St., Cambridge, Mass. 02138. *Office:* 309 Littauer Center, Harvard University, Cambridge, Mass. 02138.

CAREER: University of Kiel, Kiel, Germany, research staff, Institut fuer Weltwirtschaft, 1927-28, 1930; Chinese Government, Nanking, economic adviser, 1929; National Bureau of Economic Research, New York, N.Y., research associate, 1931; Harvard University, Cambridge, Mass., instructor, 1931-33, assistant professor, 1933-38, associate professor, 1939-45, professor of economics, 1946-53, Henry Lee Professor of Economics, 1953—, director of Harvard Economic Research Project, 1948-72. University of Manchester, Lord Simon Professor, 1951; University of California, Charles M. and Martha Hitchcock Professor, 1959. General consultant to U.S. Department of Labor, 1941-47 and 1961-65, U.S. Office of Strategic Services, 1943-45, and U.S. Department of Commerce, 1966—; consultant to United Nations Consultative Group of the Economic and Social Consequences of Disarmament, 1961.

MEMBER: American Academy of Arts and Sciences, National Academy of Sciences, American Statistical Association, American Economic Association, Econometric Society (fellow; president, 1954), American Philosophical Society, International Statistical Institute, Royal Economic Society (England), Royal Statistical Society (England; honorary fellow), British Academy (corresponding member), French Academy of Sciences (corresponding member), Society of Fellows (Harvard University; chairman and senior fellow). *Awards, honors:* Guggenheim fellowships, 1940, 1950; Order of the Cherubim, University of Pisa, 1953; Doctor Honoris Causa, University of Brussels, 1962, University of Louvain, 1971, University of Paris, 1972; Doctor of the University, University of York, England, 1967; Officer, Legion d'Honneur, 1968; Bernhard-Harms Prize in Economics, West Germany, 1970; Nobel Prize in Economics, 1973.

WRITINGS: The Structure of American Economy, 1919-29, Harvard University Press, 1941, enlarged edition published as *The Structure of American Economy, 1919-39*, Oxford University Press, 1951; (with others) *Studies in the Structure of the American Economy*, Oxford University Press, 1953; *Input-Output Economics*, Oxford University Press, 1966; *Essays in Economics: Theories and Theorizing*, Oxford University Press, 1966. Contributor to scientific journals and other periodicals in United States and abroad.

SIDELIGHTS: Leontief won the Nobel Prize for the creation of input-output economic analysis. His widely applicable system is used for budgeting and economic prediction by the United Nations, the World Bank, and over thirty countries, as well as for such specialized studies as the impact of world disarmament and waste recycling.

BIOGRAPHICAL/CRITICAL SOURCES: Forbes, January 1, 1969; *Science News*, October 27, 1973; *Newsweek*, October 29, 1973, November 5, 1973; *Time*, October 29, 1973; *Science*, November 9, 1973.

*　　　*　　　*

LEOPOLD, Nathan F. 1904-1971
(William F. Lanne, Richard A. Lawrence)

PERSONAL: Born November 19, 1904, in Chicago, Ill.; son of Nathan F. (a manufacturer) and Florence (Foreman) Leopold; married Gertrude Feldman, February 5, 1961. *Education:* Attended University of Michigan, 1921-22; University of Chicago, Ph.B., 1923, law student, 1923-24; University of Puerto Rico, M.S.W., 1961. *Religion:* Jewish. *Home:* 562 Trigo St., A-2, Santurce, Puerto Rico 00907. *Agent:* Ralph G. Newman, 18 East Chestnut St., Chicago, Ill. *Office:* Social Science Program, Department of Health, Commonwealth of Puerto Rico, San Juan, Puerto Rico.

CAREER: Taught ornithology. Spent time in prison for the kidnap-murder (with Richard Loeb) of Robert Franks in Chicago, May 22, 1924; was paroled March 13, 1958, freed March 16, 1963. Commonwealth of Puerto Rico, Department of Health, San Juan, research associate, Social Science Program, beginning 1961. Social worker, Castaner Hospital, Puerto Rico; teacher of mathematics. *Member:* American Ornithologists' Union, American Society of Tropical Medicine and Hygiene, Phi Beta Kappa, Puerto Rico Natural History Society (treasurer, 1960-62).

WRITINGS: (With James D. Watson and George Porter Lewis) *Spring Migrations Notes of the Chicago Area*, privately printed, 1922; *Life Plus Ninety-Nine Years*, Doubleday, 1958; *Checklist of Birds of Puerto Rico and the Virgin Islands*, University of Puerto Rico Press, 1963; (with

Harry E. Barnes and others) *The Future of Imprisonment in a Free Society,* St. Leonard's House, 1965. Contributor of articles, some under pseudonyms, to *Auk, Journal of Criminal Law and Criminology, American Sociological Review, Nebraska Law Journal, San Juan Review,* and *Key Issues.*

WORK IN PROGRESS: Research, under U.S. National Institutes of Health grant, into social factors in parasitic infection; an autobiography, *Grab for a Halo.*

BIOGRAPHICAL/CRITICAL SOURCES: New York Times, August 31, 1971; *Washington Post,* August 31, 1971.

(Died August 29, 1971)

*   *   *

Le PATOUREL, John Herbert 1909-

PERSONAL: Born July 29, 1909, in Guernsey, Channel Islands; son of H. A. and M. E. (Daw) Le Patourel; married Hilda Elizabeth Jean Bird (an archeologist), December 2, 1939; children: Julian Christopher, Geoffrey Noel John, Peter James, Nicolette Elizabeth Jane. *Education:* Jesus College, Oxford, B.A., 1929, M.A., D.Phil., 1934. *Home:* Westcote, Hebers Ghyll Dr., Ilkley, Yorkshire LS29 9QH, England.

CAREER: University College, University of London, London, England, 1933-45, successively assistant lecturer, lecturer, reader; University of Leeds, Leeds, England, professor of medieval history, 1945-70, research professor in medieval history, 1970—. *Awards, honors:* Honorary doctorate, University of Caen, 1957.

WRITINGS: The Medieval Administration of the Channel Islands, 1199-1399, Oxford University Press, 1937; *Documents Relating to the Manor and Borough of Leeds, 1066-1400,* Thoresby Society, 1957; (editor and author of introduction) *The Building of Castle Cornet, Guernsey,* Volume I, *The Tudor Reconstruction,* Manchester University Press, 1958; *Norman Barons,* Historical Association (London), 1966; *Ilkley Parish Church,* 2nd edition, British Publishing, 1968. Contributor of articles and reviews to *Transactions* of Royal Historical Society, and to historical journals in England, France, and the Channel Islands.

WORK IN PROGRESS: Research in the administration of lands held in France by kings of England during the Middle Ages.

*   *   *

LESTER, Reginald Mounstephens 1896-

PERSONAL: Born October 1, 1896, in Hawkhurst, Kent, England; son of Robert James and Catherine Alice Lester; married Marjorie Hermon, 1922 (died, 1948); married Ellen Grace Scott, 1950. *Education:* Educated at St. Paul's School, London, England. *Politics:* Conservative. *Religion:* Church of England. *Home:* 57 Petitor Rd., Torquay, Devonshire, England. *Office:* 5 Denison House, Vauxhall Bridge Rd., London S.W. 1, England.

CAREER: Qualified as property surveyor, 1919-20, and engaged in the estate profession, 1920-30; journalist, editor, and press officer to British concerns, 1930—. Churches' Fellowship for Psychical Study, founder and chairman, 1953—. Radio speaker on British Broadcasting Corp. programs; television appearances on "Panorama," "Tonight," and other shows; public lecturer on U.S. tour, 1964. *Military service:* British Army, Artists' Rifles, 1915-18; served in France, including Somme campaign; became captain; rejoined as staff major, Eastern Command, 1939, and served until 1945; became lieutenant colonel. *Member:* Institute of Journalists (council, 1944—; president, 1956-57), Incorporated Society of Landed Property Agents (fellow), Royal Meterological Society (fellow), Society of Authors and Playwrights, London Writer Circle (vice-president, 1939).

WRITINGS: Property Investment: A Guide to the Property Market with Practical Hints for Investors, Pitman, 1937; *The Manual of Estate Agency,* Pitman, 1939; *The Riddle of the Secret Plane* (fiction), Tuck & Sons, 1939; *Weather Prediction,* Chemical Publishing, 1940 (English edition by Hutchinson originally announced as "Weather and Climate"); *Understanding Czechoslovakia,* Pitman, 1941; *With the Commandos,* Tuck & Sons, 1943; *I'm a Parachutist,* Tuck & Sons, 1943; *Meteorology* (Part 4 of *Complete Air Training Course),* Hutchinson, 1944; *Practical Astronomy for the Forces,* Hutchinson, 1944; *The Estate Agent's Reference Handbook,* edited by H. R. Clover, Morgan, Laird, 1946; *Everybody's Weather Book,* Low, 1948; *The Householder and the Law,* Pen-in-Hand, 1949; *In Search of the Hereafter: A Personal Investigation into Life after Death,* Harrap, 1952, Funk, 1953; *Building or Buying a House: The Answer to All Your Problems,* Homefinders, 1953; *The Observer's Book of Weather,* Warne, 1955; *Towards the Hereafter: With a Special Inquiry into Spiritual Healing* (sequel to *In Search of the Hereafter),* Harrap, 1956, Citadel, 1957; (with Neville Randall) *Life after Death,* Associated Newspapers, 1960. Author of eight booklets, and of several one-act plays for British Drama League. Columnist, *Financial Times,* 1945-67. Editor at various times of *Homefinder, Property Investor, Beyond, Churches' Fellowship Quarterly Review;* co-editor, *New House* and *Sailors' News;* housing editor, *Woman's Magazine.* Contributor of articles, mainly on psychical research, weather research, houses and estates, to British magazines and newspapers.

*   *   *

LEVENSTEIN, Aaron 1910-

PERSONAL: Born November 11, 1910, in New York, N.Y.; son of Joseph and Anna (Mayers) Levenstein; married Margery Littman; children: Beth, Nora (Mrs. Miklos S. Szalavitz), Joseph. *Education:* City College (now City College of the City University of New York), A.B., 1930; New York Law School, LL.B. (later converted to J.D.), 1934. *Religion:* Jewish. *Home:* 3083 Uncas St., Mohegan Lake, N.Y. 10547. *Office:* Bernard M. Baruch College of the City University of New York, N.Y. 10010.

CAREER: Labor lawyer, 1934-40; Research Institute of America, New York, N.Y., directing editor, 1940-60; Bernard M. Baruch College of the City University of New York, professor of management, 1960—. Member, board of trustees, Freedom House; director of relief program for Bangladesh refugees, International Rescue Committee in India, 1971. *Member:* League for Industrial Democracy (executive committee), Industrial Relations Research Association.

WRITINGS: Labor Today and Tomorrow, Knopf, 1946; *Why People Work,* Crowell-Collier Press, 1962; (with William Agar) *Freedom's Advocate,* Viking, 1965; *Use Your Head,* Macmillan, 1965. Writer of television scripts. Contributor to *Look, Nation, New Republic, Personnel Psychology, Antioch Review,* and other periodicals. Editor-in-chief, *Interaction,* beginning 1971.

WORK IN PROGRESS: Research in labor relations and human relations problems in industry.

SIDELIGHTS: Levenstein has studied labor movements in developing countries of Africa and the Middle East, and in South Vietnam. He speaks French and has some command of German and Hebrew.

* * *

LEVINSON, Horace C(lifford) 1895-19(?)

PERSONAL: Born June 30, 1895, in Chicago, Ill.; son of Salmon Oliver (an attorney) and Helen (Haire) Levinson; married Alma Prescott Wells, June 23, 1921 (died April 7, 1963); children: Alma Prescott (Mrs. Edward Curran, Jr.), Ruth Bartlett. Education: Yale University, B.A., 1917; University of Chicago, Ph.D., 1922; University of Paris, Docteur de l'Universite, 1923. Politics: Independent.

CAREER: Ohio State University, Columbus, instructor in mathematics, 1923; Bernard-Hewitt & Co., director of research, 1924-26, officer and director, 1926-31; Rural Progress, Inc., Chicago, Ill., vice-president, treasurer, and director, 1934-38; L. Bamberger & Co., Newark, N.J., director of research, 1939-40, treasurer and director, 1940-46; National Academy of Sciences-National Research Council, chairman of the Committee on Operations Research, 1948-55; Arthur D. Little, Inc., consultant in operations research, 1952-54; writer and consultant. Military service: American Expeditionary Forces, Artillery, 1918-19; became captain. Member: American Mathematical Society, Sigma Xi, Tavern Club (Chicago).

WRITINGS: (With Ernest B. Zeisler) The Law of Gravitation in Relativity, University of Chicago Press, 1931; Your Chance to Win, Farrar and Rinehart, 1939, revised edition published as Chance, Luck, and Statistics: The Science of Chance, Dover, 1963; The Science of Chance, Rinehart, 1950. Contributor to technical journals.

(Deceased)

* * *

LEVY, Raphael 1900-1969

PERSONAL: Born November 4, 1900, in Baltimore, Md.; son of Max (a realtor) and Dora (Pollack) Levy; married Helen Silverman, June 30, 1929; children: Manford Harold, Jerome Seymour. Education: Johns Hopkins University, A.B., 1920, M.A., 1922, Ph.D., 1924; Universite de Paris, Certificats d'Assiduite, 1923. Politics: Democrat. Religion: Jewish. Home: 5509 Shoal Creek Blvd., Austin, Tex. 78756. Office: 316 Batts Hall, University of Texas, Austin, Tex. 78712.

CAREER: Instructor in French at Baltimore City College, Baltimore, Md., 1921-22, and at University of Wisconsin, Madison, 1924-29; University of Baltimore, Baltimore, Md., assistant professor of Romance languages, 1931-43; Louisiana State University, Baton Rouge, assistant professor of Romance languages, 1943-46; University of Texas, Austin, associate professor, 1946-62, professor of Romance languages, 1962-69 (president, 1950). Member: Modern Language Association of America, Societe des Anciens Textes Francais, South-Central Modern Language Association, Fortnightly Club. Awards, honors: Guggenheim fellow in Europe, 1929-30; American Philosophical Society award, 1939; American Council of Learned Societies grant, 1959; University of Texas Research Council grants, 1961-1965.

WRITINGS: The Astrological Works of Abraham ibn Ezra, Johns Hopkins Press, 1927; Recherches lexicographiques sur d'anciens textes francais d'origine juive, Johns Hopkins Press, 1932; Li Coronemenz Loois: Glossaire, Johns Hopkins Press, 1932; Repertoire des lexiques du vieux francais, Modern Language Association, 1937; An Introduction to Current Affairs, Wallace Press, 1939; (with Francisco Cantera) The Beginning of Wisdom, Johns Hopkins Press, 1939; Chronologie approximative de la litterature francaise du moyen age, Max Niemeyer Verlag, 1957; Contribution a la lexicographie francaise selon d'anciens textes d'origine juive, Syracuse University Press, 1960; Tresor de la langue des Juifs francais au Moyen Age, University of Texas Press, 1964.

Contributor of one hundred articles and more than seventy reviews to philological journals of twelve countries.

WORK IN PROGRESS: A comprehensive glossary of all the Old French editions in "Classiques Francais du Moyen Age."

SIDELIGHTS: Levy was conversant in French, Spanish, Italian, German, and Hebrew. He made numerous tours of Europe in the course of linguistic research along historical and evolutionary lines.

(Died, 1969)

* * *

LEVY, Rosalie Marie 1889-

PERSONAL: Born July 19, 1889, in Louisiana; daughter of Joseph and Helen (Oberdorfer) Levy. Education: Eastern College of Chiropractic, D.C., 1922; Fordham University, B.S., 1942. Religion: Catholic. Address: P.O. Box 358, Madison Square Station, New York, N.Y. 10010.

CAREER: Writer, New York, N.Y., 1919—; teacher in Catholic elementary schools, New York, N.Y., 1947-66. Travel lecturer. Founder, Catholic Guild of Israel, 1922 (now Guild of Our Lady of Sion); founder, Catholic Lay Apostle Guild, 1933.

WRITINGS: The Heavenly Road, Baltimore City Printing and Binding Co., 1919, 3rd edition, International Catholic Truth Society, 1923, 7th edition, published as What Think You of Christ?, Daughters of St. Paul, 1962; (compiler and editor) Why Jews Become Catholics: Authentic Narratives, Daughters of St. Paul, 1924, now published as Heritage Reclaimed; Heart Talks with Jesus, five series, privately printed, 1926-35, Catholic Book Publishing, 1944; Judaism and Catholicism, Daughters of St. Paul, 1927, now published as Prophetic Fulfillment; Heart Talks with Mary, two series, privately printed, 1930, 1938, Catholic Book Publishing, 1944; Stepping Stones to Sanctity: Gleanings from Spiritual Direction and Teachings (of Paul Raphael Conniff), privately printed, 1940; Thirty Years with Christ (autobiography), Daughters of St. Paul, 1942; Mary, Queen of Apostles, Daughters of St. Paul, 1950, reissued as Mary, Queen of the World; Jesus, the Divine Master, Daughters of St. Paul, 1952; St. Joseph, the Just Man, Daughters of St. Paul, 1955; The Man in Chains: St. Paul, Vessel of Election, Daughters of St. Paul, 1957; "All Generations Shall Call Me Blessed," Daughters of St. Paul, 1957; Heavenly friends, Daughters of St. Paul, 1958; (self-illustrated) Happy Moments (poems for children), Pageant Press, 1963. Writer of many booklets, pamphlets, and leaflets.

* * *

LEWIS, Arthur William 1905-1970

PERSONAL: Born November 13, 1905, in Merthyr Vale,

Glamorganshire, Wales; son of William and Mary (Richards) Lewis; married Susanna Helen Tompkins, September 2, 1933; children: Susanna Mary. *Education:* Attended University College of Wales. *Home:* 43 Fairmount Dr., Loughborough, Leicestershire, England.

CAREER: Training College for Teachers, Loughborough, Leicestershire, England, senior lecturer in craftwork, 1945-69. Fulbright exchange professor at Shasta College, Redding, Calif., 1959-60. *Awards, honors:* Judd Medallion for research into the history of bookbinding.

WRITINGS: Wood Decoration with V-Tool and Gouge, Technical Press, 1936; *Basic Bookbinding,* Dover, 1952, reissued with additional notes, 1957; *Books,* Educational Supply Association, 1952, 2nd edition, 1960; *Handsaws and Sawing,* Educational Productions, 1958; *Woodworking with Hand Tools,* Educational Productions, 1959; *Kingsway Technical Drawing,* Evans Brothers, 1962; (with Robert Winkworth Millard) *Exercises in Technical Drawing for G.C.E.,* Evans Brothers, 1963; *General Engineering Drawing,* Book 1, Evans Brothers, 1964; (with Millard) *Engineering Drawing,* Book 2 (metricated edition), Evans Brothers, 1965, reissued as *Metric Engineering Drawing,* Methuen, 1969; *A Glossary of Woodworking Terms,* Blackie & Son, 1966; (with wife, Susanna Mary Lewis) *Woodwork Drawing for G.C.E.,* Evans Brothers, 1966; *Technical Drawing,* Methuen, 1967; *Visualization Exercises in Technical Drawing,* Pergamon, 1970; *Metric Data for Craft Teachers,* Methuen, 1970; *Metric Assembly Drawing,* Methuen, 1970; *Metric Technical Drawing without Instruments,* Methuen, 1970; *Metric Woodwork Design,* Methuen, 1970.

SIDELIGHTS: Books, published in the "How Things Developed" series, was one of the "fifty beautiful books" displayed at the Frankfurt Exhibition in Germany, 1956. In 1932 Lewis was an international field hockey reserve, and represented the Amateur Athletic Association of Great Britain and Wales at the British Empire Games in London, 1934.

(Died June 6, 1970)

*   *   *

LEWIS, Joseph   1889-1968

PERSONAL: Born June 11, 1889, in Montgomery, Ala.; son of Samuel and Ray (Levy) Lewis; married Ruth Stoller Grubman, July 15, 1952. *Education:* "Self-educated" (attended public schools). *Religion:* Atheist.

CAREER: Founder and secretary of Thomas Paine Foundation, Robert G. Ingersoll Memorial Association, and American League for Separation of Church and State; founder and president of Freethinkers of America. Instigator of legal proceedings in New York State to ban use of public school buses to transport parochial pupils, to ban reading of the Bible in public schools, to ban sectarian organizations in public educational institutions, and to ban dismissal of public school pupils for religious education. *Member:* American Association for the Advancement of Science (life).

WRITINGS—All published by Freethought Press: *The Tyranny of God,* 1921; *The Bible Unmasked,* 1926; *Voltaire: The Incomparable Infidel,* 1929; *Burbank: The Infidel,* 1930; *Spain: Land Blighted by Religion,* 1933; *The Ten Commandments,* 1945; *Thomas Paine: Declaration of Independence,* 1947; *In the Name of Humanity,* 1949; *Inspiration and Wisdom from the Writings of Thomas Paine,*

1954; *The Tragic Patriot,* 1954; *An Atheist Manifesto,* 1954; *Ingersoll the Magnificent,* 1957; *The Serpents of Religion,* 1959; *Atheism,* 1960. Editor, *Age of Reason* (magazine).

WORK IN PROGRESS: Three books, *The Rebirth of Thomas Paine, The Serpents of Religion,* and *Innocent.*

SIDELIGHTS: Lewis dedicated the Borglum statue of Thomas Paine in Paris, France, 1948, a Paine statue in Morristown, N.J., 1950, in Thetford, England, 1964, and dedicated as a public memorial, 1954, the house in which Robert Ingersoll was born.

(Died, 1968)

*   *   *

LEWIS, Leon   1904-

PERSONAL: Born August 21, 1904, in Butte, Mont.; son of Lazarus M. and Vera (Rosenberg) Lewis; married Carolyn Marie Adler, December 23, 1934; children: Nancy Carol. *Education:* University of Washington, Seattle, B.S., 1925; University of Pennsylvania, M.D., 1929. *Home:* 133 Ardmore Rd., Berkeley, Calif. 94707. *Office:* Rehabilitation Center, Contra Costa County Medical Services, Martinez, Calif. 94553.

CAREER: Diplomate, National Board of Medical Examiners; certified by American Board of Internal Medicine, 1943, American Board of Industrial Hygiene, 1963. Internship and other medical posts in California, 1929-33; research fellow at University of Pennsylvania, Philadelphia, and area hospitals, 1933-34; physician in private practice in internal and industrial medicine, Newark, N.J., and New York, N.Y., 1934-44; assistant visiting physician (and later chief of Arthritic Clinic), Bellevue Hospital, and instructor in medicine at Cornell University Medical School, New York, N.Y., 1937-43; internist in private practice, Berkeley, Calif., 1946-70. University of California, Berkeley, associate professor of industrial health, School of Public Health, 1946-50; Stanford University, School of Medicine, lecturer, 1954-62. Co-director, Solano Laboratories, Berkeley, Calif., 1952-69; Fairmont Hospital, San Leandro, Calif., director of Respiratory and Rehabilitation Center, 1954-60; Herrick Memorial Hospital Berkeley, Calif., chief of Rehabilitation Service, 1965-67. Consultant on industrial health to Ministry of Health, Iran, 1952; special consultant, U.S. Public Health Service, 1959. Chairman of advisory committee on aid to the needy disabled, California State Department of Social Welfare. *Military service:* U.S. Naval Reserve, 1943-46; served on Okinawa; became commander.

MEMBER: American Academy of Industrial Hygiene, American College of Physicians (fellow), American Industrial Hygiene Association (president, Northern California section, 1950), American Medical Association, California Medical Association, California State Heart Association, Physicians Forum, Phi Beta Kappa, Sigma Xi, Alpha Omega, Delta Omega, Phi Lambda Upsilon.

WRITINGS: (Contributor) *Hospitals and Patient Dissatisfaction,* California Medical Association, 1958; (contributor) M. J. Chatton and others, editors, *Handbook of Medical Treatment,* Lange Medical Publications, 1959, and subsequent editions; (contributor) Henry Brainerd and others, editors, *Current Diagnosis and Treatment,* Lange Medical Publications, 1962; (contributor) E. F. Cheit and M. S. Gordon, editors, *Occupational Disability and Public Policy,* Wiley, 1963; (with G. G. Hirschberg and D. Thomas)

Rehabilitation: A Manual for the Care of the Disabled and Elderly, Lippincott, 1964. Contributor to *Encyclopedia of Chemical Technology* and to medical journals.

WORK IN PROGRESS: Research on rehabilitation; preparing, with G. G. Hirschberg and Patricia Vaughn, a second edition of *Rehabilitation.*

SIDELIGHTS: Lewis told CA, "I am a firm believer that 'the outside of a horse in the best thing for the inside of a man.'" Lewis has served as physician on many wilderness pack trips, most recently with Wilderness Society. He is interested in peace, social justice, an equitable system for medical care and conservation.

* * *

LEWIS, Leon Ray 1883-

PERSONAL: Born April 1, 1883, in Gilboa, Schoharie County, N.Y.; son of Charles (a farmer) and Emma (Wiltse) Lewis; married Grace Prior, June 7, 1913 (deceased); children: John Prior. *Education:* Union College, Schenectady, N.Y., B.S., 1906; Albany Law School, LL.B., 1908. *Politics:* Independent. *Religion:* Methodist. *Home:* 214 Main St., Hudson Falls, N.Y. 12839. *Agent:* John P. Lewis, 6283 67th Ct., Prince Georgetown, Riverdale, Md. 20840.

CAREER: Lawyer, Hudson Falls, N.Y., 1910—. Secretary with Allied Expeditionary Forces, Young Men's Christian Association, 1918-19. Hudson Falls School Board, member, 1929-56, president, 1939-56; former member of board of directors, New York State School Boards Association. *Member:* New York State Bar Association, Washington County Historical Society (former president), Sigma Xi.

WRITINGS: Democracy and the Law, Public Affairs Press, 1963.

* * *

LEWIS, Oscar 1914-1970

PERSONAL: Born December 25, 1914, in New York, N.Y.; son of Herman and Bertha (Biblow) Lewis; married Ruth Maslow, November 25, 1937; children: Gene L., Judy Ann. *Education:* College of the City of New York (now The City College of the City University of New York), B.S.S., 1936; Columbia University, Ph.D., 1940. *Office:* Department of Anthropology, University of Illinois, Urbana, Ill.

CAREER: Yale University, New Haven, Conn., research associate, 1942-43; U.S. Department of Justice, propaganda analyst, 1943; U.S. Department of Agriculture, social scientist, 1944-45; U.S. Department of State, visiting professor, Havana, Cuba, 1945-46; Washington University, St. Louis, Mo., associate professor of anthropology, 1946-48; University of Illinois, Urbana, professor of anthropology, 1948-70. Consultant, Ford Foundation, India, 1952-54. *Member:* American Anthropological Association, American Academy of Arts and Sciences (fellow). *Awards, honors:* Social Science Research Council summer seminar fellow, 1952; Ford Foundation, grant-in-aid, behavioral science division, 1952; National Book Award and *Saturday Review*-Anisfield-Wolf Award, 1967, for *La Vida.*

WRITINGS: Effects of White Contact upon Blackfoot Culture; With Special Reference to the Role of the Fur Trade, Augustin, 1942; *On the Edge of the Black Waxy: A Cultural Survey of Bell County, Texas,* Washington University, 1948; *Aspects of Land Tenure and Economics in a Mexican Village,* Middle American Research Institute, Tulane University, 1949; *Life in a Mexican Village: Tepoztlan Restudied,* University of Illinois Press, 1951; (with Harvant Singh Dhillon) *Group Dynamics in a North-Indian Village: A Study of Factions,* New Delhi Programme Evaluation Organisation Planning Commission, 1954; (with Victor Barnouw) *Village Life in Northern India: Studies in a Delhi Village,* University of Illinois Press, 1958; *Five Families: Mexican Case Studies in the Culture of Poverty,* Basic Books, 1959.

Tepoztlan: Village in Mexico, Holt, 1960; *Children of Sanchez: Autobiography of a Mexican Family,* Random House, 1961; *Pedro Martinez: A Mexican Peasant and His Family,* Random House, 1964; *La Vida,* Random House, 1966; *A Study of Slum Culture: Backgrounds for La Vida,* Random House, 1968; *A Death in the Sanchez Family,* Random House, 1969; *Anthropological Essays,* Random House, 1970.

WORK IN PROGRESS: A series of posthumous studies based on data gathered in Cuba by Oscar Lewis before his death. The materials are being prepared for publication by his wife, Ruth M. Lewis, with Susan M. Rigdon, Douglas Butterworth, and other assistants.

SIDELIGHTS: "Many Americans, thanks to the anthropologists, know more about the culture of some isolated tribe in New Guinea, with a total population of 500 souls," noted Lewis in *Five Families,* "than about the way of life of millions of villagers in India or Mexico and other underdeveloped nations which are destined to play so crucial a role in the international scene." Saul Bellow interpreted this remark "as a reproach to those of his colleagues who are still investigating terms of kinship among the Paiute—what does it profit me to learn how to address the cousins of my mother-in-law in that tongue?—and who shun the majority of mankind. [Lewis] has decided that the lives of peasants and of dwellers in the slums of Mexico City would repay close scrutiny, and he is right about that. His results are valuable and, to me, fascinating." Using a tape recorder, Lewis to a large extent let the poor write their own books. Michael Harrington, the sociologist, noted: "The exciting thing about *Children of Sanchez,* the fact which makes it a new point of departure in its field, is its humanity, its quality of projecting the individual, agonizing voice of the poor as they describe their own plight. This is a real accomplishment, original and full of substance." Harrington also thought that *La Vida,* a first-person account of a Puerto Rican mother and her grown children in San Juan and New York, was "unquestionably one of the most important books published in the United States" in 1967.

Even though *Five Families, Children of Sanchez,* and *La Vida* are anthropological studies, they have been treated by the critics as works of literature. *Time* called *Children of Sanchez* "a work of art created by reality itself, an edited record of fact that comes closer than most contemporary fiction to the force of literature." Similarly, Nat Hentoff said of *La Vida:* "As seldom happens in nonfiction descriptions of the poor, the people . . . have an actuality, a vividness, and an impact that will reverberate in the mind, I suspect, in the disturbing and complex ways in which characters in a superior novel keep coming back unbidden."

In his acceptance speech for the National Book Award, Lewis said that one of the major objectives of his work had been "to bridge the communication gap between the very poor and the middle-class personnel—teachers, social workers, doctors, priests and others—who bear the major responsibility for carrying out the anti-poverty programs. ... I have tried to provide a deeper understanding of the poor, their individuality and the great variety in their life styles so that all the poor are not lumped together in a similar, blurred homogeneous mass. In this connection, I have called attention to the distinction between poverty and the culture of poverty...." In his preface to *La Vida,* Lewis discussed his "culture of poverty" concept as a way of life, passed on from generation to generation, that is more difficult to eliminate than poverty itself. This culture transcends regional, urban-rural, and even national differences. Some of its traits are "the absence of childhood as a specially prolonged and protected stage in the life cycle, early initiation into sex, free unions or consensual marriages, a relatively high incidence of the abandonment of wives and children, ... [and] lack of privacy.... People with a culture of poverty are provincial and locally oriented and have very little sense of history. They know only their own troubles, their own local conditions, their own neighborhood, their own way of life. Usually they do not have the knowledge, the vision, or the ideology to see the similarities between their problems and those of their counterparts elsewhere in the world." Not all the poor, however, are involved in the culture of poverty. Lewis cited the lower castes of India, the Jews of Eastern Europe, and the present-day Cubans. In Havana, he saw that "the physical aspect of the slum had changed very little, ... but I found much less of the despair, apathy, and hopelessness which are so diagnostic of urban slums in the culture of poverty. They expressed great confidence in their leaders and hope for a better life in the future. The slum itself was now highly organized, with block committees, educational committees, party committees. The people had a new sense of power and importance." Lewis maintained, therefore, that "any movement, be it religious, pacifist, or revolutionary, which organizes and gives hope to the poor and effectively promotes solidarity and a sense of identification with larger groups destroys the psychological and social core of the culture of poverty."

Two of his books have come under attack. *Children of Sanchez* created a national scandal in Mexico and led to the dismissal of Dr. Arnold Orflia from his position as head of the publishing firm, El Fondo de Cultura Economica, an organization with which he had been affiliated for 17 years. And leading members of the Puerto Rican community bitterly criticized *La Vida* for giving a distorted image of their way of life. Lewis praised Random House for their courage in publishing the book and noted that the Puerto Rican politicians "seem more concerned about the Puerto Rican image than about a deeper understanding of the lives and problems of the poor."

BIOGRAPHICAL/CRITICAL SOURCES: Reporter, October 1, 1959; *Time,* September 1, 1961; *Commonweal,* November 17, 1961; *World Journal Tribune,* November 16, 1966; *New Yorker,* March 4, 1967; *New York Times,* March 5, 1967, March 9, 1968; *Detroit Free Press,* March 12, 1967; *Newsweek,* March 20, 1967; *Scientific American,* Volume 221, October, 1969.

(Died December 16, 1970)

*   *   *

LEWIS, R. Duffy 1908-

PERSONAL: Born August 26, 1908, in New York, N.Y.; son of Samuel and Jennie D. (Bach) Lewis; married Minna

Margulies, December 29, 1935; children: Donald Duffy, Jane Nancy. *Education:* Columbia University, B.A., 1929, LL.B., 1931. *Office:* 1 Dolma Rd., Scarsdale, N.Y. 10583.

CAREER: May & Jacobson, Attorneys, New York, N.Y., attorney, 1931-32; Alexander's Department Stores, New York, N.Y., 1932-59, became executive vice-president, later director; merchandise consultant in Scarsdale, N.Y., 1959—. Lecturer on retailing at universities and associations. Director of Lortogs, Inc. *Member:* National Retail Merchants Association (director, merchandising division, 1959), Infants', Children's & Teens' Wear Buyers Association (founder; president, 1945; honorary president), National Platform Association, Tau Epsilon Phi, Columbia University Club, Elmwood Country Club.

WRITINGS: How to Keep Merchandising Records, Fairchild, 1948, revised edition published as *How to Keep Merchandising Records: A Manual for Apparel and Dry Goods Merchants on the Profitable Use of Store Records,* 1949, 3rd edition published as *How to Keep Merchandising Records: A Manual for All Retailers on the Profitable Use of Merchandising Records,* 1954, 4th edition, 1960; (with Dorothy Stote) *How to Build an Infants' and Girls' Wear Business: A Manual for Retailers and Prospective Shop Owners,* Hobson Book Press, 1946, revised edition published as *How to Build an Infants', Girls' and Teens' Wear Business: A Manual for Retailers and Prospective Shop Owners,* Fairchild, 1949, 3rd edition published as *How to Build an Infants', Children's and Sub-Teens' Business: A Manual for Retailers, Large and Small,* 1956; (with Jonas Norman Lewis) *What Every Retailer Should Know About the Law,* Fairchild, 1951, revised edition, 1963. Also author of *Lewis Merchandise Control Kit,* published by Fairchild. Columnist for *Women's Wear Daily,* 1959-61; columnist for Haire Publications, 1962-64.

*   *   *

LEWIS, Ronello B. 1909-

PERSONAL: Born December 11, 1909, in Corvallis, Ore.; son of Claude I. (a professor) and Marie (Berry) Lewis; married Marguerite Troudt, August, 1934; children: Phyllis Lewis Mason, Paul. *Education:* University of Oregon, B.A., 1931, M.B.A., 1934. *Religion:* Congregationalist. *Home and office:* Pecksland Rd., Greenwich, Conn. 06830.

CAREER: Held various positions with Montgomery Ward, 1932-41, with Butler Bros., 1941-49; controller, Radio Corporation of America, 1949-53; vice-president and comptroller, Olin Mathieson Chemical Corp., 1953-57; partner, E. F. Hutton & Co. (investment brokers), 1957-60; self-employed management consultant, Greenwich, Conn., 1960—.

WRITINGS—All published by Prentice-Hall: Accounting Reports for Management, 1957, *Financial Analysis for Management,* 1959, *Profit Planning for Management,* 1960, *Financial Controls for Management,* 1961, *Management Control Techniques for Improving Profits,* 1962.

*   *   *

LEWTY, Marjorie 1906-

PERSONAL: Born April 8, 1906; daughter of James Alroy and Mabel (Cox) Lobb; married Richard Arthur Lewty (a dental surgeon), April 7, 1933; children: Simon, Deborah. *Education:* Attended schools in Liverpool, England. *Home:* 42 Heath Ter., Leamington Spa, Warwickshire, England. *Agent:* E. P. S. Lewin & Partners, 7 Chelsea Embankment, London S.W. 3, England.

CAREER: District Bank Ltd., Liverpool, England, secretary, 1923-33. *Member:* Society of Authors, Romantic Novelists Association.

WRITINGS—All novels, published by Mills & Boon: *Never Call it Loving*, 1958; *The Million Stars*, 1959; *The Imperfect Secretary*, 1959; *The Lucky One*, 1961; *This Must Be for Ever*, 1962; *Alex Rayner, Dental Nurse*, 1965; *Dental Nurse at Denley's*, 1968; *Town Nurse—Country Nurse*, 1970 (also published by Pocket Books, 1970). Contributor of about one hundred short stories, and stories for children to periodicals.

WORK IN PROGRESS: The Extraordinary Engagement.

AVOCATIONAL INTERESTS: Psychology, astrology, music, art, drama.

* * *

LEYS, Wayne A(lbert) R(isser) 1905-1973

PERSONAL: Surname rhymes with "peace"; born June 29, 1905, in Bloomington, Ill.; son of John Albert (a businessman) and Stella (Risser) Leys; married Helen Benson, August 26, 1930; children: Portia (Mrs. Albert Sonnenfeld), Carolyn (Mrs. Baxter Moyer). *Education:* Illinois Wesleyan University, A.B., 1926; University of Chicago, Ph.D., 1930. *Politics:* Democrat. *Religion:* United Church of Christ. *Home:* Route 1 (High Pines), Makanda, Ill. 62958. *Office:* Department of Philosophy, Southern Illinois University, Carbondale, Ill. 62901.

CAREER: Central YMCA Community College, Chicago, Ill., instructor, 1932-35, associate professor, 1935-37, professor of philosophy, 1937-45; Roosevelt University, Chicago, Ill., professor of philosophy, 1945-63, dean of faculties, 1945-55, vice-president of university, 1949-55, dean of Graduate Division, 1955-63; Southern Illinois University, Carbondale, professor of philosophy, 1963-73. Visiting lecturer at Johns Hopkins University, 1950, Northwestern University, 1954; visiting professor at University of Michigan, 1955; U.S. Department of State cultural exchange lecturer, 1962. Member of public panel, National War Labor Board, 1943-45, of labor panel, American Arbitration Association, 1946-73. Consultant to Operations Research Office, Johns Hopkins University, 1953-60. Trustee of Roosevelt University, 1945-50, 1953-59; member of National Commission on Educational Organizations, National Conference of Christians and Jews, 1949-50.

MEMBER: American Philosophical Association (chairman of committee to advance original work, 1957-73, and executive committee of Western division, 1965-73), American Society for Public Administration, American Association for the United Nations, American Association of University Professors, Illinois Agricultural Association, Phi Kappa Phi, Cliff Dwellers Club (Chicago; vice-president 1950-51). *Awards, honors:* Research grants from Rockefeller Foundation, 1950-51, 1958-59, from Fund for Adult Education and National Institute of Labor Education, 1959-61.

WRITINGS: The Religious Control of Emotion, Long & Smith, 1932; *Ethics and Social Policy*, Prentice-Hall, 1941; *Ethics for Policy Decisions*, Prentice-Hall, 1952; (with Charner M. Perry) *Philosophy and the Public Interest*, American Philosophical Association, 1959; (with Peter Senn) *Teaching Ethics in Labor Education*, National Institute of Labor Education, 1963; (with P. S. S. Rama Rao) *Gandhi and America's Educational Future*, Southern Illinois University Press, 1969.

Contributor: L. A. Cook, editor, *College Programs in Intergroup Relations*, American Council on Education, 1950; J. B. Gittler, editor, *Understanding Minority Groups*, Wiley, 1956; C. J. Friedrich, editor, *Responsibility*, Liberal Arts Press, 1960; Friedrich, editor, *The Public Interest*, Atherton, 1962; S. Mailick and E. Van Ness, editors, *Concepts and Issues in Administrative Behavior*, Prentice-Hall, 1962; H. Cleveland, editor, *Ethics and Bigness*, Harper, 1962; M. B. Parsons, editor, *Perspectives in the Study of Politics*, Rand McNally, 1968.

Contributor to professional journals. Contributing editor, *Christian Century*, 1956-58.

WORK IN PROGRESS: A book on political philosophy.

AVOCATIONAL INTERESTS: Farming and painting.

(Died March 7, 1973)

* * *

LIEBERMAN, Arnold (Leo) 1903-

PERSONAL: Born October 13, 1903, in Ukraine, Russia; son of Leo (an engineer) and Sophie (Olkhovsky) Lieberman; married Hilda Kahan; August 27, 1933; children: Mary Ellen Lieberman Nerlove, Maxine Adele Lieberman Rockoff, David L. *Education:* University of Chicago, S.B., 1924, Ph.D., 1931; Rush Medical College, M.D., 1928. *Politics:* "Usually Democratic." *Religion:* Hebrew. *Home:* 1270 Fifth Ave., New York, N.Y. 10029.

CAREER: Cook County Hospital, Chicago, Ill., intern, 1927-29; Rush Medical College, Chicago, Ill., faculty member, 1929-47; Northwestern University Medical School, Chicago, Ill., faculty, 1931-47; Tucson Medical Center, Tucson, Ariz., physician, 1946-53; private practice of internal medicine, New York, N.Y., 1956—; staff member of Mt. Sinai Hospital, St. Clare's Hospital, and Medical Arts Center Hospital. Formerly affiliated with Brooklyn-Cumberland Medical Center and New York University Medical Center. *Military service:* U.S. Army, 1928-44; became captain. *Member:* American Medical Association, American Association for the Advancement of Science, American Physiological Society, College of Angiology (fellow), American Society of Internal Medicine (fellow), New York Academy of Sciences, Phi Beta Kappa, Sigma Xi.

WRITINGS: Case Capsules: The Droll, Diverting, Devilish, Definitely Different, C. C Thomas, 1964. Contributor of book reviews and well over one hundred articles to medical and other journals. Member of translation board, Federation of American Societies for Experimental Biology.

* * *

LIEBERS, Ruth 1910-

PERSONAL: Born December 31, 1910, in New York, N.Y.; daughter of Samuel and Lena (Langman) Lampert; married Arthur Liebers (a writer), December 22, 1952. *Education:* Attended Maxwell Training School for Teachers; other courses at College of City of New York (now City College of the City University of New York), New York University, and Hunter College (now Hunter College of the City University of New York). *Home:* Halsey Lane, Remsenburg, Long Island, N.Y.

CAREER: New York City (N.Y.) Board of Education, former classroom teacher and project assistant in elementary school study, consultant for Bank Street College of Education workshop in the public schools, 1962-70. Consultant to Silver Burdett "Music for Living" series. *Member:* Women's National Book Association.

WRITINGS: I Can Count, I Can Draw, Golden Press, 1958; (with Lillian Rothenburg) *Stevie Finds a Way*, Abingdon, 1958; (with Rothenburg) *Hector Goes to School*, Abingdon, 1963. Contributor to *Book of Knowledge*. Contributor of short stories to *Humpty Dumpty*. Former associate editor of teacher edition of Scholastic Magazines publications for three elementary grades.

* * *

LIGON, Ernest M(ayfield) 1897-

PERSONAL: Born April 27, 1897, in Iowa Park, Tex.; son of Robert Leonard and Alice (Waggoner) Ligon; married Lois Agnes Wood, June 30, 1925 (deceased). *Education:* Texas Christian University, B.A., 1921, M.A., 1921; Yale University, B.D., 1924, Ph.D., 1927. *Home:* Wade Lupe Apartments, Jefferson House, Apt. 68, 15 Lafayette St., Schenectady, N.Y. 12305. *Office:* Character Research Project, Union College, 10 Nott Ter., Schenectady, N.Y. 12308.

CAREER: Connecticut College, New London, assistant professor of psychology, 1927-29; Union College, Schenectady, N.Y., assistant professor, 1929-39, associate professor, 1939-44, professor of psychology, 1944-62, chairman of department, 1943-62, founder-director of Character Research Project, 1925—. International Council of Religious Education, vice-chairman, later chairman of research section, 1946-48. Expert consultant to Secretary of War, 1942-45. *Member:* American Psychological Association (fellow), Sigma Xi. *Awards, honors:* LL.D., Texas Christian University, 1948.

WRITINGS: A Comparative Study of Certain Incentives in Learning of the White Rat (monograph), Johns Hopkins Press, 1929; *The Psychology of Christian Personality*, Macmillan, 1935; *Their Future Is Now: The Growth and Development of Christian Personality*, Macmillan, 1939; *A Greater Generation*, Macmillan, 1948; *Dimensions of Character*, Macmillan, 1956; *Parent Roles: His and Hers*, Character Research Project, Union College, c.1959; (with Leona Jones Smith) *The Marriage Climate: A Book of Home Dynamics*, Bethany Press, 1963. Contributor of articles to journals.

* * *

LINCOLN, Victoria 1904-

PERSONAL: Born October 23, 1904, in Fall River, Mass.; daughter of Jonathan Thayer and Louise Sears (Cobb) Lincoln; married Isaac Watkins, 1927; married Victor Lowe (a professor of philosophy at Johns Hopkins University), April 3, 1934; children: (first marriage) Penelope Thayer (Mrs. Donald McKay); (second marriage) Thomas Cobb, Louise Lincoln. *Education:* Radcliffe College, A.B., 1926 ("subsequently finished work for M.A., at Radcliffe and University of Marburgh-Germany, but instead of writing a thesis I wrote a detective story and lived happy ever after as an A.B."). *Politics:* Democrat. *Home:* 3947 Cloverhill Rd., Baltimore, Md. 21218. *Agent:* Harold Ober Associates, Inc., 40 East 49th St., New York, N.Y. 10017.

CAREER: Full-time author. Teacher of writing courses at Johns Hopkins University and at summer schools. *Awards, honors:* Edgar Allan Poe best fact crime book Award from Mystery Writers of America, 1967, for *A Private Disgrace*.

WRITINGS: Swan Island Murders, Farrar & Rinehart,

1930; *February Hill*, Farrar & Rinehart, 1934; *Grandmother and the Comet*, Rinehart, 1944; *The Wind at My Back*, Rinehart, 1946; *Celia Amberley*, Rinehart, 1950; *Out From Eden*, Rinehart, 1951; *The Wild Honey*, Rinehart, 1953; *A Dangerous Innocence*, Rinehart, 1958; *Charles* (biography of Dickens), Little, Brown, 1962; *Desert Water: Seven Stories*, Little, Brown, 1963; *Everyhow Remarkable*, Crowell-Collier Press, 1967; *A Private Disgrace: Lizzie Borden by Daylight*, Putnam, 1967. Short stories anthologized in collections. Contributor of short stories, articles, and poems to magazines, including *Harper's*, *Atlantic Monthly*, *New Yorker*, *Vogue*, *Harper's Bazaar*, *Ladies' Home Journal*, *McCall's*, *Redbook*.

SIDELIGHTS: Miss Lincoln told *CA:* "My last three years have been spent largely in travel (Spain and England mostly) and in libraries; this was in connection with projected work on St. Theresa of Avila. I speak fluent substandard French and worse German; I have never been east of Syria, north of Scotland or south of Mexico. I am happiest by the sea; and in large cosmopolitan cities full of strangers who want to talk and can speak basic English, German, or French.... I have been a chain-reader since the age of three and a writer of sorts since I was four.

"Art uses the beauty of disciplined form to quicken man's awareness of the reality outside his own skin, to quicken his own sense of the living importance of that reality. And it fails either by stale or weak disciplines, or by self-enclosed narcissism. To know and to try is not necessarily to accomplish, and I have sometimes forgotten my purpose...."

Some of Miss Lincoln's fiction has been dramatized (by others) for Broadway, films, and television.

* * *

LINDER, Ivan H. 1894-

PERSONAL: Born August 17, 1894, in Franklin County, Neb.; married Martha Kelso, June 11, 1913; children: Howard K., Medric I. *Education:* Kearney State College, diploma, 1918; University of Nebraska, A.B., 1923, A.M., 1925; Stanford University, graduate study. *Home:* 2551 Carmichael Way, Apt. 5, Carmichael, Calif. 95608.

CAREER: Superintendent of schools, Bayard, Neb., 1916-20, Havelock, Neb., 1921-25; Sacramento City College, Sacramento, Calif., instructor, 1926-28; high school vice-principal in Sacramento, Calif., 1928-36, principal in Palo Alto, Calif., 1936-53; Palo Alto Unified School District, Palo Alto, Calif., assistant superintendent, 1953-57; Colorado State College (now University of Northern Colorado), Greeley, professor of education, 1957-59. Summer instructor at Stanford University, University of the Pacific, Colorado State College (now University of Northern Colorado), and San Jose State College (now California State University). Member, Palo Alto City Council, 1942-50. *Member:* California Teachers Association, California Association of Secondary School Administrators, California Association of School Administrators, Rotary Club (president, Palo Alto, 1942).

WRITINGS: (With Henry M. Gunn) *Secondary School Administration, Problems and Practices*, C. E. Merrill, 1963. Contributor of articles to ten periodicals and professional journals. Author of syllabus on secondary school administration, and on "Counseling and Guidance," both privately distributed.

LINDESMITH, Alfred Ray   1905-

PERSONAL: Born August 3, 1905, in Owatonna, Minn.; son of David Ray and Louise (Priebe) Lindesmith; married Gertrude L. Wollaeger, 1930; children: Karen. Education: Columbia University, M.A., 1930; University of Chicago, Ph.D., 1936. Home: 515 South Rose Ave., Bloomington, Ind. 47401. Office: Indiana University, Bloomington, Ind. 47401.

CAREER: Indiana University, Bloomington, began as instructor, now professor of sociology. Military service: U.S. Army Air Forces, 1943-46; became first lieutenant. Member: American Sociological Association, American Association of University Professors, Society for the Study of Social Problems (president, 1960-61), Phi Beta Kappa.

WRITINGS: Opiate Addiction, Principia, 1947, reissued as Addiction and Opiates, Aldine, 1968; (with Anselm L. Strauss) Social Psychology, Dryden Press, 1949, 3rd edition, Holt, 1968; (editor with Karl Schuessler and Albert Cohen) Edwin Hardin Sutherland, The Sutherland Papers, Indiana University Press, 1956; The British System of Narcotics Control (originally published in Law and Contemporary Problems, winter, 1957), Duke University, School of Law, 1957; The Addict and the Law, Indiana University Press, 1965; (editor with Strauss) Readings in Social Psychology, Holt, 1969. Contributor of articles to professional journals.

*   *   *

LINDGREN, Ernest H.   1910-1973

PERSONAL: Born October 3, 1910, in London, England. Education: University of London, B.A. (honors), 1933. Office: National Film Archive, 81 Dean St., London W1V 6AA, England.

CAREER: National Film Archive, London, England, curator, 1935-73; British Film Institute, London, England, deputy director, 1964-73. Member: British Kinematograph Society (fellow). Awards, honors: Officer, Order of the British Empire.

WRITINGS: (With others) Twenty Years of British Film, Falcon Press, 1947; The Art of the Film, Allen & Unwin, 1948, 2nd edition, Macmillan, 1963; (author of introduction) Sergei Eisenstein, Que Viva Mexico, Vision Press, 1951; A Picture History of the Cinema, Vista Books, 1960.†

(Died July, 1973)

*   *   *

LINDSAY, Ian G(ordon)   1906-1966

PERSONAL: Born July 29, 1906, in Edinburgh, Scotland; son of George Herbert (a businessman) and Helen Eliza (Turnbull) Lindsay; married Maysie Loch, January 7, 1932; children: George Hamish, Margaret Helen, Elizabeth Jane (Mrs. Airlie Bruce-Jones), Douglas Michael, David Ian, Mary Ailsa. Education: Attended Marlborough College; Trinity College, Cambridge, B.A. Home: Houston House, Uphall, West Lothian, Scotland. Office: 17 Great Stuart St., Edinburgh, Scotland.

CAREER: Ian G. Lindsay & Partners (architects), Edinburgh, Scotland, senior partner. Scottish Development Department, chief investigator on listing buildings of architectural interest, 1946-66. UNESCO consultant to Australia on preservation of buildings of architectural interest, 1962. Member of Ancient Monuments Board for Scotland, Royal Commission on the Ancient Monuments for Scot-

land, Royal Fine Art Commission for Scotland, Historic Buildings Council for Scotland; member of council, National Trust for Scotland. Governor, Edinburgh College of Art, 1952-62. Military service: British Army, Royal Engineers, 1940-45; became major. Member: Society of Antiquaries of Scotland (fellow; member of council), Royal Incorporation of Architects in Scotland (fellow), Royal Institute of British Architects (fellow), Kungl. Vitterhets Historie och Antikvitets Akademian (Sweden; foreign member). Awards, honors: Officer of the Order of the British Empire, 1956; Royal Scottish Academician, 1960.

WRITINGS: The Cathedrals of Scotland, W. & R. Chambers, 1926; Old Edinburgh, 1939, Oliver & Boyd, 1939, revised edition published as Old Edinburgh, 1944, 1944, 2nd revised edition published as Old Edinburgh, 1947, 1947; (with Ronald Gordon Cant) Old Elgin: A Description of Old Buildings, Elgin Society, 1946; (with Cant) Old Glasgow: A Description of Old Buildings, Oliver & Boyd, 1946; The Story of Pittenweem Priory, C. S. Russell, 1947; Canongate Kirk: The Kirk of Holyroodhouse, Canongate Booklets, 1947, 2nd edition, 1950; (with Cant) Old Stirling: A Description of Old Buildings, Oliver & Boyd, 1948; The Scottish Tradition in Burgh Architecture, published for the Saltire Society by Thomas Nelson, 1948; Georgian Edinburgh, Oliver & Boyd, 1948; The Scottish Parish Kirk, St. Andrews Press, 1960; (with Mary Cosh) Inverary and the Dukes of Argyll, Aldine, 1972. Contributor of articles to periodicals. Author of guide books. Editor, Quarterly, 1935-39; editor, with Ronald S. Wright, of "The Canongate Booklets," 1947-50.

AVOCATIONAL INTERESTS: Country walking, climbing, shooting, and travel.

(Died August, 1966)

*   *   *

LIPSTREU, Otis   1919-1970

PERSONAL: Second syllable of surname is pronounced "true"; born March 5, 1919, in Aubrey, Tex.; son of Otis Arthur and Lula (Keen) Lipstreu; married Elizabeth Barmes, May 25, 1946; children: Betty Lee, Mary Lou. Education: North Texas State College (now University), B.S., 1939, M.S., 1940; University of Colorado, Ed.D., 1948. Politics: Independent. Religion: Presbyterian. Home: 832 Tenth St., Boulder, Colo. 80302. Office: University of Colorado, Boulder, Colo. 80304.

CAREER: University of Colorado, Boulder, 1948-70, began as assistant professor, became professor of business management. Consulting associate with Shepherd Associates; free-lance management consultant in Rocky Mountain states. Military service: U.S. Coast Guard Reserve, 1942-46; became lieutenant junior grade. Member: Academy of Management, American Association of University Professors, Boulder Chamber of Commerce, Beta Gamma Sigma, Sigma Iota Epsilon, Rotary Club.

WRITINGS: (Editor with Burton A. Kolb) New Concepts and Current Issues in Public Utility Regulation, Peerless Publishing, 1963; (editor with James I. Doi) Guidelines for the Aspiring Professor, South-Western Publishing, 1963; (with Ceanne Mitchell and Billy Watson) Simplified Statistics, Pruett Press, 1963; (with K. A. Reed) Transition to Automation, University of Colorado Press, 1964. Contributor to business and academic journals.

(Died September 20, 1970)

LIST, Jacob Samuel 1896-1967

PERSONAL: Born June 7, 1896, in New York, N.Y.; married Helen Berger (owner of Novick-List Art Gallery); children: Davida, Murray. *Education:* Syracuse University, B.A., B.Ped., M.A., and Ph.D.

CAREER: Worked in earlier years with New York Probation Association, as psychological consultant at Auburn State Prison, Auburn, N.Y., 1920-23, and as organizer of system of remedial reading in Auburn schools; admitted to New York bar; psychotherapist in private practice, until 1954; founder of Institute of Applied Psychology, Inc. (teaching and research organization), New York, N.Y., 1940, and publisher of *Institute of Applied Psychology Review* (quarterly); chancellor of Philathea College, London, Ontario. Former lecturer in psychology at Syracuse University, Yeshiva University, and other institutions; conductor of daily radio programs, including "The Problem Doctor" and "Psychology Behind the News."

MEMBER: American Association for the Advancement of Science, American Society of International Law (director), Academy of American Poets, Authors Guild, Mason, Shrine. *Awards, honors:* D.H.L., Philathea College, 1960; citation from American Jewish Literary Foundation, 1960; grant to study the education of mentally retarded children in Puerto Rico, 1962; Eloy Alfaro International Peace Award; citation from Pope John XXIII for Italian translation of *Education for Living*; Grand Cross of Malta, 1964, for *Can You Afford Tomorrow?*.

WRITINGS: The List Method of Psychotherapy, Philosophical Library, 1960; *Education For Living*, Philosophical Library, 1962; *Living One Day At A Time*, Philosophical Library, 1962; (editor) *The Concise Dictionary of Literature*, Philosophical Library, 1963; (editor) *Major Writers of the World*, Littlefield, 1963; *Fears, Compulsions and Complexes*, Institute of Applied Psychology, 1963; *Can You Afford Tomorrow?*, Institute of Applied Psychology, 1963; *What Happened to Yesterday?*, Institute of Applied Psychology, 1963; *A Psychological Approach to Cancer*, Institute of Applied Psychology, 1964; *A Psychological Approach to Heart Disease*, Institute of Applied Psychology, 1966.

(Died August 16, 1967)

* * *

LIVERSIDGE, (Henry) Douglas 1913-

PERSONAL: Born March 12, 1913, in Swinton, Yorkshire, England; son of Henry and Sarah Ann (Foster) Liversidge; married Cosmina Pistola, September 25, 1954; children: Ann Francesca. *Religion:* Church of England. *Home:* 56 Love Lane, Pinner, Middlesex, England. *Office:* Central Office of Information, London, England.

CAREER: Left grammar school to study metallurgical chemistry at a steel plant in Sheffield, England, but quit after seven months to go into journalism; worked on various British provincial newspapers, then moved to London, England, as correspondent for *Yorkshire Post*, news editor of *Sunday Chronicle*, assistant leader writer for *Daily Mail*, London correspondent of *Continental Daily Mail* (Paris), correspondent and staff writer for Reuters, and wartime free-lance writer of anti-Nazi propaganda commentaries for British Broadcasting Corp. overseas programs; Central Office of Information, London, England, currently an editor. *Military service:* Royal Air Force; invalided out.

WRITINGS: White Horizon, Odhams, 1951; (contributor) D. Monmouth, editor, *The Breath of Life* (anthology), Books 4-5, Allen & Unwin, 1953; *The Last Continent*, Jarrolds, 1958; *The Third Front: The Strange Story of the Secret War in the Arctic*, Souvenir Press, 1960; *The Whale Killers*, Jarrolds, 1963; (contributor) Basil Clarke, *Polar Flight*, Ian Allan, 1964; *The Arctic*, F. Watts, 1967; *Saint Francis of Assisi*, F. Watts, 1968; *Lenin: Genius of Revolution*, F. Watts, 1969; *Joseph Stalin*, F. Watts, 1969; *Ignatius of Loyola, The Soldier-Saint*, F. Watts, 1970; *Arctic Exploration*, F. Watts, 1970; *British Empire and Commonwealth of Nations*, F. Watts, 1971; *The Picture Life of Elizabeth II*, F. Watts, 1971; *The Day the Bastille Fell: The Beginning of the End of the French Monarchy*, F. Watts, 1972; *The Luddites*, F. Watts, 1972.

SIDELIGHTS: As a Reuter correspondent, Liversidge was the first British journalist to visit both polar regions, in 1949-50. On the Arctic expedition (cold weather tests) he was a "guinea pig" for Dr. G. Pugh, who later joined the party which climbed Mount Everest. He traveled to Antarctica, joining an expedition which went to the relief of Sir Vivian Fuchs and his men, who were imprisoned by icefields. Besides covering news and features, he also served as a photographer. *White Horizon* is the story of the Antarctica expedition.

AVOCATIONAL INTERESTS: Art (hopes to write and illustrate children's stories); music, especially playing piano and, formerly, organ; gardening, with specialty in roses.

BIOGRAPHICAL/CRITICAL SOURCES: Books and Bookmen, October, 1967; *New Yorker*, November 4, 1967; *Young Readers Review*, October, 1969.

* * *

LIVERTON, Joan 1913-
(Joan Medhurst)

PERSONAL: Born November 16, 1913, in Bromley, Kent, England; daughter of John and Penelope Sarah (Taylor) Medhurst; married Thomas A. Liverton (an artist and lecturer), July 27, 1936; children: Jennifer Joan, Lysbeth Angela. *Education:* Attended Bromley High School for Girls, Kent College, and Bromley and Beckenham Schools of Art. *Politics:* "Very left wing Conservative." *Religion:* Roman Catholic. *Home and office:* Melai, Northiam, Sussex, England. *Agent:* A.M. Heath & Co. Ltd., 35 Dover St., London W.1, England.

CAREER: Free-lance writer. Worker with British Red Cross during World War II. *Member:* Incorporated Society of Authors, Playwrights and Composers, National Book League, International P.E.N. (Britain).

WRITINGS—All under name Joan Medhurst: *A Fragment of Beauty*, Hurst & Blackett, 1955; *Cry Innocence*, Cassell, 1957; *The Shadowed Mirror*, Cassell, 1959; *R.X. 107*, Cassell, 1960. Contributor of articles on writing, present day problems, and art to magazines.

WORK IN PROGRESS: The Bastard Blue; *Saturday Boy*, a collection of short stories about the sea; a trilogy on lion and unicorn theme, employing two sides of a family, one concerned with business, the other, art, their interconnection, signifying the lion-unicorn or male-female factor in each human.

SIDELIGHTS: Mrs. Liverton writes: "It could be said that, since I was trained as an artist and the fact that I have been married for the past 27 years to [a] watercolour painter, my approach to writing is through the eyes—as an artist, with the delving into the deeper motives of human relationships and its consequent wider effect of international relationships. This has resulted in an attempt to bring into public consciousness the cruelty which results from what might be termed regional attitudes. Attitudes being the brick wall through which understanding cannot break through, and which inevitably lead to cant and humbug in their most virilant forms—the humbug of the man who is unaware that he is a humbug. . . .

"From [tragic] personal events, . . . I came to learn that a better understanding of ones fellows results. But, thank God, the majority of human beings do not suffer intense human tragedies and so cannot learn from experience. It is the duty then, of the writer, to so communicate, via intellectual and emotional impact, a situation of involvement with the reader—that the reader himself forgets himself in the intensity of his involvement with the fictional character."†

*   *   *

LIVIE-NOBLE, Frederick Stanley 1899-1970

PERSONAL: Born February 1, 1899, in Essex, England; son of Charles (a marine engineer) and Ellen Hariet (Horne) Livie-Noble; married Mary Hall Sedgwick, February 10, 1934; children: Mary Ann. *Education:* Educated at Queens' College, Cambridge, 1918-20, Rhodes University College, Grahamstown, South Africa, 1921-23. *Religion:* Church of England. *Home and office:* Manton Plovers, Marlborough, Wiltshire, England.

CAREER: Teacher in Transvaal, South Africa, 1923-27; British National Conference on the Welfare of Youth, London, England, secretary, 1928-29; Rational Economic Foundation Ltd., London, England, secretary, 1929-30; lecturer for educational organizations, London, England, 1930-34; private practice as consultant psychologist, 1934-70; consultant to various public schools, 1940-64. Lecturer to H. M. Forces on mental hygiene, 1940-45. *Military service:* Royal Army Medical Corps and Worcestershire Regiment, 1916-18; became lieutenant. *Member:* British Psychological Association.

WRITINGS: (Editor) *The Citizen of Tomorrow*, Benn, 1929; *Balance—or Bounce?*, Sedgwick, 1934; *The School Psychologist*, Duckworth, 1947. Contributor to *South African Journal of Science, World Science Review, Journal of Africa Society*, and to British newspapers and religious journals.

WORK IN PROGRESS: Dyslexia, Laterality, and Remedial Teaching; Psychology and Spiritual Experience in Spiritual Healing.

(Died March 3, 1970)

*   *   *

LLOYD, David Demarest 1911-1962

PERSONAL: Born June 6, 1911, in New York, N.Y.; son of David and Eliza Shore (Mathews) Lloyd; married Charlotte Tuttle, 1940; children: Andrew Mathews, Louisa Tucker. *Education:* Harvard College, A.B. (summa cum laude), 1931, LL.B., 1935; Cambridge University, Lady Julia Henry fellow, 1931-32. *Politics:* Democrat. *Religion:* Episcopalian. *Home:* 2501 Ridge Road Dr., Alexandria, Va. 22302. *Agent:* Miss Andrea Lloyd, 433 West 21st St., New York, N.Y. 10011. *Office:* Morison, Murphy, Clapp & Abrams, 425 13th St. N.W., Washington, D.C. 20004.

CAREER: Attorney with Federal Communications Commission, Office of Price Administration, other government

agencies, Washington, D.C., 1935-44; Foreign Economic Administration, Washington, D.C., assistant general counsel, 1944-45; U.S. Embassy, London, England, legal adviser to economic minister and Mission for Economic Affairs, 1946; White House staff, Washington, D.C., administrative assistant to President of the United States, 1948-53; Harry S. Truman Library, Inc., Washington, D.C., executive director, 1953-62. National Conference on International Economic and Social Development, Washington, D.C., chairman, 1959-62; Albert and Mary Lasker Foundation, Washington, D.C., director, Research and Education Committee for a Free World, 1958-61; Harry S. Truman Library Institute, vice-president, 1957-62. The National Cathedral, Washington, D.C., member of organizing committee for the Christianity and Modern Man lecture series, 1947-62. *Member:* National Capitol Democratic Club (Washington; formerly on board of governors), Harvard Club (New York).

WRITINGS: Son and Stranger, Houghton, 1950; *The Sirens Let Him Go*, Bobbs-Merrill, 1960; *Spend and Survive: The Intelligent Citizen's Guide to Public Spending* (nonfiction), Bobbs-Merrill, 1960. Contributor to various magazines.

(Died December 11, 1962)

*   *   *

LLYWELYN-WILLIAMS, Alun 1913-

PERSONAL: Born August 27, 1913, in Cardiff, Glamorgan, Wales; son of David (a medical doctor) and Margaret (Price) Llewelyn-Williams; married Alis Stocker, September 10, 1938; children: Eryl and Luned (daughters). *Education:* University College of South Wales and Monmouthshire, University of Wales, B.A., 1934, M.A., 1957. *Religion:* Presbyterian. *Home:* Pen-y-Lan, Bangor, Caernarvonshire, Wales. *Office:* University College of North Wales, Bangor, Wales.

CAREER: National Library of Wales, Aberystwyth, junior librarian, 1936; British Broadcasting Corp., announcer in Cardiff, Wales, then London, England, 1936-40, talks producer in Bangor, Wales, 1946-48; University College of North Wales, Bangor, director of extramural studies, 1948—. Arts Council of Great Britain, member of Welsh committee, 1958-67; member of Central Advisory Council for Education, 1961-64; Independent Television Authority, member of Committee for Wales, 1964-67; director, Harlech Television Ltd., 1967—; member of board of management, Welsh National Theatre Company, 1967—; member of Universities Council for Adult Education. *Member:* Association of University Teachers (president, Bangor branch, 1962-63), Honourable Society of Cymmrodorion. *Awards, honors:* Sir Ellis Griffith Memorial Prize of University of Wales, 1961, for *Y Nos, y Niwl, a'r Ynys*.

WRITINGS: Cerddi, 1934-1942 (poems), W. & G. Foyle, 1944; *Pont y Caniedydd* (poems), Gee (Denbigh), 1956; *Crwydro Arfon* (title means "Wanderings in Caernarvonshire"), Llyfrau'r Dryw, 1959; *Y Nos, Y Niwl, a'r Ynys* (title means "A Study in Welsh Romanticism"), University of Wales Press, 1960; *Crwydro Brycheinoig* (title means "Wanderings in Breconshire"), Llyfrau'r Dryw, 1964; *Y Llenor a'i Gymdeithas* (annual radio lecture; title means "The Writer and His Society"), British Broadcasting Corp., 1966; *Nes na'r Hanesydd?* (literary essays), Gee, 1968.

Poems anthologized in *Oxford Book of Welsh Verse*, edited by Thomas Parry, 1962, and *Penguin Book of Welsh Verse*, translated by A. Conran, Penguin, 1967. Contributor to *Times Literary Supplement, Adult Education, Listener*, and to Welsh literary and philosophic journals.

WORK IN PROGRESS: A partly autobiographical account of a city childhood in the 1920's; a book on the marches of Wales and England.

AVOCATIONAL INTERESTS: Travel, walking, entertaining friends, and reading.

BIOGRAPHICAL/CRITICAL SOURCES: Y Llenor, XXVIII, 1949.

* * *

LOCKLEY, Lawrence Campbell   1899-1969

PERSONAL: Born November 21, 1899, in Salem, Ore.; son of Fred and Hope (Gans) Lockley; married Phyllis Harrington, 1920; married second wife, Naomi M. Hewes, November 19, 1938; children: (first marriage) Neil Harrington. *Education:* University of California, B.A. (honors), 1920, M.A., 1921; Harvard University, M.A., 1928, Ph.D., 1931. *Politics:* Republican. *Religion:* Society of Friends. *Home:* 616 Morse St., San Jose, Calif. 95126. *Office:* University of Santa Clara, Santa Clara, Calif.

CAREER: Temple University, Philadelphia, Pa., assistant professor of business administration, 1930-32, professor of marketing and head of department, 1932-35; Curtis Publishing Co., Philadelphia, Pa., market analyst with division of commercial research, 1935-42; E. I. DuPont de Nemours & Co., New York, N.Y., manager of central marketing research division, 1942-45; New York University, New York, N.Y., professor of retailing and director of research, School of Retailing, 1946-49, professor of marketing, Graduate School of Business Administration, 1949-51; University of Southern California, Los Angeles, dean of School of Commerce, 1951-59; Columbia University, New York, N.Y., visiting professor of marketing, Graduate School of Business, 1959-60; University of Santa Clara, Santa Clara, Calif., professor of business administration and chairman of department of marketing, 1960-69. Technical analyst, U.S. Bureau of the Census, 1935; served on missions to Latin America for International Cooperation Administration and Administration for International Development. Member of arbitration panels of Federal Mediation Service and American Arbitration Association.

MEMBER: American Economic Association, American Statistical Association, American Academy of Advertising, American Marketing Association (former national director and vice-president; former chapter officer in Philadelphia and California), Beta Gamma Sigma (national director and vice-president). *Awards, honors:* Eleven Freedoms Foundation awards for executive programs and for *Monthly Economic Letter.*

WRITINGS: (With former wife, Phyllis H. Lockley) *Faulty Paragraphs for Composition Classes*, Harr Wagner, 1923; (editor) Harr Wagner and Mark Keppel, *Lessons in California History*, Harr Wagner, 1924; *Making Letters Build Business*, First National Bank of Los Angeles, 1925; (with P. H. Houston) *A Road Map to Literature*, Haldeman-Julius, 1926; *Direct Mail Advertising for Life Insurance*, Pacific Mutual Life Insurance Co., 1926; *Principles of Effective Letterwriting*, McGraw, 1927, 2nd edition, 1933; *Vertical Cooperative Advertising*, McGraw, 1931; *Instructional Notes to Accompany "Principles of Effective Letter Writing"*, McGraw, 1933; (with Albert E. Haase and Isaac W. Digges) *Advertising Agency Compensation:*

Theory, Law, Practice, Association of National Advertisers, 1934.

(Contributor) A. B. Blankenship, editor, *How to Conduct Consumer and Opinion Research*, Harper, 1946; (co-author) *Marketing by Manufacturers*, Irwin, 1947, revised edition, 1950; (with Charles J. Dirksen) *Cases in Marketing*, Allyn & Bacon, 1954, 4th edition (with others), 1971; (with Lewis K. Johnson) *Sales and Marketing Management* (includes text and cases; cases by Lockley and Dirksen), Allyn & Bacon, 1957; *Operations Research: What It Is, How It Is Conducted, What It Offers Business*, National Industrial Conference Board, 1957.

Use of Motivation Research in Marketing, National Industrial Conference Board, 1960; *The Small Business Executive Evaluates Business Education*, School of Business, University of Santa Clara, 1962; (editor with Dirksen and Arthur Kroeger) *Readings in Marketing*, Irwin, 1964; (with wife, Naomi Hewes Lockley, Frank J. Thomas Gallardo, and Neftali Alvarenga Pena) *A Guide to Market Data in Central America*, Central American Bank for Economic Integration, 1964; (with others) *A Marketing Guide to Peru*, Instituto Peruano de Administracion de Empresas, 1964, 2nd edition, 1968; (contributor) Reavis Cox and others, editors, *Theory in Marketing*, American Marketing Association, 1964; (translator) Baltasar Gracian y Morales, *The Science of Success and the Art of Prudence*, University of Santa Clara Press, 1967. Writer of monographs and pamphlets on marketing topics. Contributor of almost one hundred articles, and reviews, to journals. Editor, *Journal of Retailing*, 1947-49; member of editorial board, *Journal of Marketing*, 1937-47, 1957-69.

(Died October 27, 1969)

* * *

LOEB, Gerald M(artin)   1899-1974

PERSONAL: Born July 24, 1899, in San Francisco, Calif.; son of Sol and Dahlia (Levy) Loeb; married Rose L. Benjamin, April 11, 1947.

CAREER: E. F. Hutton & Co. (investment firm), New York, N.Y., manager of statistical department, San Francisco branch, 1922-24, head of statistical department, New York, 1924-29, became partner, 1929, retired as vice-chairman and director in 1965. President, Sidney S. Loeb Memorial Foundation, Inc., New York March of Dimes, co-chairman, 1958, 1959, chairman, 1960; Trustee and member of finance committee, Danbury Hospital; trustee, Mark Twain Library, Danbury. Former director, American National Theatre and Academy; Member of visiting committee, Board of Overseers, Harvard University Graduate School of Business Administration. Visiting lecturer at various times, Harvard University, Cornell University, University of Pennsylvania, and University of Vermont summer finance forum on Wall Street. *Member:* Explorers Club, Wall Street Club, Harvard Club (Boston), City Athletic Club (New York).

WRITINGS: Battle for Investment Survival, Simon and Schuster, 1957; *Loeb's Checklist for Buying Stocks*, Simon & Schuster, 1960; *The Battle for Stock Market Profits (Not the Way It's Taught at Harvard Business School)*, Simon & Schuster, 1971. Writer of a syndicated weekly investment column.

AVOCATIONAL INTERESTS: Architecture, photography.

(Died, 1974)

LOEW, Ralph William 1907-

PERSONAL: Born December 29, 1907, in Columbus, Ohio; son of William Louis (a machinist) and Wilhelmina (Bauer) Loew; married G. Maxine Uhl, June 8, 1939; children: Carolyn Maxine, Janet Elaine. *Education:* Capital University, A.B., 1928; Wittenberg University, B.D., 1931. *Home:* 342 Depew Ave., Buffalo, N.Y. 14214. *Office:* Holy Trinity Lutheran Church, 1080 Main St., Buffalo, N.Y. 14209.

CAREER: Ordained minister of Lutheran Church, 1931; pastor in Millersburg, Ohio, 1931-36, and Washington, D.C., 1937-44; Holy Trinity Lutheran Church, Buffalo, N.Y., pastor, 1944—. Lutheran Church in America, president of Board of Missions, 1956-60, member of executive council, 1960-66, chairman of Division of World Missions and Ecumenism; delegate to Lutheran World Federation in Lund, 1947, and Helsinki, 1963; speaker at schools and conferences in Malaysia, Japan, and Hong Kong, 1959-60; British-American exchange preacher in England and Scotland, 1966 and 1972. Vice-president of New York State Council of Churches; member of board of directors of Deaconess Hospital, Community Welfare Council, and Community Action Organization, all Buffalo. *Awards, honors:* D.D., Wittenberg University, 1947; D.H.L., Susquehanna University, 1972.

WRITINGS: Hinges of Destiny, Muhlenberg Press, 1955; *The Church and the Amateur Adult,* Muhlenberg Press, 1957; *Confronted by Jesus,* Muhlenberg Press, 1957; *The Lutheran Way of Life,* Prentice-Hall, 1966. Also author of "He Is Coming Soon." Writer of weekly column, "From My Window," in *Buffalo Courier-Express,* beginning, 1952, and "Finding the Way," syndicated by Newspaper Enterprise Associates, 1960-72.

*　　*　　*

LOMAS, Charles W(yatt) 1907-

PERSONAL: Born December 27, 1907, in Green Bay, Wis.; son of Charles Wyatt (a lawyer) and Bessie (Smith) Lomas; married Eloise Gamble, August 15, 1932; children: Charles, Stephen, Barbara. *Education:* Carroll College, Waukesha, Wis., A.B., 1929; Northwestern University, M.A., 1934, Ph.D., 1940. *Religion:* Methodist. *Home:* 10551 Wilshire Blvd., Los Angeles, Calif. 90024. *Office:* Department of Speech, University of California, Los Angeles, Calif. 90024.

CAREER: High school teacher, Waukesha, Wis., 1929-35; University of Pittsburgh, Pittsburgh, Pa., instructor in speech, 1935-43; Stanford University, Stanford, Calif., assistant professor of speech, 1943-44; U.S. Office of War Information, San Francisco, Calif., chief of propaganda analysis section, 1944-45; Universtiy of Michigan, Ann Arbor, assistant professor of speech, 1945-47; University of California, Los Angeles, 1947—, began as assistant professor, now professor of speech. *Member:* Speech Association of America (vice-chairman of public address section, 1963, and chairman, 1964), Western Speech Association.

WRITINGS: (With Elise Hahn, Donald Hargis, and Daniel Vandraegen) *Basic Voice Training for Speech,* McGraw, 1952, 2nd edition, 1957; (with Ralph Richardson) *Speech: Idea and Delivery,* Houghton, 1956, 2nd edition, 1963; (contributor) J. J. Auer, editor, *Anti-Slavery and Disunion,* Harper, 1964. Contributor to speech journals. Editor, *Western Speech,* 1951-54.

WORK IN PROGRESS: Research in nineteenth-century political and social agitators, and in the rhetoric of agitation and demagoguery.

AVOCATIONAL INTERESTS: Travel and photography.

BIOGRAPHICAL/CRITICAL SOURCES: Guardian (London), October 12, 1964; *Manchester Guardian Weekly,* October 15, 1964.

*　　*　　*

LONG, Charles R(ussell) 1904-

PERSONAL: Born June 25, 1904, in Paragould, Ark.; son of Charles Alvin and Alice (Van Tassel) Long. *Education:* Attended public school in Paragould, Ark. *Home:* 7777 Gran Quivira, El Paso, Tex. 79904.

CAREER: Western Union Morse Code operator, mainly in El Paso, Tex., 1921-53.

WRITINGS: The Infinite Brain, Avalon Books, 1957; *The Eternal Man,* Avalon Books, 1964. Contributor of short stories to pulp magazines.

WORK IN PROGRESS: Around the Horn to Frisco, sea story for boys; *Accuracy First,* a novel of automation in the telegraph field.

*　　*　　*

LONG, J(ohn) C(uthbert) 1892-

PERSONAL: Born August 22, 1892, in Babylon, Long Island, N.Y.; son of John Dietrich (a minister) and Elizabeth Trott (Audoun) Long; married Mary Parsons, June 6, 1942; children: Sheila Parsons, Nicholas Trott. *Education:* Amherst College, A.B., 1914; Harvard University, graduate student, 1914-15. *Religion:* Presbyterian. *Home and office:* 7 Edgehill St., Princeton, N.J. 08540. *Agent:* Margot Johnson Agency, 405 East 54th St., New York, N.Y. 10022.

CAREER: Successively newspaper reporter, editor of automobile publication, and special correspondent for newspapers, 1915-18; National Automobile Chamber of Commerce, manager of educational department, 1920-30; concurrently member of editorial staff of *New Yorker,* 1927-30, contributing editor of *New York American,* 1928-30; Bethlehem Steel Co., manager of publications, 1930-58; Jones, Brakeley & Rockwell, New York, N.Y., chairman of board, 1958-68. War Camp Community Service, director, 1918-20. National Conference on Street and Highway Safety, member, 1925-27. *Member:* American Historical Association, American Iron and Steel Institute (chairman, public relations committee, 1956-58), Theta Delta Chi, Delta Sigma Rho; Century Association, University Club (both New York). *Awards, honors:* L.H.D., Gettysburg College, 1958; Litt.D., Nasson College, 1966.

WRITINGS: (With John D. Long) *Motor Camping,* Dodd, 1923; *Public Relations: A Handbook of Publicity,* McGraw, 1924; *Bryan, the Great Commoner,* Appleton, 1928; *Lord Jeffrey Amherst, a Soldier of the King,* Macmillan, 1933; *The Plimpton Collection of French and Indian War Items,* Amherst College, 1934; *Mr. Pitt and America's Birthright: A Biography of William Pitt, the Earl of Chatham, 1708-1778,* Frederick A. Stokes, 1940; *Long's Bible Quiz,* G. W. Stewart, Book 1, 1943, Book 2, 1951; *Roy D. Chapin,* privately printed, 1945; *The Liberal Presidents: A Study of the Liberal Tradition in the American Presidency,* Crowell, 1948; *Soldier for the King: A Story of Amherst in America,* Winston, 1954; *Maryland Adventure: A Story of the Battle of the Severn,* Winston, 1956; *George*

III: The Story of a Complex Man, Little, Brown, 1960 (published in England as *George III: A Biography*, Macdonald, 1962); (with Leonard Carmichael) *James Smithson and the Smithsonian Story*, Putnam, 1965; *The Young Revolutionaries*, John Day, 1968. Contributor of articles and reviews to national magazines.

AVOCATIONAL INTERESTS: Tennis, sea voyages, theatre.

* * *

LONGSTRETH, Edward 1894-19(?)

PERSONAL: Born July 2, 1894, in Lansdowne, Pa.; son of Charles and M. Gertrude (Heyer) Longstreth; divorced; children: Edward, Jr. *Education:* Yale University, A.B., 1916; graduate study at University of Pennsylvania. *Politics:* Democrat. *Religion:* Episcopalian. *Home:* La Jolla Palms Inn, La Jolla, Calif. *Office:* P.O. Box 736, La Jolla, Calif.

CAREER: Began as reporter for *Philadelphia Evening Bulletin*, Philadelphia, Pa., in 1919; at various times prior to 1950, magazine and radio writer, advertising man with New York agencies, actor on Broadway, lecturer, and managing editor of *Arts and Decoration*. Longstreth Enterprises (promotions), La Jolla, Calif., owner, beginning 1950. *Military service:* U.S. Army, Field Artillery, 1918-19; served in France; became second lieutenant. *Member:* Military Order of the World Wars, American Legion, Colonial Society of Pennsylvania.

WRITINGS: What We Do Now?, Simon and Schuster, 1928; *What'll We Do Next?*, Reilly & Lee, 1930; *Primer for Politics*, Housmann, 1946; *History of the U.S. in 17 Minutes*, Murray & Gee, 1952; *Decisive Battles of the Bible*, Lippincott, 1962; *The Hill of the Lord*, Lippincott, 1964; *Eight Bible Plays for Children*, Concordia, 1965.

Writer of radio episodes for "Cavalcade of America," "Main Street," "Ipana Troubadours," and other network series. Former correspondent for *Art News*; compiler of an art guide to Philadelphia; and editor of sesquicentennial number of *Archaeology*.

WORK IN PROGRESS: A biography of Queen Anne; a novel; another book on the Bible.

SIDELIGHTS: Longstreth told CA, "I like people and like few animals I can't eat. I know furniture and the arts, but never saw anything (inanimate) that I would prefer to a person."

(Deceased)

* * *

LOOMIS, Stanley 1922-1972

PERSONAL: Born December 21, 1922, in New York, N.Y.; son of Chauncey C. and Elizabeth (McLanahan) Loomis; married Virginia Lindsley; children: Craig Putnam; stepchildren: Thomas Ginoux, Reginald Ginoux, Thayer Ginoux, Claudine Ginoux. *Education:* Columbia University, B.A., 1948, M.A., 1949. *Home:* 27 Quai Anatole France, Paris VII, France, and Stockbridge, Mass. *Agent:* Littauer & Wilkinson, 500 Fifth Ave., New York, N.Y. 10036.

CAREER: Writer. *Military service:* U.S. Army, served in World War II.

WRITINGS: DuBarry: A Biography, Lippincott, 1959; *Paris in the Terror, June, 1793-July, 1794* (Book-of-the-Month Club selection), Lippincott, 1964; *A Crime of Pas-*

sion, Lippincott, 1967; *The Fatal Friendship: Marie Antoinette, Count Fersen and the Flight to Varennes* (Literary Guild selection), Doubleday, 1972.

BIOGRAPHICAL/CRITICAL SOURCES: Book Week, May 21, 1967; *New York Times Book Review*, July 9, 1967; *Observer Review*, August 11, 1968; *Spectator*, August 23, 1968; *New York Times*, December 22, 1972.

(Died December 18, 1972)

* * *

LORAND, (Alexander) Sandor 1893-

PERSONAL: Born February 12, 1893, in Hungary; came to United States in 1925; son of Joseph and Amalia (Spritz) Lorand; married Rhod Leigh (a child psychoanalyst), June 21, 1943; children: Steven. *Education:* Royal Hungarian University and Komensky University, M.D., 1919. *Home and office:* 40 Central Park S., New York, N.Y. 10019.

CAREER: Psychiatrist in private practice, New York, N.Y., 1927—. State University of New York, founder and former director of Division of Psychoanalytic Education, now professor of clinical psychiatry at Downstate Medical Center, Brooklyn. Member of board of directors, Hillside Hospital. Wartime consultant to Selective Service boards. *Member:* International Psychoanalytic Association, American Psychiatric Society, American College of Physicians (fellow), New York Psychoanalytic Society (former president), Psychoanalytic Association of New York (former president); now honorary president).

WRITINGS: The Morbid Personality: Psycho-analytical Studies in the Structure of Character and Personality, Knopf, 1931; (editor) *Psychoanalysis Today: Its Scope and Function*, Covici-Friede, 1933; *Technique of Psychoanalytic Therapy*, International Universities Press, 1946; *Clinical Studies in Psychoanalysis*, International University Press, 1950; (editor with Michael Balint) *Perversions, Psychodynamics and Therapy*, Random House, 1956; (editor with Henry I. Schneer) *Adolescents: Psychoanalytic Approach to Problems and Therapy*, Hoeber, 1961. Contributor of papers on psychiatric and psychoanalytic problems to professional journals. Managing editor, *Yearbook of Psychoanalysis*, International Universities Press, 1945-55.

WORK IN PROGRESS: A biography of Sandor Ferenczi.

AVOCATIONAL INTERESTS: Travel, figure skating, and painting.

* * *

LORD, (Doreen Mildred) Douglas 1904-

PERSONAL: Born September 25, 1904, in Portsmouth, Hampshire, England; daughter of John and Gertrude (DeTopp) Lord. *Education:* Educated privately. *Religion:* Roman Catholic. *Home:* 51 St. Chad's Ave., Portsmouth, Hampshire, England.

CAREER: Isle of Wight Times, Ryde, Isle of Wight, reporter, 1921-26; full-time writer, except for periodic secretarial jobs, 1926—. *Military service:* Women's Royal Naval Service, writer, 1939-41; invalided out. *Member:* Romantic Novelists' Association, Poetry Society, Catholic Poetry Society, Women's Press Club of London, Portsmouth Soroptimists (librarian), Portsmouth Dickens Fellowship. *Awards, honors:* Second prize, Romantic Novelists' Association, 1960, for *Yellow Flower*.

WRITINGS—All children's books except as indicated: Spirit of Wearde Hall, Carey Press, 1927; *Doreen Douglas,*

Schoolgirl, Pilgrim Press, 1933; *Joan at Seascale*, Warne, 1936; *Lynnette at Carisgate*, Epworth, 1937; *Margery the Mystery*, Epworth, 1939; *Yellow Flower* (adult novel), Ward, Locke, 1961; *Kiwi Jane*, Odhams, 1962; *The Cypress Box*, Geoffrey Chapman, 1963; *To Win Their Crown*, Geoffrey Chapman, 1963; *Children at the Court of St. Peter*, Geoffrey Chapman, 1963; (translator from the French) Henry Daniel-Rops, *The Wonderful Life of St. Paul*, Geoffrey Chapman, 1965.

Poem antholigized in *Spring Anthology*, Volume I, Mitre Press, 1963. Contributor of poems, plays, and articles to periodicals, 1927—, stories to *Guide* and *Catholic Fireside*, 1934-61, quizzes on Catholic history to *Universe*, 1960-61. Writer of radio scripts, "Five to Ten Stories" and "Silver Lining," for British Broadcasting Corp. Co-editor, *Senior Citizen*, 1963-65.

WORK IN PROGRESS: Studies on John Clare, peasant poet of Northamptonshire, and on John Pounds, pioneer of Ragged Schools, Portsmouth.

SIDELIGHTS: Miss Lord said her major interest is writing traditional poetry, "which I have to publish myself if I want it in book form!" She lived and traveled in New Zealand, 1950-52.

BIOGRAPHICAL/CRITICAL SOURCES: Presswoman, April, 1963.

* * *

LOTHIAN, John Maule   1896-1970

PERSONAL: Born May 16, 1896, in Glenfarg, Perthshire, Scotland; son of Charles Innes (a farmer) and Helen (Maule) Lothian; married Barbara I. W. Cattanach (a university assistant), July 25, 1924; children: Barbara Swan, John K. M. (died, 1962), Margaret Jean Leith. *Education:* University of Glasgow, M.A. (first class honors), 1920. *Home:* Humanity Manse, 19 College Bounds, Aberdeen, Scotland. *Office:* English Department, University of Aberdeen, Aberdeen, Scotland.

CAREER: Carnegie Research fellow in Italy, 1920-21; University of Glasgow, Glasgow, Scotland, university assistant in Italian department, 1921-22; University of Saskatchewan, Saskatoon, junior professor, 1922-32, professor of English, 1932-40, Bateman Professor and head of English department, 1940-49; University of Aberdeen, Aberdeen, Scotland, reader in English, 1949-70. External examiner in English for University of St. Andrews, 1952-56, University of Glasgow, 1957-62, University of Edinburgh, 1961-70. Member of Canadian Library Council, 1943-45, Aberdeen Public Library Board, 1952-70. Scottish Central Library Executive, 1957-70, and Scottish National Dictionary Council, 1960-70. *Military service:* British Army, gunner, 1917-19. *Awards, honors:* Honorary fellow, Yale Univeristy, 1939-40.

WRITINGS: (Editor) Shakespeare, *Henry IV*, Macmillan (Canada), 1931; (editor) Shakespeare, *A Midsummer Night's Dream*, St. Martin's, 1932; (editor) Shakespeare, *Richard II*, Oxford University Press, 1938; *King Lear: A Tragic Reading of Life*, Clarke, Irwin, 1949; (editor and author of introduction and notes) Adam Smith, *Lectures on Rhetoric and Belles Lettres*, Thomas Nelson, 1963; (compiler) *Shakespeare's Charactery: A Book of Characters from Shakespeare*, Barnes & Noble, 1966. Contributor to *Modern Language Review, Canadian Forum, Scotsman*, and other periodicals.

WORK IN PROGRESS: Editions of R. Watson's *Treatise* on *Rhetoric* and W. Greenfield's *Lectures on Rhetoric*, from the manuscripts; an edition of *Twelfth Night*, for Methuen.

AVOCATIONAL INTERESTS: Book and manuscript hunting.

BIOGRAPHICAL/CRITICAL SOURCES: Times Literary Supplement, February 9, 1967.

(Died October 31, 1970)

* * *

LOWE, Robert W.   1910-

PERSONAL: Born December 12, 1910, in New York, N.Y., son of Peter (an engineer) and Anna (Gordon) Lowe. *Education:* Columbia University, A.B., 1944, M.A., 1945; Sorbonne, University of Paris, Ph.D., 1949. *Religion:* Roman Catholic.

CAREER: Lycee Francais, New York, N.Y., instructor in modern languages, 1939-42; Lafayette College, Easton, Pa., assistant professor of French and history of music, 1946-53; University of Arizona, Tucson, assistant professor of French, 1953-58; Georgetown University, Washington, D.C., professor of French, 1958—. Director of Collegium Musicum at Georgetown University and founder and member of Georgetown String Quartet. *Military service:* U.S. Army, Military Intelligence, 1942-46, 1951-52; became captain; received Bronze Star. *Member:* Greater Washington Association of Language Teachers (president, 1961-63), Phi Mu Alpha, Pi Delta Phi. *Awards, honors:* Belgian American Educational Foundation research fellow in history of French music, Brussels, Belgium, 1956-57.

WRITINGS: Visages de France, Odyssey, 1964.

WORK IN PROGRESS: A book on the operas of Marc-Antoine Charpentier.

* * *

LOWINSKY, Edward E(lias)   1908-

PERSONAL: Born January 12, 1908, in Stuttgart, Germany; son of Leib Leopold and Clara (Rosenfeld) Lowinsky; married Gretel J. Hoffman, August 10, 1938; married second wife, Bonnie J. Blackburn, September 10, 1971; children: (first marriage) Naomi Lowinsky Dorfman, Simon Leo, Benjamin David, Joshua Michael. *Education:* Hochschule fuer Musik, Stuttgart, Germany, student, 1923-28; University of Heidelberg, Ph.D., 1933. *Home:* 7440 South Constance, Chicago, Ill. 60649. *Office:* Department of Music, University of Chicago, Chicago, Ill. 60637.

CAREER: Black Mountain College, Black Mountain N.C., assistant professor of music, 1942-47; Queens College (now Queens College of the City University of New York), Flushing, N.Y., associate professor of music, 1949-56; University of California, Berkeley, professor of music, 1956-61; University of Chicago, Chicago, Ill., Ferdinand Schevill Distinguished Professor of Music, 1961—, Colvin Research Professor, 1964-65. *Member:* American Academy of Arts and Sciences (fellow), American Musicological Society (member of council and of executive board), Society for Ethnomusicology (member of council), International Musicological Society, Belgian Musicological Society, Dutch Musicological Society, Renaissance Society of America (member of council). *Awards, honors:* Guggenheim fellow; Bollingen fellow; fellow, Institute for Advanced Study, Princeton, N.J., 1952-54; Otto Kinkeldey Award of the American Musicological Society, 1969, for *The Medici Codex of 1518*.

WRITINGS: Buch der Kindermusik, Hansen, 1933; *Orlando di Lasso's Antwerp Motet Book*, Nijhoff, 1937; *Secret Chromatic Art in the Netherlands Motet*, Columbia University Press, 1946; (editor of facsimile edition) N. Vicentino, *L'antica musica ridotta alla moderna prattica* [Rome], 1955; *Tonality and Atonality in Sixteenth-Century Music*, foreword by Igor Stravinsky, University of California Press, 1961, revised edition, 1962; *Renaissance Image of Man and the World*, Ohio State University Press, 1965; *Aspects of the Eighteenth Century*, Johns Hopkins Press, 1965; (editor) *The Medici Codex of 1518*, three volumes, University of Chicago Press, 1968. Contributor of articles to music journals in United States, France, Belgium, and Holland, and to *Journal of the History of Ideas* and *Art Bulletin*. General editor, "Monuments of Renaissance Music," University of Chicago Press, 1964—.

WORK IN PROGRESS: A book, *Orgins of Musical Expression*.

SIDELIGHTS: A reviewer for the *Times Literary Supplement* commented on *The Medici Codex of 1518*, "To an already distinguished series of modern editions of Renaissance music, whose general editor is Professor Edward Lowinsky, these three volumes of the *Medici Codex* now add abundant as well as elegant testimony regarding the particular capabilities of the prime mover and inspirer of this enterprise." The reviewer calls the books a "vast and impressive *magnum opus*, certainly the largest of Professor Lowinsky's notable contributions to scholarship so far, and the work by which he deserves to be known as an indefatigable and devoted researcher in an area of study that is ever revealing new treasures and unsuspected riches."

Lowinsky is competent in German, Dutch, French, Italian, Spanish, Greek, and Latin.

*   *   *

LOWREY, P(errin) H(olmes)   1923-1965

PERSONAL: Born November 20, 1923, in Verona, Miss.; son of Perrin and Erin (Taylor) Lowrey; married Janet Kelso, February 3, 1945; children: Anne Kelso, Mark Perrin. *Education:* University of the South, A.B., 1947; University of Chicago, A.M., 1948, Ph.D., 1956. *Agent:* Lurton Blassingame, 10 East 43rd St., New York, N.Y. 10017. *Office:* University of Chicago, Chicago, Ill. 60637.

CAREER: San Jose State College (now California State University), San Jose, Calif., instructor in English, 1949-50; Vassar College, Poughkeepsie, N.Y., assistant professor of English, 1952-57; University of Chicago, Chicago, Ill., associate professor of English, 1957-65. *Military service:* U.S. Navy, 1942-46; served aboard destroyers in the Pacific theater. *Member:* Modern Language Association of America, American Association of University Professors. *Awards, honors:* Ford Foundation fellowship, 1954-55; two writing fellowships to Yaddo, Saratoga Springs, N.Y.; Inland Steel fellowship, 1964.

WRITINGS: The Great Speckled Bird and Other Stories, Regnery, 1964. Short stories anthologized in *Stanford Short Stories*, 1951, and *O. Henry Memorial Award Prize Short Stories*, 1954, and an article in *English Institute Essays 1952*, Columbia University Press, 1954. Contributor to *Accent, Saturday Evening Post, Sewanee Review, Epoch, Perspectives, New City, Chicago Tribune, Modern Age*, and other journals.

WORK IN PROGRESS: A novel; a book on William Faulkner.

(Died June 24, 1965)

LUCAS, D(onald) W(illiam)   1905-

PERSONAL: Born May 12, 1905, in London, England; son of Frank William (a headmaster) and Ada (Blackmur) Lucas; married Mary Irene Cohen, December 20, 1933; children: Susan Elizabeth, Peter David. *Education:* King's College, Cambridge, B.A. (honors), 1927. *Politics:* Left-center. *Religion:* Agnostic. *Office:* King's College, Cambridge University, Cambridge, England.

CAREER: Cambridge University, Cambridge, England, fellow of King's College, 1929—. lecturer in classics, 1933-52, director of studies in classics, King's College, 1937-65, Perceval Maitland Laurence Reader in Classics, 1952-69. Served with British Foreign Office, 1940-44.

WRITINGS: The Greek Tragic Poets, Cohen & West, 1950, 2nd edition, 1959, Norton, 1964; *A Commentary on Aristotle's "Poetics"*, Oxford University Press, 1968.

Translator of Euripides—All published by Cohen & West: *Bacchae*, 1930, *Medea*, 1949, *Ion*, 1949, *Alcestis*, 1951, *Electra*, 1951. Contributor to *Encyclopaedia Britannica, Oxford Classical Dictionary*, and to classical journals. Editor, *Classical Quarterly*, 1953-59.

AVOCATIONAL INTERESTS: Travel, reading.

*   *   *

LUCAS, Darrel B(laine)   1902-

PERSONAL: Born September 26, 1902, in Greene, Iowa; son of Leonard and Ursula More (Whitten) Lucas; married Dorothy Elizabeth Carl, December 24, 1924; children: Ann Harriet Ried. *Education:* Iowa State University, B.S., 1922, M.S., 1923; Rutgers University, graduate study, 1925-26; New York University, Ph.D., 1928. *Politics:* Independent Republican. *Religion:* Protestant. *Home:* 20 Sunset Park, Upper Montclair, N.J. 07043. *Office:* Graduate School of Business Administration, New York University, 100 Trinity Place, New York, N.Y. 10006.

CAREER: Rutgers University, New Brunswick, N.J., instructor, 1924-27, assistant professor of agricultural engineering, 1927-29; Iowa State University, Ames, associate professor of psychology, 1929-30; New York University, New York, N.Y., associate professor, 1930-42, professor of marketing, 1942—, chairman of department, 1950—. Licensed psychologist, New York State. Consultant to Batten, Barton, Durstine & Osborn, 1943-68, A. C. Nielsen Co., 1959-64. Advertising Research Foundation, technical director, 1944-59. Co-inventor of automatic plow. *Member:* American Psychological Association (fellow), American Marketing Association, Market Research Council of New York (president, 1943-44), Copy Research Council of New York.

WRITINGS: (With C. E. Benson) *Psychology for Advertisers*, Harper, 1930; (with Paul W. Stewart and others) *A Study of the Market Characteristics and the Magazine Reading Habits of Cleveland Housewives*, Family Circle, 1943; (with Steuart Henderson Britt) *Advertising Psychology and Research: An Introductory Book*, McGraw, 1950; *How Is Your Cost Per Thousand?* (booklet), Advertising Research Foundation, 1956; (with Britt) *Measuring Advertising Effectiveness*, McGraw, 1963; (with Arno H. Johnson and Gilbert E. Jones) *The American Market of the Future*, New York University Press, 1966.

Contributor of chapters to several books, including *New Essays in Marketing Theory*, by George Fisk, Allyn & Bacon, 1971. Contributor of articles to professional publications and trade journals.

WORK IN PROGRESS: Another advertising book for trade and teaching.

AVOCATIONAL INTERESTS: His farm near Nashua, Iowa.

BIOGRAPHICAL/CRITICAL SOURCES: Times Literary Supplement, March 9, 1967.

* * *

LUCAS, Jason 1904-

PERSONAL: Born 1904, in Yorkshire, England; married Iris La Mont. *Politics:* Registered Democrat, usually votes Republican. *Religion:* Episcopalian. *Office:* c/o *Sports Afield*, 959 Eighth Ave., New York, N.Y. 10019.

CAREER: Began working career as cowboy in the mountains of Arizona; found this too confining, so became professional wolf trapper and, later, lion hunter and fisherman. Designer of fishing tackle and long-distance electric pedal release for cameras. *Wartime service:* Undercover work for U.S. Army, World War II. *Member:* Freemason (past patron of Eastern Star).

WRITINGS: Lucas on Bass Fishing, Dodd, 1947, 3rd revised and enlarged edition, 1962. Author of earlier books, all novels, published mainly in New York, England, and Australia. Contributor of short stories and serials to national magazines. Angling editor, *Sports Afield*, 1943—.

WORK IN PROGRESS: Continuous research in piscatorial matters—"which some unkindly call 'just fishing.'"

SIDELIGHTS: Lucas is a self-described life-long gypsy, with no permanent address. About his current wanderings, he writes: "It's just that my wife and I spend most of our time in a mobile home that has itchy wheels. . . . I fish the north in the summer, the south in winter. . . . [I] shoot my own photos for illustrations with long-distance electric pedal release I devised—including photos of myself with leaping fish. [I] have made many thousand such action pictures for publication." Lucas says that his fishing time has averaged well over eight hours a day, 365 days a year, for many years.

* * *

LUDLUM, Robert P(hillips) 1909-

PERSONAL: Born January 13, 1909, in Brooklyn, N.Y.; son of Walter Denton (a physician) and Irene (Daniell) Ludlum; married Ruth A. Smith, September 20, 1930; children: Susan A., Margaret D. (Mrs. Masanori Hashimoto). *Education:* Cornell University, B.A., 1930, M.A., 1932, Ph.D., 1935. *Religion:* Presbyterian. *Home:* 901 Randell Rd., Severna Park, Md. 21146. *Office:* Anne Arundel Community College, 101 College Parkway, Arnold, Md. 21012.

CAREER: Texas A&M College (now University), College Station, instructor, 1935-37, assistant professor of history and political science, 1937-39; Cornell University, Ithaca, N.Y., research associate, 1939-40; Hofstra College (now University), Hempstead, N.Y., assistant professor, 1940-42; American Association of University Professors, Washington, D.C., associate secretary, 1942-47; Antioch College, Yellow Springs, Ohio, vice-president, 1947-49; Blackburn College, Carlinville, Ill., president, 1949-65; Adelphi University, Garden City, N.Y., dean of College of Arts and Sciences, 1965-68; Anne Arundel Community College, Arnold, Md., president, 1968—. Member of Illinois State Certification Board, 1952-62; president, Presbyterian College Union, 1957-58; Federation of Illinois Colleges, vice-president, 1957-59, president, 1960-62; chairman of board, Associated Colleges of Illinois, 1961-65; U.S. State Department specialist in Israel, Pakistan, and India, 1963; member of Board of Christian Education, United Presbyterian Church in the U.S.A.

MEMBER: American Historical Association, Organization of American Historians, American Association of University Professors, Cornell Club (New York). *Awards, honors:* L.H.D., Lincoln College, Lincoln, Ill.

WRITINGS: (With Howard B. Wilder and Harriett M. Brown) *This Is America's Story*, Houghton, 1948, revised edition, 1963; (with Franklin Patterson, Eber W. Jeffery, and Allen Schick) *American Government*, Houghton, 1965. Contributor to journals.

* * *

LUDOVICI, Anthony M(ario) 1882-19(?)
(Cobbett, Huntley Paterson, David Valentine)

PERSONAL: Born January 8, 1882, in London, England; son of Albert (an artist) and Marie (Cals) Ludovici; married Elsie Finnimore Buckley, March 20, 1920 (died, 1959). *Education:* Educated privately in England and abroad. *Politics:* Conservative. *Home:* 197 Henley Rd., Ipswich, Suffolk, England.

CAREER: Started life as an artist, illustrated various books and was for some time private secretary to Auguste Rodin, but, under the influence of a schoolmaster with strong literary tastes, abandoned a career in graphic arts for one in literature. Lecturer on the philosophy of Nietzsche. *Military service:* British Artillery and Intelligence officer, 1914-19; became captain; received Order of the British Empire (military), but resigned the award after demobilization. *Member:* Society of Authors, Society of the Teachers of the Alexander Technique, Ipswich Art Club, Sesame Club, Naval and Military Club.

WRITINGS: (Illustrator) Mary Kernahan, *Nothing But Nonsense*, J. Bowden, 1898; (illustrator) Lord Alfred Douglas, *The Duke of Berwick*, L. Smithers & Co., 1899; *Who Is to Be Master of the World?: An Introduction to the Philosophy of Friedrich Nietzsche*, T. N. Foulis, 1909; (author of notes) Nietzsche, *Thus Spake Zarathustra*, T. N. Foulis, 1909; *Nietzsche: His Life and Works*, Dodge Publishing Co., 1910; *Nietzsche and Art*, Constable, 1911, J. W. Luce & Co., 1912, reprinted, Haskell House, 1971; *A Defence of Aristocracy: A Text Book for Tories*, Constable, 1915, revised edition, 1933; *Mansel Fellowes* (novel), Grant Richards, 1918; *Catherine Doyle: The Romance of a Thrice-Married Lady* (novel), Hutchinson, 1919.

Too Old for Dolls (novel), Hutchinson, 1920, Putnam, 1921; *Man's Descent from the Gods; or, The Complete Case Against Prohibition*, Knopf, 1921; *What Woman Wishes* (novel), Hutchinson, 1921; *The False Assumptions of "Democracy"*, Heath Cranton, 1921; *The Goddess That Grew Up*, Hutchinson, 1922; *Woman: A Vindication*, Knopf, 1923, new edition, Constable, 1929; *French Beans*, Hutchinson, 1923; *The Taming of Don Juan*, Hutchinson, 1924; *Lysistrata; or, Woman's Future and Future Woman*, K. Paul, Trench, Trubner & Co., 1924, Dutton, 1925; *Personal Reminiscences of Auguste Rodin*, Lippincott, 1926; *Artist's Life in London and Paris, 1870-1925*, Minton, Balch & Co., 1926; *Man: An Indictment*, Dutton, 1927; *A Defence of Conservatism*, Faber & Gwyer, 1927; *The Night-hoers; or, The Case Against Birth-Control and an*

Alternative, Jenkins, 1928; *The Sanctity of Private Property*, Heath Cranton, 1932; *The Secret of Laughter*, Constable, 1932, Viking, 1933; *Violence, Sacrifice and War*, St. James's Kin, 1933; *Health and Education Though Self-Mastery*, C. A. Watts, 1933; *Creation or Recreation*, St. James's Kin, 1934; *The Choice of a Mate*, John Lane, 1935; (with F. W. Stella Browne and Harry Roberts) *Abortion*, Allen & Unwin, 1935; *Recovery: The Quest of Regenerate National Values*, St. James's Kin, 1935; *The Future of Woman*, K. Paul, Trench, Trubner & Co., 1936; *The Truth About Childbirth: Lay Light on Maternal Morbidity and Mortality*, K. Paul, Trench, Trubner & Co., 1937, Dutton, 1938; (under pseudonym Cobbett) *The Jews, and Jews in England*, Boswell Publishing Co., 1938; (under pseudonym David Valentine) *Poets' Trumpeter* (novel), J. Cape, 1939; *English Liberalism*, English Array, 1939.

The Four Pillars of Health: A Contribution to Post-War Planning, Heath Cranton, 1945; *Enemies of Women: The Origins in Outline of Anglo-Saxon Feminism*, Carroll & Nicholson, 1948; *The Child: An Adult's Problem*, Carroll & Nicholson, 1948; *The Quest of Human Quality: How to Rear Leaders*, Rider & Co., 1952.

Religion for Infidels, Holborn Publishing Co., 1961; *The Specious Origins of Liberalism: The Genesis of a Delusion*, Britons Publishing Co., 1967.

Translator: Nietzsche, *Thoughts Out of Season*, Volume I, T. N. Foulis, 1909; Nietzsche, *The Will to Power*, T. N. Foulis, Volume I, 1909, Volume II, 1910, published in America in one volume, Macmillan, 1924; Nietzsche, *The Twilight of the Idols* [and] *The Antichrist*, T. N. Foulis, 1911; Nietzsche, *The Case of Wagner, Nietzsche Contra Wagner*, [and] *Selected Aphorisms*, T. N. Foulis, 1911; *Ecce Homo: Nietzsche's Autobiography*, T. N. Foulis, 1911, Macmillan (New York), 1930; Elizabeth Foerster-Nietzsche, *The Young Nietzsche*, Heinemann, 1912; (and author of introductory essay) Vincent van Gogh, *The Letters of a Post-Impressionist*, Constable, 1912, Houghton, 1913; Nietzsche, *Selected Letters*, Doubleday, 1921; (and editor) August Ludolf Friedrich Schaumann, *On the Road with Wellington*, Heinemann, 1924, Knopf, 1925.

Translator under pseudonym Huntley Paterson: Johannes von Guenther, *Cagliostro*, Heinemann, 1928, Harper, 1929; Alfred Neumann, *The Devil*, Knopf, 1928 (published in England as *The Deuce*, Heinemann, 1928, new and revised edition, Hutchinson, 1948); Alfred Neumann, *The Rebels*, Knopf, 1929; Joseph Delmont, *In Chains*, Hutchinson, 1929; Otto Forst de Battaglia, editor, *Dictatorship on Its Trial*, Harrap, 1930, Harcourt, 1931; Gustav Frenssen, *Otto Babendeik*, Harrap, 1930; Alfred Neumann, *Guerra*, Knopf, 1930; Felix Salten, *The Hound of Florence*, Simon & Schuster, 1930; Josef Kastein, *The Messiah of Ismir: Sabbatai Levi*, Viking, 1931; Alfred Neumann, *The Hero: The Tale of a Political Murder*, Knopf, 1931; Karl Silex, *John Bull at Home*, Harcourt, 1931; Horst Treusch von Buttlar-Brandenfeis, *Zeppelins Over England*, Harrap, 1931, Harcourt, 1932; Carl von Westheimer, *Cleopatra: A Royal Voluptuary*, Harrap, 1931; Essad-Bey, *Stalin*, Viking, 1932; Josef Kastein, *History and Destiny of the Jews*, Viking, 1933.

Contributor to *New Age, New English Weekly, Fortnightly Review, Cornhill, Hibbert Journal, South African Observer*, and other periodicals.

SIDELIGHTS: Ludovici told *CA*: "I have long been an opponent and critic of Christianity, Democracy and Anarchy in art and literature. I am particularly opposed to 'Abstract Art,' which I trace to Whistler's heretical doctrines of art and chiefly to his denial that the subject matters, his assimilation of the graphic arts and music, and his insistence on the superior importance of the composition and colour-harmony of a picture, over its representational content."

(Deceased)

*   *   *

LUDOWYK, E(velyn) F(rederick) C(harles)   1906-

PERSONAL: Born October 18, 1906, in Kandy, Ceylon; son of Evelyn Frederick and Ida May (Andree) Ludowyk; married Edith Gyomroi (a psychoanalyst), August 18, 1941. *Education:* University College, Ceylon, B.A., 1928; Cambridge University, B.A., 1932, M.A., 1934, Ph.D., 1936. *Home:* 11 Kidderpore Gardens, London N.W. 3, England.

CAREER: University of Ceylon, Peradeniya, professor of English, 1936-56; now living and writing in London, England.

WRITINGS: Marginal Comments, Ola Book Co., 1945; (editor and compiler) Robert Knox, *Robert Knox in the Kandyan Kingdom*, Oxford University Press, 1948; *The Footprint of the Buddha*, Allen & Unwin, 1958; *The Story of Ceylon*, Faber, 1962, 2nd edition, 1967, published as *A Short History of Ceylon*, Praeger, 1967; *Understanding Shakespeare*, Cambridge University Press, 1962; *The Modern History of Ceylon*, Praeger, 1966.

Editor of plays by Shakespeare, all published by Cambridge University Press: *Twelfth Night*, 1963, *Macbeth*, 1964, *The Merchant of Venice*, 1964, *Julius Caesar*, 1965, *Henry V*, 1966, *Richard II*, 1968.

*   *   *

LUNDBERG, (Edgar) Ferdinand   1905-

PERSONAL: Born April 30, 1905, in Chicago, Ill.; son of Otto Ferdinand (a business executive) and Hannah (Svendsen) Lundberg; married Elizabeth Young, September 20, 1944; children: Randolph Horner, Laurence Young. *Education:* Studied at Chicago City College, 1922-24, New York University, 1934-35; Columbia University, B.S., 1948, M.A., 1956. *Politics:* Independent. *Home:* 598 Quaker Rd., Chappaqua, N.Y. 10514.

CAREER: New York Herald Tribune, New York, N.Y., financial writer, 1927-34; U.S. War Production Board, Washington, D.C., economist, 1941-45; Twentieth Century Fund, New York, N.Y., editor, 1946-52; New York University, New York, N.Y., adjunct professor of philosophy, 1952-68. Carnegie Institute of Technology, Pittsburgh, Pa., visiting associate professor, 1956-57; Brooklyn Institute of Arts and Sciences, Brooklyn, N.Y., lecturer, 1959-60. Committee for Cultural Freedom, executive secretary, 1939-41; Conference on Methods in Philosophy and the Sciences, secretary, 1959-61. *Member:* American Philosophical Association, American Sociological Association (fellow), American Association for the Advancement of Science, New York University Faculty Club.

WRITINGS: Imperial Hearst: A Social Biography, Equinox Cooperative Press, 1936, reissued with a preface by Charles Beard, Arno, 1970; *America's Sixty Families*, Vanguard, 1937; *Who Controls Industry? And Other Questions Raised by the Critics of "America's Sixty Families,"* with a Note on the Case of Richard Whitney, Vanguard, 1938; (with Marynia F. Farnham) *Modern Woman: The Lost Sex*, Harper, 1947; *The Treason of the People*, Harper, 1954; *The Coming World Transformation*, Doubleday, 1963; *The Rich and the Super-Rich: A Study in the Power of Money Today*, Lyle Stuart, 1968, revised edition, edited and introduced by Peter Wilsher, Thomas Nelson, 1969; *Scoundrels All: Being a Fulsome Compendium of Observations, Mostly Disenchanted and Dyspeptic, About Politics and Politicians and Their Arcane Doings Down Through the Ages*, Lyle Stuart, 1968. Contributor to magazines.

WORK IN PROGRESS: Analysis of the U.S. Constitution.

SIDELIGHTS: With *Modern Woman: The Lost Sex*, published in 1947, Lundberg and Farnham diagnosed America's ills as the result of the "displacement of women from their maternal role in home and society." Margaret Mead was puzzled by the authors' "savage attack on the feminist movement.... First to label a group as victims and then excoriate them as false prophets and criminals, reveals a confusion which runs through the whole book." "What strikes me most about *Modern Woman: The Lost Sex*, is its cruelty," wrote Frederic Wertham of *New Republic*. "After all, most of what we know about women and their share of the suffering in the world is universally human and not specifically female. This book de-humanizes the whole question and treats women in a way that is belittling, unfair and fundamentally untrue. Its central fault is a total lack of social imagination." Philip Wylie believed it "the best book yet to be written about women.... Never before have certain of the basic laws of psychology been applied so discerningly to women, and to our civilized predicament."

Lundberg first attacked "the modern industrial oligarchy which dominates the United States" in *America's Sixty Families*, in which he hypothesized that there were roughly sixty families in this country which controlled government and economic conditions by virtue of their wealth. L. H. Hacker of *Nation* called it "a very important book" which placed Lundberg in the company of American "prophets."

"Lundberg's gaudy 1937 tilt at the Nation's moneyed windmills," as Frank Porter of the *Washington Post* described *America's Sixty Families*, is updated and reassessed in *The Rich and the Super-Rich: A Study in the Power of Money Today*. "His verdict [wrote Porter]: *Plus ca change, plus c'est la meme chose*. He claims America's power elite is practically the same as it was 30 years ago." Author of a book similar to Lundberg's, *Who Rules America?*, G. William Domhoff comes to "much the same conclusion" as Lundberg about financial power in the U.S. today; i.e., a large percentage of American wealth (read "control") lies with a small, static portion of the population. Several critics disagree with Lundberg's central thesis while finding his material "fascinating." Isidore Silver considers *The Rich and the Super-Rich* "a blowsy, overwrought monster of a book," which is, at the same time, "destructive of our generation's conventional wisdom; and that is something worth being." Kenneth E. Boulding of *New York Review of Books* believes "Mr. Lundberg has some important things to say" about the power structure in this country, "and a great deal of what he has to say is probably true."

America's Sixty Families has been translated into German, Dutch, Czech, and Chinese, *Modern Woman: The Lost Sex*, into Swedish and Finnish, and *The Rich and the Super-Rich* into fifteen languages, including Russian, Turkish, and Japanese.

AVOCATIONAL INTERESTS: Sailing, swimming, fishing, ice skating.

BIOGRAPHICAL/CRITICAL SOURCES: New York Times, November 21, 1937, January 26, 1947; *Saturday Review*, November 27, 1937, February 1, 1947, May 4, 1963; *Nation*, January 22, 1938, August 19, 1968; *New Republic*, February 10, 1947, October 12, 1968; *Christian Science Monitor*, April 13, 1963; *Washington Post*, August 6, 1968; *New York Review of Books*, September 12, 1968.

* * *

LUTZ, Alma 1890-

PERSONAL: Born March 2, 1890, in Jamestown, N.D.; daughter of George (a lumber company president) and Matilda (Bauer) Lutz. *Education:* Emma Willard School, graduate, 1908; Vassar College, A.B., 1912; Boston University, graduate student, 1918. *Politics:* Democrat. *Religion:* Christian Scientist. *Home:* Highmeadow, Berlin, N.Y. 12022; and 22 River St., Boston, Mass. 02108.

CAREER: Free-lance writer. Worker for women's suffrage, 1913-18. Member of advisory board, Schlesimeer Library on Women in America, Radcliffe College, 1951—; chairman of trustees, Zion Research Library for Study of Bible and History of Christian Church; board member, White House Memorial Library. Secretary, Massachusetts Committee for Equal Rights Amendment. *Member:* Authors League, American Historical Society, National Federation of Business and Professional Women's Clubs, National Woman's Party (member of national council, 1930-46, 1959—), American Association of University Women, Associated Alumnae of Vassar College, College Club and Women's City Club (both Boston). *Awards, honors:* Litt.D., Russell Sage College, 1959, for biographies of American women.

WRITINGS: Emma Willard, Daughter of Democracy, Houghton, 1929; *Mary Baker Eddy Historical House, Swampscott, Massachusetts: The Birthplace of Christian Science*, Longyear Foundation, 1935; *Mary Baker Eddy Historical House, Rumney Village, New Hampshire: The Rumney Years*, Longyear Foundation, 1940; *Created Equal: A Biography of Elizabeth Cady Stanton, 1815-1902*, John Day, 1940; (with Harriot Blatch) *Challenging Years: The Memoirs of Harriot Stanton Blatch*, Putnam, 1940; (editor) *With Love, Jane: Letters of American Women on the War Fronts*, John Day, 1945; *Susan B. Anthony: Rebel, Crusader, Humanitarian*, Beacon Press, 1959; *Emma Willard, Pioneer Educator of American Women*, Beacon Press, 1964; *Crusade for Freedom: Women of the Antislavery Movement*, Beacon Press, 1968. *Equal Rights*, contributing editor, 1933-46, regular columnist, 1938-46; contributor to *Christian Science Monitor* and to periodicals.

AVOCATIONAL INTERESTS: Golf, the outdoors, theatre, and classical music.

BIOGRAPHICAL/CRITICAL SOURCES: Christian Science Monitor, July 17, 1959, July 3, 1968; *New York Times*, July 17, 1968.

* * *

LYMAN, Albert Robison 1880-1973 (The Old Settler)

PERSONAL: Born January 10, 1880, in Fillmore, Utah; son of Platte D. (a stockman) and Adelia (Robison) Lyman; married second wife, Gladys Perkins, July 14, 1949; children: (first marriage) fifteen. *Education:* Educated in frontier district school in San Juan County, Utah, through correspondence courses and reading while riding the range, and summer study at Brigham Young University and University of Utah. *Politics:* Republican. *Religion:* Church of Jesus Christ of Latter-day Saints (Mormon). *Address:* P.O. Box 136, 29 North Third West, Blanding, Utah.

CAREER: Lyman was taken to a Utah frontier post as an infant in 1880, rode after cattle on the Pagahrit Range in his teens, and went to England as a Mormon missionary, 1899-1900; was first settler in Blanding, Utah, in 1905 (population now 1,805), taught in schools and Latter-day Saints seminaries for twenty-seven years; farmed, raised cattle, and continued to work as a missionary to five Indian tribes throughout his active life; at one time an editor and manager of *San Juan Record,* San Juan County, Utah, and writer (as a "sideline") for fifty years; devoted his last years wholly to writing and church activities.

WRITINGS: Voice of the Intangible, Deseret News Press, 1936, revised edition published as *Man to Man,* Deseret News Press, 1963; *Indians and Outlaws,* Bookcraft, 1964; *The Native Blood,* Deseret, 1964; *Outlaw of Navajo Mountain,* Deseret, 1965; *The Edge of the Cedars,* Carlton, 1965. Also the author of *The Great Adventure,* 1971, and *Trails of the Ancients,* 1972. Contributor of more than fourteen hundred articles and stories, under byline of The Old Settler, to *San Juan Record* since 1925.

WORK IN PROGRESS: Lyman once said: "It is my practice, with any heavy work, to put it away to cool, and go over it again before offering it for sale. At present I am much absorbed in revising a 100,000 word story which has been cooling since 1959. If I live long enough, I shall get two others out of the 'fridge.'"

SIDELIGHTS: Lyman told *CA:* "The main part of my writings has been with no thought or concern for publication. I began in 1904 to write what I had thought out, beyond what I had heard or read. Thirty years later it became an unfailing practice of every day ... [to record ideas on] history, science, literature, and religion. I nail the thought in shorthand when it strikes me, and type it as soon as I can. These 54 volumes are called THOTS."

The "THOTS" were the basis for six books that Lyman was holding for posthumous publication. They were, he said, of greater volume and deeper thought than his other works, dealing with religious history and principles of immortal purpose.

Lyman's decendants include 12 married children, 76 grandchildren, 175 great-grandchildren, and 18 great-great-grandchildren.

(Died November 12, 1973)

* * *

LYNCH, Patricia (Nora) 1900-1972

PERSONAL: Born June 7, 1900, in Cork City, Ireland; daughter of Timothy Patrick (a businessman) and Nora (Lynch) Lynch; married Richard Michael Fox (an author), October 31, 1922. *Education:* Educated at convent school, and at secular schools in Ireland, Scotland, England, and Belgium. *Residence:* Dublin, Ireland. *Adress:* c/o J.M. Dent & Sons Ltd., Aldine House, 10-13 Bedford St., London W.C.2, England.

CAREER: Author of children's books. *Christian Commonwealth,* London, England, staff member, writing feature stories and other articles, 1918-20. *Member:* P.E.N. (Dublin; delegate to P.E.N. Congress in Vienna), Irish Women Writers Club. *Awards, honors:* Silver Medal. Aonac Tailtean, for *The Cobbler's Apprentice;* London

Junior Book Club annual award, for *The Turf-Cutter's Donkey;* Irish Women Writers' Club annual award, for *Fiddler's Quest.*

WRITINGS: The Green Dragon, Harrap, 1925; *The Cobbler's Apprentice,* Harold Shaylor, 1930; *The Turf-Cutter's Donkey: An Irish Story of Mystery and Adventure,* Dent, 1934; Dutton, 1935; *The Turf-Cutter's Donkey Goes Visiting: The Story of an Island Holiday,* Dent, 1935, published in America as *The Donkey Goes Visiting: The Story of an Island Holiday,* Dutton, 1936; *King of the Tinkers,* Dutton, 1938; *The Turf-Cutter's Donkey Kicks Up His Heels,* Dutton, 1939; *The Grey Goose of Kilnevin,* Dent, 1939, Dutton, 1940.

Fiddler's Quest, Dent, 1941, Dutton, 1943; *Long Ears,* Dent, 1943; *Knights of God: Stories of the Irish Saints* (Children's Book Club selection), Hollis & Carter, 1945, Regnery, 1955, new edition published as *Knights of God: Tales and Legends of the Irish Saints,* Bodley Head, 1967, Holt, 1969; *Strangers at the Fair, and other Stories,* Browne & Nolan, 1945; *A Story-Teller's Childhood* (autobiographical), Dent, 1947, Norton, 1962; *The Mad O'-Haras,* Dent, 1948 published in America as *Grania of Castle O'Hara,* L.C. Page & Co. 1952; *Lisbeen at the Valley Farm, and Other Stories,* Gayfield Press, 1949.

The Seventh Pig, and Other Irish Fairy Tales, Dent, 1950, new edition published as *The Black Goat of Slievemore, and Other Irish Fairy Tales,* 1959; *The Dark Sailor of Youghal,* Dent, 1951; *The Boy at the Swinging Lantern,* Dent, 1952, Bentley, 1953; *Tales of Irish Enchantment,* Clonmore & Reynolds, 1952; *Delia Daly of Galloping Green,* Dent, 1953; *Orla of Burren,* Dent, 1954; *Tinker Boy,* Dent, 1955; *The Bookshop of the Quay,* Dent, 1956; *Fiona Leaps the Bonfire,* Dent, 1957; *Shane Comes to Dublin,* Criterion, 1958; *The Old Black Sea Chest: A Story of Bantry Bay,* Dent, 1958; *Jinny the Changeling,* Dent, 1959; *The Runaways,* Basil Blackwell, 1959.

Sally from Cork, Dent, 1960; *Ryan's Fort,* Dent, 1961; *The Golden Caddy,* Dent, 1962; *The House by Lough Neagh,* Dent, 1963; *Holiday at Rosquin,* Dent, 1964; *The Twisted Key, and Other Stories,* Harrap, 1964; *Mona of the Isle,* Dent, 1965; *The Kerry Caravan,* Dent, 1967; *Back of Beyond,* Dent, 1967.

"Brogeen" series, all published by Burke Publishing, except as indicated: *Brogeen of the Stepping Stones,* Kerr-Cross Publishing Co., 1947, *Brogeen Follows the Magic Tune,* 1952, Macmillan (New York), 1968, *Brogeen and the Green Shoes,* 1953, *Brogeen and the Bronze Lizard,* 1954, Macmillan (New York), 1970, *Brogeen and the Princess of Sheen,* 1955, *Brogeen and the Lost Castle,* 1956, *Cobbler's Luck* (short stories), 1957, *Brogeen and the Black Enchanter,* 1958, *The Stone House at Kilgobbin,* 1959, *The Lost Fisherman of Carrigmor,* 1960, *The Longest Way Round,* 1961, *Brogeen and the Little Wind,* 1962, Roy, 1963, *Brogeen and the Red Fez,* 1963, *Guests at the Beech Tree,* 1964.

WORK IN PROGRESS: A book with Isle of Man background, for Dent; another "Brogeen" book for Burke Publishing Co.

SIDELIGHTS: Her fantasies, most of them based in Ireland, have reached children of many lands. In French editions, Brogeen (a leprechaun) has been renamed Korik, a creature of Bregon folklore. Eight books have been translated into French, four into Gaelic, five into Dutch, others into German, Swedish, and Malay. *Brogeen and the Little Wind* was dramatized in six installments for the British

Broadcasting Corporation "Children's Hour," and *The Mad O'Haras* was dramatized for a television series; other stories have been adapted for radio and issued in Braille.

BIOGRAPHICAL/CRITICAL SOURCES: Junior Bookshelf, March, 1943, March, 1949; Patricia Lynch, *A Story-Teller's Childhood*, Dent, 1947. *Times Literary Supplement*, May 25, 1967; *Library Journal*, July 1969, May 1970; *Books and Bookmen*, February 1970.

(Died September 1, 1972)

*   *   *

LYON, Quinter M(arcellus) 1898-

PERSONAL: Born June 10, 1898, in Washington, D.C.; son of William Marcellus (a minister) and Fannie (Stoner) Lyon; married Ruth Beekley (a musician), September 2, 1925; children: Donna (Mrs. Gilbert Lloyd Keck), David Beekley. *Education:* George Washington University, A.B., 1920; Princeton Theological Seminary, Th.B., 1923, M.Div., 1970; Princeton University, M.A., 1923; Ohio State University, Ph.D., 1933. *Politics:* Democrat. *Religion:* Methodist. *Home:* 1370 Manzanita Ave., Chico, Calif. 95926.

CAREER: Brethren Publishing Co., Ashland, Ohio, editor-in-chief of church school literature, 1923-30; Ohio State University, Columbus, instructor in philosophy, 1930-34; MacMurray College, Jacksonville, Ill., acting professor of philosophy and religion, 1934-35; Minot State Teachers College (now Minot State College), Minot, N.D., professor of philosophy and government, 1935-47, chairman of Division of Social Science, 1938-47, dean of Senior College, 1945-47; University of Mississippi, University, associate professor, 1946-47, professor of philosophy, 1947-63, professor emeritus, 1963—; California State University, Chico, professor of philosophy, 1962-68, professor emeritus, 1968—. Fulbright professor at University of Panama, 1959-60; lecturer at University of San Andres, Bolivia, and Univeristy of San Carlos, Guatemala, 1960. Organist or minister of music at various Brethren and Methodist churches, 1914—.

MEMBER: American Philosophical Association, Metaphysical Society of America, American Association of University Professors, Southern Society for Philosophy and Psychology, Southern Society for Philosophy of Religion, Mississippi Philosophy Association (founder; president, 1949-51), Phi Delta Kappa, Phi Sigma Tau, (vice-president, 1966-68; president, 1968-71), Masons, Rotary International. *Awards, honors:* Fulbright grant, 1959-60; American Council of Learned Societies travel grant.

WRITINGS: The Great Religions, Odyssey, 1957; *Ensayos Sobre la Filosofia Social*, Panama America (Panama), 1960; *Quiet Strength from World Religions*, Harper, 1960, published as *Meditations from World Religions*, Abingdon, 1966. Contributor to professional journals in English and Spanish, and to the proceedings of Inter-American Congress of Philosophy, 1961. Associate editor of *Dialogue*.

WORK IN PROGRESS: Philosophical poetry, *Religion Comes of Age for Planet Earth*; the story of his own philosophizing; revisions of existing publications.

SIDELIGHTS: Lyon has taught, lectured, and published in Spanish.

*   *   *

LYONS, Sister Jeanne Marie 1904-

PERSONAL: Born April 1, 1904, in Baltimore, Md.; daughter of William Patrick and Mary (Carroll) Lyons. *Education:* College of Notre Dame of Maryland, B.A., 1926; Catholic University of America, M.A., 1938, Ph.D., 1940. *Home:* Maryknoll Sisters Motherhouse, Maryknoll, N.Y. 10545.

CAREER: Roman Catholic religious of Maryknoll order. Mary Rogers College, Maryknoll, N.Y., president, 1957—. *Member:* Delta Epsilon Sigma.

WRITINGS: (Translator) Reginald Garrigou-Lagrange, *The Love of God and the Cross of Jesus*, Herder, Volume I, 1947, Volume II, 1951; *Maryknoll's First Lady*, Dodd, 1964.

Contributor to *Catholic School Journal, Field Afar, Thomist, Sign*, and *Commonweal*.

*   *   *

LYTLE, Ruby (Coker) 1917-19(?)

PERSONAL: Born February 15, 1917, in Glendale, Calif.; daughter of Edgar (a plumber) and Effie (Myers) Coker; married Marcus Zearing Lytle (a mailman, and teacher of creative poetry and naturalization classes), December 17, 1942; children: Monica Hope. *Education:* Glendale Junior College (now Glendale College), student, 1935-38. *Politics:* Democrat. *Religion:* Protestant. *Home:* 2555 Encinal Ave., Montrose, Calif. 91020.

CAREER: Private secretary or office clerical worker in Glendale, Calif., 1938-42, 1946-49, in war plants and at military installation in California, 1943-46.

WRITINGS: (Self-illustrated) *What Is the Moon?* (Japanese haiku sequence), Tuttle, 1965. Contributor of articles and short stories to *Western Family* and *Young Heart*, and of some two hundred poems to *Saturday Evening Post, Opinion, American Bard, Cats, Oakland Tribune, Desert, Poetry Caravan*, and other periodicals.

WORK IN PROGRESS: "The Harp and the Willow," a book-length Pindaric ode; a book of short stories; sonnets and poems about cats; three haiku books.

SIDELIGHTS: Mrs. Lytle wrote to *CA:* "Ever since I can remember I have wanted to write more than anything else. I remember sending a dog story to the *Post* when I was nine years old. . . . I early decided to become a scientist. I devoted all my waking time toward becoming a tropical research scientist, preferably in the Amazon jungles. . . . When I was seventeen my intense interest in science and discovery of Evolution made me break violently and painfully with my religious training. I became an atheist, I thought, and then an agnostic. I delved into exotic religions, practiced Yoga, burned butter lamps, and finally decided to set up Science as my God. Years later I felt Science, too, had let me down. I worked out a practical religion of my own, based on the ethics of Christianity. . . . I made a term paper in college on Lafcadio Hearn. It made a deep impression on me—how much I did not realize until I began these little Japanese Haiku."

(Deceased)

*   *   *

LYTTLE, G(erald) R(oland) 1908-

PERSONAL: Born October 2, 1908, in Bangor, Northern Ireland; son of Roland Alexander (an advertising manager) and Margaret (Keelan) Lyttle; married Letty Todd, July 17, 1937; children: Lorna, Tony. *Education:* College of Preceptors, London, England, Associate of College of Preceptors,

1933; Trinity College, Dublin, Ireland, M.A., 1939; Queen's University and Stranmillis Training College, Belfast, Ireland, higher diploma in education, 1940. *Home:* Ashlola, Bradshaw's Brae, Newtownards, Northern Ireland. *Office:* Movilla Secondary School, Newtownards, Northern Ireland.

CAREER: Movilla Secondary School, Newtownards, Northern Ireland, headmaster, 1945—. Organizer of house-parties and "travel abroad" groups for young people; speaker at youth rallies and youth leaders' conventions.

WRITINGS: Curlews at Culver's Cove, Pickering & Inglis, 1957; *Curlews on the Continent*, Pickering & Inglis, 1962. Contributor of "Sunday School Lesson Notes" to *Christian Sunday School Magazine.* Author of series of talks on science and school journeys abroad for British Broadcasting Corp., and a series of science talks for South Africa Broadcasting Corp. Contributor of articles and short stories to magazines.

WORK IN PROGRESS: Into Orbit, Christian talks for children based on Space Age science topics; "Time for Teens," a proposed series of Christian chats with youths for broadcasting on Trans-World Radio.

AVOCATIONAL INTERESTS: Motoring, continental travel, and photography (still and cine).

* * *

LYTTON, Noel (Anthony Scawen) 1900-

PERSONAL: Succeeded father as Earl of Lytton, 1951, born April 7, 1900, in London, England; son of Neville Steven (a portrait painter) and Baroness Wentworth; married Clarissa Mary Palmer, November 30, 1946; children: Lady Caroline, Viscount John Knebworth, Honorable Roland, Lady Lucy, Lady Sarah. *Education:* Educated at Downside School and Royal Military College at Sandhurst. *Politics:* Cross bench House of Lords. *Religion:* Catholic. *Home:* Lillycombe, Porlock, Somerset, England.

CAREER: British Army, career service, 1919-46; retired as lieutenant colonel. Served in Kenya, 1922-26, as instructor in economics at Royal Military Academy at Sandhurst, 1931-35, as staff officer, War Office, 1936-39, in England, Scotland, North Africa, Italy, Yugoslavia, Greece and as chief staff officer, British Military government, Vienna, Austria, 1939-46. Farmer and forester, 1959—. Former member, Central Advisory Council for Education. *Awards, honors:* Order of British Empire (military); Greek Distinguished Service medal.

WRITINGS: The Desert and the Green (autobiography), Macdonald & Co., 1957; *Wilfrid Scawen Blunt; A Memoir by His Grandson*, Macdonald & Co., 1961; *Mickla Bendore* (novel), Macdonald & Co., 1962; *Lucia in Taormina: A Sicilian Romance*, Macdonald & Co., 1963; *The Stolen Desert: A Study of the Uhuru in North East Africa*, Macdonald & Co., 1966.

WORK IN PROGRESS: A factual study of Kenya, Somalia, and Ethopia tentatively titled *Kush.*

* * *

MAAS, Willard 1911-1971

PERSONAL: Born June 24, 1911, in Lindsay, Calif.; son of Christian John (a rancher) and Kunigunde (Von Kroells) Maas; married Marie Menken (an artist and film-maker for Time, Inc.), September, 1936 (died December, 1970); children: Stephen. *Education:* San Jose State College (now California State University), student, 1928-31; Long Island University, B.A., 1938; Columbia University, M.A., 1946. *Religion:* Episcopalian. *Home:* Penthouse, 62 Montague St., Brooklyn Heights, N.Y. *Office:* Seton Hall University, South Orange, N.J.

CAREER: Long Island University, Brooklyn, N.Y., instructor in English, 1940-53; Iona College, New Rochelle, N.Y., instructor in English, 1954-57; Wagner College, Staten Island, N.Y., assistant professor of English and director of New York City Writers Conference, 1958-63; with Seton Hall University, South Orange, N.J., 1963-71. Writer and producer of experimental films shown at American and European festivals. *Military service:* U.S. Army. *Member:* Modern Language Association of America, American Association of University Professors. *Awards, honors:* Guarantor's award, Phelan Poetry Prize from *Poetry* (magazine); film festival awards.

WRITINGS: Fire Testament (poetry), Alecestis, 1935; *Concerning the Young* (poetry), Farrar & Rinehart, 1938; (editor and author of text with Dorothy Van Ghent) *The Essential Prose*, Bobbs-Merril, 1965, alternate edition, 1966. Book reviewer for literary reviews and New York newspapers.

Films: "Narcissus"; "Image in the Snow"; others.

WORK IN PROGRESS: World Literature, with Dorothy Van Ghent.

(Died January 2, 1971)

* * *

MacALPINE, Margaret H(esketh Murray) 1907-
(Ann Carmichael)

PERSONAL: Born October 22, 1907, in Linlithgow, Scotland; daughter of William Hutchinson and Helen R. (Dunnachie) Murray; married A. M. MacAlpine (a dental surgeon), August 8, 1935; children: Roderick, Euan, Fiona. *Education:* University of Glasgow, M.A. (honors), 1930. *Home:* Moat Cottage, Newick Lane, Heathfield, Sussex, England.

CAREER: Education Authority, Glasgow, Scotland, teacher, 1935-39. Publisher's reader of children's books. *Member:* Society of Authors (London), Children's Writers Group (London).

WRITINGS: The Hand in the Bag, Faber, 1959; *Dougal and the Wee Folk*, A. S. Barnes, 1960; *The Black Gull of Corrie Lochan*, Faber, 1964, Prentice-Hall, 1965; *Anra the Storm Child*, Faber, 1965. Author of twelve full-length magazine serials and adult romantic fiction; contributor of articles for women and reviews of children's books to newspapers.

WORK IN PROGRESS: A novel set in Sussex; a magazine serial of Scottish interest.

* * *

MacCRACKEN, Henry Noble 1880-1970

PERSONAL: Born November 19, 1880, in Toledo, Ohio; son of Henry Mitchell and Catherine (Hubbard) MacCracken; married Marjorie Dodd, June 12, 1907; children: Maisry, Joy MacCracken Dawson, Calvin D., James. *Education:* New York University, A.B., 1900, A.M., 1904; Harvard University, A.M., 1905, Ph.D., 1907. *Home:* 87 New Hackensack Rd., Poughkeepsie, N.Y.

CAREER: Syrian Protestant College, Beirut, Lebanon, instructor in English, 1900-03; Yale University, New Haven, Conn., instructor in English, 1908-10, assistant professor, Sheffield Scientific School, 1910-13; Smith College, Northampton, Mass., professor of English, 1914-15; Vassar College, Poughkeepsie, N.Y., president, 1915-46, president emeritus, 1946-70. Organizer of National Junior Red Cross and director, 1917-18; president of Kosciuszko Foundation, 1925-50, honorary chairman, 1950-70; chairman of International Conference of Christians and Jews at Oxford, 1946, at Fribourg, 1948; trustee, International Institute of New York City, Inc.; National Conference of Christians and Jews, educational consultant, 1946, general secretary, 1947-48; chairman of trustees, Sarah Lawrence College, 1926-36; trustee of Mackinac College. Associate director, Marine Midland Bank. *Member:* Modern Language Association of America, Phi Beta Kappa, Psi Upsilon. *Awards, honors:* John Harvard fellow, Oxford University, 1907-1908. Honorary degrees from Brown University, New York University, Smith College, Bard College, and Lafayette College.

WRITINGS: First Year English, 1903, 2nd edition, 1905; *The Answere of Adam,* H. Hart, 1908; (with H. S. Canby and others) *English Composition in Theory and Practice,* Macmillan, 1909, 3rd edition, 1931; (editor) John Lydgate, *The Serpent of Division,* Oxford University Press, 1909, Yale University Press, 1911; (with F. Pierce and W. Durham) *An Introduction to Shakespeare,* Macmillan, 1910; (editor) *The Minor Poems of John Lydgate,* Oxford University Press, Part I: *The Lydgate Canon, Religious Poems,* 1911, Part II: *Secular Poems,* 1934, successive editions with title variations; *A Carol for Christmas,* Oxford University Press, 1912; (editor) *The College Chaucer,* Oxford University Press, 1913; (editor with Rucker Brooke and John Cunliffe) *Shakespeare's Principal Plays,* Appleton, 1914, 3rd edition, 1935; (with Helen Sandison) *Manual of Good English,* Macmillan, 1917; *John the Common Weal,* University of North Carolina Press, 1927.

(With Charles Post) *Fair Play,* Vassar College, 1942; *The Family on Gramercy Park,* Scribner, 1948; *The Hickory Limb,* Scribner, 1950; *Old Dutchess Forever! The Story of an American County,* Hastings, 1956; *Blithe Dutchess: The Flowering of an American County from 1912,* Hastings, 1958; *Prologue to Independence: The Trials of James Alexander, 1715-1756,* Heinemann, 1964. Contributor to *Atlantic Monthly, Survey, Harper's,* and other periodicals.

WORK IN PROGRESS: Research in Hudson River Valley history.

(Died May 7, 1970)

*　　*　　*

MACDONALD, Eleanor 1910-

PERSONAL: Born September 1, 1910, in Wanstead, Essex, England; daughter of F. W. (a librarian) and Frances (Glover) Macdonald. *Education:* Academie d'Epee, Paris, France, Maitre d'Armes, 1938; London School of Economics, University of London, B.A. (honors), 1947. *Religion:* Anglican. *Home:* 4 Mapledale Ave., Croydon CRO 5TA, Surrey, England.

CAREER: Free-lance journalist, and operator of fencing schools in London and Croydon, England, 1929-39; British Government, censor, 1939-45; Selfridges (department store), London, England, staff controller, 1945-47; Unilever, London, England, marketing and public relations, 1947-69; free-lance consultant for advising and helping to train professional women, 1969—. *Member:* British Institute of Management, Royal Society of Arts (fellow). *Awards, honors:* Member of Order of British Empire.

WRITINGS: (With Ian Macdonald) *The Art of Fencing,* Foulsham, 1938; (with Anita Christophersen) *Live By Beauty,* Secker & Warburg, 1960; *The Successful Women at Home and in Society,* Allen & Unwin, 1963. Writer of television and radio scripts and articles on women's issues.

SIDELIGHTS: Miss Macdonald has traveled extensively in Europe—initially for fencing and fashion, after World War II to market cosmetics—and in Africa as women's adviser for Unilever.

*　　*　　*

MACDONALD, Zillah K(atherine) 1885-
(Zillah)

PERSONAL: Born January 15, 1885, in Halifax, Nova Scotia, Canada; daughter of John Charles (a colonel) and Annie (MacLearn) Macdonald; married Colin Macdonald. *Education:* Studied at Dalhousie University and Columbia University. *Home:* 468 Riverside Dr., New York, N.Y. 10027; and (summer) Blinkbonnie, Swan's Island, Me. 04685. *Agent:* Howard Moorepark, 444 East 82nd St., New York, N.Y. 10021.

CAREER: Dalhousie University, Halifax, Nova Scotia, secretary, 1906-13; Columbia University, University Extension, General Studies, and School of Business, New York, N.Y., teacher and lecturer, 1919-49; writer for children. *Member:* Women's National Book Association, Women's Faculty Club of Columbia University.

WRITINGS: Eileen's Adventures in Wordland: The Life Story of Our Word Friends, Stokes, 1920; *Cobblecorners,* Appleton, 1926; *The Bluenose Express,* Appleton, 1928; *Spindlespooks,* Appleton, 1928; *Windywhistle,* Appleton, 1929; *Mic Mac on the Track,* Appleton, 1930; *Haunthouse,* Appleton, 1931; (under pseudonym Zillah) *Little Travelers,* Whitman Publishing, 1937; *The Tin Tin Car,* William Penn, 1937; *Two on a Tow,* Houghton, 1942; *Flower of the Fortress,* Westminster, 1944, reissued as *Prisoner in Louisbourg,* Macmillan (Toronto), 1966; *Marcia, Private Secretary,* Messner, 1949.

A Cap for Corinne, Messner, 1952 (published in England as *Nurse Fairchild's Decision,* Transworld Publishers, 1959); *Fireman for a Day,* Messner, 1952, revised edition, Melmont, 1964; *Courage to Command, a Story of the Capture of Louisbourg,* Winston, 1953; *A Tugboat Toots for Terry,* Messner, 1953, revised edition, Melmont, 1964; *The Mystery of the Piper's Ghost,* Winston, 1954; (with Josie Johnston) *Rosemary Wins Her Cap,* Messner, 1955; (with Johnston) *Roxanne, Industrial Nurse,* Messner, 1957; (with Vivian J. Ahl) *Nurse Todd's Strange Summer,* Messner, 1960.

Plays: (With Estelle Davis) "Dad's Turn"; "The Royal Romance"; (with Victor O'Dwyer) "Two Gentlemen of the Bench"; "Our John"; "The Long Box"; "The Featherfisher"; "Circumventin' Sandy"; "Markheim"; and others.

Contributor: *Day In and Day Out,* Row, Peterson & Co.; *Luck and Pluck,* Heath; *Yesterday and Today,* Silver Burdette; *Over Hill and Plain,* Silver Burdette; *With New Friends,* Silver Burdette; *Finding New Neighbors,* Ginn. Contributor of a dozen serials and several score short stories to juvenile publications, including *American Girl, Children's Activities, Child Life, Gateway, Jack and Jill, St. Nicholas, Story Parade.*

WORK IN PROGRESS: A book for girls about growing up; a book about Prince Edward Island, Canada.

MACE, C(ecil) Alec 1894-

PERSONAL: Born July 22, 1894, in Norwich, England; son of Walter (a merchant) and Mary (Mace) Mace; married Marjorie Lebus, September 29, 1922; children: David, Paul. Education: Queens' College, Cambridge, B.A., 1915, M.A., 1918. Home: Vale Farm, Hollesley, Woodbridge, England; and 105 Roebuck House, Palace St., London S.W. 1, England.

CAREER: University College (now University of Nottingham), Nottingham, England, lecturer, 1922-25; University of St. Andrews, St. Andrews, Scotland, lecturer, 1925-32; University of London, London, England, reader at Bedford College, 1932-44, professor of psychology at Birkbeck College, 1944-61, became professor emeritus of psychology. Trinity College, Cambridge University, Tarner Lecturer, 1940-41. Member: British Psychological Society (fellow; president, 1952-53), Aristotelian Society (president, 1948-49). Awards, honors: Coronation Medal; D.Litt., University of London; fellow of Birkbeck College, University of London.

WRITINGS: The Psychology of Study, Methuen, 1932, revised edition, Penguin, 1968; The Principles of Logic, Longmans, Green, 1933; Incentives—Some Experimental Studies, H.M.S.O., 1935; (editor and contributor) British Philosophy in the Mid Century, Allen & Unwin, 1957, 2nd edition, 1966. Contributor to Encyclopaedia Britannica, Chambers's Encyclopaedia, British Journal of Psychology, and other journals in philosophy and psychology field. Editor, "Methuen's Manuals of Psychology" and "Pelican Psychology Series."

WORK IN PROGRESS: Preparing Tarner Lectures for publication; a book on interviewing and being interviewed; other writings on philosophy, psychology, and education.

BIOGRAPHICAL/CRITICAL SOURCES: C. A. Mace—A Symposium (festschrift to which colleagues and pupils contributed on his retirement), Methuen, 1962.

* * *

MacFALL, Russell P(atterson) 1903-

PERSONAL: Born September 1, 1903, in Indianapolis, Ind.; son of Russell Traul (a lawyer) and Florence (McConnell) MacFall; married Lucile Chandler, July 29, 1935; children: Joyce (Mrs. David Roderick), Judith Ann, James Russell. Education: DePauw University, A.B., 1925; University of Chicago, M.A., 1931. Politics: Republican. Religion: Methodist. Home: 721 Foster St., Evanston, Ill. 60201. Agent: Lucile Sullivan, McIntosh & Otis, 18 East 41st St., New York, N.Y. 10017.

CAREER: Member of editorial staff of Indianapolis News, Indianapolis, Ind., 1925-35, and Chicago Herald and Examiner, Chicago, Ill., 1935-36; Chicago Tribune, Chicago, Ill., 1936-68, became night editor. Manuscript reader, Bobbs-Merrill Co., Inc., 1927-35. Member of Northern Illinois Rock River Conference of Methodist Church. Lecturer on gems and minerals and old children's books. Member: Midwest Mineralogical and Geological Federation (president, 1969-70), Society of Midland Authors (president, 1968-71).

WRITINGS: Gem Hunter's Guide, Science and Mechanics Publishing, 1951, 4th edition, Crowell, 1969; (with Frank J. Baum) To Please a Child (biography of L. Frank Baum, author of The Wizard of Oz), Reilly & Lee, 1961; Collecting Rocks, Minerals, Gems and Fossils, Hawthorn, 1964; Family Fun Outdoors, Crowell, 1965. Contributing editor, Earth Science.

AVOCATIONAL INTERESTS: Collecting gems, minerals, and marine shells; making jewelry, walking, beachcombing.

* * *

MacGREGOR, Alasdair Alpin (Douglas) 1899-1970 (Francis Featherstonehaugh)

PERSONAL: Born March 20, 1899; son of John MacGregor (a colonel, Indian Army, and author); married Constance Patricia Colville, July, 1958. Education: Attended George Watson's College and University of Edinburgh. Home: 48 Upper Cheyne Row, Chelsea, London S.W.3, England.

CAREER: Author, photographer, and illustrator of other books besides his own. Private secretary to Chancellor of Duchy of Lancaster and to postmaster-general, 1929-31. Stood for Parliament, 1929, 1931, 1935. Former President, League for the Prohibition of Cruel Sports. Military service: British Army, 1915-18. Member: British Humanist Association, Royal Geographical Society (fellow), Robert Louis Stevenson Club (former vice-president of London chapter).

WRITINGS—All self-illustrated with photographs, except as indicated: Behold the Hebrides!; or, Wayfaring in the Western Isles, W. & R. Chambers, 1925, 2nd edition, Ettrick Press, 1948; Over the Sea to Skye; or, Ramblings in an Elfin Isle, W. & R. Chambers, 1926; Wild Drumalbain; or, The Road to Meggernie and Glen Coe, W. & R. Chambers, 1927; Hebridean Sea Pieces, Porpoise Press, 1927; Summer Days Among the Western Isles, Thomas Nelson, 1929; A Last Voyage to St. Kilda: Being the Observations and Adventures of an Egotistic Private Secretary, Cassell, 1931; Searching the Hebrides with a Camera, Harrap, 1933; The Haunted Isles; or, Life in the Hebrides, Maclehose & Co., 1933; Somewhere in Scotland: The Western Highlands in Pen and Picture, G. Routledge & Sons, 1935, revised and enlarged edition, R. Hale, 1948; The Peat-Fire Flame: Folk-Tales and Traditions of the Highlands and Islands, Moray Press, 1937, 3rd edition, Ettrick Press, 1947; The Goat-Wife: Portrait of a Village, Heinemann, 1939, revised and enlarged edition, Museum Press, 1951.

Vanished Waters: Portrait of a Highland Childhood, Methuen, 1942; Auld Reekie: Portrait of a Lowland Boyhood, Methuen, 1943; The Turbulent Years: A Portrait of Youth in Auld Reekie, Methuen, 1945; The Western Isles, R. Hale, 1949; The Buried Barony, R. Hale, 1949; (author of text) The Scottish Countryside in Pictures, Odhams, 1950, Norton, 1962; Skye and the Inner Hebrides, R. Hale, 1953; The Ghost Book: Strange Hauntings in Britain, R. Hale, 1955; (editor and abridger) Griffith Taylor, Journeyman Taylor: The Education of a Scientist, R. Hale, 1958; Phantom Footsteps: A Second Ghost Book, R. Hale, 1959.

Percyval Tudor-Hart, 1873-1954: Portrait of an Artist, P. R. Macmillan, 1961; The Golden Lamp: Portrait of a Landlady, M. Joseph, 1964; Land of the Mountain and the Flood, M. Joseph, 1965; The Enchanted Isles: Hebridean Portraits and Memories, M. Joseph, 1967; The Farthest Hebrides, M. Joseph, 1969; Islands by the Score, M. Joseph, 1971; The Deserted Garden, and Other Collected Poems, Kingsmead Press, 1970; An Island Here and There, Kingsmead Press, 1972. Contributor to anthologies and periodicals.

SIDELIGHTS: MacGregor's third-person comments on himself: "One of the finest photographers in Britain.... [Interested in] mountaineering, &c. Has travelled widely in

East Indies, Australia, U.S.A., Canada. Has broadcast musical recitals of English and Scottish lyrics & ballads in Australia and U.S.A. A keen field geologist, and swimmer. Army long-distance running champion. One of the most prominent opponents of Vivisection, hunting, circuses, &c. in Britain.... Has been a Vegetarian since 1925." MacGregor returned his graduation diplomas to the principal of the University of Edinburgh as a protest against experiments with live animals.

The film "The Edge of the World" was based on *A Last Voyage to St. Kilda.*

AVOCATIONAL INTERESTS: Music, swimming, mountaineering, field geology, photography, and topography.

BIOGRAPHICAL/CRITICAL SOURCES: Punch, June 7, 1967; *Antiquarian Bookman*, June 1-8, 1970.

(Died April 15, 1970)

* * *

MACHOTKA, Otakar 1899-1970

PERSONAL: Born October 29, 1899, in Prague, Czechoslovakia; came to United States in 1948; son of Richard and Marie (Zelinka) Machotka; married Jarmila Mohr, August 11, 1932; children: Pavel, Georgia (Mrs. William H. Johnson), Hana. *Education:* Received B.A. from gymnasium in Prague, Czechoslovakia, 1919; Charles University, graduate study, 1919-23, Ph.D., 1926; studied at University of Strasbourg and Sorbonne, University of Paris, 1923-25; Ecole Libre des Sciences Politique, Paris, France, Diploma (honors), 1925; post-doctoral study at University of Chicago, 1934-35, and at University of Southern California. *Home:* 313 Grant Ave., Endicott, N.Y. *Office:* Harpur College, Binghamton, N.Y.

CAREER: Charles University, Prague, Czechoslovakia, assistant in sociology, 1928-29; National Statistical Office, Prague, staff member, 1929-33; University of Bratislava, Bratislava, Czechoslovakia, docent of sociology, 1933-38, associate professor, 1938-39; Charles University, professor of sociology, 1939-40, 1945-48 (during war years, when German authorities closed the universities, worked in the National Statistical Office and later in Czechoslovak Institute for Work Research); University of Political and Social Sciences, Prague, Czechoslovakia, co-founder, professor of social psychology, 1946-48, vice-president, 1947-48; visiting professor at University of Chicago, Chicago, Ill., 1948, Syracuse University, Syracuse, N.Y., 1948-49, Cornell University, Ithaca, N.Y., 1949-50; Harpur College of State University of New York, Binghamton, 1950-70, became professor of sociology, 1951, head of department of sociology and anthropology, 1955-57. Active as organizer of Czech underground movement during World War II, serving as vice-chairman of Czechoslovak Revolutionary Committee and as one of the leaders of the Czech uprising against the Germans in 1945; vice-president of Bohemia, 1945-46, and member of Bohemian government until the communist coup in Czechoslovakia in 1948. Council for Free Czechoslovakia, Washington, D.C., member of executive committee, 1953-70, alternating chairman, 1955-56. *Military service:* Czech Army, 1926-27.

MEMBER: Royal Scientific Society (Prague), National Research Council (Prague), American Sociological Association, Statistical Society, Society of Social Research (vice-president), Sokol, Torch Club. *Awards, honors:* Officier des Palmes Academiques, 1930, for work on French-Czech cultural relations; Military Cross and Medal for

Bravery, bestowed by Czechoslovakian President Benes, 1946.

WRITINGS: Mravni problem ve svetle sociologie, Orbis, 1927; (with Ullrich) *Sociologie v modernim zivote*, Orbis, 1928; *K sociologii rodiny*, Stat. Ur. Stat., 1932; *Socialne potrebne rodiny hl. m. Prahy*, Stat. Ur. Stat., 1936; *Americka sociologie*, Melantrich, 1938; *Amerika*, Melantrich, 1946; *Cesky socialism*, Melantrich, 1946; *Socialni psychologie*, Student Union (Prague), 1947; *T. G. Masaryk*, Council for Free Czechoslovakia, 1950; *The Unconscious in Social Relations*, Philosophical Library, 1964; (editor) *Prazske povstani 1945*, Council for Free Czechoslovakia, 1965; *Povidky exulantovy*, Spolecnost pro vedy a umeni (New York), 1968.

Author of several booklets on Thomas Masaryk, and of a study of the late Czech statesman (and first president) published in *Congressional Record*, 1960. Contributor of about fifty items to Czech *Masaryk Encyclopedia* and Czech *Otto Encyclopedia*, about fifty articles to newspapers and magazines, 1945-48, and about thirty articles and larger studies to scientific journals in Czechoslovakia, France, and United States. Co-founder and former co-editor, *Sociology and Social Problems* (Czechoslovakia); former contributing editor, *Sociology and Social Research.*

WORK IN PROGRESS: A study on the unconscious cognitive phenomena in social life.

SIDELIGHTS: Machotka was competent in French, German, Latin, and Greek.

(Died July 29, 1970)

* * *

MacIVER, Robert M(orrison) 1882-1970

PERSONAL: Surname is pronounced Mac-*ee*-ver; born April 17, 1882, in Stornoway, Scotland; came to United States in 1927; son of Donald Morrison and Christine MacIver; married Ethel Marion Peterkin, May 14, 1911; children: Ian Tennant Morrison (deceased), Christine Elizabeth MacIver Bierstedt, Donald Gordon. *Education:* University of Edinburgh, M.A., 1903, D.Ph., 1915; Oxford University, B.A. (double first honors in Literae Humaniores), 1907. *Home:* Heyhoe Woods, Palisades, N.Y. 10964.

CAREER: University of Aberdeen, Aberdeen, Scotland, lecturer in political science, 1907-11, lecturer in sociology, 1911; University of Toronto, Toronto, Ontario, professor of political science, 1915-22, head of department, 1922-26; Columbia University, New York, N.Y., professor of political science at Barnard College, 1927-36, Lieber Professor of Political Philosophy and Sociology, 1929-50; City of New York Juvenile Delinquency Evaluation Project, New York, N.Y., director, 1955-61; New School for Social Research, New York, N.Y., president, 1963-64, chancellor, 1965-66. Vice-chairman, Canadian War Labor Board, 1917-18. *Member:* World Academy of Arts and Science (fellow), American Sociological Society, Institute Internationale de Sociologie, Royal Society of Canada (fellow), American Academy of Arts and Sciences (fellow), American Philosophical Society (fellow), British Academy (corresponding), Phi Beta Kappa. *Awards, honors:* Litt.D., Columbia University, 1929, Harvard University, 1936, Princeton University, 1947, Jewish Theological Seminary, 1950; Woodrow Wilson Foundation Award, 1947; D.Sc., New School for Social Research, 1950; L.H.D., Yale University, 1951; LL.D., University of Edinburgh, 1952, University of Toronto, 1957; Grand Cross of the Order of the Phoenix (Greece); Kurt Lewin Memorial Award.

WRITINGS: Community: A Sociological Study, Macmillan, 1917, 3rd edition, 1924, 3rd edition reissued with a new preface, Cass, 1970; *Labor in the Changing World*, Dutton, 1919; *The Elements of Social Science*, Metheun, 1921, 9th edition, revised, 1949; *The Modern State*, Oxford University Press, 1926.

The Contribution of Sociology to Social Work, Columbia University Press for New York School of Social Work, 1931; *Society: Its Structure and Changes*, Farrar & Rinehart, 1931, revised edition published as *Society: A Textbook of Sociology*, Farrar & Rinehart, 1937, new revised edition, with Charles H. Page, published as *Society: An Introductory Analysis*, Rinehart, 1949; *Economic Reconstruction*, Columbia University Press, 1934; *Leviathan and the People*, Louisiana University Press, 1939, Kennikat, 1971; (with Moritz J. Bonn and Ralph Barton Perry) *The Roots of Totalitarianism* (addresses), American Academy of Political and Social Science, 1940; *Social Causation*, Ginn, 1942, with a new introduction, Harper, 1964; *Towards an Abiding Peace*, Macmillan, 1943; (with Salvador de Madariaga y Rojo) *World Government: Dream or Necessity?* [and] *Fundamentals of International Order* (the former by Madariaga y Rojo, the latter by MacIver), Herbert Joseph, 1946; *The Web of Government*, Macmillan, 1947, revised edition, 1965; *The More Perfect Union: A Program for the Control of Inter-Group Discrimination in the United States*, Macmillan, 1948.

The Ramparts We Guard, Macmillan, 1950; *Report on the Jewish Community Relations Agencies*, National Community Relations Advisory Council, 1951; *Democracy and the Economic Challenge* (lectures), Knopf, 1952; *Academic Freedom in Our Time*, Columbia University Press, 1955; *The Pursuit of Happiness: A Philosophy for Modern Living*, Simon & Schuster, 1955; *Juvenile Delinquency Project of the City of New York*, Juvenile Delinquency Project, 1956-58; *The Nations and the United Nations*, Manhattan Publishing, 1959; *Life: Its Dimensions and Its Bounds*, Harper, 1960; *The Challenge of the Passing Years: My Encounter with Time*, Simon & Schuster, 1962; *Power Transformed: The Age-Slow Deliverance of the Folk and Now the Potential Deliverance of the Nations from the Rule of Force*, Macmillan, 1964; *The Prevention and Control of Delinquency*, Atherton, 1966; *As a Tale That Is Told* (autobiography), University of Chicago Press, 1968; *Politics and Society*, edited by David Spitz, Atherton, 1969.

On Community, Society, and Power: Selected Writings, edited by Leon Bramson, University of Chicago Press, 1970.

Editor—All published by Commonwealth Fund Conference on Science, Philosophy, and Religion in Their Relation to the Democratic Way of Life, except as indicated: (With Lyman Bryson and Louis Finkelstein) *Approaches to Group Understanding*, 1947; (with Bryson and Finkelstein) *Conflicts of Power in Modern Culture*, 1947; (with Bryson and Finkelstein) *Learning and World Peace*, 1948; (with Bryson and Finkelstein) *Goals for American Education*, Harper, 1950; (with Bryson and Finkelstein) *Perspectives on a Troubled Decade: Science, Philosophy, and Religion, 1939-1949*, 1950; (with Bryson, Finkelstein, and Richard McKeon) *Symbols and Values: An Initial Study*, 1954; (with Bryson, Finkelstein, and Hudson Hoagland) *Symbols and Society*, 1955; (with Bryson, Finkelstein, and Clarence

H. Faust) *Aspects of Human Equality*, 1956; *New Successes of the Doctrines of the Work "The Road to Peace and Moral Democracy" by Boris Gourevitch*, Union for the Protection of the Human Person, 1959.

Editor—All published by Institute for Religious and Social Studies, Jewish Theological Seminary of America: (And contributor) *Group Relations and Group Antagonisms*, 1944; (and contributor) *Civilization and Group Relationships*, 1945; *Unity and Difference in American Life*, 1947; (and contributor) *Discrimination and National Welfare*, 1949; *Great Expressions of Human Rights: A Series of Addresses and Discussions*, 1950; *Moments of Personal Discovery*, 1952; *Conflict of Loyalties*, 1952; *The Hour of Insight: A Sequel to Moments of Personal Discovery*, 1954; *New Horizons in Creative Thinking: A Survey and Forecast*, 1954; *Great Moral Dilemmas in Literature, Past and Present*, 1956; *Integrity and Compromise: Problems of Public and Private Conscience*, 1957; *Dilemmas of Youth in America Today*, 1961; (and contributor) *The Assault on Poverty, and Individual Responsibility*, 1965.

BIOGRAPHICAL/CRITICAL SOURCES: Saturday Review, March 11, 1967, May 17, 1969; *Washington Post*, June 17, 1970; *Time*, June 29, 1970; *Publishers Weekly*, July 13, 1970; *Antiquarian Bookman*, September 7-14, 1970.

(Died June 15, 1970)

*   *   *

MACKAY, Mercedes (Isabelle) 1906-

PERSONAL: Born March 29, 1906, in Poltesco, Cornwall, England; married Robert A. Mackay (a geology consultant), May 16, 1933; children: Jacqueline Eugenie. *Education:* Central School of Speech and Drama, General School's certificate and Phonetics Association certificate; University of London, diploma. *Politics:* Liberal. *Home:* 39 Brook Green, London W.6, England; and Gardiners Farmhouse, Sandhurst, near Gloucester, England. *Agent:* David Higham Associates, 5-8 Lower John St., London W1R 4HA, England.

CAREER: Professional actress with touring and repertory companies in England, 1926-29; teacher of elocution and English, Blundellsands, England, 1929-31; former manager of radio station in Nigeria; British Broadcasting Corp., overseas commentator for West Africa, 1945-46. Transport control officer, World War II. Correspondent for *Tanganyika Standard* and newspapers in Nigeria. Lecturer. Associate, Blackfriars Settlement. *Member:* P.E.N. International, Royal African Society (council member, 1950-53; chairman of Racial Unity), Authors Association, British Commonwealth League, Nigerian Field Society, Oriental Club (associate), African Music Society.

WRITINGS: Black Argosy, Putnam, 1954; *Shining Trouble*, Heinemann, 1956; *Loons' Cry*, Heinemann, 1958. Short story anthologized in *Pick of Today's Short Stories*, edited by John Pudney, Putnam, 1955. Contributor of articles and short stories to *New Statesman, Evening News*, of articles on politics and travel to *West Africa, New Commonwealth*, and women's magazines, and of feature stories to *News Chronicle*. Former editor, *Bulletin of Racial Unity*.

WORK IN PROGRESS: A novel.

SIDELIGHTS: Mrs. Mackay has lived in, and written about, East and West Africa and Canada, traveled through Europe, America, India, Burma, Persia, Egypt, Mexico, and San Salvador. *Avocational interests:* Collecting African musical instruments.

MACKEN, Walter   1915-1967

PERSONAL: Born May 3, 1915, in Galway, Ireland; son of Walter (a carpenter) and Agnes (Brady) Macken; married Margaret Mary Kenny, February 9, 1937; children: Walter Desmond, Ultan Joseph. *Education:* Attended Catholic schools in Galway, Ireland. *Religion:* Roman Catholic. *Home:* Gort-na-ganiv, Oughterard, County Galway, Ireland. *Agent:* Harold Matson Co., Inc., 30 Rockefeller Plaza, New York, N.Y. 10020.

CAREER: Gaelic Theatre, Galway, Ireland, actor-producer-manager, 1939-48; Abbey Theatre, Dublin, Ireland, actor, 1948-51, artistic director, 1966; playwright and novelist.

WRITINGS:—All novels except as indicated: *Quench the Moon*, Viking, 1948; *Rain on the Wind* (Literary Guild selection), Macmillan, 1951; *The Bogman*, Macmillan, 1952; *The Green Hills* (short stories), Macmillan, 1956; *Sullivan*, Macmilland, 1957; *Seek the Fair Land* (Literary Guild selection), Macmillan, 1959; *The Silent People*, Macmillan, 1962; *God Made Sunday* (short stories), Macmillan, 1962; *The Scorching Wind*, Macmillan, 1964; *Island of the Great Yellow Ox* (juvenile), Macmillan, 1966; *Lord of the Mountain*, Macmillan, 1967 (published in England as *Brown Lord of the Mountain*, Macmillan, 1967); *Flight of the Doves* (juvenile), Macmillan, 1968; *The Coll Doll and Other Stories*, Macmillan, 1969. Author of short stories appearing in *The New Yorker, The Atlantic Monthly, Harper's*, and others.

Plays: *Mungo's Mansion* (produced at the Abbey Theatre, Dublin), Macmillan, 1946; *Home is the Hero* (produced at the Abbey Theatre, Dublin; produced on Broadway by the Theatre Guild, 1954), Macmillan, 1953; *Twilight of a Warrior* (produced by the Abbey Theatre, Dublin), Macmillan, 1956. Also author of four plays in Gaelic.

SIDELIGHTS: Macken acted in his own plays as well as those of others at the Abbey Theatre, on Broadway, in London, and on the screen. Of this experience he remarked, "If a person comes back and praises the actor, the playwright in him bridles. If they praise the play, the actor bridles. It's a complicated business, indeed, but it works out all right in the end and everybody has a good time. But the question always will remain unsolved. Is the actor the pain in the neck or is it the playwright?" *Flight of the Doves* was made into a movie in 1970. The film was produced and directed by Ralph Nelson whose 12-year-old daughter, Meredith, recommended the novel to him after reading it during summer vacation.

(Died April 22, 1967)

*   *   *

MACKIE, Albert D(avid)   1904-
(MacNib)

PERSONAL: Born December 18, 1904, in Edinburgh, Scotland; son of John and Caroline S. (Gibson) Mackie; married Isabella Kerray, June 1, 1931; children: John, Isabel F. (Mrs. Anthony R. Ashcroft), Carole G. (Mrs. George Henderson). *Education:* University of Edinburgh, M.A. (honors). *Politics:* Pro-Scottish Conservative. *Religion:* Episcopalian. *Home:* 27 Blackford Ave., Edinburgh, Scotland.

CAREER: News editor on papers in Kingston, Jamaica, 1928-30; *Scotsman*, Edinburgh, Scotland, sub-editor, 1930-32, leader writer, 1932-35; *Evening News*, Glasgow, Scotland, feature writer, 1935-42; *Scottish Sunday Express and Evening Citizen*, Glasgow, feature writer, 1935-46; *Evening Dispatch*, Edinburgh, Scotland, editor, 1946-54; *Picture Post*, London, England, Scottish news editor, 1955; *Scottish Daily Express and Evening News*, Edinburgh, Scotland, feature writer, 1956—. Broadcaster for British Broadcasting Corp., including North American and other overseas broadcasts. Regular lecturer to inmates in Edinburgh and Glasgow prisons. Author of daily topical rhymes in evening papers, 1935—, under pseudonym MacNib. *Member:* National Union of Journalists, Society of Authors, Royal Scots Club.

WRITINGS: Poems in Two Tongues, Darien Press, 1928; *Sing a Sang O' Scotland: A Poem in Scots*, William MacLellan, 1944; (translator) *A Call from Warsaw: An Anthology of Underground Warsaw Poetry*, J. Harasowska, 1944; *Edinburgh*, Blackie & Son, 1951; *Gentle Like a Dove*, Oliver & Boyd, 1952; *The Hearts: The Story of the Heart of Midlothian F.C.*, Stanley Paul, 1959; *The Book of MacNib: One Hundred and Sixteen of His Choicest Effusions Over the Past Twenty Years*, Castle Wynd Printers, 1960; *Industrial History of Edinburgh*, McKenzie, Vincent & Co., 1963; *Scottish Pageantry*, Hutchinson, 1967; *To Duncan Glen: A Poem*, Akros Publications, 1971.

Plays—All produced in Edinburgh at Edinburgh Gateway Theatre: "The Hogmanay Story," 1951; "Festival City," 1952; "Hame," 1954; "Sheena," 1955; "MacHattie's Hotel," 1957. Author of scripts for British Broadcasting Corp., including "Edinburgh Folk," and "Fifty Years of Show Business." Author of lyrics for theatre.

Translator of lyric poetry from many languages into Scots. Contributor of poetry to anthologies and regular column to *Scotland's Magazine*. Editor of two issues of *Lines Review* (Edinburgh).

WORK IN PROGRESS: Double Concerto, a verse novel on Edinburgh Festival; *The Day Our Haggis Died*, an autobiography.

SIDELIGHTS: Mackie is an authority on Scots (Lallans) language and dialects; he has studied Scottish Gaelic and other Celtic languages, knows French and German, and can read Russian, Italian, Spanish, Dutch, and Norwegian.

BIOGRAPHICAL/CRITICAL SOURCES: Evening Dispatch (Edinburgh), May 1, 1946; *New Statesman*, January 5, 1968; *Times Literary Supplement*, February 22, 1968.

*   *   *

MACKINLAY, Leila Antoinette Sterling   1910-
(Brenda Grey)

PERSONAL: Born September 5, 1910, in London, England; daughter of Malcolm Sterling (a singing teacher and author) and Dagny (Hansen) Mackinlay. *Education:* Attended private schools. *Politics:* Conservative. *Religion:* Anglican. *Home:* 4P Portman Mansions, Chiltern St., London W1M 1LF, England.

CAREER: Trained as a singer and actress, but turned to writing as a career, 1930—. Regent Street Polytechnic, London, England, teacher of English to foreigners, 1938-39, and for a period after the war; London County Council, panel lecturer on writing at Regent Street Polytechnic, 1938-39, teacher at various evening institutes, 1946—. Amateur drama critic for *Dancing Times*, 1935-39, *Amateur Stage*, 1946—. Publishers' reader. *Member:* Romantic Novelists' Association, National Book League (life), National Operatic and Dramatic Association (life), Royal Society of Literature.

WRITINGS: Little Mountebank, Mills & Boon, 1930; *Fame's Fetters*, Mills & Boon, 1931; *Madame Juno*, Mills & Boon, 1931; *An Exotic Young Lady*, Mills & Boon, 1932; *Willed to Wed*, Mills & Boon, 1933; (under pseudonym Brenda Grey) *Modern Micawbers*, Eldon Press, 1933; *Musical Productions*, Jenkins, 1955; (under pseudonym Brenda Grey) *Stardust in Her Eyes*, Gresham, 1964; (under pseudonym Brenda Grey) *Girl of His Choice*, Gresham, 1965; (under pseudonym Brenda Grey) *How High the Moon*, Gresham, 1966; (under pseudonym Brenda Grey) *Throw Your Bouquet*, Gresham, 1967; (under pseudonym Brenda Grey) *A Very Special Person*, Gresham, 1967; (under pseudonym Brenda Grey) *Shadow of a Smile*, Gresham, 1968; (under pseudonym Brenda Grey) *Tread Softly on Dreams*, Gresham, 1970; (under pseudonym Brenda Grey) *Son of Summer*, Gresham, 1970; *Farewell to Sadness*, R. Hale, 1970; *The Silken Purse*, R. Hale, 1970.

All published by Ward, Lock: *The Pro's Daughter*, 1934; *Shadow Lawn*, 1934; *Love Goes South*, 1935; *Into the Net*, 1935; *Night Bell*, 1936; *Young Man's Slave*, 1936; *Doubting Heart*, 1937; *Apron-Strings*, 1937; *Caretaker Within*, 1938; *Theme Song*, 1938; *Only Her Husband*, 1939; *Reluctant Bride*, 1939; *Man Always Pays*, 1940; *Woman at the Wheel*, 1940; *Ridin' High*, 1941; *None Better Loved*, 1941; *Time on Her Hands*, 1942; *Brave Live On*, 1942; *Green Limelight*, 1943; *Lady of the Torch*, 1944; *Two Walk Together*, 1945; *Piper's Pool*, 1946; *Piccadilly Inn*, 1946; *Blue Shutters*, 1947; *Echo of Applause*, 1948; *Peacock Hill*, 1948; *Restless Dream*, 1949; *Pilot's Point*, 1949.

Six Wax Candles, 1950; *Spider Dance*, 1950; *Guilt's Pavilions*, 1951; *Five Houses*, 1952; *Unwise Wanderer*, 1952; *Cuckoo Cottage*, 1953; *Midnight Is Mine*, 1954; *Fiddler's Green*, 1954; *Riddle of a Lady*, 1955; *Vagabond Daughter*, 1955; *She Married Another*, 1956; *Man of the Moment*, 1956; *She Moved to Music*, 1956; *Divided Duty*, 1957; *Mantle of Innocence*, 1957; *Love on a Shoestring*, 1958; *The Secret in Her Life*, 1958; *Seven Red Roses*, 1959; *Uneasy Conquest*, 1959; *Food of Love*, 1960; *Spotlight on Susan*, 1960; *Beauty's Tears*, 1961; *Spring Rainbow*, 1961; *Vain Delights*, 1962; *Broken Armour*, 1963; *False Relations*, 1963; *Fool of Virtue*, 1964; *Practice for Sale*, 1964; *Ring of Hope*, 1965; *No Room for Loneliness*, 1965; *An Outside Chance*, 1966; *The Third Boat*, 1967; *Mists of the Moor*, 1967; *Frost at Dawn*, 1968; *Homesick for a Dream*, 1968; *Wanted—Girl Friday*, 1968.

WORK IN PROGRESS: Teaching all levels of English literature in prison service.

AVOCATIONAL INTERESTS: Riding, driving, theatre, and reading.

* * *

MacLEOD, Beatrice (Beach) 1910-

PERSONAL: Born January 15, 1910, in Brentwood, Long Island, N.Y.; daughter of William DeVerne and Edith (Waldo) Beach; married Robert Brodie MacLeod (a professor of psychology), October 17, 1936 (died, 1972); children: Ian Fullerton (died, 1972), Alison Stuart. *Education:* Swarthmore College, B.A., 1931; Yale University, M.F.A., 1934. *Home:* 957 East State St., Ithaca, N.Y. *Office:* Telluride Association, 217 West Ave., Ithaca, N.Y.

CAREER: Director of summer stock players, "Forty-Niners," Whitefield, N.H., 1933-41; Swarthmore College, Swarthmore, Pa., director of dramatics, 1934-46; Montreal Negro Theatre Guild, Montreal, Quebec, director, 1946-48; Ithaca College, Ithaca, N.Y., assistant professor of drama,

1949-51; Tompkins County Society for Mental Health, Ithaca, N.Y., executive secretary, 1955-58; Telluride Association, Ithaca, N.Y., executive secretary, 1959—. Children's Theatre Workshop, Ithaca, N.Y., director, 1948-61, staff, 1961—. *Member:* Phi Beta Kappa.

WRITINGS: On Small Wings (juvenile), Westminster, 1961.

* * *

MacLEOD, Earle Henry 1907-

PERSONAL: Born November 9, 1907, in West Somerville, Mass.; son of Angus Alexander (an artist) and Ida Alice (MacIvor) MacLeod; married Helen Dorothy Tripp; children: Robert Alan. *Religion:* Methodist. *Home:* 1915 Wildwood, Nashville, Tenn. 37212. *Office:* 1005 18th Ave. S., Nashville, Tenn. 37212.

CAREER: Resort Publications, Michigan City, Ind., editor and publisher, 1928-31; Brinckerhoff, Inc. (advertising), Chicago, Ill., vice-president and copy chief, 1928-33; Van Hecker-MacLeod, Inc. (advertising), Chicago, Ill., vice-president, 1933-43; Methodist Church, layman in public relations posts in Chicago, Ill., and Nashville, Tenn., 1945—, director of public relations for Scarrit College. President, Chicago District Camp Ground Association, 1952-61. *Member:* National Religious Public Relations Council, Associated Church Press, Clan MacLeod, Chicago District Methodist Camp Ground Brotherhood, Nashville Art Directors Club.

WRITINGS: Prayers for Everyone, To Meet Every Need, Zondervan, 1962; *Moments for Everyone, One by One*, Zondervan, 1969. Poetry anthologized in *Contemporary American Poets, Paebar Anthology of Verse.* Contributor of verse to *Together,* articles to religious periodicals.

AVOCATIONAL INTERESTS: Photography, reading, painting, art and design, golf, horseback riding, and spectator sports.

* * *

MACMILLAN, Norman 1892-

PERSONAL: Born August 9, 1892, in Glasgow, Scotland; son of John Campbell and Jeanie (Hamilton) Macmillan; married Gladys Mary Peterkin Mitchell, November 13, 1925. *Education:* Attended Royal Technical College, Glasgow, Scotland. *Home:* Trecara Lodge, 2 Edward St., Truro, Cornwall, England.

CAREER: Consultant and test pilot for British aircraft manufacturers, 1919-23; Fairey Aviation Co., chief test pilot, 1924-30, director, 1930; Air Survey Co. Ltd., director, 1929-30; Armstrong Siddeley Development Co., consultant test pilot, and a principal foreign representative, 1931-33; free-lance writer. Instructor in Spanish army and navy flying schools, 1922; first pilot to attempt around-the-world flight, 1922; made first one-day flight between London and Sweden, 1923; first British pilot to fly over Andes Mountains, and to make official dive and floatplane spin tests. Public lecturer, and lecturer to Royal Aeronautical Society and Royal Society of Arts. *Military service:* British Army, Infantry, Belgium and France, 1914-16; Royal Flying Corps., fighter pilot in France and Italy, 1917-18; Royal Air Force, 1918-19, 1921; Royal Air Force Volunteer Reserve, wing commander, 1942-58; received Order of Officer of the British Empire, Military Cross, Air Force Cross.

MEMBER: Royal Aeronautical Society (associate fellow), Royal Society of Arts (fellow), National League of Airmen (president, 1935-38), Guild of Air Pilots and Air Navigators (founder, 1929; first warden, 1929-34; deputy master, 1934-35; liveryman, 1958—), Institution of Aeronautical Engineers (founder associate member, 1919). *Awards, honors:* Speed prize, first international light aeroplane competition, 1923; commissioned Deputy Lieutenant of Cornwall, 1951, for military services within the duchy.

WRITINGS: The Art of Flying, Duckworth, 1928; *Into the Blue,* Duckworth, 1929, revised edition, Jarrolds, 1969, Arno, 1971; *The Air Traveller's Guide to Europe,* Duckworth, 1929, published as *The Air Tourist's Guide to Europe,* Washburn, 1930; *An Hour of Aviation,* Lippincott, 1930; *The Romance of Flight,* Evans Brothers, 1935; (editor) *Sir Sefton Brancker,* Heinemann, 1935; *The Romance of Modern Exploration and Discovery,* Evans Brothers, 1936; *Freelance Pilot,* Heinemann, 1937; *The Chosen Instrument,* Bodley Head, 1938; (editor and contributor) *How We Fly,* Guild of Air Pilots, 1939.

(Editor) *Best Flying Stories,* Faber, 1940; *Air Strategy,* Hutchinson, 1941; *Air Cadet's Handbook on How to Pilot an Aeroplane,* Allen & Unwin, 1942; *The Pilot's Book on Advanced Flying,* Allen & Unwin, 1942; *The Royal Air Force in the World War,* four volumes, Harrap, 1942-50; (with Cecil J. Allen and J. V. Stone) *Railways, Ships, and Aeroplanes Illustrated,* Odhams, 1945; *Great Airmen,* G. Bell, 1955, St. Martin's, 1959; *Great Aircraft,* St. Martin's, 1960; *Tales of Two Air Wars,* G. Bell, 1963; *Great Flights and Air Adventures from Balloons to Spacecraft,* G. Bell, 1964, St. Martin's, 1965; *Wings of Fate: Strange True Tales of Vintage Flying Days,* G. Bell, 1967.

Author of *History of the Guild of Air Pilots and Air Navigators,* privately published by the Guild. Editor of "Where Shall We Go," a series of guidebooks. Contributor of articles to *Grolier's Encyclopedia,* and to *Everyman, Chambers' Journal, Times* (London), *Baillie, Blackwoods, Daily Mail, Daily News, Times Aviation Supplement,* and other newspapers, periodicals, and aviation journals in England, Germany, Australia, Italy, India, South America, and United States.

WORK IN PROGRESS: The Flying Camels, a history of the 45th Squadron, Royal Flying Corps, and Royal Air Force, 1916-63; research into early nineteenth-century British military and naval history; *Silver River,* a history; *Aero-Engines,* a history.

SIDELIGHTS: Macmillan has traveled widely in Europe, North Africa, the Middle East, Asia, and South America. *Avocational interests:* Study of humanities, geography, archaeology, anthropology, ornithology, methods of transport, history of wars, photography.

*   *   *

MACMILLAN, William Miller   1885-

PERSONAL: Born October 1, 1885, in Aberdeen, Scotland; son of John (a minister and teacher) and Elizabeth (Lindsay) Macmillan; married Mona Constance Mary Tweedie (a writer), 1934; children: Elizabeth Lindsay Macmillan Dow, John Duncan, Hugh William, Catriona Mary Miller. *Education:* Merton College, Oxford, B.A., 1906, M.A., 1920; graduate study at University of Aberdeen, 1907-09, University of Berlin, 1910. *Religion:* Church of Scotland. *Home:* Long Wittenham, Abingdon, Berkshire, England.

CAREER: Rhodes University, Grahamstown, South Africa, lecturer in history and economics, 1911-16; University

of the Witwatersrand, Johannesburg, South Africa, professor of history, 1917-34; British Broadcasting Corp., Empire intelligence, 1941-43; British Council, senior representative in West Africa, 1943-46; University of St. Andrews, St. Andrews, Scotland, director of colonial studies, 1947-54; University of West Indies, Kingston, Jamaica, acting professor of history, 1954-55; now retired. Chairman, Johannesburg Joint Council of Europeans and Africans, 1931-32; member, Advisory Committee on Education in the Colonies, 1938-41; member, Colonial Labour Advisory Committee, 1946-52; served on official mission to Tanganyika, 1950, to Bechuanaland, 1951.

MEMBER: Royal African Society (honorary life), Institut Colonial International (honorary life), Royal Society of International Affairs, Royal Commonwealth Society, Royal and Ancient Golf Club of St. Andrews. *Awards, honors:* Rhodes Scholar at Oxford University; D.Litt., University of Natal, 1962, Oxford University, 1957; Chevalier, Royal Belgian Order of the Lion.

WRITINGS: Economic Conditions in a Non-industrial South Africa Town, [Grahamstown], 1915; *The Place of Local Government in the Union of South Africa,* W. E. Horton, 1918; *South African Agrarian Problem,* Central News, 1919; *A South African Student and Soldier, Harold Edward Howse, 1894-1947,* T. M. Miller, 1920; *The Cape Colour Question: A Historical Survey,* Faber & Gwyer, 1927; *Bantu, Boer and Briton: The Making of the South African Native Problem,* Faber & Gwyer, 1929, revised and enlarged edition, Clarendon Press, 1963; *Complex South Africa: An Economic Footnote to History,* Faber, 1930; *Warning from the West Indies: A Tract for Africa and the Empire,* Faber, 1936, revised edition, Penguin, 1938; *Africa Emergent: A Survey of Social, Political, and Economic Trends in British Africa,* Faber, 1938, revised edition, Penguin, 1949; *The Road to Self-Rule: A Study in Colonial Evolution,* Faber, 1959, Praeger, 1960. Regular contributor to *New Statesman,* 1922-36, and to British Broadcasting Corp. "Colonial Commentary," 1946-52; contributor to periodicals and newspapers.

WORK IN PROGRESS: Memoirs.

SIDELIGHTS: The Road to Self-Rule was translated into Italian. Macmillan's South African historical writings were based on the previously unknown collected papers of the controversial nineteenth-century missionary, John Philip, a collection which was totally destroyed by fire in the University of Johannesburg Library in 1931.

*   *   *

MacNEIL, Neil   1891-1969

PERSONAL: Born February 6, 1891, in Boston, Mass.; son of John A. (an engineer) and Catherine (MacNeil) MacNeil; married Elizabeth Quinn, June 28, 1920; children: Neil, Mary Rose (Mrs. Hal B. Cumbaugh), Ann Elizabeth (Mrs. John S. Kramer). *Education:* St. Francis Xavier University, Antigonish, Nova Scotia, B.A., 1912. *Politics:* Republican. *Religion:* Roman Catholic. *Home:* 3233 Northeast 34th St., Fort Lauderdale, Fla.; (summer) Southampton, N.Y. *Agent:* Samuel French, Inc., 25 West 45th St., New York, N.Y. 10036.

CAREER: Daily Mail, Montreal, Quebec, city editor, 1914-16; *Gazette,* Montreal, Quebec, correspondent, 1916-18; *New York Times,* New York, N.Y., 1918-51, began as assistant national editor, successively foreign editor, night city editor, and assistant night managing editor. Hoover Commission on Reorganization (of U.S. government), editorial director, 1954-55, special assistant to the chairman, 1955-64. President, International Friends of the Antigonish Movement. Director and acting president, Parish Art Museum. *Military service:* U.S. Army, World War I; became sergeant major.

MEMBER: Catholic Institute of the Press (founder), Clan MacNeil Association of America (president emeritus), Society of the Silurians (past president), New York Athletic Club (past governor), Dutch Treat Club (past chairman), Players Club, Southampton Club, Beach Club of Southampton. *Awards, honors:* LL.D., St. Francis Xavier University, 1947, Catholic University of America, 1956; Catholic Institute of the Press Award, 1949; John O'Hara Cosgrave Medal, 1951, for distinguished service to journalism.

WRITINGS: Without Fear or Favor, Harcourt, 1940; *How to be a Newspaperman*, Harper, 1942; *An American Peace*, Scribner, 1944; *The Highland Heart in Nova Scotia*, Scribner, 1947; (with Harold Metz) *The Hoover Report, 1953-1955: What It Means to You as Citizen and Taxpayer*, Macmillan, 1956. Contributor to *Reader's Digest, Saturday Evening Post, New York Times Magazine*, and other periodicals and newspapers.

WORK IN PROGRESS: Two books, *Chester Dale and His Pictures* and *Tales from a Bull Pen*.

(Died December 30, 1969)

* * *

MADGE, John (Hylton) 1914-1968

PERSONAL: Born June 19, 1914, in Johannesburg, South Africa; son of Charles Albert (an administrator) and Barbara (Hylton-Foster) Madge; married Janet H. Glaisyer (a social scientist), October 8, 1946; children: Nicola Jane Hylton, Robert Hylton. *Education:* Attended Winchester College, 1928-33; Trinity College, Cambridge, B.A., 1936, M.A., 1942; Architectural Association, London, England, A.A. Diploma, 1942. *Home:* Parsonage Farm, Rickmansworth, Hertfordshire, England. *Office:* P.E.P., 12 Upper Belgrave St., London S.W.1, England.

CAREER: Wartime Government Research, Princes Risborough, England, research officer, 1940-44; University of Bristol, Bristol, England, research fellow in economics, 1944-52; Building Research Station, Watford, England, sociologist and principal scientific officer, 1952-60; Political and Economic Planning, London, England, deputy director, 1960-68; University College, University of London, research associate at Bartlett School of Architecture, 1965-68. Consultant to United Nations, War Office, Ministry of Public Building and Works, Building Design Partnership, and others. Committee member of Center for Planning and Regional Development, 1958-68, of Design and Industries Association, 1963-68. *Military service:* Royal Air Force, 1943-44; became flight lieutenant. *Member:* British Sociological Association (general secretary, 1953-57; treasurer, 1964-68), American Sociological Association (fellow), Royal Statistical Society (fellow), Alpha Kappa Delta, Athenaeum Club (London).

WRITINGS: The Rehousing of Britain, Pilot Press, 1945; (editor) *Tomorrow's Houses: New Building Methods, Structures and Materials*, Pilot Press, 1946; (with Rosemary Jevons) *Housing Estates: A Study of Bristol Corporation Policy and Practices Between the Wars*, Arrowsmith, 1946; *Human Factors in Housing*, Bureau of Current Affairs, 1948; *The Tools of Social Science*, Longmans,

Green, 1953; (with J. B. Dick and C. N. Craig) *A Study of Space and Water Heating in Local-Authority Flats, 1956-59*, National Building Studies, 1961; *The Origins of Scientific Sociology*, Free Press, 1962; (with J. G. Blumler) *Citizenship and Television*, Political and Economic Planning, 1967; (with Michael Smee and Ron Bloomfield) *Workbook for People in Towns: A Course of Twenty Radio Programmes on Urban Sociology*, British Broadcasting Corp., 1968.

WORK IN PROGRESS: A short book on Beatrice Webb.

BIOGRAPHICAL/CRITICAL SOURCES: Times (London), September 4, 1968.

(Died October, 1968)

* * *

MAGIDOFF, Robert 1905-1970

PERSONAL: Born December 26, 1905, in Kiev, Russia; son of Charles and Jennie Magidoff; married Nila Shevko (a lecturer), October 14, 1937. *Education:* University of Wisconsin, B.A., 1932; University of Michigan, Ph.D., 1963. *Home:* 165 East 60th St., New York, N.Y. 10022. *Agent:* Harold Matson Co., Inc., 30 Rockefeller Plaza, New York, N.Y. 10020. *Office:* New York University, 25 Waverly Pl., New York, N.Y. 10003.

CAREER: Foreign correspondent for Associated Press and National Broadcasting Co., 1935-49; free-lance writer and lecturer, 1949-58; University of Michigan, Ann Arbor, lecturer in Russian, 1958-61; New York University, New York, N.Y., assistant professor, 1961-62, associate professor, 1962-64, professor of Russian literature and chairman of Slavic department, 1965-70. Conducted full-length course on Russian literature over Columbia Broadcasting System network, 1964-65. *Member:* Modern Language Association of America, American Association of Teachers of Slavic and Eastern European Languages (vice-president, 1970; president of New York-New Jersey chapter, 1963-66), American Association of University Professors.

WRITINGS: In Anger and Pity: Report on Russia, Doubleday, 1949; *The Kremlin versus the People*, Doubleday, 1952; *Yehudi Menuhin: A Biography*, Doubleday, 1956; *Ezio Pinza*, Rinehart, 1958; *Guide to Russian Literature: Against the Background of Russia's General Cultural Development*, New York University Press, 1964; (editor of translation) *Russian Science Fiction: An Anthology*, New York University Press, 1964; (editor of translation) *Russian Science Fiction, 1968: An Anthology*, New York University Press, 1968; (with others) *Studies in Slavic Linguistics and Poetics in Honor of Boris O. Unbegaun* (editorial commentary), New York University Press, 1968; (editor and compiler) *Russian Science Fiction, 1969: An Anthology*, New York University Press, 1969. Author of play, "The Possessed," based on Dostoevski's novel, first produced in 1961.

WORK IN PROGRESS: Miracles in Words, a study of the poetic image in Boris Pasternak.

SIDELIGHTS: Magidoff spoke most Slavic languages, some German and French.

(Died February, 1970)

* * *

MAGNER, James A. 1901-

PERSONAL: Born October 23, 1901, in Wilmington, Ill.; son of James (a merchant-farmer) and Margaret (Follen)

Magner. *Education:* Campion Academy and College, student, 1917-21; St. Mary of the Lake Seminary, B.A., 1923, M.A., 1924; Urban University of Propaganda Fidei, Rome, Italy, S.T.D., 1928; Academy of St. Thomas, Rome, Italy, Ph.D., 1929. *Politics:* Democrat. *Home address:* Box 2853, 411 Seabreeze Ave., Palm Beach, Fla. 33480.

CAREER: Ordained Roman Catholic priest, 1926, elevated to domestic prelate with title of right reverend monsignor, 1957. Curate of churches in Chicago, Ill., 1929-40; Quigley Preparatory Seminary, Chicago, professor of English and Italian, 1929-40; Catholic University of America, Washington, D.C., procurator and assistant secretary-treasurer, 1940-68, manager-director of Catholic University of America Press, Catholic Education Press, 1942-68. Founder of Charles Carroll Forums, Chicago, Ill., and Washington, D.C. Conductor of annual summer tours and travel seminars, beginning, 1940.

MEMBER: Catholic Anthropological Conference (treasurer), American Catholic Historical Association, Catholic Association for International Peace, Catholic Commission on Intellectual and Cultural Affairs (executive committee, 1951-54), Institute of Ibero-American Studies, Pax Romana, Knights of Columbus, Academy of American Franciscan History (corresponding member). *Awards, honors:* Commander, Order of Isabel la Catolica (Spain); Cross of International Eloy Alfaro Foundation, St. John's University (New York); Pi Alpha Sigma Award for Latin American contributions, 1947.

WRITINGS: This Catholic Religion, Richard Mayer Associates, 1930; *For God and Democracy*, Macmillan, 1940; *Men of Mexico*, Bruce, 1942, reprinted, Books for Libraries, 1968; *The Latin America Pattern*, Catholic Students' Mission Crusade, 1943; *Personality and Successful Living*, Bruce, 1945; *The Art of Happy Marriage*, Bruce, 1947; *The Heart of the Spanish Matter*, Charles Carroll Forum (Washington, D.C.), 1950; *Mental Health in a Mad World*, Bruce, 1953; *The Catholic Priest in the Modern World*, Bruce, 1957. Contributing editor, *Extension*, 1930-36; editor, *Catholic University of America Bulletin*, 1940-56; associate editor-in-chief, *New Catholic Encyclopedia*, 1963-68.

*   *   *

MAGNUS, Samuel Woolf   1910-

PERSONAL: Born September 30, 1910, in Ekaterinoslav, Russia; son of Samuel Woolf (an engineer) and Elizabeth (Sacks) Magnus; married Anna Gertrude Shane, June 7, 1938; children: Patricia Ruth. *Education:* University College, London, B.A. (with honors), 1931. *Politics:* Liberal. *Religion:* Jewish. *Home:* 33 Apsley House, Finchley Rd., St. John's Wood, London N.W.8, England. *Office:* 2 Harcourt Building, Temple, London E.C.4Y, England.

CAREER: Called to English Bar, Gray's Inn, 1937; admitted to Bar of Northern Rhodesia, 1960; barrister-at-law in London, England, 1937-59, in Zambia (formerly Northern Rhodesia), 1959—. Member of legislative council, Northern Rhodesia, 1962-63; member of Parliament in first Northern Rhodesia legislative assembly, 1964; member of Parliament, Zambia National Assembly, 1964-68; Puisne Judge, High Court for Zambia, 1968-71; Justice of Appeal, Court of Appeal for Zambia, 1971. Retired and returned to England, June, 1971. Resumed practice at the English bar, sitting also as a Deputy Circuit Judge. *Military service:* British Army, 1940-46. *Member:* International Committee of Jurists, National Liberal Club, Honorable Society of Gray's Inn, Masons, Association of Jewish Ex-Servicemen, Rotary Club of Westminster East.

WRITINGS: (With Maurice Estrin) *The Companies Act, 1947*, Butterworth & Co., 1947; (with Estrin) *The Companies Act, 1948*, Butterworth & Co., 1948, 3rd edition published as *Companies: Law and Practice*, 1957, 1st supplement, 1961, 2nd supplement, 1964, 4th edition, 1968, 1st supplement, 1971; (with Abraham Montagu Lyons) *Advertisement Control*, Thames Bank, 1949; *Supplement to The General Law of Landlord and Tenant by Edgar Foa*, 7th edition, Thames Bank, 1950; (author of introduction and annotations) *The Leasehold Property (Temporary Provisions) Act, 1951*, Butterworth & Co., 1951; (with Estrin) *The Excess Profits Levy*, Butterworth & Co., 1952; (author of introduction and annotations) *The Housing Repairs and Rents Act, 1954*, Butterworth & Co., 1954; (author of introduction and annotations) *The Landlord and Tenant Act, 1954*, Butterworth & Co., 1954; *The Rent Act, 1957*, Butterworth & Co., 1957, supplement, 1958; (editor with Frank E. Price) *Knight's Annotated Housing Act*, C. Knight & Co., 1958.

(Editor with Laurence Tovell) *Housing Finance*, C. Knight & Co., 1960; (with Estrin) *The Companies Act, 1967*, Butterworth & Co., 1967; *The Rent Act, 1968*, Butterworth & Co., 1969, supplement, 1971; *Business Tenancies*, Butterworth & Co., 1970. Contributor to *Encyclopaedia of Forms and Precedents, Halsbury Laws and England*, 2nd and 3rd editions, and *Encyclopaedia of Court Forms*. Editor, annual supplement to *Encyclopaedia of Court Forms*, 1948-50. Contributor to law journals and newspapers.

WORK IN PROGRESS: Second supplement to *Companies: Law and Practice*, 4th edition.

*   *   *

MAGNUS-ALLCROFT, Sir Philip (Montefiore) 1906-
(Philip Magnus)

PERSONAL: Born February 8, 1906, in London, England; son of Laurie Magnus and Dora Marion (Spielman) Magnus; married Jewell Allcroft, July 14, 1943. *Education:* Wadham College, Oxford, B.A., 1929, M.A. 1958. *Politics:* Conservative. *Religion:* Church of England. *Home:* Stokesay Court, Onibury, Shropshire, England.

CAREER: British Government, London, England, assistant principal in Office of Works, 1928-29, in Ministry of Education, 1929-33, principal in charge of listing buildings of architectural and historical interest, Ministry of Town and Country Planning, 1946-50. Justice of the peace, Shropshire, England, 1952—; Shropshire Country Council, councillor, 1952—, chairman of records and planning committees; member, Ludlow Rural District Council; member, Transport Users' Consultative Committee, West Midland, 1953-63. Chairman of Governors of Altingham College and governor of Ludlow Grammar School. Trustee of National Portrait Gallery, 1970—. *Military service:* British Army, 1939-45; served in Iceland and Italy; became major. *Member:* Royal Society of Literature (fellow), P.E.N., Athenaeum Club, Beefsteak Club, and Brooks's Club (all London), Shropshire Club, Shrewsbury Hunt Club, Ludlow Race Club.

WRITINGS—Under name Philip Magnus: Edmund Burke: A Life, Transatlantic, 1939; (editor and author of introduction) Edmund Burke, *Selected Prose*, Falcon Press, 1948; (editor) *English Association Essays and Studies, 1950*, J. Murray, 1950; *Sir Walter Raleigh*, Falcon Press, 1952, Macmillan, 1956; *Gladstone: A Biography*, Dutton, 1954; *Kitchener: Portrait of an Imperialist*, J. Murray, 1958, Dutton, 1959; *King Edward the Seventh,* Dutton, 1964. Contributor of articles and reviews to *Sunday Times, Daily Telegraph, Times Literary Supplement, Spectator,* and other periodicals.

WORK IN PROGRESS: An authorized biography of Lord Salisbury, Victorian prime minister; an authorized biography of Lord Esher (1852-1930).

SIDELIGHTS: Stokesay Castle, owned by the author's wife, is open to the public and attracts twenty-five thousand visitors each year. They have traveled extensively in North and South America, the Far, Middle, and Near East, Europe, and Africa.

*   *   *

MAGSAM, Charles Michael 1907-

PERSONAL: Born November 17, 1907, in Shelbyville, Ill.; son of John and Alice (Riemke) Magsam. *Education:* Studied at St. Joseph College, Rensselaer, Ind., St. Gregory's and St. Mary's Seminary, Cincinnati, Ohio, Maryknoll Seminary, Maryknoll, N.Y., and Gregorian University, Rome, Italy. *Home:* 822 Archer Ave., Fort Wayne, Ind.

CAREER: Roman Catholic priest of Maryknoll order; missioner in Chile. Conductor of retreats for priests and nuns in East Africa, Philippines, Hong Kong, Taiwan, Japan, Korea, and Hawaii, 1959-60.

WRITINGS: Inner Life of Worship, Grail Publications, 1958; (member of editorial staff and contributor) *Maryknoll Missal,* Kenedy, 1961; *The Theology and Practice of Love,* Helicon, 1965. Contributor to religious journals.

*   *   *

MAGUINESS, W(illiam) Stuart 1903-

PERSONAL: Born October 12, 1903, in Belfast, Ireland; son of George James (a clerk) and Margaret (Gilmour) Maguinness; married Olive Dickinson (a tutor at University College, University of London), September, 1933; children: Juliet. *Education:* Trinity College, Dublin, B.A., 1926, M.A., 1930. *Home:* 25 Hillway, Highgate, London N.6, England.

CAREER: University of Manchester, Manchester, England, assistant lecturer in classics, 1927-30; University of Sheffield, Sheffield, England, lecturer in classics, 1930-46; University of London, Kings College, London, England, professor of Latin and head of classics department, 1946-72, fellow, 1966. Lecturer in Amsterdam, Leiden, Groningen, Paris, Lille, Aix-en-Provence, Athens, Rome, Lucca, Naples, Bologna, Milan, Warsaw, and Cracow; delegate to Assemblee generale of Federation des Etudes classiques in Amsterdam, Madrid, Warsaw, and London. Trustee and committee member of Sir Richard Stapley Educational Trust. *Military service:* British Home Guard, 1940-43; seconded to Admiralty, London, England, as senior administrative officer, 1941-43.

MEMBER: British Classical Association (chairman of council, 1956-64), Society for the Promotion of Roman Studies (member of council), Classical Association (vice-president), Virgil Society (past president), London Classical Society (past president).

WRITINGS: (Editor) Jean Racine, *Berenice,* Manchester University Press, 1929, 2nd edition, 1956; (editor) Virgil, *Aeneid,* Book XII, Methuen, 1953, 2nd edition, 1960; (editor with H. H. Scullard) John C. Stobart, *The Grandeur That Was Rome,* 4th edition, Hawthorn, 1961; (translator)

Pierre Grimal, *The Civilization of Rome,* Simon & Schuster, 1963; (with W. A. Goligher) *Index to the Speeches of Isaeus,* Heffer; (translator) Francois Chamoux, *The Civilization of Greece,* Allen & Unwin, 1965; (contributor) D. R. Dudley, editor, *Lucretius,* Basic Books, 1965. Contributor to other books and to *Oxford Classical Dictionary* and *Encyclopaedia Britannica;* contributor to classical journals in Europe and abroad.

SIDELIGHTS: Maguiness speaks French, Italian, and German.

*   *   *

MAHONEY, John Thomas 1905-
(Tom Mahoney)

PERSONAL: Born December 3, 1905, in Dallas, Tex.; son of James Owen (a school superintendent) and Lacy (Braden) Mahoney; married Grace Dooley, 1930 (divorced); married Caroline Bird Menuez (a writer), January 5, 1957; children: (first marriage) Grace Elizabeth; (second marriage) John Thomas, Jr. *Education:* University of Missouri, B.J., 1927. *Home:* 60 Gramercy Park, New York, N.Y. 10010; and 31 Sunrise Lane, Poughkeepsie, N.Y. 12603.

CAREER: Worked for *El Paso Post,* 1927-30, United Press, 1930-34, *Buffalo Times,* 1934-36; Fawcett Publications, New York, N.Y., editor, 1936-37; *Look,* New York, N.Y., associate editor, 1937-39; General Electric Co., Schenectady, N.Y., assistant manager, news bureau, 1939-43; Office of War Information, Overseas Branch, writer, 1943; *Fortune,* New York, N.Y., associate editor, 1943-45; public relations work with Publicity Associates, New York, N.Y., 1945-47, Young & Rubicam, Inc., New York, N.Y., 1948-56; Dudley-Anderson-Yutzy, New York, N.Y., public relations counsel, 1956-68. *Member:* National Association of Science Writers, American Medical Writers Association, History of Science Society, American Association for the Advancement of Science, Society of Magazine Writers, Authors League, Psywar Society, National Press Club, P.E.N., Overseas Press Club, American Philatelic Society, Collector's Club, Cross and Cockade, Horseless Carriage Club, Baker Street Irregulars, Connoisseurs in Murder, Sigma Delta Chi.

WRITINGS: (With Rita Hession) *Public Relations for Retailers,* Macmillan, 1949; (with Marcus Baerwald) *Gems and Jewelry Today: An Account of the Romance and Values of Gems, Jewelry, Watches and Silverware,* M. Rodd Co., 1949; *The Great Merchants: The Stories of Twenty Famous Retail Operations and the People Who Made Them Great,* Harper, 1955, new edition (with Leonard Sloane), 1966; *The Merchants of Life: An Account of the American Pharmaceutical Industry,* Harper, 1959; (with Baerwald) *The Story of Jewelry: A Popular Account of the Lure, Lore, Science, and Value of Gems and Noble Metals in the Modern World,* Abelard, 1960; *The Story of George Romney: Builder, Salesman, Crusader,* Harper, 1960; (with George Schuster) *The Longest Auto Race,* John Day, 1966; (with Barry Sadler) *I'm a Lucky One,* Macmillan, 1967; (with Ralph Greenhill) *Niagara,* University of Toronto Press, 1969. Contributor to *Reader's Digest, American Legion Magazine,* and to other periodicals.

*   *   *

MAHOOD, Ruth I. 1908-

PERSONAL: Born March 9, 1908, in Buckingham, Ill.; daughter of Samuel John and Sarah Jane (Bulington) Mahood. *Education:* Central State College (now University), Edmond, Okla., A.B., 1933; University of Colorado, M.A., 1942. *Home:* 707 South East 26th St., Edmond, Okla. 73034.

CAREER: Public school teacher in Buckingham, Ill., 1925-31, Verden, Okla., 1938-42, Los Angeles, Calif., 1942-46; Los Angeles County Museum, Los Angeles, Calif., instructor in history, 1946-54, curator of history, 1954-57, chief curator, History Division, beginning, 1958, now chief curator emeritus. City historian for Edmond, Okla., 1974—. Regional vice-president, Conference of California Historical Societies, beginning, 1959; chairman, Junior Historical Societies; member of California Governor's Heritage Preservation Commission, 1963, and Governor's History Commission, beginning, 1963. *Member:* American Association of Museums, National Trust for Historic Preservation, Western Museums League, Historical Society of Southern California, Committee to Preserve the History of Los Angeles, Film Council of Los Angeles, Kappa Delta Pi, Delta Kappa Gamma. *Awards, honors:* Award of Merit, California Historical Society, 1964; Award of Achievement, Civil War Centennial Commission, 1965.

WRITINGS: (Editor) *Adam Clark Vroman—Photographer of the Southwest*, Ritchie, 1961. Contributor to historical society proceedings and professional journals. Editor, *Newsletter* of Western Museums League, beginning, 1964.

* * *

MAIN, Mildred Miles 1898-

PERSONAL: Born December 17, 1898, in Kansas City, Mo.; daughter of David Anderson (a bridge designer) and Maud (an artist and sculptor; maiden name, Maple) Miles; married Charles O. Main; children: Winifred (Mrs. E. W. Greenfield), David R. *Education:* University of Chicago, Kindergarten-Primary Certificate, 1920; Western Illinois State Teachers College (now Western Illinois University), B.Ed., 1925; New York University, M.A., 1937; additional study at Regia Universita per Stanieri, Perugia, Italy, and Instituto Inter-Universitario, Rome, Italy. *Home:* 316 Randolph St., Maywood, Ill. 60153.

CAREER: Teacher in Ludington, Mich., 1917-18, Evanston, Ill., 1918-20; demonstration teacher at Western Illinois State Teachers College (now Western Illinois University), Macomb, 1920-25, Chicago Teachers College, Chicago, Ill., 1928-31; teacher of English at Collegio Internazionale Monte Mario, Rome, Italy, 1931-33, in Highland Park, Ill., 1933-34; supervisor at various levels, primary through junior high, in school systems of Mansfield, Ohio, 1935-37, Beloit, Wis., 1937-38, Wilmette, Ill., 1938-41. Editorial work for Scott, Foresman & Co., 1941, Field Enterprises (on *Childcraft*), 1957-58, Follett Publishing Co., 1959-63. Lecturer on the Oregon Trail. *Member:* National League of American Pen Women (president, Chicago branch, 1954-56), Daughters of the American Colonists, Daughters of the American Revolution, Order of the Eastern Star, Theta Sigma Phi.

WRITINGS: Safety Town Stories, Lyons & Carnahan Books, 1930; *Polly, Patsy, and Pat, the Safety Triplets*, Follett, 1942; (with Sam Thompson) *Footprints*, Steck, 1957; *Hail, Nathan Hale!*, Abingdon, 1965. Author of language arts workbooks. Contributor to *Today's Health, Kansas City Star, Children's Activities*, and to education journals.

MAJOR, Ralph Hermon 1884-1970

PERSONAL: Born August 29, 1884, in Clay County, Mo.; son of John Sleet and Virginia (Anderson) Major; married Margaret Jackson; children: Ralph H., Jr., John Keene, Virginia Major Thomas. *Education:* William Jewell College, A.B., 1902; Johns Hopkins University, M.D., 1910; also studied at Universities of Leipzig, Munich, and Heidelberg. *Religion:* Episcopalian. *Home:* 6105 High Dr., Praire Village, Kan. 66208. *Office:* School of Medicine, University of Kansas, Kansas City, Kan. 66103.

CAREER: Licensed to practice medicine in Kansas and Michigan; Stanford University, Palo Alto, Calif., instructor in pathology, 1913-14; University of Kansas, Lawrence, professor of pathology, 1914-18; Henry Ford Hospital, Detroit, Mich., physician, 1919-21; University of Kansas, professor of medicine, 1921-50, professor of history of medicine, 1950-70, chairman of department of medicine, 1921-50, chairman of department of history of medicine, 1950-70. Lecturer, Scripps Metabolism Clinic, 1935. *Member:* Royal Society of Medicine, American Medical Association, American Society for Clinical Investigation, Association of American Physicians, American Clinical and Climatological Association, Kansas City Country Club. *Awards, honors:* LL.D., William Jewell College, 1933; Litt.D., University of Cincinnati, 1940.

WRITINGS: The Doctor Explains, Knopf, 1931; *Classic Descriptions of Disease*, C. C Thomas, 1932, 3rd edition, revised and enlarged, 1945; *Disease and Destiny*, Appleton, 1936; *Physical Diagnosis*, Saunders, 1937, 5th edition (with Mahlon H. Delp), 1956, 6th edition, 1962; *Faiths That Healed*, Appleton, 1940; *Fatal Partners, War and Disease*, Doubleday, 1941 (published in England as *War and Disease*, Hutchinson, 1943); *A History of Medicine*, two volumes, C. C Thomas, 1954; *Disease and Destiny: Logan Clendening*, University of Kansas Press, 1958; *Memoirs of a Vanished Era*, privately printed, c.1967; *Old Ties and New*, privately printed, c.1968; *The Logan Clendening Library and Museum of the History of Medicine at the University of Kansas Medical Center*, privately printed, c. 1969. Contributor of more than two hundred articles on medicine and history of medicine to professional journals.

(Died October 15, 1970)

* * *

MALHERBE, Ernst Gideon 1895-

PERSONAL: Born November 8, 1895, in Luckhoff, Orange Free State, South Africa; son of Ernst Gideon (a minister of religion) and Engela (Rabie) Malherbe; married Janie Antonia Nel (a writer), April 5, 1922; children: Ernst, Paul, Jean (son), Betty-Jane (Mrs. R. Wells). *Education:* University of Stellenbosch, B.A. (honors), 1917, M.A., 1918; Columbia University, M.A., 1920, Ph.D., 1924; also studied in Great Britain, in the Netherlands, and Germany. *Home:* Principal's Residence, 267 King George V Ave., Durban, Natal, South Africa. *Office:* University of Natal, King George V Ave., Durban, Natal, South Africa.

CAREER: Successively teacher at Cape Town Training College, lecturer at University of Stellenbosch, and senior lecturer in education at University of Cape Town; Carnegie Poor White Commission of Research, South Africa, chief investigator, education section, 1928-32; National Bureau of Educational Social Research, Pretoria, South Africa, director, 1929-39; Union of South Africa Census and Statistics, Pretoria, director, 1939-45; University of Natal, at

Durban and Pietermaritzburg, South Africa, principal, beginning 1945, and vice-chancellor. Government Commission to Investigate Native Education in South Africa, member, 1935; Government Commission on Medical Training in South Africa, secretary, 1938; National War Histories Committee, chairman, 1945-49; Social and Economic Planning Council, member, 1946-50. *Military service:* South African Army, 1940-45; director of Military Intelligence and Army Education Services; became lieutenant colonel.

MEMBER: South African Association for Advancement of Science (president, 1950-51), South African Psychological Association. *Awards, honors:* LL.D. from Cambridge University, University of Melbourne, Queen's University, McGill University, University of Cape Town, and Rhodes University.

WRITINGS: Education in South Africa, 1652-1922, Juta, 1925; *Education and the Poor White*, Carnegie, 1929; (editor) *Educational Adaptations in a Changing Society*, Juta, 1937; *Entrance Age of University Students in Relation to Success*, van Schaik (Pretoria), 1938; *Whither Matric?*, van Schaik, 1938.

The Bilingual School, Longmans, Green, 1943; *Race Attitudes and Education*, South Africa Institute of Race Relations, 1948; *Our Universities and the Advancement of Science*, Shuter & Shooter, 1951; *The Autonomy of Our Universities and Apartheid*, University of Natal, 1957; (contributor) *South Africa: The Road Ahead*, Timmins, 1960; *Problems of School Medium in a Bilingual Country*, University of Natal, 1962; *Manpower Training: Educational Requirements for Economic Expansion*, African Institute of Race Relations, 1965; *Demographic and Sociopolitical Forces Determining the Position of English in the South African Republic*, English Academy of South Africa, 1966; *The Need for Dialogue*, South Africa Institute of Race Relations, 1967; *The Nemesis of Docility*, South African Institute of Race Relations, 1968; *Bantu Manpower and Education*, South African Institute of Race Relations, 1969. Also author of *Educational and Social Research in South Africa*, 1939, and *Education for Leadership in Africa*, 1960.

Contributor to *Year Book of Education*, Evans, 1932-56, and to *Chambers's Encyclopedia*. Contributor of articles to educational and scientific journals.

WORK IN PROGRESS: A history of education in South Africa.

AVOCATIONAL INTERESTS: Golf and swimming.

*   *   *

MALHERBE, Janie Antonia (Nel)   1897-

PERSONAL: Surname is pronounced Mal-urb-ee; born April 11, 1897, in Wolmaransstad, South Africa; daughter of Paul (a clergyman) and Mabel (Taylor) Nel; married Ernst G. Malherbe (former principal and vice-chancellor of University of Natal), April 5, 1922; children: E. G., Paul N., Jean Christian, Betty-Jane (Mrs. Randall Wells). *Education:* University of Stellenbosch, Intermediate and Junior B.A. and Teacher's Diploma, 1917; attended Columbia University, 1922-23. *Politics:* Progressive Party of South Africa. *Religion:* Dutch Reformed Church. *Home:* By-die-See, P.O. Salt Rock, Umhlali, Natal, South Africa.

CAREER: Primary and high school teacher in Ermelo, Transvaal, South Africa, 1918-22; *Die Volkstem*, Pretoria, South Africa, women's editor, 1933-35; *Die Brandwag*,

Johannesburg, South Africa, cookery editor, 1937-40; *I. C. Digest*, Afrikaans editor, 1942-44; free-lance writer, 1933—. *Military service:* South African Forces, transport driver, 1940, military intelligence, 1940-45; became captain. *Member:* Ex-Service Women's League (founding member), University Women's Association (honorary member), Royal Durban Golf and Social Club (honorary member).

WRITINGS: (Editor) *Complex Country* (first compiled as a booklet for visiting troops), Longmans, Green (London), 1944; *Predikante Prestasies en Petaljes* (biography of father-in-law; in Afrikaans), Maskew Miller, 1951; *Port Natal—A Pioneer Story*, Howard Timmins, 1965. Contributor of historical articles to Afrikaans and English publications in South Africa.

WORK IN PROGRESS: A joint biography with husband, Ernst Malherbe, commissioned by Convocation of University of Natal.

SIDELIGHTS: Mrs. Malherbe's extensive travels include five trips to Europe, three to North America, one to South America, Australia, New Zealand, Greece, and the Greek Islands.

*   *   *

MALLONE, Ronald Stephen   1916-

PERSONAL: Born June 2, 1916, in London, England; son of Anthony St. John and Georgina Helena (Bailey) Mallone; married June Ellis, October 1, 1949 (died, 1957); married Ursula Gibson, November 19, 1966; children: (first marriage) Jonathan Francis Parnell, Eirene Christina. *Education:* University of London, B.A. (first class honors), 1936; Goldsmiths' College, London, teachers' training certificate (first class), 1937. *Politics:* Fellowship Party. *Religion:* Methodist. *Home:* 141 Woolacombe Rd., Blackheath, London S.E.3, England.

CAREER: Peace News, London, England, film and drama critic and member of editorial board, 1937-39; *Christian Party Newsletter*, Birmingham, England, editor, 1941-45; *Un-Common Sense*, London, England, editor, 1945-69; Westminster College of Commerce, London, England, lecturer in English language and literature, 1955-59; *Progress*, London, England, editor, 1958-62; City of Westminster College, London, England, lecturer in literature and liberal studies, 1960—. Fellowship Party, London, England, general secretary, 1956-57, press and publicity officer, 1958—, candidate for Parliament for Woolwich West, 1959, 1964, 1966, candidate for Greenwich Borough Council, 1970, 1971. Lay preacher.

MEMBER: Royal Geographical Society (fellow), Royal Society of Teachers, Peace Pledge Union (member of executive council, 1961-62, 1964—; member of national council, 1961-62, 1963-66, 1971), Fellowship of Reconciliation, Anglican Pacifist Fellowship (founder; member of general committee, 1965-70), Cricket Society.

WRITINGS: Blood and Sweat and Tears (poems), New Vision Publications, 1942; *Whose Victory?* (poems), Christian Party, 1945; *Bread and Butter Politics*, Loverseed Press, 1969; *Gentle Conspiracy* (poems), Loverseed Press, in press. Contributor to *Poetry Today, Adelphi, New Vision, Chambers's Journal*, and to other journals and English national and provincial papers. *Colombo Weekly*, Ceylon, London correspondent, 1947, *Socialist Leader*, cricket correspondent, 1959-63, film critic, 1959—; *Kentish Express*, rugby correspondent, 1961-63; *East Kent Critic*, cricket correspondent, 1969—. Editor, *Day by Day*, 1963—.

WORK IN PROGRESS: Research on power and influence of British Press, with view to book publication; a book on Fielding; a book on early English colonization in America, India, and elsewhere; research on social influence of cinema in Britain; a book on international peace.

AVOCATIONAL INTERESTS: Singing, playing piano, listening to music (especially classical), growing flowers, watching, playing, or writing about almost all ball games.

*   *   *

MALZBERG, Benjamin   1893-

PERSONAL: Born December 2, 1893, in New York, N.Y.; son of Nathan and Anna (Elson) Malzberg; married Rose Hershberg, August 25, 1935; children: Judith, Ruth and Amy (twins). *Education:* City College (now City College of the City University of New York), New York, N.Y., B.S., 1915; Columbia University, M.A., 1917, Ph.D., 1934; graduate study at University of Paris, 1919, 1921, and at University College, London, 1920. *Home:* 33 Bancker St., Albany, N.Y. 12208. *Office:* Research Foundation for Mental Hygiene, 44 Holland Ave., Albany, N.Y. 12208.

CAREER: Statistician in Albany for New York State Department of Social Welfare, 1923-28, New York State Department of Mental Hygiene, 1928-56, Research Foundation for Mental Hygiene, 1956—. *Member:* American Association for the Advancement of Science (fellow), Psychometric Society, Population Association of America, Institute of Mathematical Statistics, American Sociological Association, New York Academy of Science.

WRITINGS: Heredity and Environmental Factors in Dementia Praecox and Manic Depressive Psychoses, State Hospital Press, 1939; *Social and Biological Aspects of Mental Disease,* State Hospital Press, 1940; *Cohort Studies of Mental Disease,* National Association for Mental Health, 1958; *Alcoholic Psychoses at Mid-Century,* Yale Center of Alcohol Studies, 1959; *Mental Disease Among Jews in New York State,* International Medical Press, 1960; *Mental Health of the Negro,* Research Foundation for Mental Hygiene, 1962; *Mental Disease Among Jews in Canada,* Research Foundation for Mental Hygiene, 1963.

*   *   *

MANDER, A(lfred) E(rnest)   1894-

PERSONAL: Born December 13, 1894, in Malvern, England. *Education:* Educated at Queen's College, Taunton, England, and University of Birmingham. *Address:* Box 1902, G.P.O., Sydney, Australia.

CAREER: Former external lecturer at University of New Zealand, Wellington; former general secretary, New Zealand Manufacturers' Federation; research officer, Australian Public Service, New South Wales; controller of new manufacturers, Australian Public Service. Conductor of evening adult education classes in New Zealand and Australia, 1940—; also conductor of adult education courses on radio and television. *Military service:* British Army, 1914-17; served in France; became captain. Australian Army, 1939-43; became major.

WRITINGS: Psychology for Everyman—and Woman, C. A. Watts, 1935, reissued as *Trying to Understand People: Psychology for Everyday Use,* Ure Smith, 1966, Taplinger, 1967; *Clearer Thinking: Logic for Everyman,* C. A. Watts, 1936, reissued as *Clearer Thinking: Logic for Everyday Use,* Ure Smith, 1966, published as *Logic for the Millions,* Philosophical Library, 1947; *Man Marches On: The New Patriotism,* C. A. Watts, 1937; *Alarming Australia* (pamphlet), Currawong Publishing Co., 1939, 2nd edition, 1943; *Something to Live For: The Fundamental Revolution,* Currawong Publishing Co., 1943; *Our Sham Democracy: How to Make It Real* (pamphlet), Harbour Newspaper and Publishing Co., 1943; *Public Enemy, the Press,* Currawong Publishing Co., 1944; *6 P.M. Till Midnight,* Rawson's Book Shop, 1945; *Common Cause for All Who Earn Their Living,* Rawson's Book Shop, 1946; *The Making of the Australians,* Georgian House, 1958; *The Christian God,* Rationalist Press, 1963.

*   *   *

MANKOWSKA, Joyce Kells Batten   1919-
(Joyce Mortimer Batten)

PERSONAL: Born November 21, 1919, in Peebles, Scotland; daughter of Harry Mortimer (an author) and Ivy Kathleen (Godfrey) Batten; married Leopold Mankowska (a company director), April 24, 1946; children: Andrew, Martin, Gillian Mary. *Education:* Attended St. Trinneans High School, Edinburgh. *Religion:* Catholic. *Home:* Arkley, Seagrove, Manor Rd., Seaview, Isle of Wight, England. *Agent:* Carl Routledge, Charles Lavell Lt., Mowbray House, Arundel St., London W.C.2, England.

CAREER: Worker during World War II as secretary of general hospital, 1939-43, member of Scottish Land Army, 1943-44, French and German interpreter on control commission to Germany, 1944-45. *Member:* Guild of St. Francis de Sales (secretary of London women's branch, 1956-63).

WRITINGS: Chang: The Life Story of a Pekingese, Moray Press, 1935; *Airborne* (poems), Montrose Press, 1944; *The Miraculous Picture of the Black Madonna, Czestochowa,* Catholic Truth Society, 1959; *Isle of Mists,* Jenkins, 1960; (editor) Harry Mortimer Batten, *Wild and Free,* Blackie & Son, 1961. Contributor of articles on Catholic topics to British, Irish, and New Zealand publications, and articles and short stories to periodicals in Great Britain.

WORK IN PROGRESS: Editing two more of her late father's unpublished manuscripts; *The Names Remain—Cornish Saints,* the first book of several based on research on Celtic period in Britain; research on Arthurian period; illustrated book on Arthur; an early history of Isle of Wight.

SIDELIGHTS: Mrs. Mankowska traveled in Europe 1938-39. *Avocational interests:* Collecting ancient wells and stone crosses, Celtic and Anglo-Saxon archaeology.

*   *   *

MANN, (Francis) Anthony   1914-

PERSONAL: Born June 10, 1914, in Bolton, England; son of Francis O. (an educator, poet, and novelist) and Marjorie (Turner) Mann; married Gertraut Eichwede, 1937; children: Ellen Antonia Mann Trautmann, Hazel Karin, Michel. *Education:* Studied at Dulwich College and in Graz, Austria; Balliol College, Oxford, B.A. (honors), 1935. *Religion:* Anglican. *Address:* c/o Lloyds Bank, 222 Strand, London, England. *Office:* c/o Daily Telegraph, Foreign News Department, 135 Fleet St., London E.C.4, England; and 4, rue de Castiglione, Paris, France.

CAREER: Daily Telegraph, London, England, correspondent, 1936—, except for period as chief European correspondent for *Sunday Telegraph,* 1961. Principal assignments included chief Berlin correspondent, 1939, Copenhagen, 1939-40, chief correspondent for Germany, 1946, for southeast Europe, based in Rome, Italy, 1952, then special correspondent in thirty-five European, Asian, and African countries, chief correspondent for southern Europe and special correspondent, 1962-65; chief Paris correspondent, 1965—. Interned in Denmark by German orders, 1940-45. Covered War Crime Trials, Berlin Air Lift, other historic events. *Member:* Institute of Journalists, Associazione della Stampa Estera, Anglo-American Press Association of Paris (vice-president). *Awards, honors:* Humboldt Medal of German Academy (Munich).

WRITINGS: Where God Laughed: The Sudan Today, Museum Press, 1954; *Well-Informed Circles,* Cassell, 1961; *Helen Zelenzny: Portrait Sculpture, 1917-1970,* Palombi (Rome), 1970. Contributor of articles to British, European, and American newspapers and magazines, and to *World Book Encyclopedia.*

AVOCATIONAL INTERESTS: Painting, drawing, photography.

*   *   *

MANNING, Thomas Davys   1898-1972

PERSONAL: Born June 30, 1898, in Hoddesdon, Hertfordshire, England; son of Thomas Davys (a physician) and Mary Anne (Coles) Manning. *Education:* Attended Weymouth College, 1905-15. *Home:* Newlands, Seaford, Sussex, England.

CAREER: Schoolmaster, beginning, 1919, became principal, 1946, Newlands, Seaford, Sussex, England. *Military service:* Royal Naval Volunteer Reserve, 1916-17, 1921-51; Royal Naval Air Service, 1917-19; became flight sub-lieutenant; retired as captain, 1951; awarded Commander, Order of the British Empire (military), 1950, Volunteer Officers Decoration. *Member:* Society for Nautical Research (council member).

WRITINGS: (With C. F. Walker) *British Warship Names,* Putnam, 1959; *The British Destroyer,* Putnam, 1961. Honorary editor of *The Mariner's Mirror,* beginning, 1961.

(Died November, 1972)

*   *   *

MANTEY, Julius Robert   1890-

PERSONAL: Born March 17, 1890, in Gannett, Idaho; son of Julius (a farmer) and Emilie (Springer) Mantey; married Mary Ethyl Caldwell, September 20, 1916. *Education:* William Jewell College, A.B., 1916; Southwestern Baptist Theological Seminary, Th.M., 1920; Southern Baptist Theological Seminary, Th.D., 1921, Ph.D., 1931. *Politics:* Republican. *Religion:* Baptist. *Home:* 414 Palmetto Rd., New Port Richey, Fla. 33552.

CAREER: Southwestern Baptist Theological Seminary, Fort Worth, Tex., teacher, 1921-22; Union University, Jackson, Tenn., professor of Greek and New Testament, 1922-25; Northern Baptist Theological Seminary, Oakbrook, Ill., professor of Greek and New Testament, 1925-60; retired, 1960. *Member:* Society of Biblical Literature and Exegesis. *Awards, honors:* D.D., Union University, 1925; achievement citation, William Jewell College, 1950.

WRITINGS: (With H. E. Dana) *A Manual Grammar of the Greek New Testament,* Macmillan, 1927, enlarged edition, 1955; (with Ernest C. Colwell) *A Hellenistic Greek Reader: Selections from the Koine of the New Testament Period* (with lexicon), University of Chicago Press, 1939; *Was Peter a Pope?,* Moody, 1947; (with others) *The Biblical Expository,* Holt, 1960; (with others) *Basic Christian Doctrines,* A. J. Holman, 1962; (with George A. Turner) *The Gospel According to John: The Evangelical Commentary,* Eerdmans, 1964. Articles in *Christianity Today, Journal of Biblical Literature,* and other religious journals.

WORK IN PROGRESS: Compiling notes on recovered meanings for Greek words used by writers during first two centuries; assisting New York Bible Society to prepare *A Contemporary Bible.*

SIDELIGHTS: The Mantey-Dana Greek grammar of 1927 increasingly is used as a text in colleges and seminaries and world-wide. *Avocational interests:* Fishing.

*   *   *

MARCEAU, LeRoy   1907-

PERSONAL: Born September 7, 1907, in Trumbull County, Ohio; son of Harry A. and Anna L. (Price) Marceau; married Irene A. Francescon, June 21, 1941; children: Carla A., Sandra E. *Education:* Ohio State University, LL.B., 1931. *Home:* 208 Sturges Rd., Fairfield, Conn. 06430.

CAREER: Admitted to Ohio bar, 1931, New York bar, 1952; private practice of law, Warren, Ohio, 1931-41; National Labor Relations Board, regional attorney in Indianapolis, Ind., and later in New Orleans, La., 1941-45; Esso Standard Oil Co., counsel, 1945-58; Exxon Corporation, counsel, New York, N.Y., 1959-72. *Member:* International Society for Labour Law & Social Legislation, Federal Bar Association.

WRITINGS: Drafting a Union Contract, Little, 1965; *Dealing With a Union,* AMA, 1969.

WORK IN PROGRESS: Understanding a Document.

*   *   *

MARELLI, Leonard R(ussell)   1933-1973

PERSONAL: Born July 20, 1933, in New York, N.Y.; son of Henry Alexander (a marine engineer) and Catherine (Walsh) Marelli; married Jennie Jenkinson, January 24, 1960; children: Russell, Richard. *Education:* Manhattan College, B.S., 1955; Columbia University, A.M., 1959; Ph.D. candidate. *Politics:* Democrat. *Religion:* Roman Catholic. *Home:* 40 First Ave., New York, N.Y. 10009. *Office:* American Language Institute, New York University, Washington Sq., New York, N.Y. 10003.

CAREER: New York, (N.Y.) Board of Education, teacher of speech and drama, 1959-60; New York University, American Language Institute, New York, N.Y., instructor in English, 1960-73. *Military service:* U.S. Air Force, 1955-58; became first lieutenant. U.S. Air Force Reserve; became captain. *Member:* Linguistic Society of America, Modern Language Association of America, American Association of University Professors, Linguistic Circle of New York.

WRITINGS: (Editor with Robert M. Grindell and Harvey Nadler) *American Readings,* McGraw, 1964.

WORK IN PROGRESS: Two textbooks for "An Intensive Course in American English" series, *Grammar* (in collaboration with Harvey Nadler) and *Pronunciation.*

(Died October, 1973)

MARGON, Lester 1892-

PERSONAL: Born January 26, 1892, in New York, N.Y.; son of Moses (a manufacturer) and Flora (Somerfeld) Margon. *Education:* Studied at various periods at Cooper Union, Columbia University, Mechanics Institute of New York, and New York University. *Home:* 1426 South Doheny Dr., Los Angeles, Calif.

CAREER: Designer of interiors and furniture. *Member:* American Institute of Interior Designers.

WRITINGS: Construction of American Furniture Treasures, Home Craftsman, 1949; *World Furniture Treasures*, Reinhold, 1954; *Masterpieces of American Furniture*, Architectural Book Publishing, 1965; *Masterpieces of European Furniture*, Architectural Book Publishing, 1968; *More American Furniture Treasures*, Architectural Book Publishing, 1971. Contributor of articles on furniture and decoration to magazines.

* * *

MARIE THERESE, Mother 1891-

PERSONAL: Secular name, Margaret Bisgood; born May 22, 1891, in London, England; daughter of Joseph John and Laura Louise (Webber) Bisgood. *Education:* Oxford University, M.A., 1914. *Home:* Convent of Holy Child Jesus, Mayfield, Sussex, England.

CAREER: Roman Catholic nun, member of Society of the Holy Child Jesus. Former grammar school teacher and lecturer at Teachers' Training College, London, England; retired from teaching, 1970.

WRITINGS—Under name in religion Mother Marie Therese: *Cornelia Connelly: A Study in Fidelity*, Burns, 1963.

* * *

MARINONI, Rosa Zagnoni 1888-1970

PERSONAL: Born January 5, 1888, in Bologna, Italy; daughter of Antero (a journalist and author) and Maria (Marzocchi) Zagnoni; married Antonio Marinoni (a professor), July 30, 1908 (deceased); children: Paul Albert, Maria Stella. *Education:* University of Arkansas, special student, 1913-16. *Religion:* Roman Catholic. *Home:* Villa Rose, Fayetteville, Ark.

CAREER: Young Men's Christian Association, assistant educational director overseas, 1918-20; poet and author, 1925—. Organizer and co-conductor of sixteen European tours; founder of Arkansas Poetry Day, 1948; former chairman of student loan fund, Arkansas Federation of Women's Clubs. *Member:* National League of American Pen Women (founder of northwest Arkansas branch), University City Poetry Club (founder, 1926), Delta Delta Delta. *Awards, honors:* Poet laureate of Arkansas by act of the legislature; poet laureate of the Ozarks.

WRITINGS—Poems: *Behind the Mask*, H. Harrison, 1927; *Red Kites and Wooden Crosses*, R. Packard & Co., 1929; *North of Laughter*, Oglethorpe University Press, 1931; *Side Show*, McKay, 1938; *Sunny Side Up*, Atheneum, 1941; *Timberline*, Torch Press, 1954; *The Ozarks and Some of Its People*, Ozark Series Press, 1956, 4th edition, 1965; *Radici al Vento* (title means "Roots to the Sky"; English-Italian parallel text), Bazzi (Milan), 1956; *The Ozarks and More of Its People*, Ozark Series Press, 1958; *The Green Sea Horse*, Golden Quill, 1964; *Lend Me Your Ears!: A Beakfull of Humorous Verse*, Ozark Series

Press, 1966; *Whoo-whoo, the "Howl" of the Ozarks says: Think and Wink!*, Ozark Series Press, 1967. Also author of *Pine Needles*, 1927, and *In Passing*, 1930, both books of poetry.

Editor: *Forty Poets*, Ozark Series Press, 1956. Also contributor of short stories, articles, epigrams, and poems to magazines in the United States, Canada, Mexico, and Europe. Associate editor, *South and West International Quarterly*.

SIDELIGHTS: Mrs. Marinoni was the mother of two children and the grandmother of eight children. Her daughter wrote *CA* that "she prized her family as one of her greatest achievements of creation."

Mrs. Marinoni was fluent in Italian; she read and understood French and Spanish.

(Died March 26, 1970)

* * *

MARK, Irving 1908-

PERSONAL: Born June 3, 1908, in New York, N.Y.; son of Philip (a retail dress merchant) and Rose (Kafko) Mark; married Edna Weissman (a high school music teacher), 1935; children: Peter Alan, Joel Jonathan. *Education:* City College (now City College of the City University of New York), A.B., (cum laude), 1929; Columbia University, A.M., 1931, Ph.D., 1940; New York Law School, LL.B., 1933. *Home:* 4084 Bedford Ave., Brooklyn, N.Y. 11229. *Office:* Monmouth College, West Long Branch, N.J. 07764.

CAREER: Admitted to New York bar, 1934; attorney in private practice, 1934—. New York (N.Y.) public schools, teacher, 1930-33; Brooklyn College (now Brooklyn College of the City University of New York), Brooklyn, N.Y., tutor, 1933-37, instructor, 1937-49, assistant professor of history, 1949-53; Columbia University, Law School, New York, N.Y., assistant to director of Project for Effective Justice, 1956-58; Adelphi University, Garden City, N.Y., assistant professor, 1963-64, associate professor of history, 1965-67; Monmouth College, West Long Branch, N.J., professor of history, 1967-73, Distinguished Professor of History, 1973, professor emeritus, 1974—. Lecturer in history at Fairleigh Dickinson University, 1956-57, and Rutgers University, 1957-63. Consultant to International Statistical Bureau, 1943-44, Adjutant General's Office, U.S. War Department, 1944-45, and Citizens Committee on Children of New York City, 1946. Professional reader for Dorothy Canfield Fisher, 1951-52. *Member:* American Historical Association, American Association of University Professors, Phi Beta Kappa. *Awards, honors:* LL.D., Monmouth College, 1973.

WRITINGS: Agrarian Conflicts in Colonial New York, 1711-1775, Columbia University Press, 1940, 2nd edition, Friedman, 1965; (editor with Eugene L. Schwaab) *The Faith of Our Fathers: An Anthology Expressing the Aspirations of the American Common Man, 1790-1860*, Knopf, 1952; *Great Debates, U.S.A.*, Silver Burdett, 1969. Contributor of articles and reviews to history, sociology, and legal journals.

WORK IN PROGRESS: A book tentatively entitled *Rebellions and Revolutions—Through the U.S. Bicentennial.*

* * *

MARKEY, Gene 1895-

PERSONAL: Born December 11, 1895, in Jackson, Mich.;

son of Eugene Lawrence (an Army colonel) and Alice (White) Markey; married fourth wife, Lucille Parker Wright, September 27, 1952; children: (prior marriage) Melinda (Mrs. Joseph Bena). *Education:* Dartmouth College, B.S., 1918; Art Institute of Chicago, student, 1919-20. *Home address:* Calumet Farm, Box 1810, Lexington, Ky.

CAREER: Writer of short stories and novels, 1919-29; motion picture writer and producer, 1929-41; novelist. *Military service:* U.S. Army, Infantry, 1917-19; became first lieutenant. U.S. Naval Reserve, 1930-55, serving on active duty, 1941-46; received Legion of Merit, Bronze Star, Navy Commendation Medal, Star of Solidarity (Italy), Legion of Honor (France); retired as rear admiral. *Member:* Army and Navy Club (Washington, D.C.), White's Club and Buck's Club (both London), Travellers Club (Paris), Knickerbocker, Brook Club, and Jockey Club (all New York), United Hunts. *Awards, honors:* L.H.D., Rollins College, 1957; honorary citizen of Kentucky, 1957.

WRITINGS: Literary Lights; A Book of Caricatures, Knopf, 1923; *Men about Town, a Book of Fifty-Eight Caricatures,* Covici-McGee, 1924; (with Charles W. Collins) *The Dark Island* (novel), Doubleday, Doran, 1928; *Stepping High* (novel), Doubleday, Doran, 1929; *The Road to Rouen* (novel), John Day, 1930; *His Majesty's Pyjamas* (novel), Covici, Friede, 1934; *Kingdom of the Spur* (novel), Ballantine, 1953; *Kentucky Pride* (novel), Random House, 1956; *Until the Morning,* Hodder & Stoughton, 1957; *That Far Paradise* (novel), McKay, 1960; *Women, Women, Everywhere* (novel), Bobbs-Merrill, 1964; *Mountbatten* (profile), Allied Flags, 1965. Also author of *The Pumpkin Coach,* 1928, *Amabel,* 1928, and *The Great Companions,* a novel, 1949.

Plays: "Right You Are," first produced in Atlantic City, 1925; (with Samuel Hoffenstein) "The Eskimo," first produced in Detroit, 1926; (with Ashton Stevens) *The Colonel's Lady* (first produced in Chicago, 1930), Dierkes Press, 1948.

Author of twelve original stories for films, including: "White Hunter," 20th Century-Fox, 1936; (with Irving Berlin) "On the Avenue," 20th Century-Fox, 1937; "You're the One," Paramount, 1941. Also author of twenty other screenplays.

WORK IN PROGRESS: Men and Others, a memoir of the war, 1941-46.

SIDELIGHTS: The Great Companions was filmed as "Meet Me at the Fair," Universal, 1953, and *His Majesty's Pyjamas,* as "Lovers in Exile." *Avocational interests:* Reading histories and biographies.

* * *

MARKHAM, Felix (Maurice Hippisley) 1908-

PERSONAL: Born February 27, 1908, in Brighton, England; son of Richard (a clergyman) and Mary (Dalzel) Markham. *Education:* Eton College, student, 1921-26; Balliol College, Oxford, Literae Humaniores (first class honours), 1929, modern history (first class honours), 1930, M.A., 1933. *Politics:* Conservative. *Religion:* Church of England. *Home:* Hertford College, Oxford, England. *Agent:* Peter Janson-Smith Ltd., 50 Westminster Palace Gardens, London S.W.1, England.

CAREER: Oxford University, Oxford, England, fellow and tutor of Hertford College, 1932-70, senior university proctor, 1946-47, university lecturer in modern history, 1947-70. Principal officer, British Ministry of Labour;

Standing Committees on Technical Personnel and Further Education. *Member:* Royal Historical Society (fellow), Oxford University Conservative Association (honorary vice-president). *Awards, honors:* Leverhulme fellow, 1961.

WRITINGS: (Editor, translator, and author of introduction) *Henri Comte de Saint-Simon, 1760-1825: Selected Writings,* Basil Blackwell, 1952, Macmillan (New York), 1953; *Napoleon and the Awakening of Europe,* English Universities Press, 1954, Collier, 1965; (contributor) John McManners and John Wallace-Hardill, editors, *France: Government and Society,* Methuen, 1957; *Napoleon,* Weidenfeld & Nicolson, 1963, New American Library, 1964; (contributor) C. W. Crowley, editor, *New Cambridge Modern History,* Volume IX: *War and Peace in an Age of Upheaval, 1793-1830,* Cambridge University Press, 1964; (editor, translator, and author of introduction) Saint-Simon, *Social Organization, The Science of Man and Other Writings,* Harper, 1964; *Oxford,* Reynal, 1967. Contributor to *Encyclopaedia of World History,* Hutchinson, 1960, and to periodicals, including *Spectator, Listener, Apollo,* and *History Today.*

WORK IN PROGRESS: Anglo-French Relations in the Nineteenth Century.

* * *

MARPLES, William F(rank) 1907-

PERSONAL: Born February 14, 1907, in Birmingham, England; became U.S. citizen, 1956; son of Percy Morris and Marianne Hilda (Coates) Marples; married Nora A. Turner, July 25, 1934; children: Jill, Jacqueline Mary (Mrs. Gerd La Mar), Lesley Ann (Mrs. Joseph A. Fischer), John Robert. *Education:* Attended King Edward's School, Birmingham, England. *Home:* 2408 Romney Rd., San Diego, Calif. 92109.

CAREER: Actuarial clerk, Birmingham, England, 1925-32; Marples Classes (correspondence tutors for actuarial examinations), Birmingham, England, principal, 1932-37; Actuarial Tuition Service, London, England, secretary, 1937-40; Duncan C. Fraser & Co. (consulting actuaries), Liverpool, England, partner, 1940-50; George B. Buck (consulting actuary), New York, N.Y., senior associate, 1950-58; Milliman & Robertson, Inc. (actuaries), Los Angeles, Calif., vice-president, 1958-61; Martin E. Segal Co., Los Angeles, Calif., vice-president, and actuary for western division, 1961-64; Alexander & Alexander, Inc., Los Angeles, consulting actuary, 1964-71; Mitchell & Kadoyama Inc., Los Angeles, vice-president, 1971-73; consulting actuary, self-employed 1973—. Speaker on pension plans to professional groups. *Military service:* British Home Guard, 1939-46; became captain.

MEMBER: American Academy of Actuaries, Institute of Actuaries (London; fellow), Society of Actuaries (associate), Conference of Actuaries in Public Practice (fellow), American Pension Conference, Western Pension Conference, Los Angeles Actuarial Club (president, 1964-65).

WRITINGS: (Contributor) Gordon A. Hosking, *Pension Schemes and Retirement Benefits,* Sweet & Maxwell, 1956; *Actuarial Aspects of Pension Security,* Homewood Press, 1965. Contributor to *Encyclopaedia Britannica* and to professional publications.

* * *

MARSH, John 1904-

PERSONAL: Born November 5, 1904; son of George

Maurice and Florence Elizabeth Ann (Blane) Marsh; married Gladys Walker, September 3, 1934; children: John, George, Mary. *Education:* Yorkshire United College, student; University of Edinburgh, M.A. (first class honors in philosophy), 1928; Oxford University, M.A., 1940, D.Phil., 1946; advanced study at University of Marburg. *Home and office:* Rannerdale Close, Buttermere, Cockermouth, Cumberland, England.

CAREER: Congregational minister. Westhill Training College, Birmingham, England, lecturer in biblical studies, 1932-34; Congregational Church, Otley, Yorkshire, England, pastor, 1934-38; Mansfield College, Oxford University, Oxford, England, 1938-49, started as tutor, became lecturer, and professor; University of Nottingham, Nottingham, England, professor of Christian theology, 1949-53; Mansfield College, Oxford University, principal, 1953-70. Chairman, Congregational Union of England and Wales, 1963-64. Adviser on religious television, Independent Television Authority, 1955-65. Moderator, Free Church Federal Council of England and Wales, 1970-71. *Awards, honors:* D.D., University of Edinburgh; Commander, Order of the British Empire, 1964.

WRITINGS: The Living God, Independent Press, 1942; (editor) *Congregationalism Today,* Independent Press, 1943; *For the Church Member,* Independent Press, 1946; *God and Time: Three Broadcast Talks,* Independent Press, 1948; (compiler with John Huxtable, Romilly Micklem, and James Todd) *Book of Public Worship,* Oxford University Press, 1948, 2nd edition, 1949; (editor with Donald Baillie) *Intercommunion: The Report of the Theological Commission,* Harper, 1952; *The Fulness of Time,* Harper, 1952; *The Significance of Evanston,* Independent Press, 1954; (translator) Ethelbert Stauffer, *New Testament Theology,* Macmillan, 1955, new edition, S.C.M. Press, 1963; *Marking Time,* Independent Press, 1955; *A Year with the Bible,* Harper, 1957; *Amos and Micah: Introduction and Commentary,* Macmillan, 1959; (translator) Rudolf Bultmann, *The History of the Synoptic Tradition,* Harper, 1963; *Theme with Variations,* Independent Press, 1963; *The Gospel of St. John,* Penguin, 1968. Editor, "Forward Books," Independent Press, 1943-44; co-editor, "Torch Bible Commentaries," S.C.M. Press, 1948—.

WORK IN PROGRESS: Commentary on Matthew, for Bles.

* * *

MARSH, John 1907-
(John Elton, John Harley, Harrington Hastings, Grace Richmond, Lilian Woodward)

PERSONAL: Born August 8, 1907, in Halifax, Yorkshire, England; son of Thomas William (a caterer) and Lilian (Woodward) Marsh; married Irene Andrew, June 1, 1938. *Education:* Attended Giggleswick School, 1922-24. *Religion:* Church of England. *Home:* 3 Claremont Ct., Queensway, London W.2, England. *Agent:* J. F. Gibson's Literary Agency, 17 Southampton Pl., London W.C.1, England.

CAREER: King George's Fund for Sailors (maritime charitable trust), London, England, press and public relations officer, 1949—; author. *Member:* International P.E.N. (fellow), Society of Authors, Crime Writers Association, Press Club (London).

WRITINGS: Maiden Armour, Stanley Paul, 1932; *Lonely Pathway,* Stanley Paul, 1933; *Return They Must,* Stanley Paul, 1934; *Body Made Alive,* Stanley Smith, 1936; *Many Parts,* Gerald G. Swan, 1946.

The Secret of the Seven Sisters, Ward, Lock, 1950; *The Brain of Paul Menoloff,* Forbes Robertson, 1953; *Cruise of the Carefree,* British Book Service, 1955; *The Young Winston Churchill,* British Book Service, 1955; *The Hidden Answer,* Gifford, 1956; *House of Echoes,* Gifford, 1956; *Murders Maze,* British Book Service, 1957; *Operation Snatch,* Gifford, 1958; *City of Fear,* Gifford, 1959.

The Reluctant Executioner, R. Hale, 1960; *Small and Deadly,* R. Hale, 1961; *Girl in a Net,* R. Hale, 1962; *The Golden Teddybear,* T. V. Boardman, 1965; *Not My Murder,* Gifford, 1967; *Monk's Hollow,* Gifford, 1968; *Master of High Beck,* R. Hale, 1969; *Hate Thy Neighbor,* R. Hale, 1969.

Under pseudonym John Elton: *The Green Plantations,* Ward, Lock, 1955.

Under pseudonym John Harley: *The Four Doctors,* R. Hale, 1960; *Doctor with Four Hands,* R. Hale, 1962; *Doctor to the House of Jasmin,* Gifford, 1967; *Doctor in Spain,* R. Hale, 1968.

Under pseudonym Harrington Hastings: *Criminal Square,* Hutchinson, 1928; *The War Dog Stirs,* Hutchinson, 1929.

Under pseudonym Grace Richmond—All published by R. Hale: *When There's Love at Home,* 1959; *June Fairley, Air Hostess,* 1960; *Too Young to Wed,* 1960; *The Touch of Your Hand,* 1961; *Marriage is Like That,* 1961; *The Greater Love,* 1962; *The Doctor's Secret,* 1962; *The Love Race,* 1967; *Love's High Places,* 1967; *Passport to Romance,* 1969; *Waters of Conflict,* 1969.

Under pseudonym Lilian Woodward; all published by R. Hale; *Nursing Assignment,* 1959; *Cruise to Romance,* 1960; *Nurse Frayne's Strange Quest,* 1960; *The Hidden Past,* 1961; *Nurse to the Maharajah,* 1961; *The Wrong Love,* 1962; *Appointment with Love,* 1962; *Love Me, Love Me Not,* 1966; *The House on the Moor,* 1967; *Love's Sweet Music,* 1968; *Flight to Romance,* 1969.

Contributor to British magazines and newspapers.

* * *

MARSHALL, Annie Jessie 1922-

PERSONAL: Born December 11, 1922, in Manchester, England; daughter of Joseph Harold and Jessie (Entwisle) Mandleberg. *Education:* University of Edinburgh, B.S., 1947; University of London, postgraduate diploma in psychology, 1957. *Address:* c/o National Westminster Bank Ltd., 358 Oxford St., London W.1, England. *Agent:* A. M. Heath & Co. Ltd., 35 Dover St., London W.1, England.

CAREER: Mental Health Services, Hobart and Melbourne, Australia, clinical psychologist, 1958-59; National Spastics Society, Bristol, England, research psychologist, 1961-63; National Association for Mental Health, Birmingham, England, research psychologist, 1963-66.

WRITINGS: Hunting the Guru in India, Gollancz, 1963; *The Abilities and Attainments of Children Leaving Junior Training Centers,* National Association for Mental Health, 1967. Contributor to professional journals.

* * *

MARSHALL, Dorothy 1900-

PERSONAL: Born March 26, 1900, in Morecambe, Lancashire, England; daughter of John Willis (a teacher) and Eva (Edge) Marshall. *Education:* Attended Girton College, Cambridge. *Politics:* Liberal. *Religion:* Church of England. *Home:* 9 Warwick House, Castle Court, Cardiff, Wales. *Office:* University College, Cathays Park, Cardiff, Wales.

CAREER: Vassar College, Poughkeepsie, N.Y., temporary instructor, 1924-25; Reigate County School for Girls, Surrey, England, senior history mistress, 1925-27; University of the Witwatersrand, Johannesburg, South Africa, visiting lecturer, 1927-28; Cambridge University, Girton College, Cambridge, England, researcher and tutor, 1928-30; University of London, Bedford College, London, England, assistant lecturer in history, 1930-34; University of Durham, Durham, England, lecturer in history, 1934-36; University of Wales, University College of South Wales and Monmouthshire, Cardiff, 1936—, became senior lecturer in department of history. Visiting lecturer, Wellesley College, 1961-62. Member: Royal Historical Society (fellow), Economic History Society, Historical Association.

WRITINGS: The English Poor in the Eighteenth Century, Routledge, 1926, reprinted, 1969; The Rise of George Canning, Longmans, Green, 1938; The English People in the Eighteenth Century, Longmans, Green, 1956; Eighteenth Century England, Longmans, Green, 1962; John Wesley, Oxford University Press, 1965; Dr. Johnson's London, Wiley, 1968. Contributor to Clarendon Biographies, Oxford University Press, 1965, and to Grolier's Book of Knowledge. Author of monographs on domestic service in eighteenth-century England.

AVOCATIONAL INTERESTS: Cooking, entertaining, and country living.

* * *

MARSHALL, E(dmund) Jesse 1888-

PERSONAL: Born January 17, 1888, in Woodford County, Ill.; son of Solomon (a farmer) and Margaret (Gilpen) Marshall; married May Weeks, February 2, 1918; children: Margaret Ann (Mrs. Michael O'Donoghue). Education: Simpson College, B.A., 1911; University of Chicago, J.D. (cum laude), 1914. Politics: Democrat. Home: Apt. 242, Martin Hotel, Sioux City, Iowa 51101. Office: Shull, Marshall, Mayne, Marks & Vizintos, 1108 Badgerow Building, Sioux City, Iowa 51101.

CAREER: University of Missouri, Law School, Columbia, assistant professor of law, 1919-20; Shull, Marshall, Mayne, Marks & Vizintos, Sioux City, Iowa, partner in general practice of law, 1940—. Director of Sioux City Stock Yards Co., and Sioux City Home Federal Savings and Loan Association. Military service: U.S. Army, Infantry, 1917-19, 1942-46; became colonel; received Army Commendation Medal. Member: American Bar Association (member of commission for uniform state laws, 1933-42), Iowa State Bar Association (chairman, committee of title standards, 1950-64), Sioux City Bar Association. Awards, honors: Award of merit, Iowa State Bar, 1956.

WRITINGS: Iowa Title Opinions and Standards, Allen Smith, 1963.

WORK IN PROGRESS: A supplement to Iowa Title Opinions and Standards.

* * *

MARSHALL, Edison 1894-1967
(Hall Hunter)

PERSONAL: Born August 29, 1894, in Rensselaer, Ind.; son of George Edward (a newspaper publisher) and Lille (Bartoo) Marshall; married Agnes Sharp Flythe, January 4, 1920; children: Edison, Jr., Nancy Silence (Mrs. Frank Robertson Motley). Education: University of Oregon, student, 1913-16. Politics: Conservative. Religion: "Spen-

cerian agnostic." Home: Breetholm, Augusta, Ga.; Freedom Farm, Waynesboro, Ga. Agent: Paul R. Reynolds & Son, 599 Fifth Avenue, New York, N.Y. 10017.

CAREER: Writer for magazine, 1916-17; free-lance writer, 1919-1967. Hunter and explorer, in earlier years, in East Africa, Alaska, Siam, China, Japan, Nepal, and other countries. Military service: U.S. Army, 1918; became second lieutenant. Member: Georgia Authors Association (trustee), Delta Tau Delta, Sigma Upsilon, Attic Club (Augusta). Awards, honors: First prize, O. Henry Memorial Awards, 1921, for "The Heart of Little Shikara"; M.A. from University of Oregon, 1941; Gold Cross, Order of Merit, University of Miami.

WRITINGS: The Voice of the Pack, Little, Brown, 1920; The Snowshoe Trail, Little, Brown, 1921; The Strength of the Pines, Little, Brown, 1921; The Heart of Little Shikara, and Other Stories, Little, Brown, 1922; Shepherds of the Wild, Little, Brown, 1922; The Sky Line of Spruce, Little, Brown, 1922; The Isle of Retribution, Little, Brown, 1923; The Land of Forgotten Men, Little, Brown, 1923; The Death Bell, Garden City Publishing Co., 1924; Seward's Folly, Little, Brown, 1924; Ocean Gold, Harper, 1925; The Sleeper of the Moonlit Ranges, Cosmopolitan, 1925; Campfire Courage, Harper, 1926; Child of the Wild, Cosmopolitan, 1926; The Deadfall, Cosmopolitan, 1927; The Far Call, Cosmopolitan, 1928; The Fish Hawk, Cosmopolitan, 1929.

The Missionary, Cosmopolitan, 1930; The Doctor of Lonesome River, Cosmopolitan, 1931; The Deputy at Snow Mountain, Kinsey, 1932; Forlorn Island, Kinsey, 1932; The Light in the Jungle, Kinsey, 1933: Ogden's Strange Story, Kinsey, 1934; The Splendid Quest, Kinsey, 1934; Dian of the Lost Land, Kinsey, 1935; Sam Campbell, Gentlemen, Kinsey, 1935; The Stolen God, Kinsey, 1936; Darzee, Girl of India, Kinsey, 1937; The White Brigand, Kinsey, 1937; The Jewel of Malabar, Kinsey, 1938.

Benjamin Blake (a Literary Guild selection), Farrar & Rhinehart, 1941; Great Smith, Farrar & Rinehart, 1943; The Upstart, Farrar & Rinehart, 1945; Shikar and Safari, Farrar, Straus, 1947; Yankee Pasha, Farrar, Straus 1947; Castle in the Swamp, Farrar, Straus, 1948; Gypsy Sixpence, Farrar, Straus, 1949.

The Infinite Woman, Farrar, Straus, 1950; Love Stories of India, Farrar, Straus, 1950; The Viking, Farrar, Straus, 1951; (under pseudonym Hall Hunter) The Bengal Tiger, Doubleday, 1952; Caravan to Xanadu, Farrar, Straus, 1953; American Captain, Farrar, Straus, 1954 (published in England as Captain's Saga, Muller, 1955); The Gentleman, Farrar, Straus, 1956; The Heart of the Hunter (memoirs), McGraw, 1956; The Inevitable Hour, Putnam, 1957; Princess Sophia, Doubleday, 1958; The Pagan King, Doubleday, 1959.

Earth Giant, Doubleday, 1960; West with the Vikings, Doubleday, 1961; The Conqueror, Doubleday, 1962; Cortez and Marina, Doubleday, 1963; The Lost Colony, Doubleday, 1964.

Writer of educational film scripts for Department of Defense during war years; appeared on television for Veterans Administration. Contributor of short stories, serials, and articles to Cosmopolitan, True, Saturday Evening Post, Harper's Bazaar, Readers' Digest, Good Housekeeping, American, outdoor magazines, and other periodicals.

SIDELIGHTS: Writing to CA several years ago, Marshall said of himself and his work, "I count myself for the last minnesinger. I read no contemporary fiction, for fear of being influenced by it. . . . I read a great deal of lyric and epic poetry; I do not even know the names of any living American poets; as far as I know the last great American poet was Stephen Vincent Benet.

"I regard *Moby Dick* as the greatest novel ever written . . . Isak Dinesen as the greatest writer of short stories in my time, and Shaw the greatest dramatist . . . *The Snows of Kilimanjaro* (and other Hemingway books) will be remembered."

"I suspect that I am an anachronism, and my career is *contre tempes*. I wrote my novels according to my concept of the novel and precisely what I wanted to write with no thought of my audience. My first obligation is to tell an exciting story, and if I can instruct and inspire as well, all to the good."

Marshall, unhappy in crowds, eschewing New York, found commercial television and modern movies almost unbearable; he relaxed with who-done-its, his favorites being those of Conan Doyle and Agatha Christie.

Five silent movies and five sound films, including "The Vikings," have been based on his books. His novels have been translated into nine European languages and went to still other countries in pre-Iron Curtain days.

(Died October 29, 1967)

*   *   *

MARSHALL, James Vance 1887-1964
(Jice Doone)

PERSONAL: Born in 1887, in Casino, New South Wales, Australia; son of James (a Presbyterian clergyman) and Agnes (Quinn) Marshall; married Isabelle Emily Sirman, June 17, 1919; children: Vance. *Education:* Completed high school in Sydney, Australia. *Politics:* "Labour (cum Socialist)." *Religion:* "Presbyterian turned Rationalist." *Home and office:* 120 Queen St., Oberon, New South Wales, Australia. *Agent:* John Johnson, 10 Suffield House, 79 Davies St., London W. 1, England.

CAREER: Bank clerk in Sydney, Australia, for two years before setting out to roam and work his way around much of the world. Successively supercargo on a tramp ship, reporter for *North China Daily News,* Shanghai, deckhand and later assistant purser on "Empress of India," employee of *Winnipeg Star,* Winnipeg, Manitoba, *Memphis Scimitar,* Memphis, Tenn., *New Orleans Picayune,* New Orleans, La., plantation worker and railroad gang boss in Central America, where he stayed for five years, sandalwood cutter in Australia, fur trader in Bering Sea, journalist in London, England, timber cutter in Blue Mountains, New South Wales, Australia, and part-time writer. During residence in England served as campaign officer for British Board of Trade, 1940-47, justice of peace on Westminster bench in World War II period, administrative officer in Commonwealth Immigration Department, 1949-57. *Awards, honors:* Civilian Medal and Scroll of Merit for civil defense rescue work during World War II.

WRITINGS: (Under pseudonym Jice Doone) *Timely Tips for New Australians,* Empire Publishing Co., 1926; *So This Is London,* Empire Publishing Co.; *The Children,* M. Joseph, 1959, published as *Walkabout,* Doubleday, 1961; *A River Ran Out of Eden,* Hodder & Stoughton, 1962, Morrow, 1963; *Jail From Within [and] The Living Dead,* Wentworth Press, 1969 (originally published 1917, and 1919, respectively). Also author of *Hitting the Iron Trail* and

Banana Zone, published by George Newnes, and an autobiography, *Whichever Way the Wind Blew.* Author of skits for English stage. Contributor of factual narratives to *World Wide Magazine,* and of articles to newspapers and magazines.

WORK IN PROGRESS: A sequel to *Walkabout;* a book about newly arrived migrants lodged in an Australian government hostel.

SIDELIGHTS: Paradoxically, Marshall, jailed in Australia during World War I for anti-war activity, was honored for rescue work during World War II. *Walkabout* has been translated into German, made into a motion picture, and included in an omnibus book published by Thomas Nelson; *So This Is London* was serialized in newspapers and magazines. Several books written by Donald Gordon Payne have been published under Marshall's name since his death; however, it has been stated that Payne is "using the name by permission of [Marshall's] family."

(Died, 1964)

*   *   *

MARSHALL, John S(edberry) 1898-

PERSONAL: Born May 25, 1898, in Fullerton, Calif.; son of John Lundy (an orchardist) and Emma Elizabeth (Gawley) Marshall; married Elizabeth Southard, May 26, 1923; children: James Edward. *Education:* Pomona College, A.B., 1921; Boston University, Ph.D., 1926; also studied at University of Basel, 1923-25, 1926, Harvard University, 1924-25, University of California, 1928, and Russian University of Prague, summers, 1935, 1936. *Politics:* Democrat. *Religion:* Episcopalian.

CAREER: Syracuse University, Syracuse, N.Y., instructor in philosophy, 1926-29; Albion College, Albion, Mich., professor of philosophy, 1929-46; University of the South, Sewanee, Tenn., professor philosophy, 1946-68, professor, Graduate School of Theology, 1948-63. *Member:* American Philosophical Association, American Association of University Professors, Southern Society for Philosophy of Religion (past president), Guild of Scholars of Episcopal Church (past president), British Institute of Philosophy, Phi Beta Kappa, Lambda Chi Alpha.

WRITINGS: (With N. O. Lossky) *Value and Existence,* Allen & Unwin, 1935; *Hookers' Polity in Modern English,* University of the South Press, 1948; *The Genius and Mission of the Episcopal Church,* Church Historical Society, 1949; *The Word Was Made Flesh,* University of the South Press, 1949; *Hooker's Theology of Common Prayer,* University of the South Press, 1953; *Hooker and the Anglican Tradition,* University of the South Press, 1963. Contributor to *Sewanee Review* and other journals. Editor, *Anglican Theological Review,* 1959-65.

*   *   *

MARSHALL, Margaret Wiley 1908-
(Margaret L. Wiley)

PERSONAL: Born April 17, 1908, in Portland, Ore.; daughter of John Thomas and Minnie (Burnett) Wiley; married Roderick Marshall, August 21, 1954; children: (stepdaughters) Janet Marshall, Lois Marshall (Mrs. Barry Sales). *Education:* Reed College, B.A., 1929, M.A., 1931; Radcliffe College, Ph.D., 1940. *Politics:* Democrat. *Religion:* Disciples of Christ. *Home:* Kelmscott Manor, Lechlade, Glos, England.

CAREER: High school teacher, Redmond, Ore., 1933-36;

Emerson College, Boston, Mass., head of English department, 1938-43; Commercial Iron Works, Portland, Ore., personnel clerk, 1943; New School for Social Research, New York, N.Y., editorial assistant, 1943-44, student adviser, 1944-46; Brooklyn College (now Brooklyn College of the City University of New York), instructor, 1946-53, assistant professor, 1953-60, associate professor, 1960-67, professor of English, 1967-71. *Member:* Modern Language Association of America, Renaissance Society, Phi Beta Kappa. *Awards, honors:* Fulbright research grant for India, 1957-58; Fulbright lectureship in India, 1958-59.

WRITINGS: (Under name Margaret L. Wiley) *The Subtle Knot: Creative Scepticism in Seventeenth-Century England,* Harvard University Press, 1952; *Studies in American Literature: Creative Scepticism in Emerson, Melville and Henry James* (monograph), University of Punjab, 1960; *Creative Sceptics,* Allen & Unwin, 1966. Contributor to academic journals in America and India.

WORK IN PROGRESS: A study of St. Augustine of Hippo as a rhetorician.

SIDELIGHTS: Mrs. Marshall traveled and lived in India for about twenty months. *Avocational interests:* Playing violin, cooking, gardening.

BIOGRAPHICAL/CRITICAL SOURCES: Sunday Oregonian, November 4, 1962.

*   *   *

MARSHALL, Max S(kidmore) 1897-

PERSONAL: Born December 20, 1897, in Lansing, Mich.; son of Charles Edward and Maud Alice (Skidmore) Marshall; married Constance Hopkin, 1922 (deceased); married Barbara G. Trask (a musician), June 22, 1957; children: (first marriage) Craig Hopkin, Joan K. (Mrs. Paul Ton), Margaret T. (Mrs. William James Micka). *Education:* University of Massachusetts, B.Sc., 1920; University of Michigan, M.A., 1922, Ph.D., 1925. *Home:* 405 Davis St., Apt. 1604, San Francisco, Calif. 94111.

CAREER: Michigan Department of Health, Lansing, research bacteriologist, 1923-27; University of California Medical Center, San Francisco, 1927-65, professor of microbiology, 1943-65; now retired. Distinguished visiting professor, Michigan State University, 1958; consultant, San Francisco Department of Public Health, 1936-52. *Military service:* U.S. Army, Quartermaster Corps, 1917-19; became second lieutenant. *Member:* American Society for Microbiology, Sigma Xi, Phi Kappa Phi.

WRITINGS: Handbook of Public Health Bacteriology and Chemistry, Stacey, 1939; *Laboratory Guide in Elementary Microbiology,* Blakiston, 1941; (with Alfred S. Lazarus and others) *Applied Medical Bacteriology,* Lea & Febiger, 1947; *Two Sides to a Teacher's Desk,* Macmillan, 1951; *Crusader Undaunted: Dr. J. C. Geiger, Private Physician to the Public,* Macmillan, 1958; *Teaching Without Grades,* Oregon State University Press, 1968. Contributor of numerous articles on microbiology, and about 160 articles on education and university life to journals, 1952-74. Member of editorial board, *Improving College and University Teaching,* Oregon State University, 1954—.

WORK IN PROGRESS: Writing further on education and university life.

*   *   *

MARSHALL, William H(arvey) 1925-1968

PERSONAL: Born October 16, 1925, in Washington, D.C.; son of Robert W. (an attorney) and Nettie (Heinline) Marshall; married Shirley E. Repp, August 20, 1949; children: Judith, Susan, Barbara. *Education:* University of Virginia, B.A., 1946, M.A., 1951; University of Pennsylvania, Ph.D., 1956. *Politics:* Liberal Democrat. *Religion:* Episcopalian. *Home:* 406 Bryn Mawr Ave., Bala Cynwyd, Pa. 19004. *Office:* Department of English, University of Pennsylvania, Philadelphia, Pa. 19104.

CAREER: University of Pennsylvania, Philadelphia, instructor, 1956-58, assistant professor, 1958-62, associate professor of English, 1962-68. Conductor of graduate seminar, Bryn Mawr College, 1964-65. *Military service:* U.S. Army, 1943-44. *Member:* Modern Language Association of America, National Council of Teachers of English, Keats-Shelley Association of America, Phi Beta Kappa. *Awards, honors:* Guggenheim fellowship, 1963-64.

WRITINGS: Some Comments on Pope and Boileau, [Iowa City], 1959; *Byron, Shelley, Hunt, and "The Liberal,"* University of Pennsylvania Press, 1960; *The Structure of Byron's Major Poems,* University of Pennsylvania Press, 1962; (author of introduction) Charlotte Bronte, *Jane Eyre,* Collier, 1962; (author of introduction) George Meredith, *The Ordeal of Richard Feverel,* Washington Square Press, 1962; (editor and author of introduction) *The Major English Romantic Poets: An Anthology,* Washington Square Press, 1964; (editor and author of introduction) *The Major Victorian Poets: An Anthology,* Washington Square Press, 1966; *The World of the Victorian Novel,* A. S. Barnes, 1967; (editor and author of introduction) Byron, *Selected Poems and Letters,* Houghton, 1968; *Wilkie Collins,* Twayne, 1970; *Romantic and Victorian,* Fairleigh Dickinson University Press, 1971. Contributor of articles to more than fifteen professional journals.

BIOGRAPHICAL/CRITICAL SOURCES: New Yorker, December 2, 1967.

(Died, 1968)

*   *   *

MARTIN, Bernard 1905-

PERSONAL: Born February 14, 1905, in Zurich, Switzerland; son of Edouard and Berthe (Picot) Martin; married Marian De-Haller, October 25, 1927 (died, 1955); married Georgina De-Haller, March 3, 1962; children: (first marriage) Francois, Laurent, Isabelle, Veronique Martin Ladame. *Education:* Universite de Lausanne, Bachelor in Theology, 1929. *Religion:* Reformed Church. *Home:* 22 bis chemin des Clochettes, 1206 Geneva, Switzerland.

CAREER: Pastor in Switzerland, at Vaulion, 1929-38, at Leysin, 1938-39, at Cathedrale de Saint-Pierre, Geneva, 1939-40, at Eaux-Vives, Geneva, 1940-61; chaplain of psychiatric hospital, Geneva, 1961-70. Member, music conservatory committee, Geneva.

WRITINGS: Le Ministere de la guerison, Labor & Fides, 1952, translation by Mark Clement published as *The Healing Ministry in the Church,* John Knox, 1960; *Veuxtu Guerir?: Reflexions sur la cure d'ame des malades,* Labor & Fides, 1963, translation by A. A. Jones published as *Healing for You,* Lutterworth, 1965, John Knox, 1966; *Si Dieu ne meurt,* Buchet-Chastel, 1964, translation by James H. Farley published as *If God Does Not Die,* John Knox, 1966.

AVOCATIONAL INTERESTS: Music, especially playing the piano.

MARTIN, Bernard (Davis) 1897-

PERSONAL: Born April 24, 1897, in Southampton, England; son of Arthur Davis Martin (an author); married Grace Powell; children: John Powell. *Education:* Attended George Watson's College. *Home:* Smockfield, Danbury, Essex, England.

CAREER: Writer. Lecturer on the history and culture of China for Cambridge University Extra-Mural Board and Workers' Educational Association. *Military service:* British Army, 1915-19. *Member:* Society of Authors, P.E.N.

WRITINGS: Over My Shoulder, Duckworth, 1935; *Strange Vigour: A Biography of Sun Yat-sen,* Heinemann, 1944, new edition, 1952, Kennikat, 1970; *The Strain of Harmony: Men and Women in the History of China,* Heinemann, 1948; *The Ancient Mariner and the Authentic Narrative,* Heinemann, 1949, revised edition published as *An Ancient Mariner: A Biography of John Newton,* Abingdon, 1961; *John Newton: A Biography,* Heinemann, 1950; *The Obscure Way* (novel), Heinemann, 1957; (editor and author of introduction with Mark Spurrell) John Newton, *The Journal of a Slave Trader,* Epworth, 1962; (with Shui Chien-Tung) *Makers of China,* Wiley, 1972.

Juvenile fiction: *The Pagoda Plot,* Thomas Nelson, 1941; *Red Treasure,* Heinemann, 1945, Viking, 1947; *The Song of the Bluebird,* Independent Press, 1954; *The Walkabout Plot,* Heinemann, 1958.

Other juveniles: *William the Silent: A Biography for Boys and Girls,* Thomas Nelson, 1943, 2nd edition, Independent Press, 1952; *China,* Thomas Nelson, 1943; *Our Chief of Men: The Story of Oliver Cromwell,* Longmans, Green, 1960; *John Newton and the Slave Trade,* Longmans, Green, 1961.

*   *   *

MARTIN, Lawrence 1895-

PERSONAL: Born August 10, 1895, in Chicago, Ill.; married Sylvia Pass (an author), November 1, 1937. *Education:* University of Chicago, Ph.B., 1923; Northwestern University, M.A., 1925; Harvard University, graduate study, 1926-27. *Politics:* Liberal Democrat. *Agent:* David M. Clay, 7 Peter Cooper Rd., New York, N.Y. 10010.

CAREER: Northwestern University, Evanston, Ill., associate professor of journalism and English, 1927-39; concurrently associate editor of *Esquire, Coronet,* and *Ken,* Chicago, Ill., 1937-39; *Chicago Times,* Chicago, Ill., chief editorial writer, 1942-43, foreign correspondent, 1943-44; New York University, New York, N.Y., lecturer in journalism, 1959-60. *Member:* Authors Guild, Phi Beta Kappa.

WRITINGS—With wife, Sylvia Martin: *Standard Guide to Mexico and the Caribbean, 1956-57,* Funk, 1956, revised edition, 1959; *The Standard Guide to Mexico, 1961-62,* Funk, 1960; *The Standard Guide to the Caribbean,* Funk, 1962; *England!: An Uncommon Guide,* McGraw, 1963; *Paris! and Its Environs: An Uncommon Guide,* McGraw, 1963; *Switzerland!: An Uncommon Guide,* McGraw, 1965; *Europe: The Grand Tour—An Uncommon Guide,* McGraw, 1967. Contributor of more than two hundred articles to periodicals.

WORK IN PROGRESS: New editions of *England!: An Uncommon Guide* and of *Europe: The Grand Tour—An Uncommon Guide.*

MARTIN, Milward Wyatt 1895-1974

PERSONAL: Born January 27, 1895, in Eatonton, Ga.; son of Thomas W. and Kate (McComb) Martin; married Mary Lee Thurman, August 20, 1938; children: (stepchildren) Mary Lee Fletcher, Dugald Angus Fletcher. *Education:* University of Georgia, A.B., 1915; Harvard University, LL.B., 1920. *Religion:* Episcopalian. *Home:* Horse Hollow Rd., Locust Valley, N.Y. 11560.

CAREER: Admitted to New York bar, 1921; Cravath, deGersdorff, Swaine & Wood, New York, N.Y., attorney, 1928-31; Allied Chemical & Dye Corp., New York, N.Y., head of law department, 1931-34; Pepsi-Cola Co., New York, N.Y., senior vice-president and head of law department, beginning 1939, director, beginning 1956. Mayor of Incorporated Village of Lattingtown, and secretary of Grenville Baker Boys Club, Inc., both Locust Valley, N.Y. *Member:* American Bar Association.

WRITINGS: Twelve Full Ounces, Holt, 1962; *Was Shakespeare Shakespeare?: A Lawyer Reviews the Evidence,* Cooper Square, 1965.

(Died July 28, 1974)

*   *   *

MARTIN, Roscoe C(oleman) 1903-1972

PERSONAL: Born November 18, 1903, in Silsbee, Tex.; son of Benjamin Wiley and Clara Lee (Mayo) Martin; married Mildred Ellis, September 2, 1926; children: Roscoe Coleman. *Education:* University of Texas, B.A., 1924, M.A., 1925; University of Chicago, Ph.D., 1932. *Home:* 224 Scottholm Ter., Syracuse, N.Y. *Office:* Department of Political Science, Syracuse University, Syracuse, N.Y.

CAREER: University of Texas, Austin, 1926-37, began as instructor, became professor of government, director of Bureau of Municipal Research, 1933-37; University of Alabama, University, professor of political science and chairman of department, 1937-49, director of Bureau of Public Administration, 1938-49; Syracuse University, Syracuse, N.Y., professor of political science, 1949-66, Maxwell Professor of Political Science, 1966-72, chairman of department, 1949-56. Visiting professor at University of California, Los Angeles, 1939, Columbia University, 1948, University of Southern California, 1950, University of California, Berkeley, 1966-67; guest lecturer at University of Puerto Rico and other universities. Chief research technician, National Resources Planning Board, 1936-37; member of U.S. National Commission for UNESCO, 1948-54, and United Nations Public Administration Mission to Brazil, 1951-52; U.S. Department of State specialist in nine foreign countries, 1963-64. Consultant to Tennessee Valley Authority, 1949-56, Federal Civil Defense Administration, 1952-53, Commission on Intergovernmental Relations, 1954-55, and Ford Foundation, 1955-56.

MEMBER: American Society for Public Administration (council member, 1941-44; vice-president, 1944-45; president, 1949-50), American Political Science Association (member of executive council, 1937-39; vice-president, 1948-49), National Civil Service League (council member, 1945-60), National Municipal League (council member, 1950-53, 1954-57), Southern Political Science Association (president, 1941-42), New York State Political Science Association (president, 1950-51), Phi Beta Kappa. *Awards, honors:* Social Science Research Council research professor, 1959-60.

WRITINGS: The People's Party in Texas: A Study in

Third Party Politics, University of Texas Press, 1933; *A Budget Manual for Texas Cities*, University of Texas Press, 1934; *The Defendant and Criminal Justice*, University of Texas Press, 1934; *Urban Local Government in Texas*, University of Texas Press, 1936; *The Growth of State Administration in Alabama*, Bureau of Public Administration, University of Alabama, 1942.

From Forest to Front Page, University of Alabama Press, 1956; (editor) *TVA: The First Twenty Years*, University of Alabama Press and University of Tennessee Press, 1956; *Grass Roots*, University of Alabama Press, 1957, 2nd edition, 1964; *Water for New York*, Syracuse University Press, 1960; (with others) *River Basin Administration and the Delaware*, Syracuse University Press, 1960; (with others) *Decision in Syracuse*, Indiana University Press, 1961; *Government and the Suburban School*, Syracuse University Press, 1962; *Metropolis in Transition*, Housing and Home Finance Agency, 1963; *The Cities and the Federal System*, Atherton, 1965; (editor) *Public Administration and Democracy*, Syracuse University Press, 1965.

Contributor: *Education for the Professions*, U.S. Office of Education, 1955; (author of introduction) *The Federal Government and the Cities*, George Washington University Press, 1961; *Guidelines for Public Administration*, University of New Mexico Press, 1961; Stephen K. Bailey, editor, *American Politics and Government*, Basic Books, 1965; *Lectures on Water Management*, Johns Hopkins Press, 1965.

Contributor to *Encyclopaedia Britannica*, *Municipal Year Book*, and to journals, with some forty articles published in America, England, and Brazil. Planned, directed, and edited some forty-five studies of state and local problems, 1933-49. Member of board of editors, *American Political Science Review*, 1941; *Journal of Politics*, book review editor, 1939-41, member of advisory editorial board, 1945-53.

(Died May 12, 1972)

* * *

MARTINET, Andre   1908-

PERSONAL: Born April 12, 1908, in Saint-Alban, Savoie, France; son of Francois Leon (a teacher) and Peronne (Bouvier) Martinet; married Jeanne Allard, April 11, 1947; children: Catherine (Mrs. Henning Hogsbro-Holm), Theresa (Mrs. Urban Hedvall). *Education:* University of Paris, Licence Agregation; University of Berlin, Doctorat es lettres, 1932. *Home:* 3, Place de la Gare, Sceaux, Seine, France. *Office:* Sorbonne, Paris, France.

CAREER: Ecole des Hautes Etudes, Paris, France, professor of general linguistics, 1938-47; Columbia University, New York, N.Y., professor of general and comparative linguistics, 1947-55; Sorbonne, University of Paris, Paris, France, professor of general linguistics, 1955—; Ecole des Hautes Etudes, professor of structural linguistics, 1957—. Scientific director, International Auxiliary Language Association, 1946-48. *Member:* Linguistics Society of America, Linguistic Circle of New York (honorary president), Societe de Linguistique de Paris (president, 1962), Philological Society (London), Royal Academy of Denmark. *Awards, honors:* Three awards from French Academie des Inscriptions et Belles-Lettres, for *La Gemination consonantique d'orgine expressive dans les languages germaniques, La Prononciation du francais contemporain,* and *Economie des changements phonetiques;* doctorates from University of Louvain and University of Turku, 1970.

WRITINGS: La Gemination consonantique d'origine expressive dans les languages germaniques, Levin & Munksgaard, 1937; *La Phonologie du mot en danois,* Klincksieck, 1937; *La Prononciation du francais contemporain,* Droz, 1945; *Initiation pratique a l'anglais,* I.A.C., 1947; *Phonology as Functional Phonetics* (lectures), Oxford University Press, 1949; (editor with Uriel Weinreich) *Linguistics Today,* Linguistic Circle of New York, 1954; *Economie des changements phonetiques: Traite de phonologie diachronique,* Francke, 1955, 2nd edition, 1964; *La Description phonologique, avec application au parler franco-provencal d'hauteville,* Droz, 1956; (with A. J. Thomson) *Practical English Grammar for Foreign Students,* Oxford University Press, 1960; *Elements de linguistique generale,* Colin, 1960, translation by Elisabeth Palmer published as *Elements of General Linguistics,* University of Chicago Press, 1966; *A Functional View of Language,* Clarendon Press, 1962; *La Linguistique synchronique: Etudes et recherches,* Presses Universitaires de France, 1965; *Manuel pratique d'allemand,* A. & J. Picard, 1965; (with others) *Structuralism,* Yale University, 1966; (editor) *Le Langage,* Gallimard, 1968; *Le Francais sans fard,* Presses Universitaires de France, 1969; (editor with wife, Jeanne Martinet, and Henriette Walter) *La Linguistique guide alphabetique,* Denoel, 1969. Editor, *Word* (journal of Linguistic Circle of New York), 1946—, *Travaux de l'Institut de Linguistique,* 1957-60, *La Linguistique,* 1965—.

AVOCATIONAL INTERESTS: Gardening.

BIOGRAPHICAL/CRITICAL SOURCES: Linguistic Studies Presented to Andre Martinet, Linguistic Circle of New York, 1968.

* * *

MARX, Erica Elizabeth   1909-1967
(Robert Manfred)

PERSONAL: Born May 12, 1909, in Streatham, London, England; daughter of Hermann (a banker) and Lisbet (Ganz) Marx. *Education:* Attended King's College, London, 1928-30. *Politics:* Independent. *Religion:* Church of England. *Home:* Danehurst, Lympne, Hythe, England.

CAREER: The Hand & Flower Press, Lympne, Hythe, England, sole publisher, 1940-63 (now defunct). Director of Les Presses de l'Hotel Sagonne, Paris, France, 1938-40, 1945-47, of Company of Nine, 1956-59, and of M Plates Ltd. (printing process); member of board of management, Poetry Book Society, 1954-57; trustee and member of executive committee, Beauchamp Lodge Residential Settlement. *Wartime service:* Women's Home Defence, Surrey, England, commandant, 1941-43. *Member:* P.E.N., Arts Theatre, Lamda, National Film Theatre Club, Institute of Contemporary Art, Asian Music Circle.

WRITINGS: (Under pseudonym Robert Manfred) *Escape from Anger,* Hand & Flower Press, 1951; *Some Poems,* Hand & Flower Press, 1955; (editor with Patric Dickinson and J. C. Hall) *P.E.N. Anthology 1955.*

WORK IN PROGRESS: Private research into radiesthesia, paraphysics, and sonic therapy in an attempt to acqure a greater understanding of the relationship between mind and matter.

SIDELIGHTS: Erica Marx was a dedicated patroness of the arts, whom the *London Times* described as "an intense intellectual spirit, gay, penetrating, loving and perceptively critical." She founded the Hand and Flower Press as a means of encouraging and assisting novice poets, charging one shilling per copy for the paperback *Poems in Pamphlet* which she published. Elena Fearn, Charles Causley, and Thomas Blackburn were among the many poets whose works appeared for the first time in book form in that series. Dame Veronica Wedgwood observed of Miss Marx, "Although she was herself a poet, she never pressed her own claim as a creative writer, so deeply did she concentrate on what she could do to help others. She brought a keen intellectual understanding, but also sympathy and conscience to all she did."

(Died March 31, 1967)

*   *   *

MARY MADELEINE, Sister   1916-1974

PERSONAL: Born April 11, 1916, in Jersey City, N.J.; daughter of John (a store manager) and Mary Ellen (Finn) Crotty. *Education:* Notre Dame College of Staten Island, B.A., 1937; Seton Hall University, M.A., 1948; Fordham University, Ph.D., 1962. *Politics:* Independent. *Home:* Englewood Cliffs College, Hudson Ter., Englewood Cliffs, N.J.

CAREER: Roman Catholic nun, member of Congregation of St. Joseph. Teacher of English literature at Catholic institutions, 1940-74; former president of Archangel College (now Englewood Cliffs College), Englewood Cliffs, N.J.; Sisters of St. Joseph, Newark, N.J., vocational directress, 1950-65, provincial councilor, 1952-64. Former chairman, Clairvaux Speakers Bureau, addressing more than two hundred organizations (mostly in New Jersey). *Member:* Modern Language Association of America, National Catholic Educational Association, American Association of Junior Colleges. *Awards, honors:* Citation from New Jersey Association of Teachers of English for *Nun Sense*.

WRITINGS: (Editor) *St. Joseph's Song Book*, Sisters of St. Joseph, 1956; (editor) *St. Joseph's Cook Book*, Sisters of St. Joseph, 1957; *Nun Sense*, Bruce, 1963; *Chasing Rainbows*, Englewood Cliffs College Press, 1974. Editor, *Evangelist* (annual), 1963. Contributor to Catholic periodicals.

AVOCATIONAL INTERESTS: Photography (prints exhibited, 1965).

(Died August, 1974)

*   *   *

MASON, Eudo C(olecestra)   1901-1969
(Otto Maurer)

PERSONAL: Born September 26, 1901, in Colchester, Essex, England; son of Ernest Nathan and Bertha Betsy (Kitton) Mason; married Esther Klara Giesecke, August 16, 1939 (died, 1966). *Education:* Oxford University, M.A. (honors in English), 1926; Jesus College, Cambridge, M.A., 1932; University of Leipzig, Dr. Phil., 1938. *Politics:* Conservative. *Religion:* Roman Catholic. *Home:* 20 Warriston Gardens, Edinburgh 3, Scotland. *Office:* Department of German, University of Edinburgh, Edinburgh, Scotland.

CAREER: Lecturer in English at University of Munster, Munster, Germany, 1926-31, University of Leipzig, Leipzig, Germany, 1932-39, University of Basel, Basel, Switzerland, 1939-46; University of Edinburgh, Edinburgh, Scotland, lecturer, 1946-51, professor of German, 1951-69. Visiting professor, University of California, Berkeley, 1963. *Member:* English Goethe Society, Holderlin-Gesellschaft, Rudolf Kassner-Gesellschaft, Edinburgh University Staff Club. *Awards, honors:* Honorary doctorate,

University of Berne, 1938; D.Litt., Oxford University, 1963; gold medal, Goethe-Institut, 1967; prize of the Deutsche Akademie fuer Sprache und Dichtung, 1967.

WRITINGS: Rilke's Apotheosis: A Survey of Representative Recent Publications on the Work and Life of R. M. Rilke, Basil Blackwell, 1938; *Lebenshaltung und Symbolik bei Rainer Maria Rilke*, Boehlau, 1939, 2nd edition, with a new postscript, Marston Press, 1964; (translator and editor) *Fuessli's Aphorismen ueber die Kunst*, Schwabe, 1944; (translator) Jan Tschichold, *An Illustrated History of Writing and Lettering*, Zwemmer, 1946; (translator) Jan Tschichold, *Chinese Poetry Paper by the Master of Ten Bamboo Hall*, Barmerlea Book Sales, 1947; *Der Zopf des Muenchhausen: Ein Skisse in Hinblick auf Rilke*, Johannes, 1949.

(Editor) *Unveroeffentlichte Gedichte von Johann Heinrich Fuessli*, Zurcher Kinstgesellschaft, 1951; (author of introductory study) *The Mind of Henry Fuseli: Selections from His Writings*, Routledge & Kegan Paul, 1951; *Rilke und Goethe*, Boehlau, 1958; *Deutsche und englische Romantik: Ein Gegenueberstellung*, Vandenhoeck & Ruprecht, 1959, 2nd edition, revised and enlarged, 1966; *Rilke, Europe, and the English-Speaking World*, Cambridge University Press, 1961; (translator, editor, and author of introduction and commentary) Johann Heinrich Fuessli, *Remarks on the Writings and Conduct of J. J. Rousseau* (in England and German), Fretz & Wasmuth, 1962; *Exzentrische Bahnen: Studien zum Dichterbewusstsein der Neuzeit* (selected essays), Vandenhoeck & Ruprecht, 1963; *Rilke* (monograph), Oliver & Boyd, 1963; (editor and translator) *A Miscellany of German and French Poetry*, Oliver & Boyd, 1963, Dufour, 1964; *Goethe's Faust: Its Genesis and Purport*, University of California Press, 1967. Contributor of articles on T. S. Eliot, Kassner, Masefield, and Rilke to Herder's *Lexikon der Weltliteratur*, and on Gundolf to the German *Shakespeare-Jahrbuch*, 1962; contributor of other articles on themes of literary criticism to English, German, and continental periodicals.

WORK IN PROGRESS: A study of James Joyce's *Finnegans Wake;* a historical survey of the poetry of nature-pantheism; a comprehensive study of Goethe.

SIDELIGHTS: Mason stated that he attempted to find a synthesis between the British and German cultural traditions. He added: "[I am] not in love with the modern world, but also not infatuated with the past." *Avocational interests:* Mountain walking, collecting wild flowers, country dancing, old children's books, and travel.

BIOGRAPHICAL/CRITICAL SOURCES: Times Literary Supplement, December 12, 1968.

(Died June 10, 1969)

*   *   *

MASSEL, Mark S.   1910-

PERSONAL: Born August 6, 1910, in New York, N.Y.; son of Jacob (a businessman) and Sophie Massel; married Jean Magnus (an economist), September 2, 1935 (died June 22, 1965); married Katharine Douglas, January 1, 1966; children: (first marriage) Lynn, Joan. *Education:* New York University, B.S., 1930, M.A. and J.D., 1933; Columbia University, postdoctoral study, 1936-37. *Home:* 2540 Massachusetts Ave. N.W., Washington, D.C. 20008.

CAREER: General manager of Massel Press and bank auditor before admission to New York Bar, 1933; consultant to several government agencies and lecturer at universities,

1933-43; U.S. War Department, Washington, D.C., civilian chief of price policy unit, 1943-44; Bell, Boyd, Marshall & Lloyd (law firm), Chicago, Ill., partner, 1944-58; Brookings Institution, Washington, D.C., senior staff member, 1958-68. Visiting professor in law and business at University of Michigan, 1964; visiting lecturer in economics and business at University of Chicago and University of California, Berkeley, 1956; visiting professor, University of Wisconsin, 1969. Member of board of directors and chairman of policy committee of Sanford Corp.; also member of board of Sanford de Mexico, Santa Cruz Industries, and Xyno Plastics Ltd. (Canada). Consultant to United Nations Conference on Trade and Development. Chairman, Panel on Foreign Wartime Policies, National Research Council. *Member:* National Academy of Sciences (chairman, Task Force on Existing Institutions), Club de la Fondation Universitaire (Brussels), Law and Society Association (member of board of trustees), American Economics Association, Cosmos Club (Washington, D.C.), Columbia University Club (New York).

WRITINGS: Business Reserves for Post-War Survival: Their Impact on Capital Adjustments, National Planning Association, 1943; *The Regulatory Process,* Brookings Institution, 1961; *Economic Analysis in Judicial Antitrust Decisions,* Brookings Institution, 1962; *Competition and Monopoly: Legal and Economic Issues,* Brookings Institution, 1962; *Models of Value Theory and Antitrust,* Brookings Institution, 1964; *Non-Tariff Barriers as an Obstacle to World Trade,* Brookings Institution, 1965. Contributor of articles to professional periodicals.

WORK IN PROGRESS: Study of the policy implications of business accounting, a review of accounting as a principal means of communication and evaluation in our society.

* * *

MASSON, Loyes 1915-1969

PERSONAL: Born December 31, 1915, on Mauritius (British island in Indian Ocean); son of Raoul (an attorney) and Paula (Mamet) Masson; married Paula Slaweska, November, 1941; children: Gregoire. *Education:* Attended Royal College of Mauritius. *Religion:* Roman Catholic. *Home:* 7 Rue Marcel Renault, Paris 17e, France.

CAREER: Boxed professionally to earn money to leave Mauritius for France; arrived in Paris, August, 1939, three days before the outbreak of war; fought in the Legion Etrangere, 1939-40, and then with the French maquis; novelist, poet, and writer of radio and television plays in France (still a British subject). *Awards, honors:* Grand Prix de la Radio, 1959, for "Le Pape"; Prix des Deux Magots, 1962, for *Le Notaire des noirs;* Prix de la Fondation Del Duca, 1962, for *Les Noces de la vanille;* Prix Kat. Hausfield, 1970, for *Des Bouteilles dans les yeux.*

WRITINGS: Deliverez-nous du mal (poetry), Seghers, 1942, 2nd edition, 1945; (with others) *Pour les Quatre Saisons,* Seghers, 1943; *Poemes d'ici,* Les Cahiers du Rhone, 1943; *Chroniques de la grande nuit* (poetry), Ides et calendes, 1943; *L'Etoile et la clef* (novel), Gallimard, 1945; *Le Requis civil* (novel), Gallimard, 1945; *Pour une eglise* (essay), Editions des Trois Collines, 1945, new edition, Bordas, 1947; *La Lumiere nait le mercredi* (poetry), Seghers, 1946; *Saint-Alias* (short stories), Editions des Trois Collines, 1947; *Tous les corsaires sont morts* (novel), Ferenczi, 1947; *L'Illustre Thomas Wilson,* Editions Bordas, 1948.

Icare; ou, le voyage (poetry), Seghers, 1950; *Les Mutins* (novel), Editions de la Paix, 1951, revised edition, Laffont, 1959; *Les Cacti,* Editions de la Paix, 1951; *Tout ce que vous demanderez* (novel), Editions de la Paix, 1952; *Quatorze poemes du coeur viellissant,* Editions Caracteres, 1952; *Poeme-dialogue de la resurrection,* Editions Caracteres, 1953; *Les Vignes de septembre* (poetry) Seghers, 1955; *Les Tortues* (novel), Laffont, 1956, translation by Antonia White published as *The Tortoises,* Chatto & Windus, 1959, Channel Press, 1962; *La Douve* (novel), Laffont, 1957; *Les Sexes foudroyes* (novel), Laffont, 1958, translation by Denise Folliot published in England as *The Barbed Wire Fence,* Chatto & Windus, 1960, translation by Folliot and Mildred Shapiro published as *The Shattered Sexes,* Channel Press, 1961.

Theatre (three plays), Laffont, 1960; *Le Notaire des noirs* (novel), Laffont, 1961, translation by Antonia White published as *Advocate of the Isle,* Knopf, 1963 (published in England as *The Whale's Tooth,* Chatto & Windus, 1963); *Les Noces de la vanille* (novel), Laffont, 1962, translation by Marthiel Mathews published as *The Overseer,* Knopf, 1964; *Lagon de la misericorde* (novel), Laffont, 1964; *La Dame des Pavoux* (poetry), Laffont, 1965; *Celebration du Rouge-gorge,* R. Morel, 1965; *Celebration de la Chouette,* R. Morel, 1966; *Les Anges noirs du Trone,* Laffont, 1967; *La Croix de la rose rouge* (poetry), R. Morel, 1969.

Des Bouteilles dans les yeux (short stories), Laffont, 1970.

Plays: "La Resurrection des corps," produced as Theatre de l'Oeuvre, 1952, adapted for television as "Tout ce que vous demanderez," 1964; "Le Pape" (radio), 1959; "Christobal de Lugo," produced on television, 1959, and at Theatre du Vieux Colombier, 1960; *Le Notaire des noirs,* adapted and produced on television, 1968; also author of other plays for French radio and television.

SIDELIGHTS: Masson was condemned to death by the Nazis in 1943 for underground activities, but escaped. Looking back, Masson commented: "In a sense I was wrong perhaps? To die then would have been a fine thing. Now I am a 'survivant.' I shall probably finish like Hemingway." After Masson's death in 1969, his widow told *CA:* "In fact he didn't, [referring to Masson's prediction that he would end like Hemingway], but was struck down by a cerebral embolism while he was alone at home in Paris busy preparing a lecture he was to give in a sanitorium in the Alps on the subject 'The Difficult Life of a Writer.'"

The demand for his novels has been increasing abroad, with four going into at least three translations and *Les Tortues, Le Notaire des noirs,* and *Les Sexes foudroyes* being published in five different countries.

BIOGRAPHICAL/CRITICAL SOURCES: Loyes Masson, presentation par Charles Moulin; choix de textes, bibliographies, portraits, facsimiles, Seghers, 1962.

(Died October 24, 1969)

* * *

MATHER, Bertrand 1914-

PERSONAL: Born April 21, 1914, in Leeds, England; son of Eli Bertrand (a company director) and Ethel (Eastwood) Mather; married Jean Barker Moorhouse, September 10, 1946; children: Christopher Paul, Pauline Anne. *Education:* University of Leeds, B.Sc. (special honours in physics), 1935, diploma in education, 1936. *Politics:* Conservative. *Religion:* Church of England. *Home:* Wentworth, Middleton Ave., Ilkley, Yorkshire, England. *Office:* J. E. Mather & Sons Ltd., 180 Upper Wortley Rd., Leeds 12, Yorkshire, England.

CAREER: Schoolmaster in Yorkshire, England, 1936-37, in Norfolk County, England, 1937-40; J. E. Mather & Sons Ltd. (wine producers and black beer brewers), Leeds, England, 1945—, now vice-chairman. Director, Barchester Bottling Co. Researcher in connection with mine warfare, British Admiralty, World War II. Member, Leeds City Council, 1951—. *Member:* National Association of British Wine Producers (chairman, 1963—), Leeds Conservative Club.

WRITINGS: Through the Mill, Ward, Lock, 1962; *Left Foot Forward,* Ward, Lock, 1963.

BIOGRAPHICAL/CRITICAL SOURCES: Yorkshire Post, March 25, 1963.

* * *

MATTHEWS, T(homas) S(tanley) 1901-

PERSONAL: Born January 16, 1901, in Cincinnati, Ohio; son of Paul Clement (an Episcopal bishop) and Elsie (Procter) Matthews; married Juliana S. Cuyler, May 16, 1925 (deceased); married Martha Gellhorn (an author and foreign correspondent), February 4, 1954 (divorced); married Pamela Peniakoff, 1964; children: (first marriage) Thomas Stanley, Jr., John Potter Cuyler, Paul, William Alexander Procter. *Education:* Princeton University, B.A., 1922; New College, Oxford, A.B., 1924, M.A., 1968. *Politics:* Independent. *Religion:* Anglican. *Home:* Cavendish Hall, Cavendish, Suffolk, England. *Agent:* Cyrilly Abels, 119 West 57th St., New York, N.Y. 10019.

CAREER: New Republic, New York, N.Y., assistant editor, 1925-27, associate editor, 1927-29; *Time,* New York, N.Y., books editor, 1929-37, executive editor, 1937-42, managing editor, 1943-49, editor, 1949-53. Trustee, Kenyon College, 1950-53. *Member:* Century Association and Coffee House Club (both New York), Reading Room (Newport); Buck's Club, Garrick Club, Athenaeum Club (all London). *Awards, honors:* L.H.D., Kenyon College; Litt.D., Rollins College.

WRITINGS: To the Gallows I Must Go, Knopf, 1931; *The Moon's No Fool,* Random House, 1936; (editor and author of introduction) *Selected Letters of Charles Lamb,* Farrar, Straus, 1956; *The Sugar Pill: An Essay on Newspapers,* Gollancz, 1957; Simon & Schuster, 1959; *Name and Address: An Autobiography,* Simon & Schuster, 1960; *O My America! Notes on a Trip,* Simon & Schuster, 1962; *The Worst Unsaid: A Book of Verse,* Anthony Blond, 1962; *Why So Gloomy?* (verse), privately printed, 1966. Contributor to *Forum, Bookman, New English Weekly, Harper's, Atlantic, New Yorker, Saturday Evening Post, Life, Guardian,* and other publications.

WORK IN PROGRESS: A biography of T. S. Eliot.

* * *

MATTHEWS, Walter Robert 1881-1973

PERSONAL: Born September 22, 1881, in London, England; son of Philip Walter (chief inspector, Bankers' Clearing House) and Sophia Alice (Self) Matthews; married Margaret Bryan, July, 1912 (died, 1963); children: M. H. (deceased), Barbara (Mrs. Martin Hebb), W. Bryan (a physician). *Education:* King's College, London, D.D. and D.Lit. *Home:* 6 Vincent Sq., London S.W. 1, England.

CAREER: Clergyman, Church of England. Curate and chaplain in London, 1908; University of London, King's College, London, England, lecturer in philosophy and dogmatic theology, 1908-18, professor of the philosophy of religion and dean, 1918-32; dean of Exeter Cathedral, Exeter, 1931-34, dean of St. Paul's Cathedral, London, 1934-67, dean emeritus, 1967-73. Chaplain to Gray's Inn, 1920, preacher, 1929; chaplain to the King, 1923-31. Boyle Lecturer, 1920-22; White Lecturer, 1927; Noble Lecturer, 1928; Wilde Lecturer, 1929; Warburton Lecturer, 1938. *Member:* Royal Society of Literature (fellow), Athenaeum Club (London). *Awards, honors:* Knight Commander of the Royal Victorian Order, 1935; Freedom Cross of King Haakon VII (Norway), 1947; Order of the White Lion, third class (Czechoslovakia), 1947; dean of Order of the British Empire, 1951; Companion of Honour, 1962; honorary fellow of King's College and of Westfield College, University of London; honorary Bencher of Gray's Inn; D.D. from University of St. Andrews, University of Glasgow, Cambridge University, University of Dublin, Trinity College (Toronto); S.T.P. from St. John's College (Winnipeg); S.T.D. from Columbia University; LL.D., University of London, 1969.

WRITINGS: (Editor) *King's College Lectures on Immortality,* University of London Press, 1920; *Studies in Christian Philosophy* (Boyle lectures), Macmillan (London), 1921, 2nd edition, 1928; *Butler's Ethical Writings in Bohn Library* (critical edition), G. Bell, 1924; *The Idea of Revelation,* Longmans, Green, 1924; (contributor) Oscar Hardman, editor, *Psychology and the Church,* Macmillan, 1925; *The Psychological Approach to Religion,* Longmans, Green, 1925; *The Gospel and the Modern Mind,* Doran, 1925; *God and Evolution,* Longmans, Green, 1926; *Some Modern Problems of Faith,* Cassell, 1928; (with others) *Dogma in History and Thought,* Nisbet, 1929.

God in Christian Experience, Harper, 1930 (published in England as *God in Christian Thought and Experience,* Nisbet, 1930, 7th edition, 1942); *The Adventures of Gabriel in His Search for Mr. Shaw,* Hamish Hamilton, 1933; *Seven Words,* Hodder & Stoughton, 1933; *God and This Troubled World,* Dutton, 1934 (published in England as *Essays in Construction,* Nisbet, 1934); *The Hope of Immortality,* S.C.M. Press, 1936, revised edition, Morehouse, 1966; *Our Faith in God,* S.C.M. Press, 1936; *The Purpose of God,* Nisbet, 1936; (editor) *The Christian Faith: Essays in Explanation and Defence,* Harper, 1936, new edition, Eyre & Spottiswoode, 1944, Books for Libraries, 1971; *Signposts to God,* S.C.M. Press, 1938; *The Teaching of Christ,* Blackie & Son, 1939.

Following Christ, Longmans, Green, 1940; *The Moral Issues of the War,* Eyre & Spottiswoode, 1940; *The Foundations of Peace,* Eyre & Spottiswoode, 1942; *What Is Man?* (broadcast addresses), J. Clarke, 1944; *Strangers and Pilgrims* (sermons), Nisbet, 1945; *Saint Paul's Cathedral in Wartime, 1939-1945,* Hutchinson, 1946; (with others) *William Temple: An Estimate and an Appreciation,* J. Clarke, 1946.

Reason in Religion (Essex Hall lecture), Lindsey Press, 1950; *The Problem of Christ in the Twentieth Century: An Essay on the Incarnation* (Maurice lectures), Oxford University Press, 1950; *The British Philosopher as Writer,* Oxford University Press, 1955; *Claude Montefiore: The Man and His Thought,* University of Southampton, 1956; *The Religious Philosophy of Dean Mansel,* Oxford University Press, 1956; *Some Christian Words,* Allen & Unwin, 1956; *The Search for Perfection,* Macmillan, 1957; (editor with W. M. Atkins) *A History of St. Paul's Cathedral and the Men Associated with It,* Pitman, 1957, new edition, J. Baker, 1964; *The Lord's Prayer: An Exposition for Today,* Hodder & Stoughton, 1958, Morehouse, 1960.

The Thirty-Nine Articles, Hodder & Stoughton, 1961.

Memories and Meanings, Hodder & Stoughton, 1970; *The Year through Christian Eyes*, Epworth, 1970.

Author of booklets; contributor of papers to other books and articles to journals.

(Died December 3, 1973)

* * *

MAURICE, David (John Kerr) 1899-
(Wunnakyawhtin U Ohn Ghine)

PERSONAL: Born September 24, 1899, in Maclean, New South Wales, Australia; son of Stuart Kerr (an accountant) and Ellen Mary (Roche) Maurice. *Education:* University of Sydney, student, 1918-20. *Religion:* Buddhist. *Home:* Rocky Point, Mossman, Queensland, Australia.

CAREER: Started as copy writer in advertising agency, later manager of several agencies; Nobel's Explosives Ltd., Rangoon, Burma, 1941, then assistant Burma propaganda officer; propaganda writer in Australia for Asia broadcasts, and other war work, 1943-45; D. Maurice Ltd. (imports), Rangoon, Burma, director, 1945-50; fruit farmer in Fairfield, New South Wales, Australia, 1950-52; Burma Government, Union Burma Buddha Sasana Council, Rangoon, editor-in-chief of *Light of the Dhamma*, 1952-59; fruit farmer, Rocky Point, Mossman, Queensland, Australia, 1961—. *Member:* Burma Buddhist Merited Association, Young Men's Buddhist Association, Abhidhamma Society (all Burma); Universal Buddhist Fellowship (Ojai, Calif.; vice-president). *Awards, honors:* Wunnakyawhtin, title and decoration conferred by Union of Burma Government for editing Buddhist magazine and for organizational work on sixth International Buddhist Synod, 1954.

WRITINGS: The Greatest Adventure (monograph), Buddhist Publication Society (Ceylon), 1961; *One's Own Good—And Another's* (monograph), Buddhist Publication Society (Ceylon), 1961; (compiler) *The Lion's Roar: An Anthology of the Buddha's Teachings*, Rider & Co., 1962, Citadel, 1967. Contributor of articles on Buddhism to newspapers in Burma, India, and Australia.

WORK IN PROGRESS: You Don't Dare.

* * *

MAURON, Charles (Paul) 1899-1966

PERSONAL: Born June 27, 1899, in St. Remy-de-Provence, France; son of Joseph and Magdeleine (Espigue) Mauron; married Alice Thelin, September 30, 1949; children: Claude, Nicolas, Sebastien. *Education:* University of Aix-Marseille, diplome d'etudes superieures de sciences physiques, 1924; Doctorat les Letters de l'Universite, 1954; University of Paris, Doctorat es Lettres, 1963. *Home:* Avenue Van Gogh, St. Remy-de-Provence, Bouches-du-Rhone, France.

CAREER: Head of laboratory at Technical Institute, Marseille, France, 1924-25, but forced by eye trouble (that resulted in total blindness by 1940) to give up post; writer, critic, and translator, 1926-66. Visiting lecturer at Oxford University, Cambridge University, and other European universities; professor of psychocriticism at University of Aix-Marseille, 1959, 1966. Mayor of St. Remy-de-Provence, 1945-59. *Wartime service:* Member of French Resistance. *Member:* Groupement d'Etudes Provencales (Society of Provencal Studies). *Awards, honors:* Chevalier of the Legion of Honor, 1951; Prix Mistral, 1953, for *Estudi*

Mistralen; Prix Lemaitais-Lariviere of the French Academy, 1961.

WRITINGS: The Nature of Beauty in Art and Literature, translated by Roger Fry, Leonard and Virginia Woolf, 1927; *Aesthetics and Psychology,* translated by Roger Fry, and Katherine John, Leonard and Virginia Woolf, 1935, Kennikat, 1970; (editor) Stephane Mallarme, *Poems,* Chatto & Windus, 1936, Oxford University Press, 1937, revised and enlarged edition, New Directions, 1951; *Mallarme l'obscur*, Denoel, 1941; *Sagesse de l'eau* (essay), R. Laffont, 1945; *L'Homme triple* (essay), R. Laffont, 1947; *Nerval et la psychocritique*, Cahiers de Sud, 1949.

Introduction a la psychanalyse de Mallarme, Editions du Baconniere, 1950, 2nd edition, 1968, translation by Archibald Henderson, Jr. and Will L. McLendon published as *Introduction to the Psychoanalysis of Mallarme,* University of California Press, 1963; *Estudi mistralen,* G.E.P., 1953; *La Structure de l'inconscient chez Van Gogh,* Psyche, 1953; *Vincent et Theo Van Gogh: Une symbiose,* Instituut voor Moderne Kunst (Amsterdam), 1953; *L'-Inconscient dans l'oeuvre et la vie de Racine* (based on doctoral thesis), Centre National de la Recherche Scientifique, c.1957; *Van Gogh au seuil de la Provence, Arles, fevrier a octobre, 1888,* Impr. Sauquet, c.1959; *Des Metaphores obsedantes au mythe personnel: Introduction a la psychocritique* (based on doctoral thesis), Jose Corti, 1962, 2nd edition, 1964; *Psychocritique de genre comique,* Jose Corti, 1964; (editor) *Mallarme par lui-meme,* Editions du Seuil, 1964; *Le Dernier Baudelaire,* Jose Corti, 1966; (with Camille Dourguin) *Lou Provencau a l'escola,* Association Pedagogique "Lou Provenccau a L'Escola," 1966; *Les Personnages du Victor Hugo,* Volume II, Club Francais du Livre, 1967; *Phedre: La Situation dramatique,* Jose Corti, 1968; *Le Theatre de Giraudoux,* Jose Corti, 1970. Translator into French of works of E. M. Forster, T. E. Lawrence, D. H. Lawrence, Virginia Woolf, K. Mansfield, and of Laurence Sterne's *Tristam Shandy.*

(Died December 5, 1966)

* * *

MAXEY, Chester Collins 1890-

PERSONAL: Born May 31, 1890, in Ellensburg, Wash.; son of Morton M. (a cattleman) and Leota (Collins) Maxey; married Elnora Campbell, June 17, 1915; children: Mrs. R. W. Alexander, Mrs. T. F. Kelly. *Education:* Whitman College, A.B., 1912; University of Wisconsin, M.A., 1914; Columbia University, Ph.D., 1919. *Home and office:* 304 East Bryant St., Walla Walla, Wash. 99362.

CAREER: Oregon State Agricultural College (now Oregon State University), Corvallis, 1914-1918, began as instructor, became assistant professor of political science; New York Bureau of Municipal Research, New York, N.Y., staff member and supervisor of Training School for Public Service, 1918-20; Western Reserve University (now Case Western Reserve University), Cleveland, Ohio, associate professor of political science, 1920-25; Whitman College, Walla Walla, Wash., Miles C. Moore Professor of Political Science, 1925-48, president, 1948-59, president emeritus, 1959—, dean of Division of Social Sciences, 1931-48, visiting professor, 1964-68. Writer and lecturer. *Member:* American Political Science Association, Phi Beta Kappa, Beta Theta Phi. *Awards, honors:* LL.D., Lewis and Clark College, 1950; L.H.D., Whitman College, 1959.

WRITINGS: County Administration, Macmillan, 1919 (also published, with a thesis note, as *County Administra-*

tion in Delaware, Macmillan, 1919); (editor) *Readings in Municipal Government*, Doubleday, 1924; *An Outline of Municipal Government*, Doubleday, 1924; *The Problem of Government*, Knopf, 1925; *Urban Democracy*, Heath, 1929; *You and Your Government*, Heath, 1931; *The American Problem of Government*, Appleton, 1934, 6th edition (with R. Y. Fluno), 1957; *Political Philosophies*, Macmillan, 1938, 2nd edition, 1948; *Marcus Whitman, 1802-1847*, Newcomen Society, 1950; *Five Centennial Papers*, Whitman College, 1959; *Bipartisanship in the United States*, Caxton, 1965; *The World I Lived In*, Dorrance, 1966. Contributor of articles and reviews to journals.

WORK IN PROGRESS: Gods and States.

*   *   *

MAXWELL, Arthur S.   1896-1970

PERSONAL: Born January 14, 1896, in London, England; came to United States, 1936; son of George Thomas and Alice Maud (Crowder) Maxwell; married Rachel E. Joyce, May 3, 1917; children: Maureen, Graham, Mervyn, Lawrence, Malcolm, Deirdre. *Education:* Educated in England. *Home:* 24301 Elise Ct., Los Altos Hills, Calif. 94022. *Office:* Pacific Press Publishing Association, Mountain View, Calif. 94040.

CAREER: Stanborough Press Ltd., Watford, Hertfordshire, England, editor of *Present Truth*, 1920-36, general manager of company, 1925-32; Pacific Press Publishing Association, editor of *Signs of the Times*, and member of board of directors, 1937-70. *Awards, honors:* D.Lett., Andrew University, 1970.

WRITINGS: After Many Days, Review & Herald, 1921; *Looking Beyond World Problems*, Stanborough Press, 1923, revised edition, 1926; *Christ's Glorious Return*, Stanborough Press, 1924; *Protestantism Imperilled!*, Stanborough Press, 1926, revised edition, Signs Publishing Co. (Australia), 1943; *Great Issues of the Ages: Has Christ a Solution?*, Stanborough Press, 1927; (editor) *The Bible and the Wonders of Our Age*, Stanborough Press, 1930; (editor) *The Bible and the Wonder of Christ's Return*, Stanborough Press, 1931; *The Mighty Hour: The Message of These Stirring Times*, Stanborough Press, 1933, 2nd edition, Signs Publishing Co., 1934; *The Book That Changed the World*, Stanborough Press, 1933; *Back to God: The Call and the Way*, Pacific Press Publishing Association, 1935, reissued as *Back to God: The World's Most Urgent Need*, 1946; *Discovering London*, Skeffington & Son, 1935; *Our Wonderful Bible*, Stanborough Press, 1935; *These Tremendous Times: What Do They Mean? Where Are We Heading?*, Review & Herald, 1938; (with W. O. Edwards) *Great Fundamentals of Our Wonderful Bible*, Pacific Press Publishing Association, c.1939.

History's Crowded Climax: Prophecy Speaks to Our Time, Pacific Press Publishing Association, 1940; *Power and Prophecy: Who Shall Rule the World*, Pacific Press Publishing Association, 1940 (published in Australia as *World Power and Prophecy: Who Shall Rule the World?*, Signs Publishing Co., 1941); *Challenge of the Tempest*, Pacific Press Publishing Association, 1941; *Qui l'emportera* (pamphlet), Rose-Hill, 1941; *War of the Worlds*, Review & Herald, 1941; *Great Prophecies for Our Time*, Pacific Press Publishing Association, 1943; *Nuestro porvenir descifrado*, Pacific Press Publishing Association, 1943; *So Little Time: The Atom and the End*, Pacific Press Publishing Association, 1946; *Forever Heaven*, Review & Herald, 1948; *Time's Last Hour*, Pacific Press Publishing Association,

1948; *God and the Future*, Review & Herald, 1952; *Christ and Tomorrow*, Review & Herald, 1952; *The Coming King: Ten Great Signs of Christ's Return*, Pacific Press Publishing Association, 1953; *Your Bible and You: Priceless Treasures in the Holy Scriptures*, Review & Herald, 1959; *You and Your Future*, Pacific Press Publishing Association, 1959.

How to Read the Bible, Review & Herald, 1960; *Your Friends, The Adventists*, Pacific Press Publishing Association, 1960; *Courage for the Crisis: Strength for Today, Hope for Tomorrow*, Pacific Press Publishing Association, 1962; *Time Running Out: New Evidence of the Approaching Climax*, Pacific Press Publishing Association, 1963; *Under the Southern Cross*, Southern Publishing, 1966; *Good News for You*, Review & Herald, 1966; *This Is the End!*, Pacific Press Publishing Association, 1967; *Man the World Needs Most*, Pacific Press Publishing Association, 1970.

Juveniles: *The Secret of the Cave: A Thrilling Mystery Story for Boys and Girls*, Pacific Press Publishing Association, 1920, revised edition, 1951; *Uncle Arthur's Bedtime Stories*, forty-eight volumes, Stanborough Press, 1924-71; *Uncle Jim's Visitors*, Pacific Press Publishing Association, 1927; *Little Angels Unawares: The Adventures of "Denver N Company Ltd."* Stanborough Press, 1930; *The Children's Hour with Uncle Arthur*, five volumes, Review & Herald, 1945-49; *Uncle Arthur's Bible Stories*, two volumes, Stanborough Press, 1949, 1953; *The Bible Story*, ten volumes, Review & Herald, 1953-57; *Uncle Arthur's Bible Book*, Review & Herald, 1968; *Uncle Arthur's Storytime*, Review & Herald, Volumes 1-2, 1970, Volume 3, 1972.

(Died November 13, 1970)

*   *   *

MAXWELL, Gilbert   1910-

PERSONAL: Born February 13, 1910, in Washington, Wilkes County, Ga.; son of Allen Tupper and Maude (Gilbert) Maxwell. *Education:* Attended Rollins College, two years. *Politics:* Democrat. *Religion:* Protestant. *Home:* 273 Northeast 54th St., Miami, Fla. 33137. *Agent:* Bertha Klausner, 71 Park Ave., New York, N.Y. 10016.

CAREER: Professional actor, 1935-39; has taught creative writing at various institutions, including University of Tampa and Lindsey Hopkins Vocational Schools, Miami, Fla., and at writers' workshops; National Broadcasting Co., New York, N.Y., associate editor of *NBC Digest*, 1946-47; Frederick Fell, Inc., New York, N.Y., managing editor, 1962-64. Free-lance editor and writer; lecturer; has made numerous radio and television appearances, and has toured with actress Claire Luce in dramatization of *Tennessee Williams and Friends*; currently director of Miami Writers' Workshop. *Awards, honors:* Two first prizes from Poetry Society of Florida, 1934; *Lyric* Magazine award for poetry, 1942; writing grants, Authors League of America, 1957-60.

WRITINGS: Look to the Lightning (poems), Dodd, 1933; *Stranger's Garment* (poems), Dodd, 1936; *The Dark Rain Falling* (poems), Press of J. A. Decker, 1942; *The Sleeping Trees* (novel), Little, Brown, 1949; *Go Looking: Poems, 1933-1953* (with foreword by Tennessee Williams), Humphries, 1954; *Tennessee Williams and Friends* (biography), World Publishing, 1965; (adaptor for stage) Oscar Wilde, "Dorian Gray," first presented in North Miami, Fla., at North Miami Playhouse, 1971. Represented in anthologies, including *Best Poems of 1958: Borestone Mountain Poetry*

Awards, edited by Lionel Stevens and others, Pacific Books, 1960. Contributor of poetry to *Harper's, Scribner's, Saturday Review, Virginia Quarterly Review, Voices, New York Times*, and others.

WORK IN PROGRESS: A biographical memoir of Tallulah Bankhead; free-lance writing.

SIDELIGHTS: Maxwell has recorded his poems for the Harvard University permanent record collection of outstanding American poets.

* * *

MAXWELL-LEFROY, Cecil Anthony 1907-

PERSONAL: Born July 7, 1907, in Bihar, India; son of Harold (a scientist) and Kathleen (O'Meara) Maxwell-Lefroy. *Education:* Cambridge University, B.A., 1928. *Religion:* Roman Catholic. *Home:* Beacon Hotel, Fleet, Hampshire, England.

CAREER: Worked for Burmah Oil Co., in Burma and India, 1928-59, general manager in Burma and chairman of partnership company with Burma government, 1954-59; now retired. *Awards, honors:* Commander of Order of the British Empire, 1959.

WRITINGS: The Land and People of Burma, A. & C. Black, 1963, Macmillan, 1964; *The Land and People of Ceylon*, Macmillan, 1964.

* * *

MAY, Arthur James 1899-1968

PERSONAL: Born January 21, 1899, in Rockdale, Pa.; son of William (a clergyman) and Mary (Mitchell) May; married Hilda Dewey Jones, June 17, 1926; children: Christopher, Stephen. *Education:* Wesleyan University, B.A., 1921; University of Pennsylvania, M.A., 1923, Ph.D., 1926. *Politics:* Independent Republican. *Home:* 78 Arvine Heights, Rochester, N.Y. 14611. *Office:* University of Rochester, Rochester, N.Y. 14627.

CAREER: Brown University, Providence, R.I., instructor, 1924-25; University of Rochester, Rochester, N.Y., instructor, 1925-26, assistant professor, 1926-29, professor of history, 1929-64, university historian, 1964-68. Lecturer at Austrian, German, and Polish universities, 1948, 1962, 1966. Correspondent for Gannett Newspaper Group, 1948, 1953, 1955, 1959, 1961-62, 1966-67. President, Friends of Rochester Public Library, 1953-55. *Military service:* U.S. Army, 1918. *Member:* American Historical Association, Phi Beta Kappa, City Club of Rochester (president, 1935-36). *Awards, honors:* Herbert Baxter Adams Prize, American Historical Association, 1952, for *The Hapsburg Monarchy, 1867-1914;* Fulbright grants, 1954-55, 1961-62; Guggenheim fellowship, 1954-55; American Council of Learned Societies grant, 1959.

WRITINGS: Contemporary American Opinion of Mid-Century Revolutions in Central Europe, University of Pennsylvania, 1927; *The Age of Metternich 1814-1848*, Holt, 1933, revised edition, 1963; *Europe and Two World Wars*, Scribner, 1947; *The Hapsburg Monarchy, 1867-1914*, Harvard University Press, 1951, new edition, 1960; *A History of Civilization*, Volume II: *Mid-Seventeenth Century to Modern Times*, Scribner, 1956, 2nd edition, 1964, one-volume edition published with *Earliest Times to Mid-Seventeenth Century* by C. Harold King, 1969; *The Passing of the Hapsburg Monarchy, 1914-1918*, two volumes, University of Pennsylvania Press, 1966, new edition, 1968; *Vienna in the Age of Franz Josef*, University of Okla-

homa Press, 1966; *Europe Since 1939*, Holt, 1966. Also author of *History of the University of Rochester*.

Contributor: *Les Printemps des Peuples*, Volume II, [Paris], 1948; *Festschrift fuer Heinrich Benedikt*, [Vienna], 1957; D. H. Thomas and L. M. Case, editors, *Guide to the Diplomatic Archives of Western Europe*, University of Pennsylvania Press, 1959; Franz Fuhrmann, *Oesterreich in alten Ansichten*, Verlag fuer Jugend und Volk, 1965; J. P. O'Grady, editor, *The Immigrant's Influence on Wilson's Peace Policies*, University of Kentucky Press, 1967. Contributor of articles on Austria to *Encyclopedia Americana*, 1961-62, and to *Collier's Encyclopedia*, 1962, 1965.

BIOGRAPHICAL/CRITICAL SOURCES: Times Literary Supplement, May 11, 1967.

(Died June 13, 1968)

* * *

MAY, James Boyer 1904-

PERSONAL: Born December 30, 1904, in Red Granite, Wis.; son of James Virgil and Viola Florence (Pickett) May; married Geraldine Elizabeth Evancheck (a buyer for a department store), December 30, 1924. *Education:* Lawrence College (now Lawrence University), student, 1921-22; Beloit College, student, 1921, 1922-23, 1926. *Politics:* Unaffiliated. *Religion:* Unaffiliated. *Home:* 1736 Westerly Ter., Los Angeles, Calif. 90026. *Office address:* Villiers Publications Ltd., P.O. Box 1068, Hollywood, Calif. 90028.

CAREER: Heywood-Wakefield Corp., Menominee, Mich., assistant manager of advertising, 1923-24; newspaper reporter and editor in Illinois and Wisconsin, 1925-34; editor of trade periodicals, Oshkosh, Wis., and Los Angeles, Calif., 1934-36; free-lance writer Los Angeles, Calif., 1937-41; State of California, Los Angeles, insurance examiner and editor of state employee publications, 1946-49; *Trace* (literary quarterly), London, England, editor, 1952-64; Villiers Publications Ltd., London, a director, 1957—. Honorary director, Scorpion Press, Lowestoft, Suffolk, England, 1964—. Conductor of radio and civic reading programs, University of Southern California, 1957-59. *Military service:* U.S. Army, 1942-45; became sergeant.

WRITINGS: Eight Years (fiction), Charipar, 1946; *For a New Era of Hate* (fiction), Alan Swallow, 1947; (editor and author of introduction) *Eight American Poets*, Villiers Publications, 1952; (translator) *Modern Greek Poems*, Villiers Publications, 1954; *Twigs as Varied Bent*, Vagrom Publications, 1954; *Selected Poems, 1950-1955*, Inferno Press, 1955; *Selected Fiction*, Villiers Publications, 1957; *Collected Later Poems*, Villiers Publications, 1957; *Little Magazines* (monograph), Walker Art Center, 1957; *Selected Essays and Criticism*, Villiers Publications, 1957; (editor with others) *Poetry Los Angeles*, Villiers Publications, 1958. Contributor to several hundred periodicals in all parts of world.

WORK IN PROGRESS: Thirteen Years of Trace; collections of poetry and criticism.

SIDELIGHTS: May estimates that he has introduced at least one hundred hitherto-unpublished writers to print in the past decade or so, but admits that he would like to devote "some share of time and energy to my own writings, other than doing editorials, articles about the writings of others, prefaces for books of others, pot-boilers, etc." *Avocational interests:* Painting, photography, collecting experimental music and modern jazz, and collecting editions of modern poetry.

BIOGRAPHICAL/CRITICAL SOURCES: Carolina Quarterly, spring, 1958.

*   *   *

MAYALL, R(obert) Newton 1904-

PERSONAL: Born July 19, 1904, in Waltham, Mass.; son of Robert Edgar (an artist) and Grace Farrar (Newton) Mayall; married Margaret Lyle Walton (an astronomer), September 18, 1927. Education: Boston Architectural Center, student, 1925-29; also attended Northeastern University, and Massachusetts Institute of Technology. Religion: Protestant. Home: 5 Sparks St., Cambridge, Mass. 02138. Office: Planning and Research Associates, 45 Bromfield St., Boston, Mass. 02108.

CAREER: In private practice as consulting engineer, Boston, Mass., 1935-45; George B. Cabot and Associates, Boston, Mass., consulting engineer, 1945-53; Planning & Research Associates, Boston, Mass., consulting engineer and director, 1953—. Secretary-treasurer and director, Philcot Corp. Member: American Society of Landscape Architects, National Association of Science Writers, American Association for the Advancement of Science, Boston Society of Civil Engineers, Boston Society of Landscape Architects, Boston Authors Club (treasurer), Canadian Club of New York.

WRITINGS—With wife, Margaret L. Mayall: Sundials: How to Know, Use and Make Them, Hale, Cushman & Flint, 1938, revised edition, Branford, 1958; Skyshooting: Hunting the Stars with Your Camera, Ronald, 1949, revised edition published as Sky-Shooting: Photography for Amateur Astronomers, Dover, 1968; (editor) William Tyler Olcott, The Field Book of the Skies, 4th edition, Putnam, 1954; (and Jerome Wyckoff) The Sky Observer's Guide: A Handbook for Amateur Astronomers, Golden Press, 1959; A Beginner's Guide to the Skies, Putnam, 1960, revised edition, Cornerstone Library, 1962; The Story of AAVSO, [Cambridge, Mass.], c.1962. Contributor of articles on general science to national magazines in United States and Canada.

*   *   *

MAYBAUM, Ignaz 1897-

PERSONAL: Born March 2, 1897, in Vienna, Austria; son of Moritz (a merchant) and Josephine (Kohn) Maybaum; married Frances Schor; children: Michael, Alisa Maybaum Jaffa. Education: University of Berlin, Ph.D., 1925. Home: 60 Whitchurch Gardens, Edgware, Middlesex, England.

CAREER: Rabbi of congregations in Germany at Bingen, 1926-28, Frankfurt-on-the-Oder, 1928-36, Berlin, 1936-39; rabbi of congregation in Edgeware, Middlesex, England, 1947-63, now minister emeritus. Lecturer in comparative religion and Jewish theology, Leo Baeck College, London, England. Military service: Austrian Army, 1915-18; became lieutenant.

WRITINGS: Parteibefreitis Judentum, Phil Verlag, 1935; Neue Jugend und Alter Glaube: Der Chaluz und der Baalhabajit in der Verantwortung von der Lehre, Philo Verlag, 1936; Man and Catastrophe, translated by Joseph Leftwich, Allenson & Co., 1941; Synagogue and Society: Jewish-Christian Collaboration in the Defence of Western Civilization, translation by Joseph Leftwich, J. H. Clarke, 1944; The Jewish Home, translation by Tilly Barnett and L. V. Snowman, J. H. Clarke, 1946; The Jewish Mission, J. H. Clarke, 1950; The Sacrifice of Isaac: A Jewish Commentary, Valentine, Mitchell, 1959; Jewish Existence, Valentine, Mitchell, 1960; The Faith of the Jewish Diaspora, Vision Press, 1962; The Office of a Chief Rabbi, Reform Synagogues of Great Britain, 1964; The Face of God After Auschwitz, Polak & Van Gennep (Amsterdam), 1965; Creation and Guilt: A Theological Assessment of Freud's Father-Son Conflict, Valentine, Mitchell, 1969.

*   *   *

MAYBERRY, Genevieve 1900-

PERSONAL: Born July 4, 1900, in Lebanon, Ore.; daughter of Winfield Scott (a teacher) and Adeline (Smith) Mayberry. Education: Attended Oregon College of Education, 1926; University of Oregon, B.S., 1941. Politics: Republican. Religion: Presbyterian. Home: 624 South Elizabeth St., Milton-Freewater, Ore. 97862.

CAREER: Elementary teacher in Oregon, 1924-37, in Wrangell, Alaska, 1937-43, Sitka, Alaska, 1943-46, Juneau, Alaska, 1946-61, and again in Oregon, 1961-65; now retired. Member: National League of American Pen Women (president, Juneau branch, 1955), National Retired Teachers Association, Pacific Northwest Writers Conference, Delta Kappa Gamma (Alaska state founder and branch president), Order for the Eastern Star (past matron).

WRITINGS: Eskimo of Little Diomede, Follett, 1961; Sheldon Jackson Junior College: An Intimate History, Board of National Missions of the Presbyterian Church, 1959; (contributor) Alaska Book, J. G. Ferguson, 1960. Contributor to Encyclopaedia Britannica; also contributor to periodicals, including Alaska Sportsman, Alaska Magazine, and to education journals.

*   *   *

MAYO, Margot 1910-

PERSONAL: Born May 30, 1910, in Commerce, Tex.; daughter of William Leonidas (a college president) and Etta (Booth) Mayo. Education: Attended private schools in New York area, Institute of Musical Art (now Juilliard School of Music), Dalcroze School of Music, Martha Graham School of Dance, New School for Social Research, and Columbia University.

CAREER: Mills College of Education, New York, N.Y., teacher of music and dance folklore, 1945—; Woodward School (nursery and elementary), Brooklyn, N.Y., teacher of music and dance, 1953—. American Square Dance Group, New York, N.Y., founder, 1934, and director, 1934—; editor of Promenade (folklore magazine), 1939-53; recorder and collector of folk music; collector of folk dances; sometime broadcaster of radio programs on folk music. Military service: U.S. Army, Women's Army Auxiliary Corps (WAC), 1943-45. Member: American Folklore Society, Society for Ethnomusicology, United Federation of Teachers, New York Folklore Society.

WRITINGS: The American Square Dance, Sentinel, 1943, revised and enlarged edition, Oak, 1964.

Collected and selected material for four folk dance albums issued by Decca Records and three albums for Decca-American Books; selected and edited "The Margot Mayo Collection of Early American Choral Pieces," Hargail Music Press; selected and wrote album notes for "Square Dances," Keynote Records. Some of folk material taped for Library of Congress, 1946, also has been issued on records.

Contributor to Sing Out!, Dance Herald, Educational Dance, and New York Folklore Quarterly.

WORK IN PROGRESS: Two Hundred Years of Dancing Masters in New York City, 1684-1884; research on the history and contributions of the Shakers and on teaching projects in connection with American folklore.

SIDELIGHTS: Margot Mayo lived for three years (winter and summer) on an all-sail schooner, sailing the Atlantic coast.

* * *

MAYOR, Beatrice ?-1971

PERSONAL: Daughter of Daniel (an international banker) and Georgina (Potter) Meinertzhagen; married R. G. Mayor, December 14, 1912 (died 1947); children: Susan, Teresa, Andreas. *Education:* Educated privately at home, and at schools in Paris. *Home:* 26 Addison Ave., London W.11, England. *Agent:* Eric Glass, 28 Berkeley Sq., London W.1, England.

CAREER: Writer. First aid nurse; public shelter worker in home for bombed out people, World War II. *Member:* Poetry Society, Author's Society, League of Dramatists, P.E.N.

WRITINGS: Poems, Allen & Unwin, 1919; *The Pleasure Garden* (four-act play), Sidgwick & Jackson, 1925; *Four Plays for Children,* Samuel French (New York), 1926; *Thirty Minutes in a Street* (one-act), Basil Blackwell, 1926; *The Stream* (novel), Putnam, 1933; *Little Earthquake* (three-act play), Fortune Press, 1939; *The Story Without an End,* John Lane, 1940; *Voices From the Crowd* (poems), Fortune Press, 1943; *Carrie et le cygne noir* (children's story), Delagrave (Paris), 1964. Also author of three plays performed on radio and one on television; author of stories for program "Children's Hour."

WORK IN PROGRESS: A book.

(Died February 15, 1971)

* * *

McBRIDE, Earl Duwain 1891-

PERSONAL: Born June 16, 1891, in Severy, Kan.; son of Aaron (a merchant) and Alameda (Tucker) McBride; married Pauline Mary Wahl, September 2, 1913; children: Polly Anna (Mrs. William K. Ishmael), Mary Frances (Mrs. Richard Tullius), Dorothy Lou (Mrs. Terrence Malloy). *Education:* University of Oklahoma, B.S., 1912; Columbia University, M.D., 1914; orthopedic courses in London, Paris, and Vienna, 1921. *Politics:* Republican. *Religion:* Methodist. *Home:* 1705 Dorchester Pl., Oklahoma City, Okla. 73120. *Office:* 605 Northwest 10th St., Oklahoma City, Okla. 73103.

CAREER: Diplomate, American Board of Orthopedic Surgery. Began career as country practioneer in Hitchcock, Okla., 1914; orthopedic surgeon in practice in Oklahoma City, Okla., 1919-65; Bone and Joint Hospital and McBride Clinic, Oklahoma City, Okla., founder and chief surgeon, 1925-65, now chief surgeon emeritus. Consultant at other hospitals. University of Oklahoma School of Medicine, Oklahoma City, clinical professor of orthopedic surgery, 1926-65. *Military service:* U.S. Army, Medical Corps, assigned to British forces, 1917-19; became captain.

MEMBER: American Academy of Orthopaedic Surgeons, American College of Surgeons, International College of Surgeons, American Medical Association, American Medical Writers' Association, American Medico-Legal Association, American Orthopaedic Association, Association of

Bone and Joint Surgeons, Oklahoma State Medical Association, Oklahoma County Medical Association (president, 1932), Oklahoma City Rotary Club (director, 1943-44), Masons, Oklahoma City Golf and Country Club. *Awards, honors:* Professor of Medicine Extraordinari, National University of Mexico, 1945.

WRITINGS: Crippled Children and Their Nursing Treatment, Mosby, 1926, 2nd edition, 1937; *Disability Evaluation,* Lippincott, 1936, 6th edition, 1963; (contributor) Paul D. Cantor, editor, *Traumatic Medicine and Surgery for the Attorney,* Butterworth, 1960. Contributor of more than seventy articles to medical journals in United States and Canada. Associate editor and contributor, *Clinical Orthopaedics.*

WORK IN PROGRESS: Surgery of the Forefoot.

* * *

McCABE, Sybil Anderson 1902-

PERSONAL: Born December 19, 1902, in Elgin, Neb.; daughter of Daniel R. (a farmer) and Laura S. (Kinney) Anderson; married Merrill L. McCabe, June 21, 1959 (died, 1969). *Education:* Nebraska State Teachers College (now Chadron State College), graduate, 1928; DePaul University, B.A., 1941; San Francisco State College (now University), M.A., 1951. *Politics:* Non-partisan. *Religion:* Congregationalist. *Home:* 438 Silverado Trail, St. Helena, Calif. 94574.

CAREER: Elementary school teacher in Elgin, Neb., 1921-25; teacher and principal in Chadron, Neb., 1925-28; junior high school teacher in Blue Island, Ill., 1928-34; Rand McNally & Co., Chicago, Ill., assistant to literature editor, 1934-40; Beckley-Cardy Co. (publishers), Chicago, Ill., editor-in-chief, 1941-50; Harr Wagner Publishing Co., San Francisco, Calif., editor-in-chief, 1950-53; Contra Costa County schools, Martinez, Calif., curriculum consultant, 1953-59; Napa County schools, Napa, Calif., director of instruction, 1959-66; consultant for University of California, San Francisco, Overseas Project in Monrovia, Liberia, West Africa, 1966-70; free-lance writer, 1971—. Special consultant, California State Department of Education. *Member:* National Education Association, California Writers Club (Berkeley).

WRITINGS—Juvenile: Surprise Fun, Beckley-Cardy, 1946; (with Helen Heffernan) *Girls and Boys at Home,* Harr Wagner, 1956; (with Heffernan) *Girls and Boys at School,* Harr Wagner, 1956; (with Heffernan) *Days' River Farm,* Harr Wagner, 1957; (with Heffernan) *Foods From Far and Near,* Harr Wagner, 1957; (with Irmagarde Richards) *California Yesterdays,* Harr Wagner, 1957; (with Richards) *California Today,* Harr Wagner, 1957; *Treasure Tanks: The Oil Refineries of Contra Costa County,* Contra Costa County Schools, 1959; *How Schools Aid Democracy,* Benefic, 1964; *How Communication Helps Us,* Benefic, 1964; *How Books and Printing Help Us,* Benefic, 1964. Writer of educational materials for schools in Liberia, West Africa. Contributor to magazines.

WORK IN PROGRESS: Two books, *Honey Bear on the Alaska Highway* and *Heart for Liberia*; an article, "Outdoor Theater in Kodiak, Alaska."

AVOCATIONAL INTERESTS: Nature, reading, cooking, interior decorating, music, and travel.

BIOGRAPHICAL/CRITICAL SOURCES: St. Helena Star, St. Helena, Napa County, Calif., May 20, 1965.

McCALEB, Walter Flavius 1873-1967

PERSONAL: Born October 17, 1873, in Benton City, Tex.; son of John Lafayette and Elizabeth (Sweeten) McCaleb; married first wife, 1901; married second wife, Edna E. Lang, 1960; children: (first marriage) Ethel, Aurora McCaleb Pitkin Walter, Laura. *Education:* University of Texas, B.Lit., 1896, M.A., 1897; University of Chicago, Ph.D., 1900. *Home:* 3711 Windsor Rd., Austin, Tex. 78703.

CAREER: Banker and writer who began career in editorial work in New York, N.Y., and Philadelphia, Pa., 1901-04; later went into banking, organizing banks for labor, and heading banks in Cleveland, Ohio, and in California and Texas. Onetime district manager of Federal Home Loan Corp., vice-president and manager of Brotherhood of Locomotive Engineers, director and vice-chairman of Federal Reserve Bank of Dallas, Tex., and officer of several life insurance firms. Special adviser to Secretary of Interior on Puerto Rico, 1937; author of law authorizing credit unions. *Military service:* U.S. Army, Intelligence, 1918; became captain. *Member:* American Historical Association, American Academy of Political and Social Science, Texas Historical Association (fellow), Authors Club (New York), Phi Beta Kappa, Nu Alpha, Cosmos Club (Washington, D.C.), City Club (Cleveland), Rancho Golf Club.

WRITINGS: The Aaron Burr Conspiracy: A History Largely from Original and Hitherto Unused Sources, Dodd, 1903, expanded edition, with an introduction by Charles Beard, Wilson-Erickson, 1936; (editor) John Reagan, *Memoirs,* Gammell, 1906; *Winnowings of the Wind,* privately printed, 1910; (editor) Rene Stourm, *Budget,* Brookings Institution, 1917; *Happy: The Life of a Bee,* Harper, 1917; *Busy: The Life of an Ant,* Harper, 1919; *Present and Past Banking in Mexico,* Harper, 1920; *The Public Finances of Mexico,* Harper, 1921; *Ring: A Frontier Dog,* Prentice-Hall, 1921; *Theodore Roosevelt,* A. & C. Boni, 1931; *Brotherhood of Railroad Trainmen,* A. & C. Boni, 1936; (editor) *Shorter Workday,* Brotherhood of Railroad Trainmen, 1937.

The Conquest of the West, Prentice-Hall, 1947; *The Spanish Missions of Texas,* with an essay by daughter, Aurora McCaleb Pitkin, Naylor, 1954, revised edition, 1961; *The Alamo,* Naylor, 1956, revised and enlarged edition, 1961; *Bigfoot Wallace,* Naylor, 1956; *William Barret Travis,* Naylor, 1957, revised edition, 1966; *Sam Houston,* Naylor, 1958, revised edition, 1967; *The Mier Expedition,* Naylor, 1959; *How Much Is a Dollar: The Story of Money and Banks,* Naylor, 1959; *Khorasan* (poem), Naylor, 1962; *New Light on Aaron Burr,* University of Texas, 1963; *Santa Fe Expedition,* Naylor, 1964; *No Port of Call, and Other Poems,* Naylor, 1964; *The Aaron Burr Conspiracy [and] A New Light on Aaron Burr,* Argosy-Antiquarian, 1966.

(Died, 1967)

* * *

McCALL, William A(nderson) 1891-

PERSONAL: Born January 9, 1891, in Wellsville, Tenn.; son of Robert R. (a miner) and Lulu T. (Wells) McCall; married Alma Huestis, 1916; married Gretchen Switzer (a school supervisor), December 21, 1937; children: (first marriage) Lois. *Education:* Cumberland College, B.S., 1911; Lincoln Memorial University, A.B., 1913; Columbia University, Ph.D., 1916. *Politics:* "Depends on candidates and

policies." *Religion:* Eclectic. *Home:* 501 Alminar Ave., Coral Gables, Fla. 33146.

CAREER: Columbia University, New York, N.Y., 1916-56, started as instructor, professor of education at Teachers College, 1923-56, professor emeritus, beginning 1956. Summer professor at University of North Carolina, George Peabody College for Teachers, Auburn University, and University of California; lecturer for several years at University of Miami, Coral Gables, Fla. Director of research, Chinese National Association for the Advancement of Education, 1922-23; director of School Health Research Project, American Child Health Association. Deviser of New York State Literacy Test and of other mental and educational tests. *Awards, honors:* Litt.D., Lincoln Memorial University.

WRITINGS: Correlation of Some Psychological and Educational Measurements, Teachers College, Columbia University, 1916; (with Thorndike and Chapman) *Ventilation in Relation to Mental Work,* Teachers College, Columbia University, 1916; *How to Measure in Education,* Macmillan, 1922, revised edition published as *Measurement,* 1939; *How to Experiment in Education,* Macmillan, 1923; (with Harold Bixler) *How to Classify Pupils,* Teachers College, Columbia University, 1928; (with Houser) *New McCall Speller,* Laidlaw, 1936; (with Marston Balch and John Herring) *You and College,* Harcourt, 1936.

(With Lelah Crabbs) *Standard Test Lessons in Reading,* Teachers College, Columbia University, 1941, 3rd edition, Teachers College Press, 1961; (editor with George Norvell) *Improve Your Reading,* Harcourt, 1942; *Cherokees and Pioneers,* Stephens Press, 1952; (with Edwin Smith) *Test Lessons in Reading-Reasoning,* Teachers College, Columbia University, 1964; (with Mary Harby) *Test Lessons in Primary Reading,* Teachers College, Columbia University, 1965; *I Thunk Me a Thaut,* Teachers College Press, 1975. Co-editor (with many collaborators) of seventy-five books or tests published in Chinese by Commercial Press, Shanghai. Editor, "Teachers' Lesson Unit Series," Teachers College, Columbia University, beginning 1931, with more than one hundred units published; author with Elda Merton, "The Merton-McCall Readers," Laidlaw, 1937-40; author with Luella Cook, "Adventures in Literature," Harcourt, 1941-42.

WORK IN PROGRESS—Several books: (With Mark Murfin) *Ten Best Steps in Teaching, Pictured Words, Cute Couplets, Do's and Dont's, Short Stories and Tall Tales, Reading Jokes, Reading-Self Guidance,* and a novel to be published posthumously titled *Yours Al(l)ways.*

SIDELIGHTS: McCall's major political interest is "designing a plan for World Government without veto, ... with vote proportional to the number of citizens in each nation with a defined amount of education or gross national product with both required for passage of all bills ... no nation permitted to vote for one of its own nationals for high executive position, thereby encouraging world statesmanship instead of national jingoism, and with all past, present and future national legislators [as] members of the World Parliament for life."

BIOGRAPHICAL/CRITICAL SOURCES: Education, September, 1964.

* * *

McCARTHY, R. Delphina (Polley) 1894-

PERSONAL: Born June 28, 1894, in Hardwick, New

Brunswick, Canada; daughter of James Frederick (a clergyman) and Katherine McLean (Noble) Polley; married Charles Knight McCarthy, September 12, 1927 (deceased); children: Katherine Delphina (deceased). *Education:* Tufts College, M.D., 1931. *Religion:* Protestant. *Home:* West Main St., Brookfield, Mass. 01506. *Agent:* Howard E. Hill, P.O. Box 628, Culver City, Calif.

CAREER: Physician in general practice, beginning, 1931. *Member:* Massachusetts Medical Society.

WRITINGS: Beyond the Clouds, Arcadia House, 1964.

WORK IN PROGRESS: Two novels.

* * *

McCLEAN, Joseph Lucius 1919-

PERSONAL: Born March 19, 1919, in Rathfriland, County Down, Ireland; son of John and Isabella (Berry) McClean. *Education:* Attended Franciscan College, County Westmeath, Ireland; University College, Galway, Ireland, B.A., 1942; St. Anthony's College, Galway, Ireland, theological studies, 1943-47. *Home:* Catholic Radio & Television Centre, Oakleigh Rd., Hatch End, Middlesex HA5 4HB, England.

CAREER: Entered Order of Friars Minor (Franciscan Order), 1938, ordained a Roman Catholic priest, 1946; *Assisi Magazine,* Dublin, Ireland, assistant editor, 1948-51, editor, 1951-63; Franciscan Monastery, Dublin, Ireland, vicar, 1954-57, guardian, 1957-63; Rutherford Comprehensive School, London, England, teacher of languages, 1964-69; Catholic Radio and Television Centre, Hatch End, Middlesex, England, warden, 1970—. Lecturer in communications, Harrow College of Further Education, 1970—. Member of national executive board, Catholic Boy Scouts of Ireland, 1963-64. *Member:* P.E.N.

WRITINGS: The Inn, Assisi Press (Dublin), 1958; *Adam and Eve,* Stockwell, 1960; *What's the Problem?,* Assisi Press (Dublin), 1962. Founder and editor of *Bethlehem: A Franciscan Book at Christmas,* published annually by Assisi Press, 1951-63. Writer or editor of devotional booklets, centenary brochures, guide books. Contributor of weekly article to *Sunday Independent* (Dublin), 1955—.

WORK IN PROGRESS: Three books, *Emigration, Teacher in the World,* and *Christian Philosophy of Life.*

AVOCATIONAL INTERESTS: Youth work, book illustration, oil painting.

* * *

McCLINTOCK, Marshall 1906-1967
(Mike McClintock; pseudonyms: Gregory Duncan, Douglas Marshall, William Starret)

PERSONAL: Born August 21, 1906, in Topeka, Kan.; son of William S. (a lawyer) and Martha B. (Whaley) McClintock; married Helene Maunsell; married second wife, Inez Bertail; married third wife, May Garelick (a writer-editor); children: Marco, Claudia, Michael. *Education:* Dartmouth College, A.B., 1926. *Address:* Box 62, Washingtonville, N.Y. 10992.

CAREER: Started as clerk, then manager, of Doubleday Book Shops, 1927-29; worked in publishing field in New York, N.Y., as salesman, later sales manager for Viking Press, 1929-36, sales manager of Heritage Press, 1936-37, sales manager and juvenile editor of Vanguard Press, 1937-40; held editorial and office posts with Artists and Writers Guild and Western Printing and Lithographing Co., New

York, N.Y., and Racine, Wis., 1940-43; Julian Messner, Inc., New York, N.Y., editor, 1945-47; *Collier's,* New York, N.Y., associate editor, 1950-51; free-lance writer.

WRITINGS: We Take to Bed, J. Cape & H. Smith, 1931; *Here Is a Book: The Story of Your Library,* Vanguard, 1939; *The Story of the Mississippi,* Harper, 1941; *The Story of New England,* Harper, 1941; *Millions of Books,* Vanguard, 1941; (adapter) Robert Bird, *Nick of the Woods,* Vanguard, 1941; *Airplanes and How They Fly: A Complete Primer of Aviation for Young Boys and Girls,* Frederick Stokes, 1943; *The Story of War Weapons,* Lippincott, 1945; (editor) *The Greystone Nature Lover's Treasury,* Greystone Press, 1947; (editor) William H. Prescott, *The Conquest of Mexico* (History Book Club selection), Messner, 1948; *Leaf, Fruit and Flower: A Nature Primer,* Chanticleer, 1948; *Let's Learn the Flowers,* Chanticleer, 1948; (editor) *Nobel Prize Treasury* (Literary Guild selection), Doubleday, 1948; (editor) *My Favorite Stories of the Great Outdoors,* Greystone Press, 1950; (editor) *Women on the Wall,* Pyramid, 1952; (editor) Richard Dana, *Two Years Before the Mast,* Pyramid, 1953; (with Alfred Carlton Gilbert) *Man Who Lives in Paradise* (Gilbert's autobiography), Rinehart, 1954; *How to Build and Operate a Model Railroad,* Dell, 1955; (with Inez McClintock) *Toys in America,* Public Affairs Press, 1961.

Under name Mike McClintock: *A Fly Went By,* Random House, 1958; *Stop That Ball!,* Random House, 1959; *David and the Giant,* Harper, 1960; *What Have I Got?,* Harper, 1961.

Under pseudonym Gregory Duncan: *March Anson and Scoot Bailey of the U.S. Navy,* Whitman, 1944; *Dick Donnelly of the Paratroops,* Whitman, 1944.

Under pseudonym Douglas Marshall: *Doctor Ben,* Gramercy Publishing Co., 1941; *Local Doctor,* Gramercy Publishing Co., 1942; *The Young Teacher,* Gramercy Publishing Co., 1943; *All in Blue,* Gramercy Publishing Co., 1945.

Under pseudonym William Starret: *Nurse Blake, U.S.A.,* Gramercy Publishing Co., 1942; *Nurse Blake Overseas,* Gramercy Publishing Co., 1943; *Nurse Blake at the Front,* Gramercy Publishing Co., 1944.

Contributor to *Saturday Evening Post, Saturday Review, Collier's,* and other magazines.

(Died, 1967)

* * *

McCOLLUM, Elmer Verner 1879-1967

PERSONAL: Born March 3, 1879, near Fort Scott, Kan.; son of Cornelius Armstrong and Martha Catherine (Kidwell) McCollum. *Education:* University of Kansas, B.A., 1903, M.A., 1904; Yale University, Ph.D., 1906. *Home:* Baltimore, Md.

CAREER: University of Wisconsin, Madison, instructor, 1907-08, assistant professor, 1908-11, associate professor, 1911-13, professor of agricultural chemistry, 1913-17; Johns Hopkins University, School of Hygiene and Public Health, Baltimore, Md., professor of biochemistry, 1917-44, professor emeritus, 1944-67, member of advisory committee of McCollum-Pratt Institute. Nutritionist for League of Nations; member of Food and Nutrition Board of National Research Council, 1942-67; member of Scientific Advisory Committee of Nutrition Foundation; consultant to U.S. and foreign government agencies.

MEMBER: American Society of Biological Chemists (president, 1927-29), American Association for the Advancement of Science, American Chemical Society, American Public Health Association, National Academy of Science, Royal Society of Arts (London; fellow), Swedish Academy of Science (foreign member), American Philosophical Society, American Association of University Professors; honorary member of other organizations and academies in Germany, Belgium, England, and United States; Phi Beta Kappa. *Awards, honors:* Howard N. Potts Gold Medal of Franklin Institute, 1921, for distinguished scientific work; John Scott Medal from City of Philadelphia, 1924; Osborne and Mendal Award of American Institute of Nutrition, 1955; Borden Federation Centenary Award, 1958; Charles F. Spencer Award of American Chemical Society, 1958; Modern Medicine Award, 1960; New York Academy of Medicine medal and citation, 1961.

WRITINGS: A Text-book of Organic Chemistry for Students of Medicine and Biology, Macmillan, 1916, 2nd revised edition, 1920; *The Newer Knowledge of Nutrition*, Macmillan, 1918, 5th edition (with Elsa Orent-Keiles and Harry G. Day), Macmillan, 1939; (with Nina Simonds) *The American Home Diet*, F. C. Mathews, 1920; (with N. Simonds) *Menus for Two Weeks*, McCall's, 1922; *The Elusive Vitamin*, W. B. Burford, 1924; (with N. Simonds) *Food, Nutrition and Health*, privately printed, 1925, 6th edition (with J. Ernestine Becker), 1947; *Water-Soluble Vitamins*, Columbia University Press, 1927; (with William H. Lapp) *Hygiene, Feeding and Management of Baby Chicks*, privately printed, 1930; *The Business Value of Research*, Institute of American Poultry Industries, 1933; (editor) *Symposium on Nutrition*, Johns Hopkins Press, 1953; *A History of Nutrition*, Houghton, 1957; *From Kansas Farm Boy to Scientist* (autobiography), University of Kansas Press, 1964.

(Died November 15, 1967)

* * *

McCREARY, W. Burgess 1894-

PERSONAL: Born March 3, 1894, in Wilkinsburg, Pa.; son of James Scott and Annie Elizabeth (Burgess) McCreary; married Tressie Fern Hittle, August 13, 1916; children: Leroy, Treva McCreary Cockerham, Lowell, Donna Mae McCreary France, Kenneth. *Education:* Anderson College, Anderson, Ind., A.B., 1955. *Politics:* Republican. *Religion:* Church of God. *Home:* 219 Central Ave., Anderson, Ind. 46012.

CAREER: Former proprietor of real estate and insurance agency, Anderson, Ind.; after retirement, served as business administrator of Park Place Church of God, Anderson, Ind. *Member:* Lions Club.

WRITINGS: One Thousand Bible Drill Questions, Gospel Trumpet, 1926; *John Bunyan, the Immortal Dreamer*, Gospel Trumpet, 1928; *Bible Quizzes and Questions*, Warner Press, 1956; *When Youth Prays*, Warner Press, 1960; *With the Passing Seasons*, Warner Press, 1965.

* * *

McCUTCHEN, Samuel Proctor 1909-1966

PERSONAL: Born December 9, 1901, in Greenville, Miss.; son of Samuel Proctor (a salesman) and Georgie (Harbison) McCutchen; married Lineta Price, June 16, 1923; children: Martha (Mrs. David W. Wilson), Proctor. *Education:* Southwestern University at Memphis, B.A.,

1922; University of Chicago, M.A., 1925, Ph.D., 1930. *Home:* 28 Hickory Dr., Maplewood, N.J. 07040. *Office:* New York University, Washington Sq., New York, N.Y. 10003.

CAREER: Teacher of social studies and principal at high schools in Mississippi, 1922-26; John Burroughs School, Clayton, Mo., instructor in social studies, 1928-36; Ohio State University, Columbus, associate in research and assistant professor, 1936-41; New York University, New York, N.Y., professor of education, 1941-66, chairman of social studies department, 1943-65, chairman of commission on doctoral study, 1945-50, director of six workshops in economic education, 1950-59, director of university's Program of Graduate Studies in Puerto Rico, 1960-61. Director, Workshop on Economic Education. Trustee, Joint Council on Economic Education, 1962-64. *Member:* National Education Association, National Council for the Social Studies (director, 1957-65; president, 1962), American Association of University Professors.

WRITINGS: (With Harry H. Giles and A. N. Zechiel) *Exploring the Curriculum: The Work of Thirty Schools from the Viewpoint of Curriculum Consultants,* Harper, 1942; (editor) "American Way" series, four volumes, Harper, 1943-45; (with Henry Wilkinson Bragdon) *History of a Free People,* Macmillan, 1954, 6th revised edition, 1967; (with George L. Fersh and Nadine I. Clark) *Goals of Democracy: A Problems Approach,* Macmillan, 1962; (editor and author of commentary with Bragdon and Stuart Gerry Brown) *Frame of Government,* Macmillan, 1962; (editor with Dorothy McClure Fraser) *Social Studies in Transition: Guidelines for Change,* National Council for the Social Studies, 1965. Contributor to *Social Education,* 1937-66.

WORK IN PROGRESS: Curriculum revision in social studies.

(Died March, 1966)

* * *

McDADE, Thomas M. 1907-

PERSONAL: Born July 2, 1907, in Brooklyn, N.Y.; son of John J. and Emma (Thieme) McDade; married Beatrice M. Clifford, March 16, 1940; children: Jared Clifford, Innes Fergus. *Education:* City College (now City College of the City University of New York), graduate in accountancy, 1928; St. John's University, Jamaica, N.Y., LL.B. (cum laude), 1931, LL.M., 1932. *Home and office:* Scotland Yard, Purchase, N.Y. 10577.

CAREER: Admitted to New York bar, 1932; Federal Bureau of Investigation, 1934-38, began as special agent, became supervisor; private practice of law in New York, N.Y., 1938-42; General Foods Corp., White Plains, N.Y., assistant controller, then controller, 1951-68, retired; private practice of criminal law, 1972—. Legal counselor to inmates of two penitentiaries. *Military service:* U.S. Army, 1942-46; served in Pacific Theater; became lieutenant colonel; received Bronze Star. *Member:* Society of Former Special Agents of the F.B.I., Mystery Writers of America, Bibliographical Society of America, Society of Connoisseurs in Murder. *Awards, honors:* Edgar Allan Poe Award ("Edgar") of Mystery Writers of America, 1961, for *The Annals of Murder.*

WRITINGS: The Annals of Murder: A Bibliography of Books and Pamphlets on American Murders from Colonial Times to 1900, University of Oklahoma Press, 1961. Contributor to *Ellery Queen's Mystery Magazine, American Book Collector, Colophon, Pennsylvania Magazine of History and Biography*, and numerous historical publications.

* * *

McDANIEL, Ruel 1896-

PERSONAL: Born August 13, 1896, in Slocum, Tex.; son of James Samuel and Nettie (Gulley) McDaniel; married wife, Gladys, April 24, 1942. *Education:* Attended Baylor University and Massachusetts Institute of Technology. *Politics:* Democrat. *Religion:* Baptist. *Home and office:* 214 Suncrest Dr., Port Lavaca, Tex. 77979. *Agent:* Annie Laurie Williams, Inc., 18 East 41st St., New York, N.Y. 10017.

CAREER: Began as newspaper reporter in Wichita Falls, Tex., 1917, and worked as reporter, member of advertising staff, or publisher of newspapers in Louisiana, North Carolina, and Texas, 1920-23; free-lance writer, 1923-29; publisher of three business magazines and editor of a farm magazine during period, 1929-47; Star Publications, Inc., president, 1947-53; full-time free-lance writer, primarily for magazines, beginning, 1953. Mayor of Port Lavaca, Tex., 1956-58. *Military service:* U.S. Navy, naval aviator, 1917-20; became ensign. *Member:* Houston Press Club, Rotary Club (local director).

WRITINGS: Vinegarroon, Southern Publishers, 1936; *Some Ran Hot*, Regional Publishing Co., 1939; *Deep Water Boy*, Golden Gate Junior Books, 1964; *One More Sunrise*, Historical [Port Lavaca, Tex.], 1965. More than eight thousand stories and articles published in some six hundred periodicals.

WORK IN PROGRESS: Pass Cavello North, an area history; *Big Catch*, a novel of the shrimping industry.

SIDELIGHTS: McDaniel was one of the early naval aviators, with the serial number 2334. *Avocational interests:* Travel, local government.

* * *

McDERMOTT, Charles J(ames) 1905-

PERSONAL: Born September 21, 1905, in Brooklyn, N.Y.; son of Charles James (a lawyer) and Mary Elizabeth (Thornton) McDermott; married Eugenie Brumley, July 2, 1932; children: Sheila (Mrs. J. Rodney Edwards), Charles J. III. *Education:* Princeton University, A.B., 1928; New York University, A.M., 1934. *Politics:* Republican. *Religion:* Episcopal. *Address:* P.O. Box 76, Remsenburg, N.Y.

CAREER: Brooklyn College (now Brooklyn College of the City University of New York), Brooklyn, N.Y., instructor in English, 1933-40; publisher of six weekly newspapers in New Jersey, 1943-57; *Long Islander*, Huntington, N.Y., co-publisher, 1947-61; *Long Island Forum*, Westhampton Beach, N.Y., publisher, 1959-64; Madison Printing Co., Madison, N.J., president, 1947—. *Member:* Princeton Club (New York), Morristown Club (New Jersey), Quoque Field Club (Long Island).

WRITINGS: (With Cyril A. Lewis) *Historic Long Island*, Long Island Forum, 1964; *History of Suffolk County*, James Heineman, 1965. Contributor of historical articles to magazines, 1940—; writer of syndicated newspaper column, "Along Long Island," 1940-42.

WORK IN PROGRESS: Research on literary Long Island.

McDONALD, Gerald D(oan) 1905-1970

PERSONAL: Born June 5, 1905, in Wilmington, Ohio; son of Frank Luman and Frances (Doan) McDonald. *Education:* Wilmington College, Wilmington, Ohio, A.B., 1927; Haverford College, M.A., 1928; Columbia University, School of Library Service, B.S., 1930. *Religion:* Society of Friends. *Home:* 36 West 10th St., New York, N.Y. 10011. *Office:* New York Public Library, Fifth Ave. and 42nd St., New York, N.Y. 10019.

CAREER: Cleveland Public Library, Cleveland, Ohio, assistant in literature division, 1928-29; New York Public Library, New York, N.Y. head of reserve room, 1931-40, chief of rare book division, 1941-45, chief of American history division, 1946-69, chief of special collections, 1969-70. Member of board of directors, National Board of Review of Motion Pictures. *Military service:* U.S. Army, 1942-45; became sergeant. *Member:* American Library Association, American Antiquarian Society, Bibliographical Society of America, American Historical Association, Friends Historical Association, Ohio Folklore Society, Grolier Club. *Awards, honors:* L.H.D., Wilmington College, 1953.

WRITINGS: Educational Motion Pictures and Libraries, American Library Association, 1942; (editor) *Living Ideas in America*, New York Library, 1954; *A Bibliography of Song Sheets*, Music Library Association, 1958; (editor) *A Way of Knowing: A Collection of Poems for Boys*, Crowell, 1959; (editor) *The Doane Family*, Doane Family Association of America, 1960; (editor) Stephen Crane, *Poems*, Crowell, 1964; (with Michael Conway and Mark Ricci) *The Films of Charlie Chaplin*, Citadel, 1965; *The Picture History of Charlie Chaplin*, Nostalgia Press, 1965. Contributor to *Dictionary of American Biography, Ohio Authors and Their Books;* also contributor to *Films in Review*, and other periodicals. Editor, *Bulletin of New York Public Library*, 1954-56; poetry consultant, *Library Journal*, 1948-58.

WORK IN PROGRESS: A study of the New Year's poems presented by newsboys to their customers, 1720-1900.

AVOCATIONAL INTERESTS: Fine printing, early film history, topical sheet music.

BIOGRAPHICAL/CRITICAL SOURCES: Bulletin of Bibliography, May-August, 1962.

(Died May 6, 1970)

* * *

McDONALD, Mary Reynolds 1888-

PERSONAL: Born March 17, 1888, in St. Louis, Mo.; daughter of John Henry and Anne (McCormack) Reynolds; married Charles Burr McDonald, 1923 (deceased, 1963); children: Patricia A., Willis Burr. *Education:* Attended Teachers College, Warrensburg, Mo., and Loretta Seminary for Young Ladies, Webster Grove, Mo.; Washington University Training School for Nurses, St. Louis, Mo., R.N., 1917. *Politics:* Republican. *Religion:* Catholic. *Residence:* Pebble Beach, Calif.

CAREER: Teacher in St. Louis County, Mo., and school nurse in Riverside County, Calif., prior to 1923.

WRITINGS: Little Stories About God, Daughters of St. Paul, 1964.

WORK IN PROGRESS: Poetry.

SIDELIGHTS: Mrs. McDonald lived in Germany when her husband, a U.S. Army officer, was stationed there, 1946-49, and in Austria one year. She has traveled extensively in Europe.

McDONOUGH, William K. 1900-

PERSONAL: Born October 20, 1900, in Portland, Me.; son of Edward J. (a medical doctor) and Alesia M. (Kohling) McDonough. *Education:* Holy Cross College, B.A., 1923; studied for priesthood at St. Mary's Seminary, Baltimore, Md. *Home and office:* 21 High St., Fairfield, Me. 04937. *Agent:* Catherine M. Neale, 45 Tudor City Pl., New York, N.Y. 10017.

CAREER: Ordained Roman Catholic priest, Baltimore, Md., 1927; now pastor of Immaculate Heart of Mary Church, Fairfield, Me. Regional chaplain, Christian Family Movement.

WRITINGS: The Mass (pamphlet), Ave Maria Press, 1962; *The Divine Family: The Trinity and Our Life in God,* Macmillan, 1963. Contributor of articles to Catholic periodicals.

WORK IN PROGRESS: This Divine World, a book on facets of Christian humanism.

* * *

McDORMAND, Thomas Bruce 1904-

PERSONAL: Born March 15, 1904, in Bear River, Nova Scotia, Canada; son of Charles Freeman (a contractor) and Maud May (Purdy) McDormand; married Irene Webb; children: Lois Ann (deceased). *Education:* Acadia University, B.A. (magna cum laude), 1929; St. Stephen's College, Edmonton, Alberta, B.D., 1935; Emmanuel College, Victoria University, Toronto, Ontario, Th.D., 1951.

CAREER: Baptist minister, serving Canadian churches, 1935-42; Baptist Convention of Ontario and Quebec, general secretary, 1948-55; Baptist Federation of Canada, general secretary, 1955-59; Acadia University, Wolfville, Nova Scotia, vice-president, 1959-61; president of Eastern Baptist College, St. Davids, Pa., and Eastern Baptist Theological Seminary, Overbrook, Pa., beginning, 1961. Member of executive committee, Baptist World Alliance, beginning, 1950; member of Board of Education and Publication, American Baptist Convention, and president of Association of School and College Administrators.

WRITINGS: The Art of Building Worship Services, Broadman, Volume I, 1941, Volume II, 1957; *The Christian Must Have an Answer,* Broadman, 1958; (with Frederic S. Crossman) *Judson Concordance to Hymns,* Judson, 1965. Editor, Canadian Baptist church school publications, 1942-48, and *Canadian Baptist,* 1947-50.

WORK IN PROGRESS: Two books, *The Family Is a School* and *Why Believe the Bible?*

* * *

McELDERRY, Bruce R. Jr. 1900-1970

PERSONAL: Born January 2, 1900, in Fairfield, Iowa; son of Bruce Robert and Alice (Foster) McElderry; married Frances Lamb, August 15, 1921; children: John Robert, Phyllis Jean McElderry Sanderson. *Education:* Grinnell College, A.B., 1921; University of Iowa, Ph.D., 1925. *Politics:* Democrat. *Religion:* United Church of Christ. *Home:* 54640 Forest Knoll Dr., Idyllwild, CA. 92349.

CAREER: High school teacher of English and Latin in Sanborn, Iowa, 1921-23; University of Wisconsin, Madison, instructor in English, 1925-26; Western Reserve University (now Case Western Reserve University), 1926-30, began as instructor, became assistant professor of English; McCann-Erickson Co. (advertising agency), New York,

N.Y., copywriter, 1931-32; State College of Washington (now Washington State University), Pullman, 1932-43, began as assistant professor, became associate professor of English; University of Southern California, Los Angeles, associate professor, 1946-50, professor of English, 1950-70. Visiting professor at New York University, 1950; University of North Carolina, 1962; University of Iowa, 1965; Columbia University, 1966. *Military service:* U.S. Marine Corps, 1918-19. U.S. Army Air Forces, 1943-46; historical officer for Air Transport Command in Europe, 1944-45; became captain. U.S. Air Force Reserve, became major. *Member:* Modern Language Association of America, American Studies Association, American Association of University Professors, Philological Association of the Pacific Coast, Phi Beta Kappa. *Awards, honors:* University of Southern California Award for creative scholarship and research, 1965; D.Litt., University of Southern California, 1968.

WRITINGS: (Author of preface) Hamlin Garland, *Main-travelled Roads,* Harper, 1956; (author of introduction) Augustus Baldwin Longstreet, *Georgia Scenes,* Sagamore Press, 1957; (author of introduction) Hamlin Garland, *Boy Life on the Prairie,* University of Nebraska Press, 1961; (editor and author of introduction and notes) Mark Twain, *Contributions to the Galaxy,* Scholars' Facsimiles, 1961; (author of introduction) Owen Chase, *Narrative of the Most Extraordinary and Distressing Shipwreck of the Whaleship Essex,* Corinth, 1963; *Thomas Wolfe,* Twayne, 1964; *Henry James,* Twayne, 1965; (editor) *The Realistic Movement in American Writing,* Volume III, Odyssey Press, 1965; (editor) *Shelley's Critical Prose,* University of Nebraska Press, 1967; *Max Beerbohm,* Twayne, 1972.

(Died December 24, 1970)

* * *

McGARRY, Daniel D(oyle) 1907-

PERSONAL: Born October 10, 1907, in Los Angeles, Calif.; son of Daniel Francis (a real estate salesman) and Ana (Doyle) McGarry; married Margaret Reddington, May 20, 1943; children: Mary Ann, Patricia Mae, Daniel Joseph, Margaret H. *Education:* St. Patrick's Seminary, Menlo, Calif., student, 1925-29; Immaculate Heart College, Los Angeles, Calif. A.B., 1932; University of California, Los Angeles, M.A., 1938, Ph.D., 1940. *Politics:* Republican. *Religion:* Roman Catholic. *Home:* 20 Parkland, Glendale, Mo. 63122. *Office:* Department of History, St. Louis University, St. Louis, Mo. 63103.

CAREER: Traveling fellow in Europe, 1939-40; instructor in history at College on Mount St. Joseph-on-the-Ohio, Mount St. Joseph, Ohio, and at Xavier University and The Athenaeum of Ohio, both Cincinnati, Ohio, 1940-43; Indiana University, Bloomington, assistant professor of European and Latin American history, 1946-50; St. Louis University, St. Louis, Mo., 1950—, began as associate professor, now professor of medieval history. Research director, Citizens for Educational Freedom. *Military service:* U.S. Marine Corps, 1943-46; became lieutenant colonel. U.S. Marine Corps Reserve, 1942-46. *Member:* American Historical Association, Mediaeval Academy of America, Phi Delta Kappa, Pi Gamma Mu.

WRITINGS: (Translator, editor, and author of introduction and notes) John of Salisbury, *The Metalogicon: A Twelfth-Century Defense of the Verbal and Logical Arts of the Trivium,* University of California Press, 1955; (with Clarence L. Hohl, Jr. and T. P. Neill) *A History of*

Western Civilization, Bruce, 1959; *The Case for Government Aid to Independent Schools*, Social Justice Central Bureau, 1961; (editor with Hohl) *Sources of Western Civilization*, two volumes, Houghton, 1962-63; (with Sarah Harriman White) *Historical Fiction Guide: Annotated, Chronological, Geographical, and Topical List of Five Thousand Selected Historical Novels*, Scarecrow, 1963; (editor with Leo Ward) *Educational Freedom and the Case for Government Aid to Students in Independent Schools*, Bruce, 1966; (with James A. Wahl) *Outline of Medieval History*, Littlefield, 1968. Contributor to *Encyclopaedia Britannica, Catholic Youth Encyclopedia, New Catholic Encyclopedia*, and to professional journals. *Educational Freedom*, associate editor, 1961-63, editor, 1963—.

* * *

McGAVIN, E(lmer) Cecil 1900-

PERSONAL: Born February 10, 1900, in Ashton, Idaho; son of Robert F. and Elizabeth (Cooper) McGavin; married Hattie Parkinson, September 20, 1922; children: Gordon, Carol, June, Carl. *Education:* Brigham Young University, A.B., 1924; University of Utah, M.A., 1926. *Politics:* Republican. *Religion:* Church of Jesus Christ of Latter-day Saints. *Home:* 1336 Roosevelt Ave., Salt Lake City, Utah 84105.

CAREER: Principal of Spanish Fork Seminary, 1928-38, of LDS Business College Institute, 1938-52.

WRITINGS: Mormonism and Masonry, Deseret, 1935, enlarged edition, Stevens & Wallis, 1947; *Christmas Bells*, Meador Publishing Co., 1937; *Paradise Revisited*, Meador Publishing Co., 1937; *U.S. Soldiers Invade Utah*, Meador Publishing Co., 1937; (with George Stewart and Dilworth Walker) *Priesthood and Church Welfare: A Study Course for the Quorums of the Melchizedek Priesthood for the Year 1939*, 2nd edition, Deseret, 1939; *Cumorah's "Gold Bible,"* Deseret, 1940; *Nauvoo, the Beautiful*, Stevens & Wallis, 1946; *The Mormon Pioneers*, Stevens & Wallis, 1947; *How We Got the Book of Mormon*, Deseret, 1960; *The Family of Joseph Smith*, Bookcraft (Salt Lake City), 1962; *The Nauvoo Temple*, Deseret, 1962.

WORK IN PROGRESS: The Mormon Bible; a three-volume work, *Early Days of Mormonism;* a revision of *The Mormon Pioneers*.

* * *

McGIFFIN, (Lewis) Lee (Shaffer) 1908-

PERSONAL: Born October 1, 1908, in Delphi, Ind.; daughter of Charles Barnes (a banker) and Daisy Lee (Lewis) Shaffer; married Norton McGiffin (a history professor), July 6, 1937 (deceased); children: Don Norton. *Education:* DePauw University, student, 1927-29; University of Alabama, B.A., 1931. *Agent:* McIntosh & Otis, Inc., 18 East 41st St., New York, N.Y. 10017.

CAREER: Fashion editor, columnist, and reporter on newspapers in Syracuse, N.Y., 1931-35, and Buffalo, N.Y., 1935-37; free-lance magazine writer, 1937—, and writer of books for children. Arlington State College, Arlington, Tex., part-time teaching assistant in social science department, 1964—. *Awards, honors:* New York Herald Tribune Children's Spring Book Festival Honor Award, 1956, for *Ten Tall Texans;* Texas Institute of Letters Juvenile Award and Theta Sigma Phi Award, 1961, for *Pony Soldier;* Theta Sigma Phi Awards, 1963, for *The Horse Hunters*, and 1964, for *A Coat for Private Patrick*.

WRITINGS—All juvenile books: *Ten Tall Texans*, Lothrop, 1956; *The Fifer of San Jacinto*, Lothrop, 1956; *Swords, Stars and Bars*, Dutton, 1958; *Rebel Rider*, Dutton, 1959; *Ride For Texas*, Dutton, 1960; *Pony Soldier*, Dutton, 1961; *High Whistle Charley*, Dutton, 1962 (published in England as *On the Trail to Sacramento*, Deutsch, 1962); *The Horse Hunters*, Dutton, 1963; *A Coat for Private Patrick*, Dutton, 1964; *The Mustangers*, Dutton, 1965; *Riders of Enchanted Valley*, Dutton, 1966; *Yankee Doodle Dandies*, Dutton, 1967; *Yankee of the Yalu*, Dutton, 1968.

Stories anthologized in *Post Short Stories*, Random House, 1956, and *Sports Alive*, Spencer Press, 1960. Contributor of adult short stories to *Saturday Evening Post, Good Housekeeping, Ladies' Home Journal*, and *This Week*, and a serialized novel to *Redbook*. Scriptwriter for radio news commentaries during World War II.

WORK IN PROGRESS: Two books.

SIDELIGHTS: Mrs. McGiffin uses a different twelve-year-old boy as a sounding board for each book manuscript before it goes to her publisher on the theory that "there is no critic more honest and frank than a twelve-year-old." A firm opponent of the idea that "Johnny can't read"; she thinks Johnny is often not given adequate time to read; also considers ten to fourteen the crucial age in reading, for "if youngsters stop then they do not start again in high school."

High Whistle Charley has been published in French, German, and Spanish editions, and *Horse Hunters* in French. Two of her *Saturday Evening Post* stories were adapted for television presentations of "G.E. Theatre."

* * *

McGOLDRICK, Edward J., Jr. 1909-1967

PERSONAL: Born April 16, 1909, in New York, N.Y.; son of Edward J. (a New York State Supreme Court justice) and Helen (Feury) McGoldrick; married Aida Welsh, October 26, 1944; children: David, Janet, Joanne. *Education:* Manhattan College, student, 1924-25; Fordham University, LL.B., 1928. *Office:* Bridge House, 912 Bronx Park South, Bronx, N.Y. 10460.

CAREER: Attorney; founder, developer of method of therapy, and executive director of Bridge House, Bronx, N.Y., a New York City Department of Welfare agency for the rehabilitation of male alcoholics, 1943-67. Consultant to New York State Committee on Alcoholism and to Truth for Youth, Inc. Lecturer on the problems of alcohol before medical, business, and civic groups in United States and Canada.

WRITINGS: Management of the Mind: How to Conquer Alcohol and Other Blocks to Successful Living, Houghton, 1954; *Conquest of Alcohol: A Handbook of Self-Therapy*, Delacorte, 1966. Writer of script for, and narrator on, two long-play records, "Conquer Your Alcoholism" and "Tormented Women," for Pathe Ltd. Contributor to newspapers and magazines, including King Features Syndicate, *Listen*, and *Health and Welfare* (Canada).

BIOGRAPHICAL SOURCES: Reader's Digest, October, 1952.

(Died November 21, 1967)

* * *

McGRATH, Earl James 1902-

PERSONAL: Born November 16, 1902, in Buffalo, N.Y.;

son of John (a businessman) and Martha (Schottin) Mc-Grath; married Dorothy Lemmon, May 12, 1944. *Education:* State University of New York at Buffalo, B.A., 1928, M.A., 1930; University of Chicago, Ph.D., 1936. *Politics:* Independent. *Religion:* Protestant. *Home:* 632 Roller Coaster Rd., Tucson, Ariz.

CAREER: State University of New York at Buffalo, member of faculty, 1928-45; University of Iowa, Iowa City, dean of College of Liberal Arts, 1945-48; University of Chicago, Chicago, Ill., professor, 1948-49; U.S. Federal Security Administration, Washington, D.C., commissioner of education, 1949-53; University of Kansas City (now University of Missouri, Kansas City), president and chancellor, 1953-56; Columbia University, Teachers College, New York, N.Y., executive officer, Institute of Higher Education, and professor of higher education, beginning 1956. Honorary professor, Peruvian National University of Engineering, 1963. Trustee and member of advisory board, Harry S. Truman Library; trustee of Antioch College, 1958-61, and Muskingum College, 1961-65, College of Insurance (N.Y.), St. Michael's College (Vt.), Buckingham University (Eng.); senior educational advisor, Lilly Endowment (Indianapolis, Ind.); visiting professor and executive director, Institute for Experimental Liberal Education. *Military service:* U.S. Naval Reserve, 1942-44; became lieutenant commander.

MEMBER: American Association of School Administrators, American Vocational Association, American Association for the Advancement of Science, National Education Association, Phi Beta Kappa, Sigma XI, Delta Chi, Phi Delta Kappa, Iota Lambda Sigma (honorary), Delta Phi Alpha, Delta Sigma Pi, Omicron Delta Kappa. *Awards, honors:* Sc.D. in Ed., Boston University, 1950; D.C.L., New York University, 1951; LL.D., Syracuse University, 1951; Litt.D., Newark State College, 1963; and thirty-seven other honorary degrees from American colleges and universities.

WRITINGS—Published by Bureau of Publications (now Teachers College Press), Teachers College, Columbia University, except as noted: (With others) *Toward General Education*, Macmillan, 1948; (editor) *Science in General Education* and three companion books, *Social Science in General Education*, *Communication in General Education*, and *The Humanities in General Education*, W. C. Brown, 1948-49.

Education in 1949, U.S. Office of Education, 1950; *Education, the Wellspring of Democracy*, University of Alabama Press, 1951; *Liberal Education in the Professions*, 1959; *The Graduate School and the Decline of Liberal Education*, 1959.

(With Edwin J. Holstein) *Liberal Education and Engineering*, 1960; *Memo to a College Faculty Member*, 1961; *Analysis of the Curricular Offerings in Several Independent Liberal Arts Colleges*, 1961; (with Willis J. Wager) *Liberal Education and Music*, 1962; (with Thad Hungate) *A New Trimester Three-Year Degree Program*, 1963; (editor with L. R. Meeth) *Cooperative Long-Range Planning in Liberal Arts Colleges*, 1964; *The Predominantly Negro Colleges and Universities in Transition*, 1965; (with Gordon Aldridge) *Liberal Education and Social Work*, 1965; (editor) *Universal Higher Education*, McGraw, 1966.

Author or co-author of other shorter monographs on education topics and survey reports. Contributor to professional journals. Editor, *Journal of General Education*.

McGREGOR, John C(harles) 1905-

PERSONAL: Born November 10, 1905, in Pontiac, Ill.; son of Lewis C. and Gertrude (Cairns) McGregor; married Alma Newhouse, 1930; children: John Robert. *Education:* University of Arizona, A.B., 1931, M.A., 1932; University of Chicago, Ph.D., 1946. *Home:* 1506 South Carle, Urbana, Ill., 61801. *Office:* University of Illinois, Urbana, Ill. 61801.

CAREER: Arizona State College (now University), Flagstaff, instructor, 1931-38, assistant professor of anthropology, 1938-42, museum director, 1938-42; Museum of Northern Arizona, Flagstaff, curator, 1931-38, archaeologist and field director, 1938-42; Illinois State Museum, Springfield, acting chief, 1942-45, administrative assistant, 1945-48; University of Illinois, Urbana, associate professor, 1942-52, professor of anthropology, 1952-73, professor emeritus, 1973—. Director of many archaeological expeditions to the Southwest and Midwest, beginning 1935; founder, Illinois Archaeological Survey, 1956, Midwestern Archaeological Conference, 1957, Illinois Highway Salvage, 1959, Illinois River Basins Salvage, 1960. *Member:* American Association for the Advancement of Science (fellow), Society for American Archaeology, American Anthropological Association, Tree Ring Society, Illinois Archaeological Survey (president, 1956-60, 1962, 1965-66), Sigma Xi.

WRITINGS: Culture of Sites Which Were Occupied Shortly before the Eruption of Sunset Crater, Museum of Northern Arizona, 1936; *Winona Village*, Museum of Northern Arizona, 1937; *How Some Important Northern Arizona Pottery Types Were Dated*, Museum of Northern Arizona, 1938; *Southwestern Archaeology*, Wiley, 1941, 2nd edition, University of Illinois Press, 1965; *Winona and Ridge Ruins*, Museum of Northern Arizona, 1941; *The Cohonina Culture of Northwestern Arizona*, University of Illinois Press, 1951; *The Pool and Irving Villages: A Study of Hopewell Occupation in the Illinois River Valley*, University of Illinois Press, 1958; *Cohonina Culture of Mt. Floyd, Arizona*, University of Kentucky Press, 1967. Contributor of articles and book reviews to professional journals and museum publications.

WORK IN PROGRESS: Studies in the prehistory of the Southwest, the prehistory of the Midwest, tree-ring dating (dendrochronology), and prehistoric ecology, physical anthropology; a semi-autobiography.

*   *   *

McGUIRE, Frances Margaret (Cheadle)

PERSONAL: Born in Glenelg, South Australia; daughter of Alfred Stanley (a wool expert) and Margaret (Loutit) Cheadle; married Dominic Paul McGuire (a diplomat and writer). *Education:* Attended University of Adelaide. *Home:* 136 Mills Ter., North Adelaide, South Australia. *Agent:* Kay Routledge Associates, Mowbray House, Norfolk St., London WC2R 2EA, England.

CAREER: Biochemist doing insulin research, Adelaide, South Australia, 1922-23; free-lance journalist, traveling at different periods in Europe, United States, Far East, New Zealand, Egypt, 1929-38; Australian delegate to League of Nations, 1939. Semi-professional garden designer. Chairman, Pioneer Women's Memorial Trust. *Member:* Dante Alighieri Society (vice-president), Lyceum Club. *Awards, honors:* Italian silver medal for cultural achievement.

WRITINGS: (With husband, Paul McGuire) *Price of Ad-*

miralty, Oxford University Press, 1944; *Twelve Tales of the Life and Adventures of Saint Imaginus*, Sheed, 1946; *The Royal Australian Navy: Its Origin, Development, and Organization*, Oxford University Press, 1948; (with Paul McGuire and Bette Arnott) *The Australian Theatre: An Abstract and Brief Chronicle in Twelve Parts*, Heinemann, 1948; (contributor) *A Time to Laugh*, Longmans, Green (New York), 1949; (adapter and author of additional chapters) John Gerard, *The Flight of the Falcon*, Longmans, Green, 1954; *September Comes In*, Heinemann, 1961; *Time in the End*, Heinemann, 1963; *Three and Ma Kelpie*, Longmans, Green, 1964; *Gardens of Italy*, Barrows, 1964; "Who Is the Ass?" (play), first produced at the Adelaide Festival of Arts, 1966. Contributor to newspapers in Adelaide and Sydney and to Australian Broadcasting Commission programs.

WORK IN PROGRESS: The Coasts of Bergamot; The Addict, a novel; *Bright Morning*.

SIDELIGHTS: Mrs. McGuire lived in Italy, 1954-59, when her husband was the Australian ambassador to that country. *Avocational interests:* Music and naval strategy.

* * *

McINTOSH, Douglas M. 1909-

PERSONAL: Born September 27, 1909, in Dundee, Scotland; son of Simon and Janie (Stuart) McIntosh; married Jean Paterson, October 14, 1939. *Education:* University of St. Andrews, B.Sc. (first class honours), and M.A., 1932, Ph.D., 1939; University of Edinburgh, B.Ed., 1935. *Religion:* Presbyterian. *Home:* Tigh-an-Droma, 22 Balwearie Gardens, Kirkcaldy, Fife, Scotland. *Office:* Moray House College of Education, Holyrood Rd., Edinburgh, Scotland.

CAREER: Fife County Council, Fife, Scotland, director of education, 1944-66; Moray House College of Education, Edinburgh, Scotland, principal, 1966—. Visiting professor of education, University of New Brunswick, 1957, 1960, 1963, 1965, 1967, 1969, 1971, 1972, 1974; president, Scottish Council for Research in Education, 1960-72; vice-chairman, Scottish Certificate of Education Examination Board, 1965—. *Member:* British Psychological Society (fellow), Royal Society of Edinburgh (fellow), Educational Institute of Scotland (fellow). *Awards, honors:* Commander of Order of the British Empire, 1961; LL.D., University of New Brunswick, 1965.

WRITINGS: Promotion from Primary to Secondary Education, University of London Press, 1948; (with Walker Mackay) *The Scaling of Teachers' Marks and Estimates*, Oliver & Boyd, 1949, revised and enlarged edition, 1962; *Educational Guidance and the Pool of Ability*, University of London Press, 1959; *Statistics for the Teacher*, Pergamon, 1963. Regular contributor to *Scottish Educational Journal* and to *Times Educational Supplement*.

Editor of series: "Principles of Objective Testing," published by Heinemann; "Test and Learn," Holmes McDougall; Lomond series of "Arithmetics," "English," "Mathematics," and "Metric Arithmetics," University of London Press; "Teaching of Handwriting," Thomas Nelson.

* * *

McKEAG, Ernest L(ionel) 1896-
(Jacque Braza, Griff, Mark Grimshaw, Pat Haynes, John King, Ramon Lacroix, Rene Laroche, Jack Maxwell, Eileen McKeay, Roland Vane)

PERSONAL: Born September 19, 1896, in Newcastle upon Tyne, England; son of John and Alice (Ingledew) McKeag; married Constance Hibbs, October 3, 1928; children: Michael, Roderick. *Education:* South Shields Marine School, Master Mariner's Certificate, 1919; also studied at Armstrong College, University of Durham. *Politics:* Labour. *Home:* Deauville Ct., London S.W. 4, England.

CAREER: British Mercantile Marine, apprentice officer, 1913-15; began career as journalist in England, 1919, working for various newspapers and for Newspaper Features Ltd., 1919-22; editor of *Northern Weekly Review* and Amalgamated Press Juvenile Publications, 1923-28; reporter and feature writer for *Daily Mirror* and *Sunday Pictorial*, London, 1943; editor, Fleetway Publications, London, 1951-61; free-lance writer, primarily of paperback books, at various periods, beginning, 1928. Parliamentary candidate (Labour) for Dover, 1929, Harwick, 1931. *Military service:* Royal Navy, 1915-19, 1939-43; became lieutenant. *Member:* London Press Club.

WRITINGS: The School Afloat, Lloyd's Publications, 1923; *Hal of the Greenwood*, Lloyd's Publications, 1923; *Fighting Through*, Lloyd's Publications, 1923; *The City of the Swamps*, Lloyd's Publications, 1923; *Stowaway Island*, Pilgrim Press, 1924; *The Boy Commander*, Pilgrim Press, 1925; *Chums of the Northern Patrol*, Aldine, 1928; *Naval Stories of the Great War*, Aldine, 1929; *Between Two Loves*, Gramol, 1929; *Princess O'Dreams*, Modern Publications, 1931; *The Man From the Gallows*, Modern Publications, 1931; *Love's Sacrifice*, Modern Publications, 1931; *Murder at Eight Bells*, Columbine Press, 1938; *A Traitor in the Fleet*, Wright & Brown, 1939.

Also author of *Butterfly of the Cabaret, Serat the Sheik, The Girl in the Purple Mask*, syndicated by Newspaper Features Ltd.; *Hurrah for the Navy, Daredevils of the Dardanelles, From Coronel to Jutland, Saunders of the Submarines, The Lost City of the Sierras, The Flying Pirate, The Fugitive Footballers, Hissed Off the Field*, all published by Aldine, 1927-31; *The Shadow in the Stables* and *Fireflint's Derby*, published by Federation Press, 1927-28; *Hugh Fancourt: Gambler, Rivals of the King, Eyes of Doom*, published by Dowgate, 1928-29; *Tangled Loves, The Sign of the Spider, Barriers Broken, Green Eyes Are Dangerous, South of Rio*, published by Fiction House, 1939-40.

Under pseudonym Jacque Braza—all published by Modern Fiction: *Moments of Madness*, 1948; *Borrowed Love*, 1948; *Virtue in Danger*, 1948; *Amorous Moments*, 1948.

Under pseudonym Griff—all with others; all published by Modern Fiction: *Rackets Incorporated*, 1948; *Only Mugs Die Young*, 1948; *Come and Get Me*, 1948; *Dope is for Dopes*, 1948; *Rub-Out Specialty*, 1948.

Under pseudonym Mark Grimshaw—with others; published by Amalgamated: *The Outlawed Detective*, 1938; *The Sign of the Grinning Dragon*, 1938.

Under pseudonym Pat Haynes—all published by Amalgamated, 1927-39: *Steel Face; The Mountie; The Outlawed Speedster; Nagashi of the Sahara; Swift of the Secret Service*.

Under pseudonym John King—published by Harborough: *Shuna, White Queen of the Jungle*, 1951; *Shuna and the Lost Tribe*, 1951.

Under pseudonym Ramon Lacroix—all with others; all published by Modern Fiction: *Room 204*, 1950; *Seduction*, 1950; *Paris Hotel*, 1950.

Under pseudonym Rene Laroche—published by Modern

Fiction: *Ladies of Leisure*, 1950; *Tragedies of Montmartre*, 1950.

Under pseudonym Jack Maxwell—all published by Amalgamated, 1928-39, except as indicated: *Invaded by Mars; The Football Toreadors; Ah Fang the Ruthless; Geraldi: Rebel of the Hills; The Scarlet Speedster; To Sweep the Seas; Black Shadow No. 1; The Phantom Raider; The Speedboat Detective; The Lone-Hand Speed Cop; The Street of Yellow Shadows; War Dogs of the White Ensign; China Patrol; From Jockey to Judge*, Federation Press, 1929; *The Outsider*, Federation Press, 1929; *Castle of No Escape*, Fleetway, 1963.

Under pseudonym Eileen McKeay—all published by Amalgamated, 1925-55, except as indicated: *The Girls Who Guarded the Crown; Shielded by the Captain; Which Loved Him Best?; Too Big for Her Boots; The Road of Romance; Forced to Seem Faithless; She Never Counted; The Secrets of Seaburn; Forced to Doubt Him; The Romany Schoolgirl; The School on the Barge; The Talisman That Brought Them Thrills; The Schoolgirl Ballerina's Quest; Hostesses of the Seaside Fun Fair; Guests of the Dancing Princess; The School of Highwayman's Heath; Gwen the Wren*, Fleetway, 1956; *Bus to Bombay*, Fleetway, 1956; *Terry's Dual Role*, Fleetway, 1956.

Under pseudonym Roland Vane—published by Federation Press, 1926-27: *Night Haunts of Paris, Passion's Plaything, Tainted, Night Haunts of Berlin, Degradation.*

Published by Gramol, 1928-29: *Cynthia Surrenders, Passionate Youth, The Girl Who Surrendered, Trapped, Silken Divans, Bitter Dregs, The Call of Passion.*

Published by Modern Fiction, 1948-50: *Bride for a Night, The Devil's Playground, Love Denied, Her Dilemma, Love for a Night.*

Published by Archer, 1949-53: *White Slaves of New Orleans, Wanton Wife, Sin Stained, Amorous Adventuress, Ladies of the Red Lamp, Vice Rackets of Soho, Willing Sinner, White Slave Racket, Woman of Montmarte, Juvenile Delinquent, Clip Joint Girl, White Slaves of the Red Lamp, The Girl from Tiger Bay.*

Also author of serials syndicated in British and other European newspapers, and more than eighty paperbacks other than those included in this bibliography. Contributor to various periodicals.

WORK IN PROGRESS: Picture stories for juvenile books to be published by Fleetway; travel features.

*   *   *

McKEAN, Dayton D(avid) 1904-

PERSONAL: Surname is pronounced McKey-an; born December 4, 1904, in Longmont, Colo.; son of Thomas Dayton and Mary Louise (Dobbins) McKean; married Margaret Elizabeth Walrod, August 27, 1931; children: Mary Margaret (Mrs. Gerard Swartz), Paul Arthur. *Education:* University of Colorado, B.A. (cum laude), 1927, M.A., 1929; Columbia University, Ph.D., 1938. *Politics:* Democrat. *Religion:* Congregational. *Home:* 1850 Folsom St., Boulder, Colo. 80302.

CAREER: Princeton University, Princeton, N.J., instructor, 1929-31, assistant professor, 1931-37; Dartmouth College, Hanover, N.H., 1937-52, began as assistant professor, professor of government, 1946-52, chairman of department of government, 1947-52; University of Colorado, Boulder, professor of political science, 1952-73, dean of Graduate

School, 1956-62. Visiting professor, Johns Hopkins University, Baltimore, Md., 1962-63. Elected to New Jersey Legislature, 1932, re-elected, 1934; deputy commissioner of finance, state of New Jersey, 1941-43; Democratic chairman, Grafton County, N.H., 1947-48, and New Hampshire state chairman, 1948-52; consultant to Alaska Constitutional Convention, 1955; member of Colorado Governor's Commission on Reapportionment, 1957-58. Political science editor, Houghton Mifflin Co., 1951-70.

MEMBER: American Political Science Association, (member of council, 1954-1955), American Association of University Professors, National Municipal League (Colorado correspondent), Western Political Science Association, Boulder Chamber of Commerce, Phi Beta Kappa, Delta Sigma Rho, Town and Gown Club (Boulder). *Awards, honors:* M.A., Dartmouth College, 1946; senior research award, Social Science Research Council, 1960; Alumni Recognition Award, University of Colorado, 1960; Norlin Medal, 1964.

WRITINGS: Pressures on the Legislature of New Jersey, Columbia University Press, 1938; *The Boss: The Hague Machine in Action*, Houghton, 1940; *Party and Pressure Politics*, Houghton, 1949; *The Integrated Bar*, Houghton, 1963. Contributor of articles and reviews to periodicals. Editorial adviser for more than thirty books on political science published by Houghton, 1951-70. Member of editorial board, *Western Political Quarterly*, 1958-61.

*   *   *

McKEE, Paul Gordon 1897-

PERSONAL: Born October 14, 1897, in Sharon, Pa.; son of George Brady (a minister) and Louella (Wickey) McKee; married Sarah Grace McCullough, December 27, 1921; children: Beverly Ann (Mrs. Rex C. Eaton, Jr.). *Education:* Monmouth College, Monmouth, Ill., 1920; State University of Iowa, M.A., 1921, Ph.D., 1924. *Religion:* Episcopal. *Home and office:* 1900 19th Ave., Greeley, Colo. 80631.

CAREER: Hanover Public Schools, Hanover, Ill., superintendent, 1921-23; Hibbing Public Schools, Hibbing, Minn., elementary school supervisor, 1924-26; Colorado State College, Greeley, professor of elementary education, 1926-62. Consultant to Scholastic Magazines, city school systems, and state departments of education; visiting instructor at universities. *Member:* International Reading Association, National Conference on Research in English, Bosworth Club, Tau Kappa Alpha, Kappa Delta Phi, Phi Delta Kappa, Denver Club, Denver Country Club. *Awards, honors:* Litt.D., Monmouth College, 1950.

WRITINGS: Teaching Spelling by Column and Context Forms, Public School Publishing Co., 1927; *Reading and Literature in the Elementary School*, Houghton, 1934; *Language in the Elementary School: Spelling, Composition, and Writing*, Houghton, 1934, revised edition, 1939; (with Beryl Parker) *Highways and Byways* Houghton, 1938; (with Harriet E. Peet and George F. Nardin) *How to Speak and Write: A Junior Handbook*, Houghton, 1940; (with Lucile Harrison and Annie McCowen) "Language for Meaning" Series, ten books, Houghton, 1941-43, revised and collated edition, eight books, 1947-48; *What Makes a Language Program Successful?*, Houghton, 1941; (editor and contributor) "English for Meaning" series (elementary textbook series), Houghton, 1942-44, 3rd edition, 1968; *The Teaching of Reading in the Elementary School*, Houghton, 1948; (with others) "Reading for Meaning" series (elementary textbook series), twelve books, Houghton, 1949-56, 4th edition, 1966; (with Harrison) *Getting Ready: A Reading Guidelines Book*, Houghton, 1955, 3rd edition, 1962; (with Harrison) *Learning Letters Sounds*, Houghton, 1957; *A Primer for Parents*, Houghton, 1957; (with William K. Durr) *Reading: A Program of Instruction for the Elementary School*, Houghton, 1966; (with Joseph Brzeinski) *The Effectiveness of Teaching Reading in Kindergarten*, Denver Public Schools, 1968. Contributor to yearbooks and professional journals.

AVOCATIONAL INTERESTS: Music, theatre, art, law, medicine, and travel.

* * *

McKENNA, Stephen 1888-1967

PERSONAL: Born February 27, 1888, in Beckenham, Kent, England; son of Leopold and Ellen (Gethen) McKenna. *Education:* Christ Church, Oxford, B.A., 1909, M.A., 1913. *Home:* Honeys, Waltham Saint Lawrence, Berkshire, England; and 11 Stone Buildings, Lincoln's Inn, London W.C.2, England. *Agent:* A. M. Heath & Co. Ltd., 35 Dover St., London W1X 4EB, England.

CAREER: Director of private limited liability company, London, England, 1910-14; Westminster School, London, temporary staff member, 1914-15; full-time writer, 1915-67. Served in British War Trade Intelligence Department, 1915-18; member of Balfour Mission to United States, 1917; served as secretary of Enemy Exports Committee of Ministry of Economic Warfare, 1939-40.

WRITINGS: The Reluctant Lover, Jenkins, 1912, John D. Winston, 1913; *Sheila Intervenes*, Jenkins, 1913, George H. Doran, 1920; *The Sixth Sense*, Chapman & Hall, 1915, George H. Doran, 1921; *Sonia: Between Two Worlds*, George H. Doran, 1917; *Ninety-Six Hours' Leave*, George H. Doran, 1917; *Midas and Son*, George H. Doran, 1919; (author of preface) Louis Marie Anne Couperus, *Old People and Things That Pass*, Butterworth & Co., 1919; *Sonia Married*, George H. Doran, 1919.

Lady Lilith, George H. Doran, 1920; *The Education of Eric Lane*, George H. Doran, 1921; *The Secret Victory*, Hutchinson, 1921, George H. Doran, 1922; *While I Remember*, George H. Doran, 1921; *The Confessions of a Well-Meaning Woman*, George H. Doran, 1922; *Tex: A Chapter in the Life of Alexander Teixeira de Mattos*, Dodd, 1922; *Soliloquy*, Hutchinson, 1922, George H. Doran, 1923; *The Commandment of Moses*, George H. Doran, 1923; *Vindication*, Hutchinson, 1923, Little, Brown, 1924; *By Intervention of Providence*, Little, Brown, 1923; *Tomorrow and Tomorrow...*, Little, Brown, 1924; *Tales of Intrigue and Revenge*, Hutchinson, 1924, Little, Brown, 1925; *An Affair of Honour*, Little, Brown, 1925; *The Oldest God*, Little, Brown, 1926; *Saviors of Society*, Little, Brown, 1926; *The Secretary of State*, Little, Brown, 1927; *Rue Reckoning*, Butterworth & Co., 1927, Little, Brown, 1928; *The Unburied Dead*, Butterworth & Co., 1928; *The Shadow of Guy Denver*, Butterworth & Co., 1928, Dodd, 1929; *Divided Allegiance*, Dodd, 1928; *Between the Lines*, Dodd, 1929; *Happy Ending*, Cassell, 1929; *The Datchley Inheritance*, Ward, Lock, 1929, Dodd, 1930.

The Redemption of Morley Darville, Dodd, 1930; *The Cast-Iron Duke*, Cassell, 1930, Dodd, 1931; *Dermotts Rampant*, Dodd, 1931; *Beyond Hell*, Chapman & Hall, 1931, Dodd, 1932; *Pandora's Box, and Other Stories*, Ward, Lock, 1932; *Superstition*, Hutchinson, 1932, Hough-

ton, 1933; *The Way of the Phoenix*, Dodd, 1932; *Magic Quest*, Hutchinson, 1933; *Namesakes*, Hutchinson, 1933; *The Undiscovered Country*, Hutchinson, 1934; *Portrait of His Excellency*, Hutchinson, 1934; *Sole Death*, Hutchinson, 1935; *While of Sound Mind*, Hutchinson, 1936; *Lady Cynthia Clandon's Husband*, Hutchinson, 1936; *Last Confession*, Hutchinson, 1937; *The Home That Jill Broke*, Hutchinson, 1937; *Breasted Amazon*, Hutchinson, 1938; *A Life for a Life*, Hutchinson, 1939.

Mean Sensual Man, Hutchinson, 1943; *Reginald McKenna, 1863-1943: A Memoir*, Eyre & Spottiswoode, 1948; *Not Necessarily for Publication*, Hutchinson, 1949; *Pearl Wedding*, Hutchinson, 1951; *Life's Eventime*, Hutchinson, 1954; *That Dumb Loving*, Hutchinson, 1957; *A Place in the Sun*, Hutchinson, 1962.

WORK IN PROGRESS: Autobiography.

AVOCATIONAL INTERESTS: Gardening, fell walking, and horse racing.

(Died September 26, 1967)

* * *

McKIBBIN, Alma E(stelle Baker) 1871-1974

PERSONAL: Born November 26, 1871, in Homer, Iowa; daughter of Alonzo (a farmer) and Stelle A. (Tucker) Baker; married Edwin Lawrence McKibbin, May 12, 1892 (died November 4, 1896); children: Lorin Wilbur (died in infancy). *Education:* Healdsburg College (now Pacific Union College), graduate of normal course, 1892. *Religion:* Seventh-day Adventist. *Home:* 525 Palo Alto Ave., Mountain View, Calif. 94041.

CAREER: Taught in first elementary church school (Seventh-day Adventist) in California, and continued regular teaching for thirty years; as a nonagenarian, still conducted Sabbath school lessons twice a week.

WRITINGS: "Bible series" (textbooks for use in Seventh-day Adventist parochial schools), Books 1-3, Pacific Press Publishing, 1909, Book 4, 1912, Book 5, 1927; *Half Hours with the Bible* (for adults), Pacific Press Publishing, 1946; *Step by Step* (autobiography), Review & Herald, 1964. Also author of a manual on teaching the Bible to children, and articles in church periodicals.

BIOGRAPHICAL/CRITICAL SOURCES: Step by Step, Review & Herald, 1964.

(Died July 16, 1974)

* * *

McKILLOP, Alan D(ugald) 1892-1974

PERSONAL: Born May 24, 1892, in Lynn, Mass.; son of Dugald McKenzie and Catherine Jane (McKinnon) McKillop; married Lorel Pruitt, August 27, 1921. *Education:* Harvard University, A.B., 1913, A.M., 1914, Ph.D., 1920. *Home:* 5519 Chaucer Dr., Houston, Tex. *Office:* Rice University, Houston, Tex.

CAREER: University of Illinois, Urbana, instructor in English, 1917-18; Rice University, Houston, Tex., instructor, 1920-24, assistant professor, 1924-30, professor of English, 1930-62, Trustee Distinguished Professor, beginning, 1962. Visiting summer professor at University of Chicago, Northwestern University, University of Texas, Johns Hopkins University, University of Minnesota, Harvard University, Indiana University, and University of Colorado, 1925-50. *Member:* Modern Language Association of America, South Central Modern Language Association (president, 1950-51), Texas Institute of Letters, Philosophical Society of Texas, Houston Philosophical Society, Phi Beta Kappa. *Awards, honors:* Guggenheim fellowship to England and France, 1928; Newberry Library fellowship.

WRITINGS: Samuel Richardson: Printer and Novelist, University of North Carolina Press, 1936; (editor with L. I. Bredvold and Lois Whitney) *Eighteenth Century Poetry and Prose,* Ronald Press, 1939, 2nd edition, 1956; *Background of Thomson's "Seasons,"* University of Minnesota Press, 1942; *English Literature from Dryden to Burns,* Appleton, 1948; *Early Masters of English Fiction,* University of Kansas Press, 1956, 2nd edition, 1968; (editor) *James Thomson: Letters and Documents,* University of Kansas Press, 1958; (editor) James Thomson, *The Castle of Indolence and Other Poems,* University of Kansas Press, 1961; (editor and author of introduction) *An Essay on the New Species of Writing Founded by Mr. Fielding, 1751,* University of California, 1962. Contributor to learned journals. Member of editorial committee, Modern Language Association of America, 1949-53.

(Died August 5, 1974)

* * *

McLANE, Paul Elliott 1907-

PERSONAL: Born July 17, 1907, in Spokane, Wash.; son of Henry and Alice (Elliott) McLane; married; children: Don Paul, Michael, Alice Marie, Patricia Ann. *Education:* Gonzaga University, A.B., 1929, M.A., 1930; University of Washington, Seattle, Ph.D., 1942. *Religion:* Catholic. *Home:* 1954 Beverly Place, South Bend, Ind. 46616. *Office:* Department of English, University of Notre Dame, Notre Dame, Ind. 46556.

CAREER: Seattle University, Seattle, Wash., 1932-46, began as instructor, became professor and head of department of English; University of Notre Dame, Notre Dame, Ind., 1946—, began as associate professor, now professor of English Literature. *Member:* Modern Language Association of America, Renaissance Society of America, American Association of University Professors. *Awards, honors:* Huntington Library fellowship, 1952-53.

WRITINGS: Spenser's Shepheardes Calender: A Study in Elizabethan Allegory, University of Notre Dame Press, 1961. Contributor of articles to *Huntington Library Quarterly, Journal of English and Germanic Philology, Studies in Philology,* and other journals.

WORK IN PROGRESS: Studies in Shakespeare and Spenser.

* * *

McLAUGHLIN, William Raffian Davidson 1908-

PERSONAL: Born July 18, 1908, in Aberdeen, Scotland; son of Hugh (a sailor) and Joan (Taylor) McLaughlin; married Ivy Wood, September 9, 1933; children: Brian Wood, Heather Wood. *Education:* Robert Gordon's Technical College, Aberdeen, Scotland, masters foreign certificate (master mariner). *Politics:* Liberal. *Religion:* Presbyterian. *Home:* 55 Bedford Rd., Aberdeen, Scotland. *Agent:* A. M. Heath & Co. Ltd., 35 Dover St., London W. 1, England.

CAREER: British Mercantile Marine, 1925—, serving as chief executive officer for Chris Salvesen & Co. (whaling firm), Leith, Scotland, 1927-50, now engaged in trading in a cargo vessel of the Mercantile Marine. During World War II was captain and commander of Atlantic convoys. Consultant in building of two post-war whale factory ships in England and executive officer on their maiden voyages to antarctic whaling grounds; sailed on numerous other expeditions to Antarctica. *Member:* Merchant Navy Officers Association.

WRITINGS: Antarctic Raider (novel), Harrap, 1960; *Call to the South: A Story of British Whaling in Antarctica,* Harrap, 1962; *So Thin Is the Line* (novel), Harrap, 1963; *Syndicate of Evil,* R. Hale, 1965. Contributor to *Wide World Magazine.*

WORK IN PROGRESS: In the Shadow of Fujyhama, a novel of smuggling; *Lambs to the Slaughter,* a humorous travel novel; *Scott of the Antarctic,* a biography.

AVOCATIONAL INTERESTS: Observing foreign customs on visits to most of the countries of the world; photography, driving, golf.†

* * *

McLAVERTY, Michael 1904-

PERSONAL: Born July 5, 1904, in Monaghan, Ireland (now Eire); married Mary Conroy, 1933; children: two sons, two daughters. *Education:* The Queen's University of Belfast, M.Sc., 1933. *Religion:* Roman Catholic. *Home:* 30 Deramore Dr., Malone Rd., Belfast, Northern Ireland.

CAREER: St. Thomas's Secondary School, Belfast, Northern Ireland, headmaster, beginning 1957, now retired. Novelist.

WRITINGS: Call My Brother Back, Longmans, Green, 1939; *Lost Fields,* Longmans, Green, 1941; *In This Thy Day,* Macmillan, 1947; *The Three Brothers,* Macmillan, 1947; *The Game Cock and Other Stories,* Devin-Adair, 1947; *Truth in the Night,* Macmillan, 1951; *School for Hope,* Macmillan, 1954; *The Choice,* Macmillan, 1958; *The Brightening Day,* Macmillan, 1965.

SIDELIGHTS: Three of McLaverty's novels have been translated into other languages.

* * *

McMENEMEY, William Henry 1905-

PERSONAL: Born May 16, 1905, in Birkenhead, England. *Education:* Merton College, Oxford, M.B., B.Ch., 1930, M.D., 1933; St. Bartholomew's Hospital, London, England, D.P.M., 1936, F.R.C.P., 1948. *Office:* National Hospitals for Nervous Diseases, Maida Vale, London W. 9, England.

CAREER: Maida Vale Hospital, London, England, pathologist and member of Institute of Neurology, 1949—.

WRITINGS: History of Worcester Royal Infirmary, Press Alliance, 1947; *James Parkinson,* Macmillan, 1955; *Pathology of Dementia and Diseases of Basal Ganglia,* Arnold, 1958, 2nd edition, 1963; *The Life and Times of Sir Charles Hastings, Founder of the British Medical Association,* Williams & Wilkins, 1959; (editor with J. P. Schade) *Selective Vulnerability of the Brain in Hypoxaemia,* Basil Blackwell, 1963. Editor, *Proceedings* of the Second International Congress of Neuropathology, Excerpta Medica Foundation, 1957. Contributor of articles on neuropathology, clinical pathology, and medical history to journals.†

* * *

McMURTRY, Robert Gerald 1906-

PERSONAL: Born February 17, 1906, in Elizabethtown, Ky.; son of Robert Terry (a public official) and Nell Lee (Bridwell) McMurtry; married Florence Louise Koberly,

December 22, 1934; children: Joyce Ellen (Mrs. Donald E. Squibb), Stephen Terry, Susan Bridwell, Linda Hoke, Jan Leslie. *Education:* Centre College, A.B., 1929. *Politics:* Republican. *Religion:* Presbyterian. *Home:* 910 West Rudisill Blvd., Fort Wayne, Ind. 46807. *Office:* Lincoln National Life Foundation, Fort Wayne, Ind.

CAREER: Lincoln National Life Foundation, Fort Wayne, Ind., librarian, 1931-34; Lincoln Memorial University, Harrogate, Tenn., administrative secretary, and director of department of Lincolniana, 1937-56, assistant professor of history, 1937-51; Lincoln National Life Foundation, director, 1956—. U.S. Information Service lecturer in southeastern Asia, 1959; public lecturer on U.S. tours two months every year. Member of board of trustees, Lincoln Memorial University. *Member:* Civil War Round Table (Chicago, New York, Fort Wayne; president, Fort Wayne), Filson Club (life), Society of Sons of the American Revolution, Allen County-Fort Wayne Historical Society, Fortnightly Club, Quest Club (Fort Wayne). *Awards, honors:* LL.D., Iowa Wesleyan College, 1946; Litt.D., Centre College, 1952; Lincoln Diploma of Honor, Lincoln Memorial University, 1957; L.H.D., Lincoln College, 1962.

WRITINGS: The Lincolns in Elizabethtown, Kentucky, Lincolniana Publishers, 1932; *Influence of Riley's Narrative Upon Abraham Lincoln,* [Indianapolis], 1934; *James Buchanan in Kentucky, 1813,* [Louisville], 1934; *The Different Editions of the "Debates of Lincoln and Douglas,"* [Springfield, Ill.], 1934; *A Series of Monographs Concerning the Lincolns and Hardin County, Kentucky,* Enterprise Press, 1938; *The Lincoln Migration from Kentucky to Indiana, 1816,* Lincolniana Publishers, c.1938; *Let's Talk of Lincoln, of His Life, of His Career, of His Deeds, of His Immortality,* Department of Lincolniana, Lincoln Memorial University, 1939; *The Kentucky Lincolns on Mill Creek,* Department of Lincolniana, Lincoln Memorial University, 1939; (compiler) *The Lincoln Log Cabin Almanac,* Department of Lincolniana, Lincoln Memorial University, 1940; *A Great Lincoln Collection,* Department of Lincolniana, Lincoln Memorial University, 1941; *Ben Hardin Helm, "Rebel" Brother-in-Law of Abraham Lincoln,* privately printed for Civil War Round Table, 1943, abridged edition published as *Confederate General Ben Hardin Helm, a Kentucky Brother-in-Law of Abraham Lincoln,* Lincoln Fellowship of Wisconsin, 1959; *Why Collect Lincolniana?,* Abraham Lincoln Book Shop, 1947; (with David J. Harkness) *Lincoln's Favorite Poets,* University of Tennessee Press, 1959; *The Harlan-Lincoln Tradition at Iowa Wesleyan College,* Lincoln Restoration Commission, 1959; *Beardless Portraits of Abraham Lincoln Painted from Life,* Public Library of Fort Wayne and Allen County, 1962; *Pugilism and Politics in Lincoln's Time,* [Fort Wayne], 1964; *Lincoln Putting on Hairs,* Lincoln National Life Insurance Co., c.1965; *Fort Wayne's Contacts with Abraham Lincoln,* Public Library of Fort Wayne and Allen County, 1966. Editor, *Lincoln Herald,* 1947-56, and *Lincoln Lore,* 1956—.

WORK IN PROGRESS: Continuing research in the field of Lincolniana.

BIOGRAPHICAL/CRITICAL SOURCES: Saturday Evening Post, February 16, 1957.

* * *

McNAIR, Malcolm P(errine) 1894-

PERSONAL: Born October 6, 1894, in West Sparta, N.Y.; son of Samuel Edwin and Harriet (Perrine) McNair; married Mary Lowe Hemenway, June 25, 1918; children: Malcolm Perrine, Jr., Robert Edwin. *Education:* Lehigh University, student, 1912-13; Harvard University, A.B., 1916, A.M., 1920. *Politics:* Republican. *Religion:* Unitarian. *Home:* Lead Mine Rd., Madison, N.H. 03849. *Office:* Harvard Graduate School of Business Administration, Soldiers Field, Boston, Mass. 02163.

CAREER: Harvard University, Graduate School of Business Administration, Cambridge, Mass., instructor, 1920-24, assistant professor, 1924-27, associate professor, 1927-31, professor of marketing, 1931-61, director of division of research, Graduate School of Business Administration, 1933-36; professor emeritus, 1961—, Lincoln Filene Professor of Retailing, 1950—. Harvard Bureau of Business Research, assistant director, 1922-29, managing director, 1927-31; conductor, Harvard study of operating results of department store margins, expenses, and profits, 1922-62. Lecturer, London School of Economics, 1931. Director emeritus, Allied Stores Corp.; director, John Wanamaker, Cambridge Trust Co., Carroll Reed Ski Shops. Honorary chairman of the board, Allerton, Berman & Dean. *Member:* National Retail Merchants Association, American Marketing Association, American Academy of Arts and Sciences, Phi Beta Kappa. *Awards, honors:* Gold Medal for distinguished service to retailing, National Retail Merchants Association, 1952; elected to Hall of Fame in Distribution, 1953; Paul D. Converse Award for advancement of science in marketing, 1953; LL.D., Northwestern University, 1962; C. E. Parlin Award in marketing, 1968.

WRITINGS: The Retail Method of Inventory, A. W. Shaw Co., 1925; (with Donald Kirk David) *Problems in Retailing,* A. W. Shaw Co., 1926; (with C. I. Gragg) *Problems in Retail Distribution,* McGraw, 1930; (with Gragg) *Problems in Retail Store Management,* McGraw, 1931; (with Gragg) *Harvard Business Reports,* Volume X, McGraw, 1931; *Expenses and Profits in the Chain Store Grocery Business in 1929,* Bureau of Business Research, Harvard University, 1931; *Expenses and Profits of Department Store Chains and Department Store Ownership Groups in 1931,* Bureau of Business Research, Harvard University, 1933; *Chain Store Expenses and Profits: An Interim Report for 1932,* Bureau of Business Research, Harvard University, 1934; (with Gragg and S. F. Teele) *Problems in Retailing* (not the same as 1926 book), McGraw, 1937; *Expenses and Profits of Limited Price Variety Chains in 1931-1936,* six volumes, Bureau of Business Research, Harvard University, 1937; (editor with Howard T. Lewis) *Business and Modern Society,* Bureau of Business Research, Harvard University, 1938; *Operating Results of Business and Specialty Stores,* nineteen volumes (1955 volume with David Carson; others sole author), Bureau of Business Research, Harvard University, 1939-41, 1943, 1945, 1947-48, 1951-60, 1962-63.

(With R. S. Meriam) *Problems in Business Economics,* McGraw, 1941; (editor with Teele and F. G. Mulhearn) *Distribution Costs: An International Digest,* Bureau of Business Research, Harvard University, 1941; (with E. P. Learned and Teele) *Problems in Merchandise Distribution,* McGraw, 1942; (with James W. Culliton) *Business Planning Now for V Day,* Commission for Post-War Readjustment, 1943; (with H. L. Hansen) *Problems in Marketing,* McGraw, 1949, 2nd edition (with M. P. Brown, D. Leighton, and W. B. England), 1957; (editor with Hansen) *Readings in Marketing,* McGraw, 1949, 2nd edition, 1956; (with A. C. Hersum) *The Retail Inventory Method and Life,*

McGraw, 1952; (editor) *The Case Method at the Harvard Business School*, McGraw, 1954; *The Economic Outlook for 1956*, [Cambridge], 1956; (with E. A. Burnham and Hersum) *Cases in Retail Management*, McGraw, 1957; (contributor) Albert B. Smith, editor, *Competitive Distribution in a Free High-Level Economy and Its Implications for the University*, University of Pittsburgh Press, 1958; 1959: *A Year of Recovery Without Boom*, National Retail Merchants Association, 1959.

The Changing Retail Scene and What Lies Ahead, [New York,] 1962; *The Department Store: Past, Present and Future*, privately printed, 1963; (with Eleanor G. May) *The American Department Store, 1920-1960*, Bureau of Business Research, Harvard University, 1963; (with William Applebaum and Walter J. Salmon) *Cases in Food Distribution*, Irwin, 1964; (with May and Erich A. Helfert) *Controllership in Department Stores*, Bureau of Business Research, Harvard University, 1965; (editor with Mira Berman) *Marketing Through Retailers*, American Management Association, 1967.

*   *   *

McNAMARA, Lena Brooke   1891-
(Evalina Mack)

PERSONAL: Born 1891, in Norfolk, Va.; daughter of David Tucker (a lawyer and judge) and Lucy (Borland) Higgins Brooke; married Aloysius Leo McNamara (deceased); children: David B., Thomas Randolph, Lucy (Mrs. J. Addison Hagan), May (Mrs. Charles K. McAlister, Jr.). *Education:* Studied at Leache-Wood Seminary, Norfolk, Va., Corcoran School of Art, and Pennsylvania Academy of Fine Arts. *Politics:* Democrat. *Religion:* Roman Catholic. *Home:* 512 Colonial Ave., Norfolk, Va. 23507.

CAREER: Professional portrait painter, exhibiting nationally; art teacher at Hermitage Foundation, Norfolk, Va., and privately in own studio; writer of mysteries, and illustrator of juvenile books and for juvenile magazines. *Member:* Mystery Writers of America, Tidewater Artists, Norfolk Society of Arts, Virginia Beach Art Association, Irene Leache Memorial.

WRITINGS—Under pseudonym Evalina Mack: *Death of a Portrait*, Arcadia House, 1952; *The Corpse in the Cove*, Arcadia House, 1955; *Death Among the Sands*, Arcadia House, 1957; *Murder in Miniature*, Arcadia House, 1959.

Under name Lena B. McNamara: *The Penance Was Death*, Bruce, 1964; *Pilgrim's End*, Ace Books, 1967.

Illustrator: *Deaux Enfants de France*, Macmillan, 1937; *Deux Enfants a la Mere*, Macmillan, 1937.

WORK IN PROGRESS: Another mystery story.

*   *   *

McNEILL, John Thomas   1885-

PERSONAL: Born July 28, 1885, in Elmsdale, Prince Edward Island, Canada; son of William Cavendish (a farmer) and Emily Lavinia (MacNeill) McNeill; married Netta Hardy, January 10, 1917 (died May 30, 1970); children: William Hardy, Leonora Isabel (Mrs. James R. Carley), Emily Elizabeth (Mrs. Ian C. Campbell). *Education:* Prince of Wales College, student, 1902-05; McGill University, B.A., 1909, M.A., 1910; Westminster Hall, Vancouver, British Columbia, B.D., 1912; graduate study at University of Edinburgh and New College, Edinburgh, 1912-13, University of Halle-Wittenberg, 1913; University of

Chicago, Ph.D., 1920. *Home:* 11 Springside Rd., Middlebury, Vt. 05753.

CAREER: Presbyterian minister; professor of church history at Knox College, Toronto, Ontario, and at Victoria University, Toronto, Ontario, 1922-27; University of Chicago, Chicago, Ill., professor of history of European Christianity, 1927-44; Union Theological Seminary, New York, N.Y., Auburn Professor of Church History, 1944-53, now professor emeritus. Visiting professor of church history at Harvard Divinity School, Garrett Biblical Institute, Perkins School of Theology, Chicago Theological Seminary, Chicago Divinity School, and other seminaries, 1953—. Member of board of directors, Foundation for Reformation Research, 1959-64. *Member:* American Society of Church History (president, 1935), American Society for Reformation Research (president, 1948). *Awards, honors:* Co-winner of Adams Prize in history, 1923, for *The Celtic Penitentials;* LL.D., Queen's University, Kingston, Ontario, 1947; D.D., University of Edinburgh, 1950; L.H.D., Duke University, 1966.

WRITINGS: The Celtic Penitentials and Their Influence on Continental Christianity, E. Champion (Paris), 1923; *The Presbyterian Church in Canada, 1875-1925*, Board of Presbyterian Church in Canada, 1925; *Unitive Protestantism: A Study in Our Religious Resources*, Abingdon, 1930, revised edition published as *Unitive Protestantism: The Ecumenical Spirit and Its Persistent Expression*, John Knox, 1964; *Makers of Christianity: From Alfred the Great to Schleiermacher*, Holt, 1935, 2nd edition published as *Makers of the Christian Tradition from Alfred the Great to Schleiermacher*, Harper, 1964; *Christian Hope for World Society*, Willett, Clarke, 1937; (editor and translator with Helena M. Gamer) *Medieval Handbooks of Penance*, Columbia University Press, 1938; (editor with Matthew Spinka and Harold R. Willoughby) *Environmental Factors in Christian History*, University of Chicago Press, 1939; *Books of Faith and Power*, Harper, 1947.

(Editor and author of introduction) John Calvin, *On God and Political Duty*, Liberal Arts Press, 1950, 2nd edition, 1956; *A History of the Cure of Souls*, Harper, 1951; *The History and Character of Calvinism*, Oxford University Press, 1954, 2nd edition, 1957; *Modern Christian Movements*, Westminster, 1954, revised edition, Harper, 1968; (editor and author of introduction) John Calvin, *On the Christian Faith*, Liberal Arts Press, 1958, 2nd edition, Bobbs-Merrill, 1964; *The Significance of the Word of God for Calvin*, privately printed, c.1959; (editor) John Calvin, *Institutes of the Christian Religion*, two volumes, Westminster, 1959. Editor with John Baillie and H. P. Van Dusen of "Library of Christian Classics," twenty-six volumes, S.C.M. Press, 1954-69. Contributor of chapters to numerous co-operative books. Contributor of more than ninety articles and about two hundred and fifty reviews to journals and encyclopedias. Acting editor, University of Chicago Press, 1943.

*   *   *

McQUEEN, Mildred Hark   1908-
(Mildred Hark)

PERSONAL: Born October 19, 1908, in LaMoure, N.D.; daughter of William F. and Mabel (Bailey) Hark; married Noel McQueen (died 1960). *Education:* College of Music, Cincinnati, Ohio, student, 1927-30; studied drama and literature under private tutors. *Politics:* Democrat. *Religion:* Church of the New Jerusalem (Swedenborgian). *Home:* 111

East Chicago Ave., Chicago, Ill. 60611. *Office:* Science Research Associates, Inc., 159 East Erie St., Chicago, Ill. 60611.

CAREER: Science Research Associates, Inc., Chicago, Ill., part-time research editor and writer of reports on guidance and educational subjects, 1952—; author of children's books and plays. *Member:* Children's Reading Round Table.

WRITINGS—With husband, Noel McQueen; under name Mildred Hark, except as indicated: *A Toast to Christmas* (one-act play), Play Club, 1946; *Special Plays for Special Days,* Plays, 1947; *The Good Luck Cat,* Medill McBride, 1950; *Modern Comedies for Young Players,* Plays, 1951; *Twenty-Five Plays for Holidays,* Plays, 1952; *Make Your Pennies Count,* Science Research Associates, 1953; *Junior Plays for All Occasions,* Plays, 1955, revised edition, 1969; *Miss Senior High* (one-act comedy), Baker's Plays, c.1957; *Teen-Age Plays for All Occasions,* Plays, 1957; *Tomorrow Is Christmas* (one-act comedy), Baker's Plays, c.1958; *A Home for Penny,* F. Watts, 1959; *Romance for Dad* (one-act comedy), Baker's Plays, c.1959; *Doll House Tea Party,* Avon, 1960; (sole author under name Mildred McQueen) *Improved Guidance for Elementary Schools* (pamphlet), Science Research Associates, 1960; (sole author under name Mildred McQueen) *Identifying and Helping Dropouts* (pamphlet), Science Research Associates, c.1961; *Mary Lou and Johnny: An Adventure in Seeing,* F. Watts, 1963.

Joint author with Noel McQueen of more than two hundred plays for children, about forty of them reprinted in twenty-one anthologies, including reading-improvement books. Contributor of plays (formerly joint authorship, now as sole author) to *Plays Magazine,* and of poems and stories to children's magazines. Author of about two hundred research reports on honors programs, creativity, dropout problem, and related subjects. Former editor with Noel McQueen, *Guidance Index.*

WORK IN PROGRESS: Children's plays; a Christmas book for young children.

SIDELIGHTS: Doll House Tea Party was translated into Finnish, Dutch, Spanish, and sold in Great Britain. *Avocational interests:* Doing water colors of children and animals, collecting children's books, cooking for friends, watching animals and birds.

BIOGRAPHICAL/CRITICAL SOURCES: Chicago Schools Journal, May-June, 1951.

*   *   *

McREYNOLDS, Edwin C(larence)   1890-1967

PERSONAL: Born April 30, 1890, in Springfield, Mo.; son of Samuel Jackson (a minister and teacher) and Cynthia Annie (Alsup) McReynolds; married Ruth Myers Fry (a teacher), June 14, 1916; children: Earl Edwin, John Samuel (deceased), Annie Ruth (Mrs. Truman Daniel Hayes), Dorothy Pearl (Mrs. Roger Edwin Edgar; deceased). *Education:* University of Oklahoma, B.A., 1922, M.A., 1924, Ph.D., 1945. *Politics:* Democrat. *Religion:* Presbyterian. *Home:* 1501 Lincoln Ave., Norman, Okla. 73069.

CAREER: High school teacher of history and government in Oklahoma City, Okla., 1922-26; Central State College (now Central State University), Edmund, Okla., associate professor of history and government, 1926-29; Coffeyville Junior College, Coffeyville, Kan., teacher of history and government, 1929-37, dean, 1934-37; Joplin Junior College,

Joplin, Mo., teacher of history and government, 1938-43; University of Oklahoma, Norman, 1945-60, began as assistant professor, professor of history, 1957-60, professor emeritus, 1960-67; Cottey College, Nevada, Mo., professor of history, 1960-66. Visiting summer professor, Southwest Missouri State College, 1963. Consultant and expert witness in Indian claims case brought by the Sac and Fox tribe of Oklahoma versus the United States, 1958. *Military service:* U.S. Army, Infantry, 1917-18.

MEMBER: American Historical Association, Organization of American Historians, Arkansas Historical Association, Missouri Historical Association, Oklahoma Historical Association, Phi Beta Kappa. *Awards, honors:* Outstanding Teaching Award, University of Oklahoma, 1954; Distinguished Service Citation, University of Oklahoma Alumni Association, 1960.

WRITINGS: Oklahoma: A History of the Sooner State, University of Oklahoma Press, 1954; *The Seminoles,* University of Oklahoma Press, 1957; (with Alice Marriott and Estelle Faulconer) *Oklahoma: The Story of Its Past and Present,* University of Oklahoma Press, 1960, revised edition, 1968; *Missouri: A History of the Crossroads State,* University of Oklahoma Press, 1962; (with John W. Morris) *Historical Atlas of Oklahoma,* University of Oklahoma Press, 1965. Contributor to *Collier's Year Book,* 1954-64.

(Died February 9, 1967)

*   *   *

McSORLEY, Joseph   1874-1963

PERSONAL: Born December 9, 1874, in Brooklyn, N.Y.; son of William and Elizabeth (McShane) McSorley. *Education:* St. John's College (now St. John's University), Brooklyn, N.Y., B.A., 1891, M.A., 1893; Catholic University of America, S.T.L., 1897.

CAREER: Entered Missionary Society of St. Paul the Apostle (Paulist Fathers), 1891; ordained priest, 1897. Parish assistant in New York, N.Y., 1897-1899; St. Thomas College, Washington, D.C., assistant master of novices, 1899-1901, master of novices, 1901-07; St. Paul the Apostle parish, New York, N.Y., in charge of Italian members, 1907-17, pastor, 1919-24; Missionary Society of St. Paul the Apostle, superior general, 1924-29; parish assistant in Toronto, Ontario, 1929-31; Missionary Society of St. Paul the Apostle, first consultor, 1946-52. *Military service:* U.S. Army, chaplain, 1918-19; became captain.

WRITINGS: The Sacrament of Duty, Paulist Press, 1909, enlarged edition, Kenedy, 1934; (translator) Hansjakob, *Grace,* B. Herder, 1913; (translator) Keppler, *More Joy,* B. Herder, 1914; (with Wedewer) *A Short History of the Catholic Church,* B. Herder, 1916; *Italian Confessions and How to Hear Them,* Paulist Press, 1916; *Be of Good Heart,* Kenedy, 1924; *A Primer of Prayer,* Longmans, Green, 1934; *Think and Pray,* Longmans, Green, 1936; (with Sheerin) *Spanish Confessions,* B. Herder, 1942; *Outline History of the Church by Centuries (From St. Peter to Pius XII),* B. Herder, 1943, 11th edition, 1961; *Meditations for Everyman,* two volumes, B. Herder, 1947, 1948; *Father Hecker and His Friends: Studies and Reminiscences,* B. Herder, 1952; *Common Sense,* Bruce, 1957. Author of pamphlets. Contributor to *Catholic Encyclopedia, Encyclopaedia Britannica, Catholic World,* and to religious and secular periodicals.

(Died July 4, 1963)

MEAD, Frank Spencer 1898-

PERSONAL: Born January 15, 1898, in Chatham, N.J.; son of Frank and Lillie (Spencer) Mead; married Judy Duryee, October 24, 1927; children: Donald Duryee, Judy Spencer. *Education:* University of Denver, A.B., 1922; studied at Episcopal Theological Seminary of Virginia, 1922-23; Union Theological Seminary, New York, N.Y., B.D., 1927. *Politics:* Independent. *Home:* 6 McKinley St., Nutley, N.J. 07110. *Office:* Fleming H. Revell Co., Old Tappan, N.J.

CAREER: Young Men's Christian Association, New York, N.Y., secretary, 1923-24; ordained Methodist minister, 1927, holding pastorates in Newark, N.J., 1927-31, and Kearny, N.J., 1931-34; *Homiletic Review*, New York, N.Y., editor, 1934; *Baptist Leader*, Philadelphia, editor, 1935-37; free-lance writer, 1938-41; *Christian Herald*, New York, N.Y., executive editor, 1942-48; Fleming H. Revell Co., New York, N.Y., and Westwood, N.J., editor, 1949—, and a director of the firm. *Military service:* U.S. Army, 1917-18. *Member:* Phi Beta Kappa, Beta Theta Pi. *Awards, honors:* Litt.D., Dickinson College, 1950.

WRITINGS: The March of Eleven Men, Bobbs, Merrill, 1932; *Who's Who in The Bible*, Harper, 1934; *See These Banners Go*, Bobbs, Merrill, 1935; *Ten Decisive Battles of Christianity*, Bobbs, Merrill, 1937; *Right Here at Home*, Friendship, 1939; *Tales from Latin America*, Friendship, 1942; *On Our Own Doorstep*, Friendship, 1948.

Handbook of Denominations in the U.S., Abingdon, 1951, 4th edition, 1966; *The Baptists*, Broadman, 1954; (with Iona Henry) *Triumph Over Tragedy*, Revell, 1957; *Joshua the Warrior*, Doubleday, 1959; (with Roy Rogers) *My Favorite Christmas Story*, Revell, 1960; (editor) *Communion Messages*, Revell, 1961; *Reaching Beyond Your Pulpit*, Revell, 1962; *Rebels With a Cause*, Abingdon, 1964; *The Encyclopaedia of Religious Quotations*, Revell, 1965. Also author of *Tarbell's Teacher's Guide* (annual), beginning 1949. Contributor to American magazines.

WORK IN PROGRESS: Research for a book in the field of church history.

AVOCATIONAL INTERESTS: Golf.

*   *   *

MEAD, Harold C(harles) H(ugh) 1910-

PERSONAL: Born September 25, 1910, in Ootacamund, South India; son of Alfred Hugh (a tea planter) and Winifred Ada (Whitby) Mead; married Kathleen Richards, April 26, 1936; children: Arthur Hugh, Henry Charles Harold. *Education:* Royal Military College, Sandhurst, 1928-30; Staff College, Camberley, P.S.C., 1941; St. Catharine's College, Cambridge, M.A., 1950. *Religion:* Anglican. *Agent:* Curtis Brown Ltd., 575 Madison Ave., New York, N.Y. 10022.

CAREER: British Army, Dorset Regiment, regular officer, 1930-47, becoming major in India, 1931-39, in England, 1939-41, posted to Singapore, 1941, prisoner of war in Siam, 1942-46; invalided out after return from Far East; worked for one year as tennis club secretary; Southampton University, Southampton, England, warden of men's hall of residence, 1951—. *Member:* Society of Authors, Crusing Association.

WRITINGS: The Bright Phoenix, M. Joseph, 1955, Ballantine, 1956; *Mary's Country*, M. Joseph, 1957. Short stories have appeared in *Saturday Evening Post* (one anthologized in *Post Stories for 1957*), and in *Argosy, Blackwood's Magazine, John Bull*, and other periodicals.

SIDELIGHTS: As a Japanese prisoner in Siam, Mead worked at forced labor on the so-called "railway of death," which, he says, is perhaps why both of his books are best understood as essays on the subject of violence. He adds that they have drawn "good, indifferent, and plain abusive" reviews.

*   *   *

MEAD, Sidney E(arl) 1904-

PERSONAL: Born August 2, 1904, in Champlin, Minn.; son of George and Alice (Pearson) Mead; married Mildred LaDue (a photographer), April 26, 1929. *Education:* University of Redlands, B.A., 1934; studied at Yale University Divinity School, 1934-36; University of Chicago Divinity School, M.A., 1938, Ph.D., 1941. *Office:* Department of Theology, University of Iowa, Iowa City, Iowa 52240.

CAREER: University of Chicago, Chicago, Ill., member of faculty of Divinity School, 1941-60, became professor of American church history, 1947, member of faculty in department of history, 1952-60; Meadville Theological School (Unitarian), Chicago, Ill., president, 1956-60; Southern California School of Theology at Claremont and Claremont Graduate School, professor of American church history, 1960-64; University of Iowa, Iowa City, professor in history department and in school of religion, 1964. Visiting professor at McCormick Theological Seminary, Garrett Biblical Institute, Chicago Lutheran Seminary, and School of Religion, State University of Iowa. Chairman of board, Pomona Valley Unitarian Society. *Member:* American Historical Association, American Society of Church History (president, 1952), Unitarian Historical Association, Organization of American Historians.

WRITINGS: Nathaniel William Taylor, 1786-1858: A Connecticut Liberal, University of Chicago Press, 1942; (contributor) H. R. Niebuhr and D. D. Williams, editors, *The Ministry in Historical Perspectives*, Harper, 1956; (contributor) John J. Murray, editor, *The Heritage of the Middle West*, University of Oklahoma Press, 1958; *The Lively Experiment: the Shaping of Christianity in America*, Harper, 1963; (contributor) Philip U. Hefner, editor, *The Future of the American Church*, Fortress, 1969. Contributor of more than fifty articles, sermons, and reviews to *Journal of Religion, Church History, Christian Century*, and similar periodicals.

WORK IN PROGRESS: A revision of William Warren Sweet's *Story of Religion in America*, for Harper; a source book for American church history; *The Genius of American Protestantism*, for Harper.

SIDELIGHTS: Mead says: "I love to teach and think the teachers are being smothered in a thickening bureaucratic fog."†

*   *   *

MEASURES, (William) Howard 1894-

PERSONAL: Born October 16, 1894, in Yeovil, Somersetshire, England; son of William Sydney and Emily Elizabeth (Veazey) Measures; married Irene d'Aoust, November 23, 1922; children: Michael. *Education:* Educated in England at Norwich School and Jamaica College. *Religion:* Anglican. *Home:* Charlcombe, 22 Main St., Aylmer East, Quebec, Canada.

CAREER: With Passenger Department of Canadian Pacific Railway, 1913-15; with Canadian Pension Commission, 1919-20; private secretary to two Prime Ministers of

Canada, Ottawa, Ontario, 1921-35; Department of External Affairs, protocol officer and chief of protocol, 1936-51; Department of the Secretary of State, director of Protocol Branch and member of Government Hospitality Committee, 1951-65. Accompanied King George VI, Queen Elizabeth II, Presidents Roosevelt and Truman, and other heads of state on tours of Canada. Adviser to Prime Minister on Canada's national flag, 1964-65; chairman, Christ Church Parish Council, 1973. *Military service:* Served 1915-18, Canadian Overseas Telecommunications Corporation. *Member:* Aylmer and District Arts Association, Royal Ottawa Golf Club. *Awards, honors:* King George V Silver Jubilee Medal, 1935; King George VI Coronation Medal, 1936; Queen Elizabeth II Coronation Medal, 1953.

WRITINGS: Styles of Address: A Manual of Usage in Writing and in Speech, Crowell, 1947, 3rd revised edition, St. Martin's Press, 1970. Writer of monographs on protocol and on the arms of Canada.

BIOGRAPHICAL/CRITICAL SOURCES: The Times, January 10, 1947; *Time,* January 3, 1949, June 12, 1950; *Standard Magazine,* July 16, 1949; *Toronto Globe,* October 1, 1949; *Mayfair,* April, 1952, September, 1958; *Ottawa Citizen,* August 22, 1964; *Holland Herald,* 1973.

* * *

MEE, John F(ranklin) 1908-

PERSONAL: Born July 10, 1908, in Ada, Ohio; son of Raymond Kirk (a farmer) and Helen F. (Hickernell) Mee; married Muriel Eileen Collins, April 5, 1941; children: Virginia Ann (Mrs. Roger G. Burns), Raymond Kirk, Marcia Joan. *Education:* Miami University, Oxford, Ohio, A.B., 1930; University of Maine, A.M., 1933; Ohio State University, Ph.D., 1959. *Politics:* Democrat. *Religion:* Presbyterian. *Home:* 507 South Jordan Ave., Bloomington, Ind. 47401. *Office:* Graduate School of Business, Indiana University, Bloomington, Ind. 47401.

CAREER: Beal College, Bangor, Me., dean, 1932-34; Ohio State University, Columbus, instructor in business administration, 1935-39; Indiana University, Bloomington, 1941—, began as assistant professor and director of placement, School of Business, became professor of management and chairman of department of management, School of Business, 1946-60, Mead Johnson Professor of Management, Graduate School of Business, 1960—, dean of Division of General and Technical Studies, 1965—. Owner and operator of livestock farm in Butler County, Ohio. Director, Richard D. Irwin, Inc. (publishers). Consultant to Executive Office of the President of the United States, 1950—, Ford Foundation, 1956—, other federal and state agencies, State of Indiana, commissioner of revenue, 1949-50, director of Tax Study Commission, 1952, member of Highway Study Commission, 1961. *Military service:* U.S. Army Air Forces, 1941-46; became colonel; awarded Legion of Merit, Bronze Star Medal.

MEMBER: Academy of Management (president, 1950), Council of Professional Education for Business (president, 1954), Society for Advancement of Management (vice-president, 1958-64), American Psychological Association. *Awards, honors:* Academy of Management—McKinsey Foundation Award, 1963, for *Management Thought in a Dynamic Economy;* LL.D., Miami University, 1964.

WRITINGS: (Editor) *Personnel Handbook,* Ronald, 1951; (with Edgar G. Williams) *Cases and Problems in Personnel and Industrial Relations,* Ronald, 1955; *The Creative Thinking Process* (pamphlet), Bureau of Business Research, Indiana University, 1956; (editor with L. L. Waters) *Management Philosophy and Process: The European Point of View,* Bureau of Business Research, Indiana University, 1956; (with Williams) *Managing a Successful Personnel Relations Program,* Bureau of Business Research, Indiana University, 1958; *Management Thought in a Dynamic Economy,* New York University Press, 1963; (with others) *14 Practical Aids to More Profitable Management,* Bureau of Business Research, Indiana University, 1965. Editor of "Management" series, Irwin; co-editor of "Behavioral Science" series, Irwin-Dorsey. Contributor to *Business Horizons, Encyclopedia of Management,* and other business and management publications.

WORK IN PROGRESS: History and development of management thought in the twentieth century.

* * *

MELZER, John Henry 1908-1967

PERSONAL: Born July 10, 1908, in Effingham, Ill.; son of Emil Frederick (owner of a flour mill) and R. Laura (Linn) Melzer; married Dorothy Garrett (an assistant professor of English), July 4, 1936; children: John T. S., Linn Garrett (son). *Education:* Concordia College (now Concordia Senior College), Ft. Wayne, Ind., diploma, 1928; Concordia Seminary, St. Louis, Mo., C.R.M., 1931; Washington University, St. Louis, Mo., teacher's certificate; Vanderbilt University, A.M., 1934, Ph.D., 1937; Yale University, graduate study, 1935. *Religion:* Methodist. *Office:* Department of Philosophy, Auburn University, Auburn, Ala.

CAREER: Ashland College, Ashland, Ohio, 1937-39, began as assistant professor, became associate professor of philosophy; The Citadel, The Military College of South Carolina, Charleston, established department of philosophy, 1939-40; Alfred University, Jamestown Junior College Extension, Jamestown, N.Y., dean and director, 1940-41; Lambuth College, Jackson, Tenn., professor of philosophy and basketball coach, 1945-46; University of Missouri, Columbia, instructor in philosophy, 1946-47; University of Kentucky, Lexington, 1947-58, began as assistant professor, became associate professor of philosophy; Auburn University, Auburn, Ala., professor of philosophy and head of department, beginning 1958. Inventor of Melzer Validascope, a logical calculator. *Member:* American Philosophical Association, Southern Society for Philosophy and Psychology, Alabama Philosophical Society (past president), Pi Kappa Alpha.

WRITINGS: An Examination of Critical Monism, University Post Publishing 1937; *A Guide to Philosophical Terminology,* University Post Publishing, 1938; *Functional Logic* (text), W. C. Brown, 1951; (contributor) *The Teaching of Philosophy,* Philosophical Conference, 1954; *Philosophy in the Classroom,* University of Nebraska Press, 1955; *Modern Functional Logic* (text), W. C. Brown, 1961; *Functionalism: An Outline of a Philosophy for Today,* Philosophical Library, 1965. Contributor of articles on education, aesthetics and logic to professional journals.

WORK IN PROGRESS: A history of philosophy in America.

AVOCATIONAL INTERESTS: Inventing gadgets; bird dogs, hunting, guns; growing fruit and nut trees; archaeology, geology, and ornithology.

(Died June, 1967)

MENDELL, Clarence W(hittlesey) 1883-1970

PERSONAL: Born June 3, 1883, in Norwood, Mass.; son of Ellis (a clergyman) and Clara (Whittlesey) Mendell; married Elizabeth Laurence, July 10, 1930; children: Elizabeth (Mrs. Charles A. Grobe, Jr.). *Education:* Yale University, B.A., 1904, M.A., 1905, Ph.D., 1910. *Politics:* Republican. *Religion:* Episcopalian. *Home:* Beacon Rd., Bethany, Conn. 06525.

CAREER: Yale University, New Haven, Conn., instructor in Latin, 1907-11, assistant professor of Greek and Latin, 1911-19, Dunham Professor of Latin Language and Literature, 1919-46, Sterling Professor, 1946-52, professor emeritus, 1952-70, dean of Yale College, 1926-37, master of Branford College, 1932-42. American Academy in Rome, resident professor, 1932-33, visiting professor, 1950, and member of board. *Military service:* U.S. Navy, 1942-47; became commander; received Legion of Merit. *Member:* American Philological Association, Phi Beta Kappa, Century Association (New York), Graduate Club and Lawn Club (both New Haven). *Awards, honors:* LL.D., Yale University, 1953; Yale Medal; Medal of American Academy in Rome.

WRITINGS—All published by Yale University Press except as indicated: *Latin Sentence Correction*, 1917; *Prometheus*, 1926; *Jeanne d'Arc at Rouen*, 1931; *Our Seneca*, 1941; *Tacitus, the Man and His Work*, 1957; *Latin Poetry: The New Poets and the Augustans*, 1965; *Latin Poetry: The Age of Rhetoric and Satire*, Archon Books, 1967; *Latin Poetry: Before and After*, Archon Books, 1970.

WORK IN PROGRESS: Various translations; the tradition of Tacitus' work.

(Died, 1970)

*   *   *

MERRICK, William 1916-1969

PERSONAL: Born November 12, 1916, in Washington, Pa.; son of James Russel and Ruth Xavier (O'Byrne) Merrick; married Sally Stevens; children: Theresa. *Education:* Ohio State University, student, 1936-40. *Home:* 11 Rue Philibert Delorme, Paris 17, France. *Agent:* Theron Raines, 244 Madison Ave., New York, N.Y. 10016.

CAREER: Writer. *Military service:* U.S. Army, 1942-45; served in southwest Pacific; became sergeant; received Purple Heart.

WRITINGS: Freedom Is a Trumpet, John Day, 1941; *One Act Plays*, John Day, 1942; (editor) *Columbia Workshop Anthology*, Columbia University Press, 1942; *The Packard Case*, Random House, 1961; *No One of That Name*, Holt, 1964.

WORK IN PROGRESS: A novel; a book of essays on cultural anthropology in modern America.

AVOCATIONAL INTERESTS: Travel.

BIOGRAPHICAL/CRITICAL SOURCES: Washington Post, February 1, 1969.

(Died January, 1969)

*   *   *

MERRILL, Edward H. 1903-

PERSONAL: Born April 7, 1903, in Yarmouth, Me.; son of Harry L. (a carpenter) and Maude (Hackett) Merrill; married Mary Hyland, June 25, 1929; children: Patricia (Mrs. Richard W. Pratt), Martha (Mrs. John B. Philbrook).

Education: Colby College, A.B., 1925; Columbia University, M.A., 1933. *Office:* School Department, Town Hall, Brookline, Mass. 02146.

CAREER: High school history teacher in Manchester, N.H., 1926-28, Framingham, Mass., 1928-30; Brookline High School, Brookline, Mass., history teacher, 1930-57, director of social studies, beginning, 1957. Summer instructor at University of North Carolina, 1944, Boston College, 1959; co-director of Summer Institute in History, Vassar College, 1960. Consultant, Educational Testing Service; reader, College Entrance Examination Board. *Member:* American Historical Association, National Council for the Social Studies, New England History Teachers Association, Massachusetts Teachers Association, Phi Beta Kappa, Boston College Alumni Association (president). *Awards, honors:* Horace Kidger Award of New England History Teachers Association.

WRITINGS: (With Wallace E. Caldwell) *World History*, Sanborn, 1949; (with Harold U. Faulkner and Tyler Kepner) *History of the American Way*, Harper, 1950, workbook, Harper, 1951; *Responses to Economic Collapse*, Heath, 1964; (with John L. Teall) *Atlas of World History*, Ginn, 1965.

*   *   *

MERRILL, Francis E(llsworth) 1904-1969

PERSONAL: Born May 21, 1904, in Fort Dodge, Iowa; son of Roy Willard (a business executive) and Anna (Farrell) Merrill; married Emily Archibald, March 30, 1934. *Education:* Dartmouth College, A.B., 1926; University of Chicago, A.M., 1934, Ph.D., 1937. *Politics:* Democrat. *Religion:* Episcopalian. *Home:* Pine Tree Rd., Norwich, Vt.

CAREER: University of Kansas, Lawrence, instructor in sociology, 1931-32; Roosevelt University, Chicago, Ill., assistant professor of sociology, 1932-35; Dartmouth College, Hanover, N.H., 1935-69, began as instructor, professor of sociology, 1946-69, U.S. government, Washington, D.C., priority specialist, War Production Board, 1941-42, intelligence officer, Board of Economic Warfare, 1942-43. Fulbright lecturer at University of Rennes and University of Aix-en-Provence, France, 1959-60, at University of Nice, 1966-67. *Member:* American Sociological Association, Society for the Study of Social Problems, Phi Beta Kappa, Alpha Delta Phi.

WRITINGS: (With Mabel A. Elliott) *Social Disorganization*, Harper, 1934, 4th edition, 1961; (with Andrew G. Truxal) *The Family in American Culture*, Prentice-Hall, 1947, 2nd edition, 1953; *Social Problems on the Home Front*, Harper, 1948; *Courtship and Marriage*, Holt, 1949, 2nd edition, 1959; (with others) *Social Problems*, Knopf, 1950; *Society and Culture*, Prentice-Hall, 1952, 4th edition, 1969. Contributor to professional journals. Former associate editor, *American Sociological Review*.

WORK IN PROGRESS: A fifth edition of *Social Disorganization*.

SIDELIGHTS: Merrill was fluent in French. *Avocational interests:* France and French culture.

(Died November, 1969)

*   *   *

MESSENGER, Elizabeth Margery (Esson) 1908-

PERSONAL: Born July 25, 1908, in Thames, New Zealand; daughter of Melvin Brown and Amy Isabel (Dodd) Esson; married Robin Montrose Messenger (operator of a citrus orchard), June 21, 1941; children: Melvin Montrose, Nicholas Alan John. *Education:* Victoria University, Wellington, New Zealand, student for two years; also studied copywriting in London, England. *Home:* Dieudonne Orchard, Box 89, Kerikeri, Bay of Islands, New Zealand. *Agent:* E. P. S. Lewin & Partners, 7 Chelsea Embankment, London S.W.3, England.

CAREER: Messrs. Saward Baker & Co. Ltd., London, England, advertising copywriter, 1933-39; London Auxiliary Ambulance Service, London, driver, 1939-45; *East Africa News Review,* Nairobi, woman's page editor, 1946-48; regular daily columnist on food subjects for *Wellington Evening Post, Christchurch Press, Dunedin Evening Star,* and *Gisborne Herald,* all New Zealand, 1948—. *Member:* Women Writers Association, Playwrights Association.

WRITINGS: Murder Stalks the Bay, R. Hale, 1958; *Material Witness,* R. Hale, 1959; *Dive Deep for Death,* R. Hale, 1959; *Light on Murder,* R. Hale, 1960; *The Wrong Day to Die,* R. Hale, 1961; *Publicity for Murder,* R. Hale, 1961; *Golden Dawns the Sun* (historical novel), R. Hale, 1962; *A Heap of Trouble,* R. Hale, 1963; *Growing Evil,* R. Hale, 1964; *You Won't Need a Coat,* R. Hale, 1964; *Uncertain Quest,* R. Hale, 1965; *The Tale of the Dozing Cat,* R. Hale, 1965.

Nonfiction: *Dine with Elizabeth: A Round-the-Year Book of Recipes,* three volumes, Blundell Brothers, 1956-61; *The Wine and Food Book: New Zealand Recipes and Menus,* Price Milburn, 1961; *American Dishes for New Zealand,* Price Milburn, 1962; *The Complete Guide to Etiquette,* Evans Brothers, 1966. Contributor to *Woman's Realm, New Zealand Mirror, My Weekly, Auckland Herald,* and other publications.

WORK IN PROGRESS: A suspense novel, *Dark Beyond the Mountain;* a second historical novel.

SIDELIGHTS: Mrs. Messenger lived in London for nineteen years, and in Madrid, Cairo, and East Africa at other periods, returning home to New Zealand with her husband and sons in 1948. Now, along with writing, she helps pick and pack oranges, mandarins, grapefruit, and passionfruit, keeps a large garden, swims, fishes, and entertains. *Avocational interests:* Reading poetry, anything and everything about the theatre, travel, and fishing.

BIOGRAPHICAL/CRITICAL SOURCES: Auckland Herald, June 2, 1962.

* * *

METZ, Lois Lunt 1906-
(Lois Lunt)

PERSONAL: Born August 25, 1906, in Nephi, Utah; daughter of George William (a druggist) and Rosie Ettie (Morgan) Lunt; married Leroy Metz, February 22, 1960. *Education:* Utah State University, B.S., 1932; graduate work at University of Utah, Brigham Young University, Utah State University, San Jose State College (now California State University, San Jose). *Home:* 7501 Circle Hill Dr., Oakland, Calif. 94605. *Office:* Castlemont High School, 8601 MacArthur Blvd., Oakland, Calif. 94605.

CAREER: Public school teacher in Nephi, Utah, 1929-30, Weston, Idaho, 1932-34, Metropolis, Nev., 1934-39, Oakland, Calif., 1945—, currently at Castlemont High School. Composer of popular and country songs. *Member:* California Teachers Association, Phi Kappa Phi.

*WRITINGS—*All under name Lois Lunt: *Dances for Your Program and Operetta,* Denison, 1948; *Program Dances for Tiny Tots: A Collection of Twelve Dance Routines,* Denison, 1957; *Hop, Skip and Sing: A Collection of Twenty-five Songs and Rhythms Based on the Interests and Activities of Children,* Denison, 1959; *Mix 'Em and Match 'Em: A Collection of Forty New Mixers and Simple Recreational Dances for Teachers and Recreational Directors,* Denison, 1961; *Action Songs and Rhythms for Children,* Denison, 1963. Contributor of articles, songs, and poems to children's magazines.

WORK IN PROGRESS: A junior high operetta, "The Time Twisters"; instructional book on marching formations; a historical novel of sixteenth-century France.

AVOCATIONAL INTERESTS: Needlework, handicrafts, and music.

* * *

MEYER, Alfred (Herman) 1893-

PERSONAL: Born February 27, 1893, in Venedy, Ill.; son of William (a miller) and Mary (Weihe) Meyer; married Lillian E. Folkers, January 30, 1926; children: Alfred W. *Education:* University of Illinois, A.B., 1921, A.M., 1923; summer study at University of Chicago and Northwestern University; University of Michigan, Ph.D., 1934. *Politics:* Democrat ("normally votes on issues and candidates"). *Religion:* Evangelical Lutheran. *Home:* 1753 Crestview Dr., Valparaiso, Ind.

CAREER: Valparaiso University, Valparaiso, Ind., 1926—, began as instructor, became professor of geography and geology, beginning 1942, professor emeritus, 1973—, head of department, beginning 1933. Summer lecturer in geography at twelve other colleges and universities; president, Valparaiso City Plan Commission, 1948-50. *Member:* American Association for the Advancement of Science (fellow), Association of American Geographers, National Council for Geographic Education (president, 1947), Indiana Academy of Science (fellow; president, 1955), Indiana Academy of the Social Sciences (president, 1957). *Awards, honors:* Distinguished Service Award, Chicago Geographical Society, 1958-59; Distinguished Service Professor Award, Valparaiso University, 1967; Distinguished Service Award, National Council for Geographic Education, 1969.

WRITINGS: (Contributor) G. T. Renner, editor, *Global Geography* (textbook), Crowell, 1944, revised edition, 1957; (with John H. Strietelmeier) *Geography in World Society* (textbook), Lippincott, 1963. Author or co-author of more than forty articles and papers in yearbooks, published proceedings, and geography and education journals.

* * *

MEYER, Carl S(tamm) 1907-1972

PERSONAL: Born March 12, 1907, in Wetaskiwin, Alberta, Canada; came to United States in 1909, became U.S. citizen in 1909; son of George J. and Lillian M. (Yehling) Meyer; married Lucille Pfeifer, July 20, 1935; children: Carol Helen (Mrs. Wesley Toepper), Robert George, Elise Lucille (Mrs. B. K. Baylis). *Education:* Concordia Seminary, St. Louis, Mo., B.D., 1930; University of Chicago, M.A., 1931, Ph.D., 1954. *Home:* 3 Seminary Ter., Clayton, Mo. 63105. *Office:* Concordia Seminary, St. Louis, Mo. 63105.

CAREER: Ordained Lutheran minister, 1930; pastor in

Rochester, Minn., 1931-34; hospital chaplain, Rochester, Minn., 1932-34; Bethany Lutheran College, Mankato, Minn., professor of social science, 1934-43; principal of Luther Institute, Chicago, Ill., 1943-53, of Luther High School North, Chicago, 1953-54; acting superintendent, Lutheran High School Association of Greater Chicago, 1950-52; Concordia Seminary, St. Louis, Mo., professor of historical theology, 1954-69, graduate professor of historical theology, 1969-72, acting academic dean, 1958-59, director of Graduate School, 1960-69. Acting executive director, Foundation for Reformation Research, 1962-64.

MEMBER: American Historical Association, American Society of Church History, American Society for Reformation Research, Renaissance Society of America, Royal Historical Society (London; fellow), Lutheran Academy for Scholarship, Phi Delta Kappa, Concordia Historical Institute. Awards, honors: D.D., Concordia Theological Seminary, Springfield, Ill., 1964; American Association for Theological Schools study grant, 1965-66; Colonel Koch Luther Medal of Concordia Historical Institute, 1973.

WRITINGS: Elizabeth I and the Religious Settlement of 1559, Concordia, 1960; (editor, author of introduction, and compiler of bibliography) Thomas Cranmer, Selected Writings, S.P.C.K., 1961; Luther's and Zwingli's Propositions for Debate, E. J. Brill, 1963; Pioneers Find Friends, Luther College Press, 1963; (editor) Moving Frontiers: Readings in the History of the Lutheran Church—Missouri Synod, Concordia, 1964; (editor and contributor) Luther for an Ecumenical Age, Concordia, 1967; The Church: From Pentecost to the Present, Moody, 1969; (with Neelak S. Tjernagel) A History of Western Christianity, Concordia, 1971; (editor) Walther Speaks to the Church: Selected Letters of C. F. Walther, Concordia, 1973; (editor with Herbert T. Mayer) The Caring God: Perspectives on Providence, Concordia, 1973. Contributor to Lutheran Encyclopedia, 2nd edition, Wycliffe Encyclopedia, and theological journals. Editor, Concordia Historical Institute Quarterly, 1956.

WORK IN PROGRESS: An investigation of Philip Melanchton's influence in England (in the sixteenth century) on education, theology, and political theory.

(Died December 17, 1972)

*　　*　　*

MEYER, Frank S(traus)　1909-1972

PERSONAL: Born May 9, 1909, in Newark, N.J.; son of Jack F. and Helene (Straus) Meyer; married Elsie Bown, October 11, 1940; children: John Cornford, Eugene Bown. Education: Princeton University, student, 1926-27; Balliol College, Oxford, B.A., 1932, M.A.; advanced study at London School of Economics, 1932-34, University of Chicago, 1934-38. Politics: Conservative Party of New York. Office: National Review, 150 East 35th St., New York, N.Y. 10016.

CAREER: National Review, New York, N.Y., senior editor, 1955-72. Vice-chairman, Conservative Party of New York. Military service: U.S. Army, 1942-43. Member: American Political Science Association, National Press Club, Boston Athenaeum, Princeton Club (New York).

WRITINGS: (With M. Stanton Evans) Freedom, Tradition, Conservatism [and] A Conservative Case for Freedom (the former by Meyer, the latter by Evans), Intercollegiate Society of Individualists, c.1961; The Moulding of Communists: The Training of the Communist Cadre,

Harcourt, 1961; In Defense of Freedom: A Conservative Credo, Regnery, 1962; (editor and contributor) What Is Conservatism?, Holt, 1964; (editor) The African Nettle: Dilemmas of an Emerging Continent, John Day, 1965; (contributor) Robert A. Goldwin, editor, Left, Right, and Center: Essays on Liberalism and Conservatism in the U.S., Rand McNally, 1965; (compiler and author of introduction with wife, Elsie Meyer) Some Comments on Southern Africa, American-African Affairs Association, c.1967; The Conservative Mainstream, Arlington House, 1969. Editorial adviser, Modern Age; co-editor, Spotlight on Africa.

WORK IN PROGRESS: The Shape of History.

SIDELIGHTS: In a review of The Conservative Mainstream, Guy Davenport writes: "Mr. Meyer . . . is a professional watchdog. He can strip an idea to its bare bones before you can say Jack Robinson, can glance down historical perspectives as easily as the rest of us down the street, and can point to the illiberality in liberal twaddle with the sureness of a cat staring at the place in the wainscoting behind which sits the mouse. Essay after essay he dissects men, ideas and passions, to show what lies hidden inside them. He is at his best tracing ideas to their source and stripping the gaudy and charismatic trappings from the thought of men like John Dewey and B. F. Skinner to have at the simple-mindedness beneath." William F. Buckley said of Meyer: "He will exasperate, raise niggling points of ideological fidelity, he will cozen, argue, plead, catechize, he will make a million more telephone calls and announce the necessity for one thousand more plenipotentiary editorial conferences: and, little by little, his profound attachment and profound understanding of the conservative position in America will get under more and more skins, even as, looking back, it is doubtful that anyone who has worked with him would say that he is untouched either by Meyer's intelligence, or by the intensity of his faith."

BIOGRAPHICAL/CRITICAL SOURCES: National Review, March 25, 1969; New York Times Book Review, May 11, 1969; New York Times, April 3, 1972.

(Died April 1, 1972)

*　　*　　*

MILES, Russell Hancock　1895-

PERSONAL: Born March 17, 1895, in Camden, N.J.; son of C. Austin and Bertha H. Miles; married Elsa Berwald (deceased); children: Virginia Miles Mesnard, Russell Hancock, Jr., Barbara Miles Bowman. Education: Syracuse University, B.Mus., 1925, M.Mus., 1930. Politics: Independent. Religion: Protestant. Home: 308 West Michigan, Urbana, Ill. 61801.

CAREER: University of Illinois, Urbana, 1922-62, became professor of music, now professor emeritus. Church organist for forty-five years, now retired; organ recitalist and composer. Military service: U.S. Army, trombonist in Cavalry Band, later Artillery Band, 1917-18. Member: American Guild of Organists, Sinfonia, Pi Kappa Lambda.

WRITINGS: Thy King Cometh! (cantata), Oliver Ditson Co., 1938; The Chambered Nautilus: Short Cantata for Mixed Voices, H. W. Gray, 1944; Elegie Heroique, Oliver Ditson Co., 1947; Johann Sebastian Bach: An Introduction to His Life and Works, Prentice-Hall, 1962; Two Lenten Chorale Preludes for Organ, H. W. Gray, 1964. Composer of more than fifty other published musical works. Contributor of book reviews and articles to music publications.

WORK IN PROGRESS: Self-Tutor in Elementary Harmonic Principles; research for a book on organ literature.

AVOCATIONAL INTERESTS: Playing poker (consistent but good loser).

* * *

MILLAR, James Primrose Malcolm 1893-

PERSONAL: Born April 17, 1893, in Edinburgh, Scotland; son of Thomas (an accountant) and Jane Lyall (Tod) Millar; married Christine Hastie (a supervisor of the postal courses department of National Council of Labour Colleges), August 11, 1923; children: Avril Vivian, Gavin Michael. *Education:* Attended Central Labour College, London, England. *Politics:* Socialist. *Religion:* Humanist. *Home:* 5 Mount Boone, Dartmouth, England.

CAREER: Started as insurance investment and management assistant in Edinburgh, Scotland; sometime head of City of Edinburgh coal control, tutor and organizer in eastern Scotland for Scottish Labour College, and general secretary of National Council of Labour Colleges. Former secretary and editor of *Plebs* and Plebs textbooks. Member of council, Scottish Institute of Adult Education. *Military service:* World War I, court-martialed as anti-militarist. *Member:* Fabian Society (London), Clerical and Administrative Workers' Union.

WRITINGS: More Production and More Poverty, Scottish Labour College, 1921; *Education for Emancipation,* National Council of Labour Colleges Publishing Society, 1922; *The Trained Mind—Trained for What?,* National Council of Labour Colleges Publishing Society, 1923; (contributor) Julian Bell, editor, *We Did Not Fight: 1914-18 Experiences of War Resisters,* Cobden-Sanderson, 1935; *Post-War Education: A Labour View,* National Council of Labour Colleges Publishing Society, 1943; *The Vest Pocket Speaker,* National Council of Labour Colleges Publishing Society, 1959; *Trade Union Education Today,* National Council of Labour Colleges Publishing Society, 1961.

WORK IN PROGRESS: A history of the British labour college movement.

* * *

MILLER, Carroll H(iram) 1907-197(?)

PERSONAL: Born April 9, 1907, in Columbus, Neb.; son of David Marsh (a farmer) and Addie Luella (Diemer) Miller. *Education:* Nebraska Wesleyan University, A.B., 1929; University of South Dakota, M.A., 1934; Colorado State College, Ed.D., 1950. *Office:* Department of Education, Northern Illinois University, DeKalb, Ill. 60115.

CAREER: Wittenberg College, Springfield, Ohio, assistant professor of psychology, 1946-48; Colorado State University, Fort Collins, Colo., professor of psychology and education and head of department, 1948-59; U.S. Office of Education, Washington, D.C., specialist in preparation of personnel workers, 1959-62; Northern Illinois University, DeKalb, professor of education, beginning 1962. Consultant to Illinois State Department of Guidance. *Member:* American Personnel and Guidance Association, American Psychological Association, Illinois Guidance and Personnel Association.

WRITINGS: Foundations of Guidance, Harper, 1961, 2nd edition, 1971; (contributor) Henry Borow, editor, *Man in a World at Work,* Houghton, 1964; *Guidance Services: An Introduction,* Harper, 1965; (compiler and editor with George D. Weigel) *Today's Guidance: A Book of Read-*

ings, Allyn and Bacon, 1970. Contributor to periodicals. Past chairman, board of editors, *Vocational Guidance Quarterly.*

AVOCATIONAL INTERESTS: Photography, fishing, travel in Canada and Alaska.

(Deceased)

* * *

MILLER, Ethel Prince 1893-

PERSONAL: Born September 6, 1893, in Yonkers, N.Y.; daughter of George Seelye (treasurer, New York Central Railroad) and Ida (Broadmeadow) Prince; married Kenneth Dexter Miller (a clergyman), April 27, 1920; children: Kenneth Dexter, Jr., Elizabeth Prince (Mrs. Franklin M. Hiteshew). *Education:* Vassar College, A.B., 1915; Columbia University, graduate student, 1916-19. *Politics:* Independent—"Democrat, really." *Religion:* Protestant. *Home:* The Barn, 59 Fairview Ave., Madison, N.J.

CAREER: Barnard College, New York, N.Y., teacher, department of psychology, 1916-19; New York (N.Y.) Police Headquarters, psychologist, 1918-19; New York State Commission for Mental Defectives, secretary, 1918-21. Lecturer on psychology, mental hygiene, and plant life. Chairman, New York Inter-Church Committee on Migrants, 1920-30; member of national board, Young Women's Christian Association, 1943-47. *Member:* American Association of University Women, League of Women Voters, Vassar Club of New York (president, 1943-47).

WRITINGS: (With husband, Kenneth D. Miller) *The People Are the City,* Macmillan, 1962. Author of brochures, and of a pamphlet on migrants, entitled *The Church Serving the Migrants,* Friendship, 1940.

* * *

MILLER, Jay W(ilson) 1893-

PERSONAL: Born September 14, 1893, in Mapleton Depot, Pa.; son of Abram K. (a farmer) and Maggie (Wilson) Miller; married E. Lillian Steinbach, December 29, 1914 (died May 2, 1967); married Evelyn R. Kulp, May 15, 1968. *Education:* Juniata College, B.E., 1910; University of Minnesota, B.S., 1924; Temple University, Ed.M., 1936, Ed.D., 1939. *Politics:* Republican. *Religion:* Methodist. *Home:* 1016 Warwick Ct., Sun City Center, Fla. 33570.

CAREER: Rural teacher, business school manager, college and high school teacher, 1910-23; University of Minnesota, Minneapolis, instructor in accounting, 1923-24; sales consultant, 1924-29; Goldey Beacom School of Business, Wilmington, Del., 1929-68, began as director of courses, president, 1951-68. Consultant, Accrediting Commission for Business Schools; member of Administrators Advisory Committee for Vocational Rehabilitation and Education, U.S. Veterans Administration.

MEMBER: National Association of Accredited Commercial Schools (former vice-president), North-Central Business Education Association (former vice-president), Business Education Research Associates (former president), Association of Independent Schools and Colleges (former president), Administrative Management Society, (former member of national board of directors), Eastern Business Teachers Association (former president), Delaware Vocational Association (former president), Delaware Business Teachers Association (former president), Masons, Delta Pi Epsilon, Phi Delta Kappa. *Awards, honors:* Diamond Merit Award of Administrative Management Society; Man of the Year Award, National Association and Council of Business Schools, 1949 and 1956; Distinguished Service Award, Accrediting Commission for Business Schools.

WRITINGS: (Editor) *Methods in Commercial Teaching*, South-Western Publishing, 1925; *Personal Efficiency* (teacher's manual), Gregg Publishing Division, 1926; *Cases in Salesmanship*, South-Western Publishing, 1930; *A Critical Analysis of the Organization, Administration and Function of the Private Business Schools of the United States*, South-Western Publishing, 1939; (with W. J. Hamilton) *The Independent Business School in American Education*, Gregg Publishing Division, 1964. Contributor of about thirty articles to periodicals, including *Journal of Business Education, Balance Sheet, Business Teacher*, and *Office Executive.*

* * *

MILLER, Kenneth Dexter 1887-

PERSONAL: Born April 27, 1887; son of Charles Dexter (a businessman) and Julia (Hope) Miller; married Ethel Anderson Prince, April 27, 1920; children: Kenneth Dexter, Jr., Elizabeth Prince Miller Hiteshew. *Education:* Attended Princeton University, 1904-08, Columbia University, 1908-09, and Union Theological Seminary, New York, N.Y., 1909-12. *Politics:* Democrat. *Home:* 59 Fairview Ave., Madison, N.J. *Office:* 105 East 22nd St., New York, N.Y.

CAREER: Presbyterian minister. Presbyterian Board of Home Missions, New York, N.Y., immigrant fellow, 1912-13; Jan Hus Neighborhood House, New York, N.Y., director 1913-17; Young Men's Christian Association, wartime secretary in Russia, 1917-19; Board of Home Missions, secretary, 1919-26; National Council of Churches, New York, N.Y., secretary, 1926-28; pastor of Presbyterian church in Madison, N.J., 1928-36; Detroit (Mich.) Presbytery, secretary, 1936-39; New York (N.Y.) City Mission Society, executive secretary and president, 1939-54; American Fund for Czechoslovak refugees, European director, 1955-58. *Member:* Chi Alpha, Ministers Club, Century Club (New York). *Awards, honors:* Czechoslovak War Cross; Order of White Lion; Th.D. from University of Prague; D.D. from Princeton University.

WRITINGS: Czechoslovaks in America, Revell, 1921; *Peasant Pioneers*, Revell, 1926, reprinted, R & E Research, 1969; *We Who Are America*, Friendship, 1945; (with wife, Ethel P. Miller) *The People Are the City*, Macmillan, 1962.

WORK IN PROGRESS: Reminiscences and Recollections: Fifty Years Experience With Czechoslovak People. 1912-62.

* * *

MILLER, Nina Hull 1894-

PERSONAL: Born January 7, 1894, in Fremont, Neb.; daughter of Arundel C. (a photographer) and Florence C. (Miller) Hull; married Glenn E. Miller (a county judge), August 12, 1921; children: Millicent (Mrs. Alberto de Sacio), Eugene Arundel. *Education:* University of Nebraska, B.A., 1920, graduate work, 1923. *Politics:* Republican. *Religion:* Protestant. *Home:* 1408 North Lincoln St., Lexington, Neb. 68850.

CAREER: Teacher in public schools of Nebraska and South Dakota, 1914-15, 1918-19, 1920-21. *Member:* Nebraska Writers Guild, Nebraska Art Association, Nebraska

State Historical Society, P.E.O. (former chapter president), Daughters of the American Revolution (former regent), Order of Eastern Star (former chapter matron), American Legion Auxiliary.

WRITINGS: Shutters West, Sage Books, 1962. Contributor of articles to hobby publications. Member of editorial staff, *National Button Bulletin.*

WORK IN PROGRESS: Preparing an historical article for a western magazine, and a family history.

AVOCATIONAL INTERESTS: Painting in oils and travel.

* * *

MILLER, Philip L(ieson) 1906-

PERSONAL: Born April 23, 1906, in Woodland, N.Y.; son of Edward B. and Marie A. (Lieson) Miller; married Catharine A. Keyes, October 9, 1943 (deceased). *Education:* Studied at Manhattan School of Music, 1923-27, and Juilliard Institute of Musical Art, 1927-29. *Home:* 129 East 10th St., New York, N.Y. 10003.

CAREER: New York Public Library, Music Division, New York, N.Y., assistant, 1927-45, assistant chief, 1946-59, chief, 1959-66. *Military service:* U.S. Army, Infantry, 1942-45. *Member:* International Association of Music Libraries, Association for Recorded Sound Collections (president, 1965—), Music Library Association (president, 1964-65), American Musicological Society, Metropolitan Opera Association, Bohemians (vice-president). *Awards, honors:* Music Library Association citation, 1966.

WRITINGS: (Editor and arranger) Thomas Augustine Arne, *Songs to the Plays of Shakespeare for Medium Voice and Piano*, Music Press, 1947; *Guide to Long Playing Records*, Volume II: *Vocal Music*, Knopf, 1955; (compiler, translator, and author of introduction) *The Ring of Words: An Anthology of Song Texts*, Doubleday, 1963. Contributor of reviews and articles to *Saturday Review* and to music journals. Senior critic, *American Record Guide.*

* * *

MILLER, William Robert 1927-1970

PERSONAL: Born July 3, 1927, in Waterloo, N.Y.; son of Roy Benson (an English teacher) and Mildred (Hollister) Miller; married Edith Lorraine Meyer (an attorney), May 7, 1949; children: Janice Carol, Brian Roy. *Education:* Columbia University, student, 1948-51; New School for Social Research, B.A., 1964. *Religion:* United Church of Christ. *Home:* 134-19 166th Place, Jamaica, Queens, N.Y. 11434. *Office: United Church Herald*, 297 Park Ave. S., New York, N.Y. 10010.

CAREER: Time, New York, N.Y., head copyboy, 1952-53; W. W. Norton & Co., Inc. (publishers), New York, N.Y., copy editor, 1954; *Forbes*, New York, N.Y., reporter, 1955; Fellowship of Reconciliation (peace organization), Nyack, N.Y., managing editor of *Fellowship*, 1956-61; *United Church Herald*, New York, N.Y., managing editor, 1962-70. *Military service:* U.S. Air Force, 1945-47. *Member:* Fellowship of Reconciliation (member of North American committee), American Civil Liberties Union, Congress of Racial Equality, New York Committee to Abolish Capital Punishment (executive committee member), Young Men's Christian Association.

WRITINGS: Bibliography of Books on War, Pacifism, Nonviolence and Related Studies, Fellowship of Reconciliation, 1960, revised edition, 1961; *Nonviolence: A Christian Interpretation,* Association Press, 1964; *The World of Pop Music and Jazz,* Concordia, 1965; (editor and author of introduction) *The New Christianity: An Anthology of the Rise of Modern Religious Thought,* Delacorte, 1967; *Martin Luther King, Jr.: His Life, Martyrdom, and Meaning for the World,* Weybright & Talley, 1968; *Goodbye, Jehovah: A Survey of the New Directions in Christianity,* Walker & Co., 1969. Author of regular monthly column on long playing records in *United Church Herald* and *Arena.* Former contributing editor of *Hi-Fi World.*

WORK IN PROGRESS: The Tragedy of Mahatma Gandhi.

SIDELIGHTS: Miller told *CA*: "My principal interest is in writing poetry; my life ambition is to achieve recognition as a serious poet. I am also interested in music, painting, psychology, history, linguistics (no competence, but dabbling in German, French, Russian), theology. I do some carpentry for my apartment. I go to films and theatre occasionally. I do virtually no light reading, carry a paperback book or the New Testament with me for subway reading, avoid newspapers except when doing research which necessitates their use—and then I follow several daily. I get more magazines than I can possibly read but at least peruse them all."

BIOGRAPHICAL/CRITICAL SOURCES: Motive, February, 1967; *Christian Century,* May 24, 1967, September 20, 1967, January 15, 1969, September 2, 1970; *New York Times Book Review,* July 9, 1967, February 16, 1969; *Best Sellers,* December 1, 1968; *Saturday Review,* May 10, 1969; *New York Times,* August 11, 1970.

(Died August 10, 1970)

* * *

MILLHAUSER, Milton 1910-

PERSONAL: Born November 3, 1910, in New York, N.Y.; son of Louis (a salesman) and Lena (Maas) Millhauser; married Charlotte Polonsky (a teacher), August 26, 1938; children: Steven, Carla. *Education:* City College (now City College of the City University of New York), New York, N.Y., B.A., 1931; Columbia University, M.A., 1933, Ph.D., 1951. *Religion:* Humanist. *Home:* 100 Carlynn Dr., Fairfield, Conn. *Office:* Department of English, University of Bridgeport, Bridgeport, Conn. 06602.

CAREER: City College (now City College of the City University of New York), New York, N.Y., instructor in English, 1931-46; Long Island University, New York, N.Y., instructor in English, 1946-47; University of Bridgeport, Bridgeport, Conn., assistant professor of English, 1947-55, associate professor, 1955-62, professor of English, 1962—. Visiting professor, Wesleyan University, Middletown, Conn., summer, 1959. *Member:* Modern Humanities Research Association, Modern Language Association of America, American Association of University Professors, Phi Beta Kappa.

WRITINGS: Just Before Darwin, Wesleyan University Press, 1959. Also author of a monograph, *Fire and Ice,* published by the Tennyson Society. Contributor to professional journals.

* * *

MILLIS, Walter 1899-1968

PERSONAL: Born March 16, 1899, in Atlanta, Ga.; son of John (an army officer) and Mary (Raoul) Millis; married Norah Kathleen Thompson, 1929; married second wife, Eugenia Benbow Sheppard (a newspaper editor and fashion columnist), May 6, 1944; children: (first marriage), Walter, Jr., Sarah (Mrs. James M. McCoy). *Education:* Yale University, B.A., 1920. *Home:* Brookville Rd., Glen Head, Long Island, N.Y. 11545.

CAREER: Editorial writer for *Baltimore News,* 1920-23, *New York Sun and Globe,* 1923-24; *New York Herald Tribune,* New York, N.Y., editorial and staff writer, 1924-54; Fund for the Republic, New York, N.Y., staff member, 1954-68. Consultant, U.S. Office of War Information, 1944-45. Trustee, Society Library, New York, N.Y., 1945-68. *Military service:* U.S. Army, Field Artillery, 1918; became second lieutenant. *Member:* American Civil Liberties Union (board member, 1955-68), American Historical Society, U.S. Naval Institute, Company of Military Historians (honorary fellow), Phi Beta Kappa, Century Club (New York), Shelter Island Yacht Club, Off-Soundings Club.

WRITINGS: Sand Castle, Houghton, 1929; *The Martial Spirit: A Study of Our War with Spain,* Houghton, 1931; (with Raymond Leslie Buell and Frank H. Simonds) *Foreign Problems Confronting the New Administration* (pamphlet), Foreign Policy Association, 1933; *The Future of Sea Power in the Pacific* (pamphlet), Foreign Policy Association, 1935; *Road to War: America, 1914-1917,* Houghton, 1935; *View with Alarm: Europe Today,* Houghton, 1937; *Why Europe Fights,* Morrow, 1940; *The Faith of an American,* Oxford University Press, 1941; *The Last Phase: Allied Victory in Western Europe,* Interim International Information Service, 1945, hardcover edition, Houghton, 1946; *This Is Pearl!: The United States and Japan—1941,* Morrow, 1947.

(Editor) James Forrestal, *Diaries,* Viking, 1951; *Arms and Men: A Study in American Military History,* Putnam, 1956 (published in England as *Armies and Men: A Study in American Military History,* J. Cape, 1958); *Communism and Civil Liberties,* Fund for the Republic, 1956; *Individual Freedom and the Common Defense,* Fund for the Republic, 1957; (with Harvey C. Mansfield and Harold Stein) *Arms and the State: Civil-Military Elements in National Policy,* Twentieth Century Fund, 1958; (editor with John Courtney Murray, and contributor) *Foreign Policy and the Free Society,* Oceana, 1958; *The Constitution and the Common Defense* (pamphlet), Fund for the Republic, 1959; *Military History,* Service Center for Teachers of History, 1961; *Permanent Peace,* Center for the Study of Democratic Institutions, 1961; *A World without War,* Center for the Study of Democratic Institutions, 1961; (with James Real) *The Abolition of War,* Macmillan, 1963; *The Demilitarized World and How to Get There,* Center for the Study of Democratic Institutions, 1964; *An End to Arms,* Atheneum, 1965; *War and Revolution Today,* Center for the Study of Democratic Institutions, 1965; (editor) *American Military Thought,* Bobbs-Merrill, 1966. Editor-at-large, *Saturday Review.*

SIDELIGHTS: Millis was a leading proponent of the view that nuclear weapons make general warfare unthinkable as an instrument of national policy; many of his later writings were on this theme. In a review of *An End to Arms,* Hans J. Morgenthau comments: "Millis is no doubt an optimist, but he is not a utopian; for the world on which he reflects ... is a world that emerges from a rational projection of certain facts of contemporary experience. He has not paid much attention to the powerful historic and social forces that counteract the rational tendencies present in contemporary world politics. But by presenting his views in so able a manner he has contributed to bringing about the world that reason requires.''

BIOGRAPHICAL/CRITICAL SOURCES: New York Times Book Review, March 7, 1965; *New York Times,* March 18, 1968; *Washington Post,* March 19, 1968; *Time,* March 29, 1968.

(Died March 17, 1968)

*   *   *

MILLS, Clarence A(lonzo)   1891-1974

PERSONAL: Born December 9, 1891, in Miami, Ind.; son of Alonzo F. (a farmer) and Margaret (Winniger) Mills; married Edith Parrett, June 22, 1915, children: Russell Clarence, Donald Harper, Marjorie Ruth (Mrs. Jack R. Porter). *Education:* Valparaiso University, student, 1913; University of South Dakota, B.A., 1917; graduate study at University of Kansas, 1917-18, University of Chicago, 1918; University of Cincinnati, Ph.D., 1920, M.D., 1922. *Politics:* Independent. *Home:* 5343 Hamilton Ave., Cincinnati, Ohio 45224.

CAREER: Teacher in South Dakota public schools, 1910-12; instructor in physiology at University of Kansas, Lawrence, 1917-18, and Marquette University, Milwaukee, Wis., 1918; University of Cincinnati Medical School, Cincinnati, Ohio, instructor in biochemistry, 1919-22, instructor in medicine, 1922-23, assistant professor of medicine, 1923-26; Peking Union Medical College, Peking, China, associate professor of medicine, 1926-28; University of Cincinnati Medical School, associate professor of medicine, 1928-30, Heady Professor of Experimental Medicine, 1930-62, professor emeritus, 1964-74. Reflectotherm, Inc. (radiant cooling and heating firm), Cincinnati, Ohio, president, 1953-74. Did climatology research in Europe, 1932, Philippines, 1934, and Panama, 1940-41. Consultant to Surgeon General, U.S. Army, 1944-45; consultant to state of California and various metropolitan cities throughout America on air pollution hazards.

MEMBER: American Medical Association, American Physiological Society, American Society of Biological Chemists, American Association of Physical Anthropologists, American Association for the Advancement of Science, Central Society of Clinical Research, Sigma Xi, Alpha Omega Alpha, Alpha Kappa Kappa, Club Panamericano de Doctores (Mexico; founder, 1946), Research Club of Cincinnati. *Awards, honors:* Ohioana Book Award in nonfiction, 1943, for *Climate Makes the Man;* LL.D., University of South Dakota, 1961.

WRITINGS: Living with the Weather, Caxton, 1934; *Medical Climatology,* C.C Thomas, 1939; *Climate Makes the Man,* Harper, 1942; *Reflective Radiant Conditioning,* Pugh Press (Cincinnati), 1952; *Air Pollution and Community Health,* Christopher, 1954; *This Air We Breathe,* Christopher, 1962; *World Power Amid Shifting Climates,* Christopher, 1963; *Published Works of Clarence A. Mills,* four volumes, privately printed, 1963. Contributor to books and to magazines and scientific journals.

WORK IN PROGRESS: Investigation of solar-lunar influences on earth weather, earthquakes, and human functions and diseases; investigations on radiant heat transfer as related to the heating or cooling of organic products and people; *Man's Environmental Predicament.*

(Died September 17, 1974)

MILLS, G(len) E(arl)   1908-

PERSONAL: Born May 10, 1908, in Minneapolis, Minn.; married, 1937; children: one. *Education:* Eastern South Dakota State Teachers College (now Dakota State College), B.S., 1930; University of Michigan, A.M., 1935, Ph.D., 1941. *Office:* School of Speech, Northwestern University, Evanston, Ill.

CAREER: University of Michigan, Ann Arbor, instructor, 1941-42; Northwestern University, Evanston, Ill., 1942—, began as instructor in public speaking, 1942, became assistant dean of School of Speech, beginning 1956, professor of speech, beginning 1957, associate dean, beginning 1964. *Member:* Speech Association of America, American Forensic Association, Central States Speech Association, Illinois Speech Association.

WRITINGS: (With J. H. McBurney) *Argumentation and Debate: Techniques of a Free Society,* Macmillan, 1951, revised edition, 1964; *Composing the Speech,* Prentice-Hall, 1952; *Reason in Controversy: An Introduction to General Argumentation,* Allyn & Bacon, 1964, 2nd edition, published as *Reason in Controversy: On General Argumentation,* 1968; (with Otto Bauer) *Guidebook for Student Speakers,* Ronald, 1966; *Message Preparation: Analysis and Structure,* Bobbs-Merrill, 1966.

*   *   *

MILLS, (William) Mervyn   1906-

PERSONAL: Born February 23, 1906, in London, England; son of William and Florence Maude (Fisher) Mills; married Mollie Crichton-Gordon (divorced); married Marie-Therese Marguerite Petitjean; children: (first marriage) Penelope Solange Mervyn; (second marriage) Peter William Mervyn, Sophie-Chantal Mervyn. *Education:* Studied at King's College, London. *Home:* 95 Priory Rd., London, N.8, England. *Office:* Air Historical Branch, Air Ministry, Queen Anne's Chambers, 41 Tothill St., Westminster, London S.W.1, England.

CAREER: Edward Arnold Publishers Ltd., London, England, publisher's assistant, 1924-29; left to live in Paris, France, writing there as a free lance and working for Agence Litteraire Internationale; writer of television plays at Alexandra Palace, 1937-39; Air Ministry, London, England, official air historian for Middle East, now senior historian, 1948—. *Military service:* Royal Air Force, 1941-46; served in Africa, Sicily, Corsica, and Greece; became squadron leader; mentioned in dispatches. *Member:* Society of Authors, National Book League, P.E.N., Television and Screen-Writers' Guild, Arts Theatre Club (London).

WRITINGS: Nelson of the Nile (four-act play), Putnam, 1933; *The Long Haul* (novel), Macmillan, 1956; *Tempt Not the Stars* (novel), Harrap, 1958; *The Winter Wind* (war novel), Cassell, 1963. Author of various Royal Air Force wartime operations histories, all Air Ministry classified publications.

Television scripts: ''Dance Without Music''; ''The Queen of Spades.'' Radio scripts: ''Mexican Gold''; ''The Skull''; ''Paul Jones''; ''The Lost World'' series; ''The Peter Simple'' series; and other programs produced by British Broadcasting Corp.

SIDELIGHTS: The Long Haul was made into a film.

*   *   *

MILOTTE, Alfred G(eorge)   1904-

PERSONAL: Born November 24, 1904, in Appleton, Wis.;

married Elma Moore Jolly, June 15, 1934. *Education:* Studied at University of Washington and Cornish Art School, both Seattle, and Art Institute of Chicago and Chicago Academy of Fine Arts. *Office:* 9710 Angeline Rd. E., Sumner, Wash. 98390.

CAREER: Began as commercial artist in Chicago, Ill.; owner and operator of photographic studio in Ketchikan, Alaska, 1934-39; professional lecturer (with wife) on Alaska, 1939-42; producer of war and educational films, 1942-45; photographer for Walt Disney's "True Life Adventure" and "People and Places" series, 1946-57; writer and film producer, 1957—. Milotte and his wife returned to the lecture circuit, 1966-69, for a tour with the film, "Background of Adventure." Films for Walt Disney include "The Grand Canyon Country and the Colorado River," 1947, "Seal Island," 1948, "Alaska Eskimo," 1950, "Beaver Valley," 1950, "Prowlers of the Everglades," 1952, "The African Lion," 1955, "Nature's Strangest Creatures" (Australia), 1959. Teacher at University of Puget Sound, winter, 1972, 1973, and trustee of university museum board. Member of Board of Allied Arts, Tacoma, 1963-66. *Awards, honors:* Several of his films for Walt Disney, including "Seal Island" and "Alaska Eskimo," won Academy of Motion Picture Arts and Sciences "Oscars"; U.S. Camera Achievement Award for "Beaver Valley."

WRITINGS: The Story of the Platypus, Knopf, 1959; *The Story of a Hippopotamus,* Knopf, 1964; (with wife, Elma Milotte) *The Story of an Alaskan Grizzly Bear,* Knopf, 1969. Illustrator (color stills) of a number of Disney nature books. Contributor to *Rotarian, Smithsonian Magazine,* and *Reader's Digest.*

WORK IN PROGRESS: A book on the personal experiences of Milotte and his wife; a television special, "Christman Nature Fantasy"; an art exhibit for Frye Art Museum, Seattle.

SIDELIGHTS: Milotte designed the structure to be built for First Church of Christ, Scientist, in Puyallup, Washington.

BIOGRAPHICAL/CRITICAL SOURCES: Rotarian, November, 1941, August, 1955; *Vogue,* February 1, 1952; *Life,* November 2, 1953; *Reader's Digest,* February, 1955, and October, 1971; *National Geographic,* August, 1963.

* * *

MINER, Charles S(ydney) 1906-

PERSONAL: Born October 6, 1906, in Windsor, Ill.; son of Thomas Daniel and Nelle (Price) Miner; married Maria W. F. Wong, July 18, 1954. *Education:* Southeastern University, Washington, D.C., LL.B., 1940. *Home:* 33 Fifth Ave., New York, N.Y. 10003.

CAREER: Maryland News, Silver Spring, Md., editor, 1932-40; Office of the Quartermaster General, Washington, D.C., chief of press section, 1940-44; *Shanghai Evening Post & Mercury,* Chungking and Shanghai, China, editor, 1945-46, editor of *Shanghai Evening Post* "Far East Letter", 1946-48; American International Companies, Shanghai, China, vice-president and China manager, 1948-56; C. V. Starr & Co., Inc., New York, N.Y., investment counsel, 1956-62; consultant to Schenley Industries, Inc. and Lewis S. Rosenstiel, 1967-71; National Alcoholic Beverage Control Association, Inc., Washington, D.C., director of public information, 1971—. War correspondent for *New York Post* and Mutual Broadcasting System during World War II, in China-Burma-India theater. *Member:* District of

Columbia bar, Overseas Press Club, National Press Club, Free and Accepted Masons.

WRITINGS: Fire Insurance Adjusting Principles and Practices, Underwriters Adjustment Co., 1961; *Adjusting Principles and Practices Under Various Casualty Policies,* Underwriters Adjustment Co., 1961; *How to Get an Executive Job after 40,* Harper, 1963. Contributor to insurance and alcoholic beverage trade publications.

WORK IN PROGRESS: A book, *Precious Jade.*

SIDELIGHTS: Miner has traveled extensively in the Far East, Europe, and the Caribbean area. He did research in Taiwan for several months, 1965-66, and in 1972.

* * *

MINER, Lewis S. 1909-

PERSONAL: Born November 18, 1909, in Waterloo, Iowa; son of Lewis S. and Marguerite (Roeschlaub) Miner; married Frederika Mueller, February 2, 1934; children: Mark S., Marcia S. *Education:* University of Minnesota, B.B.A., 1931. *Home:* 3615 Albemarle St. N.W., Washington, D.C. 20008.

CAREER: One-time music and drama critic on *St. Paul Daily News,* St. Paul, Minn., and editor of weekly sales magazine; U.S. Army, Comptroller of the Army, Washington, D.C., 1941-70, civilian systems accountant and writer and editor of army regulations on property accounting.

WRITINGS—All juvenile books: Mightier Than the Sword: The Story of Richard Harding Davis, Whitman, 1940; *Pilot on the River* (historical novel), Whitman, 1940; *Wild Waters* (Junior Literary Guild selection), Messner, 1946; *Front Lines and Headlines: The Story of Richard Harding Davis,* Messner, 1959; *King of the Hawaiian Islands, Kamehameha I,* Messner, 1963; *Industrial Genius: Samuel Slater,* Messner, 1968. Contributor of stories and articles to newspapers and magazines.

AVOCATIONAL INTERESTS: Reading, music, theatre.

BIOGRAPHICAL/CRITICAL SOURCES: Writing Books for Boys and Girls, Doubleday, 1952; *Best Sellers,* April 1, 1968.

* * *

MINNICH, Helen Benton 1892-

PERSONAL: Surname is pronounced *Min*-nick; born October 16, 1892, in Fort Scott, Kan.; daughter of Guy Potter (a university president) and Mary (Konantz) Benton; married Dwight Elmer Minnich (emeritus professor of zoology, University of Minnesota), December 30, 1922 (died September, 1965); children: Dwight Benton, Conrad Harvey. *Education:* Attended Miami University, Oxford, Ohio, one year, and Smith College, one year; University of Vermont, Ph.B. (cum laude); graduate art study in New York, N.Y., 1915-20. *Politics:* Independent. *Religion:* Unitarian. *Home:* 2447 Third Ave. S., Minneapolis, Minn. 55404.

CAREER: Occasional lecturer at the University of Minnesota, for various independent groups, and for private classes in art history. *Member:* Phi Beta Kappa.

WRITINGS: (Self-illustrated) *A Bright Book of Lights,* Frederick Stokes, 1931; (with Shojiro Nomura) *Japanese Costume and the Makers of Its Elegant Tradition,* Tuttle (Japan), for Asia Society, 1963. Contributor to *Pasadena Art Institute Bulletin* and to *House Beautiful.*

WORK IN PROGRESS: Writing a history of a collection of prints illustrative of taste and of natural history "since

Gutenberg,'' a collection of over 8000 works assembled by Mrs. Minnich and her late husband over a period of forty years.

SIDELIGHTS: Research material for book on Japanese costumes was supplied by late Shojiro Nomura, with whom Mrs. Minnich worked in Kyoto in 1920-22. As the daughter of a college president (University of Vermont, University of The Philippines, and Miami University) and the wife of a professor, she has spent her life on college campuses.

BIOGRAPHICAL/CRITICAL SOURCES: Minneapolis Star, October 8, 1970, October 28, 1970.

* * *

MINRATH, William R(ichard) 1900-

PERSONAL: Born June 14, 1900, in New York, N.Y.; son of George and Julia (Talmadge) Minrath; married Mildred Gougeon. *Education:* Columbia University, A.B., 1921, Ch.E., 1924. *Religion:* Protestant. *Home:* 13 Dublin Rd., Pennington, N.J. 08534. *Office:* D. Van Nostrand Co., Inc., 120 Alexander St., Princeton, N.J. 08540.

CAREER: Dye Products Co., Newark, N.J., chemist, 1924-25; General Chemical Co., Edgewater, N.J., chemical engineer, 1925-28; Dry Ice Co., New York, N.Y., chemical engineer, 1928-29; D. Van Nostrand Co., Inc., New York, N.Y. and Princeton, N.J., 1929-46, advertising manager, 1946-67, and vice-president, 1958-67. *Military service:* U.S. Army, 1918. *Member:* American Chemical Society, American Physical Society, American Mathematics Society, American Institute of Mining and Metallurgical Engineering, American Nuclear Society, Chemists Club.

WRITINGS—All published by Van Nostrand: (With others) *The Chemist's Dictionary,* 1951; *How to Run Your Own Business and Make It Pay,* 1956; (editor) *Van Nostrand's Practical Formulary,* 1957; (editor) *Van Nostrand's Scientific Encyclopedia,* 3rd edition, 1958; *Handbook of Business Mathematics,* 1959; *Simplified Accounting,* 1959; (editor with Edward E. Grazda) *Handbook of Applied Mathematics,* 1959, 2nd edition, 1967; (contributing editor) *International Encyclopedia of Chemical Science,* 1964.

* * *

MITCHELL, Joan Cattermole 1920-

PERSONAL: Born March 15, 1920, in London, England; daughter of A. H. (a company director) and E. O. E. (New) Mitchell; married James Cattermole (a politician), March, 1956; children: Nicholas, Jacqueline. *Education:* Oxford University, B.A., 1942; University of Nottingham, Ph.D., 1956. *Home:* 15 Ranmoor Rd., Gedling, Nottingham, England. *Office:* Economics Department, University of Nottingham, Nottingham, England.

CAREER: Ministry of Fuel and Power, London, England, economist, 1942-45; St. Anne's College, Oxford University, Oxford, England, tutor in economics, 1945-47; Board of Trade, London, England, economist, 1947-50; Labour Party, London, England, researcher, 1950-52; University of Nottingham, Nottingham, England, reader in economics, 1952—. Member, National Board for Prices and Incomes, 1965-68.

WRITINGS: The British Gas Industry, Present and Future, Fabian Publications and Gollancz, 1945; (with others) *Distribution,* Fabian Publications and Gollancz, 1946; *The Future of Private Industry,* Labour Party Press, 1951; *Britain in Crisis 1951,* Secker & Warburg, 1963; *Groundwork to Economic Planning,* Secker & Warburg, 1966; *The*

National Board for Prices and Incomes, Secker & Warburg, 1971. Contributor to *Political Quarterly, Oxford University Bulletin of Statistics,* and *The Banker.*

WORK IN PROGRESS: A work on salaries.

* * *

MITCHELL, Lane 1907-

PERSONAL: Born July 14, 1907, in Atlanta, Ga.; son of Lane (a sheriff) and Margaret (Orr) Mitchell; married Mildred Lee Morris, June 17, 1936; children: Robert Lane. *Education:* Georgia Institute of Technology, B.S., 1929; University of Illinois, M.S., 1931; graduate study at Rutgers University, 1931-32, Emory University, 1933; Pennsylvania State University, Ph.D., 1941. *Politics:* Independent. *Religion:* Independent Methodist. *Home:* 57 25th St. N.W., Atlanta, Ga. 30309. *Office:* Georgia Institute of Technology, Atlanta, Ga. 30332.

CAREER: High school teacher of English and journalism, Atlanta, Ga., 1932-34; Georgia Geological Survey, Atlanta, assistant state geologist, 1934-36; Georgia Institute of Technology, Atlanta, assistant professor, 1936-38, associate professor, 1938-41, professor of ceramic engineering, 1941-73, director of School of Ceramic Engineering, 1948-73, professor and director emeritus, 1973—. Consultant to Oak Ridge National Laboratory, 1955-73. Member of board of directors of Metallurgy-Ceramics Foundation, Southern Porcelain Co., Universal Ceramics, Inc., and Southern Christian Home. *Military service:* U.S. Naval Reserve, beginning 1943, active duty, 1943-46; now commander.

MEMBER: American Ceramic Society (fellow), National Institute of Ceramic Engineers, Georgia Engineering Society, Georgia Mineral Society (fellow; member of board), Georgia Academy of Science (fellow), Keramos (member of board), Sigma Xi, Tau Beta Pi, Phi Kappa Phi, Pi Delta Epsilon, Kappa Sigma, Ansley Golf Club. *Awards, honors:* Hewitt Wilson Award of American Ceramic Society (Southeast section), 1956; Greaves-Walker Roll of Honor, 1965.

WRITINGS: National Strategy in the Cold War, U.S. Navy, 1962; *Ceramics, Stone Age to Space Age*, Scholastic Book Services, 1963; (contributor) *Industrial Minerals and Rocks,* A.I.M.E., 1974. Contributor to professional journals, popular magazines, and newspapers.

WORK IN PROGRESS: A glossary of terms used in current political and philosophical thought; biographical work; and a biblical novel.

AVOCATIONAL INTERESTS: Mineral collecting, political discussion.

* * *

MITTELHOLZER, Edgar Austin 1909-1965

PERSONAL: Surname is pronounced Mittel-holtser; born December 16, 1909, in New Amsterdam, British Guiana; son of William Austin (an assistant town clerk) and Rosamond Mabel (Leblanc) Mittelholzer; married second wife, Jacqueline Pointer (a writer), April 27, 1960; children: (first marriage) Anna, Stefan, Griselda, Hermann; (second marriage) Leodegar. *Education:* Attended schools in British Guiana. *Politics:* Conservative. *Religion:* Personal beliefs. *Home:* Loushall House Cottage, Dippenhall, Farnham, Surrey, England. *Agent:* Rosica Colin, 4 Hereford Sq., London S.W. 7, England (translation rights only).

CAREER: Worked as customs officer, agricultural assistant, meteorological observer, cinema inspector, free lance journalist, and hotel receptionist, until 1941. Came to England in 1948, worked in book department of British Council, 1948-52. Became professional writer, 1952-65. *Awards, honors:* Guggenheim fellow, 1952.

WRITINGS: Corentyne Thunder, Eyre & Spottiswoode, 1941; *A Morning at the Office*, Doubleday, 1950; *Shadows Move Among Them*, Lippincott, 1951; *Children of Kaywana*, Day, 1952; *The Weather in Middenshot*, Day, 1952; *The Life and Death of Sylvia*, Day, 1953; *The Harrowing of Hubertus*, Day, 1954; *My Bones and My Flute*, Secker & Warburg, 1955; *Of Trees and the Sea*, Secker & Warburg, 1956; *A Tale of Three Places*, Secker & Warburg, 1957; *Kaywana Blood*, Day, 1958; *With a Carib Eye* (reminiscences), Secker & Warburg, 1958; *The Weather Family*, Secker & Warburg, 1958; *A Tinkling in the Twilight*, Secker & Warburg, 1959; *Latticed Echoes*, Secker & Warburg, 1960; *Eltonsbrody*, Secker & Warburg, 1961; *Thunder Returning*, Secker & Warburg, 1961; *The Piling of Clouds*, Putnam, 1961; *The Mad MacMullochs*, Owen Press, 1961; *The Wounded and the Worried*, Putnam, 1962; *Uncle Paul*, Macdonald & Co., 1963; *A Swarthy Boy* (autobiographical), Putnam, 1963; *The Aloneness of Mrs. Chatham*, Gibbs & Phillips, 1965; *The Jilkington Drama*, Abelard, 1965.

WORK IN PROGRESS: Two novels.

SIDELIGHTS: Shadows Move Among Them was produced on Broadway as "Climate of Eden," 1953. *Avocational interests:* Oriental occultism and everything to do with psychical research.

(Died May 6, 1965)

* * *

MIXTER, Russell Lowell 1906-

PERSONAL: Born August 7, 1906, in Williamston, Mich.; son of Floyd B. (a salesman) and Florence (Barlow) Mixter; married Emilie Claus, June 27, 1931; children: Wilbur, Joan (Mrs. Jerry Sweers), Ruth, Priscilla (Mrs. Gordon Gault). *Education:* Wheaton College, Wheaton, Ill., A.B., 1928; Michigan State University, M.S., 1930; University of Illinois, Ph.D., 1939. *Politics:* Republican. *Religion:* Protestant. *Home:* 1006 North President St., Wheaton, Ill. 60187. *Office:* Department of Biology, Wheaton College, Wheaton, Ill. 60188.

CAREER: Wheaton College, Wheaton, Ill., 1928—, professor of zoology, 1945—, chairman of Science Division, 1950-61. Lay preacher; speaker on science and religion, creation and evolution. *Member:* American Association for the Advancement of Science, American Scientific Affiliation (president, 1951-54), Illinois Academy of Science, Sigma Xi. *Awards, honors:* Alumnus of the Year, Wheaton College, 1959; Teacher of the Year, 1969.

WRITINGS: Creation and Evolution (monograph), American Scientific Affiliation, 1951; (editor) *Evolution and Christian Thought Today*, Eerdmans, 1959. Contributor to *Christian Life*. Editor, *Journal of American Scientific Affiliation*, 1964-68.

* * *

MIYAMOTO, Kazuo 1900-

PERSONAL: Born April 1, 1900, in Oloa, Hawaii; son of Torahiko and Mosa (Murayama) Miyamoto; married Sadie Seiko Omokawa, June 28, 1930; children: Gertrude Keiko (Mrs. Shigeo Natori), Victor Takashi, Eric Kiyoshi. *Education:* Stanford University, student, 1918-21; Washington

University, St. Louis, Mo., M.D., 1927; Tokyo Jikei-Kai Medical College, Ph.D., 1940. *Politics:* Republican. *Religion:* Buddhist. *Home:* 1225 Nehoa St., Honolulu, Hawaii 96822.

CAREER: General practice of medicine, Honolulu, Hawaii, 1929—. National consultant in general practice to the Surgeon General, U.S. Air Force. *Member:* American Medical Association, American Geriatrics Society, Honolulu County Medical Society.

WRITINGS: A Nisei Discovers Japan (diary), privately printed, 1957; *Hawaii: End of the Rainbow*, Bridgeway Press, 1964.

AVOCATIONAL INTERESTS: Growing orchids, especially vandas.

* * *

MOATS, Alice-Leone

PERSONAL: Born in Mexico, Distrito Federal, Mexico; daughter of Wallace Payne and Leone (Blakemore) Moats. *Education:* Attended schools in Paris, France, and Rome, Italy. *Politics:* Republican. *Religion:* Episcopalian. *Home:* Via della Polveriera, 44, Rome, Italy. *Agent:* Elizabeth Otis, McIntosh & Otis, Inc., 18 East 41st St., New York, N.Y. 10017.

CAREER: Collier's, foreign correspondent in Far East, Soviet Union, and East Africa, 1940-42; *Collier's* and *New York Herald Tribune*, foreign correspondent in Spain, 1943-44; *Newsday*, foreign correspondent in Rome, 1963-64; full-time free-lance writer at earlier periods and 1964—. *Member:* Foreign Press Club (Rome).

WRITINGS: No Nice Girl Swears, Knopf, 1933; (with mother, Leone B. Moats) *Off to Mexico*, Scribner, 1935; *Blind Date with Mars*, Doubleday, 1943; *No Passport for Paris*, Putnam, 1945; *A Violent Innocence*, Duell, Sloan & Pearce, 1951; *At Home Abroad*, Viking, 1954; *Lupescu*, Holt, 1956; *Roman Folly*, Harcourt, 1965. Contributor to *Saturday Evening Post, Ladies' Home Journal, Woman's Home Companion, American Mercury, Redbook, Cosmopolitan, Town and Country, Harper's Bazaar, Vogue, National Review*, and *American Weekly*.

WORK IN PROGRESS: A novel set in the years 1937-43.

SIDELIGHTS: Ms. Moats speaks French, Spanish, German, Italian, and some Russian.

* * *

MOHL, Ruth 1891-

PERSONAL: Born October 8, 1891, in Adrian, Minn.; daughter of Fred (a nurseryman) and Anna (Paulson) Mohl. *Education:* University of Minnesota, B.A., 1913, M.A., 1914; Columbia University, Ph.D., 1933. *Politics:* Democrat. *Religion:* Presbyterian. *Home:* 982 West California Ave., St. Paul, Minn. 55117.

CAREER: University of Minnesota, Minneapolis, instructor in English, 1914-20, 1922-23; Adelphi College (now University), Garden City, N.Y., assistant professor, 1924-30, associate professor, 1930-38, professor of English, 1938-40; Brooklyn College (now Brooklyn College of the City University of New York), Brooklyn, N.Y., assistant professor, 1948-55, associate professor of English, 1955-62; writer. *Member:* Modern Language Association of America, Renaissance Society of America, Milton Society of America (member of executive committee, 1952-56; president, 1960), Modern Humanities Research Association,

English Graduate Union of Columbia University, Phi Beta Kappa.

WRITINGS: The Three Estates in Medieval and Renaissance Literature, Columbia University Press, 1933; *Studies in Spenser, Milton, and the Theory of Monarchy*, Columbia University Press, 1949; (editor and translator) John Milton, *Commonplace Book*, Volume I of *Milton's Complete Prose*, Yale University Press, 1953; *John Milton and His Commonplace Book*, Ungar, 1969. Contributor to *Collier's Encyclopedia* and professional journals.

WORK IN PROGRESS: A book, *The Life and Work of Edmund Spenser*; research on Milton and Irenaeus.

SIDELIGHTS: Miss Mohl reads Latin, French, German, and Italian. *Avocational interests:* Gardening, and community and church activities.

*   *   *

MOHRHARDT, Foster E(dward)   1907-

PERSONAL: Born March 7, 1907, in Lansing, Mich.; son of Albert Frederick and Alice (Bennett) Mohrhardt; married Katherine Selina Kivisto, December 19, 1936; children: David England, Katri Selina. *Education:* Michigan State University, A.B., 1929; Columbia University, B.S., 1930, graduate study, 1934-35; University of Munich, diploma, 1932; University of Michigan, M.A., 1933; special courses at other universities. *Home:* 2601 South Joyce St., Arlington, Va. 22202. *Office:* Senior Program Officer, Council on Library Resources, 1 Dupont Circle, Washington, D.C. 20036.

CAREER: Library assistant, New York (N.Y.) Public Library, 1930, University of Michigan, Ann Arbor, 1931-33; Colorado State College of Education (now Colorado State College), Greeley, assistant librarian, 1933-34; Carnegie Corp. of New York, New York, N.Y., assistant to chairman of Advisory Groups on Academic Libraries, 1935-38; Washington and Lee University, Lexington, Va., university librarian, 1938-46; U.S. Department of Commerce, Washington, D.C., chief of Library and Reports Division, Office of Technical Services, 1946-47; Columbia University, New York, N.Y., visiting professor, School of Library Service, 1947-48; U.S. Veterans Administration, Washington, D.C., chief of Library Division, 1948-54; U.S. Department of Agriculture, Washington, D.C., director of National Agricultural Library, 1954-68; Council on Library Resources, Washington, D.C., program officer, 1968—. Contract consultant, Brookhaven National Laboratory (Atomic Energy Commission), 1947-48. President of board of directors, U.S. Book Exchange, 1958-60; member of national committee, American Library Resources on Southern Asia; member of board of directors, U.S. Science Information Council, Science Abstracting and Indexing Services, 1958. *Military service:* U.S. Army, 1942; U.S. Navy, 1944-45.

MEMBER: American Library Association (president), Association of Research Libraries (president), Special Libraries Association, International Association of Agriculture Libraries and Documentalists (president, 1955-68), International Federation of Library Associations (vice-president), Cosmos Club and International Club (both Washington, D.C.). *Awards, honors:* American Association for the Advancement of Science fellow, 1962; Institute of Information Sciences (London) fellow, 1962; U.S. Department of Agriculture Distinguished Service Award, 1963; International Federation of Library Associations special medal, 1972.

WRITINGS: (Compiler with others) *Library Literature*, American Library Association, 1934; *List of Books for Junior College Libraries*, American Library Association, 1938; (with Bernard M. Fry) *Guide to Information Sources in Space, Science and Technology*, Interscience, 1963; (with Kathleen Stebbins) *Personnel Administration in Libraries*, Scarecrow, 1966. Contributor to professional and scientific journals.

*   *   *

MOHRMANN, Christine A(ndrina) E(lisabeth) M(aria)   1903-

PERSONAL: Born August 1, 1903, in Groningen, The Netherlands; daughter of Benedictus (a merchant) and Agnes (Wreesman) Mohrmann. *Education:* Attended University of Utrecht, 1923-24; University of Nijmegen, doctoral degree in classical philology, 1932. *Religion:* Roman Catholic. *Home:* 40 St. Annastraat, Nijmegen, The Netherlands.

CAREER: University of Utrecht, Utrecht, The Netherlands, private university teacher, 1938-42, lecturer, 1942-53; University of Amsterdam, Amsterdam, The Netherlands, lecturer, 1946-55, professor of Vulgar Latin, early Christian Latin, medieval Latin, and late Latin, 1955—; University of Nijmegen, Nijmegen, The Netherlands, professor of early Christian Greek, Vulgar Latin, early Christian Latin, and medieval Latin, 1953—. *Member:* Comite International Permanent de Linguistes (secretary), Conseil International de la Philosophie et des Sciences Humaines (representative of CIPL), Koninklijke Nederlandse Akademie van Wetenschappen, Societe de Linguistique de Paris, Bayerische Akademie der Wissenschaften (Munich), Norske Videnskaps Akademi i Oslo, American Linguistic Society (honorary), Royal Irish Academy, Oesterreichische Akedemie Ohr Wissenschafte (Vienna). *Awards, honors:* Doctor honoris causa, University of Ireland, Universita cattolica di Milano, Universite de Nice, Universite de Gent.

WRITINGS: Die Altchristliche sondersprache in den Sermones des heiligen Augustin, Dekker & Van de Vegt (Utrecht), 1932; *Homerische spraakleer ten dienste der gymnasia*, Dekker & Van de Vegt, 1933; *Annus festivus: Het Kerkelijk jaar door een keuze uit oudchristelijke latijnsche schrijvers toegelicht*, Dekker & Van de Vegt-Standaard Boekhande (Nijmegen) 1935; (with Josef Schrijnen) *Studien zur Syntax der Briefe des heiligen Cyprian*, two volumes, Dekker & Van de Vegt, 1936-37; *De Struktur van het oudchristelijk Latin*, Dekker & Van de Vegt, 1938; (editor with P. J. Meertens and Win Roukens) Josef Schrijnen, *Collectania schrijnen*, Dekker & Van de Vegt, 1939.

(With J. Brinkhoff and R. Lagas) *Grieksche grammatika*, Schenk, 1943, 2nd edition, 1948; *Laatlatijn en middeleeuws latijn*, Het Spectrum (Utrecht), 1947; *Monumenta christiana: Bibliotheek van christelijke klassieken*, Volume I, Het Spectrum, 1948; (translator into Dutch) J. Marouzeau, *Inleiding tot het Latijn*, North-Holland Publishing, 1948. *Sint Augustinus: Preken voor het volk*, Het Spectrum, 1948.

Tertullianus, *Apologeticum en andere geschriften uit Tertullianus' voor-Montanistische tijd*, Het Spectrum, 1951; (editor, translator, and author of critical text with Bernard Botte) *L'Ordinaire de la Messe*, Editions du Cerf, 1953; *Latin vulgaire, Latin des chretiens, Latin medieval*, C. Klincksieck (Paris), 1955; (editor with D. Philberte Schmitz) Saint Benedict, *Sancti Benedicti: Regula monachorum*, Editions Maredsous, 1955; *Het Middeleeuws latijn als substraat van westeuropee cultuur*, Het Spectrum, 1956; *Liturgical Latin: Its Origins and Character* (three lectures), Catholic University of America Press, 1957; (with Frederik van der Meer) *Atlas van de oudchristelijke wereld*, Elsevier, 1958, translation by Mary F. Hedlund and H. H. Rowley published as *Atlas of the Early Christian World*, Thomas Nelson, 1958; *Etudes sur le latin des chretiens* (in French, German, and English), two volumes, Edizioni di Storia e Letteratura (Rome), 1958, 2nd edition, 1961.

The Latin of Saint Patrick (four lectures), Dublin Institute for Advanced Studies, 1961; *Jesus, Mary, and Joseph Daily Missal: Translation of the Prayers, Secrets, and Post-communions*, Benziger, 1962; (editor with Alf Sommerfelt and Joshua Whatmough) *Trends in European and American Linguistics 1930-1960*, Het Spectrum, 1962; *Etudes sur le latin des Chretiens*, Volume III, Edizione di Storia e Letteratura, 1965.

Contributor to *Winkler Prins Encyclopaedie, Lexikon fuer Theologie und Kirche,* and *Encyclopaedia Britannica.* Contributor of over 200 articles, studies, and book reviews, primarily on the language, history, and liturgy of the early Christian church to periodicals, scholarly series, and Festschriften. Editor, "Latinitas Christianorum Primaeva" (series), "Graecitas et Latinitas Christianorum Primaeva: Supplementa" (series), *Linguistic Bibliography,* and *Trends in Modern Linguistics.*

WORK IN PROGRESS: A commentary on the ordinary of the Mass; a handbook of early Christian Latin; a commentary on Book VIII of Augustine's *Confessions.*

SIDELIGHTS: Miss Mohrmann has traveled widely in Europe and North America, primarily to academic centers.

BIOGRAPHICAL/CRITICAL SOURCES: Sever Pop, *Christine Mohrmann: Notice biographique et bibliographique,* Centre International de Dialectologie Generale (Louvain), 1957; *Melanges offerts a Mademoiselle Christine Mohrmann* (includes extensive bibliography), Spectrum, 1963.

*   *   *

MONSELL, Helen Albee   1895-

PERSONAL: Born February 24, 1895, in Richmond, Va.; daughter of Robert Edwin and Anna (Brewster) Monsell. *Education:* University of Richmond, B.A., 1916; Columbia University, M.A., 1922. *Politics:* Independent. *Religion:* Presbyterian. *Home and office:* 3008-A Floyd Ave., Richmond, Va. 23221.

CAREER: High school teacher in Warrenton, Va., 1916-17; State Board of Education, Richmond, Va., secretary in high school division, 1917-20; Institute of Public Service, New York, N.Y., editorial assistant, 1920-22; Richmond College, Richmond, Va., 1922-61, began as assistant registrar, became registrar. Lecturer in children's literature, University of Richmond, 1948—, Richmond Professional Institute, 1956—. *Member:* Virginia Association of Collegiate Registrars (past president), Virginia Association for Preservation of Virginia Antiquities, Richmond League of Women Voters, Richmond Story League, Richmond Children's Books Council, Phi Beta Kappa (former chapter president). *Awards, honors:* Lit.D., University of Richmond, 1961.

WRITINGS—All published by Bobbs-Merrill, except as indicated: *The Secret of the Chestnut Tree,* 1936; *Boy of Old Virginia, Robert E. Lee,* 1937, reissued as *Robert E. Lee, Boy of Old Virginia,* 1960; *The Secret of the Gold Earring,* 1938; *Tom Jefferson: A Boy in Colonial Days,* 1939, reissued as *Tom Jefferson, Boy of Colonial Days,* 1962; *Lucy Lou Fights for Her Rights,* 1940; *Paddy's Christmas,* Knopf, 1942; *Young Stonewall, Tom Jackson,* 1942, reissued as *Tom Jackson, Young Stonewall,* 1961; *In Her Own Hands,* 1943; *Dolly Madison, Quaker Girl,* 1944; *Henry Clay, Mill Boy of the Slashes,* 1947; *The Mystery of Grandfather's Coat,* 1948; *John Marshall, Boy of Young America,* 1949; *Woodrow Wilson, Boy President,* 1950; *Susan Anthony, Girl Who Dared,* 1954, 2nd edition, 1960; *Her Own Way: The Story of Lottie Moon,* Broadman, 1958; *The Story of Cousin George,* Woman's Missionary Union, 1961; *Henry Clay, Young Kentucky Orator,* 1963; *With Patrick Henry's Help,* Broadman, 1966; *Nabby Comes to Lowell,* Golden Press, 1969.

Plays: *The Witch's Doll* (three-act), Dramatic Publishing, 1933; *Solo Flight* (three-act comedy), Dramatic Publishing, 1933; *The Moss Roses* (three-act comedy), Dramatic Publishing, 1933; *Powder Puff Girl* (three-act comedy), Baker's Plays, 1935; *Blue Ribbon Pie* (three-act comedy), Dramatic Publishing, c.1935; *His Just Desserts,* Dramatic Publishing, c.1935.

AVOCATIONAL INTERESTS: Art of story telling, collecting old and new editions of Mother Goose.

*   *   *

MOODY, Ralph Owen   1898-

PERSONAL: Born December 16, 1898, in East Rochester, N.H.; son of Charles Owen and Mary (Gould) Moody; married Edna Lucelle Hudgins, January 25, 1922; children: Charles Owen, Edna (Mrs. Philip Morales), Andrew. *Education:* Attended grade schools in New England and Colorado; studied specialized subjects at night schools. *Home:* 1124 Singingwood Ct., Walnut Creek, Calif. 94595. *Agent:* Russell & Volkening, Inc. 551 Fifth Ave., New York, N.Y. 10017.

CAREER: Rancher and cattle trader in West following World War I; gave up prospering ranch to enter business in Kansas City, Mo., and became an officer and district manager of B/G Foods, Inc. (national restaurant chain) in Missouri and later in California; retired in 1959 and now devotes entire time to writing. Chairman, Burlingame (Calif.) Library Commission. Member of advisory board, College of the Holy Names, 1958—. *Member:* Western Writers of America (former secretary-treasurer), California Writers Club (former president), Bohemian Club (San Francisco; co-chairman of library committee).

WRITINGS: Little Britches: Father and I Were Ranchers, Norton, 1950, reissued as *Little Britches,* 1962, abridged edition published as *Little Britches: Man of the Family,* edited by Egbert W. Nieman, Harcourt, 1953; *Man of the Family,* Norton, 1951; *The Fields of Home,* Norton, 1953; *Kit Carson and the Wild Frontier,* Random House, 1955 (published in England as *Kit Carson,* E. M. Hale, 1955); *The Home Ranch,* Norton, 1956; *Geronimo, Wolf of the Warpath,* Random House, 1958; *Riders of the Pony Express,* Houghton, 1958; *Wells Fargo,* Houghton, 1961; *Mary Emma & Company,* Norton, 1961; *Silver and Lead: The Birth and Death of a Mining Town,* Macmillan, 1962; *Shaking the Nickel Bush,* Norton, 1962; *American Horses,* Houghton, 1962; *The Dry Divide,* Norton, 1963; *Come on Seabiscuit,* Houghton, 1963; *The Old Trails West,* Crowell, 1963; *The Valley of the Moon* (play; first produced in San Francisco at the Bohemian Grove, July 30, 1966), Bohemian Club, 1966; *Stagecoach West,* Crowell, 1967; *Horse of a Different Color: Reminiscenses* [sic] *of a Kansas Drover* (autobiography), Norton, 1968.

WORK IN PROGRESS: The Horse in North America.

SIDELIGHTS: When he was over fifty Moody enrolled in a beginner's short story class at a San Francisco night school, ostensibly to help his daughter with a high school writing course. He admits now to another reason: "From the time I was old enough to read a story I'd wanted to write one, but had never tried, too conscious of my lack of education." When his first paper was returned the teacher had written on it, "Don't let this go for a short story—expand into a book."

The book was *Little Britches.* "I'd been a constant reader since childhood," Moody says, "led into it by my mother reading aloud to the family. And strangely, I found that I'd learned to write from reading."

His feeling for the West dates from 1906 when his family moved from a New England mill town to a Colorado ranch. At ten he had his first job away from home, as waterboy on a big cattle ranch. After his father's death the family returned East to live in Medford, Mass., but "I was banished to my grandfather's farm in Maine because I couldn't learn to be a city boy.

"I was fortunate financially (later in the West) and was anxious to marry my Medford sweetheart, but she refused to marry a farmer, so I went to Kansas City to find out if I could make a living for a family in town. I was doubly fortunate. I got the girl, still have her, and found I could get along all right in town.

"In the late 1940's we moved to California, and our daughter signed up for a course in creative writing. She came to me one evening for help on a story [and I told her] that there was a night school around the corner from one of my shops in San Francisco, that I'd drop around and see if they offered any writing courses. If they would, I'd join a class and see if I could learn anything that would help her. . . .

"My goal in writing is to leave a record of the rural way of life in this country during the early part of the twentieth century, and to point up the values of that era which I feel that we, as a people, are letting slip away from us."

BIOGRAPHICAL/CRITICAL SOURCES: New York Times Book Review, August 6, 1967, October 27, 1968; *Best Sellers,* October 1, 1968.

*   *   *

MOOMAW, Ira W.   1894-

PERSONAL: Born July 8, 1894, in Canton, Ohio; son of Peter P. (a farmer) and Alice Moomaw; married Mabel E. Winger (a teacher); children: David Robert, Richard Wilbur. *Education:* Manchester College, North Manchester, Ind., B.Sc., 1920; Ohio State University, M.Sc., 1922, Ph.D., 1933, postdoctoral study, 1939-40. *Politics:* Republican. *Religion:* Protestant.

CAREER: Went to India as an agricultural missionary for Church of the Brethren in 1934, and served there in the agriculture education field, 1934-41; Agricultural Missions, Inc. (non-denominational agency), New York, 1955-63, became consultant. *Member:* International Association of Agricultural Economists, Rural Sociological Society, Gamma Sigma Delta. *Awards, honors:* Kaisar-I-Hind Gold Medal from government of India for public service.

WRITINGS: Education and Village Improvement, Oxford University Press, 1938; *The Farmer Speaks,* Oxford University Press, 1942; *Deep Furrows,* Agricultural Missions, 1958; *To Hunger No More: A Positive Reply to Human Need,* Friendship, 1963; *Crusade against Hunger: The Dramatic Story of the Worldwide Antipoverty Crusades of the Churches,* Harper, 1966; *The Challenge of Hunger: A Program for More Effective Foreign Aid,* Praeger, 1966; *What Future for Foreign Aid?,* Friendship, 1966; *Vietnam Summons,* Brethren Service Commission, Church of the Brethren, 1967.

WORK IN PROGRESS: Researching and writing a book, *Best Hope of Earth.*

SIDELIGHTS: Moomaw's field studies on methods of providing food for the world's hungry have carried him through much of Asia, Africa, and Latin America. His thesis: the efforts likely to succeed in the long run are those which "help people to help themselves."

*   *   *

MOORE, Alma Chesnut   1901-

PERSONAL: Born September 18, 1901, in Washington, D.C.; daughter of Victor King and Olive B. (Spohr) Chesnut; married H. Moore, 1931 (divorced); children: Peter, Anthony, Christopher. *Education:* Goucher College, A.B., 1922. *Politics:* Republican. *Religion:* Presbyterian. *Home:* 5 Rockledge Rd., Hartsdale, N.Y.

CAREER: Baltimore American, Baltimore, Md., reporter and feature writer, 1922-25; American National Red Cross, public relations, 1926-28; *American Forests,* member of editorial staff, 1928-29; *Pittsburgh Press,* Pittsburgh, Pa., woman's editor, 1929-30; *Transradio Press,* woman's editor, 1935-41; free-lance writer and editor, 1945—.

WRITINGS: How to Clean Everything, Simon and Schuster, 1952, revised edition, 1961; *The Friendly Forests,* Viking, 1954, 2nd revised edition, 1968; *Betty Bissell Book of Home Cleaning,* Bantam, 1959; *The Grasses,* Macmillan, 1960.

Writer of radio program, "Women Make the News," and of free-lance articles for Sunday newspapers, NEA Service, Science Service, and magazines.

AVOCATIONAL INTERESTS: Conservation of natural resources.

*   *   *

MOORE, Chauncey O.   1895-1965

PERSONAL: Born February 22, 1895, in Protem, Mo.; son of George W. (a farmer and rancher) and Mary Ann (McIntosh) Moore; married Ethel Pauline Perry, February 9, 1922. *Education:* University of Oklahoma, B.S., 1925; Columbia University, M.A., 1929. *Politics:* Republican. *Religion:* Presbyterian. *Home:* 1821 East 31st Place, Tulsa, Okla. 74105.

CAREER: Superintendent of schools in Oklahoma towns, 1925-35, 1941-44; Federal Writers Project, Oklahoma supervisor, 1936-37; in small loan business, 1945-47; chief probation officer, Tulsa County, Okla., 1947-56; acting postmaster, Tulsa, Okla., 1956-58; Burlingame Realtors, Tulsa, Okla., salesman and agent, 1958-65. Organizer and director, Oklahoma State Folk Festivals, 1936-39. Chairman, Tulsa Children's Christmas Placement Bureau, 1947-65; member of board, Tulsa Legal Aid Bureau, 1955-56; secretary, Tulsa County Health and Welfare Association,

1956-57. *Member:* National Institute of Real Estate Brokers, Oklahoma Real Estate Association, Oklahoma State Historical Society, Tulsa County Historical Society, Phi Delta Kappa, Sigma Mu Sigma, Masons.

WRITINGS: (Compiler and editor with wife, Ethel Pauline Perry Moore) *Ballads and Folk Songs of the Southwest* (text and music), University of Oklahoma Press, 1964.

WORK IN PROGRESS: A biographical study of early pioneers of Oklahoma.

SIDELIGHTS: Moore and his wife spent more than twenty-five years collecting the folk songs sung by Oklahomans.

(Died April 11, 1965)

* * *

MOORE, Douglas Stuart 1893-1969

PERSONAL: Born August 10, 1893, in Cutchogue, N.Y.; son of Stuart Hull and Myra (Drake) Moore; married Emily Bailey, September 16, 1920; children: Mary (Mrs. Bradford Kelleher), Sarah. *Education:* Yale University, B.A., 1915, Mus.B., 1917; studied composition with Parker and Bloch in America, and with D'Indy at Schola Cantorum, Paris, France. *Home:* 464 Riverside Dr., New York, N.Y. 10027.

CAREER: Cleveland Museum of Art, Cleveland, Ohio, curator of music, 1921-25; Columbia University, New York, N.Y., associate, department of music, 1926-27, assistant professor, 1927-28, associate professor, 1928-40, professor, 1940-43, MacDowell Professor of Music, 1943-62, executive officer of department, 1940-62, professor emeritus, 1962-69. Composer. Guest conductor with Cleveland Symphony Orchestra, New York Philharmonic Orchestra, and Manhattan Orchestra. *Military service:* U.S. Navy, 1917-19; became lieutenant junior grade.

MEMBER: American Academy of Arts and Letters (president, 1959-62), National Institute of Arts and Letters (president, 1946-52), Century Association (New York). *Awards, honors:* Pulitzer traveling scholarship, 1925, for "Four Museum Pieces"; Guggenheim fellowship, 1933; honorable mention, New York Critics Circle, 1947, for "Symphony in A Major"; Pulitzer Prize in music, 1951, for "Giants in the Earth"; New York Critics Circle Award, 1958, for "The Ballad of Baby Doe"; Henry Hadley Medal, National Association of Composers and Conductors, 1960; other publication and teaching awards. Honorary Mus.Dr., Cincinnati Conservatory of Music, 1946, University of Rochester, 1948, Yale University, 1955, Adelphi University, 1958; D.H.L., Columbia University, 1963.

WRITINGS: Listening to Music, Norton, 1932, revised edition, 1963; *Madrigal to Modern Music,* Norton, 1942, revised edition published as *A Guide to Musical Styles: From Madrigal to Modern Music,* 1962; (contributor) Jacques Barzun, editor, *A History of the Faculty of Philosophy: Columbia University,* Columbia University Press, 1957.

Musical Compositions: "Four Museum Pieces" (symphony), 1922; "The Ballade of William Sycamore" (chamber music), 1926; "Pageant of P. T. Barnum" (symphonic suite), first produced in Cleveland, Ohio, April 15, 1926; "Moby Dick" (symphonic poem), 1928; "Sonata for Violin and Piano," 1929; "A Symphony of Autumn," 1930; "Overture on an American Tune," 1931; "Quartet for Strings," 1933; "Simon Legree" (choral), poem by Vachel Lindsay, first performed in 1937; "Perhaps to Dream" (choral), words by Stephen Vincent Benet, first performed in 1937; *Dedication: Motet for Six Voices* (first performed in 1937), poem by Archibald MacLeish, Arrow Music Press, 1938; *Adam Was My Grandfather,* poem by Benet, Galaxy Music, 1938; *The Devil and Daniel Webster* (folk opera in one act; first produced in New York, N.Y., May 18, 1939), book by Benet, Boosey & Hawkes, 1943; *Prayer for the United Nations,* vocal score by Benet, H. W. Gray, 1943; *Three Sonnets of John Donne: Set to Music for High Voice and Piano,* G. Schirmer, 1944; *In Memoriam* (for large orchestra), [New York], 1944; "Symphony in A Major," first produced in Paris, France, May 5, 1946, first American production, Los Angeles, Calif., January 16, 1947; *Quintet for Winds,* G. Schirmer, 1948; "White Wings" (opera), based on stage play by Philip Barry, first produced in Hartford, Connecticut, February 2, 1949; *Farm Journal: Suite for Chamber Orchestra,* C. Fischer, 1950; "Giants in the Earth" (opera), first produced in New York, N.Y., March 28, 1951; *The Ballad of Baby Doe* (opera in two acts; first produced in Central City, Colorado, July 7, 1956), libretto by John Latouche, Program Publishing, 1958; "Gallantry" (one-act musical), text by Arnold Sundgaard, first produced in New York, N.Y., March 15, 1958; *Wings of the Dove* (opera in six scenes; based on novel by Henry James; first produced by New York City Opera, October 12, 1961), libretto by Ethan Ayer, G. Schirmer, 1961; *Carry Nation* (opera in two acts; first produced in Lawrence, Kansas, April 28, 1966), libretto by William North Jayme, Galaxy Music, 1968.

Also composer of "The Headless Horseman" (high school operetta; text by Benet), "The Emperor's New Clothes" (children's opera), "Puss in Boots" (children's operetta), "The Greenfield Christmas Tree" (a Christmas entertainment); numerous other works for orchestra and chorus, chamber music, and musical scores for theatre and films.

BIOGRAPHICAL/CRITICAL SOURCES: W. H. Mellers, *Music in a New Found Land: Themes and Developments in the History of American Music,* Barrie & Rockliff, 1964, Knopf, 1965.

* * *

MOORE, E(velyn) Garth 1906-

PERSONAL: Born February 6, 1906, in London, England; son of Robert Ernest (a judge) and Hilda Mary (Letts) Moore. *Education:* Trinity College, Cambridge, B.A., 1927, M.A., 1931; Gray's Inn, Barrister-at-Law, 1928; Cuddesdon Theological College, theological student, 1962. *Office:* Corpus Christi College, Cambridge University, Cambridge, England; and 1 Raymond Buildings, Gray's Inn, London W.C. 1, England.

CAREER: Called to bar, 1928, and practiced in London, England, and on South Eastern Circuit; justice of the peace and deputy chairman of Huntingdonshire Quarter Sessions, 1948-63, of Cambridgeshire Quarter Sessions, 1950-63. Church of England, chancellor, vicar-general, and official principal of diocese of Southwark, 1948—, of Durham, 1954—, of Gloucester, 1957—; ordained priest, 1962; also currently official principal of archdeaconries of Southwark, Lewisham, Kingston-on-Thames, and Ely. Corpus Christi College, Cambridge University, Cambridge, England, fellow and director of studies in law, 1947-69; Council of Legal Education, lecturer in evidence, 1952—, in criminal procedure, 1957-69. Former tutor of Gray's Inn, lector of Trinity College, Cambridge University, and visiting professor at University of Khartoum. *Military service:* British Army, 1939-45; served with Royal Artillery and on staff of Judge Advocate General; overseas duty in Middle East and Greece; became lieutenant colonel.

WRITINGS: Kenny's Cases on Criminal Law, 8th edition, with supplement, Cambridge University Press, 1935; (contributor) *Halsbury's Laws of England, Volume 13: Ecclesiastical Law,* 3rd edition, Butterworth & Co., 1955; *An Introduction to English Canon Law,* Oxford University Press, 1967. Contributor to legal, theological, and other journals.

WORK IN PROGRESS: A book on the morality of law.

AVOCATIONAL INTERESTS: Psychical research, architecture, furniture.

*   *   *

MOORE, Ethel Pauline Perry   1902-

PERSONAL: Born July 31, 1902, in Gainesville, Tex.; daughter of John Lawrence (a merchant) and Jennie Mae (Clapp) Perry; married Chauncey O. Moore (a realtor), February 9, 1922 (died April 11, 1965). *Education:* University of Oklahoma, student, 1923-26, received B.A. and M.A.; University of Michigan, B.A. in L.S., 1949. *Politics:* Republican. *Religion:* Presbyterian. *Home:* 1821 East 31st Pl., Tulsa, Okla. 74105.

CAREER: Prague High School, Prague, Okla., English teacher and librarian, 1927-32; Will Rogers High School, Tulsa, Okla., librarian, 1946-68. *Member:* American Library Association, National Education Association, Southwestern Library Association, Oklahoma Library Association, Oklahoma Education Association, Oklahoma State Historical Society, Tulsa County Historical Society, Delta Kappa Gamma.

WRITINGS: (Compiler and editor with husband, Chauncey O. Moore) *Ballads and Folk Songs of the Southwest* (text and music), University of Oklahoma Press, 1964.

WORK IN PROGRESS: A biographical study of some early day pioneers of Oklahoma, those of the Indian Territory in particular.

*   *   *

MOORE, Everett T(homson)   1909-

PERSONAL: Born August 6, 1909, in Los Angeles, Calif.; son of Charles B. (an educator) and Caroline (Thomson) Moore; married Jean Macalister (a librarian), June 23, 1951. *Education:* Occidental College, B.A., 1931; Harvard University, M.A., 1933; University of California, Berkeley, Certificate of Librarianship, 1939. *Home:* 11320 Joffre St., Los Angeles, Calif. 90049. *Office:* Library, University of California, 405 Hilgard Ave., Los Angeles, Calif. 90024.

CAREER: University of California Library, Berkeley, librarian in reference and acquisitions department, 1939-41; University of Illinois Library, Urbana, reference assistant, 1941-42; University of California Library, Los Angeles, head of reference department, 1946-61, assistant university librarian and member of faculty of School of Library Service, 1961—. Fulbright lecturer in Japan, 1967-68; visiting faculty member at Keio University, Tokyo, Japan, and at University of Washington, Seattle. Member of board of directors, American Civil Liberties Union of Southern California, 1961—. Trustee, Public Information Service, 1970—; trustee and vice-president, Freedom to Read Foundation, 1970—. *Military service:* U.S. Army, 1942-46; became major; received Military Merit Medal (Philippines). *Member:* American Library Association (member of coun-

cil, 1962-72; chairman of publishing board, 1966-72), California Library Association (president, 1964).

WRITINGS: (With Richard Harwell) *The Arizona University Library: Report of a Survey of the Library.* American Library Association, 1959; *Issues of Freedom in American Libraries,* American Library Association, 1964. Editor, *Newsletter on Intellectual Freedom,* American Library Association, 1960-61.

*   *   *

MOORE, Francis Edward   1898-

PERSONAL: Born October 24, 1898, in Bridgewater, Mass.; son of Thomas and Winifred (Spicer) Moore; married Christine Elizabeth Kratz (a teacher), September 15, 1928; children: Francis E. *Education:* Boston University, B.B.A., 1923. *Home:* 101 Hollingsworth Ave., Braintree, Mass. 02184; and Maple Crest Farm, East Wolfeboro, N.H. 03894.

CAREER: Certified public accountant. Lybrand, Ross Bros. & Montgomery, Boston, Mass., 1923—, now account manager. Charter member, National Council for Development of Small Business. Member of executive committee, Huggins Hospital, Wolfeboro, N.H. *Member:* American Institute of Certified Public Accountants, National Association of Accountants, American Accounting Association, Data Processing Association, Massachusetts Society of Certified Public Accountants.

WRITINGS: (With Arthur Wellington Holmes) *Audit Practice Case,* 6th edition, Irwin, 1964; (with Howard F. Stettler) *Accounting Systems for Management Control,* Irwin, 1963.†

*   *   *

MOORE, Harry Estill   1897-

PERSONAL: Born January 4, 1897, in Bethany (Lickskillet), La.; son of James Francis and Mary Ellen (Pace) Moore; married Bernice Milburn (associate director of Hogg Foundation at University of Texas), November 27, 1924. *Education:* University of Texas, B.J., 1927, M.A., 1934; University of North Carolina, Ph.D., 1937. *Politics:* Democratic. *Home:* 1215 West 22½ St., Austin, Tex. 78712. *Office:* Department of Sociology, University of Texas, Austin, Tex. 78712.

CAREER: University of Texas, Austin, beginning, 1937, began as assistant professor, became professor of sociology, 1955. Director, J. W. Millard Associates; lecturer, U.S. Air Force Chaplains Instructional Program; consultant, Southern Educational Foundation. *Military service:* U.S. Army, Medical Corps, World War I. *Member:* American Sociological Association (council member, 1950-53), Southwestern Sociological Association (president, 1949-50), Southwestern Social Science Association.

WRITINGS: (With Howard W. Odum) *American Regionalism,* Henry Holt, 1938; (with Ernest R. Groves) *Introductory Sociology,* Longmans, Green, 1940; *Nine Help Themselves,* Southwestern Cooperative Program in Educational Administration, 1955; *Tornadoes over Texas,* University of Texas Press, 1958; (with Marvin Layman and Donald Mischer) *Attitudes and Knowledge Concerning Fall-Out Shelters in Austin, Texas,* Office for Civil Defense, Department of Defense, 1962; *Before the Wind,* National Academy of Sciences—National Research Council, 1963; *... And the Winds Blew,* Hogg Foundation for Mental Health, University of Texas, 1964. Contributor to sociological journals. Editor, *Southwestern Social Science Quarterly*, 1956—.

WORK IN PROGRESS: Studies on newspaper coverage of Kennedy assassination, and on cultural characteristics of areas subject to repeated danger.

AVOCATIONAL INTERESTS: Collecting elephant figurines.

* * *

MOORE, Jessie Eleanor   1886-19(?)

PERSONAL: Born December 1, 1886, in Newark, N.J.; daughter of Edwin M. (an accountant) and Jessie (Chandler) Moore. *Education:* Newark Normal School (now Kean College of New Jersey), Diploma, 1907; Columbia University, B.S., 1919, M.A., 1922; Union Theological Seminary, New York, N.Y., B.D., 1943. *Politics:* Republican. *Home:* 66 Clark Ave., Ocean Grove, N.J.

CAREER: Kindergarten teacher in Newark, N.J., public schools, 1907-18; Columbia University, Teachers College, New York, N.Y., supervisor of student practice teaching, 1921-23; Pilgrim Press, Boston, Mass., editor, 1930-47; Methodist Publishing House, Nashville, Tenn., assistant editor, 1947-57; free-lance writer and editor, and superintendent of children's work at First Methodist Church, Asbury Park, N.J., beginning 1957.

WRITINGS: The Cradle Roll Manual, Methodist Publishing House, 1921; *The Little Child and His Crayon*, Abingdon, 1922; *Vacation Church School Manual*, Bethany, 1924; *The Missionary Education of Beginners*, Missionary Education Movement, 1927; *First Bible Stories*, Nelson, 1929; *Bible Stories to Read*, Nelson, 1929; *Experiences in the Church School Kindergarten*, Pilgrim Press, 1935; (with Frances Weld Danielson) *Three Years Old: For the Nursery Class of the Church School*, revised edition, Pilgrim Press, 1936; (co-author) *Prayers for Little Children*, Rand McNally, 1937; *Welcome House*, Friendship, 1939; *A Bell for Baby Brother*, Friendship, 1944; *Children's Prayers for Every Day*, Abingdon-Cokesbury, 1949; (compiler) *Eyes for Eric, and Other Stories*, Abingdon, 1963; (compiler) *Valuable Kindling, and Other Stories*, Abingdon, 1963; *Songs in Our Bible*, Judson Press, 1966. Writer of articles on child guidance for Methodist Publishing House, beginning, 1947.

(Deceased)

* * *

MOORE, John Robert   1890-1973

PERSONAL: Born July 27, 1890, in Pueblo, Colo.; son of Matthew Henry (a minister) and Mary Eugenia (Thomas) Moore; married Alice A. Beer, August 26, 1924; children: John Robert, Jr., Joyce Elizabeth (Mrs. Robert V. Gouwens), Katherine Lea (Mrs. William E. Wilson III). *Education:* University of Missouri, A.B., 1910, A.M., 1914; Harvard University, Ph.D., 1917. *Politics:* Independent. *Religion:* Episcopalian. *Home:* 6539 Lake Rd. W., Madison, Ohio 44057.

CAREER: Teacher of English, 1910; Indiana University, Bloomington, associate professor, 1922-29, professor of English, 1929-56, library consultant in Augustan literature, 1944-61, Distinguished Service Professor, 1956-61, professor emeritus, 1961-73. Professor at Shrivenham American University in England, 1945; visiting professor at Duke University, University of West Virginia, University of North Carolina, Kent State University; Berry College,

and University of Alberta. Also taught at Southwestern University and University of Texas. Lecturer in United States, Canada, Great Britain, and Japan. *Military service:* U.S. Army, 1918; became sergeant. *Member:* Royal Society of Arts, Bibliographical Society (London), Oxford Bibliographical Society, Bibliographical Society of America, Modern Humanities Research Association, Modern Language Association of America, Shakespeare Association of America. *Awards, honors:* Senior fellow, Huntington Library, 1950-51; American Philosophical Society research grant, 1955-56; Newberry Library fellowship, 1961-62.

WRITINGS: Symphonies and Song, Four Seas Co., 1923; *The Transformation of Bottom*, Indiana University, 1926; (editor) *Representative English Dramas*, Ginn, 1929; (editor) *Representative Essays, English and American*, Ginn, 1930; (reviser) Howard Judson Hall, *Types of Poetry Exclusive of the Drama*, Ginn, 1931; *Daniel Defoe and Modern Economic Theory*, Indiana University Bookstore, 1935; *Defoe in the Pillory and Other Studies*, Indiana University Bookstore, 1939; *Defoe's Sources for Robert Drury's Journal*, Indiana University, 1943, revised edition, Haskell House 1972; (editor) Daniel Defoe, *An Essay on the Regulation of the Press*, Luttrell Society (Oxford), 1948; *The Canon of Defoe's Writings* (pamphlet), Bibliographical Society, 1956; *Daniel Defoe: Citizen of the Modern World*, University of Chicago Press, 1958; *A Checklist of the Writings of Daniel Defoe*, Indiana University Press, 1960, 2nd edition, Shoe String, 1971; *John Robert Moore: A Bibliography*, Indiana University Foundation, 1961; (editor) Daniel Defoe, *A Brief History of the Poor Palestine Refugees*, Augustan Society Reprints, 1964.

Wrote words for Shrivenham American University song, 1945, and "Song of the White Horse Vale," Boosey & Hawkes, 1946. Contributor to *Collier's Encyclopedia, New Century Cyclopedia of Names*, and *World Scope Encyclopedia;* contributor of more than 180 articles to professional journals in United States, Great Britain, Germany, and Egypt.

WORK IN PROGRESS: A critical biography of James Macpherson; a revised and enlarged edition of *A Checklist of the Writings of Daniel Defoe;* co-editing a new edition of *Defoe's History of the Union;* a dozen articles on Defoe and other writers of the early eighteenth century.

SIDELIGHTS: Moore was official spokesman at the tercentenary celebration of the birth of Daniel Defoe in Great Britain, 1960. He was especially noted for tracing and identifying many of that prolific writer's works. He also kept diaries of fifteen of his most significant trips—those that throw light on human history and literature—intending to use them in future writings.

(Died July 18, 1973)

* * *

MOORE, Walter Lane   1905-

PERSONAL: Born June 22, 1905, in Quitman, La.; son of Richard Tubbs (a farmer) and Clara (Lane) Moore; married Miriam McCall, August 1, 1927; children: Carol (Mrs. Albert Henry III), Martha, Walter, Jr. *Education:* Attended Louisiana Polytechnic Institute, Southwestern Baptist Theological Seminary, and studied briefly at other universities and at Union Theological Seminary, New York, N.Y. *Home:* 2668 Riverview Rd., Macon, Ga. 31204.

CAREER: Baptist clergyman. Worked as missionary in

Havana, Cuba; worked as a minister in Waynesboro, Ga., 1932-37, Cedartown, Ga., 1938-47, Waycross, Ga., 1947-51, and Medidan, Miss., 1951-59; Vineville Baptist Church, Macon, Ga., minister, 1959-70. Member of executive committee, Southern Baptist Convention, 1958-59; president, Georgia Baptist Convention, 1968-70. Trustee of Southwestern Baptist Theological Seminary, 1947-51, of Mercer University, 1947-51, 1960-65. *Awards, honors:* D.D., Mercer University, 1946.

WRITINGS: Courage and Confidence from the Bible, Prentice-Hall, 1951; *Outlines for Preaching*, Broadman, 1965. Contributor to *Christian Herald*, *Christian Index*, and various publications of Southern Baptist Convention.

*   *   *

MOORHOUSE, Hilda Vansittart
(Jane Vansittart)

PERSONAL: Born in Exmouth, Devonshire, England; daughter of Herbert Dobbie (a tea planter in India) and Agatha (Dobbie) Vansittart; married Brian Moorhouse, April 30, 1935; children: Michael, Ann. *Education:* Educated in English schools. *Religion:* Anglican. *Home:* Doneraile, Salterton Rd., Exmouth, Devonshire, England. *Agent:* Eric Glass Ltd., 28 Berkeley Sq., London W.1, England.

CAREER: Taught English in West Indies during World War II; lived at other periods in Shanghai, China, Ceylon, and the Azores. *Member:* Devon Association, Devon and Exeter Institution. *Awards, honors:* Barbara Cartland Award for best historical novel of 1963, for *The Devil's Wind*.

WRITINGS—All under name Jane Vansittart: So Fair a House, R. Hale, 1961; *Prelude to Mutiny*, R. Hale, 1962; *The Devil's Wind*, R. Hale, 1963; (editor) John Haddy James, *Surgeon James's Journal, 1815*, Cassell, 1964; (editor) *Katherine Fry's Book*, Hodder & Stoughton, 1966; *The So Beloved*, Hodder & Stoughton, 1967; *Adventures of the Mayflower*, R. Hale., 1970; *The Silver Swan*, R. Hale, 1971. Writer of short stories and verse.

WORK IN PROGRESS: An historical novel set in West Cornwall in 1810.

SIDELIGHTS: Mrs. Moorhouse used many letters of the period, 1840-60 and her grandmother's diaries as source material for her first two historical novels. A film script for *The Devil's Wind* has been written by Anthony Squires and Basil Appleby.

BIOGRAPHICAL/CRITICAL SOURCES: Times Literary Supplement, January 26, 1967.

*   *   *

MORAES, Frank Robert 1907-1974
(Ariel)

PERSONAL: Born November 12, 1907, in Bombay, India; son of Anthony Xavier (a civil engineer) and Henrietta (Furtado) Moraes; married Beryl DeMonte, April 19, 1937; children: Dom. *Education:* Attended St. Xavier's College, Bombay, India; Oxford University, M.A.; Lincoln's Inn, Barrister-at-Law. *Home:* D-3, Mafatlal Park, Bhulabhai Desai Rd., Bombay 26, India. *Office: Indian Express*, Mathura Rd., New Delhi 1, India.

CAREER: Times of India, assistant editor, 1938-46 (war correspondent in China and Burma, 1942-45), deputy editor, 1949-50, editor, 1950-57; *Times of Ceylon*, editor, 1946-

48; *National Standard*, editor, 1950; *Indian Express*, New Delhi, India, editor-in-chief, 1957-73. Member of Indian Cultural Delegation to China, 1952; sheriff of Bombay, 1961-62. *Member:* Press Guild of India (president), Authors Guild of the Authors League of America, Rotary Club of Bombay (past president), Cricket Club of India, Willingdon Club (Bombay), Delhi Gymkhana.

WRITINGS: (With Robert Stimson) *Introduction to India*, Oxford University Press, 1942; *The Story of India*, Noble Publishing House (Bombay), 1942; *Report on Mao's China*, Macmillan, 1953; *Jawaharlal Nehru: A Biography*, Macmillan, 1956; *Sir Purshotamdas Thakurdas*, Asia Publishing House (Bombay), 1957; *Yonder One World: A Study of Asia and the West*, Macmillan, 1958; *The Revolt in Tibet*, Macmillan, 1960; *India Today*, Macmillan, 1960; *Nehru: Sunlight and Shadow*, Jaico Publishing House (Bombay), 1964; *The Importance of Being Black*, Macmillan, 1965; (chairman of editorial board) *Science, Philosophy, and Culture*, Asia Publishing House (New York), 1968; *Witness to an Era: India 1920 to the Present Day*, Weidenfeld & Nicolson, 1973, Holt, 1974; (editor with Edward Howe) *India*, introduction by John Kenneth Galbraith, McGraw, 1974 (published in England as *John Kenneth Galbraith Introduces India*, Deutsch, 1974); *Men and Memories*, International Scholarly Book Service, 1974.

BIOGRAPHICAL/CRITICAL SOURCES: New York Times, May 4, 1974.

(Died May 2, 1974)

*   *   *

MORE, Jasper 1907-

PERSONAL: Born July 31, 1907, in London, England; son of Thomas Jasper Mytton and Norah (Browne) More; married Clare Mary Hope-Edwardes, February 10, 1944. *Education:* King's College, Cambridge, B.A., 1929. *Politics:* Conservative. *Religion:* Church of England. *Home:* Linley Hall, Bishops Castle, Shropshire, England.

CAREER: Called to the Bar, Lincoln's Inn, 1930, Middle Temple, 1931; barrister-at-law, 1929-39; British Ministry of Aircraft production, staff member, 1940-42; Shropshire County Council, member, 1958—; member of Parliament, 1960—. *Military service:* British Army, legal officer with Central Mediterranean Forces, 1943-45, legal adviser to military government of Dodecanese Islands, 1946; became lieutenant colonel. *Member:* Travellers' Club, Brooks's Club.

WRITINGS: The Saving of Income Tax, Surtax and Death Duties, Butterworth & Co., 1935, 2nd edition, 1937; *The Land of Italy*, Batsford, 1949, 3rd edition, revised, Batsford, 1953, Norton, 1962; *The Mediterranean*, Hastings House, 1956.

AVOCATIONAL INTERESTS: Shooting, fishing, riding, building, travel, and landscape gardening.†

*   *   *

MOREHEAD, Albert H(odges) 1909-1966
(Turner Hodges)

PERSONAL: Born August 7, 1909, in Chattanooga, Tenn.; son of Albert H. (a musician) and Bianca (Noa) Morehead; married Loy Claudon (an editor), January 21, 1939; children: Andrew Turner, Philip David. *Education:* Harvard University, student, 1925-27. *Politics:* Democrat. *Religion:* Presbyterian. *Home:* 444 East 52nd St., New York, N.Y. 10022. *Office:* 446 East 52nd St., New York, N.Y. 10022.

CAREER: Newspaperman in Lexington, Ky., 1922-23, Chattanooga, Tenn., 1923-35, Chicago, Ill., 1925-26, Cleveland, Ohio, 1927, Newton, Mass., 1927-28, and New York, N.Y., 1928; worked as automobile salesman and at various other jobs, 1929-30; professional gambler, 1930-32; *Bridge World,* New York, N.Y., staff writer, beginning 1932, editor, 1934-38, publisher, 1943-46. Also bridge editor of *New York Times,* 1935-63; staff writer for *Redbook,* 1943-45, *Coronet,* 1945-48, *Cosmopolitan,* 1948-52, and columnist, King Features Syndicate, 1949-53. Author and editor. Vice-president of Kem Playing Cards, Inc., 1934-37, John C. Winston Co., 1946-48. Consultant to Services of Supply, U.S. War Department, 1942-45; consultant on games to U.S. Playing Card Co., and to publishers. National Lexicographic Board, general editor, beginning 1950, president, 1952-59, chairman of board, beginning 1961. *Member:* American Society of Composers, Authors and Publishers, American Contract Bridge League (president, 1934; chairman, 1944-45; honorary member, beginning 1946).

WRITINGS: Outline of the Culbertson System, Bridge World, 1934; *How to Lead and Play,* Bridge World, 1934; *Asking Bids,* Bridge World, 1936; (with A. Sobel) *Jo-Jotte,* U.S. Playing Card Co., 1937; (with Ely Culbertson) *Five-Suit Bridge,* Bridge World, 1938; (with D. B. Tansill) *So You're Going to Sell,* Winston, 1938; (with Josephine Culbertson) *Contract Bridge for Beginners,* Winston, 1938; (with Alfred Sheinwold) *Beginners' Course,* Autobridge, 1939.

(With William J. Huske) *Teach Yourself Bridge,* Culbertson's Bridge Institute, 1940; *Bridge Today,* New York Times, 1942; *Official Book of Contract Bridge,* Winston, 1942; *Bridge the Expert Way,* Bridge World Accessories, 1943; *Gin-Rummy,* Greystone Press, 1943; *The Pocket Book of Games,* Pocket Books, 1944; *The Modern Hoyle,* Winston, 1944; (with Geoffrey Mott-Smith) *Games for Two,* Winston, 1947; (with Mott-Smith) *Hoyle with Official Rules,* Grosset & Dunlap, 1947; *1947 Bridge,* New York Times, 1947; (with Mott-Smith) *The New Quiz Book,* Penguin, 1948; (with Mott-Smith) *Signet Crossword Puzzle Book,* New American Library, 1948; (with E. Culbertson) *Contract Bridge for Everyone,* Winston, 1948; *Adultery,* University Press, 1948; (with Alfred Drake) *Gin Rummy and Canasta,* Avon Books, 1949; (with Mott-Smith) *Canasta Made Easy,* Greystone Press, 1949; (with Mott-Smith) *The Complete Book of Solitaire and Patience Games,* Longmans, Green, 1949 (published in England as *Complete Book of Patience,* Faber, 1950).

Bidding Conventions of 1951-52, New York Times, 1951; (with Richard L. Frey) *According to Hoyle,* Fawcett, 1956; *How to Win at Poker,* Matthews, 1957; *Bidding Conventions of 1959-60,* New York Times, 1959.

Digest of the New Laws of 1963, New York Times, 1963; *Morehead on Bidding,* Macmillan, 1964, revised edition, Faber, 1966; *The Complete Guide to Winning Poker,* Simon & Schuster, 1967; *Official Rules of Card Games,* 55th edition, Whitman Publishing, 1968.

Editor: (With J. Culbertson) Ely Culbertson *Culbertson's Summary,* Bridge World, 1933, later editions published by Winston; (with Huske) *Culbertson's Blue Book,* Winston, 1934; (with Louis H. Watson) *Culbertson's Self-Teacher,* Winston 1934; (with J. Culbertson) *Red Book on Play,* Winston, 1934; (with E. Culbertson) *Encyclopedia of Bridge,* Bridge World, 1935.

(With J. Culbertson) E. Culbertson, *New Gold Book: Contract Bridge Complete,* 3rd revised edition, Winston, 1941

(revised edition published in England as *Contract Bridge Complete: The Gold Book of Bidding and Play,* Faber, 1948); (with J. Culbertson) Ely Culbertson, *Summary of Contract Bridge: Improved Culbertson System, 1941,* Winston, 1941, 2nd edition published as *Culbertson's Summary of Contract Bridge: Improved Culbertson System,* Winston, 1943, 4th edition, 1954; (with J. Culbertson) *Official Book of Contract Bridge,* Winston, 1942, revised edition, 1944; *Doubletalk Crossword Puzzles,* Knopf, 1943; (with Mott-Smith) *The Penguin Hoyle,* Penguin, 1946, 5th revised edition published as *Hoyle's Rules of Games,* New American Library, 1954, 21st edition, 1963; (with Mott-Smith) *Hoyle Up-to-Date,* Winston, 1946, Grosset & Dunlap, 1970; (with J. Culbertson) Ely Culbertson, *Bidding and Play in Duplicate Contract Bridge,* Winston, 1946; (with J. Culbertson) Ely Culbertson, *Contract Bridge for Everyone,* Winston, 1948; *Laws of Contract Bridge,* Winston, 1948; *Laws of Duplicate Contract Bridge,* Winston, 1949; (with Mott-Smith, and contributor) *Encyclopedia of Games,* Greystone Press, 1949, published as *Culbertson's Hoyle* and as *Culbertson's Card Games Complete,* Hawthorn, 1950-60, as *Goren's Hoyle,* Chancellor Hall, 1960-65, and as *Official Hoyle,* Simon & Schuster, 1965 ff.

(With Frey) *How to Play Samba,* Avon, 1950; *New American Webster Dictionary,* New American Library, 1950; (with J. Culbertson) Ely Culbertson, *Point-Count Bidding,* Winston 1952; (with Mott-Smith) *Crossword Puzzles Series 1,* Morrow, 1952; *New Wonder Book Cyclopedia,* 12 volumes, Winston, 1953; (with James Morehead) *101 Favorite Hymns,* Pocket Books, 1953; *Illustrated Encyclopedia of Knowledge,* 22 volumes, 1954; (with J. Morehead) *101 Best-Loved Songs,* Pocket Books, 1954; *Home Library Encyclopedia,* 21 volumes, 1955; (with wife, Loy Morehead) *The New American Webster Handy College Dictionary,* New American Library, 1956; (with Frey and Mott-Smith) *The New Complete Hoyle,* 2nd revised edition, Garden City Books, 1956, 3rd edition, 1964; (with Oswald Jacoby) *The Fireside Book of Cards,* Simon & Schuster, 1957; *Illustrated World Encyclopedia,* 21 volumes, 1958; *New American Roget's College Thesaurus in Dictionary Form,* Grosset & Dunlap, 1958; *Literary Treasures,* four volumes, 1958, 2nd edition published as *Illustrated Library of the Literary Treasures,* Bobley Publishing, 1963, 3rd edition published as *A Treasury of Literary Masterpieces,* Grosset & Dunlap, 1969; (with Edgar Kaplan) *Complete Italian System of Winning Bridge,* Washburn, 1959.

Roget's Unabridged Thesaurus, New American Library, 1961; (with Jack Luzzatto) *Crossword Puzzle Books 1 to 7,* New American Library, 1961-65; *Contract Bridge Summary,* Macmillan, 1963; (with J. Morehead) *Best Loved Songs and Hymns,* World Publishing, 1965; (with Harold J. Blum and others) *100 Great American Novels,* New American Library, 1966; (with L. Morehead) *New American Crossword Puzzle Dictionary,* New American Library, 1967.

Editor-in-chief of *Hoyle's Rules of Games,* six series, New American Library, 1946 ff. Under pseudonym Turner Hodges, editor of Bible Story Library, Educational Book Guild, 1956, Bobbs-Merrill, 1965. Ghost author of numerous books. Author of more than 300 magazine articles.

WORK IN PROGRESS: Vocabulary Builder; 101 Great English Novels; 101 Great World Novels; Spanish-English and English-Spanish Dictionary; Russian-English and English-Russian Dictionary; French-English and English-French Dictionary.

(Died October 5, 1966)

MORGAN, B(ayard) Q(uincy) 1883-1967

PERSONAL: Born April 5, 1883, in Dorchester, Mass.; son of Miles Forrest (a librarian) and Frances (Fisher) Morgan; married Johanna Rossberg-Leipnitz, June 19, 1912 (deceased); children: Elizabeth Ann, Margaret (Mrs. H. P. Cahill, Jr.). *Education:* Trinity College, Hartford, Conn., B.A., 1904; University of Leipzig, Ph.D., 1907. *Home:* 730 Santa Maria Ave., Stanford, Calif. 94305.

CAREER: University of Wisconsin, Madison, 1907-34, began as instructor, became professor of German; Stanford University, Stanford, Calif., professor and chairman of department of German, 1934-48, emeritus professor, 1948-67. *Member:* Modern Language Association of America (executive council member, 1948-51; vice-president, 1949). American Dialect Society, American Association of Teachers of German, American Association of University Professors, National Geographic Society, American Association of Retired Persons, California State Automobile Association, Phi Beta Kappa, Alpha Chi Rho. *Awards, honors:* Co-winner of Harvard University Press Faculty prize, 1958; National Foreign Language Achievement award, National Federation of Modern Language Teachers Associations, 1958; Goethe Medal in gold, Goethe-Institute of Munich, 1963, for services to German language and culture in United States.

WRITINGS: Nature in Middle High German Lyrics (monograph), Johns Hopkins Press, 1912; *Elementary German Syntax,* Holt, 1916; *A Bibliography of German Literature in English Translation,* University of Wisconsin Press, 1922, 2nd edition, revised and enlarged, published as *A Critical Bibliography of German Literature in English Translation, 1481-1927,* Stanford University Press, 1938; (with Erwin T. Mohme) *German Review Grammar and Composition Book,* Heath, 1934; (with Walter Wadepuhl) *Minimum Standard German Vocabulary,* F. S. Crofts, 1934; *Carl Schurz,* privately printed in Germany, 1939; (with Friedrich Wilhelm Strothmann) *Reading German,* Ginn, 1943, new edition, 1950; (with Strothmann) *Shorter German Reading Grammar,* Ginn, 1952.

Editor: *German Frequency Word Book,* Macmillan, 1928; *The German Mind* (anthology), Columbia University Press, 1928; (with A. R. Hohlfeld and Max Griebsch) *Neues deutsches Liederbuch* (songbook), new and revised edition, Heath, 1931; (with Peter Hagboldt and C. M. Purin) *Graded German Readers,* University of Chicago Press, 1933-34; (with Fernando Wagner) *Deutsch Lyrik seit Rilke: An Anthology,* F. S. Crofts, 1939; (with Hagboldt and W. F. Leopold) Petri Kettenfeier Rosegger, *Das Holzknechthaus,* Heath, 1944; (with Hohlfeld) *German Literature in British Magazines, 1750-1860,* University of Wisconsin Press, 1949; (with Strothmann) *Middle High German Translations of the Summa Theologica of Thomas Aquinas,* Stanford University Press, 1950; Victor Bluethgen, *Das Peterle von Nuernberg,* Heath, 1958; (with Herbert Spiegelberg) *The Socratic Enigma: A Collection of Testimonies Through Twenty-Four Centuries,* Bobbs-Merrill, 1964.

Translator: Gerhart Hauptmann, *Phantom,* Huebsch, 1922; Hauptmann, *The Heretic of Soana,* Huebsch, 1925; Oskar Hagen, *Art Epochs and Their Leaders,* Scribner, 1927; Goethe, *Fifteen Letters . . . from . . . Switzerland in 1775,* Greenwood Press, 1949; Karl Vietor, *Goethe the Thinker,* Harvard University Press, 1950; (with E. H. Zeydel), Wolfram von Eschenbach, *The Parzival* (in verse, abridged), University of North Carolina Press, 1951; (with Zeydel)

Poems of Walther von der Vogelweide, Thrift Press, 1952; Goethe, *Iphigenia in Tauris* (in verse), Academic Reprints, 1954; (and editor) Goethe, *Faust,* Part I (in prose), Liberal Arts Press, 1954, with act V of Part II, 1957; (with Zeydel) Hartmann von Aue, *Gregorius* (in verse), University of North Carolina Press, 1955; Lessing, *Nathan in Wise* (in verse), Ungar, 1955; Joseph Eichendorff, *Memoirs of a Good-for-Nothing,* Ungar, 1955; Gottfried Keller, *A Village Romeo and Juliet,* Ungar, 1955; Theodor Storm, *Viola Tricolor, the Little Stepmother,* Ungar, 1956; Goethe, *The Sufferings of Young Werther,* Ungar, 1957; (with Clavia Goodman) Hebbel, *Francisca and Other Stories,* Anvil Books, 1957; Kleist, *The Broken Pitcher* (in verse), University of North Carolina Press, 1961; Johann Jakob Bachofen, *Walls: Res Sanctae, Res Sacrae,* Stamperia del Santuccio, 1961; Goethe, *Faust,* Part II (in prose), Bobbs-Merrill, 1964. Contributor of articles, translations, and reviews to periodicals. Managing editor, *Modern Language Journal,* 1926-30.

WORK IN PROGRESS: A supplement to *Critical Bibliography of German Literature in English Translation,* continuing the listing through 1955, for Scarecrow; a translation of Grimmelshausen, *Simplicissimus.*

SIDELIGHTS: Morgan spoke German and French, read some Dutch, Greek, Italian, Portuguese, and Spanish. His translations include a number of unpublished works, among them the first six books of Homer's *Iliad.* He looked upon proof- and copyreading as a hobby, read *PMLA* in both galley and page proof. Between the war years he conducted four tours through western Europe; beginning in 1951 he spent eight summers driving in Europe to visit German and Austrian friends. He wrote light verse, composed two string quartets, wove gifts for relatives and friends, and gardened (with special attention to roses). Since the age of 12, he acted in numerous plays, serious and humorous, German and English, operettas, musical comedies, and grand opera.

BIOGRAPHICAL/CRITICAL SOURCES: Time, January 4, 1960; *Monatshefte,* March, 1963.

(Died February, 1967)

*   *   *

MORGAN, Barton 1889-

PERSONAL: Born February 19, 1889, in Jameson, Mo.; son of Daniel Emerson and Nancy (Stowe) Morgan; married Catherine Wallace, 1914 (deceased); married Helen Green, 1932 (deceased); married Margaret Louise Barrett, 1951; children: (first marriage) Margaret Catherine (Mrs. Warren B. Sargent; deceased), Richard Barton, Harold John, Paul Emerson. *Education:* Northeast Missouri State Teachers College (now Northeast Missouri State College), B.S., 1919; Iowa State University of Science and Technology, M.S., 1922; State University of Iowa, Ph.D., 1934. *Religion:* Congregationalist. *Home:* 917 Ridgewood Ave., Ames, Iowa 50010. *Office:* Iowa State University of Science and Technology, Ames, Iowa 50010.

CAREER: Public school teacher in Missouri, Washington, Iowa, 1909-22; Iowa State Teachers College, Cedar Falls, associate professor of rural education, 1922-23; Iowa State University of Science and Technology, Ames, professor of vocational education, 1923—, director of teacher education, 1936-50. Member of President's Committee on Vocational Education, 1937, of White House Conference on Rural Education, 1944. *Member:* National Education Association (life; president of department on rural education, 1942-44),

National Society for Study of Education, American Educational Research Association, Iowa State Education Association (life; former president), Phi Delta Kappa.

WRITINGS: (Editor with J. A. Starrak) *The Nature and Purpose of Education,* Collegiate Press, 1929; *A History of the Extension Service of Iowa State College,* Collegiate Press, 1934; (with George A. Works) *The Land-Grant Colleges,* President's Committee on Education, 1939; (editor with W. H. Stacy) *Rural Life in a Changing World,* Garrard, 1947; (with Glenn E. Holmes and Clarence E. Bundy) *Methods in Adult Education,* Interstate, 1960, 2nd edition, 1963; *Golden Nuggets of Thought,* Graphic Publishing (New York), 1966.

WORK IN PROGRESS: Another revision of *Methods in Adult Education.*

AVOCATIONAL INTERESTS: Travel, golf, nature photography, and reading.

* * *

MORGAN, Edward P. 1910-

PERSONAL: Born June 23, 1910, in Walla Walla, Wash.; son of Arthur Henry and Eledice (Paddock) Morgan; married second wife, Katharine Burden, July 18, 1960; children: (first marriage) Linda; (stepdaughters) Elaine Sohier, Sage Sohier. *Education:* Whitman College, B.A. (cum laude), 1932; University of Washington, graduate student, 1932-33. *Politics:* Independent. *Office:* ABC News, 1124 Connecticut Ave., N.W., Washington, D.C.

CAREER: Correspondent for United Press, 1934-43, *Chicago Daily News* foreign service, 1943-46; *Collier's Weekly,* associate editor and roving correspondent, 1946-48; free-lance writer in Europe, 1948-50; Columbia Broadcasting System, correspondent, 1951-54, director of news for radio and television, 1954; American Broadcasting Co., news commentator, Washington, D.C., 1955—. *Member:* Radio-Television Correspondents Association (president, 1957), Overseas Writers (Washington, D.C.; president, 1961-62), American Civil Liberties Union, Phi Beta Kappa, Sigma Delta Chi, Beta Theta Pi, Federal City Club (Washington, D.C.), Century Club (New York, N.Y.). *Awards, honors:* Peabody Award, 1957, Sidney Hillman Foundation Award, 1959, Alfred I. DuPont Award, 1960, George Polk Award, 1965, and University of Missouri School of Journalism Award, 1965, all for news broadcasting; honorary Litt.D., Whitman College, 1957.

WRITINGS: This I Believe, Simon & Schuster, Volume I (editor), 1952, Volume II (contributor), 1954; (contributor) *Candidates,* Basic Books, 1960; *Clearing the Air,* Robert B. Luce, 1963; (contributor) *The Press in Washington,* Dodd, 1966.

* * *

MORGAN, Sarah (Williams) 1901-

PERSONAL: Born April 3, 1901, in Mount Carmel, Ill.; daughter of John Wesley (a grain farmer) and Vashti (Bell) Williams; married Thurman Morgan (a member of administrative staff at Texas Christian University), June 2, 1925; children: Martha Sue (Mrs. Robert F. Scott III), J. Paul. *Education:* Texas Christian University, A.B., 1925, graduate study in children's literature, 1951-53. *Politics:* Democrat. *Religion:* Protestant. *Home:* 3109 Westcliff Rd. West, Fort Worth, Tex. 76109.

CAREER: Public school teacher in Texas for about fifteen years.

WRITINGS: Cooking for Crowds: Food and Fun for Everyone, Bethany Press, 1963.

WORK IN PROGRESS: Research for a book tentatively titled *Parsonage Etiquette;* a factual book and a fictional book on chinchillas, for second and third grade children.

* * *

MORGENSTERN, Julian 1881-

PERSONAL: Born March 18, 1881, in St. Francisville, Ill.; son of Samuel and Hanna (Ochs) Morgenstern; married Helen Thorner, 1906 (deceased); children: Jean (Mrs. William A. Greenebaum). *Education:* University of Cincinnati, B.A., 1901; Hebrew Union College, became Rabbi, 1902; University of Heidelberg, Ph.D., 1904. *Home:* 766 Marshall Dr., Macon, Ga.

CAREER: Rabbi, Lafayette, Ind., 1904-07; Hebrew Union College, Cincinnati, Ohio, instructor, 1907-10, assistant professor, 1910-13, professor, 1913-49, president, 1921-47, president emeritus, 1947—, professor emeritus, 1959—. *Member:* American Oriental Society (president, 1928-29), Society of Biblical Literature (president, 1940), Central Conference of American Rabbis (secretary, 1907-15, honorary president), British Society for Old Testament Study (honorary fellow), World Union for Progressive Judaism (honorary vice-president), Hebrew Union College Alumni Association (president, 1917-18). *Awards, honors:* D.H.L., Jewish Theological Seminary of America, 1931; LL.D., University of Cincinnati, 1937; D.D., Hebrew Union College, 1947.

WRITINGS: The Doctrine of Sin in the Babylonian Religion, Vorderasiatische Gesellschaft, 1905; *The Book of Genesis: A Jewish Interpretation,* Union of American Hebrew Congregations, 1920; *Amos Studies,* Hebrew Union College, 1945; *The Ark, the Ephod and the Tent of Meeting,* Hebrew Union College, 1945; *As a Mighty Stream,* Jewish Publication Society, 1949; *The Message of Deutero-Isaiah in its Sequential Unfolding,* Hebrew Union College, 1961; *The Fire Upon the Altar,* Brill, 1963; *Rites of Birth, Marriage, Death and Kindred Occasions Among the Semites,* Hebrew Union College Press, 1966; *Some Significant Antecedents of Christianity,* Brill, 1966. Contributor of articles to *Zeitschrift fuer Assyrologie, Hebrew Union College Annual, American Journal of Theology,* and other professional journals.

BIOGRAPHICAL/CRITICAL SOURCES: Thirteen Americans, edited by L. Finkelstein, Harper, 1953.

* * *

MORKOVIN, Boris V(ladimir) 1882-1968
(Bela V. Morkovin)

PERSONAL: Born July 30, 1882, in Tver (now Kalinin), Russia; son of Vladimir Mikhail and Nadin (Belgorodsky) Morkovin; first wife deceased; married second wife, Helen Buckman, 1959; children: (first marriage) Dimitry, George, Mark. *Education:* Attended gymnasium and junior college in Tashkent, Central Asia; University of Moscow, student, 1900-02; Charles University, Ph.C., 1911; University of Southern California, Ph.D., 1929. *Home:* 881 South Bronson Ave., Los Angeles, Calif. 90005.

CAREER: Charles University, Prague, Czechoslovakia, lecturer on Russian language and literature, 1911-24; lecturer in United States on the folklore and literature of eastern Europe, under auspices of Institute of International Education, 1924-26; University of California, Berkeley, visiting professor of comparative literature, 1926; University of Southern California, Los Angeles, began as assistant professor of comparative literature, 1926, professor of speech and hearing, and research associate of Psycho-Educational Clinic, 1937-51, founding director of Hearing Clinic, 1938-51, professor emeritus, 1951-68. National Institutes of Health, researcher on work of Moscow Institute of Defectology, 1959-61, and on the training of preschool deaf children in the Soviet Union, 1965-66. Writer-producer of various series of "Life-Situation" films, used for rehabilitation in military hospitals and in training deaf and retarded children; conductor of radio and television courses on exceptional children, 1946-50. Co-founder of John Tracy Clinic, Los Angeles, 1942; founder and board member, Metropolitan Hearing Clinic, Los Angeles, 1944.

MEMBER: American Psychological Association, American Speech and Hearing Association (fellow), American Institute of Cinematography (vice-president, 1934-39), British Columbia Institute of Cinematography (honorary president, 1939-68), Phi Beta Kappa, Alpha Kappa Delta, Delta Kappa Alpha, Faculty Club (University of Southern California). *Awards, honors:* Medal from King of Denmark for work with neutral Danish Red Cross in Austria, World War I; bronze plaque, Los Angeles Community Chest, 1954, for community service in the conservation of hearing.

WRITINGS: (Under name Bela V. Morkovin) *Cseko-Rusky Slovnik* (comparative phraseology dictionary), J. Otto (Prague), 1924; *The Fundamentals of Motion Picture Production*, 2nd edition, University of Southern California Press, 1936; *Problems of Education and Social Adjustment of the Hard of Hearing and Deaf*, University of Southern California Press, 1941; (editor) *Rehabilitation and Placement of the Disabled*, California Conference of Social Work, 1943; *Kindred Group Program on Rehabilitation of Handicapped Children and Disabled Ex-servicemen and Women Workers, and Civilians*, Pacific Zone, American Society for the Hard of Hearing, 1943; (with Lucelia Moore) *A Guide to Life Situation Films for Teaching Speech and Language*, Department of Cinema, University of Southern California, 1959; (with Moore) *Through the Barriers of Deafness and Isolation*, Macmillan, 1960.

Author of booklet on aural re-education published by Coordinating Council of Societies for the Hard of Hearing in Southern California, 1946. Contributor to *Volta Review*, *World Affairs Interpreter*, *Journal of Speech and Hearing Disorders*, and other journals. Editor, *Cinema Progress*, 1934-39; reviewer, *DSH Abstracts*, beginning, 1959.

SIDELIGHTS: In 1898, Morkovin participated in a three-month horseback expedition to the remote Tien Shan Mountains, India, Afghanistan, and to ancient historical Eurasian sites. Several years later, in Moscow, he was a friend of Maxim Gorky and several other Russian writers; he recalled Gorky reading and discussing the manuscript of *Stormy Petrel* with him. This friendship was the basis for Morkovin's paper, "Young Maxim Gorky, as a Humanitarian," presented at the Academy of Science in Moscow, October, 1964. *Avocational interests:* Reading, chess, travel, the theater, music, and art.

(Died November 1, 1968)

*   *   *

MORRIS, Everett B.   1899-1967

PERSONAL: Born June 18, 1899, in New Bedford, Mass.; married Suzanne Roge, August 27, 1920; children: Marguerite (Mrs. Carl Ruroede III), Burton E. *Education:*

Educated in schools in New Bedford, Mass. *Politics:* Independent. *Religion:* Episcopalian. *Home:* 16 Monfort Rd., Port Washington, Long Island, N.Y. 11050.

CAREER: New Bedford Evening Standard, New Bedford, Mass., began as cub reporter, became city editor, 1920-27; Dartmouth High School, Dartmouth, Mass., basketball coach, 1922-27; *New York Daily News,* New York, N.Y., night sports editor, 1927-30; *New York Herald Tribune,* New York, N.Y., sports writer, 1930-42, yachting editor, 1945-56; *Modern Boating,* New York, N.Y., assistant to publisher and editor, 1957-62, editor, 1962-63; *New York Herald Tribune,* yachting editor, 1962-67. *Military service:* U.S. Navy, 1917-19, 1942-45, 1950-53; became captain, U.S. Naval Reserve, retired; received Bronze Star Medal and Commendation Pendant. *Member:* Junior Yacht Racing Association (member of governing committee, 1948-63; chairman, 1958-60), Cruising Club of America, Yacht Racing Association of Long Island Sound, New York Yacht Club, Royal Bermuda Yacht Club, Cruising Club of America, Manhasset Bay Yacht Club, Storm Trysail Club, Off Soundings Club, Essex Yacht Club. *Awards, honors:* Thomas Fleming Day special citation for outstanding reporting of America's Cup Races, 1962; Thomas Fleming Day award for excellence in boating journalism, 1963.

WRITINGS: Outboard Boating Skills, Evinrude Foundation, 1957; (author of commentary) Morris Rosenfeld, *Under Full Sail,* Prentice-Hall, 1957; (editor with Robert Coulson) *Racing at Sea,* Van Nostrand, 1959; *The Able Seaman: A Basic Book of Boating Under Sailor Power,* Harper, 1960; *Sailing for America's Cup,* Harper, 1964.

WORK IN PROGRESS: A comprehensive book on boat buying for the non-initiated.

AVOCATIONAL INTERESTS: Sailing (participated in two Bermuda races as a watch officer on sailing yachts and has engaged in international team racing), study of wine.

(Died February 14, 1967)

*   *   *

MORRIS, Katharine

PERSONAL: Born in Nottingham, England; daughter of Robert and Katharine (Dymock) Morris. *Education:* Educated privately in England. *Home:* Bleasby, Nottingham, England.

CAREER: Nursing service with British Red Cross for a period prior to 1943, with Royal Air Force, principally occupied with welfare work, 1943-52, with duty in Hamburg, Germany, 1946-47; engaged in social work and social welfare projects after leaving military service. Novelist, focusing on English country life. *Member:* Shakespeare Society (London), English Speaking Union.

WRITINGS—Novels: *New Harrowing,* Methuen, 1934; *The Vixen's Cup,* Dutton, 1951; *County Dance,* Dutton, 1953; *The House by the Water,* Macdonald & Co. 1957; *The Long Meadow,* Macdonald & Co., 1958.

AVOCATIONAL INTERESTS: Singing, poetry and dramatic readings, sculpture (bronze castings of her prize-winning bust of Coriolanus acquired by Southwark Museum and the Playhouse Theatre, Nottingham, 1965).

*   *   *

MORRISON, Lester M.   1907-

PERSONAL: Born September 18, 1907, in London, England; now U.S. citizen; son of Harold and Sophia (Beck)

Morrison; married Rita Rosenthal, May 5, 1938. *Education:* McGill University, student, 1925-29; Temple University, M.D., 1933; Guys Hospital Medical School, University of London, additional study, 1934-35. *Office:* 10921 Wilshire Blvd., Los Angles, Calif. 90024.

CAREER: Temple University, Philadelphia, Pa., instructor in medicine, 1935-44; practicing physician in internal medicine and gastroenterology, Philadelphia, Pa., 1935-44, Los Angeles, Calif., 1944—; Los Angeles County General Hospital, Los Angeles, Calif., senior attending physician, 1944—; Loma Linda University Medical School, Loma Linda, Calif., assistant professor of medicine, 1945—. Director of arteriosclerosis research unit, Loma Linda University Medical School and Los Angeles County General Hospital, 1945—. President, Los Angeles Doctors' Symphony Orchestra, 1959-60. *Member:* American College of Gastroenterology (trustee, 1961—), American College of Physicians (fellow), American Heart Association (arteriosclerosis council), American Medical Association, Los Angeles County Medical Association.

WRITINGS: Low Fat Way to Health and Longer Life, Prentice-Hall, 1958; (with Richard G. Hubler) *Trial and Triumph* (a novel), Crown, 1965. Also co-author of *Coronary Heart Disease and the Mucopolysaccharides (Glycosaminoglycans)* published by C. C Thomas. Contributor of more than one hundred articles to medical journals and medical textbooks, 1935—.

WORK IN PROGRESS: Active research in arteriosclerosis sponsored by John A. Hartford Foundation, National Institutes of Health, and Crenshaw Research Foundation.

* * *

MORROW, Glenn R(aymond) 1895-197(?)

PERSONAL: Born April 29, 1895, in Calhoun, Mo.; son of Charles Sumner and Bessie (Bronaugh) Morrow; married Dorrice Richards, 1923. *Education:* Westminster College, A.B., 1914; Louisville Theological Seminary, student, 1916-17; University of Missouri, A.M., 1918; Cornell University, Ph.D., 1921. *Home:* 515 Rutgers Ave., Swarthmore, Pa. *Office:* Department of Philosophy, University of Pennsylvania, Philadelphia, Pa.

CAREER: Westminster College, Fulton, Mo., instructor, 1914-16; Cornell University, Ithaca, N.Y., lecturer, 1922-23; University of Missouri, Columbia, 1923-29, began as assistant professor, became associate professor; University of Illinois, Urbana, professor, 1929-39; University of Pennsylvania, Philadelphia, professor of moral and intellectual philosophy, beginning 1939. *Military service:* U.S. Army Field Artillery, 1918-19; became second lieutenant. *Member:* American Philological Association, American Philosophical Association (president, western division, 1939-40; president, eastern division, 1953-54), Archaeological Institute of America. *Awards, honors:* American Field Service Fellow in France, 1921-22; LL.D., Westminster College, 1951; Guggenheim Fellow in Greece, 1952-53, 1956-57; Fulbright Fellow at Oxford, 1956-57.

WRITINGS: The Ethical and Economic Theories of Adam Smith, Longmans, Green, 1923, reprinted, A. M. Kelley, 1969; (editor and translator) *Studies in the Platonic Epistles,* University of Illinois, 1935, revised edition published as *Plato's Epistles,* Bobbs Merrill, 1962; *Plato's Law of Slavery,* University of Illinois Press, 1939; *Plato's Cretan City,* Princeton University Press, 1960; (translator and author of notes and introduction) Proclus Diadochus, *A Commentary on the First Book of Euclid's Elements,*

Princeton University Press, 1970. American editor, *Archiv fuer Geschichte der Philosophie.* Contributor to professional journals.

(Deceased)

* * *

MORSE, Charles A. 1898-

PERSONAL: Born November 22, 1898, in Worcester, Mass.; son of Albert H. and Mabel (Daniels) Morse; married Grace I. Carlson (a librarian), April 28, 1923; children: Charles A., Jr., Albert D., Gerald R. *Education:* Worcester Polytechnic Institute, student, 1918-20. *Home:* Winchester Rd., Warwick, Mass. 03470.

CAREER: Affiliated with L. S. Starrett Co., Athol, Mass., 1941-64, retired, 1964. Lecturer on local history. Selectman, Warwick, Mass., 1940-43; member of Pioneer Valley Regional School Committee, 1957-70; chairman, Warwick Revolution Bicentennial Commission, 1973—. *Military service:* U.S. Army, World War I.

WRITINGS: Biography of a Town (Warwick, Mass.), Dresser, 1963. Weekly columnist, "Stories from Here and There," *Orange Enterprise and Journal;* contributor of stories on local history and folklore to other newspapers.

WORK IN PROGRESS: Collecting material for a biography of a local Tory minister, 1775.

* * *

MORSEY, Royal Joseph 1910-

PERSONAL: Born August 2, 1910, in Minster, Ohio; son of Anton Joseph (a farmer) and Anna (Helmsing) Morsey; married Mary Trottman, August 24, 1940; children: Paul. *Education:* Ohio State University, B.Sc. in Ed., 1933, M.A., 1937, Ph.D., 1948. *Home:* 108 Winthrop Rd., Muncie, Ind. 47304. *Office:* Ball State University, Muncie, Ind. 47306.

CAREER: High school teacher in Gambier, Ohio, 1937-39, Columbus, Ohio, 1939-48; Ball State University, Muncie, Ind., began, 1948—, professor of education and English, 1958—. *Member:* National Council of Teachers of English, American Federation of Teachers, Association for Teacher Education, Indiana Council of Teachers of English (president, 1960-62), Phi Delta Kappa.

WRITINGS: A College Seminar to Develop and Evaluate an Improved High School English Program, Ball State University Press, 1961; *A Common-Sense Approach to Teaching Spelling,* Ball State University Press, 1962; *Improving English Instruction,* Allyn & Bacon, 1965, 2nd edition, 1969.

* * *

MORTON, Newton 1901-1967

PERSONAL: Born February 1, 1901, in Palmyra, N.J.; son of Thomas Ludlam and Anne (Deitz) Morton; married Laura Jones, December 1, 1928; children: Newton Ennis, Stephen Collister. *Education:* University of Pennsylvania, B.S., 1923. *Politics:* Republican. *Religion:* Congregational. *Home:* 1550 Bridge View Circle, Cuyahoga Falls, Ohio 44223. *Office:* Kent State University, Kent, Ohio.

CAREER: Pennsylvania Railroad, freight representative, 1923-44; Bridgeport Brass Co., Bridgeport, Conn., assistant traffic manager, 1944-48; National Transportation Co., Bridgeport, Conn., salesman, 1949; Kent State University, 1949-67, associate professor of transportation, 1958-67.

Registered practitioner before Interstate Commerce Commission, 1950; special master commissioner, Common Pleas Court, Summit County (Akron), Ohio. *Member:* American Society of Traffic and Transportation (founder member), Association of Interstate Commerce Commission Practitioners, Associated Traffic Clubs (associate), Delta Nu Alpha, Tau Kappa Epsilon, Alpha Phi Omega. *Awards, honors:* Ford Foundation Fellowship to Indiana University, 1961.

WRITINGS: (With Frank H. Mossman) *Industrial Traffic Management*, Ronald, 1954; (with Mossman) *Principles of Transportation*, Ronald, 1957; (with Mossman) *Logistics of Distribution Systems*, Allyn & Bacon, 1965; *The Commerce Clause: Its Inception and Its Significance*, Bureau of Business Research, Kent State University, 1966. Contributor of about forty articles to railway and other traffic journals.

WORK IN PROGRESS: Basic Transportation, a textbook; *Development of Commerce and Influence of the Commerce Clause*; a compendium of transportation terms and phrases.

AVOCATIONAL INTERESTS: Travel, spectator sports.

(Died February 20, 1967)

* * *

MORTON, W(illiam) L(ewis)   1908-

PERSONAL: Born December 13, 1908, in Gladstone, Manitoba, Canada; son of William (a farmer) and Mary (Manwaring) Morton; married Margaret Orde, August 24, 1936; children: Orde, Lionel, Anne. *Education:* University of Manitoba, B.A., 1932; Oxford University, B.A. (honors), 1934, B.Litt., 1935, M.A., 1937. *Politics:* Tory. *Religion:* Anglican. *Home and office:* Master's Lodge, Champlain College, Peterborough, Ontario, Canada.

CAREER: St. John's College, Winnipeg, Manitoba, lecturer in history, 1935-38; assistant professor of history at United College, Winnipeg, Manitoba, 1938-39, University of Manitoba, Winnipeg, 1939-40, and Brandon College, Brandon, Manitoba, 1940-42; University of Manitoba, assistant professor, 1942-45, associate professor, 1945-49, professor of history, 1949-66, chairman of department, 1950-63; Trent University, Peterborough, Ontario, professor of history and master of Champlain College, 1966-69, Vanier Professor of Canadian History, 1969—. Member of board of directors, Canadian Broadcasting Corp., 1958-64. *Military service:* Canadian Army Reserve, 1940-45; became major.

MEMBER: Canadian Historical Association, American Historical Association, Royal Society of Canada (fellow), Champlain Society. *Awards, honors:* Governor General's Literary Award in nonfiction, Canadian Authors Association, 1951, for *The Progressive Party of Canada*; Tyrrell Medal for outstanding work in Canadian history, Royal Society of Canada, 1958, for *Manitoba: A History*; LL.D., University of Toronto, 1958; D.Litt., University of New Brunswick, 1965, McGill University, 1966, University of Manitoba, 1967.

WRITINGS: Canada and the World Tomorrow, Canadian Institute of International Affairs, 1943; (editor) John Wesley Dafoe, *Voice of Dafoe*, Macmillan, 1945; (with Margaret Morton Fahrni) *Third Crossing*, Advocate Printers, 1946; *The Progressive Party in Canada*, University of Toronto Press, 1950; (author of introduction) *Eden Colvile's Letters, 1849-1852*, Hudson's Bay Record Society,

1956; (editor) *Red River Journal of Alexander Begg*, Champlain Society, 1956; *Manitoba: A History*, University of Toronto Press, 1957; *One University: A History of the University of Manitoba*, McClelland & Stewart, 1957; *The West and Confederation, 1857-1871*, [Ottawa], 1958; *The Canadian Identity*, University of Wisconsin Press, 1961; *The Kingdom of Canada*, Bobbs-Merrill, 1963; (with Margaret MacLeod) *Cuthbert Grant of Grantown*, McClelland & Stewart, 1963; *The Critical Years: The Union of British North America*, McClelland & Stewart, 1964; (editor) *Manitoba: the Birth of a Province*, Friesen Brothers, 1965. Also author of *Prepare for Peace*, Canadian Institute of International Affairs. Contributor to learned journals. Executive editor, "Canadian Centenary Series."

WORK IN PROGRESS: Works on the political history of early Canada, and on the North in Canadian history.

SIDELIGHTS: Morton is competent in French, German, Latin, and Greek.

* * *

MOSES, Elbert R(aymond), Jr.   1908-

PERSONAL: Born March 31, 1908, in New Concord, Ohio; son of Elbert Raymond (a teacher) and Martha (Miller) Moses; married Mary Sterrett, September 21, 1933; children: James E. *Education:* Wooster College, student, 1925-27; University of Pittsburgh, A.B., 1932; University of Michigan, M.Sc., 1934, Ph.D., 1936. *Politics:* Democrat. *Religion:* Methodist. *Home:* 25 Fairview Ave., Clarion, Pa. 16214.

CAREER: Falk Speech Clinic, Pittsburgh, Pa., director, 1934-35; University of North Carolina Woman's College, Greensboro, instructor in English and speech, 1936-38; Ohio State University, Columbus, assistant professor of speech, 1938-46; Eastern Illinois University, Charleston, associate professor of speech and radio, 1946-56; Michigan State University, East Lansing, assistant professor of communication skills, 1956-59; Clarion State College, Clarion, Pa., professor of speech and head of department of speech and dramatic arts, 1959-71. Fulbright lecturer, Normal College, Cebu, Philippines, 1955-56. Member of national advisory board for foreign students and teachers, U.S. Department of Health, Education, and Welfare. Delegate to international conferences on phonetics and education in Helsinki, Vienna, Tokyo, and The Hague. *Military service:* U.S. Army, 1942-46; became major. U.S. Army Reserve, 1946-60, with active duty in Korean War, 1952-53; became lieutenant colonel.

MEMBER: American Academy of Arts and Sciences; American Speech and Hearing Association, International Society of Phonetic Sciences, International Phonetic Association, Speech Association of America, American Overseas Educators Association (past president), National Association of Foreign Student Advisors, Sons of the American Revolution (secretary/treasurer, vice-president, president, Clarion), Mason, Phi Alpha Theta, Tau Kappa Alpha, Alpha Phi Omega, Sigma Alpha Eta, Pi Kappa Delta, Alpha Epsilon Rho, Phi Delta Kappa. *Awards, honors:* Alumni Fund grant, Ohio State University, 1941; phonetic research grant, Michigan State University, 1957-58.

WRITINGS: A Workbook in Persuasion, Edwards, 1939; *A History of Palatography Techniques* (monograph), Edwards, 1940; *Interpretations of a New Method in Palatography* (monograph), Edwards, 1940; *A Guide to Effective Speaking*, Alemar (Manila), 1956, revised edition, Vantage,

1957; (with Donald H. Dininny) *An Analysis of Pronunciation Errors in the Clarion-Brookville, Pennsylvania, Area,* W. Hearst (Clarion, 1964; *Phonetics: History and Interpretation,* Prentice-Hall, 1964. Contributor of some fifty articles to speech, education, religious, and other periodicals, and meditations to *Clarion Democrat.* Editor, *Illinois Speech News,* 1948, co-editor, 1949.

WORK IN PROGRESS: Writing for contemporary papers and magazines.

SIDELIGHTS: Moses speaks and reads French; reads scientific German.

* * *

MOSS, Robert (Alfred) 1903-
(Nancy Moss, Roberta Moss)

PERSONAL: Born August 21, 1903, in Nuneaton, England; son of Henry William and May Agnes Moss; married Joyce Nancy Green, July 10, 1936; children: Jeremy Royce, Mary Lillian Royce. *Education:* Educated at private schools in England. *Politics:* Liberal. *Religion:* Christian Scientist. *Home:* 110 Cumberland Rd., Shortlands, Bromley, Kent, England. *Agent:* A. M. Health & Co. Ltd., 35 Dover St., London WIX 4EB, England.

CAREER: Engall, Cox & Co. (estate agents), Cheltenham, England, clerk, 1920-25; Edward J. Burrow & Co. Ltd., Cheltenham, guide-book writer, 1924-37; free-lance writer, 1937-38; Boulton-Paul Aircraft Co. Ltd., Wolverhampton, England, cost office clerk, 1938-45; Juvenile Productions Ltd., London, England, editor, 1945-60. Teacher of popular writing classes, Kent Committee for Further Education, eight years.

WRITINGS: The House of the Hundred Heads, R. Hale, 1939; (under pseudonym Roberta Moss) *Jenny of the Fourth,* Staples, 1953; (under pseudonym Roberta Moss) *Jenny's Exciting Term,* Staples, 1954; (under pseudonym Nancy Moss) *School on the Precipice,* W. & R. Chambers, 1954; (under pseudonym Nancy Moss) *Susan's Stormy Term,* W. & R. Chambers, 1955; (under pseudonym Nancy Moss) *Strange Quest at Cliff House,* W. & R. Chambers, 1956; (under pseudonym Roberta Moss) *Shy Girl at Southdown,* Andrew Dakers, 1957; (under pseudonym Roberta Moss) *Mystery at Gull's Nest,* Andrew Dakers, 1957; (under pseudonym Nancy Moss) *The Cliff House Monster,* W. & R. Chambers, 1957; (under pseudonym Nancy Moss) *The Riddle of Cliff House,* W. & R. Chambers, 1957; *ABC in Real-Life Pictures,* Juvenile Productions, 1960; *The Golden Bar Book of Brownie Stories,* Brown, Son & Ferguson, 1961; *The Golden Ladder Book of Brownie Stories,* Brown, Son & Ferguson, 1963; (editor) *The Arrow Book of Cub Scout Stories,* Purnell & Sons, 1968; (editor) *The Challenge Book of Brownie Stories,* Purnell & Sons, 1968; (editor) *The Challenge Book of Girl Guide Stories,* Purnell & Sons, 1969; (editor) *The Venture Book of Brownie Stories,* Purnell & Sons, 1969.

Also editor of *Boys' and Girls' Cinema Clubs Annual,* and other annuals for Brownies, Girl Guides, Scouts, and Wolf Cubs. Author of television play, "The Storm Bell," and stories for British Broadcasting Corp. "Children's Hours." Contributor of short stories, serials, and picturestrip stories to children's periodicals and annuals.†

* * *

MOTTER, Alton M(yers) 1907-

PERSONAL: Born August 28, 1907, in Silver Run, Md.; son of George Edward (a farmer) and Mary Cleveland (Myers) Motter; married Lottye Elizabeth Yealy, August 14, 1929; children: Harold, Adrienne (Mrs. Warren Strandberg), Mildred (Mrs. Stanley Graham). *Education:* Gettysburg College, B.S., 1930; Gettysburg Theological Seminary, B.D., 1933, S.T.M., 1944; United Theological Seminary, D.D., 1966. *Politics:* Democrat. *Home:* 5006 Dupont Ave. S., Minneapolis, Minn. 55419. *Office:* Minnesota Council of Churches, 122 West Franklin Ave., Minneapolis, Minn. 55404.

CAREER: Lutheran minister, 1933—; Pastor in Harrisburg, Pa., 1933-46; St. Paul Area Council of Churches, St. Paul, Minn., executive secretary, 1946-51; Chicago Sunday Evening Club (forum), Chicago, Ill., executive director, 1951-55, and managing editor of *Pulpit,* 1952-55; Messiah Lutheran Church, Denver, Colo., pastor, 1955-59; Minnesota Council of Churches, Minneapolis, associate executive secretary, 1959-63, executive director, 1964—. Instructor, Chicago Lutheran Theological Seminary, 1952-53, Bethany Theological Seminary, 1954-55. Public relations coordinator, World Council of Churches, 1954; British Council of Churches, interchange preacher in England, Scotland, Holland, 1959. Press correspondent at Vatican II, 1965, at fourth assembly of World Council of Churches, Uppsala, Sweden, 1968. *Member:* Association of Council Secretaries (national vice-president, 1962-63), Religious Public Relations Council (Minneapolis; president, 1962-64).

WRITINGS—Editor: Sunday Evening Sermons: Fifteen Selected Addresses Delivered Before the Noted Chicago Sunday Evening Club, Harper, 1952; *Great Preaching Today: A Collection of 25 Sermons Delivered at the Chicago Sunday Evening Club,* Harper, 1955; *Preaching the Resurrection: 22 Great Easter Sermons,* Fortress, 1959; *Preaching the Nativity: 19 Great Sermons for Advent, Christmas, and Epiphany,* Fortress, 1961; *Preaching the Passion: Twenty-four Outstanding Sermons for the Lenten Season,* Fortress, 1964; *Preaching on Pentecost and Christian Unity: Thirty Outstanding Sermons Dealing with Themes of Pentecost and the Ecumenical Movement,* Fortress, 1966. Contributor, *Young Adult Idea Book,* Fortress. Contributor of feature articles to religious periodicals.

* * *

MOTTRAM, (Vernon) Henry 1882-19(?)

PERSONAL: Born March 14, 1882, in Tewkesbury, Gloucestershire, England; son of William (a Congregational minister) and Elizabeth (Fruen) Mottram; married Elsie Charlotte King, July 6, 1921; children: Brian Hunter, Kay Dominic, Roy Frederic. *Education:* Trinity College, Cambridge, B.A., 1904, M.A., 1907. *Politics:* Socialist. *Religion:* Quaker. *Home:* Hope Cottage, Donhead St. Mary, Shaftesbury, Dorsetshire, England.

CAREER: Trinity College, Cambridge University, Cambridge, England, fellow, 1907-11; University of Liverpool, Liverpool, England, demonstrator and lecturer on chemical physiology, 1911-14; lecturer in physiology at McGill University, Montreal, Quebec, 1914-16, and at University of Toronto, Toronto, Ontario, 1916-17; Caterham School, Surrey, England, schoolmaster, 1917-20; Lever Brothers, Port Sunlight, Cheshire, England, research worker, 1920-21; University of London, London, England, professor of physiology, 1921-44.

WRITINGS: A Manual of Histology, Dutton, 1923; *Food and the Family,* Nisbet, 1925, 6th revised edition, 1938; *The Functions of the Body: An Outline of Physiology,* Nisbet, 1926, published as *Physiology*, Norton, 1928; (with Jessie Lindsay) *Manual of Modern Cookery*, University of London Press, 1927, 7th edition, 1943; (with Winifred Mary Clifford) *Properties of Food: A Practical Textbook for Teachers of Domestic Science*, University of London Press, 1929; *Health and Hygiene*, Philip & Son, 1931; *Sound Catering for Hard Times*, Nisbet, 1932; (with Robert Hutchison) *Food and the Principles of Dietetics*, 7th edition (Mottram was not associated with earlier editions), Edward Arnold, 1933, Wood, 1938, 9th edition (with George Graham) published as Hutchison's *Food and the Principles of Dietetics*, Wood, 1940, 11th edition, Edward Arnold, 1948, Williams & Wilkins, 1956; (with Ellen M. Radloff) *Food Tables*, Edward Arnold, 1937, Longmans, Green, 1938; *Healthy Eating*, Cassell, 1940; (with A. E. Rowlett) *Our Food Today*, British Red Cross Society, 1942; *Human Nutrition*, Williams & Wilkins, 1948, 2nd edition, 1963; (with Nell St. John Heaton) *Cooking for the Sick and Convalescent: A Textbook of Dietetics*, Faber, 1951, Transatlantic, 1952.

WORK IN PROGRESS: Writing on nutrition.

SIDELIGHTS: Mottram told *CA:* "I was brought up, or brought myself up, in a rigidly scientific atmosphere, but throughout I was more than half conscious that science is not enough and now have no use for the humanist philosophy.... I wish that the scientific attitude of mind could be built into the mentality of everyone, from ministers of religion upwards (or rather downwards) to politicians."

(Deceased)

* * *

MOURANT, John A(rthur) 1903-

PERSONAL: Born November 24, 1903, in Chicago, Ill.; son of Arthur J. and Addie (Morris) Mourant; married Margaret Elinor Connors, June 16, 1928; children: Paul Rene. *Education:* University of Chicago, Ph.B., 1926, Ph.D., 1940; Harvard University, A.M., 1928. *Politics:* Republican. *Religion:* Catholic. *Home:* 547 Westview Ave., State College, Pa. 16801.

CAREER: Instructor in philosophy and economics, at DePaul University, Chicago, Ill., 1928-31, at St. Mary's College, Winona, Minn., 1931-32; Nazareth College, Rochester, N.Y., assistant professor of history and philosophy, 1932-36, assistant professor of philosophy, 1945-46; St. Xavier College, Chicago, Ill., assistant professor of philosophy and social science, 1936-44; University of Rochester, Rochester, N.Y., assistant professor of philosophy, 1945-46; Pennsylvania State University, University Park, assistant professor, 1946-49, associate professor and head of department of philosophy, 1949-53, professor of philosophy, 1953—. Exchange professor, San Diego State College, 1964-65. *Member:* American Philosophical Association, American Catholic Philosophical Association, Association for Realist Philosophy, Personalist Society, Societe Internationale pour L'Etude de la Philosphie Medievale, Catholic Commission for Culture and Intellectual Affairs (past secretary), Southern Society for the Philosophy of Religion (past president), Western Pennsylvania Philosophical Society (past president).

WRITINGS: (Editor) *Readings in the Philosophy of Religion*, Crowell, 1954; (with Luther Harshbarger and B. Kahn) *Exploring Religious Ideas: The Great Western Faiths*, Center for Continuing Liberal Education, Pennsylvania State University, 1959; (with others) *Essays in Philosophy*, Pennsylvania State University Press, 1962; *Formal Logic: An Introductory Textbook*, Macmillan, 1963; (with E. Hans Freund) *Problems of Philosophy, a Book of Readings*, Macmillan, 1964; (editor) *Introduction to the Philosophy of St. Augustine*, Pennsylvania State University Press, 1964; (contributor) Michele F. Sciacca, editor, *Les Grands Courants de la Pensee Mondiale Contemporaine*, Fischbacher, 1964; (with Luther Harshbarger) *Judaism and Christianity: Perspectives and Traditions*, Allyn & Bacon, 1968; (contributor) R. M. McInerny, editor, *New Themes in Christian Philosophy*, University of Notre Dame Press, 1968; *Augustine on Immortality*, Augustine Institute, Villanova University, 1969. Contributor of articles to *Humanitas, New Scholasticism, Journal of Philosophy, Giornale de Metafisica*, and other philosophy journals.

AVOCATIONAL INTERESTS: Amateur radio, gardening.

* * *

MOWAT, C(harles) L(och) 1911-1970

PERSONAL: Born October 4, 1911, in Oxford, England; son of R. B. (a professor) and Mary G. (Loch) Mowat; married Jo Wadham, August, 1936; children: John, Rosemary. *Education:* Attended Marlborough College, 1925-30; St. John's College, Oxford, B.A., 1934, M.A., 1937; University of Minnesota, Ph.D., 1939. *Religion:* Anglican. *Home:* Nant Dwyst, Llanfairfechan, Caernarvonshire, Wales. *Office:* University College of North Wales, Bangor, Wales.

CAREER: University of California, Los Angeles, faculty member, 1936-50; University of Chicago, Chicago, Ill., professor of English history, 1950-58; University College of North Wales, University of Wales, Bangor, professor of history, 1959—. *Member:* American Historical Association, Historical Association (England), Economic History Society, British Association for American Studies, Victorian Society. *Awards, honors:* Guggenheim fellow, 1947-48.

WRITINGS: East Florida as a British Province, 1763-1784, University of California Press, 1943, reprinted University of Florida Press, 1964; *Britain Between the Wars, 1918-1940*, University of Chicago Press, 1955; *Charity Organization Society, 1869-1913*, Methuen, 1961; *Lloyd George*, Oxford University Press, 1964; *Golden Valley Railway: Railway Enterprise on the Welsh Border in Late Victorian Times*, University of Wales Press, 1964; (editor) *The Shifting Balance of World Forces, 1898-1945* (revised edition of Volume XII of *Cambridge Modern History*, originally titled, *The Era of Violence*), Cambridge University Press, 1968; *The General Strike, 1926*, Edward Arnold, 1969; *Great Britain Since 1914*, Cornell University Press, 1971. Editor with Mary Price of "Clarendon Biographies," Oxford University Press. Contributor of articles and reviews to *Listener* and to historical journals. Editor, *Journal of Modern History*, 1956-58.

(Died June 29, 1970)

* * *

MOWRER, Edgar Ansel 1892-

PERSONAL: Born March 8, 1892, in Bloomington, Ill.; son of Rufus (a businessman) and Nell (Scott) Mowrer; married Lillian Thomson (a writer), February 8, 1916; children: Diana Jane. *Education:* Attended University of Chicago, 1910, Sorbonne, University of Paris, 1911; University of Michigan, B.A., 1913. *Politics:* Independent. *Religion:* Deist. *Residence:* Wonalancet, N.H. 03897.

CAREER: Chicago Daily News, Chicago, Ill., war correspondent in France and Belgium, 1914-15, Rome correspondent, 1915-23, chief of Berlin bureau, 1923-33, chief of Paris bureau, 1934-40, Washington correspondent, 1940-41; U.S. Office of War Information, Washington, D.C., deputy director, 1942-43; syndicated columnist on foreign affairs, 1943-69. *Member:* Washington Institute of Foreign Affairs (charter member), Freedom House, American Security Council, Authors League of America, Century Association (New York), Adventurers Club (Chicago). *Awards, honors:* Pulitzer Prize for foreign correspondence, 1933; officer of Legion of Honor.

WRITINGS: Immortal Italy, Appleton, 1922; *This American World,* Morrow, 1928; *Sinon: Or the Future of Politics,* Kegan Paul, 1930; *Germany Puts the Clock Back,* Morrow, 1933, revised edition, 1939; *The Dragon Awakes,* Morrow, 1939; (with Marthe Rajchman) *Global War: An Atlas of World Strategy,* Morrow, 1942; *The Nightmare of American Foreign Policy,* Knopf, 1948; *Challenge and Decision,* McGraw, 1950; *A Good Time to Be Alive,* Duell, Sloan & Pearce, 1959; *An End to Make-Believe,* Duell, Sloan & Pearce, 1961; *Triumph and Turmoil: An Autobiography,* Weybright, 1968; (with wife, Lillian T. Mowrer) *Umano and the Price of Lasting Peace,* Philosophical Library, 1973. Contributor to magazines. U.S. editor, *Western World,* 1956-60.

SIDELIGHTS: Mowrer, who as a journalist and author was expelled from Germany by Hitler, in 1933, from Italy by Mussolini, in 1936, and from Russia by Stalin, in 1937, told *CA*: "[I am] confident that to date the Soviet leaders have not 'evolved' but are rather encouraged in their ambition by the readiness of the U.S. and other democratic states to overlook their threats and colossal armaments in favor of 'cooperation rather than confrontation.' . . . The emotional nature of mankind has not changed nor has his fundamental instinct of self assertion, which accounts for competition, rivalry, thirst for power, sex, etc. Only ideas have changed. Hence the fundamental of civilized living remains enforced law, local, personal, provincial, national, eventually international."

*   *   *

MOYES, John Stoward 1884-

PERSONAL: Born July 25, 1884, in Koolunga, South Australia; son of John (a teacher) and Ellen Jane (Stoward) Moyes; married Helen Margaret Butler, April 22, 1909; children: Helen Margaret (Mrs. Roger Correll), John Layton, Guy Stoward, Peter Morton, Philip Richard, and Monica Mary. *Education:* University of Adelaide, B.A., 1905, M.A., 1907; Australian College of Theology, Th.L. (first class honors), 1907. *Home:* Nell Slade Lodge, Mowll Memorial Village, Castle Hill, New South Wales, 2154, Australia. *Office:* Diocesan Registry, Rusden St., Armidale, New South Wales, Australia.

CAREER: Ordained deacon, Church of England in Australia, 1907, priest, 1908; served churches in South Australia, and in Southwark, England; Bishop of Armidale, Sydney, Australia, 1929-64, retired, 1964. Deputy chancellor of University of New England, New South Wales, 1960-67. Episcopal canon, St. George's Cathedral, Jerusalem, 1962-65. *Military service:* Australian Commonwealth Forces, chaplain, 1918-20. *Awards, honors:* Dr.Theol., Australian College of Theology; D.D., Trinity College,

University of Toronto; Litt.D., University of New England, New South Wales; Companion of Most Distinguished Order of St. Michael and St. George, 1961.

WRITINGS: Marriage and Sex, Morlock Press, 1931; *Australia: The Church and the Future* (Moorhouse Lectures), Robert Dey & Son, 1941; *American Journey,* Clarendon Press, 1944; *In Journeyings Often,* Oxford University Press, 1949; *The Communist Way of Life and the Christian Answer,* Angus & Robertson, 1950; *America Revisited,* Church Publishing, 1955; *Third Time of Asking,* Anglican Press, 1959; (with the Bishop of Coventry) *Coventry Campaign,* Anglican Press, 1960; *Vietnam: Exchange of Letters between the Prime Minister, Robert Menzies, and John Moyes, and Others,* Prime Minister's Department, Australian Government, 1965. Contributor of articles on religious and social questions to *Anglican* and to secular journals.

WORK IN PROGRESS: A book of addresses; autobiography, requested by Australian Broadcasting Commission because the bishop has lived through an interesting phase of Australian history.

AVOCATIONAL INTERESTS: Cricket, music.

*   *   *

MUELDER, Walter George 1907-

PERSONAL: Born March 1, 1907, in Boody, Ill.; son of Epke Hermann and Minnie (Horlitz) Muelder; married Martha Grotewohl, June 28, 1934; children: Sonja Jane (Mrs. Paul Devitt), Helga Louise (Mrs. Kenneth Wells), Linda Ruth (Mrs. William Schell). *Education:* Knox College, B.S., 1927; Boston University, S.T.B., 1930, Ph.D., 1933. *Home:* 82 Oxford Rd., Newton Center, Mass. 02159.

CAREER: Ordained Methodist minister, 1933. Berea College, Berea, Ky., associate professor, 1934-36, professor, 1936-40; University of Southern California, Los Angeles, professor of Christian theology and Christian ethics, 1940-45; Boston University, School of Theology, Boston, Mass., dean and professor of social ethics, 1945-72, professor emeritus, 1972—. Delegate to World Conference on Faith and Order in Lund, Sweden, 1952, in Montreal, Canada, 1963, to Third Assembly of World Council of Churches, New Delhi, India, 1963, and to the Fourth Assembly, Uppsala, Sweden, 1968. Protestant observer for World Methodist Council at Second Vatican Council, 1964. Chairman of Commission on Institutionalism of Department of Faith and Order, World Council of Churches, 1955-63. Chairman of board, Ecumenical Institute, Celigny, Switzerland, 1961-68. Visiting professor at Berea College, 1972-73, and Garrett-Evangelical Theological Seminary, 1973-75. *Member:* Society for Religion in Higher Education (fellow), American Academy of Arts and Sciences (fellow), Phi Beta Kappa. *Awards, honors:* D.H.L., West Virginia Wesleyan College, 1960, Berea College, 1974; L.H.D., Claflin University, 1963, Knox College, 1969, and Boston University, 1973; S.T.D., Boston College, 1971; D.D., Colby College, 1972.

WRITINGS: (With E. S. Brightman) *Historical Outline of the Bible,* Berea College Press, 1936; (with Lawrence Sears) *The Development of American Philosophy,* Houghton, 1940, 2nd edition (with L. Sears and Anne V. Schlabach), Houghton, 1960; *Religion and Economic Responsibility,* Scribner, 1953; *In Every Place a Voice,* Board of Missions, Methodist Church of Cincinnati, 1957; *Foundations of the Responsible Society,* Abingdon, 1959; *Methodism and Society in the Twentieth Century,* Abingdon,

1961; (editor with Nils Ehrenstrom) *Institutionalism and Christian Unity,* Association Press, 1963; *Moral Law in Christian Social Ethics,* John Knox, 1966.

Contributor: *Personalism in Theology,* Boston University Press, 1943; *Liberal Learning and Religion,* Harper, 1951; *Human Destiny,* Pacific Philosophy Institute, 1951; *Church and Social Responsibility,* Abingdon, 1953; *American Income and Its Use,* Harper, 1954; *Youth in a Responsible Society,* Board of Missions of Methodist Church, 1956; *The Responsible Student,* National Methodist Student Movement, 1957.

BIOGRAPHICAL/CRITICAL SOURCES: Paul Deats, Jr., editor, *Toward a Discipline of Social Ethics: Essays in Honor of Walter George Muelder,* Boston University Press, 1972.

*   *   *

MULLEN, Robert R(odolph)   1908-

PERSONAL: Born November 24, 1908, in Alamogordo, N.M.; son of Robert Gordon (a mining engineer) and Madeline (Rodolf) Mullen; married Edna Cummings, March 13, 1937; children: Robert R., Jr., Jonathan, Christopher, Suzanne. *Education:* Attended University of Wisconsin, 1929-31, and University of Denver, 1931-33. *Politics:* Republican. *Religion:* Christian Science. *Home:* 550 Ocean Dr., Key Biscayne, Fla. 33149.

CAREER: Rocky Mountain News, Denver, Colo., reporter, 1931-35; *Christian Science Monitor,* Boston, Mass., staff correspondent, 1935-37, assistant city editor, 1937-40, editorial writer, 1940-42; Combined Boards (United States and United Kingdom) Information Committee, U.S. member, 1943-45; *Life,* New York, N.Y., editorial writer, 1945-49; Economic Cooperation Administration, Washington, D.C., director of information, 1949-52; National Citizens Committee for Educational Television, executive director, 1953-55; Robert R. Mullen Co. (public relations), Washington, D.C., chairman, 1956—. Publicity chief, Citizens for Eisenhower, 1952. *Member:* Public Relations Society of America, National Press Club, Overseas Press Club.

WRITINGS: The Latter Day Saints: The Mormons Yesterday and Today, Doubleday, 1966, (published in England as *The Mormons,* W. H. Allen, 1967). Contributor to a number of national magazines.

WORK IN PROGRESS: Causes of World War I.

*   *   *

MULLER, Siegfried H(ermann)   1902-1965

PERSONAL: Born March 24, 1902, in Berlin, Germany; son of Hermann and Frida (Marscheider) Muller; married Dolores Smith (a librarian), October 25, 1930. *Education:* Columbia University, B.S., and A.M., 1938, Ph.D., 1948. *Religion:* Protestant. *Home:* 3977 51st St., Woodside, N.Y. 11377. *Office:* Department of German, Adelphi University, Garden City, N.Y. 11530.

CAREER: Columbia University, New York, N.Y., extension instructor in German, 1937-38, instructor in German, College of Pharmacy, 1938-39; Adelphi University, Garden City, N.Y., 1939-65, began as instructor, became professor of German and chairman of department of German and general linguistics. Part-time instructor, Polytechnic Institute of Brooklyn, 1939-43, 1946, 1948-50. Director of archives, George Washington University, 1960-61. Linguistic consultant, U.S. Office of Education, 1960. *Member:* Modern Language Association of America, Linguistic So-

ciety of America, American Association of Teachers of German (past chapter president), American Association of University Professors, Geolinguistic Society of America, New York State Federation of Modern Language Teachers, Linguistic Circle of New York, Gerhart-Hauptmann-Gesellschaft.

WRITINGS: (Editor) Hermann von Baravalle, *Physik,* Heath, 1946; *Gerhart Hauptmann and Goethe,* King's Crown Press, 1949; *General Language Laboratory Manual,* privately printed, 1956; *Multi-Language Recording,* Wible Language Institute, 1961; *The World's Living Languages: Basic Facts of Their Structure, Kinship and Number of Speakers,* Ungar, 1964. Contributor to United States and German periodicals. Editorial consultant, *World Language Dictionary,* 1954; assistant editor, *German Quarterly,* 1954-64.

WORK IN PROGRESS: A multi-language food dictionary.

(Died June 10, 1965)

*   *   *

MULLINS, (George) Aloysius   1910-

PERSONAL: Born February 9, 1910; son of George and Emily (Barnham) Mullins. *Education:* Attended University of Fribourg; Collegium Angelicum, Rome, Italy, B.Th. *Home:* St. Martin's Lodge, Stoke Golding, Warwickshire, CV13 6NT England.

CAREER: Friar of Order of Preachers (Dominicans); entered order, 1929, ordained priest at Fribourg, Switzerland, 1935. Former schoolmaster, lecturer, editor, and parish priest; preacher of missions and retreats throughout England; now chaplain to Dominican Sisters. *Military service:* British Army, chaplain, 1942-47; served in North African and Italian campaigns.

WRITINGS: A Guide to the Kingdom: A Simple Handbook on the Parables, Newman, 1963; *The New Testament,* Hawthorn, 1963; *Heaven's Hostess,* Thomas More Books, 1963; *The Quiet Guest,* Catholic Printing Co. of Farnworth, 1963; *Signs and Wonders,* St. Paul Publications, 1968. Also author of *Witchcraft: A Warning,* published by Catholic Truth Society.

WORK IN PROGRESS: Two books, *Butter and Honey* and *Look to the Rock,* awaiting publishers.

*   *   *

MULLINS, Claud   1887-1968

PERSONAL: Born September 6, 1887, in London, England; son of E. Roscoe (a sculptor) and Alice (Pelton) Mullins; married Gwendolen Brandt, May 28, 1925; children: Ann (Mrs. Peter Dally), Barbara, Edwin. *Education:* Attended University College School, London, England, 1901-02, Mill Hill School, 1902-04, and studied in Germany and France, 1905-06; Gray's Inn, barrister-at-law (honors), 1912. *Politics:* Non-party. *Religion:* Independent Christian. *Home:* Glasses, Graffham, Petworth, Sussex, England.

CAREER: London County Council, London, England, clerk, 1907-12; barrister-at-law, London, 1913-31; metropolitan magistrate, London, 1931-47. Writer on aspects of law. Broadcaster in German for Voice of America, World War II; broadcaster since retirement for British Broadcasting Corp. Member of council of Magistrates' Association, 1932-62, of Midhurst Rural District Council, 1950-63; vice-president of Family Planning Association and London Marriage Guidance Council. *Military service:* British Army, 1915-19; served in Mesopotamia and India, 1917-19; became lieutenant. *Member:* Royal Commonwealth Society (fellow).

WRITINGS: London's Story, G. Bell, 1920; *The Leipzig Trials,* Witherby, 1921; *Marriage, Children and God,* Allen & Unwin, 1923; *In Quest of Justice,* J. Murray, 1931; *Crime and Psychology,* Methuen, 1943; *Why Crime?,* Methuen, 1945; *Fifteen Years Hard Labour,* Gollancz, 1948; *Are Findings Keepings? And Other Stories from the Law for Young People,* Muller, 1953; *The Sentence on the Guilty,* Justice of the Peace, 1957; *One Man's Furrow* (autobiographical), Johnson Publications, 1963. Contributor to periodicals.

(Died, 1968)

* * *

MUNCE, Ruth Hill 1898-
(Ruth Livingston Hill)

PERSONAL: Born January 24, 1898, in Philadelphia, Pa.; daughter of Franklin G. (a clergyman) and Grace (Livingston) Hill; married Gordon Munce October 19, 1923 (deceased); children: Gordon, Robert Livingston. *Education:* Swarthmore College, student, 1914-17; Wheaton College, Wheaton, Ill., B.A., 1953; Florida State University, graduate study, 1958. *Politics:* Republican. *Home:* 10348 52nd Ave. N., St. Petersburg, Fla. 33708.

CAREER: Swarthmore School of Music, Swarthmore, Pa., co-owner and teacher, 1918-40; Grace Livingston Hill Memorial School (now Keswick Christian School), St. Petersburg, Fla., founder and teacher, 1953-62.

WRITINGS: (With Grace Livingston Hill) *Mary Arden,* Lippincott, 1948; (with Hill) *Miss Lavinia's Call,* Lippincott, 1949; *Morning Is for Joy,* Lippincott, 1949; *John Neilson Had a Daughter,* Lippincott, 1950; *Bright Conquest,* Lippincott, 1951; *Jeweled Sword,* Lippincott, 1955; *The South Wind Blew Softly,* Lippincott, 1959; *This Side of Tomorrow,* Zondervan, 1962. Contributor of stories and articles to *His, Sunday School Times,* and *Eternity.*

WORK IN PROGRESS: A series on Christian Church history for teen-agers; a book on juvenile problems.

* * *

MUNDLAK, Max 1899-

PERSONAL: Born August 29, 1899, in Plonsk, Poland; son of Henry and Deborah Mundlak; married Fanny Shapiro (a volunteer social worker), October 23, 1908; children: Judith Helen (Mrs. Irvin S. Taylor). *Education:* Studied at British College of Optics, and at Ruskin College, Oxford. *Politics:* Liberal. *Religion:* "Humanism (Jewish)." *Home:* 30 B Heath Dr., London N.W.3, England. *Office:* 26 Goodge St., London W.1, England.

CAREER: Private practice as opthalmic optician. *Member:* International P.E.N. (fellow).

WRITINGS: The Nature and Mechanics of Consciousness, John Bale, 1932; *The Consequences of Philosophy: A Reply to Planck and Einstein,* John Bale, 1936; *Journey Into Morning* (novel), Staples, 1941; *Operation Survival!: The First Step,* Survival Books, 1962. Short stories and scripts for local journals and charitable organizations.

WORK IN PROGRESS: The Structure of Visual Perception; The Structure of Awareness; Journey Into Night (sequel to *Journey Into Morning*).†

MUNSON, Gorham B(ert) 1896-1969

PERSONAL: Born May 26, 1896, in Amityville, N.Y.; son of Hubert Barney (a minister) and Carrie Louise (Morrow) Munson; married Elizabeth Delza (a dancer), April 2, 1921. *Education:* Wesleyan University, Middletown, Conn., B.A., 1917. *Politics:* Independent. *Home:* Apartment 812, Hotel Wellington, 871 Seventh Ave., New York, N.Y. 10019. *Agent:* Barthold Fles Literary Agency, 507 Fifth Ave., New York, N.Y. 10017.

CAREER: English teacher, 1917-21; free-lance journalist, 1921-24; *Secession Magazine,* New York, N.Y., editor, 1922-24; managing editor of *Psychology Magazine,* 1924-26, and Grant Publications, 1926-28; editorial adviser for Doubleday, Doran & Co., 1928-30, and for Thomas Y. Crowell Co., 1934-37; Works Progress Administration, Washington, D.C., member of administrative staff, 1939-41; Greystone Press, New York, N.Y., associate editor, 1941-42; editor for Robert M. McBride Co., 1943, Prentice-Hall, 1944-48, Hermitage House, 1951-55, and Thomas Nelson & Sons, 1955-60; Fairleigh Dickenson University, Madison, N.Y., assistant professor of English, 1961-66; University of California, Davis, professor of English, 1961-69. New School for Social Research, New York, N.Y., lecturer, 1927-69. *Member:* Delta Kappa Epsilon, Players Club.

WRITINGS: Waldo Frank: A Study, Boni & Liveright, 1923; *Robert Frost: A Study in Sensibility and Good Sense,* Doran, 1927; *Destinations: A Canvass of American Literature Since 1900,* J. H. Sears & Co., 1928; *Style and Form in American Prose,* Doubleday, Doran, 1929; *The Dilemma of the Liberated: An Interpretation of Twentieth Century Humanism,* Coward, 1930; (contributor) Norman Foerster, editor, *Humanism and America: Essays on the Outlook of American Civilization,* Farrar & Rinehart, 1930; (contributor) Samuel David Schmalhausen, editor, *Behold America!,* Farrar & Rinehart, 1931; *Self-Instruction in Writing* (booklet), Home Institute, 1935; (contributor) James Laughlin, editor, *New Directions in Prose and Poetry,* New Directions, 1936; *Learn to Write for Publication* (booklet), Reader Mail, 1936; *The Psychology of Plenty,* Practical Psychology Monthly, 1937.

Twelve Decisive Battles of the Mind: The Story of Propaganda During the Christian Era, Greystone, 1942; *Money Reform Fifth Column,* News Background, 1943; *Aladdin's Lamp: The Wealth of the American People,* Creative Age Press, 1945; *The Written Word: How to Write Readable Prose,* Creative Age Press, 1949; *The Writer's Workshop Companion,* Thomas Nelson, 1951; (editor) *Best Advice on How to Write,* Hermitage House, 1952; *Penobscot: Down East Paradise,* Lippincott, 1959; *Robert Frost: Making Poems for America,* Encyclopaedia Britannica Press, 1962. Editor, *New Democracy,* 1933-39.

WORK IN PROGRESS: Memoirs of literary 1920's.

BIOGRAPHICAL/CRITICAL SOURCES: Variety, August 27, 1969; *Publishers Weekly,* September 8, 1969.

(Died August 15, 1969)

* * *

MURBARGER, Nell Lounsberry 1909-

PERSONAL: Born October 19, 1909, in Fall River County, S.D.; daughter of Harry Clement and Bessie Nell (White) Lounsberry; married Wilbur G. Murbarger, June 15, 1931 (divorced, 1939). *Education:* Tutored by mother through eighth grade; later attended schools in South Dakota, Oregon, Washington, and California. *Politics:* Republican. *Religion:* Methodist. *Home:* 1940 Maple Ave., Costa Mesa, Calif.

CAREER: Former newspaperwoman, working on *Los Angeles Examiner, Salt Lake Tribune,* and other papers in the West; editor of two California papers, *Costa Mesa Globe Herald,* 1936-39, *Newport-Balboa Press,* 1940-45; full-time free-lance writer, 1945—. Member of advisory panel, Desert Protective Council. *Member:* Western Writers of America (Los Angeles Corral), Eastern California Museum Association, Nevada Historical Society (life member), Utah Historical Society, Death Valley '49ers, Orange Coast Mineral and Lapidary Society, Night Riders Association (Elko County, Nev.). *Awards, honors:* American Association for State and Local History award of merit, 1955; National Federation of Press Women and California Association of Press Women awards, including national award for best nonfiction book of the year, 1956, for *Ghosts of the Glory Trail.*

WRITINGS: Ghosts of the Glory Trail, Desert Press, 1956; *Sovereigns of the Sage,* Desert Press, 1958; *30,000 Miles in Mexico,* Desert Press, 1961; *Ghosts of the Adobe Walls,* Westernlore, 1964. Stories included in several anthologies. Contributor of about one thousand articles to more than one hundred periodicals.

AVOCATIONAL INTERESTS: Color photography (owns library of more than fourteen thousand black and white negatives and almost ten thousand color transparencies), horseback riding, pack trips, camping, and world-wide travel.

* * *

MURDOCK, George Peter 1897-

PERSONAL: Born May 11, 1897, in Meriden, Conn.; son of George Bronson (a farmer) and Harriet Elizabeth (Graves) Murdock; married Carmen Swanson, September 4, 1925; children: Robert Douglas. *Education:* Yale University, A.B., 1919, Ph.D., 1925; Harvard University, law student, 1919-20. *Home:* Wynnewood Plaza Apartments, No. 107, Wynnewood, Pa. 19096.

CAREER: University of Maryland, College Park, instructor in sociology, 1925-27; Yale University, New Haven, Conn., began as assistant professor, associate professor of ethnology, 1928-38, professor of anthropology, 1938-60; University of Pittsburgh, Pittsburgh, Pa., Mellon Professor of Anthropology, 1960-73, professor emeritus, 1973—. Anthropological field work in British Columbia, 1932, in Oregon, 1934-35, and in Truk, 1947; chairman of Division of Behavioral Sciences, National Research Council, 1964-66. *Military service:* U.S. Army, Field Artillery, 1918; became second lieutenant. U.S. Naval Reserve, 1943-46; became commander. *Member:* American Anthropological Association (president, 1955), American Ethnological Society (president, 1952-53), Society for Applied Anthropology (president, 1947), National Academy of Sciences, American Academy of Arts and Sciences, American Sociological Association. *Awards, honors:* Viking Fund Medal in general anthropology, 1949; Thomas Henry Huxley Medal, 1971.

WRITINGS: (Translator and editor) Julius Lippert, *The Evolution of Culture,* Macmillan, 1931; *Our Primitve Contemporaries,* Macmillan, 1934; (editor) *Studies in the Science of Society,* Yale University Press, 1937; (with others) *Outline of Cultural Materials,* Institute of Human Relations, Yale University, 1938, revised edition, 1950; *Ethnographic Bibliography of North America,* Yale Anthropological Studies, 1941, 3rd edition, 1960; *Social Structure,* Macmillan, 1949; *Africa: Its Peoples and Their Cultural History,* McGraw, 1959; *Culture and Society,* University of Pittsburgh Press, 1965.

Contributor: (And editor) *Studies in the Science of Society,* Yale University Press, 1937; M. J. E. Senn, editor, *Problems of Infancy and Childhood,* Josiah Macy, Jr. Foundation, 1951; (author of foreword) Ward H. Goodenough, *Property, Kin, and Community on Truk,* Yale University Press, 1951; John H. Gillin, editor, *For a Science of Social Man,* Macmillan, 1954; B. J. Meggers, editor, *Evolution and Anthropology,* Anthropological Society of Washington, 1959; (and editor) *Social Structure in Southeast Asia,* Viking Fund Publications in Anthropology, 1960; Robert O. Tilman and Taylor Cole, editors, *The Nigerian Political Scene,* Duke University Press, 1962. Contributor of lesser sections to other books.

Author with C. S. Ford and J. W. M. Whiting of six military government and civil affairs handbooks on the Marshall, East Caroline, West Caroline, Marianas, Izu and Bonin, and Ryuku Islands, published by U.S. Navy Department, 1943-44.

Contributor of about one hundred articles and reviews to *Newsweek, Yale Review, Baltimore Evening Sun, Review of Religion, New Leader, Journal of American Forklore, American Anthropologist, Science,* and other journals. Editor, *Ethnology,* beginning 1962.

SIDELIGHTS: Murdock has traveled extensively in Oceania, Asia, Europe, and Africa, and made four trips around the world.

BIOGRAPHICAL/CRITICAL SOURCES: Ward H. Goodenough, editor, *Explorations in Cultural Anthropology,* McGraw, 1964; George P. Murdock, *Culture and Society,* University of Pittsburgh Press, 1965.

* * *

MURPHY, James M(aurice) 1932-c.1966

PERSONAL: Born July 25, 1932, in Takoma Park, Md.; son of James Maurice (an editor and writer) and Ruth (Sangster) Murphy; married Lynn Hirshman, December, 1962; children: Dion Faulkner. *Education:* Georgetown University, A.B., 1954; graduate study at University of Chicago, 1958-61, and Roosevelt University, 1963-64. *Politics:* Independent. *Religion:* Humanist. *Home:* 801 North Wabash Ave., Chicago, Ill. 60611. *Office:* Benefic Press, 10300 West Roosevelt Rd., Westchester, Ill. 60153.

CAREER: Light (magazine), Chicago, Ill., managing editor, 1957-60; Science Research Associates, Chicago, Ill., 1960-63, began as assistant editor, became associate editor; Benefic Press, Chicago, Ill., social studies editor, 1963-c.1966. *Member:* American Personnel and Guidance Association, American Civil Liberties Union, Voters for Peace.

WRITINGS—Compiler: *Handbook of Job Facts,* 3rd edition, Science Research Associates, 1963; *Directory of Vocational Training Sources,* Science Research Associates, 1964. Contributor of poems, reviews, and articles to *Critic, Poetry, Dial,* and other magazines and journals. Managing editor and co-founder of *Chicago Choice* (national literary magazine), 1960-61.

(Deceased)

* * *

MURPHY, Robert (William) 1902-1971

PERSONAL: Born August 27, 1902, in Ridley Park, Pa.;

son of William Robert (an engineer) and Mary Elizabeth (Bryant) Murphy; married Jean Warfield Whittle, March 22, 1946; children: Robert Shane, Molly Jean. *Education:* Friends Central School, Philadelphia, Pa., graduate, 1921; attended Washington and Lee University. *Politics:* Independent. *Religion:* Presbyterian. *Home:* 321 Skyline Dr., Prescott, Ariz. 86301. *Agent:* Harold Ober Associates, Inc., 40 East 49th St., New York, N.Y. 10017.

CAREER: Saturday Evening Post, Philadelphia, Pa., began as associate editor, became senior editor, 1942-62. Has conducted courses in writing at University of Indiana, University of Colorado, and University of Michigan Writers' Conferences. *Member:* Explorers Club (New York). *Awards, honors:* Dutton Animal Book award, 1964, for *The Pond.*

WRITINGS: Murder in Waiting (novel), Scribner, 1938; (with Helen Wills Moody) *Death Serves an Ace*, Scribner, 1939; *The Warm Hearted Polar Bear*, Little, Brown, 1957; *The Haunted Journey*, Doubleday, 1961; *The Peregrine Falcon*, Houghton, 1963 (published in England as *Varda, the Flight of a Falcon*, Cassell, 1964); *The Pond*, Dutton, 1964; *The Golden Eagle*, Dutton, 1965; *Wild Geese Calling*, Dutton, 1966; *The Phantom Setter, and Other Stories*, Dutton, 1966; *A Certain Island*, M. Evans, 1967; *Wild Sanctuaries: Our National Wildlife Refuges*, Dutton, 1968; *A Heritage Restored: America's Wildlife Refuges* (juvenile edition of *Wild Sanctuaries*), Dutton, 1969; *The Haunted Journey* (juvenile edition), Farrar, Straus, 1969; *The Mountain Lion*, Dutton, 1969; *The Stream*, Farrar, Straus, 1971. Contributor of forty-four short stories and numerous articles to *Saturday Evening Post* and other magazines, and to anthologies.

SIDELIGHTS: Wild Geese Calling was made into a television film. *Avocational interests:* Nature, photography, falconry, hunting, fishing, conservation, and travel.

BIOGRAPHICAL/CRITICAL SOURCES: Young Reader's Review, December, 1966; *Best Sellers*, April 1, 1969, April 1, 1971; *New York Times Book Review*, February 15, 1970; *Antiquarian Bookman*, August 2-9, 1971.

(Died July 13, 1971)

* * *

MURPHY, Robert D(aniel) 1894-

PERSONAL: Born October 28, 1894, in Milwaukee, Wis.; son of Francis Patrick and Catherine (Schmitz) Murphy; married Mildred Taylor, March 3, 1921; children: Rosemary, Mildred (Mrs. Geoffrey Pond). *Education:* Marquette Academy, graduate; University of Wisconsin, Milwaukee, student, one year; George Washington University, LL.B., 1920, LL.M., 1928. *Religion:* Roman Catholic. *Agent:* Brandt & Brandt, 101 Park Ave., New York, N.Y. 10017. *Office:* Corning Glass, 717 Fifth Ave., New York, N.Y. 10022.

CAREER: U.S. diplomat for almost four decades, now director of Corning Glass Works, Corning, N.Y., and president of Corning International. Started government career with U.S. Post Office, 1916, served as vice-consul at Zurich, Switzerland, 1921, Munich, 1921-25, consul at Seville, Spain, 1925, Paris, 1930-36, counselor of U.S. Embassy, Paris, France, 1940; effected preparations for Allied landings in North Africa, 1942, conducted negotiations for entry of French West Africa into war later that year; U.S. Political adviser for Germany, 1944, director of German and Austrian Affairs, Department of State, 1949; U.S. Ambas-

sador to Belgium, 1949-52, to Japan, 1952; assistant secretary of state for United Nations Affairs, 1953, deputy undersecretary of state, 1953, undersecretary of state for political affairs, 1959. Director of Morgan Guaranty Trust Co., Gillette Co., Japan Fund, Inc.

AWARDS, HONORS: Distinguished Service Medal (U.S. Army), 1942; Laetare Medal, University of Notre Dame, 1959; foreign decorations include Croix de Guerre with Palm, Order of Leopold, Order of the Rising Sun; honorary degrees include LL.D. from Marquette University, University of Notre Dame, Harvard University, Fordham University, New York University, Georgetown University, George Washington University.

WRITINGS: A Look at the Middle East: Background, Public Services Division, U.S. Department of State, 1957; *The Bases of Peace* (pamphlet), U.S. Department of State, 1958; *Reporting Public Problems: An Analysis of Today's Issues*, Chilton, 1960; *Diplomat Among Warriors*, Doubleday, 1964.

* * *

MURRAY, Clara Elizabeth 1894-

PERSONAL: Born June 13, 1894, in Blandford Township, Oxford County, Ontario, Canada; daughter of Robert (a farmer) and Elizabeth Anne (Diamond) Murray. *Education:* McMaster University, B.A., 1936; University of Toronto, B.Paed., 1956. *Religion:* United Church of Canada. *Home:* 79 James St. S., Hamilton, Ontario, Canada.

CAREER: Public school elementary teacher, Orillia, Ontario, 1926-30; public school teacher of retarded children, Hamilton, Ontario, 1930—.

WRITINGS: John Bunyan's Pilgrim's Progress for Devotional Reading, Baker Book, 1958, 2nd edition, 1959; *Bunyan's Christiana*, Baker Book, 1960; *Useful Knowledge about the Human Body*, Denison, 1963; *Six Famous Stories*, Eerdmans, 1964.

WORK IN PROGRESS: A book, *The Old Testament, the Gospels, the Acts, and the Revelation.*

* * *

MURRAY, George (McIntosh) 1900-1970

PERSONAL: Born December 16, 1900, in London, England; son of Samuel and Amy Mary (Poole) Murray; married Irene Helena Bill, June 4, 1927 (died, 1963); married Loris Taylor, 1967; children: (first marriage) Mary (Mrs. Jorgen Vang Andersen), John Shaw. *Education:* Attended schools in England. *Politics:* Conservative. *Religion:* Christian. *Home:* 45 Grove Way, Esher, Surrey, England. *Office: Daily Mail*, Northcliffe House, London E.C.4, England.

CAREER: Started career as journalist on *Farnham Herald*, 1923, and worked for other newspapers, 1925-33; *Daily Mail*, London, England, 1933-70, chief leader writer, 1939-70. Director of Associated Newspapers, London, 1955-70. *Member:* British Press Council (vice-chairman, 1957-59; chairman, 1959-63), Commonwealth Press Union (council member, 1964), Institute of Journalists (fellow), Garrick Club, Press Club. *Awards, honors:* Commander, Order of the British Empire, 1958.

WRITINGS: The Life of King George V, Associated Newspapers, 1935; *The Life of King Edward VIII*, Associated Newspapers, 1936; *King George VI and the Coronation*, Associated Newspapers, 1937; *The Impatient Horse* (juvenile), Ladybird Series, 1952; *The Press and the Public: The Story of the British Press Council*, Southern Illinois University Press, 1972. Contributor of articles and verse to newspapers and journals.

AVOCATIONAL INTERESTS: Gardening.

(Died November 2, 1970)

* * *

MURRELL, Elsie Kathleen Seth-Smith   1883- (Elsie K. Seth-Smith)

PERSONAL: Born May 22, 1883, in Wonersh Guildford, Surrey, England; daughter of William and Catherine Sarah (Edwards) Seth-Smith; married Arthur Frederick Murrell (a schoolmaster), February 4, 1921; children: Catherine Priscilla (Mrs. Philip Hall), Lois Frideswide (Mrs. Richard Gendall). *Religion:* Church of England. *Home:* 12 Sackville Lane, East Grinstead, Sussex, England.

WRITINGS—All under name Elsie K. Seth-Smith: *To the Shrine of Truth*, S.P.C.K., 1904; *Friedhelm*, S.P.C.K., 1905; (editor) *The Diary of Perpetua Gylpin of the Town of Croydon*, S.P.C.K., 1908; *A Son of Odin*, Jarrolds, 1909; *The Way of Little Gidding*, Allenson & Co., 1914; *Don Raimon*, S.P.C.K., 1919; *Pioneers in Africa* (play), S.P.C.K., 1920; *Sir Ranulf*, S.P.C.K., 1920; *The Firebrand of the Indies*, Macmillan, 1922; *St. Hugh of Lincoln, 1140-1200*, S.P.C.K., 1923; *St. Boniface, A.D. 679-755*, S.P.C.K., 1924; *Lemundu*, S.P.C.K., 1928; *The First Princess Margaret*, Sheldon Press, 1931.

Historical tales for older children; all under name Elsie K. Seth-Smith: *When Shakespeare Lived in Southwark*, Harrap, 1944, published in America as *Vagabonds All*, Houghton, 1946; *At the Sign of the Gilded Shoe*, Harrap, 1955; *The Black Tower*, Harrap, 1956, published in America as *The Blacktower*, Vanguard, 1957; *The Coal-Scuttle Bonnet*, Harrap, 1958; *The Fortune of Virginia*, Harrap, 1960; *The Fen Frog*, Harrap, 1964; *Selina*, Harrap, 1965; *Jonah and the Cat*, Harrap, 1967.

SIDELIGHTS: Mrs. Murrell writes historical stories for love of it, choosing familiar districts for background. Her first tale was published when she was eighteen.

* * *

MUSCHENHEIM, William   1902-

PERSONAL: Born November 7, 1902, in New York, N.Y.; son of Frederik Augustus (an engineer and hotel man) and Elsa (Unger) Muschenheim; married Elizabeth Marie Bodanzky, November 29, 1930; children: Carl Arthur, Anna Elizabeth Muschenheim Arms. *Education:* Attended Williams College, 1919-21, Massachusetts Institute of Technology, 1921-24; Behrens Master School of Architecture, Academy of Fine Arts, Vienna, Austria, M.Arch., 1929. *Politics:* Democratic. *Religion:* Agnostic. *Home:* 1251 Heatherway, Ann Arbor, Mich. *Office:* College of Architecture and Design, University of Michigan, Ann Arbor, Mich.

CAREER: Designer with Joseph, Urban & Peabody, and with Wilson & Brown, both New York, N.Y., prior to 1934; practicing architect as principal of own firm, New York, N.Y., and Ann Arbor, Mich., 1934—; University of Michigan, Ann Arbor, professor of architecture, 1950—. *Member:* American Institute of Architects (fellow), Association of Collegiate Schools of Architecture, Congres Internationale des Architectes Modernes, Alpha Rho Chi. *Awards, honors:* Second prize, international competition

for selection of architects for new Middle East Technical University buildings; Sol King Award, 1970-71, for excellent teaching in architecture.

WRITINGS: Elements of the Art of Architecture, Viking, 1964. Contributor to more than fifteen professional journals in United States and abroad.

WORK IN PROGRESS: Research on interrelationship of contemporary architectural thought and education in various parts of the world.

SIDELIGHTS: Muschenheim speaks French and German; he understands Italian and Spanish.

* * *

MUSGRAVE, Florence   1902-

PERSONAL: Born July 21, 1902, in Mount Clare, W.Va.; daughter of P. Z. and Mary Maud (Sigler) Musgrave. *Education:* Fairmont State College, B.A., 1928; New York University, M.A., 1932. *Religion:* Protestant.

CAREER: With Wheeling (W.Va.) High School, 1928-31; junior high school teacher in New Jersey, 1932-38; with Wheeling (W.Va.) Public Library, 1939-45; with Wheeling Country Day School, 1945-50; Willoughby-Eastlake (Ohio) City School System, English teacher, beginning 1954. *Member:* American Association of University Women, Delta Kappa Gamma.

WRITINGS: Mary Lizzie, Houghton, 1951; *Dogs in the Family*, Houghton, 1952; *Stars Over the Tent*, Houghton, 1952; *Oh Sarah*, Farrar, Straus, 1953; *Catherine's Bells*, Farrar, Straus, 1954; *Trailer Tribe*, Farrar, Straus, 1955; *Marged*, Farrar, Straus, 1956; *Robert E.*, Hastings, 1957; *Like a Red, Red Rose*, Hastings, 1958; *A Boy for You, A Horse for Me*, Hastings, 1959; *Sarah Hastings*, 1960; *Merrie's Miracle*, Hastings, 1962; *Two Dates for Mike*, Hastings, 1964.

WORK IN PROGRESS: A book of fiction for junior high level, with background in Hawaii.

AVOCATIONAL INTERESTS: Breeding cockers and beagles; travel.

* * *

MUSMANNO, Michael A(ngelo)   ?-1968

PERSONAL: Born near Pittsburgh, Pa.; son of Antonio and Maddelena (Castellucci) Musmanno. *Education:* George Washington University, B.A. and M.A., Georgetown University, LL.B.; advanced law degrees, including two doctorates, from National University, American University, University of Rome. *Home:* McKees Rocks, Pa. 15136. *Office:* Supreme Court of Pennsylvania, 811 City-County Building, Pittsburgh, Pa. 15219.

CAREER: Admitted to bar, 1923; trial lawyer in Philadelphia, Pa., and Pittsburgh, Pa., 1923-31; member of Pennsylvania legislature, 1929-32; judge in Pennsylvania of Allegheny County Court, 1932-34, Common Pleas Court, 1935-51, Supreme Court, 1952-68. President of U.S. Board of Forcible Repatriation in Austria; judge at International War Crimes Tribunal in Nuremberg, Germany; witness for Israeli government in Eichmann trial, 1961. *Military service:* World War I, U.S. Army, Infantry, became captain. World War II, U.S. Navy; served two years in Italy, part of that time as naval aide to Mark Clark, and six months as military governor of Sorrentine Peninsula; became rear admiral; wounded twice in action; decorations include Legion of Merit, Bronze Star, Purple Heart with cluster. *Member:*

American Legion, Veterans of Foreign Wars, Disabled American Veterans, Military Order of the Purple Heart.

WRITINGS: The Library for American Studies in Italy, [Rome], 1925; *Proposed Amendments to the Constitution* (monograph), U.S. Government Printing Office, 1929; *Black Fury*, Trinacria, 1935; *After Twelve Years* (about Sacco-Vanzetti case), Knopf, 1939; *The General and the Man* (biography of Mark W. Clark), Mondadori, 1946; *Listen to the River* (novel), Droemersche Verlagsanstalt, 1948; *War in Italy* (autobiographical), Valecchi, 1948; (contributor) Christopher G. James and others, *Something Hitler Forgot: Memorandum on Hitler's Famous Car and Other Stories*, [Washington, D.C.], 1948; *Ten Days to Die*, Doubleday, 1950; *Across the Street from the Courthouse*, Dorrance, 1954; *Justice Musmanno Dissents* (compilation), foreword by Roscoe Pound, Bobbs-Merrill, 1956; *Verdict!: The Adventures of the Young Lawyer in the Brown Suit*, Doubleday, 1958; *The Eichmann Kommandos*, Macrae, 1961; *The Death Sentence in the Case of Adolf Eichmann: A Letter to His Excellency Itzhak Ben-Zvi, President of the State of Israel, Jerusalem*, [Pittsburgh], 1962; *Man with an Unspotted Conscience: Adolf Eichmann's Role in the Nazi Mania Is Weighed in Hannah Arendt's New Book* (pamphlet), [New York], 1963; *The Sacco-Vanzetti Case*, [Lawrence, Kan.], 1963; *Was Sacco Guilty?*, [New York], 1963; *The Story of the Italians in America*, Doubleday, 1965; *Columbus Was First*, Fountainhead, 1966; *That's My Opinion*, Michie Company, 1967; *The Glory and the Dream: Abraham Lincoln, Before and After Gettysburg*, Long House, 1967. Author of articles in legal reviews and magazines.

SIDELIGHTS: Black Fury was made into a film; *Ten Days to Die*, the story of Hitler's last days, was made into a film in Germany.

BIOGRAPHICAL/CRITICAL SOURCES: New York Mirror, May 12, 1961; *New York Times*, May 16, 1961; *Philadelphia Inquirer*, May 16, 1961.

(Died October 12, 1968)

*   *   *

MUSURILLO, Herbert (Anthony Peter) 1917-1974

PERSONAL: Born June 13, 1917, in New York, N.Y.; son of Henry (a lawyer) and Rose (Capece) Musurillo. *Education:* Georgetown University, B.A., 1939; Catholic University of America, M.A., 1941; Oxford University, D.Phil., 1951; Fordham University, Ph.D., 1954. *Home:* Fordham University, New York, N.Y. 10458.

CAREER: Roman Catholic priest, member of Society of Jesus (Jesuits). Fordham University, New York, N.Y., instructor, 1941-43; Facultes universitaires Notre-Dame de la Paix, Namur, Belgium, teacher of English, 1947-48; Fordham University, 1951-55, began as instructor, became assistant professor of classical languages; Bellarmine College Jesuit Seminary, Louisville, Ky., began as associate professor, became professor of classics, 1955-62; Fordham University, professor of classical languages, 1963-74, chairman of classics department, 1967-70. Lecturer at Yale University, Oxford University, Hebrew University, and other universities. *Member:* American Philological Association, International Society of Papyrologists, Vergilian Society, Classical Association of the Atlantic States.

WRITINGS: The Problem of Ascetical Fasting in the Greek Patristic Writers, Fordham University Press, 1956; (editor and translator) Saint Methodius of Olympus, *The Symposium: A Treatise on Chastity*, Newman, 1958; (translator; editor with Jean Danielou) Saint Gregorius of Nyssa, *From Glory to Glory: Texts from Gregory of Nyssa's Mystical Writings*, Scribner, 1961; *Symbol and Myth in Ancient Poetry*, Fordham University Press, 1961; (editor) *Acta Alexandrinorum: De mortibus Alexandriae nobilium fragmenta papyracea graeca*, Teubner, 1961; *Symbolism and the Christian Imagination*, Helicon, 1962; (author of introduction and critical text) Saint Methodius, *Le Banquet*, Editions du Cerf, 1963; *Gregory of Nyssa: De vita Moysis*, E. J. Brill, 1964; (editor) Joannes Chrysostomus, *La Virginite*, Editions du Cerf, 1966; (editor and translator) *The Fathers of the Primitive Church*, New American Library, 1966; *The Light and the Darkness: Studies in the Dramatic Poetry of Sophocles*, E. J. Brill, 1967; (compiler, translator, and author of introduction) *The Acts of the Christian Martyrs*, Clarendon Press, 1972.

Also author of two radio plays and two college produced stage plays. Contributor to festschrifts, encyclopedias, and journals. Member of editorial board, *Thought*.

WORK IN PROGRESS: An analysis of Euripides' dramas.

SIDELIGHTS: Musurillo was competent in French, German, Italian, and Spanish and he read modern Greek, Russian, and Dutch. His travels included a six-month tour of Cairo, Athens, Jordan, and Istanbul in search of relevant Greek manuscripts, and a walking trip through Israel and Turkey. *Avocational interests:* Classical music, chess, hiking, swimming, occasional handball and tennis; modern art, sculpture, painting, and poetry.

(Died May 27, 1974)

*   *   *

MYERS, A(lexander) J(ohn) William 1877-

PERSONAL: Born December 17, 1877, in Lake Verd, Prince Edward Island, Canada; son of Charles (a farmer) and Margaret Sarah MacDougall (Moore) Myers; married Mae Ethel Dickenson, 1912 (died, 1948); married Helen Penelope Ramsay, August 31, 1952. *Education:* Attended Prince of Wales College; attended Presbyterian Theological College, Halifax, Nova Scotia, 1902-03, Knox Presbyterian College, Toronto, Ontario, 1903-04; Dalhousie University, B.A., 1902, M.A., 1904; Presbyterian Theological College, Halifax, Nova Scotia, B.D., 1907; Columbia University, Ph.D., 1912. *Politics:* "Liberal—usually." *Home:* 118 Lytton Blvd., Toronto 310, Ontario, Canada.

CAREER: Clergyman, United Church of Canada (formerly Presbyterian Church); minister in Black River, New Brunswick, 1905-09; Presbyterian Church of Canada, educational secretary, 1912-17; Hartford School of Religious Education, Hartford Seminary Foundation, Hartford, Conn., professor of religious education, 1917-42; minister in Belleville, Ontario, 1942-45, Toronto, Ontario, 1945-46, Wexford, Scarboro, Ontario, 1949-54, and Oriole United Church, Toronto, Ontario, 1956-57. Lecturer at Yale Divinity School, University of Connecticut, United Church Seminary, New Brunswick Theological Seminary, and Presbyterian College and Seminary of Vancouver. *Military service:* Prince Edward Island Infantry, 1898-99. *Member:* Royal Canadian Geographical Society, United Empire Loyalists' Association, Wilson MacDonald Poetry Society, Toronto Mendelssohn Choir Society, Empire Club (Toronto).

WRITINGS: The Old Testament in the Sunday School,

Teachers College, Columbia University, 1912; *Pussy Tom*, privately printed, 1913; *Boys of the Old Testament*, Religious Education Council of Canada, 1918; *Teaching Values of the Old Testament*, Pilgrim Press, 1919; *Christian Life in the Community*, Association Press, 1919; *What Is Religious Education, and Educational Evangelism*, National Sunday School Union, 1925; *Teaching Religion*, Westminster, 1928; *Christian Education in the Local Church*, Ryerson, 1929; (with Edwin E. Sundt) *The Country Church as It Is*, Revell, 1930; *Teachers of Religion*, Ryerson, 1932; *Teaching Religion Creatively*, Revell, 1932; (with Alma N. Schilling) *Living Stone: A Record and Interpretation of Riverside Church Explorations with Boys and Girls Nine to Twelve Years of Age*, Bethany Press, 1936; (with others) *Adventuring with Kwo Ying*, Church Mission House, 1937; *Horace Bushnell and Religious Education*, Manthorne & Burack, 1937; *Religion for Today: An Essay in the Philosophy of Religious Education*, Association Press, 1941; *Historical Sketch of Tabernacle United Church*, [Belleville], 1945; (editor) *Enriching Worship*, Harper, 1949; *Victory Over Death*, Bethany Press, 1956; *Children's Adventures with Nature and People*, Exposition, 1959; *God's World and God's People: Stories for Boys and Girls,* Upper Room, 1963. Co-author of several church survey reports and contributor of articles to many magazines.

WORK IN PROGRESS: A manuscript on religious education; research on Religious Education Association.

SIDELIGHTS: Teaching Religion has gone into twenty-five editions, and has been issued in Spanish and Chinese.

* * *

MYERS, Raymond E(dward) 1902-

PERSONAL: Born October 31, 1902, in Mount Vernon, Ky.; son of Marion L. (a dentist) and Lora (Thomas) Myers; married Benson Spencer, April 4, 1924. *Education:* Kentucky Wesleyan College, student, 1920-23; University of Louisville, D.D.S., 1926, B.S., 1932. *Politics:* Independent. *Religion:* Methodist. *Home:* 35 Willow Terrace Apartments, Louisville, Ky. 40204.

CAREER: Private dental practice, Louisville, Ky., 1929-32; University of Louisville, Louisville, Ky., instructor, 1926-28, assistant professor, 1929-32, professor of dentistry, 1933-69, head of department of restorative dentistry, 1933-54, dean of School of Dentistry, 1945-69, dean emeritus, 1969—. Consultant, U.S. Veterans Administration Hospital, Louisville, 1950-69; vice-president, Southern Regional Conference of Dental Deans, 1960. Member of American College of Dentists survey, National Health Service in England and Scotland, 1949. *Member:* American College of Dentists (fellow), International Association for Dental Research, American Dental Association, Kentucky Dental Association, Louisville Civil War Round Table, Phi Kappa Phi, Omicron Kappa Upsilon, Omicron Delta Kappa, Rotary, Filson Club. *Awards, honors:* Award of merit from American Association for State and Local History, 1965, for *The Zollie Tree*.

WRITINGS: The Zollie Tree, Filson Club Press, 1964. Contributor to dental journals in America and abroad.

WORK IN PROGRESS: A book, *Dear Uncle*.

* * *

MYLES, Eugenie Louise (Butler) 1905-

PERSONAL: Born September 8, 1905, in Edmonton, Alberta, Canada; daughter of Levi (a farmer) and Eugenie Torr (Settle) Butler; married Ernest Alexander Myles, April 16, 1938; children: Eileen Constance, Stanley Terrence. *Education:* University of Alberta, B.A. (honors in English), 1927; Calgary Normal School, academic certificate, 1928. *Home:* 12424 Jasper Ave., Edmonton, Alberta, Canada.

CAREER: High school teacher in Alberta, Canada, 1928-32; *Edmonton Journal*, Edmonton, Alberta, reporter-editor, 1932-38; University of Alberta, Edmonton, teaching fellow, 1963—. Edmonton Archives Board, member, 1956-62, vice-chairman, 1961-62; member of executive board, Friends of the University of Alberta, 1962—. *Member:* Canadian Authors Association (president, Edmonton branch, 1959-62), Canadian Women's Press Club (former president, Edmonton branch; former member of Alberta executive board), Alberta Historical Society (former board member), Women's University Club (former board member).

WRITINGS: (With Elsie McCall Gillis) *North Pole Boarding House*, Ryerson, 1959; (with Donalda Copeland) *Remember, Nurse*, Ryerson, 1960; *The Emperor of Peace River*, Institute of Applied Art, 1965. Contributor of stories to "Parade Readers." Contributor of short stories to Canadian Broadcasting Corporation, *Edmonton Journal* and *Country Life*, and of articles to *Edmonton Journal*, 1938-60.

WORK IN PROGRESS: Little Cayuse, a juvenile book; *Wife of the Emperor*, a biography.

* * *

NASH, Ethel Miller 1909-

PERSONAL: Born June 20, 1909, in Liverpool, England; daughter of Edmund Miller (an architect) and Lillian (Ellery) Hughes; married Arnold S. Nash (a professor), July 1, 1933; children: A. E. Keir, David Charles. *Education:* University of Liverpool, B.A. (honors), 1931; University of North Carolina, M.A., 1949. *Religion:* Episcopalian. *Home:* Bowling Creek Rd., Chapel Hill, N.C.

CAREER: City schools psychologist, Toronto, Ontario, 1942-43; University of North Carolina, Chapel Hill, marriage counselor, 1949-56, lecturer in department of sociology, 1950-56; Bowman Gray School of Medicine, Winston-Salem, N.C., assistant professor of preventive medicine and associate in obstetrics and gynecology, 1956-65; Psychiatric Associates of Chapel Hill, Inc., Chapel Hill, N.C., partner, 1964—. Member of board of directors of National Council on Family Relations and Sex Information Education Council of the United States. *Member:* American Association of Marriage Counselors (president), American Orthopsychiatric Association, American Sociological Association, North Carolina Family Life Council (past president).

WRITINGS: With This Ring, Association Press, 1942; (contributor) Emily H. Mudd and others, editors, *Marriage Counseling: A Casebook*, Association Press, 1958; (contributor) Mary Steichen Calderone, editor, *Manual of Contraceptive Practice*, Williams & Wilkins, 1964; (editor with Lucie Jessner and D. Wilfred Abse) *Marriage Counseling in Medical Practice*, University of North Carolina Press, 1964; (contributor) Richard Klemer, editor, *Counseling in Marital and Sexual Problems: A Physician's Handbook*, Williams & Wilkins, 1965.

WORK IN PROGRESS: Research in premarital counseling and marital counseling, particularly as related to physicians.

NASH, (Frederic) Ogden   1902-1971

PERSONAL: Born August 19, 1902, in Rye, N.Y.; son of Edmund Strudwick and Mattie (Chenault) Nash; married Frances Rider Leonard, June 6, 1931; children: Linell Chenault (Mrs. J. Marshall Smith), Isabel Jackson (Mrs. Frederick Eberstadt). *Education:* Attended Harvard University, 1920-21. *Residence:* Baltimore, Md.

CAREER: Poet, author; began writing light verse about 1925. Taught one year at St. George's School, Providence, R.I.; was a bond salesman on Wall Street, briefly in the mid-1920's; worked in the copy department of an advertising agency, writing streetcar ads; worked in the editorial and publicity departments of Doubleday, Doran & Co., 1925; member of *New Yorker* editorial staff for a short time, then became a full-time writer. Gave frequent lectures and readings. Appeared on radio shows, including "Information, Please!," and the Bing Crosby and Rudy Vallee hours, and on television panel shows including "Masquerade Party." *Member:* National Institute of Arts and Letters.

WRITINGS: (With Joseph Alger) *Cricket of Carador*, Doubleday, 1925; (with Christopher Morley and Cleon Throckmorton) *Born in a Beer Garden, or, She Troupes to Conquer*, Rudge, 1930; *Free Wheeling*, Simon & Schuster, 1931; *Hard Lines*, Simon & Schuster, 1931; (editor) Pelham Granville Wodehouse, *Nothing but Wodehouse*, Doubleday, 1932; *Happy Days*, Simon & Schuster, 1933; *Four Prominent So and So's* (music by Robert Armbruster), Simon & Schuster, 1934; *The Primrose Path*, Simon & Schuster, 1935; *The Bad Parents' Garden of Verse*, Simon & Schuster, 1936; *I'm a Stranger Here Myself*, Little, Brown, 1938.

The Face is Familiar: The Selected Works of Ogden Nash, Little, Brown, 1940; *Good Intentions*, Little, Brown, 1942, revised edition, Dent, 1956; *The Ogden Nash Pocket Book*, Blakiston, 1944; *Many Long Years Ago*, Little, Brown, 1945; *The Selected Verse of Ogden Nash*, Modern Library, 1946; *Ogden Nash's Musical Zoo* (music by Vladimire Dukelsky), Little, Brown, 1947; *Versus*, Little, Brown, 1949.

Family Reunion, Little, Brown, 1950; *Parents Keep Out: Elderly Poems for Youngerly Readers*, Little, Brown, 1951; *The Private Dining Room, and Other New Verses*, Little, Brown, 1953; (editor) *The Moon is Shining Bright as Day: An Anthology of Good-Humored Verse*, Lippincott, 1953; *The Pocket Book of Ogden Nash*, Pocket Books, 1954; *You Can't Get There From Here*, Little, Brown, 1957; *The Boy Who Laughed at Santa Claus* (keepsake edition), printed by Cooper & Beatty Ltd. (London), 1957; *The Christmas That Almost Wasn't*, Little, Brown, 1957; (editor) *I Couldn't Help Laughing: Stories Selected and Introduced by Ogden Nash*, Lippincott, 1957; *Verses from 1929 On*, Little, Brown, 1959 (published in England as *Collected Verse From 1929 On*, Dent, 1961); *Custard, The Dragon*, Little, Brown, 1959.

Beastly Poetry, Hallmark Editions, 1960; *A Boy is a Boy: The Fun of Being a Boy*, Watts, 1960; (editor) *Everybody Ought to Know: Verses Selected and Introduced by Ogden Nash*, Lippincott, 1961; *Custard, The Dragon and the Wicked Knight*, Little, Brown, 1961; *The New Nutcracker Suite, and Other Innocent Verses*, Little, Brown, 1962; *Girls Are Silly*, Watts, 1962; *Everyone But Thee and Me*, Little, Brown, 1962; *A Boy and His Room*, Watts, 1963; *The Adventures of Isabel*, Little, Brown, 1963; *The Untold Adventures of Santa Claus*, Little, Brown, 1964; *An Ogden*

Nash Bonanza (five volumes; contains *Good Intentions, I'm a Stranger Here Myself, Many Long Years Ago, The Private Dining Room*, and *Versus*), Little, Brown, 1964; *Marriage Lines: Notes of a Student Husband*, Little, Brown, 1964 (published in England as *Notes of a Student Husband*, Dent, 1964); *Santa Go Home: A Case History for Parents*, Little, Brown, 1967; *The Cruise of the Aardvark*, M. Evans, 1967; *The Mysterious Ouphe*, Hale, 1967; *There's Always Another Windmill*, Little, Brown, 1968; *Funniest Verses of Ogden Nash: Light Lyrics by One of America's Favorite Humorists*, Selected by Dorothy Price, Hallmark Editions, 1968; (with others) *New Comic Limericks: Laughable Poems*, Compiled by Ivanette Dennis, Roger Schlesinger, 1969; *Bed Riddance: A Posy for the Indisposed*, Little, Brown, 1970; *The Old Dog Barks Backwards*, Little, Brown, 1972; *The Animal Garden*, Deutsch, 1972.

Completed *The Scroobious Pip*, by Edward Lear, Harper, 1968. Wrote lyrics for Broadway musical, "One Touch of Venus," 1943, for Off-Broadway production, "The Littlest Revue," and for television show, "Art Carney Meets Peter and the Wolf." Wrote adaptation of Otto A. Harbach's *The Firefly*, produced under same title, MGM, 1937; author of screenplay with George Oppenheimer and Edmund L. Hartmann, "The Feminine Touch," Loew's, 1941. Wrote new verses to Saint-Saens's "Carnival of the Animals," narrated by Noel Coward, for Columbia; author of verses set to Prokofiev's "Peter and the Wolf," and Dukas's "The Sorcerer's Apprentice."

Contributor of verse to periodicals, including *New Yorker, Life, Saturday Evening Post, Holiday, Saturday Review, Harper's Atlantic, Vogue, McCall's*, and *New Republic*.

SIDELIGHTS: Nash was probably America's most popular and most frequently quoted contemporary poet, drawing large and receptive audiences. P. M. Jack once wrote that Nash was "secure in his possession of all the best and worst rhymes outside of the rhyming dictionaries." He called himself a "worsifier," and his "worses" bear the mark of a unique style—whimsical, offbeat, yet sophisticated—which he called "my individual method for concealing my illiteracy." He freely admitted to having "intentionally maltreated and man-handled every known rule of grammar, prosody, and spelling," yet the result, suggests Albin Krebs, reveals on closer examination, "a carefully thought-out metrical scheme and a kind of relentless logic." "I like the style because it gives me a mask," Nash told an interviewer for *Holiday*, a "front behind which I can hide. I can't go straight to the point about anything emotionally valid; that's one of my faults, I get ponderous. By backing off I can make the point without belaboring it."

Looking back on his writing career, Nash once remarked: "The only lines I've ever written which I think have any chance of surviving me were lines written in my unregenerate youth." Contrary to his modest estimate, Nash is widely recognized as having had few peers when it came to exposing human frailties and absurdities. He was, in Eliot Fremont-Smith's words, "a master of a kind of civility in exposing silliness that has not been much nurtured in recent decades," retaining the possibility of "a wit expressed through a friendly wink or poke." Although some of his verse was quite serious, Nash characterized the body of his work as "fortunately slightly goofy and cheerfully sour." One critic described him as a "philosopher, albeit a laughing one," expressing "the vicissitudes and eccentricitudes of domestic life as they affected an apparently gentle, somewhat bewildered man.''

BIOGRAPHICAL/CRITICAL SOURCES: New York Herald Tribune Book Review, July 14, 1957; Laura Benet, *Famous American Humorists*, Dodd, 1959; *Seventeen*, January, 1963; *Holiday*, August, 1967; Roy Newquist, *Conversations*, Rand McNally, 1967; *Life*, December 13, 1968; *New York Times*, May 20, 1971; L. B. Axford, *An Index to the Poems of Ogden Nash*, Scarecrow, 1972.†

(Died May 19, 1971)

*   *   *

NASH, Robert 1902-

PERSONAL: Born April 23, 1902, in Cork, Ireland. *Education:* Attended St. Munchin's College and Mount St. Alphonsus College, Limerick, Ireland; further education in Jesuit institutions. *Home:* Jesuit Retreat House, Rahan, Ireland.

CAREER: Entered novitiate of Society of Jesus (Jesuits), Tullamore, Ireland, 1919; ordained priest, 1931. Xavier College, Melbourne, Australia, teacher for three years prior to 1931; conductor of missions and retreats in Ireland, United States, Australia, Philippine Islands, Malaya, and Ceylon, 1933-68.

WRITINGS: Pass It on, Browne & Nolan, 1943; *Label Your Luggage*, Browne & Nolan, 1943, Spiritual Book Associates, 1945; *In the News*, Browne & Nolan, 1944; *How It's Done*, Browne & Nolan, 1945; *Send Forth Thy Light*, Newman, 1946; *Marriage: Before and After*, Browne & Nolan, 1947, Didier, 1952; *Thy Light and Thy Truth* (companion to *Send Forth Thy Light*), Newman, 1948; *Is Life Worthwhile?*, Browne & Nolan, 1949, published as *Living Your Faith*, Prentice-Hall, 1951; *The Priest at His Prie-Dieu*, Newman, 1949; *The Nun at Her Prie-Dieu*, Newman, 1950; *The Seminarian at His Prie-Dieu*, Newman, 1951; *This is Christianity*, M. H. Gill, 1952; *We Catholics* (collection of spiritual essays), M. H. Gill, 1953; *Everyman at His Prie-Dieu*, Newman, 1954; *Standing on Holy Ground* (on Nash's tour of Palestine as member of an Irish pilgrim group), Newman, 1955; (editor) *Jesuits: Biographical Essays*, Newman, 1956; *The Incurable Optimist, and Other Spiritual Essays*, M. H. Gill, 1956; *Ideals to Live By: Some of the Principles Which Moulded St. Ignatius Loyola*, M. H. Gill, 1958, published as *Ideals to Live By: A Guide to the Spiritual Exercises of St. Ignatius Loyola*, Benziger, 1959; *Down Mexico Way* (on the Roman Catholic Church in Mexico), St. Paul Publications, 1959; *God is Our Banker* (on the Cottolengo Home, Turin), St. Paul Publications, 1960; *Hello!* (collection of articles originally published in *Dublin Evening Press*), M. H. Gill, 1960; *Priests*, Mercier Press, 1961; *Christian Spain*, St. Paul Publications, 1963; *Psychology of a Catholic*, Mercier Press, 1963; *Wisdom I Ask*, M. H. Gill, 1964, Newman Press, 1965; *Ten More Priests*, Burns & Oates, 1965.

Author of about one hundred pamphlets on spiritual subjects. Regular contributor to *Dublin Sunday Press* and *Dublin Evening Press*, 1953—.

*   *   *

NEEDLES, Robert Johnson 1903-

PERSONAL: Born March 31, 1903, in Atlantic, Iowa; son of Charles Wesley and Estelle (Murray) Needles; married Irene Swartz, April 18, 1930; children: Eleanor (Mrs. Lee W. Chapin), Susan. *Education:* State University of Iowa,

Ph.G., 1924, M.D., 1930. *Politics:* Conservative. *Religion:* Protestant. *Home:* 1227 14th Ave. North, St. Petersburg, Fla. 33705. *Office:* 615 11th St. N., St. Petersburg, Fla. 33705.

CAREER: Henry Ford Hospital, Detroit, Mich., intern and resident in pathology, 1930-32; Companhia Ford do Brazil, Boa Vista, Para, Brazil, pathologist, 1932-34; Henry Ford Hospital, associate pathologist, 1934-35, associate physician, division of cardio-respiratory diseases, 1935-39; certified by American Board of Internal Medicine, 1938 (cardiovascular disease, 1942); physician in private practice, St. Petersburg, Fla., 1939—. Founding member, City Charter Group, St. Petersburg, Fla. *Military service:* U.S. Army Air Forces, Medical Corps, 1942-46; chief of examining team of Recovered Allied Military Personnel, Letterman General Hospital, 1945; became lieutenant colonel; received Letter of Commendation.

MEMBER: American College of Physicians (fellow), American College of Cardiology (fellow), American Heart Association (fellow, Council on Clinical Cardiology), American Society of Clinical Pathology (fellow), American Diabetes Association, American Rheumatism Association, American Medical Association, Association of American Physicians and Surgeons (delegate from Florida, 1962—), American Society of Internal Medicine, Florida Medical Association, Florida Society of Internal Medicine (president, 1957-58), Pinellas County Medical Association, Alpha Omega Alpha.

WRITINGS: (With Edith Stoney) *A Primer for Coronary Patients*, Appleton, 1958 (published in England as *How to Protect Your Heart*, Elek, 1958); *Your Heart and Common Sense*, Fell, 1964. Contributor of articles and papers to medical journals, and articles on political science and economics to other journals, including *National Review*, *Modern Age*, *Freeman*, *American Mercury*.†

*   *   *

NEIHARDT, John Gneisenau 1881-1973

PERSONAL: Born January 8, 1881, near Sharpsburg, Ill.; son of Nicholas Nathan (a farmer) and Alice May (Culler) Neihardt; married Mona Martinsen (a sculptor), November 29, 1908 (died, 1958); children: Enid Neihardt Fink, Sigurd Volsung, Hilda Neihardt Petri, Alice Neihardt Thompson. *Education:* Nebraska Normal College (now Nebraska State Teachers College at Wayne), diploma in science, 1897. *Politics:* Democrat. *Religion:* Unitarian. *Home:* 5835 Vine St., Lincoln, Neb. 68505; and Skyrim Farm, Route 7, Columbia, Mo. 65201. *Office:* Department of English, University of Missouri, Columbia, Mo.

CAREER: Poet and author. Lived among Omaha Indians, 1901-07, later among the Sioux; *Minneapolis Journal*, Minneapolis, Minn., literary editor, 1911-20; University of Nebraska, Lincoln, professor of poetry, 1923; *St. Louis Post-Dispatch*, St. Louis, Mo., literary editor, 1926-38; U.S. Department of Interior, Bureau of Indian Affairs, Washington, D.C., director of information at Chicago office, 1943-46, field representative, 1946-48; University of Missouri, Columbia, lecturer in English and poet-in-residence, 1949-65. Honnold Lecturer, Knox College, 1939; also lecturer at other colleges and universities.

MEMBER: International Institute of Arts and Letters (fellow), National Institute of Arts and Letters, Westerners (founding and life member), Academy of American Poets (chancellor, 1959-67), Poetry Society of America (vice-president of Middle West branch), Companion of Order of

Indian Wars of U.S. (honorary), Sigma Tau Delta. *Awards, honors:* Poetry Society of America Prize for best volume of verse, 1919, for *The Song of Three Friends*; named poet laureate of Nebraska by an act of the legislature, 1921; Gold Scroll Medal of Honor of National Poetry Center, 1936, for *The Song of the Messiah*; Friends of American Writers Foundation award for poetry, 1964; LL.D., Creighton University, 1928; Litt.D., University of Nebraska, 1917, University of Missouri, 1947, Midland Lutheran College, 1972; elected to Nebraska State Hall of Fame, 1974.

WRITINGS: The Divine Enchantment, James T. White & Co., 1900; *The Lonesome Trail*, John Lane, 1907; *A Bundle of Myrrh*, Outing Publishing Co., 1908; *Man-Song*, Mitchell Kennerly, 1909; *The River and I*, Putnam, 1910, revised edition, Macmillan, 1927; *The Dawn-Builder*, Mitchell Kennerly, 1911; *The Stranger at the Gate*, Mitchell Kennerly, 1912; *Death of Agrippina*, Poetry Magazine, 1913; *Life's Lure*, Mitchell Kennerly, 1914; *The Song of Hugh Glass*, Macmillan, 1915, annotated edition for school use, 1919; *The Quest* (collected verse), Macmillan, 1916; *The Song of Three Friends*, Macmillan, 1919, published with *The Song of Hugh Glass* in one-volume annotated edition for school use, 1924; *The Splendid Wayfaring*, Macmillan, 1920; *Two Mothers* (two one-act plays), Macmillan, 1920; *The Song of the Indian Wars*, Macmillan, 1925, annotated edition for school use, 1928; *Poetic Values—Their Reality and Our Need of Them*, Macmillan, 1925; *Collected Poems*, Macmillan, 1926; *Indian Tales and Others*, Macmillan, 1926; *Black Elk Speaks*, Morrow, 1932; *The Song of the Messiah*, Macmillan, 1935.

The Song of Jed Smith, Macmillan, 1941; *A Cycle of the West* (includes *The Song of Hugh Glass, The Song of Three Friends, The Song of the Indian Wars, The Song of the Messiah,* and *The Song of Jed Smith*), Macmillan, 1949; *When the Tree Flowered*, Macmillan, 1951 (published in England as *Eagle Voice*, Melrose, 1953); *All Is But a Beginning* (autobiography), Harcourt, Volume I, 1972.

SIDELIGHTS: A Bronze bust of Neihardt, done by his wife, was placed in the rotunda of the Nebraska capitol by an act of the state legislature in 1961; another monument stands in the city park in Wayne, Nebraska, where he lived as a boy and attended college. The Garden Club of Bancroft, Nebraska, has acquired the cottage in which he later lived and wrote as a museum of Neihardt memorabilia. The Neihardt Memorial Collection (library and papers) was established at the University of Missouri in 1964.

(Died November 3, 1973)

* * *

NEISSER, Hans P(hilip) 1895-1975

PERSONAL: The surname is pronounced "nicer"; born September 3, 1895, in Breslau, Germany; came to United States, 1933; naturalized, 1939; son of Gustave (a lawyer) and Else (Silberstein) Neisser; married Charlotte Schroeter, 1923; children: Marianne (Mrs. Frank Selph), Ulric R. *Education:* Studied at Universities of Breslau, Frieburg, and Munich; University of Breslau, Dr. Juris, 1919, Dr. Rer. Pol., 1921.

CAREER: German government, Berlin economist, 1922-27; University of Kiel, Kiel, Germany, research principal at Institute of World Economy, and lecturer, 1927-33; University of Pennsylvania, Philadelphia, professor of monetary theory, 1933-43; U.S. Office of Price Administration, Washington, D.C., principal economist, Division of Re-

search, 1942-43; New School for Social Research, New York, N.Y., professor of economics, 1943-65, professor emeritus, 1965—. Research principal, Institute of World Affairs, 1943-51; Fulbright lecturer, University of Queensland, Queensland, Australia, 1954. *Member:* Econometric Society (fellow), Royal Economic Society, American Economic Association, American Statistical Association.

WRITINGS: The Exchange Value of Money [Germany], 1927; *Some International Aspects of the Business Cycle*, University of Pennsylvania Press, 1936; (with Modigliani) *National Income and International Trade*, University of Illinois Press, 1954; *On the Sociology of Knowledge*, Heinemann, 1965. Contributor to economics and philosophy journals. Editor of *Magazin der Wirtschaft* (weekly economic magazine), 1925-26.

WORK IN PROGRESS: Research in economic dynamics.

(Died January 1, 1975)

* * *

NELSON, Clifford Ansgar 1906-

PERSONAL: Born March 2, 1906, in Minneapolis, Minn.; son of Ola Ake and Ella (Holmes) Nelson; married E. Bernice Nelson, 1933; children: Clement, Rolf, Brent. *Education:* University of Minnesota, B.A., 1926; Augustana Theological Seminary, B.D., 1929, S.T.M., 1935; University of Leipzig, student, 1929-30. *Home:* 7400 South West 70th Terrace, Miami, Fla. 33143. *Office:* St. Peter's Lutheran Church, 3360 West Flagler St., Miami, Fla. 32207.

CAREER: Augustana Lutheran Church, Minneapolis, Minn., assistant pastor, 1929-32; St. John's Lutheran Church, Rock Island, Ill., pastor, 1932-35; Gloria Dei Lutheran Church, St. Paul, Minn., pastor, 1935-60; Lutheran missionary director, Singapore, 1960-61; St. Peter's Lutheran Church, Miami, Fla., pastor, 1961—; Minnesota State Senate, chaplain, 1953-60. *Member:* Kiwanis International, Rotary Club, St. Paul Athletic Club. *Awards, honors:* Doctor of Theology from Bratislava Theological Faculty, Czechoslovakia, 1946.

WRITINGS: The Cross is the Key: A Book About the Cross for Plain, Thoughtful People, Augustana Press, 1954; *With Hearts Uplifted: Meditations on Nuggets of Scripture*, Augustana Press, 1956; (compiler with Melvin A. Hammarberg) *My Book of Prayers: A Personal Prayer Book*, Augustana Press, 1956; *Invitation to Worship: A Devotional Study of the Lutheran Liturgy*, Augustana Press, 1960; (translator) Bo Harald Giertz, *Preaching from the Whole Bible: Background Studies in the Preaching Texts for the Church Year*, Augsburg, 1967. Contributor to periodicals. Translator of many writings from Swedish, including a novel by Bo Giertz. Wrote weekly sermon page, *Lutheran Companion*, 1954-60; president of board of publications, Augustana Press, 1949-59.

AVOCATIONAL INTERESTS: Music (piano and organ performer).†

* * *

NETTL, Paul 1889-1972

PERSONAL: Born January 10, 1889, in Hohenelbe, Bohemia; came to United States, 1939; married Margaret von Gutfeld; children: Bruno; Robert von Gutfeld, Gabriele Rosenfeld (stepchildren). *Education:* University of Prague, LL.D., 1913; University of Vienna, Ph.D., 1915. *Home:* 620 South Fess Ave., Bloomington, Ind. 47401. *Office:* Indiana University, Bloomington, Ind. 47401.

CAREER: Instructor at Musicological Institute of Germany prior to 1921; University of Prague, Prague, Czechoslovakia, professor, 1921-39; Westminster Choir College, Princeton, N.J., professor, 1939-45; Indiana University, Bloomington, professor of musicology, 1946-64, professor emeritus, 1964-72. Music director of radio station in Prague, Prague II, prior to 1939.

WRITINGS: Die Wiener Tanzkompositionen in der zweiten Haelfte des siebzehnten Jahrhunderts, Gesellschaft zur Herausgabe von Denkmaelern der Tonkunst in Oesterreich, 1921; *Alte juedische spielleute und musiker*, Flesch (Prague), 1923; *Musik und tanz bei Casanova*, Gesellschaft Deutscher Buecherfreunde in Boehmen (Prague), 1924; *Beitraege zur boehmischen und maerischen Musikgeschichte*, Rohrer, 1927; *Zur Geschichte der kaiserlichen Hofmusikkapelle von 1636-1680*, four parts, Gesellschaft zur Herausgabe von Denkmaelern der Tonkunst in Oesterreich, 1929-32; *Mozart and Casanova: Eine Erzaehlung*, [Prague], 1929; *Mozart und die koenigliche kunst: Die freimaurerische grunlage der "Zauberfloete"*, Wunder (Berlin), 1932; *Das Wiener lied im zeitalter des barock*, Passer (Vienna), 1934; (editor) Rudolph Ludwig Franz Ottokar Prochazka, *Mozart in Boehmen* (revised and enlarged edition of his *Mozart in Prag*), Neumann (Prague), 1938.

The Story of Dance Music (originally written in German as *Die Musikgeschichte des Tanzes*), Philosophical Library, 1947; *The Book of Musical Documents*, Philosophical Library, 1948; *Luther and Music*, translated from the German by Frida Best and Ralph Wood, Muhlenberg Press, 1948; *Casanova und seine Zeit: Zur Kultur- und Musikgeschichte des 18. Jahrhunderts*, Bechtle (Esslingen), 1949; *Goethe und Mozart: Eine Betrachtung*, Bechtle, 1949; *Das Veilchen/The Violet: The History of a Song*, Storm, 1949; *The Other Casanova: A Contribution to Eighteenth-Century Music and Manners*, Philosophical Library, 1950; *Forgotten Musicians*, Philosophical Library, 1951; *National Anthems*, translated from the German by Alexander Gode, Storm, 1952; *Der kleine Prophet von Boehmisch-Brod: Mozart und Grimm*, Bechtle, 1953; *Beethoven Encyclopedia*, Philosophical Library, 1956, reissued as *Beethoven Handbook*, Ungar, 1967; *Musik und Freimaurerei: Mozart und die koenigliche Kunst*, Bechtle, 1956; (with Alfred Orel, Roland Tenschert, and Hans Engel) *W. A. Mozart, 1756-1956*, Fischer (Frankfurt am Main), 1956; *W. A. Mozart als Freimaurer und Mensch*, Akazien (Hamburg), 1956; *Mozart and Masonry*, Philosophical Library, 1957; *Das Prager Quartierbuch des Personals der Kroenungsoper 1723*, Rohrer (Vienna), 1957; *Beethoven und seine Zeit*, Fischer, 1958; *Georg Friedrich Haendel*, Merseburger (Berlin), 1958.

Mozart und der Tanz: Zur Geschichte des Balletts und Gesellschaftstanzes, Classen (Zurich), 1960; *Tanz und Tanzmusik: Tausend Jahre beschwingter Kunst*, Herder (Freiburg), 1962; *The Dance in Classical Music*, Philosophical Library, 1963; *Volks- und volkstuemliche Musik bei Bach, mit Tafel*, Boehlaus (Graz), 1962; *Prag im Studentenlied*, Lerche (Munich), 1964. Former music editor, *Deutsche Arbeit* (newspaper).

SIDELIGHTS: Nettl is considered a specialist in every phase of Bohemian and Moravian music; his books have been published in six languages.

BIOGRAPHICAL/CRITICAL SOURCES: Thomas Atcherson, compiler, *Bibliography of the Musicological and Literary Works of Paul Nettl*, [Bloomington, Ind.], 1957, published in German by Schonborn (Vienna), 1962.

(Died January 8, 1972)

NEUMANN, William Louis 1915-1971

PERSONAL: Born March 4, 1915, in Buffalo, N.Y.; married Doris Elaine McGlone (a teacher), December 26, 1941; children: Christopher R., Gregory A. *Education:* State University of New York at Buffalo, B.S., 1938; University of Michigan, M.A., 1939, Ph.D., 1948. *Home:* 112 Greenmeadow Dr., Timonium, Md. 21093. *Office:* Goucher College, Baltimore, Md. 21204.

CAREER: University of Hawaii, Honolulu, assistant professor of history, 1948-49; Foundation for Foreign Affairs, Washington, D.C., executive secretary, 1949-51; University of Maryland, College Park, associate professor of history, 1951-53; Goucher College, Baltimore, Md., professor of history, 1954-71, chairman, American Studies program, 1955-71. Consultant on foreign affairs to U.S. Senate, 1952-53. *Wartime service:* Conscientious objector, serving in Civilian Public Service Camps, 1941-45. *Member:* American Historical Association, American Association of University Professors, American Civil Liberties Union, Fellowship of Reconciliation, National Committee for a Sane Nuclear Policy (chairman of Baltimore chapter). *Awards, honors:* Rockefeller Foundation fellow; Volker Foundation fellow; Social Science Research Council fellow.

WRITINGS: The Genesis of Pearl Harbor, Pacifist Research Bureau, 1945; *Recognition of Governments in the Americas*, Foundation for Foreign Affairs, 1947; *Making the Peace, 1941-45: The Diplomacy of the Wartime Conferences*, Foundation for Foreign Affairs, 1950; (contributor) Alexander DeConde, editor, *Isolation and Security*, Duke University Press, 1957; (contributor) G. L. Anderson, editor, *Issues and Conflicts*, University of Kansas Press, 1959; *America Encounters Japan: Perry to MacArthur*, Johns Hopkins Press, 1963; *After Victory: Churchill, Roosevelt, Stalin, and the Making of the Peace*, Harper, 1967. Editor of *American Perspective*, 1949-51; book reviewer for *Baltimore Sun* and *Progressive* (magazine).

WORK IN PROGRESS: Nations in Adversity, studies in changing national missions in a group of nations suffering major losses of power and territory, namely Sweden, Denmark, Spain, Austria, and Great Britain.

(Died September 30, 1971)

*   *   *

NEWICK, John 1919-

PERSONAL: Born November 30, 1919, in Bristol, England. *Education:* West of England College of Art, art teacher's diploma, 1940; attended University of Bristol; received diploma of art education, 1950. *Office:* Department of Art Education, Faculty of Art, Kwame Nkrumah University, Kumasi, Ghana.

CAREER: Sidcot School, Somerset, England, art master, 1947-52; School for Training Art Teachers, College of Art and Craft, Birmingham, England, lecturer, and tutor, 1952—. Kwame Nkrumah University of Science and Technology, Kumasi, Ghana, visiting lecturer, 1962-64, reader in art education, 1963—. *Member:* National Society for Art Education (United Kingdom), Conference of Graduate Art Teacher Training Centres.

WRITINGS: Making Colour Prints: An Approach to Lino Cutting, Dryad, 1952, 3rd revised edition, 1964; *Clay and Terracotta in Education*, Dryad, 1964.

WORK IN PROGRESS: Seeking common and local aims of art education in disparate cultures of the twentieth century.

NEWMAN, Louis Israel 1893-1972

PERSONAL: Born December 20, 1893, in Providence, R.I.; son of Paul (a manufacturing jeweler) and Antonia (Hecker) Newman; married Lucile Helene Uhry, June 14, 1923; children: Jeremy, Jonathan, Daniel. *Education:* Brown University, A.B., 1913; University of California, Berkeley, M.A., 1917; Columbia University, Ph.D., 1924. *Politics:* Democrat (Independent). *Home:* 271 Central Park West, New York, N.Y. 10024. *Office:* Congregation Rodeph Sholom, 7 West 83rd St., New York, N.Y. 10024.

CAREER: Ordained rabbi, 1918; associate rabbi in New York, N.Y., 1916-24, and rabbi in San Francisco, Calif., 1924-30; Congregation Rodeph Sholom, New York, N.Y., rabbi, 1930-72. Co-worker with Vladimir Jabotinsky in Revisionist Zionist Movement; founder and honorary chairman of American Friends of a Jewish Palestine, 1939-72; official observer at United Nations for Central Conference of American Rabbis, 1946-50; founder of Academy for Liberal Judaism, New York, 1955. Trustee of Federation for Jewish Philanthropies, New York, 1935-72. *Awards, honors:* D. D. Brown University, 1942; second prize in B'nai B'rith play contest, 1944, for "Pangs of the Messiah"; second prize in Zionist Organization of America play contest, 1950, for "Son of His Generation."

WRITINGS: (With William Popper) *Studies in Biblical Parallelism*, University of California Press, 1918; *Richard Cumberland, Critic and Friend of the Jews*, Bloch Publishing, 1919; *A Jewish University in America*, Bloch Publishing, 1923; *Jewish Influence on Christian Reform Movements*, Columbia University Press, 1925, reprinted, AMS Press, 1966; (translator and compiler, with Samuel Spitz) *The Hasidic Anthology*, Scribner, 1934, subsequent editions published by Bloch Publishing and Schocken; (editor with Spitz) *The Talmudic Anthology*, Behrman, 1945; *A "Chief Rabbi" of Rome Becomes a Catholic*, Bloch Publishing, 1945; (editor with Spitz) *The Talmudic Anthology*, Behrman, 1962; *Maggidim and Hasidim: Their Wisdom*, Bloch Publishing, 1962; *The Jewish People, Faith and Life*, Bloch Publishing, 1965; (editor) *Genesis: The Student's Guide*, United Synagogue Commission on Jewish Education, 1967, teacher's supplement, 1969. Also author of History of Congregation Rodeph Sholom (1842-1965).

Poetry: *Songs of Jewish Rebirth*, Bloch Publishing, 1921; *Joyful Jeremiads*, Lantern, 1926; *Trumpet in Adversity*, Bloch Publishing, 1948.

Plays: *Pangs of the Messiah, and Other Plays, Pageants and Cantatas*, privately printed, 1957, Bloch Publishing, 1961; *The Woman at the Wall* (and other plays), Bloch Publishing, 1958; *The Little Zaddik* (three-act), Bloch Publishing, 1961; *Go North, Young Man*, Bloch Publishing, 1961; and other produced plays in the field of religious drama.

Sermons—All published by Bloch Publishing: *Anglo-Saxon and Jew*, 1923, *Sermons and Addresses*, four volumes, 1936-43, *Biting on Granite*, 1946, *Becoming a New Person*, 1950, *Living with Ourselves*, 1952, *The Search for Serenity*, 1954, *What Does God Mean to You?*, 1959. Author of a manual for newcomers to Judaism, 1940, and cantatas and oratorios for confirmation. Weekly columnist in San Francisco *Call-Bulletin*, 1925-30, writer of column, "Telling It to Gath," syndicated in Jewish newspapers.

WORK IN PROGRESS: *Roger Williams versus John Cotton: Religious Liberty versus Bible Utopias in American Personalities 1789-1846*; also writing on Joseph and David Kimchi as religious controversialists.

(Died March 9, 1972)

NEWTON, Eric 1893-1965

PERSONAL: Born April 28, 1893, in Marple, Derbyshire, England; married Isabell Aileen Vinicombe, 1915; married Stella Mary Pearce (professional name; costume historian), 1934; children: two sons. *Education:* University of Manchester, B.A., 1914, M.A., 1945. *Religion:* Agnostic. *Home:* 3 Cumberland Gardens, London W.C.1, England. *Agent:* Curtis Brown Ltd., 1 Craven Hill, London W2 3EW, England.

CAREER: L. Oppenheimer Ltd., Manchester, England, mosaic designer and craftsman, 1913-14, 1918-33; served as art critic for *Manchester Guardian*, Manchester England, 1930-47, and *Sunday Times*, London, England, 1937-51; Oxford University, Oxford, England, Slade Professor of Fine Art, 1959-60. Art adviser, Commonwealth Institute. Lecturer in United States and Canada, 1936, 1953, and 1956, on U.S. tour, 1952. *Military service:* British Army, Manchester Regiment, 1914-18; became captain. *Member:* Association Internationale des Critiques d'Art (president of British section, 1949-61), Savile Club (London). *Awards, honors:* Commander, Order of the British Empire, 1964.

WRITINGS: *The Artist and His Public*, Allen & Unwin, 1935; *Masterpieces of Figure Painting*, Studio Publications, 1936; *Christopher Wood, 1901-1930*, Heinemann, 1938, enlarged edition published as *Christopher Wood: His Life and Work*, Redfern Gallery (London), 1959; *European Painting and Sculpture*, Cassell, 1941, Penguin (New York), 1942, revised edition published as *An Introduction to European Painting*, Longmans, Green, 1943, 4th edition, Penguin, 1956; *Art for Everybody*, Longmans, Green, for British Council, 1943; *British Painting*, Longmans, Green, for British Council, 1945, revised edition, 1946; (editor) *War Through Artists' Eyes*, Transatlantic, 1945; *Drama Omnibus*, Samuel French, 1946; *British Sculpture, 1944-46*, Tiranti, 1947.

In My View (essays), Longmans, Green, 1950; *The Meaning of Beauty*, Longmans, Green, 1950; (author of critical evaluation) Charles Handley-Read, editor, *The Art of Wyndham Lewis*, Faber, 1951; *Tintoretto*, Longmans, Green, 1952; (with Maisie Cobby) *The Playmakers* (graded course in dramatic activity for primary schools), four books, Pitman, 1956; (author of preface) *Masterpieces of European Sculpture*, Abrams, 1959; *The Arts of Man: An Anthology and Interpretation of Great Works of Art*, New York Graphic Society, 1960, 2nd edition, Thames & Hudson, 1963; *The Romantic Rebellion*, Longmans, Green, 1962, St. Martins, 1963; (with William Neil) *2000 Years of Christian Art*, Harper, 1966; (with Neil) *The Christian Faith in Art*, Hodder & Stoughton, 1966; *A Guide to Teaching Poetry*, University of London Press, 1971.

Writer of booklets and brochures on painting and sculpture.

AVOCATIONAL INTERESTS: Travel abroad, painting.

(Died, 1965)

* * *

NEWTON, Peter 1906-

PERSONAL: Born May 15, 1906, in Wellington, New Zealand; son of A. Wells and Margaret (Hurst) Newton; married Margaret Dixon, September 23, 1946; children: Sally Margaret, Judith Anne, Jill Elizabeth. *Education:* Educated in New Zealand schools. *Religion:* Anglican. *Home:* Whiterock, Rangiora, New Zealand.

CAREER: New Zealand high country shepherd, sheep station manager, and sheep farmer, whose writings revolve around phases of this life. *Military service:* New Zealand Expeditionary Forces, World War II, served in Middle East; received North Africa Star and 8th Army Star.

WRITINGS: Wayleggo: Tales of Twenty Years in the Southern Mountains of New Zealand, A. H. & A. W. Reed, 1947, 2nd edition, 1953; *High Country Days*, A. H. & A. W. Reed, 1949; *High Country Journey*, A. H. & A. W. Reed, 1952; *Mesopotamia Station: A Survey of the First Hundred Years*, Timaru Herald Co. (Timaru, N.Z.), 1960; *Straggle Master* (originally announced as "This One's on Me"), A. H. & A. W. Reed, 1964; *The Boss's Story: The Problems and Pleasures of Managing a New Zealand Sheep Station*, Tri-Ocean, 1966; *Big Country of the North Island*, A. H. & A. W. Reed, 1969.

WORK IN PROGRESS: Ten Thousand Dogs, for publication by A. H. & A. W. Reed.

*   *   *

NEWTON, Robert (Henry) G(erald) 1903-

PERSONAL: Born December 29, 1903, in London, England; son of Henry Alfred and Mary Geraldine (Hamilton) Newton. *Education:* Attended Eton College and Magdalene College, Cambridge. *Home:* Pippins, Balcombe, Sussex, England. *Agent:* Joan M. Ling, 18 Southampton Pl., London W.C.5, England.

CAREER: Drama adviser to National Council of Social Service, 1933-39, Middlesex County Drama Committee, 1946-51, West Sussex County Drama Committee, 1953-66. Professional lecturer, producer, and adjudicator in England, Canada, Ceylon, India, Gibraltar, Malta, and Germany. Chairman, overseas committee, British Drama League, 1950-60. *Member:* Arts Theatre Club (London).

WRITINGS: Madonna of the Golden Hart, Deane, 1930; *Acting Improvised*, Thomas Nelson, 1937; *Acting for All: An Introduction to Informal Drama*, Thomas Nelson, 1940; *Magic and Make-Believe: An Essay Inquiring Into the Relationship Between Theatre Experience and Improvisation*, Dobson, 1949; *Show with Music: An Approach to the Practice of Musical Documentary*, Dobson, 1950; *Together in Theatre: Some Aspects of and Exercises Dealing with Relationship in the Theatre, Particularly as It Affects the Amateur Theatre*, J. Garnet Miller, 1954; (editor) *Twenty-Minute Theatre*, J. Garnet Miller, 1955; (editor) *Miller's Medley, No. 1*, J. Garnet Miller, 1959; *Exercise Improvisation* (manual), J. Garnet Miller, 1960; (editor) *Six More Plays*, J. Garnet Miller, 1961; (editor) *Miller's Medley, No. 2*, J. Garnet Miller, 1961; (editor) *Miller's Medley, No. 3*, J. Garnet Miller, 1963; *Mourning for Little Nestings*, J. Garnet Miller, 1964; *Improvisation Steps Out*, J. Garnet Miller, 1967; *A Creative Approach to Amateur Theatre* (three volumes in one; includes *Together in Theatre, Exercise Improvisation*, and *Improvisation Steps Out*), J. Garnet Miller, 1967. Also author of plays, "Cupid and Mars" (with Rodney Ackland), and "People's Pleasures." Contributor to *Drama, Amateur Stage, Town & Country Planning, Theatre & Stage, Theatre Arts Monthly, Visvabharati Quarterly*, and *Adult Education*.

WORK IN PROGRESS: Project and Practice, for J. Garnet Miller.

*   *   *

NICHOLDS, Elizabeth (Beckwith)

PERSONAL: Born in New York, N.Y.; daughter of G. S. (a minister) and Cora (Ketchum) Beckwith. *Education:* New York State College for Teachers, B.S., 1921; Radcliffe College, M.A., 1925; New York School of Social Work, certificate, 1940. *Home:* 20 Owen Brown St., Hudson, Ohio 44236. *Office:* Division of Child Welfare, Cleveland 44115.

CAREER: High school teacher in New York State, 1921-23; Department of Public Assistance, New York, N.Y., former caseworker; Department of Family and Child Welfare, Westchester County, N.Y., former assistant supervisor; Department of Welfare, Children's Division, Cooperstown, N.Y., former supervisor; Cuyahoga County Department of Welfare, Division of Child Welfare, Cleveland, Ohio, supervisor of in-service training, 1960—. *Member:* National Association of Social Workers, Child Welfare League.

WRITINGS: Thunder Hill, Doubleday, 1953; *A Primer of Social Casework*, Columbia University Press, 1960; *In-Service Casework Training*, Columbia University Press, 1966.

*   *   *

NICHOLS, Cecilia Fawn 1906-
(Nikki Nazarian)

PERSONAL: Born March 6, 1906, in Bellevue, Neb.; daughter of Robert Cleveland (a railroad engineer) and Ellen (McGinley) Nichols. *Education:* University of Omaha, B.S., 1938; also studied at University of Nebraska and University of Southern California. *Home:* 74039 Playa Vista Dr., Twentynine Palms, Calif. 92277. *Agent:* Georgia Nicholas, 161 Madison Ave., New York, N.Y. 10016.

CAREER: Omaha Bee-News, Omaha Neb., employed in classified advertising department and also assistant movie and drama critic, 1927-29; elementary and high school teacher in Nebraska and California, 1929-43, 1945-51; civil service employee at air bases in California, 1943-45, 1951-60, with posts including director of security education at Maywood Air Force Base, 1953-59; teacher of adult education classes in creative writing at Mount San Antonio College, Pomona, and other schools in San Gabriel Valley, Calif., 1960-63; free-lance writer, 1963—. Private tutoress at Canoa Ranch, Ariz. Member of Twentynine Palms Community council; recording secretary of Twentynine Palms Taxpayers Association, 1971—.

MEMBER: Armed Forces Writers League (regional director for Southern California, 1960-64; chairman of editor's jury), National Cat Protection Society, California Retired Teachers Association (recording secretary for Palm Springs desert division, 1969-71; area chairman of information and protective services, 1971—), Twentynine Palms Artists' Guild, Twentynine Palms Artists' Workshop, Twentynine Palms Women's Club (publicity chairman). *Awards, honors:* Certificate of merit, *Boy's Life*-Armed Forces Writers League contest, 1960, for short story, "A Penny's Worth of Boy"; first prize, *Writer's Notes and Quotes*, 1960, for short story, "The Secret of Success"; first prize, Pomona Writers Club, 1962, for short story, "The Man Who Went to Hell"; third place, Annual Amateur Art Show of Twentynine Palms Artists' Guild, 1972, for a modern still life.

WRITINGS: The Goat Who Ate a Cow, Bruce, 1964. Author of short stories and plays.

WORK IN PROGRESS: (under pseudonym Nikki Nazarian) *The Mystery of the Voodoo Masks; Willie of War-*

rensburg, a biographical novel based on the early life of John William Boone, the blind Negro pianist; *The Haunting Countess*, a mystery novel; *Certain Circumstances*, a book on extrasensory perception experiences.

SIDELIGHTS: "A Penny's Worth of Boy" was dramatized on the radio in 1973. Cecilia Nichols told *CA* that she is gifted with "a certain psychic sense" and can foretell future events. She explained: "I read cards and occasionally make predictions. I am not a professional reader. I read for friends only ... Some things come to me and I am suddenly filled with a sense of knowledge about an event." *Avocational interests:* Creative art—painting, woodcarving, mask-making, acting in amateur theatricals.

BIOGRAPHICAL/CRITICAL SOURCES: University of Omaha Alumni Newsletter, January, 1965.

* * *

NICHOLS, Harold 1903-

PERSONAL: Born June 7, 1903, in Philadelphia, Pa.; son of Alfred C. (a printer) and Fannie (Hallman) Nichols; married Beatrice Howarth, June 6, 1936; children: Edna May, Margaret Hallman. *Education:* Educated in Philadelphia public schools. *Politics:* Republican. *Religion:* Baptist. *Home:* 4367 Manayunk Ave., Philadelphia, Pa. 19128.

CAREER: General Electric Co., Philadelphia, Pa., 1923-68, became production control specialist; now retired.

WRITINGS: The Work of the Deacon and Deaconess, Judson, 1964.

WORK IN PROGRESS: Research into responsibilities of other church officers, and challenging areas of dedicated church service.

* * *

NICOLSON, Harold George 1886-1968

PERSONAL: Born November 21, 1886, in Tehran, Persia (now Iran); son of Arthur Nicolson, first Baron Carnock (a diplomat) and Catharine (Rowean-Hamilton) Nicolson; married Victoria Sackville-West (a poet and author), October 1, 1912 (died, 1962); children: Lionel Benedict, Nigel. *Education:* Educated at Wellington College, Berkshire, England, and Balliol College, Oxford. *Home:* Sissinghurst Castle, Cranbrook, Kent, England. *Agent:* Peter Janson-Smith Ltd., 31 Newington Green, Islington, London N16 9PU, England.

CAREER: British Diplomatic Service, 1909-29, serving at embassies in Madrid, Constantinople, Tehran, Berlin, as member of British Delegation to Paris Peace Conference, 1919, and as first secretary of Diplomatic Service, 1920; member of Parliament from West Leicester, 1935-45; author and journalist. Governor, British Broadcasting Corp., 1941-46. Chairman of committee of London Library, 1952-57; vice-chairman of executive committee, National Trust. Trustee, National Portrait Gallery, 1948-64.

MEMBER: Royal Society of Literature (fellow), Classical Association (president, 1950-51), New York Academy (honorary member), Travellers' Club, Beefsteak Club. *Awards, honors:* Companion of St. Michael and St. George, 1920; Knight Commander of Royal Victorian Order, 1953; Commander of Legion of Honor; honorary fellow, Balliol College, Oxford University; honorary doctorates from University of Athens, University of Grenoble, University of Glasgow, University of Dublin, and University of Durham.

WRITINGS: Paul Verlaine, Constable, 1921; *Sweet Waters*, Constable, 1921; *Tennyson*, Constable, 1923, Houghton, 1925, 2nd edition, Constable, 1949; *Byron: The Last Journey, April 1823-April 1824*, Constable, 1924, 3rd edition, 1948; *Swinburne*, Macmillan (London), 1926, reprinted, Archon, 1969; *Some People*, Constable, 1927, new edition, 1958; *Development of English Biography*, Harcourt, 1928.

Portrait of a Diplomatist: Sir Arthur Nicolson, First Lord Carnock, Houghton, 1930; *People and Things*, Constable, 1931; *Public Faces*, Constable, 1932, reissued with introduction by son, Nigel Nicolson, Cedric Chivers, 1968; *Peacemaking, 1919*, Houghton, 1933, revised edition, Methuen, 1964; *Curzon: The Last Phase, 1919-1925*, Houghton, 1934, new edition, Harcourt, 1939; *Dwight Morrow*, Harcourt, 1935; *Politics in the Train*, Constable, 1936; *Helen's Tower*, Constable, 1937, Harcourt, 1938; *The Meaning of Prestige* (Rede Lecture), Macmillan, 1937; *Small Talk*, Harcourt, 1937, reprinted, Books for Libraries, 1971; *Diplomacy*, Harcourt, 1939, 3rd edition, Oxford University Press, 1963, issued with new introduction, 1969; *Marginal Comment, January 6-August 4, 1939*, Constable, 1939; *Why Britain Is at War*, Penguin, 1939.

The Desire to Please: A Story of Hamilton Rowen and the United Irishmen, Harcourt, 1943; *Poetry of Byron*, Oxford University Press, 1943, reprinted, Folcroft, 1969; *Friday Mornings, 1941-44*, Constable, 1944; (editor with others) *Transactions of the Royal Society of Literature*, 3rd series, Oxford University Press, 1944-1948; (compiler with wife, Victoria Sackville-West) *Another World Than This* (anthology), M. Joseph, 1945, Transatlantic, 1949; *The Congress of Vienna: A Study in Allied Unity, 1812-1822*, Harcourt, 1946; *The English Sense of Humor: An Essay*, limited edition, Dropmore, 1946, enlarged edition published as *The English Sense of Humor, and Other Essays*, Constable, 1956, Funk, 1968; *Tennyson's Two Brothers*, Macmillan, 1947; *Comments, 1944-1948*, Constable, 1948; (with wife, Victoria Sackville-West) *Saint Joan of Arc*, revised edition, M. Joseph, 1948; *Benjamin Constant*, Doubleday, 1949; *Future of the English-Speaking World*, Jackson, Son & Co., 1949.

Some People (illustrated), Folio Society (London), 1951, with new introduction, Vintage, 1957; *King George V: His Life and Reign*, Constable, 1952, Doubleday, 1953; *Evolution of Diplomatic Method* (Chichele Lecture), Macmillan, 1954, published as *Evolution of Diplomacy*, Collier, 1962; *Good Behaviour*, Constable, 1955, Doubleday, 1956, issued with new introduction by Harold Nicolson, Beacon Press, 1960; *Journey to Java*, Constable, 1957, Doubleday, 1958; *Saint-Beuve*, Doubleday, 1957; (editor and author of introduction) H. B. Constant de Rebecque, *Aldophe [and] The Red Notebook*, Bobbs-Merrill, 1959.

The Age of Reason, 1700-1789, Constable, 1960, published as *The Age of Reason: The 18th Century*, Doubleday, 1961; *Monarchy*, Weidenfeld & Nicolson, 1962, published as *Kings, Courts, and Monarchy*, Simon & Schuster, 1962; *Diaries and Letters* (Volume I: 1930-1939, Volume II: 1939-1945, Volume III: 1945-1962), edited by Nigel Nicolson, Atheneum, 1966-68. Member of editorial staff, *Evening Standard*, 1930.

SIDELIGHTS: Books by Sir Harold, his late novelist-poet wife, and their two sons almost constitute a library in themselves. Lionel Benedict Nicholson, editor of *Burlington Magazine* since 1947, writes on art and artists; Nigel Nicolson's books include an official history of the Grenadier Guards, and several on other subjects.

BIOGRAPHICAL/CRITICAL SOURCES: Nigel Nicolson, *Portrait of a Marriage*, Atheneum, 1973.

(Died May 1, 1968)

* * *

NIEMAN, Egbert William 1909-

PERSONAL: Born June 13, 1909, in Woodville, Ohio; son of E. J. and Mary (Kaemming) Nieman; married Hilda Bright, September, 1929; children: Petra Ann (Mrs. Carlisle C. Lewis). *Education:* Capital University, student, 1926-28; Ohio State University, B.A., 1930, M.A., 1934; Western Reserve University (now Case Western Reserve University), graduate study, 1955-57. *Politics:* Independent. *Religion:* Protestant. *Home:* 24702 Duffield, Shaker Heights, Ohio 44122. *Office:* Shaker Heights Schools, 20600 Shaker Blvd., Shaker Heights, Ohio 44122.

CAREER: High school teacher of English and history, Wood County, Ohio, 1930-36; Shaker Heights (Ohio) Schools, chairman of English department, 1936-52, director of special services, 1952-55, junior high school principal, 1955—. *Member:* National Education Association, National Council of Teachers of English, National Association of Secondary School Principals, National Association for Supervision and Curriculum Development, Council on Junior High School Administration, Ohio Education Association, Phi Beta Kappa, Phi Alpha Theta.

WRITINGS: (Editor with Jacob M. Ross and Mary Rives Bowman) *Adventures for Readers* (7th and 8th grade books in "Adventures in Literature" series, including teachers' manuals and test booklets), Harcourt, 1947, Olympic edition (with Elizabeth C. O'Daly), 1958, 6th edition, 1968; (editor with George Salt) *Pleasure in Literature*, Harcourt, 1949; (editor and author of introduction) Ralph Moody, *Little Britches: Man of the Family*, Harcourt, 1953; (with Fay Greiffenberg and Louis Zahner) *The English Language: Grade Seven*, Harcourt, 1962; (with Grieffenberg and Zahner) *The English Language: Grade Eight*, Harcourt, 1962.

WORK IN PROGRESS: Revision of textbooks.

AVOCATIONAL INTERESTS: Golf, photography, travel.

* * *

NIGHTINGALE, Sir Geoffrey (Slingsby) 1904-

PERSONAL: Born November 24, 1904, in London, England; son of Thomas Slingsby (in South African civil service) and Doris E. (Collison) Nightingale; married Mary Madeleine Doyle, January, 1936; children: Jeremy. *Education:* London Hospital Medical College, London, student, 1922-28, M.R.C.S. and L.R.C.P., 1929, D.P.M., 1934. *Home:* Greenwoods, Warley Hill, Brentwood, Essex, England.

CAREER: Warley Hospital, Brentwood, Essex, England, physician superintendent, 1946—. Consultant psychiatrist to hospitals. *Military service:* British Army, Royal Army Medical Corps, 1940-45; became lieutenant colonel. *Member:* Royal Corinthian Yacht Club (Burnham), Mid-Essex Sailing Association, Royal Yachting Association.

WRITINGS: The First Hundred Years: A History of Warley Hospital, privately printed, 1953; *Dinghy Ownership*, Coles, 1956, 3rd revised edition, 1964; *Dinghy Sailing for Boys—or Girls*, Coles, 1958, 2nd edition, 1962; (with others) *Eagle Book of Ships*, Hulton Press, 1962. Contributor to *Dinghy Year Book*, 1958—. Also contributor of articles on yachting and medical subjects to journals.

SIDELIGHTS: Nightingale told *CA*: "Writing is merely a hobby, the royalties, when the tax collector has finished with them, pay for my sailing. Presently owner of a twenty-foot racing boat of Flying Fifteen Class. Other vices—salmon and trout fishing, fast cars, tennis (enthusiastic but wild). Languages (to misquote)—a little German and less French."

* * *

NISBET, Stanley (Donald) 1912-

PERSONAL: Born July 26, 1912, in Isafjord, Iceland; son of James Love (a doctor) and Isabella (Donald) Nisbet; married Helen Alison Smith (a teacher), March 28, 1942; children: Roger MacDonald, Isabel Murray. *Education:* University of Edinburgh, M.A., 1934, B.Ed., 1940. *Home:* 6 Victoria Park Corner, Glasgow G14, Scotland.

CAREER: Moray House School, Edinburgh, Scotland, teacher, 1935-39; The Queen's University of Belfast, Belfast, Northern Ireland, professor of education, 1946-51; University of Glasgow, Glasgow, Scotland, professor of education, 1951—. *Military service:* Royal Air Force, 1940-45; became flight lieutenant. *Member:* British Psychological Society, Royal Society of Edinburgh (fellow), Educational Institute of Scotland.

WRITINGS: Purpose in the Curriculum, University of London Press, 1957; *Promise and Progress: A Study of Students at the University of Glasgow in the Nineteen sixties*, University of Glasgow, 1970. Contributor to educational and psychological journals.

AVOCATIONAL INTERESTS: Walking and sailing.

* * *

NOCK, Francis J. 1905-1969

PERSONAL: Born May 13, 1905, in Titusville, Pa.; son of Albert Jay (a writer) and Agnes (Grumbine) Nock; married Marcia Van Stry, March 24, 1940. *Education:* Haverford College, A.B., 1926; New York University, M.A., 1925, Ph.D., 1934. *Office:* University of Illinois, Urbana, Ill.

CAREER: Instructor in German at Rice Institute (now University), Houston, Tex., 1929-30, University of Wisconsin, Madison, 1930-31, and New York University, New York, N.Y., 1931-40; University of Wichita, Wichita, Kan., professor of German, 1940-48; University of Illinois, Urbana, assistant professor, 1948-50, associate professor of German, 1950-69. *Member:* Modern Language Association of America, American Association of Teachers of German, American Association of University Professors.

WRITINGS: The Parzival Manuscript Gk (monograph), privately printed, 1935; *An Introduction to Scientific German*, Macmillan, 1937; (editor with Harold Lenz) *Goethe's Urfaust*, Harper, 1938; *Expository German*, Dryden Press, 1951; (with Ernest Koch) *Essentials of German*, Oxford University Press, 1957; *German Science Reader*, Heath, 1962; (editor and annotator) *Selected Letters of Albert Jay Nock*, Caxton, 1962; (translator) Carl Menger, *Problems of Economics and Sociology*, University of Illinois Press, 1963.

(Died November, 1969)

* * *

NOREN, Paul Harold Andreas 1910-

PERSONAL: Born July 10, 1910, in St. Paul, Minn.; son of

Andreas and Amanda (Olson) Noren; married Linnea Swanson, October 7, 1936 (died, 1951); married Mildred L. Holmquist, January 3, 1957; children: (first marriage) Andrea Marie (Mrs. Fred Rogers), Karen (Mrs. Roger Talle), Mary-Ellen Beth; (second marriage) Sandra Lenore (Mrs. Thomas Swanson), Stephen Charles. *Education:* Gustavus Adolphus College, A.B., 1931; Augustana Theological Seminary, Rock Island, Ill., B.D., 1934. *Home:* 7128 South Lake Shore Dr., Minneapolis, Minn. 55423. *Office:* 5025 Knox Ave. S., Minneapolis, Minn. 55419.

CAREER: Ordained to ministry of Lutheran Church, 1934. Pastor of Lutheran churches in St. Paul, Minn., 1934-38, Duluth, Minn., 1938-44, Minneapolis, Minn., 1944-53, and Denver, Colo., 1953-68; Mount Olive Lutheran Church, Minneapolis, Minn., 1968—. Lutheran Church of America, chairman of joint commission on Lutheran unity, Rocky Mountain Synod, 1961-62, vice-president and member of executive board, 1962-68, vice-president of board on college education and church vocations, 1962-64, president, 1964-66, member of executive council, 1966-68, member of board on world missions, 1968—, member of executive board, Minnesota Synod, 1968—. Chaplain, Colorado State Senate, 1963-68, Republican National Convention, 1964. President, Denver Area Council of Churches, 1962-64, Colorado Council of Churches, 1966-68; president, Governor's Committee on Respect for the Law (Colo.), 1964-68; chairman, President's Colorado Commission on Law Enforcement and Administrative Justice, 1966-68. Trustee, Swedish Medical Center, Englewood, Colo., 1953-68, Midland College, Fremont, Neb., 1966-68; chairman of board of various councils, missions, and homes for the aged and handicapped. Radio broadcaster, 1953-68; devotional telecaster, Minneapolis, Minn., 1968—. *Member:* Tau Sigma, Rotarians, Kiwanis (president, Capital City club, Denver, Colo., 1961). *Awards, honors:* D.D., Bethany College, Lindsborg, Kan., 1958; Distinguished Alumni Citation, Gustavus Adolphus College, 1962; Torch of Liberty Award, Anti-Defamation League of B'nai B'rith, 1963.

WRITINGS: Profiles of the Passion: Lenten Sermons, Augustana, 1961. Contributor to collections of sermons.

SIDELIGHTS: Noren enjoys reading and travel, having made a trip around the world, stopping in fifteen countries, in 1956. There is a Paul H. A. Noren Educational Building in Denver, Colo., named by Augustana Lutheran Church in 1965.

*   *   *

NORMAN, Sylva 1901-

PERSONAL: Born November 1, 1901, in Manchester, England; daughter of Dicran (an artist-designer) and Araxie (Arabian) Nahabedian. *Education:* Attended Queenwood School, Eastbourne, Sussex, England, 1910-18. *Politics:* Mildly radical. *Home:* 114B Barrowgate Rd., London, W.4, England.

CAREER: Author, editor, and critic. *Military service:* British Army, Auxiliary Territorial Service, 1938-40.

WRITINGS: Nature Has No Tune (novel), Hogarth, 1929; *Cat Without Substance* (novel), P. Davies, 1931; (with Edmund Blunden) *We'll Shift Our Ground* (novel), Cobden-Sanderson, 1933; (editor) *Contemporary Essays*, Mathews & Marrot, 1933, reprinted, Books for Libraries, 1968; (editor) *After Shelly*, Oxford University Press, 1934; *Mary Shelley, Novelist and Dramatist*, Oxford University Press, 1938; *Flight of the Skylark: The Development of Shelley's Reputation*, University of Oklahoma Press, 1954; *Tongues of Angels* (novel), Secker & Warburg, 1957.

Contributor to *Encyclopaedia Britannica*. Regular reviewer, specializing in English romantic writers and their Victorian offshoots, for *Times Literary Supplement* and other journals.

WORK IN PROGRESS: Editing the journals of Claude Houghton from autograph manuscript in the University of Texas Library.

AVOCATIONAL INTERESTS: Astronomy ("before the nuclear and space ages"), visiting Italy.

*   *   *

NORRIS, Leslie 1921-

PERSONAL: Born May 21, 1921, in Merthyr Tydfil, Glamorganshire, Wales; son of George William (an engineer) and Janie (Jones) Norris; married Catharine Mary Morgan (a teacher), July 31, 1948. *Education:* Attended Training College, Coventry, England, 1947-49, University of Southampton Institute of Education, 1955-58. *Politics:* Liberal. *Home:* Plas Nant, Northfields Lane, Aldingbourne, Chichester, Sussex, England. *Office:* Training College, Bognor Regis, Sussex, England.

CAREER: Assistant teacher in Yeovil, Somerset, England, 1949-52; deputy head teacher in Bath, Somerset, England, 1952-55; head teacher in Chichester, Sussex, England, 1955-58; Training College, Bognor Regis, Sussex, England, lecturer in English, 1958—. Lecturer, Institutes of Education at University of Southampton and University of Reading. *Military service:* Royal Air Force, 1940-42; invalided out. *Awards, honors:* Welsh Arts Council Award, 1968; Arts Council Award, 1969; Alice Hunt Bartlett Prize of Poetry Society, 1970, for *Ransoms*.

WRITINGS: The Tongue of Beauty, Favil Press, 1943; *Poems*, Falcon Press, 1946; *The Ballad of Billy Rose*, Northern House, 1964; *Finding Gold* (poetry), Chatto & Windus, 1967; *The Loud Winter* (poems), Triskel Press, 1967; (editor) *Vernon Watkins, 1906-1967*, Faber, 1970; *Ransoms* (poems), Chatto & Windus, 1970. Author of short radio plays for school programs of British Broadcasting Corp. Contributor of poems to poetry magazines, many of them included in anthologies.

WORK IN PROGRESS: Come Inside, an anthology of verse for schools, for Hulton; verse translations from medieval Welsh.

SIDELIGHTS: Norris told *CA*, he writes "slowly and with great pain, about six poems a year."

BIOGRAPHICAL/CRITICAL SOURCES: Punch, April 5, 1967; *London Magazine*, June, 1967; *Poetry Review*, summer, 1967; *Times Literary Supplement*, April 23, 1970.†

*   *   *

NORRIS, Louis William 1906-

PERSONAL: Born February 3, 1906, in Columbus, Ohio; son of Vernon Ward (an accountant) and Julia Gertrude (Hamilton) Norris; married Florence Cronise Howard, June 4, 1931; children: Martha Ellen, Joanna May Norris Burton. *Education:* Otterbein College, A.B., 1928; Boston University, S.T.B., 1931, Ph.D., 1937; additional graduate study at University of Berlin, 1931-32, Harvard University, 1936-37. *Politics:* Republican. *Religion:* United Methodist. *Home:* 4443 Ellicott St. N.W., Washington, D.C. 20016. *Office:* National Endowment for the Humanities, 19th and F Sts., Washington, D.C. 20506.

CAREER: Minister of Evangelical Congregational Church,

Dunstable, Mass., for six years; Baldwin-Wallace College, Berea, Ohio, began as assistant professor, became associate professor of philosophy, 1937-46, vice-president, 1939-46; DePauw University, Greencastle, Ind., professor and head of philosophy department, 1946-52, academic dean, 1950-52; MacMurray College, Jacksonville, Ill., president, 1952-60; Albion College, Albion, Mich., president, 1960-70; National Endowment for the Humanities, Washington, D.C., program officer, 1970—. Director, City Bank and Trust Co., 1965-70; director, Michigan Foundation for Advanced Research, 1965—. Former trustee of Methodist Theological School in Ohio; member of United Methodist Senate.

MEMBER: International Association of College and University Presidents, Institute of International Education (fellow), American Philosophical Association, American Association of University Professors, American Association for the Advancement of Science, National Education Association, National Association of Biblical Instructors (treasurer, 1948-51), Royal Society of Arts (fellow), Phi Beta Kappa, Rotary. *Awards, honors:* LL.D. from Otterbein College; Litt.D. from MacMurray College.

WRITINGS: The Good New Days, Bookman Associates, 1956; *Polarity: A Philosophy of Tensions Among Values,* Regnery, 1956.

Contributor: *Goals for American Education: Conference on Science, Philosophy, and Religion in Their Relation to the Democratic Way of Life,* Harper, 1950; *Perspectives on a Troubled Decade: Science, Philosophy, and Religion, 1939-1949,* Harper, 1950; J. M. Bachelor and others, editors, *Current Thinking and Writing,* third series, Appleton, 1956; *Speech: Its Techniques and Disciplines in a Free Society,* Appleton, 1961; *Syllabus for Public Speaking,* [Dubuque], 1962; *Inservice Education for School Administration,* American Association of School Administrators, c.1963; *Hospital Administration,* American Association of Hospital Administrators, 1964. Contributor of articles and reviews to various newspapers and journals, including *Religious Education, Pastor, Annals* of American Academy of Political and Social Science, *Saturday Review,* and *School and Society.*

WORK IN PROGRESS: A book, *The Professor as Leader.*

SIDELIGHTS: Norris traveled to Africa to visit Albert Schweitzer at Lambarene for a two-week period in 1961. He writes that his "major concern has been with the philosophy of education and the welfare of educational institutions of higher education."

* * *

NOTESTEIN, Wallace 1878-1969

PERSONAL: Born December 16, 1878, in Wooster, Ohio; son of J. O. (a professor) and Margaret (Wallace) Notestein; married Ada Louise Comstock, June 14, 1943. *Education:* College of Wooster, B.A., 1900; Yale University, Ph.D., 1908. *Politics:* Mugwump. *Home:* 236 Edwards St., New Haven, Conn. 06511.

CAREER: Taught at University of Kansas, 1905-07, University of Minnesota, 1908-20, Cornell University, 1920-28; Yale University, New Haven, Conn., Sterling Professor of English History, 1928-47, emeritus, 1947-69. Oxford University, associate member of All Souls College, 1931-32, Eastman Professor (university), and fellow of Balliol College, 1949-50. Member of American Commission to Nego-

tiate Peace, Paris, France, 1919. Guggenheim Foundation, member of advisory council, 1939-48.

MEMBER: American Philosophical Society, British Academy (corresponding fellow), Century Club (New York), Athenaeum Club (London). *Awards, honors:* Herbert Baxter Adams Prize in European History, 1909, for *A History of Witchcraft in England from 1558 to 1718,* Litt.D. from College of Wooster, 1923. Harvard University, 1939, University of Birmingham, 1950, Yale University, 1951; LL.D. from University of Glasgow, 1950; D.Litt. from Oxford University, 1958.

WRITINGS: A History of Witchcraft in England from 1558 to 1718, American Historical Association, 1911, reissued as *A History of Witchcraft in England,* Apollo, 1968; (editor with Albert Beebe White) *Source Problems in English History,* Harper, 1915; (compiler with Elmer E. Stoll) *Conquest and Kultur: Aims of the Germans in Their Own Words,* Committee on Public Information, 1918; (editor and author of introduction with Frances Helen Relf) *Commons Debates for 1629,* University of Minnesota Press, 1921; (editor) Simons D'Ewes, *Journal from the Beginning of the Long Parliament to the Opening of the Trial of the Earl of Strafford,* Yale University Press, 1923; *The Winning of the Initiative by the House of Commons* (Raleigh Lectures on History, British Academy), published for the British Academy by Oxford University Press, 1924; (editor with Relf and Hartley Simpson) *Commons Debates, 1621,* seven volumes, Yale University Press, 1935; *English Folk: A Book of Characters,* Harcourt, 1938; *The Scot in History,* Yale University Press, 1946; *The English People on the Eve of Colonization, 1603-1630,* Harper, 1954; *Four Worthies: John Chamberlain, Anne Clifford, John Taylor, Oliver Heywood,* J. Cape, 1956, Yale University Press, 1957; *The House of Commons, 1604-1610,* Yale University Press, 1971; *Conflict in Stuart England,* Shoe String-Archon, 1971. Contributor to Annual Report of American Historical Association, 1916, and to *Ohio Archaeological and Historical Quarterly.*

(Died February 2, 1969)

* * *

NOVAK, Joseph 1898-
(Joe Novak)

PERSONAL: Born August 9, 1898, in Butte, Mont.; son of Frank and Mary Novak; children: Jay Allan. *Education:* Loyola University of Los Angeles, law student. *Home:* 233 Barlock Ave., Los Angeles, Calif. 90049.

CAREER: Professional golf instructor at Bel Air Country Club, Los Angeles, Calif., for thirty-six years. Golf instructor on radio, 1926; instructor on television with thirteen-week course "It's Golf Time." *Member:* Professional Golfers' Association of America (former national director, secretary, and president), Bel Air Country Club (honorary life member).

WRITINGS—All under name Joe Novak: *Par Golf in 8 Steps,* Prentice-Hall, 1950; *How to Put Power and Direction in Your Golf,* Prentice-Hall, 1954; *Golf Can be an Easy Game,* Prentice-Hall, 1962; *Golf,* Hennel Lock and Harrap, 1964; *The Novak System of Mastering Golf,* Prentice-Hall, 1969. Regular contributor of articles to golf magazines.

* * *

NOYES, Morgan Phelps 1891-1972

PERSONAL: Born March 29, 1891, in Warren, Pa.; son of

Charles Henry (a judge) and Effie (Morgan) Noyes; married Marjorie Bradford Clarke, July 24, 1926; children: Sarah Clarke (Mrs. Peyton H. Mead), William Morgan. *Education:* Yale University, B.A., 1914; Union Theological Seminary, New York, N.Y., student, 1915-17, 1919-20; Columbia University, M.A., 1922. *Home:* 250 Christopher St., Upper Montclair, N.J. 07043.

CAREER: Minister, United Presbyterian Church. Minister in Dobbs Ferry, N.Y., 1920-25, Brooklyn, N.Y., 1925-32; Central Presbyterian Church, Montclair, N.J., pastor, 1932-57, pastor emeritus, 1957-72. Union Theological Seminary, New York, N.Y., associate professor of practical theology, 1945-51. Supply minister at St. Andrew's Presbyterian Church, Frognal, London, England, summers, 1950, 1954, 1962; Lyman Beecher Lecturer at Yale Divinity School, 1942. National Council of Churches, vice-chairman of department of worship and the arts, 1952-63. Union Theological Seminary, member of board of directors, 1931-45, 1951-68; Corporation of Yale University, member, 1945-59. *Member:* Century Association (New York), Graduates Club (New Haven). *Awards, honors:* D.D. from Yale University, 1938.

WRITINGS: (Editor) *Prayers for Services: A Manual for Leaders of Worship*, Scribner, 1934; *Preaching the Word of God* (Lyman Beecher Lectures, Yale Divinity School, 1942), Scribner, 1943; *Louis F. Benson, Hymnologist*, Hymn Society of America, 1955; *Henry Sloane Coffin: The Man and His Ministry*, Scribner, 1964.

Contributor: S. A. Hunter, editor, *The Music of the Gospel*, Abingdon, 1932; R. H. Read, editor, *The Younger Churchmen Look at the Church*, Macmillan, 1935; *A Half Century of Union Theological Seminary*, Scribner, 1945; Reinhold Niebuhr, editor, *This Ministry: The Contribution of Henry Sloane Coffin*, Scribner, 1945; *Sermons for the New Age*, Morehouse-Graham Co., 1948; Nolan B. Harmon, editor, *Interpreter's Bible*, twelve volumes, Abingdon, 1951-55. Contributor to *Anglican Theological Review, Religion in Life, Westminster Bookman*, and *Union Seminary Quarterly Review*.

BIOGRAPHICAL/CRITICAL SOURCES: Edgar DeWitt Jones, *The Royalty of the Pulpit*, Harper, 1951; *Presbyterian Life*, May 1, 1964.

(Died June 20, 1972)

* * *

NOYES-KANE, Dorothy 1906-
(Dorothy Noyes Sproul)

PERSONAL: Born May 20, 1906, in Baltimore, Md.; daughter of Selden Goodwin (a business executive) and Flora (Keily) Noyes; married A. E. Sproul, Jr., December 24, 1940 (divorced July, 1955); married Lawrence J. Kane, July 10, 1965; children: (first marriage) Christopher Noyes (deceased), Barbara Chamberlain. *Education:* Goddard College, B.A., 1964; Yale University, M.P.H. and M.S. (urban studies), 1966. *Politics:* Independent. *Religion:* Protestant. *Home:* 14 Charlton Hill, Hamden Conn. 06518.

CAREER: Kings County Medical Society, Brooklyn, N.Y., librarian, 1924-27; literary assistant to neuropsychiatrist, New York, N.Y., 1927-30; Lewis Waetjen Agency (advertising firm), copywriter, 1930-33; Redfield-Johnstone Agency (advertising), New York, N.Y., vice-president, 1934-36; Noyes & Sproul, Inc., New York, N.Y., vice-president, 1934-60, secretary and treasurer, 1937-60; John Slade Ely Center for Health Education Re-

search, New Haven, Conn., president, 1960-66; Southern Connecticut State College, New Haven, Conn., director of Environmental Studies Center, 1969-72. Member of board of directors, Hamden Hall Country Day School, 1950-58, National Health Council, 1958-61, Greater New York Safety Council, 1962-69, Planned Parenthood League of Connecticut, 1968-70. *Member:* World Medical Association (founding member; member of U.S. committee), Advertising Federation of America (secretary, 1959-60), American Woman's Association (vice-president; governor), National Council of Women of the United States, Association of Medical Advertising Agencies (first president, 1953-54), Advertising Women of New York (former director and treasurer). *Awards, honors:* Advertising Woman of the Year, Advertising Federation of America, 1957-58.

WRITINGS: (Under name Dorothy Noyes Sproul) *Your Child: Step by Step Toward Maturity*, Doubleday, 1963. Writer of "Your Child," regular column in *Chicago* Daily News and twenty other newspapers, 1958-61. Contributor to medical, advertising, and other trade journals.

AVOCATIONAL INTERESTS: Golf, swimming, walking.

* * *

NYANAPONIKA 1901-

PERSONAL: Lay name, Siegmund Feniger; born July 21, 1901, in Hanau, West Germany. *Education:* Attended Classical College in Germany. *Home:* Forest Hermitage, Kandy, Ceylon.

CAREER: Worked in various branches of the book trade in Germany prior to 1936; Buddhist monk in Ceylon, 1936—; Buddhist Publication Society, Kandy, Ceylon, co-founder, 1958, editor, 1958—. Participated in sixth Buddhist Synod, Rangoon, Burma, 1954-56, and served as vice-president of World Fellowship of Buddhists, 1958-61.

WRITINGS: Abhidhamma Studies: Researches in Buddhist Psychology, Frewin & Co., 1949; (editor and translator) *Satipatthana: Der Heilsweg buddhistischer Geistesschulung* (translation of the *Satipatthana Sutta*, the Tenth Discourse of the Majjhimanikaya), Verlag Christiani, 1950, 2nd edition published in English as *The Heart of Buddhist Meditation: Satipatthana—A Handbook of Mental Training Based on the Buddha's "Way of Mindfulness," with an Anthology of Relevant Texts Translated from Pali and Sanskrit*, Word of Buddha Publishing Committee (Colombo, Ceylon), 1954, 3rd edition, enlarged, Rider, 1962, Citadel, 1969, revised and enlarged German edition published as *Geistestraining durch Achtsamkeit*, Verlag Christiani, 1970; (editor and translator into German) *Sutta-Nipata* (Buddhist canonical work), Verlag Christiani, 1955; (editor and translator into German) *Der Einzige Weg* (Buddhist texts), Verlag Christiani, 1956; (editor) Nyanatikola, *Guide Through the Abhidhamma-Pitaka Being a Synopsis of the Philosophical Collection Belonging to the Buddhist Pali Canon*, 3rd edition, revised and enlarged, Buddhist Literature Society, 1957; *The Four Sublime States: Brahma-vihara*, 3rd edition, Buddhist Publication Society, 1958; *Anatta and Nibbama: Egolessness and Deliverance*, Buddhist Publication Society, 1959; (translator and author of introduction) *Buddhism and God Idea*, Buddhist Publication Society, 1962; (translator) Sobhana, *The Progress of Insight Through the Stages of Purification*, Forest Hermitage, 1965; (translator and contributor) *The Threefold Refuge*, Buddhist Publication Society, 1965; (compiler and translator) *The Life of Sariputta* (from Pali texts of Tripitaka), Buddhist Publication Society, 1966; (editor and author of introduction and notes) *The Discourse on the Snake Simile, from the Majjhima Nikaya*, Buddhist Publication Society, 1966; (translator) *Lehrreden aus der systematischen Sammlung des Pali-Kanons* (Samyutta-Nikaya 17-34), Irma Luebcke, 1967; (translator and author of introduction) *The Four Nutriments of Life: An Anthology of Buddhist Texts*, Buddhist Publication Society, 1967; *The Power of Mindfulness: An Inquiry Into the Scope of Bare Attention and the Principal Sources of Its Strength*, Buddhist Publication Society, 1968; (editor) *Pathways of Buddhist Thought* (essays from "The Wheel"), selected by M. O'C. Walshe, Allen & Unwin, 1971. Editor, "The Wheel" series and "Bodhi Leaves" series, Buddhist Publication Society.

*   *   *

OBENHAUS, Victor 1903-

PERSONAL: Born September 26, 1903, in Superior, Wis.; son of Herman F. A. and Grace (Dexter) Obenhaus; married Marion Pendleton (director of Chicago Child Care Society), July 30, 1938; children: Constance (Mrs. Arnold Goldberg), Helen (Mrs. Paul Halverson), Mark. *Education:* Oberlin College, A.B., 1925; Union Theological Seminary, New York, N.Y., B.D., 1929; Columbia University, M.A., 1929, Ed.D., 1940. *Home:* 5549 Woodlawn Ave., Chicago, Ill., 60637. *Office:* Chicago Theological Seminary, 5757 University Ave., Chicago, Ill. 60637.

CAREER: Congregational Christian Church (now United Church of Christ), ordained minister, 1929, served at churches in Cleveland, Ohio, 1929-36, in New York, N.Y., 1936-38; Pleasant Hill Academy, Pleasant Hill, Tenn., principal, 1938-44; University of Chicago, Chicago, Ill., associate professor, federated theological faculty, 1944-60; Chicago Theological Seminary, Chicago, Ill., professor of Christian ethics, 1960—, acting president, 1973—. Member of Department of Church and Economic Life, National Council of Churches; chairman of Town and Country Commission, United Church of Christ; member of board of directors, Merom Institute. *Member:* Americal Sociological Society, Rural Sociological Society, Religious Research Association (vice-president, 1960-62), American Society of Christian Ethics (president, 1967-68).

WRITINGS: The Hebrew Prophets and America's Conscience, Pilgrim Press, 1948; *The Responsible Christian*, University of Chicago Press, 1957; *The Church and Faith in Mid America*, Westminster, 1963; (with W. Widick Schroeder) *Religion in American Culture*, Free Press of Glencoe, 1964; *Ethics for an Industrial Age: A Christian Inquiry*, Harper, 1965; *The Church in Our Time*, United Church Board for Homeland Ministries, 1965; *And See the People*, Center for the Scientific Study of Religion, 1968.

WORK IN PROGRESS: Suburban Religion, with W. W. Schroeder, Thomas Sweetser, and Larry Jonos.

SIDELIGHTS: Writing in *Christian Century*, Robert Lee commented, "*Ethics for an Industrial Age* is the final volume in the 'Ethics and Economic Life' series sponsored by the National Council of Churches. Its author . . . is to be commended for tackling so ably so gigantic a subject. His work ranges over many of the key issues emerging from our new industrial society. . . . as an overview that whets one's appetite for more, this book is an admirable and fitting climax to a distinguished series."

O'CONNOR, James I(gnatius) 1910-

PERSONAL: Born July 30, 1910, in Chicago, Ill.; son of James Francis (a policeman) and Margaret (Quealy) O'Connor. *Education:* Xavier University, Cincinnati, Ohio, Litt.B., 1934, M.A., 1935; West Baden College, Ph.L., 1938, S.T.L., 1944; Catholic University of America, J.C.B., 1946; Pontifical Gregorian University, Rome, Italy, J.C.L., 1948, J.C.D., 1950. *Address:* 2345 West 56th St., Chicago, Ill. 60636.

CAREER: Entered Society of Jesus (Jesuits), 1930, ordained priest, 1943. Jesuit high school teacher, Cincinnati, Ohio, 1938-40; West Baden College, West Baden Springs, Ind., professor of canon law and rites, 1948-64; Loyola University, Bellarmine School of Theology, North Aurora, Ill., professor of canon law and rites, 1964-70; Jesuit School of Theology, Chicago, Ill., associate professor, 1970—. Guest professor of canon law at Alma College, Los Gatos, Calif. (now The Jesuit School of Theology at Berkeley), 1952, 1954, St. Mary's College, St. Marys, Kan., 1956, 1958, 1960, 1962; summer professor of canon law at colleges throughout America, 1949—. Canonical consultant, Catholic Hospital Association of America, 1953—. *Member:* Canon Law Society of America, Canadian Canon Law Society.

WRITINGS: Dispensation from Irregularities to Holy Orders, West Baden College Press, 1952; (with T. Lincoln Bouscaren) *Canon Law Digest*, Volumes IV, V, and VI, Bruce, 1958-69; *An Introduction to the Divine Office*, West Baden College Press, 1960; (with Bouscaren) *Canon Law Digest for Religious*, Volume I, and supplements, Bruce, 1964-67. Also sole author of *Canon Law Digest*, Volume VII. Contributor to *New Catholic Encyclopedia, Hospital Progress, Jurist*, and religious journals.

WORK IN PROGRESS: Collection and translation of canonical documents for future supplements to *Canon Law Digest*.

SIDELIGHTS: O'Connor studied and traveled in Europe, 1946-48.

*   *   *

O'DELL, Andrew C(harles) 1909-1966

PERSONAL: Born June 4, 1909, in Lluipaardsvlei, Transvaal, South Africa; son of Charles and Jemima O'Dell; married Q. Louise Smith, July 21, 1938; children: Duncan S., Felicity Ann. *Education:* University of London, B.Sc. (first class honors), 1930, M.Sc., 1933. *Home:* 80 St. Machar Dr., Aberdeen, Scotland. *Office:* Department of Geography, University of Aberdeen, Aberdeen, Scotland.

CAREER: University of London, Birbeck College, London, England, lecturer in geography, 1931-45; University of Aberdeen, Aberdeen, Scotland, head of department of geography, 1945-66, professor, 1951-66. British Admiralty, Naval Intelligence Division, lecturer in geography, London, England, 1941-43, and research officer, Edinburgh, Scotland, 1943-45. Referee for planning appeals, Secretary of State for Scotland, 1961-66. Member of British National Committee of Geography, 1952-66, and Highland and Islands Advisory Panel, 1963-65. Participant in radio and television broadcasts on railways, archaeology, and universities.

MEMBER: Royal Geographical Society (fellow), Royal Scottish Geographical Society (fellow; vice-president), Royal Society of Edinburgh (fellow), Business and Professional Club of Aberdeen (president). *Awards, honors:*

Marion Newbigin Medal of Royal Scottish Geographical Society, 1939.

WRITINGS: The Historical Geography of the Shetland Islands, Manson, Lerwick, 1939; *Railways and Geography*, Rinehart, 1956; 2nd edition, revised by Peter S. Richards, Hutchinson, 1971; *The Scandinavian World*, Longmans, Green, 1957; (with A. Cain) *The St. Ninian's Isle Treasure*, Aberdeen University Press, 1960; (with Kenneth Walton) *The Highlands and Islands of Scotland*, Nelson, 1962; (editor with J. Mackintosh) *The North-East of Scotland*, British Association for the Advancement of Science, 1963; (editor) *Geography: Our Earth and Its Peoples*, Grolier Society, 1967, revised edition, 1971.

WORK IN PROGRESS: Central and South Scotland; research on railway history and traffic.

SIDELIGHTS: O'Dell was the leader of archaeological excavations in the Shetland Islands and of group discovering St. Ninian's Isle treasure (largest Celtic silver collection found in Scotland) in 1958. He traveled in North America, Africa, Australasia, and extensively in the Scandinavian countries and islands. *Avocational interests:* Railway history and collecting literature on railways.

(Died June 17, 1966)

* * *

ODLUM, Doris Maude   1890-

PERSONAL: Born June 26, 1890. in Folkestone, England; daughter of Walter Edward (an accountant and company director) and Maude Gough (Hinde) Odlum. *Education:* University of London, B.A., 1915; St. Hilda's College, Oxford, M.A., 1919; Royal Free Hospital School of Medicine and St. Mary's Hospital Medical School, M.R.C.S. and L.R.C.P., 1924, D.P.M., 1926, F.R.C.Psych., 1972. *Religion:* Church of England. *Home:* Ardmor, 11 Cliff Dr., Canford Cliffs, Poole, Dorset, England. *Office:* 56 Wimpole St., London W. 1, England.

CAREER: Lady Chichester Hospital for Nervous Diseases, Hove, England, honorary consultant physician, 1928-48; Royal Victoria and West Hampshire Hospital, Bournemouth, England, honorary physician for psychiatry, 1928-48; Elizabeth Garrett Anderson Hospital, London, England, former senior consultant physician, honorary consultant physician for psychological medicine, 1955—. Emeritus consultant physician for psychological medicine, Bournemouth and West Hampshire Hospital Group; honorary psychotherapist, Marylebone Hospital for Psychiatry and Child Guidance. Lecturer. Member of Home Office Committee on Adoption, 1954. *Military service:* Women's Volunteer Reserve, 1915-18; became captain.

MEMBER: International Medical Women's Association (vice-president, 1950-54), Royal Society of Medicine (fellow), British Medical Women's Federation (president, 1952-54), British Medical Association (fellow), European League for Mental Hygiene (president, 1954-57), World Federation for Mental Health (member of executive committee, 1948-50), National Association for Mental Health (vice-president, 1946—), The Samaritans (president, 1973—).

WRITINGS: You and Your Children, Ministry of Health, 1945; *Psychology, the Nurse and the Patient*, Iliffe, 1952, 3rd edition, 1960, published in United States as *Mental Health, the Nurse and the Patient*, Lippincott, 1960; *Journey through Adolescence*, Delisle, 1957; *The Mind of Your Child*, Foyle, 1960. Contributor to *Modern Treatment Year Book*, 1949, and to medical journals.

WORK IN PROGRESS: Writing on the male predicament.

AVOCATIONAL INTERESTS: Travel, archaeology, classical studies, painting, swimming, golf.

* * *

O'DONNELL, Cyril   1900-

PERSONAL: Born December 9, 1900, in Lincoln, Neb.; son of Patrick and Catherine (McCarthy) O'Donnell; married Elizabeth McPherson, December 20, 1928; children: Elizabeth Anne O'Donnell Aitken, James, William, Douglas. *Education:* University of Alberta, B.Com, A.M.; University of Chicago, Ph.D. *Home:* 3965 Mandeville Canyon Rd., Los Angeles, Calif. 90049. *Office:* University of California, Los Angeles, Calif. 90024.

CAREER: University of California, Los Angeles, professor of business organization and policy, 1948-68, emeritus, 1968—. Consultant to domestic and foreign governments and to agencies and private firms. Everest & Jennings, International, director. *Member:* American Management Association, Academy of Management.

WRITINGS: Recent Trends in the Demand for American Cotton, University of Chicago Press, 1945; *Business Management*, University of California Press, 1951; (with Harold D. Koontz) *Principles of Management: An Analysis of Managerial Functions*, McGraw, 1955, 5th edition, 1972; (editor with Koontz) *Readings in Management*, McGraw, 1959, 2nd edition published as *Management: A Book of Readings*, 1968, 3rd edition, 1972; *Cases in General Management*, Irwin, 1961, revised edition, 1965; *The Strategy of Corporate Research*, Chandler Publishing, 1967. Contributor of articles to professional journals.

WORK IN PROGRESS: The Management of Scientists.

AVOCATIONAL INTERESTS: Anthropology.

* * *

O'DONNELL, Elliott   1872-1965

PERSONAL: Born February 27, 1872, in Clifton, Bristol, Gloucestershire, England; son of Henry (a clergyman) and Elizabeth Sarah (Harrison) O'Donnell; married Ada Caroline William, January 5, 1905 (deceased). *Education:* Attended Clifton College, Bristol, England, Queen's Service Academy, Dublin, Ireland, and Neville Dramatic Academy, London, England. *Politics:* Conservative. *Religion:* Protestant. *Address:* c/o Westminster Bank, Queen's Rd., Clifton, Bristol, Gloucestershire, England.

CAREER: Actor on stage and in films; writer, mainly about unusual phenomena and the supernatural, and lecturer and broadcaster on the same subjects in England and United States. *Military service:* British Auxiliary Army, World War I. *Member:* Society of Authors, Royal Commonwealth Society.

WRITINGS: Ghostly Phenomena, T. W. Lourie, 1910; *Byways of Ghost-Land*, Rider, 1911; *Scottish Ghost Stories*, Paul, Trench, Trubner, 1911; *The Sorcery Club*, Rider, 1912; *Werewolves*, Methuen, 1912, Small, Maynard, 1914; *The Irish Abroad*, Pitman, 1915; *Twenty Years' Experience as a Ghost Hunter*, Heath, Cranton, 1916; *The Haunted Man*, Heath, Cranton, 1917; *Haunted Places in England*, Sands, 1919; *The Menace of Spiritualism*, Stokes, 1920; *More Haunted Houses of London*, Nash & Grayston, 1920; *Ghosts Helpful and Harmful*, Rider, 1924; (editor) *Trial of Kate Webster*, Canada Law Book, 1925;

Strange Sea Mysteries, John Lane, 1926; *Strange Disappearances*, John Lane, 1927; *Confessions of a Ghost Hunter*, Butterworth, 1928; *Fatal Kisses*, J. Hamilton, 1929; *Famous Curses*, Skeffington & Sons, 1929.

The Boys' Book of Sea Mysteries, Dodd, 1930; *Great Thames Mysteries*, Selwyn, 1930; *Women Bluebeards*, Stanley Paul, 1930; *Rooms of Mystery*, P. Allan, 1931; *Ghosts of London*, P. Allan, 1932, Dutton, 1933; *Family Ghosts and Ghostly Phenomena*, Dutton, 1934; *Strange Cults and Secret Societies of Modern London*, P. Allan, 1934, Dutton, 1935; *Haunted Churches*, Quality Press, 1939; *Murder at Hide and Seek*, Coker, 1945; *Haunted Britain*, Rider, 1948.

Dead Riders, Rider, 1952; *Ghosts with a Purpose*, Roy Publishers, 1952; *Dangerous Ghosts*, Rider, 1954; *Haunted People*, Rider, 1955; *Phantoms of the Night*, Rider, 1956; *Haunted Waters*, Rider, 1957; *Trees of Ghostly Dread*, Rider, 1958; (editor and contributor) *Ghosts: Stories of the Supernatural*, Foulsham, 1959, Taplinger, 1969; *The Screaming Skulls: And Other Ghost Stories*, arranged by H. Ludlam, Foulsham, 1964, Taplinger, 1969; *The Midnight Hearse and More Ghosts*, arranged by H. Ludlam, Foulsham, 1965, Taplinger, 1969; *Elliott O'Donnell's Casebook of Ghosts*, edited by Harry Ludlam, Taplinger, 1969; *The Hag of the Dribble and Other True Ghosts*, edited by Bernhardt J. Hurwood, Taplinger, 1971.

Also author of *Dreams and Their Meanings, Animal Ghosts, Haunted Highways, Escaped From Justice, For Satan's Sake, Dinevah the Beautiful, The Unknown Depths, Some Haunted Houses of England and Wales, Haunted Houses of London, Banshees, Spiritualism Explained, Ghostland, The Devil in the Pulpit, Caravan of Crime, Hell Ships, Cornered at Last, Haunted and Hunted*, and *Adventures With Ghosts*.

Co-author of radio plays for National Broadcasting Co. Contributor to *Harmsworth's Encyclopaedia.* Also contributor to newspapers and magazines throughout English-speaking world.

SIDELIGHTS: O'Donnell once said: "I have investigated, sometimes alone, and sometimes with other people and the press, many cases of reputed hauntings. I believe in ghosts but am not a spiritualist."

(Died May 8, 1965)

*   *   *

OGG, Oscar (John) 1908-1971

PERSONAL: Born December 13, 1908, in Richmond, Va.; son of Oscar Jessie (a railroad man) and Marcie (Chappell) Ogg; married Margaret L. T. Westenberger (a partner in a department store), June 12, 1934; children: Oscar John, Margaret Louise. *Education:* University of Illinois, B.S. in Architecture, 1932. *Politics:* Democrat. *Religion:* Catholic. *Home:* Long Close Rd., Stamford, Conn. 06902. *Office:* Book-of-the-Month Club, Inc., 345 Hudson St., New York, N.Y. 10014.

CAREER: Huxley House, New York, N.Y., typographer, 1932-35; Swafford & Koehl, New York, N.Y., art director, 1935-37; free-lance book designer and calligrapher, New York, N.Y., 1937-50; Book-of-the-Month Club, Inc., New York, N.Y., vice-president and art director, 1950-71, member of board of directors, 1959-71. Lecturer, Columbia University, 1946-52. *Military service:* U.S. Army, Corps of Engineers, Intelligence, World War II. *Member:* American Institute of Graphic Arts, Society of Typographic Arts, Type Director's Club, Grolier Club, Typophiles.

WRITINGS: An Alphabet Source Book, Harper, 1940; *The 26 Letters*, Crowell, 1948, revised edition, 1971; *Lettering as a Book Art*, McKibben, 1949; *Three Classics of Italian Calligraphy*, Dover, 1953. Also author of monographs. Contributor of articles to periodicals.

BIOGRAPHICAL/CRITICAL SOURCES: New York Times, August 11, 1971; *Publishers Weekly*, August 23, 1971.

(Died August 10, 1971)

*   *   *

O'GRADY, Francis Dominic 1909-
(Frank O'Grady)

PERSONAL: Born April 24, 1909, in Sydney, New South Wales, Australia; son of John Edward (a barrister) and Margaret (Gleeson) O'Grady; married Doris Joyce Byrne, October 17, 1936; children: Peter, Francis, Margaret, David, Catherine, John. *Education:* School of Applied Advertising, Sydney, Australia, diploma; Local Government Coaching College, Sydney, Australia, certificate of town or shire clerk. *Religion:* Roman Catholic. *Home:* 21 Karilla Ave., Lane Cove, New South Wales, Australia.

CAREER: Town clerk of Erskineville, New South Wales, Australia, 1939-46, of The Glebe, New South Wales, 1946-48; City of Sydney, New South Wales, assessments officer, 1949-68; town clerk of South Sydney, New South Wales, 1968-72. *Member:* Royal Australian Historical Society (council, 1960, 1962-64, 1966-72), Association of Local Government Clerks of New South Wales (management committee, 1942-49), Municipal and Shire Council Employee's Union (vice-president of senior officers' branch, 1958-64).

WRITINGS—Under name Frank O'Grady: *The Golden Valley*, Cassell, 1955; *Goonoo Goonoo*, Cassell, 1956; *Hanging Rock*, Cassell, 1957; *No Boundary Fence*, Angus & Robertson, 1960; *Wild Honey*, Angus & Robertson, 1961; *The Sun Breaks Through*, Angus & Robertson, 1964. Contributor of short stories to *Catholic Weekly.*

AVOCATIONAL INTERESTS: Fishing, both inland and coastal.

*   *   *

OLIVER, Herman 1885-

PERSONAL: Born January 28, 1885, in John Day, Ore.; son of Joseph Cayton (a stockman) and Elizabeth (Miller) Oliver; married Eliza Laurance, February 21, 1906; children: Anna Elizabeth (Mrs. A. Wiseman). *Education:* Attended elementary school in John Day, Ore. *Politics:* Republican. *Home:* 150 Northwest Second Ave., John Day, Ore. 97845.

CAREER: Grant County Bank, John Day, Ore., president, 30 years. Member of board of directors, First National Bank, Portland, Ore., five years. Member of Oregon State Board of Higher Education, 23 years, of State Highway Commission, three and one half years; mayor of John Day, four years. *Member:* Oregon Cattlemen's Association (president, 1928-38). *Awards, honors:* D.Sc., Oregon State College, 1958; award for outstanding service to Oregon education, Eastern Oregon College, 1962.

WRITINGS: Gold and Cattle Country, Binfords, 1961, 2nd edition, 1967.

OLIVER, R(ichard) A(lexander) C(avaye)   1904-

PERSONAL: Born January 9, 1904, in Lockerbie, Scotland; son of Charles and Elizabeth (Smith) Oliver; married Annabella Margaret White (a university lecturer), August 20, 1929; children: Francis Richard, Helen Miranda (Mrs. Alastair Hetherington). *Education:* University of Edinburgh, M.A., 1925, B.Ed., 1927, Ph.D., 1933; additional study at Stanford University. *Politics:* Independent. *Home:* Waingap, Crook, Kendal, Westmorland, England.

CAREER: Carnegie Corp. of New York, researcher in Kenya, Africa, 1929-32; teacher in Scotland and England, 1933-34; Wiltshire Education Committee, Wiltshire, England, assistant education officer, 1934-36; Devon Education Committee, Devonshire, England, deputy secretary, 1936-38; University of Manchester, Manchester, England, professor of education, 1938-70, professor emeritus, 1970—. *Member:* British Psychological Society (fellow).

WRITINGS: General Intelligence Test for Africans, Government Printer (Kenya), 1932; (with Herbert R. Hamley, H. E. Field, and Keith Struckmeyer) *The Educational Guidance of the School Child,* University of London Press, 1937; *The Training of Teachers in Universities,* University of London Press, 1943; *Research in Education,* Allen & Unwin, 1946.

Booklets, all published by Joint Matriculation Board of Universities of Manchester, Liverpool, Leeds, Sheffield, and Birmingham: *A General Paper in the General Certificate of Education Examination,* 1955, *An Experimental Examination in General Studies,* 1955, *The Effectiveness of G.C.E. Advanced Level as a Criterion for University Selection,* 1960, *General Studies (Advanced) in the G.C.E.,* 1960, *General Studies (Advanced),* 1960, 1961, *An Experimental Test in English,* 1963, *Studies in a University Entrance Test in English,* 1964, *Testing English for University Entrants,* 1967. Contributor to professional journals.

WORK IN PROGRESS: Research on sixth form curricula and their results, and on tests of academic aptitude.

AVOCATIONAL INTERESTS: Gardening, painting, travel.

*   *   *

OLSEN, Edward G(ustave)   1908-

PERSONAL: Born March 26, 1908, in Portland, Ore.; son of Gustav Adolph (a merchant) and Emma (Bush) Olsen; married Faith Theresa Elliott, June 25, 1931 (died, 1947); married Pauline Walsh (a teacher), September 11, 1948; children; (first marriage) Marvin, Marcia (Mrs. Edward Kolar); (second marriage) Douglas. *Education:* Pacific University, A.B., 1930; Columbia University, M.A., 1932, Ed.D., 1937; Union Theological Seminary, B.D., 1933. *Politics:* Independent. *Religion:* Unitarian. *Home:* 317 Memory Lane, Brookings, Ore. 97415.

CAREER: Colgate University, Hamilton, N.Y., instructor in education and acting chairman of the department, 1936-41; Russell Sage College, Troy, N.Y., associate professor of education and director of School of Education, 1941-45; Office of Washington State Superintendent of Public Instruction, director of school and community relations, 1945-50; University of Texas, Austin, associate professor of educational administration, 1950-51; National Conference of Christians and Jews, Chicago, Ill., director of education 1951-66; California State University at Hayward, professor of education, 1966-73. Visiting professor at Georgia State Teachers College, University of Washington, College of

William and Mary, Western Washington State College, University of Maine, and Stanford University. Fulbright lecturer at University College of Rhodesia and Nyasaland, 1958. President, Council on Human Relations, Park Ridge, Ill., 1963—.

MEMBER: National Education Association (life), City Club (Chicago; member of board of governors, 1955-62; vice-president, 1960). *Awards, honors:* Thomas H. Wright Award of City of Chicago for work in human relations education, 1957; distinguished service award, National Community School Education Association, 1969.

WRITINGS: (Editor and compiler) *School and Community,* Prentice-Hall, 1945, revised edition, 1954; (editor) *School and Community Programs,* Prentice-Hall, 1949; (editor) *The Modern Community School,* Appleton, 1953; (editor) *The School and Community Reader: Education in Perspective,* Macmillan, 1963. Contributor to professional journals.

SIDELIGHTS: School and Community has been published in Spanish and Japanese.

*   *   *

OLSON, Charles (John)   1910-1970

PERSONAL: Born December 27, 1910, in Worcester, Mass.; son of Karl Joseph and Mary (Hines) Olson. *Education:* Wesleyan University, B.A., 1932, M.A., 1933; also studied at Yale University and Harvard University.

CAREER: Taught at Clark University, Worcester, Mass., at Harvard University, 1936-39, and at Black Mountain College, Black Mountain, N.C., serving as rector at Black Mountain, 1951-56; taught at State University of New York, Buffalo, 1963-65, and University of Connecticut, 1969. *Awards, honors:* Received two Guggenheim fellowships; grant from Wenner-Gren Foundation, 1952, to study Mayan hieroglyphic writing in Yucatan. Oscar Blumenthal-Charles Leviton Prize, 1965.

WRITINGS: Call Me Ishmael, Reynal & Hitchcock, 1947, Grove, 1958; *To Corrado Cagli* (poetry), Knoedler Gallery (New York), 1947; *Y & X* (poetry), Black Sun Press, 1948; *Letter for Melville* (poetry), Melville Society, Williams College, 1951; *This* (poem; design by Nicola Cernovich), Black Mountain College, 1952; *The Maximus Poems 1-10,* Jargon, 1953, *11-22,* Jargon, 1956, Jargon/Corinth, 1960; *Mayan Letters,* edited by Robert Creeley, Divers Press, 1953; *In Cold Hell, In Thicket,* [Dorchester, Mass.], 1953, Four Seasons Foundation, 1967; *Anecdotes of the Late War* (anti-war document), Jargon, ca.1957; *O'Ryan 2.4.6.8.10.,* White Rabbit Press, 1958; *Projective Verse* (essay), Totem Press, 1959.

The Distances (poems), Grove, 1961; *Maximus, From Dogtown I,* foreword by Michael McClure, Auerhahn, 1961; *Human Universe, and Other Essays,* edited by Donald Allen, Auerhahn, 1965; *A Bibliography on America for Ed Dorn,* Four Seasons Foundation, 1964; *Proprioception,* Four Seasons Foundation, 1965; *O'Ryan 1, 2, 3, 4, 5, 6, 7, 8, 9, 10,* White Rabbit Press, 1965; *Selected Writings,* edited by Robert Creeley, New Directions, 1966; *Stocking Cap* (story), Four Seasons Foundation, 1966; *Charles Olson Reading at Berkeley,* Coyote, 1966; *West,* Goliard Press, 1966; *The Maximus Poems IV, V, VI,* Cape Goliard, in association with Grossman, 1968; *Pleistocene Man,* Institute of Further Studies (Buffalo, N.Y.), 1968; *Causal Mythology,* Four Seasons Foundation, 1969; *Letters for Origin, 1950-1956,* edited by Albert Glover, Cape Goliard, 1969, Grossman, 1970.

Archaeologist of Morning (collected poems), Cape Goliard, 1970, Grossman, 1971, new edition, Grossman, 1973; *The Special View of History*, edited by Ann Charters, Oyez, 1970; *Poetry and Truth: Beloit Letters and Poems*, edited by George F. Butterick, Four Seasons Foundation, 1971; *Additional Prose*, edited by Butterick, Four Seasons Foundation, 1974; *The Maximus Poems, Volume III*, Grossman, 1974; *The Post Office*, Four Seasons Foundation, in press; *The Maximus Poems, Final Volume*, edited by Butterick and Charles Boer, Grossman, in press.

Author of dance-play, "Apollonius of Tyana," 1951. Work is represented in anthologies, including *The New American Poetry: 1945-1960*, edited by Donald M. Allen, Grove, 1960, and *The Norton Anthology of Modern Poetry*, edited by Richard Ellmann and Robert O'Clair, Norton, 1973. Contributor to *Twice-A-Year, Black Mountain Review, Big Table, Yugen, Evergreen Review, Origin, Poetry New York*, and other periodicals.

SIDELIGHTS: In his influential essay on projective (or open) verse Olson asserts that "a poem is energy transferred from where the poet got it (he will have some several causations), by way of the poem itself to, all the way over to, the reader. Okay. Then the poem itself must, at all points, be a high energy-construct and, at all points, an energy-discharge." Form is only an extension of content, and "right form, in any given poem, is the only and exclusively possible extension of content under hand. . . . I take it that PROJECTIVE VERSE teaches, is, this lesson, that that verse will only do in which a poet manages to register both the acquisitions of his ear *and* the pressures of his breath." Olson goes by ear, and his lines are breath-conditioned. The two halves, he says, are: "the HEAD, by way of the EAR, to the SYLLABLE/the HEART, by way of the BREATH, to the LINE." He believes "it is from the union of the mind and the ear that the syllable is born. But the syllable is only the first child of the incest of verse. . . . The other child is the LINE. . . . And the line comes (I swear it) from the breath. . . ." Robert Creeley explains thus: "What he is trying to say is that the heart is a basic instance not only of rhythm, but it is the base of the measure of rhythms for all men in the way heartbeat is like the metronome in their whole system. So that when he says the heart by way of the breath to the line, he is trying to say that it is in the line that the basic rhythmic scoring takes place. . . . Now, the head, the intelligence by way of the ear to the syllable—which he calls also 'the king and pin'—is the unit upon which all builds. The heart, then, stands, as the primary feeling term. The head, in contrast, is discriminating. It is discriminating by way of what it hears." Olson believes that "in any given poem always, always one perception must must must MOVE, INSTANTER, ON ANOTHER!" So, all the conventions that "logic has forced on syntax must be broken open as quietly as must the too set feet of the old line."

Olson has thus rejected "academic" verse, with its closed forms and alleged artifice. Back to primal things, he says. The *Times Literary Supplement* notes that "culture, civilization, history (except history as personal exploration as in Herodotus) and, above all, sociology, are dirty words for him." Olson says: "It comes to this: the use of a man, by himself and thus by others, lies in how he conceives his relation to nature. . . . If he is contained within his nature as he is participant in the larger force, he will be able to listen, and his hearing through himself will give him secrets objects share. And by an inverse law his shapes will make their own way. . . . This is not easy. Nature works from

reverence, even in her destructions (species go down with a crash). But breath is man's special qualification as animal. Sound is a dimension he has extended. Language is one of his proudest acts. . . . I keep thinking, it comes to this: culture displacing the state." M. L. Rosenthal comments: "The problem is to get back to sources of meaning anterior to those of our own state-ridden civilization and so to recover the sense of personality and of place that has been all but throttled."

Robert Duncan, in his essay "Regarding Olson's 'Maximus,'" writes: "Olson insists upon the active. Homo maximus wrests his life from the underworld as the Gloucester fisherman wrests his from the sea." Olson's striding poetic syllables, says Duncan, are "no more difficult than walking." Duncan traces Olson's aesthetics to nineteenth-century American sources: "I point to Emerson or to Dewey," writes Duncan, "to show that in American philosophy there are foreshadowings or forelightings of 'Maximus'. In this aesthetic, conception cannot be abstracted from doing; beauty is related to the beauty of a archer hitting the mark." A *Times Literary Supplement* reviewer observes that Olson's style is at times a "bouncy, get-in-with-it manner," often involving the "juxtaposition of a very abstract statement with a practical, jocular illustration of what the statement might imply." Writes Olson: "It's as though you were hearing for the first time—who knows what a poem ought to sound like? until it's thar? And how do you get it thar ezcept as you do—*you*, and nobody else (who's a poet? . . .).

Anyone familiar with contemporary poetry would agree with Robert Creeley when he calls Olson "central to any description of literary 'climate' dated 1958." Olson's influence extends directly to Creeley, Duncan, Denise Levertov, and Paul Blackburn, and, as Stephen Stepanchev notes, Olson's projective verse "has either influenced or coincided with other stirrings toward newness in American poetry." He himself owes a great deal to Ezra Pound, William Carlos Williams, and Edward Dahlberg. The scope of Olson's work is "as broad as Pound's," writes Kenneth Rexroth. It is not simple poetry, much of it being fragmentary and experimental. But it has, says Rosenthal, "the power of hammering conviction—something like Lawrence's but with more brutal insistence behind it. It is a dogmatic, irritable, passionate voice, of the sort that the modern world, to its sorrow very often, is forever seeking out; it is not a clear voice, but one troubled by its own confusions which it carries into the attack. . . ."

Olson did not consider himself "a poet" or "a writer" by profession, but rather that nebulous and rare "archeologist of morning," reminiscent of Thoreau. He wrote on a typewriter. "It is the advantage of the typewriter that, due to its rigidity and its space precisions, it can, for a poet, indicate exactly the breath, the pause, the suspensions even of syllables, the juxtapositions even of parts of phrases, which he intends. For the first time the poet has the stave and the bar a musician has had. For the first time he can, without the convention of rime and meter, record the listening he has done to his own speech and by that one act indicate how he would want any reader, silently or otherwise, to voice his work."

BIOGRAPHICAL/CRITICAL SOURCES: Black Mountain Review, number 6, 1956; *Evergreen Review*, summer, 1958; Donald M. Allen, editor, *The New American Poetry: 1945-1960*, Grove, 1960; Kenneth Rexroth, *Assays*, New Directions, 1961; *The Review*, January, 1964; M. L. Rosenthal, *The Modern Poets*, Oxford University Press,

1965; Stephen Stepanchev, *American Poetry Since 1945*, Harper, 1965; *Times Literary Supplement*, November 25, 1965; *West Coast Review*, spring, 1967; Carolyn Riley, editor, *Contemporary Literary Criticism*, Gale, Volume I, 1973, Volume II, 1974; *Olson: The Journal of the Charles Olson Archives*, University of Connecticut Library, 1974—.

(Died January 10, 1970)

*   *   *

OLSON, Sidney 1908-

PERSONAL: Born April 30, 1908, in Salt Lake City, Utah; son of Alex Peter (a locomotive engineer) and Sigrid Erika (Granberg) Olson; married Zembra Holmgren, January 16, 1937; children: Whitney Elizabeth (Mrs. Allan Clark), John Erik, Stephen Christopher. *Education:* University of Utah, student, 1925-29. *Politics:* Independent. *Religion:* Protestant. *Home:* 21 Pryer Lane, Larchmont, N.Y. 10538.

CAREER: Deseret Evening News, Salt Lake City, Utah, reporter, 1933-34; *Washington Post*, Washington, D.C., city editor and White House correspondent, 1934-39; Time, Inc., New York, N.Y., senior editor on *Time, Life, Fortune*, 1939-44, 1945-49, war correspondent, 1944-45; Paramount Pictures, Hollywood, Calif., writer, 1950; Earl Newsom & Co., New York, N.Y., employed to write charter, aims, and scope of Ford Foundation, 1950-51; Kenyon & Eckhardt (advertising), New York, N.Y., vice-president and creative supervisor, 1951-56; J. Walter Thompson Co. (advertising), New York, N.Y., vice-president and creative supervisor, 1956—.

WRITINGS: Young Henry Ford: A Picture History of the First Forty Years, Wayne State University Press, 1963. Scriptwriter for first television spectacular, "Ford Fiftieth Anniversary Show," produced by Leland Hayward, 1953. Contributor to magazines.

SIDELIGHTS: Olson has been responsible for prizewinning television commercials as a result of pioneer experimental work in the cinema.

*   *   *

ORAS, Ants 1900-

PERSONAL: Surname is pronounced *Or*-as; born December 8, 1900, in Tallinn, Estonia; son of Hans (a teacher) and Johanna Ida (Vanari) Oras; married Livia Lueues, February 28, 1931. *Education:* University of Tartu, Mag. Phil., 1923; University of Leipzig, graduate study, 1923-24; Oxford University, B.Litt., 1928. *Politics:* Anti-totalitarian. *Religion:* Lutheran. *Home:* 1226 Northwest Fourth Ave., Gainesville, Fla.

CAREER: University of Tartu, Tartu, Estonia, lecturer, 1928-33, lecturer-docent, 1933-34, professor of English, 1934-43; U.S. Embassy, Stockholm, Sweden, staff member, 1943-45; Cambridge University, Cambridge, England, extramural lecturer, 1945-46; Oxford University, Oxford, England, special assistant in Bodleian Library, 1946-49; University of Florida, Gainesville, professor of English, 1949-72, professor emeritus, 1972—. Visiting lecturer, University of Jyvaskyla, Finland, 1933, 1958; University of Helsinki, lecturer-docent, 1934, visiting professor of English, 1957-58. State Department lecturer, Finland and Sweden, 1965. *Military service:* Estonian Army, 1918-20; became sergeant.

MEMBER: Modern Language Association of America, International P.E.N. in Exile, Estonian P.E.N. (vice-president, 1946-49, 1967-72; president, 1972—), National Association of Literary Historians of Finland (foreign member), Estonian Learned Society of America, Association of Estonian Writers Abroad, Estonian Institute (University of Stockholm), South Atlantic Modern Language Association, University of Florida Language and Literary Club (president, 1961). *Awards, honors:* Visnapuu Prize, 1961, for volume of essays, *Laiemasse Ringi*, and 1965, for *Marie Under*; Florida Blue Key, 1961; first award of Estonian Culture Fund, 1971; several fellowships for travel.

WRITINGS: Milton's Editors and Commentators (1695-1801), Oxford University Press, 1931; *The Critical Ideas of T. S. Eliot*, University of Tartu Press, 1932; (editor) *Arbujad* (anthology of Estonian poets), [Tartu], 1937; *Notes on Some Miltonic Usages* (monograph), University of Tartu Press, 1938; *On Some Aspects of Shelley's Poetic Imagery* (monograph), University of Tartu Press, 1938; (with E. Lagman) *Estnisk-Svensk Ordbok*, A. Ots (Stockholm), 1945; *Baltic Eclipse*, Gollancz, 1948; (with E. Blese and A. Senn) *Storia delle Letterature Baltiche*, Nuova Accademia (Milan), 1957; *Pause Patterns in Elizabethan and Jacobean Drama*, University of Florida Press, 1960; *Laiemasse Ringi* (essays in Estonian), Vaba Eesti (Stockholm), 1961; *Marie Under*, Estonian Writers' Cooperative (Lund), 1963; *Estonian Literary Reader*, Indiana University Press, 1963; *Acht Estnische Dichter*, Vaba Eesti, 1964; *Blank Verse and Chronology in Milton*, University of Florida Press, 1966.

Translator: Seventeen volumes of poetry into Estonian, including works of Poe, Heine, Pope, Shakespeare (six plays, sonnets), Pushkin, Moliere (three plays), Goethe (three volumes), and Vergil; eleven books of prose into Estonian, including works of Mark Twain, Robert Louis Stevenson, William Thackeray, David Garnett, Bernard Shaw, Aldous Huxley, and John Masefield; verse from the English, French, Russian, Finnish, Swedish, German, and Latin for Estonian literary journals; Estonian and other poetry into English for *P.E.N. in Exile II*, London P.E.N., 1956, and *Literary Review*, spring, 1965.

Contributor of some two hundred articles and reviews to Estonian, Finnish, British, Belgian, and American literary and learned journals.

WORK IN PROGRESS: Studies in Renaissance drama and poetry, particularly in style and versification, with special concentration on Milton; studies in Romantic imagery; a critical introduction and a commentary to accompany the completed Estonian translation in quantitative hexameter of Vergil's *Aeneid*; other translations, including three of Shakespeare's tragedies; essays on Estonian literature.

SIDELIGHTS: Oras told *CA*: "[I] worry about the decline of common sense in literature. [I have] a growing absorption in the literature of the past where idealism and even heroism are still felt to be vital factors (coupled with a deeply ingrained contempt for mere 'heroic' gestures as so often seen in the extreme 'right'). Otherwise [I take] much delight in bookish life...." Oras is competent in eight languages—English, Estonian, French, Russian, Finnish, Swedish, German, and Latin.

BIOGRAPHICAL/CRITICAL SOURCES: L'Histoire General des Litterature, [Paris], 1961; *Mana*, number 1, 1961, number 3, 1964; *Arena*, spring, 1964; *Studies in Estonian Poetry and Language: In Honor of Ants Oras*, Vaba Eesti (Stockholm), 1965; *Books Abroad*, Volume 47, number 4, 1973.

ORGEL, Joseph Randolph   1902-

PERSONAL: Born December 12, 1902, in New York, N.Y.; son of Isaac Wolf (a teacher) and Frieda (Kronish) Orgel; married Ella Goldstein; children: Shelley, Phyllis Orgel Koestenbaum. *Education:* College of the City of New York (now City College of the City University of New York), B.A., 1924; Columbia University, M.A., 1926; New York University, Ph.D., 1934. *Home and office:* 2016 Avenue N., Brooklyn, N.Y. 10010.

CAREER: Abraham Lincoln High School, Brooklyn, N.Y., dean, 1933-63. Feature writer for *Brooklyn Daily Eagle, Brooklyn Times, New York Sun,* and *New York World-Telegram;* free-lance writer. Member, Metropolitan Study Council, New York, N.Y. Educational consultant. *Member:* Modern Language Association, American Jewish Historical Society, Dean's Association of the City of New York (president), New York University Graduate School Alumni (president), New York University Alumni Federation (director), Andiron Club.

WRITINGS: (With Nathan Peyser and Austin M. Works) *Graded Units of Vital English,* Oxford Book Co., 1937; (with Peyser and Daniel Krane) *Graded Units in Junior High School English,* Oxford Book Co., 1941; *English in Review: To Prepare for Terminal and Other Examinations in English, Including New York State Regents Examinations, College Entrance Board Examinations, Uniform State Board Examinations, School Examinations, Civil Service Tests, Scholarship Tests,* Oxford Book Co., 1950; (with Works) *Building Word Power,* Oxford Book Co., 1955; *English in Review, Four Years: To Prepare for New York State Regents and Other Terminal Examinations in English,* Oxford Book Co., 1956; *English in Review, Three Years: To Prepare for New York State Regents and Other Terminal Examinations in English,* Oxford Book Co., 1956; *English in Review for College Entrance Tests,* Oxford Book Co., 1957, *College Entrance Review in English Aptitude,* Educational Advisory Center, 1957; *College Entrance Review in English Composition,* Educational Advisory Center, 1957, 2nd edition, Educators Publishing Service, 1961; (with Julius Freilich and Simon L. Berman) *Succeeding in College Entrance Tests: Preparation and Practice for the Scholastic Aptitude Test—Specimen Achievement Tests* (includes introduction and verbal section by Orgel, mathematics section by Freilich and Berman), Oxford Book Co., 1959, 3rd edition, enlarged, 1966; *Reading Comprehension: A Testing Program for College Entrance Scholastic Aptitude Tests, New York State Regents Examinations, Westinghouse Science Aptitude Examinations, Other Terminal and Scholarship Examinations,* Oxford Book Co., 1960; *Unit Lessons in Vital English,* Oxford Book Co., 1962; *Writing the Composition,* Educators Publishing Service, 1962; *Preparing for American College Test Program Examinations,* Educators Publishing Service, 1963; *Enriching Your Vocabulary,* Oxford Book Co., 1963; *Vocabulary for College Entrance,* Oxford Book Co., 1963; *Comprehensive English in Review,* Oxford Book Co., 1966.

Contributor of feature articles on education to *Scholastic;* free-lance writer for various periodicals. Editor, *Weekly Review,* 1930-31; general editor, Minna and Wolf Colvin, "College Entrance Reviews in American History"; editor of other college entrance reviews and texts.

WORK IN PROGRESS: A four-volume series, "Developmental Program in Reading," for Oxford Book Co.; a ten-volume series, "Footnotes to Biography."

ORMES, Robert M.   1904-

PERSONAL: Born September 27, 1904, in Colorado Springs, Colo.; son of Manly Dayton and Jane Eleanor (Readie) Ormes; married Suzanne Viertel, September 25, 1937; children: Jonathan F., Stephanie Jean. *Education:* Colorado College, A.B., 1926, A.M., 1927. *Politics:* Democrat. *Religion:* Congregational. *Home:* 22 East Del Norte, Colorado Springs, Colo. 80907. *Office:* Colorado College, Colorado Springs, Colo. 80903.

CAREER: Colorado College, Colorado Springs, currently professor of English. U.S. Army, civilian instructor in rock-climbing and skiing. Alpinist ranger in Rocky Mountain National Park. *Member:* American Alpine Club, Colorado Mountain Club.

WRITINGS: (Editor) *Guide to the Colorado Mountains,* Sage Books, 1951, 6th edition, completely revised, 1970; *Pikes Peak Atlas,* privately printed, 1958; *Railroads and the Rockies: A Record of Lines In and Near Colorado,* Sage Books, 1963; *Colorado Skylines,* Book 1: *Front Range from the East,* [Colorado Springs], 1967. Contributor of articles to *Sports Afield, Saturday Evening Post, American Alpine Journal, National Geographic,* and to *Restaurant Management* and other trade journals.

WORK IN PROGRESS: Three other books in *Colorado Skylines* series, identifying Colorado mountains as seen from the state's roads; trail map series for state.

SIDELIGHTS: Ormes has made many ascents, some first timers, in the Colorado Rockies; he also kayaks the mountain rivers. He is something of a Latinist.

*   *   *

OSGOOD, Ernest S(taples)   1888-

PERSONAL: Born October 29, 1888, in Lynn, Mass.; son of John Crafts and Evalina (Harvey) Osgood; married Helen Kaslo (a professor of history), June 11, 1958. *Education:* Dartmouth College, A.B., 1912; University of Wisconsin, Ph.D., 1927. *Home and office:* 360½ East Bowman St., Wooster, Ohio 44691.

CAREER: Helena (Mont.) High School, instructor in history, 1914-24; University of Minnesota, Minneapolis, 1927-57, started as instructor, became professor of history, professor emeritus, 1957—; College of Wooster, Wooster, Ohio, lecturer in history, 1958-69. *Member:* American Historical Association, Organization of American Historians, Western History Association. *Awards, honors:* Guggenheim fellow, 1937-38.

WRITINGS: The Day of the Cattleman, University of Minnesota Press, 1929, University of Chicago Press, 1968; (editor) *The Field Notes of Captain William Clark, 1803-1805,* Yale University Press, 1964.

*   *   *

OSMOND, Edward   1900-

PERSONAL: Born May 6, 1900, in Orford, Suffolk, England; son of Percy Herbert (a clergyman, Church of England) and Agnes (Sadler) Osmond; married Constance M. Biggs (an author and artist under name Laurie Osmond), November 12, 1927; children: Christine Gillian. *Education:* Educated privately; studied art at The Polytechnic, London, England, 1917-24, Art Teachers Diploma, 1924, Diploma in Art History, 1924. *Home:* Downland Cottage, Lullington Close, Seaford, Sussex, England.

CAREER: Free-lance illustrator, 1928—; author, illustrator, and designer of children's books. Part-time art teacher at Hastings College of Technology, Sussex, England, and at Hornsey College of Art, London, England. *Member:* Society of Industrial Artists, Society of Authors. *Awards, honors:* Carnegie Medal of Library Association, for outstanding children's book of the year by a British subject, 1954, for *A Valley Grows Up.*

WRITINGS—All self-illustrated, some also designed: *A Valley Grows Up*, Oxford University Press, 1953; *Houses*, Batsford, 1956; *Villages*, Batsford, 1957; *Towns*, Batsford, 1958; *From Drumbeat to Ticker Tape*, Hutchinson, 1960; *The Artist in Britain*, Studio Books, 1961; *People of the Desert*, Odhams, 1963; *People of the Jungle Forest*, Odhams, 1963; *People of the Grasslands*, Odhams, 1964; *People of the Arctic*, Odhams, 1964; *People of the High Mountains*, Odhams, 1965; *People of the Lonely Islands*, Odhams, 1965; *Animals of Central Asia*, Abelard-Schuman, 1967; *Exploring Fashions and Fabrics*, Odhams, 1967. Also author of "Animals of the World" series, Clarendon Press, 1953-56, and of "Animals of Britain" series, Clarendon Press, 1959-62.

WORK IN PROGRESS: Participating in a large work, *The Arts of Mankind*, to be published by Collins.

SIDELIGHTS: Osmond writes for children of eight years and older. His theory of children's books is that they should be produced while the writer is, himself, learning about their subject matter—that this imparts some hidden excitement which may infect the reader. He thinks that ideally the book should be written, illustrated, and designed by the same person.

* * *

OSSOWSKI, Stanislaw 1897-1963

PERSONAL: Born May 22, 1897, in Poland; married Maria Niedzwiecka (a professor at University of Warsaw), July 1, 1924. *Education:* University of Warsaw, Ph.D.; also studied at Sorbonne, University of Paris, and in Great Britain as research scholar, 1933-35.

CAREER: University of Warsaw, Warsaw, Poland, privatdocent, 1933; University of Lodz, Lodz, Poland, professor of sociology, 1945-47; University of Warsaw, professor of sociology, 1947-63. *Member:* Polish Sociological Association (co-founder; president, 1957-63), International Sociological Association (vice-president, 1957-61).

WRITINGS: Podstawy Estetygi (title means "The Foundations of Aesthetics"), Kasa im. Mianowskiego, 1933, Panstwowe Wydawnictwo Naukowe (Warsaw), 1966; *Wiez Spoleczna i Dziedzictwo Krwi* (title means "Social Bond and Blood Inheritance"), Ksiazka, 1938, Panstwowe Wydawnictwo Naukowe, 1966; *Struktura Klasowa w Spolecznej Swiadomosci*, Societas Scientiarum Lodziensis, 1957, translaion by Sheila Patterson published as *Class Structure in the Social Consciousness*, Free Press, 1963; *O Osobliwosciach Nauk Spolecznych* (title means "Peculiarities of the Social Sciences"), Panstwowe Wydawnictwo Naukowe, 1962. Contributor to sociological periodicals in Poland and abroad.

BIOGRAPHICAL/CRITICAL SOURCES: Rene Koenig, "Stanislaw Ossowski, 1897-1963," *Koelner Zeitschrift fuer Soziologie und Sozial Psychology*, volume 15, number 4, 1963; *Polish Sociological Bulletin*, number 2 (8), 1963; *American Sociological Review*, October, 1964; *Cahiers Internationaux de Sociologie*, volume XXXVII, 1964.

(Died November 7, 1963)

OSTENSO, Martha 1900-1963

PERSONAL: Born September 17, 1900, in Bergen, Norway; brought to United States, 1902; daughter of Sigurd Brigt and Lena (Tungeland) Ostenso; married Douglas Durkin, December 16, 1944. *Education:* Attended University of Manitoba. *Home:* Route 6, Brainerd, Minn. *Agent:* Shirley Burke, 35 West 53rd St., New York, N.Y. 10019.

CAREER: Lived in Minnesota and South Dakota as a child and began writing as a contributor to the junior page of the *Minneapolis Journal*; later moved to Canada with parents and taught school one semester (1918) in Manitoba; returned to United States as social worker with Bureau of Charities, Brooklyn, N.Y., 1920-23; novelist and short story writer, beginning 1923. *Member:* International P.E.N., Authors League of America. *Awards, honors:* First novel, *Wild Geese*, won a national prize offered by Pictorial Review, Dodd, Mead & Co., and Famous Players-Lasky, 1925; honorary M.E., Wittenberg University.

WRITINGS—All published by Dodd, unless otherwise indicated: *A Far Land* (verse), Thomas Selzer, 1924; *Wild Geese*, 1925; *The Dark Dawn*, 1926; *The Mad Carews*, 1927; *The Young May Moon*, 1929; *The Waters Under the Earth*, 1930; *Prologue to Love*, 1931; *There's Always Another Year*, 1933; *The White Reef*, 1934; *The Stone Field*, 1937; *The Mandrake Root*, 1938; *Love Passed This Way*, 1942; *O River, Remember* (Literary Guild selection), 1943; (with Elizabeth Kenny) *And They Shall Walk*, 1943; *Milk Route*, 1948; *The Sunset Tree*, 1949; *A Man Had Tall Sons*, 1958. Writer of serials and short stories published in national magazines.

(Died, 1963)

* * *

OUSLEY, Odille 1896-

PERSONAL: Born October 19, 1896, in Macon, Ga.; daughter of Thomas R. (a farmer) and Maymie T. (Hertel) Ousley. *Education:* George Peabody College for Teachers, B.A., M.A.; summer study at Columbia University and University of Virginia. *Religion:* Methodist. *Home and office:* 407 Landover Dr., Decatur, Ga. 30030.

CAREER: Supervisor of student teaching at Atlanta Normal School, Atlanta, Ga., and State Teachers College, Slippery Rock, Pa.; University of Georgia, Athens, reading specialist; University of Georgia and Emory University, Atlanta Area Teacher Education Service, specialist in reading and children's literature. *Member:* National Society for Teachers of English, Association of Childhood Education, Association of Supervisors and Curriculum Directors, Delta Kappa Gamma, Kappa Delta Pi.

WRITINGS—All published by Ginn: (With David Russell and others) "Ginn Basic Readers" series, 1948, revised edition, 1961; (with Russell and others) "Ginn Basic Enrichment Readers" series, 1953-59; *My ABC Book*, 1962; *Mr. Bear's Bow Ties*, 1964; (compiler) *V Is for Verses* (anthology), 1964; *Cowboy Bill and the Big Umbrella*, 1965; *The Little Pig Who Listened*, 1966.

* * *

OVERSTREET, Harry Allen 1875-1970

PERSONAL: Born October 25, 1875, in San Francisco, Calif.; son of William Franklin and Julie (Detje) Overstreet; married Elsie L. Burr, May 17, 1907 (divorced);

married second wife, Bonaro W. Wilkinson (a lecturer and writer), August 23, 1932; children: (first marriage) Edmund William, Robert Howison, Allen Burr. *Education:* University of California, A.B., 1899; Balloil College, Oxford, B.Sc., 1901. *Politics:* "A free American." *Religion:* "A free American." *Home:* 3409 Fiddler's Green, Falls Church, Va.

CAREER: University of California, Berkeley, 1901-11, began as instructor, became associate professor of philosophy; City College (now City College of the City University of New York), New York, N.Y., professor of philosophy and head of department of philosophy and psychology, 1911-39, professor emeritus, 1939—. Research associate, American Association for Adult Education (now Adult Education Association of the U.S.A.), Chicago, Ill., 1939-40. Lecturer, New School for Social Research, New York, N.Y., 1924-28; extension lecturer at University of Michigan, 1945-58, and University of California, 1948-49. Director of Leadership School, Town Hall, New York, N.Y., 1940-43, trustee, 1948. *Member:* American Association for Adult Education (president, 1940-41), Phi Beta Kappa, Beta Theta Pi.

WRITINGS—All published by Norton, except as indicated: *Influencing Human Behavior*, 1925; *About Ourselves: Psychology for Normal People*, 1927; *The Enduring Quest*, 1931; *We Move in New Directions*, 1933; *A Guide to Civilized Leisure*, 1934, reprinted, Books for Libraries, 1969; *A Declaration of Interdependence*, 1937; *Let Me Think*, Macmillan, 1939; *Our Free Minds*, 1941; *The Mature Mind*, 1949; *The Great Enterprise: Relating Ourselves to the World*, 1952.

With wife, Bonaro W. Overstreet: *Town Meeting Comes to Town*, Harper, 1938; *Leaders for Adult Education*, American Association for Adult Education, 1940; *Where Children Come First*, National Congress of Parents and Teachers, 1949; *The Mind Alive*, 1954; *The Mind Goes Forth*, 1956; *What We Must Know About Communism*, 1958; *The War Called Peace: Khrushchev's Communism*, 1961; *The Iron Curtain: Where Freedom's Offensive Begins*, 1963; *The Strange Tactics of Extremism*, 1964; *The FBI in Our Open Society*, 1969.

Writer of monographs and contributor to periodicals.

(Died August 17, 1970)

*   *   *

OWEN, David (Edward) 1898-1968

PERSONAL: Born December 2, 1898, in Owatonna, Minn.; son of Ernest Jones (a teacher) and Byrd (Tuttle) Owen; married Louise Hamblen, September 12, 1922; children: Elizabeth Byrd (Mrs. Robert Shenton). *Education:* Denison University, Ph.B., 1920; Yale University, Ph.D., 1927. *Home:* 966 Memorial Dr., Cambridge, Mass. 02138.

CAREER: Yale University, New Haven, Conn., instructor, 1923-27, assistant professor of history, 1927-38; Harvard University, Cambridge, Mass., visiting lecturer, 1937-38, associate professor, 1938-46, professor of history, 1946-58, Gurney Professor of History, 1958-68, master of John Winthrop House, 1957-64, senior fellow, Society of Fellows, 1964-68. *Member:* American Academy of Arts and Sciences (fellow), American Historical Association, Economic History Association, Signet Society (Cambridge), Elizabethan Club (New Haven), Harvard Club (Boston and New York). *Awards, honors:* Social Science Research Council fellow, 1932-33; honorary L.H.D. from Denison

University, 1955, and Carnegie Institute of Technology, 1958.

WRITINGS: Imperialism and Nationalism in the Far East, Holt, 1929; *British Opium Policy in China and India*, Yale University Press, 1934, Archon Books, 1968; *English Philanthropy, 1660-1960*, Belknap Press, 1964.

WORK IN PROGRESS: A study of local government in London, England, 1855-89, before establishment of the London County Council.

SIDELIGHTS: At the time of Professor Owen's death, the *London Times* wrote, "His famous lecture on the Crystal Palace Exhibition, a showplace of British nineteenth-century industry, was an annual event at Harvard, attended by faculty colleagues and more students than his popular course in Modern English History.... His graduate seminars on topics in English history were valued by advanced students, and scholars who studied under him now are teaching English history in colleges across the country."

(Died February 13, 1968)

*   *   *

OYLER, Philip (Tom) 1879-

PERSONAL: Born May 16, 1879, in Headcorn, Kent, England. *Education:* Attended Sutton Valence School and Lincoln College, Oxford. *Religion:* Christian. *Home:* Chapou, Puybrun, Lot, France. *Agent:* Richmond Towers, 14 Essex St., London W.C. 2, England.

CAREER: Agriculturist, with most of adult life devoted to management of large estates in England and France. *Awards, honors:* M.A. from Oxford University.

WRITINGS: The Generous Earth, Hodder & Stoughton, 1951; *Feeding Ourselves*, Hodder & Stoughton, 1952; *Heart to Heart* (verses), Adlington Hall Press, 1955; *Sons of the Generous Earth*, Hodder & Stoughton, 1963. Contributor of articles on agriculture, health, and education to journals.

WORK IN PROGRESS: A book of verse.

*   *   *

PACA, Lillian Grace (Baker) 1883-

PERSONAL: Born October 20, 1883, in Jamaica, West Indies; daughter of Robert Barrington (British Army) and Susan (Middleton) Baker; married Edward Tilghman Paca, April 5, 1920; children: Robert, Francis, Richard (deceased). *Education:* Studied under private tutors. *Home:* 122½ Caledonia St., Pacific Grove, Calif. 93950. *Agent:* Marie Rodell, 141 East 55th St., New York, N.Y. 10022.

CAREER: Bird artist, whose pictures have been exhibited in United States and England. *Member:* National Audubon Society, Nature Conservancy, Wilderness Society, Defenders of Wildlife, National Wildlife Federation.

WRITINGS—Self-illustrated: *Sea Lions and Seals of California*, privately printed, 1947; *Pelican Personalities*, privately printed, 1949; *Introduction to Western Birds*, Lane, 1953; *Sea Gulls and Such*, Pacific Books, 1960; *The Royal Birds*, St. Martins, 1963. Author of illustrated newspaper column, 1950-53.

WORK IN PROGRESS: A novel, *Shining Archway; Never a Dull Moment*, autobiography; short nature stories for children.

PACK, Roger A(mbrose)   1907-

PERSONAL: Born September 12, 1907, in Ann Arbor, Mich.; son of Ambrose Clarkson and Roba (Pulcipher) Pack. *Education:* University of Michigan, A.B., 1929, A.M., 1930, Ph.D., 1934. *Office:* Department of Classical Studies, University of Michigan, Ann Arbor, Mich.

CAREER: University of Michigan, Ann Arbor, instructor in Latin, 1934-46, assistant professor, 1946-57, associate professor, 1957-65, professor of classical studies, 1965—. Visiting instructor at University of Missouri, 1935-36, and Ohio State University, 1937-38. *Military service:* U.S. Army, Counter Intelligence Corps, special agent, 1943-45. *Member:* American Philological Association, Archaeological Institute of America. *Awards, honors:* Guggenheim fellow, 1957.

WRITINGS: The Greek and Latin Literary Texts from Greco-Roman Egypt, University of Michigan Press, 1952, 2nd edition, revised and enlarged, 1965; *Artemidori Daldiani Onirocriticon Libri V,* Teubner, 1963. Contributor of articles and reviews to learned journals.

WORK IN PROGRESS: Research in medieval Latin occult texts.

*   *   *

PAINE, Philbrook   1910-

PERSONAL: Born October 17, 1910, in Dover, N.H.; son of Ralph Delahaye (an author) and Katharine (Lansing) Paine; married Serena Coe, June 30, 1937; children: Sally Lansing. *Education:* University of New Hampshire, B.A. *Politics:* Republican. *Religion:* Protestant. *Home and office:* Durham Point Rd., Durham, N.H. 03824.

CAREER: Free-lance writer. Owner, Granite State Insulating Co., Durham, N.H., 1937-41; with *New England Dairyman,* Boston, Mass., 1941-43; publicity writer for dairy industry, Boston, Mass., 1946-55. *Military service:* U.S. Army Transport Service, 1943-45.

WRITINGS: Squarely Behind the Beavers, Norton, 1963; *Report from the Village,* Norton, 1965. Regular columnist, *New Hampshire Sunday News,* 1950—. Contributor to *New Hampshire Profiles, Yachting,* and *Reader's Digest.*

*   *   *

PALESTRANT, Simon S.   1907-
(Stephen Edwards, S. P. Stevens, Paul E. Strand)

PERSONAL: Born July 8, 1907, in New York, N.Y.; son of Jacob (a tailor) and Sarah Rachel (Gross) Palestrant; married Sarah Mina Fein, June 30, 1931; children: Stephen Edward. *Education:* Attended Cooper Union Art School, Pratt Institute, and Yale University School of Drama, 1925-30; New York University, B.S., 1935; College of City of New York (now City College of City University of New York), M.S., 1937; Institute of Fine Arts, graduate study, 1938. *Home and office:* 1235 Grand Concourse, Bronx, N.Y. 10452. *Agent:* Marie Rodell & Joan Daves, Inc., 185 West End Ave., New York, N.Y. 10023.

CAREER: Scenic designer and technical director for Little Theatre Groups, Inc., in New York, New Jersey, and Pennsylvania, 1926-32; New Haven Board of Education, New Haven, Conn., instructor in commercial art, 1929-31; New York Board of Education, New York, N.Y., instructor in fine and applied art, 1931-69, chairman of art department, 1950-53. Lecturer in history of art, City University of New York and Bronx Community College, 1961-68; instructor in art for other schools and organizations. Free-lance advertising artist in New York and Connecticut, 1926-29, interior designer and consultant, New York, N.Y., 1926—. Lecturer, Treasure Tours, Inc., 1962-67; cruise lecturer, American Export Lines, 1963-66; coordinator of tours, Douglas-Ferguson Travel Ltd., 1966-70; travel consultant, M.V. International Travel Bureau Ltd., 1970—.

MEMBER: Mystery Writers of America (member of board of directors, New York chapter, 1955-57), Academy of Television Arts and Sciences, Crime Writers Association (Great Britain), United Federation of Teachers (life member), Mark Twain Society, Authors League of America, American Association of University Professors, Association of Retired Teachers, Institute of Italian Culture, Writers Guild of America—East, Smithsonian Associates.

WRITINGS: Making Block Prints, New Haven School Publications, 1930; (with T. A. Dickinson) *Working with Plastics,* Science & Mechanics Publishing, 1948; *Practical Papercrafts: Over 400 Useful and Decorative Projects for Fun and Profit,* Homecrafts, 1950; *Toymaking: 200 Projects for Fun and Profit,* Crown, 1951; *Lamps and Lampshade Making,* Homecrafts, 1951; (with Harold Schneider) *The Car Owner's "Fix-It" Guide: A Complete Handbook to Automobile Operation, Maintenance, and Repair,* Fell, 1952; *Tailoring and Dressmaking Made Easy,* Fell, 1952; *Illustrated Reference Book of Mechanisms and Devices,* [New York], 1954; *Practical Pictorial Guide to Mechanisms and Machines,* University Books, 1956.

Contributor: *Making Block Prints,* Scholastic Book Services, 1936; *The Teaching Scientist,* Biology Teachers Association, 1947; James Conto, *T.V. Owner's Guide to Operation and Repair,* Homecrafts, 1952. Author of children's plays and television scripts. Contributor to *Industrial Arts, Popular Science, Mechanix Illustrated, Canadian Hobbycrafts, Family Circle,* and other publications. Contributing editor, *Science and Mechanics,* 1948-51; consulting editor, *Young Mechanic,* 1953, *Travel Age-East.*

WORK IN PROGRESS: Games on the Go.

BIOGRAPHICAL/CRITICAL SOURCES: Bronx Home News, November 25, 1947; *Junior Arts and Crafts,* November, 1950; *House Beautiful,* February, 1951; *City College Alumnus,* December, 1951.

*   *   *

PANIKKAR, K(avalam) Madhava   1895-1963
(Chanakya, Kerala Putra)

PERSONAL: Born June 3, 1895, in Kerala, India; son of Pota and Kunji Kulti (anima) Poli; married Gouri Amma, 1919; children: Parkati Nair, Madhusudan, Devaki Nair, Haimarati Menon, Radha Mohan. *Education:* Attended Madras Christian College; Christ Church, Oxford, M.A.; Middle Temple, London, England, Barrister-at-Law. *Home:* 10 Umayal St., Alajappanajon, Madras, India. *Office:* Jammu and Kashmir University, Srinagar, Kashmir, India.

CAREER: Aligarh Muslim University, Aligarh, Uttar Pradesh, India, professor of history, 1919-22; editor of *Hindustan Times-Courier* and then secretary to the chancellor, Chamber of Princes of India, during late 1920's; political minister, Patiala State, 1933-38; prime minister, Bikaner State, 1943-48; India's Ambassador to China, 1948-52, Egypt, 1952-53, France, 1956-59; Jammu and Kashmir University, Srinagar, Kashmir, India, vice-chancellor, 1961-63.

Member of Indian delegation to United Nations General Assembly, 1947, of Indian States Reorganization Commission, 1954-55; chairman of UNESCO advisory committee, Major Project for Eastern and Western Cultural Values, 1957. President of Kerala Library Academy, 1956-61; vice-president of Indian Council of Cultural Affairs.

MEMBER: Royal India Society (vice-president), Oxford and Cambridge Club (London). *Awards, honors:* Dadablai Noaroji Award, 1960; D.Litt., Delhi University; LL.D., Aligarh Muslim University.

WRITINGS: An Introduction to the Study of the Problems of Greater-India, T. K. Swaminathan, 1916.

Sri Harsha of Kanauj: A Monograph on the History of India in the First Half of the 7th Century, D. B. Taraporevala, 1922; *An Introduction to the Study of the Relations of Indian States with the Government of India*, M. Hopkinson, 1927, 2nd edition published as *Indian States and the Government of India*, 1932; (under pseudonym Kerala Putra) *The Working of Dyarchy in India, 1919-1928*, D. B. Taraporevala, 1928; *Malabar and the Portuguese*, D. B. Taraporevala, 1929; *The Evolution of British Policy Towards Indian States 1774-1858*, S. K. Lahiri for Calcutta University, 1929.

Gulab Singh, 1792-1858, Founder of Kashmir, M. Hopkinson, 1930, 3rd edition published as *The Founding of the Kashmir State: A Biography of Maharajah Gulab Singh, 1792-1858*, Verry, 1964; (with Kailas N. Haksar) *Federal India*, M. Hopkinson, 1930; *Malabar and the Dutch*, D. B. Taraporevala, 1931; *The New Empire; Letters to a Conservative Member of Parliament on the Future of England and India*, M. Hopkinson, 1934; *The Indian Princes in Council: A Record of the Chancellorship of His Highness, the Maharajah of Patiala, 1926-31 and 1933-36*, Oxford University Press, 1936; *His Highness the Maharajah of Bikaner* (biography), Oxford University Press, 1937; *Origin and Evolution of Kingship in India*, Baroda State Press, 1938; *Hinduism and the Modern World*, Kitabistan, 1938.

Indian States, Oxford University Press, 1942; *The Future of South-east Asia: An Indian View*, Macmillan, 1943; *India and the Indian Ocean*, Macmillan, 1945, 3rd edition, Verry, 1964; *The Basis of an Indo-British Treaty*, Oxford University Press, 1946; *A Survey of Indian History*, Meridian Books, 1947, Hafner, 1949, 4th edition, Asia Publishing House (New York), 1964; (with others) *Regionalism and Security*, Indian Council of World Affairs, 1948.

(Under pseudonym Chanakya) *The Indian Revolution*, National Information and Publications (Bombay), 1951; *Asia and Western Dominance: A Survey of the Vasco de Gama Epoch of Asian History, 1498-1945*, Allen & Unwin, 1953, Day, 1954, new edition, Allen & Unwin, 1959; (compiler) Huang K'un, translator, *Modern Chinese Stories*, Ranjit, 1953; *Geographical Factors in Indian History*, B. V. Bhavan, 1954, 2nd edition, 1959; *In Two Chinas: Memoirs of a Diplomat* (autobiographical), Allen & Unwin, 1955; *Hindu Society at the Cross Roads*, Asia Publishing House (Bombay), 1955, 3rd edition, Asia Publishing House (New York), 1961; *The State and the Citizen*, Asia Publishing House (Bombay), 1956, 2nd edition, Asia Publishing House (London), 1960; *The Principles and Practice of Diplomacy*, 2nd edition, revised, Asia Publishing House (Bombay), 1956; *India and China: A Study of Cultural Relations*, Asia Publishing House (Bombay), 1957; *The Afro-Asian States and Their Problems*, Allen & Unwin, 1959, Day, 1960.

Common Sense about India, Macmillan, 1960; *A History of*

Kerala, 1498-1801, Annamalai University, 1960; *Problems of Indian Defence*, Asia Publishing House (New York), 1960; (editor) Motilal Nehru, *The Voice of Freedom: Selected Speeches*, Asia Publishing House (New York), 1961; *Revolution in Africa*, Asia Publishing House (New York), 1961; *The Determining Periods of Indian History*, B. V. Bhavan, 1962; *In Defence of Liberalism*, Asia Publishing House (New York), 1962; *The Foundations of a New India*, Allen & Unwin, 1963, Humanities, 1964; *Hinduism and the West*, Punjal University Publication Bureau, 1964; *Lectures on India's Contact with the World in the Pre-British Period*, Nagpur University Press, 1964; *Studies In Indian History*, Asia Publishing House, 1967; *Asia and Western Dominance*, Collier, 1969.

Author of other booklets in English, published in England and India, and of novels, poetry, and drama in the Malayalam language. Contributor to *Foreign Affairs* and *Nation* in America, and to Indian, English, and French journals.

(Died December 10, 1963)

*   *   *

PARANDOWSKI, Jan   1895-

PERSONAL: Born May 11, 1895, in Lwow, Poland; son of Jan and Julia (Parandowski) Parandowski; married Irene Helcel, August 8, 1925; children: Romana (Mrs. Szczepkowska), Zbigniew, Piotr. *Education:* Attended the University at Lwow. *Religion:* Roman Catholic. *Home:* Zimorowicza 4, Warsaw, Poland.

CAREER: Catholic University of Lublin, Lublin, Poland, professor of comparative literature, 1945-50. Writer. *Member:* P.E.N. International (vice-president); Polish P.E.N. (president, 1933—), Societe Europeenne de Culture (member of executive council).

WRITINGS: Antinous w aksamitnym berecie, Altenberg (Lwow), 1921, reissued as *Krol Zycia* (title means "King of Life"), Altenberg, 1930, 2nd edition Czytelnik (Warsaw), 1963; *Mitologia: Wierzenia i podania Gekowi Raymian* (title means "Mythology"), Altenberg, 1923, 11th edition, Czytelnik, 1965; *Eros na Olimpie* (title means "Eros on Olympus"), Altenberg, 1924; *Aspasia*, Altenberg, 1925; *Dwie Wiosny* (title means "Two Springs"; essay), Ossolineum (Lwow), 1927; *Dysk Olimpijski*, Gebethner i Wolf (Warsaw), 1932, 7th edition, Instytut Wydawniczy (Warsaw), 1968, translation by A. M. Malecka and S. A. Walewski published as *The Olympic Discus: A Story of Ancient Greece*, Minerva Publishing Co., 1939, new edition, Ungar, 1964; *Niebo w plomieniach* (title means "Heaven in Flames"), Roj (Warsaw), 1936, 10th edition Czytelnik, 1967; *Odwiedziny i spotkania* (title means "Meetings and Encounters"), Roj, 1938; *Trzy Znaki Zodiaku* (title means "Three Signs of the Zodiac"), Roj, 1939. *Godzina srodziemnomorska* (title means "The Mediterranean Hour"), Gebethner i Wolf, 1948; *Alchemia slowa* (title means "The Alchemy of the Word"), Gebethner i Wolf, 1949, 4th edition Czytelnik, 1965; *Zegar slonwczny* (title means "Sundial"), Czytelnik, 1952, 5th edition, 1968; *Petrarka* (title means "Petrarch"), Czytelnik, 1956; *Wojna trojanska*, Iskry (Warsaw), 1956, 4th edition, 1967; *Opowiadania: Antyk i renesans*, Nasza Ksiegarnia (Warsaw), 1956; *Dziela wybrane*, Czyteknik, 1957; *Z Antycznego swiata*, Iskry, 1958; *Podroze literackie*, Zakkad Norvdowy, 1958, 2nd edition, Ossolineum (Wroclaw), 1968; *Moj rzym* (title means "My Rome"), Pallotinum (Poznan), 1959.

Wspomnienia i sylwety, Ossolineum, 1960, 2nd edition, 1969; *Olimpijczycy* (title means "Olympic Athletes"),

Sport i Turystyka (Warsaw), 1960; *Juvenilia,* Instytut Wydawniczy, 1960; *Powrot do zycia* (title means "Return of Life"), Pallottinum, 1961; *Wrzesniowa noc* (title means "September Night"), Iskry, 1962, 3rd edition, 1968; *Kazimierz,* Sport i Turystyka, 1962; *Pizarze swiata Mickiewiczowi: Glosy wspolczesnyck pisarzy zaprosyonyck,* Czytelnik, 1962; *Greja,* Sport i Turystyka, 1962; *Kiedy bylem vecenzentem,* Artystyczni i Filmowe (Warsaw), 1963; *Luzne Kartki* (title means "Loose Leaves"), Ossolineum, 1965, 2nd edition, 1967; *Akacja* (title means "Acacia"), Czytelnik, 1967; *Szkice: Seria Druga* (essays), Instytut Wydawniczy, 1968.

Translator into Polish: Oscar Wilde, *Poesie,* [Lwow], 1924; Einhard, *Zycie Karola Wielkiego,* Zakladu Narodowego, 1950; Homer, *Wybor z odysei Homera,* Panstwowe Wydawn, 1956, 5th edition, Czytelnik, 1956; Longus, *Dafnis i Chloe,* Czytelnik, 1962. Also author of play, "Medea," published in *Dialog,* October, 1961.

WORK IN PROGRESS: Milocz (title means "love"), a novel.

SIDELIGHTS: Parandowski knows French, English, German, Italian, Russian, and ancient Greek and Latin. He has traveled throughout Europe and to South America. His writings have been translated into English, French, German, Hebrew, Serbian, Lithuanian, Czech, Slovac, Hungarian, Greek, and other languages.

BIOGRAPHICAL/CRITICAL SOURCES: George Harjan, *Jan Parandowski,* Twayne, 1971.

* * *

PARENTE, Pascal P(rosper) 1890-1971

PERSONAL: Born September 28, 1890, in San Giovanni, Benevento, Italy; came to United States, 1920, naturalized, 1930; son of Giovanni A. (an agriculturist) and Elizabeth (Lepore) Parente. *Education:* Studied at Salvatorian colleges in Tivoli and Rome, Italy, 1904-08; Gregorian University, Rome, Italy, Ph.D., 1911, J.C.B., 1914, S.T.D., 1916. *Politics:* Independent. *Home:* 9 Spring St., Cambridge, New York, N.Y. 12816.

CAREER: Ordained to Roman Catholic priesthood in Italy, 1915; professor of theology at Salvatorian seminaries in Wisconsin and Washington, D.C., 1920-31; pastoral posts in Trenton, N.J., 1931-38; Catholic University of America, Washington, D.C., faculty of School of Sacred Theology, 1938-60, professor of ascetical and mystical theology, 1947-60, dean of School of Sacred Theology, 1957-60, professor emeritus, 1960-71. Formerly public lecturer, and teacher of adult education classes in Washington, D.C. *Military service:* Italian Army 1911-12, chaplain, 1916-20; became first lieutenant.

WRITINGS: Roma Inoccidva (poems in Latin), Catholic University of America Press, 1939; *Quaestiones de Mystica Terminologia, ad mentem Pseudo-Areopagitae et sanctorum patrum,* privately printed, 1941; *The Ascetical Life,* B. Herder, 1944, revised edition, 1955; *The Mystical Life,* B. Herder, 1946; (compiler) *The Well of Living Waters: Excerpts on Spiritual Topics from the Bible, the Fathers, and the Masters of the Spirit,* B. Herder, 1948; *Spiritual Direction,* Grail, 1950, enlarged edition, St. Paul Publications, 1961; *Susanna Mary Beardsworth, the White Dove of Peace: Life, Conversion, Mysticism,* Grail, 1950; *A City on a Mountain: Padre Pio of Pietrelcina,* Grail, 1952, enlarged edition published as *Padre Pio,* AMI Press, 1968, also published as *A City on a Mountain: Padre Pio,*

AMI Press, 1968; *Schoolteacher and Saint,* Grail, 1954; *The Angels,* Grail, 1958, 2nd edition published as *Beyond Space,* St. Paul Publications, 1961; (translator from the Latin and author of commentary) *The Regimen of Health of the Medical School of Salerno,* Vantage, 1967. Contributor to *Encyclopaedia Britannica,* Catholic encyclopedias, and theological, biblical, and devotional periodicals.

WORK IN PROGRESS: A new edition of *The Ascetical Life* and *The Mystical Life,* to be published by St. Paul Publications as *Spiritual Theology,* Volume I-II; a reprint of *The Well of Living Waters,* to be published as *A Handbook of Spiritual Quotations.*

SIDELIGHTS: Parente knew no English when he arrived in America in 1920, but all of his books except two were written in English. He was competent in Latin and Greek, with some competence in Hebrew, German, French, and Spanish. *Avocational interests:* Art (drawing and painting); Italian and Latin poetry; gardening.

(Died August 10, 1971)

* * *

PARKINSON, (Frederick) Charles Douglas 1916-

PERSONAL: Born May 28, 1916, in Ilford, Essex, England; son of Frederick Charles and Sarah Louise Ellen (Hughes) Parkinson; married Alexa St. Clair Ross, March 12, 1940; children: Frederick Alexander Ian, Malcolm Ross, Richard Henry. *Education:* Attended University Tutorial College and Heatherley School of Art. *Politics:* Conservative. *Religion:* Church of England. *Home:* Knollys Cottage, Willesborough Lees, Near Ashford, Kent, England; and Marignac, Uzes 30, France. *Office:* Artist Publishing Co. Ltd., 33 Warwick Sq., London S.W. 1, England.

CAREER: Free-lance artist in London, England, 1939; Sir Isaac Pitman & Sons Ltd., London, England, publishing trainee, 1947-48; Artist Publishing Co. Ltd., London, England, editor, 1948—. Saint Catherine Press, director, 1948—; Heatherley School of Art, principal, 1956—; Helmsman Publishing Co. Ltd., editor and managing director, 1962—. *Military service:* Royal Air Force, 1940-46; became squadron leader; twice mentioned in dispatches. *Member:* International Association of Art Critics, South Eastern Federation of Art Societies (chairman), Helmsman Club (chairman), Arts Club, Chelsea Arts Club, Ashford Society of Artists (vice-president).

WRITINGS: "Artists Handbook Series," Artist Publishing Co., 1950—; (editor) *Art Review,* Artist Publishing Co., 1950, 1952, 1954, 1956, 1959; (editor) *Artist's Guide 1951,* Artist Publishing Co., 1951; *Type Identification,* Pitman, 1953; *Oils for the Beginner,* Artist Publishing Co., 1963; *Conversion of Lifeboat Hulls,* Helmsman Publishing, 1963. Contributor to art journals.

* * *

PARMET, Simon 1897-

PERSONAL: Surname originally Pergament; born October 26, 1897, in Helsinki, Finland; son of Yehuda (a merchant) and Maria (Polarsky) Pergament; married Vera Smolensky, August 18, 1918; children: Leila (Mrs. Herbert Spevak). *Education:* Studied at Imperial Conservatory, St. Petersburg (now Leningrad), 1915-17, Sibelius Academy, Helsinki, 1918-20, Stern's Conservatory, Berlin, 1920-23. *Religion:* Jewish. *Home:* Bocksbacka, Finland.

CAREER: Made debut as pianist in Helsinki, 1917; opera

conductor in Kiel, Germany, 1923-25, Hagen, Germany, 1925-27; National Opera of Finland, Helsinki, conductor, 1927-32; Finnish Broadcasting System, Helsinki, conductor of Symphonic Orchestra, 1948-53. *Member:* Sauna Club (Helsinki). *Awards, honors:* Doctor honoris causa; literary prize of City of Helsinki; literary prize of Swedish Literary Society for *Con Amore*; Finnish Oscar Prize, 1955, for music for the film "The Dollmerchant."

WRITINGS: Sibeliuksen Sinfoniat, Otava, 1955, translation by Kingsley A. Hunt published as *The Symphonies of Sibelius*, Cassell, 1959, Dufour, 1965; *Con Amore* (essays), Soderstrom, 1960; *Genom Fonsterrutan* (title means "Through the Window Pane"), Soderstrom, 1964.

WORK IN PROGRESS: Tankar om Konst och Liv (title means "Thoughts on Art and Life"), Soderstrom.

SIDELIGHTS: Parmet is competent in Swedish, German, and English in addition to his native tongue.

*   *   *

PARR, Charles McKew   1884-

PERSONAL: Born November 23, 1884, in Baltimore, Md.; son of Charles Edward (a grain exporter) and Helen B. (McKew) Parr; married Ruth Butler, June 22, 1916; children: Charles McKew, Jr. (deceased), Alexander S. *Education:* U.S. Military Academy, West Point, cadet, 1903-04; Columbia University, studied Classic Greek for four years. *Politics:* Republican. *Religion:* Roman Catholic. *Home:* Straits Rd., Chester, Conn. 06412. *Agent:* Elizabeth M. Riley, 1035 Fifth Ave., New York, N.Y. 10028. *Office:* McKew Parr Library, Chester, Conn. 06412.

CAREER: Parr Electric Co., Newark, N.J., 1919—, now chairman of board. Member of board of directors, Thomas Y. Crowell Co. (publishing firm) and Parr Marine and Export Corp. U.S. Government, special assistant to secretary of state, 1918, foreign agent for War Trade Board and Bureau of Exports, 1918, consular service in Spain and Canary Islands, 1919, senior electric consultant, War Planning Board, 1942, chairman, Industry Advisory Committee, 1952. Member of Connecticut House of Representatives, 1942-49, and of Connecticut Senate, 1950-54. Donated McKew Parr Magellan Collection to Brandeis University, 1961; chairman, Middletown Library Service Center, 1955-57, and Chester Public Library, 1955-65.

MEMBER: American Library Association, American Air Force Academy Library Association, American Geographical Society, American Historical Society, Hispanic Society of America, National Association of Electrical Distributors (member of board of directors), Sociedad de Geografia de Lisbon, Society for Nautical Research, Historical Association (London), Hakluyt Society (London), De Linschoten-Vereeniging (The Hague), Nederlandsch Historisch Scheepvart Museum (Amsterdam), Biblioteca Capitular Columbina (Seville), Bibliophile Society, Deep River Historical Society, Connecticut Library Association (chairman of board of trustees, 1953), New Jersey Historical Society, Maryland Society of Colonial Wars, New Jersey Library Association, John Carter Brown Library Association, Essex Electrical League (member of board of directors), Yale Library Association, West Point Society of New York, Sons of the American Revolution, Rotary International, Essex Club (Newark), Hartford Club, New York Athletic Club, Players Club (New York). *Awards, honors:* LL.D., University of Bridgeport, 1961; Comendador da Ordem Militar de Cristo (Portugal); commander, Order of Orange-Nassau (Netherlands).

WRITINGS: Over and Above Our Pacific, Brentano, 1941; *So Noble a Captain,* Crowell, 1953, 2nd edition published as *Ferdinand Magellan, Circumnavigator,* 1964; *Jan Van Linschoten: The Dutch Marco Polo,* Crowell, 1964; *The Voyages of David de Vries, Navigator and Adventurer,* Crowell, 1969.

WORK IN PROGRESS: Research in the Dutch exploration of Newfoundland, Maine, and Rhode Island in the sixteenth century and the parallel activities of Portuguese pioneers in New England.

*   *   *

PARSLOE, Guy Charles   1900-

PERSONAL: Born November 5, 1900, in Stroud Green, England; son of Henry Edward (a jeweler) and Emma (Gamlen) Parsloe; married Zirphie Faiers, April 6, 1929; children: Phyllida, Christopher, John. *Education:* University College, London, B.A. and M.A. (first class honors), 1921; London Day Training College, Diploma in Education, 1922. *Politics:* "Confound their politics." *Religion:* Christian. *Home:* 1 Leopold Ave., Wimbledon, London S.W. 19, England.

CAREER: University of London, University College, London, England, lecturer in history department, 1925-27; Institute of Historical Research, London, England, secretary and librarian, 1927-43; Institute of Welding, London, England, secretary, 1943-67; International Institute of Welding, London, England, secretary-general, 1948-66, vice-president, 1966-69. Secretary of welding mission to United States, Organization for European Economic Cooperation, 1953. *Member:* Royal Historical Society, Historical Association, Surrey Archaeological Society, Surrey Record Society, London Record Society, Worshipful Company of Founders of City of London (honorary freeman), Athenaeum Club. *Awards, honors:* Wheatley Medal, Library Association, 1965; honorary fellow, Institute of Welding, 1968; Edstrom Medal, Institute of Welding, 1971.

WRITINGS: The English Country Town, Longmans, Green, 1932; (major contributor) *Cambridge Bibliography of English Literature,* Cambridge University Press, 1940; *The Minute Book of Bedford Corporation, 1647-1664,* Bedfordshire Historical Record Society, 1949; *Wimbledon Village Club, 1858-1958,* Wimbledon Village Club, 1958; *Wardens' Accounts of the Worshipful Company of Founders of the City of London, 1497-1681,* Athlone Press, 1964. Editor-in-chief, *British Welding Journal,* 1954—; joint editor, *Welding in the World.*

WORK IN PROGRESS: A history of London; studies in genealogy and the development of welding technology.

*   *   *

PARSONS, Coleman O(scar)   1905-

PERSONAL: Born April 16, 1905, in Ripley, W.Va.; son of William Oscar (a lawyer) and Frances (Coleman) Parsons; married June Cohen, August 20, 1928; children: Eleanor. *Education:* Student at University of California, Los Angeles, 1923-25, University of Chicago, 1925-27; Columbia University, A.B., 1928; Yale University, Ph.D., 1931. *Politics:* Democrat. *Religion:* Protestant. *Home:* 501 West 123rd St., New York, N.Y. 10027. *Office:* Graduate School, City University of New York, New York, N.Y. 10036.

CAREER: Instructor in English at Long Island University, Brooklyn, N.Y., 1931-32, Vassar College, Poughkeepsie,

N.Y., 1933-34, American University, Washington, D.C., 1934-35, and Long Island University, 1937-41; The City University of New York, New York, N.Y., began as instructor in City College, 1941, became professor of English, 1963, supervisor of English in Evening Division, 1956-61, professor of English in Graduate School, 1962-72, visiting professor, 1972—. Visiting professor, Columbia University, summers, 1965 and 1966; researcher at National Library, Scotland, and British Museum, 1932-33, 1961-62, and 1965-66; adviser in Scottish literature to Yale University Libraries, 1973-76. Vice-president, East Meadow, N.Y., Board of Education, 1951-53; president, East Meadow Civic Association, 1953-54. *Member:* Modern Language Association of America, Edinburgh Sir Walter Scott Club, Friends of the National Libraries (Britain), Grolier Club, Andiron Club (president, 1968-72). *Awards, honors:* Hungtington Library international research fellow, 1935-36.

WRITINGS: Witchcraft and Demonology in Scott's Fiction, Oliver & Boyd, 1964; (editor) Joseph Glanvill, *Saducismus Triumphatus,* Scholars' Facsimiles, 1966; (editor) George Sinclair, *Satan's Invisible World Discovered,* Scholar's Facsimiles, 1969. Contributor of nearly one hundred articles to learned journals in the United States, England, Scotland, and Germany, including articles on Mark Twain that have appeared in *Virginia Quarterly Review, American Literature, The Twainian, South Atlantic Quarterly, Antioch Review,* and *Mississippi Quarterly.*

WORK IN PROGRESS: Articles on Scott, Blake, and Defoe.

AVOCATIONAL INTERESTS: Travel.

* * *

PASCOE, John (Dobree) 1908-1972

PERSONAL: Born September 26, 1908, in Christchurch, Canterbury, New Zealand; son of Guy Dobree (a solicitor) and Effie (Denham) Pascoe; married Dorothy G. Harding, June 22, 1940; children: Anna (Mrs. I. A. Gilmour), Sara (Mrs. Than Tun), Martha, Jane. *Education:* Canterbury University College (now University of Canterbury), law student, 1936. *Religion:* Church of England. *Home:* 289 Muritai Rd., Eastbourne, Wellington, New Zealand. *Office:* Chief Archivist, National Archives, 8-12 The Terrace, Wellington, New Zealand.

CAREER: Law clerk in New Zealand, 1928-37; New Zealand government, Wellington, civil servant, 1937-72. Government posts include illustrations editor of centennial publications, 1938-41, official photographer, Department of Internal Affairs, 1942-45, illustrations editor of New Zealand war histories, 1946-55, secretary of National Historic Places Trust, 1955-60, controller of Wildlife Branch, 1960, executive officer, Department of Internal Affairs, 1960-63, chief archivist, National Archives, 1963-72. *Member:* P.E.N., Canterbury Mountaineering Club, New Zealand Alpine Club, Tararua Tramping Club.

WRITINGS: Unclimbed New Zealand, Macmillan, 1939; *The Mountains, the Bush and the Sea,* Whitcombe & Tombs, 1950; *The Southern Alps* (guidebook), Part I, Pegasus Press, 1951; *Land Uplifted High,* Whitcombe & Tombs, 1952; (editor) Thomas Brunner, *The Great Journey,* Pegasus Press, 1952; (editor) *Mr. Explorer Douglas,* A. H. & A. W. Reed, 1957; *Great Days in New Zealand Mountaineering,* A. H. & A. W. Reed, 1958; *Great Days in New Zealand Exploration,* A. H. & A. W. Reed, 1959; *Over the Whitcombe Pass,* Whitcombe & Tombs, 1960; (author of introduction and text) Jean Bigwood and Ken-

neth Bigwood, *New Zealand in Colour* (photographs), A. H. & A. W. Reed, 1962; *The Haast is in South Westland,* A. H. & A. W. Reed, 1966; *New Zealand From the Air in Colour,* A. H. & A. W. Reed, 1968; *Of Unknown New Zealand,* John McIndoe, 1971; *Exploration New Zealand,* A. H. & A. W. Reed, 1971.

Editor, *Oxford New Zealand Encyclopedia,* Oxford University Press, 1965. Author of scripts for New Zealand Broadcasting Service. Contributor of stories, articles, and photographs to school and mountaineering journals. Book reviewer, *New Zealand Listener.*

AVOCATIONAL INTERESTS: Mountaineering.

(Died October 20, 1972)

* * *

PATERSON, John 1887-

PERSONAL: Born September 20, 1887, in Dumfriesshire, Scotland; son of John and Jane (Jack) Paterson; married Jane Wilson Wiseman, August 22, 1914; children: John Christie, Ann Wilson (Mrs. Chester Dugdale), Arthur Renwick, Walter David. *Education:* University of Glasgow, M.A. (first class honors in classics), 1910, B.D., 1914, Ph.D., 1929. *Politics:* Independent.

CAREER: Minister of Church of Scotland, 1914-30; Drew University, Madison, N.J., professor of Hebrew and Old Testament exegesis, 1930-57, became professor emeritus. Biblical lecturer at adult schools and conferences. *Member:* Glasgow University Oriental Society, Society of Biblical Literature (United States). *Awards, honors:* D.D., University of Glasgow, 1950.

WRITINGS: The Goodly Fellowship of the Prophets, Scribner, 1948; *The Praises of Israel,* Scribner, 1950; *The Book That Is Alive,* Scribner, 1954; *The Evangelistic Message of the Bible,* Tidings, 1955; *The Wisdom of Israel,* Abingdon, 1961; (general editor), Thomas Hardy, *Jude the Obscure,* Harper, 1966. Contributor of articles to *Hastings Dictionary of the Bible* and *Peake Bible Commentary.*

WORK IN PROGRESS: With W. Barclay and Hugh Anderson, *Historical Companion to the Bible.*

SIDELIGHTS: Patterson is competent in Oriental and classical languages, and in French, German, Dutch, Italian, Spanish, Danish, Norwegian, and Swedish.

* * *

PATON, Alan (Stewart) 1903-

PERSONAL: Surname rhymes with "Dayton"; born January 11, 1903, in Pietermaritzburg, South Africa; son of James (a civil servant) and Eunice (James) Paton; married Doris Olive Francis, July 2, 1928 (died October 23, 1967); married Anne Hopkins, 1969; children: (first marriage) David Francis, Jonathan Stewart. *Education:* Attended Maritzburg College, 1914-18; University of Natal, B.Sc., 1923. *Religion:* Anglican. *Address:* P.O. Box 278, Hillcrest, Natal, South Africa.

CAREER: Ixopo High School, Ixopo, Natal, South Africa, teacher of mathematics and physics, 1925-28; Maritzburg College, Pietermaritzburg, Natal, teacher of mathematics, physics, and English, 1928-35; Diepkloof Reformatory, near Johannesburg, South Africa, principal, 1935-48; Toc H Tuberculosis Settlement, Botha's Hill, Natal, honorary commissioner, 1949-58; University of Natal, Natal, president of the Convocation, 1951-55, 1957-59; founder and president, Liberal Party of South Africa (originally the Liberal Association of South Africa before emergence as a political party; declared an illegal organization, 1968), 1958-68. Non-European Boys' Clubs, president of Transvaal association, 1935-48. *Member:* Royal Society of Literature (fellow), Free Academy of Arts (Hamburg; honorary member). *Awards, honors:* Anisfield-Wolf *Saturday Review* Award, 1948, Newspaper Guild of New York Page One Award, 1949, and London Sunday *Times* Special Award for Literature, 1949, all for *Cry, the Beloved Country;* Freedom House Award (U.S.), 1960; Medal for Literature, Free Academy of Arts, 1961; C.N.A. Literary Award for the year's best book in English in South Africa, for *Hofmeyr,* 1965. L.H.D., Yale University, 1954, Kenyon College, 1962; D.Litt., University of Natal, 1968, Trent University, 1971, Harvard University, 1971, Rhodes University, 1972; D.D., University of Edinburgh, 1971.

WRITINGS: Cry, the Beloved Country, Scribner, 1948; *Too Late the Phalarope* (Book-of-the-Month Club selection), Scribner, 1953; *The Land and the People of South Africa,* Lippincott, 1955, (published in England as *South Africa and Her People,* Lutterworth, 1957), revised edition (under original title), Lippincott, 1972; *South Africa in Transition,* Scribner, 1956; *Hope for South Africa,* Praeger, 1959; *Debbie Go Home* (stories), J. Cape, 1961; *Tales From a Troubled Land* (stories), Scribner, 1961; *Hofmeyr* (biography), Oxford University Press, 1964, abridged edition published as *South African Tragedy: The Life and Times of Jan Hofmeyr,* Scribner, 1965; (with Krishna Shah) *Sponono* (play; based on three stories from *Tales From a Troubled Land*), Scribner, 1965; *Instrument of Thy Peace,* Seabury, 1968; *The Long View,* edited by Edward Callan, Praeger, 1968; *Kontakion For You Departed,* J. Cape, 1969, published as *For You Departed,* Scribner, 1969. Also author of *The People Wept,* 1957.

WORK IN PROGRESS: Planning a novel dealing with modern South Africa.

SIDELIGHTS: Paton told *CA:* "Circumstances compelled me to take a leading part in the [South African] Liberal Party. This is not a good thing for a writer. He may be 'committed,' as they say, but not that far. I would have withdrawn from politics had it not been for the actions of the Government, who have restricted the movements and activities of Liberals on the grounds that they 'further the aims of Communism.' This is called a 'banning,' and a banned person (who is usually restricted for 5 years) is never charged, never brought to court, nor can he himself contest the order. Under these circumstances I did not feel able to retire to the ivory tower, if I had one." After his last trip to the United States, Paton's passport was revoked.

W. B. Gould wrote: "Literary men with an active interest in politics are rare. . . . There are, however, a few who have used their artistry as a political weapon, and among those few, Alan Paton of South Africa is notable. . . . He believes there is a road away from destruction, and he stakes out the signposts along the road." Paton's work has been highly praised for his ability to analyze human motivation, for his sharp insight into political and social conditions, and for his reportorial accuracy. Saunders Redding wrote: "*Cry, the Beloved Country* and *Too Late the Phalarope* . . . were read for the reasons that still commend them: the revelations of the human condition; the insights into the state of man's fettered soul. Most of the stories in *Tales From a Troubled Land* will also be read for these reasons. Set in South Africa, they transcend the boundaries of place, the limitations of timeliness, and the special relationship of Afrikander white to Bantu black. They are peopled by characters sharply drawn to a scale of truth that goes beyond the particular situations in which they are involved. . . . They provide insights into the whole state of universal man. . . ."

Maxwell Anderson adapted *Cry, the Beloved Country* into an opera, *Lost in the Stars* (Sloane, 1950), with music by Kurt Weill. London Films also made a movie, "Cry, the Beloved Country," based on the novel. *Too Late the Phalarope* has also been made into a play; film and stage rights to *Kontakion For You Departed* have been sold.

BIOGRAPHICAL/CRITICAL SOURCES: Harvey Breit, *The Writer Observed,* World, 1956; *Saturday Review,* August 1, 1959; *New Republic,* September 21, 1959; *Chicago Sunday Tribune,* April 9, 1961; *New York Herald Tribune Lively Arts,* April 9, 1961; *Atlantic,* May, 1961; *Christian Century,* May 24, 1961; *New Statesman,* April 30, 1965; *New York Times,* August 11, 1965.

*   *   *

PATON, George (Whitecross) 1902-

PERSONAL: Born August 16, 1902; son of Frank Hume Lyall (a clergyman) and Clara (Heyer) Paton; married Alice Watson, July 11, 1931; children: Jeannine (Mrs. K. Mills), Heather (Mrs. M. Winneke), Elspeth, Frank. *Education:* University of Melbourne, M.A., 1925; Magdalen College, Oxford, B.A., 1928, B.C.L., 1929. *Religion:* Presbyterian. *Home:* 7 Dunraven Ave., Toorak, Victoria 3142, Australia. *Office:* University of Melbourne, Victoria, Australia.

CAREER: Barrister-at-law, Gray's Inn, 1929; University of Melbourne, Melbourne, Victoria, Australia, professor of jurisprudence, 1931-51, dean of faculty of law, 1946-51, vice-chancellor of university, 1951-68. Chairman, Royal Commission on Television in Australia, 1953-54. *Awards, honors:* Knighted, 1957; Swiney Prize, Royal Society of Arts, for *A Text Book of Jurisprudence;* LL.D., University of Glasgow, 1953, University of Sydney, 1955, University of Queensland, 1960, University of London, 1963, University of Tasmania, 1963; D.C.L., University of Western Ontario, 1958.

WRITINGS: A Text Book of Jurisprudence, Oxford University Press, 1946, 3rd edition, 1964; (with John V. W. Barry and G. Sawer) *An Introduction to the Criminal Law in Australia,* Macmillan (London), 1948; *Bailment in the Common Law,* Stevens & Sons, 1952; (editor) *The British Commonwealth: The Development of Its Laws and Constitutions,* Volume II, Stevens & Sons, 1952.

AVOCATIONAL INTERESTS: Drama and gardening.†

*   *   *

PATON, Herbert James 1887-1969

PERSONAL: Born March 30, 1887, in Abernethy, Perthshire, Scotland; son of William Macalister (a clergyman) and Jean Robertson (Millar) Paton; married Mary Sheila Todd-Naylor, 1936 (died, 1959); married Sarah Irene Macneile Dixon, April 9, 1962 (died, 1964). *Education:* University of Glasgow, M.A., 1908; Balliol College, Oxford, M.A., 1914, D.Litt., 1933. *Religion:* Church of Scotland. *Home:* Nether Pitcaithly, Bridge of Earn, Perthshire, Scotland.

CAREER: Oxford University, Oxford, England, fellow of Queen's College and praelector in classics and philosophy, 1911-27, dean of Queen's College, 1917-22, junior proctor, 1920-21; University of California, Berkeley, Laura Spelman

Rockefeller Research Fellow, 1925-26; University of Glasgow, Glasgow, Scotland, professor of logic and rhetoric, 1927-37, dean of Faculty of Arts, 1935-37; Oxford University, White's Professor of Moral Philosophy and fellow of Corpus Christi College, 1937-52, curator of Bodleian Library, 1938-52, professor emeritus, 1952-69. Visiting professor, University of Toronto, 1955; philosophical editor, Hutchinson Publishing Group's University Library. Served in Intelligence Division of British Admiralty, 1914-19, as British representative on Sub-Commission for Polish Affairs, Paris, 1919, in Research Department of Foreign Office, 1939-44. Member of executive committee, League of Nations Union, 1939-46; member of University Court, University of St. Andrews, 1953-60.

MEMBER: British Academy (fellow), Aristotelian Society (past president), Mind Association. *Awards, honors:* Fellow of Corpus Christi College, Oxford University; LL.D. from University of Glasgow, University of St. Andrews, and University of Toronto.

WRITINGS: The Good Will, Allen & Unwin, 1927; *Kant's Metaphysic of Experience: A Commentary on the First Half of the 'Kritik der reinen Vernunft,'* Allen & Unwin, 1936, Macmillan, 1961; (editor with Raymond Klibansky) *Philosophy and History,* Clarendon Press, 1936, Harper, 1963; *The Categorical Imperative: A Study in Kant's Moral Philosophy,* Hutchinson, 1947, 6th edition, Harper, 1967; (editor and translator) *The Moral Law: Kant's Groundwork of the Metaphysic of Morals,* Hutchinson, 1948, Barnes & Noble, 1967; *In Defence of Reason,* Hutchinson, 1951; *The Modern Predicament: A Study in the Philosophy of Religion* (Gifford lectures), Macmillan, 1955; (contributor) H. D. Lewis, editor, *Contemporary British Philosophy,* 3rd series, Macmillan, 1956; *The Claim of Scotland,* Humanities, 1968.

WORK IN PROGRESS: Studies on Immanuel Kant and on political philosophy.

SIDELIGHTS: In the report of Professor Paton's death the *London Times* commented, "Paton will be remembered more as a scholar than as a creative thinker, though he took an effective part in contemporary philosophical controversy at various stages in his career. His ethical theory has perhaps attracted less attention than it deserves, but there can be no question of the solidity and distinction of his work as an interpreter of Kant. The high standards of accuracy and sweeping intolerance of the second hand there exhibited were salient and salutary features of his influence on his juniors, whether pupils or colleagues, but he was too chary of enthusiasm himself to wish to arouse it in others."

Paton was competent in Greek, Latin, German, French, and Italian. *Avocational interests:* Politics (foreign and domestic), education, and reading history and biography.

(Died August 2, 1969)

* * *

PATTERSON, Eric James 1891-1972

PERSONAL: Born May 9, 1891, in Ramsey, Isle of Man, England; son of George and Euphemia (Abbey) Patterson; married Ethel Simkins (a university lecturer), July 25, 1936; children: George Benjamin. *Education:* Peterhouse College, Cambridge, B.A., 1910, M.A., 1916; additional study at University of Freiburg. *Politics:* Conservative. *Religion:* Anglican. *Home:* Stonehedge, Alphington Cross, Exeter, Devonshire, England.

CAREER: University of Liverpool, Liverpool, England,

university extension lecturer in modern history, 1914-15; Young Men's Christian Association, lecturer in France with British troops, World War I; University College of South West of England, Exeter, head of department of extra mural studies, 1920-38, head of department of international politics, 1926-38; Ashridge Bonar Law College of Citizenship, England, principal, 1938-39. Delegate, Saar Commission, 1955-56. *Military service:* Italian Army, 1917; Special Forces, 1940-42, Army education, 1942-46. *Awards, honors:* Polish Silver Academic Laurel.

WRITINGS: The International Mind, Carnegie Foundation, 1926; *Poland,* Arrowsmith, 1934; *The Man and the Hour* (Pilsudski) Methuen, 1934; *Pilsudski, Marshal of Poland,* Arrowsmith, 1935; *Yugoslavia,* Arrowsmith, 1936; *The Saar Referendum,* Council of Europe, 1958.

WORK IN PROGRESS: The Problem of Senates and Upper Chambers; Poland and the German Problem; The Eastern States of Europe; Religion and World Unity: Religious and Political Factors; Baldwin, Prime Minister of England.

(Died October, 1972)

* * *

PATTERSON, Harriet-Louise H(olland) 1903-

PERSONAL: Born November 21, 1903, in Chicago, Ill., daughter of Samuel Benjamin and Louise Jane (Holland) Patterson. *Education:* Western Reserve University (now Case Western Reserve University), A.B., 1926; specialized study at Kent State University, 1926, Union Theological Seminary, New York, N.Y., 1945, and Oberlin College, Graduate School of Theology, 1945-46. *Home:* Apartment 211, 12805 Shaker Blvd., Cleveland, Ohio 44120.

CAREER: Public lecturer in Ohio on travel and biblical history, 1933-38; ordained minister of Disciples of Christ Church, 1941; minister in Chesterland, Ohio, 1944-53; Maupintour Associates (travel agents), Lawrence, Kan., associate, and director of tours to Middle East and Holy Land, 1951-66. Instructor in Old Testament, Schauffler College, 1952-54; member of board of directors, Heritage of America Foundation; consultant on Bible lands, Gotaas World Travel, 1969-73. *Member:* Disciples of Christ Historical Society (former trustee), Pi Tau Chi.

WRITINGS: How to Understand Your Bible Better, W. A. Wilde, 1934; *Enjoy the Bible's Beauty,* W. A. Wilde, 1938; *Around the Mediterranean with My Bible,* W. A. Wilde, 1941, 2nd edition, Judson, 1947; *Come With Me to the Holy Land,* Judson, 1963, revised edition, 1969; *Traveling through Turkey,* Judson, 1969. Contributor to *Christian Science Monitor, Christian Century Pulpit, Church Management,* and *Woman's Home Companion.* Also illustrator of *Family Heritage Bible* published by Illustrated World Publishing Co.

SIDELIGHTS: Miss Patterson has made more than seventy trips to the Middle East and Europe since 1935, and five world tours, two South American tours, three tours of Africa below the Sahara, and two tours of South Pacific areas.

* * *

PATTON, Arch 1908-

PERSONAL: Born January 11, 1908, in New York, N.Y.; son of Henry Deford and Edna (Archibald) Patton; married second wife, Marion Hutton, 1959; children: (first marriage) Leslie Sprague. *Education:* Colgate University, B.S.,

1929; Harvard University, graduate student, 1931. *Home:* 205 East 63rd St., New York, N.Y. *Office:* McKinsey & Co., Inc., 270 Park Ave., New York, N.Y.

CAREER: Vick Chemical Co., New York, N.Y., economist, 1940-42; R. Hoe & Co., New York, N.Y., assistant to president, 1943-46; Wilbur-Suchard Chocolate Co., Lititz, Pa., vice-president of sales, 1946-49; McKinsey & Co., New York, N.Y., management consultant and director, beginning 1951. *Member:* Harvard Club, Fifth Avenue Club, Harbor View Club (all New York).

WRITINGS: Men, Money and Motivation, McGraw, 1961, published as *What is an Executive Worth?,* 1963. Contributor of over forty articles on executive compensation, administration, management organization, and related topics to *Fortune, Harvard Business Review,* and other periodicals.

* * *

PATTON, James W(elch) 1900-

PERSONAL: Born September 28, 1900, in Rutherford County, Tenn.; son of James Wesley (a merchant and farmer) and Elizabeth (Welch) Patton; married Carlotta Dorothea Petersen (a college teacher), June 25, 1930; children: Emilie Frances (Mrs. Sanders de Luca). *Education:* Vanderbilt University, A.B., 1924; University of North Carolina, A.M., 1925, Ph.D., 1929. *Politics:* Democrat. *Religion:* Episcopalian. *Home:* 614 East Franklin St., Chapel Hill, N.C. 27514. *Office:* 504 Hamilton Hall, University of North Carolina, Chapel Hill, N.C. 27514.

CAREER: Georgia State Woman's College, Valdosta, professor of history, 1925-27; The Citadel, Charleston, S.C., associate professor of history, 1929-30; Wittenberg College, Springfield, Ohio, assistant professor of history, 1930-31; Converse College, Spartanburg, S.C., professor and head of department of history, 1931-42; North Carolina State College, Raleigh, professor and head of department of history and political science, 1942-48; University of North Carolina, Chapel Hill, professor of history 1948—, director of Southern Historical Collection of Manuscripts, 1948-66.

MEMBER: English-Speaking Union (president, Raleigh-Durham-Chapel Hill branch, 1966-70), American Historical Association, Society of American Archivists, Organization of American Historians, Southern Historical Association (secretary-treasurer, 1939-48; president, 1956), Historical Society of North Carolina (president, 1966), North Carolina Literary and Historical Association (president, 1964), Phi Beta Kappa, Phi Kappa Phi.

WRITINGS: Unionism and Reconstruction in Tennessee, 1860-1869, University of North Carolina Press, 1934; (with Francis B. Simkins) *The Women of the Confederacy,* Garrett & Massie, 1936; (editor) *Minutes of the Greenville Ladies Association in Aid of the Volunteers of the Confederate Army,* Duke University Press, 1937; (editor) *Messages, Addresses, and Public Papers of Governor Luther H. Hodges,* three volumes, Council of State of North Carolina, 1960-63.

Contributor: Fletcher M. Green, editor, *Essays in Southern History Presented to J. G. de Roulhac Hamilton,* University of North Carolina Press, 1949; Thomas D. Clark, editor, *Travels in the Old South, a Bibliography,* Volume III, University of Oklahoma Press, 1959; R. C. Simonini, editor, *Education in the South: Institute of Southern Culture Lectures at Longwood College,* Longwood College (Farmville, Va.) 1959. Also contributor to

Dictionary of American Biography, 1928-37, *Dictionary of American History,* 1940, *Collier's Encyclopedia,* and *American People's Encyclopedia.*

WORK IN PROGRESS: Editing the Civil War diary of Mrs. Catherine Devereux Edmondston, 1860-65.

* * *

PAULL, Raymond Allan 1906-1972

PERSONAL: Born September 3, 1906, in Melbourne, Australia; son of William Henry and Annie (Wilkens) Paull; married Christine Rosalind Trood (a medical practitioner), August 25, 1938; children: Jon Alan Trood, Vivienne Christine Trood (Mrs. Norman Jones). *Education:* Attended Canterbury School, Melbourne, Australia. *Home:* Qeleya Point, Lami, Suva, Fiji. *Office:* Radio Australia, Melbourne, Australia.

CAREER: Member of literary staff of *Argus,* Melbourne, Australia, 1933-38, of *Advertiser,* Adelaide, Australia, 1938-39; News Department, Australian Broadcasting Commission, deputy chief sub-editor of Radio Australia, 1939-63; Fiji Broadcasting Commission, Suva, news editor, 1963-72. War correspondent in Southwest Pacific, 1944-45; in charge of Australian domestic short-wave "News for the Inland," 1947-50; press officer, first South Pacific Conference, Nasinu, Fiji, 1950. *Military service:* Australian Army, Infantry, 1942-44. *Member:* Australian Institute of International Affairs, Australian Journalists' Association, National Trust of Australia; Melbourne Cricket Club and Victorian Club (both Melbourne); Fiji Defence and Union Clubs (both Suva).

WRITINGS: (Contributor) *Historical Records of the Queen's Own Cameron Highlanders, 1932-48,* Volume I, W. Blackwood, 1952; *Retreat from Kokoda,* Heinemann, 1958; *Old Walhalla: Portrait of a Gold Town,* Cambridge University Press, 1963. Contributor to *Australian Historical Studies.* Contributor of articles to *Australasian Post* and *Desiderata.*

WORK IN PROGRESS: Welfare in the South Pacific, for Heinemann; research on central Asia.

AVOCATIONAL INTERESTS: History, Australian aboriginal art, cricket, and Australian rules football.

(Died September, 1972)

* * *

PEARSON, Norman Holmes 1909-

PERSONAL: Born April 13, 1909, in Gardner, Mass.; son of Chester Page (a merchant) and Fanny Holmes (Kittredge) Pearson; married Susan Silliman Bennett, February 21, 1941; children: (stepdaughters) Susan (Mrs. James M. Addiss), Elizabeth B. Tracy. *Education:* Yale University, B.A., 1932, Ph.D., 1941; Magdalen College, Oxford, A.B., 1932, M.A., 1941; University of Berlin, graduate student, 1933. *Religion:* Congregationalist. *Home:* 39 Goodrich St., Hamden, Conn. 06517. *Office:* Hall of Graduate Studies, Yale University, New Haven, Conn. 06520.

CAREER: Yale University, New Haven, Conn., instructor, 1941-42, assistant professor, 1946-51, associate professor, 1951-58, professor of English and American studies, 1958—, chairman of department of American studies, 1957-67; Visiting fellow, Huntington Library, 1948; president of Bryher Foundation, 1949-52; chancellor, Academy of American Poets, 1964—; counsellor, Smithsonian Institution, 1966—, visiting professor, University of Kyoto and

Doshisha University, 1970; adviser, American Council of Learned Societies. *Wartime service:* U.S. Office of Strategic Services, civilian, 1942-46; decorated Medal of Freedom (United States), Medaille de la Reconnaissance and Chevalier de la Legion d'honneur (France), Knight of St. Olaf, First Class (Norway), Knight of Dannebrog, First Class (Denmark). *Member:* English Institute (chairman, 1948), College English Association (president of New England branch, 1951-52; national vice-president, 1955-56), Modern Language Association of America, American Studies Association (president of New England branch, 1965-66; national president, 1968), Connecticut Academy (vice-president, 1963—), Essex Institute, Grolier Club and Century Association (both New York), Elizabethan Club (New Haven). *Awards, honors:* Guggenheim fellowships, 1948-49, 1956-57.

WRITINGS: (Editor) *Complete Novels and Selected Tales of Nathaniel Hawthorne*, Random House, 1937; (editor with William Rose Benet) *Oxford Anthology of American Literature*, Oxford University Press, 1938; (editor) Henry David Thoreau, *Walden*, Rinehart, 1948.

(Editor with W. H. Auden) *Poets of the English Language*, five volumes, Viking, 1950, revised edition published as *Poets of the English Language*, Volume I: *Medieval and Renaissance Poets: Langland to Spenser*, Volume II: *Elizabethan and Jacobean Poets: Marlowe to Marvell*, Volume III: *Restoration and Augustan Poets: Milton to Goldsmith*, Volume IV: *Romantic Poets: Blake to Poe*, Volume V: *Victorian and Edwardian Poets: Tennyson to Yeats*, all 1957; (editor) James Fenimore Cooper, *The Pathfinder*, Random House, 1952; *Four Studies* (in English), Stamperia Valdonega (Milan), 1962; *American Literature* (English with Japanese notes), edited, with notes by Shinji Takuwa, Eihosha (Tokyo), 1964; *Some American Studies* (English with Japanese notes), edited, with notes by Takuwa, Apollon-sha (Kyoto), 1964; *American Literary Fathers* (English with Japanese notes), edited, with notes by Takuwa, Apollon-sha, 1965; *The History of American Literature* (English with Japanese notes), edited, with notes by Takuwa, revised and enlarged edition, Eihosha, 1967; (compiler) *Decade: A Collection of Poems from the First Ten Years of the Wesleyan Poetry Program*, Wesleyan University Press, 1969.

Writer of introductions to other books and of pamphlets; reviewer for journals. Member of editorial board, *New England Galaxy* and *Essex Institute Quarterly*.

WORK IN PROGRESS: Editing two books, *Complete Letters of Hawthorne*, and Hawthorne's *French and Italian Journals*.

AVOCATIONAL INTERESTS: Collecting manuscripts and rare books; Viking and Eskimo archaeology, especially in Greenland; problems of literary property rights and executorship.

* * *

PEGGE, C(ecil) Denis 1902-

PERSONAL: Born 1902, in Briton Ferry, South Wales. *Education:* Magdalene College, Cambridge, M.A., 1928. *Address:* c/o Barclays Bank Ltd., Benet St., Cambridge, England.

CAREER: Cambridge University, Cambridge, England, teacher of engineering, 1940-51, general secretary of Educational Film Council, 1946-55; Institute of Experimental Psychology, Oxford, England, researcher on film and simu-

lacrics, 1960-61; writer. Producer of films independently as well as in university work. *Member:* Society of Authors.

WRITINGS: Construction (novel), J. Cape, 1930; *Bombay Riots* (film poem), Scholartis Press, 1932; *Obsidian* (poems), Scholartis Press, 1934; *The Fire* (poems), Williams & Norgate, 1943; *The Flying Bird* (poems), MacLellan, 1955; *Tribute and Other Poems*, Semaphore Publications, 1966. Poems represented in anthology, *Fear No More: A Book of Poems for the Present Time by Living English Poets*, Cambridge University Press, 1941. Contributor of poems and stories to periodicals, including *Poetry Review* and *Blackwood's Magazine*; also contributor to British Broadcasting Corp. "Midland Poets" programs. Writer of articles on film art, history, humanist thought, and research for journals.

WORK IN PROGRESS: As the Pigeons Fly, a collection of poems.

* * *

PEGIS, Jessie Corrigan 1907-

PERSONAL: Born May 13, 1907, in Milwaukee, Wis.; daughter of Walter Dickson (a lawyer) and Jessie (Donaldson) Corrigan; married Anton C. Pegis (a professor of philosophy), August 5, 1931; children: Charles, Richard, Sylvia, Marina, Gerard, Jessica. *Education:* University of Wisconsin, student, 1923-25; Marquette University, M.A., 1929. *Religion:* Roman Catholic. *Home:* 140 Elm Ridge Drive, Apt. 1614, Toronto, Ontario M6B 1B1, Canada.

CAREER: High school teacher of English and Latin, Eureka, S.D., 1929-31.

WRITINGS: Chrysalis Songs, Marquette University Press, 1928; (editor) *The Children's Book of Prayers and Hymns*, Samuel Lowe, 1944; (editor with Sharon Banigan) *Hear Our Prayer* (Catholic version), Samuel Lowe, 1946; *A Practical Catholic Dictionary*, Hanover, 1957; *Best Friends* (juvenile), Hastings, 1964. Contributor of verse and short stories to magazines.

WORK IN PROGRESS: A juvenile book.

* * *

PENDELL, Elmer 1894-

PERSONAL: Born July 28, 1894, in Waverly, N.Y.; son of George Grant (a newspaperman) and Ida (Harris) Pendell; married Lucille Hunt (head librarian at Gallaudet College), October 11, 1930 (divorced, 1946); children: Martha Jane (Mrs. James E. Griffin). *Education:* George Washington University, LL.B., 1917; University of Oregon, B.S., 1921; University of Chicago, M.A., 1923; Cornell University, Ph.D., 1929. *Politics:* Conservative. *Home:* 206 West Mountain Ave., Jacksonville, Ala. 36265.

CAREER: Started as high school teacher in Klamath County, Ore.; college teacher of economics and sociology, at various levels, at Cornell University, Ithaca, N.Y., 1923-25, 1928-29, University of Nevada, Reno, 1925-26, University of Arkansas, Fayetteville, 1926-27, Oklahoma Agriculture and Mechanical College (now Oklahoma State University), Stillwater, 1929-30, University of Oregon, Eugene, 1931-32, Oregon Normal School (now Oregon College of Education), Monmouth, Ore., 1932-33, and Pennsylvania State College (now University), 1933-44; Republican National Committee, Washington, D.C., economic analyst, 1944-45; Baldwin-Wallace College, Berea, Ohio, assistant professor of economics, 1946-54; Ashtabula County Historical Society, Jefferson, Ohio, executive secretary, 1954-55;

Jacksonville State College (now University), Jacksonville, Ala., associate professor of economics 1957-65. Visiting professor of economics, Olivet College, 1956-57. *Military service:* U.S. Army, Infantry, 1917-19; attached to Air Service, 1918-19; became first lieutenant; received Distinguished Service Cross and Purple Heart. *Member:* Legion of Valor of the U.S.

WRITINGS: (Editor and contributor) *Society Under Analysis: An Introduction to Sociology,* Cattell Press, 1942; (with Guy Irving Burch) *Population Roads to Peace or War,* Population Reference Bureau, 1945, revised edition published as *Human Breeding and Survival,* Penguin, 1947; *Population on the Loose,* Funk, 1951; *The Next Civilization,* privately printed, 1960; (editor) *Wisdom to Guide You: Sayings Selected and Commented On,* privately printed, 1960; *Sex Versus Civilization,* Noontide, 1967.

WORK IN PROGRESS: A book dealing with birth rate differences as a major cause of the fall of civilizations.

* * *

PENDLETON, Winston K. 1910-

PERSONAL: Born November 27, 1910, in Tampa, Fla.; son of Winston Kent (a minister) and Daisy (Watt) Pendleton; married Gladys Henderson, September 14, 1950; children: Philip Lamar, Winston K. III. *Education:* Transylvania College (now University), A.B., 1934. *Politics:* Democrat. *Religion:* Disciples of Christ. *Home and office:* Windermere, Fla.

CAREER: Eustis News, Eustis, Fla., publisher and editor, 1946-49; self-employed public relations consultant, Washington, D.C., 1950-62; Universal Dynamics Corp., Alexandria, Va., vice-president and sales manager, 1962-65; now retired. Public speaker and writer, mostly on humorous topics. *Military service:* U.S. Army, 1942-46; served in European theater; became major; received U.S. General's Citation, Polish Cross of Valor, French Croix de Guerre avec Palme. *Member:* Masons, Shrine, Rotary International (district governor, 1959-60).

WRITINGS: Pursuit of Happiness: A Study of the Beatitudes, Bethany, 1963; *2121 Funny Stories and How to Tell Them,* Bethany, 1964; *Aw Stop Worryin',* Bethany, 1966; *How to Win Your Audience with Humor,* Simon & Schuster, 1969. Writer of newspaper column, "Washington See-Saw," 1953-63; also writer of book reviews, titled "Book Browsing with Win Pendleton," for radio, television, and newspapers.

WORK IN PROGRESS: A book of humor for teen-agers.

* * *

PENTREATH, A(rthur Godolphin) Guy C(arleton) 1902-

PERSONAL: Surname is accented on second syllable; born March 30, 1902, in Bermuda; son of Arthur Godolphin (a priest, Church of England) and Helen (Guy-Carleton) Pentreath; married Lesley Cadman, December 21, 1926; children: Michael, David, Prisilla Pentreath Boddington. *Education:* Magdalene College, Cambridge, 1921-24, Wescott House Theological College, 1924-26, M.A. (Cambridge). *Home:* Wooden Walls, Dock Lane, Beaulieu, Hampshire, England. *Agent:* (Lectures) Foyles Lecture Agency, 125 Charing Cross Rd., London W. 2, England.

CAREER: Church of England, ordained deacon, 1928, priest, 1929. Michaelhouse School, Natal, South Africa, chaplain and assistant classics master, 1928-30; Westmin-

ster School, London, England, master of King's scholars, 1930-34; headmaster of St. Peter's College, Adelaide, South Australia, 1934-44, of Wrekin College, Wellington, England, 1944-51, of Cheltenham College, Cheltenham, England, 1952-59, retiring, 1959; residentiary canon of Rochester Cathedral, 1959-65. Lecturer on Greece, throughout England and on cruises to Greece; organizer of lectures in London by other authorities on classical and archaeological topics; broadcaster on British and Australian radio and television. *Member:* Hellenic Travellers Club (honorary secretary, 1958—).

WRITINGS: Rochester Cathedral, Pitkin, 1962; *Hellenic Traveller,* Crowell, 1964.

SIDELIGHTS: Pentreath has made more than fifty trips to Greece. *Avocational interests:* Sailing.

* * *

PERCIVAL, Walter 1896-

PERSONAL: Born July 31, 1896, in England; son of Joseph Ashton and Jane Ann (Jameson) Percival; married Elsie Street, August 2, 1927. *Education:* University of Manchester, B.A. (first class honors), 1922; Sorbonne, University of Paris, M.A., 1929. *Home:* 46 Belgrave Rd., Seaford, Sussex, England.

CAREER: French master at schools in Durham and London, England, 1924-37; Hornsey County School, London, England, headmaster, 1938-52; Tollington School, London, England, headmaster, 1952-60. Co-operative Holidays Association, resident secretary, 1921-26; University of London, examiner in French, 1962—. *Military service:* British Army, 1915-19. *Member:* Hornsey Schools Music Association (chairman, 1947-49), United Nations Association, Seaford Chess Club, Eastbourne and District Post Rotarians (vice-president, 1964, 1968-69), Lewes Liberal Association (president).

WRITINGS: (With L. G. Newton) *Chantons!,* Stainer & Bell, 1933; (with Newton) *Chantons Encore,* Stainer & Bell, 1934; (with Newton) *Five Carols for Christmas,* Stainer & Bell, 1935; *Five Little French Plays,* University of London Press, 1939; (with Erich Lewy) *English, a Handbook for the Foreigner,* Longmans, Green, 1947; *Mountain Memories,* Jacey Printers, 1962. Librettist, "Paradise Lost" (oratorio), with music by L. G. Newton. Contributor to *Contemporary Review.*

* * *

PEROSA, Sergio 1933-

PERSONAL: Born November 27, 1933, in Chioggia (Venice), Italy; married Alberta Bardella, August 8, 1960. *Education:* Ca'Foscari University, Doctor's Degree, 1957; Princeton University, postdoctoral study, 1957-58. *Home:* San Polo 1865, Venice, Italy. *Office:* Ca'Foscari University, Venice, Italy.

CAREER: Ca'Foscari University, Venice, Italy, lecturer in English, 1958-63, lecturer, 1963-68, professor of American literature and chairman of English department, 1968—; University of Trieste, Trieste, Italy, lecturer in English, 1961-66. *Member:* International Association of University Professors of English, Fulbright Association, Associazione Scrittori Veneti, Ateneo Veneto, Instituto Veneto di Scienze, Letters e Arti, European Advisory Committee, Salzburg Semino. *Awards, honors:* Fulbright fellowship; Lyly fellowship; Salzburg Seminar fellowship; Harvard International Seminar fellowship; American Council of Learned Societies fellowship.

WRITINGS: L'arte di F. Scott Fitzgerald, Edizione Storia e Letteratura, 1961 (English translation, *The Art of F. Scott Fitzgerald*, University of Michigan Press, 1965); (translator and author of introduction) Herman Melville, *L'uomo di fiducia*, Neri Pozza, 1961; (author of introduction) Emily Dickinson, *Poesie*, Nuova Accademia, 1961; (translator and author of introduction) Henry James, *La fonte sacra*, Neri Pozza, 1963; (editor and author of introduction and notes) Washington Irving, *Sketches and Tales*, Mursia, 1963; *La vie della narrativa americana*, Mursia, 1965; *Il teatro nord-americano*, Vallardi, 1966; (editor and author of introduction and notes) William Shakespeare, *Antony and Cleopatra*, Adriatica, 1968; (translator and author of introduction and notes) John Berryman, *Omaggio a Mistress Bradstreet*, Einaudi, 1969; *Storia della letteratura inglesse*, Volume I, Fabbri, 1969; *Antologia della letteratura inglesse*, Volume I, Fabbri, 1969; (translator and author of introduction and notes) Robert Penn Warren, *Racconto del Tempo e altre poesie*, Einaudi, 1971; (author of introduction) F. Rolfe, *Don Renato*, Longanesi, 1971; (translator and author of introduction and notes) John Berryman, *Canti del sogno e altre poesie*, Einaudi, in press. Contributor of essays on English and American literature to scholarly journals in Italy and the U.S. Book reviewer for English literature, *Il Resto del Carlino* (Bologna), 1966-69, *Il Corriere della Sera* (Milan), 1969—. Editor, *Annali di Ca'Foscari* (tri-quarterly), 1970—.

WORK IN PROGRESS: A critical study of Henry James, publication expected in 1975; an anthology of twentieth-century American poetry, publication expected in 1975.

* * *

PERRUCHOT, Henri 1917-1967

PERSONAL: Born January 27, 1917, in Montceau-les-Mines, Saone-et-Loire, France; son of Adrien (a railway officer) and Lucie (Bertrand) Perruchot; married Georgette Cuisinier, December 9, 1939. *Education:* Universite d'Aix-en-Provence, licence es lettres, 1941. *Home:* 24 rue Saint-Louis-en-l'Isle, Paris IV, France.

CAREER: Writer. *Military service:* French Army, 16e Regiment de Tirailleurs Senegalais, 1939-40. *Member:* Societe des Gens de Lettres de France, Syndicat des Ecrivains. *Awards, honors:* Chevalier de la Legion d'honneur; Chevalier de l'Ordre des arts et des lettres; Prix Charles-Blanc de l'Academie francaise, in 1961 for *La Vie de Manet*, in 1962 for *La Vie de Gauguin;* Grand Prix litteraire de la ville de Paris, 1963, for the entirety of his work.

WRITINGS: Le Maitre d'homme (novel), Jean Vigneau, 1946; *Patrice* (tale), Robert Cayla, 1947; *Port-Royal* (essay), Le Livre de Paris, 1947; *Gauguin* (monograph), Le Sillage, 1948; *Les Grotesques* (novel), Les 13 Epis, 1948; *Sous la lumiere noire* (short stories), Les 13 Epis, 1948; *L'Heroine* (poems), La Presse a Bras, 1948; *Introduction a l'epiphanisme* (essay), Le Sillage, 1949; *Le Theatre rose et noir de Jean Anouilh,* Gand Imprint, 1949; *Quatre poems pour l'heroine,* A l'Eveil de l'Homme, 1950; *La Haine des Masques* (essay), La Table Ronde, 1955; *Le Douanier Rousseau* (monograph), Editions Universitaires, 1957; *Le Corbusier,* Editions Universitaires, 1958; *La France et sa jeunesse* (essay), Hachette, 1958; *Montherlant* (essay), Gallimard, 1959, *Montefeltro, Duc d'Urbin* (essay), La Table Ronde, 1960; *Dix grands peintres: De Manet a Rouault* (essay), Gautier-Languereau, 1961; *Eduard Manet,* Barnes & Noble, 1962; *L'Art modern a travers le monde* (essay), Hachette, 1963; *Manet,* Bibliotheque Mara-

bout, 1964; *La peinture,* Hachette, 1965; *Cezanne,* Hachette, 1966.

"Art et Destin," all originally published by Hachette in France; translations by Humphrey Hare published as indicated: *La Vie de Van Gogh,* 1955, new edition, 1966; *La Vie de Cezanne,* 1956, translation published as *Cezanne,* Perpetua Books, 1961, World Publishing, 1962; *La Vie de Toulouse-Lautrec,* 1958, translation published as *Toulouse-Lautrec,* Perpetua Books, 1960, World Publishing, 1961; *La Vie de Manet,* 1959, translation published as *Manet,* Perpetua Books, 1962, World Publishing, 1963; *La Vie de Gauguin,* 1961, translation published as *Gauguin,* Perpetua Books, 1963, World Publishing, 1964; *La Vie de Renoir,* 1964; *La Vie de Seurat,* 1966. Editor, *Jardin des Arts.* Contributor to *Grand Dictionnaire Larousse* and to periodicals, including *Les Nouvelles litteraires, Le Figaro litteraire, La Revue des deux mondes, Realites, Larousse mensuel, La Revue de Paris.*

WORK IN PROGRESS: More books in the multi-volume "Art and Destiny" series; planned for the near future are lives of Rodin, Modigliani, and Picasso.

SIDELIGHTS: Perruchot wrote to *CA:* "I have always written, and I would not know how to do anything else but write. If I would not have been able to write, I would most certainly be dead. My life is restricted to my work. I live almost like a monk and do not go either to the movies, the theater, or concerts. It is only rarely that I accept an invitation, no matter what the nature of it might be. In short, I work from twelve to fifteen hours every day. Why should I seek entertainment? I am entrenched in all that I work at; I live my work with passion. Entertainment would be nothing but *ennui* for me. I live in solitude with the 1485 personages of the 'Art and Destiny' series. The appellations criticism bestows upon me are mounting up: for example, 'the Balzac of biography' (Yves Sjoberg), 'the Maigret of art history' (J.-P. Crespelle in *France-Soir*), 'The Plutarch of contemporary painting' *(Bulletin critique du livre francais),* and so on." His works have been translated into eleven languages.

BIOGRAPHICAL/CRITICAL SOURCES: Tableau de chasse, by R. P. Pirard, Editions Universitaires, 1961; *Henri Perruchot et le Destin Humain,* by Tristan Maya, Syntheses, 1963; *Henri Perruchot, l'homme et l'oeuvre,* by Vial, Maya, and Vandiest, Editions les Debats, 1963.†

(Died February 17, 1967)

* * *

PERRY, Louis B(arnes) 1918-

PERSONAL: Born March 4, 1918, in Los Angeles, Calif.; son of Louis Henry (a restaurant owner) and Julia (Stoddard) Perry; married Genevieve Patterson, February 8, 1942; children: Robert Barnes, Barbara Anne, Donna Lou. *Education:* University of California, Los Angeles, B.A., 1938, M.A., 1940, Ph.D., 1950; Yale University, graduate study, 1941. *Religion:* Congregational. *Home:* 515 Boyer Ave., Walla Walla, Wash. *Office:* Whitman College, Walla Walla, Wash.

CAREER: Pomona College, Claremont, Calif., member of faculty, 1947-59, assistant to president, 1955-57, professor of economics, 1955-59; Wagenseller & Durst, Los Angeles, Calif., investment counselor and broker, 1951-59; Whitman College, Walla Walla, Wash., president, 1959—. Research coordinator, Southern California Research Council, 1952-54; consultant, Carnegie Corp. Survey of Business Education, 1957-58. Member of board of directors of Walla Walla United Fund, 1959-62, of Chamber of Commerce, 1962—, of Community Service Council, 1963—. *Military service:* U.S. Army, 1941-46; became major; received Army Commendation Medal. U.S. Army Reserve, 1946—; now lieutenant colonel (inactive Reserve).

MEMBER: American Economic Association, Association of American Colleges (member of committee on liberal education, 1962—), Western Economic Association (member of executive committee, 1958-60), Southern California Economic Association (secretary-treasurer, 1949-50; vice-president, 1950-51; president, 1951-52), Phi Beta Kappa, Phi Delta Kappa, Pi Gamma Mu, Artus, Rotary International. *Awards, honors:* LL.D., Pacific University, 1964.

WRITINGS: (With others) *Our Needy Aged*, Henry Holt, 1954; (with brother, Richard S. Perry) *A History of the Los Angeles Labor Movement, 1911-1941*, University of California Press, 1963. Contributor to business, finance, education, and labor journals.

AVOCATIONAL INTERESTS: Outdoor activity "of a pressure-relieving nature," including upland bird hunting, stream fishing, and skiing.

* * *

PERRY, Octavia Jordan 1894-

PERSONAL: Born April 21, 1894, in Orange County, N.C.; daughter of Archibald Currie (a physician) and Octavia (Stroud) Jordan; married Charles W. Perry, April 16, 1919. *Education:* University of North Carolina Woman's College, Greensboro, B.Ed., 1916. *Politics:* Democrat. *Religion:* Presbyterian. *Home:* 1207 North Rotary Dr., High Point, N.C.

MEMBER: Historical Book Club of North Carolina (Greensboro), North Carolina Presbyterian Historical Society (Raleigh), Synod of North Carolina (Raleigh), Canterbury Study Club (High Point), Priscilla Club (High Point), and Mid-Week Garden Club (High Point).

WRITINGS: History of First Presbyterian Church of High Point, N.C., Hall Print, 1959; *My Head's High from Proudness*, Blair, 1963; *Saga of Strouds and Strodes* (genealogy), [Baltimore], 1966; *These Jordons Were Here* (genealogy), J. G. Stevenson, 1969. Also author of unpublished juvenile novels: *The Indian Bracelet, The Tuggles Family*, and *Flowerland Lays.*

WORK IN PROGRESS: A historical novel based on the life of Theodosia Burr Alston, entitled *The Baroness of Hobcaw*; an odyssey of the Lost Colony; *Robbie*, a story.

* * *

PERSON, Peter P. 1889-

PERSONAL: Born January 7, 1889, in Cooperstown, N.D.; son of Per (Hodal) and Margaret (Olson) Person; married Florence Couleur (a teacher), June 12, 1926. *Education:* Union Theological College, Chicago, Ill., B.Th., 1921; University of Chicago, B.Ph., 1925; Northwestern University, M.A., 1928; Harvard University, Ed.D., 1941. *Home:* 6158 North Moody, Chicago, Ill. 60646.

CAREER: North Park College, Chicago, Ill., member of staff, 1921-57. Ordained clergyman, Evangelical Covenant Church.

WRITINGS: An Introduction to Christian Education, Baker Book, 1958; *The Minister in Christian Education,*

Baker Book, 1960; *The Church and Modern Youth,* Zondervan, 1963.

WORK IN PROGRESS: Crossroads, a novel.

* * *

PETRIE, Alexander 1881-

PERSONAL: Born October 26, 1881, in Banffshire, Scotland; son of Thomas (a millwright) and Jane Ann (Allan) Petrie; married Robina Donald Rule, July 11, 1911; children: Ruby Margaret (Mrs. Graham Scott), Barbara Allan (Mrs. Howard Swan). *Education:* University of Aberdeen, M.A., 1903; Trinity College, Cambridge, B.A., 1907. *Politics:* United Party of South Africa. *Religion:* Presbyterian. *Home:* Victoria Club, Longmarket St., Pietermaritzburg, Natal, Republic of South Africa.

CAREER: University of Aberdeen, Aberdeen, Scotland, lecturer in Greek, 1908-10; Natal University College (now University of Natal), Pietermaritzburg, Natal, Republic of South Africa, professor of classics, 1910-48, professor emeritus, 1948—. *Member:* Victoria Club (Pietermaritzburg). *Awards, honors:* D.Litt., University of Natal, 1950.

WRITINGS: A Latin Reader, for Matriculation and Other Students, Oxford University Press, 1918; *Introduction to Roman History, Literature and Antiquities*, Oxford University Press, 1918, 3rd edition, 1963; (compiler) *Poems of South African History, A.D., 1497-1910*, Oxford University Press, 1919; (editor) *The Speech Against Leocrates*, Cambridge University Press, 1922; *Introduction to Greek History, Antiquities and Literature*, Oxford University Press, 1932, 2nd edition, 1962.

* * *

PEYTON, Karen (Hansen) 1897-196(?)

PERSONAL: Born October 16, 1897, in Duluth, Minn.; daughter of Christian and Siri (Tweeden) Hansen; divorced; children: Alan Morrison. *Education:* Attended schools in Duluth, Minn. *Religion:* Protestant. *Home:* 2805 South Ninth St., Arlington, Va. 22204. *Agent:* Miss Patricia Lewis, 200 West 34th St., New York, N.Y. 10001. *Office:* U. S. Coast Guard, 1300 E St., Washington, D.C. 20025.

CAREER: U.S. government employee, Washington, D.C., from 1938, legislative reference assistant, Office of the Commandant, U.S. Coast Guard, from 1954.

WRITINGS: The World So Fair, Chilton, 1963; *Love Song,* Chilton, 1964. Author of several short stories and many government articles.

WORK IN PROGRESS: Short stories; a novel, *The Vermillion Tree.*

(Deceased)

* * *

PFAFFENBERGER, Clarence J. 1889-1967

PERSONAL: Born April 25, 1889, in Brownstown, Ind.; son of Newton J. (a farmer) and Anna Louisa (Meyer) Pfaffenberger; married Juanita Glidden, January 20, 1924; children: Helenjoy, Kathleen (Mrs. Paul Kokezas). *Education:* Attended New Mexico Baptist College, 1909-10, University of Southern California, 1911-13, 1916-17, and University of California, Berkeley, intermittently, 1926-42. *Politics:* Democrat. *Religion:* Presbyterian. *Home:* 1446 Fifteenth Ave., San Francisco, Calif. *Office:* Guide Dogs for the Blind, Inc., P.O. Box 1200, San Rafael, Calif.

CAREER: American Trading Company, traveling representative in Central and South America, 1919-21; Frank Reid Motor Co., Modesto, Calif., sales and advertising manager, 1921-24; Genuine Electrical Sales and Equipment Co., president, 1924-26; San Francisco (Calif.) public schools, teacher of journalism, 1928-55; Dogs for Defense, regional director, 1942-48; Guide Dogs for the Blind, Inc., San Rafael, Calif., vice-president, 1946-67. American Kennel Club licensed breed, obedience, and field trial judge. Conductor of classes in dog behavior and in use and care of dogs. Military service: U.S. Army, 1917-19. Member: American Spaniel Club, English Springer Spaniel Field Trial Club, Northern California Field Trial Club, San Francisco Dog Training Club, Stockton English Spaniel Training Club. Awards, honors: "Fido" award as Dog Man of the Year, 1957; Guide Dogs Plaque for distinguished service to Guide Dogs for the Blind, Inc., 1958; Guggenheim fellowship to Roscoe B. Jackson Memorial Laboratory to evaluate and improve guide-dog puppy testing and training; Dog Writers Association of America award for best technical dog book, 1963, for New Knowledge of Dog Behavior.

WRITINGS: Training Your Spaniel, Putnam, 1946, revised edition, Howell Book, 1963; New Knowledge of Dog Behavior, Howell Book, 1963. Contributor of articles, columns, and sections to dog journals and to magazines, including American Field, Ladies' Home Journal, American Kennel Club Gazette, Argosy, Field and Stream, and American Weekly.

WORK IN PROGRESS: Principal investigator of research project, "Factors in the Success of Guide Dogs for the Blind," under U.S. Department of Health, Education, and Welfare research grant, 1961-66.

(Died September 9, 1967)

*   *   *

PHARES, Ross (Oscar) 1908-

PERSONAL: Born March 9, 1908, in Hornbeck, La.; son of James Kirk (a physician) and Sally (Gipson) Phares; married Eunice Elizabeth Russell, December 15, 1942. Education: Louisiana College, B.A., 1927; Peabody College for Teachers, M.A., 1929; postgraduate study at George Peabody College for Teachers, University of Chicago, Vanderbilt University, National University of Mexico. Residence: Houston, Tex. Agent: Edith Margolis, Lenniger Literary Agency, Inc., 437 Fifth Ave., New York, N.Y. 10016.

CAREER: High school principal, Sabine Parish, La.; parish supervisor of music, Winn Parish, La.; East Texas Baptist College, Marshall, professor of English and chairman of the division of languages and literature; Centenary College of Louisiana, Shreveport, director of publicity; in public relations and editor of various publications, Houston, Tex.; Rice University, Houston, Tex., editor of university publications; now full-time writer. Military service: U.S. Air Force, 1942-46; became officer. Member: Louisiana Historical Society, Texas Institute of Letters.

WRITINGS: Reverend Devil, a Biography of John A. Murrell, Pelican, 1941; Cavalier in the Wilderness: The Story of the Explorer and Trader Louis Juchereau de St. Denis, Louisiana State University Press, 1952; Texas Tradition, Holt, 1954; Bible in Pocket, Gun in Hand: The Story of Frontier Religion, Doubleday, 1964. Contributor to Texas Handbook and History of Natchitoches. Writer

and editor for commercial publications; author of three syndicated newspaper columns; contributor to magazines.

WORK IN PROGRESS: Two books.

AVOCATIONAL INTERESTS: Music (plays piano), tennis, and travel.

*   *   *

PHILLIPS, Emma Julia 1900-

PERSONAL: Born March 26, 1900, in Brownsburg, Ind.; daughter of John Wilbur and Arvia (Harbison) Phillips. Education: Indiana University, A.B. (with distinction), 1923, A.M., 1934, graduate study, 1956-58, Ph.D., 1967; University of Grenoble, Certificat d'etudes francaises and Diplome de hautes etudes, 1936; additional study at Western Reserve University (now Case Western Reserve University). Home: 313 South E St., Lake Worth, Fla.

CAREER: High school teacher in Indiana and Illinois, 1923-26, 1928-41; instructor in English, French, and Spanish at Centerville Community College, Centerville, Iowa, 1941-43, Itasca Junior College, Coleraine, Minn., 1943-46, Hazleton Campus of Pennsylvania State University, 1946-52, Palm Beach Junior College, Lake Worth, Fla., beginning 1958. Member: American Association of University Women, Phi Beta Kappa, Pi Lambda Theta.

WRITINGS: A Review of English Fundamentals, Holt, 1962.

AVOCATIONAL INTERESTS: Music, literature, travel.

*   *   *

PHILLIPS, Loretta (Hosey) 1893-

PERSONAL: Born April 17, 1893, in Southbridge, Mass.; daughter of William Joseph (a building contractor) and Katherine (Dempsey) Hosey; married Prentice Phillips (an artist and writer), December 23, 1917. Education: Attended Connecticut public schools and Norwich Art School, Norwich, Conn. Politics: Independent. Religion: Catholic. Home: 1060 Main St., Apt. 317, Worcester, Mass. 01603.

CAREER: Former fashion artist and illustrator of books for children; now writer-illustrator in collaboration with husband, Prentice Phillips.

WRITINGS: (With husband, Prentice Phillips) Two Silly Kings, Steck, 1964. Illustrator, with husband, of more than twenty books for children. The Phillipses also are creators of a panel feature, "They Made the Headlines," which appeared on alternate weeks in the Worcester Sunday Telegram for twenty years, and contributors of other illustrated features to Boston daily and Sunday newspapers, and to juvenile publications.

WORK IN PROGRESS: A picture book for children, Mother Goody and Doctor Smart; illustrated articles for New England Galaxy and Good Old Days (magazines).

*   *   *

PHILLIPS, Prentice 1894-

PERSONAL: Born May 15, 1894, in Plainfield, Conn.; son of Warren Winfield (a farmer) and Flora Bertha (Card) Phillips; married Loretta Hosey (a free-lance artist and writer), December 23, 1917. Education: Attended public schools in Plainfield, Conn. Politics: Independent. Religion: Catholic. Home: 1060 Main St., Apt. 317, Worcester, Mass. 01603.

CAREER: Commercial artist, owner and operator of art studio and advertising agency; free-lance writer and illustrator; former lecturer and teacher of cartooning and commercial art at Worcester Junior College, Worcester, Mass.

WRITINGS: (With wife, Loretta Phillips) *Two Silly Kings*, Steck, 1964. Illustrator with wife of more than twenty books for children. The Phillipses also are creators of a panel feature "They Made the Headlines," which appeared on alternate weeks in the *Worcester Sunday Telegram* for twenty years, and contributors of other illustrated features to Boston daily and Sunday newspapers and to juvenile publications.

WORK IN PROGRESS: A picture book for children, *Mother Goody and Doctor Smart*; illustrated articles for *New England Galaxy* and *Good Old Days* (magazines).

* * *

PICAZO, Jose 1910-

PERSONAL: Born July 2, 1910, in Madrid, Spain; son of Jose and Juana (Guillen) Picazo. *Education:* Universidades de Madrid y Oviedo, Licenciado en Derecho (LLB.), 1931. *Home:* Flat 6, Mere Park, Victoria Rd., Liverpool, England. *Office:* Liverpool Polytechnic, Faculty of Humanities and Social Studies, Tithebarn St., Liverpool, England.

CAREER: British Broadcasting Corp., London, England, Spanish commentator and broadcaster, 1940-43; The Polytechnic, London, England, lecturer in Spanish, 1943-49; Liverpool College of Commerce (now incorporated in Liverpool Polytechnic), Liverpool, England, 1949—, began as senior lecturer, became principal lecturer in Spanish language and literature. Examiner in Spanish to Cambridge University, 1955—. *Member:* Institute of Linguists (fellow; member of council), Royal Society of Arts (fellow), Spanish Society (Liverpool; chairman, 1949—). *Awards, honors:* Spanish insignia of Knight Commander of the Order of Civil Merit, in recognition of his work for Spanish studies.

WRITINGS: Spanish Irregular Verbs, Redman, 1944; (editor with C. E. Eckersley) *Essential English-Spanish Dictionary*, Longmans, Green, 1948; *El Folklore espanol*, Hirschfeld Brothers, 1953. General editor of French, Italian, German, and Spanish editions of *G.C.E. Examinations Papers for Translation*, University of London Press, 1958, and of French, German, and Spanish editions of *B. A. Examination Papers for Translation*, University of London Press, 1961. Founding editor of *El Clarin* (Anglo-Spanish educational and literary magazine published by College of Commerce, Liverpool), 1949—.

SIDELIGHTS: Picazo is fluent in Spanish, English, and French.

* * *

PICKETT, J(arrell) Waskom 1890-

PERSONAL: Born February 21, 1890, near Jonesville, Tex.; son of Leander Lycurgus (a minister and author) and Ludie (Day) Pickett; married Ruth Robinson, July 27, 1916; children: Elizabeth (Mrs. Henry Lacy), Miriam (Mrs. William Gould), Margaret (Mrs. John Sagan), Douglas. *Education:* Asbury College, Wilmore, Ky., A.B., 1907, A.M., 1908. *Politics:* Democrat. *Home:* 301 Parkwood Dr., Glendale, Calif. 91202.

CAREER: Methodist minister; Vilonia College, Vilonia, Ark., instructor in Latin and Greek, 1908-09; Taylor University, Upland, Ind., assistant professor of New Testament and Greek, 1909-10; Methodist Church, missionary pastor in Lucknow, India, 1910-14, district superintendent,

Arrah, India, 1916-23, editor and secretary of Regional Christian Council, 1925-29, secretary of National Christian Council of India, 1929-35, Bishop of Bombay, 1936-45, Bishop of Delhi, 1945-56; Boston University, Boston, Mass., professor of missions, 1957-60. Counselor in evangelism for Board of Missions for Asia, Africa, and Latin America, 1957-61. Consultant to Constitution Drafting Committee of Republic of India; organizer and leader of Christian Relief Committee in Delhi and North India during disturbances following partition; representative of Prime Minister Nehru in preliminary discussions with President Truman leading to wheat sales to avert famine in India, 1950. Investigator of missions in forty countries for Board of Missions and other organizations. Former president of National Christian Council, of Delhi Regional Christian Council, of Medical Council of Methodist Church in India, and of Council of Christian Education in India, 1936-56; former chairman of board of trustees, United Christian Schools of the Punjab, Union Mission Tuberculosis Sanitarium and Clara Swan Hospital; former member of board of governors, Isabella Thoborn College, Lucknow Christian College, Baring Union Christian College and Vellore Christian Medical College.

MEMBER: Asiatic Society of Bengal, Theological Society of Bombay, Church History Association of India, Pakistan and Ceylon. *Awards, honors:* D.D. from Ashbury College, 1925; LL.D. from Ohio Northern University, 1944.

WRITINGS: Christian Mass Movements in India: A Study with Recommendations, Abingdon, 1933; (with D. A. McGavran and G. H. Singh) *Christian Missions in Mid-India*, Lucknow Publishing (Lucknow, India), 1936, 3rd revised edition issued as *Church Growth and Group Conversion*, 1956; *Christ's Way to India's Heart*, S.C.M. Press, 1937; *The Dynamics of Church Growth*, Abingdon, 1963. Also contributor to *Moving Millions*, 1938, and *Lands of Witness and Decision*, 1957. Contributor to church periodicals, including *World Outlook*, *World Dominion* (London), *United Church Herald* (India), *Christian Advocate*. Editor, *Indian Witness*, 1925-29.

SIDELIGHTS: The Dynamics of Church Growth has been published in twelve languages.

* * *

PICKLES, M(abel) Elizabeth 1902-
(Elizabeth Burgoyne)

PERSONAL: Born August 19, 1902, in Halifax, Yorkshire, England; daughter of Angus and Sarah Jane (Keighley) Pickles. *Education:* Private study of music; A.R.C.M., 1924, L.R.A.M., 1927. *Politics:* "Usually vote Conservative." *Religion:* Church of England. *Home:* 94 Park Hill, Carshalton, Surrey, England.

CAREER: Private teacher of pianoforte in Halifax, Yorkshire, England, 1924-29, in Carshalton, Surrey, England, 1946—. During World War II worked for British War Office, Foreign Office, and Ministry of Information, and for British Broadcasting Corp. *Member:* Incorporated Society of Musicians, Society of Authors.

WRITINGS—All under pseudonym Elizabeth Burgoyne: *Travail* (fiction), Stanley Paul, 1934; *Road Royal* (fiction), Stanley Paul, 1935; *Carmen Sylva, Queen and Woman*, Eyre & Spottiswoode, 1941; *Gertrude Bell, from her Personal Papers, 1889-1914*, Benn, Volume I, 1958, Volume II, 1961.

WORK IN PROGRESS: Autobiography.

SIDELIGHTS: Miss Pickles writes: "[I] am very much concerned with liberty for the individual, noise abatement, homes (*not* institutions) for old people; but believing in individual effort I prefer to give what help I can to people known to me or near to me. I abhor all committees. I now prefer to read about foreign countries, and to make music in my own home." *Avocational interests:* Gardening and country walks.

*   *   *

PIERCY, Josephine Ketcham 1895-

PERSONAL: Born September 27, 1895, in Indianapolis, Ind.; daughter of Joseph William and Mary (Ketcham) Piercy. *Education:* The Western College for Women (now The Western College), student, 1914-16; Indiana University, A.B., 1918, M.A., 1919; Columbia University, M.A., 1922; Yale University, Ph.D., 1937. *Religion:* American Baptist. *Home:* 708 Ballantine Rd., Bloomington, Ind.

CAREER: Indiana University, Bloomington, instructor, 1926-40, assistant professor, 1940-50, associate professor, 1950-64, professor of English, 1964—. *Member:* Modern Language Association of America, College English Association, American Association of University Professors, Phi Beta Kappa, Theta Sigma Phi, Kappa Alpha Theta.

WRITINGS: Modern Writers at Work, Macmillan, 1930; *Studies in Literary Types in Seventeenth-Century America,* Yale University Press, 1939, 2nd edition, 1969; *Anne Bradstreet,* Twayne, 1965; (author of introduction) Anne Bradstreet, *The Tenth Muse,* Facsimile & Reprints, 1965; (author of introduction) Cotton Mather, *Bonifacius or Essays to Do Good,* Facsimile & Reprints, 1967; (author of introduction) Mather, *Christian Philosophy,* Facsimile & Reprints, 1969. Contributor to *Encyclopaedia Britannica,* 1974; also contributor of articles on seventeenth-century America to periodicals, including *New England Quarterly* and *Indiana University Review.*

AVOCATIONAL INTERESTS: Travel, seeing Broadway plays, and gardening.

*   *   *

PINNER, Erna 1896-

PERSONAL: Born January 27, 1896, in Frankfurt am Main, Germany; daughter of Oscar (a surgeon) and Anna (Roos) Pinner. *Education:* Educated privately, and at Academie Ransson, Paris, France. *Religion:* Jewish. *Home:* 3 Cleve House, Cleve Rd., London N.W. 6, England.

CAREER: Emigrated to England in 1935; author, and illustrator of animal life.

WRITINGS—Self-illustrated: Curious Creatures, J. Cape, 1951, Philosophical Library, 1953; *Born Alive,* J. Cape, 1959, Dodd, 1960; *Merkwurdiges aus dem Tierreich,* Kemper Verlag, 1964. Contributor to *Die Weltwoche, Die Tat, Naturwissenschaftliche-Rundschau.*

SIDELIGHTS: Books have been published in French, Danish, German, and Dutch editions.

BIOGRAPHICAL/CRITICAL SOURCES: Deutsche Exil-Literatur, 1933-45, Verlag Lambert Schneider, 1962, enlarged edition, 1970.

*   *   *

PINTO, Edward Henry 1901-1972

PERSONAL: Born July 12, 1901, in London, England; son of Jonathan Henry and Diamond May (Lee) Pinto; married Eva Levy, March 7, 1945 (died March, 1972). *Education:* Attended St. Paul's School, London, England. *Office:* Oxhey Woods House, Oxhey Dr., Northwood, Middlesex, England.

CAREER: Engaged in the building, decorating, and furnishing trades with the Bovis Holdings Group of companies in England, 1921-64, serving more than thirty years of that time as managing director of Compactom Ltd., and subsidiaries, and then as technical design and development consultant to the Bovis Holdings Group. Designed furniture, fitments, and decorative accessories for private homes on all continents, and for hotels, ships, and trains; during World War II was in charge of timber economy for the British Ministry of Works; in the post-war years specialized in the design of prefabricated partitioning and furniture for offices. Writer and lecturer on modern and antique furnishings, and on design and construction, 1945-72. Originator of Guild Mark Scheme and former chairman of Guild Mark committee; former chairman of London and South Eastern Furniture Manufacturers Association.

MEMBER: Royal Society of Arts (fellow), Freeman of City of London, Liveryman of the Worshipful Company of Turners, Worshipful Company of Furniture Manufacturers (founding member; former master).

WRITINGS: Wood Adhesives, Spon, 1948, popular edition, 1955; *Treen,* Batsford, 1949; (with wife, E. R. Pinto) *Care of Woodwork in the Home,* Benn, 1954; *Wooden Bygones of Smoking and Snuff Taking,* Hutchinson, 1961; *The Craftsman in Wood,* G. Bell, 1962; *The History of the Worshipful Company of Furniture Makers,* privately printed, 1964; *Treen and Other Wooden Bygones: An Encyclopedia and Social History,* G. Bell, 1969; (with E. R. Pinto) *Turnbridge and Scottish Souvenir Woodware,* G. Bell, 1970.

Contributor to *Furnisher's Encyclopaedia,* 1953, to *The Concise Encyclopaedia of Antiques,* Volume IV, 1959. Author of more than five hundred articles in British and American periodicals, including *Connoisseur, Antiques Review, Antiques, Country Life, Times* (London), *Ideal Home, Building Digest, British Plastics, Timber News.*

SIDELIGHTS: Almost one hundred thousand persons from all over the world have visited the Pintos' private collection of wooden bygones. They had received something like five thousand inquiries a year for information about the collection, which was open to the public four afternoons a week, April through September. Pinto began assembling it more than forty years ago.

(Died May 10, 1972)

*   *   *

PIPPETT, (Winifred) Aileen 1895-

PERSONAL: Born July 9, 1895, in London, England; daughter of Charles Henry (a clerk) and Eliya Alice (Searle) Side; married Roger Samuel Pippett (a literary critic, editor, and reader for Book-of-the-Month Club; died September 20, 1962). *Education:* Attended London School of Economics and Political Science. *Home:* 11 West Eighth St., New York, N.Y. 10011.

CAREER: Atlantic Transport Line, London, England, clerical positions, 1914-20; *Daily Herald,* London, England, editorial work, 1920-34; Odham's Press Ltd., London, England, editorial work, 1934-38; Marshall Field's Committee for English Children, New York, N.Y., receptionist and interviewer, 1940; Downtown Community School, New York, N.Y., executive assistant, 1941-45; Book-of-the-Month Club, New York, N.Y., reader, 1962—. *Member:* International P.E.N., National Society of Operative Printers and Assistants (London; former member of executive board), National Union of Journalists (London).

WRITINGS: The Moth and the Stars (biography of Virginia Woolf), Little, 1955, reprinted, Kraus Reprint, 1969. Contributor to *New York Times, Saturday Review, Vogue, Harper's.*

WORK IN PROGRESS: Criticism, biography, and fiction.

AVOCATIONAL INTERESTS: Child education and welfare, psychology, comparative religion, world affairs, law (strictly as an amateur).

*   *   *

PISK, Paul A(madeus) 1893-

PERSONAL: Born May 16, 1893, in Vienna, Austria; came to United States in 1936, naturalized in 1942; son of Ludwig (an attorney) and Jennie (Pollock) Pisk; married Irene Hanna; children: George. *Education:* University of Vienna, Ph.D.; Vienna Conservatory of Music, state music teacher's diploma and conductor's diploma. *Religion:* Presbyterian. *Home:* 2724 Westshire Dr., Los Angeles, Calif. 90068. *Office:* Department of Music, California State University, Northridge, Calif.

CAREER: People's University, Vienna, Austria, head of music department, 1922-34; teacher of theory at New Vienna Observatory, Vienna, Austria, 1925-26, at Austro-American Conservatory Mondsee, Salzburg, Austria, 1931-33; University of Redlands, Redlands, Calif., professor of music, 1937-50, director of School of Music, 1948-50; University of Texas, Austin, professor of music, 1951-63; Washington University, St. Louis, Mo., professor of music, 1963-72; California State University, Northridge, professor of music, 1972—. Pianist, appearing in International Music Festivals in Salzburg, Prague, Vienna, in Germany, and in United States; composer of orchestral, vocal, chamber music, and piano works; lecturer on music, and broadcaster. *Member:* American Musicological Society, American Composers Alliance, Renaissance Society of America, American Music Center.

WRITINGS: (With G. Adler) *Handbuch der musik Geschichte*, Hesse, 1930; *Denkmaler der Tonkunst in Austria*, four volumes, Austrian State Publishers, 1935-1961; (with Homer Ulrich) *History of Music and Musical Style*, Harcourt, 1963. Musical works published in Austria, Germany, Uruguay, and by ten publishers in United States. Contributor of articles and reviews to musical journals.

*   *   *

PITCHER, Gladys 1890-
(Betsy Adams, Barbara Wentworth, Ann Weston)

PERSONAL: Born December 11, 1890, in Belfast, Me.; daughter of Elbridge Simmons (a music teacher) and Emma B. (a music teacher; maiden name, Pitcher) Pitcher. *Education:* Studied piano and violincello privately, 1907-12; New England Conservatory of Music, diploma (with honors), 1911, additional study, 1911-12, 1922. *Politics:* Republican. *Religion:* Congregationalist. *Home and office:* 1 Northport Ave., Belfast, Me. 04915.

CAREER: High school music teacher in Chelsea, Mass., 1912-13; Beloit College, Beloit, Wis., chairman of music department and acting dean of women, 1917-19; music edu-

cator in public schools at Passaic, N.J., 1920-21, Bennington, Vt., 1922-24, Manchester, N.H., 1924-25; C.C. Birchard & Co. (publishers of music and music textbooks), Boston, Mass., began as member of editorial staff, 1925, editor-in-chief, 1946-56; free-lance composer, arranger, editor, and consultant, 1956—. Member of board of managers, Boston Port and Seaman's Society, 1956-63. *Member:* National Music Education Association, American Musicological Society, Music Educators National Conference, Bookbuilders of Boston (chairman, 1950; chairman of workshop, 1950-51), Boston Music Publishers Association, Victoria Society of Maine Women, Pi Kappa Lambda, Alpha Chi Omega, Boston Art Club, University Club (Boston), Belfast Business Women's Club, Traveller's Club.

WRITINGS: (Editor with Theresa Armitage and Peter W. Dykema) *Merry Music*, C. C. Birchard, 1939, 2nd edition, 1943; (editor with Armitage and Dykema) *Our Songs*, C. C. Birchard, 1939, new edition, 1952; (editor with Armitage and Dykema) *We Sing*, C. C. Birchard, 1940; (editor with others) *Our First Music*, C. C. Birchard, 1941; (editor with others) *Our Land of Song*, C. C. Birchard, 1942; (compiler) *Music Everywhere: Songs of Texas with Accompaniments*, C. C. Birchard, 1948; *Playtime in Song: Folk Songs in Simple Dance and Play Patterns*, M. Witmark, 1959; (arranger) *People and Song*, Harold Flammer, 1960; (editor, compiler, and arranger) *30 Old and New Christmas Carols*, G. Schirmer, 1960-61; *Not Too High, Not Too Low*, Harold Flammer, 1961; *Long Wharf Songs*, Willis Music Co., 1962; *The Bay Book*, Willis Music Co., 1964; *Day of Gladness* (Christmas cantata), Willis Music Co., 1968. Managing editor, "A Singing School" series of music textbooks, C. C. Birchard, 1936-40. Consultant, "This Is Music," Allyn & Bacon, 1959—.

WORK IN PROGRESS: Choral octavo numbers.

AVOCATIONAL INTERESTS: Sketching and sailing.

*   *   *

PITTER, Ruth 1897-

PERSONAL: Born November 7, 1897, in Ilford, Essex, England; daughter of George and Louisa R. (Murrell) Pitter. *Education:* Attended secondary school in London, England. *Politics:* "None, I go for the best *man. Religion:* Anglican. *Home and office:* 71 Chilton Rd., Long Crendon, Aylesbury, Bucks, England.

CAREER: War Office, London, England, temporary clerk, 1916-18; Walberswick Peasant Pottery Co., Walberswick, Suffolk, and London, England, painter, 1918-30; Deane & Forester, Chelsea, London, England, working partner, painting gift goods and furniture, 1930—. *Awards, honors:* Hawthornden Prize, 1937, *A Trophy of Arms;* Heinemann Award, 1954, for *The Ermine;* Queen's Gold Medal for Poetry, 1955, for general merit.

WRITINGS—Poems: First Poems, C. Palmer, 1920; *First and Second Poems* (preface by Hilaire Belloc), Doubleday, 1930; *Persephone in Hades*, privately printed, 1931; *A Mad Lady's Garland* (foreword by John Masefield, preface by Belloc), Cresset, 1934, Macmillan, 1935; *A Trophy of Arms* (preface by James Stephens), Macmillan, 1936, new edition, 1937; *The Spirit Watches*, Cresset, 1939, Macmillan, 1940; *The Rude Potato*, Cresset, 1941; *The Bridge*, Cresset, 1945, Macmillan, 1946; *On Cats*, Cresset, 1947; *Urania*, Ambassador, 1951; *The Ermine*, Cresset, 1953; *Poems 1926-66*, Barrie & Rockcliff, 1968, published as *Collected Poems*, Macmillan, 1969. Contributor to various periodicals.

WORK IN PROGRESS: More poems.

SIDELIGHTS: In his review of *Poems 1926-66* in *Books and Bookmen*, Derek Stafford quotes Miss Pitter "'I think a real poem, however simple its immediate content, begins and ends in mystery.'" Noting that her first poem was published in *New Age* when she was only fourteen, he adds: "Miss Pitter is melodious and eloquacious—a mystically-minded writer with a healthy respect for the hard facts.... Her pinioned longing to possess the transcendental is beautifully balanced by a lovely earthy humor."

Miss Pitter wrote *CA*: "I face a peculiar dilemma. I am 'square,' and can't bear the 'with-it.' But somehow the 'with-it' makes the 'square' seem out of focus anyway. Result suspension, and liability not to care; can always grow cabbage or make a cake. Not literary, hate paper and fight to keep it down." As for membership organizations, they are "carefully avoided. I lurk in undergrowth."

Recordings of her poems are available at the libraries of Yale and Harvard.

* * *

PLATTEN, Thomas George 1899-

PERSONAL: Born August 1, 1899, in Great Yarmouth, England; son of George and Florence (Smith) Platten; married Alice Mary Dixon, August 23, 1934; children: Christopher, Felicity Platten Belward, Geoffrey, Margaret, David. *Education:* St. John's College, Cambridge, B.A., 1922, M.A., 1927. *Home:* High St., Lower Brailes, Banbury, England.

CAREER: Ordained deacon of Church of England, 1923, priest, 1924; St. Chrysostom's Church, Manchester, England, curate, 1923-27; Trinity College, Kandy, Ceylon, assistant master, 1928-32; College of St. Mark and St. John, Chelsea, London, England, chaplain and tutor, 1932-36; Madras Christian College, Madras, India, professor of physics, 1936-46; St. Peter's College, Saltley, Birmingham, England, principal, 1947-68.

WRITINGS: Christianity and Mental Healing: An Answer to the Claims of Christian Science, Macmillan, 1928; *The Growth of the Kingdom: Lessons on Christian History*, Heffer, 1928; *The Odyssey of Israel: The Story of the Old Testament for Modern Readers*, Macmillan, 1936; "The Living Faith" series, published by University of London Press: *Jesus and His People*, 1959, *The Promised King*, 1959, *Messengers of the Kingdom*, 1960, *Believing and Living*, 1961; *A Faith for Today*, University of London Press, 1965; *The Word and the World*, University of London Press, 1967. Regular reviewer of religious books, *Teacher*.

* * *

POIS, Joseph 1905-

PERSONAL: Born December 25, 1905, in New York, N.Y.; son of Adolph and Augusta (Lesser) Pois; married Rose Tomarkin, June 24, 1928; children: Robert August, Marc Howard. *Education:* University of Wisconsin, A.B., 1926; University of Chicago, M.A., 1927, Ph.D., 1929; Chicago-Kent College of Law (now incorporated in Illinois Institute of Technology), LL.B., 1934. *Home:* 825 Morewood Ave., Pittsburgh, Pa. 15213.

CAREER: J. L. Jacobs & Co. (management consultants and engineers), Chicago, Ill., member of staff, 1929-35; admitted to Illinois bar, 1934; Public Administration Service, Chicago, Ill., general field supervisor, 1935-38; U.S. Bureau of Old Age and Survivors Insurance, Washington,

D.C., chief of administrative studies section, 1938-39; U.S. Bureau of the Budget, Executive Office of the President, Washington, D.C., chief of Administrative and Fiscal Reorganization Section, 1939-42; J. L. Jacobs & Co., junior partner, 1946-47; Signode Steel Strapping Co., Chicago, Ill., 1947-61, began as counsel and assistant to the president, became vice-president, treasurer, and director; State of Illinois, Springfield, director of finance, 1951-53; University of Pittsburgh, Pittsburgh, Pa., professor of public administration, 1961—, acting dean of Graduate School of Public and International Affairs, 1973—. Part-time instructor or lecturer at Cornell University, University of California, University of Wisconsin, and other schools; member of Advisory Committee on International Organization, U.S. State Department, 1962-65; consultant to other government departments and agencies, including Economic Cooperation Administration, 1948, Department of Defense, 1954, U.S. Agency for International Development, 1965; consultant to Brookings Institution, 1962-63, governor of Virgin Islands, 1964; member of executive committee, Taxpayers Federation of Illinois, 1953-61; Metropolitan Housing and Planning Council of Chicago, vice-president, 1955-56, president, 1956-57. Member of citizens committee of University of Illinois, 1955-60, Chicago Board of Education, 1956-61, citizens board of University of Chicago, 1958—, and Pittsburgh Board of Public Education, 1973—. *Military service:* U.S. Coast Guard Reserve, active duty, 1942-46; became captain.

MEMBER: American Academy of Political and Social Science, American Accounting Association, American Bar Association, American Political Science Association, American Society for Public Administration, National Association of Accountants, Federal Bar Association, Financial Executives Institute, Royal Institute of Public Administration (United Kingdom), Allegheny County Bar Association.

WRITINGS: (With Edward M. Martin and Lyman S. Moore) *The Merit System in Illinois*, Joint Committee on the Merit System (Chicago), 1935; *Public Personnel Administration in the City of Cincinnati*, 1936; *Kentucky Handbook of Financial Administration*, 1937; *Financial Administration in the Michigan State Government*, 1938; (author of appendix) David T. Stanley and others, *Professional Personnel for the City of New York*, Brookings, 1963; *The School Board Crisis: A Chicago Case Study*, Educational Methods, 1964. Contributor to social science and other professional journals.

* * *

POLACK, Albert Isaac 1892-

PERSONAL: Born April 4, 1892, in Bristol, England; son of Joseph and Sophia (Isaac) Polack; married Beatrice Cohen, April 30, 1922; children: Benjamin, Irene Polack Aitman, Patricia, Ernest. *Education:* Attended Clifton College; Cambridge University, M.A., 1919. *Politics:* Liberal. *Religion:* Judaism. *Home:* 24 Sandy Lodge Way, Northwood, Middlesex, England. *Office:* Council of Christians and Jews, 41 Cadogan Gardens, London, England.

CAREER: Schoolmaster at Taunton School, Somerset, England, 1920-23, at Clifton College, Bristol, England, 1923-49; Council of Christians and Jews, London, England, education officer, 1949—. *Military service:* Royal Engineers, 1914-19; became first lieutenant. *Member:* Royal Commonwealth Society.

WRITINGS: Tolerance: Can It Be Taught?, Council of

Christians and Jews, 1951, 3rd edition, 1960; (with W. W. Simpson) *Jesus in the Background of History,* Cohen & West, 1957, R. M. McBride Co., 1959.

WORK IN PROGRESS: With W. W. Simpson, *A Short History of Post-Biblical Judaism.*

* * *

POLK, Mary   1898-

PERSONAL: Born December 15, 1898, in Warrenton, N.C.; daughter of Tasker (a lawyer) and Eliza (Jones) Polk; married Frank Gibbs, December 15, 1921 (deceased); children: Mary Tasker (Mrs. Barnaby McAuslan), Frank. *Education:* Columbia University, student, 1919, 1920, 1921. *Politics:* "Southern Democrat." *Religion:* Episcopalian. *Home:* Main St., Warrenton, N.C. 27589.

CAREER: Part-time librarian.

WRITINGS: The Way We Were, Blair, 1962. Contributor of poetry and short stories to *Harper's Bazaar* and other magazines.

WORK IN PROGRESS: My Dooryard Birds.

AVOCATIONAL INTERESTS: Painting.

* * *

POLLACK, Ervin H(arold)   1913-1972

PERSONAL: Born April 19, 1913, in St. Louis, Mo.; son of Jacob M. (a contractor) and Tillie (Padratzik) Pollack; married Lydia Irene Weiss (a teacher), June 12, 1940; children: Jay R., Joan N. *Education:* Attended St. Louis University, 1932-35; Washington University, St. Louis, Mo., LL.B., 1939; Columbia University, graduate study, 1939-41. *Home:* 2276 Hoxton Ct., Columbus, Ohio 43221. *Office:* Ohio State University, 1659 North High St., Columbus, Ohio 43201.

CAREER: Admitted to Missouri bar, 1939; Hays, Podell & Schulman, New York, N.Y., librarian, 1942; U.S. Office of Price Administration, Washington, D.C., secretary, 1942-47; Ohio State University, Columbus, assistant professor of law, 1947-50, associate professor, 1950-54, professor, 1954-72, law librarian 1947-59, director of research services, 1959-72. Consultant to Office of Economic Stabilization, 1951, Library of Congress, 1959-64, and to various law libraries. Trustee of Ohio Legal Center, 1961-72, fellow of Ohio State Bar Association Foundation 1964-72. *Member:* American Association of Law Libraries (president 1958-59), American Association for Legal and Political Philosophy, International Association for Philosophy of Law and Social Philosophy, American Bar Association, Ohio Bar Association, Ohio Association of Law Libraries (president, 1949-51), Order of the Coif.

WRITINGS: (Editor) *Ohio Court Rules Annotated,* Dennis, 1949; *Legal Research and Materials* (Ohio edition), Allen Smith, 1950; *Ohio Unreported Judicial Decisions Prior to 1823,* Allen Smith, 1952; *Fundamentals of Legal Research,* Foundation Press, 1956, 3rd edition, 1967; (editor) *Brandeis Reader,* Oceana, 1956. Editorial director, Office of Price Administration service and desk books, 1942-47. Contributor to legal and library journals.

WORK IN PROGRESS: Two books on jurisprudence.

(Died June 9, 1972)

* * *

POLLARD, James E(dward)   1894-

PERSONAL: Born October 25, 1894, in Chambersburg,

Pa.; son of James Joseph and Anna Mary (Eby) Pollard; married Marjorie O. Pearson, 1918 (died, 1945); married Founta Davis Greene, 1947; children: (first marriage) Mary Margaret (Mrs. Richard C. Dale), David Edward; stepchildren: Charles N. Greene, Jr. *Education:* Ohio State University, B.A., 1916, M.A., 1917, Ph.D., 1939. *Politics:* Republican. *Religion:* Congregationalist. *Home:* 2033 Bedford Rd., Columbus, Ohio. *Office:* Ohio State University, 1858 Neil Ave., Columbus, Ohio.

CAREER: Assistant city editor in Canton, Ohio, 1917, and copy editor for Associated Press, 1917-19; *Ohio State Journal,* Columbus, assistant city editor and telegraph editor, 1920-23; Ohio State University, Columbus, director of news bureau, 1923-33, associate professor, 1932-34, acting director of School of Journalism, 1934-38, professor and director of School of Journalism, 1938-58, professor of journalism and university historian, 1958-65, professor emeritus, 1965—. Staff member, U.S. Civil Service Commission, 1937; visiting instructor, University of Southern California, summer, 1940. *Military service:* U.S. Army, 1917, 1918-19; served in France and Germany.

MEMBER: Association for Education in Journalism, Ohioana Library Association, Kappa Tau Alpha, Pi Delta Epsilon, Pi Kappa Alpha, Sigma Delta Chi. *Awards, honors:* Sigma Delta Chi award for research in journalism, 1947; Ohioana Award in biography from Ohioana Library Association, 1956, for *William Oxley Thompson*; distinguished service award, Ohio State University, 1965.

WRITINGS: History, 47th U.S. Infantry, Seaman & Peters, 1920; *The Journal of Jay Cooke,* Ohio State University Press, 1935; *Principles of Newspaper Management,* McGraw, 1937; (with E. M. Martin) *Newspaper Laws of Ohio,* Ohio State University Press, 1937; *The Newspaper as Defined by Law,* Ohio State University Press, 1940; (coauthor) *History of the State of Ohio,* Volume VI, Heer Printing, 1941; (editor) *Index of Public Notice Laws of the Forty-Eight States,* two volumes, Ohio State University, 1942; *The Presidents and the Press,* Macmillan, 1947, Octagon Books, 1973.

History of The Ohio State University, 1873-1948, Ohio State University Press, 1952; (with E. M. Martin) *Ohio Newspaper and Publication Laws,* Ohio State University Press, 1954; *William Oxley Thompson: Evangel of Education* (biography), Ohio State University Press, 1955; *Ohio State Athletics, 1879-1959,* Ohio State University Press, 1959; *Military Training in the Land-Grant Colleges,* Association of State Universities and Land-Grant Colleges, 1964; *The Presidents and the Press—Truman to Johnson,* Public Affairs, 1964; *The Bevis Administration,* privately printed, Part I (1940-45), 1971, Part II (1945-56), 1972.

Writer of pamphlets on newspapers and the law. Contributor to *Dictionary of American Biography, Encyclopedia Americana.* Also contributor to professional journals and other periodicals. Editor of *Ohio Newspaper,* 1935-60.

* * *

POPKIN, John William   1909-

PERSONAL: Born October 6, 1909, in Winnipeg, Manitoba, Canada; son of John and Charlotte Popkin; married; wife's name, Elizabeth; children: John David James. *Education:* Brandon College, B.A., 1929; Queen's University, Kingston, Ontario, B. Comm., 1930; McGill University, M.A., 1936. *Religion:* Anglican. *Residence:* Montreal, Quebec, Canada.

CAREER: Sun Life Assurance Co. of Canada, Montreal, Quebec, economist, 1956—. Director of Canadian School Trustees Association, 1964—; president of Quebec Association of Protestant School Boards, 1964. *Military service:* Royal Canadian Air Force, navigation instructor, World War II. *Member:* Canadian Political Science Association.

WRITINGS: Non-Merchandise Transactions Between Canada and the United States, National Planning Association and Private Planning Association, 1963. Contributor of articles on business outlook to magazines.

*   *   *

POPPLETON, Marjorie 1895-

PERSONAL: Born April 29, 1895, in London, England; daughter of George and Mary Elizabeth (Lang) Poppleton. *Education:* Attended Maria Grey Training College, London, National Froebel Union Higher Certificate, 1917; Merrill-Palmer Institute, Detroit, Mich., graduate course in child development, 1927. *Religion:* Church of England. *Home:* Avebury, Near Marlborough, Wiltshire, England.

CAREER: Teacher of juniors at schools in England, 1917-23, 1924-26; British Home for Austrian Children, Liezen, Styria, Austria, interpreter and secretary, 1923-24; Childrens' Community Center, New Haven, Conn., staff member, 1926-27; Belmont Country Day School, Belmont, Mass., head, 1927-28; University of Toronto, St. George's School for Child Study (now Institute of Child Study), Toronto, Ontario, secretary, 1928-47.

WRITINGS: (With J. M. Waterman) *We Go to Nursery School*, Morrow, 1935; *Where's Patsy?*, Oxford University Press (Toronto), 1946; *Ten Tales for the Very Young*, University of London Press, 1952; *Rumpelstiltskin Told Again* (play), privately published, 1962. Contributor of short stories to children's magazines and articles for parents to adult periodicals.

WORK IN PROGRESS: Another book for very young children.

SIDELIGHTS: Stories from *Ten Tales for the Very Young* were broadcast in Australia and New Zealand, 1962-64.

*   *   *

POSEY, Walter B(rownlow) 1900-

PERSONAL: Born October 22, 1900, in Smyrna, Tenn.; son of Wilson Yandell (a merchant and farmer) and Myrtle (Omohundro) Posey; married Margaret Grisham, September 1, 1926; children: Blythe (Mrs. Jack Pearce Ashmore, Jr.). *Education:* University of Chicago, Ph.B., 1923; Vanderbilt University, M.A., 1930, Ph.D., 1933. *Religion:* Methodist. *Home:* 1107 Oxford Rd., N.E., Atlanta, Ga. 30306.

CAREER: Cumberland University, Lebanon, Tenn., instructor in economics, 1923-25; Birmingham-Southern College, Birmingham, Ala., assistant professor, 1925-28, associate professor, 1928-32, professor of history and head of department, 1932-43; Agnes Scott College, Decatur, Ga., professor of history and head of department, 1943-70; Emory University, Atlanta, Ga., professor of history, 1948-69. Exchange professor, University of Hawaii, 1939-40; instructor, Shrivenham American University, England, 1945; civilian lecturer in Europe for U.S. Army, 1946; instructor in Germany and England for University of Maryland Overseas Program, 1953-54.

MEMBER: American Historical Association, Southern Historical Association (member of executive council, 1934-36), Organization of American Historians (member of executive council, 1938-41), Phi Beta Kappa, Lambda Chi Alpha. *Awards, honors:* L.H.D. from Birmingham-Southern College, 1955.

WRITINGS: The Development of Methodism in the Old Southwest, Weatherford Printing, 1933; *The Presbyterian Church in the Old Southwest, 1778-1838*, John Knox, 1952; (co-editor) *Travels in the Old South*, Volume II, University of Oklahoma Press, 1956; *The Baptist Church in the Lower Mississippi Valley, 1776-1845*, University of Kentucky Press, 1957; *Religious Strife on the Southern Frontier*, Louisiana State University Press, 1965; *Frontier Mission: A History of Religion West of the Southern Appalachians to 1861*, University of Kentucky Press, 1966. Member of board of editors of Southern Historical Association, 1938-42.

WORK IN PROGRESS: Religion in the Old South.

*   *   *

POSIN, Daniel Q. 1909-

PERSONAL: Born August 13, 1909, in Turkestan; came to United States in 1918, naturalized in 1927; son of Abram and Anna (Izritz) Posin; married Frances Schweitzer, 1934; children: Daniel Q., Jr., Kathryn. *Education:* University of California, Berkeley, A.B., 1932, A.M., 1934, Ph.D., 1935. *Home:* 726 Crestview Dr., Millbrae, Calif. 94030. *Office:* San Francisco State University, San Francisco, Calif. 94132.

CAREER: University of California, Berkeley, instructor in physics, 1932-37; University of Panama, Panama City, professor, 1937-41; Montana State University, Missoula, professor, 1941-44, chairman of department of physics and mathematics, 1942-44; Massachusetts Institute of Technology, Cambridge, staff member of Radiation Laboratory, 1944-47; North Dakota State College, Fargo, professor of physics and chairman of department, 1946-55; DePaul University, Chicago, Ill., professor of physics, 1956-67; San Francisco State University, San Francisco, Calif., professor of physical science, 1967—, chairman of department of interdisciplinary science, 1969—. Science lecturer on Columbia Broadcasting System radio and television, and on WTTW, Chicago (educational television), 1956-67, conducted American Broadcasting System television series, "Dr. Posin's Universe"; director of Schwab Space Age Science Lecture Program at Museum of Science and Industry, Chicago; science consultant, *World Book Encyclopedia, Encyclopaedia Britannica, Jr., Compton's Yearbook*, Borg Warner Science Hall, Allied Chemical Science Hall, Columbia Broadcasting System; chairman of education committee, Chicago Heart Association, 1963-67; trustee, Leukemia Society. *Member:* American Physical Society (fellow), American Association for the Advancement of Science, Phi Beta Kappa, Sigma Xi. *Awards, honors:* Six Emmy Awards from National Academy of Television Arts and Sciences, including awards as best educator in television and conductor of best educational program, James T. Grady Award from American Chemical Society, 1972.

WRITINGS: Mendeleyev: The Story of a Great Scientist, McGraw, 1948; *I Have Been to the Village*, privately printed, 1948; *Out of This World*, Popular Mechanics, 1949; *What is a Star*, Benefic Press, 1961; *What is Chemistry*, Benefic Press, 1961; *What is a Dinosaur*, Benefic Press, 1961; *Physics: Its Marvels and Mysteries*, Whitman, 1961; *Chemistry for the Space Age*, Lippincott, 1961, revised edition, with Marc Shampo, Lippincott, 1964; *Experiments and Exercises in Chemistry*, Lippincott, 1961; *What is Electronic Communication*, Benefic Press, 1961; *Dr. Posin's Giants: Men of Science*, Row, Peterson, 1961; *What is Matter*, Benefic Press, 1962; *What is Energy*, Benefic Press, 1962; *Life Beyond Our Planet*, McGraw, 1962; *Man and the Desert*, Lyons & Carnahan, 1962; *Man and the Sea*, Lyons & Carnahan, 1963; *Man and the Earth*, Lyons & Carnahan, 1963; *Man and the Jungle*, Lyons & Carnahan, 1963; *Find Out! First Step to the Future*, Whitman, 1964; *Science in the Age of Space*, Quadrangle, 1965; *Exploring and Understanding Rockets and Satellites*, Benefic Press, 1967. Contributor to *Physical Review*, *Chemtech*, and *Today's Health*.

*   *   *

POST, C(harles) Gordon   1903-

PERSONAL: Born November 22, 1903, in San Juan, Puerto Rico; son of Charles Gordon (an architect) and Lottie (Munson) Post; married Emily Dohme, December 3, 1927; children: Claudia (Mrs. John Hannah), Regan (Mrs. Robert Leydenfrost), Antonia (Mrs. Brooks Fiske), Olivia (Mrs. Preston M. Fiske). *Education:* Johns Hopkins University, A.B., 1925, Ph.D., 1933; London School of Economics and Political Science, University of London, postgraduate study, 1930. *Politics:* Republican. *Religion:* Unitarian. *Home:* Wells Rd., Aurora, N.Y. 13026. *Office:* Macmillan Hall, Wells College, Aurora, N.Y. 13026.

CAREER: Johns Hopkins University, Baltimore, Md., instructor in political science, 1931-33; Vassar College, Poughkeepsie, N.Y., instructor, 1933-36, assistant professor, 1936-42, associate professor, 1942-48, professor of political science and chairman of the department, 1948-69. Summer professor at Barnard College, Colgate University, Johns Hopkins University, and Cornell University; Campbell Visiting Professor of Government, Wells College, 1969-71.

WRITINGS: The Supreme Court and Political Questions, Johns Hopkins Press, 1936; (editor with Emerson David Fite) *Cases on the Constitution,* Vassar College, 1937; (with Fite) *Syllabus: American Federal Government, British Government,* Vassar College, 1937; (with Henry Noble MacCracken) *Fair Play: An Introduction to Race and Group Relations,* privately printed, 1942; *Introduction to Government Syllabus,* Vassar College, 1946; (editor with Frances P. De Lancy and Fredryc R. Darby) *Twenty Cases on the Constitution for an Introductory Course in American Government,* Vassar College, 1946, revised edition published as *Basic Constitutional Cases,* Oxford University Press, 1948; (editor) *Calhoun's Disquisition of Government,* Bobbs-Merrill, 1957; (editor and author of introduction) *Significant Cases in British Constitutional Law,* Liberal Arts Press, 1957; *An Introduction to the Law,* Prentice-Hall, 1963.

WORK IN PROGRESS: A study on the right to privacy.

AVOCATIONAL INTERESTS: English literature.

*   *   *

POST, Gaines   1902-

PERSONAL: Born March 7, 1902, in Haskell, Tex.; son of Henry S. (a banker) and Rachel (Ballard) Post; married Katherine Rike, July 6, 1935; children: John Frederic, Gaines, Jr. *Education:* University of Texas, B.A., 1924; Harvard University, M.A., 1925, Ph.D., 1931; Ecole des

Chartes, Paris, France, advanced study, 1927-28. *Politics:* Independent. *Religion:* Protestant. *Home:* 408 North Ave. E., Haskell, Tex. 79521.

CAREER: Harvard University, Cambridge, Mass., instructor and tutor in history, 1929-35; University of Wisconsin, Madison, assistant professor, 1935-38, associate professor, 1938-41, professor of history, 1941-64; Princeton University, Princeton, N.J., professor of history, 1964-70; professor emeritus, 1970—. Institute for Advanced Study, Princeton, N.J., fellow, 1959-60. *Member:* Mediaeval Academy of America (fellow), American Academy of Arts and Sciences (fellow), American Historical Association, Heidelberg Akademie der Wissenschaften (corresponding member). *Awards, honors:* Fulbright award for research in France, 1951-52; Guggenheim fellowship, 1939-40, 1955-56.

WRITINGS: Studies in Medieval Legal Thought: Public Law and the State, Princeton University Press, 1964. Contributor of articles on medieval learning to learned journals.

WORK IN PROGRESS: Further studies of medieval public law.

*   *   *

POTTER, John Mason   1907-

PERSONAL: Born April 25, 1907, in Bridgton, Me.; son of Charles Henry (a mailman) and J. Maud (Downs) Potter; married Mary Louise Dowdell, June 9, 1935; children: Mary Louise. *Education:* Boston University, student, 1927; Harvard University, extension courses, 1929-30. *Religion:* Methodist. *Home:* 611 East State St., Ithaca, N.Y. *Office:* Department of English, Hunter College of City University of New York, 695 Park Ave., New York, N.Y. 10021.

CAREER: Boston Globe, Boston, Mass., writer, 1928-46; Robert Playfair Associates (public relations), Boston, Mass., vice-president, 1946-47; *Boston Post,* Boston, Mass., feature writer, 1947-56; Harvard University, Cambridge, Mass., assistant news director, 1956-57; Cornell University, Ithaca, N.Y., news director, 1957-64; Ithaca College, Ithaca, N.Y., became director of public information; now member of faculty, Hunter College of City University of New York, New York, N.Y. Instructor in journalism, Massachusetts University Extension, 1945-46, Boston University, 1953-54. Former chairman, Ivy League Public Relations committee. *Member:* American Public Relations Association, Boston Newspaper Guild (former vice-president), Cambridge Press Club (former president). *Awards, honors:* National citation of Education Writers Association, 1954.

WRITINGS: Quiz Me Again, Boston Newspaper Guild, 1945; *Thirteen Desperate Days,* Obolensky, 1964; *Plots Against Presidents,* Astor-Honor, 1968. Contributor of articles to *Saturday Evening Post, Coronet, Venture, Boston Business,* and *Esplanade.*

WORK IN PROGRESS: A book on the Battle of Midway; a book on Charles Read, Confederate naval officer.†

*   *   *

POTTS, George Chapman   1898-

PERSONAL: Born January 6, 1898, in Cumberland, England; son of Joseph and Alice Eliza (Chapman) Potts; married Dorothy Gallimore (a languages mistress), May 15, 1928; children: John Andrew, Judith Mary (Mrs. R. Bean). *Education:* Attended Caterham School, Oxford University, and Cuddesdon Theological College; B.A., 1921, M.A., 1925. *Home:* 164 Shenley Fields Rd., Birmingham, England.

CAREER: Clergyman, Church of England. Rector in Distington, Cumberland, England, 1930-37, in Wetheral, Carlisle, England, 1937-40; vicar of Casterton, Westmorland, England, and chaplain of Casterton School, 1945-50; Birmingham Parish Church, Birmingham, England, lecturer, 1950-69. Birmingham Cathedral, honorary canon, 1966-69, canon emeritus, 1969—. Diocesan examiner in religious education for County of Cumberland and Westmorland; evangelistic missions in Britain, Canada, and United States. Artist, exhibiting annually at shows in London and Birmingham. *Military service:* British Army, senior chaplain; mentioned in dispatches. *Member:* Birmingham Water-Colour Society (president, 1963), Royal Birmingham Society of Artists (member of council).

WRITINGS: *Know Your Bible (How to Make a Start)*, Coram Publishers, 1956, revised edition published as *A Beginner's Modern Bible Background*, Hodder & Stoughton, 1964, also published as *Background to the Bible: An Introduction*, Harper, 1966.

WORK IN PROGRESS: *Adventures in the Old Testament; Adventures in the New Testament.*

AVOCATIONAL INTERESTS: Mountaineering in Britain and the Alps, gardening and exhibiting in garden shows.

*   *   *

POUCHER, William Arthur   1891-

PERSONAL: Born November 22, 1891, in Horncastle, England; son of John and Rachel (Dixon) Poucher; married Elsie Dorothy Wood; children: John. *Education:* Attended University of London. *Politics:* Conservative. *Religion:* Wesleyan. *Home and office:* 4 Heathfield, Reigate Heath, Surrey, England.

CAREER: Consulting chemist in London, England, 1923-29; Yardley & Co. Ltd., London, England, chief perfumer, 1929-59; now retired. *Military service:* Royal Army Medical Corps, 1914-19; served in Europe; became captain. *Member:* Pharmaceutical Society (fellow), Royal Photographic Society (fellow), Reform Club. *Awards, honors:* Gold medal award, Society of Cosmetic Chemists, 1954.

WRITINGS: *Perfumes and Cosmetics, with Especial Reference to Synthetics*, Chapman & Hall, 1923, 2nd edition published as *Perfumes, Cosmetics and Soaps*, two volumes, Chapman & Hall, 1925-26, Van Nostrand, 1926, 7th edition, three volumes, Van Nostrand, 1959; *Eve's Beauty Secrets*, Chapman & Hall, 1926.

Travel books; all with photographs and illustrations by the author: *Lakeland Through the Lens, a Ramble Over Fell and Dale*, Chapman & Hall, 1940; *Snowdonia Through the Lens, Mountain Wanderings in Wildest Wales*, Chapman & Hall, 1941; *Lakeland Holiday*, Chapman & Hall, 1942; *Snowdon Holiday*, Chapman & Hall, 1943; *Scotland Through the Lens, Loch Tulla to Lochaber*, Chapman & Hall, 1943; *Escape to the Hills*, Country Life, 1943, revised edition, 1952; *Highland Holiday, Arran to Ben Cruachan*, Chapman & Hall, 1945; *Lakeland Journey*, Chapman & Hall, 1945; *Peak Panorama, Kinder Scout to Dovedale*, Chapman & Hall, 1946; *The Backbone of England*, Country Life, 1946; *A Camera in the Cairngorms*, Chapman & Hall, 1947; *Over Lakeland Fells*, Chapman & Hall, 1948, Scribner, 1949; *The Surrey Hills*, Chapman & Hall, 1949; *Wanderings in Wales*, Country Life, 1949; *The Magic of Skye*, Scribner, 1949.

Lakeland Scrapbook, Chapman & Hall, 1950; *The Magic of the Dolomites*, Country Life, 1951; *Journey Into Ireland*, Transatlantic, 1953; *The North-Western Highlands*, Country Life, 1954; *West Country Journey*, Country Life,

1957; *The Lakeland Peaks: A Pictorial Guide to Walking in the District and to the Safe Ascent of Its Principal Mountain Groups*, Constable, 1960, 4th revised edition, 1971; *The Welsh Peaks: A Pictorial Guide to Walking in This Region and to the Safe Ascent of Its Principal Mountain Groups*, Constable, 1962, 3rd revised edition, 1970; *Climbing with a Camera: The Lake District*, Transatlantic, 1963; *The Scottish Peaks: A Pictorial Guide to Walking in This Region and to the Safe Ascent of Its Most Spectacular Mountains*, Constable, 1964, 2nd revised edition, 1971; *The Peaks and Pennines from Dovedale to Hadrian's Wall: A Pictorial Guide to Walking in the Region and to the Safe Ascent of Its Hills and Moors*, Constable, 1966. Contributor to *Country Life, Scotland's Magazine*, English climbing journals, and to English and American perfume and cosmetic journals.

WORK IN PROGRESS: An 8th edition of *Perfumes, Cosmetics and Soaps.*

*   *   *

POWDERMAKER, Hortense   1900-1970

PERSONAL: Born December 24, 1900, in Philadelphia, Pa.; daughter of Louis (a businessman), and Minnie (Jacoby) Powdermaker. *Education:* Goucher College, B.A., 1920; University of London, Ph.D., 1928. *Agent:* Mavis McIntosh, McIntosh, McKee & Dodds, 30 East 60th St., New York, N.Y. 10022. *Residence:* Berkeley, Calif.

CAREER: Yale University, New Haven, Conn., research associate, Institute of Human Relations, 1931-37; Queens College (now Queens College of the City University of New York), Flushing, N.Y., member of faculty, 1938-67, organized department of anthropology and sociology, 1938, professor of anthropology, 1954-67. Visiting lecturer or professor at University of California, Los Angeles, Columbia University, University of Minnesota, and New School for Social Research. Trustee, Goucher College, 1958-61. Field work in Southwest Pacific, 1929, rural Mississippi, 1932, Hollywood, 1946, and Africa, 1953-54. *Member:* American Anthropological Association (past member of council), American Ethnological Society (president, 1946-47), African Studies Association. *Awards, honors:* Fellowships from Australian National Research Council, 1929-30, U.S. National Research Council, 1930-31, Social Science Research Council, 1933-34, Wenner-Gren Foundation for Anthropological Research, 1947-48, Guggenheim Foundation, 1953-54; Sc.D. from Goucher College, 1957.

WRITINGS: *Life in Lesu: The Study of a Melanesian Society*, Norton, 1933, reissued, 1971; *After Freedom: A Cultural Study in the Deep South*, Viking, 1939, reissued with new preface, Russell, 1968; *Probing Our Prejudices*, Harper, 1944; *Hollywood, the Dream Factory: An Anthropologist Studies the Movie Makers*, Little, Brown, 1950; *Copper Town: Changing Africa, the Human Situation on the Rhodesian Copperbelt*, Harper, 1962; *Stranger and Friend: The Way of an Anthropologist* (autobiographical), Norton, 1966. Writer of articles and papers on anthropology.

(Died June 15, 1970)

*   *   *

POWELL, Clarence Alva   1905-

PERSONAL: Born April 28, 1905, in McMinnville, Tenn.; son of William Bruce (a contractor) and Katherine Elizabeth (Larsen) Powell; married Bertha Latendresse, March

1, 1928; children: Norma Bertha (Mrs. R. W. Johnson). *Education:* Educated in public schools, under private tutors, and through university extension courses. *Politics:* Republican. *Office:* Ford Motor Co., 3001 Miller Rd., Dearborn, Mich. 48120.

CAREER: Ford Motor Co., Dearborn, Mich., purchasing agent, 1939-49, new models coordinator, 1950—. *Member:* Oklahoma Historical Society. *Awards, honors:* Keats-Shelley Memorial Prize (London), 1941.

WRITINGS: Industrial Sonnets, Glass Hill, 1950; *Experiment* (essay), Alan Swallow, 1959; *Atom and Evil,* Hemlock Press, 1961; *Parable* (poetry), Golden Quill, 1962; *Seven* (poetry), Windfall Press, 1964; *The Rose Garden* (poetry), Golden Quill, c.1965; *The Fire Bridge* (fable), Windfall Press, c.1965; *Acoustics,* Atlantis Editions, 1966. Contributor of poetry, short stories, articles, essays, and translations from the French to more than 100 literary reviews and other periodicals in United States, Canada, England, Scotland, New Zealand, France, Denmark, Japan, Brazil, Honduras, India; contributor of articles and fiction to newspapers and trade journals. Former editor, Experiment Press.

WORK IN PROGRESS: Research for writing on Indian Territory and the Southwest, German legends, Roman ruins, ancient castles, churches; a novel; a short story collection; two collections of poetry.

AVOCATIONAL INTERESTS: Fishing, deer hunting, reading, and classical music.

* * *

POWELL, John Roland   1889-

PERSONAL: Born September 2, 1889, in London, England; son of A. H. (a minister) and Jane (Matilda) Powell; married Olive Hilary Gordon Majendie. *Education:* Queen's College, Cambridge, M.A., 1915.

CAREER: Ordained clerk in holy orders, Church of England, 1913; curate of St. Mary's, Peterborough, 1913-15, St. George's, Hanover Square, 1915-21, St. Anne's, Limehouse, 1921-31; vicar of Holy Innocents, Kingsbury, 1931-34, St. Barnabas, Honerton, 1934-43; rector of Harpsden, 1943-50; retired. *Military service:* British Army, chaplain, 1917-19; served with Egyptian Expeditionary Force. *Member:* Navy Records Society (vice-president of council, 1965), Nautical Research Society. *Awards, honors:* Julian Cornbelt's Prize, 1956, for essay, "The Navy in the English Civil War."

WRITINGS: (editor) *Letters of Robert Blake,* Navy Records Society's Publications, 1937; (editor) *The Journal of John Weale,* Navy Records Society's Publications, 1952; *The Navy in the English Civil War,* Archon Books, 1962; (editor with E. K. Timings) *Documents Relating to the Civil War: 1642-1648,* Navy Records Society's Publications, 1963; (editor with E. K. Timings) *The Rupert and Monck Letter Book, 1666,* Navy Records Society's Publications, 1969. Contributor to *Mariners Mirror* and *Irish Sword.*

* * *

POWER, Michael   1933-

PERSONAL: Born July 16, 1933, in Pietermaritzburg, South Africa; son of Michael John and Patricia (St. George) Power. *Education:* University of Natal, B.A. (English), 1952; Oriel College, Oxford, B.A. (law), 1955. *Home:* P. O. Box 48, Orange Grove, Johannesburg, South Africa. *Agent:* Curtis Brown Ltd., 1 Craven Hill, London W2 3EW, England. *Office:* Niven, Norton, Glyn & Coetzee & Associates, P. O. Box 8774, Johannesburg, South Africa.

CAREER: Anglo American Corp. of South Africa Ltd., (mining and finance), Johannesburg, public relations officer, 1956-62; Niven, Norton, Glyn, Coetzee & Associates (public relations consultants), Johannesburg, South Africa, director, 1962—.

WRITINGS: Holiday, Cassell, 1962; *A Gathering of Golden Angels,* Cassell, 1963.

AVOCATIONAL INTERESTS: Reading, swimming, tennis, motion pictures, and travel.

BIOGRAPHICAL/CRITICAL SOURCES: Sunday Times, (Johannesburg), July 29, 1962.†

* * *

POWER, Richard   1928-1970
(Risteard de Paor)

PERSONAL: Born February 24, 1928, in Dublin, Ireland; son of Patrick Joseph (a bank official) and Kathleen May (Murphy) Power; married Ann Lowry Colvill, November 5, 1955; children: Patrick Joseph, Robert Victor, John Milo, Frances Mary. *Education:* Trinity College, Dublin, B.A., 1953; State University of Iowa, M.F.A., 1960. *Religion:* Catholic. *Home:* 16, Ardagh Ave., Blackrock, County Dublin, Ireland. *Agent:* Candida Donadio, Russell and Volkening, 551 Fifth Ave., New York, N.Y. 10017.

CAREER: Civil servant with Irish civil service, Dublin Castle, 1946-58, and Custom House, Dublin, Ireland, 1960-70; has written film scripts for departmental documentaries. Lecturer at State University of Iowa, 1959-60. Worked as builder's laborer in Birmingham, England, 1955. Has had some acting and other stage experience with several Dublin groups, including Dublin University Players and the Studio Theatre; worked in summer theater on Cape Cod. *Awards, honors:* Club Leabhar (Gaelic Book Club) award, 1957, for *Ull i mBarr an Gheagain;* first prize, Cork International Film Festival, 1962.

WRITINGS: Ull i mBarr an Gheagain (in Gaelic), Sairseal agus Dill, 1959; *The Land of Youth,* Dial, 1964; *The Hungry Grass,* Dial, 1969. Two one-act plays have been produced in the Abbey Theatre. Contributor of short stories and drama reviews to *Dial, Dubliner, The Bell, Saturday Book, Irish Times,* and *Daily Iowan,* and in Gaelic to *Comhar and Feasta.* Former editor, *Comhar.*

WORK IN PROGRESS: A novel, *A Man of War;* a television script in Gaelic for Telefis Eireann.

SIDELIGHTS: Power wrote to *CA:* "In my early twenties I travelled most of western Europe, mainly by hitchhiking, once working my passage by tending horses on a cargoboat. I also travelled with my family in the [United] States in a fifteen-year-old Ford, camping out.... My writing is done in the evenings. Though I have never lived, except for short periods, in the Irish countryside, I draw most of my material from there. The Power family is a large and close-knit one, living in the Decies, the 'Power country' of County Waterford and through them I am in touch with the life of that area, which I intend to use as the background to my novels." His books are, to varying degrees, based on his experiences on the Aran Islands and in Birmingham, England, where he worked in the company of Aran emigrants.

BIOGRAPHICAL/CRITICAL SOURCES: Saturday Review, May 31, 1969; Time, June 6, 1969; New Yorker, August 30, 1969; Variety, February 25, 1970.

(Died February 12, 1970)

* * *

POWLEY, Edward Barzillai 1887-1968

PERSONAL: Born October 15, 1887, in Narborough, Norfolk, England; son of James (a farmer) and Anna Elizabeth (Hodson) Powley; married Hilda Mary Reeder, 1914 (died, 1960); married Florence Mary Pomeroy (an author), February 25, 1962. Education: King's College, London, B.A.; Balliol College, Oxford, B.Litt. and D. Phil.; University of Liverpool, M.A. Politics: Independent. Home: The Old Rectory, Grafham, Huntingdonshire, England.

CAREER: Schoolmaster in Lancaster, England, 1919-20, in Lincolnshire, England, 1922-25 (also farmed in Norfolk at same time); Merchant Taylors' School, Crosby, Lancashire, England, librarian, 1925-51. H. M. Borstal Institution, Gaynes Hall, Huntingdonshire, England, part-time organizer of education, 1953-57. County councillor, Huntingdonshire, England, 1954-65. Minister of Transport's Committee on Rural Bus Services, member, beginning 1959. Deputy traffic commissioner, Eastern Counties. Inaugurated Cromwell Museum, Huntingdon, England, 1962. Military service: Royal Navy, 1914-18. Member: Royal Historical Society (fellow), Authors' Club, Pepys Club (chairman).

WRITINGS: The English Navy in the Revolution of 1688 (forward by Earl Jellicoe), Cambridge University Press, 1928; Vicisti Galilaee? or Religion in England, Routledge, 1931; (compiler) A Hundred Years of English Poetry, Cambridge University Press, 1931; (editor) The Laurel Bough (English epical verse, 1380-1932), G. Bell, 1934; The House of de la Pomerai (Berry Pomeroy, Devon) 1066-1719: The Annals of The Family, with appendix post-1719, Liverpool University Press, 1944; Poems 1914-60, Muller, 1961; Catalogue of Cromwell Museum, Alden Press, 1965; The Naval Side of King William's War, 16th/26th November 1688–14th June 1690, Archon Books, 1972.

AVOCATIONAL INTERESTS: Gardening, travel by rail.

(Died February 7, 1968)

* * *

POWLEY, Florence Mary Pomeroy 1892-
(Florence Mary Pomeroy)

PERSONAL: Born October 26, 1892, in Kingston-upon-Hull, England; daughter of John James and Mary Jane (Pearce) Pomeroy; married Edward B. Powley (a schoolmaster, now retired; author). Education: Attended Ecole Normale, Orleans, France; University of London, B.A. (honors), 1914. Religion: Agnostic. Home: The Old Rectory, Grafham, Huntingdon, England.

CAREER: Assistant mistress at schools in Peterborough and Newport, England, 1914-19; Wolsey Hall (correspondence college), Oxford, England, tutor in French, beginning 1919. Deputy assistant censor, British Postal and Telegraph Censorship, 1939-45.

WRITINGS—Under name Florence Mary Pomeroy: Tristan and Iseult (epic poem in twelve books), Bodley Head, 1958. Contributor to A Hundred Years of English Poetry, Cambridge University Press, 1931.

WORK IN PROGRESS: A play about Andre Chenier.

PRATT, Julius W(illiam) 1888-

PERSONAL: Born February 25, 1888, in Piedmont, S.D.; son of William McLain and Sophia (Rand) Pratt; married Louisa Gabriella Williamson, June 7, 1919; children: William Winston, Walden Penfield. Education: Davidson College, A.B., 1908; University of Chicago, M.A., 1914, Ph.D., 1924. Home: 65 Evans St., Williamsville, N.Y. 14221.

CAREER: U.S. Naval Academy, Annapolis, Md., began as instructor, became assistant professor of English and history, 1916-24; Rutgers University, New Brunswick, N.J., assistant professor of history, 1924-26; University of Buffalo (now State University of New York at Buffalo), professor of American history, 1926-58. Visiting professor at Salzburg Seminar in American Studies, 1952; Fulbright professor at University of Munich, 1956; visiting professor at various institutions before and since retirement, including University of Notre Dame, 1964-69. Member: American Historical Association, American Association of University Professors, Organization of American Historians, Buffalo and Erie County Historical Society, Phi Beta Kappa. Awards, honors: LL.D., Davidson College, 1963, University of Notre Dame, 1967.

WRITINGS: Expansionists of 1812, Macmillan, 1925; Friends or Enemies?, University of Chicago Press, 1935, revised edition, 1939; Expansionists of 1898: The Acquisition of Hawaii and the Spanish Islands, Johns Hopkins Press, 1936; America's Colonial Experiment: How the United States Gained, Governed, and in Part Gave Away a Colonial Empire, Prentice-Hall, 1950; The Mantle of George Washington, University of Buffalo, 1953; A History of United States Foreign Policy, Prentice-Hall, 1955, Cooper Square, 1964; Challenge and Rejection: The United States and World Leadership, 1900-1921, Macmillan, 1967, reissued as America and World Leadership, 1900-1921, Collier, 1970. Contributor to Dictionary of American Biography, Dictionary of American History, and to historical periodicals.

* * *

PRESTON, Ivy (Alice) Kinross 1914-

PERSONAL: Born November 11, 1914, in Timaru, Canterbury, New Zealand; daughter of Andrew (a farmer) and Lily (Ward) Kinross; married Percival Edward James Preston (a farmer), October 14, 1937 (died, 1956); children: David Robin, Peter Ronald, Diane Jeane, Lynnette Ruth. Education: Attended schools in Canterbury, New Zealand. Politics: Labour. Religion: Presbyterian. Home: 95 Church St., Timaru, New Zealand.

CAREER: Novelist. Member: New Zealand Women Writers Society, Romantic Novelists' Association (London), Timaru Writers Guild.

WRITINGS: The Silver Stream (autobiography), Pegasus Press, 1959; Where Ratas Twine, Wright & Brown, 1960; None So Blind, Wright & Brown, 1961; Magic in Maoriland, Wright & Brown, 1962; Rosemary for Remembrance, R. Hale, 1962; Island of Enchantment, R. Hale, 1963; Tamarisk in Bloom, R. Hale, 1963; Hearts Do Not Break, R. Hale, 1964; The Blue Remembered Hills, R. Hale, 1965; The Secret Love of Nurse Wilson, R. Hale, 1966; Enchanted Evening, R. Hale, 1966; Hospital on the Hill, R. Hale, 1967; Nicolette, R. Hale, 1967; Red Roses for a Nurse, R. Hale, 1968; Ticket of Destiny, R. Hale, 1969; April in Westland, R. Hale, 1969; A Fleeting Breath, R. Hale, 1970, Beagle Books, 1971; Interrupted Journey, R.

Hale, 1970, Beagle Books, 1971; *Portrait of Pierre*, R. Hale, 1970, Beagle Books, 1971; *Petals in the Wind*, R. Hale, 1971. Contributor of short stories and articles to *New Zealand Playdate, New Zealand Farmer, Arena, New Zealand Home Journal*, and other magazines. Author of radio scripts.

WORK IN PROGRESS: A novel with a Canadian setting, for R. Hale.

SIDELIGHTS: Mrs. Preston told *CA:* "I write my books in longhand, then type the final copy with one finger, rather slow, but I get there. With four teenagers living at home, I find it impossible to spend as much time at my typewriter as I would like, but try to produce two books a year." She went to work at fifteen, wrote first book after she was forty.

BIOGRAPHICAL/CRITICAL SOURCES: Ivy Preston, *The Silver Stream*, Pegasus Press, 1959; *New Zealand Weekly News*, July 15, 1959; *Christchurch Star*, December 1, 1960; *New Zealand Women's Weekly*, January 23, 1963; *Timaru Herald*, July 7, 1963, December 12, 1963.

*   *   *

PRESTON, James   1913-
(Ronald James)

PERSONAL: Born July 26, 1913, in Ballarat, Victoria, Australia; son of Ernest and Elsie (Button) Preston; married Bonnie Jean Campbell, August 4, 1938; children: Fay Diane, Gail Francis, Ronald James. *Education:* Educated in Australian state schools. *Religion:* Church of Christ. *Home:* 4 Reserve Rd., Beaumaris 3193, Melbourne, Australia. *Agent:* Laurence Pollinger Ltd., 18 Maddox St., London W.1, England. *Office:* Council of Fire & Accident Underwriters, 335 Flinders Lane, Melbourne, Australia.

CAREER: Former prison warden, farmer in Queensland, and clerical worker in Australia; Council of Fire & Accident Underwriters, Melbourne, Australia, public relations officer, 1953—. Represented Australia at Asian Writers Conference in Manila, 1962. *Military service:* Royal Australian Air Force, served in New Guinea area, 1939-45; became sergeant. *Member:* Quill Club of Australia (organizing secretary for annual writers' convn), P.E.N. (secretary, Melbourne Centre).

WRITINGS: Valley of No Escape, John Long, 1961; *The Empty Years*, Cresset, 1962; *Prison Feud*, John Long, 1962; *The Killer Came Riding*, John Long, 1963; *Axes of Hate*, John Long, 1963; *Shattered Steel*, John Long, 1964; *Breakdown*, John Long, 1965; *Goal in Conflict*, John Long, 1966; *Crashout*, John Long, 1968; *Murder at Sundown*, John Long, 1968; *The Ring of the Axe*, Lansdowne Press, 1968; *Bushfire*, John Long, 1969; *Death Takes Revenge*, John Long, 1970; *Power Failure*, John Long, 1971; *Jeedarra Country*, Rigby (Adelaide), 1971. Contributor of more than three hundred short stories and articles to Australian magazines. Suburban newspaper columnist for ten years.

WORK IN PROGRESS: Theirs Is the Kingdom; Point of No Return; and *The House That Jim Built.*

AVOCATIONAL INTERESTS: Archery and entomology.

BIOGRAPHICAL/CRITICAL SOURCES: Books and Bookmen, March, 1970.

PRICE, Francis Wilson   1895-1974
(Frank W. Price)

PERSONAL: Born February 25, 1895, in Kashing, Chekiang Province, China; son of missionary parents, Philip Francis and Esther (Wilson) Price; married Essie McClure, June 14, 1923; children: Mary Virginia (Mrs. Raymond E. Miller), Frank W., Jr. (a physician). *Education:* Early education in China; Davidson College, B.A., 1915; Yale University, B.D., 1922, Ph.D., 1938; Columbia University, M.A., 1923. *Home:* Hillcrest Lane, Morningside Heights, Lexington, Va.

CAREER: Began career in Nanking, China, as school principal, 1915-17, then became secretary for Young Men's Christian Association, 1917-18; Chinese Labor Corps, welfare secretary in France, 1918-19; ordained to ministry of Presbyterian Church in U.S., 1922; Presbyterian Board of World Missions, Nashville, Tenn., missionary to China, 1932-52, serving as professor at Nanking Theological Seminary, 1932-48, teacher at other universities, and as missionary secretary of Church of Christ in China, 1948-50; detained in China by Communist regime until 1952; New Monmouth Presbyterian Church, Lexington, Va., pastor, 1953-56; Missionary Research Library, New York, N.Y., director, 1956-61, retired, 1961; National Council of Churches of Christ in U.S.A., research secretary, Division of Foreign Missions, 1956-61; Mary Baldwin College, Staunton, Va., professor of international studies, 1961-65. Moderator of General Assembly of Presbyterian Church in the U.S., 1953-54; member of Columbia University Seminar on Modern East Asia. *Wartime service:* Relief work and liaison service in Free China, 1939-45; decorated for service.

MEMBER: Association for Asian Studies, Phi Beta Kappa, Sigma Upsilon, Rotary. *Awards, honors:* D.D. from Davidson College, 1940; decorated by National Government of China for wartime service, 1945; Distinguished Service Citation, Agricultural Missions, Inc., 1955.

WRITINGS: (Translator) Sun Yat-sen, *San min chu i: Three Principles of the People*, Commercial Press (Shanghai), 1927; (with Miao Chu-seng) *Religion and Character in Christian Middle Schools in China*, China Christian Educational Association (Shanghai), 1929; (editor with Yi-fang Wu) *China Rediscovers Her West: A Symposium*, Missionary Education Movement, 1940; (co-editor) *China Fights On*, China Publishing, 1941; *The Rural Church in China*, Kelly & Walsh (Shanghai), 1941, 2nd edition, Agricultural Missions, 1948; *We Went to West China*, Presbyterian Board of World Missions, 1943; (translator) Chiang Kai-shek, *Resistance and Reconstruction*, 2nd section, Harper, 1943; *China: Twilight or Dawn*, Friendship, 1948; *As the Lightning Flashes* (James Sprunt lectures), John Knox, 1948; (translator) *Chinese Christian Hymns*, Presbyterian Board of World Missions, 1953; *Marx Meets Christ*, Westminster, 1957; (compiler) *Africa South of the Sahara: A Selected and Annotated Bibliography of Books in the Missionary Research Library*, Missionary Research Library, 1961; *History of Nanking Theological Seminary*, Foundation for Theological Education in Southeast Asia, 1963. Contributor to magazines and journals. Editor of Missionary Research Library research bulletins, 1956-61.

WORK IN PROGRESS: A book for use in Asian theological schools, *The Church in Rural Society.*

(Died January 9, 1974)

PRICE, George (Henry) 1910-19(?)
(Rhys Price)

PERSONAL: Born July 14, 1910, in Ebbw Vale, Wales; son of Albert (a steelworker) and Elizabeth (Wilkinson) Price; married Charlotte Scholz, April 10, 1948; children: Stephen. *Education:* University of Wales, B.A. (honors), 1935, B.D. (double distinction), 1938, M.A., 1952; University of Basel, graduate study, 1938-39. *Office:* University of Alberta, Edmonton, Alberta, Canada.

CAREER: Minister of Baptist church in Bridgend, Glamorganshire, Wales, 1947-64; University of Alberta, Edmonton, assistant professor, department of philosophy, beginning 1964. President, South Wales Baptist Association, 1955-56; mayoral chaplain, Bridgend, 1947-48, 1958-59; chaplain, British Legion, 1947-64. *Military service:* British Army, chaplain, 1939-47; became major.

WRITINGS: (Under pseudonym Rhys Price) *One In a Million,* Hutchinson, 1944; *The Narrow Pass: A Study of Kierkegaard's Concept of Man,* McGraw, 1963.

WORK IN PROGRESS: A "restatement" of Charles S. Peirce; a new development of existentialism beyond the present limits imposed by its major representatives.

AVOCATIONAL INTERESTS: Painting in oils.

(Deceased)

* * *

PRICE, Miles O(scar) 1890-1968

PERSONAL: Born July 31, 1890, in Plymouth, Ind.; son of Emanuel (a building contractor) and Mary Jane (Dickson) Price; married Fannie J. Elliott, January 3, 1915; children: Miles Macy (deceased), Mary Dunsdon (Mrs. Peter J. Franco). *Education:* University of Chicago, S.B., 1914; University of Illinois, B.L.S., 1922; Columbia University, LL.B., 1938. *Politics:* Independent Republican. *Home:* 15 Third St., N.E., Washington, D.C. 20003. *Office:* Association of American Law Schools, 1521 New Hampshire Ave., N.W., Washington, D.C. 20036.

CAREER: Chief of Library divisions at University of Chicago, Chicago, Ill., 1910-14, and at University of Illinois, Urbana, 1914-22; U.S. Patent Office, Washington, D.C., librarian, 1922-29; Columbia University, New York, N.Y., law librarian and professor of law, 1929-61. Consultant to Duke University Law School, 1961-62, and Library of Congress, 1962-64; director of Association of American Law Schools library project (compiling annotated lists of books on all topics of interest to law school libraries), 1964-65. *Member:* Association of American Law Schools, American Library Association (member of council, 1924-25, 1933-37), Special Libraries Association (member of executive board, 1930-31), American Association of Law Librarians (president, 1945-46), District of Columbia Library Association (president, 1924-25), member of bar of State of New York. *Awards, honors:* LL.D. from Temple University, 1954.

WRITINGS: (Compiler) *Subject Headings in Anglo-American and International Law used in the Dictionary Catalog of the Law Libraries,* Columbia University School of Library Service, 1927; (editor with Dorsey W. Hyde, Jr.) *Handbook of Washington's Informational Resources,* District of Columbia Library Association, 1928; (compiler) *Catalog for a Law Library of 15,000 Volumes,* Columbia University School of Library Service, 1942; *Practical Manual for Standard Legal Citations,* Oceana, 1950, 3rd revised edition, 1970; (with Harry Bitner) *Effective Legal Research: A Practical Manual of Law Books and Their Use,* Little, 1953, 3rd revised edition, 1969; (with Harry Bitner) *Problems for Effective Legal Research,* Prentice-Hall, 1954, 4th revised edition, Little, 1970. Contributor to *Journal of Patent Office Society, American Political Science Review,* and other legal and library periodicals.

SIDELIGHTS: Prince retired the second time at the close of 1965 to a "life of intellectual prostitution"—indexing law books. He had his first job at the age of ten, began to work full time at thirteen, and shortly before his seventy-fifth birthday flew to Los Angeles on a six-week consulting job, then to New York to appear on a panel at the American Association of Law Libraries convention. He read in German, French, Italian, Spanish, and Russian.

(Died August 18, 1968)

* * *

PRICE, Morgan Philips 1885-1973

PERSONAL: Born January 29, 1885, in Gloucestershire, England; son of William Edwin (a major, British Army, and member of Parliament) and Margaret (Philips) Price; married Elise Balster, August 1, 1919; children: Tania (Mrs. William Rose), William Philips Peter. *Education:* Trinity College, Cambridge, M.A. (honors). *Religion:* Unitarian. *Home:* The Grove, Taynton, near Gloucestershire, England.

CAREER: Traveled in central Asia, Siberia, and Middle East, 1908-14; *Manchester Guardian* (now *Guardian*), Manchester, England, correspondent in Russia, 1914-18; *Daily Herald,* London, England, correspondent in Berlin, Germany, 1919-23; switched from Liberal to Labour Party in 1919, ran as Labour candidate for Parliament for Gloucestershire, 1922-24; member of Parliament (Labour) for Whitehaven Division of Cumberland, 1929-31, for Forest of Dean and West Gloucestershire, 1935-39, serving as Forestry Commissioner, 1942-45, Charity Commissioner, 1945-50; Price Walker & Co. (timber importers), Gloucestershire, England, director, 1933-73, chairman, 1962-73. Farmed five hundred acres and managed woodlands of own estate at Taynton, Gloucestershire, England, 1924-59. Justice of the peace. *Member:* Royal Geographical Society (fellow).

WRITINGS: Siberia, Methuen, 1912; *Diplomatic History of the War,* Allen & Unwin, 1914; *War and Revolution in Asiatic Russia,* Allen & Unwin, 1918; *The Soviet: The Terror and Intervention,* Socialist Publication Society, 1918; *My Reminiscences of the Russian Revolution,* Allen & Unwin, 1921; *Germany in Transition,* Labour Publishing, 1923; *Economic Problems of Europe,* Allen & Unwin, 1928; *America after Sixty Years,* Allen & Unwin, 1936; *Hitler's War and Eastern Europe,* Macmillan, 1940; *Russia through the Centuries: The Historical Background of the U.S.S.R.,* Allen & Unwin, 1943; *Russia, Red or White,* Low, 1948; *Through the Iron-Laced Curtain: A Record of a Journey Through the Balkans in 1946,* Sampson Low, Marston & Co., 1949; *A History of Turkey: From Empire to Republic,* Macmillan, 1956, 2nd edition, 1961; *Russia, Forty Years On: An Account of a Visit to Russia and Germany in the Autumn of 1959,* Allen & Unwin, 1961; *My Three Revolutions,* Allen & Unwin, 1969.

WORK IN PROGRESS: An autobiography, and an account of the Parliamentary careers of his forebears.

SIDELIGHTS: Price said: "My writings on Russia were very sympathetic to the Russian Revolution from 1917 to 1922, after which they became more objective."

(Died September, 1973)

PRICE, R(ichard) G(eoffrey) G(eorge) 1910-

PERSONAL: Born September 1, 1910, in London, England; son of George Lewis (a legal civil servant) and Jessie May (Cowper) Price; married Ellen Susan Margaret Artlett, April 3, 1943 (died, 1971). *Education:* Jesus College, Oxford, M.A., 1933; Institute of Education, University of London, diploma, 1934. *Home:* Lower Brook Bank, 28A, Lucastes Ave., Haywards Heath, Sussex RH16 1JX, England. *Agent:* A. P. Watt & Son, 26/28 Bedford Row, London WC1R 4HL, England.

CAREER: Shoreham Grammar School and Ordingly College, Sussex, England, assistant master, 1935-47; free-lance journalist, 1947—; *Punch* literary critic, 1949—. *Member:* Society of Authors, Savage Club, Punch Table.

WRITINGS: A History of Punch, Collins, 1957; *How to Become Headmaster,* Blond, 1960; *Survive with Me,* Blond, 1962. Contributor of articles and reviews to *Punch, Atlantic Monthly, Christian Science Monitor, Times Literary Supplement, Times Educational Supplement,* and other periodicals and newspapers.

*　　*　　*

PRICHARD, Katharine Susannah 1883-

PERSONAL: Born 1883, in Levuka, Fiji; daughter of Tom Henry (editor of *Fiji Times*) and Edith Isabel (Fraser) Prichard; married Hugo Throssell (an Army captain), 1919; children: Ric Prichard. *Education:* Educated in Australia schools. *Home:* Greenmount, West Australia.

CAREER: Grew up in Australia, except for one period in Tasmania, and had first short stories published at eleven; later journalist for newspapers in Melbourne and Sydney and other Australian publications, and free-lance journalist in London, England, 1908, 1912-16; fiction writer in Australia, 1916—. *Awards, honors:* Hodder & Stoughton prize of 1,000 pounds, 1924, for *The Pioneers; Art in Australia* prize, 1924, for short story, "The Grey Horse"; *Triad* award for a three-act Australian play, 1927, for *Brumby Innes; Bulletin* (Sydney) prize of 500 pounds, 1928, for *Coonardoo.*

WRITINGS: The Pioneers, Hodder & Stoughton, 1915, revised edition, Angus & Robertson, 1963; *Windlestraws,* Holden & Hardingham, 1917; *The Black Opal,* Heinemann, 1921; *Working Bullocks,* Viking, 1927; *The Wild Oats of Han* (juvenile), Angus & Robertson, 1928, revised edition, Lansdowne Press, 1968; *Coonardoo, the Well in the Shadow,* J. Cape, 1929, Norton, 1930; *Haxby's Circus: The Lightest, Brightest Little Show on Earth,* J. Cape, 1930, published as *Fay's Circus,* Norton, 1931; *Earth Lover* (poems), Sunnybrook Press, 1930; *Kiss on the Lips, and Other Stories,* J. Cape, 1932; *The Real Russia,* Modern Publishers, 1934; (with others) William Moore and T. I. Moore, editors, *Best Australian One-Act Plays,* Angus & Robertson, 1937; *Intimate Strangers,* J. Cape, 1937.

Brumby Innes (three-act play), Paterson's Printing Press, 1940; *Moon of Desire,* J. Cape, 1941; (editor with others) *Australian New Writing 1943-45,* Current Books, 1943-45; *Potch and Colour* (short stories), Angus & Robertson, 1944; *The Roaring Nineties: A Story of the Goldfields of Western Australia,* J. Cape, 1946; *Golden Miles,* J. Cape, 1948; *Winged Seeds,* J. Cape, 1950; *N'goola, and Other*

Stories, Australasian Book Society, 1959; *Child of the Hurricane* (autobiography), Angus & Robertson, 1963; *On Strenuous Wings,* edited by Joan Williams, Seven Seas Publishers, 1965; *Happiness: Selected Short Stories,* Angus & Robertson, 1967; *Subtle Flame,* Australasian Book Society, 1967; *Moggie and Her Circus Pony,* F. W. Cheshire, 1967. Anthologized in *The World's Greatest Short Stories,* Crown.

SIDELIGHTS: Miss Prichard's books have been translated into twelve languages, including Russian, Latvian, Hungarian, Slovak, Afrikaans, Armenian, and Chinese. *The Pioneers* was made into a motion picture in 1926.

*　　*　　*

PRINZ, Joachim 1902-

PERSONAL: Born May 10, 1902, in Burkhardsdorf, Germany; came to United States in 1937, naturalized in 1944; son of Joseph and Nani (Berg) Prinz; married Lucie Horovitz, 1925 (died, 1931); married Hilde Goldschmidt, May 24, 1932; children: (first marriage) Lucie Berkowitz; (second marriage) Michael, Jonathan J., Deborah M. *Education:* University of Berlin and University of Breslau, student, 1922-23; University of Giessen, Ph.D., 1923; Jewish Theological Seminary, Rabbi, 1925. *Home:* 306 Elmwynd Dr., Orange, N.J. 07050. *Office:* Temple B'nai Abraham, 621 Clinton Ave., Newark, N.J. 07108.

CAREER: Rabbi for Jewish Community of Berlin, Germany, from 1926 until expulsion by Gestapo, 1937; public lecturer in United States, 1937-39; Temple B'nai Abraham, Newark, N.J., rabbi, 1939—. Member of executive board, World Jewish Congress, 1946; president, American Jewish Congress, 1958—. *Awards, honors:* D.D., Hebrew Union College (now Hebrew Union College-Jewish Institute of Religion), 1960.

WRITINGS: Juedische Geschichte, Verlag fuer Kulturpolitik, 1931; *Illustrierte Juedische Geschichte,* Brandus, 1933; *Die Geschichten der Bible: Der Juedischen jugend neu erzaehlt,* Erich Reiss, 1934; *Wir Juden,* Erich Reiss, 1934; *Der Freitagabend,* Brandus, 1935; *Die Reiche Israel und Juda Geschichten der Bibel: Der Juedischen Jugend neu erzaehlt,* Erich Reiss, 1936; *Das Leben im Ghetto,* Erwin Lowe, 1937; *Heroes y principes Hebreos,* Editorial Israel, 1941; *Cartes Cartilor,* Editura Socec & Co., 1946; *The Great Jewish Books,* edited by Samuel Caplan and Harold U. Ribalow, Horizon Press, 1952; *The Dilemma of the Modern Jew,* Little, Brown, 1962; *Popes from the Ghetto; A View of Medieval Christendom,* Horizon Press, 1966; *The Secret Jews,* Random House, 1973. Member of editorial board, *Judaism,* 1958—.

*　　*　　*

PRITCHARD, Leland J(ames) 1908-

PERSONAL: Born February 20, 1908, in McClleland, Iowa; son of James Edward (a clergyman) and Dora (Baumker) Pritchard; married Helen Von Behren, August 12, 1933; children: John, Thomas. *Education:* Cornell College, Mount Vernon, Iowa, A.B., 1929; Syracuse University, A.M., 1930; University of Chicago, graduate study, 1932-33; University of Illinois, Ph.D., 1941. *Home:* 1725 Mississippi, Lawrence, Kan. 66044. *Office:* Department of Economics, Summerfield Hall, University of Kansas, Lawrence, Kan. 66044.

CAREER: University of Kansas, Lawrence, 1942—, began as assistant professor, now professor of economics, chairman of the department of economics, 1956-62. *Member:* American Economic Association, American Finance Association, American Association of University Professors (member of national council, 1954-56), Midwest Economics Association (president, 1963-64), Phi Beta Kappa. *Awards, honors:* Appointed Fulbright lecturer at Middle East Technological University, Ankara, Turkey, 1962.

WRITINGS: Money and Banking, Houghton, 1958, 2nd edition, 1964.

Contributor: Dean Chalmers Carson, editor, *Banking and Monetary Studies,* Irwin, 1963; Marshall Dana Ketchum and L. T. Kendall, editors, *Readings in Financial Institutions,* Houghton, 1965; H. A. Wolf and R. C. Doenges, editors, *Readings in Money and Banking,* Appleton, 1965. Contributor of articles to finance and economic journals.

BIOGRAPHICAL/CRITICAL SOURCES: Cornell College Alumnus, May, 1964.

*　　*　　*

PRITCHARD, Sheila (Edwards) 1909-

PERSONAL: Born May 10, 1909, in Detroit, Mich.; daughter of Calita Elvin (a Methodist minister) and Mable (Cobb) Edwards; married Robert Otis Pritchard (an engineer with Michigan Bell Telephone Co.), September 1, 1927; children: Robert Otis, Neil E. *Education:* Attended Wayne (now Wayne State) University, 1946. *Address:* Route 1, Box 212, Bonita Springs, Fla. 33923.

CAREER: Michigan Bell Telephone Co., Detroit, Mich., service supervisor, 1935-44; Detroit Adventure, University Center for Adult Education, Detroit, Mich., staff member, 1961-62; Michigan State University, Oakland (now Oakland University), Rochester, Mich., Writer's Conference staff member, 1963-65; University Center for Adult Education, teacher of creative writing and poetry, 1965. Regular participant, Wayne State University radio and television broadcasts, 1955-65; has worked as a judge of literary contests, Wayne State University, Detroit, Mich., 1958, 1964-65. Has done volunteer work with American Red Cross as nurses' aid, 1940-54, and the Mayor's Committee on Skid-Row Problems, Detroit, Mich., 1959-65. *Member:* Detroit Women Writers.

WRITINGS: (Contributor) John Hall Wheelock, editor, *Poets of Today, Volume V,* edited by John Hall Wheelock, Scribner, 1958. Poems have appeared in *Accent, Antioch Review, Approach, Arizona Quarterly, Botteghe Oscure, Georgia Review, Kenyon Review, Poetry, Sewanee Review,* and other periodicals. Two hours of her readings were taped by Wayne State University in 1963 and are now in the Library of Congress (Washington, D.C.).

WORK IN PROGRESS: One book of poetry, tentatively titled *For a New Song.*

*　　*　　*

PROSKE, Beatrice (Irene) Gilman 1899-

PERSONAL: Born October 31, 1899, in Thornton, N.H.; daughter of Milan J. and Alice May (Hazeltine) Gilman; married Herbert Proske, August 19, 1935; children: Cynthia Anna (Mrs. Edward J. Maestro). *Education:* Simmons College, B.S., 1920. *Home:* 2 Lincoln Ave., Ardsley, N.Y. 10502.

CAREER: Hispanic Society of America, New York, N.Y., staff member, 1920-23, curator of sculpture, 1923—.

Member: Real Academia de Bellas Artes y Ciencias Historicas de Toledo, Real Academia de Bellas Artes de Santa Isabel de Hungria de Seville, Societe Francaise d'-Archeologie, Hispanic Society of America (honorary corresponding secretary, 1948—). *Awards, honors:* Hispanic Society of America Sorolla Medal, 1937, Sculpture Medal, 1953, membership medal, 1970.

WRITINGS: Gregorio Fernandez, Hispanic Society of America, 1926; *Catalogue of Sculpture ... in the Collection of The Hispanic Society of America,* Hispanic Society of America, 1930-32, revised edition, 1968; *Brookgreen Gardens; Sculpture,* Brookgreen Gardens, Volume I, 1943, Volume II, 1955; *Robert A. Baillie, Carver of Stone,* Brookgreen Gardens, 1946; *Castilian Sculpture: Gothic to Renaissance,* Hispanic Society of America, 1951; *Henry Clews, Jr., Sculptor,* Brookgreen Gardens, 1953; *Pompeo Leoni: Work in Marble and Alabaster in Relation to Spanish Sculpture,* Hispanic Society of America, 1956; *Juan Martinez Montanes, a Commission for Santo Domingo,* Hispanic Society of America, 1960; *Archer Milton Huntington,* Hispanic Society of America, 1963; *Juan Martinez Montanes, Sevillian Sculptor,* Hispanic Society of America, 1967. Contributor of articles to *Notes Hispanic, Archivo Espanol de Arte, Connoisseur, Arts in Virginia,* and *Gazette des Beaux-Arts.*

*　　*　　*

PUGH, Samuel F(ranklin) 1904-

PERSONAL: Born June 4, 1904, in Bowling Green, Mo.; son of Clyde R. and Harriett A. (Wicks) Pugh; married Catherine J. Buchanan, April 10, 1932; children: Cathleen (Mrs. William L. Erickson), Larry S. *Education:* University of Puget Sound, A.B., 1929; The College of the Bible (now Lexington Theological Seminary), Lexington, Ky., B.D., 1935; graduate study at Pacific School of Religion, 1936, and University of Southern California, 1944. *Home and office:* 6940 East 10th St., Indianapolis, Ind. 46219.

CAREER: Ordained to ministry of Disciples of Christ (Christian Church), 1932. Pastor of churches in Watsonville, Hollister, El Monte, and Sacramento, Calif., 1932-52; Disciples of Christ, Indianapolis, Ind., director of local church life, 1952-61, editor of *World Call,* 1961-71. Member of Disciples of Christ Commission on Christian Literature, 1952-61, of Commission on Brotherhood Restructure, 1961-71; member of publication committee, Bethany Press, 1955-65. *Member:* Religious Public Relations Council. *Awards, honors:* D.Litt., Culver-Stockton College, 1962; Award for Excellence from the Associated Church Press.

WRITINGS: Between-Time Meditations (verse), Bethany, 1954; *Women's Place in the Total Church,* Bethany, 1957; *The Church's Ministry to the Homebound,* Bethany, 1958; (editor) *Primer for New Disciples,* Bethany, 1963. Writer of booklets and pamphlets. Contributor of articles and verse to religious periodicals; columnist, "Toward a Better Church," *Christian,* 1953-61; columnist, "Lift Up Your Hearts," *World Call,* 1972-74.

WORK IN PROGRESS: A book of inspirational and religious verse, *Morning and Evening; Read Aloud Verses for Children.*

*　　*　　*

PUGSLEY, Clement H. 1908-

PERSONAL: Born September 23, 1908, in England; son of Frederick John (in advertising) and Ellen (Besley) Pugsley;

married, wife's maiden name Trounson; children: Margaret Patricia (Mrs. Henry Stansbury), Ruth Elaine, David Philip. *Education:* Educated at Bristol Grammar School and Harley Victoria College. *Politics:* Liberal. *Home:* All Saints Rd., Bromsgrove, Worcestershire, England.

CAREER: Methodist minister. *Military service:* Royal Navy, chaplain.

WRITINGS: After This Manner, Epworth, 1952; *A Preachers Prayer Book,* Epworth, 1959; *A Prayer Book for Women,* Epworth, 1961; *In Sorrow's Lone Hour,* James, 1963, Abingdon, 1964.

*   *   *

PULLIAS, Earl V(ivon)   1907-

PERSONAL: Surname is pronounced *Pull*-i-as; born March 12, 1907, in Castalian Springs, Tenn.; son of John Grey (a farmer) and Margaret (Leath) Pullias; married Pauline Boyce, December, 1929; children: Calvin Moffatt, John Malcolm. *Education:* Cumberland University, B.A., 1928; University of Chicago, M.A., 1931; Duke University, Ph.D., 1936; University of London and Oxford University, postdoctoral study, 1937-38. *Politics:* Democrat. *Religion:* Church of Christ. *Home:* 7422 Brighton Ave., Los Angeles, Calif. 90047.

CAREER: High school teacher of English, Richard City, Tenn., 1928-30; Duke University, Durham, N.C., instructor, 1936-37; Pepperdine College, Los Angeles, Calif., professor of pyschology, 1937-57, dean of faculty, 1940-57; University of Southern California, Los Angeles, professor of higher education, 1958—. Psychological counselor, licensed to practice in California. Member of survey team to University of Teheran, International Cooperation Administration. Los Angeles County Board of Education, member, 1954—, president, 1956-57, 1962-63, 1967-68. *Member:* American Educational Research Association, National Education Association, American Psychological Association, California Teachers Association (chairman of commission of higher education), Los Angeles County Psychological Association (fellow), Phi Beta Kappa, Kappa Delta Pi, Pi Gamma Mu.

WRITINGS: Variability in Results from New-Type Achievement Tests, Duke University Press, 1937; (editor) *Christian Courtship and Marriage,* Pepperdine College Press, 1946; *Some Special Responsibilities of Accrediting Agencies* (pamphlet), [Washington, D.C.], 1958; (with Aielene Lockhart and others) *Toward Excellence in College Teaching,* W. C. Brown, 1963; *A Search for Understanding: Thoughts on Education and Personality in a Time of Transition,* W. C. Brown, 1965; (with James D. Young) *A Teacher Is Many Things,* Indiana University Press, 1968. Contributor of articles to educational and psychological journals.

WORK IN PROGRESS: A book on contemporary values, tentatively titled *A Search for Fundamentals;* a monograph on factors influencing excellence in college teaching.

BIOGRAPHICAL/CRITICAL SOURCES: Earl V. Pullias, *A Search for Understanding,* W. C. Brown, 1965.

*   *   *

PULLING, Christopher Robert Druce   1893-
(Christopher Druce)

PERSONAL: Born August 26, 1893, in England; son of Alexander (a barrister-at-law) and Margaret Elen (Bealey) Pulling; married Eleanor Lois Sacre (a justice of the peace),

May 21, 1938; children: Simon Alexander Christopher. *Education:* Trinity College, Cambridge, B.A., 1915. *Politics:* Conservative. *Religion:* Church of England. *Home:* 4 Holmesdale Rd., Kew Gardens, Richmond, Surrey, England.

CAREER: Called to bar, London, England, 1924; Commissioner of Police of the Metropolis, New Scotland Yard, London, England, member of staff, 1919-54; retired. Seconded to Ministry of Home Security, 1942-45. Lecturer on the history of Scotland Yard, Sherlock Holmes, and Victorian and Edwardian music hall songs and singers. Freeman of City of London and liveryman of Merchant Taylors' Company. *Military service:* British Army, King's Royal Rifle Corps, 1914-18; lieutenant. *Member:* Music Hall Society, Oxford and Cambridge Club, Paternosters Luncheon Club, Players Theatre Club, Musgrave Ritualists (honorary member; New York).

WRITINGS: (Under pseudonym Christopher Druce) *Eccles Entertainers* (fiction), Bodley Head, 1924; (under pseudonym Christopher Druce) *Victorian Lays Relayed* (parodies), A. B. Campbell, 1935; *They Were Singing,* Harrap, 1952; *The Police* (careerbook), R. Hale, 1962; *Mr. Punch and the Police,* Butterworth & Co., 1964. Writer of radio scripts for "Song Scrapbook" programs, 1948-54. Contributor to *Chambers's Encyclopaedia, Oxford Junior Encyclopaedia* and *World Book Encyclopedia.* Also contributor to *Times* (London) and to *Punch.*

WORK IN PROGRESS: Two illustrated books, tentatively titled *The Seaside Holiday in England* and *The London Cab Driver;* further research on Victorian and Edwardian popular song.

AVOCATIONAL INTERESTS: Going to the theater and amateur theatricals; photography, walking, riding, and skiing.

*   *   *

PURDOM, Charles B(enjamin)   1883-1965

PERSONAL: Born October 15, 1883, in London, England; son of Benjamin and Margaret (Newington) Purdom; married Lilian Antonia Cutlar, July 9, 1912; children: Ronan Hugh (deceased), Philip Campden (deceased), Edmund Cutlar, Barbara (Mrs. Roger de Pourtales). *Home:* 39 Woodland Rise, Welwyn Garden City, Hertfordshire, England.

CAREER: Letchworth Magazine, Letchworth, Hertfordshire, England, editor, 1906-07; First Garden City, Letchworth, Hertfordshire, England, accountant, 1907-15; Welwyn Garden City, Hertfordshire, England, finance director, 1919-28; editor in London, England, of *Everyman,* 1928-32, *Theatregoer,* 1933, *New Britain,* 1933-34. International Housing and Town-Planning Federation, secretary, 1919-35, treasurer, 1935-38; joint secretary, London Theatre Council, 1939-40; former member, Welwyn Garden City Urban District Council. *Military service:* British Expeditionary Force, Infantry, 1915-18. *Member:* British Actors' Equity (secretary, 1939-40), Town Planning Institute (honorary), National Union of Journalists (honorary), Junior Philatelic Society (honorary), Critics' Circle (London; member of council, 1928-65).

WRITINGS: (With Charles Lee) *The Garden City Pantomine, 1910,* Dent, 1910; (with Lee) *The Garden City Pantomine, 1911,* Dent, 1911; *The Garden City: A Study in the Development of a Modern Town,* Dent, 1913; *The Garden City After the War,* privately printed, 1917; (editor) *Town*

Theory and Practice, Benn, 1921; *The Building of Satellite Towns*, Dent, 1925, 2nd edition, 1949; *Producing Plays*, Dutton, 1930, 3rd revised edition, 1951; (author of introduction and notes) *The Swan Shakespeare*, Dutton, 1930; (editor) *Everyman at War*, Dutton, 1930; *A Plan of Life*, Dent, 1932, 2nd edition, 1939; *The Perfect Master* (biography), Williams & Norgate, 1937.

The New Order, Dent, 1941; *Britain's Cities Tomorrow*, King, Littlewood, 1942; *How Should We Rebuild London?*, Dent, 1945, 2nd edition, 1946; *Economic Wellbeing*, Nicholson & Watson, 1948; *Producing Shakespeare*, Pitman, 1950; *Drama Festivals and Their Adjudication*, Dent, 1951; *Life Over Again* (essay in autobiography), Dent, 1951; *The Crosby Hall "Macbeth,"* Dent, 1951; *Harley Granville Barker*, Barrie & Rockliff, 1955, Harvard University Press, 1956; (editor) *God to Man and Man to God*, Gollancz, 1955; (editor) *Bernard Shaw's Letters to Granville Barker*, Theatre Arts, 1957; *The Letchworth Achievements*, Dent, 1963, Hillary, 1966; *What Happens in Shakespeare: A New Interpretation*, John Baker, 1963, Roy, 1964; *A Guide to the Plays of Bernard Shaw*, Crowell, 1963; *The God-Man: The Life, Journeys and Work of Meher Baba*, Allen & Unwin, 1964, Sheriar Press, 1971.

WORK IN PROGRESS: Playwriting Today.

(Died July 8, 1965)

* * *

PURKISER, W(estlake) T(aylor) 1910-

PERSONAL: Born April 28, 1910, in Oakland, Calif.; son of Jacob Taylor (a police officer) and May Frances (Naismith) Purkiser; married Arvilla Mae Butler, July 24, 1930; children: Joyce Mae (Mrs. Clinton W. Ingram), Joanne Lois (Mrs. Darrel K. Gumm), Sharon Lee. *Education:* Pasadena College, A.B., 1930; University of Southern California, M.A., 1939, Ph.D., 1948. *Politics:* Republican. *Home:* 9433 Reeder Rd., Overland Park, Kan. 66214.

CAREER: Church of the Nazarene, ordained minister, 1932. Pastor of Nazarene churches in Riverside, Bellflower, and Corning, Calif., 1930-37; Pasadena College, Pasadena, Calif., professor of philosophy, 1937-48, dean, 1943-45, vice-president, 1945-48, president, 1948-57; Nazarene Theological Seminary, Kansas City, Mo., professor of biblical theology, 1957-60; Nazarene Publishing House, Kansas City, Mo., editor of *Herald of Holiness*, 1960—. *Member:* Phi Beta Kappa, Kappa Phi Kappa.

WRITINGS—All published by Beacon Hill Press, except as indicated: *Know Your Old Testament*, 1947; *Conflicting Concepts of Holiness: Some Current Issues in the Doctrine of Sanctification*, 1953; (editor) *Exploring the Old Testament*, 1955; *Security: The False and the True*, 1956; *Beliefs That Matter Most*, 1959; (editor) *Exploring the Christian Faith*, 1960; *Adventures in Truth*, 1960; *Leviticus-Deuteronomy*, Light and Life Press, 1961; *Sanctification and Its Synonyms: Studies in the Biblical Theology of Holiness*, 1961; *The Message of Evangelism: The Saving Power of God*, 1963; *Joel-Micah*, Light and Life Press, 1963; *Spiritual Gifts: Healing and Tongues*, 1964; *The New Testament Image of the Ministry*, 1969.

WORK IN PROGRESS: Commentary on Psalms, for "Beacon Bible Commentary" series; *Old Testament Theology.*

* * *

PUTZ, Louis J. 1909-

PERSONAL: Born June 1, 1909, in Simbach, Germany; came to United States in 1923; son of Ludwig (a railroad engineer) and Anna (Leidmann) Putz. *Education:* University of Notre Dame, A.B., 1932; Grand Seminaire du Mans, theology study, 1932-35; Institut Catholique de Paris, L.S.T., 1936. *Home:* University of Notre Dame, Notre Dame, Ind. 46556. *Office:* Boxes 507, 596, Notre Dame, Ind.

CAREER: Ordained Roman Catholic priest, Paris, April 11, 1936. University of Notre Dame, Notre Dame, Ind., associate professor of theology, 1940—. President of Fides Publishers, 1952—; rector of Moreau Theological Seminary, 1966-72; director, Family Life Services for diocese of Fort Wayne and South Bend, 1972—; founder and director of Young Christian Students; co-founder of Christian Family Movement; director of Catholic Action Office, Notre Dame, Ind. *Awards, honors:* LL.D., Portland University, 1959.

WRITINGS: (With Francois Louvel) *Signs of Life*, Fides, 1953; (editor) *The Catholic Church, U.S.A.*, Fides, 1956; *The Modern Apostle*, Fides, 1957; *The Lord's Day*, Fides, 1963; (editor with James M. Lee) *Seminary Education in a Time of Change*, Fides, 1965; (with others) *Apostolic Dimensions of the Religious Life*, University of Notre Dame Press, 1966. Associate editor, *Perspectives*, 1959—.

SIDELIGHTS: Father Putz organized Harvest House, an organization to serve the elderly with church centers, a community living housing operation, and an adult education center.

* * *

PYM, Barbara (Mary Crampton) 1913-

PERSONAL: Born June 2, 1913, in Oswestry, Shropshire, England; daughter of Frederic Crampton (a solicitor) and Irena (Thomas) Pym. *Education:* St. Hilda's College, Oxford, B.A. (honors), 1934. *Religion:* Church of England. *Home:* Barn Cottage, Finstock, Oxford, England.

CAREER: Novelist. *Africa* (journal of International African Institute), London, England, assistant editor, 1958—. *Military service:* Women's Royal Naval Service, serving in England and Italy, 1943-46. *Member:* Society of Authors, P.E.N.

WRITINGS—Novels: *Some Tame Gazelle*, J. Cape, 1950; *Excellent Women*, J. Cape, 1952; *Jane and Prudence*, J. Cape, 1953; *Less Than Angels*, J. Cape, 1955, Vanguard, 1956; *A Glass of Blessings*, J. Cape, 1958; *No Fond Return of Love*, J. Cape, 1961.

AVOCATIONAL INTERESTS: Reading, domestic life, and cats.

* * *

PYM, Dora Olive (Ivens) 1890-

PERSONAL: Born December 10, 1890, in Harboro' Parva, Warwickshire, England; daughter of William (a timber merchant) and Sarah (Walker) Ivens; married Thomas Wentworth Pym (a clergyman), July 15, 1918 (deceased); children: Nancy (Mrs. C. P. Silver), Michael Tom, Christopher, Mary. *Education:* Girton College, Cambridge, classical tripos, 1913, M.A., 1944, researcher, 1914-15. *Religion:* Church of England. *Home:* 591 Finchley Rd., London NW3 7BS, England.

CAREER: University of London, Westfield College, London, England, temporary classical lecturer, 1916; Cambridge University, Girton College, Cambridge, England, classical lecturer, 1916-18, director of classical studies, 1918; part-time teacher of classics at Clifton High School, Bristol, England, and other schools, 1930-46; University of Bristol, Bristol, England, part-time lecturer in education, 1933-46, full-time lecturer, 1946-56. *Member:* Classical Association (life member), Joint Association of Classical Teachers (honorary member).

WRITINGS: Readings from the Literature of Ancient Rome, Harrap, 1921; *Readings from the Literature of Ancient Greece,* Harrap, 1924; *Salve per Saecula—A Latin Reader,* Harrap, 1936; *Outlines for Teaching Greek Reading,* J. Murray, 1946, enlarged edition, 1961; *Tom Pym: A Portrait,* Heffer, 1952; (with Nancy Silver) *Alive on Men's Lips—An Anthology of Rome and the Latin Language,* Harrap, 1953, new edition, Centaur Books, 1964; *Free Writing,* University of London Press, 1956; *The Tragedy of Dido and Aeneas,* Rivingtons, 1970. Contributor to educational journals.

SIDELIGHTS: Mrs. Pym speaks Italian, French, some German and modern Greek, and is studying Russian "to re-experience elementary learning."

*　　*　　*

QUASIMODO, Salvatore   1901-1968

PERSONAL: Surname is accented on second syllable; born August 20, 1901, in Modica, Sicily, Italy; son of Gaetano (a state inspector) and Clotilde (Ragusa) Quasimodo; married Maria Cumani (a dancer), 1948; children: Orietta, Alessandro. *Education:* Polytechnic study in Rome, Italy. *Religion:* Roman Catholic. *Home:* Corso Garibaldi 16, Milan, Italy.

CAREER: Worked as a technical designer for a construction firm, 1920-24, and in hardware store, 1924-26; junior official in the State Civil Engineers Bureau, traveling in Calabria, Sardinia, and Lombardy, Italy, 1926-29; began writing seriously, and worked briefly as a secretary for the publishing house of Mondadori in Milan during 1929; *Il Tempo* (magazine), Milan, Italy, assistant editor and drama critic, 1938-40; Giuseppe Verdi Conservatory, Milan, Italy, professor of Italian literature, 1941-64. *Member:* Accademia Nazionale di Luigi Cherubini (Florence; corresponding member), Academy of American Arts and Sciences, Akademi der Kuenste zu Berlin, Academie Internationale des Sciences Politiques de Geneve, Accademia Italiana di Scienze Biologiche e Morali. *Awards, honors:* Etna-Taormina International Poetry Prize (shared with Dylan Thomas), 1953; Tor Margana Prize; Viareggio Prize, 1958, for *La terra impareggiabile;* Nobel Prize for Literature, 1959; laureate (honoris causa), Universita di Messina.

WRITINGS: Acque e terre, Edizioni di Solaria (Florence), 1930; *Oboe sommerso,* Circoli (Genoa), 1932; *Odore di eucalyptus e altri versi,* Antico Fattore (Florence), 1933; *Erato e Apollion,* Scheiwiller (Milan), 1936; *Poesie,* Primi Piani (Milan), 1938; *Ed e subito sera,* Mondadori, 1942, 5th edition, 1971; *Con il piede straniero sopra il cuore,* Costume (Milan), 1946; *Giorno dopo giorno,* Mondadori, 1947, 7th edition, 1961; *La vita non e sogno,* Mondadori, 1949, 7th edition, 1966; (libretto) *Billy Budd,* Suvini e Zerboni, 1949; *Il falso e vero verde: Con undiscorso sulla poesia,* Mondadori, 1956, 4th edition, 1961; *La terra impareggiabile,* Mondadori, 1958, 5th edition, 1962; *Poesie scelte,* edited by Roberto Sanesi, Guanda (Parma), 1959; *Petrarca e il sentimento della solitudine,* All'insegna del pesce d'oro (Milan), 1959; *Tutte le poesie,* Mondadori, 1960, 8th edi-

tion, 1970; (libretto) *L'amore di Galatea,* Edizioni Teatro Massimo (Palermo), 1960; *Il poeta e il politico e altri saggi,* Schwarz, 1960; *Scritti sul teatro,* Mondadori, 1961; *Xavier Bueno,* Edizioni Galleria Santa Croce, *Nove poesie,* Franco Riva (Verone), 1963; *Dare a avere: 1959-1965* (poems), Mondadori, 1966; (author of introduction) Domenico Cantatore, *Cantatore,* Maestre (Rome), 1968; *Un anno di Salvatore Quasimodo: Lettere aperte,* Immordino, 1968; *Le opere: Poesia, prosa, traduzioni,* edited by Guido di Pino, Unione tipograficoeditrice torinese, 1968; *Le lettere d'amore di Quasimodo,* edited by Guido Le Noci, Apollinaire, 1969; *Poesie e discorsi sulla poesia,* edited by Gilberto Finzi, Mondadori, 1971.

Translator into Italian: Lirici Greci, Edizioni di Corrente, 1940; 7th edition, Mondadori, 1963; Virgil, *Il fiore delle Georgiche,* Gentile (Milan), 1942; Catullus, *Carmina,* [Milan], 1945; Homer, *Traduzioni dall' Odissea,* Rosa e Ballo, 1945; The Bible, *Il Vangelo secondo Giovanni,* Gentile, 1946; John Ruskin, *La Bibbia di Amiens,* Mondadori, 1946; Aeschylus, *Le coefore* (also see below), Bompiani, 1946; Sophocles, *Edipo re* (also see below), [Florence], 1946; Shakespeare, *Romeo e Giulietta,* Mondadori, 1948; Shakespeare, *Macbeth,* Einaudi (Turin), 1952; Shakespeare, *Riccardo III,* Mondadori, 1952; Pablo Neruda, *Poesie,* Einaudi, 1952, 3rd edition, 1967; Sophocles, *Elettra* (also see below), Mondadori, 1954; Catullus, *Canti,* Mondadori, 1955; Shakespeare, *La tempesta,* Einaudi, 1956; Moliere, *Tartuffe,* [Milan], 1957; e. e. cummings, *Poesie scelte* (also see below), All'insegna del Pesce d'oro, 1957; Shakespeare, *Otello,* Mondadori, 1958; Ovid, *Dalle metamorfosi,* All'insegna del Pesce d'oro, 1959; Euripides, *Ecuba,* Mondadori, 1963; Conrad Aiken, *Mutevoli pensieri* (also see below), Scheiwiller (Milan), 1963; *Tragici greci* (includes *Le coefore, Elettra, Edipo re*), Mondadori, 1963; Shakespeare, *Drammi,* Mondadori, 1963—; Euripides, *Eracle,* Mondadori, 1966; Shakespeare, *Antonio e Cleopatra,* Mondadori, 1966; *Dall' Antologia Palatina,* Mondadori, 1968; Homer, *Iliade: Episodi scelti,* Mondadori, 1968; Yves Lecomte, *Il gioco degli astragali,* Moneta (Milan), 1968; (and compiler) *Da Aiken e Cummings* (includes *Mutevoli pensieri* and *Poesie scelte*), Mondadori, 1968; *Leonida di Taranto* (with essay by Carlo Bo), Lacarta, 1969, limited edition (translations only, edited by Guido Noci), Apollinaire, 1970; (and editor) Paul Eluard, *Donner a voir,* Mondadori, 1970.

Editor: (with L. Anceschi) *Lirici minori del XIII e XIV secolo,* [Milan], 1941; *Lirica d'amore italiana,* Schwarz, 1957; *Poesia italiana del dopoguerra,* Schwarz, 1958; *Fiore dell'Antologia Palatina,* Guanda (Bologna), 1958; Tudor Arghezi, *Poesie,* Mondadori, 1966; Michel Angelo Buonarroti, *L'opera completa de Michelangelo pittore,* Rizzoli, 1966, 5th edition, 1969.

Translations of his works into English: The Selected Writings of Salvatore Quasimodo, edited and translated by Allen Mandelbaum, Farrar, Straus, 1960; *Salvatore Quasimodo: Poems,* Wesleyan University, 1960; *The Poet and the Politician: And Other Essays,* translated by Thomas Bergin and Sergio Pacifici, Southern Illinois University Press, 1964; *Selected Poems,* translated by Jack Bevan, Penguin, 1965; *To Give and to Have: And Other Poems,* translated by Edith Farnsworth, H. Regnery, 1969; *Debit and Credit,* translated by Jack Bevan, Anvil Press Poetry, 1972.

Translated work included in many anthologies, including *1001 Poems of Mankind,* compiled by Henry W. Wells, Tupper & Love, 1953; *The Promised Land and Other*

Poems, edited by Sergio Pacifici, Vanni, 1957; *The Penguin Book of Italian Verse*, edited by George Kay, Penguin, 1958.

SIDELIGHTS: "His voice is not only unique in contemporary European poetry," wrote Francis Golffing, "but it is a voice of rarest distinction: absolutely free of rhetorical inflation, at once generous and fastidious, *'unfashionable'* yet representative of an entire generation. . . . Quasimodo is the least vapid of poets, even as he is one of the purest by those exigent standards to which Mallarme, Rilke, and Valery have accustomed us." C. M. Bowra noted that Quasimodo "writes with an unusual sensibility about nature and with a keen understanding about the more elusive moods of the human spirit. He never says too much or tries to pass beyond the limits of his themes. He is intimate, discerning, sensitive, but he has not yet found the extraordinary power which is all the more impressive for being held in strict control and is now his most characteristic gift." The simplicity of his free verse was deceptive. A reviewer in the *Yale Review* wrote: "At first glance [his] poetry may seem somewhat minor and monotonous. . . . However, some careful examination will reveal Quasimodo's rare gift for delicacy of phrasing and tightness of structure."

His early poems tended to be subjective and nearly experimental. Though his work showed great continuity through the years, after 1940 it became less personal, more aware of external events. Bowra wrote: "Quasimodo is a classical poet who has absorbed the best modern devices and combines order, economy and clarity with a full measure of inventive surprise. Though he eschews the more traditional forms of Italian verse and in his earlier work favored short lines, his work has now an impressive, majestic movement which owes not a little to the great masters of his language. . . . [He now stands] in his own strength as a poet who is both Italian and European, both contemporary and universal."

BIOGRAPHICAL/CRITICAL SOURCES—Periodicals: *Saturday Review*, November 7, 1959, June 11, 1960; *New York Times Book Review*, November 15, 1959, July 3, 1960; *Reporter*, December 10, 1959; *Christian Science Monitor*, June 9, 1960; *New York Herald Tribune Book Review*, July 10, 1960; *Yale Review*, September, 1960; *Books Abroad*, winter, 1960; *London Magazine*, December, 1960.

Books: Annamaria Angioletti, *E fu subito sera*, Marotta (Naples), 1969; *Birolli, x. Beuno, Cantatore, De Chirico, Esa D'albisola, Fabbri, Manzu, Marino C., Mastroianni, Migneco, Rossello, Rossi, Sassu, Sotilis, Unsellini, Tamburi visti da Salvatore Quasimodo*, Edizioni Trentadue (Milan), 1969.

(Died June 14, 1968)

* * *

QUINN, Herbert F(urlong) 1910-

PERSONAL: Born February 11, 1910, in Montreal, Quebec, Canada; son of James Patrick and Margaret (Furlong) Quinn; married Evelyn Hessian (a social worker), June 4, 1955; children: Kevin Herbert. *Education:* Sir George Williams University, B.A., 1942; McGill University, M.A., 1946; Columbia University, Ph.D., 1959. *Home:* 3789 Royal Ave., Montreal H4A 2M3, Canada. *Office:* Concordia University, 1455 Maisonneuve Blvd. W., Montreal 107, Quebec, Canada.

CAREER: Sir George Williams University, Montreal, Quebec, part-time lecturer, 1942-46, lecturer, 1946-47, assistant professor, 1947-49, associate professor, 1949-55, professor of political science beginning, 1955; now professor of political science, Concordia University, Montreal, Quebec. *Member:* Canadian Political Science Association (executive council, 1949-51), American Political Science Association. *Awards, honors:* Canada Council senior fellowship, 1966-67.

WRITINGS: The Union Nationale: A Study in Quebec Nationalism, University of Toronto Press, 1963. Contributor to *Canadian Encyclopaedia*, 1966, and to *Culture*, *Dalhousie Review*, *Queen's Quarterly*, and political science journals.

WORK IN PROGRESS: Evolution of Political Parties in the French Third Republic, 1870-1940, publication expected in 1975.

* * *

QURESHI, Ishtiaq Husain 1903-

PERSONAL: Born November 20, 1903, in Patiali, India; son of Sadiq Husain (a civil servant) and Altafunnisa (Ali) Qureshi; married Nayab Begam, July 5, 1925; children: Saiyid Afsar (son). *Education:* St. Stephen's College, Delhi University, B.A. (honors), 1926, M.A., 1928; Sydney Sussex College, Cambridge, Ph.D., 1939. *Politics:* Liberal. *Religion:* Islam. *Home:* Zeba Manzar, Shahid-1.c.-Millat Rd., Sharafabad, Karachi 5, Pakistan. *Office:* University of Karachi, Karachi 32, Pakistan.

CAREER: Delhi University, Delhi, India, lecturer at St. Stephen's College, 1928-40, university reader, 1940-42, professor of history, 1943-47; University of Punjab, Lahore, Pakistan, professor of history, 1948-49; Pakistan government, deputy minister, 1949, minister of state, 1950-51, cabinet minister, 1952-54; Central Institute of Islamic Research, director, 1960-61; University of Karachi, Karachi, Pakistan, vice-chancellor, 1961—. Visiting professor of history, Columbia University, 1955-60. *Member:* Pakistan Institute of International Affairs (member of council), Pakistan Historical Society (president), Pakistan Political Science Association (president), Institute of Central and West Asian Studies (president).

WRITINGS: The Administration of the Sultanate of Delhi, S. M. Ashraf, 1942, 4th edition, Pakistan Historical Society, 1958; *The Development of Islamic Culture in India*, S. M. Ashraf, 1946; *The Future Development of Islamic Policy*, S. M. Ashraf, 1946; *The Pakistani Way of Life*, Praeger, 1956, 2nd edition, 1957; *The Muslim Community of the Indo-Pakistan Subcontinent, 610-1947: A Brief Historical Analysis*, Mouton & Co., 1962; *Aspects of the History, Culture and Religions of Pakistan: A Series of Lectures*, South-East Asia Treaty Organization, 1963; *The Struggle for Pakistan*, University of Karachi, 1965, 2nd edition, 1969; *The Administration of the Mughul Empire*, University of Karachi, 1966; (editor) *A Short History of Pakistan*, four volumes, University of Karachi, 1967. Also author of *Pakistan, an Islamic Democracy*.

Contributor to *Sources of Indian Tradition*, 1955; *History of Freedom Movement*, 1956; *Traditions, Values and Socio-Economic Development*, 1961; *Foreign Policies in a World of Change*, 1963. Contributor to learned journals. Member of editorial board, *History of Freedom Movement* and *Journal of Pakistan Historical Society*.

WORK IN PROGRESS: The Role of the Ulema in the Freedom Movement.

SIDELIGHTS: Qureshi speaks Urdu, English, Persian, and reads Arabic, French, and Italian. *Avocational interests:* Poetry; gardening, especially growing plants experimentally which normally do not grow in Pakistan.

*   *   *

RADHAKRISHNAN, Sarvepalli   1888-

PERSONAL: Born September 5, 1888, at Tiruttani, Madras, India; son of S. Veeraswami; married S. Sivakamamma, May, 1903 (deceased); children: one son, five daughters. *Education:* Madras University, M.A., 1909; Oxford University, M.A., 1936. *Home:* 30 Edward Elliot Rd., Madras, India.

CAREER: Madras University, Presidency College, Madras, India, assistant professor, 1911-16, professor of philosophy, 1916-18; Mysore University, Mysore, India, professor of philosophy, 1918-21; Calcutta University, Calcutta, India, Calcutta George V Professor of Philosophy, 1921-39; Oxford University, Oxford, England, Spalding Professor of Eastern Religions and Ethics, 1936-52, professor emeritus, 1952—; Indian Ambassador to Soviet Union, 1949-52; Vice-President of Republic of India, 1952-62, president, 1962-67. Vice-chancellor of Andhra University, 1931-36, Banares Hindu University, 1939-48; chancellor of Delhi University, 1953-62. Leader of Indian delegation to UNESCO, 1946-52, chairman of executive board, 1948-49, president of General Conference, 1953-54, 1958.

MEMBER: British Academy (honorary fellow), Royal Society of Literature (fellow), Royal Asiatic Society of Bengal (honorary fellow), P.E.N. (president of India branch, 1949—; vice-president of international organization, 1956—). *Awards, honors:* Knighted, 1931; German Order pour le Merite, 1954; honorary fellow, All Souls College, Oxford; Order of Merit, 1963; honorary degrees from University of London, Oxford University, Cambridge University, and from more than fifty other universities.

WRITINGS: The Essentials of Psychology, Oxford University Press, 1912; *The Philosophy of Rabindranath Tagore*, Macmillan, 1918, Indian edition, Good Companions (Baroda), 1961; *The Reign of Religion in Contemporary Philosophy*, Macmillan, 1920; *Indian Philosophy*, Allen & Unwin, Volume I, 1923, Volume II, 1927; *The Philosophy of the Upanisads*, Allen & Unwin, 1924, 2nd edition, 1935; *The Hindu View of Life*, Allen & Unwin, 1927; *The Religion We Need*, Benn, 1928; *The Vedanta According to Samkara and Ramanuja*, Allen & Unwin, 1928; *Kalki or the Future of Civilization*, Kegan Paul & Co., 1929, 2nd edition, 1934.

An Idealist View of Life, Allen & Unwin, 1932; *East and West in Religion*, Allen & Unwin, 1933; *Freedom and Culture*, G. A. Natesan & Co., (Madras), 1936; *Contemporary Indian Philosophy*, Allen & Unwin, 1936; *The Heart of Hindusthan*, G. A. Natesan & Co., 1936; *Guatama—the Buddha*, Oxford University Press, 1938; *Eastern Religious and Western Thought*, Oxford University Press, 1939; *Introduction to Mahatma Gandhi* (essays and reflections), Allen & Unwin, 1939; *India and China*, Hind Kitabs (Bombay), 1944; *Education, Politics and War*, International Book Service (Poona), 1944; *Is This Peace?*, Hind Kitabs, 1945; *Religion and Society*, Allen & Unwin, 1947; *The Bhagavadgita*, Allen & Unwin, 1948; *Great Indians*, Hind Kitabs, 1949.

The Dhammapada, Oxford University Press, 1950; *The Principal Upanisads*, Allen & Unwin, 1953; *Occasional*

Speeches and Writings, First Series, Publications Division, Government of India, 1956, Second Series, 1960, combined edition, First and Second Series, 1960, Third Series, 1963; *The Brahma Sutra; The Philosophy of Spiritual Life*, Allen & Unwin, 1960; *Fellowship of the Spirit*, Center for the Study of World Religions, Harvard Divinity School, 1961; *President Radhakrishnan's Speeches and Writings*, Publications Division, Government of India, 1965; *Radhakrishnan on Nehru*, Publications Division, Government of India, 1965; *Religion in a Changing World*, Allen & Unwin, 1967. Contributor to *Encyclopaedia Britannica* and to *Hibbert Journal, Mind*, and other philosophy journals.

*   *   *

RAE, (Margaret) Doris

PERSONAL: Born in Newcastle upon Tyne, England; daughter of John and Jessie (McKay) Rae. *Education:* Attended private and council schools in England. *Politics:* Conservative. *Religion:* Church of England. *Home:* 79 Cheviot View, Ponteland, Northumberland, England.

CAREER: Administration of Justice, Newcastle upon Tyne, England, currently chief clerk and cashier to justices.

WRITINGS—All published by R. Hale, except as indicated: *Sings the Nightingale*, Hurst & Blackett, 1956, *The Whispering Wind*, 1958, *Flame on the Peaks*, 1958, *Journey into Paradise*, 1959, *Painted Waters*, 1959, *The Music and the Splendour*, 1959, *Golden Dawn*, 1960, *The Rowans Are Red*, 1960, *The Lying Jade*, 1961, *The Flowering Summer*, 1961, *Serenade to a Nurse*, 1962, *The Gossamer Web*, 1962, *Bright Particular Star*, 1962, *The Shadow and the Sun*, 1963, *Enchantment in the Snow*, 1963, *Highland Nurse*, 1964, *Blue Is the Lake*, 1964, *Blaze of Gladness*, 1965, *Magic Spring*, 1965, *The Painted Fan*, 1966, *The Constant Star*, 1966, *Echo of Romance*, 1967, *The Golden Hours*, 1968, *Flame of the Forest*, 1969, *The Joyous Prelude*, 1971.

WORK IN PROGRESS: A novel set in Scotland.

AVOCATIONAL INTERESTS: Reading, history, travel, theatre, opera, ballet, music, walking, collecting miniatures, china, and ivory. •

*   *   *

RAFTERY, Gerald (Bransfield) 1905-

PERSONAL: Born October 30, 1905, in Elizabeth, N.J.; son of Timothy Edward (an attorney) and Mary (Bransfield) Raftery; married Eleanor M. Murnin, August 5, 1933. *Education:* Seton Hall University, A.B., 1929; New York University, M.A., 1937; Columbia University, library courses. *Politics:* Independent Democrat. *Religion:* Roman Catholic. *Home address:* R.D. 2, Arlington, Vt. 05250.

CAREER: Elizabeth (N.J.) Board of Education, junior high school teacher, 1930-46, librarian, 1947-64; Martha Canfield Memorial Library, Arlington, Vt., librarian, 1964—. *Military service:* U.S. Army, Signal Intelligence Service, 1942-45; served in European theatre; became sergeant; received five battle stars.

WRITINGS: Gray Lance (juvenile), Morrow, 1950; *Snow Cloud* (juvenile), Morrow, 1951; *Copperhead Hollow* (juvenile), Morrow, 1952; *City Dog* (juvenile), Morrow, 1953; *Twenty-Dollar Horse* (juvenile), Messner, 1955; *The Natives Are Always Restless*, Vanguard, 1964; *Slaver's Gold* (juvenile), Vanguard, 1967. Author of weekly column, "If I May Say So," in *Bennington Banner* (Vermont) and *Berkshire Eagle* (Pittsfield, Mass.), 1966—.

WORK IN PROGRESS: An adult comic novel.

SIDELIGHTS: Four of Raftery's juvenile books have been published in England, Holland, Germany, and Sweden.

* * *

RAMASWAMY, Mysore 1902-

PERSONAL: Born April 27, 1902, in Tumkur, Mysore State, India; son of Sir M. N. Krishna Rau (senior member of Executive Council and officiating dewan of Mysore State) and Gundamma; married Sarojamma, 1924; children: Malathi (Mrs. B. V. Jaya Rao), Shantha (Mrs. R. Ramachandry); Jayasimha, Narendra, and Bharatha (sons). *Education:* University of Bangalore, B.A., 1923; Madras University, B.L., 1925. *Religion:* Hindu. *Home:* 1 Kankanhalli Rd., Bangalore 4, Mysore State, India.

CAREER: High Court of Mysore, India, advocate, 1925—; Supreme Court of India, senior advocate, 1953—; Delhi University, Delhi, India, 1960-65, became professor of constitutional law and dean of Faculty of Law. Exchange scholar at Stanford University, School of Law, under U.S. Department of State International Educational Exchange Program, 1955-56.

WRITINGS: The Law of the Indian Constitution, Longmans, Green, 1938; *Distribution of Legislative Powers in the Future Indian Federation,* Longmans, Green, 1944; *Fundamental Rights,* Indian Council of World Affairs, 1946; *The Commerce Clause in the Constitution of the United States,* Longmans, Green, 1948; *The Creative Role of the Supreme Court of the United States,* Stanford University Press, 1956. Contributor to law journals in Canada, United States, Australia, and India.

SIDELIGHTS: The Creative Role of the Supreme Court of the United States has been translated into Indonesian and Urdu.

* * *

RAMSKILL, Valerie Patricia Roskams (Carole Brooke)

PERSONAL: Born in Plymouth, Devonshire, England; daughter of Leslie Jack and Dorothy Eleanor (Croker) Roskams; married Herbert Ramskill (a businessman and theatrical producer). *Education:* Attended schools in London, Sussex, and Surrey, England. *Home:* Armadale, Mellor Brow, Mellor, near Blackburn, Lancasterhire, England.

CAREER: Peterborough Standard, Peterborough, England, reporter. *Member:* Royal National Life Boat Institution.

WRITINGS—All under pseudonym Carole Brooke: *Light and Shade,* John Long, 1947; *To Reach the Heights,* John Long, 1948; *Devils' Justice,* John Long, 1948; *Simon and Monica,* John Long, 1950; *As Others See Us,* John Long, 1952; *The Changing Tide,* John Long, 1952; *Bitter Summer,* John Long, 1954; *No Other Destiny,* John Long, 1955; *The Way of Life,* John Long, 1956; *The Day Returns,* John Long, 1957; *To Each His Own,* Hurst & Blackett, 1958; *Shadow of the Past,* Hurst & Blackett, 1960; *For Promised Joy,* Hurst & Blackett, 1962; *This Day's Madness,* Hurst & Blackett, 1962; *Till All the Seas,* Hurst & Blackett, 1964; *Deceivers Ever,* Hurst & Blackett, 1965. Contributor of short stories to *Heiress.*

WORK IN PROGRESS: A novel.

AVOCATIONAL INTERESTS: The country, animals, reading (particularly history and biographies), travel, and theatre-going.

* * *

RAND, Frank Prentice 1889-

PERSONAL: Born November 8, 1889, in Worcester, Mass.; son of John Prentice (a physician) and Harriet (Anderson) Rand; married Margarita S. Hopkins, August 17, 1916. *Education:* Williams College, A.B., 1912; Amherst College, M.A., 1915. *Religion:* Protestant. *Home:* Mount Pleasant, Amherst, Mass. 01002.

CAREER: University of Maine, Orono, instructor in English, 1913-14; University of Massachusetts, Amherst, began as instructor, 1914, professor of English, 1933-60, head of department, 1933-55, acting dean, School of Liberal Arts, 1948-55. Trustee of Cushing Academy and Jones Library. *Military service:* U.S. Medical Corps, 1918-19; became sergeant first class. *Member:* College English Association (director, 1939-40), Shakespeare Association of America, Modern Language Association of America, Phi Kappa Phi, Delta Sigma Rho, University Club (Winter Park, Fla.). *Awards, honors:* L.H.D., University of Massachusetts, 1955, Williams College, 1956.

WRITINGS: Tiamat, and Other Verses, Kingsbury, 1917; *Garlingtown* (verse), Cornhill Publishing Co., 1918; *John Epps* (play; first produced by Roister Doisters at Massachusetts Agricultural College [now University of Massachusetts], June, 1921), Kingsbury, 1921; (translator with Dan F. Waugh) *Crumpled Leaves of Old Japan,* 1922; *Phi Sigma Kappa, a History, 1872-1923,* Council of Phi Sigma Kappa, 1923; *Doctor Ben of Butter Hill,* Cornhill Publishing Co., 1923; *Sidney* (play; first produced by Roister Doisters at Massachusetts Agricultural College, 1925), Roister Doisters, Massachusetts Agricultural College, 1925; "Our Lady Cushing" (play), first produced at Cushing Academy, 1925; *In the Octagon* (three-act play), Row, Peterson, 1927; *Yesterdays at Massachusetts State College, 1863, 1933,* Associate Alumni, Massachusetts State College, 1933; (self-illustrated) *Heart O'Town,* privately printed, 1945; *The Village of Amherst, a Landmark of Light,* Amherst Historical Society, 1958; *The Story of David Grayson,* Jones Library, 1963; *The Myth and Magic of David Grayson,* Jones Library, 1963; *Cushing Academy, 1865-1965,* Cushing Academy, 1965; *Wordsworth's Mariner Brother,* Newell Press, 1966; *The Jones Library in Amherst, 1919-1969,* Jones Library, 1969. Editor, *Signet* (Phi Sigma Kappa), 1914-29.

SIDELIGHTS: Rand has been the director of fifty full-length plays for the Roister Doisters. *Avocational interests:* Painting, bird-carving, and mask-making.

* * *

RANDALL, Clarence Belden 1891-1967

PERSONAL: Born March 5, 1891, in Newark Valley, N.Y.; son of Oscar Smith (a storekeeper) and Esther Clara (Belden) Randall; married Emily Fitch Phelps, August 18, 1917; children: Mary (Mrs. J. Gordon Gilkey, Jr.), Miranda (Mrs. Lemuel B. Hunter). *Education:* Harvard University, A.B., 1912, LL.B., 1915. *Politics:* Republican. *Religion:* Episcopalian. *Home:* 700 Blackthorn Rd., Winnetka, Ill. *Office:* Inland Steel Co., 30 West Monroe St., Chicago, Ill.

CAREER: Admitted to Michigan bar, 1915. Attorney in

Ishpeming, Mich., 1915-25; Inland Steel Co., Chicago, Ill., assistant vice-president in charge of raw materials, 1925-30, vice-president, 1930-48, assistant to president, 1948, president, 1949-53, chairman of board of directors, 1953-56, became honorary director of the company. Director of Chicago Burlington & Quincy Railroad Co., 1955-63 and of Bell & Howell Co., 1956-63. U.S. government posts include: member of Business Advisory Council, U.S. Department of Commerce, 1951-57; chief or member of special missions to Turkey, 1953, 1956; special consultant to President Eisenhower on foreign economic policy, 1954-56, and special assistant to the President, 1956-61; chairman of Council on Foreign Economic Policy, 1956-61; advisory committee on International Business Problems for the State Department, 1963-67. General chairman, Chicago Community and War Fund Campaign, 1944; director, National War Fund, 1944-45. Trustee of University of Chicago, 1936-61, Wellesley College, 1946-49, and Chicago Natural History Museum, 1946-61; member of Harvard Board of Overseers, 1947-53. Godkin Lecturer, Harvard University, 1938; Charles R. Walgreen Foundation Lecturer, University of Chicago, 1954; Fund for Adult Education Lecturer, Harvard University, 1956; Regents Lecturer, University of California, 1962. *Military service:* U.S. Army, Infantry, 1917-19; served in France; became captain.

MEMBER: American Academy of Arts and Sciences (fellow), American Ornithologists Union (associate), American Philosophical Society, Chicago Heart Association (vice-chairman of board of directors), Phi Beta Kappa, Delta Upsilon, Association of Harvard Clubs (president, 1937-38), Harvard Alumni Association (president, 1949), Commercial Club, Chicago Club, University Club, and Mid-Day Club (all Chicago), Indian Hill Country Club (Winnetka), Metropolitan Club (Washington, D.C.), Union Interalliee (Paris).

AWARDS, HONORS: D.Eng. from Michigan College of Mining and Technology, 1947, Rose Polytechnic Institute, 1952; LL.D. from Northeastern University, 1948, University of Michigan, 1953, Brown University, 1954, Dartmouth College, 1954, Harvard University, 1954, Kenyon College, 1954, Northwestern University, 1955, Colby College, 1956, Amherst College, 1957, Lake Forest College, 1957, Knox College, 1963, Beloit College, 1964; D. Bus. Adm. from Denison University, 1953; L.H.D. from National College of Education, 1960; J.S.D. from Suffolk University, 1963. American Iron and Steel Institute Medal, 1932, honorary citation, 1952; Lane Memorial Award, Lane Technical High School, 1948; honorary member, Chippewa Indian Tribe, 1951; Patriotic Service Award, Sons of the American Revolution, Illinois Society, 1952; Phi Beta Kappa Association of Chicago Distinguished Service Award, 1952; Tau Kappa Alpha Speaker-of-the-year Award, 1952; National Association of Manufacturers "Man of the Year" Award, 1952; Freedoms Foundation Honor Medal, 1952, for article, "Free Enterprise Is Not a Hunting License" in *Atlantic Monthly*, 1953, for *Freedom's Faith*, 1955, for article, "The American Pharisee" in *Kiwanis Magazine;* Colonial Dames of America Award, 1953, for *A Creed for Free Enterprise*, 1954, for *Freedom's Faith;* Captain Robert Dollar Memorial Award of National Foreign Trade Council, 1954; Business Statesman of the Year Award, National Sales Executives, 1954; Chicago Merit Award, Rotary Club of Chicago, 1955; Distinguished Service Award, National Society of Delta Sigma Rho, 1956; Medal of Honor, Theodore Roosevelt Association, 1956; American Metal Market Distinguished Service Award, 1956; World Under-

standing Award, Chicago Council on Foreign Relations, 1958; U.S. Chamber of Commerce "Great Living American" Award, 1960; American College of Hospital Administrators "Executive of the Year" Award, 1961; Award for Business Statesmanship, Harvard Business School of Chicago, 1961; American Heart Association "Heart-of-the-Year" Award, 1962; Presidential Medal of Freedom, 1963; other awards for civic and national service.

WRITINGS: (With Roger N. Baldwin) *Civil Liberties and Industrial Conflict*, Harvard University Press, 1938; *A Creed for Free Enterprise*, Atlantic-Little, Brown, 1952; *Freedom's Faith*, Atlantic-Little, Brown, 1953; *A Foreign Economic Policy for the United States*, University of Chicago Press, 1954; *Over My Shoulder*, Atlantic-Little, Brown, 1956; *The Communist Challenge to American Business*, Atlantic-Little, Brown, 1958; *The Folklore of Management*, Atlantic-Little, Brown, in association with Dun & Bradstreet, 1961; *A Businessman Looks at Government Pay*, National Civil Service League, 1962; *Sixty-Five Plus*, Atlantic-Little, Brown, 1963; *Making Good in Management*, McGraw, 1964; *Adventures in Friendship*, Atlantic-Little, Brown, 1965; *The Executive in Transition*, McGraw, 1967. Contributor to magazines.

(Died August 4, 1967)

*   *   *

RANKIN, Daniel S(tanislaus)   1895-1972

PERSONAL: Born February 23, 1895, in New Orleans, La.; son of Roland O. and Anna M. (Hanney) Rankin. *Education:* Catholic University of America, B.A., 1919, M.A., 1928; University of Pennsylvania, Ph.D., 1932. *Home:* Bishop's House, 5078 Warwick Ter., Pittsburgh, Pa. 15213. *Office:* 60, rue d'Assas, Paris 6, France.

CAREER: Ordained Roman Catholic priest, diocese of Pittsburgh, 1919; U.S. Navy, chaplain, 1942-53, retired as commander; historical researcher in France and England, 1956-72; American Students' and Artists' Center, Paris, France, director, 1958-72. Discoverer of unknown manuscripts relating to Joan of Arc era; lecturer on Joan of Arc on U.S. tour, 1964-65. *Awards, honors:* University of Pennsylvania fellowship for European study, 1932-33.

WRITINGS: Kate Chopin and Her Creole Stories, University of Pennsylvania Press, 1932; (editor and translator with Claire Quintal) *The First Biography of Joan of Arc*, University of Pittsburgh Press, 1964; (with Quintal) *Letters of Joan of Arc*, Pittsburgh Diocesan Council of Catholic Women, 1969. Contributor of articles and reviews to *New York Herald Tribune, New York Sun, Commonweal, America, Saturday Review, Catholic Educational Review, Month* (London), and *Sign*.

WORK IN PROGRESS: Joan of Arc and the Pope, for Yale University Press; *Joan of Arc Indicted;* and a third book, *Joan of Arc and Paris*, including author's discovery of diplomatic correspondence between Charles VII and the Duke of Burgandy.

(Died May 25, 1972)

*   *   *

RANKIN, Karl Lott   1898-

PERSONAL: Born September 4, 1898, in Manitowoc, Wis.; son of Emmet Woollen (a clergyman) and Alberta (Lott) Rankin; married Pauline Jordan, October 3, 1925. *Education:* Studied at California Institute of Technology, 1917-19, Federal Polytechnic, Zurich, Switzerland, 1920-

21; Princeton University, C.E., 1922. *Politics:* Republican. *Religion:* Congregationalist. *Home:* South Bridgton, Me. 04009; (winter) c/o American Embassy, Athens 602, Greece.

CAREER: Near East Relief, construction superintendent in Armenia, 1922-25; Berlant Development Co., Linden, N.J., manager, 1925-27; U.S. Department of Commerce, foreign commerce officer, 1927-39; U.S. Department of State, Foreign Service officer, 1939-61, ambassador, 1953-61; retired. Assigned to diplomatic and consular posts in Prague, 1927, Athens and Tirana, 1932, Brussels, 1939, Belgrade, 1940, Cairo, 1941 (interned in Manila by Japanese before officially taking Cairo post), Cairo, 1944, Athens and Belgrade, 1944-46, Vienna, 1946-47, and Athens, 1947-49; consul general, Canton, 1949, and Hong Kong, 1949; minister and charge d'affairs, Taipei, Formosa, 1950-53; Ambassador to China, 1953-57; Ambassador to Yugoslavia, 1958-61. Trustee, Pierce College, Athens, Greece. *Military service:* U.S. Navy, active duty, 1918. U.S. Naval Reserve; lieutenant commander, 1937.

MEMBER: American Society of Civil Engineers (life), Phi Kappa Sigma, Dial (Princeton), Cosmos Club (Washington, D.C.), Princeton Club of New York, Royal Yacht Club (Athens). *Awards, honors:* LL.D., Bowdoin College and Bates College.

WRITINGS: China Assignment, University of Washington Press, 1964.

* * *

RAUSHENBUSH, Esther (Mohr) 1898-

PERSONAL: Born November 22, 1898, in Seattle, Wash.; daughter of Maurice (a merchant) and Ann (Suransky) Mohr; married Carl Raushenbush (a labor economist), April 17, 1935; children: John. *Education:* University of Washington, Seattle, A.B., 1921, M.A., 1922; post-graduate study at Cambridge University, British Museum, and Radcliffe College. *Home:* 54 Morningside Dr., New York, N.Y.

CAREER: Teacher of English at University of Washington, Seattle, 1922-23, Wellesley College, Wellesley, Mass., 1924-25, and Barnard College and Columbia University, 1928-35; Sarah Lawrence College, Bronxville, N.Y., teacher of English, 1935-46, 1957-62, dean, 1946-57, director of Center for Continuing Education, 1962-65, acting dean, 1964-65, president, 1965-69, president emeritus, 1969—. Consultant in planning New College (an experimental division) of Hofstra University, 1957-58; Trustee of Sarah Lawrence College, 1958-61. Member of education subcommittee, President's Commission on the Status of Women, and of advisory council, National Institutes of Health; senior advisor, John Hay Whitney Foundation, 1971—.

AWARDS, HONORS: Litt.D., Russell Sage College, 1962; L.H.D., Women's Medical College of Pennsylvania, 1965, Skidmore College, 1965; Alumnus Summa Laude Dignatus, University of Washington, Seattle.

WRITINGS: (Editor) *Psychology for Individual Education,* Columbia University Press, 1942; *Literature for Individual Education,* Columbia University Press, 1942; (contributor) *A Graduate Program in an Undergraduate College,* Wesleyan University Press, 1956; (editor with Lois Murphy, and contributor) *Achievement in the College Years: A Record of Intellectual and Personal Growth,* Harper, 1960; *The Student and His Studies,* Wesleyan

University Press, 1964; (contributor) *Unfinished Journey: Issues in American Education,* preface by Lyndon B. Johnson, Day, 1968. Writer of pamphlets on education for women. Contributor to *Harper's* and *Educational Record.*

* * *

RAVEN, Frithjof Andersen 1907-1966

PERSONAL: Born January 18, 1907, in Cincinnati, Ohio; son of Kristn Andersen (a civil engineer) and Emily (Schaeffer) Raven; married Margaret Whitcomb, November 27, 1947. *Education:* University of Washington, Seattle, B.A., 1934, Normal Diploma, 1935, M.A., 1939; George Washington University, Ph.D., 1944. *Politics:* Southern Democrat. *Religion:* Episcopalian. *Home:* 317 Lee St., Starkville, Miss. 39762. *Office:* Mississippi State University, State College, Miss. 39762.

CAREER: High school and junior college teacher, 1935-37; University of Washington, Seattle, instructor in German, 1939-40; U.S. Navy, David W. Taylor Model Basin, Carderock, Md., civilian research analyst, 1941-46; Massachusetts Institute of Technology, Cambridge, assistant professor of modern languages, 1946-50; University of Alabama, Tuscaloosa, assistant professor, 1950-51, associate professor, 1951-52, professor of German, 1953-65; Mississippi State University, Starkville, professor of modern languages and comparative Indo-European linguistics, 1965-66. Adjunct professor of Spanish, George Washington University, 1944-46; Fulbright research professor, University of Marburg, 1956-57; visiting professor, Wake Forest College, 1962-63. Consultant to U.S. Navy, 1946-63.

MEMBER: Modern Language Association of America, Linguistic Society of America, Mediaeval Academy of America, American Dialect Society, American Academy of Arts and Sciences, South Atlantic Modern Language Association, Institute Verein der Germanisten. *Awards, honors:* Distinguished Civilian Service Award and Citation from U.S. Navy, 1945; Alabama Research Commission grants-in-aid, 1953, 1955, 1956, 1960, 1962, 1963.

WRITINGS: (Translator) H. Neuber, *Theory of Notch Stresses,* Edwards Brothers, 1945; (with A. M. Feiler and A. Jespersen) *An Annotated Bibliography of Cavitation,* U.S. Navy, 1945; (translator) R. Fuchs, *Cycles of Gas Turbines and Attempts to Actually Produce Them,* U.S. Navy, 1945; *Die schwachen Verben des Althochdeutschen,* W. Scmitz, 1963-67, University of Alabama Press, 1964—; (editor with Wolfram Karl Legner and James Cecil King) *Germanic Studies in Honor of Edmund Henry Sehrt,* University of Miami Press, 1968.

Translator of some thirty scientific reports from the German, French, and Dutch for publication by Taylor Model Basin, U.S. Navy, 1948-52, some of them running to booklength. Contributor of articles, monographs, reviews and abstracts to *Hispania, Monatshefte, Bataviana, Chemical and Engineering News, Erasmus,* and other scholarly journals.

WORK IN PROGRESS: Translating Wilhelm von Humboldt's *Uber die Verschiedenheit des menschlichen Sprachbaues,* for University of Alabama Press; revising Old High German period of Korner's *Bibliographisches Handbuch,* for Francke Verlag; translating with E. Scott Barr, Poggendorff's *Geschichte der Physik.*

SIDELIGHTS: Raven was competent in modern, old, and middle High German, modern and old French, modern and old Spanish, Italian, Dutch, Norwegian, Swedish, Gothic, Old Icelandic, Old and Middle English, vulgar and medieval Latin, and Sanskrit. *Avocational interests:* Tennis, trout fishing, travel.

(Died, 1966)

* * *

READ, Cecil B(yron) 1901-1972

PERSONAL: Born January 11, 1901, in Lewis, Iowa; son of Byron Justus (a teacher) and Mattie (Burns) Read; married Mabel Marie Culbert, 1928 (died, 1931); married Marguerite Williams (a secretary), April 20, 1935; children: (first marriage) Byron Joseph; (second marriage) Barbara Janet (Mrs. Russell J. Hayes), Beverly Jean. *Education:* Colorado College, Colorado Springs, A.B., 1927; Princeton University, A.M., 1928; University of Colorado, Boulder, M.S., 1935; Colorado State College (now University of Northern Colorado), Ph.D., 1938. *Politics:* Republican. *Religion:* Methodist. *Home:* 304 North Brown, Mount Pleasant, Mich. 48858.

CAREER: Princeton University, Princeton, N.J., instructor in mathematics, 1928-29; Taft School, Watertown, Conn., master in mathematics, 1929-31; Genessee Wesleyan Junior College, Lima, N.Y., head of department of mathematics, 1931-32; University of Wichita, Wichita, Kan., 1932-62, began as assistant professor, became professor of mathematics and head of department, 1940-62; Central Michigan University, Mount Pleasant, professor of history of mathematics, 1962-72. Visiting lecturer, Colorado State College, 1937; visiting professor, Baylor University, 1962; visiting lecturer in mathematics under sponsorship of Mathematical Association of America. *Member:* American Mathematical Society, Mathematical Association of America (regional governor, 1955-58), National Council of Teachers of Mathematics, Central Association of Science and Mathematics Teachers (member of board; president, 1960-61), Michigan Council of Teachers of Mathematics, Phi Beta Kappa.

WRITINGS: (With others) *Mathematics of Finance*, Pitman, 1952; *Manual of Statistics*, University of Wichita Press, 1956; (with others) *College Algebra*, Pitman, 1963; (with Amy King) *Pathways to Probability*, Holt, 1963. Writer of over three hundred book reviews and 150 articles, principally on mathematics. Mathematics editor, *School Science and Mathematics*; former editor, *Reviews and Evaluation* and *Mathematics Teacher*.

WORK IN PROGRESS: A bibliography of articles on the history of mathematics.

(Died June 5, 1972)

* * *

REAMAN, George Elmore 1889-1969

PERSONAL: Surname is pronounced *Ray*-man; born July 22, 1889, in Concord, Ontario, Canada; son of George (a farmer) and Martha Ann (White) Reaman; married Flora Green, July 22, 1914; children: Elaine. *Education:* University of Toronto, B.A., 1911, M.A., 1913; McMaster University, graduate study, 1916; Queen's University, Kingston, Ontario, Canada, B.Paed., 1917; Cornell University, Ph.D., 1920. *Religion:* Protestant.

CAREER: Teacher in secondary schools, 1913-19; Young Men's Christian Association, Toronto, Ontario, educational director, 1923-24; Boys' Training School, Bowmanville, Ontario, superintendent, 1924-32; Glen Lawrence

School, Toronto, Ontario, principal, 1932-39; Ontario Agricultural College, Guelph, professor and head of English department, 1939-54; University of Waterloo, Waterloo, Ontario, director of adult education and dean of men, 1954-63, university representative at Doon School of Fine Arts, 1963-69. President of board, Young Men's Christian Association, Guelph, Ontario, 1952-54. *Member:* International Platform Association (president, 1950-51), English Speaking Union (founder and honorary president, Waterloo-Wellington branch), Canadian Historical Association, Pennsylvania German Society, Pennsylvania German Folklore Society, Ontario Genealogical Society (president, 1962-69), Pennsylvania German Folklore Society of Ontario (president, 1952-62), London Huguenot Society (England: fellow), Arts and Letters Club (Toronto; life). *Awards, honors:* Fellow, Carl Schurz Memorial Foundation; Centennial Medal, Government of Canada, 1967; LL.D., University of Waterloo, 1969.

WRITINGS: English for New Canadians, National Council YMCA (Toronto), 1919; *The New Citizen: Modern Language Instruction*, Macmillan, 1921; *Our Canada*, Ryerson, 1923; *English Grammar for New Canadians*, Longmans, Green, 1931; *Child Guidance for Parents and Teachers*, Longmans, Green, 1933; *The Personality Rating Chart*, Clarke, Irwin, 1936; *History of the Holstein-Friesian Breed in Canada*, Collins, 1946; *Speak the Speech...the Technique of Public Speaking and Radio Speaking*, McClelland & Stewart (Toronto), 1947; *The Trail of the Black Walnut*, Herald Press, 1957; *The Trail of the Huguenots in Europe, the United States, South Africa and Canada*, Thomas Allen, 1964, Genealogical Publishing, 1966; *The Trail of the Iroquois Indians: How the Iroquois Nation Saved Canada from the British Empire*, Barnes & Noble, 1967; *A History of Agriculture in Ontario*, two volumes, Ontario Department of Agriculture and Food, 1970. Contributor of articles to newspapers and magazines.

WORK IN PROGRESS: History of Vaughan Township.

AVOCATIONAL INTERESTS: Music, travel.

(Died December 7, 1969)

* * *

REED, James F(red) 1909-

PERSONAL: Born July 19, 1909, in Pittsburgh, Pa.; son of Fred John (in clerical work) and Elsie (Shields) Reed. *Education:* University of Pittsburgh, A.B., 1932, M.A., 1935, LL.B., 1939, J.D., 1966; graduate study at University of Wisconsin, 1936, 1938, Northwestern University, 1959-60. *Politics:* Independent. *Religion:* Christian. *Home:* 2713 Dippen Ave., Pittsburgh, Pa. 15226. *Office:* Pittsburgh Board of Education, Sheraden Blvd., Pittsburgh, Pa. 15204.

CAREER: University of Pittsburgh, Pittsburgh, Pa., instructor in history, 1931-39; Carnegie Institute of Technology (now Carnegie-Mellon University) and Margaret Morrison College, Pittsburgh, Pa., instructor, 1939-41; Pennsylvania Merchandising Institute, Ambridge, director, 1948-49; U.S. Department of Labor, Pittsburgh, Pa., inspector, 1950; Pittsburgh Board of Public Education, Pittsburgh, Pa., instructor in world history and economics, 1951—, instructional coordinator, 1966—. Instructor, Educational Television Station WQED, 1954-57. Church organist and choir director, 1931—. *Member:* American Academy of Political and Social Science, American Association of University Professors, National Education Association, Omicron Delta Kappa, Phi Alpha Theta.

WRITINGS—Reviser: Ray Osgood Hughes and C.H.W. Pullen, *Eastern Lands: A Text in Social Studies,* Allyn & Bacon, 1959, new edition, 1966; Ray Osgood Hughes and C. H. W. Pullen, *Western Lands: A Text in Social Studies,* Allyn & Bacon, 1962, new edition, 1967; (with Pullen) Ray Osgood Hughes, *Today's Problems: Social, Political, and Economic Issues Facing America,* Allyn & Bacon, 1962, new edition, 1967.

WORK IN PROGRESS: Research for a world history text at the junior college level; research for a biography of Thomas Wakley, member of Parliament, circa 1850; a continuing revision of *Eastern Lands, Western Lands,* and *Today's Problems.*

AVOCATIONAL INTERESTS: Music.

* * *

REEVE, Frank D(river)   1899-1967

PERSONAL: Born June 7, 1899, in Ogden, Utah; son of John James (a railroader) and Ellen Barbara (Driver) Reeve. *Education:* University of New Mexico, B.A., 1925, M.A., 1928; University of Texas, Ph.D., 1937. *Home:* 1808 Las Lomas Rd. N.E., Albuquerque, N.M. 87106. *Office:* University of New Mexico, Library 211, Albuquerque, N.M. 87106.

CAREER: University of New Mexico, Albuquerque, 1927-67, began as assistant in history and political science, became professor, 1947, research professor of history, 1962-64, professor emeritus, 1964-67. History consultant to U.S. Government in Navaho Land Claim Case. Member of committee on appointments of Cowboy Hall of Fame and Museum, 1958-67, of New Mexico Civil War Centennial Commission, 1961-65, of New Mexico Selective Service Board Number 1, 1962-67. *Member:* American Historical Association, American Civil Liberties Union, American Association of University Professors, Mississippi Valley Historical Association, New Mexico Historical Association, New Mexico Art League (president, 1937).

WRITINGS: (Contributor) J. C. Knode, editor, *Foundations of an American Philosophy of Education,* Van Nostrand, 1942; *New Mexico: Yesterday and Today,* Division of Research, Department of Government, University of New Mexico, 1946; (editor with Clinton E. Brooks) James Augustus Bennett, *Forts and Forays: A Dragoon in New Mexico,* University of New Mexico Press, 1948; *A Letter to Clio,* University of New Mexico Press, 1956; *History of New Mexico,* three volumes, Lewis Historical Publishing, 1961; *New Mexico, a Short, Illustrated History,* Sage Books, 1964; (with Alice Ann Cleaveland) *New Mexico, Land of Many Cultures,* Pruett, 1969. Also contributor to *Texas Handbook of History,* Texas State Historical Association. Contributor to *Encyclopaedia Britannica, World Book Encyclopedia, Encyclopedia Americana, Britannica Book of the Year,* 1937-61, and to historical periodicals. Editor, *New Mexico Historical Review,* 1946-64.

WORK IN PROGRESS: A history of the Navaho Nation.

(Died, 1967)

* * *

REEVE, Wilfred D.   1895-

PERSONAL: Born February 7, 1895, in Liverpool, England; son of William and Ellen (Jeal) Reeve; married, February 23, 1923, wife's maiden name Cox. *Education:* Studied privately, and attended London School of Economics and Political Science, 1920-23. *Home:* 31A Brunswick Sq., Hove, East Sussex, England.

CAREER: Royal Thai government, Thailand, adviser to Ministry of Finance, 1930-40, 1946-49; Republic of Korea, economic adviser to prime minister, 1952-57; government of Tunisia, economic planning expert, 1957-58. *Military service:* British Army, 1916-19 and 1940-43; became acting lieutenant colonel; decorated Chevalier de la Legion d'Honneur (France), Knight, Grand Cross Crown of Thailand, and Commander, Order of White Elephant (Siam).

WRITINGS: Public Administration in Siam, Royal Institute of International Affairs, 1951; *The Republic of Korea: A Political and Economic Study,* Oxford University Press, 1963.

AVOCATIONAL INTERESTS: Travel, fly-fishing, and bridge.

* * *

REEVES, Dorothea D(resser)   1901-

PERSONAL: Born December 18, 1901, in Cambridge, Mass.; daughter of Horatio Willis (an author) and Alice (Reed) Dresser; married Charles H. Reeves, August 29, 1925; children: Philip, Dorcas (Mrs. Arthur H. Rohn, Jr.). *Education:* Vassar College, student, 1920-22; Radcliffe College, A.B., 1924; Drexel Institute of Technology, B.S. in L.S., 1938. *Politics:* Independent. *Religion:* Protestant. *Office:* Harvard Business School, Boston, Mass. 02163.

CAREER: Swarthmore College, Swarthmore, Pa., assistant librarian, 1938-46; Kress Library of Business and Economics, Harvard University, Boston, Mass., assistant, 1946-56, assistant curator, 1956-61, curator, 1961-68. *Member:* American Library Association. League of Women Voters, Boston Shakespeare Club.

WRITINGS: Sir Richard Gough and His Broadside Collection, 1956; (editor and compiler) *Resources for the Study of Economic History,* Harvard University Press, 1961; (editor) *Catalogue of Kress Library of Business and Economics, 1918-1948,* Kress Library, 1964, supplement, *1473-1848,* 1967; *Come All for the Cure-all: Patent Medicines, Nineteenth Century Bonanza,* [Cambridge], 1967. Contributor to *Business History Review* and library periodicals.

AVOCATIONAL INTERESTS: Gardening.

* * *

REGIS, Sister Mary   1908-

PERSONAL: Born July 17, 1908, in Los Angeles, Calif.; daughter of George L. (an attorney) and Clara (Karmer) Reynolds. *Education:* Immaculate Heart College, B.A., 1933; University of Southern California, Library Credential, 1943; Catholic University of America, M.S. in L.S., 1953. *Politics:* Democrat. *Home:* 5515 Franklin Ave., Los Angeles, Calif.

CAREER: Roman Catholic nun, member of California Institute of the Sisters of Immaculate Heart of Mary, 1931—. Immaculate Heart College, Los Angeles, Calif., librarian, 1940-62, dean of Library School, 1953-58, director of public relations, 1962-67, professor of library science, 1967—. *Member:* American Library Association, Catholic Library Association, American College Public Relations Association, Special Libraries Association, California Library Association, Delta Phi Mu.

WRITINGS: (Editor) *Catholic Bookman's Guide,* Hawthorn, 1962. Contributor to library journals.

WORK IN PROGRESS: A revision of *Catholic Bookman's Guide;* research in library histories.

REHDER, Jessie Clifford   1908-1967

PERSONAL: Born April 29, 1908, in Wilmington, N.C.; daughter of Will (a florist) and Jessie (Stewart) Rehder. *Education:* Randolph-Macon Woman's College, A.B., 1929; Columbia University, M.A., 1931; attended University of North Carolina, 1941-42. *Religion:* Lutheran. *Home:* 817 Old Pittsboro, Chapel Hill, N.C. 27514. *Office:* English Department, University of North Carolina, Chapel Hill, N.C. 27514.

CAREER: University of North Carolina, Chapel Hill, instructor, 1947-61, associate professor of English, 1961-67. *Member:* Southeast Modern Language Associations.

WRITINGS: The Nature of Fiction, University of North Carolina Press, 1948; (editor) *Adventures in Reading,* University of North Carolina Extension Library, 1949; *Remembrance Way* (novel), Putnam, 1956; *The Young Writer at Work,* Odyssey, 1962; (editor) *The Young Writer at Chapel Hill,* Department of English, University of North Carolina, 1962; (editor) *The Story at Work: An Anthology,* Odyssey, 1963; (editor) *Chapel Hill Carousel,* University of North Carolina Press, 1967; (with Wallace Kaufman) *The Act of Writing,* Odyssey, 1969.

(Died February 3, 1967)

*   *   *

REID, Charles K(er) II   1912-19(?)

PERSONAL: Born October 8, 1912, in Philadelphia, Pa.; son of Clive Monk (a coffee and tea importer) and Mary (Hayward) Reid; married Allis Merriam Beaumont, August 18, 1945; children: Anne Beaumont (Mrs. T. L. Dews), Charles K. III, William Bruce, Douglas Ker. *Education:* Attended Germantown Friends School for twelve years, and took evening courses at University of Pennsylvania. *Home:* 24 Mountain View Dr., West Hartford, Conn. 06117. *Office:* Life Insurance Agency Management Association, 170 Sigourney St., Hartford, Conn. 06105.

CAREER: Chartered life underwriter, beginning 1948. Union Central Life of Ohio, agent in Philadelphia, Pa., and Wilmington, Del., 1935-41; Connecticut General Life Insurance Co., agent in Philadelphia, Pa., and Wilmington, Del., 1942-43; U.S. Air Force, personal affairs consultant, 1943-45; U.S. Veterans Administration, Washington, D.C., assistant director of National Service Life Insurance conservation, 1945-47; Lincoln National Life of Indiana, assistant general agent in Washington, D.C., 1947-53; Life Insurance Agency Management Association, Hartford, Conn., senior consultant, 1953-57, associate director of company relations, beginning 1958. *Member:* American Society of Chartered Life Underwriters (chapter president, Hartford, Conn., 1956-57), American Risk and Insurance Association, National Association of Life Underwriters, Hartford Life Underwriters Association, Hartford Golf Club, City Club, Avon Country Club.

WRITINGS: (With Harry S. Redeker) *Life Insurance Settlement Options,* Little, 1957, 2nd revised edition, Irwin, 1964. Author, editor, or reviser of Life Insurance Agency Management Association booklets, courses, and other publications.

(Deceased)

*   *   *

REID, James Macarthur   1900-1970
(Colin Walkinshaw)

PERSONAL: Born May 26, 1900, in Paisley, Scotland; son of John Fulton (a businessman) and Agnes Fletcher (Gibb) Reid; married Rebecca Black Ballingall (died, 1962); children: Marion (Mrs. William G. A. Craig), Jean Margaret, Andre Arneil. *Education:* University of Glasgow, M.A., 1920; Lincoln College, Oxford, B.A., 1922. *Politics:* Scottish Nationalist. *Religion:* Church of Scotland. *Home:* 33 Polnoon St., Eaglesham, near Glasgow, Scotland.

CAREER: Bulletin, Glasgow, Scotland, assistant editor, 1931-36; *Glasgow Herald,* Glasgow, Scotland, assistant editor, 1936-43; *Bulletin,* editor, 1943-55; *Saltire Review,* Edinburgh, Scotland, editor, 1956-58. Church of Scotland, member of Church and Nation Committee, convener of Scottish Interests Sub-Committee. Chairman, Glasgow Buildings Guardian Committee. *Member:* Royal Institute of International Affairs, Saltire Society (former honorary secretary, president, and vice-president). *Awards, honors:* Newdigate Prize, 1922, for poem, "Mount Everest"; Scottish Arts Council award for *Traveller Extraordinary.*

WRITINGS: Mount Everest (poem), Basil Blackwell, 1922; *The Sons of Aethne* (novel), Blackwood, 1923; (under pseudonym Colin Walkinshaw) *The Scots Tragedy,* Routledge, 1934; *The History of the Clydesdale Bank, 1838-1938,* Blackie, 1938; *Modern Scottish Literature,* Saltire Society, 1945; *Glasgow,* Batsford, 1957; *Scotland Past and Present,* Oxford University Press, 1957; *Kirk and Nation,* Skeffington & Sons, 1960; (editor) *Scottish Short Stories,* Oxford University Press, 1963; *The Case for Charlotte Square,* National Trust for Scotland, 1963; *James Lithgow, Master of Work,* Hutchinson, 1964; *A History of the Merchants House of Glasgow,* T. L. Grahame Reid, 1967; *Traveller Extraordinary: The Life of James Bruce of Kinnaird,* Norton, 1968; *Scotland's Progress: The Survival of a Nation,* Eyre & Spottiswoode, 1971. Contributor of regular weekly column on international affairs to *British Weekly,* and contributor of articles to *Scottish Field, Life and Work,* and other periodicals.

WORK IN PROGRESS: Research on the records of the Merchants House of Glasgow, a guild; a study on the influence on Scottish literature of union with England in 1707; a study on the probable effect on modern society of the abandonment of the H-bomb.

SIDELIGHTS: Reid traveled in most countries of western Europe, in the United States (with bicycle), in Russia, Yugoslavia, and Egypt, "watching the world becoming more comfortable, much more dangerous, possibly less intelligent." *Avocational interests:* Architecture, chamber music, gardening.

BIOGRAPHICAL/CRITICAL SOURCES: Listener, August 15, 1968; *Times Literary Supplement,* September 12, 1968.

(Died, 1970)

*   *   *

REID, Leslie Hartley   1895-

PERSONAL: Born November 17, 1895, in Masulipatam, India; son of Robert Newby Hartley and Dora (Mais) Reid; married Beatrice Wilburn, September 22, 1922. *Education:* University of Toronto, B.Sc.F., 1922; University of London, B.A. (extramural), 1930. *Home:* Chapel Cottage, Thornborough, Buckingham, England. *Agent:* David Higham Associates Ltd., 76 Dean St., London W. 1, England.

CAREER: Ontario Forestry Branch, Toronto, assistant forester, 1922-28; Stowe School, Stowe, Buckinghamshire,

England, tutor, 1943-58. Teachers Training College, Bletchley, Buckinghamshire, England, lecturer in English literature, 1956-58. *Military service:* British Army, Royal Field Artillery, 1915-18; became lieutenant. Home Guard, 1940-45. *Member:* Fauna Preservation Society, British Trust for Ornithology.

WRITINGS: The Rector of Maliset, Dent, 1924; *Saltacres*, Dent, 1926; *Trevy the River*, Dent, 1928; *Cauldron Bubble*, Gollancz, 1935; *Earth's Company*, J. Murray, 1958, published as *The Sociology of Nature*, Penguin, 1962. Contributor to *Contemporary Review, Quarterly Review, Field, Countryman*, and *Scottish Field*.

* * *

REID, Louis Arnaud 1895-

PERSONAL: Born February 18, 1895, in Ellon, Scotland; son of Alexander Humphrey (a clergyman) and Margaret (Cornfute) Reid; married Gladys Kate Bignold, 1920; married second wife, Frances Mary Horton (a university lecturer), 1957; children: (first marriage) two sons; (second marriage) two stepdaughters. *Education:* University of Edinburgh, M.A., D.Litt.; University of Wales, Ph.D. *Address:* 50 Rotherwick Rd., London N.W. 11, England.

CAREER: University College of Wales, Aberystwyth, lecturer in philosophy, 1919-26; University of Liverpool, Liverpool, England, independent lecturer in philosophy, 1926-32; University of Durham, Armstrong College (now University of Newcastle), Newcastle upon Tyne, England, professor of mental and moral philosophy, 1932-47; University of London, London, England, professor of philosophy of education, 1947-62, became professor emeritus, 1962—. Visiting professor at Stanford University, 1927, University of British Columbia, 1951, University of Oregon, 1962-63, and Chinese University of Hong Kong, 1966-67. *Member:* Mind Association, Aristotelian Society, P.E.N., Philosophy of Education Society (president), Athenaeum.

WRITINGS: Knowledge and Truth, Macmillan, 1923; *A Study in Aesthetics*, Allen & Unwin, 1931, Greenwood Press, 1973; *Creative Morality*, Allen & Unwin, 1937; *Preface to Faith*, Allen & Unwin, 1939; *Rediscovery of Belief*, Lindsey Press, 1944; *Ways of Knowledge and Experience*, Oxford University Press, 1961; *Philosophy and Education*, Heinemann, 1962, Random, 1965; *Meaning in the Arts*, Humanities, 1969. Contributor to learned journals.

* * *

REINFELD, Fred 1910-1964
(Edward Young)

PERSONAL: Born January 27, 1910, in New York, N.Y.; son of Barnett and Rose (Pogrozelsky) Reinfeld; married Beatrice Levine, December 10, 1932; children: Don, Judith. *Education:* Attended New York University and City College of the City University of New York. *Politics:* Independent. *Religion:* Jewish.

CAREER: Author, 1932-64. At brief intervals held positions as accountant and editor of *Chess Review;* chess instructor, extension course at New York University in the 1950's; chess consultant, Dover Publications. *Member:* American Numismatic Society, American Numismatic Association, Marshall Chess Club (New York; honorary). *Awards, honors:* Thomas Edison Foundation Award, 1959, for *The Great Dissenters*.

WRITINGS: (With I. Chernev) *Chess Strategy and Tactics*, Black Knight, 1933, new edition, McKay, 1946; (editor, with Reuben Fine) *A. Alekhine vs. E. D. Bogoljubow, World's Chess Championship*, McKay, 1934; (editor, with Fine) *Dr. Lasker's Chess Career, Part I, 1889-1914*, Black Knight, 1935; (editor) *The Book of the Cambridge Springs International Tournament, 1904*, Black Knight, 1935; *The Elements of Combination Play in Chess*, Black Knight, 1935, 2nd edition, Capitol Publishing, 1950; (with Harold Phillips) *Book of the Warsaw 1935 International Chess Team Tournament*, Black Knight, 1936; (editor) V. Sozin, *Chess Combinations and Traps*, Black Knight, 1936; (annotator) Edgard Colle, *Colle's Chess Masterpieces*, Black Knight, 1936; (editor) *Book of the Margate 1935 Tournament*, Black Knight, 1936; (editor) *Botvinnik's Best Games, 1927-34*, Black Knight, 1937; (editor) *Instructive and Practical Endings from Master Chess*, Black Knight, 1937; (editor, with S. Bernstein) *Kemeri Tournament, 1937*, privately printed, 1938; (editor and translator) M. Euwe, *From My Games, 1920-37*, Bell, 1938; *Chess Mastery by Question and Answer*, McKay, 1939, 3rd edition, Collier, 1962.

Practical End-Game Play, McKay, 1940, published as *Reinfeld on the End-Game in Chess*, Dover, 1957; (editor) P. Keres, *Best Games of Chess, 1931-40*, Bell, 1941, McKay, 1942; *Immortal Games of Capablanca*, Horowitz & Harkness, 1942; *Chess for Amateurs*, McKay, 1943, revised edition, Pitman, 1954; *Chess Quiz*, McKay, 1945, republished as *Win at Chess*, Dover, 1958; *Chess by Yourself*, McKay, 1946, new edition published as *Learn Chess from the Masters*, Dover, 1956; (editor) James Mason, *Principles of Chess*, McKay, 1946, new edition, Dover, 1960; *Botvinnik, the Invincible*, McKay, 1946; (editor) Emanuel Lasker, *Common Sense in Chess*, revised edition, McKay, 1946; (editor) Lasker, *Manual of Chess*, new edition, McKay, 1947; (editor) Siegbert Tarrasch, *Best Games of Chess*, McKay, 1947; (with Samuel Reshevsky) *Learn Chess Fast*, McKay, 1947; (editor, with Bernstein) Mason, *The Art of Chess*, revised edition, McKay, 1947, new edition, Dover, 1958; *Challenge to Chessplayers*, McKay, 1947, republished as *How to Force Checkmate*, Dover, 1958; (editor) Aron Nimzowitsch, *My System*, revised edition, McKay, 1947; *British Chess Masters, Past and Present*, Bell, 1947; *How to Play Better Chess*, Pitman, 1948, new edition, Hanover House, 1961; (editor) *Nimzovich, the Hypermodern*, McKay, 1948, 2nd edition published as *Hypermodern Chess, as Developed in the Games of Its Greatest Exponent, Aron Nimzovich*, Dover, 1958; (editor) Charles Dickens, *Oliver Twist*, Pocket Books, 1948; *Relax with Chess and Win in 20 Moves*, Pitman, 1948, republished as *Chess: Win in 20 Moves or Less*, Crowell, 1962; (with Chernev) *Winning Chess*, Simon & Schuster, 1948; (with Chernev) *The Fireside Book of Chess*, Simon & Schuster, 1949; (editor) Keres, *Best Games of Chess, 1931-1948*, 2nd edition, McKay, 1949, Dover, 1960; *The Unknown Alekhine, 1905-1914*, Pitman (New York), 1949, republished as *The Development of a Chess Genius; 100 Instructive Games of Alekhine*, Dover, 1959; (editor) E. A. Znosko-Borovsky, *How Not to Play Chess*, Dover, 1949.

(Editor) Edgard Colle, *51 Brilliant Chess Masterpieces*, 2nd edition, Capitol Publishing, 1950; *A Treasury of British Chess Masterpieces*, Chatto & Windus, 1950, 2nd edition, Dover, 1962; (with I. A. Horowitz) *How to Think Ahead in Chess*, Simon & Schuster, 1951; (editor) R. Spielmann, *Art of Sacrifice in Chess*, McKay, 1951; (editor) *The Treasury of Chess Lore*, McKay, 1951; (with David Alfred Boehm, pseudonym for Robert V. Masters) *Coinometry*, Sterling, 1952, revised edition, 1958, republished as *Coin Collecting*,

1960, revised edition, 1964; (editor) Richard Coles, *Epic Battles of the Chessboard*, McKay, 1952; (with Horowitz) *How to Improve Your Chess*, Dutton, 1952; *The Human Side of Chess*, Pellegrini & Cudahy, 1952, also published as *The Great Chess Masters and Their Games*, Sterling, 1952, revised edition, Hanover House, 1960; (with Horowitz) *First Book of Chess*, Sterling, 1952; *Second Book of Chess*, Sterling, 1953 (published in England as *Improving Your Chess*, Faber, 1954); *The Complete Chess Player*, Prentice-Hall, 1953; (with Masters) *Blazer the Bear*, Sterling, 1953; *Treasury of the World's Coins*, Sterling, 1953, 2nd revised edition, 1967; *Third Book of Chess*, Sterling, 1954 (published in England as *Chess: How to Play the White Pieces*, Foulsham, 1955); (with Horowitz) *First Book of Chess, with Pocket Chessboard*, Barnes & Noble, 1954; *How to be a Winner at Chess*, Hanover House, 1954; (with Horowitz) *Chess Traps, Pitfalls, and Swindles*, Simon & Schuster, 1954; *Coin Collectors' Handbook*, Sterling, 1954, 10th edition, 1965; *Commemorative Stamps of the U.S.A.*, Crowell, 1954, new edition, Crowell, 1956; *Chess*, Eyre, 1954; *Treasures of the Earth*, Sterling, 1954, revised and published as *Picture Book of Rocks and Minerals*, 1963; *Fourth Book of Chess*, Sterling, 1955 (published in England as *Chess: How to Play the Black Pieces*, Foulsham, 1955); *Fifth Book of Chess*, Sterling, 1955 (published in England as *Chess: How to Win When You're Ahead*, Foulsham, 1956); *Sixth Book of Chess*, Sterling, 1955 (published in England as *Chess: How to Fight Back*, Foulsham, 1956); *1001 Brilliant Chess Sacrifices and Combinations*, Sterling, 1955, republished as *1001 Chess Sacrifices and Combinations*, Barnes & Noble, 1959; *1001 Ways to Checkmate*, Sterling, 1955; *Improving Your Chess, With Pocket Chessboard*, Barnes & Noble, 1955; *Uranium and Other Miracle Metals*, Sterling, 1955, revised edition, 1959.

Seventh Book of Chess, Sterling, 1956; *They Almost Made It*, Crowell, 1956; (with Horowitz) *The Macmillan Handbook of Chess*, Macmillan, 1956; *Young Charles Darwin*, Sterling, 1956; *How to Play Chess Like a Champion*, Hanover House, 1956; *A Catalogue of the World's Most Popular Coins*, Sterling, 1956, 2nd revised edition, edited by Burton Hobson, Doubleday, 1971; *Cash for Your Coins*, Sterling, 1956, revised edition, 1957; *How to Beat Your Opponent Quickly*, Sterling, 1956 (published in England as *Chess: How to Beat Your Opponent Quickly*, Foulsham, 1957); *Why You Lose at Chess*, Simon & Schuster, 1956; *How to Get More Out of Chess*, Hanover House, 1957; *Eighth Book of Chess*, Sterling, 1957 (published in England as *Chess: How to Play the Queen Pawn Openings and Other Close Games*, Foulsham, 1958); *How to Play Top-Notch Checkers*, Sterling, 1957, also published as *How to Play Checkers*, Barnes & Noble, 1957; *How to Win Chess Games Quickly*, (includes *Eighth Book of Chess*), Barnes & Noble, 1957; *Miracle Drugs and the New Age of Medicine*, Sterling, 1957, revised edition, 1962; *The Story of Paper Money, Including Catalogue of Values*, Sterling, 1957, revised edition, 1960, republished as *A Simplified Guide to Collecting American Paper Money*, Hanover House, 1960; *Reinfeld Explains Chess*, Sterling, 1957, revised edition published as *Chess Explained*, 1960 (published in England as *Chess: Reinfeld Explains Chess*, Foulsham, 1958); *Fun With Stamp Collecting*, Doubleday, 1957; *Complete Book of Chess Openings*, Sterling, 1957; *Trappers of the West*, Crowell, 1957; *How to Build a Coin Collection*, Sterling, 1958, 2nd revised edition, edited by Hobson, 1972; *The Secret of Tactical Chess*, Crowell, 1958; *Rays: Visible and Invisible*, Sterling, 1958, revised

edition published as *An Introduction to Electronics*, Cornerstone Library, 1963; *Complete Book of Chess Stratagems*, Sterling, 1958, republished as *The Complete Book of Chess Tactics*, Doubleday, 1961; *Complete Book of Chess Openings* (combines the *Seventh Book of Chess*, and the *Eighth Book of Chess*), Barnes & Noble, 1958; *Chess in a Nutshell*, Hanover House, 1958; *Attack and Counterattack in Chess* (combines the *Third Book of Chess*, the *Fourth Book of Chess*, and part of *Improving Your Chess*), Barnes & Noble, 1958; *Chess for Children*, Sterling, 1958, 2nd edition, Mayflower, 1959; *Chess Victory, Move By Move*, Sterling, 1959; *The Complete Chess Course*, Hanover House, 1959; *Creative Chess*, Sterling, 1959; *The Great Dissenters, Guardians of Their Country's Laws and Liberties*, Crowell, 1959, enlarged edition, Bantam, 1964; *A New Approach to Chess Mastery*, Hanover House, 1959; *The Story of Civil War Money*, Sterling, 1959; *The Way to Better Chess*, Macmillan, 1959.

(Editor) C. Mansfield, *101 Chess Puzzles and How to Solve Them*, Sterling, 1960; (editor) *How to Use Algebra in Everyday Life*, Sterling, 1960; (under pseudonym Edward Young) *A Beginner's Guide to Stamp Collecting*, Ottenheimer Publishers, 1960; (editor) Philip Walsingham Sergeant, *Championship Chess*, revised edition, Sterling, 1960; *The Chess Masters on Winning Chess*, Hanover House, 1960; *The Easiest Way to Learn Chess*, Simon & Schuster, 1960; (with Christopher Churchill Chamberlain) *Coin Dictionary and Guide*, Sterling, 1960; *How to be a Winner at Checkers*, Hanover House, 1960; *The Real Book About Whales and Whaling*, Doubleday, 1960; *What's New in Science*, Sterling, 1960, revised edition, 1964; *Chess Strategy for Offense and Defense*, Barnes & Noble, 1961; *Great Brilliancy Prize Games of the Chess Masters*, Collier, 1961; *The Modern Fundamentals of Chess*, Kaye & Ward, 1961, republished as *Better Chess*, 1968; (editor) R. Wade, *Chess Tactics for Beginners*, Sterling, 1961; *A Catalogue of European Coins*, Oak Tree Press, 1961; *Chess for Young People*, Holt, 1961; *Chess is an Easy Game*, Sterling, 1961; *Great Short Games of the Chess Masters*, Collier, 1961; *The Real Book About Famous Battles*, Doubleday, 1961; *Winning Chess Openings*, Hanover House, 1961; *The Joys of Chess*, Hanover House, 1961; *A Treasury of American Coins*, Hanover House, 1961; *A Chess Primer*, Dolphin Books, 1962; (with Hobson) *Pictorial Guide to Coin Conditions*, Sterling, 1962, revised edition, edited by Hobson, Doubleday, 1968; *How to Play Winning Chess*, Bantam, 1962; *Improving Your Chess Skills*, Encyclopaedia Britannica Press, 1963; (with Hobson) *Manual for Coin Collectors and Investors*, Sterling, 1963, revised edition, Bantam, 1965; *Great Moments in Chess*, Doubleday, 1963; (with Hobson) *Picture Book of Ancient Coins*, Sterling, 1963; *Picture Book of Atomic Science*, Sterling, 1963; (with Hobson) *U.S. Commemorative Coins and Stamps*, Sterling, 1964; *Pony Express*, Collier, 1964; *The Biggest Job in the World: The American Presidency*, Crowell, 1964; *Strategy in the Chess Endgame*, Cornerstone Library, 1964; *Beginner's Guide to Winning Chess*, Follett, 1964; *Great Games by Chess Prodigies*, Macmillan, 1967; *Stamp Collectors' Handbook*, Doubleday, 1970; (adapted from the author's work) Beatrice Reinfeld, *Two Weeks to Winning Chess*, Doubleday, 1971.

Also author of *Chicago 1937 Tournament*, privately printed, and *Course in the Elements of Modern Chess Strategy*, Black Knight, and editor of *Semmering-Baden Tournament, 1937*, privately printed, and P. Keres, *Best Games, 1937*, privately printed.

Contributor to *World Book Encyclopedia;* consultant for *American College Dictionary,* Random.

SIDELIGHTS: Reinfeld was twice New York State chess champion in the 1930's, retiring from serious tournament play in 1942. His books on chess, numismatics, philately, checkers, and science, and his biographies for young people are on many recommended lists in their respective fields, and have been translated into Spanish, French, Portuguese, Japanese, German, Bengali, and Italian.

BIOGRAPHICAL SOURCES: New York Times, May 30, 1964, June 17, 1964; *Coin World,* June 17, 1964; *Chess Review,* July, 1964; *Publishers' Weekly,* July 27, 1964.†

(Died May 29, 1964)

*   *   *

REMER, Theodore G.   1899-

PERSONAL: Born August 15, 1899, in Chicago, Ill.; son of Louis John and Rose (Noyck) Remer; married Annetta Leon, November 11, 1926; children: Rita Louise (Mrs. Robert S. Mendelsohn), Michael David. *Education:* Chicago-Kent College of Law (now part of Illinois Institute of Technology), LL.B., 1926; John Marshall Law School, J.D., 1929. *Politics:* Republican. *Religion:* Jewish. *Office:* 1 First National Plaza, Chicago, Ill. 60670.

CAREER: Admitted to Illinois bar, 1926; attorney in private practice, Chicago, Ill., 1926-43; corporation secretary, director-general, and counsel, 1943-57; Union Carbide Corporation, Chicago, attorney and executive, 1957-64; attorney in private practice, Chicago, 1964—. Former secretary and trustee, Illinois Institute of Technology, Chicago-Kent College of Law; former member of general counsel and member of board of governors, Chicago Heart Association; former director, LaRabida-Jackson Park Sanitarium. *Member:* American Bar Association, Illinois Bar Association, Society of Midland Authors, Friends of Literature, Chicago Bar Association, and Boswell Club (Chicago).

WRITINGS: (Editor) *Serendipity and the Three Princes: From the Peregrinaggio of 1557,* University of Oklahoma Press, 1965. Contributor of feature story to *Chicago Daily News.*

WORK IN PROGRESS: Clybourn Junction and *The Jewish Ghetto.*

*   *   *

RENNIE, James Alan   1899-1969
(Morton Cleland, Boone Denver, Maxwell MacFee)

PERSONAL: Born January 29, 1899, in Scotland; married Elizabeth Claire MacWalter Silander, April 28, 1931; children: Elizabeth Pamela (deceased). *Education:* Studied at Glasgow School of Art, 1919-22. *Religion:* Church of Scotland. *Home:* Ballintian, Cromdale, near Grantown-on-Spey, Moray, Scotland. *Agent:* David Higham Associates Ltd., 5-8 Lower John St., London W1R 4HA, England.

CAREER: Ran away from school at fifteen and falsified age to join the British Army; after World War I spent several years roaming about on four continents, working at sugar planting in Mozambique, East Africa, as a cowboy in Alberta, Canada, and exploring in the Canadian Arctic; theatrical manager and impresario in London's West End during late 1920's and early 1930's; professional writer in England, 1935-41, in Scotland, 1944-69. British Legion (Scotland), Delegate to Highlands and Islands Area Council, 1954-69. *Military service:* British Army, 1914-19; wounded three times; mentioned in dispatches. Royal Air Force, 1941-44; retired as flying officer (invalided out). *Member:* Society of Antiquaries (fellow), Society of Authors, Radiowriters Association.

WRITINGS—Nonfiction: *In the Steps of the Clansmen,* Rich & Cowan, 1951; *In the Steps of the Cavaliers,* Rich & Cowan, 1954; *Romantic Strathspey: Its Lands, Clans and Legends,* R. Hale, 1956; *The Scottish People, Their Clans, Families and Origins,* Hutchinson, 1960; *Past Horizons* (autobiography; Adventurers Book Club selection), Jarrolds, 1962.

Fiction under name J. Alan Rennie: *The Trail of the Wendigo,* Muller, 1937; *The Riddle of Rainbow Mountain,* Muller, 1938; *The Footstool of the Moon,* Hurst & Blackett, 1938; *Golden Midnight,* Quality Press, 1946; *Aces Run Wild,* Quality Press, 1950; *The Forest Gods Sing,* Quality Press, 1953; *Guns of Brazos,* Quality Press, 1954; *Maverick Blood,* Benn, 1956; *Dead Man's Saddle,* Benn, 1957; *Sonora Hits Horizon,* R. Hale, 1964; *Buckskin Bolero,* R. Hale, 1966.

Under pseudonym Boone Denver: *Pay-Off at Eagle Butte,* R. Hale, 1956; *West of Sunset,* R. Hale, 1964; *The Gunman's Way,* R. Hale, 1965.

Juveniles: *The Little Giant Who Needed Sunshine,* Blackie & Son, 1953; *'Coonie' the Bandit,* Blackie & Son, 1958.

Film musicals: "Happy Days Are Here Again," A.T.P., 1935; "Sing While You're Dancing," Continental Films, 1936. Writer of radio plays, serials, stories, and talks for British Broadcasting Corp., 1936-69.

Contributor of serials under pseudonym Morton Cleland, humor under pseudonym Maxwell MacFee, and of articles to magazines and newspapers, including *Scots Magazine, Toronto Star Weekly, This Week, Chambers's Magazine,* and *Corrierra della Serra*; also contributor of cartoons to *London Opinion,* 1920-22.

WORK IN PROGRESS: A nonfiction historical book, *The Flowering of the Rose*; continuation of forty-years of researching into the history of the Scottish Gael.

AVOCATIONAL INTERESTS: Fishing, shooting, hill-walking, landscape photography.

(Died September 14, 1969)

*   *   *

REPP, Arthur C(hristian)   1906-

PERSONAL: Born July 7, 1906, in New York, N.Y.; son of Christian (a builder) and Barbara (Wetzler) Repp; married Minnie Elnora Witt (now a secretary-clerk), June 4, 1930; children: Arthur C., Jr., Mildred Louise Repp Neibacher, Dorothy Ruth Repp Meszaros. *Education:* Attended Concordia Collegiate Institute, Bronxville, N.Y., 1919-25; Concordia Seminary, St. Louis, Mo., student, 1925-29, B.D., 1945; St. Mary's University of San Antonio, M.A., 1940; St. Louis University, postgraduate study, 1943-44; Washington University, St. Louis, Mo., Ph.D., 1951. *Politics:* Independent. *Home:* 7531 Warner Ave., Richmond Heights, Mo. 63117.

CAREER: Ordained minister of Lutheran Church, 1929; pastor in San Antonio, Tex., 1929-43; Lutheran Church-Missouri Synod, Board of Parish Education, St. Louis, Mo., executive secretary, 1943-45; Concordia Seminary, Clayton, Mo., professor of religious education, 1945-74, academic dean, 1952-69, vice-president for academic affairs, 1969-72. Member of curriculum commission for theological education, Lutheran Church-Missouri Synod, 1953-62; Concordia Historical Institute, board member, 1946-69, president, 1950-69.

WRITINGS: (Editor and contributor) *100 Years of Christian Education*, Concordia, 1947; (contributor) *The Pastor at Work*, Concordia, 1960; (contributor) *Toward a More Excellent Ministry*, Concordia, 1964; *Confirmation in the Lutheran Church*, Concordia, 1964. Contributor to Lutheran periodicals. Member of editorial staff, *Lutheran Witness*, 1949-52; *Concordia Historical Institute Quarterly*, associate editor, 1946-50, 1956—, editor, 1950-56.

*   *   *

ReQUA, Eloise Gallup 1902-

PERSONAL: Born December 1, 1902, in Chicago, Ill.; daughter of William Bruyn (a grain commission merchant) and Susan Eloise (Gallup) ReQua. *Education:* Bryn Mawr College, A.B., 1924; School of International Studies, Geneva, Switzerland, 1928; graduate student, Bryn Mawr College, University of Chicago. *Home:* 999 Lake Shore Dr., Chicago, Ill. 60611. *Office:* 660 N. Wabash Ave., Chicago, Ill. 60611.

CAREER: Library of International Relations, Chicago, Ill., founder, director, 1932—. Founder of Children's International Library, Century of Progress Exposition, Chicago, Ill. (later given to University of Chicago), 1933; assistant in publicity office, Bryn Mawr College, 1934-35; International House, served on board of governors in Chicago, and organized World Trade Reference Library in New Orleans, 1946. *Member:* Special Libraries Association (chairman of public relations committee, 1945-46), American Political Science Association, Society of Woman Geographers, National Society of Colonial Dames, Illinois League of Women Voters. *Awards, honors:* Eloy Alfaro International Foundation medal, 1959.

WRITINGS: (With Jane Statham) *The Developing Nations: A Guide to Information Sources*, Gale, 1965.

*   *   *

REUSS, Frederick G(ustav) 1904-

PERSONAL: Born July 5, 1904, in Wurzburg, Bavaria, Germany; came to United States in 1938; son of Joseph (a judge) and Hedwig (Mohr) Reuss; married Mathilda Spiekermann, December 6, 1933; children: Peter Joseph, Ursula Elizabeth. *Education:* Studied at University of Munich, 1922-25, M.A., 1927; attended University of Kiel, 1925-26; University of Wurzburg, Ph.D., 1929; Catholic University of America, A.M., 1939. *Religion:* Roman Catholic. *Home:* 309 Windover Rd., Baltimore, Md. 21218. *Office:* Department of Economics, Goucher College, Towson, Md. 21204.

CAREER: Ministries of Finance and Transportation, Berlin, Germany, economist, 1929-34; Victoria Life Insurance Co., Berlin, Germany, assistant manager, 1934-38; U.S. Social Security Administration, Washington, D.C., analyst, 1943-46; Goucher College, Towson, Md., professor of economics, 1946—. *Member:* American Economic Association, American Association of University Professors, American Finance Association.

WRITINGS: (Contributor) John Jay Corson and J. W. McConnell, *Economic Needs of Older People*, Twentieth Century Fund, 1956; (with others) *Money and Banking*, Pitman, 1957; *Fiscal Policy for Growth without Inflation:*

The German Experiment, Johns Hopkins Press, 1963. Contributor to economics and finance journals.

WORK IN PROGRESS: A book on fiscal policy.

*   *   *

RICE, Cy 1905-1971

PERSONAL: Born May 22, 1905, in Kansas City, Mo.; son of Seymour (an advertising man) and Blanche (Judah) Rice; married Kathryn Shepard, June 2, 1961. *Education:* Attended University of Missouri, 1923, Washington University, St. Louis, Mo., 1924-25. *Home:* 1971 DeMille Dr., Los Angeles, Calif. 90027. *Agent:* Alex Jackinson, 55 West 42nd St., New York, N.Y. 10036; and Earl Mills, 9006 Burton Way, Beverly Hills, Calif. 90211.

CAREER: Former reporter for *Kansas City Star*, Kansas City, Mo., and *Burlington Daily News*, Burlington, Vt., and owner of a weekly newspaper in Schroon Lake, N.Y.; free-lance writer. *Military service:* U.S. Navy, combat correspondent, 1942-45; received Asiatic Pacific Ribbon with two battle stars, Philippine Liberation Ribbon with one battle star.

WRITINGS: (With Sam Balter) *One for the Book of Sports*, Citadel, 1955; (with Pancho Gonzales) *Man with a Racket*, A. S. Barnes, 1959; (with Ted Husing) *My Eyes Are in My Heart*, Geis, 1959; (with Nora Eddington Flynn Haymes) *Errol and Me*, New American Library, 1960; *Cleopatra in Mink*, Paperback Library, 1962; *Defender of the Damned: Gladys Towles Root*, Citadel, 1964, reissued as *Get Me Gladys!: The Poignant Memoirs of America's Most Famous Lady Criminal-Lawyer*, Holloway, 1966; (with Lafayette Fresco Thompson) *Every Diamond Doesn't Sparkle*, McKay, 1964; (with Chester Wander) *Winning at Gin*, Stackpole, 1965; *Inside the Dodgers*, Holloway, 1966; *Children in Danger: The Molesters*, with an essay by J. Edgar Hoover, Holloway, 1967; *Nick the Greek, King of the Gamblers*, Funk, 1969; (with Carlotta Monti) *W. C. Fields and Me*, Prentice-Hall, 1971. Author of television scripts for Ralph Edwards Productions. Contributor to *Argosy, Coronet, Bluebook*, and other magazines.

AVOCATIONAL INTERESTS: Fishing, spectator sports, and collecting pipes.

BIOGRAPHICAL/CRITICAL SOURCES: Variety, May 5, 1971, September 1, 1971; *Washington Post,* August 27, 1971.

(Died August 23, 1971)

*   *   *

RICH, (Ora) Everett 1900-

PERSONAL: Born September 22, 1900, in Centerville, Kan.; son of Arthur (a farmer) and Fanny Bell (Eddy) Rich; married Lillian Louise Sexton, March 7, 1942; children: Phyllis Ailene Rich Spicer. *Education:* Kansas State Teachers College, B.S., 1924; University of Kansas, M.A., 1932; Western Reserve University (now Case Western Reserve University), Ph.D., 1940. *Home:* 1430 State St., Emporia, Kan. 66801.

CAREER: Kansas State Teachers College, Emporia, superintendent of printing, 1924-36, instructor, 1936-39, assistant professor, 1939-42, associate professor, 1942-44, professor of English, 1944-65, professor emeritus, 1965—, head of department of English, 1945-58. Visiting instructor, Western Reserve University (now Case Western Reserve

University), 1936-38. Trustee of Emporia State College Endowment Association and William Allen White Foundation. *Member:* College English Association, National Council of Teachers of English, Kansas Association of Teachers of English (honorary life), Kansas State Historical Society, Sigma Tau Gamma. *Awards, honors:* Outstanding teacher award and distinguished alumni award, Kansas State Teachers College; distinguished alumni award, Sigma Tau Gamma.

WRITINGS: William Allen White, the Man from Emporia, Farrar & Rinehart, 1941; (editor) *The Heritage of Kansas: Selected Commentaries on Past Times,* University of Kansas Press, 1960. Contributor of more than 200 feature stories to *Kansas City Star,* mainly on writers and books; occasional contributor to professional journals. Section editor of "From the Library Shelves," in *Kansas Teacher,* 1934-35, and of "Stories from the Book Shelf," in *Kansas City Star,* 1953-57. Founder and first editor of "Emporia State College Research Series," and of *Kansas Heritage.*

* * *

RICHARDS, Joe 1909-

PERSONAL: Born January 10, 1909, in New York, N.Y.; son of Bernard G. Richards; divorced; children: Seth John, Susan Rachel. *Education:* Studied at Columbia University Extension and Art Students League. *Home:* 631 Warren Lane, Key Biscayne, Fla. 33149.

CAREER: Artist. Work exhibited in Maritime Service shows at U.S. museums, 1942-44, at Carnegie International, 1948, in one-man shows at galleries in Charleston, S.C., Philadelphia, Pa., and New York, 1940-59, in retrospective one-man shows at Lowe Gallery, University of Miami, 1960, Art Alliance, Philadelphia, Pa., 1961. Holder of two patents on process of transfering live art to motion picture film. *Wartime service:* U.S. Marine Corps, U.S. Merchant Marine, U.S. Army Transportation Corps; became captain. *Member:* Masters, Mates, and Pilots, Artists' Equity.

WRITINGS: (Self-illustrated) *Princess—New York,* Bobbs-Merrill, 1956. Contributor of sea stories to boating magazines, and experimental writing to *Time.*

WORK IN PROGRESS: Tug-o-War.

SIDELIGHTS: Richard's painting, "Jury Rig," was presented to President Roosevelt by Admiral Emory Land and now hangs in the Franklin Delano Roosevelt Memorial Library at Hyde Park. He sailed the Mediterranean in the Princess in 1971.

BIOGRAPHICAL/CRITICAL SOURCES: Art Digest, October 1, 1949; *Saturday Review,* April 6, 1957.

* * *

RICHARDSON, Evelyn M(ay Fox) 1902-

PERSONAL: Born May 16, 1902, in Shag Harbour, Nova Scotia, Canada; daughter of Arthur Douglas (a teacher) and Hattie (Larkin) Fox; married Morrill Richardson (a lightkeeper), August 14, 1926 (died, 1974); children: Anne Gordon Richardson Wickens, Laurie (deceased), Elizabeth Richardson Smith. *Education:* Dalhousie University, student, two years. *Religion:* Baptist. *Home:* R.R. 1, Barrington, Nova Scotia, Canada.

CAREER: Spent thirty-five years (1929-64) as the lightkeeper's wife on Bon Portage Island, three miles off the coast of Nova Scotia; wrote about life on Bon Portage, where the Richardsons were the only family until 1955, in her first book, *We Keep a Light;* transferred her interest in local history to the mainland where the Richardsons built a retirement home on property granted in 1770 to the grandmother of John Howard Payne ("Home Sweet Home"). *Member:* Canadian Authors Assocciation. *Awards, honors:* Governor General's Literary Award in non-fiction, 1946, for *We Keep a Light;* Ryerson Fiction Award, 1953, for *Desired Haven.*

WRITINGS: We Keep a Light, Ryerson, 1945 (published in England under title *We Bought an Island,* Christopher Johnson, 1953), published as *We Bought an Island,* Macrae Smith, 1954; *Desired Haven* (novel), Macrae Smith, 1953; *No Small Tempest* (novel), Ryerson, 1957; *My Other Islands* Christopher Johnson, 1960; *Living Island,* Ryerson, 1964. Occasional writer of radio scripts. Contributor to *Yankee, Down East, Atlantic Advocate, Dalhousie Review* and *Nova Scotia Historical Quarterly.*

* * *

RICHARDSON, Isla Paschal 1886-1971

PERSONAL: Born July 30, 1886, in McMinnville, Tenn.; daughter of John Monroe (a professor) and Sallie (Sanders) Paschal; married Thomas Edward Richardson, June 15, 1911 (died, 1945); children: Isla (Mrs. Thurel J. Poe). *Home:* 210 West Hogan, Tullahoma, Tenn. 37388.

CAREER: Writer. *Member:* Poetry Society of Tennessee, National Society of Arts and Letters.

WRITINGS: My Heart Waketh: Poems, Humphries, 1947; *Wind Among the Pines, and Other Poems,* Humphries, 1949; (self-illustrated) *My Bed-Time Game* (collection of poetry and stories for children), Story Book Press, 1949; *In Beauty's Presence, and Other Poems,* Humphries, 1952; *Against All Time* (poetry), Humphries, 1958; *Along the Way, and Other Poems,* Humphries, 1963; (self-illustrated) *My Feathered Friend* (juvenile poems), Royal Publishers, 1963; (self-illustrated) *When Springtime Comes,* Royal Publishers, 1964.

Plays: *That's What They All Say* (one-act), Eldridge Publishing, 1929; *Doughnuts* (two-act), Eldridge Publishing, 1929; *The Prominent Author* (one-act), Eldridge Publishing, c.1930; *Uncle Bob's Bride* (one-act), Samuel French, 1934; *The Cancelled Debt* (one-act), Baker's Plays, 1934; *Just Another Day,* Eldridge Publishing, 1935; *Too Much Static* (one-act comedy), Samuel French, 1936; *The Message* (one-act), Falmouth Publishing House, 1949.

Poetry anthologized in *The Golden Flute: An Anthology of Poetry for Young Children,* edited by Alice Hubbard and Adeline Babbitt, John Day, 1932; *Poems for the Very Young Child,* edited by Dolores Knippel, Whitman, 1932; *Between the Book Ends,* edited by Frank Alden Russell, Morrow, 1943; *All The Best Dog Poems: An Anthology of Poetry About Dogs,* edited by Edwin Burtis, Crowell, 1946. Also contributor of juvenile poems set to music to *Singing and Rhyming,* Ginn, *We Sing and Dance,* Ginn, and *Let's Read Together,* Row, Peterson & Co. Contributor of poems, articles, and stories to more than seventy magazines, including *Good Housekeeping, Better Homes and Gardens, Woman's Weekly, Judge, Ideals, Home Life, Together, Jack and Jill, Radio Mirror.* Tennessee editor, *North America Book of Verse.*

(Died January 10, 1971)

RICHARDSON, Laurence E(aton) 1893-

PERSONAL: Born December 10, 1893, in Concord, Mass.; son of Henry Preston (a naturalist) and Maria (Smith) Richardson; married Anne Atwater Weed, June 24, 1922; children: Barbara Weed Richardson Keyes, Nancy Eaton Richardson Carr, Jane Roger Richardson Pearson. *Education:* Harvard University, S.B., 1916. *Politics:* Republican. *Home:* 363 Barrett's Mill Rd., Concord, Mass. 01742.

CAREER: Executive positions in various manufacturing activities, 1916-60; now retired. *Military service:* U.S. Army, Field Artillery, 1917-19, Corps of Military Police, 1942-45; became captain. *Member:* New England Botanical Club.

WRITINGS: Concord at the Turn of the Century, Concord, Antiquarian Society, 1961; *Concord River,* Barre, 1964; *Concord Chronicle, 1865-1899,* privately printed, 1967.

WORK IN PROGRESS: A biography of Minot Pratt.

*   *   *

RICHTER, J. H(ans) 1901-

PERSONAL: Family name is Richter-Altschaffer; born June 23, 1901, in Vienna, Austria; son of Johannes F. and Lucie (Altschaffer) Richter-Altschaffer; married Luba Orina (an economist), October 22, 1938. *Education:* University of Berlin, M.A., 1936, Ph.D., 1936. *Home:* 6110 Old Dominion Dr., McLean Va. 22101.

CAREER: U.S. government, Washington, D.C., and abroad, economic adviser to Departments of Agriculture, State, and Defense, 1926-62; Tobacco Associates, Inc., Washington, D.C., director of European office in Brussels, Belgium, 1963; International Federation of Agricultural Producers, consultant, 1964, director of North American office, Washington, D.C., 1965-71. *Member:* American Economic Association. *Awards, honors:* Superior Service Award from U.S. government.

WRITINGS: Theory and Technique of Correlation Analysis, Paul Parey, 1932; *Economic Theory of Public Investment,* Duncker & Humblot, 1936; *Agricultural Protection and Trade,* Praeger, 1964. Contributor to professional journals.

*   *   *

RICKETTS, Viva Leone (Harris) 1900-

PERSONAL: Born August 15, 1900, near LaRue, Ohio; daughter of John Elmer and Anna (Dell) Harris; married Van Arthur Ricketts; children: Lawrence Ervan. *Politics:* Independent Republican. *Religion:* Methodist. *Home address:* Route 3, Box 3-N, Brooksville, Fla. 33512.

CAREER: Radio Station WAIU (now WBNS), Columbus, Ohio, program announcer, 1930-32; free-lance writer of western and outdoor stories for pulp magazines, 1934-42; now free-lance writer, primarily about dogs. Ohio publicity and radio director, American Legion Auxiliary, 1932-33.

WRITINGS: (With J. E. Fox) *Pet Pomeranian [and] The Health of Your Dog* (the former by Ricketts, the latter by Fox), All-Pets Books, 1954, 2nd edition, 1956; *The Complete Miniature Pinscher* (Part II by Milo G. Denlinger, revised by Merrick), Denlinger's, 1957, 2nd edition (Part II: *General Care and Training of Your Dog,* by Elsworth C. Howell and others, published in 1963 as *The Howell· Book of Dog Care and Training*), Howell Book, 1972; *The*

New Complete Pomeranian (Part II: *General Care and Training of Your Dog* by Denlinger, revised by Merrick), Howell Book, 1962, expanded edition (with Part II by Denlinger, Merrick, and Howell), 1965; *Operation of a Successful Kennel,* Gaines Dog Research Foundation, 1964; *All About Toy Dogs: Their Care in Sickness and Health, Feeding, Training, Breeding, and the History and Character of Each Breed,* Howell Book, 1965, revised edition, 1969; *The New Miniature Pinscher,* Howell Book, in press. Contributor of more than 200 articles to pet periodicals, including *Dog World, A.K.C. Pure Bred Dogs, Italian Greyhound, English Dog World,* and *Pomeranian Review.* Women's editor, *Ohio Legion News.*

*   *   *

RIENITS, Rex 1909-1971

PERSONAL: Born April 17, 1909, in Dubbo, New South Wales, Australia; son of Oswald Guenther (a civil servant) and Marion Evelyn Maie (Cramp) Rienits; married Dorothea (Thea) Gilchrist (a writer), August 11, 1955. *Education:* Educated in schools in New South Wales, Australia. *Religion:* Nominally Anglican. *Home:* 20 Margaretta Ter., Chelsea, London S.W. 3, England. *Agent:* Harvey Unna Ltd., 79 Baker St., London W. 1, England.

CAREER: Journalist on Australian newspapers, 1928-47; free-lance writer, mainly in London, England, 1947-71. Television drama editor, Australian Broadcasting Commission, 1959-61. *Member:* British Screen and Television Writers Guild, Crime Writers Association.

WRITINGS: Who Would Be Free, Invincible Press, 1944; *Eureka Stockade,* Convoy Press, 1949; *Assassin for Hire,* Muller, 1952; (with wife, Thea Rienits) *Early Artists of Australia,* Angus & Robertson, 1963; *Stormy Petrel,* Muller, 1964 (with Thea Rienits) *The Voyages of Captain Cook,* Hamlyn, 1968; (with Thea Rienits) *A Pictorial History of Australia,* Hamlyn, 1969; *James Cook,* Oxford University Press, 1969; (with Thea Rienits) *Discovery of Australia,* Hamlyn, 1969. Author of film scripts, and radio and television plays and series.

WORK IN PROGRESS: "Bread and butter" writing for radio and television; research and writing with wife, Thea Rienits, of a social history of early Van Diemens Land (New Tasmania), Australian Commonwealth literary fellowship.

AVOCATIONAL INTERESTS: Collecting early Australiana and Pacificana.

(Died April 30, 1971)

*   *   *

RISER, Wayne H. 1909-

PERSONAL: Born August 29, 1909, in Earlham, Iowa; son of John (a farmer) and Mabel (Tichenor) Riser; married Beth McGauley (an instructor at Child Development Institute, Bryn Mawr College), May 25, 1946. *Education:* Iowa State College (now Iowa State University of Science and Technology), D.V.M., 1932, M.S. in Veterinary Pathology, 1945; additional study at Oxford University and Royal Veterinary College, Stockholm, Sweden, 1963. *Home:* 2212 Stone Ridge Lane, Villanova, Pa. *Office:* School of Veterinary Medicine, University of Pennsylvania, Philadelphia, Pa. 19104.

CAREER: Diplomate of American College of Veterinary Pathologists. Private practice as veterinarian, Glenwood, Iowa, 1932-37, as operator of Riser Small Animal Clinic,

Des Moines, Iowa, 1937-46; *North American Veterinarian*, Evanston, Ill., editorial and research work, 1946-49; Riser Animal Hospital, Skokie, Ill., veterinarian, 1949-60; University of Pennsylvania, School of Veterinary Medicine, Philadelphia, research assistant professor, 1961—. Lecturer in department of pathology, Northwestern University Medical School, 1950-62. Research fellow in orthopedic diseases, Armed Forces Institute of Pathology, 1960-63.

MEMBER: American Veterinary Medical Association (vice-chairman of council on education), American Animal Hospital Association (secretary, 1949-59; president, 1960-61), World Association of Small Animal Specialists, (president, 1950-63; senior vice-president, 1963), World Small Animal Veterinary Association (past president), Midwest Small Animal Association (past president), Phi Kappa Tau, Philadelphia Rotary Club. *Awards, honors:* Michigan State University Centennial Award, 1955; American Veterinary Medical Association practitioner-research award, 1957; National Institute of Health research grantee, 1960—.

WRITINGS: (Contributor) H. P. Hoskins and J. V. Lacroix, editors, *Canine Surgery* (textbook), North American Veterinarian, 1949; *Planning Your Animal Hospital*, American Animal Hospital Association, 1950; *Your Future in Veterinary Medicine*, Rosen, 1963; (contributor) E. J. Catcott, editor, *Feline Medicine and Surgery*, American Veterinary Publications, 1964; (contributor) Robert W. Kirk and others, editors, *Current Veterinary Therapy*, Saunders, 1964-65. Editorial consultant to *Veterinary Medicine*, 1958—, *Journal of Small Animal Practice* (England), 1960—, *Small Animal Clinician, 1961–*.

WORK IN PROGRESS: Continuing research on orthopedic pathology and canine hip dysplasia, under National Institute of Health grant.

* * *

ROACH, Helen P(auline) 1903-

PERSONAL: Born June 30, 1903, in St. Joseph, Mo.; daughter of Marcus S. and Mary Margaret (McConville) Roach. *Education:* Hunter College (now Hunter College of the City University of New York), A.B., 1924; Columbia University, M.A., 1928, Ph.D., 1948. *Religion:* Catholic. *Home:* 333 East 41st St., New York, N.Y. 10017.

CAREER: New York City Public Schools, New York, N.Y., teacher, 1924-29; Hunter College (now Hunter College of the City University of New York), New York, N.Y., substitute instructor in speech, 1929-30; Brooklyn College (now Brooklyn College of the City University of New York), 1931-69, began as instructor, became associate professor of speech and theatre. First apprentice director, American Shakespeare Festival, 1955. Appointed by Mrs. Richard Nixon to serve on a five-member commission to establish a White House record library. *Member:* Speech Association of America, Society for Theatre Research, American Association of University Professors, American Association of University Women. *Awards, honors:* Visiting research fellow, Radcliffe College, 1960-61.

WRITINGS: History of Speech Education at Columbia College, 1754-1940, Bureau of Publications, Teachers College, Columbia University, 1950; *Spoken Record Collection*, Department of Speech and Theatre, Brooklyn College, 1959; *Spoken Records*, Scarecrow, 1963, 3rd edition, 1970. Contributor of articles to speech and teaching journals.

ROBERTS, Bleddyn J(ones) 1906-

PERSONAL: Born April 21, 1906, in Ruabon, Denbighshire, Wales; son of Thomas Jones and Sophia (Davies-Jones) Roberts; married Miriam Eluned (a medical doctor), April 20, 1944. *Education:* University College of North Wales, B.A., 1928, B.D., 1934, M.A., 1936, D.D., 1951; University of Leipzig, graduate study, 1929-31. *Home:* Bryn Teg, Menai Bridge, Anglesey, Wales.

CAREER: Ordained minister, Presbyterian Church of Wales, 1936. University of Manchester, Manchester, England, assistant lecturer in Hebrew, 1934-36; University College of North Wales, Bangor, assistant lecturer in Hebrew, 1936-37; United Presbyterian Theological College, Aberystwyth, Wales, professor of Hebrew, 1937-46; University College of North Wales, senior lecturer in Biblical studies, 1946-51, professor of Hebrew, 1951—. Committee member, Palestine Exploration Fund. *Member:* Society for Old Testament Studies (president, 1964), Society for New Testament Study, Association of British Orientalists, Royal Asiatic Society.

WRITINGS: Patrymau Llenyddol y Beibl, Brython Press, 1950; *The Old Testament Text and Versions*, University of Wales Press, 1951; *Some Observations on the Dead Sea Scrolls* [Manchester], 1952; *The Dead Sea Scrolls and Old Testament Scripture*, [Manchester], 1953; *Sgroliau'r Mor Marw*, University of Wales Press, 1956; *The Second Isaiah Scroll from Qumran*, [Manchester], 1959; *Diwinyddiaeth yr Hen Destament*, University of Wales Press, 1965; *Son am Achub*, Gwasg Prifysgol Cymru, 1965; *Proffwyd Gofidiau*, Argaffty'r Methodistiad Calfinaidd, 1967. Contributor to theological and other journals in England and Germany.

WORK IN PROGRESS: Directing a new translation of the Bible in Welsh; books on Old Testament text and versions, and on the Dead Sea scrolls.

* * *

ROBERTS, Denys (Tudor Emil) 1923-

PERSONAL: Born January 19, 1923, in London, England; son of William David (a barrister) and Dorothy Elizabeth (Morrison) Roberts; married Brenda St. Clair Marsh, 1949; children: Nigel Charles Emil, Amanda Karin Patricia. *Education:* Wadham College, Oxford, B.A., 1948, M.A., 1949, B.C.L., 1949. *Home:* High Point, Beaucroft Lane, Colehill, Wimburne, Dorset, England. *Agent:* A. P. Watt & Son, 26/28 Bedford Row, London W.C.2, England. *Office:* Attorney-General's Chambers, Central Government Offices, Hong Kong.

CAREER: Barrister-at-law, Lincoln's Inn, 1950; barrister in private practice, London, England, 1950-53; Crown counsel, Nyasaland, 1953-59; attorney-general, Gibraltar, 1960-62; solicitor-general, Hong Kong, 1962-66, attorney-general, 1966—. *Military service:* British Army, Royal Artillery, 1942-46; became captain. *Awards, honors:* Order of the British Empire, 1960; Commander of the Order of the British Empire, 1970.

WRITINGS: Smuggler's Circuit, Methuen, 1954; *Beds and Roses*, Methuen, 1956; *The Elwood Wager*, Methuen, 1957; *The Bones of the Wajingas*, Methuen, 1959; *How to Dispense with Lawyers*, Muller, 1964.

* * *

ROBERTS, Dorothy James 1903-
(Peter Mortimer)

PERSONAL: Born September 5, 1903, in Elizabeth,

W.Va.; daughter of James A. (an oil producer) and Anna (Rogers) Roberts. *Education:* Barnard College, B.A., 1925; University of Wisconsin, graduate study, 1932-35. *Home and office:* 569 Patricia Lane, Palo Alto, Calif. 94303.

CAREER: Author.

WRITINGS: (With K. A. Smallzried) *More Than You Promise*, Harper, 1942; *Man of Malice Landing*, Macmillan, 1943; *A Durable Fire*, Macmillan, 1945; *The Mountain Journey*, Appleton, 1947; *Marshwood*, Appleton, 1949; *The Enchanted Cup*, Appleton, 1953; *Launcelot My Brother*, Appleton, 1954; *Missy*, Appleton, 1957; *Return of the Stranger*, Appleton, 1958; *With Night We Banish Sorrow*, Little, Brown, 1960; *Fire in the Ice*, Little, Brown, 1961; *Kinsmen of the Grail*, Little, Brown, 1963.

* * *

ROBERTS, Sydney (Castle) 1887-1966

PERSONAL: Born April 3, 1887, in Birkenhead, England; son of Frank (a civil engineer) and Mary Cowell (Castle) Roberts; married Irene Wallis (died, 1932); married Marjorie Swann, November 10, 1938; children: John (deceased), Mary (deceased), Nan (Mrs. Graham Hooper). *Education:* Pembroke College, Cambridge, B.A., 1909, M.A., 1913. *Religion:* Church of England. *Home:* 21 West Rd., Cambridge, England.

CAREER: Cambridge University Press, Cambridge, England, secretary, 1922-48; Cambridge University, master of Pembroke College, 1948-58, vice-chancellor of university, 1949-51. Vice-president of International Association of Universities, 1950-55; chairman of British Film Institute, 1952-56, of Cinematograph Films Council, 1954-64, of Committee of Enquiry into Public Libraries, and Dr. Johnson's House. Widely known as investigator of chronology and other matters relating to Sherlock Holmes and Dr. Watson. *Military service:* British Army, Suffolk Regiment, lieutenant, 1915-19; wounded at Ypres, 1917.

MEMBER: Royal Society of Literature (fellow), Library Association (honorary fellow; president, 1953), English Association (president 1963), Athenaeum Club (London). *Awards, honors:* Knighted, 1958; honorary LL.D., University of St. Andrews; L.H.D., Brown University.

WRITINGS: The Story of Doctor Johnson: Being an Introduction to Boswell's Life, Cambridge University Press, 1919; *A History of the Cambridge University Press, 1521-1921*, Cambridge University Press, 1921; *Doctor Johnson in Cambridge: Essays in Boswellian Imitation*, Putnam, 1922; *Samuel Johnson: Writer*, Dial, 1926; *Lord Macaulay: The Pre-eminent Victorian*, J. Johnson and Oxford University Press, 1927; *The Charm of Cambridge*, A. & C. Black, 1927; *An Eighteenth-Century Gentleman and Other Essays*, Cambridge University Press, 1930; *Doctor Watson: Prolegomena to the Study of a Biographical Problem, with a Bibliography of Sherlock Holmes*, Faber, 1931; *Introduction to Cambridge: A Brief Guide to the University from Within*, Cambridge University Press, 1934; *Doctor Johnson*, Duckworth, 1935.

Zuleika in Cambridge, Heffer, 1941, Macmillan, 1942; *British Universities*, Macmillan, 1947; *Holmes and Watson: A Miscellany*, Oxford University Press, 1953; *Samuel Johnson*, Longmans, Green, for the British Council, 1954; *The Evolution of Cambridge Publishing*, Cambridge University Press, 1956; *Doctor Johnson and Others*, Cambridge University Press, 1958; *Adventures With Authors* (memoirs), Cambridge University Press, 1966.

Editor: James Boswell, *Journal of a Tour to Corsica and Memoirs of Pascal Paoli*, Cambridge University Press, 1923; Hester L. Piozzi, *Anecdotes of Samuel Johnson: During the Last Twenty Years of His Life*, Cambridge University Press, 1925; Thomas Browne, *Christian Morals, with the Life of the Author by Samuel Johnson*, Cambridge University Press, 1927; Izaak Walton, *Lives of Donne and Herbert*, Cambridge University Press, 1928; A. L. Attwater, *Pembroke College, Cambridge: A Short History*, Cambridge University Press, 1936; (and author of introduction) A. T. Quiller-Couch, *Memories and Opinions: An Unfinished Autobiography*, Cambridge University Press, 1945; Harold H. Child, *Essays and Reflections*, Cambridge University Press, 1948; *History of Brighton College*, compiled by George P. Burstow and M. B. Whittaker, Brighton College, 1957; (and author of introduction) Max Beerbohm, *The Incomparable Max: A Selection*, Heinemann, 1962.

Translator: Andre Maurois, *Aspects of Biography*, Appleton, 1929; Francois de La Rochefoucauld, *Frenchmen in England, 1784*, Macmillan, 1933.

Compiler: *A Picture Book of British History*, three volumes, Cambridge University Press, 1914-32; *English Association Essays and Studies*, Oxford University Press, 1937-41.

Publications also include essays and lectures. Contributor to *Encyclopaedia Britannica*, *Dictionary of National Biography*, and *Chambers's Encyclopaedia*.

(Died July 21, 1966)

* * *

ROBERTS, Warren Aldrich 1901-

PERSONAL: Born November 28, 1901, in Galva, Iowa; son of Charles Edward Burr and Edith May (Aldrich) Roberts; married Blanche Elizabeth Wylie, July 26, 1926; children: Jean Katharine, Caroline Elizabeth (Mrs. William Conklin), Harriet Edith. *Education:* Gooding College, B.A., 1924; University of Idaho, M.A., 1928; Harvard University, Ph.D., 1932. *Politics:* Republican. *Religion:* Episcopalian. *Home:* 410 Crawford St., Crawfordsville, Ind. 47933. *Office:* Department of State, Washington, D.C. 20525.

CAREER: Member of economics faculty at University of Idaho, Moscow, 1929-30, at University of Arizona, Tucson, 1933-37; Western Reserve University (now Case Western Reserve University), Cleveland College, Cleveland, Ohio, chairman of department of economics, 1937-44; with U.S. Department of State, Washington, D.C., 1942-47, foreign service officer, 1962-64; Wabash College, Crawfordsville, Ind., professor of economics and political science, 1947—, chairman of department, 1948-49. Technical adviser, United Nations Conference on International Organization, San Francisco, 1945; adviser to U.S. representative on United Nations Security Council, 1946; public member of Department of State inspection team in Central America, 1962, and member of U.S. delegation at Inter-America Economic and Social Conference, Mexico City, 1962. Consultant on public finance at various times to Idaho, Arizona, Minnesota. Director of Indiana Special Committee on Public Education, 1954.

MEMBER: American Political Science Association, American Economics Association, American Society of International Law, American Society of Political and Legal Philosophy, Midwest Political Science Association. *Awards, honors:* Guggenheim fellow in mine economics and taxation, 1940-41.

WRITINGS: Arizona Tax Problems, University of Arizona, 1935; *State Taxation of Metallic Deposits,* Harvard University Press, 1944; (contributor) Carl Friedrich, editor, *Nomos II,* Liberal Arts Press, 1957; (contributor) Friedrich, editor, *Nomos III,* 1958. Contributor to economic periodicals.

WORK IN PROGRESS: Aspects of World Order.

* * *

ROBERTSON, Edith Anne (Stewart)   1883-19(?)

PERSONAL: Born January 10, 1883, in Scotland; daughter of Robert and Jane Louisa (Faulds) Stewart; married James Alexander Robertson, 1919 (died, 1955); children: Alison Mary (Mrs. Charles Mathews), Beryl Jenette (Mrs. Eric Barnes), Lesley Anne (Mrs. Donald Parry). *Education:* Educated at Glasgow High School for Girls and privately, at home and abroad. *Politics:* Liberal. *Religion:* Pre-Reformation.

CAREER: Author and poet. Former president, St. Katherine's Girls Club, Aberdeen, Scotland; founder, Shiprow Tavern (working man's non-licensed club and tavern), Aberdeen. *Member:* Society of Authors, P.E.N., Saltire Society. *Awards, honors:* First prize in world competition for best poem in Scots tongue on occasion of Robert Burns bicentenary; second prize from *Scotsman* for best poem in Scots tongue.

WRITINGS: Songs of Pilgrimage and Battle, Headley Brothers, 1916; *The Life and Letters of St. Francis Xavier,* Headley Brothers, 1917; *Poems: Second Book,* Headley Brothers, 1919; *He Is Become My Song, Carmen Jesu Nazareni,* Macmillan, 1930; *Francis Xavier, Knight Errant of the Cross, 1506-1552,* S.C.M. Press, 1930; (translator) *Poems frae the Suddron o Walter de la Mare Made Ower intil Scots,* M. Macdonald, 1955; *Voices frae the City o Trees,* M. Macdonald, 1955; *Collected Ballads and Poems in the Scots Tongue,* Aberdeen University Press, 1967; (translator) *Translations into the Scots Tongue of Poems by Gerard Manley Hopkins,* Aberdeen University Press, 1968; *Forest Voices, and Other Poems in English,* Aberdeen University Press, 1969. Also author of a historical play, "Lady Jonet Douglas." Contributor of poetry to newspapers and magazines.

WORK IN PROGRESS: The Journal of an Unquiet King, about James V of Scotland; ballads and poems in Scots.

(Deceased)

* * *

ROBERTSON, Thomas Anthony   1897-

PERSONAL: Born November 22, 1897, in Los Mochis, Sinaloa, Mexico; son of Louis (a Danish sailor, later a farmer) and Elizabeth (Bunker) Robertson; married Dorothy May Utt, January 25, 1919; children: Alan, Jean, Leigh, Rae, Merilie, Thomas, Jr. *Education:* Attended public high school in Santa Ana, Calif., 1913-1917. *Religion:* Protestant. *Home:* Apartado Postal 50, San Miguel Village, El Sauzal, Baja California, Mexico.

CAREER: Has worked as farmer; Liga Agricola Occidental Mexicana (agricultural cooperative), director, 1920-25; California Farm Bureau Federation, chairman of vegetable growers department, 1933-39; American National Foods, Inc., vice-president, 1935-39; California Agricul-

tural Prorate Commission, member of board of directors, 1935-39; Civil Service Commission, Ventura County, Calif., chairman, 1944-45. President of Simi Valley M.E. Community Church Brotherhood, Ventura County, Calif., 1929-31. *Member:* Masons.

WRITINGS: A Southwestern Utopia, Ward Ritchie, 1947, revised edition, Anderson & Ritchie, 1964; (translator) *The Saga of Cabeza de Vaca,* Ensenada Hello (Mexico), 1963. Also translator of *Triumphs of Our Saintly Faith among People the Most Savage and Barbarous of the New Orb,* three volumes, 1967, originally written in 1645 by the Padre Provincial of Mexico.

WORK IN PROGRESS: A history, in Spanish and English, of Lower California and its missions.

SIDELIGHTS: Robertson grew up in an American colony in Mexico, the son of a former Danish sailor who had been around Cape Horn and around the world four times in the days of sailing ships. Robertson describes his father as a tireless worker and fisherman, "and my early days were spent ocean fishing, hunting, horseback riding, and seeing the life of Mexicans and Indians."

* * *

ROBINSON, Alan R(onald)   1920-

PERSONAL: Born April 3, 1920, in Southampton, Hampshire, England; son of Walpole Allen (a businessman) and May (a teacher; maiden name, Bryant) Robinson. *Education:* University of London, B.A. (with first class honors in German), 1944, B.A. (Swedish), 1966; Oxford University, Dip. Ed., 1945; University of Edinburgh, Ph.D., 1950. *Home and office:* University College of Wales, Aberystwyth, Cardiganshire, Wales.

CAREER: Assistant master at Merchant Taylors' School, Rickmansworth, Hertfordshire, England, 1945-46, and at Haberdashers' Aske's School, Hampstead, London, England, 1946-47; British Foreign Office, London, England, inspector, German section, 1947-48; University College of Wales, Aberystwyth, Cardiganshire, lecturer in German, 1950-67, and in Swedish language and literature, 1954-67; University of Guelph, Guelph, Ontario, professor of German, 1967-71; University College of Wales, professor of German and head of German, Swedish, and Russian Department, 1971—. Visiting professor at McGill University, 1963. *Military service:* British Army, 1940-42. *Member:* Council for the Protection of Rural Wales (county branch vice-president, 1959—) Council for the Protection of Rural England, National Trust, Southampton Civic Trust (founder, 1962), Tramway Museum Society, Paddle Steamer Preservation Society (founder, 1959; president, 1962—).

WRITINGS—Editor: Theodor, Fontane, *Grete Minde,* Methuen, 1955; Albrecht Goes, *Das Brandopfer,* Harrap, 1958; Carl Zuckmayer, *Der Seelenbraeu,* Harrap, 1960; *"Am I My Brother's Keeper?": The Literary and Pastoral Mission of Albrecht Goes,* University of Wales Press, 1973. Contributor of articles on Fontane and Goes, and of reviews to *Modern Languages, German Life and Letters,* and *Modern Language Review.*

WORK IN PROGRESS: A critical study of Theodor Foantane, for Methuen.

AVOCATIONAL INTERESTS: Protecting beautiful areas of countryside and coast in Britain; studying the history of transportation, especially tramways, light railways, and paddle steamers; travel; country walks.

ROBINSON, Howard 1885-

PERSONAL: Born July 17, 1885, in Redwood Falls, Minn.; son of James Bostwick and Adele M. (Chapman) Robinson; married Jennie Wrenn, July 22, 1931; children: Hester Adele, Arthur H. *Education:* Hamline University, B.A., 1908; Union Theological Seminary, New York, N.Y., B.D., 1911; Columbia University, M.A., 1911, Ph.D., 1916. *Home:* 75 Elmwood Pl., Oberlin, Ohio.

CAREER: McGill University, Wesleyan Theological College, Montreal, Quebec, 1911-15, became professor of church history; Carleton College, Northfield, Minn., 1916-24, became professor of history; Miami University, Oxford, Ohio, professor of history, 1924-35, dean of College of Arts and Sciences, 1930-35; Ohio State University, Columbus, professor of history, 1935-37; Oberlin College, Oberlin, Ohio, professor of history, 1937-50, professor emeritus, 1950—, dean of the College, 1948-49. Fulbright lecturer, University of Queensland, 1951-52; visiting summer professor at University of Minnesota, Columbia University (twice), University of Illinois, Indiana University, University of Missouri, University of Michigan, Western Reserve University (now Case Western Reserve University), and Clark University.

MEMBER: American Historical Association, Royal Historical Society (fellow and life member), Society of Postal Historians (London; charter member), Postal History Society, Ohio Academy of History (honorary life member; president, 1935), Phi Beta Kappa. *Awards, honors:* LL.D. from Hamline University, 1930; Schuyler Prize of American Historical Society, 1951, for *History of the British Post Office.*

WRITINGS: Development of the British Empire, Houghton, 1924, revised edition, 1936; *History of Great Britain*, Houghton, 1927; (with others) *Essays in Intellectual History Dedicated to James Harvey Robinson*, Harper, 1929; *Bayle the Sceptic*, Columbia University Press, 1931; *History of the British Post Office*, Princeton University Press, 1948; *Britain's Post Office*, Oxford University Press, 1953; *History of the Post Office in New Zealand*, Verry, 1964; *Carrying British Mails Overseas*, New York University Press, 1964.. Also contributor to *Encyclopedia of Social Sciences* and *Compton's Pictured Encyclopedia.* Charter member of board of editors of *Journal of Modern History.*

AVOCATIONAL INTERESTS: Collecting old and rare books; photography, and traveling.

* * *

ROBISON, Mabel Otis 1891-

PERSONAL: Born May 4, 1891, in Granite Falls, Minn.; daughter of John L. (a grain buyer) and Sarah (Painter) Otis; married Cleatus Robison (separated); children: Arthur, Jean (Mrs. Harold King), Charles. *Education:* Attended University of Minnesota. *Religion:* Protestant. *Home:* 1034 South Coast Blvd., La Jolla, Calif. 92037.

CAREER: Free-lance writer. Former teacher of creative writing in adult education classes in Minneapolis, Minn., and privately. *Member:* Pot Boilers (San Diego).

WRITINGS: Charcoal Faces, Bruce, 1956; *Pioneer Panorama: A Story of St. Anthony and Minnesota in the Turbulent Years of Growth from 1853-1866*, Denison, 1957; *Minnesota Pioneers: Word Pictures of Famous Characters and Interesting Events in the Story of Minnesota*, Denison, 1958; (with Phillips E. Osgood) *Straight Tongue: A Story of Henry Benjamin Whipple, First Episcopal Bishop of Min-*

nesota, Denison, 1958; (with Rae Oetting) *Camping and Outdoor Cooking*, Denison, 1958; *Mystic Wonderlands*, Denison, 1959; *Frank H. Krusen, M.D., Pioneer in Physical Medicine and Rehabilitation*, Denison, 1963; (with Joe Dell Garcia) *Come Along to Mexico*, Denison, 1965; *The Hole in the Mountain*, Dodd, 1966; *Come Along to Canada*, Denison, 1967; *Come Along to South Africa*, Denison, 1969. Author of several hundred short stories and articles in *American Forests, Jack and Jill, Golden Magazine*, and other magazines.

WORK IN PROGRESS: A Minnesota historical book of the period 1954-58; a fictionalized biography of Audubon; *The Great Plan*; *Years of Expectation*; *Dillers' Landing.*

* * *

ROBO, Etienne 1879-

PERSONAL: Born May 9, 1879, in Lorient, France; son of Etienne Robo (a naval officer). *Education:* St. Anne's College, Auray, France, B.A., 1895. *Home:* 32 Orchard Rd., Bromley, Kent, England.

CAREER: Roman Catholic priest. St. Joan of Arc Parish, Farnham, Surrey, England, founder, builder, and rector, 1930-51; now retired. *Military service:* French Army, World War I.

WRITINGS: A Little History of the Abbey of S. Mary of Waverley, E. W. Langham, 1928; *Medieval Farnham: Everyday Life in an Episcopal Manor*, E. W. Langham, 1935; *The Story of a Catholic Parish: St. Joan's Farnham*, E. W. Langham, 1938; *St. Joan, the Woman and the Saint*, Burns & Oates, 1947, revised edition, Sands & Co., 1959; *The Holiness of Joan of Arc*, Catholic Truth Society (London), 1951; *Two Portraits of St. Therese of Lisieux*, Regnery, 1955, revised and enlarged edition published as *Two Portraits of St. Teresa of Lisieux*, Newman, 1957; *Ancient Prayers and Modern Devotions*, Clonmore & Reynolds, 1957; *In the Margins of the Gospel*, Sands & Co., 1963, Newman, 1964.

WORK IN PROGRESS: Autobiography, entitled *Rough Stone and Chisel—Years of Formation.*

* * *

RODGERS, Betsy (Aikin-Sneath) 1907-

PERSONAL: Born August 29, 1907, in Paignton, Devonshire, England; daughter of Francis and Louise (Langworthy Baker) Aikin-Sneath; married Sir John Rodgers (a member of Parliament), December 23, 1930; children: Tobias, Piers. *Education:* St. Hugh's College, Oxford, B.A., 1929, M.A.; University College, London, Ph.D., 1933. *Religion:* Church of England. *Home:* Dower House, Groombridge, Kent, England.

CAREER: Author. Justice of the peace.

WRITINGS: Comedy in Germany, Clarendon Press, 1936; *Cloak of Charity*, Methuen, 1949; *Georgian Chronicle*, Methuen, 1958. Contributor to *Encyclopaedia Britannica, London Mercury, Modern Language Review, Contemporary Review.*

SIDELIGHTS: Lady Rodgers speaks French, German, and Spanish. *Avocational interests:* Country life and sport, including fox hunting and beagling.

* * *

RODGERS, John (Charles) 1906-

PERSONAL: Born October 5, 1906, in York, England; son

of Charles (an antique dealer) and Maud Mary (Hodgson) Rodgers; married Betsy Aikin-Sneath, 1931; children: John Fairie Tobias, Andrew Piers Wingate. *Education:* Attended St. Peter's, York, England, and Ecole des Roches in France; Keble College, Oxford, M.A., 1947. *Politics:* Conservative. *Religion:* Church of England. *Home:* The Dower House, Groombridge, Kent, England; and 72 Berkeley House, Hay Hill, London W.1, England. *Office:* J. Walter Thompson Co. Ltd., 40 Berk Rd., Bromley, Kent, England.

CAREER: Mary Ward Settlement, London, England, subwarden, 1929-30; University of Hull, Hull, England, lecturer and administrative assistant, 1930-31; J. Walter Thompson Co. Ltd., London, England, member of staff, 1931-36, director, 1936-60, deputy chairman, 1960-70. Founder and chairman, British Market Research Bureau Ltd., 1933-54; director, History Today Ltd., 1952—; chairman, New English Library Ltd., 1960-70. Member of Parliament, Sevenoaks Division of Kent, 1950—, serving as parliamentary private secretary to Viscount Eccles, 1951-57, minister at Board of Trade, 1958-60. Temporary civil servant, World War II, serving successively in Ministry of Information, Ministry of Production, and Foreign Office, 1941-45. Member of court of assistants, Worshipful Company of Masons, of York Civic Trust. Freeman, City of London. Count of University of Kent at Canterbury, Royal College of Art, and City University. *Member:* Royal Society of Arts (fellow), Royal Statistical Society (fellow), Incorporated Statisticians (fellow), Brooks's Club, Royal Thames Yacht Club. *Awards, honors:* Created a Baronet, 1964.

WRITINGS: Mary Ward Settlement, Late Passmore Edwards Settlement: A History, 1891-1931, Edwards Museum, 1931; *The Old Public Schools of England,* Scribner, 1938; *The English Woodland,* Batsford, 1941, Scribner, 1946; *English Rivers,* Batsford, 1948; *York,* Batsford, 1951; (editor and author of preface and notes) Thomas Gray, *Poems,* Grey Walls Press, 1953.

With others; all published by Conservative Political Centre: *Industry Looks at the New Order,* 1941; *One Nation,* 1950; *Change Is Our Ally,* 1954; *Capitalism—Strength and Stress,* 1958; *Monopoly and the Public Interest,* 1963; *The Atlantic Community,* 1963. Author of political pamphlets. Contributor of articles to *Adelphi, Criterion, History Today, Spectator,* and other periodicals.

AVOCATIONAL INTERESTS: Theatre, travel, and reading.

* * *

ROEPKE, Wilhelm (Theodor) 1899-1966

PERSONAL: Born October 10, 1899, in Schwarmstedt, Germany; son of Wilhelm (a doctor) and Martha (Rechten) Roepke; married Eva Fincke, April 21, 1923; children: Barthold, Ilse Roepke Berger, Renate Roepke Begaud. *Education:* Various universities, receiving Dr. rer. pol., 1921. *Religion:* Lutheran. *Office:* Graduate Institute of International Studies, University of Geneva, Geneva, Switzerland.

CAREER: University of Marburg, Marburg, Germany, privatdozent, 1922-24; University of Jena, Jena, Germany, associate professor, 1924-28; University of Graz, Graz, Austria, professor, 1928-29; University of Marburg, professor, 1929-33; University of Istanbul, Istanbul, Turkey, professor, 1933-37; University of Geneva, Graduate Institute of International Studies, Geneva, Switzerland, professor,

1937-66. Visiting professor in U.S. five times, under auspices of Rockefeller Foundation. Economic adviser to Adenauer government, Bonn, Germany, 1950. *Military service:* World War I; received Iron Cross. *Member:* American Economic Association, Swiss Economic Association, Royal Economic Society, Institut de France (corresponding). *Awards and honors:* D.Litt., Columbia University, 1954; Dr. es Sciences Politiques, University of Geneva, 1959; Grand Cross of Merit of Federal Republic of Germany.

WRITINGS: Geld und Aussenhandel, S. Fischer (Jena), 1925; *Finanzwissenschaft,* Spaeth & Linde (Berlin), 1929; *Die Theorie der Kapitalbildung,* J. C. Mohr (Tuebingen), 1929; *Der Weg des Unheils,* S. Fischer, 1931, translation published as *What's Wrong with the World?,* Dorrance, 1932; *Weltwirtschaft, eine Notwendigkeit der deutschen Wirtschaft,* J. C. Mohr, 1932; *Krise und Konjunktur,* Quelle & Meyer (Heidelberg), 1932, translation and adaptation by Vera C. Smith published as *Crises and Cycles,* Hodge & Co., 1936; *German Commercial Policy,* Longmans, Green, 1934; *Die Lehre von der Wirtschaft,* J. Springer (Vienna), 1937, 11th edition, E. Rentsch (Zurich), 1968, translation by Patrick M. Boarman published as *Economics of the Free Society,* Regnery, 1963.

Die Gesellschaftskrisis der Gegenwart, E. Rentsch, 1942, 5th edition, 1948, translation by Annette Jacobsohn and Peter Schiffer Jacobsohn published as *The Social Crisis of our Time,* University of Chicago Press, 1950; *International Economic Disintegration,* Macmillan (New York), 1942; *Civitas humana: Grundfragen der Gesellschafts und Wirtschaftsreform,* E. Rentsch, 1944, 2nd edition, 1946, translation by Cyril Spencer Fox published as *Civitas Humana, a Humane Order of Society,* Hodge & Co., 1948, British Book Centre, 1950; *Die Deutsche Frage,* E. Rentsch, 1945, 3rd edition, revised and enlarged, 1948, translation by E. W. Dickes published as *The German Question,* Allen & Unwin, 1946, revised and enlarged American edition published as *The Solution of the German Question,* Putnam, 1947; *Internationale Ordnung,* E. Rentsch, 1945, 2nd edition, revised and enlarged, published as *Internationale Ordnung—Heute,* 1954, translation by Gwen E. Trinks, Joyce Taylor and Cicely Kaufer published as *International Order and Economic Integration,* D. Reidel Publications, 1959, Circa Publications, 1960; *Die Krise des Kollektivismus,* Kurt Desch (Munich), 1947; *Das Kulturideal des Liberalismus,* Gerhard Schulte-Bulmke (Frankfurt), 1947.

Ist die deutsche Wirtschaftspolitik richtig?: Analyse und Kritik, Verlag W. Kohlhammer (Stuttgart), 1950; *Mass und Mitte,* E. Rentsch, 1950; *The Problem of Economic Order,* [Cairo], 1951; *The Economics of Full Employment: An Analysis of the U.N. Report on National and International Measures for Full Employment,* American Enterprise Association, 1952; (with others) *Kommt der vierte Mensch?,* Europa Verlag (Stuttgart), 1952; (with others) *Aufbau eines neuen Europa: Fuenf Aufsaetze ueber wirtschaftliche? Zusammenarbeit,* Grunewald Verlag (Berlin), 1953; (with J. Hunerman and E. Muller) *Wirtschaftsethik Heute: Drei Reden an jeden,* Furche-Verlag (Hamburg), 1956; *Welfare, Freedom, and Inflation,* Pall Mall, 1957, University of Alabama Press, 1964; *Freie Welt und Totalitarismus,* Angelsachsen Verlag (Breman), 1957; (with others) *Hat der Westen Eine Idee?,* Martin Hoch (Ludwigsburg), 1957; *Ein Jahrzehnt sozialer Marktwirtschaft in Deutschland und seine Lehren,* Verlag fuer Politik und Wirtschaft (Cologne), 1958; *Jenseits von Angebot und Nachfrage,* E. Rentsch, 1958, 3rd edition, revised, 1961, translation by Elizabeth

Henderson published as *A Humane Economy: The Social Framework of the Free Market*, Regnery, 1960; *Gegen die Brandung: Zeugnisse eines Gelehrtenlebens unserer Zeit*, edited by Albert Hunold, E. Rentsch, 1959, translation by Henderson published as *Against the Tide*, Regnery, 1969; *L'Economie mondiale aux XIXe et XXe siecles*, Librarie E. Droz (Geneva), 1959.

Derwirtschaftliche Standort des Buchhaendlers, Schweizerisches Vereinssortiment (Olten), 1960; *Economia y libertad* (lectures originally in English but published first in Spanish), Foro de la libre Empresa (Buenos Aires), 1960; (author of introduction) *Einige Gedanken zum Thema: Die Kommunistische Gefahr, die Entwicklungslaender und wir*, 3rd edition, P. Haupt (Bern), 1961; (with others) *Entwicklungslaender, Wahn und Wirklichkeit*, E. Rentsch, 1961; (with others) *Politik fuer uns alle oder fuer die Interessenten?*, Martin Hoch, 1961; *Wirrnis und Wahrheit: Ausgewaehlte Aufsaetze*, E. Rentsch, 1962; *Europa in der Welt von heute: Vortrag gehalten von dem Handels- und Industrieverein Thun*, W. Kebser (Thun), 1962; *The Crisis of European Economic Integration*, Swiss Credit Bank (Zurich), 1963; *Wort und Wirkung*, edited by Walter Hoch, Martin Hoch, 1964; (with others) *Ein Neuer Anlauf in der Gesellschafts- und Wirtschaftspolitik*, Martin Hoch, 1964; *South Africa, an Attempt at a Positive Appraisal*, Information Service of South Africa, c.1965; *Fronten der Freiheit: Wirtschaft, Internationale Ordnung, Politik*, edited by Hans Otto Wesemann and Grete Schleicher, Seewald (Stuttgart), 1965, 2nd edition, 1966; (with others) *Die Schweiz und die Integration des Westens*, Schweizer Spiegel (Zurich), 1965; (with others) *Was Muessen wir fuer die freie Welt tun?*, Martin Hoch, 1965; *Torheiten der Zeit*, Christiana-Verlag (Zurich), 1966; (contributor) Paul Koenig, editor, *Die Schweiz unterwegs, 1798-?: Ausgewaehlte Geschichtssehreibung und Deutung*, Thomas-Verlag (Zurich), 1969.

WORK IN PROGRESS: Autobiography.

SIDELIGHTS: Roepke was fluent in German, French, English, Italian, and Latin, and had a reading knowledge of Spanish and Dutch. He traveled in the United States, South America, Far East, and Africa.

AVOCATIONAL INTERESTS: Gardening, mountaineering, skiing, collecting old books and prints.

BIOGRAPHICAL/CRITICAL SOURCES: Gegen die Brandung, E. Rentsch, 1959.

(Died, 1966)

*   *   *

ROFE, (Fevzi) Husein 1922-

PERSONAL: Born May 3, 1922, in Manchester, England; son of Albert Clement (a merchant) and Suzanne (Blieck) Rofe. *Education:* Attended Shrewsbury School; School of Oriental Studies, University of London, intermediate B.A. in Middle Eastern languages, 1946, 1957, B.A. (general), 1969. *Religion:* Islam. *Home:* c/o Asian Development Bank, Manila, Philippines.

CAREER: London School of Languages, London, England, teacher, 1945-46; British Consulate, Tetuan, Corocco, interpreter, 1947-49; teacher in government secondary schools, Djokjakarta, Indonesia, 1950-54; Turkish Lycee, Nicosia, Cyprus, teacher, 1955-56; University of Hong Kong, Hong Kong, language tutor, 1959-65; Asian Development Bank, Manila, Philippines, head of translation service, 1970—. Simultaneous interpreter for Junior

Chamber of Commerce International Congress, Hong Kong, 1962; occasional translator for U.N. agencies in Europe. Travel consultant to Holland-America Line, 1970—. *Military service:* Royal Air Force, 1940-45; became sergeant; received Africa Star. *Member:* Association Internationale de Traducteurs de Conference, Mongolia Society, Royal Asiatic Society (fellow).

WRITINGS: Evolution of Islam, Ashraf, 1952; *Path of Subud*, Rider, 1959; *Reflections on Subud*, Humanity Publishing, 1961; (with T. C. Lai) *Things Chinese*, Swindon (Hong Kong), 1971; (contributor) Don McLean, editor, *The Changing Orient*, Angus & Robertson, in press; *Bali, Serasia* (Hong Kong), in press. Contributor of articles to magazines and journals in Europe and Asia, including *Tropical Fish Hobbyist, Islamic Review, Pet Industry, Far Eastern Economic Review, Lookeast, Orientations*, and *Golden Guide to South East Asia*.

WORK IN PROGRESS: Studies and related photography in Southeast Asia.

SIDELIGHTS: Rofe is competent in English, German, Dutch, French, Italian, Spanish, Portuguese, Arabic, Turkish, Persian, Malay, Indonesian, Cantonese, Japanese, and Mongol. *Avocational interests:* Spiritual disciplines, tropical fish culture, photography and cinematography, travel, Asian culture, and Egyptology.

*   *   *

ROMAINE, Lawrence B. 1900-
(The Weathercock)

PERSONAL: Born October 13, 1900, in Morristown, N.J.; son of William Jones and Rose C. M. (Bond) Romaine; married Elizabeth Frederika DiZerega (a bookkeeper and ornithologist), August 28, 1930 (deceased); children: Elizabeth Park, William Thornton. *Education:* Williams College, B.A., 1923. *Politics:* "Vote for the best man." *Religion:* Episcopalian. *Home and office:* Weathercock House, Middleborough, Mass. 02346.

CAREER: Worked at one time for New York Trust Co., *New York World*, and for realty and other firms in New York, N.Y.; former newspaper representative with John B. Woodward; Weathercock House, Middleboro (officially Middleborough), Mass., operator of antiques business, and out-of-print Americana and American trade catalogues business (mail only), 1933—. Curator of Middleborough Historical Association museum. *Member:* Early American Industries Association, Society for the Preservation of New England Antiquities.

WRITINGS: The Weathercock Crows (rhymes and jingles), Weathercok House, 1955; *Narrative of Captivities of James Van Horne*, Weathercock House, 1957; *From Cambridge to Champlain, March 18 to May 5, 1776*, Weathercock House, 1957; *A Guide to American Trade Catalogs, 1744-1900*, Bowker, 1960. Contributor of several hundred articles to *Antiques*, antiquarian periodicals, newspapers, and to historical society periodicals. Editor, *Middleborough Antiquarian*.

*   *   *

RONAN, Thomas Matthew 1907-
(Tom Ronan)

PERSONAL: Born November 11, 1907, in Perth, Western Australia; son of Denis James and Julia (Richardson) Ronan; married Mary Elizabeth Kearins; children: Nicholas, Brian, Kevin, Pamela, Niall, Kimberley, Erla,

Damian. *Education:* Attended Aquinas College, Perth, Western Australia. *Politics:* Australian Labour Party. *Religion:* Roman Catholic. *Home:* Springvale, Katherine, Northern Territory, Australia.

CAREER: Worked for Gregory & Co. (pearlers and traders), Broome, Western Australia, 1923-27, for Connor, Coherty & Durack (graziers), Wyndham, Western Australia, 1933-37, 1944-50, for Council of Scientific and Industrial Research, Katherine, Northern Territory, Australia, 1950-56; farmer and writer, 1956—. Member, Northern Territory Legislative Council, 1954-55; chairman, Northern Territory Tourist Board, 1963—. Secretary of Katherine branch, Australian Primary Producers Union, 1953-59, 1961—. *Military service:* Australian Imperial Forces, 1940-44. *Awards, honors:* Commonwealth Jubilee Literary prize, 1951, for *Vision Splendid.*

WRITINGS—Under name Tom Ronan: *Strangers on the Ophir,* Dymocks, 1946; *Vision Splendid* (novel), Macmillan, 1954; *Moleskin Midas,* Cassell, 1956, published as *Rogue Yates,* Putnam, 1957; *The Pearling Master,* Cassell, 1958; *Only A Short Walk,* Cassell, 1961; *Deep of the Sky: An Essay in Ancestor Worship,* Cassell, 1962; *Packhorse and Pearling Boat: Memories of a Misspent Youth,* Cassell, 1964; *Once There Was a Bagman: A Memoir,* Cassell, 1966. Contributor to Australian periodicals and newspapers, including *20th Century, Bulletin* (Sydney), *Hoofs and Horns, Territorian.*

WORK IN PROGRESS: Two more books of memoirs, *On the Stone Outside Mat Wilson's Store* and *And Nobody Cared for Me.*

SIDELIGHTS: Ronan writes: "Other than six broken years at school and four on active service in the army, my life since childhood has been spent in the less settled areas of Australia. In my earlier books I wrote of life on pearling boats, alongside the campfires of cattle camps, across the counter of wayside stores and shanties. Then I started on a sequence of factual narratives to cover the lifetimes of my father and myself, 1860-1945 against the background of the wide, empty land on which both of us have spent our lives through choice."

About his interest in people, he says that "it is a happy paradox that in an environment where there are so few, we meet more in numbers and in diversity of character and background than we would in a city apartment or suburban villa."

BIOGRAPHICAL/CRITICAL SOURCES: People, September, 1952.

* * *

ROOD, Allan 1894-

PERSONAL: Born October 10, 1894, in Turner Junction (now West Chicago), Ill.; son of Hebert Hamlin (a clergyman) and Orthonette (Brown) Rood; married Helen Wheeler Jackson, April 30, 1944; children; Charles Martin, Gerald Day. *Education:* Hillsdale College, student, 1912-14; Oberlin College, A.B., 1916; Harvard University, M.B.A., 1924. *Politics:* Independent. *Religion:* Protestant. *Home and office:* Winter St., Lincoln, Mass. 01751.

CAREER: Allyn & Bacon (textbook publishers), Boston Mass., bookman, 1916-18, 1919-22, assistant office manager, Chicago, Ill., 1924-26; advertising representative of *Magazine of Business,* 1926-29, *Business Week,* 1929-31; account executive and writer with advertising agencies in Cleveland, Ohio, 1931-39; McGraw-Hill Publishing Co.,

New York, N.Y., 1939-46, became associate district manager and Boston branch manager; Horton Noyes Co. (advertising agency), Providence, R.I. director of marketing, 1946-48; Harvard University Graduate School of Business Administration, Boston, Mass., director of placement, 1948-54, placement consultant, 1954-62, faculty member, 1953-61; consultant in executive placement and writer, beginning 1962. *Military service:* U.S. Army, 1918-19; became second lieutenant, Officers Reserve Corps. *Member:* Harvard Club (Boston). *Awards, honors:* Gordon A. Hardwick Award of the Middle Atlantic Placement Association, 1962, for article, "The Paradox of Effective Recruiting," in *Journal of College Placement.*

WRITINGS: Job Strategy: Preparing for Effective Placement in Business and Industry, McGraw, 1961; *Realizing Your Executive Potential,* McGraw, 1965.

AVOCATIONAL INTERESTS: Books and reading; sports.

BIOGRAPHICAL/CRITICAL SOURCES: Journal of College Placement, February, 1962, and December, 1962.

* * *

ROOT, E(dward) Merrill 1895-1973

PERSONAL: Born January 4, 1895, in Baltimore, Md.; son of Edward Tallmadge (a minister) and Georgiana (Merrill) Root; married Alsa Voorhees Landon, June 8, 1922; married second wife, Dorothy Jewel MacNab, November 22, 1969; children: (first marriage) Georgiana Merrill (Mrs. Melvin Pine). *Education:* Amherst College, A.B., 1917; also studied at University of Missouri, 1917-18, Andover Theological Seminary, 1919-20. *Politics:* Independent Conservative. *Religion:* Society of Friends (Quaker). *Home:* R.R. 1, Thompson, Conn. 06277.

CAREER: Earlham College, Richmond, Ind., assistant professor, 1920-29, professor of English, 1929-60. Poet, essayist, and lecturer. *Member:* Authors League of America, Phi Beta Kappa.

WRITINGS—Poetry: *Lost Eden,* Unicorn Press, 1927; *Bow of Burning Gold,* Packard & Co., 1929; *Dawn is Forever,* Packard & Co., 1938; *Before the Swallow Dares,* Packard & Co., 1947; *The Seeds of Time,* Falmouth, 1950; *Ulysses to Penelope,* Golden Quill, 1951; *Out of Our Winter,* Golden Quill, 1956; *The Light Wind Over,* Golden Quill, 1958; *Shoulder the Sky,* Golden Quill, 1962; *Of Perilous Seas,* Golden Quill, 1964; *Like White Birds Flying,* Golden Quill, 1969; *Children of the Morning,* Golden Quill, 1974.

Prose: *The Way of All Spirit,* Packard & Co., 1940; *Frank Harris: A Biography,* Odyssey, 1947; *Collectivism on the Campus,* Devin, 1955; *Brainwashing in the High Schools,* Devin, 1958; *America's Steadfast Dream,* Western Islands, 1971.

Contributor of poems to about forty anthologies and texts. Also contributor of poems, reviews, and articles to periodicals in United States and abroad. Poetry editor of *Quaker Life* (Richmond, Ind.), and *American Opinion* (Belmont, Mass.).

SIDELIGHTS: "My chief interest is poetry. I am also deeply interested in philosophy, and regard it as most important to restore a sense of quality, value, and meaning, in literature and in life. My emphasis is on affirmation, and a valid *yes* to life. We have traveled widely in the United States, and once to Mexico. I am interested in fishing, hunting, motoring. I prefer life in the country."

(Died October 26, 1973)

ROSE, Harold Wickliffe 1896-

PERSONAL: Born November 4, 1896; son of Wickliffe (a director general of Rockefeller Foundation and president of General Education Board) and Ella (Sadler) Rose; married Elizabeth Leeming, June 9, 1923; children: Stephen Wickliffe, Michael Lewis. *Education:* Attended St. Alban's School, 1914-15; Harvard University, A.B., 1919. *Politics:* Republican. *Religion:* Episcopalian. *Home and office:* Sharon, Conn. 06069.

CAREER: Began career with Packard Motor Co. of New York; cotton buyer for mills group, North Adams, Mass., 1921-24; American Viscose Corp., started as southern sales manager, New York, N.Y., 1924, Charlotte, N.C., 1925-32, sales manager, rayon staple, 1935-42, coordinator of research and planning at main office, Wilmington, Del., 1942-46, general assistant to president at main office, Philadelphia, Pa., 1946-53; Linen Thread Co., Inc., New York, N.Y., and Paterson, N.J., president and general manager, 1953-57, director, 1953-61; Dolphin Jute Mills, Paterson, N.J., president and director, 1956-57; textile consultant, 1957—. Member of U.S. Department of State Textile Mission to Japan, 1946; made other surveys of textile industries in Great Britain, Mexico, South America, and East Pakistan. Lecturer and photographer. President and member of board, American Tariff League, 1945-55; Textile Research Institute, member of board, 1945-51, chairman, 1945-48. Trustee, Philadelphia Museum of Art, 1945-54; member of board, School of Industrial Art, Philadelphia, 1947-50. *Military service:* U.S. Naval Reserve, 1917-21; became lieutenant junior grade.

MEMBER: National Audubon Society, Housatonic Color-camera Club, Sharon Historical Society; Harvard Club and Century Association (both New York).

WRITINGS: The Story of Rayon, 3rd edition, Moore Press, 1937; *Britanny Patrol: The Story of the Suicide Fleet,* Norton, 1937; (self-illustrated, photographs) *The Rayon and Synthetic Fiber Industry of Japan,* Textile Research Institute, 1946; *The Protection of Our Productivity* (address), American Tariff League, 1947; (with others) *Industrial Opportunities for Peru,* Arthur D. Little, 1960; (with others) *Industrial Survey of East Pakistan,* Arthur D. Little, 1961; (self-illustrated, photographs and maps) *The Colonial Houses of Worship in America: Built in the English Colonies Before the Republic, 1607-1789, and Still Standing,* Hastings House, 1964. Author of reports and monographs on textile matters, several of them published as pamphlets; contributor of short stories to *Sea Stories,* articles to *Modern Industry, Cotton,* and other textile and trade journals.

AVOCATIONAL INTERESTS: Radio, music, conversation, birds, gardening, and history.

* * *

ROSE, Homer C. 1909-1967

PERSONAL: Born October 30, 1909, in Augusta, Wis.; son of Harold S. and Ethel (Palms) Rose; married Mary Gough (a teacher), May 23, 1941; children: Patricia, Katherine, Michael. *Education:* Stout State College (now University of Wisconsin, Stout), B.S., 1931; Iowa State University of Science and Technology, M.S., 1937; New York University, postgraduate study, 1937-38. *Home:* 7128 Roosevelt Ave., Falls Church, Va. 22042. *Office:* Training Di-

vision, Federal Aviation Agency, Ninth and Independence, Washington, D.C.

CAREER: High school teacher of industrial education in Augusta, and West Allis, Wis., 1931-39; Southern Illinois University, Carbondale, instructor in industrial education, 1939-42; Federal Aviation Agency, Washington, D.C., 1946-67, became chief of Training Program Development. *Military service:* Began with U.S. Army, 1941; transferred to U.S. Navy, serving during World War II as naval officer; became commander in naval reserve. *Member:* American Vocational Association, American Society of Training Directors, National Education Association, Epsilon Pi Tau. *Awards, honors:* Distinguished Service Award, University of Wisconsin, Stout; Lousche Award, Epsilon Pi Tau, 1957; American Society of Training Directors, authors award, 1965.

WRITINGS: The Instructor and His Job, American Technical Society, 1961; *The Development and Supervision of Training Programs,* American Technical Society, 1964, 2nd edition published as *The Instructor and his Job,* 1966. Author of more than one hundred articles on industrial education, photography, and education administration.

WORK IN PROGRESS: On the Job Training.

AVOCATIONAL INTERESTS: Inventing, building, metal and wood crafts, and photography.

(Died November 27, 1967)

* * *

ROSENBLATT, Bernard A. 1886-

PERSONAL: Born June 15, 1886, in Poland; son of Louis Y. (a merchant) and Mary (Hachnoci) Rosenblatt; married Gertrude Goldsmith, June 3, 1914 (died October 9, 1955); children: David B., Jonathan J. *Education:* Columbia University, A.B., 1908; LL.B., 1909. *Politics:* Democrat. *Religion:* Jewish.

CAREER: Attorney in private practice, New York, N.Y.; New York Magistrates Court, New York, N.Y., justice, 1921. Chairman of board of Tiberias Hot Springs; director of Israel Land Development Co., Migdal Insurance Co., and Rassco Israel Corp. Began career as active Zionist by organizing first high school and college Zionist societies in America; became vice-president and member of executive committee of Zionist Organization of America, 1920-46; first American representative on World Zionist Executive, 1921-23; launched first Jewish bond drive; organizer and developer of American Zion Commonwealth; president of Jewish National Fund of America and Keren Hayesod (later a division of United Jewish Appeal), Yievich National Fund in United States, 1923-27, and Palestine Foundation Fund in United States, 1941-46. *Member:* American Bar Association, Federation of American Zionists (honorary secretary, 1911-15).

WRITINGS: The Social Commonwealth, Lincoln Publishing Co., 1914; *Social Zionism,* Public Publishing Co., 1919; *Federated Palestine and the Jewish Commonwealth,* 1943; *American Bridge to Israel Commonwealth,* Farrar Straus, 1959; *Two Generations of Zionism: Recollections of an American Zionist,* Shengold, 1967. Contributor of articles to Zionist periodicals.

SIDELIGHTS: Rosenblatt has traveled to Israel nearly every year since the end of World War II, serving on committees for economic development.

ROSENSTOCK-HUESSY, Eugen   1888-1973

PERSONAL: Born July 6, 1888, in Berlin, Germany; son of Theodor (a banker) and Paula (Rosenstock) Rosenstock; married Margrit Huessy, 1914 (died September 1, 1959); children: Johannes Paul Theodor. *Education:* University of Heidelberg, Juris Doctor, 1909, Ph.D., 1923. *Religion:* Congregationalist. *Home:* Four Wells, Norwich, Vt. 05055.

CAREER: University of Leipzig, Leipzig, Germany, privatdozent in constitutional and civil law, 1912; *Damler Werkzeitung*, Stuttgart, Germany, editor, 1919; head of Akademie der Arbeit, Frankfurt am Main, Germany, 1921; University of Darmstadt, Darmstadt, Germany, reader, 1923; University of Breslau, Breslau, Germany, professor of law, 1923-34; Harvard University, Cambridge, Mass., Kuno Francke Professor, 1934-36; Dartmouth College, Hanover, N.H., professor of social philosophy, 1935-57, professor emeritus 1957-73. Guest professor, University of Goettingen, Goettingen, Germany, 1950; professor at University of California, Los Angeles, 1959. Also taught at Oxford University, Oxford, England, University of Muenster, Muenster, Germany, and University of Cologne, Cologne, Germany; University of California, Santa Cruz and Santa Barbara, staff member, 1965-66.

Founded Deutsche Schule fuer Volksforschung und Erwachsenenbildung, 1925, Loewenberger Work Camps, 1928-30. At the request of President Roosevelt, founded Camp William James in Vermont, for the training of Civilian Conservation Corps leaders, 1940. *Military service:* German Army, 1910-12, 1914-18; awarded Iron Cross. *Member:* World Association of Adult Education (vicechairman, 1929-34). *Awards, honors:* Doctor of Theology, University of Muenster, 1958; Dr.Phil., University of Cologne, 1961.

WRITINGS: Herzogsgewalt und Friedensschutz, M. & H. Marcus, 1910; *Ostfalens Rechtsliteratur unter Friedrich II*, H. Boehlau, 1912; *Koenigshaus und Staemme in Deutschland zwischen 911 und 1250*, F. Meiner Verlag, 1914; *Die Hochzeit des Krieges und der Revolution*, Patmos-Verlag, 1920; (with Eberhard Sauer and Hans Ehrenberg) *Osteuropa und wir: Das Problem Russland*, Neuwerkverlag, 1921; (with Martin Gruenberg and Eugen May) *Werkstattaussiedlung*, J. Springer, 1922; (with Richard Koch) *Paracelsus: Fuenf Buecher ueber die unsichtbaren Krankheiten*, Fromanns Verlag, 1923; *Zerfall und Ordnung des Industrievolks*, Carolus-Druckerei, 1923, revised edition published as *Abbau der politischen Luege*, 1924; *Angewandte Seelenkunde*, Roether-Verlag, 1924; *Soziologie* (also see below), Volume I: *Die Kraefte der Gemeinschaft*, W. de Gruyter, 1925, revised edition published as *Die Uebermacht der Raeume*, W. Kohlhammer, 1956, 2nd revised edition, 1958, Volume II: *Die Vollzahl der Zeiten*, W. Kohlhammer, 1958; (with Werner Picht) *Im Kampf um die Erwachsenenbildung*, Quelle & Meyer, 1926; *Lebensarbeit in der Industrie und Aufgaben einer europaeischen Arbeitsfront*, J. Springer, 1926; *Vom Industrierecht*, H. Sack, 1926; (with Joseph Wittig) *Das Alter der Kirche*, L. Schneider, 1927-28; *Die Schranke des Sozialpolitikers*, C. H. Beck, 1929; *Politische Reden: Vierklang aus Volk, Gesellschaft, Staat and Kirche*, L. Schneider, 1929.

Menschenmacht und Massenmacht, C. H. Beck, 1930; (with Carl Dietrich von Trotha) *Das Arbeitslager*, E. Diederichs, 1931; *Die Europaeischen Revolutionen*, E. Diederichs, 1931; *Arbeitsdienst—Heeresdienst?*, E. Diederichs, 1932; *Out of Revolution*, Morrow, 1938; reprinted as *Out of Revolution: Autobiography of Western Man*, Argo, 1969;

The Christian Future or the Modern Mind Outrun, Scribner, 1946, reprinted, Harper, 1966; *The Multiformity of Man*, Beachhead, 1949; *The Driving Power of Western Civilization*, Beacon, 1950; *Der Atem des Geistes*, Verlag der Frankfurter Hefte, 1951; *Heilkraft und Wahrheit*, Evangelisches Verlagswerk, 1952; *Frankreich-Deutschland: Mythos oder Anrede*, Kaethe Vogt, 1957; *Das Geheimnis der Universitaet*, W. Kohlhammer, 1958; *Die Sprache des Menschengeschlechts: Eine leibhaftige Grammatik in vier Teilen* two volumes, L. Schneider, 1963-65 (also see below); *Dienst auf dem Planeten: Kurzweil und Langeweile im Dritten Jahrtausend*, W. Kohlhammer, 1965; *Die Interims des Rechts*, Four Wells, 1964; *Mihi est propositum: Ein autobiographischer Versuch*, L. Schneider, 1966; *Die Umwandlung: Die Umwandlung des Wortes Gottes in der Sprache des Menschengeschlects* (includes enlarged excerpts from *Soziologie* and *Die Sprache des Menschengeschlects*), L. Schneider, 1968; *Ja und Nein: Autobiographische Fragmente*, L. Schneider, 1968; *Judaism Despite Christianity* (letters between Rosenstock-Huessy and Franz (Rosenzweig), University of Alabama Press, 1969; *I am an Impure Thinker*, introduction by W. H. Auden, Argo, 1970; *Speech and Reality*, Argo, 1970. Contributor of articles to professional journals and to general periodicals.

WORK IN PROGRESS: Studies in economics, religious and secular; research on speech and language.

SIDELIGHTS: In 1962, the Eugen Rosenstock-Huessy Society was formed for the purpose of spreading his teachings. The Society has members in the United States and Europe.

AVOCATIONAL INTERESTS: Classics, Egyptology, medieval history, mountaineering, horseback riding, raising horses.

BIOGRAPHICAL/CRITICAL SOURCES: Bibliography-Biography: Eugen Rosenstock-Huessy, privately printed in New York, N.Y., 1959.

*   *   *

ROSS, Frances Aileen   1909-

PERSONAL: Born September 20, 1909, in New Glasgow, Nova Scotia, Canada; daughter of Francis Allen (a clergyman) and Christina (Sutherland) Ross; married John E. Dodge (a conservation educator), December 22, 1951. *Education:* Acadia University, A.B., Simmons College, B.Sc.; Columbia University, M.A. *Politics:* Republican. *Religion:* Presbyterian. *Home address:* RFD 1, Center Harbor, N.H. 03226.

CAREER: Norwich Free Academy, Norwich, Conn., teacher of history, 1931-47; Pine Manor Junior College, Wellesley, Mass., teacher of history, 1947-52; Laconia School District, Laconia, N.H., director of adult education, 1954-64. *Member:* New Hampshire Council on World Affairs (member of board, 1959-61; secretary, 1961-65), League of Women Voters of Laconia (member of board, 1959-62; president, 1962-64; member of state board, 1964-69).

WRITINGS: The Land and People of Canada, Lippincott, 1947, revised edition, 1964 (published in England as *Canada and Her People*, Lutterworth, 1958).

*   *   *

ROSSER, Neill A(lbert)   1916-1973

PERSONAL: Born October 8, 1916, in Broadway, N.C.;

son of T. Raymond (a farmer) and Mary (Mims) Rosser; married Grace Lee Byers (a teacher), May 9, 1943; children: Donald Paul, Phona LaNae. *Education:* Presbyterian Junior College, Maxton, N.C., A.A., 1935; Maryville College, Maryville, Tenn., A.B. (cum laude), 1939; Harvard University, Ed.M., 1947; University of Denver, Ed.D., 1952. *Politics:* Democrat. *Religion:* Methodist. *Home:* 215 Markham Dr., Chapel Hill, N.C. *Office:* School of Education, University of North Carolina, 121 Peabody Hall, Chapel Hill, N.C.

CAREER: Fort Lupton (Colo.) public schools, high school principal, 1947-51; University of Illinois, Champaign, assistant professor, 1951-54, research associate at Institute for Research on Exceptional Children, 1954-55; Raleigh (N.C.) public schools, director of instruction, 1955-59; University of North Carolina, Chapel Hill, associate professor of education, 1959-69, professor of educational psychology and chairman of department of specialized professional services, 1969-73, professor of guidance and mental health, 1973. President, Raleigh (N.C.) Family Service Organization; executive director, Governor's Study Commission on the Public School System, 1967-68. *Military service*: U.S. Army Air Forces, active duty, 1941-45; became captain, U.S. Air Force Reserve, 1945-65; retired as lieutenant colonel. *Member:* American Psychological Association, National Education Association, Association for Student Teaching, National Society for the Study of Education, North Carolina Psychological Association (fellow), North Carolina Education Association (president of University of North Carolina unit), Phi Kappa Delta, Optimist Club.

WRITINGS: Personal Guidance, Holt, 1964; *Personal Health*, Holt, 1965. Contributor to education journals and popular periodicals.

WORK IN PROGRESS: Educational Psychology.

(Died June 5, 1973)

*   *   *

ROTH, Henry   1906-

PERSONAL: Born February 8, 1906, in Tysmenica, Austria-Hungary; son of Herman (a waiter) and Leah (Farb) Roth; married Muriel Parker (an elementary school principal), October 7, 1939; children: Jeremy, Hugh. *Education:* College of the City of New York (now City College of the City University of New York), B.S., 1928. *Politics:* Unaffiliated. *Religion:* None. *Home:* 741 Chavez Rd., Albuquerque, N.M. 87107. *Agent:* Roslyn Targ Literary Agency, 325 East 57th St., New York, N.Y. 10022.

CAREER: Roth says: "in writing and idleness [New York, N.Y.]," 1929-38; with Works Progress Administration (WPA), 1939; substitute high school teaching, Bronx, N.Y., sporadically, 1939-41; precision metal grinder, New York, N.Y., 1941-45, Providence, R.I., and Boston, Mass., 1945-46; taught in a one-room school in Maine, 1947-48; Augusta State Hospital, Augusta, Me., attendant, 1949-53; waterfowl farmer, 1953-63; tutor in math, and occasionally Latin, 1956-65. *Awards, honors:* Grant from National Institute of Arts and Letters, 1965; Townsend Harris Medal, City College of the City University New York, 1965; D. H. Lawrence fellowship, 1968.

WRITINGS: Call It Sleep (novel), Ballou, 1934, 2nd edition with a history by Harold U. Ribalow, a critical introduction by Maxwell Geismar, and a personal appreciation by Meyer Levin, Pageant, 1960, Avon, 1964 (same edition published in England with a foreword by Walter Allen, M.

Joseph, 1963). Contributor to *Commentary, Midstream, New Yorker,* and short story anthologies.

WORK IN PROGRESS: In an interview with David Bronsen, Roth said that his revival of interest in Israel after the 1967 war gave him "a place in the world and an origin. Having started to write, it seemed natural to go on from there, and I have been writing long hours every day since then. I am not yet sure what it is leading to, but it is necessary and is growing out of a new allegiance, an adhesion that comes from belonging." He wrote *CA:* "The surge of partisanship awakened by the '67 war broke the hold of an ossified radicalism."

SIDELIGHTS: First published almost 40 years ago, *Call It Sleep* received laudatory reviews, Alfred Hayes calling it "as brilliant as Joyce's *Portrait of the Artist,* but with a wider scope, a richer emotion, a deeper realism." The book went into two printings (4,000 copies) and disappeared, leading an underground existence until republication by Pageant in 1960, as a result of the interest of the critic, Harold Ribalow. In 1956, *The American Scholar* asked certain notable critics to list the most neglected books of the past twenty-five years. Alfred Kazin and Leslie Fiedler both chose *Call It Sleep*, making it the only book named twice. On October 25, 1964, Irving Howe's front-page review of *Call It Sleep* in the *New York Times Book Review* marked the first time such space was devoted to a paperback reprint. Howe described the book as "one of the few genuinely distinguished novels written by a 20th-century American, [one which] achieves an obbligato of lyricism such as few American novels can match.... Intensely Jewish in tone and setting, *Call It Sleep* rises above all the dangers that beset the usual ghetto novel: it does not deliquesce into nostalgia, nor sentimentalize poverty and parochialism. The Jewish immigrant milieu happens to be its locale, quite as Dublin is Joyce's and Mississippi Faulkner's."

The story line of the novel concerns the slum life of a young boy. Haskel Frankel has written, however, that to offer *Call It Sleep* as a tale about "a period in the life of an immigrant Jewish boy in the slums of New York's Lower East Side ... is to offer a synopsis on a par with Roz Russell's plot summation of *Moby Dick* in the musical *Wonderful Town:* 'It's about this whale.'"

Howe believes that Roth is especially successful in the way he uses the mind of the young boy. "Yet the book is not at all the kind of precious or narrowing study of a child's sensibility that such a description might suggest. We are locked into the experience of a child, but are not limited to his grasp of it." Roth acknowledges the autobiographical qualities of the novel, but emphasizes the methods he used in manipulating events remembered from his childhood. "I was working with characters, situations and events that had in part been taken from life, but which I molded to give expression to what was oppressing me. To a considerable extent I was drawing on the unconscious to give shape to remembered reality. Things which I could not fully understand but which filled me with apprehension played a critical role in determining the form of the novel."

Many critics disagree about the central theme or purpose of *Call It Sleep*. James Ferguson feels that it "is essentially the story of the development of a religious sensibility. Its implications are far more profoundly theological, even metaphysical, than they are social." In *Proletarian Writers of the Thirties,* Gerald Green suggests that Roth did have some social motivation in writing the novel. "Unlike the fashionable terrorists, Roth never loses hope, even if salvation speaks to us through cracked lips.'' And Walter Allen sees the book as ''the most powerful evocation of the terrors of childhood ever written. We are spared nothing of the rawness of cosmopolitan slum life.''

Roth once said that ''the man who wrote that book at the age of 27 is dead. I am a totally different man.'' Some years ago he started another novel. Maxwell Perkins at Scribners thought it was brilliant and gave him an advance, but Roth was dissatisfied and destroyed the manuscript.

Boston University, which is starting a collection of manuscripts and materials on American Jewish literature, is beginning with a Henry Roth Collection. But the man whose only reaction to the front-page book review was ''Why?'' continues to be unassuming. To *CA* he wrote simply: ''I find my greatest pleasure in matrimony, mathematics and puttering about the premises, in that order; [I] am daily compelled to admiration at the miracle of my wife.''

BIOGRAPHICAL/CRITICAL SOURCES: New York Times Book Review, October 25, 1964; *Saturday Review*, November 21, 1964; Walter Allen, *The Modern Novel*, Dutton, 1965; *Life*, January 8, 1965; Daniel Madden, editor, *Proletarian Writers of the Thirties*, Southern Illinois University Press, 1968; *Twentieth Century Literature*, January, 1969; *Partisan Review*, #2, 1969; *New York Times*, April 15, 1971; Carolyn Riley, editor, *Contemporary Literary Criticism*, Volume III, Gale, 1975.

* * *

ROUSE JONES, Lewis 1907-

PERSONAL: Born October 1, 1907, in Surrey, England; son of Bernard Edward (a publisher) and Edith Anne (Rouse) Jones; married Dorothy Smith, 1938; children: Isabel Ann. *Education:* Merton College, Oxford, B.A. and B.C.L., 1931. *Home:* 14 Tubbenden Lane, Orpington, Kent, England. *Office:* Board of Trade, Victoria St., London S.W. 1, England.

CAREER: Barrister-at-law in government service, London, England, 1941—. Legal adviser to government of Ghana on Volta River Project, 1954-62.

WRITINGS: Magistrates' Courts: Jurisdiction Procedure and Appeals, Sweet & Maxwell, 1953.

WORK IN PROGRESS: A book on law as it actually affects people—how it operates in society, what use people make of its creations, and why.

AVOCATIONAL INTERESTS: Typography (prints as a hobby), playing the flute.

* * *

ROUTH, C(harles) R(ichard) N(airne) 1896-

PERSONAL: Born August 17, 1896, in Blackheath, London, England; son of Henry Lloyd and Alice Margaret (Nairne) Routh. *Education:* Christ Church, Oxford, M.A., 1921. *Politics:* Conservative. *Religion:* Church of England. *Home:* Charlecote Park, Warwick, England.

CAREER: Eton College, Windsor, England, successively master, housemaster, and then senior history master, 1921-57; National Trust for Places of Historic Interest or Natural Beauty, Warwick, England, curator, beginning, 1957. Trustee of Shakespeare Birthplace Trust. *Military service:* British Army, Rifle Brigade, 1915-19. *Member:* Historical Association (vice-president), Junior Carlton Club (London).

WRITINGS: They Saw It Happen: An Anthology of Eyewitnesses' Accounts of Events in British History, 1485-1688, Basil Blackwell, 1956, Macmillan, 1957; (general editor) *Who's Who in History*, Volume I: *British Isles, 55 B.C. to 1485*, Barnes & Noble, 1960, (and author) Volume II: *England, 1485 to 1603*, Barnes & Noble, 1964, Volume III: *England, 1603-1714*, Basil Blackwell, 1965, Barnes & Noble, 1966; (compiler) *They Saw It Happen in Europe: An Anthology of Eyewitnesses' Account of Events in European History, 1450-1600*, Basil Blackwell, 1965, Barnes & Noble, 1966.

AVOCATIONAL INTERESTS: Stalking deer; music, architecture, and Siamese cats.

* * *

ROWELL, Henry T(hompson) 1904-

PERSONAL: Born March 12, 1904, in Stamford, Conn.; son of Edward Everett and Ruth (Thompson) Rowell; married Tanja Ramm, February 21, 1931; children: Louisa (Mrs. Bruce L. Stark), Margit Ruth. *Education:* Yale University, A.B., 1926, Ph.D., 1933. *Office:* Department of Classics, Johns Hopkins University, Baltimore, Md.

CAREER: Yale University, New Haven, Conn., instructor in classics, 1931-35, assistant professor of Latin, 1935-40; Johns Hopkins University, Baltimore, Md., professor of Latin, beginning, 1940, chairman of department of classics, beginning, 1946. American Academy in Rome, professor-in-charge of summer sessions, 1937-39, professor-in-charge, School of Classical Studies, 1961-63, trustee, beginning, 1946. American Council of Learned Societies, delegate, 1953-55. *Military service:* U.S. Army, Corps of Military Police, 1942-45; served in Mediterranean, Southwest Pacific, and Middle Pacific theaters; became lieutenant colonel; received Philippine Liberation Medal, five battle stars. *Member:* Archaeological Institute of America (president, 1953-56), American Philological Association, German Archaeological Institute (corresponding member), L'Hirondelle Club (Ruxton, Md.), Hamilton Street Club, Yale Club of New York. *Awards, honors:* Litt.D. from University of the South, 1958; Cavaliere Ufficiale della Corona d'Italia.

WRITINGS: (Editor) J. Carcopino, *Daily Life in Ancient Rome*, Yale University Press, 1940; *Rome in the Augustan Age*, University of Oklahoma Press, 1962; (editor with Don C. Allen) *The Poetic Tradition: Essays on Greek, Latin and English Poetry*, Johns Hopkins Press, 1968. Contributor of articles on Latin literature and the Roman Army to professional journals. Editor-in-chief, *American Journal of Philology*, beginning, 1946.

* * *

ROY, James A(lexander) 1884-

PERSONAL: Born April 27, 1884, in Kirriemuir Angus, Scotland; son of William (a clergyman) and Elizabeth (MacTavish) Roy; married Helen Maud Mary Talbot, 1917 (marriage dissolved, 1952); married Margaret Gordon Fleming, July 30, 1952. *Education:* Attended Universities of Edinburgh, Giessen, and Marburg; M.A. (first class honors in English), 1906. *Politics:* Conservative. *Religion:* Presbyterian. *Home:* 17 South Learmonth Gardens, Edinburgh, Scotland. *Agent:* Harold Matson Co., Inc., 30 Rockefeller Plaza, New York, N.Y. 10020.

CAREER: University of St. Andrews, St. Andrews, Scotland, lecturer in English, 1908-20; Queen's University at

Kingston, Kingston, Ontario, 1920-50, began as assistant professor, became associate professor, then professor of English, lecturer in Scottish literature, 1944-45. Visiting professor at University of Giessen, 1922, at Universities of Gottingen, Berlin, and Munster, 1935-37, and at Queen's University at Kingston, 1960. Member of staff, Paris Peace Conference, 1919, of Allied Commission of Control, Teschen, Silesia, 1919. Former chairman, Eastern Ontario Drama Festival. *Military service:* British Army, Artillery, Intelligence, and attached as educational officer to General Headquarters, 1914-19; became captain; mentioned in dispatches. *Member:* Royal Commonwealth Society (former chairman, Edinburgh branch), Victoria League in Scotland (member of council), Canada Club of Edinburgh (chairman). *Awards, honors:* Plaque of honorable mention, City of Kingston.

WRITINGS: (Editor) *The Dream of the Rood*, Bagster, 1910; *Cowper and His Poetry*, Harrap, 1914; *Pole and Czech in Silesia*, John Lane, 1921; *Christ in the Strand and Other Poems*, Jackson Press, 1922; *The Breaking of the Bridge* (one-act play), Jackson Press, 1923; *Joseph Howe: A Study in Achievement and Frustration*, Macmillan (Canada), 1935; *James Matthew Barrie, an Appreciation*, Jarrolds, 1937, Scribner, 1938; *Is There a Scottish Literature?*, Queen's University at Kingston, 1945; *Forbes of Culloden* (lecture), Queen's University at Kingston, 1945; *The Heart Is Highland*, McClelland & Stewart, 1947; *The Scot and Canada*, McClelland & Stewart, 1947; *Kingston, the King's Town*, McClelland & Stewart, 1952; (contributor) Malcolm Mackenzie Ross, editor, *Our Sense of Identity: A Book of Canadian Essays*, Ryerson, 1954. Contributor to *Scottish Field, Edinburgh Review, Toronto Quarterly, Times Literary Supplement,* and *Dalhousie Review.*

AVOCATIONAL INTERESTS: Collecting books and antiques; fishing, and motoring.

*   *   *

ROZWENC, Edwin C(harles) 1915-1974

PERSONAL: Born May 21, 1915, in Dover, N.J.; son of Stephen and Stanislawa (Tesarz) Rozwenc; married Harriet E. Strong, September 1, 1940; children: Emily Ann, Stephen Andrew, Johathan Strong. *Education:* Amherst College, B.A., 1937; Columbia University, M.A., 1938, Ph.D., 1941. *Politics:* Republican. *Religion:* Congregationalist. *Home:* 85 Dana St., Amherst, Mass. *Office:* Department of History, Amherst College, Amherst, Mass.

CAREER: Cornell College, Mount Vernon, Iowa, instructor in history and social science, 1940-42; Clark University, Worcester, Mass., assistant professor of history, 1942-46; Amherst College, Amherst, Mass., associate professor, 1946-52, professor of history, 1952-57, Dwight Morrow Professor, 1957-74. Visiting summer professor, Columbia University, 1945, 1947, 1948. *Member:* American Historical Association, American Studies Association, Academy of Political Science, American Association of University Professors, Phi Beta Kappa, Tau Kappa Alpha. *Awards, honors:* Fellow, Foundation for the Advancement of Education, 1954.

WRITINGS: Cooperatives Come to America, Hawkeye-Record Press, 1941; (contributor) H. H. Quint and others, editors, *Main Problems of American History*, Dorsey, 1964; (with Thomas Lyons) *Realism and Idealism in Wilson's Peace Program*, Heath, 1965; (with A. Wesley Roehm) *The Entrepreneur in the Gilded Age*, Heath, 1965; (with Kenneth Lindfors) *Containment and the Origins of*

the Cold War, Heath, 1967; (with Thomas Lyons) *Reconstruction and the Race Problem*, Heath, 1968; (compiler with Kenneth Lindfors) *The United States and the New Imperialism, 1898-1912*, Heath, 1968; (with Martin W. Sandler and Edward C. Martin) *The People Make a Nation*, Allyn & Bacon, 1971; (compiler with Martin W. Sandler and Edward C. Martin) *The Restless Americans: The Challenge of Change in American History*, Xerox College Publications, 1972; *The Making of American Society: An Institutional and Intellectual History of the United States*, Allyn & Bacon, 1972.

Editor: Slavery as a Cause of the Civil War, Heath, 1949, revised edition, 1963; *The New Deal—Revolution or Evolution?*, Heath, 1949, revised edition, 1959; *Roosevelt, Wilson and the Trusts*, Heath, 1950; *Reconstruction in the South*, Heath, 1952; (and contributor) *The Northampton Book* (tercentenary history) [Northampton], 1953; (and contributor) *Teachers of History*, Cornell University Press, 1954; *Compromise of 1850*, Heath, 1957; *The Causes of the American Civil War*, Heath, 1961; *The Meaning of Jacksonian Democracy*, Heath, 1963; (with Thomas T. Lyons) *Presidential Power in the New Deal*, Heath, 1963; (with Frederick E. Bauer) *Liberty and Power in the Making of the Constitution*, Heath, 1963; (with A. Wesley Roehm) *The Status Revolution and the Progressive Movement*, Heath, 1963; (and author of introduction) *Ideology and Power in the Age of Jackson*, New York University Press, 1964; (with Donald P. Schultz) *Conflict and Consensus in the American Revolution*, Heath, 1964; (with Wayne A. Frederick) *Slavery and the Breakdown of the American Consensus*, Heath, 1964; (with Frederick E. Bauer, Jr.) *Democracy in the Age of Jackson*, Heath, 1965; (with John C. Matlon) *Myth and Reality in the Populist Revolt*, Heath, 1966.

Contributor of articles and reviews to *American Quarterly, William and Mary Quarterly, New England Quarterly*, and articles to Vermont periodicals.

(Died March 5, 1974)

*   *   *

RUBEL, Maximilien 1905-

PERSONAL: Born October 10, 1905, in Czernowitz, Austria-Hungary (now Ukraine; son of Meyer and Freude (Schifter) Rubel; married Mariane Gruman, 1945; children: Nathalie, Nicolas, Georges. *Education:* University of Czernowitz, licenta in filozofie, licenta in drept, 1928-30; Sorbonne, University of Paris, licencie es lettres, 1933, docteur es lettres, 1954. *Office:* Centre d'etudes sociologiques, 82 rue Cardinet, Paris XVII, France.

CAREER: National Centre of Scientific Research, Paris, France, professor of research sociology, 1947—. *Member:* Sociology Society of France, Institute of French Social History.

WRITINGS: (Editor, translator, annotator, and author of introduction) Karl Marx, *Pages choisies pour une ethique socialiste*, M. Riviere & Cie, 1948, 2nd edition, Payot, 1970; (editor and author of introduction and notes with T. B. Bottomore) Karl Marx, *Selected Writings in Sociology and Social Philosophy*, C. A. Watts, 1956; *Bibliographie des oeuvres de Karl Marx*, M. Riviere & Cie, 1956, supplement, 1960; *Karl Marx, essai de biographie intellectuelle*, M. Riviere & Cie, 1957, 2nd edition, 1970; *Karl Marx devant le bonapartisme*, Mouton & Co., 1960; (editor) Karl Marx, *Oeuvres, Economie*, Gallimard, Volume I, 1963, new edition, 1965, Volume II, 1968; *Marx-Chronik: Daten zu Leben und Werk,* Carl Hanser Verlag (Munich), 1968. Contributor of articles to sociological journals. Editor, "Etudes de marxologie," 1959.

WORK IN PROGRESS: Editing Volume III, Karl Marx, *Oeuvres, Economie,* for Gallimard; editing Karl Marx and Friedrich Engels, *Die Russische Kommune: Kritik eines Mythos,* for Carl Hanser Verlag.

BIOGRAPHICAL/CRITICAL SOURCES: Times Literary Supplement, September 21, 1956; *Le Contrat Social,* July, 1957; *Ost-Probleme,* XIV, Number 4, 1962; *Le Figaro litteraire,* October 12, 1963.

* * *

RUBIN, Isadore 1912-1970

PERSONAL: Born June 5, 1912, in Wilmington, Del.; son of Morris (a grocer) and Anna (Salkind) Rubin; married Phyllis Cooper (a teacher), April 23, 1937; children: Jo Anne Uziel, Daniel Uziel. *Education:* City College (now City College of the City University of New York), B.A., 1932, M.S., 1933; New York University, Ph.D., 1962. *Home:* 651 Vanderbilt St., Apartment 5C, Brooklyn, N.Y. 10018. *Office: Sexology,* 154 West 14th St., New York, N.Y. 10011.

CAREER: Sexology (magazine), New York, N.Y., managing editor, 1956-70. *Military service:* U.S. Army, 1943-45; became sergeant. *Member:* Society for Scientific Study of Sex (fellow), Sex Information and Education Council of the United States (past treasurer), American Association of Marriage Counselors, National Council on Family Relations. *Awards, honors:* Mediterranean Theater winner in U.S. Army essay contest on "What Victory Means to Me."

WRITINGS: (With L. Cark) *150 Sex Questions and Answers,* Health Publications, 1961; *Sexual Life After Sixty,* Basic Books, 1965; (editor) *Homosexuals Today,* Health Publications, 1965; (editor with Lester A. Kirkendall) *Sex in the Adolescent Years: New Directions in Guiding and Teaching Youth,* Association Press, 1968; (editor with Kirkendall) *Sex in the Childhood Years: Expert Guidance for Parents, Counselors and Teachers,* Association Press, 1970. Contributor to *Journal of Marriage and the Family, Medical Times,* and *Journal of Association of Women College Deans and Counselors.*

WORK IN PROGRESS: Conflicting Sex Ethics.

(Died July 31, 1970)

* * *

RUBIN, Jacob A. 1910-1972
(J. Odem)

PERSONAL: Born July 1, 1910, in Podwoloczyska, Austria; emigrated to Israel; came to United States, 1953; son of Michael I. (a banker) and Esther (Schmierer) Rubin; married Aliza Sass (an attorney; now director of a school), July 10, 1938; children: Nira Stephanie (Mrs. Joel P. Silverman), Edna. *Education:* University of Lemberg, law graduate, 1928; Institute of Diplomatic Studies, Lemberg, M.A., 1932, Dr. juris, 1935; also studied archeology at Sorbonne, University of Paris, and political science at New School for Social Research. *Religion:* Jewish. *Home:* 124 West 93rd St., New York, N.Y. 10025. *Office:* Authentic Publications, 39 Murray St., New York, N.Y. 10007.

CAREER: Journalist, 1935-72. Former editor of *Tribuna Narodowa,* Cracow, Poland, *Palestine Observer,* Pales-

tine, and Tel-Aviv, Israel, Zins News Service, New York; free-lance United Nations correspondent; correspondent for *Yediyoth Hayon* (daily), Tel Aviv, and for *Aonde Vamos,* Brazil. Deputy member, First State Council, Israel. Director, Jewish National Fund Foundation of Greater New York, land-development arm of World Zionist Organization in Israel. Lecturer on international affairs and contemporary Israel. *Military service:* British Army, Jewish Brigade Group, 1940-46; mentioned in dispatches. *Member:* Overseas Press Club, United Nations Correspondents Association (chairman, Gold Club Fund, 1962-63).

WRITINGS: Minority Problems of Postwar Europe, Dubiner, 1939; *Youth at the Crossroads,* Dubiner, 1939; *At the Gates of Hades,* Palestine Observer, 1946; (co-author) *Soldiers and Statesmen,* Avinoam, 1952; *Country Without a Curtain,* Lamkor, 1953; (with Meyer Barkai) *Pictorial History of Israel,* Yoseloff, 1958, revised edition, 1961; *Pictorial History of the United Nations,* foreword by U Thant and others, Yoseloff, 1962, revised edition, 1963; *Your Hundred Billion Dollars: The Complete Story of American Foreign Aid,* Chilton, 1964; *Partners in State-Building: American Jewry and Israel,* Diplomatic Press, 1969; *True/False About Israel,* published for the American Zionist Federation by Herzl Press, 1972. Editorial consultant on book series, "Knowledge for All"; editor, Authentic Publications, 1964-72.

WORK IN PROGRESS: At the Crossroads of Via Maris; Towards the Islands of the Sea; Partners in State Building; Colonialism—The Myth, the Truth, the End; a novel on meeting the Communist challenge with working title, *From the Jordan to the Rhine.*

AVOCATIONAL INTERESTS: Study of archeology and comparative history.

(Died December 28, 1972)

* * *

RUGH, Belle Dorman 1908-

PERSONAL: Born June 8, 1908, in Beirut, Lebanon; daughter of Harry Gaylord (a physician) and Mary (Dale) Dorman; married Douglas Rugh (a professor), July 11, 1934; children: Elizabeth Patricia, Mary Dorman, June Caroline. *Education:* Vassar College, B.A., 1929; Columbia University, M.A., 1932. *Religion:* Congregationalist. *Home:* 62 Burwood Rd., Wethersfield, Conn. 06109.

CAREER: Teacher at Ahliah School, Beirut, Lebanon, 1929-30; Beirut Junior College for Women, Beirut, instructor in English, 1931-34; Yenching University, Peiping, China, instructor in English, 1934-36; Central Connecticut State College, New Britain, instructor in English, 1946-55; Beirut College for Women, Beirut, instructor in English, 1955-56; Central Connecticut State College, instructor in English, 1962—. *Member:* East Haddam (Conn.) Writers Group. *Awards, honors:* First prize, *New York Herald Tribune* Children's Spring Book Festival Awards, 1955, for *Crystal Mountain.*

WRITINGS: Crystal Mountain, Houghton, 1955; *The Path Above the Pines,* Houghton, 1962; *The Lost Waters,* Houghton, 1967.

* * *

RUSSELL, Arthur (Wolseley) 1908-

PERSONAL: Born April 2, 1908, in Watford, England; son of Frederick Montagu (an engineer) and Winifred (Wolseley) Russell; married Anne Pendleton (a playwright),

June 3, 1936; children: Nicholas, Juliet. *Education:* Attended University of New Zealand, 1926-27. *Politics:* Liberal. *Home:* 85 Elstree Rd., Bushey Heath, Hertfordshire, England. *Agent:* Curtis Brown Ltd., 1 Craven Hill, London W.2 3E.W., England.

CAREER: British Broadcasting Corp., London, England, editor and producer, specializing in production of Shakespeare for short-wave transmission, 1935-64; playwright, poet, and antique dealer, 1964—. *Member:* Society of Authors.

WRITINGS—Plays, all with wife, Anne Russell; all published by H. F. W. Dean & Sons, except when noted: *The Wedding at Pemberley*, 1949; *The Last Victory*, 1953; *In Need of Support*, 1954; *Really Isabella*, 1955; *Mute Witness*, Evans Brothers, 1956.

Poetry: *In Idleness of Air*, Scorpion Press, 1960; *Ice on the Live Rail*, Scorpion Press, 1963.

Editor: *Ruth Pitter: Homage to a Poet*, Dufour, 1969.

AVOCATIONAL INTERESTS: Bookbinding and woodcarving.

*   *   *

RUSSELL, Bertrand (Arthur William)   1872-1970

PERSONAL: Born May 18, 1872, in Trelleck, Monmouthshire, England; son of Lord John (Viscount Amberley) and Katherine (Stanley) Russell; married Alys Whitall Pearsall Smith, 1894 (divorced, 1921; died, 1951); married Dora Winifred Black, 1921 (divorced, 1935); married Patricia Helen Spence, 1936 (divorced, 1952); married Edith Finch, 1952; children: (second marriage) John Conrad, Katharine Jane; (third marriage) Conrad Sebastian Robert. *Education:* Trinity College, Cambridge, M.A. (first class honors), 1894. *Politics:* Formerly member of Liberal Party, then of Labour Party for 51 years. *Religion:* Agnostic. *Home:* Plas Penrhyn, Penrhyndeudraeth, Merionethshire, Wales.

CAREER: Succeeded brother as 3rd Earl of Russell, Viscount Amberley, 1931; honorary attache at British Embassy in Paris, 1894; fellow and lecturer at Trinity College, Cambridge University, 1894-1916 (dismissed for his opposition to World War I, and sentenced to four and one-half months in prison); Harvard University, Cambridge, Mass., temporary professor, 1914; National University of Peking, Peking, China, professor of philosophy, 1920-21; co-founder and director, with wife Dora Russell, of Beacon Hill School (an experimental school for children), Sussex, England, 1927-32; University of Chicago, Chicago, Ill., lecturer, 1938; University of California, Los Angeles, professor of philosophy, 1939-40; appointed William James Lecturer in Philosophy at Harvard University, and professor of philosophy at City College of New York (latter appointment withdrawn over controversy surrounding his beliefs); Barnes Foundation, Merion, Pa., lecturer on history of culture, 1941-42; stood for Parliament as Liberal candidate, 1907, and as Labour candidate, 1922 and 1923. *Member:* Royal Society (fellow), Athenaeum Club. *Awards, honors:* Nicholas Murray Butler Medal, 1915; Sylvester Medal of Royal Society, 1934; British Order of Merit, 1949; Nobel Prize for Literature, 1950; Kalinga Prize, 1957; Sonning Foundation Prize (Denmark), 1960.

WRITINGS: German Social Democracy, Longmans, Green, 1896, Simon & Schuster, 1966; *An Essay on the Foundations of Geometry*, University Press (Cambridge), 1897, Dover, 1957.

A Critical Exposition of the Philosophy of Leibnitz, University Press (Cambridge), 1900, new edition, Allen & Unwin, 1937; *The Principles of Mathematics*, Volume I (no further volumes published), University Press (Cambridge), 1903, 2nd edition, Norton, 1938, reprinted, 1964.

(With Alfred North Whitehead) *Principia Mathematica*, University Press (Cambridge), Volume I, 1910, 2nd edition, 1935, Volume II, 1912, 2nd edition, 1927, Volume III, 1913, 2nd edition, 1927, 2nd edition in three volumes, 1950; *Philosophical Essays*, Longmans, Green, 1910, reissued as *Mysticism and Logic*, 1918, revised edition published under original title, Allen & Unwin, 1966, Simon & Schuster, 1967; *Anti-Suffragist Anxieties*, People's Suffrage Federation, 1910; *The Problems of Philosophy*, H. Holt, 1912; *Our Knowledge of the External World as a Field for Scientific Method in Philosophy*, Open Court, 1914, 2nd edition, Norton, 1929, reprinted, New American Library, 1960; *The Philosophy of Bergson*, Bowes, 1914; *Scientific Method in Philosophy*, Clarendon, 1914; *War: The Offspring of Fear* (pamphlet), Union of Democratic Control, 1915; *Why Men Fight*, Century, 1916, reprinted, Books for Libraries, 1971 (published in England as *Principles of Social Reconstruction*, Allen & Unwin, 1916, reprinted, 1960); *The Policy of the Entente, 1904-14*, National Labour Press, 1916; *Justice in War-time*, Open Court, 1916, reprinted, Haskell, 1974; *Political Ideals*, Century, 1917, reprinted, Simon & Schuster, 1964; *Roads to Freedom: Socialism, Anarchism, and Syndicalism*, Allen & Unwin, 1918, revised edition, 1919, published as *Proposed Roads to Freedom: Socialism, Anarchism, and Syndicalism*, H. Holt, 1919, reprinted under British title, Barnes & Noble, 1966; *Introduction to Mathematical Philosophy*, Allen & Unwin, 1919, Simon & Schuster, 1971.

Bolshevism: Practice and Theory, Harcourt, 1920, published in England as *The Practice and Theory of Bolshevism*, Allen & Unwin, 1920, 2nd edition, 1949, Simon & Schuster, 1964; *The Analysis of Mind*, Macmillan, 1921, reprinted, Humanities, 1958; *The Problem of China*, Century, 1922; *Free Thought and Official Propaganda*, B. W. Huebsch, 1922; *A Free Man's Worship*, T. B. Mosher, 1923; (with wife Dora Russell) *The Prospects of Industrial Civilization*, Century, 1923, 2nd edition, Allen & Unwin, 1960; *The ABC of Atoms*, Dutton, 1923, 4th edition, Routledge & Kegan Paul, 1932; (contributor) Freda Kirchway, *Styles in Ethics*, A. & C. Boni, 1924; *Icarus, Or, The Future of Science*, Dutton, 1924; (debate with Scott Nearing) *Bolshevism and the West*, Macmillan, 1924; (contributor) J. H. Muirhead, editor, *British Philosophy*, Macmillan, Volume I, 1924; *How to Be Free and Happy*, Rand School of Social Science, 1924; *The ABC of Relativity*, Harper, 1925, 3rd revised edition, Allen & Unwin, 1969; *What I Believe*, Dutton, 1925; (contributor) Frederich A. Lange, *The History of Materialism*, 3rd edition, Harcourt, 1925; *Education and the Good Life*, Boni & Liveright, 1926, reprinted, 1970 (published in England as *On Education Especially in Early Childhood*, Allen & Unwin, 1926); *Why I Am Not a Christian* (also see below), Watts, 1927, Freethought Press Association, 1940; *The Analysis of Matter*, Harcourt, 1927, with new introduction by Lester E. Denonn, Dover, 1954; *Philosophy*, Norton, 1927 (published in England as *An Outline of Philosophy*, Allen & Unwin, 1927), published under British title, World Publishing, 1961; *Selected Papers of Bertrand Russell*, Modern Library, 1927; (contributor) Charles A. Beard, editor, *Whither Mankind*, Longmans, Green, 1928; *Skeptical Essays*, Norton, 1928, reprinted, Barnes & Noble, 1961; *Marriage and Morals*, Liveright, 1929, 2nd edition, Unwin Books, 1961, reprinted, Liveright, 1970; (contributor) Baker Brownell, editor, *Man and His World*, Van Nostrand, Volume XII, 1929; (with others) *If I Could Preach Just Once*, Harper, 1929, reissued as *If I Had Only One Sermon to Preach*, 1932; *A Liberal View of Divorce*, Haldeman-Julius, 1929.

The Conquest of Happiness, Book League of America, 1930, reprinted, Liveright, 1971; *Has Religion Made Useful Contributions to Civilization?*, Haldeman-Julius, 1930; (with others) *Divorce*, Day, 1930 (published in England as *Divorce as I See It*, Douglas, 1930); (debate with John Cowper Powys) *Is Modern Marriage a Failure?*, Discussion Guild, 1930; (contributor) N. A. Crawford and K. A. Menninger, *The Healthy-Minded Child*, Coward, 1930; *The Scientific Outlook*, Norton, 1931, 2nd edition, Allen & Unwin, 1962; *Education and the Modern World*, Norton, 1932 (published in England as *Education and the Social Order*, Allen & Unwin, 1932); (contributor) Charles W. Morris, *Six Theories of Mind*, University of Chicago Press, 1932; (contributor) Will Durant, editor, *On the Meaning of Life*, Ray Long & Richard R. Smith Inc., 1932; (contributor) M. Adams, editor, *Science in the Changing World*, Appleton, 1933; *Freedom Versus Organization, 1814-1914*, Norton, 1934, reprinted, 1962 (published in England as *Freedom and Organization, 1814-1914*, Allen & Unwin, 1934, parts 1 and 2 reissued as *Legitimacy Versus Industrialism, 1814-1848*, 1965); (contributor) Sidney Hook, editor, *The Meaning of Marx*, Farrar, Straus, 1934; (contributor) A. B. Brown, editor, *Great Democrats*, Nicholson, 1934; (contributor) R. S. Loomis and D. L. Clark, editors, *Modern English Readings*, Farrar, Straus, 1934; *In Praise of Idleness, and Other Essays*, Norton, 1935, reprinted, Simon & Schuster, 1972; *Religion and Science*, H. Holt, 1935, reprinted, Oxford University Press, 1961; *Determinism and Physics* (Earl Grey Memorial Lecture), The Librarian, Armstrong College, 1936; *Which Way to Peace?*, M. Joseph, 1936; (editor with wife Patricia Russell) *The Amberley Papers: The Letters and Diaries of Bertrand Russell's Parents*, two volumes, Norton, 1937, reprinted, Simon & Schuster, 1967; (with others) *Dare We Look Ahead?* (Fabian Lectures), Macmillan, 1938; (contributor) E. A. Walter, editor, *Toward Today*, Scott, 1938; *Power: A New Social Analysis*, Norton, 1938, reprinted, 1969; (contributor) *Encyclopaedia and Unified Science*, University of Chicago Press, Volume I, 1938; (contributor) *What Is Happiness?*, H. C. Kinsey & Co., 1939; (contributor) Clifton Fadiman, editor, *I Believe: The Personal Philosophies of Certain Eminent Men and Women of Our Time*, Simon & Schuster, 1939; (contributor) Paul Arthur Schlipp, editor, *The Philosophy of John Dewey*, Northwestern University Press, 1939; (contributor) *Calling America*, Harper, 1939.

An Inquiry Into Meaning and Truth, Norton, 1940, reprinted, Allen & Unwin, 1966; (contributor) R. N. Anshen, editor, *Freedom: Its Meaning*, Harcourt, 1940; (contributor) Schlipp, editor, *The Philosophy of George Santayana*, Northwestern University Press, 1940; (with others) *Invitation to Learning*, Random, 1941; *Let the People Think*, Watts, 1941, 2nd edition, Rationalist Press Association, 1961; (with others) *New Invitation to Learning*, Random House, 1942; *How to Become a Philosopher: The Art of Rational Conjecture*, Haldeman-Julius, 1942; *How to Become a Logician: The Art of Drawing Inferences*, Haldeman-Julius, 1942; *How to Become a Mathematician: The Art of Reckoning*, Haldeman-Julius, 1942; *An Outline of Intellectual Rubbish: A Hilarious Catalogue of Organized and Individual Stupidity*, Haldeman-Julius, 1943;

(contributor) *Palestine: Jewish Commonwealth in Our Times*, Zionist Organization of America, 1943; *How to Read and Understand History*, Haldeman-Julius, 1943; (contributor) P. A. Schilpp, *The Philosophy of Bertrand Russell*, Tudor, 1944; (contributor) Ben Raeburn, editor, *Treasury for the Free World*, Arco, 1945; *A History of Western Philosophy and Its Connection With Political and Social Circumstances From the Earliest Times to the Present Day*, Simon & Schuster, 1945, new edition, Allen & Unwin, 1961; (with others) *Among the Great*, N. M. Tripathi (Bombay), 1945; *Physics and Experience* (Henry Sidgwick Lecture), Cambridge University Press, 1946; *Ideas That Have Harmed Mankind*, Haldeman-Julius, 1946; *Ideas That Have Helped Mankind*, Haldeman-Julius, 1946; *Is Materialism Bankrupt?*, Haldeman-Julius, 1946; *Is Science Superstitious?*, Haldeman-Julius, 1947; *Philosophy and Politics*, Cambridge University Press, for National Book League, 1947; *Human Knowledge: Its Scope and Limits*, Simon & Schuster, 1948; *Authority and the Individual*, Simon & Schuster, 1949, reprinted, AMS Press, 1968.

Unpopular Essays, Allen & Unwin, 1950, Simon & Schuster, 1951, reprinted, Simon & Schuster, 1966; *The Impact of Science on Society*, Columbia University Press, 1951, reprinted, AMS Press, 1968; (with others) *The Impact of America on European Culture*, Beacon, 1951; (contributor) *The Western Tradition*, Beacon, 1951; (contributor) *Worth Reading*, New York Times Co., 1951; *New Hopes for a Changing World*, Simon & Schuster, 1951, reprinted, Minerva Press, 1968; *The Wit and Wisdom of Bertrand Russell*, Beacon, 1951; *Bertrand Russell's Dictionary of Mind, Matter, and Morals*, Philosophical Library, 1952, reprinted, 1965; *How Near is War?*, D. Ridgway, 1952; *What Is Freedom?*, Batchworth Press, 1952; *Satan in the Suburbs, and Other Stories*, Simon & Schuster, 1953; *What Is Democracy?*, Batchworth Press, 1953; *The Good Citizen's Alphabet* (also see below), Gaberbocchus Press, 1953, Philosophical Library, 1958; *History as an Art*, Hand and Flower Press, 1954; *Human Society in Ethics and Politics*, Allen & Unwin, 1954, Simon & Schuster, 1955, reprinted, New American Library, 1962; *Nightmares of Eminent Persons, and Other Stories*, Bodley Head, 1954, Simon & Schuster, 1955; (contributor) Wallace Brockway, editor, *High Moment: Stories of Supreme Crisis in the Lives of Great Men*, Simon & Schuster, 1955; *Portraits From Memory and Other Essays*, Simon & Schuster, 1956; *John Stuart Mill*, Oxford University Press, 1956; *Logic and Knowledge: Essays, 1901-1950*, Macmillan, 1956; (contributor) Hugh Trevor-Roper, editor, *Why I Oppose Communism: A Symposium*, Phoenix House, 1956; *Why I Am Not a Christian and Other Essays on Religion and Related Subjects*, Simon & Schuster, 1957, 7th edition, 1963; *Understanding History, and Other Essays*, Philosophical Library, 1957; *The Vital Letters of Russell, Khrushchev, Dulles*, MacGibbon & Kee, 1958; *Bertrand Russell's Best: Silhouettes in Satire*, Allen & Unwin, 1958, New American Library, 1961; *The Will to Doubt*, Philosophical Library, 1958; (author of introduction) Ludwig Wittgenstein, *Logiko-filosofskii traktat*, Izd-vo inostrannoi litry (Moscow), 1958; *Wisdom of the West: A Historical Survey of Western Philosophy in Its Social and Political Setting*, Doubleday, 1959, reprinted, Fawcett, 1966; *The Philosophy of Logical Atomism* (lectures), Department of Philosophy, University of Minnesota, 1959; *My Philosophical Development*, Simon & Schuster, 1959; *The Future of Science*, Philosophical Library, 1959; *Common Sense and Nuclear Warfare*, Simon & Schuster, 1959, reprinted, AMS Press, 1968.

Bertrand Russell Speaks His Mind, World Publishing, 1960; *On Education*, Allen & Unwin, 1960; *Basic Writings, 1903-1959*, Simon & Schuster, 1961; *Education of Character*, Philosophical Library, 1961; *Fact and Fiction*, Allen & Unwin, 1961, Simon & Schuster, 1962; *Has Man a Future?*, Simon & Schuster, 1962; *Essays in Skepticism*, Philosophical Library, 1963; *Unarmed Victory*, Simon & Schuster, 1963; (with Stafford Cripps and Reinhold Niebuhr) *Que es, hoy, la democracia?*, Centro de Estudios y Documentacion Sociales (Mexico), 1964; *On the Philosophy of Science*, Bobbs-Merrill, 1965; (author of introduction) Harold Dicker, *The Bell of John Donne*, Intrepid Press, 1965; *Appeal to the American Conscience*, Bertrand Russell Peace Foundation, 1966; *War Crimes in Vietnam*, Monthly Review Press, 1967; *The Autobiography of Bertrand Russell*, Volume I: *1872-1914*, Little, Brown, 1967, Volume II: *1914-1944*, Little, Brown, 1968, Volume III: *1944-1969*, Simon & Schuster, 1969; (with others) *Nacionalidad Oprimida*, Ediciones Mordejai Anilevich (Montevideo, Uruguay), 1968; *The Art of Philosophizing and Other Essays*, Philosophical Library, 1968; *Dear Bertrand Russell: A Selection of His Correspondence with the General Public, 1950-1968*, Houghton, 1969.

The Good Citizen's Alphabet; And, History of the World in Epitome, Gaberbocchus, 1970; (editor with Jean-Paul Sartre) *Das Vietnam-Tribunal*, Rowohlt, 1970; (with others) *Ladislas Reymont, Romain Rolland [and] Bertrand Russell*, A Gregory, 1971; *Atheism: Collected Essays*, Arno, 1972; *The Collected Stories of Bertrand Russell*, Simon & Schuster, 1972.

Contributor to *Encyclopaedia Britannica*, and to *Mind, Independent Review, Edinburgh Review, American Journal of Mathematics, Hibbert Journal, Monist, Atlantic, Unpopular Review, International Journal of Ethics, American Scholar, Dial, New Republic, Nation, Saturday Review, Virginia Quarterly Review, Spectator, New Statesman, Esquire, American Mercury, Harper's, New Leader, Listener, New York Times Magazine, Science Digest, Look*, and other publications.

SIDELIGHTS: Russell's biographer, Alan Wood, wrote that "less than halfway through [Russell's] career he had already achieved immortality; his place was secure as a thinker who had made the greatest advances in logic since Greek times." Wood also wrote that Russell was "a philosopher without a philosophy.... He started by asking questions about mathematics and religion and philosophy, and he went on to question accepted ideas about war and politics and sex and education, setting the minds of men on the march, so that the world could never be quite the same as if he had not lived." Russell himself once declared: "Science is what you know, philosophy is what you don't know." In a letter (1918) he wrote: "I want to stand at the rim of the world and peer into the darkness beyond, and see a little more than others have seen, of the strange shapes of mystery that inhabit that unknown night...." He later admitted the impossibility of definitely knowing very much at all: "I have been painfully forced to the belief that nine-tenths of what is regarded as philosophy is humbug. The only part that is at all definite is logic, and since it is logic, it is not philosophy."

Believing that "a philosophy which is to have any value should be built upon a wide and firm foundation of knowledge that is not specifically philosophical," he came to philosophy through other disciplines. He was an inquisitive child. Wood reports that at the age of five, "informed that the earth was round, he refused to believe it, but began digging a hole in the garden to see if he came out in Australia." At eleven he began to study Euclid and developed a passion for mathematics. Then he studied history ("History has always interested me more than anything else except philosophy and mathematics," Russell once remarked.), literature, and finally philosophy, always seeking some impersonal truth—examining the arguments favoring different religions, rejecting personal immortality, turning to Kant and Hegel, and by 1898 abandoning them both. "I wanted certainty," he wrote, "in the kind of way in which people want religious faith." "And yet I am unable to believe that, in the world as known, there is anything that I can value outside human beings, and, to a much lesser extent, animals. Not the starry heavens, but their effects on human percipients, have excellence; to admire the universe for its size is slavish and absurd; impersonal non-human truth appears to be a delusion." He came to realize, in effect, that "the non-human world is unworthy of worship."

His best known works are *A History of Western Philosophy* and *Principia Mathematica*. The latter, written with Alfred North Whitehead, has become a classic in its field, though Wood wrote that "probably not more than twenty people have read it right through." Russell's output was prodigious, and his special gift was a lucid and witty style that makes him the most readable of philosophers. He once remarked: "I'm paid by the word so I always use the shortest words possible." He did do some pot-boiling, having, he said, no "lofty feelings" about it. But his work was always precise, having been thoroughly planned before he set it down on paper. In 1930 he said: "I dictate at full speed, just as fast as the stenographer can go.... I do three thousand words a day. I plan to work only in the morning. If I haven't done my stint, I sometimes go on working into the afternoon...." He claimed he never revised. To authors he offered this advice: "Never alter anything you write—especially if someone else asks you to."

His diminutive physical appearance had been likened to that of a gnome and to "a sophisticated koala bear" (the latter description particularly flattered him). Once, in China, he nearly died of pneumonia, and, as a result of the confusion in England about his condition, he had the unique pleasure of reading his own obituaries. (At the age of 70 he wrote his own obituary in which he said his life, "for all its waywardness, had a certain anachronistic consistency.") Beatrice Webb called him a dissector of persons and a demolisher of causes, and Jean Nichod once said that Russell's statements had "that slightly ludicrous quality which comes from being true." He espoused many unpopular causes, not the least of these being free love. As for family relationships, he once wrote: "There is no greater reason for children to honour parents than for parents to honour children, except that while the children are young, the parents are stronger than the children. The same thing, of course, happened in the relations of men and women. It was the duty of wives to submit to husbands, not of husbands to submit to wives. The only basis for this view was that if wives could be induced to accept it, it saved trouble for their husbands."

Russell regarded the "good life" as one "inspired by love and guided by knowledge." And one that includes tobacco, he might have added. Some time ago he said: "When I was young I was told that smoking would shorten my life: after sixty years of smoking, it hasn't shortened much.... Anyway I get much more pleasure from smoking than I would from a few more years in decrepitude. I smoke heavily and only stop to sleep or eat.''

As the grandson of Lord John Russell and of Lord Stanley of Alderly, Russell was long associated with notable people. He personally knew Henri Bergson, George Santayana, Aldous Huxley, John Maynard Keynes, and D. H. Lawrence, and was the teacher of Ludwig Wittgenstein and T. S. Eliot. He disagreed with many of his friends and acquaintances, especially with those philosophers who believe that the world is a unity. "The most fundamental of my intellectual beliefs," he wrote, "is that this is rubbish. I think the universe is all spots and jumps, without unity, without continuity, without coherence or orderliness or any of the other properties that governesses love. Indeed, there is little but prejudice and habit to be said for the view that there is a world at all. . . .''

He had always been involved with many things at any given time. At the age of 89 he was again jailed, this time for helping to plan a demonstration advocating unilateral disarmament and refusing to keep the Queen's peace. He said: "What I want is some assurance before I die that the human race will be allowed to continue.''

Of the last volume of Russell's autobiography, Sidney Hook wrote in the *New York Times Book Review:* "Anyone who has spent more than a few hours in Russell's company during his prime will sense the failure of this autobiography to reflect his genius. He was without peer as a brilliant conversationalist. There was an unfailing play of common sense, profundity and puckish wit in his treatment of the most diverse themes. Others could have made careers out of the crumbs of his table talk. Here he appears as a figure of wooden virtue, violating by his dogmatism, self-righteousness and touches of malice key principles of his own decalogue of liberal commandments. . . . The greatness of Russell . . . lies not in his political thought but in his contributions to philosophy and logic. There was a dramatic appropriateness in his envy of Socrates. Russell's life has been nobler than this portrait from memory suggests. Some day, let us hope, a proper biography will do justice to it.''

In 1968, McMaster University purchased Russell's collection of private papers for a reported $600,000.

BIOGRAPHICAL/CRITICAL SOURCES: George Santayana, *Winds of Doctrine,* Scribner, 1913; P. E. B. Jourdain, editor, *The Philosophy of Mr. Bertrand Russell,* Open Court, 1918; J. Jorgensen, *Bertrand Russell,* Levin, 1935; John Dewey and H. M. Kallen, editors, *The Bertrand Russell Case,* Viking, 1941; P. A. Schilpp, editor, *The Philosophy of Bertrand Russell,* Tudor, 1944, 3rd edition, Harper, 1963; H. W. Leggett, *Bertrand Russell,* Philosophical Library, 1950; Alan Dorward, *Bertrand Russell: A Short Guide to His Philosophy,* Longmans, Green, for the British Council, 1951; C. A. Fritz, *Bertrand Russell's Construction of the External World,* Humanities, 1952; Alan Wood, *Bertrand Russell: The Passionate Skeptic,* Simon & Schuster, 1958; L. W. Aiken, *Bertrand Russell's Philosophy of Morals,* Humanities, 1963; E. D. Klemke, editor, *Essays on Bertrand Russell,* University of Illinois Press, 1971; A. J. Ayer, *Russell and Moore,* Harvard University Press, 1971; D. F. Pears, *Bertrand Russell and the British Tradition in Philosophy,* Vintage, 1971.

(Died February 2, 1970)

RUSSELL, Maurine (Fletcher) 1899-

PERSONAL: Born December 8, 1899, in Canton, Ill.; daughter of Edwin Newton (a stockbroker) and Frances (Robbins) Fletcher; married Clark Wayne Russell (a dentist), July 15, 1922. *Education:* Studied at University of Denver for three years; College of Speech Arts, Denver, Colorado, graduate, 1938. *Politics:* Republican. *Religion:* Christian Scientist.

CAREER: College of Speech Arts, Denver, Colo., occasional speech teacher. Recorder (on tape) of college-level textbooks for the blind, 1961-69. *Member:* Colorado Authors League (secretary-treasurer), Daughters of the American Revolution, Denver Woman's Press Club (president), Friends of the Public Library (Denver), Sigma Kappa. *Awards, honors:* Three-time winner of Top Hand Award of Colorado Authors League.

WRITINGS: (With Billie M. Eschenburg) *Contemporary Letter Writing for Every Woman,* Hearthside, 1962, revised edition, 1971. Contributor of short stories, and articles on travel, personality, and historical subjects to periodicals.

WORK IN PROGRESS: Research for juvenile historical novel.

AVOCATIONAL INTERESTS: Collecting paperweights, pincushion dolls, pattern goblets, Meissen china, and miniatures; golf, skating, swimming, and fishing.

BIOGRAPHICAL/CRITICAL SOURCES: Colorado Editor, March, 1952.

* * *

RUSSELL, Ronald (Stanley) 1904-

PERSONAL: Born May 29, 1904, in Cardiff, Wales; son of James Stanley and Margaret (Jones) Russell; married Ena Glendenning Forrester; children: Jillian Margaret, Ronald Charles Forrester. *Education:* Attended Haileybury and Imperial Service College; Gonville and Caius College, Cambridge, B.A., 1925, M.A., 1929. *Politics:* Conservative. *Religion:* Anglican. *Home:* 29 Acacia Rd., London N.W.8, England.

CAREER: Newcastle Chronicle Ltd., Newcastle upon Tyne, England, journalist, 1929-31; Reuters Ltd., London, England, journalist, 1931-35; Mining Association of Great Britain, London, England, lecturer, 1936-39; Empire Economic Union, London, England, research secretary, 1946-51. Member of Parliament for Wembley South, 1950—. *Military service:* Royal Artillery, 1939-45; became captain. *Member:* Institute of Journalists. *Awards, honors:* Knighted, 1964.

WRITINGS: (Compiler) *Britain's Commercial Treaty Position,* Empire Economic Union, 1946; *Imperial Preference: Its Development and Effects,* Empire Economic Union, 1947; *Government Bulk Buying,* Empire Economic Union, 1948; *Tariff Preferences in Western Europe,* Empire Economic Union, 1949; *Surplus or Shortage?: A Survey of the Commodity Situation,* Empire Economic Union, 1950; (editor) *Empire and Commonwealth Yearbook,* Volumes 1-2, Rolls House, 1952-53, Volumes 3-9, Newman Neame, 1954-61, Volume 10 published as *British Commonwealth Yearbook,* MacGibbon & Kee, 1963.

* * *

RUSSO, Giuseppe Luigi 1884-
(Joseph Louis Russo)

PERSONAL: Born October 12, 1884, in Naples, Italy; son

of Federico Franco (a banker) and Concetta (Fiorentino) Russo; married Margherita Alessandri, September 28, 1927. *Education:* Liceo Garibaldi (Naples), A.B., 1903; attended University of Naples Law School, 1903-06; Columbia University, A.M., 1915, Ph.D., 1921. *Politics:* Republican. *Religion:* Roman Catholic. *Home:* Via Tasso 480, Naples, Italy.

CAREER: Columbia University, New York, N.Y., instructor, 1913-16; Hamilton College, Clinton, N.Y., assistant professor of French and Italian, 1919-21; Allegheny College, Meadville, Pa., associate professor of French and Italian, 1921-24; University of Wisconsin, Madison, professor of Italian language and literature, 1924-49, professor emeritus, 1949—. *Military service:* Italian Army, field artillery, 1916-19; became first lieutenant; received War Cross. *Member:* Modern Language Association of America, American Association of Teachers of Italian.

WRITINGS—All under name Joseph Louis Russo; all published by Heath, except as indicated: *Lorenzo da Ponte, Poet and Adventurer,* Columbia University Press, 1922; *Elementary Italian Grammar,* 1927, new edition, 1929 (published in England as *Practical Italian Grammar,* 1927); (editor and author of introduction and notes) Luigi Pirandello, *Cosi e—se vi pare,* 1930; *Nel paese del sole* (Italian reader), 1934; *First Year Italian,* 1937; *Second Year Italian,* 1941; *Present Day Italian,* 1947; *Sotto un cielo azzurro* (Italian reader), 1952; (editor and author of introduction, notes, and exercises) Carlo Goldoni, *I Rusteghi,* 1955; *La Lingua inglese d'Oggi,* Carlo Signorelli, 1955; *Primo corso d'italiano,* 1960; *Secondo corso d'italiano,* 1961; *Corso integrale d'italiano,* 1963. Contributor to *Italy and the Italians in Washington's Time,* Italian Publishers, 1934.

WORK IN PROGRESS: An Autobiography.

SIDELIGHTS: Russo has traveled extensively, and speaks and writes French, German, and Spanish, reads Latin and ancient Greek. *Avocational interests:* Photography, moving pictures, philately.

BIOGRAPHICAL/CRITICAL SOURCES: New York Times, October 23, 1921, April 23, 1922, November 5, 1922, February 3, 1924; *American,* July, 1922; *Musical America,* September 16, 1923; *America,* January 27, 1923; *Modern Philology,* November, 1923.

* * *

RYAN, Patrick J. 1902-

PERSONAL: Born December 3, 1902, in Litchfield, Minn.; son of Patrick Phillip and Johanna (Cassady) Ryan. *Education:* College of St. Thomas, B.A., 1923; Catholic University, S.T.B., 1927. *Home:* 3839 Massachusetts Ave., Washington, D.C. 20016.

CAREER: Roman Catholic priest; ordained, 1927, named domestic prelate with title of monsignor, 1947; served in U.S. Army, 1928-58; became major general; entered Chaplains Corps after one year as a parish priest; served in office of Chief of Chaplains, 1945-48, 1952-54, chief of Chaplains, 1954-58. Executive vice-president, *Catholic Digest. Member:* Military Chaplains Association of the U.S.A. (president), Association of the United States Army, Military Order of the World Wars, American Legion, Knights of Columbus. *Awards, honors*—Military: Distinguished Service Medal, Bronze Star, Legion of Merit, and Army Commendation Ribbon (United States); Order of British Empire and British Service Medal (Great

Britain); Legion of Honor (France); Medal of War (Brazil); Order of Crown, Bronze Medal of Valor with Star (Italy).

WRITINGS: A Soldier Priest Talks to Youth, Random House, 1963.

* * *

SABINE, Ellen S. (Borcherding) 1908-

PERSONAL: Born February 23, 1908, in New York, N.Y.; daughter of George William (an accountant) and Julia (Schwickart) Borcherding; married William H. W. Sabine (an author and publisher), July 2, 1937. *Education:* Studied at New York School of Fine and Applied Arts, 1924-25, Pratt Institute, 1925-27. *Religion:* Protestant. *Home:* 21-A Yorkshire Court, Lakehurst, N.J. 08733.

CAREER: Free-lance advertising, newspaper, and magazine artist in New York, N.Y., 1932-37, 1946-52, in London, England, 1937-46; free-lance designer of printed fabrics, 1952-56; teacher of adult education classes in art at Young Womens' Christian Association Central Branch, New York, N.Y., 1948-73, and in adult education program, Floral Park, N.Y., 1956-59. *Member:* Esther Stevens Brazer Guild of Historical Society of Early American Decoration.

WRITINGS: American Antique Decoration, Van Nostrand, 1956; *American Folk Art,* Van Nostrand, 1958; *Early American Decorative Patterns,* Van Nostrand, 1962.

WORK IN PROGRESS: Further research in American antique decoration technique and patterns.

* * *

SADLER, Christine 1908-

PERSONAL: Born April 7, 1908, in Silver Point, Tenn.; daughter of Philip Edley (a construction worker) and Frances (Williams) Sadler; married Richard L. Coe (a theater editor for the *Washington Post*), May 4, 1946. *Education:* George Peabody College for Teachers, B.S., 1928; Columbia University, M.S., 1937. *Politics:* Democrat. *Home:* 2713 Dumbarton Ave. N.W., Washington, D.C. 20007. *Agent:* Bella Linden, 110 East 59th St., New York, N.Y. 10022.

CAREER: Nashville Banner, Nashville, Tenn., reporter, 1930-36; *Washington Post,* Washington, D.C., successively district news reporter, rotogravure editor, Sunday editor, National News Bureau staffer, 1937-46; *McCall's,* Washington, D.C., Washington editor, 1944-70. Defense Advisory Committee on Women in the Services, member, 1956-59; member of board of trustees, George Peabody College for Teachers. *Member:* Women's National Press Club (president, 1941-42), American Newspaper Women's Club, Theta Sigma Phi.

WRITINGS: America's First Ladies, Macfadden, 1963; *Children in the White House,* Putnam, 1967. Author of guidebook for History and Technology Building, Smithsonian Institution.

WORK IN PROGRESS: The Women of Congress.

AVOCATIONAL INTERESTS: Gardening, painting, American history, reading, travel.

BIOGRAPHICAL/CRITICAL SOURCES: New York Times Book Review, September 17, 1967.

* * *

SAILOR, Merlin F(orrest) 1906-

PERSONAL: Born November 18, 1906, in Cascade, Iowa;

son of George Durrell and Edith Sailor; married Ethel May Jung, November 24, 1930; children: David, Karen Sailor Carey, Paula Noel. *Education:* Attended Cornell College, Mount Vernon, Iowa, 1924-26; University of Nebraska, LL.B., 1930. *Religion:* Methodist. *Office:* Phillips Petroleum Co., P.O. Box 51185, Lafayette, La.

CAREER: Practiced law in Lisbon and Marshalltown, Iowa, 1930-42; Phillips Petroleum Co., Lafayette, La., leaseman, beginning 1945. *Military service:* U.S. Navy, 1942-45; became lieutenant junior grade. U.S. Naval Reserve, 1945-63; retired as lieutenant commander, 1963. *Member:* National Association of Professional Landmen.

WRITINGS: You Might Strike Oil, University of Oklahoma Press, 1965. Occasional contributor of features and light verse to newspapers.

WORK IN PROGRESS: Study of the Andean civilizations.

* * *

ST. BRUNO, Albert Francis 1909-
(Frank Bruno)

PERSONAL: Born September 1, 1909, in Sydney, Australia; son of Antoine Francis and Mary (Hopkinson) St. Bruno; married Edith Carter, August 18, 1937; children: Randall, Louis Donald Antony. *Education:* Attended schools in Australia and New Zealand. *Politics:* Liberal, "no extremes either way." *Home:* 19 Savage St., Westmere, Auckland, New Zealand. *Agent:* Kurt Singer, P.O. Box 3668, Fullerton, Calif. 92634; and W. B. Wallace Ltd., P.O. Box 30022, Takapuna, Auckland, New Zealand.

CAREER: Former law clerk, journalist, professional fighter, cartoonist, hobo, seaman, soldier, editor, scriptwriter; now novelist. *Military service:* New Zealand Army, 2nd Division, 1939-42.

WRITINGS—All under pseudonym Frank Bruno; all published by R. Hale: *The Hellbuster*, 1959, *Black Noon at Ngutu*, 1960, *Fury at Finnegan's Folly*, 1962, *The Black Pearl*, 1962, *Cockeye Kerrigan*, 1963, *Yellow Jack's Island*, 1963, *Riggermortis*, 1966.

WORK IN PROGRESS: Long Green Graveyard, about the Maori wars in New Zealand; *On the Wallaby*, book of experiences as hobo around Australia in the thirties.

* * *

SALINGER, Herman 1905-

PERSONAL: Born December 23, 1905, in St. Louis, Mo.; son of Isadore (a broker and cannery executive) and Florence (Treichlinger) Salinger; married Marion Georgette Casting, November 29, 1941; children: (previous marriage) Timothy Madison; (current marriage) Jill Hudson (Mrs. F. Duane Lankin), Wendy Lang, Jennifer Wilson. *Education:* Princeton University, A.B., 1927; Stanford University, M.A., 1929; graduate study at University of Berlin, 1929-30, and University of Cologne, 1930-31; Yale University, Ph.D., 1937; University of Wisconsin, postdoctoral study, summers, 1951-53. *Politics:* Democrat, *Religion:* Episcopal. *Home:* 3444 Rugby Rd., Hope Valley, Durham, N.C. 27707. *Office:* Duke University, Durham, N.C.

CAREER: Princeton University, Princeton, N.J., instructor in German, 1932-35; University of Wisconsin, Madison, instructor in German, 1937-42; University of Kansas City (now University of Missouri), Kansas City, assistant professor of German, 1946-47; Grinnell College,

Grinnell, Iowa, 1947-55, became professor of German; Duke University, Durham, N.C., professor of German, 1955—, chairman of department, 1955-70, chairman of program in comparative literature, 1972—. Visiting summer lecturer, University of Wisconsin, 1954, 1957. *Military service:* U.S. Army Air Forces, 1942-46; became captain.

MEMBER: American Association of Teachers of German, Modern Language Association of America, South Atlantic Modern Language Association, American Comparative Literature Association, International Arthur Schnitzler Research Association (secretary-treasurer, 1961-72), Masons, Phi Beta Kappa. *Awards, honors:* Badge of Honor Poetry Prize, 1942; Roanoke-Chowan Poetry Award for best book by a North Carolina poet, 1963, for *A Sigh Is the Sword*; Alex von Humboldt Foundation fellow, 1971.

WRITINGS: (Editor) *An Index to the Poems of Rainer Maria Rilke*, University of Wisconsin Press, 1942; (translator) Heinrich Heine, *Germany: A Winter's Tale*, L. B. Fischer, 1944; *Angel of Our Thirst: Poems*, James B. Decker Press and Grinnell College Press, 1950; *Twentieth Century German Verse: A Selection*, Princeton University Press, 1952; (editor with Haskell M. Block) *Creative Vision: European Writers on Their Art*, Grove, 1960; (translator) Rudolf Hagelstange, *Ballad of the Buried Life*, University of North Carolina Press, 1962; (editor with Herbert Reichert) *Studies in Arthur Schnitzler*, University of North Carolina Press, 1963; *A Sigh Is the Sword: Poems*, McNally & Loftin, 1963; (translator) Karl Krolow, *Poems Against Death*, Charioteer Press, 1969. Contributor of articles to *Modern Austrian Literature*, *Lyrica Germanica*, and *Comparitive Drama*. Member of editorial board, *University of Kansas City Review*, 1946-47, *South Atlantic Quarterly*, 1956-66.

WORK IN PROGRESS: Heinrich Heine: A Critical Introduction, completed and awaiting publication in a periodical.

AVOCATIONAL INTERESTS: Swimming, fishing; Confederate history, especially the life of Robert E. Lee.

BIOGRAPHICAL SOURCES: University of Kansas City Review, spring, 1947.

* * *

SALISBURY, Edward J(ames) 1886-

PERSONAL: Born April 16, 1886, in Harpenden, Hertfordshire, England; son of James Wright (a company director) and Eliza (Stimpson) Salisbury; married Mabel Elwin-Coles, 1919 (died, 1956). *Education:* University College, London, B.Sc., 1908, D.Sc., 1913. *Home:* Croindene, Strandway, Felpham, Sussex, England.

CAREER: East London College, London, England, senior lecturer, 1914-18; University of London, London, England, lecturer at University College, 1918-24, university reader in plant ecology, 1924-29, Quain Professor of Botany at University College, 1929-43; Royal Botanic Gardens, Kew, Surrey, England, director, 1943-56. Fullerton Professor of Physiology, Royal Institution, 1947-52. Member of Agricultural Research Council, 1940-44, of Scientific Advisory Committee to Cabinet, 1943-45; vice-chairman of Agricultural Improvement Council, 1944-56. Member of University Grants Committee, 1944-49; former governor of Royal Holloway College and Queen Mary College, both University of London; trustee of Rothamstah Experimental Station.

MEMBER: Royal Society (fellow; vice-president, 1943, 1948-55; biological secretary, 1945-55), Royal Horticultural

Society (vice-president), Linnean Society (fellow; vice-president, 1928), British Ecological Society, Marine Biological Association, Sussex Naturalists Trust (president), Bee Research Association (president), Institute of Biology (honorary fellow). *Awards, honors:* Veitchian Gold Medal, 1936; Companion, Order of the British Empire, 1939; Royal Medal of Royal Society, 1945, knighted 1946; Victoria Medal of Honour, Royal Horticultural Society, 1953. Honorary LL.D. from University of Edinburgh and University of Glasgow; honorary fellow of University College and Queen Mary College, University of London.

WRITINGS: (With Felix E. Fritsch) *An Introduction to the Study of Plants*, G. Bell, 1914, 9th edition, 1928; (with Fritsch) *Elementary Studies in Plant Life*, G. Bell, 1915, 8th edition, 1926; (with Fritsch) *An Introduction to the Structure and Reproduction of Plants*, G. Bell, 1920, 2nd edition, 1927; (with Fritsch) *Botany for Medical Students*, G. Bell, 1921, 3rd edition, 1928; *The East Anglian Flora*, Norwich, 1933; *The Living Garden*, G. Bell, 1935, Macmillan (New York), 1936; (with Fritsch) *Plant Form and Function*, G. Bell, 1938.

The Reproductive Capacity of Plants, G. Bell, 1942; *Flowers of the Woods*, Penguin, 1946; *Downs and Dunes*, G. Bell, 1952; *The Biology of Garden Weeds*, Royal Horticultural Society, 1952; *Weeds and Aliens*, Collins, 1961. Contributor to scientific journals. Co-editor, *Science Progress*, 1930-62.

WORK IN PROGRESS: Studies on reproduction and biology of British species of plants.

SIDELIGHTS: Salisbury told *CA*: "I have travelled for botanical purposes in South Africa and in Australia, and of course on the Continent of Europe, but most of my personal researches have been concerned with species found wild in Britain."

*   *   *

SAMARTHA, S(tanley) J(edidiah)   1920-

PERSONAL: Born October 7, 1920, in Karkal, Mysore State, India; son of Lucas Joshia (a minister) and Sahadevi (Soans) Samartha; married Iris Furtado (a high school teacher), January 2, 1947; children: Usha and Prabha (daughters), Ravi (son). *Education:* Madras University, B.A., 1941; Serampore University, B.D., 1945; Union Theological Seminary, New York, N.Y., S.T.M., 1950; Hartford Seminary Foundation, graduate study, 1950-51, 1957-58, Ph.D., 1958; Basel University, graduate study, 1951-52. *Religion:* Protestant. *Home:* 7, Chemin des Palettes, 1212 Grand Lancy, Geneva, Switzerland. *Office:* 150 Route de Ferney, 1211 Geneva, Switzerland.

CAREER: Assistant pastor, Udipi, Mysore State, India, 1945-47; Basel Mission Theological Seminary, Mangalore, Mysore State, lecturer, 1947-49, principal, 1952-60; United Theological College, Bangalore, Mysore State, professor of philosophy and the history of religions, and director of department of research and postgraduate studies, 1960-65; Serampore College, West Bengal, India, principal and professor, 1966-68; World Council of Churches, Geneva, Switzerland, director, Program on Dialogue with People of Living Faiths and Ideologies, 1968—. Young Men's Christian Association, Bangalore, Mysore State, member of board, 1960-65, president, 1961-63; member of committee for training, National Council for India; Fulbright visiting professor, Park College, Parkville, Mo., 1965-66. *Member:* Institute of World Culture (Bangalore), Indian Philosophical Congress.

WRITINGS: The Hindu View of History: Classical and Modern, Christian Institute for the Study of Religion and Society (Bangalore), 1959; (editor with Nalini Devanandan) Paul David Devanandan, *I Will Lift Up Mine Eyes Unto the Hills: Sermons and Bible Studies,* Christian Institute for the Study of Religion and Society, 1963; *Introduction to Radhakrishnan: The Man and His Thought,* Association Press, 1964; *Hindus vor dem universalen Christus.* Evangelisches Verlagswerk GMBH (Stuttgart), 1970, translation published as *The Hindu Response to the Unbound Christ: Towards a Christology in India,* in press; (editor) *Dialogue Between Men of Living Faiths,* World Council of Churches, 1971; (editor) *Living Faiths and the Ecumenical Movement,* World Council of Churches, 1971; (contributor) J. Robert Nelson, editor, *No Man is Alien,* E. J. Brill, 1971. Contributor to *Dictionary of Christian Mission,* and to religious journals. General editor of "Christian Students' Library," a basic theological textbook series, published by Serampore College Senate, 1962-66.

SIDELIGHTS: Samartha has a working knowledge of New Testament Greek, German, and Sanskrit.

*   *   *

SAMUELS, Ernest   1903-

PERSONAL: Born May 19, 1903, in Chicago, Ill.; son of Albert and Mary (Kaplan) Samuels; married Jayne Newcomer, August 24, 1938; children: Susanna (Mrs. Helmut Epp), Jonathan, Elizabeth. *Education:* University of Chicago, Ph.B., 1923, J.D., 1926, M.A., 1931, Ph.D., 1942. *Politics:* Independent. *Home:* 3116 Park Place, Evanston, Ill. 60201. *Office:* English Department, Northwestern University, Evanston, Ill. 60201.

CAREER: Admitted to the bar of Texas and of Illinois; attorney at law in El Paso, Tex., 1928-30, in Chicago, Ill., 1933-37, as partner in Samuels & Samuels; State College of Washington (now Washington State University), Pullman, instructor in English, 1937-39; Northwestern University, Evanston, Ill., instructor in English, 1942-46, assistant professor, 1946-49, associate professor, 1949-54, professor of English, 1954—, Franklyn Bliss Snyder Professor of English, 1970—, chairman of department, 1964—. Visiting associate professor, University of Chicago, 1950; Fulbright lecturer in American literature to the Belgian universities, 1958-59; first holder of the Bing Chair in English and American Literature, University of Southern California, 1966-67. Member of advisory committee for the publication of the Adams papers; member of Commission of Scholars, Illinois Board of Higher Education. *Member:* Modern Language Association, American Studies Association, National Council of Teachers of English, American Association of University Professors, Massachusetts Historical Society. *Awards, honors:* Guggenheim fellowship, 1955-56; Bancroft Prize, Columbia University, and Francis Parkman Prize, Society of American Historians, both 1959, for *Henry Adams: The Middle Years*; Pulitzer Prize in biography, 1965, for the three-volume *Henry Adams.*

WRITINGS: The Young Henry Adams (first in a trilogy), Harvard University Press, 1948; *Henry Adams: The Middle Years* (2nd in the trilogy), Harvard University Press, 1958; *Henry Adams: The Major Phase* (3rd in the trilogy), Harvard University Press, 1964; (editor) Henry Adams, *History of the United States of America During the Administrations of Jefferson and Madison,* abridged edition, University of Chicago Press, 1967. Author of introduction to Henry Adams's *Democracy,* and *Esther* (both novels), and to *Chartres*. Member of editorial board, *American Literature*. Contributor to *Major American Writers*, Harcourt, 1962, and to *American Quarterly, Nation, American Literature, Christian*, and *Lincoln Herald*.

WORK IN PROGRESS: Editing the correspondence of Henry Adams and Bernard Berenson; a biography of Bernard Berenson; an annotated edition of *The Education of Henry Adams*.

AVOCATIONAL INTERESTS: Skiing, camping, travel.

BIOGRAPHICAL/CRITICAL SOURCES: Saturday Review, November 8, 1958; *Chicago Sunday Tribune*, November 23, 1958; *New England Quarterly*, March, 1959; *Reporter*, December 17, 1964; *Virginia Quarterly Review*, winter, 1965; *Canadian Forum*, March, 1968.

* * *

SANDERS, Gerald D(eWitt) 1895-

PERSONAL: Born July 1, 1895, in Chesterfield County, S.C. *Education:* Wofford College, A.B. and A.M., 1918; Cornell University, Ph.D., 1922. *Residence:* Methodist Home, Box 327, Orangeburg, S.C. 29115.

CAREER: Cornell University, Ithaca, N.Y., instructor in English, 1919-23; University of Arizona, Tucson, 1923-28, began as assistant professor, became professor; Eastern Michigan University, Ypsilanti, head of English department, 1928-52; owner and publisher of *Sylvester Local*, Sylvester, Ga., and *Claxton Enterprize*, Claxton, Ga., 1952-57. Visiting summer professor of English at Cornell University, Duke University, and University of Colorado; professor of English, Shrivenham American University, 1945; special adviser to U.S. Army Air Forces, 1946. *Military service:* U.S. Army, 27th Division, World War I; became sergeant. *Member:* Modern Language Association of America, Phi Beta Kappa.

WRITINGS: Elizabeth Gaskell, Cornell University Press, 1929, reprinted, Russell, 1971; (with others) *Chief Modern Poets of England and America*, Macmillan, 1929, 5th edition published as *Chief Modern Poets of Britain and America*, 1970, paperback edition published in two volumes, 1962, 2nd edition, 1970; (editor with Frederick C. Prescott) *Introduction to American Prose*, Crofts, 1932; (editor with Prescott) *Introduction to American Poetry*, Crofts, 1933; *A Poetry Primer*, Rinehart, 1935, reprinted, 1960; (editor with Walter H. French) *The Reader's Macaulay*, American Book Co., 1936; *Unified English Composition*, Appleton, 1942, (subsequent editions with others) 4th edition, 1966; *A Shakespeare Primer*, Rinehart, 1950.

* * *

SAUNDERS, Aretas (Andrews) 1884-

PERSONAL: Born November 15, 1884, in Avon, Conn.; son of George Augustus and Isabel T. (Andrews) Saunders; married Grace E. Adams, August 12, 1916; children: Stanley Burdette (deceased). *Education:* Yale University, Ph.B., 1907, graduate study in forestry, 1907-08. *Politics:* Usually Republican. *Religion:* Congregational. *Home address:* Box 141, Canaan, Conn. 06018.

CAREER: Employed by U.S. Forest Service, 1908-13; high school biology teacher, Bridgeport, Conn., 1913-48. *Member:* American Ornithologists Union (fellow). *Awards, honors:* American Philosophical Society grant to travel and study bird song.

WRITINGS: A Distributional List of the Birds of Montana, Cooper Ornithological Club, 1921; *Bird Song*, University of the State of New York (Albany), 1929; *Butterflies of the Allegany State Park*, University of the State of New York, 1932; *A Guide to Bird Songs: Descriptions and Diagrams of the Songs and Singing Habits of the Land Birds of Northeastern United States*, Appleton, 1935, 2nd edition, Doubleday, 1951; *Ecology of the Birds of Quaker Run Valley, Allegany State Park, New York*, University of the State of New York, 1936; *Studies of Breeding Birds in the Allegany State Park*, University of the State of New York, 1938; *Summer Birds of the Allegany State Park*, University of the State of New York, 1942; *The Lives of Wild Birds*, Doubleday, 1954, 2nd edition published as *An Introduction to Bird Life for Bird Watchers*, Dover, 1964. Contributor to *Encyclopedia of Biological Science*.

WORK IN PROGRESS: Songs and Calls of American Birds; Insects, a book designed to show that majority of insects are useful and to combat use of pesticides; autobiography, *On Being a Naturalist*.

* * *

SAUNDERS, Blanche 1906-

PERSONAL: Born September 12, 1906, in Easton, Me.; daughter of Abram E. (a clergyman) and Fidelia Saunders. *Education:* Attended Stockbridge School of Agriculture, Stockbridge, Mass., for two years. *Home:* Old Post Rd., Bedford, N.Y. *Agent:* McIntosh & Otis, Inc., 18 East 41st St., New York, N.Y. 10017.

CAREER: Farmer, swimming instructor, kennel manager, and former owner (for eight years) of poodle-clipping shop in New York, N.Y.; self-employed kennel owner and instructor of dog obedience classes, 1942—. Exhibitor at dog shows; dog show judge and conductor of training clinics throughout United States and Canada, and in New Zealand, Venezuela, and Trinidad; producer of six sound films about dogs. Guest on radio and television programs, including "To Tell the Truth." *Member:* Honorary member of nine obedience clubs in United States and South America. *Awards, honors:* Film based on *Training You to Train Your Dog* was named best film on dogs for 1963 by Dog Writers Association of America; other awards from National Dog Welfare Guild and dog magazines.

WRITINGS: Training You to Train Your Dog, Doubleday, 1946, revised edition, 1965; (with Jeanette Cross) *The Standard Book of Dog Care: 1001 Questions Answered*, Greystone Press, 1952, revised edition, 1957, published as *The New Standard Book of Dog Care and Training: 1001 Questions Answered*, 1962. *The Complete Book of Dog Obedience*, Prentice-Hall, 1954, 3rd edition, Howell Books, 1969; *Grooming and Showing Instructions*, Denlinger, 1956, revised edition published as *How to Trim, Groom, and Show Your Dog*, Howell Book, 1963; *The Complete Novice Obedience Manual*, Denlinger, 1958, 3rd edition, Howell Books, 1969; *The Complete Open Obedience Course*, Howell Book, 1961, 2nd edition, Howell Books, 1969; (with Jeanette Wallace Cross) *The New Standard Book of Dog Care and Training*, Greystone Press, 1962; *The Complete Utility Obedience Course with Tracking*, Howell Book, 1961, revised edition, 1969; *Dog Training for Boys and Girls*, Howell Book, 1962; *Dog Care for Boys and Girls*, Howell Book, 1964. Also author of *The Story of Obedience*.

BIOGRAPHICAL SOURCES: New Yorker, November 24, 1951.

SAUNDERS, Roy 1911-

PERSONAL: Born January 5, 1911, in Swansea, Wales; son of Christopher and Margaret (Rees) Saunders; married Irene Perkins (a teacher), August 19, 1939; children: Gareth. *Education:* Cardiff College of Art, A.T.D., 1934. *Home:* 63 Wenallt Rd., Rhiwbina, Cardiff, Wales.

CAREER: Art master, Cardiff, Wales, 1935—. Extramural lecturer, University College of South Wales and Monmouthshire, Cardiff. Nature photographer, with films shown on television networks. *Member:* West Wales Naturalists Trust, South Wales Sheepdog Trials Association, Glamorgan Naturalists Trust, Cardiff Naturalists Society.

WRITINGS: (Self-illustrated) *Sheepdog Glory,* Deutsch, 1954; (self-illustrated) *Craig of the Welsh Hills,* Oldbourne, Duell, Sloane & Pearce, 1959; (self-illustrated) *Drovers Highway,* Oldbourne, 1959; *The Escuminac Disaster,* Oldbourne, 1960; *Queen of the River,* Oldbourne, 1961; *The Raising of the Vasa: The Rebirth of a Swedish Galleon,* Oldbourne, 1962.

WORK IN PROGRESS: A book on nature conservation sites in Britain.

AVOCATIONAL INTERESTS: Skiing, bird watching, sheep dog trials, and travel.†

* * *

SAVAGE, Frances Higginson (Fuller) 1898-

PERSONAL: Born January 1, 1898, in New York, N.Y.; daughter of Robert Higginson (a writer) and Bessie Adams (Clagett) Fuller; married Howard James Savage, June 23, 1923; children: Cordelia Fuller (Mrs. Gerald Gaskell), Maud Fuller. *Education:* Bryn Mawr College, B.A., 1919. *Politics:* Independent. *Religion:* Protestant. *Home:* 150 Brewster Rd., Scarsdale, N.Y. 10583.

CAREER: Bryn Mawr College, Bryn Mawr, Pa., instructor in English, 1922-23. Poet. *Member:* Poetry Society of America, New York Women Poets (president, 1958-61), Pen and Brush Club (New York). *Awards, honors:* First prize for poetry, *Bronxville Villager,* 1944; *Lyric* Award, 1954, 1966; *Lyric* New England Prize, 1965; *Lyric* monthly prize, 1967; Love Prize, Poetry Society of Georgia, 1967.

WRITINGS—Poetry: *Bread and Honey,* privately printed, 1939; *A Pinch of Salt,* privately printed, 1941; *Winter Nocturne,* Golden Quill, 1963; *Postscript to Spring, and Other Poems,* Golden Quill, 1967. Poems included in seven anthologies. Contributor of verse to newspapers and national periodicals, including *New York Herald Tribune, New York Times, Ladies' Home Journal, New Yorker, Atlantic Monthly, Lyric.*

WORK IN PROGRESS: A book of verse.

AVOCATIONAL INTERESTS: Drawing and painting.

* * *

SAYRE, Leslie C. 1907-

PERSONAL: Born January 4, 1907, in Globe, Ariz.; son of Sydney (an electrical engineer) and Mary Helena (Bawden) Sayre; married Josephine Adair Jackson, January 10, 1956; children: Carol Jeanne (Mrs. William Clark), William K., Ruth E., Mary Elanor. *Education:* Wayne University (now Wayne State University), A.B., 1931; Northwestern University, M.A., 1934; Garrett Biblical Institute, B.D., 1934; Iliff Seminary, Th.D., 1935. *Politics:* Independent. *Home:* 95 Glenwood, Leonia, N.J. 07605. *Office:* Intermedia, 475 Riverside Dr., New York, N.Y. 10027.

CAREER: Ordained Methodist minister, 1934. Detroit Annual Conference, Detroit, Mich., minister, 1934-37; Springer Institute, Katanga, Belgian Congo, director, 1937-42; Friendship Press, New York, N.Y., editor, 1946-54; Kailua Methodist Church, Kailua, Hawaii, minister, 1954-59; National Council of Churches, New York, N.Y., literacy-literature staff, 1959—. *Member:* Kiwanis.

WRITINGS: Africans on Safari, Friendship, 1952; (editor) *Where There Is Life* (pictures), Friendship, 1953; *This Rocket Called Freedom,* Friendship, 1964; *Christian Publishers Handbook,* Lit-Lit, 1966. Also author of *Focus: What's New in Mission?,* published by Friendship.

* * *

SAYRES, Alfred Nevin 1893-19(?)

PERSONAL: Surname rhymes with "cares"; born December 9, 1893, in Lancaster, Pa.; son of Edwin Pinkerton (a merchant) and Lura May (Cocklin) Sayres; married Carrie A. Pugh, May 11, 1918; children: R. Gardner (deceased), Dorothy Jane (Mrs. Ned M. Cohen). *Education:* Franklin and Marshall College, A.B., 1914; Lancaster Theological Seminary, B.D., 1917; Union Theological Seminary, New York, N.Y., S.T.B., 1918. *Politics:* Independent. *Home:* 1939 Bloomingdale Ave., Lancaster, Pa. 17601.

CAREER: Ordained minister, Evangelical and Reformed Church (now United Church of Christ), 1917; pastor in Harrisburg, Pa., 1918-23, and Lansdale, Pa., 1923-44; Evangelical and Reformed Church, Board of Christian Education and Publication, Philadelphia, Pa., president, 1934-44, executive secretary, 1944-45; Lancaster Theological Seminary, Lancaster, Pa., professor of practical theology, 1946-61. Trustee, Catawba College, 1951-66; secretary, Lancaster County Board of Assistance, beginning, 1961. *Member:* Phi Beta Kappa.

WRITINGS: (With others) *Windows of Worship,* Christian Education Press, 1941; (with others) *Gates of Beauty,* Christian Education Press, 1945; (with Robert Stanger) *March on with Strength,* Christian Education Press, 1953; (with others) *Pathways of Prayer,* Christian Education Press, 1953; *That One Good Sermon,* United Church Press, 1963. Writer of church curriculum materials, and contributor to denominational journals.

(Deceased)

* * *

SCANLON, Kathryn I(da) 1909-

PERSONAL: Born May 12, 1909, in Yonkers, N.Y.; daughter of Edward J. (a businessman) and Ida (Johnstone) Scanlon; married John J. Carlin (a professor of chemistry and science), June 13, 1953 (deceased 1968). *Education:* Fordham University, B.S. in Ed., 1934, M.A., 1936, Ph.D., 1956. *Religion:* Roman Catholic. *Home:* 1304 New York Ave., Brooklyn, N.Y. 11203.

CAREER: New York City (N.Y.) Bureau of Research Laboratory, bacteriologist, 1930-32; New York City (N.Y.) Board of Education, teacher of biology and general science, 1932-34; Rosemont College, Rosemont, Pa., head of education department, 1936-46; Villanova College, Villanova, Pa., part-time teacher of English, 1943-45; Fordham University, School of Education, New York, N.Y., part-time teacher of secondary education, 1945-46, director of teacher education, 1946—, now Director of Field Services and Teacher Certification, and professor of secondary education. Metropolitan New York City Commission on Teacher Education and Professional Standards, member of executive committee; Latin American Institute, member of board of advisers. *Member:* National Education Association (executive committee, New York chapter), American Association of University Professors, American Association of Student Teachers, Association for Supervision and Curriculum Development, National Association for Advancement of Education, New York Academy of Public Education, New York State Teachers Association.

WRITINGS: Basic Facts of Principles of Elementary Education, Collier, 1963; *Secondary Education: Basic Facts for Examination Review,* Collier, 1967. Contributor of articles to educational journals.

AVOCATIONAL INTERESTS: Photography, gardening, swimming, tennis, travel, and retreat to home in Catskill Mountains.

* * *

SCHAEFER, Jack Warner 1907-

PERSONAL: Born November 19, 1907, in Cleveland, Ohio; son of Carl Walter (a lawyer) and Minnie Luella (Hively) Schaefer; married Eugenia Hammond Ives, August 26, 1931 (divorced December, 1948); married Louise Wilhide Deans, June, 1949; children: (first marriage) Carl, Christopher, Susan, Jonathan; (stepchildren) Sharon, Stephani, Claudia. *Education:* Oberlin College, A.B., 1929; Columbia University, graduate study, 1929-30. *Home:* 1719 San Cristobel, Albuquerque, N.M. 87104. *Agent:* Harold Matson Co., Inc., 22 East 40th St., N.Y. 10020.

CAREER: United Press, reporter and office man, 1930-31; Connecticut State Reformatory, assistant director of education, 1931-38; *New Haven Journal-Courier,* New Haven, Conn., associate editor, 1932-39, editor, 1939-42; *Baltimore Sun,* Baltimore, Md., editorial writer, 1942-44; *Norfolk Virginian-Pilot,* Norfolk, Va., associate editor, 1944-48; *Shoreliner,* editor, 1949; Lindsay Advertising Co., New Haven, Conn., associate, 1949; free-lance writer, 1949—. *Awards, honors: Old Ramon* was chosen as an American Library Association Notable book.

WRITINGS—All published by Houghton, except as indicated: *Shane,* 1949; *First Blood,* 1953; *The Big Range* (short stories), 1953; *The Canyon,* 1953; *The Pioneers* (short stories), 1954; *Company of Cowards,* 1957; *The Kean Land* (short stories), 1959; *Old Ramon,* 1960; *The Plainsmen,* 1963; *Monte Walsh,* 1963; *The Great Endurance Horse Race,* Stagecoach, 1963; *Stubby Pringle's Christmas,* 1964; *Heroes Without Glory: Some Goodmen of the Old West,* 1965; *Collected Stories,* 1966; *New Mexico,* Coward-McCann, 1967; *The Short Novels,* 1967; *Mavericks,* 1967. Also author of screenplay, "Jinglebob," and special material on which the film "The Great Cowboy Race" is based. Contributor of short stories to magazines. Editor and publisher, *Theatre News,* 1935-40, *Movies,* 1939-41.

SIDELIGHTS: Shane was filmed by Paramount in 1953, and a film of *Monte Walsh* was produced in 1970.

* * *

SCHELLENBERG, Theodore R. 1903-19(?)

PERSONAL: Born February 24, 1903, in Harvey County, Kan.; son of Abraham Lohrenz (a newspaperman) and Sarah (Schroeder) Schellenberg; married Alma Groening, August 26, 1927; children: Paul Herbert, Karl Abraham.

Education: Tabor College, student, 1924-26; University of Kansas, A.B., 1928, A.M., 1930; University of Pennsylvania, Ph.D. 1934. *Home address:* Route 1, Box 11, Broad Run, Va. 22014.

CAREER: American Council of Learned Societies and Social Science Research Council Joint Committee on Materials for Research, executive secretary, Cleveland, Ohio, 1934-35; archives and records posts with U.S. government, Washington, D.C., 1935-63, as deputy examiner, National Archives, 1935-38, chief of Department of Agriculture Archives, 1938-45, records officer, Office of Price Administration and War Production Board, 1945-48, director of archival management, National Archives and Records Service, 1950-56, assistant Archivist of the United States, 1957-63. Fulbright lecturer in Australia and New Zealand, 1954; professorial lecturer and adjunct professor at The American University, 1955-61; director of summer courses in archival management, 1959-61; also director of summer courses at University of Texas, 1960, University of Washington, 1962, 1966, and Columbia University, 1965. Rockefeller Foundation consultant in Trinidad and Tobago, 1958; U.S. Department of State specialist in South America, 1960; director of Inter-American Archival Seminar, 1961; consultant to Jamaican government, 1965.

MEMBER: Society of American Archivists (chairman of committee on international relations, 1955-60; chairman of committee on education and training, beginning 1964), American Historical Association (chairman of committee on historical source materials, 1936-38), American Association for State and Local History, International Archives Council (honorary member); also honorary member of archivist associations in Mexico, Peru, and Venezuela; Phi Beta Kappa, Phi Delta Kappa, Pi Sigma Alpha. *Awards, honors:* Merit citation, National Civil Service League, 1955; Meritorious Service Award, General Services Administration, 1957; Waldo Gifford Leland Prize of Society of American Archivists.

WRITINGS: Modern Archives: Principles and Techniques, University of Chicago Press, 1956; *Manual de arquivas,* National Archives of Brazil, 1959; *Tecnicas descriptivos de archivos,* University of Cordoba Press, 1961; *Documentos publicos & privados: Arranjo e descripto,* National Archives of Brazil, 1963; *The Management of Archives,* Columbia University Press, 1965. Contributor to archival and historical journals.

SIDELIGHTS: Schellenberg had a speaking knowledge of German, and reading knowledge of French, Spanish, and Dutch. *Modern Archives: Principles and Techniques* has been published in Australia, Cuba, Germany, and Israel.

(Deceased)

* * *

SCHLAUCH, Margaret 1898-

PERSONAL: Born September 25, 1898; daughter of William Storb and Margaret (Brosnahan) Schlauch. *Education:* Columbia University, A.B., 1918, M.A., 1919, Ph.D., 1927. *Home:* Brzozowa 10 m. 12, Warsaw, Poland. *Office:* Department of English Philology, University of Warsaw, Warsaw, Poland.

CAREER: New York University, New York, N.Y., instructor, 1924-27, assistant professor, 1927-31, associate professor, 1931-40, professor, 1940-50; University of Warsaw, Warsaw, Poland, professor, 1951—. *Member:* Mediaeval Academy of America, Modern Language Association of America, Polish Academy of Sciences (corresponding member; neophilological committee), English Society of Hiroshima University (honorary). *Awards, honors:* Officer's rank for scholarly work, Order of Polonia Restituta, 1958; Icelandic Order of the Falcon, 1968.

WRITINGS: Chaucer's Constance and Accused Queens, New York University Press, 1927; *Medieval Narrative: A Book of Translations*, Prentice-Hall, 1928; *The Saga of the Volsungs*, Norton, 1930; *Romance in Iceland*, Princeton University Press, 1933; *The Gift of Tongues*, Viking, 1942; *Three Icelandic Sagas* (two texts), Princeton University Press, 1950; *English Medieval Literature*, Polish Scientific Publishers, 1956; *Modern English and American Poetry*, C. A. Watts, 1956; *The English Language in Modern Times*, Polish Scientific Publishers, 1959; *Antecedents of the English Novel*, Polish Scientific Publishers, 1963; *Language and the Study of Languages Today*, Polish Scientific Publishers, 1967, Oxford University Press, 1968. Contributor of articles to professional journals in the United States, England, and Poland. Writer of introductions to anthologies and brochures in fields of medieval comparative literature and linguistics, 1923—.

WORK IN PROGRESS: A popular introduction to the Old Icelandic sagas, to be published in Polish.

* * *

SCHLESINGER, Alfred Cary 1900-

PERSONAL: Born February 17, 1900, in College Point, N.Y.; son of Alfred Henry and Mary (Jones) Schlesinger; married Ethel S. Towne, June 29, 1929; children: Alfred Towne (deceased), Charles Towne, Richard Cary. *Education:* Williams College, B.A., 1921; Princeton University, M.A., 1923, Ph.D., 1924. *Politics:* Independent Democrat. *Religion:* Protestant. *Residence:* Williamstown, Mass. 01267.

CAREER: Williams College, Williamstown, Mass., instructor, became assistant professor of classics, 1924-35; Oberlin College, Oberlin, Ohio, assistant professor, 1935-47, associate professor, 1947-60, professor of classics, beginning 1960. Annual professor, American School of Classical Studies at Athens, Greece, 1952-53. *Military service:* U.S. Army Reserve, Field Artillery, 1919-37; became first lieutenant. *Member:* American Philological Association, Archaeological Institute of America, American Association of University Professors, Classical Association of the Middle West and South, Ohio Classical Conference (president, 1947-48), Phi Beta Kappa, Oberlin Rotary Club (president, 1958-59).

WRITINGS: (Editor with E. T. Sage) *Livy XII*, Heinemann, 1938; (editor) *Livy XIII*, Heinemann, 1951; (editor with Sage and R. M. Geer) *Livy XIV*, Heinemann, 1953; *Boundaries of Dionysus*, Harvard University Press, 1963. Contributor to *Classical Journal, American Journal of Philology, Transactions of American Philological Association*, and *Classical World*.

SIDELIGHTS: Schlesinger is competent in German, French, ancient Greek and Latin; he has reading knowledge of modern Greek.

* * *

SCHLIMBACH, Alice (Paula) 1898-

PERSONAL: Born September 29, 1898, in St. Trudpert, Germany; daughter of Carl Conrad (a business manager) and Lina (Erdrich) Schlimbach. *Education:* Teacher's Sem-

inary, Wuerttemberg, Germany, Teacher's Diploma, 1922; Rutgers University, M.A., 1932; New York University, Ph.D., 1940. *Home:* 156 Medford Lees, Medford, N.J. 08055.

CAREER: Rutgers University, Douglass College, New Brunswick, N.J., 1929-64, began as instructor, became professor of German and director of German Language House, professor emeritus, 1964—. *Member:* Modern Language Association of America (life), American Association of Teachers of German (life), American Association on Emeriti, National Retired Teachers Association.

WRITINGS: Kinder lernen Deutsch, Max Hueber, 1964; (editor with Erna Kritsch) *Moderne Erzaehlungen*, Appleton, 1964; *Lehrerhandbuch*, Max Hueber, 1966.

WORK IN PROGRESS: Lichtenberg and Hogarth; research in eighteenth-century literature in Germany and England.

BIOGRAPHICAL/CRITICAL SOURCES: American German Review, spring, 1954.

* * *

SCHMID, Mark J(oseph) 1901-19(?)

PERSONAL: Born December 1, 1901, in Jordan, Ore.; son of Matthias and Bernadine Schmid. *Education:* Mount Angel College, B.A., 1923; University of Rome, Ph.D., 1926; University of Washington, Seattle, post-doctoral study.

CAREER: Entered Benedictine Order, 1922, ordained Roman Catholic priest, 1928. Mount Angel Seminary, St. Benedict, Ore., librarian, 1936-52, professor of philosophy and head of department, beginning 1939. *Member:* Catholic Library Association (Northwest chairman, 1936-39), Catholic Philosophical Association (Northwest secretary-treasurer, 1939-44). *Awards, honors:* Silver Jubilee Award from Catholic Library Association (Northwest branch).

WRITINGS: Talks on Religion, Benedictine Press, 1932; *Meet After Death?*, Benedictine Press, 1934; *The Solution is Easy*, Pustet, 1942; *Sublimity: Story of an Oregon Countryside, 1850-1950*, Library Bookstore, 1951; *Mary, Full of Grace*, St. Paul Publications, 1961. Writer of film script, "They Heard the Angels Sing," for Clune Studios. Editor of *St. Joseph Magazine*, 1929-34.

WORK IN PROGRESS: A book, *A Little Below Angels*.

AVOCATIONAL INTERESTS: Landscape photography, fruit horticulture, and travel.

(Deceased)

* * *

SCHMIDT, John 1905-1969

PERSONAL: Born October 30, 1905, in Rotterdam, Netherlands; son of Johan Rudolf (a factory worker) and Dirkje (Been) Schmidt; married Zelma Hattie Dennison, May 10, 1934; children: Lucille T. (Mrs. Robert E. Doxey), Juliana M. (Mrs. Michael Scott), Zelma Ann. *Education:* Wittenberg College, A.B., 1928, B.D., 1931; University of Leipzig, graduate study, 1930; Lutheran School of Theology, Maywood, Ill., M.S.T., 1941. *Politics:* Independent Republican. *Home:* 121 Caesar Blvd., Williamsville, N.Y. 14221. *Office:* St. John Lutheran Church, 6540 Main St., Williamsville, N.Y. 14221.

CAREER: Lutheran minister in Detroit, Mich., 1931-38, and Blacksburg, Va., 1938-40; Lutheran Theological Southern Seminary, Columbia, S.C., teacher of homiletics, missions, and exposition, 1940-46; minister in Toledo, Ohio, 1946-51; Lutheran World Federation, Service to Refugees, senior representative in Frankfurt, Germany, 1951-52, director in Geneva, Switzerland, 1952-53; minister in Columbus, Ohio, 1953-58; St. John Lutheran Church, Williamsville, N.Y., minister, 1958-69. United Lutheran Church in America, former member of Board of Publications and Board of Foreign Missions. *Member:* Torch Club. *Awards, honors:* Litt.D. from Roanoke College.

WRITINGS: (Translator) Karl Heim, *The Living Fountain*, Zondervan, 1936; (translator) Karl Heim, *The Gospel of the Cross*, Zondervan, 1937; *The Cross Destroys*, Zondervan, 1937; *Strange Evangelists*, Zondervan, 1939; *The Riches of His Grace*, American Tract Society, 1940; *In His Care*, Muhlenberg Press, 1941; *Letter to Corinth*, Muhlenberg Press, 1947; *The Lutheran Confessions*, Fortress, 1956; (translator) William J. Kooiman, *Luther and the Bible*, Fortress, 1961; (translator) Karl Heim, *The Nature of Protestantism*, Fortress, 1963; *They Welcomed the Child*, Augsburg, 1965. Contributor to religious periodicals.

WORK IN PROGRESS: A book of sermons; a book on the content of preaching.

AVOCATIONAL INTERESTS: Philately.

(Died May, 1969)

* * *

SCHNEIDER, Elisabeth Wintersteen 1897-

PERSONAL: Born September 7, 1897, in Salt Lake City, Utah; daughter of Anton and Mary (Robinson) Schneider. *Education:* Smith College, A.B., 1920; University of Pennsylvania, M.A., 1926, Ph.D., 1933; Oxford University, graduate study, 1930-31. *Politics:* Democratic. *Religion:* Protestant. *Home:* 924 Jimeno Rd., Santa Barbara, Calif. 93103. *Office:* Department of English, University of California, Santa Barbara, Calif. 92706.

CAREER: Temple University, Philadelphia, Pa., instructor, 1926-33, assistant professor, 1933-39, associate professor, 1939-45, professor of English, 1945-64; University of California, Santa Barbara, visiting professor of English, 1964—. *Member:* Modern Language Association of America, American Association of University Professors, College English Association (board of directors, 1959-61; vice-president, 1961-63; president, 1963-64), Modern Humanities Research Association, Phi Beta Kappa. *Awards, honors:* Modern Language Association of America award for article, "The Wreck of the Deutschland," 1966.

WRITINGS: The Aesthetics of William Hazlitt: A Study of the Philosophical Basis of His Criticism, University of Pennsylvania Press, 1933, 2nd edition, 1952; *Aesthetic Motive,* Macmillan, 1939; (editor) *Samuel Taylor Coleridge: Selected Poetry and Prose,* Holt, 1951; *Coleridge, Opium, and Kubla Khan,* University of Chicago Press, 1953; (contributor) Carolyn and Lawrence Houtchens, editors, *English Romantic Poets and Essayists: A Review of Research and Criticism,* Modern Language Association of America, 1957, revised edition, published for Modern Language Association of America by New York University Press, 1966; (editor with Albert L. Walker and Herbert E. Childs) *The Range of Literature: An Introduction to Prose and Verse,* American Book Co., 1960, 3rd edition, Van Nostrand, 1972; *Poems and Poetry,* American Book Co., 1964; *The Dragon in the Gate: Studies in the Poetry of G. M. Hopkins,* University of California Press, 1968. Contributor of articles to literary journals, including *PMLA.*

WORK IN PROGRESS: A monograph on T. S. Eliot, tentatively entitled "Prufrock and After."

AVOCATIONAL INTERESTS: Music and gardening.

* * *

SCHNEIDER, Isidor 1896-

PERSONAL: Born August 25, 1896, in Austria-Hungary; brought to United States in 1902, became American citizen; son of Hyman (a tailor) and Sarah (Rothman) Schneider; married Helen Berlin (a self-employed editor); children: Emily Shachter. *Education:* City College of New York (now City College of the City University of New York), student, four years. *Politics:* Independent. *Home and office:* 35 West 92nd St., New York, N.Y. 10025.

CAREER: Doubleday, Page and Co., New York, N.Y., advertising department, 1919-23; Boni & Liveright, New York, N.Y., advertising manager, 1923-28; Macauley Co., New York, N.Y., editor, 1929-33; free-lance writer and editor, 1963—. *Awards, honors:* Guggenheim fellowships, 1935 and 1937.

WRITINGS: Dr. Transit (novel), Boni & Liveright, 1926; *The Temptation of Anthony and Other Poems,* Boni & Liveright, 1927; *Comrade-Mister and Other Poems,* Equinox Press, 1934; *From the Kingdom of Necessity* (novel), Putnam, 1935; *The Judas Time* (novel), Dial, 1947; (translator) *The Autobiography of Maxim Gorky,* Citadel, 1952; (editor) *The World of Love,* Braziller, 1964; (editor) *The Enlightenment: The Culture of the Eighteenth Century,* Braziller, 1965. Contributor to anthologies and yearbooks, and to periodicals. Correspondence and papers in Columbia University collections.

WORK IN PROGRESS: A novel; a book of criticism, tentatively titled *The Functions of Literature*; a volume of reminiscences on writers, critics, and publishers of the last fifty years, tentatively titled *The Literary Life.*

* * *

SCHNEIDERS, Alexander A(loysius) 1909-1968

PERSONAL: Born February 2, 1909, in Sioux City, Iowa; son of Mathias (a shoemaker) and Mary (Mootz) Schneiders; married Glen Ogle, August 11, 1934; children: Ronald, Sandra, Anne, Paul, Mary, Eileen (Mrs. Peter McHugh), Gregory. *Education:* Creighton University, Ph.B., 1930; Georgetown University, M.A., 1931, Ph.D., 1934. *Politics:* Democrat. *Religion:* Roman Catholic.

CAREER: National Archives, Washington, D.C., personnel assistant, 1935-36; Loyola University, Chicago, Ill., instructor, 1936-39, assistant professor of psychology and director of student personnel, 1939-45; University of Detroit, Detroit, Mich., associate professor, 1945-48, professor of psychology, 1948-53, director of department, 1945-53; Fordham University, New York, N.Y., professor of psychology and director of psychological services, 1953-61; Boston College, Chestnut Hill, Mass., professor of psychology, 1961-68. Marriage counselor and psychotherapist. *Member:* Inter-American Society of Psychologists, American Psychological Association, Academy of Psychologists in Marriage Counseling, American Catholic Psychological Association (president, 1952-53), New England Psychological Association, Massachusetts Psychological Association, Sigma Xi. *Awards, honors:* Family Action Award of National Catholic Welfare Conference, 1951.

WRITINGS: Outline of Rational Psychology, University Lithoprinters, 1941; *Introductory Psychology,* Rinehart,

1951; *Psychology of Adolescence*, Bruce, 1951; *Personal Adjustment and Mental Health*, Rinehart, 1955; *Personality Development and Adjustment in Adolescence*, Bruce, 1960; *The Anarchy of Feeling*, Sheed, 1963; *Personality Dynamics and Mental Health*, Holt, 1965; *Adolescents and the Challenge of Maturity*, Bruce, 1965; (with others) *Counseling the Adolescent*, Chandler, 1967. Contributor to *World Book Encyclopedia*, 1959, and *New Catholic Encyclopedia*, 1965. Editor or co-editor of proceedings of workshops and institutes.

AVOCATIONAL INTERESTS: Travel, reading, movies, selected television programs, and the legitimate theater.

(Died September 30, 1968)

* * *

SCHREIBER, Daniel 1909-

PERSONAL: Born April 18, 1909, in New York, N.Y.; son of Salaman (a businessman) and Millie (Einstoss) Schreiber; married Bernice Lewin, August 13, 1935; children: Selina (Mrs. Peter B. Morris), Lenore, Scott. *Education:* New York University, B.S., 1930; Brooklyn Law School, LL.B., 1937; City College (now City College of the City University of New York), M.S., 1945. *Politics:* Democrat. *Religion:* Jewish.

CAREER: New York (N.Y.) Board of Education, principal in secondary schools, 1950-59, coordinator of Higher Horizons Program, 1959-61; National Education Association, Washington, D.C., director of School Dropouts Project, 1961—. Consultant to Ford Foundation and Carnegie Corp. Member of advisory board of Community Talent Search, of New York Mayor's Inter-Agency Stay-In School Committee, of Council of Southern Mountains, and of Educational Seminar of Institute for Policy Studies. *Member:* American Association of School Administrators, National Association of Secondary-School Principals, National Education Association, Society for the Experimental Study of Education, American Personnel and Guidance Association, New York City Junior High School Principals Association.

WRITINGS—Editor: *The School Dropout*, National Education Association, 1964; (with B. Kaplan) *Guidance and the School Dropout*, National Education Association, 1964; *Holding Power–Large City School Systems*, National Education Association, 1964; *Profile of the School Dropout*, Random House, 1968. Contributor of articles to educational periodicals.

WORK IN PROGRESS: Design for Dropout Studies; a second book, *Role of the Teacher in the Urban Depressed Area School*.

AVOCATIONAL INTERESTS: Jewelry-making and wood turning.

* * *

SCHRIFTGIESSER, Karl 1903-

PERSONAL: Born November 12, 1903, in Boston, Mass.; son of Berthold (a reporter) and Hetty B. (Row) Schriftgiesser; married Ruth Mansfield (a reporter), 1928; children: Mrs. Peter Irvine. *Education:* Attended Roxbury Latin School and Goddard Seminary. *Politics:* Democrat. *Religion:* Episcopalian. *Home:* Londonderry, Vt. 05148. *Office:* Committee for Economic Development, 711 Fifth Ave., New York, N.Y. 10022.

CAREER: Member of editorial staffs of *Boston Post,*

Boston Evening Transcript, Washington Post, New York Times, and *Newsweek,* 1920-50; free-lance writer, 1950-56; Committee for Economic Development (non-partisan private organization), New York, N.Y., and Washington, D.C., editor and assistant information director, 1956—. *Member:* American Political Science Association, American Newspaper Guild (honorary), National Press Club (Washington, D.C.); Overseas Press Club and Coffee House (both New York).

WRITINGS: Families, Howell, Soskin, 1940; *The Amazing Roosevelt Family, 1613-1942,* Funk, 1942; *Oscar of the Waldorf,* Dutton, 1943; *The Gentleman from Massachusetts: Henry Cabot Lodge,* Little, Brown, 1944; *This Was Normalcy: An Account of Party Politics During Twelve Republican Years, 1920-1932,* Little, Brown, 1948; *The Lobbyists: The Art and Business of Influencing Lawmakers,* Little, Brown, 1951; *The Farmer from Merner: The Biography of George J. Mecherla and a History of the State Farm Insurance Companies of Bloomington, Illinois,* Random House, 1955; *Business Comes of Age,* Harper, 1960; *Business and the American Government,* Luce, 1964; *Business and Public Policy: The Role of the Committee for Economic Development, 1942-1967,* Prentice-Hall, 1967. Contributor to *Atlantic, New Republic, New Yorker, Saturday Review, New York Times,* and other periodicals.

* * *

SCHRODER, John Henry Erle 1895-

PERSONAL: Born October 24, 1895, in Hokitika, New Zealand; son of John Frederick William and Mary (Muller) Schroder; married Marjorie Winsome Young; children: Frederick Thomas Mark. *Education:* Canterbury College, University of New Zealand, B.A., 1918, M.A., 1920. *Religion:* Church of England. *Home:* 5 Wesley Rd., Wellington C.1, New Zealand.

CAREER: English master, Christchurch, New Zealand, 1919-26; assistant editor of *Sun,* Christchurch, 1927-29, of *Press,* Christchurch, 1929-49; New Zealand Broadcasting Service, Wellington, assistant director, 1949-50, director, 1959-62; Victoria University of Wellington, Wellington, conductor of tutorial classes in English literature, beginning 1962. University of Canterbury, member of council, 1928-46, chairman, 1945-47; University of New Zealand, member of senate, 1947-49. Member of National Council of Adult Education, Literary Fund Advisory Committee, Arts Advisory Committee, Queen Elizabeth II Arts Council, and Indecent Publications Tribunal.

WRITINGS: Remembering Things, Dent, 1938; *Second Appearances,* A. H. & A. W. Reed, 1959; *The Street and Other Verses,* Pegasus, 1962; *The Ways of Words,* Pegasus, 1969.

WORK IN PROGRESS: Light verse, reminiscences of boyhood in a very isolated township.

* * *

SCHROEDER, Eric 1904-

PERSONAL: Born November 20, 1904, in Dale, Cheshire, England; son of William Lawrence (a minister) and Catherine (Fargher) Schroeder; married Margaret Forbes, September 27, 1930; children: Gay Murray, Mark Cabot Waldo. *Education:* Attended Corpus Christi College, Oxford, 1923-27. *Home:* 9 Follen St., Cambridge, Mass. 02138.

CAREER: Harvard University, Fogg Museum, Cambridge, Mass., keeper of Islamic art, beginning 1938. Former director and secretary, Boston Center for Adult Education; secretary, Ralph Waldo Emerson Memorial Association.

WRITINGS: Architecture of the Early Islamic Period, Oxford University Press, 1938; *Architecture of the Seljuq Period*, Oxford University Press, 1938; (editor with R. Ettinghausen) *Iranian and Islamic* Art, University Prints, 1941; *Persian Miniatures in the Fogg Museum of Art*, Harvard University Press, 1942; *Muhammad's People*, Bond Wheelright, 1955; *Visions of Element and Other Poems*, Bond Wheelwright, 1963. Contributor to *Collier's Encyclopedia, Encyclopedia of the Arts, Oxford Poetry, Ars Islamica*, and other periodicals.

WORK IN PROGRESS: Investigation of the astrological Zodiac, and analysis of its distinct actions in single degrees.

SIDELIGHTS: Schroeder speaks French, and a little Arabic, Persian, and German. *Avocational interests:* Painting—held an exhibition at Margaret Brown Gallery, Boston, 1949; horse-training.

* * *

SCHUMANN, Elizabeth Creighton 1907-

PERSONAL: Born December 17, 1907, in Nashville, Tenn.; daughter of Wilbur Foster (a civil engineer and contractor) and Amelia (Dudley) Creighton; married William Anderson Spickard (died, 1950); married Fred Schumann (chairman of electrical engineering department, Vanderbilt University), May 29, 1960; children: (first marriage) Anderson, Amelia (Mrs. Robert P. Watson), Elizabeth. *Education:* Ward-Belmont School, student, 1923-25; Vanderbilt University, student, 1925-27; Goucher College, B.A., 1929. *Religion:* Presbyterian. *Home:* 3502 Amanda Ave., Nashville, Tenn. 37215.

CAREER: Nashville Banner, Nashville, Tenn., part-time society reporter, 1952-59. *Member:* Vanderbilt Woman's Club, Centennial Club, Junior League, Kappa Alpha Theta, Wayside Garden Club.

WRITINGS: The Secret of Big Skookum (youth book), Abingdon, 1963. Author of skits and radio scripts.

WORK IN PROGRESS: A girls' book about Guatemala in 1891, for Abingdon; a short novel, short stories, and articles.

* * *

SCHUYLER, Robert Livingston 1883-1966

PERSONAL: Born February 26, 1883, in New York, N.Y.; son of Montgomery (a journalist and architectural critic) and Katharine (Livingston) Schuyler; married Sara V. D. Keller, October 19, 1907 (deceased); children: Virginia (Mrs. Cassius Clay Halstead). *Education:* Columbia University, A.B., 1903, A.M., 1904, Ph.D., 1909. *Politics:* Democrat. *Home:* 253 Alexander St., Rochester, N.Y. 14607.

CAREER: Yale University, New Haven, Conn., instructor in history, 1906-10; Columbia University, New York, N.Y., lecturer, then assistant professor, 1910-11, associate professor, 1911-24, professor of history, 1924-42, Gouverneur Morris Professor of History, 1942-51, Gouverneur Morris Professor emeritus, 1951-66. Visiting professor at Yale University, 1926, Hobart College, 1953-54, University of Houston, 1962. *Member:* American Historical Association (president, 1951), American Philosophical Society,

Century Association, Conference on British Studies, Phi Beta Kappa. *Awards, honors:* L.H.D., Union College, 1937; Litt.D., Columbia University, 1954; John F. Lewis Prize of American Philosophical Society, 1954, for essay, "British Imperial Theory and American Territorial Policy."

WRITINGS: The Transition in Illinois from British to American Government, Columbia University Press, 1909, AMS Press, 1966; *A Syllabus of American History,* Columbia University Press, 1913; *The Constitution of the United States: An Historical Survey of Its Formation,* Macmillan, 1923; *Parliament and the British Empire: Some Constitutional Controversies Concerning Imperial Legislative Jurisdiction,* Columbia University Press, 1929; (editor) *Josiah Tucker: A Selection from His Economic and Political Writings,* Columbia University Press, 1931; (reviser) George Burton Adams, *A Constitutional History of England,* Henry Holt, 1934; *The Fall of the Old Colonial System: A Study in British Free Trade, 1770-1870,* Oxford University Press, 1945; (editor with Herman Ausubel) *The Making of English History,* Dryden Press, 1952; (with Corinne C. Weston) *British Constitutional History Since 1832,* Van Nostrand, 1957; (editor) *Frederic William Maitland, Historian: Selections from His Writings,* University of California Press, 1960; (editor with Weston) *Cardinal Comments in British History,* Van Nostrand, 1961. Contributor of essays, articles, and reviews to journals and other publications. Managing editor: *Political Science Quarterly,* 1919-21; "Columbia Studies in History, Economics and Public Law," 1923-28; *American Historical Review,* 1936-41; *Dictionary of American Biography,* 1954-58.

WORK IN PROGRESS: Selecting essays, articles, reviews, and other of his writings over the past fifty years, to be published as a collection.

(Died August 15, 1966)

* * *

SCHWIEBERT, Ernest G(eorge) 1895-

PERSONAL: Surname is pronounced *Swee*-bert; born October 17, 1895, in Deshler, Ohio; son of Fred H. and Emma (Freytag) Schwiebert; married Joyce Gayle Tustin (a historian), August 20, 1930 (deceased); children: Ernest George, Jr. *Education:* Capital University, B.A., 1921, seminary diploma, 1924; Ohio State University, M.A., 1923; University of Chicago, graduate study, 1925-26; Cornell University, Ph.D., 1930. *Politics:* Independent. *Religion:* Lutheran. *Home:* 104 Library Place, Princeton, New Jersey 08540.

CAREER: Capital University, Columbus, Ohio, instructor in history, 1923-25; St. Olaf College, Northfield, Minn., assistant professor of history, 1926-27; Valparaiso University, Valparaiso, Ind., professor of history and head of department of social science, 1930-46; Wittenberg College, Springfield, Ohio, professor of history, 1947-50, on leave serving with U.S. State Department in Germany and as Gast Professor at University of Erlangen, 1948-50; U.S. Air Force, Washington, D.C., scientific historian, 1951-65; University of Iowa, Iowa City, professor of history, 1965-66; University of Florida, Gainesville, professor of history, 1966-67; Lutheran Theological Seminary, Gettysburg, Pa., professor of history, 1967-68; Folger Shakespeare Library, consultant, 1970; Princeton Theological Seminary, fellow, 1974—. Summer lecturer at University of Michigan, 1935, 1938; visiting professor at Carleton College, 1943-44, Northwestern University, 1946-47. Executive director of

Foundation for Reformation Research, 1958-63. *Military service:* U.S. Army, American Expeditionary Forces, 1918-19.

MEMBER: American Historical Association, American Society of Church History, (president, 1946-47), American Society for Reformation Research (co-founder; first president, 1946-48), Jahrbuch der Luthergesellschaft, International Luther Congress, Renaissance Society of America. *Awards, honors:* Martha Kinney Cooper Ohioana Library Book Award for best biography of the year, 1951, for *Luther and His Times.*

WRITINGS: Reformation Lectures Delivered at Valparaiso University, [Valparaiso, Indiana], 1937; *Luther and His Times,* Concordia, 1950; *A History of U.S. Air Force Ballistic Missiles,* Praeger, 1965; (contributor) Carl S. Meyer, editor, *Luther for an Ecumenical Age,* Concordia, 1967. Contributor to *Library Quarterly, Church History,* and *Archiv fuer Reformationschichte.*

WORK IN PROGRESS: A revision of *Luther and His Times; Luther and the Universities;* studies in medieval paleography.

SIDELIGHTS: Schwiebert reads and speaks German fluently. He surveyed European libraries in fourteen countries for the Foundation for Reformation Research in 1959; with the aid of European teams organized in Germany and Switzerland, some 750,000 pages of rare Reformation materials were put on microfilm for research use in America. *Avocational interests:* Trout fishing.

*   *   *

SCOTT, Robert Lee, Jr. 1908-

PERSONAL: Born April 12, 1908, in Macon, Ga.; son of Robert Lee and Ola (Burckhalter) Scott; married Catharine Green, September 1, 1934; children: Robin Lee (Mrs. Bruce Fraser). *Education:* United States Military Academy, B.S., 1932; National War College, M.S., 1954. *Politics:* Republican. *Religion:* Episcopalian. *Home:* Phoenix Towers, 2201 North Central Ave., Phoenix, Ariz. 85004. *Office:* Sun Life Assurance Company of Canada, Montreal, Quebec, Canada.

CAREER: Career officer with U.S. Air Force; Commanding Officer, 23rd Fighter Group, "Flying Tigers," China, under General Claire Lee Chennault, 1942-43; served as Commander, Williams Air Force Base, jet training center, and Luke Air Force Base, both in Arizona; U.S. Air Force, director of information, 1955-57; retired after thirty years in 1957, as brigadier general; received two Silver Stars, three Distinguished Flying Crosses, British Flying Cross, Distinguished Service Cross, Chinese Order Cloud Banner, Chinese Hum-Whei, and Ten Star Dragon. Lecturer on anti-Communism, 1957-60. *Member:* Military Order of the World Wars, Falcon Society, Fourteenth Air Force Association, American Fighter Ace Association, Association of Graduates, United States Military Academy, Professional Hunters Association of East Africa (honorary).

WRITINGS: God Is My Co-Pilot, Scribner, 1943; *Damned To Glory,* Scribner, 1944; *Runway to the Sun,* Scribner, 1945; *Between the Elephant's Eyes,* Dodd, 1954; *Look of the Eagle,* Dodd, 1955; *Samburu,* Dodd, 1957; *Tiger in the Sky,* Ballantine, 1959; *Flying Tiger: Chennault of China,* Doubleday, 1959; *Boring A Hole in the Sky,* Random House, 1961. Contributor to *The Diplomat.*

BIOGRAPHICAL/CRITICAL SOURCES: The Diplomat, October, 1961.

SCOTT-MONCRIEFF, George (Irving) 1910-

PERSONAL: Born April 9, 1910, in Edinburgh, Scotland; son of Colin William (a clergyman) and Constance (Lunn) Scott-Moncrieff; married Agnes Shearer, March, 1934 (died, 1943); married Eileen Ward, January 20, 1962; children: (first marriage) Lesley Jean (Mrs. M. Peter Findlay), Colin Michael, Gavin Charles; (second marriage) Ian James, Alan More, Simon Hew, Colin Charles. *Education:* Self-educated. *Politics:* Scottish Nationalist. *Religion:* Catholic. *Home:* Traquair Mill, Innerleithen, Peeblesshire, Scotland.

CAREER: New Alliance, Edinburgh, Scotland, editor, 1939-45; Scottish Council of the National Buildings Record, Edinburgh, Scotland, secretary, 1941-45. *Member:* Royal Institute of Architects (Scotland; honorary associate), Society of Authors, Scottish Arts Club. *Awards, honors:* Atlantic Award, 1947; Arts Council Award, 1954.

WRITINGS: Cafe Bar, Wishart, 1932; *Tinkers' Wind: The Saga of a Cheapjack,* Wishart, 1933; (editor and author of introduction) *Scottish Country* (fifteen essays by Scottish authors), Lawrence & Wishart, 1935; (with Robert Gibbings) *A Book of Uncommon Prayer* (includes woodcuts by Gibbings, verses by Scott-Moncrieff), Methuen, 1936; (editor) *The Stones of Scotland,* Batsford, 1938; *The Lowlands of Scotland,* Scribner, 1939, 3rd edition, 1949; (with Eric Parker) *Landmarks Given to the People* (includes "In England and Wales," by Parker, and "In Scotland," by Scott-Moncrieff), Longmans, Green, 1946; *Edinburgh,* Batsford, 1947, 3rd edition, Oliver & Boyd, 1965, International Publications Service, 1966; *Looking at Scottish Buildings,* Serif, 1947; *Death's Bright Shadow,* Wingate, 1948; (author of introduction and captions) Robert M. Adam, *Scotland: Rivers and Streams,* Hopetown Press, 1948; *Living Traditions of Scotland,* published for Council of Industrial Design, Scottish Committee, by H.M.S.O., 1951; *The Scottish Islands,* Batsford, 1952, 2nd edition, Oliver & Boyd, 1961, Simmons-Boardman, 1964; *Fotheringhay* (three-act play), Mercat Cross, 1953; *Burke Street,* Paterson, 1956; *Scotland's Dowry,* preface by Her Majesty, Queen Elizabeth, the Queen Mother, published for National Trust for Scotland by Paterson, 1956; *Catholic Edinburgh,* Catholic Truth Society of Scotland, 1957; (author of prologue and text) *Presenting Edinburgh—The Royal Burgh: Thirty Photographic Studies of Old and New Edinburgh,* Oliver & Boyd, 1958; *This Day* ("reflections on one man's spiritual life"), Hollis & Carter, 1959, Helicon, 1960; *The Mirror and the Cross: Scotland and the Catholic Faith,* Burnes & Oates, 1960, Helicon, 1961; (author of introduction and text) *Scotland: Land of Colour,* Simmons-Boardman, 1961; (with A. F. Kersting) *Portrait of Edinburgh: A Selection of Photographs* (includes photographs by Kersting, text by Scott-Moncrieff), Batsford, 1961; *Scottish Border Abbeys,* H.M.S.O., 1964; *The Beauty of Scotland in Colour,* Batsford, 1965, Soccer, 1966.

Plays: "Fiddler Calls the Tune"; "Just the Thing"; "The Alchemist's Daughter"; "Blood Upon the Rose"; other plays for the theatre, radio, and television. Contributor of articles and reviews to *Glasgow Herald, Tablet, Month, Times Literary Supplement,* and other newspapers and journals.

*   *   *

SCOUTEN, Arthur Hawley 1910-

PERSONAL: Born February 15, 1910, in Baton Rouge, La.; son of Oren Miller (a clergyman) and Margaret (Frasier) Scouten; married Josephine Rebecca Bradshaw; children: Margaret, Ellen Bradshaw, Robert Edward Lee. *Education:* Louisiana State University, B.A., 1935, M.A., 1938, Ph.D., 1942. *Politics:* Democrat. *Religion:* Baptist. *Home:* Callao, Va. *Office:* 207 College Hall, University of Pennsylvania, Philadelphia, Pa.

CAREER: University of Texas, Austin, instructor in English, 1943-46; Auburn University, Auburn, Ala., assistant professor of English, 1946-47; University of Pennsylvania, Philadelphia, associate professor, 1950-60, professor of English, beginning 1960. *Member:* Society for Theatre Research, Modern Language Association of America, American Association of University Professors. *Awards, honors:* Fellow, Folger Shakespeare Library, 1952; Ford Foundation fellow, 1953-54; Guggenheim fellow, 1954-55.

WRITINGS: (Editor, with Leo Hughes) *Ten English Farces*, University of Texas Press, 1948, reprinted, Books for Libraries, 1970; (contributor of Part 3) *The London Stage*, two volumes, Southern Illinois University Press, 1961; (editor) Teerink Herman, *A Bibliography of The Writings of Jonanthan Swift*, 2nd edition (Scouten was not connected with original edition), University of Pennsylvania Press, 1963; (contributor of Part 1, with Emmett Avery and William B. VanLennep) *The London Stage*, one volume, Southern Illinois University Press, 1965. Contributor of about thirty articles on Swift, Defoe, and on London theaters to learned journals.

WORK IN PROGRESS: Stage history of London theaters in the eighteenth century.

AVOCATIONAL INTERESTS: American Civil War.

* * *

SCULL, Florence Doughty 1905-

PERSONAL: Born June 16, 1905, in Somers Point, N.J.; daughter of James English and Ada (Doughty) Scull. *Education:* Trenton Normal School, student, 1922-24; Columbia University, B.S., 1931, M.A., 1934; graduate study at University of California, Berkeley, Rutgers University, and Columbia University. *Home:* 41 East Meyran Ave., Somers Point, N.J. 18244.

CAREER: Elementary school teacher in New Jersey and Connecticut, 1924-34; superintendent of schools, Somers Point, N.J., 1934-46; elementary school principal, New Brunswick, N.J., 1946-64. *Member:* National Education Association (life member), American Association of University Women, Daughters of the American Revolution, New Jersey Historical Society, New Jersey Education Association, New Jersey Retired Educators Association, New Jersey Audubon Society, Historical Society of Pennsylvania, Atlantic County (N.J.) Historical Society, Art Center (Atlantic City).

WRITINGS: *Bear Teeth for Courage*, Van Nostrand, 1964.

WORK IN PROGRESS: A Time to Remember, the story of an English lad indentured to a New Jersey manufacturer in 1775, completed and awaiting publication; *John Dickinson Sounds the Alarm.*

* * *

SEATON, Don Cash(ius) 1902-

PERSONAL: Born January 31, 1902, in Canton, Ill.; son of C. M. C. and Anna (M.) Seaton; married Louise Shoop, 1928. *Education:* University of Illinois, B.S., 1925, M.A.,

1936; Columbia University, graduate study, summer, 1938; New York University, Ed.D., 1947. *Religion:* Presbyterian. *Office:* University of Kentucky, Lexington, Ky. 40506.

CAREER: University of Illinois, Champaign, assistant professor and track coach, 1933-37; Illinois State Department, Springfield, state director of health, physical education, and safety, 1937-42; New York (N.Y.) Public Schools, fellow and coordinator of safety education, 1945-47; University of Kentucky, Lexington, head of department of physical education, 1947—. *Military service:* U.S. Navy, 1942-45; became lieutenant commander. *Member:* American Association for Health, Physical Education, and Recreation (fellow), College of Sports Medicine (fellow), National Track Coaches Association, American Association of University Professors, College Physical Education Association, Phi Delta Kappa, Delta Theta Epsilon, Sigma Chi Fraternity, United Cerebral Palsy Association (member of board), Kentucky Rehabilitation Center (member of board), Rotary International (member of board), Lexington Country Club, Spindletop Hall, University Faculty Club. *Awards, honors:* Distinguished service award, Kentucky Association for Health, Physical Education, and Recreation; Southern District honor award, American Association for Health, Physical Education, and Recreation.

WRITINGS: (Co-author) *Safety in the World of Today,* Beckley-Cardy, 1941; *Safety in Sports,* Prentice-Hall, 1948; (with others) *Physical Education Handbook,* Prentice-Hall, 1951, 4th edition, with teacher's guide, 1965, 5th edition, 1969; (co-author) *Safety Challenges You,* Beckley-Cardy, 1953; (with others) *Basic Book of Sports,* Prentice-Hall, 1956; (with Herbert J. Stack and Bernard I. Loft) *The Administration and Supervision of Safety Education,* Macmillan, 1968. Contributor of articles to professional journals.

* * *

SEAVER, George (Fenn) 1890-

PERSONAL: Born July 23, 1890, in Cheltenham, England; son of William (a clergyman) and Emily (Parsonage) Seaver. *Education:* St. Edmund Hall, Oxford, M.A., 1912; University of London, B.D., 1925; University of Dublin, D.Litt., 1948. *Home:* Donegal, Ireland.

CAREER: Assistant native commissioner, Northern Rhodesia, 1919-24; ordained to ministry of Church of England, 1925; St. Aidan's College, Birkenhead, England, lecturer, 1933-42; dean of Ossory and rector of Kilkenny, 1950-57; canon of St. Patrick's Cathedral, Dublin, Ireland, 1951-57; University of Dublin, Dublin, Ireland, deputy professor of Biblical Greek, 1958. *Military service:* British Army, Army Service Corps and Infantry, attached to Royal Air Force, 1914-18; lieutenant. Royal Observer Corps, 1939-45. *Member:* Royal Irish Academy, Royal Geographical Society (fellow), Royal Institute of Antiquaries in Ireland (fellow).

WRITINGS: Bam: The Story of An African Boy, Oxford University Press, 1925; *Edward Wilson of the Antarctic,* J. Murray, 1933, reprinted, 1963; *Edward Wilson: Nature-Lover,* J. Murray, 1937, Dutton, 1938; *"Birdie" Bowers of the Antarctic,* J. Murray, 1938; *Scott of the Antarctic,* J. Murray, 1940; (with N. Cantlie) *Sir James Cantlie,* J. Murray, 1939; *Albert Schweitzer: Christian Revolutionary,* J. Clarke, 1944, Harper, 1946, revised edition, A. & C. Black, 1955, Harper, 1956; *Albert Schweitzer: The Man and His Mind,* Harper, 1947, 6th definitive edition, A. & C. Black, 1969; *The Faith of Edward Wilson,* J. Murray, 1948, reprinted, 1957; *Albert Schweitzer: A Vindication*, J. Clarke, 1950, Beacon, 1951.

Nicolas Berdyaev: An Introduction to His Thought, Harper, 1950; *Francis Younghusband: Explorer and Mystic*, J. Murray, 1952; *David Livingstone: His Life and Letters*, Harper, 1957; (with Coleman Jennings) *Tales of Brother Douglas*, Mowbray & Co., 1960; *John Allen Fitzgerald Gregg: Archbishop*, Faith Press, 1963; *Apsley Cherry-Garrard: A Memoir*, Chatto & Windus, 1965; (author of introduction) Apsley Cherry-Garrard, *The Worst Journey in the World*, new edition, Chatto & Windus, 1965.

SIDELIGHTS: Seaver is competent in Latin, Greek, and Hebrew. He has traveled in central Africa, on the Continent, in Canada, and the United States. *Avocational interests:* Philosophy and poetry.

*   *   *

SEBALD, William J(oseph) 1901-

PERSONAL: Born November 5, 1901, in Baltimore, Md.; son of Frank Joseph (a physician) and Elizabeth (Buerkholz) Sebald; married Edith Frances deBecker, May 14, 1927. *Education:* Attended Baltimore Polytechnic Institute; U.S. Naval Academy, B.Sc., 1922; University of Maryland, LL.B., 1933 (later converted to J.D.). *Home:* 245 Spring Line Dr., Naples, Fla. 33940. *Agent:* Collins-Knowlton-Wing, Inc., 60 East 56th St., New York, N.Y. 10022.

CAREER: U.S. Navy, commissioned officer, 1922-30, assigned as language officer, U.S. Embassy, Tokyo, Japan, 1925-28; resigned from Navy and entered law school, 1930; private practice of law, Kobe, Japan, 1933-39, Washington, D.C., 1939-41; returned to active duty with U.S. Navy, 1941-45, organized and headed Combat Intelligence Division for Pacific Area, 1943-45, and became captain; U.S. Department of State, special assistant in Auxiliary Foreign Service, 1945-47, career officer in Foreign Service, 1947-61, with posts as chief of Diplomatic Section, General Headquarters, Supreme Commander of the Allied Powers in Japan (SCAP) deputy for the Supreme Commander and chairman of Allied Council for Japan, 1947-52, U.S. political adviser to SCAP, with personal rank of ambassador, 1950-52, U.S. Ambassador to Burma, 1952-54, deputy assistant Secretary of State for Far Eastern Affairs, Washington, D.C., 1954-57, and Ambassador to Australia, 1957-61; resigned ambassadorship, 1961, and retired from Foreign Service. Japanese adviser to U.S. delegation, Japanese Peace Conference, San Francisco, 1951; Far Eastern adviser to U.S. delegation, Southeast Asia Treaty Organization (SEATO) Conference, Manila, 1954. Member of Maryland, District of Columbia, and U.S. Supreme Court bars.

MEMBER: Asiatic Society of Japan (former president), Japan-American Society of Washington (former president), Washington Institute of Foreign Affairs, American Foreign Service Association, U.S. Naval Academy Alumni Association (life member), Masons, Naples Yacht Club. *Awards, honors*—Military: Legion of Merit, World War II. Civilian: First Class Order of the Rising Sun with Grand Cordon (Japan), 1962; LL.D., University of Maryland, 1949.

WRITINGS: (Translator and annotator) *Civil Code of Japan*, J. L. Thompson, 1934; (translator and annotator) *Criminal Code of Japan*, Japan Chronicle Press, 1936; *A Selection of Japan's Emergency Legislation*, Japan Chronicle Press, 1937; *Principal Tax Laws of Japan*, Japan

Chronicle Press, 1938; *Commercial Code of Japan*, U.S. Army, 1945; (with Russell Brines) *With MacArthur in Japan*, Norton, 1965; (with C. Nelson Spinks) *Japan: Prospects, Options, and Opportunities*, American Enterprise Institute, 1967. Also author of unpublished work, "Burma Diary," 1972.

SIDELIGHTS: Sebald is fluent in Japanese and German; visited every country of the Far East in an official capacity (traveled widely in Asia at other times in an unofficial capacity), has traveled extensively in Europe, and went to Antarctica in 1958.

*   *   *

SEDGWICK, Walter (Bradbary) 1885-

PERSONAL: Born August 16, 1885, in Hyde, Cheshire, England; married Muriel Roberts; children: Monica. *Education:* Hertford College, Oxford, M.A., 1909. *Residence:* Scarborough, England.

CAREER: Began as lecturer in classics at University of Bristol, Bristol, England, 1908; senior classical master at Stockport Grammar School, Stockport, Cheshire, England, 1908-14, at Wyggeston Grammar School, Leicester, England, 1914-45; lecturer in classics at University of Leicester, Leicester, England, 1934-50, University of Manchester, Manchester, England, 1950-54. *Member:* Classical Association, Lancashire Dialect Society, Scarborough Chamber Music Club, Leicester Chamber Music Club.

WRITINGS: (Editor) Petronius, *Cena Trimalchionis* [and] Seneca, *Apocolocyntosis*, Clarendon Press, 1925, 2nd edition, 1950; *Johannis Historia* (Latin reader), G. Bell, 1931; (editor) Plautus, *Amphitruo*, Manchester University Press, 1960. Contributor of nearly one hundred articles on classical, patristic, and medieval authors, and comparative literary criticism to English, American, German, Dutch, French, and Belgian journals. Former editor of *Ensemble*, a journal of Leicester Chamber Music Club.

WORK IN PROGRESS: Textual criticism of Tertullian.

*   *   *

SEEMAN, Elizabeth (Brickel) 1904-

PERSONAL: Born May 2, 1904, in Chicago, Ill.; daughter of William Henry (a realtor) and Anna Florence (Perin) Brickel; married Ernest Albright Seeman (a writer), May 22, 1937. *Education:* Attended Cincinnati Art Academy and Art Student's League, New York, N.Y. *Home address:* Tumblin' Creek, R.D. 2, Erwin, Tenn. 37650.

CAREER: Onetime commercial artist, working mainly on greeting card designs, in Cincinnati, Ohio, New York, N.Y., and Chicago, Ill.; now writer, subsistence farmer, and keeper of library for mountain children. *Awards, honors:* Honor Award, *New York Herald Tribune* Children's Spring Book Festival, 1961, for *The Talking Dog and the Barking Man*.

WRITINGS: The Talking Dog and the Barking Man (children's book), F. Watts, 1961; *In the Arms of the Mountain* (autobiographical), Crown, 1961.

WORK IN PROGRESS: Children's stories; a boy's adventure story, based on research in survival techniques and on the archaeology of the Southwest; a short story for adults.

SIDELIGHTS: Elizabeth Seeman lived on a Colorado cattle ranch as a child, and has spent more than twenty years in a cabin far back in the Smoky Mountains. The

Seemans maintain a library in their cabin for mountain children; books for the library have been received from school children, teachers, and librarians all over the country. *Avocational interests:* Hiking, canoeing, international politics, everyday people; Smoky Mountain folklore, history, and plants.

BIOGRAPHICAL/CRITICAL SOURCES: Scholastic, September 30, 1965, and May 6, 1966.

* * *

SEGGER, Sydney Walter 1902-19(?)

PERSONAL: Born February 22, 1902, in Norwich, Norfolk, England; son of Alfred Bitting (a printing house secretary) and Ellen (Williment) Segger; married Phyllis Sutcliffe, April 7, 1932; children: Jennifer, Patricia Joy. *Education:* Corpus Christi College, Cambridge, B.A. (honors), 1924, M.A., 1927. *Religion:* Nonconformist. *Home:* 42 Glenferness Ave., Bournemouth, Hampshire, England.

CAREER: Modern language master at Dauntsey's School, Wiltshire, England, 1925-28. Mill Hill School, London, 1928-42, and Oundle School, Peterborough, Northhamptonshire, 1943-45; British Broadcasting Corp., London, England, supervisor of information bureau, Monitoring Service, 1942-43; Bournemouth School, Bournemouth, England, head of modern language department, 1945-60. Visiting summer instructor at University of Strasbourg, 1925, University of Tours, 1926, 1927, and University of Lausanne, 1937. *Member:* Royal Society of St. George, Organization Scolaire Franco-Britannique (director of Bournemouth group, 1948-58), Cercle Francais de Bournemouth (president, 1946-48), Linguists Club (London). *Awards, honors:* Officier d'Academie (France).

WRITINGS: (With H. P. Monclin) *Model French Proses for Scholarship Candidates,* University of London Press, 1952; *Themes Modeles,* Cambridge University Press, 1964.

WORK IN PROGRESS: A book of advanced French composition.

(Deceased)

* * *

SELLERS, Robert Victor 1894-

PERSONAL: Born October 18, 1894, in Scholes, Cleckheaton, Yorkshire, England; son of Richard and Martha Ann (Bolland) Sellers; married Irene Oesterley, April 14, 1931; children: Rosemary (Mrs. Llewelyn Arthur Rhys), Susan. *Education:* St. Catharine's College, Cambridge, B.A., 1916; Wells Theological College, B.D., 1927, D.D., 1939. *Home:* Slade Cottage, Maddocks Slade, Burnham-on-Sea, Somersetshire, England.

CAREER: Began as school master; ordained deacon, Church of England, 1917, priest, 1920; assistant curate and vicar in Yorkshire, England, 1919-31; St. Augustine's House, Reading, Berkshire, England, warden, 1931-48; King's College, University of London, London, England, professor of theology, 1948-55, fellow, 1954—; Wells Cathedral, Wells, Somersetshire, England, chancellor and canon, 1955-61, treasurer, 1955, prebendary of Wiveliscombe, 1955—. Select preacher, Cambridge University, 1941, 1957; Boyle Lecturer, 1950-52.

WRITINGS: Eustathius of Antioch, Cambridge University Press, 1928; *Two Ancient Christologies,* S.P.C.K., 1940; *The Council of Chalcedon,* S.P.C.K., 1953. Contributor to theological journals.

WORK IN PROGRESS: Primitive Christological traditions.

* * *

SELLEW, Gladys 1887-

PERSONAL: Born July 29, 1887, in Cincinnati, Ohio; daughter of Ralph Hooker and Rachel Ella (Moore) Sellew. *Education:* University of Cincinnati, A.B., 1918, B.S. (School of Nursing and Health), 1920, M.A., 1921; Catholic University of America, Ph.D., 1938. *Politics:* Republican. *Religion:* Catholic. *Home:* 280 Elm St., Oberlin, Ohio 44074.

CAREER: University and hospital teaching and nursing administrative posts in Cincinnati and Cleveland, Ohio, 1920-30; Cook County School of Nursing, Chicago, Ill., assistant dean of nursing and pediatric service, 1930-33; Catholic University of America, Washington, D.C., staff of department of sociology, 1935-42; College of St. Catherine, St. Paul, Minn., director of department of nursing, 1942-47; Rosary College, River Forest, Ill., began as associate professor, became professor and chairman of department of sociology and social work, 1947-56; University of Maryland, College Park, professor of pediatric nursing, 1956-58. Visiting lecturer at University of Maryland, 1947-56, University of Pennsylvania, 1959.

WRITINGS: Pediatric Nursing. Including the Nursing Care of the Well Infant and Child, Saunders, 1926, 4th edition published as *The Child in Nursing,* 1936, 5th edition published as *Nursing of Children,* 1942, 6th edition (with Sister Annette Walters and Sister Ann Harvey), 1948, 7th edition (with Mary F. Pepper), 1953; *A Textbook of Ward Administration,* Saunders, 1930; *A Deviant Social Situation: A Court,* Catholic University of America, 1938; (with Paul H. Furfey) *Sociology and Social Problems in Nursing Service,* Saunders, 1941, 4th edition published as *Sociology and Its Use in Nursing Service,* 1957, 5th edition, 1962; (with C. J. Nuesse) *A History of Nursing,* Mosby, 1946, 3rd edition (with Sister Mary Ethelreda Ebel), 1955; (with Florence M. Gipe) *Ward Administration and Clinical Teaching,* Mosby, 1949; (with Furfey and William T. Gaughan) *An Introduction to Sociology,* Harper, 1958; (with Dorothy R. Marlow) *Textbook of Pediatric Nursing,* Saunders, 1961, 2nd edition, 1965. Contributor to *American Journal of Nursing.*

SIDELIGHTS: Miss Sellew created a fifteen-house, low-cost housing project in Oberlin, Ohio.

* * *

SEN GUPTA, Rajeswar 1908-

PERSONAL: Born February 1, 1908, in Goila, Barisal, Bengal, India; son of Hari Charan (an estate owner) and Khiroda Sundari Das Gupta) Sen Gupta; married Santi Lata, September 2, 1935; children: Ranu, Suchitra, Malobika (daughters); Dipak (son). *Education:* Brojo Mohan College, University of Calcutta, B.Sc. (with distinction), 1930; University of Manchester, B. Sc. Tech., and associate of Manchester College of Science and Technology, 1936. *Religion:* Hindu. *Home:* Dudhwala Bungalow, 15/221 Civil Lines, Kampur, Uttar Pradesh, India.

CAREER: Benares Cotton and Silk Mills Ltd., Benares, India, apprentice, then supervisor, 1931-33; Mahalaxmi Cotton Mills Ltd., Palta, West Bengal, India, weaving master, 1936-37; Rampooria Cotton Mills Ltd., Serampore, West Bengal, India, weaving master, 1937-38; Ashoka Mills

Ltd., Ahmedabad, India, in charge of weaving department, 1938-41; Government of India Defence Production Organisation, Chief Inspectorate of Textiles and Clothing, Kanpur, India, senior scientific officer, 1941-66. Examiner in textiles for Indian universities and institutes; Indian Standard Institute, member of textile subcommittees, 1952-66. *Member:* Scientific Workers' Association, Science and Technology Society, Textile Institute (Manchester, England), Textile Association (India; managing committee, northern India branch, 1957—).

WRITINGS: Weaving Calculations, D. B. Taraporevala & Sons, 1944, 5th edition, revised and enlarged, 1971; *Yarn Preparation,* Popular Prakashan, Volume I, 1951, 2nd edition, revised and enlarged, 1963, Volume II, 1954, 2nd edition, revised and enlarged, 1970; *Weaver's Pocket Book,* Popular Prakashan, 1954, 2nd edition, revised and enlarged, 1962. Contributor to *Textile India* and to other textile journals. Editor, 14th and 24th issues of *All India Textile Conference,* Textile Association (India).

*   *   *

SENSABAUGH, George Frank 1906-

PERSONAL: Born July 15, 1906, in Dublin, Tex.; son of Leonidas Franklin (an educator) and Effie (Frank) Sensabaugh; married Elizabeth Kathryn Ake, December 20, 1938; children: George Frank, Jr., David Ake. *Education:* Vanderbilt University, B.A., 1928; University of North Carolina, M.A., 1930, Ph.D., 1934. *Politics:* Democrat. *Religion:* Methodist. *Home:* 1350 Byron St., Palo Alto, Calif.

CAREER: Stanford University, Stanford, Calif., instructor, 1935-37, assistant professor, 1937-43, associate professor, 1943-47, professor of English, 1947-71, professor emeritus, 1971—, acting executive head of department, 1955-56. Visiting summer professor at University of Texas, 1947, University of California, 1950; member of advisory committee, Conference on College Composition and Communication, 1959. *Member:* Modern Language Association of America, American Academy of Political and Social Science, Renaissance Society of America, Milton Society of America, Philological Association of the Pacific Coast. *Awards, honors:* Fellow of Henry E. Huntington Library, 1942, 1950-51; Guggenheim fellow, 1944-45; Fellow of Folger Library, 1963.

WRITINGS: The Tragic Muse of John Ford, Stanford University Press, 1944, reprinted, Benjamin Blom, 1965; (with V. K. Whitaker) *Purposeful Prose,* Holt, 1951; *That Grand Whig, Milton,* Stanford University Press, 1952, reprinted, Benjamin Blom, 1967; (editor and contributor) *The Study of English in California Schools,* Stanford University Press, 1952; *Milton in Early America,* Princeton University Press, 1964. Contributor to *World Book Encyclopedia.* Member of editorial board of *Studies in English Literature.*

*   *   *

SEWNY, Kathryn Wiehe 1909-

PERSONAL: First syllable of surname rhymes with "dew"; born April 8, 1909, in New York, N.Y.; daughter of Theodore Charles (a businessman) and May (Baird) Wiehe; married Vahan D. Sewny (an artist and writer), November 25, 1933. *Education:* Wellesley College, A.B., 1929; Columbia University, B.S. in L.S., 1930. *Office:* Columbia University Press, 2960 Broadway, New York, N.Y.

CAREER: Columbia University, School of Library Service, New York, N.Y., reviser, 1930-31; New School for Social Research, New York, N.Y., librarian, 1931-32; Brooklyn College Library, Brooklyn, N.Y., head of cataloging, 1932-37; Columbia University, School of Library Service, head reviser, 1938-40, curator, 1940-48, editorial assistant, 1948-50; City College Library, New York, N.Y., assistant to librarian, 1951-55; Columbia University Press, New York, N.Y., editor, beginning 1956. *Member:* American Library Association, New York Library Association, New York Library Club.

WRITINGS: (With W. E. Weld) *Herbert E. Hawkes,* Columbia University Press, 1958; (editor with William F. Bernhardt) *Granger's Index to Poetry: Supplement,* 5th edition, (Sewny was not associated with earlier editions), Columbia University Press, 1967. Editor, with Edwin N. Iino, of *Directory of Social and Health Agencies of New York City,* Columbia University Press, 1956, sole editor of 1958, 1960, 1962, and 1965 editions.

*   *   *

SEYMOUR, Alta Halverson

PERSONAL: Born in Deer Park, Wis.; daughter of Gilbert (a merchant) and Matilda (Finke) Halverson; married George Seymour (an economic consultant), June 12, 1922; children: Jean (Mrs. Robert Gardner). *Education:* University of Minnesota, B.A., 1921, M.A., 1923. *Home:* 12 Elizabeth Ct. W., Oak Park, Ill. 60302.

CAREER: Former owner and manager of public stenographic company in Pasadena and Los Angeles, Calif.; free-lance writer, mainly of juveniles. *Member:* Chicago Children's Reading Round Table, Nineteenth Century Club (Oak Park, Ill.; chairman of literature department, 1943-44), Phi Beta Kappa, Lambda Alpha Psi, Delta Phi Lambda. *Awards, honors:* Honorable mention, Midland Authors, for *Toward Morning,* as one of three best juveniles from Middle West in 1961.

WRITINGS: Timothy Keeps a Secret, Grosset, 1939; *On the Edge of the Fjord* (Junior Literary Guild selection), Westminster, 1944; *Galewood Crossing,* Westminster, 1945; *The Tangled Skein* (Junior Literary Guild selection), Westminster, 1946; *A Grandma for Christmas,* Westminster, 1946; *At Snug Harbor Inn,* Westminster, 1947; *The Secret of the Hidden Room,* Westminster, 1948; *The Christmas Stove: A Story of Switzerland,* Follett, 1951; *Arne and the Christmas Star* (about Norway), Follett, 1952; *The Christmas Donkey* (France), Follett, 1953; *Kaatje and the Christmas Compass* (Holland), Follett, 1954; *The Top o' Christmas Morning: A Story of Ireland,* Follett, 1955; *Erik Christmas Camera* (Sweden), Follett, 1956; *When the Dikes Broke,* Follett, 1958; *Toward Morning: A Story of the Hungarian Freedom Fighters,* Follett, 1961; *Charles Steinmetz,* Follett, 1965.

Operettas with Helen Wing: "The Inn of the Golden Cheese"; "Mulligan's Magic"; "Going to the Fair"; "The Lemonade Stand." Contributor of serials, short stories, and articles to magazines for children; contributor of historical and biographical articles to *Christian Science Monitor* and to periodicals.

WORK IN PROGRESS: A biography of John Muir; a collection of Christmas Stories.

SIDELIGHTS: Excerpts from Mrs. Seymour's books have been published in school readers and dramatized on radio and television, and her books have been translated into

Italian, Spanish, and Dutch, and issued in Braille. She speaks German and Norwegian, reads Spanish, some Greek. *Avocational interests:* Weaving, gardening, refinishing antiques, reading, making room-size braided rugs, travel.

BIOGRAPHICAL/CRITICAL SOURCES: Chicago Schools Journal, May-June, 1951; *Christian Science Monitor,* May 21, 1952; *Oak Leaves,* Oak Park, Ill., November 22, 1956.

* * *

SHANKLAND, Peter Macfarlane 1901-

PERSONAL: Born June 15, 1901, in London, England; son of Robert (a shipowner) and Hilda (Macfarlane) Shankland; married third wife, Marion Ehlers (a potter), October 1, 1960; children: (second marriage) John, Catherine; (third marriage) Michael, David. *Education:* Attended Highgate School, London, England, and Fettes College, Edinburgh, Scotland. *Home:* 9 Market St., Poole, Dorsetshire, England.

CAREER: Director of documentary film production in British Zone of Germany, 1949-53; producer of documentary films for International Labour Office and other organizations, 1954-59; Anglo-Continental School of English, Bournemouth, England, teacher of English and English literature, 1959—. Lecturer in Germany and England on documentary films and English literature; official delegate of British Film Producers Association to international film festivals. *Military service:* Royal Naval Volunteer Reserve, 1940-45; became lieutenant; received Order of the British Empire (military). *Member:* Royal Naval Volunteer Reserve Club (London).

WRITINGS: The Phantom Flotilla: The Story of the Naval Africa Expedition, 1915-16, Collins, 1968.

With Anthony Hunter: *Malta Convoy,* Washburn, 1961, also published in *Three Great Sea Stories,* Collins, 1968; *Dardanelles Patrol,* Scribner, 1964.

WORK IN PROGRESS: Several books on British naval history, spanning the period from the eighteenth century through World War II.

SIDELIGHTS: Malta Convoy has been translated into seven languages.

BIOGRAPHICAL/CRITICAL SOURCES: Paul Rotha, *Documentary Film,* Faber, 1952.

* * *

SHAW, Carleton Ford 1908-

PERSONAL: Born July 28, 1908, in Goshen, Mass.; son of Alonzo Benjamin (an electrical engineer) and Clara Helen (Thatcher) Shaw; married Madelin Vivian Means (a shoe stitcher); children: Mrs. John E. Lynch, Jr., Alan Edward, Laurel Thatcher. *Education:* Special study with Sidney Cox in modern American and British poetry, at Cummington School of the Arts, 1933, 1936-37; attended Bread Loaf Writers Conference, 1965. *Politics:* Registered Democrat. *Religion:* Roman Catholic. *Home:* 15 North Common St., North Brookfield, Mass. 01535.

CAREER: Has worked as semi-skilled laborer, shipfitter, truck driver, farm hand, working stiff, and school custodian-janitor. Served in Massachusetts State Guard, 1941-44.

WRITINGS: Desperado (38 poems), Barre Publishers, 1965.

WORK IN PROGRESS: Two books of poetry.

AVOCATIONAL INTERESTS: Collecting classical recordings (Beethoven, Berlioz, Bruckner and Mahler), climbing mountains in Vermont and New Hampshire.

BIOGRAPHICAL SOURCES: Worcester, Mass., *Sunday Telegram,* March 21, 1965.

* * *

SHAW, Charles (Green) 1892-1974

PERSONAL: Born May 1, 1892, in New York, N.Y.; son of Charles Green (a merchant) and Eva (Morris) Shaw. *Education:* Yale University, Ph.B., 1914; Columbia University, study of architecture, 1914-15. *Home:* 340 East 57th St., New York, N.Y. 10022. *Agent:* (Art) Bertha Schaefer, 41 East 57th St., New York, N.Y.

CAREER: Free-lance writer of prose, 1916-31, contributing to *Vanity Fair, Bookman, Smart Set, Harper's Bazaar,* and other magazines; took up painting while living in Paris, 1932, and began a second literary phase as a poet in 1954 (aged 62). Work as an artist exhibited in thirty one-man shows, principally in New York, and in museums, galleries, and traveling exhibitions throughout the United States and western Europe, in Honolulu, and Japan; represented in the permanent collections of Museum of Modern Art, Musee de l'Art (Paris), Metropolitan Museum of Art, Boston Museum of Fine Arts, Whitney Museum of Modern Art, Chicago Institute of Art, and other metropolitan museums; also illustrated books and designed posters and magazine covers. *Military service:* U.S. Army, officer with American Expeditionary Forces, 1917-18.

MEMBER: Federation of Modern Painters and Sculptors, American Abstract Artists, Poetry Society of America, Poetry Society (London), Artists Equity Association, Nantucket Art Association (formerly member of executive committee), Newport Art Association, Century Association (New York). *Awards, honors:* First prize, Nantucket Art Association, 1958.

WRITINGS: Heart in a Hurricane, Brentano, 1927; *The Low Down,* Holt, 1928; *Night Life,* Day, 1930; *Lady by Chance,* Macaulay, 1931; *New York—Oddly Enough,* Farrar, Rinehart, 1938; *Giant of Central Park,* W. R. Scott, 1940; *It Looked Like Spilt Milk,* Harper, 1945; *Into the Light* (poetry), Fine Editions, 1959; *Image of Life* (poetry), Poets of America Publishing Co., 1962; *Time Has No Edge: A Poetry Collection,* William-Frederick, 1966; *Moment of the Now: A Poetry Collection,* Profile Press, 1969. Articles (v.s.) also have appeared in *Connoisseur, House and Garden, Antiques, New Yorker,* and *Life;* some twelve hundred poems have been published in *Poetry Digest, New York Herald Tribune, Literary Review, Trace,* and in other publications.

Illustrator: *The Milk That Jack Drank,* W. R. Scott, 1945; *Dark is Dark,* W. R. Scott, 1947; *Winter Noisy Book,* Harper, 1949; Elsa Pedersen, *Petticoat Fisherman,* Atheneum, 1969; Harold W. Felton, *James Weldon Johnson,* Dodd, 1971.

SIDELIGHTS: Shaw lived for many years in London and Paris. He assembled and owned the C. G. Shaw Theatrical Print Collection.

(Died April 2, 1974)

* * *

SHAW, Earl Bennett 1889-

PERSONAL: Born March 18, 1889, in Monroe, Iowa; son

of William Henry (a physician) and Flora (Corr) Shaw; married Sophia Halsted, June 17, 1940. *Education:* Washington University, St. Louis, Mo., B.B.A., 1927, M.S., 1929; Clark University, Ph.D., 1933. *Home:* 46 Elm St., Worcester, Mass. 01609.

CAREER: Massachusetts State College at Worcester (now Worcester State College), professor of geography and head of department, 1933-59, became professor emeritus; Assumption College, Worcester, Mass., professor of geography, 1959-72, professor emeritus, 1972—. Visiting professor, University of Puerto Rico, 1932-33, 1940; head of geographical branch, U.S. Office of Strategic Services, U.S. Army University, England, 1945-46; Fulbright lecturer, Ibrahim University, Egypt, 1952-53. *Military service:* U.S. Army, 1917-19; became sergeant. *Member:* Association of American Geographers, National Council for Geographic Education (former president), other geographical societies. *Awards, honors:* Jane Smith Award of National Geographic Society, 1949; Distinguished Service Award, National Council for Geographic Education, 1960; honorary Doctor of Science, Assumption College, 1970.

WRITINGS: (Reviser) Ellsworth Huntington and S. W. Cushing, *Principles of Human Geography*, 6th edition (Shaw was not associated with earlier editions), Wiley, 1951; *World Economic Geography*, Wiley, 1955; *Anglo-America*, Wiley, 1959; *Fundamentals of Geography*, Wiley, 1965.

Contributor: William H. Haas, editor, *The American Empire*, University of Chicago Press, 1940; S. Van Valkenburg, editor, *America at War*, Prentice-Hall, 1942; Fred E. Dohrs and others, editors, *Outside Readings in Geography*, Crowell, 1955; G. Etzel Pearcy, *World Political Geography*, Crowell, 1957; John Wesley Morris, editor, *Methods of Geographic Instruction*, Blaisdell, 1968.

Editor of half a dozen films for Coronet Films. Contributor of more than a hundred professional and popular articles on geography to periodicals and newspapers.

WORK IN PROGRESS: A revised edition of *Anglo-America*; popular articles on geography for newspapers and magazines.

SIDELIGHTS: Shaw has traveled on every continent except Antarctica for study and research. *Avocational interests:* Sports, music.

* * *

SHAW, Ronald D. M. 1883-

PERSONAL: Born October 7, 1883, in London, England; son of Alexander Croft (a clergyman) and Mary Anne (Cattell) Shaw; married Elizabeth May Walter, November 22, 1911 (deceased). *Education:* Attended Ecole de l'Etoile du Matin, and International School, Tokyo, Japan; Oxford University, M.A., 1921, D.D., 1929. *Address:* c/o Hongkong and Shanghai Bank, London, England.

CAREER: Clergyman, Church of England. Missionary and teacher in Japan, 1906-38, lecturing in department of religion at St. Paul's University, Tokyo; has served with British Imperial Censorship, Bermuda, 1940-41, with U.S. Office of War Information, 1942-45; translated Japanese in California for U.S. Navy, U.S. Treasury Department, U.S. Senate Committee on Un-American Activities, 1949-50.

WRITINGS: Seisan Shikibun Chushaku, Nippon Seikokwai Shuppansha, 1918; *Enlightenment and Salvation*, Williams & Norgate, 1930; (translator and editor) *The Blue*

Cliff Records, M. Joseph, 1961; (translator) Ekaku, *The Embossed Tea Kettle*, Allen & Unwin, 1963.

* * *

SHEEHAN, Sister Helen 1904-

PERSONAL: Born July 25, 1904, in Manchester, N.H.; daughter of John A. (in insurance) and Georgia M. (Beebe) Sheehan. *Education:* Trinity College, Washington, D.C., A.B., 1924; Simmons College, B.S. in L.S., 1926. *Politics:* Republican. *Office:* Trinity College, Washington, D.C. 20017.

CAREER: Roman Catholic religious, member of Sisters of Notre Dame de Namur. *Manchester Mirror*, Manchester, N.H., staff member, 1924-25; Manchester (N.H.) Public Library, branch librarian, 1926-30; Cathedral Library, Manchester, N.H., librarian, 1930-31; high school teacher in New England, 1931-34; Trinity College, Washington, D.C., librarian, 1934-72, college budget officer, officer, 1972—. Consultant on high school and college libraries. Chairman, Workshop on Small College Libraries, Philadelphia, Pa., 1965. *Member:* American Library Association, Association of College and Research Libraries, Catholic Library Association (member of executive board, 1959-65, 1967-73; president, 1969-71). *Awards, honors:* Papal medal, Pro Ecclesia et Pontifice, 1965; Alumni Achievement Award, Simmons College, 1973.

WRITINGS: (With Winifred Tuttle) *Seventy-Five Years of the City Library*, Clarke (Manchester, N.H.), 1929; *The Small College Library*, Newman, 1963, 2nd edition, 1969. Contributor to library journals. Member of editorial board, *CULS*, 1963-65, *Choice*, 1965-71, chairman, 1966-69; *Library College Journal*, 1967-72.

WORK IN PROGRESS: Research on experimental colleges and on budgetary problems.

SIDELIGHTS: Sister Helen has some competence in French, German, and Spanish.

* * *

SHEFFY, Lester Fields 1887-

PERSONAL: Born March 27, 1887, in Henrietta, Tex.; married. *Education:* Southwestern University, Georgetown, Tex., A.B., 1911; University of Texas, M.A., 1915; University of Chicago, graduate study, 1923-24. *Religion:* Methodist.

CAREER: West Texas State University, Canyon, 1918-57, began as instructor, became professor of history and head of department. *Member:* Texas State Historical Association (fellow), Panhandle-Plains Historical Society (life member; president, 1920-21, 1948-49). *Awards, honors:* Lit.D., Austin College, Sherman, Tex., 1937; Writers' Roundup Award, 1964.

WRITINGS: The Life and Times of Timothy Dwight Hobard, 1855-1935, Russell Stationery 1950; *Texas*, Banks Upshaw & Co., 1954; *The Francklyn Land and Cattle Company: A Panhandle Enterprize, 1882-1957*, University of Texas Press, 1963. Contributor of articles to periodicals. Editor of *Panhandle-Plains Historical Review*, 1930-48, associate editor, 1948-54.

WORK IN PROGRESS: The Colonization of White Deer Lands, 1885-1935.

* * *

SHEPHARD, John (Brownlow) 1900-

PERSONAL: Born August 17, 1900, in Hever, England;

son of Herbert Brownlow (a farmer) and Eleanor (Williams) Shephard; married to Avis Ashdown, April 20, 1926; children: one son (deceased), and Avis Elizabeth Taylor, Anne Goghlan, Joan Savory. *Education:* Attended Royal Military College at Sandhurst, 1918-20. *Home:* Little Stream, Swartberg, East Griqualand, Republic of South Africa.

CAREER: Regular officer in British Army, 1920-26, and in Indian Army, 1926-48; became lieutenant colonel. *Member:* Wild Life Society of Southern Africa, Zoological Society of Southern Africa, Natal Bird Club.

WRITINGS: Rooinek's Ride, Longmans, Green, 1950; *Land of the Tikoloshe*, Longmans, Green, 1953; *Check List of Birds of Swartberg District*, Percy Fitzpatrick Institute of African Ornithology, 1962. Contributor of numerous articles to South African newspapers, magazines, and to programs of South African Broadcasting Corp.

WORK IN PROGRESS: A travel book on Italy; a book on East Griqualand.

* * *

SHEPHERD, Robert Henry Wishart 1888-1971

PERSONAL: Born May 25, 1888, in Invergowrie, Perthshire, Scotland; son of Matthew Moncrieff and Isabella (MacEwen) Shepherd; married Mary Shearer Goodfellow, June 4, 1918; children: Isabella (Mrs. Athol Bernard Armstrong Bursey), Elizabeth. *Education:* University of St. Andrews, student, 1911-14; University of Edinburgh, M.A., 1915; University of the Witwatersrand, Lit.D., 1942.

CAREER: Ordained minister of Church of Scotland (Presbyterian). Began as missionary to South Africa, 1918; Lovedale Missionary Institution, Alice, Cape Province, South Africa, chaplain, 1927-42, principal, 1942-55; minister of Alice and Fort Beaufort Presbyterian churches, Cape Province, South Africa, 1956-68. Director, Lovedale Press, Alice, Cape Province, South Africa, 1927-58; moderator of General Assembly, Church of Scotland, 1959-60; president, Christian Council of South Africa, 1956-60. Member of British government advisory commission on Central Africa (Monckton Commission), 1960. *Awards, honors:* Carnegie Corp. grant to investigate Negro literature in United States, 1934; D.D. from University of Edinburgh, 1947, Rhodes University (South Africa), 1965; Queen's Coronation Medal, 1953.

WRITINGS: The Bantu, United Free Church of Scotland Publications Committee, 1925; *The Humanism of Jesus*, J. Clarke, 1926; *Under the Oaks* (sermons), Lovedale Press, 1933; *Literature for the South African Bantu*, Carnegie Corp. Visitors' Grants Committee, 1936; *Children of the Veld*, J. Clarke, 1937.

Though Mountains Shake (sermons), Marshall, Morgan & Scott, 1940; *Lovedale, South Africa, The Story of a Century*, Lovedale Press, 1940; *Lovedale and Literature for the Bantu: A Brief History and a Forecast*, Lovedale Press, 1945, reprinted, Negro Universities Press, 1970; (with B. G. Paver) *African Contrasts*, Oxford University Press (Cape Town), 1947; *Where Aloes Flame: South African Sketches*, Lutterworth, 1948; (editor) *Brownlee John Ross: His Ancestry and Some Writings*, Lovedale Press, 1948; *A South African Medical Pioneer: The Life of Neil Macvicar, M.D.*, Lovedale Press, 1952; (with Horton Davies) *South African Missions, 1800-1950: An Anthology*, Nelson, 1954; *Abazibaluleyo noKubhaliweyo ngesi Ntv. Iguqulelwe esi-Xhoseni B. B. Mdledle*, Lovedale Press, 1960; (editor) James Henderson, *Forerunners of Modern Malawi*, Lovedale Press, 1968.

Contributor to *South African Dictionary of Biography*. Also contributor of articles on missionary and African affairs to *Glasgow Herald* and other newspapers and periodicals. Editor, *South African Outlook*, 1932-63.

WORK IN PROGRESS: Editing two volumes, *Letters of James Henderson, D.D., Missionary to Central Africa, 1895-1905*, and *Letters of James Henderson, D.D., Principal of Lovedale Missionary Institution, South Africa, 1906-1930*.

SIDELIGHTS: Shepherd has traveled widely in southern and central Africa, in the United States, and in Australia, visiting aborigines missions. He is competent in Xhosa, a South African vernacular language.

BIOGRAPHICAL/CRITICAL SOURCES: South African Outlook, December, 1941, November, 1958; *Scotsman*, February 19, 1959; *Evening Citizen*, Glasgow, Scotland, May 16, 1959; *Daily Mail*, Glasgow, Scotland, May 16, 1959.

(Died June 22, 1971)

* * *

SHEPPARD, Lila (Brooks) 1906-

PERSONAL: Born January 3, 1906, in Ilion, N.Y.; divorced; children: Frances (Mrs. Richard Hirlemann), Judith (Mrs. Clyde Burnett). *Education:* Syracuse University, B.S., 1956; Cornell University, graduate study, 1960. *Home:* 103 East Marshall St., Ithaca, N.Y.

CAREER: Ithaca (N.Y.) Board of Education, elementary teacher, beginning 1944. Fulbright exchange teacher to New Zealand, 1960-61; exchange teacher in San Francisco, Calif., 1964-65. *Member:* National Education Association, National League of American Pen Women, Overseas Teachers' Association, New York State Teachers Association, Ithaca Teachers Association, Ithaca Writers Association (former president).

WRITINGS: Dancing on the Desk Tops, Harper, 1960; *The Story of New Zealand*, McCormick-Mathers, 1967. Author of monograph on classroom climate published by Harper. Contributor of about one hundred articles to popular and educational magazines, including several in New Zealand periodicals, and of occupational briefs to Chronicle Guidance Publications.

WORK IN PROGRESS: Collaborating with Margaret Phillips on *Mental Health Techniques for Elementary School Teachers*; stories for children; social studies books for elementary grades.

* * *

SHEREK, Henry 1900-1967

PERSONAL: Born April 23, 1900, in London, England; son of Bernard (a theatrical producer) and Marguerite Sherek; married Honorable Kathleen Boscawen, April 27, 1937. *Education:* Early education at schools in Germany and Switzerland; also attended St. John's College, Cambridge. *Politics:* "Citizen of the world." *Religion:* Church of England.

CAREER: British theatrical impresario. Except for war years, has been connected with the London theater for more than three decades, and with television since 1937; producer or manager of more than one hundred productions in London, New York, and Paris, and at Berlin and Edinburgh Festivals, beginning 1945; hits include "Idiot's Delight" (London), "Edward, My Son" (London and New

York), "The Cocktail Party" (London and New York), "The Confidential Clerk" (London, New York, Paris, and Edinburgh Festival), "Saint Joan" (London), "Under Milk Wood" (London, New York, and Edinburgh Festival), "The Playboy of the Western World" (London); produced one of the earliest television revues, in 1937; produced twenty-four plays for British Broadcasting Corp., 1957-59, and appeared on television with some regularity himself. *Military service:* British Army, 1915-19, 1940-44; became major. *Member:* Garrick Club.

WRITINGS: Not in Front of the Children, Heinemann, 1959.

SIDELIGHTS: In the late 1950's Sherek was described by a writer for the *Times* of London as a "formidable combination of the conscious humorist, the man of action, and the connoisseur—tall and Falstaffian in appearance.... in spirit, though born a few years too late, Edwardian."

Despite the Edwardian air, Sherek was a close student of Group Theatre acting when it was an innovation in America, introduced T. S. Eliot and Dylan Thomas to London and Broadway audiences, and has been identified with contemporary drama throughout his career. He collected modern art as well as Sevres porcelain, wintered in Kenya, and viewed the world beyond the stage with high interest: "Everyone in the theatre thinks it is the whole of life, whereas really it's a reproduction."

BIOGRAPHICAL/CRITICAL SOURCES: Times, London, England, October 14, 1958.

(Died September 23, 1967)

*   *   *

SHERIF, Muzafer 1906-

PERSONAL: Born July 29, 1906, in Odemis, Izmir, Turkey; married Carolyn Wood (a social psychologist), December 29, 1945; children: Sue, Joan, Ann. *Education:* American International College, Izmir, B.A., 1927; University of Istanbul, M.A., 1929; Harvard University, M.A., 1932; Columbia University, Ph.D., 1935. *Office:* Department of Sociology, Pennsylvania State University, University Park, Pa. 16802.

CAREER: Gaza Institute, Turkey, assistant professor of psychology, 1937-39; University of Ankara, Ankara, Turkey, assistant professor of psychology, 1939-44, professor of psychology, 1944; Princeton University, Princeton, N.J., U.S. Department of State Fellow, 1945-47; Yale University, New Haven, Conn., resident fellow in psychology, 1947-49; University of Oklahoma, Norman, professor, 1949-60, research professor of psychology, 1960-65, director of Institute of Group Relations, 1955-65, consulting professor in department of psychiatry, School of Medicine, 1954-65; Pennsylvania State University, University Park, distinguished visiting professor, 1965-66, professor of sociology, 1966-72, professor emeritus, 1972—. Visiting professor, University of Texas, 1958-59; Ford Visiting Professor, University of Washington, 1960. *Member:* American Psychological Association (fellow; council member, 1963-65), American Sociological Association, Society for the Psychological Study of Social Issues, American Orthopsychiatric Association, American Association of University Professors, Sigma Xi. *Awards, honors:* Rockefeller Fellow, 1935-36; Kurt Lewin Memorial Award from Society for Psychological Study of Social Issues, 1967.

WRITINGS: A Study of Some Social Factors in Perception, Archives of Psychology, 1935; *The Psychology of*

Social Norms, Harper, 1936; (with Hadley Cantril) *The Psychology of Ego-Involvements,* Wiley, 1947; *An Outline of Social Psychology,* Harper, 1948, 2nd revised edition (with wife, Carolyn W. Sherif) published as *Social Psychology,* 1969.

(Editor) *Social Psychology at the Crossroads,* Harper, 1951; (editor) *Group Relations at the Crossroads,* Harper, 1953; (with Carolyn W. Sherif) *Groups in Harmony and Tension,* Harper, 1953; (editor) *Emerging Problems in Social Psychology,* University of Oklahoma, Book Exchange, 1957; (with others) *Intergroup Conflict and Cooperation: The Robber Cave Experiment,* Institute of Group Relations, University of Oklahoma, revised edition, 1961; (with Carl I. Hovland) *Social Judgment: Assimilation and Contrast Effects in Communication and Attitude Change,* Yale University Press, 1961; (editor) *Intergroup Relations, and Leadership,* Wiley, 1962; (with Carolyn W. Sherif) *Reference Groups: An Exploration into Conformity and Deviation of Adolescents,* Harper, 1964; (with Carolyn W. Sherif and R. Nebergall) *Attitude and Attitude Change,* Saunders, 1964; (editor with Carolyn W. Sherif) *Problems of Youth: Transition to Adulthood in a Changing World,* Aldine, 1965; *In Common Predicament: Social Psychology of Intergroup Conflict and Cooperation,* Houghton, 1966 (published in England as *Group Conflict and Cooperation: Their Social Psychology,* Routledge & Kegan Paul, 1967); *Social Interaction, Process and Products: Selected Essays,* Aldine, 1967; (editor with Carolyn W. Sherif) *Interdisciplinary Relationships in the Social Sciences,* Aldine, 1969.

Contributor: K. Bigelow, editor, *Cultural Groups and Human Relations,* Columbia University Press, 1951; *The Social Welfare Forum* (Lindeman Memorial Lecture), National Conference of Social Work, Columbia University Press, 1956; J. Peatman and E. L. Hartley, editors, *Festschrift for Gardner Murphy,* Harper, 1960; B. Bass and I. Berg, editors, *Conformity and Deviation,* Harper, 1961; *Study of the Status and Development of Psychology in the United States,* McGraw, for American Psychological Association, 1963; S. B. Sells, editor, *Stimulus Dimensions Accounting for Behavior Variance,* Ronald, 1963; W. W. Charters and N. L. Gage, editors, *Readings in the Social Psychology of Education,* Allyn & Bacon, for Society for the Psychological Study of Social Issues, 1963.

Also contributor to psychology and sociology journals and to published conference proceedings.

WORK IN PROGRESS: Research on groups and attitudes of their members, supported by National Science Foundation, Rockefeller Foundation, and U.S. Department of Health, Education, and Welfare.

*   *   *

SHIELS, W(illiam) Eugene 1897-

PERSONAL: Born February 2, 1897, in Cincinnati, Ohio; son of Charles Francis and Ida (Shrimpton) Shiels. *Education:* Gonzaga University, A.B., 1922; St. Louis University, M.A., 1927; University of California, Ph.D., 1933. *Home and office:* Xavier University, Victoria Parkway, Cincinnati, Ohio 45207.

CAREER: Entered Order of Society of Jesus (Jesuits), 1916, ordained Roman Catholic priest, 1929; Loyola University, Chicago, Ill., instructor, 1930-31, assistant professor, 1935-36, associate professor of history, 1936-42; St. Johns University, Toledo, Ohio, assistant professor of history, 1934-35; University of Detroit, Detroit, Mich., associate professor of history, 1944-46; Xavier University, Cincinnati, Ohio, professor of history, 1946—, chairman of department, 1946-65. *Member:* American Catholic Historical Association, American Jesuit Historical Conference, U.S. Catholic Historical Society, American Historical Association, Mississippi Valley Historical Association. *Awards, honors:* Canisius Research fellowship, 1958-59.

WRITINGS: Gonzalo de Tapia, U.S. Catholic Historical Society, 1934; *History of Europe,* Loyola University Press, 1941; (with others) *Greater America,* University of California Press, 1945; *King and Church,* Loyola University Press, 1961. Contributor of articles and reviews to historical journals. Associate editor, *Mid-America,* 1935—, *America,* 1942-44, *Latin America,* 1944.

* * *

SHIPPEY, Frederick Alexander 1908-

PERSONAL: Born August 21, 1908, in Rensselaer County, N.Y.; son of William D. (a molder foreman) and Jennie (Rankin) Shippey; married Melda B. Haynes, June 17, 1938; children: Melda Jean (Mrs. David A. Pike), Stuart Haynes. *Education:* Syracuse University, A.B., 1935; Yale University, B.D., 1938; Northwestern University, Ph.D., 1947; University of Paris, postdoctoral study, 1960-61. *Home:* 52 Fairview Ave., Madison, N.J. 07940. *Office:* Drew University, Madison, N.J.

CAREER: Ordained Methodist minister, 1938. Pastor of churches in Connecticut and New York, 1938-44; The Methodist Church, New York, N.Y., superintendent of department of research and surveys, 1944-53; Drew University, Madison, N.J., professor of sociology of religion, 1950—, acting dean of department of theological sociology, 1967—. Research consultant, The Methodist Church, 1956-60; visiting professor, Boston University, Emory University, Texas Christian University. *Member:* American Sociological Association (fellow), American Academy of Political and Social Science (fellow), Religious Research Association, Society for the Scientific Study of Religion (fellow), American Association of University Professors, Kiwanis Club. *Awards, honors:* Distinguished Editors award from Religious Research Association, 1965.

WRITINGS: Church Work in the City, Abingdon, 1952; *Selected Work Documents: Six Research Studies,* for the Commission for Study and Action on the Jurisdictional System, the Methodist Church, 1960; *Protestantism in Suburban Life,* Abingdon, 1964. Contributor of articles to religious and sociological periodicals. Member of editorial board, 1965—, *Review of Religious Research,* and editor.

WORK IN PROGRESS: Research studies, including clique structure of religious groups, effects of social class upon religion, and French sociology of religion.

* * *

SHOEMAKER, Leonard Calvin 1881-

PERSONAL: Born April 22, 1881, in Rosita, Colo.; son of Hiram Calvin (a farmer) and Elvira (Hurt) Shoemaker; married Augusta May Swigart, December 2, 1906; children: Cecil Richard, Leslie Erman. *Politics:* Republican. *Religion:* Methodist. *Home:* 2148 South Downing St., Denver, Colo. 80210.

CAREER: U.S. Forest Service, forester, 1913-43, now retired. *Member:* National Association of Retired Civil Employees, Colorado Historical Society, Denver Westerners Posse, Masons, Elks, Modern Woodmen of America, Eastern Star.

WRITINGS: Saga of a Forest Ranger, University of Colorado Press, 1958; *Roaring Fork Valley,* Sage Books, 1958; *Pioneers of the Roaring Fork,* Sage Books, 1965. Author of poetry booklet, 1965. Scriptwriter for U.S. Forest Service radio program, "Uncle Sam's Forest Rangers," 1934-35. Contributor of articles, poems, and radio skits to Forest Service bulletins; also contributor of articles to popular magazines and to fraternal papers.

WORK IN PROGRESS: A novel of Western conflict and romance; poetry booklets; research and articles about western Colorado history.†

* * *

SHOEMAKER, Richard H(eston) 1907-1970

PERSONAL: Born April 5, 1907, in Cynwyd, Pa.; son of Richard Martin and Susan E. L. (Heston) Shoemaker; married Helen Louise Rose, November 23, 1936; children: Richard Martin. *Education:* William Penn Charter School, student, 1918-25; University of Pennsylvania, A.B., 1935; Columbia University, B.S. in L.S., 1938; Washington and Lee University, M.A., 1941. *Office:* Graduate School of Library Service, Rutgers University, New Brunswick, N.J. 08903.

CAREER: Washington and Lee University, Lexington, Va., assistant librarian, then chief librarian, 1939-47; Rutgers University, New Brunswick, N.J., librarian of Newark colleges, 1947-59, professor of library service, 1959-70. *Member:* American Library Association, Bibliographical Society of America, American Association of University Professors, Special Libraries Association, New Jersey Library Association, American Civil Liberties Union. *Awards, honors:* Carnegie fellow, 1958.

WRITINGS: (Compiler with Ralph R. Shaw) *American Bibliography: A Preliminary Checklist for 1801-1819,* nineteen volumes, Scarecrow, 1958-63, *Title Index,* 1965, *Addenda, List of Sources, Library Symbols,* 1965, *Corrections and Author Index,* 1966; (editor) *A Checklist of American Imprints,* Scarecrow, Volumes 2-4; *For 1821-1823,* 1967-68, Volume 5: *For 1824,* 1969, Volume 6: *For 1825,* 1969, Volume 7: *For 1826,* 1970, Volume 8: *For 1827,* 1970, Volume 9 (with Gayle Cooper): *For 1828,* 1971, Volume 10: *For 1829,* 1970. Contributor to *Library Resources and Technical Services.*

(Died March 3, 1970)

* * *

SHULMAN, Charles E. 1904-1968

PERSONAL: Born July 25, 1904, in Berdichev, Ukrainian Soviet Socialist Republic; son of Maurice (a salesman) and Rachel (Nemirow) Shulman; married Avis Clamitz (a writer and lecturer), June 27, 1927; children: Deborah. *Education:* Ohio Northern University, LL.B., 1920; University of Cincinnati, graduate study, 1922-23; University of Chicago, Ph.B., 1924, M.A., 1927; Hebrew Union College, Cincinnati, Ohio, Rabbi, 1927. *Office:* Riverdale Temple, West 246th St. and Independence Ave., Bronx, N.Y.

CAREER: Rabbi in Johnstown, Pa., 1926-27, Wheeling, W.Va., 1927-31; North Shore Congregation Israel, Glencoe, Ill., rabbi, 1931-47; Riverdale Temple, Bronx, N.Y., rabbi, 1947-68. Member of chaplaincy commission, National Jewish Welfare Board; member of executive committee, American Jewish Congress; traveling representative to Europe, North Africa, and Israel for United Jewish Appeal, 1952-53. Lecturer in United States and abroad. *Military service:* U.S. Navy, chaplain, 1943; served in Southwest Pacific; became lieutenant commander; received Navy Commendation Medal. *Member:* National Association of Jewish Chaplains (past president), Chicago Rabbinical Association (past president) Urban League of Greater New York (chairman of Bronx advisory committee), New York Board of Rabbis (member of executive committee), Anti-Defamation League of Metropolitan New York (member of religious advisory committee). *Awards, honors:* LL.D. from Ohio Northern University, 1954; D.D. from Hebrew Union College, Cincinnati, Ohio, 1956; George Washington Medal of Freedoms Foundation, 1953, 1954, 1955, 1957, 1963, and 1965.

WRITINGS: Problems of the Jews in the Contemporary World, Argus, 1936; *Europe's Conscience in Decline*, Argus, 1939; *What It Means to Be a Jew*, Crown, 1960.

Pamphlets: *Religion's Message to a War-torn World*, 1942; *The Test of a Civilization*, 1947; *A People That Did Not Die*, 1956; *The Best Years of Our Lives*, 1958.

Sermons anthologized in *World's Best Sermons.* Contributor to religious and secular periodicals. Chairman of editorial board, *The American Zionist* and the *Reconstructionist.*

WORK IN PROGRESS: The Modern World of the Jew; Religion in an Age of Anxiety.

SIDELIGHTS: During World War II, Shulman, the only rabbi among some 225 chaplains attached to the Seventh Fleet, traveled constantly between Australia and the Philippines with the greater part of the Southwest Pacific for his parish. He continued to travel, especially in Europe, Israel, and North Africa, studying the problems of the Jewish people.

(Died June 2, 1968)

*   *   *

SIBLEY, Elbridge   1903-

PERSONAL: Born September 19, 1903, in Worcester, Mass.; son of Willis Emory (a lawyer) and Marion E. (Chapin) Sibley; married Elizabeth LaBarre, September 7, 1927; children: John LaBarre, Willis E., Marion (Mrs. Lawrence Gushee), Abigail Sibley Morin. *Education:* Amherst College, A.B., 1924; Columbia University, Ph.D., 1930. *Home:* 216 Melbourne Ave., Mamaroneck, N.Y. 10543.

CAREER: Near East Survey, New York, N.Y., assistant staff director, 1926-27; New York City (N.Y.) Health Department, vital statistician, 1927; Fisk University, Nashville, Tenn., professor of statistics, 1928-30; Tennessee Department of Public Health, Nashville, statistician, 1928-32; Bowdoin College, Brunswick, Me., assistant, later associate professor of sociology, 1932-40; U.S. Bureau of the Budget, Washington, D.C., social statistician, 1940-44; Social Science Research Council, New York, N.Y., executive associate, 1944-70. Visiting professor, University of Massachusetts, Amherst, 1973. *Member:* American Sociological Association, American Statistical Association, Population Association of America, Cosmos Club (Washington, D.C.).

WRITINGS: (With F. A. Ross and C. L. Fry) *The Near East and American Philanthropy*, Columbia University Press, 1929; *Differential Mortality in Tennessee*, Fisk University Press, 1930; *Recruitment, Selection, and Training of Social Scientists*, Social Science Research Council,

1948; *Support for Independent Scholarship and Research*, Social Science Research Council, 1951; *The Education of Sociologists in the United States*, Russell Sage Foundation, 1963.

*   *   *

SICKMAN, Laurence C(halfant) S(tevens)   1906-

PERSONAL: Born August 27, 1906, in Denver, Colo.; son of D. Vance and May Ridding (Fuller) Sickman. *Education:* Harvard University, A.B. (cum laude), 1930. *Home:* 901 East 47th St., Kansas City, Mo. 64110. *Office:* Nelson-Atkins Gallery, 4525 Oak St., Kansas City, Mo. 64111.

CAREER: Harvard-Yenching Fellow, Peking, China, 1930-35; Nelson-Atkins Gallery of Art, Kansas City, Mo., curator of oriental art, 1935-45, vice-director, 1946-53, director, 1953—. Harvard University, Fogg Arts Museum, resident fellow and lecturer on oriental art, 1937-39. *Military service:* U.S. Air Corps, Combat Intelligence, 1942-45; served in England, India, and China; received Legion of Merit. *Member:* Association of American Art Museum Directors (vice-president, 1963-64; president, 1964-65), Chinese Art Society of America (board of governors, 1948—), College Art Association of America (board of governors, 1963-67), American Association of Museums (council), Association for Asian Studies, Japan Society, American Oriental Society, Rotary Club, Kansas City Country Club, River Club.

WRITINGS: (Editor) *The University Prints*, Oriental Art, Series O, *Early Chinese Art*, Section II, University Prints, 1938; (with Alexander Soper) *The Art and Architecture of China*, Penguin, 1956, 3rd edition, 1968; (editor) *Chinese Calligraphy and Painting in the Collection of John M. Crawford, Jr.*, Pierpont Morgan Library, 1962, also published as *Catalogue of the Exhibition of Chinese Calligraphy and Painting in the Collection of John M. Crawford, Jr.*, Pierpont Morgan Library, 1962. Contributor of articles to journals of oriental art. Editor, *Archives* of the Chinese Art Society of America.

*   *   *

SIEWERT, Frances E. (Cornelius)   1881-

PERSONAL: Born March 7, 1881, in Cornelius, Ore.; daughter of Thomas E. (a penal official) and Emma C. (Smith) Cornelius; married Samuel A. Siewert, May 26, 1903 (deceased); children: Carmen Elizabeth (deceased). *Education:* Attended Pacific University; Willamette University, B.L., 1901, M.A., 1906; Napierville Seminary and Schuykill Seminary, B.D., 1911; additional study at Kansas State University and University of Indiana. *Home:* 1574 Paloma St., Pasadena, Calif. 91104.

CAREER: Bible history teacher (interdenominational) in Seattle, Wash., 1911-13, Denver, Colo., 1914-19, Kansas, 1920-29, Warsaw, Ind., 1930-37, Whittier, Calif., 1938-46. Biblical researcher for ministers and religious publications, 1934-52. *Awards, honors:* D.Litt. from Wheaton College, for translation of *The Amplified New Testament.*

WRITINGS—Editor and translator: (From Greek) *The Amplified New Testament*, Zondervan, 1958; (from Hebrew) *The Amplified Old Testament*, Zondervan, Volume II, 1962, Volume I, 1964, both books reissued together as *The Amplified Bible; Containing the Amplified Old Testament and the Amplified New Testament*, Zondervan, 1965. Editor of religious books written by clergyman.

WORK IN PROGRESS: A book of conversational studies in the Old Testament.

SIDELIGHTS: Mrs. Siewert was the first woman in America to receive a B.D. degree. Granting of the degree was delayed three years because of Naperville Seminary charter provisions; finally credits were transferred to Schuylkill Seminary which did not have the restraining clause against giving a B.D. degree to a woman.

* * *

SILVER, Rollo G(abriel) 1909-

PERSONAL: Born June 27, 1909, in New York, N.Y.; son of Stanley Gabriel (a merchant) and Anna (Newman) Silver; married Alice Gindin, June 9, 1933. *Education:* Brown University, Ph.B., 1931; Boston University, M.A., 1941; Simmons College, B.S., 1948. *Home:* 105 Mt. Vernon St., Boston, Mass. 02108.

CAREER: Peabody Institute, Boston, Mass., reference librarian, 1948-50; Simmons College, Boston, Mass., assistant professor, 1950-53, associate professor, 1953-60, professor of library science, 1960-65. Lecturer. Fellow of Boston University and Boston University Library. *Military service:* U.S. Army, 1943-45. *Member:* American Antiquarian Society, Bibliographical Society of America (member of advisory committee), Society of Printers (former president), Friends of Boston University Library (former president), Grolier Club, Double Crown Club (London), Phi Beta Kappa (honorary).

WRITINGS: Boston Book Trade, 1800-1825, New York Public Library, 1949; (editor with Clarence Gohdes) Walt Whitman, *Faint Clews & Indirections*, Duke University Press, 1949; (with Hellmut Lehmann-Haupt and Lawrence C. Wroth) *The Book In America*, 2nd edition (Silver was not associated with earlier edition), Bowker, 1951; *Baltimore Book Trade, 1800-1825*, New York Public Library, 1953; *Typefounding in America, 1787-1825*, University Press of Virginia, 1965; *The American Printer, 1787-1825*, University Press of Virginia, 1967. Contributor to journals.

* * *

SILVERTHORN, J(ames) E(dwin) 1906-

PERSONAL: Born October 20, 1906, in Stillwater, Okla.; son of Sherman Ulyses (a merchant) and Nettie (Myer) Silverthorn; married Thelma Rentfrow (a teacher), August 26, 1930; children: James Edwin II. *Education:* Oklahoma State University, B.S., 1937, M.S., 1941; Indiana University, Ed.D., 1955. *Politics:* Democrat. *Religion:* Methodist. *Home:* Route 4, Stillwater, Okla.

CAREER: Oklahoma State University, Stillwater, beginning 1945, former head of department of office management, now professor emeritus. Consultant to U.S. Air Force, Gulf Oil Co., and Rural Electrification Administration. *Member:* Administrative Management Society, Business Education Association, Mountain-Plains Business Education Association, Oklahoma Business Education Association, Pi Omega Pi, Delta Pi Epsilon.

WRITINGS: Basic Typewriting, Oklahoma State University Press, 1949; *Word Division Manual*, South-Western Publishing, 1958; *College Spelling*, South-Western Publishing, 1959; *College Vocabulary Building*, South-Western Publishing, 1964. Contributor to professional journals.

* * *

SILVESTER, Victor

PERSONAL: Born in Wembley, Middlesex, England; son of John William (a clergyman) and Katherine (Hudson) Silvester; married Dorothy Newton; children: Victor. *Education:* Attended St. John's School, Leatherhead, England. *Religion:* Church of England. *Office:* Victor Silvester Organization, 111 Baker St., London W. 1, England.

CAREER: Leader of dance band, Victor Silvester and His Ballroom Orchestra, playing under contract with British Broadcasting Corp., London, England, 1937—, and recording for Columbia Records. Broadcasts include weekly worldwide request program on BBC General Overseas Service and the "Television Dancing Club," both running continuously, 1948—. Chairman of Victor Silvester Entertainments Ltd., Victor Silvester Ballroom Enterprises Ltd., and Victor Silvester-Oscar Grasso Productions Ltd. *Military service:* British Army, 1915-19; became lieutenant; received Italian Bronze Medal for valor. *Member:* Imperial Society of Dancing (president). *Awards, honors:* Order of the British Empire, 1962, for services to ballroom dancing; winner of world's dancing championship.

WRITINGS: The Art of the Ballroom, Jenkins, 1936; *Theory and Technique of Ballroom Dancing*, Jenkins, 1938; *Dancing is My Life* (autobiography), Heinemann, 1958; *Modern Dancer's Handbook*, Jenkins, 1960; *Modern Ballroom Dancing*, 56th edition, Jenkins, 1965; (with Walter Whitman) *The Complete Old Time Dancer*, Jenkins, 1967.

SIDELIGHTS: Silvester received Columbia Record Platinum Disc for the sale of thirty million single records.

* * *

SIMEON, Mother Mary 1888-

PERSONAL: Born October 19, 1888, in Kent, England. *Education:* Educated at boarding school in Sussex, England, and studied violin for four years in Germany and England. *Home:* Convent of the Holy Child Jesus, Killiney, County Dublin, Ireland.

CAREER: Roman Catholic nun, member of Society of the Holy Child Jesus. Headmistress, 1927-39, later teacher, in Mayfield, and Sussex, England.

WRITINGS: Christ's Way, Douglas Organ, 1947; *Simon Called Peter*, Browne & Nolan, 1958; *Personalities in the Gospel Story*, Bruce, 1963; *If Any Man Thirst*, Bruce, 1964. Also author of religious pamphlets, several of them published in United States.

* * *

SIMON, Martin P(aul William) 1903-1969

PERSONAL: Born February 16, 1903, in Angelica, Wis.; son of T. F. (a farmer) and Eleanor (Elbert) Simon; married Ruth Tolzmann, September 8, 1926; children: Paul, Arthur. *Education:* Concordia College, Milwaukee, Wis., graduate (with honors), 1922; Concordia Seminary, St. Louis, Mo., B.D., 1926; University of Oregon, M.A., 1931, D.Ed., 1953. *Politics:* Democrat.

CAREER: Lutheran minister. Missionary in China, 1926-28; pastor in Eugene, Ore., 1928-38; *Christian Parent*, editor and publisher in Eugene, Ore., 1938-46, in Highland, Ill., 1946-57; Scripture Press, Wheaton, Ill., editor of *Christian Parent*, 1957-61; writer, assistant pastor, pastor, 1962-69. *Member:* National Council of Family Relations.

WRITINGS: Bible Readings for the Family Hour, Moody, 1954; (with Allan H. Jahsmann) *Little Visits with God*, Concordia, 1957; (with Jahsmann) *More Little Visits with God*, Concordia, 1961; *Daily Family Devotions for the*

Whole Family, Christian Life Publishing, 1963; *Points for Parents: A Book to Help Parents Understand and Guide Their Children*, Zondervan, 1963; *How to Know and Use Your Bible*, Zondervan, 1963; *Glad Moments with God*, Zondervan, 1964; *Meeting Current Family Problems*, edited by Oscar E. Feucht, Concordia, 1966. Contributor and consulting editor, *Lutheran Digest*; columnist, *Lutheran Layman*.

WORK IN PROGRESS: Bible Story Devotions, for Standard Press.

(Died September 23, 1969)

*   *   *

SIMONDS, William Adams 1887-19?

PERSONAL: Born September 19, 1887, in Central City, Neb.; son of Henry Austin (an educator) and Elizabeth (Goodnough) Simonds; married Marjory Muncaster, 1909 (died, 1919); married Teresa Callahan, 1920 (died, 1947); married Marie Callahan Fitts, April 14, 1948; children: (first marriage) William, Jr., Henry Austin, Dwight Chandler, Bruce Thomas; (second marriage) Vance Charles, Betty (Mrs. Henry Tuttle). *Education:* University of Washington, Seattle, student, 1908-11. *Politics:* Republican. *Religion:* Episcopalian. *Home:* 10810 El Dorado Dr., Sun City, Ariz. 85351.

CAREER: Seattle Daily Times and *Seattle Sunday Times*, Seattle, Wash., successively reporter, automotive editor, and assistant city editor, 1912-16; *Northwest Motor*, Seattle, Wash., managing editor, 1916-22; Ford Motor Co., 1922-45, regional advertising manager, Seattle, Wash., 1922-26, in Dearborn, Mich., as editor of *Ford News*, 1926-42, director of Greenfield Village, 1933-42, public relations director for Willow Run Bomber Plant, 1942-45; N. W. Ayer & Son, advertising and public relations in Honolulu, Hawaii, 1946-58; University of Hawaii, lecturer on public relations, 1953-57. Lecturer on Ford, Edison, and Hawaii; technical adviser on Edison films, Metro-Goldwyn-Mayer, 1939-40. President of Dearborn Community Forum, 1936-37; chairman of Dearborn Civil Service Commission, 1937-40. *Member:* Public Relations Society of America, Hawaii Public Relations Society, Sigma Delta Chi. *Awards, honors:* M.A. from Wayne State University, 1940.

WRITINGS: Henry Ford, Motor Genius, Doubleday, 1929; (with Fred L. Black) *From the Ground Up*, Doubleday, 1930; *A Boy with Edison*, Doubleday, 1931; *Edison: His Life, His Work, His Genius*, Bobbs-Merrill, 1934; *Henry Ford and Greenfield Village*, Frederick A. Stokes, 1938; *Henry Ford: His Life, His Work, His Genius*, Bobbs-Merrill, 1943, revised edition, Clymer, 1946 (published in England as *Henry Ford: A Biography*, M. Joseph, 1946); *Kamaaina: A Century in Hawaii*, privately printed, 1949; *The Hawaiian Telephone Story*, Hawaiian Telephone Co., 1958. Editor of *Menlo Park Reminiscences*, three volumes by Francis Jahl, published by Henry Ford.

WORK IN PROGRESS: Community Life in Retirement; fiction.

(Deceased)

*   *   *

SIMONINI, R(inaldo) C(harles), Jr. 1922-1967

PERSONAL: Born February 11, 1922, in Baltimore, Md.; son of Rinaldo Charles (a businessman) and Wilmeth (Geyer) Simonini; married Juanita Thorne Evans, February 1, 1944; children: Diane Marie, R. Charles III. *Education:*

Johns Hopkins University, A.B., 1943; University of North Carolina, A.M., 1946, Ph.D., 1949. *Home:* 304 Buffalo St., Farmville, Va. 23901.

CAREER: University of North Carolina, Chapel Hill, instructor in English, 1946-47; Washington College, Chestertown, Md., professor and chairman of department of English, 1948-50; East Carolina College, Greenville, N.C., professor of English, 1950-51; Longwood College, Farmville, Va., professor and chairman of department of English, speech, and dramatic art, 1951-67. Fulbright research professor at University of Florence, Italy, 1953-54; American Council of Learned Societies fellow at Linguistic Institute, summer, 1958; visiting professor of English at University of North Carolina, summer, 1962. *Military service:* U.S. Naval Reserve, 1943-45; became lieutenant s.g. *Member:* National Council of Teachers of English (member of commission on the English language, 1961-64; director, 1963-66), Modern Language Association of America, Shakespeare Association of America, American Dialect Society, Renaissance Society of America, American Association of University Professors, Linguistic Society, South Atlantic Modern Language Association, College English Association of North Carolina, Virginia, and West Virginia (president, 1956-57), Virginia Association of Teachers of English (president, 1956-58).

WRITINGS: Italian Scholarship in Renaissance England, University of North Carolina Press, 1952; (editor) *John Florio's Second Frutes*, Scholars Facsimiles & Reprints, 1953; *The Universities of Italy*, American Association of University Professors, 1955; (editor) John K. Bettersworth and others, *Education in the South* (lectures), Longwood College, 1959; (editor and author of preface) *Southern Writers: Appraisals in Our Time*, University Press of Virginia, 1964. Contributor to *American Speech, Language Learning, Studies in Philology, Shakespeare Quarterly, Modern Language Journal, Italica*, and other journals. Editor, *Virginia English Bulletin*, 1960-67.

WORK IN PROGRESS: A study of linguistic principles influencing divided usage in present-day English.

(Died April 3, 1967)

*   *   *

SIMPSON, George Gaylord 1902-

PERSONAL: Born June 16, 1902, in Chicago, Ill.; son of Joseph Alexander (a lawyer) and Helen Julia (Kinney) Simpson; married Lydia Pedroja, February 2, 1923 (divorced, 1938); married Anne Roe (a psychologist), May 27, 1938; children: (first marriage) Helen (Mrs. Wolf Vishniac), Gaylord (Mrs. Frank Bush; deceased), Joan (Mrs. James Burns), Elizabeth. *Education:* University of Colorado, student, 1918-19, 1920-22; Yale University, Ph.B., 1923, Ph.D., 1926. *Politics:* Democrat. *Religion:* "Nondogmatic." *Office:* Department of Geosciences, University of Arizona, Tucson, Ariz. 85721.

CAREER: American Museum of Natural History, New York, N.Y., field assistant, 1924, assistant curator, 1927, associate curator, 1928-42, curator of fossil mammals, 1942-59, chairman of department of geology and paleontology, 1944-58; Columbia University, New York, N.Y., professor of vertebrate paleontology, 1945-59; Harvard University, Cambridge, Mass., Alexander Agassiz Professor of Vertebrate Paleontology, 1959-70; University of Arizona, Tucson, professor, 1967—. Special lectureships at Princeton University, Harvard University, Yale University, University of California, Columbia University, and other universities, 1946-63. Collected fossil animals on thirteen expeditions to New Mexico between 1924-57, in Patagonia, 1930-31, 1933-34, Venezuela, 1938-39, Brazil, 1954-55, 1956, Spain, 1960, East Africa, 1961, and on other field trips abroad and in Southwestern United States. *Military service:* U.S. Army, 1942-44; became major.

MEMBER: American Society of Zoologists (president, 1964), Geological Society of America (fellow), Society for the Study of Evolution (president, 1946), Society of Systematic Zoology (president, 1962-63), Society of Vertebrate Paleontology (president 1942-43), American Academy of Arts and Sciences (fellow; councillor, 1960-63), American Philosophical Society (fellow; councillor, 1946-49), National Academy of Sciences (fellow), Academia de Ciencias (Venezuela, Brazil, Argentina), Sociedad Cientifica Argentina (corresponding member), Accademia Nazionale die Lincei (Italy); foreign member of Royal Society, Linnean Society, and Zoological Society (all London).

AWARDS, HONORS: Lewis Prize, American Philosophical Society, 1942; National Academy of Sciences, Thompson Medal, 1943, and Elliott Medal, 1944, 1961; Gaudry Medal, Societe Geologique de France, 1947; Hayden Medal, Philadelphia Academy of Sciences, 1950; Penrose Medal, Geological Society of Belgium, 1953; Darwin-Wallace Medal, Linnean Society of London, 1958; Darwin Plakette, Deutsche Akademie Leopoldina, 1959; Darwin Medal, Royal Society of London, 1962; National Medal of Science, 1965. Sc.D. from Yale University, 1946, Princeton University, 1947, University of Durham, 1951, Oxford University, 1951, University of New Mexico, 1954, University of Chicago, 1959, Cambridge University, 1965, York University, 1966; LL.D., University of Glasgow, 1951; Dr. h.c., University of Paris, 1965.

WRITINGS: A Catalogue of the Mesozoic Mammalia in the Geological Department of the British Museum, British Museum, 1928; (contributor) *Memoirs of the Peabody Museum of Yale University*, Volume III, Yale University Press, 1929; *Attending Marvels: A Patagonian Journal*, Macmillan, 1934; *The Fort Union of the Crazy Mountain Field, Montana, and Its Mammalian Faunas*, U.S. National Museum, 1937; (with wife, Anne Roe) *Quantitative Zoology*, McGraw, 1939, revised edition (with Anne Roe and Richard Lewontin), Harcourt, 1960; *Los Indios Kamarakotos*, Revista de Fomento (Caracas), 1940; *Tempo and Mode in Evolution*, Columbia University Press, 1944; *The Principles of Classification and a Classification of Mammals*, American Museum of Natural History, 1945; *The Beginning of the Age of Mammals in South America*, Part I, American Museum of Natural History, 1948; *The Meaning of Evolution*, Yale University Press, 1949, revised and abridged edition, New American Library 1951, revised edition, Yale University Press, 1967.

Horses: The Story of the Horse Family in the Modern World and Through Sixty Million Years of History, Oxford University Press, 1951, published with new preface, Anchor Books, 1961; *Life of the Past* (an introduction to paleontology), Yale University Press, 1953; *The Major Features of Evolution*, Columbia University Press, 1953; *Evolution and Geography* (Condon Lectures), Oregon State System of Higher Education, 1953; (with Carlos de Paula Cauto) *The Mastodonts of Brazil*, American Museum of Natural History, 1957; (with C. S. Pittendrigh and L. H. Tiffany) *Life: An Introduction to Biology*, Harcourt, 1957, revised edition (with William S. Beck), 1965; (editor with Anne Roe) *Behavior and Evolution*, Yale University Press, 1958; *Principles of Animal Taxonomy*, Columbia

University Press, 1961; *This View of Life: The World of an Evolutionist*, Harcourt, 1964; *The Geography of Evolution* (collected essays), Chilton, 1965; *Biology and Man*, Harcourt, 1969.

Published articles, reports, and essays total over six hundred.

WORK IN PROGRESS: Principles and Philosophy of Evolution; monographic studies of mammals; a book on penguins, recent and fossil.

SIDELIGHTS: Tempo and Mode in Evolution has been translated into French, German, Russian, and other languages, and *The Meaning of Evolution* into eleven languages, including Persian, Japanese, and Finnish.

* * *

SIMPSON, Ian J(ames) 1895-

PERSONAL: Born December 24, 1895, in Monymusk, Aberdeenshire, Scotland; son of Alexander Wilson (a schoolmaster) and Catherine (Milne) Simpson; married Muriel Dohm, June 2, 1923; children: Jenny C. (Mrs. Alastair D. S. Fowler). *Education:* Attended Robert Gordon's College, 1911-14; University of Aberdeen, M.A., 1920, Ed.B., 1922, Ph.D., 1942. *Home:* 8 Wilton Rd., Edinburgh, EH16 5NX, Scotland.

CAREER: Hermitage School, Helensburgh, Scotland, principal teacher of English, 1931-62; now retired.

WRITINGS: Idle Hands (play), H. F. W. Deane & Sons, 1931; *Education in Aberdeenshire before 1872*, University of London Press, 1947. Writer of British Broadcasting Corp. feature program, "O Sing a New Song," 1948. Contributor of articles on literary and historical topics to *Scotsman, Glasgow Herald, Scottish Educational Journal*, and other journals and newspapers.

* * *

SIMPSON, Kemper 1893-

PERSONAL: Born April 7, 1893, in Chattanooga, Tenn.; son of Saul (a capitalist) and Flora (Kemper) Simpson, *Education:* Attended Baltimore City College, 1907-10; Johns Hopkins University, A.B., 1914, Ph.D., 1917.

CAREER: U.S. Federal Trade Commission, Washington, D.C., economist, 1918-21; Princeton University, Princeton, N.J., assistant professor of economics, 1923; U.S. Tariff Commission, Washington, D.C., economist and adviser abroad, 1924-29; Goldman Sachs Trading Corp., economist, 1929-31; consulting economist for banks, importers, and foreign industries, 1931-34; U.S. Securities and Exchange Commission, Washington, D.C., economic adviser, 1934-37; U.S. Board of Economic Warfare, Washington, D.C., onetime chief of Iberian section; Economic Cooperation Administration, Washington, D.C., onetime economic adviser to Greece; now retired and writing. Member of President Roosevelt's original "Brain Trust," 1932.

WRITINGS: The Capitalizaton of Good Will, Johns Hopkins Press, 1921; *Economics for the Accountant*, Appleton, 1921; *Introduction to World Economics*, Harper, 1934; *The Margin Trader: A Study in Trade in Securities and Insecurity in Trade*, Harper, 1938; *Big Business, Efficiency, and Fascism: An Appraisal of the Efficiency of Large Corporations and of Their Threat to Democracy*, Harper, 1941; *Uncommon Men* (poems), Agathon Press, 1963. Contributor of articles to economic journals. Editor and compiler of numerous government reports.

WORK IN PROGRESS: The Common Man, a novelette study of the debunking of a so-called liberal by Washington Society.

* * *

SKARSTEN, Malvin O. 1892-

PERSONAL: Born September 28, 1892, in Crookston, Minn.; son of Rasmus A. and Mary (Eide) Skarsten; married Naomi I. Johnson (deceased); children: Phyllis Skarsten Dixon, Margaret Skarsten Alexander. *Education:* University of Minnesota, B.A., 1925, M.A., 1926; Colorado State College (now University of Northern Colorado), D.Ed., 1944. *Religion:* Protestant. *Home:* 3601 Reder St., Rapid City, S.D. 57701.

CAREER: Teacher in elementary and high schools in Minnesota, 1909-11, 1918-21; superintendent of schools, Williams, Minn., 1922-24; Black Hills Teachers College (now Black Hills State College), Spearfish, S.D., director of student teaching, 1926-44; Pacific University, Forest Grove, Ore., successively director of admissions, registrar, director of Graduate School, head of Division of Education, 1944-62. *Member:* Phi Delta Kappa, Kappa Delta Pi.

WRITINGS: George Drouillard: Hunter and Interpreter, Arthur H. Clark, 1964. Contributor of articles to *Kadelpian Review*, *Educational Administration and Supervision*, *Association of American Colleges Bulletin*, *Travel*, and *St. Nicholas*. Also author of *The Least of These*, an autobiography being considered for publication, and *Their Hearts Were Right*, a tribute to the Indians who helped Lewis and Clark. Contributor to a multi-volume series on early Rocky Mountain men, published by Arthur H. Clark.

WORK IN PROGRESS: Two novels for juveniles, *The Long Journey* and *A Daughter of the Real People*.

* * *

SKINNER, Charles Edward 1891-

PERSONAL: Born April 24, 1891, in Licking County, Ohio; son of Morris Allen and Martha Leota (Loughman) Skinner; married Mary Ethel Shuman, August 5, 1917; children: Charles Edward, Jr., William James. *Education:* Ohio University, B.S. in Ed., 1914; Cornell University, graduate study, 1914; University of Chicago, M.A., 1916; Columbia University, postgraduate study, 1922-23; New York University, Ph.D., 1923. *Home:* 703 West Church St., Galion, Ohio 44833.

CAREER: Ohio University, Athens, began as instructor, became assistant professor of psychology, 1914-17; Mount Union College, Alliance, Ohio, professor of psychology and philosophy, 1919-20; Indiana State College, Indiana, Pa., professor of education, 1920-22; Miami University, Oxford, Ohio, professor of education, 1923-25; New York University, New York, N.Y., assistant professor, 1925-28; associate professor, 1928-30, professor of education, 1930-56, professor emeritus, 1956—. Distinguished visiting professor, Southern Illinois University, 1956-58, 1959-65; visiting professor, Kent State University, 1958-59, Otterbein College, and Slippery Rock State College, 1965-66, and Westminster College, 1966-67; lecturer at Western Reserve University (now Case-Western Reserve University), 1958-59. *Military service:* U.S. Army, Infantry, 1917-19; became second lieutenant.

MEMBER: American Psychological Association (fellow), National Society of College Teachers of Education, Phi Beta Kappa, Kappa Delta Pi (laureate member), Phi Delta

Kappa. *Awards, honors:* New York University Alumni Meritorious Service Medallion.

WRITINGS: (With Benson, Lough, and West) *Psychology for Teachers*, Ginn, 1926, revised edition, 1933; (editor with I. M. Gast and H. C. Skinner) *Readings in Educational Psychology*, Appleton, 1926; (with Paul Vining West) *Psychology for Social and Religious Workers*, Century, 1930; (with Otis William Caldwell and J. W. Tietz) *Biological Foundations of Education*, Ginn, 1931; *Good Manners for Young Americans*, Beckley-Cardy, 1932; (editor with others) *Readings in Psychology*, Farrar & Rinehart, 1935; (editor with others) *Educational Psychology*, Prentice-Hall, 1936, 4th edition, 1959; (editor with G. T. Buswell and others) *Readings in Educational Psychology*, Farrar & Rinehart, 1937; (editor with R. Emerson Langfitt and others) *An Introduction to Modern Education*, Heath, 1937; (with others) *Psychology in Everyday Living*, Heath, 1938; (editor with Paul Andrew Witty, Rose H. Alschuler and others) *Mental Hygiene in Modern Education*, Farrar & Rinehart, 1939.

(Editor with Philip Lawrence Harriman and others) *Child Psychology, Child Development, and Modern Education*, Macmillan, 1941; (with Harriman and L. L. Greenwood) *Psychology in Nursing Practice*, Macmillan, 1942, revised edition (with Lester Donald Crow and A. V. Crow), 1954; (editor with others) *Elementary Educational Psychology*, Prentice-Hall, 1945, revised edition published as *Essentials of Educational Psychology*, 1958. Author with others of "Story and Study Reading" Series, seven books with manuals, B. F. Johnson, 1928-29. Occasional contributor to education and psychology journals.

* * *

SLADEN, Norman St. Barbe   ?-1969
(Rodney Bullingham, Dennis Montclair)

PERSONAL: Married Violet Mabel Thorpe; children: David, Ruth (Mrs. J. E. B. Marsh). *Education:* Educated in London, Paris, and Germany. *Home:* 5 Daver Court, London, W.5, England. *Agent:* Robert Sommerville, 14 Norfolk St., London, W.C. 2, England.

CAREER: Head of a department in a banker's office, London and New York, 1923-31; served in confidential departments of British government for many years; was head of a securities department of the Board of Trade Clearing Office, 1922; formerly London editor, *Livingstone Mail*, Rhodesia, South Africa; founder of the Sladen Literary Service (now discontinued); former chairman of the Authors' Insurance Association Ltd., London, England. Former assistant secretary of the Society of Civil Servants. *Military service:* British Army, 1917; second lieutenant. *Member:* Royal Society of Literature (life fellow), Royal Commonwealth Society (fellow), Institute of Journalists, British Legion, Authors' Club (London; secretary), Freeman of the City of London, Freeman of the Worshipful Company of Merchant Tailors.

WRITINGS: Ark: Or a New Industrial Era, Williams & Norgate, 1932; *The Real Le Queux*, Nicholson & Watson, 1938; *Wake Up, Anglicans!*, Lifestream Publications, 1947; *The Complete Crossword Reference Book*, Syndicate Publishing, 1949; *Personalities of the Twentieth Century*, Odhams, 1951; (translator) *My Uncle and the Cure*, Cassell, 1957, Vanguard, 1958. Former literary critic, *Commonwealth and Empire Review*. Contributor to *British Weekly* and to other periodicals.

(Died July 28, 1969)

SLANEY, George Wilson 1884-
(George Woden, George Wouil)

PERSONAL: Born September 1, 1884, in Wednesbury, England; son of George (an engineer) and Anne (Wilson) Slaney; married Edith M. Tomkinson, June 29, 1914 (deceased); children: Noel (Mrs. G. Moules). *Education:* Attended University of London; additional study in France and Germany. *Religion:* Protestant. *Home:* 182 King's Park Ave., Glasgow S.4, Scotland. *Agent:* Austin Wahl Agency, Chicago, Ill.

CAREER: Studied engineering, but abandoned that career to become a journalist and artist; schoolmaster in Glasgow, Scotland, 1909-48; novelist, beginning, 1913. Lecturer on European affairs and World War II for British Ministry of Information. *Member:* Scottish P.E.N. (president, 1944-47).

WRITINGS—All published by Hutchinson, except as indicated; under pseudonym George Wouil: *Sowing Clover*, 1913, new edition under pseudonym George Woden, 1934; *Paul Moorhouse*, 1914; *The New Dawn*, 1915.

Under pseudonym George Woden: *Little Houses*, Dutton, 1919; *The Wrenfield Mystery*, Leonard Parsons, 1923; *The Great Cornelius*, J. Murray, 1926; *The Gates of Delight*, J. Murray, 1927; *This Way to Fortune*, 1929; *The Parson and Clerk*, Benn, 1930; *Mungo*, 1932; *Love and Let Love*, 1934; *Our Peter*, 1934; *Upside-Turvydown*, 1934; *Tannenbrae*, 1935; *Othersmith*, 1936; *Perhaps Young Man*, 1936; *The Baillie's Tale*, 1937; *The Cathkin Mystery*, 1937; *Happiness Has No Story*, 1938; *Holiday Adventure*, 1939; *Voyage Through Life*, 1940; *Dusk for Dreams*, 1941; *The Queer Folk Next Door*, 1942; *The Golden Lion*, 1944; *Ruffy and Sons*, 1945; *Messenger-at-Arms*, 1947; *The Lovers' Tale*, 1948; *The Puzzled Policeman*, 1949; *Helen Enchanted*, 1950; *Mystery of the Amorous Music Master*, 1951; *Simonetta*, 1952.

Plays: "The Money's the Thing," produced at Scottish National Players, Glasgow, 1921; "Thistledown," produced at Court Theater, London, 1923. Contributor of poetry and prose to *Cornhill* and other periodicals.

WORK IN PROGRESS: Short stories.

SIDELIGHTS: Slaney speaks French, German, Italian. *Avocational interests:* Travel, music, gardening, cooking.

* * *

SLATER, Robert (Henry) Lawson 1896-

PERSONAL: Born February 8, 1896, in Newcastle upon Tyne, England; son of Harry Lawson (a merchant) and Jane Elizabeth (Lawson) Slater; married Alys Lennox Graham Simpson, September 8, 1929; children: John G. L., C. Peter R. L. *Education:* Cambridge University, M.A., 1928; Columbia University, Ph.D., 1948. *Home:* Georgeville, Quebec, Canada (summer). *Mailing address:* Ecumenical Institute, 97 St. George St., Toronto, Ontario, Canada.

CAREER: Ordained priest, Church of England, 1925; chaplain, and lecturer in logic at Rangoon University, Rangoon, Burma, 1929-36; Union Theological Seminary, New York, N.Y., visiting lecturer in comparative religion, 1947-49; McGill University, Montreal, Quebec, professor of systematic theology, 1949-50; Diocesan Theological College, Montreal, Quebec, principal, 1950-58; Harvard University, Cambridge, Mass., professor of world religions, 1959-64, founder and director of Center for Study of World Religions. Lecturer on history of religion, American Council of Learned Societies, 1959. *Military service:* Senior chaplain to the forces, British Army in India, 1942-46. *Member:* American Society for the Study of Religions, American Oriental Society, Society for the Scientific Study of Religion. *Awards, honors:* D.D., Montreal Diocesan Theological College.

WRITINGS: God of the Living, Scribner, 1938; *God and Human Suffering*, Epworth, 1940; *Guns through Arcady: Burma and the Burma Road*, Angus & Robertson, 1941; *Paradox and Nirvana*, University of Chicago Press 1951; *Can Christians Learn from Other Religions?*, Seabury, 1963; *World Religions and World Community*, Columbia University Press, 1963; (with Hywel D. Lewis) *World Religions: Meeting Points and Major Issues*, C. A. Watts, 1966, published as *The Study of Religions: Meeting Points and Major Issues*, Penguin, 1969. Contributor of chapters and introductions to books edited by others.

SIDELIGHTS: Slater told *CA:* "Following retirement from Harvard [I was] awarded a grant which will enable me to travel in Africa, Asia, etc. during the next two years or so, and write as the Spirit moves me, if the Spirit does."

"Always have been a scribbler.... In youth was a newspaper correspondent and twice or thrice have come near to publishing a novel, but have ended by writing out of my depth, on Paradox, and now (mainly) on world religions and world peace."

* * *

SLOAN, Harold Stephenson 1887-

PERSONAL: Born November 23, 1887, in Brooklyn, N.Y.; son of Alfred Pritchard (a merchant) and Katharine (Meade) Sloan; married Bertha Florey, September 14, 1910; children: Alvin Florey. *Education:* Columbia University, B.S., 1909, A.M., 1926. *Politics:* Democrat. *Religion:* Unitarian Universalist. *Home:* 880 Fifth Ave., New York, N.Y. 10021. *Office:* 22 East 72nd St., New York, N.Y. 10021.

CAREER: DeCamp and Sloan Manufacturing Co., Newark, N.J., general manager, 1909-25; teacher of economics, Brooklyn, N.Y., 1925-27, of history at New Jersey State Normal School, Newark, 1927-29; Montclair State College, Upper Montclair, N.J., associate professor of economics, 1929-36; New York University, New York, N.Y., adjunct professor of economics, 1936-58; Fairleigh Dickinson University, Rutherford, N.J., director of research, 1958—. Executive director, Alfred P. Sloan Foundation, 1938-47; president, Institute for Instructional Improvement, 1960—. Visiting lecturer in economics, Columbia University, 1945-64; professor of economics, Association of American States, Bogota, Colombia, 1959; consultant in Peru, U.S. Agency for International Development, 1963; trustee, Fairleigh Dickinson University, 1964—. *Member:* Authors Guild. *Awards, honors:* LL.D., University of Denver, 1946; D.Sc., Fairleigh Dickinson University, 1960.

WRITINGS: Today's Economics, Prentice-Hall, 1938; *Farming in America*, Harper, 1947; (with Arnold J. Zurcher) *Dictionary of Economics*, Barnes & Noble, 1949; (with Harold F. Clark) *Classrooms in the Factories*, New York University Press, 1960; (with Clark) *Classrooms in the Stores*, Roxbury Press, 1962; (with Clark) *Classrooms in the Military*, Teachers College, Columbia University, 1964; (with Clark) *Classrooms on Main Street*, Teachers College, Columbia University, 1966. Author of articles on economics.

WORK IN PROGRESS: Studies on electro-mechanical aids to learning.

*   *   *

SLOAN, Raymond Paton   1893-

PERSONAL: Born December 12, 1893, in Brooklyn, N.Y.; son of Alfred Pritchard (an importer) and Katharine (Mead) Sloan; married Mabel V. MacArthur, November 20, 1916. *Education:* Brooklyn Preparatory Institute, student, 1908-11. *Home:* 19 East 72nd St., New York, N.Y. 10021. *Office:* 36 East 70th St., New York, N.Y. 10021.

CAREER: Automobile Topics, New York, N.Y., member of editorial staff, 1920-33; *Modern Hospital*, Chicago, Ill., editor, 1933-53; Alfred P. Sloan Foundation, New York, N.Y., vice-president, 1953—; writer and lecturer. Special lecturer, Columbia University, 1945—; president and chairman of board, Modern Hospital Publishing Co., 1953-58. Member of board of trustees of five hospitals in metropolitan New York and Waterville, Me. *Member:* American Hospital Association (honorary member), American College of Hospital Administrators (honorary fellow), Metropolitan Club and Sky Club (both New York), The Creek (Locust Valley, N.Y.), Tavern Club (Chicago). *Awards, honors:* D.H.L., Colby College, 1946; LL.D., St. Lawrence University, 1954; Dr. Social Welfare, Women's Medical College of Pennsylvania, 1958; La Grande Medaille d'Argent de laville de Paris, City of Paris, 1961; brother, Order of Hospital of St. John (London).

WRITINGS: Hospital Color and Decoration, Physicians' Record Co., 1944; *This Hospital Business of Ours*, Putnam, 1952; *On a Shoestring and a Prayer*, Doubleday, 1964; *Today's Hospital*, Harper, 1966. Contributor of articles on hospital and health topics to professional journals.

WORK IN PROGRESS: Two books, a biography, and a history of a hospital.

SIDELIGHTS: Sloan is fluent in French (he has lectured in French in France and Canada).

*   *   *

SLOANE, Joseph C(urtis)   1909-

PERSONAL: Born October 8, 1909, in Pottstown, Pa.; son of Joseph Curtis (a businessman) and Julia (Moss) Sloane; married Marjorie Merrill, December 14, 1934; children: Janet, Margaret Merrill. *Education:* Princeton University, A.B., 1931, M.F.A., 1934, Ph.D., 1949. *Politics:* Democrat. *Religion:* Presbyterian. *Home:* Morgan Creek Rd., Chapel Hill, N.C. 27514.

CAREER: University of North Carolina, Chapel Hill, chairman of art department and director of Ackland Art Center, 1959—. North Carolina Museum of Art, trustee, 1962—. *Military service:* U.S. Naval Reserve, served in Pacific theater, 1943-46; became lieutenant commander; received Naval Commendation Ribbon. *Member:* American Society for Aesthetics, College Art Association of America (past president), North Carolina State Art Society (past president), National Council of the Arts in Education (president, 1969-71). *Awards, honors:* Senior Fulbright research grant, 1952-53.

WRITINGS: French Painting Between the Past and the Present: Artists, Critics, and Traditions, from 1848 to 1870, Princeton University Press, 1951; *Paul Marc Joseph Chenavard, Artist of 1848*, University of North Carolina Press, 1962. Contributor to *Arts, Art Bulletin, Art Quarterly, Journal of Aesthetics and Art Criticism, Gazette des Beaux Arts*, and other periodicals.

WORK IN PROGRESS: A Guide to Art History, publication expected by Norton.

*   *   *

SMALLENBURG, Harry W.   1907-

PERSONAL: Born August 25, 1907, in Buffalo, N.Y.; son of Harry Russell and Mary C. (Piall) Smallenburg; married Carol Thornton (a college professor), August 23, 1940; children: Harry, John, Carol Ann, Robert. *Education:* University of Buffalo, A.B., 1928; University of Southern California, M.S., 1935, Ed.D., 1943. *Home:* 840 South Sunset Canyon, Burbank, Calif.

CAREER: Teacher in Buffalo, N.Y., 1928-33; Burbank, Calif., city schools, junior high teacher and counselor, 1936-38, principal, 1939-41, director of research, 1939-44; Office of Los Angeles County, Superintendent of Schools, Los Angeles, Calif., director of Division of Research and Guidance, 1944—. University of Southern California, adjunct professor, 1960—. Visiting professor at University of California, Los Angeles, 1957-60, University of Southern California, 1959, State University of New York College at Buffalo 1960-61; lecturer at other universities in California and at University of Hawaii.

MEMBER: American Psychological Association (fellow; also member of Western and California branches), American Personnel and Guidance Association (member of executive council, 1955-57), American School Counselor Association (president, 1957-58), American Educational Research Association, Association for Supervision and Curriculum Development (California president, 1951-52), National Vocational Guidance Association, American Association of School Administrators, National Congress of Parents and Teachers (chairman for mental health, 1961-64; member of California advisory board, 1952-55), California Association of School Psychologists and Psychometrists, Phi Delta Kappa, Burbank Optimist Club (president, 1944).

WRITINGS: (With Ruth Martinson) *Guidance in Elementary Schools*, Prentice-Hall, 1958; (with Emery Stoops and others) *Guidance Services, Organization and Administration*, McGraw, 1959.

Co-author of four handbooks on guidance published by California Test Bureau, 1948-60, and of handbooks for National Congress of Parents and Teachers, and California Congress. Contributor to educational and counseling journals. Member of editorial board, *Personnel and Guidance*, 1958-61, *School Counselor*, 1958-63, and *California Journal of Educational Research*, 1958-63.

*   *   *

SMART, Charles Allen   1904-1967

PERSONAL: Born November 30, 1904, in Cleveland, Ohio; son of George (an editor) and Lucy (Allen) Smart; married Margaret Warren Hussey, January 1, 1935. *Education:* Harvard University, A.B., (cum laude), 1926. *Politics:* Democrat. *Home:* Oak Hill, Dun Rd., Chillicothe, Ohio 45601.

CAREER: Doubleday, Page & Co. and Doubleday, Doran (publishers), New York, N.Y., editorial assistant, 1927-30; Choate School, Wallingford, Conn., instructor in English, 1932-34; farmer, 1934-42; Ohio University, Athens, writer-in-residence, 1946-54. Author, 1930-67. *Military service:* U.S. Naval Reserve, 1942-45; served in Normandy invasion; became lieutenant. *Member:* Authors Guild of the

Authors League of America, Ohio Historical Society (honorary life), Ohio University Alumni Association (honorary life). *Awards, honors:* Ohioana Library Association medal for best biography of the year by an Ohio writer, 1964, for *Viva Juarez!*

WRITINGS: New England Holiday (novel), Norton, 1931; *The Brass Cannon* (novel), Norton, 1933; *R.F.D.* (essays), Norton, 1938 (published in England as *The Adventures of an American Farmer*, Oxford University Press, 1938); *Rosscommon* (novel), Random House, 1940; *Wild Geese and How to Chase Them* (essays), Random House, 1941; *Sassafras Hill* (novel), Random House, 1947; *The Green Adventure* (play), Ohio University Press, 1954; *At Home in Mexico* (essays), Doubleday, 1957; *Viva Juarez!*, Lippincott, 1963; *The Long Watch*, World Publishing, 1968.

SIDELIGHTS: Two of his books have been published in England, and others in Australia, Sweden, and Latin America. The author and his wife have spent most winters since 1953 in Mexico. *Avocational interests:* Drawing and painting.

BIOGRAPHICAL/CRITICAL SOURCES: New York Times, March 14, 1967; *Best Sellers*, June 1, 1968.

(Died March 11, 1967)

* * *

SMART, Harold R(obert) 1892-

PERSONAL: Born May 4, 1892, in Searsport, Me.; son of William Dyer (a carpenter) and Jeanne (Porteus) Smart; married Francis Goodfellow, August 11, 1952; children: Jeanne (Mrs. Jack Bagby). *Education:* Wesleyan University, Middletown, Conn., B.S., 1915; Cornell University, M.A., 1921, Ph.D., 1923. *Politics:* Independent. *Religion:* Protestant. *Home:* 396 Arlington, Acton, Mass. 01720.

CAREER: Hill School, Pottstown, Pa., instructor in French, 1919-20; University of North Carolina, Chapel Hill, assistant professor of philosophy, 1923-24; Cornell University, Ithaca, N.Y., assistant professor, 1924-39, associate professor of philosophy, 1939-60, assistant to dean of College of Arts and Sciences, 1947-50, professor emeritus, 1960—. *Military service:* U.S. Army, 1917-19; became sergeant. *Member:* American Philosophical Association, Phi Beta Kappa, Phi Kappa Phi.

WRITINGS: The Philosophical Presuppositions of Mathematical Logic, Cornell University Press, 1925; (editor and author of bibliography) James Edwin Creighton, *Studies in Speculative Philosophy*, Macmillan, 1925; *The Logic of Science*, Appleton, 1931; (reviser and contributor) James Edwin Creighton, *Introductory Logic*, 5th edition, revised, Macmillan, 1932; *Philosophy and Its History*, Open Court, 1963. Contributor to philosophy journals. Member of editorial board, *Philosophical Review*, 1924—.

* * *

SMITH, Alfred Edward 1895-1969

PERSONAL: Born June 3, 1895, in England; son of Alfred William (a butcher) and Ella (Thomas) Smith; married Dorothy May Berry, August 8, 1920; children: Christopher Colin, Brenda Margaret. *Education:* Brighton Training College, student, 1913-14. *Politics:* Socialist. *Home:* 11 Wellington Rd., Bognor Regis, England.

CAREER: Schoolmaster in Brighton, England, 1919-36; headmaster in Brighton, England, 1936-46; Bognor Regis Training College, Bognor Regis, England, senior lecturer in English, 1946-55; retired 1955. *Military service:* British Army, 1914-19. *Member:* Sussex Archaeological Society.

WRITINGS: Reading with Understanding, four books, McDougall's Educational Co., 1935-55; *Reading, Writing and Appreciation*, McDougall's Educational Co., 1941; *Practical Everyday Reading*, four books, McDougall's Educational Co., 1942-63; *Let's Talk*, McDougall's Educational Co., 1949; "Challenge Books," twenty-six books, McDougall's Educational Co., 1951-69; *English in the Modern School*, Methuen, 1954, 2nd edition, revised, 1957, reissued with corrections, 1966; *Test and Teach*, McDougall's Educational Co., 1958; *Express Yourself*, four books, J. Murray, 1959-61; (compiler) *The Living Word: An Anthology of Passages for Reading Aloud*, Methuen, 1966.

WORK IN PROGRESS: Book of junior English tests.

AVOCATIONAL INTERESTS: Medieval archaeology; pottery.

(Died April 15, 1969)

* * *

SMITH, Cordelia Titcomb 1902-

PERSONAL: Born November 6, 1902, in Bath, Me.; daughter of Fred Evans and Katrina (Beals) Titcomb; married James Ambler Smith, 1930 (deceased); children: Sally (Mrs. James Fenton), Margaret (Mrs. George Inglis). *Education:* Simmons College, B.L.S., 1926; Western Reserve University (now Case Western Reserve University), certificate in library work with children, 1929. *Religion:* Christian Science. *Home:* 122½ West Wayne, Maumee, Ohio 43537.

CAREER: Cuyahoga County Library, Cleveland, Ohio, branch librarian, 1926-29; Cleveland Public Library, children's and school librarian, 1929-36; Fenn College Library, Cleveland, cataloger, 1937-41; Morley Library, Painesville, Ohio, children's librarian and cataloger, 1947-48; Kirtland School District Library, Willoughby, Ohio, school and public librarian, 1948-55; Lucas County Library, Maumee, Ohio, director of work with young people, 1955-70; retired, 1970. Girl Scouts of America, day camp director, 1943, 1944, county board member, 1944-45. *Member:* American Library Association, Ohio Library Association, Pan Pacific and Southeast Asia Women's Association (delegate to international conference, 1964), League of Women Voters (Maumee; secretary, 1960—), International Institute (Toledo).

WRITINGS: (With John P. Morse) *Paul Bunyan in Geauga County*, privately printed, 1946; (contributor) M. Jerry Weiss, *An English Teacher's Reader*, Odyssey, 1962; (editor) *Great Science Fiction Stories*, Dell, 1964.

* * *

SMITH, Datus C(lifford), Jr. 1907-

PERSONAL: Born May 3, 1907, in Jackson, Mich.; son of Datus C. and Marion (Houston) Smith; married Dorothy Hunt, 1931; children: Sandra (Mrs. Robert G. Auchincloss), Karen. *Education:* Princeton University, B.S., 1929. *Home:* 29 Wilson Rd., Princeton, N.J. 08540. *Office:* Room 5600, 30 Rockefeller Plaza, New York, N.Y. 10020.

CAREER: Princeton University, Princeton, N.J., graduate manager of student employment, 1929-30, held title of associate professor, 1943-47, professor, 1947-53; with Princeton University Press, 1930-53, director, 1942-53; Franklin Publications Inc., New York, N.Y., president, 1952-67; JDR 3rd Fund, Inc., vice-president, 1967—. Member of U.S.

National Commission for UNESCO, 1964-70. Lecturer on book publishing, Radcliffe College and New York University. Member, Borough of Princeton Board of Education; trustee, Asia Society, International School Service, Center for Applied Linguistics. *Member:* Association of American University Presses (president, 1947-48), Publishers Lunch Club (president, 1956-57), American Book Publishers Council (board of directors, 1948-51), National Book Committee. *Awards, honors:* M.A., Princeton University, 1958.

WRITINGS: American Books in the Non-Western World: Some Moral Issues, New York Public Library, 1958; *The Land and People of Indonesia*, Lippincott, 1961, revised edition, 1968; (compiler with William E. Spaulding) *Books in West Africa*, Franklin Publications, 1963; (with others) *A Guide to Book-Publishing*, Bowker, 1966. Contributor to *Atlantic Monthly, Saturday Review, Publishers Weekly, Foreign Affairs*, and other periodicals.

SIDELIGHTS: Smith's major interest is in international book publishing. As for claiming the title of author, he says he "just happened to write a book."

*   *   *

SMITH, Dick   1908-1974

PERSONAL: Born September 9, 1908, in Milford, Tex.; son of Jesse Richard (a rancher) and Bettie (Parkes) Smith. *Education:* University of Texas, B.A., 1930, M.A., 1931; Harvard University, M.A., 1938, Ph.D., 1939. *Religion:* Episcopalian. *Home:* 746 North Neblett, Stephenville, Tex. 76402. *Office:* Box 2006, Tarleton Station, Stephenville, Tex. 76402.

CAREER: Tarleton State College, Stephenville, Tex., dean of men, 1933, instructor, 1934-39, assistant professor, 1939-45, associate professor, 1945-46, professor of political science, 1946-74, head of department of social science, 1947-67. Visiting lecturer at University of Texas, North Texas State University, and Southern Methodist University. *Member:* American Political Science Association, American Historical Association, Organization of American Historians, Southwestern Political Science Association, Southern Political Science Association, Pi Sigma Alpha.

WRITINGS: How Bills Become Laws in Texas, Institute of Public Affairs, University of Texas, 1945, 3rd edition, 1970; *Layman's Guide to Texas State Administrative Agencies*, Institute of Public Affairs, University of Texas, 1945, 2nd edition, 1954; (with Stuart A. MacCorkle) *Texas Government*, McGraw, 1949, 6th edition, 1968; *Texas New Mental Health Code*, Institute of Public Affairs, University of Texas, 1957; *Constitutional Revision in Texas*, Institute of Public Affairs, University of Texas, 1961; *Medical Care for Indigent Aged*, Institute of Public Affairs, University of Texas, 1963. Contributor to government and social science journals. Member of board of editors, *Southwestern Social Science Quarterly*, 1952-59.

(Died January 6, 1974)

*   *   *

SMITH, Ethel Sabin   1887-

PERSONAL: Born July 25, 1887, in Windsor, Wis.; daughter of Samuel Wells (a farmer) and Ernestine Sophia (Espenett) Sabin; married Willard M. Smith (a college professor), July 29, 1922 (deceased). *Education:* University of Wisconsin, B.A., 1908, M.A., 1914; University of Illinois,

Ph.D., 1916. *Politics:* Democrat. *Home:* 5203 Alum Rock, San Jose, Calif. 95127.

CAREER: University of Illinois, Urbana, assistant in English, 1916-17; Bryn Mawr College, Bryn Mawr, Pa., associate in philosophy and psychology, 1917-22; Mills College, Oakland, Calif., professor of philosophy and psychology, 1922-53, professor emeritus, 1953—. Cottey College, Nevada, Mo., guest professor of philosophy, 1960-61. *Member:* American Association of University Professors (second vice-president, 1945-48), American Association of University Women (president of Oakland branch, 1956-57).

WRITINGS: The Dynamics of Aging, Norton, 1956; *Passports at Seventy*, Norton, 1961; *A Furrow Deep and True*, Norton, 1964; *God and Other Gods*, Exposition, 1973. Contributor of articles to magazines and professional journals.

SIDELIGHTS: Mrs. Smith lived in Europe while on sabbatical with her husband in 1932, and has traveled around the world twice by cargo ship. *The Dynamics of Aging* has been translated into Swedish and Japanese.

*   *   *

SMITH, Eugene Waldo   1905-

PERSONAL: Born July 29, 1905, in Everett, Mass.; son of Arthur Edgar (in engineering) and Effie V. (Moore) Smith; married Beatrice L. Hughes, October 6, 1928; children: Grace Smith Leonard, David Arthur. *Politics:* Republican. *Religion:* Congregational. *Home:* 424 Lebanon St., Melrose, Mass. 02176. *Office:* Bernitz Furnace Appliance Co., 150 Causeway St., Boston, Mass. 02114.

CAREER: Bernitz Furnace Appliance Co., Boston, Mass., assistant treasurer. *Member:* Steamship Historical Society of America, World Ship Society.

WRITINGS: Trans-Atlantic Passenger Ships, Past and Present, G. H. Dean, 1947; *Trans-Pacific Passenger Ships* (includes appendix to *Trans-Atlantic Passenger Ships, Past and Present*), G. H. Dean, 1953; *Passenger Ships of the World, Past and Present*, G. H. Dean, 1963.

WORK IN PROGRESS: Coastal Liners of the World, Past and Present.

AVOCATIONAL INTERESTS: All forms of transportation.

*   *   *

SMITH, Eunice Young   1902-

PERSONAL: Born June 10, 1902, in LaSalle, Ill.; daughter of Arthur Merriman (a railroad commerce agent) and Katherine Genevieve (Whitmarsh) Young; married Stuyvesant C. Smith (a research engineer), June 17, 1927; children: Stuyvesant Chadwick, Sharon Katherine (Mrs. Herbert Kane). *Education:* Attended Rosary College, 1920, Lake View Commercial Art School, Chicago, Ill., 1921, Indiana University Extension, 1935-36, and Academy of Fine Arts, Chicago, Ill., 1945. *Home and office:* 15026 Dragoon Trail, Mishawaka, Ind.

CAREER: Writer and illustrator of children's books and illustrator of film strips. *Member:* Authors League, American Association of University Women, Children's Aid Society, Children's Reading Round Table of Chicago.

WRITINGS—Self-illustrated: The Jennifer Wish, Bobbs-Merrill, 1949; *The Jennifer Gift*, Bobbs-Merrill, 1950; *Moppet*, Whitman, 1950; *The Jennifer Prize*, Bobbs-Merrill, 1951; *Jennifer is Eleven*, Bobbs-Merrill, 1952;

Denny's Story, Whitman, 1952; *Sam's Big Worry*, Whitman, 1953; *Jennifer Dances*, Bobbs-Merrill, 1954; *The House with the Secret Room*, Bobbs-Merrill, 1956; *The Little Red Drum*, Whitman, 1961; *Where From?*, Rand McNally, 1962; *High Heels for Jennifer*, Bobbs-Merrill, 1964; *Where To, Tillie Turtle?*, Bobbs-Merrill, 1964; *Shoon, Wild Pony of the Moors*, Bobbs-Merrill, 1965; *To Each a Season*, Bobbs-Merrill, 1965; *The Knowing One*, Meredith, 1967.

Illustrator: *The Children's Treasury*, Consolidated Book Publishers, 1947; *Merry Christmas Book*, Whitman, 1948; *Merry Songs*, Follett, 1949; *Come and Hear*, Follett, 1952; *Fun for Chris*, Whitman, 1956. Also illustrator of *Mother's Day in the Meadow*, Consolidated Book Publishers.

Illustrator of film strips: "Paddy's Christmas"; "Mrs. Squirrel and Her Family"; "Mrs. Cottontail and Her Springtime Family"; "The Friendly Beasts at Jesus' Manager."

Contributor of stories and poems to *Humpty Dumpty's Magazine*.

WORK IN PROGRESS: A series of etched portraits of Chaucer's Canterbury pilgrims.

SIDELIGHTS: Mrs. Smith's books have been translated into French and German, and published in England. *Avocational interests:* Conservation of America's natural resources and wildlife.

* * *

SMITH, Harvey K(ennedy)   1904-1968

PERSONAL: Born August 21, 1904, in Rye, N.Y.; son of Alfred Gilbert (a steamship executive) and Charlotte (Williams) Smith; married Virginia Maria Mancini (a nurse), September 11, 1938. *Education:* Yale University, Ph.B., 1929, M.F.A., 1948. *Politics:* Ticketsplitter. *Home:* 1762 Linden St., New Haven, Conn. 06511. *Office:* University Theatre, Yale University, New Haven, Conn.

CAREER: Yale University, School of Drama, New Haven, Conn., assistant professor of stage lighting, beginning 1950. Consultant to architects and to school, university, and community theaters. *Member:* American Education Theatre Association, Illuminating Engineering Society, U.S. Institute of Theatre Technicians, United Scenic Artists (lighting associate).

WRITINGS: (With W. Oren Parker) *Scene Design and Stage Lighting*, Holt, 1962, 3rd edition, 1974.

(Died, 1968)

* * *

SMITH, Herbert F. A.   1915-1969

PERSONAL: Born October 17, 1915, in Green's Harbour, Newfoundland; son of Robert S. (a minister) and Dora (Fields) Smith; married Bettie Winsor, December 28, 1940; children: Judith (Mrs. Steven Gerlach), Wesley, Stephen, Gloria, Patricia, David. *Education:* McGill University, B.A., 1937; University of Michigan, M.A. 1943, Ph.D., 1951. *Home:* R.R. 5, Edwardsville, Ill. *Office:* Southern Illinois University, Edwardsville, Ill.

CAREER: Teacher in Montreal, Quebec, 1937-41; principal in high schools in Quebec, 1941-46; high school science teacher in 1946-49; Mankato State College, Mankato, Minn., 1949-57, began as instructor, became associate professor of education; Southern Illinois University, Carbondale, 1957-64, began as associate professor, became professor of education; Southern Illinois University, Edwards-

ville, professor of education, 1964-69. *Member:* National Education Association, Association for Student Teaching, American Association of University Professors, Phi Delta Kappa.

WRITINGS: (With Clarence D. Samford and others) *Secondary Education*, W. C. Brown, 1963; (with Polter and Moss) *Photo Situations*, Burgess, 1963; *Secondary School Teaching: Modes for Reflective Thinking*, W. C. Brown, 1964. Contributor of about thirty-five articles to education journals.

WORK IN PROGRESS: Focus on Family Living.

(Died August 30, 1969)

* * *

SMITH, J(ames) L(eonard) B(rierley)   1897-1968

PERSONAL: Born September 26, 1897, in Graaff Reinet, Cape Province Republic of South Africa; married second wife, Mary Margaret Macdonald (scientific associate in ichthyology), April 14, 1938; children: (first marriage) Robert Brierley, Cecile Brierley, Shirley Brierley; (second marriage) William Macdonald. *Education:* Victoria College, University of South Africa, B.A., 1917; University of Stellenbosch, M.Sc., 1918; Selwyn College, Cambridge, Ph.D, 1922. *Office:* Department of Ichthyology, Rhodes University, Grahamstown, Republic of South Africa.

CAREER: Rhodes University, Grahamstown, Republic of South Africa, lecturer, then associate professor of organic chemistry, 1923-45, research professor, 1946-68. South African Council for Scientific and Industrial Research, Pretoria, research fellow in ichthyology, 1946-68. Conductor of numerous expeditions to remote areas of western Indian Ocean and eastern coastline of Africa, 1946-56, including flight to Comoro Islands to rescue the second coelacanth, 1952. *Military service:* South African Army, East African Campaign, 1915-16.

WRITINGS: A Simplified System of Organic Identification, Nasionale Pers, 1940; (with M. Rindl) *Numerical and Constitutional Exercises in Organic Chemistry*, Metheun, 1941; *A System of Qualitative Inorganic Analysis*, Nasionale Pers, 1941, 4th edition, 1950; *The Sea Fishes of Southern Africa*, Central News Agency (Johannesburg), 1949, 4th edition, 1961; "Old Fourlegs," the Story of the Coelacanth, Longmans, Green, 1956; *The Search Beneath the Sea*, Henry Holt, 1956; (with wife, Margaret M. Smith) *Fishes of Seychelles*, Department of Ichthyology, Rhodes University 1963; (with M. M. Smith) *Fishes of the Tsitsikama Coastal National Park*, National Parks Board of Trustees of the Republic of South Africa, 1966.

Author of thirty bulletins (purely scientific), Rhodes University Ichthyological Publications, 1956-64. Regular contributor to *Field and Tide*; contributor of scientific papers to professional journals and popular articles to magazines all over the world.

WORK IN PROGRESS: Continued investigation of fishes in western Indian Ocean for reports in Rhodes University Ichthyological Bulletins.

SIDELIGHTS: Smith was the first man to identify and trace the coelacanth, a fish believed extinct for 40 million years. His book *Search Beneath the Sea* was translated for publication in German, French, Estonian, Slovak, Dutch, and Afrikaans. As a research scientist, Smith regarded his more popular writings as a means of providing scientific information in understandable language for the layman, "who after all is the man who pays for scientific research."

(Died January 7, 1968)

SMITH, J(oseph) Russell 1874-1966

PERSONAL: Born February 3, 1874, in Lincoln, Va.; son of Thomas R. and Ellen H. Smith; married Henrietta Stewart, June 16, 1898; children: Newlin Russell, James Stewart, Thomas Russell. *Education:* University of Pennsylvania, B.S., 1898, Ph.D., 1903; University of Leipzig, graduate study, 1901-02. *Religion:* Society of Friends. *Home:* 550 Elm Ave., Swarthmore, Pa.

CAREER: George School, Newtown, Pa., instructor in history, 1896-99; Isthmian Canal Commission, economic investigator, 1899-1901; University of Pennsylvania, Wharton School of Finance and Commerce, Philadelphia, instructor in commerce, 1903-06, assistant professor of geography and industry, 1906-09, professor of industry, 1909-19; Columbia University, New York, N.Y., professor of economic geography, 1919-44, professor emeritus, 1944-66. Operator of a commercial nursery in Round Hill, Va. *Member:* Association of American Geographers (president, 1941-42), Cosmos Club (Washington, D.C.), Franklin Inn Club (Philadelphia). *Awards, honors:* Harmon Foundation Prize, 1927; Cullum Medal of American Geographic Society, 1956; Sc.D. from Columbia University, 1929, University of Pennsylvania, 1957.

WRITINGS: The Organization of Ocean Commerce, University of Pennsylvania Press, 1905; *Ocean Freight Rates,* Ginn, 1906; *The Ocean Carrier,* Putnam, 1908; *The Story of Iron and Steel,* Appleton, 1908; *Industrial and Commercial Geography,* Holt, 1913, 5th edition (with M. Ogden Philips and Thomas R. Smith), Holt, 1960; *The Elements of Industrial Management,* Lippincott, 1915; *Commerce and Industry,* Holt, 1916, 2nd revised edition, 1925 (published in England as *Industry and Commerce,* Constable, 1916, 2nd revised edition, 1925); *The World's Food Resources,* Holt, 1919; *Influence of the Great War Upon Shipping,* Oxford University Press, 1919.

Human Geography, Winston, Volume I (with John M. Foote), 1921, Volume II (with Margaret J. McCoy and Edwin W. Adams), 1922, 2nd edition, 1939; *North America, Its People and the Resources, Development, and Prospects of This Continent as an Agricultural, Industrial, and Commercial Area,* Harcourt, 1925, 4th edition (with Phillips and Smith), 1960; *Home Folks,* Winston, 1927, 2nd edition, 1939; *Tree Crops,* Harcourt, 1929, 2nd edition, Devin-Adair, 1950.

Our Neighboring Continents, Winston, 1930; *Our State and North America,* Winston, 1930; *World Folks,* Winston, 2nd edition, 1945; *World-Picture Building,* P. Garrigue, 1930; *American Lands and Peoples,* Winston, 1932, 2nd edition, 1946; *Foreign Lands and Peoples,* Winston, 1933, 2nd edition published as *Our Neighbors in Europe and Asia,* 1935, 3rd edition, under original title, 1945; *Human Use Geography,* two volumes, Winston, 1934, 2nd edition, 1939; *New York: The Empire State,* Winston, 1934; *Other World Neighbors,* Winston, 1934, 2nd edition, 1942; *Our Country and Northern Neighbors,* Winston, 1934, 2nd edition, 1946; *Our European Neighbors,* Winston, 1934, 2nd edition, 1946; *Our Industrial World,* Winston, 1934, 2nd edition, 1948; *New Jersey: People, Resources, and Industries of the Garden State,* Winston, 1935; *California: Life, Resources, and Industries of the Golden State,* California State Department of Education, 1936; *Men and Resources: A Study of North America and Its Place in World Geography,* Harcourt, 1937.

The Devil of the Machine Age, Harcourt, 1941, 2nd edition published as *Abundance: the Devil of the Machine Age,* Walnut Lane Press, 1949; *West Virginia: Life, Resources,*

Industries of the Mountain State, Winston, 1942; *Geography and World War II,* Winston, 1943, 2nd edition, 1944; (with Frank E. Sorenson) *Neighbors Around the World,* Winston, 1947, 2nd edition, 1952; (with Sorenson) *Our Neighbors at Home,* Winston, 1947, 2nd edition, 1954; (with Sorenson) *Neighbors in the Americas,* Winston, 1948, revised edition, 1957; (with Sorenson) *Neighbors in the United States and Canada,* Winston, 1951, revised edition, 1957; *How to Graft Nut Trees,* Soil and Crops Research Institute, 1962.

Also author of *Commerce and Transportation,* published by University of Pennsylvania Press; *Geography of Europe, Asia, Africa, for Elementary Schools,* Winston; *World Geography for Elementary Schools,* Winston; *Geography of the Americas for Elementary Schools,* Winston.

Editor of world map series, Denoyer-Geppert, published annually, 1952-56. Contributor of papers to published yearbooks, conference proceedings, and symposia.

WORK IN PROGRESS: A high school geography textbook.

BIOGRAPHICAL/CRITICAL SOURCES: V. M. Rowley, *J. Russell Smith, Geographer, Educator, and Conservationist,* University of Pennsylvania Press, 1964.

(Died February 26, 1966)

*   *   *

SMITH, Leslie F(rancis) 1901-

PERSONAL: Born June 30, 1901, in Plumstead, Kent, England; son of Frank Hugh and Kathleen Mary (Connors) Smith; married Liv Lundevall, 1932; children: Joan (Mrs. William S. Borden). *Education:* Attended Oxford University, 1923-25; University of Glasgow, M.A. (honors in classics), 1926; Columbia University, A.M., 1929, Ph.D., 1940. *Politics:* Democrat. *Home:* 1715 South Pickard, Norman, Okla. 73069. *Office:* History Department, University of Oklahoma, Norman, Okla. 73069.

CAREER: Columbia University, New York, N.Y., lecturer in Greek and Latin, 1929-36, instructor in history of education at Teachers College, 1929-35; University of Maine, Orono, assistant professor of classics, 1938-47; University of Oklahoma, Norman, associate professor, 1947-59, professor of history, 1959-71, professor emeritus, 1971—. Visiting lecturer, University of Dublin, 1970. *Member:* Renaissance Society of America, Norwegian Historical Association, Phi Kappa Phi. *Awards, honors:* Fulbright research award to Oslo, Norway, 1954-55.

WRITINGS: Thesaurus Linguae Latinae Epigraphicae, Volume II, Columbia University Press, 1935-36; *The Genuineness of the Ninth and Third Letters of Isocrates,* privately printed, 1940; (contributor) Matthew Anthony Fitzsimons and others, editors, *The Development of Historiography,* Stackpole, 1954; *Modern Norwegian Historiography,* Norwegian Universities Press, 1962. Contributor to *Studies in the Renaissance, Classical Philology,* and other journals.

WORK IN PROGRESS: Working on manuscripts of unpublished Italian humanists of the latter part of the fifteenth century.

SIDELIGHTS: Smith is competent in Greek, Latin, Norwegian, German, Italian, Spanish, and French; and can read Russian ("not as well as others"), and modern Greek.

SMITH, Margaret Ruth 1902-

PERSONAL: Born February 23, 1902, in Wallace, W.Va.; daughter of Flavius Josephus (a merchant) and Mary Alice (Meredith) Smith. *Education:* Goucher College, A.B., 1924; Columbia University, A.M., 1929, Ph.D., 1937. *Religion:* Protestant. *Home and office:* 3060 Pharr Court North N.W., Atlanta, Ga. 30305.

CAREER: Junior high school teacher in Trenton, N.J., 1924-25, in Fairmont, W.Va., 1925-26; West Chester State College, West Chester, Pa., assistant dean of women, 1926-28; University of Michigan, Ann Arbor, social director of Martha Cook Building, 1929-34; Northwest Missouri State College, Maryville, director of personnel for women, 1937-40; Wayne State University, Detroit, Mich., director of student activities, 1940-46, associate admissions officer, 1946-52, research analyst, 1952-64, research analyst emeritus, 1964—; educational consultant in Atlanta, Ga., 1964—. Member of regional interviewing committee, Committee for Interchange of Teachers, Federal Security Agency, 1948-64; member of subcommittee on financial aid information and guidance, College Scholarship Service, College Entrance Examination Board, 1966—.

MEMBER: American Personnel and Guidance Association, American College Personnel Association, Association for Higher Education, American Educational Research Association, National Association of Women Deans and Counselors, American Association of University Women, Pi Lambda Theta (chairman of national finance committee, 1955-57; parliamentarian of national council, 1963), Delta Kappa Gamma, Kappa Delta Pi.

WRITINGS: Student Aid—Bases of Selection of Students to Whom Loans, Scholarships, and Fellowships Are Awarded in a Graduate School of Education, Teachers College, Columbia University, 1937; (with Esther Lloyd-Jones) *A Student Personnel Program for Higher Education*, McGraw, 1938; (contributor) Percy Friars Valentine, editor, *The American College*, Philosophical Library, 1949, (editor with Lloyd-Jones) *Student Personnel Work as Deeper Teaching*, Harper, 1954; (editor) *Guidance-Personnel Work: Future Tense*, Teachers College, Columbia University, 1966. Writer of reports on research studies and contributor to journals in her field. Member of editorial board, *Journal of College Student Personnel* (quarterly of American College Personnel Association), 1959-62, and chairman of ACPA Commission on Student Personnel Monographs, 1962-66; member of publications committee, American Personnel and Guidance Association, 1962-66, and member of editorial committee for *Review of Educational Research*, April, 1963.

* * *

SMITH, Rhea Marsh 1907-

PERSONAL: Given name rhymes with "day"; born April 19, 1907, in Celina, Tex.; son of J. Fred (a realtor) and Lula Alexander (Miller) Smith; married Dorothy Lockhart (director of exhibitions at an art gallery, Winter Park, Fla.), June 5, 1932. *Education:* Southern Methodist University, B.A., 1926; Princeton University, M.A., 1929; University of Pennsylvania, Ph.D., 1937. *Politics:* Democrat. *Religion:* Presbyterian. *Home:* 600 Elizabeth Dr., Winter Park, Fla.

CAREER: Instructor in history at Southern Methodist University, Dallas, Tex., 1928-29, and University of Texas, Austin, 1929-30; Rollins College, Winter Park, Fla., began as assistant professor, 1930, professor of history,

1942-72. *Military service:* U.S. Army, Signal Corps, 1943-46; became major. U.S. Army Reserve, 1946-62; now colonel (retired). *Member:* Phi Beta Kappa, Kappa Alpha, Pi Sigma Alpha, Pi Gamma Mu, Phi Alpha Theta. *Awards, honors:* Cervantes Medal of Hispanic Institute, 1938; Rollins College Decoration of Honor, 1949; Hamilton Holt Medal, 1974.

WRITINGS: The Day of the Liberals in Spain, University of Pennsylvania Press, 1938; *Spain: A Modern History*, University of Michigan Press, 1965. Contributor to *Americana Annual*, and to historical journals.

SIDELIGHTS: Smith speaks Spanish, and reads Spanish, French, German, Portuguese.

* * *

SMITH, Robert S(idney) 1904-1969

PERSONAL: Born June 13, 1904, in Waterbury, Conn.; son of Leslie James (a machinist) and Laura Grace (Rouse) Smith; married Lucille Mulholland, August 2, 1932; children: Frances Smith Vaughan, Laurence. *Education:* Amherst College, A.B., 1927, A.M., 1928; Duke University, Ph.D., 1932. *Home:* 2236 Cranford Rd., Durham, N.C. 27706. *Office:* Duke University, Durham, N.C.

CAREER: Duke University, Durham, N.C., instructor, 1932-38, assistant professor, 1938-45, associate professor, 1945-48, professor of economics, 1948-69, chairman of department of economics and business administration, 1964-68. Visiting professor at University of Costa Rica, 1945, University of San Carlos, Guatemala, 1949, University of North Carolina, 1955-56; lecturer in Spanish at various Latin-America institutions, under auspices of U.S. Department of State, 1956, 1957, 1965. Honorary consul, Republic of Guatemala, 1955-63. *Member:* American Economic Association, Economic History Association, Southern Economic Association. *Awards, honors:* Guggenheim fellow, 1942; Ford Foundation faculty research fellow, 1959-60.

WRITINGS: The Spanish Guild Merchant, Duke University Press, 1940; *Mill on the Dan: A History of the Dan River Mills*, Duke University Press, 1960; (editor with F. T. DeVyer) *Economic Systems and Public Policy: Essays in Honor of Calvin Bryce Hoover*, Duke University Press, 1966. Also contributor to *Cambridge Economic History of Europe* published by Cambridge University Press. Member of editorial boards, *Hispanic American History Review*, 1947-53, *Southern Economic Journal*, 1959-62, *South Atlantic Quarterly*, 1960-66, and *Business History Review*, 1966-69.

WORK IN PROGRESS: Research in the Central American Common Market (materials being prepared for posthumous publication by co-author, W. T. Wilford); research in the history of Spanish economics.

(Died March 23, 1969)

* * *

SMITH, Ronald Gregor 1913-1968
(Sam Browne, Ronald Maxwell)

PERSONAL: Born April 17, 1913, in Edinburgh, Scotland; son of George Henry (a civil servant) and Helen (Wilson Dea) Smith; married Katherina Elisabeth Helena Wittlake, June 13, 1947. *Education:* University of Edinburgh, M.A., 1934, B.D., 1938; graduate study at University of Munich, 1934-35, University of Marburg, 1937, University of Copenhagen, 1938. *Home:* 5 The University, Glasgow, Scotland.

CAREER: Church of Scotland, minister in Selkirk, 1939-44; Control Commission for Germany, Bonn, university education control officer, 1946-47; Student Christian Movement Press, London, England, managing director and editor, 1947-56; University of Glasgow, Glasgow, Scotland, Primarius Professor of Divinity, 1956-68. Lecturer in Europe, United States, Australia. *Military service:* British Army, chaplain, 1944-46; became captain. *Member:* Athenaeum (London). *Awards, honors:* D.D. from University of Edinburgh and University of Marburg, both 1963.

WRITINGS: D. H. Lawrence in Essays and Literature, Oliver & Boyd, 1936; (under pseudonym Ronald Maxwell) *Still Point: An Essay in Living*, Nisbet, 1943; (under pseudonym Sam Browne) *Back from the Front*, Oliver & Boyd, 1947; *The Thought of Martin Buber*, Ridgeway House, 1949; (editor) *The Enduring Gospel: A Symposium Written in Honor of Hugh Martin* (essays), A. R. Allenson, 1950; (editor) Karl Barth, *Against the Stream: Shorter Post-War Writings, 1946-52*, translated by E. M. Delacour and Stanley Godman, Philosophical Library, 1954; *The New Man: Christianity and Man's Coming of Age*, Harper, 1956; (contributor) *Festschrift fuer Rudolf Bultmann*, Mohr, 1964; *Secular Christianity*, Harper, 1966; (editor with Wolf-Dieter Zimmerman) *I Knew Dietrich Bonhoeffer: Reminiscences by His Friends*, Collins, 1966, Harper, 1967; *Martin Buber*, Carey Kingsgate Press, 1966, John Knox, 1967; (compiler and author of introduction) *World Come of Age*, Fortress, 1967 (published in England as *World Come of Age: A Symposium on Dietrich Bonhoeffer*, Collins, 1967); *The Whole Man: Studies in Christian Anthropology*, Westminster, 1969 (published in England as *The Free Man: Studies in Christian Anthropology*, Collins, 1969); *The Doctrine of God*, edited by A. D. Galloway and Katherina Gregor Smith, Westminster, 1970.

Translator: (And editor) Martin Buber, *I and Thou*, Scribner, 1937, 2nd edition, enlarged, 1958; (and editor) Karl Barth, *The Germans and Ourselves*, Nisbet, 1945; (and editor) Martin Buber, *Between Man and Man*, Routledge & Kegan Paul, 1947, Macmillan, 1948, reissued with an introduction by Smith, Collins, 1961; (and author of introduction) Karl Jaspers, *The European Spirit*, S.C.M. Press, 1948, Macmillan, 1949; (with wife, Katherina Gregor Smith) Egon Caesar Conte Corti, *The Destruction and Resurrection of Pompeii and Herculaneum*, Routledge & Kegan Paul, 1951; (with K. Gregor Smith) Walter Eichrodt, *Man in the Old Testament*, Regnery, 1951; (translator with K. Gregor Smith) Willy Kramp, *The Prophecy*, S.C.M. Press, 1952; Martin Buber, *Right and Wrong: An Interpretation of Some Psalms*, S.C.M. Press, 1952, also published with Buber's *Images of Good and Evil*, translated by Michael Bullock, as *Good and Evil: Two Interpretations*, Scribner, 1953; (with K. Gregor Smith) Ethelbert Stauffer, *Christ and the Caesars: Historical Sketches*, Westminster, 1955; (and editor) *J. G. Hamann, 1730-1788: A Study in Christian Existence, with Selections from His Writings*, Harper, 1960; Gerhard Ebeling, *The Nature of Faith* (lectures), Collins, 1961, Muhlenberg Press, 1962; Dietrich Bonhoeffer, *The Communion of Saints: A Dogmatic Inquiry into the Sociology of the Church*, revised edition, Harper, 1963 (published in England as *Sanctorum Communio: A Dogmatic Inquiry into the Sociology of the Church*, Collins, 1963); (and editor) Soeren Kierkegaard, *The Last Years: Journals, 1853-1855*, Harper, 1965.

General editor, with John Marsh, of *Torch Bible Commentaries*, Mansfield College, Oxford, 1948; editor, *Scottish Periodicals*, 1948; editor, "Library of Philosophy and Theology," S.C.M. Press, 1955-56. Contributor of articles to *Christian Scholar, Listener, Theology Today*, and other publications.

BIOGRAPHICAL/CRITICAL SOURCES: Motive, February, 1967; *Christian Science Monitor*, March 9, 1967; *Christian Century*, July 12, 1967.

(Died October, 1968)

*   *   *

SMITH, Talbot 1899-

PERSONAL: Born October 11, 1899, in Fayette, Mo.; son of Franklin C. and Mary (Major) Smith; married Lola E. Hamlen, 1921; children: Barbara Jean Capps, Talbot Michael. *Education:* U.S. Naval Academy, B.S., 1920; University of Michigan, M.S. in Chemical Engineering, 1927, J.D., 1934. *Religion:* Episcopalian. *Home:* 2011 Day St., Ann Arbor, Mich. 48104. *Office:* 802 Federal Building, Detroit, Mich. 48226.

CAREER: Commissioned ensign, U.S. Navy, 1920; advanced through grades to lieutenant, senior grade, 1926; retired, 1931. Admitted to Michigan Bar, 1934; practiced law in Detroit, Mich., 1934-37; University of Missouri, Columbia, professor of law, 1937-41; University of California, Berkeley, professor of law, 1946-47; practiced law in Ann Arbor, Mich., 1947-55; Justice, Supreme Court of Michigan, Lansing, 1955-62; U.S. District Judge, Detroit, Mich., 1962—. U.S. Government, Office of Price Administration, World War II, served on staff drafting the Price Act, and assisted in setting up Office of Price Administration; member of Governor's committee, Michigan Anti-Subversive Legislation Study Commission, 1950; member, Michigan Corrections Commission, 1953-55. *Member:* U.S. Naval Academy Alumni Association, Michigan Bar Association, Phi Beta Kappa, Masons, Order of Coif.

WRITINGS: Lawyer, Macmillan, 1961. Contributor to law reviews.†

*   *   *

SMITHELLS, Roger (William) 1905-
(Sebastian Cash)

PERSONAL: Born April 2, 1905, in Stafford, England; son of Edwin and Amy (Cohen) Smithells; married Anabel Doreen Boscawen, December 22, 1928; children: Jancis Elinor, Julian Boscawen, Roger David. *Education:* Attended Sorbonne, University of Paris. *Home:* Tree Cottage, 23 Shackstead Lane, Godalming GU7 1RL, England. *Office:* Roger Smithells Ltd., 9 Great Chapel St., London W. 1, England.

CAREER: Mayfair Press Ltd., London, England, managing director, 1935-39; Pennant Press Ltd., London, managing director, 1938-45; London School of Interior Decoration, London, founder and director, 1936-39; Roger Smithells Ltd., London, managing director, 1955—; Sebastian Cash Travel and Holiday Features, London, director, 1958—. *Member:* Guild of British Travel Writers (past chairman). *Awards, honors:* Thomson Travel Award for Journalism, 1972.

WRITINGS: (With S. John Woods) *The Modern Home*, F. Lewis, 1936; *Modern Small Country Houses*, Country Life, 1936; *Country Life Book of Small Houses*, Country Life, 1939; *Make Yourself at Home*, Royle Publications, 1946; (editor) *Better Homes Book*, News of the World, 1948; *Fabrics in the Home*, Jenkins, 1950; *Interiors in Color*, Batsford, 1960; (editor) *A Truthful Guide to*

Package Holiday Resorts, Dickens Press, 1968. Editor of *Decoration*, 1935-39, *House and Garden Design*, 1939, *Electrical Housekeeping* (bi-annual).

Under pseudonym Sebastian Cash: *Holidays Abroad*, Take-Home-Books; *Unusual Holidays*, Take-Home-Books.

Travel editor of *Woman's Realm*, *Ideal Home*. Contributor to *Guardian*, *Sunday Times* (London), *Observer* (London), and other periodicals and newspapers.

SIDELIGHTS: Smithells wrote: "Have all my life taken a great interest in improving old houses. . . . Have occupied twenty-two homes (at one time the score was twenty homes in twenty years). Keen gardener, and keen but bad painter." In recent years Smithells has visited thirty-two European, African, and Middle Eastern countries collecting holiday information; his magazine readers' holiday information service answers about twenty-five thousand inquiries annually.

BIOGRAPHICAL/CRITICAL SOURCES: Daily Mail (London), October 28, 1950, April 13, 1957; *Housewife*, September, 1951.

* * *

SMYSER, H(amilton) M(artin)   1901-

PERSONAL: Born July 28, 1901, in Delaware, Ohio; son of William Emory (a college dean) and Elisabeth (Craig) Smyser; married Jane Worthington (a professor), March 24, 1949. *Education:* Attended Wesleyan University, Middletown, Conn., 1919-20; Ohio Wesleyan University, A.B., 1923; Ohio State University, M.A., 1924; Harvard University, Ph.D., 1932. *Politics:* Independent. *Religion:* Protestant. *Home:* 5 North Ridge Rd., New London, Conn. 06320. *Office:* Connecticut College, New London, Conn. 06320.

CAREER: Ohio University, Athens, assistant professor of English, 1925-26; Harvard University, Cambridge, Mass., instructor in English, 1929-34; Connecticut College, New London, assistant professor, 1934-38, associate professor, 1938-45, professor of English, 1945-68, professor emeritus, 1968—. Chairman of department, 1950-52, 1954-55, 1961-66. Visiting summer lecturer at Harvard University, 1946-49 and 1968, University of California, Berkeley, 1950, Northwestern University, 1951. *Member:* Modern Language Association of America, Mediaeval Academy of America (fellow; president, 1969-71).

WRITINGS: Footnotes and Bibliographies: A Style Sheet, Harvard Co-op Society, 1934, revised edition, 1940; (editor) *The Pseudo-Turpin*, Mediaeval Academy of America, 1937; (translator with F. P. Magoun, Jr.) *Survivals in Old Norwegian*, Connecticut College Book Shop, 1941; (with Magoun) *Walter of Aquitaine*, Connecticut College, 1950. Assistant editor, *Speculum*, 1947-69.

WORK IN PROGRESS: Studies in Chaucer's language.

* * *

SNELL, Bruno   1896-

PERSONAL: Born June 18, 1896, in Hildesheim, Germany; son of Otto and Anna (Struckmann) Snell; married Herta Schrader, 1925; children: Barbara (Mrs. Horst Leptin), Cornelia (Mrs. Martin Sperlich). *Education:* Studied at Universities of Edinburgh, Leiden, Berlin, Munich, and Goettingen; Dr.Phil., 1922. *Home:* Heimhuder Strasse 80, Hamburg 13, Germany.

CAREER: University of Pisa, Pisa, Italy, lector, 1925; University of Hamburg, Hamburg, Germany, privatdocent, 1925-31, professor of classics, 1931-60. *Member:* Classical academies of Goettingen, Berlin, Munich, Vienna, London, Lund, and Athens. *Awards, honors:* Dr.Phil., University of Aarhus; D.Litt., University of Leeds, Oxford University, and University of Southampton.

WRITINGS: (Editor) *Bacchylides*, Teubner, 1934, 4th edition, 1961; *Die Entdeckung des Geistes*, Claassen, 1946, 3rd edition, 1955; *Der Aufban der Sprache*, Claassen, 1952, 2nd edition, 1961; (editor) *Pindarus*, Teubner, 1953; *Griechische Metrik*, Vandenhoeck & Ruprecht (Zurich), 1953, 3rd edition, 1962; *Poetry and Society*, Indiana University Press, 1961; *Scenes from Greek Drama*, University of California Press, 1964; (editor) *Fragmenta Tragicorum Graecorum*, Vandenhoeck & Ruprecht, 1971.

* * *

SNOW, Dorothy Mary Barter   1897-

PERSONAL: Born July 30, 1897, in London, England; daughter of Frank Trevelyan (a clergyman, Church of England) and Laura Anna (an author and editor; maiden name, Barter) Snow. *Education:* King's College, London, B.Sc. (honors in zoology), B.D.; St. Anne's College, Oxford, B.Litt. *Religion:* Church of England (Evangelical).

CAREER: Teacher of divinity and science at schools in England, 1926-48; St. Michael's House (theological college for women), Oxford, England, principal, beginning, 1948. Member of committees for St. Mary's and St. Paul's Teacher Training colleges, Cheltenham, England, and member of council of Fernhill Manor School, New Milton, England. Member of Convocation of University of London and Oxford University; associate of King's College, University of London. *Member:* Society of Authors, Society of Women Journalists, Oxford Beekeeper's Association, Oxford Guild of Handweavers (chairman), Tyndale Fellowship, Campers' Club.

WRITINGS: The Long Pursuit, Pickering & Inglis, c.1926; *David, Tony, and the Bees*, Christian Literature Crusade, c.1928; *Into a Far Country*, Christian Literature Crusade, c.1939; (author with her sisters) *The Joyous Servant: The Life Story of Laura Anna Barter Snow*, Oliphants, 1941; *Fiddlers Three*, Pickering & Inglis, 1953. Contributor to periodicals. Editor of *You and I* (women's monthly magazine), 1937-56.

WORK IN PROGRESS: A novel.

SIDELIGHTS: Dorothy Snow has a working knowledge of French, New Testament Greek, Old Testament Hebrew, and some German.

AVOCATIONAL INTERESTS: Beekeeping, weaving, spinning, and general crafts; and swimming, sailing, and horseback riding.

* * *

SODERBERG, Percy Measday   1901-1969
(S. E. Archer, George Measday, G. R. Seebord, Peter Underhill)

PERSONAL: Born March 15, 1901, in Whitstable, Kent, England; son of Edward Percy (a schoolmaster) and Louisa (Corbin) Soderberg. *Education:* Attended Goldsmiths' College, University of London, and University of Grenoble. *Religion:* Church of England. *Home:* 9, Varndean Gardens, Brighton, Sussex, England.

CAREER: Headmaster of boarding school; broadcaster; author.

WRITINGS: Cat Breeding and General Management, Cassell, 1948; *Your Cat: A Useful Handbook for All Cat Lovers*, Cassell, 1951; *A.B.C. of Cat Diseases*, All-Pets Books, 1952, T.F.H. Publications, 1967; *Tropical Fish and Aquaria*, Cassell, 1953; *Popular Pet Keeping*, Elliot, 1953; *Foreign Birds for Cage and Aviary*, four volumes, Book 1: *Care and Management*, Book 2: *Waxbills, Weavers, Whydahs*, Book 3: *Finches*, Book 4: *Buntings, Cardinals, Lovebirds, Mannikins*, Cassell, 1956, T.F.H. Publications, 1963; *The Care of Your Cat*, edited by Margaret Pinney, Harper, 1957; *Pedigree Cats: Their Varieties, Breeding and Exhibition*, Cassell, 1958.

Under pseudonym S. E. Archer: *Faeries Hither!* (poems), Stockwell, 1935. Also author of other books under pseudonyms. Contributor of articles to *All Pets, Our Cats*, and other British and American magazines.

(Died July 6, 1969)

* * *

SORENSON, Marian 1925-1968

PERSONAL: Born May 13, 1925, in Elyria, Ohio; daughter of Nels Christian and Doris (Leuzler) Sorenson. *Education:* Ohio State University, B.A., 1948. *Religion:* Christian Science. *Home:* 300 42nd St., Bradenton, Fla.

CAREER: Christian Science Monitor, Boston, Mass., staff writer and editorial assistant, 1950-56; free-lance writer. *Member:* National Audubon Society, National Wildlife Federation, American Forestry Association, Wilderness Society.

WRITINGS: (With Allen S. Hitch) *Conservation and You*, Van Nostrand, 1964. Contributor of regular column on conservation to *Christian Science Monitor*.

(Died March 17, 1968)

* * *

SOTH, Lauren (Kephart) 1910-

PERSONAL: Surname rhymes with "both"; born October 2, 1910, in Sibley, Iowa; son of Michael Ray (a school superintendent and newspaper editor) and Virginia Mabel (Kephart) Soth; married Marcella Shaw Van, June 5, 1934; children: John Michael, Sara Kathryn (Mrs. James Leroy Hoogenakker), Melinda (Mrs. Jack Fribley). *Education:* Iowa State University of Science and Technology, B.S., 1932, M.S., 1938. *Politics:* Democrat. *Religion:* Episcopalian. *Home:* State Farm Rd., West Des Moines, Iowa. *Office: Register* and *Tribune*, Locust St., Des Moines 4, Iowa.

CAREER: Iowa State University of Science and Technology, Ames, 1933-47, began as instructor, became associate professor of economic information; *Register* and *Tribune*, Des Moines, Iowa, editorial writer, 1947-50, assistant editor of editorial pages, 1950-54, editor of editorial pages, 1954—. Principal agricultural economist, Office of Price Administration, Washington, D.C., 1942; chairman, committee on agriculture, National Planning Association, 1954—; member of board of directors, Resources for the Future, 1965—, and of National Advisory Commission on Food and Fiber, 1966-67. Member of editorial group studying economic recovery in Europe and activities of U.S. Economic Cooperation Administration, 1951, of first agricultural delegation to the Soviet Union, 1955, and of

newspaper editors delegation to Soviet Union, 1962. *Military service:* U.S. Army, Artillery, 1942-46; served in Leyte and Okinawa campaigns; became major; received Bronze Star.

MEMBER: American Society of Newspaper Editors, National Conference of Editorial Writers (chairman, 1961), American Agricultural Association, (fellow), American Agricultural Economic Association, American Economic Association, Council on Foreign Relations, Sigma Delta Chi, Beta Theta Pi, Alpha Zeta, Phi Kappa Phi, Cosmos Club (Washington, D.C.), Des Moines Club, Hyperion Field Club. *Awards, honors:* Pulitzer Prize for editorial writing, and Headliners Club Award for editorials inviting Russian farm delegation to United States, both 1956; Reuben Brigham Award, Agricultural College Editors Association, 1966.

WRITINGS: Farm Trouble, Princeton University Press, 1957; *An Embarrassment of Plenty*, Crowell, 1965. Writer of pamphlet, "Agriculture in an Industrial Society," Holt, 1965. Contributor of articles on agriculture and economics to farm journals and popular magazines. Editor, *Agricultural Situation*, U.S. Department of Agriculture, 1936-37.

SIDELIGHTS: Soth's Pulitzer Prize-winning editorial, "If the Russians Want More Meat," suggesting that a Soviet delegation visit Iowa farms to "get the low-down on raising high-quality cattle, hogs, sheep, and chickens," appeared in February, 1955. The Soviet government formally accepted this citizen-invitation within the month, and agreed to an exchange tour by U.S. farmers and economists.

* * *

SOWDEN, Lewis 1905-

PERSONAL: Born March 24, 1905, in Manchester, England; son of Jacob (a draper) and Anna (Mofson) Sowden; married Dora Levitt (a film and music critic), 1936. *Education:* University of the Witwatersrand, B.A., 1925, B.A. (honors), 1926, M.A., 1930. *Politics:* Liberal. *Religion:* Jewish. *Address:* P.O. Box 7145, Jerusalem, Israel. *Agent:* A. P. Watt & Son, 26-28 Bedford Row, London WCIR 4HI, England.

CAREER: Began as reporter on *Rand Daily Mail* and *Sunday Times*, Johannesburg, South Africa, became literary editor, *Rand Daily Mail*, 1935, drama critic, assistant editor, literary critic, 1945-66, in charge of drama, books, production, and foreign news, 1962-66. Free-lance writer in Europe, 1946-50. Chosen by U.S. Department of State as member of Multinational Journalists Project at Indiana University, 1961-62. *Member:* South African Society of Journalists (president, 1939, 1941), P.E.N. (chairman, South African chapter, 1953-55; delegate to six international congresses), Sigma Delta Chi.

WRITINGS: The Union of South Africa, Doubleday, 1943; *The Charmed Fabric* (poems), Fortune Press, 1943; *The Man Who Was Emperor* (novel), R. Hale, 1946; *Lady of Coventry* (novel), R. Hale, 1950; *The King of High Street* (novel), R. Hale, 1950; *Tomorrow's Comet* (novel), R. Hale, 1951; *Family Cromer* (novel), R. Hale, 1952; *Poems with Flute*, R. Hale, 1955; *The Crooked Bluegum*, Bodley Head, 1955; *Kop of Gold*, Afrikaanse Pers-Boekhanael, 1956; *Poems on Themes Drawn from the Bible*, R. Hale, 1960; *Both Sides of the Mask: The World of Muriel Alexander*, Howard Timmins, 1964; *The Land of Afternoon: The Story of a White South African*, McGraw, 1968.

Plays produced: "The Fugitives," London, 1934; "The

man in Checks," Johannesburg, 1935; "Red Rand," Johannesburg, 1937; "The Gold Earth," Johannesburg, 1944; "Ramses the Rich," British Broadcasting Corp., 1956; "The Kimberley Train," Johannesburg, 1958. Poetry published in *Poetry Review, Poetry of Today*, and other periodicals. Co-editor, *South African P.E.N. Year Book.*

SIDELIGHTS: Sowden writes: "'The Kimberley Train' was first play to deal frankly with color problem on South African stage and had over one hundred performances in Johannesburg and other towns. [I] made [an] unofficial intervention at United Nations General Assembly in New York, November, 1961, to protest against South African government's racialist policies and was ejected. Subsequently deprived of passport and press card by South African government." Sowden left South Africa for Israel on an "exit-only" passport in 1966. *Avocational interests:* Playing eighteenth-century music on the recorder.†

BIOGRAPHICAL/CRITICAL SOURCES: Punch, October 16, 1968; *Christian Century*, July 16, 1969.

* * *

SOWERBY, A(rthur) L(indsay) M(cRae) 1899-
(Lindsay McRae)

PERSONAL: Born January 2, 1899, in Harrow-on-the-Hill, Middlesex, England; son of Arthur Lichfield and Alice (Hutchison) Sowerby; married Ruth Margaret Adams; married second wife, Delia Helen Hunt, June 24, 1938. *Education:* Trinity College, Oxford, B.A., 1920; University College, London, M.Sc., 1924. *Politics:* Anti-Socialist. *Religion:* "Nominal Anglican." *Home:* Flat K, 70 Ladbroke Grove, London W.11, England.

CAREER: University College, University of London, London, England, assistant lecturer, department of chemistry, 1920-30; A.C. Cossor Ltd., London, chief development engineer, 1930-35; Iliffe & Sons Ltd. (publishers), London, technical editor of *Amateur Photographer*, 1936-44, editor, 1944-63, editor-in-chief, 1963-64. Technical consultant, R. G. Lewis Ltd. (photographic dealer). *Member:* Royal Photographic Society (council member, 1948-70; president, 1956-58; honorary fellow), Deutsche Gesellschaft fuer Photographie (corresponding member), London Salon of Photography.

WRITINGS: Foundations of Wireless, Iliffe Books, 1936, 3rd edition, 1941; *Dictionary of Photography and Reference Book for Amateur and Professional Photographers*, 15th edition, Iliffe Books, 1939, 19th edition, 1962; (editor and translator with others) Dick Boer, *The Complete Amateur Photographer*, Iliffe Books, 1947, 7th edition, revised and enlarged, 1958. Contributor to *Amateur Wireless* and *Wireless World.*

AVOCATIONAL INTERESTS: Seaside sun bathing.

BIOGRAPHICAL/CRITICAL SOURCES: Amateur Photographer, November 6, 1963.

* * *

SPEARS, Dorothea (Johnson) 1901-

PERSONAL: Born July 23, 1901, in Webster City, Iowa; daughter of Eben Samuel (a bishop) and Sarah (Tilsley) Johnson; married Frank Sydney Spears (an artist), December 15, 1932; children: Colin Graham Botha, Darlow Graham Botha, Hilary Peter, Michael John. *Politics:* Progressive (South Africa). *Home:* 1 Airlie Close, Willow Rd., Constantia, Cape Province, Republic of South Africa.

CAREER: Writer. *Member:* P.E.N., Soroptimist Club of Cape of Good Hope (president, 1962-64), Civil Service Club (lady associate), Zeekoe Vlei Yacht Club.

WRITINGS: My Friend (verse), Epworth, 1925; *Sunshine and Shadows from the South*, Fortune Press, 1929; *Van Riebeeck: A Song of Tomorrow*, Maskew Miller, 1952; *No Common Day*, Howard Timmins, 1962. Contributor to *Cape Times, Country Life, Poetry Review*. Author of radio scripts for South African Broadcasting Corp.

WORK IN PROGRESS: Pioneers, a book of poetry; *The Unacceptable Prophet*, a novel.

SIDELIGHTS: Dorothea Spears told *CA:* "Early writing chiefly lyrical; later work philosophical. My belief: One God, one human race (on this planet, anyway)." She has lived in South Africa since 1919, returned to United States, 1920, 1949, and 1963.

* * *

SPENCER, Steven M. 1905-

PERSONAL: Born July 3, 1905, in Omaha, Neb.; son of Guy R. (a cartoonist) and Josephine (McNulty) Spencer; married Mary Sears, September 19, 1928; children: Steven S., Douglas M. S., C. David. *Education:* Attended University of Montana, 1923-24, University of Omaha, 1924-26; University of Pennsylvania, A.B., 1928. *Home:* 100 Yale Ave., Swarthmore, Pa. *Agent:* Brandt & Brandt, 101 Park Ave., New York, N.Y. 10017.

CAREER: Philadelphia Evening Bulletin, Philadelphia, Pa., reporter and science editor, 1927-41; DuPont de Nemours & Co., Wilmington, Del., science writer, 1942-46; *Saturday Evening Post*, New York, N.Y., science writer and editor, 1945-69; *Reader's Digest*, Pleasantville, N.Y., writer, 1969—. Member of advisory council, U.S. Public Health Service, National Institute of Allergy and Infectious Diseases, 1963-67.

MEMBER: National Association of Science Writers (president, 1948), American Association for the Advancement of Science. *Awards, honors:* Harvard University, Nieman fellow, 1939-40; George Westinghouse-American Association for the Advancement of Science Prize for distinguished science writing in magazines, 1947, for "New Hope for the Anemic"; Albert Lasker Medical Journalism Award, 1956, for "Mystery of the Blinded Babies"; Howard W. Blakeslee Award of American Heart Association, 1957, for "They Repair Damaged Hearts"; National Association for Mental Health Award, 1958, for "They Befriend the Mentally Ill" and, 1962, for series, "The Menningers of Kansas."

WRITINGS: Wonders of Modern Medicine, McGraw, 1953; (with wife, Mary S. Spencer) *Outposts of Medicine*, Friendship, 1963. Writer of more than 125 articles for *Saturday Evening Post*, several reprinted in *Reader's Digest*, and co-author with wife of articles on medical missions in *Presbyterian Life.*

SIDELIGHTS: Spencer wrote a series of articles on the British health scheme in 1949, another on the work of the Pan American Sanitary Bureau in 1956, covered the United Nations Atoms for Peace Conference in Geneva, 1958, and traveled to medical missions in Southeast Asia and Africa for the series of articles co-authored with his wife. His *Wonders of Modern Medicine* has been translated into Spanish and Italian.

SPERRY, Armstrong W. 1897-

PERSONAL: Born November 7, 1897, in New Haven, Conn.; son of Sereno Cark (a business executive) and Nettie (Alling) Sperry; married Margaret Mitchell, June 12, 1930; children: Susan, John Armstrong. *Education:* Studied at Yale School of Fine Arts, 1918, Art Students League, New York, N.Y., 1919-21, Academie Colarossis, Paris, France, 1922. *Home:* 10 Buell, Hanover, N.H. 03755. *Office:* Bridgman Building, Hanover, N.H. 03755.

CAREER: Started as illustrator, turned to writing, and began combining the two as writer-illustrator of children's books, 1932—. *Military service:* U.S. Navy, 1917. *Awards, honors:* John Newbery Medal for most distinguished contribution to literature for American children, 1941, for *Call It Courage; New York Herald Tribune* Children's Spring Book Festival award, 1944, for *Storm Canvas;* Boys' Clubs of America Junior Book Award, 1949, for *The Rain Forest.*

WRITINGS—All self-illustrated, except as otherwise noted: *One Day with Manu,* John C. Winston, 1933; *One Day with Jambi in Sumatra,* John C. Winston, 1934; *One Day with Tuktu, an Eskimo Boy,* John C. Winston, 1935; *All Sail Set: A Romance of the "Flying Cloud,"* John C. Winston, 1936; *Wagons Westward: The Old Trail to Sante Fe,* John C. Winston, 1936; *Little Eagle, a Navajo Boy,* John C. Winston, 1938; *Lost Lagoon: A Pacific Adventure,* Doubleday, 1939.

Call It Courage, Macmillan, 1940; *The Boy Who Was Afraid,* Lane, 1942; *Coconut, the Wonder Tree,* Macmillan, 1942; *Bamboo, the Grass Tree,* Macmillan, 1942; *No Brighter Glory,* Macmillan, 1942; *Storm Canvas,* John C. Winston, 1944; *Hull-Down for Action,* Doubleday, 1945; *The Rain Forest,* Macmillan, 1947; *Danger to Windward,* John C. Winston, 1947; *Black Falcon: A Story of Piracy and Old New Orleans,* John C. Winston, 1949.

The Voyages of Christopher Columbus, Random House, 1950; (compiler and author of introduction) *Story Parade: A Collection of Modern Stories for Boys and Girls* (gold book), John C. Winston, 1951; *River of the West: The Story of the Boston Men,* illustrated by Henry C. Pitz, John C. Winston, 1952; *Thunder Country,* Macmillan, 1952; *John Paul Jones, Fighting Sailor,* Random House, 1953; *Captain Cook Explores the South Seas,* Random House, 1955 (revised British edition published as *All About Captain Cook,* W. H. Allen, 1960); *Pacific Islands Speaking,* Macmillan, 1955; *Frozen Fire,* Doubleday, 1956; *All About the Arctic and Antarctic,* Random House, 1957; *South of Cape Horn: A Saga of Nat Palmer and Early Antarctic Exploration,* John C. Winston, 1958; *All About the Jungle,* Random House, 1959.

The Amazon, River Sea of Brazil, Garrard, 1961; *Great River, Wide Land: The Rio Grande Through History,* Macmillan, 1967.

Illustrator: Helen T. Follett, *Stars to Steer By,* Macmillan, 1934; Florence C. Means, *Shuttered Windows,* Houghton, 1938; Clara I. Judson, *Boat Builder: The Story of Robert Fulton,* Scribner, 1940; James Cloyd Bowman, *Winabojo, Master of Life,* Albert Whitman, 1941; Helen T. Follett, *House Afire!,* Scribner, 1941; Marion Florence Lansing, *Nicholas Arnold, Toolmaker,* Doubleday, 1941; Edith Berrien, *Dogie Boy,* Albert Whitman, 1943; Howard Pease, *Thunderbolt House,* Doubleday, 1944; Trevor Lloyd, *Sky Highways: Geography from the Air,* Houghton, 1945; Howard Pease, *Jungle River,* Doubleday, 1948; Allen Chaffee, adapter, *Story of Hiawatha,* Random House, 1951.

WORK IN PROGRESS: Research for a book about the American Southwest.

SIDELIGHTS: Sperry told *CA:* "From the beginning of my career it has been my conviction that no writer should ever write down to children. He should tell his story clearly, in a supple prose that leaves his reader—young or old—wondering, 'What happens next?' Children have imagination enough to grasp almost any idea and respond to it if it is presented to them honestly, and without a patronizing pat on the head."

Sperry speaks French and Tahitian. He spent two years in the French-owned islands of the South Pacific, and the themes for many of his books have come from this experience. He now spends most of the year in New Hampshire, the summers at his farm in Vermont, and wanders at intervals through Europe, across America, and to the West Indies in search of new ideas.

*   *   *

SPIEL, Hilde (Maria) 1911-

PERSONAL: Born October 19, 1911, in Vienna, Austria; daughter of Hugo F. (a scientist) and Marie (Gutfeld) Spiel; married Peter de Mendelssohn (a writer), October 30, 1936; married second husband, Hans Flesch Edler von Brunningen (a writer), February 7, 1971; children: (first marriage) Christine, Anthony Felix. *Education:* Vienna University, Doctor of Philosophy, 1936. *Politics:* Independent. *Religion:* Roman Catholic. *Home:* Cottagegasse 65/II/3, Vienna XIX, Austria. *Agent:* Dagmar Henne, Seestrasse 6, Munich, Germany.

CAREER: Writer. Works in broadcasting, mainly for Norddeutscher Rundfunk, RIAS Berlin and Bayerischer Rundfunk. *Member:* P.E.N. *Awards, honors:* Julius Reich Prize (Vienna), 1933, for *Kati auf der bruecke;* honorary professorship, awarded by presdent of Austrian Republic; Cross of Merit, first class, awarded by president of Federal Republic of Germany.

WRITINGS: Kati auf der bruecke (novel), Paul Zsolnay, 1933; *Verwirrung am Wolfgangsee* (novel), R. A. Hoeger, 1935, reissued with slight alterations as *Sommer am Wolfgangsee,* Rowohlt, 1961; *Flute and Drums* (novel), Hutchinson, 1939; *Der Park und die Wildnis, zur Situation der neueren englischen Literatur* (essays), C. H. Beck, 1953; (author of text) Elisabeth Niggemeyer, *London: Stadt, Menschen, Augenblicke* (book of illustrations), Sueddeutscher, 1956; *Sir Laurence Olivier,* Rembrandt, 1958; *Welt im Widerschein* (essays), C. H. Beck, 1960; (compiler and author of introduction) *England erzaehlt: Achtzehn Erzaehlungen,* S. Fischer, 1960; *The Darkened Room* (novel), Methuen, 1961; *Fanny von Arnstein; oder, Die Emanzipation: Ein Frauenleben an der Zeitenwende, 1758-1818* (biography), S. Fischer, 1962; (editor and author of commentary and documentation) Shakespeare, *Koenig Richard III,* Ullstein, 1964; (editor and author of introduction) *Der Wiener Kongress in Augenzeugenberichten,* Karl Rauch, 1965, 3rd edition, 1966, translation by Richard H. Weber published as *The Congress of Vienna: An Eyewitness Account,* Chilton, 1968; (author of introduction) Franz Vogler, *Verliebt in Doebling: Die Doerfer unter dem Himmel* (book of illustrations), Verlag fuer Jugend und Volk, 1965; *Lisas Zimmer* (novel), Nymphenburger, 1965; *Rueckkehr nach Wien* (diary), Nymphenburger, 1968; (translator with Otto Breicha and Georg Eisler) *Ver sacrum: Neue Hefte fuer Kunst und Literatur,* Verlag Jugend und Volk, 1969; (editor) *Wien/Spektrum einer*

Stadt, Nymphenburger, 1971. Contributor to *New Statesman, Times Literary Supplement, Guardian, Frankfurter Allgemeine Zeitung, Monat, Weltwoche, Sueddeutsche Zeitung,* and other periodical publications.

* * *

SPITTEL, Richard Lionel 1881-1969

PERSONAL: Born December 9, 1881, in Ceylon; son of Frederick George and Zilia (Jansz) Spittel; married Claribel Frances van Dort, 1911 (deceased); children: Christine (Mrs. A. McN. Wilson). *Education:* Educated in Ceylon and London, England; F.R.C.S., 1910. *Home:* Wycherley, Buller's Rd., Colombo, Ceylon. *Agent:* John Farquharson Ltd., 18 Red Lion Sq., London W.C. 1, England.

CAREER: General Hospital, Colombo, Ceylon, surgeon, 1910-35, consulting surgeon after retirement in 1935. *Member:* Wild Life Protection Society (Ceylon; former president), Rotary Club (Colombo; former president). *Awards, honors:* Commander of Order of the British Empire, 1942; Companion of St. Michael and St. George, 1950.

WRITINGS: A Basis of Surgical Ward Work [Colombo, Ceylon], 1915; *A Preliminary Course of Surgery,* Butterworth, 1918; *Paraugi of Ceylon,* Bailliere, 1923; *Framboesia Tropica* (medical), Butterworth, 1923; *Wild Ceylon,* Colombo Apothecaries, 1924, 3rd edition, General Publishers (Ceylon), 1945; *Essentials of Surgery,* 1932; *Far-Off Things,* Colombo Apothecaries, 1933, 2nd edition, Colombo Book Centre, 1957; *Savage Sanctuary,* Rich & Cowan, 1941; *Vanished Trails: The Last of the Veddas,* Oxford University Press, 1950; *Where the White Sambhur Roams* (novel), Hodder & Stoughton, 1951, abridged edition, adapted by D. J. Carpenter, Macmillan, 1957, published as *Savage Island,* Criterion, 1959; *Leaves of the Jungle* (poems) [Ceylon], 1953; *Wild White Boy* (novel), Phoenix House, 1958; (with Christine Wilson) *Brave Island,* Lake House Investments (Ceylon), 1966.

AVOCATIONAL INTERESTS: Anthropology, wildlife preservation.

(Died September 3, 1969)

* * *

SPITZER, Herbert Frederick 1906-

PERSONAL: Born September 20, 1906, in Brenham, Tex.; married Lois Hess, 1931; children: Martha Clatterbaugh, Anna Quandt, John. *Education:* North Texas State Teachers College (now North Texas State University), B.S., 1930; Ohio University, M.A., 1932; University of Iowa, Ph.D., 1938. *Home:* 330 West Main St., West Branch, Iowa 52358 (summer); and 109 Spanish Oak Dr., Georgetown, Tex. 78626 (winter).

CAREER: University of Iowa, Iowa City, 1938-68, became professor of education. Member of editorial staff, Armed Forces Institute, Washington, D.C., 1942-44; visiting professor, University of Texas, 1968-70, University of Oregon, 1971-72. *Member:* National Society for the Study of Education, National Council of Teachers of Mathematics, American Association of School Administrators, Association for Student Teaching, National Education Association, American Educational Research Association.

WRITINGS: The Teaching of Arithmetic, Houghton, 1948, 4th edition, 1967; *Practical Classroom Procedures for Enriching Arithmetic,* Webster Publishing, 1956; (with others) *Exploring Arithmetic,* Grades 1-8, Webster Publish-

ing, 1958-62, workbooks, 1959-62; *Enrichment of Arithmetic,* McGraw, 1964. Also author of published tests for basic skills, Houghton, 1943, and study skills, World Book Co., 1952; author or co-author of thirteen educational films issued by Coronet Instructional Films and Bureau of Audio-Visual Instruction, University of Iowa. Contributor to educational yearbooks and journals.

AVOCATIONAL INTERESTS: Gardening, travel.

* * *

SPOONER, Frederick Percy 1898-

PERSONAL: Born October 9, 1898, in Kimberley, South Africa; son of Frederick (a merchant) and Maria (Kirsten) Spooner; married Louise Frida Wolff, December, 1927; children: Margaret Ann Spooner Beekhuis. *Education:* University of Stellenbosch, B.Sc., 1919. *Politics:* Progressive. *Religion:* Protestant. *Home:* 602 Villa d'Este, Beach Rd., Sea Point, Republic of South Africa.

CAREER: Articled to Deloitte Plender Griffiths Annan (chartered accountants), South Africa, 1922-24, chartered accountant, 1924; Department of Commerce and Industries, Pretoria, South Africa, economic adviser, 1930-44; managing director of Fisheries Development Corp. of South Africa Ltd., 1945-52, and several other private fishing companies in South Africa, 1952-58; managing director of Tristan Investments Propriety Ltd., 1962-64. Member of board of directors of Sugar Co. Ltd. and Moreland Estates Ltd., 1952-68. *Member:* Economic Society of South Africa (secretary, 1934-37), Society of Accountants and Auditors, City Club (Cape Town). *Awards, honors:* Coronation Medal, 1937.

WRITINGS: South African Predicament, J. Cape, 1960. Contributor of articles to *Condenser.*

SIDELIGHTS: Spooner told CA, "[I] am not really a writer. [I] wrote the book to give people outside South Africa an indication of the problems (race relations) as seen by a worried South African."

* * *

SPOONER, (Glenda) Victoria Maude (Graham) 1897-

PERSONAL: Born August 5, 1897, in Poona, India; daughter of Sir Frederick and Lady Irene (Campbell) Graham; married Hugh Spooner, June 8, 1934 (died, 1935). *Politics:* Conservative. *Religion:* Presbyterian. *Home:* Brookside Farm, Ascot, Berkshire, England. *Agent:* E.P.S. Lewin & Partners, 7 Chelsea Embankment, London S.W.3, England.

CAREER: Great Eight (illustrated newspaper), London, England, head representative, fourteen years; *Popular Flying,* London, England, managing director, 1930-35. Judge and breeder of show ponies; authority and writer on horses and ponies; holds diploma from British Horse Society. *Member:* Ponies of Britain Club (co-founder; chairman, 1952—), British Horse Society (member of council).

WRITINGS: Victoria Glencairn (novel), Heinemann, 1935; *Royal Crusader: The Autobiography of a Horse,* Latimer House, 1948; *The Earth Sings,* Latimer House, 1950; *The Perfect Pest,* J. Cape, 1951; *Minority's Colt,* Cassell, 1952; *The Silk Purse,* Cassell, 1953; *Instructions in Ponymastership,* Museum Press, 1955, 4th edition, revised, 1962; (editor) Dorothy Brooke, *For Love of Horses: The Diaries of Mrs. Geoffrey Brooke,* Old War Horse Memorial Hospital, 1960; *Pony Trekking,* Museum Press, 1961,

Sportshelf, 1961; *Riding*, Museum Press, 1964, published as *Step-by-Step Riding*, Arco, 1965; *The Handbook of Showing: Basic Conformation, Defects, Unsoundness, Breeds, Types, Horse and Pony Socs, Breeding, Showing in Hand and Under Saddle, Judges and Judging, and a Complete Guide to Show Organization*, Pitman, 1968.

*   *   *

SPRING, (Robert) Howard 1889-1965

PERSONAL: Born February 10, 1889, in Cardiff, Wales; son of William Henry and Mary Spring; married Marion Ursula Pye, 1920; children: David, Michael. *Education:* Self-educated. *Home:* The White Cottage, Falmouth, Cornwall, England. *Agent:* David Higham Associates Ltd., 5-8 Lower John St., Soho, London WIR 4HA, England.

CAREER: Reporter for *South Wales Daily News*, then with *Yorkshire Observer*, 1911-15, *Manchester Guardian* (now *Guardian*), 1919-31; *Evening Standard*, London, England, book critic, 1931-38; author, 1931-65.

WRITINGS: Darkie and Company, Oxford University Press, 1932; *Shabby Tiger*, Collins, 1934, Covici-Friede, 1935; *Rachel Rosing*, Hillman-Curl, 1936; *Sampson's Circus*, Faber, 1936; *Book Parade*, Constable, 1938, Kennikat, 1970; *My Son, My Son!*, Viking, 1938 (published in England as *O Absalom*, Collins, 1938); *Heaven Lies About Us: A Fragment of Infancy*, Viking, 1939; *Tumbledown Dick: All People and No Plot*, Faber, 1939, Viking, 1940.

All They Like Sheep, Collins, 1940; *Fame Is the Spur*, Viking, 1940, new edition, Collins, 1956; (with Herbert Morrison and E. M. Delafield) *This War We Wage*, Emerson Press (autobiographical), Constable, 1942; *Hard Facts*, Viking, 1944; *And Another Thing . . .* (autobiographical), Harper, 1946; *Dunkerley's* (sequel to *Hard Facts*), Collins, 1946, Harper, 1947; *There Is No Armour*, Harper, 1948; *Christmas Honeymoon*, St. Hugh's Press, 1949; *Christmas Awake* (chapter of *Tumbledown Dick*), St. Hugh's Press, 1949.

The Houses in Between, Collins, 1951, Harper, 1952; *Jinny Morgan* (three-act play), Evans Brothers, 1952; *A Sunset Touch*, Harper, 1953; *Three Plays* (contains *Jinny Morgan, The Gentle Assassin*, and *St. George at the Dragon*), Collins, 1953; *These Lovers Fled Away*, Harper, 1955; *Time and the Hour*, Harper, 1957; *All the Day Long*, Collins, 1959, Harper, 1960.

I Met a Lady, Harper, 1961; *Winds of the Day*, 1964.

The Autobiography of Howard Spring (contains *Heaven Lies Above Us, In the Meantime*, and *And Another Thing . . .*), Collins, 1972.

(Died May 3, 1965)

*   *   *

SPRINGER, Otto 1905-

PERSONAL: Born March 18, 1905, in Aalen, Wuerttemberg, Germany; came to United States in 1930, naturalized, 1944; son of Julius (superintendent, German state railroads) and Else (Bammesberger) Springer; married Anne Marie Breur, 1932; married second wife, Herta Fischer-Colbrie, March 23, 1959; children (first marriage) Wolfgang Ernest, John Ulrich; (second marriage) Leonore Barbara. *Education:* Attended Protestant theological seminaries in Germany, 1919-23; University of Tuebingen, student, 1923-24, 1925-28, Ph.D., 1927; other study at University of Berlin, 1924-25, University of Munich, 1925, University of Upsala,

1928, University of Iceland, 1948. *Religion:* Protestant. *Home:* 1311 Pine Rd., Rosemont, Pa. *Office:* 737 Williams Hall, University of Pennsylvania, Philadelphia, Pa. 19174.

CAREER: Research fellow in England, Scotland, Sweden, and Norway, 1928-29; Wheaton College, Norton, Mass., head of German department, 1932-36; University of Kansas, Lawrence, chairman of department of Germanic languages, 1936-40; University of Pennsylvania, Philadelphia, professor of Germanics, 1940—, chairman of department, 1946-59, dean of College of Arts and Sciences, 1959-68, vice-provost, 1963-68. *Military service:* U.S. Army, war mission to Germany, 1945; held assimilated rank of lieutenant colonel. *Member:* Mediaeval Academy of America (fellow), Modern Language Association of America, Linguistic Society of America (vice-president, 1954), American Association of Teachers of German, Institut fuer Deutsch Sprache (Mannheim; corresponding member), Phi Beta Kappa.

WRITINGS: Die Flussnamen Wuerttembergs und Badens, W. Kohlhammer, 1930; *Die Nordische Renaissance in Skandinavien*, W. Kohlhammer, 1936; (editor and translator) Jakob Walter, *A German Conscript with Napoleon: Recollections of the Campaigns of 1806-1807, 1809, and 1812-13*, University of Kansas Press, 1938; (editor) Ernst Jockers, *Mit Goethe: Gesammelte Aufsaetze*, C. Winter (Heidelberg), 1957; (contributor) Roger S. Loomis, editor, *Arthurian Literature in the Middle Ages: A Collaborative History*, Oxford University Press, 1959; (editor-in-chief) *Langenscheidts Enzyklopaedisches Woerterbuch der Englischen und Deutschen Sprache, Englisch-Deutsch*, Langenscheidt, Volume I, 1962, Volume II, 1963; (contributor) *Thomson-Festschrift: Research Studies*, University of Washington Press, 1964; (contributor) Werner Betz and others, editors, *Taylor Starck: Festschrift*, Humanities, 1965. Compiler of Americana-Germanica bibliographies for *American-German Review*, annually, 1947-57, for PMLA, annually, 1957-65. Contributor to *Standard Reference Encyclopedia*, Funk, 1959—, and contributor of articles and reviews to professional journals in United States and Germany.

WORK IN PROGRESS: Research for special papers in the field of medieval German literature, Germanic linguistics, dialect geography, and Old Germanic epigraphy.

*   *   *

STAGEBERG, Norman C(lifford) 1905-

PERSONAL: Surname is pronounced *Stag*-e-berg; born April 7, 1905, in Owatonna, Minn.; son of Andrew N. and Marie (Larsen) Stageberg; married Alma Rosenberger, June 21, 1937. *Education:* University of Minnesota, B.S., 1926; University of Iowa, M.A., 1932; University of Wisconsin, Ph.D., 1946; also studied at Harvard University, Yale University, and University of Chicago. *Home:* 2210 Tremont St., Cedar Falls, Iowa 50613.

CAREER: State College of Iowa (now University of Northern Iowa), Cedar Falls, assistant professor, 1946-53, associate professor, 1953-56, professor of English, 1956-71. Visiting professor of English at University of Rhode Island. *Military service:* U.S. Army Air Forces, 1942-46, 1951-53; became captain. *Member:* Linguistic Society of America, Modern Language Association of America, National Council of Teachers of English, Teachers of English to Speakers of Other Languages, International Linguistic Association. *Awards, honors:* Fulbright professor in Holland, 1954-55.

WRITINGS: (Editor with Wallace L. Anderson) *Poetry as Experience*, American Book Co., 1952; *Using Grammar to Improve Writing*, State College of Iowa, 1953, revised edition, 1966; (editor with Anderson) *Introductory Readings on Language*, Holt, 1962, 3rd edition, 1970; (with Louis E. Glorfeld and D. Lauerman) *A Concise Guide for Writers*, Holt, 1963, 2nd edition, 1969; *An Introductory English Grammar*, Holt, 1965, 2nd edition, 1971; (compiler with Anderson) *Readings on Semantics*, Holt, 1967. Contributor to *Encyclopedia of Education*.

SIDELIGHTS: Stageberg is interested in pidgin languages and in the teaching of English as a foreign language; he claims "varying degrees of incompetence" in French, Chinese, Dutch, Italian, and other languages. *Avocational interests:* History of music, fine arts, Mexican artifacts.

* * *

STAHL, Le Roy 1908-
(George E. Sheldon, Kirk Wood)

PERSONAL: Born April 18, 1908, in DeWitt, Iowa; son of John H. and Sadie (Carson) Stahl; married Esther Louise Mace (a teacher), July 18, 1935. *Education:* Attended Minneapolis Institute of Arts, Northwestern College of Speech Arts, Minneapolis, Minn. *Politics:* Liberal Republican. *Religion:* Congregational. *Home:* 315 23rd St. N., Great Falls, Mont. 59401. *Agent:* Frieda Fishbein, Room 318, 353 West 57th St., New York, N.Y. 10019.

CAREER: KFBB (radio-television station) Great Falls, Mont., copy editor, program director, salesman, and television station manager, 1941-55; freelance writer, 1955—. Advertising and information consultant for various firms and associations in Great Falls. *Member:* Advertising Association of the West, Great Falls Rotary Club (past director), Advertising Club of Great Falls (past president and director).

WRITINGS—Humor and drama; all published by Northwestern Press except as otherwise noted: *Impromptu Vaudeville Burlesques: A Collection of Five Novelty Stunts*, 1932, *Big Game: A Farce in One Act*, 1934, *Bits of Fun: A Collection of Eight Comedy Sketches*, 1934, *Hot Biscuits: A Farce in One Act*, 1934, *Amateur Revue*, 1936, *The Five Star Minstrel Book: Suggestions and Material for Staging a Complete Minstrel Show*, 1938, *Hearty Laughs: A Collection of Three-Minute Sketches*, 1938, *The High School Minstrel Book: Suitable Minstrel Material for High School Presentation*, 1938, *The Circus Queen: A Comedy Drama in Three Acts*, 1939, *Doctor Jack: A Drama*, Eldridge Entertainment House, 1940, *More Hearty Laughs: A Collection of Three-Minute Sketches*, 1940, *It Happened to Sweeney: A Comedy of Youth in One Act*, 1941, *The Landmarks of Time: A Series of Simply Presented Assembly Sketches*, 1941, *The Varsity Minstrels: A Stream-Lined Potpourri of Scholastic Mirth and Melody*, 1941, *Peppy Puppet Plays: A Collection of Puppet Plays*, Denison, 1950, (with Van Chalmers) *Laugh Hits: A Collection of Short Sketches for Laugh Purposes*, Denison, 1964.

Other: *Simplified Stagecraft*, Northwestern Press, c.1938, reissued as *The Simplified Stagecraft Manual*, Denison, 1962; *The Marionette Handbook*, Northwestern Press, 1938; *Simplified Make-up*, Northwestern Press, 1938; (with wife, Esther L. Mace) *Simplified Stage Costuming*, Northwestern Press, 1939; (with Mace) *Producing the High School Play: A Handbook of Complete Directions for Staging the Amateur Play*, Northwestern Press, 1940; *How to be a Successful Emcee*, Denison, 1953; *The Art of Pub-*

licity, Denison, 1962; (with Effa E. Preston) *The Master Puppet Book: A Collection of Suitable Plays with Complete Instructions About How to Make and Operate Puppets*, Denison, 1965. Contributor of articles to newspapers and magazines.

WORK IN PROGRESS: Two non-fiction works, one on the impact of television, and the other on school public relations.

* * *

STAMP, L(aurence) Dudley 1898-1966

PERSONAL: Born March 9, 1898, in London, England; son of Charles (a company director) and Clara (Evans) Stamp; married Elsa Clara Rea, May 5, 1923 (died, 1962); children: Bryan Unett Dudley. *Education:* King's College, University of London, B.Sc. (first class honors in geology), 1917, M.Sc., 1919, B.A. (first class honors in geography) and D.Sc., 1921; London School of Economics and Political Science, D.Lit., 1948. *Religion:* Church of England. *Home:* Ebbingford Manor, Bude, Cornwall, England; and 93 Sloane St., London S.W.1, England.

CAREER: Yomah Oil Co. and Indo-Burma Petroleum Co., geologist, 1921-23; University of Rangoon, Rangoon, Burma, professor of geology and geography, 1923-26; University of London, London School of Economics and Political Science, London, England, Sir Ernest Cassell Reader in Economic Geography, 1926-45, professor of geography, 1945-48, research professor, 1948-58, professor emeritus and honorary lecturer, 1958-66. Soil erosion researcher in North and South America, 1933-34, West Africa, 1937, Burma, 1938; chief adviser on rural land utilization to British Ministry of Agriculture, 1942-55; member of Royal Commission on Common Land, 1955-58; United Kingdom permanent delegate on land use to United Nations Food and Agriculture Organization, beginning 1955; member of numerous governmental committees on land resources. *Military service:* Royal Engineers, 1917-19; served in France and Belgium; became lieutenant.

MEMBER: International Geographical Union (vice-president, 1949-52, 1956-60; president, 1952-56; former director of world land use survey), Royal Geographical Society (vice-president, 1958-62; president, beginning 1963), Royal Society of Arts (vice-president, 1954-56), Institute of British Geographers (president, 1956), Geographical Association (president, 1950; member of board of trustees), Institute of Grocers (president, 1960-63), Town Planning Institute (honorary member), Nature Conservancy (chairman for England, beginning 1963).

AWARDS, HONORS: Gold Medal, Mining and Geological Institute of India, 1922; Medaille Gosselet, Societes des Sciences (Lille), 1923; Companion, Order of the British Empire, 1946; Founder's Medal, Royal Geographical Society, 1949; Daly Medal, American Geographical Society, 1950; Darwin Medal (Union of Soviet Socialist Republics); Vega Medal (Sweden), 1954; Tokyo Geographical Society Medal, 1957, Scottish Geographical Medal, Royal Society of Geographers of Scotland, 1964; LL.D., Clark University, 1955, University of Edinburgh, 1961; honorary Ekon. D., University of Stockholm, 1959; D.Sc., University of Warsaw, 1962, University of Exeter, 1965; created Knight Bachelor, 1965.

WRITINGS: *An Introduction to Stratigraphy: British Isles*, T. Murby, 1923, 3rd edition revised, 1957; *The Vegetation of Burma from an Ecological Standpoint*, Thacker, Spink, 1924; (with Frederick G. French) *A Geography of*

Burma for Schools, Longmans, Green, 1924; *Longmans Regional Geographies of India*, Part IV, *India, Burma and Ceylon*, Longmans, Green, 1926; *An Intermediate Commercial Geography*, Longmans, Green, 1927, 12th edition, 1966; (with wife, Elsa C. Rea Stamp) *Geographical Exercises*, Longmans, Green, 1928, 2nd edition revised, 1937; (with E. C. R. Stamp) *Longmans Geographical Exercise Book*, Longmans, Green, 1928, 2nd edition, 1937; *The World: A General Geography*, 1929 (some North American editions with George H. T. Kimble, other regional editions with James N. Jamieson and Archibald G. Price), 18th edition, 1966; *Asia: An Economic and Regional Geography*, Dutton, 1929, 12th edition, 1967, reprinted in part as *India, Pakistan, Ceylon and Burma*, Metheun, 1957.

A Regional Geography for Higher Certificate and Intermediate Courses (later editions published as *A Regional Geography for Advanced and Scholarship Courses*), Part I, "The Americas," Part II (with Stanley H. Beaver), "Africa," Part III, "Australia and New Zealand," Part V [sic], "Europe and the Mediterranean," Longmans, Green, 1930, 13th edition, 1957, component parts also published separately under individual titles, 1961-68; *Real Life Geography*, two books, G. Gill, 1931; *An Agricultural Atlas of Ireland*, G. Gill, 1931; *Chisholm's Handbook of Commercial Geography*, Longmans, Green, (editor) 11th edition, 1928, (author) 13th edition, 1937, 18th edition, 1966; (with Arthur J. Newman) *The New Age West Indian Geographies*, Longmans, Green, 1932 ff.; (with Beaver) *The British Isles: A Geographic and Economic Survey*, Longmans, Green, 1933, 6th edition, 1971; *High School Geography*, Longmans, Green, 1933; *Smaller World Geography*, Longmans, Green, 1933, 2nd edition, 1951, also issued in three parts published as "New Age Geographies," Senior Series, 1930, 2nd edition, 1939; (with M. L. Mukerji) *Essentials of Commercial Geography*, Longmans, Green, 1933; *An Intermediate Geography* (incorporating parts of *An Intermediate Commercial Geography* and *A Regional Geography*), Longmans, Green, 1934, new edition, 1954; *India and World Studies*, John Long, 1935; *Secondary School Geography*, Section I, *The Three Southern Continents, North America and Eurasia*, Longmans, Green, 1935; *Concise Geography of the World*, Longmans, Green, 1936, new edition published as *Longmans Matriculation Geography*, 1941; *A Commercial Geography*, Longmans, Green, 1936, 9th edition, 1973; *Physical Geography and Geology*, Longmans, Green, 1938, 2nd edition, 1953; *A New Geography of India, Burma and Ceylon*, Longmans, Green, 1939; (with Leonard S. Suggate and others) *Europe and the British Isles*, Longmans, Green, 1939, new edition, Harlow, Longmans, 1969.

An Introduction to Commercial Geography, Longmans, Green, 1940, 4th edition, 1965 (adaptation for Canadian schools, with Kimble, published as *An Introduction to Economic Geography*, 1949); *The Face of Britain*, Longmans, Green, for British Council, 1940, revised edition, 1956; *Britain's Structure and Scenery*, Collins, 1946, 6th edition, 1967; *The Land of Britain and How It Is Used*, Longmans, Green, for British Council, 1946, 3rd edition, 1962; *The Land of Britain: Its Use and Misuse*, Longmans, Green, with Geographical Publications, 1948, 3rd edition, 1962; (with Gerwyn E. D. Lewis) *The Malayan Geographies for Today*, Longmans, Green, 1949 ff., 3rd edition, 1959 ff.

British Commonwealth, Longmans, Green, 1951; *The Earth's Crust: A New Approach to Physical Geography and Geology*, Crown, 1951, Harrap, 1964; *Land for To-*

morrow: The Underdeveloped World, Indiana University Press, 1952, revised edition published as *Land for Tomorrow: Our Developing World*, 1969 (published in England as *Our Undeveloped World*, Faber, 1953, 3rd edition, revised by Audrey N. Clark, published as *Our Developing World*, Faber, 1968); *Africa: A Study in Tropical Development*, Wiley, 1953, 3rd edition (with W. T. W. Morgan), 1972; (with B. G. Nene) *Textbook of Geography for Higher Secondary Schools*, Longmans, Green, 1953; *Man and the Land*, Collins, 1955, 3rd edition, 1969; (with Suggate) *The Southern Continents* (including "Australia and New Zealand," "South America," and "Africa"), Longmans, Green, 1957, component parts also published separately under individual titles in various editions.

Applied Geography, Penguin, 1960; (with William G. Goskins) *The Common Lands of England and Wales*, Collins, 1963; *Some Aspects of Medical Geography* (University of London Heath Clark lectures), Oxford University Press, 1964; *The Geography of Life and Death*, Collins, 1964; *Land Use Statistics of the Countries of Europe*, Geographical Publications, 1965; *Nature Conservation in Britain*, Collins, 1969. Also author, with E. C. R. Stamp, of "New Age Geographies," Junior Series, Longmans, Green, 1930, 2nd edition, 1939.

Editor: Elsa C. Rea Stamp, *The Practical Atlas of Modern Geography*, 3rd edition, G. Gill, 1931, new edition, 1948; *Oxford and Cambridge Geography*, new edition, G. Gill, 1933; D. D. M. Gooneratne, *Ceylon: The Land of the Sinhalese*, John Long, 1933; *Slovene Studies*, Le Play Society, 1933; John Thornton, *Physical Geography* (originally published as *Primary Physical Geography*, 1896), revised edition, Longmans, Green, 1936; (with Thomas Herdman) *Discovering Geography* (incorporating adaptations from *Geography for Today* and *An Introduction to Commercial Geography*), Longmans, Green, 1938 ff.; (with Sidney W. Wooldridge) *London Essays in Geography: Rodwell Jones Memorial Volume*, Harvard University Press, 1951, Books for Libraries, 1969; *Natural Resources, Food and Population in Inter-Tropical Africa*, Geographical Publications, 1956; *The World Land Use Survey*, Geographical Publications, 1956 ff.; *A History of Land Use in Arid Regions*, UNESCO, 1961; *A Glossary of Geographical Terms*, Wiley, 1961, 2nd edition, 1966; *Dictionary of Geography*, Wiley, 1966 (also published as *Longmans Dictionary of Geography*); *The Faber Atlas*, 5th edition revised, 1971.

Series editor: "University Geographical Series," Longmans, Green, 1927 ff.; (with L. S. Suggate, and others at various times, and contributor) "Geography for Today" series, Longmans, Green, 1937-71; (and contributor) "The Land of Britain: The Report of the Land Utilisation Survey of Britain," Geographical Publications, 1937 ff.; (with James M. M. Fisher and others) "The New Naturalist," Collins, 1945 ff.; (with Fisher and others) "New Naturalist Monographs," Collins, 1948 ff.

Author of booklets and pamphlets. Contributor to encyclopedias and to geography, geology, and botany journals.

SIDELIGHTS: A select bibliography of Stamp's writings, deposited in the University of London Library, lists more than 380 items, excluding reviews, encyclopedia articles, and notes, and takes up more than 93 quarto pages.

Reviewing one of Stamp's last books, Stephen Mullin commented in the *New Statesman*, "It is a mellow book, as one might expect from a great and much-loved geographer, whose real affection for the English countryside gave added point to a concise and valuable account of what is still one of the most compact areas of varied habitat in the world.'' Mullin noted Stamp's ''success in influencing government policies, most notably as vice-chairman of the Scott Report on Land Utilisation,'' as well as ''his own characteristic modesty in assessing his own role....''

Stamp lectured and traveled in most of the countries of the world. *Avocational interests:* Philately.

BIOGRAPHICAL/CRITICAL SOURCES: Ian Niall, *The Way of a Countryman*, Collins, 1964; *Land Use and Resources: Studies in Applied Geography: A Memorial Volume to Sir Dudley Stamp*, Institute of British Geographers, 1968.

(Died August 8, 1966)

* * *

STANDING, Edwin (Mortimer) 1887-

PERSONAL: Born September 18, 1887, in Tananarive, Madagascar; came to United States, 1962; son of Herbert Fox (a Quaker missionary) and Lucy (Glynn) Standing. *Education:* University of Leeds, B.Sc.; Cambridge University, Diploma in Education; additional study at University of Freiburg. *Politics:* Conservative. *Religion:* Roman Catholic (convert, 1923). *Home:* Mount St. Vincent, 4831 35th Ave. S.W., Seattle, Wash. 98126.

CAREER: Teacher and author; worked in collaboration with Maria Montessori, 1921-51, in Rome, London, Edinburgh, and Dublin, as her assistant in teacher training courses, also helping with teaching of religion to children.

WRITINGS: Maria Montessori: Her Life and Work, Hollis & Carter, 1957, Academy Library Guild, 1959; *The Montessori Method: A Revolution in Education*, Academy Library Guild, 1962, reissued as *The Montessori Revolution in Education*, Schocken, 1966; (editor) Maria Montessori and others, *The Child in the Church*, Academy Library Guild, 1964, 2nd edition, Catechetical Guild, 1965. Contributor to *Atlantic, Sower, Irish Rosary, America, Times* (London), and to educational journals.†

* * *

STANFIELD, Nancy Fisher Clay 1905-

PERSONAL: Born September 30, 1905, in Nuneaton, Warwickshire, England; daughter of Richard and Catherine Elizabeth (Fisher) Clay; married Dennis Percival Stanfield (with Forestry Research Office, Nigeria), March 18, 1948. *Education:* Attended Cheltenham Ladies College; Royal College of Art, A.R.C.A., 1927, teaching certificate, 1928. *Religion:* Church of England. *Home:* The Oasis, Great Comp. Boro Green, Kent, England; and c/o Department of Forest Research, Ibadan, West Nigeria.

CAREER: Leicester College of Art, Leicester, England, art teacher and embroidery specialist, 1928-45; Exhall Teacher Training College, Exhall, England, senior lecturer in crafts, 1945-47; lecturer in teacher training colleges in West Nigeria, and art teacher in St. Anne's School, Ibadan, Nigeria, 1954-63. Broadcaster on arts and crafts, Ibadan.

WRITINGS: Art for African Schools, Evans Brothers, 1955; *A Handbook of Art Teaching for Tropical Schools*, Evans Brothers, 1958.

WORK IN PROGRESS: Research into Nigerian crafts.†

* * *

STANFORD, Alfred (Boller) 1900-

PERSONAL: Born February 12, 1900, in East Orange, N.J.; son of Joseph Marsh and Mary N. (Boller) Stanford; married Dorothy Janet Taylor, September, 1922; married second wife, Berenice Langton, March 2, 1953; children: (first marriage) John, Peter M. *Education:* Amherst College, B.A., 1921. *Home:* 433 Gulf St., Milford, Conn. 06461.

CAREER: Former sailor and officer in U.S. Merchant Marine, and editor and publisher of *Boats*; *New York Herald Tribune*, New York, N.Y., second vice-president and advertising director, 1949-51; *Milford Citizen*, Milford, Conn., publisher, 1954—. Trustee, Marine Historical Association, Mystic, Conn. *Military service:* U.S. Naval Reserve, 1942-45; became captain; received Legion of Merit and Croix de Guerre. *Member:* Cruising Club of America (former commodore), Off Soundings Club.

WRITINGS: Groundswell, Appleton, 1922; *A City Out of the Sea*, Appleton, 1924; *Invitation to Danger*, Appleton, 1925; *Navigator—the Story of Nathaniel Bowditch*, Morrow, 1927; *Men, Fish and Boats*, Morrow, 1930; *Pleasures of Sailing*, Simon & Schuster, 1943; *Force Mulberry*, Morrow, 1953; *Mission in Sparrow Bush Lane*, Morrow, 1966. Contributor of articles and short stories to magazines.

WORK IN PROGRESS: A novel based on a Caribbean island, and another book about Benjamin Franklin in Paris.

AVOCATIONAL INTERESTS: Off-shore sailing.

* * *

STANLEY, Nora Kathleen Begbie Strange 1885-
(Nora K. Strange)

PERSONAL: Born September 11, 1885, in Bombay, India, of Scotch-Irish ancestry; daughter of William Lumisden and R. F. (Cobbold) Strange; married Edward Gower Stanley, December 5, 1922 (deceased). *Education:* Educated in English schools. *Politics:* Conservative. *Religion:* Church of England. *Home:* 5 Rugby Ct., Rugby Rd., Worthing, Sussex, England. *Agent:* Curtis Brown Ltd., 1 Craven Hill, London W2 3EW, England.

CAREER: Secretary in Nairobi and Kenya, 1913-19, one of first women to work in business offices in East Africa; novelist, using Kenya as the setting for most of her books, 1924—.

WRITINGS—All under name Nora K. Strange: Latticed Windows, Stanley Paul, 1924; *An Outpost Wooing: A Romance of East Africa*, Stanley Paul, 1924; *A Wife in Kenya*, Stanley Paul, 1925; *Blondes Prefer Gentlemen*, Stanley Paul, 1926, reissued as *Blondes Prefer Gentlemen: A Satire–The Ingenious Diary of an Amateur, by an Englishwoman*, Ogilvie, 1926, reissued as *Confessions of an Amateur Blonde*, 1928; *Cynthia Abroad*, Stanley Paul, 1927; *Kenya Calling*, Stanley Paul, 1928; *Kenya Dawn*, Stanley Paul, 1929.

Mistress of Ceremonies, Stanley Paul, 1930; *Her Serenity*, Stanley Paul, 1931; *Courtship in Kenya*, Stanley Paul, 1932; *Kenya Noon*, Wright & Brown, 1933; *Kenya Today*, Stanley Paul, 1934; *Autumn Meeting*, Wright & Brown, 1934; *The Morning Mist: A Romance of Kenya*, Wright & Brown, 1935; *The Listening Earth*, Hutchinson, 1936; *It's Deep Beyond the Reef*, Hutchinson, 1937; *Miss Wiston Goes Gay*, Hutchinson, 1938; *Youth Comes to Kenya*, Hutchinson, 1938.

To Everything There is a Season, Hutchinson, 1940; *Imperial Mountain*, Hutchinson, 1941; *Reflections of Rowena*, Muller, 1941; *Judy*, Hutchinson, 1942; *Testimony of Three*, Hutchinson, 1944; *Sanctuary*, Hutchinson, 1945; *The Re-*

luctant Nymph, Hutchinson, 1946; *Jenny*, Hutchinson, 1947; *Jacobean Tapestry* (on Sir Robert Strange and His Family), Stanley Paul, 1947; *Paul and Olivia*, Hutchinson, 1948; *The Compassionate Lovers*, Hutchinson, 1949.

Until the Tree Blossoms, Hutchinson, 1950; *The Sunflower Scarf*, Hutchinson, 1951; *Portrait of Shirley*, Hutchinson, 1951; *The Invaluable Miss Logan*, Hutchinson, 1952; *The Silent Grove*, Hutchinson, 1954; *I Am Caterina*, Hutchinson, 1955; *Beneath the Thorn Tree*, Hutchinson, 1956; *Courtship of Daniel Hurcott*, Hutchinson, 1957; *Clinton Heritage*, Hurst & Blackett, 1958; *Escape to Elysia*, Hurst & Blackett, 1959.

Ann's Story, Hurst & Blackett, 1960; *A Touch of Earth*, Hurst & Blackett, 1961; *The Honourable Miss*, Hurst & Blackett, 1962; *Husband of Caroline*, Hurst & Blackett, 1962; *Firefly*, Hurst & Blackett, 1964; *The Secret Stair*, Hurst & Blackett, 1965; *The Merivale Twins*, Hurst & Blackett, 1966; *The Quiet Girl*, Hurst & Blackett, 1967; *The Rector's Daughter*, Hurst & Blackett, 1968; *Amelia*, Hurst & Blackett, 1969.

The Blue Daffodil, Hurst & Blackett, 1970.

Contributor of short stories and serials to *Woman's Weekly*.

* * *

STEARNS, Raymond Phineas   1904-1970

PERSONAL: Born January 11, 1904, in Canton, Ill.; son of W. Clark (a farmer) and Catherine (Stimeling) Stearns; married Mary Elizabeth Scott, 1927; married second wife, Josephine Bunch, September 8, 1947; children: (first marriage) Peter Nathaniel, Sarah Elizabeth; (second marriage) Susan, Catherine, Martha. *Education:* Illinois College, A.B., 1927; Harvard University, M.A., 1931, Ph.D., 1934; postdoctoral study at University of London, 1934-35. *Politics:* Democrat. *Religion:* Episcopalian. *Home:* 403 Bradley Lane, Normal, Ill. 61761.

CAREER: Teacher in Illinois elementary and high schools, 1922-23, 1927-29; Social Science Research Council, postdoctoral fellow, 1934-36; Lake Forest College, Lake Forest, Ill., professor of history and head of department, 1936-37; University of Illinois, Urbana, assistant professor, 1937-42, associate professor, 1942-48, professor of history, 1947-70. Fulbright lecturer at University of Ghent, 1959. Institute of Early American History and Culture, Williamsburg, Va., member of council, 1947-53. *Member:* American Historical Association, American Antiquarian Society, American Society of Church History, History of Science Society (council), Massachusetts Historical Society, Pennsylvania Historical Society (honorary), Phi Beta Kappa, Phi Alpha Theta, Harvard Club (Chicago). *Awards, honors:* Frank S. Brewer Award of American Society of Church History, 1940, for *Congregationalism in the Dutch Netherlands;* Medal of University of Ghent, 1959; National Science Foundation research grant, London, England, 1967-68; National Book Award in science, 1971, for *Science in the British Colonies of America*.

WRITINGS: Congregationalism in the Dutch Netherlands: The Rise and Fall of the English Congregational Classes, 1621-1635, American Society of Church History, 1940; *The Pageant of Europe: Sources and Selections from the Renaissance to the Present Day*, Harcourt, 1947, revised edition, 1961; (editor and contributor) Edwin William Pahlow, *Introduction to World History: Man's Great Adventure*, revised edition, Ginn, 1949; *James Petiver, Pro-*

moter of Natural Science, American Antiquarian Society, 1953; *The Strenuous Puritan: Hugh Peters, 1598-1660*, University of Illinois Press, 1954; (with others) *A History of the World*, two volumes, Rand McNally, 1960; (with G. F. Frick) *Mark Catesby, the Colonial Audubon*, University of Illinois Press, 1961; (editor) Martin Lister, *A Journey to Paris in the Year 1698*, University of Illinois Press, 1967; *Science in the British Colonies of America*, University of Illinois Press, 1970. Contributor to history journals in United States and England. Member of board of editors, *William and Mary Quarterly*, 1948-51, *Historian*, 1955-61.

WORK IN PROGRESS: A study of the Royal Society of London and the American colonies; textbooks on modern Europe and early America.

AVOCATIONAL INTERESTS: Fishing and gardening.

(Died November 15, 1970)

* * *

STEELE, Fletcher   1885-1971

PERSONAL: Born June 7, 1885, in Rochester, N.Y.; son of John Mason (a lawyer) and Mary (Lampert) Steele. *Education:* Williams College, B.A., 1907; graduate study at Harvard University. *Home:* 20 Monroe Ave., Pittsford, N.Y.

CAREER: Landscape architect, Boston, Mass., working on projects in many sections of the United States, 1910-62. American Red Cross, served in Europe, World War I. *Member:* American Society of Landscape Architects (fellow), Garden Club of America (member-at-large), Les Amateurs de Jardins, and other professional societies.

WRITINGS: Design in the Little Garden, Atlantic Monthly Press, 1924; *Gardens and People*, Houghton, 1963. Contributor of articles to magazines.

(Died, 1971)

* * *

STEELE, Harwood R(obert) E(lmes)   1897-

PERSONAL: Born May 5, 1897, in Fort Macleod, Alberta, Canada; son of Sir Samuel Benfield (a major general) and Maye (deLotbiniere-Harwood) Steele. *Education:* Educated privately and at Highfield School, Hamilton, Ontario. *Home:* 20 Brant St., Orillia, Ontario, Canada; White Lodge, Dunchurch near Rugby, England.

CAREER: Author and journalist. Canadian Pacific Railway, assistant press representative, 1923-25; Canadian (government) Arctic Expedition, historian, 1925; lecturer on Royal Canadian Mounted Police in Canada and United States, 1928-30, lecturer on same subject and others in England and Canada, beginning, 1945. Canadian Broadcasting Corp., military adviser, 1937-39. *Military service:* Canadian and British armies, 1914-18, serving three years in France; became captain; mentioned in dispatches and received Military Cross. British Army, 1939-45, serving in England, Ireland, India, Assam, and Burma; mentioned in dispatches; became lieutenant colonel. *Member:* Royal Commonwealth Society, Royal Geographical Society (fellow), Society of Authors, Savage Club (London).

WRITINGS: Cleared for Action (naval poems), T. Fisher Unwin, 1914; *The Canadians in France, 1915-18*, Dent, 1920; *Spirit of Iron* (novel), Doubleday, Doran, 1923; *I Shall Arise* (novel), Hodder & Stoughton, 1926; *The Ninth Circle* (novel), Burt, 1927; *Policing the Arctic* (history), Jarrolds, 1934; *To Effect an Arrest* (short stories), Jarrolds,

1946; *Ghosts Returning* (novel), Ryerson, 1950; *The Marching Call* (juvenile about father's early life with Royal Canadian Mounted Police), Nelson, 1955; *The Red Serge* (short stories), Ryerson, 1961; *RCMP: Royal Canadian Mounted Police*, Grossman, 1968.

Co-author of guide book for King George VI on his Canadian tour, 1939. Writer of radio plays for Canadian Broadcasting Corp. and British Broadcasting Corp. Contributor of short stories and articles to *Maclean's Magazine* and to British and Canadian newspapers.

* * *

STEFFERUD, Alfred (Daniel) 1903-

PERSONAL: Born May 17, 1903, in Kenyon, Minn.; son of Edvart Elias (a farmer) and Hilda (Haugen) Stefferud; married Doris H. Roberts, March 31, 1932 (died, 1958); children: David R., John A., Christine (Mrs. Leonard Jacoby III). *Education:* St. Olaf College, B.A. (high honors), 1925; additional study at University of Iowa, summers, 1926-27, American Academy in Rome, summer, 1929, University of Berlin, 1935, University of Vienna, 1936-37. *Religion:* Society of Friends. *Home:* 62 Lincoln Park, Amersham, Buckinghamshire HP7 9HD, England.

CAREER: High school English and Latin teacher in Highmore, S.D., 1925-27, Kemper Military School, Boonville, Mo., 1927-30; Associated Press, reporter in Des Moines, Iowa, 1930-31, foreign news editor, New York, N.Y., 1932-34, foreign correspondent in Berlin, Germany, 1934-36, with Southwest Europe bureau, Vienna, Austria, 1936-38; U.S. Department of Agriculture, Washington, D.C., writer and editor, *Land Policy Review*, Bureau of Agricultural Economics, 1938-40; *Time*, New York, N.Y., contributing editor, 1941-42; U.S. Office of War Information, editor and writer in London, England, 1943-44, New York, N.Y., 1944-45; U.S. Department of Agriculture, editor of "Yearbooks of Agriculture," 1945-65; U.S. Department of Agriculture Graduate School, faculty member, teaching English and Latin, 1938-40, and again, beginning, 1958. Lecturer at seminars, conferences, and colleges. Member of executive committee, Friends World Committee; secretary, Group on Christian Theology and Ethics of Man-Nature Resources.

MEMBER: American Institute of Graphic Arts, Federal Editors Association, Sons of Norway, Nordmanns Forbundet, Creative Crafts Council (chairman), Design Weavers, Potomac Craftsmen, Arts Club, Cosmos Club. *Awards, honors:* Superior Service Award, U.S. Department of Agriculture, 1951; Distinguished Alumnus Award, St. Olaf College, 1955.

WRITINGS: How to Know the Wildflowers, Henry Holt, 1950, 2nd edition, New American Library, 1951; (editor) *The Wonderful World of Books*, Houghton, 1953, 8th edition, New American Library, 1964; *The Wonders of Seeds*, Harcourt, 1956; (editor) *Birds In Our Lives*, U.S. Government Printing Office, 1966; (editor) *Uncle Sam's Household Hints*, Bantam, 1967.

"Yearbooks of Agriculture" edited: *Science in Farming*, 1943-47, *Grass*, 1948, *Trees*, 1949, *Crops in Peace and War*, 1950-51, *Insects*, 1952, *Plant Diseases*, 1953, *Marketing*, 1954, *Water*, 1955, *Animal Diseases*, 1956, *Soil*, 1957, *Land*, 1958, *Food*, 1959, *Power to Produce*, 1960, *Seeds*, 1961, *After a Hundred Years*, 1962, *A Place to Live*, 1963, *Farmer's World*, 1964, *Consumers All*, 1965.

Contributor to *World Encyclopedia, Parents' Magazine,*

New York Times, Red Cross Journal, and other publications. Consulting editor, *Waterfowl Tomorrow*, 1964; consulting editor, Fish and Wildlife Service, 1964; editor, *Friends Journal*, 1968-72.

WORK IN PROGRESS: Books on natural history and agricultural history.

SIDELIGHTS: Stefferud has reading knowledge of German, French, and Norwegian.

* * *

STEINBERG, S(igrid) H(enry) 1899-1969

PERSONAL: Born August 3, 1899, in Goslar, Germany; son of Adolf (a merchant) and Emmi (Romer) Steinberg; married Christine von Pape, July 25, 1923; children: Eric. *Education:* Attended University of Munich, University of Leipzig, and University of London; Ph.D., 1922. *Politics:* Conservative. *Religion:* Church of England. *Home:* 182 Stoneleigh Park Rd., Ewell, Surrey, England.

CAREER: University of Leipzig, Leipzig, Germany, reader in history, 1925-33; Courtauld Institute of Art, University of London, London, England, research student, 1935-39; Sedbergh School, Yorkshire, England, assistant master, 1940-44; *Chambers's Encyclopaedia*, London, England, assistant editor, 1946-50; *The Statesman's Year-Book*, London, editor, 1946-69. *Military service:* British liaison officer with U.S. Office of War Information, 1944-45. *Member:* Royal Historical Society, Bibliographical Society.

WRITINGS: (Editor) *Die Geschichtswissenschaft der Gegenwart is Selbstdarstellungen*, F. Meiner, 1925-26; (with wife, Christine Steinberg von Pape) *Die Bildnisse Geistlicher und weltlicher fuersten und Herren*, B. G. Teubner, 1931; *Die Goslarer stadtschreiber und ihr einfluss auf die Ratspolitik bis zum anfang des 15. jahrhunderts*, Goslar, 1933; *Bibliografie zur Geschichte des deutschen Portraets*, Diepenbroick-Grueter & Schulz, 1934; *A One-Year German Course*, Macmillan, 1939; *Historical Tables*, Macmillan, 1939, 8th edition, St. Martin's, 1966; *A Short History of Germany*, Cambridge University Press, 1944, Macmillan, 1945; (editor) *Fifteen German Poets*, Macmillan, 1945, St. Martin's, 1956, 5th edition, St. Martin's, 1962; (editor) *Cassell's Encyclopaedia of Literature*, Cassell, 1953, published as *Cassell's Encyclopaedia of World Literature*, Funk, 1954; *Five Hundred Years of Printing*, Penguin, 1955, 2nd edition, 1962; (editor) *A New Dictionary of British History*, St. Martin's, 1963, 2nd edition (with I. H. Evans and others) published as *Steinberg's Dictionary of British History*, 1964; *The "Thirty Years' War" and the Conflict for European Hegemony*, Edward Arnold, 1966, Norton, 1967. Contributor of articles to periodicals.

BIOGRAPHICAL/CRITICAL SOURCES: Times Literary Supplement, April 13, 1967; *Times* (London), January 30, 1969, February 5, 1969.

(Died January 28, 1969)

* * *

STEINER, Lee R. 1901-

PERSONAL: Born November 18, 1901, in Superior, Wis.; daughter of Harry and Sarah (Skolnik) Rabinowitz; married Alfred Steiner, 1935 (died, 1939); married Samuel Melitzer (a former mining engineer), April 22, 1949. *Education:* University of Minnesota, B.A., 1924; Smith College, M.S., 1929. Training in clinical psychology at Institute for Juvenile Research, 1929-31; training in psychotherapy with Alfred Adler. Antioch College, Ph.D., 1972. *Office:* 45 West 81st St., New York, N.Y. 10024.

CAREER: Psychologist and consultant in personal problems, in private practice, Chicago, 1932-35, New York, N.Y., 1935—. Institute for Interpersonal Research, New York, N.Y., founder and director of research, 1947—. Psychiatrist and social worker, Institute of Juvenile Research, Chicago, 1931-33; University of Chicago, instructor, 1931-32, director of training program, 1932-33; special lecturer, Illinois Society Mental Hygiene, 1933-34; instructor, Fordham University, 1935-36; discussion leader, Child Study Association of America, 1937-38; instructor, Rand School of Social Science, 1939-40, Rutgers University, 1940-44, Hunter College (now Hunter College of the City University of New York), 1944-48, College of William and Mary, 1945, and Queens College (now Queens College of the City University of New York), 1948-49. Radio lecturer, with network programs, 1938-42; producer and moderator of forum, "Psycologically Speaking," WEVD University of the Air, 1948—; lecturer to private groups, 1932—.

MEMBER: International Radio and Television Society, American Psychological Association, Academy of Psychologists in Marital Counseling (founder and president, 1959—), American Women in Radio and Television, American Association of University Professors, Eastern Psychological Association, New York State Psychological Association.

WRITINGS: Where Do People Take Their Troubles, Houghton, 1945; *A Practical Guide for Troubled People*, Greenberg, 1952; *Make the Most of Yourself*, Prentice-Hall, 1954; *Understanding Juvenile Delinquency*, Chilton, 1960; *Romantic Marriage: The Twentieth-Century Illusion*, Chilton, 1963. Ghost writer and editor of psychological books and articles; author of radio scripts. Contributor to *Book of Knowledge*, a monthly column to *Best Years*, 1955, and a column to *True Love*, 1961—; reviewer for other periodicals.

*   *   *

STEINHAUS, Arthur H.   1897-1970

PERSONAL: Born October 4, 1897, in Chicago, Ill.; son of Henry D. (a physician) and Rosa (Dahler) Steinhaus; married Eva Kunzmann, June 23, 1921; children: Robert A. *Education:* University of Chicago, S.B., 1920, M.S., 1925, Ph.D., 1928; George Williams College, B.P.E., 1921, M.P.E., 1926. *Religion:* Baptist. *Home:* 308 Highland Ave., East Lansing, Mich. 48823.

CAREER: George Williams College, Chicago, Ill., instructor, 1920-28, professor of physiology, 1928-63, Oscar G. Mayer Distinguished Service Professor of Psychophysiology, 1963-65, dean of college, 1954-62, dean emeritus, 1962-70; Chicago College of Osteopathy, Chicago, Ill., distinguished service professor of physiology, 1965-66; Michigan State University, East Lansing, professor of health and physical education, 1966-70. Chief of Division of Physical Education and Health Activities, U.S. Office of Education, 1944; civilian adviser, U.S. Navy, 1945-47. Lecturer at Baptist Missionary Training College, 1934-45, Northwestern University, 1948-49, and University of Southern California, 1965; Fulbright professor in Germany, 1955, and at Tokyo University, 1962-63; visiting summer professor at other universities in United States and Canada; lecturer in Europe, Asia, Africa, and Australasia.

MEMBER: American Academy of Physical Education (fellow; president, 1943-45), American Association for Health, Physical Education and Recreation (fellow; vice-president, 1947-48), American Public Health Association

(fellow), American College of Sports Medicine (fellow; vice-president, 1956), Society of Fellows in Physical Education, American Medical Writers' Association, Society for Psychophysiological Research, National Education Association, Federation Internationale d'Education Physique (vice-president, 1966-70), Federation Internationale Medico-Sportive, Mid American Society of Physical Medicine and Rehabilitation, Phi Delta Kappa, Phi Epsilon Kappa, Sigma Xi.

AWARDS, HONORS: Guggenheim fellowship for study in Europe, 1931-32; Roberts-Gulick Memorial Award of Physical Education Society of YMCAs of North America, 1940; William G. Anderson Award of American Association for Health, Physical Education and Recreation, 1951; Clarke Hetherington Award of American Academy of Physical Education, 1963; Honor Award of American College of Sports Medicine, 1965.

WRITINGS: Tobacco and Health, Association Press, 1939; *More Firepower for Health Education*, U.S. Government Printing Office, 1945; (with others) *Research Methods Applied to Health, Physical Education and Recreation*, American Association for Health, Physical Education and Recreation, 1949, 2nd edition, 1959; *How to Keep Fit and Like It*, Dartnell, 1957, 3rd edition, 1963; (with others) *L'Education Physique dans le Monde*, Editions Biere, 1961; *Toward an Understanding of Health and Physical Education*, W. C. Brown, 1963; (with Jeanne E. Norris) *Teaching Neuromuscular Relaxation*, George Williams College, 1964. Contributor to *Yearbook* of American Association of Health, Physical Education and Recreation, 1962. About two hundred articles have appeared in research and professional journals in America and Germany, and in popular magazines such as *Coronet* and *Look*. Member of editorial board, *Journal of Physical Education*.

(Died, 1970)

*   *   *

STEPHEN, Parel Lukose   1898-

PERSONAL: Born April 26, 1898, in Kottayam, Kerala, India; son of Parel Lukos and Aleyamma (Mannoor Thomas) Lukose; married Annamma Thatchet Neendoor, May 1921; children: Thomas, Molly Jacob, Litty Joseph, Baby Thomas. *Education:* Madras Christian College, M.A., 1922. *Religion:* Romo-Syrian Catholic. *Home:* Parel House, Kottayam, Kerala, India.

CAREER: Professor of English at St. Xavier's College, University of Madras, Madras, India, 1924-1951, at St. Thomas College, University of Madras, 1951-1953, at Nirmala College, University of Kerala, Trivandrum, Kerala State, 1953-1955, at Bishop Chulaparambil Memorial College, Kottayam, 1955-63. University of Kerala, honorary reader in English, 1949-54; member of senate and academic council, University of Madras.

WRITINGS: Correct Everyday English, D. B. Taraporevala, 1945, 4th edition, 1963; Shakespeare's *Othello* (critical edition), House of Knowledge, 1959; *1001 Famous Proverbs and Sayings*, D. B. Taraporevala, 1964; *Bishop Chulaparambil* (biography), C. M. Press, 1969. Translator of *Ammayum Makulum* (life of St. Therese's mother). Contributor of articles and book reviews to journals.

WORK IN PROGRESS: A book of idioms; Malayalam short stories.

STEPHENSON, Gilbert T(homas) 1884-1972

PERSONAL: Born December 17, 1884, in Pendleton, N.C.; son of James Henry (a farmer) and Susan (Fleetwood) Stephenson; married Grace Morris White; children: Thomas W., James Henry. *Education:* Wake Forest College, A.B., 1902, A.M., 1904; Harvard University, A.M., 1906, LL.B., 1910. *Politics:* Democrat. *Religion:* Baptist. *Home and office:* Warren Place, Pendleton, N.C.

CAREER: Admitted to North Carolina bar, 1910; practicing lawyer in Winston-Salem, N.C., 1910-19; Wachovia Bank and Trust Co., Winston-Salem, N.C., successively secretary, assistant trust officer, and vice-president, 1919-29; Equitable Trust Co., Wilmington, Del., vice-president in charge of trust department, 1929-36, director, 1929-51; American Bankers Association, Graduate school of Banking, New York, N.Y., member of faculty, 1935-50. Owner and operator of plantation, Warren Place, Pendleton, N.C.; also connected with T. B. Stephenson & Sons (farmers), Pendleton, 1914-72. Member of North Carolina Awards Commission. *Member:* Rotary International, Ruritan, Watauga Club, Quill and Grill Club, Roanoke-Chowan Group. *Awards, honors:* D.C.L., Wake Forest College, 1955.

WRITINGS: Race Distinctions in American Law, Appleton, 1910, reprinted, Johnson Reprint, 1970; *War Savings Campaign in North Carolina*, War Savings Committee (Winston-Salem), 1919; (with A. H. Eller) *Guide Posts in Preparing Wills*, Wachovia Bank and Trust Co., 1919; *The Business Relations Between God and Man—a Trusteeship*, Sunday School Board, Southern Baptist Convention, 1921; *The Pastor Beloved*, Sunday School Board, Southern Baptist Convention, 1925; *Living Trusts*, Crofts, 1926, 2nd edition, 1937; *Wills*, Crofts, 1930; *Life Story of a Trustman*, Crofts, 1930; *English Executor and Trustee Business*, Harper, 1930; *What a Life Insurance Man Should Know About Trust Business*, Crofts, 1932; *The American System of Trust Business*, American Bankers Association, 1936.

Trust Business in Common-Law Countries, American Bankers Association; *Your Family and Your Estate*, Prentice-Hall, 1949; *Estates and Trusts*, Crofts, 1949, 4th edition, Appleton, 1965; *Drafting Wills and Trust Agreements—Administrative Provisions*, Little, Brown, 1952; *Drafting Wills and Trust Agreements: Dispositive Provisions*, Little, Brown, 1954; (with wife, Grace W. Stephenson) *We Came Home to Warren Place*, Alfred Williams & Co., 1958; *Reflections of a Trustman*, American Bankers Association, 1960; *The Trust Business as a Career*, Fiduciary Publishers, 1965.

Author of "Studies in Trust Business," four series, American Bankers Association, 1938-40; series of fourteen law school lectures, "Working Provisions of Wills and Trust Agreements," also was published by American Bankers Association, 1937-50.

WORK IN PROGRESS: The living at Warren Place in the 1890's and in the 1960's.

(Died June 9, 1972)

* * *

STERN, William B(ernhard) 1910-1972

PERSONAL: Born March 12, 1910, in Wuerzburg, Germany; son of Bruno (a lawyer) and Frida (Hellmann) Stern; married Ruth Harriet Yarnell, 1942; children: Philinda Caroline Stern Denson. *Education:* University of Wuerzburg, Dr. iur. utr., 1933. *Office:* Los Angeles County Law Library, 301 West First St., Los Angeles, Calif. 90012.

CAREER: University of Chicago Law School Library, Chicago, Ill., cataloger, 1937-39; Los Angeles County Law Library, Los Angeles, Calif., foreign law librarian and head cataloger, 1939-45, foreign law librarian, 1945-72. Deputy county clerk in charge of archival materials, Los Angeles, Calif. Instructor of Peace Corps law trainees for Ethiopia, summers, 1964 and 1965. *Member:* International Association of Law Libraries (secretary, 1959-62; president, 1962-65), American Association of Law Libraries (member of executive board, 1954-58), American Society of International Law, American Foreign Law Association, Association Internationale pour l'Enseignement du Droit Compare, Sierra Club, Town Hall (Los Angeles).

WRITINGS: (Contributor) *The California Family Lawyer*, Continuing Education of the Bar, California, 1963; (contributor) *Russia and the Soviet Union*, University of Chicago Press, 1965; (compiler with Joseph L. Andrews and others) *The Law in the United States of America: A Selective Bibliographical Guide*, New York University Press, 1965. Contributor to *American Journal of International Law*, *American Political Science Review*, *Library Quarterly*, and a dozen other law and library journals in America, Mexico, and Spain. Editor, *Law Library Journal*, 1953-54.

SIDELIGHTS: Stern was competent in French, German, Spanish, Latin, and classical Greek. *Avocational interests:* Music.

(Died September 27, 1972)

* * *

STEVENS, Frances Isted 1907-
(Fae Hewston Stevens)

PERSONAL: Born December 3, 1907, in Wedderburn, Victoria, Australia; daughter of Ernest (a farmer) and Maude (Huggins) Hewston; married Ernest Albert Stevens (a farmer), April 4, 1953; children: Lexie (Mrs. Edward Koch). *Education:* Attended state schools in Australia. *Politics:* Liberal. *Religion:* Church of England. *Home:* Glenburnie, Diggora West, Victoria, Australia.

CAREER: Music teacher in Victoria, Australia, 1923-30; mothercraft nurse, Melbourne, Victoria, Australia, 1935-50. *Member:* P.E.N., Red Cross Country Womens Association of Australia.

*WRITINGS—*Under name Fae Hewston Stevens: *Koronglea Cobbers*, Ward, Lock, 1961; *Koronglea Ponies*, Ward, Lock, 1962; *Koronglea Holidays*, Ward, Lock, 1963; *Koronglea Adventures*, Ward, Lock, 1965; *Koronglea Twins*, Ward, Lock, 1967; (with Elizabeth O'Brien) *Then the Water Wheel Turned: A History of Lockington and District, 1867-1967*, Rochester Shire Council, 1967; *Smoke from the Hills: A Story of the Boort District 1836-1968*, Boort Historical Society, 1969. Author of ten novelettes and a radio serial; weekly columnist, *Bendigo Advertiser;* contributor of short stories to other Australian newspapers.

WORK IN PROGRESS: Another "Koronglea" book; arrangement of aboriginal Australian legends, illustrated by daughter, Lexie Koch.

* * *

STEVENS, Georgiana G(erlinger) 1904-

PERSONAL: Born October 24, 1904, in Portland, Ore.; daughter of George Theodore (a business executive) and Irene (Hazard) Gerlinger; married Harley Crawford Stevens, February 21, 1935 (died December, 1959). *Education:* University of California, Berkeley, A.B., 1926. *Religion:*

Protestant. *Home:* 1641 Green St., San Francisco, Calif. 94123.

CAREER: Office of Strategic Services, Washington, D.C., writer, 1944-45; U.S. Department of State, Office of Intelligence Research, Washington, D.C., research analyst, 1945-46; lived in Lebanon, 1946-47; writer on Middle East affairs. Member of board, Middle East Institute, Washington, D.C., and Near East Foundation, New York; trustee of World Affairs Council of Northern California, and Mills College.

WRITINGS: The Jordan River Valley, International Conciliation, 1956; (editor) *The United States and the Middle East*, Prentice-Hall, 1963; *Egypt: Yesterday and Today*, Holt, 1964; *Jordan River Partition*, Hoover Institution, 1965. Contributor to *Economist* (London), *Middle East Journal*, and *Atlantic Monthly*.

WORK IN PROGRESS: Articles on current Middle East politics and on the United Nations in the Middle East.

* * *

STEVENS, Sylvester K(irby)   1904-1974

PERSONAL: Born July 10, 1904, in Harrison Valley, Pa.; son of Herbert C. (a farmer) and Anna (Outman) Stevens; married Crescence Miller, June 22, 1926; children: James Harry. *Education:* Pennsylvania State College (now University), A.B., 1926, M.A., 1927; Columbia University, Ph.D., 1945. *Politics:* Republican. *Religion:* Lutheran. *Home:* 20 Center Dr., Camp Hill, Pa. *Office:* William Penn Memorial Building, Harrisburg, Pa.

CAREER: Pennsylvania State College (now University), University Park, 1926-37, began as instructor, became assistant professor of history; Commonwealth of Pennsylvania, Harrisburg, state historian, 1937-56; Pennsylvania Historical and Museum Commission, Harrisburg, executive director, 1956-72. *American Heritage*, business manager, 1950-54, member of editorial board, 1954-74, member of board of directors, beginning 1954. Executive secretary, Pennsylvania Federation of Historical Societies, 1937-72; National Park Service, member of advisory board of Historic Sites Survey, and member of Consulting Committee on Historic Sites and Buildings; chairman of President's Advisory Council on Historic Preservation, 1967-74; member of boards of trustees, Harrisburg Area College Center, and South Central Pennsylvania Educational Television Corp.

MEMBER: Association of Historic Sites Administrators (president, 1958-60; chairman of board of directors, 1960-66), American Association for State and Local History (president, 1946-50; treasurer, 1950-62; member of council, 1960-71), Manuscript Society of America (vice-president, 1949-53), Pennsylvania Historical Association (president, 1948-51; member of council), Theta Chi, Phi Gamma Mu, Delta Sigma Rho, Torch Club. *Awards, honors:* Litt.D., Lebanon Valley College, 1953; L.H.D., Susquehanna University, 1961; LL.D., Moravian College, 1962; Distinguished Alumnus Award, 1966; Award of Merit, American Association for State and Local History, 1969.

WRITINGS: (With Donald H. Kent) *Wilderness Chronicles of Northwestern Pennsylvania*, Pennsylvania Historical Commission, 1941; (editor with Kent) J. C. B., *Travels in New France*, Pennsylvania Historical Commission, 1941; *Local History and Winning the War*, American Association for State and Local History, 1942; *American Expansion in Hawaii, 1842-1898*, Archives Publishing, 1945, Rus-

sell & Russell, 1968; *Pennsylvania at War*, Pennsylvania Historical Commission, 1946; *Pennsylvania: Titan of Industry*, three volumes, Lewis Historical Publishing, 1948; (editor with Kent) *Papers of Colonel Henry Bouquet*, Pennsylvania Historical Commission, 1951; (with R. W. Cordier and others) *Exploring Pennsylvania*, three volumes, Harcourt, 1953, 3rd edition, 1968; *Pennsylvania: The Keystone State*, two volumes, American Historical Publishing, 1956; *Pennsylvania: Birthplace of a Nation*, Random House, 1964; *Pennsylvania: A Guide to Localized History*, Teachers College Press, 1965; *Pennsylvania: The Heritage of a Commonwealth*, four volumes, American Historical Co., 1968; *The Pennsylvania Colony*, Collier, 1970; *Portrait of Pennsylvania*, Doubleday, 1970.

Also writer of numerous bulletins and pamphlets on Pennsylvania history. Member of editorial advisory boards of Franklin Papers, Alexander Hamilton Bicentennial Commission, and *Pennsylvania History* (magazine).

WORK IN PROGRESS: The Susquehanna: A Study in Local History; The Delaware: A Study in Local History.

AVOCATIONAL INTERESTS: Golf, travel.

(Died January 16, 1974)

* * *

STEVENSON, Adlai E(wing)   1900-1965

PERSONAL: Born February 5, 1900, in Los Angeles, Calif.; son of Lewis Green (assistant general manager of *Los Angeles Examiner*, later Secretary of State of Illinois) and Helen Louise (Davis) Stevenson; married Ellen Borden, December 1, 1928 (divorced, 1949); children: Adlai Ewing, Borden, John Fell. *Education:* Princeton University, B.A., 1922; Harvard University, law student, 1922-24; Northwestern University, J.D., 1926. *Home:* Libertyville, Ill.

CAREER: Began work on the *Daily Pantagraph*, the Bloomington (Ill.) newspaper founded by his great grandfather, in 1924; admitted to Illinois bar in 1926, but traveled in central Europe and Russia as a newspaper correspondent before practicing law with Cutting, Moore & Sidley, Chicago, Ill., 1927-33; special counsel, Agricultural Adjustment Administration, Washington, D.C., 1933-34; assistant general counsel, Federal Alcoholic Control Administration, Washington, D.C., 1934; partner in law firm of Sidley, Austin, Burgess & Smith, Chicago, Ill., 1934-41; special assistant to Secretary of the Navy Frank Knox, 1941-44; special assistant to Secretary of State Edward Stettinius, working on organization of the United Nations, 1945; U.S. minister and chief of U.S. delegation to Preparatory Commission of the United Nations in London, 1945, senior adviser to U.S. delegation at first meeting of the General Assembly in London, and alternate delegate to General Assembly in New York, 1946, 1947; governor of Illinois, 1948-52; drafted by Democratic National Convention to run for President in 1952 and again in 1956 (losing both times to Dwight D. Eisenhower); returned to law practice as partner in firm of Stevenson, Rifkind & Wirtz, Chicago, Ill., and Paul, Weiss, Rifkind, Wharton & Garrison, New York, N.Y., 1955-60; U.S. Ambassador to United Nations, with cabinet rank, 1960-65. Member or head of a number of U.S. missions and delegations to foreign countries, 1943-65; personal representative of President John F. Kennedy on South American tour, 1961, to lay the groundwork for Alliance for Progress program. *Military service:* U.S. Naval Reserve, 1918.

MEMBER: Illinois, Chicago, New York, Riverdale, N.Y., and Washington (D.C.) Bar associations, Onwentsia Club (Lake Forest, Ill.), Century Association and Knickerbocker Club (New York), Metropolitan Club (Washington, D.C.), Chicago Club. *Awards, honors:* Distinguished Service Award, Department of the Navy, 1945; honorary degrees from Harvard University, Princeton University, Oxford University, Northwestern University, Columbia University, McGill University, and a number of other American and foreign universities and colleges; also honored by Jewish Theological Seminary of America with establishment of Adlai E. Stevenson Foundation (for study of ethics), 1961; Stevenson Chair in International Politics established in his honor, 1966, by Brandeis University.

WRITINGS: Major Campaign Speeches of Adlai E. Stevenson, Random House, 1953; *Call to Greatness,* Harper, 1954; *What I Think,* Harper, 1956; *The New America,* Harper, 1957; *Friends and Enemies: What I Learned in Russia,* Harper, 1959; *Putting First Things First,* Random House, 1960; *Looking Outward: Years of Crisis at the United Nations,* edited by Robert L. and Selma Schiffer, Harper, 1963; *An Ethic for Survival: Adlai Stevenson Speaks on International Affairs, 1936-1965,* edited by Michael H. Prosser, Morrow, 1969.

SIDELIGHTS: In 1947, Stevenson decided to enter politics as a career and, in 1948, he won the Illinois gubernatorial election by 572,000 votes, the largest plurality in the history of the state. Stevenson, reversing the phrase, "home town boy makes good," said of himself, "good home town makes boy." In the 17 years that followed, he held nearly a dozen advisory and executive positions. John Fischer, in a summary of Stevenson's career, wrote: "Stevenson's achievement, it seems to me, was to change the timbre of American political life. He made politics intellectually respectable once again."

One of Stevenson's principal assets was his ability to speak with wit and eloquence, both extemporaneously and from notes. Many believed that he wrote all of his own speeches, but he employed, according to Fischer, the biggest battalion of ghost writers of any candidate in recent times. One of Stevenson's first head writers was Arthur Schlesinger, Jr. Later he enlisted the services of Kenneth Galbraith, Eric Hodgins, John Bartlow Martin, and John Fischer. But, Fischer added, "he was a better craftsman than any of the writers who helped him, and they all knew it."

Stevenson's eloquence is reflected in his books, which have been received as the only American political writings since those of Lincoln to rate as literature. (A. A. Berle, *Saturday Review*). E. D. Canham said that "[Stevenson's] speeches are themselves mostly of high quality, the subject matter is interesting and important and sometimes fraught with real drama, and the eloquence and wit of Adlai Stevenson give them unique savor.... No meretricious ghostly flavor pervades them. They are first-rate advocacy, filled now with indignation and now with magnanimity. The best of them will not be forgotten." G. W. Johnson called him "intelligent, provocative, [and] stylistically charming," and A. W. Hearn commented: "Adlai Stevenson's utterances are consistently worth hearing.... His own morality neither floats free, detached from facts, nor is it an icing plastered over predetermined policy. It is rather the compass which gives consistency to a twisting course through perilous waters...." Walter Lippmann wrote of Stevenson: "...the kind of American that Americans themselves and the great mass of mankind would like to think Americans are."

On September 9, 1965, President Johnson unveiled the Adlai Stevenson commemorative stamp, describing Stevenson as one who "skillfully and beautifully helped shape the dialogue of 20th-century democracy." The issue date, October 23rd, was selected to coincide with the 20th anniversary of the founding of the United Nations on October 24th. An international committee to assist in the creation of an Adlai E. Stevenson Institute for International Affairs was announced on January 5, 1966, by Adlai E. Stevenson III.

AVOCATIONAL INTERESTS: Hunting pheasants with a 20 gauge shotgun; caring for his "melancholy" Dalmation, Artie (King Arthur); riding, tennis, travel, books, good paintings.

BIOGRAPHICAL/CRITICAL SOURCES—Books: Bessie R. James and Mary Waterstreet, compilers, *The Wit and Wisdom of Stevenson of Illinois,* Schuman, 1952; John Bartlow Martin, *Adlai Stevenson,* Harper, 1952; Noel F. Busch, *Adlai Stevenson of Illinois,* Farrar, Strauss & Young, 1952; Elizabeth S. Ives and Hildegarde Dolson, *My Brother Adlai,* Morrow, 1956; Kenneth S. Davis, *A Prophet in His Own Country,* Doubleday, 1957, revised edition, published as *The Politics of Honor: A Biography of Adlai E. Stevenson,* Putnam, 1967; Stuart Gerry Brown, *Conscience in Politics,* Syracuse University Press, 1961; Leon A. Harris, *The Fine Art of Political Wit,* Dutton, 1964; Stuart Gerry Brown, *Adlai E. Stevenson: A Short Biography,* Baron's Woodbury Press, 1965; Lillian Ross, *Adlai Stevenson,* Lippincott, 1966; Herbert J. Muller, *Adlai Stevenson: A Study of Values,* Harper, 1967; Richard J. Walton, *Remnants of Power: The Tragic Last Years of Adlai Stevenson,* Coward, 1968.

Periodicals: *Time* (cover story), January 28, 1952; *New Republic,* April 11, 1960; *Saturday Review,* May 28, 1960; *Christian Century,* July 27, 1960; *New York Times Book Review,* October 27, 1963; *New York Times,* July 22, 1965, August 3, 1965, September 10, 1965, and December 15, 1965; *Harper's,* November, 1965.

(Died July 14, 1965)

*   *   *

STEVENSON, Dorothy E(mily) 1892-1973

PERSONAL: Born 1892, in Edinburgh, Scotland; daughter of David Alan (a civil engineer) and Anne (Roberts) Stevenson; married James Reid Peploe (a major, British Army), 1916; children: Robert, Rosemary, John. *Education:* Privately educated in England and France. *Religion:* Episcopal Church of Scotland. *Agent:* Curtis Brown Ltd., 1 Craven Hill, London, W2 3EW, England.

CAREER: Novelist. Dumfriesshire Girl Guides Association, president. *Awards, honors:* Boston University created a D. E. Stevenson Room in their library and several of her books were made selections of the Christian Herald Family Bookshelf.

WRITINGS: Peter West, Chambers, 1929; *Miss Buncle's Book,* Jenkins, 1934; *Golden Days,* Jenkins, 1936; *Miss Buncle, Married,* McClelland, 1936, Farrar & Rinehart, 1937; *Smouldering Fire,* Jenkins, 1936, Farrar & Rinehart, 1938; *The Empty World,* Jenkins, 1936, published as *A World in Spell,* Farrar & Rinehart, 1939; *Divorced From Reality,* Jenkins, 1937, published as *Miss Dean's Dilemma,* Farrar & Rinehart, 1938; *The Story of Rosabelle Shaw,* Chambers, 1937, Farrar & Rinehart, 1939; *The Baker's Daughter,* Farrar & Rinehart, 1938 (published in England as *Miss Bun the Baker's Daughter*, Collins, 1940); *The Green Money*, Farrar & Rinehart, 1939.

All published by Farrar & Rinehart except as indicated: *Alister and Co.* (poems), 1940; *The English Air*, 1940; *Rochester's Wife*, 1940; *Mrs. Tim of the Regiment* (diary of officer's wife), 1940; *Mrs. Tim Carries On*, 1941; *Crooked Adam*, 1942; *Celia's House*, 1943; *The Two Mrs. Abbotts*, 1943; *It's Nice to Be Me* (children's poems), Methuen, 1943; *Listening Valley*, 1944; *The Four Graces*, 1946.

All published by Rinehart: *Kate Hardy*, 1947; *Mrs. Tim Gets a Job*, 1947; *Vittoria Cottage*, 1949; *Young Mrs. Savage*, 1949; *Music in the Hills*, 1950; *Shoulder the Sky*, 1951 (published in England as *Winter and Rough Weather*, Collins, 1951); *Mrs. Tim Flies Home*, 1952; *Five Windows*, Rinehart, 1953; *Blow the Wind Southerly*, Rinehart, 1954 (published in England as *Charlotte Fairlie*, Collins, 1954); *Amberwell*, 1955; *Summerhills* (sequel to *Amberwell*), 1956; *The Tall Stranger*, 1957; *Anna and Her Daughters*, 1958; *Still Glides the Stream*, 1959.

All published by Holt: *The Musgraves*, 1960; *Bel Lamington*, 1961; *Fletchers End*, 1962; *The Blue Sapphire*, 1963; *Katherine Wentworth*, 1964; *The Marriage of Katherine*, 1965 (published in England as *Katherine's Marriage*, Collins, 1965); *The House on the Cliff*, 1966; *Sarah Morris Remembers*, 1967; *Sarah's Cottage*, 1968; *Gerald and Elizabeth*, 1969; *The House of the Deer*, 1971.

Omnibus volumes: *Mrs. Tim* (containing *Mrs. Tim of the Regiment* and *Golden Days*), Collins, 1941; *Miss Buncle* (containing *Miss Buncle's Book* and *Miss Buncle, Married*), Holt, 1964.

Writer of serials, poems, and features for journals in Britain and America.

SIDELIGHTS: Virtually all of Dorothy Stevenson's novels have been published both in England and America and reissued in paperback by Fontana in London and Popular Library in the United States. Some have been published in other Commonwealth nations, and translated into German, Dutch, Danish, Swedish, Norwegian, and Spanish. *Avocational interests:* Archaeology, social work, sports, and visiting old castles and Roman roads in Scotland.

(Died December 30, 1973)

*   *   *

STEWART, Edith Hamilton 1883-

PERSONAL: Born April 14, 1883, in Lynn, Mass.; daughter of David (a custom tailor) and Wilhelmina (Reid) Hamilton; married Alfred H. Stewart, April 12, 1912 (deceased). *Religion:* Episcopalian. *Home:* 1002 East Eighth St., Goodland, Kan. 67735.

CAREER: As a young woman, Mrs. Stewart spent five years as a singer, dancer, and actress with an Australian opera company, touring from Vladivostok to Calcutta, and another three years in Shanghai, China. Later, she was rancher and chick hatchery operator in western Kansas, a radio announcer for thirteen years, linotype operator, newspaper columnist, trapper, and served as deputy sheriff.

WRITINGS: I, Me, My, We (autobiography), Alan Swallow-Big Mountain Press, 1963.

*   *   *

STEWART, Hal D(ouglas) 1899-

PERSONAL: Born March 7, 1899, in Glasgow, Scotland; son of Ralph R. (a lieutenant colonel) and Elizabeth J. D. (Mason) Stewart; married Jean D. Stuart (an actress), June 2, 1925. *Education:* Attended schools in Scotland. *Politics:* Conservative. *Religion:* Church of Scotland. *Home:* 12 Goodwin's Ct., London WC2N 4LL, England.

CAREER: Henry J. Stewart & Bro. Ltd., Glasgow, Scotland, director, 1920-37; Howard & Wyndham Repertory Co., Glasgow and Edinburgh, Scotland, stage director, 1938; Colchester Repertory Co., Colchester and Clacton, England, producer, 1938-39. Worked for various companies in London, England, as stage director, 1945-55; Players Ventures Ltd., London, England, general manager, 1954—. With Reunion Theatre Association, 1945-50, West End Stagemanagement Association, 1954—, former chairman of both associations. *Military service:* Territorial Army, 1917-45; Royal Artillery, 1917-19, 1939-45; became lieutenant colonel. Awarded Territorial Decoration, Netherlands Bronze Lion. *Member:* P.E.N., Players' Theatre Club, Arts Theatre Club, Green Room Club (London), Western Club (Glasgow).

WRITINGS: Stagecraft from the Stage Director's Point of View, Pitman, 1949; *Stage Management*, Pitman, 1957. Contributor to *Theatre & Stage*.

Plays—all in one act, except where indicated; all published by Brown, Son, and Ferguson, except where indicated: *More Things*, Nelson, 1929; *Rizzio's Boots*, Nelson, 1930; *The Home Front*, Nelson, 1932; *The Blind Eye*, Nelson, 1932; *Mrs. Watson's Window*, 1932; *The Nineteenth Hole*, 1933; *John Brown's Body*, 1933; *A Month of Sundays* (full length), 1933; *Trade Union*, 1934; *Mrs. Watson at Bay*, 1935; *Fire Policy*, 1935; *The Crime in the Club House*, French, 1935; *Southward Ho!*, 1936; *The Causeway Comic*, 1936; *Tommy Turnbull's Trousers*, 1937; *The Beannachy Bomb* (full length), 1937; *Window Pains*, French, 1938; *The County Calls* (full length), Deane, 1949 (presented in London under title "Lacking a Title," 1951); *Ladies Only*, 1951; *Henry Hereafter*, Evans, 1958; *Robbers Rendezvous*, 1967.

Unpublished plays—all full length: "The Left Boot," produced at Lyceum Theatre (Edinburgh), 1928; "Out of Court," produced at Lyric Theatre (Glasgow), 1937; "The First Victoria," produced at Embassy Theatre (London), 1950.

SIDELIGHTS: Broadcast versions of "A Month of Sundays," "The Beannachy Bomb," "Out of Court," and many of the one-act plays were performed by the British Broadcasting Co.; "The Crime in the Club House" was televised in the United States in the thirties.

*   *   *

STEYERMARK, Julian A(lfred) 1909-

PERSONAL: Born January 27, 1909, in St. Louis, Mo.; son of Leo L. (a merchant) and Mamie (Isaacs) Steyermark; married Cora Shoop, September 1, 1939. *Education:* Washington University, St. Louis, Mo., A.B., 1929, M.S., 1930, Ph.D., 1933; Harvard University, M.A., 1931. *Office:* Instituto Botanico, Apartado 2156, Caracas, Venezuela.

CAREER: Missouri Botanical Garden, St. Louis, research assistant, 1934, member of expedition to Panama, 1934-35; high school biology instructor, University City, Mo., 1935-36; Chicago Natural History Museum, Chicago, Ill., assistant curator of herbarium, 1937-47, associate curator, 1947-49, curator, 1950-58; Venezuela Ministry of Agriculture botanist at Instituto Botanico, Caracas, beginning 1959. Taxonomist and ecologist, U.S. Forest Service, summers 1936-37; visiting professor, Southern Illinois University, 1958. Leader or member of botanical expeditions to Guatemala, Panama, Ecuador, Venezuela, and other Latin American countries. Botanical consultant, Eli Lilly & Co. Nature Conservancy, member of Missouri board of directors, 1955-56, chairman of Illinois committee for preservation of Volo and Wauconda Bogs, 1956-57; visiting curator, New York Botanical Gardens, 1961-65, 1968-69.

MEMBER: International Association of Plant Taxonomists, American Association for the Advancement of Science (fellow), Botanical Society of America, American Society of Plant Taxonomists, Ecological Society of America, America Fern Society, New England Botanical Society, Sociedad Venezolana de Ciencias Naturales (honorary), honorary member of naturalist societies in North, Central, and South America, Barrington Natural History Society (president, 1947-53), Torrey Botanical Club. *Awards, honors:* Honorary research associate, Missouri Botanical Gardens, 1947-58; special plaque for botanical achievement, Washington University, St. Louis, Mo., 1954; National Science Foundation grant, 1958-59; Order of Quetzal (Guatemala), 1961, for work on flora of Guatemala; Order Andres Bello (Venezuela); Amigos Venezuela, 1972; other distinguished service awards.

WRITINGS: Spring Flora of Missouri, Missouri Botanical Garden, 1940; (with P. C. Standley) *Flora of Guatemala*, Chicago Natural History Museum, 1946-59; (contributor) *Flora of Venezuela*, Chicago Natural History Museum, eight volumes, 1953-57; *Vegetational History of the Ozark Forest*, University of Missouri Press, 1959; *Flora of Missouri*, Iowa State University Press, 1963. Contributor of about three hundred articles on plant life discoveries to periodicals.

WORK IN PROGRESS: Rubiaceae of Venezuela, for Venezuela Ministry of Agriculture; articles on new species discovered in Venezuela, for botanical journals.

SIDELIGHTS: Steyermark speaks and reads Spanish, reads Latin, German, and French. *Avocational interests:* Playing piano, all types of music, tennis, swimming, and hiking.

* * *

STILLMAN, Frances (Jennings) 1910-

PERSONAL: Born January 22, 1910, in Detroit, Mich.; daughter of Harry Francis (an industrialist) and Esther (Munger) Jennings; married E. Clark Stillman (an educator), September 28, 1932. *Education:* University of Michigan, A.B., 1931, A.M., 1932. *Religion:* Episcopalian. *Home:* 24 Gramercy Park, New York, N.Y. 10003.

CAREER: Free-lance writer, editor and translator, 1933—; City University of New York, New York, N.Y., lecturer in English, Hunter College, 1959—, Brooklyn College, 1964—. *Member:* American Association of University Women (first vice president, New York City branch, 1959-63; board of directors, New York City branch, 1963—). *Awards, honors:* Avery and Jule Hopwood Award for poetry, University of Michigan.

WRITINGS: Oriental Love Poems, Crowell, 1951; (translator with husband, E. Clark Stillman) *Lyra Belgica* (French and Flemish poetry of Belgium), Belgian Information Center (New York), 1963; (with Jane S. Whitfield) *The Poet's Manual and Rhyming Dictionary*, Crowell, 1965.

Contributor of poetry to magazines and newspapers, including *Saturday Evening Post*, *Poetry*, *New Republic* and *New York Times*. Also has done translations of poetry from the French, Dutch, German, and Latin for anthologies and periodicals.

WORK IN PROGRESS: A translation from the Dutch of Roger d'Hulst's *Flemish Tapestries*; *Pictorial Imagery in the Poetry of Edmund Spenser*.

SIDELIGHTS: Mrs. Stillman lived in Europe, 1933-39, and 1945-48, and visits there frequently. The Stillmans collect African traditional sculpture, especially Congolese; their collection was exhibited at the Museum of Primitive Art in New York for four months during the winter of 1965-66.

* * *

STILLWELL, Norma Jamieson 1894-

PERSONAL: Born February 25, 1894, in Burlingame, Kan.; daughter of William George (a merchant) and Lena (Munger) Jamieson; married Jerry E. Stillwell (a technical editor in the oil industry), January 1, 1917 (died September 4, 1959). *Education:* University of Kansas, A.B., 1916. *Home:* 6306 Prospect, Dallas, Tex. 75214.

CAREER: High school teacher of English in Eskridge, Kan., 1916, and junior high school teacher in Bartlesville, Okla., 1919-20. Collector and recorder of bird songs; speaker at schools and garden clubs on birds, trees, wildflowers, and conservation; nature counselor to Dallas Girl Scouts, Boy Scouts, and Campfire Girls. Member of advisory board, Texas Roadside Council, 1940-48. *Member:* American Ornithologists' Union, Texas Ornithological Society (board member, 1963-64), Dallas Audubon Society.

WRITINGS: Key and Guide to Woody Plants of Dallas County, privately printed, 1939, Proctor-Adams, 1965; *Bird Songs: Adventures and Techniques in Recording the Songs of American Birds*, Doubleday, 1964. Collector and recorder, with husband, Jerry E. Stillwell, of three long-playing records of bird songs, "Bird Songs of Dooryard, Field and Forest," 1952, 1953, 1956. Writer of nature columns for *Dallas News*, 1930-35; contributor to *Nature* and *Wilson Bulletin*. Editor of *Texas Ornithological Society Newsletter*, 1965—.

SIDELIGHTS: Lifelong amateur naturalists and conservationists, Mrs. Stillwell and her husband spent twelve retirement years traveling all over America to record the songs of wild birds. Their three records were part of an album, "National Network of American Bird Songs."

BIOGRAPHICAL/CRITICAL SOURCES: Frontiers (publication of Academy of Natural Science of Philadelphia), December, 1954; *Audubon Magazine*, March-April, 1960.

* * *

STIRLING, Anna Maria Diana Wilhelmina (Pickering) 1865-1965 (Percival Pickering)

PERSONAL: Born August 26, 1865, in London, England; daughter of Percival Andree (Queen's counsellor and county attorney general) and Anna Maria Wilhelmina (Spencer-Stanhope) Pickering; married Charles G. Stirling, 1901. *Home:* Old Battersea House, 30 Vicarage Crescent, Battersea, London S.W.11, England.

CAREER: Writer.

WRITINGS: Coke of Norfolk and His Friends, two volumes, John Lane, 1908, 2nd edition, one volume, 1912; *Annals of a Yorkshire House*, John Lane, 1911; *Macdonald of the Isles*, J. Murray, 1913, John Day, 1914; (compiler) *The Letter-Bag of Lady Elizabeth Spencer-Stanhope*, John Lane, 1913; *A Painter of Dreams* (biographical studies), John Lane, 1916; *The Hothams*, Jenkins, 1918; *Pages and Portraits from the Past: Memoirs of Admiral Sir William Hotham, G.C.B.*, 1919; *William De Morgan and His Wife*, Holt, 1922; *Life's Little Day*, Butterworth & Co., 1925; *The Richmond Papers*, Heinemann, 1926; *Fyvie Castle: Its Lairds and Their Times*, J. Murray, 1928; *The Ways of Yesterday: Being the Chronicles of the Way Family from 1307-1885*, Butterworth & Co., 1930; (editor) Stephen Terry, *Diaries of Dummer*, Unicorn Press, 1934; *Life's Mosaic*, Unicorn Press, 1934; *Victorian Sidelights*, Benn, 1954; *The Merry Wives of Battersea and Gossip of Three Centuries*, R. Hale, 1956; *Ghosts Vivisected*, R. Hale, 1957, Citadel, 1958; *Odd Lives*, P. R. Macmillan, 1959; *A Scrapheap of Memories* (autobiographical), P. R. Macmillan, 1960; *Stirling Tales and Strange Jests of History*, P.R.M. Publishers, 1961.

Fairy tales: *The Adventures of Prince Almero; The Queen of the Goblins*.

Novels under pseudonym Percival Pickering: *A Life Awry*, Bliss & Co., 1893; *A Pliable Marriage*, Osgood & Co., 1895; *The Spirit is Willing*, Bliss, Sards & Co., 1898; *Toy Gods*, John Long, 1904.

SIDELIGHTS: Mrs. Stirling lived in Old Battersea House, built by Sir Christopher Wren in the early eighteenth century, and there collected Pre-Raphaelite paintings, especially those of her sister, Evelyn DeMorgan, as well as the pottery of her brother-in-law, William DeMorgan.

BIOGRAPHICAL/CRITICAL SOURCES: New Daily, February 2, 1963.†

(Died August 11, 1965)

*   *   *

STIVER, Mary Weeden 1909-

PERSONAL: Born February 18, 1909, in Bristol Township, Morgan County, Ohio; daughter of Converse Thomas (a farmer and switchboard telephone man) and Amelia Mary (Tiemann) Weeden; married Lawrence Hahn Stiver (a sheet-metal layout worker), March 26, 1939; children: James LeRoy, Robert Hanson, Lawrence Wilfred. *Education:* Attended University of Michigan, 1929-30; Michigan State Normal College (now Eastern Michigan University), B.S. in Education, 1933; graduate work in special education. *Politics:* Registered Democrat. *Religion:* "Confirmed Lutheran (to Quaker sympathies)."

CAREER: Second grade teacher, North Lima, Ohio, 1934-38.

WRITINGS: Lonely Hills (poetry chapbook), Clarendon Press, 1961; *Brief Argument* (poetry), Hawk and Whippoorwill Press, 1964.

WORK IN PROGRESS: Poetry.

AVOCATIONAL INTERESTS: Homemaking, raising children, gardening, nature, letter-writing, and reading.

*   *   *

STONE, Mildred Fairbanks 1902-

PERSONAL: Born May 21, 1902, in Bloomfield, N.J.; daughter of Franklin A. (a salesman) and Ida Louise (Gara-

brant) Stone. *Education:* Vassar College, A.B., 1924. *Politics:* Republican. *Religion:* Baptist. *Home:* 23 Clarendon Pl., Bloomfield, N.J. 07003.

CAREER: Mutual Benefit Life Insurance Co., Newark, N.J., 1925-68, assistant secretary (officer), 1934-68; retired, 1968—. Trustee of Bloomfield United Fund, 1939-67, of Mountainside Hospital, Montclair, N.J., 1952-64; member of Bloomfield Board of Education, 1954-64. *Member:* American Society of Chartered Life Underwriters (past president of Newark chapter), National Audubon Society, American Forestry Association, American Association of University Women (past president of Bloomfield branch), New Jersey Historical Society, New Jersey Audubon Society, Bloomfield Friends of the Library, Vassar Club of Essex County, Phi Beta Kappa. *Awards, honors:* Bloomfield Outstanding Citizen Award, 1956; Newark Chartered Life Underwriters' Distinguished Service Award, 1961.

WRITINGS: A Short History of Life Insurance, Insurance Research & Review Co., 1942; (editor) *Life Underwriting: A Career for Women*, Insurance Research & Review Co., 1942; *Better Life Insurance Letters*, National Underwriter Co., 1950; *Since 1845: A History of the Mutual Benefit Life Insurance Company*, published for Mutual Benefit Life Insurance Co. by Rutgers University Press, 1957; *The Teacher Who Changed an Industry* (biography of S. S. Huebner), Irwin, 1960; *A Calling and Its College: A History of the American College of Life Underwriters*, Irwin, 1963.

*   *   *

STONOR, Oliver 1903-
(E. Morchard Bishop, Morchard Bishop)

PERSONAL: Born July 3, 1903, in Teddington, Middlesex, England. *Home:* Velthams, Morebath, near Tiverton, Devonshire, England.

CAREER: Author, journalist, and critic.

WRITINGS: The End of Mr. Davidson (novel), Heinemann, 1932; *A First Book of Synonyms* (reference), Routledge & Kegan Paul, 1963; (editor of revised British edition) Joseph Jordan, *The Awful Spellers Dictionary*, Wolfe, 1964.

Under pseudonym E. Morchard Bishop: *Two for Joy* (novel), J. Cape, 1938.

Under pseudonym Morchard Bishop—novels, except as indicated: *Aunt Betty*, J. Cape, 1939; *The Green Tree and the Dry*, J. Cape, 1939; *The Star Called Wormwood*, Gollancz, 1941; *The Song and the Silence*, Gollancz, 1947; *Valerie*, Gollancz, 1948; *Blake's Hayley: The Life, Works, and Friendships of William Hayley* (biography), Gollancz, 1951, Books for Libraries, 1972.

Also contributor to *Two Romantic Painters*, by Eric and Joan Stevens, published in 1974.

Editor, and author of introduction under pseudonym Morchard Bishop: *The Poetical Works of Shelley*, Macdonald & Co., 1949; James Boswell, *The Journal of a Tour to Corsica*, Williams & Norgate, 1951; *The Autobiography of Arthur Machen*, Richards Press, 1951; Samuel Rogers, *Recollections of Table-Talk*, Richards Press, 1952; Samuel Taylor Coleridge, *Complete Poems*, Macdonald & Co., 1954; Morley Roberts, *The Private Life of Henry Maitland*, Richards Press, 1958; Arthur Machen, *Hieroglyphics*, Unicorn Press, 1961.

Contributor to encyclopedias, and to *Times Literary Sup-*

plement, *New Statesman*, *Cornhill*, *John O'London's*, *Reader's Digest*, and other periodicals. Assisted in preparing for publication *The Notebooks of Samuel Taylor Coleridge*, Routledge & Kegan Paul.

WORK IN PROGRESS: Editing Arthur Machen's *Table-Talk*; editing *Memoir of James Smethan*, by his wife.

* * *

STOPFORD, Robert Wright 1901-

PERSONAL: Born February 20, 1901, in Liverpool, England; son of John William and Ethel (Wright) Stopford; married Winifred Sophia Morton, 1935 (killed during Battle of Britain, 1942); married Kathleen Mary Holt, 1945; children: (first marriage) Patrick, John; (second marriage) Catherine. *Education:* Hertford College, Oxford, B.A., 1924, M.A., 1927. *Home address:* Stockbridge, Hampshire S020 6RO, England.

CAREER: Clergyman, Church of England, ordained, 1932. Schoolmaster in England, 1924-34; principal of Trinity College, Kandy, Ceylon, 1934-40, and Achimota College, Ghana, 1940-45; rector of Chipping Barnet, England, 1946-47; moderator of Church of England training colleges, 1947-52; secretary of Church Assembly Schools Council, 1952-55; Bishop of Fulham, 1955-56; Bishop of Peterborough, 1956-61; Bishop of London, 1961-73; Vicar General of the Episcopal Church in Jerusalem and the Middle East, 1973—. Chaplain to the Queen, 1952-55; dean of H. M. Chapels Royal, 1961; Privy Counsellor, 1961. Chairman, Church of England Board of Education, 1958-73; Churchill fellow, Westminster College, Fulton, Mo., 1969. *Awards, honors:* Knight Commander, Royal Victorian Order; Commander, Order of the British Empire, 1949, prelate, Order of the British Empire, 1961; D.D. and D.C.L., University of Durham, 1951; honorary fellow, Hertford College, Oxford University, 1956; D.D. (Lambeth), 1957; fellow of King's College, University of London, 1965; D.D. from University of London, 1965, Westminster College, 1966, and College of William and Mary (Virginia), 1968.

WRITINGS: (With M. VC. Jeffreys) *Play Production*, Longmans, Green, 1928; (with others) *The Anglican Communion*, Oxford University Press, 1948; *Church School and Life*, Oxford University Press, 1949; *No Man Liveth for Himself*, Bles, 1964.

* * *

STOPPELMAN, Frans 1921-
(Francis Stopelman, Francis Stoppelman)

PERSONAL: Born January 9, 1921, in Amsterdam, Netherlands; son of Lodewijk and Hermanda (van Brink) Stoppelman. *Education:* School of Photography, Lausanne, Switzerland, graduate. *Home:* P.O. Box 7008, Amsterdam Z-II, Netherlands.

CAREER: Pix, Inc., New York, N.Y., correspondent, seventeen years; photographer and writer. *Member:* Netherlands Press Photographers Association, International Focus Salon (honorary). *Awards, honors:* Gold medal and award for best color picture of Olympic Games, Mexican Press Club, 1968.

WRITINGS: *La Republica Dominicana*, Instituto Dominicano del Libro, 1959; *Jamaica*, Benn, 1962; *Mexico on the Move*, Libreria Anglo Americana, 1970. Contributor to *Life*, *Quick*, *Paris Match*, *Focus*, *Der Spiegel*, *Panorama*, *Het Vrije Volk*, *Revue*, *New York Times*, *New York Herald Tribune*, and other periodicals and newspapers.

WORK IN PROGRESS: Latin America.

AVOCATIONAL INTERESTS: Spearfishing, skiing, swimming, sailing, reading, doing nothing.

BIOGRAPHICAL/CRITICAL SOURCES: *Camera* (English International Edition), July, 1953.

* * *

STRAIN, Dudley 1909-

PERSONAL: Born June 27, 1909, in Pomeroy, Wash.; son of Joseph Albert (a rancher) and Sallie (Allen) Strain; married Helen Irene McClay, July 17, 1938; children: Ann (Mrs. C. W. Hoffmann, Jr.), Keith, *Education:* Butler University, A.B., 1935; American School of Oriental Research, Jerusalem, graduate study, 1935; Yale Divinity School, B.D., 1936, M.A., 1939; Union Theological Seminary, New York, N.Y., additional study. *Politics:* Democrat. *Home:* 3216 42nd St., Lubbock, Tex. 79413. *Office:* 2323 Broadway, Lubbock, Tex. 79401.

CAREER: Minister, Disciples of Christ. Minister in Salem, Ore., 1942-53; minister of First Christian Church, Lubbock, Tex., 1953—. Short-term missioner in Japan, summer, 1963. Member of board of directors of United Fund, Young Men's Christian Association, Family Service Association, Salvation Army, all Lubbock, Tex., and of Texas Governor's Commission on Alcoholism. *Awards, honors:* D.D., Texas Christian University, 1958.

WRITINGS: *The Measure of a Minister*, Bethany, 1964.

* * *

STRASSER, Bernard Paul 1895-
(P.W., Silvanus)

PERSONAL: Born March 21, 1895, in Windsheim, Bavaria, Germany; son of Peter (a courthouse official) and Pauline (Strobel) Strasser. *Education:* Humanistisches Gymnasium, Metten, Bavaria, B.A., 1915; advanced study at University of Munich, University of Wuerzburg, and at Theologische Hochschule, Regensburg, Bavaria; equivalent M.A., 1923. *Home:* St. Joseph Nursing Home, Norfolk, Neb. 68701.

CAREER: Entered Roman Catholic Benedictine Order in Metten, Germany, 1919, ordained priest, 1923; Humanistisches Gymnasium, Metten, Bavaria, Germany, professor and prefect of studies, 1923-35; St. Gallus Stift, Bregenz, Austria, professor, 1935-36; fled Gestapo in 1935 to refuge in Benedictine monastery in Luxembourg, and thence to Belgium, Portugal, and finally to the United States in 1940; St. John's University, Collegeville, Minn., professor of French and German, 1940-50; St. Mary's Church, Primrose, Neb., administrator, 1950-63; St. Henry's Church, Howells, Neb. Chaplain at St. Joseph Nursing Home, Norfolk, Neb. *Military service:* German Army, Artillery, 1915-18; became lieutenant; received Iron Cross and Verwundeten Abzeichen (Purple Heart).

WRITINGS: *Vom Erleben des Kirchenjahres*, Abbaye de Cleryaux, 1939, revised translation published as *With Christ Through the Year: The Liturgical Year in Word and Symbols*, Bruce, 1947; *The Dews of Tabor: Light and Strength for Our Every Day*, Exposition, 1960.

Booklets: *Beichte gut!*, Abbaye de Metten, translation published as *Make a Good Confession!*, Bopp; *Family Blessing*, Family Life Bureau, 1948; *Love's Sorrowful Journey*, Bopp, 1961. Also writer of *A Footnote to the History of Germany* (apologia for brothers, Gregor and Otto Strasser), privately printed, 1950. Contributor of articles to Catholic newspapers, magazines, and journals in Germany, Luxembourg, Austria, and United States, writing under pseudonyms of P.W. and Silvanus in Hitler days. Editor, *Alt und Jung Metten* (quarterly of Humanistisches Gymnasium, Metten), 1926-35.

SIDELIGHTS: Strasser published *A Footnote to the History of Germany* about his politically prominent brothers to correct "erroneous and misleading stories." Gregor Strasser was killed by Hitler's agents in 1934, a year after Otto Strasser fled Germany to eventual exile in Nova Scotia, Canada. *Avocational interests:* History, stamp collecting, music.

*   *   *

STRATON, Hillyer H(awthorne)   1905-

PERSONAL: Surname is pronounced *Strayt*-on; born April 11, 1905, in Waco, Tex.; son of John Roach (a clergyman) and Georgia (Hillyer) Straton; married Alice Aven; children: Sylvia, Carter. *Education:* Mercer University, A.B., M.A., 1926; Columbia University, graduate study, 1926; Eastern Baptist Theological Seminary, B.D., 1928, Th.M., 1929, Th.D., 1933; Harvard University, special studies, 1947, 1949, 1956. *Politics:* Independent. *Home:* 166 Hawthorne St., Malden, Mass. 02148. *Office:* 493 Main St., Malden, Mass. 02148.

CAREER: Minister of First Baptist Church, Muncie, Ind., 1930-38, Detroit, Mich., 1938-45, Malden, Mass., 1945—. Chairman, Citizens Action Committee, Malden, Mass., 1962-64. *Member:* Ministers' Club of Boston (secretary, 1957—). *Awards, honors:* D.D., Kalamazoo College, 1949, Mercer University, 1956.

WRITINGS: Peter: The Man Jesus Made, Zondervan, 1938; *Baptists: Their Message and Mission*, Judson, 1941; *Thinking Where Jesus Thought*, Bethany Press, 1945; *Preaching the Miracles of Jesus*, Abingdon, 1950; *Solving Life's Problems: Methods of The Master*, Bethany Press, 1954; *A Guide to the Parables of Jesus*, Eerdmans, 1959; *Prayers in Public*, Judson, 1963. Contributor of articles to religious journals.

WORK IN PROGRESS: A book about his father, *John Roach Straton: Prophet of Social Righteousness*.

AVOCATIONAL INTERESTS: Travel, photography, and lecturing.

*   *   *

STRATTON, William David   1896-

PERSONAL: Born April 17, 1896, in Grand Rapids, Mich.; son of William Wesley and Nettie (Barnahrdt) Stratton; married Lucille Neville, May 15, 1920; children: John N., David W. *Religion:* Roman Catholic. *Home:* 1835 West Grove Center St., West Covina, Calif. 91790.

CAREER: Rural school teacher in Montana, 1914-17; assistant bank cashier in Sidney, Mont., 1918-21; hardware buyer in Minnesota and California, 1922-60; now retired. Former professional pianist. *Military service:* U.S. Army, World War I.

WRITINGS: Tutka of the Barren Grounds, Criterion, 1963; (with wife, Lucille Stratton) *Wild Wings Over the Marshes*, Golden Gate, 1964.

WORK IN PROGRESS: Wild Wings Over the Arctic, for Golden Gate; *Wild Wings Over the Desert; Trouble at Snake Canyon*.

STRAUSS, (Mary) Lucille Jackson   1908-
(Lucille Jackson)

PERSONAL: Born September 8, 1908, in Pittsburgh, Pa.; daughter of Robert Wallace (a salesman) and Mary Elizabeth (Kreimendahl) Jackson; married Jerome Strauss, December 23, 1955. *Education:* Chatham College, B.A., 1930; Pennsylvania State University, M.S., 1931. *Politics:* Republican. *Religion:* Presbyterian. *Home:* 520 West Nittany Ave., State College, Pa. 16801.

CAREER: Pennsylvania State University, University Park, mineral industries librarian, 1931-41; Vanadium Corp. of America, Research and Development Laboratory, Bridgeville, Pa., librarian, 1941-48; Pennsylvania State University, chemistry and physics librarian, 1948—. Consultant to industrial firms on organization of technical libraries. *Member:* Special Libraries Association (chapter director, 1945-46; chairman of national non-serials publication committee, 1954-55), American Chemical Society (secretary, division of chemical literature, 1955-57), Chemical Society (London), American Association of University Women, Iota Sigma Pi (chapter president, 1950; national director, 1968—), Sigma Delta Epsilon (chapter president, 1951). *Awards, honors:* Special achievement award of Special Libraries Association, 1964, for *Technical Libraries: Their Organization and Management*.

WRITINGS: (Editor and contributor under name Lucille Jackson) *Technical Libraries: Their Organization and Management*, Special Libraries Association, 1951; (with Irene M. Strieby and Alberta L. Brown) *Scientific and Technical Libraries: Their Organization and Administration*, Interscience, 1964, 2nd edition, Wiley, 1972. Writer of pamphlets on special library topics under name Lucille Jackson. Contributor to library journals.

*   *   *

STREET, Arthur George   1892-1966
(James Brian)

PERSONAL: Born April 7, 1892, in Wilton, Salisbury, England; son of Henry (a farmer) and Sarah Anne (Butte) Street; married Vera Florence Foyle, 1918; children: Pamela (Mrs. David McCormick). *Education:* Attended Dauntsey's School, Wiltshire, England. *Home:* Mill Farm, South Newton, Salisbury, Wiltshire, England.

CAREER: Emigrated to Canada and worked as farm laborer in Manitoba, 1911-14; farmed with father near Wilton, Salisbury, England, 1914-17, and took over farm in 1918; free-lance writer and journalist (as well as farmer), 1932-1966. Lecturer on agricultural topics at schools and universities in Britain, and in Canada and United States, 1937; broadcaster of talks on the countryside. *Member:* Edinburgh University Agricultural Society (honorary president, 1935), Savage Club and Farmers Club (both London), Salisbury Club.

WRITINGS: Farmer's Glory, Faber, 1932; *Strawberry Roan*, Faber, 1932; *Country Days*, Faber, 1933; *Hedge Trimmings*, Faber, 1933; *Thinking Aloud*, Faber, 1934; *The Endless Furrow*, Faber, 1934; *Land Everlasting*, Bodley Head, 1934; *To Be a Farmer's Boy*, Faber, 1935 (republished as *Farming: How to Begin*, Faber, 1939); *Country Calendar*, Eyre, 1935; *Moonraking*, Eyre, 1936; *The Gentleman of the Party*, Faber, 1936; *Farming England*, Scribner, 1937; *Already Walks To-morrow*, Faber, 1938; *A Year of My Life*, Eyre, 1939.

A Crook in the Furrow, Faber, 1940; *Wessex Wins*, Faber,

1941; *Round the Year on a Farm*, Oxford University Press, 1941; *Harvest by Lamplight*, Faber, 1941; *From Dusk Till Dawn*, Harrap, 1943; *Hitler's Whistle*, Eyre, 1943; *Ditchampton Farm*, Eyre, 1946; *Holdfast*, Faber, 1946; *Landmarks*, Eyre, 1949.

Wheat and Chaff (includes *Hedge Trimmings*, *Country Days*, and *Thinking Aloud*), Faber, 1950; *In His Own Country* (includes *Country Calendar*, *Moonraking*, *A Year of My Life*, *Hitler's Whistle*, and *Ditchampton Farm*), Eyre & Spottiswoode, 1950; *Shameful Harvest*, Faber, 1952; *Kittle Cattle*, M. Joseph, 1954; *Feather-Bedding*, Faber, 1954; *Master of None*, Faber, 1956; *Sweetacres*, M. Joseph, 1956; *Bobby Bocker*, M. Joseph, 1957.

Cooper's Crossing, R. Hale, 1962; (under pseudonym James Brian) *Fair Enough*, R. Hale, 1962; *Fish and Chips*, R. Hale, 1964; *Johnny Cowslip*, R. Hale, 1964.

Regular feature writer for *Farmers Weekly*; advisory editor, *Country Fair*.

AVOCATIONAL INTERESTS: Game shooting, salmon and trout fishing, contract bridge.

(Died July 21, 1966)

* * *

STREET, Mattie (Waters) 1896-

PERSONAL: Born December 19, 1896; daughter of John Birch (a farmer) and Elizabeth (Beck) Waters; married Wesley Street, May 6, 1925; children: Philip. *Education:* Attended high school in Blackfoot, Idaho, and continued education through correspondence and extension courses. *Politics:* "Flexible." *Religion:* Unitarian Universalist. *Home:* 1001 Southwest 28th St., Pendleton, Ore. 97801.

CAREER: Secretarial work in Portland, Ore., and Blackfoot, Idaho, 1915-25. Country correspondent at various times for six newspapers. *Member:* National Writers Club, Oregon State Poetry Association, Idaho Poets and Writers Guild.

WRITINGS: Open Range and Open Doors (poetry), Big Mountain Press, 1964. Contributor to magazines and newspapers.

WORK IN PROGRESS: A book of poetry with proposed title, *Water Under the Bridge*; research for a book on early life in the West.

SIDELIGHTS: Mrs. Street told *CA:* "My avocation at present is writing. I find it an interesting occupation for my retirement years, motivated by the fact that I can no longer do hard work. I think too much of our current literature contains obscenity and hope to see improvement in this respect soon. I am interested in traveling in the great open spaces of the west."

BIOGRAPHICAL/CRITICAL SOURCES: Oregon Farmer, June 20, 1961, and February 21, 1963.

* * *

STRIEBY, Irene Macy 1894-

PERSONAL: Born September 6, 1894, in Converse, Ind.; daughter of Milton D. (a merchant) and Mary O. (Hunt) Macy; married A. Wright Strieby, December 25, 1917 (died, 1927); children: Robert Milton. *Education:* Brenau College, A.B., 1916; University of North Carolina, B.S. in L.S., 1933. *Home:* 2550 Cold Spring Rd., Indianapolis, Ind. 46222.

CAREER: High School teacher, 1916-18; Riverside Military Academy, Gainesville, Ga., and Hollywood, Calif., librarian and publicity director, 1929-32; Lilly Research Laboratories, Indianapolis, Ind., librarian, 1934-56, archivist and consultant, 1956-59; independent consultant on business libraries and archives, 1956—. Columbia University, instructor in library science, summer, 1957. Council of National Library Associations, member of joint committee on library education, 1949—; U.S. Book Exchange, vice-president, 1948-50, director, 1950-52. National Library Week, Indiana chairman, 1959-60.

MEMBER: Special Libraries Association (first vice-president, 1940-41, 1946-47; president, 1947-48; director, 1948-49), Medical Library Association (honorary life member), American Library Association, Society of American Archivists, Daughters of the American Revolution, National Society Colonial Dames XVII Century, Indiana Association for Adult Education (treasurer and director, 1945-47), Indiana Association for History of Medicine (secretary-treasurer, 1940-43), Indiana State Historical Society, Indiana Library Association (honorary life), Delta Delta Delta, Indiana Button Society (president). *Awards, honors:* Special Libraries Association award for significant professional achievement, 1956.

WRITINGS: (Contributor) Lucille Jackson, editor, *Technical Libraries: Their Organization and Management*, Special Libraries Association, 1951; (with Lucille Jackson Strauss and Alberta L. Brown) *Scientific and Technical Libraries: Their Organization and Administration*, Interscience, 1964, 2nd edition, Wiley, 1972. Assistant editor and contributor, Remington's *Practice of Pharmacy*, 12th edition, 1960. Contributor to library symposia, and contributor of about thirty-five articles to library, business, and historical journals. Member of editorial advisory committee, *Indiana Quaker Records*.

WORK IN PROGRESS: Compiling history of the Richard Haynes family (1763-1850); assisting with revision of a book on chemical process industries.

AVOCATIONAL INTERESTS: Local history, genealogy; collecting antiques, rare buttons, and china pitchers; gardening.

* * *

STUART, Graham H. 1887-

PERSONAL: Born January 27, 1887, in Cleveland, Ohio; son of Graham W. (an engineer) and Annie (Gill) Stuart; married Agnes Wright, August 27, 1918; children: Jean Stuart Frost, Ann Stuart Orloff. *Education:* Western Reserve University (now Case Western Reserve University), A.B., 1908; Alliance Francaise, Paris, France, diplome, 1911; Ecole Libre des Sciences Politiques, Paris, France, advanced study, 1913-14; University of Wisconsin, M.A., 1918, Ph.D., 1919. *Politics:* Republican. *Religion:* Protestant. *Home:* 450 Santa Rita, Palo Alto, Calif. *Office:* Department of Political Science, Stanford University, Stanford, Calif.

CAREER: Stanford University, Stanford, Calif., began as assistant professor, 1923, professor of political science, 1928-52, now professor emeritus. Carnegie Professor of International Relations at Universities of Toulouse, Poitiers, and Montpellier, in France, 1929-30; professor at Johns Hopkins University School of Advanced International Studies, Washington, D.C., 1952-53, at School of American Studies, Salzburg, Austria, 1954; visiting professor at University of Washington, Seattle, summers, 1927, 1932, 1940, at Hague Academy of International Law,

1934, and Institut de Hautes Etudes Internationales, Geneva, Switzerland, 1937. Adviser to U.S. Department of State, 1942-43, and to U.S. minister in Tangier, 1946.

MEMBER: American Society of International Law, American Political Science Association, Institute of World Affairs (life member; member of executive committee), Phi Beta Kappa, Alpha Tau Omega, Cosmos Club (Washington, D.C.). *Awards, honors:* Citation, State of Florida for outstanding contributions to inter-American relations; LL.D. from Western Reserve University, 1948.

WRITINGS: French Foreign Policy, Century Co., 1921; *Latin America and the United States*, Appleton, 1922, 5th edition, 1955; *The Governmental System of Peru*, Carnegie Institute of Washington, 1925; *The International City of Tangier*, Stanford University Press, 1931, 2nd edition, 1955; *American Diplomatic and Consular Practice*, Appleton, 1936, 2nd edition, 1952; (editor) *U.S. Foreign Policy*, University of Southern California, 1947; (editor) *Conflict of Two Worlds*, University of Southern California, 1949; *The Department of State*, Macmillan, 1949. Editor of "Stanford Books in World Politics," 1924-52.

WORK IN PROGRESS: Preparing 6th edition of *Latin America and the United States*, with James L. Tigner.

SIDELIGHTS: Stuart told *CA* that he is particularly interested in the Foreign Service. He was studying in Paris at L'Ecole Libre des Sciences Politiques, preparing for the Foreign Service, when World War I erupted and closed the Service for four years in Europe. In his teaching career, Stuart specialized in preparing students for the Foreign Service. More than fifty of his students entered the Service or the State Department, and a dozen became ambassadors.

*   *   *

STUART-JONES, Edwyn Henry   1895-19(?)

PERSONAL: Born September 1, 1895, in Oxford, England; son of Sir Henry (principal of University College of Wales) and Ileen (Vaughan) Stuart-Jones; married Susanne Myfanwy Long-Price, July 11, 1929; children: Crystal Ileen Margaret Stuart-Jones Wijesurira, Edwyn Anthony Lawrance. *Education:* Attended Royal Naval College, Osborne, England, 1908-1910, and Royal Naval College, Dartmouth, 1910-1912. *Religion:* Church of England. *Home:* The Dell, Milton Lane, Wells, Somersetshire, England.

CAREER: Career officer in Royal Navy, beginning as cadet in 1908, and invalided from service with rank of lieutenant, 1922; manufacturer's agent for paint company in England, 1924-39; also involved in gold mining operations in Wales and with an explosives manufacturing company in Rhodesia, 1926-29; recalled to active duty with Royal Navy, 1939-46, retiring with rank of commander; manufacturer's agent for paint company, from 1946 until his retirement. *Awards, honors:* Decorated by Belgium and Denmark.

WRITINGS: An Invasion That Failed, Basil Blackwell, 1950; *The Last Invasion of Britain*, University of Wales Press, 1950. Contributor to *Dock Leaves* and *Anglo-Welsh Review*.

WORK IN PROGRESS: A Vanished Treaty, a book of short stories, mostly with Welsh background.

AVOCATIONAL INTERESTS: Anything to do with Wales and Ireland; history and literature in general (with emphasis on French literature); the English author, George Borrow.

(Deceased)

STUBER, Stanley I(rving)   1903-
(M. Nott Erasmus)

PERSONAL: Born August 24, 1903, in Gardiner, Me.; son of Benjamin F. (an agent for United Shoe Co.) and Edith (Henderson) Stuber; married Helen Hill, June 15, 1927; children: Roscoe Vernon, Sylvia (Mrs. Walker Heap), Lois (Mrs. Kenneth Spitzer). *Education:* Bates College, A.B., 1926; Rochester Theological Seminary, B.D., 1928; Colgate-Rochester Divinity School, Th.M., 1929. *Politics:* Independent. *Home:* 74 Burma Rd., Wyckoff, N.J. *Office:* 165 Burton Ave., Hasbrouck Heights, N.J. 07604.

CAREER: Ordained Baptist minister, 1928. Pastor in Maine and New York, 1924-37; Clifton Springs Sanitarium and Clinic, Clifton Springs, N.Y., chaplain-consultant, 1938-41; Northern Baptist Convention (now American Baptist Convention), New York, N.Y., national publicity secretary, 1941-45, executive secretary, World Relief Commission, 1942-49, national director of public relations, 1945-49; Japan International Christian University Foundation, New York, N.Y., executive secretary, 1950-56; Council of Churches of Greater Kansas City, Kansas City, Mo., general secretary, 1956-60; Missouri Council of Churches, Jefferson City, Mo., executive director, 1961-64; Association Press, New York, N.Y., director, 1964—. Member and special counselor, Department of National Religious Radio, National Council of Churches, 1945-55; member of board of directors, Religion in American Life; official observer at Second Vatican Council in Rome, 1962-65; Ecumenical minister, Bergan County Council of Churches, 1969—; president, New Jersey Council of Organizations, 1972-73. *Member:* United Nations Association (president of New Jersey Division, 1972-73), Religious Public Relations Council (New York; life member), Rotary Club (honorary member). *Awards, honors:* D.D. from Keuka College, 1946.

WRITINGS—All published by Association Press, except as indicated: *The Living Water*, 1927; *How We Got Our Denominations*, 1928, 2nd revised edition, 1965; *Treasury of the Christian Faith*, 1948; *Public Relations Manual*, Doubleday, 1951; *The Christian Reader*, 1952; *Primer on Roman Catholicism for Protestants*, 1953; *Basic Christian Writings*, 1957; *How Protestants Differ from Roman Catholics*, 1961; *Who We Are*, Commission of Army Chaplains, 1962; (editor) *The Illustrated Bible and Church Handbook*, 1966; (with Claud D. Nelson) *Implementing Vatican II in Your Community: Dialogue and Action Manual Based on the Sixteen Documents of the Second Vatican Council*, Guild Press, 1967; *Human Rights and Fundamental Freedoms*, 1968. Contributor to *Christian Century*, *Forum*, and other religious periodicals. Former editor, *Baptist World*.

WORK IN PROGRESS: First Amendment Freedoms and *The Bicentenial*.

*   *   *

SUCHMAN, Edward A(llen)   1915-197?

PERSONAL: Born December 5, 1915, in New York, N.Y.; son of Joseph (a businessman) and Sadie (Silverstein) Suchman; married Janet Malkin, 1939; married second wife, Elaine Markley (a psychologist), June 22, 1958; children: (first marriage) Susan, Lucille; (second marriage) Mark, Sara. *Education:* Cornell University, A.B., 1936, M.A., 1937; Columbia University, Ph.D., 1947.

Home: 1175 York Ave., New York, N.Y. 10021. *Office:* University of Pittsburgh, Pittsburgh, Pa.

CAREER: Princeton University, Radio Research Project, Princeton, N.J., research assistant, 1937-39; Columbia University, Office of Radio Research, New York, N.Y., executive officer and research director, 1940-42; U.S. War Department, Research Branch, senior research associate, 1942-46; Cornell University, Ithaca, N.Y., professor and sometime executive officer, department of sociology and anthropology, 1947-58; New York City (N.Y.) Department of Health, director of social science activities, 1958-63; University of Pittsburgh, Pittsburgh, Pa., professor of sociology, 1963-7?. Consultant to U.S. Public Health Service and Puerto Rico Department of Health; member of advisory committee on rehabilitation, Association for the Aid of Crippled Children, 1959-63; member of Mayor's Committee on Narcotics Addiction, New York City Department of Hospitals, 1960-63; member of evaluation committee, Congress of International Society for the Welfare of Cripples, 1960-61.

MEMBER: American Public Health Association (fellow), American Sociological Association (fellow; chairman of medical sociology section, 1965), Sociological Research Association, American Association for Public Opinion Research, American Association of University Professors. *Awards, honors:* Rockefeller Foundation fellow, 1939-40; Social Science Research Council fellow, 1946-47; Ford Foundation research award, 1956; U.S. Public Health Service fellow, 1958.

WRITINGS: (With S. A. Stouffer and others) *The American Soldier*: Volume I, *Adjustment During Army Life*, Volume IV, *Measurement and Prediction*, Princeton University Press, 1949; (with Doby and others) *An Introduction to Social Research*, Stackpole, 1954; (with M. Rosenberg) *Occupations and Values*, Free Press of Glencoe, 1958; (with J. Dean and R. Williams) *Desegragation: Propositions and Research Suggestions*, Anti-Defamation League, 1958; (with R. Goldsen and others) *What College Students Think*, Van Nostrand, 1960; (with A. Scherzer) *Current Research in Childhood Accidents*, Association for the Aid of Crippled Children, 1960; *Sociology and the Field of Public Health*, Russell Sage, 1963; (with W. Haddon and D. Klein) *Accident Research: Methods and Approaches*, Harper, 1964; (with R. Williams and J. Dean) *Strangers Next Door*, Prentice-Hall, 1964; *An Experimental Study of Accident Prevention Among Sugar Cane Workers in Puerto Rico*, Office of Research, Department of Health, 1966; *Evaluative Research: Principles and Practice in Public Service and Social Action Programs*, Russell Sage, 1967; *The Relationship Between Poverty and Educational Deprivation*, Office of Education, 1968.

WORK IN PROGRESS: With G. James and J. Elinson, *Evaluation in Public Health*, for Russell Sage.

(Deceased)

*   *   *

SUGDEN, Mark 1902-

PERSONAL: Born February 11, 1902, in Leek, Staffordshire, England; son of F. L. (a silk manufacturer) and F. G. (King) Sugden; married Margaret-Esther Chambers; children: Peter, Michael. *Education:* University of Dublin, M.A., 1926. *Politics:* Conservative. *Religion:* Church of England. *Home:* Boringdon, Dartmouth, Devonshire, England.

CAREER: Trinity College, Glenalmond, Perthshire, Scotland, master, 1926-31; Royal Naval College, Dartmouth, Devonshire, England, head of modern language department, 1949-64. Fellow of the Woodard Schools Foundation. Member of Dartmouth Youth Council. *Member:* Devonshire Squash Racquets Association (president). *Awards, honors:* Member, Order of the British Empire, 1963.

WRITINGS: (With Gerry Hollis) *Rugger—Do It This Way*, J. Murray, 1946, 2nd edition, 1961.

SIDELIGHTS: Sugden speaks French and Spanish. *Avocational interests:* Golf and gardening.

*   *   *

SUMMERS, Festus P(aul) 1895-

PERSONAL: Born March 2, 1895, near Lockwood, W.Va.; son of Paul Jones (a farmer) and Julia (Cutlip) Summers; married Helen Page, December 22, 1922; children: Jane Maxwell (Mrs. Robert J. Wygal, Jr.). *Education:* Concord Normal School (now Concord College), diploma, 1917; West Virginia University, A.B., 1923, Ph.D., 1933; University of Chicago, A.M., 1927; Columbia University, graduate study, 1927-28. *Home:* 8 Elgin St., Morgantown, W.Va. 26505. *Office:* Department of History, West Virginia University, Morgantown, W.Va. 26505.

CAREER: Teacher, principal and superintendent of schools in West Virginia, 1911-15, 1917-18, 1922-26; Morris Harvey College, Barboursville, W.Va., professor and chairman of department of history, 1928-31; West Virginia University, Morgantown, archivist and lecturer, 1935-39, associate professor, 1939-46, professor of history, 1946—, chairman of department, 1947-62. West Virginia War History Commission, chairman, 1943-53; West Virginia Centennial Commission, member, 1957-63. *Military service:* U.S. Army, 1918-19; became second lieutenant. U.S. Officers Reserve Corps, Infantry, 1919-39; became captain.

MEMBER: American Historical Association, Southern Historical Association, Organization of American Historians, West Virginia Historical Society (president, 1943-44), Authors League, American Association of University Professors, American Military Institute, Phi Beta Kappa, Phi Delta Theta, Rotary Club, Mountain Club (West Virginia University), XX Club (Morgantown). *Awards, honors:* Hayes Foundation fellow in American history, 1940-42; D.Litt., Marshall University, 1963, Morris Harvey College, 1965; L.H.D., Concord College, 1967.

WRITINGS: Johnson Newlon Camden: A Study in Individualism, Putnam, 1937; *The Baltimore and Ohio in the Civil War*, Putnam, 1939; *William L. Wilson and Tariff Reform* (biography), Rutgers University Press, 1953; (editor) William L. Wilson, *Cabinet Diary, 1896-1897*, University of North Carolina Press, 1957; (reviser with Charles Henry Ambler) *West Virginia, the Mountain State*, 2nd edition, Prentice-Hall, 1958; (editor) William L. Wilson, *A Borderland Confederate*, University of Pittsburgh Press, 1962; (editor with Elizabeth Cometti) *The Thirty Fifth State: A Documentary History of West Virginia*, West Virginia University Library, 1966. Contributor to *Junior Encyclopaedia Britannica*, *Encyclopedia Americana*, *World Book Encyclopedia*, and to historical journals.

WORK IN PROGRESS: Mr. Lincoln's Lifeline: The Baltimore and Ohio; West Virginia University, 1867-1967: A History.

SUNNERS, William 1903-
(Lee Keith, Weston Satterly)

PERSONAL: Born August 11, 1903, in New York, N.Y.; son of George and Bertha (Catcher) Sunners; married Rebecca Yates, June 19, 1926; children: Harold, Marilyn. *Education:* Attended Hunter College (now Hunter College of City University of New York), 1925-29, and New York University, 1929-31. *Politics:* Democrat. *Home:* 4216 Quentin Rd., Brooklyn, N.Y. 11234.

CAREER: Board of Education, New York, N.Y., teacher, 1929—. Consultant and adviser for advertising agencies and newspaper syndicates. *Member:* National Contesters Association (secretary, 1939), Printing Teachers Guild (New York; acting secretary, 1932), New York Contest Club (president, 1940).

WRITINGS: American Slogans, Paebar Co., 1949; *How to Win Prize Contests*, Arco, 1950; *How to Solve Rebus Puzzles*, Arco, 1950; (editor) *Picture Encyclopedia*, Research Book Co., 1950; *How to Coin Winning Names*, Arco, 1951; *Irregular and Unusual Plurals*, Research Book Co., 1951; (under pseudonym Lee Keith) *Out-of-the-Place Words*, Research Book Co., 1951; *Categories of Famous People and Places for Unicorn-American Puzzle Contests*, Research Book Co., 1952; (under pseudonym Lee Keith) *How to Solve Contest Picture Puzzles*, Research Book Co., 1952; (under pseudonym Lee Keith) *Positional Words*, two volumes, Research Book Co., 1952; *How to Solve and Construct Unicorn and American Puzzles and Tie-Breakers*, Research Book Co., 1953; (under pseudonym Weston Satterly) *Complete Contest Course*, Arco, 1958; *How to Solve Magic and Cartoon Puzzles*, Arco, 1959; *How to Write Prize Winning Jingles*, Arco, 1961; *How to Write Prize Winning Statements*, Arco, 1961; *How and Where to Find the Facts: An Encyclopedic Guide to All Types of Information*, Arco, 1963.

WORK IN PROGRESS: Encyclopedia of Nicknames; With Pun and Ink; It Happened Today.

*   *   *

SUTHERLAND, Arthur Eugene, Jr. 1902-1973

PERSONAL: Born February 9, 1902, in Rochester, N.Y.; son of Arthur Eugene (a lawyer) and Eleanor (Reed) Sutherland; married Margaret Adams, September 10, 1927 (died January, 1958); married Mary Genung Kirk, February 21, 1959; children: (first marriage) David Adams, Peter Adams, Eleanor Reed (Mrs. David C. Lukens), Prudence. *Education:* Wesleyan University, Middletown, Conn., A.B., 1922; Harvard University, LL.B., 1925. *Politics:* Republican. *Religion:* Episcopalian. *Home:* 12 Berkeley St., Cambridge, Mass. 02138. *Office:* Harvard Law School, Cambridge, Mass. 02138.

CAREER: Staff member with American Commission for Near East Relief, Asia Minor and Thrace, 1919; admitted to New York State bar, 1926; attorney in private practice, Rochester, N.Y., 1926-41; Cornell University, Ithaca, N.Y., professor of law, 1945-50; Harvard University, Cambridge, Mass., professor of law, 1950-55, Bussey Professor of Law, 1955-70, professor emeritus, 1970-73, acting master of Lowell House, 1965-66. Secretary to U.S. Supreme Court Justice Oliver Wendall Holmes, 1927-28; delegate, New York State Constitutional Convention, 1938; Fulbright lecturer, Oxford University, 1956; Purrington visiting professor, Mount Holyoke College, 1958-59; member, New York State Commission on Elementary and Sec-

ondary Education, 1969-71; trustee, Mount Holyoke College. *Military service:* U.S. Army, 1941-45; served in Europe and the Mediterranean; became colonel; awarded Legion of Merit with cluster, Bronze Star, Order of the British Empire, Croix de guerre (twice), Czechoslovakian War Cross, Ouissam Alaouite (Morocco), Volontari della Liberta (Italy). U.S. Army Reserve, retired as colonel.

MEMBER: American Academy of Arts and Sciences (fellow), American Law Institute, American Bar Association, New York State Bar Association. *Awards, honors:* Ford Foundation travel grants to Ghana, 1959 and 1962; J.S.D. from Suffolk University, 1960.

WRITINGS: (With others) *Cases and Materials on Commercial Transactions*, Foundation, 1951; *Constitutional Law: Cases and Problems*, Little, Brown, 1952; *The Law and One Man Among Many*, University of Wisconsin Press, 1956; *Constitutionalism in America*, Blaisdell, 1965; *Apology for Uncomfortable Change*, Macmillan, 1965; *The Church Shall Be Free: A Glance at Eight Centuries of Church and State*, University Press of Virginia, 1965; *The Law at Harvard*, Harvard University Press, 1967; (editor) *The Path of Law From 1967* (proceedings), Harvard University Press, 1968. Contributor to legal journals.

(Died March 8, 1973)

*   *   *

SUTHERLAND, Lucy Stuart 1903-

PERSONAL: Born June 21, 1903, in Geelong, Victoria, Australia; daughter of Alexander Charles (a civil engineer and public servant) and Margaret Mabel (Goddard) Sutherland. *Education:* University of the Witwatersrand, M.A., 1925; Somerville College, Oxford, B.A., 1927, M.A., 1930, D.Litt., 1954. *Politics:* Conservative. *Religion:* Church of England. *Home:* 59 Park Tower, Oxford University, Oxford, England.

CAREER: Oxford University, Oxford, England, fellow and tutor in economics, history, and politics at Somerville College, 1927-45; British Civil Service, assistant auditor, Board of Trade, Whitehall, London, England, 1940-45; Oxford University, Oxford, principal for Lady Margaret Hall, 1945-71. *Member:* British Academy (fellow), Royal Society of Arts (fellow). *Awards, honors:* Commander, Order of the British Empire, 1947; Litt.D., Cambridge University, 1963; LL.D., Smith College, 1964; received honorary degrees from Glasgow University, University of Kent, University of Keele, and Queen's University of Belfast; emeritus fellow, Leverhulme Trust Fund; honorary fellow of Somerville College and of Lady Margaret Hall, Oxford.

WRITINGS: A London Merchant 1695-1776, Oxford University Press, 1932; (editor with M. McKisack) M. V. Clarke, *Mediaeval Representation and Comment*, Macmillan, 1936; (editor with H. Cam and M. Coate) A. E. Levett, *Studies in Manorial History*, Oxford University Press, 1938; *The East India Company in Eighteenth Century Politics*, Oxford University Press, 1952; (editor) *The Correspondence of Edmund Burke*, Volume II, Cambridge University Press, 1960. Contributor of articles to *Times Literary Supplement* and to professional journals.

WORK IN PROGRESS: The City of London in Eighteenth Century Politics; eighteenth-century volume of the history of the University of Oxford.

SUTHERLAND, R(ussell) Galbraith 1924-

PERSONAL: Born July 14, 1924, in Dunedin, New Zealand; son of George James and Janet Ritchie (Donald) Sutherland. *Education:* University of Otago, Bachelor of Dental Surgery. *Home:* Clarkville, Canterbury, New Zealand. *Office:* 272 High St., Christchurch, New Zealand.

CAREER: Dental surgeon, Norwegian Health Department, 1954-57, Christchurch, New Zealand, 1957-63. *Member:* New Zealand Dental Association, New Zealand Antarctic Society.

WRITINGS: Land of the Bog-Cotton, Hodder & Stoughton, 1960. Contributor to *New Zealand Listener*, *Weekly News*, *Otago Daily Times*, *Bergens Tiden*, and to New Zealand Broadcasting Service.

WORK IN PROGRESS: Research on the period of settlement in Southland of New Zealand from 1864-1910 for novel; radio play for New Zealand Broadcasting Corp.

AVOCATIONAL INTERESTS: Farming.

*   *   *

SUTHERLAND, (William) Temple (Gairdner) 1906-

PERSONAL: Born March 24, 1906, in Dundee, Scotland; son of Lewis Robertson (a pathologist) and Helen (Gairdner) Sutherland; married Thelma Chadwick, August 12, 1930 (died, 1965); married Gwenifer Ann Griffiths, April 8, 1967. *Religion:* Presbyterian. *Home:* 137 Moana Ave., Tahunanui, Nelson, New Zealand.

CAREER: Varied career as farm laborer, truck driver, road-metalling contractor, and gold miner; now writer.

WRITINGS: The Golden Bush, M. Joseph, 1953; *Green Kiwi*, M. Joseph, 1956; *The Silver Fern: A Journey in Search of New England*, A. H. & A. W. Reed, 1959; *Maui and Me: A Search for a Fisherman's El Dorado*, A. H. & A. W. Reed, 1963; *The Sixty Million Muster*, A. H. & A. W. Reed, 1966, Tri-Ocean, 1967.

*   *   *

SVARLIEN, Oscar 1906-

PERSONAL: Born March 25, 1906, in Overhalla, Norway; son of Johan Hoyer (a postman) and Charlotte (Kolberg) Svarlien; married Mattie Stinson, June 7, 1942; children: John. *Education:* University of Washington, Seattle, B.A., 1937, M.A., 1939; University of North Carolina, Ph.D., 1942. *Politics:* Democrat. *Religion:* Lutheran. *Home:* 4120 Northwest 39th Rd., Gainesville, Fla. 32601. *Office:* Department of Political Science, University of Florida, Gainesville, Fla.

CAREER: Appalachian State College, Boone, N.C., teacher of social sciences, 1941-42; Library of Congress, Washington, D.C., social science analyst, 1942-46; University of Florida, Gainesville, associate professor of political science, 1946-55, professor, 1955—. *Member:* American Political Science Association, American Society of International Law (executive council, 1962-65), American Association for the United Nations (vice-president, Gainesville chapter, 1965), Consular Law Society (honorary member), London Institute of World Affairs, American Association of University Professors. *Awards, honors:* Knight's Cross, First Class of the Royal Order of Saint Olav (Norway), 1966.

WRITINGS: An Introduction to the Law of Nations, McGraw, 1955; *The Eastern Greenland Case in Historical Perspective*, University of Florida Press, 1964. Contributor to *A Dictionary of the Social Sciences*, and *World Book Encyclopedia*. Contributor of articles to legal journals on the laws of human rights, of the sea, of outer space, and of territorial claims in the polar regions.

SIDELIGHTS: Svarlien speaks and writes German, Norwegian, Swedish, and Danish; reads and understands French and Spanish.

BIOGRAPHICAL/CRITICAL SOURCES: Normanns Forbundet, January, 1964.

*   *   *

SWARTZLOW, Ruby Johnson 1903-

PERSONAL: Born July 18, 1903, in Fond du Lac, Wis.; daughter of Uriah L. and Anna (Butler) Johnson; married Carl R. Swartzlow (National Park Service naturalist and ranger, now retired), August 12, 1925; children: Joan (Mrs. John McDougal). *Education:* Lawrence College, Appleton, Wis., A.B., 1924; University of Missouri, A.M., 1933. *Religion:* United Methodist. *Home:* 6346 Diamond Ave., Paradise, Calif. 95969.

CAREER: Teacher of history in high schools in Wisconsin, 1924-28, Klamath Falls, Ore., 1935-36, Omaha, Neb., 1946-52, and in adult education classes in Paradise, Calif., 1960—. *Member:* American Association of University Women, National League of American Pen Women (president, 1970-72, Butte County Branch), California Historical Society, Butte County Historical Society (board of directors, 1961—; president, 1964; member of advisory committee), Colusi County Historical Society, Phi Beta Kappa. *Awards, honors:* Award of Merit, Butte County Historical Society, 1967; Teacher-Historian Award of Merit, Conference of California Historical Societies, 1968.

WRITINGS: Lassen—His Life and Legacy, Loomis Museum Association, 1964; (editor and contributor) *Butte Remembers*, National League of American Pen Women, 1973. Editor and contributor, *Tales of the Paradise Ridge* (periodical); contributor to *Missouri Historical Review*, *California Historical Quarterly*, and *Diggins*.

WORK IN PROGRESS: Research for historical articles on Paradise Ridge.

SIDELIGHTS: Swartzlow became interested in the life of Peter Lassen while living at Lassen Volcanic National Park, where husband was the park naturalist, 1935-46; did further Lassen research at Library of Congress and National Archives and Bancroft Library in Berkeley, Calif.

*   *   *

SWIFT, Howard W. 1908-

PERSONAL: Born November 24, 1908, in Thomaston, Me.; married (wife's name Avie E.), March 24, 1951. *Education:* Studied at Long Island Agricultural and Technical Institute and Royal Botanical Garden, Kew, England; other courses at Boston University and Columbia University. *Religion:* Episcopalian. *Home:* 2330 Euclid Heights Blvd., Cleveland Heights, Ohio 44106. *Office:* Garden Center of Greater Cleveland, East Blvd. at Euclid Ave., Cleveland, Ohio 44106.

CAREER: New York Botanical Garden, Bronx Park, New York, N.Y., assistant curator of education, 1934-42; salesman for florist, San Francisco, Calif., 1942-43, for W. Atlee Burpee Co., 1946-47; Peter Henderson, Stumpp & Walter (seedsmen), New York, N.Y., retail store manager, 1950-52; New York Botanical Garden, assistant curator of education, 1954-62; Garden Center of Greater Cleveland, Cleveland, Ohio, associate director, 1962—. *Military service:* U.S. Army Air Corps, 1943-45, served in Australia. *Member:* Association of Kew Gardeners in America (current president), Dahlia Society, Men's Garden Club of Cleveland, Cleveland Museum of Art.

WRITINGS: (With others) *Getting Acquainted with Nature*, J. G. Ferguson, 1962; *The Wonderful World of Plants and Flowers*, Home Library Press, 1963. Contributor to *American Handyman, Journal of New York Botanical Garden*. Editor, *Garden Center Bulletin* (Cleveland, Ohio).

AVOCATIONAL INTERESTS: Photography.

*   *   *

SWIRE, Otta F(lora Macdonald Lois)   1898-1973

PERSONAL: Born December 7, 1898, in London, England; daughter of Sir William Woodthorpe (a barrister and historian) and Flora Macdonald (Robertson) Tarn; married Roger Swire (a British Army officer, now a retired colonel), December 9, 1931; children: Flora Macdonald Otta Evelyn (Mrs. F. P. E. Gardner), Herbert. *Education:* Educated privately. *Politics:* Conservative. *Religion:* Episcopalian. *Home:* Orbost, near Dunvegan, Isle of Skye, Scotland.

CAREER: British War Office, Military Intelligence, 1917-19 (mentioned in dispatches twice); Bermuda Censorship Office, examiner, 1940-41; professional flower grower, 1946-58. Volunteer worker with Girl Guides, 1923-45, St. John's Ambulance Brigade, 1930-31, Bermuda Women's Auxiliary Corps, 1939-41, Civil Defence, 1941-43, and Women's Voluntary Services, 1943-45.

WRITINGS: Skye, the Island and Its Legends, Oxford University Press, 1953; *The Highlands and Their Legends*, Oliver & Boyd, 1964; *The Inner Hebrides and Their Legends*, Collins, 1964; *The Outer Hebrides and Their Legends*, Oliver & Boyd, 1965.

Contributor to *Statistical Account of Scotland*. Also contributor of articles to newspapers and periodicals.

WORK IN PROGRESS: Traditions of Windsor Castle, and *A Dictionary of Plant Lore*, with husband, Roger Swire.

SIDELIGHTS: Mrs. Swire lived in Italy as well as Bermuda, traveled extensively in Europe, Canada, United States, South America, and West Indies, and visited Iceland, parts of Australia and Asia, and the Near East. Reads French, knows some Spanish and Italian. *Avocational interests:* Collecting legends, gardening.

(Died, January 2, 1973)

*   *   *

SZIGETI, Joseph   1892-1973

PERSONAL: Born September 5, 1892, in Budapest, Hungary; son of Adolf (a musician) and Dorah (Faktor) Szigeti; married Wanda Ostrowska, 1919; children: Irene Szigeti Magaloff. *Education:* Studied at Academy of Music, Budapest, Hungary. *Home:* Le Crepon, Baugy s/Clarens, Vaud, Switzerland.

CAREER: Made concert debut at Royal Academy, Budapest, Hungary, at age of eleven, later played in Germany, and in London, England; toured Continent, 1912; professor of violin at Geneva Conservatory, Geneva, Switzerland, 1919-24; made U.S. debut as soloist with Philadelphia Orchestra, 1925, then played in Carnegie Hall; has since appeared with major orchestras throughout America, on two

world tours, a tour in Japan, 1953, in South America, 1954. Radio, television, and recording artist. *Awards, honors:* Officer, French Legion of Honor; Commander, Belgium Order of Leopold; Officer, Hungarian Order of Merit; honorary doctorate, Acadia University.

WRITINGS: With Strings Attached: Reminiscences and Reflections, Knopf, 1947, 2nd edition, revised and enlarged, 1967; (contributor) *Conflict and Creativity*, McGraw, 1962; *A Violinist's Notebook*, Duckworth, 1964; *Szigeti on the Violin*, Cassell, 1969, Praeger, 1970.

Composer: *Cadenza to the First Movement of Violin Concerto No. 3 (G Major) by W. A. Mozart*, Carl Fischer, 1937; (composer of original cadenzas for concert version) *Concerto in D Minor* (by Giuseppe Tartini), Carl Fischer, 1943.

Arranger: Sergei Prokofiev, *Sonata in F Minor, for Violin and Piano*, Leeds Music Corp., 1948; Johann Sebastian Bach, *Concerto in G Minor, for Violin and Piano*, Peters, 1949; *The Ten Beethoven Sonatas for Piano and Violin*, edited by Paul Rolland, American String Teachers Association, 1965, enlarged edition published in German as *Beethovens Violinwerke: Hinweise fuer Interpreten und Hoerer*, translated by Brigitte and Helmut Kaufmann, Atlantis Verlag, 1965.

BIOGRAPHICAL/CRITICAL SOURCES: Roland Gelatt, *The Music Makers: Some Outstanding Musical Performers of Our Day*, Knopf, 1953; Kurt Blaukopf, *Die Grossen Virtuosen*, A. Niggli & W. Verkauf, c.1954; *Bookman's Yearbook*, 1970; *Washington Post*, February 22, 1973.

(Died February 19, 1973)

*   *   *

TAFT, Pauline Dakin   1891-

PERSONAL: Born July 23, 1891, in Cherry Valley, N.Y.; daughter of Leonard (a banker) and Jessie (Messmore) Dakin; married Arthur Irving Taft (a college professor), August 31, 1916 (deceased); children: Margaret. *Education:* Attended Wilkes-Barre Institute, Wilkes-Barre, Pa., and Oberlin College. *Politics:* Democrat. *Religion:* Congregationalist. *Home:* 915 East Ridge Village Dr., Miami, Fla. 33157.

CAREER: Lecturer at art museums and to historical societies and women's clubs on "Social Life in the 1880's" and "Life and Laughter in the Elegant Eighties" (illustrating lectures with photographs taken by father, Leonard Dakin), 1948-65. Professional trainer of leaders for Girl Scouts of America during 1930's.

WRITINGS: The Happy Valley: The Elegant Eighties in Upstate New York, Syracuse University Press, 1965.

AVOCATIONAL INTERESTS: Music, poetry, nature (chiefly ornithology), and travel.

*   *   *

TAPLIN, Walter   1910-

PERSONAL: Born August 4, 1910, in Southampton, England; son of Ernest and Eveline (Wareham) Taplin; married Susan Ross, 1942; children: Oliver Paul, John Quentin, Jessica, Mark James, Julia. *Education:* University College, Southampton, England, B.Com., 1933; Queen's College, Oxford, B.A., 1936, M.A., 1957. *Home:* Kent Hatch Lodge, Crockham Hill, Edenbridge, Kent, England.

CAREER: University College (now University of Southampton), Southampton, England, tutor organizer for adult education, 1936-38; *Economist*, London, England, assistant editor, 1938-40; statistician with Ministry of Food, later with Offices of the War Cabinet, London, England, 1940-45; *Spectator*, London, England, assistant editor, 1946-53, editor, 1953-54; British Broadcasting Corp., London, England, advisor, 1954-55; Iron and Steel Bcard, London, England, senior economist, 1955-56; London School of Economics and Political Science, University of London, London, England, research fellow in advertising and promotional activity, 1957-61; *Accountancy*, London, England, editor, 1961—. *Member:* Reform Club (London).

WRITINGS: Britain's New Economy, Canadian Institute of International Affairs, 1956; *Advertising* (pamphlet), Newman Neame, 1958; *Advertising: A New Approach*, Hutchinson, 1960, revised edition, Little, Brown, 1963; *Advertising Appropriation Policy* (monograph), Institute of Practitioners in Advertising, 1960; *The Origin of Television Advertising in the United Kingdom*, Pitman, 1961; (with J. C. Carr) *History of the British Steel Industry*, Harvard University Press, 1962. Author of radio scripts for British Broadcasting Corp., Canadian Broadcasting Co., and Australian Broadcasting Corp. Contributor to British journals.

SIDELIGHTS: Taplin is a frequent visitor to the United States; he aims at "mid-Atlantic nationality."

* * *

TATE, Merle W(esley)   1903-

PERSONAL: Born November 29, 1903, in Salem, Ill., son of Orville W. and Lily (Chassells) Tate; married Agnes Z. Bruihl, December 23, 1927; children: Margaret Ruth (Mrs. S. G. Owen), Rowena Mary (deceased). *Education:* Central Wesleyan College, Warrenton, Mo., A.B., 1926; University of Montana, M.A., 1943; Harvard University, Ed.M., 1946, Ed.D., 1947. *Home:* 2502 Leisure Lane, Leesburg, Fla. 32748.

CAREER: Teacher and athletic coach in Montana and Idaho public high schools, 1926-35; Gooding (Idaho) public schools, superintendent, 1935-44; Hamilton College, Clinton, N.Y., associate professor of education, 1946-49; University of Pennsylvania, Philadelphia, professor of education, 1949-65; Lehigh University, Bethlehem, Pa., professor of education, 1966-74, professor emeritus, 1974—. Research professor, University of Iowa, 1960-61; visiting summer professor, University of Maine; visiting professor, Inter-American University of Puerto Rico, 1972-73. *Member:* American Association for the Advancement of Science (fellow), American Educational Research Association, American Statistical Association.

WRITINGS: Statistics in Education, Macmillan, 1955; (with R. C. Clelland) *Nonparametric and Shortcut Statistics*, Interstate, 1957; (with Barbara Stanier and Berj Harootunian) *Differences between Good and Poor Problem Solvers*, University of Pennsylvania Press, 1959; (with S. M. Brown) *Tables for Comparing Related Percentages*, University of Pennsylvania Press, 1964; *Statistics in Education and Psychology*, Macmillan, 1965. Contributor to professional journals.

WORK IN PROGRESS: Revision of books.

AVOCATIONAL INTERESTS: Chess, carpentry, gardening.

* * *

TATFORD, Brian F(rederick) B(arrington)   1927-
PERSONAL: Born September 29, 1927, in Wembley, Mid-

dlesex, England; son of Frederick Albert and Grace (Vince) Tatford; married Helene Moulin-Racine, October 22, 1960; children: Laurent-Frederic, Nathania. *Education:* Attended Whitgift Middle School; London School of Economics, University of London, B.Sc. (honors), 1951; London Institute of Education, University of London, postgraduate certificate, 1952; Alliance Francaise, Paris, France, diplome de langue Francaise, 1952; University of Grenoble, Doctorat, 1958, Conseiller d'Education Populaire, 1967. *Religion:* Evangelical. *Home:* L'Eau Vive, 63, rue St. Gabriel, Lille, Nord, France.

CAREER: Lycees Montaigne, Louis le Grand, Paris, France, assistant, 1952-55; Instituts Britannique et Hautes Etudes d'Interpretariat, Paris, France, professeur of economic geography and English, 1953-56; Institut de Geographie Alpine, Grenoble, France, research fellow, 1957; GATT (General Agreement on Trade and Tariff), Geneva, Switzerland, research assistant, 1958; currently director, Association de l'Eau Vive (Christian youth social center), Lille, France, President, Films Moody, France, 1961—. Charge de cours, Faculte de Theologie de Vaux.

WRITINGS: The ABC of London Transport Services, Ian Allan, 1944; *The ABC of Irish Locomotives*, Ian Allan, 1945; *The Story of British Railways*, Low, 1946, Macdonald & Co., c.1950; *Un Facteur d'Investissement dans l'Economie Alpine*, University of Grenoble Press, 1958; *So Near and Yet So Far*, Echoes of Service, 1963. French correspondent, *Christian Newspaper*.

WORK IN PROGRESS: A Biblical geography of Palestine.

AVOCATIONAL INTERESTS: Tennis and skiing.

* * *

TATHAM, C. Ernest   1905-

PERSONAL: Born February 13, 1905, in Canada; son of Charles G. (a minister) and Edna E. (Stovel) Tatham; married Louise Lough, 1964; children: Ruth (Mrs. Dewitt Nottage), Lois (Mrs. Ron Clark), Grace (Mrs. Michael Kemp), David, Paul. *Education:* Toronto Bible College, graduate. *Home:* 737 Teal Way, North Palm Beach, Fla. 33408.

CAREER: Evangelical Protestant minister in Lakefield, Ontario, 1930-44, in Toronto, Ontario, 1944-57, in Boca Raton, Fla., 1958-61, in North Palm Beach, Fla., 1961—. Conducts daily broadcast in Florida. *Member:* Royal Geographic Society (fellow).

WRITINGS: Waiting for the Sunrise, Loizeaux Brothers, 1934; *He Lives!: Seven Studies of the Resurrection Appearances of the Lord Jesus Christ*, Pickering & Inglis, 1939, Loizeaux Brothers, c.1945; *Beginning Over Again, and Other Papers*, Loizeaux Brothers, c.1945; *The Messianic Psalms*, Emmaus Bible School, 1946; *Daniel Speaks Today*, Pickering & Inglis, 1948; *Old Testament Survey*, Emmaus Bible School, 1949; *Elijah*, Loizeaux Brothers, 1950; *The Holy Spirit at Work*, Emmaus Bible School, 1957; *Bible Prophecy: Twelve Studies for Earnest Bible Students*, Emmaus Bible School, 1964; *Matthew*, Emmaus Bible School, 1966. Columnist, *Sun Press*, Lake Park, Fla. Contributor to religious journals.

BIOGRAPHICAL/CRITICAL SOURCES: Kenyon Review, January, 1966; *Virginia Quarterly Review*, autumn, 1967; *Poetry*, June, 1968; *London Magazine*, June, 1968, September, 1970; *Hudson Review*, autumn, 1968; *Jewish Quarterly*, winter, 1968-69.

TATTERSALL, M(uriel Joyce) 1931-
(Elizabeth Waud)

PERSONAL: Born December 21, 1931, in Preston, Lancashire, England; daughter of Alfred Joseph and Dorothy (Parkinson) Tattersall. *Education:* University of London, B.A. (with honors), 1953; University of Birmingham, M.Ed., 1965. *Religion:* Church of England. *Home:* 27 Green Dr., Penwortham, Preston, Lancashire, England.

CAREER: Hillary Street County Secondary School, Walsall, Staffordshire, England, school mistress, 1954-55, head of biology department, 1955-61, head of modern languages department, 1961-65; Bingley College of Education, lecturer, 1965-69; West Midlands College of Education, senior tutor, 1969—.

WRITINGS: (Under pseudonym Elizabeth Waud) *Easter Meeting* (juvenile), Harrap, 1959.

WORK IN PROGRESS: Research for M.Phil. degree.

SIDELIGHTS: Miss Tattersall is fluent in French, fairly good in German, has a "nodding acquaintance" with Spanish, Italian, and Provencal, and knows all Romance languages at the medieval stage. *Avocational interests:* Music, especially grand opera; foreign travel, history, cooking, theatre, gardening.

*   *   *

TAYLOR, Earl Aulick 1904-1965

PERSONAL: Born February 12, 1904, in Temple, Tex.; son of James G. and Annie (Simmons) Taylor; married Johnnie Smoot, June 2, 1926; children: Stanford Earl, Terance Smoot. *Education:* University of Texas, B.A., 1928, M.A., 1929, graduate study, 1931; University of Chicago, graduate study, 1935-36; New York University, Ed.D., 1943.

CAREER: High school teacher and principal in Texas, 1925-26 and 1928-35; American Optical Co., reading research, 1935-39; New York University, New York, N.Y., teacher of reading and psychology courses, 1941-43; Taylor Center for Controlled Reading and Research (originally Washington Square Reading Center; later, Reading and Study Skills Center), New York, N.Y., co-founder, 1941, director, 1942-65, co-founder of Amackassin extension boarding facility, Blairstown, N.J., 1952; New School for Social Research, New York, N.Y., member of faculty, 1962-65. Co-developer of Ophthalmograph, Metronoscope, Controlled Reader, and Prism-Reader. *Member:* American Association of School Administrators, National Education Association (life member), American Association of University Professors, American Academy of Optometry, Phi Delta Kappa, Beta Sigma Kappa. *Awards, honors:* Gold Medal of Distinguished Service Foundation of Optometry, 1937.

WRITINGS: Controlled Reading: A Correlation of Diagnostic, Teaching, and Corrective Techniques, University of Chicago Press, 1937; (with Stanford E. Taylor) *A Basic Vocabulary*, Washington Square Reading Center, 1949; (with Taylor and Helen Frackenpohl) *Basic Vocabulary*, Washington Square Reading Center, 1951; (with Harold A. Solan) *Functional Readiness and School Adjustment*, Reading and Study Skills Center, 1955, revised edition, 1956; *Visual Training with the Prism Reader*, Educational Developmental Laboratories, 1957, revised edition, 1964; *The Functional Readiness Questionnaire and Maladjustment*, Reading and Study Skills Center, 1958; *Juvenile Delinquency and Functional Readiness*, Reading and Study

Skills Center, 1958; *Eyes, Visual Anomalies, and the Fundamental Reading Skill*, Reading and Study Skills Center, 1959, 2nd edition published as *The Fundamental Reading Skill: As Related to Eye-Movement Photography and Visual Anomalies*, C. C Thomas, 1966; *Meeting the Increasing Stresses of Life: A Multiple-Therapy Approach in Education*, C. C Thomas, 1963; *A Manual of Visual Presentation in Education and Training*, Pergamon, 1966. Contributor of articles to professional journals.

*   *   *

TAYLOR, Frank J. 1894-1972

PERSONAL: Born October 8, 1894, in Wessington Springs, S.D.; son of John S. (a painter) and Ellen (Stobbs) Taylor; married Katherine Ames, June 30, 1919; children: James F. (deceased), Paul A., Robert W. *Education:* Stanford University, student, 1914-17. *Politics:* Maverick. *Religion:* Protestant. *Home:* 12871 West Sunset Dr., Los Altos, Calif. *Office:* P.O. Box J., Los Altos, Calif. 94022.

CAREER: Free-lance magazine writer, West Coast staff writer for *Reader's Digest*. War correspondent, World War I and II. *Member:* San Francisco Press Club, Bohemian Club (San Francisco).

WRITINGS: (With Horace M. Albright) *"Oh, Ranger,"* Dodd, 1928; (with Ruth D. Taylor) *Our U.S.A.: A Gay Geography*, Little, Brown, 1935; (with Lawton Wright) *Democracy's Air Arsenal*, Duell, Sloan & Pearce, 1947; (with Earl M. Welty) *Black Bonanza*, McGraw, 1950; *High Horizons*, McGraw, 1951; (with Neill C. Wilson) *Southern Pacific*, McGraw, 1951; (with Wilson) *The Earth Changers*, Doubleday, 1957; (compiler and editor with Robert G. Putnam and Phillip G. Kettle) *A Geography of Urban Places: Selected Readings*, Methuen, 1970; (compiler and editor with Putnam and Kettle) *Pollution: The Effluence of Affluence*, Methuen, 1971. Contributor to *Saturday Evening Post*, *Collier's*, *Country Gentlemen*, and other magazines.

AVOCATIONAL INTERESTS: Experimental gardening, tree-growing, photography.

(Died October 23, 1972)

*   *   *

TAYLOR, Jed H(arbottle) 1902-

PERSONAL: Born January 26, 1902, in Columbia, S.C.; son of Edward B. (an engineer) and Ada V. (Harbottle) Taylor; married Ruth Bolton (in nursing education), April 12, 1939; children: Susan Vassar. *Education:* Syracuse University, B.S.B.A., 1924; Columbia University, B.S.L.S., 1931; Boston University, M.A., 1951; University of Pennsylvania, graduate study, 1951-52, and summers. *Politics:* Democrat. *Religion:* Methodist. *Home:* 64 College Ave., Mansfield, Pa.

CAREER: In insurance business, 1924-30; Mechanics Institute, New York, N.Y., assistant librarian, 1931-35; Civilian Conservation Corps, library service in New York State, New York City, and New England, 1938-46; *Congressional Quarterly*, Washington, D.C., library consultant, 1946-48; Suffolk University, Boston, Mass., associate librarian, 1948-49; Boston University, Boston, Mass., librarian with Bureau of Public Administration, 1950-51; University of Pennsylvania, Philadelphia, research assistant, 1951-52; University of Baltimore, Baltimore, Md., librarian, 1952-53; Dickinson College, Carlisle, Pa., head of technical services, 1953-60; Mansfield State College, Mansfield, Pa., reference librarian, 1960—. *Member:* American Library Association, American Association of University Professors, Pennsylvania Library Association, Pi Gamma Mu.

WRITINGS: Organization of C.C.C. Camp Library Reading Rooms, American Association for Adult Education, 1938; (editor with Lashley G. Harvey) *Bibliography of State and Local Government in New England*, Boston University Press, 1951; *Vocal and Instrumental Music in Print*, Scarecrow, 1965. Contributor to professional journals.

WORK IN PROGRESS: Study of criteria and methods of book indexing.

*   *   *

TAYLOR, Roland   1907-

PERSONAL: Born March 27, 1907, in Whitehaven, Cumberland, England; son of Hermon and Annie (Mitchell) Taylor; married Ethel Wilkinson; children: Alan Maurice, David Brian. *Education:* Attended county school in England. *Politics:* Liberal. *Religion:* Congregationalist. *Home and office:* 62 Loop Rd. N., Whitehaven, Cumberland, England.

CAREER: Cutter in retail and wholesale clothing trade in England, 1924—. *Member:* Cumbrian Literary Group, Lake District Ramblers Association (area president).

WRITINGS: Selected Walks in Lake District, Lake District Ramblers Association, 1946, 7th edition, 1961; *Rambles and Scrambles in Western Lakeland*, Warne, 1947; *Guide to Lake District*, Geographia, 1950; *Walkers Guide to Newlands*, Lake District Ramblers Association, 1963; *Walkers Guide to Langdale*, Lake District Ramblers Association, 1964. Also editor with W. J. Robinson of "Lakeland Rambler" series, 1960-70. Weekly columnist for *West Cumberland Times and Star*; editor of *Lakeland Rambler*.

*   *   *

TAYLOR, Ron(ald) W(illiam)   1922-

PERSONAL: Born 1922, in Sydney, Australia; son of Henry Coppin and Minnie Ethel (Stewart) Taylor; married Flora Margaret Fraser, 1944; children: Jeanette. *Education:* Studied at Australasian Missionary College, 1939-40, Sydney Sanitarium and Hospital, 1941-44, and University of Sydney, 1944. *Home:* Tamavua, Suva, Fiji Islands. *Office:* Central Pacific Union Mission, Box 270, Suva, Fiji Islands.

CAREER: Seventh-day Adventist Church, pastor in New Zealand, 1945-46, medical missionary in Samoa, 1946-52, principal of Vailoa College, Samoa, 1952-56, denominational secretary in Melbourne, Australia, 1956-61, denominational president in Samoa, 1961-62. President, Central Pacific Union Mission, 1963-64.

WRITINGS: Polynesian Paradise, Pacific Press, 1960. Contributor to *Reader's Digest* (Australian edition), *Australasian Record*, and to daily newspapers.

AVOCATIONAL INTERESTS: Photography.

*   *   *

TELFER, William   1886-1968

PERSONAL: Born January 16, 1886, in Rochester, England; son of Andrew (a schoolmaster) and Annie Emily (Bayly) Telfer. *Education:* Clare College, Cambridge, B.A., 1908, M.A., 1916, B.D., 1932, D.D., 1937. *Home:* Langton, Upper St., Ann's Rd., Faversham, Kent, England.

CAREER: Church of England, ordained deacon, 1909, priest, 1910; missioner at Clare College Mission, London, England, 1909-14, 1917-18; vicar of All Saints, Rotherhithe, 1919-21; Cambridge University, Cambridge, England, fellow of Clare College, 1921-46, dean of Clare College, 1923-46, university lecturer in divinity, 1926-51, Ely Professor of Divinity, 1944-46, master of Selwyn College, 1946-56; canon of Ely Cathedral, 1944-46, became canon emeritus. *Military service:* British Army, chaplain, 1914-17; received Military Cross, 1915.

WRITINGS: The Treasure of Sao Roque, S.P.C.K., 1932; *Cyril of Jerusalem and Nemesius of Emesa*, S.C.M. Press, 1955; *The Forgiveness of Sins*, S.C.M. Press, 1959; *The Office of a Bishop*, Darton, Longman & Todd, 1962. Contributor to encyclopedias and theological journals.

WORK IN PROGRESS: A history of Faversham Grammar School.

(Died January 13, 1968)

*   *   *

TELLER, Edward   1908-

PERSONAL: Born January 15, 1908, in Budapest, Hungary; came to United States in 1935, naturalized in 1941; son of Max (a lawyer) and Ilona (Deutch) Teller; married Augusta Harkanyi, February 26, 1934; children: Paul, Susan Wendi. *Education:* Studied at Karlsruhe Technical Institute, Karlsruhe, Germany, 1926-28, University of Munich, 1928-29; University of Leipzig, Ph.D., 1930. *Home:* 1573 Hawthorne Ter., Berkeley, Calif. 94708. *Office:* Lawrence Radiation Laboratory, P.O. Box 808, Livermore, Calif. 94550.

CAREER: Research associate at University of Leipzig, Leipzig, Germany, 1929-31, and University of Gottingen, Gottingen, Germany, 1931-33; Rockefeller Foundation fellow at University of Coppenhagen, Copenhagen, Denmark, 1934; University of London, London, England, lecturer in physics, 1934-35; George Washington University, Washington, D.C., professor of physics, 1935-41; Columbia University, New York, N.Y., professor of physics, 1941-42; physicist for Manhattan Engineer District at University of Chicago, Chicago, Ill., 1942-43, and Los Alamos Scientific Laboratory, Los Alamos, N.M., 1943-46; University of Chicago, professor of physics, 1946-52, on leave as assistant director of Los Alamos Scientific Laboratory, 1949-52; University of California, professor of physics at Berkeley, 1953-60, professor of physics-at-large, 1960-70, chairman of department of applied science, Davis-Livermore, 1963-66, consultant to Livermore branch, University of California Radiation Laboratory, 1952-53, associate director of Lawrence Radiation Laboratory, Livermore, 1954—, director of Lawrence Radiation Laboratory, 1958-60. Early researcher in thermonuclear reactions; helped develop atomic bomb, and worked on development and function of other nuclear weapons after Hiroshima (including the hydrogen bomb); currently concerned with peaceful applications of nuclear energy. Director, Thermo Electron Corp.; member of President's Foreign Intelligence Advisory Board; member of scientific advisory board, U.S. Air Force; member of general advisory committee, U.S. Atomic Energy Commission, 1956-58; member of board of directors, Defense Intelligence School and Naval War College; member of other committees, councils, and advisory boards.

MEMBER: National Academy of Sciences, American Nuclear Society (fellow), American Physical Society (fellow), American Academy of Arts and Sciences, American Ordnance Association, American Geophysical Union, Society of Engineering Science, International Platform Association. *Awards, honors:* Joseph Priestley Memorial Award, Dickinson College, 1957; Albert Einstein Award, 1959; General Donovan Memorial Award, 1959; Midwest Research Institute Award, 1960; Living History Award from Research Institute of America, 1960; Thomas E. White Award, 1962; Enrico Fermi Award, 1962. Honorary degrees: D.Sc., Yale University, 1954, University of Alaska, 1959, Fordham University, 1960, George Washington University, 1960, University of Southern California, 1960, St. Louis University, 1960, Rochester Institute of Technology, 1962, University of Detroit, 1964, Clemson University, 1966, Clarkson College, 1969; LL.D., Boston College, 1961, Seattle University, 1962, University of Cincinnati, 1962, University of Pittsburgh, 1963; L.H.D., Mount Mary College, 1964.

WRITINGS: (With J. H. Hibben) *Raman Effect and Its Chemical Applications*, Reinhold, 1939; (with F. O. Rice) *The Structure of Matter*, Wiley, 1949; (with A. L. Latter) *Our Nuclear Future*, Criterion, 1958; *Basic Concepts of Physics*, Part I, California Book Co., 1960; (with Allen Brown) *The Legacy of Hiroshima*, Doubleday, 1962; *The Reluctant Revolutionary*, University of Missouri Press, 1964; (with G. W. Johnson, W. K. Talley, and G. H. Higgins) *The Constructive Uses of Nuclear Explosives*, McGraw, 1968.

* * *

THALER, Alwin 1891-

PERSONAL: Born January 10, 1891, in Hamburg, Germany; son of Adolf and Rosa (von Halle) Thaler; married Harriet Page Albright, August 14, 1920; children: Richard Winston, Roderick Page. *Education:* Adelphi College, B.A., 1912; Columbia University, M.A., 1914; Harvard University, Ph.D., 1918. *Religion:* Episcopalian. *Home:* 2115 Terrance Ave., Knoxville, Tenn. 37916.

CAREER: Instructor in English at Adelphia College (now Adelphi University), Garden City, N.Y., 1912-13, at Northwestern University, Evanston, Ill., 1913-16; University of California, Berkeley, assistant professor of English, 1920-23; University of Tennessee, Knoxville, professor of English, 1923-61, now professor emeritus. Visiting professor of English, Stanford University, 1925, University of North Carolina, 1952, Emory University, 1961-63, and Tennessee Wesleyan College, 1964; visiting summer professor at Harvard University, University of California, University of Texas, University of Minnesota, and Adelphi University. *Military service:* U.S. Navy, 1918-19.

MEMBER: Modern Language Association of America (former chairman, advisory committee and Shakespeare Group), Shakespeare Association of America, American Association of University Professors, South Atlantic Modern Language Association, Tennessee Philological Association (president, 1955-56), Tennessee Folklore Society, Phi Kappa Phi, Irving Club. *Awards, honors:* Sheldon traveling fellow, Harvard University, 1919-20; Guggenheim traveling fellow, 1929-30; Litt.D., Adelphi University, 1967.

WRITINGS: *Shakespeare to Sheridan: A Book About the Theatre of Yesterday and To-day*, Harvard University Press, 1922; *Shakespeare's Silences*, Harvard University Press, 1929; (editor and author of introduction and notes with Charles Mills Gayley) *Representative English Comedies*, Volume IV: *Dryden and His Contemporaries: Cowley to Farquhar*, Macmillan, 1936; *Shakespeare and Democracy*, University of Tennessee Press, 1941; *Liberal Education for Democracy* (address), Division of University Extension, University of Tennessee, 1945; *Shakespeare and Sir Philip Sidney: The Influence of "The Defense of Poesy,"* Harvard University Press, 1947; (editor with Richard Beale Davis) *Tennessee Studies in Literature*, Volumes I-VII, University of Tennessee Press, 1956-62; (editor with Norman Sanders) *Shakespearean Essays*, University of Tennessee Press, 1964; *Shakespeare and Our World*, University of Tennessee Press, 1966.

BIOGRAPHICAL/CRITICAL SOURCES: *Studies in Honor of John C. Hodges and Alwin Thaler*, University of Tennessee Press, 1961; *South Atlantic Quarterly*, summer, 1967.

* * *

THATCHER, Dorothy Southwell 1903-

PERSONAL: Born September 5, 1903, in Sunderland, Durham, England; daughter of William John (an engineer with the Air Ministry) and Annie (a teacher; maiden name, McNeil) Southwell; married George Slessor Thatcher (a civil servant in Malaya), February, 1929 (divorced); children: Rosemary Thatcher (Mrs. Leonard Bullen). *Education:* Educated privately and took special courses at Bede School, Sunderland, England. *Politics:* Impartial, usually Conservative. *Religion:* Protestant. *Home:* 254 Holly Lodge Mansions, Highgate, London N. 6, England. *Office:* British Association of Malaysia, 522 Grand Buildings, Trafalgar Sq., London W.C. 2, England.

CAREER: British Association of Malaysia, London, England, columnist, *Malaysia*, beginning, 1946. London correspondent, *Straits Times*, Malaya, 1950-57. Volunteer worker for hospitals, Girl Guides, other organizations in Malaya prior to World War II.

WRITINGS: *Pai Naa*, edited by Robert Cross, Constable, 1959. Writer of scripts for British Broadcasting Corp. Contributor to *Animals*, *Blackwood's Magazine*, *Mariner's Mirror*, *Eastern World*, *Times* (London), and other magazines and newspapers.

WORK IN PROGRESS: A book about her forebearers who were privateers and tea clipper owners; a first-person account about Malaya between the wars up to the time of the Japanese invasion; a play.

SIDELIGHTS: Dorothy Thatcher speaks Malay. She commented to *CA*: "[I have been a] keen flyer since childhood. . . . love ships and the sea. Before being crippled (by arthritis) enjoyed ballroom dancing and tennis. Rotten golfer! Pastimes now reading and writing and a good film—theatre when in funds!"

* * *

THAYER, Emma R(edington) Lee 1874-1973
(Lee Thayer)

PERSONAL: Born April 5, 1874, in Troy, Pa.; daughter of Edgar James and Janie (Pomeroy) Lee; married Henry W. Thayer, 1909. *Education:* Attended Cooper Art School and Pratt Institute Art School. *Home:* 2315 Durant Ave., Berkeley, Calif. 94704.

CAREER: Associated Artists, New York, N.Y., interior decorator, 1890-96; Decorative Designers, New York,

N.Y., director, 1896-1932; writer, 1919-73. *Member:* California Writers Club, Berkeley Women's City Club, Town and Gown Club.

WRITINGS—Under name Lee Thayer: *When Mother Lets Us Draw*, Moffat, Yard, 1916; *The Mystery of the Thirteenth Floor*, Century Co., 1919; *The Unlatched Door*, Century Co., 1920; *That Affair at "The Cedars,"* Doubleday, 1921; *Q. E. D.*, Doubleday, 1922; *The Sinister Mark*, Doubleday, 1923; *The Puzzle*, Hurst & Blackett, 1923; *The Key*, Doubleday, 1924; *Doctor S.O.S.*, Doubleday, 1925; *Poison*, Doubleday, 1926; *Alias Dr. Ely: Peter Clancy's New Impersonation*, Doubleday, 1927; *The Darkest Spot*, Sears, 1928; *Dead Men's Shoes*, Sears, 1929.

They Tell No Tales, Sears, 1930; *The Last Shot*, Sears, 1931; *Set a Thief*, Sears, 1931 (published in England as *To Catch a Thief*, Hurst & Blackett, 1932); *The Glass Knife*, Sears, 1932; *The Scrimshaw Millions*, Sears, 1932; *Counterfeit*, Sears, 1933 (published in England as *The Counterfeit Bill*, Hurst & Blackett, 1934); *Hell-Gate Tides*, Sears, 1933; *The Second Bullet*, Sears, 1934 (published in England as *The Second Shot*, Hurst & Blackett, 1935); *Dead Storage*, Dodd, 1935; *Sudden Death*, Dodd, 1935 (published in England as *Red-Handed*, Hurst & Blackett, 1936); *The Death Weed*, Hurst & Blackett, 1935; *Dark of the Moon*, Dodd, 1936 (published in England as *Death in the Gorge*, Hurst & Blackett, 1937); *Dead End Street, No Outlet*, Dodd, 1936 (published in England as *Murder in the Mirror*, Hurst & Blackett, 1936); *Last Trump*, Dodd, 1937; *A Man's Enemies*, Dodd, 1937; *Ransom Racket*, Dodd, 1938; *That Strange Sylvester Affair*, Dodd, 1938 (published in England as *The Strange Sylvester Affair*, Hurst & Blackett, 1939); *This Man's Doom*, Hurst & Blackett, 1938; *Lightning Strikes Twice*, Dodd, 1939; *Stark Murder*, Dodd, 1939.

Guilty, Dodd, 1940; *X Marks the Spot*, Dodd, 1940; *Hallowe'en Homicide*, Dodd, 1941; *Persons Unknown*, Dodd, 1941; *Murder Is Out*, Dodd, 1942; *Murder on Location*, Dodd, 1942; *Accessory after the Fact*, Dodd, 1943; *Hanging's Too Good*, Dodd, 1943; *Five Bullets*, Dodd, 1944; *A Plain Case of Murder*, Dodd, 1944; *Accident, Manslaughter or Murder?*, Dodd, 1945; *A Hair's Breadth*, Dodd, 1946; *The Jaws of Death*, Dodd, 1946; *Murder Stalks the Circle*, Dodd, 1947; *Out, Brief Candle!*, Dodd, 1948; *Pig in a Poke*, Dodd, 1948 (published in England as *A Clue for Clancy*, Hurst & Blackett, 1950); *Evil Root*, Dodd, 1949.

Within the Vault, Dodd, 1950 (published in England as *Death Within the Vault*, Hurst & Blackett, 1951); *Too Long Endured*, Dodd, 1950; *Do Not Disturb*, Dodd, 1951; *Guilt-Edged*, Dodd, 1951 (published in England as *Guilt-Edged Murder*, Hurst & Blackett, 1953); *Blood on the Knight*, Dodd, 1952; *Clancy's Secret Mission*, Hurst & Blackett, 1952; *The Prisoner Pleads "Not Guilty,"* Dodd, 1953; *Dead Reckoning*, Dodd, 1954 (published in England as *Murder on the Pacific*, Hurst & Blackett, 1955); *No Holiday for Death*, Dodd, 1954; *Who Benefits?*, Dodd, 1955 (published in England as *Fatal Alibi*, Hurst & Blackett, 1956); *Guilt Is Where You Find It*, Dodd, 1957; *Still No Answer*, Dodd, 1958 (published in England as *Web of Hate*, John Long, 1959); *Two Ways to Die*, Dodd, 1959.

Dead on Arrival, Dodd, 1960; *And One Cried Murder*, Dodd, 1961; *Dusty Death: Peter Clancy and Wigger Solve a Unique Case*, Dodd, 1966 (published in England as *Death Walks in Shadow*, John Long, 1966).

(Died November 18, 1973)

THIELE, Edwin R(ichard) 1895-

PERSONAL: Born September 10, 1895, in Chicago, Ill.; son of Gustav (a nurse) and Lucia (Wirsing) Thiele; married Lorena Stone, June 20, 1920; married Margaret Rositer, July 22, 1962; children: Lorwin. *Education:* Emmanuel Missionary College, B.A., 1918; Nanking University, graduate study, 1920-22; University of Chicago, M.A., 1937, Ph.D., 1943. *Home:* 33274 La Colina Dr., Porterville, Calif. 93257.

CAREER: Seventh-Day Adventist minister, Holly, Mich., 1918-20; Signs of the Times Publishing House, Shanghai, China, editor, 1922-34, manager, 1935-36; Emmanuel Missionary College, Berrien Springs, Mich., instructor in religion, 1937-43, chairman of department, 1943-63. *Member:* American Oriental Society, American Schools of Oriental Research, Society of Biblical Literature. *Awards, honors:* D.D., Andrews University, 1965.

WRITINGS: The Mysterious Numbers of the Hebrew Kings, University of Chicago Press, 1951, revised edition, Eerdmans, 1966. Contributor to religious and oriental studies journals.

WORK IN PROGRESS: Further studies in Old Testament chronology and the chronology of the ancient Near East.

SIDELIGHTS: Thiele is proficient in German and Chinese.

* * *

THIMAN, Eric Harding 1900-

PERSONAL: Born September 12, 1900, in Ashford, England; son of Israel Phoebus (a minister) and Muriel Kate (Harding) Thiman; married Clare Madeline Arnold, August 25, 1928. *Education:* Educated privately in piano, organ, and violin; University of London, Mus.D., 1927. *Religion:* Congregational. *Home:* 7 Edmunds Walk, London N. 2, England.

CAREER: Royal Academy of Music, London, England, professor of harmony and composition, 1931—; University of London, London, England, dean of faculty of music, 1956—. Organist at Park Chapel, London, 1927-57, at City Temple, London, 1958—; organist for choral and orchestral concerts elsewhere. Examiner for Royal Schools of Music (including tours of South Africa, Australia, and New Zealand), and for University of London; adjudicator at music festivals in England, Scotland, Ireland, and Hong Kong. Composer of church and secular cantatas, instrumental works, anthems, and school music. *Member:* Royal College of Organists (fellow; council member).

WRITINGS: A Guide to Elementary Harmony, Curwen & Sons, 1941; *Practical Free Counterpoint*, Curwen & Sons, 1947; *Musical Form for Examination Students*, Curwen & Sons, 1950; *The Beginning Organist*, Ascherberg, Hopwood & Crew, 1954; *Improvisation on Hymn-Tunes*, Novello & Co., 1957. Musical compositions published in England by Augener, Cramer, Elkin, Arnold, Oxford University Press, Paterson & Co., Keith Prowse, and Boosey & Hawkes, in United States by H. W. Gray, Oliver Ditson, and Schirmer.

* * *

THOMAS, Cornelius Dickinson 1920-1972
(T. N. T., Neal Thomas)

PERSONAL: Born August 20, 1920, in Miami, Fla.; son of

Cornelius and Wilna Victoria (Dickinson) Thomas; married Zelda Rothschild, August 20, 1946; children: Cornelius D., Wilna V., Thomas Pickett, Robert P. *Education:* University of North Carolina, A.B., 1942, M.A.C.A., 1954; also studied at University of California, Berkeley, 1943, and University of Miami, Coral Gables, Fla., 1952. *Home:* Clarendon Plantation, Winnabow, N.C. 28479. *Agent:* Ruth White, Southport, N.C.

CAREER: Formerly professor of art, Ashland Art Center, University of North Carolina, Chapel Hill. Charles Towne Preservation Trust, Winnabow, N.C., director, beginning, 1965. Professional artist, exhibiting in one-man shows at Raleigh State Art Museum, N.C., Parma Gallery, New York, N.Y., and Artists' Gallery, New York. Director of St. John's Art Gallery, beginning, 1950. *Military service:* U.S. Naval Reserve, 1943-46; became lieutenant. *Member:* Society for the History of Discoveries, Naval Historical Foundation, Hakluyt Society, Society for the Preservation of Antiquities (life member), Augustan Society, Huguenot Society, Brunswick County Historical Society (president and historian, 1951-56).

WRITINGS: Wilmington, Harbinger, 1945; *James Forte: A 17th-Century Settlement*, Clarendon Imprint, 1959; *Map of the Lower Cape Fear River and Coast of Brunswick County, N.C.*, Charles Towne Preservation Trust, 1960; *Tales of the Cape Fear Blockade*, Clarendon Imprint, 1960; *Carolina Lords Proprietors' Account of Disbursements and Receipts*, Clarendon Imprint, 1963; *Letters from the Colonel's Lady*, Clarendon Imprint, 1965. Writer of television scripts. Contributor of art reviews to newspapers.

WORK IN PROGRESS: A photographic history of Fort Fisher; a book on the Dickinson family; research on seventeenth-century Cape Fear River in Carolina history; searching for John Locke's Carolina papers and other seventeenth-century material about Carolina, especially on the founding of Charleston.

(Died January 9, 1972)

*   *   *

THOMAS, David Winton   1901-1970

PERSONAL: Born January 26, 1901, in London, England; son of David John (a priest, Church of England) and Sarah (Thomas) Thomas; married Edith Higgins, December 20, 1932; children: David John Winton, Arthur Barry Winton, Judith Mary Winton. *Education:* St. John's College, Oxford, M.A., 1926. *Home:* 4 Grantchester Rd., Cambridge, England.

CAREER: University of Durham, Durham, England, professor of Oriental languages, 1930-38; Cambridge University, Cambridge, England, Regius Professor of Hebrew, 1938-68, fellow of St. Catharine's College, 1943-70. *Member:* Society for Old Testament Study (president, 1953).

WRITINGS: The Recovery of the Ancient Hebrew Language, Cambridge University Press, 1939; *"The Prophet" in the Lachish Ostraca*, Tyndale Press, 1946; (editor) *Essays and Studies Presented to Stanley Arthur Cook*, Taylor's Foreign Press, 1950; (editor and contributor with Martin Noth) *Wisdom in Israel and in the Ancient Near East*, E. J. Brill (Leiden), 1955; (with others) *The Bible Today: Historical, Social and Literary Aspects of the Old and New Testament*, Eyre & Spottiswoode, 1955, Harper, 1956; (editor) *Documents from Old Testament Times*,

Thomas Nelson (London), 1958, Harper, 1961; *The Hebrew Bible Since Claude Montefiore* (lecture), Liberal Jewish Synagogue (London), 1958; (editor with W. D. McHardy) *Hebrew and Semitic Studies: Presented to Godfrey Rolles Driver*, Oxford University Press, 1963; *The Text of the Revised Psalter: Notes*, S.P.C.K., 1963; (editor) *Archaeology and Old Testament Study: Jubilee Volume of the Society for Old Testament Study, 1917-1967*, Oxford University Press, 1967; *Understanding the Old Testament* (lecture), Athlone Press, 1967. Contributor of articles to professional journals in England and abroad.

WORK IN PROGRESS: Semitic studies.

AVOCATIONAL INTERESTS: Music, reading, and walking.

(Died June, 1970)

*   *   *

THOMAS, George Leicester, Jr.   1907-

PERSONAL: Born July 9, 1907, in Adamstown, Md.; son of George Leicester and Louise Pearl (Brown) Thomas; married Virginia Louise Brosius (a public relations director); children: George Leicester III, Charles Brosius. *Education:* Franklin and Marshall College, B.A. and D.Sc. *Politics:* Democrat. *Religion:* United Church of Christ. *Home address:* Route 9, Box 87, Frederick, Md. 21701.

CAREER: Manager of Three Springs Fisheries, Thomas Supply Co., and Lilypons Canning Co., all Lilypons, Md., 1927-66. Holder of patent for method of shipping live fish; numerous plant patents. Co-director and member of Finance Committee, Ursinus College. Director, Security Credit Corp., Security Home Mortgage Co., First Abstract Co. *Member:* Civitan Club, Torch Club, Cotillion Club of Frederick, Kenwood Golf and Country Club and Congressional Country Club (both Washington, D.C.).

WRITINGS: Garden Pools, Water-Lilies, and Goldfish, Van Nostrand, 1958, reissued as *Goldfish Pools, Water-Lilies, and Tropical Fishes*, T.F.H. Publications, 1966. Contributor of articles to *New York Times*.

WORK IN PROGRESS: Research on algae, fish culture, and aquatics.

*   *   *

THOMAS, Henri (Joseph Marie)   1912-

PERSONAL: Born December 7, 1912, in Anglemont, France; son of Joseph and Mathilde (Bailly) Thomas; married Jacqueline le Beguec, November 17, 1957; children: Nathalie. *Education:* Lycee Henri IV, Paris, France, student, 1932-36; University of Strasbourg, degrees in German and Russian languages. *Politics:* "Very much averse to 'Progressism." *Home:* 9 Place Saint Andre des Arts, Paris 6, France.

CAREER: Writer. British Broadcasting Corp., London, England, program assistant, West European braodcast, 1948-58; Brandeis University, Waltham, Mass., professor of French literature, 1958-60; Gallimard (publisher), Paris, France, member of department of German translations. *Awards, honors:* Prix Sainte-Beuve, 1956, for *La Cible*; Prix Medicis, 1960, for *John Perkins*; Prix Femina, 1961, for *Le Promontoire*.

WRITINGS: Le Seau a charbon (novel), Gallimard, 1940; *Travaux d'aveugle* (poetry and prose), Gallimard, 1941; *Le Precepteur* (novel), Gallimard, 1942; *Signe de vie* (poetry), Gallimard, 1944; *La Vie ensemble* (novel), Gallimard, 1945;

Le Monde absent (poetry), Gallimard, 1947; *Le Porte a faux* (essays), Editions de Minuit, 1948; *Nul desordre* (poetry), Gallimard, 1950; *Les Deserteurs* (novel), Gallimard, 1951; *La Cible* (short stories), Gallimard, 1955; *La Nuit de Londres* (novel), Gallimard, 1956.

John Perkins, suivi d'Un Scrupule (novel), Gallimard, 1960; *La Derniere annee* (novel), Gallimard, 1960; *Histoire de Pierrot et quelques autres* (short stories), Gallimard, 1960; *Le Promontoire* (novel), Gallimard, 1961; *La Chasse aux tresors* (criticism), Gallimard, 1961; *Deplacements* (essays), 1963; (editor) Henri Constant de Rebecque, *Le Cahier rouge, Cecile, Adolphe*, Club des Librairies de France, 1963; *Sous le lien du temps* (poetry and prose), Gallimard, 1963; *Le Parjure* (novel), Gallimard, 1964; (editor) Armand Robin, *Le Monde d'une voix* (poetry), Gallimard, 1968; (with Andre Pieyre de Mandiargues) *Le Marechal [et] Guillain Siroux* (the former by Pieyre de Mandiargues, the latter by Thomas), Galerie Inna Salomon, 1968; *La Relique* (novel), Gallimard, 1969; *Tristan le depossede* (on Tristan Corbiere), Gallimard, 1972.

Translator into French: Goethe, *Torquato Tasso*, Gallimard, c.1940; Ernst Juenger, *Sur les Falaises de marbre*, Gallimard, c.1940; Ernst Juenger, *Le Coeur aventureux*, Gallimard, c.1940; Ernst Juenger, *Le Mur du temps*, Gallimard, c.1940; Pushkin, *La Roussalka*, Editions du Seuil, 1950; Pushkin, *Le Convive de Pierre*, Editions du Seuil, 1950; Shakespeare, *The Sonnets of Shakespeare, Titus Andronicus, Antony and Cleopatra*, and *Henry IV, Part 2*, Club Francais du Livre, 1950-60; William Faulkner, *Proses, poesies et essais critiques de jeunesse*, Gallimard, 1966.

WORK IN PROGRESS: A novel, *Des Secrets pour changer la vie*; a critique, *Le Retour de Leon Paul Farque*.

BIOGRAPHICAL/CRITICAL SOURCES: L'Express, August 18-24, 1969.

* * *

THOMAS, Paul 1908-

PERSONAL: Born July 18, 1908, in Melur, Kerala State, India; son of Uthup and Theresa (Vadakunchery) Thomas; married Rose Varkey (a gynecologist), January 24, 1946; children: Mary, George Rajan. *Education:* Studied at Government High School, Chalakudi, India. *Religion:* Syrian Christian. *Home:* V/202 East Fort, Trichru-5, Kerala State, India.

CAREER: St. Joseph's School, Melur, India, teacher, 1926-27; North Western Railway, Karachi, India, traffic officer, 1928-40; Bombay Port Trust, assistant manager, 1941-56; full-time writer, 1957—. *Member:* Indo-American Society (Bombay), Rotary Club (Trichur: vice-president).

WRITINGS: Women and Marriage in India, Allen & Unwin, 1939; *Epics, Myths and Legends of India: A Comprehensive Survey of the Sacred Lore of the Hindus and Buddhists*, Taraporevala, 1942, 12th edition, 1961; *Hindu Religion, Customs and Manners: Describing the Customs and Manners, Religious, Social and Domestic Life, Arts and Sciences of the Hindus*, Taraporevala, 1947, 4th edition, revised, 1961.

Christians and Christianity in India and Pakistan: A General Survey of the Progress of Christianity in India From Apostolic Times to the Present Day, Macmillan, 1954; *Kama Kalpa; or, the Hindu Ritual of Love: A Survey of the Customs, Festivals, Rituals and Beliefs Concerning Marriage, Morals, Women, the Art and Science of Love and Sex Symbolism in Religion in India from Remote Antiquity to the Present Day*, Taraporevala, 1956, 11th edition, 1969; *The Story of the Cultural Empire of India: A Survey of the Development of Indian Culture and Its Expansion Abroad*, Joseph Thomasons, 1959; *Colonists and Foreign Missionaries of Ancient India*, Joseph Thomasons, 1963; *Indian Women Through the Ages: A Historical Survey of the Position of Women and the Institutions of Marriage and Family from Remote Antiquity to the Present Day*, Asia Publishing House, 1964; *Churches in India*, Publications Division, Ministry of Information and Broadcasting, Government of India, 1964; *Incredible India*, Taraporevala, 1966; *The March of Free India*, Joseph Thomasons, 1968; *The Theology of Chakkarai*, Christian Institute for the Study of Religion and Society, 1968; *Kama Kalha*, Taraporevala, 1969; *Humour, Wit and Satire from Indian Classics*, Joseph Thomasons, 1969; *Festivals and Holdiays of India*, Taraporevala, in press. Contributor to *World Book Encyclopedia, Illustrated Weekly of India, March of India*.

WORK IN PROGRESS: A History of Religion.

* * *

THOMAS, Rollin G. 1896-19?

PERSONAL: Born December 17, 1896, in Anamosa, Iowa; son of George A. and Emily (Fisher) Thomas; married Dorothy Erb, September 10, 1925; children: John F., Emily J. (Mrs. Charles W. Terrell). *Education:* Cornell College, Mount Vernon, Iowa, A.B., 1919; University of Chicago, M.A., 1923, Ph.D., 1930. *Religion:* Methodist. *Home:* 636 Rose, West Lafayette, Ind. *Office:* Department of Economics, Purdue University, Lafayette, Ind.

CAREER: Purdue University, Lafayette, Ind., assistant professor, 1925-38, professor of economics, 1938-65, professor emeritus, beginning, 1965. Visiting professor Bowling Green State University, 1965-66. Member of board of directors, West Lafayette Public Library, 1942-63. *Member:* American Economic Association, Midwest Economic Association, Midwest Economic Association, Indiana Academy of Social Sciences.

WRITINGS: Modern Banking, Prentice-Hall, 1937; *Our Modern Banking and Monetary System*, Prentice-Hall, 1942, 4th edition, 1964.

(Deceased)

* * *

THOMAS, Sewell 1884-

PERSONAL: Born February 24, 1884, in Denver, Colo.; son of Charles Spaulding (a lawyer) and Emma (Fletcher) Thomas; married Marie Louise Wade, April 10, 1912; children: Lenore Marie (Mrs. John T. Stoddart). *Education:* Pomfret School, student; Columbia University, Engineer of Mines, 1906. *Politics:* Republican. *Home:* 2101 East Fourth Ave., Denver, Colo. 80206.

CAREER: Self-employed consulting mining engineer. *Member:* American Institute of Mining and Metallurgical Engineers, American Mining Congress.

WRITINGS: Silhouettes of Charles S. Thomas, Colorado Governor and United States Senator, Caxton, 1959; *Yaqui Gold* (novel), Swallow, 1963. Contributor of miscellaneous technical articles to professional journals.

WORK IN PROGRESS: Memoirs.

AVOCATIONAL INTERESTS: Wood carving and all sorts of wood work; bridge.

THOMMEN, George S. 1896-

PERSONAL: Born February 7, 1896, in Basel, Switzerland; son of Paul Louis and Elizabeth (Saeuberlin) Thommen; married Suzanne Louise Baschlin, September 1, 1923. Education: Attended High Real (junior college) in Basel, Switzerland. Religion: Protestant.

CAREER: Owner and president of export-import business, New York, N.Y., beginning, 1945. Lecturer on rhythmic cycles in life to clubs and professional groups. Member: Foundation for the Study of Cycles, Society for the Investigation of Recurring Events, Academy of Sciences and Academy of Nutrition (both Middletown, N.Y.).

WRITINGS: Is This Your Day? How Biorhythm Helps You Determine Your Life Cycles, Crown, 1964.

WORK IN PROGRESS: A study of industrial loss and accident prevention through tracing of cyclical and rhythmical behavior.

*   *   *

THOMPSON, Claude Holmes 1908-

PERSONAL: Born September 21, 1908, in Bethlehem, Md.; son of James Peyton (a Methodist preacher) and Elsie (Thomas) Thompson; married Sue Lovelace (a teacher), September 6, 1932; children: Marilyn Carter (Mrs. Robert Casey), Mary Sue (Mrs. C. W. Stevenson), Nanci Ann (Mrs. William Youngblood). Education: Asbury College, A.B., 1932; studied at University of Maryland, 1937-38, Virginia Theological Seminary, Alexandria, 1939-40; Drew Theological Seminary, B.D., 1943, Ph.D., 1949. Home: 1307 Harvard Rd. N.E., Atlanta, Ga. 30306.

CAREER: Methodist minister, 1932—, holding pastorates in Delaware, Maryland, and New Jersey, 1932-46; Asbury Theological Seminary, Wilmore, Ky., professor of Christian doctrine, 1947-50; Candler School of Theology, Emory University, Atlanta, Ga., professor of Christian doctrine, 1951-55, professor of systematic theology, 1951—. Member: Society of Biblical Literature and Exegesis, American Association of University Professors, Theta Phi. Awards, honors: Pilling fellowship from Drew University for study at Oxford University and University of Edinburgh, 1946-47.

WRITINGS: Theology of the Kerygma: A Study of Primitive Preaching, Prentice-Hall, 1962. Regular contributor to Methodist church school publications.

WORK IN PROGRESS: A survey of current theology.

*   *   *

THOMPSON, Frances C(lements) 1906-

PERSONAL: Born April 2, 1906, in Milton, Ontario, Canada; daughter of William Bradford and Bertha Frances (Deacon) Clements; married F. Wesley Thompson (public relations manager, Bell Telephone Co. of Canada), June 23, 1928; children: David, Madeline, Robert. Education: Victoria College, University of Toronto, B.A., 1927. Politics: Liberal. Religion: United Church of Canada. Home: 50 Indian Valley Trail, Port Credit, Ontario, Canada.

CAREER: Writer. Member: University Women's Club (Port Credit; publicity chairman, 1955-57), Mississauga Historical Society. Awards, honors: Honorable mention, Macmillan of Canada contest for children's stories, 1962.

WRITINGS: The Travel Tea (one-act play), Pioneer Drama Service, 1961; Danger in the Coves, St. Martin's, 1963; Escape From Grand Pre, Macmillan, 1966. Contrib-

utor to Toronto Globe and Mail, Toronto Telegram, Financial Post, Family Herald, Chatelaine, Onward, Port Credit Weekly.

WORK IN PROGRESS: A play about the Acadians; a play about a Toronto family in the early 1900's.

AVOCATIONAL INTERESTS: Early Canadian furniture and glass; music, art, and theatre.

*   *   *

THOMPSON, Harlan H. 1894-
(Stephen Holt)

PERSONAL: Born December 25, 1894, in Brewster, Kan.; son of William Lewis (a rancher) and Clara Cornelia (Shultz) Thompson; married Gail Gertrude Friend, May 31, 1960; children: (former marriage) Charlotte, James Van De Water (deceased), Harlan Trenholm, Barbara (Mrs. Charles F. Wheeler). Education: University of Southern California, student, 1917-19. Politics: Republican. Religion: Methodist. Home and office: 1160 Oakwood Dr., San Marino, Calif. 91108. Agent: William Morris Agency, Beverly Hills, Calif.

CAREER: Writer. Owner TX Ranch, Alberta, Canada. Member: P.E.N. (international president, 1958-59), California Writers Guild, Westerners (Los Angeles Corral), Commonwealth Club (San Francisco). Awards, honors: Boys' Clubs of America gold medal, 1948, for Prairie Colt; Commonwealth Club juvenile silver medal, 1957, for Spook, the Mustang.

WRITINGS—Under pseudonym Stephen Holt: Wild Palomino, Longmans, Green, 1946; Prairie Colt, Longmans, Green, 1947; Phantom Roan (Junior Literary Guild selection), Longmans, Green, 1949; Whistling Stallion, Longmans, Green, 1951; Stormy, Longmans, Green, 1955; We Were There with the California Forty Niners, Grosset, 1956; We Were There with the California Rancheros, Grosset, 1960; Ranch Beyond the Mountains, Longmans, Green, 1961.

Under name Harlan Thompson: Star Roan, Doubleday, 1952; Spook, the Mustang (Junior Literary Guild selection), Doubleday, 1956; Outcast Stallion of Hawaii, Doubleday, 1957. Contributor of short stories to national periodicals.

WORK IN PROGRESS: Lasso Land—Six Famous Ranchers of the World, for McKay; Ride a Red Horse, for McGraw; Hawaiian Fire Ranch; and a novel, Reach for Heaven.

*   *   *

THOMPSON, Helen M. (Smith) 1903-

PERSONAL: Born March 2, 1903, in Rock Rapids, Iowa; daughter of Burton R. (an inventor) and Alpha R. (Wright) Smith; married John Vincent Thompson, September 2, 1930. Education: Drake University, A.B., 1926; Claremont Graduate School, M.A., 1950; grauate study at University of California, Los Angeles, University of Southern California, and University of Wisconsin. Politics: "Votes for the individual." Religion: Protestant. Office: Thompson Reading Clinic, Chapman College, Orange, Calif.

CAREER: Educator, beginning, 1925, teaching in country school and at all levels from primary grades to college; Chapman College, Orange, Calif., associate professor of psychology and education, and director of Thompson Reading Clinic, beginning, 1959. Consultant to schools and colleges in California and Montana. *Member:* International Council of Psychologists, American Psychological Association, Association for Childhood Education International, American Research Association, National Education Association, California Psychological Association, Pi Lambda Theta, Delta Kappa Gamma, Kappa Kappa Gamma.

WRITINGS: SWIERL: A Plan for Better Reading, Vantage, 1956; *The Art of Being a Successful Student*, Washington Square, 1964.

WORK IN PROGRESS: A ten-year research study on low metabolic efficiency and its relation to reading retardation; a book, *The K's Get Ready to Read.*

* * *

THOMPSON, Stanbury Dugard 1905-

PERSONAL: Born May 22, 1905, in Nottingham, England; son of Wellington James and Rosamund Edith (Wheatley) Thompson; married Norah Amelia Nind, May 22, 1926; children: Robert Dugard, Stella Caroline. *Education:* Educated in English schools. *Religion:* Church of England. *Home:* 20 William Rd., Stapleford, Nottingham, England.

CAREER: Composer, 1924—. H.M. Welsh Guards, London, England, violoncello and clarinet player, 1931-45; antiquarian bookseller, Stapleford, Nottingham, England, 1945—.

WRITINGS: Memoirs of de Tallard (poem), Stockwell, 1929; *Marchente, and Other Poems*, Stockwell, 1931; *The Story of Jenny Diver: A Memoir of a Famous Female Criminal*, Stockwell, 1942; *True Ghost Stories*, Stockwell, 1942; *The Incomparable Jenny: A Tale of Old London*, Stockwell, 1943; *Ghost Stories*, Stockwell, 1944, enlarged edition, 1948, 2nd series, Thompson & Co., 1957, 3rd series, Thompson & Co., 1958; *Glimpses into a Vanished Age: Some Talks on the Eighteenth Century*, Stockwell, 1946; *The Black Shadow* (novel), privately printed, 1951; (editor) *The Journal of John Gabriel Stedman, 1744-1797, Soldier and Author, Including an Authentic Account of His Expedition to Surinam in 1772*, Mitre Press, 1962, Heinman, 1963; *Tales of the Supernatural: A Collection of Weird and Uncanny Stories* (contains *Ghost Stories*, 1st, 2nd, and 3rd series), Thompson & Co., 1963; *John Gabriel Stedman: A Study of His Life and Times*, Thompson & Co., 1966. Published music includes a cello solo, two marches, and five piano compositions.

AVOCATIONAL INTERESTS: Collecting antiques and old manuscripts.

* * *

THOMPSON, William Bernard 1914-

PERSONAL: Born April 6, 1914, in Prestwich, Lancashire, England; son of William Bernard and Hilda Mary (Hudson) Thompson; married Marianne Kilvert-Minor-Adams, December 30, 1947; children: Michael William, Ann Catharine, Philip Kilvert. *Education:* University of Manchester, B.A., 1935. *Religion:* Anglican. *Home:* Woodlands, Otley, Yorkshire LS21 3HB, England. *Office:* Department of Education, University of Leeds, Leeds, Yorkshire LS2 9JT, England.

CAREER: City Grammar School, Sheffield, England, senior Latin master, 1938-44; Service Civil International, Egypt and Italy, relief and rehabilitation work, 1944-46; Sidcot School, Somerset, England, classics master, 1946-48; King Edward VI School, Southampton, England, head of the classical side, 1949-56; University of Leeds, Leeds,

Yorkshire, England, lecturer, 1956-69, senior lecturer in education, 1969—. Visiting professor, University of Minnesota, 1966. Assistant examiner, Cambridge University and Northern Universities Joint Matriculation Board. Governor of Bretton Hall Teachers' College and of various schools; member, Ripon Diocesan Education Council; member of advisory panel, Cambridge School Classics Project; curator, National Collection of Greek and Latin School Textbooks.

MEMBER: Classical Association (member of council, 1958-61), Joint Association of Classical Teachers (member of committee, 1962-64; deputy to honorary secretary, 1965—), Association for the Reform of Latin Teaching, National Association of Governing Bodies of Aided Grammar Schools (member of executive committee), National Centre for Classical Studies (secretary), Colloquium Didacticum Classicum (British delegate, 1969; member of British committee, 1971), Society of Saints Mary and Aidan (York; fellow; member of working party on educational policy, 1969—).

WRITINGS: Greece and Rome on Postage Stamps, Wilding & Son, 1947; *Classical Novels: A Catalogue of Novels Dealing with the People and Events of Greece and Rome*, Wilding & Son, 1966; (with J. D. Ridge) *Catalogue of the National Collection of Greek and Latin School Textbooks: Part One*, Leeds Institute of Education, 1970. Contributor of articles to *Greece and Rome*, *Didaskalos*, *Rucksack*, *Didactica Classica Gandensia*, *Speech and Drama*, *Latin Teaching*, and to educational journals.

WORK IN PROGRESS: The Influence of the Reformed Pronunciation of Latin on the Pronunciation of English; Ediscenda, a collection of passages from Latin verse and prose to be committed to memory and spoken aloud; *An Anthology of Yorkshire Latin; Classics in Colleges of Education.*

* * *

THOMSON, Arthur Alexander (Malcolm) 1894-1968

PERSONAL: Born April 7, 1894, in Harrogate, Yorkshire, England; son of Alexander (a businessman) and Helen (Howieson) Thomson; married Beatrice Maude VanHee, August 22, 1917 (died, 1963); children: Noel Ann (Mrs. John Antony Hill). *Education:* King's College, London, B.A., 1921. *Religion:* Church of England. *Home:* 26 Alma Sq., London N.W.8, England. *Agent:* John Farquharson Ltd., 15 Red Lion Sq., London W.C.1, England.

CAREER: Writer. British civil servant, London, England, 1940-63, serving in Air Ministry, 1940-43, Ministry of Information, 1943-46, Central Office of Information, 1946-63; senior information officer at time of retirement, 1963. *Military service:* British Army, 1914-19; became temporary captain. *Member:* P.E.N. International, Society of Authors, Cricket Society (president, 1963-68), Savage Club (London). *Awards, honors:* Member of the British Empire, 1966.

WRITINGS: Cheerio!: The Army of Today, Cassell, 1917.

The Records of Reggie, Jenkins, 1924; *Bumbledinky*, Mills & Boon, 1925; *Sweet Cicely*, Jenkins, 1926; *Meet Mr. Huckabee!*, Mills & Boon, 1926; *Marigold Cottage*, Jenkins, 1927; *The Exploits of Piccolo*, Jenkins, 1927; *The World of Billiam Wissold*, Hurst & Blackett, 1927; *Trust Tilty*, Jenkins, 1928; *Mary Gets the Vote*, Newnes, 1928; *Steeple Thatchby*, Jenkins, 1928; *O Petrina!*, Jenkins, 1929.

The Happy Windmill, Jenkins, 1930; *Dorinda Darling!*,

Jenkins, 1930; *Let's See the Lowlands*, Jenkins, 1930; *According to Alfie*, Jenkins, 1930; *The Burns We Love* (biography), foreword by G. K. Chesterton, Jenkins, 1931; *Let's See the Highlands*, Jenkins, 1931; *The Lilac Maid*, Jenkins, 1931; *Fay of the Ring: A Circus Story*, Jenkins, 1932; *The Breezy Coast: Berwick to John O'Groats*, Jenkins, 1932; *Heart's Content*, Jenkins, 1933; *Borders of Enchantment*, Jenkins, 1933; *Out of Town* (poetry), Jenkins, 1935; *The Exquisite Burden*, Jenkins, 1935; *Written Humour*, A. & C. Black, 1936; *Bijou Merle*, Jenkins, 1936; *Reggie Goes Rural*, Jenkins, 1937; (with Ashley Sterne) *Listener's Licence*, Jenkins, 1938; *Strolling Commentaries*, Jenkins, 1938; *What a Picture!*, Jenkins, 1939.

Cottage Loaf, Jenkins, 1944; (with Falkland C. Cary) *Burning Gold* (play), Samuel French, 1945, novelized version, Jenkins, 1946; (with Cary) *Ladysfingers*, Jenkins, 1947; (with Cary) *Murder at the Ministry* (play), Samuel French, 1945, novelized version, Jenkins, 1947; *Bed of Rose's*, Jenkins, 1949.

(With Cary) *But Once a Year* (novel), Jenkins, 1951; *Highland Welcome*, Jenkins, 1951, Roy, 1956; *Cricket My Pleasure*, Museum Press, 1953; *Spanish Chariot*, Jenkins, 1953; *Cricket My Happiness*, Museum Press, 1954; *Rugger My Pleasure*, Museum Press, 1955; *Great Men of Kent*, Bodley Head, 1955; *Pavilioned in Splendour* (essays on cricket), Museum Press, 1956; (with John Henry Wardle) *Happy Go Johnny*, R. Hale, 1957; *The Great Cricketer: W. G. Grace*, R. Hale, 1957, new edition, Hutchinson, 1968; *Odd Men In: A Gallery of Cricket Eccentrics*, Museum Press, 1958; (with Dorothy Middleton) *Lugard in Africa* (biography), R. Hale, 1959, International Publications, 1966; *Hirst and Rhodes* (cricket biography), Epworth, 1959.

Cricket Bouquet: Comedy and Character in the Counties, Museum Press, 1961; *Cricket: The Golden Ages*, Stanley Paul, 1961; *Hutton and Washbrook* (cricket biography), Epworth, 1963; *When I Was a Lad*, Epworth, 1964; *Cricket: The Great Captains*, Stanley Paul, 1965; (editor) Harold Vincent Mackintosh, *By Faith and Work: The Autobiography of the Rt. Hon. the First Viscount of Mackintosh of Halifax*, Hutchinson, 1966; *Anatomy of Laughter*, Epworth, 1966; *Cricket: The Wars of the Roses*, Pelham Books, 1967; *Cricketers of My Times*, Stanley Paul, 1967; *Vintage Elevens* (completed by Danzil Batchelor), Pelham Books, 1969.

Co-author with Ashley Sterne of six musical comedy scripts for British Broadcasting Corp., 1933-38. Writer of columns, "Cigarette Papers" in *People*, 1924-48, and "Strolling Commentaries" in *Radio Times*, 1933-46. Contributor of articles to *Punch* and *Passing Show*.

BIOGRAPHICAL/CRITICAL SOURCES: London Times, June 3, 1968.

(Died June 2, 1968)

*   *   *

THORNING, Joseph F(rancis) 1896-

PERSONAL: Born April 25, 1896, in Milwaukee, Wis.; son of Cully Michael (a shipbuilder) and Julia Theresa (Hallissey) Thorning. *Education:* Attended Marquette Academy, 1910-14; College of the Holy Cross, B.A., 1918; St. Louis University, M.A., 1922; Catholic University of America, Ph.D. 1931; Georgian University, S.T.D., 1933; additional study at Oxford University and Sorbonne, University of Paris. *Politics:* Democrat. *Home:* St. Joseph's-on-Carrollton Manor, Box 345, Frederick, Md. 21701. *Office:* c/o *World Affairs*, 4000 Albemarle St. N.W., Washington, D.C. 20016.

CAREER: Ordained a Roman Catholic priest, 1928. Loyola University, Chicago, Ill., professor, 1922-25; Georgetown University, Washington, D.C., professor of sociology and acting dean of Graduate School, 1934-36; Mount St. Mary's Seminary and College, Emmitsburg, Md., chairman of department of sociology, 1936-44; St. Joseph's-on-Carrollton Manor, Frederick, Md., rector, 1946—; now professor of Latin American history at Marymount College, Arlington, Va. Director of inter-American seminars at University of San Marcos, Lima, Peru, 1941, at University of Havana, Havana, Cuba, 1942, University of Havana and National University of Mexico, 1943; special adviser to U.S. senatorial delegation at tenth Inter-American Conference, Caracas, Venezuela, 1954; consultant to congressional committees on Latin American matters.

MEMBER: U.S. Catholic History Society, Catholic Association for International Peace, American Peace Society (director), Pi Gamma Mu, Mediaevalists (Chicago; honorary member), Charles Carroll Forum, Metropolitan Club and Congressional Country Club (both Washington, D.C.), Maryland Club (Baltimore). *Awards, honors:* Fourteen decorations from foreign countries, including Grand Cross, Order of Alfonso the Wise and Grand Cross, Order of Isabella the Catholic (both Spain), 1945, Cross of Boyaca (Columbia); Military Order of Christ (Portugal), 1959, Order of the Sun (Peru), National Order of Merit (Ecuador), 1945, Francisco de Miranda (Venezuela), Constellation of the Southern Cross (Brazil), 1956, honorary D.D., Catholic University of Chile, 1944, J.U.D., University of Santo Domingo, 1954; fellow, American Geographical Society; honorary fellow, Historical and Geographical Institute of Brazil.

WRITINGS: Religious Liberty in Transition, Catholic University of America Press, 1931; *A Primer of Social Justice*, Paulist Press, 1940; *Builders of the Social Order*, Catholic Literary Guild, 1941; *Miranda: World Citizen*, University of Florida Press, 1952. Also author of several pamphlets on international relations, and religious subjects. Associate editor for international relations, *Thought*, 1935-36; associate editor of *World Affairs*, 1946—. Former European correspondent of *America* and National Welfare Conference News Service; Washington correspondent of *America*, 1935-36, and of *Sign*; special correspondent, Religious News Service.

WORK IN PROGRESS: Spain in America, a survey of public opinion in the United States with reference to the Spanish Civil War and its aftermath in the successful movement to re-establish full diplomatic relations between the United States and Spain.

SIDELIGHTS: Thorning has been invited by Congress to give the invocation at all official celebrations of Pan American Day on Capitol Hill since 1944. His interest in international relations has led to travels in almost every part of the world; he is competent in Spanish, French, Portuguese, German, Italian, Latin and Greek. He has been elected to the Gallery of Living American Authors. *Avocational interests:* Swimming, tennis.

BIOGRAPHICAL/CRITICAL SOURCES: Register, national edition, March 17, 1963; *Congressional Record*, April 17, 1964.

THORNTON, Willis 1900-

PERSONAL: Born March 10, 1900, in Cleveland, Ohio; married Eugenia Mackiernan, 1935. Education: Western Reserve University (now Case Western Reserve University), A.B., 1921, M.A., 1953. Home: 2855 Coventry Rd., Shaker Heights, Ohio.

CAREER: Scripps-Howard Newspapers, editor and writer in Cleveland, Ohio, and Washington, D.C., for 25 years; Press of Case Western Reserve University, Cleveland, Ohio, former director. Military service: U.S. Army Air Forces, World War II; became captain.

WRITINGS: Almanac for Americas, Chilton, 1941; The Nine Lives of Citizen Train, Chilton, 1948; (editor) The Best of Life (anthology), Houghton, 1950; Newton D. Baker and His Books, Western Reserve University Press, 1954; Fable, Fact and History, Chilton, 1957; The Liberation of Paris, Harcourt, 1962.

*   *   *

THURSTAN, Violetta

PERSONAL: Born in Hastings, Sussex, England; daughter of Edward Paget (a physician, traveler, and writer) and Anna (Reid) Thurstan. Education: Educated privately in England, France, and Germany; University of St. Andrews, L.L.A. (honors in aesthetics and fine arts); also studied tapestry, weaving, and designing in Sweden. Politics: Conservative. Religion: Roman Catholic. Home: Old Mill House, The Square, Penryn, Cornwall, England.

CAREER: War work as representative of Order of St. John of Jerusalem in Belgium and Russia, 1914-18, in Universities Ambulance Unit in Spain during Spanish Civil War; Women's Royal Naval Service, officer, 1939-44; Allied Commission for Austria, staff officer, P.O.W. and Refugee Department, Klagenfurt, 1945-49; Allied Commission for Austria, commandant of refugee hospital, Carinthia, Greece, 1946-49. Designer and craftsman in textiles, with work exhibited in London, Berlin, Cairo; former director of Bedouin industries for Egyptian government; arts and crafts consultant at other periods in Albania and Denmark. Member: Royal Geographical Society (fellow), Designer and Craftsman Society, Les Arts Decoratifs Paris. Awards, honors: Military Medal, 1914, and other decorations for war work.

WRITINGS: Field Hospital and Flying Column: Being the Journal of an English Nursing Sister in Belgium and Russia, Putnam, 1915; The People Who Run: Being the Tragedy of the Refugees in Russia, Putnam, 1916; A Text Book of War Nursing, Putnam, 1917; The Use of Vegetable Dyes for Beginners, Dryad, 1930, 13th edition issued as The Use of Vegetable Dyes, 1972; A Short History of Decorative Textiles and Tapestries, Pepler & Sewell, 1934, 3rd edition, Favil Press, 1972; Weaving Patterns of Yesterday and Today, Dryad, 1936; Weaving Without Tears, Museum Press (London), 1956; Stormy Petrel, Dawson and Goodall, 1964; The Foolish Virgin, Marazion Press, 1966. Contributor of series of articles on the dye plants of Egypt to Egyptian Horticultural Review, another series to Weavers' Journal; also contributor to Spectator, Time and Tide, Outlook, and to historical journals.

WORK IN PROGRESS: A history of European tapestry.

SIDELIGHTS: Miss Thurstan has traveled extensively in Mediterranean countries, Russia, and Lapland. She was made a fellow of the Royal Geographical Society for journeys in the Libyan Desert. She is fluent in French, German, and Spanish, competent in Italian, and speaks some Russian and Swedish.

*   *   *

THUT, I(saac) N(oah)

PERSONAL: Born in Columbus Grove, Ohio; son of Noah O. (a farmer) and Emma (Niswander) Thut; married J. Marguerite Callow, July 2, 1932; children: Paul Douglas. Education: College of Wooster, B.S., 1929; University of Buffalo (now State University of New York at Buffalo), M.Ed., 1938; Ohio State University, Ph.D., 1940. Religion: Protestant.

CAREER: Ohio State University, Columbus, instructor, 1940-41; University of New Hampshire, Durham, associate professor, 1941-45; University of Connecticut, Storrs, professor of education, 1945-72, professor emeritus, 1972—. Consultant to U.S. Office of Education and Agency for International Development. Military service: U.S. Coast Guard, Temporary Reserves, 1943-45. Member: Association for Higher Education, Comparative Education Society (director, 1965-68), History of Education Society, Philosophy of Education Society, John Dewey Society (executive secretary, 1948-57; board of directors), Connecticut Education Association (president, department of higher education, 1962-64), Rotary International.

gs;)with J. Raymond Gerberich) Foundations of Method for Secondary Schools, McGraw, 1949; The Story of Education: Philosophical and Historical Foundations, McGraw, 1957; (with Don Adams) Educational Patterns in Contemporary Societies, McGraw, 1964. Contributor to published survey reports on Ohio schools, to Westminister Dictionary of Christian Education, 1962, The Year Book of Education (London), 1965, proceedings of educational conferences, and education journals.

*   *   *

TICKNER, Fred(erick James) 1902-

PERSONAL: Born December 29, 1902, in Brighton, England; son of Frederick Windham (a schoolmaster) and Mary Ellen (Higginson) Tickner; married Lucy Winifred James, May 19, 1931; children: Judith Ann (Mrs. Hayward Rose Alker). Education: Balliol College, Oxford, B.A., 1925, M.A., 1951, B. Litt., 1952. Home: 322 Wellington Rd., Delmar, N.Y. 12054. Office: Graduate School of Public Affairs, State University of New York at Albany, Albany, N.Y. 12203.

CAREER: General Post Office, Great Britain, telecommunications controller for Welsh and Border Counties Region, 1940-44, assistant secretary, 1944-49; H.M. Treasury, Great Britain, director of training and education, 1950-52; United Nations, New York, N.Y., deputy director of Public Administration Division, 1952-62; State University of New York, Albany, professor of political science, Graduate School of Public Affairs, 1962—, dean of graduate school, 1967-70. Member of national advisory council for education in industry and commerce, British Ministry of Education, 1950-52, and of board of economic studies, University of London, 1950-62. Member of United Nations Mission in Congo, 1961; representative of United Nations on other missions and committees. Member: American Political Science Association, American Society for Public Administration, Royal Institute of Public Administration, East India and Sports Club (London). Awards, honors: Commander, Order of the British Empire.

WRITINGS: (Editor) *Earlier English Drama from Robin Hood to Everyman*, Thomas Nelson, 1926, American edition, revised by Thomas Whitfield Baldwin, 1929, new and enlarged edition published as *Earlier English Drama, from Robin Hood to the Second Play of the Shepherds*, 1931; (editor) *Shakespeare's Predecessors: Selections from Heywood, Udall, Sackville and Norton, Lyly, Kyd, Greene, and Marlowe*, Thomas Nelson, 1929; (editor) *Restoration Dramatists: Selections from Dryden, Etheredge, Otway, Congreve, Vanbrugh, and Farquhar*, Thomas Nelson, 1930; (adapter) Jonathan Swift, *Dwarfs and Giants: Being Selections from Gulliver's Travels*, Thomas Nelson, 1930; (adapter) Alexander Dumas, *Prisoner's Treasure* (adapted from *The Count of Monte Cristo*), Thomas Nelson, 1930; (editor) Jean Froissart, *A Shorter Froissart: Being Selections from "The Chronicles,"* Thomas Nelson, 1930; (adapter) Edward Bulwer Lytton, *Warwick the King-Maker* (adapted from *The Last of the Barons*), Thomas Nelson, 1931; (editor) *A Shorter Milton*, Thomas Nelson, 1935; (editor) *An Anthology of Modern Historical Fiction*, Thomas Nelson, 1938; *Modern Staff Training: A Survey of Training Needs and Methods of Today*, University of London Press, 1952; *Technical Cooperation*, Hutchinson, 1965, Praeger, 1966; *Training in Modern Society: An International Review of Training Practices and Procedures in Government and Industry*, Graduate School of Public Affairs, State University of New York at Albany, 1967. Contributor to professional journals, Editor, *Post Office Magazine*, 1934-36.

WORK IN PROGRESS: The European in the East Indies 1495-1825.

* * *

TILLEY, Ethel 1894-

PERSONAL: Born December 12, 1894, in Bellevue, Pa.; daughter of J. Frank (secretary of Pittsburgh Coal Exchange) and Dollie (Smashey) Tilley. *Education:* Ohio Wesleyan University, A.B., 1922; Boston University, A.M., 1926, Ph.D., 1936. *Politics:* Democrat. *Religion:* Methodist. *Office:* Meredith College, Raleight, N.C. 27611.

CAREER: Hastings College, Hastings, Neb., professor of philosophy and psychology and dean of women, 1937-43; Sullins Junior College, Bristol, Va., professor of philosophy and Bible, 1944-46; Greensboro College, Greensboro, N.C., dean of students, 1946-48; Brenau College, Gainesville, Ga., professor of philosophy and psychology, 1948-51; Meredith College, Raleigh, N.C., professor of philosophy and psychology, 1951—. Former professional musician as piano player and soprano soloist. Member, Raleigh (N.C.) Little Theatre. *Member:* American Psychological Association, American Philosophical Association, American Association for Advancement of Science (fellow), Interamerican Society of Psychology, International Council of Psychologists, Society of Biblical Literature and Exegesis, American Academy of Religion, American Association of University Women, North Carolina Academy of Science, North Carolina Art Society, North Carolina Literary and Historical Society, Raleigh Woman's Club, Phi Beta Kappa.

WRITINGS: Paul, an Early Pioneer, Pilgrim Press, 1949; *Christians in Our Community*, Pilgrim Press, 1951; *The Book of the Ages*, published for the Cooperative Publication Association by Abingdon, 1956, 2nd edition, 1962; *Jesus is His Name*, published by the Cooperative Publica-

tion Association by Westminster, 1958; *The Church: What It Is and What It Does*, Methodist Board of Education, 1961; *He Was Called Jesus*, Westminster, 1963. Writer of Sunday school texts for United Presbyterian Church in the U.S.A., United Church, Methodist Church; contributor of articles, stories, verse to religious magazines.

WORK IN PROGRESS: A life of Jesus for eight-and-nine-year olds, for Methodist Board of Education; a book of devotions; short stories.

* * *

TILLOTSON, Geoffrey 1905-1969

PERSONAL: Born June 30, 1905, in Nelson, Lancashire, England; son of John Henry and Annie (Peacock) Tillotson; married Kathleen Mary Constable (Hildred Carlisle Professor of English at Bedford College, University of London), November 21, 1933; children: Edmund, Harry. *Education:* Balliol College, Oxford, B.A. (honors), 1927, B. Litt., 1930, M.A., 1931. *Home:* 23 Tanza Rd., London N.W. 3, England. *Office:* Birkbeck College, Malet St., London W.C. 1, England.

CAREER: University of London, London, England, successively assistant lecturer, lecturer, and reader in English at University College, 1931-44, professor of English literature at Birkbeck College, 1944-69. Served with Ministry of Aircraft Production, 1940-44. Visiting lecturer at Harvard University, 1948. Governor of City Literary Institute, 1952-69. *Member:* American Academy of Arts and Sciences (honorary foreign member), Charles Lamb Society (president, 1955-69).

WRITINGS: On the Poetry of Pope, Clarendon Press, 1938; *Twickenham Pope*, Volume II, Methuen, 1940; (editor) Pope's *Rape of the Lock*, Methuen, 1941, 3rd edition, Yale University Press, 1962; *Bibliography of Michael Drayton*, Shakespeare Head Press, 1941; *Essays in Criticism and Research*, Cambridge University Press, 1942, revised edition, Archon Books, 1967.

Criticism and the Nineteenth Century, Athlone Press, 1951, reprinted, Archon Books, 1967; *Thackeray the Novelist*, Cambridge University Press, 1957; *Newman*, Reynard Library, Hart-Davis, 1957; *Pope and Human Nature*, Clarendon Press, 1958.

Augustan Studies, Athlone Press, 1961; *Thackeray: The Novelist*, Methuen, 1963; *Augustan Poetic Diction*, Athlone Press, 1964; (with wife, Kathleen Tillotson) *Mid-Victorian Studies*, Athlone Press, 1965; (editor) Cardinal John Henry Newman, *Prose and Poetry*, Harvard University Press, 1965; *The Continuity of English Poetry from Dryden to Wordsworth*, University of Nottingham Press, 1967; (editor with Donald Hawes) *Thackeray: The Critical Heritage*, Barnes & Noble, 1968; (editor with Paul Fussell, Jr. and Marshall Waingrow) *Eighteenth-Century English Literature*, Harcourt, 1969; *The Moral Poetry of Pope*, Folcroft, 1969; (editor and author of preface) James Blair Leishman, *Milton's Minor Poems*, Hutchinson, 1969, University of Pittsburgh Press, 1971.

(Author of introduction) Hardwicke Drummond Rawnsley, *Reminiscences of Wordsworth Among the Peasantry of Westmorland*, Dillon, 1970; (editor and author of introduction with Brian Jenkins) Samuel Johnson, *The History of Rasselas, Prince of Abissinia*, Oxford University Press, 1971.

Contributor to periodicals.

WORK IN PROGRESS: A volume in *Oxford History of*

English Literature; in collaboration with his wife, *Mid-Victorian Studies.*

AVOCATIONAL INTERESTS: All the arts, and especially Mozart's music.

(Died, 1969)

* * *

TILTMAN, Ronald Frank 1901-
(Ronald Fraser)

PERSONAL: Born April 24, 1901, in London, England; son of Frank and Ada (Rose) Tiltman; married Mary Bowers, March 23, 1929; children: Janette. *Education:* Attended Durham House School. *Politics:* Conservative. *Religion:* Church of England.

CAREER: Civil servant in various British government departments, 1921-61; author and free-lance journalist, 1921—. *Member:* Radio Association of Great Britain (general secretary).

WRITINGS: Radio Log and Distant Reception Manual, Fleetgate, 1926; *Wireless Without Worry,* Seeley Service, 1927; *Televsion for the Home,* Hutchinson, 1927; *ABC of Broadcast Reception,* Drane, 1928; *ABC of Television,* Drane, 1929; *Baird of Television: The Life Story of John Logie Baird,* Seeley Service, 1933; *Television Really Explained,* Foulsham & Co., 1952. Writer of television scripts, 1926—. Contributor of articles to journals in United States and England. First acting editor, *Television,* 1928; editor, *Broadcast Reception Annual,* 1932; former wireless editor, *Sphere.*

WORK IN PROGRESS: Best of Both Worlds, autobiography of forty-year dual career; a second biography of John Logie Baird, British television pioneer.†

* * *

TIMMERS, J(an) Joseph M(arie) 1907-

PERSONAL: Born March 25, 1907, in Sittard, The Netherlands; son of J. Theophile J.M. (a chemist) and Bertha (Lanckohr) Timmers. *Education:* Attended Canisius College (Nijmegen, The Netherlands); Catholic Univerisity (Nijmegen), doctorate, 1942. *Religion:* Roman Catholic. *Home:* Papenstraat 13, Maastricht, The Netherlands.

CAREER: Archiepiscopal Museum, Utrecht, The Netherlands, curator, 1942-46; Bonnefantenmuseum, Maastricht, The Netherlands, director, 1946-71; Episcopal Museum, Maastricht, The Netherlands, director, 1946-71; Catholic University, Nijmegen, The Netherlands, professor of the history of art, 1948-55; Jan van Eyck Academy, Maastricht, The Netherlands, director, 1955-65, and professor of the history of art, 1948—. *Member:* Centre International d'Etudes Romanes, Maatschappij der Nederlandse Letterkunde, Istituto di Studi Romani, Membre associe etranger de l'Academie Royale d'Archeologie de Belgique, Rotary Club (Maastricht).

WRITINGS: Gerard Lairesse, H.J. Paris, 1942; *Kerkelijke Monumentenzorg,* Het Spectrum, 1943; *De Religieuse Schilderkunst,* In den Toren, 1947; *Symboliek en Iconographie der Christelijke Kunst,* Romen en Zonen, 1947; *Houten Beelden, de Houtsculptuur in de Noordelijke Nederlanden tijdens de la te Middeleeuwen,* Contact, 1949; *De Sint Servaaskerk te Maastricht,* Het Spectrum, 1955; *Atlas van de Nederlandse Beschaving,* Elsevier, 1957, 2nd edition, 1964, translation by Mary J. Hedlund, published as *A History of Dutch Life and Art,* Nelson, 1959; *Schoonheid langs de grote Wegen van Italie,* Elsevier, 1958.

Rome en omstreken, Elsevier, 1960, 3rd edition, 1968; *St. Servatius' Noodkist en de Heiligdomsvaart,* Crouzen, 1962; *Oude Schoonheid in Limburg,* Leiter-Nypels, 1962, 2nd edition, 1968; *Spiegel van twintig Eeuwen,* Elsevier, 1963; *Kleine Atlas van de Nederlandse Beschaving,* Elsevier, 1963; *Atlas van het Romaans,* Elsevier, 1965, translation by author, published as *A Handbook of Romanesque Art,* Nelson, 1969; *De Kunst van het Maasland,* Van Gorcum, 1971; *De Glorie van Nederland,* Elsevier, 1972; *Christelijke Symboliek en Iconografie,* Unieboek, 1974. Contributor of columns to *Elseviers Weekblad* and *Limburgs Dagblad.*

WORK IN PROGRESS: De Kunst van het Maasland (volume II), for Van Gorcum; *Atlas van de Nederlandse Beschaving,* revised edition for Elsevier; *Rome en omstreken,* 4th edition for Elsevier.

SIDELIGHTS: Works by Timmers have been translated into French and German. Fields of professional interest include the history of architecture, topography of Rome, and Italy and its art.

* * *

TINKER, Edward Larocque 1881-1968

PERSONAL: Born September 12, 1881, in New York, N.Y.; son of Henry Champlin and Louise (Larocque) Tinker; married Frances McKee Dodge, 1916 (deceased). *Education:* Columbia University, A.B., 1902; New York University, LL.B., 1905; University of Paris, Docteur de l'universite, 1932. *Politics:* Republican. *Religion:* Episcopalian. *Home and office:* 550 Park Ave., New York, N.Y. 10021.

CAREER: Admitted to New York bar, 1905, served as counsel for Legal Aid Society in New York, N.Y., 1906-07, as assistant district attorney, New York, N.Y., 1908-11; resigned to travel in Mexico and eventually settled in El Paso, Tex.; began to study and write about Creole Louisiana after his marriage to New Orleans resident, extended his interest to South America; was president of Tinker Foundation, founded to promote better understanding between the Americas. Lecturer at National University of Mexico under auspices of Carnegie Endowment for International Peace, 1943, in Argentina and Uruguay under U.S. Department of State exchange program, 1945. At one time, literary columnist, "New Editions Fine and Otherwise," *New York Times.* Member of advisory council, School of International Affairs, Columbia University; trustee of Museum of the City of New York, French Institute of United States, Hispanic Society of America, other institutions and organizations. *Military service:* U.S. Navy, World War I; became lieutenant junior grade.

MEMBER: Society of American Historians, American Academy of Political and Social Science, Spanish Institute (vice-president), National Institute of Social Sciences (vice-president), American Bible Society (member of board of managers), Uruguayan-American Society (founder; president emeritus), Council on Foreign Relations, Northwestern Council for Latin American and Inter-American Studies, Pan-American Society, English-Speaking Union, Union Club, University Club, Piping Rock Club, Coffee House Club, Dutch Treat Club, Paris-American Club.

AWARDS, HONORS: Palmes Academiques (France), 1933; Chevalier of the Legion of Honor (France), 1939; Order de Mayo al Merito (Argentina), 1959; Americas Foundation Award for promoting unity among New World nations, 1962; Knight Commander, Order of Queen Isabella (Spain), 1963; Medal of Alliance Francaise, 1964, for improving Franco-American relations. LL.D. from Middlebury College, 1949, Columbia University, 1963; Docteur de la Universidad de Madrid, 1955.

WRITINGS: *Lafcadio Hearn's American Days*, Dodd, 1924; *Toucoutou*, Dodd, 1928; (with wife, Frances Tinker) *Old New Orleans*, Appleton, 1930; *Les Cenelles*, Colophon, 1930; *Les Ecrits de Langue Francaise en Louisiana au 19e Siecle* (bio-bibliography), Champion (Paris), 1932; *The Palingenesis of Craps*, Press of the Wooly Whale, 1933; *Bibliography of French Newspapers and Periodicals of Louisiana*, American Antiquarian Society, 1933; *Gombo: The Creole Dialect of Louisiana*, American Antiquarian Society, 1936; *The Cult of the Gaucho and the Creation of a Literature*, American Antiquarian Society, 1947; *The Pennells*, [New York], 1951; *Los Jinetes de las Americas y la literatura por ellos inspirada*, Guillermo Kraft Limitada, 1952, translated by the author, published as, *The Horsemen of the Americas and the Literature They Inspired*, Hastings, 1953, 2nd revised edition, University of Texas Press, 1967; *Creole City*, Longmans, Green, 1953; *The Life and Literature of the Pampas*, University of Florida Press, 1961; *Corridos and Calaveros*, University of Texas Press, 1961; *Centaurs of Many Lands*, University of Texas Press, 1964; *The Splendid Spectacle of Portuguese Bull Fighting*, Encino Press, 1967.

Author of pamphlets and monographs on other subjects.

WORK IN PROGRESS: Bullfighting in Portugal.

SIDELIGHTS: Tinker dated his interest in Latin America from boyhood days, when his parents brought him a charro outfit from Mexico. Later he was struck by the fact "that the gaucho of Argentina, the huaso of Chile, the llanero of Venezuela, and the North American cowboy were as much alike as Fords off the assembly line" and decided that nations producing men so similar should be bridged to better understanding. The books and other materials he collected to promote this understanding have been exhibited at the Library of Congress, New York Public Library, and at universities; now the collection belongs to the University of Texas, where it is housed in its own Hall of the Horsemen of the Americas.

BIOGRAPHICAL/CRITICAL SOURCES: Edward Larocque Tinker, *The Horsemen of the Americas and the Literatures They Inspired*, Hastings, 1953; *Corral Dust*, July, 1960; *New York Times*, July 7, 1968.

(Died July 6, 1968)

* * *

TOD, Osma Gallinger 1898-
(Osma Palmer Couch, Osma Couch Gallinger)

PERSONAL: Born January 18, 1898; daughter of William Edward (a minister) and Alice (Hoyt) Palmer; married second husband, James Rowlands Tod (a marine surveyor) July 31, 1960; children: (previous marriage) Josephine Alice Couch (Mrs. Salvatore Del Deo). *Education:* Wellesley College, student, 1913-16; also studied at Juilliard School of Music, two years. *Politics:* Republican. *Religion:* Unitarian. *Home and office:* 319 Mendoza Ave., Coral Gables, Fla. 33134.

CAREER: Organized and conducted Craft Industries of Michigan (now Hartland Area Crafts), Hartland, Mich., 1933-44; organized and conducted Creative Crafts, East Berlin, Pa., 1944-60; now conducts private school of weaving, Coral Gables, Fla. Craft writer and lecturer. *Member:*

Wellesley College Alumnae Club (Coral Gables), Soroptimist Club.

WRITINGS—Under name Osma Palmer Couch: *Basket Pioneering*, Judd Publishing Co., 1933, revised edition published under name Osma Couch Gallinger, 1940, 3rd edition, 1947; *Embroidery in Wools*, Pitman, 1933, reissued under name Osma Gallinger Tod as *Wool Stitchery*, Gramercy Publishing Co., c.1970.

Under name Osma Couch Gallinger: *The Game of Weaving, with First Lessons in the Craft*, International Textbook Co., 1938; (with Oscar H. Benson) *Hand Weaving with Reeds and Fibers*, Pitman, 1948; *The Joy of Hand Weaving*, International Textbook Co., 1950, 2nd edition published under name Osma Gallinger Tod, Van Nostrand, 1964; (with daughter, Josephine Couch Del Deo) *Rug Weaving for Everyone*, Bruce, 1957.

Under name Osma Gallinger Tod: *Handweaving Hints for Everyone: A Collection of Short Cuts and Finishes for the Handweaver*, [Guernsey, Pa.] c.1964; *Manual of Helpful Hints for Handweavers*, [Coral Gables], c.1969.

Contributor of more than three hundred articles to *McCall's*, *Better Homes and Gardens*, *Woman's Home Companion*, *National Decorative Trade Journal*, *Country Gentleman*, *Woman's Day*, *New York Herald Tribune*, *Detroit News*, and other periodicals and newspapers. Editor and publisher, *Shuttle Service*, thirty-one years.

AVOCATIONAL INTERESTS: Music.

* * *

TODD, Herbert Eatton 1908-

PERSONAL: Born February 22, 1908, in London, England; son of Henry Graves (a headmaster) and Minnie Elizabeth Todd; married Bertha Joyce Hughes (died, 1968); children: Jonathan (died, 1964), Mark, Stephen, *Education:* Christ's Hospital, Horsham, England, student, 1919-25. *Politics:* Conservative. *Religion:* Church of England. *Home:* St. Nicholas, 2 Brownlow Rd., Berkhamsted, Hertfordshire, England. *Agent:* Winant Towers Ltd., 1 Furnival St., London E.C.4, England.

CAREER: Houlder Brothers Ltd., London, England, shipping clerk, 1925-27; British Foreign and Colonial Corp., London, England, investment clerk, 1927-29; Bourne & Hollingsworth Ltd., London, England, hosiery underbuyer, 1929-31; F. G. Wigley & Co. Ltd., London, England, traveler, later director, 1931—. Children's Book Week storyteller in libraries and schools, 1953—; broadcaster of "Bobby Brewster" stories on radio and television; broadcaster of children's musical programs; performer in local operatic productions, 1945-62. *Military service:* Royal Air Force, 1940-45; became squadron leader. *Member:* Berkhamsted Amateur Operatic and Dramatic Society (choir master, 1948-52; chairman, 1956-60; president, 1961—).

WRITINGS—"Bobby Brewster" series; all published by Brockhampton Press, except as indicated: *Bobby Brewster and the Winkers Club*, Edmund Ward, 1949; *Bobby Brewster*, 1954; *Bobby Brewster–Bus Conductor*, 1955; *Bobby Brewster's Shadow*, 1956; *Bobby Brewster's Bicycle*, 1957; *Bobby Brewster's Camera*, 1959; *Bobby Brewster's Wallpaper*, 1961; *Bobby Brewster's Conker*, 1963; *Bobby Brewster, Detective*, 1964; *Bobby Brewster's Potato*, Brockhampton Press, 1964; *Bobby Brewster and the Ghost*, 1966; *Bobby Brewster's Kite*, 1967; *Bobby Brewster's Scarecrow*, 1968; *Bobby Brewster's Torch*, 1969; *Bobby Brewster's Balloon Race*, 1970; *Bobby Brewster's Typewriter*, 1971.

Musical works: (With Capel Annand) *Blackbird Pie* (play for children), Boosey & Hawkes, 1956; five adult musical revues and ten children's musical programs produced by British Broadcasting Corp., 1949-57.

WORK IN PROGRESS: A story for *Bad Boy's Book*, edited by Ellen Colwell; *Bobby Brewster's Bee*.

* * *

TOMASIC, D(inko) A(nthony) 1902-

PERSONAL: Born April 23, 1902, in Yugoslavia; son of Francis (a teacher) and Veronica (Cvjetisa) Tomasic; married Carol Greening, September 22, 1957; children: Veronika, Francis, Anthony. *Education:* University of Zagreb, D.J., 1927; postdoctoral study at University of Paris, 1929-30, and at Columbia University, University of Chicago, and University of California, 1932-35. *Home:* 2101 Covenanter Dr., Bloomington, Ind. 47401. *Office:* Indiana University, Bloomington, Ind.

CAREER: University of Zagreb, Faculty of Law, Zagreb, Yugoslavia, 1935-40, began as docent, became professor of sociology; Washington University, St. Louis, Mo., visiting professor, 1941; Lawrence College, Appleton, Wis., associate professor, 1942-43; Indiana University, Bloomington, associate professor, 1943-55, professor of area studies, 1955-56, professor of political science, 1956-72, professor emeritus, 1972—. Chief of research and analysis, Institute of Foreign Trade, Belgrade, Yugoslavia, 1930-32. Member of council of Institute of Economics, Zagreb, Yugoslavia, 1939-40. Diplomatic aide in Montreal and New York for Yugoslav Government in Exile, 1941-43. Consultant to U.S. State Department, 1943-45. Project officer, U.S. Air Force, Air University, 1950-52. Chief of research, Radio Free Europe, Munich, 1957-58. *Member:* American Sociological Association, American Association for Advancement of Slavic Studies, American Association of University Professors, Society for European Culture (Venice, Italy), Croatian Historical Academy (Rome), Croatian-American Academy. *Awards, honors:* Prize for best essay on political history of Croatia, Association of Croatian Writers; Hoover Senior Fellowship in Slavic Studies, Stanford University, 1947-49.

WRITINGS: Zakoni Porasta Stanovnistva, Geca Kon (Belgrade), 1929; *Pobacaj sa Gledista Sociologije*, Obnova (Zagreb), 1930; *Drustveni Razvitak Hrvata* (title means "Social Development of the Croatian People"), Hrvatska Naklada (Zagreb), 1937; *Politicki Razvitak Hrvata* (title means "Political Development of the Croatian People"), Hrvatska Naklada, 1938; *Svjetski Mir na Novim Drustenim Osnovama* (title means "World Peace Based on New Social Foundations"), Selijacka Sloga (Zagreb), 1940; *Personality and Culture in Eastern European Politics*, George Stewart, 1948; *The Impact of Russian Culture on Soviet Communism*, Free Press of Glencoe, 1953; *Some Problem Areas in Communist Society*, Institute of Eastern European Studies, Indiana University, 1954; *National Communism and Soviet Strategy*, Public Affairs, 1957; *The Communist Leadership and Nationalism in Czechoslovakia*, Institute of Ethnic Studies (Washington, D.C.), 1960; *The Problem of Unity of World Communism*, Slavic Institute, Marquette University, 1962. Contributor to *Encyclopedia Americana* and *Slavonic Encyclopedia*; also contributor of more than sixty articles to professional journals, including *Canadian Slavic Studies*, *Slavic Review*, *Journal of Human Relations*, and *American Journal of Sociology*. Member of editorial board, *Croatian Encyclopedia*, 1939-40, and *Slavonic Encyclopedia*.

WORK IN PROGRESS: A book, *Cultural Sources of Maoism*.

SIDELIGHTS: Tomasic told *CA*: "In studying a society, I view it as a totality of inter-relationships of cultural, economic, and political developments. My purpose is to understand such a society in its totality and on that basis to identify the basis of its future development." Tomasic was active in the Croatian peasant movement, 1935-40, and blacklisted by the Nazis, 1940. He engaged in anti-Nazi and pro-Allied activities among Yugoslav immigrants in the United States, 1940-45. Tomasic is competent in Serbo-Croatian, French, and Italian.

* * *

TOMASSON, Katherine 1895-

PERSONAL: Born December 21, 1895, in Nottingham, England; daughter of William Hugh (chief constable of Nottinghamshire) and Eliza (Lees) Tomasson. *Education:* Privately educated. *Politics:* Conservative. *Religion:* Church of England.

CAREER: County Police Headquarters, Nottingham, England, secretarial work, 1917-18; Broxtowe Division of Nottinghamshire, England, Women's Conservative Association, honorary divisional secretary, 1924-25, Conservative agent, 1939-45. Volunteer worker in general and bye-elections, in England and Scotland. Charted Battlefield of Culloden for National Trust for Scotland, 1959. *Member:* Forty-Five Association (former member of council).

WRITINGS: The Jacobite General (biography of Lord George Murray) Blackwood, 1958; (with Francis Buist) *The Battles of the '45*, Macmillan, 1962; *The Bonnie Hoose*, privately printed, 1963. Contributor of articles and reviews to *Chamber's Magazine*, and to local papers and historical journals. Writer of series of historical articles, "Byegone Broxtowe," 1938-39.

WORK IN PROGRESS: Prince Charlie's Dukes, a book on the lives of his generals, the Dukes of Atholl and Perth; *'Forty-Five Stories*, a collection of hitherto little-known stories of the Rising; a novel.

AVOCATIONAL INTERESTS: Sports, the theatre, films, Gilbert and Sullivan, Highland concerts and pipe music, drawing, painting, reading history, biographies, historical novels, and topographical books, travel.

* * *

TORRES-RIOSECO, Arturo 1897-1971

PERSONAL: Born October 18, 1897, in Talca, Chile; came to United States, 1918; son of Domingo and Juana (Rioseco) Torres; married Rosalie Godt, June 19, 1949. *Education:* University of Chile, B.A., 1916; University of Minnesota, M.A., 1924, Ph.D., 1931. *Home:* 106 Forest Lane, Berkeley, Calif. 94708. *Office:* Spanish Department, University of California, Berkeley, Calif. 94720.

CAREER: Newspaperman in New York, N.Y., 1918-19; Williams College, Williamstown, Mass., instructor in Spanish, 1920-21; University of Minnesota, Minneapolis, instructor in Romance languages, 1921-24; University of Texas, Austin, associate professor of Latin American literature, 1925-28; University of California, Berkeley, 1928-69, chairman of Spanish department, 1956-61, 1964-65. Rockefeller scholar in Latin America, 1943. Special adviser to U.S. Department of State at United Nations session, San Francisco, Calif., 1945. *Member:* American Association of Teachers of Spanish, Instituto Internacional, Profesores

Literatura Iberoamericana, Hispanic Society of America, Mexican Academy of Letters, Academy of Panama, Phi Beta Kappa. *Awards, honors:* Cross of Vasco Nunez de Balboa (Panama), 1946.

WRITINGS: Latin American Secondary Schools (monograph), Pan American Union, 1920; *Walt Whitman*, Garcia Monge, 1922; *Precursores del modernismo*, Talleres Calpe, 1925, 2nd edition published as *Precursores del modernismo: Estudios criticos y antologia*, Las Americas, 1963; *Jose Ingenieros*, University of Texas Press, 1926; *Essentials of Spanish*, Doubleday, 1927, Texas editon, 1932, new Texas edition, 1936; *Poemas ineditos de Fr. Manuel de Navarrete*, Bibliofilos Mexicanos, 1929.

Ruben Dario: Casticismo y americanismo, Harvard University Press, 1931; *Ausencia* (poems), Imprenta Universitaria (Santiago), 1932; *La Poesia lirica mexicana*, Imprenta Universitaria (Santiago), 1933; *El Libro de buen humor*, Henry Holt, 1933; *Bibliografia de la novela mexicana*, Harvard University Press, 1933; (with Ralph E. Warner) *Bibliografia de la poesia mexicana*, Harvard University Press, 1934; *Mar sin tiempo* (poems), Fabula, 1935; (with Raul Silva-Castro) *Ensayo de bibliografia de la literatura chilena*, Harvard University Press, 1935; *La Moderna poesia mexicana*, Imprenta Universitaria (Santiago), 1936; *Luis Cane*, privately printed, 1936; (with Edwin Seth Morby) *Cartilla mexicana*, Crofts, 1938; *La Novela en la America hispana*, University of California Press, 1939; *Novelistas contemporaneos de America*, Nascimento, 1939.

Grandes novelistas de la America hispana, two volumes, University of California Press, Volume 1, 1941, Volume 2, 1943, 2nd edition of both volumes, 1949; *The Epic of Latin American Literature*, Oxford University Press, 1942, 3rd edition, 1956; (with Edwin Bray Place) *Contemporary Spanish Grammar*, Oxford University Press, 1943; (with Luis Monguio) *Lector hispanoamericano*, Heath, 1944; *Vida y poesia de Ruben Dario*, Emece, 1944; *Expressao literaria do Novo Mundo*, Casa do Estudante, 1945; *Veintidos poemas*, Revista Ibero Americana, 1945; *La Gran literatura iberoamericana*, Emece, 1945, 3rd edition published as *Nueva historia de la gran literatura iberoamericana*, 1960, 6th edition, 1967, published in America as *Historia de la literatura iberoamericana*, Las Americas, 1965; *Vida, pasion y muerte de Ruben Dario*, Emece, 1945; *Poesias*, introduction by Gabriela Mistral, O Globo, 1945; (translator) Walt Whitman, *La Ultima vez que florecieron las lilas en el patio*, [Mexico], 1946; *California Adventure*, California Book Club, 1947; *Elegias* (poems), [Mexico], 1947; *New World Literature: Tradition and Revolt in Latin America*, University of California Press, 1949; *The Family in Latin America*, Harper, 1949.

El Frijolito salton, Heath, 1953; *Ensayos sobre literatura latinoamericana*, University of California Press, first series, 1953, second series, 1958; *Contemporary English, French, and Spanish Literatures*, California Book Club, 1954; *Pajaro herido* (poem), Philobiblion, 1955; *Cautiverio* (poetry anthology), Ediciones de Andrea, 1955; *Breve historia de la literatura chilena*, Ediciones de Andrea, 1956; *Relatos chilenos*, Harper, 1956; *Madurez de la muerte* (poem), Castalia, 1959.

Aventura mexicana, Harper, 1960; *Autobiografia* (poem), Papeles de Son Armadans, 1962; *Gabriela Mistral: Una Profunda amistad, un dulce recuerdo*, Castalia, 1962; *Aspects of Spanish American Literature*, University of Washington Press, 1963; *Panorama de la literatura iberoameri-

cana*, Zig-Zag, 1964; *La Hebra en la aguja*, Cultura, 1965; *Antologia general*, Fondo de Cultura Economica, 1969.

Editor: *En el encantamiento* (poems), Garcia Monge, 1921; (and author of introduction) *Chilean Short Stories*, Prentice-Hall, 1929; (and author of introduction and notes with Nila Flaten) Manuel Linares Rivas, *Camino adelante* (two-act comedy), Macmillan, 1930; *Antologia de la literatura hispanoamericana*, Crofts, 1930, 2nd edition, 1941; (and author of introduction and notes) *Mexican Short Stories*, Prentice-Hall, 1932; (with Albert R. Lopez) Ricardo Becerro de Bengoa, *El Recien nacido*, Oxford University Press, 1937; *Canto a Espana viva* (poems), M.N. Lira, 1941; Estanislao del Campo, *Fausto*, Harper, 1947; *Antologia de poetas precursores del modernismo*, Pan American Union, 1949; *Antologia poetica*, University of California Press, 1949; *La Novela iberoamericana*, University of New Mexico Press, 1952; *Llama de amor viva*, Revista Ibero Americana, 1955; (with Juan B. Rael) *Antolgia escolar de la poesia mexicana*, privately printed, 1960; *Short Stories of Latin America*, translated by Zoila Nelken and Rosalie Torres-Rioseco, Las Americas, 1963. Contributor of nearly one thousand articles to American, Latin American, and European journals. Former editor of *Revista Iberoamericana; co-editor of* Revista Hispanica Moderna.

(Died November 4, 1971)

*   *   *

TOURS, Hugh Berthold 1910-

PERSONAL: Born July 16, 1910, in London, England; son of Henry John (a stockbroker) and Louisa Canning (Davies) Tours; married second wife, Mary Adelina Broackes, March 20, 1948; children: (first marriage) Caroline Gay (Mrs. Jeremy King). *Education:* Aldenham School, student, 1924-28. *Religion:* Church of England. *Home:* 15 Cresswell Pl., London S.W. 10, England.

CAREER: Bank of England, London, 1928-69, began as probationary clerk, became deputy superintendent, archives section. *Military service:* Royal Naval Volunteer Reserve, 1941-46; became lieutenant. *Member:* Modern Society of Model Engineers.

WRITINGS: Parry Thomas, Designer-Driver, Batsford, 1959; *The Life and Letters of Emma Hamilton*, Gollanez, 1963, Hillary, 1965. Contributor to *Old Lady* (Bank of England quarterly magazine), *Autocar*, and *Profile*.

*   *   *

TOWLE, Joseph W(alter) 1909-

PERSONAL: Born December 13, 1909, in Potosi, Mo.; son of Joseph Walter (a merchant) and Frances (Sloane) Towle; married Patience Ellwood, June 16, 1934; children: Rolfe (Mrs. Richard King Teague), J. Ellwood, Amy Hopkins. *Education:* Lehigh University, A.B., 1932; Northwestern University, M.B.A., 1938, Ph.D., 1948. *Politics:* Liberal Republican. *Religion:* Christian Scientist. *Home:* Route 3, Chesterfield, Mo. *Office:* School of Business, Washington University, St. Louis, Mo.

CAREER: Began career with Montgomery Ward & Co. in Kansas City, Mo., and in Chicago, Ill., 1933-41; Bodine Electric Co., Chicago, personnel manager, 1942-45; Booz, Allen & Hamilton (management consultants), Chicago, part-time staff member, 1945-46; Northwestern University, Evanston, Ill., 1946-54, became associate professor of management; Washington University, St. Louis, Mo., professor of management, 1954—, acting dean, 1967-68. Participant in management development and business education programs in Chile, South Korea, England, other countries in Europe; editorial adviser in management field for Houghton Mifflin Co. *Member:* American Economic Association, American Management Association, American Society of Training Directors, Academy of Management (fellow; president, 1960), Society for Advancement of Management (fellow; president of Chicago chapter, 1953-54).

WRITINGS: (With W. R. Spriegel) *Retail Personnel Management*, McGraw, 1951; (editor and contributor) *Ethics and Standards in American Business*, Houghton, 1964; (with S. H. Schoen and R. Hilgert) *Problems and Policies in Personnel Management: A Casebook*, Houghton, 1965, revised edition, 1972.

AVOCATIONAL INTERESTS: Farming, sports, travel.

* * *

TOWNER, Donald C. 1903-

PERSONAL: Born March 2, 1903, in Eastbourne, England; son of William Albert (a schoolmaster) and Grace (Bernard) Towner. *Education:* Royal College of Art, A.R.C.A. *Home:* 8 Church Row, Hampstead, London N.W. 3, England.

CAREER: Artist, doing mostly landscapes, but also portraits, and church and flower paintings, many purchased for municipal galleries in England. *Member:* English Ceramic Circle (honorary secretary, 1949-68).

WRITINGS: Handbook of Leeds Pottery, Leeds Corp., 1951; *English Cream-coloured Earthenware*, Faber, 1957; *The Leeds Pottery*, Cory, Adams & Mackay, 1963; (with others) *World Ceramics*, edited by Robert J. Charleston, McGraw, 1968. Contributor to art periodicals, including *Apollo*, *Connoisseur*, *Cahiers de la Ceramique*, and *Transactions of the English Ceramic Circle*. Honorary editor, *Transactions of the English Ceramic Circle*, 1959—.

WORK IN PROGRESS: A book, *English Creamware*.

BIOGRAPHICAL/CRITICAL SOURCES: "Donald Towner, a Painter of London," *Studio*, July, 1935.

* * *

TOYE, John Francis 1883-1964

PERSONAL: Born January 27, 1883, in Winchester, England; son of Arlingham James and Alice Fayres (Coates) Toye; married Anna Huston Miller, April 27, 1914. *Education:* Attended Winchester College and Trinity College, Cambridge. *Home:* 36 Via de Bardi, Florence, Italy.

WRITINGS: (With Xavier Marcel Boulestin) *The Swing of the Pendulum*, Eveleigh Nash, 1911; *Diana and Two Symphonies*, Heinemann, 1913; *The Well-Tempered Musician: A Musical Point of View*, preface by Hugh Walpole, Methuen, 1925, Knopf, 1926; *Guiseppe Verdi: His Life and Works*, Knopf, 1931; *Rossini: A Study in Tragi-Comedy*, Knopf, 1934, new edition, 1947; (contributor) A. L. Bacharach, *The Musical Companion*, Gollancz, 1940; *The King's, and Other English* (lecture), Rodriquez & Cia (Rio de Janeiro), 1944; *For What We Have Received: An Autobiography*, Knopf, 1948; *Italian Opera*, Parrish, 1952; *Truly Thankful?: A Sequel to an Autobiography*, Arthur Barker, 1957.

(Died October 13, 1964)

TRAUGER, Wilmer K(ohl) 1898-

PERSONAL: Born September 12, 1898, in Revere, Pa.; son of Milton D. and Annie E. (Kohl) Trauger; married Carrie Leonora Strock (an art teacher), June 27, 1930; children: Roberta S. (Mrs. Richard Blackmer). *Education:* Keystone State Normal School (now Kutztown State College), student, 1915-17; Gettysburg College, A.B., 1922, A.M., 1923; Harvard University, A.M., 1926, Ph.D., 1940. *Politics:* Republican. *Religion:* Protestant. *Home:* 9 Broad St., Potsdam, N.Y. 13676.

CAREER: State University of New York, Potsdam, 1927—, now chairman of English department. *Military service:* U.S. Army, 1918. *Member:* National Council of Teachers of English, National Education Association, Phi Beta Kappa, Kappa Phi Kappa.

WRITINGS: Language Arts in Elementary schools, McGraw, 1963. Contributor to professional journals and general periodicals.

WORK IN PROGRESS: A textbook on writing, for college freshmen.†

* * *

TRAVERS, Louise Allderdice 1891-

PERSONAL: Born September 20, 1891, in Pittsburgh, Pa.; daughter of Taylor (a steel manufacturer) and Ellen Forde (Hansell) Allderdice; married Edward S. Travers (a clergyman), 1913 (died, 1942); married Kenneth T. Barnaby, 1959 (died, 1962); children: Jane (Mrs. Burrows Sloan), Eleanor (Mrs. John W. Mettler), Edward S., Jr. *Education:* Miss Masters School, Dobbs Ferry, N.Y., student, 1905-07. *Politics:* Republican. *Religion:* Episcopal. *Home:* 1201 Brookwood Dr., Tallahassee, Fla. 32303.

CAREER: Travelers' Aid, New York, N.Y., supervisor of volunteers at Grand Central Station and Pennsylvania Station during World War II; Joe McDougalls (Scottish imports), traveling saleswoman, eight years; originator of shell decoupage (sea shells as flowers in shadow boxes); lecturer to garden clubs on sea shells. *Member:* American Malacological Union, New York Shell Club, Pittsburgh Junior League (charter member), Rhinebeck Garden Club, Millbrook Garden Club.

WRITINGS: The Romance of Shells, in Nature and Art, Barrows, 1962.

WORK IN PROGRESS: Research and writing on sea shells.

* * *

TRENEER, Anne 1891-

PERSONAL: Born January 30, 1891, in Gorran, Cornwall, England; daughter of Joseph (a schoolmaster) and Susan (Nott) Treneer. *Education:* Exeter University College, B.A., 1918, M.A., 1922; Lady Margaret Hall, Oxford, B.Litt., 1932. *Agent:* A. P. Watt & Son, Hastings House, Norfolk St., London W.C. 2, England.

CAREER: Camborne Grammar School, Cornwall, England, English mistress, 1918-29; King Edward's High School, Birmingham, England, English mistress, 1932-48. *Member:* P.E.N. (London), Society of Authors.

WRITINGS: The Sea in English Literature from Beowulf to Donne, University Press of Liverpool, 1926; *Charles M. Doughty: A Study of His Prose and Verse*, J. Cape, 1935; *This World's Bliss* (verse), privately printed, 1942; *Schoolhouse in the Wind* (autobiography), J. Cape, 1944, 3rd edition, 1953; *Cornish Years* (autobiography), J. Cape, 1949; *Happy Button, and Other Stories*, Westaway Books, 1950; *A Stranger in the Midlands* (autobiography), J. Cape, 1952; *The Mercurial Chemist: A Life of Sir Humphry Davy*, Methuen, 1963. Contributor to *Penguin New Writing*, 1950.

WORK IN PROGRESS: Invitation to Bermuda: an enlarged edition of *This World's Bliss*.†

* * *

TRENT, Robbie 1894-

PERSONAL: Born February 15, 1894, in Wolf Creek, Meade County, Ky.; daughter of Robert Ross (a farmer) and Sarah Ruth (Parr) Trent. *Education:* Studied at University of Louisville, University of Wisconsin, and George Peabody College for Teachers. *Politics:* Mostly Democratic. *Religion:* Baptist. *Home and office:* 2313 Golf Club Lane, Nashville, Tenn. 37215.

CAREER: Baptist Sunday School Board, Nashville, Tenn., children's editor, 1929-59. National Council of Churches, member of lessons committees and Children's Division. *Member:* League of American Pen Women (former president). *Awards, honors:* Litt.D., Georgetown College, Georgetown, Ky.

WRITINGS: Your Child and God, Willett, Clark, 1941, revised edition, Harper, 1952; *A Book about Me*, Broadman, 1942; *Susan*, Viking, 1944; *The Faith We Share*, Broadman, 1947; *Bible Stories*, Whitman, 1947; *The First Christmas*, Harper, 1948; *A Star Shone*, Westminster, 1948; *To Church We Go*, Wilcox & Follett, 1948; *In the Beginning*, Westminster, 1949; *Stories of Jesus*, Whitman, 1950; *Always There Is God*, Abingdon, 1950; *A Year of Junior Programs*, Broadman, 1950; *They Saw Jesus*, Broadman, 1952; *What Is God Like?* (poems), Harper, 1953; *A Boy's Friend*, Whitman, 1953; *I Can Tell God Things*, Broadman, 1954; *Daily Discoveries*, Harper, 1955; *The Little Old Lady*, Broadman, 1958; *Jesus' First Trip*, Broadman, 1961; *The Boy's Lunch*, Abingdon, 1964; (with Howard P. Colson) *Basic Christian Beliefs* (adult textbook), Sunday School Board of Southern Baptist Convention, 1964; *How the Bible Came to Us*, Broadman, 1964; *The Life of Jesus*, Broadman, student's book, 1964, teacher's book, 1965; *Cubby's World: Story of a Baby Bear*, Abingdon, 1966.

Also author of *The Basket Boat*, published by Whitman; editor or co-editor of numerous religious textbooks and teacher's guides, all published by Sunday School Board of Southern Baptist Convention, 1960-62.

SIDELIGHTS: Miss Trent's books have been reprinted in England, and translated into Chinese, Korean, and Danish.

* * *

TREVASKIS, John 1911-1968

PERSONAL: Born February 11, 1911, in West Bromwich, England; son of John B. T. and Annie (Whitmore) Trevaskis; married Enid Lewis, December 16, 1939; children: Gillian Nan, Linden Dorice. *Education:* St. Catherine's College, Oxford, M.A., 1933. *Home:* 62 High View, Pinner, Middlesex, England. *Office:* Evans Brothers Ltd., Montague House, Russell Sq., London W.C.1, England.

CAREER: Schoolmaster, 1933-45; W. & R. Chambers Ltd. (publishers), Edinburgh, Scotland, an editor, 1945-46; Evans Brothers Ltd. (publishers), London, England, an editor, 1946-68. *Military service:* British Army, Royal Artillery, 1940-45; became major.

WRITINGS—All published by Evans Brothers, unless otherwise indicated: *Junior English*, two books, W. & R. Chambers, 1947; *Exercise in Punctuation*, 1950; (with Alexander M. MacDonald) *Step by Step Arithmetics*, Gilmour & Dean, 1952; (with Emlyn Davies) *Visual English, Secondary Series*, four books, 1954, *Junior Series*, four books, 1957; (with Davies) *Visual English Practice*, four books, 1960; (with Patrick Pringle) *Pictorial and Practical English*, four books, 1963; *Exercises in Using Your Dictionary*, 1964; (with Robin Hyman) *Boy's and Girls' First Dictionary*, 1967; (with Hyman) *Visual Words*, 1967; (with Hyman) *Words for Spelling*, 1967; (with Hyman) *Working with Words*, 1967. Contributor of articles to *Schoolmaster* and *Teacher's World*, 1935-39.

(Died December, 1968)

* * *

TREVELYAN, Katharine 1908-
(Katharine Goetsch-Trevelyan)

PERSONAL: Born May 7, 1908, in Westminster, London, England; daughter of Sir Charles Philips (a privy councillor) and Mary Katharine (Bell) Trevelyan; married Georg Goetsch, March 29, 1932 (deceased); children: Erika Karla (Mrs. Robin Lees), Elisabeth (Mrs. Steven Greenfield), Katharine Mary (Mrs. Jeremy Chapple). *Education:* Studied privately at home, and at Sidcot School, Somerset, England; attended Somerville College, Oxford, 1929, and Girton College, Cambridge, 1930-31. *Politics:* Liberal with leftish tendencies. *Religion:* Church of England. *Home:* Godshill, Fordingbridge, Hampshire, England. *Agent:* Christy & Moore Ltd., 52 Floral St., Covent Garden, London W.C.2, England.

MEMBER: Anthroposophical Society of Great Britain, Institute for Comparative Studies of History, Philosophy, and the Sciences.

WRITINGS: (Under name Katharine Goetsch-Trevelyan) *Unharboured Heaths*, Selwyn & Blount, 1934; *Fool in Love*, Gollancz, 1962, published in America as *Through Mine Own Eyes: The Autobiography of a Natural Mystic*, Holt, 1963. Adapter of the story, "Little Ida's Flowers," published in *Hans Andersen Fairy Tales*, Collins, 1944. Contributor of stories and articles to British Broadcasting Corp. Home Service.

SIDELIGHTS: Mrs. Trevelyan lists her interest as "world religions," and adds: "I live alone in a small hut in New Forest, Hampshire. I am interested in the possibilities of communication of human and Divine in prayer, meditation, etc."

* * *

TRIVAS, A(lexander) Victor 1894-1968

PERSONAL: Born July 9, 1894, in St. Petersburg (now Leningrad), Russia; came to United States in late 30's; son of Alexander (a musician) and Marie (Haskel) Trivas; married Mary Schneerson, March 20, 1919; children: Irene. *Education:* Academy of Fine Arts, St. Petersburg, Russia, graduated as architect, 1917. *Home:* 315 East 72nd St., New York, N.Y.

CAREER: Originally an artist and art director for films in Russia; free-lance film writer and director. *Awards, honors:* Academy Award (Oscar) nomination for "The Stranger."

WRITINGS: (With Charles O'Neal) *The Thirty-Second Day*, Doubleday, 1964.

Author of screenplays, occasionally with others, including: "Niemandsland" (title means "No Man's Land"); "Song of the Street"; "The Mayor's Dilemma"; "Where the Sidewalk Ends"; "The Secret of Convict Lake"; "The Head"; "Song of Russia"; "The Stranger."

SIDELIGHTS: Trivas fled Russia to Germany where he wrote the screenplay for "Niemandsland," a film later destroyed by the Hitler regime. He later fled to France, and thence to the United States.

(Died April 12, 1968)

* * *

TRONCHIN-JAMES, (Robert) Nevil   1916-

PERSONAL: Born September 17, 1916, in London, England; son of W. Warwick (a surgeon) and Mary (Froude) James; married second wife, Jill (Caroline) Tinsley, June 27, 1961; children: (first marriage) Geoffrey, Christopher, Nevil; (second marriage) Michele. *Education:* Attended Marlborough College; Middlesex Hospital, University of London, L.R.C.P., M.R.C.S.; other study at Universities of London and Munich. *Religion:* Protestant. *Address:* c/o Lloyds Bank Lt., 222 Strand, London W.C.2, England. *Agent:* A. P. Watt & Son, 10 Norfolk St., London W.C.2, England.

CAREER: Institute of Living, Hartford, Conn., psychiatrist, 1947; International Refugee Organization, U.S. Zone of Austria, senior medical officer, 1948-50; independent consultant on organization, structure, and communications in England, 1950—. Chairman, Planned Instruction Ltd. (non-profit organization in field of programmed learning and teaching machines), London, England. Lecturer in industrial administration, University of Manchester, 1961—. *Military service:* Royal Air Force, 1939-46; neuropsychiatrist, 1942-46; became squadron leader. *Member:* Royal Society of Medicine (fellow), Institute of Directors (fellow), Reform Club, Savile Club (all London).

WRITINGS: Master of Others, Cassell, 1961; *Arbitrary Retirement*, Cassell, 1962; *Ministry of Procreation*, R. Hale, 1968. Contributor to *British Medical Journal, Manager, Journal of British Psychological Society, Guardian*, and other journals.

WORK IN PROGRESS: A book tentatively titled *Me and the Code*, on the social significance of the difference between the civil and common law; a television series, "Social Changes with Ageing."

* * *

TROUP, Cornelius V.   1902-

PERSONAL: Born February 7, 1902, in Brunswick, Ga.; son of Washington Davis (a barber) and Sarah Virginia (Whitsey) Troup; married Katye Celeste Murphy, June 20, 1931; children: Cornelius, Jr., Kenneth, Elliott. *Education:* Morris Brown College, A.B., 1925; Atlanta University, M.A., 1937; Ohio State University, Ph.D., 1947. *Religion:* Baptist. *Home:* 167 Howard St. N.E., Atlanta, Ga. 30317.

CAREER: Morris Brown College, Atlanta, Ga., head of commercial department and accountant, 1925-27; Risley High School, Brunswick, Ga., principal, 1928-39; Fort Valley State College, Fort Valley, Ga., professor of education, registrar, 1939-45, president, 1945-66; Coppin State College, Baltimore, Md., director of talent research project, 1966-67; National Urban League, counselor, Southern Regional Office, 1967—. Frontiers International, chapter president, 1962-63. *Member:* National Education Associa-

tion (life member), Alpha Kappa Mu, Phi Delta Kappa, Phi Beta Sigma (former national vice-president), Masons. *Awards, honors:* LL.D., Wilberforce University, 1949, Morris Brown College, 1959, Atlanta University, 1965.

WRITINGS: Distinguished Negro Georgians, Royal, 1962. Poems anthologized in *Ebony Rhythm*, edited by Beatrice M. Murphy, Exposition, 1948, and in *Negro Voices, Music Unheard*, and *Badge of Honor*. Contributor to educational journals. Editor of *Crescent* (publication of Phi Beta Sigma).†

* * *

TRUEBLOOD, Paul Graham   1905-

PERSONAL: Born October 21, 1905, in Macksburg, Iowa; son of Charles Elmer and Adele (Graham) Trueblood; married Helen Churchill, August 19, 1931; children: Anne Brodzky, Susan (Mrs. Larry A. Stuart). *Education:* Willamette University, A.B., 1928; Duke University, A.M., 1930, Ph.D., 1935. *Politics:* Independent. *Religion:* Quaker and Methodist. *Home and office:* 2635 Bolton Ter. South, Salem, Ore. 97302. *Agent:* Timothy Seldes, 551 Fifth Ave., New York, N.Y. 10017.

CAREER: Friends University, Wichita, Kan., instructor, 1931-34; Mohonk School for Boys, Lake Mohonk, N.Y., head of English studies, 1935-37; University of Idaho, Moscow, instructor in English, 1937-40; Stockton College and College of the Pacific, Stockton, Calif., associate professor of English, 1940-46; University of Washington, Seattle, assistant professor of English, 1947-52; University of Oregon, Eugene, visiting professor of English, 1954-55; Willamette University, Salem, Ore., professor of English, and chairman of department, 1955-70, professor emeritus, 1971—. Byron consultant, University of Chicago Press, 1950-51; visiting lecturer, University of British Columbia, 1963. Participant in First International Byron Seminar, Cambridge University, 1974. *Member:* Modern Language Association of America, Keats-Shelley Association of America, Byron Society (founding member of American committee), American Association of University Professors, Philological Association of the Pacific Coast (member of executive committee, 1964). *Awards, honors:* Pendle Hillfellow, 1934-35; American Council of Learned Societies scholar, 1952-53.

WRITINGS: The Flowering of Byron's Genius: Studies in Byron's Don Juan, Stanford University Press, 1945, revised edition, Russell, 1962; *Lord Byron*, Twayne, 1969. Contributor to *Saturday Review, Keats-Shelley Journal, Byron Journal*, and other periodicals.

WORK IN PROGRESS: Byron: Romantic Realist, a book on Byron's political influence in early nineteenth-century Europe, completion expected in 1976; a travel book on literary and historical scenes and sites in Europe.

SIDELIGHTS: Trueblood spent sabbatical year, 1964-65, following Byron's trail from England to Greece; traveled and wrote in Europe (chiefly Greece), 1971-72. *Avocational interests:* Vocal and piano music, swimming, mountain climbing, dramatics.

* * *

TRUMPER, Hubert Bagster   1902-
(Hubert Bagster)

PERSONAL: Born December 27, 1902, in Market Rasen, Lincolnshire, England; son of Oscar Bagster and Annie (Smith) Trumper; married Frances Greener, February 12,

1929; children: Gillian Trumper Wilson, Michael Bagster, Fanny Lou Trumper Copping. *Education:* Queens' College, Cambridge, B.A., 1923, B.Chir., 1926, M.A. and M.B., 1929. *Religion:* Church of England. *Home:* Upper Dulas, Cusop, Hay-on-Wye, Herefordshire, England. *Office:* Compton House, Hay-on-Wye, Herefordshire, England.

CAREER: General Hospital, Birmingham, England, successively house surgeon, house physician, resident anaesthetist, 1926-28; Canadian Pacific Line, ship's surgeon, 1928; practiced medicine in Birmingham, 1928-30; Imperial Chemical Industries, labor manager of Medical Office, 1930-39, personnel manager, 1946-49; general practice of medicine, Hay-on-Wye, England, 1949—. *Military service:* Royal Army Medical Corps, 1939-46; became lieutenant colonel. *Member:* British Medical Association (chairman, Herefordshire branch, 1963-64), Royal Society of Medicine.

WRITINGS—Under pseudonym Hubert Bagster: *Country Practice*, Deutsch, 1957, published in America as *Gallstones and Ghosts*, Simon & Schuster, 1958; *Doctor's Weekend*, Simon & Schuster, 1960.

WORK IN PROGRESS: A book on the Armstrong Case of 1921, to be published by Harrap; a novel; a book similar to *Doctor's Weekend*.

AVOCATIONAL INTERESTS: Reading, fishing, shooting, criminology, witchcraft, and travel.

* * *

TRYON, W(arren) S(tenson) 1901-

PERSONAL: Born October 15, 1901, in Middletown, Conn.; son of Charles Warren and Lucy (Stenson) Tryon; married Rachel Keller, September 1, 1925; children: Jeremy Warren, Jonathan Stedman. *Education:* Dartmouth College, A.B., 1923; Harvard University, A.M., 1924, Ph.D., 1931; also attended Institut de Touraine, 1930. *Politics:* Democrat. *Religion:* Episcopalian. *Home:* 71 Granite St., Rockport, Mass. 01966; and Boqueron, Puerto Rico.

CAREER: Instructor in American history at University of Iowa, Iowa City, 1924-25, at Ohio State University, Columbus, 1925-26; Simmons College, Boston, Mass., assistant professor, 1927-32, associate professor of American history, 1932-47; Boston University, Boston, Mass., professor of American history, 1947-68. Visiting professor of history and chairman of the department, Universidad Interamericana de Puerto Rico, San German, 1969. Treasurer, Pigeon Hill Quarry Associates, Rockport, Mass., 1945-56. *Member:* American Academy of Arts and Sciences (fellow), American Historical Association, Organization of American Historians, New England Pan American Society, New York Historical Society. *Awards, honors:* Guggenheim fellow in history, 1946-47; Shell Oil Co. award for best faculty publication at Boston University, 1963, for *Parnassus Corner, the Life of James T. Fields.*

WRITINGS: (Editor and author of introduction and notes with William Charvat) *The Cost Books of Ticknor & Fields, and Their Predecessors, 1832-1858*, Bibliographical Society of America, 1949; (editor) *A Mirror for Americans: Life and Manners in the United States, 1790-1870, as Recorded by American Travelers*, University of Chicago Press, Volume I: *Life in the East*, 1952, Volume II: *Cotton Kingdom*, 1952, Volume III: *Frontier Moves West*, 1952; (editor) *My Native Land* (abridged edition of *A Mirror for Americans: Life and Manners in the United States, 1790-*

1870, as Recorded by American Travelers), University of Chicago Press, 1961; *Parnassus Corners: A Life of James T. Fields, Publisher to the Victorians*, Houghton, 1963. Also author of "The Old Corner," *Boston Globe*, 1964. Contributor of articles to *American Literature*, and to regional historical journals, and book reviews to magazines and newspapers.

WORK IN PROGRESS: A book about American expatriates in Paris from 1776 to 1930.

SIDELIGHTS: For thirty years Tryon has collected first editions of major New England writers and has seen this collection installed in the restored Old Corner Bookstore in Boston, now declared a national shrine. He has studied and traveled extensively in western Europe, Central America, and the West Indies. *Avocational interests:* Examining Mayan ruins in Yucatan and Guatemala.

* * *

TULCHIN, Lewis 1905-1971

PERSONAL: Born September 4, 1905, in Russia; son of Hyman (owner of retail store) and Esther (Lubin) Tulchin; married Ruth Hallen (a receptionist), May 2, 1952; children: Robert Seymore. *Education:* Studied in New York, N.Y., at Music Settlement and Cooper Union; New York University, Certificate in Education, 1965. *Residence:* Jackson Heights, N.Y. *Office:* New York Institute of Photography, New York, N.Y.

CAREER: Formerly theatrical and fashion photographer; New York Institute of Photography, New York, N.Y., lecturer, 1953-71. *Military service:* U.S. Army, Signal Corps, 1941. *Awards, honors:* Two first prizes and two second prizes, Guild of Professional Photographers, 1947-50.

WRITINGS: The Nude in Photography, Ziff-Davis Publishing, 1949; *Photographing the Nude*, A. S. Barnes, 1962; *Lighting in Portraiture*, Greystone Press, 1963; *The Photography of Women*, A. S. Barnes, 1964; *Creative Figure Photography*, A. S. Barnes, 1967. Contributor to photography magazines, 1941-52.

(Died, 1971)

* * *

TUNICK, Stanley B(loch) 1900-

PERSONAL: Born March 6, 1900, in New York, N.Y.; son of Abraham (an insurance man) and Mary (Bloch) Tunick; married Mildred P. Superior, June 26, 1942; children: Andrew Jeffrey, Richard David. *Education:* City College (now City College of the City University of New York), A.B., 1919, M.B.A., 1923; St. Lawrence University, LL.B., 1928 (converted to J.D.); New York University, Ph.D., 1938. *Home:* 300 Seminole Ave., Palm Beach, Fla. 33480; and 252 DeMott Ave., Rockville Centre, N.Y. 11570. *Office:* Tunick & Platkin, 2 Park Ave., New York, N.Y. 10016.

CAREER: Certified public accountant, states of New York, New Jersey, Pennsylvania, and Florida; admitted to New York bar, 1929, tax court, 1934, Federal bar, 1945. Accountant and auditor, mainly for motion picture industry, 1920-26; on staffs of certified public accountants, 1926-28; private practice as certified public accountant, beginning, 1928, as partner of Tunick & Platkin, New York, N.Y., 1941—; practicing attorney, 1929—. Bernard M. Baruch School of Business and Public Administration of the City College (now Bernard M. Baruch College of the

City University of New York), member of faculty, 1931-62, began as instructor, professor of accounting, 1951-62, chairman of department, 1956-62, professor emeritus, 1962—. Officer of New York firms, including treasurer, Thirty Third Equities, 1948—, vice-president, Kamber Management, 1957—, treasurer-secretary, Abstan Realty Corp., 1963—. New York State Board of CPA Examiners, member, 1962-70, secretary, 1964-65, vice-chairman, 1965-67, chairman, 1967-69. City College of the City University of New York, Trustee of Students Aid Association, 1955—, and director of City College Fund, 1967—. Trustee of Camp Loyaltown, 1966—; treasurer of Wallace S. Whittaker Foundation, 1962—. *Military service:* U.S. Army, 1918. U.S. Army, 1942-46; became lieutenant colonel; received Commendation Medal; U.S. Army Reserve, 1946-56.

MEMBER: American Institute of Certified Public Accountants, American Accounting Association, National Panel of Arbitrators, American Arbitration Association, Accountants Club of America, New York State Society of Certified Public Accountants (director, 1948-51; treasurer, 1951-53; vice-president, 1955-56), Phi Beta Kappa, Beta Alpha Psi, Beta Gamma Sigma, Phi Delta Kappa, Delta Pi Epsilon, Iota Theta, Town Club, Lancers Club (treasurer, 1966—), 100 Club (president, 1971-72). *Awards, honors:* Alumni Service Medal, City College, 1940; annual award of New York State Society of Certified Public Accountants, 1965; Townsend Harris Medal, City College Alumni, 1966; 125th Anniversary Medal, City College of the City University of New York, 1973.

WRITINGS: (With Emanuel Saxe) *Fundamental Accounting—Theory and Practice*, Prentice-Hall, 1950, 3rd edition, 1963; *The Key Facts of Basic Accounting*, Books I-III, Data Guide, 1961-65. Contributing editor, "New York Tax Course," Prentice-Hall, 1939-62; consulting editor, "Federal Tax Course," Prentice-Hall, 1955-65.

AVOCATIONAL INTERESTS: Amateur magician; stamp and coin collector; painting.

* * *

TUNNER, William H. 1906-

PERSONAL: Born July 14, 1906, in Elizabeth, N.J.; son of Joseph and Fanny (Schantz) Tunner; married Sarah Margaret Sams (deceased); married second wife, Ann Hamilton, June 18, 1951; children: (first marriage) William Sams; (second marriage) H. Suzanne. *Education:* U.S. Military Academy, B.S., 1928. *Home:* Hockley Farm, Ware Neck, Va. *Agent:* Bill Berger Associates, Inc., 535 East 72nd St., New York, N.Y. 10021.

CAREER: Commissioned second lieutenant, U.S. Army, 1928, retired as lieutenant general, U.S. Air Force, 1960. Commanding general of Air Transport Command, Ferrying, 1942-44, India-China Division, 1944-45, commander of Combined Airlift Task Force, Berlin, 1948-49, and of Combat Cargo Command, Korean Airlift, 1950; deputy commander of Air Material Command, 1951-53; commander-in-chief of U.S. Air Force, Europe, 1953-57; deputy chief of staff, Operations, U.S. Air Force Headquarters, 1957-58; commander of Military Air Transport Service, 1958-60. Director, Seaboard-World Airlines; consultant, Douglas Aircraft. *Awards, honors*—Military: Distinguished Service Cross, Distinguished Service Medal (four times), Companion of the Bath (England), Grand Knight of Merit (Italy), and other foreign decorations.

WRITINGS: Over the Hump, Meredith, 1964.

AVOCATIONAL INTERESTS: Farming and gardening.

* * *

TURK, Frances (Mary) 1915-

PERSONAL: Born April 14, 1915, in Huntingdon, England; daughter of Francis Leonard (an accountant) and Elizabeth (Dalton) Turk. *Education:* Attended school in Huntingdon, England. *Religion:* Church of England. *Home:* Hillrise, Buckden, Huntingdon, England.

CAREER: Secretarial work in Huntingdon, England, 1931-35, in Godmanchester, England, 1936-40; Women's Land Army, Huntingdon, assistant county secretary, 1940-48; Women's Voluntary Services, Huntingdon, county secretary, 1950-61. Member, Huntingdon County Library Committee, 1950—. *Member:* Romantic Novelists Association (founder member), National Book League, Huntingdon Federation of Women's Institutes (member of executive committee, 1949—; vice-chairman, 1963-68; president, 1968-71), Huntingdon Music and Arts Society (vice-chairman, 1956—), Buckden Women's Institut (*former president*).

WRITINGS—All published by Wright & Brown, except as indicated: *Paddy O'Shea*, 1937; *Doctor Periwinkle*, 1937; *The Song of the Nightingale*, 1938; *The Precious Hours*, 1938; *The Rector, Bless Him*, 1938; *Paradise Street*, 1939; *Green Garnet*, 1940; *Lovable Clown*, 1941; *Dear Professor*, 1941; *Angel Hill*, 1942; *Candle Corner*, 1943; *Wideawake*, 1943; *The Five Grey Geese*, 1944; *The House of Heron*, 1945; *Ancestors*, 1947; *Jerninghams*, 1948; *Three Bags Full*, 1949; *Salutation*, 1949.

Time and Tranquillity, 1950; *The Small House at Ickley*, 1951; *The Gentle Flowers*, 1952; *The Lovely Things*, 1952; *The Laughing Fox*, 1953; *The Heart of a Rose*, 1954; *The Dark Wood*, 1954; *The Glory and the Dream*, 1955; *The Fruit of the Vine*, 1955; *Dinny Lightfoot*, 1956; *The Jagged Edge*, 1956; *No Through Road*, 1957; *A Vain Shadow*, 1957; *The House in Orange Street*, 1958; *The White Swan*, 1958; *The Land of Beulah*, 1959; *The Temple of Fancy*, 1959.

Journey to Eternity, 1960; *A Time to Know*, 1960; *A Man Called Jeremy*, 1961; *The Golden Leaves*, 1961; *The Secret Places* (Foyle's Romantic Book Club choice), 1962; *The Living Fountains*, 1962; *A Lamp from Murano*, 1963; *The Mistress of Medlam*, 1963; *A Flush of Scarlet*, 1963; *A Visit to Marchmont*, 1964; *The Guarded Heart*, 1964; *The Summer Term*, 1965; *The Sour-Sweet Days*, 1965; *Goddess of Threads*, 1966; *The Rectory at Hay*, 1966; *Lionel's Story*, 1966; *Legacy of Love*, 1967; *The Flowering Field*, 1967; *The Martin Widow*, 1968; *The Lesley Affair*, 1968; *Fair Recompense*, 1969.

For Pity, for Anger, R. Hale, 1970; *The Absent Young Man*, R. Hale, 1971; *Whispers*, R. Hale, 1972.

Contributor of children's short stories to *Family Herald*, poems and short stories to *Land Girl, Huntingdonian, Woman's Way*, and *Peterborough Evening Telegraph*, and articles to *Cambridgeshire, Huntingdon and Peterborough Life*. County press correspondent, *Home and Country*, 1955-66.

AVOCATIONAL INTERESTS: Painting in oil and water colors, and drawing in ink (painted county page in book presented to Queen Elizabeth at the time of her marriage), handicrafts, gardening, reading, and local history.

TURNER, Clair (Elsmere) 1890-

PERSONAL: Born April 28, 1890, in Harmony, Me.; son of Fred Orrison (a physician) and Mary Frances (Chalmers) Turner; married Naomi E. Cocke, December 24, 1924; children: Mary Frances Turner Bonk, Frederick Clair. *Education:* Bates College, A.B., 1912; Harvard University, M.A., 1913, M.P.H., 1948; Massachusetts Institute of Technology, Dr.P.H., 1928; Boston University, Ed.M., 1944. *Home:* 19 Village Lane, Arlington, Mass. 02174.

CAREER: Bates College, Lewiston, Me., instructor in biology, 1913-14; Massachusetts Institute of Technology, Cambridge, 1914-44, began as instructor, became professor of public health and head of department, 1943-44; Institute of Inter-American Affairs, Washington, D.C., chief health education officer, 1944-45; University of California, Berkeley, professor of health education, 1945-46; National Foundation for Infantile Paralysis, New York, N.Y., assistant to president, 1946-58; World Health Organization, Geneva, Switzerland, chief of health education, 1962-64. Lecturer at universities and colleges in United States and abroad. Consultant to Metropolitan Life Insurance Co., 1924-62, Eastman Teaching Films, 1928-33, Chinese Ministry of Health and Education, 1936, government of Iran, 1948-49, to UNESCO, 1962-65, and to school systems in four states. Technical adviser in health education, League of Red Cross Societies, 1958-62. Trustee, Bates College, 1922—. *Military service:* U.S. Public Health Service, sanitary engineer, 1917-19, became first lieutenant; U.S. Army, Sanitary Corps Reserve, 1924-34; became major.

MEMBER: International Union for Health Education (first president, 1951-56; honorary president, 1969—), World Federation of Education Association (chairman of health section, 1927-40), American Public Health Association (fellow; member of governing council, 1928-30, 1942; member of executive board, 1928-29, 1933-35), American School Health Association (fellow; president, 1942-43), Society of Public Health Educators (first president, 1950-51), American Medical Association (associate fellow), American Academy of Arts and Sciences (fellow), American Academy of Physical Education (fellow), American Association for Health, Physical Education and Recreation (fellow), Philippine Public Health Association (honorary), New England Health Education Association (honorary president, 1924—). *Awards, honors:* Sc.D., Bates College, 1927; Howe Award, American School Health Association, 1949; Medal of City of Paris, 1953; Prentiss Award, 1953; gold medal, National Academy of Medicine (France), 1958; Grand Cross of Order of Merit (German Federal Republic), 1959; Lemuel Shattuck Award, 1969.

WRITINGS: (With William Rice) *Hygiene, Dental and General,* Mosby, 1920; (with J. W. M. Bunker) *Personal Hygiene for Nurses,* Mosby, 1924; *Personal and Community Health,* Mosby, 1925, 14th edition, 1971; (with Grace T. Hallock) *Louis Pasteur,* Heath, 1928; (with Hallock) *Edward Jenner,* Heath, 1928; (with Hallock) *Edward Livingstone Trudeau,* Heath, 1929; *Principles of Health Education,* Heath, 1932, 2nd edition, 1939; (with Ellen L. Lytle) *The Nature of Bacteria: A Description of Units of Work,* Metropolitan Life Insurance Co. Press, c.1932; *Personal Hygiene,* Mosby, 1937; (with others) *Community Organization for Health Education,* American Public Health Association, 1941; (with Elizabeth McHose) *Effective Living,* Mosby, 1941, 3rd edition, Prentice-Hall, 1950; *School Health and Health Education,* Mosby, 1947, 2nd

edition (with C. Morley Sellery and Sara Louise Smith), 1957, 6th edition, 1970; *Community Health Educator's Compendium of Knowledge,* Mosby, 1951; (with Hallock) *Florence Nightingale and the Founding of Professional Nursing,* Metropolitan Life Insurance Co., c.1959; *Planning for Health Education in Schools,* UNESCO (Paris), 1962; *Test Manual to Accompany the Twelfth Edition of "Personal and Community Health,"* Mosby, 1963.

"Malden Health" series, juveniles, published by Heath: (With Georgie B. Collins) *Health,* 1924, 3rd edition, 1937; (with Collins) *Cleanliness and Health,* 1926, 3rd edition, 1937; (with Collins) *Community Health,* 1928, revised edition, 1935; (with Hallock) *The Voyage of Growing Up,* 1928, revised edition, 1935; *Physiology and Health,* 1929, revised edition, 1935; (with Jeanie M. Pinckney) *In Training for Health,* 1929, revised edition, 1935; (with Collins and Nell Josephine Morgan) *Home Nursing and Child Care,* 1930, revised edition, 1939; (with Morgan and Alice Beckwith) *The Jay Family,* Heath, 1936.

"Health, Safety, Growth" series, published by Heath: (With C. E. Burton) *Building Healthy Bodies,* 1941; (with Juanita McD. Melchior and Grace Voris Curl) *Cleanliness and Health Protection,* 1941; (with Melchior and Curl) *Gaining Health,* 1941; (with Hallock) *Growing Up,* 1941; (with Curl and Frances W. Clough) *Keeping Safe and Well,* 1941; (with Burton and Curl) *Working for Community Health,* 1941.

Author of scripts for ten Eastman teaching films. Contributor of more than 250 articles to professional journals.

SIDELIGHTS: Turner's books have been translated into Spanish, Chinese, Japanese, Italian, Thai, Nepalese, and Arabic. He has traveled in seventy-seven countries on five continents.

* * *

TURNER, Henry Ernest William 1907-

PERSONAL: Born January 14, 1907, in Sheffield, Yorkshire, England; son of Henry Frederick Richard (a commercial traveler) and Ethel (Hitchcock) Turner; married Constance Parker Haythornthwaite, July 11, 1936; children: Christopher Hugh, Mark Richard Haythornthwaite. *Education:* St. John's College, Oxford, B.A. (first class honors), 1929; Wycliffe Hall, B.A. (first class honors in theology), 1931, B.D., 1940, D.D., 1955. *Home:* 14, The College, Durham, England.

CAREER: Anglican minister. Lincoln College, Oxford University, Oxford, England, fellow, chaplain, and tutor, 1935-51; University of Durham, Durham, England, Lightfoot Professor of Divinity, 1951-58, Van Mildert Professor of Divinity, 1958—, head of department of theology, 1958—; Durham Cathedral, Durham, England, canon, 1951—. Bampton Lecturer, Oxford University, 1954.

WRITINGS: The Life and Person of Jesus Christ, S.P.C.K., 1951; *Why We Believe in Jesus Christ,* S.P.C.K., 1952; *The Patristic Doctrine of Redemption: A Study of the Development of the Doctrine During the First Five Centuries,* Mowbray, 1952; *Jesus, Master and Lord: A Study in the Historical Truth of the Gospels,* Mowbray, 1953, 2nd edition, 1957; *The Pattern of Christian Truth: A Study in the Relations Between Orthodoxy and Heresy in the Early Church,* Mowbray, 1954; *Why Bishops? Their Origin, Functions, and Traditions,* Church Information Board, 1955; *The Meaning of the Cross,* Morehouse-Gorham Co., 1959; (with Hugh Montefiore) *Thomas and the Evangelists*, Allenson, 1962; *Historicity and the Gospels: A Sketch of Historical Method and Its Application to the Gospels*, Mowbray, 1963; (author of introduction) *The Articles of the Church*, Mowbray, 1964. Contributor to theology journals.

WORK IN PROGRESS: Gospel Criticism and Patristic Theology.

* * *

TURNER, Sheila 1906-

PERSONAL: Born July 15, 1906, in Eastbourne, Sussex, England; daughter of Charles McLellan (a publisher) and Nora (Bayford-Holmes) Turner; married George Adams Tilney (a retired naval officer), August 8, 1962; children: Susannah Storm-Turner. *Education:* Attended Malvern Girls' College and Oxford University. *Politics:* Conservative. *Religion:* Church of England. *Home:* Symonds Farm House, Childrey, Wantage, Berkshire, England. *Office:* Turner & Price Ltd., Childrey, Wantage, Berkshire, England.

CAREER: Dairy cattle farmer in Somersetshire, Sussex, and Berkshire, England; Turner & Price Ltd. (mail order firm specializing in luxury foodstuffs, tea, and coffee), Wantage, Berkshire, England, managing director, beginning, 1932. Driver in London for Mechanized Transport Corps, World War II.

WRITINGS: Over the Counter: A Year in the Village Shop, Macdonald & Co., 1960, Holt, 1963; *This is Private*, Macdonald & Co., 1962; *A Farmer's Wife*, Macdonald & Co., 1963, published as *Farmer Takes a Wife*, Holt, 1964; *The Farm at King's Standing*, Macdonald & Co., 1964, published as *A Little Place Called King's Landings: A Novel*, Holt, 1965; *Honestly the Country!*, Macdonald & Co., 1965. Contributor to *Punch*; stories broadcast by British Broadcasting Corp. and in Finland.

* * *

TURTON-JONES, Edith Constance (Bradshaw) 1904-1968
(Susan Gillespie)

PERSONAL: Born September 27, 1904; married John Wyntoun Turton-Jones (a group captain, Royal Air Force, now retired). *Education:* Educated at home by governess, and at private schools in England, Australia, France. *Politics:* Conservative. *Religion:* Church of England. *Home:* Alburgh House, Alburgh, Harleston, Norfolk, England. *Agent:* A. P. Watt & Son, Hastings House, Norfolk St., Strand, London, W.C.2, England.

CAREER: Author. *Member:* National Book League (London).

WRITINGS—All under pseudonym Susan Gillespie; all published by Bles, unless otherwise indicated: *The Story of Christine*, Loval Dickson, 1933; *The Rajah's Guests*, 1935; *Cantonment*, 1936; *Government House*, 1937; *Take My Youth*, 1938; *The Man He Was*, 1939; *They Went to Karathia*, 1940; *The Promotion of Fools*, 1942; *North From Bombay*, 1944; *Himalayan View*, 1947.

Clash by Night, Hutchinson, 1950; *Carillon in Bruges*, Hutchinson, 1952; *Janet Firbright*, Hutchinson, 1953; *The Dutch House*, 1955; *The Martyr*, 1956; *The Grandson*, 1957; *The Victors*, 1959; *The Day the Soldier Died*, 1960; *The Neighbour*, 1961; *Diamonds in the Night*, 1962; *The Young Green Blade*, 1963; *The Frozen Lake*, 1964; *A Summer at Home*, 1965; *A Matter of Conscience*, 1966; *Mother's Day*, 1967; *Women of Influence*, 1968.

Contributor of short stories to *New Yorker*, *Argosy* (England), and *Punch*, and to London editions of *Vogue* and *Good Housekeeping*.

BIOGRAPHICAL/CRITICAL SOURCES: Good Housekeeping (London), November, 1940; *Books and Bookmen*, February, 1969.

(Died March, 1968)

* * *

TUSHNET, Leonard 1908-1973

PERSONAL: Born November 26, 1908, in Newark, N.J.; son of Samuel (a hatter) and Lena (Schoenbrunn) Tushnet; married Fannie Brandchaft (a psychiatric social worker), July 2, 1939; children: Judith Tushnet Broder, Naida Tushnet Bagenstos, Mark V. *Education:* New York University, B.S., 1928, M.D., 1932. *Home:* 572 Prospect St., Maplewood, N.J. *Office:* 662 18th Ave., Irvington, N.J.

CAREER: Physician in general practice, Irvington, N.J., 1932-66. *Military service:* U.S. Army, Medical Corps, World War II; became first lieutenant. *Member:* Academy of Medicine of New Jersey, Essex County Medical Society.

WRITINGS: To Die with Honor, Citadel, 1965; *The Uses of Adversity*, Yoseloff, 1965; *The Medicine Men*, Paperback Library, 1972; *The Pavement of Hell*, St. Martin, 1973. Work included in *Best American Short Stories of 71*, edited by Martha Foley, Houghton, 1971. Contributor of articles to *Eucharist*, *Chicago Jewish Forum*, and *Journal of History of Medicine*; also contributor of short stories to periodicals, including *New Mexico Quarterly*, *Mosaic*, *Forum*, and *Fantasy and Science Fiction*.

WORK IN PROGRESS: Two novels, *The Elevator* and *The Little Black Bag*.

AVOCATIONAL INTERESTS: Various facets of Jewish life, particularly in America.

(Died November 28, 1973)

* * *

TUVE, Rosemond 1903-1964

PERSONAL: Born November 27, 1903, in Canton, S.D., daughter of Anthony G. (president of Augustana College, then located in Canton, S.D.) and Ida (a music instructor at Augustana College; maiden name, Larsen) Tuve. *Education:* University of Minnesota, B.A., 1924; Johns Hopkins University, graduate study, 1926-28; Somerville College, Oxford University, graduate study, 1928-29; Bryn Mawr College, M.A., 1925, Ph.D., 1931. *Politics:* Democrat. *Home:* Bettws-Y-Coed, Yarrow and Marion Aves., Bryn Mawr, Pa. *Office:* English Department, University of Pennsylvania, Philadelphia, Pa.

CAREER: Member of faculty of Goucher College, Baltimore, Md., 1926-28, Vassar College, Poughkeepsie, N.Y., 1929-32; Connecticut College, New London, professor of English, 1934-62; University of Pennsylvania, Philadelphia, professor of English, 1963-64. Instructor at Bryn Mawr School for Women Workers in Industry, three summers; visiting lecturer in English at University of Minnesota, 1952, at Harvard University, 1956-57; NATO visiting professor of English at Aarhus University, Denmark, 1960; visiting professor at Princeton University, 1961. On leave for work abroad, 1932-34, 1948-49; Fulbright senior research fellow at Oxford University, 1957-58.

MEMBER: American Academy of Arts and Sciences (fellow), Mediaeval Academy, American Association of University Professors, International Association of University Professors of English, English Institute, Modern Language Association of America (member of executive council), Renaissance Society of America, International Federation of University Women, Phi Beta Kappa. *Awards, honors:* Litt.D. from Augustana College, 1952, Wheaton College, 1957, Mount Holyoke College, 1959, Carleton College, 1961; Dr. Hum. Litt. from Syracuse University, 1962; Rosemary Crawshaw Prize for English Literature of British Academy for *Elizabethan and Metaphysical Imagery*, 1949; Achievement Award of American Association of University Women, 1955; American Council of Learned Societies award, 1960.

WRITINGS: Seasons and Months: Studies in a Tradition of Middle English Poetry, Librairie Universitaire (Paris), 1933, Folcroft Library Editions, 1971; (author of introduction) Marcellus Palingenius, *The Zodiake of Life,* [New York], 1947; *Elizabethan and Metaphysical Imagery: Renaissance Poetic and Twentieth-Century Critics,* University of Chicago Press, 1947; *A Reading of George Herbert,* University of Chicago, 1952; *Images and Themes in Five Poems by Milton,* Harvard University Press, 1957; *Allegorical Imagery: Some Mediaeval Books and Their Posterity,* Princeton University Press, 1966; *Essays by Rosemond Tuve: Spenser, Herbert, Milton,* edited by Thomas P. Roche, Jr., Princeton University Press, 1970. Contributor of articles to learned journals.

BIOGRAPHICAL/CRITICAL SOURCES: D. Bethurum, ''Vignette,'' *PMLA,* June, 1960; *New York Times,* December 22, 1964; *Yale Review,* spring, 1967; *Comparative Literature,* winter, 1967; *New York Review of Books,* June 6, 1968.

(Died December, 1964)

*   *   *

TYLECOTE, Mabel (Phythian) 1896-

PERSONAL: Born February 4, 1896, in Manchester, England; daughter of John Ernest (a lecturer and author) and Ada P. (Crompton) Phythian; married Frank Edward Tylecote (a professor emeritus of medicine), February 6, 1932 (died, 1967); children: John Phythian; (stepchildren) Ronald Frank, Doreen Marjorie Tylecote Simes. *Education:* University of Manchester, B.A., 1919, Ph.D., 1930; University of Wisconsin, graduate student, 1919-20. *Politics:* Labour. *Home:* 1 Rusholme Gardens, Wilmslow Road, Manchester M14 5LG, England.

CAREER: Huddersfield Technical College, Huddersfield, Yorkshire, England, lecturer in history, 1920-24; University of Manchester, Manchester, England, assistant lecturer in history, 1926-30; Elvington Settlement, Kent, England, warden, 1930-32. Lecturer, Workers' Educational Association, 1920-51; part-time lecturer, University of Manchester Joint Committee for Adult Education, 1935-51. Parliamentary candidate, 1938, 1945, 1950, 1951, 1955. Member of Manchester City Council, 1940-51, co-opted member of education committee, beginning 1951; member of Stockport Borough Council, 1956-63. University of Manchester, court member, beginning 1945, council member, beginning 1960, court member of Institute of Science and Technology, beginning 1960.

MEMBER: National Federation of Community Associations (president, 1958-61; vice-president, beginning 1961), Workers' Educational Association (vice-president, 1960-68), Association of Art Institutions (chairman, 1960-61),

National Institute of Adult Education (chairman of executive committee, 1961-64), Manchester and Salford Council of Social Service (vice-president, beginning 1968), Union of Lancashire and Cheshire Institutes (vice-president, beginning 1969).

WRITINGS: The Education of Women at Manchester University, 1883-1933, Manchester University Press, 1941; *The Mechanics Institutes of Lancashire and Yorkshire before 1851,* Manchester University Press, 1957; *The Future of Adult Education,* Fabian Society, 1960. Contributor to social and educational journals.

WORK IN PROGRESS: Editing grandparents' love letters, illustrating life in Lancastershire and Yorkshire in the 1840's.

*   *   *

TYLER, John Ecclesfield (?)-1966

PERSONAL: Born in England; son of Thomas W. (a manufacturer) and Florence M. F. (Allen) Tyler; married Mary Winder, January, 1933; children: Anne F., Ruth C., Maud A. *Education:* St. John's College, Oxford, M.A., 1922. *Home:* Wickham Green, Sandygate, Sheffield 10, Yorkshire, England.

WRITINGS: The Alpine Passes: The Middle Ages, 962-1250, Basil Blackwell, 1930; *The Struggle for Imperial Unity, 1868-1895,* Longman's, Green, 1938; *The British Army and the Continent, 1904-1914,* Edward Arnold, 1938; *A Short History of America,* W. & R. Chambers, 1940; *Anglo-American Relations* (pamphlet), Historical Association (London), 1942; *Great Britain, the United States and the Future,* Stevens & Sons, 1947. Contributor of articles and reviews to British and American historical periodicals.

WORK IN PROGRESS: A book on British military and strategic policy, 1919-39; a history of Swiss Alpine passes; a book on the American Revolution.

AVOCATIONAL INTERESTS: Golf and Alpine travel.

(Died May 17, 1966)

*   *   *

UGARTE, Francisco 1910-1969

PERSONAL: Born February 19, 1910, in Hellin, Spain; son of Javier (a mining engineer) and Micaela (Cristobal) Ugarte; married Mercedes Precioso, September 27, 1935; children: George, Michael. *Education:* Instituto del Cardenal Cisneros, Bachiller, 1929; University of Madrid, Doctor in Law, 1939. *Religion:* Catholic. *Home:* 2 Dana Rd., Hanover, N.H. 03755. *Office:* Dartmouth College, Hanover, N.H. 03755.

CAREER: American Embassy, Madrid, Spain, custodian, 1936-39, member of staff, Office of War Information, 1940-46; Dartmouth College, Hanover, N.H., instructor, 1946-49, assistant professor, 1949-53, professor of Spanish, 1953-69. Visiting professor, Colby-Swarthmore School of Languages, summers, 1948-51, Western Reserve University, 1955. Carnegie fellow in humanities and Spanish, University of Chicago, 1951-52. *Member:* Modern Language Association of America, American Association of Teachers of Spanish and Portuguese, American Association of University Professors. *Awards, honors:* M.A., Dartmouth College, 1953.

WRITINGS: (Translator into Spanish) Carlton J. H. Hayes, *A Generation of Materialism,* Espasa-Calpe (Madrid), 1944-45; (with Foster E. Guyer) *Platicas y temas:*

Sobre la America Espanola, Heath, 1952; *Espana y su civilizacion,* Odyssey, 1952, 2nd edition, 1965; (editor) Jose Ruiz Martinez, *Dos Comedias de Azorin,* Houghton, 1952; *Beginning Spanish,* Odyssey, 1955; *Gramatica Espanola de repaso,* Odyssey, 1958, 2nd edition, 1969; *Panorama de la civilizacion Espanola,* Odyssey, 1963; *Elementary Spanish: A Conversational Approach,* Odyssey, 1967.

*   *   *

UPHAUS, Willard Edwin 1890-

PERSONAL: Born November 27, 1890, in Ridgeville, Ind.; son of Samuel (a farmer) and Mary (Kayser) Uphaus; married Ola Hawkins Dudley. *Education:* Earlham College, student, 1913-14; Indiana University, A.B., 1917; Yale University, A.M., 1922, Ph.D., 1925. *Politics:* "Progressive, not affiliated with any party." *Religion:* Methodist. *Home:* 66 Edgewood Ave., New Haven, Conn. 06511.

CAREER: National Religion and Labor Foundation, New Haven, Conn., executive secretary, 1934-51; World Fellowship, Inc., New Haven, Conn., and Conway, N.H., executive director. Was a central figure in a civil liberty case that eventually reached the U.S. Supreme Court, as the result of his conviction for contempt of court in connection with the membership roster of World Fellowship Center in New Hampshire; spent 1960 in a New Hampshire county jail. Sponsor of American Institute for Marxist Studies; co-chairman of Citizens Committee for Constitutional Liberties. *Member:* Society for Religion in Higher Education, Fellowship of Reconciliation, World Council of Peace, Methodist Federation for Social Action, Phi Delta Kappa.

WRITINGS: (With Hugh Hartshorne and Helen R. Stearns) *Standards and Trends in Religious Education,* Yale University Press, 1933; *Commitment* (autobiography), McGraw, 1963.

BIOGRAPHICAL SOURCES: Willard Uphaus, *Commitment,* McGraw, 1963.

*   *   *

UPJOHN, Everard M(iller) 1903-

PERSONAL: Born November 7, 1903, in Scranton, Pa.; son of Hobart Brown (an architect) and Margaret (Miller) Upjohn; married Florence Davol, June 14, 1927; children: Richard Vassall, Amy Putnam. *Education:* Harvard University, A.B., 1925, M. Arch., 1929. *Religion:* Episcopalian. *Home:* 47-06 U Meadow Lakes, Hightstown, N.J. 08520.

CAREER: University of Minnesota, Minneapolis, assistant professor of fine arts and founder of department, 1929-35; Columbia University, New York, N.Y., associate, 1935-37, assistant professor, 1937-41, associate professor, 1941-51, professor of art history, 1951-70, professor emeritus, 1970—. Matthews Lecturer, Metropolitan Museum of Art, 1941-42, 1959. *Military service:* U.S. Naval Reserve, 1943-46; became lieutenant commander.

WRITINGS: Richard Upjohn, Architect and Churchman, Columbia University Press, 1939; (with P. S. Wingert and J. G. Mahler) *History of World Art,* Oxford University Press, 1949, revised edition, 1958; (with John P. Sedgwick) *Highlights,* Holt, 1963. Contributor of articles on history of art and architecture to professional journals and encyclopedias. Editorial adviser for art and architecture, *Grolier Encyclopedia,* 1958, *Richards Topical Encyclopedia,* 1959.

URE, Peter 1919-1969

PERSONAL: Born July 12, 1919, in Birkenhead, England; son of James Matthew (a headmaster) and Elsie Mai (Overton) Ure. *Education:* Birkenhead School, student, 1928-36; University of Liverpool, B.A., 1940, M.A., 1944. *Office:* The University, Newcastle upon Tyne 1, England.

CAREER: University of Newcastle upon Tyne, Newcastle upon Tyne, England, lecturer in English language and literature, 1947-58, senior lecturer, 1958-60, Joseph Cowen Professor of English Language and Literature, 1960-69. *Military service:* Conscientious Objector; served in Friends' Ambulance Unit, 1942-46; welfare officer in Greece, U.N. Relief and Rehabilitation Administration, 1946. *Member:* Newcastle Literary and Philosophical Society (vice-president, 1967-69).

WRITINGS: Towards a Mythology: Studies in the Poetry of W. B. Yeats, University Press of Liverpool, 1946, Russell, 1967; *William Shakespeare: The Problem Plays—Troilus and Cressida; All's Well That Ends Well; Measure for Measure; Timon of Athens,* published for the British Council by Longmans, Green, 1961, revised edition, 1964; *Shakespeare and the Inward Self of the Tragic Hero* (inaugural lecture), University of Durham, 1961; *Yeats the Playwright: A Commentary on Character and Design in the Major Plays,* Barnes & Noble, 1963; *Yeats,* Oliver & Boyd, 1963, published in America as *W. B. Yeats,* Grove, 1964; *Yeats and the Shakespearian Moment,* Queen's University Institute of Irish Studies, 1969.

Editor: *Seventeenth-Century Prose, 1620-1700,* Penguin, 1956; *New Arden Edition of Shakespeare's Richard II,* 4th edition, revised, Harvard University Press, 1956, 5th edition, 1961; John Eachard, *Mr. Hobbs's State of Nature Considered in a Dialogue Between Philautus and Timothy,* University Press of Liverpool, 1955; John Ford, *The Chronicle History of Perkin Warbeck: A Strange Truth,* Methuen, 1968; *Shakespeare: Julius Caesar: A Casebook* (critical essays), Macmillan, 1969, Aurora, 1970.

Contributor to *Stratford-upon-Avon Studies, Review of English Studies, Modern Language Review, Philological Quarterly,* and other journals.

WORK IN PROGRESS: Editing Shakespeare's *Two Noble Kinsmen.*†

(Died June 30, 1969)

*   *   *

URWICK, Lyndall Fownes 1891-

PERSONAL: Born March 3, 1891, in North Malvern, Worcestershire, England; son of Sir Henry and Annis (Whitby) Urwick; married Joan Wilhelmina Bedford, 1924; married Helen B. F. Warrand, 1941; children: Naomi June Urwick Biddlecombe, Alan Bedford, John Lyndall, Gillian Annis. *Education:* New College, Oxford, B.A., 1913, M.A., 1919. *Politics:* Liberal. *Religion:* Anglican. *Home:* 83 Kenneth St., Longueville, New South Wales, Australia. *Office:* Urwick, Orr & Partners Ltd., London S.W.1, England.

CAREER: In family business, Fownes Bros. & Co. (glove manufacturers), Worcester, England, 1913-14, 1918-20; Rowntree & Co. Ltd. (confectioners), York, England, 1922-28, became organizing secretary; International Management Institute, Geneva, Switzerland, director, 1928-33; Urwick, Orr & Partners Ltd. (management consultants), London, England, chairman, 1934-63, managing partner, 1945-51, life director, 1963—. Consultant in organization to

H.M. Treasury, 1940-42; chairman, Ministry of Education Committee on Education for Management, 1945-47; member, United Kingdom Advisory Committee on Education for Management, 1961. Visiting professor at University of Toronto, 1951, University of New South Wales, 1963; lecturer at University of California, 1953, 1959, University of Minnesota, 1955, for American Society of Mechanical Engineers, 1952, 1960. *Military service:* British Army, 1914-18; became major; mentioned in dispatches three times, awarded Order of British Empire and Military Cross. British Army, Petroleum Warfare Department, 1942-44; became lieutenant colonel.

MEMBER: British Institute of Management (founder member; fellow; vice-chairman of council, 1947-52; member of council, 1956-57), International Academy of Management (charter fellow; member of governing board), American Academy of Management (fellow, 1973—), American Management Association (life member), Royal Society of Arts (fellow), Institution of Mechanical Engineers (companion), Institution of Production Engineers, Royal Institute of Public Administration, Society for Advancement of Management (United States), Management Consultants Association (council member, 1957—), Institutional Management Association (president, 1956-59), European Federation of Management Consultants Association (president, 1960-61), British Association for Advancement of Science (life member), American Society of Mechanical Engineers (life member), Bombay Management Association (honorary fellow).

AWARDS, HONORS: Knight first class, Order of St. Olaf of Norway, 1948; Gold Medal of International Committee for Scientific Management, 1951; Wallace Clark International Management Gold Medal Award, 1955; Henry Laurance Gantt Gold Medal, 1961; Taylor Key, 1963.

WRITINGS: (With C. H. Northcott, Oliver Sheldon, and J. W. Wardropper) *Factory Organization*, Pitman, 1928; (with others) *Organizing a Sales Office*, Gollancz, 1928, 2nd edition, Pitman, 1937; *The Meaning of Rationalization*, Nisbet & Co., 1929; *Europe—U.S.A.: Distribution Problems*, U.S. Chamber of Commerce, 1931; *Management of Tomorrow*, Nisbet & Co., 1933.

(Editor with Henry C. Metcalf) *Dynamic Administration: The Collected Papers of Mary Parker Follett*, Pitman, 1941; *Business Administration* (lectures), Institute of Industrial Administration, 1945; (with E. F. L. Brech) *The Making of Scientific Management*, Pitman, Volume II, 1946, Volume III, 1948, Volume I, 1949; *The Elements of Administration*, 2nd edition, Pitman, 1947; (editor with Luther Gulick) *Papers on the Science of Administration*, 2nd edition, Institute of Public Administration, 1947; (editor and author of introduction) *Freedom and Co-ordination: Lectures in Business Organization by Mary Parker Follett*, Pitman, 1949; *The Need Is Urgent to Make Leadership a Reality* (lectures), University of Toronto Press, 1952; *Management Education in American Business*, American Management Association, 1954; (editor) *The Golden Book of Management*, Newman Neame, 1956; *The Pattern of Management*, University of Minnesota Press, 1956; *Leadership in the Twentieth Century*, Pitman, 1957.

Writer of other shorter studies published by British Institute of Management, American Management Association, Institute of Labour Management, and Institute of Personnel Management. Contributor to periodicals.

WORK IN PROGRESS: The Elements of Organization, and an autobiography.

SIDELIGHTS: Urwick speaks French; travels frequently in the United States and in many other countries between England and Australia.

* * *

USSHER, (Percival) Arland 1899-

PERSONAL: Born September 9, 1899, in London, England; son of Beverley and Emily (Jebb) Ussher; married Emily Whitehead, May, 1925; children: Henrietta Owen (Mrs. Gerald Arland Staples). *Education:* Educated at Trinity College, Dublin, and St. John's College, Cambridge. *Politics:* Liberal. *Religion:* Protestant. *Home:* 18 Green Rd., Blackrock, Dublin, Ireland.

CAREER: Author and critic, living in Waterford and Dublin, Ireland, and traveling abroad at some periods. *Member:* Irish Academy of Letters, Philosophical Society and Metaphysical Society (both Dublin).

WRITINGS: (Translator in verse from the Gaelic) *The Midnight Court*, preface by W. B. Yeats, J. Cape, 1926; *Cainnt an Tsean Shaoghail* ("Old World Speech"), Government Publications Office, 1942; *Postscript on Existentialism, and Other Essays*, Sandymount Press, 1946; *The Twilight of the Ideas, and Other Essays*, Sandymount Press, 1948; *Cursai an Tsean-Shaoghail* (title means "Life on a Farm in the Old World"), Government Publications Office, 1948; *The Face and Mind of Ireland*, Devin, Adair, 1950; *The Magic People*, Devin, Adair, 1952; *Three Great Irishmen*, Gollancz, 1952, Devin, Adair, 1953; *Alphabet of Aphorisms*, Dolmen Press, 1953; *Journey Through Dread*, Darwen Finlayson, 1955, Devin, Adair, 1956; (with Carl von Metzradt) *Enter These Enchanted Woods*, Dolmen Press, 1955; *The Thoughts of Wi Wong*, Dolmen Press, 1955; *The 22 Keys of the Tarot*, Dolmen Press, 1957; *Spanish Mercy*, Gollancz, 1960; *Sages and Schoolmen*, Dolmen Press, 1967. Contributor to *New English Weekly, Adelphi, Dublin Magazine*, and other periodicals.

WORK IN PROGRESS: A journal, *Letters to Myself.*

SIDELIGHTS: Ussher describes his writing as reflecting "different facets of a private philosophy—especially in relation to national characters, cultures, and languages."

* * *

VALE, (Henry) Edmund (Theodoric) 1888-1969
(John Bledlow)

PERSONAL: Born September 9, 1888, in Holywell, Flintshire, Wales; son of William Theodoric (a rector) and Catherine Emma (Buxton) Vale; married Ruth Madeline Hutchings (an artist), June 4, 1924; children: Robert Edmund, Richenda Mary Vale Acheson, Anna Mary Vale Devereux. *Education:* St. John's College, Cambridge, B.A., 1913, M.A., 1919. *Politics:* Conservative. *Religion:* Church of England. *Home:* Nant Ffrancon, near Bangor, North Wales.

CAREER: Author. *Military service:* Royal Corps of Signals, 1914-18; Royal Signals, 1939-45; became captain.

WRITINGS: *Echoes from the Northland*, Frank H. Morland, 1908; *Pixie Pool* (verse and stories), Heffer, 1911; *Elfin Chaunts and Railway-Rhythms* (verse), Mathews & Marrot, 1914; *By Shank and By Crank* (travel), W. Blackwood, 1924; *Porth Smuggler* (novel), Thomas Nelson, 1926; *The Track of the Irish Mail*, McCorquodale & Co., 1927; *The Track of the Royal Scot*, McCorquodale & Co., 1928; *The Track of the Twenty-fives, St. Pancras to Manchester*, McCorquodale & Co., 1928; *Along the Viking Border*, McCorquodale & Co., 1928.

Roc, a Dog's Eye View of War, Dutton, 1930; *Shipshape; or, Sea-legs without Tears,* Dutton, 1931, enlarged edition, Dent, 1934; *The Offing* (novel), Dent, 1932; *See for Yourself: A Field-book of Sight-Seeing,* Dent, 1933, revised edition, 1947; *Drake, a Game of the Sea,* Ross & Co., 1934; *Local Colour: A Landscape Analysis for Sightseers,* Dent, 1934; *The World of Wales,* Dent, 1935; *The Seas and Shores of England,* Scribner, 1936, 2nd edition, Batsford, 1950; *Northern England and the Lakes,* Scribner, 1937 (published in England as *North Country,* Batsford, 1937); *How to See England,* Methuen, 1937, Dutton, 1938; *The Way of Ships,* Scribner, 1938; *Straw into Gold: An Account of the Doings of a Worker in Ideas from the Armistice of '18 to the Crisis of '38* (autobiography), Methuen, 1939; *How to Look at Old Buildings,* Batsford, 1940; *Curiosities of Town and Countryside,* Batsford, 1940, Scribner, 1941; *Ancient England: A Review of Monuments and Remains in Public Care and Ownership,* Batsford, 1941; *Trust House Story,* Trust Houses, 1949, revised edition, 1952; *Shropshire,* R. Hale, 1949.

The World of Cotton, R. Hale, 1951; *Churches,* Batsford, 1954, Macmillan, 1955; *Abbeys and Priories,* Batsford, .1955, Macmillan, 1956; (author of text) A. F. Kersting, *A Portrait of English Churches,* Batsford, 1956, Norton, 1961; (author of text under pseudonym John Bledlow) A. F. Kersting, *The Heritage of England in Color,* Studio Publications, 1956; (author of introduction) Kurt Peter Karfeld, *England in Colour,* Studio Publications, 1956; *Cathedrals,* Macmillan, 1957; (under pseudonym John Bledlow) *The Cotswolds in Color,* Batsford, 1957; *Cambridge and Its Colleges,* new edition, Methuen, 1959; *The Mail-Coach Men of the Late Eighteenth Century,* Cassell, 1960, Augustus M. Kelley, 1967; *The Harveys of Hayle: Engine Builders, Shipwrights, and Merchants of Cornwall,* Barton, 1966; *An Outline of English Architecture,* Collins, 1966; (editor) *Snowdonia,* H.M.S.O., 1968.

Contributor: *Cambridge Poets, 1900-1913,* Heffer, 1913; *Essays of the Year, 1930-31,* Argonaut Press, 1931; *The Beauty of Britain,* Batsford, 1935; Clough Williams-Ellis, editor, *Britain and the Beast,* Dent, 1937; Tom Stephenson, editor, *Romantic Britain,* Odhams, 1937; *Introducing Britain* (radio scripts), Allen & Unwin, 1938; *Mainly Personal,* London Times, 1958.

Author of commercial books, including a railroad series, and *Ships of the Narrow Seas: A General Guide to Ireland,* and others on subjects related to travel. Also author of four published indoor games. Contributor to *Blackwood's Magazine, Cornhill, Observer, Field, Country Life, Times, Guardian,* and other magazines and newspapers. General editor, Methuen's "Little Guide" series.

BIOGRAPHICAL/CRITICAL SOURCES: Times Literary Supplement, March 2, 1967; *London Times,* March 19, 1969, March 24, 1969.

(Died March 15, 1969)

* * *

VAN COEVERING, Jan Adrian 1900-
(Jack Van Coevering)

PERSONAL: Born March 12, 1900, in Herwynen, Netherlands; son of Nicolaas Gerrit (a shoe merchant) and Jenneke (Vander Wal) Van Coevering; married, wife's name, Lucina, June 6, 1927; children: Grieta. *Education:* Calvin College, student, two years; University of Michigan, A.B., 1926. *Politics:* Independent. *Religion:* Presbyterian. *Home*

and office: 6150 Commerce Rd., Orchard Lake, Mich. 48033.

CAREER: Grand Rapids Herald, Grand Rapids, Mich., reporter, 1927-30; *Detroit Free Press,* Detroit, Mich., wildlife editor, 1931—. *Member:* Outdoor Writers Association of America (president and chairman of board, 1959), Izaak Walton League of America (honorary life), Michigan Outdoor Writers Association (president), Michigan Academy of Science, Arts and Letters, Michigan Audubon Society, Wilson Ornithological Society. *Awards, honors:* First honor roll award, Izaak Walton League of America, 1948; Academy merit award, Detroit Sportsmen's Congress, 1948; first award, National Association of Conservation, Education and Publicity, 1949; television "Oscar," 1950, and "best quality outdoor writing" award, 1963, Michigan Outdoor Writers Association; medal of honor, Fishing and Hunting Hall of Fame, 1951.

WRITINGS: Real Boys and Girls Go Birding, Lippincott, 1939; *A-Hiking We Will Go,* Lippincott, 1941; *Fishing for Fun,* Van Coevering Productions, 1950; (with Fred Bear) *Fun with Bow and Arrow,* Van Coevering Productions, 1953; *Tips and Tricks for Outdoor Folks,* Van Coevering Productions, 1959; *Catch Fish Even If You Don't Know How,* Van Coevering Productions, 1963. Contributor of articles to *Sports Afield, Outdoor Life, Field and Stream, Saturday Evening Post, Holiday, True,* and *Animals.* Consultant, *Sports Afield,* 1940-41. Producer, television show, "Woods and Waters," 1945-50, and syndicated television series, "Adventure Out of Doors."

AVOCATIONAL INTERESTS: Taking motion pictures in color for lectures and television programs, and travel.

* * *

VANDERBILT, Cornelius, Jr. 1898-1974

PERSONAL: Born April 30, 1898, in New York, N.Y.; son of Cornelius and Grace Graham (Wilson) Vanderbilt; married Rachel Littleton, April 29, 1920 (divorced November 26, 1927); married Mary Weir Logan, July, 1928 (divorced August, 1931); married Helen Varner Anderson, January 4, 1935 (divorced December, 1940); married Feliza Pablos, September 3, 1946 (divorced April 29, 1948); married Patricia Murphy Wallace, September 2, 1948 (divorced June, 1953); married Ann Needham, 1957 (divorced May, 1960); married Mary Lou Gardner Bristol, November 4, 1967. *Education:* Attended Pine Lodge School (Lakewood, N.J.), 1907-09, Das Colonel (Bad Nauheim, Germany), 1909-11, The Priory (Malvern, England), 1911-12, St. Pauls School (Concord, N.H.), 1912-16, and Harstrom's Tutoring School (Norwalk, Conn.), 1916-17. *Politics:* Democrat-Liberal. *Religion:* Episcopalian. *Home address:* Vanderbilt Ranch, Box 654, Reno, Nev. *Agent:* H. N. Swanson, Inc., 8523 Sunset Blvd., West Hollywood, Calif. 90069. *Office:* Vagabonding with Vanderbilt, 7103 Florida, Chevy Chase, Md. 20015.

CAREER: New York Herald, New York, N.Y., reporter, 1919-20; *New York Times,* New York, N.Y., legislative and Washington correspondent, 1921-23; Vanderbilt Newspapers, Inc., Los Angeles and San Francisco, Calif., and Miami, Fla., editor and publisher, 1923-28; *New York Mirror,* New York, N.Y., associate managing editor, 1928-31; with Democratic National Committee, and presidential agent for Franklin D. Roosevelt, New York, N.Y., 1933-40; *New York Post* Syndicate, New York, N.Y., travel columnist, 1944-49; Vagabonding with Vanderbilt, Reno, Nev., editor and publisher, 1950-54; Vanderbilt Enterprises, New York, N.Y., president, film division, 1961-64.

Vice-president: Street Railway Advertising of the World, 1922-30; Subway Ads, 1922-30; Barron G. Collier Advertising Agency, 1922-30; Collier-Florida Hotels, 1922-30; American Hotel Corp., 1922-30; United Hotels of America, 1922-30; General Outdoor Advertising, 1922-30; Freddie Benham Public Relations Co., 1922-30; Russel G. Birdwell Public Relations Co., 1943-50; Airtronics International Co., 1955-60; Cal-Val Airtronics, 1956-61. Federal Bureau of Investigation, undercover agent in Asia, Europe, Central and South America, 1938-41. Military aide-de-camp to Governor Miller, New York, N.Y., 1923-28; press officer, New York City Civil Defense, 1952-53. Sergeant, Nevada State Police, 1926-36; assistant deputy sheriff, Washoe County, Nev., 1945-64. Lecturer, 1929-61. Radio news commentator, Radio Corp. of America, 1936-38. *Military service:* U.S. Army, 1917-19, served as dispatch driver, Twenty-Seventh Division, American Expeditionary Forces, 1918; became sergeant of transportation; received French Croix de la Croix Rouge. U.S. Army Reserve, 1920-44; became colonel. U.S. Army, Intelligence Corps., General Staff, served as inspector general of North Atlantic-Metropolitan Military District, 1941-43; became major. New York National Guard, 1923-25; became captain.

MEMBER: Landmark Society of the United States, Society of the Cincinnati (Rhode Island division), National Geographic Society, National Press Club, Historical Society of Pennsylvania, Union Club of New York, Knickerbocker Club, New York Yacht Club, Berlin (West Germany) Yacht Club, Sittin', Starin' and Rockin' Club (Stamford, Conn.), Cave des Roys (Los Angeles). *Awards, honors:* Abdon Calderon, Ecuador, 1940; distinguished service cross, Federal Bureau of Investigation, 1941.

WRITINGS: Personal Experience of a Cub Reporter, Sully, 1922; *Personal Experiences of a Legislative Correspondent,* Sully, 1922; *Personal Experiences of a Washington Correspondent,* Sully, 1923; *Reno,* Macaulay, 1929; *Park Avenue,* Macaulay, 1930; *Palm Beach,* Macaulay, 1931; *Symposium of Public Opinion on Japanese-American Question,* Bernays, 1934; *Farewell to Fifth Avenue,* Simon & Schuster, 1935; *A Woman of Washington,* Dutton, 1937; *Children of Divorce,* Simon & Schuster, 1939; *Too Many Wives,* Simon & Schuster, 1940; *Vanderbilt's European Travel Directory,* Intercontinental Associates, 1954; *The Living Past of America: A Pictorial Treasury of Our Historic Houses and Villages That Have Been Preserved and Restored,* Crown, 1955; *Queen of the Golden Age: The Fabulous Story of Grace Wilson Vanderbilt,* McGraw, 1956 (published in England as *The Vanderbilt Feud,* Hutchinson, 1957); *Let's Visit Our Historic Places,* Birk, c.1956; *Man of the World: My Life on Five Continents,* Crown, 1959; *Ranches and Ranch Life in America,* Crown, 1968. Writer of a number of scenarios for Fox Films and United Artists, 1940-55.

WORK IN PROGRESS: Three books, *Newport* (R.I.), to be published by Little, Brown, *Who Was Who in U.S. Society,* for Hutchinson, and *Vagabonding Around the World.*

SIDELIGHTS: Vanderbilt traveled extensively—at times by trailer—all over the world except in Southeast Asia. He crossed the Atlantic 158 times, the Pacific forty-six times, and went around the world twelve times. *Avocational interests:* Stamp collecting, mountaineering, trailering, photography, extra sensory perception, astrology, and the unknown.

(Died July 7, 1974)

van der PLOEG, Johannes P(etrus) M(aria) 1909-

PERSONAL: Born July 4, 1909, in Nijmegen, Netherlands; son of Harke Antonius and Petronella Anna (Snijers) van der Ploeg. *Education:* Dominicans, Zwolle, Netherlands, student, 1927-30; Paris Dominicans "Le Saulchoir," student, 1931-32; Collegio Angelico, Rome, Italy, D.Theol., 1936, Doctor S. Scripturae, 1946; studied at Ecole Biblique Francaise Jerusalem. *Home:* Driehuizerweg 145, Nijmegen, Netherlands. *Office:* Catholic University, Institutes for Theology and Semitics, Nijmegen University, Nijmegen, Netherlands.

CAREER: Ordained Roman Catholic priest of Dominican order, July 6, 1932. Lecturer on Old Testament introduction and Hebrew, Dominican Monastery, Zwolle, Netherlands, 1934-37, and Dominican Monastery "Albertinum," Nijmegen, Netherlands, 1938-51; Catholic University of Nijmegen, Nijmegen, Netherlands, professor of Old Testament exegesis and Hebrew, 1951—. Vice-president, apostolate for the reunion of churches, Utrecht. *Member:* Royal Dutch Academy of Sciences.

WRITINGS: Les Chants du Serviteur de Jahve, Gabalda, 1936; *Oud-Syrisch monniksleven,* E. J. Brill, 1942; (translator and editor) *Spreuken,* Romen & Zonen, 1952; (translator and editor) *Prediker,* Romen & Zonen, 1953; *De Kerk en Israel,* Gooi & Sticht, 1954, translation published as *The Church and Israel,* Blackfriars Publications, 1956; *Vondsten in de woestijn van Juda,* Het Spectrum, 1957, 4th edition, 1970, translation by Kevin Smyth published as *The Excavations at Qumran: A Survey of the Judaean Brotherhood and Its Ideas,* Longmans, Green, 1958; (translator and author of introduction and notes) *Le Rouleau de la guerre,* E. J. Brill, 1959; *La Secte de Qumran et les origines du Christianisme,* Desclee, De Brouwer, 1959; *Mens tegenover mens in het Oude Testament,* Dekker & Van de Vegt, 1960; *Bij-belverklaring te Qumran,* Noord-Hollandsche, 1960; (editor) *Le Targum de Job de la grotte XI de Qumran,* Noord-Hollandsche, 1962; *Une Theologie de l'Ancien Testament: Est-elle possible?,* Publications Universitaires de Louvain, 1962; (translator and editor) *De Psalmen,* Romen & Zonen, 1963; (translator and editor) *De Boeken van het Oude Testament,* Volume I, Romen, c.1970. Contributor of articles to religious journals. Editor, "Studies on the Texts of the Desert of Judah," E. J. Brill, 1957.

WORK IN PROGRESS: Research on the Scrolls of the Dead Sea, found in the Desert of Judah near Qumran.

SIDELIGHTS: Van der Ploeg has traveled extensively; his first journey was to Palestine in 1947. Since then he has traveled to the countries of the Near East, and to Kerala, India, to study Christian problems, 1963-64.†

*   *   *

VAN DEVENTER, Fred 1903-1971

PERSONAL: Born December 5, 1903, in Tipton, Ind.; son of Joseph and Allie (Rood) Van Deventer; married Florence Rinard; children: Nancy, Robert. *Education:* Attended Butler University. *Home:* 133 Mansgrove Rd., Princeton, N.J.

CAREER: Newsman with Hearst Universal News Services, Chicago, Ill., 1924-28, and identified with radio and television, 1942-71; news broadcaster for Mutual Broadcasting System, 1960-65. *Awards, honors:* D.Litt., Rider College, 1945; L.H.D., Franklin and Marshall College, 1953; D.B.A., Lawrence Institute of Technology, 1954.

WRITINGS: Parade to Glory (story of the Shriners), Morrow, 1959, 4th revised edition, Pyramid Books, 1969; *Cruising New Jersey Tidewater: A Boating and Touring Guide*, Rutgers University Press, 1964.

WORK IN PROGRESS: Updated editions of *Parade to Glory* and *Cruising New Jersey Tidewater.*

(Died, 1971)

* * *

VANDIVER, Edward P(inckney), Jr. 1902-

PERSONAL: Born October 16, 1902, in Anderson, S.C.; son of Edward Pinckney (a banker) and Sudie (Watson) Vandiver. *Education:* Furman University, B.A., 1922; University of North Carolina, M.A., 1928, Ph.D., 1931. *Home:* 703 East Calhoun St., Anderson, S.C. 29621.

CAREER: Mississippi College, Clinton, associate professor of English, 1929-30; Mary Baldwin College, Staunton, Va., professor of English and chairman of department, 1931-47; Mercer University, Macon, Ga., professor of English and chairman of department, 1947-48; Erskine College, Due West, S.C., professor of English and chairman of department, 1948-49; Furman University, Greenville, S.C., professor of English, 1949-66. *Member:* Modern Language Association of America, Shakespeare Association of America, American Association of University Professors, South Atlantic Modern Language Association.

WRITINGS: Highlights of Shakespeare's Plays (selections from twenty-three plays, with explanation, summary, comment, and emphasis on famous quotations), Barron's, 1965.

WORK IN PROGRESS: A new and enlarged edition of *Highlights of Shakespeare's Plays* (with selections from twenty-six plays).

AVOCATIONAL INTERESTS: Walking; Gilbert and Sullivan music.

* * *

VAN ITALLIE, Philip H. 1899-

PERSONAL: Born September 25, 1899, in Amsterdam, Netherlands; son of Benjamin and Sarah J. (de Jongh) Van Itallie; married Frances E. Gaines (a technical editor), July 12, 1941 (deceased); children: Philip Karel, Frederick Judd. *Education:* Polytechnic Institute of Brooklyn, B.S., 1926, M.S., 1942. *Home:* 341 McClenaghan's Mill Rd., Wynnewood, Pa. 19096. *Agent:* Oliver Swan, Paul R. Reynolds & Son, 599 Fifth Ave., New York, N.Y. 10017.

CAREER: Topics Publishing Co., New York, N.Y., technical editor of *Drug Topics* and *Drug Trade News,* 1932-45; Wyeth Laboratories (pharmaceutical manufacturers), Radnor, Pa., editor of *Pulse of Pharmacy,* 1945-65. *Member:* American Pharmaceutical Association.

WRITINGS: How to Live with a Hearing Handicap, Eriksson, 1963. Contributor of columns and articles to drug trade journals. Translator and abstractor for *Biological Abstracts.*

SIDELIGHTS: Van Itallie is competent in Dutch, German, French, Spanish, Italian, and Portuguese; he is now engaged in self-study of Russian. *Avocational interests:* Painting.

VAN LIERDE, John 1907-
(Peter Canisius Van Lierde)

PERSONAL: Born April 22, 1907, in Hasselt, Belgium; son of Henry (founder of a commercial firm) and Susan (Sevriens) Van Lierde. *Education:* Augustinian Seminary (Nijmegen, Holland), student of philosophy and theology; earned doctorate degree in theology, Angelicum (Rome, Italy), licenciate degree in Scriptural studies, Biblical Institute (Rome), and diploma in organ-playing (Holland). *Home and office:* Vatican City, Italy.

CAREER: Scripture lecturer in Holland, 1936-37; St. Monica's International College, Rome, Italy, 1937-51, lecturer in Scripture, patrology, and liturgy, director of plainsong choir, vice-rector, later rector; now Bishop, Titular of Porphyreon, and head of the Sacrarium, including the Papal Lipsanoteca and liturgical treasury. Vicar General of the Pope for the Vatican City. Lecturer, especially at Ascetical Centre at Sestri Levante, and at "The Studium" of Catholic Action in Italy. President, Sestri Levante Ascetical Center. *Awards, honors:* State honors from Luxemburg, Holland, Belgium, Austria, Spain, Germany, and Italy; Grand Cross of the Order of the Holy Sepulchre, Jordan.

WRITINGS: Doctrina S. Augustini circa dona Spiritus Sancti, St. Rita Verlag, 1935; *Roeping tot Levenstaat,* Spectrum, 1941; (contributor) *Novant'anni delle Leggi Mendelianne,* [Rome], 1956; *The Holy See at Work,* Hawthorn, 1962; (contributor) *Staatslexicon,* Herder, 1962; *Le Senat de l'Eglise: Le Sacre College,* Fayard, 1963. Manuscripts: "Handleiding van de Gregoriaanse Zang," 1933; "Spiritualiteit van de Orde der Augustijnen," 1934; "La perfezione cristiana e il servizio sociale," 1953. Contributor to annual publications of the Sestri Levante Ascetical Center, 1958-71.

WORK IN PROGRESS: A long article on Vatican Secretariat of State for a book on the Vatican by Christopher Hollis.

SIDELIGHTS: Van Lierde knows Dutch, French, Spanish, Italian, German, English, Russian, and classical languages. Peter Canisius Van Lierde is the name he uses in religion. *Avocational interests:* Music, art, and travel.

* * *

van OVERBEEK, Johannes 1908-

PERSONAL: Born January 2, 1908, in Schiedam, Netherlands; came to United States in 1933, naturalized in 1942; son of Johannes Marinus (a business executive) and Elisabeth (Vos) van Overbeek; married Mathilde van Aarem, 1933 (deceased); married Thelma Taylor, 1948; children: (first marriage) Robert, Barbara; (second marriage) Thomas, Marina, Frederick, William. *Education:* University of Leiden, B.S., 1928; University of Utrecht, M.S. (cum laude), 1932, Ph.D. (cum laude), 1933. *Home:* Route 6, Old Oakdale Rd., Modesto, Calif. 95350.

CAREER: California Institute of Technology, Pasadena, assistant professor of biology, 1934-43; Institute of Tropical Agriculture, Mayaguez, Puerto Rico, assistant director and head of plant physiology, 1943-47; Shell Development Co., Modesto, Calif., chief plant physiologist, 1947—. Honorary professor, College of Agriculture, Mayaguez, Puerto Rico, 1943-47. Consultant in agricultural research to Colorado State University and U.S. Department of Agriculture Cotton Experimental Station. Operator of commercial vineyard in California. Lecturer at scientific and popular levels on botanical subjects.

MEMBER: American Association for the Advancement of Science (fellow), American Society of Plant Physiologists (secretary of western division, 1941-42; chairman of division, 1943), American Institute of Biological Sciences, Botanical Society of America, Society of General Physiologists, Royal Dutch Botanical Society, Society for Experimental Biology (London), Western Society of Naturalists, Sigma Xi. *Awards, honors:* Doctorate in agronomy, State Institute of Agronomy, Gambloux, Belgium.

WRITINGS: (With I. Velez) *Planta Tropicales*, University of Puerto Rico Press, 1950; *The Lore of Living Plants*, National Science Teachers Association, 1964.

Contributor: D.E.H. Frear, *Agricultural Chemistry*, Van Nostrand, 1950; F. S. Koog, *Plant Growth Substances*, University of Wisconsin Press, 1951; H. B. Tukey, *Plant Regulators in Agriculture*, Wiley, 1954; R. L. Wain, *The Chemistry and Mode of Action of Plant Growth Substances*, Academic Press, 1956; R. M. Klein, *Plant Growth Regulations*, Iowa State University Press, 1961; W. Ruhland, *Encyclopedia of Plant Physiology*, Springer, 1961; Leslie J. Audus, editor, *The Physiology and Biochemistry of Herbicides*, Academic Press, 1964. Contributor to scientific journals and author of popular articles on botany.

WORK IN PROGRESS: Research on the growth of plants.

* * *

Van SAHER, Lilla 1912-1968

PERSONAL: Born March 18, 1912, in Budapest, Hungary; came to U.S., 1940; daughter of Bernard (a professor of philosophy) and Maria Regina Alexander; married A. E. Van Saher (a lawyer; divorced, 1949); children: Alex, Stella. *Education:* Attended Chemin du Miremont, Geneva, Switzerland, 1922-30, Sorbonne, Ecole de Medicine, Paris, France, 1930-32, and Reinhardt School of Acting, Berlin, Germany, 1932-33. *Politics:* Democrat. *Religion:* Orthodox Catholic. *Home:* Apartment 12T, 333 East 79th St., New York, N.Y. 10021. *Agent:* Margot Johnson Agency, 405 East 54th St., New York, N.Y. 10022.

CAREER: Model and film actress in Europe, appearing in Seven German films, in leading role in "Grain au Vent," directed by Jean·Renoir; writer. Correspondent for Bonniers Magazines and *Svensk Damtidning,* both Stockholm, Sweden. Ambulance driver and translator during World War II. *Member:* Dramatists Guild of Authors League of America, P.E.N. *Awards, honors:* Made honorary brigadier general during World War II.

WRITINGS: The Echo (novel; Basic Book Club selection), Dutton, 1947; *Macamba* (Book-of-the-Month Club recommendation), Dutton, 1949; *Three Days with Aira* (play), Kurt Desch, 1959; *Exotic Cookery*, World Publishing, 1964. Author of film script, "Girls are Here to Stay," sold to Twentieth-Century Fox, 1962, and of an unpublished play, "The Beach Story: The Story of One Night and Two People," 1962. Translator of scientific books into English. Contributor of travelogues, short stories, and exotic recipes to magazines abroad.

WORK IN PROGRESS: An anthology of case histories, for Bantam; *Mirrors Are Lonely,* a novel; a series of articles for *Gourmet.*

SIDELIGHTS: Mrs. Van Saher had been around the world twice, but islands were her major travel interest. She knew French, German, Dutch, Flemish, English, and Hungarian. *Avocational interests:* Psychology, gardening, Siamese cats, psychological research about monkeys.†
(Died July 15, 1968)

van ZWOLL, James A. 1909-

PERSONAL: Born November 15, 1909, in Rochester, N.Y.; son of John (an accountant) and Adriana (vander Pijl) van Zwoll; married Philippine M. Boeye (an artist), March 19, 1949; children: Arthur W., Adrienne M., Jacqueline J. *Educaton:* Grand Rapids Junior College, Associate in Science of Engineering, 1931; Calvin College, B.A., 1933, M.A., 1937; University of Michigan, Ph.D., 1942. *Politics:* Republican-independent. *Religion:* Presbyterian. *Home:* 11504 Orebaugh Ave., Silver Spring, Md. 20902.

CAREER: Port Huron (Mich.) Board of Education, assistant superintendent of schools, 1942-46; University of Michigan, Ann Arbor, lecturer, 1946-47; University of Iowa, Iowa City, assistant professor, 1947-48; University of Maryland, College Park, 1948—, now professor of school administration. Consultant to Division of Higher Education, U.S. Department of Health, Education, and Welfare, 1951-58. *Military service:* U.S. Naval Reserve, 1943-46; became lieutenant. *Member:* American Academy of Political and Social Science, American Association of School Administrators, American Educational Research Association, National Education Association, National Society for the Study of Education, Association for Higher Education.

WRITINGS: (Contributor) David Trout, editor, *The Education of Teachers*, Michigan Cooperative Teacher Education Study, 1943; (with Arthur B. Moehlman) *School Public Relations*, Appleton, 1957; *School Personnel Administration*, Appleton, 1964. Contributor to professional journals.

WORK IN PROGRESS: Research in school pay increments unrelated to competence factors.

SIDELIGHTS: van Zwoll speaks Dutch, some French and German, *Avocational interests:* Travel.

* * *

VARLEY, Dimitry V. 1906-

PERSONAL: Born' February 10, 1906, in Russia; son of Vladimir and Maria Varley; married Bessie Schoenberg (a college director of dance). *Education:* Columbia University, B.S., 1928, M.A., 1930. *Home:* 9 McIntyre St., Bronxville, N.Y. 10708.

CAREER: With New York State Department of Labor, 1932-33, New York State Unemployment Insurance, 1934-37; research director, advisory council, 1937-42; with United Nations Relief and Rehabilitation Administration (UNRRA), 1944-46. Ceramist, 1952—has exhibited in Connecticut, New York, Kansas, Virginia. *Military service:* U.S. Army, 1942-44.

WRITINGS: Whirly Bird (juvenile), Knopf, 1961.

WORK IN PROGRESS: Queenie, The Singing Seal.

AVOCATIONAL INTERESTS: Philately, gardening.

* * *

VAUGHAN, Agnes Carr 1887-

PERSONAL: Born February 1, 1887, in Richland, N.J.; daughter of Alexander S. (a minister) and Ida Elizabeth (Pettit) Vaughan. *Education:* Galloway College, B.A., 1907; University of Michigan, M.A., 1910, Ph.D., 1917. *Politics:* Republican. *Religion:* Presbyterian. *Home:* 70 La

Salle St., Apartment 14A, New York, N.Y. 10027. *Agent:* McIntosh & Otis, Inc., 18 East 41st St., New York, N.Y. 10017.

CAREER: Wells College, Aurora, N.Y., assistant professor of Greek, 1918-24; Smith College, Northampton, Mass., 1926-52, began as assistant professor, became professor of Greek. Member of managing committee, American School in Athens. *Member:* American Philological Association, American Archaeological Association, Women's Faculty Club of Columbia University. *Awards, honors:* University of Michigan fellow in Greek, Bryn Mawr College, 1915-16.

WRITINGS: Madness in Greek Thought and Custom, Furst, 1919; (adapter and translator) *Lucian Goes A-Voyaging* (adapted from Lucian's *Vera Historia*), Knopf, 1930; *Evenings in a Greek Bazaar,* Knopf, 1932; *Within the Walls,* Macmillan, 1935; *Akka, Dwarf of Syracuse,* Longmans, Green, 1940; *The Genesis of Human Offspring: A Study in Early Greek Culture,* Smith College Trustees, 1945; *The House of the Double Axe: The Palace at Knossos,* Doubleday, 1959; *Bury Me in Ravenna: A Novel of the Fifth Century Based on the Life of Galla Placidia, Gothic Queen and Roman Empress,* Doubleday, 1962; *Those Mysterious Etruscans,* Doubleday, 1964; *Zenobia of Palmyra,* Doubleday, 1967.

SIDELIGHTS: Research and study for Miss Vaughan's books have led to extensive travel, with stays in Greece, Italy, and Paris and shorter visits to museums in other countries, in pursuit of her chief interests of archaeology and ancient life.

BIOGRAPHICAL/CRITICAL SOURCES: Literary Times, May-June, 1967.†

*　　*　　*

VEACH, William B. Templeton 1896-

PERSONAL: Born February 14, 1896; son of Frank Hollister (an inventor) and Katherine (Brier) Veach. *Education:* Attended Philips Exeter Academy; studied music privately. *Politics:* Independent. *Religion:* Episcopal. *Home and office:* Bonnetable, Sarthe, France. *Agent:* John Schaffner, 425 East 51st St., New York, N.Y. 10022.

CAREER: American vice-consul in Canton, China, and Colombo, Ceylon, 1921-25; Guide Dogs for the Blind, San Francisco, Calif., executive vice-president, 1940-46. *Military service:* U.S. Army, Infantry; served in France during World War I.

WRITINGS: (With Helen Evans Brown) *A Book of Curries and Chutneys,* Ritchie, 1963; (with Brown) *An Amphitryon's Cook Book,* Little, Brown, 1964; (with Brown) *A Bon Vivant's Cookbook: A Collection of Fine Foreign and American Recipes,* Little, Brown, 1965. Contributor to *Vogue, Town and Country, Christian Science Monitor,* and San Francisco newspapers.

WORK IN PROGRESS: An opera, "Swan White," after a libretto by Strindberg.†

*　　*　　*

VERRAL, Charles Spain 1904-
(George L. Eaton)

PERSONAL: Born November 7, 1904, in Highfield, Ontario, Canada; son of George William and Kate E. (Peacocke) Verral; married Jean Mithoefer, March 19, 1932; children: Charles Spain, Jr. *Education:* Attended Upper

Canada College, 1919-23, and Ontario College of Art, 1923-26. *Religion:* Episcopalian. *Home:* 79 Jane St., New York, N.Y. 10014. *Office: Reader's Digest,* 380 Madison Ave., New York, N.Y. 10017.

CAREER: Free-lance commercial artist, New York, N.Y., 1927-30; Clayton Publications, New York, N.Y., an editor, 1930-33, art director, 1933-35; free-lance writer, New York, N.Y., 1935-62, with some editorial positions, including biographies editor for *Harper Encyclopedia of Science,* 1961-62; Reader's Digest Association, New York, N.Y., editor-writer for General Books, 1962—. *Member:* Mystery Writers of America, Authors League of America. *Awards, honors:* Bureau of Intercultural Education short story contest prize, 1947, for "The Miracle Quarterback."

WRITINGS: Captain of the Ice, Crowell, 1953; *Champion of the Court,* Crowell, 1954; *Men of Flight: Conquest of the Air,* Aladdin Books, 1954; *The King of the Diamond,* Crowell, 1955; *Mighty Men of Baseball,* Aladdin Books, 1955; *High Danger,* Sterling, 1955; *The Wonderful World Series,* Crowell, 1956; *Walt Disney's The Great Locomotive Chase,* Simon & Schuster, 1956; *Annie Oakley, Sharpshooter,* Simon & Schuster, 1957; *Lassie and the Daring Rescue,* Simon & Schuster, 1957; *Brave Eagle,* Simon & Schuster, 1957; *Broken Arrow,* Simon & Schuster, 1957; *The Lone Ranger and Tonto,* Simon & Schuster, 1957; *Rin-Tin-Tin and the Outlaw,* Simon & Schuster, 1957; *Lassie and Her Day in the Sun,* Simon & Schuster, 1958; *Cheyenne,* Simon & Schuster, 1958; *Walt Disney's Andy Burnett,* Simon & Schuster, 1958; *Play Ball,* Simon & Schuster, 1958; *Zorro,* Simon & Schuster, 1958; *Smoky the Bear,* Simon & Schuster, 1958; *Rin-Tin-Tin and the Hidden Treasure,* Simon & Schuster, 1959; *Zorro and the Secret Plan,* Simon & Schuster, 1959; *Walt Disney's The Shaggy Dog,* Simon & Schuster, 1959.

The Winning Quarterback, Crowell, 1960; *The Case of the Missing Message,* Golden Press, 1960; *Smoky the Bear and His Animal Friends,* Golden Press, 1960; *The Flying Car,* Golden Press, 1961; *Jets,* Prentice-Hall, 1962; *Go! The Story of Outer Space,* Prentice-Hall, 1962; *Robert Goddard: Father of the Space Age,* Prentice-Hall, 1963. Short stories anthologized in collections published by American Book Co., Harcourt, Holt, and Watts. Author of 25 book-length "Bill Barnes" air adventure stories in *Air Trails,* and some 150 short stories, novelettes and articles to *Boys' Life, Argosy, This Week, American Boy, Clues,* and other magazines, 1935-52. Continuity writer for national syndicated adventure newspaper strip, "Hap Hopper," 1941-47. Script writer for radio program, "Mandrake the Magician," 1940-41.

WORK IN PROGRESS: A juvenile mystery, for Golden Press.

AVOCATIONAL INTERESTS: Amateur magician; cartooning and painting.

*　　*　　*

VESTER, Horatio 1906-

PERSONAL: Born August 25, 1906, in Jerusalem, Palestine; son of Frederick (a company director) and Bertha (Spafford) Vester; married Valentine Richmond (an author), April 1, 1938; children: Paul Richmond, Nicholas George Spafford. *Education:* Phillips Academy, Andover, Mass., diploma, 1927; studied at Columbia University, 1927-30, at American University of Beirut, 1932-33; Gray's Inn, London, England, barrister-at-law, 1935. *Home:* 141 Old Church St., London S.W. 3, England; American Colony, Jerusalem, Israel. *Office:* Francis Taylor Building, Temple, London E.C. 4, England.

CAREER: Joined the Oxford Circuit, practicing almost entirely in commercial and industrial law in London, England, 1946-62, retired, 1962. Chairman of American Colony Ltd. and American Colony Hotels Ltd., Jerusalem, Israel, of Vester & Co. Ltd., London, England, and Beirut, Lebanon, and of Sloan Flats Ltd., London. Also chairman of Anna Spafford Memorial Children's Hospital, Jerusalem. *Member:* Chelsea Arts Club (London).

WRITINGS: (With A. H. Gardner) *Trade Unions and the Law*, Methuen, 1955; (with Gardner) *Trade Union Law and Practice*, Sweet & Maxwell, 1959; *Industrial Injuries*, two volumes, Sweet & Maxwell, 1961.

AVOCATIONAL INTERESTS: The history and archaeology of the Middle East.

* * *

VIGUERS, Ruth Hill   1903-1971
(Ruth A. Hill)

PERSONAL: Born July 24, 1903, in Oakland, Calif.; daughter of Everett Merril (a clergyman) and Alfarata (Kimball) Hill; married Richard Thomson Viguers (a hospital administrator), June 2, 1937 (died, 1969); children: Deborah Hill, Susan Thomson and Doris Kimball (twins). *Education:* Willamette University, A.B., 1924; University of Washington, Seattle, B.S. in L.S., 1926. *Politics:* Democrat. *Religion:* Methodist.

CAREER: Children's librarian at Seattle (Wash.) Public Library, 1926-27, New York (N.Y.) Public Library, 1927-29; International Institute for Girls, Madrid, Spain, organizer of library and librarian, 1929-31; American Library, Paris, France, head of children's department, 1932-36; Boone Library School, Wuchang, China, instructor in library science, 1936-37; New York Public Library, assistant superintendent of work with children, 1937-43; Simmons College, School of Publication, Boston, Mass., lecturer in children's literature, 1949-70, also instructor in library science; *Horn Book* (magazine), Boston, Mass., editor, 1958-67. Lecturer and storyteller. Judge, *New York Herald Tribune* Children's Spring Book Festival, 1958, Book World Spring Festival, 1965, *Boston Globe* Children's Book Award, 1967-68; delegate, Golden Anniversary White House Conference on Children and Youth, 1960; Caroline H. Hewins lecturer, Boston, 1955; Anne C. Moore lecturer, New York Public Library, 1962; Miriam A. Wessel lecturer, Detroit, 1965; lecturer, University of Hawaii, 1968; member of board of directors, International Institute for Girls in Spain, Friends of Wellesley (Mass.) Free Library; member of editorial advisory board, Open Court Publishing Co. *Member:* American Library Association, Women's National Book Association, National League of American Pen Women, New England Library Association, Massachusetts Library Association. *Awards, honors:* Ed.D. from Portia Law School, 1965; Alumni Citation Award, Willamette University, 1967; Constance Linsay Skinner Award, Women's National Book Association, 1968; Distinguished Alumni Award, University of Washington, 1969.

WRITINGS: (Under name Ruth A. Hill, with Elsa de Bondelli) *Children's Books from Foreign Languages*, Wilson, 1936; (with Cornelia Meigs, Anne Eaton, and Elizabeth Nesbitt) *A Critical History of Children's Literature*, Macmillan, 1953, revised edition, 1969; (with Marcia Dalphin and Bertha Nahony Miller) *Illustrations of Children's*

Books, 1946-56, Horn Book, 1958; *Margin for Surprise: About Books, Children, and Librarians*, Little, Brown, 1964.

(Died February 3, 1971)

* * *

VIVEASH, Cherry Jacqueline Lee   1929-

PERSONAL: Born December 3, 1929, in London, England; daughter of F. S. C. and Dorothy (Herbert) Viveash. *Education:* Privately educated. *Religion:* Baha'i World Faith. *Home:* 6 Hyde Abbey Flats, Hyde St., Winchester, Hampshire, England.

CAREER: Secretary.

WRITINGS: *Walking by Night* (poems), Stockwell, 1956; *Tales from the Ballet* (juvenile), George Ronald, 1958. Contributor of book reviews, poems, and articles to *Art Quarterly* and *Science of Thought Review.*

WORK IN PROGRESS: A book of poems.

BIOGRAPHICAL/CRITICAL SOURCES: Chichester Observer, Chichester, England, February 24, 1961.

* * *

VOYCE, Arthur   1889-

PERSONAL: Born July 5, 1889, in Russia; became U.S. citizen. *Education:* Carnegie Institute of Technology, architecture student, 1913-15, 1919-20; University of California, Berkeley, A.B. in L.S., 1921. *Home:* 302 Silver Ave., San Francisco, Calif. 94112.

CAREER: Worked in the field of architecture in Chicago, Ill., and San Francisco, Calif., 1922-47; writer and researcher on Soviet art and architecture, beginning, 1947. *Member:* American Association for the Advancement of Slavic Studies. *Awards, honors:* Senior fellow in Slavic studies at Hoover Institution, Stanford University, 1947-51; grants from American Philosophical Society, 1952-53, 1954, Social Science Research Council, 1956-57, 1959-60, Inter-University Committee on Travel Grants, for travel in Soviet Union, 1958, 1961, American Council of Learned Societies, 1964-65.

WRITINGS: Russian Architecture: Trends in Nationalism and Modernism, Philosophical Library, 1948; *The Moscow Kremlin: Its History, Architecture, and Art Treasures*, University of California Press, Berkeley, 1954; *Moscow and the Roots of Russian Culture*, University of Oklahoma Press, 1964; *The Art and Architecture of Medieval Russia*, University of Oklahoma Press, 1967. Contributor to *Encyclopaedia Britannica* and *The American Peoples Encyclopedia Yearbook* and to art, architecture, and political science journals.

WORK IN PROGRESS: The Art and Architecture of Modern Russia; St. Petersburg.

SIDELIGHTS: Voyce lived and studied in France and Italy for two years. He is fluent in Russian, and has working knowledge of French and German.

* * *

VYVYAN, C(lara) C(oltman Rogers)   1885-

PERSONAL: Born September 28, 1885, in Australia; taken to England at age of two; daughter of Edward Powys and Charlotte (Williams) Rogers; married Sir Courtenay Bouchier Vyvyan, 1929 (died, 1941). *Education:* London School of Economics and Political Science, degree in social science (with distinction), 1913. *Home:* Trelowarren, Helston, Cornwall, England. *Agent:* Curtis Brown Ltd., 1 Craven Hill, London W2 3EW, England.

CAREER: Writer. *Member:* P.E.N.

WRITINGS: Cornish Silhouettes, Bodley Head, 1924; *Echoes in Cornwall,* Bodley Head, 1926; *Gwendra Cove, and Other Cornish Sketches,* Jordan & Sons, 1931; (compiler) *Bird Symphony* (anthology), J. Murray, 1933; *Cornish Cronies,* Channing Press, 1937; *Our Cornwall,* Westaway Books, 1948; *Amateur Gardening,* Museum Press, 1951; *The Dead Smile* (novel), Carroll & Nicholson, 1952; *The Old Place,* Museum Press, 1952; *The Scilly Isles,* R. Hale, 1953; *Down the Rhone on Foot,* P. Owen, 1955; *Temples and Flowers: A Journey to Greece,* P. Owen, 1955; *The Helford River,* P. Owen, 1956; *On Timeless Shores: Journeys in Ireland,* P. Owen, 1957; *Cornish Year,* P. Owen, 1958; *Random Journeys,* P. Owen, 1960; *Arctic Adventure,* P. Owen, 1961; *Roots and Stars: Reflections on the Past,* P. Owen, 1962; *Coloured Pebbles* (reminiscences), P. Owen, 1964; *Journey Up the Years,* P. Owen, 1966; *Nothing Venture,* P. Owen, 1967; *Letters from a Cornish Garden,* foreword by Daphne du Maurier, M. Joseph, 1972. Contributor of articles on travel, gardening, and Cornwall to *Guardian, Irish Times, Times, Blue Peter, Canadian Geographical Journal, Royal Geographical Journal, West Briton, Hibbert Journal,* and *Cornhill.*

WORK IN PROGRESS: A continuation of her autobiography.

* * *

WACKERBARTH, Marjorie

PERSONAL: Surname is pronounced Walkerbarth; born in Rockford, Iowa; daughter of Francis Miles (a lawyer) and Lillian (Stout) Graham; married Carl Wackerbarth (owner of an insurance agency), November 2, 1925; children: James Carl, Graham. *Education:* Attended University of Iowa, 1918-19, and Columbia University, 1921-23. *Politics:* Republican. *Religion:* Presbyterian. *Home:* 4122 Linden Hills Blvd., Minneapolis, Minn.

CAREER: Foreign translator (French, Spanish, and Portuguese) for Hart-Parr Tractor Co., Charles City, Iowa, prior to marriage; free-lance writer, 1945—. *Member:* National League of American Pen Women (president of Minneapolis branch, 1952-55; Minnesota president, 1955-58).

WRITINGS: (With mother, Lillian S. Graham) *Party Fun for Boys and Girls,* Prentice-Hall, 1952; (with Graham) *Games for All Ages and How to Use Them,* Denison, 1959; (with Graham) *Bobby Discovers Garden Friends* (insects), Denison, 1960; (with Graham) *Successful Parties and How To Give Them,* Denison, 1961; *Bobby Discovers Bird Watching,* Denison, 1963; *Bobby Learns about Butterflies,* Denison, 1964; *Bobby Learns about Squirrels,* Denison, 1966; *Bobby Learns about Woodland Babies,* Denison, 1968.

Contributor of about 350 stories and articles, most of them in collaboration with Lillian S. Graham, to *Redbook, True, Holiday, Look, McCall's, Better Homes and Gardens, American Home, Farm Journal, Toronto Star, Jack and Jill,* and other magazines and newspapers.

WORK IN PROGRESS: Research for two more nature books in "Bobby" series.

SIDELIGHTS: A collaboration that started as a hobby ended in 1961 with the death of Lillian S. Graham, just three months shy of her ninetieth birthday. One of the

Wackerbarth-Graham stories, "If I Needed a Roof Tonight," was translated into Russian for *America Illustrated,* a U.S. government publication sent overseas.

BIOGRAPHICAL SOURCES: Christian Science Monitor, June 3, 1952.

* * *

WADE, Francis C(larence) 1907-

PERSONAL: Born November 11, 1907, in Whitesboro, Tex.; son of George Henry (a hardware retailer) and Jennie (Ligon) Wade. *Education:* St. Mary's College, St. Mary's, Kan., student, 1924-25; Gonzaga University, A.B., 1931; St. Louis University, M.A., 1932, S.T.L., 1939. *Home:* 1131 West Wisconsin Ave., Milwaukee, Wis. 53233. *Office:* Department of Philosophy, Marquette University, Milwaukee, Wis. 53233.

CAREER: Ordained Roman Catholic priest, member of Society of Jesus (Jesuits). Campion High School, Prairie du Chien, Wis., history instructor, 1932-35; Rockhurst College, Kansas City, Mo., chairman of division of philosophy and theology, 1943-45; Marquette University, Milwaukee, Wis., assistant professor, 1948-54, associate professor of philosophy, 1954—, assistant chairman of department, 1956—. Member of planning committee and chairman of leader training, Great Books Program, Milwaukee, Wis., 1954-60. *Member:* American Catholic Philosophical Association (member of executive committee, 1952-54), Metaphysical Society of America, Jesuit Philosophical Association (president, 1957).

WRITINGS: (Translator, and author of introduction and notes) *Outlines of Logic,* Marquette University Press, 1955; 2nd edition, 1962; *Teaching and Morality,* Loyola University Press, 1963; (translator, and author of introduction with Lottie H. Kendzierski) Tommaso de Vio, *Commentary on Being and Essence,* Marquette University Press, 1964. Contributor to religious and philosophical publications.

WORK IN PROGRESS: A book, *For Concerned Parents.*

* * *

WADE, Rosalind Herschel 1909-
(Catharine Carr)

PERSONAL: Born September 11, 1909, in London, England; daughter of Harry H. (an Army officer and member of the League of Nations secretariat) and Kathleen Adelaide Wade; married William Kean Seymour (a poet, novelist, and critic); children: Philip Herschel Kean, Gerald William Herschel Kean. *Education:* Educated privately in Ireland, Denmark, and other countries where father was stationed. *Religion:* Church of England. *Home:* White Cottage, Old Alresford, Hampshire, England. *Agent:* Curtis Brown Ltd., 1 Craven Hill, London W2 3EW, England.

CAREER: Novelist, 1931—. Stage manager for Repertory Players, London, in early career. Currently organizer and conductor with husband of creative writing courses at Moor Park College, Farnham, Surrey, England. *Member:* P.E.N. (London committee, 1934-38), Poetry Society (council, 1962-66), National Book League (council, 1962—), Society of Women Writers and Journalists (chairman, 1962-64; vice-president, 1965), West Country Writers Association (committee, 1953-64). *Awards, honors:* Silver Cup from Society of Women Writers and Journalists for best published work of 1947, for *Present Ending.*

WRITINGS: Children, Be Happy!, Gollancz, 1931; *Kept*

Man, Dutton, 1933; *Pity the Child!,* Chapman & Hall, 1934; *Shadow Thy Dream,* Chapman & Hall, 1934; *A Fawn in a Field,* Collins, 1935; *Men Ask for Beauty,* Collins, 1936; *Treasure in Heaven,* Collins, 1937; *Fairweather Faith,* Cassell, 1940; *Man of Promise,* Cassell, 1941; *Bracelet for Julia,* Cassell, 1942; *Pride of the Family,* Cassell, 1943; *Present Ending,* Cassell, 1946; *As the Narcissus,* Macdonald & Co., 1946; *The Widows,* Macdonald & Co., 1948; *The Raft,* Macdonald & Co., 1950; *The Falling Leaves,* Macdonald & Co., 1951; *Alys at Endon,* Macdonald & Co., 1953; *The Silly Dove,* Macdonald & Co., 1953; *Cassandra Calls,* Macdonald & Co., 1954; *Come Fill the Cup,* Macdonald & Co., 1955, Pantheon, 1956; *Morning Break,* Macdonald & Co., 1956; *Mrs. Jamison's Daughter,* Hutchinson, 1957; *The Grain Will Grow,* Hutchinson, 1959; *The Will of Heaven,* Hutchinson, 1960; *A Small Shower,* R. Hale, 1961; *The Ramerson Case,* R. Hale, 1962; *New Pasture,* R. Hale, 1965; *The Vanished Days,* R. Hale, 1966; *The Stroke of Seven,* Heinemann, 1967; *Ladders,* R. Hale, 1968; *The Umbrella,* R. Hale, 1970; *The Golden Bowl,* R. Hale, 1971. Also author with K. G. Newham, of *Tap Dancing in 12 Easy Lessons,* McKay, 1936.

Under pseudonym Catharine Carr—All published by Jenkins, except as otherwise noted: *English Summer,* 1954; *Lovers in the Sun,* 1955; *The Spinning Wheel: City of Cardiff High School for Girls, 1895-1955,* Western Mail & Echo, 1955; *Heart-Tide,* 1956; *The Richest Gift,* 1956; *A Dream Come True,* 1957; *It Must Be Love,* 1959; *In Search of a Dream,* 1960; *The Shining Heart,* 1961; *The Golden City,* 1963.

Contributor to *Books and Bookmen* and *Poetry Review.* Editor, *Contemporary Review* (incorporating *Fortnightly Review*), 1971—.

WORK IN PROGRESS: An autobiography; studies on George Eliot, her poetry and novels; studies on Thomas Hardy, and on Parton Street poets; writing on David Gascoyne, George Barker, Dylan Thomas, and others.

* * *

WAELDER, Robert 1900-1967

PERSONAL: Born February 20, 1900, in Vienna, Austria; son of Joseph (a business executive) and Helene (Mautner) Waelder; married Jennie Pollack, 1930 (divorced, 1943); married Elsie L. Martens (a social worker), July 27, 1946; children: (first marriage) Dorothea (Mrs. Emanuel S. Hellman), Marianne (Mrs. Arndt R. Von Hippel); (second marriage) David M., Catherine B. *Education:* University of Vienna, Ph.D., 1922.

CAREER: Vienna Psychoanalytical Institute, Vienna, Austria, instructor, 1925-38; Boston Psychoanalytical Institute, Boston, Mass., lecturer, 1938-41; Bryn Mawr College, Bryn Mawr, Pa., lecturer in psychiatric information, 1941-42; Philadelphia Psychoanalytical Institute, Philadelphia, Pa., training and supervising analyst, 1946-50; Institute of Philadelphia Association for Psychoanalysis, Philadelphia, Pa., training and supervising analyst, 1950-67; Jefferson Medical College, Philadelphia, Pa., professor of psychoanalysis, 1962-67; Center for Advanced Psychoanalytic Studies, Princeton, N.J., member of faculty, 1961-67. *Member:* American Psychoanalytic Association, International Psychoanalytic Association, American Psychological Association, Pennsylvania Psychological Society.

WRITINGS: Psychological Aspects of War and Peace, Geneva Research Center (Switzerland), 1939; (editor)

Living Thoughts of Sigmund Freud, Longmans, Green, 1941; *Basic Theory of Psychoanalysis,* International Universities, 1960; *Psychoanalytic Avenues to Art,* International Universities, 1965; *Progress and Revolution: A Study of the Issues of Our Age,* International Universities, 1967.

WORK IN PROGRESS: Collected Papers: Psychoanalysis and Social Science.

(Died, 1967)

* * *

WAITE, William W(iley) 1903-

PERSONAL: Born September 10, 1903, in Toledo, Ohio; son of William Henry Waite and Katharine (Wiley) Waite; married Grace McCastline Smith (a psychotherapist), September 14, 1927; children: William McCastline, Maria Morison. *Education:* Columbia University, A.B., 1924, M.A., 1926. *Religion:* Episcopal. *Home:* 445 Riverside Dr., New York, N.Y. 10027.

CAREER: New Jersey Bell Telephone Co., staff, line, and engineering supervisor, 1926-39, employment and training supervisor, 1940-41; Columbia University, New York, N.Y., associate professor, 1947-53, professor of industrial engineering, 1954—, chairman of department, 1953-62, 1965-68. Fulbright professor of industrial relations, University of Istanbul, 1953; visiting professor at University of Michigan, 1947, University of Belgrade, 1960, and Robert College (Turkey), 1967. Consultant to Agency for International Development, U.S. Department of State, in Japan, 1952, Mexico, 1955, 1959, Yugoslavia, 1960, Turkey, 1965, and Peru, 1966, 1967. Consulting management engineer; labor arbitrator. *Military service:* U.S. Army, 1942-46; became lieutenant colonel; received Army Commendation Ribbon. *Member:* American Society of Mechanical Engineers, Phi Gamma Delta, Tau Beta Pi, Alpha Pi Mu, Overseas Press Club of America.

WRITINGS: A Management Casebook, Department of Industrial Engineering, Columbia University, 1948; *Personnel Administration,* Ronald, 1952; (with R. T. Livingston) *The Manager's Job,* Columbia University Press, 1960; *Personnel Administration* (new book), Regents Publishing Co., 1964. Contributor to technical and scientific periodicals.

* * *

WAKSMAN, Selman A(braham) 1888-1973

PERSONAL: Surname rhymes with "box-man"; born July 22, 1888, in Priluka, near Kiev, Russia; came to United States, 1910, naturalized, 1916; son of Jacob and Fradia (London) Waksman; married Deborah Mitnik, August 5, 1916; children: Byron Halsted. *Education:* Rutgers University, B.S., 1915, M.S., 1916; University of California, Berkeley, Ph.D., 1918. *Home:* 16 Logan Lane, River Rd., Piscataway, N.J. 08904. *Office:* Institute of Microbiology, Rutgers University, New Brunswick, N.J. 08903.

CAREER: Rutgers University, New Brunswick, N.J., lecturer in soil microbiology and microbiologist at Experiment Station, 1920-25, associate professor, 1925-30, professor of microbiology, 1930-58, professor emeritus, 1958-73, head of department of microbiology, 1940-58, director of Institute of Microbiology, 1949-58, director of Institute of Microbiology, 1949-58. Woods Hole Oceanographic Institution, organizer of Division of Marine Bacteriology, 1931, marine bacteriologist, 1931-42, trustee, 1942-73. Head of research teams that isolated a number of new antibiotics, including actinomycin, 1940, streptomycin, 1943, and neomycin, 1948. Consultant to U.S. Department of Agriculture, U.S. Navy, National Research Council, Office of Scientific Research and Development, and other public and private agencies. Lecturer before scientific bodies in America and abroad. Founder (with wife) and president of Foundation for Microbiology.

MEMBER: American Society for Microbiology (president, 1942), National Academy of Sciences, American Academy of Arts and Sciences, American Society of Agronomy (vice-president, 1930-32), International Society of Soil Sciences (president of commission on soil microbiology, 1927-35), French Academy of Sciences (foreign associate), honorary member of other foreign academies and societies; Phi Beta Kappa, Sigma Xi, Alpha Zeta.

AWARDS, HONORS: Albert and Mary Lasker Award of American Public Health Association, 1948; Amory Award of American Academy of Arts and Sciences, 1948; Page One Award, 1949; American Phamaceutical Manufacturers Award, 1949; Leeuwenhoek Medal of Netherlands Academy of Sciences, 1950; Nobel Prize in physiology and medicine, 1952; Order of Merit of the Rising Sun (Japan), 1952; Variety Clubs Humanitarian Award, 1953; Great Cross of Public Health (Spain), 1954; American Trudeau Medal, 1961; Order of Southern Cross (Brazil), 1963; Commander, French Legion of Honors; and other awards. Honorary D.Sc. from Rutgers University, 1943, University of Liege, 1946, Princeton University, 1947, University of Madrid, 1950, Rhode Island State College, 1950, University of Athens, 1952, Pennsylvania Military College, 1953, Philadelphia College of Pharmacy, 1953, Brandeis University, 1954, Hebrew University of Jerusalem, 1958, University of Strasbourg, 1958, Jacksonville University, 1959, University of Pavia, 1961, Hahnemann Medical College, 1962, University of Brazil, 1963.

WRITINGS: (With W. C. Davison) *Enzymes: Properties, Distribution, Methods, and Applications*, Williams & Wilkins, 1926; *Principles of Soil Microbiology*, Williams & Wilkins, 1927, 2nd edition, 1932; (with E. B. Fred) *Laboratory Manual of General Microbiology*, McGraw, 1928; (with R. L. Starkey) *The Soil and the Microbe*, Wiley, 1931; *Humus: Origin, Chemical Composition, and Importance in Nature*, Williams & Wilkins, 1936, 2nd edition, 1938; *The Peats of New Jersey and Their Utilization*, Department of Conservation and Development, State of New Jersey, Part I, 1942, Part II, 1943; *Microbial Antagonisms and Antibiotic Substances*, Commonwealth Fund, 1945, 2nd edition, 1947; *The Literature on Streptomycin, 1944-1948*, Rutgers University Press, 1948, 2nd edition published as *The Literature on Streptomycin, 1944-1952*, 1952; (editor) *Streptomycin: Its Nature and Practical Application*, Williams & Wilkins, 1949.

The Actinomycetes: Their Nature, Occurrence, Activities, and Importance, Chronica Botanica, 1950; *Soil Microbiology*, Wiley, 1952; (editor) *Neomycin: Nature, Formation, Isolation, and Practical Application*, Rutgers University Press, 1953; *Sergei Nikolaevitch Winogradsky: The Story of a Great Bacteriologist*, Rutgers University Press, 1953; (with H. A. Lechevalier) *Guide to the Classification and Identification of the Actinomycetes and Their Antibiotics*, Williams & Wilkins, 1953; *My Life with the Microbes* (autobiographical), Simon and Schuster, 1954; (editor) *Perspectives and Horizons in Microbiology: A Symposium*, Rutgers University Press, 1955; (editor with others) *Neomycin*, Williams & Wilkins, 1958; *The Actinomycetes*, Williams & Wilkins, Volume I: *Nature, Occurrence, and Activities*,

1959, Volume II: *Classification, Identification, and Descriptions of Genera and Species*, 1961, Volume III: (with Lechevalier) *The Antibiotics of Actinomycetes*, 1962; *The Brilliant and Tragic Life of W.M.W. Haffkine, Bacteriologist*, Rutgers University Press, 1964; *The Conquest of Tuberculosis*, University of California Press, 1964; (with Robert L. Starkey and Richard Donovick) *Microbiology in New Jersy: Origins and Developments*, American Society for Microbiology, 1965; *Jacob G. Lipman*, Rutgers University Press, 1966; *The Actinomycetes: A Summary of Current Knowledge*, Ronald, 1967; *Actinomycin: Nature, Formation, and Activities*, Interscience Publishers, 1968.

Also author of research reports published in the U.S. Department of Agriculture *Journal of Agricultural Research*. Contributor of more than four hundred articles to scientific journals.

SIDELIGHTS: In 1941 Dr. Waksman coined the term "antibiotic" to describe penicillin and other newly-discovered wonder drugs. Waksman, with his team of researchers at Rutgers University, isolated streptomycin in 1943 after a four-year study of 10,000 microbes. The discovery of streptomycin, the first effective antibiotic against tuberculosis, earned Waksman the Nobel Prize in 1952.

The patent held by Waksman and his associates on streptomycin has been called one of the "ten letter patents that shaped the world." Three of their other antibiotics are also used extensively in the treatment of infectious diseases of men, animals, and plants. The bulk of the royalties obtained from patents on streptomycin and neomycin were used in support of the Institute of Microbiology at Rutgers. Waksman's personal share was used mainly to establish the Foundation for Microbiology, which supports research and publications at various institutions. He and his wife also endowed a scholarship at Rutgers for an immigrant student or the child of immigrants.

My Life with the Microbes has been translated into several languages, including Japanese, Spanich, Serbo-Croatian, and Polish; it was also published in England. Other Waksman books have been translated into Russian, French, and German.

BIOGRAPHICAL/CRITICAL SOURCES: My Life with the Microbes, Simon and Schuster, 1954; H. Boyd Woodruff, editor, *Scientific Contributions of Selman A. Waksman: Selected Articles Published in Honor of His Eightieth Birthday*, Rutgers University, 1968.

(Died August 16, 1973)

* * *

WALCOTT, Robert 1910-

PERSONAL: Born January 24, 1910, in Boston, Mass.; son of Robert (a lawyer and judge) and Mary T. (Richardson) Walcott; married Rosamond Pratt, June 18, 1938; children: Robert, Jr., Rebecca, Joseph Pratt. *Education:* Harvard University, A.B. (magna cum laude), 1931, M.A., 1932, Ph.D., 1938. *Politics:* Democrat. *Religion:* Episcopalian. *Home:* 1559 Burbank Rd., Wooster, Ohio 44691. *Office:* College of Wooster, Wooster, Ohio 44691.

CAREER: Harvard University, Cambridge, Mass., Bayard Cutting traveling fellow, 1934-35, Rogers traveling fellow, 1935-36, instructor and tutor, 1938-41; Westminster College, New Wilmington, Pa., instructor in history, 1942; Raytheon Manufacturing Co., Waltham, Mass., laboratory technician and technical writer, 1942-45; Black Mountain College, Black Mountain, N.C., instructor in history, 1945-

46; College of Wooster, Wooster, Ohio, associate professor, 1949-52, professor of history, 1952—. *Member:* American Historical Association (chairman of Robert Livingston Schuyler Prize committee), Anglo-American Conference of Historians, Midwestern Conference on British Historical Studies (president, 1964-65), Royal Historical Society (fellow). *Awards, honors:* Fulbright award for research in United Kingdom, 1953-54; Social Science Research Council grant-in-aid, 1955-57.

WRITINGS: (With D. K. Clark and others) *Essays in Modern English History in Honor of W. C. Abbott*, Harvard University Press, 1941; *English Politics in the Early Eighteenth Century*, Harvard University Press, 1956. Contributor of articles to *Collier's Encyclopedia*; also contributor to periodicals, including *New England Quarterly, Journal of British Studies, Atlantic Monthly*, and *Virginia Law Quarterly*.

WORK IN PROGRESS: A study of the London mercantile community, particularly London merchants engaged in overseas trade, 1685-1714.

* * *

WALDORF, Paul D(ouglass) 1908-

PERSONAL: Born January 13, 1908, in Syracuse, N.Y.; son of Ernest Lynn (a Methodist preacher) and Flora (Irish) Waldorf; married Rosina Thomas (a teacher), August 29, 1931; children: Mary Rosina, Thomas Ernest. *Education:* Baker University, A.B., 1929; University of Kansas, M.A., 1930; Northwestern University, Ph.D., 1948. *Religion:* Methodist. *Home:* 216 Branson St., Mankato, Minn. *Office:* Department of Foreign Languages, Mankato State College, Mankato, Minn.

CAREER: Teacher at University of Arizona, Tucson, 1930-31, Wentworth Military Academy, Lexington, Mo., 1931-33, McKendree College, Lebanon, Ill., 1933-36, Fort Hays State College, Hays, Kan., 1936-42, and Denison University, Granville, Ohio, 1945-47; Mankato State College, Mankato, Minn., chairman of department of foreign languages, 1947—. *Member:* American Association of University Professors, Alpha Mu Gamma, Phi Sigma Iota, Lions Club.

WRITINGS: Veraneo en Mexico, Dodd, 1964. Contributor to *Texas Quarterly*.

* * *

WALKERLEY, Rodney Lewis (de Burgh) 1905-
(Athos, Grande Vitesse)

PERSONAL: Born April 2, 1905, in Oundle, Northamptonshire, England; son of George Youngs (a civil servant) and Agnes (Bourke) Walkerley; married Jean Sievwright Bailey (a former fashion model), April 18, 1957. *Education:* Attended Mount St. Mary's Jesuit College, Derbyshire, England. *Politics:* Conservative. *Religion:* Catholic. *Home:* 6 Mill Bank, Tewkesbury, Gloucestershire, England.

CAREER: Bank clerk, 1922-25; *Motor Sport* (magazine), London, England, joint editor, 1926-28; Temple Press Ltd., London sports editor of *Light Car*, 1928-34, of *Motor*, 1928-58; free-lance author and journalist, 1958—. *Military service:* Royal Army Service Corps, instructor in mechanical transport at officer training units, 1940-42, attached to War Office, 1943-45; became staff captain. *Member:* British Racing Drivers Club, Bugatti Owners Club (pennant holder), Guild of Motoring Writers. *Awards, honors:* Journalists' plaque from French Minister of Tourisme, Alpine Rally, 1953.

WRITINGS: Grands Prix 1934-1939, Motor Racing Publications, 1948, revised edition, 1950; (compiler) *The Motor Yearbook*, Temple Press, 1949-57; *Motoring Abroad*, Temple Press, 1950; *More Motoring Abroad*, Temple Press, 1954; *Take Your Car Abroad*, Temple Press, 1958; *Moments That Made Racing History*, Temple Press, 1959, Sports Car Press, 1960; *Races That Shook the World*, Sports Car Press, 1959; *Come Motor Racing With Me*, Muller, 1961; *Motor Racing Facts and Figures*, Batsford, 1961, Bentley, 1962; *Brooklands to Goodwood: Fifty Years of the B.A.R.C.*, Foulis & Co., 1961; *With Your Car in Switzerland and Northern Italy*, Muller, 1961; *Automobile Racing*, Temple Press, 1962; *Sports Car Today*, Arthur Barker, 1962; *Racing Cars Today*, Arthur Barker, 1962, Sportshelf, 1965; (translator with Lyon Benzimra) Gianni Marin and Andrea Mattei, *The Motor Car: An Illustrated History*, Anthony Blond, 1962; (editor) *Famous Motor Races*, Muller, 1963; *The Motor Industry as a Career*, Batsford, 1963, Sportshelf, 1965; *Famous Motor Cars of the World*, Muller, 1964; *Sussex Pubs*, Hastings House, 1966; *Racing Car Design*, Weidenfeld & Nicolson, 1966.

WORK IN PROGRESS: Famous Motorists; Memoirs of a Motoring Journalist; Motor Museums of Europe; The House on the Square, a novel.

* * *

WALLACE, Paul A(nthony) W(ilson) 1891-

PERSONAL: Born October 31, 1891, in Cobourg, Ontario, Canada; son of Francis Huston (a professor at Victoria College, University of Toronto) and Johanna (Wilson) Wallace; married Dorothy Eleanor Clarke, July 23, 1919; children: Anthony Francis Clarke, David Harold. *Education:* University of Toronto, B.A., 1915, M.A., 1923, Ph.D., 1925. *Politics:* Democrat. *Religion:* Presbyterian. *Home:* 1027 Drexel Hills Blvd., New Cumberland, Pa. 17070.

CAREER: Instructor in English at University of Alberta, Edmonton, 1919-22, and University of Toronto, Toronto, Ontario, 1922-25; Lebanon Valley College, Annville, Pa., professor of English, 1925-49; Pennsylvania Historical and Museum Commission, Harrisburg, historian, 1949-65; Lebanon Valley College, fellow in the humanities, 1965—. *Military service:* Canadian Army, dispatch rider with Canadian Expeditionary Force, 1916-18. *Member:* American Historical Association, Pennsylvania Historical Association, Pennsylvania Folklore Society, Historical Society of Pennsylvania, Franklin Inn Club (Philadelphia). *Awards, honors:* Litt.D. from Muhlenberg College; L.H.D. from Moravian College.

WRITINGS: Baptiste Larocque: Legends of French Canada, Musson, 1923; *The Twist and Other Other Stories*, Ryerson, 1923; (editor) *Selections from Sam Slick*, Ryerson, 1923; (editor) Anna Jameson, *Winter Studies and Summer Rambles in Canada*, McClelland & Stewart, 1923; *Conrad Weiser, 1696-1760: A Friend of Colonist and Mohawk*, University of Pennsylvania Press, 1945; *The White Roots of Peace*, University of Pennsylvania Press, 1946.

The Muhlenbergs of Pennsylvania, University of Pennsylvania Press, 1950; *Thirty Thousand Miles with John Heckewelder*, University of Pittsburgh Press, 1958; (with Katherine B. Shippen) *Milton S. Hershey*, Random House, 1959; *Indians in Pennsylvania*, Pennsylvania Historical and Museum Commission, 1961; *Pennsylvania, Seed of a Nation*, Harper, 1962; *Lloyd Mifflin; Painter and Poet of the Susquehanna*, Pennsylvania Historical and Museum Commission, 1965; *Indian Paths of Pennsylvania*, Pennsylvania

Historical and Museum Commission, 1966; *Lebanon Valley College: A Centennial History*, Lebanon Valley College, 1966. Contributor to historical journals. Editor of *Pennsylvania History*, 1951-57.

WORK IN PROGRESS: A pamphlet on the Daniel Boone Homestead in Berks County, Pa.

AVOCATIONAL INTERESTS: Canoeing in northern Ontario, mountaineering in Switzerland and the Canadian Rockies, motoring.

*   *   *

WALLENSTEIN, Meir   1903-

PERSONAL: Born May 13, 1903, in Jerusalem. Palestine; son of Shimon and Sarah Wallenstein; married Sara Shoshanah Rabby, September, 1946. *Education:* Teachers' Training College, Jerusalem, Palestine, student; Training College, Jerusalem, Palestine, student; University of Manchester, M.A., 1935, Ph.D., 1937. *Religion:* Jewish. *Home:* 6, Zlocisti St., Tel-Aviv, Israel.

CAREER: University of Manchester, Manchester, England, lecturer in modern Hebrew, 1941-45, lecturer, 1945-57, senior lecturer, 1957-61, reader in medieval and modern Hebrew, 1961-72; University Bar Ilan, Ramat-Gan, Israel, professor of Hebrew literature with special reference to medieval Hebrew manuscripts, 1972—. Advisory member, Hebrew Language Academy, Jerusalem; honorary director of Hebrew studies, King David High School, Manchester, England. *Member:* Royal Asiatic Society, Society for Old Testament Study, Tarbut Society (Manchester; chairman).

WRITINGS: (Editor with E. Robertson) *Melilah*, Manchester University Press, 1955; *Some Unpublished Piyyutim from the Cairo Genizah*, Manchester University Press, 1956; *The Nezer and the Submission in Suffering Hymn from the Dead Sea Scrolls*, Nederlans Historisch-Archaeologisch Instituut in het Nabije Oosten, 1957. Contributor to *Manchester Guardian, Leshonenu, Molad, Bulletin of the John Ryland Library*, and to journals in his field. Co-editor, *Melilah*.

WORK IN PROGRESS: Letters and Poetry of Mosheh Yehudah Abbas; several monographs.

BIOGRAPHICAL/CRITICAL SOURCES: Haaretz, Tel-Aviv, August 16, 1963.

*   *   *

WALMSLEY, Leo   1892-1966

PERSONAL: Born September 29, 1892, in Shipley, Yorkshire, England; son of James Ulric (an artist) and Jane Cohu (Dodd) Walmsley; married Margaret Bell-Little, 1931 (divorced, 1955); married Stephanie Gurbins; children: (first marriage) Anna (Mrs. Richard Scott), Henrietta (Mrs. William Lagarde), Simon, Patrick (deceased), Shawn; (second marriage) Selina. *Education:* Attended schools in England. *Religion:* Christian Humanist. *Home:* Bramblewick, Passage St., Fowey, Cornwall, England.

CAREER: Curator of Marine Biological Station at Robin Hood's Bay, Yorkshire, England, 1913-14; naturalist on filming expedition to Timbuktu, West Africa, 1918; fulltime writer, 1919-66. *Military service:* British Army, East Yorkshire Regiment, 1914-15, Royal Flying Corps, flying officer observer in German East Africa, 1916-18; received Military Cross, mentioned in dispatches four times.

WRITINGS: Flying and Sport in East Africa, W. Blackwood, 1920; *The Silver Blimp* (boys' book), Thomas Nel-

son, 1921; *The Lure of Thunder Island*, Jenkins, 1923; *The Green Rocket*, Jenkins, 1926; *Toro of the Little People*, George H. Doran, 1926; *Three Fevers*, Knopf, 1932; *Pahntom Lobster*, J. Cape, 1933; *Foreigners*, J. Cape, 1935, Meredith, 1968; *Sally Lunn*, Macmillan, 1937; *Love in the Sun* (Book Society choice), Collins, 1939, Doubleday, 1940; *Fisherman at War*, Doubleday, 1941; *British Poets and Harbors*, Collins, 1942; *So Many Loves*, Collins, 1944, new edition, 1969, published as *Turn of the Tide*, Doubleday, 1945; *Sally Lunn* (play), Collins, 1947; *Master Mariner*, Collins, 1948; *Lancashire and Yorkshire*, Collins, 1951; *Invisible Cargo*, M. Joseph, 1952; *The Golden Waterwheel*, Collins, 1954; *The Happy Ending*, Collins, 1957; *Sound of the Sea*, Collins, 1959; *Paradise Creek*, Collins, 1963; *Angler's Moon: Memoirs of Fish, Fishing and Fishermen*, Hamish Hamilton, 1965. Also author of "Home Is the Sailor" (television play), 1963. Contributor of articles and short stories to *Adventure, National Geographic*, and other publications in Europe and the United States.

WORK IN PROGRESS: Television plays.

SIDELIGHTS: Love in the Sun, a best seller, appeared in five foreign language editions.

BIOGRAPHICAL/CRITICAL SOURCES: Saturday Review, January 18, 1969; *Books and Bookmen*, October, 1969.†

(Died June, 1966)

*   *   *

WALTER, Dorothy Blake   1908-
(Katherine Blake, Kay Blake, Katherine Ross)

PERSONAL: Born June 6, 1908, in Stroud, Okla.; daughter of T. J. and L. Beulah (Henry) Blake; married Edwin C. Walter (Dean of Academic Administration, Columbia Union College), 1935; children: Linda Katherine. *Education:* St. Helena Hospital School of Nursing, St. Helena, Calif., R.N., 1934; Pacific Union College, B.S., 1959. *Home:* 922 Kenbrook Dr., Wheaton (Silver Spring), Md. 20902. *Office:* Columbia Union College, Takoma Park, Md. (Washington, D.C.) 20012.

CAREER: Elementary teacher at schools in Oklahoma and Texas, 1927-31; St. Helena Sanitarium and Hospital, St. Helena, Calif., nurse and supervisor, 1934-35; elementary teacher at schools in California and Indiana, 1936-42; La Sierra College, Riverside, Calif., secretary, 1942-45; Pacific Union College, Angwin, Calif., secretary, 1945-46, administrative assistant, 1946-63, assistant to Director of Graduate Study, 1963-65, instructor in English and writing, 1965-68; textbook writer and editor, 1968-70; Columbia Union College, Takoma Park, Md., assistant director of admissions, 1970—. Free-lance writer.

WRITINGS: Worship Time: A Book of Stories, Finger Plays, and Poems for Children, Pacific Press Publishing Association, 1961. Also author of ten health and science elementary textbooks and teacher's guides, published by Pacific Press Publishing Association, 1968-70. One-time writer of regular page, "Fun and Health," in *Life and Health*. Contributor, under various pseudonyms, of fifteen serials and nearly one thousand poems, stories, and articles to newspapers and periodicals, including juvenile Sunday School publications and *Farm Journal, Hearthstone, Children's Activities, Child Life*.

WORK IN PROGRESS: Stories and verses; a book on writing for juveniles.

SIDELIGHTS: There is a complete collection of Dorothy

Blake Walter manuscripts, both published and unpublished, at Boston University Libraries. *Avocational interests:* Drawing and painting, reading, collecting classical records and cooking recipes, travel.

BIOGRAPHICAL/CRITICAL SOURCES: Life and Health, August, 1960.

*   *   *

WALTON, Alfred Grant   1887-1970

PERSONAL: Born October 17, 1887, in Kalamazoo, Mich.; son of David and Margaret (Thomson) Walton; married Mary Isabel Ingell, January 1, 1916; children: Carolyn I. (Mrs. John Thayer Taintor), Gloria L. (Mrs. Burton Knust), Alfred Grant, Jr. *Education:* Oberlin College, A.B., 1911; Columbia University, A.M., 1913; Oberlin Theological Seminary, B.D., 1914. *Politics:* Republican. *Home:* 750 East 18th St., Brooklyn, N.Y. 11230.

CAREER: Ordained Congregational minister, 1914. Pastor in Stamford, Conn., 1917-31, in Springfield, Mass., 1931-34, in Brooklyn, N.Y., 1934-64. Captain in American Red Cross, Paris, 1916-18. Network broadcaster, Federal Council of Churches, 1935-39; president of board of Home Missions, Congregational Christian Churches, 1944-48; member of board of directors, Protestant Council of Brooklyn, beginning, 1944; Indus-Home for the Blind, trustee, beginning, 1937, vice-president, beginning, 1964; trustee of Brooklyn Eye and Ear Hospital, 1944-54, and Brooklyn Public Library, beginning, 1956. *Awards, honors:* D.D. from Oberlin College, 1926; LL.D. from American International College, 1935; L.H.D. from Kalamazoo College, 1941.

WRITINGS: Stamford Historical Sketches, Cunningham Press, 1922; *This I Can Believe,* Harper, 1935; *Highways to Happiness,* Harper, 1939; *Life Is What You Make It,* Revell, 1942; *Living Waters,* National Printing Co., 1946; *Walking With God,* Pilgrim Press, 1948; *Lyrics for Living,* Golden Quill, 1963. Also writer of pamphlets, booklets of poems, and articles.

(Died July 9, 1970)

*   *   *

WARD, R(ichard) H(eron)   1910-1969

PERSONAL: Born May 23, 1910, in Chesham Bois, Buckinghamshire, England; son of Arthur Harry (a master lapidary) and Grace (Silsby) Ward; divorced. *Education:* Studied at Stowe School, Buckinghamshire, England, 1924-28, at Sorbonne, University of Paris, 1928-29, at Royal Academy of Dramatic Art, London, England, 1929. *Politics:* "Radical of no party." *Religion:* "Christian of no church." *Home:* 17 Bell Rd., Haslemere, Surrey, England.

CAREER: Actor with English Players, Paris, France, 1929-30, with American Players, Paris, 1930, with British theatre companies, 1930-69, including Pilgrim Players, Oxford, England, 1940-41. Founder and director, Adelphi Players, 1941-46; member of council of management, Century Theatre, 1961-69. Occasional producer for Compass Players, Adelphi Guild Theatre, and Century Theatre, 1946-69. Literature secretary, Peace Pledge Union, 1936-40. *Member:* Society of Authors, League of British Dramatists, Religious Drama Society.

WRITINGS: The Compelled Hero (novel), J. Cape & H. Smith, 1931; *The Spring Term Is Over* (novel), Jarrolds, 1933; *The Progress to the Lake,* Nicholson & Watson, 1934; *The Powys Brothers: A Study,* John Lane, 1935; *The*

Sun Shall Rise, Nicholson & Watson, 1935; (editor) *Ten Peace Plays,* Dent, 1938; *William Somerset Maugham,* Bles, 1937; *What Is Non-Violent Technique?,* Publicity Unit, 1938; *The Human Factor,* Peace Pledge Union, 1939; *The Encounter* (poems), Andrew Dakers, 1948; *God's Absence, God's Return,* Ridgeway & Shorn, 1950; *Twenty-Three Poems,* Hand & Flower Press, 1952; *The Leap in the Dark* (novel), Gollancz, 1954; *A Gallery of Mirrors: Memoirs of Childhood, Boyhood, and Early Youth,* Gollancz, 1956; *A Drug-Taker's Notes,* Gollancz, 1957; (editor) Robert Brooks Simpkins, *New Light on the Eyes,* Vincent Stuart, 1958; *The Wilderness* (novel; first in the trilogy "Variations on a Theme"), Cassell, 1958; (translator) Eugene Labiche and Edouard Martin, *A Trip Abroad,* Mermaid Dramabook, 1959; *The Offenders* (second in the trilogy), Cassell, 1960; *The Life of Cassie Pearson* (novel), Cassell, 1962; *The Hidden Boy: The Work of C. A. Joyce,* Cassell, 1962; *The Conspiracy* (third in trilogy), Cassell, 1964; *Names and Natures: Memoirs of Ten Men,* Gollancz, 1968; *The Prodigal Son: Some Comments on the Parable,* Gollancz, 1968; *Angles of Vision: Three Longer Poems,* Fernhurst Press, 1968.

Published plays: *An Experiment in Fear* (one-act), Samuel French, 1933; *Holy Family* (nativity play in verse), Adelphi Players, 1942, revised edition with preface, S.P.C.K., 1950; *The Destiny of Man* (in verse), Adelphi Players, 1943; *Faust in Hell* (one-act), Samuel French, 1944; *The Prodigal Son* (in verse), Religious Drama Society, 1944, revised edition, S.P.C.K., 1952; *The Figure on the Cross* (in verse), S.P.C.K., 1947; *The Wise and Foolish Virgins,* Religious Drama Society, 1949; *The Builders,* S.P.C.K., 1959; *The Lost Sheep* (comedy), S.P.C.K., 1960; *The Wanderer,* S.P.C.K., 1962.

Produced plays: "Flora Whiteley"; "Of Gods and Men"; "The Landing Party"; "The Years and the Days"; "The Barbarian Invasion"; "The Westward Journey" (radio); "The Murder of Chatterton" (radio). Editor of monthly radio program, "Apollo in the West," British Broadcasting Corp., 1951-52. Contributor to *Time and Tide, Adelphi, Listener, Radio Times,* and other periodicals.

BIOGRAPHICAL/CRITICAL SOURCES: Stage, January 1, 1970; *Variety,* January 21, 1970.

(Died December, 1969)

*   *   *

WARDELL, Phyl(lis Robinson)   1909-

PERSONAL: Born October 21, 1909, in Christchurch, New Zealand; daughter of James Ernest Boyd and Mary Margaret (Cook) Robinson; married Thomas William Rae Wardell, December 21, 1935; children: William Michael, Lynne Margaret. *Education:* Educated in New Zealand. *Home:* 192 Salisbury St., Christchurch, New Zealand.

MEMBER: P.E.N.

WRITINGS—Juvenile fiction: *Gold at Kapai,* A. H. & A. W. Reed, 1960; *The Secret of the Lost Tribe of Te Anau,* A. H. & A. W. Reed, 1962; *Passage to Dusky,* Parrish, 1967. Writer of serials for radio in Australia and New Zealand.

WORK IN PROGRESS: Several books; commissioned radio and television scripts.

SIDELIGHTS: Mrs. Wardell's books have been published in England, Germany, and Holland.

WARE, Jean (Jones) 1914-

PERSONAL: Born December 17, 1914, in Rangoon, Burma; daughter of Elias Henry (with Indian Civil Service) and Maur Olwen (Evans) Jones; married Arthur Gordon Ware, March 2, 1943 (died July 19, 1943); children: Nicholas Gordon. *Education:* University College of North Wales, B.A. (honors), 1936; King's College, London, graduate study, 1936-37. *Religion:* Church of England. *Home:* 3 Tanysgafell, Bethesda, Bangor, Caernarvonshire, Wales. *Agent:* Curtis Brown Ltd., 13 King St., Covent Garden, London WC2E 8HU, England.

CAREER: Dumfries Standard, Dumfries, Scotland, junior reporter, 1937; North Wales Chronicle Group, staff reporter, 1937-41; secretary to regional committee for adult education in H.M. Forces, 1941-43; teacher for Polish Resettlement Corps under Worker's Education Association extramural scheme, 1946-48; free-lance journalist, with permanent commissions for British Broadcasting Corp. and *Liverpool Daily Post,* 1948—. Lecturer to clubs and societies. North Wales representative, British Council, 1952-55. *Member:* North Wales Naturalists' Trust (publicity officer, 1963-64), Caernarvonshire Historical Association, French Society (University College of North Wales).

WRITINGS: Campau Dic (Welsh reader), Hughes & Son, 1952; *Rowdy House,* Faber, 1962. Contributor of articles to magazines and journals, a regular weekly column and book reviews to *Daily Post,* 1950—, and children's plays, adult features, talks, and short stories to British Broadcasting Corp. Former editor, Welsh edition of "Woman's Hour," and interviewer for British Broadcasting Corp.

WORK IN PROGRESS: A biography of a Welsh centenarian, Griffith Evans, M.D., 1835-1935.

SIDELIGHTS: Mrs. Ware lives in a tiny Welsh cottage made of slate, by a mountain river in Snowdonia.†

*   *   *

WARFEL, Harry R(edcay)   1899-1971

PERSONAL: Born March 21, 1899, in Reading, Pa.; son of Wyatt William and Kate (Redcay) Warfel; married Ruth Evelyn Farquhar, April 15, 1922 (died June 24, 1961); married Elizabeth Warner Sturges, June 11, 1962. *Education:* Bucknell University, A.B., 1920, A.M., 1922; Columbia University, A.M., 1924; University of North Carolina, graduate study, 1924-25; Yale University, Ph.D., 1932. *Politics:* Democrat. *Religion:* Baptist. *Home:* 1605 Northwest 14th Ave., Gainesville, Fla. *Office:* Anderson Hall, University of Florida, Gainesville, Fla.

CAREER: St. John's School, Manlius, N.Y., master, 1920-21; Bucknell University, Lewisburg, Pa., instructor, 1921-25, assistant professor, 1925-34, associate professor of English, 1934-35; University of Maryland, College Park, professor of English, 1935-43; U.S. Department of State, Washington, D.C., 1943-46, became assistant chief, Division of International Exchange of Persons; Bucknell University, administrative officer, 1946-47. Pennsylvania Military College, Chester, professor of English and head of department, 1947-48; University of Florida, Gainesville, professor of English, beginning, 1948. Consulting editor, American Book Co., 1942-55, general editor and proprietor, Scholars' Facsimiles & Reprints, 1948-71. Fulbright lecturer, Philipps University, 1953-54. Director, American Humanities Center for Liberal Education, 1955-71.

MEMBER: Modern Language Association of America, American Dialect Society, College English Association (president, 1959), National Council of Teachers of English. *Awards, honors:* Sterling research fellow at Yale University, 1934-35; Alumni Award from Bucknell University, 1958, for meritorious achievement.

WRITINGS: Noah Webster: Schoolmaster to America, Macmillan, 1936; (with E. G. Mathews and J. C. Bushman) *American College English: A Handbook of Usage and Composition,* American Book Co., 1949; *Charles Brockden Brown: American Gothic Novelist,* University of Florida Press, 1949; *The Demies: A History,* Delta Sigma Fraternity, 1949; *American Novelists of Today,* American Book Co., 1951; *Who Killed Grammar?,* University of Florida Press, 1952; (with D. J. Lloyd) *American English in Its Cultural Setting,* Knopf, 1956; *Language: A Science of Human Behavior,* Howard Allen, 1962; *From Irving to Steinbeck,* University of Florida Press, 1972.

Editor: (With R. H. Gabriel and S. T. Williams) *The American Mind: Selections from the Literature of the United States,* American Book Co., 1937, revised edition, 1947, 2nd revised edition published in 2 volumes, 1963; *Sketches of American Policy by Noah Webster,* Scholars' Facsimiles, 1937; (with G. H. Orians) *American Local-Color Stories,* American Book Co., 1941; (with E. W. Manwaring) *Of the People,* Oxford University Press, 1942; C. B. Brown, *The Rhapsodist and Other Uncollected Writings,* Scholars' Facsimiles, 1943; (with H. Brickell and D. G. Poore) *Cuentistas Norteamericanos,* W. M. Jackson, 1946; *Dissertations on the English Language by Noah Webster,* Scholars' Facsimiles, 1951; *Letters of Noah Webster,* Library Publishers, 1953; *Studies in Walt Whitman's Leaves of Grass,* Scholars' Facsimiles, 1953; James Gates Percival, *Uncollected Letters,* University of Florida Press, 1959.

Contributor to professional journals. Member of editorial board, *Century Cyclopedia of Names,* and *American Speech.*

WORK IN PROGRESS: Two books, *The Art of Walt Whitman* and *The Structure of Literature.*

SIDELIGHTS: Warfel once wrote to *CA:* "My earliest scholarly interest was in tracing American literary nationalism. In 1935 I enlarged the scope of my work to include the whole of American intellectual progress as it related to literature. Since 1952 I have been most concerned with the nature of the mechanism of language, especially as it relates to the structure of literature. My theory of functionality is probably the first attempt to explain all language manifestations by a single principle: literary art gains its effects by the harmonious interplay of six language systems."

(Died, 1971)

*   *   *

WARLIMONT, Walter   1894-

PERSONAL: Born October 3, 1894, in Osnabrueck, Germany; son of Louis and Anna (Rinck) Warlimont; married Anita, Baroness von Kleydorff, March, 1927; children: Christa (Baroness von Kittlitz), Dorothee Warlimont Racky, Wolfgang W. *Education:* Attended schools and military institutions in Germany. *Religion:* Roman Catholic. *Home:* Herzogweg 16, Gumund am Tegernsee, Bavaria, West Germany.

CAREER: German Army, Artillery and General Staff officer, 1913-45; retired with rank of lieutenant general.

WRITINGS: (Contributor) H. A. Jacobsen and J. Rohwer, editors, *Entscheidungsschlachten des 2 Weltkriegs,* Bernard & Greafe, 1959; *Im Hauptquartier der deutschen*

Wehrmacht, Bernard & Greafe, 1962, translation by R. H. Barry published as *Inside Hitler's Headquarters, 1939-45*, Praeger, 1964.

SIDELIGHTS: Warlimont is competent in English, French, and Spanish.

* * *

WARMAN, (William) Eric 1904-

PERSONAL: Born September 23, 1904, in London, England; son of William and Margaret (Dent) Warman; divorced; children: Jean Warman Simpson. *Education:* Attended Westminster City School, London, England. *Office:* Editorial Consultants Ltd., 56 Grosvenor St., London W.1, England.

CAREER: Books for Pleasure Group, London, England, director, 1949-60; Editorial Consultants Ltd., London, England, managing director, 1960—; Consortium Publications, London, England, partner, 1960—. Theo Cowan Ltd. (public relations), London, England, director, 1962—; Soundguide Ltd., London, England, chairman, 1963—. *Member:* Society of Authors, Crime Writers' Association, P.E.N., Savile Club (London).

WRITINGS: No Place for the Young, Fortune Press, 1934; *Relative to Murder*, Harrap, 1941; *Pattern for Murder*, Harrap, 1943; *Soft at the Centre*, Dakers, 1953; (with M. Moisewitsch) *Royal Ballet on Stage and Screen*, Heinemann, 1960; (editor with Tom Vallance) *Westerns: A Preview Special*, Golden Pleasure Books, 1964; *These Same Men*, Whiting & Wheaton, 1966. Editor, *Preview Film Album*, 1951-60, 1962-63.

WORK IN PROGRESS: A novel.

AVOCATIONAL INTERESTS: Psychology and psychoanalysis.

* * *

WARNER, Kenneth (Lewis) 1915-
(Dighton Morel)

PERSONAL: Born April 10, 1915, in Gosport, Hampshire, England; son of Frederick George (a shoemaker) and Caroline (Weedon) Warner; married Elfriede Krawatzo, October 24, 1953; children: Jennifer, Susan, Gabriele, Isabel. *Education:* Nelson Hall Training College, teaching diploma, 1947. *Home:* Ludwig-Hofer-Str. 2, Stuttgart 1, West Germany. *Agent:* Curtis Brown Ltd., 1 Craven Hill, London W2 3EW, England. *Office:* Ernst Klett Verlag, Rotebuhlstrasse 77, Stuttgart 1, West Germany.

CAREER: Teacher in Gosport, Hampshire, England, 1933-36; British Army, education officer, 1936-45; 1948-52, becoming captain; Ernst Klett (educational publishers), Stuttgart, Germany, literary adviser and editor of English-language publications, 1954—. Novelist.

WRITINGS—Under pseudonym Dighton Morel: *Moonlight Red*, Secker & Warburg, 1960; *The Little Perisher*, Secker & Warburg, 1961; *Autumn Fair*, Secker & Warburg, 1962; *The Son*, Secker & Warburg, 1963.

Under own name: *Tom and Jenny*, M. Joseph, 1964; *A Question of Living*, M. Joseph, 1966. Writer of English-language educational aids.

WORK IN PROGRESS: A novel with a German setting, to be published under his own name.

SIDELIGHTS: Warner has aspired to a writing career since the age of eighteen, but it was not until after going to

work in Germany that he wrote seriously. His first four books, written under a pseudonym, were moderately well-received; he felt, however, that they represented "a complete stage in the development of my work," and when *Tom and Jenny*, entirely different from any of his other work, was completed he decided to publish it under his real name.

Film rights to *Tom and Jenny*, are being sold to Pinewood Studios in England.

* * *

WARSAW, Irene

PERSONAL: Born in Kawkawlin, Mich.; daughter of Herman A. and Auguste (Malzahn) Warsaw. *Education:* Attended public schools in Bay City, Mich.; also attended Bread Loaf Writers' Conferences, Middlebury, Vt., 1951-64. *Politics:* Republican. *Religion:* Presbyterian. *Home:* 1309 Sixth St., Bay City, Mich. 48076. *Office:* Peoples National Bank & Trust Co. of Bay City, Bay City, Mich.

CAREER: Peoples National Bank & Trust Co. of Bay City, Bay City, Mich., private secretary, 1935-50, trust officer, 1950—, vice-president, 1972—. Lecturer on poetry; staff member of various writers' conferences. *Member:* National League of American Pen Women, American Academy of Poets, National Federation of Poetry Societies, Poetry Society of Michigan, Pennsylvania Poetry Society, Detroit Women Writers' Club, Poets' Study Club of Terre Haute, League of Women Voters.

WRITINGS: A Word in Edgewise (collection of light verse), Golden Quill, 1964. Writer of lyrics for sacred music and prayer responses. Contributor of hundreds of pieces of poetry and prose humor to magazines and newspapers, including *Saturday Evening Post, Good Housekeeping, McCall's, Wall Street Journal, Better Homes and Gardens, Look, Christian Science Monitor, Atlantic Monthly.*

* * *

WASHBURNE, Carleton W(olsey) 1889-

PERSONAL: Born December 2, 1889, in Chicago, Ill.; son of George Foote (a physician) and Marion (Foster) Washburne; married Heluiz Chandler (a writer), September 15, 1912 (deceased); children: Margaret Joan (Mrs. Donald K. Marshall), Beatrice (Mrs. John E. Visher), Chandler. *Education:* University of Chicago, A.Sc., 1910; Hahemann Medical College, student, 1910-11; Stanford University, B.A., 1912; University of California, Berkeley, Ed.D., 1918. *Politics:* Usually Democrat. *Religion:* Quaker.

CAREER: Teacher in Los Angeles County and Tulare, Calif., 1912-14; San Francisco State Normal School (now San Francisco State University), San Francisco, Calif., instructor, 1914-19; Winnetka, Ill., public schools, superintendent, 1919-43; U.S. Information Service, director for North Italy, 1946-48; UNESCO, educational reconstruction specialist, 1948-49; Brooklyn College (now Brooklyn College of the City University of New York), director of teacher education and Graduate Division, 1949-60; Michigan State University, East Lansing, Distinguished Professor, teaching part-time, beginning, 1961. Writer on educational subjects. Director of Louisiana school survey, 1941-42; participant in international conferences on education. Member of board of Michigan Area Office, American Friends Service Committee. *Military service:* U.S. Army, 1943-46; director of Education Subcommission; became lieutenant colonel; received Legion of Merit.

New Education Fellowship (international president, 1947-55), American Educational Research Association (vice-president, 1925), National Society for Study of Education, Progressive Education Association (president, 1936-40). *Awards, honors:* Ped.D., University of Messina; Litt.D., Newark State College; Grande Bene Merito, University of Rome; decorated by Italy and Cambodia.

WRITINGS: (With Myron Stearns) *New Schools in the Old World*, Day, 1926; (with Gray and Mabel Vogel) *A Survey of the Winnetka Public Schools*, Public School Publishing Co., 1926; (with Vogel and others) *Winnetka Graded Book List*, American Library Association, 1926, published as *What Children Like to Read*, Rand-McNally, 1926; (with Stearns) *Better Schools*, Day, 1928; *Adjusting the School to the Child*, World Book, 1932; *Remakers of Mankind*, Day, 1932; (with Vivian Weedon and others) *The Right Book for the Right Child*, Day, 1933, 3rd edition, 1943.

A Living Philosophy of Education, Day, 1940; *Louisiana Looks at Its Schools*, Louisiana Survey Commission, 1942; *What Is Progressive Education?*, Day, 1952 (published in England as *Schools Aren't What They Were: A Book for Parents and Others*, Heinemann, 1953); *The World's Good: Education for World-Mindedness*, Day, 1954; *La Formazione dell' Insegnati Stati Uniti*, La Nuova Italia, 1958; *Winnetka, Un Esperimento Pedagogico*, La Nuova Italia, 1960, published (with S. P. Marland, Jr.) as *Winnetka: The History and Significance of an Educational Experiment*, Prentice-Hall, 1963. Contributor to journals.

Textbooks: (With wife Heluiz Chandler Washburne) *The Story of The Earth*, Century, 1916; *Common Science*, World Book Co., 1920; *Individual Speller*, World Book Co., 1924; (with Olivia Youngquist) *My Reading Book; My Sound Book; My Other Reading Book*, Rand McNally, 1926-30; (with others) "Washburne Individual Arithmetic Series," World Book Co., 1927-30; (with Vivian Weedon) *Winnetka Speed Practice and Tests in Arithmetic*, Winnetka Individual Materials, 1930; (with H. C. Washburne and Frederick Reed) *The Story of Earth and Sky*, Appleton, 1933. Editor, "Winnetka Language Series," 1941, "Functional Arithmetic Series," 1943, and, with W. W. Beatty, "Social Study Series," Rand McNally, 1928-40.

WORK IN PROGRESS: A book with tentative title, *Thresholds of Understanding*.

SIDELIGHTS: Washburne has studied educational systems and lectured on all continents except Antarctica. Many of his books have been translated into Spanish, Italian, Japanese, Chinese, Danish, and Polish.

* * *

WASHBURNE, Heluiz Chandler   1892-

PERSONAL: Born January 25, 1892, in Cincinnati, Ohio; daughter of Charles Colby (a civil engineer) and Julia (Davis) Chandler; married Carleton W. Washburne (a professor and writer), September 15, 1912; children: Margaret Joan (Mrs. D. K. Marshall), Beatrice (Mrs. John E. Visher), Chandler. *Education:* Attended School of Industrial Arts and Women's School of Design, both Philadelphia, Pa. *Politics:* Democrat. *Religion:* Quaker. *Home and office:* 2248 Kent St., Okemos, Mich. 48864.

CAREER: Carson, Pirie, Scott & Co. (department store), Chicago, Ill., home fashion adviser, 1928-30; *Chicago Daily News*, Chicago, Ill., travel columnist, 1940-42; free-lance writer. *Member:* League of Women Voters, Women's International League.

WRITINGS: Letters to Channy: A Trip Around the World, (Junior Literary Guild selection), Rand McNally, 1932; (with husband, Carleton W. Washburne, and Frederick Reed) *Stories of the Earth and Sky* (Junior Literary Guild selection), Appleton, 1933; *Little Elephant Catches Cold*, Whitman, 1937; *Little Elephant's Christmas*, Whitman, 1938; *Little Elephant's Picnic*, Whitman, 1939; *Fridl, a Mountain Boy*, Winston, 1939; *Rhamon, a Boy of Kashmir*, Whitman, 1939; (with Anauta Blackmore) *Land of the Good Shadows: The Life Story of Anauta, an Eskimo Woman*, John Day, 1940; *Little Elephant Visits the Farm*, Whitman, 1941; (with Blackmore) *Children of the Blizzard* (Junior Literary Guild selection), John Day, 1952; *Tomas Goes Trading*, John Day, 1959. Contributor of articles to *Britannica Junior Encyclopaedia*.

SIDELIGHTS: Mrs. Washburne has lived in Italy, Mexico, and Cambodia, and traveled in Europe frequently, and in China, Japan, Korea, India, Russia, the Near East, Africa, South America, and Australia. *Letters to Channy* has been published in England and Poland, and *Children of the Blizzard* in Denmark, Germany, Sweden, Japan, and England.

* * *

WASHINGTON, (Catherine) Marguerite Beauchamp 1892-1972
(Anne Beaton, Pat Beauchamp, Pat Beauchamp Washington)

PERSONAL: Born in 1892 in Warwick Bridge, near Carlisle, England; daughter of Cranston (a woolen manufacturer) and Beatrice (Thompson) Waddell; married Peter Washington, July 27, 1922; children: Timothy John Clulow, Ralph Peter. *Education:* Studied at University of Lausanne; Royal Academy of Music, London, England, A.R.C.M. and L.R.A.M.; Cordon Bleu, Paris, France, school certificate. *Politics:* Conservative. *Religion:* Protestant. *Home:* Broadwath House, Heads Nook, near Carlisle, Cumberland, England.

CAREER: Served in France and Belgium as volunteer ambulance driver for First Aid Nursing Yeomanry, 1915-17; College of Modern Housekeeping, chief lecturer and publicity expert, 1934-38; Chelsea Polytechnic, Chelsea, London, England, lecturer and demonstrator of cookery, 1938-39; British Broadcasting Corp., London and Newcastle, England, and Edinburgh, Scotland, broadcaster on various subjects, 1938-72; officer in charge of canteen unit at Polish camp, Coetquidan, France, 1940, escaped to England three weeks after Dunkirk; lecturer on tour of United States for Paderewski Hospital, Edinburgh, Scotland, and British War Relief, 1940-41; Polish Hostel for Soldiers, Edinburgh, Scotland, organizer, directress, 1942-48. *Member:* Womens Transport Service Club (life). *Awards, honors:* Croix de Guerre silver star (France); Order of Merit with bar and Croix Civique (Belgium); Krucz Zalugi, military class (Poland); Bronze Medal, Frankfurt International Food and Cookery Exhibition, 1956, for *Success Cookery*.

WRITINGS: (Under name Pat Beauchamp) *Fanny Goes to War*, J. Murrary, 1919, revised edition published as *Fanny Went to War*, G. Routledge & Sons, 1940; *Eagles in Exile*, Maxwell, Love, & Co., 1942; (under pseudonym Anne Beaton) *Success Cookery*, Dobson, 1952. Contributor of articles on cookery, travel, and personal experiences to magazines.

WORK IN PROGRESS: A novel; articles; a television play.

SIDELIGHTS: Mrs. Washington spoke fluent French, average German, Spanish, and Polish, and had studied Russian. *Avocational interests:* Travel, entertaining, organizing, driving a car, riding horseback, interior decorating, water color painting, politics, and people.

(Died December 25, 1972)

* * *

WATERMAN, Leroy 1875-1972

PERSONAL: Born July 4, 1875, in Pierpont, Ohio; son of Hadley A. (a farmer) and Louisa (Lombard) Waterman; married Mabelle Walrath, July 24, 1906 (died May 7, 1966); children: Dorothea Lydia (Mrs. George Ragland, Jr.), Donald Leroy (died, 1932). *Education:* Hillsdale College, A.B., 1898, B.D., 1900; graduate study at Oxford University, 1900-1902, and University of Berlin, 1906-1907; University of Chicago, Ph.D., 1912. *Politics:* Independent. *Home:* 1835 Vinewood Blvd., Ann Arbor, Mich.

CAREER: Baptist clergyman. Hillsdale College, Divinity School, Hillsdale, Mich., professor of Hebrew language and literature, 1902-1910; Meadville Theological School, Meadville, Pa., professor of Old Testament and history of religion, 1913-15; University of Michigan, Ann Arbor, professor of Semitics and head of department of Oriental languages and literatures, 1915-45, professor emeritus, 1945-72. Extension lecturer on biblical subjects, 1945-65, American Schools of Oriental Research, Bagdad, Iraq, annual professor, 1928-29; University of Michigan Mesopotamian archaeological expedition, director, 1929-32. Member of translation committee (American translation) of the Bible, 1922-27, of Revised Standard Version of the Bible translation committee, 1938-52. President of Michigan Council of Churches, 1937-42.

MEMBER: American Oriental Society (life member; president, 1936-37), National Association of Biblical Instructors, Society of Biblical Literature and Exegesis (president, 1946), Society for Old Testament Study, American Association for the Advancement of Science Royal Asiatic Society, Palestinian Oriental Society. *Awards, honors:* D.Litt., Hillsdale College, 1925; D.D., Butler University Divinity School, 1961.

WRITINGS: (Translator) *Business Documents of the Hammurapi Period from the British Museum,* Luzac, 1916; (Editor and translator) *Royal Correspondence of the Assyrian Empire,* four volumes, University of Michigan Press, 1930-36, reprinted, Johnson Reprint, 1972; *Preliminary Report upon the Excavations at Tel Umar, Iraq, Conducted by the University of Michigan and the Toledo Museum of Art,* University of Michigan Press, 1931; *Preliminary Report of the University of Michigan Excavations at Sepphoris, Palestine, in 1931,* University of Michigan Press, 1937; *Religion Faces the World Crisis,* Ann Arbor Press, 1943 (translator) *The Song of Songs,* University of Michigan Press, 1948; *The Religion of Jesus,* Harper, 1952; *The Historical Jesus: Hope of Mankind,* Exposition, 1955; *Forerunners of Jesus,* Philosophical Library, 1959; *Religion's Role in Tomorrow's World,* American Press, 1963. Contributor to *Michigan Quarterly Review.*

SIDELIGHTS: Waterman was competent in the ancient languages, Accadian, Aramaic, Assyrian, Greek, Hebrew, Latin, and in modern French and German.

(Died May 9, 1972)

WATERSTON, Albert 1907-

PERSONAL: Born October 28, 1907, in New York, N.Y.; married Edith Somerfleck, April 18, 1931; children: John, Naomi. *Education:* New York University, A.B., 1937; Columbia University, A.M., 1939. *Home:* 7117 Braeburn Pl., Bethesda, Md. 20034.

CAREER: In consumer goods industries on manufacturing, wholesale, and retail levels, 1927-37; Governmental Affairs Institute, Washington, D.C., director of Agricultural Sector Implementation Project, 1927—; U.S. government, 1941-47, served with Office of Price Administration and later with Foreign Economic Administration, 1941-45, also served as economic adviser to U.S. delegation of Allied Reparations Commission in Paris and Berlin, 1945-46, and as vice-president of Virgin Island Co., Department of Interior, 1946-47; International Bank for Reconstruction and Development, Washington, D.C., 1947-72, began as senior loan officer, later served as adviser on planning organization in Development Advisory Service, and finally as senior lecturer in Economic Development Institute; The American University, Washington, D.C., professor of economics, 1970—. Visiting lecturer at University of Pittsburgh, 1960-61, Vanderbilt University, summer, 1963, and El Colegio de Mexico, 1965. *Member:* American Economic Association, American Society for Public Administration, Society for International Development, Phi Beta Kappa, Phi Kappa Phi.

WRITINGS:—All published by Johns Hopkins University Press: (With Raul Ortiz Mena, Victor Urquidi, and Jonas Haralz) *Economic Development of Mexico,* 1953; *Planning in Morocco,* 1962; *Planning in Yugoslavia,* 1962; *Planning in Pakistan,* 1963; *Development Planning: Lessons of Experience,* 1965.

SIDELIGHTS: Waterston is fluent in Spanish, and speaks passable German, French, and Italian.

* * *

WATKINS, Vernon Phillips 1906-1967

PERSONAL: Born June 27, 1906, in Maesteg, South Wales; son of William and Sarah (Phillips) Watkins; married Gwendoline Mary Davies, October 2, 1944; children: Rhiannon Mary, Gareth Vernon, William Tristan David, Dylan Valentine, Conrad Meredith. *Education:* Attended Magdalene College, Cambridge, 1924-25. *Religion:* Church of England. *Home:* The Garth, West Cliff, Pennard, near Swansea, Glamorgan, Wales.

CAREER: Lloyds Bank Ltd., St. Helens Rd., Swansea, Glamorgan, Wales, clerk, 1925-66. Visiting professor of poetry at University of Washington, Seattle, 1964, 1967; Gulbenkian fellow of poetry, University College of Swansea, 1966. *Military service:* Royal Air Force, 1941-46. *Member:* Royal Society of Literature (fellow). *Awards, honors:* Levinson Prize, 1953; Guinness Poetry Prize, 1957, for "The Tributary Seasons"; D.Litt., University of Wales.

WRITINGS—Poetry: *Ballad of the Mari Lwyd, and Other Poems,* Faber, 1941, 2nd edition, 1947; *The Lamp and the Veil,* Faber, 1945; *The Lady with the Unicorn,* Faber, 1948; *Selected Poems,* New Directions, 1948; *The Death Bell,* New Directions, 1954; *Cypress and Acacia,* New Directions, 1959; *Affinities,* New Directions, 1962; *Selected Poems,* New Directions, 1967 (published in England as *Selected Poems, 1930-1960,* Faber, 1967); Owen Evans, compiler, *Kathleen Raine and Vernon Watkins,* Pergamon,

1968; Kathleen Raine, editor, *Uncollected Poems,* Enitharmon Press (London), 1969; *Fidelities,* New Directions, 1969; *Vernon Watkins and Jon Silkin,* Longmans, Green, 1969; *Poesie* (text in English and Italian; Italian translation by Roberto Sanesi), Guanda (Parma), 1968; *Elegiac Sonnet* (text in English and Italian; Italian translation by Roberto Sanesi), M'Arte Edizioni (Milan), 1970.

Other: (Translator) Heinrich Heine, *The North Sea,* New Directions, 1951; (editor and author of introduction) Dylan Thomas, *Letters to Vernon Watkins,* New Directions, 1957; (editor) *Landmarks and Voyages* (poetry supplement), Poetry Book Society (London), 1957; (author of foreword) Dylan Thomas, *Adventures In the Skin Trade,* Ace Books, 1961.

SIDELIGHTS: Alan Brownjohn said of the poet: "Friendship with Dylan Thomas, and certain affinities of theme with the younger poet, helped to link the late Vernon Watkins decisively with the Forties neo-Romantics. When the Forties mode lost favour, his reputation lost ground with the rest. He was Welsh, he tended to get excited and rhapsodic about nature, and he admired some of the mystics and sages adopted by the New Apocalypse. . . . And his uncompromising pursuit of poetry as a sacred and honourable vocation didn't exactly impress Fifties poets busy being sceptical, robust and ironic. . . . Yet his was, by any standards, a major talent; and the publication of *Fidelities,* his last and perhaps his best book, should help to correct a persistent underestimation." His work is perhaps best exemplified in Kathleen Raines' words: "Not Yeats himself could spin those gossamer lines, strung with their words like perfect spheres of dew, that characterise Vernon Watkins' finest lyrics; yet that gossamer is held by forces strong and coterminous with the universe. All his best poems seem . . . like parts of a single poem; his elegies flow into an affirmation of rebirth, his poems for a birth or a christening are rooted in the world of the dead within the rocks, and out of the graves flowers grow for some epithalamion, or foals are born to the shadowy *mari.* He sought always, as in his Ballad of the *Mari,* a unity of vision which should include life, death and rebirth; but in his work the theme is not doctrine, but experienced in a manner wholly poetic." Miss Raines also says: "He was a perfectionist, never allowing any poem short of attainable perfection to appear in print; he has left unpublished more poems than he ever passed for publication." Although Douglas Dunn called Watkin's ideas about life and literature "simply and totally at odds with most of the trends in the modern world," he continued: "Watkin's poetry as a whole is a process of remembering a time when song and the synthesizing visionary experience were not only acceptable in literature but were a part of the perfect life. We may call this activity 'post-romantic,' but we cannot deny that it is often moving, beautiful, and above all, in a literary if not a social context, useful."

A *London Times* obituary stated: "With the exception of war service in the R.A.F. [Watkins] spent his life as a clerk in Lloyds Bank (he had a fund of stories relating to this slightly incongruous employment), and, at least to the outsider, never experienced the slightest difficulty in reconciling this routine occupation with complete immersion in writing poems. He had written over a thousand poems before his first pieces were printed in Wales in 1936."

BIOGRAPHICAL/CRITICAL SOURCES: New Statesman, January 4, 1963, December 13, 1968; *Times Literary Supplement,* February 1, 1963, December 19, 1968; *Library Journal,* July, 1963; *New York Times Book Review,* No-

vember 24, 1963; *London Times,* October 10, 1967; *Poetry Review,* Spring, 1968; *London Magazine,* October, 1969; *Poetry,* March, 1970.

(Died October 8, 1967)

* * *

WATSON, Donald Stevenson 1909-

PERSONAL: Born October 28, 1909, in Greenwood, British Columbia, Canada; son of James L. (an educator) and Roberta (Stevenson) Watson; married Liselotte Bunge (an attorney), October 4, 1935; children: Margot (Mrs. Thomas A. Zener), Wendy. *Education:* University of British Columbia, B.A., 1930; University of California, Berkeley, Ph.D., 1935. *Home address:* Route 2, Box 1850, Port Angeles, Wash. 98362.

CAREER: George Washington University, Washington, D.C., 1935-72, professor of economics, 1948-72, executive head of department, 1945-51, 1956-60. Visiting professor, University of Hawaii, 1964. Consultant, U.S. Operations Research Office, 1950-60; consultant to other government agencies, research organizations, business firms, and trade associations.

WRITINGS: (With A. E. Burns) *Government Spending and Economic Expansion,* American Council on Public Affairs, 1940; (with Burns and A. C. Neal) *Modern Economics,* Harcourt, 1948, 2nd edition, 1953; *Economic Policy: Business and Government,* Houghton, 1960; *Price Theory and Its Uses,* Houghton, 1963, 3rd revised edition, 1972; (editor) *Price Theory in Action: A Book of Readings,* Houghton, 1965, 3rd revised edition, 1973. Contributor to economics journals.

* * *

WATSON, E(lliot) L(ovegood) Grant 1885-1970

PERSONAL: Born June 14, 1885, in England; son of Regenald Grant and Lucy (Fuller) Watson; married Katharine Grant Hamnay; children: Bridget Grant, Josephine Watson Spence. *Education:* Trinity College, Cambridge, Natural Science Tripos (first class honors), 1909. *Politics:* Conservative, "if I don't see too much of them." *Home:* 9 Woodbury Ave., Petersfield, England. *Agent:* David Higham Associates Ltd., 5-8 Lower John St., London W1R 4HA, England.

CAREER: Zoologist on ethnological expedition among aborigines of northwest Australia, 1909-10; returned to England, 1910, and began to write novels under influence and encouragement of Joseph Conrad; had long psychoanalysis under Jungian influence in 1930's and later practiced as a psychotherapist.

WRITINGS: Where Bonds Are Loosed, Knopf, 1913; *The Mainland,* Duckworth, 1917, Knopf, 1919; *Shadow and Sunlight,* Knopf, 1919; *The Other Magic,* Knopf, 1921; *The Desert Horizon,* Knopf, 1923; *Innocent Desires,* J. Cape, 1924, Books for Libraries, 1970; *English Country,* J. Cape, 1924; *Daimon,* Liveright, 1925; *The Contracting Circle,* Liveright, 1926; *Moses, the Lord of the Prophets,* Butterworth & Co., 1929, Liveright, 1930.

With the Australian Aborigines, Phillips & Co., 1930; *Moonlight in Ur,* Noel Douglas, 1932; *The Common Earth,* Dent, 1932; *It's Up to You,* Noel Douglas, 1933; *The Partners,* Gollancz, 1934, published as *Lost Man,* Harper, 1934; *The Nun and the Bandit,* Smith & Durrell, 1935; *Enigmas of Natural History,* Cresset, 1936; *More Enigmas of Natural History,* Cresset, 1937; *Mysteries of*

Natural History, Frederick Stokes, 1937; *Country Holiday,* Thomas Nelson, 1938; *A Mighty Man of Valour,* Duckworth, 1939; *Man and His Universe,* Hutchinson, 1940; *Priest Island,* Smith & Durrell, 1940; (editor) *Nature Abounding,* Faber, 1941, new edition, 1951; *Walking with Fancy,* Country Life, 1943; *But to What Purpose,* Cresset, 1946; *The Leaves Return,* Country Life, 1947; *Wonders of Natural History,* Pleiades Books, 1947; *Departures* (essays), Pleiades Books, 1948; *Profitable Wonders,* Country Life, 1949, Scribner, 1950.

Some Aspects of Instinctive Life, Guild of Pastoral Psychology, 1954; *What to Look for in Winter,* Wills & Hepworth, 1959; *What to Look for in Summer,* Wills & Hepworth, 1960; *What to Look for in Autumn,* Wills & Hepworth, 1960; *What to Look for in Spring,* Wills & Hepworth, 1961; *Nature's Changing Course,* Hutchinson, 1961; *The Mystery of Physical Life,* Abelard, 1964; *Animals in Splendor,* Baker Publishers, 1967, Horizon Press, 1968; *Journey Under the Southern Stars,* Abelard, 1968. Contributor of short stories and articles to anthologies and periodicals.

SIDELIGHTS: Watson considered *The Mystery of Physical Life* (given the blessing of C. G. Jung) the most important—and most controversial—of his forty-odd books. "Rather surprised," he commented when *Saturday Evening Post* accepted a resume of one of the chapters for "Adventures of the Mind" series.

BIOGRAPHICAL/CRITICAL SOURCES: New York Review of Books, November 21, 1968.†

(Died May 21, 1970)

*   *   *

WATSON-WATT, Robert A(lexander)   1892-1973

PERSONAL: Born April 13, 1892, in Brechin, Angus, Scotland; son of Patrick Watson (a master carpenter) and Mary Small (Matthew) Watt; married Margaret Robertson, 1916 (divorced, 1952); married Jean Smith, November 2, 1952 (died, 1964); married Katherine Trefusis-Forbes, 1966 (died, 1971); stepchildren: (second marriage) Anthony Drew, Dennie (Mrs. D. Reburn). *Education:* University College, Dundee, University of St. Andrews, B.Sc. (special distinction), 1912. *Politics:* Liberal-Labour. *Agent:* Matie Molinaro, 44 Douglas Crescent, Toronto, Ontario, Canada.

CAREER: Chief developer of radar (acronym for "radio detecting and ranging"). University College, Dundee, University of St. Andrews, Scotland, assistant to professor of physics, 1912-21; British government posts in meteorology, radio, and radar, 1915-52, including meteorologist-in-charge, Royal Aircraft Establishment, South Farnborough, 1917-23, superintendent of radio department, National Physical Laboratory, Teddington, 1933, deputy chairman of Radio Board, War Cabinet, 1943-45. Consultant to Axe Science Corp., Tarrytown, N.Y., and Sterling Forest International Research Center, Tuxedo, N.Y., beginning, 1959. Inventor of "Huff Duff," instantaneous high frequency radio direction finder (proposed 1916, made effective, 1923). Lecturer on international affairs, and on science and technology.

MEMBER: Institute of Physics (fellow; former treasurer), Royal Society (fellow), Institute of Navigation (former president), Royal Meteorological Society (former president), Institute of Radio Engineers (United States; former vice-president), Deutsche Gesellschaft fuer Ortung und

Navigation (honorary), Athenaeum Club (London). *Awards, honors:* Companion of the Bath, 1941; knighted, 1942; awarded 50,000 pounds sterling by Royal Commission on Awards to Inventors for his work on radar; Medal for Merit (United States), 1946; Hughes Medal of Royal Society; Elliott Cresson Medal of Franklin Institute, 1957. LL.D., University of St. Andrews, 1943; D.Sc., University of Toronto, 1943, University of Laval, 1952.

WRITINGS: (With J. F. Herd and L. H. Bainbridge-Bell) *The Cathode Ray Oscillograph in Radio Research,* H.M.S.O., 1933; *Through the Weather House,* P. Davies, 1935; *Three Steps to Victory,* Odhams, 1957; *The Pulse of Radar* (autobiography), Dial, 1959; *Man's Means to His End,* C. N. Potter, 1961. Contributor of articles and papers on meteorology, radio, radar, sociology, science, and government to journals.

WORK IN PROGRESS: Writing on current problems of international policy, world conflict and world peace, science, technology, and the ecology of man.

SIDELIGHTS: Watson-Watt lived for a time in Tuxedo, N.Y., and in Canada. He was a traveler in fifty-five countries, doing research in England, Canada, United States, Egypt, Sudan, Ceylon, and in the Mediterranean and Indian Oceans. He spoke, and lectured in, English, French, and German.

(Died in Inverness, Scotland, December 5, 1973)

*   *   *

WEAR, Theodore G(raham)   1902-
(Ted Graham Wear)

PERSONAL: Surname rhymes with ear; born 1902, in Joplin, Mo.; son of Theodore Graham and Marie (Price) Wear; married Ruth Girard (a television actress), November 30, 1951. *Education:* Columbia University, student, 1920-22; University of Kansas, A.B., 1924. *Religion:* Protestant. *Home:* 41 Central Park W., New York, N.Y. 10023.

CAREER: State Journal, Topeka, Kan., began as reporter, became city editor, 1925-40; Kansas Industrial Development Commission, Topeka, Kan., public relations, 1940-42; "March of Time" (cinema), New York, N.Y., staff writer, 1949-51; free-lance writer, 1951—. *Military service:* U.S. Army Reserve, 1925-62; on active duty, 1942-47; lieutenant colonel (retired). *Member:* Screen Directors International Guild (charter), American Numismatic Society, American Numismatic Association, Ancient Coin Club of America, Retired Officers Association, Phi Kappa Psi, Phi Alpha Tau. *Awards, honors:* Christopher Award for best radio play, 1953, for "Proclaim Liberty," in National Broadcasting Co. "Inheritance Series"; certificate of merit of Selective Service System, 1962.

WRITINGS—All under name Ted Graham Wear, except as otherwise noted: *Brownie Makes the Headlines* (juvenile), Messner, 1953; *Strange Moneys of the World: A Story of the Unusual Objects That Have Served Man as Money Through the Centuries,* Kay Coin Service Corp., 1957; *Coin Collecting in a Nutshell,* Doubleday, 1963; (under name Ted G. Wear) *Ancient Coins: How to Collect for Fun and Profit,* Doubleday, 1965.

Writer of "March of Time" films, including "Nation's Mental Health," "Where's the Fire," "The American Customer," "Man with a Mission," and a feature length adaptation of Vannevar Bush's *Modern Arms and Free Men* under title "If Moscow Strikes"; author of six stories and television scripts for "Hallmark Hall of Fame," National Broadcasting Corp., 1952-54, eight scripts for "Inheritance Series," National Broadcasting Corp., 1953-54, more than seventy-five motion picture scripts for U.S. Army, 1954-64; also writer of series of sixty-five radio scripts for U.S. Treasury children's program, "Bill Squirrel," and for "It's Time," week-end radio series, American Broadcasting Corp., 1955-56.

Contributor of articles and photographs to *Life, Newsweek, Time, American Artist, Business Week, Health Industry, Numismatic Scrapbook Magazine,* and other magazines.

AVOCATIONAL INTERESTS: Modern and ancient coins, photography (still and motion picture), model railroading.

* * *

WEATHERALL, Norman Leigh   1902-

PERSONAL: Born December 11, 1902, in London, England; children: one son, one daughter. *Home:* Torcroft, Dukes Wood Ave., Gerrard Cross, Buckinghamshire, England.

CAREER: Free-lance writer. *Military service:* Royal Air Force, 1941-45.

WRITINGS: (Reviser) James Bazley, *Coarse Fishing,* Witherby, 1942, 2nd revised edition, Witherby, 1954; *Pike Fishing,* Witherby, 1961.†

* * *

WEAVER, Bertrand   1908-1973

PERSONAL: Born September 27, 1908, in Union City, N.J.; son of W. Alfred (a bookkeeper) and Jennie C. (Weldon) Weaver. *Education:* Studied at Holy Cross Seminary, Dunkirk, N.Y., and St. Ann's Monastery-Seminary, Scranton, Pa. *Home:* 1239 St. Ann's St., Scranton, Pa. 18504.

CAREER: Roman Catholic priest, member of Passionists order, 1934-73; preacher for retreats for clergy, religious orders, and parish missions. First preacher selected for the Paulist Father's weekly radio program; director, Passionist Father's radio and television programs of St. Ann's Monastery, 1965-72. *Awards, honors:* Catholic Book Publisher's "Book of the Month" award, 1960, for *Joy.*

WRITINGS: His Cross in Your Life, Alba, 1960; *Joy,* Sheed, 1964. Contributor of approximately 250 articles and reviews to periodicals, including *Catholic World, America, Reader's Digest,* and *Sign.*

WORK IN PROGRESS: Making notes for possible book on experiences during thirty-one years as a priest.

(Died August 29, 1973)

* * *

WEBER, Lenora Mattingly   1895-1971

PERSONAL: Born October 1, 1895, in Dawn, Mo.; daughter of Thomas Connelly and Mary Agnes (Bradley) Mattingly; married Albert Herman Weber (a football and basketball coach), September 20, 1916 (deceased); children: Harry Albert, William Herman (deceased), Rosemary Louise (Mrs. Lyle L. Liggett), David Edward, Lawrence Mattingly (deceased), Thomas Wesley. *Education:* Took about two years of special courses at University of Denver. *Politics:* Democrat. *Religion:* Roman Catholic. *Home and office:* 1611 Adams, Denver, Colo. 80206. *Agent:* Brandt & Brandt, 101 Park Ave., New York, N.Y. 10017.

CAREER: Author for almost forty years, writing books for teen-agers and short stories for adult magazines. *Member:* Colorado Authors' League (president, 1940), Denver Woman's Press Club. *Awards, honors:* Four Top Hand Awards from Colorado Authors' League, for short stories.

WRITINGS—All published by Crowell, except as shown: *Wind on the Prairie,* Little, Brown, 1929; *The Gypsy Bridle,* Little, Brown, 1930; *Podgy and Sally, Co-eds,* Barse & Co., 1930; *Wish in the Dark,* Little, Brown, 1931; *Mr. Gold and Her Neighborhood House,* Little, Brown, 1933 (published in England as *Mister Gold,* Putnam, 1934); *Rocking Chair Ranch,* Houghton, 1936.

Sing for Your Supper, 1941; *Happy Landing,* 1941; *Meet the Malones,* 1943; *Riding High,* 1946; *Beany Malone,* 1948; *Leave it to Beany!* (Junior Literary Guild selection), 1950; *Beany and the Beckoning Road,* 1952; *My True Love Waits,* 1953; *Beany Has a Secret Life,* 1955; *Make a Wish for Me,* 1956; *Happy Birthday, Dear Beany,* 1957; *The More the Merrier,* 1958; *Bright Star Falls,* 1959.

Welcome Stranger, 1960; *Pick a New Dream,* 1961; *Tarry Awhile,* 1962; *Something Borrowed, Something Blue,* 1963; *Don't Call Me Katie Rose,* 1964; (with Greta Hilb) *For Goodness Sake!* (cookbook), Sage, 1964; *The Winds of March: A Katie Rose Story,* 1965; *A New and Different Summer,* 1966; *I Met a Boy I Used to Know,* 1967; *Angel in Heavy Shoes,* 1968; *Come Back Wherever You Are,* 1969; *How Long Is Always?,* 1970; *Hello, My Love Goodbye,* 1971; *Sometimes A Stranger,* 1972; *Beany Malone Cookbook,* 1972.

Contributor to *Saturday Evening Post* and other magazines. Writer for over 20 years, of monthly column in *Extension.*

SIDELIGHTS: A writer may write a story to put over one of his favorite themes," wrote Mrs. Weber. "For instance, in my girls' book, *Meet the Malones.* The theme of that came from two quotations from Emerson; one, 'What wilt thou? quoth God; take it and pay for it,' and the other, closely aligned in thought, 'The highest price you can pay for a thing is to get it for nothing.' The Malone family (Beany was my favorite) came into being to prove that Emerson was right." Her audience shares this favoritism for Beany and still enjoys the numerous sequels to *Meet the Malones.* Although the series has been called highly improbable at times, it is thought to be "good solid stuff with real values" [Kirkus]. "As the Malones sift their values of living," wrote E. L. Buell, "older girls will find their family crises full of humor and revealing bits of characterization; and if the story occasionally verges on the sentimental this is more than offset by the tonic tone of the whole."

BIOGRAPHICAL/CRITICAL SOURCES: New York Times Book Review, October 17, 1943; *Kirkus,* February 15, 1948.

(Died January 29, 1971)

* * *

WEBSTER, Randolph Wyatt   1900-

PERSONAL: Born November 18, 1900, in Rushville, Ind.; son of William W. (a farmer) and Mary L. (Wyatt) Webster; married Esther I. Dawson, May 21, 1920; married second wife, Leona C. Stoppel, March 22, 1955; children: (first marriage) Randolph W., Jr., Esther Dawson (deceased). *Education:* University of Michigan, B.S., 1928, M.A., 1930, Ph.D., 1940. *Politics:* Republican. *Religion:* Methodist. *Home address:* P.O. Box 17, Okemos, Mich. 48864.

Office: 211 Men's Intramural Building, East Lansing, Mich. 48823.

CAREER: University of Michigan, Ann Arbor, instructor in health and physical education and supervisor of intramural sports, 1929-40; West Virginia University, Morgantown, associate professor, 1940-43, professor of physical education, 1945-47, acting dean of School of Physical Education and Athletics, 1943-44; Michigan State University, East Lansing, professor of health, physical education and recreation, 1947-70, professor emeritus, 1970—, coordinator of physical education program and personnel, men's intramural, 1955-70. U.S. Office of Education, member of National Health Committee, 1943-44; Michigan Department of Public Instruction, chairman of Health Education Committee, 1950-51. *Military service:* U.S. Army, Medical Service Corps, 1944-45; became major. U.S. Army Reserve, 1945-55, retiring as lieutenant colonel.

MEMBER: American Association for Health, Physical Education and Recreation (fellow; chairman of intramural sports division, 1941, and college recreation division, 1944), College Physical Education Association, American College of Sports Medicine (fellow), Michigan Association for Health, Physical Education and Recreation (president, 1952-53; executive secretary, 1970-73), Society of Mayflower Descendents, Phi Epsilon Kappa, Phi Delta Kappa, Sigma Delta Psi, Kiwanis Club, Masons. *Awards, honors:* Distinguished Service Award from Michigan Association for Health, Physical Education and Recreation, 1962.

WRITINGS: (With E. D. Mitchell, A. A. James, John Johnstone, and Earl N. Riskey) *Sports for Recreation*, A. S. Barnes, 1936, revised edition, 1952; *Philosophy of Physical Education*, W. C. Brown, 1965. Author of booklet on teaching square dancing, published by College of Education, Michigan State University, 1958, and co-author of a curriculum study for West Virginia elementary schools and several military manuals on physical reconditioning and recreation. Tape recordings include "Recreational Folk and Square Dancing," 1958, and "Teaching Square Dancing," 1959, both with instructions, calls, and music.

Contributor of about thirty articles to professional journals. Member of editorial board, *Physical Educator*, 1951-54, and *News* (publication of Michigan Association for Health, Physical Education and Recreation), 1959-60; member of editorial committee, *College Education Quarterly*, 1955-60.

AVOCATIONAL INTERESTS: Photography, rifle shooting, golf, and travel.

*   *   *

WEBSTER, S(tanley) Eric   1919-1971

PERSONAL: Born November 20, 1919, in Ripon, Yorkshire, England; son of Stanley Anthony (a master draper) and Winifred Adela (Smith) Webster; married Marjorie Susan Bottomley, February 25, 1950, children: Tessa Jane, Stephen Alexander, Jessica Mary. *Education:* Jesus College, Oxford, M.A., 1946. *Home:* Quarry Bank, Quarry Woods, Marlow, Buckinghamshire, England. *Office:* Alfred Pemberton Ltd., 29 Marylebone Rd., London N.W.1, England.

CAREER: Alfred Pemberton Ltd. (advertising), London, England, creative director. Reed Marketing Personnel Ltd., director. Ashridge Management College, Berkhamsted, Hertfordshire, England, outside lecturer, 1964-71. *Military service:* British Army, Royal Artillery, 1939-46; served in Middle East and North Africa; captured, 1942,

escaped, 1943, recaptured, 1944, and held as prisoner of war in Germany, 1945; became lieutenant.

WRITINGS: How to Win the Business Battle, J. Murray, 1964, Coward, 1965. Editor of *Pemberton Quarterly*, and writer of articles for that periodical that have been reprinted in more than forty other publications in Great Britain, Australia, Belgium, Southern Rhodesia, and United States; American journals carrying reprints include *Advertising Age*, *Management Review*, *Supervisory Management*, and *Armed Forces Management*.

WORK IN PROGRESS: A book on management subjects.

SIDELIGHTS: Webster spoke varying amounts of German, French, and Italian.

(Died December, 1971)

*   *   *

WEEKS, Edward J(oseph)   1902-

PERSONAL: Born April 5, 1902, in London, England; son of George (a civil servant) and Harriet (Oxenham) Weeks; married Dorothy Prince, April 18, 1925; children: Kenneth Frederick. *Education:* University of London, B.Sc., 1921, M.Sc., 1923, Ph.D., 1924, M.A., 1927. *Religion:* Church of England. *Home:* 24 Norbury Dr., Lancing, England.

CAREER: Master, later deputy head of Battersea Grammar School; County Borough of Croydon, England, inspector, later chief inspector, 1945-62; University of London, London, England, tutorial lecturer in psychology, 1945—, tutor post in graduate education, Goldsmiths' College, 1962—.

WRITINGS: (With W. Glassey) *Educational Development of Children*, University of London Press, 1950; (with N. L. Houslop) *Fundamental Science*, University of London Press, Volume I, 1955, Volume II, 1956, Volume III, 1958, Volume IV, 1963.

*   *   *

WEIGAND, Hermann J(ohn)   1892-

PERSONAL: Born November 17, 1892, in Philadelphia, Pa.; son of Herman A. (a minister) and Ottilie (Rumpff) Weigand; married Frances Rhoades, February 2, 1916 (divorced); married Mary Koenig (a professor), March 28, 1961; children: Erika (deceased). *Education:* University of Michigan, A.B., 1913, Ph.D., 1916. *Religion:* Humanist. *Home:* 40 Trumbull St., New Haven, Conn. 06510.

CAREER: University of Michigan, Ann Arbor, instructor in German, 1914-18; University of Pennsylvania, Philadelphia, 1919-29, began as instructor, became professor of German; Yale University, New Haven, Conn., 1929-61, began as professor, became Sterling Professor of Germanic Literature, now professor emeritus. Visiting professor, University of Massachusetts, 1961-69; also visiting professor at University of California, Berkeley, Harvard University, University of Wisconsin, and University of Colorado. *Member:* Modern Language Association of America (president, 1966), Phi Beta Kappa. *Awards, honors:* Guggenheim fellow, 1956; University of Michigan Alumni Medal, 1967; Knight Commander's Cross of Order of Merit, West Germany, 1967; L.H.D., University of Colorado, 1968.

WRITINGS: The Modern Ibsen: A Reconsideration, Holt, 1925; *Thomas Mann's Novel Der Zauberberg: A Study*, Appleton, 1933, revised edition published as *The Magic Mountain: A Study of Thomas Mann's Novel, Der*

Zauberberg, University of North Carolina Press, 1964; (editor, translator, and author of introduction) *Goethe's Wisdom and Experience*, Pantheon, 1949; *Three Chapters on Courtly Love in Arthurian France and Germany: Lancelot-Andreas Capellanus-Wolfram von Eschenbach's Parzival*, University of North Carolina Press, 1956; (editor) Herman Broch, *Die Schuldlosen: Roman in elf Erzaehlungen*, Deutscher Taschenbuch Verlag, 1965; *Surveys and Soundings in European Literature*, edited by A. Leslie Wilson, Princeton University Press, 1966; *Faehrten und Funde*, A. Francke, 1967; *Wolfram's Parzival: Five Essays with an Introduction*, edited by Ursula Hoffmann, Cornell University Press, 1969. Contributor of about one hundred essays, literary and philological, in English and German, to American and European periodicals.

SIDELIGHTS: Weigand speaks German; reads Latin, Greek, French, Italian, and Scandinavian languages. His main interest is medieval and modern literature. Weigand has been legally blind since 1962.

BIOGRAPHICAL/CRITICAL SOURCES: Yale Review, summer, 1967.

* * *

WEINBERG, Julius R(udolph) 1908-1971

PERSONAL: Born September 3, 1908, in Zanesville, Ohio; son of Solomon (a merchant) and Dolores (Chase) Weinberg; married Ilse Hildegard Heimann, June, 1938; children: Marilyn, Mark. *Education:* Ohio State University, B.A., 1931, M.A., 1932; Cornell University, Ph.D., 1935. *Religion:* Jewish. *Home:* 584 Park Lane, Madison, Wis. 53705. *Office:* Institute for Research in the Humanities, University of Wisconsin, Madison, Wis. 53706.

CAREER: Cornell University, Ithaca, N.Y., instructor in philosophy, 1937-38; University of Cincinnati, Cincinnati, Ohio, instructor, later assistant professor of philosophy, 1941-47; University of Wisconsin, Madison, 1947-71, began as assistant professor, became professor of philosophy, 1954. *Member:* American Philosophical Association (past president of Western division). *Awards, honors:* Elizabeth Clay postdoctoral fellow, 1938-39; American Council of Learned Societies grant, 1940-41; National Science Foundation grant, 1962; Guggenheim Foundation grant, 1965-66.

WRITINGS: An Examination of Logical Positivism, Routledge & Kegan Paul, 1936; *Nicolaus of Autrecourt: A Study in 14th Century Thought*, Princeton University Press, 1948; *A Short History of Medieval Philosophy*, Princeton University Press, 1964; *Abstraction, Relation and Induction: Three Essays in the History of Thought*, University of Wisconsin Press, 1965; *Ideas and Concepts*, Marquette University Press, 1970; (compiler with Keith E. Yandell) *Problems in Philosophical Inquiry*, Holt, 1971.

SIDELIGHTS: Weinburg's first book, *An Examination of Logical Positivism* was translated into Italian, 1950, into Spanish, 1959, and reissued in England as a paperback, 1960.

(Died January 17, 1971)

* * *

WEINRAUCH, Herschel 1905-
(Grigory Vinokur)

PERSONAL: Born January 7, 1905, in Sarne, near Kiev, Russia (now in Ukranian Soviet Socialist Republics); came to U.S., 1948; naturalized citizen, 1953; son of Benjamin (a teacher) and Sheva (Kravitz) Vinokur; married Tillie Young (a teacher), November 20, 1948 (died, 1953). *Education:* Attended Second Moscow University, 1930-31, and Institute of People's Education, Odessa, 1931-33. *Politics:* Democrat. *Religion:* Jewish. *Home:* 141 West 73rd St., New York, N.Y. 10023.

CAREER: Editor of cultural division of *Biro-Bidjaner Shteren* (Yiddish newspaper), and assistant director of local radio programs in Biro-Bidjan, Jewish Autonomous Region, Soviet Russia (Asia), 1933-37. Free-lance writer. *Military service:* Soviet Army, 1941-45; became lieutenant. *Member:* Workmen's Circle and P.E.N. (both of New York).

WRITINGS: In Aufkum, Government Publishing Co., (Moscow), 1932; *Tige Berg*, Government Publishing Co. (Minsk), 1936; *Der Ershter Yeger*, Government Publishing Co. (Minsk), 1940; *Dos Yingel Fun Ochrimora*, Government Publishing Co. (Minsk), 1941; *Blut auf der Zun*, Rausen Brothers, 1950; *Durch Ziban Fierin*, Rausen Brothers, 1951; *Commissars* (in Yiddish), [Buenos Aires], 1962, published as *The Commissar*, under pseudonym Grigory Vinokur, Twayne, 1965. Also author of *Adamism*, a collection of essays. *A Hanging in Pumir*, a novel about life in Soviet border area, and *A Grain of Salt*, a collection of short stories and essays on Jewish life in Soviet Russia, Israel, and America.

WORK IN PROGRESS: Corn on the Grave, a novel about five-hundred years of Russian Jewry, completion expected in 1975.

* * *

WEINSTEIN, Michael 1898-

PERSONAL: Born July 12, 1898, in London, England; son of Bernard (a jeweler) and Helena (Stern) Weinstein; married Betty Levin, June 22, 1935. *Education:* Attended Chelsea Polytechnic, London, England. *Religion:* Jewish. *Home:* 27 Manor Dr., Wembley, Middlesex, England.

CAREER: Jeweler and gemologist, London, England, beginning, 1920. *Military service:* British Army, 1917-19; served in France, Belgium, and Italy; became lieutenant. *Member:* Gemological Association of Great Britain (fellow), British Jewelers Association.

WRITINGS: Precious and Semi-Precious Stones, Pitman, 1928; *The World of Jewel Stones*, Sheridan, 1958. Contributor to trade journals.

* * *

WEISENBURGER, Francis Phelps 1900-

PERSONAL: Born October 31, 1900, in Defiance, Ohio; son of Francis Peter (a pharmacist) and Abbie (Phelps) Weisenburger; married Helen Carter, September 1, 1928; children: Elizabeth Ann (Mrs. Harry D. Weckesser). *Education:* University of Michigan, A.B., 1922, M.A., 1923, Ph.D., 1929. *Politics:* Democrat. *Religion:* Presbyterian. *Home:* 99 Aldrich Rd., Columbus, Ohio 43214. *Office:* Department of History, Ohio State University, 216 North Oval Dr., Columbus, Ohio 43210.

CAREER: Ohio State University, Columbus, instructor, 1924-29, assistant professor, 1929-38, associate professor, 1938-46, professor of history, beginning 1946. *Member:* American Historical Association, Organization of American Historians, American Association of University Professors, Ohio Academy of History, Ohio Historical Society (honorary life member), Faculty Club (Columbus). *Awards, honors:* Ohioana Library Association citation, 1965.

WRITINGS: (With E. H. Roseboom) *History of Ohio*, Prentice-Hall, 1934, enlarged edition published as *A Sesquicentennial History of Ohio*, Ohio Historical Society, 1953; *A Life of Charles Hammond, First Great Journalist of the Old Northwest*, Ohio Historical Society, 1934; *A Life of John McLean*, Ohio State University Press, 1937; *The Passing of the Frontier*, Ohio Historical Society, 1941; *A Brief History of Urbana University*, Urbana University Press, 1951; *Ordeal of Faith: The Crisis of Church-Going America*, Philosophical Library, 1959; *Triumph of Faith: Contributions of the Church to American Life, 1865-1900*, William Byrd Press, 1962; *Idol of the West: The Fabulous Career of Rollin M. Daggett*, Syracuse University Press, 1965; *Ohio: A Guide to Localized History*, Teachers College Press, 1965.

Contributor to *Dictionary of American Biography*, *Dictionary of American History*, *Encyclopedia Americana*, and to history journals. Member of board of editors at various times, *Mississippi Valley Historical Review* and *Ohio History*.

WORK IN PROGRESS: A revision of *History of Ohio*.

*   *   *

WELCH, George Patrick   1901-
(Patrick Welch)

PERSONAL: Born April 10, 1901, in Boston, Mass.; son of Patrick and Anna (McGuinness) Welch; married Janet Underhill, May 11, 1938; children: Janet Raymer (Mrs. Wiley R. Reynolds; stepdaughter), Patricia (Mrs. Alfred J. Lister), George Patrick, Jr., Richard Skeffington. *Education:* Attended Harvard University. *Politics:* Independent. *Home:* Garden of the Gods Club, Colorado Springs, Colo. *Agent:* Ad Schulberg Agency, 300 East 57th St., New York, N.Y. 10022.

CAREER: Investment banking business, 1923-38; U.S. Army, 1942-56, retiring as colonel. Served in Africa, Middle East, Japan, and in Korea where he commanded an artillery battalion at the Inchon landing and assault on Seoul, received Legion of Merit with two oak leaf clusters, Air Medal, Korean Medal with four battle stars, Order of the British Empire (military), Republic of Korea Presidential Citation. *Member:* Lotos Club and New York Athletic Club (both New York), Army-Navy Club (Washington, D.C.), Army-Navy Country Club (Arlington, Va.), Cheyenne Mountain Country Club (Colorado Springs).

WRITINGS: (Under name Patrick Welch) *Final Hosting* (historical novel), Stokes, 1940; *Britannia—The Roman Conquest and Occupation of Britain*, Wesleyan University Press, 1963. Author of play, "Assignment in Judea," produced by Florida State University Theater, 1961. Contributor to *Military Review* and of occasional book reviews to other periodicals.

WORK IN PROGRESS: Tacitus and Agricola—A Roman Kinship, an attempt to establish the background that led to Tacitus' writing the biography of his father-in-law, to fill in the archeological discoveries that have corrected errors, and to provide a colloquial translation of *Agricola* with appropriate commentary to introduce Latin students and others to Tacitus.

SIDELIGHTS: Welch's travels, military and otherwise, have covered the United States, most of Europe, north Africa, the Middle East, Japan, and Korea. He is fluent in French, speaks "poor" German, reads Latin.

WELCH, Herbert   1862-1969

PERSONAL: Born November 7, 1862, in New York, N.Y.; son of Peter Ambrose (a merchant) and Mary L. (Loveland) Welch; married Adelaide Frances McGee, June 3, 1890 (died, 1958); children: Dorothy McGee (Mrs. Anthony F. Blanks), Eleanor Loveland. *Education:* Polytechnic Institute of Brooklyn, student, 1877-82; Wesleyan University, Middletown, Conn., B.A., 1887, M.A., 1890, D.D., 1902; Drew Theological Seminary (now Drew University), B.D., 1890; Oxford University postdoctoral study, 1902-03. *Home:* 520 West 100th St., New York, N.Y. 10025.

CAREER: Pastor of Methodist churches in New York, N.Y., and vicinity, and in Middletown, Conn., 1890-1905; president of Ohio Wesleyan University, Delaware, 1905-1916; bishop of Methodist Episcopal Church, 1916-36, serving as resident bishop in Japan and Korea, 1916-28, Pittsburgh, Pa., 1928-32, Shanghai, China, 1932-36, Boston, Mass., 1938-39 (after official retirement, 1936). Chairman of Methodist Commission for Overseas Relief, 1940-48; vice-president and director of Church World Service, 1946-48; member of numerous religious, educational, and public service committees. Trustee of Wesleyan University, 1901-06, 1937-59; also former trustee of Ohio Wesleyan University and Drew University, and member of governing boards of Chinese universities and seminaries. Carol Gardner Foundation Lecturer in the College of Physicians and Surgeons, Columbia University, 1962.

MEMBER: Phi Beta Kappa, Psi Upsilon, Masons. *Awards, honors:* Order of Sacred Treasure (Japan), 1928; Medal of Republic of Korea, 1952; Honor Citation, Republic of China, 1952; Poe Medal, Ohio Wesleyan University, 1957; Golden Jubilee Award, Polytechnic Institute of Brooklyn, 1960; numerous other citations. Honorary degrees include LL.D. from Wesleyan University, 1906, Northwestern University, 1910, University of Vermont, 1911, and Ohio Wesleyan University, 1924; D.D. from Boston University, 1938; L.H.D. from Drew University, 1966.

WRITINGS: (Editor, and author of introduction) *Selections from the Writings of John Wesley*, 1901; (with others) *The Christian College*, Methodist Book Concern, 1916; *That One Face*, Cokesbury, 1925; *College Lectures* (in Korean), 1935; *Men of the Outposts*, Abingdon, 1937, Books for Libraries, 1969; *As I Recall My Past Century* (autobiography), Abingdon, 1962. Contributor to Methodist and other religious magazines.

(Died April 4, 1969)

*   *   *

WELFLE, Richard A.   1901-

PERSONAL: Surname is pronounced Well-flee; born January 30, 1901, in Hamler, Ohio. *Education:* St. Louis University, M.A., 1926; theology studies in India, 1929-33. *Home:* St. Xavier's, Patna, Bihar, India.

CAREER: Entered Roman Catholic order of Society of Jesus (Jesuits), at Florissant, Mo., 1920; ordained priest at Kurseong, India, 1933. Went to India as Jesuit scholastic, 1929, and taught English, Latin, and Greek at Khrist Raja High School, Bettiah, 1930-31; preacher of missions and retreats throughout India, 1937-47; Patna Mission, Patna, India, mission superior, 1947-53; Sacred Heart Novitiate for the Society of Jesus, Digha Ghat, Patna, India, master of novices, beginning, 1960.

WRITINGS: The Ruined Temple, Benzinger, 1935; *Blood on the Mountain*, Benziger, 1937; *Greater than the Great Mogul*, Ranchi Press (India), 1939; *Pieces of India*, Loyola University Press (Chicago), 1963. Writer of pamphlets; contributor of articles and poems to Catholic periodicals.

WORK IN PROGRESS: An adventure story, *To the Dark Lagoon*, set in Malabar in southern India.

SIDELIGHTS: Welfle wrote his first adventure story, *Ruined Temple* (also published in Spanish and Dutch), after coming upon a dilapidated Hindu temple in the jungle at the foot of the mountains on the border of Nepal, then a forbidden kingdom closed to foreigners.

Both of Welfle's brothers also became Jesuits; one, F. E. Welfle was president of John Carroll University, 1946-56.

BIOGRAPHICAL/CRITICAL SOURCES: Mary Kiely, *New Worlds to Live*, Pro Parvulis Book Club, 1946.

* * *

WELLS, Kenneth McNeill   1905-

PERSONAL: Born July 22, 1905, in Mitchel, Ontario, Canada; son of John Page (a merchant) and Jessie (McNeill) Wells; married Ethel Lucille Oille (an artist), March 22, 1937; children: Arden (Mrs. Frank Moretti). *Education:* Educated privately and at University of Western Ontario. *Agent:* M. Molinaro, 44 Douglas Crescent, Toronto, Ontario, Canada.

CAREER: After leaving the University of Western Ontario, spent a year in London, England, reading in museums, then went to Paris, France, where first book was published; became a journalist on return to Canada, working for newspapers in London and Toronto, Ontario; since then art critic, columnist, bee-farmer, lecturer, yachtsman, author, and self-described international tramp. *Military service:* Canadian Army, World War II; became captain. *Member:* Royal Canadian Yacht Club.

WRITINGS: Absit Omen (poems), Titus, 1937; *The Owl Pen*, Dent, 1947; (editor) Peter McArthur, *In Pastures Green* (memorial edition), Dent, 1947; *By Moonstone Creek*, Dent, 1949; *Up Mendonte Way*, Dent, 1951; *By Jumping Cat Bridge*, Heinemann, 1953; *Cruising the Georgian Bay*, British Book Service, 1958, revised and enlarged edition, 1961; *Cruising the Trent-Severn Waterway*, British Book Service, 1959, revised and enlarged edition, McClelland & Stewart, 1964; *Cruising the North Channel*, British Book Service, 1960; *Trailor Boating Where the North Begins*, British Book Service, 1961; *The Moonstruck Two*, McClelland & Stewart, 1964; *Cruising the Rideau Waterway*, McClelland & Stewart, 1965; *The Owl Pen Reader*, Doubleday, 1969.

WORK IN PROGRESS; The Goats of Father Peabody, a novel; *Songs of Dead Seasons*, collected poems.

SIDELIGHTS: Wells told *CA:* "Spent some wasted years inventing, designing, and putting together what, much to my surprise, became generally recognized as the most advanced and most modern small honey processing plant on the North American continent. Distributed Owl Pen Honey . . . Lost interest when the inventing and developing phase was over. Passed it into other hands and went in an eighteen-foot outboard on a wintertime cruise down the Mississippi and around the Gulf of Mexico. Would like to have a million. Am not enough of a damned fool to waste a lifetime getting it."

Wells lived for five years on his own yacht, "Sea Owl,"

and cruised some fifty thousand miles. He has a new ship, "Saugeen Witch," and says he hopes to do his last writing aboard her at age ninety-nine. "If the wind is blowing and the sea is up, I shall write a poem. If the sea is flat and dull, I shall write a prose bit for a magazine with a national circulation (if any be still extant)."

* * *

WELTMANN, Lutz   1901-

PERSONAL: Born February 15, 1901, in Elbing, East Prussia, Germany (now Elbing, Poland); went to England, 1939; son of Jaques (a merchant) and Emma (Blumberg) Weltmann; married Beryl Elizabeth Hopper, March 16, 1940; children: Austin Jaques. *Education:* University of Berlin, student; University of Freiburg, Ph.D., 1924; University of London, teacher's diploma, 1944. *Politics:* Liberal. *Religion:* Jewish. *Home:* 35 Glencairn Dr., Ealing, London W.5, England.

CAREER: Rudolf Mosse Newspapers, Berlin, Germany, drama and literary critic, 1919-33; associated with Barnowski Theatres, Berlin, Germany, 1920-26, Rudolf Beer Theatres, Vienna, Austria, 1923-44; assistant master of grammar schools in Erith, England, 1944-49, Ealing, England, 1949-52; Leyton Grammar School, Leyton, England, master of modern languages, 1960—. Secretary, Kleist Foundation, 1925-33; member, Committee in Support of German Literature, 1927-33. *Military service:* British Army, Royal Pioneer Corps, 1940-43; received France Star. *Member:* P.E.N. (German and British centers).

WRITINGS: Kathe Dorsch, Paul List, 1929; (translator) Victor Gollancz, *Aufbruch und Begegnung*, Bertelsmann, 1954; (contributor) *Handbuch der Deutschen gegenwarts Literatur*, Nymphenburger, 1964. Co-editor, *Literatur*, 1927-32, *Open Gate*, 1950-52, *Goethe Year*, 1949; London cultural correspondent, *Europe*, 1958—.

WORK IN PROGRESS: Shakespeare und der englische Geist, 1564-1964; books on T. S. Eliot and Christopher Fry.

SIDELIGHTS: Weltmann is competent in English, German, French, Latin, Greek, Italian, and Spanish.

BIOGRAPHICAL/CRITICAL SOURCES: Rhein-Neckar-Zeitung (Heidelberg), February 9, 1961; *Aufbau* (New York), February 10, 1961; *All Gemeine Wochenzeitung der Juden in Deutschland*, February 17, 1961.†

* * *

WENDEL, Francois Jean   1905-19(?)

PERSONAL: Born June 30, 1905, in Strasbourg, France; son of Louis and Jeanne (Siegfried) Wendel; married Eveline Belin, June 6, 1930; children: Jean-Daniel, Dominique, Pierre-Louis, Jean-Luc. *Education:* Faculte de Droit, Strasbourg, Docteur en Droit, 1928; Faculte de Theologie Protestante, Strasbourg, Licencie en Theologie, 1942, Docteur en Theologie, 1948. *Home:* 16, rue de l'Observatoire, Strasbourg, France. *Office:* Faculte de Theologie Protestante, Palais Universitaire, Strasbourg, France.

CAREER: Society of Friends of the University, Strasbourg, France, secretary general, 1936-38; School of Protestant Theology, Strasbourg, France, master of conferences, 1938-49, professor, 1950-53, titular professor, beginning, 1953, dean, beginning, 1958; Institute of Political Studies, Strasbourg, France, professor of history and political theory, beginning, 1945; Archives and Municipal Library of Strasbourg, director, 1946-48. Member of council of University of Strasbourg, beginning, 1956. *Awards, honors:* Chevalier de la Legion d'Honneur, 1960; Commandeur des Palmes Academiques, 1964; honorary doctorates from University of Muenster and University of Uppsala.

WRITINGS: Le Mariage a Strasbourg a l'epoque de la Reforme, Imprimerie Alsacienne, 1928; *L'Eglise de Strasbourg 1532-1535,* Presses Universitaires de France, 1942; *Calvin: Sources et evolution de sa pensee religieuse,* Presses Universitaires de France, 1950, translation by Philip Maret, published as *Calvin: The Origins and Development of His Religious Thought,* Harper, 1963; *Martin Bucer: Resume sommaire de la doctrine chretienne,* Presses Universitaires de France, 1951; *Martini Buceri Opera Omnia,* Volume XV, Presses Universitaires de France, 1954.

WORK IN PROGRESS: An edition of the works (Latin) of Martin Bucer; research on Erasmus and Calvin, and on medieval and reformation history.

(Deceased)

*   *   *

WENTWORTH, Harold   1904-

PERSONAL: Born February 15, 1904, in Homer, N.Y. *Education:* Cornell University, B.S., 1927, M.A., 1929, Ph.D., 1934. *Religion:* Episcopalian.

CAREER: Cornell University, Ithaca, N.Y., instructor in English, 1928-29, 1930-34; West Virginia University, Morgantown, instructor in English, 1934-39, assistant professor of English, 1939-44; Temple University, Philadelphia, Pa., associate professor of English, 1944-48; Pennsylvania State University, University Park, professor of English, 1946-47; Blackburn College, Carlinville, Ill., visiting distinguished professor of English, beginning, 1960. *Member:* Modern Language Association of America.

WRITINGS: American Dialect Dictionary, Crowell, 1944; (editor with Stuart Berg Flexner) *Dictionary of American Slang,* Crowell, 1960, 2nd edition, 1967; *Poems, 1920-1960,* Homer Press, 1961. Assistant editor, *Webster's New International Dictionary,* 2nd edition, Merriam, 1934-60; consulting editor, *Words: The New Dictionary,* Grosset, 1947-49, later editions published as *The Grosset Webster Dictionary,* 1957, 1966.

*   *   *

WERTH, Alexander   1901-1969

PERSONAL: Born February 4, 1901, in St. Petersburg (now Leningrad), Russia; married Freda Helen Lendrum, 1931; married second wife, Aline B. Dawson, 1947; children: (first marriage) Nancy (Mrs. Leonard Gabrysch); (second marriage) Nicholas. *Education:* University of Glasgow, M.A. (first class honors), 1922. *Politics:* Labour party. *Religion:* Lutheran. *Home:* 13 rue Herold, Paris 1, France.

CAREER: Began career as journalist with newspapers in Glasgow, Scotland, 1923-26; Columbia University Council in the Social Sciences, assistant, Paris, France, 1927-28; Paris correspondent for *Glasgow Herald,* 1929-32, *Manchester Guardian,* 1932-40, *New Statesman,* 1949-53; Moscow correspondent for *Sunday Times* and British Broadcasting Corp., 1941-47; University of Manchester, Manchester, England, Simon research fellow, 1953-55; *Nation,* New York, N.Y., European correspondent, 1955-69. Visiting professor of modern history, Ohio State University, 1957.

WRITINGS: France in Ferment, Jarrolds, 1934; *Which Way France?,* Harper, 1937 (published in England as *The Destiny of France,* Hamish Hamilton, 1937); *France and Munich, Before and After the Surrender,* Harper, 1939; *The Last Days of Paris; a Journalist's Diary,* Hamish Hamilton, 1940; *Moscow War Diary,* Knopf, 1942 (published in England as *Moscow '41,* Hamish Hamilton, 1942); *The Twilight of France, 1933-1940; a Journalist's Chronicle,* Harper, 1942; *Leningrad,* Knopf, 1944; *The Year of Stalingrad, an Historical Record and a Study of Russian Mentality, Methods and Policies,* Hamish Hamilton, 1946, Knopf, 1947; *Musical Uproar in Moscow,* Turnstile Press, 1949.

France, 1940-1955, Henry Holt, 1956, revised edition, Beacon, 1966; *The Strange History of Pierre Mendes-France and the Great Conflict Over French North Africa,* Barrie Books, 1957, published as *Lost Statesman, the Strange Story of Pierre Mendes-France,* Abelard, 1958; *America in Doubt,* R. Hale, 1959; *The DeGaulle Revolution,* R. Hale, 1960; *The Khrushchev Phase: The Soviet Union Enters the Decisive Sixties,* R. Hale, 1961, published as *Russia under Khrushchev,* Hill & Wang, 1962; *Russia at War, 1941-45,* Dutton, 1964. *DeGaulle: A Political Biography,* Simon & Schuster, 1966; *Russia: Hopes and Fears,* Simon & Schuster, 1969; *DeGaulle,* Bruguera, 1969.

Russia: The Post War Years, Taplinger, 1971.

Translator: M. G. Rozanov, *Diary of a Communist Schoolboy,* Harcourt, 1928; S. A. Tolstaia, *Diary of Tolstoy's Wife,* two volumes, Gollancz, 1928, 1929; Rozanov; *Diary of a Communist Undergraduate,* Harcourt, 1929; Leon Blum, *Peace and Disarmament,* J. Cape, 1932.

AVOCATIONAL INTERESTS: Playing the piano.

(Died March 5, 1969)

*   *   *

WEST, Elmer D.   1907-

PERSONAL: Born September 13, 1907, in Spencer, W.Va.; son of Homer E. and Katherine (Dalton) West; married Dorothy Barton (a teacher), September 13, 1931; children: Deborah (Mrs. Robert Zipf), Penelope Jane. *Education:* Ohio University, A.B., 1930; Western Reserve University (now Case Western Reserve University), graduate study, 1934; Harvard University, Ed.M., 1934, Ed.D., 1935. *Home:* 1511 Live Oak Dr., Silver Springs, Md.

CAREER: Simmons College, Boston, Mass., instructor in psychology, 1933-34; Woodbury Perkins School, Boston, instructor in psychology, 1932-34; Stoneleigh College (now Stoneleigh-Burnham School), Greenfield, Mass., provost, 1935-37, instructor in psychology, director of projects, and dean, 1937-43; University of New Hampshire, Durham, associate professor, and director of admissions, counseling, and placement, 1946-48; American Institute of Research, Pittsburgh, Pa., deputy director for reasearch and administration, 1948-55; American Council on Education, Washington, D.C., special associate, 1955; National Security Agency, Washington, D.C., 1955-56; American Council on Education, director of office of statistical information and research, 1956-64; Joint Graduate Consortium (five universities participating), Washington, D.C., executive secretary, 1964-72; retired. Lecturer, Lehigh University, summer school, 1934. American Board of Examiners in Professional Psychology, diplomate in couseling. *Military service:* U.S. Naval Reserve, 1943-46; became lieutenant.

MEMBER: American Association for the Advancement of

Science (fellow), American Psychological Association (fellow), Association for Higher Education of the National Education Association, Midwestern Psychological Association, Maryland Psychological Association (fellow), District of Columbia Psychological Association, Phi Delta Kappa, Psi Chi.

WRITINGS: Background for a National Scholarship Policy, American Council on Education, 1956; *Financial Aid to the Undergraduate*, American Council on Education, 1964.

Contributor: *Critical Requirements for Research Personnel: A Study of the Observed Behaviors of Personnel in Research Laboratories; The Adolescent: A Book of Readings; The University Calendar; Partners in Education; A Feedback System for Human Error Information.*

Editor of three American Council on Education annual publications, *Report on Questionnaires, Report on Current Institutional Research*, and *A Fact Book on Higher Education, 1958-64.*

Contributor of articles and reviews to more than fifteen journals and bulletins, mainly in education field.

*　　*　　*

WEST, Gordon 1896-

PERSONAL: Born March 7, 1896, in London, England; son of James (a landowner) and Margaret (Hope) West. *Education:* Studied at London School of Economics and Political Science. *Politics:* Liberal. *Religion:* Agnostic. *Home:* 1562 Greenford Rd., Greenford, near London, Middlesex, England. *Office:* 17 John Adam St., London W.C.2, England.

CAREER: One-time editor of publications and acting director of propaganda for Liberal Party in England; *Westminster Gazette*, foreign correspondent, 1926-27; *Advertising World*, editor, 1929-30; *Daily Sketch*, London, England, foreign editor, 1941-45; *World Tobacco*, London, England, editor, beginning, 1963. *Military service:* Royal Navy, World War I. *Member:* Place Names Society of Great Britain, Savage Club.

WRITINGS: Ambling in Albania, Alston Rivers, 1926; *Immortality* (short stories), Alston Rivers, 1926; *Jogging Round Majorca*, Alston Rivers, 1929; *Bus to the Sahara*, Gifford, 1939; *Dancing Debutante* (novel), Hamish Hamilton, 1939; *Murder for Charity* (novel), Cherry Tree Library, 1943; *The History of Smoking*, Industrial Newspapers, 1953; *All About Cigars*, Industrial Newspapers, 1962; *All About Pipes*, Industrial Newspapers, 1962. Contributor to *Daily Mail, Daily Express*, and to other newspapers and magazines.

WORK IN PROGRESS: Research in the world's tobacco industry; research on the origin of place names.

SIDELIGHTS: West toured the United States with presidential candidates Alfred E. Smith and Herbert Hoover in 1928 to study election methods for David Lloyd George. *Avocational interests:* "Swimming, laughing at life. An enthusiastic felinophile with a passion for cats (has six); taught one to respond to words in three languages representing objects of special interest to cats."

*　　*　　*

WEST, Muriel (Leitzell) 1903-19?

PERSONAL: Born May 18, 1903, in Portland Mills, Pa.; daughter of Peter Wilson (a physician) and Minnie (Muzzer) Leitzell; married Donald Wilson West (an author and a teacher of English), January 21, 1935; children: Petra Wilson Phaby, Timothy. *Education:* University of Wisconsin, B.A., 1924; University of Arkansas, M.A., 1955, Ph.D., 1957. *Home:* 404 Cherry Ct., Carbondale, Ill. 62901. *Office:* Southern Illinois University, Carbondale, Ill. 62901.

CAREER: Worked at advertising, publicity, research, and copywriting jobs in New York, 1924-30; Arkansas College, Batesville, associate professor of English, 1956-57; Southern Illinois University, Carbondale, assistant professor of English, beginning, 1957. *Member:* Modern Language Association of America, Modern Humanities Research Association, Renaissance Society of America, Society for the Study of Alchemy and Early Chemistry.

WRITINGS: (Editor) *A Stormy Night with "The Turn of the Screw"*, Frye and Smith, 1964. Contributor of poetry and literary articles to *PMLA, Ambix, New Mexico Quarterly, Comparative Literature, Explicator*, and other journals.

WORK IN PROGRESS: What Chaucer Knew about Alchemy, a study of "Canon's Yeoman's Tale"; a study of the significance of alchemical imagery in the works of Donne, Webster, and others.

(Deceased)

*　　*　　*

WEST, Richard S(edgewick), Jr. 1902-1968

PERSONAL: Born June 30, 1902, in Nashville, Tenn.; son of Richard S. and Edith Mae (Morris) West; married Marie McElreath (a teacher), September 4, 1928; children: Charles Vernon. *Education:* Vanderbilt University, B.A., 1925; Yale University, M.A., 1928. *Politics:* Democrat. *Home:* 213 North Glen Ave., Annapolis, Md. *Office:* U.S. Naval Academy, Annapolis, Md.

CAREER: Mississippi State College for Women, Columbus, instructor in English, 1926-27; U.S. Naval Academy, Annapolis, Md., 1928-68, began as instructor, became professor in the department of English, history, and government. Chairman of Anne Arundel county chapter of American National Red Cross, 1945-47. Principal, West Tutorial School. *Member:* American Historical Association, Modern Language Association of America, Phi Beta Kappa.

WRITINGS: The Second Admiral: A Life of David Dixon Porter, Coward, 1937; *Gideon Welles: Lincoln's Navy Department*, Bobbs-Merrill, 1943; (co-author) *American Sea Power Since 1775*, Lippincott, 1947; *Admirals of American Empire*, Bobbs-Merrill, 1948, reprinted, Greenwood Press, 1971; *Mr. Lincoln's Navy*, Longmans, Green, 1957; *Lincoln's Scapegoat General: A Life of Benjamin F. Butler*, Houghton, 1965.

WORK IN PROGRESS: History of Amphibious Warfare; a biography of Admiral David Glasgow Farragut.

AVOCATIONAL INTERESTS: Painting (large numbers of West's paintings have been sold; some have also been donated to local nursing centers).

(Died February 13, 1968)

*　　*　　*

WESTFELDT, Lulie 1896-

PERSONAL: Born December 6, 1896, in New Orleans, La.; daughter of Patrick McLoskey and Louise (Ogden)

Westfeldt. *Education:* Newcomb College, Tulane University, B.A., 1917. *Politics:* Democrat. *Religion:* Episcopalian.

CAREER: In earlier years in Louisiana worked for the Consumer's League as a lobbyist for a child labor bill, wrote pamphlets on job analysis for Orleans Parish School Board, did research work on children in agriculture for National Child Labor Committee, and worked as a factory inspector in New Orleans; teacher of F. Matthias Alexander's work (a technique of psycho-physical education), in New York, N.Y. *Member:* Emergency Civil Liberties Committee, Cosmopolitan Club (both New York); Phi Beta Kappa.

WRITINGS: F. Matthias Alexander, The Man and His Work, Allen & Unwin, 1964.

AVOCATIONAL INTERESTS: Gardening at summer cottage in Vermont; animals (has a cat and pony); painting.

* * *

WESTPHAL, Barbara Osborne 1907-

PERSONAL: Born January 31, 1907, in San Fernando, Calif.; daughter of Howard Edgerly and Jessie (Barber) Osborne; married Henry Joseph Westphal (a minister), July 11, 1927; children: Halcyon Alicia (Mrs. Keith Alden Rhodes), Arthur Eugene, Melbert Chester. *Education:* Pacific Union College, B.A., 1933; M.A., San Jose State College (now California State University), 1968. *Religion:* Seventh-day Adventist. *Home:* 482 North Snell, Sonora, Calif. 95370.

CAREER: Teacher of English in Uruguay, 1940-44; teacher of English or Spanish in California schools, 1944-48, 1954-55, in Florida schools, 1958-60, 1963-64, in Texas schools, 1964-66; Sonora High School, Sonora, Calif., librarian, 1966-72. *Member:* Audubon Society.

WRITINGS: A Bride on the Amazon, Review & Herald, 1948; *Gold, Silver, and Spice,* Pacific Press Publishing Association, 1951; *Mexican Nuggets,* Review & Herald, 1956; *Ana Stahl of the Andes and Amazon,* Pacific Press Publishing Association, 1960; *These Fords Still Run,* Pacific Press Publishing Association, 1962; *John, the Intrepid: Missionary on Three Continents,* Review & Herald, 1968; *Crazy Pigs and Other Bible Stories,* Review & Herald, 1968. Managing editor of church paper, *Inter-American Divisional Messenger,* 1954-58.

WORK IN PROGRESS: With the God-Men: The Story of La Malinche of Mexico.

SIDELIGHTS: Mrs. Westphal lived in South American countries for eighteen years, in Mexico for five years, and in Central America for one year. *Avocational interests:* Bird watching (has over 1000 birds on life list).

* * *

WHALLEY, Dorothy 1911-
(Dorothy Cowlin)

PERSONAL: Born August 16, 1911, in England; daughter of William Henry and Beatrice Helena (Exton) Cowlin; married Ronald Harry Whalley (a schoolmaster), April 12, 1941; children: Virginia. *Education:* University of Manchester, B.A., 1931. *Politics:* Labour. *Home:* Aconbury, Larpool Dr., Whitby, Yorkshire, England.

WRITINGS—Under name Dorothy Cowlin; all published by J. Cape: *Penny to Spend,* 1941; *Winter Solstice,* 1942; *The Holly and the Ivy,* 1950; *The Slow Train Home,* 1951;

Rowanberry Wine, 1952; *An End and a Beginning,* 1954; *Draw the Well Dry,* 1955; *The Pair of Them,* 1956.

Biographies for young people, under name Dorothy Cowlin: *Greenland Seas: The Story of Scoresby, the Whaler,* Edward Arnold, 1965; *A Woman in the Desert: The Story of Gertrude Bell,* Muller, 1967; *Elizabeth Barrett Browning,* Muller, 1968; *Cleopatra, Queen of Egypt,* Wayland, 1970.

SIDELIGHTS: Mrs. Whalley believes the novel phase of writing is over, due largely to a "change in taste that has occurred in England between the early fifties and the present. [I] may continue work for children [since] I have not yet learned to write scripts for television and probably never shall."

BIOGRAPHICAL/CRITICAL SOURCES: Books and Bookmen, February, 1969.

* * *

WHEAT, Cathleen Hayhurst 1904-

PERSONAL: Born May 3, 1904, in Terre Haute, Ind.; daughter of Joseph Owen (a physician) and Maude (McKinney) Hayhurst; married Shepherd Deloney Wheat (an attorney), June 17, 1926; children: Gail Wheat Scantlin (deceased). *Education:* University of Chicago, M.A., 1925; University of Minnesota, LL.B., 1935; University of California, Ph.D., 1945. *Politics:* Democrat. *Religion:* Methodist. *Home:* 1636 Mandeville Canyon Rd., Los Angeles, Calif. 90049. *Office:* 306 Royce Hall, University of California, Los Angeles, Calif.

CAREER: University of California, Los Angeles, member of faculty, 1942-72.

WRITINGS: Clear and Effective Writing, Appleton, 1955; *Building Writing Skills,* Houghton, 1965. Contributor of articles on literary research to *Huntington Library Quarterly, Philological Quarterly,* and other journals.

WORK IN PROGRESS: Books about her travels.

SIDELIGHTS: Mrs. Wheat has travelled around the world seven times. She has visited South America, twice, Africa, Australia, and Europe.

* * *

WHEATLEY, Richard C(harles) 1904-

PERSONAL: Born August 21, 1904, in Handsworth, Birmingham, England; son of Frank (a manufacturer) and Minnie (Foulds) Wheatley; married Dorothy G. Terry, June 16, 1940. *Education:* Attended King Edward's Grammar School, Aston, Birmingham, England. *Politics:* Conservative. *Religion:* Church of England. *Home:* Wentworth Lodge, Knowle Lane, Lichfield, Staffordshire, England.

CAREER: Richard Wheatley & Son Ltd. (leather goods and fishing tackle manufacturers), Walsall, England, director, 1922-66; retired, 1966—. *Member:* Vintage Sports Car Club, Bentley Drivers Club, Twenty Ghost Club.

WRITINGS: (With Brian Morgan) *The Restoration of Vintage and Thoroughbred Cars,* Batsford, 1957, published as *The Restoration of Antique and Classic Cars,* Bentley, 1964, 3rd edition, under original title, Batsford, 1969; (with Morgan) *Antique and Classic Cars: Their Maintenance and Operation,* Bentley, 1964 (published in England as *The Maintenance and Driving of Vintage Cars,* Batsford, 1964).

AVOCATIONAL INTERESTS: Amateur engineering, vintage motor cars, antiques, and shooting.

WHEATLEY, Vera (Semple)

PERSONAL: Born in Surrey, England; married A. R. Wheatley (died, 1973); children: Daphne (Mrs. A. J. F. Doulton), Garth. *Education:* Educated privately. *Home:* Greenacre, Orchard Way, Esher, Surrey, England. *Agent:* A. M. Heath & Co., Ltd., 35 Dover St., London W. 1, England.

CAREER: Writer ("almost all my life").

WRITINGS—Novels, except as indicated: *This, My Singing* (verse), Erskine Macdonald, 1919; *This, My Dreaming* (verse), Hodder & Stoughton, 1923; *Devices and Desires*, Dutton, 1926; *The Happy Medium*, Dutton, 1927; *The Enchanting Danger*, Dutton, 1928; *Single-Handed*, J. Murray, 1931; *Miraculous Bread*, J. Murray, 1932; *Saturday at Hazeldines*, Thornton Butterworth, 1935, Dutton, 1936; *No Stepping Backward*, Thornton Butterworth, 1936, Dutton, 1937; *Mixed Foursomes: A Saga of Golf in Verse*, Thornton Butterworth, 1936.

The Old Superb, Stanley Paul, 1945; *A Candle of Understanding*, Stanley Paul, 1947; *No Month but May*, Stanley Paul, 1949; *And All for Love*, R. Hale, 1957; *The Life and Work of Harriet Martineau* (biography), Secker and Warburg, 1957; *The Time of Roses*, R. Hale, 1959; *The Time to Tell*, R. Hale, 1961; *Living with Lauretta*, R. Hale, 1962; *Love Has Many Tongues*, R. Hale, 1964; *Always the Wetherby Girls*, R. Hale, 1966.

Children's books: *Into the Picture Screen*, J. Murray, 1931; *Lilias Next-Door*, Blackie & Son; *Lilias Goes to School*, Partridge & Co.; *Summer with the Morrisons*, Cassell, 1954.

Plays: *Scandal at Barchester* (adapted from *The Last Chronicle of Barset*, a novel by Anthony Trollope; produced in London, 1944), Samuel French, 1946. Also author of one-act radio play, "Elevenses," produced by British Broadcasting Corp., 1940.

WORK IN PROGRESS: A book on the English novel with tentative title, *The Novel in the Middle*.

* * *

WHIPPLE, Dorothy 1893-

PERSONAL: Born February 26, 1893, in Blackburn, Lancashire, England; daughter of Walter (an architect) and Ada (Cunliffe) Stirrup; married Alfred Henry Whipple, August 1, 1917. *Education:* Studied at convents in England and France. *Religion:* Church of England. *Home:* 3 Whinfield Pl., Blackburn, Lancashire, England. *Agent:* David Higham Associates Ltd., 76 Dean St., Soho, London W. 1, England.

CAREER: Author. *Member:* Society of Authors.

WRITINGS: Young Anne (novel), J. Cape, 1927; *High Wages* (novel), J. Murray, 1929; *Greenbanks* (novel; Book Society choice), Farrar & Rinehart, 1929, J. Murray, 1932; *They Were Sisters* (novel; Book Society choice), J. Murray, 1943, Macmillan, 1944; *They Knew Mr. Knight* (novel), J. Murray, 1934; *The Great Mr. Knight* (novel), Farrar & Rinehart, 1934; *On Approval* (short stories), 1935; *The Other Day* (autobiography), M. Joseph, 1936, Macmillan, 1950; *The Priory* (novel; Book Society choice), Macmillan, 1939; *After Tea* (short stories), J. Murray, 1941; *Every Good Deed* (novel), J. Murray, 1946; *Because of the Lockwoods* (novel; People's Book Club selection), Macmillan, 1949; *Someone at a Distance* (novel), J. Murray, 1953; *Wednesday, and Other Short Stories*, M. Joseph, 1961; *Random Commentary* (autobiography), M. Joseph, 1966.

Children's books: *The Tale of a Very Little Tortoise*, Warne, 1962; *The Smallest Tortoise of All*, Warne, 1964; *The Little Hedgehog*, Ladybird Series, 1965.

SIDELIGHTS: They Knew Mr. Knight and *They Were Sisters* were filmed in England, 1945. *Avocational interests:* Cooking, gardening, and animals.

* * *

WHIPPLE, Fred Lawrence 1906-

PERSONAL: Born November 5, 1906, in Red Oak, Iowa; son of Harry Lawrence and Celestia (Macfarland) Whipple; married Dorothy Woods, 1928 (divorced, 1935); married Babette Frances Samuelson, August 20, 1946; children: (first marriage) Earle Raymond; (second marriage) Dorothy Sandra, Laura. *Education:* Occidental College, student, 1923-24; University of California, Los Angeles, B.A., 1927; University of California, Berkeley, Ph.D., 1931. *Home:* 35 Elizabeth Rd., Belmont, Mass. 02178. *Office:* Smithsonian Astrophysical Observatory and Harvard College Observatory, 60 Garden St., Cambridge, Mass. 02138.

CAREER: Harvard University, Cambridge, Mass., member of staff of Harvard College Observatory, 1931—, member of faculty, 1932—, professor of astronomy, 1950—, Phillips Professor of Astronomy, 1968—, chairman of department, 1949-56, director of Radio Meteor Project, 1957—; Smithsonian Astrophysical Observatory, Cambridge, Mass., director, 1955—. U.S. Office of Scientific Research and Development, research associate, 1942-45; U.S. Rocket and Satellite Research Panel, member, 1946—; U.S. Air Force, member of Scientific Advisory Board, 1953-62, associate adviser to board, 1963-67; National Aeronautics and Space Administration, director or consultant for various programs and projects, 1958—, member of Space Sciences Working Group on Orbiting Astronomical Observatories, 1959—; U.S. House of Representatives, special consultant, Committee on Science and Astronautics, 1960—. International Geophysical Year, chairman of Technical Panel on Rocketry, 1955-59; National Science Foundation, chairman of Advisory Panel on Astronomy, 1954-55; National Academy of Sciences, National Research Council, member of Space Science Board, 1958—. Inventor of tanometer and meteor bumper.

MEMBER: International Academy of Astronautics (scientific advisory committee, 1962—), International Astronomical Union (member or officer of commissions, 1932—), International Scientific Radio Union (national committee, United States), National Academy of Science, Committee on Space Research (member of working groups), American Astronomical Society (fellow; vice-president, 1948-50), American Astronautical Society (fellow; vice-president, 1962—), American Geophysical Union (fellow), American Institute of Aeronautics and Astronautics, American Rocket Society (fellow), American Standards Association, Royal Society of Sciences (Belgium; corresponding member), Royal Society of Arts (London; Benjamin Franklin Fellow, 1968—), Royal Astronomical Society (London; associate, 1970), American Academy of Arts and Sciences, American Association for the Advancement of Science, American Meteoritical Society, American Meteorological Society, American Philosophical Society, Astronomical Society of the Pacific, Phi Beta Kappa, Sigma Xi, Cosmos Club (Washington, D.C.), Examiner Club (Boston).

AWARDS, HONORS: Donohue Medals for independent discovery of six new comets; Presidential Certificate of Merit and Exceptional Service Award of U.S. Air Force for scientific work; J. Lawrence Smith Medal of National Academy of Sciences for research on meteors, 1949; medal for astronomical research, University of Liege, 1960; Space Flight Award of American Astronautical Society, 1961; Esnault-Pelterie Award (France); Distinguished Civilian Service Award, presented June 12, 1963, by President John F. Kennedy; Space Pioneers Medallion, for contributions to Federal Space Program, 1968; NASA Public Service Award, for contributions to OAO 2 development, 1969; NASA Public Service Group Achievement Award, for significant contribution to success of Apollo Program, 1969; Leonard Medal, 1970. Honorary degrees: M.A., Harvard University, 1945; D.Sc., American International College, 1958, Temple University, 1961; D.Litt., Northwestern University, 1961; LL.D., C. W. Post College of Long Island University, 1962.

WRITINGS: Earth, Moon and Planets, Blakiston Co., 1942, revised 3rd edition, Harvard University Press, 1968; *History of the Solar System,* Astrophysical Observatory, Smithsonian Institution, 1964; (with Richard B. Southworth and Carl S. Nilsson) *Studies in Interplanetary Particles,* Astrophysical Observatory, Smithsonian Institution, 1967; (editor with Charles Lundquist) *Smithsonian Astrophysical Observatory Star Atlas of Reference Stars and Nonstellar Objects,* M.I.T. Press, 1969. Writer of *Annual Review of Astronomy and Astrophysics,* 1965-69; contributor to *Comments on Astrophysics and Space Physics,* 1968—; contributor to *Encyclopaedia Britannica.* Writer of scientific papers published in professional journals and of popular articles on astronomical subjects. Editor, *Harvard Announcement Cards,* 1952-60; associate editor, *Astrophysical Journal,* 1952-54, and *Astronomical Journal,* 1954-56, 1964—; editor, *Smithsonian Contributions to Astrophysics,* 1956—; regional editor, *Planetary and Space Science,* 1958—; member of editorial board, *Space Science Reviews,* 1961—, and *Earth and Planetary Letters,* 1966—.

* * *

WHITBY, Henry Augustus Morton 1898-1969

PERSONAL: Born September 24, 1898, in Colchester, Essex, England; son of Henry D'arcy (a physician) and Edith Morton (Festing) Whitby; married Marie Augusta Krauss, July 19, 1954; children: Francis James Hurley. *Education:* St. Bartholomew's Hospital Medical College, London, M.R.C.S. and L.R.C.P., 1924. *Politics:* Independent Conservative. *Religion:* Catholic. *Home:* 12a Prince Edward Mansions, Pembridge Sq., London W.2, England.

CAREER: Medical posts between 1924-42 included surgeon lieutenant commander, British Navy, resident surgical officer at hospitals in England, assistant colonial surgeon in Falkland Islands, surgeon and radiologist in British Guiana, surgical registrar at London Lock Hospital and chief urological assistant at West London Hospital, London, England; Stanger Hospital, Natal, South Africa, surgeon and research worker on cancer detection, 1955-57; resumed private practice and research in England, 1957-59; retired from private practice, 1959, to found Cancer Prevention Detection Center, London, England, and serve as its director, 1959-69. Consulting surgeon to St. Margaret's Clinic for Tumours, London, England; consulting urologist to St. Mary's Hospital, Natal, South Africa, 1945-69. World-wide lecturer on cancer. *Military service:* British Army, Cavalry, World War I; surgeon, Springfield Military Hospital, Durban, South Africa, World War II. *Member:* Royal Society

of Medicine, (fellow), British Association of Urological Surgeons, British Medical Association, Authors Society.

WRITINGS: Theory of Life, Disease and Death, Cutler, 1945; *Investigations of Disease,* Cutler, 1951; *When Body Controls Mind,* Knox (Durban), 1952; *A Surgeon's Adventures,* Johnston Publications, 1959; *Courage Her Passport* (biography), Muller, 1963; (with Marie Augusta Krauss) *Cancer: Its Prevention and Early Detection,* Clair Press, 1964; *Preservation of Health,* Thorsons, 1967; *Bio-electronic Detection of Cancer and Other Diseases: Methods of Diagnosing Symptomless Disease,* C. C. Thomas, 1967. Contributor of articles to medical journals.

WORK IN PROGRESS: Electronic research into the early detection of cancer.

(Died, 1969)

* * *

WHITCOMB, Jon 1906-

PERSONAL: Born June 9, 1906, in Weatherford, Okla.; son of Lemley Preston and Melissa (Hull) Whitcomb. *Education:* Ohio Wesleyan University, student, 1923-27; Ohio State University, B.A., 1928. *Address:* Box 1027, Darien, Conn. 06821.

CAREER: Radio-Keith-Orpheum theatres, poster artist in Chicago, Ill., 1928-29; advertising artist in Cleveland, Ohio, 1930-34; Charles E. Cooper, Inc. (advertising art), New York, N.Y., vice-president, 1935—. Artist and illustrator. Cover artist for *Cosmopolitan;* illustrator for *Ladies' Home Journal, McCall's,* and other magazines. *Military service:* U.S. Navy, 1942-45; became lieutenant junior grade. *Member:* Society of Illustrators, New York Athletic Club. *Awards, honors:* Elected to Society of Illustrators Hall of Fame, 1973.

WRITINGS—All self-illustrated: *Pom-Pom's Christman,* Holt, 1959; *All About Girls,* Prentice-Hall, 1962; *Coco, the Far-Out Poodle,* Random House, 1963. Contributor of regular column and articles to *Cosmopolitan,* 1947-52.

* * *

WHITE, Dorothy Shipley

PERSONAL: Born in Philadelphia, Pa.; daughter of Samuel Richards (a banker) and Agnes (Evans) Shipley; married Thomas Raeburn White (a lawyer), January 12, 1924 (deceased); children: David, Dorothy (Mrs. Michael Gaus), Stephen. *Education:* Bryn Mawr College, B.A.; Temple University, B.F.A., Columbia University, M.A., University of Pennsylvania, Ph.D. *Religion:* Unitarian. *Home:* 717 Glengarry Rd., Chestnut Hill, Philadelphia, Pa.

CAREER: Member of administrative staff at Bryn Mawr College, Bryn Mawr, Pa., one year before marriage; painter and sculptor. Chairman, Bryn Mawr College Summer School of Nursing, 1941-44; chairman of Red Cross Arts and Skills unit, Valley Forge Hospital, 1943-45; University of Pennsylvania, associate trustee and member of advisory commission to the dean of the College for Women, and summer school lecturer, first session, 1965. Member of board, Philadelphia College of Art, New School of Music, and Womens Medical College. *Member:* Academie des Sciences d'Outre-Mer, Comite Universitaire pour l'Etude des Idees Gaulliennes, Alumni of the Graduate School of Arts, University of Pennsylvania (president, 1956-58), Cosmopolitan Club (Philadelphia; president, 1928-30). *Awards, honors:* Athenaeum Prize, 1964, for *Seeds of Discord.*

WRITINGS: Seeds of Discord: DeGaulle, Free France and the Allies, Syracuse University Press, 1964. Contributor to *Orbis, Espoir*, and *Philadelphia Bulletin*.

WORK IN PROGRESS: A book on DeGaulle's influence in the decolonization of Black Africa.

SIDELIGHTS: Dorothy White speaks French, reads Italian and German.

* * *

WHITE, Eric Walter 1905-

PERSONAL: Born September 10, 1905, in Bristol, England; son of Percy Walter and Ethelind Charlotte (Chambers) White; married Edith Dorothy Swinburne, December 15, 1939; children: Sarah Swinburne. *Education:* Attended Clifton College; Balliol College, Oxford, B.A., 1927. *Home:* 21 Alwyne Rd., London N.1, England.

CAREER: Private teacher, Germany, 1928-29; League of Nations, Geneva, Switzerland, staff member in minute-writing and translation section, 1929-33; National Council of Social Service, London, England, staff member in rural department, 1935-42; Council for the Encouragement of Music and the Arts, London, England, assistant secretary, 1942-45; Arts Council of Great Britain, London, assistant secretary, 1945-71, literature director, 1966-71. *Awards, honors:* Awarded Commander Order of the British Empire, 1966.

WRITINGS: The Room, and Other Poems, 1921-1926, High House Press, 1927; *Parnassus to Let: An Essay About Rhythm in the Films*, L. & V. Woolf, 1928, Arno, 1970; *Stravinsky's Sacrifice to Apollo*, Hogarth Press, 1930; *Walking Shadows: An Essay on Lotte Reiniger's Silhouette Films*, Hogarth Press, 1931; *Wander Birds* (tale), Perpetua Press, 1934; *The Little Chimney Sweep*, White & White, 1936; *Stravinsky: A Critical Survey*, Lehmann, 1947, Philosophical Library, 1948; (editor) *Entertain Yourselves*, revised edition, National Council of Social Service, 1949; *Benjamin Britten: A Sketch of His Life and Works*, Boosey & Hawkes, 1949, 3rd edition, revised and enlarged, published as *Benjamin Britten: His Life and Operas*, University of California Press, 1970; *The Rise of English Opera*, introduction by Benjamin Britten, Philosophical Library, 1951; (author of introduction) Martin Huerlimann, *London: Ein Bildband*, Atlantis, 1956; *A Tarot Deal* (poems), Scorpion Press, 1962; (editor) *Fifteen Poems for William Shakespeare*, Trustees and Guardians of Shakespeare's Birthplace, 1964; (translator) Robert Siohan, *Stravinsky*, Hillary, 1965; *Stravinsky: The Composer and His Works*, University of California Press, 1966.

WORK IN PROGRESS: A new history of English opera, and an account of the Arts Council of Great Britain (1945-72).

BIOGRAPHICAL/CRITICAL SOURCES: Times Literary Supplement, February 16, 1967; *Listener*, March 16, 1967; *London Magazine*, May, 1967.

* * *

WHITE, Leslie Turner 1903-19?

PERSONAL: Born May 12, 1903, in Ottawa, Ontario, Canada; son of George Whitfield and Sarah (Turner) White; married Helen Vera Dudley (a high school teacher), November 3, 1947; children: Edward Allen, Helen Joan, Leslie Turner, Jr., Mary Katherine. *Politics:* Liberal Democrat. *Home:* White Anchors Farm, R.R.1, Montross, Va. *Agent:* Paul R. Reynolds & Son, 599 Fifth Ave., New York, N.Y. 10017.

CAREER: Law enforcement officer in California, 1924-32, began as a ranger, later served as a policeman in Ventura City, Calif., and finally as a detective in office of district attorney, Los Angeles, Calif.; full-time writer, beginning, 1932. *Member:* Authors Guild, National Model Railroad Association (president of mid-eastern region, 1956-58), Tidewater Beef Cattle Association (president, 1950-56), Westmoreland County Farm Bureau (president, 1954-56).

WRITINGS—Novels, except as indicated: *Me, Detective* (autobiography), Harcourt, 1936; *Harness Bull*, Harcourt, 1937; *Homocide*, Harcourt, 1938; *River of No Return*, Macrae Smith, 1941; *Five Thousand Trojan Horses*, World's Work, 1943; *Look Away, Look Away*, Random House, 1943; *Six Weeks South of Texas*, World's Work, 1948; *Lord Johnnie*, Crown, 1949.

Magnus the Magnificent, Crown, 1950; *The Highland Hawk*, Crown, 1952; *Sir Rogue*, Crown, 1954; *The Winged Sword*, Morrow, 1955; *Monsieur Yankee*, Morrow, 1957; *Profane Junction*, Morrow, 1958; *Log Jam*, Doubleday, 1959; *Lord Fancy*, Doubleday, 1960; *Scorpus the Moor*, Doubleday, 1962; *Scale Model Railroading* (nonfiction), Nelson, 1964; *Wagons West*, Doubleday, 1964; *His Majesty's Highlanders*, Crown, 1964.

Former script writer for motion pictures in Hollywood. Contributor of over five hundred articles, novelettes, serials, and short stories to magazines, including *Reader's Digest, Saturday Evening Post, Collier's, Liberty, Red Book, Cosmopolitan, Argosy, Adventure*, and many pulp magazines.

SIDELIGHTS: Three of White's books, *Harness Bull, Look Away, Look Away*, and *Lord Johnnie* were made into films. Fourteen of his books have been published in England and many have been book club selections.

(Deceased)

* * *

WHITE, William A(nthony) P(arker) 1911-1968 (Anthony Boucher, H. H. Holmes, Herman W. Mudgett)

PERSONAL: Born August 21, 1911, in Oakland, Calif.; son of James Taylor (a physician) and Mary Ellen (a physician; maiden name, Parker) White; married Phyllis Mary Price (a librarian), May 19, 1938; children: Lawrence Taylor, James Marsden. *Education:* Attended Pasadena Junior College, 1928-30; University of Southern California, B.A., 1932; University of California, Berkeley, M.A., 1934. *Politics:* Democrat. *Religion:* Roman Catholic. *Home:* 2643 Dana St., Berkeley, Calif. 94704. *Agent:* Willis Kingsley Wing, 24 East 38th St., New York, N.Y. 10016.

CAREER: Writer and editor, 1934—. Co-founder, editor, *Magazine of Fantasy and Science Fiction*, 1949-58; editor, *True Crime Detective*, 1952-53, "Mercury Mysteries," 1952-55, "Dell Great Mystery Library," 1957-60, and "Collier Mystery Classics," 1962-68; author of weekly review column, "Criminals at Large," in *New York Times Book Review*, 1951-68, and reviewer for *Ellery Queen's Mystery Magazine*, 1948-50, 1957-68. Theater and music critic for *United Progressive News*, Los Angeles, Calif., 1935-37; science fiction-mystery reviewer for *San Francisco Chronicle*, 1942-47, and, under pseudonym H. H. Holmes, for *Chicago Sun-Times*, 1949-50, and *New York Herald Tribune*, 1951-63. Opera reviewer for *Opera News*, 1961-68, and Canadian Broadcasting Co. Scriptwriter for "Sherlock Holmes" and "Gregory Hood" radio programs,

1945-48; originator of "Golden Voice" program of historical records, Pacifica Radio, Berkeley, Calif., 1949-68, also aired on New York and Los Angeles stations, and "Escape," a bi-weekly radio book review, 1961-68; conductor of television program, "Introduction to Opera," KQED-TV, San Francisco, Calif., 1960. California State Democratic Party, member of central committee, 1948-52.

MEMBER: Mystery Writers of America (president, 1951); Crime Writers Association; Baker Street Irregulars; Elves, Gnomes, and Little Men's Science Fiction Chowder and Marching Society; San Francisco Opera Guild; National Collegiate Players, Scowrers and Molly Maguires of San Francisco, Phi Beta Kappa. *Awards, honors:* Edgar Allan Poe Award (Edgar) of Mystery Writers of America for best mystery criticism of year, 1946, 1950, 1953.

WRITINGS—Under pseudonym Anthony Boucher: *The Case of the Seven of Calvary*, Simon & Schuster, 1937; *The Case of the Crumpled Knave*, Simon & Schuster, 1939; *The Case of the Baker Street Irregulars*, Simon & Schuster, 1940; *The Case of the Solid Key*, Simon & Schuster, 1941; *The Case of the Seven Sneezes*, Simon & Schuster, 1942; *Ellery Queen, A Double Profile*, Little, Brown, 1951; *Far and Away* (short stories), Ballantine, 1955.

Under pseudonym H. H. Holmes: *Nine Times Nine*, Duell, Sloan & Pearce, 1940; *Rocket to the Morgue*, Duell, Sloan & Pearce, 1942.

Editor, under pseudonym Anthony Boucher: *The Pocket Book of True Crime Stories*, Pocket Books, 1943; *Great American Detective Stories*, World Publishing, 1945; *Four-and-Twenty Bloodhounds*, Simon & Schuster, 1950; *The Best from Fantasy and Science Fiction*, Little, Brown, annually, 1952-53, Doubleday, annually, 1954-59; *A Treasury of Great Science Fiction*, Doubleday, 1959; *The Quintessence of Queen*, Random House, 1962; *The Quality of Murder*, Dutton, 1962; *Best Detective Stories of the Year*, Dutton, annually, 1963-68 (selections from these years, chosen and edited by Jeanne F. Bernkopf, published as *Boucher's Choice: A Collection of Anthony Boucher's Favorites from Best Detective Stories of the Year*, Dutton, 1969).

Author of introductions to some thirty other books; contributor of stories and novelettes to more than forty anthologies. Stories also have appeared in *Esquire, Playboy, Astounding Science Fiction, Galaxy, Adventure,* and other magazines. Writer of several hundred radio shows.

SIDELIGHTS: A *New York Times* writer said of Boucher in 1968: "In the special world of writers and readers of mystery and science-fiction books and stories, Anthony Boucher occupied a pre-eminent place, for his encyclopedic knowledge of those genres and for his ability to express his learning with pithy wit."

Boucher, as White was almost entirely known, once explained as his reason for choosing a second name "that the Library of Congress lists 75 books by authors named William White." He told *CA*: "Outside of crime, I guess my major interests are, in no fixed order, opera, poker, and women (including my wife), with frequent competition from spectator sports (football, basketball, track, rugby, gymnastics), food when not dieting, wine, brandy, silent films, comic strips, Elizabethan drama, Catholic liturgy, and collecting historic vocal recordings (have some six thousand 78s)." While indicating that he was going on with editing and reviewing, Boucher added a footnote: "I keep taking an oath that I shall eventually get back to creative writing; sometime it'll stick."

Boucher translated from the French, Spanish, and Portuguese for *Ellery Queen's Mystery Magazine*, had a working knowledge of German and Italian, "plus Church Latin and a very little Russian."

BIOGRAPHICAL/CRITICAL SOURCES: New York Times, May 1, 1968; *Washington Post*, May 2, 1968; *Newsweek*, May 13, 1968; *New York Times Book Review*, October 6, 1968, November 9, 1969; *Saturday Review*, September 27, 1969.

(Died April 29, 1968)

* * *

WHITEHOUSE, Elizabeth S(cott) 1893-1968

PERSONAL: Born July 15, 1893, in Springfield, Mass.; daughter of John Joseph (a factory foreman) and Marion Beatrice (Hommel) Whitehouse. *Education:* Boston University, B.S.S. and B.R.E., 1924; University of Pennsylvania, M.S. in Ed., 1942. *Religion:* Baptist. *Home:* 816 Woodbrook Lane, Plymouth Valley, Norristown, Pa. 19401.

CAREER: Methodist Board of Religious Education, Boston, Mass., director of religious education, 1922-26; Presbyterian Board of Christian Education, Philadelphia, Pa., editor of children's publications, 1926-42; Bapist Junior College, Bryn Mawr, Pa., teacher of education, and field director, 1942-58.

WRITINGS: Kingdom Stories for Juniors, Revell, 1927; *Followers of Jesus*, Westminster, 1942; *The Nursery Department at Work*, Judson, 1944; *Opening the Bible to Children*, Bethany, 1945; *The Children We Teach*, Judson, 1950; *Jesus, Friend and Teacher*, Westminster, 1957; *Victory at Dawson's Glade*, Bethany, 1964; *Bible Stories to Tell*, Judson, 1967; *There's Always More*, Judson, 1969; *My Window World*, Judson, 1969. Author of pamphlets, stories, magazine articles, and curriculum materials.

WORK IN PROGRESS: A book of inspirational writings.

SIDELIGHTS: Miss Whitehouse, victim of a stroke and broken hip in 1948, used crutches from then on. She kept office hours for writing (9 a.m. to noon), and managed considerable travel.

(Died October 31, 1968)

* * *

WHITFIELD, George J(oshua) N(ewbold) 1909-

PERSONAL: Born June 2, 1909, in Sunderland, Durham, England; son of Joshua Newbold and Eva (Johnson) Whitfield; married April 3, 1937 (wife is a medical practitioner); children: Ann (Mrs. Alan C. Teuten), Diana (Mrs. David C. Siggers), George Hugh. *Education:* King's College, University of London, B.A., 1930, A.K.C., 1930, M.A., 1935. *Home:* Chesterfield House, Broad Lane, Hampton, Middlesex, England.

CAREER: Hymers College, Hull, England, senior English master, 1937-43; Tavistock Grammar School, Devon, England, headmaster, 1944-46; Stockport School, Cheshire, England, headmaster, 1947-50; Hampton Grammar School, Middlesex, England, headmaster, 1950-58. Church of England, ordained deacon, 1962, priest, 1963, general secretary of Board of Education, 1969—. Chairman of religious knowledge committee, Associated Examining Board; president of Headmasters' Association, 1967. *Member:* Royal Commonwealth Society, Athenaeum.

WRITINGS: (Editor) *Teaching Poetry,* Oxford University

Press, 1937; *An Introduction to Drama*, Oxford University Press, 1938, 2nd edition, 1963; *God and Man in the Old Testament*, S.C.M. Press, 1949; (editor) *Poetry in the Sixth Form*, Macdonald & Co., 1950; *Philosophy and Religion: An Introduction to Some Questions of Belief*, Religious Education Press, 1955. Contributor of articles to *British Journal of Educational Studies* and *I Problemi Della Pedogogia*.

WORK IN PROGRESS: Research in current theological developments and their significance in Christian education.

* * *

WHITING, Percy H(ollister) 1880-

PERSONAL: Born April 10, 1880, in Great Barrington, Mass.; son of John Fred (a druggist) and Annie Louise (Hitchcock) Whiting; married Elise Warren Polk, 1909; married second wife, Genevieve Bearmore, October 19, 1946; children: (first marriage) Percy H., Jr., Dorothy Polk (Mrs. T. G. Howland). *Education:* Attended Harvard University, 1898-99, and Vanderbilt University, 1900-02. *Politics:* Republican. *Religion:* Episcopal. *Residence:* Montrose, Ala.

CAREER: Sports editor on newspapers in Nashville and Memphis, Tenn., and Atlanta, Ga., 1902-13; *Comfort* (mail order magazine), Augusta, Me., advertising manager, 1913-18; Central Maine Power Co., Augusta, Me., manager of securities department, 1918-23; Henry L. Doherty & Co., New York, N.Y., general retail sales manager, securities department, 1923-27; P. H. Whiting & Co., Inc., New York, N.Y., president, 1927-32; W. R. Bull & Co., New York, N.Y., vice-president, 1933-37; Dale Carnegie Institute, New York, N.Y., began 1937, managing director, 1943-52, managing director of Dale Carnegie Sales Courses, 1952-60. *Member:* Sales and Marketing Executives of Mobile, New York Sales Executive Club (charter member).

WRITINGS: The Five Great Rules of Selling, McGraw, 1947; *How to Speak and Write with Humor*, McGraw, 1959; *The Five Great Problems of Salesmen and How to Solve Them*, McGraw, 1965. Contributor to newspapers and trade magazines.

* * *

WHITMAN, W(illiam) Tate 1909-

PERSONAL: Born October 26, 1909, in Boaz, Ala.; son of Edward Fenno (a cotton buyer) and Jane (Street) Whitman; married Luisita Dye, August 12, 1936; children: Melinda, Ernestine. *Education:* Duke University, A.B., 1929, M.A., 1933, Ph.D., 1943. *Religion:* Methodist. *Home:* 1533 Emory Rd., N.E., Atlanta, Ga. 30306. *Office:* School of Business Administration, Emory University, Atlanta, Ga. 30322.

CAREER: University Motors, Inc., Durham, N.C., accountant, 1934-36; The Citadel, Charleston, S.C., assistant professor of business administration, 1936-47; Duke University, Durham, N.C., instructor in economics, 1939-40; Emory University, Atlanta, Ga., associate professor, 1947-50, professor, 1950-60, Charles Howard Candler Professor of Economics, 1960—. *Member:* American Economic Association, Industrial Relations Research Association, American Association of University Professors, Southern Economic Association (executive committee member, 1959-61; vice-president, 1962-63), Beta Gamma Sigma, Alpha Kappa Psi, Delta Tau Delta.

WRITINGS: (With C. S. Cottle) *Investment Timing: The Formula Plan Approach*, McGraw, 1953; (with Cottle) *Corporate Earning Power and Market Valuation: 1935-1955*, Duke University Press, 1959; (with Frank Charvat) *Marketing Management: A Quantitative Approach*, Simmons-Boardman, 1964; (editor with Melvin L. Greenhut) *Essays in Southern Economic Development*, University of North Carolina Press, 1964.

* * *

WHITNEY, Byrl A(lbert) 1901-

PERSONAL: Born June 19, 1901, on a farm in Cherokee County, Iowa; son of Chester Alanson (a farmer) and Edith Adell (Forsythe) Whitney; married Juanita Cleone Welty (a schoolteacher), September 21, 1926; children: Alanson Welty. *Education:* University of Iowa, B.A., 1923; George Washington University, LL.B., 1928.

CAREER: Member of District of Columbia and U.S. Supreme Court bars. Brotherhood of Railroad Trainmen, director of education and research, 1930-63, assistant general counsel, 1949-50. Certified professional parliamentarian. Holder of patents for phonograph record holder and lawn mower-cleaner. *Member:* Adult Education Association of the U.S.A., American Institute of Parliamentarians, American Federation of Teachers.

WRITINGS: The Practical Chart and Handbook of Parliamentary Motions, Especially Adapted for Ready Reference in Business Meetings, The Economic Adverting Company, 1923; *Parliamentary Guide and Practical Chart*, Lyons & Carnahan, 1926; *Whitney's Parliamentary Procedure*, Robert B. Luce, 1962; *Please Come to Order! A New Approach to Efficient Group Decision-Making*, Turnpike Press, 1966. Contributor to magazines. Editor, *Trainman News* (weekly tabloid), 1950-54.

WORK IN PROGRESS: A treatise on rules for personal conduct.

* * *

WHITTICK, Arnold 1898-

PERSONAL: Born May 17, 1898, in Ilford, Essex, England; son of John and Alice (Palmer) Whittick; married Helen Isobel Miller (an editor), February 8, 1930; children: Gillian Margaret (Mrs. Brian Pitt). *Education:* University of London, diploma in history of art, 1927; attended various London art schools. *Home:* 4 Netherwood, Gossops Green, Crawley, Sussex, England.

CAREER: Turned from painting to writing on aspects of architecture and design. London County Council lecturer on appreciation of art and architecture, London Literary Institutes, London, England, 1930-39; lecturer on architecture, art, housing, and reconstruction, Central Advisory Council on Education among H.M. Forces, World War II. Founder and president, Beckenham Planning Group. *Military service:* British Army, served in France as signaller in Infantry, 1916-18. *Member:* Royal Society of Arts (fellow), Royal Institute of Philosophy, British Society of Aesthetics (founder member), Town and Country Planning Association (council member). *Awards, honors:* Leverhulme Research Award to complete three-volume work on *European Architecture in the Twentieth Century*.

WRITINGS: Symbols for Designers, Crosby Lockwood & Son, 1935, Gale, 1972; *History of Cemetery Sculpture, Volume I: Ancient Times to the Norman Conquest*, Mineral Publications, 1938; *Eric Mendelsohn*, Faber, 1940, 2nd edition, F. W. Dodge Corp., 1956; *Civic Design and the Home,* Faber, 1943; *The Small House Today and Tomorrow,* Crosby Lockwood & Son, 1947, 2nd edition, Hill, 1957; *War Memorials,* Country Life, 1947; *European Architecture in the Twentieth Century,* Crosby Lockwood & Son, Volume I, 1950, Volume II, 1953; *Symbols, Signs and Their Meaning,* Branford, 1960, 2nd edition published as *Symbols, Signs and Their Meaning and Uses in Design,* Hill, 1970; (with Frederic Osborn) *The New Towns: The Answer to Megalopolis,* introduction by Lewis Mumford, McGraw, 1963, revised edition, M.I.T. Press, 1969. Editor, *Building Materials and Components,* 1945-64, *Muck Shifter and Public Works,* 1946-63, and *Pottery and Glass.* Editor and contributor, *Encyclopedia of Urban Planning,* McGraw, 1973. Contributor to *Encyclopaedia of Modern Architectures* and to *Times* (London).

WORK IN PROGRESS: The third volume of *European Architecture in the Twentieth Century*; third and enlarged edition of *The New Towns*; *Woman into Citizen,* a history of the woman's movement in the twentieth century.

AVOCATIONAL INTERESTS: The arts of poetry, painting, sculpture, and music.

* * *

WHYTE, Fredrica (Harriman) 1905-

PERSONAL: Born August 9, 1905, in Hampton, Iowa; daughter of Frederick Alvin and Irma (Hemingway) Harriman; married Robert Whyte (a mining and civil engineer), September 22, 1938; children: Irma Elizabeth. *Education:* Sorbonne, University of Paris, student, 1926-27; University of Michigan, A.B., 1928, A.M., 1937; graduate study at University of Poitiers and University of Bordeaux, 1935; University of Southern California, M.S. in L.S., 1958. *Politics:* Republican. *Religion:* Christian Scientist. *Residence:* Long Beach, Calif.

CAREER: University High School, Ann Arbor, Mich., teacher of French, 1930-36; Long Beach (Calif.) Public Library, librarian, 1958—, now curator of Casa de Rancho Los Cerritos Library.

WRITINGS: Whyte's Atlas Guide, Scarecrow, 1962. Contributor of articles on New Guinea, Australia, and on library topics to local publications.

WORK IN PROGRESS: Heads of States in Modern Times.

SIDELIGHTS: Mrs. Whyte lived in France two years, in New Guinea and Australia, 1937-53.

* * *

WHYTE, Lancelot Law 1896-1972

PERSONAL: Born November 4, 1896, in Edinburgh, Scotland; married Eva Korner, 1947. *Education:* Cambridge University, M.A. *Home:* 93 Redington Rd., London N.W. 3, England.

CAREER: Scientist in industry, 1923-27; worked with an investment bank, financing new inventions, 1931-39; Power Jets Ltd., chairman and managing director, 1936-41; worked for Ministry and Supply, London, England, 1941-45; writer and lecturer, 1945-72. *Military service:* British Army, 1916-18; became lieutenant; served in France; received Military Cross. *Awards, honors:* Rockefeller Fellowship, 1928-29.

WRITINGS: Archimedes, or the Future of Physics, Kegan Paul, 1927, Norton, 1928; *Critique of Physics,* Norton,

1931; *The Next Development in Man,* Cresset, 1944, Henry Holt, 1948; *Everyman Looks Forward,* Cresset, 1946, Henry Holt, 1948; *The Unitary Principle in Physics and Biology,* Henry Holt, 1949; (editor) *Aspects of Form,* Pelligrini & Cudahy, 1951, revised edition, American Elsevier, 1968; *Accent on Form,* Harper, 1954, reprinted, Greenwood Press, 1973; *The Unconscious Before Freud,* Basic Books, 1960; *The Atomic Problem,* Allen & Unwin, 1961; (editor) *R. J. Boscovich, 1711-1787: Studies of His Life and Work,* Allen & Unwin, 1961; *Essay on Atomism, From Democritus to 1960,* Wesleyan University Press, 1961; (editor) *Roger Joseph Boscovich, S.J., F.R.S., 1711-1787: Studies of his Life and Work on the 250th Anniversary of his Birth,* foreword by Sir Harold Hartley, Fordham University Press, 1961; *Focus and Diversions,* Braziller, 1963; *Internal Factors in Evolution,* Braziller, 1965; *The Universe of Experience,* Harper, in press.

WORK IN PROGRESS: Vistas, collected essays.

(Died, 1972)

* * *

WICKENS, Delos D(onald) 1909-

PERSONAL: Born October 6, 1909, in Rochester, N.Y.; son of Vallance Albert (a physician) and Margaret (Gibson) Wickens; married Carol Hedberg (a research associate), November 6, 1937; children: Thomas Dow, Christopher Dow. *Education:* Centre College of Kentucky, A.B., 1931; University of North Carolina, M.A., 1933, Ph.D., 1937. *Home:* 218 Leland Ave., Columbus, Ohio 43214. *Office:* Ohio State University, 1945 North High St., Columbus, Ohio 43210.

CAREER: Ohio State University, Columbus, instructor in psychology, 1937-39; University of Colorado, Boulder, assistant professor, 1939-40; Oberlin College, Oberlin, Ohio, instructor, 1940-41; University of Wisconsin, Madison, assistant professor, 1941-46; Ohio State University, associate professor, 1946-47, professor of psychology, 1947—. Member of National Defense Research Committee, 1943-45; consultant to Research and Development Board, 1948-52, to National Science Foundation Panel on Psychology, 1956-59; member of Committee on Fulbright Awards in Psychology, 1959-61.

MEMBER: American Psychological Association (fellow), Society of Experimental Psychologists, Psychonomic Society, American Academy of Arts and Sciences (secretary, 1949-51; council member, 1960-61), Midwestern Psychological Association (president, 1958).

WRITINGS: (With W. L. Valentine) *Experimental Foundations of General Psychology,* 3rd edition, Rinehart, 1949; (contributor) *Kentucky Symposium: Learning Theory, Personality Theory, and Clinical Research,* Wiley, 1954; (with D. R. Meyer) *Psychology,* Dryden Press, 1955, revised edition, Holt, 1961; (contributor) C. N. Cofer and Barbara Musgrave, editors, *Verbal Behavior and Verbal Learning; Problems and Processes,* McGraw, 1963; *Conditioned Suppression as an Index of Perceptual Selection: Final Report,* College of Education, Ohio State University, 1964. Co-author of research bulletins for U.S. Air Force and project reports for U.S. Department of Commerce. Contributor of about forty articles to psychology journals. Associate editor, *Journal of Experimental Psychology.*

* * *

WIECKING, Anna M. 1887-1973

PERSONAL: Born December 6, 1887, in Mankato, Minn.;

daughter of Hermann R. (a merchant) and Emma (Kerndt) Wiecking. *Education:* University of Minnesota, B.A., 1914; Columbia University, M.A., 1915; University of Iowa, Ph.D., 1933. *Politics:* Independent. *Religion:* Liberal. *Home:* 506 Byron St., Mankato, Minn. 56001.

CAREER: Public School teacher in Minnesota, 1907-12; Michigan State Normal College (now Eastern Michigan University), Ypsilanti, supervisor of teaching, 1915-17; Mankato State Normal School (now Mankato State College), Mankato, Minn., supervisor of teaching, 1917-33, principal of college elementary school, 1933-52, professor and supervisor, 1952-56. Former secretary of Blue Earth county chapter of American National Red Cross. *Member:* National Education Association, American Association of University Women, Minnesota Education Association, Blue Earth County Historical Association (former secretary), Pi Lambda Theta.

WRITINGS: Education Through Manual Activities, Ginn, 1928; *Blue Earth County from 1700-1900*, Mankato Free Press, 1957; *Helping Children to be Better Citizens*, Denison, 1960; *As We Once Were*, Markitek (Mankato, Minn.), 1971. Writer of educational materials, and contributor to yearbooks, magazines, and newspapers.

SIDELIGHTS: Miss Wiecking spoke, read, and wrote German.

(Died, 1973)

* * *

WIENER, Philip P(aul) 1905-

PERSONAL: Surname pronounced *Wee*-ner. Born July 8, 1905, in New York, N.Y.; son of Elias and Sophia (Lorman) Wiener; married Gertrude Schler, August 24, 1934; children: Leonard, Marjorie. *Education:* City College of New York (now City College of the City University of New York), B.S., 1925; Columbia University, M.A., 1926, additional study, 1927-29; University of California, Berkeley, graduate study, 1926-27; University of Paris, graduate study; University of Southern California, Ph.D., 1931. *Home:* Oak Hill, N. 418, Narberth, Pa. 19072. *Office:* Temple University, Philadelphia, Pa. 19122.

CAREER: New York City high schools, teacher of mathematics and sciences, 1927-29; City College of New York (now City College of the City University of New York), New York, N.Y., instructor in philosophy, 1933-42, assistant professor, 1943-48, associate professor, 1949-53, professor of philosophy, 1953-68, chairman of department, 1959-68; Temple University, Philadelphia, Pa., professor of philosophy, 1968—. Visiting professor or lecturer at Harvard University, 1936, Smith College, 1943-44, Columbia University, 1947, Claremont Graduate School, 1950, University of Michigan, 1954, University of Minnesota, 1955. Supervisor of adult education, W.P.A. Project, New York, N.Y., 1932-33. Fulbright lecturer in philosophy, University of Lille and University of Bordeaux, 1953-54; senior scholar, East-West Center, University of Hawaii, 1962-63. Executive officer, City University of New York, 1960-66. *Member:* American Association for the Advancement of Science (fellow), Peirce Society (president, 1958-59), American Philosophical Society, History of Science Society, International Society for the History of Ideas (vice-president), Mind Association, British Society for Philosophy of Science, International Conference on Unified Science, Conference on Methods in Philosophy and Science (president, 1960-61), Phi Beta Kappa. *Awards, honors:* University of Brussels and University of Liege medal; Institute of

International Education, University of Paris field service fellow in philosophy, 1931-32; American Philosophical Society Penrose award, 1946-47; D.H.L., Kenyon College, 1961.

WRITINGS: (Translator) Jean Nicod, *Foundations of Geometry and Induction,* Harcourt, 1930; (editor with Daniel Jay Bronstein and Y. H. Krikorian) *Basic Problems of Philosophy,* Prentice-Hall, 1947, 3rd edition, 1963; *Evolution and the Founders of Pragmatism,* foreword by John Dewey, Harvard University Press, 1949; (editor) Gottfried Wilhelm Leibnitz, *Selections,* Scribner, 1951; (editor with Frederick H. Young) *Studies in the Philosophy of Charles Sanders Peirce,* first series, Harvard University Press, 1952; (editor) *Readings in the Philosophy of Science: Introduction to the Foundations and Cultural Aspects of the Sciences,* Scribner, 1953; (translator) Pierre M. M. Duhem, *Aim and Structure of Physical Theory,* Princeton University Press, 1954; (editor with Aaron Noland) *Roots of Scientific Thought: A Cultural Perspective,* Basic Books, 1957; (editor) Charles Sanders Peirce, *Values in a Universe of Chance: Selected Writings of Charles S. Peirce,* Stanford University Press, 1958, reissued as *Selected Writings,* Dover, 1966; (editor with Noland) *Ideas in Cultural Perspective,* Rutgers University Press, 1962; (editor of revised English edition) Hajime Nakamura, *Ways of Thinking of Eastern Peoples: India, China, Tibet, Japan,* East-West Center Press, 1964; (editor with Paul O. Kristeller) *Renaissance Essays, from the Journal of the History of Ideas,* Harper, 1968. Co-founder, executive editor, *Journal of the History of Ideas,* 1940—; editor-in-chief, *Dictionary of the History of Ideas,* published by Scribner, 1967-71. Contributor to *Journal of Philosophy, Philosophical Review,* and to other professional journals.

* * *

WIKSELL, Wesley 1906-

PERSONAL: Born January 7, 1906, in Kiron, Iowa; son of Nels (a minister) and Alice (Lundberg) Wiksell; married Jean Starr (a consultant in puppetry to Junior Leagues of America), December 20, 1934; children: Weslie Ann (Mrs. Philip Priest), Audre Jean. *Education:* Tabor College, student, 1924-26; University of Iowa, B.A., 1929, M.A., 1931; Louisiana State University, Ph.D., 1935; postdoctoral study at University of Wisconsin, 1935, University of London, 1939, Columbia University, 1942, University of Chicago, 1943. *Politics:* Democrat. *Religion:* Methodist. *Home:* 532 Stanford Ave., Baton Rouge, La. *Office:* Department of Speech, Louisiana State University, Baton Rouge, La.

CAREER: High school teacher in Newcastle, Neb., 1927-28; Stephens College, Columbia, Mo., professor of speech, 1929-47, chairman of Communications Division, 1934-47; Louisiana State University, Baton Rouge, professor of speech, 1947—. Visiting professor of speech at University of Missouri, 1946, University of Hawaii, 1955. Special lecturer on communication in business for American Management Association, Sales and Marketing Executives, and other groups and businesses; professional lecturer to management, service, and educational organizations throughout America. *Member:* National Society for the Study of Communication (vice-president, 1959; president, 1960), National Council of Teachers of English, Association for Higher Education, Alpha Tau Omega, Alpha Sigma Lambda, Kiwanis Club (Baton Rouge board).

WRITINGS: Your Conversation, John Swift, 1941; *Do*

They Understand You?, Macmillan, 1961; *How to Conduct Meetings*, Harper, 1966. Contributor of more than fifty articles to professional journals.

WORK IN PROGRESS: A programed manual with films, *How to Solve Problems in Groups*; *The Use of Parliamentary Procedure in Meetings at Grand Portage, 1800.*

AVOCATIONAL INTERESTS: Puppetry and canoeing.

* * *

WILBUR, Marguerite Eyer 1889-

PERSONAL: Born October 14, 1889, in Evanston, Ill.; daughter of Clarendon Bennet (a lawyer) and Cora (Knowlton) Eyer; married Van Rensselaer Wilbur, April 26, 1919 (died 1962); married Harvey Taylor, January, 1963. *Education:* Stanford University, B.A., 1913; University of Southern California, M.A., 1918, graduate study. *Politics:* Republican. *Religion:* Protestant. *Home:* 656 Park Lane, Santa Barbara, Calif. 93108.

CAREER: Writer. *Member:* California Historical Society (board member), Santa Barbara Museum of Art (board member), Music Academy of the West (board member), National Society of Arts and Letters, P.E.N., Pen and Brush Club (New York), Fine Arts Club (Santa Barbara).

WRITINGS: The East India Company and the British Empire in the Far East, Richard Smith, 1945, Russell, 1970; *John Sutter, Rascal and Adventurer*, Liveright, 1949; *Immortal Pirate: The Life of Sir Francis Drake*, Hastings House, 1951; *The Unquenchable Flame: The Life of Philip II*, Hastings House, 1952; *Thomas Jefferson, Apostle of Liberty*, Liveright, 1962.

Editor: Edwin Bryant, *What I Saw in California*, Fine Arts Press, 1936; (and author of foreword) Alonzo Delano, *Old Block's Sketch Book*, Fine Arts Press, 1947; Walter Colton, *Three Years in California*, Stanford University Press, 1949; Frank Marryat, *Mountains and Molehills*, Stanford University Press, 1952; George Vancouver, *Vancouver in California, 1792-1794*, Dawson's Book Shop, 1954.

Editor and translator: *A Frenchman in the Gold Rush: The Journal of Ernest de Massey, Argonaut of 1849*, California Historical Society, 1927; Miguel Venegas, *Juan Maria de Salvatierra of the Company of Jesus, Missionary in the Province of New Spain, and Apostolic Conqueror of the Californias*, Arthur Clark, 1929; Ludwig Emil Salvator, *Los Angeles in the Sunny Seventies: A Flower from the Golden Land*, B. McCallister & Jake Zeitlin, 1929; Raveneau de Lussan, *Buccaneer of the Spanish Main and First French Filibuster of the Pacific: A Translation into English of His Journal of a Voyage into the South Seas in 1684, and the Following years with the Filibusters*, Arthur Clark, 1930; (and author of notes) Sigismundo Taraval, *The Indian Uprising in Lower California, 1734-1737*, Quivira Society (Los Angeles), 1931, Arno, 1967; Eugene Duflot de Mofras, *Travels on the Pacific Coast*, two volumes, Fine Arts Press, 1937; Heinrich Lienhard, *A Pioneer at Sutter's Fort, 1846-1850: The Adventures of Heinrich Lienhard*, Calafia Society, 1941; Alexandre Dumas, *The Journal of Madame Giovanni*, Liveright, 1944; Alexandre Dumas, *A Gil Blas in California*, Hammond, 1947, Fine Arts Press, 1948.

AVOCATIONAL INTERESTS: Travel, gardening, music.

* * *

WILBUR, William H(ale) 1888-

PERSONAL: Born September 24, 1888, in Palmer, Mass.; son of John (a physician) and Edith (Smart) Wilbur; married Laura Girard Schieffelin, September 8, 1923; children: Mary S. (Mrs. L. H. Cummings), William H., Jr. (deceased). *Education:* Haverford College, student, 1907-08; U.S. Military Academy, B.S., 1912; graduate of Ecole Speciale Militaire, Saint Cyr, France, 1921, Ecole Superieure de Guerre, Paris, France, 1924, Command and General Staff College, 1932, Army War College, 1935. *Politics:* Republican. *Religion:* Presbyterian.

CAREER: U.S. Army, commissioned second lieutenant in 1912, served on active duty until retired as brigadier general in 1947; Cook County Jail, Chicago, Ill., warden, 1950. Also in import-export business as Far East representative, 1947-49. Major Army assignments included chief of staff, Sixth Corps Area, 1940-41, commanding officer of 60th Infantry, Fort Bragg, N.C., 1941-42, other command assignments in North Africa and Salerno campaigns. Lecturer on education subjects and world affairs throughout United States. Member, Chicago Crime Commission, beginning, 1954; director, Defenders of American Liberties, beginning, 1962. *Member:* Military Order of the World Wars, Order of Lafayette, Rotary (honorary), Kiwanis (honorary), Army and Navy Club (Washington, D.C.). *Awards, honors*—Military: Medal of Honor, Silver Star, Bronze Star, Legion of Merit (two), Combat Infantryman's Badge; Knight Commander, Order of Saints Maurice and Lazarus (Italy); Ouissam Alaouite (Morocco).

WRITINGS: Guideposts to the Future, Regnery, 1954; *Russian Communism: A Challenge and a Fraud*, Caxton, 1964; *Freedom Must Not Perish*, privately printed, 1964.

WORK IN PROGRESS: The Making of Young George Washington.

SIDELIGHTS: Wilbur speaks French and German, some Russian and Spanish.

* * *

WILBURN, Ralph G(lenn) 1909-

PERSONAL: Born May 10, 1909, in Emporia, Kan.; son of Eddie Joshua and Alura (Schnelle) Wilburn; married Mary Louise Hayes, December 24, 1928; children: Betty Louise (Mrs. Robert O. Koontz), Leta Marie (Mrs. Keith E. Shattuck). *Education:* University of California, Berkeley, A.B., 1939; University of Chicago Divinity School, M.A., 1942, Ph.D., 1945; postdoctoral study at University of Heidelberg, 1954-55, and Yale University, 1962-63. *Politics:* Democrat. *Home:* Manor 3336-1E, Punta Alta, Laguna Hills, Calif. 92653. *Office:* 213 Wilkinson Hall, Chapman College, Orange, Calif.

CAREER: Ordained minister of Disciples of Christ, 1951. Pastor in Chicago, Ill., 1939-44; George Pepperdine College, Los Angeles, Calif., associate professor, 1944-46, professor of religion, 1946-51; Phillips University, Graduate Seminary, Enid, Okla., professor of historical theology, 1951-57; The College of the Bible (now Lexington Theological Seminary), Lexington, Ky., professor of historical theology, 1957-69, dean, 1961-69; now at Chapman College, Orange, Calif. Pastor in Los Angeles, Calif., 1945-51; interim minister, American Protestant Community Church, Bad Godesberg, and consultant to U.S. Army Chaplaincy in Germany, 1954-55; member of Commission on Theology and Unity of the Christian Church of Disciples of Christ. *Member:* American Academy of Religion (Pacific Coast Division), American Theological Society, National Association of Biblical Instructors (president, 1951), Association of Disciples for Theological Discussion (president, 1960-63).

WRITINGS: Schleiermacher's Conception of Grace Viewed in Historical Relations, University of Chicago Press, 1945; (contributor) *Christian Courtship and Marriage*, Pepperdine College Press, 1946; *Christianity vs. Legalism*, Associated Publishers (Los Angeles), 1949; *The Prophetic Voice in Protestant Christianity*, Bethany, 1956; (editor) *The Reconstruction of Theology*, Bethany, 1963; *The Historical Shape of Faith*, Westminster, 1966; *The Interrelationship Between Theology and Science*, University of Nebraska, 1967. Contributor to *Americana Annual*, 1961-63, and to *World Vision Bible*; contributor of about sixty articles and reviews to religious journals. Member of editorial council, *Encounter*.

WORK IN PROGRESS: Current Intellectual Frontiers of the Christian Faith.

* * *

WILES, Roy McKeen 1903-19(?)

PERSONAL: Born October 15, 1903, in Truro, Nova Scotia, Canada; son of James Albert (a locomotive engineer) and Katherine Ellen (McKeen) Wiles; married Olwen Gertrude Jones, August 8, 1928; children: Evan Stuart, David McKeen. *Education:* Dalhousie University, B.A., 1927; Harvard University, A.M., 1928, Ph.D., 1935. *Politics:* Conservative. *Religion:* Anglican. *Home:* 863 Falcon Blvd., Burlington, Ontario, Canada. *Office:* McMaster University, Hamilton, Ontario, Canada.

CAREER: University of Alberta, Edmonton, lecturer in English, 1928-31; McMaster University, Hamilton, Ontario, assistant proeessor, 1935-39, associate professor, 1939-48, professor of English, beginning 1948, head of department, 1960-62, chairman of department, 1962-67. Visiting professor, Bowling Green State University, 1967-68. Organist and choirmaster at churches in Edmonton, Alberta, 1929-31, and Sydney, Nova Scotia, 1934; organizer and conductor of McMaster University choirs, 1935-54. Lay reader and warden of lay readers, Anglican Diocese of Niagara.

MEMBER: International Federation for Modern Languages and Literatures, International Association of University Professors of English, Royal Society of Canada (fellow), Humanities Association of Canada (secretary-treasurer, 1950-52; president, 1952-54), Humanities Research Council of Canada (chairman, 1960-62), Association of Canadian University Teachers of English (president, 1965-66), Modern Humanities Research Association, Modern Language Association of America, Johnson Society of the Great Lakes Region (president, 1964-65), Oxford Bibliographical Society. *Awards, honors:* Canada Council senior fellowship, 1958-59; Twentieth Anniversary Medal of Humanities Research Council of Canada, 1964.

WRITINGS: Scholarly Reporting in the Humanities, Humanities Research Council of Canada, 1951, 4th edition, University of Toronto Press, 1968; *Serial Publication in England Before 1750*, Cambridge University Press, 1957; *Freshest Advices: Early Provincial Newspapers in England*, Ohio State University Press, 1965; *The Humanities in Canada: Supplement to December 31, 1964*, University of Toronto Press, 1966. Contributor of articles and reviews to literary and other scholarly journals.

WORK IN PROGRESS: A book on social life in provincial England in the eighteenth century.

SIDELIGHTS: Wiles toured with Harvard Glee Club during his college days. In later years since traveled to the Arctic, Australia, and a number of points between.

(Deceased)

WILKE, Ulfert (Stephan) 1907-

PERSONAL: Surname is pronounced "Wilkie"; born July 14, 1907, in Bad Toelz, Germany; son of Rudolf and Mally (Brandes) Wilke; married Dorothy Kehl (a mechanical draftsman), 1947; children: Christopher, Nicholas, Karen Alexis. *Education:* Studied in Germany, Paris, and at Harvard University; University of Iowa, M.A., 1947. *Religion:* Lutheran. *Home:* R.R. #3, Solon, Iowa 52333. *Agent:* Wittenborn & Co., 1018 Madison Ave., New York, N.Y. 10028. *Office:* University of Iowa Museum of Art, Iowa City, Iowa 52240.

CAREER: Artist, and teacher of painting. Former director of art associations in Kalamazoo, Mich., and Springfield, Ill.; University of Iowa, Iowa City, assistant professor of art, 1947; University of Louisville, Louisville, Ky., associate professor , 1948-61, professor of art, 1961-62; Rutgers University, New Brunswick, N.J., became professor of painting at Douglass College, beginning, 1962; now director of the University of Iowa Museum of Art. Visiting professor at University of Georgia, 1955-56, University of British Columbia, summer, 1961. Painted in Japan, 1958, in Rome, 1959-61. Work hung in Guggenheim Museum, Cleveland Museum, Hanover Museum in Germany, Los Angeles County Museum, and in other public and private collections; exhibitor at one-man shows in America and abroad. *Military service:* U.S. Army, 1942-45. *Awards, honors:* Albrecht Durer Prize in Germany, 1928, and other awards for paintings; Guggenheim fellowships, 1959-60, 1960-61.

WRITINGS: Music to be Seen, Erewhon Press, 1956; *Fragments from Nowhere*, Kuroyama Press (Kyoto), 1958; *One, Two, and More*, Kuroyama Press, 1960. Contributor to art journals.

AVOCATIONAL INTERESTS: Abstract calligraphy, collecting primitive art, and Zen writings.

* * *

WILKINSON, Lorna Hilda Kathleen 1909-
(Lorna Deane)

PERSONAL: Born 1909, in Plumstead, London, England; daughter of Henry John (a woodworker) and Hilda (Minter) Gibbs; married Philip John Wilkinson (a barrister-at-law), 1928 (divorced, 1932). *Education:* Educated in state schools. *Religion:* Church of England. *Address:* c/o Westminster Bank Ltd., 31 Cheapside, London E.C.2, England.

CAREER: Legal clerk in London, England, 1926-33; worked for City of London Medical Auxiliary, London, 1933-47; H.M. Treasury, London, stenographer, 1961—. Volunteer telephonist, Auxiliary Fire Service, London, 1938-42; volunteer member, Kensington Civil Defence Corps, London, 1950—. *Member:* Society of Authors (life member), Wig and Pen Club (life member).

WRITINGS—All published under pseudonym Lorna Deane by MacDonald & Co.: *The Solitary Reaper*, 1944; *Strawberry Street*, 1946; *Portrait of a Man*, 1947.

Plays—All Published by Festival Plays: *Buttercup Hole*, 1952, *Portrait of Anna*, 1953, *Mixed Chartreuse*, 1955, *The Monkey-Bread* (comedy), 1956, *Private Apartments*, 1958.

Contributor of series of articles to *Sunday Chronicle* (London), 1955, poems, short stories, and articles to *Decachord*, *View Points, Poetry of Today, Congregational Monthly*, and other periodicals; occasional reviewer of books and plays.

WORK IN PROGRESS: A novel, *No Witness for the Defence;* an autobiography, *Death is the Enemy.*

*   *   *

WILLEM, John M. 1909-

PERSONAL: Born November 1, 1909, in Milwaukee, Wis.; son of John M. and Emma (Gunther) Willem; married Lois Hedrick, July 2, 1942; children: Susan Willem Martinson, Ann (Mrs. James S. Martin), Wendy Logan, John III. *Education:* Lawrence University, B.S., 1931; Northwestern University, M.S., 1932. *Politics:* Republican. *Religion:* Methodist. *Home:* 225 Elderfields Rd., Manhasset, N.Y. 11030. *Office:* West Indies & Caribbean Developments Ltd., Two Park Ave., Manhasset, N.Y. 11030.

CAREER: J. Walter Thompson Co. (advertising agency), New York, N.Y., senior vice-president and chairman of business development program, 1945-61; Indiana University, Business School, Bloomington, associate faculty member, 1957-59; West Indies & Caribbean Developments Ltd., New York, N.Y., president and managing director of companies in West Indies, 1961—. Appointed to U.S. Assay Commission, 1957. President of board of trustees, Methodist Hospital, Brooklyn, N.Y. *Member:* American Numismatic Association (fellow), Canadian Numismatic Association, Sociedad Numismatica de Mexico, University Club (New York). *Awards, honors:* Distinguished Alumni Award, Lawrence University, 1974.

WRITINGS: The United States Trade Dollar: America's Only Unwanted, Unhonored Coin, privately published, 1959, Whitman Publishing Co., 1965. Contributor to numismatic and economics journals.

WORK IN PROGRESS: History of Canadian National (West Indies) Steamships Ltd., for Canadian National Railways.

*   *   *

WILLIAMS, Cecil B(rown) 1901-1966

PERSONAL: Born October 27, 1901, in Spring Creek, W.Va.; son of Isaac and Mary Elizabeth (Brown) Williams; married Frances Ell (died December, 1958); married Mary Elizabeth Waits, October 27, 1961; children: (first marriage) Philip C., James I. *Education:* Oklahoma State University, B.S., 1926, M.S., 1927; University of Chicago, Ph.D., 1933. *Religion:* Disciples of Christ. *Home:* 2521 Highview Ter., Fort Worth, Tex. 76109. *Office:* Texas Christian University, Fort Worth, Tex. 76129.

CAREER: McPherson College, McPherson, Kan., associate professor of English, 1926-28; Oklahoma State University, Stillwater, assistant professor, 1928-30, professor of English, 1946-59; De Paul University, Chicago, Ill., 1930-45, began as instructor, became professor of English; Texas Christian University, Fort Worth, professor of English and chairman of department, 1960-66, director of graduate research studies in American literature. Lecturer, Northwestern University, 1944-46; Fulbright lecturer, University of Hamburg, 1959-60. Participant in writers' conferences. *Member:* Modern Language Association of America (life), National Council of Teachers of English, American Studies Association, Conference on College Composition and Communications, South Central Modern Language Association (president, 1961-62), Texas Conference of College Teachers of English, Poetry Society of Texas, Poetry Society of Oklahoma, Phi Kappa Phi, Pi Gamma Mu, Pi

Kappa Delta. *Awards, honors:* Friends of Literature award for poetry, 1944, for *In Time of War.*

WRITINGS: (Editor) Robert Montgomery Bird, *Nick of the Woods,* American Book Co., 1939; (with Allan H. Stevenson) *A Research Manual,* Harper, 1940, 3rd edition (sole author) published as *A Research Manual for College Studies and Papers,* 1963; *In Time of War: Sonnets for America,* Torch Press, 1943; *Effective Business Writing,* Ronald, 1947, 2nd edition (with John Ball), 1953, 3rd edition (with E. Glenn Griffin) published as *Effective Business Communication,* Ronald, 1966; *Studies in American Literature Since 1850: Four Critical Essays,* Oklahoma Agricultural and Mechanical College, 1951; *Paradise Prairie* (novel), John Day, 1953; (with Ball) *Report Writing,* Ronald, 1955; *Oklahoma* (verse), Oklahoma State University Press, 1957; (with Ball) *College Writing,* Ronald, 1957; *Regionalism in American Literature,* Quelle & Meyer, 1962; *Henry Wadsworth Longfellow* (biography and criticism), Twayne, 1964. Contributor of chapters to books and articles to periodicals. Editor of *College Composition and Communications,* 1959-60.

AVOCATIONAL INTERESTS: Golf and gardening.†

(Died September 6, 1966)

*   *   *

WILLIAMS, Edward K. 1923-1966

PERSONAL: Born April 4, 1923, in New York, N.Y.; son of Arthur Lewis and Martha (Wallach) Williams; married Bettine Martha Harlow, August 28, 1954; children: Bradford Harlow, Paul Arthur. *Education:* Williams College, A.B., 1943; Columbia University, M.D., 1951. *Politics:* Republican. *Religion:* Episcopal. *Home:* 624 Dorchester Rd., San Mateo, Calif. 94402.

CAREER: Physician, specializing in internal medicine and diseases of the chest, in private practice, San Mateo, Calif., 1955-66. Stanford University, Stanford, Calif., assistant professor of clinical medicine, 1955-66; College of San Mateo, San Mateo, Calif., health education instructor, 1961-66. Lecturer to lay groups. *Military service:* U.S. Naval Reserve, 1943-45; became lieutenant junior grade. *Member:* American Medical Association, American College of Chest Physicians (associate fellow), American Public Health Association (fellow), California Medical Association, California Council on Smoking and Health (chairman, 1965-66), San Mateo County Medical Society.

WRITINGS: (With Irwin and Staton) *Health for Better Living,* C. E. Merrill, 1964. Writer of news column, "Health Tips," distributed by California Medical Association, and of articles for laymen on health topics.

WORK IN PROGRESS: Writing and producing "Modern Medicine," series of thirty-two forty-five minute television programs, explaining medical topics to college students and lay audiences.

(Died, 1966)

*   *   *

WILLIAMS, Eirlys O(lwen) (Eirlys Trefor)

PERSONAL: Born of Welsh parents in Lancashire, England; married Trefor Williams (a tobacconist), 1940; children: Nan M. *Education:* Trained as a nurse. *Home:* Ardwyn, Barmouth, Merioneth, North Wales.

CAREER: Formerly a nurse; now husband's partner as tobacconist and news agent. Rural Community Council, member of drama committee. *Member:* Writers Guild of Great Britain (associate member), Bermo Arts Club (founder; chairman for three years; dramatic producer).

WRITINGS: (Under pseudonym Eirlys Trefor) *Light Cakes for Tea,* Hutchinson, 1958. Also author of radio play, "Mr. Watkyn," and of book, *Woman in a Valley of Stones.* Contributor of plays and several stories and talks to British Broadcasting Corp., and of articles and stories to *Wales, Anglo-Welsh Review, Country Quest,* and other magazines.

WORK IN PROGRESS: A book, *The Mali Morgan*; a television play, *The Anniversary.*

* * *

WILLIAMS, John Stanley 1925-

PERSONAL: Born December 26, 1925, in Plymouth, Devonshire, England; son of William John (a sales manager) and Margaret Janet (Thomas) Williams; married Rona Mary Thomas (a speech therapist); children: Felicity Jane. *Education:* Brasenose College, Oxford, B.A. (with honors), 1951, M.A. (with honors), 1956. *Home:* Ashcroft, Abbots Rd., Abbots Langley, Hertfordshire, England.

CAREER: Barclays Bank Ltd., London, England, university trainee, 1951-53; Pye Radio Ltd., Cambridge, England, sales office manager, 1953-54; Humanitas Books Ltd., London, England, sales manager, 1954-55; Queen Elizabeth's Grammar School, Blackburn, England, teacher of English, 1955-58; Watford Grammar School, Watford, England, teacher of English, 1958-66; Grove Hill Grammar School, Hemel Hempstead, England, teacher of English, 1966—. *Military service:* British Army, 1945-48; became warrant officer, second class.

WRITINGS—Novels: On the Way Out, Hutchinson, 1962; *Death Is a Lizard,* Hutchinson, 1963; *The God-Seeker,* Hutchinson, 1966; *The Spinsters,* Hutchinson, 1967.

WORK IN PROGRESS: A novel, tentatively titled *Down Among the Dead Men*; a novel, *An Aspect of Love*; short stories.

BIOGRAPHICAL/CRITICAL SOURCES: Punch, November 22, 1967.†

* * *

WILLIAMS, Walter G(eorge) 1903-

PERSONAL: Born June 26, 1903, in England; came to United States, 1921; son of Walter Brooks (a grocer) and Amy T. S. (Griffiths) Williams; married Mary Esther Buchanan, June 26, 1929; children: Walter John, Amy Ruth (Mrs. Roger Gohring), George Buchanan, Eva Rose (Mrs. Troy Andersen), Edwin Ross. *Education:* Mount Union College, A.B., 1928; Garrett Theological Seminary, B.D., 1931; University of Chicago, Ph.D., 1934. *Politics:* Republican. *Home:* 1370 South Downing St., Denver, Colo. 80210. *Office:* Iliff School of Theology, 2201 South University, Denver, Colo. 80210.

CAREER: Ordained to Methodist ministry, 1931; University of Chicago, Chicago, Ill., instructor in Semitic languages, 1933-35; pastor of churches in Ohio, 1935-42; Baldwin-Wallace College, Berea, Ohio, instructor in religion, 1936-37; Iliff School of Theology, Denver, Colo., professor of Old Testament, 1942—, dean of students, 1950-61.

Visiting professor at Garrett Theological Seminary, summers, 1936, 1954, Union Theological Seminary, Matanzas, Cuba, 1957; lecturer at American School of Oriental Research, Jerusalem, 1951, 1961; lecturer at sixteen theological seminaries in Far East, 1962. Member of World Methodist Council; member of Methodist Church Commission on Ecumenical Consultation, and advisory member of Commission on Worship. *Member:* American Academy of Religion, Society of Biblical Literature (council member, 1963-65), American Association of University Professors. *Awards, honors:* Litt.D., Mount Union College, 1951.

WRITINGS: A Handbook of Worship for Ministers, Iliff School of Theology, 1944, 3rd edition, Iliff Students Bookstore, 1963; *The Books of the Law,* Abingdon-Cokesbury, 1945; *Adventures in Bible Discovery,* Graded Press, 1948; *The Prophets, Pioneers to Christianity,* Abingdon, 1956; *Archaeology in Biblical Research,* Abingdon, 1965. Regular writer of lesson material for Methodist Publishing. Contributor to *Harper's Dictionary of Biblical Biography, Interpreters' Dictionary of the Bible,* and *World Book of Knowledge*; contributor of some forty articles to *American Journal of Semitic Languages,* other journals, and to religious periodicals.

WORK IN PROGRESS: Continuing excavations at Dhiban, Jordan, in association with William H. Morton.

* * *

WILLIAMSON, Claude C(harles) H. 1891-19(?) (Felix Hope)

PERSONAL: Born December 27, 1891, in England; son of Horace and Fanny (Luthcke) Williamson. *Education:* University College and King's College, London, honors diploma in English literature, 1920. *Politics:* Conservative. *Home:* 11 Dock St., London E. 1, England.

CAREER: Teacher in English schools, 1914-19; entered Congregation of Oblates of St. Charles, ordained Roman Catholic priest, 1926. *Member:* Royal Geographical Society (fellow), Royal Historical Society (fellow), Royal Society of Literature (fellow).

WRITINGS—All published by Grant-Richards except as indicated: Human Concerns, Stockwell, 1915; *Some Aspects of Men and Things,* 1915; *Writers of Many Centuries,* 1918; *Writers of Three Centuries, 1789-1914,* 1920; *Greek Aesthetics,* 1921; *The Concept of History,* 1922.

Stations of the Cross, Burns & Oates, 1937; (editor) *Great Catholics,* Nicholson & Watson, 1938, Macmillan, 1939; (compiler) *Readings on the Character of Hamlet, 1661-1947,* Allen & Unwin, 1950, Gordian, 1972; (compiler) *Letters From the Saints,* Philosophical Library, 1958; (editor) *Great True Stories of the Islands,* Arco, 1961. Under pseudonym Felix Hope, contributor of more than 120 articles to about 60 English and American magazines and journals.

(Deceased)

* * *

WILLIAMSON, Joseph 1895-

PERSONAL: Born June 15, 1895, in London, England; son of George (a shipwright) and Lucy Rebecca (Payne) Williamson; married Audrey Hollist Barnes, November 1, 1927; children: Joy (Mrs. Barrie Williams), Lucy (Mrs. John Woolfenden), Tony. *Education:* Studied at Knutsford Ordination Test School, 1919-21, St. Augustine's Theological College, Canterbury, England, 1921-25. *Home and of-*

fice: High Spray, Marine Dr. West, West Wittering, Chichester, Sussex, England.

CAREER: Ordained priest, Church of England, 1925; attached to Grahamstown Cathedral, Grahamstown South Africa, 1928-32; rector of parishes in Warwickshire, Suffolk, and Norfolk, England, 1932-52; St. Paul's, London, England, rector, 1952-62; Wellclose Square Fund Ltd., London, chaplain and founder, 1958-65. *Military service:* British Army, 1914-18; served in France. Chaplain of Forces, 1940-46; served as chaplain of Detention Barracks on Gibraltar for twenty months.

WRITINGS: Father Joe: The Autobiography of Joseph Williamson of Poplar and Stepney, Hodder & Stoughton, 1963, published as *Father Joe,* Abingdon, 1964; *Friends of Father Joe,* Hodder & Stoughton, 1965.

AVOCATIONAL INTERESTS: Travel and sawing wood.†

*   *   *

WILLIAMSON, Rene de Visme 1908-

PERSONAL: Born May 28, 1908, in Chicago, Ill.; son of Hiram Parker (a professor) and Alice (de Visme) Williamson; married Virginia Hardgrove Sutherland, September 12, 1936; children: Parker Trevilian, Warren Ligon, Roger Leigh. *Education:* Rutgers University, A.B., 1931; Harvard University, A.M., 1932, Ph.D., 1935, studied at University of Munich, summer, 1932, and University of Berlin, summer, 1933. *Politics:* Democrat. *Religion:* Presbyterian. *Home:* 3234 Fritchie Dr., Baton Rouge, La. 70809. *Office:* 237 Stubbs Hall, Louisiana State University, Baton Rouge, La.

CAREER: Faculty member at Princeton University, Princeton, N.J., 1935-37, Davidson College, Davidson, N.C., 1937-44, Beloit College, Beloit, Wis., 1944-45; University of Tennessee, Knoxville, professor of government, 1945-54; Louisiana State University, Baton Rouge, professor of government 1954—, past chairman of department. Visiting summer professor at University of Michigan, 1949, Western Reserve University (now Case Western Reserve University), 1950, University of Nebraska, 1957, Vanderbilt University, 1960, 1962, Johns Hopkins University, 1963, Duke University, 1965, University of Natal, South Africa, 1969. Presbyterian Church in the U.S., visiting professor at South American universities under auspices of Board of Christian Education, 1956, chairman of General Assembly's Advisory Committee on Higher Education, 1958-65, member of General Assembly's Permanent Universities Committee, 1960-63, and of General Assembly's Permanent Theological Committee, beginning 1966. Member of board of directors, Southwestern University, 1968-72.

MEMBER: American Political Science Association (executive council member 1959-61), American Association of University Professors, Southern Political Science Association (president, 1959-60), Phi Beta Kappa.

WRITINGS: The Politics of Planning in the Oil Industry under the Code, Harper, 1936, *Culture and Policy: The United States and the Hispanic World,* University of Tennessee Press, 1949; (editor with Lee S. Greene) *Five Years of British Labour, 1945-50: A Symposium,* Kallman, 1950; *Independence and Involvement: A Christian Re-Orientation in Political Science,* Louisiana State University Press, 1964. Contributor to political science and other journals. Editor, *Journal of Politics,* 1949-53.

SIDELIGHTS: Williamson speaks French, Spanish, and German.

*   *   *

WILLISON, George F(indlay) 1896-1972

PERSONAL: Born July 24, 1896, in Denver, Colo.; son of Robert (an architect) and Anna (Brunton) Willison; married Florence Hauser, 1928; children: Malcom. *Education:* Studied at University of Colorado, A.B., 1918, Oxford University, 1920-23, Sorbonne, University of Paris, 1924. *Home:* South Hill, R.D. 3, Ballston Spa, N.Y.

CAREER: Newspaperman in Denver, Colo., and New York, N.Y., 1925-27; St. John's College, Annapolis, Md., head of classics department, 1928; Hessian Hills School, Croton-on-Hudson, N.Y., teacher, 1929-35, acting director, 1934; Federal Writers Project, writer in Provincetown, Mass., later national editor-in-chief, Washington, D.C., 1936-41; writer for Civil Aeronautics Administration, Washington, D.C., 1942-43, Democratic National Committee, Washington, D.C., 1944-45, Department of Public Information, United Nations, New York, N.Y., 1950; member of Senator Estes Kefauver's presidential campaign staff, 1952, 1955, of governor's executive chamber staff, State of New York, 1955-59; director of public information/relations for New York (N.Y.) Commission on Intergroup Relations, 1959-60, and New York (N.Y.) Department of Commerce and Public Events, 1961-62. *Military service:* U.S. Army, Machine Gun Corps, 1918. *Awards, honors:* Rhodes Scholar.

WRITINGS: Here They Dug Gold, Brentano, 1931, revised edition, 1946; *Why Wars are Declared,* Basic Books, 1935; (editor) *Let's Make a Play,* Harper, 1940; *Saints and Strangers: Being the Lives of the Pilgrim Fathers and Their Families, With Their Friends and Foes; And an Account of Their Posthumous Wanderings in Limbo, Their Final Resurrection and Rise to Glory, and the Strange Pilgrimages of Plymouth Rock,* Reynal & Hitchcock, 1945, Time, Inc., 1964, revised and abridged edition, published as *Saints and Strangers,* Ballantine, 1965, published in England as, *Saints and Strangers: The Story of the "Mayflower" and the Plymouth Colony,* Heinemann, 1966; *Behold Virginia: The Fifth Crown. Being the Trials, Adventures and Disasters of the First Families of Virginia, the Rise of the Grandees and the Eventual Triumph of the Common and Uncommon Sort in the Revolution,* Harcourt, 1951; (editor) *The Pilgrim Reader: The Story of the Pilgrims as Told by Themselves and Their Contemporaries, Friendly and Unfriendly,* Doubleday, 1953; *The History of Pittsfield, Massachusetts, 1916-1955,* [Pittsfield, Mass.], 1957; *Our Pilgrim Fathers,* Ballantine, 1965; *Patrick Henry and His World,* Doubleday, 1969.

Contributor to *Unforgettable Americans,* Channel, 1960; *American Heritage Cookbook and Illustrated History of American Eating and Drinking,* Simon & Schuster, 1964, and other books. Also contributor to *Book of Knowledge,* and to magazines and critical journals.

WORK IN PROGRESS: A life of Tom Paine.

(Died July 30, 1972)

*   *   *

WILSON, Dale 1894-

PERSONAL: Born September 20, 1894, in Corder, Mo.; son of William (a merchant) and Martha Susan (Fisher) Wilson; married Kathleen F. Flynn, May 15, 1923. *Educa-*

tion: University of Missouri, B.J., 1916. *Home:* 12 Rockwell Lane, Sarasota, Fla.

CAREER: Milwaukee Journal, Milwaukee, Wis., 1923-60, started as copy editor, became Sunday and feature editor. *Military service:* U.S. Navy, World War I. *Member:* Sigma Delta Chi.

WRITINGS: (With wife, Kathleen F. Wilson, and Will C. Conrad) *The Milwaukee Journal: The First 80 Years,* University of Wisconsin Press, 1964. Editor, *Milwaukee County Historical Society Messenger,* 1950-55.

* * *

WILSON, Frank (Avray) 1914-

PERSONAL: Born May 5, 1914, in Vacoas, Mauritius; son of Albert James (a sugar manufacturer) and Anna (D'-Avray) Wilson; married Higford Eckbo, April 28, 1936; children: Wendy-Ann Wilson Holzbog, Raymond, Jason, Norman. *Education:* Attended Brighton College; St. John's College, Cambridge, M.A., 1937. *Religion:* Agnostic. *Home:* 30 Edwardes Sq., London W.8, England.

CAREER: Overseas Sugar Co., Colony of Mauritius, manager, 1937-39, 1947-48; member of research unit in tropical nutrition, 1944-46; professional painter, 1948—. *Military service:* British Army, 1939-45; became captain. *Member:* P.E.N.

WRITINGS: Food for the Golden Age, Daniel Co., 1954; *Art into Life: An Interpretation of Contemporary Trends in Painting,* Centaur Press, 1958; *Art as Understanding: A Painter's Account of the Last Revolution in Art and Its Bearing on Human Existence as a Whole,* Routledge & Kegan Paul, 1963. Also author of film script, "The New Painting."

WORK IN PROGRESS: Research into the biological and anthropological aspects of world art.

BIOGRAPHICAL/CRITICAL SOURCES: Apollo, February, 1960, March, 1961; *The British Imagination,* Atheneum, 1961; *Avray Wilson—Illustrated,* Centaur Press, 1961; *Quadrum,* No. 14.†

* * *

WILSON, Frank J. 1887-1970

PERSONAL: Born May 19, 1887, in Buffalo, N.Y.; son of John F. and Mary A. (McGreevy) Wilson; married Judith M. Barbaux. *Education:* Attended University of Buffalo one year. *Politics:* Republican. *Religion:* Catholic. *Home:* 2910 Tennyson St., N.W., Washington, D.C. 20015.

CAREER: U.S. Treasury, Washington, D.C., investigator and special agent, 1918-36, chief of U.S. Secret Service, 1936-47. Consultant to U.S. Atomic Energy Commission, 1947-48, U.S. Air Force, 1949. National president, Senior Citizens for Dick Nixon, 1960. *Member:* U.S. Treasury Agents Association, National Association of Retired Civil Employees, International Association of Chiefs of Police (honorary life member), Chief Constables of Canada (honorary life member), Knights of Columbus (honorary life member), National Press Club. *Awards, honors:* Order of Cloud and Banner (China), Order of Saint Olaf (Norway).

WRITINGS: (With Beth Day) *Special Agent: A Quarter Century with the Treasury Department and the Secret Service,* Holt, 1965 (published in England as *Special Agent: Twenty-five Years with the U.S. Treasury Department and Secret Service,* Muller, 1966). Contributor of articles on crime prevention, juvenile delinquents, counterfeiting, and

protection of the President, to magazines, including *Collier's.*

WORK IN PROGRESS: Secret Service Stories, a book of important cases of the U.S. Secret Service since establishment in 1865.

SIDELIGHTS: Columbia Pictures film, "Undercover Man," 1949, was based on one of Wilson's articles published by *Collier's* in 1947.

(Died June 22, 1970)

* * *

WILSON, Ivor (Arthur) 1924-

PERSONAL: Born August 30, 1924, in Grimsby, England; son of Baron and Rita (Green) Wilson; married Marjorie Berry (a lecturer), March 17, 1945; children: Keren, Ian Roger. *Education:* Attended City Training College, Sheffield, England, and College of Art, Hull, England; University of London, B.Sc. (honors in economics). *Home:* 139 Newland Park, Hull, Yorkshire, England.

CAREER: Art teacher, Hull, England, 1947-56; Jervis County High School, Hull, head of department of social studies, 1956-61; College of Commerce, Hull, lecturer in economics and government, 1961—, head of department of Soviet economic studies, 1973—. Consultant and commentator on government on local radio station. *Military service:* British Navy, Fleet Air Arm, 1943-47; became lieutenant pilot. *Member:* Economics Association, Government Lecturers Society.

WRITINGS: But Not For Love, Collins, 1962; *That Feeds on Men,* Collins, 1963; *Lilies That Fester,* Collins, 1964; *Empty Tigers,* Collins, 1965. Radio plays; all broadcast by British Broadcasting Corp.: "Take Any Day," 1969; "Insufficient Evidence," 1970; "Fly in Amber," 1970; "Over the Hills and Far Away," 1971; "Our John," 1971; "Time to Go Home," 1972; "Who Walks Alone," 1972; "Save a Slice of Ham for Me," 1972; "Never Miss a Bargain," 1973. Contributor of a one-act play to Heinemann's "Windmill" series. Contributor of occasional articles to *Government Lectures Bulletin* and *Perspective.*

WORK IN PROGRESS: Radio scripts; drama.

AVOCATIONAL INTERESTS: Drawing and painting.

BIOGRAPHICAL/CRITICAL SOURCES: Hull Daily Mail, August 8, 1962; *Yorkshire Post,* August 9, 1962.

* * *

WILSON, James Orville 1895-

PERSONAL: Born May 3, 1895, in Avoca, Ark.; son of James N. (a farmer) and Genia (McConnell) Wilson; married Lillie Anne Johnson, September 11, 1917; children: John A., Morris V., Harold B., Eugene H. *Education:* Pacific Union College, B.A., 1931; SDA Seminary (now part of Andrews University), M.A., 1953. *Address:* P.O. Box 246, Bolton, N.C. 28423.

CAREER: Missionary to Burma and India, 1922-52; Atlantic Union College, South Lancaster, Mass., teacher of Burmese, 1943-46; missionary to Israel, with residence in Jerusalem, 1954-56. *Military service:* U.S. Air Service, American Expeditionary Forces, 1917-19.

WRITINGS: Cheer Up, World: It's Better Ahead, Review & Herald, 1962; *Who Has Your Allegiance?,* Southern Publishing, 1965. Editor of *Kin Saung* (Watchman, a Burmese magazine), 1932-36.

WILSON, James Vernon 1881-
(Jim Wilson)

PERSONAL: Born January 29, 1881, in Cheltenham, Gloucester, England; son of Edward T. (a medical doctor) and Mary (Whishaw) Wilson; married Norah Crump (deceased); children: Edward Patrick, John Michael, Joan Mary Wilson Williams. *Education:* Attended Cheltenham College; Gonville and Caius College, Cambridge, B.A., 1904, M.A., 1907. *Home:* 3 Salisbury Rd., Batford, Harpenden, Hertfordshire, England. *Office:* Guild of Health, Edward Wilson House, 26 Queen Anne St., London W.1, England.

CAREER: Clergyman, Church of England; curate in Stoke on Trent, England, 1904-12; vicar in Wolverhampton and Burslem, England, 1912-33; curate in St. Albans, England, 1934-42, concurrently chaplain of Napsbury Mental Hospital, 1937-42; St. Mary the Virgin Church, London, England, vicar, 1942-47; Guild of Health, London, chaplain, 1947-58. Alderman, St. Pancres Borough Council, 1945-47. *Military service:* British Army, chaplain, 1916-17; became captain.

WRITINGS—All under name Jim Wilson: *Healing Through the Power of Christ,* James Clarke, 1946; *Redemption of the Common Life,* Dobson, 1950; *First Steps in Meditation for Young People,* James Clarke, 1956; *Father Jim's Silver Lining Radio Talks,* James Clarke, 1958; *Growth in Prayer,* James Clarke, 1960; *Go Preach the Kingdom, Heal the Sick,* James Clarke, 1962. Author of pamphlets on Christian healing, published by Guild of Health.

SIDELIGHTS: Headquarters of organization for which he writes is named in honor of Wilson's older brother, Edward, who died with Captain Scott and his companions after reaching the South Pole in 1912.†

*   *   *

WILWERDING, Walter Joseph 1891-1966

PERSONAL: Surname is pronounced *Will*-wording; born February 13, 1891, in Winona, Minn.; son of John (a mill owner) and Albertine (Muller) Wilwerding; married Nan Barrett, November 30, 1916 (died February, 1932); married Sylvia Grace Novotny, May 23, 1933. *Education:* Studied at Minneapolis Art School, 1910-15. *Politics:* Republican. *Home:* 5644 Chowen Ave. S., Edina, Minn. 55410.

CAREER: Art Instruction Schools, Minneapolis, Minn., vice-president and director of education, 1948-61; painter of animal life; writer and illustrator. Made expeditions to Africa to study and paint animals, 1929, 1933, 1953; has also sketched in Europe, Alaska, and the American West; paintings exhibited at one-man shows in New York, Chicago, Los Angeles, Minneapolis, and other cities. *Member:* Society of Animal Artists (vice-president, 1956-58), American Geographical Society (fellow), Association of Professional Artists (Minneapolis).

WRITINGS: (Self-illustrated) *Jangwa, the Story of Jungle Prince,* Macmillan, 1935; (self-illustrated) *Keema of the Monkey People,* Macmillan, 1936; (self-illustrated) *Punda the Tiger Horse,* Macmillan, 1937; (self-illustrated) *Tembo the Forest Giant,* Macmillan, 1939; *Animal Drawings and Painting,* Watson, 1946, revised edition, Dover, 1956; (self-illustrated) *Book of Wild Beasts*, Putnam, 1963; *The Cats in Action,* Foster Art Service, 1963; *How to Draw and Paint Hoofed Animals,* Foster Art Service, 1964; *How to Draw and Paint Animal Textures,* Foster Art Service,

1965; (self-illustrated) *The Big One: A Second Book of Wild Beasts*, Putnam, 1966.

Also editor with Lee S. Preston of Minneapolis Art Instruction manuals, 1953-59. Regular contributor of articles and illustrations to *Sports Afield,* 1930-66. Also writer of articles and short stories for *Field and Stream, Boy's Life, This Week, Blue Book, Nature, Jack and Jill, Story Parade,* and *Audubon Magazine.*

SIDELIGHTS: Wilwerding spoke German and KiSwahili.

(Died September 19, 1966)

*   *   *

WINCH, Michael Bluett 1907-

PERSONAL: Born December 6, 1907, in London, England; son of Arthur Bluett and Elsie Winch. *Education:* Trinity College, Cambridge, B.A., 1929. *Home:* Boughton-Monchelsea Place, near Maidstone, Kent, England.

CAREER: British Foreign Service, attache in Warsaw, Brussels, and Athens, 1931-33; Reuter's, member of editorial staff, 1934-35; *Christian Science Monitor,* correspondent in Poland and central Europe, 1936-39; British Broadcasting Corp. European Service, director of Slav and Portuguese broadcasts, 1939-43; British Foreign Service, London, Moscow, Warsaw, Bonn, 1943-54.

WRITINGS: Republic for a Day: An Eye-Witness Account of the Carpatho-Ukraine Incident, R. Hale, 1939; *Introducing Germany,* Methuen, 1958, revised edition, International Publications Service, 1967; *Introducing Belgium,* International Publications Service, 1964; *The World in Colour: Austria,* includes photographs by Kees Scherer, Follett, 1968. Contributor of articles on foreign affairs and travel to monthly and quarterly periodicals.

*   *   *

WINCHELL, Constance M(abel) 1896-

PERSONAL: Born November 2, 1895, in Northampton, Mass.; daughter of Joseph E. and Inez (Bliss) Winchell. *Education:* University of Michigan, B.A., 1918; Columbia University, M.S., 1930. *Home address:* Box 642, R.D. 2, New Paltz, N.Y. 12561.

CAREER: Central High School, Duluth, Minn., librarian, 1918-19; Merchant Marine Service, New York, N.Y., assistant in lighthouse division, 1920; University of Michigan Library, Ann Arbor, reviser in cataloging department, 1920-21, reference assistant, 1921-23; American Library, Paris, France, head cataloger, 1924-25; Columbia University Libraries, New York, N.Y., reference assistant, 1925-33, assistant reference librarian, 1933-41, reference librarian, 1941-62. *Member:* American Library Association, Association of College and Reference Libraries, Kappa Alpha Theta. *Awards, honors:* Isadore Gilbert Mudge citation, 1960, from the reference services division, American Library Association.

WRITINGS: Locating Books for Interlibrary Loan, Wilson, 1930; (with Isadore G. Mudge) *Reference Books of 1929: An Informal Supplement to Guide to Reference Books,* American Library Association, 1930; (with Mudge) *Reference Books of 1931-1933; Third Informal Supplement to Guide to Reference Books,* American Library Association, 1931; (with Mudge) *Guide to Reference Books,* American Library Association, 6th edition, 1936, sole author of 7th edition, 1951, and 8th edition, 1967, sole author of three supplements to 6th edition, 1941, 1944, 1947, (with O. A.

Johnson) first supplement to 7th edition, 1954, sole author of second supplement, 1956, (with others) author of third supplement, 1960, fourth supplement, 1963.

BIOGRAPHICAL/CRITICAL SOURCES: College and Research Libraries, July, 1960, September, 1962, July, 1967; *Choice,* November, 1967.

* * *

WINDER, George Herbert 1895-

PERSONAL: Born December 24, 1895, in Wellington, New Zealand; son of George and Florance (Hackney) Winder; married Dove Hunter, December 21, 1936. *Education:* Victoria College, University of New Zealand, law professional, 1923. *Politics:* "Libertarian." *Religion:* Church of England. *Home:* Springhead Farm, Crowborough, Sussex, England.

CAREER: Solicitor of the Supreme Court of New Zealand, 1923-27; farmer, 1932-63; free-lance writer, 1950—. *Member:* Royal Economics Society, Institute of Journalists, National Liberal Club (London). *Awards, honors:* First prize for magazine article, *World's Press News,* 1959.

WRITINGS: (With Cluny MacPherson) *Delusion of Protection,* Angus & Robertson, 1929; *The Menace of the Planned Economy,* Society of Individualists, 1943; *Milk Marketing: An Experiment in Collectivism,* Society of Individualists and National League for Freedom, 1945; *British Farming and Food,* City Press (London), 1953; (editor) *Greetings to Freemen: An Anthology,* Freedom First, 1953; *The Free Convertibility of Sterling,* Batchworth Press, 1955; *Are British Farmers Doomed?: The Only Solution,* City Press, 1958; *How "Tick" Ticks,* Newman Neame, 1959; *A Short History of Money,* Newman Neame and Institute of Economic Affairs, 1959; (contributor) *Atlantic Ocean Fisheries,* Fishing News, 1961; *Modern Rural Rides,* Hutchinson, 1964. Contributor of articles to *City Press, Freeman,* and *Christian Economist.* Editor, *Free Trader,* 1950—.

WORK IN PROGRESS: History of Money.

AVOCATIONAL INTERESTS: Riding.†

* * *

WINDSOR-RICHARDS, Arthur (Bedlington) 1904-

PERSONAL: Born 1904, in Eccles, England; married Audrey Mary Adams. *Education:* Educated in English schools. *Politics:* Conservative. *Home:* Little Roof, Lymington, Hampshire, England. *Agent:* A. M. Heath & Co. Ltd., 35 Dover St., London W1X 4EB, England.

CAREER: Journalist and naturalist.

WRITINGS: Tiercel the Peregrine, Warne, 1948; *Merry Brown Hare,* Hutchinson, 1957; *And the Running of the Deer,* Hutchinson, 1959; *Vix, the Story of a Fox Cub,* Benn, 1960; *Where the Rushes Grow Green,* Hutchinson, 1960; *Birds of the Lonely Lake,* Benn, 1961; *There Came the Little Foxes,* Hutchinson, 1961; *The Nature Detectives,* Hutchinson, 1962; *The Cabin in the Woods,* Friday Press, 1963; *Look at British Wild Animals,* Hamish Hamilton, 1964; *The Wild White Swan,* Friday Press, 1965; *The Island of Whispering Rocks,* Hutchinson, 1965; (with William Thatcher) *Caring for Your Cat,* W. & G. Foyle, 1966, Arco, 1972; *Of Hidden Depths,* Gifford, 1966; (with P. Joyce) *Great Nature Stories,* Benn, 1967. Contributor to *Sunday Express* (London) and other periodicals.

AVOCATIONAL INTERESTS: Yachting and gardening.

WINEBRENNER, D(aniel) Kenneth 1908-

PERSONAL: Born June 5, 1908, in Pitcairn, Pa.; son of Daniel H. and Margery (Smith) Winebrenner; married Miriam Fleming, 1934; children: D(aniel) Kenneth, Jr., James Edward. *Education:* Carnegie Institute of Technology, student, 1926-28; Pennsylvania State College, Indiana, Pa., B.S. in Art Ed., 1933; Columbia University, M.A., 1939, Ed.D., 1951. *Politics:* Independent Republican. *Religion:* Methodist. *Home:* 400 Woodland Dr., Buffalo, N.Y. 14223.

CAREER: East Huntington Township Junior-Senior High School, Alverton, Pa., art teacher, 1933-36; Senior High School, Reading, Pa., art teacher, 1936-39; State University of New York College at Buffalo, professor of art, 1939—. Consultant, Army Special Services Crafts Program in Europe. Chairman, Independent Town Party, 1955—. Civilian defense policeman. *Member:* International Society for Education Through Art, National Committee on Art Education (member, council of directors, 1960—; chairman, 1963-64), National Art Education Association (editorial board, 1963—), American Association of University Professors, National Education Association, Eastern Arts Association (member of council, 1957-61), York State Craftsmen, Kenmore Art Society, Buffalo Society of Artists, Buffalo Craftsmen (chairman, 1958-59), Phi Delta Kappa, Kappa Delta Pi, Sigma Tau Gamma.

WRITINGS: Jewelry Making as an Art Expression, International Textbook, 1953; *Readings in Art Education,* International Textbook, 1964. Editor, *School Arts,* 1953-63, *Education Through Art,* 1963—.

* * *

WING, Frances (Scott) 1907-
   (Frances V. Scott)

PERSONAL: Born April 25, 1907, in Weldon, N.C.; daughter of Walter Lee (an accountant) and Gertrude (Grossmann) Scott; married Charles Sewall Wing, Jr. (owner of a plastics company), September 29, 1951. *Education:* Wellesley College, A.B., 1928. *Home:* 2020 Chippewa Pl., Sarasota, Fla. *Agent:* McIntosh & Otis, Inc., 18 East 41st St., New York, N.Y. 10017.

CAREER: Harvard University, Graduate School of Business Administration, Boston, Mass., research and editorial work, 1928-41; Bureau of National Affairs, Inc., Washington, D.C., assistant managing editor of *Labor Relations Reporter,* and other publications, 1941-51, member of board of directors, Washington Newspaper Guild, chairman of collective bargaining committee, 1943-45. *Member:* National Guild of Decoupeurs (lifetime honorary member), Sarasota Art Association, Old Colony Women's Club (Bourne, Mass.; vice-president).

WRITINGS: (Under name Frances V. Scott, with D. H. Davenport) *An Index to Business Indices,* Business Publications, 1937; *The Complete Book of Decoupage,* Coward, 1965.

* * *

WINGFIELD DIGBY, George Frederick 1911-

PERSONAL: Born March 2, 1911, in Sherborne, Dorsetshire, England; son of F. J. B. and Gwendolyn (Fletcher) Wingfield Digby; married Cornelia Keitler (a painter), October 1, 1935; children: Frederick (deceased). *Education:* Trinity College, Cambridge, English literature tripos (second class); also studied at Sorbonne, University of

Paris, and in Vienna. *Home:* 72 Palace Gardens Ter., London W.8, England. *Office:* Victoria and Albert Museum, London S.W.7, England.

CAREER: Victoria and Albert Museum, London, England, Department of Textiles, assistant keeper, 1934-37; Jamaica College, Jamaica, West Indies, history master, 1941-45; Victoria and Albert Museum, keeper of Department of Textiles, 1947-72, keeper emeritus, 1972—.

WRITINGS: French Tapestries, Batsford, 1951; (with E. H. Carter and R. N. Murray) *History of the West Indian Peoples,* four volumes, Thomas Nelson, 1951-56, 2nd edition, 1960-64; *The Work of the Modern Potter in England,* J. Murray, 1952; *Meaning and Symbol in Three Modern Artists: Edvard Munch, Henry Moore, Paul Nash,* Faber, 1955; *Symbol and Image in William Blake,* Clarendon Press, 1957; (contributor) Frank Stenton, editor, *The Bayeux Tapestry,* Phaidon Press, 1957; *Elizabethan Embroidery,* Faber, 1963, Yoseloff, 1964; *Lucie Rie: A Retrospective Exhibition of Earthenware, Stoneware and Porcelain, 1926-1967,* Arts Council, 1967; *The Devonshire Hunting Tapestries,* H.M.S.O., 1972. Contributor of articles to *Burlington Magazine, Connoisseur,* and other periodicals, and of papers to Brussels Colloque International, 1959, and Colston Research Society Papers, 1960.

* * *

WINN, Laura Rocke 1902-

PERSONAL: Born November 24, 1902, in Hickman, Neb.; daughter of John Christian (a farmer) and Mary (Steinke) Rocke; married Joseph William Winn, June 10, 1932. *Education:* Summer study and special courses at University of California, Berkeley, at Madison College, Madison College, Tenn., at Santa Ana College, Denton State College, and Southwestern Union College. *Religion:* Seventh-day Adventist. *Address:* P.O. Box 26, Keene, Tex. 76059.

CAREER: Piano teacher in home. *Member:* National Guild of Piano Teachers.

WRITINGS: Margie Asks Why, Southern Publishing, 1963.

WORK IN PROGRESS: Study for a possible sequel to *Margie Asks Why.*

SIDELIGHTS: Mrs. Winn's first attempt at writing was her book, published when she had passed sixty.

* * *

WINNICOTT, Donald (Woods) 1896-1971

PERSONAL: Born 1896, in Plymouth, England; son of Sir Frederick (a merchant) and Elizabeth Martha (Woods) Winnicott; married Elsie Clare Nimmo Britton (a psychoanalyst), 1951. *Education:* Jesus College, Cambridge, 1914-18, St. Bartholomew's Hospital Medical College, University of London, 1919-23. *Religion:* "Militant Protestant-agnostic." *Home:* 87 Chester Sq., London S.W. 1, England.

CAREER: Paddington Green Children's Hospital, London, England, physician, 1923-62. *Member:* Royal College of Physicians (fellow), British Psycho-Analytical Society (former president), British Psychological Society (former chairman of medical section), British Paediatric Association, Royal Society of Medicine (former chairman of pediatric section), honorary member of other societies, including Philadelphia Psychiatric Society.

WRITINGS: Clinical Notes on Disorders of Childhood, Heinemann, 1931; *The Child and the Family: First Relationships,* Basic Books, 1957; *The Child and the Outside World: Studies in Developing Relationships,* Basic Books, 1957; *Mother and Child: A Primer of First Relationships,* Basic Books, 1957; *Collected Papers: Through Pediatrics to Psycho-Analysis,* Basic Books, 1958; (with others) *Psychoanalysis and Contemporary Thought,* Hogarth, 1958, Grove, 1959, reprinted, Books for Library Press, 1971; *The Family and Individual Development,* Basic Books, 1965; *The Maturational Processes and the Facilitating Environment: Studies in the Theory of Emotional Development* (collected papers), International Universities, 1965; *The Child, the Family, and the Outside World,* Penguin Books, 1965; *Playing and Reality,* Tavistock Publications, 1971; *Therapeutic Consultations in Child Psychiatry,* Basic Books, 1971.

WORK IN PROGRESS: Psycho-Analytic Treatment of a Little Girl; Theory of Human Growth (tentative title); collections of papers.

(Died January 28, 1971)

* * *

WINTER, Michael Morgan 1930-

PERSONAL: Born April 9, 1930, in Croydon, Surrey, England; son of Wilfrid Simeon Arthur and Kathleen Mary (Lloyd) Winter. *Education:* Educated at St. George's College and St. John's Seminary, Surrey, England, and School of Oriental and African Studies, University of London. *Home:* The Presbytery, Between Streets, Cobham, Surrey, England. *Agent:* A. M. Heath & Co. Ltd., 35 Dover St., London W1X 4EB, England.

CAREER: Roman Catholic priest. Assistant priest at Wimbledon, Surrey, England; lecturer in fundamental theology, St. John's Seminary, Wonersh, Surrey, England; assistant priest at Cobham, Surrey, England. *Member:* Vernacular Society of Great Britain (former chairman).

WRITINGS: St. Peter and the Popes, Darton, Longman & Todd, 1960. Contributor of articles on theology, liturgy, and religious sociology to periodicals.†

* * *

WINTERS, Janet Lewis 1899-
(Janet Lewis)

PERSONAL: Born August 17, 1899, in Chicago, Ill.; daughter of Edwin Herbert (a novelist, poet, and teacher) and Elizabeth (Taylor) Lewis; married Yvor Winters (a writer and professor of English), June 22, 1926 (died January, 1968); children: Joanna Winters Thompson, Daniel Lewis. *Education:* Lewis Institute, A.A., 1918; University of Chicago, Ph.B., 1920. *Home:* 143 West Portola Ave., Los Altos, Calif. 94022. *Agent:* Curtis Brown Ltd., 60 East 56th St., New York, N.Y. 10022.

CAREER: Novelist and poet. After college worked for short periods at American consulate in Paris, France, as proofreader for *Redbook* in Chicago, Ill., and as teacher at Lewis Institute, Chicago, Ill.; resident of Santa Fe, N.M., 1923-27, California, 1927—. Stanford University, visiting lecturer in creative writing, 1960, 1966, 1967, 1970; lecturer at writer's workshops at University of Missouri, 1952, University of Denver, 1956. *Member:* Authors League of America, American Society of Composers, Authors and Publishers, National Association for the Advancement of Colored People (life member). *Awards, honors:* Shelley

Memorial Award for poetry, 1948; Commonwealth Club of California Gold Medal, 1948, for *The Trial of Soren Qvist*; Guggenheim fellowship in creative writing for research in Paris, 1950-51; Friends of American Writers award, for *The Invasion: A Narrative of Events Concerning the Johnston Family of St. Mary's.*

WRITINGS—Under name Janet Lewis: *The Indians in the Woods* (poetry), Monroe Wheeler Manikin I (series), 1922; *The Friendly Adventures of Ollie Ostrich* (juvenile), Doubleday, 1923; *The Wheel in Midsummer* (poetry), Lone Gull, 1927; *The Invasion: A Narrative of Events Concerning the Johnston Family of St. Mary's*, Harcourt, 1932; *The Wife of Martin Guerre* (novel), Colt, 1941, 2nd edition, Rapp & Carroll, 1967; *Against a Darkening Sky* (novel), Doubleday, 1943; *The Earth-Bound, 1924-1944* (poetry), Wells College Press, 1946; *Good-Bye, Son, and Other Stories*, Doubleday, 1946; *The Trial of Soren Qvist* (novel), Doubleday, 1947; *Poems 1924-1944*, A. Swallow, 1950; *The Ghost of Monsieur Scarron* (novel), Doubleday, 1959; *Keiko's Bubble* (juvenile), Doubleday, 1961.

Wrote libretto for adaptation of *The Wife of Martin Guerre*, produced under same title at Juilliard School of Music, 1956, at San Francisco State College (now San Francisco State University), 1960, and at the University of Washington, 1967. Contributor of short stories, poetry, and reviews to *New Yorker, New Republic, McCall's, Poetry, Revue de Paris*, and other magazines. An editor, *Gyroscope*, 1929-30.

SIDELIGHTS: "An exquisite book," wrote Emily Maxwell about *Keiko's Bubble*, "written in prose that has the clarity and hard smoothness and delicate coloring of a glass float." Four composers have written settings for Mrs. Winters' poem, "Lullee, Lullay." Excerpts from the opera, "The Wife of Martin Guerre," were recorded by Composer's Recordings; and Mrs. Winters can be heard reading her own poems on a Library of Congress recording.

BIOGRAPHICAL/CRITICAL SOURCES: Critique, winter, 1964-65; *Times Literary Supplement,* June 22, 1967.

*   *   *

WINTERS, (Arthur) Yvor   1900-1968

PERSONAL: Born October 17, 1900, in Chicago, Ill.; son of Harry Lewis and Faith Evangeline (Ahnefeldt) Winters; married Janet Lewis (a writer), June 22, 1926; children: Joanna Winters Thompson, Daniel Lewis. *Education:* Attended University of Chicago, 1917-18; University of Colorado, A.B. and A.M., 1925; Stanford University, Ph.D., 1934. *Home:* 143 West Portola Ave., Los Altos, Calif. 94022. *Office:* Department of English, Stanford University, Stanford, Calif. 94305.

CAREER: Taught in coal camps of Madrid and Los Cerillos, N.M., two years; University of Idaho, Moscow, instructor in French and Spanish, 1925-27; Stanford University, Stanford, Calif., instructor, 1928-37, assistant professor, 1937-41, associate professor, 1941-49, professor of English, 1949-61, Albert Guerard Professor of Literature, 1961-66. *Member:* American Association of University Professors, National Association for the Advancement of Colored People (life), American Academy of Arts and Sciences (fellow), American Civil Liberties Union (for Northern California), Phi Beta Kappa (resigned). *Awards, honors:* Oscar Blumenthal Prize of *Poetry* Magazine, 1945; National Institute of Arts and Letters award, 1952; University of Chicago Harriet Monroe Poetry Award, 1960-61; Bollingen Prize, 1960, for *Collected Poems*; Guggenheim

grant, 1961-62; Brandeis University Creative Arts award for poetry, 1963; National Endowment for the Arts grant, 1967.

WRITINGS—Poetry: *The Immobile Wind*, M. Wheeler, 1921; *The Magpie's Shadow*, Musterbookhouse, 1922; *The Bare Hills*, Four Seas Co., 1927; *The Proof*, Coward, 1930; *The Journey*, Dragon Press, 1931; *Before Disaster*, Tryon Pamphlets, 1934; *Poems*, Gyroscope Press, 1940; *To the Holy Spirit*, California Poetry Folios, 1947; *Three Poems*, Cummington Press, 1950; *Collected Poems*, A. Swallow, 1952, revised edition, 1960; *The Early Poems of Yvor Winters, 1920-1928*, A. Swallow, 1966.

Prose, and works edited: *Notes on the Mechanics of the Poetic Image*, [Vienna], 1925; (with Frances Theresa Russell) *The Case of David Lamson: A Summary*, Lamson Defense Committee, 1934; *Primitivism and Decadence: A Study of American Experimental Poetry*, Arrow Editions, 1937; (editor) *Twelve Poets of the Pacific*, New Directions, 1937; *Maule's Curse: Seven Studies in the History of American Obscurantism*, New Directions, 1938; *The Anatomy of Nonsense*, New Directions, 1943; *Edwin Arlington Robinson*, New Directions, 1946; *In Defense of Reason*, Swallow Press, 1947, 3rd revised edition, A. Swallow, 1960; (editor) Elizabeth Daryush, *Selected Poems*, Swallow Press, 1948; (editor) *Poets of the Pacific, Second Series*, Stanford University Press, 1949; *The Function of Criticism: Problems and Exercises*, A. Swallow, 1957, 2nd edition, 1966; (contributor) Irving Howe, editor, *Modern Literary Criticism*, Beacon Press, 1958; *On Modern Poets: Stevens, Eliot, Ransom, Crane, Hopkins, Frost*, Meridian Books, 1959; *The Poetry of W. B. Yeats* (pamphlet), A. Swallow, 1960; *The Poetry of J. V. Cunningham* (pamphlet), A. Swallow, 1961; *The Brink of Darkness* (pamphlet), A. Swallow, c.1965; (contributor) Paul J. Alpers, editor, *Elizabethan Poetry: Modern Essays in Criticism*, Oxford University Press, 1967; *Forms of Discovery: Critical and Historical Essays on the Forms of the Short Poem in English*, A. Swallow, 1967; (compiler with Kenneth Fields) *Quest for Reality: An Anthology of Short Poems in English*, Swallow Press, 1969.

Represented in many anthologies, including *Robert Frost: A Collection of Critical Essays*, edited by James Melville Cox, Prentice-Hall, 1962, *A Dial Miscellany*, edited by William Wasserstrom, Syracuse University Press, 1963, and *The Structure of Verse: Modern Essays on Prosody*, edited by Harvey Seymour Gross, Fawcett, 1966.

Contributor to *Poetry, New Republic, Gyroscope, MS, Hudson Review, Dial, Transition, American Caravan, Modern Verse, New Mexico Quarterly, Southern Review, American Literature, Kenyon Review, Sewanee Review, American Scholar, Arizona Quarterly*, and other publications. Co-editor, *Gyroscope*, 1929-30; western editor, *Hound and Horn*, 1932-34.

SIDELIGHTS: Allen Tate once commented on Winters the poet thus: "If he has been neglected—when he has not been ignored—the reasons are not hard to find. He has conducted a poetic revolution all his own that owes little or nothing to the earlier revolution of Pound and Eliot, and that goes back to certain great, likewise neglected Tudor poets for metrical and stylistic models." Winters commented to *CA*: "Tate is wrong about this, but in general my admirers have read me as carelessly as my detractors." Winters deals in strict rhymes and formal metrics, maintaining detachment from his subject in the process. If his poetry is cold, it is "that burning cold that belongs to ice," writes Babette Deutsch. In *Poetry in Our Time* she observes: "His small output testifies to the rigor of his craftsmanship and to his belief that a poem, being 'a full and definitive account of a human experience,' is 'an act of moral judgment.' His songs and sonnets, a sheaf of his longer pieces, are fired with the moral passion of this absolutist."

Winters writes, says William Troy, "like a combination of a medieval scholastic and a New England divine." ("Twaddle," said Winters.) Keith F. McKean asserts that "Winters defends reason and warns against certain aspects of romantic philosophy," and explains Winters's approach thus: "First, Winters believes, the critic should record any historical or biographical data necessary to understand the mind and the method of the author; second, he should analyze the literary theories that are relevant to the work; third, he must make a critique of the paraphrasable content; and fourth, he must make a critique of the feelings motivated by the experience; and last of all, he must judge the work."

Though his approach to literature has been called "narrow" and "dogmatic," he has, as Troy admits, sharpened the focus on certain problems and formulated useful distinctions. Poet Hayden Carruth has the highest praise for him: ". . . I admire Winters, and what he has done for American literature; no one else could have done it—I mean aside from his own poems, some of which are superb. There's no one like him for making a simple declarative sentence crackle under your eyes like a burning apple-bough. Such magnificent wrath. . . . Of course, Winters is as insane as the rest of us, but he has made a whole career out of covering it up. . . . Winters is able to *prove*—demonstrate irrefutably with step-by-step arguments and copious illustrations from line and stanza—that our favorite poets are idiots, and in the process show us just why we like them so much. . . ."

Winters recorded his poems for the Library of Congress and the Yale Series of Recorded Poets.

BIOGRAPHICAL/CRITICAL SOURCES: Bookman, June, 1928; *Nation,* February 20, 1937; Reed Whittemore, *The Fascination of the Abomination,* Macmillan, 1939; *New Republic,* July 12, 1943, March 2, 1953, March 2, 1968; *New York Times Book Review,* August 24, 1947; Stanley Edgar Hyman, *The Armed Vision,* Knopf, 1948; *South Atlantic Quarterly,* April, 1951; C. I. Glicksberg, *American Literary Criticism, 1900-1950,* Hendricks House, 1951; F. O. Matthiessen, *Responsibilities of the Critic,* Oxford University Press, 1952; Babette Deutsch, *Poetry in Our Time,* Columbia University Press, 1952; Louis Bogan, *Selected Criticism: Prose, Poetry,* Noonday, 1955; John Paul Pritchard, *Criticism in America,* University of Oklahoma Press, 1956; *Poetry,* August, 1958; *New Statesman,* September 24, 1960; *Spectator,* July 1, 1960; Keith F. McKean, *The Moral Measure of Literature,* A. Swallow, 1961; H. T. Moore, editor, *The World of Lawrence Durrell,* Southern Illinois University Press, 1962; Howard Nemerov, *Poetry and Fiction: Essays,* Rutgers University Press, 1963; *Commonweal,* October 20, 1967; *American Quarterly,* fall, 1967; *New Leader,* December 4, 1967; *New York Review of Books,* February 29, 1968; *Hudson Review,* summer, 1968; *Partisan Review,* summer, 1968; *Criticism,* fall, 1968; *Southern Review,* winter, 1969; *Centennial Review,* fall, 1970.

(Died January 25, 1968)

WISE, John E(dward) 1905-1974

PERSONAL: Born May 21, 1905, in Washington, D.C.; son of George A. and Mary Edith (Ward) Wise. *Education:* Georgetown University, A.B., 1926; Woodstock College, M.A., 1931; St. Louis University, graduate study; Fordham University, Ph.D., 1946. *Home and office:* Loyola College, Baltimore, Md.

CAREER: Member of Society of Jesus, 1926; ordained priest, 1937; Georgetown University, Washington, D.C., dean of freshman, 1939-43; Loyola College, Baltimore, Md., dean of Evening College, 1945-49, organizer of Graduate Division, 1949; University of Scranton, Scranton, Pa., dean, 1949-50; Georgetown University, Washington, D.C., professor of religion, 1950-52; Loyola College, Baltimore, Md., professor of education, 1952-74. Member of Governor's Commission on the Needs of Higher Education in Maryland, 1953-55; member of Citizens Planning and Housing Association, Baltimore, and of Walters Gallery of Art. *Military service:* U.S. Army Reserve, Infantry, 1926-31, became second lieutenant. *Member:* History of Education Society, Comparative Education Society, Maryland Association for Higher Education (former president), Baltimore Association for Adult Education (former president). *Awards, honors:* LL.D., College of Notre Dame of Maryland, 1963.

WRITINGS: The Nature of the Liberal Arts, Bruce, 1947; *The History of Education: An Analytic Survey from the Age of Homer to the Present Time,* Sheed, 1964; (with R. B. Nordberg and D. J. Reitz) *Methods of Research in Education,* Heath, 1966.

(Died June 21, 1974)

*   *   *

WISEMAN, Francis Jowett 1905-

PERSONAL: Born May 21, 1905, in Horton Ribblesdale, Yorkshire, England; son of Joseph (a farmer) and Alice (Jowett) Wiseman; married Alice Joan Reade, July 30, 1931 (died, 1972). *Education:* Attended Sidney Sussex College, Cambridge (second class honors in classical tripos). *Religion:* Church of England. *Home:* 4 Cranbrook Ct., Fleet, Hampshire, England.

CAREER: Wolverhampton Grammar School, Wolverhampton, Staffordshire, England, teacher of Latin and Greek, 1927-44; St. Peter's School, Yorkshire, England, teacher of Latin, Greek, and local history, 1944-65. Lecturer for National Trust. *Member:* Yorkshire Philosophical Society (member of council, 1955-62), Roman Society (London).

WRITINGS: Roman Spain, G. Bell, 1956; *The Recent History of St. Peter's School, York,* Herald Printers, 1968.

WORK IN PROGRESS: Outlines of Local History.

SIDELIGHTS: Wiseman speaks French and Spanish. *Avocational interests:* Golf and cricket.

*   *   *

WISLOFF, Carl Johan Fredrik 1908-

PERSONAL: Born December 31, 1908, in Drammen, Norway; son of Fredrik (a civil engineer) and Dagny (Waalmann) Wisloff; married Ingrid Brun, October 13, 1934; children: Sigurd, Ingrid, Kari, Finn. *Education:* Free Faculty of Theology (Church of Norway), Cand. theol, 1931; University of Oslo, Dr., 1958. *Home:* Laaveveien 52, Oslo 6, Norway.

CAREER: Minister, Church of Norway, in Oslo, Norway, 1932-40, in Birkenes, 1940-47; Free Faculty of Theology (Church of Norway), headmaster of department of practical theology, 1947-60, professor of church history, 1960—. *Member:* International Fellowship of Evangelical Students (president).

WRITINGS: Jeg vet pa hvem jeg tror, Lunde, 1946; *Ordet fra Guds munn,* Lutherstiftelsen, 1951; *Nattverd og Messe,* Lutherstiftelsen, 1957 (translation by Joseph M. Shaw published as *The Gift of Communion,* Augsburg, 1964); *Politikk og Kristendom,* Lunde, 1961; *Norsk Kirkehistorie I,* Lutherstiftelsen, 1966; *Norsk Kirkehistorie III,* Lutherstiftelsen, 1971; *Ordet om Korset,* Lunde, 1973.

* * *

WITCUTT, William Purcell 1907-

PERSONAL: Born August 12, 1907, in Hull, Yorkshire, England; son of William Thomas and Charlotte (Purcell) Witcutt. *Education:* University of Birmingham, LL.B., 1928. *Politics:* Tory. *Home:* Wimbish Vicarage, Saffron Walden, Essex, England.

CAREER: Roman Catholic priest, serving in diocese of Birmingham, England, as curate of churches in Birmingham, 1934-38, Leek, 1938-41, parish priest of Wappenbury with Princethorpe, 1941-48. Anglican priest, serving in diocese of Chelmsford, England, as curate of East Ham, 1949-58, rector of Foulness, 1958-63, vicar of Wimbish with Thunderley, 1963—. *Member:* Society for Propagation of Christian Knowledge (propaganda advisory committee).

WRITINGS: The Dying Lands: A Fifty Years' Plan for the Distressed Areas, Distributist League, 1937; *Catholic Thought and Modern Psychology,* Burns, Oates, & Washbourne, 1943; *Blake: A Psychological Study,* Hollis & Carter, 1946, Kennikat, 1966; *Return to Reality,* S.P.C.K., 1954, Macmillan, 1956; *The Rise and Fall of the Individual,* Macmillan, 1958.

WORK IN PROGRESS: Research into the archetypes of the unconscious mind, entitled *The Prophetic Dream: A Study of the Book of Changes.*

AVOCATIONAL INTERESTS: Gardening, dogs.†

* * *

WOLF, Miriam Bredow 1895-
(Miriam Bredow)

PERSONAL: Born March 10, 1895, in Brooklyn, N.Y.; daughter of Alfred Albert (a businessman) and Anita (Adkins) Bredow; married Heinrich F. Wolf (a medical doctor), August 2, 1932. *Education:* Junior College (Vevey, Switzerland), student, 1913-14; Sorbonne, University of Paris, extension courses. *Politics:* Liberal. *Religion:* Lutheran. *Home:* 227 East 57th St., New York, N.Y. 10022.

CAREER: Secretary, U.S. Consular Service, Buenos Aires, Argentina, 1919-21, American Embassy, Paris, France, 1921-22, Dr. Trigant Burrow, New York, N.Y., 1929-43; Eastern School for Physicians' Aides, New York, N.Y., assistant director, 1943-59, director, 1959-60. *Member:* American Association of Medical Technology Schools (secretary-treasurer, 1952-55), New York Council of Adult Education, Private Vocational Schools Association of New York (member, board of directors, 1952-60).

WRITINGS—Under name Miriam Bredow: *Handbook for the Medical Secretary,* McGraw, 1943, 5th edition published as *Medical Secretarial Procedures,* 1966; *The Medical Assistant,* McGraw, 1958, 3rd edition, 1971.

WORK IN PROGRESS: A sixth edition of *Medical Secretarial Procedures*; an article or book dealing with medical-technical education.

AVOCATIONAL INTERESTS: The theatre, music, reading, and travel.

* * *

WOLFE, Herbert S(now) 1898-

PERSONAL: Born September 14, 1898, in Parkville, Mo.; son of Arthur L. (a college professor) and Gertrude (Snow) Wolfe; married Mary Willard, September 1, 1932; children: William Willard, Mary Ellen (Mrs. Robert E. Bieder). *Education:* Park College, A.B., 1918; Trinity College, Dublin, graduate study, 1920-21; University of Chicago, M.S., 1925, Ph.D., 1930. *Religion:* Presbyterian. *Home:* 2115 Northwest Seventh Lane, Gainesville, Fla. 32603.

CAREER: University of Kentucky, Lexington, assistant professor of botany, 1921-24; West Virginia University, Morgantown, assistant professor of botany, 1926-29; Florida Agricultural Experiment Station, Homestead, horticulturist in charge, 1930-38; University of Florida, Gainesville, professor of horticulture, 1938-55, professor of fruit crops, 1955-64, professor emeritus, 1964—. Technical adviser in tropical horticulture for USAID, Lima, Peru, 1968-69. *Member:* American Association for the Advancement of Science (fellow), American Society for Horticultural Science, Florida State Horticultural Society (vice-president, 1937-45), Gainesville Philharmonic Society (president, 1943-45, 1961-62), Rotary Club (president, Homestead, Fla., 1935-37), Sigma Xi.

WRITINGS: (With E. W. Garris) *Southern Horticulture Management,* Lippincott, 1948; (with J. V. Watkins) *Your Florida Garden,* University of Florida Press, 1954, 5th edition, 1968; (with Watkins and T. Mack) *Five Hundred Answers to Florida Garden Questions,* University of Florida Press, 1957; (with L. W. Ziegler) *Citrus Growing in Florida,* University of Florida Press, 1961, 2nd edition, 1974; (with Watkins and Mack) *1001 Answers to Florida Garden Questions,* University of Florida Press, 1962.

SIDELIGHTS: Wolfe reads and speaks ("with modest ability") Spanish, German, French, and Italian.

AVOCATIONAL INTERESTS: Playing the violin.

* * *

WOLLE, Muriel Sibell 1898-

PERSONAL: Surname is pronounced *Wol*-le; born April 3, 1898, in Brooklyn, N.Y.; daughter of Harry Gardner (an architect) and Florence (Underwood) Sibell; married Francis Wolle (an ordained priest of the Episcopal Church), October 26, 1945. *Education:* New York School of Fine and Applied Art, diploma, 1920; New York University, B.S., 1928; University of Colorado, M.A., 1930. *Politics:* Democrat. *Religion:* Episcopalian. *Home:* 500 Mohawk Dr., No. 204, Boulder, Colo.

CAREER: College of Industrial Arts (now Texas Woman's University), Denton, Tex., instructor in art, 1920-23; New York School of Fine and Applied Art (now Parsons School of Design), New York, N.Y., instructor in art, 1923-26; University of Colorado, Boulder, assistant professor, 1926-29, associate professor, 1929-36, professor of art, 1936-66, head of department, 1936-47. Artist, exhibiting in one-woman shows and in collections. Lecturer (with slides made from her own sketches) on ghost mining towns of the West. Member of board of directors of Boulder County

Visiting Nurse Association, 1958-63; member of Episcopal Diocesan Commission on Arts and Architecture; member of Governor's Committee on Historic Preservation, 1968—; member of Colorado Centennial-Bicentennial Heritage Commission, 1972.

MEMBER: National Association of Women Artists, Colorado Education Association (state chairman of art section, 1936-39), Westerners (Denver Posse), Colorado Authors Guild, Soroptimist Club (Boulder president, 1956), Ghost Town Club of Colorado (honorary), Colorado Mountain Club (honorary), Denver Woman's Press Club, Delta Phi Delta (former national first vice-president; laureate member). *Awards, honors:* Silver Medal for watercolor, Kansas Midwestern Annual Art Show, 1934; Eloise Egan Prize for watercolor, National Association of Women Painters and Sculptors, 1935; Norlin Medal for distinguished achievement, University of Colorado, 1957; Stearns Award, University of Colorado, 1966; ten grants-in-aid and three faculty fellowships for travel to mining camps and research in their history.

WRITINGS—All self-illustrated: *Ghost Cities of Colorado,* privately printed, 1933; *Cloud Cities of Colorado,* privately printed, 1934; *Stampede to Timberline,* privately printed, 1949, Swallow Press, 1968; (with Barnard Hewitt and Jacob F. Foster) *Play Production, Theory and Practice,* Lippincott, 1952; *The Bonanza Trail,* Indiana University Press, 1953; *Montana Pay Dirt,* Sage Books, 1963. Columnist in *Mining World,* 1945-55, self-illustrated articles in *Design, Brand Book, Ford Times,* and various Colorado periodicals.

WORK IN PROGRESS: Continued research in mining history, and completion of more than nine hundred sketches of Colorado mining camps.

SIDELIGHTS: The Bonanza Trail was selected by the Carnegie Corp. as one of the 350 books most descriptive of life in America for inclusion in collections sent to libraries in the British Dominians and other countries where the English language is read.

BIOGRAPHICAL/CRITICAL SOURCES: American Soroptimist, March, 1956, January, 1963; *Denver Post,* November 10, 1957.

* * *

WOOD, G(eorge) R(obert) Harding   1878-1968

PERSONAL: Born June 23, 1878, in Cork, Ireland. *Education:* Studied at Christ's College, Cambridge, 1906-09, Wycliffe Hall, Oxford, 1909-10. *Home:* 16 Belsize Ct., Hampstead, London N.W.3, England.

CAREER: Former vicar, Holy Trinity Church, Hampstead, London, England; conductor of "Enjoy Your Bible" campaigns in the British Isles, Sweden, Canada, and United States, 1946-68. *Member:* Authors' Club.

WRITINGS: Enjoy Your Bible, Walter, 1949; *St. Paul's First Letter,* Walter, 1950; *Learning and Living the Christian Life,* Walter, 1953; *A Year With Our Lord,* National Sunday School Union, 1954; *Things Jesus Did and Said,* National Sunday School Union, 1955; *God and the Children,* Paternoster, 1955; *Pentecost—and After,* National Sunday School Union, 1956; *The Saviour of the World,* National Sunday School Union, 1957; *A Year with the Old Testament,* National Sunday School Union, 1960; *Through the Bible Day by Day,* Walter, 1960; *A Bird's-eye View of the Bible,* two volumes, Marshall, Morgan & Scott, 1960; *Talking with Children about God,* Walter, 1962; *A Little*

Posy of Poetry, Walter, 1963; *The Lordship of Christ: A Study in Verbal Inspiration,* Walter, 1965; *Are You Listening Children?: 52 Sunday Talks to Boys and Girls,* Walter, 1965. Contributor of articles to religious periodicals. Writer of Sunday School lesson books.

(Died, 1968)

* * *

WOODFORD, Frank B(ury)   1903-1967

PERSONAL: Born February 27, 1903, in Detroit, Mich.; son of Fred VanRensslealear (a broker) and Florence (Bury) Woodford; married Mary-Kirk MacKinnon, November 14, 1929; children: Susan, Arthur M. *Education:* University of Pennsylvania, B.S., 1925. *Politics:* Independent. *Religion:* Episcopalian. *Home:* 14161 Warwick Rd., Detroit, Mich. 48223.

CAREER: Detroit Free Press, Detroit, Mich., reporter, 1931-44, editorial writer, 1944-56, chief editorial writer, 1956-62; City of Detroit, deputy treasurer, 1962-67. Author. *Member:* The National Conference of Editorial Writers, The Detroit Press Club, Friends of the Library (Detroit), Detroit Historical Society, Algonquin Club (Detroit), Delta Tau Delta.

WRITINGS: A Telescope on Mars, privately printed, 1925; *Lewis Cass: the Last Jeffersonian,* Rutgers University Press, 1950; *Yankees in Wonderland* (monograph), Wayne State University, 1951; *Mr. Jefferson's Disciple,* Michigan State University Press, 1953; *We Never Drive Alone,* Automobile Club of Michigan, 1958; (with Alfred Hyma) *Gabriel Richard,* Wayne State University Press, 1958; *Introduction to Mighty Mac,* Wayne State University Press, 1958; *Law Day U.S.A.,* State Bar of Michigan, 1961; *Father Abraham's Children,* Wayne State University Press, 1961; *Alex J. Groesbeck: Portrait of a Public Man,* Wayne State University Press, 1962; (with Philip P. Mason) *Harper of Detroit,* Wayne State University Press, 1964; *Parnassus on Main Street: A History of the Detroit Public Library,* Wayne State University Press, 1965; (with son, Arthur M. Woodford) *All Our Yesterdays: A Brief History of Detroit,* Wayne State University Press, 1969.

Contributor of articles to *The Sunday New York Times.* Member of the editorial board, *Detroit Free Press.*

(Died June 17, 1967)

* * *

WOODWARD, Grace Steele   1899-
(Marion S. Doane)

PERSONAL: Born September 14, 1899, in Joplin, Mo.; daughter of John Thomas and Dora Elizabeth (Sims) Steele; married Guy Hendon Woodward (an attorney), September 8, 1920; children: John A., Robert Louis. *Education:* Attended University of Missouri, 1917-18, University of Oklahoma, 1918-19, extension division, 1943-54, Columbia University, 1919-20, Middlebury College, two sessions, Tulsa University, one session. *Home:* 2622 East 33rd Place, Tulsa, Okla. 74105.

CAREER: Author of non-fiction historical books. *Member:* Daughters of the American Colonists, Daughters of the American Revolution, Thomas Gilcrease Institute of American History and Art, Association for Preservation of Virginia Antiquities, Arts Club of Washington (D.C.), Tuesday Writers (Tulsa, Okla.). *Awards, honors:* First prize from Oklahoma State Writers, for *Pocahontas.*

WRITINGS: *The Man Who Conquered Pain: A Biography of William Thomas Green Morton,* Beacon, 1962; *The Cherokees,* University of Oklahoma Press, 1963; *Pocahontas* (biography), University of Oklahoma Press, 1969. Contributor of articles to *Parents' Forecast, Kansas City Star,* and *Tulsa World.*

WORK IN PROGRESS: Historical work on World War II.

AVOCATIONAL INTERESTS: Travel, gardening, and French cooking.

BIOGRAPHICAL/CRITICAL SOURCES: *Tulsa World,* February 16, 1962, September 13, 1962, October 14, 1962, October 13, 1963; *Muskogee-Phoenix,* September 23, 1962; *Boston Sunday Globe,* October 14, 1962; *Personal Book Guide,* November, 1962; *Watchman Examiner,* November 22, 1962; *Townsman,* November 22, 1962; *Bulletin* of the Tulsa County Medical Society, December, 1962; *Charleston* (W.Va.) *Sunday Gazette,* December 16, 1962; *Current Medical Digest,* January, 1963; *Joplin Globe,* February 24, 1963; *Webb City Sentinel,* March 15, 1963; *American Journal of the Medical Sciences,* April, 1963; *Atlanta-Journal Constitution,* April 7, 1963; *Kansas City Times,* May 1, 1963; *Dental Students Magazine,* May 19, 1963; *Anesthesiology,* May-June, 1963; *Oklahoma Today,* Spring, 1963; *Saturday Review,* June 15, 1963; *Northside News,* July 4, 1963; *Anesthesia and Analgesia,* July-August, 1963; *Colonial Courier,* August 1, 1963; *Bixby Bulletin,* October 18, 1963; *Tulsa Herald,* Volume 34, number 3; *Book World,* September 28, 1969.

* * *

WOODWORTH, G(eorge) Wallace 1902-1969

PERSONAL: Born November 6, 1902, in Boston, Mass.; son of George Loomis (a private secretary) and Ruth Smith (Beckford) Woodworth; married Evelyn Barnes, December 20, 1928; children: Ellery Beckford, Harriet Tilden (Mrs. Albin C. Koch). *Education:* Harvard University, A.B., 1924, A.M., 1926. *Politics:* Republican. *Religion:* Episcopalian. *Home:* 8 Francis Ave., Cambridge, Mass. 02138. *Office:* Department of Music, Harvard University, Cambridge, Mass. 02138.

CAREER: Harvard University, Cambridge, Mass., 1926-69, professor of music, 1946-69; former college organist, conductor, and choirmaster of Harvard Glee Club and Radcliffe Choral Society. Visiting lecturer at universities. Guest conductor of choral and orchestral concerts; music director of First International University Choral Festival, Lincoln Center, New York, 1965. Trustee of Fisk University and New England Conservatory of Music. *Member:* American Academy of Arts and Sciences (fellow; council member, 1965-69), American Musicological Society, College Music Society (first president, 1958-60), Phi Beta Kappa. *Awards, honors:* Litt.D., Miami University, Oxford, Ohio, 1955; Mus.D., New England Conservatory of Music, 1958, University of Hartford, 1963; Harvard Glee Club Medal; Moremus Award for distinguished service to American music; Founders Award from Radcliffe College, 1969.

WRITINGS: *The World of Music,* Harvard University Press, 1964. Editor of "Harvard-Radcliffe Choral Music," published by Schirmer. Contributor to music journals.

(Died July 18, 1969)

WOODWORTH, G(eorge) Walter 1903-

PERSONAL: Born March 1, 1903, in Delphos, Kan.; son of George W. (a farmer) and Lillie (Davis) Woodworth; married Elizabeth Cunningham, September 4, 1926. *Education:* Kansas Wesleyan University, A.B., 1924; University of Kansas, M.A., 1925; University of Michigan, Ph.D., 1932. *Politics:* Republican. *Religion:* Congregational. *Office:* Amos Tuck School of Business Administration, Dartmouth College, Hanover, N.H. 03755.

CAREER: University of Michigan, Ann Arbor, instructor in economics, 1925-30; Dartmouth College, Hanover, N.H., assistant professor, 1930-38, professor of finance, 1938-52; University of Michigan, School of Business Administration, professor of finance, 1952-59; University of Illinois, Urbana, Fred M. Bailey Memorial Professor of Finance, 1959-62; Dartmouth College, Amos Tuck School of Business Administration, Leon E. Williams Professor of Finance and Banking, beginning, 1962. Public interest director, Federal Home Loan Bank of Boston, 1951-52; trustee, Dartmouth Savings Bank, 1936-52. *Member:* American Economic Association, American Finance Association, Phi Beta Kappa, Delta Sigma Pi, Rotary Club. *Awards, honors:* D. Bus. Admin., Kansas Wesleyan University, 1950.

WRITINGS: (With R. D. Kilborne) *Principles of Money and Banking,* McGraw, 1937; *The Monetary and Banking System,* McGraw, 1950; *The Detroit Money Market, 1934-55,* University of Michigan Press, 1956; *The Money Market and Monetary Management,* Harper, 1965, 2nd edition, 1972; *The Management of Cyclical Liquidity of Commercial Banks,* Bankers Publishing, 1967.

* * *

WOOLFE, H(arold) Geoffrey 1902-

PERSONAL: Born May 19, 1902, in London, England; married Ivy Maxine Hyman, March 26, 1931; children: John, Elisabeth (Mrs. David Kahn). *Education:* University College School, Hampstead, London, student; Trinity Hall, Cambridge, M.A., 1925. *Politics:* Liberal. *Home:* 18 The Pryors, East Heath Rd., London N.W. 3, 1 BS, England.

CAREER: Barrister, 1924-33; solicitor, 1933-68; barrister, 1969—. South Bucks Liberal Association, first chairman and president, 1949-55; Watford Liberal Association, president, 1959-60; Hampstead Liberal Association, president, 1966-70. *Military service:* Royal Air Force, pilot officer, 1940. *Member:* National Playing Fields Association (honorary county legal consultant, 1970—).

WRITINGS: *The Junior Branch: Being an Episodic Account of a Short Period in the Life of a Young Scholar,* P. R. Macmillan, 1959; *Married to a Lawyer,* P. R. Macmillan, 1962. Play, "Come to Meet the Bride" (re-titled "A Gambler in Brides"), produced at Strand Theatre and Embassy Theatre, London. Contributor of satirical articles to *Punch.*

* * *

WOOLLEY, Geoffrey Harold 1892-1968

PERSONAL: Born May 14, 1892, in London, England; son of George Herbert and Sarah (Cathcart) Woolley; married Janet Beatrix Culme-Seymour (died, 1943); married Elcie Elisabeth Nichols, June 12, 1945; children: (second marriage) Geoffrey Nicholas. *Education:* Attended St. John's School, Leatherhead, England; Queen's College, Oxford,

B.A., 1919, M.A., 1920, diploma in theology (with distinction); Cuddesdon College, Oxford, graduate studies. *Home:* Hunters Barn, West Chiltington, Pulborough, Sussex, England.

CAREER: Clergyman, Church of England. Rugby School, Rugby, England, assistant master, 1920-23; vicar of Monk Sherborne, England, 1923-27; Harrow School, Harrow, England, chaplain and master, 1927-39; vicar of Harrow, England, 1944-52; rector of West Grinstead, Sussex, England, 1952-58. Select preacher at Cambridge University, Westminster Abbey, St. Paul's Cathedral. Director of School Empire Tours to Australia, 1926, Canada, 1928-39. Institute of Christian Education, member of committee, 1927-39. *Military service:* British Army, 1914-1919; received Victoria Cross, Military Cross, twice mentioned in dispatches. British Army, chaplain, 1940-49; became major; received Order of the British Empire. *Member:* Royal Commonwealth Society.

WRITINGS: The Epic of the Mountains (poem), Basil Blackwell, 1929; *Fear and Religion,* Benn, 1930; *A Journey to Palestine* (poems), Basil Blackwell, 1935; *A Pocket Book of Prayers for Those on Active Service and for Those at Home,* S.C.M. Press, 1940; *Sometimes a Soldier* (autobiography), Benn, 1963. Also author of *The Hill-Top and Other Poems,* H. Toc. Contributor to *Harrow Lectures on Education.*

WORK IN PROGRESS: A book, *About Christian Education;* a revised edition of *A Pocket Book of Prayers;* stories for children.†

(Died December 10, 1968)

*   *   *

WORCESTER, Gurdon Saltonstall   1897-

PERSONAL: Born December 7, 1897, in Philadelphia, Pa.; son of Elwood (a clergyman) and Blanche (Rulison) Worcester; married Natalie Shipman (a writer), May 18, 1934. *Education:* Harvard University, A.B., 1920. *Religion:* Protestant. *Home:* High St., Gloucester, Mass. 01930. *Agent:* Maurice Crain, Inc., 18 East 41st St., New York, N.Y. 10017. *Office:* 10 Mitchell Place, New York, N.Y. 10017.

CAREER: Consulting psychologist in private practice, New York, N.Y., 1932-60; writer and inventor, 1960—. Sheraton Plaza, Boston, Mass., director. *Military service:* U.S. Army, 1918-19; became second lieutenant.

WRITINGS: (With wife, Natalie Shipman) *Way of the Heart,* Greystone Press, 1941; (with Natalie Shipman) *Perchance to Dream,* Prentice-Hall, 1946; *The Singing Flute,* Obolensky, 1963.

WORK IN PROGRESS: A novella; a book for children ages six to nine.†

*   *   *

WORDEN, William L.   1910-

PERSONAL: Born January 15, 1910; son of Ralph K. and Lizbeth Worden; married Evelyn Williams, March 1, 1934; children: W. Nikolaus. *Education:* Drake University, B.A., 1930; University of Washington, Seattle, courses in fiction. *Home:* 9015 Haddin Way, Bellevue, Wash. 98004. *Agent:* H. N. Swanson, Inc., 8523 Sunset Blvd., Los Angeles, Calif. 90069. *Office:* Boeing Co., Seattle, Wash.

CAREER: Associated Press, writer and editor on West Coast and overseas, 1934-41, war correspondent, 1941-45,

1950-52; *Saturday Evening Post*, Philadelphia, Pa., war correspondent, 1941-45, 1950-52, and contract writer, 1951, 1955-56; free-lance journalist and fiction writer at other periods, 1945-59; Boeing Co., Seattle, Wash., publicist, 1959—. *Member:* Alpha Tau Omega, Sigma Delta Chi, Foreign Correspondents Club (Tokyo), Meydenbauser Bay Yacht Club (Bellevue, Wash.). *Awards, honors:* Distinguished Service Award, Drake University and Alumni Association, 1958.

WRITINGS: (With William Dean) *General Dean's Story,* Viking, 1954. Contributor of two hundred articles and approximately eighty short stories and novelettes to magazines.

*   *   *

WOYTINSKY, Emma S(hadkhan)   1893-1969

PERSONAL: Born April 15, 1893, in Witebsk, Russia; daughter of Savely W. (a builder) and Bertha (Kensen) Shadkhan; married Wladimir S. Woytinsky (an economist and writer), July, 1917 (died June, 1960). *Education:* Educated in Russia at Bestugef Women's College, St. Petersburg (now Leningrad), 1909-14, and in France at Sorbonne, University of Paris, 1920-22, Ecole des Hautes Etudes, 1933-34. *Home:* 5324 39th St., N.W., Washington, D.C. 20015.

CAREER: Economist and writer in Germany; came to United States in 1935; continued collaborative work with husband in Social Science Research Council study on social security, 1940-41; economist with Board of Economic Warfare (later Foreign Economic Administration) and U.S. Department of State, 1942-47; professional writer, primarily on economics. Joint lecturer with husband for U.S. Department of State and India Ministry of Education on tour of Far East, 1955-56, and for Department of State on tour of Latin-American countries, 1957-58.

WRITINGS—All with husband, Wladimir S. Woytinsky, except as noted: *Die Welt in Zahlen* (title means "The World in Figures"), seven volumes, Rudolf Mosse (Berlin), 1924-28; *Zehn Jahre Neues Deutschland* (title means "Ten Years of New Germany"), Rudolf Mosse, 1929; (sole author) *Die Kommunalverwaltung Gross-Berlin* (title means "Municipal Problems of Metropolitan Berlin"), E. Laubsche, 1929; *Earnings and Social Security in the United States,* Social Science Research Council, 1943; *World Population and Production, Trends and Outlook,* Twentieth Century, 1953, 2nd edition, 1955; *World Commerce and Governments, Trends and Outlook,* Twentieth Century, 1955; *Lessons of the Recessions,* Public Affairs, 1959; (editor) *So Much Alive: The Life and Works of W. S. Woytinsky,* Vanguard, 1962; (sole author) *Two Lives in One* (autobiography), Praeger, 1965; (sole author) *Profile of the U.S. Economy: Survey of Growth and Change,* Praeger, 1967. Translator from the Russian: *La Democratie Georgienne* (title means "Democracy in Georgia"), Alcan Levy (Paris), 1922; W. S. Woytinsky, *Der Erste Sturm* (title means "The First Storm"; memoirs), Buchergilde (Berlin), 1931; W. S. Woytinsky, *Wehe den Besiegten* (title means "Woe to the Defeated"; memoirs), Bucherglide, 1933; W. S. Woytinsky, *Market and Prices,* Kelley, 1964. Contributor to *Encyclopaedia Britannica* and to several journals.

SIDELIGHTS: Mrs. Woytinsky was proficient in French, German, Spanish, and knew a little Italian. Her travels covered most countries of Europe and Central America, and many of Asia and South America, as well as almost all the national parks in the United States. Mrs. Woytinsky climbed mountains (in earlier years) in the French, Swiss, and Italian Alps, in Norway, Germany, Canada, and America.

BIOGRAPHICAL SOURCES: Two Lives in One, Praeger, 1965.

(Died April 13, 1968)

* * *

WRIGHT, (Julia) Celeste Turner 1906-

PERSONAL: Born of American parents, on March 17, 1906, in St. John, New Brunswick, Canada; daughter of George Howard (a merchant) and Viola (Kelley) Turner; married Vedder Allen Wright (an investor), June 26, 1933 (divorced, 1970); children: Vedder Allen, Jr. *Education:* University of California, Los Angeles, A.B., 1925; University of California, Berkeley, M.A., 1926, Ph.D., 1928. *Religion:* Episcopalian. *Home:* 1001 "D" St., Davis, Calif. 95616. *Office:* English Department, University of California, Davis, Calif. 95616.

CAREER: University of California, Davis, 1928—, began as instructor, became professor of English in 1948, chairman of English department, 1928-55, faculty research lecturer, 1963. *Member:* Modern Language Association of America, Renaissance Society of America, Poetry Society of America, Phi Beta Kappa, Faculty Club (Davis campus). *Awards, honors:* Reynolds Lyric award, 1964, for "State of Preservation"; University of California, Institute for Creative Arts writing fellowships, 1961, 1965, 1970; Poetry Society of America prizes, 1966-67; Eva M. Bradway award, 1970, for "Minor Medici."

WRITINGS: Anthony Mundy: An Elizabethan Man of Letters, University of California, 1928; *Etruscan Princess, and Other Poems*, A. Swallow, 1964. Contributor to *Yale Review, Harper's, Poetry, PMLA, Studies in Philology, Philological Quarterly*, and other publications.

WORK IN PROGRESS: A second volume of poetry; a collection of her studies of warlike women and other female worthies in Elizabethan England.

* * *

WRIGHT, Frances Fitzpatrick 1897-

PERSONAL: Born June 26, 1897; daughter of Robert Harrison and Roberta (Johnson) Fitzpatrick; married George W. Wright, December 8, 1918 (died April 8, 1956); children: Ann Puryear Bagley, Roberta Wright Martin, George Francis. *Education:* Attended public schools in Phoenix, Ariz., and Gallatin, Tenn. *Politics:* Independent but currently Democrat. *Religion:* Catholic convert. *Home:* Faraway Hills, Gallatin, Tenn. 37066.

CAREER: Free-lance writer. Formerly lesson writer for Baptist Sunday School Board, Nashville, Tenn., for twenty years. Gallatin Library Board member. *Member:* Women's National Book Association, Association for Preservation of Tennessee Antiquities, Hermitage Association, Review Club (past president). *Awards, honors:* Voted most popular *American Girl* author.

WRITINGS—All juvenile books: *Lucy Ellen*, Farrar & Rinehart, 1940; *Lucy Ellen's College Days*, Farrar & Rinehart, 1943; *Lucy Ellen's Heydey*, Farrar & Rinehart, 1945; *Secret of the Old Sampey Place*, Abingdon, 1946; *Your Loving Sister, Pat Downing*, Holt, 1948; *Number Eleven Poplar Street*, Abingdon, 1948; *Surprise at Sampey Place,*

Abingdon, 1950; *Poplar Street Park*, Abingdon, 1952; *Sam Houston* (biography), Abingdon, 1953; *Daybreak at Sampey Place*, Abingdon, 1954; *Andrew Jackson* (biography), Abingdon, 1958; *American Girl Book of Pat Downing Stories*, Random House, 1963; *Bless Your Bones, Sammy*, Abingdon, 1968.

Contributor of articles and short stories to religious and farm periodicals, and of several articles to *Spur* and *Saturday Evening Post*.

SIDELIGHTS: Some of Mrs. Wright's stories have been put in Braille, several reprinted in textbooks. Her early writings for the Baptist Sunday School Board have been translated into Chinese and Portuguese.

* * *

WRIGHT, Ione Stuessy 1905-

PERSONAL: Born March 12, 1905, in La Grange, Ill.; daughter of Samuel (a realtor and builder) and Augusta H. (Ek) Stuessy; married Victor A. Wright (an airlines pilot), July 21, 1926; children: Yvonne (Mrs. Robert P. Hunter), Clyde Lee, Beverly (Mrs. William G. Lacey), Keith Albert. *Education:* University of Richmond, B.A., 1926; University of California, Berkeley, M.A., 1937, Ph.D., 1940. *Religion:* Baptist. *Home:* 485 Northeast 94th St., Miami, Fla. 33138. *Office address:* University of Miami, Box 8134, Coral Gables, Fla. 33134.

CAREER: University of Miami, Coral Gables, Fla., associate professor, 1946-59, professor of history, beginning, 1959. *Member:* American Historical Association, American Association of University Women, Conference on Latin American History, Southern Historical Association, Mortar Board, Phi Beta Kappa, Phi Alpha Theta.

WRITINGS: Voyages of Alvaro de Saavedra Ceron, 1527-1529, University of Miami Press, 1951. Editor, *Journal of Inter-American Studies*.

WORK IN PROGRESS: Research on the Scots' venture in colonization in Darien in the 1690's.

* * *

WRIGHT, Mary Pamela Godwin 1917-
(Mary Bawn)

PERSONAL: Born February 16, 1917, in Chippenham, Wiltshire, England; daughter of Edgar William (a farmer) and Beatrice Alice (Gready) Godwin; married Vivian Goldsworth Bawn, August 20, 1947 (died March 31, 1961); married Robert Edgar Wright (a farmer), October 3, 1961. *Education:* Attended Bath Domestic Science College. *Politics:* Conservative. *Religion:* Spiritualist. *Home:* East Sands, Little Cheverell, Divizes, Wiltshire, England.

CAREER: Teacher of domestic science, 1938-49.

WRITINGS—Under name Mary Bawn; all published by R. Hale: *Scarlet for Tartan*, 1958; *Son of the Robber Clan*, 1958; *Price of Rebellion*, 1959; *Lady Jean's Feather*, 1960; *The Stone at Drumaroo*, 1960; *Against the Tide*, 1960; *Pass of the Foxes*, 1961; *Rogue Tide*, 1962; *Galleons Grave*, 1963; *Brother's Blood*, 1964; *Thunder of Cavaliers*, 1964; *Men of the Bay*, 1965.

AVOCATIONAL INTERESTS: History, gardening, travel, animals.†

* * *

WRIGHT, Michael R(obert) 1901-

PERSONAL: Born December 3, 1901, in London, England; son of Sir Robert Samuel (a judge) and Meriel (Chermside) Wright; married Esther Ursula Long, April, 1934; children: Jeremy, Nicholas. *Education:* Balliol College, Oxford, B.A. (honors), 1924. *Religion:* Church of England. *Home:* 4 Whitehall Court, London S.W.1, England.

CAREER: British Foreign Service, 1926-63, with posts at embassies in Washington, D.C., 1926-30, Paris, 1936-40, Cairo, 1940-43, Washington, D.C., 1943-46; member of staff of Special Commissioner in South-East Asia, 1946-47; assistant Under-Secretary of State, British Foreign Office, 1947-50; Ambassador to Norway, 1951-54, Ambassador to Iraq, 1954-58; delegate to Nuclear Test Ban Conference, Geneva, Switzerland, 1959-62, Ten Nation Disarmament Conference, 1960, Eighteen Nation Disarmament Conference, 1962-63. Director of Guinness Mahon Holdings Co., London. Broadcaster on disarmament questions. *Member:* Royal Geographical Society (fellow), Save the Children Federation, Anglo-Norse Society, St. James Club, Norske Club. *Awards, honors:* Companion of St. Michael and St. George, 1945, Knight Commander, 1951, Knight Grand Cross, 1958; Order of Rafidain (Iraq).

WRITINGS: Disarm and Verify, Praeger, 1964. Contributor of articles on disarmament to magazines and the press.

AVOCATIONAL INTERESTS: Skiing, fishing.

* * *

WRIGHT, Philip Arthur   1908-

PERSONAL: Born June 4, 1908, in Hawstead, Suffolk, England; son of Willoughby William and Ellen (Honeywood) Wright; married Amy Newton; children: John Newton, Christine Mary. *Education:* Chadacre Agricultural Institute, diploma, 1924; St. Andrew Theological College, student. *Home:* The Vicarage, Woodford Bridge, Roxwell, Essex, England.

CAREER: Farmer, 1924-31; Church Army Captain, 1931-33; clerk in Holy Orders, Church of England, 1938; vicar of Littlebury, England, 1945-54; vicar of Woodford Bridge, England, 1954; vicar of Roxwell, England, 1965—. Commentator for annual London carthorse parade and van horse parade. *Military service:* British Army, chaplain, 1944-46; Territorial Army, chaplain, 1946—; received Order of British Empire. *Member:* National Traction Engine Club of Great Britain (chairman), Guild of Agricultural journalists (chaplain).

WRITINGS: Our Daily Bread: A Form of Prayer for Agriculture, Epworth, 1945; (self-illustrated) *Ploughshare and Pulpit,* Hart, 1947; *Padre Calling!* (18 talks), Paul & Mathew, 1948; *Joining Up?* (tract), Churchman Publishing Co., 1950; *Traction Engines,* A. & C. Black, 1959; *Old Farm Implements,* A. & C. Black, 1961; *Old Farm Tractors,* A. & C. Black, 1962. Occasional contributor of articles to *Country Life, Farmers' Weekly, Smallholder, Farm and Country, Church Times,* and other periodicals.†

* * *

WRISTON, Henry M(erritt)   1889-

PERSONAL: Born July 4, 1889, in Laramie, Wyo.; son of Henry Lincoln (a Methodist minister) and Jennie Amelia (Atcheson) Wriston; married Ruth Colton Bigelow, 1914 (deceased); married Marguerite Woodworth, June 28, 1947; children: (first marriage) Barbara, Walter Bigelow. *Education:* Wesleyan University, A.B., 1911, A.M., 1912; Harvard University, Ph.D., 1922. *Religion:* Methodist. *Home:* 12 Beekman Place, New York, N.Y. 10022.

CAREER: Wesleyan University, Middletown, Conn., instructor, 1914-17, associate professor, 1917-19, professor of history, 1919-25; Lawrence College, Appleton, Wis., president, 1925-37; Institute of Paper Chemistry, Appleton, Wis., director and founder, 1929-37; Brown University, Providence, R.I., president, 1937-55; American Assembly (Columbia University), New York, N.Y., executive director, 1955-58, president, 1958-62, chairman, 1962-65. Member of board of trustees of Northwestern Mutual Life Insurance Co., 1942—; public governor of New York Stock Exchange, 1950-52. Chairman of Secretary of State's Public Committee on Personnel, 1954-55, of President's Commission on National Goals, 1961. Trustee of World Peace Foundation, 1939-52, of Carnegie Endowment for International Peace, 1943-54. President of United Campaign of Community Chests, Rhode Island, 1941-46; vice-president of National War Fund, 1943-46.

MEMBER: American Academy of Arts and Science (fellow), American Historical Association, Council on Foreign Relations (president, 1951-64, honorary president, 1964—), American Political Science Association, American Society for International Law, Phi Beta Kappa, Century Association (New York). *Awards, honors:* Commander, Order of the British Empire; thirty honorary degrees, including LL.D. from Harvard University, Princeton University, New York University, Rutgers Universtiy, Wesleyan University, Williams College, University of Southampton (England), and Lit.D. from Wesleyan University and Columbia University.

WRITINGS: War Chest Practice, State of Connecticut, 1918; *Report of the Connecticut State Council of Defense,* State of Connecticut, 1919; *Executive Agents in American Diplomacy,* Johns Hopkins Press, 1929, reissued as *Executive Agents in American Foreign Relations,* Peter Smith, 1967; *The Nature of a Liberal College,* Lawrence College Press, 1937; *College Students and the war,* National Policy Committee, 1940; *Prepare for Peace,* Harper, 1941; *Challenge to Freedom,* Harper, 1943; *Strategy of Peace,* World Peace Foundation, 1944; *Diplomacy in a Democracy,* Harper, 1956; *Wriston Speaking: A Selection of Addresses,* Brown University Press, 1957; *Academic Procession: Reflections of a College President,* Columbia University Press, 1959; *Rugged Individualism,* Brunswick Publishing Co., 1960; *Policy Perspectives,* Brown University Press, 1964; (contributor) John Plank, editor, *Cuba and the United States: Long-Range Perspectives* (essays), Brookings Institution, 1967. Also author of several pamphlets on Brown University structure, housing, etc. Contributor of articles to professional journals. Member of editorial advisory board, *Foreign Affairs.*

BIOGRAPHICAL/CRITICAL SOURCES: A Mike Wallace Interview with Henry M. Wriston (produced by ABC), Fund for the Republic (New York), c.1953.

* * *

WYNDHAM, Everard Humphrey   1888-

PERSONAL: Born December 4, 1888, in London, England. *Education:* Attended Eton College and Royal Military College at Sandhurst. *Politics:* Conservative. *Home:* Caversfield, Bicester, Oxfordshire, England.

CAREER: British Army, 1908-42; became colonel; received Military Cross.

WRITINGS: A Backward Glance, Clowes, 1948; (contributor) *The World War,* Volumes III-IV, Caxton, 1951; *The First Household Cavalry Regiment,* Gale & Poldon, 1952.

Contributor of articles on the military situation in Europe to *Army Quarterly* for seventeen years.

* * *

WYNESS, (James) Fenton 1903-

PERSONAL: Born August 15, 1903, in Aberdeen, Scotland; son of John Morrison (a company secretary) and Alice Gordon (Fenton) Wyness. *Education:* Gray's School of Art, Aberdeen, Scotland, D.A., 1926; School of Architecture, Aberdeen, Scotland, A.R.I.B.A., 1927. *Home:* 45 Salisbury Ter., Aberdeen, Scotland.

CAREER: Gray's School of Art, Aberdeen, Scotland, lecturer in architectural history, 1928; architect in private practice, Aberdeen, Scotland, 1929—. County commissioner, Boy Scouts, 1936. *Member:* Gray's School of Art F.P. Club (honorary president, 1930, 1953, 1954), Deeside Field Club (president, 1962-71). *Awards, honors:* Knight of the Order of St. John, 1965.

WRITINGS: A Buchan Tower-house, Buchan Field Club, 1943; *A Book of Legends,* W. & W. Lindsay, 1943; *North-Eastern Journey,* W. & W. Lindsay, 1943; "County Series of Local Histories," nine volumes, Aberdeenshire County Council, 1948-57; *Kincardineshire,* Encyclopaedia Britannica, 1956; *Balmoral Castle,* Historical Publications, 1957; *Birkhall,* Historical Publications, 1957; *Templars' Park,* Waverley Press, 1962; *City by the Grey North Sea: Aberdeen,* Reid & Son, 1965; *Royal Valley: The Story of the Aberdeenshire Dee,* Reid & Son, 1968; *Spots from the Leopard,* Impulse Publications, 1971. Also author of several brochures on regional history. Contributor of articles to *Scotsman, Scotland's Magazine,* and other publications. Honorary editor, *Deeside Field,* 1945-59.

WORK IN PROGRESS: A book on witchcraft in northeast Scotland.

SIDELIGHTS: Wyness designed a series of Royal Deeside plaids.

* * *

WYON, Olive 1890-19?

PERSONAL: Born in 1890, in London, England. *Education:* Five years' study of theology at Church of Scotland Missionary College, Seley Oak Colleges, and King's College, London. *Religion:* Anglican. *Home:* 19a Trumpington St., Cambridge, England.

CAREER: Professional writer on religions and theological subjects. Young Womens Christian Association, Birmingham, England, education secretary, one year; *World Dominion* (now *Frontier*), assistant editor, seven years; Church of Scotland Missionary College, Edinburgh, began as tutor, became principal, 1948-54. Study secretary, Conference on Church, Community and State, Oxford, England, 1936-37, and World Council of Churches, Geneva, Switzerland, 1947-48. *Member:* Royal Institute for International Affairs, Society for New Testament Study, Theological Society. *Awards, honors:* D.D. from University of Aberdeen, 1948.

WRITINGS: (With J. R. Coates and others) *The Gospel of the Cross,* Macmillan, 1918; *An Eastern Palimpsest: A Brief Survey of the Religious Situation in Turkey, Syria, Palestine, Transjordania, Egypt,* World Dominion Press, 1927; *William Lockhart* (pamphlet), Livingstone Bookshop, 1928; *The Dawn Wind: A Picture of Changing Conditions Among Women in Africa and the East,* S.C.M. Press, 1931; *Radiant Freedom: The Story of Emma Pieczynska,*

Lutterworth, 1939; *The Church and World Peace* (pamphlet), Embassies of Reconciliation, 1940; *The School of Prayer,* S.C.M. Press, 1943, Westminster, 1944, 10th edition, S.C.M. Press, 1962, Macmillan, 1963; *The Three Windows: The Story of Ann Hunter Small,* James Clarke, 1953; *The Altar Fire: Reflections on the Sacrament of the Lord's Supper,* Westminster, 1954 (published in England as *The Altar Fire: Reflections on the Sacrament of the Eucharist,* S.C.M. Press, 1954); *Consider Him: Three Meditations on the Passion Story,* S.C.M. Press, 1956, Abingdon, 1957; *Prayers for Unity Through the Christian Year,* Book 2, Edinburgh House Press, 1956; *On the Way: Reflections on the Christian Life,* Westminster, 1958; *The Grace of the Passion,* S.C.M. Press, 1959, Fortress, 1965; *Prayer,* Muhlenberg Press, 1960; *Living Springs: New Religious Movements in Western Europe,* Westminster, 1962; *Teachings Toward Christian Perfection, Introducing Three Spiritual Classics,* Board of Missions, Methodist Church, 1963, reissued as *Desire for God: A Study of Three Spiritual Classics—Francois Fenelon, "Christian Perfection"; John Wesley, "Christian Perfection"; Evelyn Underhill, "The Spiritual Life,"* Collins, 1966; (editor) *The World's Christmas* (stories by various authors, retold by Wyon), S.C.M. Press, 1964, Fortress, 1965.

Translator: Paul Seippel, *Huguenot Saint of the Twentieth Century: The Life of Adele Kamm,* Revell, 1914 (published in England as *A Living Witness: The Life of Adele Kamm,* Hodder & Stoughton, 1914); Friedrich Heiler, *The Gospel of Sadhu Sundar Singh,* abridged edition, Oxford University Press, 1927; Ernst Troeltsch, *The Social Teaching of the Christian Churches,* two volumes, Macmillan, 1931; Ernst Curtius, *The Civilization of France,* Macmillan, 1932; Maurice Goguel, *The Life of Jesus,* Macmillan, 1933; Carl G. A. von Harnack, *A Scholar's Testament,* Nicholson & Watson, 1933; Heinrich E. Brunner, *The Mediator,* Lutterworth, 1934; Heinrich E. Brunner, *The Divine Imperative,* Lutterworth, 1936, Macmillan, 1937; (with Denzil Patrick) Nils Ehrenstroem, *Christian Faith and the Modern State,* Willett, 1937; Heinrich E. Brunner, *Man in Revolt,* Scribner, 1939; Heinrich E. Brunner, *Revelation and Reason,* S.C.M. Press, 1947; Heinrich E. Brunner, *Christian Doctrine of God,* Westminster, 1950; (and author of introduction) Hanns Lilje, *The Valley of the Shadow,* Muhlenberg Press, 1950; Jacques Ellul, *The Presence of the Kingdom,* S.C.M. Press, 1951, Westminster, 1952; Hanns Lilje, *The Last Book of the Bible,* Muhlenberg Press, 1957; Leopold Malevez, *The Christian Message and Myth: The Theology of Rudolf Bultmann,* S.C.M. Press, 1958, Newman, 1960; Maurice Goguel, *Jesus and the Origins of Christianity,* Harper, 1960; Helmut Gollwitzer, *The Dying and the Living Lord,* Muhlenberg Press, 1960; Suzanne Dietrich, *Free Men,* Westminster, 1961. Contributor of articles to *Spectator* and to religious periodicals.

WORK IN PROGRESS: New Testament theology and translations.

SIDELIGHTS: Wyon lived for prolonged periods in Germany, France, Switzerland, and the Netherlands, traveled extensively in the Middle East and Europe, with more recent travels concerned with Christian unity, and spoke French, German, Dutch, and Italian. *Avocational interests:* Drawing, designing embroidery, painting.

(Deceased)

* * *

WYZANSKI, Charles E(dward), Jr. 1906-

PERSONAL: Born May 27, 1906, in Boston, Mass.; son of

Charles E. and Maude (Joseph) Wyzanski; married Gisela Warburg, July 23, 1943; children: Charles Max, Anita Henrietta. *Education:* Harvard University, A.B. (magna cum laude), 1927, LL.B. (magna cum laude), 1930. *Religion:* Jewish. *Home:* 39 Fayerweather St., Cambridge, Mass. *Office:* U.S. Courthouse, Room 1500, Boston, Mass. 02109.

CAREER: Admitted to Massachusetts bar, 1931; law secretary to U.S. Circuit Court judges, 1930-32; U.S. Department of Labor, Washington, D.C., solicitor, 1933-35; U.S. Department of Justice, Washington, D.C., special assistant to Attorney General, 1935-37; Ropes, Gray, Boyden & Perkins, partner, 1938-41; U.S. District Court, Boston, Mass., judge, 1941-65, chief judge, 1965-71, senior judge 1971—. Member of committee of experts, International Labor Organization, Geneva, 1945-53; member of National Defense Mediation Board, 1941; copyright expert for UNESCO in Paris, 1949, and Washington, D.C., 1950. Lecturer at Harvard University, 1942-43, 1949-50; visiting professor at Massachusetts Institute of Technology, 1948-50. Trustee of Phillips Exeter Academy, 1944-54, of Ford Foundation, president of board of overseers, Harvard University, 1953-57.

MEMBER: American Law Institute (council member, 1943—), American Academy of Arts and Sciences, Phi Beta Kappa, Harvard Society of Fellows (honorary senior fellow), Century Association (New York), Athenaeum Club (London); Harvard Club and Tavern Club (both Boston). *Awards, honors:* LL.D., University of Pennsylvania, 1953, Carleton College, 1953, Tufts University, 1953, Swarthmore College, 1956, Brandeis University, 1956, Harvard University, 1958, Clark University, 1963, Washington University, 1974.

WRITINGS: Whereas: A Judge's Premises, Atlantic-Little, Brown, 1965.

* * *

YAHUDA, Joseph 1900-

PERSONAL: Born July 29, 1900, in Jerusalem, Israel; son of Isaac Ezekiel (a bookseller, scholar, and author) and Vida (Ashreky) Yahuda; married Cecile Friend, January 11, 1925. *Education:* Attended College St. Joseph, Cairo, Egypt; King's College, London, LL.B. *Religion:* Jewish. *Home:* 3 Hare Ct., Temple, London E.C. 4, England. *Office:* English Bar, 3 King's Bench Walk, London E.C. 4, England.

CAREER: Barrister-at-law, London, England, 1933—. *Member:* Authors' Club.

WRITINGS: La Palestine Revisitee, privately printed, 1929; *Law and Life According to Hebrew Thought*, Oxford University Press, 1932; *This Democracy*, Pitman, 1937; *Bio-Economics*, Pitman, 1938; *New Biology and Medicine*, St. Catherine Press, 1951; *Truth and Freedom*, St. Catherine Press, 1953; *An Original Interpretation of Masonry*, Masonic Record, 1954. Contributor of articles to legal journals.

WORK IN PROGRESS: Hebrew Is Greek, a book which attempts to demonstrate that both the Aramaic and the Hebrew of the Old Testament are pure Greek and that the barrier between Semitic and Arian languages is artificial.

AVOCATIONAL INTERESTS: The Bible, biology, and thinking.

YELVERTON, Eric Esskildsen 1888-1964

PERSONAL: Born June 24, 1888, in London, England; son of Max Kai (an engineer) and Fanny (Hicks) Esskildsen; married Nina Brudenell, June 9, 1920; children: David Eric. *Education:* Attended St. Paul's School, London, England; Trinity College, Dublin, B.A., 1911; Christ's College, Cambridge, B.A., 1911, M.A., 1914; St. Edmund Hall, Oxford, M.A. ad eundem, 1914, B.D., 1917, D.D., 1924. *Home:* 22 Crossmead Ave., New Milton, Hampshire, England.

CAREER: Ordained a deacon of the Church of England, 1911, priest, 1912; assistant curate in London and Bristol, England, 1911-18; Royal Army, Chaplains' Department, regular chaplain, 1918-45; Church of England Men's Society, London, England, traveling and general secretary, 1945-52. Served with Army in France, 1918, in England and Egypt, 1920-38, East Africa, 1914-43, Palestine, 1943, with General Headquarters, Allied Armies, in Italy, 1944; retired as chaplain to the forces first class (colonel); received Order of British Empire (military), 1919.

WRITINGS: The Mass in Sweden: Its Development from the Latin Rite from 1531 to 1917, Henry Bradshaw Society, 1920; (translator) *The Swedish Rite*, Macmillan, 1921; (translator and editor) *The Manual of Olavus Petri*, S.P.C.K., 1953; *An Archbishop of the Reformation: Laurentius Petri Nericius, Archbishop of Uppsala, 1531-73*, Epworth, 1958, Augsburg, 1959. Contributor of articles to religious journals.†

(Died July 17, 1964)

* * *

YEO, Cedric Arnold 1905-

PERSONAL: Surname rhymes with "no"; born September 10, 1905, in Port Hill, Prince Edward Island, Canada; son of Herbert (a farmer) and Mary Jane Yeo; married second wife, Rosetta Sexton, November 16, 1962; children: (first marriage) Helen M. (Mrs. Michael Chew), Janet Clark (Mrs. Norman Johansen), John Arnold Clark, Tammy Lynn Hall. *Education:* Dalhousie University, B.A., 1929; Yale University, Ph.D., 1933; University of Chicago, postdoctoral study, 1962. *Politics:* Democrat. *Religion:* Episcopalian. *Home:* 909 Vickers Dr., Richmond, Ky. 40475. *Office:* Eastern Kentucky University, Richmond, Ky. 40475.

CAREER: Dalhousie University, Halifax, Nova Scotia, lecturer in classics at King's College (now University of King's College), 1931-32, 1936-39, university lecturer, 1939-40; King's Collegiate School, Windsor, Nova Scotia, Latin master, 1936-37; The Citadel, Charleston, S.C., associate professor of history, 1940-53; Memphis State University, Memphis, Tenn., associate professor of classics, 1955-57; Alice Lloyd College, Pippa Passes, Ky., professor of history, 1961-64; Eastern Kentucky State College (now University), Richmond, professor of history, 1965—. *Member:* American Historical Association, American Philosophical Society, American Association of University Professors.

WRITINGS: (Contributor) Fritz M. Heichelheim, editor, *Manual for the Teaching of Classical Subjects*, American Classical League, 1958; (with Heichelheim) *A History of the Roman People*, Prentice-Hall, 1962. Contributor to *Transactions* of Huguenot Society of South Carolina and American Philological Association, and to classical and historical journals.

WORK IN PROGRESS: "The influence of the Fourth Christian Century on Later Historiography," and *Aufstieg und Niedergang der Roemischen Welt*, completion expected 1976.

SIDELIGHTS: Yeo is competent in Latin, Greek, German, French, and Italian.

* * *

YODER, Sanford Calvin 1879-

PERSONAL: Born December 5, 1879, near Iowa City, Iowa; son of Christian S. and Anna (Swartzendruber) Yoder; married Emma Stutzman, September 23, 1903; children: Myron Sanford, Anna Marguerite (Mrs. David Zimmerly), Etta LaVerne (Mrs. C. M. Hostetler). *Education:* University of Iowa, A.B.; Northern Baptist Theological Seminary, B.D.; Winona Lake Theological Seminary, M.A.; Gordon School of Theology and Missions, S.T.D., 1939. *Politics:* Republican. *Home:* 1801 South Main St., Goshen, Ind.

CAREER: Ordained Mennonite minister, 1911; ordained bishop, 1913; pastor in Kalona, Iowa, 1912-24; Goshen College, Goshen, Ind., president, 1924-40, professor of Bible, 1940-52. Mennonite Board of Missions and Charities, secretary, 1923-44, president, 1944-48. *Member:* Phi Alpha Chi. *Awards, honors:* D.D., Northern Baptist Seminary, 1936; named Alumnus of the Year, Winona School of Theology, 1962.

WRITINGS—All published by Mennonite Publishing House: *Down South America Way*, 1919; *Brief Outline of Bible Study*, 1928; *For Conscience Sake: A Study of Mennonite Migrations as a Result of the First World War*, 1940; *Old Testament Poetry*, 1948; *Eastward to the Sun*, 1952; *Horsetrails Along the Desert*, 1954; *Things That Remain*, 1955; *The Days of My Years*, 1959; *He Gave Some Prophets*, 1964.

* * *

YOUNG, Douglas (Cuthbert Colquhoun) 1913-1973

PERSONAL: Born June 5, 1913, in Tayport, Scotland; son of Stephen (a businessman) and Margaret S. (Black) Young; married Helena Gossaree Auchterlonie (an artist-potter), August 24, 1943; children: Clara, Joanna. *Education:* University of St. Andrews, M.A., 1934; New College, Oxford, graduate study, 1934-38. *Home:* Makarsbield, Tayport, Fife, Scotland.

CAREER: University of St. Andrews, St. Andrews, Scotland, senior lecturer in Greek, beginning, 1947; University of North Carolina, Chapel Hill, Paddison Professor of Greek, 1970-73. Visiting professor, University of Minnesota, 1963-64.

WRITINGS: Auntran Blads, MacLellan, 1943; *A Braird o Thristles*, MacLellan, 1947; *Chasing an Ancient Greek*, Hollis & Carter, 1950; (editor) *Scottish Verse, 1851-1951*, Nelson, 1952; *The Puddocks* (Scots verse translation of Aristophanes), privately printed, 1958; *The Burdies* (Scots verse translation of Aristophanes), privately printed, 1958; *The Burdies* (Scots verse translation of Aristophanes), privately printed, 1959; (editor) *Theognis*, Teubner, 1961; *Edinburgh in the Age of Scott*, University of Oklahoma Press, 1965; *Scotts Burds and Edinburgh Reviewers* (pamphlet), M. MacDonald (Edinburgh), 1966; *Edinburgh in the Age of Reason*, Edinburgh University Press, 1967; *St. Andrews: Town and Gown, Royal and Ancient*, Cassell, 1969; *Scotland*, Cassell, 1971.

WORK IN PROGRESS: English verse translations of *Oresteia* of Aeschylus, with brief commentary for adult

beginners in Greek; English verse translation of Euripides' *Hippolytus*.

AVOCATIONAL INTERESTS: Scottish history and literature, European travel, American affairs.

(Died October 24, 1973)

* * *

YOUNG, Edward J(oseph) 1907-1968

PERSONAL: Born November 29, 1907, in San Francisco, Calif.; son of Edward Eyestone (an architect) and Julia (Tharp) Young; married Lillian G. Riggs, July 25, 1935; children: Lillian Jean (Mrs. Richard B. Gaffin), Davis Alan. *Education:* Stanford University, B.A., 1929; Westminster Theological Seminary, B.D., and Th.M., 1935; Dropsie College, Ph.D., 1943. *Politics:* Republican. *Home:* 2450 Edge Hill Rd., Huntingdon Valley, Pa. 19006.

CAREER: Ordained Presbyterian minister, 1935. Westminster Theological Seminary, Philadelphia, Pa., instructor, 1936-39, assistant professor, 1939-46, professor of Old Testament, 1946-68. Orthodox Presbyterian Church, member of Committee on Christian Education, 1937-68, moderator of General Assembly, 1956. *Member:* American Oriental Society, Society of Biblical Literature and Exegesis, Evangelical Theological Society. *Awards, honors:* Dropsie College Alumni Award.

WRITINGS: Study Your Bible: A Self Study Course for Bible Believing Christians, Eerdmans, 1934; *The Prophecy of Daniel, a Commentary*, Eerdmans, 1949; *An Introduction to the Old Testament*, Eerdmans, 1949, revised edition, 1960; *Arabic for Beginners*, Eerdmans, 1950; *My Servants, the Prophets*, Eerdmans, 1952; *Isaiah Fifty-Three, a Devotional and Expository Study*, Eerdmans, 1952; *Studies in Isaiah*, Eerdmans, 1954; *The Messianic Prophecies of Daniel*, Eerdmans, 1954; *Thy Word Is Truth: Some Thoughts on the Biblical Doctrine of Inspiration*, Eerdmans, 1957; *The Study of Old Testament Theology Today*, Clarke & Co., 1958, Revell, 1959; *Daniel's Vision of the Son of Man*, Tyndale Press, 1958; *Who Wrote Isaiah?*, Eerdmans, 1958; *Jesus Christ, the Servant of the Lord*, Evangelical Library, c.1959; *Old Testament Hebrew for Beginners*, privately printed, 1960; *Studies in Genesis One*, Presbyterian & Reformed, 1964; (author of introduction, exposition, and notes) *The Book of Isaiah*, Eerdmans, Volume I, 1965, Volume II, 1970, Volume III, 1971; *Psalm 139: A Devotional and Expository Study*, Banner of Truth Trust, 1965; *Genesis 3: A Devotional and Expository Study*, Banner of Truth Trust, 1966.

SIDELIGHTS: Young read most modern European languages and spoke several. *Avocational interests:* Playing the cello.

(Died, 1968)

* * *

YOUNG, Frank Carl 1907-

PERSONAL: Born September 1, 1907, in Philadelphia, Pa.; son of Louis Richard (a carpenter and builder) and Clara (Vogel) Young. *Education:* Attended public schools in Bucks County and Philadelphia, Pa. *Religion:* Protestant. *Address:* c/o Arcadia House, 419 Park Ave. South, New York, N.Y. 10016.

CAREER: Stock and accounting clerk for firms in Philadelphia, Pa., 1925-28, 1933-37; Ledger Syndicate, Philadelphia, Pa., newspaper advertising clerk and short story writer, 1929-30; free-lance writer of fiction, Philadelphia, Pa., 1930—.

WRITINGS: The Stagecoach Trail, Arcadia House, 1964, R. Hale, 1966. Author of short stories and novelettes in magazines, including All Western, Lariat, Wild West Weekly, Star Western, Western Romances.

*   *   *

YOUNG, Leontine R. 1910-

PERSONAL: Born March 29, 1910, in Palmyra, N.Y.; daughter of Sanford and Genevieve Young. Education: University of Denver, A.B., 1933; Columbia University, M.S., 1944, Doctor of Social Welfare, 1963. Religion: Protestant. Home: 381 Broad St., Newark, N.J. 07104. Agent: Marie Rodell, 145 East 49th St., New York, N.Y. 10017. Office: Child Service Association, 284 Broadway, Newark, N.J. 07104.

CAREER: Caseworker or consultant for federal, state, and private agencies in Nebraska, 1934-37, Hawaii, 1938-40; New York Children's Aid Society, New York, N.Y., supervisor of treatment center for adolescent girls, 1940-43; Inwood House for Unmarried Mothers, New York, N.Y., casework supervisor, 1943-45; Columbia University, School of Social Work, New York, N.Y. began as assistant professor, became associate professor, 1945-52; Ohio State University, School of Social Administration, Columbus, professor in casework, 1952-60; Child Service Association, Newark, N.J., executive director, 1960—; Rutgers University, New Brunswick, N.J., visiting professor of social work, 1960—. Conductor of summer institutes at other universities. Member: American Association of Social Workers.

WRITINGS: The Treatment of Adolescent Girls in an Institution, Child Welfare League of America, 1945; Out of Wedlock, McGraw, 1954; Wednesday's Children: A Study of Child Neglect and Abuse, McGraw, 1964; Life Among the Giants, McGraw, 1966. Contributor to magazines and professional journals.

WORK IN PROGRESS: Studies on the disorganized and culturally deprived families of the urban areas, with special reference to the widespread educational failure of the children.

AVOCATIONAL INTERESTS: Theatre, music, reading history and mysteries, good food, gardening, photography.

*   *   *

YOUNG, Louise Merwin 1903-

PERSONAL: Born September 5, 1903, in East Palestine, Ohio; daughter of Charles Lewis (a newspaper publisher) and Estella (Meek) Merwin; married Ralph Aubrey Young (a monetary economist for Federal Reserve Board), September 5, 1925; children: Merwin Crawford, Anne Alexandra (Mrs. Roger N. Pierce), Ralph Aubrey, Jr. Education: Ohio Wesleyan University, B.A., 1925; University of Pennsylvania, M.A., 1927, Ph.D., 1939; University of Berlin, postgraduate study, 1930-31. Politics: Democrat (usually). Religion: Methodist. Home: 2836 Chesapeake St. N.W., Washington, D.C. 20008.

CAREER: Independent researcher and free-lance writer, Philadelphia, Pa., 1935-46; Library of Congress, Washington, D.C., consultant, preparing archives of League of Women Voters for Manuscript Division, 1950-52; American University, Washington, D.C., adjunct professor, 1954-57, associate professor, 1957-61, professor of English,

1961-71. Visiting scholar, Radcliffe Institute for Independent Study, 1968; resident, Rockefeller Foundation Bellagio Center, Italy, fall, 1973. Trustee, Ohio Wesleyan University, 1950-55. Pennsylvania vice-president and regional director, League of Women Voters, 1942-46; consultant, Radcliffe Women's Archives, 1952—. Member: Modern Language Association of America, American Historical Association, American Political Science Association, American Association of University Women.

WRITINGS: Thomas Carlyle and the Art of History, University of Pennsylvania Press, 1939, Octagon, 1972; (with Harold Alderfer) Know Pennsylvania: Your Local and State Government, Telegraph Press, 1946, 2nd edition, revised by Elizabeth Smedley, published as Know Pennsylvania: A Handbook of Basic Information, Penns Valley Publishers, 1951; (editor) Women's Opportunities and Responsibilities, American Academy of Political and Social Science, 1947; Understanding Politics: A Practical Guide for Women, Pellegrini & Cadahy, 1950. Contributor of articles and book reviews to scholarly periodicals. Contributor, Notable American Women: A Biographical Dictionary, 1960—.

WORK IN PROGRESS: Editing and annotating the letters of Ethel Sturges Dummer, Chicago philanthropist, with possibility of a full biography resulting; a study of the adaptations and modifications in political institutions as a result of women's emergence.

*   *   *

YOUNG, Marguerite

PERSONAL: Born in Indianapolis, Ind.; daughter of Chester Ellis (a salesman) and Fay (Knight) Young. Education: Attended Indiana University; Butler University, B.A., 1930; University of Chicago, M.A., 1936; graduate work at University of Iowa. Home: 375 Bleecker St., New York, N.Y.

CAREER: Writer. Has taught at Indiana University, University of Iowa, Columbia University, Fairleigh Dickinson University, New School for Social Research, Fordham University, and Seton Hall University. Awards, honors: Grants from American Association of University Women, National Institute of Arts and Letters, 1946, Guggenheim Foundation, 1948, Rockefeller Foundation, and Newberry Library.

WRITINGS: Prismatic Ground (poetry), Macmillan, 1937; Moderate Fable (poetry), Reynal & Hitchcock, 1945; Angel in the Forest (account of Utopian community at New Harmony), Reynal & Hitchcock, 1945, new edition with preface by Mark Van Doren, Scribner, 1966; Miss MacIntosh, My Darling (novel), Scribner, 1965.

WORK IN PROGRESS: Two biographies, Harp Song for a Radical and Little Orphant Annie Man.

SIDELIGHTS: Miss MacIntosh, My Darling, eighteen years in the writing, has been hailed as a masterpiece and its author has been compared to James Joyce and Marcel Proust. William Goyen calls the book "a mammoth epic, a massive fable, a picaresque journey, a Faustian quest and a work of stunning magnitude and beauty."

The novel deals with the nature of dreams and reality. Richard Ellmann writes: ". . . Miss Young explores with single-minded passion the residual questions in all fiction, including the validity of dreams, the deception of appearances, the confusion of identities, and the multiplicity of selves that cluster in each seemingly integral being." The tenuous fibers of reality permeated with dream-states has been explained by Miss Young: "Every sentence in my book has to do with one of four categories of the dream-world everyone inhabits. Sometimes reality is a dream that crumbles before your eyes. As when someone you deeply love is taken from you, and everything you cherished suddenly vanishes. Sometimes the reality you thought was a dream turns out to be real. You might see an elephant walking down the road. You think you are dreaming, but it turns out an elephant has escaped from the circus and *is* walking down the road. Sometimes a dream is a dream. Knowing this fact is the difference between being sane and crazy. And the greatest tragedy of all is when reality turns out to be reality and the unbelievable thing must be faced as true. As when a man walks in to his wife at breakfast and tells her what she knew all along but pretended was a dream, that he has fallen in love with someone else and wants a divorce."

Those who, like William Goyen, praise the technique used in *Miss MacIntosh, My Darling* consider the style to be "the very theme itself." Marion Simon writes: "The language and even the length of this book are as important to the creation of Miss Young's vision as are the many and secret lives of the novel's characters. Long convoluted sentence follows long convoluted sentence. Images are drawn and redrawn, pounded into shape again and again, but never twice into exactly the same shape.... There is no sure ground in Miss Young's vision where the reader may set a steady foot." Goyen believes the force and vigor displayed are almost unique in American fiction: "... we have come upon a strong, deep loudness, a full-throated outcry, a literature of expanse and daring that makes most of our notable male writers look like a motorcycle gang trying to prove a kind of literary masculinity."

BIOGRAPHICAL/CRITICAL SOURCES: New York Times Book Review, September 12, 1965; *Book Week*, September 12, 1965; *New Republic*, October 2, 1965; *America*, October 2, 1965; *National Observer*, October 4, 1965; *New York Times*, October 15, 1965; *Detroit Free Press*, October 24, 1965; *New York Review of Books*, November 25, 1965; Roy Newquist, *Conversations*, Rand McNally, 1967.

* * *

YOUNG, Whitney M(oore), Jr. 1921-1971

PERSONAL: Born July 31, 1921, in Lincoln Ridge, Ky.; son of Whitney M. and Laura (Ray) Young; married Margaret Buckner, January 2, 1944; children: Marcia, Lauren. *Education:* Kentucky State College, B.S., 1941; Massachusetts Institute of Technology, graduate student, 1942-44; University of Minnesota, M.A. in Social Work, 1947. *Religion:* Unitarian. *Home:* 29 Mohegan Pl., New Rochelle, N.Y. *Office:* National Urban League, 14 East 48th St., New York, N.Y. 10017.

CAREER: Urban League, Omaha, Neb., executive secretary, 1950-53; University of Nebraska, Lincoln, instructor in School of Social Work, 1950-54; Creighton University, Omaha, Neb., instructor, 1951-53; Atlanta University, Atlanta, Ga., dean of School of Social Work, 1954-61; National Urban League, New York, N.Y., executive director, 1961-71. Member of President's Committee on Youth Employment, President's Committee on Equal Opportunity in the Armed Forces, of Advisory Committee on Juvenile Delinquency, U.S. Department of Justice, and of Advisory Committee, Bureau of Public Assistance and Children's Bureau, U.S. Department of Health, Education, and Welfare. *Awards, honors:* Florina Lakser Award ($1,000) for outstanding achievement in field of social work, 1959; LL.D. from Agriculture and Technical College of North Carolina, 1961, Tuskegee Institute, 1963.

WRITINGS: To Be Equal, McGraw, 1964; *Beyond Racism: Building an Open Society*, McGraw, 1969. Writer of column, "To Be Equal," which was carried in thirty-five daily and weekly newspapers.

SIDELIGHTS: Describing Young's work, Roy Wilkins said: "Young hammered at employment for blacks, and at education and at training programs for minorities.... Perhaps Young was a bridge between the two races at a most abrasive period in their lives together. The old whites, and those younger ones who wanted to keep the old ways, could not abide the angry young Negroes who were through, forever, with the old ways, crass or subtle. And the old blacks, timidly aware of their shortchanging at every turn, but aware, too, of the powerlessness of the group, shuddered at the truth of the basic complaints of their young, but shuddered more at the wild rhetoric and the predictable violence among the undisciplined.

"Young was busy in this time of turmoil with building his National Urban League to minister to the needs of his people and of the nation ... A measure of his success in the ceaseless quest for racial justice is found in the attendance of 6,000 persons at his funeral—the largest in the 40-year history of the Riverside Church in New York City. None present could quarrel with the minister's description of him: 'tenacious in his beliefs and winsome in their presentation'."

Young died in Lagos, Nigeria while attending a conference on the development of a diologue between the West and Black Africa.

Elizabeth Lee Haseldon wrote of Young's last book: "This is an important book, beautifully integrated! A blend of pragmatism and idealism, it is written clearly, pungently, factually, with an undercurrent of burning urgency and controlled anger. *Beyond Racism* makes a meaningful whole of the fragmented, confused pieces of the racial picture in America; it combines diagnosis with prescription; and it is based on the belief that an open, integrated society is both possible and preferable to racial separatism."

(Died March 11, 1971)

* * *

YUAN, T'ung-li 1895-1965

PERSONAL: Born March 23, 1895, in Peking, China; married Ruth Hui-hsi Yuan; children: Ching, Cheng, Tsing. *Education:* Columbia University, A.B., 1922; New York State Library School, B.L.S., 1923; graduate study, Institute of Historical Research, University of London, 1923-24. *Home:* 1723 Webster St. N.W., Washington, D.C. 20011. *Office:* Library of Congress, Washington, D.C. 20540.

CAREER: National University of Peking, Peking, China, professor of bibliography, 1925-27; Metropolitan Library of Peking, librarian, 1926-29; National Library of Peking, associate director, 1929-42, director, 1942-48; Stanford Research Institute, Menlo Park, Calif., chief bibliographer, 1951-53; Library of Congress, Washington, D.C., member of staff, 1957-65. Lecturer on bibliography, National Normal University, Peking, 1927-29. Member, administrative council, National Palace Museum, 1925-48; member, Chinese National Commission for Preservation of Antiquities, 1928-48; member, Chinese National Commission for

UNESCO, 1949-65. *Member:* American Oriental Society, Association for Asian Studies, Royal Central Asian Society, Bibliographical Society (London), Oxford Bibliographical Society. *Awards, honors:* Columbia University, university medal for excellence, 1934; LL.D., University of Pittsburgh, 1945.

WRITINGS: Economic and Social Development of China: A Bibliographical Guide, Human Relations Area Files, 1956; (editor) *Kuo hui t'u shu kuan ts'ang chung-kuo shan pan shu lu* (catalog of rare Chinese books), Library of Congress, 1957; *China in Western Literature: A Continuation of Cordier's Bibliotheca Sinica,* Far Eastern Publications, Yale University, 1958; *Russian Works on China, 1918-1960, in American Libraries,* Far Eastern Publications, Yale University, 1961; *A Guide to Doctoral Dissertations by Chinese Students in America, 1905-1960,* Sino-American Cultural Society, 1962; *Doctoral Dissertations by Chinese Students in Great Britain and Northern Ireland, 1916-1961,* Chinese Culture (Taipei), 1962; (compiler with Hajime Watanabe) *Classified Bibliography of Japanese Books and Articles Concerning Sinkiang, 1886-1962,* [Tokyo], 1962; *Bibliography of Chinese Mathematics, 1918-1960,* privately printed, 1963; (compiler) *Russo-Chinese Treaties and Agreements Relating to Sinkiang 1851-1949,* U.S. Joint Publications Research Service, 1964; *A Guide to Doctoral Dissertations by Chinese Students in Continental Europe, 1907-1962,* Chinese Culture, 1964, Chinese-American Education Foundation, 1967; (translator) Aleksandr Genrikhovich Jomini, *I-li Chiao she ti o fang wen chien,* 1966. Managing editor, *Quarterly Bulletin of Chinese Bibliography,* 1934-48.

WORK IN PROGRESS: Bibliography of Chinese Turkestan; Bibliography of Chinese Art and Archaeology.

(Died, 1965)

*　*　*

ZAGOREN, Ruby 1922-1974

PERSONAL: Born December 9, 1922, in New Britain, Conn.; daughter of Louis Solace (a farmer-machinist) and Marie (Klaz) Zagoren; married Samuel Silverstein (a science teacher), December 25, 1946; children: Zona Finley, Grant Merlin. *Education:* Connecticut College, B.A., 1943. *Home:* Felicity Lane, Torrington, Conn. 06790.

CAREER: Hartford Courant, Hartford, Conn., reporter, 1943-46; free-lance writer. Teacher of creative writing in adult education courses. Publicity chairman, Torrington Community Chest. *Member:* Connecticut College Club of Litchfield County (president), Litchfield Hills Audubon Society (publicity chairman).

WRITINGS: Meandering Meditations, Kaleidograph Press, 1939; *New England Sampler,* Golden Quill, 1965; *Israel, My Israel,* Gray-Zone Publishers, 1968; *Venture for Freedom: The True Story of an African Yankee,* World Publishing Co., 1969; *Chaim Weizmann: First President of Israel,* Garrard, 1972. Contributor to more than a hundred periodicals, including *Saturday Evening Post, Good Housekeeping, House Beautiful, Ladies' Home Journal, Prairie Schooner, Calcutta Review* (India), and *University Review.* Free-lance feature writer for *Hartford Times,* Hartford, Conn., 1935-74.

WORK IN PROGRESS: Anne Frank's Testament, poems on Jewish themes; *A Catskill Story,* a novel; *I Never Thought That Fire Could Fly,* poems about birds.

AVOCATIONAL INTERESTS: Travel—including a 10,000-mile camping trip in 1962; bird watching—has seen 254 different species.

(Died June 9, 1974)

*　*　*

ZELDNER, Max 1907-

PERSONAL: Born August 25, 1907, in Brest Litovsk, Poland (now in Union of Soviet Socialist Republics); son of Aaron David (a rabbi) and M. Toibe (Leff) Zeldner; married Fannie Brody (a librarian), July 3, 1933; children: Adina (Mrs. Arthur Nadelhaft), Miriam (Mrs. Ionel Klipper). *Education:* Teachers Institute, Yeshiva University, diploma, 1927; New York University, B.S., 1931; Harvard University, graduate study, 1931; Columbia University, M.A., 1933, graduate study. *Religion:* Jewish. *Home:* 35 West 82nd St., New York, N.Y. 10024.

CAREER: Yeshiva University, New York, N.Y., instructor in Hebrew at Teachers Institute, 1934-35, in German at Yeshiva College, 1935-37; teacher of Hebrew, German, and French in high schools, New York, N.Y., 1937-58; Fort Hamilton High School, Brooklyn, N.Y., chairman of department of foreign languages, 1958-61; William Howard Taft High School, New York, N.Y., chairman of department of foreign languages, 1961-72. Instructor at School of Education, Yeshiva University, 1948-64, Queens College (now Queens College of the City University of New York), 1949-50, and Herzliah Hebrew Teachers Institute, 1949-58; visiting assistant professor of education at Stern College of Yeshiva University, 1958; Hunter College (now Hunter College of the City University of New York), 1960-61. *Member:* Association of Chairmen in New York City High Schools, Association of Foreign Language Chairmen of New York City, Histadruth Ivrith of America.

WRITINGS: (Editor with George Epstein) *Modern Hebrew Literature,* Hebrew Publishing Co., 1948; *Bibliography of Methods and Materials of Teaching Hebrew in the Light of Modern Language Methodology,* Jewish Education Committee of New York, 1951, 2nd enlarged edition, 1953; *Bible Teaching: A Bibliography of Methods, Materials and Model Lessons,* American Association for Jewish Education, 1960. Contributor of about fifty articles to Anglo-Jewish, Hebrew, education, and language periodicals.

AVOCATIONAL INTERESTS: Music, folk dancing, silversmithing, and travel.

*　*　*

ZIEMER, Gregor (Athalwin) 1899-

PERSONAL: Born May 24, 1899, in Columbia, Mich.; son of Robert (a minister) and Adele (Grabau) Ziemer; married Edna Wilson (a teacher), May 30, 1926; children: Patricia (Mrs. William Eadie). *Education:* University of Illinois, B.A., 1922; University of Minnesota, M.A., 1923; University of Berlin, Ph.D., 1934. *Politics:* Independent. *Religion:* Lutheran. *Home:* 26950 Spring Creek Rd., Palos Verdes Peninsula, Calif. *Agent:* Anita Diamant, 51 East 42nd St., New York, N.Y. 10017.

CAREER: Teacher in government schools, Philippine Islands, 1926-28; American School, Berlin, Germany, founder and headmaster, 1928-39; WLW, Cincinnati, Ohio, newscaster, 1942-44; Town Hall, New York, N.Y., director of education, 1945-60; WRVA, Richmond, Va., newscaster, 1948-50; International Enterprises, Inc., Philadelphia, Pa., vice-president for public relations, 1949-50; American Foundation for the Blind, Inc., New York, N.Y., director of public education, 1952-64. Public lecturer on international affairs and other topics, sometimes appearing in dialogue lectures with wife, Edna Ziemer. Writer and producer of radio and television shows. *Military service:* U.S. Army, lieutenant colonel with Fourth Armored Division in Europe, 1945. *Member:* American Public Relations Association (now Public Relations Society of America; president, New York chapter, 1960), Overseas Press Club (member of board, 1950), Association of Radio-Television News Analysts (secretary, 1948), Kappa Delta Phi, American Legion. *Awards, honors:* Silver Anvil Award of American Public Relations Association, 1956, 1958, 1960.

WRITINGS: Two Thousand and Ten Days of Hitler, Harper, 1941; *Education for Death: The Making of the Nazi*, Oxford University Press, 1942, reprinted, Octagon, 1972; (with wife, Edna Ziemer) *Whirlaway Hopper*, Bobbs-Merrill, 1962. Also author of *Too Old For What*. Contributor of articles to *Collier's, Reader's Digest, Saturday Evening Post, Good Housekeeping, Mademoiselle*. One of his books was adapted for the motion picture, "Hitler's Children"; author of six television plays and of radio shows.

WORK IN PROGRESS: A humorous novel on experiences with Fourth Armored Division in World War II; two historical novels, *The Brigand of Montserrat* and *The Halfbreed*.

* * *

ZORACH, William   1887-1966

PERSONAL: Born February 28, 1887, in Eurburg, Lithuania; brought to United States at the age of four; son of Aaron and Toba (Bloch) Zorach; married Marguerite Thompson, 1912; children: Tessim, Dahlov. *Education:* Studied at Cleveland School of Art, at Arts Students League and National Academy of Design in New York, and then in Paris, 1910-12.

CAREER: Exhibiting artist, 1910-66, and instructor at Art Students League, New York, N.Y., 1929-66. Painted in oils, 1910-18, then turned to watercolors and sculpture; work shown at more than twenty one-man shows throughout United States, 1924-60, including Art Institute of Chicago, 1938, Dallas Museum of Fine Arts, 1945, Pasadena Art Institute and San Francisco Museum, 1946, Detroit Institute of Art, 1947; retrospective shows at Whitney Museum of American Art, 1959, and at a series of shows at Downtown Gallery, New York; represented in permanent collections of Metropolitan Museum of Art, Museum of Modern Art, Philadelphia Museum of Art, Cleveland Museum, and in other museums and institutions in thirty American cities; executor of sculpture for Benjamin Franklin Post Office, Washington, D.C., and for the facade of the Mayo Clinic, Rochester, N.Y.; executor of "Spirit of the Dance," Radio City Music Hall, New York, N.Y.

MEMBER: National Institute of Arts and Letters (vice-president, 1955-57), Sculptors Guild. *Awards, honors:* Logan Medal and award ($1,500) for sculpture, Art Institute of Chicago, 1931; Logan Medal and purchase prize, 12th International Watercolor Exhibition, Art Institute of Chicago, 1932; Avery Award for sculpture, Architectural League, 1939; George D. Widner Memorial Gold Medal, Pennsylvania Academy of Fine Arts, 1961; National Institute of Arts and Letters Gold Medal for sculpture, 1961. M.S., from Bowdoin College, 1958; D.F.A., Colby College, 1961, and Bates College, 1964.

WRITINGS: Zorach Explains Sculpture, American Artists Group, 1947, 2nd edition, Tudor, 1960; *Art is My Life* (autobiography) World Publishing, 1967. Contributor of articles to *Art Digest, American Artist, Arts*, and other art journals. Sculpture and paintings shown in books, museum publications, magazines, and newspapers, including *Art in America*, 1939, *London Studio, Survey, International Studio, Outlook, Esquire, Design, Life, New York Times*, and *Christian Science Monitor*.

BIOGRAPHICAL/CRITICAL SOURCES: Magazine of Art, April and May, 1941; *American Artist*, April, 1958; John I. H. Bauer, *William Zorach*, Praeger, 1959.

(Died, 1966)